COLLEGE ATLAS OF THE WORLD

NATIONAL GEOGRAPHIC, WASHINGTON, D.C.

VP and Publisher	*Jay O'Callaghan*
Executive Editor	*Ryan Flahive*
Assistant Editor	*Laura Kelleher*
Editorial Assistant	*Courtney Nelson*
Marketing Manager	*Emily Streutker*
Marketing Assistant	*Nicole Ferrato*
Media Editor	*Lynn Pearlman*

Library of Congress Cataloging in Publication data
is available upon request.

ISBN-13: 978-0-471-74117-6

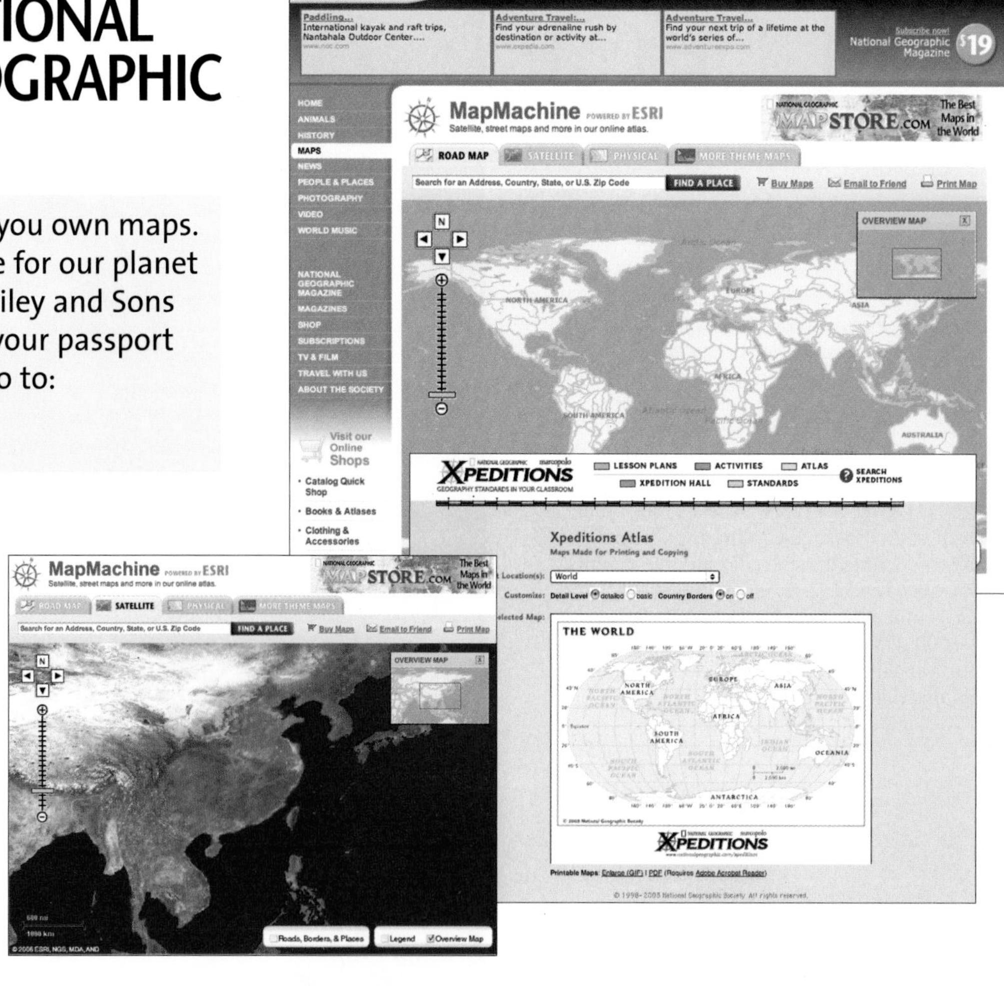

Explore the World! Research and make you own maps. Learn how you can be involved and care for our planet Earth. National Geographic and John Wiley and Sons will help you start your adventure. For your passport to the World of Maps and Geography go to: www.wiley.com/college/atlas

- MapMachine
  www.nationalgeographic.com/maps
- XPEDITIONS
  www.nationalgeographic.com/xpeditions/atlas/

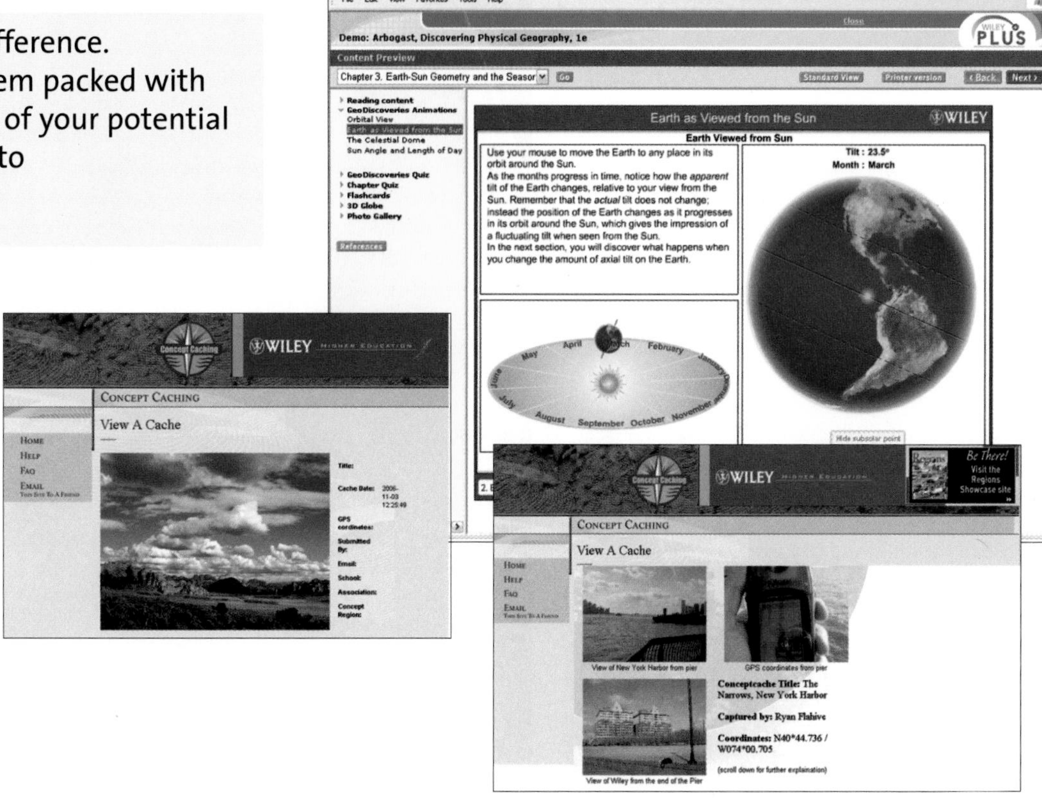

You have the potential to make a difference. Wiley**PLUS** is a powerful online system packed with features to help you make the most of your potential and get the best grade you can! Go to www.wiley.com/college/atlas

- Wiley**PLUS**
- GeoDiscoveries
  www.wiley.com/college/geodiscoveries
- ConceptCaching
  www.ConceptCaching.com

COLLEGE ATLAS OF THE WORLD

Founded in 1888, the National Geographic Society is one of the largest nonprofit scientific and educational organizations in the world. It reaches more than 285 million people worldwide each month through its official journal, NATIONAL GEOGRAPHIC, and its four other magazines; the National Geographic Channel; television documentaries; radio programs; films; books; videos and DVDs; maps; and interactive media. National Geographic has funded more than 8,000 scientific research projects and supports an education program combating geographic illiteracy.

For more information, please call
1-800-NGS LINE (647-5463)
or write to the following address:
National Geographic Society
1145 17th Street N.W.
Washington, D.C. 20036-4688 U.S.A.

Log on to nationalgeographic.com;
AOL Keyword: NatGeo.

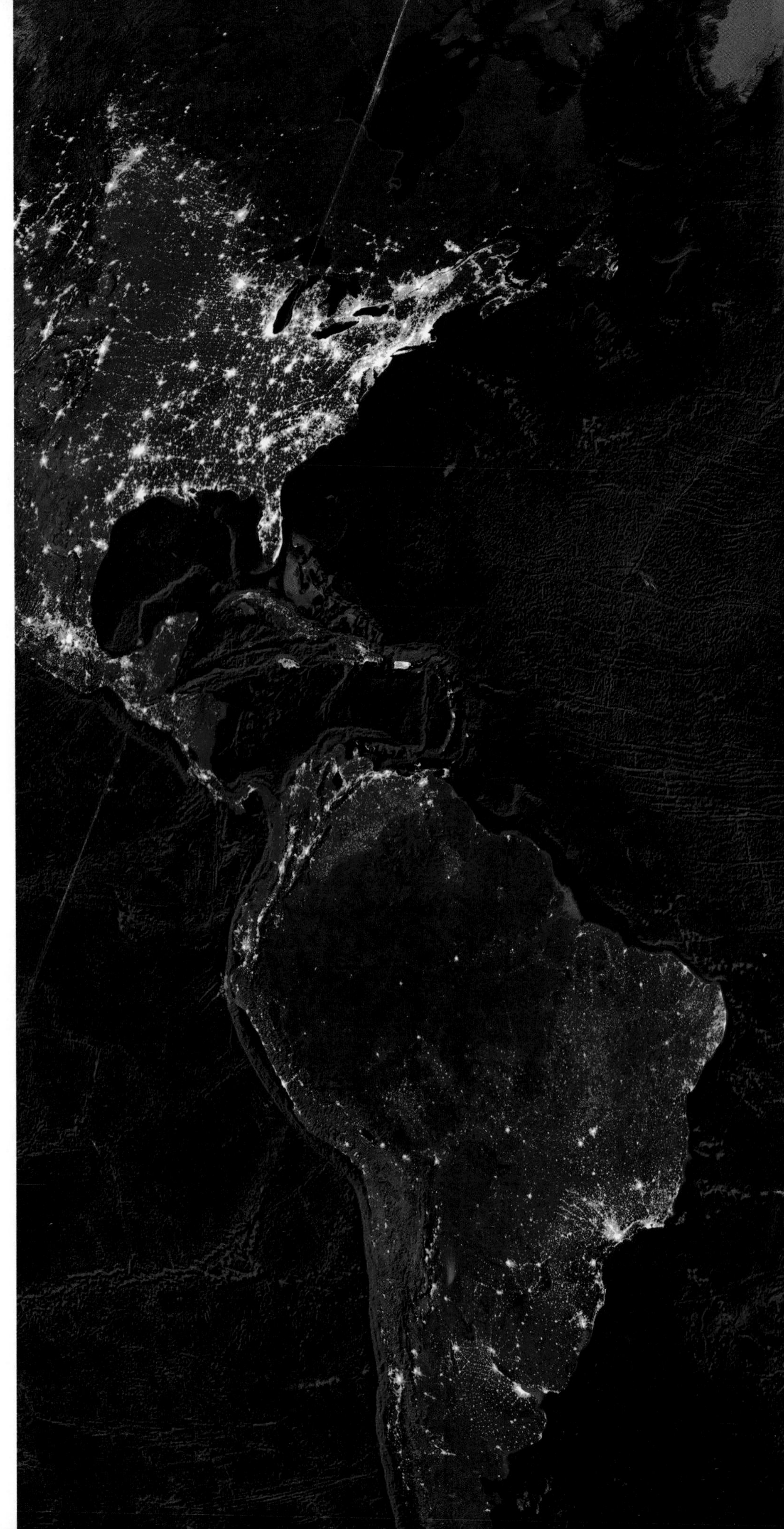

PREFACE

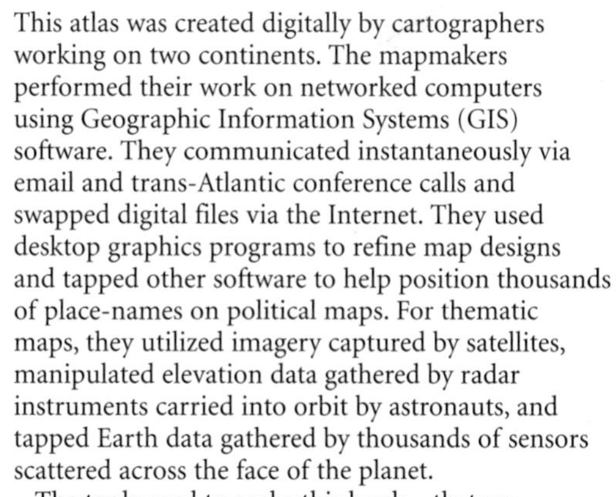

This atlas was created digitally by cartographers working on two continents. The mapmakers performed their work on networked computers using Geographic Information Systems (GIS) software. They communicated instantaneously via email and trans-Atlantic conference calls and swapped digital files via the Internet. They used desktop graphics programs to refine map designs and tapped other software to help position thousands of place-names on political maps. For thematic maps, they utilized imagery captured by satellites, manipulated elevation data gathered by radar instruments carried into orbit by astronauts, and tapped Earth data gathered by thousands of sensors scattered across the face of the planet.

The tools used to make this book—that we cartographers take for granted as standard methods of the trade—would have been considered almost miraculous by the gentlemen who founded the National Geographic Society in 1888 on a late winter evening in Washington, D.C. Among their ranks were Alexander Graham Bell, inventor of the telephone, and John Wesley Powell, leader of the first expedition through the rapids of the Grand Canyon.

The mission the founders articulated for the fledgling Society was "the increase and diffusion of geographic knowledge." They sensed, perhaps, that the Age of Exploration was drawing to a close and that scientific inquiry would replace discovery and conquest. They likely surmised that a globe whose limits were finite would require conservation and stewardship. They no doubt recognized that new mass communication technologies, including telephony and photography, could be used to spread knowledge.

They would have been visionaries indeed if they could have foreseen how the next century's new information technologies would transform geography itself. The cumulative revolution wrought by computers, satellite and aerial photography, global positioning systems satellites, GIS, and the Internet turned geographers from the relatively passive pursuits of observing and documenting the planet to the active endeavors of analysis, synthesis, prediction, and decision making. Geography can now assimilate and present—in its unique expression, cartography—a vast array of high-quality information, giving us an incomparable basis for understanding our world and taking action in it. Bell and Powell would be thrilled.

Today, scientists, businesspeople, soldiers, policy makers, and informed citizens of every country on Earth tap geographic knowledge via their computers, laptops, handheld devices—and modern atlases. The book in your hands is a conduit to a complex and nuanced view of the world you are entering. In time, you will take the world itself into your hands—to preserve, improve, and make safer and more prosperous.

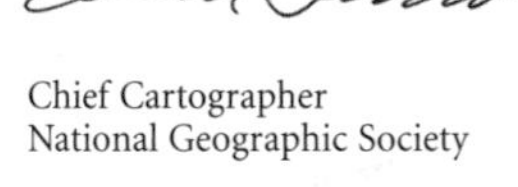

Chief Cartographer
National Geographic Society

INTRODUCTION

5 Preface
8 Geographic Index
10 Using This Atlas
12 Mapping the Earth
14 World From Above
16 Geospatial Concepts

THE WORLD

20 Physical World
22 Political World
24 Tectonics
26 Geomorphology
28 Earth's Surface
30 Climate
32 Weather
34 Biosphere
36 Water
38 Land Cover
40 Biodiversity
42 Land Use
44 Human Population
46 Population Trends
48 Cultures
50 Health & Literacy
52 Economy
54 Food
56 Trade & Globalization
58 Transportation
60 Communication
62 Energy
64 Defense & Conflict
66 Environment
68 Protected Lands

NORTH AMERICA

72 Physical & Political
74 Natural World
76 Human World
78 Economic World

UNITED STATES

80 Physical U.S.
82 Political U.S.
84 U.S. Natural World
86 U.S. Human World
88 U.S. Economic World
90 Northwestern U.S.
92 Southwestern U.S.
94 Northeastern U.S.
96 Southeastern U.S.
98 Alaska, U.S.
99 Hawai'i, U.S. & Principal Hawaiian Islands

REGIONS OF THE UNITED STATES

100 Puget Sound & Central California Coast
101 Southern California
102 Southern Great Lakes
103 Western Gulf Coast
104 Southern New England
105 Peninsular Florida

CANADA, MEXICO & OTHER REGIONS OF NORTH AMERICA

106 Canada
108 Western Canada
110 Central Canada
111 Maritime Canada
112 Mexico
114 Central Mexico
115 Central America
116 Caribbean
118 Bermuda & the West Indies

SOUTH AMERICA

122 Physical & Political
124 Natural World
126 Human World
128 Economic World
130 Northern
132 Central
134 Southern

REGIONS OF SOUTH AMERICA

136 Northern Andes
137 Altiplano
138 Southeastern Brazil
139 River Plate Region

EUROPE

142 Physical & Political
144 Natural World
146 Human World
148 Economic World
150 Western
152 Northern
154 Northeastern
156 Southern
158 Southeastern
160 Russia

REGIONS OF EUROPE
162 Central England
163 Low Countries
164 Northeastern & Southern Spain
165 Rhone Valley
166 Baltic States
167 Ruhr & Po Valleys
168 Western Balkans
169 Central Russia

ASIA

172 Physical & Political
174 Natural World
176 Human World
178 Economic World
180 Western
182 Southwestern
184 Central
186 South Central
188 Southern
190 Eastern
192 Southeastern

REGIONS OF ASIA
194 Eastern Mediterranean
195 Caucasus Region
196 Persian Gulf & Strait of Malacca
197 Fergana & Ganges Valleys
198 Eastern China
200 Korean Peninsula
201 Central Japan
202 Indochina
203 Philippines

AFRICA

206 Physical & Political
208 Natural World
210 Human World
212 Economic World
214 Western
216 Northeastern
218 Central
220 Southern

REGIONS OF AFRICA
222 Coastal West Africa
224 Central Rift Valley
226 Nile Valley
227 South Africa

AUSTRALIA & OCEANIA

230 Physical & Political
232 Natural World
234 Human World
236 Economic World
238 Oceania

ISLANDS OF OCEANIA
240 New Zealand & Polynesia
242 Micronesia & Melanesia

POLAR REGIONS

246 Arctic
248 Antarctic

OCEANS

252 Pacific & Atlantic
254 Indian & Arctic, Oceans Around Antarctica

WORLD FACTS

258 Demographic Information
260 Demographic Information
262 Demographic Information
264 Socioeconomic Information
266 Socioeconomic Information
268 Socioeconomic Information
270 Geographic Information: Comparisons & Conversions
272 Glossary: Geographic Terms & Abbreviations
274 Index
380 Acknowledgments
382 Sources & Credits

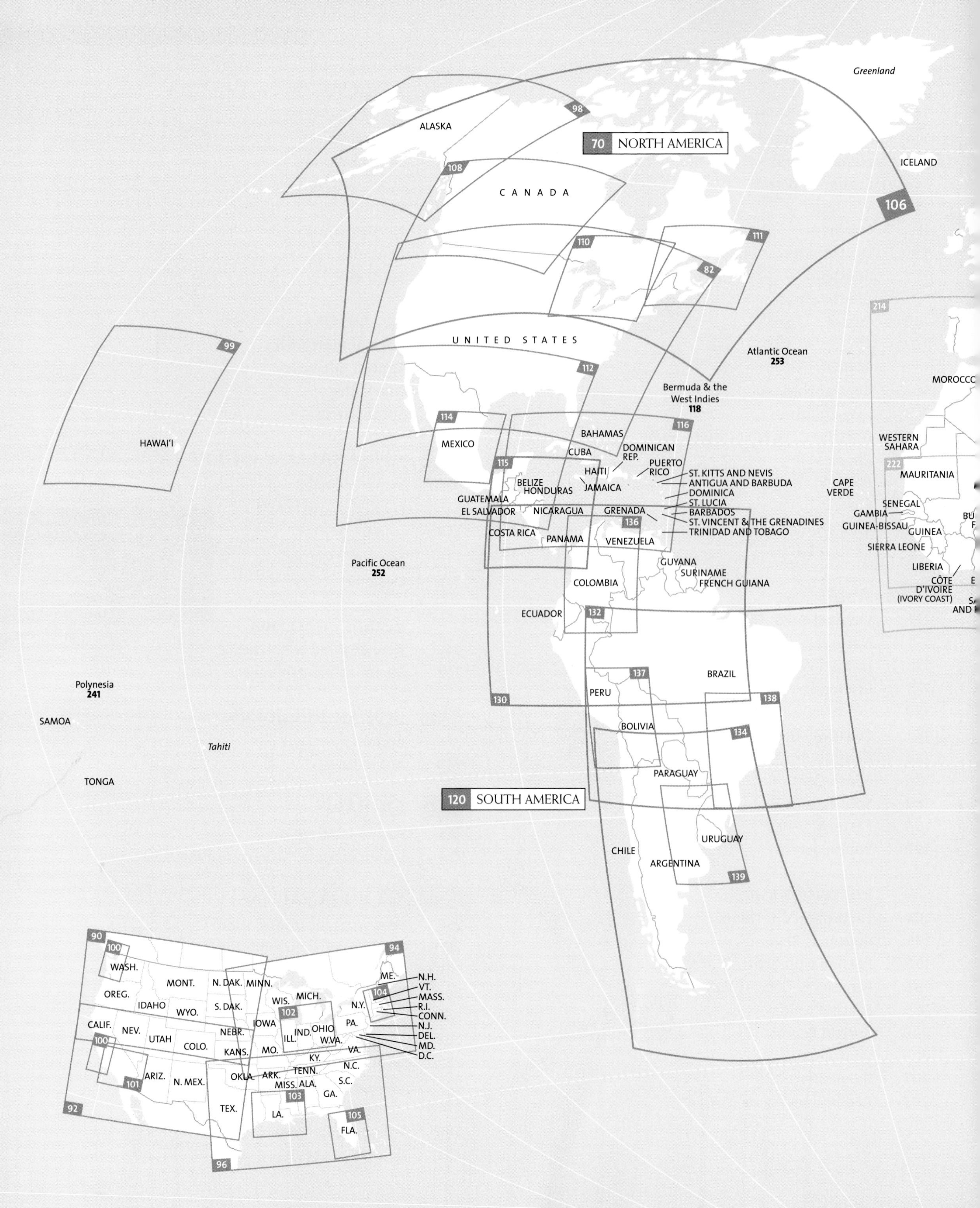
Greenland
ALASKA
98
70 NORTH AMERICA
ICELAND
108
CANADA
106
110
111
82
214
99
UNITED STATES
Atlantic Ocean
253
MOROCCO
112
Bermuda & the
West Indies
118
HAWAI'I
114
MEXICO
BAHAMAS
116
CUBA
DOMINICAN
REP.
WESTERN
SAHARA
222
115
HAITI
PUERTO
RICO
ST. KITTS AND NEVIS
ANTIGUA AND BARBUDA
MAURITANIA
BELIZE
HONDURAS
JAMAICA
DOMINICA
CAPE
VERDE
GUATEMALA
ST. LUCIA
SENEGAL
EL SALVADOR
NICARAGUA
GRENADA
BARBADOS
GAMBIA
ST. VINCENT & THE GRENADINES
136
GUINEA-BISSAU
GUINEA
COSTA RICA
TRINIDAD AND TOBAGO
PANAMA
VENEZUELA
SIERRA LEONE
GUYANA
Pacific Ocean
252
SURINAME
LIBERIA
COLOMBIA
FRENCH GUIANA
CÔTE
D'IVOIRE
(IVORY COAST)
ECUADOR
132
BRAZIL
Polynesia
241
137
PERU
130
138
SAMOA
BOLIVIA
134
Tahiti
PARAGUAY
TONGA
120 SOUTH AMERICA
URUGUAY
CHILE
ARGENTINA
139
90
94
100
WASH.
ME.
N.H.
MONT.
N. DAK.
MINN.
VT.
104
OREG.
MASS.
IDAHO
S. DAK.
WIS.
MICH.
N.Y.
R.I.
WYO.
102
CONN.
IOWA
PA.
CALIF.
N.J.
NEV.
NEBR.
OHIO
100
UTAH
ILL.
IND.
DEL.
W.VA.
COLO.
MD.
KANS.
MO.
VA.
D.C.
KY.
N.C.
TENN.
ARIZ.
ARK.
OKLA.
N. MEX.
MISS.
ALA.
S.C.
101
GA.
103
92
TEX.
LA.
105
FLA.
96

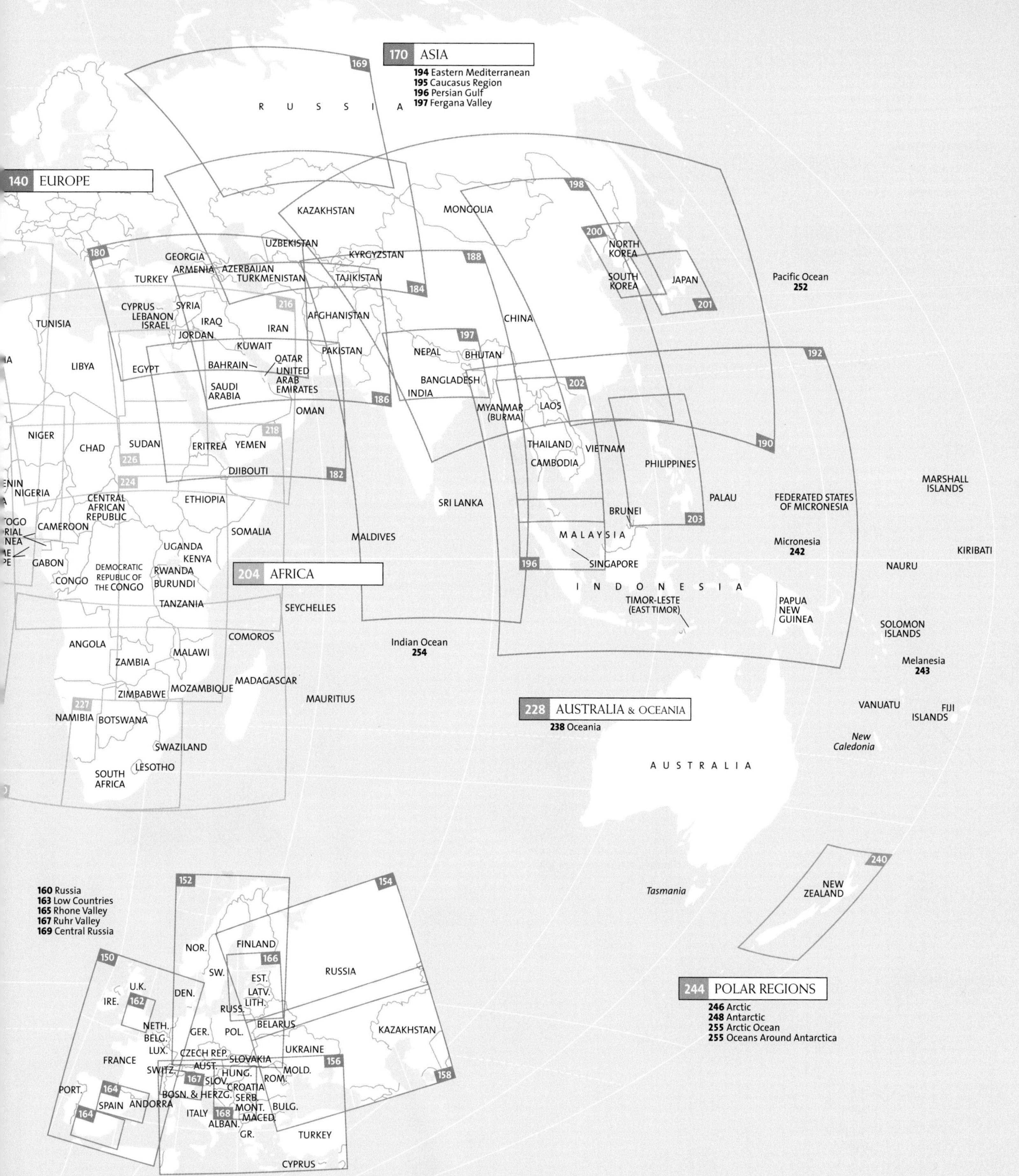

170 ASIA
194 Eastern Mediterranean
195 Caucasus Region
196 Persian Gulf
197 Fergana Valley
140 EUROPE
204 AFRICA
228 AUSTRALIA & OCEANIA
238 Oceania
244 POLAR REGIONS
246 Arctic
248 Antarctic
255 Arctic Ocean
255 Oceans Around Antarctica
160 Russia
163 Low Countries
165 Rhone Valley
167 Ruhr Valley
169 Central Russia
Pacific Ocean
252
Indian Ocean
254
Micronesia
242
Melanesia
243
RUSSIA
KAZAKHSTAN
MONGOLIA
UZBEKISTAN
KYRGYZSTAN
GEORGIA
ARMENIA
AZERBAIJAN
TURKMENISTAN
TAJIKISTAN
TURKEY
NORTH KOREA
SOUTH KOREA
JAPAN
CYPRUS
LEBANON
ISRAEL
SYRIA
IRAQ
JORDAN
IRAN
AFGHANISTAN
CHINA
TUNISIA
KUWAIT
PAKISTAN
NEPAL
BHUTAN
LIBYA
EGYPT
BAHRAIN
QATAR
UNITED ARAB EMIRATES
SAUDI ARABIA
BANGLADESH
INDIA
OMAN
MYANMAR (BURMA)
LAOS
NIGER
CHAD
SUDAN
ERITREA
YEMEN
THAILAND
VIETNAM
CAMBODIA
PHILIPPINES
DJIBOUTI
NIGERIA
CENTRAL AFRICAN REPUBLIC
ETHIOPIA
SRI LANKA
BRUNEI
PALAU
FEDERATED STATES OF MICRONESIA
MARSHALL ISLANDS
CAMEROON
SOMALIA
MALDIVES
MALAYSIA
KIRIBATI
UGANDA
KENYA
GABON
CONGO
DEMOCRATIC REPUBLIC OF THE CONGO
RWANDA
BURUNDI
SINGAPORE
NAURU
INDONESIA
TANZANIA
SEYCHELLES
TIMOR-LESTE (EAST TIMOR)
PAPUA NEW GUINEA
SOLOMON ISLANDS
ANGOLA
ZAMBIA
MALAWI
COMOROS
ZIMBABWE
MOZAMBIQUE
MADAGASCAR
MAURITIUS
VANUATU
FIJI ISLANDS
NAMIBIA
BOTSWANA
New Caledonia
SWAZILAND
AUSTRALIA
SOUTH AFRICA
LESOTHO
Tasmania
NEW ZEALAND
NOR.
FINLAND
SW.
EST.
LATV.
LITH.
RUSS.
RUSSIA
U.K.
IRE.
DEN.
NETH.
BELG.
LUX.
GER.
POL.
BELARUS
KAZAKHSTAN
FRANCE
CZECH REP.
SLOVAKIA
UKRAINE
SWITZ.
AUST.
SLOV.
HUNG.
MOLD.
ROM.
PORT.
SPAIN
ANDORRA
BOSN. & HERZG.
CROATIA
SERB.
MONT.
BULG.
ITALY
MACED.
ALBAN.
GR.
TURKEY
CYPRUS

POLITICAL MAP SYMBOLS

BOUNDARIES

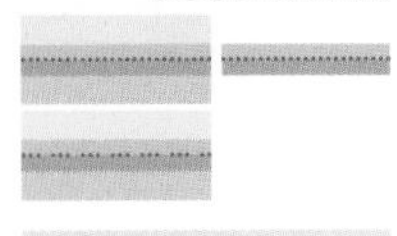

Defined

Disputed or undefined

Offshore line of separation

CITIES

Capitals

Towns

TRANSPORTATION

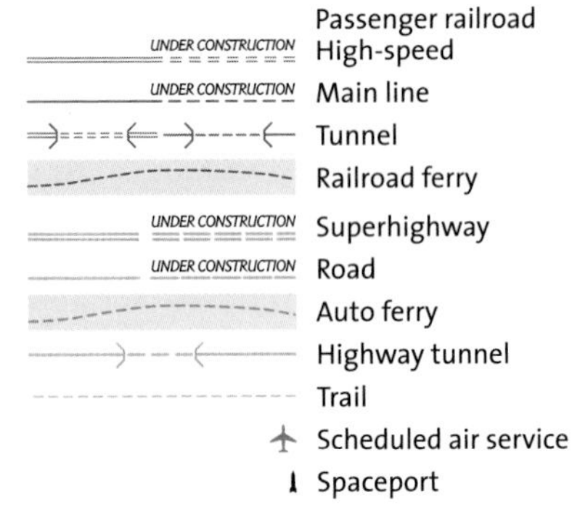

Passenger railroad

High-speed

Main line

Tunnel

Railroad ferry

Superhighway

Road

Auto ferry

Highway tunnel

Trail

Scheduled air service

Spaceport

WATER FEATURES

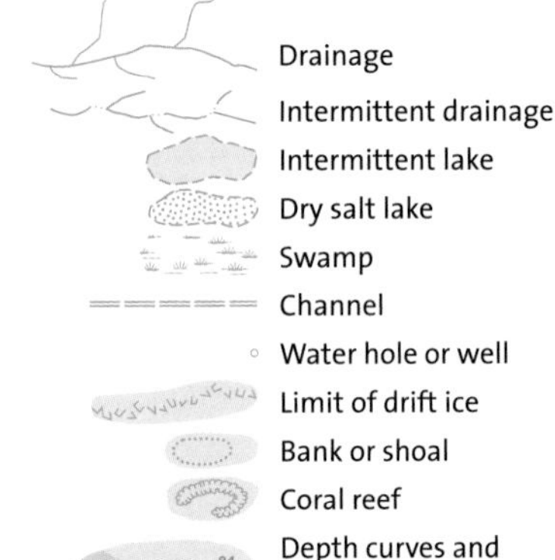

Drainage

Intermittent drainage

Intermittent lake

Dry salt lake

Swamp

Channel

Water hole or well

Limit of drift ice

Bank or shoal

Coral reef

Depth curves and soundings in meters

Falls or rapids

PHYSICAL FEATURES

Tundra

Relief

Crater

Lava and volcanic debris

8850 (29035 ft) Elevation in meters

Pass

Sand

Below sea level

Ice shelf

Glacier

CULTURAL FEATURES

Dam

Wall

Park

Site

Ruin

Battle

Oil field

Oil pipeline

Canal

BOUNDARIES AND POLITICAL DIVISIONS

Red dots:
Claimed boundary; India claims the entire region of Kashmir—including areas now controlled by Pakistan and China

Broken boundary dots:
Disputed boundary; the line of control, a cease-fire line dating back to 1972, separates Indian and Pakistani forces

Single color band:
Internal country boundary

Double color band:
International boundary

Internal region type:
In this case, Punjab, a state of India

Most political boundaries depicted in this *Atlas* are stable and uncontested. Those that are disputed receive special treatment. Disputed areas are shown in a gray color, including the Palestinian territories (West Bank and Gaza Strip) and separatist states still claimed by other countries.

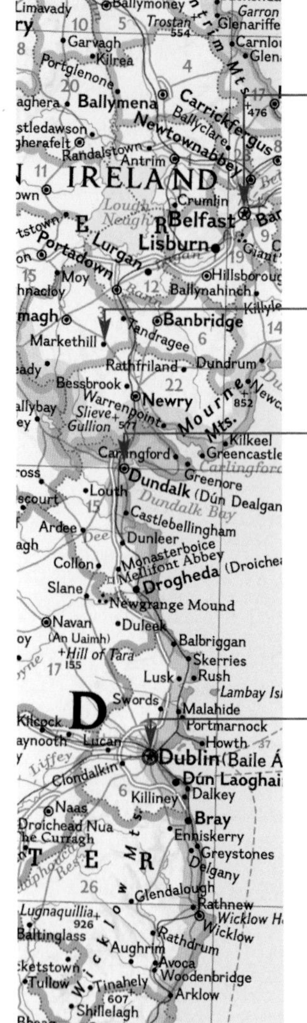

CITIES AND TOWNS

Star with ring:
Administrative capital for internal regions, such as provinces, states, and territories in Australia, Canada, Mexico, United Kingdom, and the United States

Small type and town spot:
City or town with fewer than 100,000 people

Bull's-eye:
Administrative capital for internal regions in most countries and for dependent territories

Star with double ring:
National capital; larger type size shows Dublin as a city between 100,000 and one million people

The regional political maps that form the bulk of this *Atlas* depict four categories of cities or towns. The largest cities, over five million, are shown in capital letters (for example, **LONDON**).

WORLD THEMATIC MAPS

Thematic maps show the spatial distribution of physical or cultural phenomena in a way that is graphically illuminating and useful. This thematic map on language was created by National Geographic Maps, using a combination of data on subjects such as cultures, linguistics, and migrations, as well as consultation with experts. Thematic maps also use quantitative sources in the presentation of topics such as economics or health.

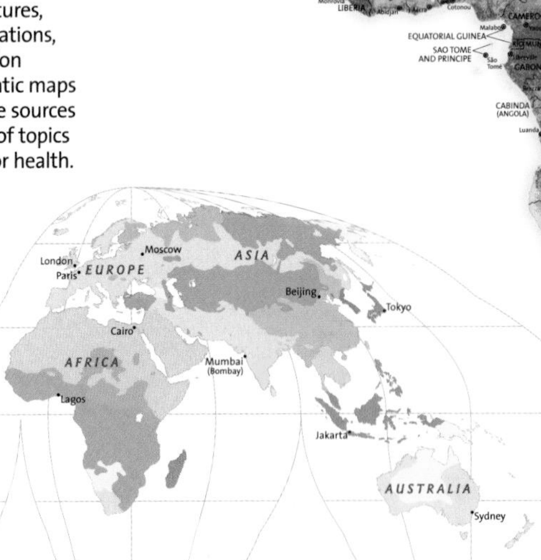

CONTINENTAL THEMATIC MAPS

This Atlas contains three spreads of thematic maps for each continent covering human, natural, and economic topics. The map shown here of Africa's vegetation, derived from satellite imagery, on-the-ground analysis, and population data for urban areas, was compiled using data from the University of Maryland Global Land Cover Facility.

TRANSPORTATION

Dashed red line: Trail or track

Red line: Road or highway

Double red line: Superhighway; this includes interstates, motorways, and other limited-access highways

Plane symbol: Airport with scheduled service

Dark gray line: Passenger railroad

Double gray line: High-speed passenger railroad

Red dots: Intracoastal waterway

Dashed red line in water: Car or passenger ferry

Superhighways and roads produce a dense network as they crisscross the Philadelphia area, but good roads and highways are rare in many parts of the world.

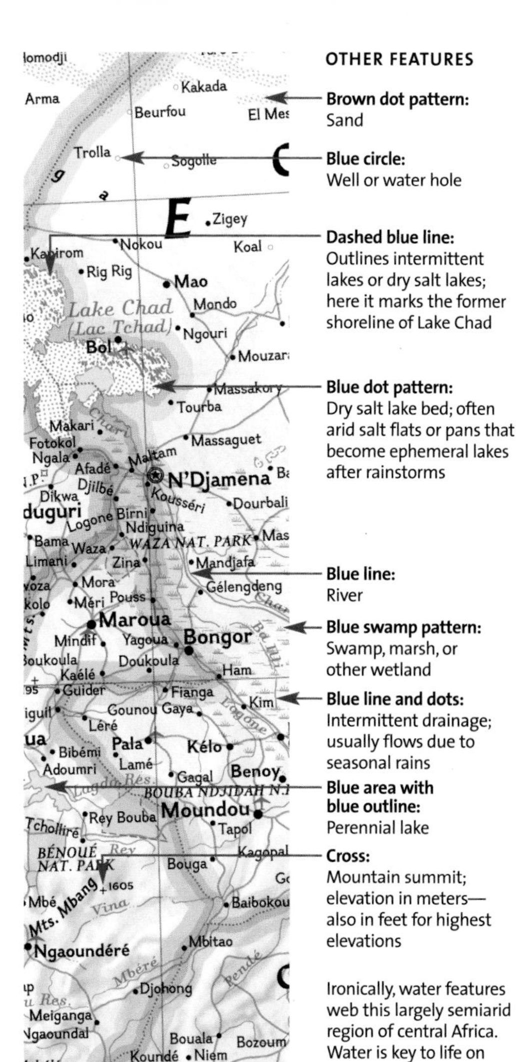

OTHER FEATURES

Brown dot pattern: Sand

Blue circle: Well or water hole

Dashed blue line: Outlines intermittent lakes or dry salt lakes; here it marks the former shoreline of Lake Chad

Blue dot pattern: Dry salt lake bed; often arid salt flats or pans that become ephemeral lakes after rainstorms

Blue line: River

Blue swamp pattern: Swamp, marsh, or other wetland

Blue line and dots: Intermittent drainage; usually flows due to seasonal rains

Blue area with blue outline: Perennial lake

Cross: Mountain summit; elevation in meters—also in feet for highest elevations

Ironically, water features web this largely semiarid region of central Africa. Water is key to life on Earth. Lack of water can lead to desertification and human migration.

"When people at a party ask me where I'm from and I say Morocco, the conversation often comes to a complete halt. Even if they know nothing about my country, people could ask where it is. Then they might ask me about its languages or religions or its physical appearance."

Twenty-four year-old Amine Elouazzani, who recently graduated from an American college, could be describing how to use the *National Geographic Collegiate Atlas of the World.* A well-educated person should know how to ask good questions and be able to read, understand, and appreciate maps. Use the political and thematic maps in this Atlas to orient yourself to the world at present and to inform your direction for the future.

The maps in the political, or reference, section of this Atlas show international boundaries, cities, national parks, road networks, and other features. They are organized by continent, and each section begins with an overview of the continent's physical and human geography. In the index, most entries are keyed to place-names on the political maps, citing the page number, followed by their geographic coordinates. The thematic maps at the front of the Atlas explore topics in depth, revealing the rich patchwork and infinite interrelatedness of our changing planet. In selecting from the vast storehouse of knowledge about the Earth, the Atlas editors relied upon proven data sources, such as the World Health Organization, United Nations, World Wildlife Fund, Bureau of the Census, and U.S. Department of Commerce.

Maps inform us, feed our curiosity, and help us shape our inquiry in spatial and temporal terms. They enable us to move beyond our boundaries and engage in conversation with each other.

GRAPHS, CHARTS, AND TABLES

Conveying relationships, facts, and trends quickly and efficiently is the work of these types of displays. They are diagrams that compare information in visual form. Three common types are the bar graph, the line graph, and the circle (or pie) chart. This Atlas uses all three conventions. The bar graph below, from the Health & Literacy thematic spread, compares male and female literacy rates for a range of countries and in relation to world averages. The viewer gains immediate insight not only into the level of literacy in a society but also into the relative value and status accorded to women. These graphic presentations summarize complex data and are most valuable when they generate deep and penetrating inquiry.

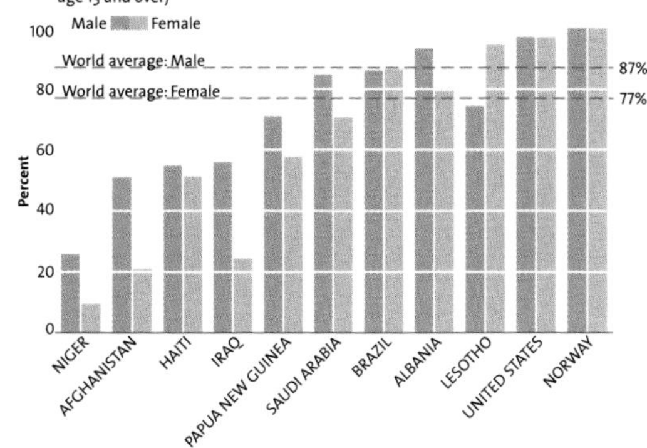

GeoBytes

UNIQUE SPECIES
Madagascar and the Indian Ocean islands are home to many species found nowhere else. Of the region's 13,000 plant species, more than 89% are endemic, meaning that is the only place on Earth they live.

FRAGILE POPULATIONS
Nearly half of the world's tortoises and freshwater turtles are threatened.

HUMAN HEALTH
Medicines derived from plants and animals are the primary source of health care for 80% of the world's population.

ECONOMIC VALUE
Scientists estimate that ecosystems worldwide provide goods and services, such as nutrient recycling and waste treatment, valued at more than $20 trillion a year.

EXTINCTION RISK
One in every eight birds and one in every four mammals face a high risk of extinction in the near future.

BEETLEMANIA
Beetles are the most diverse life-form on Earth. More than a thousand different kinds can live on a single tree in the forests of South America.

TEXT AND GEOBYTES

A blue box on each spread is headed GeoBytes—short, striking facts chosen on a need-to-know or fun-to-know basis. Each thematic spread is introduced with a text block that discusses the theme and alludes to the graphic presentations. Each map or graphic is anchored by explanatory text for a complete and coherent unit.

OTHER UNIQUE FEATURES

The Atlas employs a variety of images and mapping techniques to express data. A cartogram, for instance, depicts the size of an object, such as a country, in relation to an attribute, not geographic space. Grounded in research by the Population Reference Bureau, this cartogram represents countries by unit of population, with only a suggestive nod to geographical location. An economic cartogram shows the relative prosperity of the countries of the world. In both cases, editors chose cartograms as the most visually striking way to convey the information.

On a map showing the distribution of human population, LandScan global population databases were used, as the most reliable and visually striking tool. While this Atlas is distinguished by its thematic maps, individual thematic maps are, in turn, distinguished by the number of variables analyzed. For example, a thematic map on economy shows Gross Domestic Product by agriculture, manufacturing, and services. Another on land cover parses out pasture, cropland, and forest.

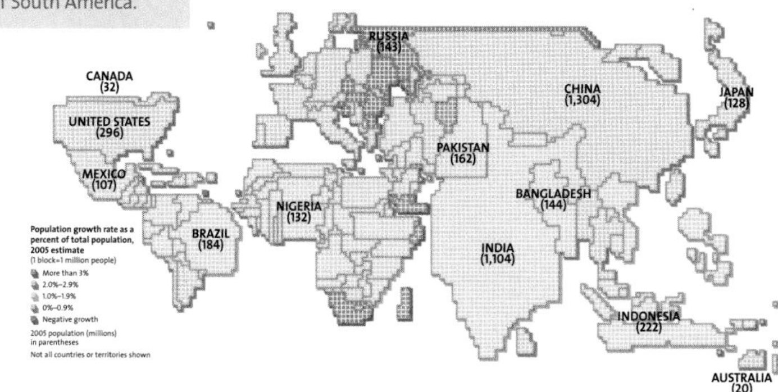

MAP SCALE RELATIONSHIPS IN THIS ATLAS

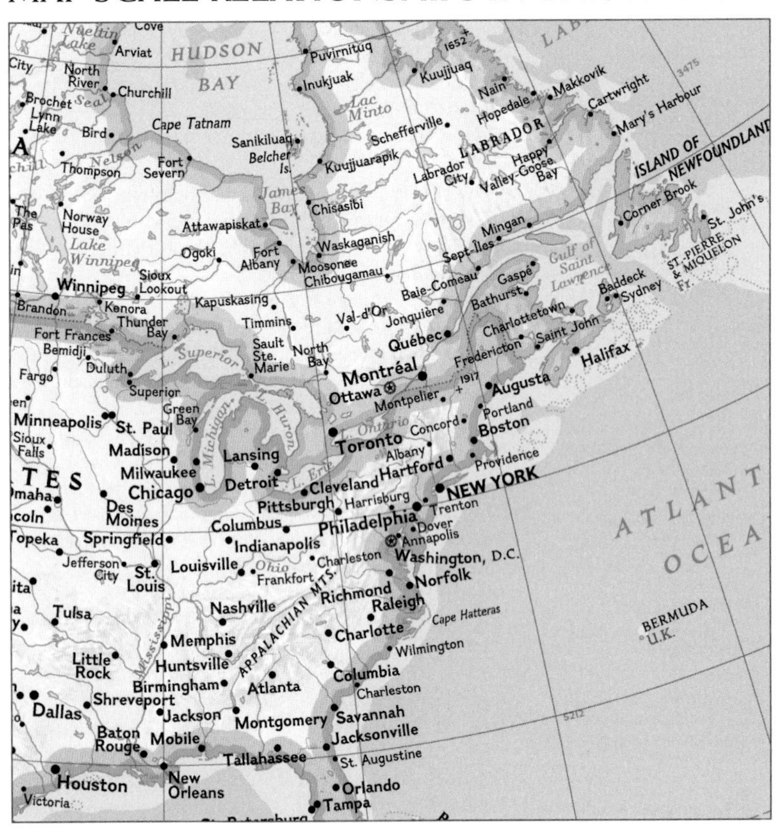

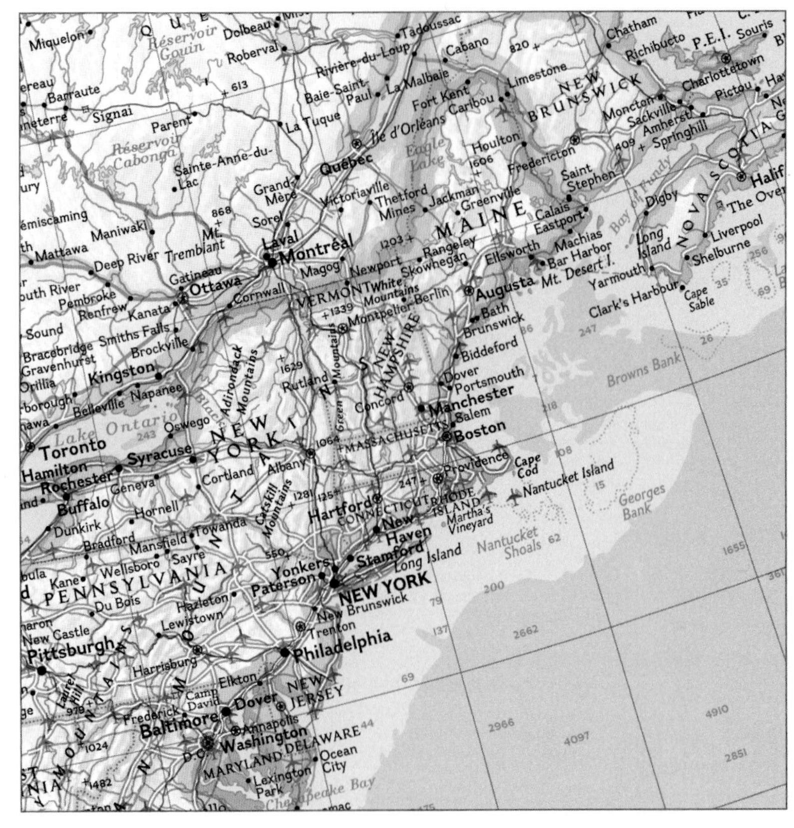

MAP PROJECTIONS

▲ **LAMBERT AZIMUTHAL EQUAL-AREA**
Distortion away from the center makes this projection a poor choice for world maps but useful for fairly circular regions. It is used on the Trade & Globalization spread, pages 56-57, in the Income Group, 2005, map.

▼ **ORTHOGRAPHIC**
Designed to show Earth as seen from a distant point in space, the orthographic is usually used to portray hemispheres. Distortion at the edges, however, compresses landmasses.

▲ **ALBERS CONIC EQUAL-AREA**
The Albers is a good format for mapping mid-latitude regions that are larger east to west than north to south. Most maps of the United States in the Atlas appear on this projection.

▲ **AZIMUTHAL EQUIDISTANT**
Mapmakers can choose any center point, from which directions and distances are true, but in outer areas shapes and sizes are distorted. On this projection, Antarctica, the Arctic Ocean, and several continents appear.

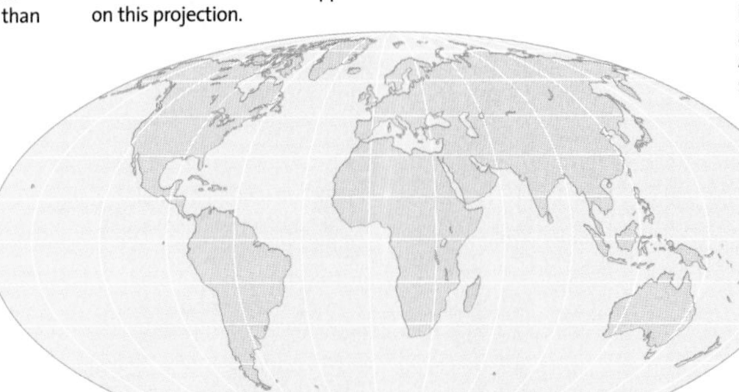

▲ **MOLLWEIDE**
In 1805, Carl B. Mollweide, a German mathematician, devised this elliptical equal-area projection that represents relative sizes accurately but distorts shapes at the edges. Many thematic maps in the Atlas use the Mollweide.

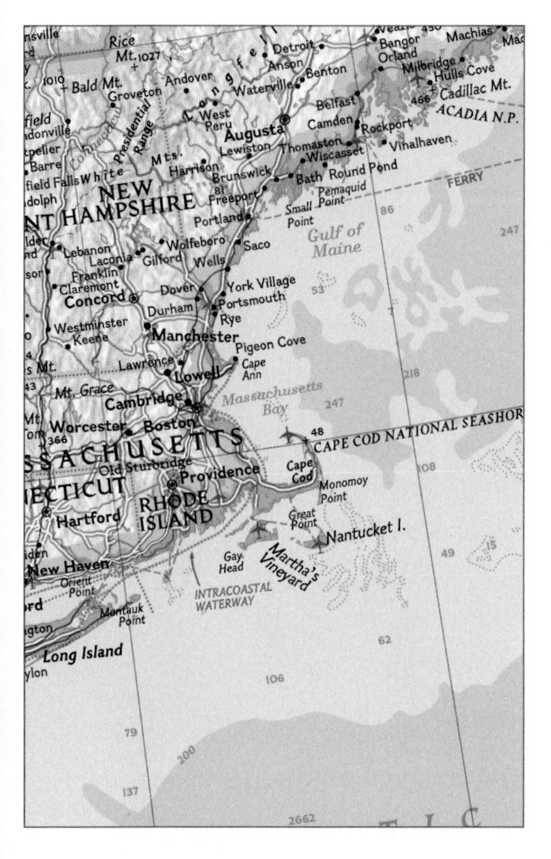

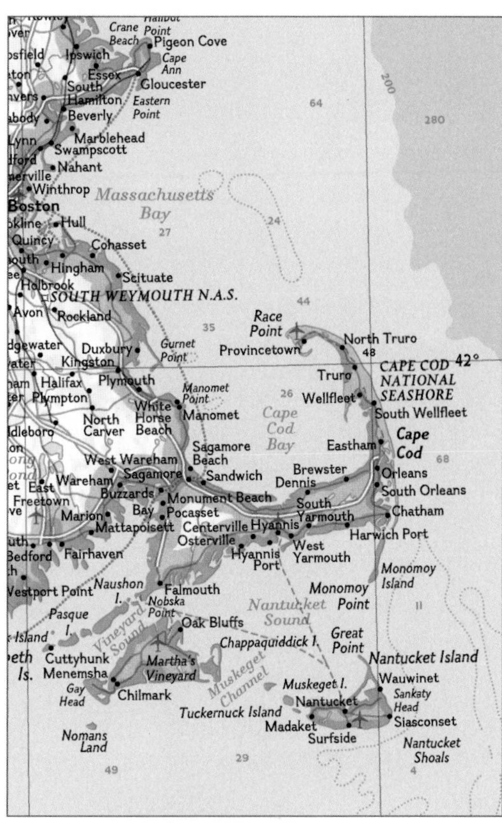

Map scale describes the relationship between distance on a map and distance on the ground. It is usually presented as a ratio or fraction in any of three ways. Verbal scale is a written description of scale, such as "one centimeter equals 100 kilometers," meaning one centimeter on the map is equal to 100 kilometers on the ground. A graphic scale is a bar or line with tick marks showing units such as kilometers or miles that graphically represent scale. A representative fraction (RF) or ratio scale indicates how much the size of a physical area was reduced to fit on the map by showing the relationship between one unit on the map and one unit of the same length on the ground. For example, if the scale is in centimeters and reads 1:10,000,000 (or 1/10,000,000), then each centimeter on the map represents 100 kilometers on the ground.

Political maps in this Atlas were created in a range of scales from global cartographic databases that merged data from maps NGS created in the past. These "seamless" databases give NGS the ability to map anywhere in the world at an appropriate scale.

From left to right, these four maps illustrate the relationship between the scale of a map and the area shown. The area shown decreases as scale increases, while the level of detail shown increases. Smaller scale maps such as the U.S. map on the far left (1:36,000,000) show more area but only the largest features are visible. Large scale maps, such as the map of Cape Cod (1:1,750,000), show a small area but in greater detail.

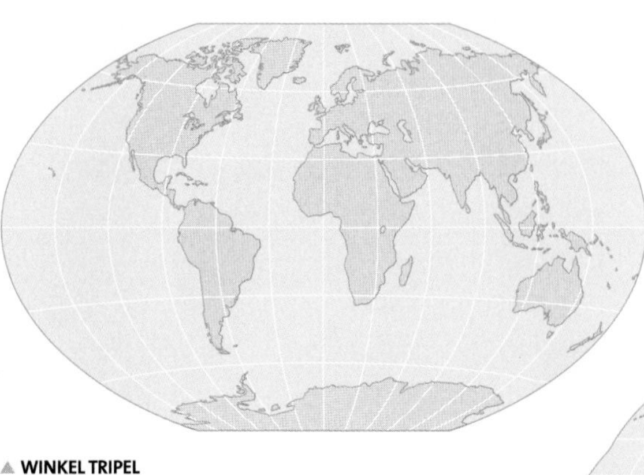

▲ **WINKEL TRIPEL**
First developed by Oswald Winkel in 1921, this "tripel" projection avoids the congestion and compression of polar areas that are common to many projections. The shapes of countries and islands closely resemble their true shapes as one would see on a globe.

▼ **INTERRUPTED GOODE HOMOLOSINE**
To minimize distortion of shape and preserve horizontal scale, this projection interrupts the globe. Its equal-area quality makes it suitable for mapping distributions of various kinds of information.

▶ **BUCKMINSTER FULLER**
Also known as the "Dymaxion map," this projection created by Richard Buckminster Fuller in the mid-20th century mostly retains the relative size of each part of the globe. Because the continents are not split, one can better see the interconnectedness of the Earth's landmasses.

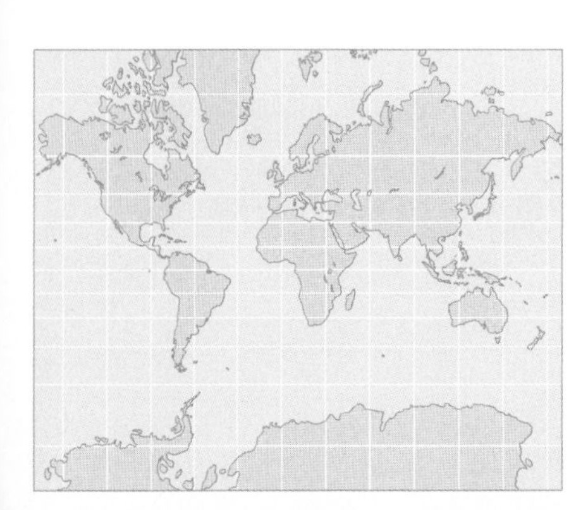

◀ **MERCATOR**
Named for Gerardus Mercator, the Flemish geographer who invented it in 1569, this most famous of all map projections was intended for navigation. Useful for showing constant bearings as straight lines, the Mercator greatly exaggerates areas at higher latitudes.

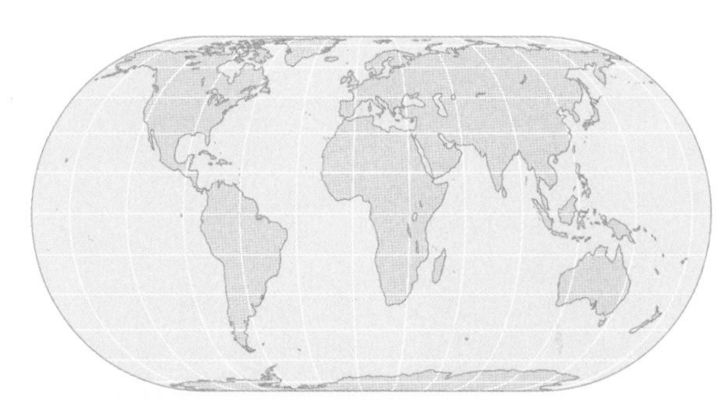

◀ **ECKERT EQUAL-AREA**
Produced by German educator Max Eckert, this projection represents the Poles by a line one-half the length of the Equator. Polar regions are less compressed than on elliptical projections; low-latitude landmasses are elongated.

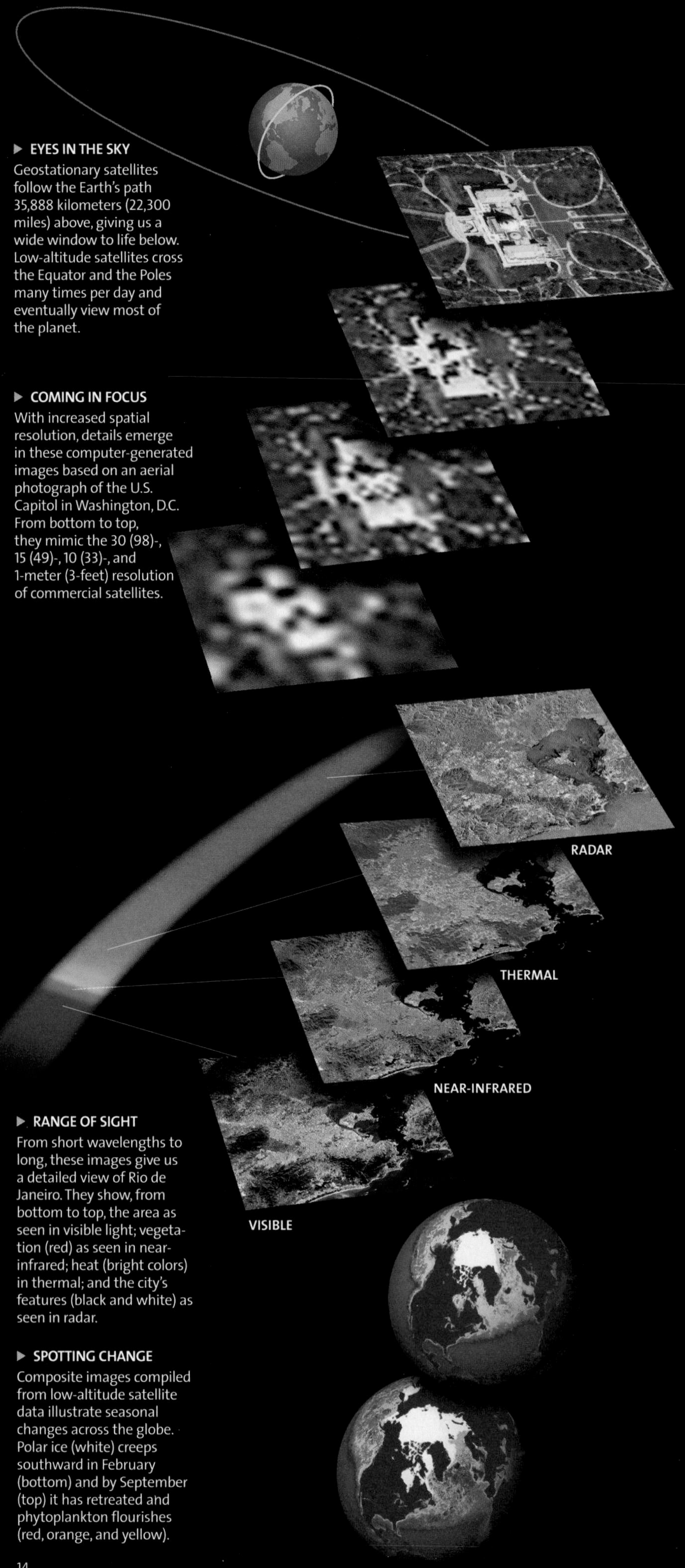

▶ EYES IN THE SKY
Geostationary satellites follow the Earth's path 35,888 kilometers (22,300 miles) above, giving us a wide window to life below. Low-altitude satellites cross the Equator and the Poles many times per day and eventually view most of the planet.

▶ COMING IN FOCUS
With increased spatial resolution, details emerge in these computer-generated images based on an aerial photograph of the U.S. Capitol in Washington, D.C. From bottom to top, they mimic the 30 (98)-, 15 (49)-, 10 (33)-, and 1-meter (3-feet) resolution of commercial satellites.

▶ RANGE OF SIGHT
From short wavelengths to long, these images give us a detailed view of Rio de Janeiro. They show, from bottom to top, the area as seen in visible light; vegetation (red) as seen in near-infrared; heat (bright colors) in thermal; and the city's features (black and white) as seen in radar.

▶ SPOTTING CHANGE
Composite images compiled from low-altitude satellite data illustrate seasonal changes across the globe. Polar ice (white) creeps southward in February (bottom) and by September (top) it has retreated and phytoplankton flourishes (red, orange, and yellow).

The human eye sees only a tiny fraction of the spectrum of electromagnetic radiation that illuminates the world, a narrow band known as "visible" radiation. With the aid of remote sensing, we are able to view a wider range of that spectrum, including infrared, thermal, and microwave bands. From space, we are also able to view large expanses of the Earth, as well as small areas, in great detail. From an altitude of 730 kilometers (454 miles), Landsat 7 can view features as small as 15 meters (49 feet) across. Scientists use remote-sensing satellite data to understand global processes on the Earth's surface, in the oceans, and in the lower atmosphere.

This mosaic image of North America illustrates some of the types of remotely sensed data that scientists have access to today. The eastern third of the continent shows clusters of light on the Earth's surface visible from space at night, helping us better understand urbanization and population density. False-color is used in the middle of the continent to show surface-feature classes. Reds and purples represent different classes or types of vegetation; blues show arid land. Images like this are useful for environmental monitoring. The westernmost part of the continent is in true color. The greener areas are more densely vegetated and less populated. Vibrant colors of the oceans represent sea-surface temperature. Areas in red are the warmest; the blues are the coolest.

To create this image, data were extracted from a number of datasets—the Advanced Very High Resolution Radiometer (AVHRR), the Moderate Resolution Imaging Spectroradiometer (MODIS), and versions 4, 5, and 7 of the Landsat Enhanced Thematic Mapper (ETM). The base of the image was enhanced with shaded relief produced from Shuttle Radar Topography Mission (SRTM) digital elevation model (DEM) data.

IMAGE BY ROBERT STACEY, WORLDSAT INTERNATIONAL INC.

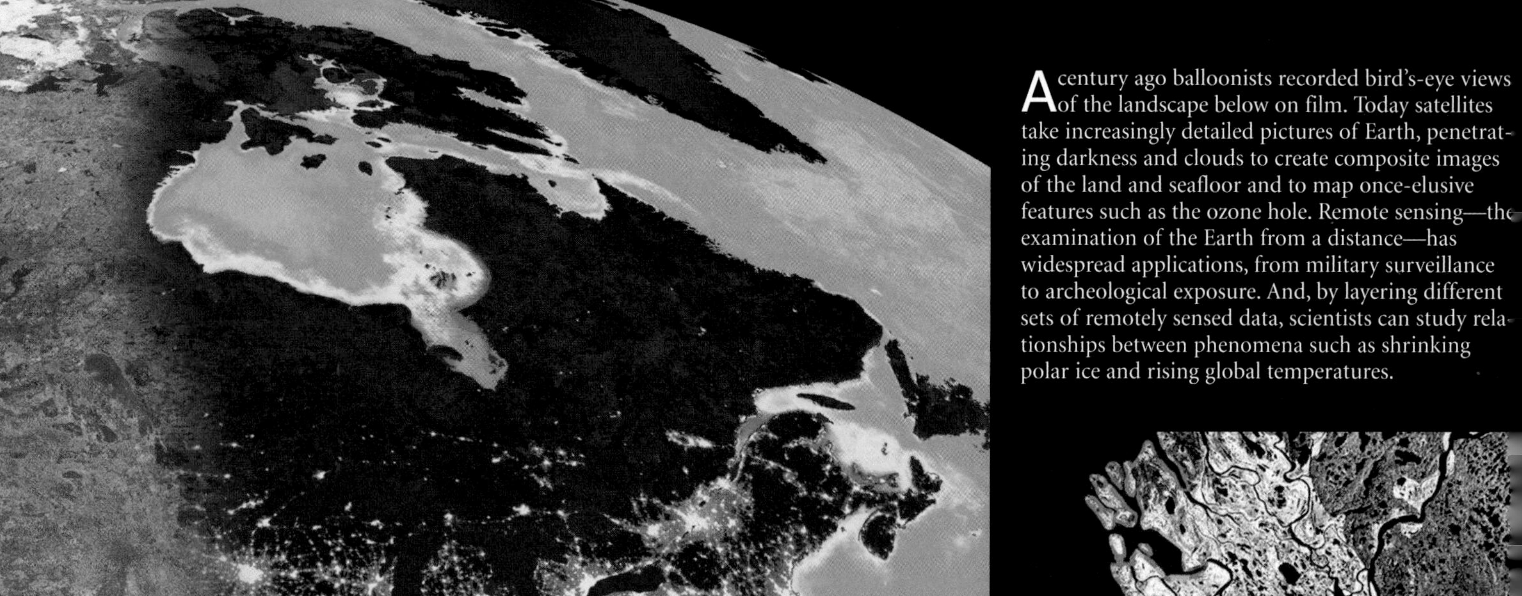

A century ago balloonists recorded bird's-eye views of the landscape below on film. Today satellites take increasingly detailed pictures of Earth, penetrating darkness and clouds to create composite images of the land and seafloor and to map once-elusive features such as the ozone hole. Remote sensing—the examination of the Earth from a distance—has widespread applications, from military surveillance to archeological exposure. And, by layering different sets of remotely sensed data, scientists can study relationships between phenomena such as shrinking polar ice and rising global temperatures.

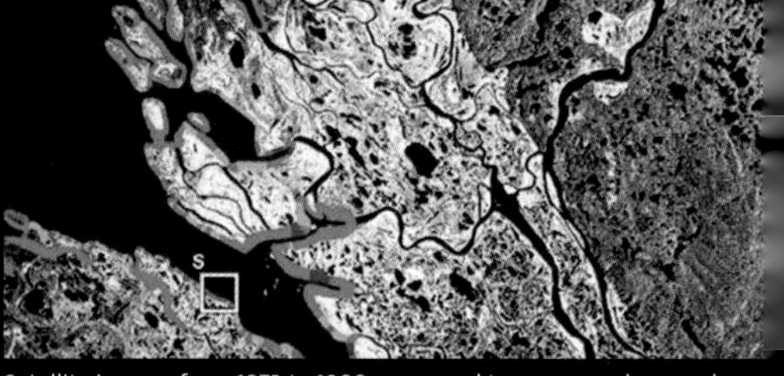

Satellite images from 1973 to 1999 were used to measure change along Canada's Beaufort Sea coastline, an area highly sensitive to erosion. This image illustrates areas of rapid erosion (red), moderate erosion (orange), no detectable erosion (green), and accretion (blue).

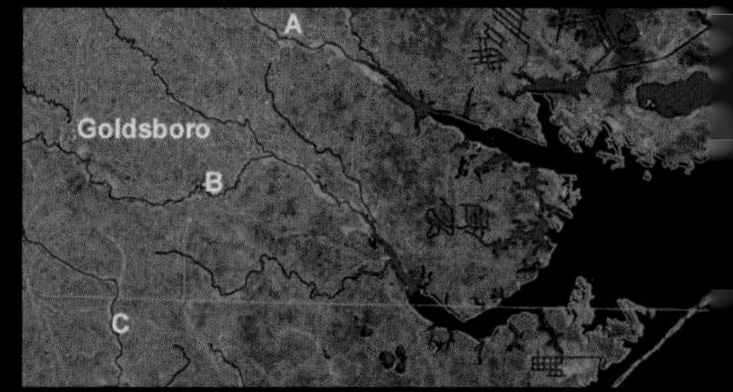

This image shows the widespread flooding that occurred throughout North Carolina in late September 1999 after the region was hit by Hurricanes Dennis and Floyd. Flooded areas are shown in light blue, rivers in dark blue, roads in red, and the coastline in green.

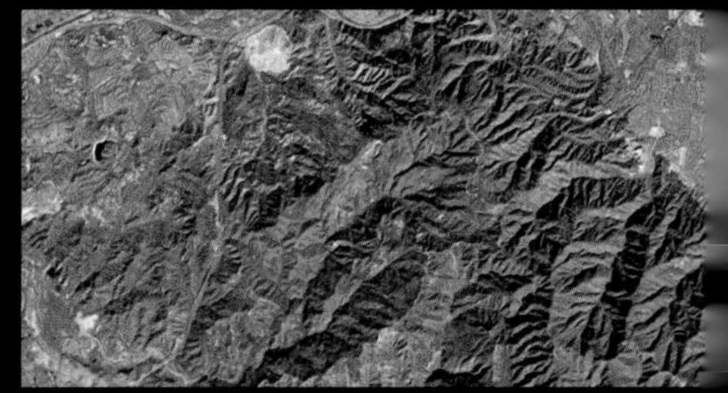

Nearly 4,450 hectares (11,000 acres) burned in the February 2006 Sierra fire in Orange County, California. Deep red tones in the center of this Landsat image show the burned areas on February 12th, the day the fire was contained.

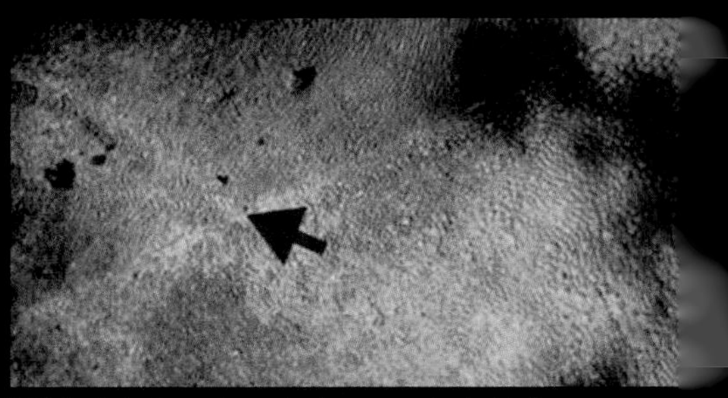

With the help of remote-sensing imagery, archeologists have identified ancient footpaths in the Arenal Region of Costa Rica. These 2,500-year-old footpaths are being used to study the prehistoric religious, economic, political, and social organization of the region.

UNDERSTANDING OUR WORLD THROUGH GIS

Geographic Information Systems (GIS) is a digitally organized collection of computer hardware, software, methodology, and data assemblage and storage. GIS supports the capture, manipulation, and analysis of place-based information. A highly adaptable tool, GIS provides the means to store and display geographic data and to analyze and describe patterns, distributions, and phenomena. Because so many human and environmental issues can be usefully considered in geographic terms, GIS is becoming increasingly common across a range of enterprises. Foresters use GIS data to inventory trees. Epidemiologists model and predict the spread of disease. Policy makers, environmentalists, and city planners employ GIS technologies to analyze issues and provide dramatic visualizations for matters ranging from wildfire management in the western United States to the rates of suburban sprawl in India's burgeoning cities. The attraction of GIS comes from the magnitude of its analytical capabilities that, in turn, derive from once-unimaginable powers of manipulation of spatial data to suit specific needs. For example, a table with latitude/longitude coordinates of car crashes can be overlaid with a road network to route emergency service vehicles and estimate their arrival time. Combine the crash incident database with other geospatial data, such as terrain, weather, transportation infrastructure, or socioeconomic characteristics, and traffic planners can determine contributing factors to accidents and recommend preventative action. More and more, GIS is the analytical tool for understanding patterns and processes that affect our lives.

Vector data (point)

Vector data (line)

Vector data (polygon)

Raster data (relief)

Raster data (population density classes)

Vector and raster data combined (physical)

Vector and raster data combined (political)

◄ **GEOGRAPHIC DATA LAYERS**
GIS enables the layering of data. Vector data represents precise location in terms of a point (a city or airport, for example), a line (roadways, rivers, boundaries), or a polygon (an enclosed area such as a body of water or a protected area category). Raster data presents continuous data (such as elevation) or classes of data (for example, population densities) that cover the area in pixels, the discrete elements that make up an image. Vector and raster data are geographically referenced, allowing for overlay.

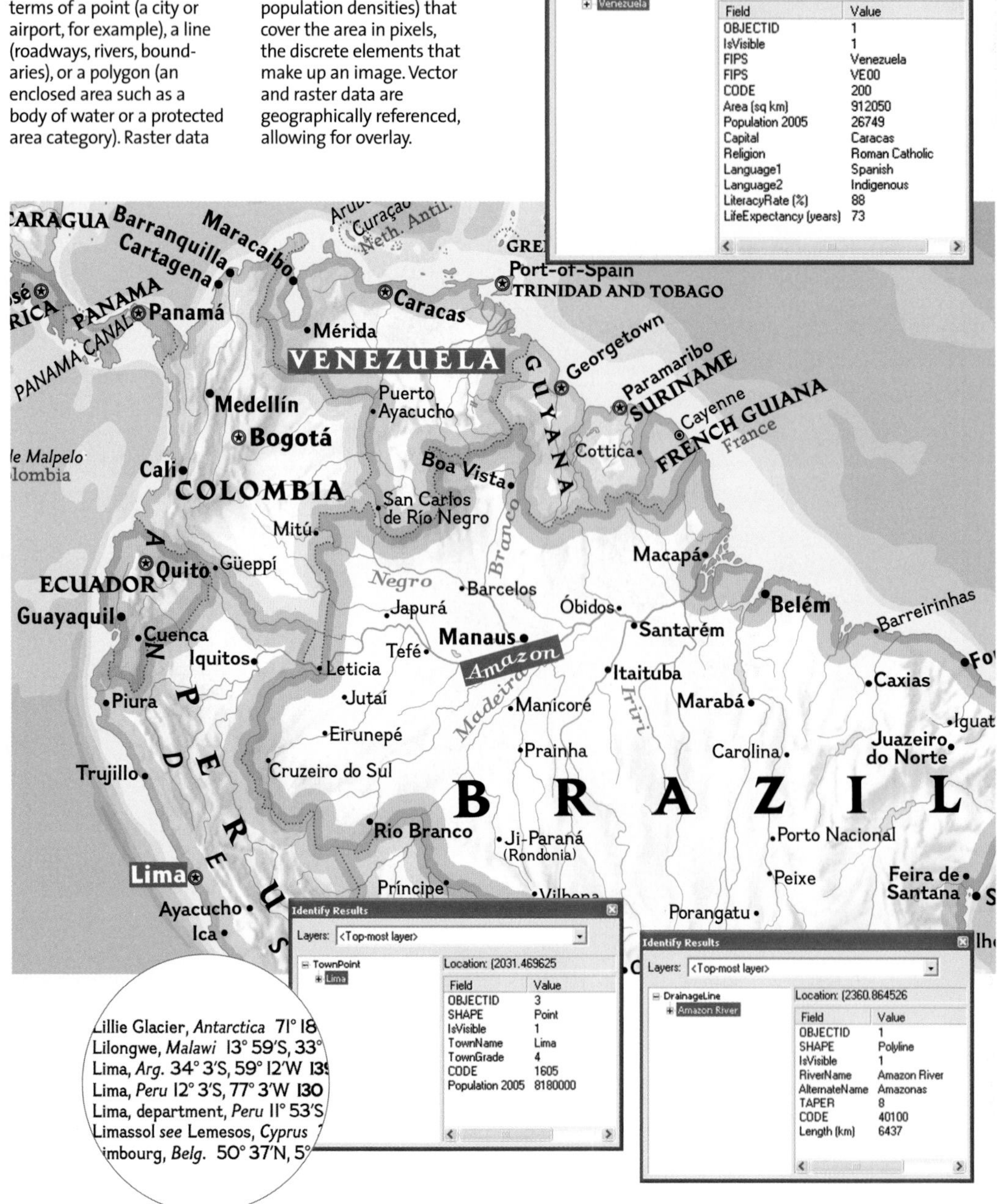

▲ **GIS DATA STRUCTURE**
GIS data have both spatial and attribute components. Spatial components are mapped features, such as the cities and rivers on this map of South America. Attribute components consist of stored data, as shown in the windows above. Attribute components might include, for example, socioeconomic characteristics of a city. GIS correlates spatial and attribute data, creating overlays that reveal geospatial relationships. Another use of GIS is digital indexing, which constituted a major advance over laborious and error-prone manual compilation. This Atlas used customized GIS software to coordinate place-names with latitude and longitude (bubble).

GEOSPATIAL CONCEPTS

At the dawn of the Age of Exploration, the problem facing mapmakers was a dearth of information. With geospatial data flowing from satellite imagery, aerial photography, on-the-ground surveying, quantitative data, and archival records, the challenge for cartographers became how to manage a wealth of information. Geographic Information Systems (GIS), a sophisticated and versatile digital tool set with a wide range of applications, provides a solution. The data management capabilities of this digital technology make geospatial information readily available for analysis, modeling, and mapping. Scientists use GIS to inventory plant and animal species in their native habitats. Disaster relief managers identify at-risk areas and evacuation routes. The 2004 U.S. presidential election marked the first time that GIS software was used to collate and present near-real-time voting tallies. While GIS allows the layering of information, on-board and handheld Global Positioning System (GPS) devices pinpoint location. Today, geospatial concepts permeate ordinary life to an extraordinary degree.

URBAN PLANNING

GIS can be used to inventory and visualize urban land use patterns. The strict code of zoning laws and classifications common to cities and towns requires an accurate database management system. GIS can not only manage the zoning database but can also portray the data in a map. Such visualization can help clarify development issues, plan resource allocations, or identify park and open space needs. Maps with specific GIS overlays can provide common ground for discussion in public forums that may address questions of, for example, school zones, land ownership, or sprawl.

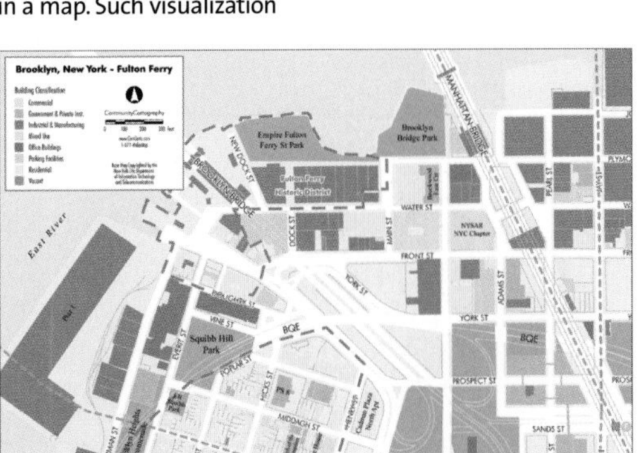

TRANSPORTATION

Many applications of GIS exist within the transportation sector and work particularly well when coupled with the pinpoint accuracy of Global Positioning System (GPS) technology. Freight shipping companies frequently turn to GIS to estimate arrival times of their trucks, using real-time traffic information, digital representations of nationwide transportation infrastructure, and GPS information. Individual drivers have become accustomed to using GIS and GPS for finding directions and avoiding traffic jams.

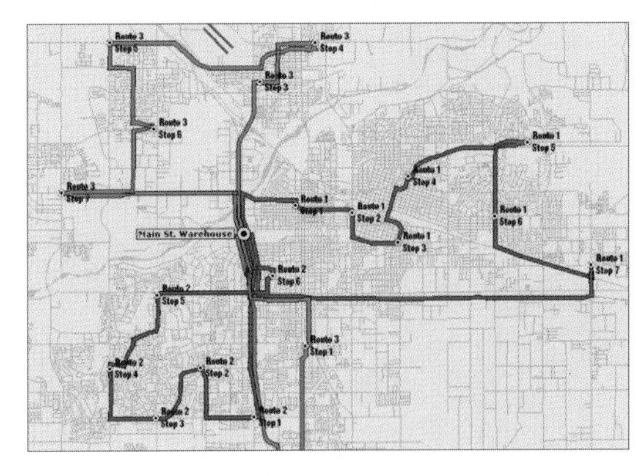

EMERGENCY MANAGEMENT

In emergency management, GIS can be used to model potential disasters, track real-time weather, plan and adjust evacuation routes, define disaster areas, and inventory damage. Predicting and tracking wildfire helps fire management crews plan and allocate resources. GIS can show the before-and-after appearance of the land affected by a disaster, which can help recovery and show how to plan ahead for next time.

DEMOGRAPHICS & CENSUS

The U.S. Census Bureau stores demographic and socioeconomic data at numerous levels, even at the county, tract, or city-block level. Applying spatial analysis techniques to such archival data can reveal patterns, trends, and distributions. The findings can be put to various uses, including encouraging economic development or indicating the results of elections.

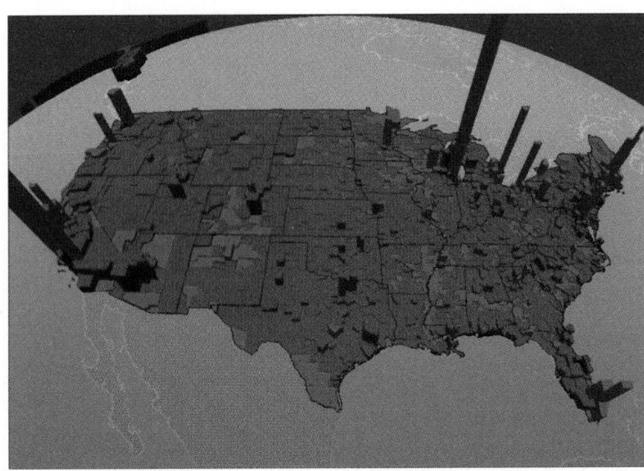

HEALTH

During the 2002-03 SARS outbreak in China, an Internet GIS server allowed for the rapid collection and dissemination of data to health officials and the public. This application tracked the spread of the disease, detected patterns, and distributed accurate information. GIS is currently being used to monitor the H5N1 strain of avian flu around the world, combining outbreaks with pertinent data such as wildfowl migration routes and locations of poultry farms.

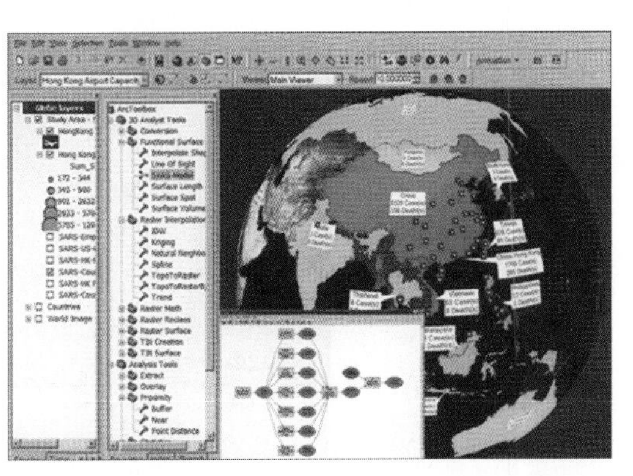

CONSERVATION

Mapping the effects of human population growth and deforestation on Asian elephant habitat highlights the versatility of GIS. Satellite images, demographic data, and elephant locations derived from radio tracking and GPS yielded a comprehensive database and visualization of elephant viability in Myanmar (formerly Burma). The study demonstrated that the rate of deforestation caused by human population growth was lower here than in most countries of Southeast Asia and that as a result elephant populations were less affected .

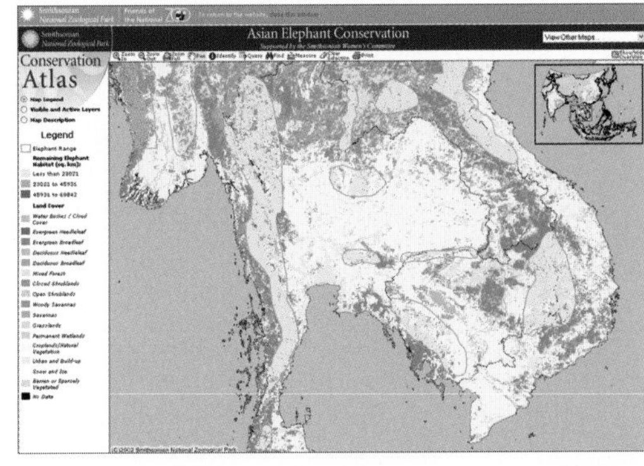

GeoBytes

BORN IN THE SIXTIES
GIS is a young field, having its beginnings in the 1960s, during the so-called Quantitative Revolution in Geography.

GIS IN COLLEGE
Some 200 universities and colleges offer majors or courses in GIS, with most but not all in Geography departments.

GIS AT WORK
The list of professions that utilize GIS continues to grow and now includes agriculture, archaeology, banking, biology, cartography, civil engineering, ecology, economics, forestry, health care, meteorology, public policy and safety, transportation, urban planning, and utilities.

GIS IN OIL AND GAS
The oil and gas industries use GIS, often combining satellite imagery and radar scans of the Earth's surface to "see through the ground" for new discoveries.

IN SERVICE TO OTHERS
After Hurricanes Katrina and Rita in 2005, nearly a thousand GIS professionals volunteered to gather field data and use GIS to aid recovery on the U.S. Gulf Coast.

MORE THAN MAPS
Anything with a spatial dimension can be recorded, stored, analyzed, and visualized within GIS.

GIS AND GPS TOGETHER
GIS, along with GPS, is used in archaeology to inventory artifacts and digitally recreate ancient sites.

DATA DATA DATA
Local, state, and federal governments are the major producers of GIS data.

HIGH MAINTENANCE
The collection and maintenance of data are the most expensive activities in GIS, sometimes running into the tens of millions of dollars for a field such as transportation asset management.

Earth was born of an agglomeration of dust and rock, gravity sucking ever more fragments into its mass as the young planet wobbled in its orbital path. Early on, an infant planet about the size of Mars struck Earth. With the aggregation of solid particles from the impact, the Moon took shape. Earth stabilized in its orbit around the Sun. A bombardment of comets and asteroids pocked the Moon; Earth absorbed meteor hits with little visible impact. Continents drifted and collided, oceans filled the basins. Another great agent of change, life in the form of massive colonies of photosynthesizing cyanobacteria pumped oxygen into the atmosphere. Oxygen-breathing organisms evolved on land. Now humans—all six billion and more—have become a major force. Our burning of fossil fuels pumps carbon dioxide, a major greenhouse gas, into the atmosphere and heats the planet. Industrial and agricultural chemicals, human effluent, and rubbish pollute land, air, and water. Travel, more common and speedier than ever before, spreads ideas, commerce, culture, alien plant and animal species, and diseases at an unprecedented rate. Resources of food and fuel are unevenly distributed. Ideologies clash; turmoil and wars devastate societies. Yet good will, learning, and ingenuity may be marshaled to mitigate adverse consequences. Earth goes forward on its own course and in its own time. The adventure continues, and geography helps to write the record.

HUMAN FOOTPRINT COURTESY OF WILDLIFE CONSERVATION SOCIETY

THE

PHYSICAL REGIONS

This artist-rendered relief map depicts Earth's landforms above and below the surface of the ocean. Major mountain systems are shaded to emphasize their elevation. The Himalaya tower over India's Ganges plain; the Andes and Rocky Mountains reign over the Americas. All are dwarfed by the Mid-Atlantic Ridge, a submarine mountain range that stretches from Iceland to near Antarctica.

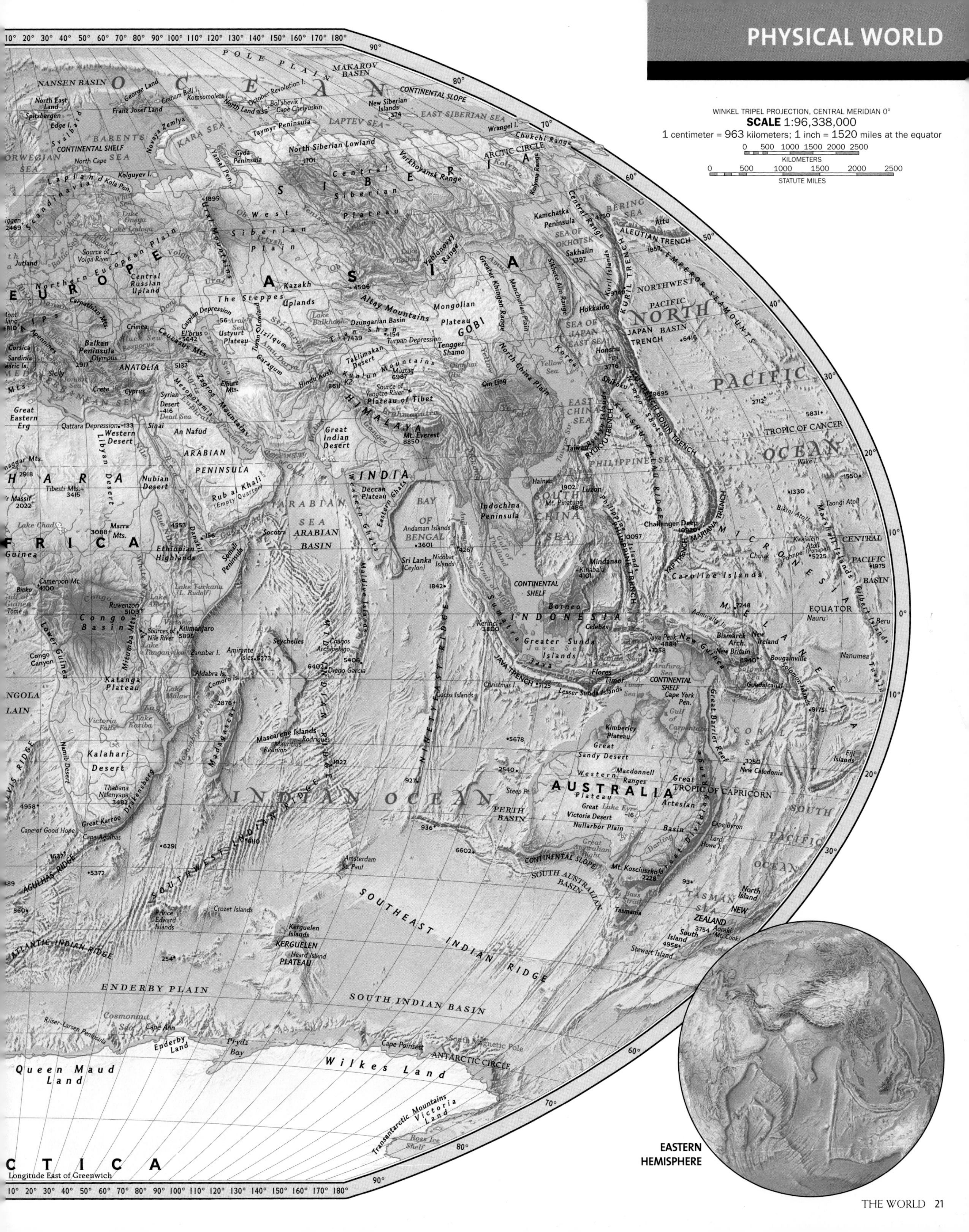
WINKEL TRIPEL PROJECTION, CENTRAL MERIDIAN 0°
SCALE 1:96,338,000
1 centimeter = 963 kilometers; 1 inch = 1520 miles at the equator
0 500 1000 1500 2000 2500
KILOMETERS
0 500 1000 1500 2000 2500
STATUTE MILES
POLE PLAIN
MAKAROV BASIN
NANSEN BASIN
OCEAN
CONTINENTAL SLOPE
North East Land
Spitsbergen
Edge I.
Svalbard
George Land
Franz Josef Land
Graham Bell I.
Komsomolets I.
October Revolution I.
Bol'shevik I.
Cape Chelyuskin
North Land
New Siberian Islands
EAST SIBERIAN SEA
Wrangel I.
LAPTEV SEA
Taymyr Peninsula
KARA SEA
BARENTS SEA
CONTINENTAL SHELF
Novaya Zemlya
NORWEGIAN SEA
North Cape
Kolguyev I.
Yamal Pen.
Gyda Peninsula
North Siberian Lowland
Chukchi Range
ARCTIC CIRCLE
Kolyma Range
Verkhoyansk Range
Central Siberian Plateau
SIBERIA
Lapland
Kola Pen.
Scandinavia
Lake Onega
Lake Ladoga
Ural Mountains
West Siberian Plain
BERING SEA
Kamchatka Peninsula
SEA OF OKHOTSK
Sakhalin
Central Range
Attu
ALEUTIAN TRENCH
EMPEROR SEAMOUNTS
Jutland
Source of Volga River
Northern European Plain
Central Russian Upland
EUROPE
ASIA
Yablonovyy Range
Greater Khingan Range
Manchurian Plain
Sikhote Alin Range
Kuril Islands
KURIL TRENCH
NORTHWEST PACIFIC BASIN
NORTH
Hokkaido
SEA OF JAPAN (EAST SEA)
JAPAN BASIN
JAPAN TRENCH
Honshu
Fuji
Kazakh Uplands
The Steppes
Altay Mountains
Mongolian Plateau
GOBI
Lake Balkhash
Dzungarian Basin
Tian Shan
Turpan Depression
Caspian Depression
Carpathian Mts.
ALPS
Crimea
El'brus
Caucasus Mts.
Ustyurt Plateau
Qizilqum
Garagum
Taklimakan Desert
Kunlun Mountains
Muztag
Tengger Shamo
North China Plain
Korea
Yellow Sea
Corsica
Sardinia
Balkan Peninsula
Olympus
Apennines
Sicily
ANATOLIA
Crete
Cyprus
Elburz Mts.
Zagros Mountains
Mesopotamia
Hindu Kush
K2
Source of Yangtze River
Plateau of Tibet
Qin Ling
EAST CHINA SEA
Shikoku
KYUSHU-PALAU RIDGE
BONIN TRENCH
PACIFIC
Great Eastern Erg
Syrian Desert
Dead Sea
Qattara Depression
Western Desert
Libyan Desert
Sinai
An Nafūd
HIMALAYA
Mt. Everest
Great Indian Desert
Taiwan
RYUKYU TRENCH
PHILIPPINE SEA
TROPIC OF CANCER
OCEAN
Wake I.
ARABIAN PENINSULA
INDIA
Nubian Desert
Tibesti Mts.
SAHARA
Rub al Khali (Empty Quarter)
Deccan Plateau
Western Ghats
Eastern Ghats
BAY OF BENGAL
Hainan
Luzon
Mt. Pinatubo
Indochina Peninsula
SOUTH CHINA SEA
PHILIPPINE TRENCH
Challenger Deep
MARIANA TRENCH
MICRONESIA
Bikini Atoll
Taongi Atoll
Marshall Islands
Lake Chad
Marra Mts.
AFRICA
Guinea
Ethiopian Highlands
Danakil
Socotra
ARABIAN SEA
ARABIAN BASIN
Andaman Islands
Nicobar Islands
Sri Lanka (Ceylon)
Gulf of Thailand
Strait of Malacca
Mindanao
Kinabalu
YAP TRENCH
Chuuk
Pohnpei
Kwajalein Atoll
CENTRAL PACIFIC BASIN
Caroline Islands
Somali Peninsula
Lake Turkana (L. Rudolf)
Cameroon Mt.
Bioko
Gulf of Guinea
São Tomé
Congo Basin
Ruwenzori
Lake Albert
Lake Victoria
Sources of Nile River
Kilimanjaro
Maldive Islands
CONTINENTAL SHELF
Borneo
INDONESIA
Sumatra
Kerinci
Celebes
Admiralty Is.
MELANESIA
EQUATOR
Nauru
Beru
Gilbert Islands
Lower Guinea
Congo Canyon
Mitumba Mts.
Lake Tanganyika
Zanzibar I.
Amirante Isles
Seychelles
Chagos Archipelago
Diego Garcia
MID-INDIAN RIDGE
NINETYEAST RIDGE
Greater Sunda Islands
Java Sea
Java
JAVA TRENCH
Flores
Timor
Lesser Sunda Islands
Jaya Peak
New Guinea
Bismarck Arch.
New Ireland
New Britain
Bougainville
Solomon Islands
Guadalcanal
Nanumea
Tuvalu
Katanga Plateau
Aldabra Is.
Comoro Is.
Lake Malawi
Lake Kariba
Victoria Falls
Mozambique Channel
Madagascar
Christmas I.
Cocos Islands
Arafura Sea
CONTINENTAL SHELF
Cape York Pen.
Gulf of Carpentaria
Great Barrier Reef
ANGOLA PLAIN
Mascarene Islands
Mauritius
Rodrigues
Réunion
Kimberley Plateau
Great Sandy Desert
CORAL SEA
Fiji Islands
New Caledonia
Kalahari Desert
Namib Desert
WALVIS RIDGE
Thabana Ntlenyana
Drakensberg
Great Karroo
Cape of Good Hope
Cape Agulhas
INDIAN OCEAN
SOUTHWEST INDIAN RIDGE
Steep Pt.
PERTH BASIN
AUSTRALIA
Western Plateau
Macdonnell Ranges
Great Artesian Basin
TROPIC OF CAPRICORN
Great Dividing Range
Lake Eyre
Great Victoria Desert
Nullarbor Plain
Cape Byron
Lord Howe I.
SOUTH PACIFIC OCEAN
Great Australian Bight
CONTINENTAL SLOPE
Darling
Mt. Kosciuszko
Amsterdam
St. Paul
AGULHAS RIDGE
SOUTHEAST INDIAN RIDGE
SOUTH AUSTRALIAN BASIN
Bass Strait
Tasmania
TASMAN SEA
North Island
NEW ZEALAND
South Island
Aoraki (Mt. Cook)
Stewart Island
Crozet Islands
Prince Edward Islands
Kerguelen Islands
KERGUELEN PLATEAU
Heard Island
ATLANTIC-INDIAN RIDGE
ENDERBY PLAIN
SOUTH INDIAN BASIN
Cosmonaut Sea
Riiser-Larsen Peninsula
Cape Ann
Enderby Land
Prydz Bay
Cape Poinsett
South Magnetic Pole
ANTARCTIC CIRCLE
Queen Maud Land
Wilkes Land
Transantarctic Mountains
Victoria Land
Ross Ice Shelf
ANTARCTICA
Longitude East of Greenwich
EASTERN HEMISPHERE

POLITICAL BOUNDARIES

The world is divided into 193 independent countries, with colors on the map showing the extents of national sovereignty. International boundaries only occasionally mark true cultural boundaries; they are more often a complex artifact of colonialism, conquest, religious conversion, and conflict. The political map is a useful but all-too-neat construct for a bewilderingly complicated world.

WINKEL TRIPEL PROJECTION, CENTRAL MERIDIAN 0°
SCALE 1:96,338,000
1 centimeter = 963 kilometers; 1 inch = 1520 miles at the equator
0 500 1000 1500 2000 2500
KILOMETERS
0 500 1000 1500 2000 2500
STATUTE MILES
Longitude East of Greenwich
R U S S I A
K A Z A K H S T A N
M O N G O L I A
C H I N A
I N D I A
I N D O N E S I A
A U S T R A L I A
I N D I A N O C E A N
PACIFIC OCEAN
SOUTH PACIFIC OCEAN
TROPIC OF CANCER
TROPIC OF CAPRICORN
EQUATOR
ARCTIC CIRCLE
ANTARCTIC CIRCLE
Date Line
SOUTH INDIAN BASIN
ATLANTIC - INDIAN RIDGE
SOUTHWEST INDIAN RIDGE
SOUTHEAST INDIAN RIDGE
MID-INDIAN RIDGE
NINETYEAST RIDGE
Winter Extent of Sea Ice
South Magnetic Pole
WILKES LAND
VICTORIA LAND
TRANSANTARCTIC MOUNTAINS
ENDERBY LAND
ANTARCTIC REGION
0 600 km
0 600 mi
Azimuthal Equidistant Projection
• Research station
ANTARCTICA
WEST ANTARCTICA
EAST ANTARCTICA
South Pole
Queen Maud Land
Weddell Sea
Ross Sea
Ross Ice Shelf
Vinson Massif 4897 (16067ft)
Ellsworth Mts.
Polar Plateau
Amundsen-Scott U.S.

HISTORICAL EARTH AND TECTONICS

Cataclysms such as volcanoes and earthquakes, which occur most often along plate boundaries, capture attention, but the tectonic movement that underlies them is imperceptibly slow. How slow? The Mid-Atlantic Ridge, for example, which is being built up by magma oozing between the North American and African plates, grows at about the speed of a human fingernail.

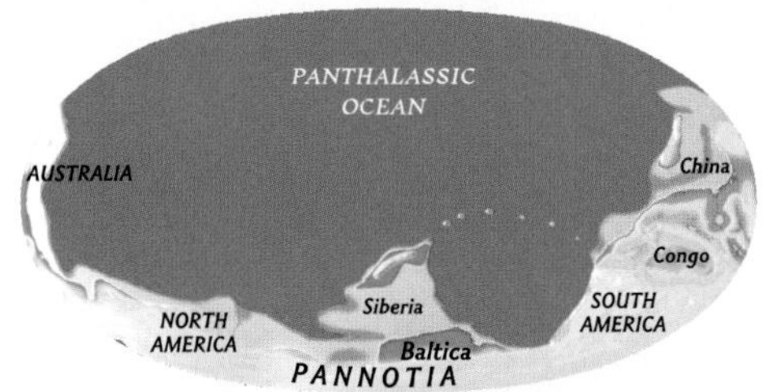

600 MILLION YEARS AGO
A supercontinent, known as Rodina, split apart, and oceans filled the basins. Fragments collided, thrusting up mountain ranges. Glaciers spread, twice covering the Equator. A new polar supercontinent, Pannotia, formed.

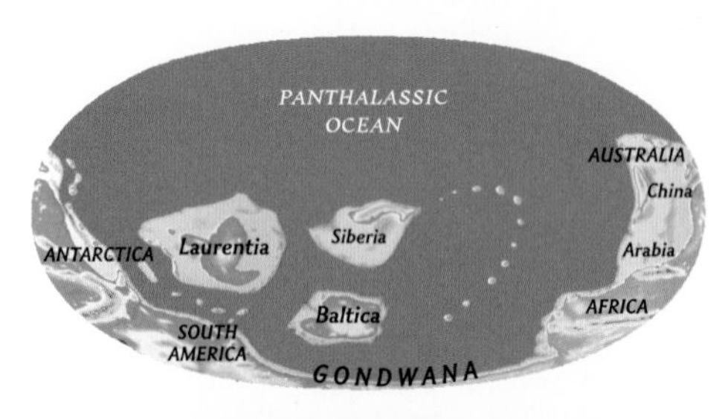

500 MILLION YEARS AGO
A breakaway chunk of Pannotia drifted north, splitting into three masses—Laurentia (North America), Baltica (northern Europe), and Siberia. In shallow waters, the first multicellular animals with exoskeletons appeared, and the Cambrian explosion of life took off.

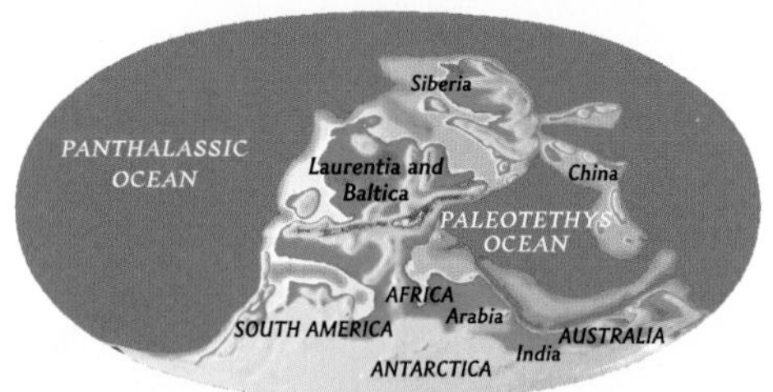

300 MILLION YEARS AGO
Laurentia collided with Baltica and later with Avalonia (Britain and New England). The Appalachian mountains arose along the edge of the supercontinent, Pangaea, as a new ice age ensued.

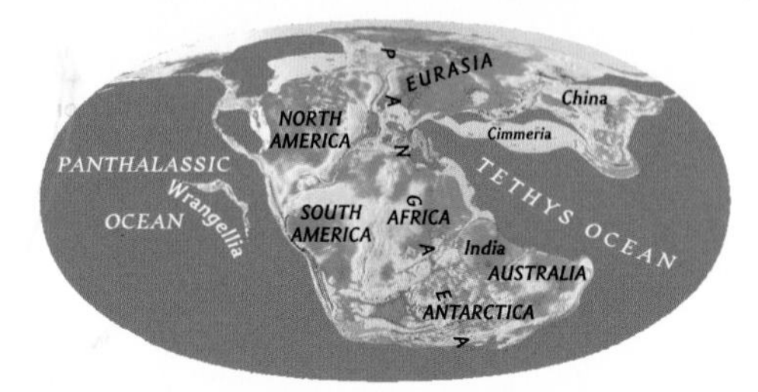

200 MILLION YEARS AGO
Dinosaurs roamed the Pangaean land mass, which stretched nearly from Pole to Pole and almost encircled Tethys, the oceanic ancestor of the Mediterranean Sea. The Pacific's predecessor, the immense Panthalassic Ocean, surrounded the supercontinent.

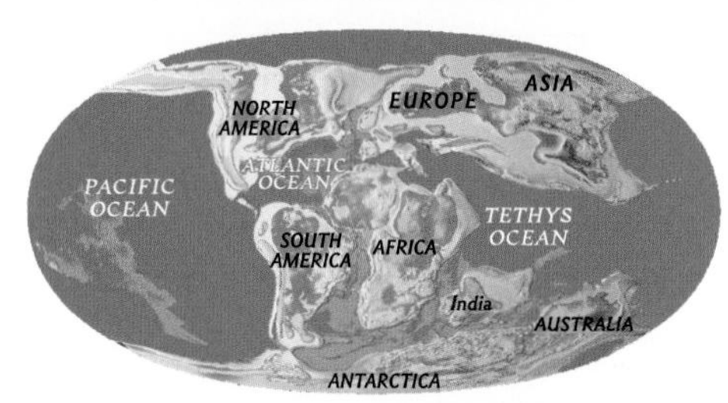

100 MILLION YEARS AGO
Pangaea broke apart. The Atlantic poured in between Africa and the Americas. India split away from Africa, and Antarctica and Australia were stranded near the South Pole.

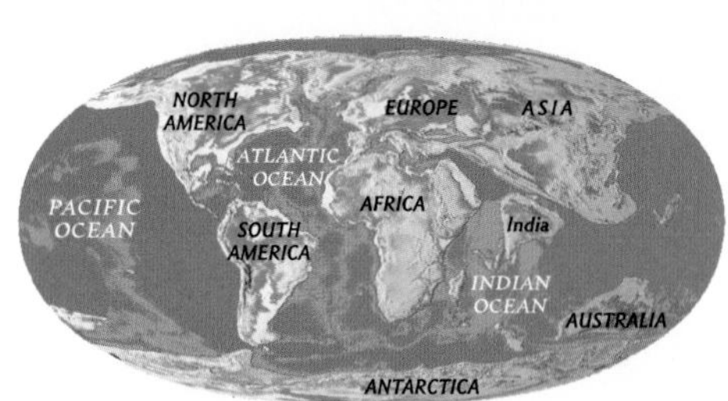

50 MILLION YEARS AGO
A meteorite wiped out the dinosaurs. Drifting continental fragments collided—Africa into Eurasia, pushing up the Alps; India into Asia, raising the Himalaya. Birds and once-tiny mammals began to fill the ecological niche vacated by dinosaurs.

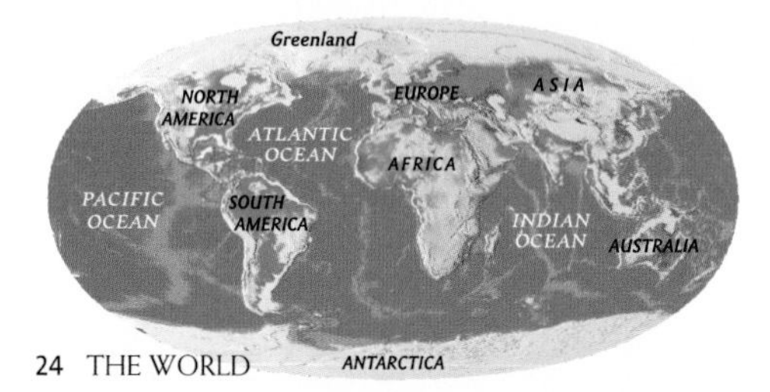

PRESENT DAY
Formation of the Isthmus of Panama and the split of Australia from Antarctica changed ocean currents, cooling the air. Ice sheets gouged out the Great Lakes just 20,000 years ago. Since then, warmer temperatures have melted ice, and sea levels have risen.

Tectonic feature
Plate boundary
- Divergent
- Convergent
- Transform zone

Plate motion
- Divergent (arrow length proportional to plate motion speed)
- Convergent
- Hot spot

Major tectonic event in the last 100 years
Earthquake
- Ten deadliest
- Ten costliest
- Other

Volcanic eruption
- Notable
- Known during the past 10,000 years

1.

1. SEAFLOOR SPREADING
Adjacent oceanic plates slowly diverge, at the rate of a few centimeters a year. Along such boundaries—the Mid-Atlantic Ridge and the East Pacific Rise—molten rock (magma) pours forth to form new crust (lithosphere).

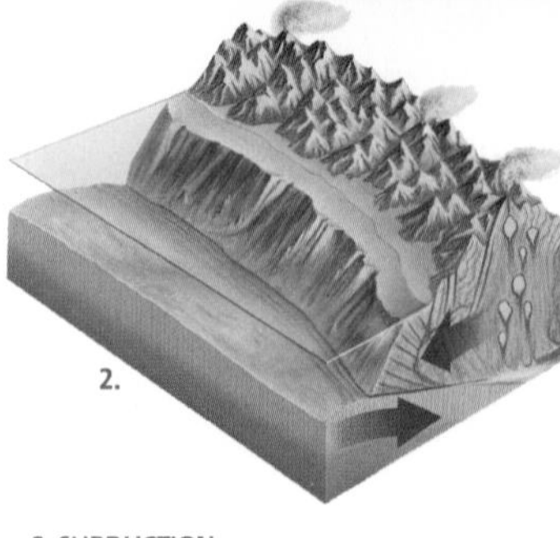

2. SUBDUCTION
When two massive plates collide, the older, colder, denser one—usually the oceanic plate meeting a continental plate—takes a dive. Pushed into the interior of the Earth, it is transformed into molten material that may rise again in volcanic eruption. Subduction also causes earthquakes, raises coastal mountains, and creates island arcs such as the Aleutians and the Lesser Antilles.

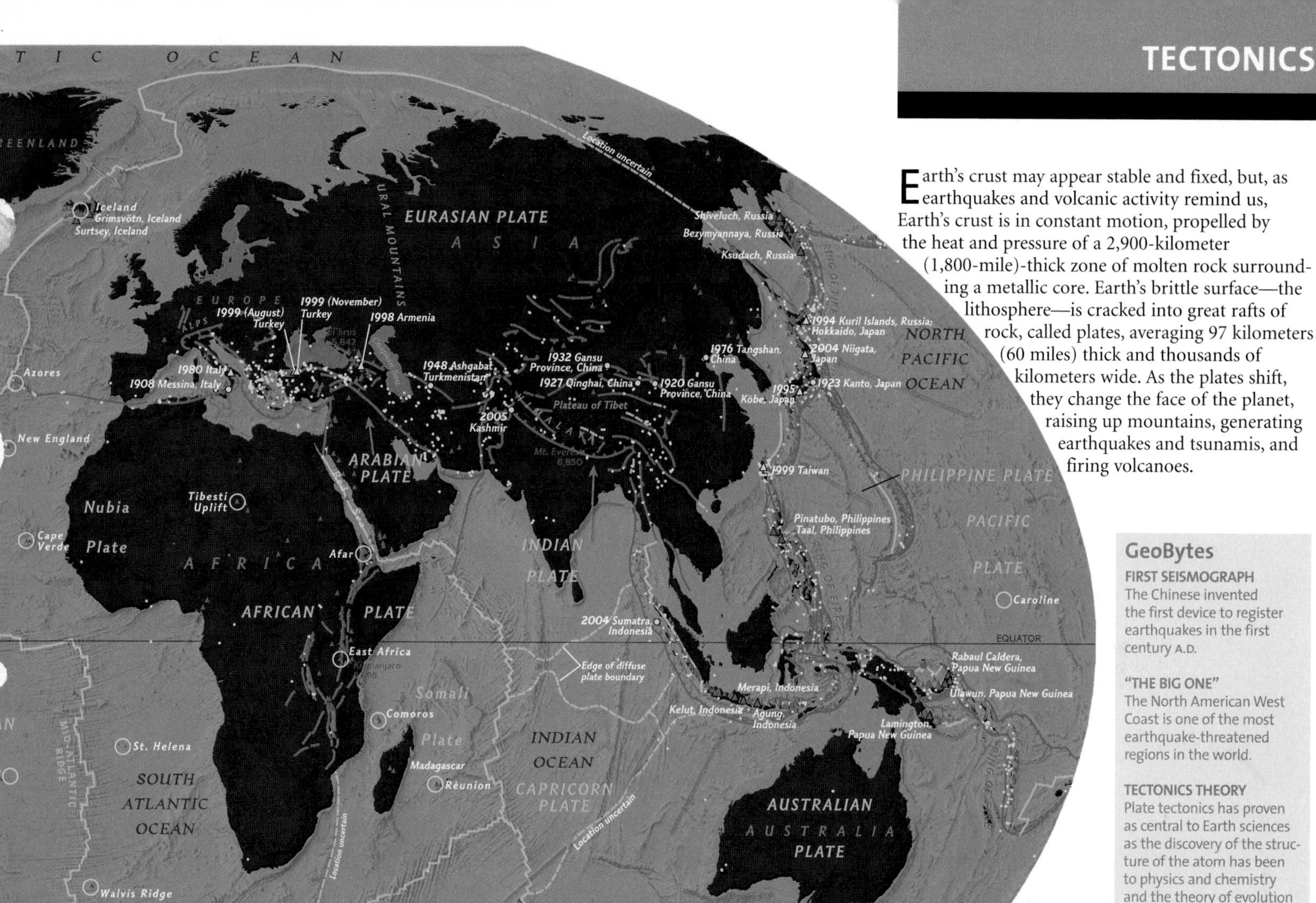

Earth's crust may appear stable and fixed, but, as earthquakes and volcanic activity remind us, Earth's crust is in constant motion, propelled by the heat and pressure of a 2,900-kilometer (1,800-mile)-thick zone of molten rock surrounding a metallic core. Earth's brittle surface—the lithosphere—is cracked into great rafts of rock, called plates, averaging 97 kilometers (60 miles) thick and thousands of kilometers wide. As the plates shift, they change the face of the planet, raising up mountains, generating earthquakes and tsunamis, and firing volcanoes.

GeoBytes

FIRST SEISMOGRAPH
The Chinese invented the first device to register earthquakes in the first century A.D.

"THE BIG ONE"
The North American West Coast is one of the most earthquake-threatened regions in the world.

TECTONICS THEORY
Plate tectonics has proven as central to Earth sciences as the discovery of the structure of the atom has been to physics and chemistry and the theory of evolution to biology.

NEW NEIGHBORS
Moving slowly to the northwest, the Pacific plate carries a sliver of California, including Los Angeles, which will become a suburb of San Francisco—in a few million years.

RISKY BEHAVIOR
Today, 500 million people live within striking distance of 550 or so active volcanoes.

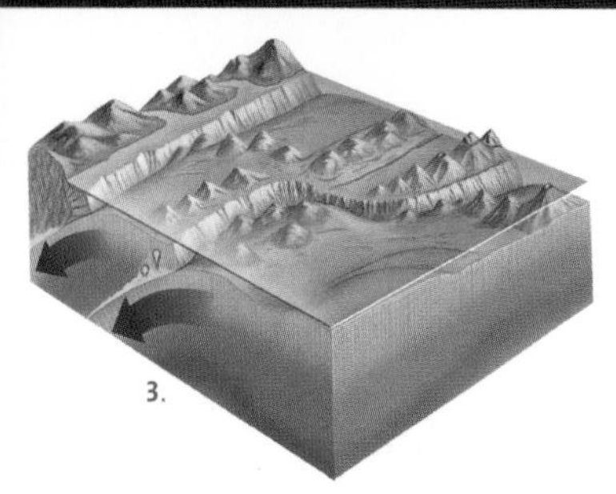

3. ACCRETION
As ocean plates advance on continental edges or island arcs and slide under them, seamounts on the ocean floor are skimmed off and pile up in submarine trenches. The buildup can fuse with continental plates, as most geologists agree was the case with Alaska and much of western North America.

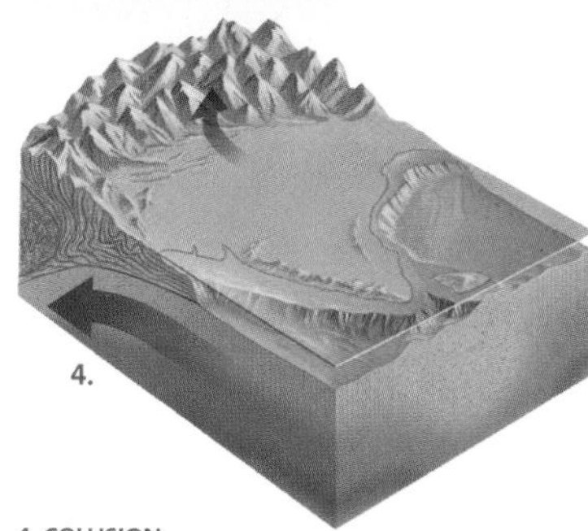

4. COLLISION
When continental plates meet, the resulting forces can build impressive mountain ranges. Earth's highest landforms—the Himalaya and adjacent Tibetan Plateau—were born when the Indian plate rammed into the Eurasian plate 50 million years ago.

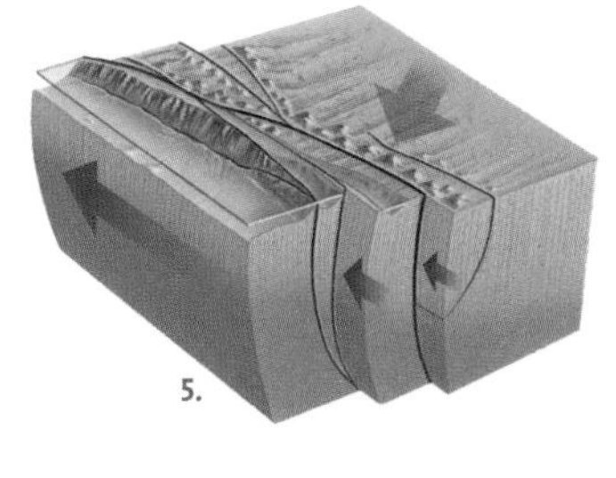

5. FAULTING
Boundaries at which plates slip alongside each other are called transform faults. An example is California's San Andreas fault, which accommodates the stresses between the North American and Pacific plates. Large and sudden displacements—strike-slip movements—can create high-magnitude earthquakes.

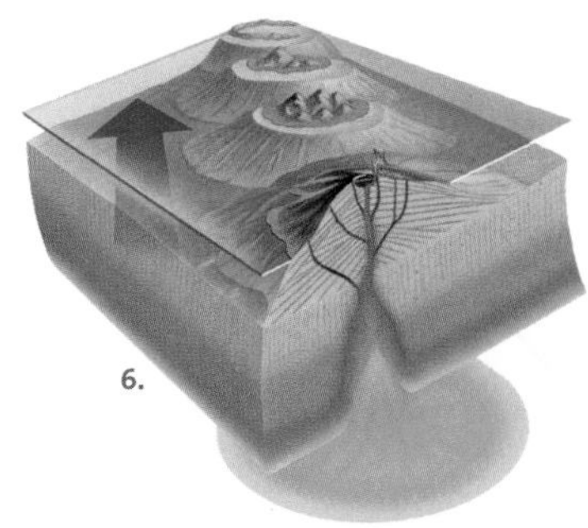

6. HOT SPOTS
A column of magma rising from deep in the mantle, a hot spot is a thermal plume that literally burns a hole in Earth's rocky crust. The result? Volcanoes, geysers, and new islands. Eruptions occur at plate boundaries, such as in Iceland and the Galápagos, as well as within plates, such as the volcanoes of Hawai'i and the geysers of Yellowstone.

EOLIAN LANDFORMS
Sand dunes

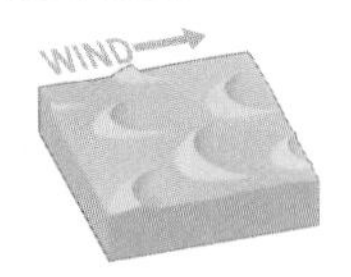

BARCHAN
The most common type of sand dune, the points of these crescent-shaped dunes lie downwind.

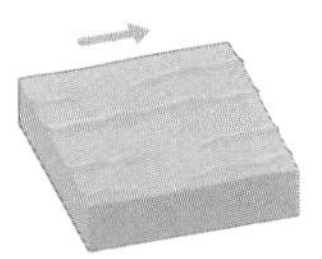

LONGITUDINAL
These are narrow, lengthy sand ridges that lie parallel to the prevailing wind direction.

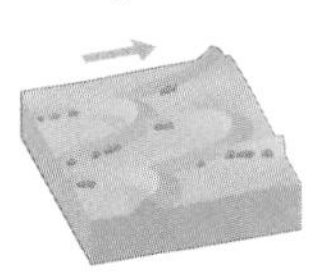

PARABOLIC
Similar in shape to barchans, the points of these crescent-shaped dunes lie upwind.

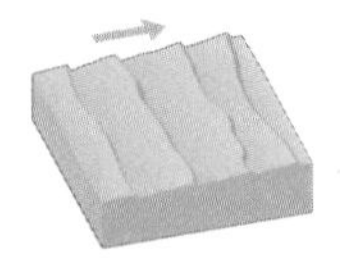

TRANSVERSE
Looking like sandy sea waves, these dunes form perpendicular to the prevailing wind.

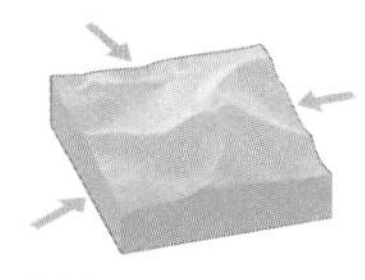

STAR
Formed by winds blowing from many directions, these pyramidal sand mounds grow upward.

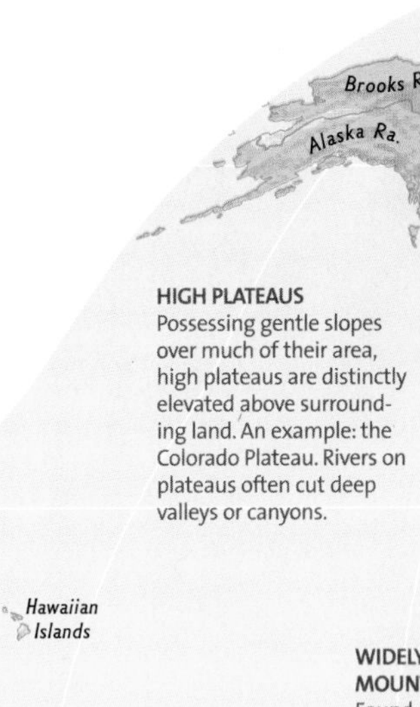

ICE SHEETS
These dome-shaped masses of glacier ice cover Greenland and Antarctica today. Glaciers blanketed most of Canada 12,000 years ago.

HIGH PLATEAUS
Possessing gentle slopes over much of their area, high plateaus are distinctly elevated above surrounding land. An example: the Colorado Plateau. Rivers on plateaus often cut deep valleys or canyons.

PLAINS
The legacy of exogenic forces after millions of years, these gently sloping regions result from eroded sediments that are transported and deposited by glaciers, rivers, and oceans.

WIDELY SPACED MOUNTAINS
Found, for instance, in the Great Basin in the U.S., this feature consists of heavily eroded mountains, where the eroded material fills the adjacent valleys.

MOUNTAINS
Mountains are formed by tectonic folds and faults and by magma moving to the surface. Mountains exhibit steep slopes, form elongated ranges, and cover one-fifth of the world's land surface.

LANDFORMS OF THE WORLD
The map shows the seven landforms that make up the Earth.

Major landform types
- Mountains
- Widely spaced mountains
- High plateaus
- Hills and low plateaus
- Depressions
- Plains
- Ice sheets

GeoBytes

LOESS PLATEAU, CHINA
The thickest known loess (windblown silt) deposits are 335 meters (1,100 feet) deep. The plateau possesses fertile soil and high cliffs.

GANGES RIVER DELTA
The world's largest delta is formed by the Ganges and Brahmaputra Rivers. Its area is about the size of Ireland.

PERU–BOLIVIA ALTIPLANO
Second only to Tibet's plateau in elevation and extent, the Altiplano is a basin 4,000 meters (13,000 feet) high.

LAKE BAIKAL, RUSSIA
This lake lies in the planet's deepest fault-generated trough, a rift about 9 kilometers (5.6 miles) deep.

LANDFORMS

VOLCANIC
1. Crater Lake, Oregon
The caldera, now filled by Crater Lake, was produced by an eruption some 7,000 years ago.

VOLCANIC
2. Misti Volcano, Peru
A stratovolcano, or composite volcano, it is composed of hardened lava and volcanic ash.

VOLCANIC
3. Mount Fuji, Japan
Japan's highest peak at 3,776 meters (12,388 feet), Mt. Fuji is made up of three superimposed volcanoes.

EXOGENIC
4. Isle of Skye, Scotland
A pinnacle of basalt lava, known as the Old Man of Storr, resulted from millions of years of erosion.

KARST
5. Southern China
Steep-sided hills, or tower karst, dominate a karst landscape,where rainfall erodes limestone rock.

FLUVIAL LANDFORMS

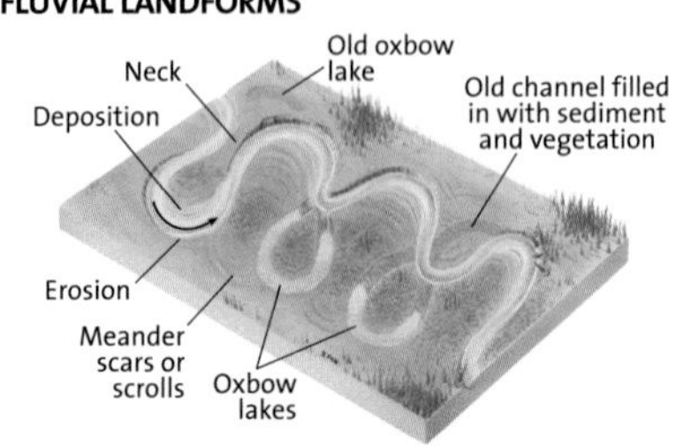

▲ **MEANDERS**
Meanders are the smooth, rounded bends of rivers that increase in size as a floodplain widens. Meanders form as faster currents erode the river's outer banks while adding sediment to the inner banks. Erosion eventually cuts off the meander, creating an oxbow lake. Floods can suddenly change a river's course.

GLACIAL LANDFORMS

▼ **GLACIAL**
Glaciers fill river valleys and bury them in ice. Ice sheets, including the ones that covered parts of North America and Europe, can be hundreds of meters thick. Migrating glacial ice transforms preglacial topography as it grinds away rock in its path. Debris, carried by the ice, is deposited when the glacier stops advancing—further changing the terrain.

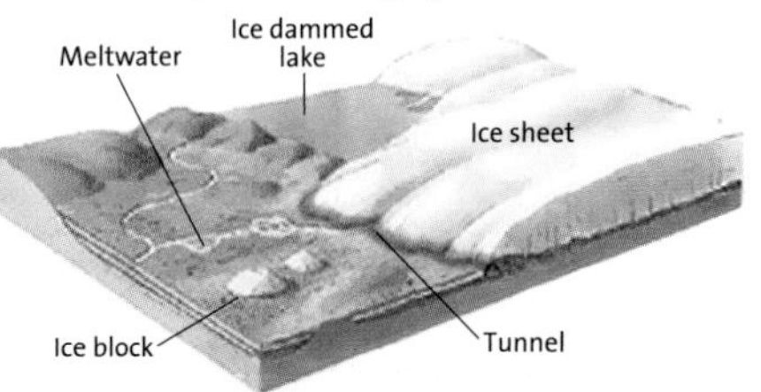

Esker formed by stream under ice sheet
Drumlin shaped by overriding glacier
Kettle lakes formed when ice blocks melt
Terminal moraines formed at margins of ice

▲ **POSTGLACIAL**
Mountain glaciers leave behind sharp-edged ridges and steep-sided valleys—causing waterfalls to plunge down sheer slopes. Areas that were covered with ice sheets, such as the Canadian Shield, exhibit stony soils, lowlands dotted with lakes, and grooved bedrock surfaces.

What are the many forces that mold the landforms on Earth's surface? Geomorphology is the science that studies the various relief features and the forces that form them. Endogenic forces (internal processes within the planet) produce folding, faulting, and magma movement in the Earth's crust. Subsidence in the crust causes depressions, and uplift builds mountains and plateaus. Exogenic (external) forces hold sway on the surface of the planet. In a process known as weathering, ice, water, and organisms like plant roots break down rock. Weathered rock material is carried great distances by rivers, glaciers, and other erosional agents. These forces of nature are usually gradual, often taking millions of years, but heavy rains and high winds can transform a landscape in a matter of hours. Human activities such as deforestation and poor farming practices, however, can rapidly accelerate soil erosion.

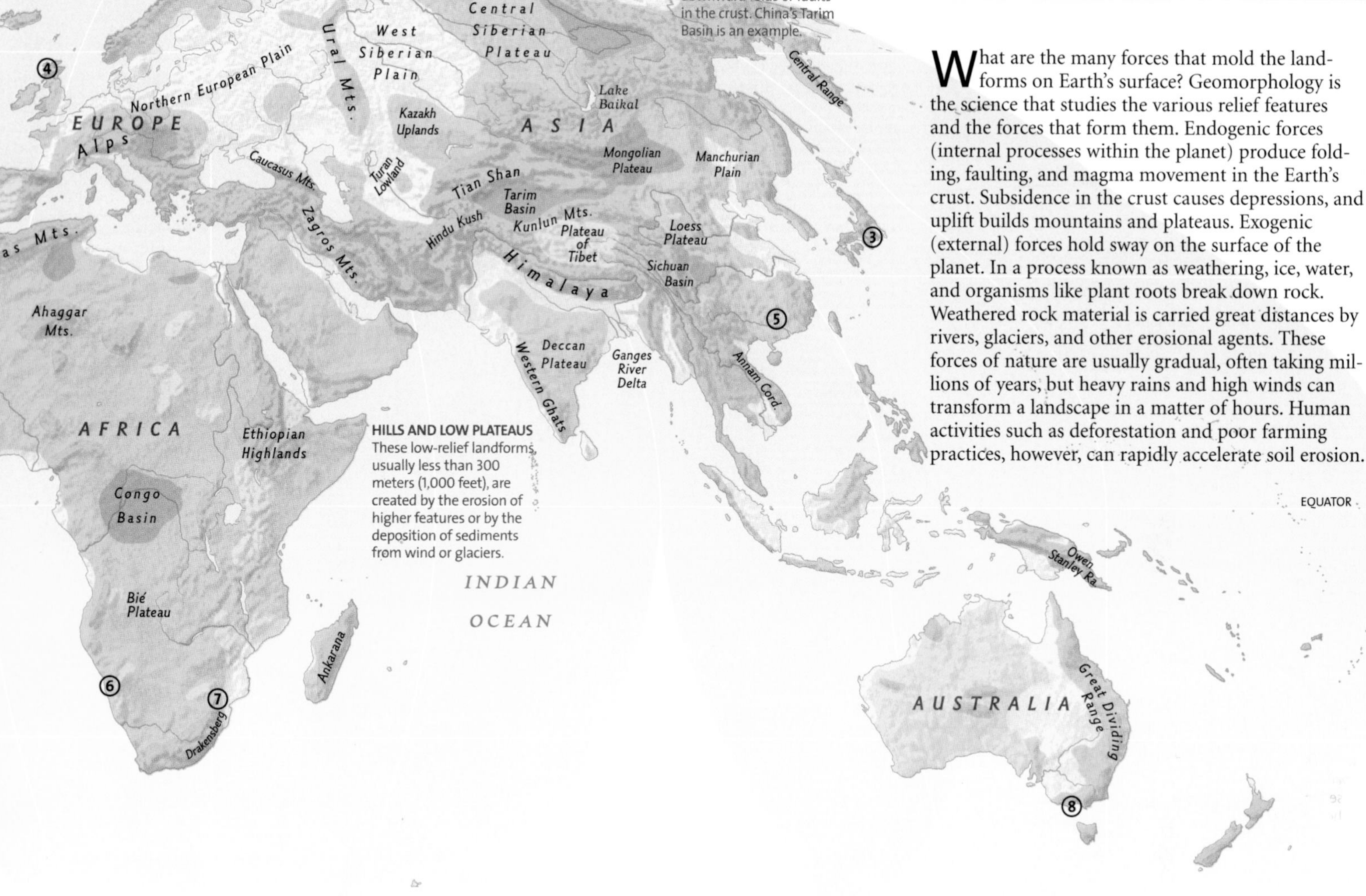

EOLIAN
6. Namibia, Africa
Arid conditions and windstorms combine to build some of the tallest sand dunes in Africa.

FLUVIAL
7. Blyde River Canyon, Africa
South Africa's Blyde River carved a steep, colorful canyon some 800 meters (2,600 ft) deep.

COASTAL
8. Victoria, Australia
Ocean waves erode coastal cliffs, leaving behind sea stacks made of more resistant rock.

POSTGLACIAL
9. Kejimkujik, Nova Scotia
Drumlins, shaped by overriding glaciers, are elliptical mounds paralleling past glacial movement.

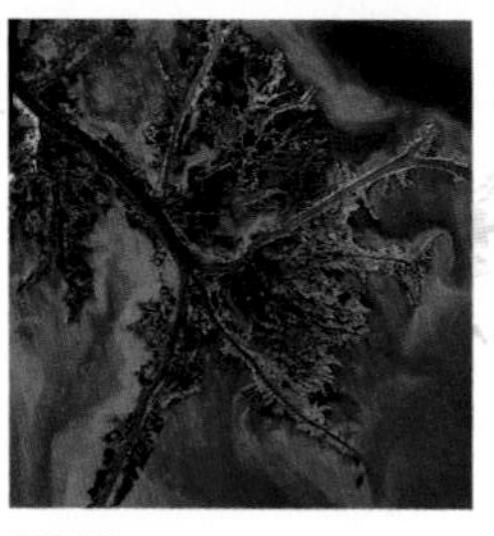

FLUVIAL
10. Mississippi River Delta
Deltas result from the deposition of river sediments and vary in shape and size depending on discharge, currents, and waves.

OTHER LANDFORMS
11. Meteor Crater, Arizona
Some 150 visible impact craters exist on Earth; others may have eroded away or been covered.

▲ **EOLIAN LANDFORMS**
Eolian (from Aeolus, the Greek god of the winds) describes landforms shaped by the wind, and it works best as a geomorphic agent when wind velocity is high—and moisture and vegetation are low. Desert dunes are the most common eolian landform. During the last glaciation, however, strong winds carried vast clouds of silt that were deposited as loess (a fine-grained, fertile soil).

▲ **WATERSHEDS**
The map above shows the watersheds, or drainage basins, of Earth's largest river systems. Rivers rise in mountains or plateaus, eroding and depositing sediments along their entire length. Erosional landforms created by rivers include mesas and canyons; depositional (aggradational) landforms include levees and deltas.

▲ **ICE AGES**
A glacier is a mass of ice moving slowly down a slope or valley. Glacial ice that spreads over vast non-mountainous areas is known as an ice sheet. For millions of years ice sheets have gone through cycles of advancing over continents—and then melting back. The most recent glacial period ended some 10,000 years ago.

□ Maximum glaciation 20,000 years ago

Present-day

□ Projected sea level rise: 13m (43ft)

▲ SEA LEVEL CHANGES

Earth's hydrologic cycle shows that oceans expand as ice sheets melt and that oceans contract as glaciers grow. Global sea level 20,000 years ago was about 125 meters (410 feet) lower than today—when ice sheets covered much of North America, and the continental shelf was above water. We currently live in an interglacial period (a time of relatively warmer global temperatures). In recent geologic history, global sea level was up to 6 meters (20 feet) higher than today's levels. A future 13-meter (43-foot) rise in sea level, caused primarily by ice sheet melting, would flood areas in the United States affecting about a quarter of the population, mainly in the Gulf and East Coast states.

▶ A SLICE OF EARTH

A cross-section shows that the oceanic crust includes plains, volcanoes, and ridges. The abyssal plains, deepest parts of the the oceanic floor, can reach greater than 3,000 meters (9,840 feet) beneath the surface of the ocean. Underwater volcanoes are called seamounts if they rise more than 1,000 meters (3,300 feet) above the seafloor. The Mid-Atlantic Ridge is a vast submarine mountain range beneath the Atlantic Ocean. Surrounding most continents is an underwater extension of the landmass known as a continental shelf—a shallow, submerged plain. Continental slopes connect the continental shelf with the oceanic crust in the form of giant escarpments that can descend some 2,000 meters (6,600 feet).

▼ EARTH'S HIGHS AND LOWS

This computer-generated image of the Earth is a digital elevation model—color-coded to show elevation differences. The image was derived from satellite altimetry and shipboard echo-sounding measurements. The deepest point, Challenger Deep at 10,920 meters (35,827 feet) below sea level, is dark blue , while the highest point, Mount Everest at 8,850 meters (29,035 feet) above sea level, is brown. Antarctica, the world's highest continent thanks to its thick ice sheet, shows up in shades of red, with a 2,300 meters (7,546 feet) average elevation. Also red is Greenland's ice sheet, about one-eighth the size of Antarctica's. Green expanses highlight lowland areas, and the adjacent aqua-hued regions reveal underwater continental shelves.

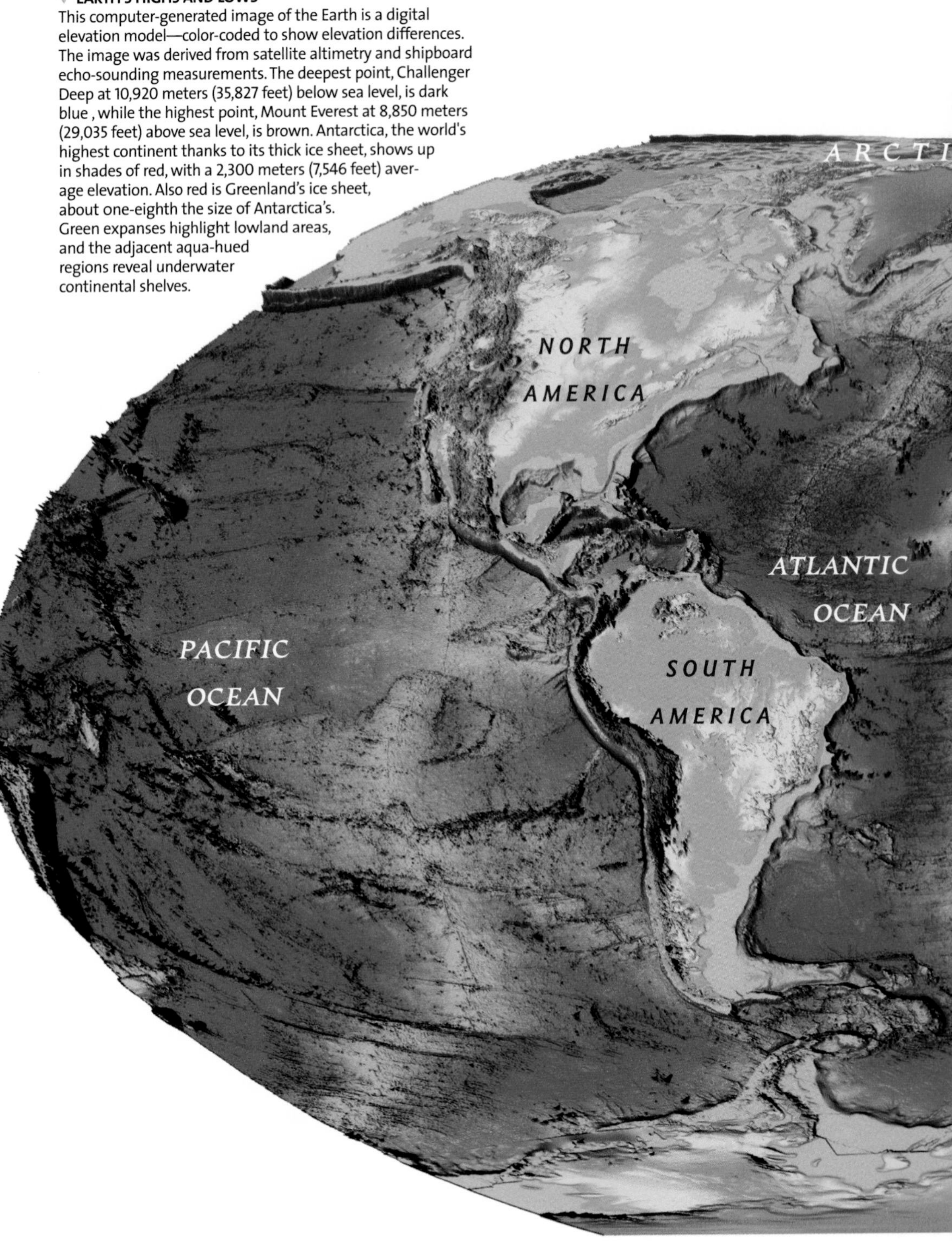

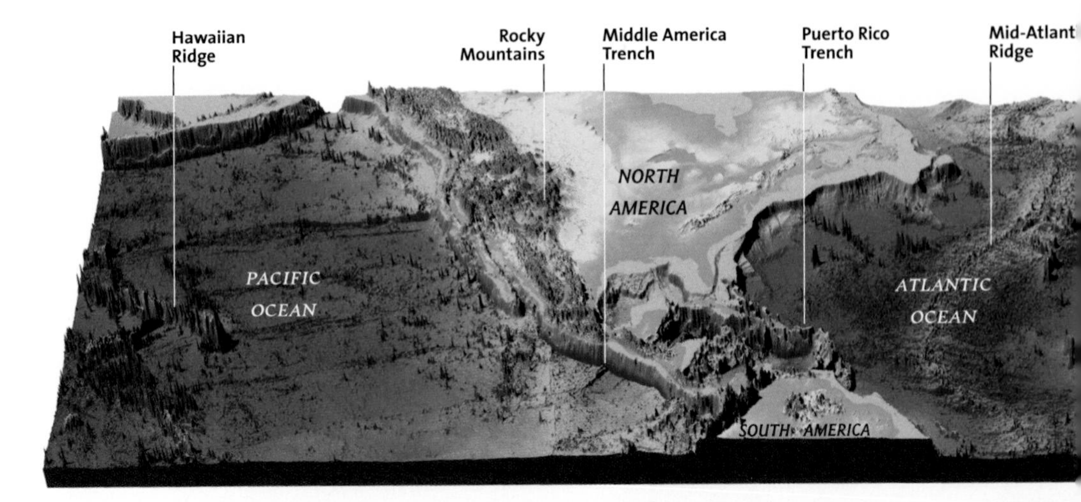

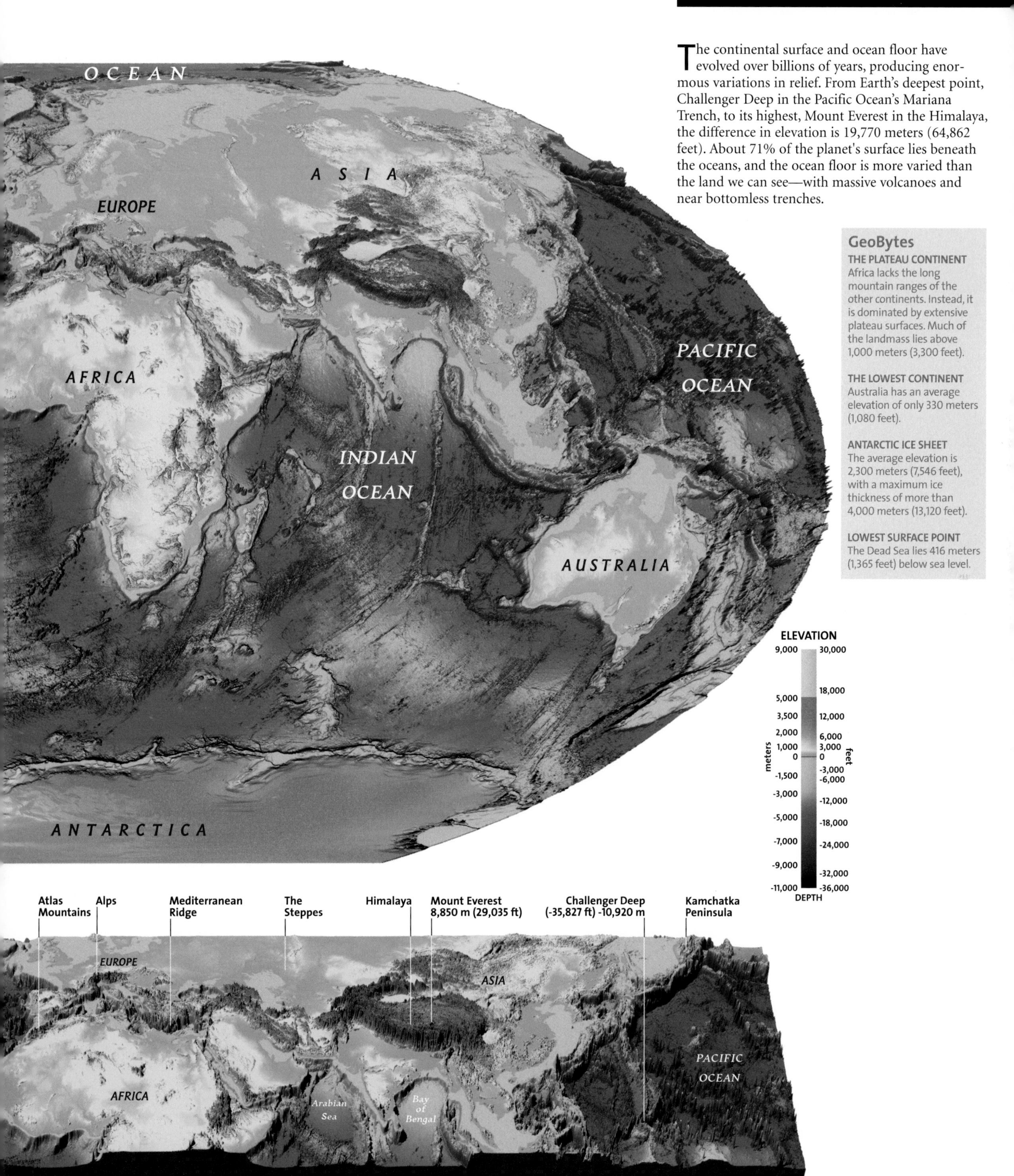

The continental surface and ocean floor have evolved over billions of years, producing enormous variations in relief. From Earth's deepest point, Challenger Deep in the Pacific Ocean's Mariana Trench, to its highest, Mount Everest in the Himalaya, the difference in elevation is 19,770 meters (64,862 feet). About 71% of the planet's surface lies beneath the oceans, and the ocean floor is more varied than the land we can see—with massive volcanoes and near bottomless trenches.

GeoBytes

THE PLATEAU CONTINENT
Africa lacks the long mountain ranges of the other continents. Instead, it is dominated by extensive plateau surfaces. Much of the landmass lies above 1,000 meters (3,300 feet).

THE LOWEST CONTINENT
Australia has an average elevation of only 330 meters (1,080 feet).

ANTARCTIC ICE SHEET
The average elevation is 2,300 meters (7,546 feet), with a maximum ice thickness of more than 4,000 meters (13,120 feet).

LOWEST SURFACE POINT
The Dead Sea lies 416 meters (1,365 feet) below sea level.

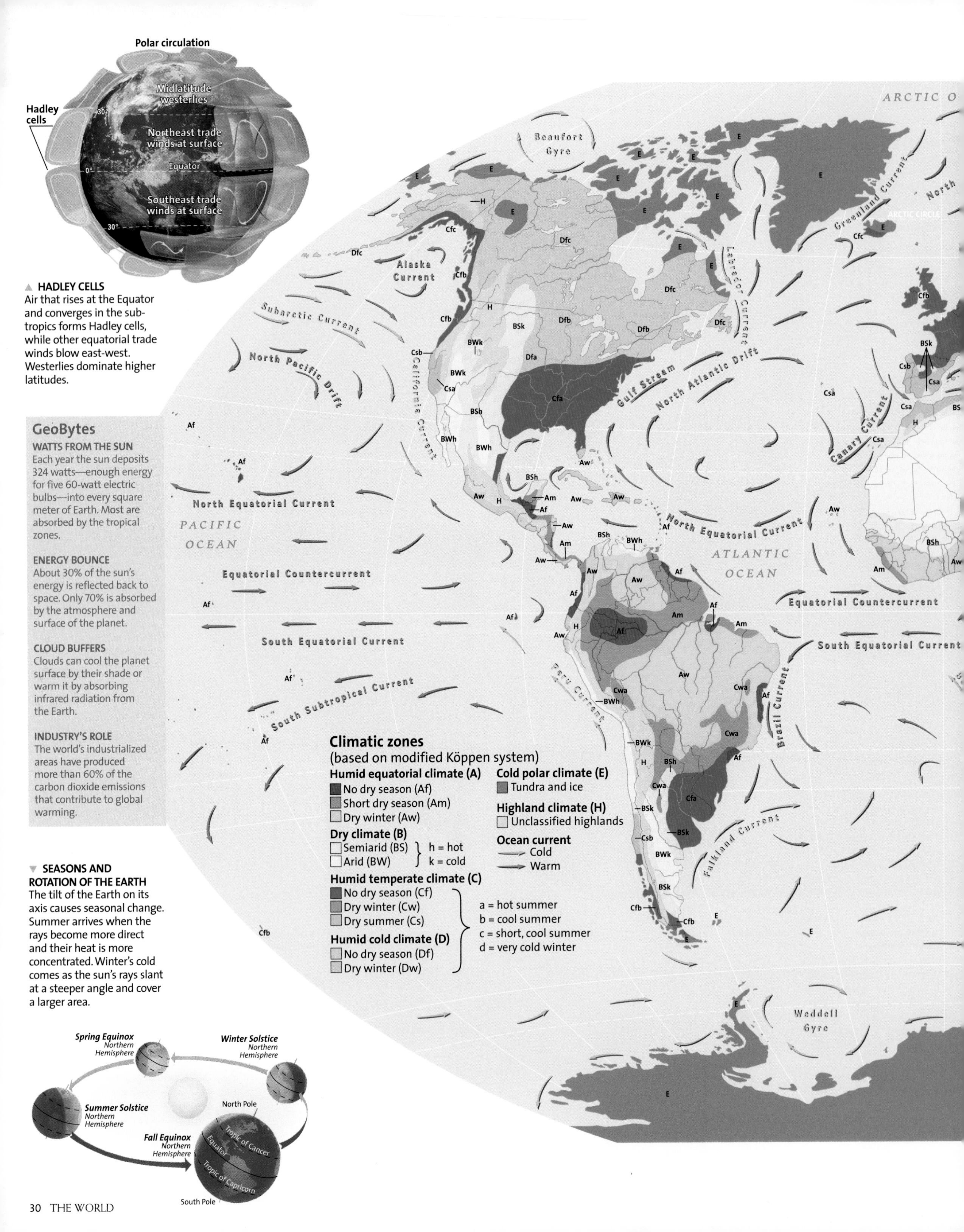

▲ **HADLEY CELLS**
Air that rises at the Equator and converges in the subtropics forms Hadley cells, while other equatorial trade winds blow east-west. Westerlies dominate higher latitudes.

GeoBytes

WATTS FROM THE SUN
Each year the sun deposits 324 watts—enough energy for five 60-watt electric bulbs—into every square meter of Earth. Most are absorbed by the tropical zones.

ENERGY BOUNCE
About 30% of the sun's energy is reflected back to space. Only 70% is absorbed by the atmosphere and surface of the planet.

CLOUD BUFFERS
Clouds can cool the planet surface by their shade or warm it by absorbing infrared radiation from the Earth.

INDUSTRY'S ROLE
The world's industrialized areas have produced more than 60% of the carbon dioxide emissions that contribute to global warming.

▼ **SEASONS AND ROTATION OF THE EARTH**
The tilt of the Earth on its axis causes seasonal change. Summer arrives when the rays become more direct and their heat is more concentrated. Winter's cold comes as the sun's rays slant at a steeper angle and cover a larger area.

From Arctic desert to equatorial rain forest, climate is the average of the elements of weather over time and dictates conditions for the viability of life. Climatic patterns are established primarily by the energy of the sun and the distribution of solar radiation, which is greatest at the Equator and least at the Poles, and is modified by altitude and distance from the sea. The Köppen system used here classifies Earth's climatic zones based on precipitation, temperature, and vegetation. These zones can shift over time. In recent decades, human activities, such as the burning of fossil fuels that increase greenhouse gases in the atmosphere, are contributing to worldwide temperature variations.

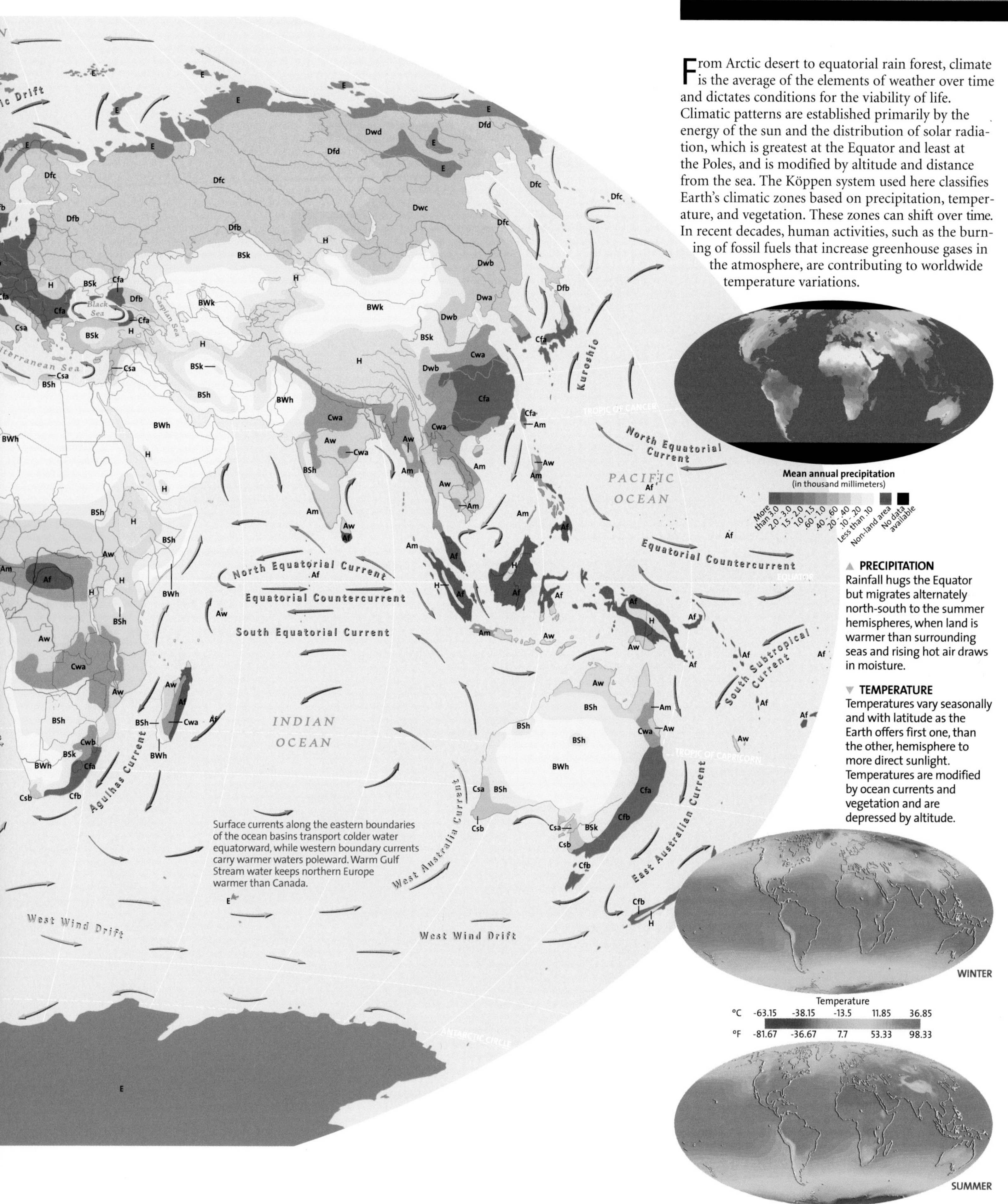

Surface currents along the eastern boundaries of the ocean basins transport colder water equatorward, while western boundary currents carry warmer waters poleward. Warm Gulf Stream water keeps northern Europe warmer than Canada.

▲ **PRECIPITATION**
Rainfall hugs the Equator but migrates alternately north-south to the summer hemispheres, when land is warmer than surrounding seas and rising hot air draws in moisture.

▼ **TEMPERATURE**
Temperatures vary seasonally and with latitude as the Earth offers first one, than the other, hemisphere to more direct sunlight. Temperatures are modified by ocean currents and vegetation and are depressed by altitude.

TRACKING WEATHER PATTERNS

PRESSURE AND PREDOMINANT WINDS

The sun's direct rays shift from south of the Equator in January to north in July, creating large temperature differences over the globe. These, in turn, lead to air density differences and the creation of high and low pressure areas. Winds result from air attempting to equalize these pressure differences, but the influence of the rotating planet deflects them from a straight line path.

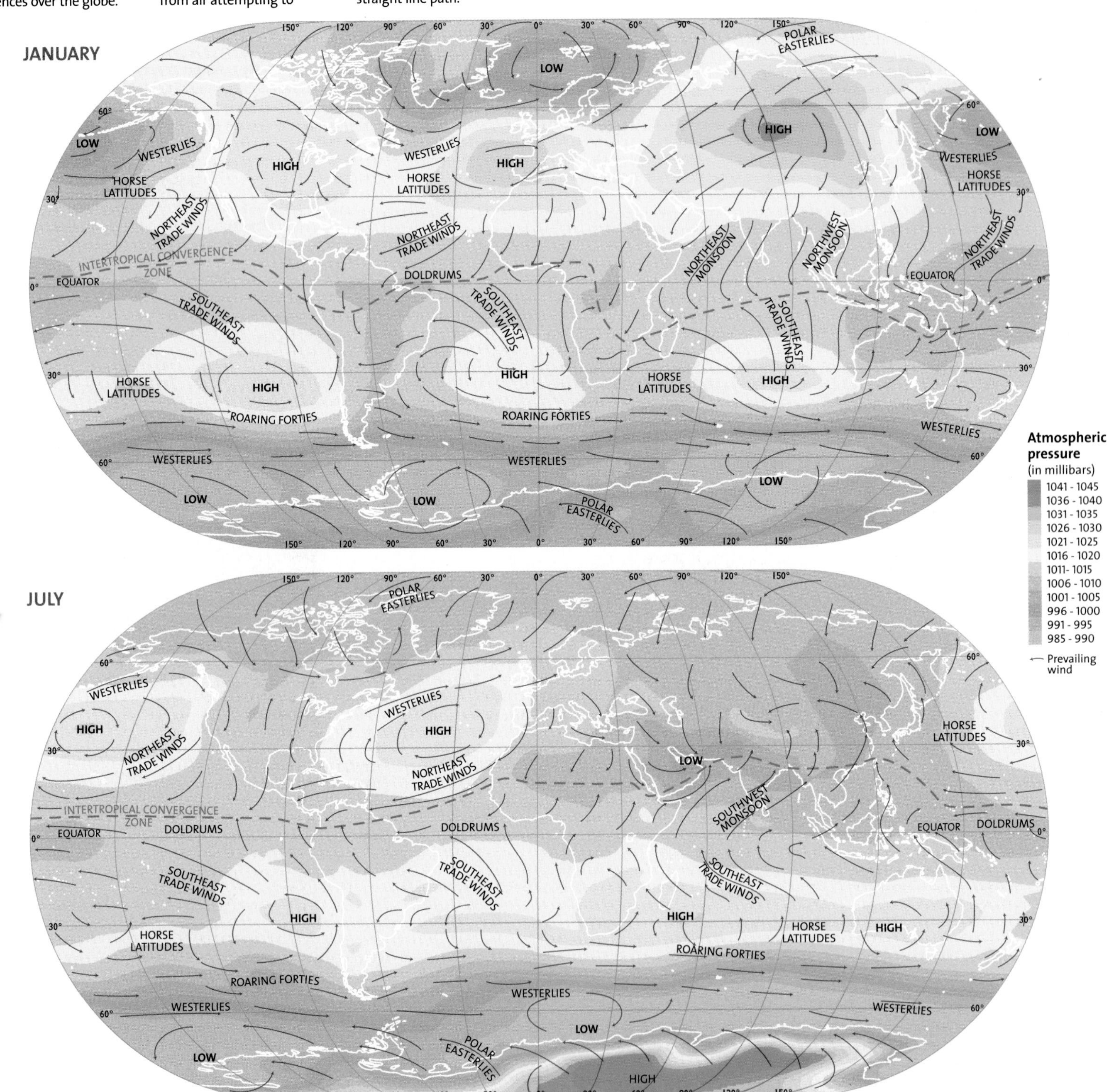

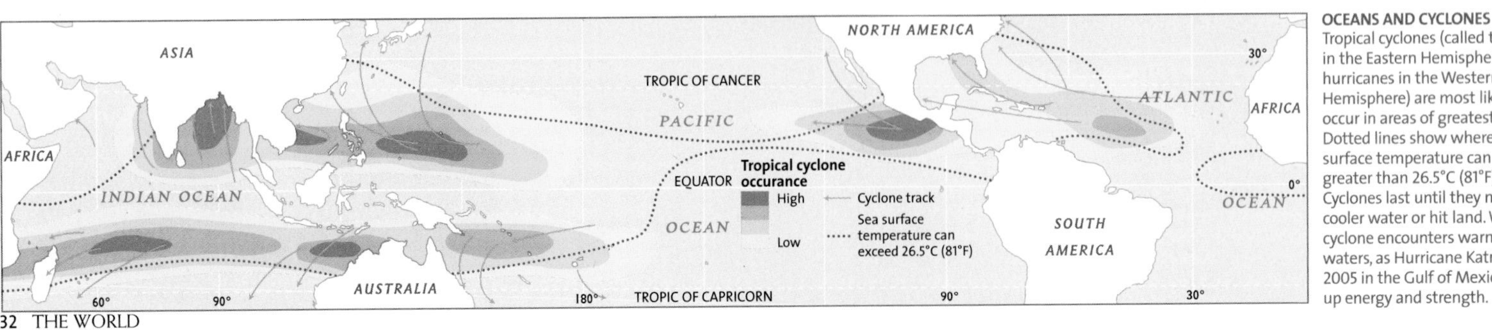

OCEANS AND CYCLONES

Tropical cyclones (called typhoons in the Eastern Hemisphere and hurricanes in the Western Hemisphere) are most likely to occur in areas of greatest heating. Dotted lines show where the sea surface temperature can be greater than 26.5°C (81°F). Cyclones last until they move over cooler water or hit land. When a cyclone encounters warmer waters, as Hurricane Katrina did in 2005 in the Gulf of Mexico, it picks up energy and strength.

Weather is the state of the atmosphere—as indicated by temperature, moisture, wind speed and direction, and barometric pressure—at a specific time and place. Although still frustratingly difficult to predict, weather acts in some known patterns. Variations in ocean temperatures off the South American coast influence storm formation and rainfall around the globe. Jet streams that speed around the planet can usher in winter storms. And the right combination of warm water, wind, and energy from heated water vapor can cook up lethal hurricanes and typhoons that can overwhelm shorelines and cities.

GeoBytes

CHRISTMAS GIFTS
El Niño, The Child, is named for the Christ Child, because the oceanic temperature rise traditionally comes around Christmas.

MONSIEUR CORIOLIS
The Coriolis Effect, the apparent force exerted on winds and ocean currents by the rotation of the earth, was first described by Gastave-Gaspard Coriolis, a French mathematician, in 1835.

SUPER STORMS
One hurricane during its life cycle can expend as much energy as 10,000 nuclear bombs.

BIG STORMS
Frontal systems are the most common weather feature in the mid-latitudes and give precipitation to large, populated areas of the globe. Most occluded fronts have a life of 3 to 6 days.

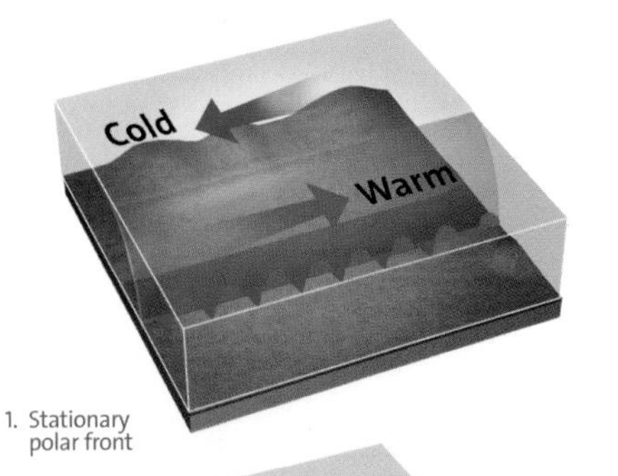

1. Stationary polar front

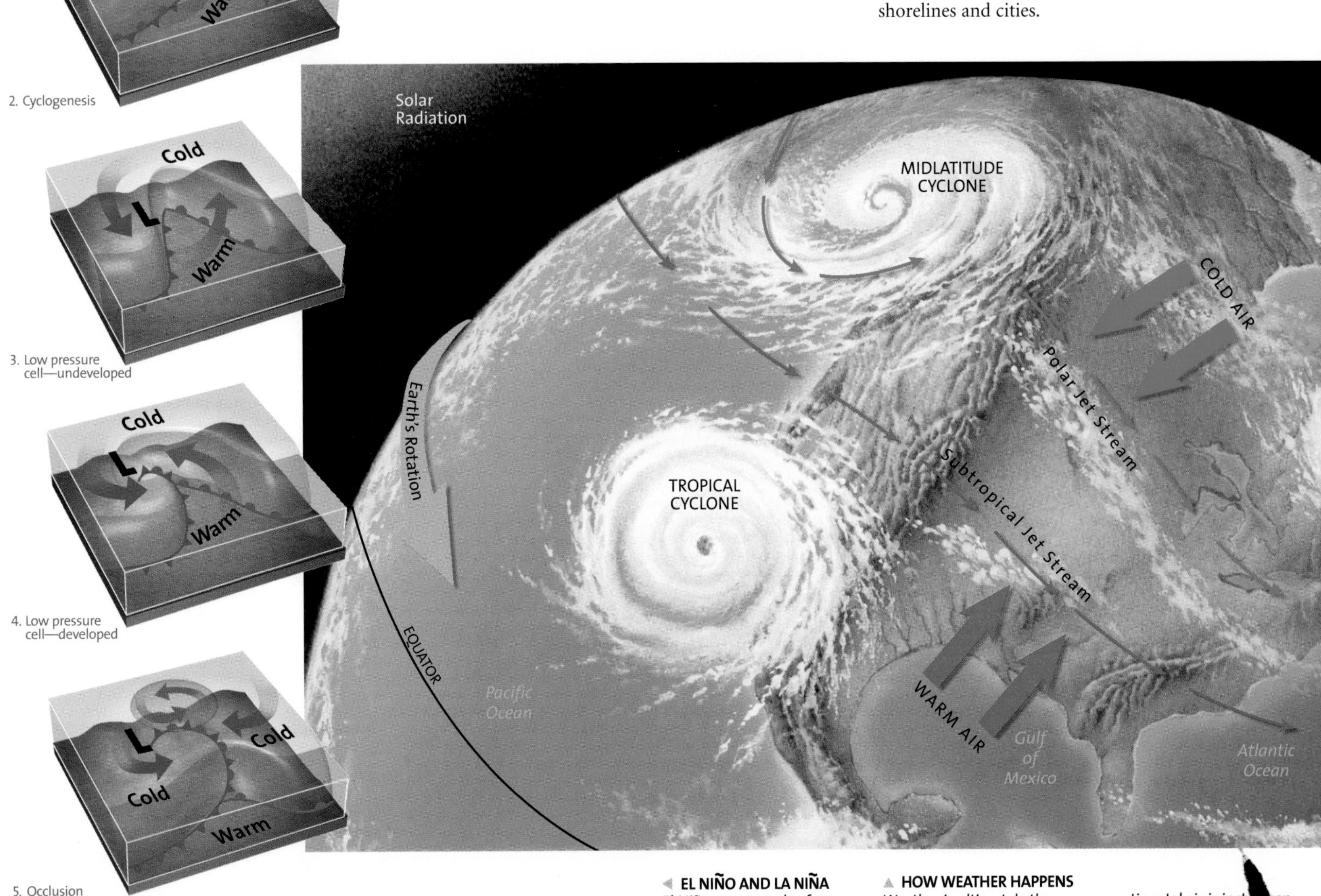

2. Cyclogenesis

3. Low pressure cell—undeveloped

4. Low pressure cell—developed

5. Occlusion

▲ FORMATION OF A MID-LATITUDE CYCLONE
Mid-latitude cyclones are found between 35° and 70° of latitude in the zone of the westerly winds. Most are occluded fronts. (1) Characterized by intense, heavy precipitation, cold polar air—with a boundary known as a front—meets warm tropical air. (2) A wave develops along the frontal boundary as the opposing air masses interact. Cyclogenesis (the birth of a cyclone) begins. (3) The faster-moving cold air forces the warm air to lift above the cold. (4) Full rotation develops, counter-clockwise in the Northern Hemisphere and clockwise in the Southern Hemisphere. (5) Complete occlusion occurs as the warm air, fully caught-up by the cold air, has been lifted away from the surface. Because the warm air is completely separated from the surface, the characteristics of the cold air are felt on the ground in the form of unsteady, windy, and wet weather.

Sea surface height anomaly
cm -12 -8 -4 0 4 8 12
in -5 -3 -2 0 2 3 5

◄ EL NIÑO AND LA NIÑA
El Niño, an anomaly of sea-surface height or "relief" of the sea, brings warm water to South America's west coast, leading to severe short-term changes in world weather. La Niña, a cooling of those waters, has opposite effects.

▲ HOW WEATHER HAPPENS
Weather is ultimately the atmospheric response to unequal inputs of solar energy over the globe, as a surplus of heat in low latitudes is transferred to higher latitudes by air motion and by mid-latitude storms. Part of that dynamic are jet streams—rivers of westerly winds speeding as fast as 400 kph (250 mph) in the upper atmosphere, which are also instrumental in the genesis of storms: The Polar Front Jet, which snakes along the front between Arctic and warmer continental air, is inst[illegible]en-tal in the formation a[illegible] direction of cyclonic N[illegible] Pacific winter storms; t[illegible] Subtropical Jet blows a[illegible] the boundary of tropic[illegible] circulation cells and c[illegible]al also abet storm formation, bringing warm, moist air and precipitation into the continent. Weather patterns are also influenced by the different properties of oceans and continents to absorb or reflect heat, which creates pressure differences that give rise to moving air masses.

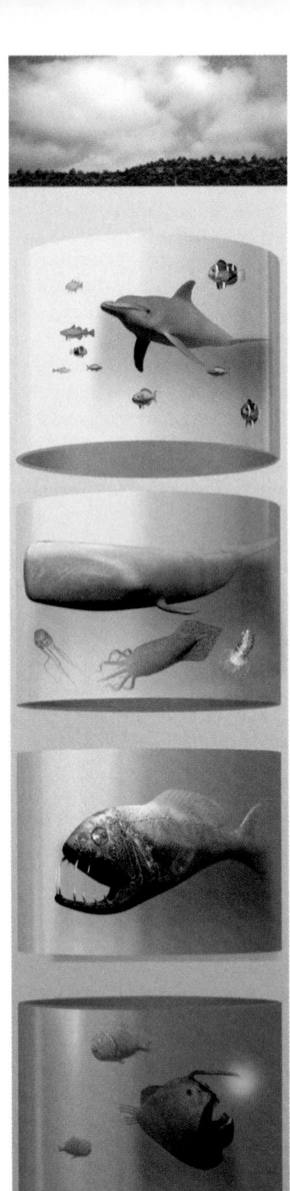

OUR LAYERED OCEAN
With depth, the ocean's five layers get colder, darker, saltier, denser, and more devoid of life.

200 meters (660 feet)
The epipelagic is the sunlit zone where photosynthesis by plants can take place and where the vast majority of all marine animals live.

1,000 meters (3,300 feet)
Only some light penetrates the mesopelagic, or twilight zone. Thus no plants grow, but large fish and whales hunt and bioluminescent fish first appear.

3,960 meters (13,000 feet)
No light reaches the midnight zone, or bathypelagic, but sperm whales and rays are known to hunt here for food.

6,100 meters (20,000 feet)
Pressure is crushing in the abyssopelagic, or abyss zone, home to bizarre angler fish and invertebrates such as sponges and sea cucumbers.

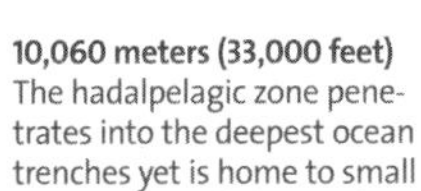

10,060 meters (33,000 feet)
The hadalpelagic zone penetrates into the deepest ocean trenches yet is home to small crustaceans called isopods.

Marine Sediments
The vast majority of the Earth's biologically fixed carbon lies in marine sediments trapped at the bottom of the seas. Carbon deposits from past eras are seen in current landforms upthrust from the oceans, such as the white cliffs of Dover.

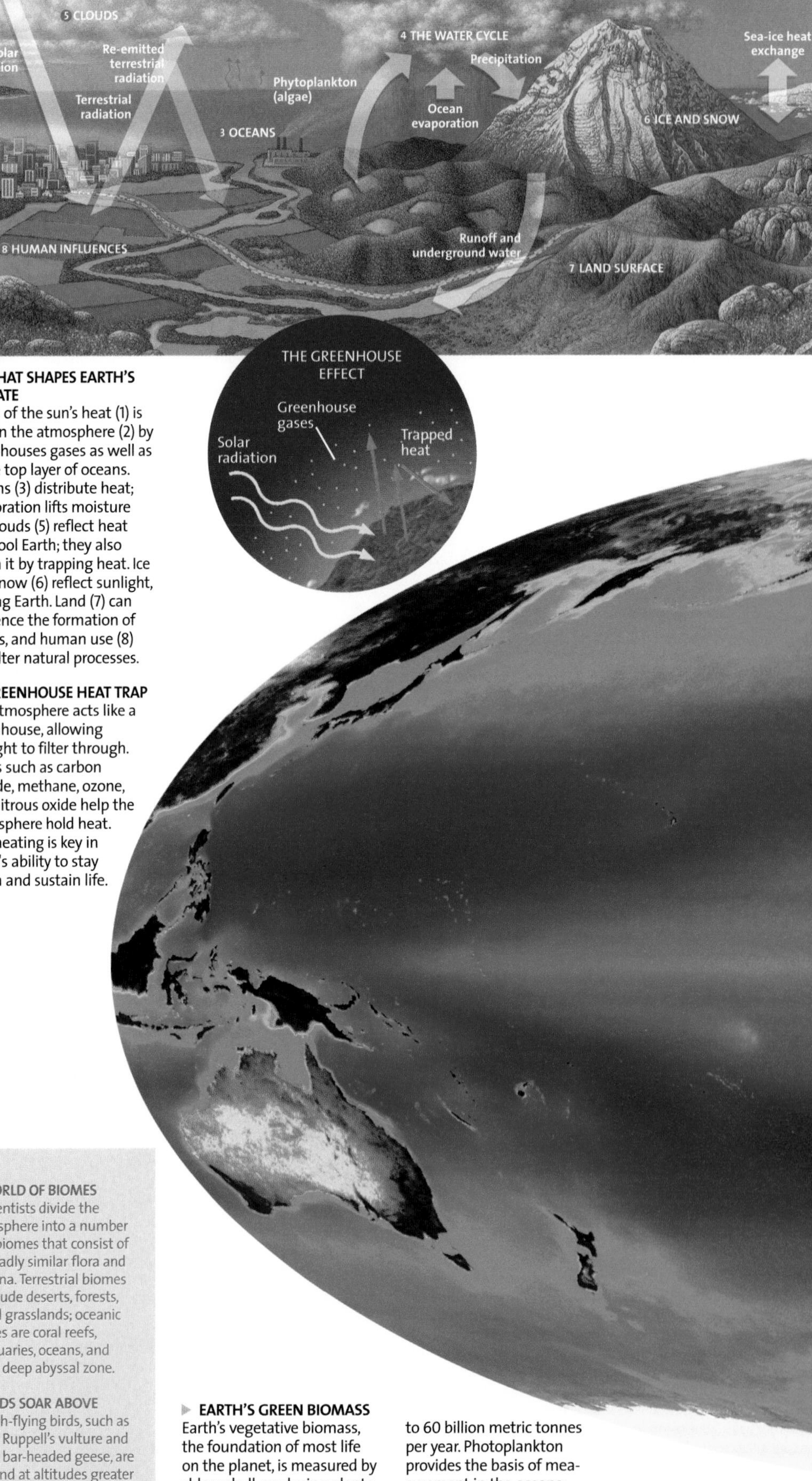

WHAT SHAPES EARTH'S CLIMATE
Much of the sun's heat (1) is held in the atmosphere (2) by greenhouses gases as well as in the top layer of oceans. Oceans (3) distribute heat; evaporation lifts moisture (4). Clouds (5) reflect heat and cool Earth; they also warm it by trapping heat. Ice and snow (6) reflect sunlight, cooling Earth. Land (7) can influence the formation of clouds, and human use (8) can alter natural processes.

GREENHOUSE HEAT TRAP
The atmosphere acts like a greenhouse, allowing sunlight to filter through. Gases such as carbon dioxide, methane, ozone, and nitrous oxide help the atmosphere hold heat. This heating is key in Earth's ability to stay warm and sustain life.

GeoBytes

BIOGENESIS
The evolution of the biosphere is thought to have begun some 3.5 billion years ago.

A NEW SCIENCE
In 1926 a Soviet scientist, Vladimir I. Vernadsky, argued that human reason is capable of ensuring the sustainability of the biosphere.

BOTTOM BIOMASS
The microbes that live deep beneath the Earth's surface could exceed all animal and plant life on the surface by biomass.

WORLD OF BIOMES
Scientists divide the biosphere into a number of biomes that consist of broadly similar flora and fauna. Terrestrial biomes include deserts, forests, and grasslands; oceanic ones are coral reefs, estuaries, oceans, and the deep abyssal zone.

BIRDS SOAR ABOVE
High-flying birds, such as the Ruppell's vulture and the bar-headed geese, are found at altitudes greater than Mt. Everest's nearly 9,140 meters (30,000 feet).

EARTH'S GREEN BIOMASS
Earth's vegetative biomass, the foundation of most life on the planet, is measured by chlorophyll-producing plants. Both land and sea process an equal amount of carbon—50 to 60 billion metric tonnes per year. Photoplankton provides the basis of measurement in the oceans; green-leaf mass on land.

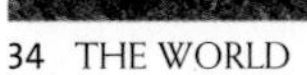

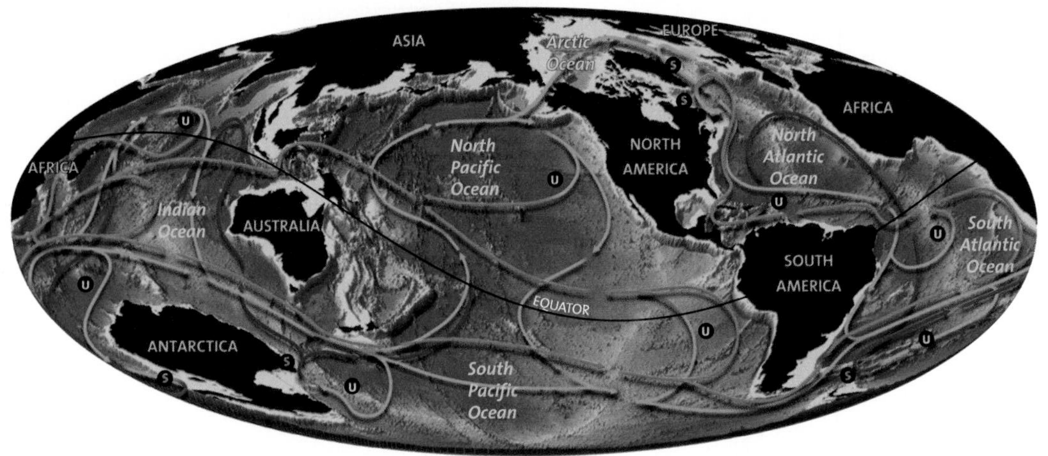

▲ **OCEAN CIRCULATION**
Ocean circulation, driven by wind, density, and Earth's rotation, conveys heat energy around the globe. Tropical surface waters move toward the Poles, cool, sink, and loop around to upwell near the Equator. The Gulf Stream, for example, warms northern Europe. Other, density-driven currents flow vertically to replenish deeper waters.

Ocean circulation
- Warmer than 3.5°C (38.3°F)
- 1°C – 3.5°C
- Cooler than 1°C (33.8°F)

S Sinking
U Upwelling

The biosphere is Earth's thin layer of life. Containing all known life in the solar system, the biosphere, if viewed from miles above the planet, would be at a scale no thicker than this page. Although the biosphere is 19 kilometers (12 miles) from top to bottom, the bulk of it ocean depths, most living things occupy a three-kilometer-wide (two-mile-wide) band extending from the sunlit ocean layer to the snowline of high mountains. The biosphere—and its communities of plants and animals—interacts with the other key spheres of physical geography: the lithosphere, Earth's solid outer crust; the atmosphere, the layer of air above; and the hydrosphere, the oceans and all water on and within Earth. The ecosystems of the biosphere are in constant flux as the planet turns, as weather and climate shift, and as the human impacts of forestry, agriculture, and urbanization affect the fundamental components of the biosphere—carbon dioxide and other gases, water, and the photosynthesis of plants.

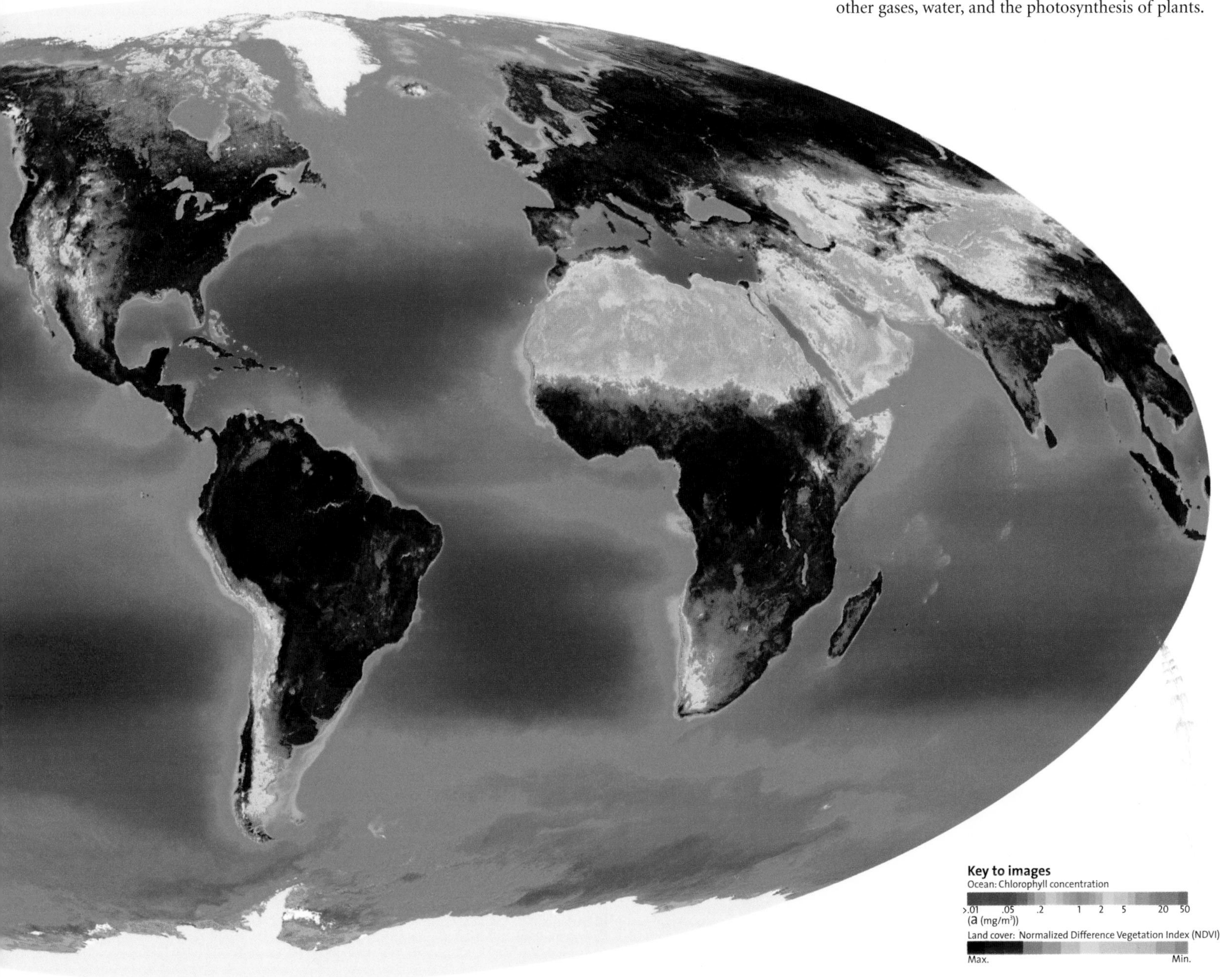

Key to images
Ocean: Chlorophyll concentration
>.01 .05 .2 1 2 5 20 50
(a (mg/m³))
Land cover: Normalized Difference Vegetation Index (NDVI)
Max. Min.

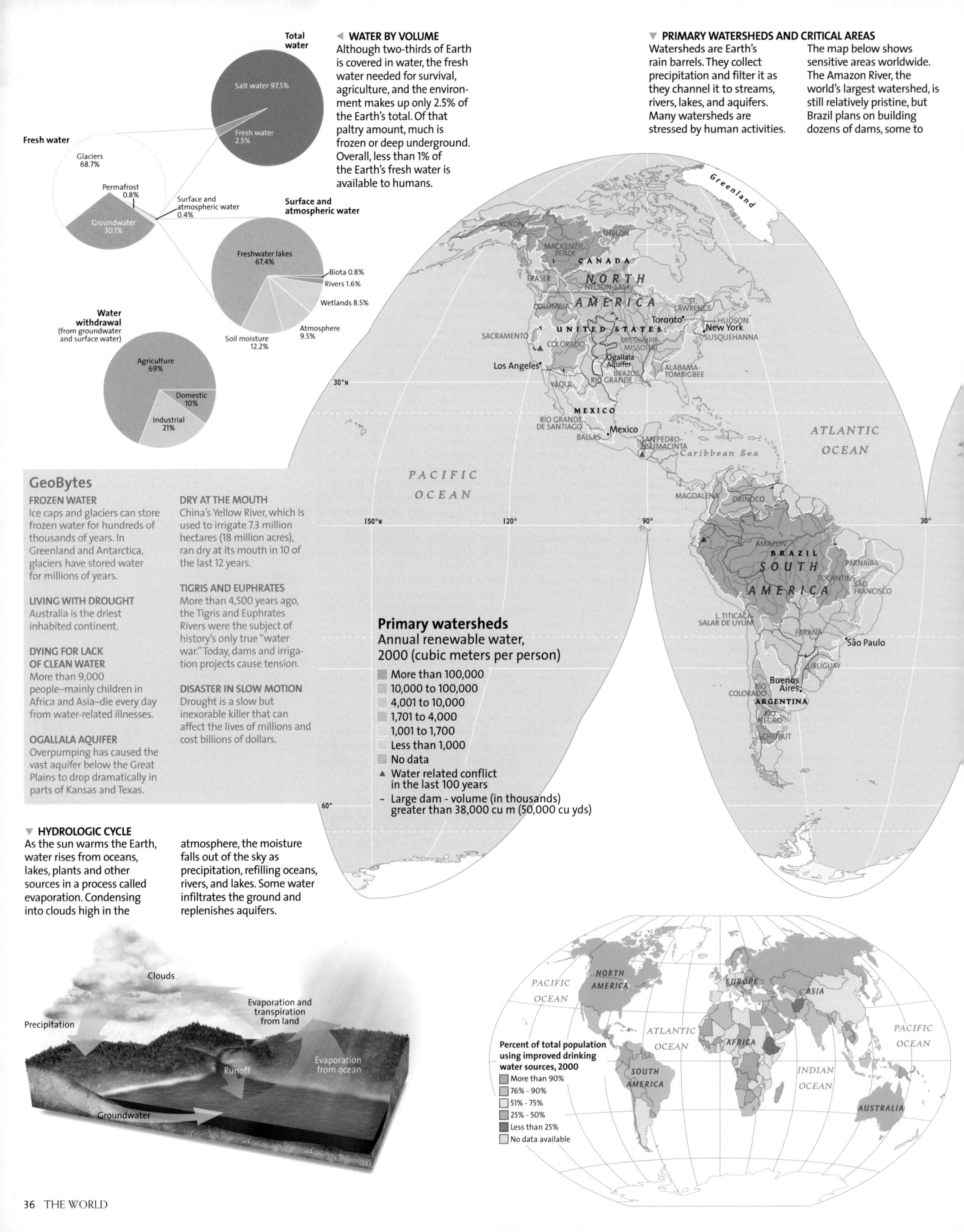

WATER BY VOLUME

Although two-thirds of Earth is covered in water, the fresh water needed for survival, agriculture, and the environment makes up only 2.5% of the Earth's total. Of that paltry amount, much is frozen or deep underground. Overall, less than 1% of the Earth's fresh water is available to humans.

PRIMARY WATERSHEDS AND CRITICAL AREAS

Watersheds are Earth's rain barrels. They collect precipitation and filter it as they channel it to streams, rivers, lakes, and aquifers. Many watersheds are stressed by human activities. The map below shows sensitive areas worldwide. The Amazon River, the world's largest watershed, is still relatively pristine, but Brazil plans on building dozens of dams, some to

GeoBytes

FROZEN WATER
Ice caps and glaciers can store frozen water for hundreds of thousands of years. In Greenland and Antarctica, glaciers have stored water for millions of years.

LIVING WITH DROUGHT
Australia is the driest inhabited continent.

DYING FOR LACK OF CLEAN WATER
More than 9,000 people–mainly children in Africa and Asia–die every day from water-related illnesses.

OGALLALA AQUIFER
Overpumping has caused the vast aquifer below the Great Plains to drop dramatically in parts of Kansas and Texas.

DRY AT THE MOUTH
China's Yellow River, which is used to irrigate 7.3 million hectares (18 million acres), ran dry at its mouth in 10 of the last 12 years.

TIGRIS AND EUPHRATES
More than 4,500 years ago, the Tigris and Euphrates Rivers were the subject of history's only true "water war." Today, dams and irrigation projects cause tension.

DISASTER IN SLOW MOTION
Drought is a slow but inexorable killer that can affect the lives of millions and cost billions of dollars.

HYDROLOGIC CYCLE

As the sun warms the Earth, water rises from oceans, lakes, plants and other sources in a process called evaporation. Condensing into clouds high in the atmosphere, the moisture falls out of the sky as precipitation, refilling oceans, rivers, and lakes. Some water infiltrates the ground and replenishes aquifers.

power aluminum smelters. In Africa and Asia, lack of access to water and water-related diseases are the main problems. In Europe and the Middle East, overuse, pollution, and disagreement over diverting water are the major challenges. Hope rests in better planning and community-scale projects.

It's as vital to life as air. Yet fresh water is one of the rarest resources on Earth. Only 2.5% of Earth's water is fresh, and of that the usable portion for humans is less than 1% of all fresh water, or 0.01% of all water on Earth. Water is constantly recycling through Earth's hydrologic cycle. But population growth and pollution are combining to make less and less available per person per year, while global climate change adds new uncertainty. Efficiency, conservation, and technology can help ensure that the water you absorb today will still be usable and clean hundreds of years from now.

◄ ACCESS TO FRESH WATER
Access to clean fresh water is critical for human health. Yet, in many regions, potable water is becoming scarce because of heavy demands and pollution. Especially worrisome is the poisoning of aquifers—a primary source of water for nearly a third of the world—by sewage, pesticides, and heavy metals.

▼ GLOBAL IRRIGATED AREAS AND WATER WITHDRAWALS
Since 1970, global water withdrawals have correlated with the rise in irrigated area. Some 70% of withdrawals are for agriculture, mostly for irrigation that helps produce 40% of the world's food.

Freshwater withdrawal as a percentage of total water utilization, 2000

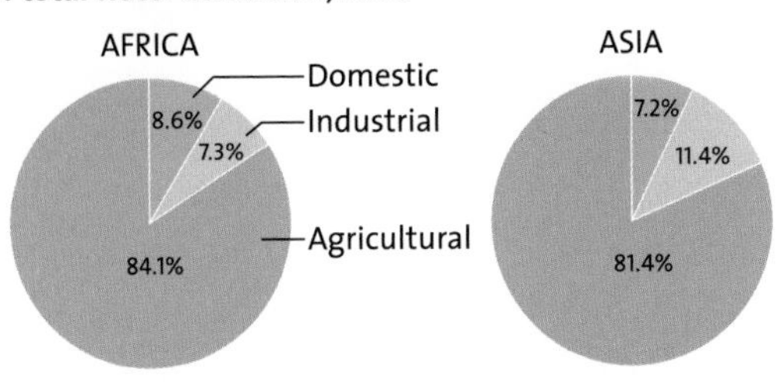

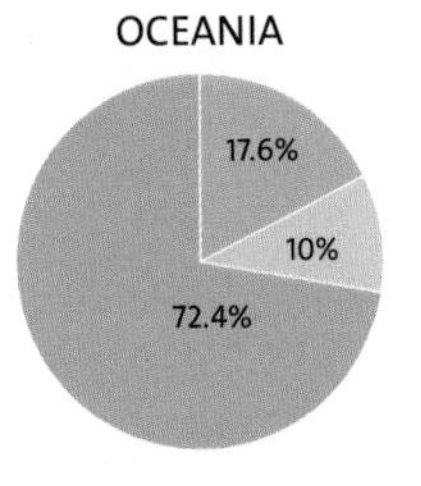

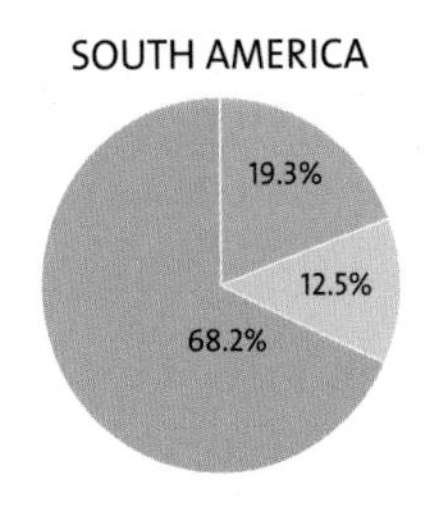

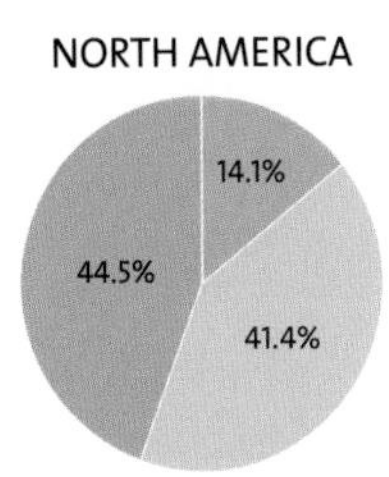

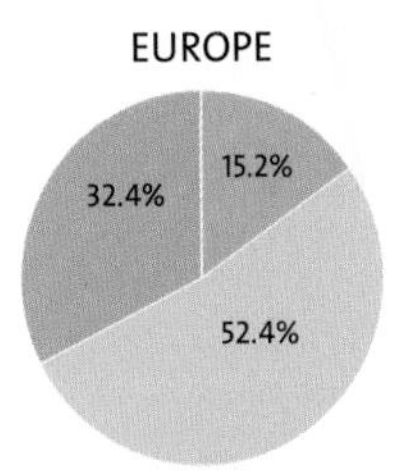

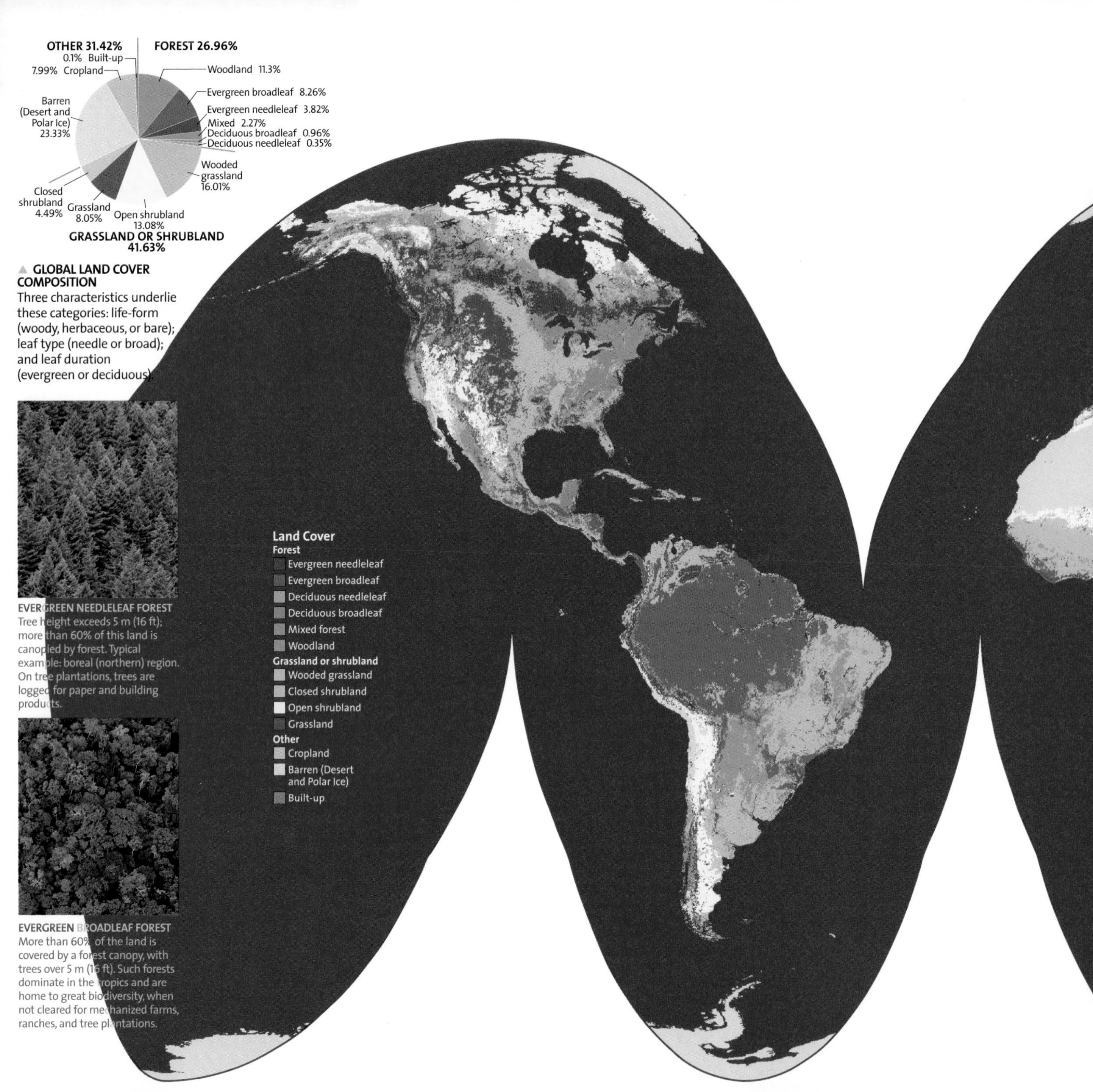

▲ GLOBAL LAND COVER COMPOSITION
Three characteristics underlie these categories: life-form (woody, herbaceous, or bare); leaf type (needle or broad); and leaf duration (evergreen or deciduous).

EVERGREEN NEEDLELEAF FOREST
Tree height exceeds 5 m (16 ft); more than 60% of this land is canopied by forest. Typical example: boreal (northern) region. On tree plantations, trees are logged for paper and building products.

EVERGREEN BROADLEAF FOREST
More than 60% of the land is covered by a forest canopy, with trees over 5 m (16 ft). Such forests dominate in the tropics and are home to great biodiversity, when not cleared for mechanized farms, ranches, and tree plantations.

DECIDUOUS NEEDLELEAF FOREST
A forest canopy covers more than 60% of the land; tree height exceeds 5 m (16 ft). This class is dominant only in Siberia, taking the form of larch forests.

DECIDUOUS BROADLEAF FOREST
More than 60% of the land is covered by a forest canopy; tree height exceeds 5 m (16 ft). In temperate regions, much of this forest has been converted to cropland.

MIXED FOREST
Both needle and deciduous types of trees appear. This type is largely found between temperate deciduous and boreal evergreen forests.

WOODLAND
Land has herbaceous or woody understory; trees exceed 5 m (16 ft) and may be deciduous or evergreen. Highly degraded in long-settled human environments, such as in West Africa.

WOODED GRASSLAND
Woody or herbaceous understories are punctuated by trees. Examples are African savannah as well as open boreal borderland between trees and tundra.

CLOSED SHRUBLAND
Found where prolonged cold or dry seasons limit plant growth, this cover is dominated by bushes or shrubs not exceeding 5 m (16 ft). Tree canopy is less than 10%.

Satellite data provide the most reliable picture of global vegetative cover over time. Few natural communities of plants and animals have remained the same; most have been altered by humans. The "natural" vegetation reflects what would grow there, given ideal conditions.The map at left is based on a year of global satellite imagery from the Advanced Very High Resolution Radiometer (AVHRR) at a spatial resolution of one kilometer. By recording the data at different wavelengths of the electro-magnetic spectrum, scientists can derive land cover type through spectral variation. Changes in vegetation are captured in the satellite record, contributing to a rich data bank for Earth studies in areas such as conservation, biodiversity assessments, and land resource management.

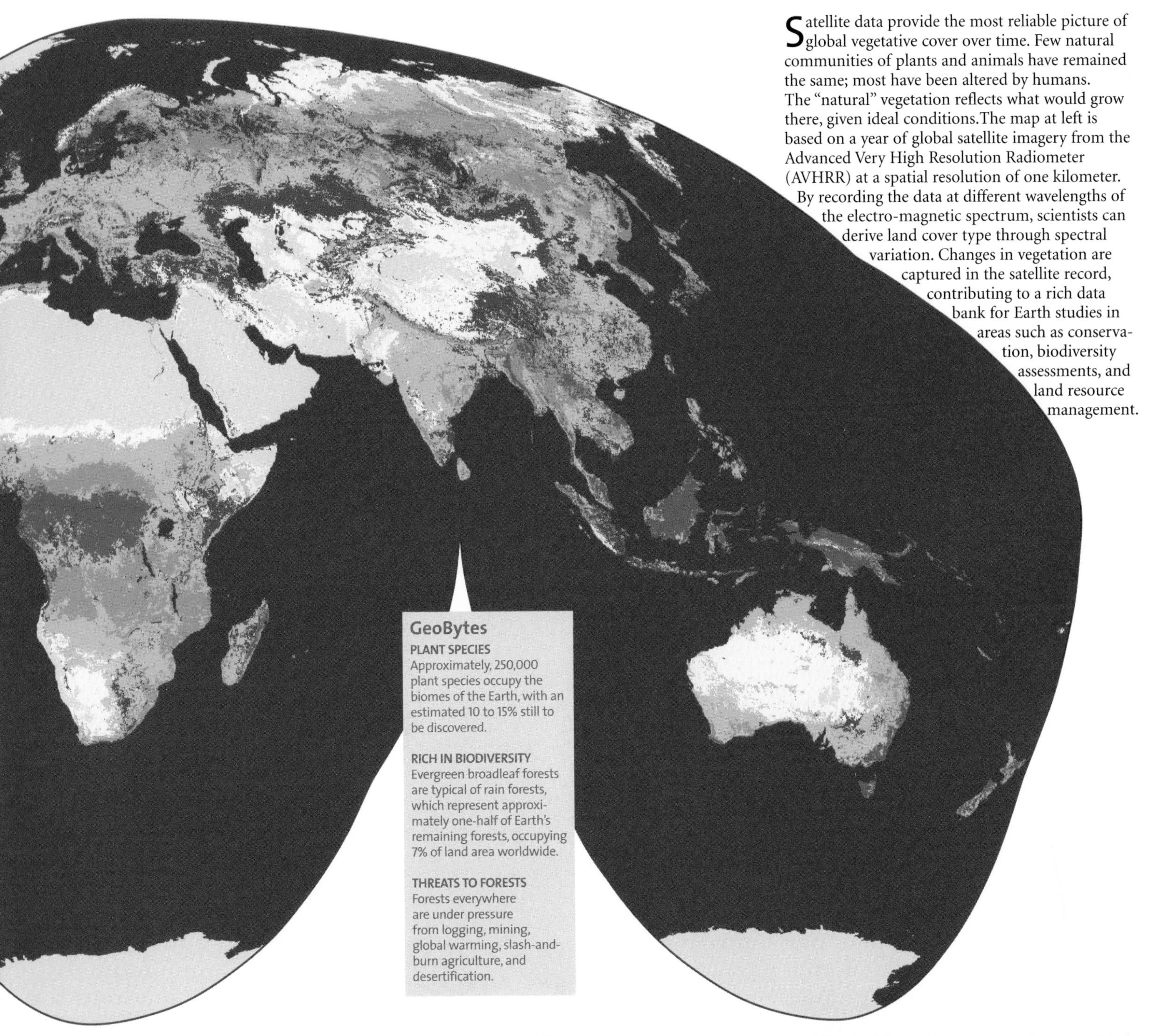

GeoBytes

PLANT SPECIES
Approximately, 250,000 plant species occupy the biomes of the Earth, with an estimated 10 to 15% still to be discovered.

RICH IN BIODIVERSITY
Evergreen broadleaf forests are typical of rain forests, which represent approximately one-half of Earth's remaining forests, occupying 7% of land area worldwide.

THREATS TO FORESTS
Forests everywhere are under pressure from logging, mining, global warming, slash-and-burn agriculture, and desertification.

OPEN SHRUBLAND
Shrubs are dominant, not exceeding 2 m (6.5 ft) in height. They can be evergreen or deciduous. This type occurs in semiarid or severely cold areas.

GRASSLAND
Occurring in a wide range of habitats, this landscape has continuous herbaceous cover. The American Plains and central Russia are the premier examples.

CROPLAND
Crop-producing fields constitute over 80% of the land. Temperate regions are home to large areas of mechanized farming; in the developing world, plots are small.

BARREN (DESERT)
The land never has more than 10% vegetated cover. True deserts, such as the Sahara, as well as areas succumbing to desertification, are examples.

BUILT-UP
This class was mapped using the populated places layer that is part of the "Digital Chart of the World" (Danko, 1992). It represents the most densely inhabited areas.

BARREN (POLAR ICE)
Permanent snow cover characterizes this class, the greatest expanses of which are in the polar regions, as well as on high elevations in Alaska and the Himalaya.

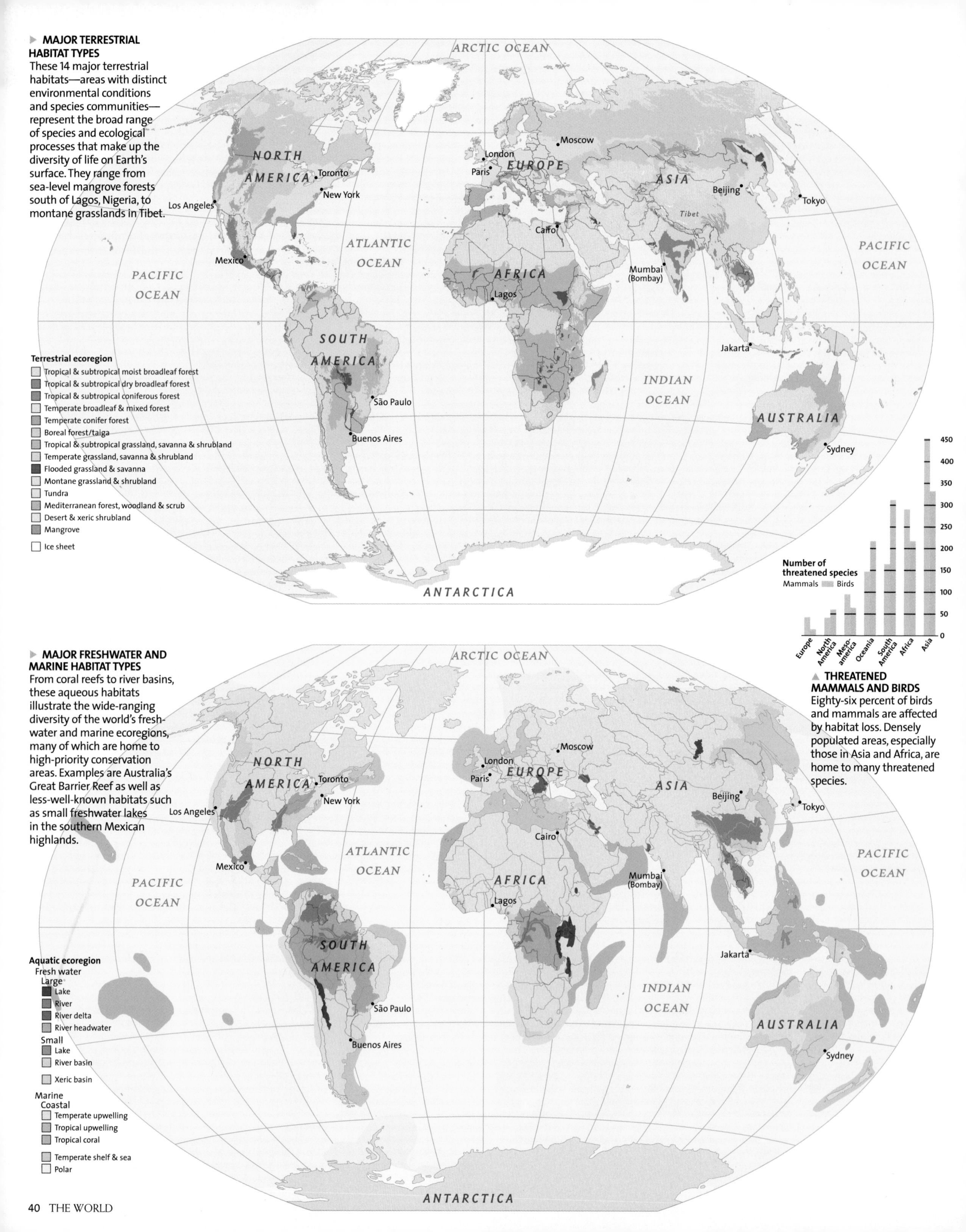

MAJOR TERRESTRIAL HABITAT TYPES
These 14 major terrestrial habitats—areas with distinct environmental conditions and species communities—represent the broad range of species and ecological processes that make up the diversity of life on Earth's surface. They range from sea-level mangrove forests south of Lagos, Nigeria, to montane grasslands in Tibet.

THREATENED MAMMALS AND BIRDS
Eighty-six percent of birds and mammals are affected by habitat loss. Densely populated areas, especially those in Asia and Africa, are home to many threatened species.

MAJOR FRESHWATER AND MARINE HABITAT TYPES
From coral reefs to river basins, these aqueous habitats illustrate the wide-ranging diversity of the world's freshwater and marine ecoregions, many of which are home to high-priority conservation areas. Examples are Australia's Great Barrier Reef as well as less-well-known habitats such as small freshwater lakes in the southern Mexican highlands.

Biodiversity refers to the rich variety of life among the world's living organisms and the ecological communities they are part of. It includes the number of different species, the genetic diversity within species, and the ecosystems in which species live. Some areas, such as coral reefs, are replete with diversity; others, like the polar regions, are noted for their lack of diversity. The biodiversity of any given place is shaped by biogeographic conditions including local and regional climate, latitude, range of habitats, evolutionary history, and biological productivity—a place's capacity to generate and support life. Out of the estimated 5 to 30 million species that exist, only 1.9 million species have been named. Experts estimate that species are becoming extinct at a rate of 100 to 1,000 times higher than might be expected from natural extinction, akin to a mass extinction. Humans rely on the world's diverse assets for survival—food, medicine, clean air, drinkable water, habitable climates—yet it is our activities that pose the greatest threat to the world's biodiversity.

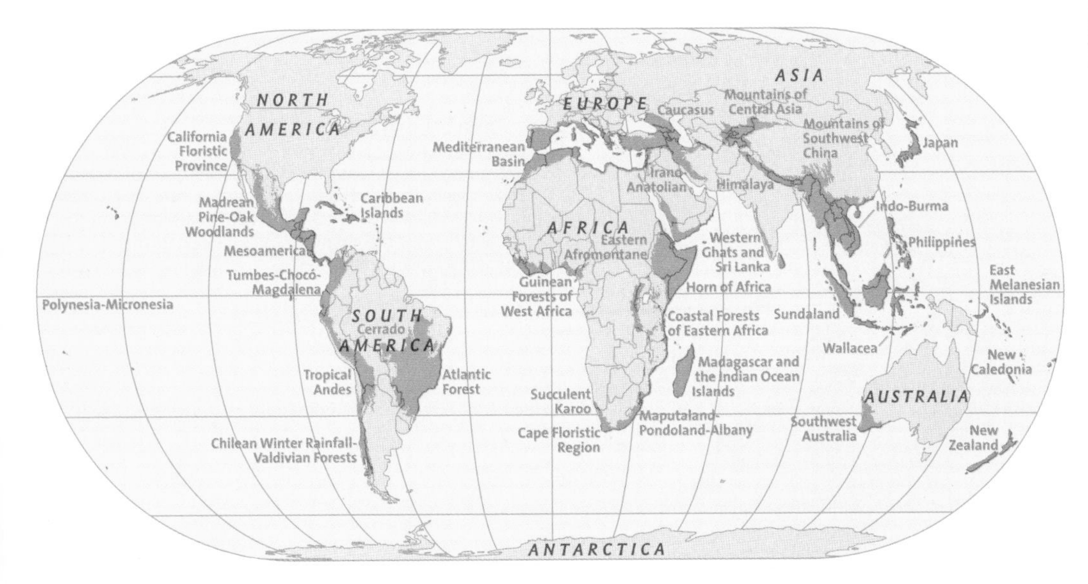

BIODIVERSITY HOTSPOTS
What areas are vital for conserving biodiversity? Conservation International identified 34 "hotspots," defined as habitat holding at least 1,500 endemic plant species and having lost 70% of its original extent.

THREATS TO BIODIVERSITY
The greatest threats to biodiversity—habitat loss and fragmentation, invasion of non-native species, pollution, and unsustainable exploitation—are all caused by human economic activity and population growth.

NORTH AMERICA, SOUTH AMERICA, EUROPE, ASIA, AFRICA, AUSTRALIA, ANTARCTICA
Los Angeles, Toronto, New York, Mexico, London, Paris, Moscow, Cairo, Lagos, Mumbai (Bombay), Beijing, Tokyo, Jakarta, São Paulo, Buenos Aires, Sydney

Projected status of biodiversity, 1998–2018
- Critical and endangered
- Threatened
- Relatively stable/intact

GeoBytes

UNIQUE SPECIES
Madagascar and the Indian Ocean islands are home to many species found nowhere else. Of the region's 13,000 plant species, more than 89% are endemic, meaning that is the only place on Earth they live.

FRAGILE POPULATIONS
Nearly half of the world's tortoises and freshwater turtles are threatened.

HUMAN HEALTH
Medicines derived from plants and animals are the primary source of health care for 80% of the world's population.

ECONOMIC VALUE
Scientists estimate that ecosystems worldwide provide goods and services, such as nutrient recycling and waste treatment, valued at more than $20 trillion a year.

EXTINCTION RISK
One in every eight birds and one in every four mammals face a high risk of extinction in the near future.

BEETLEMANIA
Beetles are the most diverse life-form on Earth. More than a thousand different kinds can live on a single tree in the forests of South America.

1. THE BERING SEA
The Bering Sea, separating Alaska and Russia, is one of the world's most diverse marine environments. Polar bears, seals, sea lions, walruses, whales, enormous populations of seabirds, and more than 400 species of fish, crustaceans, and mollusks live in this ecoregion. It is also home to one of the world's largest salmon runs. Global warming, pollution, overfishing, and mining are major threats to this region's biodiversity.

2. SOUTHEASTERN U.S. RIVERS AND STREAMS
From Appalachian streams to saltwater marshes along the Atlantic and Gulf coasts, this ecoregion harbors hundreds of species of fish, snails, crayfish, and mussels. A single river in the region, the Cahaba River in Alabama, has more fish species per mile than any other river in North America. Population growth and increasing streamside development, dams, and water diversion for irrigation are long-term threats.

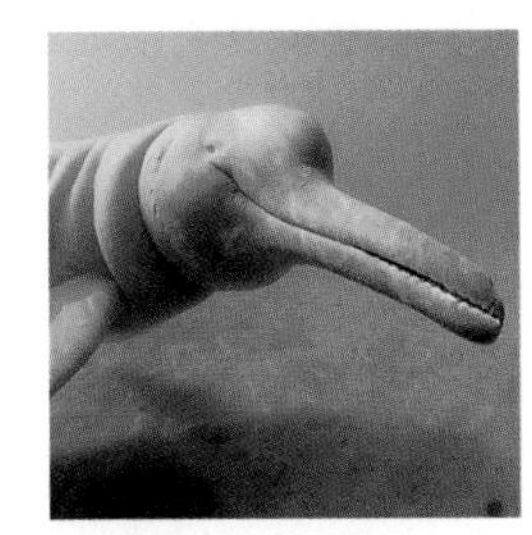

3. THE AMAZON RIVER AND FLOODED FORESTS
More than 3,000 species of freshwater fish and many mammals, including the pink river dolphin, inhabit this ecoregion. The Amazon Basin is Earth's largest watershed and is noted for having the world's largest expanse of seasonally flooded forests, habitat for a wide array of migratory species. Selective logging and the conversion of floodplains for ranching and agricultural use are threats to the region.

4. RIFT VALLEY LAKES
This cluster of freshwater and alkaline lakes spread across East Africa's Great Lakes region. It is home to nearly 800 species of cichlid fishes, all derived from a common ancestor, a process called species radiation. These radiations are an extraordinary example of evolutionary adaptation. The lakes also provide important bird habitat—half of the world's flamingo population lives here. Threats to the region include deforestation, pollution, and the spread of non-native species.

5. EASTERN HIMALAYAN BROADLEAF AND CONIFER FORESTS
Snaking across the lowlands and foothills of the Himalaya, this ecoregion supports a remarkable diversity of plants and animals, including endangered mammals such as the clouded leopard, Himalayan black bear, and the golden langur. These sub-alpine forests are also a significant endemic bird area. Because forests are slow to regenerate, conversion to cropland and timber extraction are serious threats to this region's biodiversity.

6. SULU-SULAWESI SEAS
Extensive coral reefs, mangroves, and seagrass beds make this one of the richest habitats for reef animals and plants in the world. More than 450 species of coral, six of the world's eight species of marine turtles, and numerous species of fish, sharks, and whales live in this marine ecoregion between Indonesia, Malaysia, and the Philippines. These reefs continue to be threatened by coastal erosion, pollution, and overfishing.

GeoBytes

SHRINKING FORESTS
Since 1700, nearly 20% of Earth's forests and woodlands have disappeared.

CARBON DIOXIDE EMISSIONS
Land use has contributed to 35% of human-caused carbon dioxide emissions over the last 150 years.

URBANIZING POPULATION
Urban areas cover roughly 3% of the Earth and house half of the world's population.

LAND USE PATTERNS
Data from satellite imagery and ground-based records show the impact land use has on the Earth. Food production has had the greatest impact—croplands and pastures now cover nearly 40% of the Earth's surface. Increasing urbanization is poised to alter the landscape further.

New data show how humans have transformed the face of the Earth from virgin forests and grasslands to croplands, pastures, and cities.

More disturbed — Cropland
Less disturbed
More disturbed — Pasture

Built-up area

Highly degraded land from agriculture or overgrazing

Largest urban agglomerations, 2005

Population
- More than 10 million (Megacity)
- 5-10 million

Image area

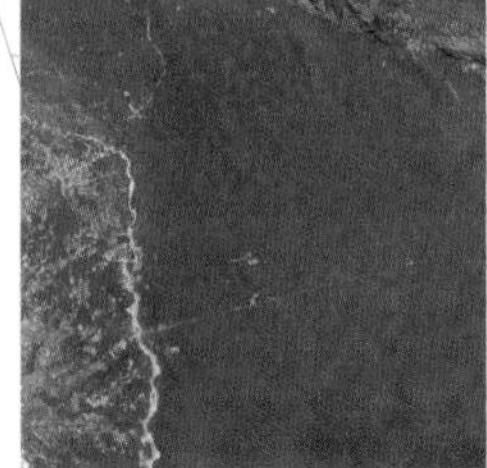

1. DEFORESTATION
These images show the progression of deforestation and increasing agricultural development in Bolivia. The first image (1975) shows a large expanse of solid red, representing tropical dry forest, to the east of Bolivia's second largest city, Santa Cruz. The other two images (1992 and 2000, respectively) show an increasing number of open patches representing small communities and soybean fields, depicted as light-colored rectangles, in areas that were once forested.

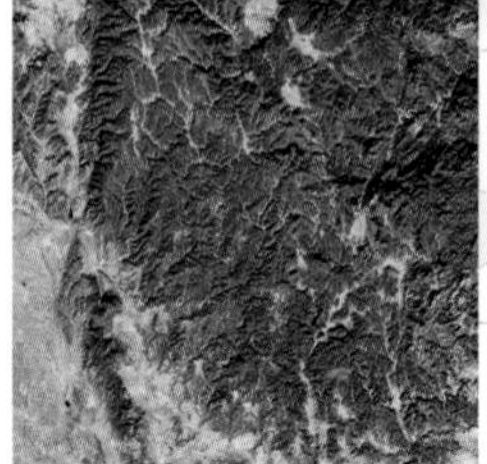

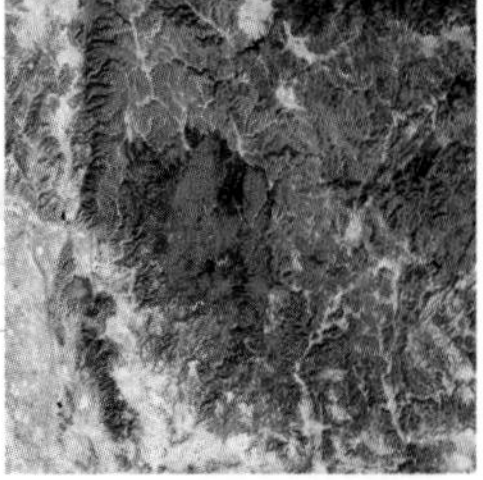

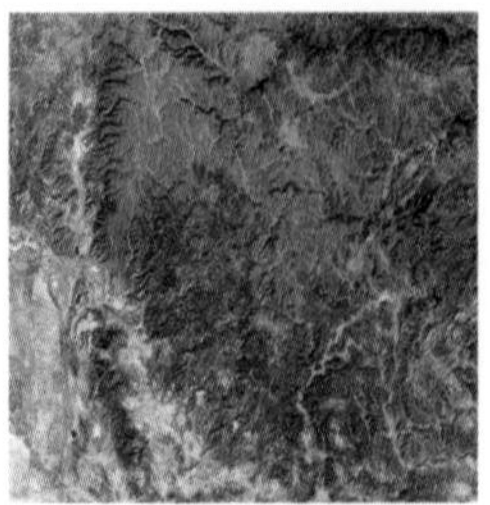

2. FIRE
Fire can have a devastating and immediate impact on the landscape. In 1999, the Black Hills of South Dakota were covered with vegetation, shown in green, and relatively free of fire damage. The second and third images show the same area after the Jasper fire of 2000 destroyed nearly 34,000 hectares (84,000 acres) and a smaller fire burned an additional 5,260 hectares (13,000 acres) in 2002, both shown in red. It will take decades for the area to recover.

The intensification of agriculture, increasing consumption of natural resources, and a global trend toward urbanization, partnered with swift population growth, are dramatically transforming Earth's landscape. Practices associated with land use vary widely across the globe, but most fulfill human needs such as food and shelter while having an often negative impact on the natural world, such as climate change, loss of biodiversity, and degradation of soil and water. Lessening these negative impacts is critical to the preservation of the natural world and ultimately to human survival.

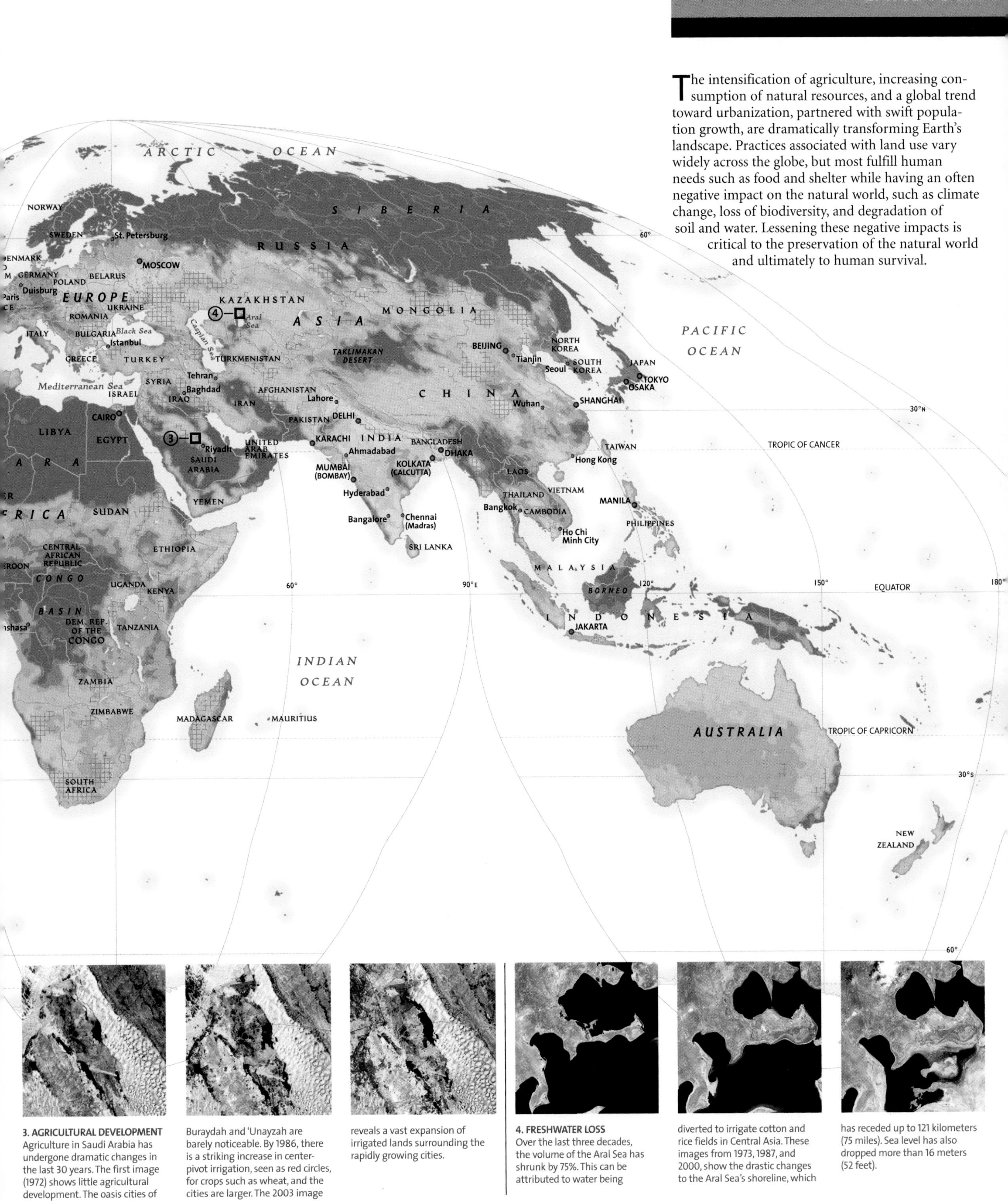

3. AGRICULTURAL DEVELOPMENT
Agriculture in Saudi Arabia has undergone dramatic changes in the last 30 years. The first image (1972) shows little agricultural development. The oasis cities of Buraydah and 'Unayzah are barely noticeable. By 1986, there is a striking increase in center-pivot irrigation, seen as red circles, for crops such as wheat, and the cities are larger. The 2003 image reveals a vast expansion of irrigated lands surrounding the rapidly growing cities.

4. FRESHWATER LOSS
Over the last three decades, the volume of the Aral Sea has shrunk by 75%. This can be attributed to water being diverted to irrigate cotton and rice fields in Central Asia. These images from 1973, 1987, and 2000, show the drastic changes to the Aral Sea's shoreline, which has receded up to 121 kilometers (75 miles). Sea level has also dropped more than 16 meters (52 feet).

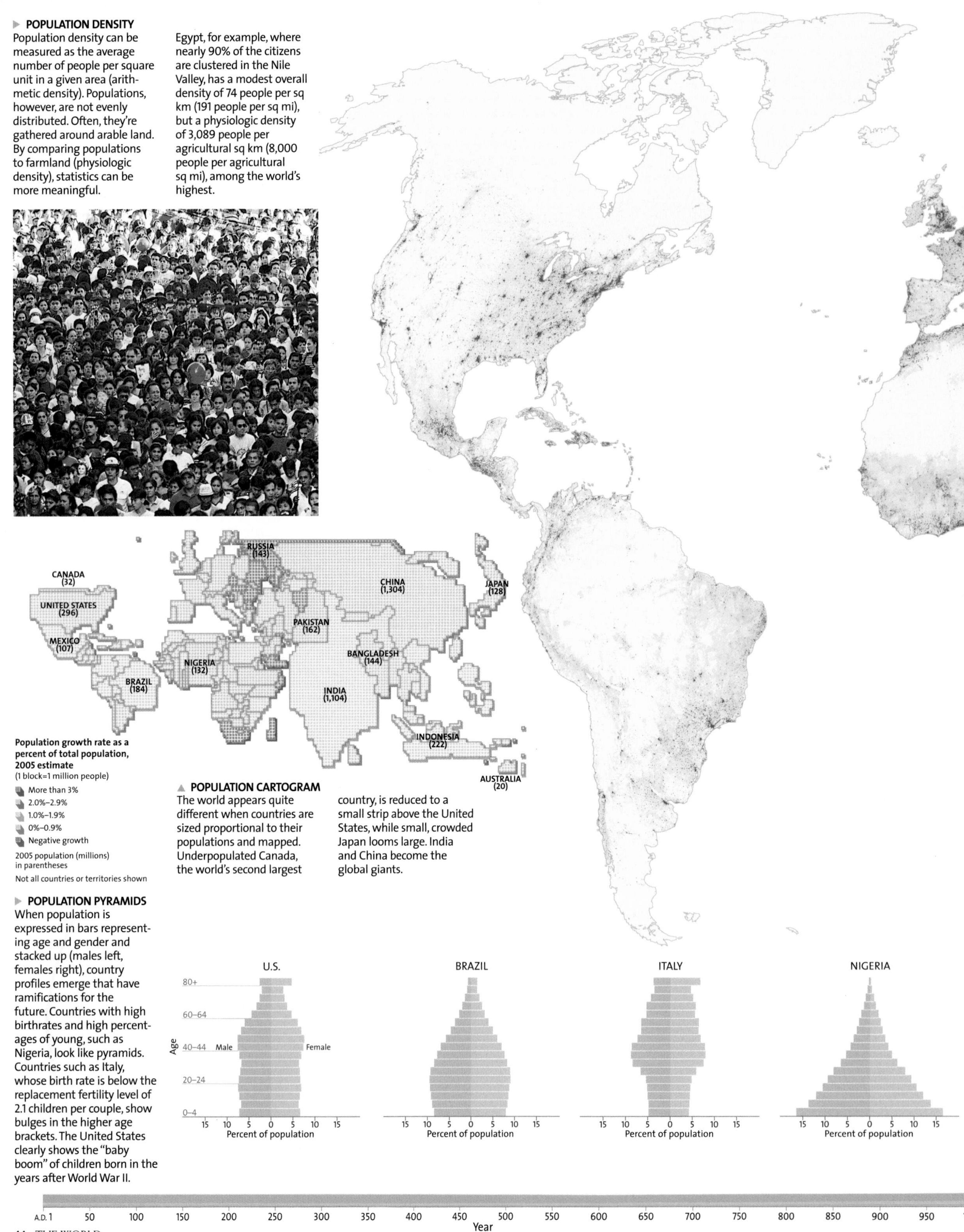

POPULATION DENSITY
Population density can be measured as the average number of people per square unit in a given area (arithmetic density). Populations, however, are not evenly distributed. Often, they're gathered around arable land. By comparing populations to farmland (physiologic density), statistics can be more meaningful. Egypt, for example, where nearly 90% of the citizens are clustered in the Nile Valley, has a modest overall density of 74 people per sq km (191 people per sq mi), but a physiologic density of 3,089 people per agricultural sq km (8,000 people per agricultural sq mi), among the world's highest.

POPULATION CARTOGRAM
The world appears quite different when countries are sized proportional to their populations and mapped. Underpopulated Canada, the world's second largest country, is reduced to a small strip above the United States, while small, crowded Japan looms large. India and China become the global giants.

POPULATION PYRAMIDS
When population is expressed in bars representing age and gender and stacked up (males left, females right), country profiles emerge that have ramifications for the future. Countries with high birthrates and high percentages of young, such as Nigeria, look like pyramids. Countries such as Italy, whose birth rate is below the replacement fertility level of 2.1 children per couple, show bulges in the higher age brackets. The United States clearly shows the "baby boom" of children born in the years after World War II.

Geographers approach the study of human populations, or demography, from a spatial perspective, asking why density, distribution, resources, births, deaths, and migrations vary from place to place. Earth's population, now at 6.5 billion, grows by 80 million a year, or 1.2% annually. The bulk of the increase occurs in developing countries in Asia, Africa, and Latin America. Physiologic density—the number of people per unit of agricultural land—shows concentrations in Asia, in particular in China and India; in Europe, from Britain into Russia; along the eastern seaboard of the United States; and in West Africa in Nigeria and along the Nile Valley.

GeoBytes

COUNTING HEADS
Most governments conduct a population census every ten years, although the process is expensive and accuracy is difficult to attain for most.

PACKED NEIGHBORHOODS
The most densely populated place in the world is Macau, a Chinese Special Administrative Region, with 18,960 people per sq km (47,400 people per sq mi). The least dense is Greenland.

IOWA VS. BANGLADESH
Bangladesh's rural population density is up to 12,950 per sq km (5,000 per sq mi) in an area the size of Iowa. In Iowa, the figure is fewer than 145 per sq km (55 per sq mi).

SHEER NUMBERS
The most populated country is the People's Republic of China, with 1.3 billion. The least populated jurisdiction is Pitcairn Island in the Pacific, with 46 people.

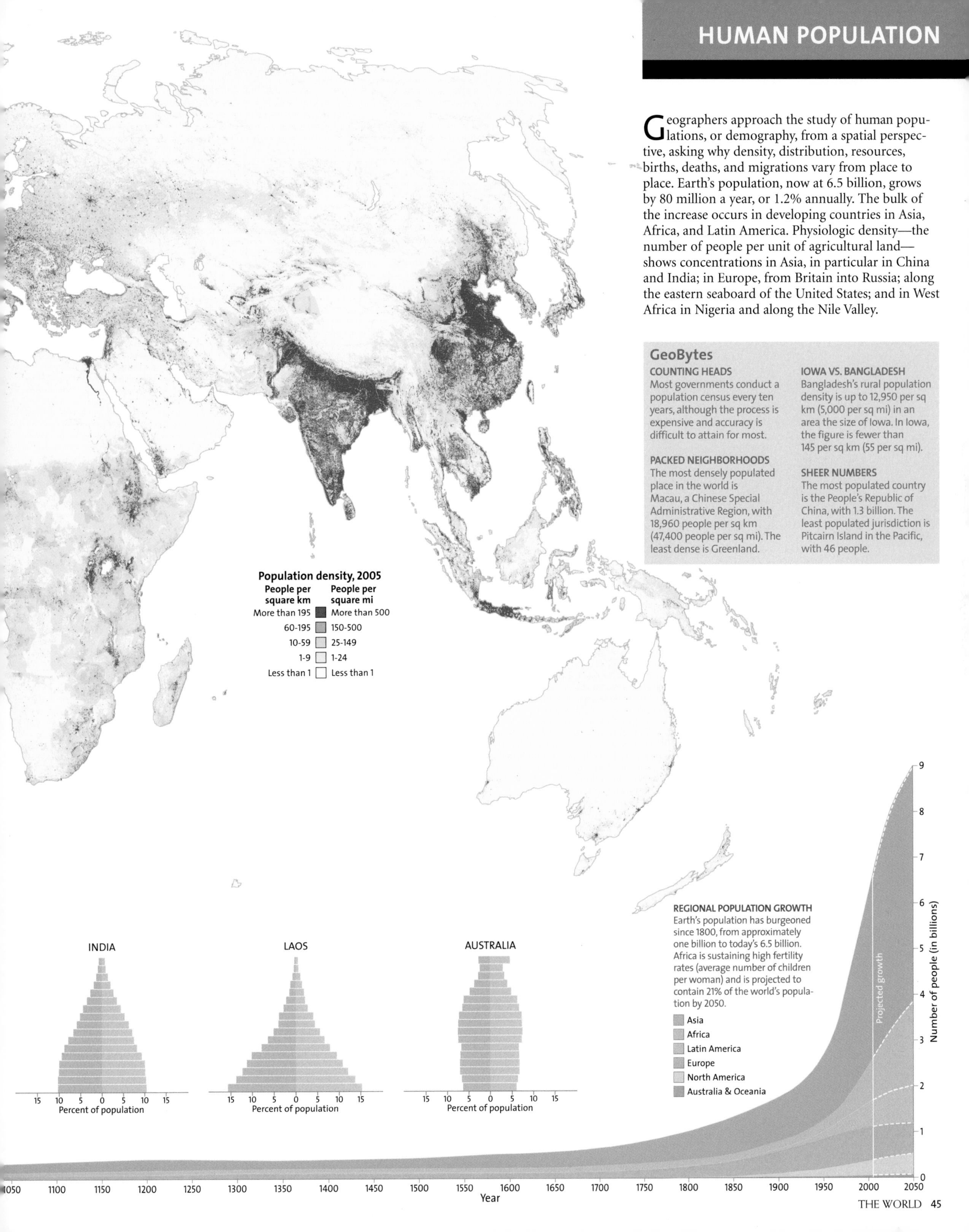

REGIONAL POPULATION GROWTH
Earth's population has burgeoned since 1800, from approximately one billion to today's 6.5 billion. Africa is sustaining high fertility rates (average number of children per woman) and is projected to contain 21% of the world's population by 2050.

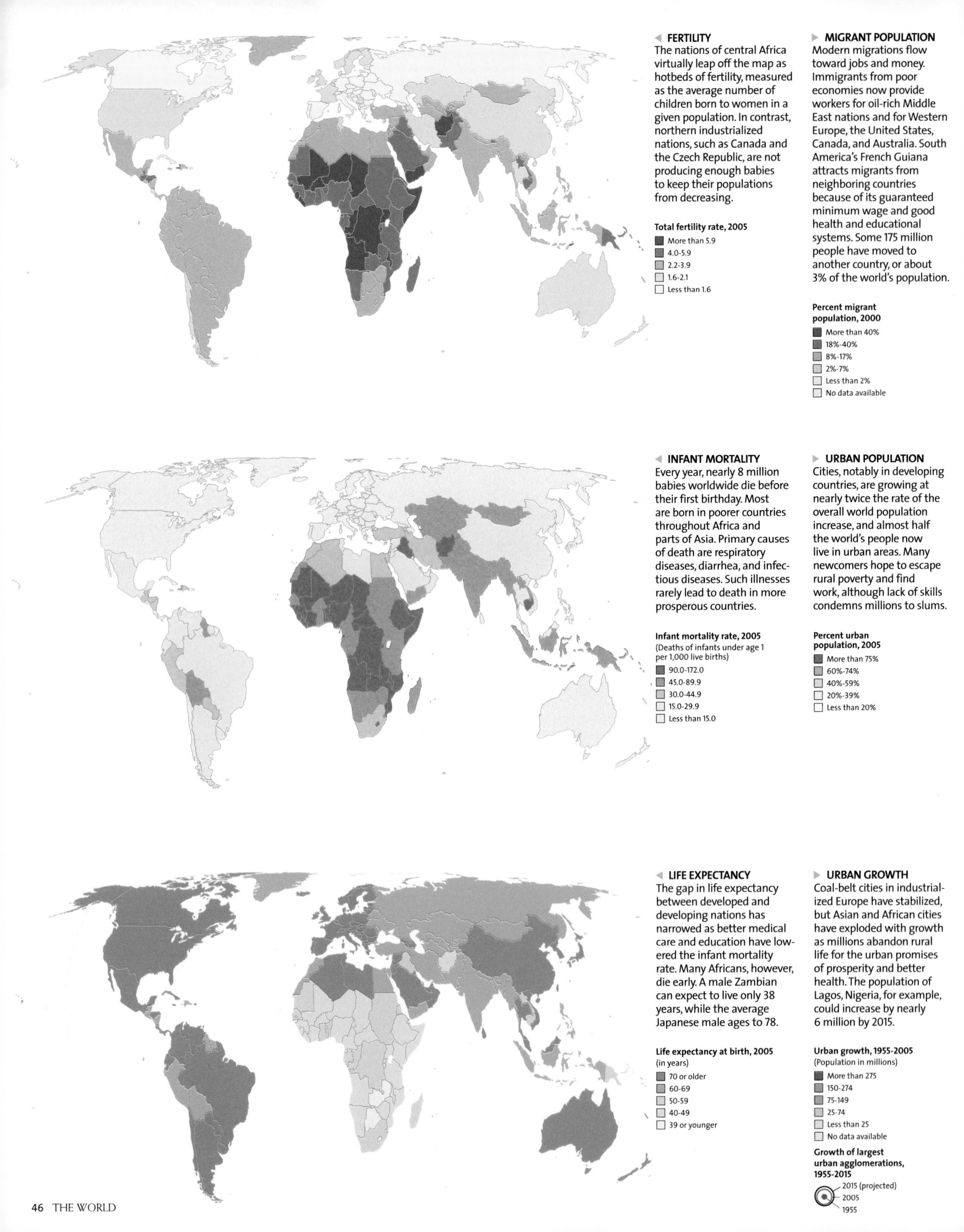

FERTILITY

The nations of central Africa virtually leap off the map as hotbeds of fertility, measured as the average number of children born to women in a given population. In contrast, northern industrialized nations, such as Canada and the Czech Republic, are not producing enough babies to keep their populations from decreasing.

Total fertility rate, 2005

- More than 5.9
- 4.0-5.9
- 2.2-3.9
- 1.6-2.1
- Less than 1.6

MIGRANT POPULATION

Modern migrations flow toward jobs and money. Immigrants from poor economies now provide workers for oil-rich Middle East nations and for Western Europe, the United States, Canada, and Australia. South America's French Guiana attracts migrants from neighboring countries because of its guaranteed minimum wage and good health and educational systems. Some 175 million people have moved to another country, or about 3% of the world's population.

Percent migrant population, 2000

- More than 40%
- 18%-40%
- 8%-17%
- 2%-7%
- Less than 2%
- No data available

INFANT MORTALITY

Every year, nearly 8 million babies worldwide die before their first birthday. Most are born in poorer countries throughout Africa and parts of Asia. Primary causes of death are respiratory diseases, diarrhea, and infectious diseases. Such illnesses rarely lead to death in more prosperous countries.

Infant mortality rate, 2005
(Deaths of infants under age 1 per 1,000 live births)

- 90.0-172.0
- 45.0-89.9
- 30.0-44.9
- 15.0-29.9
- Less than 15.0

URBAN POPULATION

Cities, notably in developing countries, are growing at nearly twice the rate of the overall world population increase, and almost half the world's people now live in urban areas. Many newcomers hope to escape rural poverty and find work, although lack of skills condemns millions to slums.

Percent urban population, 2005

- More than 75%
- 60%-74%
- 40%-59%
- 20%-39%
- Less than 20%

LIFE EXPECTANCY

The gap in life expectancy between developed and developing nations has narrowed as better medical care and education have lowered the infant mortality rate. Many Africans, however, die early. A male Zambian can expect to live only 38 years, while the average Japanese male ages to 78.

Life expectancy at birth, 2005
(in years)

- 70 or older
- 60-69
- 50-59
- 40-49
- 39 or younger

URBAN GROWTH

Coal-belt cities in industrialized Europe have stabilized, but Asian and African cities have exploded with growth as millions abandon rural life for the urban promises of prosperity and better health. The population of Lagos, Nigeria, for example, could increase by nearly 6 million by 2015.

Urban growth, 1955-2005
(Population in millions)

- More than 275
- 150-274
- 75-149
- 25-74
- Less than 25
- No data available

Growth of largest urban agglomerations, 1955-2015

- 2015 (projected)
- 2005
- 1955

POPULATION TRENDS

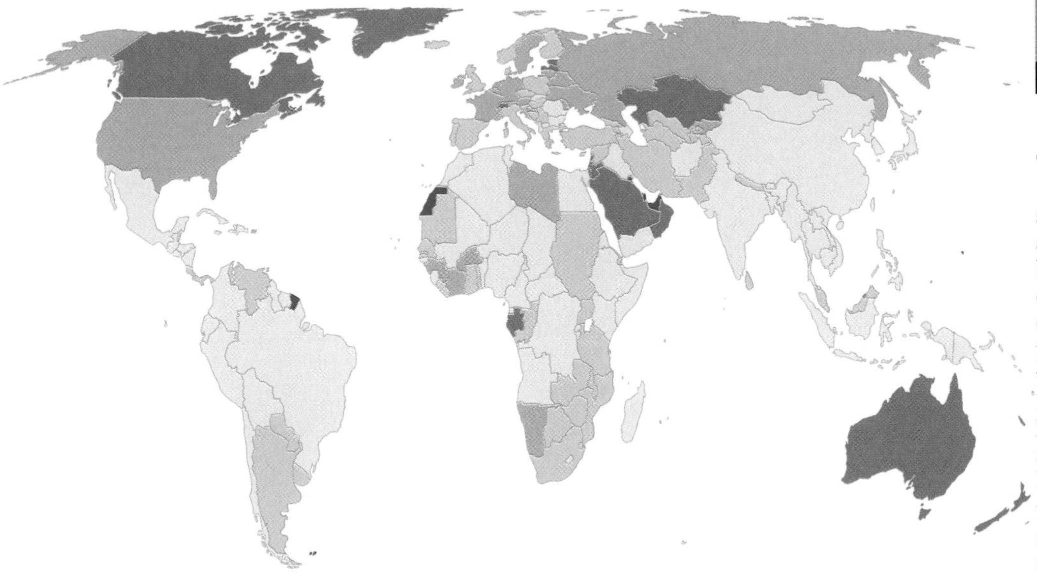

The 21st century will witness substantial world population growth, even as the rate of growth slows, total fertility rates decline, and populations age. Sheer numbers will increase simply because the base population is so great; the benchmark figure of 6 billion was reached in October 1999. By mid-century, up to 10 billion humans may be sharing the planet. Of the 80 million people being added each year, some 90% are born into developing countries. In some African and Muslim countries, one key to limiting growth is improving the status of women and their access to education and contraception. By 2050, the elderly could constitute 22% of the world's population, affecting economies, savings, employment, and health care. The toll of AIDS in sub-Saharan Africa and adult male mortality in some Eastern European countries are disturbing trends. In the future, cities will grow, and more people will cross international boundaries in search of employment and security.

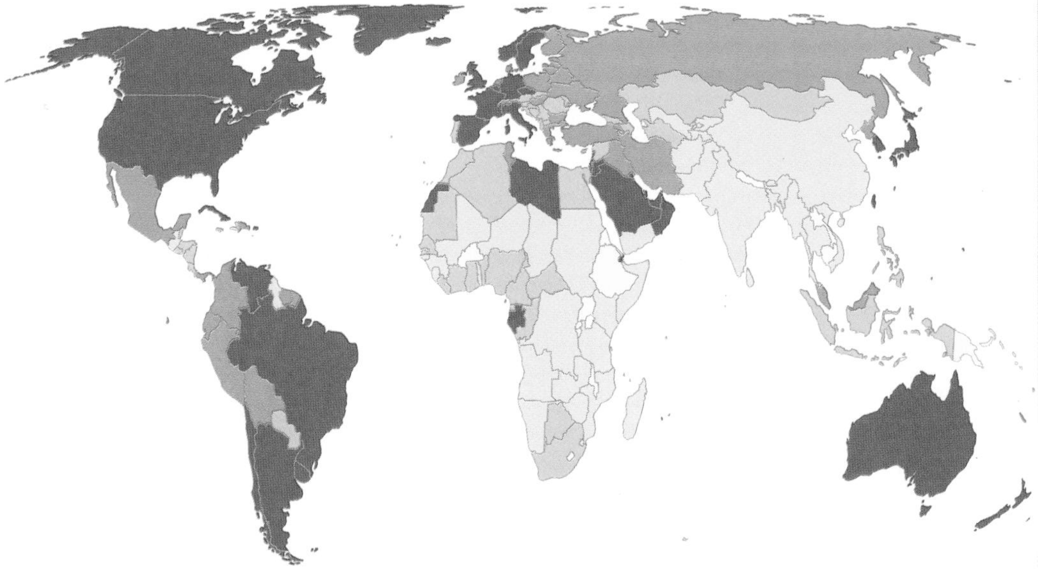

GeoBytes

PEOPLE THROUGH TIME
The total number of humans born since 50,000 B.C. is 106 billion.

FAST FORWARD
Today the world gains one billion people every 11 years. With current growth rates, world population could reach 10 billion by 2050.

SIX BILLION STRONG
At the beginning of the 21st century, world population stood at 6.4 billion people, or an estimated 6% of the total who have ever lived.

SMALL CITIES
Pre-Industrial Age cities were comparatively small. Rome, the largest city of antiquity, had only 350,000 people.

NATIVITY DISCREPANCY
The death rate of mothers during childbirth in developing countries is 22 times higher than that of women in the developed world.

MOST CHILDREN
In 2005, the the highest fertility rate in the world was in Niger, where women averaged eight children.

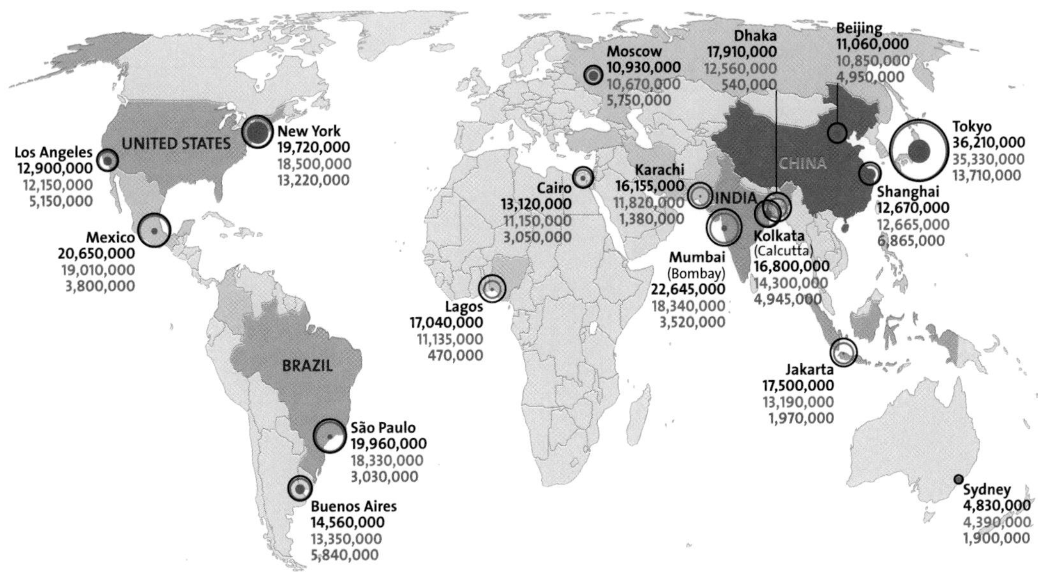

MOST POPULOUS COUNTRIES, Mid-2005

1	China	1,303,701,000
2	India	1,103,596,000
3	United States	296,483,000
4	Indonesia	221,932,000
5	Brazil	184,184,000
6	Pakistan	162,420,000
7	Bangladesh	144,233,000
8	Russia	143,025,000
9	Nigeria	131,530,000
10	Japan	127,728,000

MOST DENSELY POPULATED PLACES, Mid-2005

		Population density per sq km	(sq mi)
1	Macau	18,960	(47,400)
2	Monaco	16,500	(33,000)
3	Singapore	6,509	(16,847)
4	Hong Kong	6,338	(16,400)
5	Gibraltar	4,143	(9,667)
6	Vatican City	1,995	(3,990)
7	Malta	1,282	(3,320)
8	Bermuda	1,170	(2,952)
9	Bahrain	1,020	(2,639)
10	Maldives	987	(2,557)

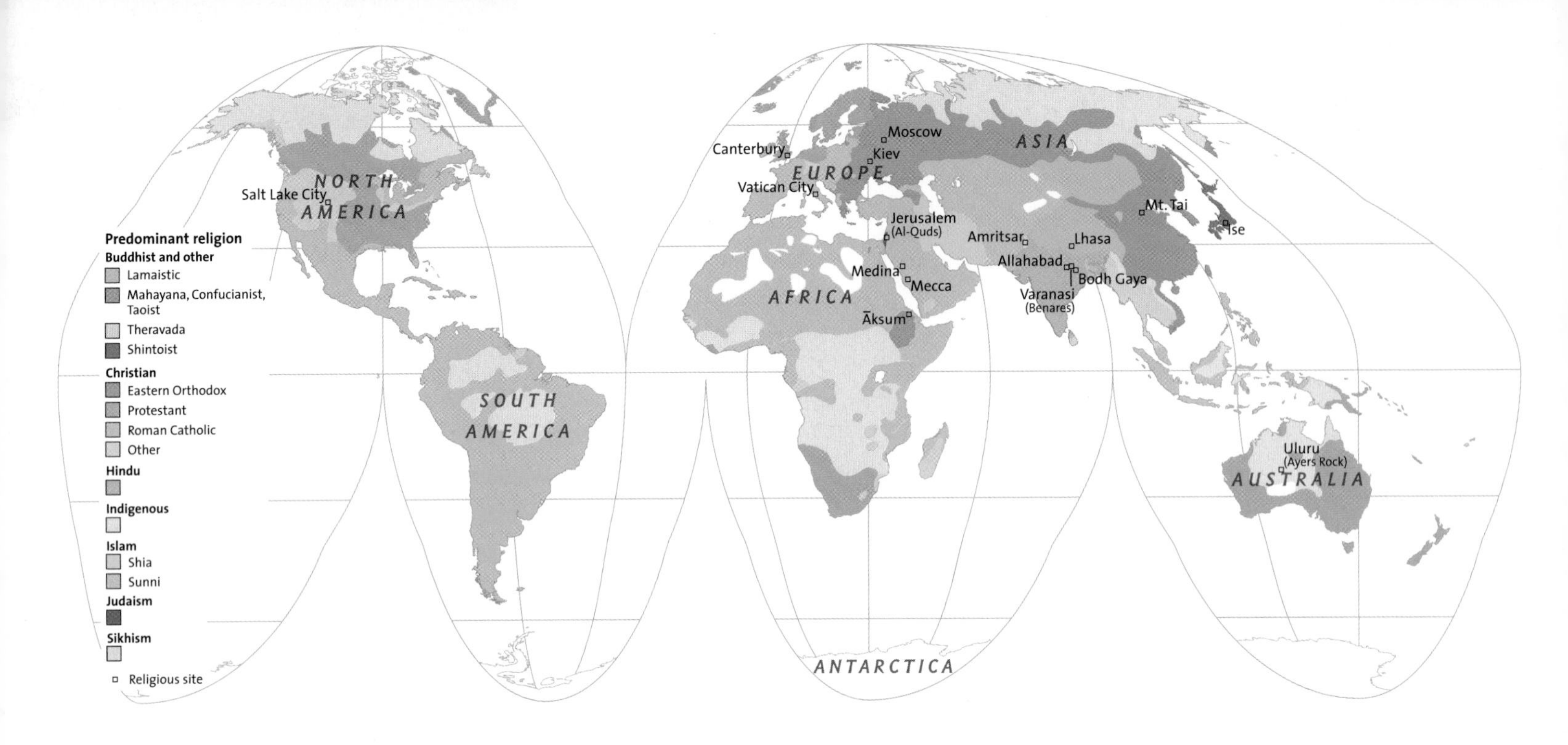

▼ WORLD LANGUAGES

Indo-European languages dominate the West, and English has become the language of aviation and technology. But a global language is not yet at hand. More people speak Mandarin Chinese than speak English, Spanish, German, and French combined. Half of the 6,000 languages in the world today are spoken by fewer than 10,000 people; a quarter by fewer than a thousand. Only a score are on the tongues of millions. After Mandarin Chinese and English, Hindi ranks third.

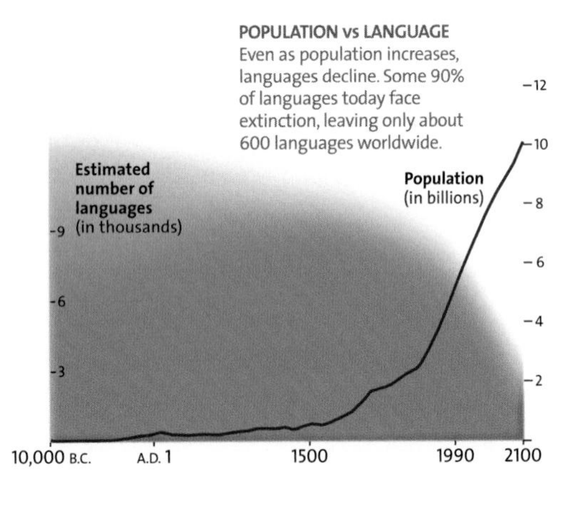

POPULATION vs LANGUAGE
Even as population increases, languages decline. Some 90% of languages today face extinction, leaving only about 600 languages worldwide.

▲ MAJOR RELIGIONS

Christianity, spread mostly by European conquest, has the most adherents of the five major religions, but a resurgent Islam has blossomed on the African-Asian axis. Hinduism and Buddhism today maintain wide blocs of the faithful in Asia, while the homeland of Judaism in Israel is a beleaguered bastion.

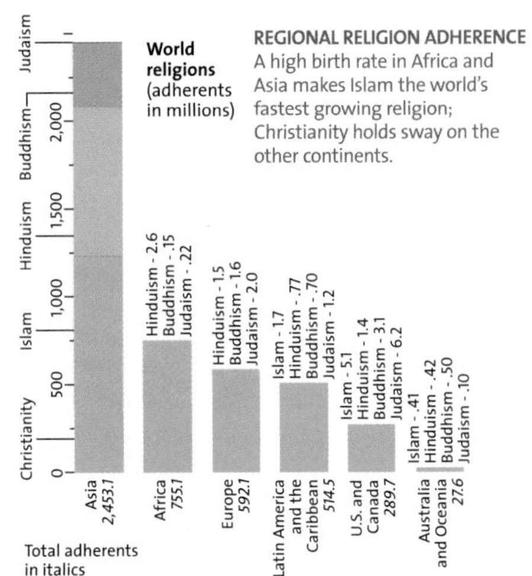

REGIONAL RELIGION ADHERENCE
A high birth rate in Africa and Asia makes Islam the world's fastest growing religion; Christianity holds sway on the other continents.

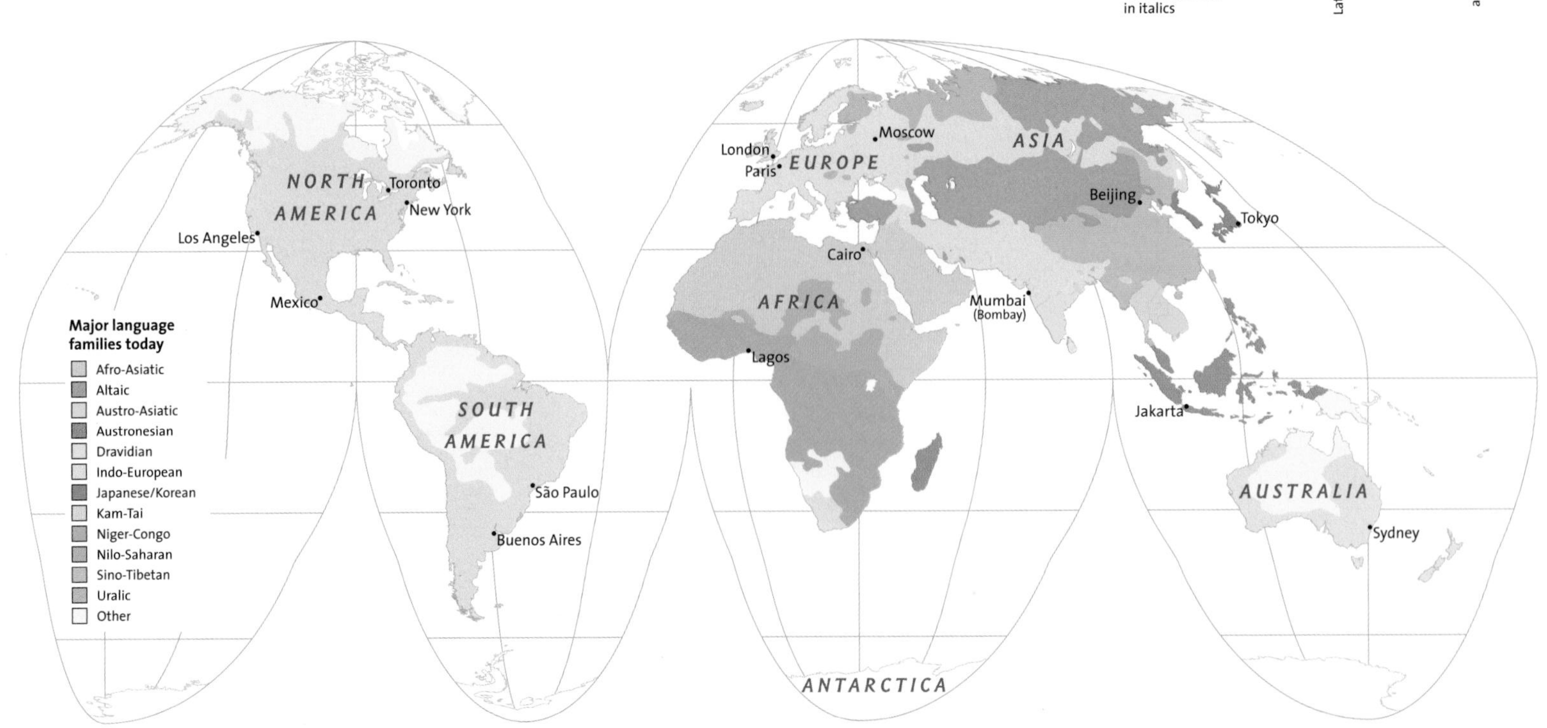

From the food we eat to the values we cherish, culture is at the heart of how we live and understand our human world. Not just a collection of customs, rituals, or artifacts, culture is a complex building up of ideas, innovation, and ideologies. Distinct cultures emerged in river valleys, along coastlines, on islands, and across land masses, as humans spread to every continent but Antarctica. Conquest and trade helped dominant cultures to expand. Today, electronic communication, transportation networks, and economic globalization bring major cultures closer. Cultural perceptions can play a part in misunderstanding and conflict. Yet cultures arose in the first place in response to a human need for stability and progress.

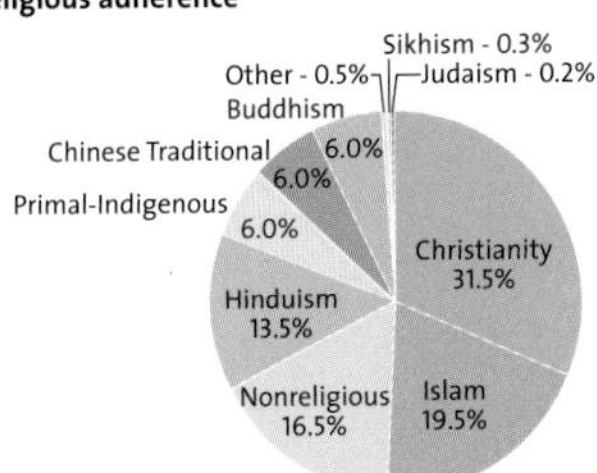

RELIGIOUS ADHERENCE
The classification of religion and adherents has changed over time. In Western thought and early "world-religion" writing, three religions were recognized: Judaism, Christianity, and Paganism. As Eastern history was more understood, other faiths were added to the list of world religions. Around 1800, the "big five" religions were classified as Judaism, Christianity, Islam, Hinduism, and Buddhism. Most recently, nonreligious has been added as an important segment.

GeoBytes

FIRST URBANITES
The Sumerians developed the first city on the broad alluvial plain of the Tigris and Euphrates Rivers.

ACROSS THE STRAIT
Walking dry-shod across a land bridge, ancestors of Native Americans crossed into present-day Alaska from Siberia more than 14,000 years ago.

A TROVE OF LANGUAGES
Papua New Guinea is home to more than 800 languages.

CHINA KEPT OUTSIDERS OUT
The rulers of ancient China were so fearful of external influences that they shut off their kingdom for centuries. The quarantine led to technological stagnation.

STONE TOOLS IN AN AGE OF EXPLORATION
In Australia, Africa, South America, and India's Andaman and Nicobar Islands, European explorers found indigenous people living with Stone Age technology.

SATELLITE IMAGES OF HOLY SITES
The Old City of Jerusalem surrounds Al' Aqsa Mosque and the Dome of the Rock (left). Al' Aqsa is the second oldest mosque in Islam after the Kaaba in Mecca and is third in holiness after the mosques in Mecca and Medina. It holds up to 400,000 worshippers at one time. The shrine of the Dome of the Rock, built in A.D. 692, commemorates the Prophet Muhammad's ascension to heaven. Also visible is the Western (Wailing) Wall of the Jews, the holiest site in the Jewish world. Part of the retaining wall supporting the Temple of Jerusalem built by Herod in 20 B.C., it is visited by Jews from all over the world. Here, too, is the Via Dolorosa, the traditional route of Christ's crucifixion. Christians pray along the route. The streets of Mecca huddle around the Kaaba (center), Islam's holiest shrine. At Allahabad, the Ganges and Yamuna Rivers (right) draw over 30 million Hindus to bathe in their waters during the Maha Kumbh Mela, the largest gathering of human beings ever recorded.

OLD CITY OF JERUSALEM, ISRAEL

MECCA, SAUDI ARABIA

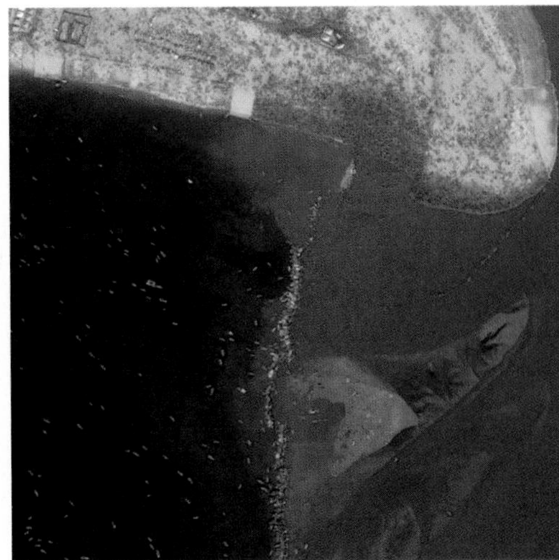
ALLAHABAD, INDIA

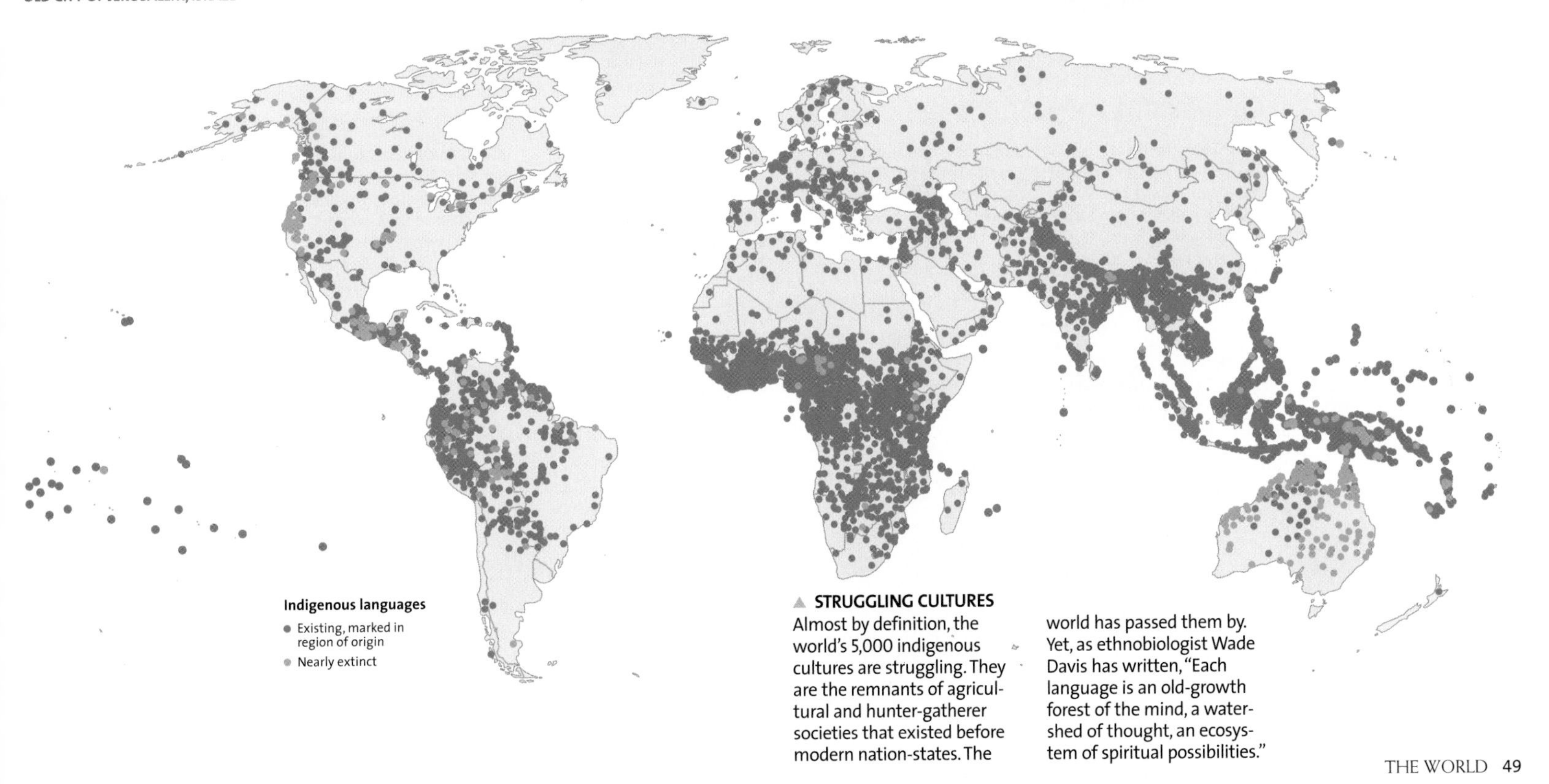

▲ **STRUGGLING CULTURES**
Almost by definition, the world's 5,000 indigenous cultures are struggling. They are the remnants of agricultural and hunter-gatherer societies that existed before modern nation-states. The world has passed them by. Yet, as ethnobiologist Wade Davis has written, "Each language is an old-growth forest of the mind, a watershed of thought, an ecosystem of spiritual possibilities."

Causes of deaths as a percentage of world totals, 2002 estimates

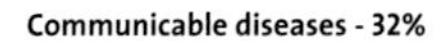

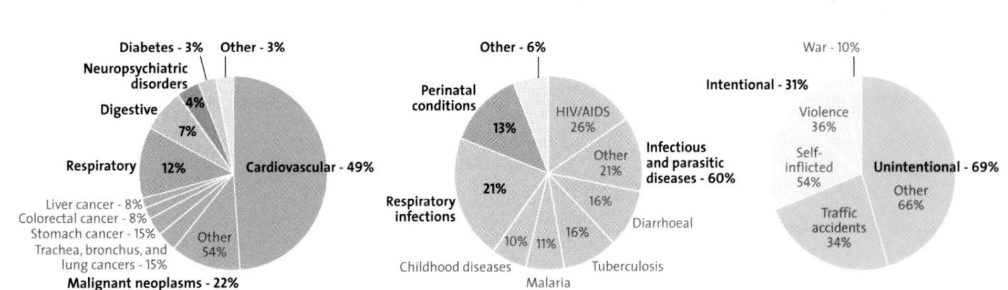

▲ HOW DO PEOPLE DIE?

Nearly one-third of those who die each year succumb to communicable diseases such as tuberculosis and HIV/AIDS, especially in developing nations where treatment is lacking. In deaths from injuries, suicide accounts for as many as war and violence combined. The aging populations of more developed nations more often die from noncommunicable, chronic conditions such as cardiovascular diseases and cancers.

GeoBytes

WHAT IS AN EPIDEMIC?
An epidemic is a sudden outbreak of disease in an area that leads to a high percentage of cases and possibly a large number of deaths.

WHAT IS A PANDEMIC?
A pandemic is an outbreak of disease that spreads over a wide area, possibly even the entire globe.

A WEIGHTY PROBLEM
The percentage of overweight young Americans has more than tripled since 1980. Among Americans aged 6 to 19, 16% (more than 9 million) are considered overweight.

FEAR OF BIRD FLU
A new virus strain found in chickens, wild birds, and cats raises concerns that a mutation might lead to human-to-human contagion, sparking a worldwide pandemic.

KWASHIORKOR
A protein deficiency, this disease kills thousands of children in tropical and subtropical parts of the world.

TRACHOMA
In Africa and parts of Latin America and Asia, this painful and blinding fly-borne disease threatens 70 million, mainly poor women and children living in unsanitary conditions.

▼ CARDIOVASCULAR DISEASE

Cardiovascular diseases—heart diseases and stroke—seem to be by-products of the more affluent lifestyle that afflicts the developed world, especially in Russia and Eastern Europe. Stress, alcohol abuse, smoking, inactivity, and diets lacking in fruits and vegetables and rich in cholesterol and saturated fats are risk factors that exacerbate the diseases that kill some 17 million people a year, nearly one-third of all deaths.

▼ HIV/AIDS

Acquired Immunodeficiency Syndrome (AIDS) came to the world's attention in the 1980s. Since then, more than 25 million people have died of the disease, which is carried by the Human Immunodeficiency Virus (HIV). Although HIV/AIDS symptoms can be stabilized by modern drugs, 40 million people remain infected at the end of 2005. Many of these live in countries where poverty, denial, lack of health-delivery systems, and drug production and patent problems limit access to prevention and treatment strategies.

NORTH AMERICA
EUROPE
ASIA
AFRICA
SOUTH AMERICA
AUSTRALIA

Percentage of adults (ages 15-49) living with HIV/AIDS, 2003
- 20.0% - 38.0%
- 10.0% - 19.9%
- 5.0% - 9.9%
- 2.0% - 4.9%
- 0.1% - 1.9%
- No data available

▼ DOCTORS WITHIN BORDERS

A shortage of physicians is critical in sub-Saharan African countries. Liberia and Eritrea, for example, had only three doctors for every 100,000 people in 2004. In contrast, Italy had 606, and Cuba, where health care is centralized, had 590. Now the gap between haves and have-nots is widening as many formerly socialist countries decentralize health care and physicians emigrate from poor societies to wealthier.

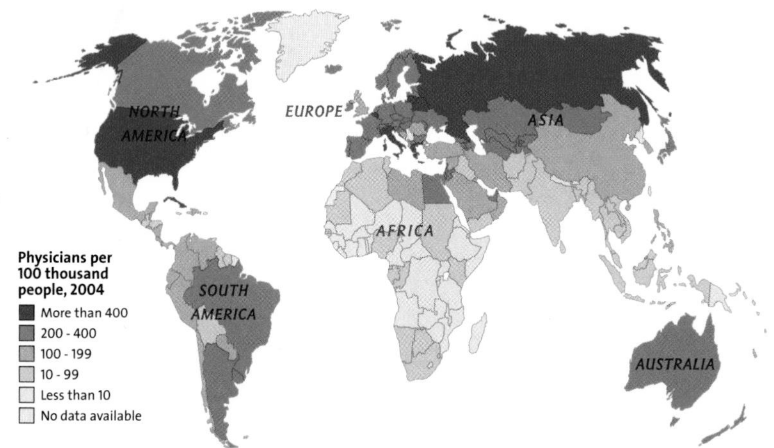

▼ MALARIA RAVAGES TROPICS

Malaria is a mostly tropical, parasitic disease transmitted from human to human by mosquito bites. Worldwide, over 500 million people suffer from illness caused by the malaria parasite. In sub-Saharan Africa exposure to malaria-infected mosquitoes is so intense that over a million people die each year. Use of insecticide-treated mosquito nets and new drugs to alleviate the disease will continue to make a difference while scientists work to develop an effective vaccine.

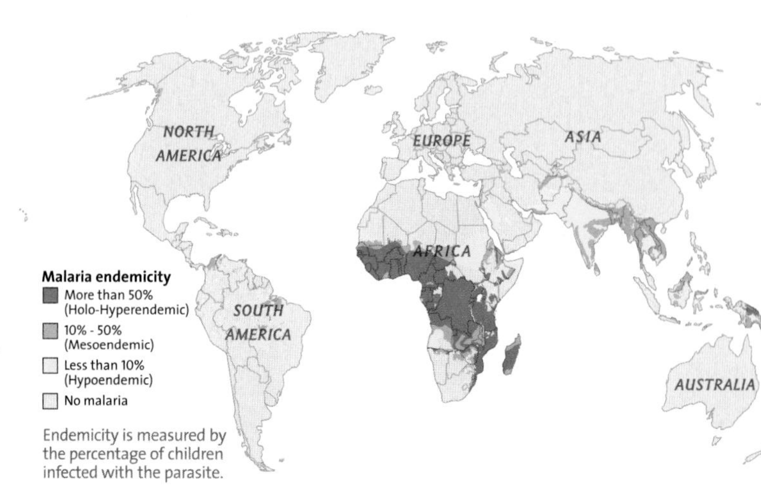

Endemicity is measured by the percentage of children infected with the parasite.

HEALTH & LITERACY

Developed and developing nations show major differences in the rates and causes of death, with AIDS the most significant difference. Cardiovascular disease, the major cause of death in the developed world, is an increasing contributor to mortality in developing nations. Closely tied to health measurements are literacy rates—the percentage of a population who can read—mainly because literacy is an indicator of the reach and effectiveness of a nation's educational system. Educating girls and women improves health indices not only for females but for families. Girls' education makes a difference—in lowered infant mortality and overall mortality rates and in increased rates at which health care is sought.

NORTH AMERICA
EUROPE
ASIA
AFRICA
SOUTH AMERICA
AUSTRALIA

Calorie supply per capita, 2002
- More than 3,500
- 3,000 - 3,499
- 2,500 - 2,999
- Less than 2,500
- No data available

CALORIE CONSUMPTION
How many calories do people need to stay healthy? At least 2,500 a day. But Afghans consume a paltry 1,523 a day, and one-third of sub-Saharan African children are undernourished. In wealthy countries, such as the United States, high calorie intake means a high rate of obesity—a risk factor for heart disease, diabetes, and cancer. Middle-income countries, such as Mexico and Brazil, are beginning to confront their own epidemics of obesity.

NORTH AMERICA
EUROPE
ASIA
AFRICA
SOUTH AMERICA
AUSTRALIA

Percentage of population undernourished, 2000-02
- 51% - 75%
- 26% - 50%
- 11% - 25%
- 2.5% - 10%
- Less than 2.5%
- No data available

HUNGER
Although the world produces 20% more food than its population can consume, nearly a billion people suffer from chronic hunger, a condition provoked by drought, war, social conflicts, and inept public policy. Some five million children under age five die each year from lack of food. In sub-Saharan Africa, where desertification has overtaken agricultural lands and there is little irrigation, drought precedes famine.

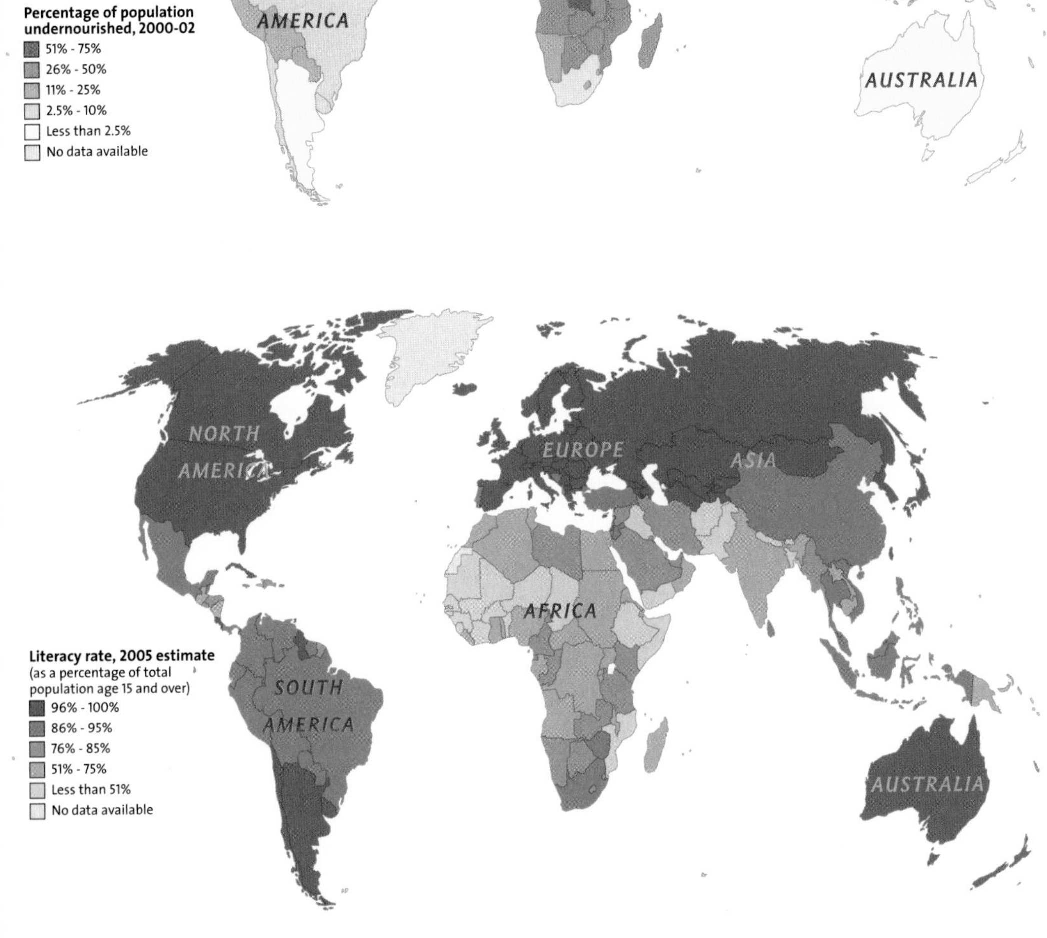

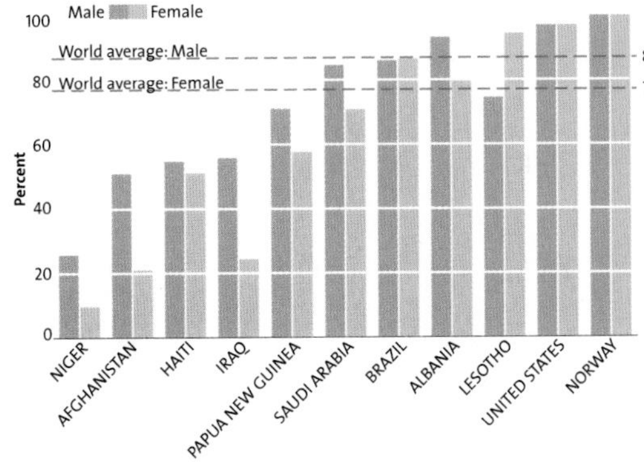

LITERACY
A nation's success depends on an educated population; thus illiteracy remains strongly tied to poverty. In some regions of Asia, Africa, and the Middle East, women suffer much higher rates of illiteracy than men, a reflection of a systematic social bias against them and a denial or discouragement of women's access to education.

CURRENT GDP POPULATION DATA
Cartograms are value-by-area maps. As a graphic representation that depicts the size of an object (such as a country) in relation to an attribute (such as Gross Domestic Product or GDP per capita), cartograms do not delineate geographic space but rather express a thematic relationship. In the cartogram at right, each block represents one hundred U.S. dollars. With some geographical facsimile, countries are associated with neighboring countries and land masses, but the size of an individual country is related to its Gross Domestic Product per capita, that is, the value of final goods and services produced within a country in a year, divided by population. Luxembourg, a tiny inland area, is the giant among the nations of the world in terms of GDP per capita, at $58,900. The United States is next, at $40,100. Russia ranks a middling 82, at $9,800, in GDP per capita. Ranked 231 and 232 are Malawi and Timor-Leste (East Timor), at $600 and $400, respectively.

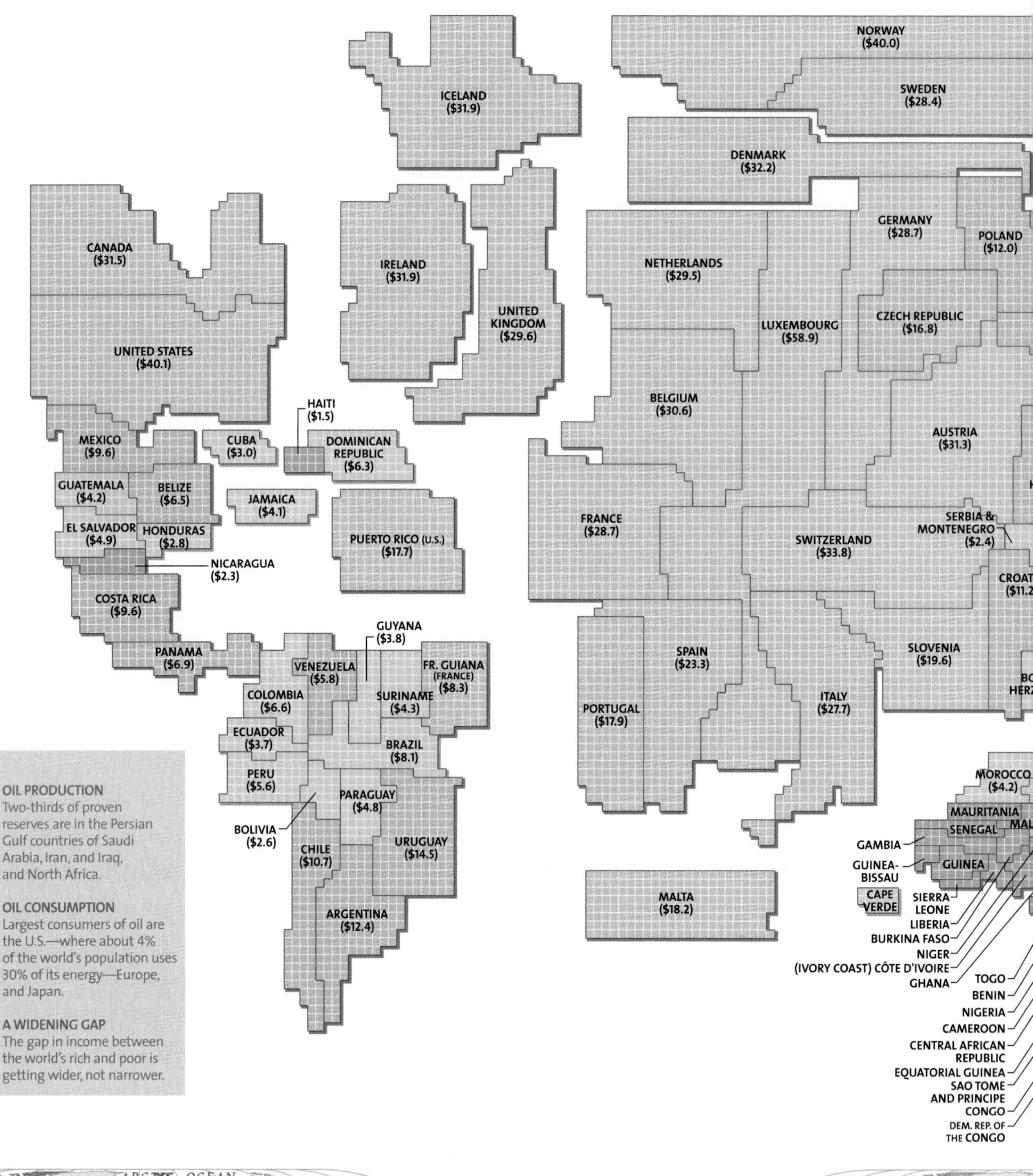

GeoBytes

HUNTING AND GATHERING
This mode of production supported people for more than 95% of the time humans have lived on Earth.

NEOLITHIC REVOLUTION
Around 10,000 B.C., agriculture ushered in settled societies and increasing populations.

FIVE COUNTRIES
The largest deposits of strategic minerals, essential to industry, are concentrated in Canada, the U.S., Russia, South Africa, and Australia.

OIL PRODUCTION
Two-thirds of proven reserves are in the Persian Gulf countries of Saudi Arabia, Iran, and Iraq, and North Africa.

OIL CONSUMPTION
Largest consumers of oil are the U.S.—where about 4% of the world's population uses 30% of its energy—Europe, and Japan.

A WIDENING GAP
The gap in income between the world's rich and poor is getting wider, not narrower.

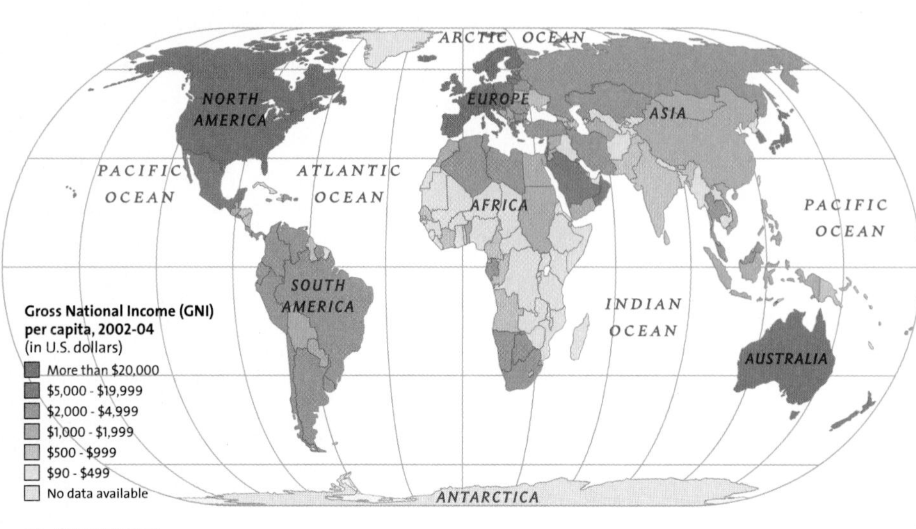

GROSS NATIONAL INCOME
Broad terms such as First or Third World, or the global North-South divide, conceal as much as they reveal. Yet the division between the haves and the have-nots is real. One measurement is Gross National Income at Purchasing Power Parity (GNI PPP), which measures a currency's buying power based on U.S. dollars. In 2004, GNI PPP ranged from Norway's high of $36,690 to a low of $500 in Sierra Leone.

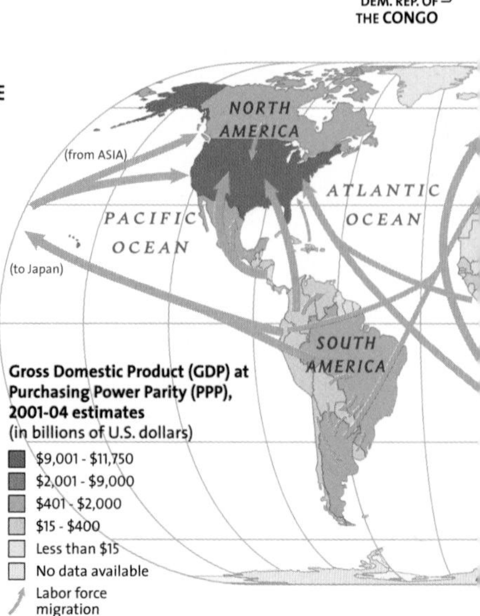

The world's economies are increasingly interrelated. The exchange of farm products, natural resources, manufactured goods, and services benefits trading partners by allowing them to sell what they best produce at home and buy what is economical for them to purchase from overseas. Regional trade is on the rise, as agreements among countries offer each other preferential access to markets, improving the economy of neighboring blocs of countries and the general standard of living. Nevertheless, the stark difference between high- and low-income countries is apparent in a cartogram, which depicts quantitative data not dependent on scale or area. Dominant economies generally occupy the Northern Hemisphere. Oil-rich countries in the Middle East hold their own. The burden of poverty falls mainly on countries in sub-Saharan Africa and in Asia.

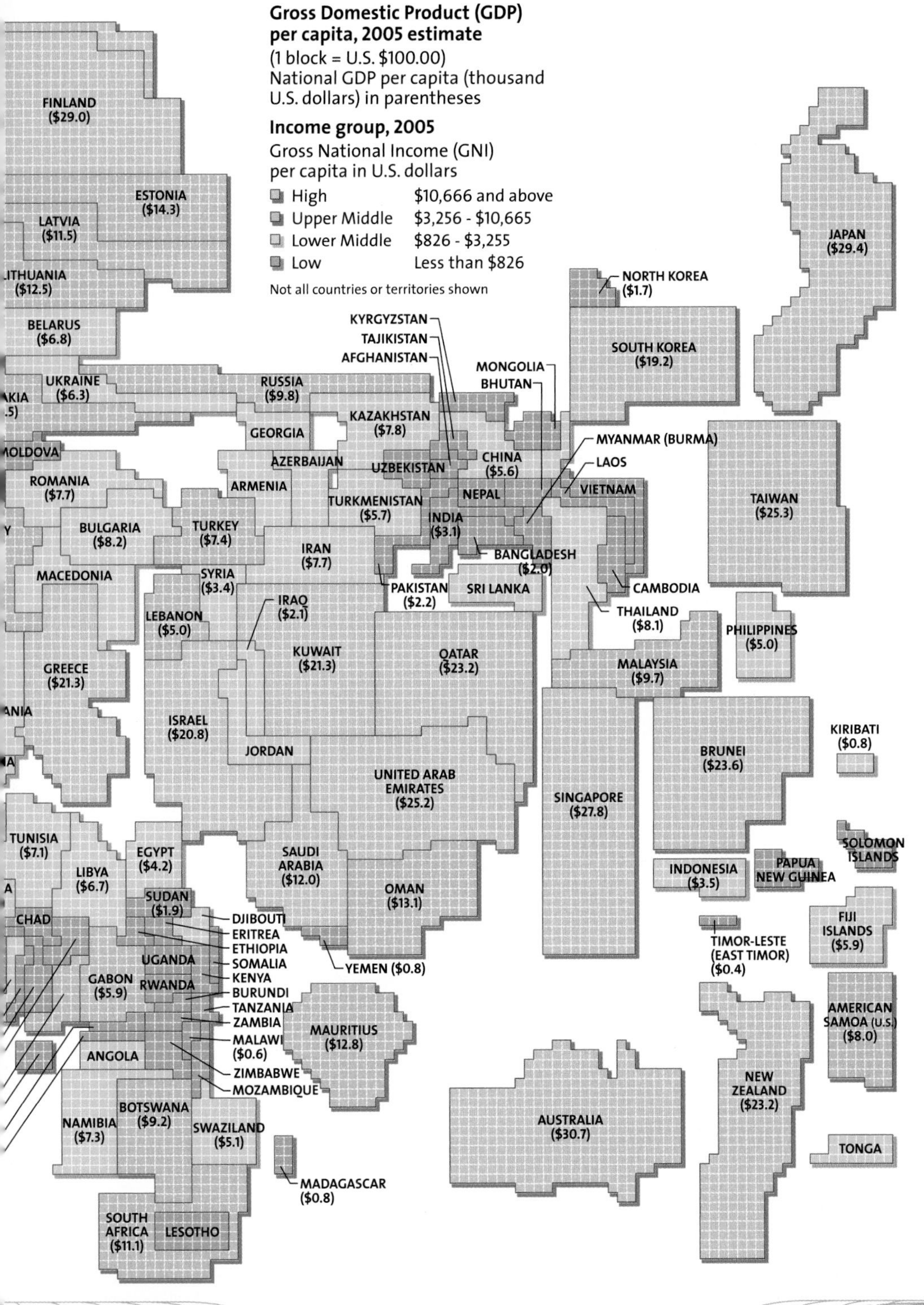

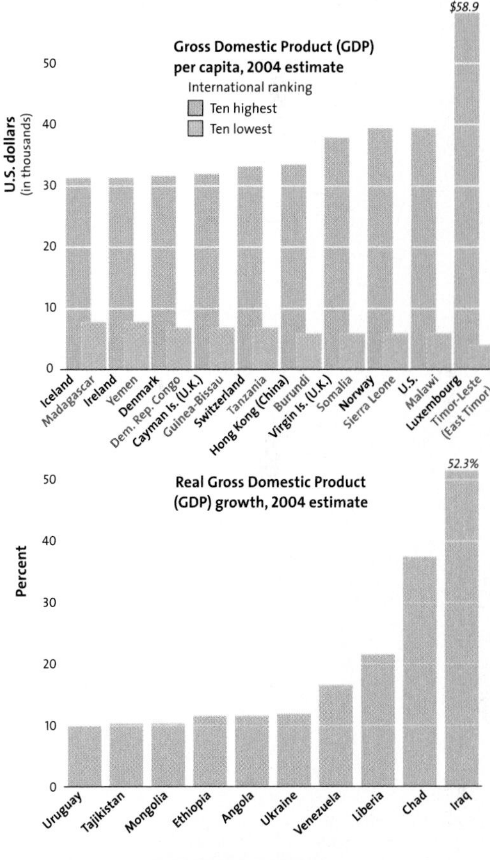

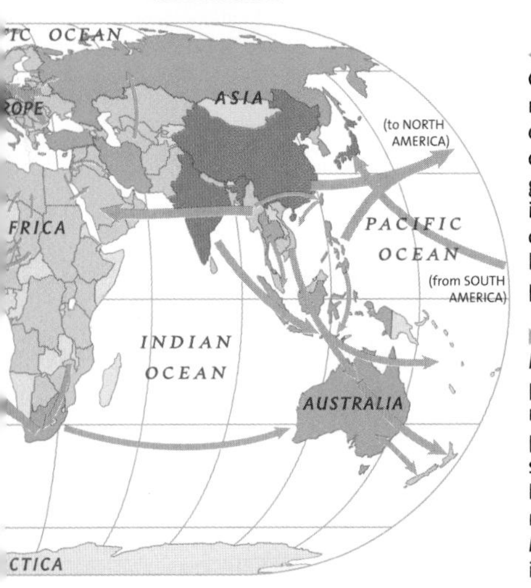

LABOR MIGRATION Globalization has made migration from low GDP countries to high GDP counties easier, but integrating this new labor force into the social fabric of destination countries has become a major public policy issue.

WORLD EMPLOYMENT Manufacturing–the production of goods from raw materials–long powered industrialized societies such as the U.S., Europe, and Japan, now more service oriented. Manufacturing is increasingly important in developing economies.

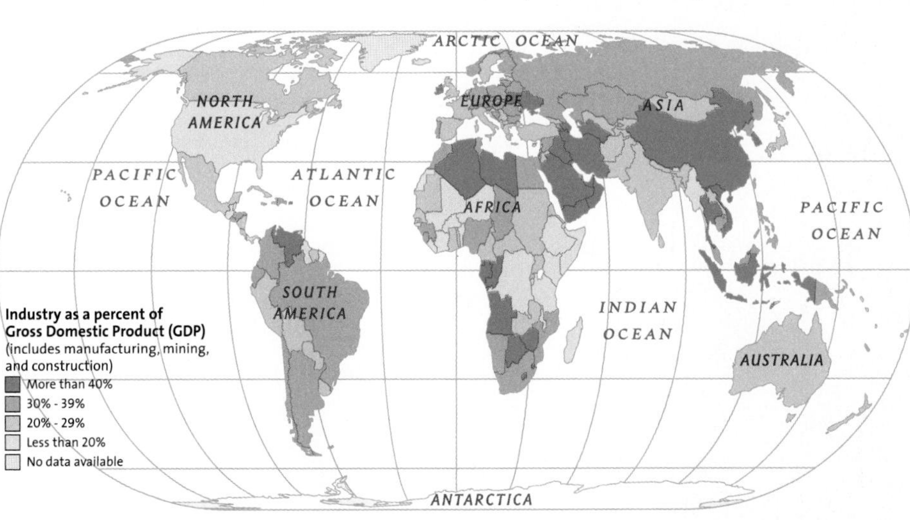

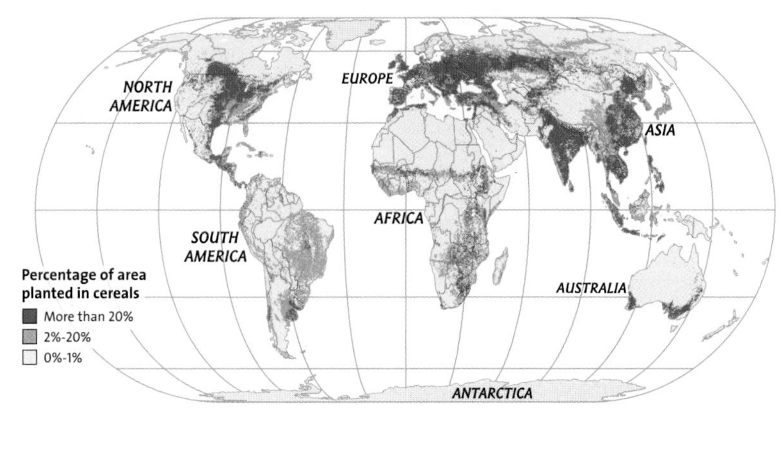

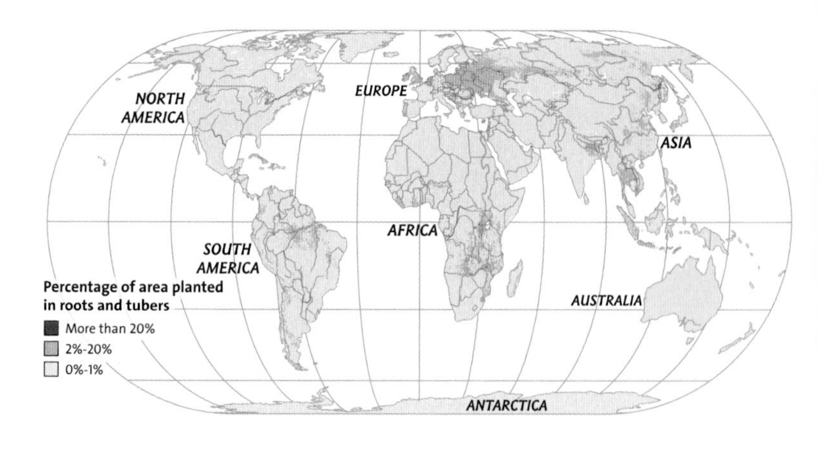

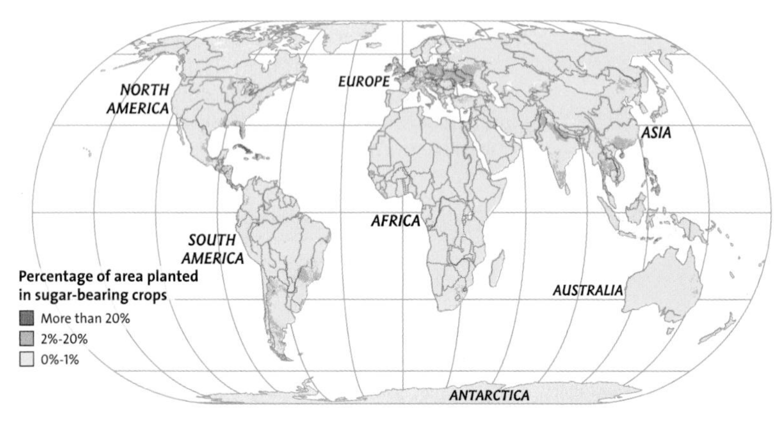

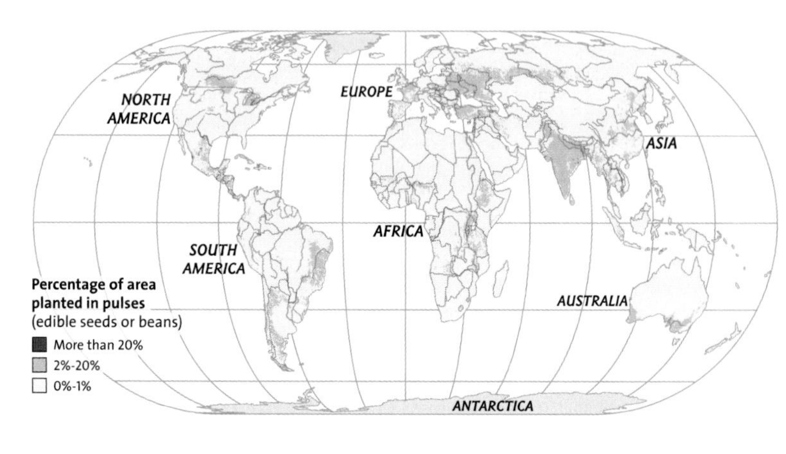

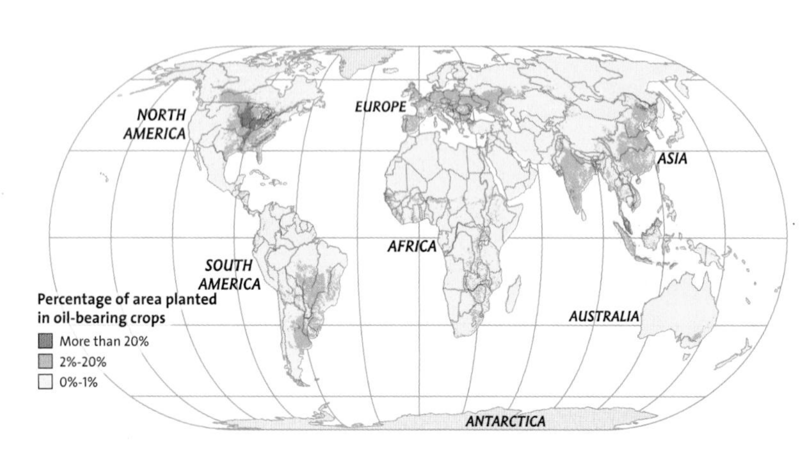

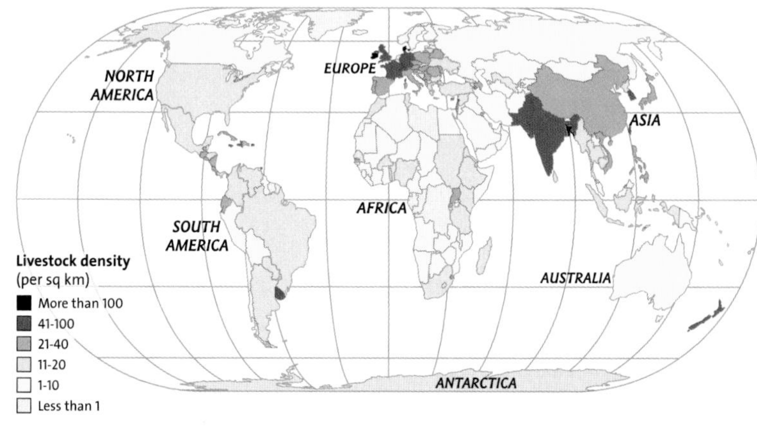

▲ **CEREALS**
Cereal grains, including barley, maize, millet, rice, rye, sorghum, and wheat, are agricultural staples across the globe. They cover 61% of the world's cultivated land and contribute more calories and protein to the human diet than any other food group.

▲ **SUGAR-BEARING CROPS**
Our taste for sweetness is met by two sugar-bearing crops: sugarcane and sugar beets. Sugarcane is grown in the subtropics, mostly in the Caribbean and Florida. Sugar beets thrive in the temperate latitudes of the Northern Hemisphere, primarily in Europe.

▲ **OIL-BEARING CROPS**
Major oil-bearing crops—soybeans, groundnuts, rapeseed, sunflower, and oil palm fruit—account for 10% of the total calories available for human consumption. Asia and the Americas are the largest producers of these crops, with soybeans contributing the greatest share.

▲ **ROOTS AND TUBERS**
Although cultivation of tubers such as cassava, potatoes, sweet potatoes, taro, and manioc makes up less than 5% of the world's harvested area, these foods are staples across the globe and are critical to subsistence farming in Africa, Asia, and Latin America.

▲ **PULSES**
Pulses—the edible seeds of legumes such as dry beans, chick-peas, and lentils—have two to three times as much protein as most cereals. They are cultivated broadly, but nearly 90% of the world's crop is consumed in developing countries.

▲ **ANIMAL PRODUCTS**
Consumption of meat, milk, and eggs, all high-protein foods, is unequal across the globe. Wealthier industrialized nations consume 30% more meat than developing nations. With population growth, rising incomes, and urbanization, worldwide demand for animal products is increasing.

◄ **MAIZE**
Corn, or maize, was domesticated 6,000 years ago in Mexico. It is now intensively grown in the United States, China, along Africa's Rift Valley, and throughout Eastern Europe. Although it remains a staple food, more than 70% of the world's harvest is for animal feed.

◄ **WHEAT**
Wheat—the most widely grown cereal—is cultivated across the globe. Most of it is grown, however, in the temperate latitudes of the Northern Hemisphere. Wheat, mainly in baked goods, is a major source of calories for more than half of the world's population.

◄ **RICE**
Rice plays a dominant role in the agriculture and diet of Asia. Nearly 90% of the world's rice is consumed and produced in Asia, mostly on small family farms. Larger scale commercial cultivation of rice takes place in the southern United States, southern Australia, and the Amazon Basin.

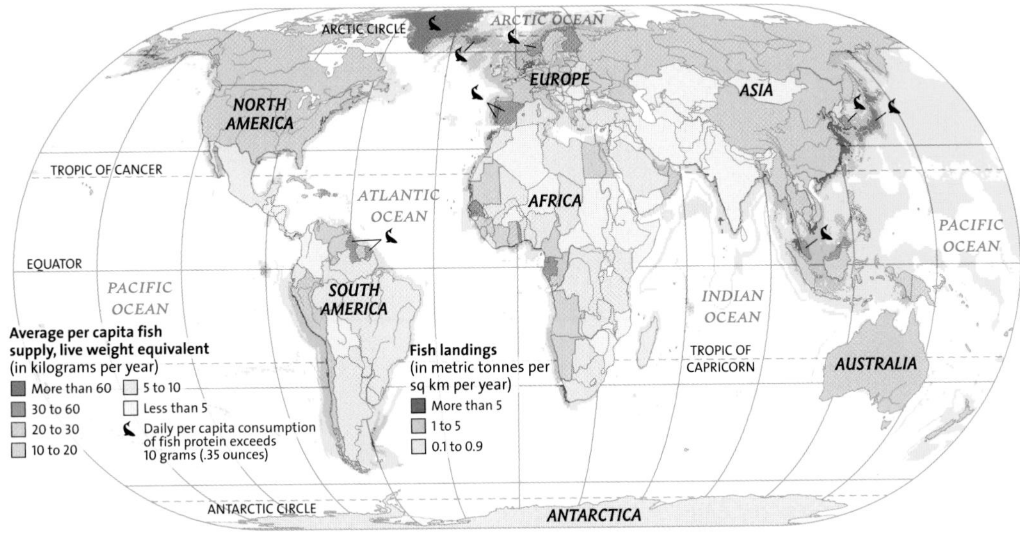

FISHERIES AND AQUACULTURE

Fish is a vital source of protein for much of the world. Yet the world's primary fisheries are under stress from overfishing and environmental degradation. The tonnage of fish caught in the wild has remained relatively stable over the past five years, while tonnage of fish produced by aquaculture has increased markedly. Aquaculture, primarily in freshwater environments, now accounts for more than 30% of total fish production. China leads in aquaculture production, growing more than two-thirds of all farm-raised fish.

More than 850 million people worldwide do not have access to adequate food. Hunger, found across the globe and even in the richest countries, is chronic in rural areas of the developing world, places not always well suited for agriculture or managed for sustainable yield. Other countries with climates and soils better suited to agriculture, such as the United States, grow and consume far more food than is required to meet the needs of their populations. We are faced with closing this gap between the hungry and the overfed at a time when the world's population, mostly in developing countries, is expected to grow by three billion over the next 50 years. Lack of space for cropland expansion, climate change, and environmental stresses such as deforestation, desertification, and erosion add to the challenge of agricultural management and productivity.

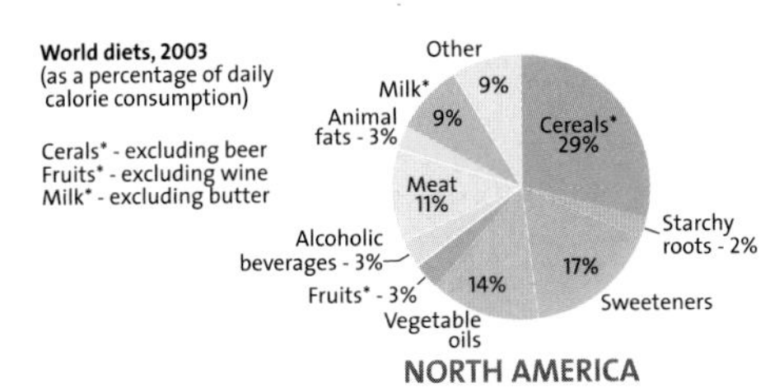

EUROPE

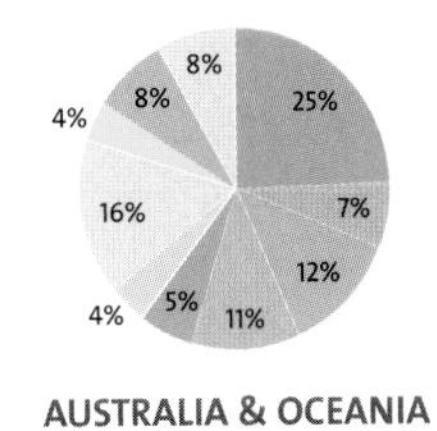

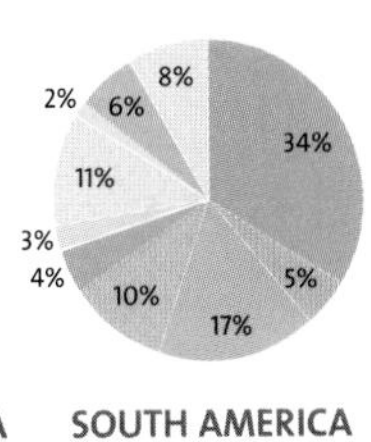

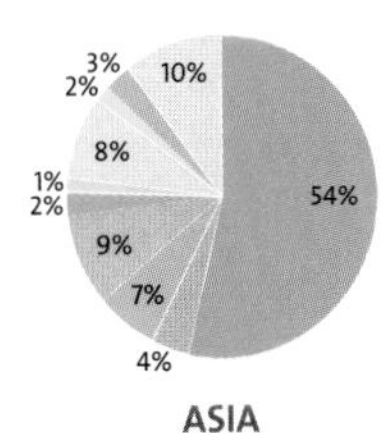

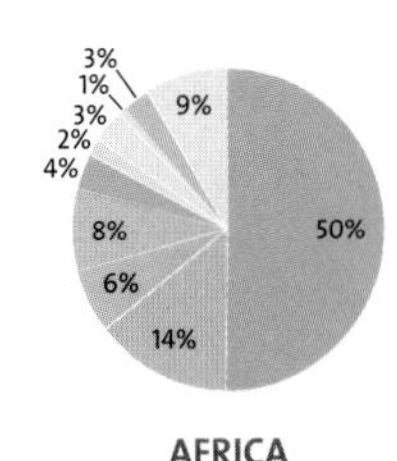

WHAT THE WORLD EATS

The foods people eat vary widely and are chosen on the basis of availability, income, and cultural preference. Cereals, arguably the most significant food source worldwide, make up a large percentage of diets in Africa and Asia. High caloric foods—sugars, meats, and oils—make up a significant portion of diets in Oceania, the Americas, and Europe.

GENETICALLY MODIFIED AGRICULTURE

Planting of genetically modified (GM) or "biotech" crops, mainly soybeans, corn, cotton, and canola, is still conservative but on the rise despite continued debate over ecological impacts and human health hazards. GM crops first became an industry in 1996. Some 75% of GM planting today is in countries such as the United States, Argentina, Canada, and Brazil. Some developing nations are beginning to grow GM crops in hopes of increasing output in areas where traditional crops do not meet the needs of the population.

DISTRIBUTION OF CROPS

The distribution of the world's staple crops varies across the globe. Wheat, maize, and barley thrive in the temperate climates of the United States, Europe, and Australia, whereas sugarcane is better suited to the tropical climate of the Caribbean. Rice thrives in high rainfall areas of Asia, and drought-resistant crops such as millet and sorghum are staples of drier places, such as the Sahel on the southern fringe of the Sahara Desert in Africa.

U.S. 49.8 million ha (123.1 million acres)
ROMANIA 100,000 ha (250,000 acres)
CHINA 3.3 million ha (8.2 million acres)
AUSTRALIA 300,000 ha (250,000 acres)
SOUTH AFRICA 500,000 ha (1.2 million acres)
ARGENTINA 17.1 million ha (42.3 million acres)

Biotech cropland, 2005 (in million hectares)
More than 10
2.5-10
0.5-2.49
0.1-0.49
Less than 0.1
No data available

Principle biotech crop
Canola
Cotton
Maize
Papaya
Rice
Soybean
Squash

PERCENTAGE OF WORLD CROP PRODUCTION BY REGION

Highest producers		Lowest producers	
Conterminous U.S. 87%		**Caribbean 60%**	
Maize	28%	Sugarcane	36%
Wheat	26%	Maize	8%
Soybean	24%	Pulses*	6%
Cotton	5%	Rice	6%
Sorghum	4%	Cassava	4%
Central Asia 87%		**Eastern Africa 59%**	
Wheat	51%	Maize	27%
Barley	23%	Pulses*	10%
Cotton	9%	Sorghum	9%
Millet	2%	Cassava	8%
Rye	2%	Rice	5%
Australia & New Zealand 85%		**East Asia 57%**	
Wheat	51%	Rice	20%
Barley	18%	Wheat	17%
Pulses*	11%	Maize	12%
Sorghum	3%	Soybean	5%
Sugarcane	2%	Rapeseed	3%
Southern Africa 84%		**Southern Europe 51%**	
Maize	54%	Wheat	21%
Wheat	15%	Barley	16%
Sunflower	6%	Maize	6%
Sorghum	5%	Sunflower	6%
Sugarcane	4%	Pulses*	2%

*Pulses-edible seeds or beans

GeoBytes

AGRICULTURAL HEARTLANDS
The world's largest agricultural areas are in China, Australia, the United States, Kazakhstan, the Russian Federation, Brazil, Argentina, India, and Saudi Arabia.

GM CROPS
Nearly 30% of the world's total area of soybeans, maize, cotton, and canola is planted with genetically modified (GM) varieties.

UNEQUAL CONSUMPTION
On average, people in North America and Europe consume more than 3,000 calories per day, whereas people in some African countries consume barely half that. In countries such as Eritrea, the Democratic Republic of the Congo, and Burundi, up to 70% of the population is undernourished.

TRADE BLOCS

Common interests encourage neighboring countries to form trade blocs to benefit from increased trade and growth. Trade blocs steer a course between protectionism and unbridled capitalism. Such agreements fall into two classes: free trade zones, such as NAFTA (North American Free Trade Agreement), which removes internal tariffs but allows participants to set external tariffs; and customs unions, such as the EU (European Union), in which all agree to common outside tariffs.

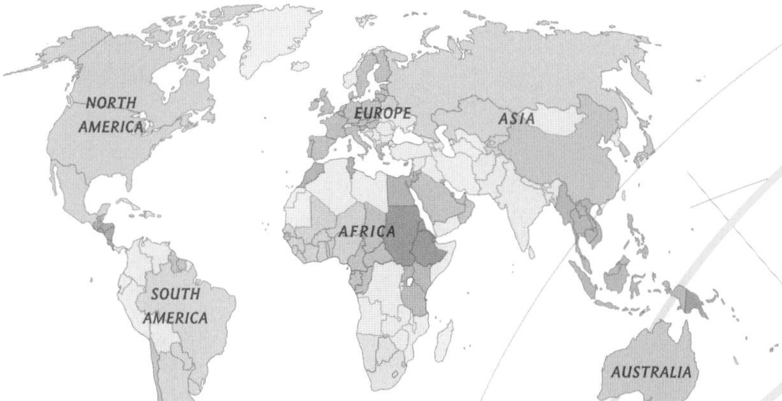

Most active regional trade blocs, 2005

- Agadir Agreement
- Andean Community
- APEC - Asia-Pacific Economic Cooperation
- ASEAN - Association of Southeast Asian Nations
- CACM - Central American Common Market
- CARICOM - Caribbean Community and Common Market
- CEMAC - Economic and Monetary Community of Central Africa
- COMESA - Common Market for Eastern and Southern Africa
- EAC - East African Community
- ECOWAS - Economic Community of West African States
- EU - European Union
- EurAsEC - Eurasian Economic Community
- GCC - Gulf Cooperation Council
- MERCOSUR - Southern Common Market
- NAFTA - North American Free Trade Agreement
- PARTA - Pacific Regional Trade Agreement
- SAARC - South Asian Association for Regional Cooperation
- SACU - Southern African Customs Union
- Not an active bloc member

GeoBytes

LARGEST TRADE BLOC
The European Union (EU) member states account for nearly one-third of the global economy, making the EU the largest economic body in the world.

LARGEST ECONOMY
The country with the largest economy is the United States, with an income of more than $12 trillion.

LARGEST ASIAN ECONOMY
Japan has the world's second largest economy at $4.7 trillion—the biggest in Asia.

LARGEST EUROPEAN ECONOMY
Germany maintains the largest economy in Europe, with a national income of more than $2.4 trillion.

LARGEST SOUTH AMERICAN ECONOMY
The Brazilian economy, which exceeds $550 billion, dominates South America.

WORLD DEBT

Debt hinders many developing countries. The World Bank classifies countries by debt level. A country with debt at or above 80% of its gross national income (GNI) is classified as severely indebted and in danger of defaulting on loans.

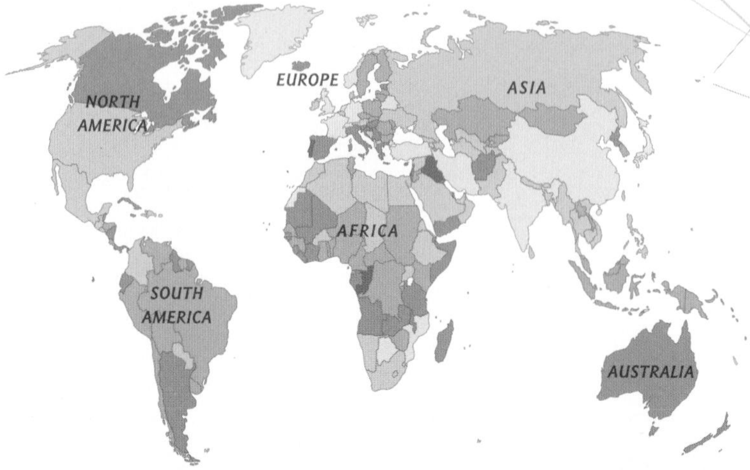

Estimated external debt as a percentage of Gross Domestic Product (GDP) at Purchasing Power Parity, 2002-04 estimates
(GDP PPP based upon U.S. dollars)

- More than 100%
- 30% - 100%
- 15% - 29%
- 5% - 14%
- Less than 5%
- No data available

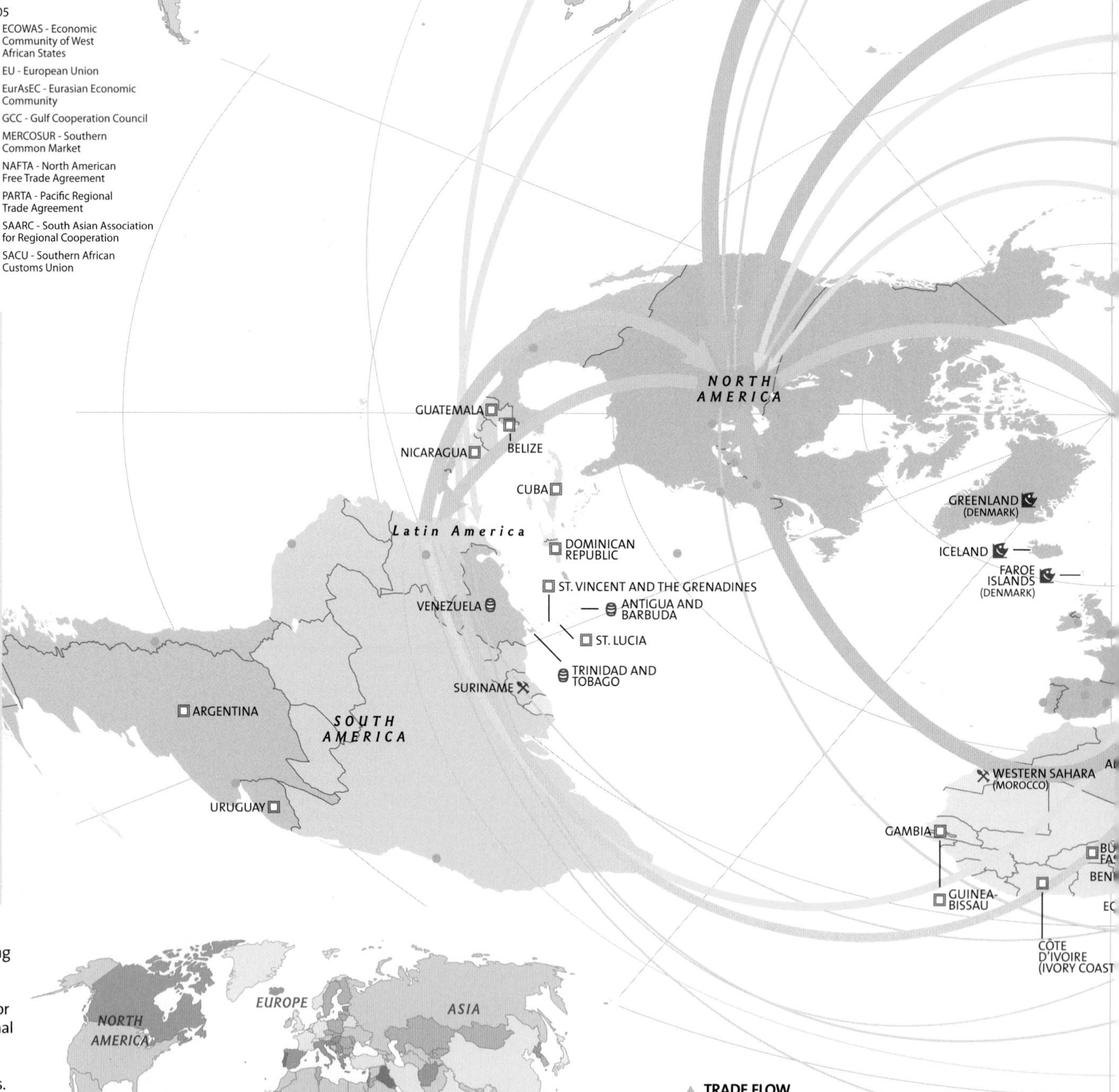

TRADE FLOW

International trade of goods is a major avenue of globalization. The arrows above show the value of trade between major regions of the world. More than half of world trade occurs between high-income areas such as Japan, the United States, and Western Europe. Trade is increasing, however, between these high-income countries and developing countries in Asia, South America, and Africa. Lowered trade barriers offer opportunities for low-income countries, although still limited. Labor-intensive merchandise, such as textiles, can be produced and exported at a low cost from developing nations. Trade in agricultural commodities is a key issue between developing and high-income countries. Two billion families in the world make a living from farming. About 60 countries are dependent on commodities for more than 40% of their export income—in some African countries the figure is 80%. Stormy meetings of the World Trade Organization (WTO) focus on making the European Union (EU) and the United States end subsidies to their farmers to increase trade opportunities for developing nations.

NEW ZEALAND
VANUATU
SOLOMON ISLANDS
FEDERATED STATES OF MICRONESIA
AUSTRALIA
INDONESIA
BRUNEI
ASIA
NORWAY
KAZAKHSTAN
UZBEKISTAN
PAKISTAN
TURKMENISTAN
IRAN
AZERBAIJAN
KUWAIT
UNITED ARAB EMIRATES
OMAN
EUROPE
MOLDOVA
HUNGARY
SYRIA
IRAQ
Middle East
QATAR
BAHRAIN
SAUDI ARABIA
YEMEN
LIBYA
ETHIOPIA
RÉUNION (FRANCE)
CHAD
UGANDA
MADAGASCAR
RWANDA
BURUNDI
NIGERIA
AFRICA
CONGO
GABON
MALAWI
DEM. REP. OF THE CONGO
ZAMBIA
ANGOLA
BOTSWANA
LESOTHO

Income Group, 2005
Gross National Income (GNI) per capita in U.S. dollars

High	$10,066 and above
Upper middle	$3,256 - $10,065
Lower middle	$826 - $3,255
Low	Less than $826
No data available	

Interregional merchandise trade
(in billions of U.S. dollars)

- $240 and above
- $120 - $240
- $60 - $119
- $30 - $59
- $5 - $29
- Less than $5

Stock exchange (World Federation of Exchanges member)

Single-commodity-dependent economy
(commodity comprising more than 40 percent of total exports)

- Agriculture
- Cotton
- Crude oil and petroleum products
- Fishing
- Gems, metals, and minerals
- Machinery and equipment
- Textiles and apparel

TRADE & GLOBALIZATION

To multinational corporations, globalization means that products can be produced in multiple locations and distributed worldwide. To consumers, globalization means lower prices. To governments, globalization can mean job losses, multinational mergers, and price-fixing cartels. While the benefits of globalization have not been universally shared, it has been a force in bringing economic growth. The World Trade Organization (WTO) works with governments and international organizations to regulate trade and reduce economic inequality among countries. Global integration increases the flow of trade, capital, information, and people across borders by reducing or eliminating trade restrictions and customs barriers. Globalization presents both challenges and opportunities—for new markets, jobs, and export-led growth.

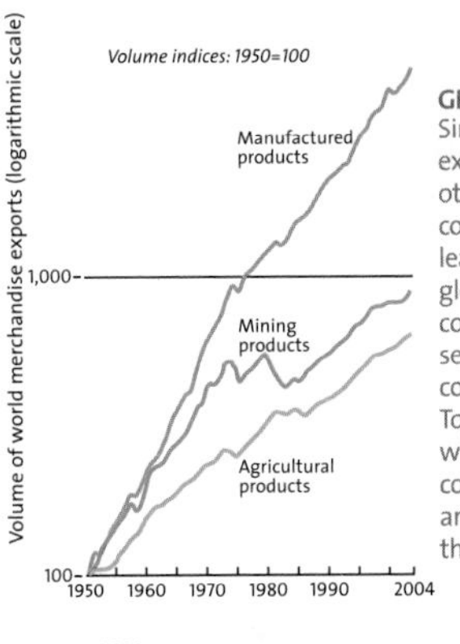

GROWTH OF TRADE
Since World War II, manufactured exports have grown faster than other products. Transnational corporations are the primary leaders of the growth and globalization of trade. These companies locate factories and sell products outside their country of origin. For example, Toyota has 12 plants in Japan, with 53 manufacturing companies in 27 other countries, and it sells vehicles in more than 170 countries.

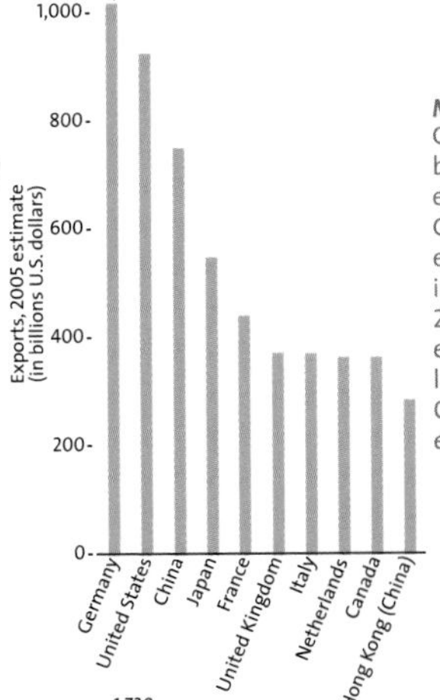

MERCHANDISE EXPORTS
China has risen quickly to become the third-largest exporter of merchandise after Germany. China's growth rate exceeds that of any large industrial country. From 2000 to 2004, the value of merchandise exports grew by 24% annually, largely due to the undervalued Chinese currency that makes exports cheap.

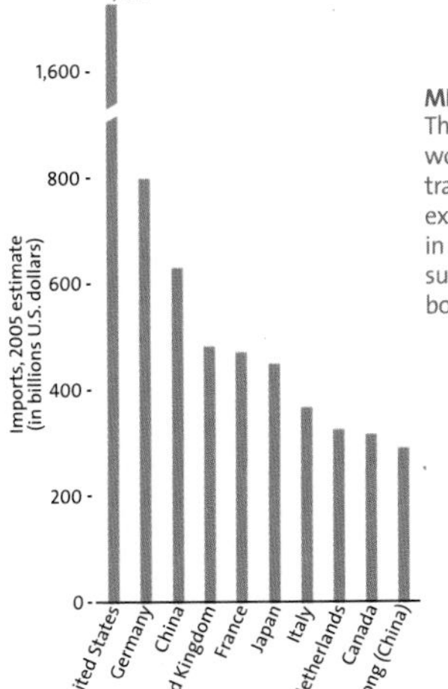

MERCHANDISE IMPORTS
The United States is by far the world's largest importer—the U.S. trade deficit (more imports than exports) approached $725 billion in 2005. China's growing trade surplus is fueling an economic boom in that country.

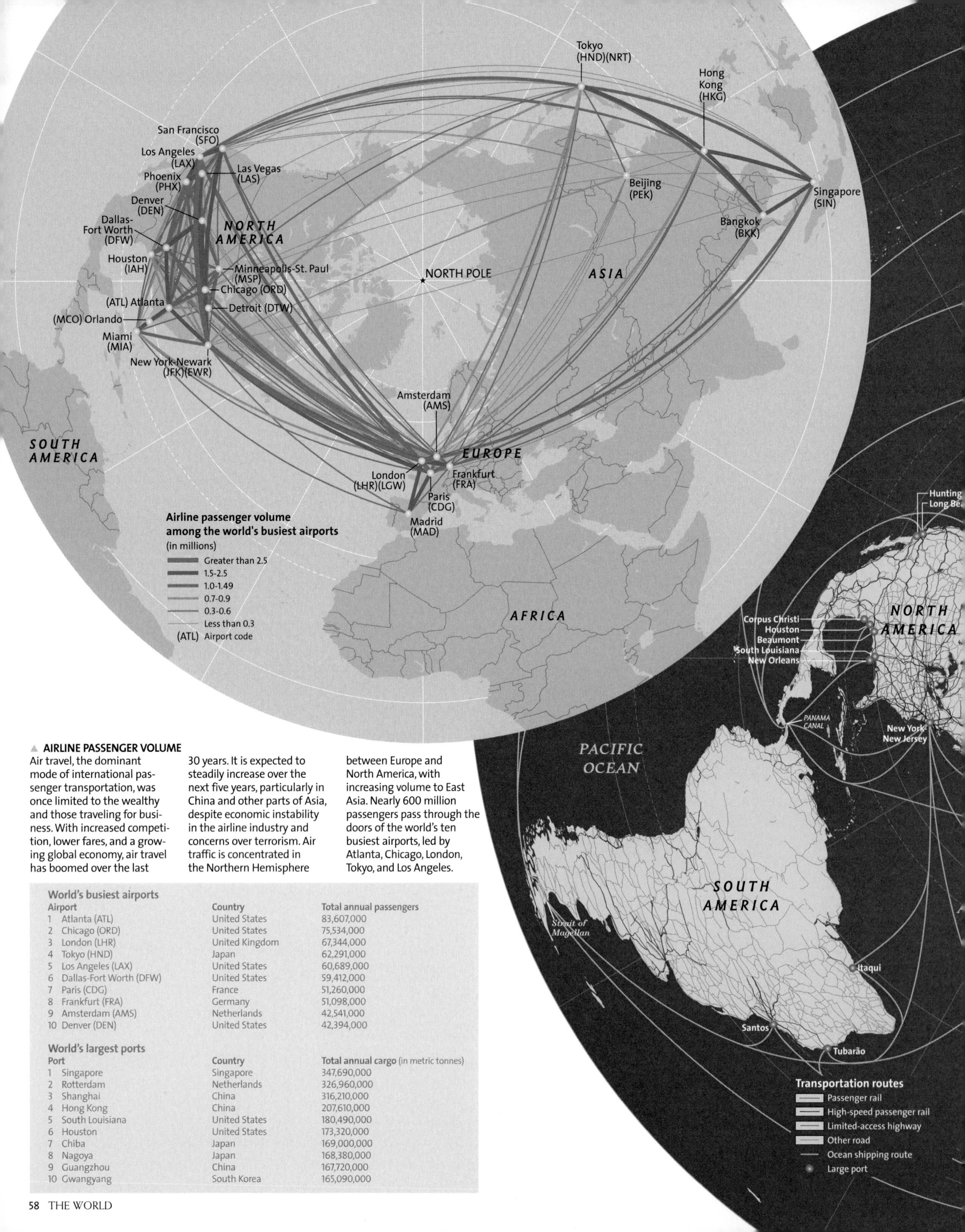

▲ **AIRLINE PASSENGER VOLUME**

Air travel, the dominant mode of international passenger transportation, was once limited to the wealthy and those traveling for business. With increased competition, lower fares, and a growing global economy, air travel has boomed over the last 30 years. It is expected to steadily increase over the next five years, particularly in China and other parts of Asia, despite economic instability in the airline industry and concerns over terrorism. Air traffic is concentrated in the Northern Hemisphere between Europe and North America, with increasing volume to East Asia. Nearly 600 million passengers pass through the doors of the world's ten busiest airports, led by Atlanta, Chicago, London, Tokyo, and Los Angeles.

World's busiest airports

Airport	Country	Total annual passengers
1 Atlanta (ATL)	United States	83,607,000
2 Chicago (ORD)	United States	75,534,000
3 London (LHR)	United Kingdom	67,344,000
4 Tokyo (HND)	Japan	62,291,000
5 Los Angeles (LAX)	United States	60,689,000
6 Dallas-Fort Worth (DFW)	United States	59,412,000
7 Paris (CDG)	France	51,260,000
8 Frankfurt (FRA)	Germany	51,098,000
9 Amsterdam (AMS)	Netherlands	42,541,000
10 Denver (DEN)	United States	42,394,000

World's largest ports

Port	Country	Total annual cargo (in metric tonnes)
1 Singapore	Singapore	347,690,000
2 Rotterdam	Netherlands	326,960,000
3 Shanghai	China	316,210,000
4 Hong Kong	China	207,610,000
5 South Louisiana	United States	180,490,000
6 Houston	United States	173,320,000
7 Chiba	Japan	169,000,000
8 Nagoya	Japan	168,380,000
9 Guangzhou	China	167,720,000
10 Gwangyang	South Korea	165,090,000

Throughout history, the movement of goods and people linked places and their economies. Early transport was undertaken on foot or by animals such as horses and camels. Long distances were traveled over water by pole and current-propelled boats, then by oar and later by sail. With the introduction of mechanical means of transport—steamboats, railroad locomotives, and eventually automobiles and airplanes—movement from place to place accelerated rapidly. Speed, efficiency, and safety are some of the metrics of modern transportation systems. Today, people and goods move quickly about the world via a web of land, sea, and air networks that together keep the global economy humming.

GeoBytes

SAVING TIME BY CANAL
With the opening of the Suez Canal in 1869, the journey from London to Mumbai (Bombay) shrunk from nearly six months to about two months.

SAVING TIME BY TRAIN
First launched in Japan in 1964, high-speed trains can carry passengers at speeds exceeding 300 kph (186 mph). Europe, East Asia, and the U.S. have adopted fast trains to provide national, inter-urban transport.

◄ **TRANSPORTATION ROUTES** Nearly all of the world's freight headed for international destinations is transported via ships in standardized containers. These sealed metal containers have dramatically altered the face of international freight transport. They are designed to be easily transferred from one mode of transport to another, for instance, from a ship to a train, thereby increasing efficiency and reducing cost. As with passenger airline traffic, maritime freight traffic is concentrated. The largest 10 ports, led by Singapore, Rotterdam, Shanghai, Hong Kong, and South Louisiana, handle more than 50% of global freight traffic.

COMMUNICATIONS SATELLITES

Although satellites do not have the voice and data carrying capacity of fiber-optic cables, they remain a vital component of global communication services. They serve large geographic areas, making them well-suited to television and radio broadcasting, maritime and aeronautical communications, emergency services, and fleet management. In areas underserved by landlines, including much of Asia and Africa, they provide mobile phone service and Internet connectivity.

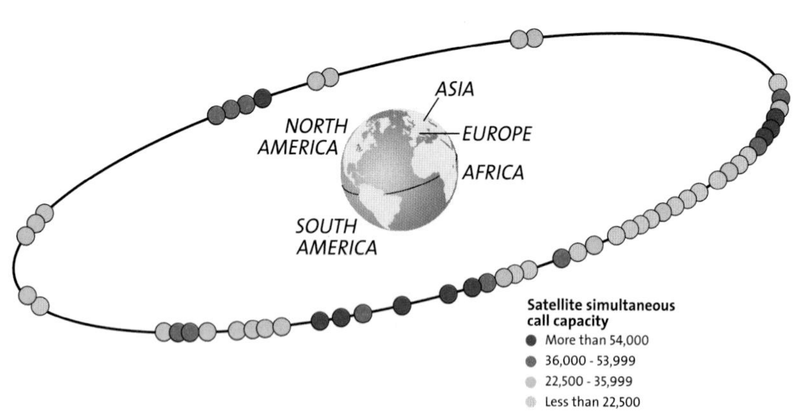

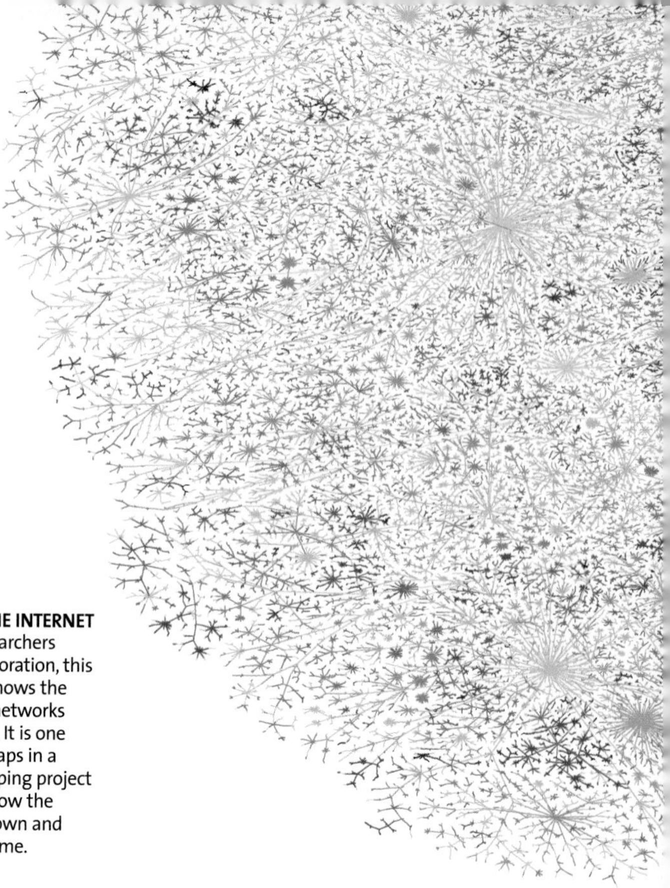

MAPPING THE INTERNET

Created by researchers at Lumeta Corporation, this tree-like map shows the paths of most networks on the Internet. It is one of a series of maps in a long-term mapping project documenting how the Internet has grown and changed over time.

INTERNET EXPLOSION

With more than one billion users worldwide, the Internet is a powerful, if unequally distributed, form of global communication. The U.S. leads in Internet usage, with about one-fifth of all users. In 2005, China displaced Japan for the second-highest number of users, but the 100 million Chinese users represent fewer than 10% of the county's population.

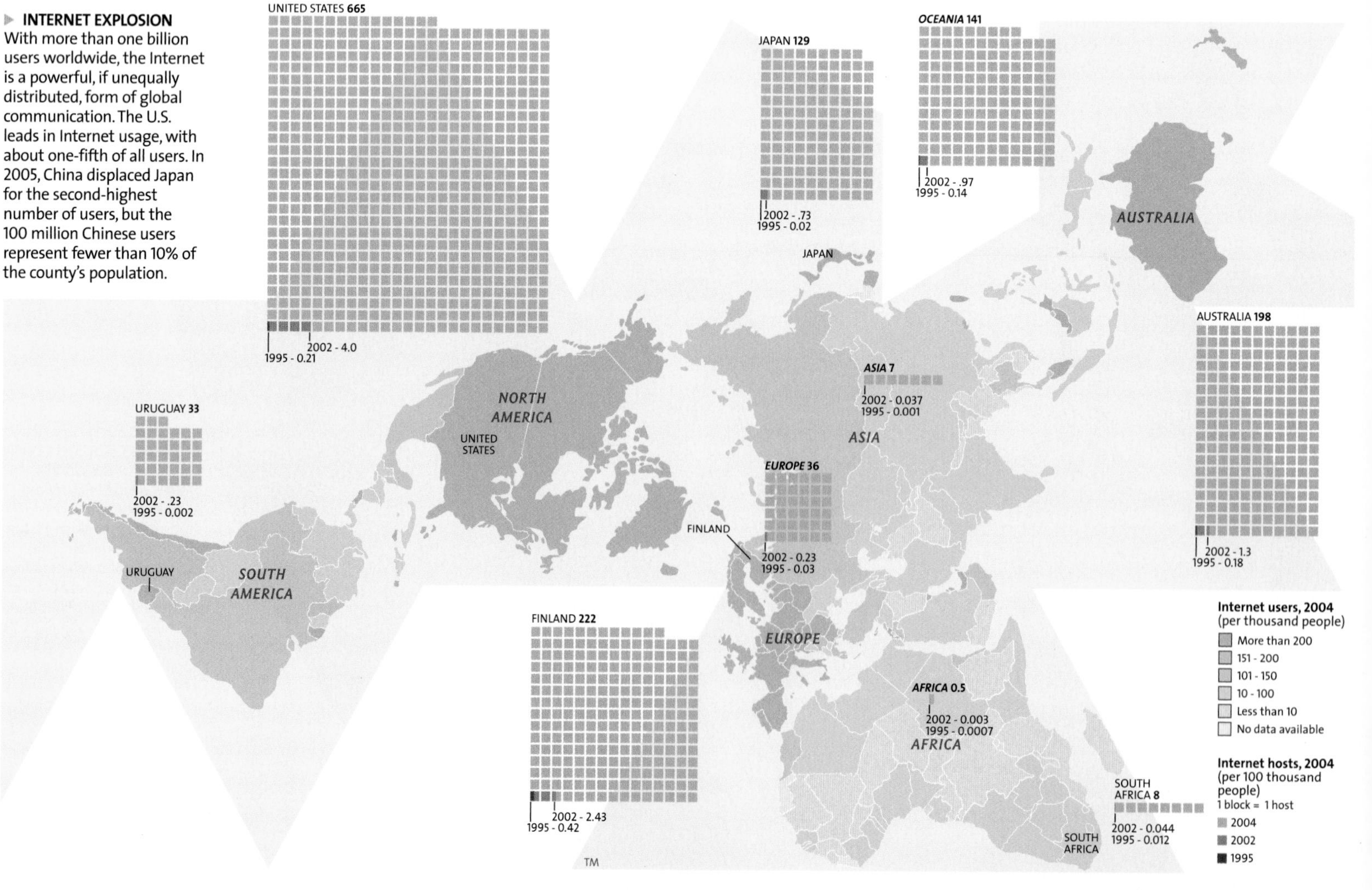

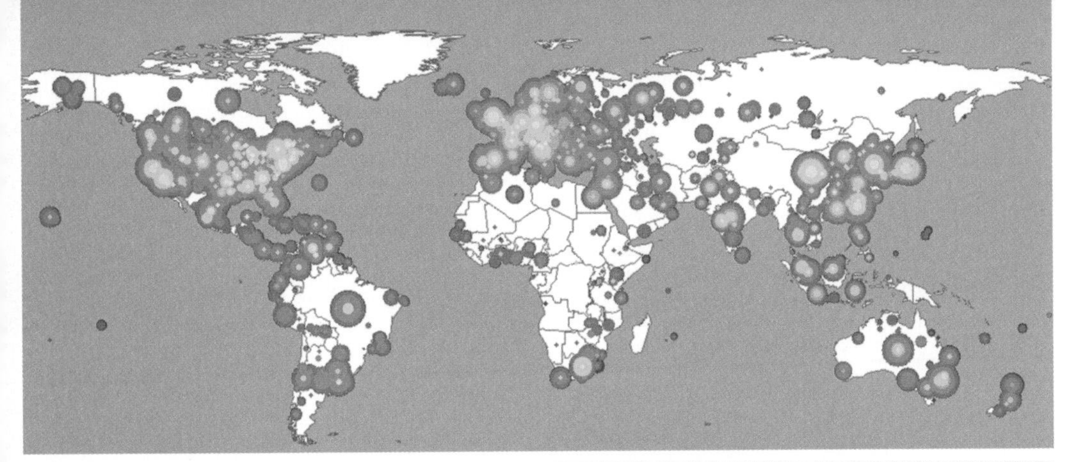

▲ **SPREAD OF A COMPUTER VIRUS**
This map shows the spread of the CodeRed worm on July 19, 2001, which disproportionately affected small businesses and home users. Some 360,000 computers were infected, spreading in early (yellow), middle (orange), and late (red) zones. Clearly, not all software programs are benign. Programs designed to intentionally disrupt, damage, or interfere with computer functions, files, and data are commonly referred to as computer viruses. Much like human-spread viruses, they range in complexity, severity and speed of transmission. One particularly fast-spreading type of virus is called worms. They spread themselves automatically by controlling other software programs such as email.

GeoBytes

EXPLOSIVE GROWTH
In 1981, the Internet had barely more than 200 host computers. Today there are more than 400 million, with millions more being added every month.

MOBILE WORLD
More than 75% of the world's population lives within range of a mobile phone network, whereas only 50% have access to a fixed-line telephone.

TV AND RADIO
In the last thirty years, television viewers in the developing world have multiplied 55 fold. The number of radios per 1,000 habitants has more than doubled.

U.S. OWNS THE SKIES
The United States owns more than half of the world's satellites, with Russia a distant second. Other satellite holders include Japan and China. Satellites serve a mix of civilian, commercial, and military uses.

Advances in and widespread use of communication technologies have quickly changed the face of international communication. Enormous amounts of data can be shared nearly instantaneously, and voice communication is now possible across much of the globe. Neither would have been possible a few decades ago when nearly all telecommunication services were carried over copper wire. The Internet has fostered entrepreneurship, helped open new markets, created new industries and jobs, and provided accessibility to and sharing of vast amounts of information. Cellular phones have made voice communication a reality for many who previously had no access to land-line phone service. And without the widespread network of fiber-optic cables, the rapid transmission of volumes of data and crystal-clear voice communication—hallmarks of international communication today—would not be possible. Although these technologies have helped foster communication and economic activity across the globe, they are not truly global. Many areas, both in the developed and developing world, do not have access to these technologies, creating a divide between the digital haves and have-nots.

▶ **CONNECTING THE PLANET**
The world is increasingly connected by underground and undersea fiber-optic cables and cellular networks. Fiber-optic cables allow for lightening-fast transmission of email, data, and voice calls, whereas cellular technology has extended phone service to parts of the world previously without any land-line service, including rural regions in Asia and Africa.

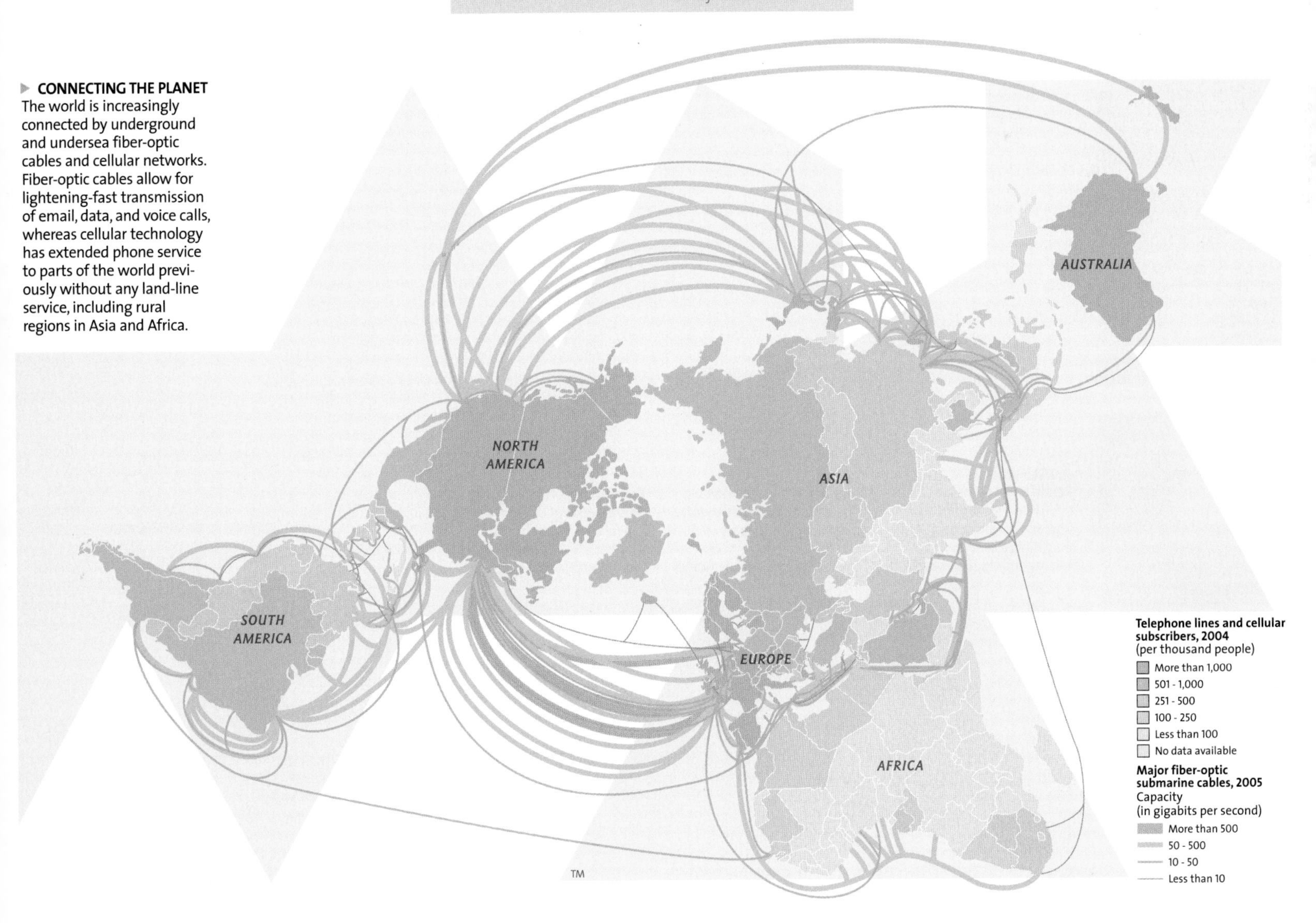

ENERGY CONSUMPTION

The use and availability of primary energy resources are unequally distributed across the globe. More than 86% of energy consumed globally is from nonrenewable fossil fuels—coal, oil, and natural gas. Consumption of these fuels is greatest in industrialized nations, with the U.S. using up nearly one-quarter. Developing countries, especially those in sub-Saharan Africa, rely on more traditional sources of energy, such as firewood and dung.

HYDROPOWER

NUCLEAR

SOLAR

WIND

GEOTHERMAL

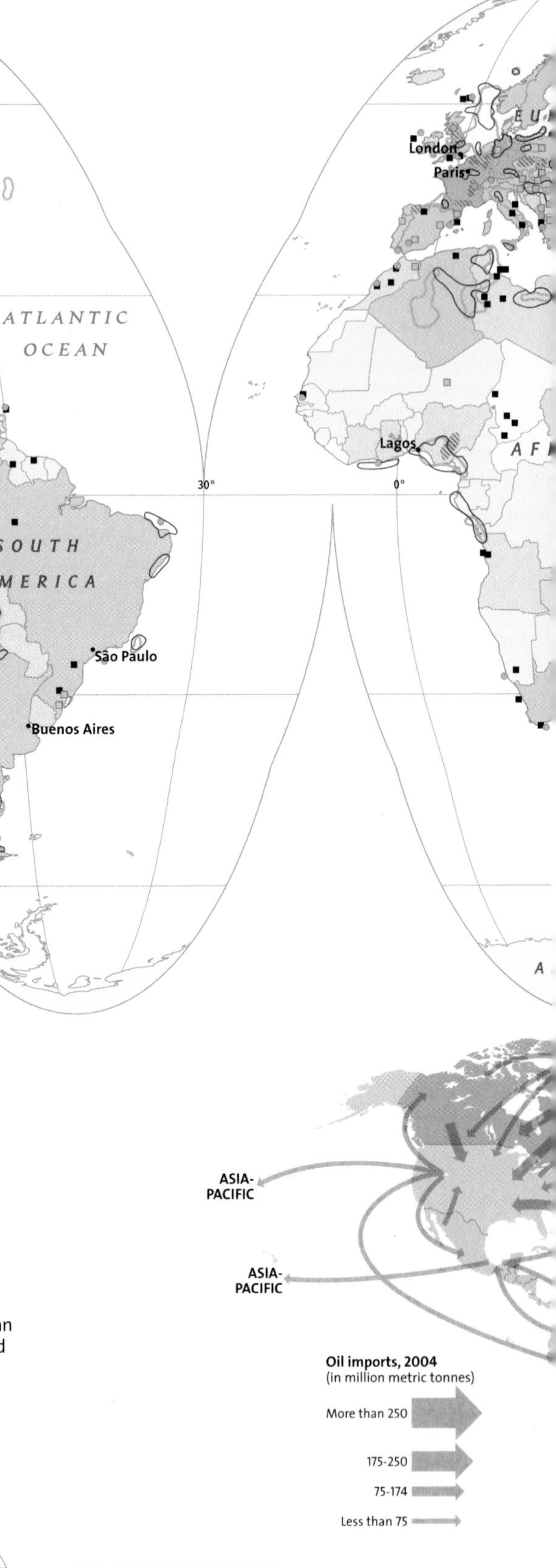

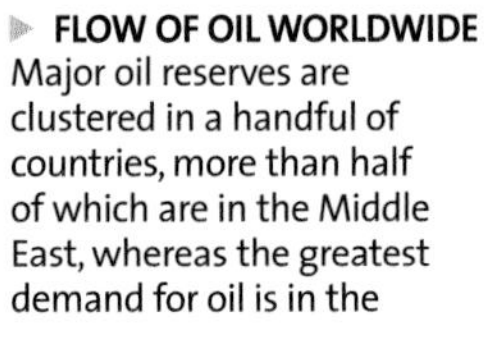

ALTERNATIVE ENERGIES

Hydropower provides nearly 18% of the world's electricity, but it is limited to countries with adequate water resources, and it poses threats to local watersheds. **Nuclear energy** makes up 17% of the Earth's electricity, but few countries have adopted it because of potential environmental risks and waste disposal issues. **Solar** and **wind energy** are inexhaustible and are the focus of new energy technologies and research. **Geothermal energy** is efficient but limited to countries with ready sources of hot ground water, such as Iceland.

RENEWABLE ENERGY

Renewable sources of energy—geothermal, solar, and wind—make up a small percentage of the world's energy supply. They have a significant impact, however, on local and regional energy supplies, especially for electricity, in places such as the U.S., Japan, and Germany. These sources of energy can be regenerated or renewed in a relatively short time, whereas fossil fuels form over geologic time spans.

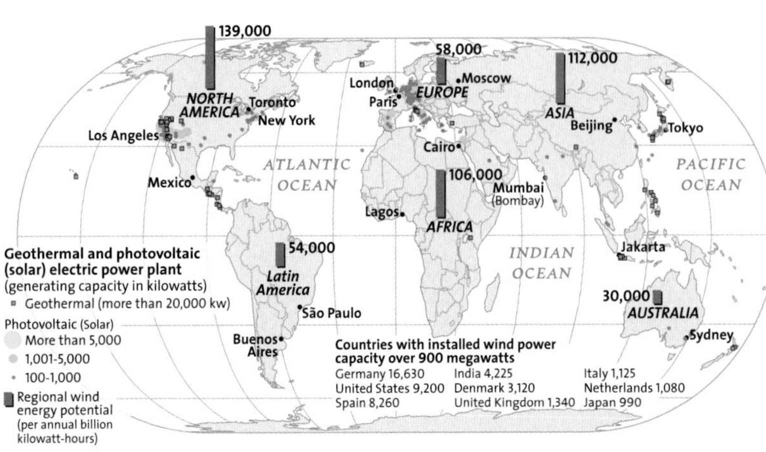

FLOW OF OIL WORLDWIDE

Major oil reserves are clustered in a handful of countries, more than half of which are in the Middle East, whereas the greatest demand for oil is in the United States, Europe, Japan, and China. Other major oil exporters include the Russian Federation, Norway, Venezuela, and Mexico.

ENERGY

Energy enables us to cook our food, heat our homes, move about our planet, and run industry. Everyday the world uses some 320 billion kilowatt-hours of energy—equivalent to each person burning 22 lightbulbs nonstop, and over the next century demand may increase threefold. Consumption is not uniform across the globe. People in industrialized countries consume far greater amounts of energy than those in developing countries. The world's energy supply is still fossil-fuel based, despite advances in alternative energy sources. To meet demand, many countries must import fuels, making the trade of energy a critical, often volatile global political issue. Instability where most oil is found—the Persian Gulf, Nigeria, Venezuela—make this global economic powerline fragile. Insatiable demand where most energy is consumed—the U.S., Japan, China, India, Germany—makes national economies increasingly dependent. Furthermore, extraction and use of fossil fuel have serious environmental effects, such as air pollution and global warming. The challenge for the future? Reducing reliance on fossil fuels, developing alternative energies to meet demand, and mediating the trade-offs between the environment and energy.

GeoBytes

LACK OF ACCESS
More than two billion people, mostly in the developing world, do not have access to electricity. Increasingly, small-scale wind and solar projects bring power to poor rural areas.

WINDS OF CHANGE
Worldwide, wind supplies less than 1% of electric power, but it is the fastest growing source, especially in Europe. Denmark gets 20% of its electricity from wind.

POWER OF THE SUN
Near Leipzig, Germany, some 33,000 photovoltaic panels produce up to five megawatts of power. It is one of the world's largest solar arrays.

GOING NUCLEAR
France gets 78% of its electricity from nuclear power. Developing nations, such as China and India, are building new reactors to reduce pollution and meet soaring energy demands.

GROWING PAINS
China is fueling its economic growth with huge quantities of coal, and it suffers from energy-related environmental problems. China is second only to the United States in greenhouse gas emissions that contribute to global warming.

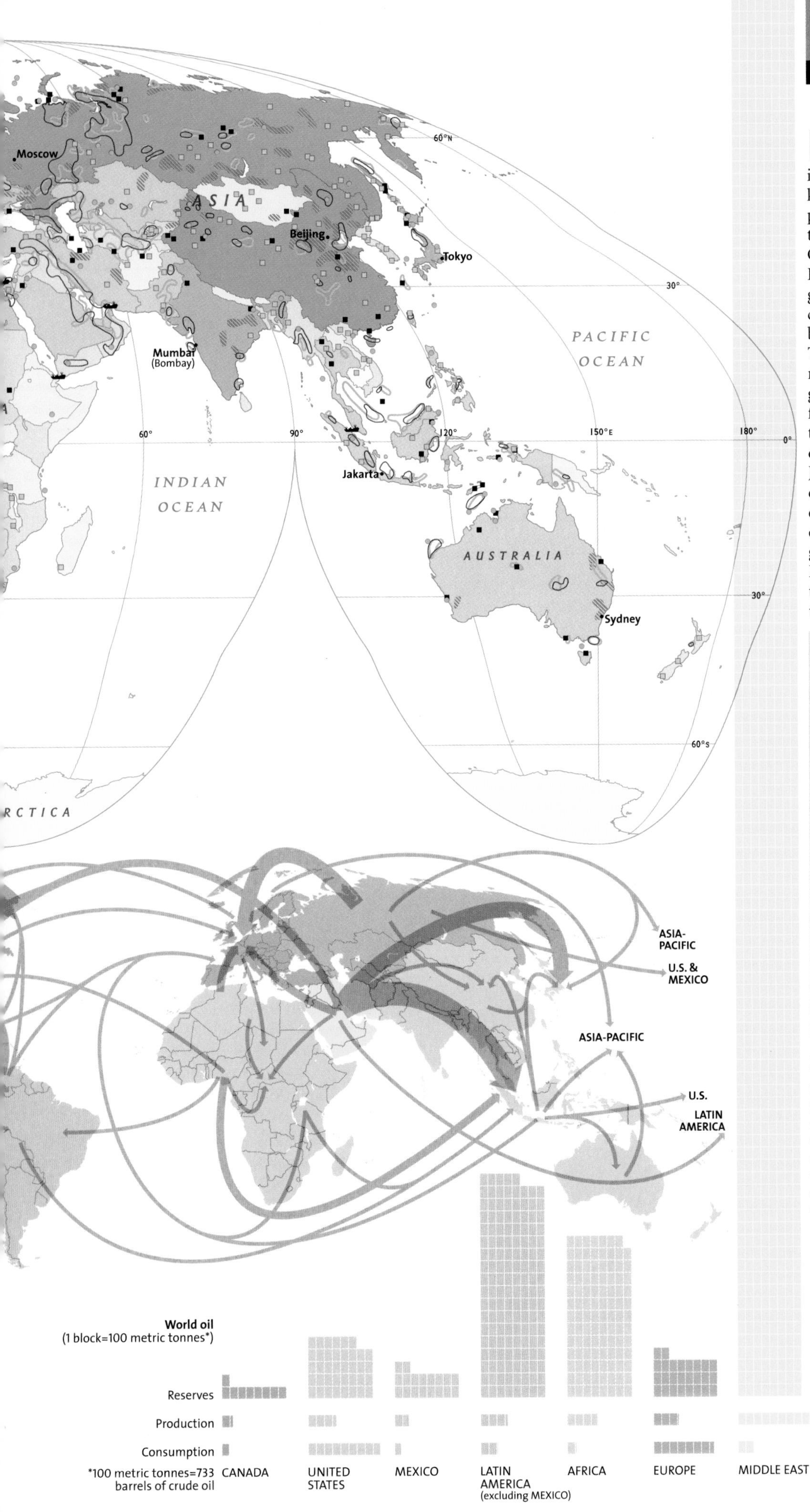

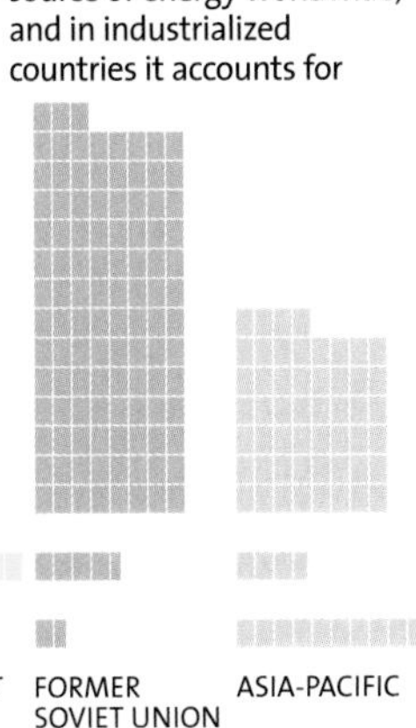

◄ **WORLD OIL SUPPLY**
The world's hunger for oil is insatiable, but the supply is finite and unequally distributed, making it one of the world's most valuable commodities. It is the leading source of energy worldwide, and in industrialized countries it accounts for more than one-third of all energy consumed. Pressure on the world's oil supply continues to mount as both industrialized and developing countries grow more dependent on it to meet increasing energy needs.

▼ FLIGHT FROM CONFLICT

By the end of 2004, the number of refugees worldwide reached an estimated 9.2 million, and the flows of people uprooted from their homes because of war, violence, and oppression showed no sign of abating in 2005. The bar graph below indicates the scale of refugee displacement and sanctuary. In Colombia, decades of conflict have led to a vast number of internal displaced persons (IDPs), shown by the brown bar. The blue bar shows the number of Colombians who have fled their homes. Large numbers of Afghans are displaced internally (brown bar) and have left the country. Pakistan has given residence to many (brown bar). Germany and the United States shelter refugees from around the world (brown bars).

United Nations High Commission for Refugees trucks evacuate people from Srebrenica during the Bosnian conflict in 1993.

Uprooted people, 2005

Country of origin

Residency

Number of people (in thousands)

1,000

500

100

0

Canada, Costa Rica, Cuba, El Salvador, Guatemala, Haiti, Mexico, Nicaragua, United States — NORTH AMERICA

Colombia, Ecuador, Peru, Venezuela — SOUTH AMERICA

Albania, Austria, Belarus, Belgium, Bosnia and Herzegovina, Bulgaria, Croatia, Cyprus, Denmark, Estonia, Finland, France, Germany, Greece, Hungary, Ireland, Italy, Latvia, Macedonia, Moldova, Netherlands, Norway, Poland, Romania, Russia, Serbia and Montenegro, Spain, Sweden, Switzerland, Ukraine, United Kingdom — EUROPE

Algeria, Angola, Benin, Burundi, Cameroon, Central African Republic, Chad, Congo, Côte d'Ivoire (Ivory Coast), Democratic Republic of the Congo, Djibouti, Egypt, Eritrea, Ethiopia, Gabon

NORTH AMERICA

SOUTH AMERICA

▶ MEASURING DEMOCRACY

Democracy surged in the 1990s as Eastern and Central European states emerged from the Soviet Union, while Latin Americans tossed out many of their autocrats. Belarus remained belligerently repressive, but only Cuba, North Korea, Laos, Vietnam, and the People's Republic of China cling officially to Communism. Africa and parts of Asia are dominated by autocracies and anocracies (a mixture of democratic and authoritarian), while some populist South American regimes again flirt with strong-man quasi-democratic rule.

Military expenditure as a percentage of Gross Domestic Product (GDP)

- More than 9%
- 5% - 9%
- 3% - 4.9%
- 1.5% - 2.9%
- Less than 1.5%
- No data available
- ▪ Military service required

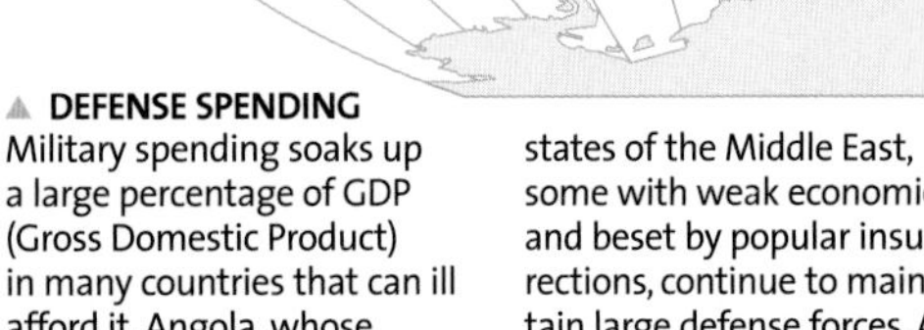

Biological weapons possession

- Known
- Possible
- Possible offensive research program

▲ DEFENSE SPENDING

Military spending soaks up a large percentage of GDP (Gross Domestic Product) in many countries that can ill afford it. Angola, whose 26-year-old civil war ended in 2002, is awash in arms. The states of the Middle East, some with weak economies and beset by popular insurrections, continue to maintain large defense forces. A resurgent China flexes new military muscle. The United States spends as much on defense as the rest of the world combined. More than 80 nations, headed by both democracies and totalitarian governments, require military service of their youth.

▲ BIOLOGICAL WEAPONS

Only a small volume of a toxic biological agent, if properly dispersed, could cause massive casualties in a densely populated area. Moreover, its manufacture could be virtually undetectable, as only a small facility is needed, and much of the material and equipment has legitimate medical and agricultural use. Although only about 8 countries have offensive biological weapons programs, that number is expected to grow with the increased international flow of technology, goods, and information.

Regime type, 2005

Autocratic

Governed by an authoritarian leader

Anocratic

Government in transition between autocratic and democratic rule

Democratic

Governed by the people through representatives

No data available

Active military, 2005 (personnel in thousands)

More than 1,000

250 - 1,000

50 - 249

10 - 49

Less than 10

No active military

In the 21st century, the threat of war between sovereign nations has largely given way to war within states—conflicts between aggrieved religious, tribal, or ethnic groups. Even more sinister threats involve forces unattached to sovereign states—globally dispersed ideological cadres, loyal to no government, whose use of new communication technologies makes them elusive. Not since Iraq rolled into Kuwait in 1991 has one nation tried to forcibly incorporate another, although the United States and its coalition of allies, in response to the September 11, 2001, attacks by the radical Islamists of al Qaeda, have invaded both Afghanistan and Iraq. The shock waves have dispersed millions of refugees into Pakistan, Iran, and Western Europe. Even as the Cold War superpowers disarm, nuclear proliferation by unstable governments remains alarmingly possible.

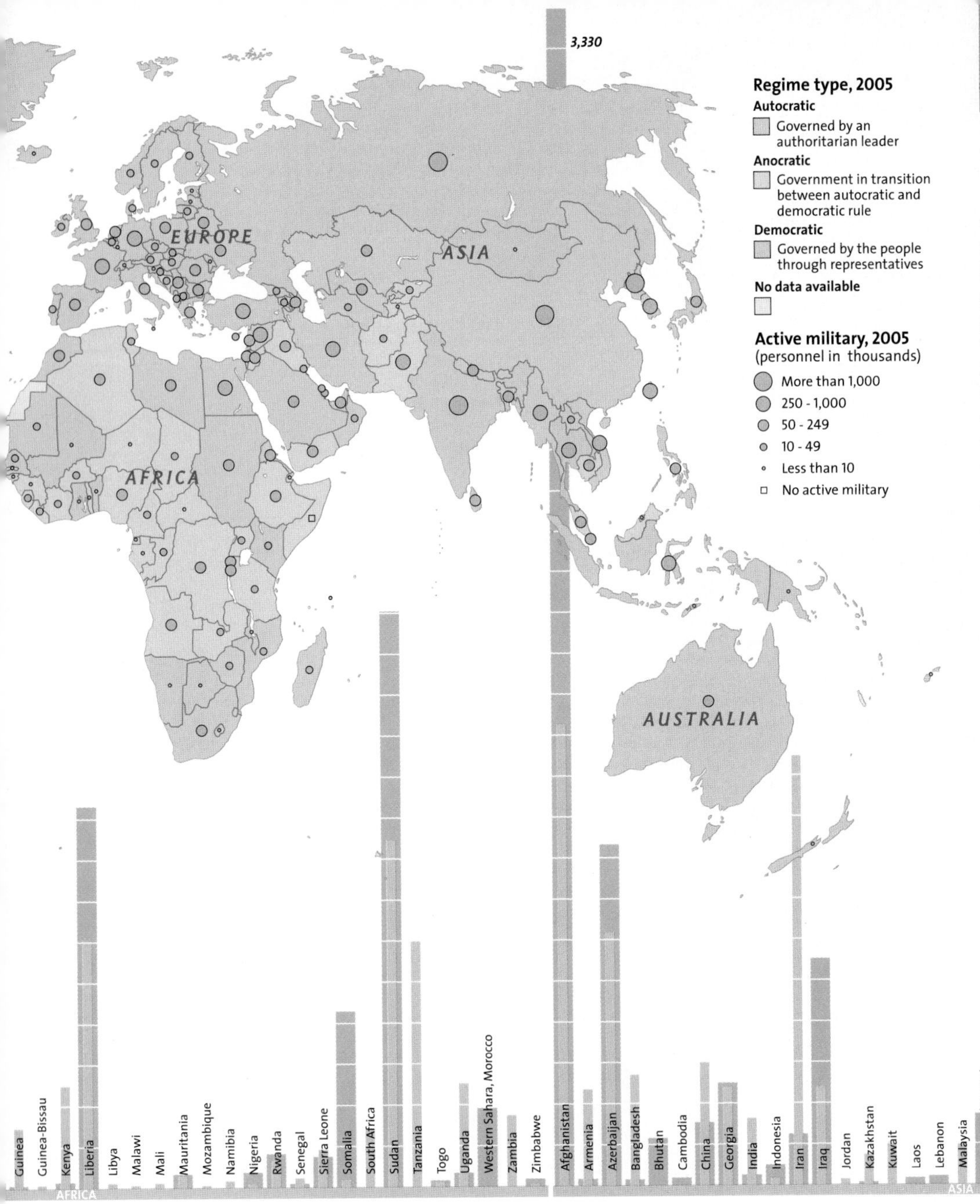

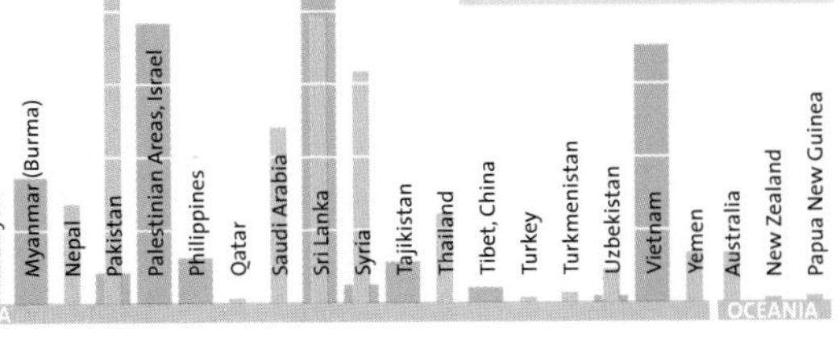

GeoBytes

NEVER AGAIN?
Atomic weapons have been used only in World War II—in 1945 by the United States against Japan.

BIO-WEAPON SCARE
Envelopes containing the biological agent anthrax were mailed only months after 9/11, killing five.

CHECHNYA IN RUINS
Two protracted wars by Russia against its recalcitrant territory of Chechnya have created another platform for Muslim extremists.

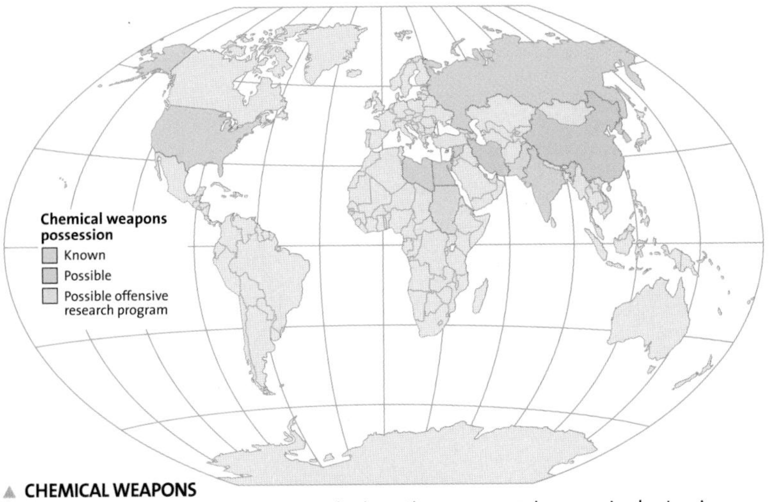

Chemical weapons possession

Known

Possible

Possible offensive research program

Nuclear weapons possession

Known

Potential (Capable of developing weapons or had a weapons program)

Possible offensive research program

▲ CHEMICAL WEAPONS
Only 9 sovereign nations, including the United States, Russia, South Korea, and India, acknowledge chemical weapon stockpiles, but little doubt remains that additional countries and subnational groups also have them. Under the Chemical Weapons Convention (CWC), member countries are scheduled to destroy stockpiles by 2007, although Russia and the United States have received extensions. Terror groups seldom acknowledge international treaties, and materials for chemical weapons are readily available to those who would have them.

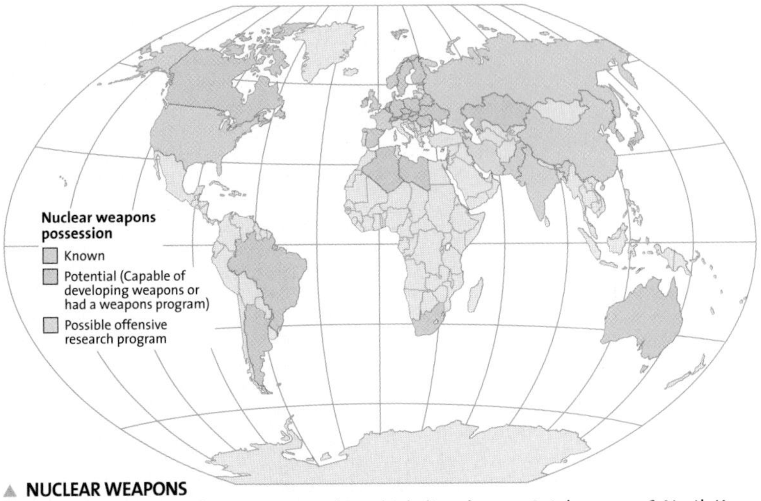

▲ NUCLEAR WEAPONS
The United States, United Kingdom, China, France, and Russia remain the world's only declared nuclear weapon states under the Nuclear Non-Proliferation Treaty, but Pakistan and India have conducted nuclear tests, and Israel is believed also to possess arsenals. Libya recently gave up its nuclear program, and Belarus, Kazakhstan, and Ukraine all relinquished Soviet nuclear weapons on their territories. But on October 9, 2006, North Korea tested a nuclear weapon. Iran, another country with nuclear ambitions, is enriching uranium and building its first nuclear power plant.

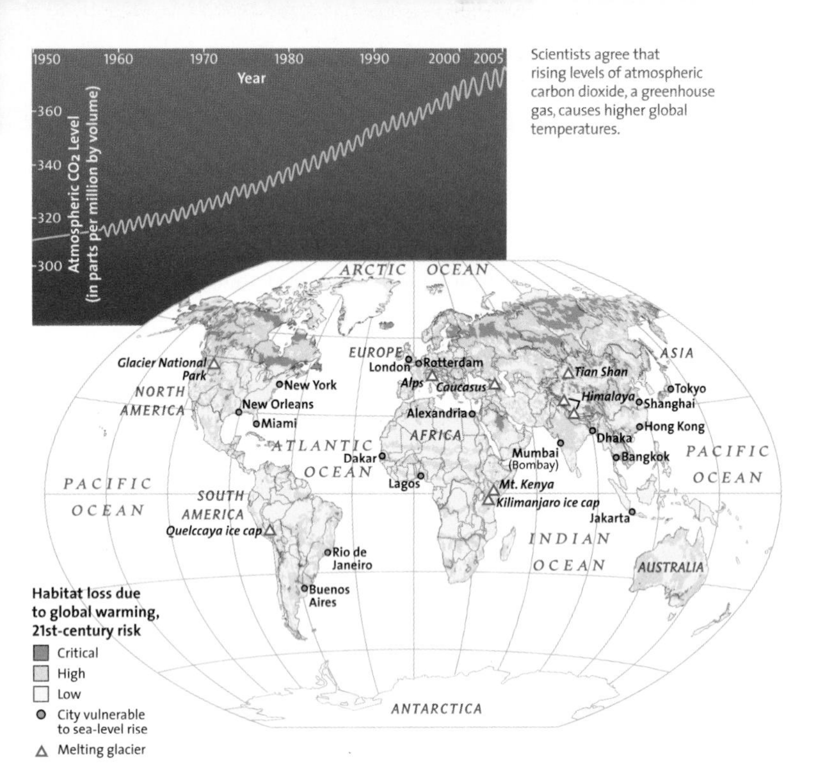

Scientists agree that rising levels of atmospheric carbon dioxide, a greenhouse gas, causes higher global temperatures.

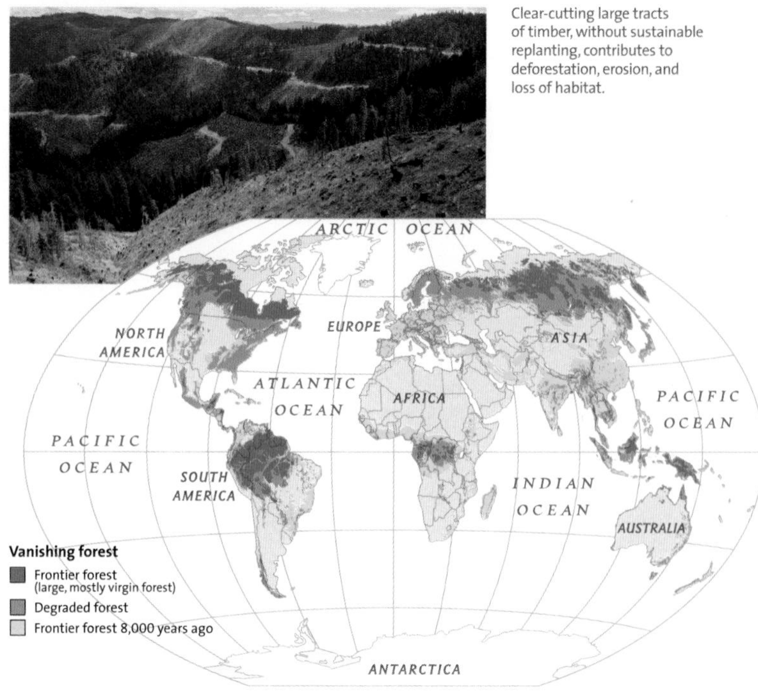

Clear-cutting large tracts of timber, without sustainable replanting, contributes to deforestation, erosion, and loss of habitat.

▲ GLOBAL WARMING

Temperatures across the world are increasing at a rate not seen at any other time in the last 10,000 years. Although climate variation is a natural phenomenon, human activities that release carbon dioxide and other greenhouse gases into the atmosphere—industrial processes, fossil fuel consumption, deforestation, and land use change—are contributing to this warming trend. Scientists predict that if this trend continues, one-third of plant and animal habitats will be dramatically altered and more than one million species will be threatened with extinction in the next 50 years. And even small increases in global temperatures can melt glaciers and polar ice sheets, raising sea levels and flooding coastal cities and towns.

▲ DEFORESTATION

Of the 13 million hectares (32 million acres) of forest lost each year, mostly to make room for agriculture, more than half are in South America and Africa, where many of the world's tropical rain forests and terrestrial plant and animal species can be found. Loss of habitat in such species-rich areas takes a toll on the world's biodiversity. Deforested areas also release, instead of absorb, carbon dioxide into the atmosphere, contributing to global climate change. Deforestation can also affect local climates by reducing evaporative cooling, leading to decreased rainfall and higher temperatures.

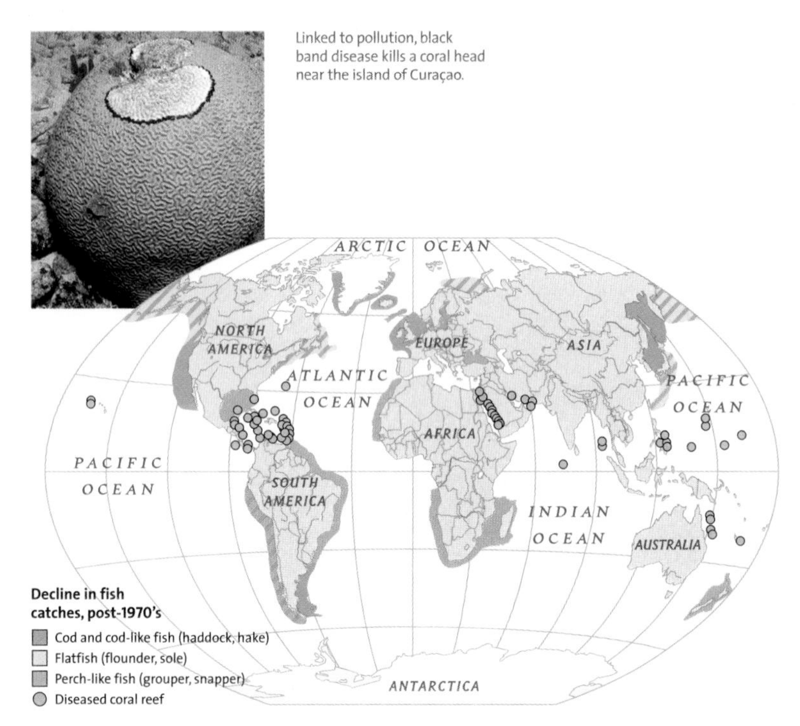

Linked to pollution, black band disease kills a coral head near the island of Curaçao.

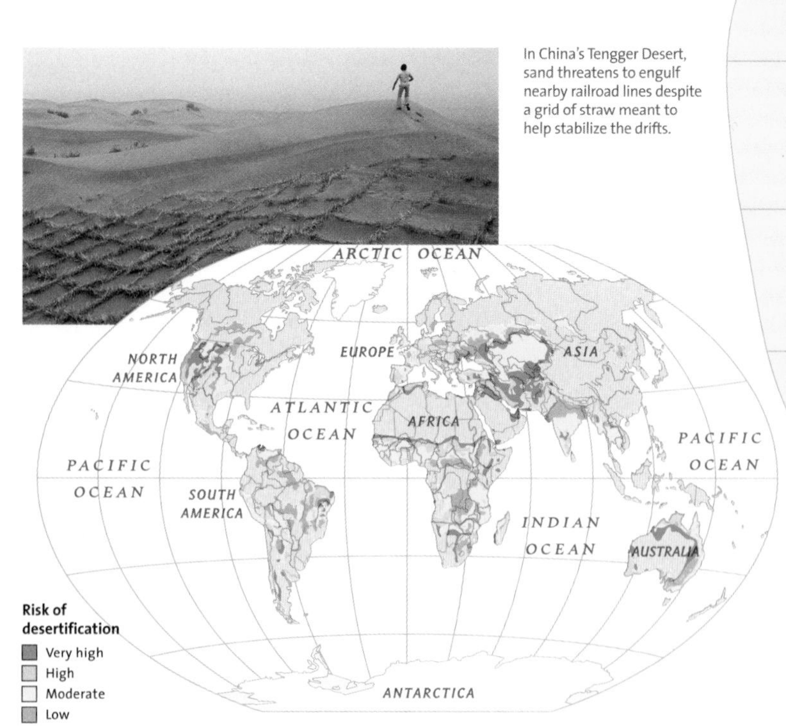

In China's Tengger Desert, sand threatens to engulf nearby railroad lines despite a grid of straw meant to help stabilize the drifts.

▲ THREATENED OCEANS

Oceans cover more than two-thirds of the Earth's surface and are home to at least half of the world's biodiversity, yet they are the least understood ecosystems. The combined stresses of overfishing, pollution, increased carbon dioxide emissions, global climate change, and coastal development are having a serious impact on the health of oceans and ocean species. Over 70% of the world's fish species are depleted or nearing depletion, and 50% of coral reefs worldwide are threatened by human activities.

▲ DESERTIFICATION

Climate variability and human activities, such as grazing and conversion of natural areas to agricultural use, are leading causes of desertification, the degradation of land in arid, semiarid, and dry subhumid areas. The environmental consequences of desertification are great—loss of topsoil, increased soil salinity, damaged vegetation, regional climate change, and a decline in biodiversity. Equally critical are the social consequences—more than 2 billion people live in and make a living off these dryland areas, covering about 41% of Earth's surface.

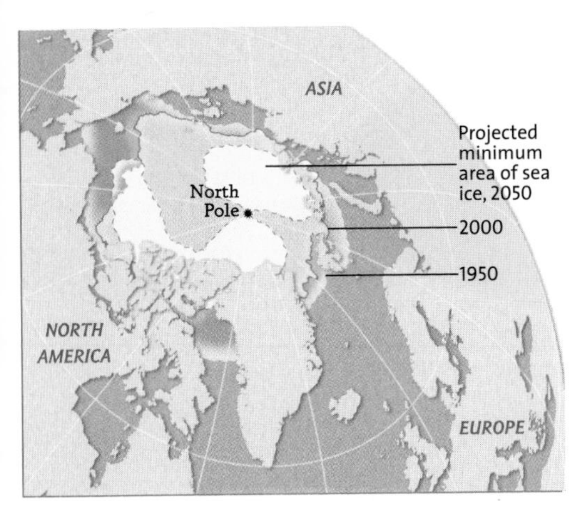

POLAR ICE CAP
Over the last 50 years, the extent of polar sea ice has noticeably decreased. Since 1970 alone, an area larger than Norway, Sweden, and Denmark combined has melted. This trend is predicted to accelerate as temperatures rise in the Arctic and across the globe.

GeoBytes

ACIDIFYING OCEANS
Oceans are absorbing an unprecedented 20 to 25 million tonnes (22 to 28 millions tons) of carbon dioxide each day, increasing the water's acidity.

ENDANGERED REEFS
Some 95% of coral reefs in Southeast Asia have been destroyed or are threatened.

RECORD TEMPERATURES
The 1990s were the warmest decade on record in the last century.

WARMING ARCTIC
While the world as a whole has warmed nearly 0.6°C (1°F) over the last hundred years, parts of the Arctic have warmed 4 to 5 times as much in only the last 50 years.

DISAPPEARING RAIN FORESTS
Scientists predict that the world's rain forests will disappear within the next one hundred years if the current rate of deforestation continues.

OIL POLLUTION
Nearly 1.3 million tonnes (1.4 million tons) of oil seep into the world's oceans each year from the combined sources of natural seepage, extraction, transportation, and consumption.

ACCIDENTAL DROWNINGS
Entanglement in fishing gear is one of the greatest threats to marine mammals.

A FAREWELL TO FROGS?
Worldwide, almost half of the 5,700 named amphibian species are in decline.

With the growth of scientific record keeping, observation, modeling, and analysis, our understanding of Earth's environment is improving. Yet even as we deepen our insight into environmental processes, we are changing what we are studying. At no other time in history have humans altered their environment with such speed and force. Nothing occurs in isolation, and stress in one area has impacts elsewhere. Our agricultural and fishing practices, industrial processes, extraction of resources, and transportation methods are leading to extinctions, destroying habitats, devastating fish stocks, disturbing the soil, and polluting the oceans and the air. As a result, biodiversity is declining, global temperatures are rising, polar ice is shrinking, and the ozone layer continues to thin.

POLLUTION
No corner of the earth is immune to pollution, be it in the air, soil, or water. Concentrations of pollution can be found in the industrial centers of North America, Europe, and, increasingly, Asia—and areas downwind or downstream from them. Shipping routes are sources of pollution, from oil spills to garbage dumpings.

OZONE DEPLETION
First noted in the mid-1980s, the springtime "ozone hole" over the Antarctic continues to grow. With sustained efforts to restrict chlorofluorocarbons (CFCs) and other ozone-depleting chemicals, scientists have begun to see what they hope is a leveling off in the rate of depletion. Stratospheric ozone shields the Earth from the sun's ultraviolet radiation. Thinning of this protective layer puts people at risk for skin cancer and cataracts. It can also have devastating effects on the Earth's biological functions.

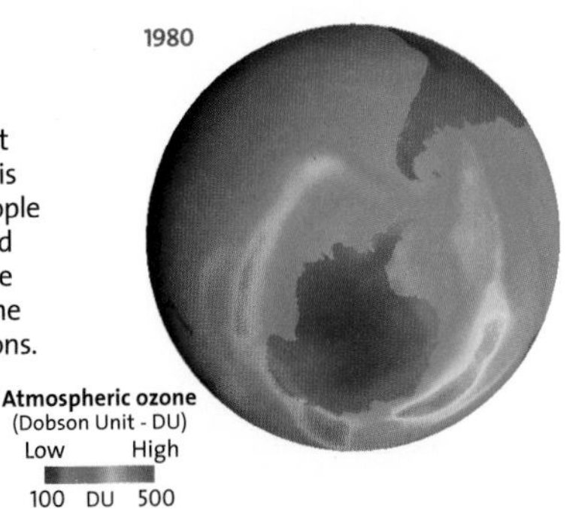

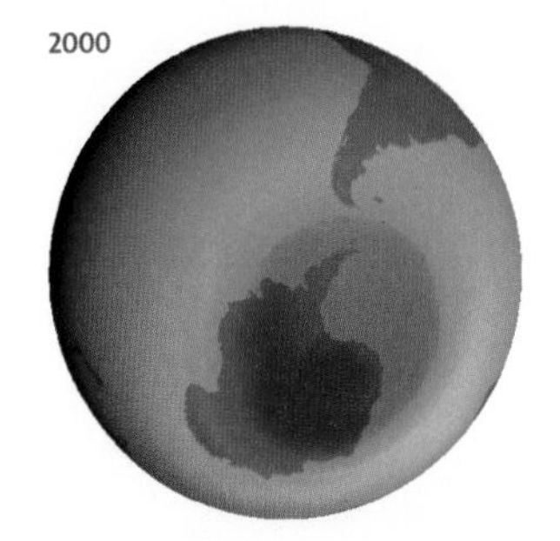

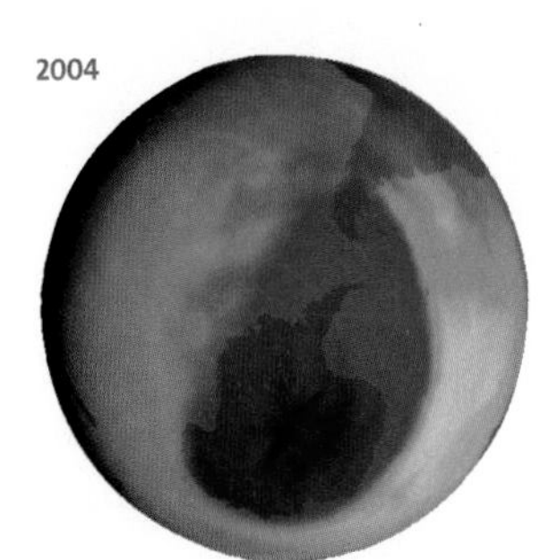

GeoBytes

LARGEST NATIONAL PARK
North East Greenland National Park, Greenland, 972,000 sq km (375,000 sq mi)

LARGEST MARINE PARK
Northwestern Hawaiian Islands Marine National Monument, U.S., 360,000 sq km (140,000 sq mi)

LARGEST TROPICAL FOREST PARK
Tumucumaque National Park in the Brazilian Amazon 24,135 sq km (9,319 sq mi)

BIODIVERSITY HOTSPOTS
Conservation International identifies world regions suffering from a severe loss of biodiversity.

WORLD HERITAGE SITES
The United Nations Educational, Scientific, and Cultural Organization (UNESCO) recognizes natural and cultural sites of "universal value."

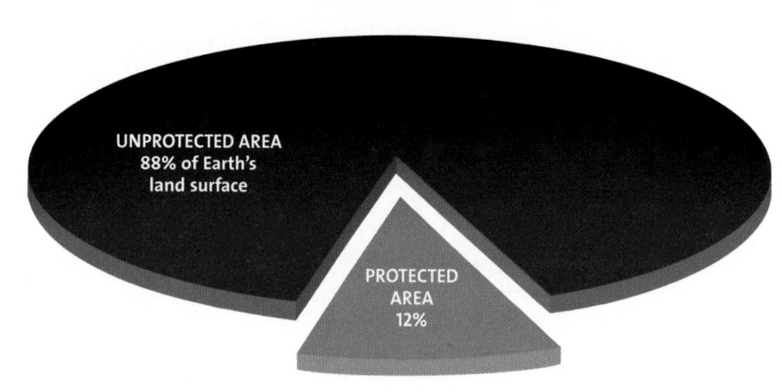

PERCENTAGE PROTECTED
Protected areas worldwide represent 12% of the Earth's land surface, according to the U.N. Environmental Programme World Conservation Monitoring Centre. Only 0.5% of the marine environment is within protected areas—an amount considered inadequate by conservationists because of the increasing threats of overfishing and coral reef loss worldwide.

HAWAI'I VOLCANOES NATIONAL PARK, HAWAI'I
The park includes two of the world's most active volcanoes, Kilauea and Mauna Loa. The landscape shows the results of 70 million years of volcanism, including calderas, lava flows, and black sand beaches. Lava spreads out to build the island, and seawater vaporizes as lava hits the ocean at 1,149°C (2,100° F). The national park, created in 1916, covers 10% of the island of Hawai'i and is a refuge for endangered species, like the hawksbill turtle and Hawaiian goose. It was made a World Heritage site in 1987.

GALÁPAGOS NATIONAL PARK, ECUADOR
Galápago means tortoise in Spanish, and at one time 250,000 giant tortoises roamed the islands. Today about 15,000 remain, and three of the original 14 subspecies are extinct—and the Pinta Island tortoise may be extinct soon. In 1959, Ecuador made the volcanic Galápagos Islands a national park, protecting the giant tortoises and other endemic species. The archipelago became a World Heritage site in 1978, and a marine reserve surrounding the islands was added in 2001.

WESTERN UNITED STATES
An intricate public lands pattern—including national forests, wilderness areas, wildlife refuges, and national parks such as Arches (above)—embraces nearly half the surface area of 11 western states. Ten out of 19 World Heritage sites in the United States are found here. It was in the West that the modern national park movement was born in the 19th century with the establishment of Yellowstone and Yosemite National Parks.

MADIDI NATIONAL PARK, BOLIVIA
Macaws may outnumber humans in Madidi, Bolivia's second largest national park, established in 1995. A complex community of plants, animals, and native Indian groups share this 18,900-sq-km (7,300-sq-mi) reserve, part of the Tropical Andes biodiversity hotspot. Indigenous communities benefit from ecotourism.

AMAZON BASIN, BRAZIL
Indigenous peoples help manage reserves in Brazil that are linked with Jaú National Park. The park and reserves are part of the Central Amazon Conservation Complex, a World Heritage site covering more than 60,000 sq km (23,000 sq mi). It is the largest protected area in the Amazon Basin and one of the most biologically rich regions on the planet.

ARCTIC REGIONS
Polar bears find safe havens in Canadian parks, such as on Ellesmere Island, and in Greenland's huge protected area—Earth's largest—that preserves the island's frigid northeast. In 1996 countries with Arctic lands adopted the Circumpolar Protected Areas Network Strategy and Action Plan to help conserve ecosystems. Today 15% of Arctic land area is protected.

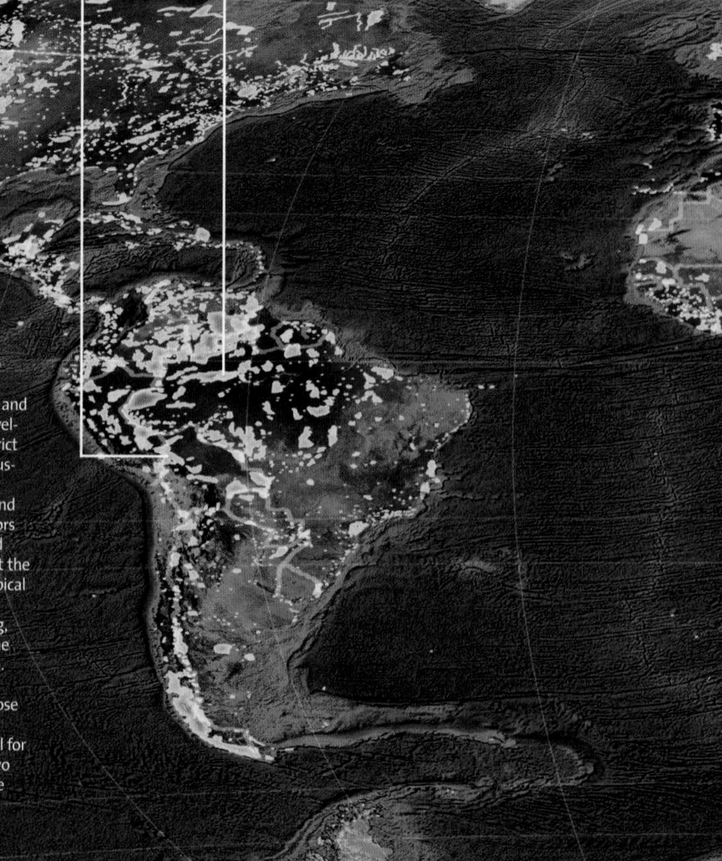

PROTECTED AREAS WORLDWIDE
What are protected areas? Most people agree that such territories are dedicated to protecting and maintaining biodiversity and are often managed through legal means. Yellowstone National Park, established in 1872, is often cited as the start of the modern era of protected areas. From a mere handful in 1900, the number of protected areas worldwide now exceeds 104,790, covering more than 20 million sq km (7.7 million sq mi). North America claims the most protected land of any region, amounting to almost 18% of its territory. South Asia, at about 7%, has the least amount of land under some form of protection. Not all protected areas are created or managed equally, and management categories developed by IUCN range from strict nature reserve to areas for sustainable use. Management effectiveness varies widely and can be affected by such factors as conservation budgets, and political stability. Throughout the world—but especially in tropical areas—protected areas are threatened by illegal hunting, overfishing, pollution, and the removal of native vegetation. Countries and international organizations no longer choose between conservation and development; rather the goal for societies is to balance the two for equitable and sustainable resource use.

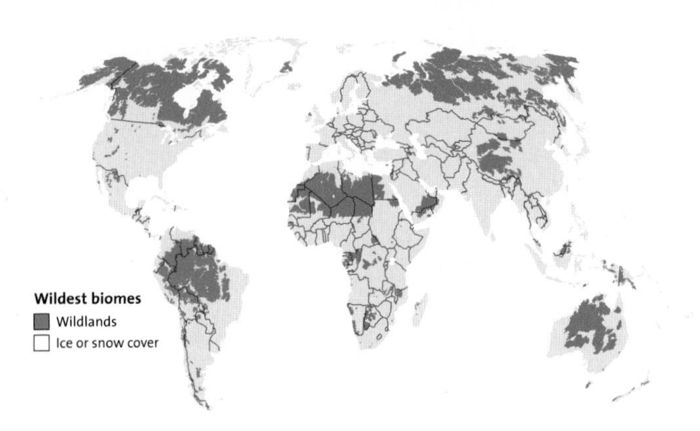

WILDEST AREAS
Although generally far from cities, the world's remaining wild places play a vital role in a healthy global ecosystem. The boreal (northern) forests of Canada and Russia, for instance, help cleanse the air we breathe by absorbing carbon dioxide and providing oxygen. With the human population increasing by an estimated one billion over the next 15 years, many wild places could fall within reach of the plow or under a cloud of smog.

For millennia, lands have been set aside as sacred ground or as hunting reserves for the powerful. Today, great swaths are protected for recreation, habitat conservation, biodiversity preservation, and resource management. Some groups may oppose protected spaces because they want access to resources now. Yet local inhabitants and governments are beginning to see the benefits of conservation efforts and sustainable use for human health and future generations.

SAREKS NATIONAL PARK, SWEDEN
This remote 1,970-sq-km (760-sq-mi) park, established in 1909 to protect the alpine landscape, is a favorite of backcountry hikers. It boasts some 200 mountains more than 1,800 m (5,900 ft), high, narrow valleys, and about 100 glaciers. Sareks forms part of the Laponian Area World Heritage site and has been a home to the Saami (or Lapp) people since prehistoric times.

AFRICAN RESERVES
Some 120,000 elephants roam Chobe National Park in northern Botswana. Africa has more than 7,500 national parks, wildlife reserves, and other protected areas, covering about 9% of the continent. Protected areas are under enormous pressure from expanding populations, civil unrest and war, and environmental disasters.

WOLONG NATURE RESERVE, CHINA
Giant pandas freely chomp bamboo in this 2,000-sq-km (772-sq-mi) reserve in Sichuan Province, near the city of Chengdu. Misty bamboo forests host a number of endangered species, but the critically endangered giant panda—among the rarest mammals in the world—is the most famous resident. Only about 1,600 giant pandas exist in the wild.

KAMCHATKA, RUSSIA
Crater lakes, ash-capped cones, and diverse plant and animal species mark the Kamchatka Peninsula—a World Heritage site—located between the icy Bering Sea and Sea of Okhotsk. The active volcanoes and glaciers form a dynamic landscape of great beauty, known as "The Land of Fire and Ice." Kamchatka's remoteness and rugged landscape help fauna flourish, producing record numbers of salmon species and half of the Steller's sea-eagles on Earth.

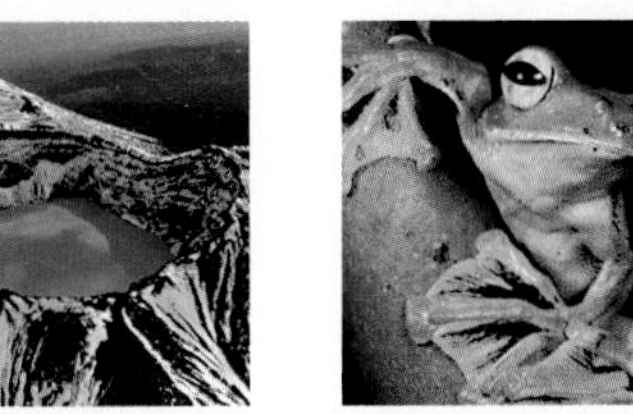

GUNUNG PALUNG NATIONAL PARK, INDONESIA
A tree frog's perch could be precarious in this 900-sq-km (347-sq-mi) park on the island of Borneo, in the heart of the Sundaland biodiversity hotspot. The biggest threat to trees and animals in the park and region is illegal logging. Gunung Palung contains a wider range of habitats than any other protected area on Borneo, from mangroves to lowland and cloud forests. A number of endangered species, such as orangutans and sun bears, depend on the dense forests.

AUSTRALIA & NEW ZEALAND
Uluru, a red sandstone monolith (formerly known as Ayers Rock), and the vast Great Barrier Reef, one of the largest marine parks in the world, are outstanding examples of Australia's protected areas—which make up more than 10% of the country's area and conserve a diverse range of unique ecosystems. About a third of New Zealand is protected, and it is a biodiversity hotspot because of threats to flightless native birds, such as the kakapo and kiwi. Cats, stoats, and other predators, introduced to New Zealand by settlers, kill thousands of birds each year.

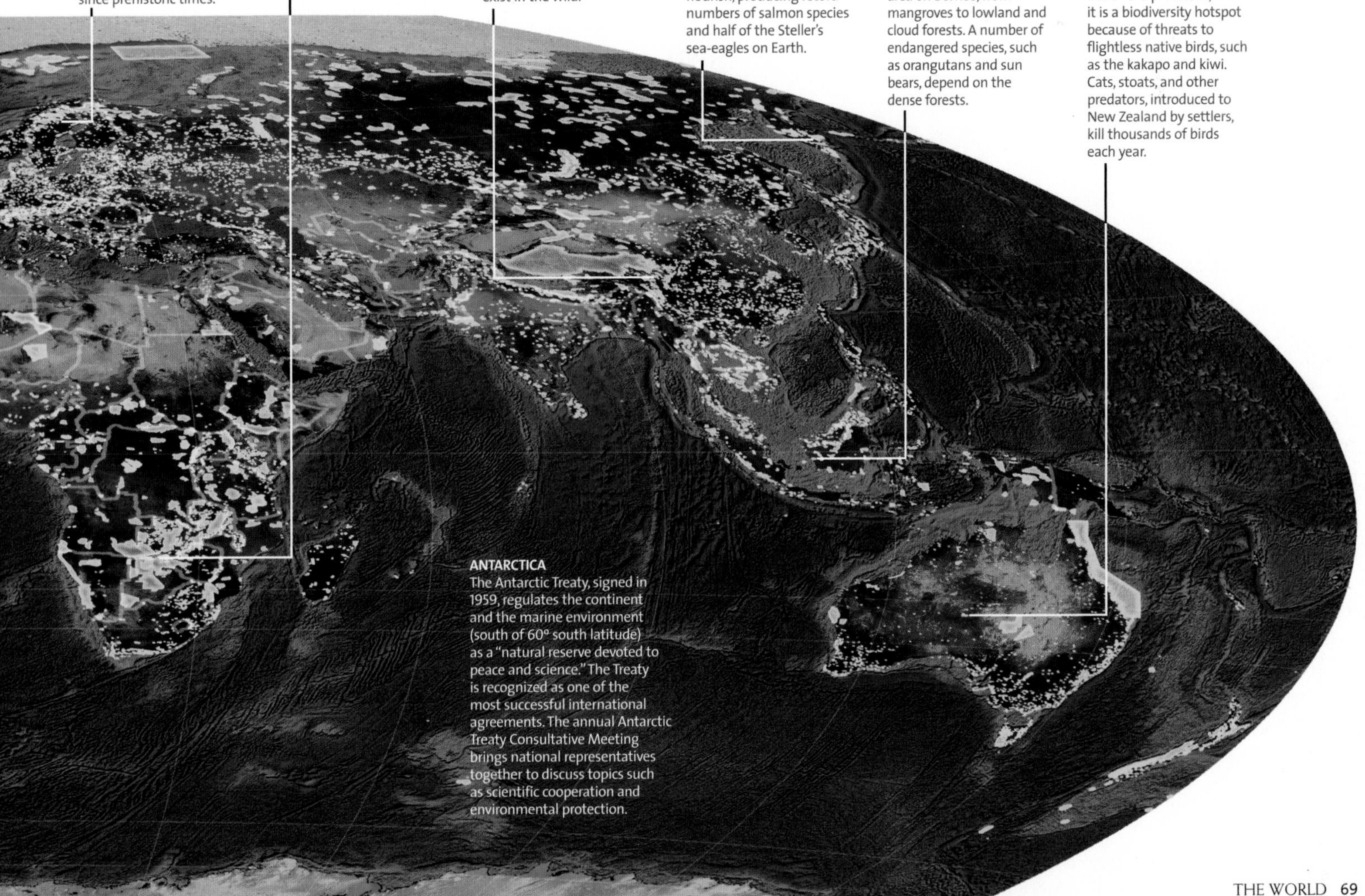

ANTARCTICA
The Antarctic Treaty, signed in 1959, regulates the continent and the marine environment (south of 60° south latitude) as a "natural reserve devoted to peace and science." The Treaty is recognized as one of the most successful international agreements. The annual Antarctic Treaty Consultative Meeting brings national representatives together to discuss topics such as scientific cooperation and environmental protection.

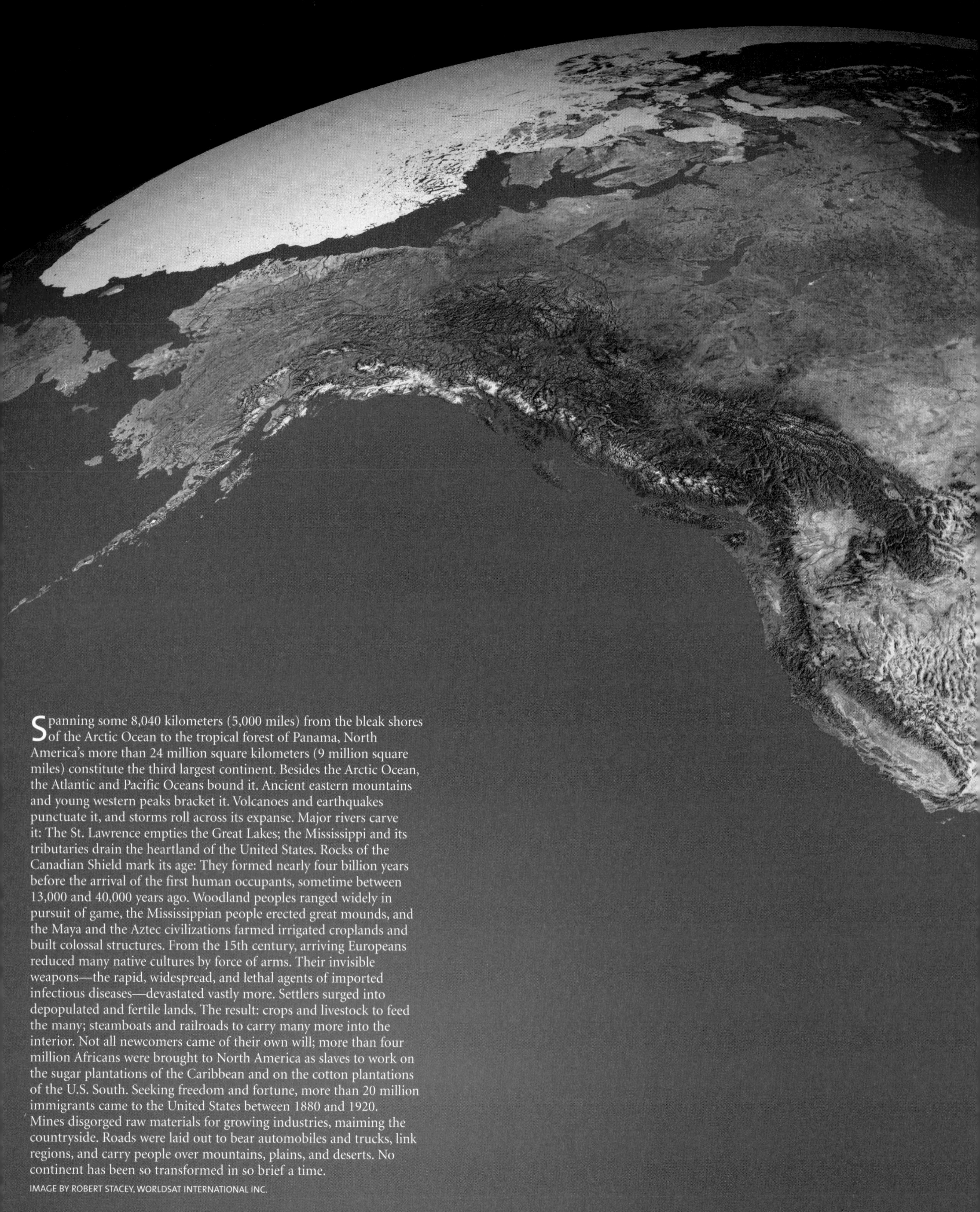

Spanning some 8,040 kilometers (5,000 miles) from the bleak shores of the Arctic Ocean to the tropical forest of Panama, North America's more than 24 million square kilometers (9 million square miles) constitute the third largest continent. Besides the Arctic Ocean, the Atlantic and Pacific Oceans bound it. Ancient eastern mountains and young western peaks bracket it. Volcanoes and earthquakes punctuate it, and storms roll across its expanse. Major rivers carve it: The St. Lawrence empties the Great Lakes; the Mississippi and its tributaries drain the heartland of the United States. Rocks of the Canadian Shield mark its age: They formed nearly four billion years before the arrival of the first human occupants, sometime between 13,000 and 40,000 years ago. Woodland peoples ranged widely in pursuit of game, the Mississippian people erected great mounds, and the Maya and the Aztec civilizations farmed irrigated croplands and built colossal structures. From the 15th century, arriving Europeans reduced many native cultures by force of arms. Their invisible weapons—the rapid, widespread, and lethal agents of imported infectious diseases—devastated vastly more. Settlers surged into depopulated and fertile lands. The result: crops and livestock to feed the many; steamboats and railroads to carry many more into the interior. Not all newcomers came of their own will; more than four million Africans were brought to North America as slaves to work on the sugar plantations of the Caribbean and on the cotton plantations of the U.S. South. Seeking freedom and fortune, more than 20 million immigrants came to the United States between 1880 and 1920. Mines disgorged raw materials for growing industries, maiming the countryside. Roads were laid out to bear automobiles and trucks, link regions, and carry people over mountains, plains, and deserts. No continent has been so transformed in so brief a time.

IMAGE BY ROBERT STACEY, WORLDSAT INTERNATIONAL INC.

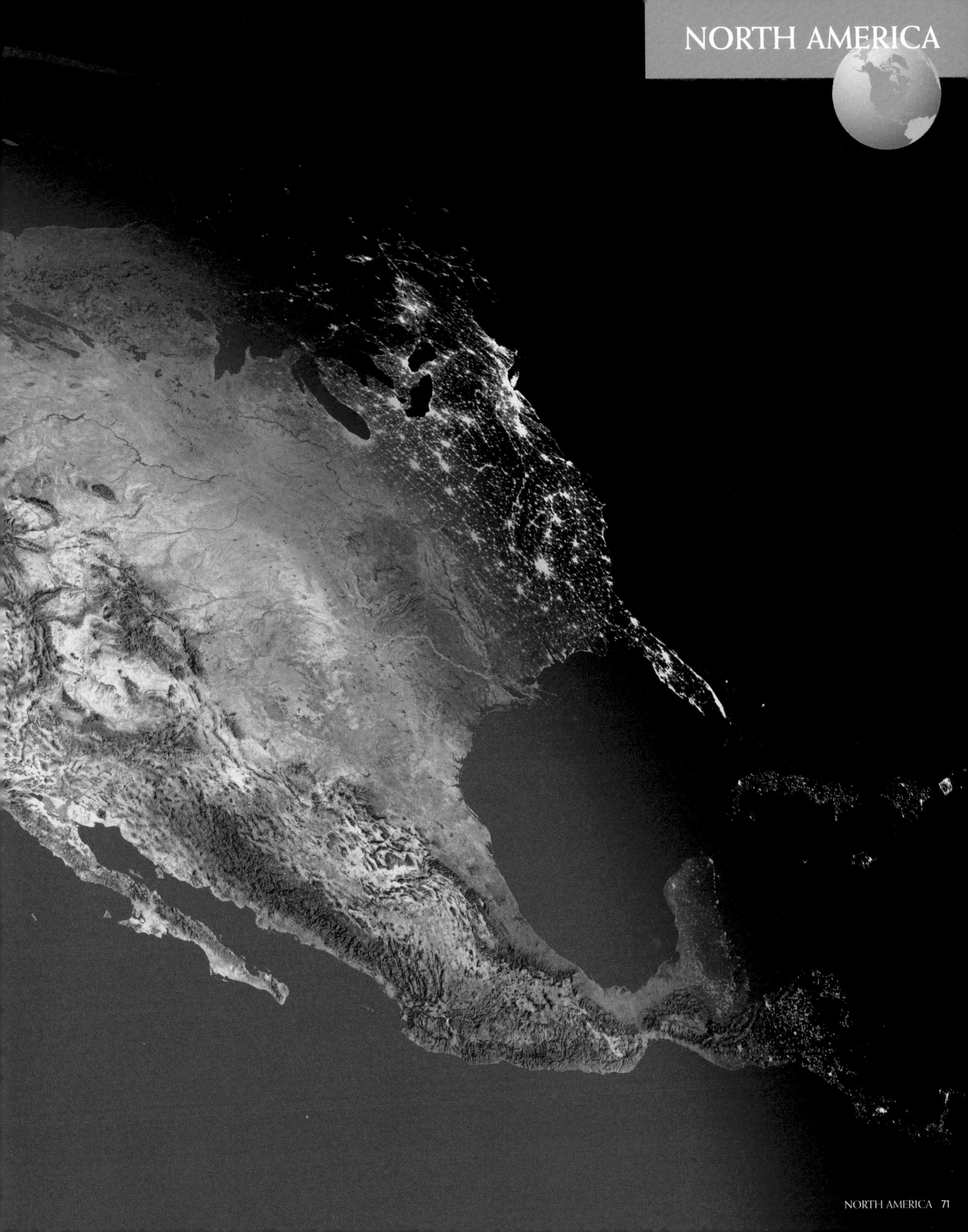
NORTH AMERICA

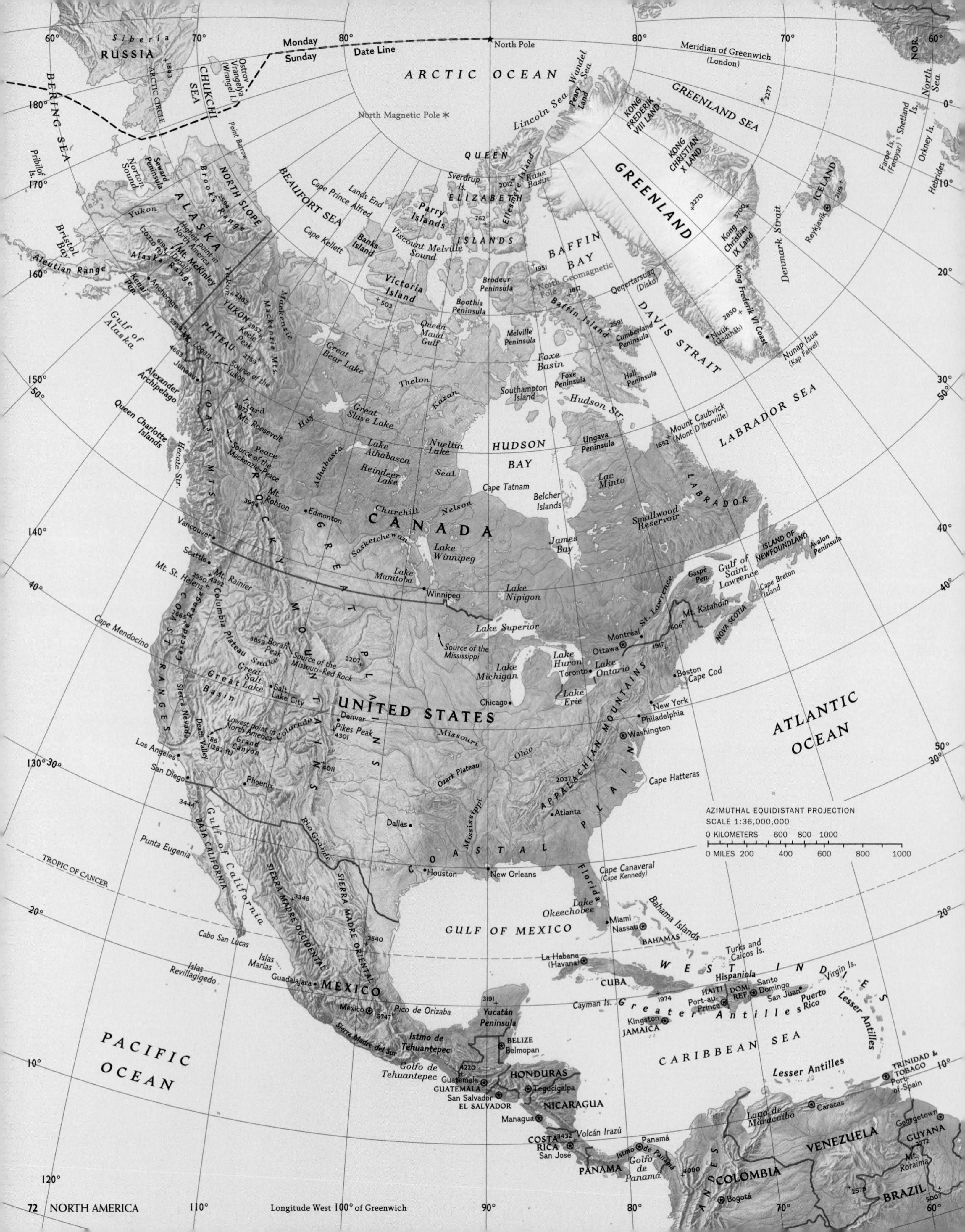

RUSSIA
Siberia
ARCTIC CIRCLE
Ostrov Vrangelya (Wrangel I.)
CHUKCHI SEA
BERING SEA
Monday
Sunday
Date Line
North Pole
ARCTIC OCEAN
North Magnetic Pole
Meridian of Greenwich (London)
Lincoln Sea
Wandel Sea
Peary Land
GREENLAND SEA
KONG FREDERIK VIII LAND
KONG CHRISTIAN X LAND
GREENLAND
Kong Christian IX Land
Kong Frederik VI Coast
Denmark Strait
ICELAND
Reykjavík
Faroe Is. (Føroyar)
Shetland Is.
Orkney Is.
Hebrides
North Sea
NOR.
Pribilof Is.
Seward Peninsula
Norton Sound
Point Barrow
NORTH SLOPE
Brooks Range
ALASKA
Yukon
Bristol Bay
Aleutian Range
Alaska Range
Mt. McKinley (Denali)
Highest point in North America
Kenai Pen.
Anchorage
Gulf of Alaska
BEAUFORT SEA
Cape Prince Alfred
Lands End
Cape Kellett
Banks Island
Viscount Melville Sound
Parry Islands
Sverdrup Is.
QUEEN ELIZABETH ISLANDS
Ellesmere Island
Kane Basin
BAFFIN BAY
North Geomagnetic Pole
Qeqertarsuaq (Disko)
Nuuk (Godthåb)
Nunap Isua (Kap Farvel)
DAVIS STRAIT
Baffin Island
Cumberland Peninsula
Hall Peninsula
Brodeur Peninsula
Boothia Peninsula
Victoria Island
Queen Maud Gulf
Melville Peninsula
Foxe Basin
Foxe Peninsula
Southampton Island
Hudson Str.
LABRADOR SEA
Mount Caubvick (Mont D'Iberville)
Ungava Peninsula
HUDSON BAY
Lac Minto
LABRADOR
Smallwood Reservoir
Belcher Islands
Cape Tatnam
James Bay
ISLAND OF NEWFOUNDLAND
Avalon Peninsula
Gulf of Saint Lawrence
Gaspé Pen.
Cape Breton Island
NOVA SCOTIA
Mt. Katahdin
YUKON PLATEAU
Yukon
Mackenzie
Mackenzie Mts.
Keele Peak
Mt. Logan
Source of the Yukon
Juneau
Alexander Archipelago
Queen Charlotte Islands
Hecate Str.
COAST MTS.
Liard
Mt. Roosevelt
Peace
Source of the Mackenzie-Peace
Great Bear Lake
Great Slave Lake
Thelon
Kazan
Hay
Nueltin Lake
Lake Athabasca
Athabasca
Reindeer Lake
Seal
Churchill
Nelson
Mt. Robson
Edmonton
CANADA
Saskatchewan
Lake Winnipeg
Lake Manitoba
Winnipeg
Lake Nipigon
ROCKY MOUNTAINS
GREAT PLAINS
Vancouver
Seattle
Mt. Rainier
Mt. St. Helens
COAST RANGES
Cascade Range
Columbia
Columbia Plateau
Cape Mendocino
Borah Peak
Snake
Source of the Missouri-Red Rock
Great Salt Lake
Salt Lake City
Great Basin
Sierra Nevada
Death Valley
Lowest point in North America
Grand Canyon
Colorado
Los Angeles
San Diego
Phoenix
Denver
Pikes Peak
UNITED STATES
Missouri
Source of the Mississippi
Lake Superior
Lake Huron
Lake Michigan
Lake Ontario
Lake Erie
Toronto
Ottawa
Montréal
St. Lawrence
Boston
Cape Cod
Chicago
New York
Philadelphia
Washington
APPALACHIAN MOUNTAINS
Ohio
Ozark Plateau
Mississippi
Cape Hatteras
Atlanta
COASTAL PLAIN
Dallas
Houston
New Orleans
Rio Grande
Florida
Cape Canaveral (Cape Kennedy)
Lake Okeechobee
Miami
ATLANTIC OCEAN
AZIMUTHAL EQUIDISTANT PROJECTION
SCALE 1:36,000,000
0 KILOMETERS 600 800 1000
0 MILES 200 400 600 800 1000
TROPIC OF CANCER
Punta Eugenia
BAJA CALIFORNIA
Gulf of California
SIERRA MADRE OCCIDENTAL
SIERRA MADRE ORIENTAL
Cabo San Lucas
Islas Revillagigedo
Islas Marías
Guadalajara
MEXICO
México
Pico de Orizaba
Sierra Madre del Sur
Istmo de Tehuantepec
Golfo de Tehuantepec
GULF OF MEXICO
Yucatán Peninsula
BELIZE
Belmopan
Nassau
BAHAMAS
Bahama Islands
Turks and Caicos Is.
La Habana (Havana)
CUBA
WEST INDIES
Cayman Is.
Greater Antilles
Hispaniola
HAITI
Port-au-Prince
DOM. REP.
Santo Domingo
San Juan
Puerto Rico
Virgin Is.
Lesser Antilles
Kingston
JAMAICA
CARIBBEAN SEA
TRINIDAD & TOBAGO
Port-of-Spain
PACIFIC OCEAN
Guatemala
GUATEMALA
San Salvador
EL SALVADOR
HONDURAS
Tegucigalpa
NICARAGUA
Managua
COSTA RICA
San José
Volcán Irazú
PANAMA
Panamá
Istmo de Panamá
Golfo de Panamá
Lago de Maracaibo
Caracas
VENEZUELA
Georgetown
GUYANA
Mt. Roraima
COLOMBIA
ANDES
Bogotá
BRAZIL
Longitude West 100° of Greenwich

North Pole
Monday
Sunday
Date Line
ARCTIC OCEAN
North Magnetic Pole
RUSSIA
BERING SEA
CHUKCHI SEA
ARCTIC CIRCLE
BEAUFORT SEA
GREENLAND SEA
GREENLAND
(KALAALLIT NUNAAT)
Denmark
QUEEN ELIZABETH ISLANDS
Parry Islands
Victoria Island
Baffin Island
BAFFIN BAY
DAVIS STRAIT
Denmark Strait
ICELAND
Reykjavík
Faroe Is. (Føroyar) Denmark
UNITED KINGDOM
ALASKA
NORTH SLOPE
Anchorage
Gulf of Alaska
Alexander Archipelago
Queen Charlotte Is.
COAST MTS.
CANADA
ROCKY MTS.
HUDSON BAY
Hudson Strait
LABRADOR SEA
LABRADOR
ISLAND OF NEWFOUNDLAND
Gulf of Saint Lawrence
ST.-PIERRE & MIQUELON Fr.
Vancouver
Edmonton
Calgary
Winnipeg
Ottawa
Montréal
Québec
Toronto
Halifax
UNITED STATES
Seattle
Portland
San Francisco
Los Angeles
San Diego
Salt Lake City
Denver
Chicago
Detroit
NEW YORK
Boston
Philadelphia
Washington, D.C.
Atlanta
Dallas
Houston
New Orleans
Miami
SIERRA NEVADA
APPALACHIAN MTS.
ATLANTIC OCEAN
BERMUDA U.K.
AZIMUTHAL EQUIDISTANT PROJECTION
SCALE 1:36,000,000
0 KILOMETERS 600 800 1000
0 MILES 200 400 600 800 1000
TROPIC OF CANCER
GULF OF MEXICO
BAHAMAS
Nassau
TURKS & CAICOS U.K.
CUBA
La Habana (Havana)
CAYMAN IS. U.K.
JAMAICA
Kingston
HAITI
Port-au-Prince
DOM. REP.
Santo Domingo
PUERTO RICO U.S.
San Juan
Virgin Is. U.S. & U.K.
ST. KITTS AND NEVIS
ANTIGUA AND BARBUDA
GUADELOUPE France
DOMINICA
MARTINIQUE Fr.
ST. LUCIA
BARBADOS
ST. VINCENT AND THE GRENADINES
GRENADA
TRINIDAD AND TOBAGO
CARIBBEAN SEA
Aruba Neth.
Curaçao Neth. Antilles
MEXICO
MÉXICO
Monterrey
Guadalajara
BAJA CALIFORNIA
SIERRA MADRE OCCIDENTAL
SIERRA MADRE ORIENTAL
Gulf of California
BELIZE
GUATEMALA
EL SALVADOR
HONDURAS
Tegucigalpa
NICARAGUA
Managua
COSTA RICA
San José
PANAMA
Panamá
PACIFIC OCEAN
COLOMBIA
BOGOTÁ
VENEZUELA
Caracas
GUYANA
Georgetown
BRAZIL
Longitude West 100° of Greenwich

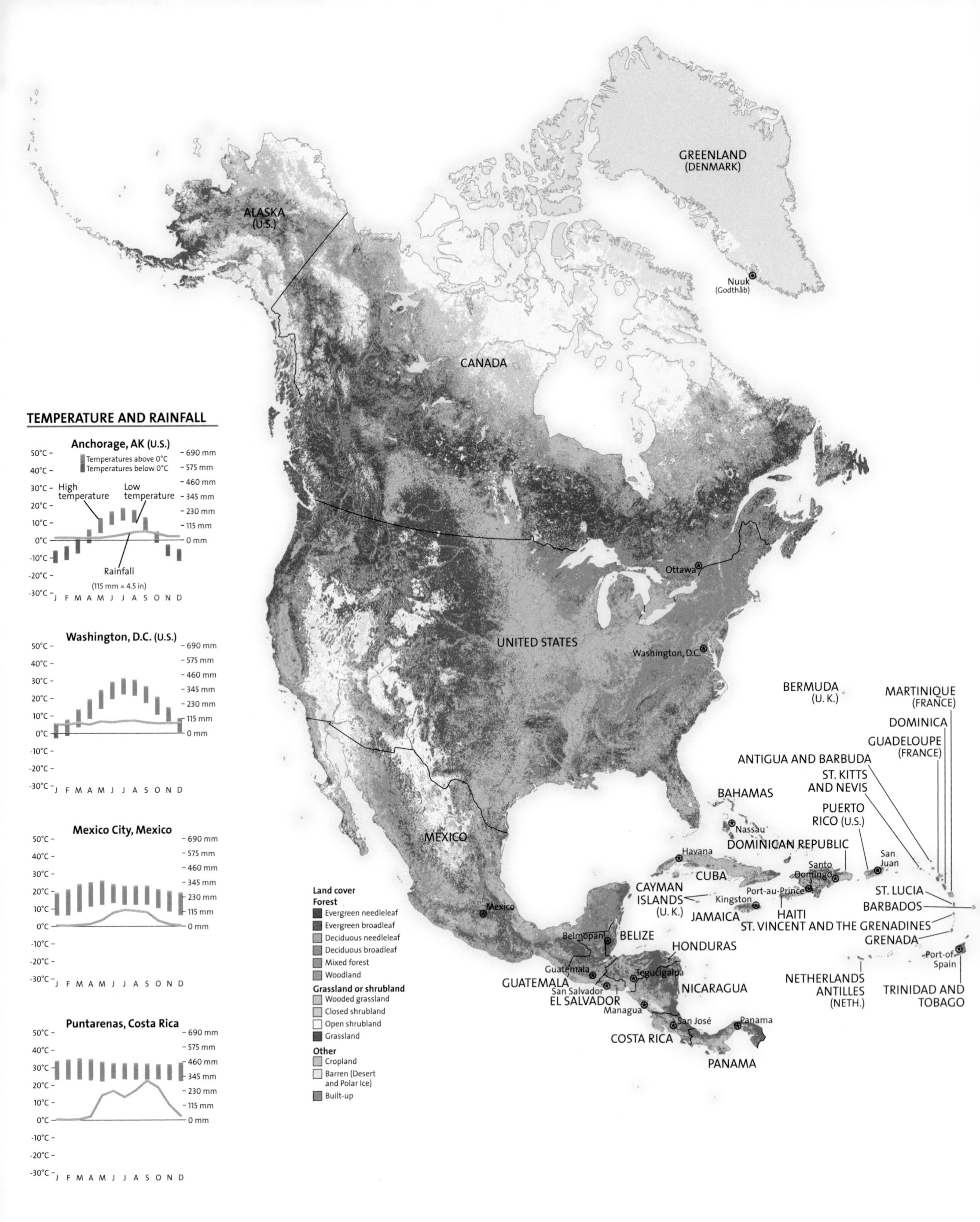

GREENLAND
(DENMARK)
Nuuk
(Godthåb)
ALASKA
(U.S.)
CANADA
Ottawa
UNITED STATES
Washington, D.C.
MEXICO
Mexico
BERMUDA
(U. K.)
MARTINIQUE
(FRANCE)
DOMINICA
GUADELOUPE
(FRANCE)
ANTIGUA AND BARBUDA
ST. KITTS
AND NEVIS
BAHAMAS
Nassau
PUERTO
RICO (U.S.)
DOMINICAN REPUBLIC
Havana
CUBA
Santo
Domingo
San
Juan
CAYMAN
ISLANDS
(U. K.)
Kingston
JAMAICA
Port-au-Prince
HAITI
ST. LUCIA
BARBADOS
ST. VINCENT AND THE GRENADINES
GRENADA
Port-of-
Spain
Belmopan
BELIZE
HONDURAS
Guatemala
GUATEMALA
Tegucigalpa
San Salvador
EL SALVADOR
NICARAGUA
Managua
NETHERLANDS
ANTILLES
(NETH.)
TRINIDAD AND
TOBAGO
San José
Panama
COSTA RICA
PANAMA
TEMPERATURE AND RAINFALL
Anchorage, AK (U.S.)
Temperatures above 0°C
Temperatures below 0°C
High
temperature
Low
temperature
Rainfall
(115 mm = 4.5 in)
50°C
40°C
30°C
20°C
10°C
0°C
-10°C
-20°C
-30°C
690 mm
575 mm
460 mm
345 mm
230 mm
115 mm
0 mm
J F M A M J J A S O N D
Washington, D.C. (U.S.)
Mexico City, Mexico
Puntarenas, Costa Rica
Land cover
Forest
Evergreen needleleaf
Evergreen broadleaf
Deciduous needleleaf
Deciduous broadleaf
Mixed forest
Woodland
Grassland or shrubland
Wooded grassland
Closed shrubland
Open shrubland
Grassland
Other
Cropland
Barren (Desert
and Polar Ice)
Built-up

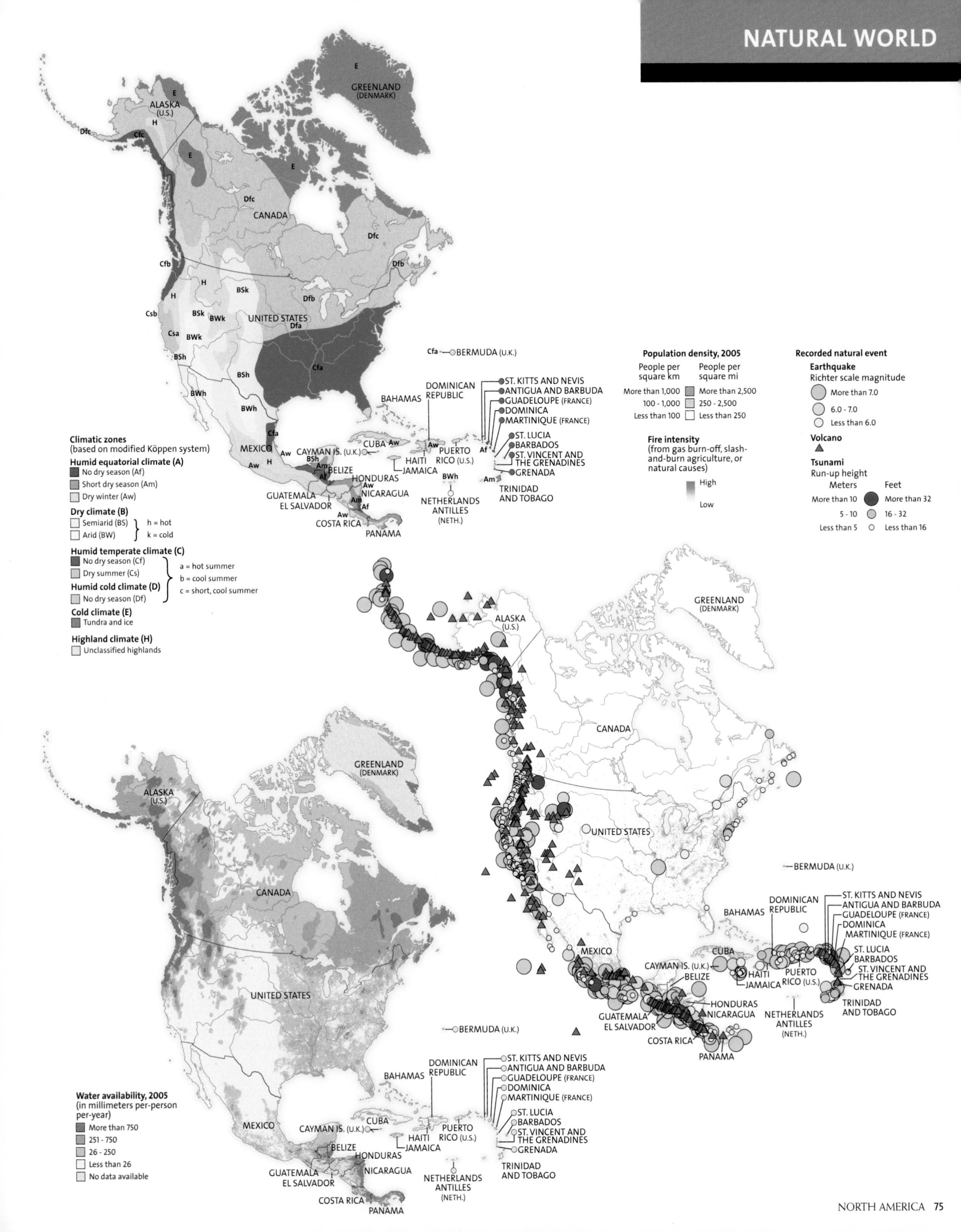
GREENLAND
(DENMARK)
ALASKA
(U.S.)
CANADA
UNITED STATES
MEXICO
BERMUDA (U.K.)
BAHAMAS
CUBA
CAYMAN IS. (U.K.)
HAITI
JAMAICA
DOMINICAN REPUBLIC
PUERTO RICO (U.S.)
NETHERLANDS ANTILLES (NETH.)
ST. KITTS AND NEVIS
ANTIGUA AND BARBUDA
GUADELOUPE (FRANCE)
DOMINICA
MARTINIQUE (FRANCE)
ST. LUCIA
BARBADOS
ST. VINCENT AND THE GRENADINES
GRENADA
TRINIDAD AND TOBAGO
BELIZE
HONDURAS
GUATEMALA
EL SALVADOR
NICARAGUA
COSTA RICA
PANAMA
E
H
Dfc
Cfc
Dfb
Cfb
Csb
Csa
BSk
BWk
BSh
BWh
Dfa
Cfa
Aw
Am
Af
Climatic zones
(based on modified Köppen system)
Humid equatorial climate (A)
No dry season (Af)
Short dry season (Am)
Dry winter (Aw)
Dry climate (B)
Semiarid (BS)
Arid (BW)
h = hot
k = cold
Humid temperate climate (C)
No dry season (Cf)
Dry summer (Cs)
a = hot summer
b = cool summer
c = short, cool summer
Humid cold climate (D)
No dry season (Df)
Cold climate (E)
Tundra and ice
Highland climate (H)
Unclassified highlands
Population density, 2005
People per square km
People per square mi
More than 1,000
More than 2,500
100 - 1,000
250 - 2,500
Less than 100
Less than 250
Fire intensity
(from gas burn-off, slash-and-burn agriculture, or natural causes)
High
Low
Recorded natural event
Earthquake
Richter scale magnitude
More than 7.0
6.0 - 7.0
Less than 6.0
Volcano
Tsunami
Run-up height
Meters
Feet
More than 10
More than 32
5 - 10
16 - 32
Less than 5
Less than 16
Water availability, 2005
(in millimeters per-person per-year)
More than 750
251 - 750
26 - 250
Less than 26
No data available

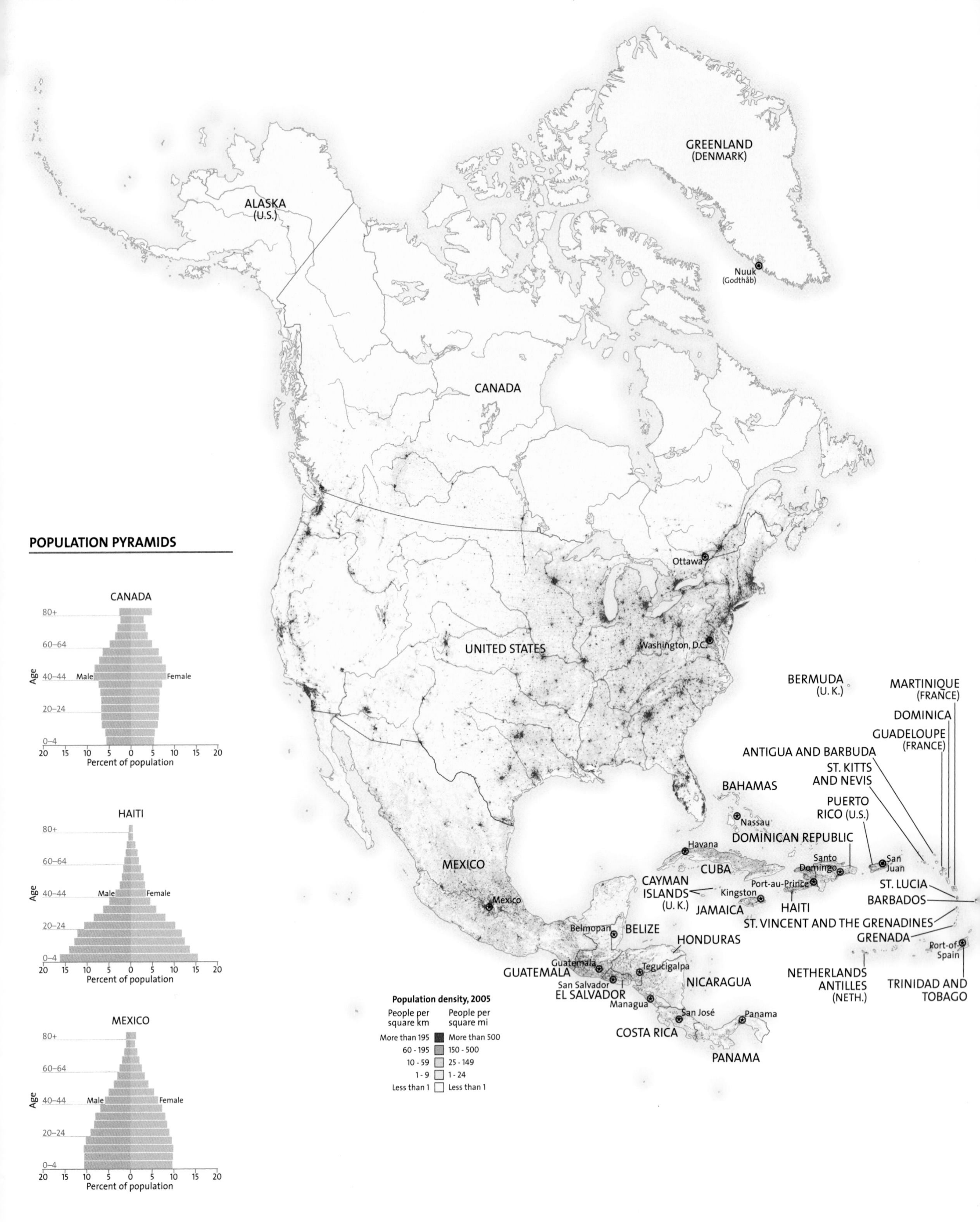

GREENLAND
(DENMARK)
Nuuk
(Godthåb)
ALASKA
(U.S.)
CANADA
Ottawa
UNITED STATES
Washington, D.C.
BERMUDA
(U. K.)
MARTINIQUE
(FRANCE)
DOMINICA
GUADELOUPE
(FRANCE)
ANTIGUA AND BARBUDA
ST. KITTS
AND NEVIS
BAHAMAS
Nassau
PUERTO
RICO (U.S.)
DOMINICAN REPUBLIC
Havana
Santo
Domingo
San
Juan
CUBA
MEXICO
CAYMAN
ISLANDS
(U. K.)
Kingston
Port-au-Prince
JAMAICA
HAITI
ST. LUCIA
BARBADOS
ST. VINCENT AND THE GRENADINES
GRENADA
Mexico
Belmopan
BELIZE
HONDURAS
Port-of-
Spain
Guatemala
GUATEMALA
Tegucigalpa
San Salvador
EL SALVADOR
NICARAGUA
Managua
NETHERLANDS
ANTILLES
(NETH.)
TRINIDAD AND
TOBAGO
San José
Panama
COSTA RICA
PANAMA
Population density, 2005
People per square km
People per square mi
More than 195
More than 500
60 - 195
150 - 500
10 - 59
25 - 149
1 - 9
1 - 24
Less than 1
Less than 1
POPULATION PYRAMIDS
CANADA
HAITI
MEXICO
Age
80+
60–64
40–44
20–24
0–4
Male
Female
20 15 10 5 0 5 10 15 20
Percent of population

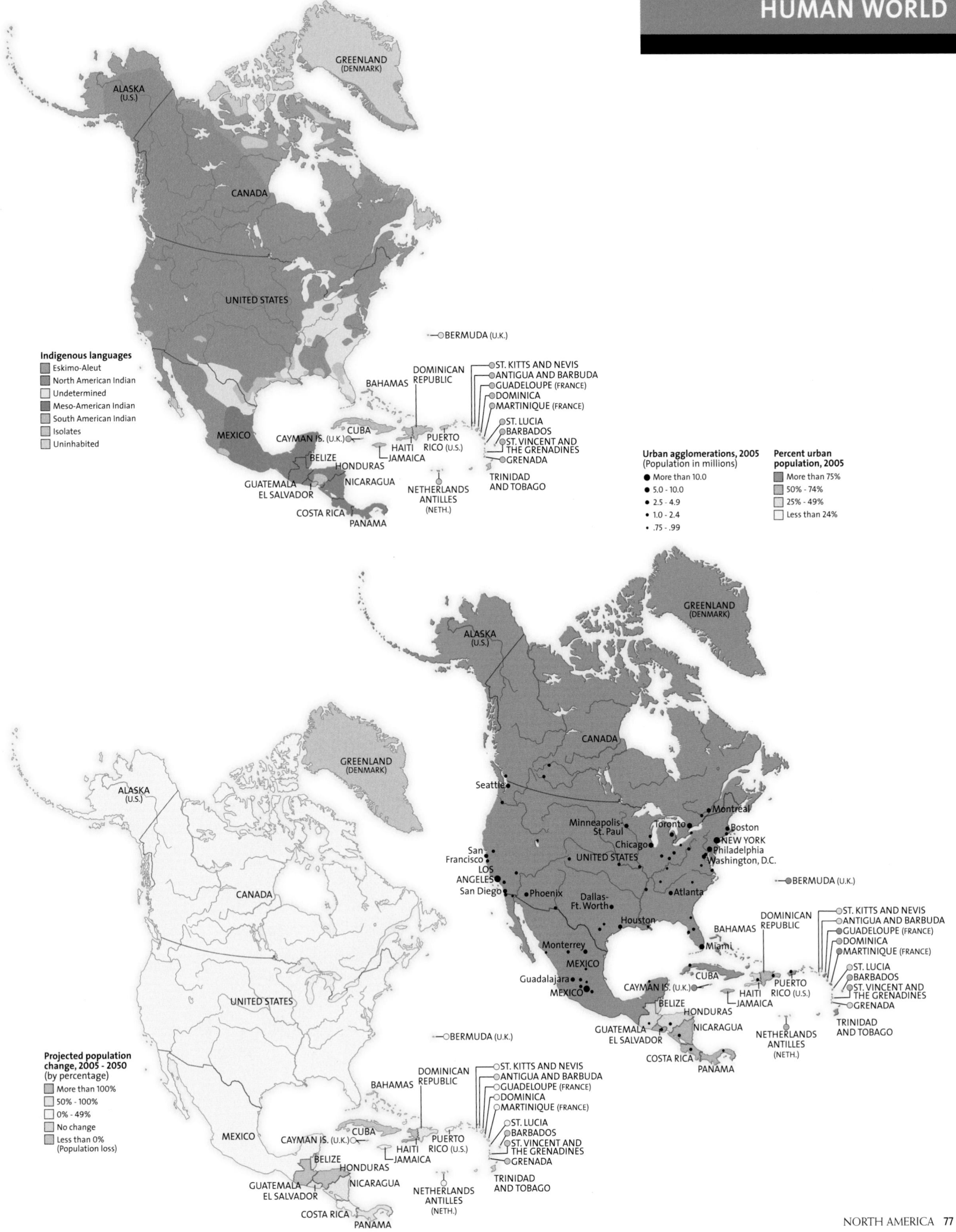
GREENLAND (DENMARK)
ALASKA (U.S.)
CANADA
UNITED STATES
BERMUDA (U.K.)
Indigenous languages
Eskimo-Aleut
North American Indian
Undetermined
Meso-American Indian
South American Indian
Isolates
Uninhabited
MEXICO
BAHAMAS
DOMINICAN REPUBLIC
ST. KITTS AND NEVIS
ANTIGUA AND BARBUDA
GUADELOUPE (FRANCE)
DOMINICA
MARTINIQUE (FRANCE)
ST. LUCIA
BARBADOS
ST. VINCENT AND THE GRENADINES
GRENADA
CUBA
CAYMAN IS. (U.K.)
HAITI
JAMAICA
PUERTO RICO (U.S.)
BELIZE
HONDURAS
NICARAGUA
GUATEMALA
EL SALVADOR
COSTA RICA
PANAMA
NETHERLANDS ANTILLES (NETH.)
TRINIDAD AND TOBAGO
Urban agglomerations, 2005
(Population in millions)
More than 10.0
5.0 - 10.0
2.5 - 4.9
1.0 - 2.4
.75 - .99
Percent urban population, 2005
More than 75%
50% - 74%
25% - 49%
Less than 24%
Seattle
Montreal
Toronto
Minneapolis-St. Paul
Boston
NEW YORK
Philadelphia
Washington, D.C.
Chicago
San Francisco
LOS ANGELES
San Diego
Phoenix
Dallas-Ft. Worth
Houston
Atlanta
Miami
Monterrey
Guadalajara
MEXICO
Projected population change, 2005 - 2050
(by percentage)
More than 100%
50% - 100%
0% - 49%
No change
Less than 0%
(Population loss)

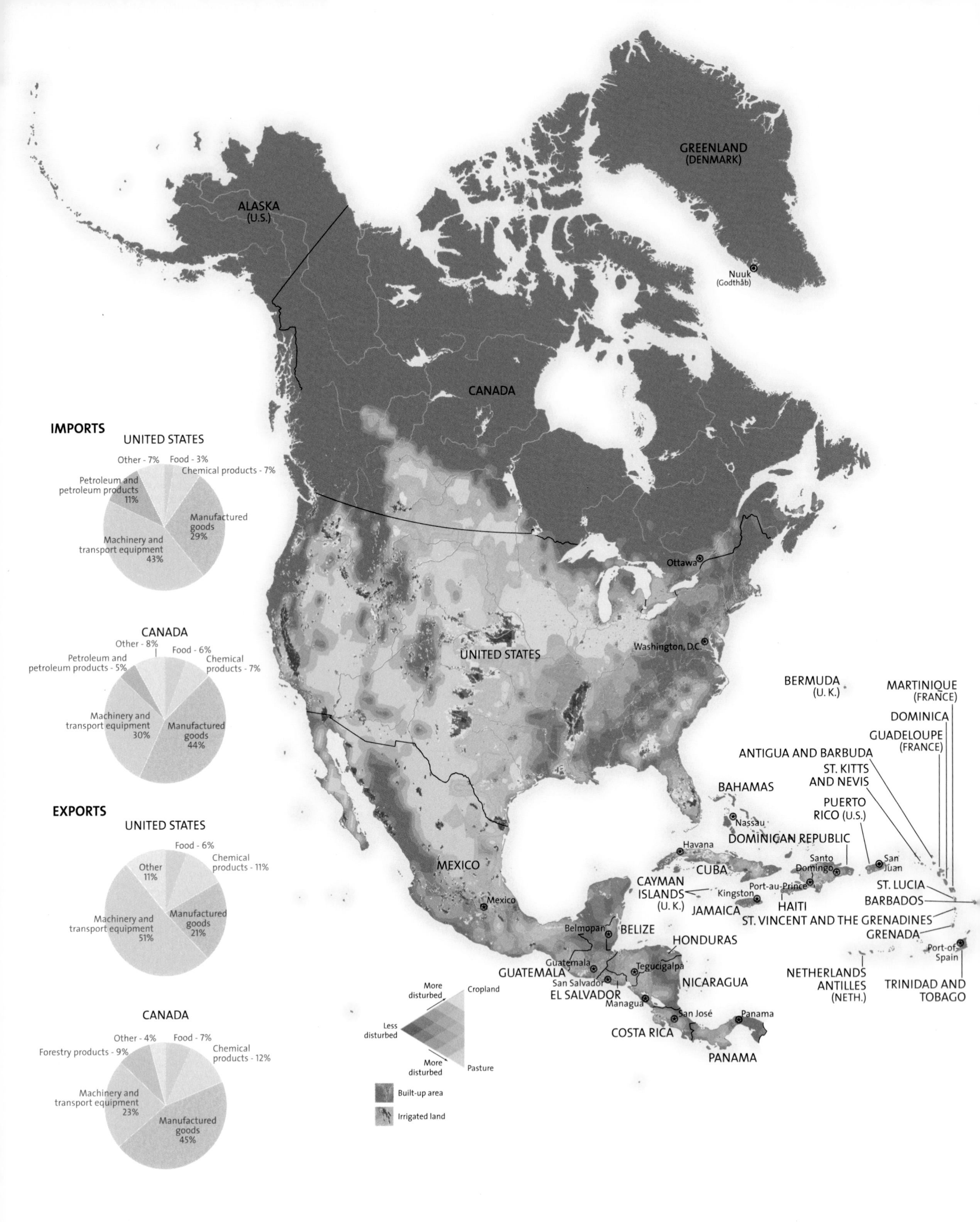

GREENLAND
(DENMARK)
Nuuk
(Godthåb)
ALASKA
(U.S.)
CANADA
Ottawa
UNITED STATES
Washington, D.C.
MEXICO
Mexico
BERMUDA
(U. K.)
MARTINIQUE
(FRANCE)
DOMINICA
GUADELOUPE
(FRANCE)
ANTIGUA AND BARBUDA
ST. KITTS
AND NEVIS
BAHAMAS
Nassau
PUERTO
RICO (U.S.)
DOMINICAN REPUBLIC
Havana
CUBA
Santo
Domingo
San
Juan
CAYMAN
ISLANDS
(U. K.)
Kingston
Port-au-Prince
ST. LUCIA
BARBADOS
JAMAICA
HAITI
ST. VINCENT AND THE GRENADINES
GRENADA
Belmopan
BELIZE
HONDURAS
Port-of-
Spain
Guatemala
Tegucigalpa
GUATEMALA
San Salvador
EL SALVADOR
NICARAGUA
NETHERLANDS
ANTILLES
(NETH.)
TRINIDAD AND
TOBAGO
Managua
San José
Panama
COSTA RICA
PANAMA
More
disturbed
Cropland
Less
disturbed
More
disturbed
Pasture
Built-up area
Irrigated land
IMPORTS
UNITED STATES
Other - 7%
Food - 3%
Chemical products - 7%
Petroleum and
petroleum products
11%
Manufactured
goods
29%
Machinery and
transport equipment
43%
CANADA
Other - 8%
Food - 6%
Petroleum and
petroleum products - 5%
Chemical
products - 7%
Machinery and
transport equipment
30%
Manufactured
goods
44%
EXPORTS
UNITED STATES
Food - 6%
Chemical
products - 11%
Other
11%
Manufactured
goods
21%
Machinery and
transport equipment
51%
CANADA
Other - 4%
Food - 7%
Forestry products - 9%
Chemical
products - 12%
Machinery and
transport equipment
23%
Manufactured
goods
45%

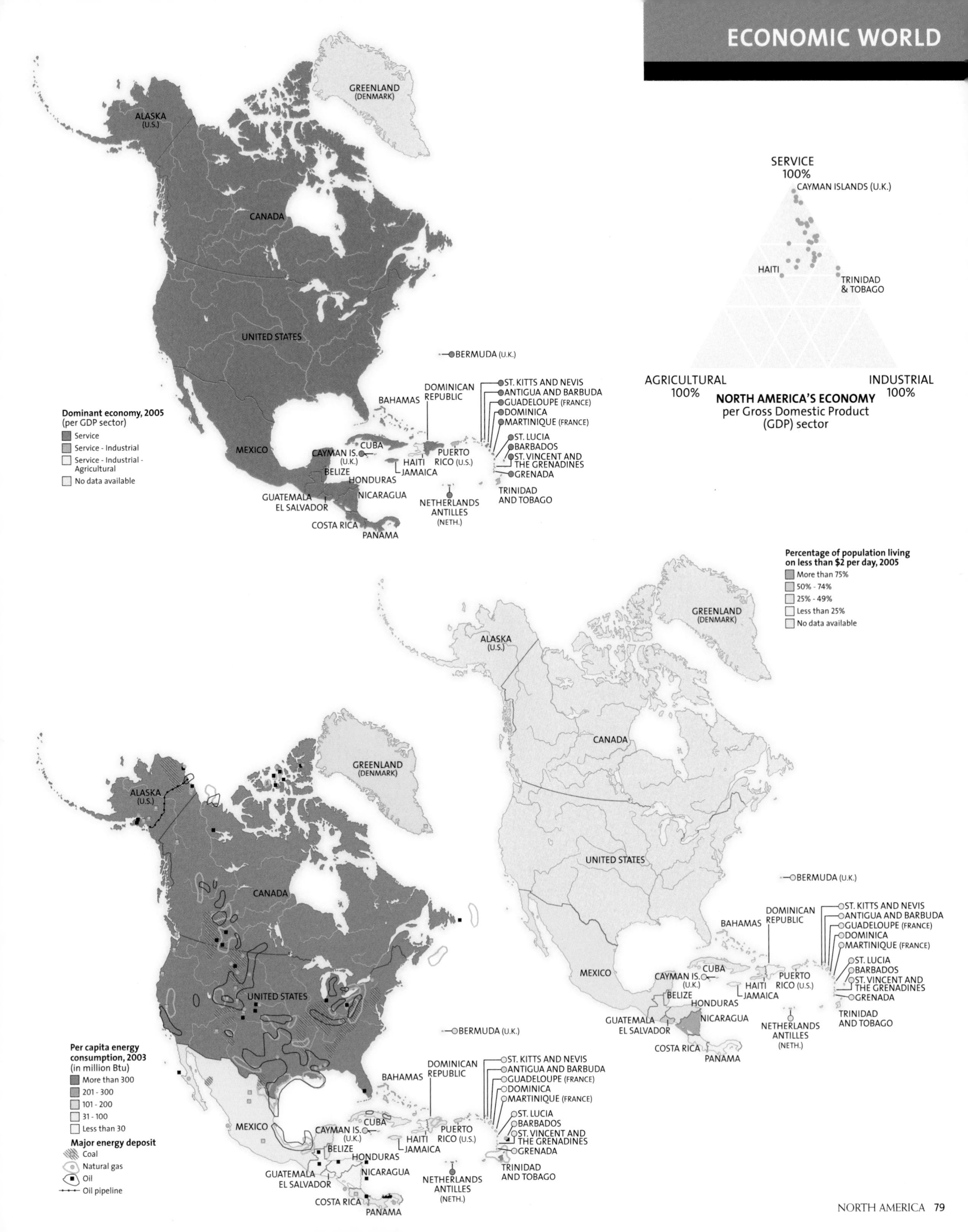
GREENLAND
(DENMARK)
ALASKA
(U.S.)
CANADA
UNITED STATES
MEXICO
BERMUDA (U.K.)
BAHAMAS
DOMINICAN REPUBLIC
ST. KITTS AND NEVIS
ANTIGUA AND BARBUDA
GUADELOUPE (FRANCE)
DOMINICA
MARTINIQUE (FRANCE)
ST. LUCIA
BARBADOS
ST. VINCENT AND THE GRENADINES
GRENADA
TRINIDAD AND TOBAGO
CUBA
CAYMAN IS. (U.K.)
HAITI
PUERTO RICO (U.S.)
JAMAICA
BELIZE
HONDURAS
NICARAGUA
GUATEMALA
EL SALVADOR
COSTA RICA
PANAMA
NETHERLANDS ANTILLES (NETH.)
Dominant economy, 2005
(per GDP sector)
Service
Service - Industrial
Service - Industrial - Agricultural
No data available
SERVICE
100%
CAYMAN ISLANDS (U.K.)
HAITI
TRINIDAD & TOBAGO
AGRICULTURAL
100%
INDUSTRIAL
100%
NORTH AMERICA'S ECONOMY
per Gross Domestic Product
(GDP) sector
Percentage of population living on less than $2 per day, 2005
More than 75%
50% - 74%
25% - 49%
Less than 25%
No data available
Per capita energy consumption, 2003
(in million Btu)
More than 300
201 - 300
101 - 200
31 - 100
Less than 30
Major energy deposit
Coal
Natural gas
Oil
Oil pipeline

PACIFIC OCEAN
WASHINGTON
OREGON
CALIFORNIA
NEVADA
IDAHO
MONTANA
WYOMING
UTAH
COLORADO
ARIZONA
NEW MEXICO
NORTH DAKOTA
SOUTH DAKOTA
NEBRASKA
KANSAS
OKLAHOMA
TEXAS
MEXICO
CAN
Str. of Georgia
Str. of Juan de Fuca
Cape Flattery
Mt. Olympus
2428
Puget Sd.
Olympia
Cape Disappointment
4392 Mt. Rainier
2550 Mt. St. Helens
Mt. Hood 3425
Columbia
Snake
Salem
Willamette
John Day
Blue Mountains
Wallowa Mountains
Cape Blanco
Harney Basin
Great Sandy Desert
Cape Mendocino
Klamath Mountains
4317 Mt. Shasta
3015 Eagle Pk.
Warner Mts.
Black Rock Desert
Point Arena
Sacramento
Sacramento Valley
Pyramid Lake
Donner Pass 2160
Carson City
L. Tahoe
Point Reyes
San Francisco Bay
Monterey Bay
Point Sur
San Joaquin
Diablo Range
Santa Lucia Range
Mt. Whitney
4418 (14494 ft)
Highest point in 48 contiguous United States
4006
Boundary Peak
Death Valley
-82 (-282 ft)
Lowest point in North America
Mojave Desert
Point Buchon
Santa Barbara Chan.
San Miguel
Santa Rosa
Santa Cruz
Channel Islands
San Nicolas
Santa Catalina
San Clemente
Gulf of Santa Catalina
Palomar Mt.
Salton Sea
Imperial Valley
Colorado
Great Basin
Shoshone Mts.
Monitor Range
Schell Creek Ra.
Great Salt Lake Desert
Great Salt Lake
Salt Lake City
Wasatch Ra.
Kings Pk. 4123
Uinta Mountains
Green
Sevier
Fremont
Lake Powell
Lake Mead
Colorado Plateau
2447 Mt. Trumbull
Grand Canyon
Painted Desert
San Francisco Mt. 3851
Mogollon Rim
Baldy Pk. 3476
Phoenix
Sonoran Desert
Gila Desert
Pend Oreille L.
Bitterroot Range
Clearwater Mts.
Salmon
Salmon River Mountains
Boise
3859 Borah Pk.
Snake River Plain
Snake River Plateau
Shoshone Falls
Bear River Ra.
Targhee Pass 2156
Yellowstone L.
Source of the Missouri–Red Rock
Flathead L.
Helena
Rocky Mountains
Bears Paw Mts.
Milk
Missouri
Fort Peck Lake
Musselshell
Yellowstone
Granite Peak 3901
Bighorn Mountains
Absaroka Range
Grand Teton 4197
Wind River Ra.
4207
Tongue
Powder
Little Missouri
Belle Fourche
Great Divide Basin
Laramie Mountains
Laramie Pk. 3131
Medicine Bow Mts.
Cheyenne
Front Range
Denver
Mt. Elbert 4399
4301 Pikes Peak
Sawatch Ra.
Uncompahgre Plateau
Source of the Rio Grande
San Juan Mts.
4372
Sangre de Cristo Mountains
Santa Fe
Pecos
Rio Grande
San Andres Mts.
Sacramento Mts.
Guadalupe Peak 2667
Red Bluff Lake
Llano Estacado
Cap Rock Escarpment
Black Mesa 1516
Great Plains
Souris
Lake Sakakawea
Sheyenne
Red River of the North
Lake Ashtabula
Badlands
765
Bismarck
Heart
1069 White Butte
Grand
Moreau
Lake Oahe
Geographical Center of the 50 United States
Cheyenne
Pierre
Lake Sharpe
James
Black Hills
Harney Peak 2207
White
Lake Francis Case
Niobrara
Missouri
Elkhorn
Sand Hills
N. Platte
S. Platte
Platte
Loup
Lincoln
Republican
Solomon
Geographical Center 48 Contiguous United States
Smoky Hills
Smoky Hill
Kansas
Arkansas
Red Hills
Cimarron
N. Canadian
Canadian
Washita
Wichita Mts. 756
Oklahoma City
Red
Brazos
Edwards Plateau
Pecos
Austin
Colorado
Amistad Res.
San Antonio
Rio Grande
Nueces
Baffin B.
Falcon Lake
Flint
132° 129° 126° 123° 120° 117° 114° 111° 108° 105° 102° 99°
48° 45° 42° 39° 36° 33° 30° 27° 24°

Lake Superior
Isle Royale
Keweenaw Peninsula
Eagle Mt. 701
Mesabi Ra.
Lower Red L.
Leech Lake
Mille Lacs L.
St. Paul
Timms Hill 595
WISCONSIN
Lake Winnebago
Madison
Wisconsin
Mississippi
Menominee
Wolf
Upper Peninsula
Strs. of Mackinac
Lake Michigan
MICHIGAN
Lower Peninsula
Muskegon
Saginaw Bay
Grand
Lansing
Lake St. Clair
Lake Huron
Georgian Bay
Lake Ontario
Niagara Falls
Lake Erie
St. Lawrence
NEW YORK
Finger Lakes
Albany
Catskill Mountains
Adirondack Mountains
Lake Champlain
Mt. Marcy 1629
Mt. Mansfield 1339
Montpelier
Green Mountains
VT.
N.H.
White Mts.
Mt. Washington 1917
Concord
Connecticut
Merrimack
Mt. Katahdin 1606
Moosehead Lake
MAINE
Augusta
Mt. Desert I.
Gulf of Maine
Boston
MASS.
Providence
R.I.
Cape Cod
Nantucket I.
Martha's Vineyard
Hartford
CONN.
Hudson
Long Island Sd.
Long Island
New York
Trenton
NEW JERSEY
Pine Barrens
Delaware
PENNSYLVANIA
Harrisburg
Susquehanna
Allegheny
Dover
DEL.
Delaware Bay
Annapolis
MARYLAND
Washington D.C.
Chesapeake Bay
Chincoteague Bay
Potomac
Mt. Davis 1024
WEST VIRGINIA
Charleston
VIRGINIA
James
Richmond
Cape Charles
Great Dismal Swamp
Albemarle Sound
Roanoke
Tar
Pamlico Sound
Neuse
Cape Hatteras
Raleigh
NORTH CAROLINA
Cape Lookout
Cape Fear
Pee Dee
Mt. Mitchell 2037
Great Smoky Mts.
Clingmans Dome 2025
Blue Ridge
Piedmont
SOUTH CAROLINA
Columbia
Santee
Savannah
Atlanta
GEORGIA
Ocmulgee
Oconee
Altamaha
Sea Islands
Okefenokee Swamp
Suwannee
Tallahassee
Flint
L. Seminole
Chattahoochee
Apalachee Bay
Cape San Blas
FLORIDA
Cape Canaveral
Kissimmee
Peace
Lake Okeechobee
Tampa Bay
Charlotte Harbor
Cape Romano
The Everglades
Biscayne Bay
Cape Sable
Florida Keys
Dry Tortugas
Marquesas Keys
Straits of Florida
BAHAMAS
TROPIC OF CANCER
ATLANTIC OCEAN
Gulf of Mexico
IOWA
Cedar
Iowa
Des Moines
Charles Mound 376
Rock
ILLINOIS
Illinois
Springfield
Kaskaskia
Wabash
INDIANA
Indianapolis
Campbell Hill 472
OHIO
Columbus
Scioto
Maumee
Gt. Miami
Ohio
KENTUCKY
Frankfort
Kentucky
Lake Cumberland
Cumberland
Black Mt. 1263
Lake Barkley
Kentucky Lake
Nashville
TENNESSEE
Tennessee
Clinch
Cumberland Plateau
Allegheny Mountains
Appalachian Mountains
Woodall Mountain
Coosa
Cheaha Mt. 734
ALABAMA
Montgomery
Alabama
Tombigbee
Black Belt
Mobile Bay
Pensacola Bay
MISSISSIPPI
Jackson
Pearl
Yazoo
Mississippi
Mississippi Sd.
Breton Sound
Mississippi River Delta
Timbalier Bay
Marsh I.
LOUISIANA
Baton Rouge
Lake Pontchartrain
Red
Sabine
Driskill Mt. 163
Galveston Bay
ARKANSAS
Little Rock
Ouachita Mountains
Lake Ouachita
Ouachita
Saline
Boston Mountains
Magazine Mt. 839
White
Black
St. Francis
MISSOURI
Jefferson City
Missouri
Osage
Lake of the Ozarks
Harry S. Truman Res.
Taum Sauk Mt. 540
Ozark Plateau
Central Lowland
Coastal Plain
LAMBERT CONFORMAL CONIC PROJECTION
SCALE 1:12,000,000
0 KILOMETERS 200 300
0 MILES 100 200 300
Longitude West 93° of Greenwich
90°
87°
84°
81°
78°
75°
72°
45°
42°
39°
36°
33°
30°
27°
24°

PACIFIC OCEAN
BRITISH COLUMBIA
ALBERTA
SASKATCHEWAN
MANITOBA
WASHINGTON
OREGON
IDAHO
MONTANA
NORTH DAKOTA
SOUTH DAKOTA
WYOMING
NEVADA
UTAH
COLORADO
NEBRASKA
KANSAS
CALIFORNIA
ARIZONA
NEW MEXICO
OKLAHOMA
TEXAS
MEXICO
SONORA
CHIHUAHUA
COAHUILA
NUEVO LEÓN
SINALOA
DURANGO
ZACATECAS
TAMAULIPAS
BAJA CALIFORNIA
BAJA CALIFORNIA SUR
COLORADO PLATEAU
GREAT PLAINS
SIERRA NEVADA
ROCKY MOUNTAINS
COAST MOUNTAINS
SIERRA MADRE OCCIDENTAL
SIERRA MADRE ORIENTAL
Mojave Desert
Painted Desert
Llano Estacado
Vancouver Island
Vancouver
Surrey
Victoria
Calgary
Regina
Winnipeg
Seattle
Tacoma
Spokane
Portland
Salem
Boise
Helena
Salt Lake City
Provo
Reno
Sacramento
San Francisco
Oakland
San Jose
Stockton
Fresno
Bakersfield
Los Angeles
Long Beach
San Bernardino
San Diego
Tijuana
Mexicali
Las Vegas
Phoenix
Mesa
Tucson
Albuquerque
Denver
Aurora
Colorado Springs
Pueblo
Cheyenne
El Paso
Ciudad Juárez
Chihuahua
Lubbock
Amarillo
Oklahoma City
Wichita
Abilene
San Antonio
Austin
Laredo
Nuevo Laredo
Monterrey
Saltillo
Torreón
Gómez Palacio
Hermosillo
Ciudad Obregón
Los Mochis
Culiacán
La Paz
TROPIC OF CANCER
132° 129° 126° 123° 120° 117° 114° 111° 108° 105° 102° 99°
48° 45° 42° 39° 36° 33° 30° 27° 24°

ATLANTIC OCEAN

Gulf of Mexico

BAHAMAS

LAMBERT CONFORMAL CONIC PROJECTION
SCALE 1:12,000,000

0 KILOMETERS 200 300

0 MILES 100 200 300

93° Longitude West 90° of Greenwich 87° 84° 81° 78° 75°

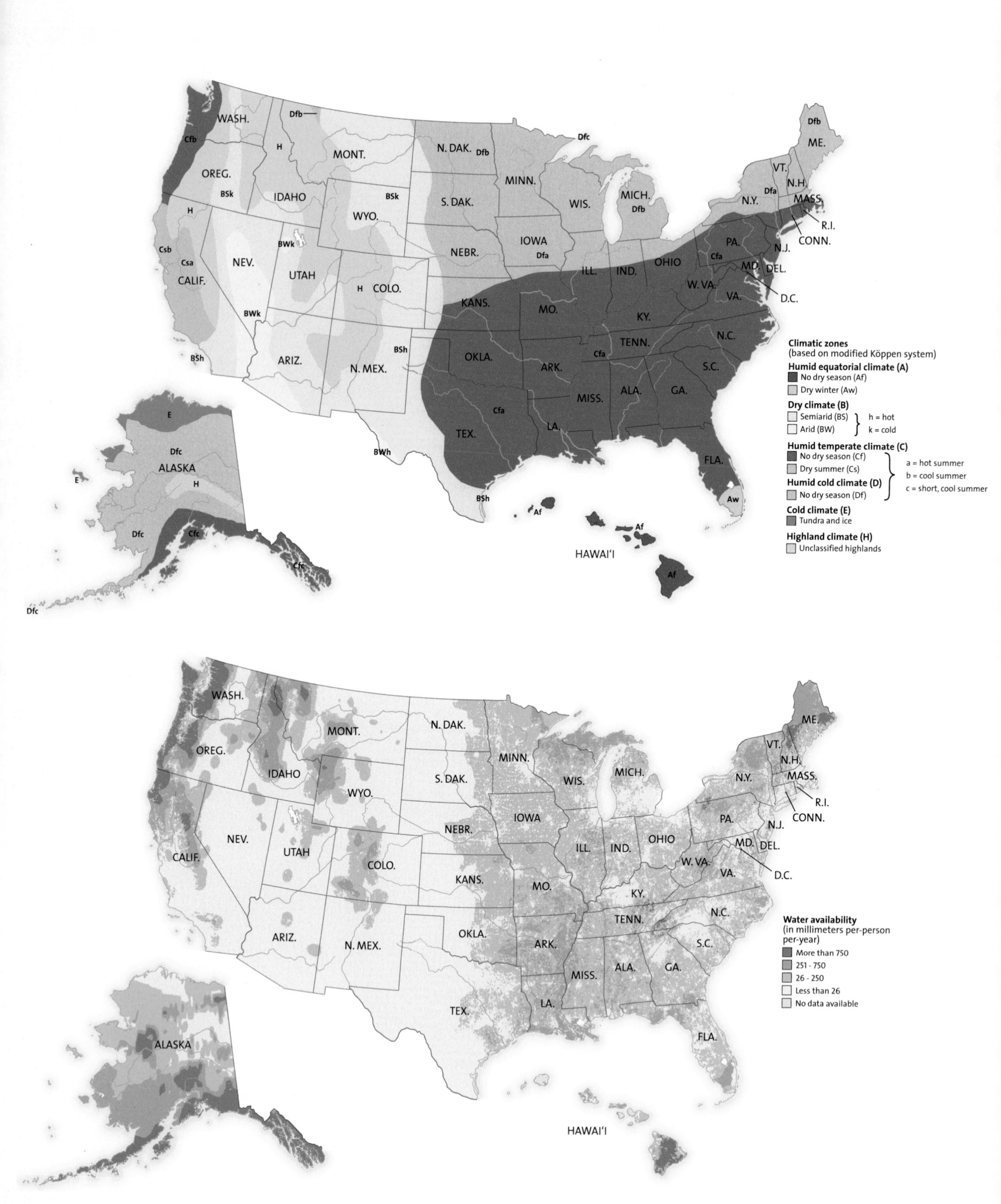
WASH.
OREG.
CALIF.
NEV.
IDAHO
MONT.
WYO.
UTAH
COLO.
ARIZ.
N. MEX.
N. DAK.
S. DAK.
NEBR.
KANS.
OKLA.
TEX.
MINN.
IOWA
MO.
ARK.
LA.
WIS.
ILL.
MICH.
IND.
OHIO
KY.
TENN.
MISS.
ALA.
GA.
FLA.
S.C.
N.C.
VA.
W. VA.
PA.
N.Y.
N.J.
DEL.
MD.
D.C.
CONN.
R.I.
MASS.
VT.
N.H.
ME.
ALASKA
HAWAI'I
Cfb
Dfb
H
BSk
Csb
Csa
BWk
BSh
BWh
Dfc
Dfa
Cfa
Aw
Af
E
Cfc
Climatic zones
(based on modified Köppen system)
Humid equatorial climate (A)
No dry season (Af)
Dry winter (Aw)
Dry climate (B)
Semiarid (BS)
Arid (BW)
h = hot
k = cold
Humid temperate climate (C)
No dry season (Cf)
Dry summer (Cs)
Humid cold climate (D)
No dry season (Df)
a = hot summer
b = cool summer
c = short, cool summer
Cold climate (E)
Tundra and ice
Highland climate (H)
Unclassified highlands
WASH.
OREG.
CALIF.
NEV.
IDAHO
MONT.
WYO.
UTAH
COLO.
ARIZ.
N. MEX.
N. DAK.
S. DAK.
NEBR.
KANS.
OKLA.
TEX.
MINN.
IOWA
MO.
ARK.
LA.
WIS.
ILL.
MICH.
IND.
OHIO
KY.
TENN.
MISS.
ALA.
GA.
FLA.
S.C.
N.C.
VA.
W. VA.
PA.
N.Y.
N.J.
DEL.
MD.
D.C.
CONN.
R.I.
MASS.
VT.
N.H.
ME.
ALASKA
HAWAI'I
Water availability
(in millimeters per-person per-year)
More than 750
251 - 750
26 - 250
Less than 26
No data available

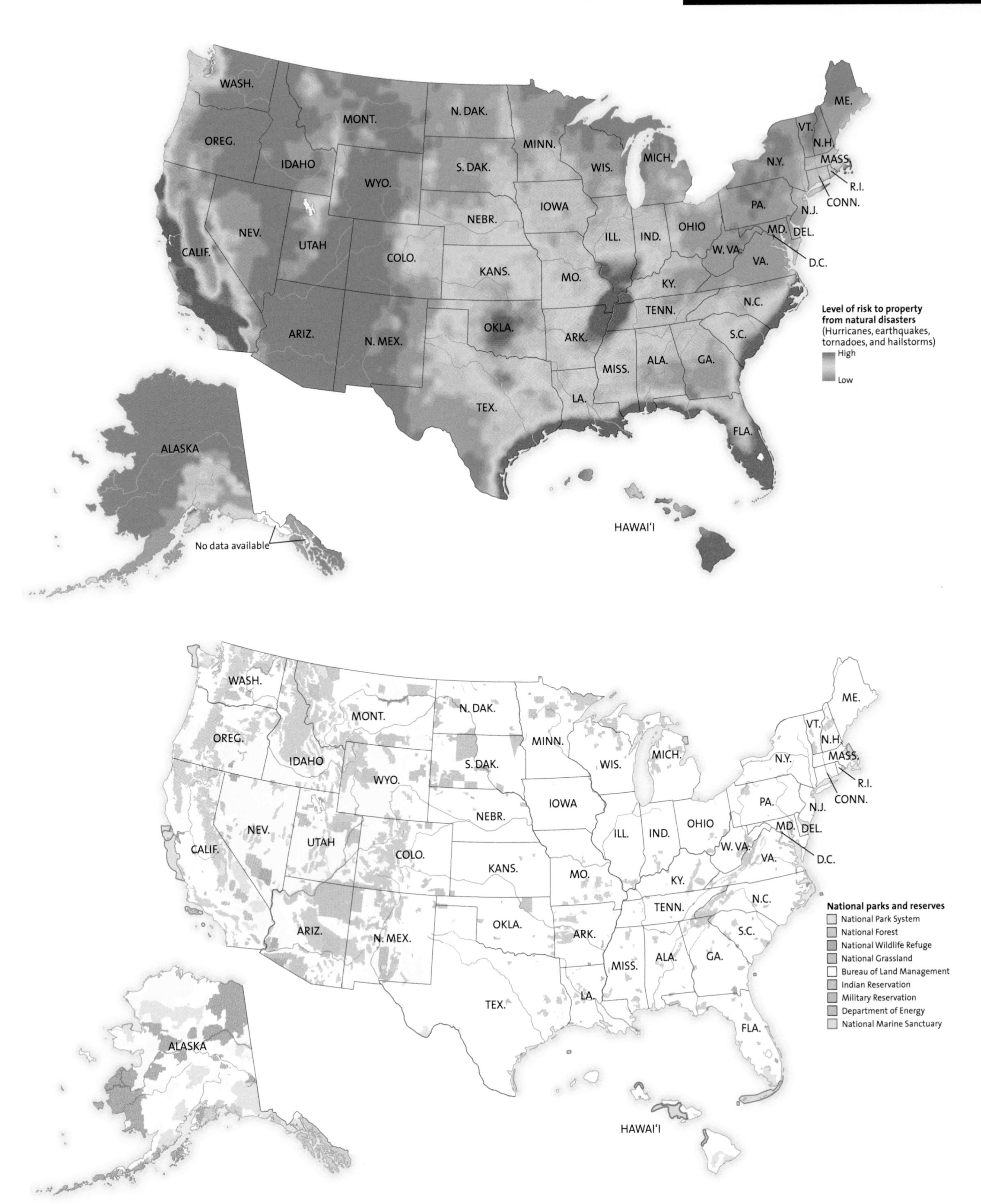

WASH.
MONT.
N. DAK.
ME.
OREG.
IDAHO
WYO.
S. DAK.
MINN.
WIS.
MICH.
VT.
N.H.
MASS.
N.Y.
R.I.
CONN.
PA.
N.J.
IOWA
NEBR.
NEV.
UTAH
CALIF.
COLO.
KANS.
ILL.
IND.
OHIO
MD.
DEL.
W. VA.
VA.
D.C.
MO.
KY.
TENN.
N.C.
OKLA.
ARK.
ARIZ.
N. MEX.
S.C.
MISS.
ALA.
GA.
TEX.
LA.
FLA.
ALASKA
HAWAI'I
No data available
Level of risk to property from natural disasters
(Hurricanes, earthquakes, tornadoes, and hailstorms)
High
Low
National parks and reserves
National Park System
National Forest
National Wildlife Refuge
National Grassland
Bureau of Land Management
Indian Reservation
Military Reservation
Department of Energy
National Marine Sanctuary

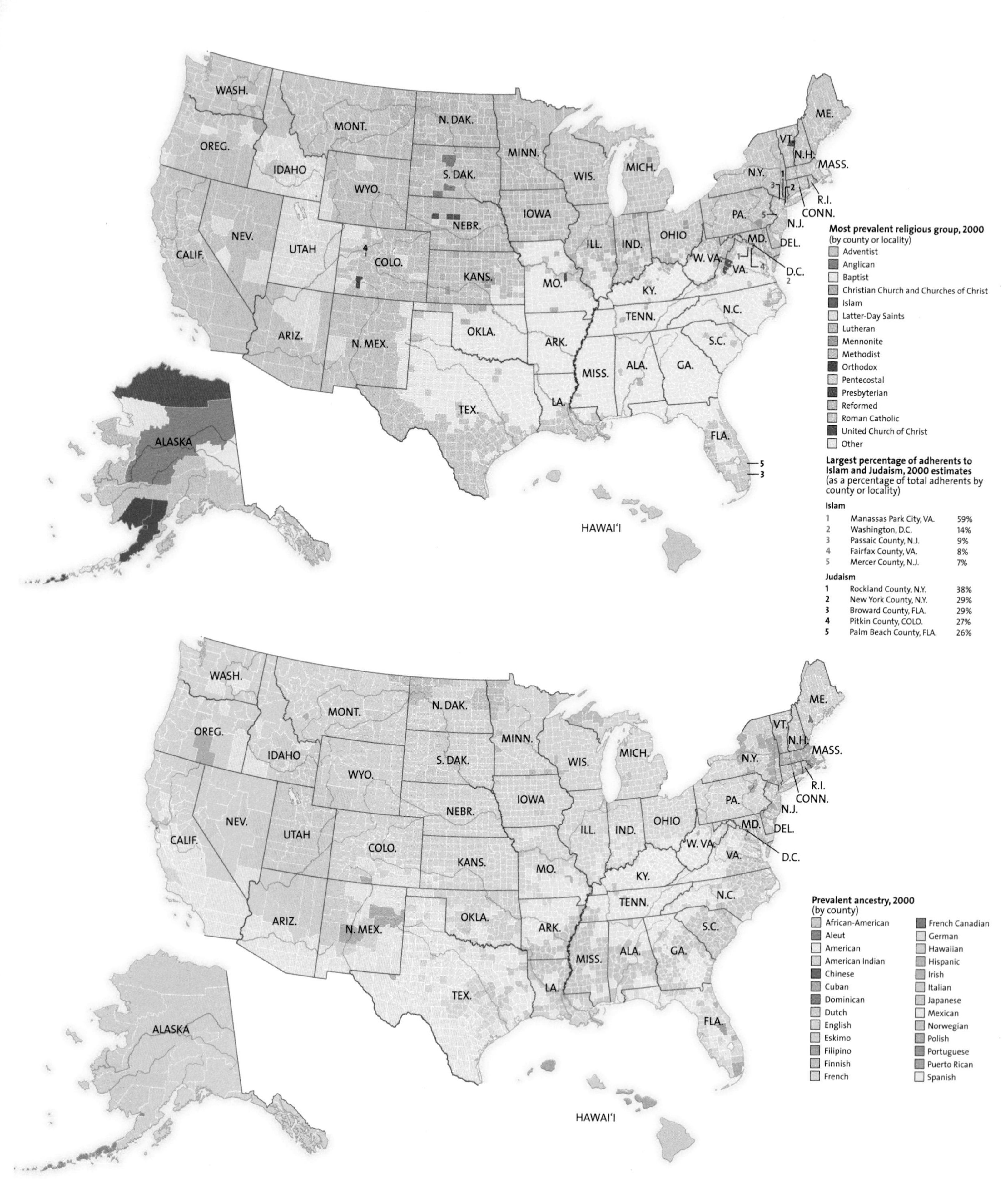
WASH.
OREG.
CALIF.
IDAHO
NEV.
MONT.
WYO.
UTAH
COLO.
ARIZ.
N. MEX.
N. DAK.
S. DAK.
NEBR.
KANS.
OKLA.
TEX.
MINN.
IOWA
MO.
ARK.
LA.
WIS.
ILL.
MICH.
IND.
OHIO
KY.
TENN.
MISS.
ALA.
GA.
FLA.
S.C.
N.C.
VA.
W. VA.
MD.
DEL.
D.C.
PA.
N.J.
N.Y.
CONN.
R.I.
MASS.
VT.
N.H.
ME.
ALASKA
HAWAI'I
Most prevalent religious group, 2000
(by county or locality)
Adventist
Anglican
Baptist
Christian Church and Churches of Christ
Islam
Latter-Day Saints
Lutheran
Mennonite
Methodist
Orthodox
Pentecostal
Presbyterian
Reformed
Roman Catholic
United Church of Christ
Other
Largest percentage of adherents to Islam and Judaism, 2000 estimates
(as a percentage of total adherents by county or locality)
Islam
1 Manassas Park City, VA. 59%
2 Washington, D.C. 14%
3 Passaic County, N.J. 9%
4 Fairfax County, VA. 8%
5 Mercer County, N.J. 7%
Judaism
1 Rockland County, N.Y. 38%
2 New York County, N.Y. 29%
3 Broward County, FLA. 29%
4 Pitkin County, COLO. 27%
5 Palm Beach County, FLA. 26%
WASH.
OREG.
CALIF.
IDAHO
NEV.
MONT.
WYO.
UTAH
COLO.
ARIZ.
N. MEX.
N. DAK.
S. DAK.
NEBR.
KANS.
OKLA.
TEX.
MINN.
IOWA
MO.
ARK.
LA.
WIS.
ILL.
MICH.
IND.
OHIO
KY.
TENN.
MISS.
ALA.
GA.
FLA.
S.C.
N.C.
VA.
W. VA.
MD.
DEL.
D.C.
PA.
N.J.
N.Y.
CONN.
R.I.
MASS.
VT.
N.H.
ME.
ALASKA
HAWAI'I
Prevalent ancestry, 2000
(by county)
African-American
Aleut
American
American Indian
Chinese
Cuban
Dominican
Dutch
English
Eskimo
Filipino
Finnish
French
French Canadian
German
Hawaiian
Hispanic
Irish
Italian
Japanese
Mexican
Norwegian
Polish
Portuguese
Puerto Rican
Spanish

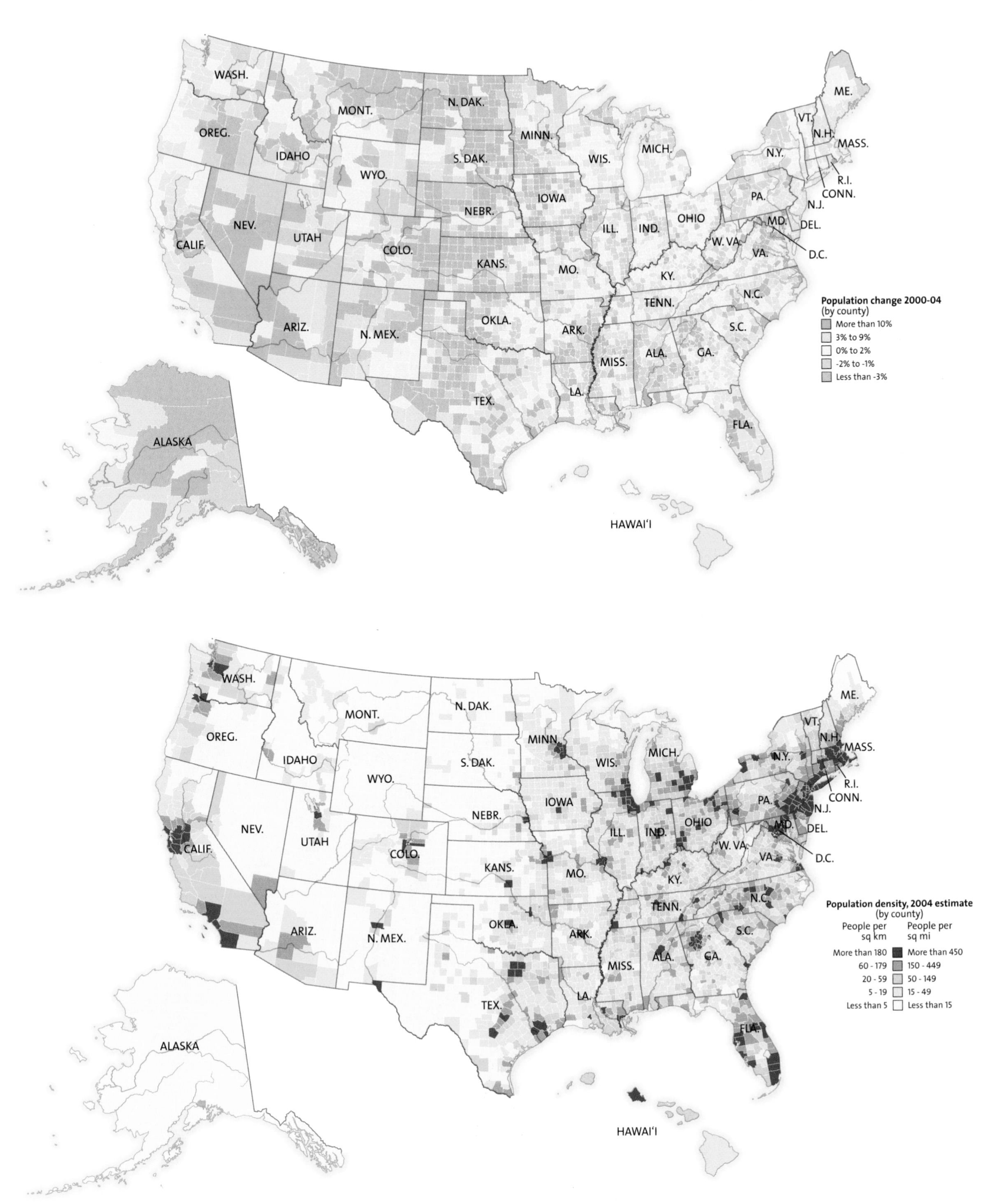

WASH.
OREG.
CALIF.
NEV.
IDAHO
MONT.
WYO.
UTAH
ARIZ.
COLO.
N. MEX.
N. DAK.
S. DAK.
NEBR.
KANS.
OKLA.
TEX.
MINN.
IOWA
MO.
ARK.
LA.
WIS.
ILL.
MICH.
IND.
OHIO
KY.
TENN.
MISS.
ALA.
GA.
FLA.
S.C.
N.C.
VA.
W. VA.
PA.
N.Y.
VT.
N.H.
ME.
MASS.
R.I.
CONN.
N.J.
DEL.
MD.
D.C.
ALASKA
HAWAI'I
Population change 2000-04
(by county)
More than 10%
3% to 9%
0% to 2%
-2% to -1%
Less than -3%
Population density, 2004 estimate
(by county)
People per sq km
People per sq mi
More than 180
60 - 179
20 - 59
5 - 19
Less than 5
More than 450
150 - 449
50 - 149
15 - 49
Less than 15

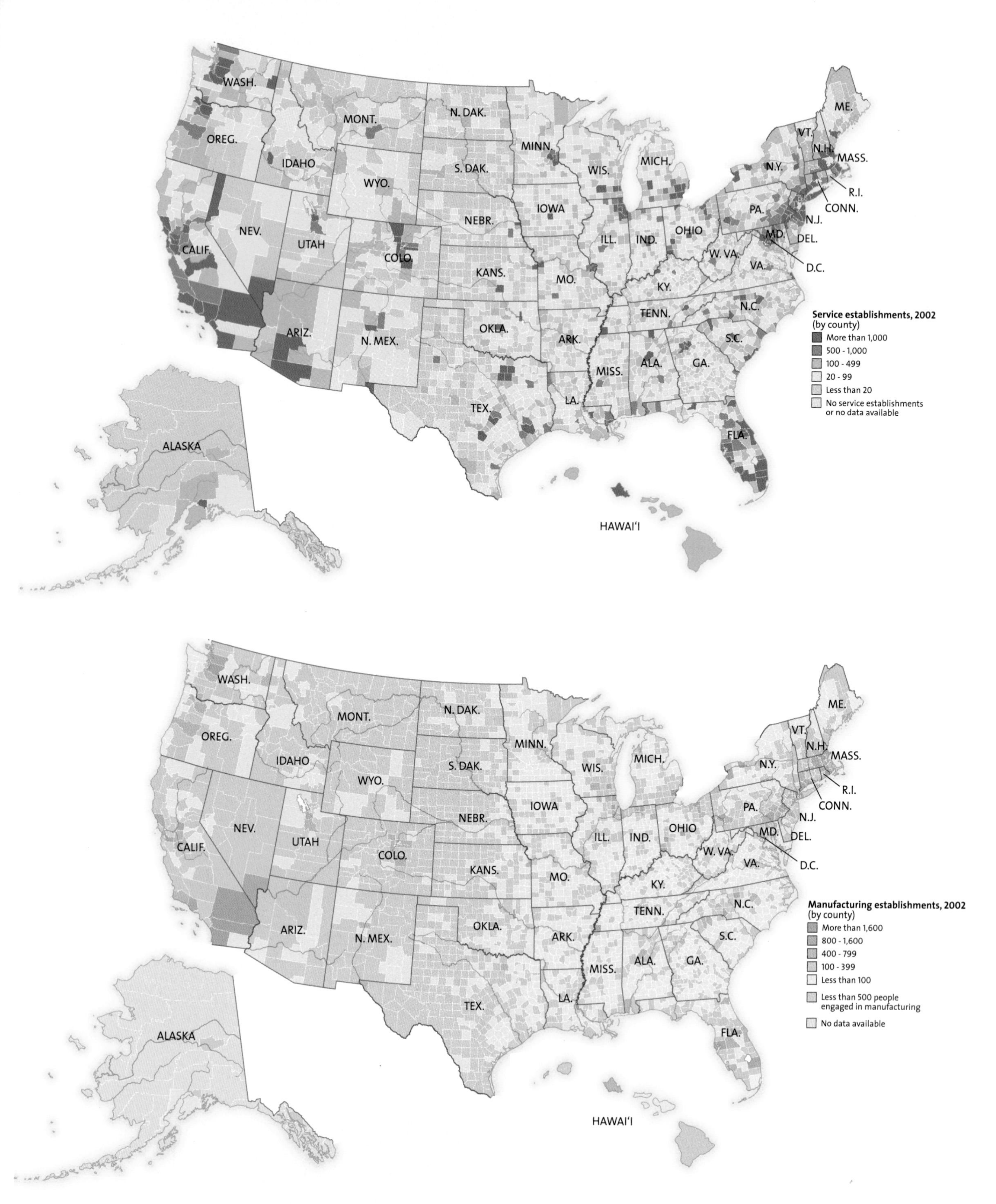
WASH.
OREG.
CALIF.
NEV.
IDAHO
MONT.
WYO.
UTAH
COLO.
ARIZ.
N. MEX.
N. DAK.
S. DAK.
NEBR.
KANS.
OKLA.
TEX.
MINN.
IOWA
MO.
ARK.
LA.
WIS.
ILL.
MICH.
IND.
OHIO
KY.
TENN.
MISS.
ALA.
GA.
FLA.
S.C.
N.C.
VA.
W. VA.
MD.
DEL.
D.C.
PA.
N.J.
N.Y.
CONN.
R.I.
MASS.
VT.
N.H.
ME.
ALASKA
HAWAI'I
Service establishments, 2002
(by county)
More than 1,000
500 - 1,000
100 - 499
20 - 99
Less than 20
No service establishments or no data available
WASH.
OREG.
CALIF.
NEV.
IDAHO
MONT.
WYO.
UTAH
COLO.
ARIZ.
N. MEX.
N. DAK.
S. DAK.
NEBR.
KANS.
OKLA.
TEX.
MINN.
IOWA
MO.
ARK.
LA.
WIS.
ILL.
MICH.
IND.
OHIO
KY.
TENN.
MISS.
ALA.
GA.
FLA.
S.C.
N.C.
VA.
W. VA.
MD.
DEL.
D.C.
PA.
N.J.
N.Y.
CONN.
R.I.
MASS.
VT.
N.H.
ME.
ALASKA
HAWAI'I
Manufacturing establishments, 2002
(by county)
More than 1,600
800 - 1,600
400 - 799
100 - 399
Less than 100
Less than 500 people engaged in manufacturing
No data available

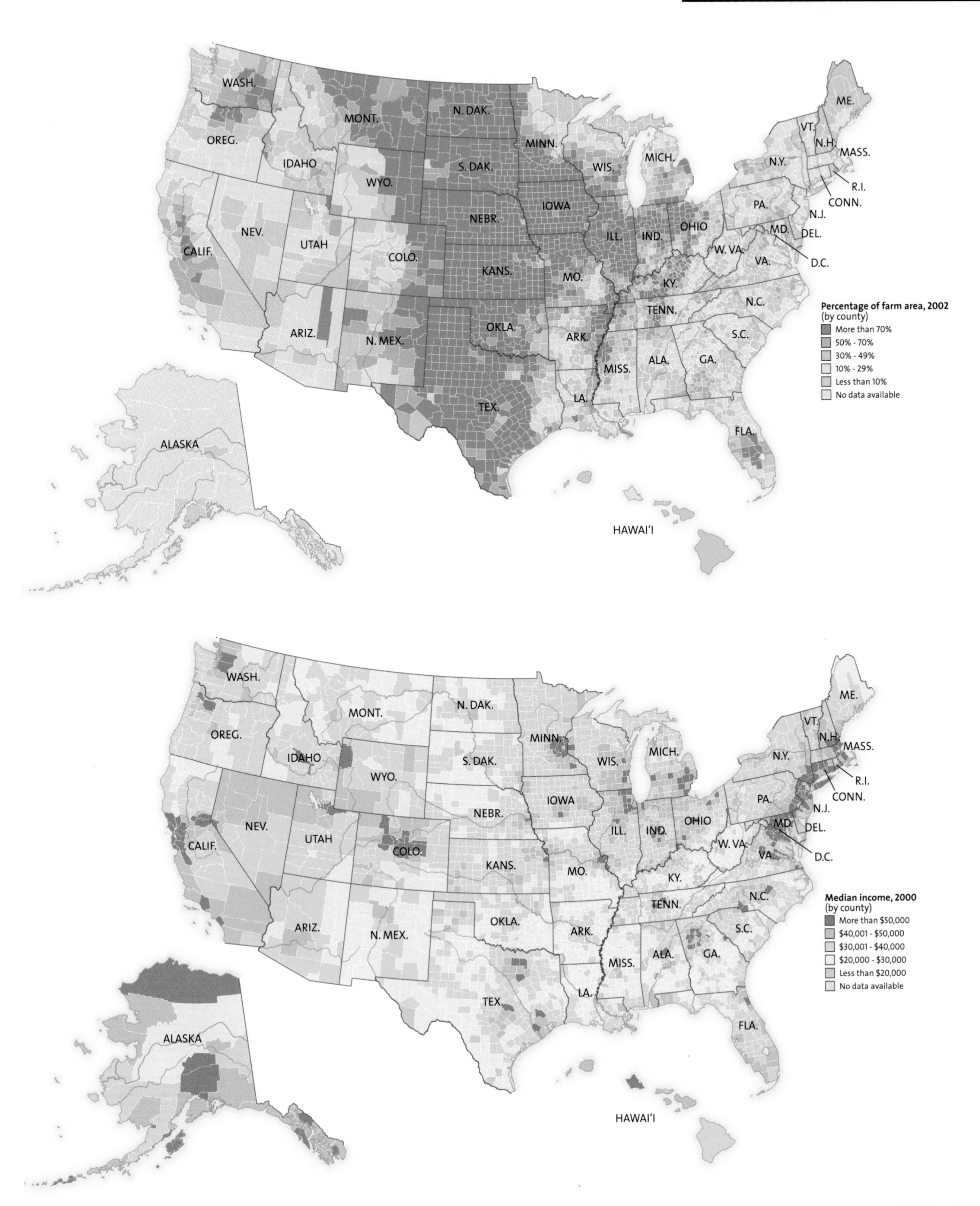
WASH.
OREG.
CALIF.
NEV.
IDAHO
MONT.
WYO.
UTAH
ARIZ.
COLO.
N. MEX.
N. DAK.
S. DAK.
NEBR.
KANS.
OKLA.
TEX.
MINN.
IOWA
MO.
ARK.
LA.
WIS.
ILL.
MICH.
IND.
OHIO
KY.
TENN.
MISS.
ALA.
GA.
FLA.
S.C.
N.C.
VA.
W. VA.
PA.
N.Y.
VT.
N.H.
ME.
MASS.
R.I.
CONN.
N.J.
DEL.
MD.
D.C.
ALASKA
HAWAI'I
Percentage of farm area, 2002
(by county)
More than 70%
50% - 70%
30% - 49%
10% - 29%
Less than 10%
No data available
Median income, 2000
(by county)
More than $50,000
$40,001 - $50,000
$30,001 - $40,000
$20,000 - $30,000
Less than $20,000
No data available

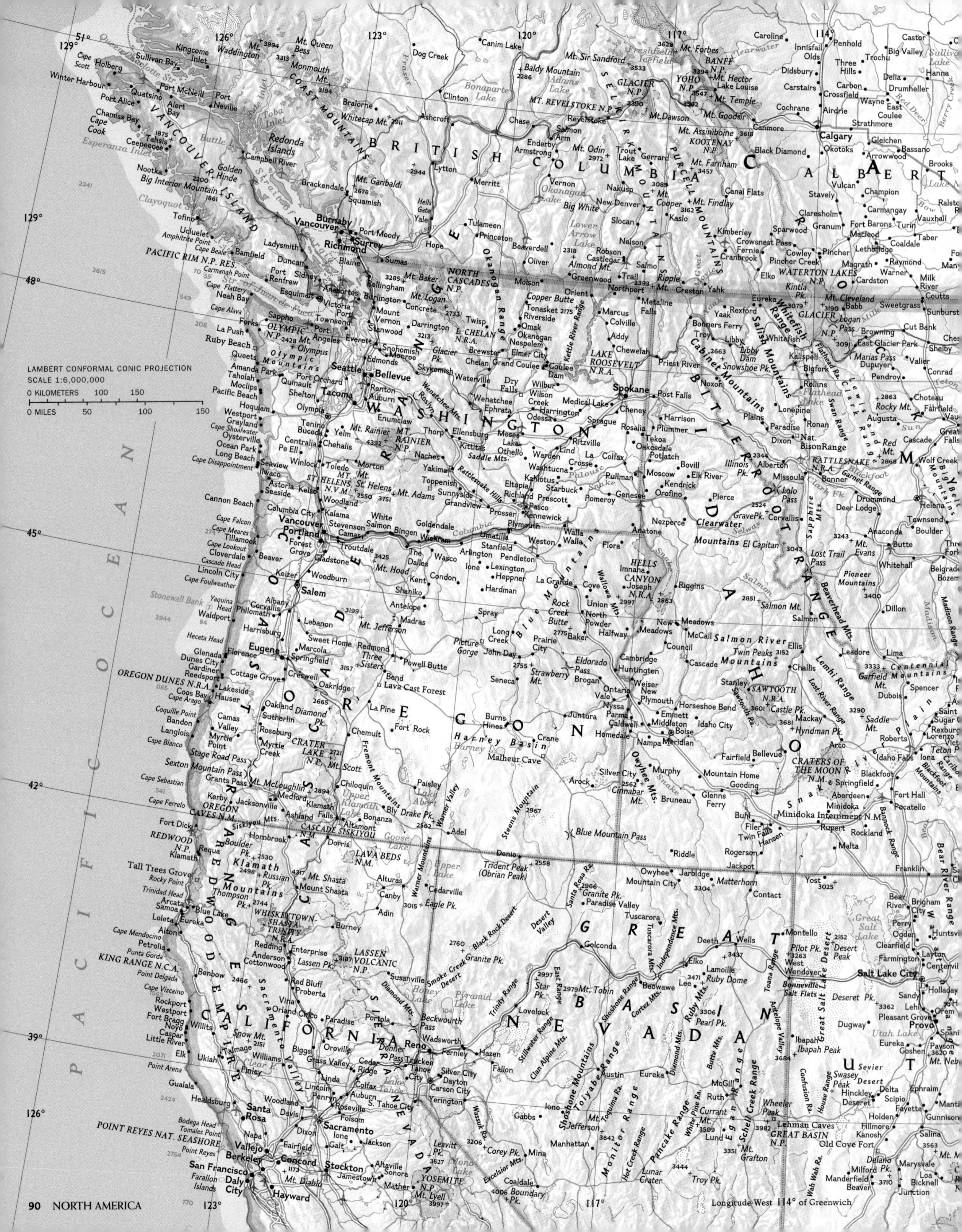
LAMBERT CONFORMAL CONIC PROJECTION
SCALE 1:6,000,000
0 KILOMETERS 100 150
0 MILES 50 100 150
PACIFIC OCEAN
BRITISH COLUMBIA
ALBERTA
WASHINGTON
OREGON
IDAHO
MONTANA
CALIFORNIA
NEVADA
UTAH
GREAT BASIN
VANCOUVER ISLAND
COAST MOUNTAINS
CASCADE RANGE
SIERRA NEVADA
KLAMATH MOUNTAINS
BITTERROOT RANGE
PACIFIC RIM N.P. RES.
OLYMPIC N.P.
NORTH CASCADES N.P.
MT. RAINIER N.P.
CRATER LAKE N.P.
REDWOOD N.P.
LASSEN VOLCANIC N.P.
YOSEMITE N.P.
GLACIER N.P.
BANFF N.P.
YOHO N.P.
KOOTENAY N.P.
MT. REVELSTOKE N.P.
WATERTON LAKES N.P.
GREAT BASIN N.P.
OREGON DUNES N.R.A.
HELLS CANYON N.R.A.
SAWTOOTH N.R.A.
CRATERS OF THE MOON N.M.
LAVA BEDS N.M.
OREGON CAVES N.M.
POINT REYES NAT. SEASHORE
KING RANGE N.C.A.
Vancouver
Victoria
Seattle
Tacoma
Spokane
Portland
Salem
Eugene
Boise
Calgary
Reno
Sacramento
San Francisco
Salt Lake City
Stonewall Bank
Harney Basin
Longitude West 114° of Greenwich

OREGON
IDAHO
NEVADA
CALIFORNIA
UTAH
ARIZONA
GREAT BASIN
MOJAVE DESERT
SONORAN DESERT
PACIFIC OCEAN
CHANNEL ISLANDS
BAJA CALIFORNIA
GOLFO DE CALIFORNIA
Desierto de Altar
COAST RANGES
SIERRA NEVADA
CASCADE RANGE
GREAT VALLEY
REDWOOD N.P.
LAVA BEDS N.M.
WHISKEYTOWN-SHASTA-TRINITY N.R.A.
LASSEN VOLCANIC N.P.
KING RANGE N.C.A.
YOSEMITE N.P.
KINGS CANYON N.P.
SEQUOIA N.P.
DEATH VALLEY N.P.
PINNACLES NAT. MON.
CARRIZO PLAIN NAT. MON.
CALIFORNIA COASTAL NAT. MON.
MONTEREY BAY NATIONAL MARINE SANCTUARY
CALIFORNIA SPACEPORT
DRYDEN FLIGHT RESEARCH CENTER
MOJAVE NATIONAL PRESERVE
JOSHUA TREE N.P.
SANTA ROSA AND SAN JACINTO MTS. N.M.
SANTA MONICA MOUNTAINS N.R.A.
CHANNEL ISLANDS N.P.
LAKE MEAD N.R.A.
GRAND CANYON-PARASHANT NAT. MON.
GRAND CANYON N.P.
GREAT BASIN N.P.
ZION N.P.
BRYCE CANYON N.P.
GRAND STAIRCASE-ESCALANTE NAT. MON.
VERMILION CLIFFS N.M.
WUPATKI N.M.
AGUA FRIA NAT. MON.
IRONWOOD FOREST NAT. MON.
ORGAN PIPE CACTUS NAT. MON.
CONSTITUCIÓN DE 1857 N.P.
SIERRA DE SAN PEDRO MÁRTIR N.P.
San Francisco
Oakland
Berkeley
Daly City
Fremont
Hayward
Sunnyvale
Santa Clara
San Jose
Sacramento
Stockton
Modesto
Fresno
Bakersfield
Santa Rosa
Vallejo
Concord
Salinas
Reno
Carson City
Las Vegas
Henderson
Santa Clarita
Lancaster
Palmdale
Oxnard
Thousand Oaks
Simi Valley
Burbank
Los Angeles
Long Beach
Anaheim
Huntington Beach
Irvine
Ontario
San Bernardino
Riverside
Oceanside
Escondido
San Diego
Chula Vista
Tijuana
Mexicali
Ensenada
Salt Lake City
West Valley City
Provo
Phoenix
Glendale
Scottsdale
Mesa
Peoria
Tempe
Chandler
Yuma
Pioneer Seamount
Guide Seamount
Davidson Seamount
Rodriguez Seamount
San Juan Seamount
Ranger Bank
Isla Cedros
Bahía Sebastián Vizcaíno
Isla Ángel de la Guarda
Isla Tiburón
Mt. Whitney 4418 (14494 ft)
Mt. Shasta 4317
Lassen Pk. 3187
126°
123°
120°
117°
114°
39°
36°
33°
30°
LAMBERT CONFORMAL CONIC PROJECTION
SCALE 1:6,000,000
0 KILOMETERS 100 150
0 MILES 50 100 150
Longitude West 117° of Greenwich

MANITOBA
NORTH DAKOTA
SOUTH DAKOTA
NEBRASKA
KANSAS
OKLAHOMA
MINNESOTA
IOWA
MISSOURI
ARKANSAS
WISCONSIN
ILLINOIS
INDIANA
MICHIGAN
KENTUCKY
TENN.
ONTARIO
Lake Superior
Lake Michigan
Lake Nipigon
Upper Red Lake
Lower Red Lake
Leech Lake
Mille Lacs L.
Lake of the Woods
Green Bay
Thunder Bay
Duluth
Superior
Minneapolis
St. Paul
Sioux Falls
Fargo
Grand Forks
Omaha
Lincoln
Des Moines
Cedar Rapids
Kansas City
Topeka
Wichita
Tulsa
Springfield
St. Louis
Madison
Milwaukee
Chicago
Rockford
Peoria
Joliet
Aurora
Naperville
Gary
South Bend
Fort Wayne
Indianapolis
Evansville
Louisville
Lexington
Cincinnati
Dayton
Columbus
Toledo
Ann Arbor
Lansing
Grand Rapids
Flint
Detroit
Independence
Overland Park
Clarksville
VOYAGEURS N.P.
ISLE ROYALE N.P.
PUKASKWA N.P.
APOSTLE ISLANDS N.L.
PICTURED ROCKS N.L.
SAINT CROIX N.S.R.
OZARK N.S.R.
MAMMOTH CAVE N.P.
LAND BETWEEN THE LAKES
BUFFALO NAT. RIVER
BIG S. FORK N.R. & REC. AREA
SLEEPING BEAR DUNES
Mesabi Range
Vermilion Ra.
Sawtooth Mountains
Gogebic Range
Huron Mts.
Porcupine Mts.
Cuyuna Range
OZARK PLATEAU
CUMBERLAND PLATEAU
Saint Francois Mountains
Taum Sauk Mt.
Timms Hill
Rib Mt.
Charles Mound
Eagle Mt.
Mt. Arvon
Missouri
Mississippi
Ohio
Wisconsin
Wabash
99°
96°
93°
90°
87°
84°
48°
45°
42°
39°
36°

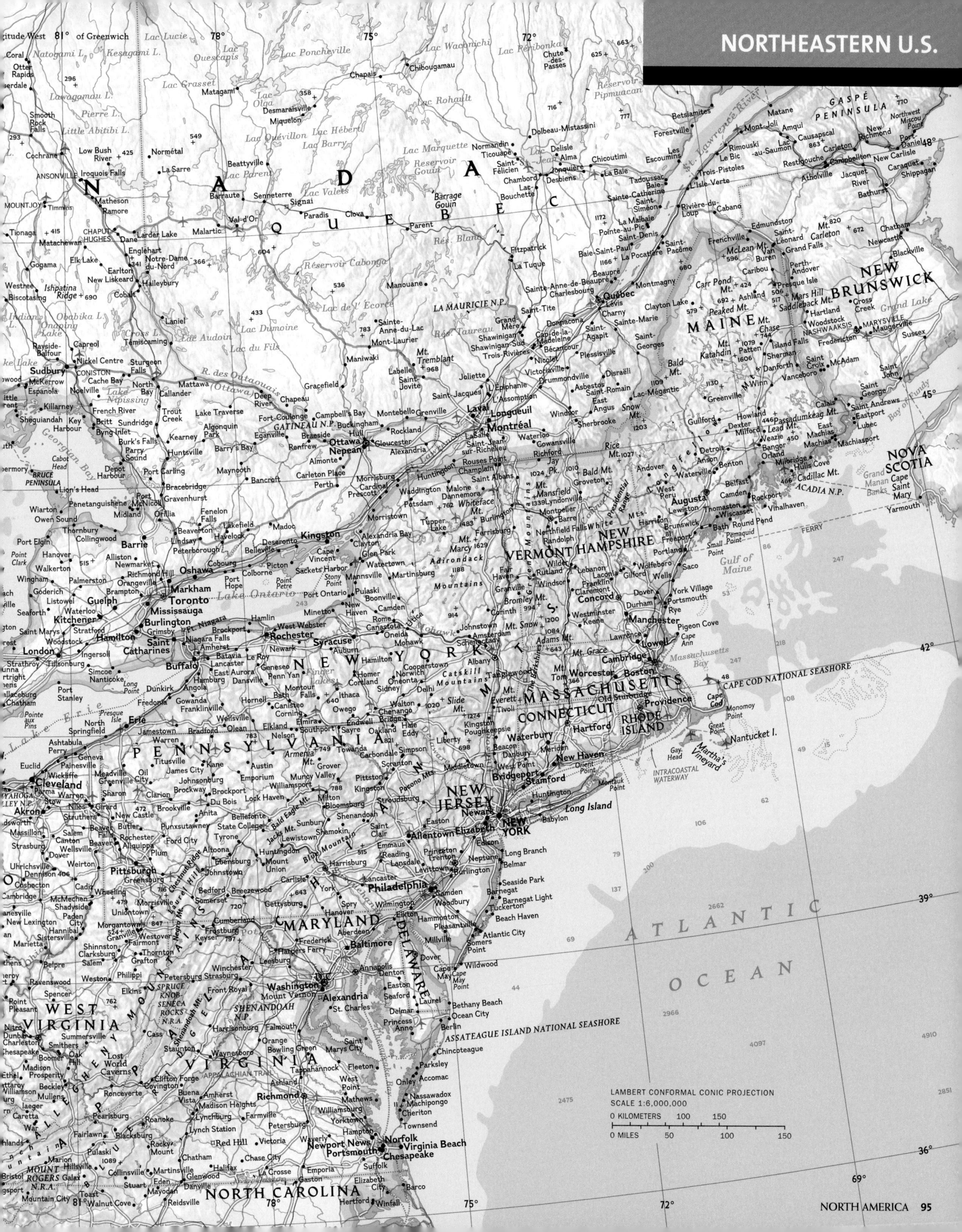
NORTHEASTERN U.S.
CANADA
QUEBEC
ONTARIO
NEW BRUNSWICK
NOVA SCOTIA
GASPÉ PENINSULA
MAINE
VERMONT
NEW HAMPSHIRE
MASSACHUSETTS
RHODE ISLAND
CONNECTICUT
NEW YORK
NEW JERSEY
PENNSYLVANIA
DELAWARE
MARYLAND
WEST VIRGINIA
VIRGINIA
NORTH CAROLINA
ATLANTIC OCEAN
Gulf of Maine
Bay of Fundy
Lake Ontario
Lake Erie
Georgian Bay
Long Island
Cape Cod
Nantucket I.
Martha's Vineyard
Adirondack Mountains
Catskill Mountains
White Mts.
Green Mountains
The Berkshires
Blue Mountain
Allegheny Mountains
Appalachian Mountains
APPALACHIAN TRAIL
Chesapeake Bay
Delaware Bay
St. Lawrence River
CAPE COD NATIONAL SEASHORE
ASSATEAGUE ISLAND NATIONAL SEASHORE
ACADIA N.P.
SHENANDOAH N.P.
LA MAURICIE N.P.
GATINEAU N.P.
INTRACOASTAL WATERWAY
Montréal
Québec
Ottawa
Toronto
Boston
NEW YORK
Philadelphia
Baltimore
Washington D.C.
Pittsburgh
Buffalo
Albany
Hartford
Providence
Augusta
Concord
Montpelier
Harrisburg
Trenton
Richmond
Norfolk
LAMBERT CONFORMAL CONIC PROJECTION
SCALE 1:6,000,000
0 KILOMETERS 100 150
0 MILES 50 100 150
Longitude West 81° of Greenwich
78°
75°
72°
69°
48°
45°
42°
39°
36°

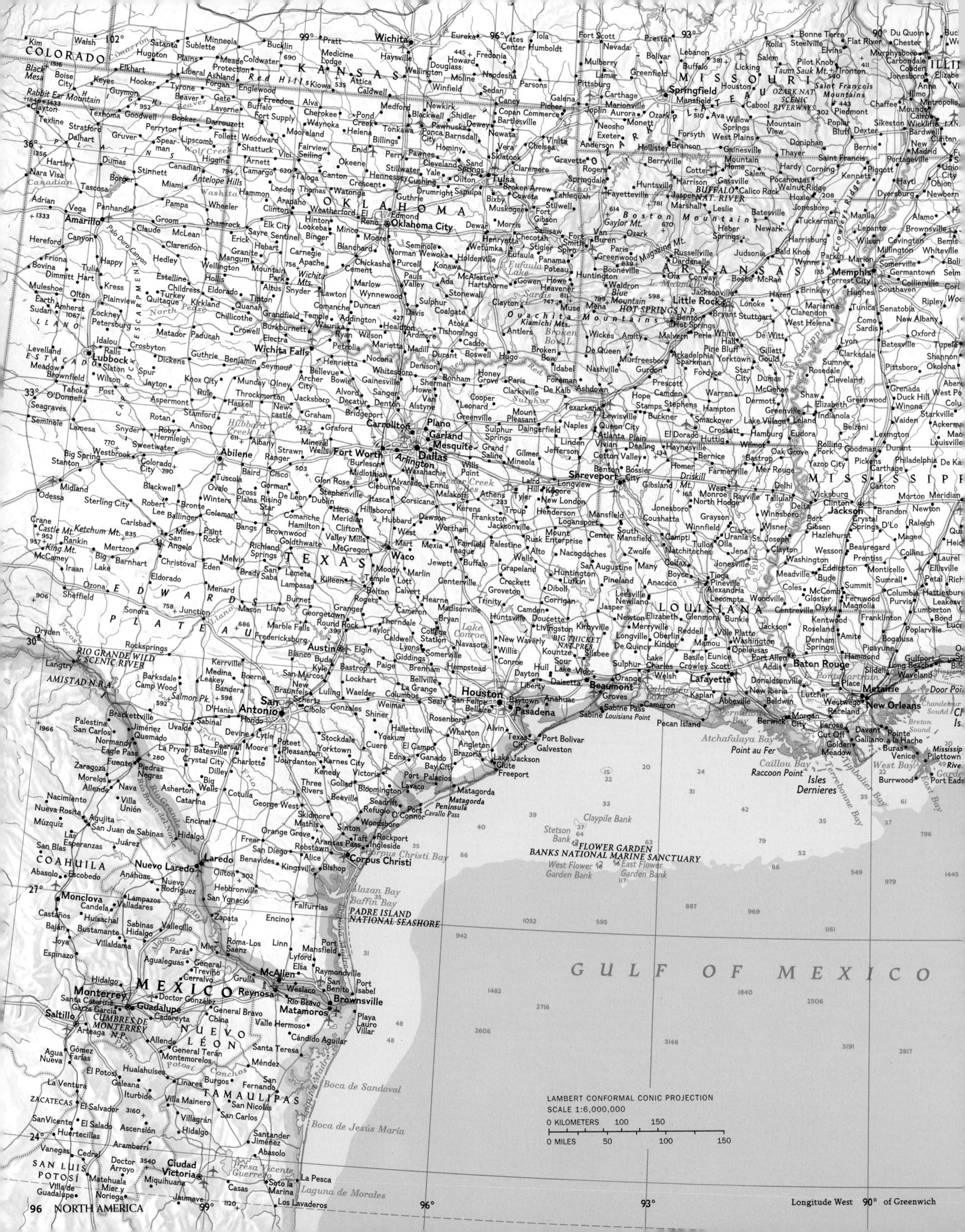
COLORADO
KANSAS
MISSOURI
OKLAHOMA
ARKANSAS
TEXAS
LOUISIANA
MISSISSIPPI
COAHUILA
NUEVO LEÓN
TAMAULIPAS
SAN LUIS POTOSÍ
MEXICO
GULF OF MEXICO
EDWARDS PLATEAU
OZARK PLATEAU
Boston Mountains
Ouachita Mountains
Wichita
Tulsa
Oklahoma City
Amarillo
Lubbock
Wichita Falls
Abilene
Fort Worth
Dallas
Arlington
Garland
Mesquite
Plano
Carrollton
Waco
Austin
San Antonio
Houston
Pasadena
Beaumont
Corpus Christi
Laredo
Nuevo Laredo
McAllen
Reynosa
Brownsville
Matamoros
Monterrey
Guadalupe
Saltillo
Monclova
Ciudad Victoria
Shreveport
Little Rock
Memphis
Jackson
Baton Rouge
Lafayette
Metairie
New Orleans
Springfield
PADRE ISLAND NATIONAL SEASHORE
FLOWER GARDEN BANKS NATIONAL MARINE SANCTUARY
BIG THICKET NAT. PRES.
HOT SPRINGS N.P.
BUFFALO NAT. RIVER
OZARK NAT. SCENIC RIVERWAYS
RIO GRANDE WILD & SCENIC RIVER
AMISTAD N.R.A.
CUMBRES DE MONTERREY N.P.
LAMBERT CONFORMAL CONIC PROJECTION
SCALE 1:6,000,000
0 KILOMETERS 100 150
0 MILES 50 100 150
Longitude West 90° of Greenwich

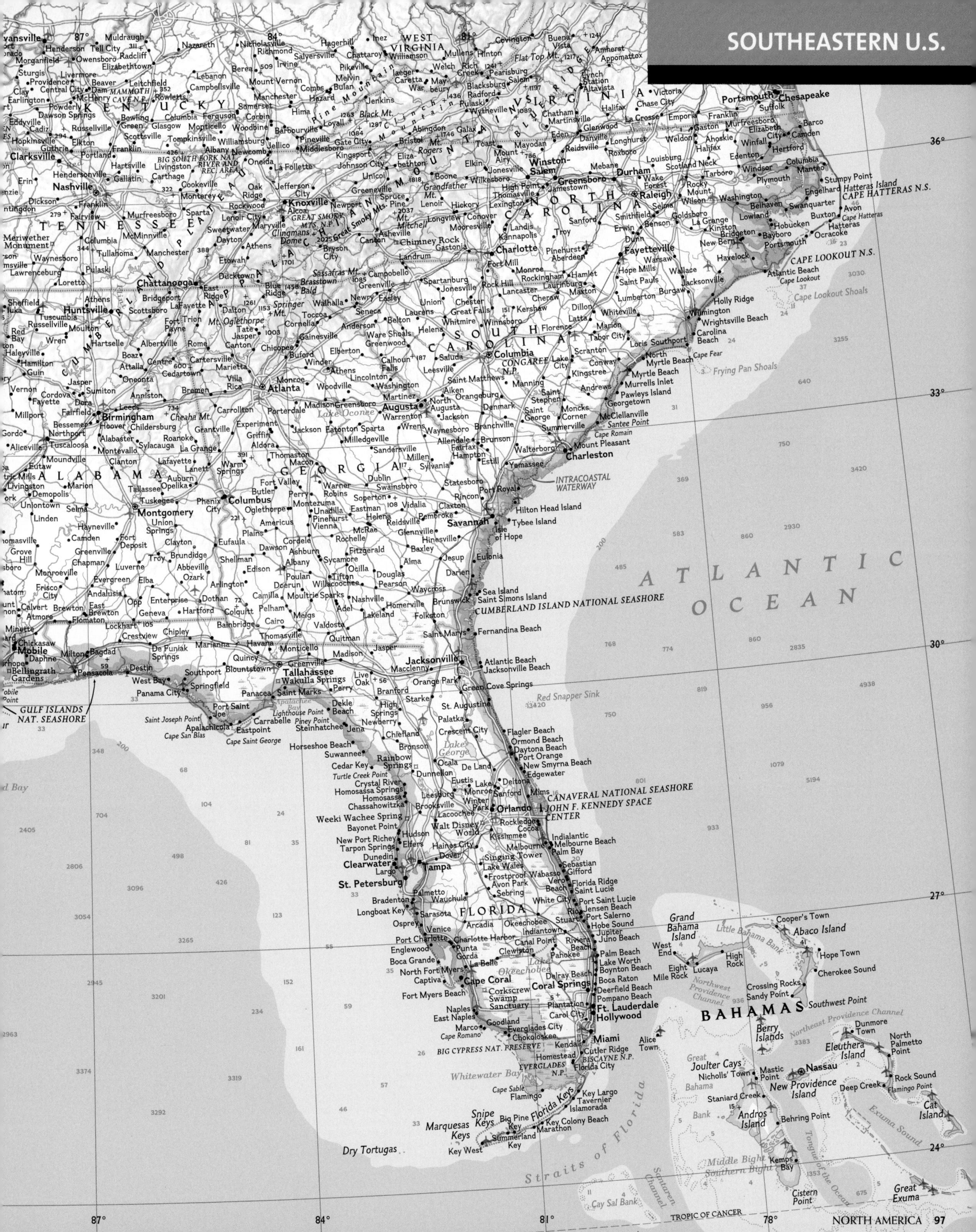

SOUTHEASTERN U.S.

KENTUCKY
TENNESSEE
NORTH CAROLINA
SOUTH CAROLINA
GEORGIA
ALABAMA
FLORIDA
WEST VIRGINIA
VIRGINIA
BAHAMAS

ATLANTIC OCEAN

Straits of Florida

ALASKA, U.S.
ALBERS CONIC EQUAL-AREA PROJECTION
SCALE 1:10,000,000
0 KILOMETERS 200 300
0 MILES 100 200 300
ARCTIC OCEAN
PACIFIC OCEAN
Beaufort Sea
Chukchi Sea
Bering Sea
Gulf of Alaska
UNITED STATES
ALASKA
CANADA
RUSSIA
YUKON
NORTHWEST TERRITORIES
BRITISH COLUMBIA
NUNAVUT
NORTH SLOPE
BROOKS RANGE
ALASKA RANGE
KUSKOKWIM MOUNTAINS
Chugach Mountains
Wrangell Mountains
St. Elias Mountains
COAST MOUNTAINS
Mackenzie Mountains
Selwyn Mountains
Ogilvie Mountains
Richardson Mountains
SEWARD PENINSULA
KENAI PENINSULA
ALASKA PENINSULA
Aleutian Islands
Fox Islands
Pribilof Islands
Shumagin Islands
Kodiak Island
Anchorage
Fairbanks
Juneau
Nome
Barrow
Date Line
Monday
Sunday
ARCTIC CIRCLE
153° Longitude West 150° of Greenwich

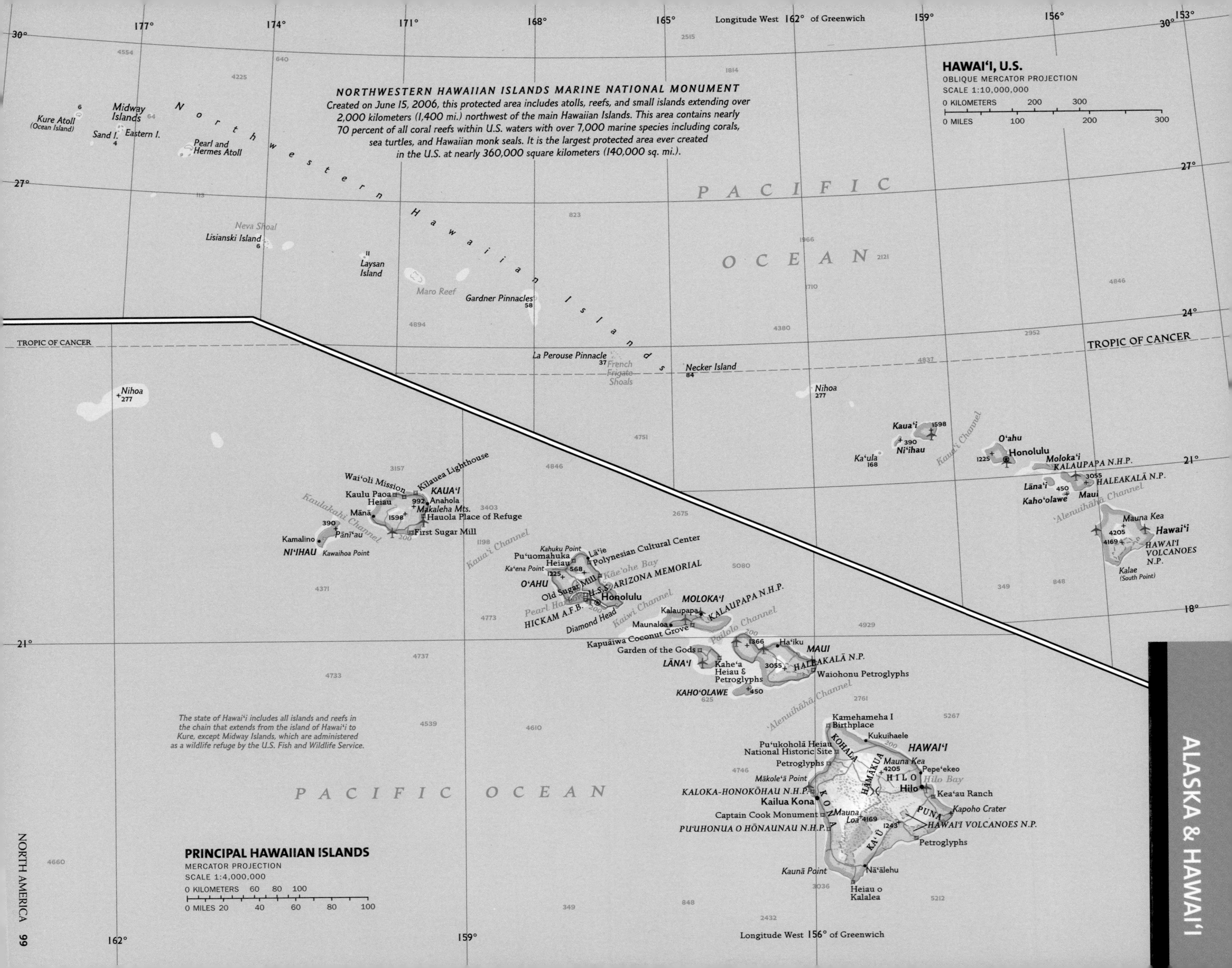
HAWAI'I, U.S.
OBLIQUE MERCATOR PROJECTION
SCALE 1:10,000,000
NORTHWESTERN HAWAIIAN ISLANDS MARINE NATIONAL MONUMENT
Created on June 15, 2006, this protected area includes atolls, reefs, and small islands extending over 2,000 kilometers (1,400 mi.) northwest of the main Hawaiian Islands. This area contains nearly 70 percent of all coral reefs within U.S. waters with over 7,000 marine species including corals, sea turtles, and Hawaiian monk seals. It is the largest protected area ever created in the U.S. at nearly 360,000 square kilometers (140,000 sq. mi.).
PRINCIPAL HAWAIIAN ISLANDS
MERCATOR PROJECTION
SCALE 1:4,000,000
The state of Hawai'i includes all islands and reefs in the chain that extends from the island of Hawai'i to Kure, except Midway Islands, which are administered as a wildlife refuge by the U.S. Fish and Wildlife Service.
PACIFIC OCEAN
Northwestern Hawaiian Islands
TROPIC OF CANCER
Longitude West 162° of Greenwich
Longitude West 156° of Greenwich
Kure Atoll (Ocean Island)
Midway Islands
Sand I.
Eastern I.
Pearl and Hermes Atoll
Lisianski Island
Neva Shoal
Laysan Island
Maro Reef
Gardner Pinnacles
La Perouse Pinnacle
French Frigate Shoals
Necker Island
Nihoa
Kaua'i
Ni'ihau
Ka'ula
O'ahu
Honolulu
Moloka'i
Lāna'i
Kaho'olawe
Maui
Hawai'i
Mauna Kea
Kalae (South Point)
KALAUPAPA N.H.P.
HALEAKALĀ N.P.
HAWAI'I VOLCANOES N.P.
Kaua'i Channel
'Alenuihāhā Channel
Kaulakahi Channel
Kaiwi Channel
Pailolo Channel
Kamalino
Kawaihoa Point
Pānī'au
Mānā
Kaulu Paoa Heiau
Wai'oli Mission
Kilauea Lighthouse
Anahola
Makaleha Mts.
Hauola Place of Refuge
First Sugar Mill
Ka'ena Point
Kahuku Point
Pu'uomahuka Heiau
Lā'ie
Polynesian Cultural Center
Kāe'ohe Bay
ARIZONA MEMORIAL
Old Sugar Mill
HICKAM A.F.B.
Diamond Head
Kapuāiwa Coconut Grove
Maunaloa
Kalaupapa
Garden of the Gods
Kahe'a Heiau & Petroglyphs
Ha'iku
Waiohonu Petroglyphs
Kamehameha I Birthplace
Kukuihaele
Pu'ukoholā Heiau National Historic Site
Petroglyphs
Mākole'ā Point
Kailua Kona
KALOKA-HONOKŌHAU N.H.P.
Captain Cook Monument
PU'UHONUA O HŌNAUNAU N.H.P.
Kaunā Point
Heiau o Kalalea
Nā'ālehu
Kapoho Crater
Kea'au Ranch
Pepe'ekeo
Hilo
Hilo Bay
KOHALA
HĀMĀKUA
KONA
KA'Ū
PUNA
Mauna Loa

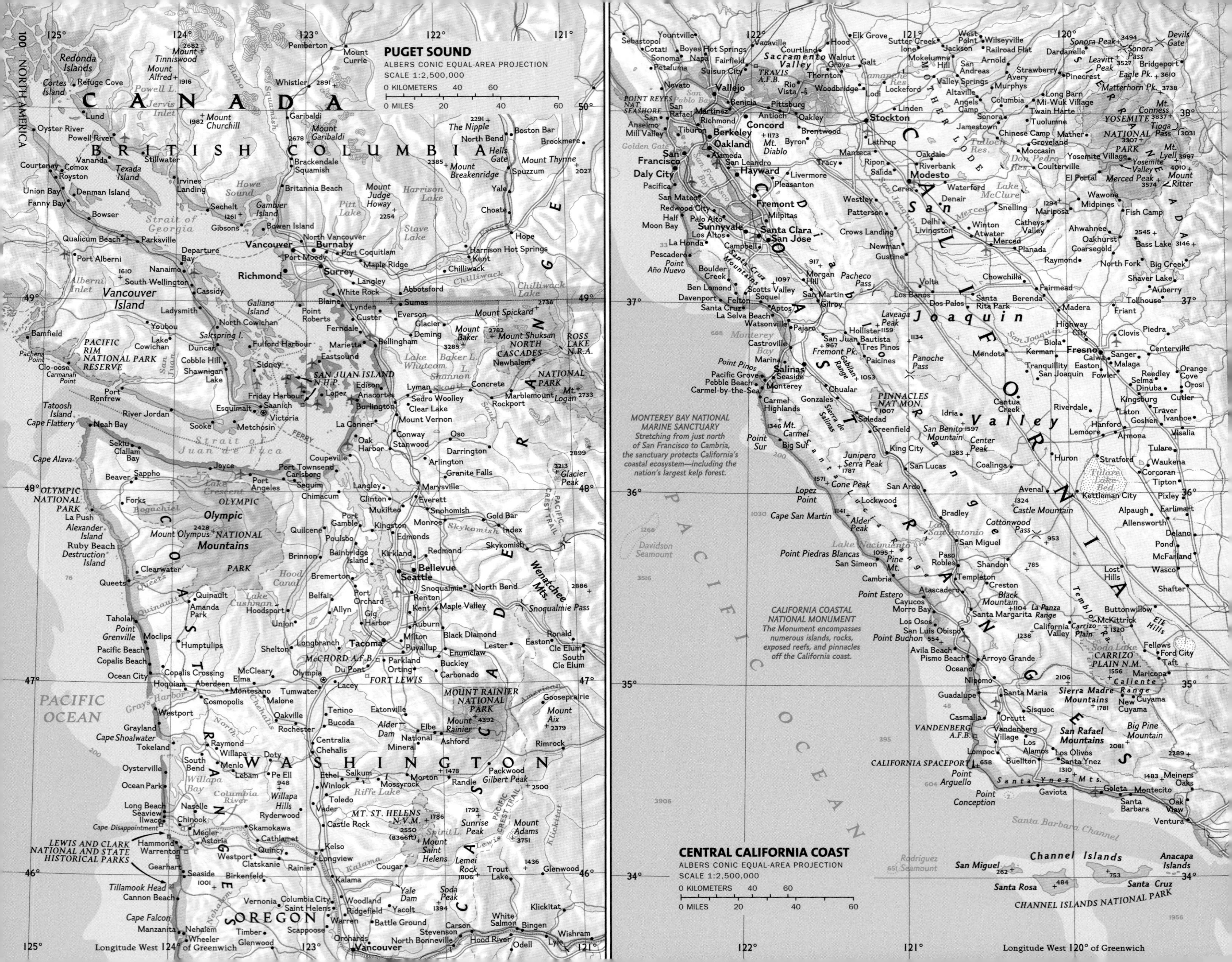
PUGET SOUND
ALBERS CONIC EQUAL-AREA PROJECTION
SCALE 1:2,500,000
0 KILOMETERS 40 60
0 MILES 20 40 60
CANADA
BRITISH COLUMBIA
WASHINGTON
OREGON
COAST RANGES
CASCADE RANGE
PACIFIC OCEAN
Vancouver Island
Strait of Georgia
Strait of Juan de Fuca
Puget Sound
Olympic Mountains
OLYMPIC NATIONAL PARK
PACIFIC RIM NATIONAL PARK RESERVE
SAN JUAN ISLAND N.H.P.
NORTH CASCADES NATIONAL PARK
ROSS LAKE N.R.A.
MOUNT RAINIER NATIONAL PARK
MT. ST. HELENS N.V.M.
LEWIS AND CLARK NATIONAL AND STATE HISTORICAL PARKS
PACIFIC CREST TRAIL
Wenatchee Mts.
Vancouver
Victoria
Seattle
Tacoma
Bellevue
Olympia
Everett
Bellingham
Vancouver
Mount Rainier 4392
Mount Baker 3285
Mount Olympus 2428
Mount Saint Helens 2550 (8366ft)
Mount Adams 3751
Longitude West 124° of Greenwich
CENTRAL CALIFORNIA COAST
ALBERS CONIC EQUAL-AREA PROJECTION
SCALE 1:2,500,000
0 KILOMETERS 40 60
0 MILES 20 40 60
CALIFORNIA
COAST RANGES
SIERRA NEVADA
San Joaquin Valley
MOTHER LODE
PACIFIC OCEAN
MONTEREY BAY NATIONAL MARINE SANCTUARY
Stretching from just north of San Francisco to Cambria, the sanctuary protects California's coastal ecosystem—including the nation's largest kelp forest.
CALIFORNIA COASTAL NATIONAL MONUMENT
The Monument encompasses numerous islands, rocks, exposed reefs, and pinnacles off the California coast.
POINT REYES NAT. SEASHORE
YOSEMITE NATIONAL PARK
PINNACLES NAT. MON.
CARRIZO PLAIN N.M.
VANDENBERG A.F.B.
CALIFORNIA SPACEPORT
CHANNEL ISLANDS NATIONAL PARK
Channel Islands
Santa Barbara Channel
San Francisco
Oakland
San Jose
Sacramento
Stockton
Modesto
Fresno
Salinas
Monterey
Santa Barbara
Longitude West 120° of Greenwich

SOUTHERN CALIFORNIA
ALBERS CONIC EQUAL-AREA PROJECTION
SCALE 1:2,500,000
0 KILOMETERS 40 60
0 MILES 20 40 60
Longitude West 119° of Greenwich
UTAH
NEVADA
ARIZONA
CALIFORNIA
MEXICO
BAJA CALIFORNIA
GREAT BASIN
SIERRA NEVADA
COAST RANGES
MOJAVE
DESERT
Sonoran Desert
Colorado Desert
PACIFIC OCEAN
Santa Barbara Channel
San Pedro Channel
Gulf of Santa Catalina
Channel Islands
CHANNEL ISLANDS NATIONAL PARK
DEATH VALLEY N.P.
MOJAVE NATIONAL PRESERVE
JOSHUA TREE NATIONAL PARK
LAKE MEAD NATIONAL RECREATION AREA
GRAND CANYON-PARASHANT NAT. MON.
SEQUOIA N.P.
KINGS CANYON N.P.
CARRIZO PLAIN N.M.
EDWARDS A.F.B.
NELLIS A.F.B.
CAMP PENDLETON M.C.B.
Salton Sea
Lake Mead
Lake Havasu
Black Mountains
Spring Mts.
Panamint Range
Argus Range
Inyo Mountains
San Gabriel Mts.
San Bernardino Mts.
Chocolate Mts.
Bullion Mountains
Old Woman Mountains
Tehachapi Mts.
Diablo Range
Temblor Range
Sierra Madre Mts.
San Rafael Mts.
Santa Ynez Mts.
Los Angeles
San Diego
Las Vegas
Bakersfield
Fresno
Santa Barbara
Riverside
San Bernardino
Palm Springs
Barstow
Needles
Yuma
Mexicali
Tijuana
Long Beach
Anaheim
Santa Ana
Oxnard
Lancaster
Palmdale
Visalia
Kingman
Henderson
San Clemente
Santa Catalina
Santa Cruz
Santa Rosa
San Miguel
San Nicolas
Anacapa Is.

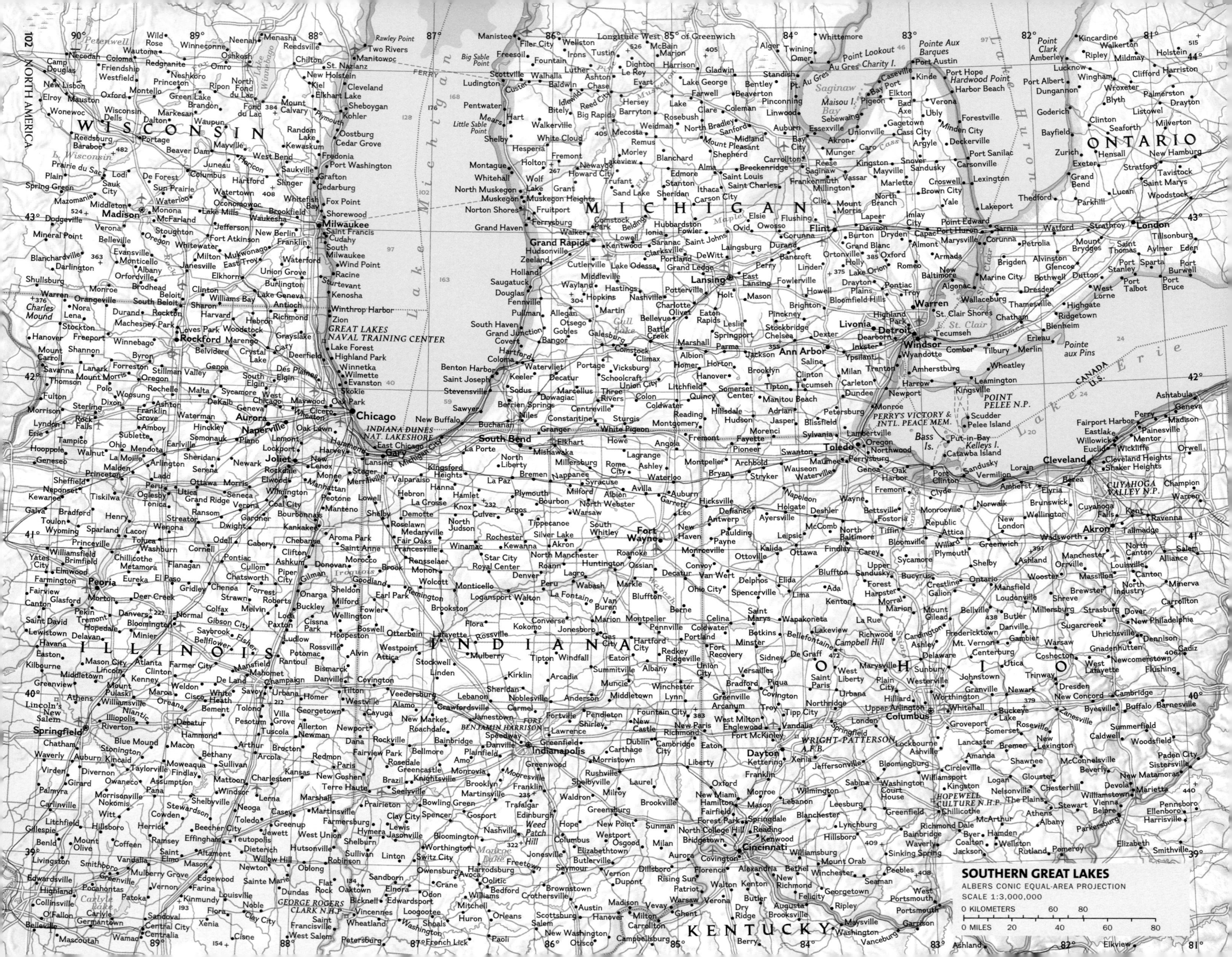
SOUTHERN GREAT LAKES
ALBERS CONIC EQUAL-AREA PROJECTION
SCALE 1:3,000,000
0 KILOMETERS 60 80
0 MILES 20 40 60 80
ONTARIO
MICHIGAN
WISCONSIN
ILLINOIS
INDIANA
OHIO
KENTUCKY
Lake Huron
Lake Michigan
Lake Erie
Saginaw Bay
Chicago
Milwaukee
Detroit
Cleveland
Toledo
Columbus
Cincinnati
Indianapolis
Fort Wayne
Dayton
Grand Rapids
Lansing
Madison
Rockford
Peoria
Springfield
South Bend
Akron
London
Windsor
Flint
Ann Arbor
CUYAHOGA VALLEY N.P.
INDIANA DUNES NAT. LAKESHORE
GREAT LAKES NAVAL TRAINING CENTER
PERRY'S VICTORY & INTL. PEACE MEM.
POINT PELEE N.P.
WRIGHT-PATTERSON A.F.B.
HOPEWELL CULTURE N.H.P.
GEORGE ROGERS CLARK N.H.P.
Longitude West 85° of Greenwich

WESTERN GULF COAST
ALBERS CONIC EQUAL-AREA PROJECTION
SCALE 1:3,000,000
0 KILOMETERS 60 80
0 MILES 20 40 60 80
GULF OF MEXICO
ARKANSAS
LOUISIANA
MISSISSIPPI
ALABAMA
TEXAS
FLA.
Longitude West 90° of Greenwich
New Orleans
Baton Rouge
Jackson
Shreveport
Houston
Mobile
Beaumont
Lafayette
Galveston
Pasadena
Metairie
JEAN LAFITTE N.H.P. & PRESERVE
GULF ISLANDS NATIONAL SEASHORE
SABINE NATIONAL WILDLIFE REFUGE
BIG THICKET NATIONAL PRESERVE
JOHNSON SPACE CENTER
VICKSBURG N.M.P.
FORT POLK
BARKSDALE A.F.B.
KEESLER A.F.B.
FORT MORGAN
FLOWER GARDEN BANKS NATIONAL MARINE SANCTUARY
Chandeleur Islands
Lake Pontchartrain
Isles Dernieres
Marsh Island
Galveston Island
Mississippi River Delta
Atchafalaya Bay
Terrebonne Bay
Timbalier Bay
Chandeleur Sound
Breton Sound
Toledo Bend Reservoir
Sam Rayburn Reservoir
Claypile Bank
Stetson Bank
East Flower Garden Bank
West Flower Garden Bank

SOUTHERN NEW ENGLAND
ALBERS CONIC EQUAL-AREA PROJECTION
SCALE 1:1,750,000
0 KILOMETERS 10 20 30 40 50
0 MILES 10 20 30 40 50
ATLANTIC OCEAN
Gulf of Maine
Massachusetts Bay
Cape Cod Bay
Long Island Sound
Block Island Sound
Rhode Island Sound
Nantucket Sound
Vineyard Sound
Muskeget Channel
NEW YORK
VERMONT
NEW HAMPSHIRE
MAINE
MASSACHUSETTS
CONNECTICUT
RHODE ISLAND
NEW JERSEY
LONG ISLAND
Adirondack Mountains
Green Mountains
White Mountains
Longfellow Mts.
Appalachian Mountains
Lake Champlain
Lake George
Lake Winnipesaukee
Sebago Lake
Quabbin Res.
Isles of Shoals
Cape Ann
Cape Cod
CAPE COD NATIONAL SEASHORE
Martha's Vineyard
Nantucket Island
Elizabeth Is.
Block Island
FIRE ISLAND NATIONAL SEASHORE
GATEWAY NAT. RECREATION AREA
SARATOGA NATIONAL HISTORICAL PARK
ST.-GAUDENS N.H.S.
FORT DEVENS
SOUTH WEYMOUTH N.A.S.
BRUNSWICK N.A.S.
NAVAL SUBMARINE BASE
INTRACOASTAL WATERWAY
APPALACHIAN NAT. SCENIC TRAIL
LONG TRAIL
Mount Washington
Mount Marcy 1629
Whiteface Mountain
Mount Mansfield 1339
Mt. Greylock 1064
Mt. Monadnock 965
Augusta
Concord
Montpelier
Boston
Providence
Hartford
Albany
Manchester
Worcester
Springfield
Portland
Burlington
Cambridge
New Haven
Bridgeport
Stamford
Waterbury
Lowell
Waltham
Yonkers
NEW YORK
Jersey City
44°
43°
42°
41°
74°
73°
72°
71°
70°
Longitude West 72° of Greenwich

PENINSULAR FLORIDA
ALBERS CONIC EQUAL-AREA PROJECTION
SCALE 1:2,500,000
0 KILOMETERS 40 60
0 MILES 20 40 60
Longitude West 81° of Greenwich
83°
82°
81°
80°
29°
28°
27°
26°
25°
FLORIDA
ATLANTIC OCEAN
GULF OF MEXICO
BAHAMAS
Straits of Florida
Florida Keys
Dekle Beach
Salem
Piney Point
Steinhatchee
Jena
Mallory Swamp
Shamrock
Cross City
Old Town
Horseshoe Beach
Horseshoe Cove
Suwannee
Suwannee Sound
Cedar Key
Waccasassa Bay
Fort White
Brooker
Hampton
High Springs
Alachua
Waldo
Keystone Heights
Newberry
Gainesville
Melrose
Trenton
Archer
Hawthorne
Chiefland
Micanopy
Bronson
McIntosh
Island Grove
Otter Creek
Williston
Reddick
Citra
Fairfield
Gulf Hammock
Anthony
Silver Springs
Rainbow Springs
Ocala
Dunnellon
Turtle Creek Pt.
Yankeetown
Inglis
Crystal River
Crystal Bay
Homosassa Springs
Homosassa
Chassahowitzka
Beverly Hills
Inverness
Floral City
Belleview
Oklawaha
Weirsdale
Wildwood
Coleman
Bushnell
Webster
Center Hill
Weeki Wachee
Weeki Wachee Spring
Brooksville
Spring Hill
Hudson
Bayonet Point
New Port Richey
Elfers
Tarpon Springs
Palm Harbor
Dunedin
Clearwater
Largo
Pinellas Park
St. Petersburg
Gulfport
Mullet Key
Tampa
Tampa Bay
Brandon
Gibsonton
MACDILL A.F.B.
Wimauma
Parrish
Palmetto
Ellenton
Bradenton
Bradenton Beach
Longboat Key
Oneco
Sarasota
Fruitville
Bee Ridge
Siesta Key
Osprey
Venice
North Port
Englewood
Port Charlotte
Charlotte Harbor
Punta Gorda
Placida
Gasparilla Island
Boca Grande
Pine Island
Saint James City
Captiva
Captiva Island
Sanibel Island
Fort Myers Beach
Fort Myers
North Fort Myers
Cape Coral
Bonita Springs
North Naples
Naples
East Naples
Marco
Goodland
Cape Romano
Ten Thousand Is.
Trilby
Lacoochee
Saint Leo
Dade City
Land O'Lakes
Zephyrhills
Thonotosassa
Plant City
Dover
Mulberry
Lakeland
Auburndale
Eagle Lake
Winter Haven
Haines City
Davenport
Homeland
Bradley Junction
Bowling Green
Wauchula
Zolfo Springs
Manatee
Myakka City
Peace
Arcadia
Nocatee
Fort Ogden
Lake Wales
Babson Park
Frostproof
Avon Park
Sebring
Lake Istokpoga
Lake Placid
Venus
Palmdale
Caloosahatchee
La Belle
Lehigh Acres
Immokalee
Corkscrew Swamp Sanctuary
Sunniland
Big Cypress Swamp
BIG CYPRESS NATIONAL PRESERVE
Ochopee
Everglades City
Chokoloskee
CASTILLO DE SAN MARCOS N.M.
Anastasia Island
St. Augustine
Red Snapper Sink
FORT MATANZAS N.M.
Elkton
Hastings
Marineland
Palatka
East Palatka
Pomona Park
Welaka
Crescent City
Georgetown
Palm Coast
Flagler Beach
Bunnell
Ormond by the Sea
Seville
Lake George
Ormond Beach
Holly Hill
Daytona Beach
Pierson
South Daytona
Barberville
Port Orange
De Leon Springs
De Land
Lake Helen
New Smyrna Beach
Orange City
Edgewater
DeBary
Deltona
Oak Hill
Eustis
Tavares
Lake Monroe
Sanford
CANAVERAL N.S.
Leesburg
Mount Dora
Mosquito Lagoon
Zellwood
Apopka
Casselberry
Mims
Groveland
Ocoee
Pine Hills
Winter Park
Titusville
Christmas
Clermont
Orlando
JOHN F. KENNEDY SPACE CENTER
Cape Canaveral (Cape Kennedy)
Cape Canaveral
Walt Disney World
Lake Buena Vista
Cocoa
Merritt Island
Kissimmee
Rockledge
Cocoa Beach
PATRICK A.F.B.
Saint Cloud
Holopaw
Satellite Beach
Indialantic
Melbourne
Melbourne Beach
Palm Bay
Singing Tower
Kenansville
Sebastian
Fellsmere
Wabasso
Gifford
Vero Beach
FLORIDA'S TURNPIKE
Florida Ridge
Saint Lucie
Basinger
Kissimmee
Fort Pierce
White City
Port Saint Lucie
Hutchinson Island
Okeechobee
Rio
Jensen Beach
Stuart
Port Salerno
Hobe Sound
Indiantown
SAINT LUCIE CANAL
Jupiter
Juno Beach
Lake Okeechobee
Canal Point
Palm Beach Gardens
Lake Park
Pahokee
Bryant
Moore Haven
Clewiston
Riviera Beach
West Palm Beach
Palm Beach
Lake Harbor
Belle Glade
South Bay
Palm Springs
Lake Worth
Lantana
Boynton Beach
Delray Beach
Boca Raton
Okaloacoochee Slough
Coral Springs
Deerfield Beach
Pompano Beach
Lighthouse Point
Lauderdale Lakes
Oakland Park
Plantation
Fort Lauderdale
Davie
Hollywood
Miramar
Hallandale
Carol City
North Miami
Hialeah
Miami
Miami Beach
Coral Gables
Key Biscayne
Kendall
Perrine
BISCAYNE N.P.
Biscayne Bay
Cutler Ridge
Homestead
Florida City
EVERGLADES N.P.
Everglades
Old Rhodes Key
Ponce de Leon Bay
Whitewater Bay
Cape Sable
Flamingo
Plantation Key
Florida Bay
Key Largo
Tavernier
Islamorada
Lower Matecumbe Key
Long Key
Key Colony Beach
Marathon
INTRACOASTAL WATERWAY
Sugarloaf Key
Snipe Keys
Perky
Big Pine Key
Summerland Key
Key West
Marquesas Keys
DRY TORTUGAS N.P.
Dry Tortugas
Mangrove Cay
Crishy Swash
West End Point
West End
Grand Bahama Island
Freeport
Eight Mile Rock
Lucaya
Pinders Point
Great Isaac
Little Isaac
East Isaac
North Bimini
Alice Town
Bimini Islands
South Bimini
Gun Cay
North Cat Cay
South Cat Cay
Ocean Cay
Brown's Cay

ARCTIC OCEAN
BEAUFORT SEA
BERING SEA
Bristol Bay
GULF OF ALASKA
PACIFIC OCEAN
QUEEN ELIZABETH
PARRY ISLANDS
ALASKA
NORTH SLOPE
Brooks Range
Alaska Range
Chugach Mts.
Mt. McKinley (Denali) 6194
Anchorage
Kenai Peninsula
Alaska Peninsula
Kodiak Island
Fairbanks
Nome
YUKON
Whitehorse
Dawson
Mackenzie Mountains
Selwyn Mts.
NORTHWEST TERRITORIES
Yellowknife
Great Slave Lake
Great Bear Lake
Victoria Island
Banks Island
Prince of Wales I.
Melville I.
Bathurst I.
CANADA
BRITISH COLUMBIA
COAST MOUNTAINS
ROCKY MOUNTAINS
Columbia Mountains
Cassiar Mountains
Queen Charlotte Is.
Vancouver Island
Vancouver
Victoria
Prince George
Kamloops
ALBERTA
Edmonton
Calgary
Jasper N.P.
Banff N.P.
SASKATCHEWAN
Saskatoon
Regina
Lake Athabasca
MANITOBA
Winnipeg
Lake Winnipeg
UNITED STATES
WASHINGTON
Seattle
Spokane
Mt. Rainier
OREGON
Portland
Salem
Crater Lake N.P.
CALIFORNIA
San Francisco
Sacramento
San Jose
Reno
SIERRA NEVADA
NEVADA
GREAT BASIN
IDAHO
Boise
MONTANA
Helena
Billings
WYOMING
Yellowstone N.P.
Grand Teton N.P.
UTAH
Salt Lake City
COLORADO
NORTH DAKOTA
Bismarck
SOUTH DAKOTA
Pierre
Black Hills
NEBRASKA
Lincoln
Omaha
Des Moines
Minneapolis

GREENLAND (KALAALLIT NUNAAT)
BAFFIN BAY
DAVIS STRAIT
LABRADOR SEA
ATLANTIC OCEAN
HUDSON BAY
NUNAVUT
QUEBEC
ONTARIO
NEWFOUNDLAND AND LABRADOR
NEW BRUNSWICK
NOVA SCOTIA
PRINCE EDWARD I.
MAINE
NEW YORK
PENNSYLVANIA
MICHIGAN
WISCONSIN
ILLINOIS
INDIANA
OHIO
Ellesmere Island
Devon Island
Bylot I.
BAFFIN ISLAND
AUYUITTUQ NATIONAL PARK
SIRMILIK NATIONAL PARK
Melville Peninsula
Southampton I.
Coats I.
Mansel Island
Foxe Basin
Foxe Peninsula
Hudson Strait
Ungava Bay
James Bay
Akimiski I.
Belcher Is.
LABRADOR
ISLAND OF NEWFOUNDLAND
I. d'Anticosti
Gulf of St. Lawrence
Gaspé Peninsula
Cape Breton I.
Sable Island Nova Scotia
Gulf of Maine
Lake Superior
Lake Michigan
Lake Huron
Lake Erie
Lake Ontario
Lake Nipigon
Iqaluit
Nuuk (Godthåb)
Kuujjuaq
Schefferville
Labrador City
Goose Bay
St. John's
Halifax
Québec
Montréal
Ottawa
Toronto
Hamilton
Buffalo
Rochester
Detroit
Chicago
Milwaukee
Cleveland
Pittsburgh
Boston
Providence
Hartford
NEW YORK
Philadelphia
Baltimore
Augusta
Fredericton
Charlottetown
Thunder Bay
AZIMUTHAL EQUIDISTANT PROJECTION
SCALE 1:16,000,000
0 KILOMETERS 300 400
0 MILES 100 200 300 400
Longitude West 66° of Greenwich

WESTERN CANADA
ALBERS CONIC EQUAL-AREA PROJECTION
SCALE 1:6,000,000
0 KILOMETERS 100 150
0 MILES 50 100 150
YUKON
BRITISH COLUMBIA
ALBERTA
ALASKA
WASHINGTON
IDAHO
PACIFIC OCEAN
VANCOUVER ISLAND
QUEEN CHARLOTTE ISLANDS
GWAII HAANAS NAT. PARK RES. AND HAIDA HERITAGE SITE
GLACIER BAY NAT. PARK AND PRESERVE
MISTY FIORDS NAT. MON.
JASPER NAT. PARK
BANFF NAT. PARK
GLACIER N.P.
MOUNT REVELSTOKE N.P.
KOOTENAY NAT. PARK
WATERTON GLACIER INTERNATIONAL PEACE PARK
NORTH CASCADES NAT. PARK
OLYMPIC NAT. PARK
PACIFIC RIM N.P. RESERVE
NAHANNI NAT. PARK RESERVE
Queen Charlotte Sound
Hecate Strait
Dixon Entrance
Strait of Juan de Fuca
Seattle
Vancouver
Victoria
Prince Rupert
Juneau
Whitehorse
Longitude West

NUNAVUT
HUDSON BAY
NORTHWEST TERRITORIES
CANADA
SASKATCHEWAN
MANITOBA
ONTARIO
MINNESOTA
NORTH DAKOTA
MONTANA
UNITED STATES
WOOD BUFFALO NATIONAL PARK
WAPUSK NATIONAL PARK
FORT PRINCE OF WALES NATIONAL HISTORICAL PARK
YORK FACTORY NATIONAL HISTORIC SITE
PRINCE ALBERT NAT. PARK
BATOCHE N.H.S.
RIDING MOUNTAIN NATIONAL PARK
GRASSLANDS NATIONAL PARK
GLACIER N.P.
WATERTON LAKES
UPPER MISSOURI RIVER BREAKS N.M.
FORT UNION TRADING POST N.H.S.
KNIFE RIVER INDIAN VILLAGES N.H.S.
MINOT A.F.B.
GRAND FORKS A.F.B.
Lake Athabasca
Lake Winnipeg
Lake Manitoba
Lake Winnipegosis
Reindeer Lake
Wollaston Lake
Churchill
Edmonton
Saskatoon
Regina
Winnipeg
Brandon
Prince Albert
North Battleford
Moose Jaw
Swift Current
Yorkton
Lloydminster
Flin Flon
The Pas
Thompson
Uranium City
Fort McMurray
Fort Chipewyan
Fort Resolution
Minot
Williston
Grand Forks
Havre
Glasgow
Medicine Hat
Lethbridge
111°
108°
105°
102°
99°
96°
93°
57°
54°
51°
48°

CENTRAL CANADA
ALBERS CONIC EQUAL-AREA PROJECTION
SCALE 1:6,000,000
0 KILOMETERS 100 150
0 MILES 50 100 150
CANADA
QUEBEC
ONTARIO
NUNAVUT
JAMES BAY
UNITED STATES
MINNESOTA
WISCONSIN
MICHIGAN
ILLINOIS
INDIANA
OHIO
PENNSYLVANIA
NEW YORK
IOWA
VT.
MASS.
CONN.
NEW JERSEY
LAKE SUPERIOR
LAKE MICHIGAN
LAKE HURON
LAKE ERIE
LAKE ONTARIO
GEORGIAN BAY
Thunder Bay
Sudbury
Toronto
Ottawa
Montréal
Detroit
Chicago
Milwaukee
Cleveland
Buffalo
Duluth
Green Bay
Grand Rapids
Kingston
London
Hamilton
Syracuse
Rochester
Toledo
Madison
Peoria
Cedar Rapids
Fort Wayne
Akron
Erie
NEW YORK
Sault Sainte Marie
Moosonee
ISLE ROYALE N.P.
PUKASKWA N.P.
PICTURED ROCKS NATIONAL LAKESHORE
SLEEPING BEAR DUNES N.L.
APOSTLE ISLANDS N.L.
VOYAGEURS N.P.
LA MAURICIE N.P.
BRUCE PENINSULA N.P.
GEORGIAN BAY ISLANDS N.P.
POINT PELEE N.P.
CUYAHOGA VALLEY N.P.
SAINT CROIX NATIONAL SCENIC RIVERWAY
Adirondack Mountains
Catskill Mts.
ALLEGHENY MTS.
APPALACHIAN MOUNTAINS

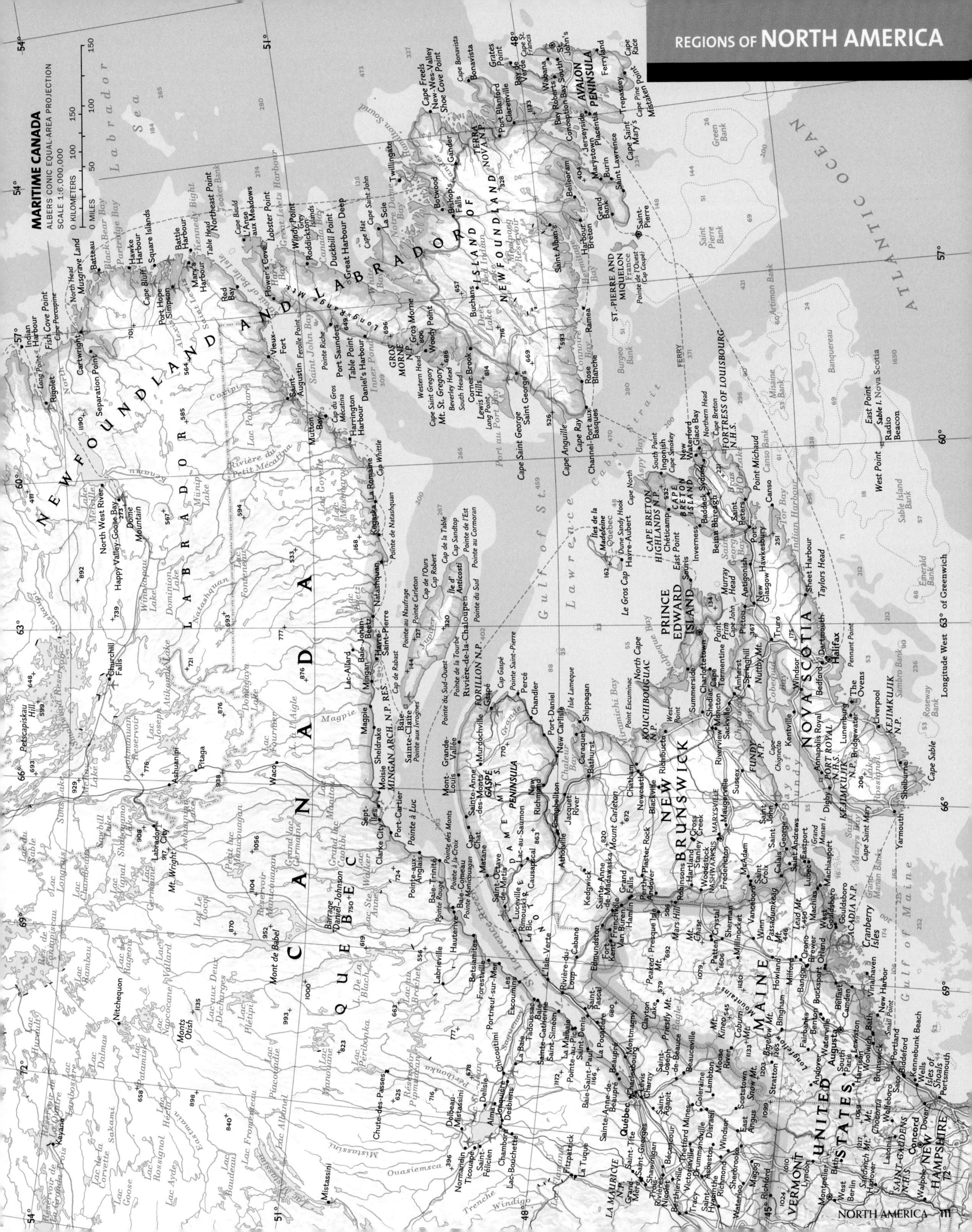
MARITIME CANADA
ALBERS CONIC EQUAL-AREA PROJECTION
SCALE 1:6,000,000
0 KILOMETERS 50 100 150
0 MILES 50 100 150
NEWFOUNDLAND AND LABRADOR
LABRADOR
ISLAND OF NEWFOUNDLAND
QUEBEC
CANADA
NEW BRUNSWICK
NOVA SCOTIA
PRINCE EDWARD ISLAND
CAPE BRETON ISLAND
GASPÉ PENINSULA
AVALON PENINSULA
ST.-PIERRE AND MIQUELON France
UNITED STATES
MAINE
NEW HAMPSHIRE
VERMONT
ATLANTIC OCEAN
Labrador Sea
Gulf of St. Lawrence
Bay of Fundy
Gulf of Maine
Cabot Strait
Strait of Belle Isle
Anticosti
Halifax
St. John's
Québec
Fredericton
Charlottetown
Augusta
Concord
Longitude West of Greenwich

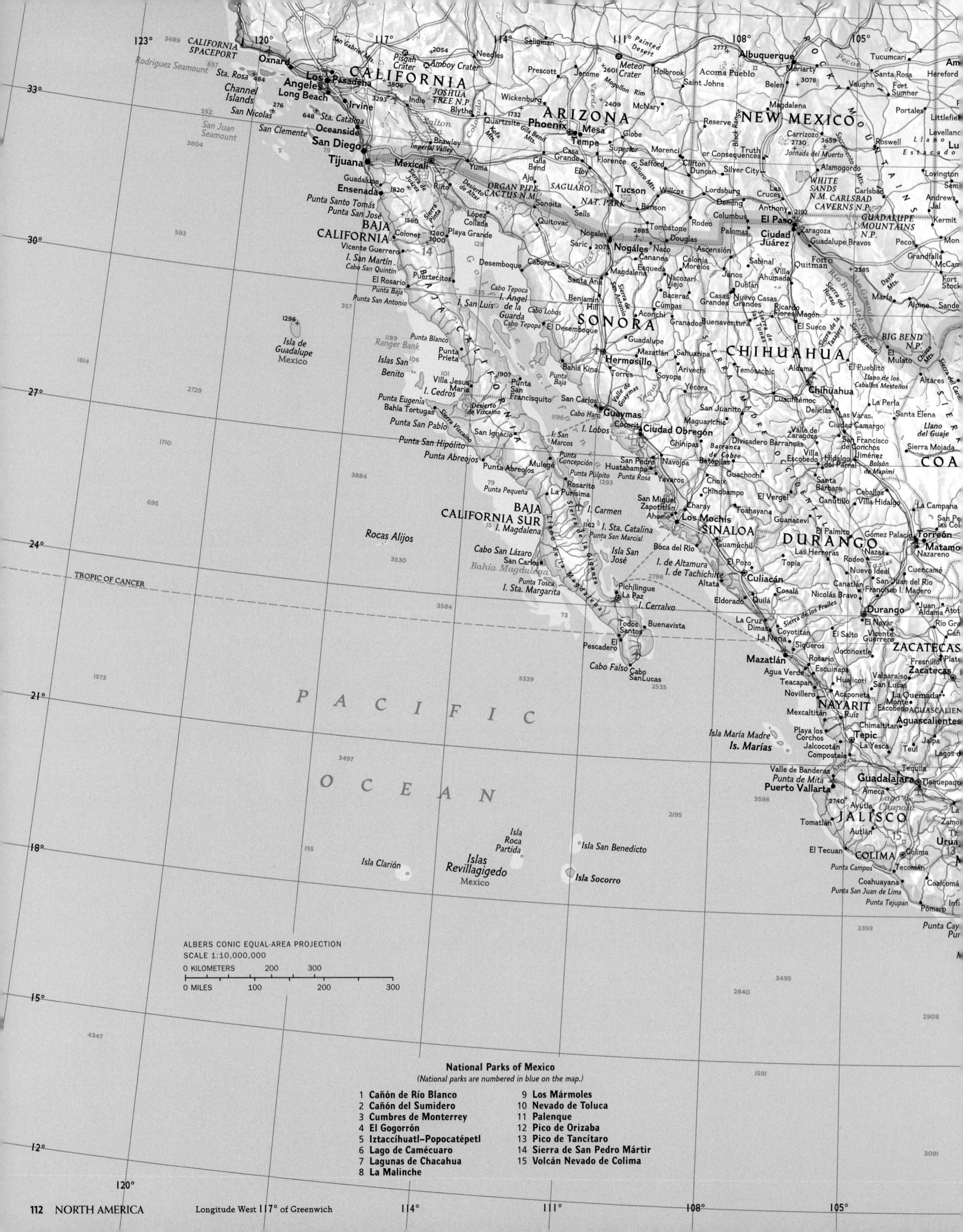

National Parks of Mexico

(National parks are numbered in blue on the map.)

1 Cañón de Río Blanco
2 Cañón del Sumidero
3 Cumbres de Monterrey
4 El Gogorrón
5 Iztaccíhuatl–Popocatépetl
6 Lago de Camécuaro
7 Lagunas de Chacahua
8 La Malinche
9 Los Mármoles
10 Nevado de Toluca
11 Palenque
12 Pico de Orizaba
13 Pico de Tancítaro
14 Sierra de San Pedro Mártir
15 Volcán Nevado de Colima

National Parks and Biotopes of Guatemala
(Protected areas are numbered in blue on the map.)
16 Sierra del Lacandón
17 Laguna del Tigre-Río Escondido
18 Laguna del Tigre
19 Mirador
20 Dos Lagunas
21 Río Azul
22 Tikal
UNITED STATES
OKLAHOMA
ARKANSAS
MISSISSIPPI
ALABAMA
GEORGIA
LOUISIANA
TEXAS
FLORIDA
MEXICO
NUEVO LEÓN
TAMAULIPAS
SAN LUIS POTOSÍ
HIDALGO
TLAXCALA
PUEBLA
VERACRUZ
GUERRERO
OAXACA
TABASCO
CHIAPAS
CAMPECHE
YUCATÁN
QUINTANA ROO
GUATEMALA
BELIZE
HONDURAS
EL SALVADOR
NICARAGUA
CUBA
GULF OF MEXICO
ATLANTIC OCEAN
Caribbean Sea
CAMPECHE BANK
TROPIC OF CANCER
YUCATÁN PENINSULA
Golfo de Tehuantepec
Gulf of Honduras
CAYMAN IS. U.K.
George Town
Oklahoma City
Memphis
Little Rock
Huntsville
Birmingham
Montgomery
Jackson
Shreveport
Dallas
Fort Worth
Austin
Houston
San Antonio
Corpus Christi
Baton Rouge
New Orleans
Mobile
Tallahassee
Jacksonville
Savannah
Orlando
Tampa
St. Petersburg
Miami
Key West
Brownsville
Matamoros
Monterrey
Saltillo
Nuevo Laredo
Laredo
Ciudad Victoria
Tampico
Poza Rica
Veracruz
Orizaba
Puebla
Toluca
MÉXICO
Acapulco
Oaxaca
Coatzacoalcos
Villahermosa
Tuxtla Gutiérrez
Tapachula
Campeche
Mérida
Cancún
Chetumal
Belmopan
Guatemala
Quetzaltenango
San Salvador
San Miguel
Tegucigalpa
San Pedro Sula
La Ceiba
Managua
La Habana (Havana)
Matanzas
Cienfuegos
Pinar del Río
Padre Island
PADRE ISLAND NATIONAL SEASHORE
EVERGLADES N.P.
Florida Keys
Dry Tortugas
Isla de Lobos
I. Cozumel
Isla Mujeres
Arrecife Alacranes
Islas Santanilla (Swan Islands) Honduras
Cayos Miskitos
Islas del Maíz
HALF MOON CAY NATURAL MONUMENT RESERVE
CHIQUIBUL N.P.
VOLCÁN MASAYA N.P.
99°
96°
93°
90°
87°
84°
30°
27°
24°
21°
18°
15°
12°

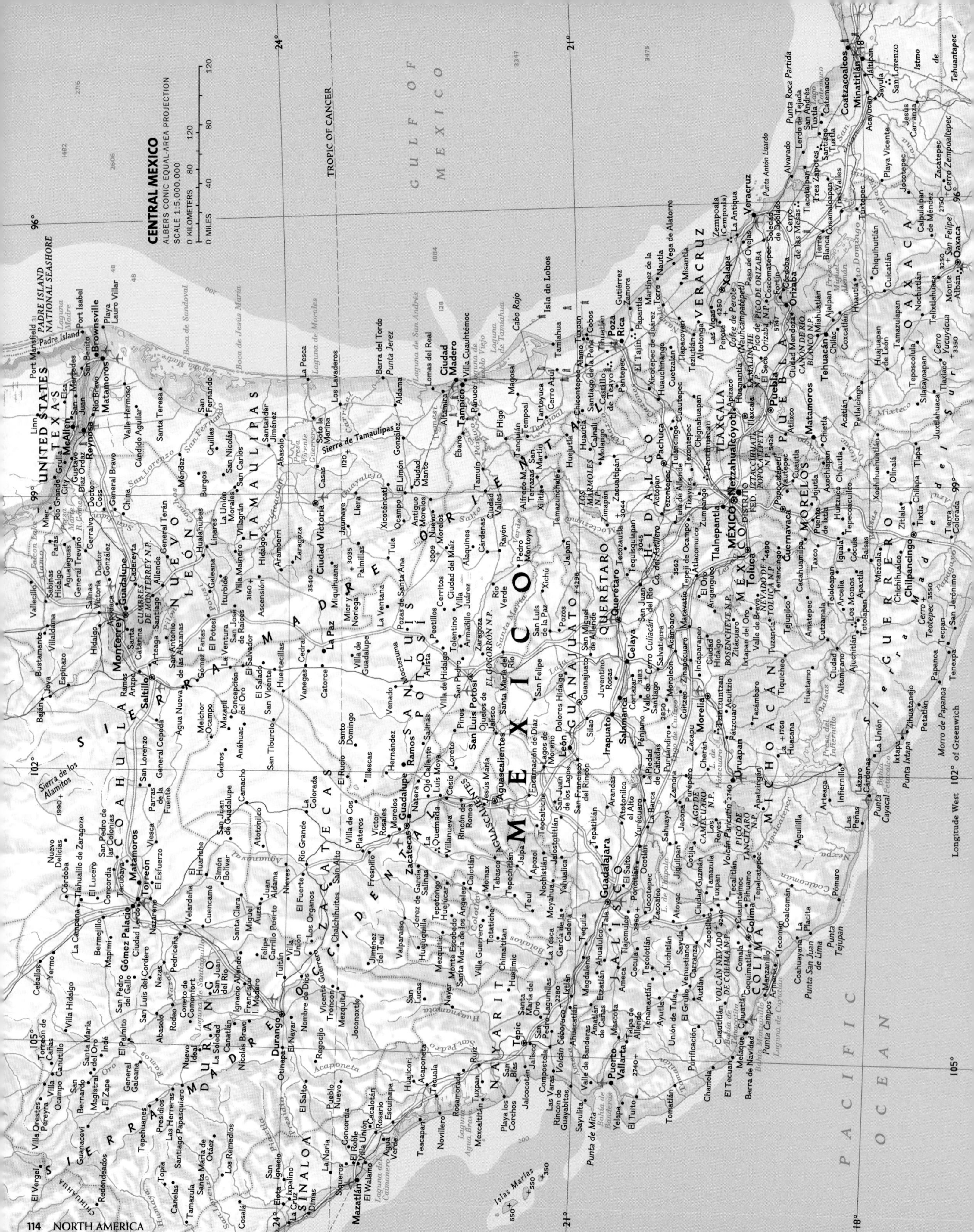

CENTRAL MEXICO

ALBERS CONIC EQUAL-AREA PROJECTION
SCALE 1:5,000,000

0 KILOMETERS 40 80 120
0 MILES 40 80 120

El Vergel
Villa Orestes Pereyra
Villa Ocampo
Torreón de Cañas
Canutillo
105°
Ceballos
Yermo
Villa Hidalgo
Nuevo Delicias
Córdoba
1990
Sierra de los Alamitos
102°
Bajan
Joya
Bustamante
Villaldama
Espinazo
Vallecillo
Sabinas Hidalgo
Falcon Lake
Parás
Agualeguas
General Treviño
Mier
Río Grande City
99°
Linn
Grulla
UNITED STATES
TEXAS
McAllen
Elsa
Mercedes
Port Mansfield
PADRE ISLAND NATIONAL SEASHORE
Padre Island
Laguna Madre
Port Isabel
San Benito
Brownsville
Playa Lauro Villar
96°
1482
2716
2606
48
CHIHUAHUA
Guanaceví
San Bernardo
Magistral
Santa María del Oro
Indé
El Zape
Redondeados
La Campana
Tlahualilo de Zaragoza
El Lucero
Bermejillo
Mapimí
Concordia
San Pedro de las Colonias
Tacubaya
COAHUILA
Gómez Palacio
Ciudad Lerdo
Matamoros
Torreón
Nazareno
El Esfuerzo
Viesca
Parras de la Fuente
San Lorenzo
General Cepeda
Ramos Arizpe
Saltillo
Arteaga
Monterrey
Apodaca
Guadalupe
Santa Catarina
CUMBRES DE MONTERREY N.P.
Santiago
Cadereyta
Allende
Hidalgo
Salinas Victoria
Doctor González
Cerralvo
Doctor Coss
Gustavo Díaz Ordaz
Reynosa
San Juan
Río Bravo
Matamoros
General Bravo
China
Valle Hermoso
Cándido Aguilar
General Terán
Santa Teresa
CENTRAL MEXICO
El Palmito
General Galeana
San Pedro del Gallo
San Luis del Cordero
Tepehuanes
Presidios
Topia
Las Herreras
Canelas
Santiago Papasquiaro
Tamazula
Abasolo
Rodeo
Nazas
Pedriceña
Nuevo Ideal
Coneto de Comonfort
Laguna de Santiaguillo
Santa María de Otáez
DURANGO
La Soledad
San Juan del Río
Canatlán
Los Remedios
Cosalá
Velardeña
El Huariche
Cuencamé
Simón Bolívar
Santa Clara
Miguel Auza
Juan Aldama
Ignacio Allende
Nicolás Bravo
Francisco I. Madero
San Juan de Guadalupe
Camacho
Atotonilco
Agua Nueva
Melchor Ocampo
Mazapil
Concepción del Oro
Cedros
Anáhuac
Gómez Farías
El Potosí
La Ventura
San José de Raíces
El Salvador
San Antonio de las Alazanas
Galeana
Iturbide
Hualahuises
Linares
Montemorelos
NUEVO LEÓN
Méndez
Burgos
Cruillas
San Fernando
Laguna Madre
Boca de Sandoval
La Unión
San Nicolás
San Carlos
Villa Mainero
Villagrán
3160
Hidalgo
Ascensión
TAMAULIPAS
Boca de Jesús María
San Tiburcio
San Vicente
El Salado
Huertecillas
Durango
Otinapa
Tuitán
Villa Unión
El Nayar
Nombre de Dios
Felipe Carrillo Puerto
Nieves
El Fuerte
Río Grande
La Colorada
24°
Elota
San Ignacio
Ixpalino
La Cruz
SINALOA
Dimas
El Salto
Regocijo
Vicente Guerrero
Los Organos
Troncon
ZACATECAS
Chalchihuites
Saín Alto
Vanegas
Cedral
Catorce
La Paz
Aramberri
Zaragoza
3540
Ciudad Victoria
Casas
Presa Vicente Guerrero
Abasolo
Santander Jiménez
Soto la Marina
La Pesca
Laguna de Morales
Los Lavaderos
La Noria
Pueblo Nuevo
Mezquital
Joconoxtle
Siqueros
Concordia
El Roble
Villa Unión
Mazatlán
El Walamo
Cacalotán
Rosario
Escuinapa
Agua Verde
Laguna del Caimanero
El Rucio
Santo Domingo
Villa de Cos
Plateros
Illescas
Villa de Guadalupe
Miquihuana
Mier y Noriega
3035
Palmillas
Jaumave
Llera
1120
Sierra de Tamaulipas
TROPIC OF CANCER
Jiménez del Teul
Fresnillo
Víctor Rosales
Morelos
Zacatecas
Guadalupe
Hernández
Ramos
Venado
Moctezuma
SAN LUIS POTOSÍ
La Ventana
Pozas de Santa Ana
Tula
Xicoténcatl
Ocampo
El Limón
González
Barra del Tordo
Punta Jerez
Aldama
Huajicori
Acaponeta
Tecuala
Teacapan
Novillero
Rosamorada
Laguna Agua Brava
Mexcaltitán
Tuxpan
Ruiz
San Lucas
Huejuquilla
Valparaíso
Jerez de García Salinas
Tepetongo
Huejúcar
Mezquitic
Monte Escobedo
Santa María de los Ángeles
Villa Guerrero
Colotlán
Totatiche
Momax
Tabasco
La Quemada
Villanueva
Rincón de Romos
Natera
Ojo Caliente
Luis Moya
Cosío
Loreto
Salinas
Arista
Peotillos
Villa de Hidalgo
Cerritos
Tolentino
Ciudad del Maíz
Villa Juárez
Armadillo
Antiguo Morelos
Ciudad Mante
2009
Nuevo Morelos
Alaquines
Laguna de San Andrés
Lomas del Real
Altamira
Ciudad Madero
Tampico
Villa Cuauhtémoc
Laguna de Pueblo Viejo
GULF OF MEXICO
1884
128
NAYARIT
Chimaltitán
Huajimic
Playa los Corchos
San Blas
Tepic
Jalcocotán
Jalisco
Santa María del Oro
Compostela
San Pedro Lagunillas
Islas Marías
650
550
350
200
AGUASCALIENTES
Jesús María
Aguascalientes
Tepechitlán
Jalpa
Teul
Apozol
MEXICO
Pinos
San Luis Potosí
Ojuelos de Jalisco
EL GOGORRÓN N.P.
San Pedro
Zaragoza
Santa María del Río
Río Verde
Cárdenas
Ciudad Valles
Tamuín
Ébano
Pánuco
Rayón
El Higo
Laguna de Tamiahua
Magosal
Cabo Rojo
Pedro Montoya
Alfredo M. Terrazas
Xilitla
San Martín
Tanquián
Tempoal
Tantoyuca
Cerro Azul
Tamiahua
Isla de Lobos
3347
Las Varas
Rincón de Guayabitos
Volcán Ceboruco
2280
Ixtlán
La Yesca
García de la Cadena
Moyahua
Nochistlán
Teocaltiche
Yahualica
Jalostotitlán
Encarnación de Díaz
Lagos de Moreno
San Juan de los Lagos
San Francisco del Rincón
León
San Felipe
Dolores Hidalgo
San Luis de la Paz
Xichú
Pozos
GUANAJUATO
4296
Jalpan
Tamazunchale
Huejutla
Chicontepec
Álamo
Tuxpan
Cobos
21°
Sayulita
Punta de Mita
Ahuacatlán
Valle de Banderas
Bahía de Banderas
Magdalena
Tequila
Amatlán de Cañas
Etzatlán
Ahualulco
Tala
Guadalajara
Tepatitlán
Arandas
Silao
Guanajuato
San Miguel de Allende
Irapuato
Juventino Rosas
QUERÉTARO
Querétaro
LOS MÁRMOLES N.P.
Zimapán
Huautla
Calnali
Molango
Santiago de la Peña
Tihuatlán
Castillo de Teayo
Poza Rica
Pantepec
Puerto Vallarta
Mascota
Talpa de Allende
Yelapa
El Tuito
2740
Ameca
Tlajomulco
JALISCO
Cocula
El Salto
Atotonilco el Alto
Salamanca
Celaya
Tecozautla
3044
Zacualtipán
Gutiérrez Zamora
Tenamaxtlán
Tecolotlán
2960
Poncitlán
Ocotlán
Yurécuaro
La Piedad de Cabadas
Pénjamo
Cortazar
3183
Valle de Santiago
Cerro Culiacán
Salvatierra
San Juan del Río
Tequisquiapan
3045
HIDALGO
Co. del Astillero
Actopan
Pachuca
El Tajín
Papantla
Martínez de la Torre
Nautla
Vega de Alatorre
Ayutla
Unión de Tula
Tomatlán
Juchitlán
Jocotepec
Zacoalco
L. de Chapala
La Barca
Sahuayo
Jiquilpan
Zamora
Puruándiro
2850
Lago de Cuitzeo
Moroleón
Acámbaro
3562
Tezontepec
Tulancingo
Xicotepec de Juárez
Huauchinango
Cuetzalan
Atoyac
Sayula
El Grullo
Venustiano Carranza
Autlán
Purificación
Chamela
Cotija
Jacona
Purépero
Zacapu
Cuitzeo
Zinapécuaro
Maravatío
Tepeji de Ocampo
Tula de Allende
Tizayuca
Tezontepec
Cuautepec
Tlapacoyan
Misantla
Ciudad Guzmán
Tamazula
Zapotiltic
Tuxpan
4240
LAGO DE CAMÉCUARO N.P.
Los Reyes
Cherán
Morelia
Indaparapeo
Atlacomulco
Zumpango
Teotihuacán
Chignahuapan
Teziutlán
Altotonga
VERACRUZ
Cuautitlán
VOLCÁN NEVADO DE COLIMA N.P.
Bahía de Tenacatita
El Tecuan
Melaque
Cihuatlán
Barra de Navidad
Bahía Manzanillo
Comala
Coquimatlán
Colima
Cuauhtémoc
Tecalitlán
Pihuamo
Volcán Paricutín
2740
PICO DE TANCÍTARO N.P.
L. de Pátzcuaro
Tzintzuntzan
Pátzcuaro
Acuitzio
Uruapan
Ciudad Hidalgo
El Oro
Angangueo
BOSENCHEVE N.P.
Zitácuaro
Tlalnepantla
MÉXICO
Netzahualcóyotl
TLAXCALA
Apizaco
Huamantla
Las Vigas
Perote
4250
Cofre de Perote (Nauhcampatépetl)
Xalapa
Zempoala (Cempoala)
La Antigua
Punta Campos
Manzanillo
Armería
COLIMA
Tepalcatepec
Apatzingán
Tecomán
Laguna de Cuyutlán
Coalcomán
Tacámbaro
MICHOACÁN
Ixtapan del Oro
Valle de Bravo
NEVADO DE TOLUCA N.P.
Toluca
DISTRITO FED.
IZTACCÍHUATL-POPOCATÉPETL N.P.
4690
5426
Tlaxcala
LA MALINCHE N.P.
Puebla
El Seco
Pico de Orizaba
PICO DE ORIZABA N.P.
5747
Coscomatepec
Fortín
Córdoba
Orizaba
Paso de Ovejas
Veracruz
Soledad de Doblado
Punta Antón Lizardo
Cerro de las Mesas
Alvarado
Punta Roca Partida
Coahuayana
La Placita
Punta San Juan de Lima
Punta Tejupan
Aguililla
La Huacana
1768
Tuzantla
Tiquicheo
Tenancingo
Tejupilco
Cuernavaca
Popocatépetl
Yautepec
Cuautla
Atlixco
PUEBLA
Ciudad Mendoza
CAÑÓN DE RÍO BLANCO N.P.
Miahuatlán
Tlacotalpan
Lerdo de Tejada
San Andrés Tuxtla
Tres Zapotes
Santiago Tuxtla
Laguna Catemaco
Catemaco
Pómaro
Arteaga
Infiernillo
Presa del Infiernillo
Huetamo
Amatepec
Cacahuamilpa
MORELOS
Taxco
Puente de Ixtla
Jojutla
Axochiapan
Matamoros
Chietla
Tehuacán
Chilac
Ajalpan
Presa Miguel Alemán
Tierra Blanca
Cosamaloapan
Tres Valles
Coatzacoalcos
Minatitlán
PACIFIC OCEAN
18°
Las Peñas
Lázaro Cárdenas
Ciudad Altamirano
Cutzamala
Teloloapan
Arcelia
Los Monos
Ajuchitlán
Totolapan
Apaxtla
Iguala
Cocula
Huitzuco
Tepecoacuilco
Chiautla
Acatlán
Petlalcingo
Huautla
Coxcatlán
Santo Domingo
Tuxtepec
Acayucan
Jáltipan
Punta Cayacal
Bahía Petacalco
La Unión
Ixtapa
Punta Ixtapa
Zihuatanejo
Petatlán
GUERRERO
Sierra Madre del Sur
Mezcala
Balsas
Xochihuehuetlán
Chichihualco
Chilpancingo
Olinalá
Zitlala
Chilapa
Tixtla
Tlapa
Huajuapan de León
Tamazulapan
Teposcolula
Silacayoapan
Juxtlahuaca
Tlaxiaco
Cerro Yucuyácua
3350
Nochixtlán
Telixtlahuaca
3250
Monte Albán
Oaxaca
San Felipe
OAXACA
Chiquihuitlán
Cuicatlán
Calpulalpan de Méndez
2750
Cerro Zempoaltepec
Jocotepec
Playa Vicente
Jesús Carranza
Sayula
San Lorenzo
Istmo de Tehuantepec
Morro de Papanoa
Papanoa
Tecpan
Tenexpa
Cerro Teotepec
3550
San Jerónimo
Tierra Colorada
Zacatepec
105°
Longitude West 102° of Greenwich
99°
96°
3475

CENTRAL AMERICA
ALBERS CONIC EQUAL-AREA PROJECTION
SCALE 1:8,000,000
0 KILOMETERS 120 160 200
0 MILES 40 80 120 160 200
GULF OF MEXICO
PACIFIC OCEAN
CARIBBEAN SEA
Greater Antilles
MEXICO
YUCATÁN
PENINSULA
CAMPECHE
QUINTANA ROO
TABASCO
CHIAPAS
BELIZE
GUATEMALA
HONDURAS
EL SALVADOR
NICARAGUA
COSTA RICA
PANAMÁ
COLOMBIA
CUBA
HAITI
JAMAICA
CAYMAN ISLANDS
United Kingdom
SAN ANDRÉS Y PROVIDENCIA
Colombia
Golfo de Panamá
Gulf of Honduras
Bahía de la Ascensión
Islas Santanilla (Swan Islands) Honduras
Islas de la Bahía Honduras
Cayos Miskitos
N.W. Rocks Colombia
Pedro Cays Jamaica
Morant Cays Jamaica
Managua
Tegucigalpa
San Salvador
Guatemala
San José
Panamá
Belmopan
Kingston
Barranquilla
Cartagena
Medellín
Montería
Santiago de Cuba
George Town
Grand Cayman
Little Cayman
U.S. NAVAL BASE GUANTANAMO BAY
Isla del Coco Costa Rica
Longitude West 84° of Greenwich

Gulf of Mexico
TROPIC OF CAPRICORN
FLORIDA
UNITED STATES
Port Charlotte
Arcadia
Stuart
West Palm Beach
Fort Myers
Belle Glade
Sanibel Island
Naples
BIG CYPRESS NAT. PRESERVE
Delray Beach
Pompano Beach
Fort Lauderdale
Hollywood
Miami
Cape Romano
Everglades City
Homestead
EVERGLADES N.P.
Ponce de Leon Bay
Cape Sable
Key Largo
Marquesas Keys
Key West
Florida Keys
Marathon
Little Abaco Island
Cooper's Town
Grand Bahama I.
Freeport
High Rock
Tilloo Cay
Moore's I.
Abaco Island
Bimini Islands
Southwest Point
Berry Islands
Nassau
New Providence
Eleuthera Island
Rock Sound
Williams I.
Flamingo Point
Little San Salvador
Andros Island
Big Wood Cay
Exuma Sound
Kemps Bay
Gt. Guana Cay
Cistern Point
Great Exuma
Little Exuma
Deadman's Cays
Dog Rocks
Elbow Cays
Cay Sal Bank
Santaren Channel
Damas Cays
Anguilla Cays
GREAT BAHAMA BANK
Long Cay
La Habana (Havana)
GUANABACOA
Archipiélago de Sabana
Matanzas
Corralillo
Cayo Sta. María
La Esperanza
Artemisa
LA HABANA
MATANZAS
Quemado de Güines
Colón
VILLA CLARA
PINAR DEL RÍO
Pinar del Río
Los Palacios
Península de Zapata
Caibarién
Cayo Coco
Arch. de Camagüey
Ciudad Sandino
Mantua
Santa Clara
CIEGO DE ÁVILA
Cruces
Cabaiguán
Cienfuegos
CIENFUEGOS
Sancti Spíritus
SANCTI SPÍRITUS
Bolivia
Ciego de Ávila
Cayo Romano
Cayo Guajaba
Cayo Sabinal
Cabo de San Antonio
Cabo Francés
Cayos de San Felipe
Punta Francés
Nueva Gerona
Arch. de los Canarreos
Cayo Largo
Cayos de Dios
Cayo del Rosario
I. DE LA JUVENTUD
CAMAGÜEY
Camagüey
Minas
CUBA
LAS TUNAS
Gibara
Cayos Ana María
Cayo Bretón
Cayos Cinco Balas
Cayo Grande
Cayo Anclitas
Contramaestre
Punta Macurijes
Guáimaro
Las Tunas
Holguín
HOLGUÍN
Santa Cruz del Sur
Guayabal
Bayamo
GRANMA
SANTIAGO DE CUBA
Niquero
Sierra Maestra
Cabo Cruz
Santiago de Cuba
GREATER
Little Cayman
West End Point
CAYMAN ISLANDS U.K.
George Town
Grand Cayman
Montego Bay
St. Ann's Bay
North Negril Point
South Negril Point
Browns Town
Port Maria
Northeast Point
Port Antonio
Morant Point
Savanna-la-Mar
JAMAICA
Spanish Town
Kingston
Great Pedro Bluff
The Alley
Portland Point
CARIBBEAN
Islas Santanilla (Swan Islands) Honduras
Half Moon Reefs
North West Rocks Colombia
SAN ANDRÉS Y PROVIDENCIA
Isla de Providencia Colombia
Roncador Bank
Isla de San Andrés Colombia
Islas del Maíz Nicaragua
I. del Maíz Grande (Great Corn Island) Nicaragua
Isla Pérez
Arrecife Alacránes
CAMPECHE BANK
Bancos Ingleses
Banco Nuevo
Cayos Arcas
Isla Holbox
Cabo Catoche
Punta Holohit
Punta Yalkubul
Dzilam de Bravo
Progreso
Chelem
El Cuyo
Dzonot Carretero
Chiquilá
Isla Mujeres
I. Cancún
Cancún
Sisal
Hunucmá
Dzibilchaltún
Mérida
Izamal
Tizimín
Umán
Espita
Maxcanú
Acancéh
Pisté
Valladolid
Chichén Itzá
Cobá
Puerto Morelos
Punta Molas
Isla Cozumel
Calkiní
Mayapán
Muna
Uxmal
Ticul
Tepich
Tulum
Jaina
Peto
Tihosuco
Punta Celarain
Campeche
YUCATÁN
Hopelchén
Dzuiché
Edzná
Punta Allen
Vigia Chico
Champotón
Dzibalchén
Felipe Carrillo Puerto
MEXICO
CAMPECHE
QUINTANA ROO
YUCATÁN PENINSULA
Punta Herrero
Sabancuy
Escárcega
Majahual
Centenario
Becán
Xpuhil
Calderitas
Cayo Norte
Banco Chinchorro
Cayo Lobos
Kohunlich
Chetumal
Monclova
Ramonal
Orange Walk
Bahía de Chetumal
Balancán
Calakmul
Cuello
Altun Ha
Ambergris Cay
TABASCO
El Mirador
San Pedro
Tenosique
Carmelita
Dos Lagunas
Hill Bank
Belize City
Turneffe Is.
El Ceibo
Uaxactún
TIKAL N.P.
Tikal
Piedras Negras
Flores
San Ignacio
Belmopan
Northern Cay
Lighthouse Reef
Yaxchilán
PETÉN
BELIZE
Dangriga
HALF MOON CAY NATURAL MONUMENT RESERVE
Bonampak
La Libertad
CHIQUIBUL N.P.
Glover Reef
CHIAPAS
Seibal
Maya Mts.
Jonathan Point
Naj Tunich
Placentia Point
Isla de Roatán
Isla de Guanaja
Santa Amelia
San Luis
Monkey River Town
Islas de la Bahía
Gulf of Honduras
Sarstoon
GUATEMALA
Livingston
Puerto Barrios
Puerto Cortés
Punta Sal
Isla de Utila
Cabo Camarón
Trujillo
La Ceiba
Tela
PICO BONITO N.P.
Payas
Brus Laguna
Barra Patuca
Cobán
Sierra de los Cuchumatanes
San Pedro Sula
Quimistán
Quiriguá
El Progreso
Olanchito
Sierra de las Minas
La Lima
Yoro
San Esteban
Laguna de Caratasca
Sierra Madre
Zacapa
Guálan
SIERRA DE AGALTA N.P.
Wampusirpi
Puerto Lempira
Cabo Falso
Chimaltenango
Chiquimula
Copán
Manto
San Francisco de la Paz
Cabo Gracias a Dios
Guatemala
Las Minas
HONDURAS
Juticalpa
Bilwaskarma
Escuintla
Jutiapa
MONTECRISTO N.P.
Comayagua
Villa de San Antonio
PATUCA N.P.
Ninayeri
Cayos Miskitos
Chiquimulilla
Santa Ana
La Esperanza
Ahuachapán
San José
Sonsonate
EL SALVADOR
LA TIGRA N.P.
Tegucigalpa
Bocay
Punta Gorda
Dákura
Cojutepeque
Bonanza
Tuapí
Puerto Cabezas
San Salvador
San Miguel
Nacaome
San Lorenzo
Murra
Kilambé
Siuna
Puerto El Triunfo
Punta San Juan
Golfo de Fonseca
Choluteca
Yalagüina
Kuikuina
Punta Cosigüina
Potosí
Somotillo
Estelí
Jinotega
Prinzapolka
Matagalpa
Puerto Morazán
La Trinidad
San Pedro del Norte
La Barra
NICARAGUA
Chinandega
León
Lago de Managua
Laguna de Perlas
Managua
Tipitapa
La Libertad
Rama
Haulover
Masaya
VOLCÁN MASAYA N.P.
Granada
Acoyapa
Bluefields
Casares
Rivas
Lago de Nicaragua
I. del Venado
San Jorge
Punta Gorda
Punta Mono (Monkey Point)
San Juan del Sur
PACIFIC OCEAN
Cabo Santa Elena
SANTA ROSA N.P.
Peñas Blancas
La Cruz
San Carlos
El Castillo de Las Concepción
San Juan del Norte
Golfo de Papagayo
Liberia
Altamira
Tortuguero
TORTUGUERO N.P.
Sardinal
Cabo Velas
Cañas
COSTA RICA
Parismina
Nicoya
Esparza
Punta Guiones
Puntarenas
Puerto Limón
San José
Cartago
CAHUITA N.P.
Cabo Blanco
Golfo de Nicoya
Golfo de los Mosquitos
CHIRRIPÓ N.P.
Sixaola
I. Colón
Isla Bastimentos
I. Cayo Agua
Portobelo
PORTOBELO N.P.
Colón
El Porvenir
Archipiélago de San Blas
Punta Judas
LA AMISTAD N.P.
I. Popa
Cusapin
SOBERANÍA N.P.
CHAGRES N.P.
Ciudad Cortés
Palmar Sur
Bahía de Coronado
Santa Catalina
PANAMA
Panamá
Lago Bayano
Ailigandí
Punta Llorona
Golfito
Cañas Gordas
OMAR TORRIJOS N.P.
La Pintada
Golfo de Panamá
Chimán
Cabo Tiburón
Puerto Jiménez
Punta Banco
Antón
I. del Rey
Puerto Obaldía
CORCOVADO N.P.
Puerto Armuelles
ANTIOQUIA
Barranquilla
Puerto Colombia
ATLÁNTICO
Cartagena
Turbaco
Bahía de Barbacoas
SUCRE
Carmen de Bolívar
Tolú
Sincelejo
Lorica
CÓRDOBA
Montería
Planeta Rica
ALBERS CONIC EQUAL-AREA PROJECTION
SCALE 1:8,000,000
0 KILOMETERS 40 80 120 160 200
0 MILES 40 80 120 160 200
Red circled numbers are reference keys to larger scale maps on page 118.

Longitude West 72° of Greenwich
69°
66°
63°
24°
21°
18°
15°
12°
9°
ATLANTIC OCEAN
San Salvador (Watling)
Samana Cay
Plana Cays (French Cays)
Mayaguana I.
TURKS AND CAICOS ISLANDS
U.K.
East Caicos
West Caicos
Caicos Is.
Turks Islands
Cockburn Town
Little Inagua Island
Great Inagua Island
Ambergris Cays
Mouchoir Passage
Matthew Town
Baracoa
Punta de Maisí
Île de la Tortue
HISPANIOLA
Cabo Isabela
Monte Cristi
Jean-Rabel
Anse-à-Foleur
Cap-à-Foux
Anse-Rouge
Cap-Haïtien
HAITI
Dessalines
Saint-Marc
I. de la Gonâve
Pointe Ouest
Anse-à-Galets
Hinche
Grande Cayemite
Massif de la Hotte
Port-au-Prince
Miragoâne
Jacmel
Les Cayes
Côtes-de-Fer
Port-Piment
Imbert
Puerto Plata
Cabo Francés Viejo
Abreú
Bahía Escocesa
Mao
Santiago
San Francisco de Macorís
Cordillera Central
Cabo Cabrón
Cabo Samaná
Samaná
Cabo San Rafael
DOMINICAN REPUBLIC
Sabana de La Mar
El Macao
Comendador
San Juan
Santo Domingo
Higüey
Cabo Engaño
Neiba
Azua
Baní
Duvergé
Cabral
Barahona
Nizao
San Pedro de Macorís
La Romana
Isla Saona
Isla Beata
Cabo Beata
Punta Higüero
I. Mona P.R.
Mayagüez
Cabo Rojo
San Germán
Utuado
San Juan
Cayey
Ponce
PUERTO RICO
United States
Vieques P.R.
Charlotte Amalie
St. Thomas
St. John
Tortola
Virgin Gorda
Anegada
U.K. Virgin Gorda
BRITISH VIRGIN ISLANDS U.K.
Road Town
U.S. VIRGIN ISLANDS U.S.
St. Croix
Christiansted
Sombrero
ANGUILLA U.K.
The Valley
St. Martin France & Neth. Antilles
St.-Barthélemy France
Gustavia
Saba Neth. Antilles
St. Eustatius Neth. Antilles
Barbuda
ANTIGUA AND BARBUDA
Basseterre
Nevis
St. John's
Antigua
ST. KITTS AND NEVIS
Montserrat
Plymouth
MONTSERRAT U.K.
Guadeloupe Passage
LEEWARD ISLANDS
GUADELOUPE France
Grande-Terre
La Désirade
Basse-Terre
Pointe-à-Pitre
Marie-Galante
Les Saintes
Dominica Passage
DOMINICA
Roseau
Martinique Passage
Mgne. Pelée
Sainte-Marie
Martinique
Fort-de-France
MARTINIQUE France
Pointe d'Enfer
St. Lucia Channel
ST. LUCIA
Castries
St. Vincent Passage
ST. VINCENT AND THE GRENADINES
Kingstown
Bequia
Canouan
Union
Carriacou
GRENADA
Hillsborough
St. George's
Pt. Salines
WINDWARD ISLANDS
Speightstown
Bridgetown
BARBADOS
LESSER ANTILLES
ANTILLES
CARIBBEAN SEA
MONTSERRAT
Eruptions from Soufriere Hills volcano since 1995 have forced the evacuation of southern Montserrat—including its capital, Plymouth.
NETHERLANDS ANTILLES
The Netherlands Antilles consist of the islands of Curaçao and Bonaire off Venezuela and Saba, St. Eustatius, and southern St. Martin (St. Maarten) in the Leeward Islands. Aruba separated from the Netherlands Antilles in 1986.
Punta Gallinas
Bahía Honda
Bahía de Portete
ARUBA Neth.
Oranjestad
NETHERLANDS ANTILLES
Curaçao
Bonaire
Willemstad
Península de Paraguaná
Islas de Aves Venez.
Islas Los Roques Venez.
ARCHIPIÉLAGO LOS ROQUES N.P.
Netherlands
Venezuela
Cayo Grande
La Blanquilla
Los Hermanos
Cabo de la Vela
Península de la Guajira
Puerto López
Uribia
Riohacha
Santa Marta
GUAJIRA
Paraguaipoa
Golfo de Venezuela
Punto Fijo
Punta Cardón
MÉDANOS DE CORO N.P.
Puerto Cumarebo
Coro
La Vela de Coro
FALCÓN
Mirimire
Chichiriviche
MORROCOY N.P.
Tucacas
San Rafael
Mara
Dabajuro
Churuguara
Valledupar
Maracaibo
Puerto Mirando
Santa Rita
Rosario
Cabimas
Lagunillas
Sierra de Perijá
Caracolí
CÉSAR
Machiques
PERIJA N.P.
ZULIA
Lago de Maracaibo
Mene Grande
TRUJILLO
Trujillo
Valera
Betijoque
Bobures
Encontrados
El Banco
MAGDALENA
COLOMBIA
BOLÍVAR
NORTE DE SANTANDER
MÉRIDA
Mérida
Cordillera de Mérida
BARINAS
Barinas
LARA
Carora
Barquisimeto
El Tocuyo
Acarigua
PORTUGUESA
Guanare
YARACUY
San Felipe
CARABOBO
Valencia
Puerto Cabello
Los Teques
VARGAS
La Guaira
Caracas
CAPITAL DIST.
MIRANDA
Maracay
ARAGUA
San Carlos
COJEDES
San Juan de los Morros
Ortiz
El Sombrero
VENEZUELA
El Calvario
Grico
Calabozo
El Baúl
GUÁRICO
AGUARO-GUARIQUITO N.P.
Río Chico
Altagracia de Orituco
NUEVA ESPARTA
La Asunción
I. de Margarita
I. Cubagua
I. Coche
Cumaná
SUCRE
Guanta
Barcelona
Puerto Píritu
Naricual
Aragua de Barcelona
San Mateo
Anaco
Zaraza
Nipa
Leona
El Pao
Oficina
ANZOÁTEGUI
Ciudad Bolívar
Soledad
Carúpano
Río Caribe
Península de Paria
Gulf of Paria
Maturín
MONAGAS
Pedernales
MARIUSA N.P.
Punta Araguapiche
Tucupita
Coporito
Barrancas
Curiapo
DELTA AMACURO
Sierra de Imataca
San José de Amacuro
Mabaruma
Morawhanna
Waini Point
GUYANA
Tobago
Charlotteville
Canaan
TRINIDAD AND TOBAGO
Galera Point
Macuro
Port-of-Spain
San Fernando
Trinidad
Delaware Bank

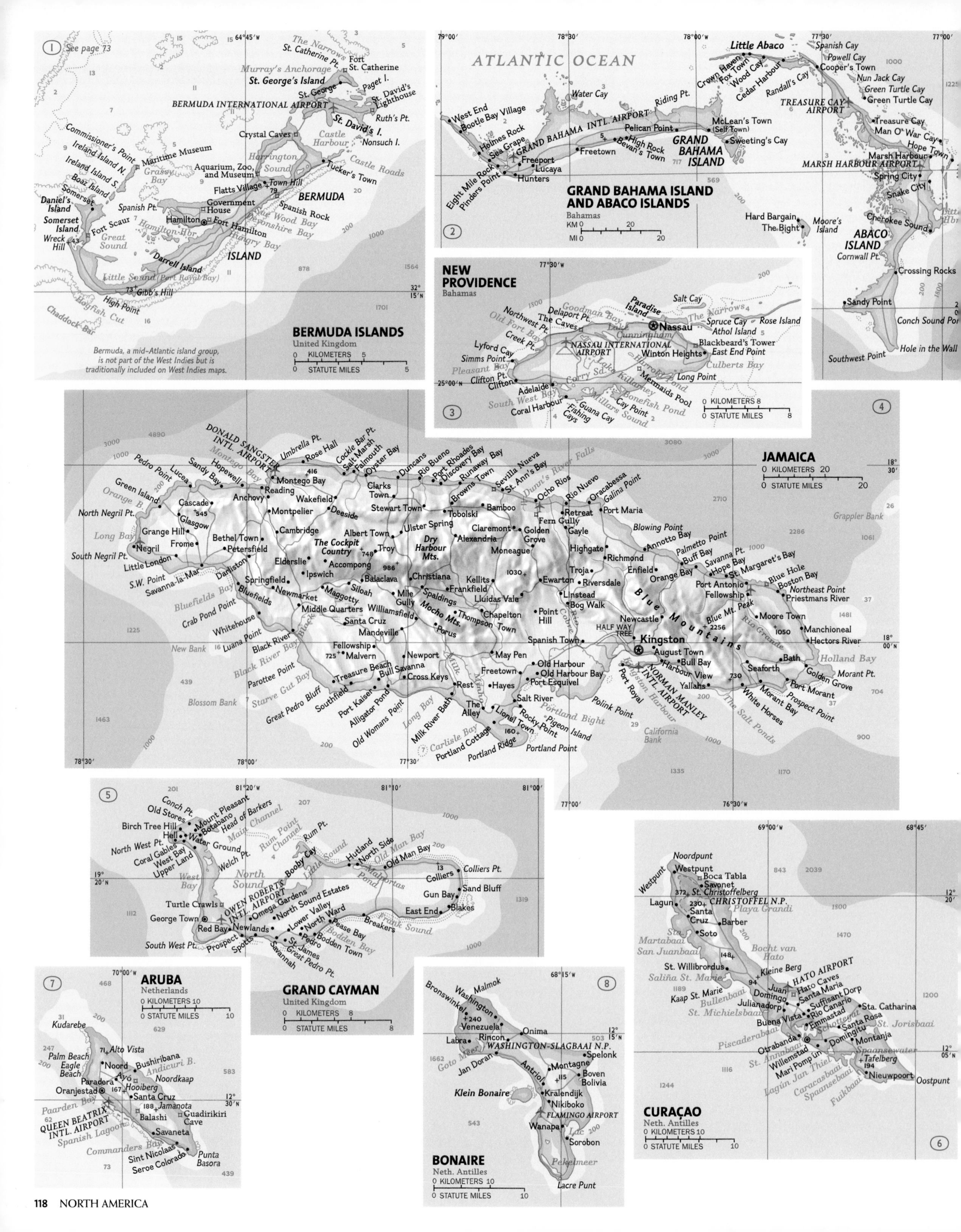

1
See page 73
BERMUDA ISLANDS
United Kingdom
KILOMETERS 5
STATUTE MILES 5
Bermuda, a mid-Atlantic island group, is not part of the West Indies but is traditionally included on West Indies maps.
The Narrows
St. Catherine Pt.
Fort St. Catherine
Murray's Anchorage
St. George's Island
St. George
Paget I.
St. David's Lighthouse
BERMUDA INTERNATIONAL AIRPORT
St. David's I.
Ruth's Pt.
Crystal Caves
Castle Harbour
Nonsuch I.
Commissioner's Point
Ireland Island N.
Ireland Island S.
Maritime Museum
Grassy Bay
Harrington Sound
Aquarium, Zoo, and Museum
Castle Roads
Tucker's Town
Boaz Island
Somerset
Daniel's Island
Somerset Island
Wreck Hill
Flatts Village
Town Hill
Government House
Spanish Pt.
Hamilton
Fort Hamilton
Hamilton Hbr.
BERMUDA
Spanish Rock
Devonshire Bay
Hungry Bay
Fort Scaur
Great Sound
Darrell Island
ISLAND
Little Sound (Port Royal Bay)
Gibb's Hill
High Point
Hogfish Cut
Chaddock Bar
32° 15′N
64°45′W
2
ATLANTIC OCEAN
GRAND BAHAMA ISLAND AND ABACO ISLANDS
Bahamas
KM 0 20
MI 0 20
Little Abaco
Spanish Cay
Powell Cay
Cooper's Town
Nun Jack Cay
Green Turtle Cay
Crown Haven
Fox Town
Wood Cay
Cedar Harbour
Randall's Cay
TREASURE CAY AIRPORT
Treasure Cay
Man O' War Cay
Hope Town
Marsh Harbour
MARSH HARBOUR AIRPORT
Spring City
Snake City
Water Cay
Riding Pt.
West End
Bootle Bay Village
GRAND BAHAMA INTL. AIRPORT
Pelican Point
McLean's Town (Self Town)
Sweeting's Cay
Holmes Rock
Sea Grape
Freeport
Lucaya
Hunters
Eight Mile Rock
Pinders Point
Freetown
High Rock
Bevan's Town
GRAND BAHAMA ISLAND
Hard Bargain
The Bight
Moore's Island
Cherokee Sound
ABACO ISLAND
Cornwall Pt.
Crossing Rocks
Sandy Point
Conch Sound Pt.
Hole in the Wall
Southwest Point
79°00′ 78°30′ 78°00′W 77°30′ 77°00′
3
NEW PROVIDENCE
Bahamas
KILOMETERS 8
STATUTE MILES 8
Paradise Island
Salt Cay
The Narrows
Nassau
Spruce Cay
Rose Island
Athol Island
Goodman Bay
Northwest Pt.
Delaport Pt.
The Caves
Old Fort Bay
Creek Pt.
Lake Cunningham
NASSAU INTERNATIONAL AIRPORT
Blackbeard's Tower
East End Point
Winton Heights
Lyford Cay
Simms Point
Pleasant Bay
Clifton Pt.
Clifton
Lake Killarney
Culberts Bay
Long Point
Adelaide
South West Bay
Coral Harbour
Fishing Cays
Guana Cay
Cay Point
Mermaids Pool
Bonefish Pond
Millars Sound
25°00′N
77°30′W
4
JAMAICA
KILOMETERS 20
STATUTE MILES 20
DONALD SANGSTER INTL. AIRPORT
Montego Bay
Umbrella Pt.
Rose Hall
Cockle Bar Pt.
Salt Marsh
Falmouth
Oyster Bay
Duncans
Rio Bueno
Port Rhoades
Discovery Bay
Runaway Bay
Browns Town
Sevilla Nueva
St. Ann's Bay
Dunn's River Falls
Ocho Rios
Rio Nuevo
Oracabessa
Galina Point
Port Maria
Pedro Point
Lucea
Sandy Bay
Hopewell
Green Island
Orange B.
Cascade
Anchovy
Reading
Wakefield
Clarks Town
Stewart Town
Tobolski
Bamboo
Retreat
Fern Gully
Gayle
North Negril Pt.
Glasgow
Montpelier
Deeside
Ulster Spring
Claremont
Golden Grove
Blowing Point
Annotto Bay
Long Bay
Grange Hill
Bethel Town
Cambridge
Albert Town
Dry Harbour Mts.
Alexandria
Moneague
Highgate
Palmetto Point
Buff Bay
Negril
Frome
Petersfield
The Cockpit Country
Troy
Richmond
Savanna Pt.
Hope Bay
St. Margaret's Bay
South Negril Pt.
Little London
Darliston
Elderslie
Accompong
Enfield
Orange Bay
Port Antonio
Blue Hole
Boston Bay
S.W. Point
Savanna-la-Mar
Springfield
Ipswich
Balaclava
Christiana
Kellits
Ewarton
Troja
Riversdale
Northeast Point
Priestmans River
Fellowship
Bluefields Bay
Bluefields
Newmarket
Maggotty
Siloah
Mile Gully
Spaldings
Frankfield
Lluidas Vale
Linstead
Bog Walk
Blue Mountains
Crab Pond Point
Middle Quarters
Williamsfield
Mocho Mts.
Chapelton
Point Hill
Newcastle
Blue Mt. Peak
Moore Town
Whitehouse
Santa Cruz
Thompson Town
Manchioneal
Luana Point
Black River
Mandeville
Porus
Spanish Town
HALF WAY TREE
Kingston
Rio Grande
Hectors River
New Bank
Black River Bay
Fellowship
Malvern
Newport
May Pen
August Town
Bull Bay
Holland Bay
Parottee Point
Treasure Beach
Bull Savanna
Old Harbour
Old Harbour Bay
Harbour View
Seaforth
Bath
Golden Grove
Morant Pt.
Starve Gut Bay
Cross Keys
Freetown
Port Esquivel
Hayes
Yallahs
Port Morant
Great Pedro Bluff
Southfield
Port Kaiser
Alligator Pond
Rest
Salt River
Port Royal
NORMAN MANLEY INTL. AIRPORT
Kingston Harbour
Polink Point
White Horses
Morant Bay
Prospect Point
Blossom Bank
Old Womans Point
Long Bay
Milk River Bath
The Alley
Lionel Town
Rocky Point
Portland Bight
Pigeon Island
California Bank
The Salt Ponds
Carlisle Bay
Portland Cottage
Portland Ridge
Portland Point
Grappler Bank
18° 30′
18° 00′N
78°30′ 78°00′ 77°30′ 77°00′ 76°30′W
5
GRAND CAYMAN
United Kingdom
KILOMETERS 8
STATUTE MILES 8
Conch Pt.
Old Stores
Mount Pleasant
Botabano
Head of Barkers
Main Channel
Birch Tree Hill
Hell
Water Ground
Rum Point Channel
Rum Pt.
North West Pt.
Coral Gables
West Bay
Upper Land
Welch Pt.
Booby Cay
Little Sound
Hutland
North Side
Old Man Bay
Colliers Pt.
West Bay
North Sound
Meagre Bay Pond
Colliers
Sand Bluff
Turtle Crawls
OWEN ROBERTS INTL. AIRPORT
Omega Gardens
North Sound Estates
Gun Bay
East End
Blakes
George Town
Red Bay
Newlands
Lower Valley
North Ward
Breakers
Frank Sound
South West Pt.
Prospect
Spotts
Pedro
Pease Bay
Bodden Bay
Bodden Town
St. James
Savannah
Great Pedro Pt.
19° 20′N
81°20′W 81°10′ 81°00′
6
CURAÇAO
Neth. Antilles
KILOMETERS 10
STATUTE MILES 10
Noordpunt
Westpunt
Boca Tabla
Savonet
St. Christoffelberg
ST. CHRISTOFFEL N.P.
Playa Grandi
Lagun
Santa Cruz
Barber
Soto
Sta. Martabaai
San Juanbaai
Bocht van Hato
St. Willibrordus
Saliña St. Marie
Kleine Berg
HATO AIRPORT
Hato Caves
Kaap St. Marie
Juan Domingo
Santa Maria
Suffisant Dorp
Rio Canario
Julianadorp
Bullenbaai
St. Michielsbaai
Buena Vista
Emmastad
Sta. Catharina
Schottegat
Santa Rosa
St. Jorisbaai
Piscaderabaai
Otrabanda
Dominguito
Montanja
St. Annabaai
Willemstad
Mari Pomp'un
Spaanse water
Tafelberg
Lagún Jan Thiel
Caracasbaai
Spaansebaai
Fuikbaai
Nieuwpoort
Oostpunt
69°00′W 68°45′
12° 20′
12° 05′N
7
ARUBA
Netherlands
KILOMETERS 10
STATUTE MILES 10
Kudarebe
Alto Vista
Palm Beach
Eagle Beach
Noord
Bushiribana
Andicuri B.
Noordkaap
Paradera
Ayó
Hooiberg
Oranjestad
Santa Cruz
Paarden Bay
Jamanota
Balashi
Guadirikiri Cave
QUEEN BEATRIX INTL. AIRPORT
Spanish Lagoon
Savaneta
Commanders Bay
Sint Nicolaas
Seroe Colorado
Punta Basora
70°00′W
12° 30′N
8
BONAIRE
Neth. Antilles
KILOMETERS 10
STATUTE MILES 10
Malmok
Bronswinkel
Washington
Venezuela
Labra
Rincon
Onima
WASHINGTON-SLAGBAAI N.P.
Spelonk
Goto Meer
Jan Doran
Antriol
Montagne
Boven Bolivia
Klein Bonaire
Kralendijk
Nikiboko
FLAMINGO AIRPORT
Wanapa
Lac
Sorobon
Pekelmeer
Lacre Punt
68°15′W
12° 15′N

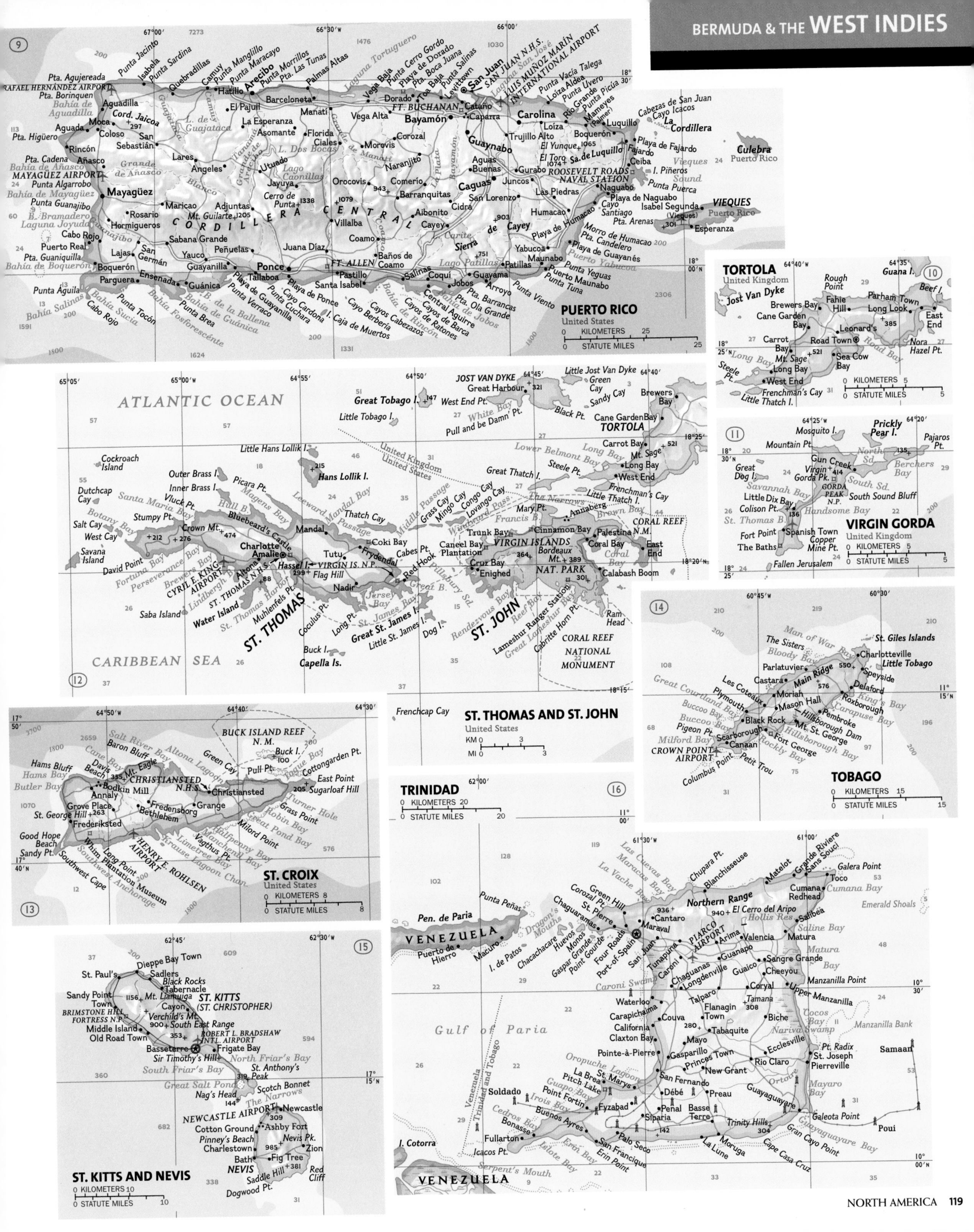
PUERTO RICO
United States
KILOMETERS 25
STATUTE MILES 25
San Juan
SAN JUAN N.H.S.
LUIS MUÑOZ MARÍN INTERNATIONAL AIRPORT
RAFAEL HERNÁNDEZ AIRPORT
MAYAGÜEZ AIRPORT
Mayagüez
Arecibo
Bayamón
Carolina
Caguas
Guaynabo
Ponce
Culebra
Puerto Rico
VIEQUES
Puerto Rico
Vieques Sound
La Cordillera
CORDILLERA CENTRAL
Sierra de Cayey
FT. BUCHANAN
FT. ALLEN
ROOSEVELT ROADS NAVAL STATION
Aguadilla
Aguada
Rincón
Añasco
Cabo Rojo
Boquerón
Guánica
Guayanilla
Yauco
Santa Isabel
Salinas
Guayama
Arroyo
Patillas
Maunabo
Yabucoa
Humacao
Naguabo
Ceiba
Fajardo
Luquillo
Loíza
Trujillo Alto
Caparra
Cataño
Dorado
Vega Alta
Vega Baja
Manatí
Barceloneta
Hatillo
Camuy
Quebradillas
Isabela
Moca
San Sebastián
Lares
Utuado
Adjuntas
Jayuya
Orocovis
Morovis
Corozal
Naranjito
Comerío
Barranquitas
Aibonito
Cidra
Cayey
Coamo
Villalba
Juana Díaz
San Germán
Lajas
Sabana Grande
Maricao
Hormigueros
Rosario
Juncos
Gurabo
Las Piedras
San Lorenzo
Aguas Buenas
Esperanza
Isabel Segunda (Vieques)
El Yunque
Sa. de Luquillo
ATLANTIC OCEAN
CARIBBEAN SEA
ST. THOMAS AND ST. JOHN
United States
ST. THOMAS
ST. JOHN
Charlotte Amalie
CYRIL E. KING AIRPORT
VIRGIN ISLANDS NAT. PARK
CORAL REEF NATIONAL MONUMENT
CORAL REEF N.M.
Great Tobago I.
Little Tobago I.
Hans Lollik I.
Little Hans Lollik I.
JOST VAN DYKE
TORTOLA
Great Thatch I.
Little Thatch I.
Water Island
Saba Island
Savana Island
Buck I.
Capella Is.
Great St. James I.
Little St. James I.
Red Hook
Cruz Bay
Coral Bay
East End
Ram Head
Frenchcap Cay
TORTOLA
United Kingdom
Road Town
Jost Van Dyke
Guana I.
Beef I.
West End
Sea Cow Bay
Long Look
East End
VIRGIN GORDA
United Kingdom
Spanish Town
GORDA PEAK N.P.
Prickly Pear I.
Mosquito I.
The Baths
Fallen Jerusalem
TOBAGO
Scarborough
CROWN POINT AIRPORT
Charlotteville
Little Tobago
St. Giles Islands
Speyside
Roxborough
Plymouth
Main Ridge
ST. CROIX
United States
Christiansted
Frederiksted
HENRY E. ROHLSEN AIRPORT
BUCK ISLAND REEF N. M.
CHRISTIANSTED N.H.S.
Whim Plantation Museum
ST. KITTS AND NEVIS
ST. KITTS (ST. CHRISTOPHER)
NEVIS
Basseterre
Charlestown
ROBERT L. BRADSHAW INTL. AIRPORT
NEWCASTLE AIRPORT
BRIMSTONE HILL FORTRESS N.P.
Mt. Liamuiga
Nevis Pk.
TRINIDAD
Port-of-Spain
San Fernando
PIARCO AIRPORT
Arima
Chaguanas
Couva
Point Fortin
Rio Claro
Sangre Grande
Northern Range
El Cerro del Aripo
Gulf of Paria
Serpent's Mouth
Dragon's Mouths
Pitch Lake
Galeota Point
VENEZUELA
Pen. de Paria
NORTH AMERICA

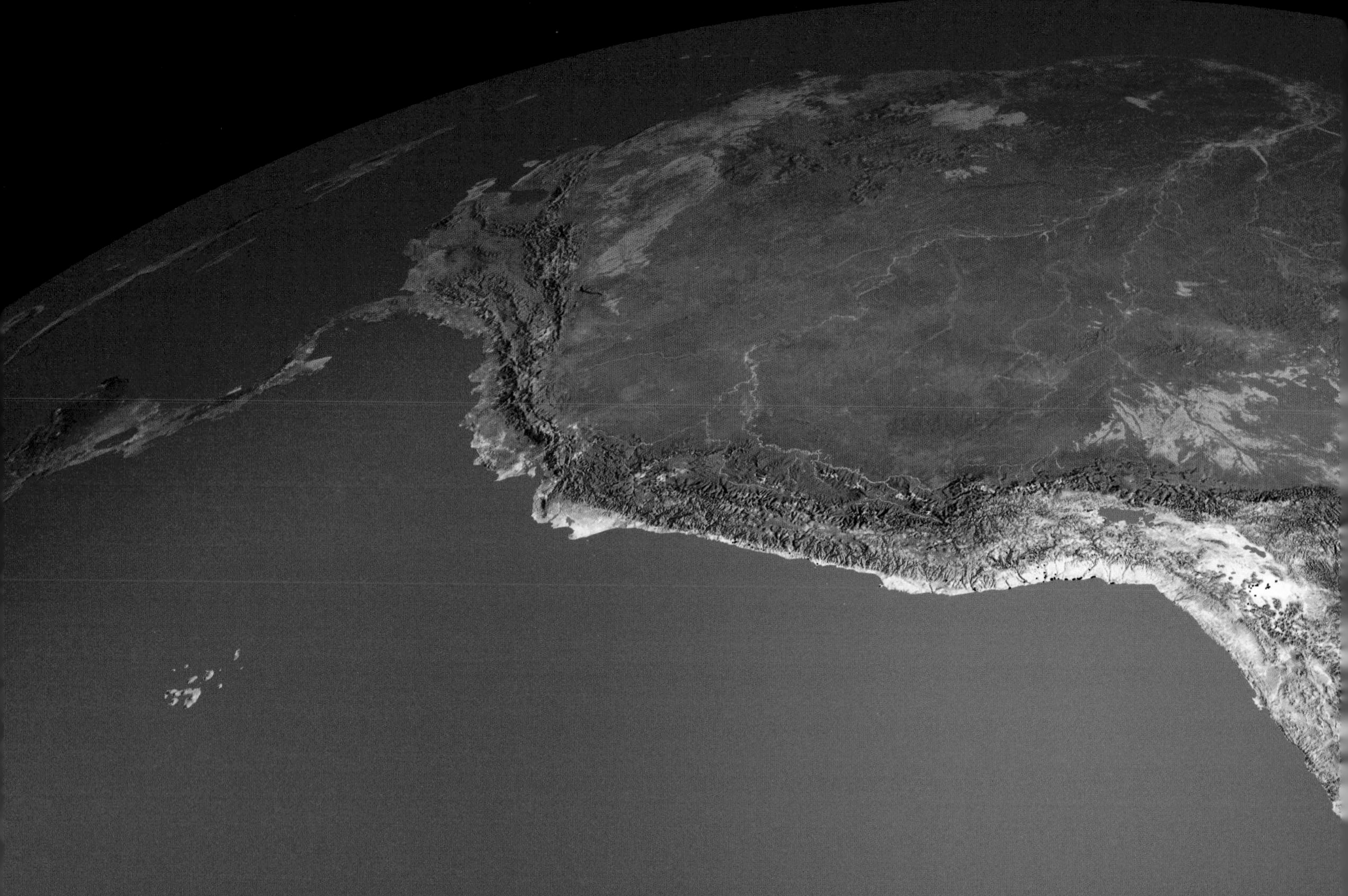

Two features dominate South America: the Andes, extending 7,242 kilometers (4,500 miles), is the world's longest and second highest mountain range; the Amazon—the world's largest river by volume and, at 6,437 kilometers (4,000 miles), the second longest—flows through the largest, most biologically rich rain forest on Earth. Some of the people in the Amazon Basin are among the least touched by the modern world, although the press of logging, agriculture, and settlement has devastated much of the forest and its scattered inhabitants. Other South American features also stand out. The Pantanal, spanning parts of Brazil, Paraguay, and Bolivia with flooded grasslands and savannas, is 17 times the size of the Florida Everglades and home to a kaleidoscopic diversity of plant and animal life. The vast grassy plains of the Argentine Pampas nourish livestock, but the Atacama Desert of Chile supports little life. Its dry, clear, thin air, however, makes it ideal for astronomical observatories. In the Andes, the Inca empire expanded between 1438 and 1527, stretching from modern Colombia to western Argentina. Weakened by internal dissension, the Inca succumbed to Francisco Pizarro's forces in 1533. Spaniards looted its golden treasures and forced native slave labor to work gold and silver mines; Portuguese overlords imported millions of slaves from Africa to work Brazilian plantations. Not until the early 19th century under Simón Bolívar, the Liberator of the Americas, did the desire for independence coalesce and rebellion spread rapidly. Yet even after the colonial period, strife continued during the 20th century with coups, civil wars, and cross-border disputes. Today mining of industrial mineral ores, fishing, forestry, petroleum extraction, and commercial agriculture support the continent's economies, but prosperity does not reach all its people. Populist leaders in countries such as Venezuela and Bolivia are raising their voices, while indigenous peoples' activists are gaining new influence.

IMAGE BY ROBERT STACEY, WORLDSAT INTERNATIONAL INC.

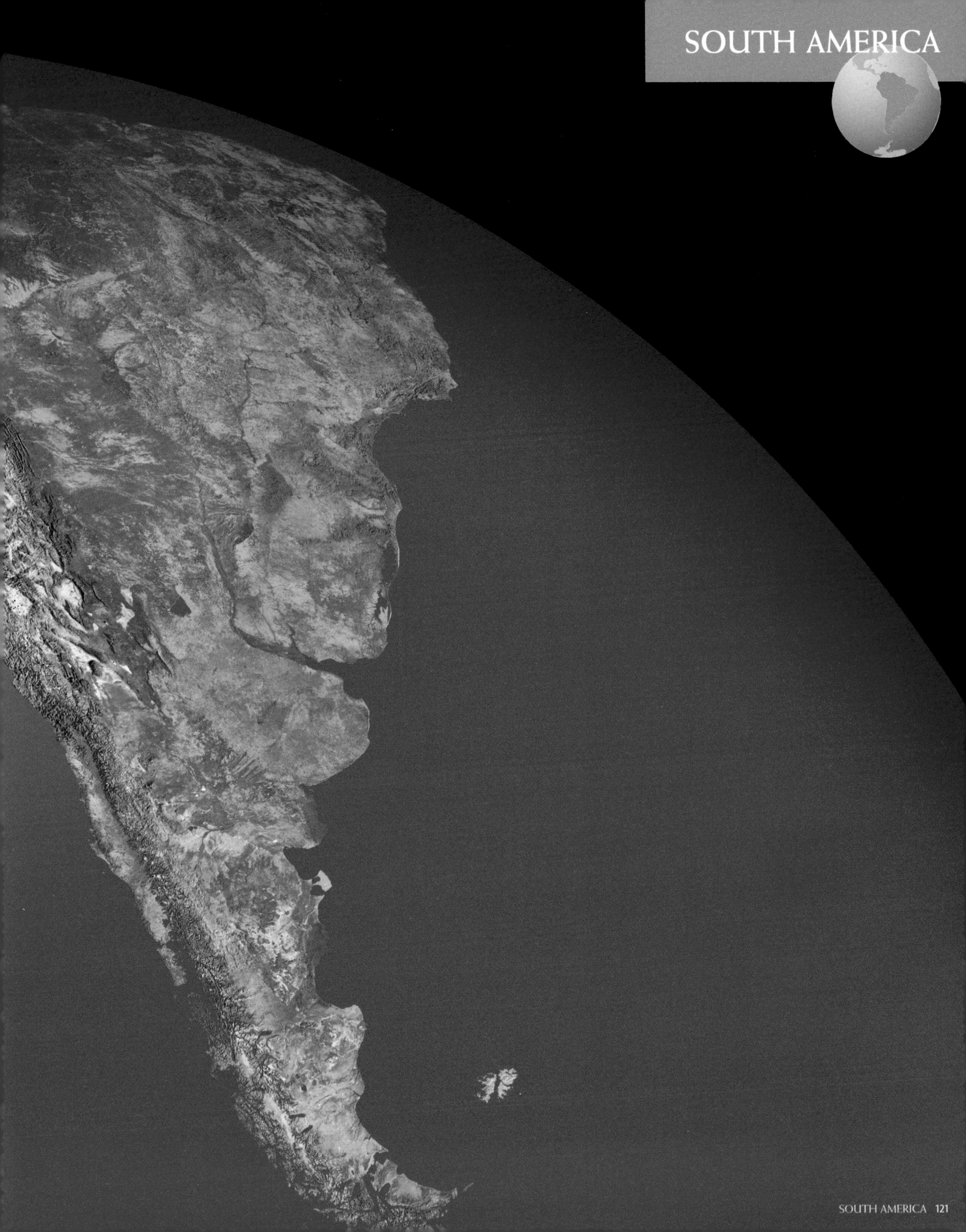

SOUTH AMERICA

Caribbean Sea
GUATEMALA
HONDURAS
Coco
EL SALVADOR
Tegucigalpa
NICARAGUA
Managua
Volcán Irazú
3412
3819
San José
COSTA RICA
PANAMA
Panamá
Golfo de Panamá
Barranquilla
5775
Golfo de Venezuela
Maracaibo
Lago de Maracaibo
Lesser Antilles
Isla de Margarita
Caracas
Port-of-Spain
TRINIDAD AND TOBAGO
Orinoco River Delta
VENEZUELA
LLANOS
Angel Falls
GUIANA HIGHLANDS
2772
Mt. Roraima
GUYANA
Georgetown
Paramaribo
SURINAME
FRENCH GUIANA
Cayenne
5007
Serra de Tumucumaque
2579
Source of the Orinoco
4080
Medellín
Bogotá
COLOMBIA
Cali
5750
3014
Pico de Neblina
Cabo Norte
Mouths of the Amazon
ILHA DE MARAJÓ
Belém
Baía de São Marcos
Quito
EQUATOR
ECUADOR
Caquetá
AMAZON
Putumayo
Napo
Manaus
Pará
Amazon
Guayaquil
Golfo de Guayaquil
Galápagos Islands
Amazon (Solimões)
Madeira
Javari
Juruá
Selvas
Tapajós
Iriri
Araguaia
Parnaíba
Fortaleza
Ponta do Calcanhar
Punta Pariñas
Marañón
BASIN
Purus
Aripuanã
Xingu
Punta Negra
Ucayali
Juruena
BRAZIL
Teles Pires
Araguaia
Tocantins
Recife
Nev. Huascarán
6768
PERU
Lima
Mamoré
BRAZILIAN
Salvador
6425
Source of the Amazon
Nev. Coropuna
Lago Titicaca
1995
PLANALTO DO MATO GROSSO
La Paz
BOLIVIA
Brasília
Goiânia
HIGHLANDS
Pantanal
Sucre
Belo Horizonte
2890
Bandeira
PACIFIC
Atacama Desert
CHILE
Gran Chaco
PARAGUAY
Campos
Cabo Frio
Rio de Janeiro
São Paulo
TROPIC OF CAPRICORN
Volcán Llullaillaco
6723
Asunción
Iguazú Falls
Curitiba
Isla San Félix
Isla San Ambrosio
6880
Cerro Ojos del Salado
OCEAN
Paraná
Ríos
Cerro del Toro
Salinas Ambargasta
Salinas Grandes
Cabo de Santa Marta Grande
Córdoba
Porto Alegre
Entre
Uruguay
Highest point in South America
Lagoa dos Patos
Cerro Aconcagua
6960 (22834 ft)
URUGUAY
Islas Juan Fernández
Santiago
Pampas
Buenos Aires
Montevideo
Río de la Plata
Bahía Samborombón
ATLANTIC OCEAN
ARGENTINA
4709
Volcán Domuyo
Negro
Bahía Blanca
Golfo San Matías
PENÍNSULA VALDÉS
Patagonia
Archipiélago de los Chonos
Golfo San Jorge
Península de Taitao
1372
Cabo Tres Puntas
Lowest point in South America
Laguna del Carbón
-105 (-344 ft)
Bahía Grande
ANDES
West Falkland
Stanley
East Falkland
Strait of Magellan
Falkland Islands
Tierra del Fuego
Scotia Sea
Cape Disappointment
South Georgia
Cabo de Hornos (Cape Horn)
Longitude West 50° of Greenwich
ATLANTIC OCEAN
AZIMUTHAL EQUIDISTANT PROJECTION
SCALE 1:31,000,000
0 KILOMETERS 600 800
0 MILES 200 400 600 800
90°
80°
70°
60°
40°
10°
0°
20°
30°
50°
100°

ATLANTIC OCEAN
PACIFIC OCEAN
Caribbean Sea
EQUATOR
TROPIC OF CAPRICORN
GUATEMALA
HONDURAS
EL SALVADOR
NICARAGUA
Tegucigalpa
Puerto Cabezas
León
Managua
Granada
Bluefields
Vol. Irazú
Pto. Limón
Colón
San José
COSTA RICA
PANAMA
Panamá
David
Puerto Armuelles
Golfo de Panamá
ST. LUCIA
ST. VINCENT & THE GRENADINES
BARBADOS
GRENADA
TRINIDAD AND TOBAGO
Port-of-Spain
Aruba
Neth.
Bonaire
Curaçao
Neth. Antilles
Amuay
Barranquilla
Cartagena
Santa Marta
Maracaibo
Puerto Cabello
La Guaira
Caracas
Cumaná
Maturín
Mérida
Montería
Cúcuta
Bucaramanga
Ciudad Bolívar
Ciudad Guayana
Morawhanna
VENEZUELA
Angel Falls
Georgetown
Nieuw Amsterdam
GUYANA
Lethem
Paramaribo
SURINAME
St.-Laurent du Maroni
Cayenne
FRENCH GUIANA
France
Oiapoque
Calçoene
Amapá
Cabo Norte
Bailique
Macapá
Mt. Roraima
Lueria
Puerto Ayacucho
Bello
Medellín
Manizales
Ibagué
BOGOTÁ
Villavicencio
Buenaventura
Cali
COLOMBIA
Guaviare
Orinoco
San Carlos
Pico de Neblina
Boa Vista
Caracaraí
Novo Paraíso
Calamar
Mitú
Popayán
Tumaco
San Lorenzo
Esmeraldas
Pasto
Güeppí
Quito
Ibarra
ECUADOR
Chimborazo
Manta
Portoviejo
Guayaquil
Cuenca
Machala
Tumbes
Loja
Galápagos Islands (Archipiélago de Colón)
Ecuador
Puerto Baquerizo Moreno
Talara
Punta Pariñas
Paita
Piura
Punta Negra
Chiclayo
Tarapoto
Cajamarca
Pacasmayo
Trujillo
Salaverry
Chimbote
PERU
Huaraz
Huánuco
Cerro de Pasco
LIMA
Callao
Huancayo
Huancavelica
Ayacucho
Machu Picchu
Cusco
Pisco
Abancay
Ica
Nasca
Nev. Coropuna
Juliaca
Arequipa
Matarani
Moquegua
Tacna
Arica
Pucallpa
Contamana
Iquitos
Leticia
Putumayo
Napo
Marañón
Ucayali
La Pedrera
Japurá
Fonte Boa
Tefé
São Paulo de Olivença
Solimões (Amazonas)
Coari
Jutaí
Juruá
Javari
Eirunepé
Cruzeiro do Sul
Canutama
Lábrea
Manicoré
Humaitá
Prainha
Purus
Boca do Acre
Calama
Madeira
Porto Velho
Rio Branco
Guajará-Mirim
Ji-Paraná
Cobija
Riberalta
Puerto Maldonado
Príncipe da Beira
Vilhena
Trinidad
Mamoré
L. Titicaca
La Paz
BOLIVIA
Cochabamba
Oruro
Potosí
Sucre
Santa Cruz
San José de Chiquitos
Corumbá
Salar de Uyuni
Camiri
Tarija
Pisagua
Barcelos
Carvoeiro
Negro
Branco
Manaus
Parintins
Itacoatiara
Óbidos
Monte Alegre
Gurupá
Santarém
Itaituba
Borba
Jacareacanga
Barra do São Manuel
Cachimbo
Tapajós
Juruena
Xingu
Iriri
Amazonas
Chaves
ILHA DE MARAJÓ
Curralinho
Belém
Abaetetuba
Bragança
São Luís
Tucuruí
Marabá
Imperatriz
Araguaína
Conceição do Araguaia
Carolina
Pedro Afonso
Araguaia
Tocantins
BRAZIL
Bacabal
Teresina
Camocim
Parnaíba
Sobral
Fortaleza
Aracati
Caxias
Ipu
Crateús
Mossoró
Iguatu
Ponta do Calcanhar
Natal
João Pessoa
Campina Grande
Patos
Juazeiro do Norte
Recife
Garanhuns
Caruaru
Petrolina
Juazeiro
Arapiraca
Maceió
Penedo
Propriá
Aracaju
Estância
Alagoinhas
Feira de Santana
Salvador (Bahia)
Ilhéus
Itabuna
Jequié
Barra Mansa
Xique Xique
Porto Nacional
Barreiras
Peixe
Sítio do Mato
Carinhanha
Vitória da Conquista
Januária
Canavieiras
Itaúba
Sinop
Parecis
PLANALTO DO MATO GROSSO
Mato Grosso
Cáceres
Cuiabá
Porangatu
Anápolis
Goiânia
Brasília
Rio Verde
Pirapora
Montes Claros
Diamantina
Caravelas
Governador Valadares
Araguari
Uberlândia
Uberaba
Curvelo
Belo Horizonte
Coxim
Campo Grande
São José do Rio Preto
Ribeirão Preto
Araçatuba
Bauru
Bandeira
Juiz de Fora
Vitória
Campos
Volta Redonda
Nova Friburgo
Londrina
Campinas
Sorocaba
SÃO PAULO
Santos
RIO DE JANEIRO
Curitiba
Iguape
Paranaguá
Joinville
Florianópolis
Imbituba
Tubarão
Passo Fundo
Caxias do Sul
Porto Alegre
Pelotas
Rio Grande
Bagé
Iguazú Falls
Villarrica
Posadas
PARAGUAY
Concepción
Asunción
Mariscal Estigarribia
Aguaray
Gran Chaco
Formosa
Resistencia
Corrientes
Tocopilla
Calama
Mejillones
Antofagasta
San Salvador de Jujuy
Taltal
Volcán Llullaillaco
Diego de Almagro
Chañaral
Caldera
Cerro Ojos del Salado
San Miguel de Tucumán
Santiago del Estero
Belén
Catamarca
La Rioja
Huasco
Sarco
Cerro del Toro
La Serena
Ovalle
CHILE
Los Vilos
Cerro Aconcagua
Valparaíso
Santiago
Rancagua
Curicó
Talca
Chillán
Concepción
Los Ángeles
Temuco
Zapala
Valdivia
Osorno
Puerto Montt
Ancud
San Carlos de Bariloche
Isla Grande de Chiloé
Esquel
Archipiélago de los Chonos
Puerto Aisén
Balmaceda
Monte San Valentín
Las Heras
El Calafate
Yacimiento Río Turbio
Puerto Natales
Punta Arenas
Isla San Félix
Isla San Ambrosio
Chile
Islas Juan Fernández
San Juan
Mendoza
San Luis
San Rafael
Córdoba
Río Cuarto
ARGENTINA
Mercedes
Goya
Uruguaiana
Salto
Paysandú
Paraná
Rosario
URUGUAY
Treinta-y-Tres
Rocha
Montevideo
Buenos Aires
Río de la Plata
Pehuajó
Santa Rosa
Olavarría
Tandil
Tres Arroyos
Mar del Plata
Necochea
Bahía Blanca
Pampas
Neuquén
Río Colorado
Viedma
Golfo San Matías
Puerto Madryn
PENÍNSULA VALDÉS
Rawson
Camarones
Golfo San Jorge
Comodoro Rivadavia
Cabo Tres Puntas
Puerto Deseado
Puerto San Julián
Puerto Santa Cruz
Puerto Coig
Patagonia
Administered by United Kingdom (claimed by Argentina)
Stanley
Falkland Islands (Islas Malvinas)
U.K.
Manantiales
ISLA GRANDE DE TIERRA DEL FUEGO
Río Grande
Ushuaia
Cabo de Hornos (Cape Horn)
Scotia Sea
South Georgia I.
U.K.
AZIMUTHAL EQUIDISTANT PROJECTION
SCALE 1:31,000,000
0 KILOMETERS 600 800
0 MILES 200 400 600 800
Longitude West 90° of Greenwich
100°
90°
80°
70°
60°
50°
40°
30°
20°
10°
0°

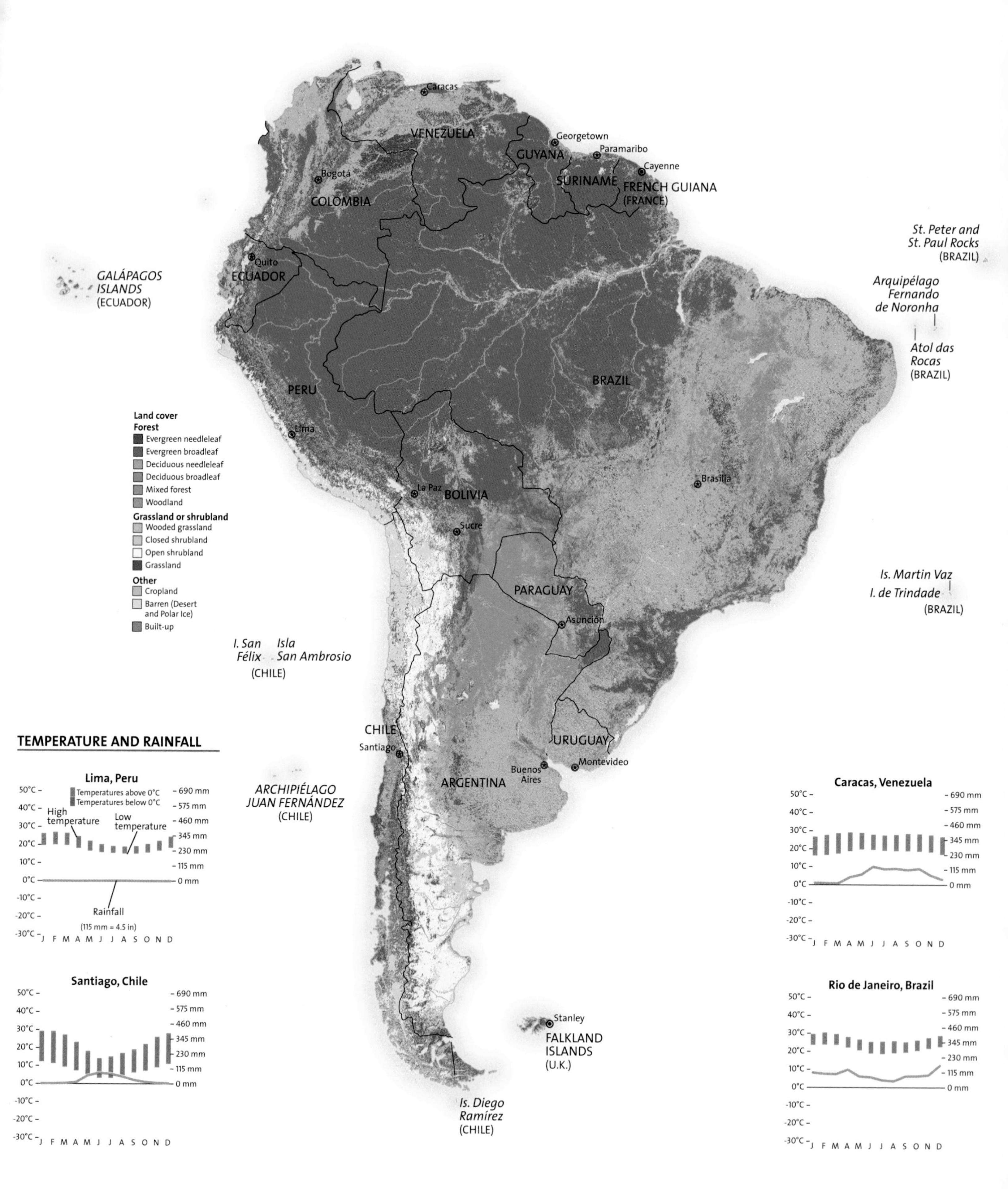
Caracas
VENEZUELA
Georgetown
GUYANA
Paramaribo
SURINAME
Cayenne
FRENCH GUIANA
(FRANCE)
Bogotá
COLOMBIA
Quito
ECUADOR
GALÁPAGOS ISLANDS
(ECUADOR)
St. Peter and St. Paul Rocks
(BRAZIL)
Arquipélago Fernando de Noronha
Atol das Rocas
(BRAZIL)
PERU
BRAZIL
Lima
Brasília
La Paz
BOLIVIA
Sucre
PARAGUAY
Asunción
Is. Martin Vaz
I. de Trindade
(BRAZIL)
I. San Félix
Isla San Ambrosio
(CHILE)
CHILE
Santiago
URUGUAY
Montevideo
Buenos Aires
ARGENTINA
ARCHIPIÉLAGO JUAN FERNÁNDEZ
(CHILE)
Stanley
FALKLAND ISLANDS
(U.K.)
Is. Diego Ramírez
(CHILE)
Land cover
Forest
Evergreen needleleaf
Evergreen broadleaf
Deciduous needleleaf
Deciduous broadleaf
Mixed forest
Woodland
Grassland or shrubland
Wooded grassland
Closed shrubland
Open shrubland
Grassland
Other
Cropland
Barren (Desert and Polar Ice)
Built-up
TEMPERATURE AND RAINFALL
Lima, Peru
Temperatures above 0°C
Temperatures below 0°C
High temperature
Low temperature
Rainfall
(115 mm = 4.5 in)
50°C 40°C 30°C 20°C 10°C 0°C -10°C -20°C -30°C
690 mm 575 mm 460 mm 345 mm 230 mm 115 mm 0 mm
J F M A M J J A S O N D
Santiago, Chile
Caracas, Venezuela
Rio de Janeiro, Brazil

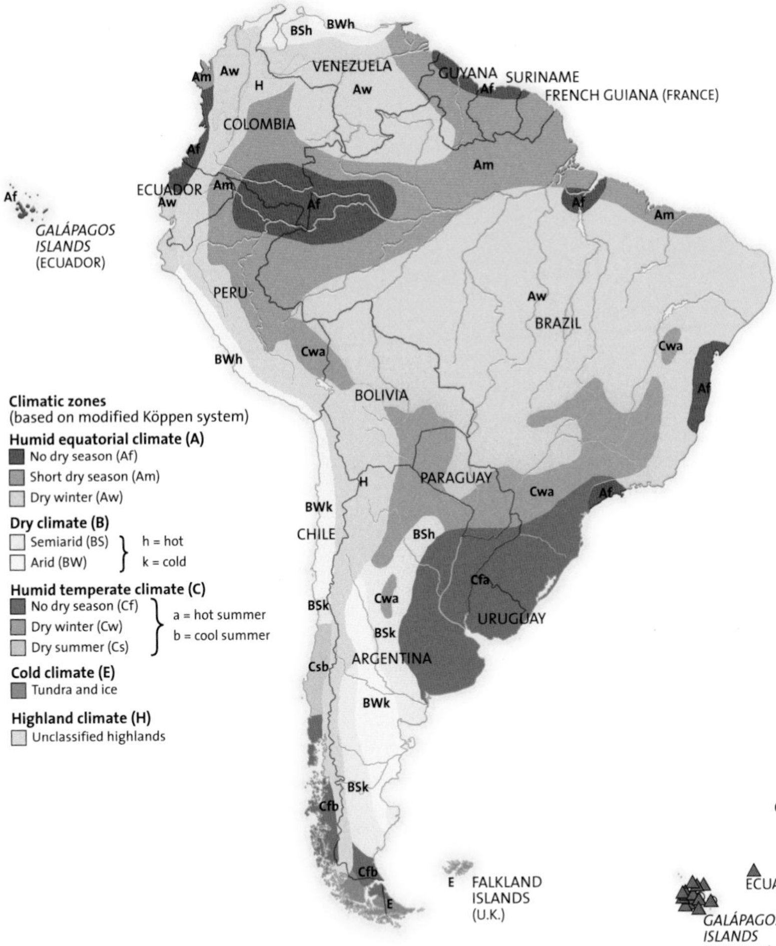

BSh BWh
VENEZUELA GUYANA SURINAME FRENCH GUIANA (FRANCE)
Am Aw H Aw Af
COLOMBIA
Af
ECUADOR Am Aw Af Am Af Am
GALÁPAGOS ISLANDS (ECUADOR)
PERU
Aw
BRAZIL
BWh Cwa Cwa Af
BOLIVIA
H PARAGUAY Cwa Af
BWk
CHILE BSh
Cfa
BSk Cwa URUGUAY
BSk
Csb ARGENTINA
BWk
BSk
Cfb
Cfb
E
E FALKLAND ISLANDS (U.K.)

Climatic zones
(based on modified Köppen system)

Humid equatorial climate (A)
- No dry season (Af)
- Short dry season (Am)
- Dry winter (Aw)

Dry climate (B)
- Semiarid (BS)
- Arid (BW)

h = hot
k = cold

Humid temperate climate (C)
- No dry season (Cf)
- Dry winter (Cw)
- Dry summer (Cs)

a = hot summer
b = cool summer

Cold climate (E)
- Tundra and ice

Highland climate (H)
- Unclassified highlands

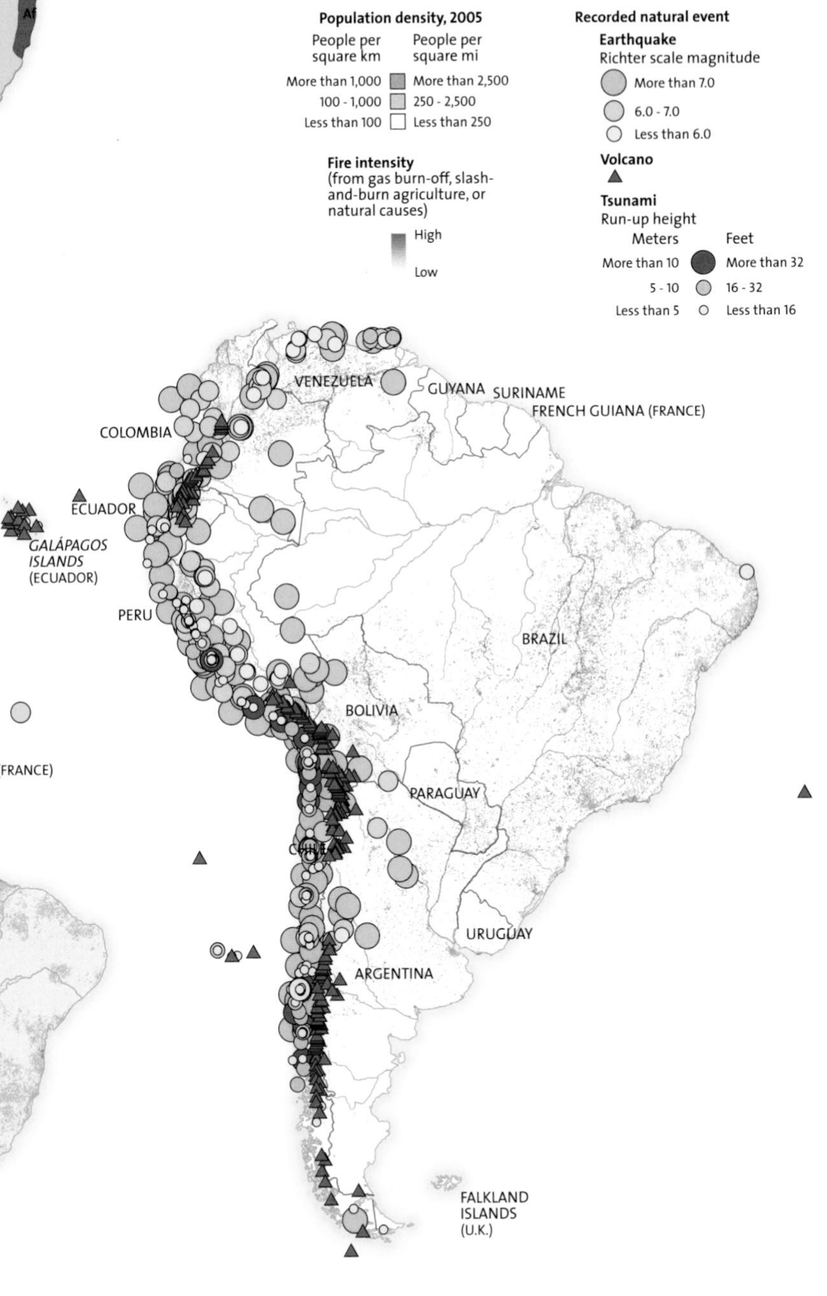

Population density, 2005

People per square km	People per square mi
More than 1,000	More than 2,500
100 - 1,000	250 - 2,500
Less than 100	Less than 250

Fire intensity
(from gas burn-off, slash-and-burn agriculture, or natural causes)
High
Low

Recorded natural event

Earthquake
Richter scale magnitude
- More than 7.0
- 6.0 - 7.0
- Less than 6.0

Volcano

Tsunami
Run-up height

Meters	Feet
More than 10	More than 32
5 - 10	16 - 32
Less than 5	Less than 16

VENEZUELA GUYANA SURINAME FRENCH GUIANA (FRANCE)
COLOMBIA
ECUADOR
GALÁPAGOS ISLANDS (ECUADOR)
PERU
BRAZIL
BOLIVIA
PARAGUAY
CHILE
URUGUAY
ARGENTINA
FALKLAND ISLANDS (U.K.)

VENEZUELA GUYANA SURINAME FRENCH GUIANA (FRANCE)
COLOMBIA
ECUADOR
GALÁPAGOS ISLANDS (ECUADOR)
PERU
BRAZIL
BOLIVIA
PARAGUAY
CHILE
URUGUAY
ARGENTINA
FALKLAND ISLANDS (U.K.)

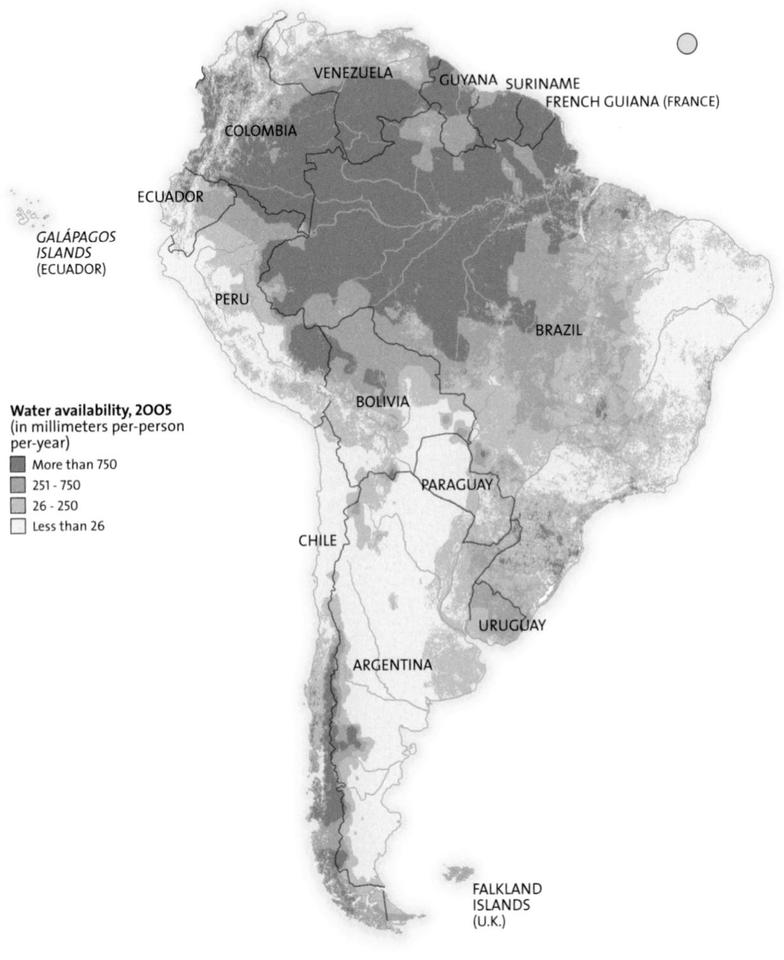

Water availability, 2005
(in millimeters per-person per-year)
- More than 750
- 251 - 750
- 26 - 250
- Less than 26

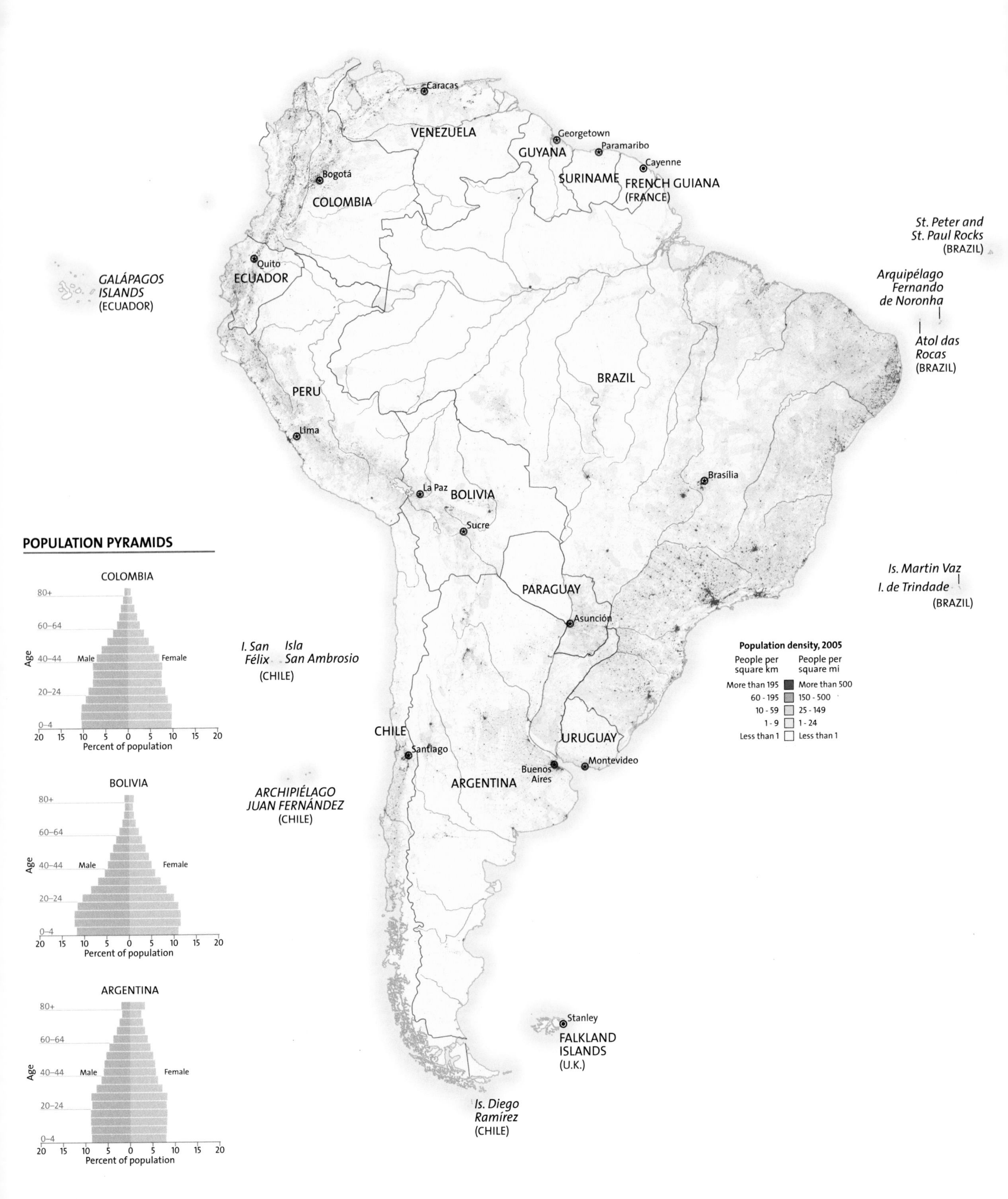
Caracas
VENEZUELA
Georgetown
Paramaribo
GUYANA
Cayenne
SURINAME
FRENCH GUIANA
(FRANCE)
Bogotá
COLOMBIA
St. Peter and
St. Paul Rocks
(BRAZIL)
Quito
ECUADOR
GALÁPAGOS
ISLANDS
(ECUADOR)
Arquipélago
Fernando
de Noronha
Atol das
Rocas
(BRAZIL)
BRAZIL
PERU
Lima
Brasília
La Paz
BOLIVIA
Sucre
POPULATION PYRAMIDS
COLOMBIA
80+
60–64
Age
40–44
Male
Female
20–24
0–4
20 15 10 5 0 5 10 15 20
Percent of population
PARAGUAY
Is. Martin Vaz
I. de Trindade
(BRAZIL)
Asunción
I. San
Félix
Isla
San Ambrosio
(CHILE)
Population density, 2005
People per square km
People per square mi
More than 195
More than 500
60 - 195
150 - 500
10 - 59
25 - 149
1 - 9
1 - 24
Less than 1
Less than 1
CHILE
URUGUAY
Santiago
Montevideo
Buenos Aires
ARGENTINA
BOLIVIA
ARCHIPIÉLAGO
JUAN FERNÁNDEZ
(CHILE)
ARGENTINA
Stanley
FALKLAND
ISLANDS
(U.K.)
Is. Diego
Ramírez
(CHILE)

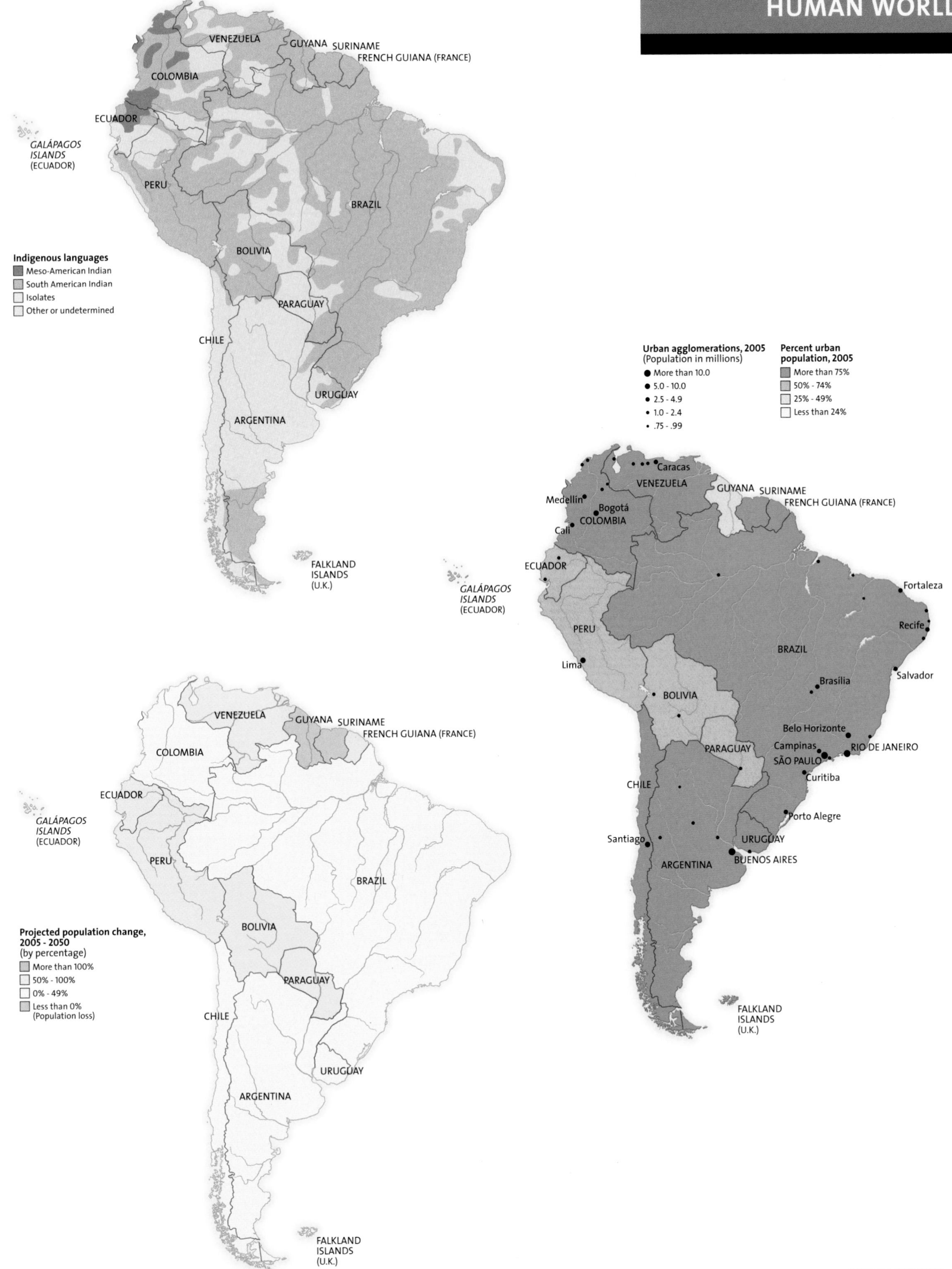
VENEZUELA
GUYANA
SURINAME
FRENCH GUIANA (FRANCE)
COLOMBIA
ECUADOR
GALÁPAGOS ISLANDS (ECUADOR)
PERU
BRAZIL
BOLIVIA
PARAGUAY
CHILE
URUGUAY
ARGENTINA
FALKLAND ISLANDS (U.K.)
Indigenous languages
Meso-American Indian
South American Indian
Isolates
Other or undetermined
Urban agglomerations, 2005
(Population in millions)
More than 10.0
5.0 - 10.0
2.5 - 4.9
1.0 - 2.4
.75 - .99
Percent urban population, 2005
More than 75%
50% - 74%
25% - 49%
Less than 24%
Caracas
Medellín
Bogotá
Cali
Fortaleza
Recife
Lima
Salvador
Brasília
Belo Horizonte
Campinas
SÃO PAULO
RIO DE JANEIRO
Curitiba
Porto Alegre
Santiago
BUENOS AIRES
Projected population change, 2005 - 2050
(by percentage)
More than 100%
50% - 100%
0% - 49%
Less than 0% (Population loss)

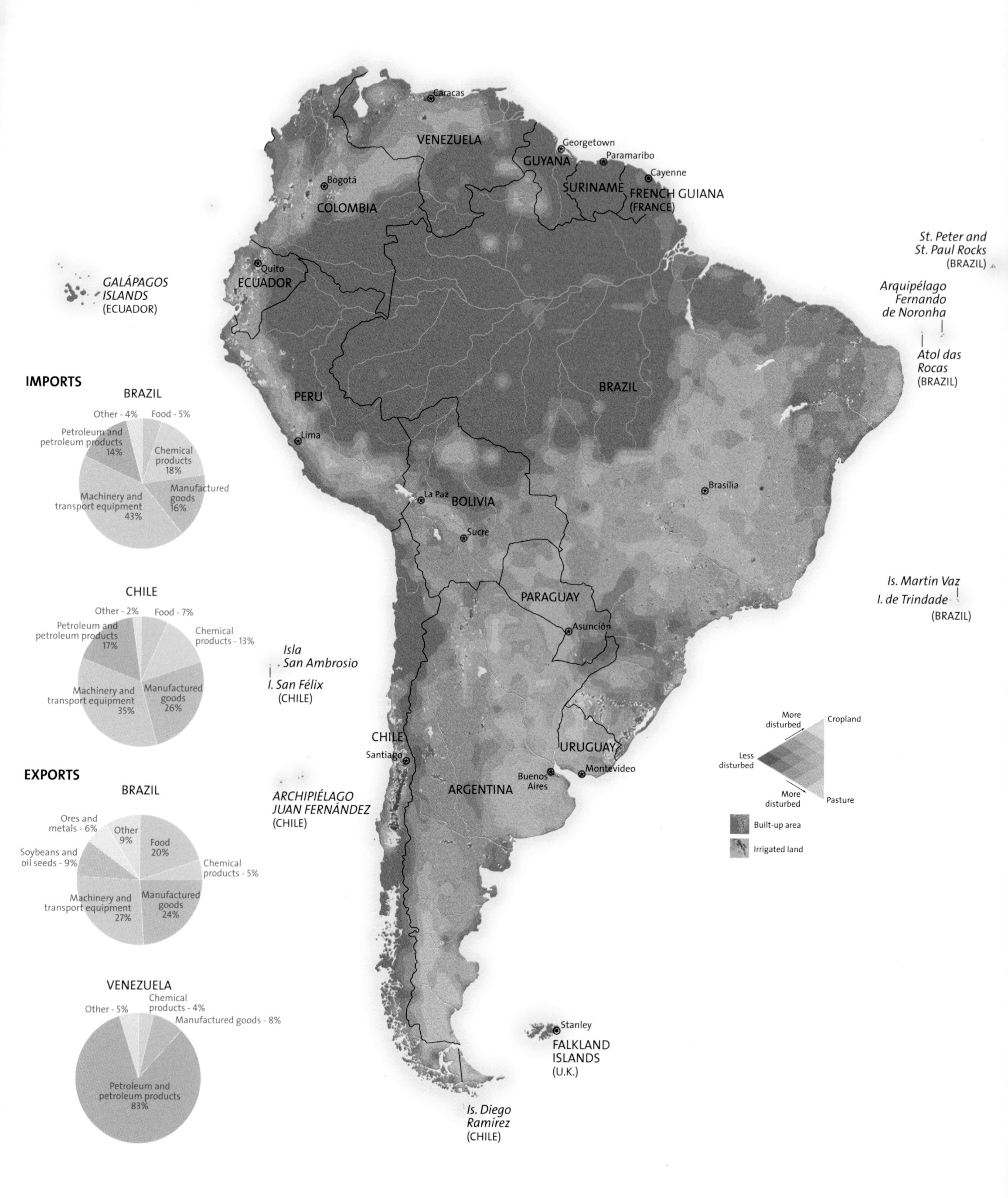

Caracas
VENEZUELA
Georgetown
GUYANA
Paramaribo
Cayenne
SURINAME
FRENCH GUIANA
(FRANCE)
Bogotá
COLOMBIA
St. Peter and
St. Paul Rocks
(BRAZIL)
GALÁPAGOS
ISLANDS
(ECUADOR)
Quito
ECUADOR
Arquipélago
Fernando
de Noronha
Atol das
Rocas
(BRAZIL)
IMPORTS
BRAZIL
Other - 4%
Food - 5%
Petroleum and
petroleum products
14%
Chemical
products
18%
Manufactured
goods
16%
Machinery and
transport equipment
43%
PERU
BRAZIL
Lima
Brasília
La Paz
BOLIVIA
Sucre
CHILE
Other - 2%
Food - 7%
Petroleum and
petroleum products
17%
Chemical
products - 13%
Machinery and
transport equipment
35%
Manufactured
goods
26%
PARAGUAY
Asunción
Is. Martin Vaz
I. de Trindade
(BRAZIL)
Isla
San Ambrosio
I. San Félix
(CHILE)
CHILE
Santiago
URUGUAY
Buenos
Aires
Montevideo
ARGENTINA
More
disturbed
Cropland
Less
disturbed
More
disturbed
Pasture
Built-up area
Irrigated land
EXPORTS
BRAZIL
ARCHIPIÉLAGO
JUAN FERNÁNDEZ
(CHILE)
Ores and
metals - 6%
Other
9%
Food
20%
Soybeans and
oil seeds - 9%
Chemical
products - 5%
Machinery and
transport equipment
27%
Manufactured
goods
24%
VENEZUELA
Chemical
products - 4%
Other - 5%
Manufactured goods - 8%
Petroleum and
petroleum products
83%
Stanley
FALKLAND
ISLANDS
(U.K.)
Is. Diego
Ramírez
(CHILE)

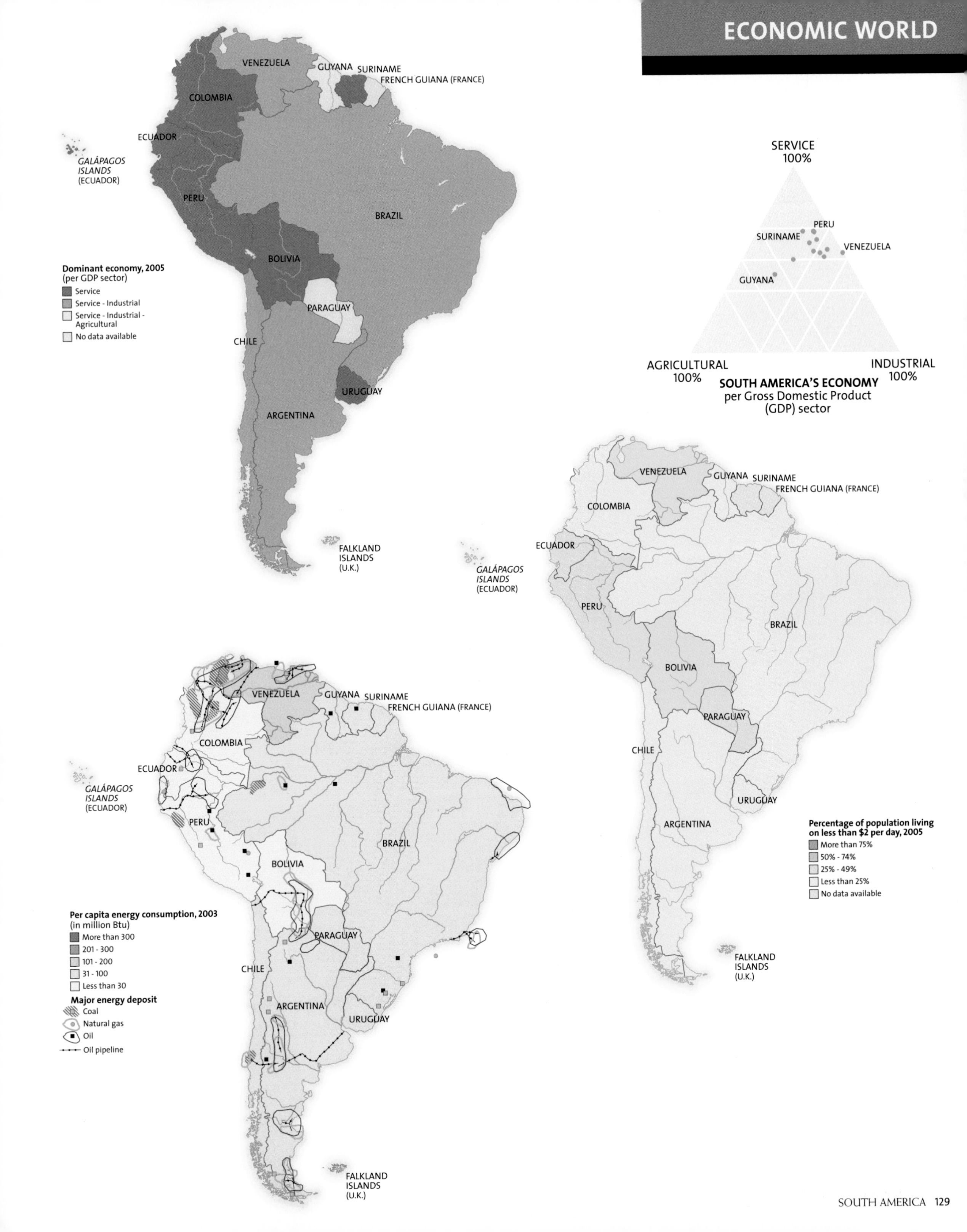
VENEZUELA
GUYANA
SURINAME
FRENCH GUIANA (FRANCE)
COLOMBIA
ECUADOR
GALÁPAGOS ISLANDS (ECUADOR)
PERU
BRAZIL
BOLIVIA
PARAGUAY
CHILE
URUGUAY
ARGENTINA
FALKLAND ISLANDS (U.K.)
Dominant economy, 2005
(per GDP sector)
Service
Service - Industrial
Service - Industrial - Agricultural
No data available
SERVICE 100%
PERU
SURINAME
VENEZUELA
GUYANA
AGRICULTURAL 100%
INDUSTRIAL 100%
SOUTH AMERICA'S ECONOMY
per Gross Domestic Product (GDP) sector
Percentage of population living on less than $2 per day, 2005
More than 75%
50% - 74%
25% - 49%
Less than 25%
No data available
Per capita energy consumption, 2003
(in million Btu)
More than 300
201 - 300
101 - 200
31 - 100
Less than 30
Major energy deposit
Coal
Natural gas
Oil
Oil pipeline

ADMINISTRATIVE AREAS OF VENEZUELA AND THEIR CAPITALS
(Numbered in blue where not labeled on map)
1 Aragua (Maracay)
2 Capital District (Caracas)
3 Miranda (Los Teques)
4 Vargas (La Guaira)
AZIMUTHAL EQUIDISTANT PROJECTION
SCALE 1:12,000,000
0 KILOMETERS 200 300
0 MILES 100 200 300
Longitude West 81° of Greenwich
PACIFIC OCEAN
CARIBBEAN
EQUATOR
GALÁPAGOS ISLANDS
(Archipiélago de Colón)
Ecuador
I. Darwin
I. Wolf
Isla Pinta
Isla Marchena
Isla Genovesa
I. Isabela
I. San Salvador
I. Fernandina
Isla Santa Cruz
Isla San Cristóbal
Puerto Villamil
Puerto Ayora
Puerto Baquerizo Moreno
Puerto Velasco Ibarra
I. Santa María
Isla Española
Isla del Coco
Costa Rica
I. de Malpelo
Colombia
NICARAGUA
COSTA RICA
PANAMA
COLOMBIA
ECUADOR
PERU
EL SALVADOR
HONDURAS
SAN ANDRÉS Y PROVIDENCIA
Managua
San José
Panamá
BOGOTÁ
Quito
LIMA
Medellín
Cali
Barranquilla
Cartagena
Guayaquil
Cúcuta
Maracaibo
Trujillo
Chiclayo
Piura
Iquitos
Cusco
Callao
Huancayo
Ica
Chimbote
Cuenca
Machala
Loja
Pucallpa
Huánuco
Cajamarca
Bucaramanga
Santa Marta
San Cristóbal
CORDILLERA DE LOS ANDES
ANTIOQUIA
SANTANDER
ARAUCA
CASANARE
META
GUAVIARE
CAQUETÁ
PUTUMAYO
AMAZONAS
LORETO
SAN MARTÍN
LA LIBERTAD
ANCASH
HUÁNUCO
PASCO
JUNÍN
LAMBAYEQUE
PIURA
TUMBES
NARIÑO
CAUCA
TOLIMA
HUILA
CHOCÓ
ZULIA
Golfo de Panamá
Golfo de Guayaquil
Golfo de los Mosquitos
Golfo de Venezuela
Lago de Nicaragua

66°
63°
60°
57°
54°
12°
9°
6°
3°
0°
SEA
ANTILLES
WINDWARD ISLANDS
Castries
ST. LUCIA
Kingstown
ST. VINCENT AND THE GRENADINES
Bridgetown
BARBADOS
Tobago Basin
GRENADA
St. George's
Is. de Aves Venez.
Is. Los Roques Venez.
Isla Blanquilla Venez.
ARCHIPIÉLAGO LOS ROQUES N.P.
Bonaire Basin
NUEVA ESPARTA
La Asunción
Charlotteville
Tobago
TRINIDAD AND TOBAGO
Galera Point
Port-of-Spain
Gulf of Paria
San Fernando
Trinidad
Isla La Tortuga
I. de Margarita
Isla Coche
MOCHIMA N.P.
Chichiriviche
Tucacas
Caracas
Petare
La Guaira
Río Chico
Caraico Basin
Puerto La Cruz
Barcelona
Cumaná
SUCRE
Caripito
Los Teques
Maracay
San Juan de los Morros
San Mateo
Maturín
Pedernales
MARIUSA N.P.
Punta Araguapiche
San Carlos
Ortiz
Valle de la Pascua
Zaraza
MONAGAS
Nipa
El Calvario
Grico
Saban
Leona
Tucupita
DELTA AMACURO
Calabozo
GUÁRICO
ANZOÁTEGUI
Barrancas
Curiapo
San José de Amacuro
AGUARO-GUARIQUITO N.P.
Santa Cruz
Ciudad Bolívar
Ciudad Guayana
Morawhanna
Shell Beach
Hosororo
Mabaruma
San Fernando de Apure
Cabruta
Caicara
Orinoco
El Pao
Guri Dam
Serranía de Imataca
Matthew's Ridge
Port Kaituma
Charity
VENEZUELA
Guachara
Cunaviche
1863
Cerro Mato
Aripao
Co. Bolívar
802
Ciudad Piar
Guasipati
El Callao
El Perú
Tumeremo
Surama
Calceta
Suddie
Wakenaam I.
Parika
Georgetown
Buxton
El Dorado
Cuyuni
Peaima Falls
Serranía de La Cerbatana
Puerto Páez
BOLÍVAR
Co. Venamo
1890
Bartica
Rosignol
New Amsterdam
Puerto Carreño
Puerto Ayacucho
CANAIMA N.P.
Auyán Tepui
2957
Issano
Linden
Mara
Corriverton
Totness
Nieuw Amsterdam
Pointe Isère
Mana
Skeldon
Paramaribo
Meerzorg
Albina
Saint-Laurent du Maroni
GUYANAIS SPACE CENTER
Samariapo
Morganito
1672
Co. Chanaro
Urimán
La Gran Sabana
Pakaraima Mountains
Mt. Roraima
2772
Mt. Ayanganna
2042
Mahdia
Ituni
Matapi
Brokopondo
Brownsweg
Saint-Jean
Sinnamary
Kourou
Cayenne
Rémire
JÁUA SARISARIÑAMA N.P.
Cerro Curutú
MONTE RORAIMA N.P.
GUYANA
Van Blommestein Meer
Délices
Roura
Pointe Béhague
San Vicente
Cacuri
Santa Elena
1136
Kurupukari
Grand Santi
Régina
Cabo Orange
Ponta do Mosquito
2260
Cerro Yumari
1999
Ser. Quiniguia
2499
Wonotobo Vallen
975
Hendrik Top
Atabapo
YAPACANA N.P.
DUIDA-MARAHUACA N.P.
Sierra Pacaraima
Apoteri
SURINAME
FRENCH GUIANA
Saint-Georges
Oiapoque
Cabo Cassiporé
Santa Bárbara
Co. Marahuaca
2579
Conceição do Maú
Annai
Kumaka
Wilhelmina Geb.
1230
Granbori
Benzdorp
France
CABO ORANGE N.P.
La Esmeralda
PARIMA-TAPIRAPECÓ NATIONAL PARK
Uraricoera
Lethem
Malavate
Camopi
Vila Velha
Victorino
AMAZONAS
Serra Parima
Boa Vista
Kayser Geb.
Oronoquekamp
Cunani
Maroa
Mucajaí
Pico Redondo
Sa. do Apiaú
Sa. do Mucajaí
Sa. Grande (Carauna)
439
Boundary claimed by Suriname
495
635
Euca
Calçoene
Cejal
Capibara
Platanal
Aishalton
Serra de Tumucumaque
541
Amapá
Ilha de Maracá
Cerro Caparro
Solano
RORAIMA
Sa. Acaraí
TUMUCUMAQUE N.P.
Cabo Norte
San Felipe
San Carlos de Río Negro
SERRANÍA DE LA NEBLINA N.P.
Caracaraí
Kamoa Mountains
Tacalé
AMAPÁ
Ponta Grossa
I. Bailique
Bailique
El Carmen
Cucuí
Sa. Imeri
Sa. Tapirapecó
734
Cafuini
Merirumã
Serra do Navio
Teresinha
Porto Grande
I. Curuá
Ferreira Gomes
I. Janaucu
São José de Anauá
Maloca
315
Içana
Pico 31 de Março
PICO DA NEBLINA N.P.
Cachoeira dos Índios
Vila Conceição
Macapá
I. Caviana
Ilha Mexiana
EQUATOR
Taraquá
São Gabriel da Cachoeira
Sa. Curicuriari
500
Tapurucuará
Tomar
Porto Santana
Mazagão
I. Camaleão
Cabo Maguari
Boiaçu
San Antonio da Cachoeira
Afuá
Santa Cruz do Arai
Soure
Salinópolis
Ilha de Marajó
Salvaterra
Maracanã
Primavera
Bragança
Cabo Gurupi
I. da Trauira
Barcelos
Tiago
Mapuera
Munguba
Itatupã
Anajás
Viseu
Moura
Carvoeiro
Sa. Parauaquara
Almeirim
Boca do Jari
Muaná
Belém
Castanhal
Maraã
Japurá
Represa da Balbina
Santa Maria
Oriximiná
Cipoal
Prainha
359
Porto de Moz
Breves
Curralinho
Abaetetuba
Capitão Poço
Turiaçu
Cametá
Camiranga
JAÚ NATIONAL PARK
Mirapinima
Faro
Juruti
Óbidos
Alenquer
Monte Alegre
Portel
Tonantins
Fonte Boa
Ilhas Macuapanim
Arquipélago das Anavilhanas
Tauapeçaçu
Urucará
Urucurituba
Albano
Nhamundá
Alter do Chão
Belterra
Santarém
Curuá
Carvalho
Mocajuba
Canindé
Santa Maria
Manaus
Silves
Itacoatiara
Parintins
Freguesia do Andirá
Independência
Senador José Porfírio
Ilha Grande de Jutaí
Santo Antônio do Içá
Alvarães
Manacapuru
Amatari
Careiro
Autazes
Barreirinha
Ilha Tupinambarana
Maués
Cataurara
Boim
Aveiro
229
Vitória
Altamira
Maloca Timbé
Serra da Desordem
São Paulo de Olivença
Jutaí
Tefé
Solimões (Amazonas)
Anamã
Anori
Codajás
Nova Olinda do Norte
Sa. Urubuquara
Tucuruí
Renascença
Coari
Beruri
Axinim
Canumã
Mucajá
AMAZÔNIA N.P.
Brasília Legal
Itaituba
PARÁ
Santa Inês
Serra do Tiracambu
AMAZONAS
Borba
Vista Alegre
Paga Conta
Porto Alegre
Remansão
Jatobal
Açailândia
Carauari
Aruajá
Novo Aripuanã
Tabuleiro
Belo Horizonte
Itupiranga
São João do Araguaia
Imperatriz
Tambaqui
Santa Helena
BRAZIL
Marabá
Marari
São Romão
Penha do Tapaua
Purus
Arimã
Manicoré
Laje
Serra dos Carajás
São Raimundo do Araguaia
Araguatins
Grajaú
Constância dos Baetas
Canumã
Araras
Tocantinópolis
Canutama
São Félix do Xingu
Porto Franco
São Geraldo do Araguaia
640
Serra Negra
100
Paraíso
Serra da Seringa
Lábrea
100
Natal
Barra do São Manuel
Manuelzinho
Araguaína
Carolina
Riachão
Prainha
Canudos
Mamoriá
Crato
Pauini
Guajarraã
Humaitá
Sumaúma
Cachoeira do Tareraimbu
Gradaús
Filadélfia
Balsas
Calama
Santa Júlia
Serra do Cachimbo
Palmeirante
Boca do Curuquetê
Foz do Jamari
Conceição do Araguaia
Couto Magalhães
Itacajá
Samaúma
Boca do Acre
Porto Velho
Barracão do Barreto
Serra dos Gradaús
MARANHÃO
Araras
Cachoeira do Rebojo
92
Cachoeira das Sete Quedas
Cachimbo
Araguacema
Guaraí
Pedro Afonso
Tasso Fragoso
Serra do Penitente
Riozinho
Caritianas
Santana do Araguaia
Miracema do Norte
Santa Filomena
Rio Branco
Manoa
Abunã
Fortaleza
Ariquemes
Aripuanã
Serra do Estrondo
Tocantínia
Bom Destino
Vila Murtinho
Jaru
Serra do Norte
Serra dos Apiacás
Santana
Gilbués
Santa Rosa
Villa Bella
Yata
Serra dos Pacaás Novos
Serra da Providência
Santa Teresinha
ARAGUAIA NATIONAL PARK
Palmas
Novo Acordo
PIAUÍ
Brasiléia
Bella Flor
Las Piedras
Moreno
Conquista
RONDÔNIA
Ji-Paraná (Rondonia)
Rancho de Caça dos Tapiúnas
Morro do Sinal
Posto Alto Maniçauã
Macaúba
TOCANTINS
Cristalândia
Chapada das Mangabeiras
Pedra de Amolar
Porto Nacional
Formosa do Rio Prêto
PANDO
Ivón
Sena
PACAÁS NOVOS NATIONAL PARK
503
Pimenta Bueno
Porto dos Gaúchos
MATO GROSSO
Santa Isabel do Morro
Almas
Carmen
San Lorenzo
Apere
Mayo Mayo
Príncipe da Beira
Maloca de Indios
Sinop
Natividade
Caripare
Gurupi
Peixe
870
Puerto Heath
Serra do Tombador
Serra Formosa
Serra dos Caiabis
Serra do Roncador
Alvorada
BAHIA
LA PAZ
Pedras Negras
Vilhena
BOLIVIA
Mateguá
Utiariti
Lucas
Porto Artur
Paranã
Arraias
Campos Belos
186
São Miguel do Araguaia
Serra Dourada
Yata
Exaltación
Lago Rogagua
BENI
Puerto Villazón
NOEL KEMPFF MERCADO N.P.
Puerto Saucedo
Yacuma
Bandeirante
Estrêla do Norte
GOIÁS
SANTA CRUZ
51°
48°
ATLANTIC OCEAN

COLOMBIA
AMAZONAS
VAUPÉS
RORAIMA
LORETO
PERU
ACRE
PANDO
RONDONIA
BRAZIL
MATO GROSSO
MADRE DE DIOS
JUNÍN
UCAYALI
HUANCAVELICA
AYACUCHO
CUSCO
APURÍMAC
PUNO
AREQUIPA
MOQUEGUA
TACNA
LA PAZ
BENI
BOLIVIA
SANTA CRUZ
COCHABAMBA
ORURO
CHUQUISACA
POTOSÍ
TARIJA
TARAPACÁ
ANTOFAGASTA
ATACAMA
CHILE
JUJUY
SALTA
ARGENTINA
TUCUMÁN
CATAMARCA
LA RIOJA
SANTIAGO DEL ESTERO
CHACO
FORMOSA
SANTA FE
CORRIENTES
MISIONES
PARAGUAY
MATO GROSSO DO SUL
RIO GRANDE DO SUL
PACIFIC OCEAN
TROPIC OF CAPRICORN
CORDILLERA DE LOS ANDES
Manaus
Santarém
Itaituba
Porto Velho
Rio Branco
Iquitos
Pucallpa
Cusco
Juliaca
Arequipa
Tacna
Arica
La Paz
Cochabamba
Oruro
Sucre
Potosí
Santa Cruz
Trinidad
Cuiabá
Campo Grande
Dourados
Asunción
Formosa
Corrientes
Resistencia
Posadas
Foz do Iguaçu
Salta
San Miguel de Tucumán
Santiago del Estero
Catamarca
Antofagasta
Calama
Iquique
Chañaral
Caldera
Copiapó
Tarija
Cobija
Puerto Maldonado
Machu Picchu
Lago Titicaca
Salar de Uyuni
JAÚ N.P.
AMAZÔNIA N.P.
SERRA DO DIVISOR N.P.
MANU N.P.
BAHUAJA-SONENE N.P.
MADIDI N.P.
NOEL KEMPFF MERCADO N.P.
PACAÁS NOVOS N.P.
ISIBORO SÉCURE N.P.
CARRASCO ICHILO N.P.
AMBORÓ N.P.
KAA-IYA NATIONAL PARK
DEFENSORES DEL CHACO N.P.
PANTANAL MATOGROSSENSE N.P.
EMAS N.P.
IGUAÇU N.P.
LLULLAILLACO N.P.
Serra do Cachimbo
Serra dos Parecis
Serra do Roncador
3°
6°
9°
12°
15°
18°
21°
24°
27°
72°
69°
66°
63°
60°
57°
54°
75°

Belém
Castanhal
Bragança
Viseu
Abaetetuba
Cametá
Capitão Poço
I. Mangunça
Cururupu
Camiranga
Guimarães
ALCANTARA LAUNCH CENTER
LENÇÓIS MARANHENSES N.P.
São João de Cortes
São Luís
I. de São Luís
Primeira Cruz
I. do Caju
I. das Canárias
Ponta dos Patos
Parnaíba
Camocim
Granja
Acaraú
Ilha Grande de Santa Isabel
Morros
Rosário
Viana
Penalva
Arari
Itapecuru Mirim
Urbano Santos
Morrinhos
Sobral
Paracuru
Caucaia
Fortaleza
Maranguape
Tucuruí
Maloca
Timbé
Santa Inês
Chapadinha
Brejo
Porto
Bacabal
Coelho Neto
Piracuruca
Ipu
Tianguá
Peritoró
Codó
Pedreiras
Caxias
Barras
Piripiri
Cascavel
Pacajus
Fortim
Aracati
Baturité
Canindé
União
Campo Maior
Ipueiras
MARANHÃO
Timon
Teresina
Oiticica
Tamboril
Quixadá
Russas
Mossoró
Presidente Dutra
Barra do Corda
CEARÁ
Independência
RIO GRANDE DO NORTE
Macau
Ponta do Calcanhar
Touros
Ceará Mirim
Natal
Atol das Rocas Brazil
Arquipélago de Fernando de Noronha Brazil
Marabá
São Raimundo
Araguatins
Grajaú
Remansão
Jatobal
Itupiranga
Represa de Tucuruí
Serra do Gurupi
Serra do Tiracambu
Tocantinópolis
Porto Franco
São Geraldo do Araguaia
Colinas
Parnarama
Regeneração
Amarante
Mirador
Pastos Bons
Guadalupe
Barão de Grajaú
Floriano
Oeiras
Benedito Leite
Loreto
Carolina
Riachão
Balsas
Araguaína
Filadélfia
Uruçuí
PIAUÍ
Picos
Fronteiras
Tauá
Iguatu
Orós
Jucás
Lavras da Mangabeira
Icó
Juazeiro do Norte
Crato
Cajazeiras
Sousa
Pombal
Patu
Caicó
Currais Novos
Jardim do Seridó
Macaíba
Goianinha
Arês
Canguaretama
Guarabira
Rio Tinto
João Pessoa
PARAÍBA
Chapada do Araripe
Simplício Mendes
Jaicós
Conceição
Palmeirante
Conceição do Araguaia
Couto Magalhães
Itacajá
Canto do Buriti
Eliseu Martins
Paulistana
Parnamirim
Bodocó
Flores
Sertânia
Sumé
Paulista
Olinda
Recife
Caruaru
Arcoverde
Salgueiro
Cabrobó
São João do Piauí
Bom Jesus
Serra Dois Irmãos
Serra Bom Jesus da Gurguéia
Tasso Fragoso
Guaraí
Serra do Estrondo
Chapada das Mangabeiras
Serra do Penitente
Serra do Uruçuí
Alto Parnaíba
Santa Filomena
Miracema do Norte
Caracol
São Raimundo Nonato
Rajada
Petrolândia
Macururé
PERNAMBUCO
Ribeirão
Palmares
Garanhuns
Inajá
Palmeira dos Índios
Curaçá
Juazeiro
Glória
Paulo Afonso
Porto de Pedras
TOCANTINS
Palmas
Gilbués
Remanso
Pilão Arcado
Represa de Sobradinho
Serra de Itiúba
Uauá
Piranhas
ALAGOAS
Arapiraca
Maceió
Novo Acordo
Cristalândia
Macaúba
ARAGUAIA N.P.
Porto Nacional
Pedra de Amolar
Serra da Tabatinga
Serra do Estreito
Ibiraba
Jeremoabo
SERGIPE
Propriá
Penedo
Ponta do Manguinho
Senhor do Bonfim
Ribeira do Pombal
Itabaiana
São Cristóvão
Aracaju
Formosa do Rio Prêto
Ibipetuba
Barra
Xique Xique
Queimadas
Tucano
Itabaianinha
Estância
Almas
Natividade
Cariparé
Serra do Boqueirão
Morpará
Irecê
Jacobina
Miguel Calmon
Serrinha
Chapada Diamantina
Gurupi
Peixe
Jupaguá
Ipupiara
Inhambupe
Conde
Alagoinhas
Barreiras
Ibotirama
Rui Barbosa
Feira de Santana
Brejolândia
BAHIA
Itaberaba
Santo Amaro
Muritiba
Candeias
Alvorada
Paranã
Campos Belos
Paratinga
Ibitiara
Lençóis
Itaeté
Maragogipe
Salvador (Bahia)
Arraias
Santana
Bom Jesus da Lapa
Piatã
Maracás
I. de Itaparica
São Miguel do Araguaia
Porangatu
Santa Maria da Vitória
Coribe
Valença
Estrêla do Norte
Cavalcante
Nova Roma
Serra do Ramalho
Riacho de Santana
Ituaçu
Jequié
I. de Boipeba
Mara Rosa
Posse
Guanambi
Caetité
Serra Dourada
Niquelândia
São Luís do Tocantins
Carinhanha
Malhada
Brumado
Ipiaú
São João da Aliança
Sítio da Abadia
Manga
Caculé
Vitória da Conquista
Ubaitaba
Ceres
Goianésia
Uruana
Serra Bonita
GRANDE SERTÃO VEREDAS N.P.
Januária
Condeúba
Monte Azul
Itambé
Ibicaraí
Itapetinga
Camacan
Brasília
Formosa
DISTRITO FED.
Itaberaí
Urucuia
São Francisco
Janaúba
Salinas
Pedra Azul
Canavieiras
Belmonte
Unaí
Mirabela
Almenara
Santa Cruz Cabrália
Inhumas
Anápolis
Trindade
Goiânia
Silvânia
Cristalina
PLANALTO DO BRASIL
Montes Claros
Jequitinhonha
MONTE PASCOAL N.P.
Mte. Pascoal
Araçuaí
Cumuruxatiba
ATLANTIC OCEAN
Pires do Rio
Paracatu
Minas Novas
Machacalis
Ponta da Baleia
Pontalina
Guarda Mor
João Pinheiro
Pirapora
Buenópolis
Serra do Chifre
Prado
Teófilo Otoni
Nanuque
Morrinhos
Ipameri
Catalão
MINAS GERAIS
Caravelas
Ibirapuã
Itumbiara
Alegre
Patos de Minas
Corinto
Arquipélago dos Abrolhos
Araguari
Tupaciguara
Peçanha
Serra dos Aimorés
Chavesilândia
Uberlândia
Curvelo
Mantena
São Mateus
Conceição da Barra
Ituiutaba
Patrocínio
Governador Valadares
Conselheiro Pena
Prata
Araxá
Ibiá
Abaeté
Linhares
Sete Lagoas
Luz
Frutal
Uberaba
João Monlevade
Baixo Guandu
Colatina
Divinópolis
Belo Horizonte
Aracruz
Colômbia
Formiga
Itaúna
Franca
São José do Rio Preto
Barretos
Piuí
Passos
Ponte Nova
Muniz Freire
ESPIRITO SANTO
Vitória
Campo
Oliveira
Conselheiro Lafaiete
Ubá
Muriaé
Guarapari
Catanduva
Lavras
Guaxupé
Barbacena
Ribeirão Preto
Juiz de Fora
Miracema
Itapemirim
Machado
Varginha
São Carlos
Pirajuí
Caxambu
Leopoldina
Campos
Trindade
Ilhas Martin Vaz
Brazil
Pouso Alegre
Araras
Três Rios
Lagoa Feia
Bauru
Jaú
Limeira
Itajubá
Resende
RIO DE JANEIRO
Macaé
Assis
SÃO PAULO
Campinas
Nova Iguaçu
Niterói
Cabo Frio
Jacarézinho
Piraju
Sorocaba
Jundiaí
Jacareí
Parati
Rio de Janeiro
SERRA DA BOCAINA N.P.
Itapetininga
São Paulo
Itararé
São Vicente
Santos
Ilha de São Sebastião
Serra do Paranapiacaba
Registro
Itanhaém
TROPIC OF CAPRICORN
Castro
Apiaí
Iguape
Ponta Grossa
Antonina
Curitiba
São José dos Pinhais
Lapa
São Francisco do Sul
Mafra
I. de São Francisco
Jaraguá do Sul
Tijucas
Florianópolis
Bom Retiro
São José
Serra do Mar
Imbituba
Laguna
Criciúma
Praia Grande
AZIMUTHAL EQUIDISTANT PROJECTION
SCALE 1:12,000,000
0 KILOMETERS 200 300
0 MILES 100 200 300
Longitude West 45° of Greenwich
48°
45°
42°
39°
36°
33°
30°
27°
3°
6°
9°
12°
15°
18°
21°
24°

BRAZIL
PARAGUAY
URUGUAY
ARGENTINA
BOLIVIA
CHILE
PERU
PACIFIC OCEAN
TROPIC OF CAPRICORN
Longitude West 60° of Greenwich
MATO GROSSO DO SUL
MINAS GERAIS
GOIÁS
SÃO PAULO
PARANÁ
SANTA CATARINA
RIO GRANDE DO SUL
MISIONES
CORRIENTES
ENTRE RÍOS
SANTA FE
CHACO
FORMOSA
SANTIAGO DEL ESTERO
TUCUMÁN
SALTA
JUJUY
CATAMARCA
LA RIOJA
SAN JUAN
CÓRDOBA
SAN LUIS
MENDOZA
LA PAMPA
BUENOS AIRES
NEUQUÉN
RÍO NEGRO
SANTA CRUZ
CHUQUISACA
TARIJA
POTOSÍ
ORURO
COCHABAMBA
TARAPACÁ
ANTOFAGASTA
ATACAMA
COQUIMBO
MAULE
BÍO-BÍO
LA ARAUCANÍA
Desierto de Atacama
Asunción
SÃO PAULO
Curitiba
Porto Alegre
Montevideo
Buenos Aires
Rosario
Córdoba
Santiago
Valparaíso
Mendoza
Mar del Plata
Bahía Blanca
Antofagasta
Salta
San Miguel de Tucumán
Florianópolis
Campo Grande
Sucre
Santos
Concepción
Talcahuano
Valdivia
Osorno

ATLANTIC OCEAN
SCOTIA SEA
WEDDELL SEA
Drake Passage
SOUTH GEORGIA
U.K.
Willis Islands
Annenkov I.
Cape Disappointment
Shag Rocks
Black Rock
South Orkney Islands
Coronation I.
Laurie I.
Signy I.
Inaccessible Is.
Administered by United Kingdom
(claimed by Argentina)
Falkland Islands
(Islas Malvinas)
Stanley
Macbride Head
Cape Dolphin
E. Falkland
W. Falkland
Sea Lion Islands
Jason Islands
Lively I.
Weddell I.
New I.
Beauchêne Island
Barren Island
Burdwood Bank
Elephant I.
Clarence I.
Gibbs I.
Seal Is.
S. Shetland Is.
Smith Island
Snow I.
Livingston I.
Greenwich I.
Nelson I.
Deception I.
Low Island
Tower I.
Joinville I.
D'Urville I.
Moody Point
Danger Is.
Vega I.
James Ross I.
Seymour I.
Snow Hill I.
Robertson I.
ANTARCTIC PENINSULA
ANTARCTICA
Brabant I.
Anvers I.
Melchior Is.
Palmer Arch.
CHUBUT
SANTA CRUZ
TIERRA DEL FUEGO
Comodoro Rivadavia
Rawson
Puerto Deseado
Golfo San Jorge
Bahía Grande
Río Gallegos
Punta Arenas
Ushuaia
Cabo San Juan
Isla de los Estados
(Staten Island)
Is. Wollaston
CABO DE HORNOS N.P.
Cabo de Hornos
(Cape Horn)
I. Navarino
Isla Grande de Chiloé
Islas Guaitecas
Arch. de los Chonos
PENÍNSULA VALDÉS
Cabo Dos Bahías
Cabo Tres Puntas
Cabo Blanco
Bahía de los Nodales
I. Madre de Dios
I. Duque de York
Arch. Reina Adelaida
Grupo Evangelistas
I. Desolación
I. Sta. Inés
Islas Gilbert
Golfo de Penas
Península Tres Montes
AZIMUTHAL EQUIDISTANT PROJECTION
SCALE 1:12,000,000
0 KILOMETERS 200 300
0 MILES 100 200 300

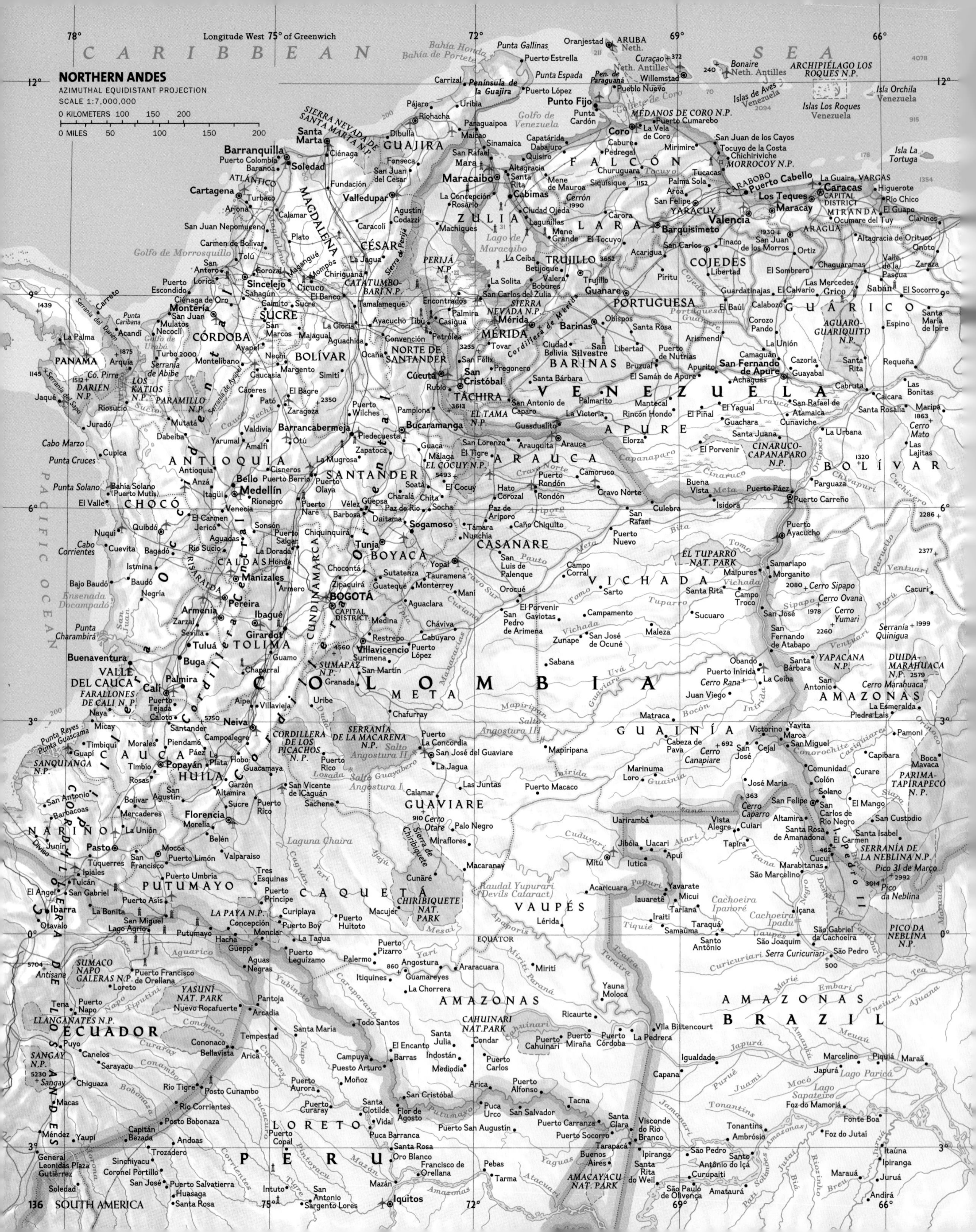

NORTHERN ANDES
AZIMUTHAL EQUIDISTANT PROJECTION
SCALE 1:7,000,000
0 KILOMETERS 100 150 200
0 MILES 50 100 150 200
Longitude West 75° of Greenwich
78°
72°
69°
66°
12°
9°
6°
3°
0°
CARIBBEAN SEA
PACIFIC OCEAN
COLOMBIA
VENEZUELA
ECUADOR
PERU
BRAZIL
PANAMA
ARUBA Neth.
Oranjestad
Curaçao Neth. Antilles
Willemstad
Bonaire Neth. Antilles
ARCHIPIÉLAGO LOS ROQUES N.P.
Islas Los Roques Venezuela
Isla Orchila Venezuela
Islas de Aves Venezuela
Isla La Tortuga
Bahía Honda
Bahía de Portete
Punta Gallinas
Puerto Estrella
Punta Espada
Península de la Guajira
Pen. de Paraguaná
Golfo de Venezuela
Golfo de Morrosquillo
Golfo de Urabá
Punto Fijo
Punta Cardón
Pueblo Nuevo
MÉDANOS DE CORO N.P.
Coro
La Vela de Coro
Puerto Cumarebo
SIERRA NEVADA DE SANTA MARTA N.P.
GUAJIRA
Riohacha
Uribia
Maicao
Paraguaipoa
Santa Marta
Barranquilla
Soledad
Ciénaga
Cartagena
ATLÁNTICO
MAGDALENA
Valledupar
CÉSAR
Sierra de Perijá
PERIJÁ N.P.
CATATUMBO-BARÍ N.P.
Maracaibo
Cabimas
Lago de Maracaibo
ZULIA
FALCÓN
LARA
Barquisimeto
YARACUY
CARABOBO
Puerto Cabello
Valencia
Maracay
Los Teques
Caracas
CAPITAL DISTRICT
La Guaira, VARGAS
MIRANDA
ARAGUA
MORROCOY N.P.
San Juan de los Cayos
Tucacas
COJEDES
San Carlos
TRUJILLO
Trujillo
Guanare
PORTUGUESA
MÉRIDA
Mérida
SIERRA NEVADA N.P.
Cordillera de Mérida
Barinas
BARINAS
GUÁRICO
AGUARO-GUARIQUITO N.P.
San Fernando de Apure
APURE
TÁCHIRA
San Cristóbal
Cúcuta
NORTE DE SANTANDER
EL TAMA N.P.
Guasdualito
Arauca
ARAUCA
EL COCUY N.P.
CINARUCO-CAPANAPARO N.P.
Puerto Páez
Puerto Carreño
BOLÍVAR
Puerto Ayacucho
EL TUPARRO NAT. PARK
VICHADA
CASANARE
Yopal
BOYACÁ
Tunja
Sogamoso
SANTANDER
Bucaramanga
Barrancabermeja
ANTIOQUIA
Medellín
Bello
CHOCÓ
Quibdó
CÓRDOBA
Montería
SUCRE
Sincelejo
BOLÍVAR
RISARALDA
Pereira
CALDAS
Manizales
QUINDÍO
Armenia
CUNDINAMARCA
BOGOTÁ
CAPITAL DISTRICT
TOLIMA
Ibagué
Girardot
VALLE DEL CAUCA
Cali
Buenaventura
Palmira
Tuluá
Buga
FARALLONES DE CALI N.P.
CAUCA
Popayán
HUILA
Neiva
META
Villavicencio
SUMAPAZ N.P.
SERRANÍA DE LA MACARENA N.P.
CORDILLERA DE LOS PICACHOS N.P.
GUAVIARE
San José del Guaviare
GUAINÍA
Puerto Inírida
CAQUETÁ
Florencia
CHIRIBIQUETE NAT. PARK
VAUPÉS
Mitú
NARIÑO
Pasto
Ipiales
Tumaco
SANQUIANGA N.P.
PUTUMAYO
Mocoa
LA PAYA N.P.
AMAZONAS
CAHUINARI NAT. PARK
AMACAYACU NAT. PARK
Leticia
Tabatinga
Iquitos
LORETO
YASUNÍ NAT. PARK
LLANGANATES N.P.
SANGAY N.P.
Sangay
SUMACO NAPO GALERAS N.P.
Tena
Puyo
Macas
Ibarra
Otavalo
Tulcán
Nueva Loja
Puerto Francisco de Orellana
Cordillera Occidental
Cordillera Central
Cordillera Oriental
LOS ANDES
Serranía de Abibe
PARAMILLO N.P.
LOS KATIOS N.P.
DARIÉN N.P.
Cabo Corrientes
Punta Solano
Cabo Marzo
AMAZONAS
YAPACANA N.P.
DUIDA-MARAHUACA N.P.
PARIMA-TAPIRAPECÓ N.P.
SERRANÍA DE LA NEBLINA N.P.
PICO DA NEBLINA N.P.
Pico da Neblina
Pico 31 de Março
Cerro Marahuaca
Rio Negro
Japurá
Solimões
Amazonas
Río Meta
Río Orinoco
Río Caquetá
Río Putumayo
Río Napo
Río Guaviare
Río Vaupés
Río Apaporis
Río Inírida
EQUATOR

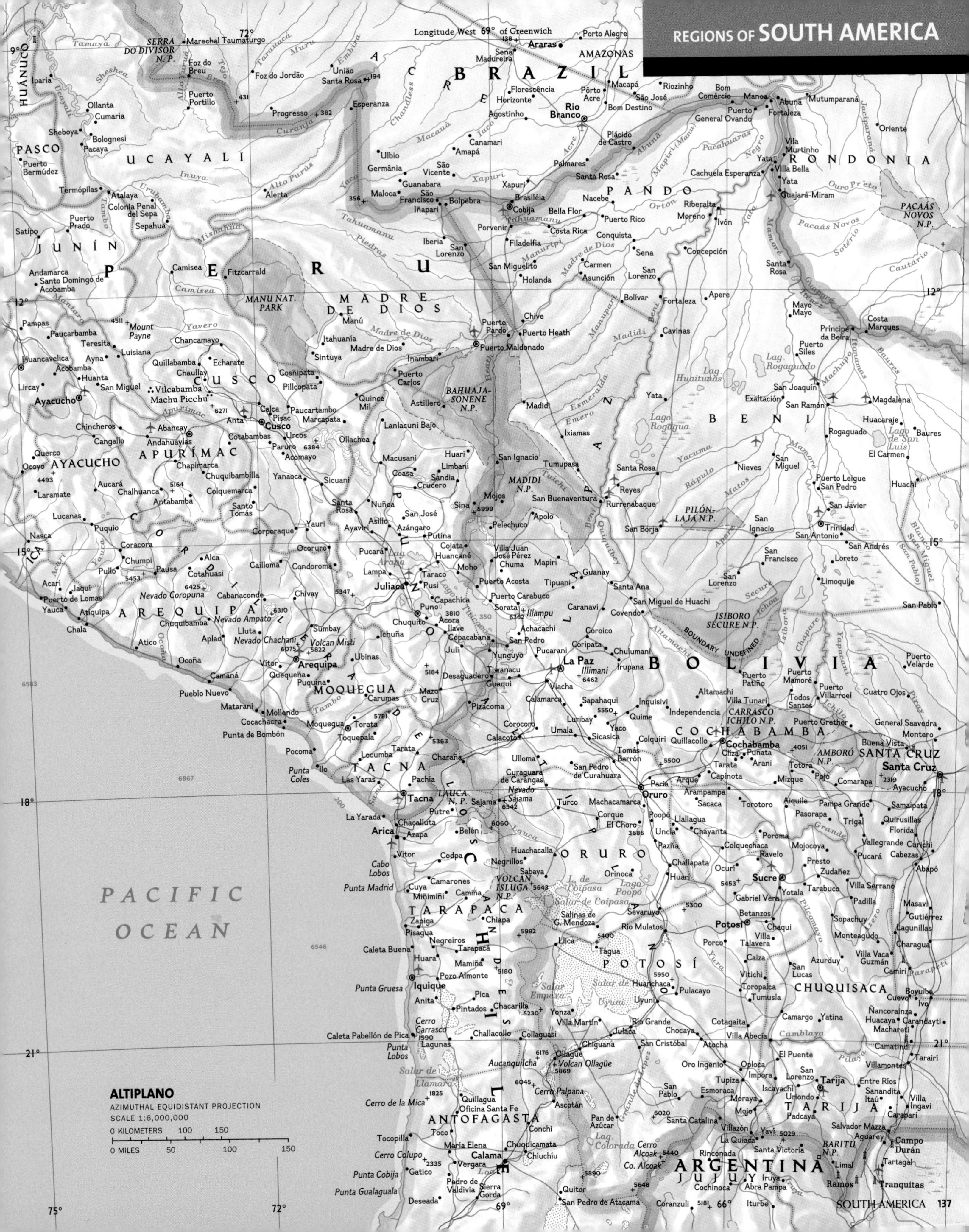

ALTIPLANO
AZIMUTHAL EQUIDISTANT PROJECTION
SCALE 1:6,000,000
0 KILOMETERS 100 150
0 MILES 50 100 150
Longitude West 69° of Greenwich
72°
75°
69°
66°
9°
12°
15°
18°
21°
PACIFIC OCEAN
BRAZIL
PERU
BOLIVIA
ARGENTINA
HUÁNUCO
PASCO
UCAYALI
JUNÍN
ACRE
AMAZONAS
RONDONIA
PANDO
MADRE DE DIOS
CUSCO
APURÍMAC
AYACUCHO
ICA
AREQUIPA
MOQUEGUA
TACNA
PUNO
LA PAZ
BENI
COCHABAMBA
SANTA CRUZ
ORURO
POTOSÍ
CHUQUISACA
TARIJA
TARAPACA
ANTOFAGASTA
JUJUY
CORDILLERA OCCIDENTAL
SERRA DO DIVISOR N.P.
MANU NAT. PARK
BAHUAJA-SONENE N.P.
MADIDI N.P.
PILÓN-LAJA N.P.
ISIBORO SECURE N.P.
BOUNDARY UNDEFINED
CARRASCO ICHILO N.P.
AMBORÓ N.P.
PACAÁS NOVOS N.P.
LAUCA N.P.
VOLCAN ISLUGA N.P.
BARITU N.P.
Marechal Taumaturgo
Porto Alegre
Araras
Sena Madureira
Foz do Breu
Foz do Jordão
União
Santa Rosa
Puerto Portillo
Iparia
Ollanta
Cumaría
Sheboya
Bolognesi
Pacaya
Puerto Bermúdez
Progresso
Esperanza
Florescência
Horizonte
Porto Acre
Macapá
São José
Riozinho
Bom Comércio
Manoa
Abunã
Mutumparaná
Rio Branco
Bom Destino
Puerto General Ovando
Fortaleza
Oriente
Agostinho
Canamari
Amapá
Plácido de Castro
Vila Murtinho
Ulbio
Germânia
São Vicente
Palmares
Santa Rosa
Cachuela Esperanza
Villa Bella
Yata
Guajará-Mirim
Termópilas
Atalaya
Colonia Penal del Sepa
Sepahua
Alerta
Guanabara
Maloca
São Francisco
Iñapari
Bolpebra
Xapuri
Brasiléia
Cobija
Bella Flor
Nacebe
Riberalta
Moreno
Ivón
Puerto Rico
Puerto Prado
Satipo
Porvenir
Costa Rica
Filadelfia
Conquista
Sena
Iberia
San Lorenzo
Concepción
Santa Rosa
Andamarca
Santo Domingo de Acobamba
Camisea
Fitzcarrald
San Miguelito
Holanda
Carmen
Asunción
San Lorenzo
Bolívar
Fortaleza
Apere
Mayo Mayo
Costa Marques
Príncipe da Beira
Puerto Siles
Pampas
Paucarbamba
Teresita
Luisiana
Mount Payne
Manú
Itahuania
Sintuya
Madre de Dios
Chive
Puerto Pardo
Puerto Heath
Puerto Maldonado
Inambari
Cavinas
Lag. Huñtunas
Lag. Rogaguado
Huancavelica
Acobamba
Ayna
Huanta
San Miguel
Lircay
Ayacucho
Chancamayo
Quillabamba
Echarate
Chaullay
Vilcabamba
Machu Picchu
Cosñipata
Pillcopata
Puerto Carlos
Quince Mil
Astillero
Madidi
Yata
San Joaquín
Exaltación
San Ramón
Magdalena
Calca
Pisac
Cusco
Anta
Paucartambo
Marcapata
Chincheros
Abancay
Andahuaylas
Cangallo
Cotabambas
Urcos
Paruro
Acomayo
Ollachea
Lanlacuni Bajo
Ixiamas
Lago Rogagua
Huacaraje
Rogaguado
Lago de San Luis
Baures
El Carmen
Querco
Ocoyo
Chapimarca
Chuquibambilla
Macusani
Huari
Limbani
San Ignacio
Tumupasa
Santa Rosa
Nieves
San Miguel
Puerto Leigue
San Pedro
Huachi
Laramate
Aucará
Chalhuanca
Antabamba
Colquemarca
Santo Tomás
Yanaoca
Sicuani
Coasa
Sandia
Crucero
Mojos
San Buenaventura
Reyes
Rurrenabaque
Santa Rosa
Nuñoa
San José
Sina
San Javier
Trinidad
Lucanas
Puquio
Yauri
Asillo
Azángaro
Ayaviri
Putina
Pelechuco
Apolo
San Borja
San Ignacio
San Antonio
Nasca
Corporaque
Ocoruro
Pucará
Cojata
Huancané
Villa Juan José Pérez
Chuma
Mapiri
San Andrés
Coracora
Chumpi
Alca
Cotahuasi
Cailloma
Condoroma
Lampa
Taraco
Moho
San Francisco
Loreto
Pullo
Pausa
Guanay
Tipuani
Lorenzo
Limoquije
Acarí
Jaquí
Puerto de Lomas
Yauca
Atiquipa
Chala
Nevado Coropuna
Cabanaconde
Chivay
Juliaca
Pusi
Puerto Acosta
Santa Ana
San Miguel de Huachi
San Pablo
Capachica
Puerto Carabuco
Sorata
Illampu
Caranavi
Covendo
Nevado Ampato
Chuquibamba
Puno
Chuquito
Acora
Ilave
Achacachi
Coroico
Coripata
Chulumani
Irupana
Puerto Velarde
Lluta
Aplao
Atico
Nevado Chachani
Volcan Misti
Sumbay
Ichuña
Copacabana
San Pedro
Pucarani
La Paz
Illimani
Ocoña
Vitor
Arequipa
Quequeña
Ubinas
Juli
Yunguyo
Tiwanacu
Desaguadero
Guaqui
Puerto Patiño
Altamachi
Puerto Mamoré
Puerto Villarroel
Cuatro Ojos
Camaná
Puquina
Mazo Cruz
Viacha
Calamarca
Sapahaqui
Inquisivi
Independencia
Villa Tunari
Todos Santos
Puerto Grether
General Saavedra
Pueblo Nuevo
Carumas
Pizacoma
Luribay
Quime
Yaco
Montero
Buena Vista
Matarani
Mollendo
Cocachacra
Punta de Bombón
Moquegua
Torata
Toquepala
Corocoro
Calacoto
Umala
Sicasica
Colquiri
Quillacollo
Cochabamba
Cliza
Punata
Arani
Santa Cruz
Pocoma
Ilo
Punta Coles
Locumba
Tarata
Charaña
Ulloma
Tomás Barrón
Tarata
Capinota
Totora
Pojo
Comarapa
Las Yaras
Pachia
Curaguara de Carangas
San Pedro de Curahuara
Paria
Oruro
Arque
Mizque
Ayacucho
Tacna
Nevado Sajama
Sajama
Putre
Turco
Machacamarca
Arampampa
Sacaca
Torotoro
Aiquile
Pampa Grande
Samaipata
La Yarada
Chacalluta
Arica
Azapa
Belén
Corque
El Choro
Poopó
Llallagua
Uncía
Chayanta
Pasorapa
Trigal
Quirusillas
Florida
Vallegrande
Curichi
Vitor
Codpa
Huachacalla
Negrillos
Pazña
Colquechaca
Poroma
Mojocoya
Pucará
Cabezas
Cabo Lobos
Sabaya
Orinoca
Challapata
Ocurí
Ravelo
Presto
Zudañez
Abapó
Punta Madrid
Cuya
Camarones
Miñimiñi
Camiña
Lago de Coipasa
Salar de Coipasa
Lago Poopó
Huari
Sucre
Yotala
Tarabuco
Villa Serrano
Zapiga
Chiapa
Salinas de G. Mendoza
Sevaruyo
Gabriel Vera
Padilla
Masavi
Gutiérrez
Pisagua
Río Mulatos
Betanzos
Potosí
Chaqui
Sopachuy
Lagunillas
Caleta Buena
Negreiros
Tarapacá
Llica
Tagua
Villa Talavera
Porco
Monteagudo
Charagua
Huara
Mamiña
Caiza
Villa Vaca Guzmán
San Lucas
Azurduy
Camiri
Iquique
Pozo Almonte
Punta Gruesa
Salar de Empexa
Salar de Uyuni
Huanchaca
Pulacayo
Vitichi
Toropalca
Tumusla
Boyuibe
Cuevo
Ivo
Anita
Pica
Pintados
Chacarilla
Uyuni
Yonza
Villa Martín
Río Grande
Cotagaita
Camargo
Yatina
Ñancorainza
Huacaya
Carandayti
Macharetí
Cerro Carrasco
Caleta Pabellón de Pica
Lagunas
Challacollo
Collaguasi
Julaca
Chocaya
Villa Abecia
Camatindi
Punta Lobos
Chiguana
San Cristóbal
Atocha
El Puente
Tarairí
Aucanquilcha
Ollagüe
Volcan Ollagüe
Oro Ingenio
Oploca
Impora
Villamontes
Salar de Llamara
Tupiza
San Lorenzo
Tarija
Entre Ríos
Cerro de la Mica
Quillagua
Oficina Santa Fe
Cerro Palpana
Ascotán
San Pablo
Esmoraca
Iscayachi
Uriondo
Sanandita
Villa Ingavi
Itaú
Mojo
Padcaya
Caraparí
Conchi
Pan de Azúcar
Santa Catalina
Villazón
Salvador Mazza
Aguarey
Tocopilla
Toco
La Quiaca
Yavi
Campo Durán
María Elena
Chuquicamata
Lag. Colorada
Cerro Alcoak
Co. Alcoak
Rinconada
Santa Victoria
Cerro Colupo
Gatico
Vergara
Calama
Chiuchiu
Limal
Tartagal
Punta Cobija
Pedro de Valdivia
Sierra Gorda
Iruya
Abra Pampa
Cochinoca
Ramos
Tranquitas
Punta Gualaguala
Deseada
Quitor
San Pedro de Atacama
Coranzuli
Iturbe
Tamaya
Sheshea
Ucayali
Tarauacá
Muru
Embira
Chandless
Macauã
Iaco
Curanja
Alto Purús
Inuya
Urubamba
Tambo
Mishahua
Tahuamanu
Piedras
Manuripi
Madre de Dios
Orton
Beni
Madidi
Manupari
Esmeralda
Emero
Yacuma
Rápulo
Matos
Mamoré
Guaporé
Yata
Abunã
Mapiri
Pacahuaras
Negro
Ouro Preto
Pacaás Novos
Sotério
Cautário
Baures
Machupo
Itonamas
Blanco
San Miguel
San Pablo
Secure
Ichoa
Isiboro
Chapare
Yapacani
Ichilo
Piray
Grande
Azero
Pilcomayo
Parapeti
Pilaya
Camblaya
Tarija
Pirai
Apurímac
Mantaro
Yavero
Heath
Tuichi
Quiquibey
Altamachi
Tambo
Ocoña
Acarí
Yauca
Camisea
Acre
Xapuri
Yaco
Lauca
Loa
Salar de Pica
Grande de Lipez
Sama
Tusi

SOUTHEASTERN BRAZIL
AZIMUTHAL EQUIDISTANT PROJECTION
SCALE 1:7,000,000
0 KILOMETERS 100 150 200
0 MILES 50 100 150 200
ATLANTIC
OCEAN
TROPIC OF CAPRICORN
Longitude West 45° of Greenwich
B R A Z I L
TOCANTINS
BAHIA
GOIÁS
MATO GROSSO
MATO GROSSO DO SUL
MINAS GERAIS
SÃO PAULO
PARANÁ
SANTA CATARINA
RIO GRANDE DO SUL
RIO DE JANEIRO
ESPÍRITO SANTO
DISTRITO FEDERAL
PLANALTO
Serra do Espinhaço
Serra do Roncador
Espigão Mestre
CHAPADA DOS VEADEIROS
CHAPADA DIAMANTINA N.P.
GRANDE SERTÃO VEREDAS N.P.
EMAS N.P.
SERRA DA CANASTRA N.P.
SERRA DA BOCAINA NAT. PARK
IGUAÇU N.P.
SÃO JOAQUIM N.P.
MONTE PASCOAL N.P.
Três Marias Dam
Jurumirim Dam
Pico de Itambé
Brasília
Goiânia
Anápolis
Belo Horizonte
Uberlândia
Uberaba
Montes Claros
Governador Valadares
Teófilo Otoni
Vitória da Conquista
Vitória
Vila Velha (Espírito Santo)
Cariacica
Colatina
Linhares
Cachoeiro do Itapemirim
Campos
Macaé
Cabo Frio
Niterói
RIO DE JANEIRO
Duque de Caxias
Nova Iguaçu
Nova Friburgo
Volta Redonda
Barra Mansa
Resende
Petrópolis
Juiz de Fora
Barbacena
Divinópolis
Sete Lagoas
Sabará
Varginha
Pouso Alegre
Poços de Caldas
Passos
Patos de Minas
Araguari
Ribeirão Preto
Franca
Barretos
Catanduva
São José do Rio Preto
Araraquara
São Carlos
Rio Claro
Araras
Limeira
Piracicaba
Campinas
Jundiaí
SÃO PAULO
Santo André
Santos
São Vicente
São José dos Campos
Taubaté
Guaratinguetá
Pindamonhangaba
Sorocaba
Itapetininga
Itu
Botucatu
Jaú
Bauru
Marília
Presidente Prudente
Londrina
Maringá
Apucarana
Ponta Grossa
Guarapuava
Cascavel
Curitiba
São José dos Pinhais
Paranaguá
Joinville
Jaraguá do Sul
Blumenau
Itajaí
Florianópolis
São José
Criciúma
Praia Grande
Lages
Passo Fundo
Chapecó
Rio Verde
Jataí
Catalão
Itumbiara
Ipatinga
Linhares
Jequié
Ilhéus
Atlantic Ocean

RIVER PLATE REGION

AZIMUTHAL EQUIDISTANT PROJECTION

SCALE 1:6,000,000

0 KILOMETERS 100 150

0 MILES 50 100 150

Longitude West 57° of Greenwich

The second smallest continent with the exception of Australia, Europe has a population density second only to Asia. Its name comes from Europa, a Phoenician woman who, according to Greek myth, was seduced by the god Zeus and carried off to Crete. From the Ural Mountains in the east to peninsulas and islands in the west, Europe has had an influence in the world that far outweighs its size: From the continent's seaports in Portugal, Spain, Italy, England, France, and Holland, Europeans set out in the last 600 years and left their imprint throughout the world. The Minoan, Greek, and Roman societies that gave rise to Western civilization were Mediterranean kin and sometimes antagonists to, among others, Phoenicia, Tyre, Judea, Egypt, and Carthage. The welter of peoples, nations, philosophies, religions, arts, and customs that make up Europe and, in the 19th and 20th centuries, the various "isms"—national-, imperial-, Marx-, Nazi-, and others—kept Europe in flux throughout its history, from the fall of Rome to the jittery cold peace that followed World War II. While numerous rivers and plains gave passage for commerce and conquest, the mountain fastnesses of the Pyrenees and Alps and hard passages of the North Sea and English Channel stood as barriers against invaders. The tendency of Europe to fracture has been mended by cooperative enterprises such as the economic Common Market, followed by the European Union. The EU now has 25 members, including eight former Soviet Bloc countries, and five applicants. While members maintain open borders to each other, and 12 countries use a common currency, the Euro, the adoption of a common constitution has been rejected by voters in France and the Netherlands. Difficulties in assimilating, employing, and acculturating immigrants from former colonial states and Muslim countries challenge European societies, long steeped in democratic ideas of equality and free expression.

IMAGE BY ROBERT STACEY, WORLDSAT INTERNATIONAL INC.

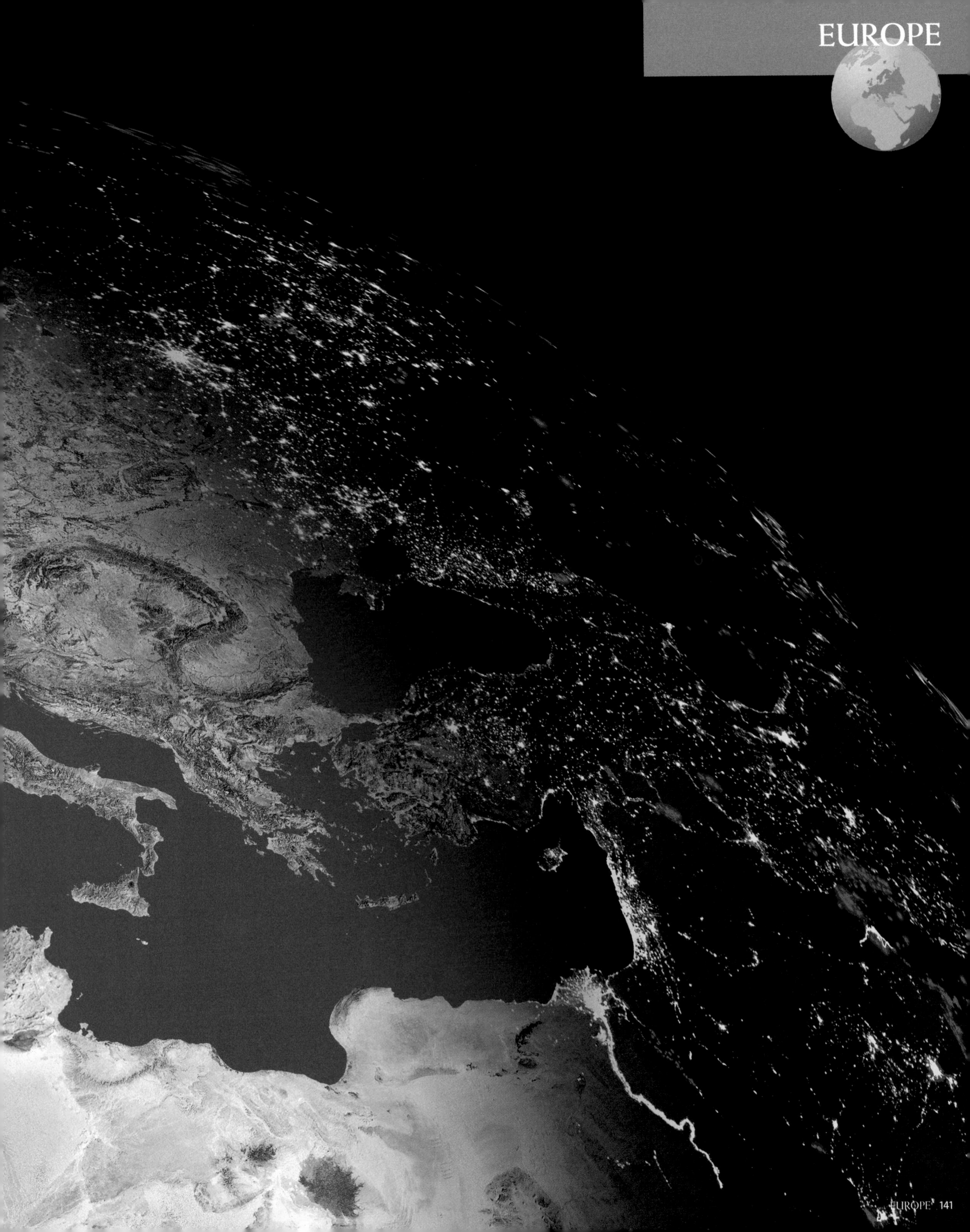

AZIMUTHAL EQUIDISTANT PROJECTION
SCALE 1:23,000,000
0 KILOMETERS 400 600
0 MILES 200 400 600
ATLANTIC OCEAN
NORWEGIAN SEA
NORTH SEA
BARENTS SEA
BALTIC SEA
GULF OF BOTHNIA
BLACK SEA
CASPIAN SEA
MEDITERRANEAN SEA
ADRIATIC SEA
IONIAN SEA
TYRRHENIAN SEA
BAY OF BISCAY
CELTIC SEA
ARCTIC CIRCLE
Meridian of Greenwich (London)
ICELAND
FAROE ISLANDS
BRITISH ISLES
UNITED KINGDOM
IRELAND
NORWAY
SWEDEN
FINLAND
DENMARK
ESTONIA
LATVIA
LITHUANIA
BELARUS
POLAND
GERMANY
NETHERLANDS
BELGIUM
FRANCE
SPAIN
PORTUGAL
SWITZERLAND
AUSTRIA
CZECH REPUBLIC
SLOVAKIA
HUNGARY
ROMANIA
BULGARIA
MOLDOVA
UKRAINE
RUSSIA
SIBERIA
ITALY
SLOVENIA
CROATIA
BOSNIA AND HERZEGOVINA
SERBIA
MONTENEGRO
ALBANIA
MACEDONIA
GREECE
TURKEY
CYPRUS
GEORGIA
ARMENIA
AZERBAIJAN
KAZAKHSTAN
UZBEKISTAN
TURKMENISTAN
IRAN
IRAQ
SYRIA
LEBANON
ISRAEL
JORDAN
KUWAIT
SAUDI ARABIA
EGYPT
LIBYA
TUNISIA
ALGERIA
MOROCCO
WESTERN SAHARA
MAURITANIA
MALTA
CORSICA
SARDINIA
SICILY
CRETE
BALEARIC ISLANDS
Reykjavík
London
Paris
Madrid
Lisboa (Lisbon)
Roma (Rome)
Berlin
Oslo
Stockholm
Helsinki (Helsingfors)
København (Copenhagen)
Warszawa (Warsaw)
Moskva (Moscow)
Sankt-Peterburg (Saint Petersburg)
Kyiv (Kiev)
Minsk
Rīga
Vilnius
Tallinn
Praha (Prague)
Wien (Vienna)
Budapest
Bucureşti (Bucharest)
Beograd (Belgrade)
Sofiya (Sofia)
Athína (Athens)
Ankara (Angora)
İstanbul (Constantinople)
Tehrān (Tehran)
Baghdād
Dimashq (Damascus)
Beyrouth (Beirut)
El Qâhira (Cairo)
Ţarābulus (Tripoli)
Tunis
Alger (Algiers)
Rabat
URAL MOUNTAINS
Caucasus Mountains
Carpathian Mts.
Pyrenees
ATLAS MOUNTAINS
Zagros Mountains
Caspian Depression
SYRIAN DESERT
Grand Erg Occidental
Grand Erg Oriental
Longitude East 20° of Greenwich

AZIMUTHAL EQUIDISTANT PROJECTION
SCALE 1:23,000,000
0 KILOMETERS 400 600
0 MILES 200 400 600
A commonly accepted division between Asia and Europe – here marked by a green line – is formed by the Ural Mountains, Ural River, Caspian Sea, Caucasus Mountains, and the Black Sea with its outlets, the Bosporus and Dardanelles.
ATLANTIC OCEAN
NORWEGIAN SEA
NORTH SEA
BARENTS SEA
BALTIC SEA
GULF OF BOTHNIA
BAY OF BISCAY
CELTIC SEA
MEDITERRANEAN SEA
BLACK SEA
CASPIAN SEA
ADRIATIC SEA
TYRRHENIAN SEA
IONIAN SEA
ARCTIC CIRCLE
Meridian of Greenwich (London)
Longitude East 10° of Greenwich
ICELAND
IRELAND
UNITED KINGDOM
NORWAY
SWEDEN
FINLAND
LAPLAND
DENMARK
ESTONIA
LATVIA
LITHUANIA
BELARUS
POLAND
GERMANY
NETH.
BELG.
LUX.
FRANCE
SWITZ.
AUSTRIA
CZECH REPUBLIC
SLOVAKIA
HUNGARY
ROMANIA
MOLD.
UKRAINE
RUSSIA
KAZAKHSTAN
UZBEKISTAN
TURKMENISTAN
BULGARIA
SERBIA
CROATIA
BOSNIA AND HERZEGOVINA
MONTENEGRO
ALBAN.
MACED.
GREECE
TURKEY
GEORGIA
ARM.
AZERBAIJAN
SYRIA
LEB.
ISRAEL
JORDAN
IRAQ
IRAN
KUWAIT
SAUDI ARABIA
EGYPT
LIBYA
TUNISIA
ALGERIA
MOROCCO
PORT.
SPAIN
ITALY
MALTA
CYPRUS
LONDON
Paris
Madrid
Lisboa (Lisbon)
Roma (Rome)
Berlin
Wien (Vienna)
MOSKVA (MOSCOW)
Sankt-Peterburg (St. Petersburg)
İSTANBUL (CONSTANTINOPLE)
EL QÂHIRA (CAIRO)

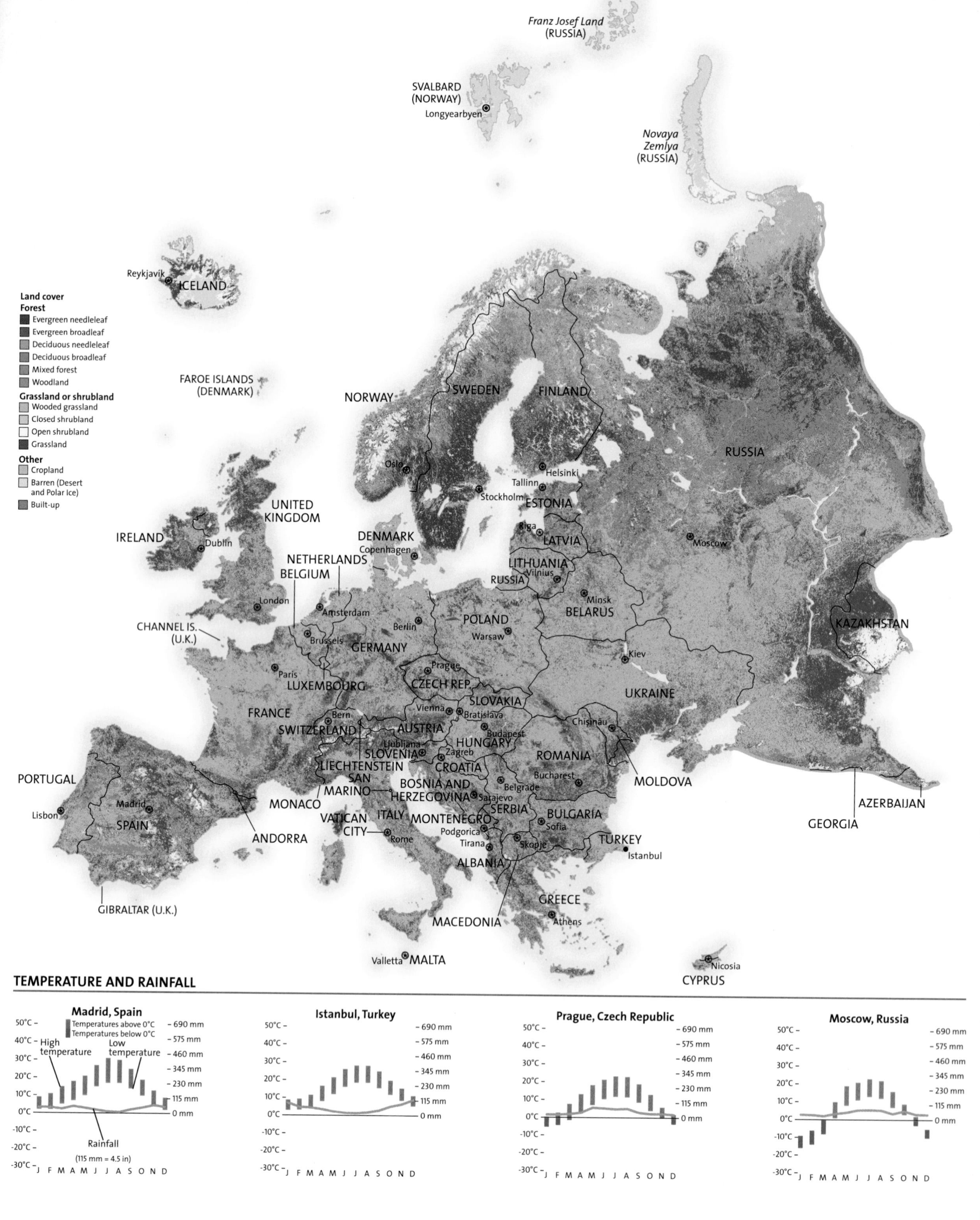
Franz Josef Land
(RUSSIA)
SVALBARD
(NORWAY)
Longyearbyen
Novaya
Zemlya
(RUSSIA)
Reykjavík
ICELAND
Land cover
Forest
Evergreen needleleaf
Evergreen broadleaf
Deciduous needleleaf
Deciduous broadleaf
Mixed forest
Woodland
Grassland or shrubland
Wooded grassland
Closed shrubland
Open shrubland
Grassland
Other
Cropland
Barren (Desert and Polar ice)
Built-up
FAROE ISLANDS
(DENMARK)
NORWAY
SWEDEN
FINLAND
RUSSIA
Oslo
Helsinki
Tallinn
Stockholm
ESTONIA
UNITED
KINGDOM
IRELAND
Dublin
DENMARK
Copenhagen
Riga
LATVIA
Moscow
NETHERLANDS
BELGIUM
LITHUANIA
Vilnius
RUSSIA
London
Amsterdam
Minsk
BELARUS
Berlin
POLAND
Warsaw
CHANNEL IS.
(U.K.)
Brussels
GERMANY
KAZAKHSTAN
Kiev
Paris
Prague
LUXEMBOURG
CZECH REP.
SLOVAKIA
UKRAINE
FRANCE
Vienna
Bratislava
Bern
Chişinău
SWITZERLAND
AUSTRIA
Budapest
HUNGARY
Ljubljana
SLOVENIA
Zagreb
ROMANIA
LIECHTENSTEIN
CROATIA
PORTUGAL
SAN
MARINO
BOSNIA AND
HERZEGOVINA
Bucharest
Belgrade
MOLDOVA
Madrid
MONACO
Sarajevo
SERBIA
AZERBAIJAN
Lisbon
SPAIN
VATICAN
CITY
ITALY
MONTENEGRO
BULGARIA
Sofia
GEORGIA
Podgorica
ANDORRA
Rome
Tirana
Skopje
TURKEY
Istanbul
ALBANIA
GIBRALTAR (U.K.)
GREECE
MACEDONIA
Athens
Valletta
MALTA
Nicosia
CYPRUS
TEMPERATURE AND RAINFALL
Madrid, Spain
Temperatures above 0°C
Temperatures below 0°C
High
temperature
Low
temperature
Rainfall
(115 mm = 4.5 in)
Istanbul, Turkey
Prague, Czech Republic
Moscow, Russia
50°C
40°C
30°C
20°C
10°C
0°C
-10°C
-20°C
-30°C
690 mm
575 mm
460 mm
345 mm
230 mm
115 mm
0 mm
J F M A M J J A S O N D

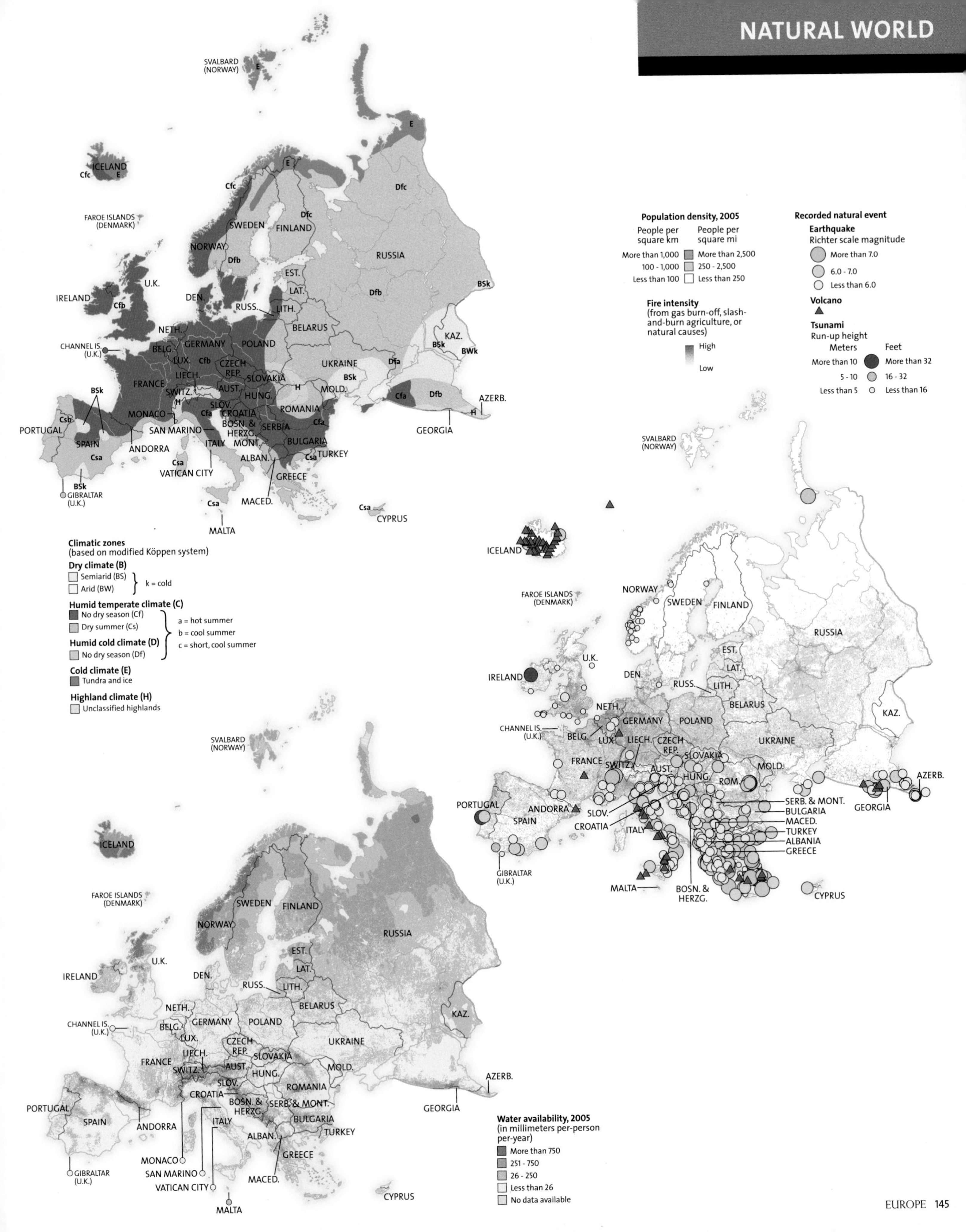
NATURAL WORLD
SVALBARD (NORWAY)
ICELAND
FAROE ISLANDS (DENMARK)
NORWAY
SWEDEN
FINLAND
RUSSIA
IRELAND
U.K.
DEN.
EST.
LAT.
LITH.
RUSS.
BELARUS
KAZ.
NETH.
CHANNEL IS. (U.K.)
BELG.
GERMANY
POLAND
LUX.
CZECH REP.
UKRAINE
LIECH.
SLOVAKIA
FRANCE
SWITZ.
AUST.
HUNG.
MOLD.
ROMANIA
SLOV.
CROATIA
MONACO
BOSN. & HERZG.
SERBIA
SAN MARINO
MONT.
BULGARIA
PORTUGAL
SPAIN
ANDORRA
ITALY
ALBAN.
TURKEY
VATICAN CITY
GREECE
GIBRALTAR (U.K.)
MACED.
MALTA
CYPRUS
GEORGIA
AZERB.
Cfc
E
Dfc
Dfb
Cfb
BSk
BWk
Dfa
Cfa
Csb
Csa
H
Climatic zones
(based on modified Köppen system)
Dry climate (B)
Semiarid (BS)
Arid (BW)
k = cold
Humid temperate climate (C)
No dry season (Cf)
Dry summer (Cs)
a = hot summer
b = cool summer
c = short, cool summer
Humid cold climate (D)
No dry season (Df)
Cold climate (E)
Tundra and ice
Highland climate (H)
Unclassified highlands
Population density, 2005
People per square km
People per square mi
More than 1,000
More than 2,500
100 - 1,000
250 - 2,500
Less than 100
Less than 250
Fire intensity
(from gas burn-off, slash-and-burn agriculture, or natural causes)
High
Low
Recorded natural event
Earthquake
Richter scale magnitude
More than 7.0
6.0 - 7.0
Less than 6.0
Volcano
Tsunami
Run-up height
Meters
Feet
More than 10
More than 32
5 - 10
16 - 32
Less than 5
Less than 16
ROM.
SERB. & MONT.
MACED.
ALBANIA
SERB. & MONT.
Water availability, 2005
(in millimeters per-person per-year)
More than 750
251 - 750
26 - 250
Less than 26
No data available

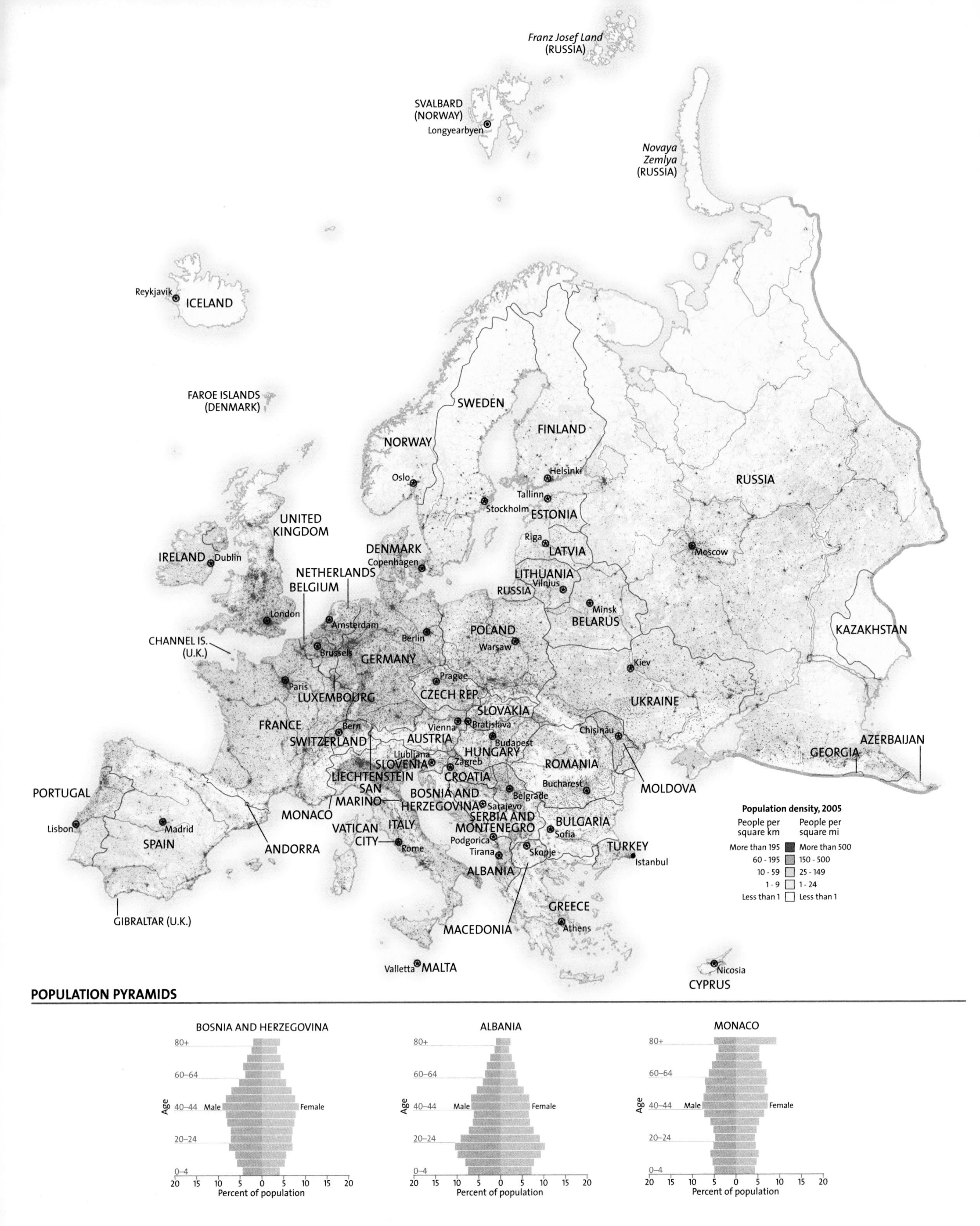

Franz Josef Land
(RUSSIA)
SVALBARD
(NORWAY)
Longyearbyen
Novaya
Zemlya
(RUSSIA)
Reykjavík
ICELAND
FAROE ISLANDS
(DENMARK)
SWEDEN
FINLAND
NORWAY
Helsinki
Oslo
RUSSIA
Tallinn
Stockholm
ESTONIA
UNITED
KINGDOM
Riga
LATVIA
DENMARK
IRELAND
Dublin
Copenhagen
Moscow
NETHERLANDS
LITHUANIA
BELGIUM
Vilnius
RUSSIA
Minsk
London
BELARUS
Amsterdam
Berlin
POLAND
KAZAKHSTAN
CHANNEL IS.
(U.K.)
Warsaw
Brussels
GERMANY
Kiev
Prague
Paris
LUXEMBOURG
CZECH REP.
UKRAINE
SLOVAKIA
FRANCE
Bern
Vienna
Bratislava
Chişinău
SWITZERLAND
AUSTRIA
Budapest
AZERBAIJAN
Ljubljana
HUNGARY
GEORGIA
Zagreb
SLOVENIA
ROMANIA
LIECHTENSTEIN
CROATIA
SAN
MARINO
BOSNIA AND
HERZEGOVINA
Belgrade
Bucharest
MOLDOVA
PORTUGAL
Sarajevo
MONACO
SERBIA AND
MONTENEGRO
BULGARIA
Madrid
Lisbon
VATICAN
CITY
ITALY
Podgorica
Sofia
SPAIN
Rome
Tirana
Skopje
TURKEY
Istanbul
ANDORRA
ALBANIA
GREECE
GIBRALTAR (U.K.)
MACEDONIA
Athens
Valletta
MALTA
Nicosia
CYPRUS
Population density, 2005
People per square km
People per square mi
More than 195
More than 500
60 - 195
150 - 500
10 - 59
25 - 149
1 - 9
1 - 24
Less than 1
Less than 1
POPULATION PYRAMIDS
BOSNIA AND HERZEGOVINA
ALBANIA
MONACO
80+
60–64
40–44
20–24
0–4
Age
Male
Female
20 15 10 5 0 5 10 15 20
Percent of population

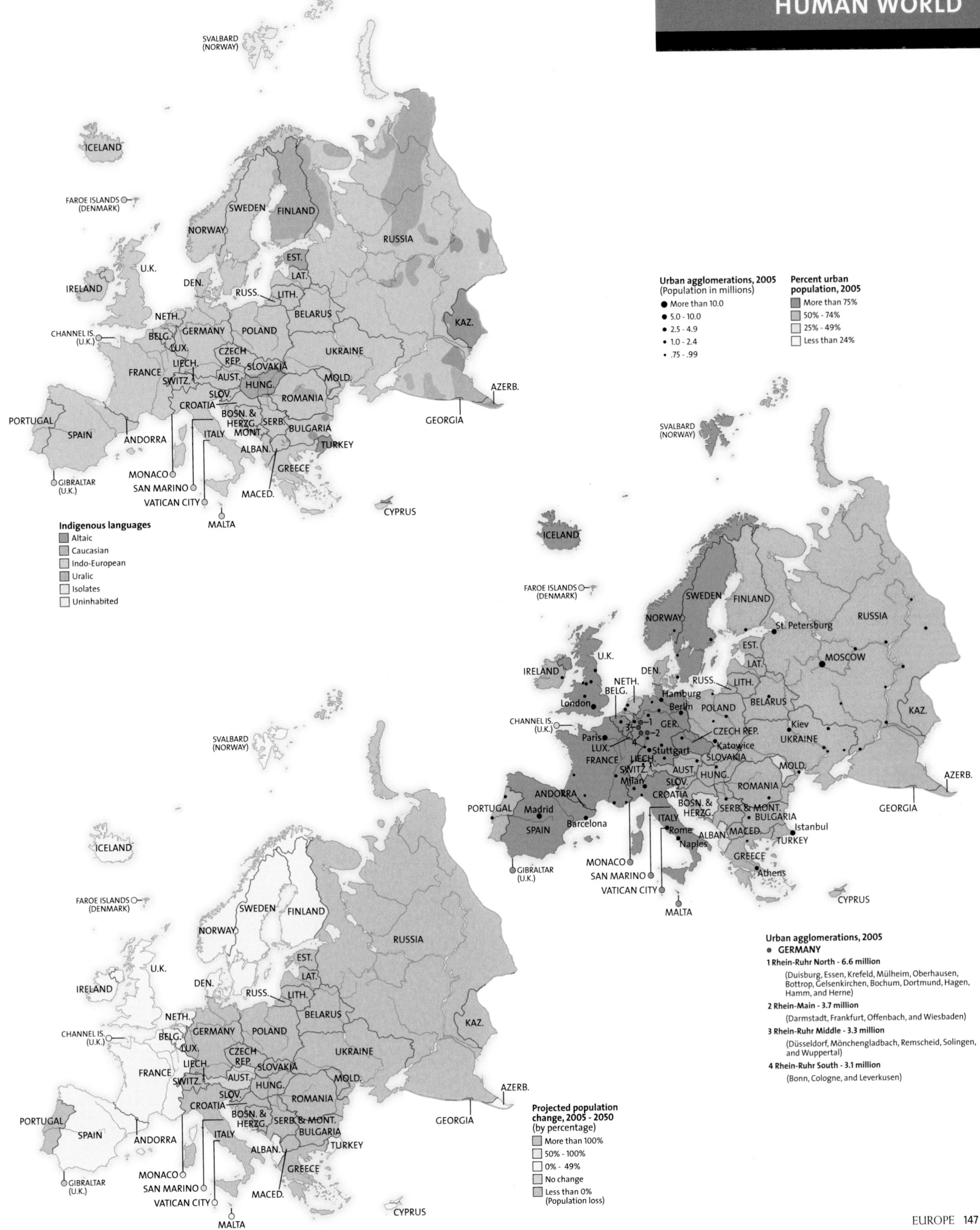
SVALBARD (NORWAY)
ICELAND
FAROE ISLANDS (DENMARK)
SWEDEN
FINLAND
NORWAY
RUSSIA
U.K.
EST.
LAT.
IRELAND
DEN.
RUSS.
LITH.
NETH.
BELARUS
KAZ.
CHANNEL IS. (U.K.)
BELG.
GERMANY
POLAND
LUX.
CZECH REP.
UKRAINE
LIECH.
SLOVAKIA
FRANCE
SWITZ.
AUST.
MOLD.
HUNG.
SLOV.
ROMANIA
AZERB.
CROATIA
BOSN. & HERZG.
SERB.
MONT.
PORTUGAL
SPAIN
ANDORRA
ITALY
BULGARIA
GEORGIA
TURKEY
ALBAN.
GREECE
MACED.
MONACO
SAN MARINO
VATICAN CITY
GIBRALTAR (U.K.)
CYPRUS
MALTA
Indigenous languages
Altaic
Caucasian
Indo-European
Uralic
Isolates
Uninhabited
Urban agglomerations, 2005
(Population in millions)
More than 10.0
5.0 - 10.0
2.5 - 4.9
1.0 - 2.4
.75 - .99
Percent urban population, 2005
More than 75%
50% - 74%
25% - 49%
Less than 24%
St. Petersburg
MOSCOW
Hamburg
Berlin
London
GER.
Paris
Stuttgart
Katowice
Kiev
Milan
Madrid
Barcelona
Rome
Naples
Istanbul
Athens
SERB. & MONT.
Urban agglomerations, 2005
GERMANY
1 Rhein-Ruhr North - 6.6 million
(Duisburg, Essen, Krefeld, Mülheim, Oberhausen, Bottrop, Gelsenkirchen, Bochum, Dortmund, Hagen, Hamm, and Herne)
2 Rhein-Main - 3.7 million
(Darmstadt, Frankfurt, Offenbach, and Wiesbaden)
3 Rhein-Ruhr Middle - 3.3 million
(Düsseldorf, Mönchengladbach, Remscheid, Solingen, and Wuppertal)
4 Rhein-Ruhr South - 3.1 million
(Bonn, Cologne, and Leverkusen)
Projected population change, 2005 - 2050
(by percentage)
More than 100%
50% - 100%
0% - 49%
No change
Less than 0%
(Population loss)

Franz Josef Land
(RUSSIA)
SVALBARD
(NORWAY)
Longyearbyen
Novaya
Zemlya
(RUSSIA)
Reykjavik
ICELAND
FAROE ISLANDS
(DENMARK)
SWEDEN
FINLAND
NORWAY
Oslo
Helsinki
Tallinn
Stockholm
ESTONIA
RUSSIA
UNITED
KINGDOM
Riga
LATVIA
Moscow
IRELAND
Dublin
DENMARK
Copenhagen
NETHERLANDS
LITHUANIA
BELGIUM
Vilnius
RUSSIA
Minsk
BELARUS
London
Amsterdam
Berlin
POLAND
KAZAKHSTAN
CHANNEL IS.
(U.K.)
Warsaw
Brussels
GERMANY
Kiev
Prague
Paris
LUXEMBOURG
CZECH REP.
UKRAINE
SLOVAKIA
AZERBAIJAN
FRANCE
Bern
Vienna
Bratislava
Chișinău
GEORGIA
SWITZERLAND
AUSTRIA
Budapest
HUNGARY
Ljubljana
SLOVENIA
Zagreb
ROMANIA
LIECHTENSTEIN
CROATIA
SAN
MARINO
Bucharest
MOLDOVA
PORTUGAL
BOSNIA AND
HERZEGOVINA
Belgrade
MONACO
Sarajevo
SERBIA
BULGARIA
Lisbon
Madrid
VATICAN
CITY
ITALY
MONTENEGRO
Sofia
SPAIN
Rome
Podgorica
TURKEY
ANDORRA
Tirana
Skopje
Istanbul
ALBANIA
GREECE
GIBRALTAR (U.K.)
MACEDONIA
Athens
Valletta
MALTA
Nicosia
CYPRUS
More
disturbed
Cropland
Less
disturbed
More
disturbed
Pasture
Built-up area
Irrigated land
IMPORTS
GERMANY
Petroleum and
petroleum products - 8%
Other
8%
Food
6%
Chemical
products - 10%
Machinery
and transport
equipment
38%
Manufactured
goods
30%
UNITED KINGDOM
Petroleum and
petroleum products - 4%
Other
6%
Food - 6%
Chemical
products - 10%
Machinery
and transport
equipment
46%
Manufactured
goods
28%
EXPORTS
FRANCE
Other - 6%
Beverages - 3%
Food
8%
Chemical
products
14%
Machinery
and transport
equipment
45%
Manufactured
goods
24%
GERMANY
Medical and
pharmaceutical
products - 2%
Food - 3%
Other
8%
Chemical
products - 12%
Machinery
and transport
equipment
52%
Manufactured
goods
23%

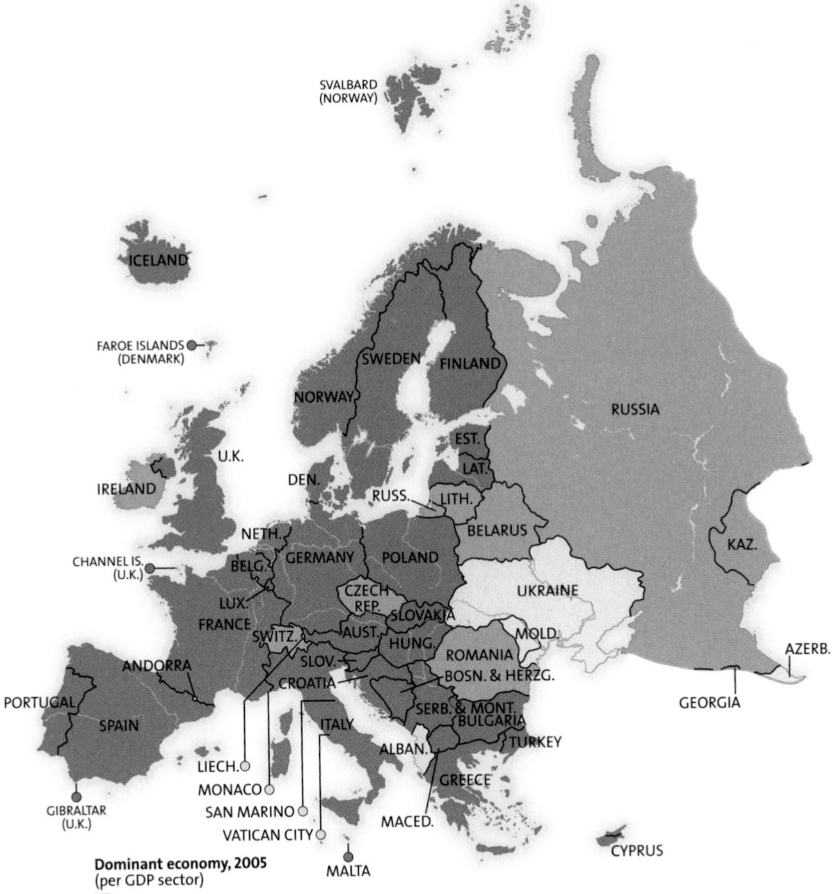

SERVICE 100%

GUERNSEY, CHANNEL IS. (U.K.)

IRELAND

ALBANIA

AGRICULTURAL 100%

INDUSTRIAL 100%

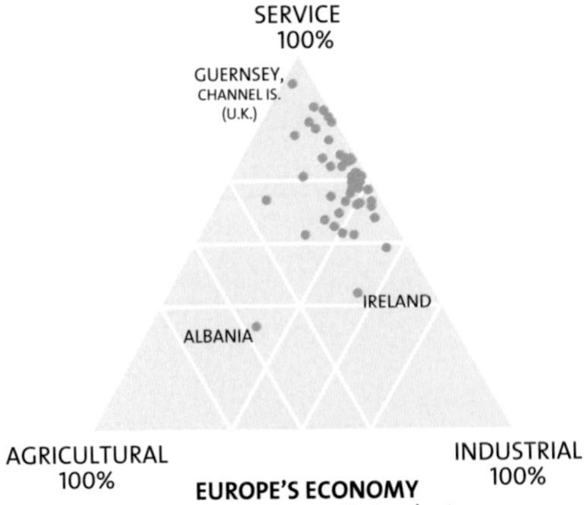

EUROPE'S ECONOMY
per Gross Domestic Product (GDP) sector

Dominant economy, 2005
(per GDP sector)

- Service
- Service - Industrial
- Service - Industrial - Agricultural
- No data available

Percentage of population living on less than $2 per day, 2005

- More than 75%
- 50% - 74%
- 25% - 49%
- Less than 25%
- No data available

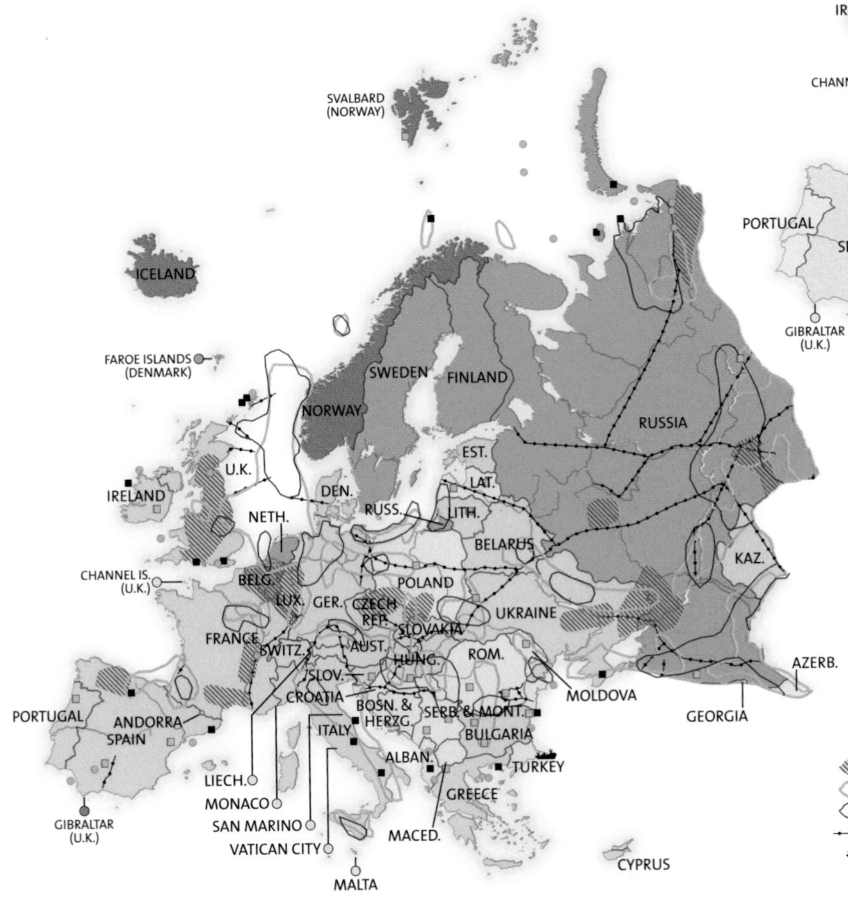

Per capita energy consumption, 2003
(in million Btu)

- More than 300
- 201 - 300
- 101 - 200
- 31 - 100
- Less than 30
- No data available

Major energy deposit

- Coal
- Natural gas
- Oil
- Oil pipeline
- Oil transit chokepoint

NORWAY
SWEDEN
DENMARK
GERMANY
NETHERLANDS
BELGIUM
LUX.
FRANCE
UNITED KINGDOM
GREAT BRITAIN
SCOTLAND
ENGLAND
WALES
NORTHERN IRELAND
IRELAND
NORTH SEA
Celtic Sea
ATLANTIC OCEAN
ENGLISH CHANNEL (LA MANCHE)
Irish Sea
Skagerrak
Kattegat
Meridian of Greenwich (London)
Outer Hebrides
Inner Hebrides
Channel Islands
Isles of Scilly
Aran Is.
Blasket Is.
Skellig Rocks
Dogger Bank
North Frisian Islands
East Frisian Is.
West Frisian Is.
LONDON
Edinburgh
Glasgow
Dublin
Belfast
Cork
Amsterdam
Rotterdam
Bruxelles (Brussels)
Paris
Hamburg
Bremen
Aberdeen
Manchester
Liverpool
Birmingham
Cardiff

AZIMUTHAL EQUIDISTANT PROJECTION
SCALE 1:6,000,000
0 KILOMETERS 100 150
0 MILES 50 100 150
Bay of Biscay
MEDITERRANEAN SEA
Balearic Sea
Alboran Sea
BALEARIC ISLANDS
Golfe du Lion
Golfo de Valencia
Golfo de Cádiz
PORTUGAL
SPAIN
ITALY
ANDORRA
MONACO
MOROCCO
ALGERIA
U.K. GIBRALTAR
GALICIA
ASTURIAS
CANTABRIA
BASQUE COUNTRY
NAVARRA
LA RIOJA
ARAGON
CATALONIA
CASTILE AND LEON
MADRID
CASTILE LA MANCHA
EXTREMADURA
VALENCIA
MURCIA
ANDALUSIA
POITOU-CHARENTES
LIMOUSIN
AUVERGNE
RHÔNE-ALPES
AQUITAINE
MIDI-PYRÉNÉES
PROVENCE-ALPES-CÔTE D'AZUR
Madrid
Lisboa (Lisbon)
Porto (Oporto)
Barcelona
Valencia
Sevilla (Seville)
Zaragoza
Bilbao
Málaga
Granada
Córdoba
Murcia
Alicante
Palma de Mallorca
Mallorca (Majorca)
Menorca (Minorca)
Ibiza
Bordeaux
Toulouse
Marseille
Montpellier
Toulon
Nice
Lyon
Genève
Torino (Turin)
Alger (Algiers)
Tanger (Tangier)
Tétouan (Tetuán)
FERRY
Longitude West 3° of Greenwich
Longitude East 3° of Greenwich

BARENTS SEA
NORWEGIAN SEA
GULF OF BOTHNIA
BELOYE MORE (WHITE SEA)
RUSSIA
FINLAND
SWEDEN
NORWAY
ARCTIC CIRCLE
Meridian of Greenwich (London)
15° Longitude East 18° of Greenwich
AZIMUTHAL EQUIDISTANT PROJECTION
SCALE 1:6,000,000
0 KILOMETERS 50 100 150
0 MILES 50 100 150
Lofoten
Vesterålen
Murmansk
Sankt-Peterburg (St. Petersburg)
Helsinki (Helsingfors)
Oulu (Uleåborg)
Tampere (Tammerfors)
Turku (Åbo)
Trondheim
Bergen
Umeå
Gävle
Åland (Ahvenanmaa)

ESTONIA
LATVIA
LITHUANIA
BELARUS
UKRAINE
POLAND
GERMANY
DENMARK
CZECH REPUBLIC
SLOVAKIA
AUSTRIA
HUNGARY
ROMANIA
NETHERLANDS
NORTH SEA
BALTIC SEA
KATTEGAT
SKAGERRAK
Gulf of Riga
KALININGRAD

SWEDEN
FINLAND
ESTONIA
LATVIA
LITHUANIA
BELARUS
POLAND
UKRAINE
KALININGRAD OBLAST
EAST PRUSSIA
GULF OF BOTHNIA
GULF OF FINLAND
BALTIC SEA
Gulf of Riga
Irbe Strait
KOL'SKIY POLUOSTROV
BELOYE MORE (WHITE SEA)
Onezhskiy Zaliv
Kandalakshskiy Zaliv
Onezhskaya Guba
Dvinskaya Guba
Solovetskiye Ostrova
Ladozhskoye Ozero (L. Ladoga)
Onezhskoye Ozero
Chudskoye Ozero (L. Peipus)
Ozero Il'men'
Rybinskoye Vdkhr.
KARELIYA
ARKHA
VOLO
NOVGOROD
PSKOV
TVER'
YAROSLAVL'
MOSKVA
SMOLENSK
KALUGA
TULA
BRYANSK
OREL
LIPETSK
RYAZAN
VLADIMI
IVAN
TAMB
Valdayskaya Vozvyshennost'
WHITE SEA-BALTIC CANAL
VOLGA-BALTIC WATERWAY
MOSCOW CANAL
ÅLAND (AHVENANMAA)
Hiiumaa (Dagö)
Saaremaa (Ösel)
GOTSKA SANDÖN N.P.
OULANKA N.P.
LAHEMAA N.P.
GAUJA N.P.
ŽEMAITIJA N.P.
KURŠIU NERIJA N.P.
AUKŠTAITIJA N.P.
TRAKAI N.P.
DZŪKIJA N.P.
BELOWEZSKAYA PUSHCHA N.P.
MURMANSK
Arkhangel'sk
Severodvinsk
Petrozavodsk
Sankt-Peterburg (St. Petersburg) (Leningrad)
Helsinki (Helsingfors)
Espoo (Esbo)
Turku (Åbo)
Tampere (Tammerfors)
Oulu (Uleåborg)
Umeå
Tallinn (Reval)
Tartu
Riga
Daugavpils
Vilnius
Kaunas
Klaipėda
Šiauliai
Panevėžys
Minsk
Hrodna
Brest
Homyel'
Mahilyow
Vitsyebsk
Pskov
Velikiy Novgorod
Velikiye Luki
Smolensk
Tver'
MOSKVA (MOSCOW)
Yaroslavl'
Vologda
Cherepovets
Rybinsk
Kaluga
Tula
Bryansk
Orel
Ryazan'
Vyborg
Kotka
Kolpino
Mariehamn
Luleå
Tornio (Torneå)
15°
18°
21°
24°
27°
30°
33°
36°
39°
63°
60°
57°
54°

AZIMUTHAL EQUIDISTANT PROJECTION
SCALE 1:6,000,000
0 KILOMETERS 100 150
0 MILES 50 100 150
ARCTIC CIRCLE
NENETS
KOMI
KHANTY-MANSI
YAMAL-NENETS
YUGYD VA NATIONAL PARK
ARKHANGEL'SK
KOSTROMA
KIROV
PERM'
SVERDLOVSK
UDMURTIYA
MARIY-EL
NIZHNIY NOVGOROD
CHUVASHIYA
TATARSTAN
BASHKORTOSTAN
CHELYABINSK
KURGAN
MORDOVIYA
UL'YANOVSK
PENZA
SAMARA
ORENBURG
KAZAKHSTAN
QOSTANAY
Timanskiy Kryazh
Pechorskaya Nizmennost'
Severnyye Uvaly
URAL MOUNTAINS
Privolzhskaya Vozvyshennost'
Syktyvkar
Kirov
Perm'
Yekaterinburg
Chelyabinsk
Ufa
Kazan'
Nizhniy Novgorod
Cheboksary
Izhevsk
Ul'yanovsk
Samara
Tol'yatti
Saransk
Penza
Magnitogorsk
Naberezhnyye Chelny
Nizhniy Tagil
Sterlitamak
Salavat
Ukhta
Kotlas
Serov
Berezniki
of Greenwich

GERMANY
BAVARIA
AUSTRIA
SWITZERLAND
LIECH.
FRANCE
SLOVAKIA
HUNGARY
SLOVENIA
CROATIA
SLAVONIA
BOSNIA AND HERZEGOVINA
SERBIA
MONTENEGRO
KOSOVO
MACEDONIA
ALBANIA
GREECE
ITALY
TUNISIA
ALGERIA
MALTA
CORSE
CORSICA
SARDEGNA
SARDINIA
SICILIA
SICILY
TUSCANY
UMBRIA
LATIUM
ABRUZZI
MOLISE
CAMPANIA
APULIA
BASILICATA
CALABRIA
MARCHES
EMILIA-ROMAGNA
LIGURIA
PIEDMONT
LOMBARDY
VENETO
TRENTINO-ALTO ADIGE
FRIULI-VENEZIA GIULIA
VALLE D'AOSTA
APENNINES
DALMATIA
Ligurian Sea
TYRRHENIAN SEA
ADRIATIC SEA
IONIAN SEA
MEDITERRANEAN SEA
Golfo di Genova
Golfo di Manfredonia
GOLFO DI TARANTO
Gulf of Gabes
Malta Channel
Roma (Rome)
Napoli (Naples)
Milano (Milan)
Torino (Turin)
Venezia (Venice)
Firenze (Florence)
Genova (Genoa)
Bologna
Palermo
Bari
Cagliari
Catania
Messina
Trieste
Ljubljana
Zagreb
Sarajevo
Beograd (Belgrade)
Budapest
Wien (Vienna)
Bratislava
München (Munich)
Tunis
Valletta
AZIMUTHAL EQUIDISTANT PROJECTION
SCALE 1:6,000,000
0 KILOMETERS 100 150
0 MILES 50 100 150
Longitude East 21° of Greenwich

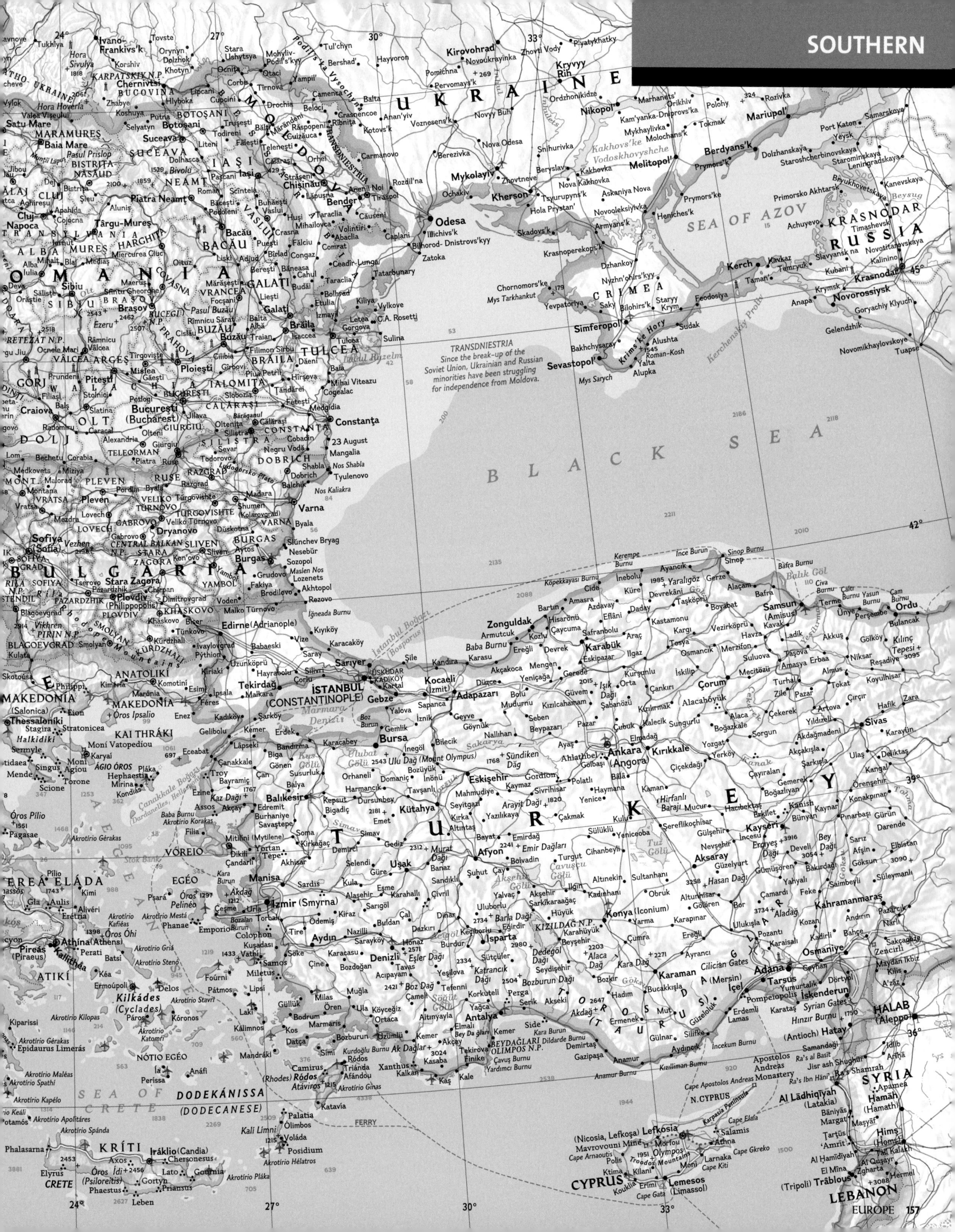

TRANSDNIESTRIA
Since the break-up of the Soviet Union, Ukrainian and Russian minorities have been struggling for independence from Moldova.

POLAND
BELARUS
UKRAINE
MOLDOVA
ROMANIA
BULGARIA
TURKEY
RUSSIA
GR.
BLACK SEA
SEA OF AZOV
CRIMEA
TRANSDNIESTRIA
ABKHAZIA
SMOLENSK
KALUGA
TULA
RYAZAN'
BRYANSK
OREL
LIPETSK
KURSK
BELGOROD
VORONEZH
ROSTOV
KRASNODAR
ADYGEYA
KUZEY ANADOLU DAĞLARI
Minsk
Kyiv (Kiev)
Chişinău
Bucureşti (Bucharest)
ISTANBUL (CONSTANTINOPLE)
MOSKVA
Odesa
Kharkiv
Sevastopol'
Simferopol'
Rostov na Donu
Krasnodar
Constanţa
Varna
Burgas
Samsun (Amisus)
Trabzon
Sochi
Sokhumi
AZIMUTHAL EQUIDISTANT PROJECTION
SCALE 1:6,000,000
0 KILOMETERS 50 100 150
0 MILES 50 100 150
Longitude E

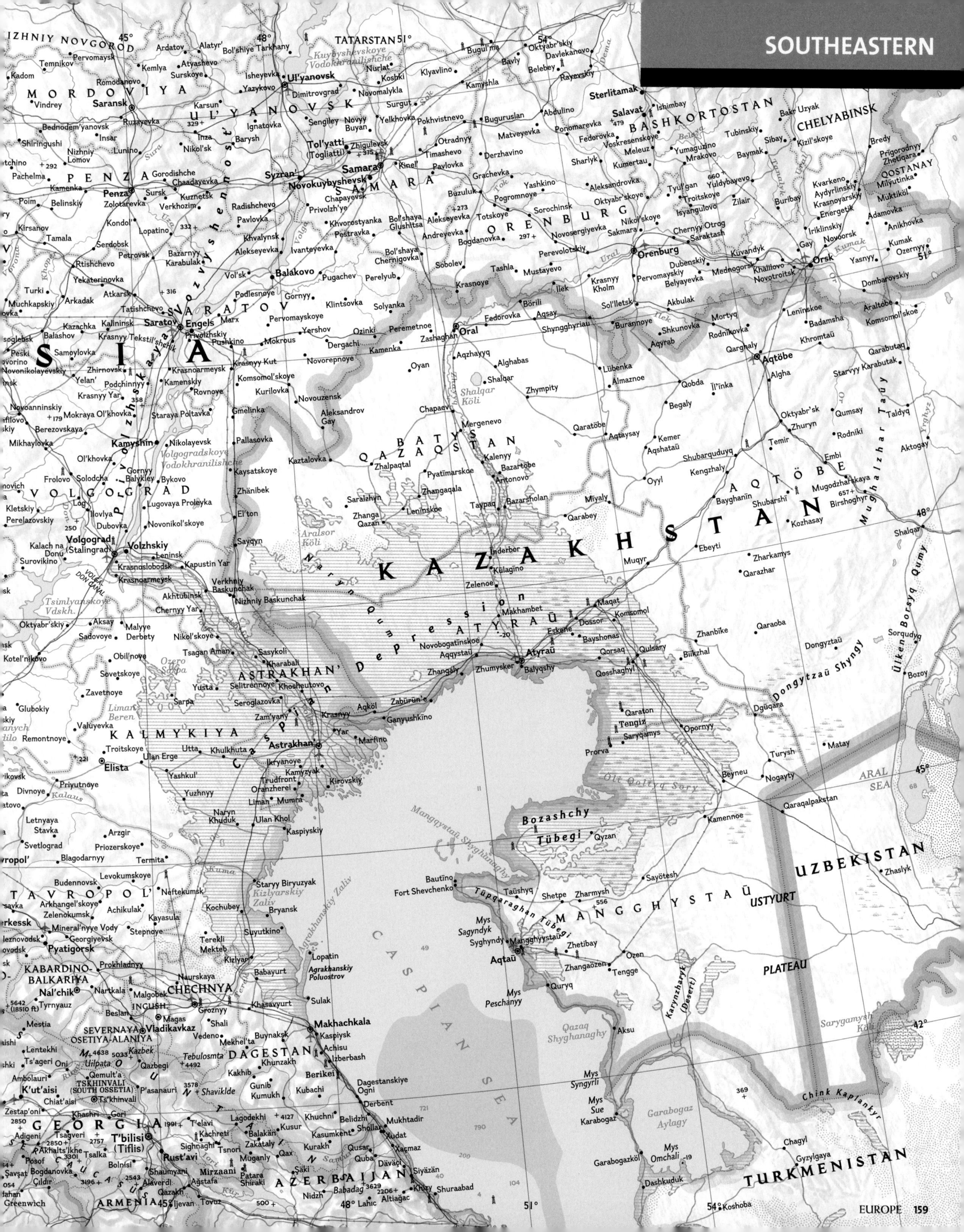

MORDOVIYA

UL'YANOVSK

PENZA

SAMARA

ORENBURG

BASHKORTOSTAN

CHELYABINSK

QOSTANAY

SARATOV

VOLGOGRAD

ASIA

QABATYS QAZAQSTAN

AQTÖBE

KAZAKHSTAN

ATYRAŪ

ASTRAKHAN'

KALMYKIYA

Caspian Depression

Naryn Qum

STAVROPOL'

KABARDINO-BALKARIYA

CHECHNYA

INGUSH.

SEVERNAYA OSETIYA-ALANIYA

DAGESTAN

GEORGIA

ARMENIA

AZERBAIJAN

CAUCASUS

CASPIAN SEA

MANGGHYSTAŪ

UZBEKISTAN

TURKMENISTAN

USTYURT PLATEAU

ARAL SEA

GREENLAND SEA
NORWEGIAN SEA
NORTH SEA
ARCTIC CIRCLE
SVALBARD
Norway
ZEMLYA FRANTSA IOSIFA
(FRANZ JOSEF LAND)
Russia
BARENTS SEA
GULF OF BOTHNIA
BALTIC SEA
NORWAY
SWEDEN
FINLAND
DENMARK
NETH.
GERMANY
POLAND
LITHUANIA
LATVIA
ESTONIA
BELARUS
UKRAINE
CRIMEA
Sea of Azov
BLACK SEA
KARELIYA
NOVAYA ZEMLYA
KARA SEA
NENETS
KOMI
YAMAL-NENETS
KHANTY-MANSI
Zapadno Sibirskaya Ravnina
R U
SVERDLOVSK
BASHKORTOSTAN
TATARSTAN
UDMURT
MORDOVIYA
KALMYKIYA
Caucasus Mountains
GEORGIA
ARMENIA
AZERBAIJAN
Caspian Depression
CASPIAN SEA
Ustyurt Plateau
KAZAKHSTAN
Kazakh Uplands
BAYKONUR COSMODROME
Aral Sea
UZBEKISTAN
Qizilqum
Garagum
TURKMENISTAN
KYRGYZSTAN
TAJIKISTAN
AFGHAN.
IRAN
KHORASAN
Elburz Mts.
ALTAY
GORNO-ALTAY
KHAKASIYA
TYVA
XINJIANG UYGUR
TIAN SHAN
Moyynqum
Oslo
Stockholm
Helsinki
Tallinn
Riga
Vilnius
Minsk
Warszawa (Warsaw)
Berlin
Hamburg
København (Copenhagen)
Amsterdam
Kyiv (Kiev)
Moskva (Moscow)
Sankt-Peterburg (Saint Petersburg)
Arkhangel'sk (Archangel)
Murmansk
Nizhniy Novgorod
Kazan'
Samara
Volgograd (Stalingrad)
Rostov na Donu
Astrakhan'
Perm'
Yekaterinburg
Chelyabinsk
Ufa
Orenburg
Omsk
Novosibirsk
Tomsk
Krasnoyarsk
Barnaul
Kemerovo
Novokuznetsk
Tyumen'
Surgut
Nizhnevartovsk
Salekhard
Noril'sk
Astana
Qaraghandy
Almaty
Bishkek
Toshkent (Tashkent)
Samarqand
Dushanbe
Ashgabat
Mashhad
Tehran
Bakı (Baku)
Tbilisi
Yerevan
Ürümqi
Hami
North Pole

TWO-POINT EQUIDISTANT PROJECTION
SCALE 1:20,000,000
0 KILOMETERS 300 400 500
0 MILES 200 300 400 500
Administrative subdivisions of Russia are outlined on the map; where they are not labeled, they bear the same name as their capitals. Subdivisions in the Caucasus are on plate 195.
KURIL ISLANDS
The southern Kuril Islands of Iturup (Etorofu), Kunashir (Kunashiri), Shikotan, and the Habomai group were lost by Japan to the Soviet Union in 1945. Japan continues to claim these Russian-administered islands.
Date Line
Sunday
Monday
ARCTIC OCEAN
NOVOSIBIRSKIYE OSTROVA (NEW SIBERIAN ISLANDS)
OSTROVA ANZHU
EAST SIBERIAN SEA
NORTHERN SEA ROUTE
LAPTEV SEA
CHUKCHI SEA
Ostrov Vrangelya (Wrangel I.)
CHUKOTSKIY
ANADYRSKIY ZALIV
BERING SEA
ALEUTIAN ISLANDS
United States
Near Islands
Rat Islands
KORYAKSKIY
KAMCHATKA
Komandorskiye Ostrova (Commander Is.)
SEA OF OKHOTSK
KURIL ISLANDS (KURIL'SKIYE OSTROVA)
Khrebet Cherskogo
Verkhoyanskiy Khrebet
SAKHA (YAKUTIYA)
SIBERIA
Stanovoy Khrebet
AMUR
BURYATIYA
OSTROV SAKHALIN
SAKHALIN
HOKKAIDŌ
JAPAN
HONSHŪ
SEA OF JAPAN (EAST SEA)
PACIFIC OCEAN
Khrebet Sikhote Alin'
HEILONGJIANG
JILIN
LIAONING
HEBEI
NEI MONGOL
CHINA
MONGOLIA
GOBI
NORTH KOREA
SOUTH KOREA
Yakutsk
Magadan
Petropavlovsk Kamchatskiy
Anadyr'
Khabarovsk
Vladivostok
Blagoveshchensk
Chita
Irkutsk
Ulan Ude
Ulaanbaatar (Ulan Bator)
Harbin
Changchun
Shenyang
P'yŏngyang
SEOUL
TOKYO
Sapporo
Yuzhno Sakhalinsk
longitude East 102° of Greenwich

CENTRAL ENGLAND
ALBERS CONIC EQUAL-AREA PROJECTION
SCALE 1:1,750,000
0 KILOMETERS 30 40 50
0 MILES 10 20 30 40 50
NORTH SEA
IRISH SEA
WALES
ENGLAND
Meridian of Greenwich (London)
Longitude West 2° of Greenwich
LONDON
Birmingham
Manchester
Liverpool
Leeds
Sheffield
Bristol
Cardiff (Caerdydd)
Nottingham
Leicester
York
Carlisle
Newcastle under Lyme
Stoke on Trent
Oxford
Cambridge
Norwich
Southampton
Portsmouth
Brighton
PEAK DIST. NAT. PARK
YORKSHIRE DALES NAT. PARK
LAKE DIST. NAT. PARK
NORTH YORK MOORS NAT. PARK
SNOWDONIA NATIONAL PARK
BRECON BEACONS NAT. PARK
EXMOOR NAT. PARK
The Wash
Bristol Channel
Lincoln Heights
Chiltern Hills
Cotswold Hills
Cambrian Mountains
Berwyn
The Weald
South Downs
North Downs
Salisbury Plain
Mendip Hills
Blackdown Hills
Cleveland Hills
EAST ANGLIA
THE FENS
THE WOLDS

LOW COUNTRIES

ALBERS CONIC EQUAL-AREA PROJECTION

SCALE 1:2,500,000

0 KILOMETERS 40 80

0 MILES 20 40 60 80

Longitude East 4° of Greenwich

NORTHEASTERN SPAIN
ALBERS CONIC EQUAL-AREA PROJECTION
SCALE 1:3,250,000
0 KILOMETERS 60 80
0 MILES 20 40 60 80
SOUTHERN SPAIN
ALBERS CONIC EQUAL-AREA PROJECTION
SCALE 1:3,250,000
0 KILOMETERS 60 80
0 MILES 20 40 60 80
BAY OF BISCAY
FRANCE
PYRENEES
SPAIN
ANDORRA
CATALONIA
ARAGON
NAVARRA
BASQUE COUNTRY
CANTABRIA
LA RIOJA
CASTILE AND LEON
CASTILE LA MANCHA
MADRID
VALENCIA
BALEARIC ISLANDS
BALEARIC SEA
MEDITERRANEAN SEA
EXTREMADURA
ANDALUSIA
MURCIA
ALBORAN SEA
ATLANTIC OCEAN
ALGERIA
GIBRALTAR U.K.
Longitude West 1° of Greenwich
Longitude East 1° of Greenwich
Longitude West 2° of Greenwich

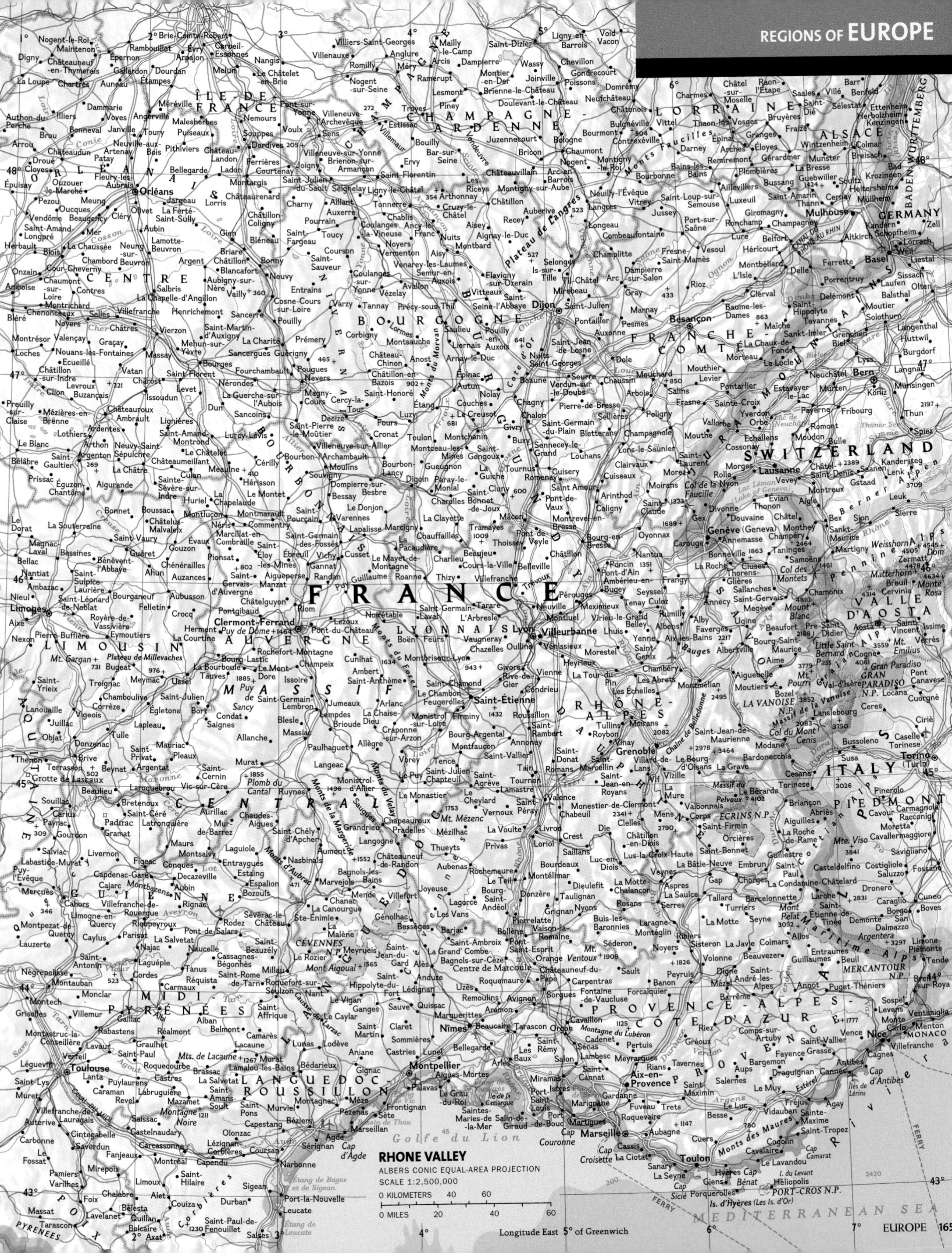
RHONE VALLEY
ALBERS CONIC EQUAL-AREA PROJECTION
SCALE 1:2,500,000
0 KILOMETERS 40 60
0 MILES 20 40 60
FRANCE
SWITZERLAND
GERMANY
ITALY
MONACO
ÎLE DE FRANCE
CHAMPAGNE - ARDENNE
LORRAINE
ALSACE
FRANCHE - COMTÉ
BOURGOGNE
CENTRE
ORLÉANAIS
NIVERNAIS
BOURBONNAIS
AUVERGNE
LIMOUSIN
MASSIF CENTRAL
LYONNAIS
RHÔNE - ALPES
DAUPHINÉ
SAVOY
VALLE D'AOSTA
PIEDMONT
AQUITAINE
GUIENNE
MIDI - PYRÉNÉES
LANGUEDOC - ROUSSILLON
PROVENCE - CÔTE D'AZUR
PROVENCE
FOIX
BADEN-WÜRTTEMBERG
JURA MOUNTAINS
Monts Faucilles
Plateau de Langres
Monts du Morvan
Monts du Forez
Monts de la Margeride
Monts du Vivarais
CÉVENNES
Causse du Larzac
Pennine Alps
Berner Alpen
Graian Alps
Cottian Alps
Maritime Alps
Monts des Maures
Plateau de Millevaches
Golfe du Lion
MEDITERRANEAN SEA
Riviera
Lake of Geneva
Paris
Orléans
Dijon
Besançon
Basel
Bern
Genève (Geneva)
Lausanne
Lyon
Villeurbanne
Saint-Étienne
Grenoble
Clermont-Ferrand
Limoges
Toulouse
Montpellier
Nîmes
Avignon
Aix-en-Provence
Marseille
Toulon
Nice
Torino (Turin)
Mulhouse
Mont Blanc
Matterhorn
Mte. Viso
Mt. Ventoux
Mont Aigoual
Puy de Dôme
Mt. Mézenc
Plomb du Cantal
Longitude East 5° of Greenwich

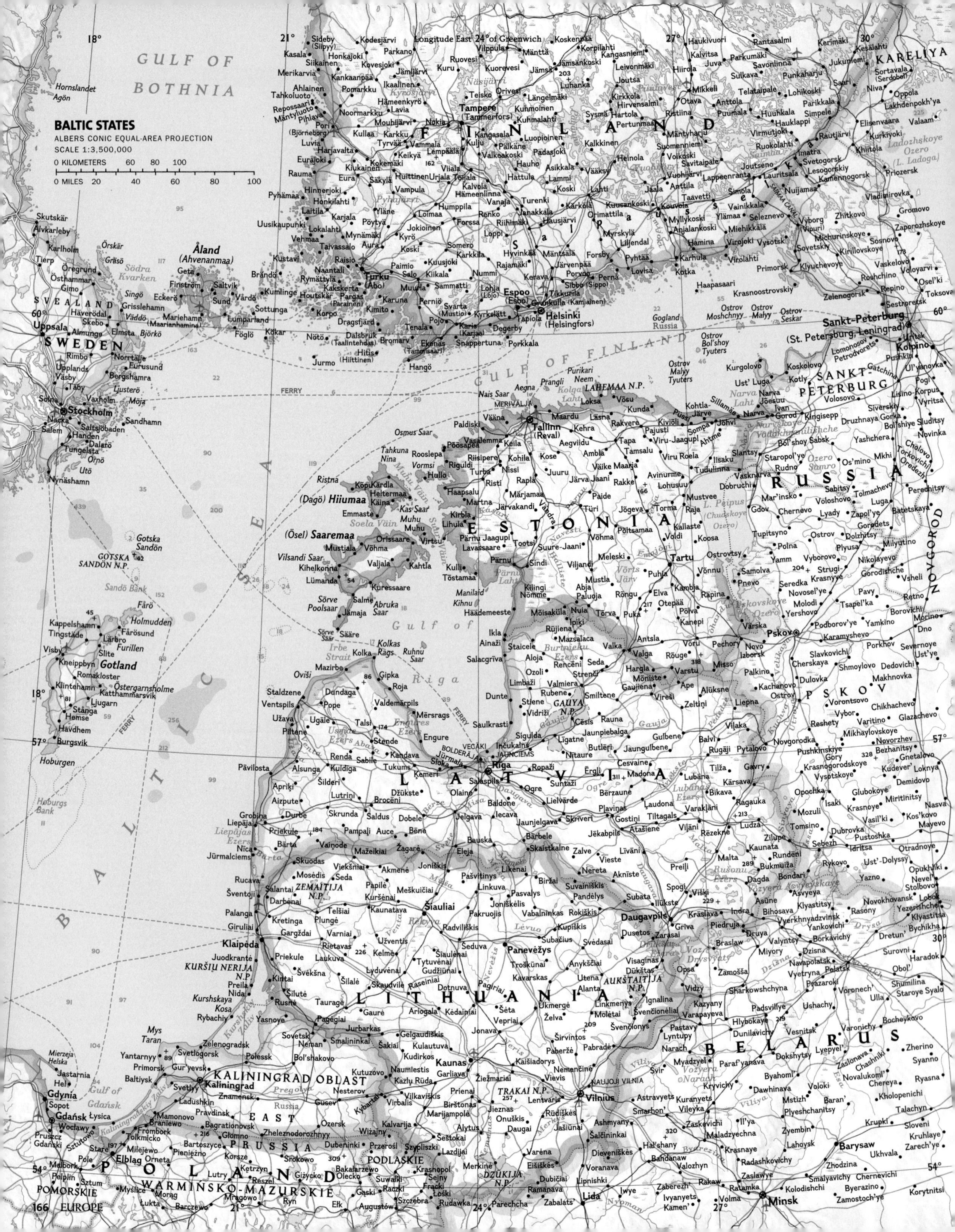

BALTIC STATES
ALBERS CONIC EQUAL-AREA PROJECTION
SCALE 1:3,500,000
0 KILOMETERS 20 40 60 80 100
0 MILES 20 40 60 80 100
Longitude East 24° of Greenwich
GULF OF BOTHNIA
GULF OF FINLAND
BALTIC SEA
Gulf of Riga
FINLAND
SWEDEN
SVEALAND
ESTONIA
LATVIA
LITHUANIA
BELARUS
RUSSIA
POLAND
KARELIYA
SANKT-PETERBURG
NOVGOROD
PSKOV
KALININGRAD OBLAST
EAST PRUSSIA
POMORSKIE
WARMIŃSKO-MAZURSKIE
PODLASKIE
Åland (Ahvenanmaa)
Gotland
(Dagö) Hiiumaa
(Ösel) Saaremaa
GOTSKA SANDÖN N.P.
LAHEMAA N.P.
GAUYA N.P.
ZEMAITIJA N.P.
KURŠIŲ NERIJA N.P.
AUKŠTAITIJA N.P.
TRAKAI N.P.
DZŪKIJA N.P.
Ladozhskoye Ozero (L. Ladoga)
L. Peipus (Chudskoye Ozero)
Helsinki (Helsingfors)
Stockholm
Tallinn (Reval)
Riga
Vilnius
Minsk
Sankt-Peterburg (St. Petersburg, Leningrad)
Kaliningrad
Kaunas
Tartu
Pskov
Daugavpils
Klaipėda
Šiauliai
Panevėžys
Turku (Åbo)
Tampere (Tammerfors)
Gdańsk
Gdynia
FERRY

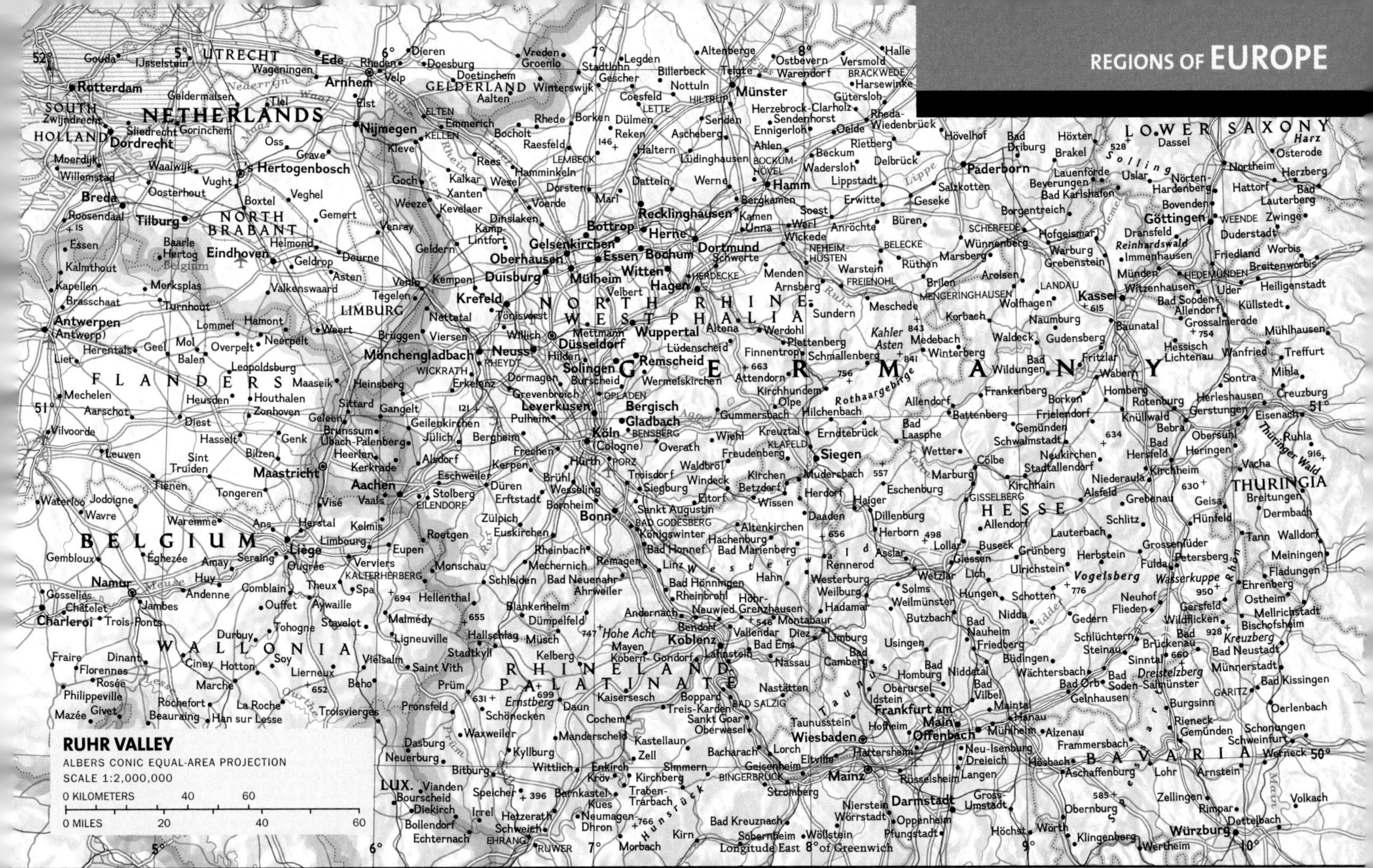
RUHR VALLEY
ALBERS CONIC EQUAL-AREA PROJECTION
SCALE 1:2,000,000
0 KILOMETERS 40 60
0 MILES 20 40 60
NETHERLANDS
SOUTH HOLLAND
NORTH BRABANT
LIMBURG
GELDERLAND
FLANDERS
BELGIUM
WALLONIA
LUX.
NORTH RHINE-WESTPHALIA
GERMANY
LOWER SAXONY
HESSE
THURINGIA
RHINELAND-PALATINATE
BAVARIA
Rotterdam
Utrecht
Arnhem
Nijmegen
Eindhoven
Antwerpen (Antwerp)
Liège
Maastricht
Aachen
Köln (Cologne)
Düsseldorf
Duisburg
Essen
Dortmund
Bochum
Münster
Bonn
Koblenz
Wiesbaden
Mainz
Frankfurt am Main
Darmstadt
Würzburg
Kassel
Paderborn
Siegen
Longitude East 8° of Greenwich

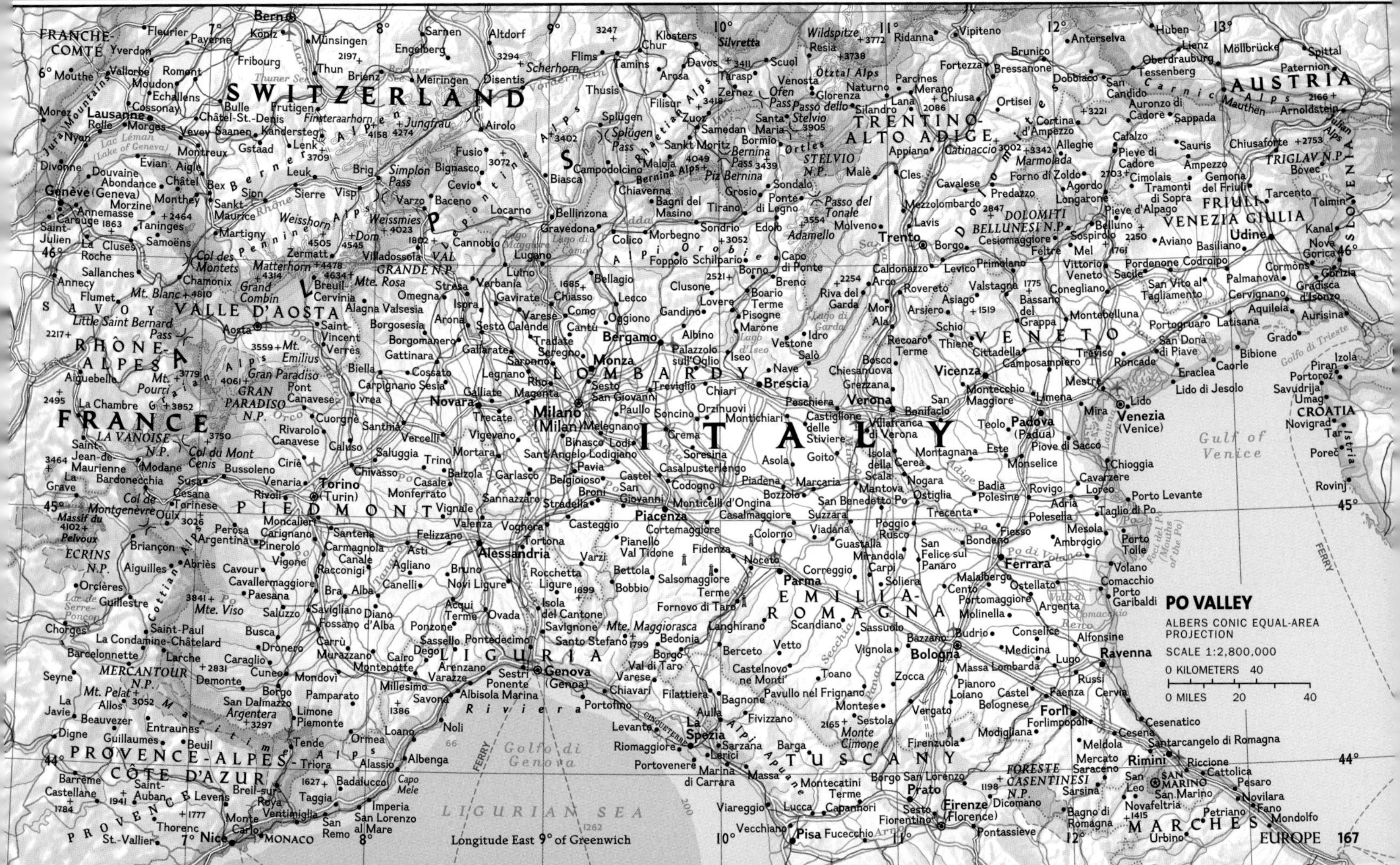
PO VALLEY
ALBERS CONIC EQUAL-AREA PROJECTION
SCALE 1:2,800,000
0 KILOMETERS 40
0 MILES 20 40
SWITZERLAND
AUSTRIA
FRANCE
ITALY
CROATIA
SLOVENIA
FRANCHE-COMTÉ
RHÔNE-ALPES
PROVENCE-ALPES-CÔTE D'AZUR
VALLE D'AOSTA
PIEDMONT
LOMBARDY
TRENTINO-ALTO ADIGE
VENETO
FRIULI-VENEZIA GIULIA
LIGURIA
EMILIA-ROMAGNA
TUSCANY
MARCHES
Riviera
Gulf of Venice
Golfo di Genova
LIGURIAN SEA
Bern
Lausanne
Genève (Geneva)
Torino (Turin)
Milano (Milan)
Genova (Genoa)
Bologna
Venezia (Venice)
Verona
Padova (Padua)
Firenze (Florence)
Longitude East 9° of Greenwich

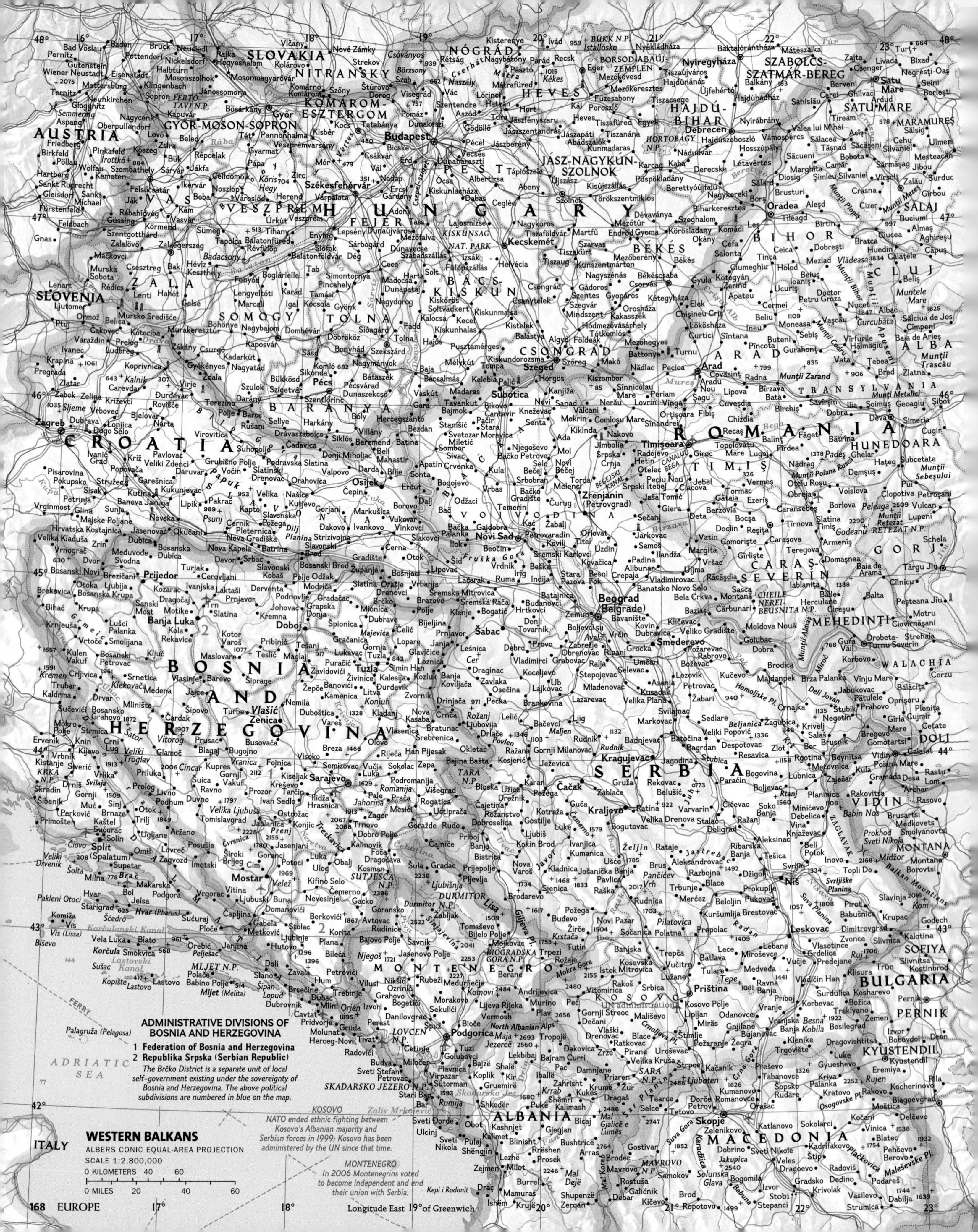
WESTERN BALKANS
ALBERS CONIC EQUAL-AREA PROJECTION
SCALE 1:2,800,000
0 KILOMETERS 40 60
0 MILES 20 40 60
ADMINISTRATIVE DIVISIONS OF BOSNIA AND HERZEGOVINA
1 Federation of Bosnia and Herzegovina
2 Republika Srpska (Serbian Republic)
The Brčko District is a separate unit of local self-government existing under the sovereignty of Bosnia and Herzegovina. The above political subdivisions are numbered in blue on the map.
KOSOVO
NATO ended ethnic fighting between Kosovo's Albanian majority and Serbian forces in 1999; Kosovo has been administered by the UN since that time.
MONTENEGRO
In 2006 Montenegrins voted to become independent and end their union with Serbia.
AUSTRIA
SLOVAKIA
HUNGARY
SLOVENIA
CROATIA
ROMANIA
BOSNIA AND HERZEGOVINA
SERBIA
MONTENEGRO
KOSOVO
ALBANIA
MACEDONIA
BULGARIA
ITALY
ADRIATIC SEA
Longitude East 19° of Greenwich

CENTRAL RUSSIA
ALBERS CONIC EQUAL-AREA PROJECTION
SCALE 1:10,000,000
0 KILOMETERS 200 300
0 MILES 100 200 300
ARCTIC CIRCLE
NORTHERN SEA ROUTE
R U S S I A
S I B E R I A
Zapadno Sibirskaya Ravnina
URAL MTS.
YAMAL-NENETS
KHANTY-MANSI
KRASNOYARSK
EVENK
TOMSK
NOVOSIBIRSK
KEMEROVO
ALTAY
OMSK
TYUMEN'
KURGAN
SVERDLOVSK
CHELYABINSK
PERM'
KOMI
NENETS
ARKHANGEL'SK
VOLOGDA
KIROV
UDMURTIYA
MARIY-EL
TATARSTAN
BASHKORTOSTAN
ORENBURG
SAMARA
UL'YAN.
KAZAKHSTAN
PAVLODAR
SOLTÜSTIK QAZAQSTAN
AQMOLA
QOSTANAY
MURMANSK
KOL'SKIY POLUOSTROV
Poluostrov Yamal
Gydanskiy Poluostrov
Obskaya Guba
Baydaratskaya Guba
Ostrov Kolguyev
O. Vaygach
White Sea
YUGYD VA N.P.
Gora Narodnaya
Novosibirsk
Omsk
Yekaterinburg
Chelyabinsk
Perm'
Ufa
Kazan'
Samara
Orenburg
Tomsk
Barnaul
Surgut
Nizhnevartovsk
Arkhangel'sk (Archangel)
Syktyvkar
Kirov
Izhevsk
Tyumen'
Kurgan
Pavlodar
Magnitogorsk
Nizhniy Tagil
Salekhard
Khanty Mansiysk
Longitude East 78° of Greenwich

o large and so diverse—covering almost two-thirds of Earth's land surface and inhabited by 60% of humanity—Asia is as much a world s a continent. Earth's most violent tectonic collision continues here, as he Indian subcontinent rams into Asia and thrusts up the Himalaya nd the Tibetan Plateau. The resulting land demarcation has effectively solated large sections of Asia from each other and, in particular, has ept the two most populous countries—China and India, which etween them contain half the continent's population—as counter- veights to one another, demographically, culturally, economically, and olitically. Asia's vast landmass embraces a wide range of terrain and eoples, from the lightly populated steppes of central Russia to the leserts of the contentious Middle East, from the perilous floodplain of angladesh to the teeming western islands of the Indonesian archipela- go. Home to the faiths of Judaism, Christianity, Islam, Hinduism, uddhism, Taoism, Shintoism—and more tongues than religions—the ontinent supports both megacities and Shangri-La pockets of solitude. Once primarily a source of raw materials and crops such as rubber, tin, etroleum, timber, and rice, Asia now manufactures goods, from chil- lren's toys to high-end electronics, that flood the rest of the world. apan led the economic boom. China, India, Korea, Singapore, and oth- rs are extending it. Prosperity remains elusive for less-developed coun- ries, such as Afghanistan and Timor-Leste (East Timor), which have er-capita incomes only one-fourth of that in the region overall. Other egional issues include cross-border migration, trafficking of people nd drugs, trans-boundary spread of diseases, spillover of conflicts, and ooming environmental hazards.

MAGE BY ROBERT STACEY, WORLDSAT INTERNATIONAL INC.

ASIA

TWO-POINT EQUIDISTANT PROJECTION
SCALE 1:49,000,000
0 KILOMETERS 1000
0 MILES 400 600 800 1000
ARCTIC OCEAN
PACIFIC OCEAN
INDIAN OCEAN
ATLANTIC OCEAN
North Pole
Date Line
Sunday
Monday
ARCTIC CIRCLE
TROPIC OF CANCER
EQUATOR
Meridian of Greenwich (London)
Longitude East 110° of Greenwich
RUSSIA
SIBERIA
CENTRAL SIBERIAN PLATEAU
WEST SIBERIAN PLAIN
NORTHERN EUROPEAN PLAIN
URAL MOUNTAINS
KAZAKHSTAN
Kazakh Uplands
MONGOLIA
GOBI
ALTAY MOUNTAINS
CHINA
PLATEAU OF TIBET
KUNLUN MOUNTAINS
ALTUN SHAN
TAKLIMAKAN DESERT
HIMALAYA
INDIA
DECCAN PLATEAU
Western Ghats
Eastern Ghats
Great Indian Desert
PAKISTAN
AFGHAN.
IRAN
Zagros Mountains
IRAQ
SAUDI ARABIA
ARABIAN PENINSULA
Ar Rub' al Khālī (Empty Quarter)
YEMEN
OMAN
TURKEY
Anatolia (Asia Minor)
SYR.
JORDAN
ISRAEL
LEBANON
CYPRUS
EGYPT
Western Desert
Eastern Desert
SUDAN
Nubian Desert
ERITREA
DJIBOUTI
ETHIOPIA
Ethiopian Highlands
SOMALIA
KENYA
TANZANIA
MADAGASCAR
LIBYA
CYRENAICA
TUNISIA
ALGERIA
SPAIN
PORTUGAL
FRANCE
ITALY
GREECE
GER.
POLAND
UKRAINE
BELARUS
FINLAND
SWEDEN
NORWAY
SCANDINAVIA
U.K.
IRE.
Caucasus Mts.
JAPAN
NORTH KOREA
SOUTH KOREA
TAIWAN
PHILIPPINES
PHILIPPINE ISLANDS
MYANMAR (BURMA)
THAILAND
LAOS
CAMBODIA
VIETNAM
INDOCHINA PENINSULA
MALAY PENINSULA
MALAYSIA
SINGAPORE
BRUNEI
SUMATRA
JAVA
Borneo
Celebes
INDONESIA
NEW GUINEA
AUSTRALIA
GREATER SUNDA ISLANDS
LESSER SUNDA ISLANDS
TIMOR LESTE (EAST TIMOR)
SRI LANKA
MALDIVES
SEYCHELLES
COMOROS
BANGLADESH
NEPAL
BHUTAN
KASHMIR
Bay of Bengal
Arabian Sea
Andaman Sea
South China Sea
East China Sea
Yellow Sea
Sea of Japan (East Sea)
Sea of Okhotsk
Bering Sea
Philippine Sea
Caspian Sea
Black Sea
Red Sea
Mediterranean Sea
Persian Gulf
Gulf of Aden
Gulf of Oman
Kara Sea
Barents Sea
Laptev Sea
East Siberian Sea
Norwegian Sea
North Sea
Baltic Sea
Celebes Sea
Sulu Sea
Banda Sea
Flores Sea
Timor Sea
Arafura Sea
Java Sea
Moskva (Moscow)
Beijing (Peking)
Tōkyō (Tokyo)
Shanghai
Hong Kong
New Delhi
Karachi
Mumbai (Bombay)
Colombo
Dhaka
Kathmandu
Yangon (Rangoon)
Krung Thep (Bangkok)
Hanoi
Manila
Jakarta
Kuala Lumpur
Ulaanbaatar (Ulan Bator)
Astana
Tehrān
Baghdād
Ar Riyāḑ (Riyadh)
El Qâhira (Cairo)
İstanbul (Constantinople)
Ankara (Angora)
Kyiv
Mt. Everest (Qomolangma Sagarmatha)
World's highest point
Lake Baikal
World's deepest lake
Kamchatka Peninsula
Kuril Islands
Aleutian Islands
Sakhalin
Hokkaido
Honshu
Kyushu
Shikoku
Ryukyu Islands
Hainan
Novaya Zemlya
Svalbard
Zemlya Frantsa Iosifa (Franz Josef Land)
Sev. Zemlya (North Land)
Novosibirskiye Ostrova (New Siberian Islands)

A commonly accepted division between Asia and Europe—here marked by a green line—is formed by the Ural Mountains, Ural River, Caspian Sea, Caucasus Mountains, and the Black Sea with its outlets, the Bosporus and Dardanelles.
TWO-POINT EQUIDISTANT PROJECTION
SCALE 1:49,000,000
0 KILOMETERS 1000
0 MILES 400 600 800 1000
North Pole
Date Line
Sunday
Monday
Meridian of Greenwich (London)
Longitude East 110° of Greenwich
ARCTIC OCEAN
PACIFIC OCEAN
INDIAN OCEAN
ATLANTIC OCEAN
TROPIC OF CANCER
ARCTIC CIRCLE
EQUATOR
Aleutian Islands
Bering Sea
Sea of Okhotsk
Philippine Sea
South China Sea
East China Sea
Arabian Sea
Bay of Bengal
Andaman Sea
Celebes Sea
Java Sea
Banda Sea
Arafura Sea
RUSSIA
SIBERIA
URAL MOUNTAINS
KAZAKHSTAN
MONGOLIA
ALTAY MTS.
GOBI
INNER MONGOLIA
CHINA
PLATEAU OF TIBET
TAKLIMAKAN DESERT
HIMALAYA
INDIA
PAKISTAN
AFGHAN.
IRAN
IRAQ
SAUDI ARABIA
YEMEN
OMAN
TURKEY
UKRAINE
JAPAN
NORTH KOREA
SOUTH KOREA
TAIWAN
PHILIPPINES
INDONESIA
MALAYSIA
THAILAND
MYANMAR (BURMA)
CAMBODIA
LAOS
VIETNAM
SRI LANKA
MALDIVES
EGYPT
SUDAN
ETHIOPIA
SOMALIA
KENYA
TANZANIA
LIBYA
FRANCE
SPAIN
ITALY
GREECE
AUSTRALIA
MOSKVA (MOSCOW)
BEIJING (PEKING)
TŌKYŌ (TOKYO)
SEOUL
SHANGHAI
HONG KONG
DELHI
MUMBAI (BOMBAY)
Kolkata (Calcutta)
KRUNG THEP (BANGKOK)
JAKARTA
SINGAPORE
TEHRĀN
ISTANBUL
LONDON
Chagos Archipelago (Oil Islands) British Indian Ocean Territory
SEYCHELLES
MADAGASCAR
COMOROS

TEMPERATURE AND RAINFALL

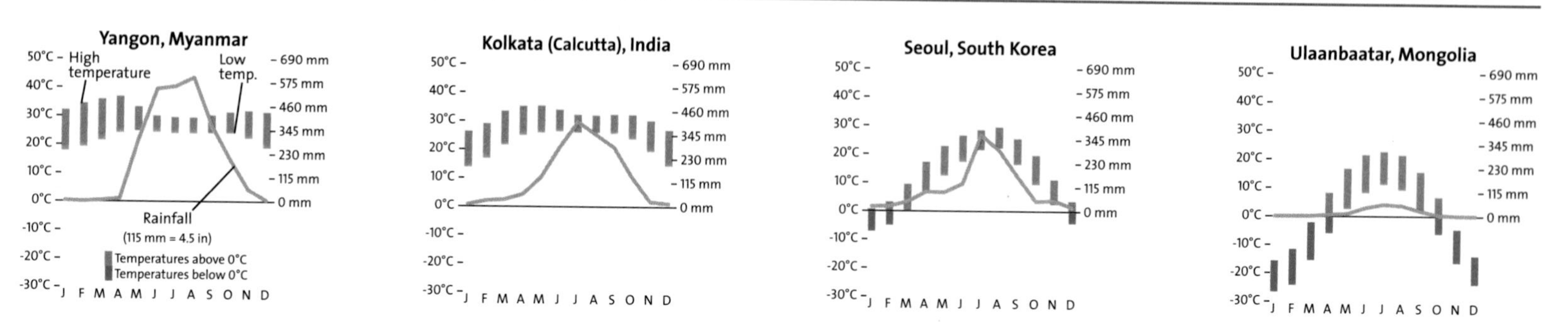

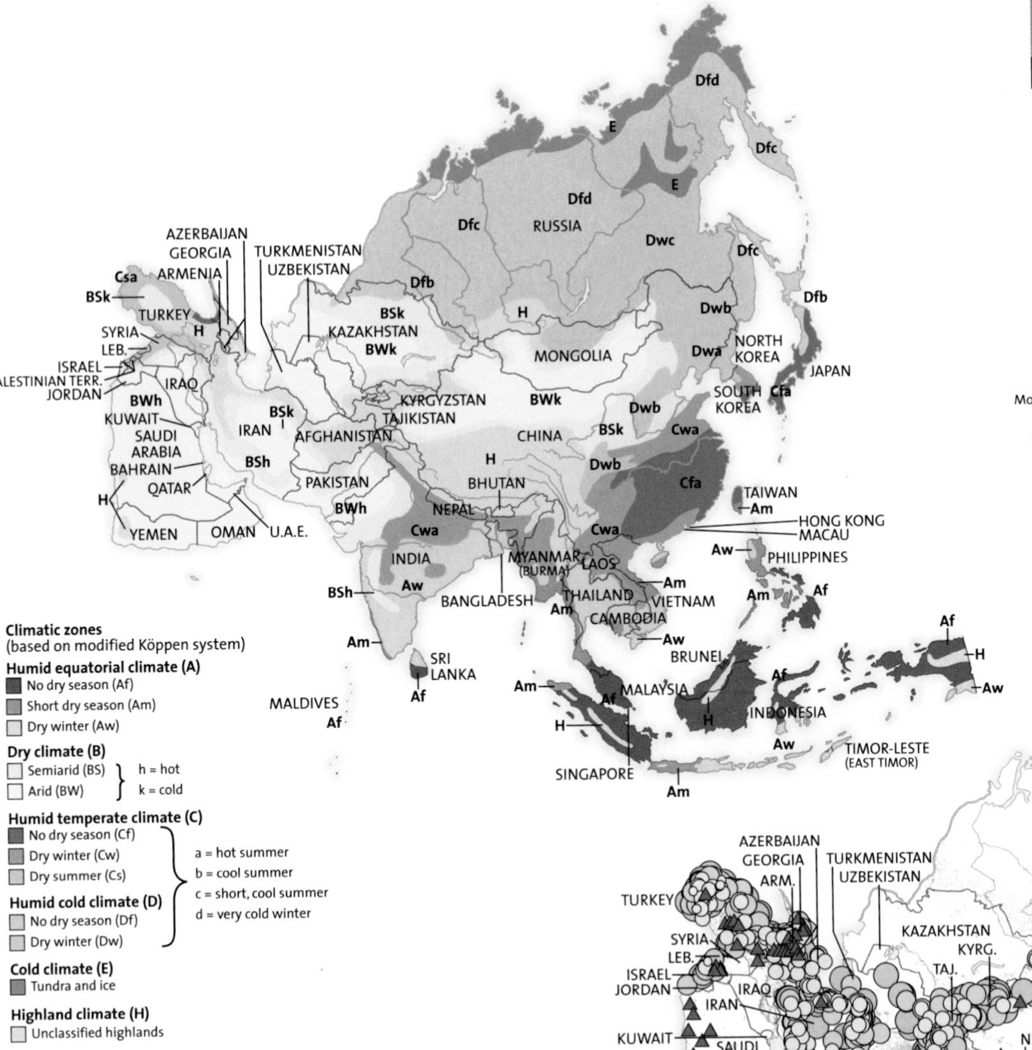

Climatic zones
(based on modified Köppen system)

Humid equatorial climate (A)
- No dry season (Af)
- Short dry season (Am)
- Dry winter (Aw)

Dry climate (B)
- Semiarid (BS)
- Arid (BW)

h = hot
k = cold

Humid temperate climate (C)
- No dry season (Cf)
- Dry winter (Cw)
- Dry summer (Cs)

Humid cold climate (D)
- No dry season (Df)
- Dry winter (Dw)

a = hot summer
b = cool summer
c = short, cool summer
d = very cold winter

Cold climate (E)
- Tundra and ice

Highland climate (H)
- Unclassified highlands

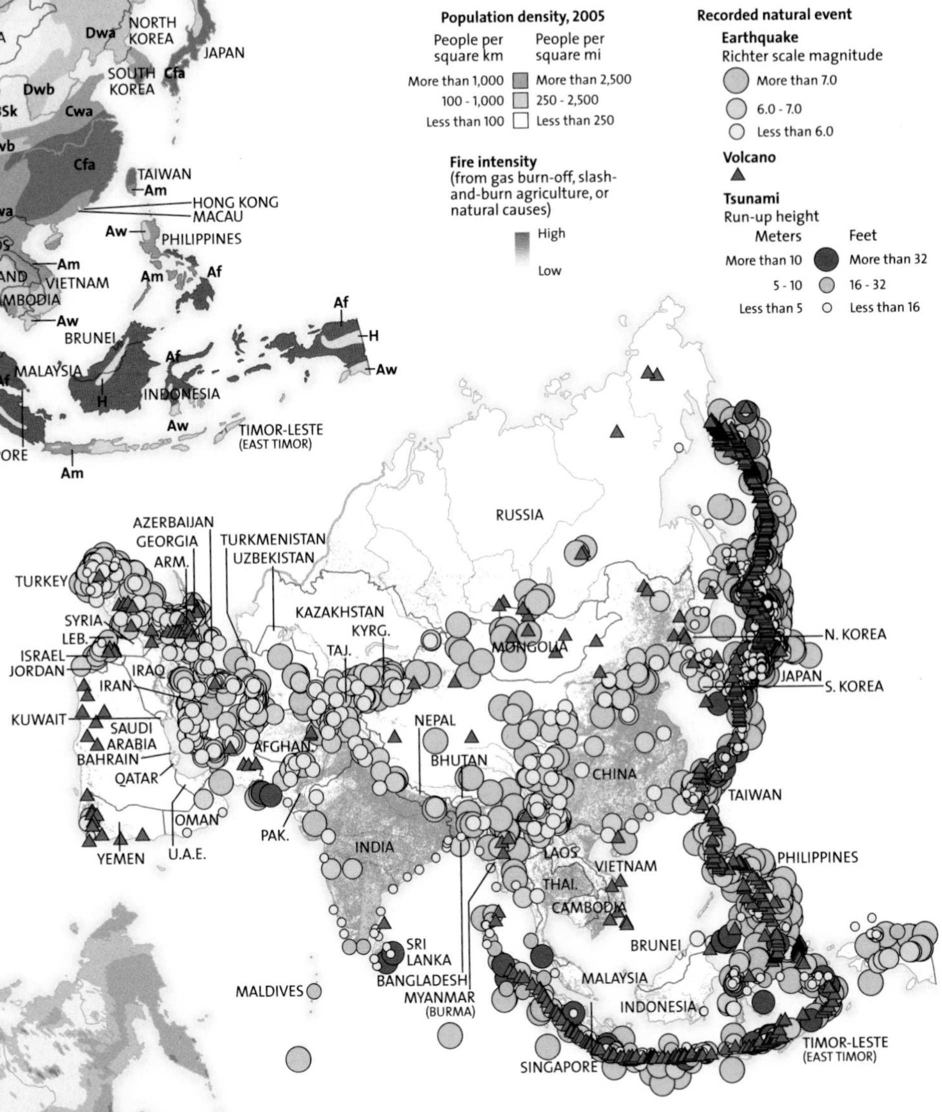

Population density, 2005

People per square km	People per square mi
More than 1,000	More than 2,500
100 - 1,000	250 - 2,500
Less than 100	Less than 250

Fire intensity
(from gas burn-off, slash-and-burn agriculture, or natural causes)
High
Low

Recorded natural event

Earthquake
Richter scale magnitude
- More than 7.0
- 6.0 - 7.0
- Less than 6.0

Volcano

Tsunami
Run-up height

Meters	Feet
More than 10	More than 32
5 - 10	16 - 32
Less than 5	Less than 16

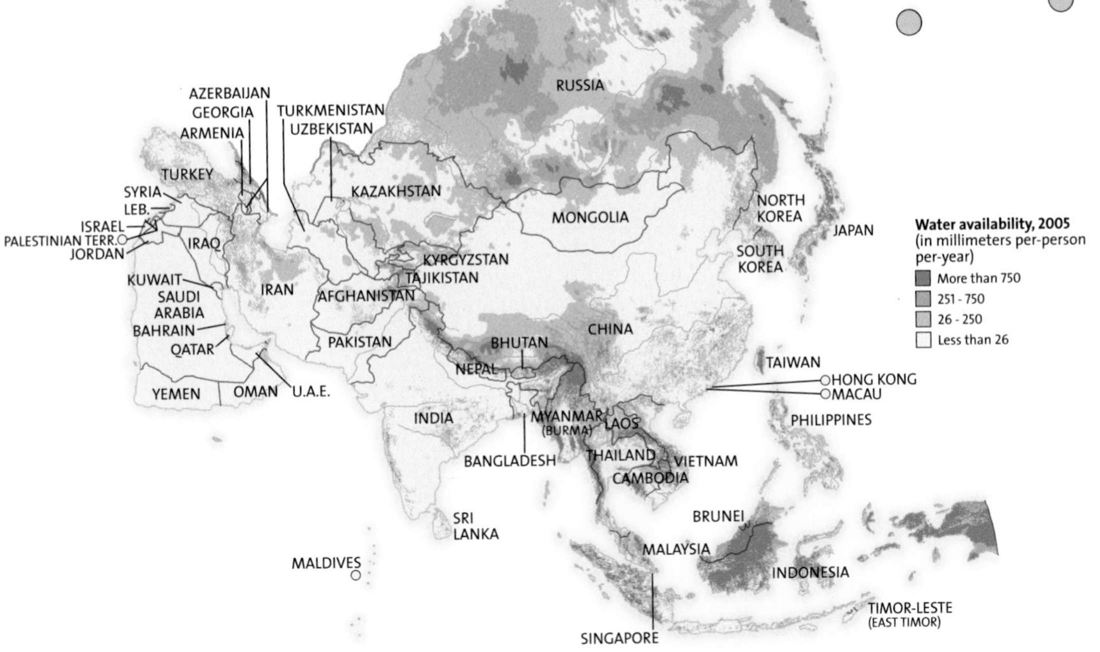

Water availability, 2005
(in millimeters per-person per-year)
- More than 750
- 251 - 750
- 26 - 250
- Less than 26

POPULATION PYRAMIDS

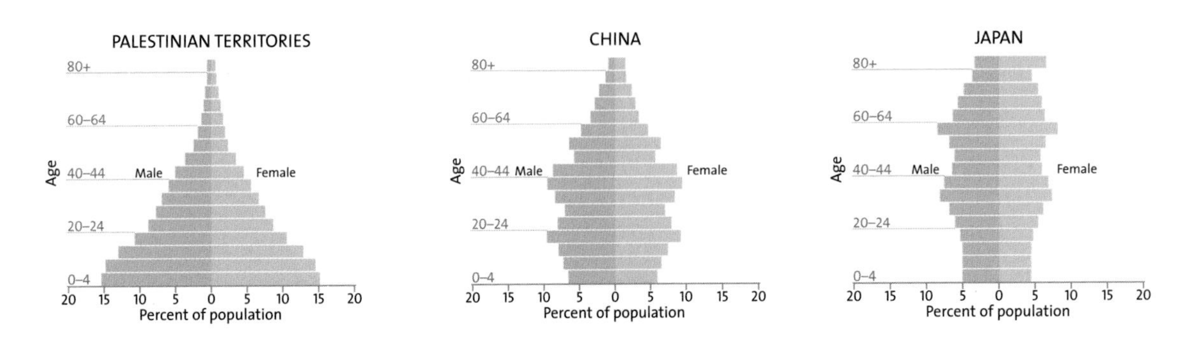

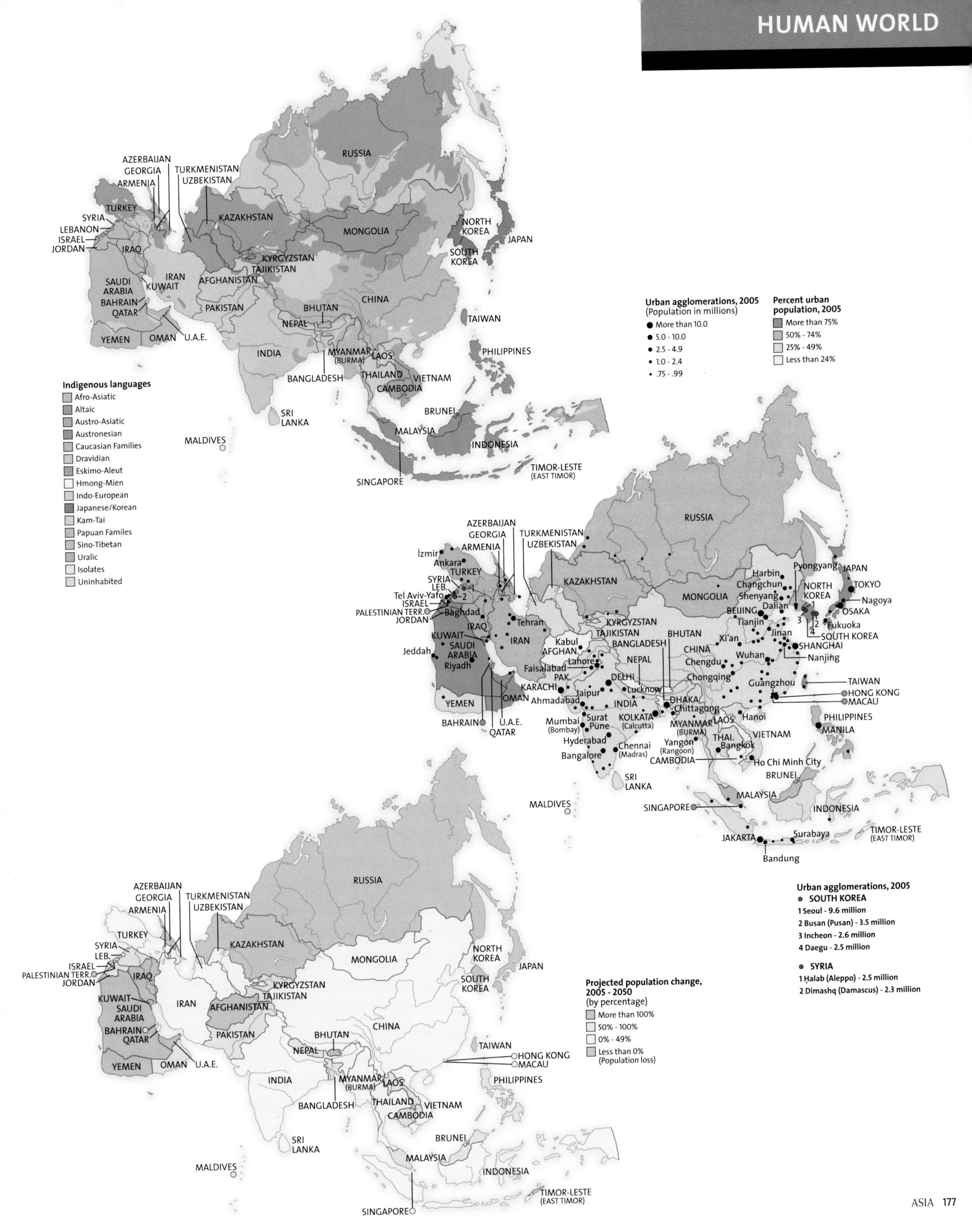

RUSSIA
AZERBAIJAN
GEORGIA
ARMENIA
TURKMENISTAN
UZBEKISTAN
TURKEY
SYRIA
LEBANON
ISRAEL
JORDAN
IRAQ
KAZAKHSTAN
MONGOLIA
NORTH KOREA
SOUTH KOREA
JAPAN
KYRGYZSTAN
TAJIKISTAN
IRAN
KUWAIT
SAUDI ARABIA
BAHRAIN
QATAR
AFGHANISTAN
PAKISTAN
NEPAL
BHUTAN
CHINA
TAIWAN
YEMEN
OMAN
U.A.E.
INDIA
MYANMAR (BURMA)
LAOS
PHILIPPINES
BANGLADESH
THAILAND
VIETNAM
CAMBODIA
SRI LANKA
BRUNEI
MALAYSIA
MALDIVES
INDONESIA
TIMOR-LESTE (EAST TIMOR)
SINGAPORE
Indigenous languages
Afro-Asiatic
Altaic
Austro-Asiatic
Austronesian
Caucasian Families
Dravidian
Eskimo-Aleut
Hmong-Mien
Indo-European
Japanese/Korean
Kam-Tai
Papuan Familes
Sino-Tibetan
Uralic
Isolates
Uninhabited
Urban agglomerations, 2005
(Population in millions)
More than 10.0
5.0 - 10.0
2.5 - 4.9
1.0 - 2.4
.75 - .99
Percent urban population, 2005
More than 75%
50% - 74%
25% - 49%
Less than 24%
İzmir
Ankara
Tel Aviv-Yafo
LEB.
PALESTINIAN TERR.
Baghdad
Tehran
Jeddah
Riyadh
Kabul
AFGHAN.
Lahore
Faisalabad
PAK.
KARACHI
Ahmadabad
Jaipur
DELHI
Lucknow
Mumbai (Bombay)
Surat
Pune
KOLKATA (Calcutta)
Hyderabad
Bangalore
Chennai (Madras)
DHAKA
Chittagong
Yangon (Rangoon)
THAI.
Bangkok
Hanoi
Ho Chi Minh City
Harbin
Changchun
Shenyang
Dalian
BEIJING
Tianjin
Jinan
Xi'an
Pyongyang
TOKYO
Nagoya
OSAKA
Fukuoka
SHANGHAI
Nanjing
Wuhan
Chengdu
Chongqing
Guangzhou
HONG KONG
MACAU
MANILA
JAKARTA
Bandung
Surabaya
Urban agglomerations, 2005
SOUTH KOREA
1 Seoul - 9.6 million
2 Busan (Pusan) - 3.5 million
3 Incheon - 2.6 million
4 Daegu - 2.5 million
SYRIA
1 Ḥalab (Aleppo) - 2.5 million
2 Dimashq (Damascus) - 2.3 million
Projected population change, 2005 - 2050
(by percentage)
More than 100%
50% - 100%
0% - 49%
Less than 0% (Population loss)

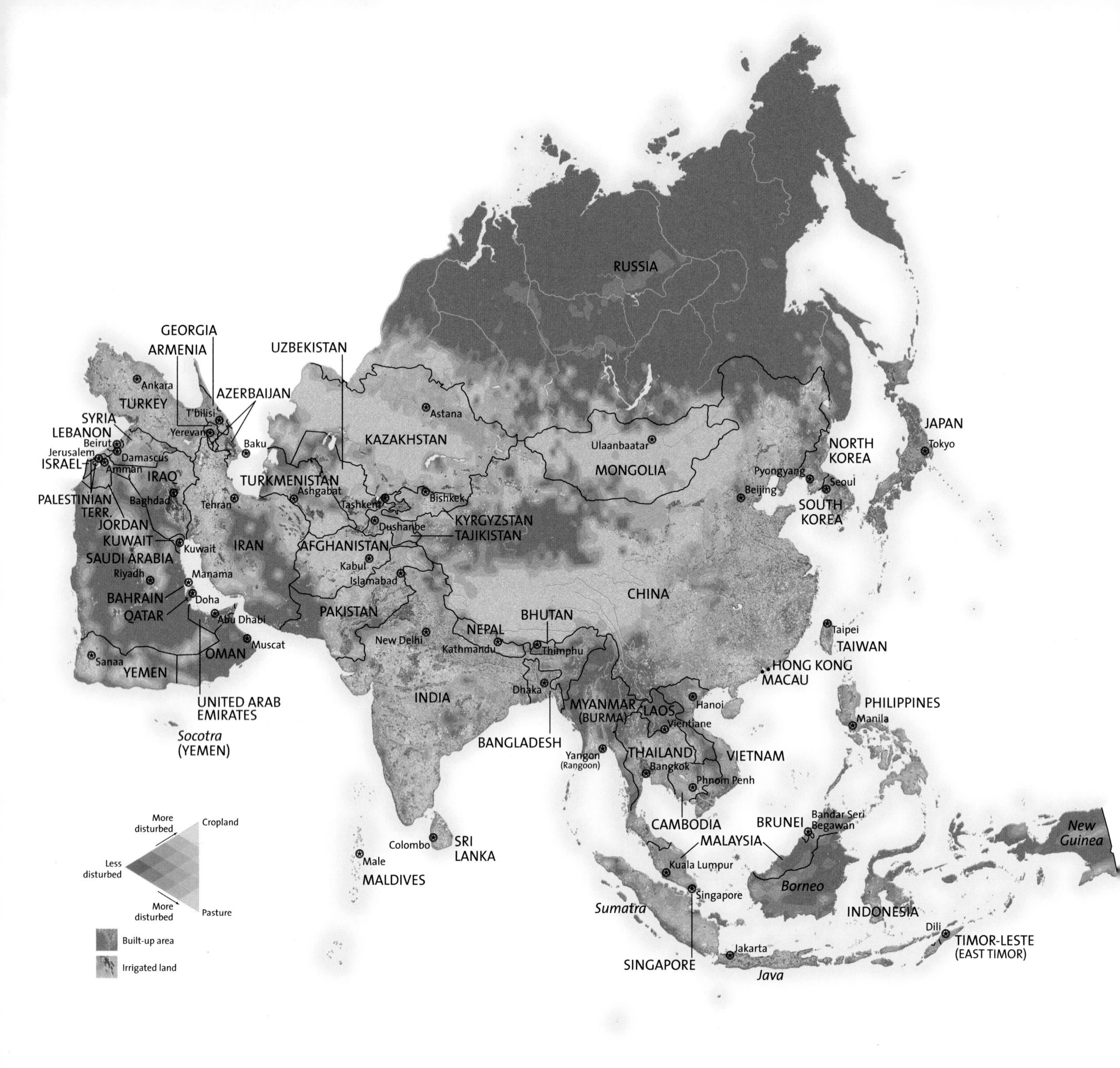
RUSSIA
GEORGIA
ARMENIA
UZBEKISTAN
AZERBAIJAN
TURKEY
Ankara
SYRIA
LEBANON
Beirut
Jerusalem
ISRAEL
Damascus
Amman
IRAQ
T'bilisi
Yerevan
Baku
KAZAKHSTAN
Astana
Ulaanbaatar
MONGOLIA
JAPAN
Tokyo
NORTH KOREA
Pyongyang
Seoul
SOUTH KOREA
Beijing
TURKMENISTAN
Ashgabat
Tashkent
Bishkek
KYRGYZSTAN
TAJIKISTAN
Dushanbe
PALESTINIAN TERR.
Baghdad
Tehran
JORDAN
KUWAIT
Kuwait
IRAN
AFGHANISTAN
SAUDI ARABIA
Riyadh
Manama
Kabul
Islamabad
BAHRAIN
Doha
QATAR
Abu Dhabi
PAKISTAN
CHINA
BHUTAN
NEPAL
Muscat
OMAN
Sanaa
YEMEN
New Delhi
Kathmandu
Thimphu
Taipei
TAIWAN
HONG KONG
MACAU
UNITED ARAB EMIRATES
Socotra (YEMEN)
INDIA
Dhaka
MYANMAR (BURMA)
LAOS
Hanoi
PHILIPPINES
Manila
Vientiane
BANGLADESH
Yangon (Rangoon)
THAILAND
VIETNAM
Bangkok
Phnom Penh
CAMBODIA
BRUNEI
Bandar Seri Begawan
New Guinea
Colombo
SRI LANKA
MALAYSIA
Male
MALDIVES
Kuala Lumpur
Borneo
Singapore
Sumatra
INDONESIA
Dili
TIMOR-LESTE (EAST TIMOR)
Jakarta
SINGAPORE
Java
More disturbed
Cropland
Less disturbed
More disturbed
Pasture
Built-up area
Irrigated land

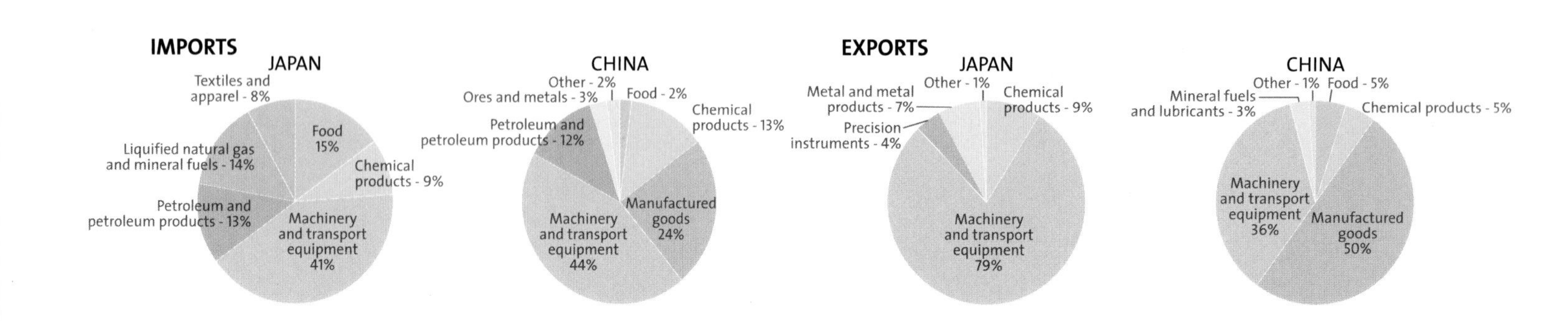
IMPORTS
JAPAN
Textiles and apparel - 8%
Food 15%
Liquified natural gas and mineral fuels - 14%
Chemical products - 9%
Petroleum and petroleum products - 13%
Machinery and transport equipment 41%
CHINA
Other - 2%
Ores and metals - 3%
Food - 2%
Chemical products - 13%
Petroleum and petroleum products - 12%
Manufactured goods 24%
Machinery and transport equipment 44%
EXPORTS
JAPAN
Metal and metal products - 7%
Other - 1%
Chemical products - 9%
Precision instruments - 4%
Machinery and transport equipment 79%
CHINA
Other - 1%
Food - 5%
Mineral fuels and lubricants - 3%
Chemical products - 5%
Machinery and transport equipment 36%
Manufactured goods 50%

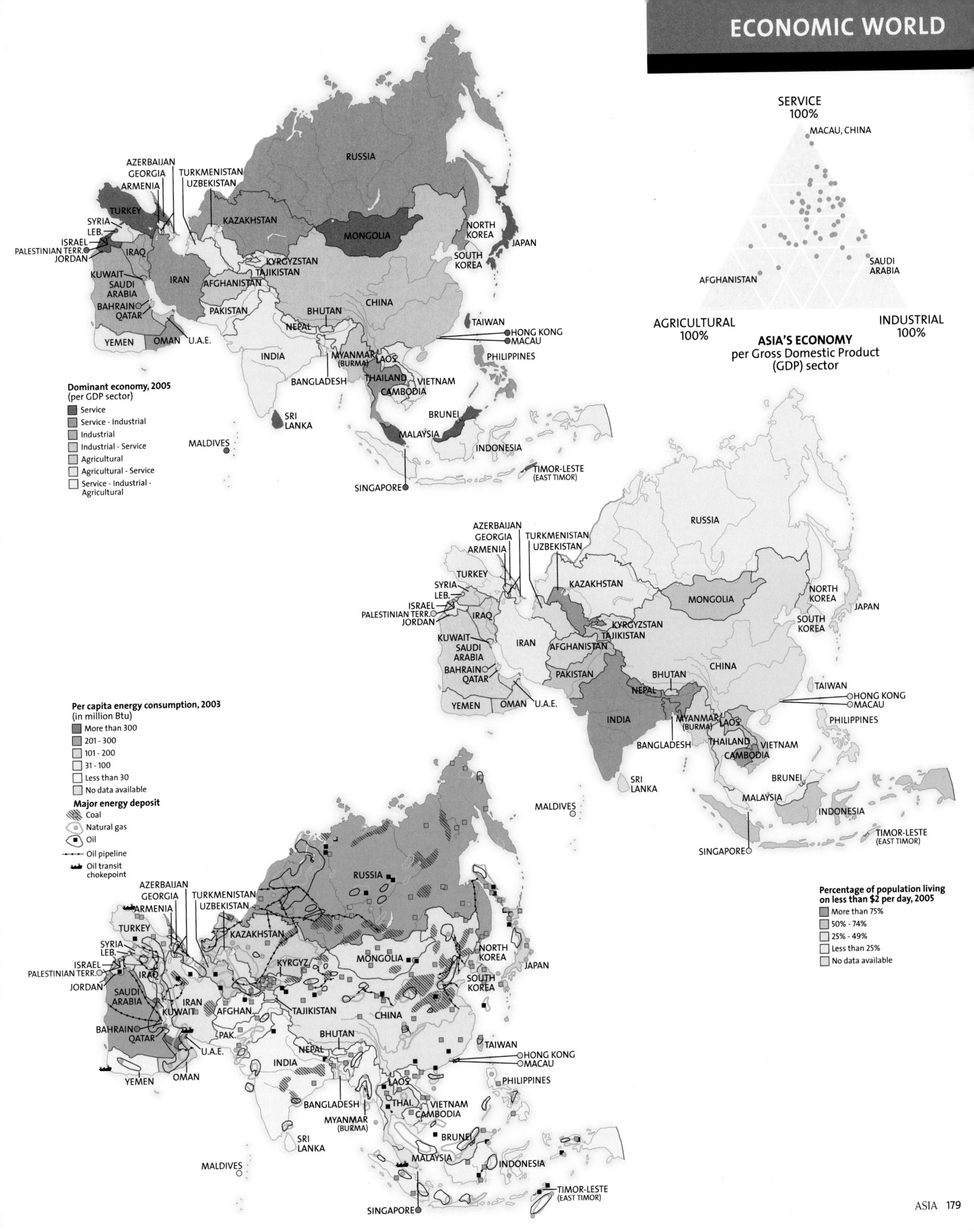
SERVICE
100%
MACAU, CHINA
AFGHANISTAN
SAUDI ARABIA
AGRICULTURAL
100%
INDUSTRIAL
100%
ASIA'S ECONOMY
per Gross Domestic Product (GDP) sector
Dominant economy, 2005
(per GDP sector)
Service
Service - Industrial
Industrial
Industrial - Service
Agricultural
Agricultural - Service
Service - Industrial - Agricultural
Per capita energy consumption, 2003
(in million Btu)
More than 300
201 - 300
101 - 200
31 - 100
Less than 30
No data available
Major energy deposit
Coal
Natural gas
Oil
Oil pipeline
Oil transit chokepoint
Percentage of population living on less than $2 per day, 2005
More than 75%
50% - 74%
25% - 49%
Less than 25%
No data available
RUSSIA
AZERBAIJAN
GEORGIA
ARMENIA
TURKMENISTAN
UZBEKISTAN
TURKEY
SYRIA
LEB.
ISRAEL
PALESTINIAN TERR.
JORDAN
IRAQ
KAZAKHSTAN
MONGOLIA
NORTH KOREA
SOUTH KOREA
JAPAN
KYRGYZSTAN
TAJIKISTAN
KUWAIT
SAUDI ARABIA
IRAN
AFGHANISTAN
BAHRAIN
QATAR
PAKISTAN
CHINA
BHUTAN
NEPAL
TAIWAN
HONG KONG
MACAU
U.A.E.
YEMEN
OMAN
INDIA
MYANMAR (BURMA)
LAOS
PHILIPPINES
BANGLADESH
THAILAND
VIETNAM
CAMBODIA
SRI LANKA
BRUNEI
MALDIVES
MALAYSIA
INDONESIA
TIMOR-LESTE (EAST TIMOR)
SINGAPORE
KYRGYZ.
AFGHAN.
PAK.
THAI.

Longitude East 30° of Greenwich
ROMANIA
SERBIA
BULGARIA
MACEDONIA
GREECE
TURKEY
CRIMEA
UKRAINE
BLACK SEA
Simferopol'
Sevastopol'
Constanța
Varna
Burgas
Sofiya (Sofia)
Skopje
Plovdiv
Edirne (Adrianople)
Thessaloníki
ISTANBUL (CONSTANTINOPLE)
Marmara Denizi
Tekirdağ
Bursa
Zonguldak
Sinop
Samsun (Amisus)
Trabzon
Ordu
Krasnodar
Sochi
ABKHAZIA
Sukhumi (Sukhum)
ABKHAZIA
Separatist defeated Georgian troops to gain control of this region in 1993—negotiations continue on resolving the conflict.
Ankara (Angora)
Eskişehir
Kütahya
Balıkesir
Çanakkale
Edremit
Manisa
İZMİR (SMYRNA)
Aydın
Denizli
Afyon
Konya (Iconium)
Kayseri
Sivas
Erzincan
Erzurum
Malatya
Elazığ
Diyarbakır
Batman
Mardin
Gaziantep
Şanlıurfa (Edessa)
Adana
İçel (Mersin)
İskenderun
Hatay (Antioch)
Antalya
Antalya Körfezi
Alanya (Coracesium)
Anamur
Silifke
AEGEAN SEA
SEA OF CRETE
Athína (Athens)
Peloponnesus
KIKLÁDES
Dodecanese
Kríti (Crete)
Ródos (Rhodes)
Kárpathos
CYPRUS
NORTHERN CYPRUS
Lefkosia (Lefkoşa, Nicosia)
Lemesos
Pafos
LAMBERT CONFORMAL CONIC PROJECTION
SCALE 1:8,000,000
0 KILOMETERS 120 160 200
0 MILES 40 80 120 160 200
MEDITERRANEAN SEA
SYRIA
Ḩalab (Aleppo)
Al Lādhiqīyah (Latakia)
Ḩamāh (Hamath)
Ḩimş (Homs)
Ar Raqqah
Trâblous (Tripoli)
Beyrouth (Beirut)
LEBANON
Dimashq (Damascus)
Haifa
Tel Aviv-Yafo
Jerusalem (Yerushalayim, Al Quds)
WEST BANK
GAZA STRIP
ISRAEL
Be'er Sheva
Negev
JORDAN
'Ammān
Az Zarqā'
Irbid
Petra
Wādī as Sirḩān
SAUDI
An Nafūd
Tabūk
El Iskandarîya (Alexandria)
Dumyât (Damietta)
Bûr Sa'îd (Port Said)
SUEZ CANAL
El Mahalla el Kubra
Tanta
Zagazig
El Mansûra
EL QÂHIRA (CAIRO)
El Giza
Memphis
El Suweis (Suez)
SINAI
Gebel Mûsa (Mount Sinai)
Gulf of Suez
Gulf of Aqaba
EGYPT
Libyan Plateau
Libyan Desert
Western Desert
Eastern Desert
Munkhafad el Qaṭṭâra (Qattara Depression)
Siwa
El Faiyûm
Beni Suef
El Minya
Asyûṭ
Sohâg
Qena
RED SEA
The Brothers
AL HIJAZ (HEJAZ)
LIBYA

KAZAKHSTAN
UZBEKISTAN
TURKMENISTAN
AZERBAIJAN
ARMENIA
GEORGIA
IRAN
IRAQ
KUWAIT
BAHRAIN
QATAR
U.A.E.
OMAN
AFGHANISTAN
ARABIA
CASPIAN SEA
PERSIAN GULF
GULF OF OMAN
Strait of Hormuz
SOUTH OSSETIA
A 1992 cease-fire ended fighting between Ossetians and Georgians, but with no political settlement.
NAGORNO-KARABAKH
Since a cease-fire in 1994 ethnic Armenians in Azerbaijan's Nagorno-Karabakh region have exercised autonomous control over the region. International mediation to resolve the conflict continues.
CAUCASUS MOUNTAINS
Caspian Depression
USTYURT PLATEAU
MANGGHYSTAU
Garabogaz Aylagy
Garagum
Turan Lowland
Köpetdag Mountains
Reshteh-ye Alborz (Elburz Mountains)
Zagros Mountains
Dasht-e Kavir (Salt Desert)
Dasht-e Lut
KHORASAN
Kūh-e Dīnār
Qolleh-ye Damāvand 5671
TEHRAN
Tabrīz
Mashhad
Eşfahān (Isfahan)
Shīrāz
Kermān
Yazd
Qom (Qum)
Hamadān (Ecbatana)
Kermānshāh
Ahvāz (Ahwaz)
Abādān
Bandar-e 'Abbās
Baghdād
Al Başrah
Al Kuwayt (Kuwait)
Al Manāmah (Manama)
Bakı (Baku)
Yerevan
T'bilisi (Tiflis)
Aşgabat (Ashgabat)
Nukus
Daşoguz
Aqtaū
Makhachkala
Groznyy
Vladikavkaz
Nal'chik
Persepolis
-28 (-92 ft)
45°
48°
51°
54°
57°
42°
39°
36°
33°
30°
27°

EGYPT
SINAI
Gebel el Tîh
Gebel el 'Igma
Gebel Mûsa (Mt. Sinai)
RAS MUHAMMED N.P.
Gulf of Suez
Gulf of Aqaba
ISRAEL
JORDAN
IRAQ
KUWAIT
SAUDI ARABIA
An Nafūd
Jabal Shammar
At Taysīyah
Ad Dahnā'
Al Qaşīm
Ḩarrat al 'Uwayrid
Ḩarrat Khaybar
Ḩarrat Rahaţ
Ḩarrat al Kishb
Sahl Rakbah
Ḩarrat Nawāşif
Ḩarrat al Buqūm
Nafūd ad Dahy
'Urūq ar Rumaylah
Jabal Tuwayq
Wādī ad Dawāsir
Tihāmat ash Shām
'Asīr
RED SEA
The Brothers
Gezaîr Marir (Mirear)
Siyal Islands
Mukawwar Island
Suakin Arch.
Dahlak Arch.
Dahlak Kebir
Massawa Channel
Jazā'ir Farasān
Bāb al Mandab
GULF OF ADEN
Eastern Desert
Nubian Desert
Lake Nasser
Lake Nubia
Boundary claimed by Sudan
SUDAN
NORTHERN
RIVER NILE
KHARTOUM
KASSALA
GEZIRA
GEDAREF
WHITE NILE
SINNAR
BLUE NILE
UPPER NILE
S. KORDOFAN
ERITREA
ETHIOPIA
TIGRAY
AMHARA
AFAR
DINDER NAT. PARK
DJIBOUTI
YEMEN
Tana Hāyk'
Cairo
Helwân
El Faiyûm
Beni Suef
El Minya
Asyût
Sohâg
Qena
Luxor
Aswân
Abu Simbel
Wadi Halfa
Port Sudan
Suakin
Atbara
Khartoum
Khartoum North
Omdurman
Kassala
Kosti
Asmara
Massawa
Gonder
Bahir Dar
Mek'elē
Djibouti
Al 'Aqabah
Tabūk
Al Wajh
Yanbu' al Baḩr
Al Madīnah (Medina)
Jeddah
Makkah (Mecca)
Aţ Ţā'if
Ar Riyāḑ
Ḩā'il
Buraydah
Jīzān
Abhā
Najrān
Al Ḩudaydah
Şan'ā' (Sanaa)
Ta'izz
'Adan (Aden)
30°
33°
36°
39°
42°
45°
27°
24°
21°
18°
15°
12°

IRAN
PAKISTAN
BALUCHISTAN
UNITED ARAB EMIRATES
OMAN
QATAR
BAHRAIN
YEMEN
SOMALIA
PERSIAN GULF
GULF OF OMAN
ARABIAN SEA
ADEN
TROPIC OF CANCER
Zagros Mountains
Rub' al Khālī
(Empty Quarter)
ZUFĀR
BOUNDARY UNDEMARCATED
BOUNDARY UNDEFINED
Strait of Hormuz
Gulf of Bahrain
Kermān
Shīrāz
Persepolis
Bandar-e Būshehr
Bandar-e 'Abbās
Sa'īdābād (Sīrjan)
Hāmūn-e Jaz Mūrīān
Hāmūn-i-Māshkel
Ad Dammām
Al Manāmah (Manama)
Ad Dawḥah (Doha)
Ghawar Oil Field
Sharjah
(Dubai) Dubayy
Abū Ẓaby (Abu Dhabi)
Al 'Ayn
Masqaṭ (Muscat)
Maṭraḥ
Ra's al Ḥadd
Jazīrat Maṣīrah (Masira)
Khalīj Maṣīrah
Ra's al Madrakah
Ghubbat Ṣawqirah
Kuria Muria Is.
Al Ḥallānīyah
Salālah
Mirbāṭ
Ra's Fartak
Ghubbat al Qamar
Al Mukallā
Socotra (Suquṭrá) Yemen
Hadīboh
'Abd al Kūrī Yemen
Al Ikhwān (The Brothers)
Cape Gwardafuy
Gwadar
Chābahār
Jāsk
Ra's Musandam
Ghaba North
Saih Nihayda
Qarn Alam
Fahud
Natih
Umm as Samīm
Al Ḥadīdah (meteorite craters)
LAMBERT CONFORMAL CONIC PROJECTION
SCALE 1:8,000,000
0 KILOMETERS 120 160 200
0 MILES 40 80 120 160 200
51° 54° 57° 60° 63°
27° 24° 21° 18° 15° 12°

RYAZAN'
LIPETSK
MORDOVIYA
TATARSTAN
UL'YANOVSK
TAMBOV
PENZA
SAMARA
BASHKORTOSTAN
CHELYABINSK
VORONEZH
SARATOV
ORENBURG
VOLGOGRAD
BATYS QAZAQSTAN
QOSTANAY
AQTÖBE
ATYRAŪ
ROSTOV
KALMYKIYA
ASTRAKHAN'
STAVROPOL'
CHECHNYA
INGUSH.
SEVERNAYA OSETIYA-ALANIYA
DAGESTAN
GEORGIA
AZERBAIJAN
ARM.
NAGORNO-KARABAKH
MANGGHYSTAŪ
QORAQALPOG'ISTON (KARAKALPAKSTAN)
UZBEKISTAN
TURKMENISTAN
IRAN
QYZYLORDA
R U S S I A
K A Z A
URAL MTS.
Privolzhskaya Vozvyshennost'
Caspian Depression
Naryn Qum
CASPIAN SEA
Caucasus Mts.
Mughalzhar Taūy
Ülken Borsyq Qumy
Dongyztaū Shyngy
Aral Mangy Qaraqumy
Ustyurt Plateau
Karynzharyk (Desert)
Chink Kaplankyr
Garagum
Turan Lowland
Qizilqum
Aralqum
Reshteh-ye Alborz (Elburz Mountains)
Kopetdag Mts.
Apsheron Yarymadasy
Bozashchy Tübegi
Tüpqaraghan Tübegi
Tülen Araldary
Qazaq Shyghanaghy
Garabogaz Aylagy
Türkmenbaşy Aylagy
Kuybyshevskoye Vodokhranilishche
Volgogradskoye Vodokhranilishche
VOLGA-DON CANAL
GARAGUM CANAL
Railroad Ferry
ARAL SEA
North Aral Sea
BAYKONUR COSMODROME Russian-administered
Once the world's fourth largest lake, the Aral Sea today is less than half its 1960 extent. Soviet-era irrigation canals divert river water—causing the sea to shrink and changing the former lake bed into a desert. A UN study predicts the Aral Sea could disappear by 2018.
Lipetsk
Tambov
Saransk
Ul'yanovsk
Penza
Togliatti
Samara
Naberezhnyye Chelny
Nizhnekamsk
Al'met'yevsk
Ufa
Miass
Chelyabinsk
Sterlitamak
Salavat
Magnitogorsk
Saratov
Engels
Balakovo
Orenburg
Orsk
Novotroitsk
Aqtöbe
Rūdnyy
Volgograd (Stalingrad)
Volzhskiy
Astrakhan'
Atyraū
Elista
Groznyy
Vladikavkaz
Makhachkala
Derbent
T'bilisi (Tiflis)
Gäncä
Sumqayıt
Bakı (Baku)
Aqtaū
Fort Shevchenko
Nukus
Daşoguz
Türkmenbaşy
Balkanabat
Aşgabat (Ashgabat)
Türkmenabat (Chärjew)
Buxoro (Bukhara)
Tabrīz
Ardabīl
Rasht
Zanjān
Qazvīn
Bojnūrd
Gorgān
Āmol
Marāgheh
Oral
Qazaly
Bayqongyr (Baykonur, Leninsk)
Kazbek 5033
Ural
Volga
Don
Khoper
Kuma
Terek
Zhayyq
Samara
Belaya
Ilek
Emba
Sarygamysh Köli
Aralsor Köli
Shalqar Köli
Sumbar
Atrak
Qezel Owzan
54°
51°
48°
45°
42°
39°
36°
57°
60°
63°

TYUMEN
OMSK
NOVOSIBIRSK
Novosibirsk
Omsk
Barnaul
Biysk
Prokop'yevsk
KHAKASIYA
TYVA (TUVA)
ALTAY
GORNO-ALTAY
UVS
MONGOLIA
BAYAN-ÖLGIY
SOLTÜSTIK QAZAQSTAN
Kökshetaū
AQMOLA
PAVLODAR
Pavlodar
Ekibastuz
Astana
Qaraghandy
Temirtaū
Semey (Semipalatinsk)
Öskemen (Ust' Kamenogorsk)
SEMIPALATINSK NUCLEAR TEST SITE (closed in 1991)
Degelen
SHYGHYS QAZAQSTAN
Zaysan Köli
Rubtsovsk
Gora Belukha 4506
Altay
Tarbaghatay Zhotasy
Tacheng (Qoqek)
Karamay
Junggar Pendi (Dzungarian Basin)
Dzungarian Gate
Ebinur Hu
Alaköl
Bole
Shihezi
Changji
Ürümqi
Fukang
KAZAKH UPLANDS
QARAGHANDY
Balqash
Balqash Köli
Saryesik-Atyraū Qumy
ALMATY
Almaty
Taldyqorghan
Yining (Gulja)
Boharo Shan
BETPAQDALA
ZHAMBYL
Moyynqum
Qaratau Zhotasy
ONGTÜSTIK QAZAQSTAN
Taraz
Shymkent
Bishkek
ALA-ARCHA N.P.
Kyrgyz Range
Ysyk-Köl
TIAN SHAN
Khan Tängiri (Khan Tengri) 6995
Jengish Chokusu (Pobedy Peak, Victory Peak) 7439
KYRGYZSTAN
Toktogul Reservoir
Kök Shal Tau (Kakshaal Range)
Naryn
XINJIANG UYGUR (SINKIANG)
CHINA
TARIM PENDI
TAKLIMAKAN SHAMO
Aksu
Baicheng
Korla
Kuqa
Toshkent (Tashkent)
Chirchiq
UGAM-CHATKAL N.P.
Angren
Namangan
Andijon
Osh
Farg'ona
Qo'qon
Fergana Valley
Olmaliq
Khujand
Jizzax
Samarqand
ZAAMIN N.P.
Turkestan Range
Zarafshon Range
Alay Mts.
Turugart Pass
Kashi (Kashgar)
Lenin Peak 7134
Qullai Ismoili Somoni (Communism Peak) 7495
Kongur Shan 7719
Muztagata 7546
Uzbel Shankou
Kulma Pass
TAJIKISTAN
Dushanbe
Pamirs
Jaman Pass
AFGHANISTAN
Shache (Yarkant)
Yecheng (Kargilik)
Hotan
Qiemo (Qargan)
LAMBERT CONFORMAL CONIC PROJECTION
SCALE 1:8,000,000
0 KILOMETERS 120 160 200
0 MILES 40 80 120 160 200
69°
72°
75°
78°
81°
84°
51°
48°
45°
42°
39°
36°

TURKEY
KURDISTAN
ARMENIA
AZERBAIJAN
NAGORNO-KARABAKH
CASPIAN SEA
SYRIA
JORDAN
IRAQ
IRAN
KUWAIT
SAUDI ARABIA
BAHRAIN
QATAR
UNITED ARAB EMIRATES
OMAN
PERSIAN GULF
MESOPOTAMIA
Syrian Desert
Al Hamad
An Nafūd
Ad Dahnā'
Aş Şummān
Nafūd ad Dahy
Jabal Shammar
Al Qaşīm
Jabal Ţuwayq
Ad Dibdibah
Şaḩrā' al Ḩijārah
Reshteh-ye Alborz (Elburz Mountains)
Zagros Mts.
Dasht-e Kavīr (Salt Desert)
FARS
KHORASAN
BOUNDARY UNDEMARCATED
BOUNDARY UNDEFINED
Railroad Ferry
Apsheron Yarymadasy
Strait of Hormuz
Dawḩat Salwá
Khawr Duwayhin
Dijlah (Tigris)
Al Furāt (Euphrates)
Tharthār Lake
Razzaza Lake
Van Gölü
Daryācheh-ye Orūmīyeh
Daryācheh-ye Tashk
Daryācheh-ye Bakhtegān
Hawr al Hammār
Ramādī Barrage
Dokan Dam
Darbandi Khan Dam
Bakhma Dam
Uly Balkan Gershi
Erzincan
Erzurum
Sarıkamış
Horasan
Ağrı (Karaköse)
Yerevan
Gäncä
Sumqayıt
Bakı (Baku)
Sabunçu
Divriği
Malatya
Elazığ
Bingöl
Malazgirt
Patnos
Erciş
Muş
Ahlat
Tatvan
Bitlis
Van
Diyarbakır
Adıyaman
Siirt
Batman
Siverek
Midyat
Mardin
Gaziantep
Nizip
Şanlıurfa (Edessa)
Viranşehir
Cizre
Al Qāmishlī
Ceylanpınar
Yüksekova
Şemdinli
Stepanakert (Xankändi)
Naxçıvan
Khvoy
Tabrīz
Ardabīl
Orūmīyeh (Urmia)
Marāgheh
Rasht
Bandar-e Anzalī
Zanjān
Qazvīn
Karaj
Tajrīsh
TEHRĀN
Rey
Āmol
Bābol
Sārī
Qā'emshahr
Gorgān
Türkmenbaşy
Balkanabat (Nebitdag)
Gazanjyk
Gyzylarbat
Ekerem
Chaloyuk
Astara
Lankäran
Salyan
Neftçala
Al Mawşil (Mosul)
Arbīl
Zakho
Dahūk
As Sulaymānīyah
Karkūk (Kirkūk)
Sanandaj
Kermānshāh
Hamadān (Ecbatana)
Qom (Qum)
Arāk
Kāshān
Malāyer
Borūjerd
Khorramābād
Īlām
Baghdād
Al Fallūjah (Fallujah)
Ar Ramādī
Hīt
Ar Rutbah
Ar Raqqah
Dayr az Zawr
Al Mayādīn
Tadmur
Abū Kamāl
Al Qā'im
Sāmarrā'
Ba'qūbah
Karbalā'
Babylon
Al Ḩillah
Al Kūt
An Najaf (Najaf)
Ad Dīwānīyah
Al 'Amārah
An Nāşirīyah (Nasiriyah)
Al Başrah (Basra)
Al Qurnah
Al Fāw
Ābādān
Khorramshahr
Ahvāz (Ahwāz)
Dezfūl
Shūshtar
Masjed Soleymān
Khomeynīshahr
Najafābād
Eşfahān (Isfahan)
Shahr-e Kord
Qomsheh
Yazd
Ardakān
Shīrāz
Persepolis
Kāzerūn
Bandar-e Būshehr
Khārk
Gach Sārān
Bandar-e Deylam
Sa'īdābād (Sīrjān)
Bandar-e 'Abbās
Qeshm
Lār
Bandar-e Lengeh
Kīsh
Al Kuwayt (Kuwait)
Al Aḩmadī
Wafra
Ḩafar al Bāţin
King Khalid Military City
Ḩā'il
Buraydah
'Unayzah
Ar Rass
Al Majma'ah
Ar Riyāḑ (Riyadh)
Al Kharj
Ad Dammām
Al Khubar
Al Qaţīf
Ra's Tannūrah
Al Jubayl
Al Hufūf (Hofuf)
Ghawar Oil Field
Al Manāmah (Manama)
Ad Dawḩah (Doha)
Dukhān
Umm Sa'īd
Abū Z̧aby (Abu Dhabi)
Dubayy (Dubai)
Sharjah
Al 'Ayn
Jabal Ḩafīt
Liwa
Ţurayf
Al Jawf
Sakākah
Dawmat al Jandal
Badanah
'Ar'ar
Rafḩā'
An Nabk Abū Qaşr
Aţ Ţā'if
'Afīf
Zalim
As Sikr
As Salmān
Nukhayb
Jabal 'Unayzah
Sharjah
Kumzār
Khaşab
Jabal Rāf
Mahd adh Dhahab
Aş Şufūq
Bu Hasa
Zarrārah
Shaybah
Umm az Zumūl
Bi'r Fardān
Yabrīn
Ḩaraḑ
Al Kharfah
39°
42°
45°
48°
51°
54°
36°
33°
30°
27°
24°

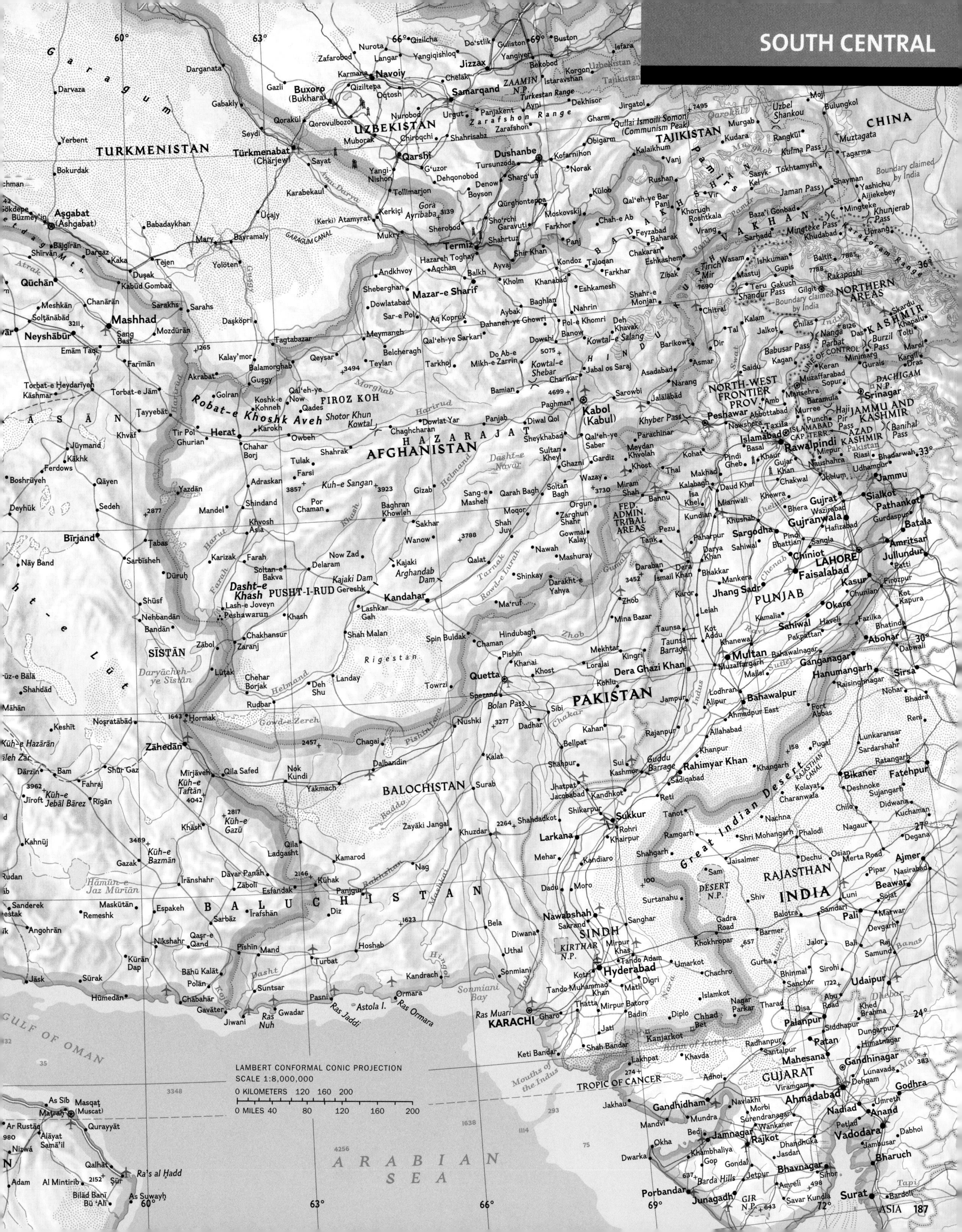

LAMBERT CONFORMAL CONIC PROJECTION
SCALE 1:8,000,000
0 KILOMETERS 120 160 200
0 MILES 40 80 120 160 200

TURKMENISTAN
UZBEKISTAN
TAJIKISTAN
CHINA
AFGHANISTAN
PAKISTAN
INDIA
KASHMIR
NORTHERN AREAS
NORTH-WEST FRONTIER PROV.
FED. ADMIN. TRIBAL AREAS
ISLAMABAD CAP. TERR.
AZAD KASHMIR
JAMMU AND KASHMIR
PUNJAB
BALOCHISTAN
SINDH
RAJASTHAN
GUJARAT
SĪSTĀN
HAZARAJAT
BALUCHISTAN
TROPIC OF CANCER
GULF OF OMAN
ARABIAN SEA

63° 66° 69° 72° 75° 78° 81° 84° 87° 90° 93° 96° 99°
39° 36° 33° 30° 27° 24° 21° 18°

UZBEKISTAN
KAZ.
Toshkent (Tashkent)
Olmaliq
Qizilqum
Qizilcha
Sirdaryo
Nurota
Langar
Do'stlik
Zafarobod
Navoiy
Jizzax
Gulistan
Taboshar
Yangiyer
Gazli
Qiziltepa
Gizhduvan
Buxoro (Bukhara)
Samarqand
Qorakul
Qorovulbozor
ZAAMIN N.P.
Zarafshon Range
Konibodom
Isfara
Sükh
Uzb.
Korgon
Fergana Valley
Andijon
Osh
Farg'ona
KYRGYZSTAN
Kara-Köl
Kazarman
Kara-Ünkür
Ooruk-Tam
At-Bashy
Chatyr-Tash
Turugart Pass
Kök-Aygyr
Güicho
Kyzyl-Korgon
Ulugqat
Muborak
Qarshi
Shahrisabz
Zarafshon
Dekhisor
Gharm
Khodzhatau
Lenin Pk.
7134
Simhana
Uzbel Pass
Sayat
Yangi-Nishon
G'uzor
Dushanbe
Kofarnihon
TAJIKISTAN
Tollimarjon
Boysun
Sharg'un
Denow
Norak
Garagum
Kerkiçi
Qüghontepa
Kulob
Atamyrat
TURKM.
Mukry
Sherobod
Shahrtuz
Garavuti
Kelef
Termiz
Andkhvoy
Aqcheh
Ayvaj
Panj
Shir Khan
Sheberghan
Balkh
Mazar-e Sharif
Kholm
Kondoz
Dowlatabad
Sar-e Pol
Aybak
Pol-e Khomri
Baghlan
Aq Kopruk
Batamorghab
3494
Belcheragh
Teylan
Tarkhoj
Dowshi
Khavak
Qades
Shotor Khun Kowtal
Bamian
Banow
Deh
Charikar
Chaghcharan
Diwal Qol
Shahrak
Tulak
3857
AFGHANISTAN
Kabol (Kabul)
4699
Sultan Kheyl
Gardiz
Wazay
Ghazni
3923
Por Chaman
Gizab
Sang-e Masheh
Baghran
Khowleh
Sakhar
3788 Shah Juy
Mogor
Orgun
FEDERALLY ADMINISTERED TRIBAL AREAS
Now Zad
Wanow
Kajaki
Qalat
Nawah
Mashuray
Wana
Gereshk
Lashkar Gah
Kandahar
Shinkay
Ma'ruf
Darakht-e Yahya
Tank
Daraban
Shah Malan
Spin Buldak
Chaman
Mina Bazar
Hindubagh
Zhob
Rigestan
Landay
Pishin
Khanai
Khost
Mekhtar
Quetta
Spezand
Bolan Pass
Sibi
Kohlu
Dera Ghazi Khan
Muzaffargarh
Chagai
Nushki
3277
Dadhar
Kalat
Bellpat
Kahan
Rajanpur
Kharan
BALOCHISTAN
Shahpur
Sui
Kashmor
Surab
Jacobabad
Shikarpur
2264
Zayaki Jangal
Khuzdar
Nag
Larkana
Mehar
Sukkur
Rohri
Khairpur
Dadu
Moro
Kandiaro
1623
Bela
Nawabshah
Uthal
Diwana
Sonmiani
Sonmiani Bay
Kandrach
Ras Ormara
SINDH
KIRTHAR N.P.
Kotri
Hyderabad
KARACHI
Badin
Thatta
Jati
Shah Bandar
Keti Bandar
Lakhpat
Kanjarkot
Umarkot
Chhachro
Diplo
Nagar Parkar
Khokhropar
100
Surtanahu
Sam
DESERT N.P.
Shiv
657
Barmer
Gurha
274
Khavda
Adhoi
TROPIC OF CANCER
1638
1114
293
75
3147
3456

HINDU KUSH
Boundary claimed by India
BADAKHSHAN
Baharak
Eshkashem
Farkhar
Chakaran
Khorugh
Vanj
Rushan
Sasyk Kel
Kudara
Murghob
Pamirs
Kulma Pass
Jaman Pass
Uzbel Shankou
Tagarma
Tokhtamysh
Yashichu
Aijiekebey
Sarhadd
Vrang
Wasam
Baltit
7788
Karakoram Range
Gilgit
Teru
Askole
Jalkot
Dir
Tal
Asmar
Narang
Jalalabad
Mardan
Peshawar
NORTHERN AREAS
NORTH-WEST FRONTIER PROV.
KASHMIR
LINE OF CONTROL
7742
AKSAI CHIN
Tolti
Marol
Kagan
Muzaffarabad
ISLAMABAD CAPITAL TERR.
Islamabad
Rawalpindi
Thal
Uri
Srinagar
Dras
Khalatse
AZAD KASHMIR
JAMMU AND KASHMIR
Riasi
Banihal Pass
Jammu
Samba
Umasi La
Kilar
Mianwali
Daud Khel
Bhera
Kundian
Darya
Khan
Sargodha
Sialkot
Gujranwala
Batala
Gurdaspur
Faisalabad
LAHORE
Amritsar
Sangla
Kasur
Karor
Leiah
Kot Addu
Sahiwal
Okara
Ludhiana
Jalandhar
Hoshiarpur
PUNJAB
PAKISTAN
Multan
Pakpattan
Fazilka
Abohar
Patiala
Ganganagar
Sirsa
Hanumangarh
Bahawalpur
Mailsi
Ahmadpur East
Fort Abbas
Rahimyar Khan
Allahabad
Khanpur
Reti
Tanot
Charanwala
Shri
Great Indian Desert
158
Pugal
Bikaner
Nohar
Jaisalmer
Phalodi
Dechu
Chilo
Nagaur
Jodhpur
RAJASTHAN
Pali
Balotra
Jalor
Bhinmal
Sojat
Marwar
Bali
Sirohi
Devgarh
Udaipur
Palanpur
Disa
Patan
Chhad Bet
Santalpur
Viramgam
Gandhinagar
Gandhidham
Mandvi
Navlakhi
Bedi
Okha
Dwarka
GUJARAT
Ahmadabad
Nadiad
Anand
Dehgam
Himatnagar
Godhra
Dahod
Jambusar
Vadodara
Porbandar
Gop
Gondal
Jetpur
498
GIR N.P.
Junagadh
Mangrol
Mahuva
Kodinar
Daman and Diu
Diu
DAMAN AND DIU
Daman (Damão)
DADRA AND NAGAR HAVELI
Silvassa
Bharuch
Surat
Navsari
Valsad
Mahim
Thane
Kalyan
(BOMBAY) MUMBAI
Srivardhan
Harnai
Roha
Wai
Pune
Satara
Lonavli
Junnar
Rahuri
Sirur
892
Sholapur
Barsi
Bir
Parli
Kallam
Latur
Bidar
Homnabad
Akalkot

Kashi (Kashgar)
Artux
Bachu
Shufu
Yopurga
Akto
Moji
Yengisar
Markit
Khunjerab Pass
Shache (Yarkant)
Zepu
Yecheng
Akmeqit
Pishan
Moyu
Hotan
Lop Qira
5466
Tekiliktag
7282
Muztag
Karakax
Dahongliutan
Karakoram Pass
Boundary claimed by Pak.
Boundary claimed by India
Shukpa
Kunzang
7672
Pamzal
4226
Chushul
Changmar
Domar
Wujiang
Zapug
Tsaka La
Nyoma Rap
8596
Gê'gyai
Hanle
Shiquanhe
7026
Gar
Boundary claimed by China
Garyarsa
Zanda
Thaga Pass
Namgia
Sutak
Manali
Kullu
Simla
HIMACHAL PRADESH
Nagar
Rampur
Chandigarh
CHANDIGARH
Dehra Dun
UTTARANCHAL
Rishikesh
Ambala
Kaithal
Karnal
Jakhal
HARYANA
Hisar
Sonipat
Bhiwani
Saharanpur
Chandpur
Nagina
DELHI
New Delhi
Amroha
Pilibhit
Jhunjhunun
Pilani
Reni
Sikar
1052
Alwar
Palwal
Chandausi
Bareilly
Lakhimpur
Hathras
Aligarh
Budaun
Sri Madhopur
Bharatpur
Agra
Jaipur
Chatsu
Lalsot
Bandikui
Etawah
Makrana
Kishangarh
Tonk
Karauli
Morena
Jora
Lashkar
Gohad
Aron
Datia
Jhansi
Sawai Madhopur
Shahabad
Bundi
Kota
Baran
Singoli
Nimbahera
Bhanpura
Ashoknagar
Guna
Khilchipur
Nimach
Dungarpur
Jaora
Ratlam
Alot
Nagda
Shajapur
Sehore
Ujjain
Dewas
Indore
Bhopal
881
Mhow
Makrai
Itarsi
Sanawad
Harsud
Bhikangaon
Khandwa
1325
Chikalda
Burhanpur
953
Jalgaon
Achalpur
Amla
Amravati
Dhule
Bhusawal
Akot
Akola
Malegaon
Chikhli
Nasik
Yeola
Jalna
Yavatmal
Pusad
606
Wani
Warora
MAHARASHTRA
Sailu
Parbhani
Nanded
Adilabad
Nizamabad
Bitoli
Nirmal
Atmakur
Bijapur
Karimnagar
Warangal
Medak
Nekonda
Parkal
Secunderabad
Tandur
INDRAVATI N.P.
935
Mul
Dhanora
Wardha
Sambalpur
Nagpur
Saoner
PENCH N.P.
Seoni
Gondia
Balhar
Mandla
Nainpur
SATPURA N.P.
Jabalpur
Sagar (Saugor)
Umaria
Bina
Lalitpur
Chhatarpur
Mahoba
Manikpur
Banda
Satna
Maihar
MADHYA PRADESH
INDIA

Uprang
Tashkurgan
Karamiran Shankou
6717 Aktag
Andir
Kunlun Shan
Keriya
Keriya Shankou
Yutian
Minfeng
Andirlangar
Hadilik
Tatrang
Qiemo
TAKLIMAKAN SHAMO
XINJIANG UYGUR (SINKIANG)
Wensu
Aksu
Awat
Aral
Akqi
Kalpin
Sanchakou
Taxkan
Tarim
Baicheng (Bay)
Xayar
Luntai
Korla
Yuli
Tikanlik
Xingdi
Loulan Yiji
Argan
Lop Nur
Araqi
Ruoqiang
Miran
ALTUN SHAN
Waxxari
Qarqan
6161
Ayakkum Hu
Aqqikkol Hu
Karamiran
6987
Muztag
Bukadaban Feng
6860
Hoh Xil Shan
CHINA
QING ZANG GAOYUAN
Chagdo Kangri
6148
Lungdo
Margai Caka
Dogai Coring
5200
KASHMIR
India and Pakistan both claim Kashmir—a disputed region of some 10 million people. India administers only the area south of the line of control; Pakistan controls northwestern Kashmir. China took eastern Kashmir from India in a 1962 war.
Qagcaka
Oma
Gêrzê
Ngoqumaima
6300
Yibug Caka
Zhaxi Co
Nganglong Kangri
6714
Ngangla Ringco
Tangra Yumco
Lhazhong
Coqên
Lunggar
Nyima
4495
Siling Co
Baingoin
Nam Co
TIBET
XIZANG
Xainza
Kangmar
Barga
Lipu Lekh Pass
6715
Paryang
Gangdisê Shan
Zhongba
Saga
Gyirong
Xaitongmoin
Ngamring
Tingri
6482
Gyangzê
Bainang
Rinbung
Namling
Lhasa
Qüxü
Dagzê
Zhanang
Nêdong
Gyaca
Nagarzê
Lhünzê
Comai
Cona
Maizhokunggar
Lhünzhub
Dolungdêqên
Gamba
Kangmar
7088
Xaitongmoin
Shey-Phoksundo N.P.
Baitadi
Baijnath
Jumla
Dailekh
2446
Tibrikot
8167
Dhangadhi
Jajarkot
HIMALAYA
NEPAL
Mt. Everest (Sagarmatha, Qomolangma) 8850 (29035 ft)
SAGARMATHA N.P.
MAKALU-BARUN N.P.
Gorkha
Kunchha
Kathmandu
ROYAL CHITWAN N.P.
Butwal
Jarwa
Bhairahawa
Uska
Raxaul
Birganj
Dhankuta
Dharan
Biratnagar
Karsiyang
Darjiling
SIKKIM
Gangtok
Kalimpang
Thimphu
JIGME DORJI N.P.
BHUTAN
Mongar
Shemgang
Tashigang
Bomdila
Itanagar
Dibrugarh
Tinsukia
Ledo
Digboi
Lhozhag
Singye Dzong
Gasa
Jalpaiguri
Koch Bihar
Dinajpur
Rangpur
Saidpur
Barpeta
Guwahati
Tezpur
Balipara
Golaghat
Dispur
ASSAM
MEGHALAYA
Shillong
Jowai
Tura
Lumding
Dimapur
Kohima
NAGALAND
Naga Hills
Imphal
MANIPUR
Haflong
Karimganj
Silchar
Habiganj
Sylhet
BANGLADESH
Bogra
Rajshahi
Tangail
Dhaka
Narayanganj
Jessore
Khulna
Barisal
Chandpur
Agartala
TRIPURA
Aizawl
MIZORAM
Mizo Hills
Lunglei
Rangamati
Chittagong
Bandarban
Kutubdia
Maiskhal
Chakaria
Nazir Hat
Mouths of the Ganges
Kolkata (Calcutta)
Basirhat
Contai
Navadwip
Baharampur
WEST BENGAL
Bankura
Asansol
Medinipur
Kharagpur
Baleshwar
Bhadrakh
Palmyras Point
False Point
Jajpur
Cuttack
Bhubaneshwar
Konarak
Puri
Brahmapur
Tekkali
Narasannapeta
Srikakulam
Vizianagaram
Vishakhapatnam
Parvatipuram
Jagdalpur
Kotapad
Rayagada
Bastar
Bissameuttack
Asika
Ganjam
Tangi
ORISSA
Balangir
Deobhog
Bargarh
Sambalpur
Rairakhol
Nawapara
Pithora
Raipur
Bhilai
Balod
Pauni
CHHATTISGARH
Bhatapara
Bemetara
Bilaspur
Korba
Champa
1043
Kalnai
Jharsuguda
Lahara
Pal
1117
1188
1165
Udala
Malayagiri
Raurkela
Simdega
Gumla
Khunti
Ranchi
Dhanbad
JHARKHAND
Deoghar
Dumka
Pakaur
Bhagalpur
Katihar
Araria
Saharsa
Balurghat
Bihar Sharif
Gaya
Sasaram
Daltenganj
Dudhi
Robertsganj
Varanasi (Banaras)
Ramnagar
Chakia
Rewa
Beohari
Sonhat
Kothi
Bharatpur
Anuppur
Jashpurnagar
1142
BIHAR
Patna
Ara
Chhapra
Siwan
Motihari
Dumra
Jaunpur
Azamgarh
Deoria
Gorakhpur
Tanda
Nawabganj
Sultanpur
Rae Bareli
Fatehpur
Lucknow
Unnao
Kanpur
Hamirpur
Rath
UTTAR PRADESH

QINGHAI
Golmud
Nomhon
Qaidam Pendi
Dulan
Ulan
Delingha
Tianjun
5030
Toson Hu
Muri
Har Hu
5808
Da Qaidam
Iqe
Lenghu
Suhai Hu
Obo Liang
Xorkol
Mangnai Zhen
Youshashan
Aral
Mangnai
Chalengkou
Tart
Naij Gol
Kunlun Shankou
Gyaring Hu
5730
Madoi
Wudaoliang
Bayan Har Shan
Bayan Har Shankou
Qumarlêb
Zhidoi
Xümatang
Qingshuihe
Chindu
Gyêgu
Sêrxü
Zadoi
Dainkog
Nangqên
Ulan Ul Hu
Beilu
Tuotuo
Wuli
Tanggulashan
6800
Wenquan
Tanggula Shankou
Tanggula Shan
Source of the Yangtze
Yag
Pagnag
Dongqiao
Nyainrong
Sogxian
Baqên
Biru
Banbar
Dêngqên
Riwoqê
Qamdo
Jomda
Qu'nyido
Ngamda
Gonjo
Zhag'yab
Nagqu
Nyainqentanglha Shan
Lhari
Yi'ong
Lhorong
Tangmai
Bomi
Baxoi
Zogang
Nyingchi
Mêdog
Mainling
Bruini
Boundary claimed by China
Chengele
ARUNACHAL PRADESH
Nangxian
Longju
Mara
Taipudia
Nizamghat
Anili
Tezu
Tawai
Walong
Zayü
5881
Takum
Hachi
Khonsa
McMAHON LINE
Konglu
Sumprabum
Yammaw
Shaduzup
Maingkwan
Mogaung
Kamaing
Layshi
Ukhrul
Hommalinn
Mohnyin
Mawlu
Shwegu
Thaungdut
Palel
Tamu
Indaw
Katha
Kawlinn
Pinlebu
Tigyaing
Mawlaik
Masein
Kalay-wa
Ye-u
Kanbalu
Mogok
Namtu
Tazé
MYANMAR (BURMA)
Pyin-Oo-Lwin
Mandalay
Kyaukse
Sagaing
Yinmabin
Pakokku
Myingyan
Gantgaw
Falam
Badupi
Paletwa
3053
Saw
Chauk
Yawnghwe
Yamethinn
Hsi-hseng
Tatkon
Leiway
Pyinmanaa
Sa-koi
Thawatti
Taungoo
Paungde
Pyu
Minhla
Nyaunglebin
Mon
Bago
Taikkyee
Kyeintali
Gwa
Bawmi
Thabaung
Myohaung
Buthidaung
Maungdaw
Ukhiya
Teknaf
Sittwe
Dalet
An
Hunters Bay
Man Aung
Taunggok
Lamu
Cheduba I.
Arakan Yoma
57
73
1033
1532
2061
3383

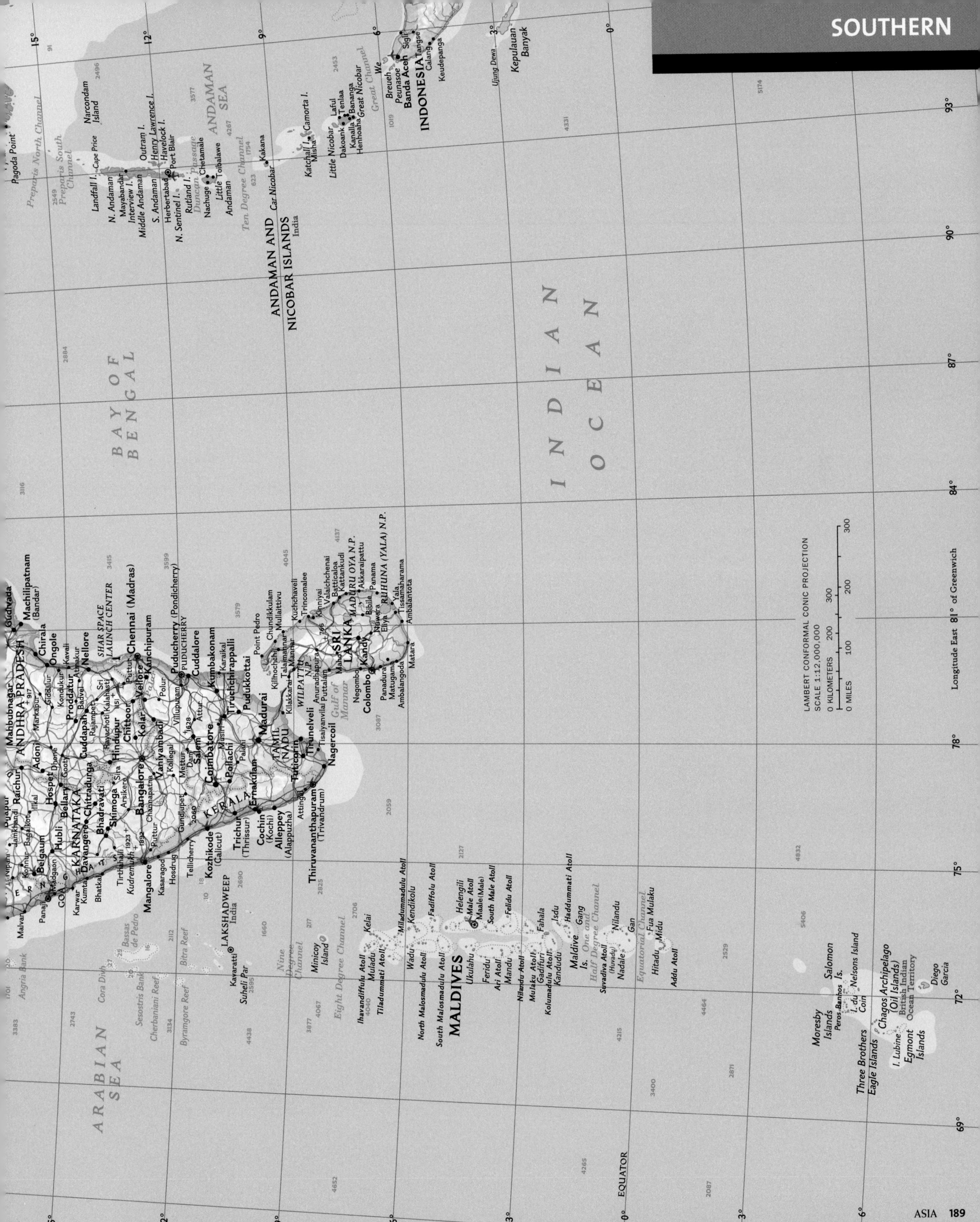

BAY OF BENGAL

ANDAMAN SEA

ARABIAN SEA

INDIAN OCEAN

ANDAMAN AND NICOBAR ISLANDS
India

ANDHRA PRADESH

KARNATAKA

KERALA

TAMIL NADU

GOA

PUDUCHERRY

LAKSHADWEEP
India

SRI LANKA

MALDIVES

INDONESIA

Chagos Archipelago (Oil Islands)
British Indian Ocean Territory

Chennai (Madras)

Bangalore

Puducherry (Pondicherry)

Madurai

Coimbatore

Cochin (Kochi)

Thiruvananthapuram (Trivandrum)

Kozhikode (Calicut)

Mangalore

Colombo

Kandy

Trincomalee

Jaffna

Port Blair

Banda Aceh

Male

Diego Garcia

Gulf of Mannar

Nine Degree Channel

Eight Degree Channel

One and Half Degree Channel

Equatorial Channel

Ten Degree Channel

Duncan Passage

Preparis North Channel

Preparis South Channel

Great Channel

SHAR SPACE LAUNCH CENTER

EQUATOR

LAMBERT CONFORMAL CONIC PROJECTION
SCALE 1:12,000,000

0 KILOMETERS 100 200 300

0 MILES 100 200 300

Longitude East 81° of Greenwich

KAZAKHSTAN
Kazakh Uplands
Astana
Pavlodar
Ekibastuz
Temirtau
Qaraghandy
Qarqaraly
Zhezqazghan
Qarsaqbay
BAYKONUR COSMODROME
Russian-administered
Bayqongyr (Baykonur, Leninsk)
Zhosaly
Syr Darya
Qyzylorda
Shieli
Qarataū Zhotasy
Moyynqum
Moyynty
Balqash
Balqash Köli
Saryshaghan
Saryesik-Atyraū Qumy
Qizilqum
Toshkent (Tashkent)
Türkistan
Shymkent
Taraz
Shū
Qapshaghay
Taldyqorghan
Lepsi
Matay
Aqtoghay
Ayaköz
Zharma
Semey (Semipalatinsk)
Öskemen (Ust' Kamenogorsk)
Ridder (Leninogorsk)
Zyryanovsk
Kökpekti
Zaysan Köli
Tarbaghatay Zhotasy
Slavgorod
Mikhaylovskiy
Mayqayyn
Rubtsovsk
Barnaul
Novokuznetsk
Prokop'yevsk
Aleysk
Biysk
Gorno Altaysk
ALTAY
KEMEROVO
KHAKASIYA
Abakan
Minusinsk
Krasnoturansk
Artemovsk
Abaza
Sayanogorsk
KRASNOYARSK
GORNO-ALTAY
TYVA (TUVA)
Kyzyl
Saryg Sep
Toora Khem
Systyg Khem
Kosh-Agach
Erzin
Nizhneudinsk
Neroy
IRKUTSK
Zima
Cheremkhovo
UST'-ORDA BURYAT
Ust' Ordynskiy
Angarsk
Irkutsk
Kultuk
Slyudyanka
Orlik
Turt
Ulan Ude
Kachug
Ust' Barguzin
Ozero Baykal
Severobaykal'sk
Karam
Hövsgöl Nuur
Hatgal
Zakamensk
Naushki
Sühbaatar
Mörön
Selenge
Ulaangom
Ölgiy
Har Us Nuur
Hyargas Nuur
Hovd (Dund-Us)
Uliastay
Hangayn Nuruu
Altay
Bulgan
Hunt
Tsetserleg
Ulaanbaatar (Ulan Bator)
Baruunharaa
Dzuunmod
MONGOLIA
ALTAY MTS.
Bayanhongor
Arvayheer
Choyr
Mandalgovĭ
Talshand
Bulgan
Arguut
Ulaanjirem
Buyant Ovoo
Saynshand (Buyant-Uhaa)
Dalandzadgad
Nomgon
Ergel
Edrengiyn Nuruu
Altay
Tsetsegnuur
Bürenhayrhan
Ertai
Fuhai
Tacheng (Qoqek)
Dzungarian Gate
Karamay
Junggar Pendi (Dzungarian Basin)
Kuytun
Ürümqi
Bogda Feng
Turpan (Turfan)
Turpan Depression
Hami (Kumul)
Barkol
Weiya
Zharkent
Yining
Almaty
Bishkek
KYRGYZSTAN
Karakol
Naryn
Bazar-Kurgan
Osh
Andijon
Namangan
Qo'qon
Khujand
UZBEKISTAN
TAJIKISTAN
Dushanbe
Qullai Ismoili Somoni (Communism Peak)
Jengish Chokusu (Pobedy Peak, Victory Peak)
TIAN SHAN
Aksu
Kuqa
Luntai
Hejing
Korla
Murgab
Pamirs
Feyzabad
AFGHAN.
HINDU KUSH
Kashi (Kashgar)
Kongur Shan
Akto
Muztagata
Taxkorgan
Shache (Yarkant)
Pishan (Guma)
Hotan
Yutian
Minfeng
Qiemo
Qarqan
Argan
Lop Nur
Tarim
TAKLIMAKAN SHAMO
XINJIANG UYGUR
SINKIANG
Ejin Qi
JIUQUAN SPACE LAUNCH CENTER
Anxi
Dunhuang
Yumen (Laojunmiao)
Jiayuguan
Shuangchengzi
ALTUN SHAN
KUNLUN SHAN
Lenghu
Qilian Shan
Zhangye
GANSU
Hanggin Houqi
INNER
Baotou
Wuhai
Minqin
Wuwei
Pingluo
Yinchuan
Wuzhong
Zhongwei
NINGXIA HUIZU
Da Qaidam
Qaidam Pendi
Har Hu
QINGHAI
Ulan
Golmud
Xining
Dulan
Qinghai Hu
Guide
Linxia
Lanzhou
Dingxi
Longxi
Tianshui
Baoji
SHAANXI
Xi'an (Sian)
Pingliang
Qingyang
Muztag
Hoh Xil Shan
Kunlun Shankou
Bayan Har Shankou
Bayan Har Shan
Maqên Gangri
Huang (Yellow)
Tongtian (Yangtze)
Dogai Coring
QING ZANG GAOYUAN
XIZANG (TIBET)
Tanggula Shan
Tanggula Shankou
Tangra Yumco
Xainza
Gangdisê Shan
Ngangiong Kangri
Gar
AKSAI CHIN
Boundary claimed by Pak.
Boundary claimed by India
Boundary claimed by China
K2 (Godwin Austen, Qogir)
Karakoram Range
KASHMIR
Gilgit
Nanga Parbat
Kyber Pass
Peshawar
PAKISTAN
Islamabad
Rawalpindi
Srinagar
Leh
Jammu
Gujranwala
Jhang Sadr
Sialkot
Faisalabad
LAHORE
Jalandhar
Ludhiana
Patiala
Simla
Ambala
Dehra Dun
Saharanpur
Nanda Devi
Great Indian Desert
DELHI
New Delhi
Meerut
Moradabad
Rampur
Bareilly
Aligarh
Mathura
Agra
Jaipur
Ajmer
Tonk
Gwalior
Jhansi
Datia
Kota
Guna
Shahjahanpur
Lucknow
Kanpur
Faizabad
Gorakhpur
Allahabad
Varanasi (Banaras)
Ganga (Ganges)
Rewa
Son
Bhopal
Murwara
Jabalpur
Chhindwara
Seoni
Nagpur
Amravati
Akola
Bhandara
Bilaspur
Raipur
Raigarh
Chandrapur
Nizamabad
Karimnagar
Hyderabad
EASTERN GHATS
Jeypore
Salur
Vizianagaram
Vishakhapatnam
Rajahmundry
Kakinada (Cocanada)
Yanam
Vijayawada
Guntur
Machilipatnam
Nellore
Mahanadi
Cuttack
Puri
Brahmapur
INDIA
Patna
Gaya
Bhagalpur
Darbhanga
Hazaribag
Ranchi
Jamshedpur
Barddhaman
Kolkata (Calcutta)
NEPAL
Dhaulagiri
Kathmandu
Lalitpur
Mt. Everest (Qomolangma, Sagarmatha)
(29035 ft)
HIMALAYA
Xigazê
Gyangzê
Lhasa
Gongbo'gyamda
Nyainqêntanglha Shan
Baqên
Yarlung Zangbo (Brahmaputra)
Nu (Salween)
Lancang (Mekong)
Qamdo
Dêgê
Garzê
Batang
Gangtok
Shiliguri
Thimphu
BHUTAN
Kangto
Boundary claimed by China
Dibrugarh
Teju
Zayü
Putao
Goalpara
Shillong
Guwahati
Brahmaputra
Naga Hills
Chindwin
Imphal
Maingkwan
Sylhet
Rajshahi
BANGLADESH
Dhaka
Khulna
Mizo Hills
Chittagong
BAY OF BENGAL
Sittwe
Kyaukphyu
Cheduba I.
Arakan Yoma
Mt. Victoria
MYANMAR (BURMA)
Mandalay
Ayeyarwady
Kalemyo
Shwebo
Monywa
Hsipaw
Lashio
Katha
Bhamo
Myitkyina
Mawlite
Pyinmanaa
Loikaw
Taungoo
Pyay
Hinthada
Tengchong
Baoshan
Dali
Luxi
Lincang
Jinggu
Pu'er
Simao
YUNNAN
Kunming
Yiliang
Yuxi
Gejiu
Mengzi
Wenshan
Panzhihua
Jinsha (Yangtze)
Xichang
XICHANG SPACE LAUNCH CENTER
Zhongdian
Gongga Shan
SICHUAN
Chengdu
Ya'an
Leshan
Zigong
Yibin
Luzhou
Neijiang
CHONGQING
CHONGQING SHI
Nanchong
Mianyang
Langzhong
Wanxian
Fengjie
Hanzhong
Ankang
Zunyi
Zhijiang
Zhaotong
Guiyang
Zhenyuan
GUIZHOU
Anshun
Huize
Zhanyi
Xingyi
Liping
Dushan
Yishan
GUANGXI ZHUANGZU
Bose
Laibin
Nanning
Chongzuo
Ningming
Litang
Lang Son
Lao Cai
Dien Bien
Hoa Binh
Hanoi
Haiphong
Nam Dinh
VIETNAM
Beihai
Gulf of Tonkin
Xuwen
Haikou
HAINAN
Dongfang
Muang Sing
Xam Nua
LAOS
Louangphrabang
Xiangkhoang
DOI LUANG N.P.
Pai
Mekong
THAILAND
Lampang
Phrao
Uttaradit
Vientiane
Vinh

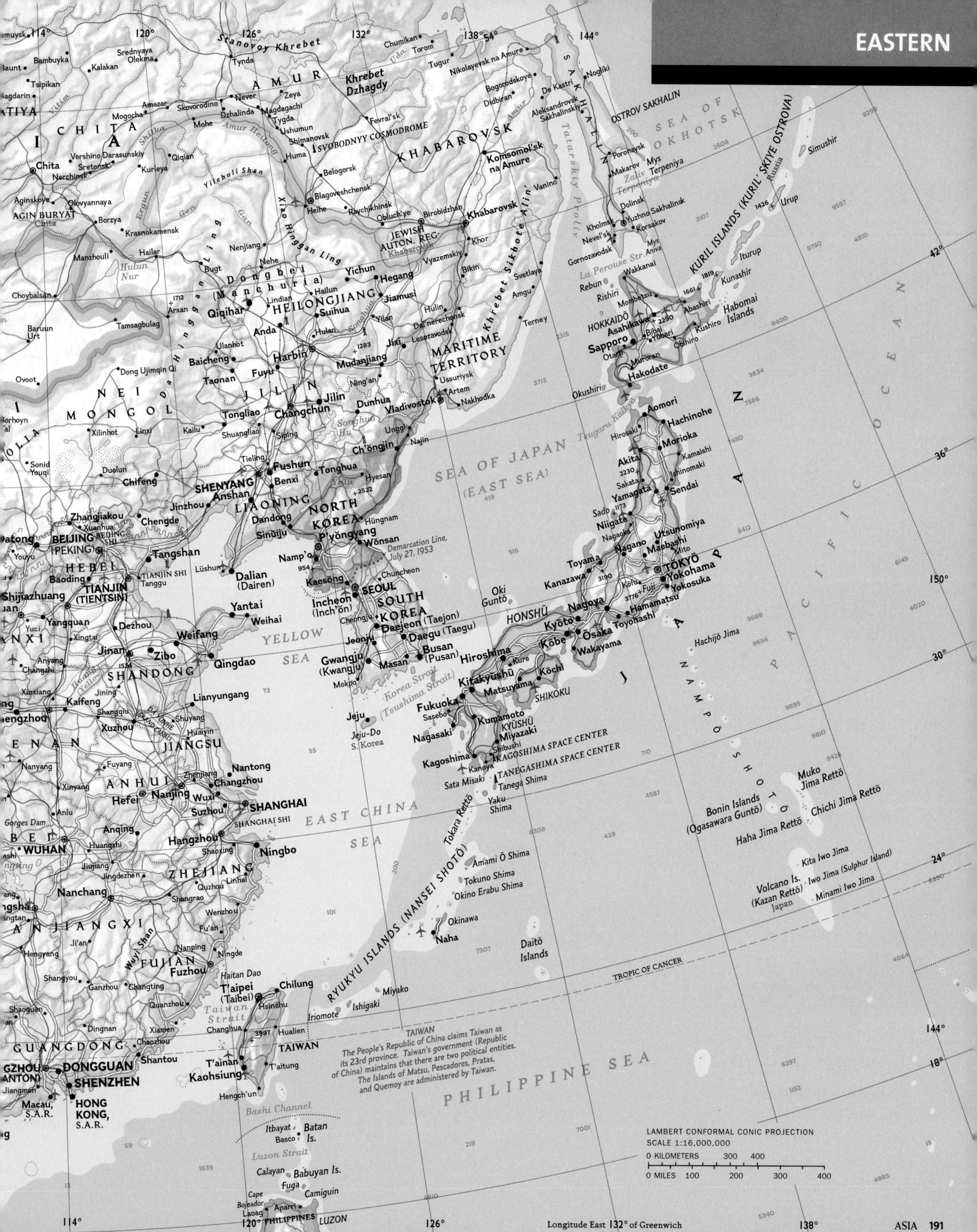
Stanovoy Khrebet
Tynda
AMUR
Khrebet Dzhagdy
Chumikan
Torom
Tugur
Nikolayevsk na Amure
SAKHALIN
Nogliki
Bogorodskoye
De Kastri
Aleksandrovsk Sakhalinskiy
OSTROV SAKHALIN
SEA OF OKHOTSK
Srednyaya Olekma
Bambuyka
Kalakan
Tsipikan
Bagdarin
CHITA
Mogocha
Amazar
Skovorodino
Never
Zeya
Magdagachi
Dzhalinda
Tygda
Shimanovsk
Ushumun
Fevral'sk
SVOBODNYY COSMODROME
KHABAROVSK
Chita
Vershino Darasunskiy
Sretensk
Nerchinsk
Qiqian
Kurleya
Yilehuli Shan
Huma
Belogorsk
Komsomol'sk na Amure
Poronaysk
Mys Terpeniya
Zaliv Terpeniya
Simushir
KURIL ISLANDS (KURIL'SKIYE OSTROVA)
Aginskoye
Olovyannaya
AGIN BURYAT
Borzya
Krasnokamensk
Blagoveshchensk
Heihe
Raychikhinsk
Obluch'ye
Birobidzhan
Khabarovsk
Vanino
Tatarskiy Proliv
Dolinsk
Yuzhno Sakhalinsk
Kholmsk
Nevel'sk
Korsakov
Urup
Russia
JEWISH AUTON. REG.
Khor
Manzhouli
Hailar
Hulun Nur
Nenjiang
Nehe
Xiao Hinggan Ling
Bugt
Dongbei (Manchuria)
Yichun
Hegang
Jiamusi
Vyazemskiy
Bikin
Khrebet Sikhote Alin'
Svetlaya
Amgu
Terney
Gornozavodsk
La Perouse Str.
Mys Aniva
Wakkanai
Rebun
Rishiri
Mombetsu
Iturup
Kunashir
Choybalsan
Arxan
Qiqihar
HEILONGJIANG
Suihua
Lindian
Yilan
Hulin
Dal'nerechensk
Lesozavodsk
HOKKAIDŌ
Asahikawa
Abashiri
Habomai Islands
Kushiro
Obihiro
Bibai
Yubari
Sapporo
Otaru
Muroran
Hakodate
Baruun Urt
Tamsagbulag
Anda
Hulan
Harbin
Jixi
Mudanjiang
MARITIME TERRITORY
Ulanhot
Baicheng
Dong Ujimqin Qi
Taonan
Fuyu
Ning'an
Ussuriysk
Artem
Nakhodka
Vladivostok
Ovoot
NEI MONGOL
JILIN
Jilin
Dunhua
Tongliao
Changchun
Xilinhot
Linxi
Kailu
Shuangliao
Siping
Unggi
Najin
Ch'ŏngjin
Okushiri
Aomori
Hachinohe
Hirosaki
Morioka
Kamaishi
Akita
Ishinomaki
Sakata
Yamagata
Sendai
Sonid Youqi
Duolun
Chifeng
Tieling
Fushun
Benxi
Tonghua
Hyesan
SHENYANG
Anshan
LIAONING
NORTH KOREA
SEA OF JAPAN (EAST SEA)
Tsugaru Kaikyō
Jinzhou
Zhangjiakou
Xuanhua
Chengde
Dandong
Sinŭiju
Hŭngnam
P'yŏngyang
Wŏnsan
Demarcation Line, July 27, 1953
Sado
Niigata
Nagaoka
Utsunomiya
Datong
BEIJING (PEKING)
BEIJING SHI
Tangshan
HEBEI
Nampo
Kaesŏng
Chuncheon
Toyama
Nagano
Maebashi
Mito
Kanazawa
TŌKYŌ
Yokohama
Yokosuka
Kōfu
Fuji
Baoding
TIANJIN (TIENTSIN)
TIANJIN SHI
Tanggu
Lüshun
Dalian (Dairen)
SEOUL
SOUTH KOREA
Incheon (Inch'ŏn)
Cheongju
Daejeon (Taejon)
Oki Guntō
HONSHŪ
Nagoya
Hamamatsu
Toyohashi
Shijiazhuang
Yuci
Yangquan
Dezhou
Yantai
Weihai
Weifang
YELLOW SEA
Daegu (Taegu)
Jeonju
Kyōto
Ōsaka
Kobe
Wakayama
Hachijō Jima
Jinan
Zibo
Qingdao
Anyang
Changzhi
SHANDONG
Gwangju (Kwangju)
Busan (Pusan)
Masan
Mokpo
Hiroshima
Kure
Kōchi
SHIKOKU
Matsuyama
Kitakyūshū
Korea Strait (Tsushima Strait)
Xinxiang
Kaifeng
Jining
Shangqiu
Lianyungang
Zhengzhou
Xuzhou
Shuyang
Huaiyin
Jeju
Jeju-Do S. Korea
Fukuoka
Sasebo
Kumamoto
KYŪSHŪ
Miyazaki
Nagasaki
Kagoshima
Kanoya
Shibushi
KAGOSHIMA SPACE CENTER
TANEGASHIMA SPACE CENTER
HENAN
JIANGSU
Nantong
Zhenjiang
Changzhou
Fuyang
Nanyang
Xinyang
ANHUI
Hefei
Nanjing
Wuxi
Suzhou
SHANGHAI
SHANGHAI SHI
Sata Misaki
Tanega Shima
Yaku Shima
Muko Jima Rettō
Bonin Islands (Ogasawara Guntō)
Chichi Jima Rettō
Haha Jima Rettō
NAMPŌ SHOTŌ
EAST CHINA SEA
Anlu
Anqing
Gorges Dam
WUHAN
Huangshi
Hangzhou
Shaoxing
Ningbo
Jiujiang
Jingdezhen
ZHEJIANG
Quzhou
Linhai
Nanchang
Shangrao
Wenzhou
Tokara Rettō
Amami Ō Shima
Tokuno Shima
Okino Erabu Shima
Kita Iwo Jima
Iwo Jima (Sulphur Island)
Volcano Is. (Kazan Rettō) Japan
Minami Iwo Jima
JIANGXI
Fu'an
Ji'an
Wuyi Shan
Nanping
Ningde
Hengyang
RYUKYU ISLANDS (NANSEI SHOTŌ)
Okinawa
Naha
Daitō Islands
FUJIAN
Fuzhou
Haitan Dao
Shangyou
Ganzhou
Changting
T'aipei (Taibei)
Chilung
Hsinchu
Miyako
Ishigaki
Iriomote
TROPIC OF CANCER
Quanzhou
Taiwan Strait
Shaoguan
Xiamen
Dingnan
Changhua
Hualien
TAIWAN
The People's Republic of China claims Taiwan as its 23rd province. Taiwan's government (Republic of China) maintains that there are two political entities. The Islands of Matsu, Pescadores, Pratas, and Quemoy are administered by Taiwan.
GUANGDONG
Chaozhou
Shantou
T'ainan
T'aitung
Kaohsiung
PHILIPPINE SEA
GUANGZHOU (CANTON)
DONGGUAN
SHENZHEN
Jiangmen
Macau, S.A.R.
HONG KONG, S.A.R.
Hengch'un
Bashi Channel
Itbayat
Basco
Batan Is.
Luzon Strait
Calayan
Babuyan Is.
Fuga
Camiguin
Cape Bojeador
Laoag
Aparri
PHILIPPINES
LUZON
PACIFIC OCEAN
JAPAN
LAMBERT CONFORMAL CONIC PROJECTION
SCALE 1:16,000,000
0 KILOMETERS 300 400
0 MILES 100 200 300 400
Longitude East 132° of Greenwich
114°
120°
126°
132°
138°
144°
54°
42°
36°
150°
30°
24°
18°

C H I N A
INDIA
BANGLADESH
Dhaka
Khulna
Chittagong
Sylhet
Naga Hills
3826
Imphal
Mizo Hills
ALAUNGDAW KATHAPA N.P.
Mt. Victoria
3053
MYANMAR (BURMA)
Myitkyina
Bhamo
Katha
Mawlite
Kalemyo
Shwebo
Monywa
Hsipaw
Lashio
Mandalay
Myingyan
Sittwe
Kyaukphyu
Pyinmanaa
Loikaw
Taungoo
Pyay
Arakan Yoma
Cheduba I.
BAY OF BENGAL
Pathein
Insein
Yangon (Rangoon)
Mawlamyine
Gulf of Martaban
Dawna Ra.
Preparis North Channel
North Andaman
Middle Andaman
ANDAMAN IS.
India
South Andaman
Little Andaman
Ten Degree Channel
NICOBAR ISLANDS
India
Camorta I.
Little Nicobar
Great Nicobar
Great Channel
ANDAMAN SEA
Mergui Archipelago
Mali Kyun
Kadan Kyun
Myeik
Isthmus of Kra
Ranong
Takua Pa
Ko Phuket
Phuket
Kantang
Dali
Baoshan
Tengchong
Luxi
Kunming
Yiliang
Yuxi
YUNNAN
Lincang
Jinggu
Pu'er
Simao
Gejiu
Mengzi
Wenshan
Lao Cai
GUIZHOU
Zhanyi
Xingyi
Dushan
GUANGXI ZHUANGZU
Yishan
Liuzhou
Laibin
Bose
Nanning
Litang
Chongzuo
Lang Son
Ningming
Beihai
Maoming
Zhanjiang
Xuwen
Haikou
Gulf of Tonkin
HAINAN
Dongfang
Sanya
1867
HUNAN
JIANGXI
Wuyi Shan
Shangyou
Ganzhou
Changting
Fuzhou
FUJIAN
Quanzhou
Xiamen
Shaoguan
Lianxian
Dingnan
GUANGDONG
GUANGZHOU (CANTON)
DONGGUAN
SHENZHEN
Jiangmen
Macau S.A.R.
HONG KONG, S.A.R.
Shantou
Chaozhou
EAST
Haitan Dao
T'aipei
Hsinchu
Changhua
Taiwan Strait
Hualien
T'ainan
Kaohsiung
T'aitung
3997
Hengch'un
Bashi Channel
VIETNAM
Hanoi
Haiphong
Nam Dinh
Hoa Binh
Dien Bien
Muang Sing
Xam Nua
LAOS
Louangphrabang
Xiangkhoang
2818
Vientiane
Udon Thani
CUC PHUONG N.P.
Vinh
Mui Ron
Quang Tri
Hue
BACH MA N.P.
Da Nang
Savannakhet
Mukdahan
Ban Xénô
Saravan
Attapu
Kon Tum
2598
Play Ku
An Khe
Qui Nhon
Tuy Hoa
YOK DON N.P.
Nha Trang
2405
Cam Ranh
Phan Rang
Di Linh
CAT TIEN N.P.
Ho Chi Minh City (Saigon)
Can Tho
Long Xuyen
Go Cong
Soc Trang
Ca Mau
Con Son
DOI LUANG N.P.
Pai
Chiang Mai
2565
Lampang
Phrae
Uttaradit
MAE PING N.P.
Tak
Phitsanulok
NAM NAO N.P.
THAILAND
Nakhon Ratchasima
Ubon Ratchathani
THAP LAN N.P.
KHAO YAI N.P.
Ayutthaya
Dawei
KRUNG THEP (BANGKOK)
Chachoengsao
Dangrek Range
VIRACHEY N.P.
Angkor
Siem Reap
Battambang
Sattahip
CAMBODIA
Kratie
KAENG KRACHAN N.P.
1744
Phnom Penh
PHNOM BOKOR N.P.
Kompong Som
Ream
Dao Phu Quoc
GULF OF THAILAND
Ko Samui
Surat Thani
Mui Bai Bung
Songkhla
Pattani
Kota Baharu
Alor Setar
George Town
Pinang
Butterworth
Tanah Merah
Kuala Terengganu
Taiping
Ipoh
Tahan
2190
TAMAN NEGARA N.P.
Kuala Dungun
Chukai
MALAY PENINSULA
Kuantan
Kuala Lumpur
Putrajaya
Seremban
Malacca
Muar
Johor Bahru
SINGAPORE
Singapore
Strait of Malacca
MALAYSIA
Sabang
Banda Aceh
2140
Sigli
Julu Rayeu
Idi
Langsa
Calang
2985
Meulaboh
Panjang
Binjai
Medan
GUNUNG LEUSER N.P.
Pematangsiantar
Tanjungbalai
Simeulue
Kep. Banyak
SIBERUT N.P.
NIAS
Sibolga
886
Telukdalem
Natal
2912
EQUATOR
Tanahmasa
Pini
Kep. Batu
Tanahbala
Bukittinggi
Padang
Sawahlunto
Taluk
BUKIT TIGAH PULUH N.P.
SIBERUT N.P.
Siberut
Sipura
KEPULAUAN MENTAWAI
Kerinci
3800
Inderapura
KERINCI SEBLAT N.P.
Jambi
Lais
Bengkulu
3159
Lahat
Muaraenim
Manna
Baturaja
Krui
Pegunungan Barisan
Enggano
BUKIT BARISAN SELATAN N.P.
Dumai
Bengkalis
Sebanga
Pekanbaru
Lirik
Bintan
Tanjungpinang
KEP. RIAU
KEP. LINGGA
Lingga
Kotadabok
BERBAK N.P.
Pangkalpinang
Muntok
Bangka
Palembang
Toboali
Selat Gelasa
Belitung (Billiton)
Tanjungpandan
Kep. Natuna Besar
Binjai
Natuna Besar
Kep. Anambas
Kep. Natuna Selatan
Indonesia
Kep. Karimata
Paracel Is.
Administered by China (Claimed by Vietnam)
SOUTH CHINA SEA
SPRATLY ISLANDS
SPRATLY ISLANDS
The scattered islands and reefs called the Spratly Islands are claimed by Brunei, China, Malaysia, the Philippines, Taiwan, and Vietnam. The Spratlys possess rich fishing grounds and potential oil.
North Luconia Shoals
MALAYSIA
Malaysia includes peninsular Malaysia, Sarawak, and Sabah; the capital is Kuala Lumpur.
Itbayat
Basco
Calayan
Babuyan
Fuga
Cape Bojeador
Laoag
Aparri
Vigan
Ilagan
Sierra Madre
San Fernando
Baguio
LUZON
Dagupan
Cabanatua
Tarlac
Quezon City
Manila
Cavite
San Pablo
Batangas
Calapan
MINDORO
Calamian Group
El Nido
Pandan
Iloilo
Dumaran
Puerto Princesa
PANAY
Cagayan Is.
PALAWAN
2100
Balabac
Balabac Strait
SULU SEA
Kudat
Banggi
Cagayan Sulu I.
Zamboanga
Isabela
KINABALU PARK
Kinabalu
4101
Kota Kinabalu
CROCKER RANGE N.P.
Sandakan
Bandar Seri Begawan
Beaufort
Bandar Labuan (Victoria)
Lahad Datu
Tawi Tawi
Jolo
Sulu Archipelago
BRUNEI
Seria
SABAH
GUNUNG MULU N.P.
Tawau
Tanahmerah
Malinau
Tarakan
Bintulu
Baram
SARAWAK
Igan
Oya
Sibu
Sarikei
Kapit
KAYAN-MENTARANG N.P.
Tanjungselor
Maratua
BOGANI NANI WARTABONE
2987
Kong Kemul
2053
Tanjungredep
Tg. Mangkalihat
Saratok
Kuching
Sambas
Singkawang
1701
Niut
Serian
Putussibau
Menyapa
2000
GUNUNG BENTUANG N.P.
Sangkulirang
KUTAI N.P.
Bontang
Mempawah
Sintang
BORNEO (KALIMANTAN)
Pontianak
Kapuas
Nangapinoh
Raya
2278
Purukcahu
BUKIT BAKA-BUKIT RAYA N.P.
Muaratewe
Samarinda
GUNUNG PALUNG N.P.
Maya
Balikpapan
Ketapang
Barito
Tanahgrogot
Sampit
Kandangan
Pangkalanbuun
TANJUNG PUTING N.P.
Banjarmasin
Kualakapuas
Martapura
Kotabaru
Laut
MAKASSAR STRAIT
GREATER
INDONESIA
SUNDA ISLANDS
Tolitoli
Buol
Tilamuta
Tinombo
Sabang
Donggala
Teluk Tomini
LORE LINDU N.P.
Uebonti
Poso
SULAWESI (CELEBES)
Mamuju
Palopo
Majene
3455
Parepare
Kolaka
Teluk Bone
Maros
Ujungpandang (Makassar)
Bulukumba
Bantaeng
Kabaena
Selayar
Muna
CELEBES SEA
JAVA SEA
Kep. Laut Kecil
Kep. Masalumbu
WAY KAMBAS N.P.
Tanjungkarang-Telukbetung
Serang
JAKARTA
Cirebon
Pekalongan
Semarang
UJUNG KULON N.P.
Sukabumi
Bandung
3428
Kudus
Tuban
Madura
Pamekasan
Kep. Kangean
Cilacap
Surakarta
Kediri
Surabaya
JAVA
Malang
3676
Semeru
Banyuwangi
BALI SEA
Kalao
Denpasar
ALAS PURWO NATIONAL PARK
BALI
LOMBOK
3726
Mataram
Moyo
SUMBAWA
Raba
FLORES SEA
Reo
FLORES
LESSER SUNDA ISLANDS
Waikabubak
Waingapu
SUMBA
Sawu
INDIAN OCEAN
Christmas Island
Australia
LAMBERT CONFORMAL CONIC PROJECTION
SCALE 1:16,000,000
0 KILOMETERS 300 400
0 MILES 100 200 300 400
90°
96°
102°
108°
114°
120°
24°
18°
12°
6°
0°
6°
12°

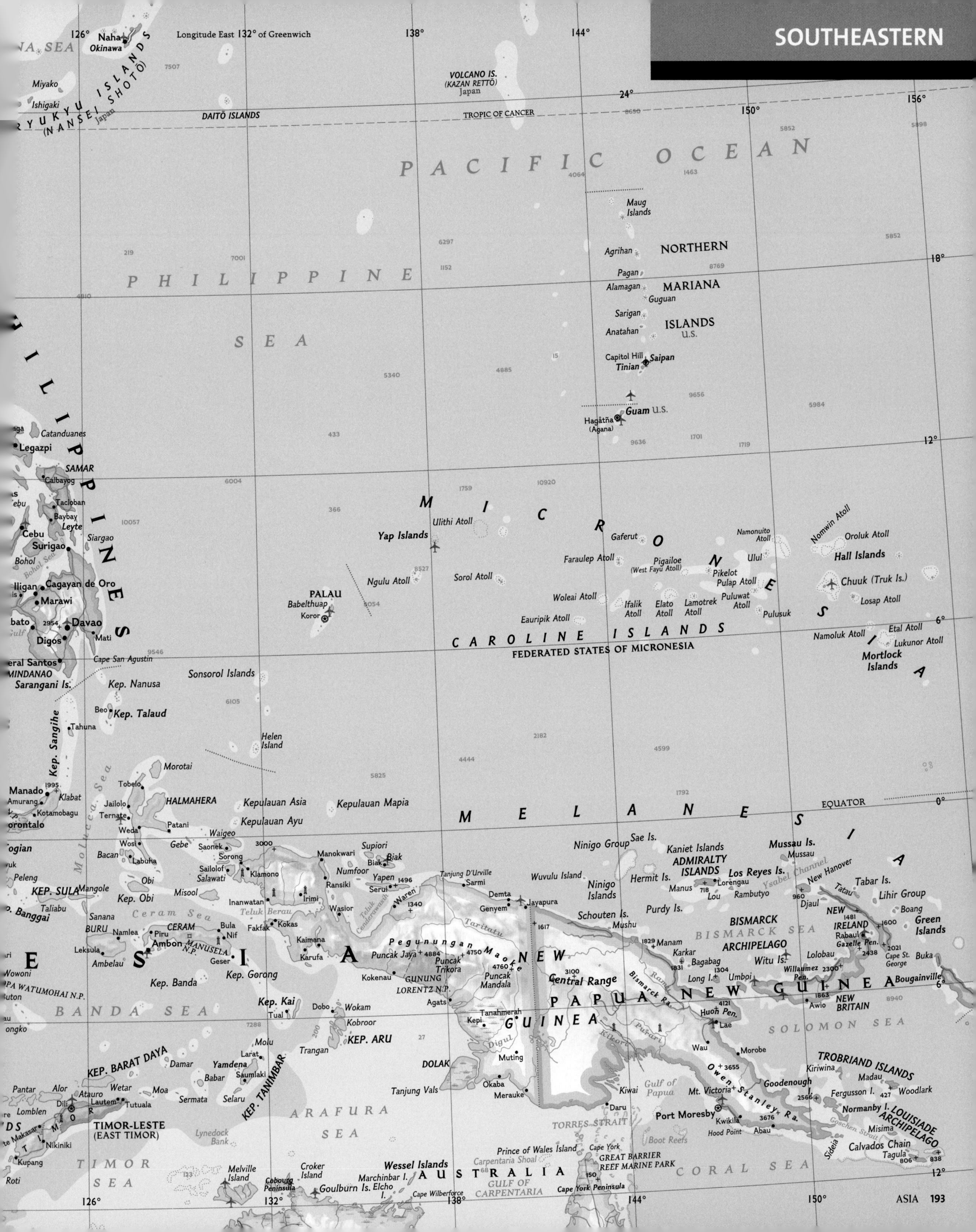
Longitude East 132° of Greenwich
PACIFIC OCEAN
PHILIPPINE SEA
TROPIC OF CANCER
VOLCANO IS.
(KAZAN RETTŌ)
Japan
DAITŌ ISLANDS
RYUKYU ISLANDS
(NANSEI SHOTŌ)
Naha
Okinawa
Miyako
Ishigaki
NORTHERN MARIANA ISLANDS
U.S.
Maug Islands
Agrihan
Pagan
Alamagan
Guguan
Sarigan
Anatahan
Capitol Hill
Saipan
Tinian
Guam U.S.
Hagåtña
(Agana)
MICRONESIA
CAROLINE ISLANDS
FEDERATED STATES OF MICRONESIA
Ulithi Atoll
Yap Islands
Ngulu Atoll
Sorol Atoll
Gaferut
Faraulep Atoll
Pigailoe
(West Fayu Atoll)
Namonuito Atoll
Ulul
Pikelot
Pulap Atoll
Nomwin Atoll
Oroluk Atoll
Hall Islands
Chuuk (Truk Is.)
Losap Atoll
Woleai Atoll
Ifalik Atoll
Elato Atoll
Lamotrek Atoll
Puluwat Atoll
Pulusuk
Eauripik Atoll
Namoluk Atoll
Etal Atoll
Lukunor Atoll
Mortlock Islands
PALAU
Babelthuap
Koror
Sonsorol Islands
Helen Island
Kep. Nanusa
Kep. Talaud
Beo
Tahuna
Kep. Sangihe
PHILIPPINES
Catanduanes
Legazpi
SAMAR
Calbayog
Tacloban
Baybay
Leyte
Cebu
Surigao
Siargao
Bohol
Bohol Sea
Iligan
Cagayan de Oro
Marawi
Davao
Mati
Digos
MINDANAO
Sarangani Is.
Cape San Agustin
Morotai
Tobelo
HALMAHERA
Jailolo
Ternate
Weda
Patani
Manado
Klabat
Amurang
Kotamobagu
Gorontalo
Molucca Sea
Kepulauan Asia
Kepulauan Mapia
Kepulauan Ayu
Waigeo
Gebe
Saonek
Sorong
Bacan
Labuha
Obi
Kep. Obi
Misool
Salawati
Klamono
Peleng
KEP. SULA
Mangole
Taliabu
Banggai
Sanana
BURU
Namlea
CERAM
Ceram Sea
Piru
Bula
Nif
Ambon
MANUSELA N.P.
Geser
Leksula
Ambelau
Kep. Banda
Kep. Gorong
Kep. Kai
Tual
BANDA SEA
Wowoni
RAWA WATUMOHAI N.P.
MELANESIA
EQUATOR
Manokwari
Supiori
Biak
Numfoor
Yapen
Serui
Waren
Ransiki
Inanwatan
Teluk Berau
Fakfak
Kokas
Irimi
Wasior
Teluk Cenderawasih
Kaimana
Karufa
Pegunungan Maoke
Puncak Jaya
Puncak Trikora
Puncak Mandala
GUNUNG LORENTZ N.P.
Kokenau
Agats
Taritatu
Tanjung D'Urville
Sarmi
Demta
Genyem
Jayapura
Tanahmerah
Kepi
Digul
Muting
Okaba
Merauke
Dobo
Wokam
Kobroor
KEP. ARU
Trangan
DOLAK
Tanjung Vals
Molu
Larat
Yamdena
KEP. TANIMBAR
Saumlaki
Selaru
Damar
Babar
Sermata
KEP. BARAT DAYA
Wetar
Moa
Alor
Atauro
Pantar
Dili
Lautem
Tutuala
Lomblen
TIMOR
TIMOR-LESTE
(EAST TIMOR)
Nikiniki
Kupang
Roti
TIMOR SEA
ARAFURA SEA
Lynedock Bank
Melville Island
Cobourg Peninsula
Croker Island
Goulburn Is.
Marchinbar I.
Elcho I.
Wessel Islands
Cape Wilberforce
AUSTRALIA
GULF OF CARPENTARIA
Carpentaria Shoal
Prince of Wales Island
Cape York
Cape York Peninsula
GREAT BARRIER REEF MARINE PARK
TORRES STRAIT
Boot Reefs
CORAL SEA
Daru
Kiwai
Gulf of Papua
NEW GUINEA
PAPUA NEW GUINEA
Wuvulu Island
Ninigo Group
Ninigo Islands
Sae Is.
Kaniet Islands
Hermit Is.
ADMIRALTY ISLANDS
Manus
Lorengau
Lou
Rambutyo
Los Reyes Is.
Mussau Is.
Mussau
Ysabel Channel
New Hanover
Tabar Is.
Lihir Group
Tatau
Djaul
Boang
NEW IRELAND
Green Islands
Rabaul
Gazelle Pen.
Cape St. George
Buka
Bougainville
Schouten Is.
Mushu
Purdy Is.
BISMARCK ARCHIPELAGO
BISMARCK SEA
Manam
Karkar
Bagabag
Long I.
Umboi
Witu Is.
Lolobau
Willaumez Pen.
Awio
NEW BRITAIN
Central Range
Bismarck Ra.
Ramu
Huon Pen.
Lae
Wau
Morobe
Kikori
Purari
SOLOMON SEA
Owen Stanley Ra.
Mt. Victoria
Port Moresby
Kwikila
Hood Point
Abau
TROBRIAND ISLANDS
Kiriwina
Madau
Woodlark
Goodenough I.
Fergusson I.
Normanby I.
LOUISIADE ARCHIPELAGO
Goschen Strait
Misima
Calvados Chain
Sideia
Tagula
126°
132°
138°
144°
150°
156°
24°
18°
12°
6°
0°

EASTERN MEDITERRANEAN
ALBERS CONIC EQUAL-AREA PROJECTION
SCALE 1:2,250,000
0 KILOMETERS 40 60
0 MILES 20 40 60
Longitude East 33° of Greenwich
DIVIDED CYPRUS
Cyprus was partitioned in 1974 following a coup backed by Greece and an invasion by Turkey. The island is composed of a Greek Cypriot south with an internationally recognized government and a Turkish Cypriot north (gray) with a government recognized only by Turkey. The UN patrols the dividing line and works toward reunification of the island.
PALESTINE
The bounds of the historical region of Palestine have varied through time, but it is generally agreed that the land between the Mediterranean Sea and the Jordan River constitutes its core.
WEST BANK & GAZA STRIP
Captured by Israel in the 1967 Six Day War, a 1993 peace agreement gives areas of the West Bank and Gaza limited Palestinian autonomy. The future for these autonomous areas and 3 million Palestinians is subject to Israeli–Palestinian negotiations.
MEDITERRANEAN
SEA
CYPRUS
NORTHERN CYPRUS
Kyreneia Range
Troodos Mountains
Lefkosia (Nicosia, Lefkoşa)
Lemesos (Limassol)
AKROTIRI (WESTERN) SOVEREIGN BASE AREA
U.K. Base
DHEKELIA (EASTERN) SOVEREIGN BASE AREA
U.K. Base
Karpasia Peninsula
Cape Apostolos Andreas
LEBANON
Beyrouth (Beirut)
Trâblous (Tripoli)
SYRIA
Dimashq (Damascus)
Al Lādhiqīyah (Latakia)
Ḩamāh (Hamath)
Ḩimş (Homs)
GOLAN HEIGHTS
ISRAEL
Jerusalem (Yerushalayim, Al-Quds)
Tel Aviv-Yafo
Hefa (Haifa)
WEST BANK
GAZA STRIP
(Gaza) Ghazzah
PALMACHIM AIR BASE
JORDAN
Ammān (Philadelphia)
Az Zarqā'
SYRIAN DESERT
Dead Sea
Sea of Galilee
NEGEV
EGYPT
SINAI
Bûr Sa'îd (Port Said)
Ismâ'ilîya
Suez Canal
Be'ér Sheva' (Beersheba)
Eilat
32° 33° 34° 35° 36° 37°
35° 34° 33° 32° 31°

CAUCASUS REGION
ALBERS CONIC EQUAL-AREA PROJECTION
SCALE 1:4,000,000
0 KILOMETERS 20 40 60 80 100
0 MILES 20 40 60 80 100
SOUTH OSSETIA
A 1992 cease-fire ended fighting between Ossetians and Georgians, but with no political settlement.
NAGORNO-KARABAKH
Since a cease-fire in 1994 ethnic Armenians in Azerbaijan's Nagorno-Karabakh region have exercised autonomous control over the region. International mediation to resolve the conflict continues.
ABKHAZIA
Separatists defeated Georgian troops to gain control of this region in 1993—negotiations continue on resolving the conflict.
KAZAKHSTAN
RUSSIA
GEORGIA
ARMENIA
AZERBAIJAN
TURKEY
IRAN
IRAQ
SYRIA
CASPIAN SEA
BLACK SEA
CAUCASUS MOUNTAINS
KURDISTAN
DAGESTAN
CHECHNYA
INGUSHETIYA
KABARDINO-BALKARIYA
KARACHAYEVO-CHERKESIYA
KRASNODAR
STAVROPOL'
SEVERNAYA OSETIYA-ALANIYA (NORTH OSSETIA)
TSKHINVALI (SOUTH OSSETIA)
ABKHAZIA
NAGORNO-KARABAKH
NAXÇIVAN
Caspian Depression
Makhachkala
Groznyy
Vladikavkaz
T'bilisi (Tiflis)
Yerevan
Bakı (Baku)
Sumqayıt
Gäncä
Gyumri
Sokhumi (Sukhum)
Bat'umi
Trabzon
Erzurum
Van
Tabrīz
Rasht
Ardabīl
Orūmīyeh (Urmia)
Daryācheh-ye Orūmīyeh (Lake Urmia)
Ağrı Dağı (Mount Ararat)
Diyarbakır
Al Mawşil (Mosul)
R.R. FERRY
Longitude East 48° of Greenwich

PERSIAN GULF
ALBERS CONIC EQUAL-AREA PROJECTION
SCALE 1:6,000,000
0 KILOMETERS 100 150
0 MILES 50 100 150
Longitude East 54° of Greenwich
IRAQ
KUWAIT
IRAN
SAUDI ARABIA
BAHRAIN
QATAR
UNITED ARAB EMIRATES
OMAN
PERSIAN GULF
GULF OF OMAN
Strait of Hormuz
Gulf of Bahrain
Kūhhā-ye Zāgros
Zagros Mountains
FARS
Ad Dahnā
Historically and most commonly known as the Persian Gulf, this body of water is referred to by some as the Arabian Gulf.
Ābādān
Al Kuwayt (Kuwait)
Shīrāz
Persepolis
Bandar-e Būshehr
Bandar-e 'Abbās
Ad Dammām
Al Manāmah (Manama)
Ad Dawḩah (Doha)
Abū Z̧aby (Abu Dhabi)
Dubayy (Dubai)
Sharjah
Ar Riyāḑ (Riyadh)
Al Hufūf (Hofuf)
Ghawar Oil Field
Masqaţ (Muscat)
Sa'īdābād (Sīrjan)
Bandar-e Lengeh
Qeshm
Hormoz
Tunb Is.
Zirkūh
Al Fujayrah
Al 'Ayn
Al Buraymī
BOUNDARY UNDEFINED
FERRY
STRAIT OF MALACCA
ALBERS CONIC EQUAL-AREA PROJECTION
SCALE 1:8,000,000
0 KILOMETERS 120 160 200
0 MILES 40 80 120 160 200
Longitude East 105° of Greenwich
ANDAMAN SEA
SOUTH CHINA SEA
Gulf of Thailand
INDIAN OCEAN
Strait of Malacca
THAILAND
MALAY PENINSULA
MALAYSIA
INDONESIA
SUMATRA
SINGAPORE
Songkhla
Kota Baharu
Alor Setar
George Town
Ipoh
Kuala Lumpur
Kuala Terengganu
Kuantan
Seremban
Malacca
Johor Bahru
Medan
Banda Aceh
Pekanbaru
Padang
Siberut
Nias
Simeulue
Danau Toba
TAMAN NEGARA NAT. PARK
GUNUNG LEUSER NAT. PARK
KERINCI SEBLAT N.P.
BUKIT TIGAH PULUH NAT. PARK
BERBAK N.P.
SIBERUT N.P.
Kep. Natuna Besar
Natuna Besar
Kep. Anambas
Kepulauan Natuna Selatan
Kepulauan Riau
Kepulauan Lingga
Bintan
Singkep
Borneo (Kalimantan)
Pontianak
EQUATOR

FERGANA VALLEY
ALBERS CONIC EQUAL-AREA PROJECTION
SCALE 1:4,500,000
0 KILOMETERS 60 80 100 120
0 MILES 40 60 80 100 120
KAZAKHSTAN
ONGTÜSTIK QAZAQSTAN
UZBEKISTAN
KYRGYZSTAN
TAJIKISTAN
TURKMENISTAN
AFGHANISTAN
CHINA
Qizilqum
Fergana Valley
Turkestan Range
Zarafshon Range
Alay Mountains
Pamirs
BADAKHSHAN
UGAM-CHATKAL NAT. PARK
ZAAMIN NAT. PARK
GARAGUM CANAL
Aydar Köl
Toktogul Res.
Qayroqqum Res.
Qarokŭl
Longitude East 69° of Greenwich
Toshkent (Tashkent)
Shymkent
Samarqand
Buxoro (Bukhara)
Navoiy
Jizzax
Qarshi
Turkmenabat (Chärjew)
Dushanbe
Khujand
Andijon
Namangan
Farg'ona
Marg'ilon
Qo'qon
Osh
Olmaliq
Angren
Chirchiq
Gulistan
Sirdaryo
Yangiyer
Termiz
Kulob
Qŭrghonteppa
Kuybishevskiy
Murgab
Karakul'
Sary-Tash
Daroot-Korgon
Lenin Peak 7134
Qullai Ismoili Somoni (Communism Peak) 7495
Uzbel Shankou
Kyzyl-Suu
Naryn
Arys
Temir
Qyzylorda
Tomdibuloq
Zarafshon
Muruntau
Gazli
Karmana
Kattaqo'rg'on
Urgut
Panjakent
Ayni
Istaravshan (Ŭroteppa)
Isfara
Gharm
Jirgatol
Khorog
Rushan
Vanj
Kalaikhum
Tursunzoda
Hisor
Varzob
Yovan
Norak
Vose
Sherobod
Boyson
Denow
Sarıyab
Kerkiçi
Atamyrat (Kerki)
Dostlux
Burdalyk
Karabekaul
Sayat
Kitob
Shahrisabz
Yakkabog'
Muborak
Kashkadar'ya
Gora Ayribaba 3139
Adelunga Toghi 4301
GANGES VALLEY
ALBERS CONIC EQUAL-AREA PROJECTION
SCALE 1:8,000,000
0 KILOMETERS 120 160 200
0 MILES 40 80 120 160 200
Longitude East 84° of Greenwich
CHINA
XIZANG
NEPAL
INDIA
BHUTAN
BANGLADESH
HIMALAYA
Gangdise Shan
MOUNT EVEREST Straddling the Nepal-China border, the mountain is called Sagarmatha in Nepal and Qomolangma in China.
Mt. Everest (Sagarmāthā) (Qomolangma) 8850
Yarlung Zangbo (Brahmaputra)
Mapam Yumco
La'nga Co
Tangra Yumco
Ngangzê Co
Yamzho Yumco
Puma Yumco
PUNJAB
HARYANA
DELHI
UTTARANCHAL
UTTAR PRADESH
RAJASTHAN
MADHYA PRADESH
BIHAR
JHARKHAND
CHHATTISGARH
ORISSA
WEST BENGAL
SIKKIM
ASSAM
MEGHALAYA
TRIPURA
ARUNACHAL PRADESH
CHANDIGARH
CORBETT N.P.
RARA N.P.
SHEY-PHOKSUNDO N.P.
ROYAL CHITWAN N.P.
SAGARMATHA N.P.
MAKALU-BARUN N.P.
JIGME DORJI N.P.
THRUMSING LAN N.P.
ROYAL MANAS N.P.
PALAMAU N.P.
SATPURA N.P.
TROPIC OF CANCER
Nanda Devi 7817
Dhaulagiri 8167
Lipu Lekh Pass
Pêdo Pass
Gya La Pass
Rabga Pass
Bum La
Kathmandu
Pokhara
Thimphu
Dhaka
Delhi
New Delhi
Chandigarh
Dehra Dun
Lucknow
Kanpur
Agra
Jaipur
Gwalior
Bhopal
Indore
Jabalpur
Allahabad
Varanasi (Banaras)
Patna
Ranchi
Kolkata (Calcutta)
Darjiling
Gangtok
Guwahati
Shillong
Agartala
Chittagong
Khulna
Rajshahi
Jessore
Comilla
Mymensingh
Sylhet
Bareilly
Moradabad
Meerut
Aligarh
Mathura
Bharatpur
Gorakhpur
Muzaffarpur
Gaya
Bhagalpur
Dhanbad
Jamshedpur
Bilaspur
Korba
Satna
Sagar
Lalitpur
Jhansi
Saga
Zhongba
Tingri
Shigatse
Dhangadhi
Nepalganj
Biratnagar
Bay of Bengal
Haldia
Kharagpur
Medinipur
Asansol
Bankura
Ujjain
Dewas
Kota
Tonk
Sikar
Alwar
Hisar
Karnal
Ambala
Patiala
Bhatinda
Sirsa
Bhiwani

RUSSIA
MONGOLIA
NORTH KOREA
SOUTH KOREA
HEILONGJIANG
JILIN
LIAONING
HEBEI
SHANXI
SHAANXI
SHANDONG
NINGXIA HUIZU
BEIJING SHI
TIANJIN SHI
DONGBEI (MANCHURIA)
NEI MONGOL
GOBI
Da Hinggan Ling
ORHON
BULGAN
DARHAN-UUL
SELENGE
HENTIY
CENTRAL
EASTERN
SÜHBAATAR
GOVĬSÜMBER
MIDDLE GOVĬ
EAST GOVĬ
SOUTH GOVĬ
SOUTH HANGAY
BO HAI
YELLOW SEA
Korea Bay
Liaodong Wan
Mouth of the Yellow River
Demarcation Line, July 27, 1953
Great Wall
105°
108°
111°
114°
117°
120°
123°
126°
129°
48°
45°
42°
39°
36°
Ulaanbaatar (Ulan Bator)
Darhan
Erdenet
Ingettolgoy
Bulgan
Hüremt
Höshööt
Maanit
Nart
Baruunharaa
Orhontuul
Züünharaa
Tünchel
Mandal
Ihsuuj
Dund-Urt
Lün
Har Horin (Karakorum)
Hujirt
Arvayheer
Bumbat
Ongi
Sangiyn Dalay
Önjüül
Dzogsool
Amardalay
Mandalgovĭ
Rashaant
Hashaat
Sharhulsan
Doloon
Öldzeyte Suma
Üydzin
Baruunsuu
Dalandzadgad
Tsoohor
Nomgon
Hörh Uul
1763
1865
2825
Engershand
Dzuunmod
2800
Bayan
Ögöömör
Darhan
Choyr
Tsomog
Har Ayrag
Argatay
Böhöt
Buyant Ovoo
Saynshand (Buyant-Uhaa)
Öldziyt
Töhöm
1424
Dzüünbayan
Ulaan-Uul
Nüden
Hövsgöl
Agaruut
Ergel
Sulanheer
Ihbulag
Borhoyn Tal
Erenhot
Gora Burun
2519
Shibertuy
Menza
Bukukun
Mangut
Khapcheranga
Sümiyn Bulag
Dashbalbar
Övör-Ereen
Bayan-Ovoo
Onon
Bayan Uul
Naranbulag
Eg
Bulag
Hentiy
Uldz
Höövör
Herlenbayan
Tsagaanders
Choybalsan
Han Uul
Dundbürd
Berh
Idermeg
Bayan Ovoo
Öndörhushuu
Hanhöhiy
Mörön
Avraga
Öndörhaan
Kerulen
Tuul
Bayasgalant
Haylaastay
Baruun Urt
Buyant
Delgerhet
Hongor
Shireet
Havirga
Dzotol
Chonogol
Ovoot
1778
Shiliyn Bogd Uul
Dzüünbulag
Tamsagbulag
1247
Jargalant
Buyr Nuur
Herlen
Orxon
539
Zabaykal'sk
Manzhouli
Xin Barag Youqi
Xin Barag Zouqi
Chen Barag Qi
Hailar
Hailar
Yakeshi
Ewenkizu Zizhiqi
Orqohan
Mianduhe
Bugt
Bila
Zalantun
Songling
Taiping Ling
1712
Yirshi
Arxan
Chaor
855
Jalaid Qi
Ulanhot
Nungnain Sum
Dong Ujimqin Qi
Huolin Gol
Xi Ujimqin Qi
1949
1224
Abag Qi
Xilinhot
Sonid Zuoqi
Sonid Youqi
Qagan Nur
Qagan Nur
Ondor Sum
Huanggangliang
2029
Dalai Nur
Hexigten Qi
Linxi
Bairin Youqi
Bairin Zuoqi
Ar Horqin Qi
Jarud Qi
Horqin Youyi Zhongqi
Tuquan
Ongniud Qi
Xar Moron
Chifeng
Yuanbaoshan
Aohan Qi
Naiman Qi
Hure Qi
Kailu
Tongliao
Horqin Zuoyi Houqi
Horqin Zuoyi Zhongqi
Shuangliao
Kangping
Zhangwu
Faku
Liao
Tieling
Fuxin
Beipiao
Chaoyang
Xinmin
SHENYANG
Fushun
Benxi
Liaoyang
Anshan
Yingkou
Haicheng
Jinzhou
Jinxi
Xingcheng
Suizhong
Qinhuangdao
Changli
Tangshan
Leting
Fengning
Chengde
Luanping
Longhua
Kuancheng
1270
Zunhua
Yutian
Pingquan
Lingyuan
Jianping
Harqin Qi
Ningcheng
Jianchang
Kuizhuang
Luanxian
Duolun
1754
Weichang
Taibus Qi
Zhenglan Qi
Zhengxiangbai Qi
Xianghuang Qi
Huade
Kangbao
Guyuan
Shangdu
Zhangbei
Shangyi
Xinghe
Zhangjiakou
Xuanhua
Huailai
Zhuolu
2870
BEIJING (PEKING)
Miyun
Changping
Daxing
Tongxian
Jixian
Langfang
Wuqing
TIANJIN (TIENTSIN)
Hangu
Tanggu
Huanghua
Cangzhou
Baoding
Dingzhou
Dingxing
Anxin
Gaoyang
Hejian
Jinghai
Anguo
Wangdu
Shijiazhuang
Xinji
Hengshui
Dezhou
Nangong
Xingtai
Handan
Linqing
Liaocheng
Jinan
Zibo
Weifang
Tai'an
1524
Laiwu
Linyi
Rizhao
Qingdao
Yantai
Weihai
Penglai
Longkou
Huangxian
Laiyang
Jimo
Laoshan
Lianyun
Lianyungang (Xinpu)
Zaozhuang
Heze
Jining
Qufu
Kaifeng
Zhengzhou (Chengchow)
Luoyang
Sanmenxia
Lingbao
Xinxiang
Anyang
1619
Hebi
Jiaozuo
Jiyuan
Jincheng
Changzhi
Gaoping
Taiyuan
Yuci
TAIYUAN SPACE LAUNCH CENTER
Yangquan
Xinzhou
Datong
Shuozhou
Fengzhen
Jining
Hohhot
Wuchuan
2174
Baotou
2187
Huang (Yellow)
Dongsheng
Linhe
Wuhai
Zhuozi Shan
2149
Shizuishan (Dawukou)
Shizuishan
Yinchuan
Lingwu
Wuzhong
Qingtongxia
Zhongwei
Helan Shan
3556
Guyuan
Pingliang
Baiyin
Lanzhou
Tianshui
Baoji
Xi'an
Weinan
Tongchuan
Hancheng
Yan'an
Yulin
Linfen
Houma
Yuncheng
Xiaoyi
Jiexiu
Migang Shan
2942
1935
3058
1440
1156
923
1131
1845
757
1060
1397
Dandong
Sinŭiju
Ji'an
Kanggye
Manp'o
Changjin Res.
Yalu
P'yŏngyang
Namp'o
Songnim
Sariwŏn
Haeju
Kaesŏng
Wŏnsan
SEOUL
Incheon (Inch'ŏn)
Cheonan
Gunsan
Gwangju (Kwangju)
Mokpo
Haenam
Harbin
Acheng
Shangzhi
Qiqihar
Daqing
Anda
Zhaodong
Suihua
Hailun
Bei'an
Wudalianchi
Tieli
Yichun
Changchun
Jilin
Siping
Liaoyuan
Meihekou
Tonghua
Hunjiang
Dunhua
Huadian
Gongzhuling
Baicheng
Taonan
Da'an
Fuyu
Zhaoyuan
Shuangcheng
Yingcheng
Jiutai
Dalian (Dairen)
Lüshun
Wafangdian
Zhuanghe
Xiuyan
Fengcheng
Kuandian
Sunwu
Nenjiang
Longzhen
Nehe
Nemor
Gen
Nen
Dedu
Morin Dawa
Keshan
Laha
Yi'an
Arun Qi
Gannan
Fuyu
Baiquan
Nianzishan
Longjiang
Ang'angxi
Lindian
Dorbod
Wangkui
Qinggang
Suileng
Qing'an
Youhao
Cuiluan
Tailai
Zhenlai
Zhaozhou
Hulan
Bayan
Tonghe
Mulan
Binxian
Yanshou
Yuquan
Wuchang
Sanchahe
Yushu
Shulan
Qian Gorlos
Qian'an
Tongyu
Nong'an
Dehui
Heilinzi
Changling
Shuangyang
Jiaohe
Huangnihe
Songhua Hu
Yitong
Panshi
Huinan
Lishu
Dongfeng
Xifeng
Kaiyuan
Liuhe
Jingyu
Fusong
Baihe
Qingyuan
Xinbin
Linjiang
Yŏngjŏ
Tianshifu
Heishan
Beizhen
Liaozhong
Ch'osan
Gaixian
Donggou
Gushan
Xinjin
Jinzhou
Sŏnch'ŏn
Anju
Sunch'ŏn
P'yŏngsŏng
Okp'yong
Tŏkch'ŏn
Ich'ŏn
Anak
Changyŏn
Ongjin
Baengnyeongdo
Ansan
Anseong
Seosan
Ganggyeong
Gochang
Hampyeong
Gangjin
Wando
Soheuksando
Changxing Dao
Xizhong Dao
Chengshan Jiao
Sanggou Wan
Dingzi Gang
Fushan
Muping
Wendeng
Rongcheng
Shidao
Qixia
Yexian
Pingdu
Jiaozhou
Zhucheng
Jiaonan
Wulian
Juxian
Junan
Tancheng
Xinyi
Pixian
Jiawang
Weishan
Tengxian
Zouxian
Pingyi
Yinan
Yishui
Xinwen
Yiyuan
Boxing
Huantai
Guangrao
Binzhou
Kenli
Zhanhua
Wudi
Yanshan
Huimin
Dongguang
Linyi
Yucheng
Pingyin
Dongping
Juye
Dingtao
Jinxiang
Shanxian
Dangshan
Caoxian
Daming
Nanle
Fanxian
Puyang
Huaxian
Cixian
Quzhou
Wu'an
Neiqiu
Julu
Xinhe
Hunyuan
Yangyuan
Huairen
Shanyin
Yingxian
Shanyincheng
Fanshi
Daixian
Ningwu
Shenchi
Wutai
Dingxiang
Jingle
Lanxian
Xingxian
Baode
Pianguan
Pinglu
Qingshuihe
Horinger
Liangcheng
Tumd Zuoqi
Tumd Youqi
Togtoh
Shiguaigou
Guyang
Darhan Muminggan Lianheqi
Bayan Obo
Siziwang Qi
Qahar Youyi Zhongqi
Qahar Youyi Houqi
Zhuozi
Urad Zhongqi
Urad Houqi
Urad Qianqi
Hanggin Houqi
Wuyuan
Dengkou
Hails
Adun Gol
Jartai
Bayan Mod
Wuda
Lasengmiao
Otog Qi
Hanggin Qi
Jungar Qi
Ejin Horo Qi
Uxin Qi
Hengshan
Jingbian
Dingbian
Yanchi
Alxa Zuoqi
Pingluo
Huangqiquiao
Taole
Xincheng
Yongning
Zhongning
Dongzhen
Tongxin
Haiyuan
Xiji
Longde
Jingyuan
Huining
Dingxi
Tongwei
Qin'an
Gangu
Longxi
Zhuanglang
Lingtai
Qingyang
Huachi
Heshui
Zhenyuan
Chongxin
Qianyang
Longxian
Qianxian
Binxian
Xunyi
Yaoxian
Chunhua
Fuping
Pucheng
Sanyuan
Lintong
Huangling
Yijun
Yichuan
Jixian
Xiangning
Ganquan
Fuxian
Yanchang
Yanchuan
Qingjian
Zichang
Ansai
Zhidan
Wuqi
Suide
Zizhou
Mizhi
Jiaxian
Shenmu
Fugu
Wubu
Linxian
Fenyang
Jiaokou
Shilou
Puxian
Hongtong
Huoxian
Fenxi
Anze
Qinxian
Pingyao
Taigu
Qingxu
Loufan
Fangshan
Yuxian
Jingxing
Zhangzi
Quwo
Xinjiang
Yuanqu
Anyi
Dali
Pinglu
Mianchi
Mixian
Changzheng
Jingtai
Gaolan
Yuzhong
Lixian
Xihe
Dangchang
Wugong
Caijiapo
Taibai
Fen
Luo
Yellow
Sanggan
Hutuo
Luan

EASTERN CHINA
ALBERS CONIC EQUAL-AREA PROJECTION
SCALE 1:8,000,000
0 KILOMETERS 120 160 200
0 MILES 40 80 120 160 200
Longitude East 114° of Greenwich
TAIWAN
The People's Republic of China claims Taiwan as its 23rd province. Taiwan's government (Republic of China) maintains that there are two political entities. The islands of Matsu, Pescadores, Pratas, and Quemoy are administered by Taiwan.
EAST CHINA SEA
PHILIPPINE SEA
SOUTH CHINA SEA
TROPIC OF CANCER
Gulf of Tonkin
JAPAN
Ryukyu Islands (Nansei Shotō)
SHANGHAI
SHANGHAI SHI
ANHUI
HENAN
HUBEI
HUNAN
JIANGXI
ZHEJIANG
FUJIAN
GUANGDONG
GUANGXI ZHUANGZU
GUIZHOU
SICHUAN
CHONGQING SHI
GANSU
HAINAN
VIETNAM
PHILIPPINES
TAIWAN
WUHAN
CHONGQING
GUANGZHOU (CANTON)
HONG KONG
HONG KONG (XIANGGANG) S.A.R.
Macau
MACAU (AOMEN) S.A.R.
SHENZHEN
T'aipei (Taibei)
Hanoi
Nanning
Changsha
Nanchang
Hangzhou
Fuzhou
Guiyang
Hefei
Nanjing
Haikou
Wuyi Shan
Three Gorges Dam
Taiwan Strait
Bashi Channel
Balintang Channel
Pratas Reef
Formosa Reefs
Leizhou Wan
Dao Bach Long Vi (Nightingale Island) Vietnam

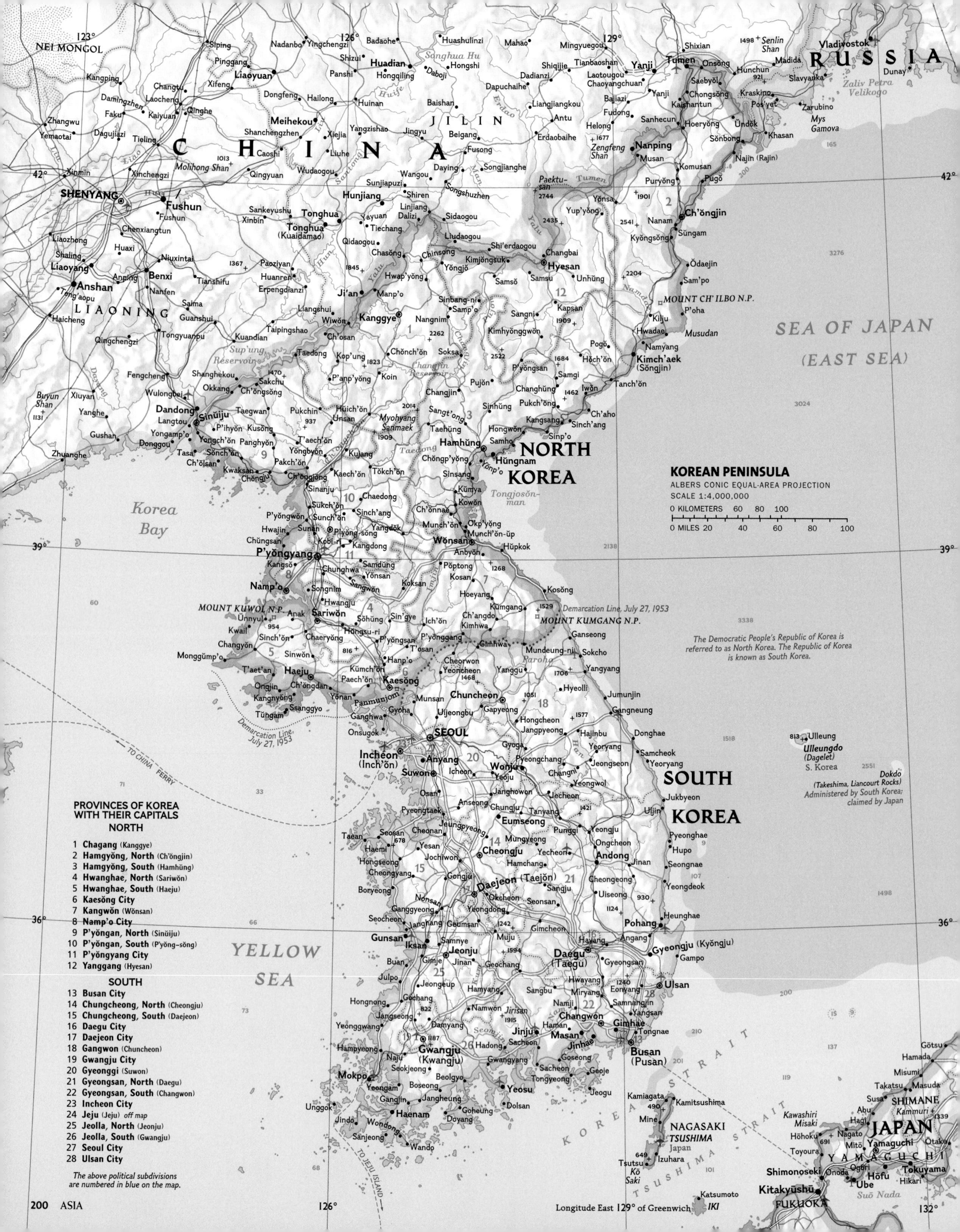
KOREAN PENINSULA
ALBERS CONIC EQUAL-AREA PROJECTION
SCALE 1:4,000,000
0 KILOMETERS 20 40 60 80 100
0 MILES 20 40 60 80 100
PROVINCES OF KOREA WITH THEIR CAPITALS
NORTH
1 Chagang (Kanggye)
2 Hamgyŏng, North (Ch'ŏngjin)
3 Hamgyŏng, South (Hamhŭng)
4 Hwanghae, North (Sariwŏn)
5 Hwanghae, South (Haeju)
6 Kaesŏng City
7 Kangwŏn (Wŏnsan)
8 Namp'o City
9 P'yŏngan, North (Sinŭiju)
10 P'yŏngan, South (P'yŏng-sŏng)
11 P'yŏngyang City
12 Yanggang (Hyesan)
SOUTH
13 Busan City
14 Chungcheong, North (Cheongju)
15 Chungcheong, South (Daejeon)
16 Daegu City
17 Daejeon City
18 Gangwon (Chuncheon)
19 Gwangju City
20 Gyeonggi (Suwon)
21 Gyeongsan, North (Daegu)
22 Gyeongsan, South (Changwon)
23 Incheon City
24 Jeju (Jeju) off map
25 Jeolla, North (Jeonju)
26 Jeolla, South (Gwangju)
27 Seoul City
28 Ulsan City
The above political subdivisions are numbered in blue on the map.
The Democratic People's Republic of Korea is referred to as North Korea. The Republic of Korea is known as South Korea.
CHINA
RUSSIA
JAPAN
NORTH KOREA
SOUTH KOREA
JILIN
LIAONING
NEI MONGOL
SEA OF JAPAN (EAST SEA)
YELLOW SEA
Korea Bay
KOREA STRAIT
TSUSHIMA STRAIT
Demarcation Line, July 27, 1953
MOUNT KUMGANG N.P.
MOUNT KUWOL N.P.
MOUNT CH'ILBO N.P.
Ulleungdo (Dagelet) S. Korea
Dokdo (Takeshima, Liancourt Rocks) Administered by South Korea; claimed by Japan
TO CHINA FERRY
TO JEJU ISLAND
SHENYANG
P'yŏngyang
SEOUL
Incheon (Inch'ŏn)
Busan (Pusan)
Daegu (Taegu)
Daejeon (Taejŏn)
Gwangju (Kwangju)
Ulsan
Hamhŭng
Wŏnsan
Ch'ŏngjin
Kaesŏng
Panmunjom
Vladivostok
Kitakyūshū
FUKUOKA
NAGASAKI
TSUSHIMA
SHIMANE
YAMAGUCHI
123°
126°
129°
132°
42°
39°
36°
Longitude East 129° of Greenwich

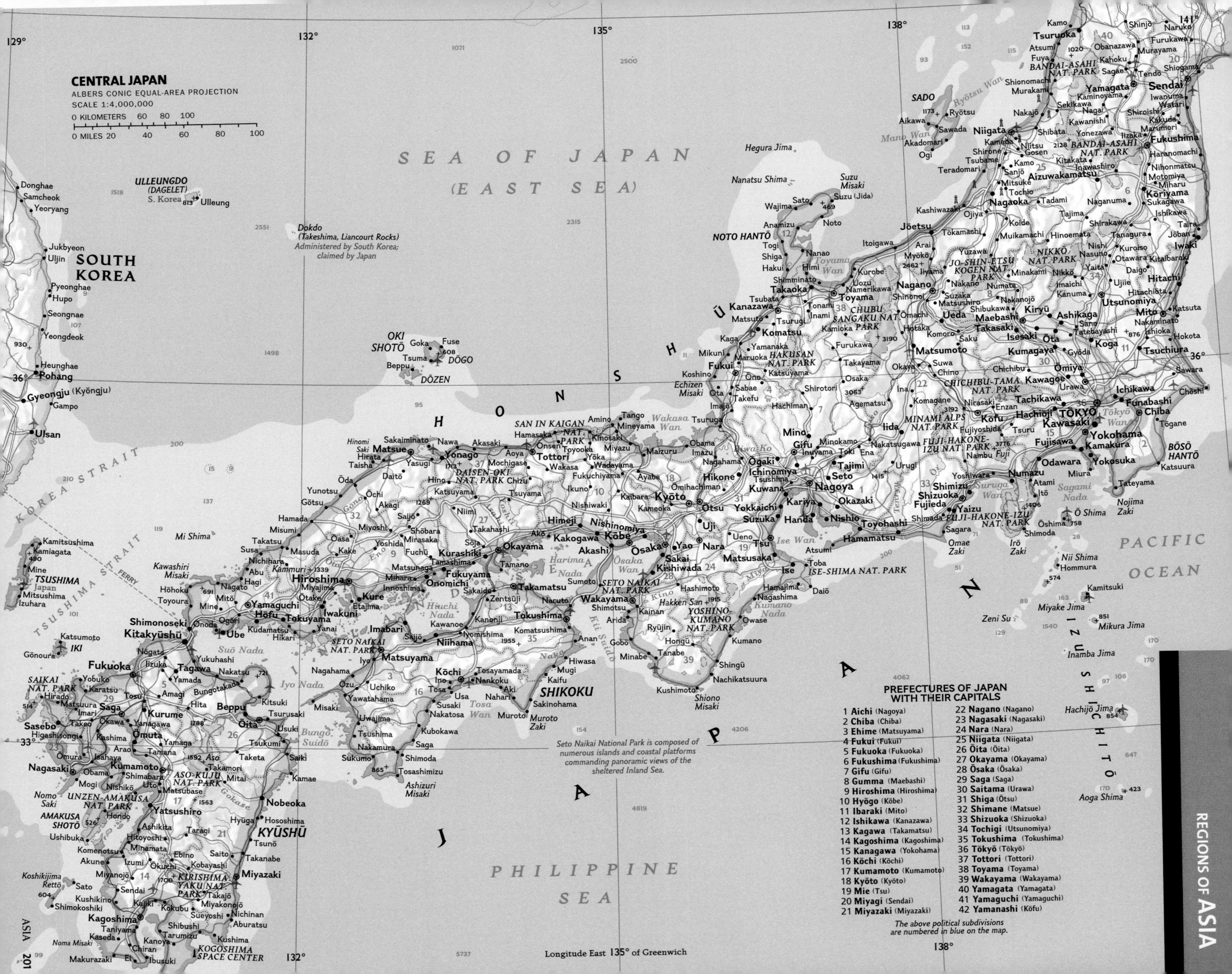

CENTRAL JAPAN
ALBERS CONIC EQUAL-AREA PROJECTION
SCALE 1:4,000,000
0 KILOMETERS 60 80 100
0 MILES 20 40 60 80 100
SEA OF JAPAN
(EAST SEA)
PACIFIC OCEAN
PHILIPPINE SEA
JAPAN
HONSHŪ
SHIKOKU
KYŪSHŪ
SOUTH KOREA
KOREA STRAIT
TSUSHIMA STRAIT
ULLEUNGDO (DAGELET) S. Korea
Dokdo (Takeshima, Liancourt Rocks) Administered by South Korea; claimed by Japan
OKI SHOTŌ
NOTO HANTŌ
IZU SHICHITŌ
Seto Naikai National Park is composed of numerous islands and coastal platforms commanding panoramic views of the sheltered Inland Sea.
Longitude East 135° of Greenwich
Tōkyō
Ōsaka
Kyōto
Nagoya
Yokohama
Kōbe
Hiroshima
Fukuoka
Kitakyūshū
Sendai
Niigata
Kagoshima
PREFECTURES OF JAPAN WITH THEIR CAPITALS
1 Aichi (Nagoya)
2 Chiba (Chiba)
3 Ehime (Matsuyama)
4 Fukui (Fukui)
5 Fukuoka (Fukuoka)
6 Fukushima (Fukushima)
7 Gifu (Gifu)
8 Gumma (Maebashi)
9 Hiroshima (Hiroshima)
10 Hyōgo (Kōbe)
11 Ibaraki (Mito)
12 Ishikawa (Kanazawa)
13 Kagawa (Takamatsu)
14 Kagoshima (Kagoshima)
15 Kanagawa (Yokohama)
16 Kōchi (Kōchi)
17 Kumamoto (Kumamoto)
18 Kyōto (Kyōto)
19 Mie (Tsu)
20 Miyagi (Sendai)
21 Miyazaki (Miyazaki)
22 Nagano (Nagano)
23 Nagasaki (Nagasaki)
24 Nara (Nara)
25 Niigata (Niigata)
26 Ōita (Ōita)
27 Okayama (Okayama)
28 Ōsaka (Ōsaka)
29 Saga (Saga)
30 Saitama (Urawa)
31 Shiga (Ōtsu)
32 Shimane (Matsue)
33 Shizuoka (Shizuoka)
34 Tochigi (Utsunomiya)
35 Tokushima (Tokushima)
36 Tōkyō (Tōkyō)
37 Tottori (Tottori)
38 Toyama (Toyama)
39 Wakayama (Wakayama)
40 Yamagata (Yamagata)
41 Yamaguchi (Yamaguchi)
42 Yamanashi (Kōfu)
The above political subdivisions are numbered in blue on the map.

INDOCHINA
ALBERS CONIC EQUAL-AREA PROJECTION
SCALE 1:8,000,000
0 KILOMETERS 120 160 200
0 MILES 40 80 120 160 200
Longitude East 105° of Greenwich
Indochina refers historically to French Indochina, which comprised Vietnam, Laos, and Cambodia. Physical geographers extend the region to include Thailand, Myanmar (Burma), and peninsular Malaysia.
TROPIC OF CANCER
CHINA
YUNNAN
GUANGXI ZHUANGZU
HAINAN
MYANMAR (BURMA)
LAOS
THAILAND
CAMBODIA
VIETNAM
MALAYSIA
INDONESIA
ANDAMAN SEA
GULF OF THAILAND
SOUTH CHINA SEA
Gulf of Tonkin
Bay of Bengal
Strait of Malacca
Mergui Archipelago
MALAY PENINSULA
Isthmus of Kra
Dangrek Range
Dawna Range
Three Pagodas Pass
Plain of Jars
Tonle Sap
Mekong
Hainan
Mandalay
Yangon (Rangoon)
Bago
Pathein
Kunming
Kaiyuan
Gejiu
Nanning
Beihai
Zhanjiang
Haikou
Sanya
Hanoi
Haiphong
Nam Dinh
Vinh
Hue
Da Nang
Qui Nhon
Nha Trang
Da Lat
Bien Hoa
Ho Chi Minh City (Saigon)
My Tho
Can Tho
Vung Tau
Rach Gia
Bac Lieu
Viangchan (Vientiane)
Louangphrabang
Savannakhet
Chiang Mai
Chiang Rai
Nakhon Sawan
Nakhon Ratchasima (Khorat)
Khon Kaen
Udon Thani (Udorn)
Ubon Ratchathani
Saraburi
Pathum Thani
Nonthaburi
KRUNG THEP (BANGKOK)
Samut Prakan
Chon Buri
Rayong
Battambang
Siem Reap
Angkor
Phnom Penh
Surat Thani (Ban Don)
Nakhon Si Thammarat
Songkhla
Phuket
Ko Samui
Alor Setar
Sungai Petani
George Town
Kota Baharu
Kuala Terengganu
Banda Aceh
Con Son

PHILIPPINES
ALBERS CONIC EQUAL-AREA PROJECTION
SCALE 1:7,000,000
0 KILOMETERS 100 150 200
0 MILES 50 100 150 200
SPRATLY ISLANDS
The scattered islands and reefs called the Spratly Islands are claimed by Brunei, China, Malaysia, the Philippines, Taiwan, and Vietnam. The Spratlys possess rich fishing grounds and potential oil.
PHILIPPINES
SOUTH CHINA SEA
PHILIPPINE SEA
Sulu Sea
Celebes Sea
SPRATLY ISLANDS
Batan Islands
Basco
Luzon Strait
Balintang Channel
Babuyan Islands
Babuyan Channel
Vereker Banks
Tungsha Tao (Pratas I.)
Stewart Seamount
Macclesfield Banks
Scarborough Shoal
Dreyer Banks
Benham Seamount
LUZON
Mayraira Point
Cape Bojeador
Bangui
Claveria
Santa Ana
Aparri
Iligan Point
Laoag
San Nicolas
Batac
Espiritu
Bacarra
Abulug
Kabugao
Buguey
Valley Head
Mount Sicapoo
Cabugao
Bangued
Vigan
Narvacan
Tuguegarao
Baguio Point
Divilacan Bay
Aubarede Point
Candon
Santa Cruz
Bangar
Bacnotan
San Fernando
Lubuagan
Bontoc
Ilagan
Roxas
Palanan
NORTHERN SIERRA MADRE NATIONAL PARK
Mount Pulog
Bayombong
Sierra Madre
Lingayen Gulf
Cape Bolinao
Baguio
Dagupan
Lingayen
San Carlos
Santa Cruz
Masinloc
Palauig
Tarlac
San Jose
Cuyapo
Victoria
Baler
Casiguran
Cape San Ildefonso
Cape Encanto
Cabanatuan
Gapan
Angeles
San Fernando
San Narciso
Olongapo
Malolos
Quezon City
Manila
Cavite
Bataan Peninsula
Corregidor
Manila Bay
Lag. de Bay
Polillo Islands
Lamon Bay
Jose Panganiban
Paracale
Daet
San Miguel Bay
San Pablo
Santa Cruz
Lucena
Batangas
Lipa
Tayabas Bay
Ragay Gulf
Naga
Mt. Isarog
Mayon Volcano
Iriga
Ligao
Legazpi
Pandan
Yog Point
Panganiban (Payo)
Catanduanes
Virac
Lubang Island
Boac
Marinduque
Mulanay
Paluan
Calapan
Mount Halcon
Pola
Mamburao
Santa Cruz
Sablayan
Mount Baco
MINDORO
Roxas
San Jose
Mindoro Strait
Tablas Strait
Burias
Sibuyan
Sorsogon
Gubat
Magallanes
Bulan
Ticao
Allen
Catarman
Palapag
SAMAR
Oras
Romblon
Sibuyan
Tablas
Santa Fe
Sibuyan Sea
Masbate
Masbate
Cataingan
Calbayog
Busuanga
Bintuan
Culion
Calamian Group
Nabas
Pandan
Kalibo
Roxas
Wright
Sulat
Catbalogan
Calbiga
Visayan Sea
Culasi
Mount Nangtud
PANAY
Ajuy
Carigara
Basey
General MacArthur
Guiuan
Tacloban
Leyte Gulf
El Nido
Malampaya Sound
Cuyo Islands
Cuyo
Taytay
Imuruan Bay
Cadiz
Bogo
Borbon
Ormoc
LEYTE
Alimodian
Iloilo
San Jose
Bacolod
Dao
CEBU
Cebu
Baybay
Sogod
Loreto
Dinagat
La Carlota
Isabela
San Carlos
NEGROS
Saint Bernard
Roxas
Cleopatra Needle
Ulugan Bay
Panay Gulf
BOHOL
Siargao
Dapa
Puerto Princesa
PALAWAN
Cauayan
Sipalay
Hinoba-an
Tanjay
Guindulman
Tagbilaran
Surigao
Placer
Aborlan
Inagauan
Birong
Cagayan Islands
Bayawan
Oslob
Dumaguete
Bohol Sea
L. Mainit
Mambajao
Mt. Hilonghilong
Lanuza
Quezon
Aboabo
Malabuñgan
Siquijor
Siaton
Zamboanguita
Buenavista
Salay
Butuan
Bonobono
Brooke's Point
Tubbataha Reefs
Gingoog
Lianga
Canipaan
Cape Buliluyan
Rio Tuba
Dipolog
Baliangao
Oroquieta
Cagayan de Oro
Hinatuan
Manukan
Iligan Bay
Iligan
Bislig
Sindangan
Liloy
Ozamis
Tubod
Marawi
Malaybalay
Lingig
Cateel
Lake Lanao
MINDANAO
Balabac
Balabac
Balabac Strait
Pagadian
Compostela
Siocon
Kabasalan
Alicia
Illana Bay
Kibawe
Baganga
Tagum
Caraga
Margosatubig
Malabang
Carmen
Maco
Sibuco
Sibuguey Bay
Moro Gulf
Cotabato
Davao
Babak
Manay
Zamboanga
Datu Piang
Mount Apo
Lupon
Mati
Basilan Strait
Digos
Padada
Isabela
Lamitan
Basilan
Buluan
Isulan
Lebak
Davao Gulf
Koronadal
Palimbang
Tupi
General Santos
Cape San Agustin
Kiamba
Glan
Jose Abad Santos
Sarangani Bay
Tinaca Point
Sarangani Islands
Miangas (Palmas)
INDONESIA
Kepulauan Nanusa
Kepulauan Karakaralong
Reed Tablemount
Lys Shoal
Loaita Bank
Tizard Bank
Union Reefs
Brown Bank
Seahorse Shoal
Carnatic Reef
Sabina Shoal
Commodore Reef
Investigator Shoal
Banggi
Cagayan Sulu I.
Sikuati
Kudat
Senaja
Kota Belud
Bandau
Tandik
Tanjong Sugut
KINABALU PARK
Kinabalu
Tuaran
Labuk Bay
Sugut
Kota Kinabalu
Ranau
Sandakan
Tambunan
CROCKER RANGE N.P.
MALAYSIA
Beaufort
Bingkor
Pintasan
Lamag
Sukau
Melalap
Lintang
Brunei Bay
Weston
Pinangah
SABAH
Lahad Datu
Bandar Seri Begawan
BRUNEI
Padas
Darvel Bay
Pangutaran
Pangutaran Group
Jolo
Jolo
Parang
Luuk
Tapul
Siasi
Tawi Tawi
Sulu Archipelago
Sibutu Passage
Bongao
Longitude East 123° of Greenwich
117°
120°
123°
126°
21°
18°
15°
12°
9°
6°

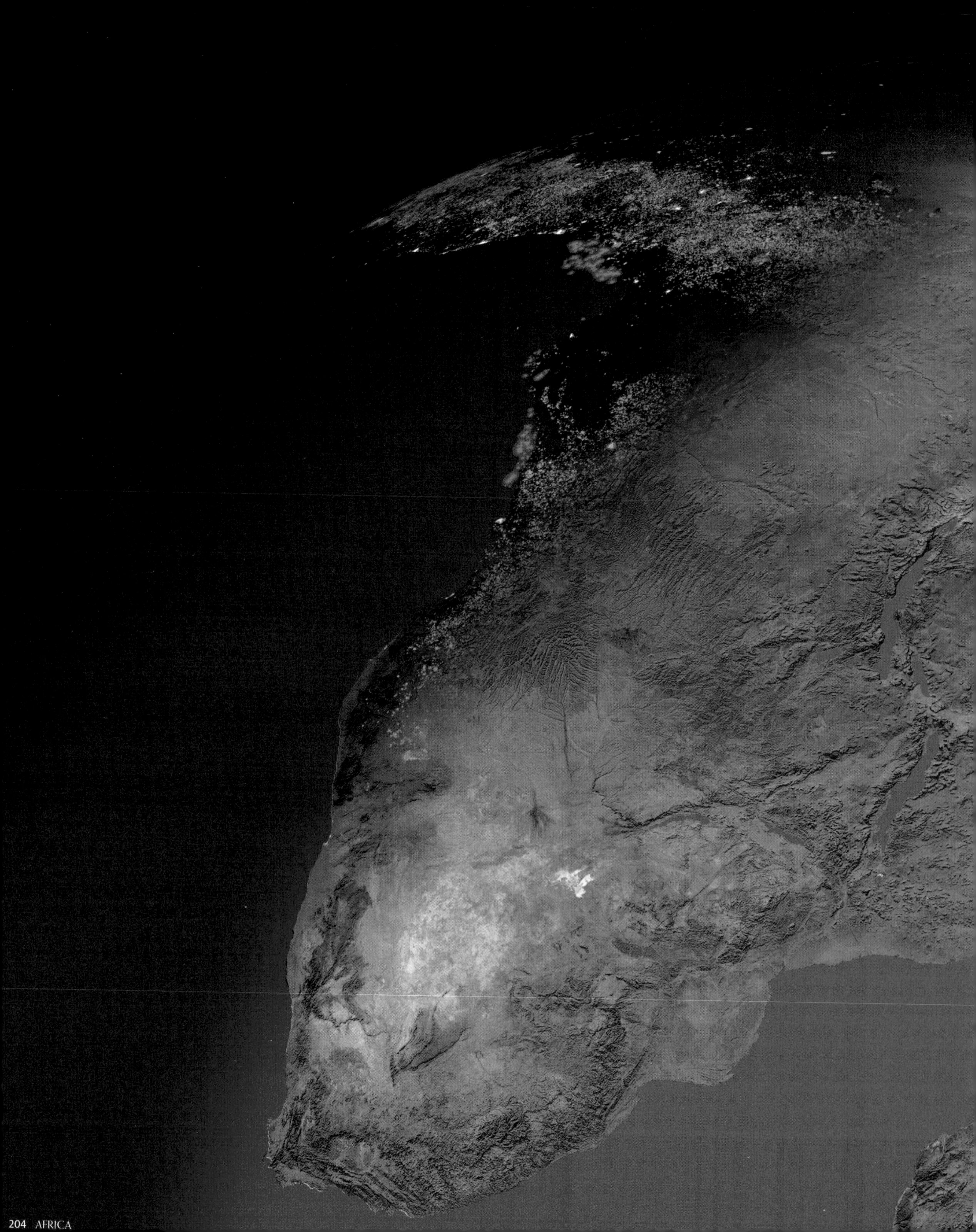

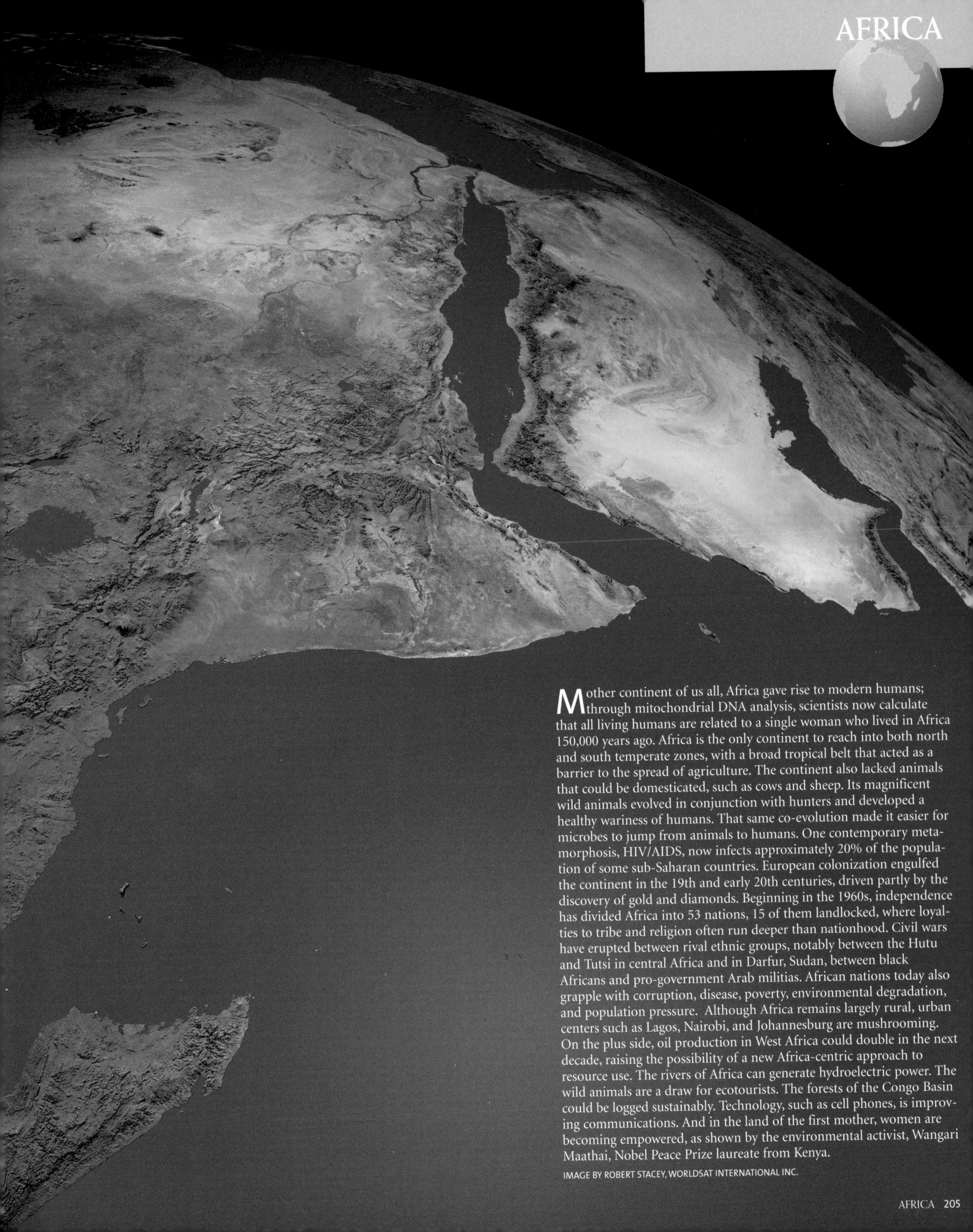

Mother continent of us all, Africa gave rise to modern humans; through mitochondrial DNA analysis, scientists now calculate that all living humans are related to a single woman who lived in Africa 150,000 years ago. Africa is the only continent to reach into both north and south temperate zones, with a broad tropical belt that acted as a barrier to the spread of agriculture. The continent also lacked animals that could be domesticated, such as cows and sheep. Its magnificent wild animals evolved in conjunction with hunters and developed a healthy wariness of humans. That same co-evolution made it easier for microbes to jump from animals to humans. One contemporary metamorphosis, HIV/AIDS, now infects approximately 20% of the population of some sub-Saharan countries. European colonization engulfed the continent in the 19th and early 20th centuries, driven partly by the discovery of gold and diamonds. Beginning in the 1960s, independence has divided Africa into 53 nations, 15 of them landlocked, where loyalties to tribe and religion often run deeper than nationhood. Civil wars have erupted between rival ethnic groups, notably between the Hutu and Tutsi in central Africa and in Darfur, Sudan, between black Africans and pro-government Arab militias. African nations today also grapple with corruption, disease, poverty, environmental degradation, and population pressure. Although Africa remains largely rural, urban centers such as Lagos, Nairobi, and Johannesburg are mushrooming. On the plus side, oil production in West Africa could double in the next decade, raising the possibility of a new Africa-centric approach to resource use. The rivers of Africa can generate hydroelectric power. The wild animals are a draw for ecotourists. The forests of the Congo Basin could be logged sustainably. Technology, such as cell phones, is improving communications. And in the land of the first mother, women are becoming empowered, as shown by the environmental activist, Wangari Maathai, Nobel Peace Prize laureate from Kenya.

IMAGE BY ROBERT STACEY, WORLDSAT INTERNATIONAL INC.

ATLANTIC OCEAN
Azores (Açores)
Bay of Biscay
Cabo Fisterra
FRANCE
Lyon
Marseille
Bern
SWITZ.
LIECH.
AUST.
GER.
CZECH. REP.
(Pressburg) Bratislava
SLOVAKIA
Wien (Vienna)
Budapest
HUNGARY
SLOVENIA
Ljubljana
Zagreb
CROATIA
BOSN. & HERZG.
Sarajevo
SERB.
Beograd (Belgrade)
ROM.
București (Bucharest)
BULGARIA
Sofiya (Sofia)
MOLD.
Chișinău
UKRAINE
Carpathian Mts.
Danube
Sea of Azov
CRIMEA
Black Sea
RUSSIA
Caspian Sea
KAZ.
UZB.
Caucasus Mts.
GEORGIA
Tbilisi (Tiflis)
ARM.
AZERB.
Naxçivan
TURK.
Pyrenees
ANDORRA
MONACO
SAN MARINO
Corsica
VATICAN CITY
Roma (Rome)
ITALY
Adriatic Sea
MONT.
Podgorica
Skopje
MACED.
(Tirana) Tiranë
ALBAN.
2917
GREECE
Athína (Athens)
Aegean Sea
Peloponnesus
İstanbul (Constantinople)
Bursa
Ankara (Angora)
TURKEY
İzmir (Smyrna)
Konya
Adana
Lake Van
Lake Urmia
Elburz Mts.
Tehrān
IRAN
Eşfahān (Isfahan)
Shīrāz
PORTUGAL
(Lisbon) Lisboa
Madrid
SPAIN
Barcelona
Sardinia
Balearic Islands
Cabo de São Vicente
Sicily
3315 Etna
MALTA Valletta
Mediterranean Sea
Strait of Gibraltar
Gibraltar
Alger (Algiers)
Tunis
Crete
CYPRUS
N. CYPRUS
Lefkosia (Lefkoşa, Nicosia)
Halab (Aleppo)
SYRIA
Beyrouth (Beirut)
Dimashq (Damascus)
LEBANON
ISRAEL
Jerusalem
'Ammān
JORDAN
Baghdād
IRAQ
Tigris
Madeira Islands
Rabat
Casablanca
ATLAS MOUNTAINS
MOROCCO
4165 Jebel Toubkal
TUNISIA
Tarābulus (Tripoli)
968
Gulf of Sidra
TRIPOLITANIA
CYRENAICA
El Iskandarîya (Alexandria)
El Qâhira (Cairo)
Suez Canal
SINAI
2285
KUWAIT
Al Kuwayt (Kuwait)
Persian Gulf
Canary Islands (Islas Canarias)
3718
Cap Boujdour
Grand Erg Occidental
Grand Erg Oriental
Hamada de Tinrhert
ALGERIA
LIBYA
FEZZAN
Libyan Desert
Western Desert
EGYPT
Eastern Desert
Nile
133
HEJAZ
SAUDI ARABIA
NAJD
Al Manāmah (Manama)
BAHRAIN
QATAR
Ad Dawhah (Doha)
Ar Riyāḑ (Riyadh)
WESTERN SAHARA
TROPIC OF CANCER
Erg Iguidi
Erg Chech
SAHARA
El Djouf
Ahaggar (Hoggar)
Jebel 'Uweinat (Al 'Uwaynat)
654
1893
Lake Nasser
Red Sea
1419
Nubian Desert
Jeddah
Al Hadīdah (meteorite craters)
Ar Rub' al Khālī (Empty Quarter)
Cap Blanc
Cap Timiris (Mirik)
MAURITANIA
Nouakchott
Ténéré
Tibesti (Tibesti Mountains)
3415 Emi Koussi
BORKOU
1310 Ennedi
Aïr (Aïr Massif)
MALI
SAHEL
NIGER
872
YEMEN
Şan'ā'
3760
ERITREA
Asmara
-166
Sénégal
Dakar
SENEGAL
Niger
Omdurman
Khartoum
Blue Nile
Banjul
GAMBIA
GUINEA-BISSAU
Bissau
952
Bamako
Niamey
CHAD
Lake Chad
Jebel Marra 3088
SUDAN
4231
DJIBOUTI
Djibouti
-156 (-512 ft)
Gulf of Aden
Lowest point in Africa
2408
Ouagadougou
BURKINA FASO
N'Djamena
1613
Lake Tana
GUINEA
Conakry
Freetown
SIERRA LEONE
BENIN
NIGERIA
Abuja
TOGO
GHANA
CÔTE D'IVOIRE (IVORY COAST)
Yamoussoukro
1752
Monrovia
LIBERIA
Abidjan
Lomé
Accra
Lagos
Porto-Novo
Cotonou
1960
CENTRAL AFRICAN REPUBLIC
Ādīs Ābeba (Addis Ababa)
ETHIOPIA
Ogadēn
White Nile
Cape Palmas
Cape Three Points
Gulf of Guinea
Malabo
CAMEROON
Yaoundé
Bangui
Ubangi
Bomu
Lotagipi Swamp
Lake Turkana (Lake Rudolf)
SOMALIA
Juba
Muqdisho (Mogadishu)
EQ. GUINEA
Príncipe
SAO TOME AND PRINCIPE
São Tomé
EQUATOR
Annobón
Libreville
GABON
CONGO
Congo
CONGO BASIN
DEMOCRATIC REPUBLIC OF THE CONGO
UGANDA
Kampala
5109
KENYA
5199 Mt. Kenya
Nairobi
Lake Victoria
RWANDA
Kigali
BURUNDI
Bujumbura
Sources of the Nile
Kilimanjaro
5895 (19340 ft)
Highest point in Africa
1015
Brazzaville
Kinshasa (Léopoldville)
Meridian of Greenwich (London)
CABINDA Angola
Mitumba Mountains
Lake Tanganyika
Dodoma
Dar es Salaam
TANZANIA
SEYCHELLES
Aldabra Islands
Farquhar Group
Cosmoledo Group
Luanda
KATANGA PLATEAU
Source of the Congo
Lake Malawi (Lake Nyasa)
Cabo Delgado
Moroni
Glorioso Is.
COMOROS
Cap d'Ambre
Mayotte
2620
ANGOLA
MALAWI
Lilongwe
2419
3000
ZAMBIA
Lusaka
Massif du Tsaratanana
2876
Zambezi
Lake Kariba
Harare
ZIMBABWE
MOZAMBIQUE
Mozambique Channel
MADAGASCAR
Antananarivo
2642
Cape Fria
NAMIBIA
Okavango Delta
Brandberg 2573
Palgrave Point
Windhoek
NAMIB DESERT
BOTSWANA
KALAHARI DESERT
TROPIC OF CAPRICORN
Gaborone
2128
Pretoria (Tshwane)
Johannesburg
Maputo
Mbabane
SWAZILAND
Lobamba
Ponta da Barra
Cap Sainte Marie
1957
SOUTH AFRICA
2202
Orange (Oranje)
Bloemfontein
Maseru
LESOTHO
Drakensberg
Cape Saint Lucia
AZIMUTHAL EQUIDISTANT PROJECTION
SCALE 1:37,000,000
0 KILOMETERS 600 800 1000
0 MILES 200 400 600 800 1000
INDIAN OCEAN
Cape Columbine
Cape Town
Cape of Good Hope
Cape Agulhas
Tristan da Cunha Group
Longitude East 30° of Greenwich

ATLANTIC OCEAN
Azores (Açores) Portugal
Ponta Delgada
FRANCE
Paris
Rennes
La Rochelle
Bordeaux
Bay of Biscay
A Coruña
Cabo Fisterra
Vigo
Ourense
Bilbao
Lyon
Marseille
MONACO
ANDORRA
Valladolid
Madrid
Barcelona
PORTUGAL
Coimbra
Lisboa (Lisbon)
Setúbal
Cabo de São Vicente
SPAIN
Córdoba
Murcia
Palma
Balearic Is. Sp.
Málaga
Cartagena
Cádiz
Strait of Gibraltar
GIBRALTAR U.K.
Corsica Fr.
Ajaccio
Sardinia Italy
Cagliari
GER.
Wien (Vienna)
CZECH REP.
SLOVAKIA
Bratislava (Pressburg)
Budapest
HUNGARY
AUST.
LIECH.
SWITZ.
Bern
Milano (Milan)
SLOV.
Ljubljana
Zagreb
CROATIA
BOSN. & HERZG.
Sarajevo
SAN MARINO
Pisa
ITALY
VATICAN CITY
Roma (Rome)
Adriatic Sea
Napoli (Naples)
MONT.
Podgorica
SERB.
Beograd (Belgrade)
ROM.
București (Bucharest)
Constanța
Iași
MOLD.
Chișinău
UKR.
Yalta
Black Sea
BULGARIA
Sofiya (Sofia)
MACED.
Skopje
ALBAN.
Tiranë (Tirana)
GREECE
Athína (Athens)
Aegean Sea
Crete
Iráklio
Sicily
Catania
Valletta
MALTA
ISTANBUL (CONSTANTINOPLE)
İzmit
Bursa
Samsun
Sivas
Ankara (Angora)
TURKEY
Konya
Antalya
Adana
Trabzon
RUSSIA
GEORGIA
T'bilisi (Tiflis)
ARM.
AZERB.
Naxçıvan
Caspian Sea
Türkmenbaşy
Balkanabat
Aşgabat (Ashgabat)
Ardabīl
Tabrīz
Rasht
Orūmīyeh
Elburz
TEHRĀN
Qazvīn
Kirkūk
Hamadān
Qom
IRAN
Eşfahān (Isfahan)
Ḩalab (Aleppo)
SYRIA
Idlib
Euphrates
N. CYPRUS
Lefkosia (Lefkoşa, Nicosia)
CYPRUS
Beyrouth (Beirut)
LEBANON
Dimashq (Damascus)
ISRAEL
'Ammān
Jerusalem
JORDAN
IRAQ
Baghdād
An Najaf
Al Başrah (Basra)
Shīrāz
KUWAIT
Al Kuwayt (Kuwait)
Persian Gulf
Al Jawf
NAJD
Al Manāmah (Manama)
BAHRAIN
QATAR
Ad Dawhah (Doha)
Ar Riyāḑ (Riyadh)
U.A.E.
Al Madīnah
Al Ḩillah
SAUDI ARABIA
Aţ Ţā'if
Jeddah
As Sulayyil
Mediterranean Sea
Funchal
Ilhas Desertas
Madeira Islands Portugal
Casablanca
Rabat
ATLAS MTS.
Safi
Essaouira
MOROCCO
Marrakech
Agadir
Alger (Algiers)
Oran
Annaba
Tunis
Sfax
Gabès
TUNISIA
Djelfa
Laghouat
Béchar
Ghardaïa
Ouargla
Beni Abbès
El Goléa
Ţarābulus (Tripoli)
Mişrātah
Surt
Banghāzī (Benghazi)
Shaḩḩāt
Ajdābiyā
El Iskandarîya (Alexandria)
El Gîza
EL QÂHIRA (CAIRO)
Suez Canal
SINAI
Elat
Sīwa
Canary Islands (Islas Canarias) Spain
Las Palmas
Tarfaya
Goulimine
Tabelbala
Tindouf
Cap Boujdour
Al Farciya
WESTERN SAHARA Morocco
Bir Mogreïn
TROPIC OF CANCER
Ad Dakhla
Cap Barbas
Nouadhibou
Techla
Fdérik
Timimoun
Ghadāmis
I-n-Amenas
Reggane
Aoulef
I-n-Salah
ALGERIA
Arak
Mount Tahat
Illizi
Ghāt
Djanet
Tamanrasset
Silet
Taoudenni
SAHARA
Hūn
Sawkanah
Umm al 'Abīd
LIBYA
Marzūq
Tmassah
Awjilah
CYRENAICA
Al Jawf
EGYPT
Asyūt
Gemsa
Qena
El Khârga
Aswân
Lake Nasser
Nile
Jebel 'Uweinat (Al 'Uwaynat)
Yanbu' al Baḩr
Halayeb
Red Sea
Wadi Halfa
Boundary claimed by Sudan
AOZOU STRIP
Aozou
Toummo
Djado
MAURITANIA
Cap Timiris (Mirik)
Ouadane
Nouamrhar
Akjoujt
Tidjikdja
Tessalit
Araouane
Boû Djébéha
Ti-n-Zaouâtene
MALI
Nouakchott
St.-Louis
Rosso
Kaédi
Kiffa
Néma
Tombouctou
Gao
Niger
Nioro du Sahel
Nara
Dakar
SENEGAL
Banjul
GAMBIA
Kayes
Ziguinchor
Bissau
Kédougou
Bamako
Koulikoro
Ségou
Mopti
GUINEA-BISSAU
Labé
GUINEA
Boké
Conakry
Kankan
Sikasso
BURKINA FASO
Ouagadougou
Niamey
Kabala
Freetown
SIERRA LEONE
Nzérékoré
Korhogo
CÔTE D'IVOIRE (IVORY COAST)
Bawku
Tamale
GHANA
TOGO
BENIN
Kandi
Parakou
Monrovia
LIBERIA
Yamoussoukro
Kumasi
Lomé
Accra
Abidjan
Cotonou
Porto-Novo
Cape Palmas
Gulf of Guinea
Aneÿ
Bilma
Aïr (Aïr Massif)
NIGER
Ménaka
Ingal
Agadez
Tahoua
Tânout
Maradi
Katsina
Nguigmi
Lake Chad
Gusau
Zaria
Kano
Kaduna
NIGERIA
Abuja
Makurdi
Idah
Enugu
LAGOS
Port Harcourt
BORKOU
Ounianga Kébir
Faya-Largeau
Fada
CHAD
N'Djamena
Maiduguri
Maroua
Mubi
Yola
Mbé
Ngaoundéré
Bamenda
Bouar
CAMEROON
Biltine
Abéché
Ati
Sarh
Moundou
Am Timan
Birao
Chari
CENTRAL AFRICAN REPUBLIC
Ndélé
Sibut
Bambari
Bangassou
Bangui
Berbérati
Nola
Bomu
DARFUR
El Fasher
Nyala
Gabras
Kafia Kingi
SUDAN
Dongola
Argo
Karima
Merowe
Abu Hamed
Ed Debba
Ed Damer
Atbara
Omdurman
Khartoum
Shendi
Wad Medani
Gedaref
Kadugli
Renk
Kodok
Melut
Malakal
Raga
Wau
Ler
Akobo
Rumbek
Tambura
Bor
Juba
Towot
Maridi
Suakin
Port Sudan
Tokar
ERITREA
Asmara
Agordat
Mek'elē
Gonder
Lake Tana
Bahir Dar
Debre Mark'os
Ādīs Ābeba (Addis Ababa)
ETHIOPIA
Ogadēn
Imī
Alem
Yirga
Nagelē
Majī
Arba Minch'
Dolo Bay
Beledweyne
Jīzān
Khamīs Mushayţ
Al Qunfudhah
YEMEN
Şan'ā'
Ta'izz
'Adan
Sayḩūt
Al Mukallā
Gulf of Aden
DJIBOUTI
Djibouti
SOMALILAND
Hargeysa
Eyl
PUNTLAND
K'orahē
Hilalaya
Boundary undemarcated and in dispute
Xarardheere
Mereeg
SOMALIA
Shebele
Merca (Marka)
Muqdisho (Mogadishu)
Baraawe
Jamaame
Kismaayo
Bura
BIOKO
Malabo
Ebolowa
Yaoundé
EQ. GUINEA
RIO MUNI
Príncipe
SAO TOME AND PRINCIPE
São Tomé
Oyem
Ouesso
Makokou
Libreville
GABON
CONGO
Mossaka
Mbandaka
Annobón Eq. Guinea
Port-Gentil
Iguéla
Tchibanga
Franceville
Setté Cama
Mayumba
Brazzaville
Pointe-Noire
Angola CABINDA
Cabinda
Boma
Kinshasa (Léopoldville)
Inongo
Bandundu
Gemena
Congo
Ubangi
Uele
Bumba
Buta
Lisala
Basankusu
Kisangani
Isiro
Arua
Bunia
Ikela
DEMOCRATIC REPUBLIC OF THE CONGO
Kananga
Mbuji-Mayi
Kalemie
Kahemba
Chitato
KATANGA
Pweto
Lake Mweru
Kolwezi
Lubumbashi
Nimule
Gulu
UGANDA
Jinja
Kampala
Lake Turkana (Lake Rudolf)
Marsabit
Wajir
Dif
KENYA
Mt. Kenya
Lake Victoria
Kigali
RWANDA
BURUNDI
Bujumbura
Kigoma
Nairobi
Kilimanjaro
Arusha
Malindi
Tabora
Dodoma
Lamu
Kaambooni
Tanga
Dar es Salaam
Lake Tanganyika
TANZANIA
Iringa
Mbala
Mbeya
Kilwa Kivinje
Songea
Lindi
Kasama
Mansa
Mpika
Lake Malawi (Lake Nyasa)
MALAWI
Marrupa
Lichinga
Lilongwe
Nacala
Nampula
Moçambique
Uíge
Ambriz
Luanda
Malanje
Caungula
Saurimo
Sandoa
Dondo
Calulo
Cacolo
Porto Amboim
Luena
Sumbe
Lobito
Kuito
Benguela
Lucira
ANGOLA
Macondo
Chingola
Zambezi
Luanshya
Kabwe
ZAMBIA
Kuvango
Mussuma
Lubango
Namibe
Tombua
Baía dos Tigres
Foz do Cunene
Humbe
Xangongo
Mavinga
Mongu
Lusaka
Lake Kariba
Kariba
Harare
Tete
Mutarara
MOZAMBIQUE
Quelimane
Chinde
Moma
Cape Fria
Ondangwa
Dirico
Livingstone
ZIMBABWE
Sesfontein
Tsumeb
Grootfontein
Bulawayo
Gweru
Beira
Nova Mambone
Palgrave Point
NAMIBIA
Windhoek
BOTSWANA
Palapye
Swakopmund
Walvis Bay
Rehoboth
NAMIB DESERT
KALAHARI DESERT
Gaborone
Lobatse
Massangena
Limpopo
Inhambane
Ponta da Barra
Xai-Xai
Maputo
Pretoria (Tshwane)
Mbabane
Johannesburg
Lobamba
SWAZILAND
Maltahöhe
Keetmanshoop
Lüderitz
Welkom
Vryheid
Alexander Bay
Warmbad
Bloemfontein
Maseru
LESOTHO
Durban
Cape Saint Lucia
Port Nolloth
Prieska
SOUTH AFRICA
Garies
Calvinia
Queenstown
Umzimvubu
Lambert's Bay
Saldanha
Cape Columbine
Mossel Bay
George
Bhisho
East London
Port Alfred
Port Elizabeth
Cape Town
Hermanus
Cape Agulhas
Namaqua Seamount
Vema Seamount
Wüst Seamount
Wyandot Seamount
Tristan da Cunha Group
Walters Shoal
SEYCHELLES
Aldabra Islands
Cosmoledo Group
Farquhar Group
Glorioso Is. France
Cap d'Ambre
Moroni
COMOROS
Andoany
Mayotte Fr.
Pemba
Mahajanga
Antalaha
Marovoay
Ambatondrazaka
Maintirano
Belo-Tsiribihina
Antananarivo
Antsirabe
MADAGASCAR
Manja
Morombe
Fianarantsoa
Manakara
Farafangana
Vangaindrano
Toliara
Ampanihy
Bekily
Androka
Tôlañaro
Cap Sainte Marie
Mozambique Channel
INDIAN OCEAN
ATLANTIC OCEAN
EQUATOR
TROPIC OF CAPRICORN
Meridian of Greenwich (London)
Longitude East 30° of Greenwich
AZIMUTHAL EQUIDISTANT PROJECTION
SCALE 1:37,000,000
0 KILOMETERS 600 800 1000
0 MILES 200 400 600 800 1000

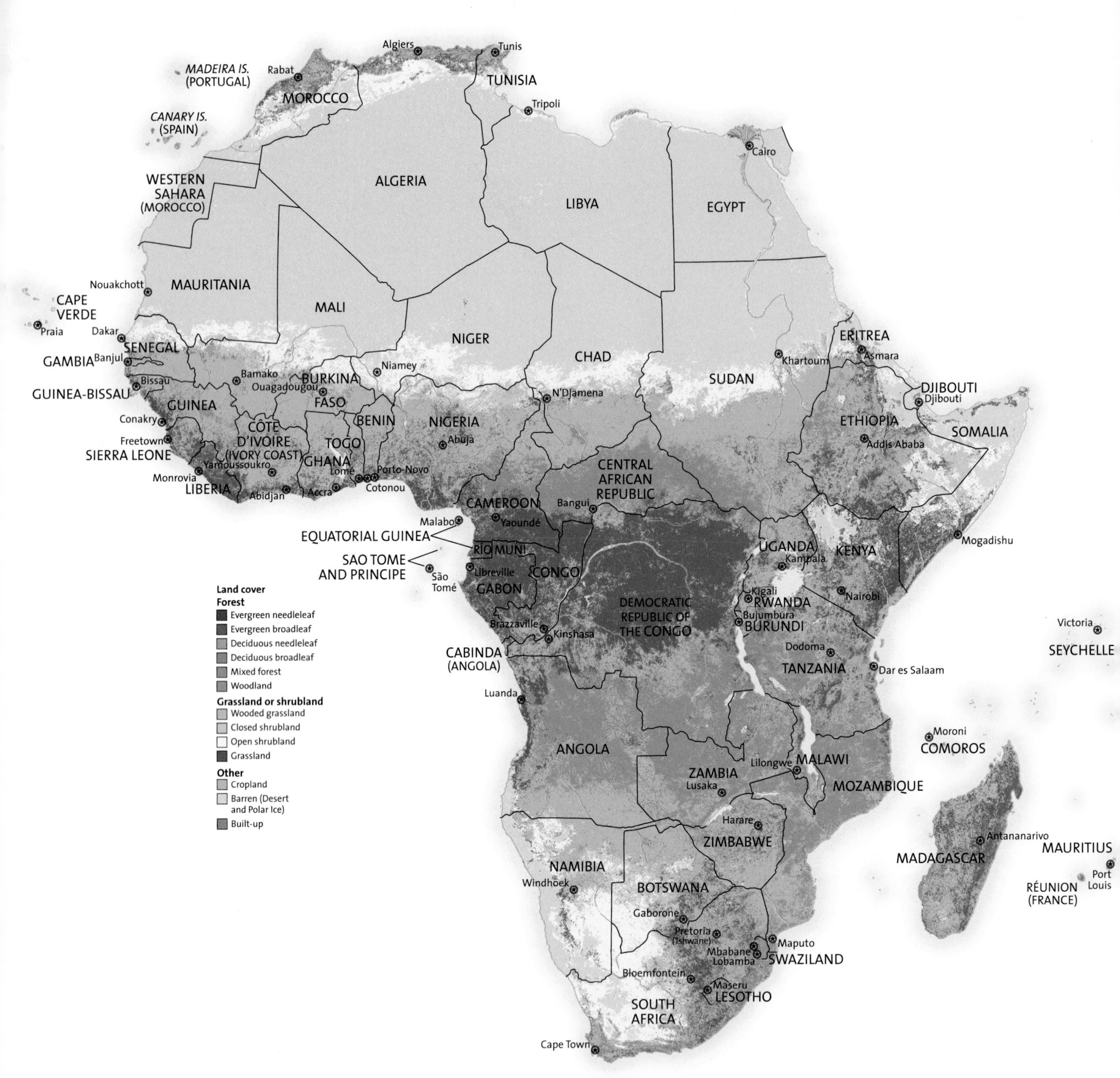

TEMPERATURE AND RAINFALL

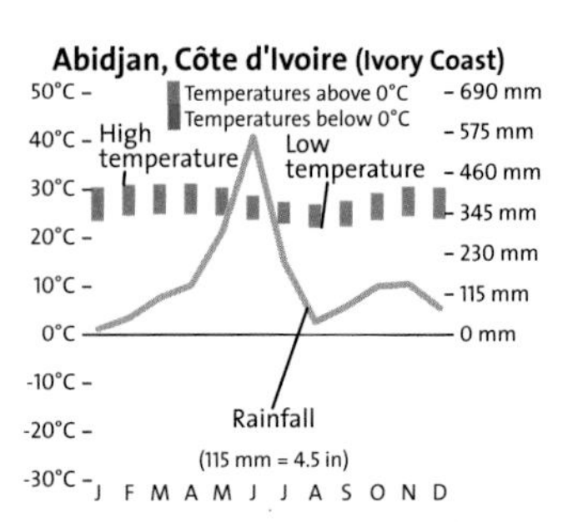

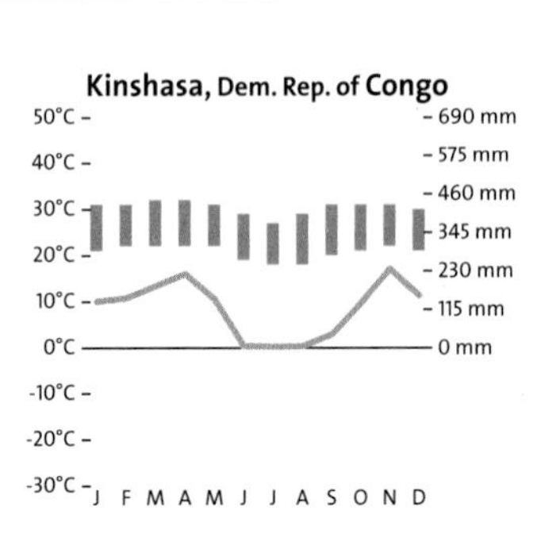

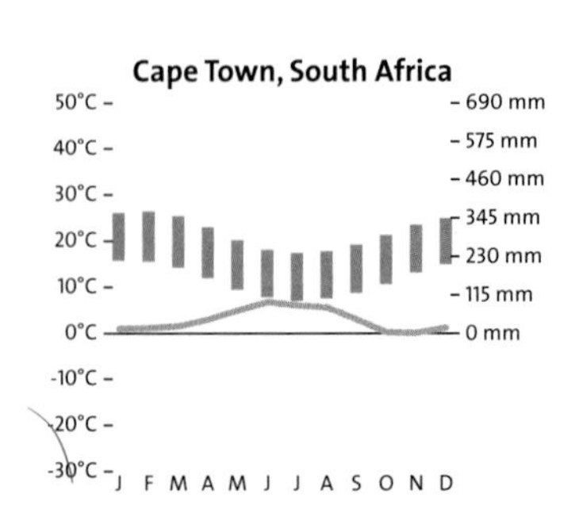

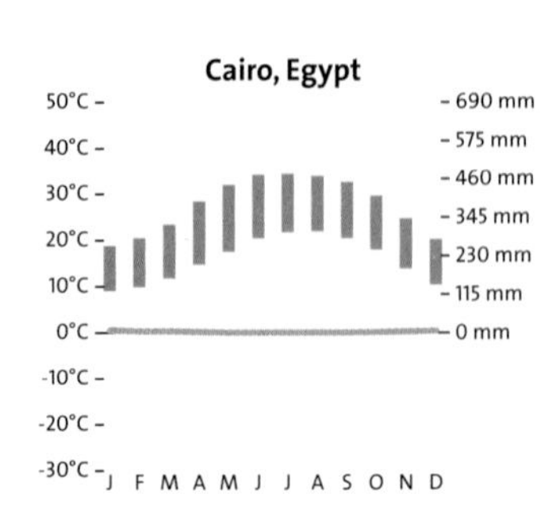

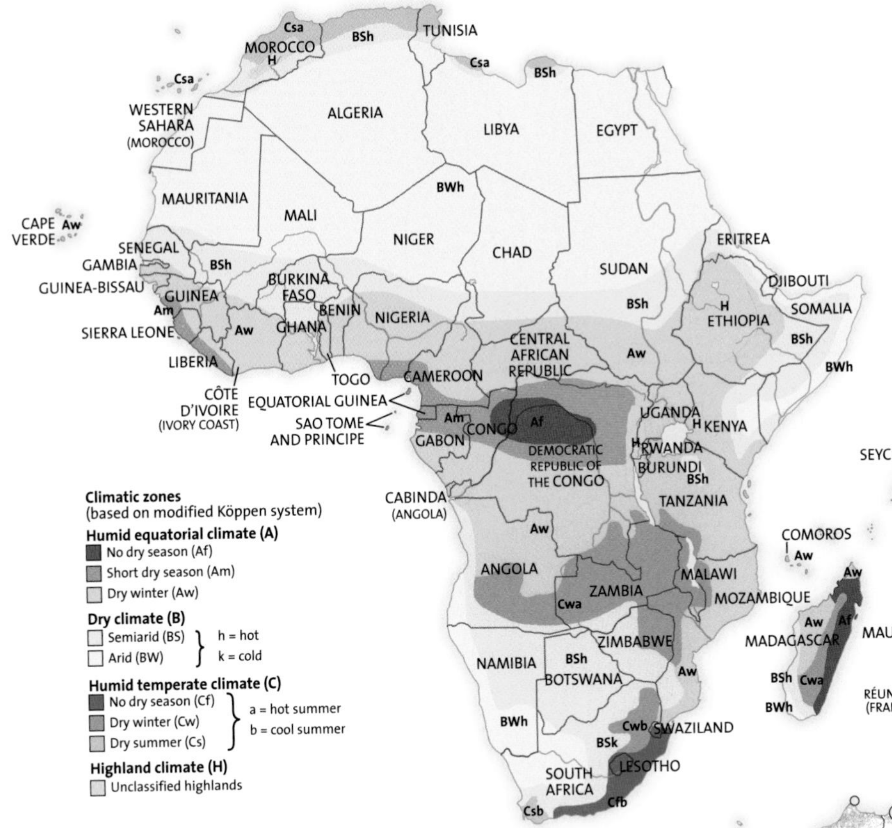

Climatic zones
(based on modified Köppen system)

Humid equatorial climate (A)
- No dry season (Af)
- Short dry season (Am)
- Dry winter (Aw)

Dry climate (B)
- Semiarid (BS)
- Arid (BW)

h = hot
k = cold

Humid temperate climate (C)
- No dry season (Cf)
- Dry winter (Cw)
- Dry summer (Cs)

a = hot summer
b = cool summer

Highland climate (H)
- Unclassified highlands

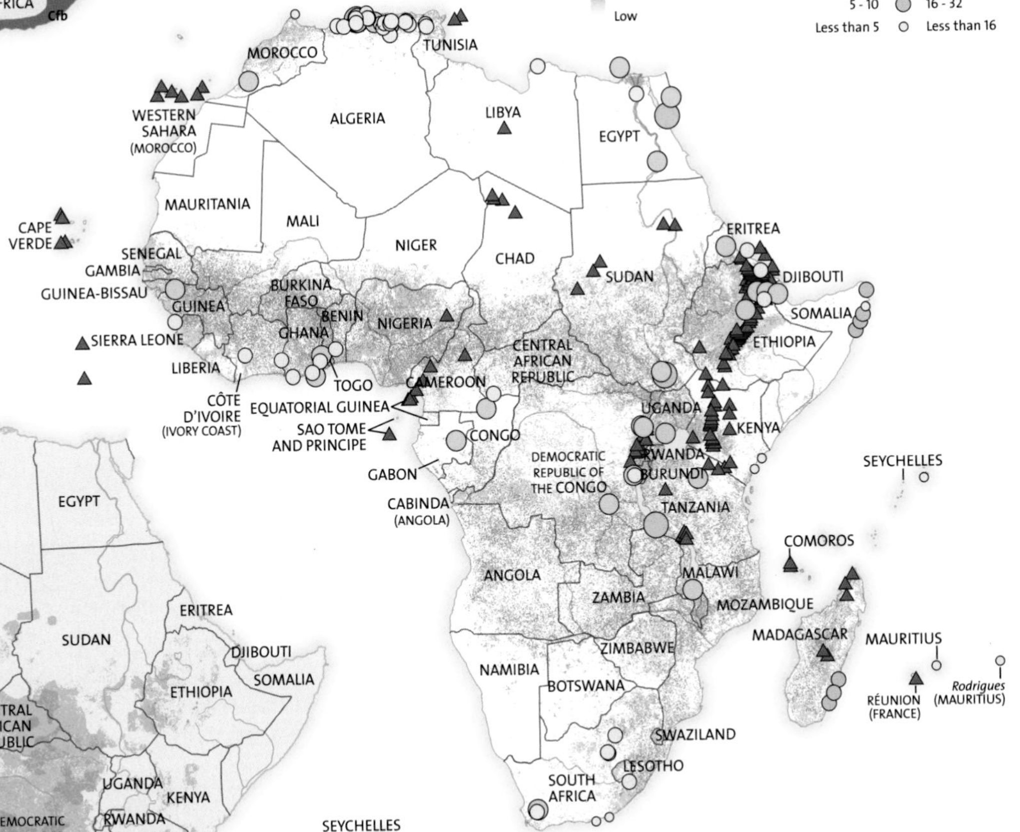

Population density, 2005

People per square km	People per square mi
More than 1,000	More than 2,500
100 - 1,000	250 - 2,500
Less than 100	Less than 250

Fire intensity
(from gas burn-off, slash-and-burn agriculture, or natural causes)

High

Low

Recorded natural event

Earthquake
Richter scale magnitude
- More than 7.0
- 6.0 - 7.0
- Less than 6.0

Volcano

Tsunami
Run-up height

Meters	Feet
5 - 10	16 - 32
Less than 5	Less than 16

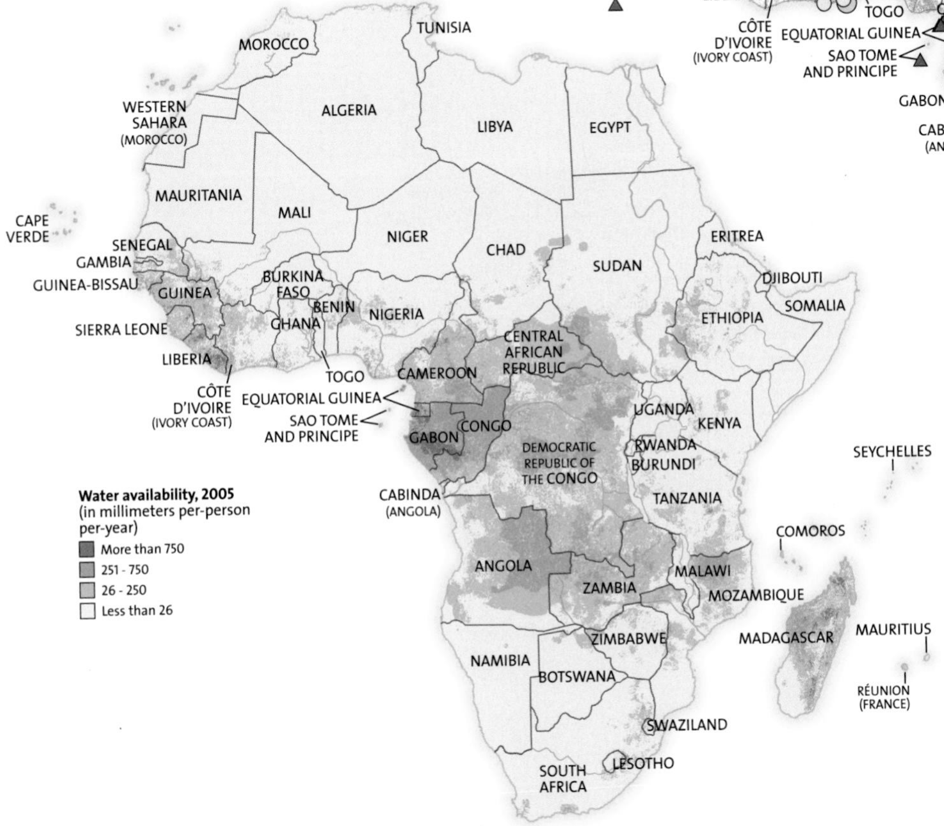

Water availability, 2005
(in millimeters per-person per-year)
- More than 750
- 251 - 750
- 26 - 250
- Less than 26

POPULATION PYRAMIDS

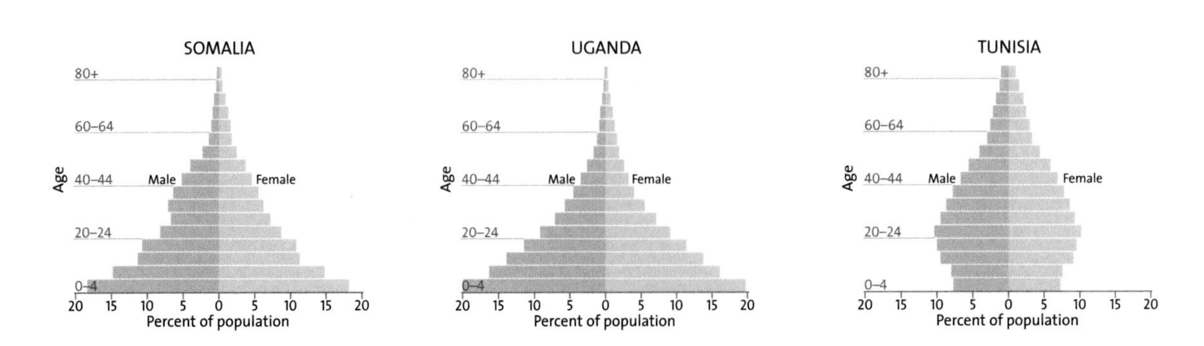

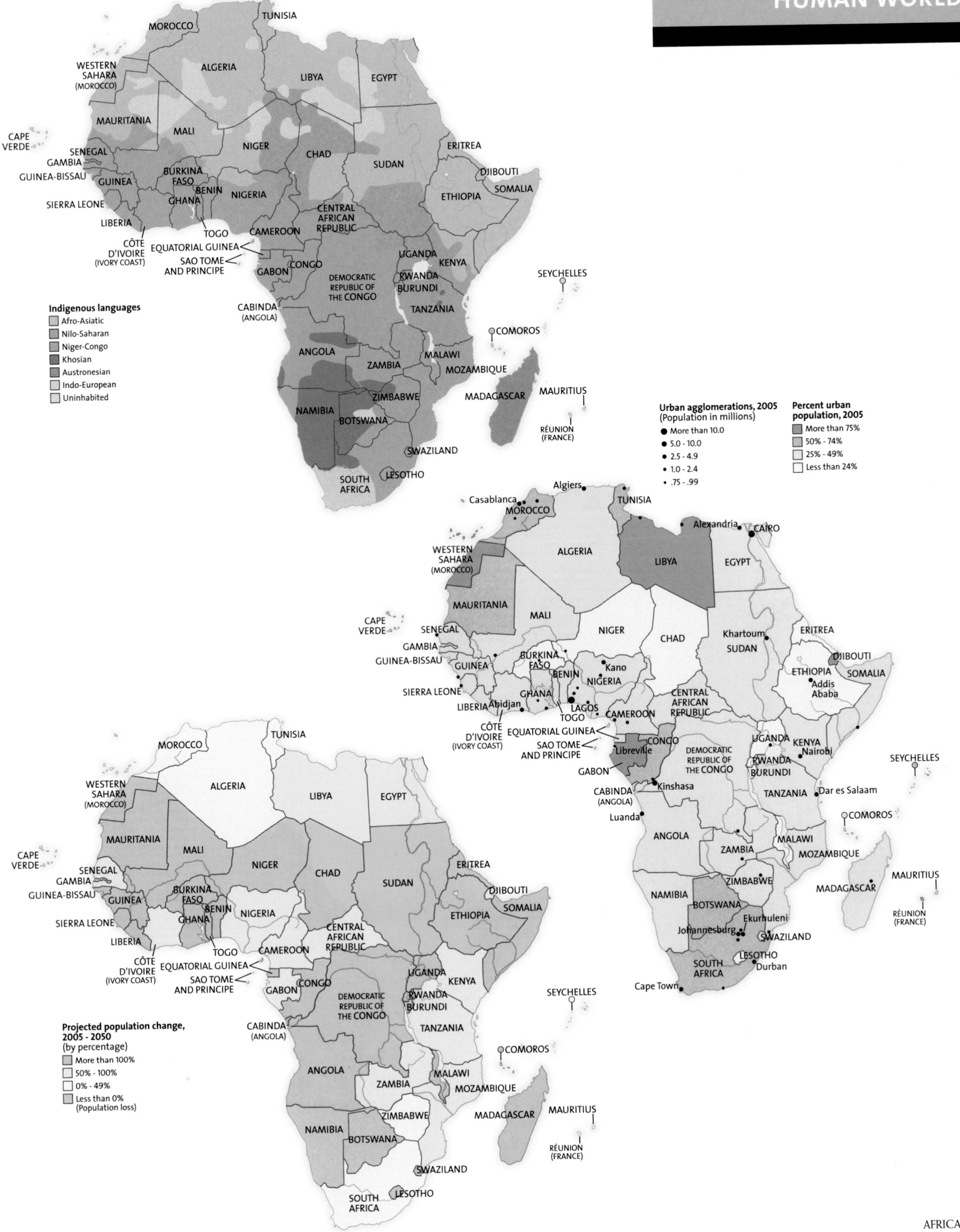
Indigenous languages
Afro-Asiatic
Nilo-Saharan
Niger-Congo
Khosian
Austronesian
Indo-European
Uninhabited
Urban agglomerations, 2005
(Population in millions)
More than 10.0
5.0 - 10.0
2.5 - 4.9
1.0 - 2.4
.75 - .99
Percent urban population, 2005
More than 75%
50% - 74%
25% - 49%
Less than 24%
Projected population change, 2005 - 2050
(by percentage)
More than 100%
50% - 100%
0% - 49%
Less than 0% (Population loss)
MOROCCO
TUNISIA
WESTERN SAHARA (MOROCCO)
ALGERIA
LIBYA
EGYPT
MAURITANIA
MALI
CAPE VERDE
SENEGAL
GAMBIA
GUINEA-BISSAU
GUINEA
SIERRA LEONE
LIBERIA
CÔTE D'IVOIRE (IVORY COAST)
BURKINA FASO
GHANA
TOGO
BENIN
NIGER
NIGERIA
CHAD
SUDAN
ERITREA
DJIBOUTI
SOMALIA
ETHIOPIA
CENTRAL AFRICAN REPUBLIC
CAMEROON
EQUATORIAL GUINEA
SAO TOME AND PRINCIPE
GABON
CONGO
CABINDA (ANGOLA)
DEMOCRATIC REPUBLIC OF THE CONGO
UGANDA
KENYA
RWANDA
BURUNDI
TANZANIA
SEYCHELLES
COMOROS
ANGOLA
ZAMBIA
MALAWI
MOZAMBIQUE
MADAGASCAR
MAURITIUS
RÉUNION (FRANCE)
ZIMBABWE
NAMIBIA
BOTSWANA
SWAZILAND
LESOTHO
SOUTH AFRICA
Algiers
Casablanca
Alexandria
CAIRO
Khartoum
Kano
LAGOS
Abidjan
Addis Ababa
Libreville
Kinshasa
Nairobi
Dar es Salaam
Luanda
Ekurhuleni
Johannesburg
Durban
Cape Town

MADEIRA IS. (PORTUGAL)
CANARY IS. (SPAIN)
MOROCCO
Rabat
Algiers
Tunis
TUNISIA
Tripoli
Cairo
WESTERN SAHARA (MOROCCO)
ALGERIA
LIBYA
EGYPT
MAURITANIA
Nouakchott
CAPE VERDE
Praia
MALI
NIGER
CHAD
SUDAN
ERITREA
Asmara
Khartoum
DJIBOUTI
Djibouti
SOMALIA
ETHIOPIA
Addis Ababa
Dakar
SENEGAL
GAMBIA
Banjul
Bissau
GUINEA-BISSAU
GUINEA
Conakry
Freetown
SIERRA LEONE
Monrovia
LIBERIA
Bamako
Ouagadougou
BURKINA FASO
Niamey
CÔTE D'IVOIRE (IVORY COAST)
Yamoussoukro
Abidjan
GHANA
Accra
TOGO
Lomé
BENIN
Porto-Novo
Cotonou
NIGERIA
Abuja
N'Djamena
CENTRAL AFRICAN REPUBLIC
Bangui
CAMEROON
Yaoundé
Malabo
EQUATORIAL GUINEA
RÍO MUNI
SAO TOME AND PRINCIPE
São Tomé
Libreville
GABON
CONGO
Brazzaville
Kinshasa
DEMOCRATIC REPUBLIC OF THE CONGO
UGANDA
Kampala
KENYA
Nairobi
Mogadishu
Kigali
RWANDA
Bujumbura
BURUNDI
Dodoma
TANZANIA
Dar es Salaam
Victoria
SEYCHELLES
CABINDA (ANGOLA)
Luanda
ANGOLA
ZAMBIA
Lusaka
Lilongwe
MALAWI
MOZAMBIQUE
Moroni
COMOROS
Harare
ZIMBABWE
Antananarivo
MADAGASCAR
MAURITIUS
Port Louis
RÉUNION (FRANCE)
NAMIBIA
Windhoek
BOTSWANA
Gaborone
Pretoria (Tshwane)
Maputo
Mbabane
Lobamba
SWAZILAND
Bloemfontein
Maseru
LESOTHO
SOUTH AFRICA
Cape Town
More disturbed
Cropland
Less disturbed
More disturbed
Pasture
Built-up area
Irrigated land

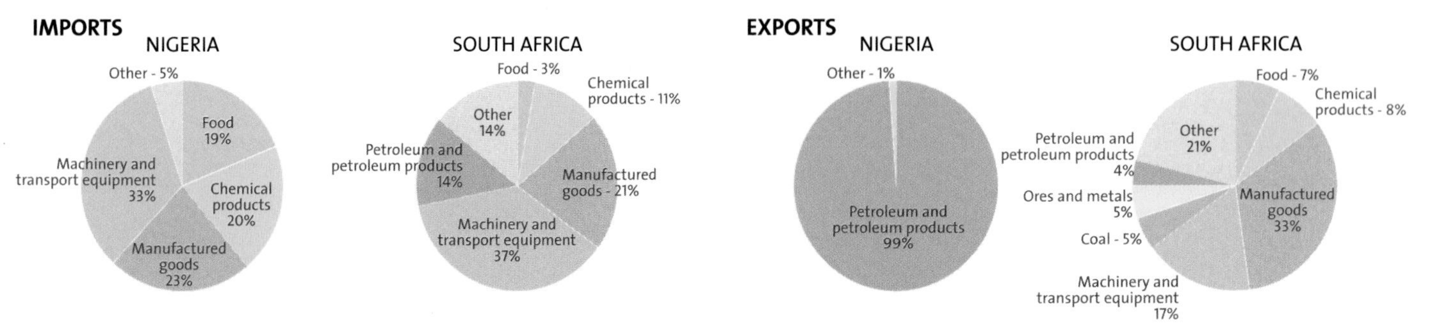
IMPORTS
NIGERIA
Other - 5%
Food 19%
Chemical products 20%
Manufactured goods 23%
Machinery and transport equipment 33%
SOUTH AFRICA
Food - 3%
Chemical products - 11%
Manufactured goods - 21%
Machinery and transport equipment 37%
Petroleum and petroleum products 14%
Other 14%
EXPORTS
NIGERIA
Other - 1%
Petroleum and petroleum products 99%
SOUTH AFRICA
Food - 7%
Chemical products - 8%
Manufactured goods 33%
Machinery and transport equipment 17%
Coal - 5%
Ores and metals 5%
Petroleum and petroleum products 4%
Other 21%

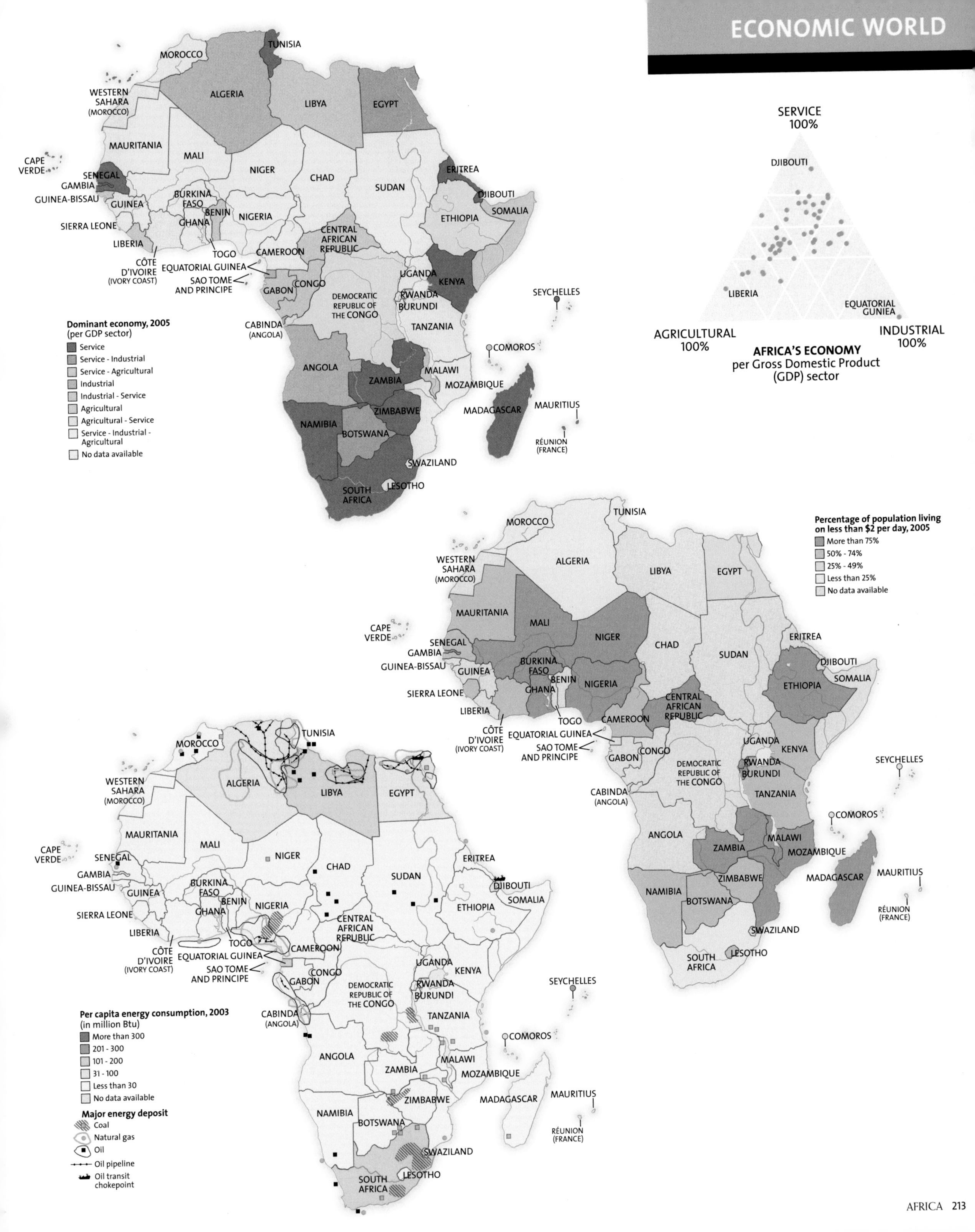
Dominant economy, 2005
(per GDP sector)
Service
Service - Industrial
Service - Agricultural
Industrial
Industrial - Service
Agricultural
Agricultural - Service
Service - Industrial - Agricultural
No data available
SERVICE
100%
AGRICULTURAL
100%
INDUSTRIAL
100%
DJIBOUTI
LIBERIA
EQUATORIAL GUNIEA
AFRICA'S ECONOMY
per Gross Domestic Product
(GDP) sector
Percentage of population living on less than $2 per day, 2005
More than 75%
50% - 74%
25% - 49%
Less than 25%
No data available
Per capita energy consumption, 2003
(in million Btu)
More than 300
201 - 300
101 - 200
31 - 100
Less than 30
No data available
Major energy deposit
Coal
Natural gas
Oil
Oil pipeline
Oil transit chokepoint
MOROCCO
TUNISIA
WESTERN SAHARA (MOROCCO)
ALGERIA
LIBYA
EGYPT
MAURITANIA
MALI
NIGER
CHAD
SUDAN
CAPE VERDE
SENEGAL
GAMBIA
GUINEA-BISSAU
GUINEA
BURKINA FASO
BENIN
NIGERIA
GHANA
SIERRA LEONE
LIBERIA
TOGO
CÔTE D'IVOIRE (IVORY COAST)
CAMEROON
CENTRAL AFRICAN REPUBLIC
ERITREA
DJIBOUTI
SOMALIA
ETHIOPIA
EQUATORIAL GUINEA
SAO TOME AND PRINCIPE
GABON
CONGO
DEMOCRATIC REPUBLIC OF THE CONGO
UGANDA
KENYA
RWANDA
BURUNDI
TANZANIA
SEYCHELLES
CABINDA (ANGOLA)
COMOROS
ANGOLA
ZAMBIA
MALAWI
MOZAMBIQUE
ZIMBABWE
MADAGASCAR
MAURITIUS
NAMIBIA
BOTSWANA
RÉUNION (FRANCE)
SWAZILAND
SOUTH AFRICA
LESOTHO

24° 21° 18° 15° 45° 12° 9° 6° 3° 0° 3° 6° 9° 12°

BAY OF BISCAY

Bordeaux Arcachon Mont-de-Marsan Biarritz Pau Tarbes Lourdes Agen Montauban Cahors Rocamadour Rodez Toulouse FRANCE Alès Nîmes Avignon Orange Gap Digne Arles Sète Béziers Narbonne Marseille Îles d'Hyères Cannes Riviera MONACO San Remo Cuneo Savona Genova (Genoa) La Spezia Pisa Livorno ITALY Forlì Rimini SAN MARINO Arezzo Siena Perugia Piombino Terni Viterbo Civitavecchia VATICAN CITY Roma (Rome) Elba Capraia Cap Corse Bastia Corte Montecristo CORSICA France Mte. Cinto Ajaccio 2136 Sartène Porto-Vecchio Bonifacio Tyrrhenian Sea 2858 2546 2677

PYRENEES Pamplona (Iruña) 2017 Aneto 3404 ANDORRA Figueres Perpignan Cap de Creus Girona Lleida Manresa Mataró Terrassa Barcelona Reus Tarragona Tortosa Cap de Tortosa

Cabo Ortegal Ferrol Viveiro Cabo de Peñas Gijón Mieres A Coruña Santiago de Compostela Cabo Fisterra Lugo Sarria Ponferrada 2648 Picos de Europa León Astorga Monforte Pontevedra Vigo Ourense Tui Valença Braga Bragança Viana do Castelo Guimarães Vila Real Matosinhos Porto (Oporto) Aveiro Viseu Cabo Mondego Figueira da Foz Guarda Covilhã Tejo Nazaré Fátima Peniche Abrantes Santarém Portalegre (Lisbon) Lisboa Montijo Barreiro Setúbal Évora Elvas Cabo de Sines Sines Beja Portimão Faro Cabo de São Vicente PORTUGAL

Santander Bilbao Vitoria Gasteiz Burgos Logroño Tudela Palencia Soria Medina de Rioseco Valladolid Zamora Medina del Campo Medinaceli Calatayud Zaragoza Duero 2316 1492 Salamanca Segovia Ávila Madrid Guadalajara Molina de Aragón Teruel 2019 Talavera de la Reina Aranjuez SPAIN Cáceres Trujillo Mérida Badajoz 2592 Ciudad Real Puertollano Almendralejo Alcázar de San Juan Cuenca Utiel Daimiel Tomelloso Manzanares Valdepeñas Albacete Valencia Alzira Castelló de la Plana Sagunto Villena Hellín Alcoy Dénia Cabo de La Nao Alicante Elche (Elx) Cieza Murcia Lorca Cartagena La Unión Mazarrón Águilas Sierra Morena 1323 Andújar Linares Úbeda Baeza Vila de Moura Córdoba Écija Lucena Jaén (Seville) Sevilla Huelva Utrera Antequera Granada 3481 Motril Almería Cabo de Gata Sanlúcar de Barrameda Málaga Jerez de la Frontera Cádiz Algeciras GIBRALTAR U.K.

Cases Velles de Formentor 1445 357 Menorca (Minorca) Manacor Palma de Mallorca Mallorca (Majorca) Ibiza (Iviza) 475 Cabrera Formentera BALEARIC ISLANDS MEDITERRANEAN SEA 2132 2726 2651 2597 2791

I. Asinara Olbia Sassari Ozieri Capo Comino Nuoro SARDINIA Italy Oristano 1834 Tortolì Terralba Cagliari Capo Carbonara Carbonia Sant' Antioco Capo Teulada Capo Spartivento 39° 36° 33° 30° 27° 24° 21°

Jalitah I. Ras el Abiadh Bizerte Ras el Tib Tunis Hammam Lif Grombalia Nabeul Beja El Kef Qalaa Kebira Zaghouan Sousse Mahdia Qairouan Tala Kasserine Msaken Qerqenah Is. Sfax Gharbi I. Jerba I. Feriana Gafsa 1165 Sekhira Ghraiba Metlaoui Gabes Kebili Nefta Zarzis Medenine Ben Gardane TUNISIA Bir Ghoumrassen Romane Borj el Kessira Dehibat Wāzin Nālūt

Collo Annaba (Bône) Souk Ahras 'Aïn M'lila Constantine Kabylie 2308 Dellys El Harrach Alger (Algiers) Blida Médéa Bouira Sétif Bordj bou Arreridj M'Sila Sidi Aïssa Barika Batna Timgad 2326 1544 Arris Monts des Nementcha Djebel Onk Biskra Oumache Ouled Djellal Negrine Redeyef El Meghaier Guemar El Oued Touggourt Mouiat el Behima Beressof Cherchell Chlef Miliana Sidi Lakhdar Mostaganem Arzew Relizane Tissemsilt 'Aïn el Hadjel Bou Saâda Ksar Chellala Mers el Kebir Oran Mascara Tiaret Saïda 'Aïn Deheb Djelfa 1570 Messaad Ksar el Hirane Djamaa Tlemcen Râs el Ma Hauts Plateaux Aflou 2008 Laghouat El Bayadh Nili Tilrhemt Dzioua Oujda El Aïoun Berguent Debdou El Aricha Mecheria Brezina Hassi R'mel Guerara Berriane El Hadjira 'Aïn Sefra 2236 Naama Tendrara Bou Arfa Djeniene bou Rezg El Mahfoura Ghardaïa Zelfana Metlili Chaamba Benoud El Hobra Ouargla Hassi bou Zid Sidi bou Haous Sidi el Hadj bou Haous Figuig Saharan Atlas Hassi Taïeb Hassi Messaoud El Borma Rhourd el Baguel Messdar Biar Zahr Sif Fatima Tiaret Fort Saint Dirj Ghadamis LIBYA

Alborán Sp. Melilla Sp. Ceuta Spain Cap Spartel Martil (Tangier) Tanger Tétouan Asilah Larache Ksar el Kebir Er Rif 2456 Rhafsaï Souk el Arba du Rharb Taourirt Guercif Taza Tahala (Port Lyautey) Kenitra Rabat (Fez) Fès Meknès Sefrou El Hajeb 3340 Azrou Casablanca Mohammedia (Fedala) El Jadida (Mazagan) Nouasser Settat Khouribga Moyen Atlas Outat Oulad el Hajj Missour Matarka Oualidia Cap Beddouza Boujad El Ksiba Ksabi Talsint Mengoub Beni Tajit Rich Youssoufia Safi Beni Mellal Cap Hadid El Kelaa Chemaïa des Srarhna Azilal 4071 Assoul Goulmima Boudenib Kenadsa Béchar Menouarar Taghit Marrakech Aït Ourir Jebel Sarhro Erfoud Rissani Alnif Cap Sim Chichaoua Imi n Tanout Asni Jeb. Toubkal 4165 Tamanar Cap Rhir Agadir Inezgane High Atlas Agdz 2712 Zagora Tazzarine Oglat Beraber Tamgrout Hamada du Guir Hamaguir Igli Beni Abbes MOROCCO

Aït Baha 1635 Tissint Foum Zguid Tagounit Hassi Chefaïa Zerhamra Hassi Zegdou Ougarta Guerzim Oulad Saïd Kerzaz Talmine Ksabi Charouine Tiznit Tafraout Tata Akka Sidi Ifni Bou Izakarn Cap Drâa Tan-Tan Assa Jebel Ouarkziz Bou Akba Hassi Targant Tinfouchy Khorb el Ethel Rhemilès Hamada du Drâa Ben Zohra Chouikhia Tindouf Tilemsoun Messeïed Amot Tarfaya Cap Juby Dawra Al Haggounia Al Mahbas Laayoune Dchira Jdiriya Hawza Al Farciya Dayet el Khadra 'Aouinet Bel Egrâ Iguidi Mcherrah Boubout Bordj Flye Sainte Marie Bir el Hadjaj Lemsid Cap Boujdour Boujdour Smara Boukra Aridal Awfist Amasine Lamjaybir Aglat Jrayfiya Bir Lahmar Tfaritiy Al Bir Lahlou Aïn Ben Tili Galtat Zemmour 360 Nwayfadh Skaymat Cnalwa Agmar Bir Mogreïn Bir Bel Guerdâne Tourassine Bir Lemouissat 'Ayoûn 'Abd el Mâlek Bir el Khzaïm Touila El Milhas El Mzereb Cheïkria Chegga Eglab Regbat Yetti 2421 Chenachane Grizim Bir Ould Brini Bir ed Deheb Toufourine Tazadite Tni Haïa

Grand Erg Occidental Hassi Guern el Guessaa Hassi Allal el Hadjar Hassi Berkane El Gassi El Agreb Hassi Touareg 'Aïn Taïba Hassi Djafou Hassi Fokra Hassi Ouchene Hassi Nechou El Homeur Tabelkoza Hassi Erg Sedra Hassi Inifel Hassi bou Khechba Grand Erg Oriental Hassi Tartrat Hassi Imoulaye Timellouline Tinrhert Ohanet Hassi bel Guebbour Fort Miribel Hassi Tabaloulet Hassi I-n-Sokki Hamada de Tinrhert Tin Fouye Hassi Tanezrouft I-n-Amenas Tiguentourine Edjeleh Ouan Taredert El Maïz Oufrane Plateau du Tademaït 'Aïn Souf El Atimine Hassi Mdakane El Kseibat El Mansour Sbaa Adrar I-n-Belbel Hassi Moungar Sidi el Hadj Zaoui Bordj Omar Driss Hassi Tabelbalet El Adeb Larache ALGERIA Tazzait Hassi Issaouane Ta-n-Kena Titaf Bou Ali Sali Aoulef I-n-Rahr Foggaret el Arab 'Aïn Azaz Reggane Taourirt Tit Tidikelt Salah Hassi Tiguentourine Hassi Habadra 'Aïn Tiguift Mouilah Hassi I-n-Belrem I-n-Azaoua Hassi Koussane Amguid TASSILI-N-AJJER Tassili-n-Ajjer NATIONAL PARK Tarat Feuet Ghât Dider Tadjmout 1680 Arak 2327 Garet el Djenoun Anou Meniet Zaouatallaz Djebel Telerhteba 2455 Asedjrad Erg I-n-Afarag I-n-Eker Ideles Tiririne Ould Mouloud Erg-n-Ataram 1450 I-n-Amguel Mount Tahat 2918 AHAGGAR N.P. Abalessa Silet Ahaggar Tarhaouhaout Tadjetaret Ti-n-Taourdi Erg Tidjidit Tayarte Adrar I-n-Hihaou 1188 I-n-Ebeggi Tanezrouft-n-Ahenet Anti-m-Misaou Ilaferh Tamada Abreuvoir Assiou (Azéo) Sobti El Mahia I-n-Dagouber Aïn Cheikr 376

El Mhabes 460 Zednes Karêt 'Oglât ed Daoud Terhazza Oumm el A'sel 'Erg el Ahmar Aouker El Mreïti Agueraktem Hamada Safia Bir Chali Hamada el Haricha Atokila 'Oglât el Fersig Taoudenni Azigzane El Guettâra Mléhas Bir Zreïgat Eddaré El Mrâyer Khnâchich Tazouikert El Hank MAURITANIA

Bir Tinkardad Mijek Oglât d'Admamlalmat Zouîrât Fdérik 915 Hammami Oglats de Mkhaïzira Tourine Aouchich Arhreïjît Makteïr El Moueïla Awaday Char 647 Awsard Aghwinit Zoug Techla Aghaylas Imlily Argoub Ad Dakhla Tamayya Sebeta Rabt Bir Anzarane Cap Barbas Bir Gandouz Adrar Sotuf WESTERN SAHARA Morocco

Ilhas Desertas Pico do Facho 1862 517 Pico Ruivo MADEIRA IS. Portugal Ilhas Selvagens (Salvage Islands) Portugal CANARY ISLANDS (ISLAS CANARIAS) Spain Alegranza Lanzarote Haría 671 689 Fuerteventura Gran Tarajal 807 Las Palmas 1949 Gran Canaria La Palma 2426 Sta. Cruz de Tenerife Tenerife 3718 Gomera 1487 Hierro (Ferro)

ATLANTIC

3425 892 6326 200 1798 2074 5422 5708 3542 5603 1628 3272 4973 5502 4641 2346 86 4252 4100 4997 4107 1128 86 1066 2200 161 4510 3383 3438 4259 150 3294 902 2756 3923

TROPIC OF CANCER

Western Sahara, formerly Spanish Sahara, was divided by Morocco and Mauritania in 1976. Morocco has administered the territory since Mauritania's withdrawal in August 1979. The United Nations does not recognize this annexation, and Western Sahara remains in dispute.

MAURITANIA
MALI
NIGER
SENEGAL
GAMBIA
GUINEA-BISSAU
GUINEA
SIERRA LEONE
LIBERIA
CÔTE D'IVOIRE (IVORY COAST)
BURKINA FASO
GHANA
TOGO
BENIN
NIGERIA
SAHEL
SAO TOME AND PRINCIPE
Nouakchott
Dakar
Banjul
Bissau
Conakry
Freetown
Monrovia
Bamako
Ouagadougou
Niamey
Yamoussoukro
Abidjan
Accra
Lomé
Porto-Novo
Abuja
LAGOS
São Tomé
GULF OF GUINEA
OCEAN
Bight of Benin
Gold Coast
Ivory Coast
Grain Coast
Slave Coast
Cape Palmas
Cape Three Points
Cap Vert
Arquipélago dos Bijagós
Annobón Eq. Guinea
Meridian of Greenwich (London)
Longitude West 3° of Greenwich
Longitude East 3° of Greenwich
EQUATOR
LAMBERT CONFORMAL CONIC PROJECTION
SCALE 1:12,000,000
0 KILOMETERS 200 300
0 MILES 100 200 300

LAMBERT CONFORMAL CONIC PROJECTION
SCALE 1:12,000,000
0 KILOMETERS 200 300
0 MILES 100 200 300
IONIAN SEA
MEDITERRANEAN
SICILY
ITALY
MALTA
GREECE
Sea of Crete
Kríti (Crete)
ALGERIA
TUNISIA
LIBYA
EGYPT
NIGER
CHAD
NIGERIA
CAMEROON
CENTRAL AFRICAN REPUBLIC
SUDAN
SAHARA
SAHEL
ATLAS MOUNTAINS
Libyan Desert
Western Desert
Grand Erg Oriental
Grand Erg Occidental
Hamada de Tinrhert
Tassili-n-Ajjer
Tibesti (Tibesti Mts.)
AOZOU STRIP
Plateau du Djado
Grand Erg de Bilma
'Erg du Ténéré
Aïr (Aïr Massif)
BORKOU
Ennedi
DARFUR
NORTHERN DARFUR
WESTERN DARFUR
SOUTHERN DARFUR
WESTERN KORDOFAN
NORTHERN
Khalīj Surt (Gulf Of Sidra)
Gulf of Gabes
TROPIC OF CANCER
Ṣaḥrā' Marzūq
Kalanshiyū
Sarīr Tibasti
Mesach Mellet
Țarābulus (Tripoli)
Banghāzī (Benghazi)
Tunis
Constantine
Sabhā
N'Djamena
Kano
Abuja
Zinder
Maradi
Abéché
Maiduguri
Garoua
Kaduna

TURKEY
SYRIA
CYPRUS
LEBANON
ISRAEL
JORDAN
IRAQ
IRAN
KUWAIT
BAHRAIN
QATAR
UNITED ARAB EMIRATES
OMAN
SAUDI ARABIA
YEMEN
ERITREA
ETHIOPIA
DJIBOUTI
SOMALIA
SOMALILAND
PUNTLAND
RED SEA
GULF OF ADEN
INDIAN OCEAN
PERSIAN GULF
SYRIAN DESERT
An Nafūd
Ar Rub' al Khālī (Empty Quarter)
TEHRAN
Baghdād
Dimashq (Damascus)
Beyrouth (Beirut)
'Ammān
Jerusalem
Tel Aviv-Yafo
Ar Riyāḍ (Riyadh)
Jeddah
Makkah (Mecca)
Al Madīnah (Medina)
Ṣan'ā' (Sanaa)
'Adan (Aden)
Asmara
Djibouti
Khartoum
Omdurman
Port Sudan
Kuwait
Al Manāmah (Manama)
Ad Dawḥah (Doha)
Abū Ẓaby (Abu Dhabi)
Dubayy
Sharjah
Eṣfahān (Isfahan)
Shīrāz
Kermān
Yazd
Mosul
Al Baṣrah
Halab (Aleppo)
Adana
Konya
Socotra
Cape Gwardafuy
KHARTOUM
KASSALA
GEZIRA
GEDAREF
SINNAR
WHITE NILE
BLUE NILE
UPPER NILE
RIVER NILE
SINAI

NIGER
CHAD
NIGERIA
CAMEROON
CENTRAL AFRICAN REPUBLIC
EQUATORIAL GUINEA
SAO TOME & PRINCIPE
GABON
CONGO
DEMOCRATIC REPUBLIC OF THE CONGO
ANGOLA
MALI
ATLANTIC OCEAN
Gulf of Guinea
Libyan Desert
Erg du Ténéré
Rio Muni on the mainland and the islands of Bioko, Annobón, Corisco, and the Elobeies constitute the independent country of Equatorial Guinea.
N'Djamena
Abuja
Yaoundé
Bangui
Libreville
Malabo
São Tomé
Brazzaville
Kinshasa (Léopoldville)
Luanda
WESTERN DARFUR
NORTHERN DARFUR
SOUTHERN DARFUR
ORIENTALE
MANIEMA
KASAÏ-ORIENTAL
KASAÏ-OCCIDENTAL
BANDUNDU
KATANGA
EQUATEUR
BAS-CONGO
KINSHASA
CABINDA
ZAIRE
UÍGE
BENGO
LUANDA
CUANZA NORTE
MALANJE
LUNDA NORTE
LUNDA SUL
Longitude East 9° of Greenwich

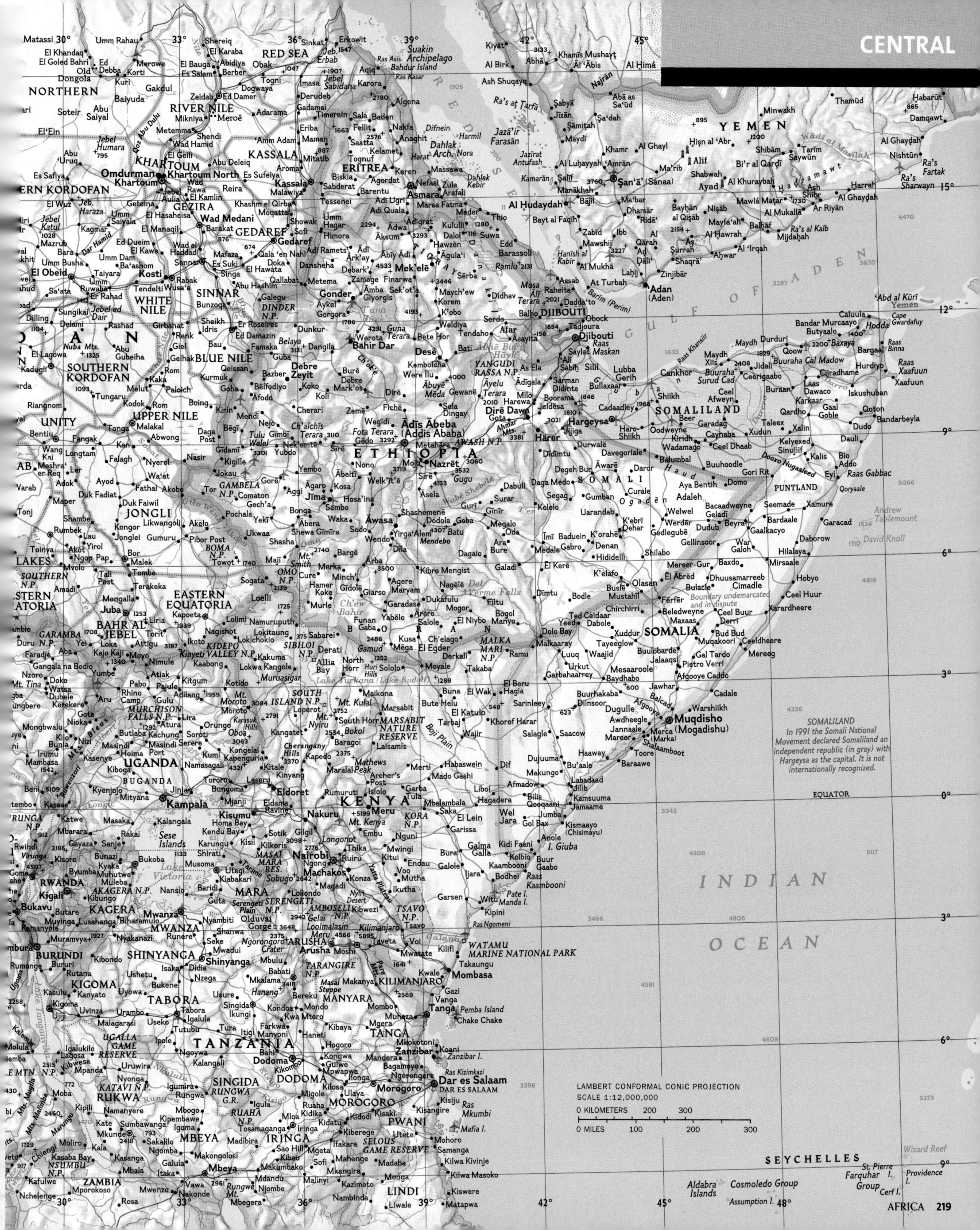
RED SEA
GULF OF ADEN
INDIAN OCEAN
NORTHERN
RIVER NILE
KHARTOUM
KASSALA
GEZIRA
GEDAREF
SINNAR
WHITE NILE
BLUE NILE
SOUTHERN KORDOFAN
UPPER NILE
UNITY
JONGLI
EASTERN EQUATORIA
BAHR AL JEBEL
ERITREA
ETHIOPIA
DJIBOUTI
YEMEN
SOMALILAND
PUNTLAND
SOMALIA
KENYA
UGANDA
RWANDA
BURUNDI
TANZANIA
SEYCHELLES
Khartoum
Omdurman
Asmara
Addis Ababa
Djibouti
Şan'ā' (Sanaa)
Adan (Aden)
Hargeysa
Muqdisho (Mogadishu)
Nairobi
Kampala
Kigali
Dodoma
Dar es Salaam
Mombasa
EQUATOR
SOMALILAND
In 1991 the Somali National Movement declared Somaliland an independent republic (in gray) with Hargeysa as the capital. It is not internationally recognized.
Boundary undemarcated and in dispute
LAMBERT CONFORMAL CONIC PROJECTION
SCALE 1:12,000,000
0 KILOMETERS 200 300
0 MILES 100 200 300

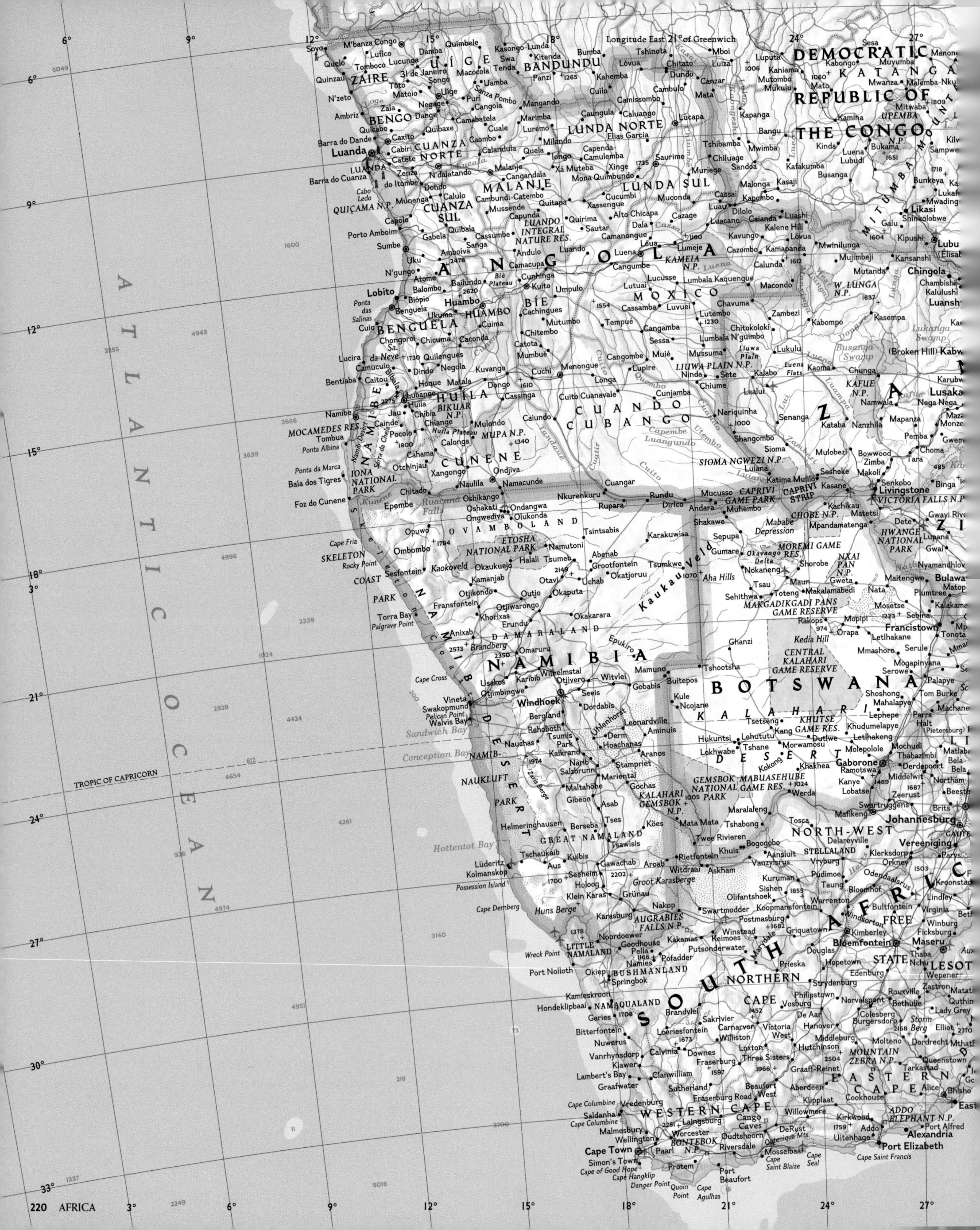

Longitude East 21° of Greenwich
ATLANTIC OCEAN
TROPIC OF CAPRICORN
DEMOCRATIC REPUBLIC OF THE CONGO
KATANGA
ANGOLA
NAMIBIA
BOTSWANA
SOUTH AFRICA
ZAMBIA
ZAIRE
UÍGE
BANDUNDU
BENGO
CUANZA NORTE
LUANDA
LUNDA NORTE
LUNDA SUL
MALANJE
CUANZA SUL
BENGUELA
HUAMBO
BIÉ
MOXICO
HUÍLA
NAMIBE
CUNENE
CUANDO CUBANGO
OVAMBOLAND
DAMARALAND
GREAT NAMALAND
KALAHARI
KALAHARI DESERT
NAMIB DESERT
SKELETON COAST PARK
NAMIB-NAUKLUFT PARK
NORTH-WEST
FREE STATE
NORTHERN CAPE
WESTERN CAPE
EASTERN CAPE
NAMAQUALAND
BUSHMANLAND
LITTLE NAMALAND
CAPRIVI STRIP
LESOTHO
Luanda
Lobito
Huambo
Namibe
Windhoek
Walvis Bay
Swakopmund
Lüderitz
Gaborone
Francistown
Livingstone
Lusaka
Chingola
Lubumbashi
Johannesburg
Vereeniging
Kimberley
Bloemfontein
Maseru
Port Elizabeth
East London
Cape Town
Cape of Good Hope
Cape Agulhas
ETOSHA NATIONAL PARK
CENTRAL KALAHARI GAME RESERVE
GEMSBOK NATIONAL PARK
KALAHARI GEMSBOK N.P.
MAKGADIKGADI PANS GAME RESERVE
MOREMI GAME RES.
CHOBE N.P.
HWANGE NATIONAL PARK
KAFUE N.P.
AUGRABIES FALLS N.P.
ADDO ELEPHANT N.P.
MOUNTAIN ZEBRA N.P.
BONTEBOK N.P.
IONA NATIONAL PARK
MUPA N.P.
BIKUAR N.P.
QUIÇAMA N.P.
KAMEIA N.P.
LIUWA PLAIN N.P.
SIOMA NGWEZI N.P.
VICTORIA FALLS N.P.
Okavango Delta
Hottentot Bay
Sandwich Bay
Conception Bay
6° 9° 12° 15° 18° 21° 24° 27° 30° 33°
3° 6° 9° 12° 15° 18° 21° 24° 27°

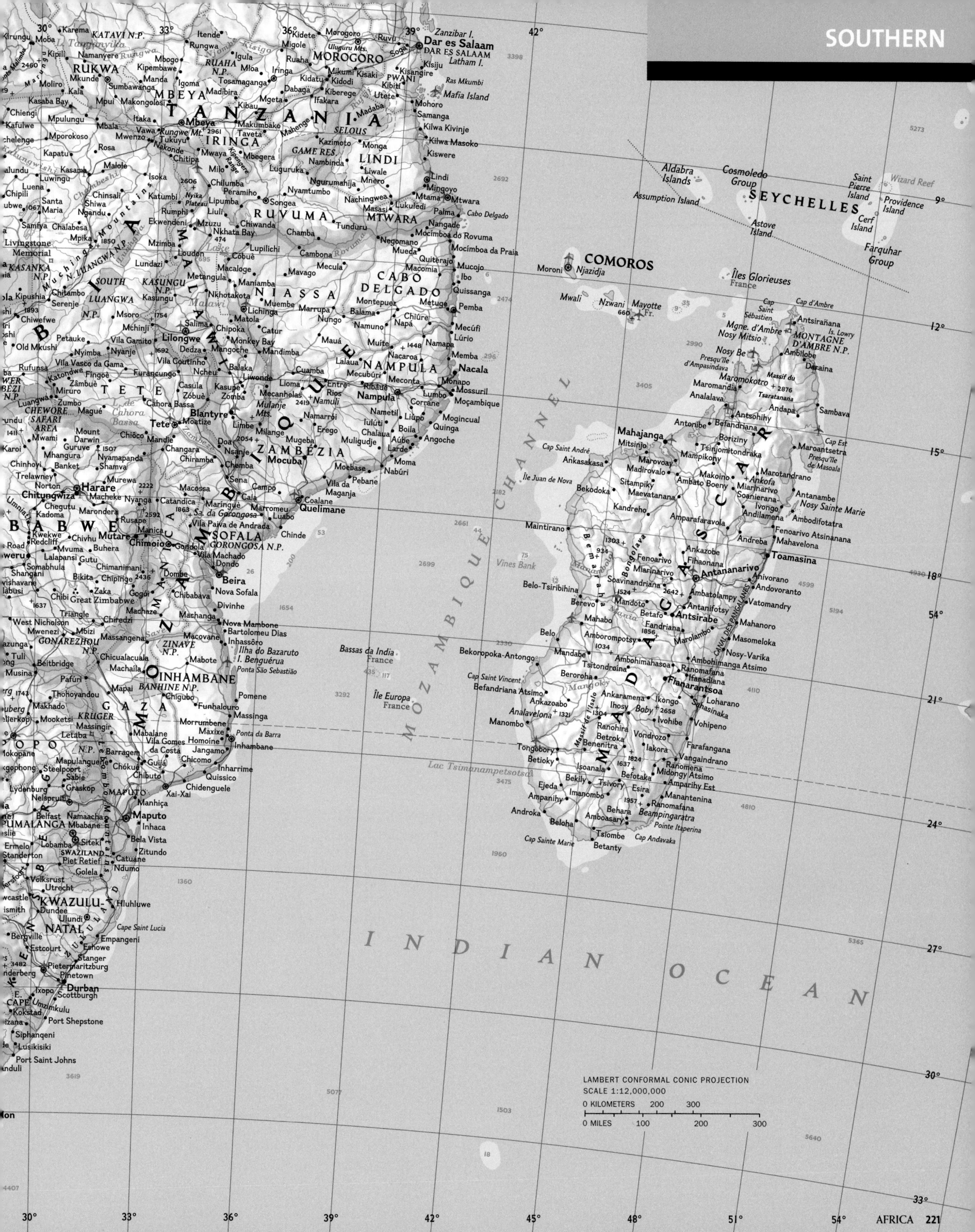
TANZANIA
Dar es Salaam
DAR ES SALAAM
MOROGORO
Zanzibar I.
Mafia Island
MBEYA
IRINGA
RUKWA
LINDI
MTWARA
RUVUMA
MALAWI
Lilongwe
Blantyre
MOZAMBIQUE
NIASSA
CABO DELGADO
NAMPULA
ZAMBÉZIA
TETE
SOFALA
MANICA
INHAMBANE
GAZA
MAPUTO
Maputo
Beira
Quelimane
Nampula
Nacala
Pemba
ZIMBABWE
Harare
Mutare
SWAZILAND
Mbabane
KWAZULU-NATAL
Durban
MPUMALANGA
COMOROS
Moroni
Njazidja
Mwali
Nzwani
Mayotte
SEYCHELLES
Aldabra Islands
Cosmoledo Group
Assumption Island
Astove Island
Providence Island
Farquhar Group
Îles Glorieuses
MADAGASCAR
Antananarivo
Toamasina
Mahajanga
Fianarantsoa
Antsirabe
Antsiranana
Tsiombe
MOZAMBIQUE CHANNEL
Bassas da India
Île Europa
Île Juan de Nova
INDIAN OCEAN
LAMBERT CONFORMAL CONIC PROJECTION
SCALE 1:12,000,000
0 KILOMETERS 200 300
0 MILES 100 200 300

COASTAL WEST AFRICA
ALBERS CONIC EQUAL-AREA PROJECTION
SCALE 1:8,000,000
0 KILOMETERS 120 160 200
0 MILES 40 80 120 160 200
MAURITANIA
SENEGAL
GAMBIA
GUINEA-BISSAU
GUINEA
SIERRA LEONE
LIBERIA
CÔTE D'IVOIRE
(IVORY COAST)
WESTERN SAHARA Morocco
ATLANTIC OCEAN
Nouakchott
Dakar
Banjul
Bissau
Conakry
Freetown
Monrovia
Bamako
Yamoussoukro
Abidjan
Nouadhibou
Cap Blanc
Baie du Lévrier
BANC D' ARGUIN N.P.
Cap Timiris
Saint-Louis
Cap Vert
Thiès
Kaolack
Ziguinchor
Cap Roxo
Arquipélago dos Bijagós
Îles Tristao
Cap Verga
Îles de Los
Banana Islands
Turtle Islands
Sherbro Island
Yawri Bay
Grain Coast
Ivory Coast
Cape Palmas
Harper
Azefal
Akchâr
Adrar
Ouarane
El Djouf
Trarza
Tagant
Assaba
Aoukâr
Hodh
Affollé
Fouta Djallon
Loma Mts.
Nimba Mts.
MOUNT SANGBE N.P.
TAÏ N.P.
MARAHOUE N.P.
COMOÉ N.P.
NIOKOLO-KOBA N.P.
BADIAR N.P.
BOUCLE DU BAOULÉ N.P.
DELTA DU SALOUM N.P.
KIANG WEST N.P.
D'ASAGNY N.P.
Atar
Akjoujt
Kiffa
Néma
Kayes
Kankan
Labé
Korhogo
Bouaké
Daloa
Bobo Dioulasso
Ségou
Mopti
Djenné
Longitude West 6° of Greenwich
18°
15°
12°
9°
6°
3°
21°

ALGERIA
NIGER
NIGERIA
BENIN
TOGO
GHANA
BURKINA FASO
CAMEROON
EQUATORIAL GUINEA
BIOKO
GULF OF GUINEA
Bight of Benin
Slave Coast
Gold Coast
Cape Three Points
Cape Saint Paul
Niger Delta
Palm Point
Lake Chad (Lac Tchad)
Lake Volta
Adrar des Iforas
Tassili Oua-n-Ahaggar
Tamesna
Talak
Aïr (Aïr Massif)
Massif de Tarazit
Ténéré
'Erg du Ténéré
Ténéré du Tafassâsset
Kaouar
Azaouagh
Tagama
Damergou
Damagarim
Adar Doutchi
Manga
Koutous
Gourma
Mossi
Borgou
Tanezrouft
Timétrine
"W" NATIONAL PARK
PENDJARI N.P.
KABORE-TAMBI N.P.
KERAN N.P.
FAZAO-MALFAKASSA N.P.
MOLE N.P.
DIGYA N.P.
BUI N.P.
KAINJI LAKE N.P.
YANKARI N.P.
GASHAKA-GUMTI N.P.
FARO RESERVE
CROSS RIVER N.P.
KORUP N.P.
Cameroon Mt. 4100
Malabo
Niamey
Ouagadougou
Lomé
Accra
Cotonou
Porto-Novo
Abuja
LAGOS
Ibadan
Kano
Kaduna
Zaria
Sokoto
Maiduguri
Jos
Ilorin
Benin City
Port Harcourt
Calabar
Enugu
Onitsha
Douala
Yaoundé
Kumasi
Tamale
Sekondi-Takoradi
Parakou
Djougou
Agadez
Zinder
Maradi
Tahoua
Gao
Kidal
Bilma
Garoua
Bamenda
Meridian of Greenwich (London)
Longitude East 6° of Greenwich
0°
3°
6°
9°
12°
15°
18°

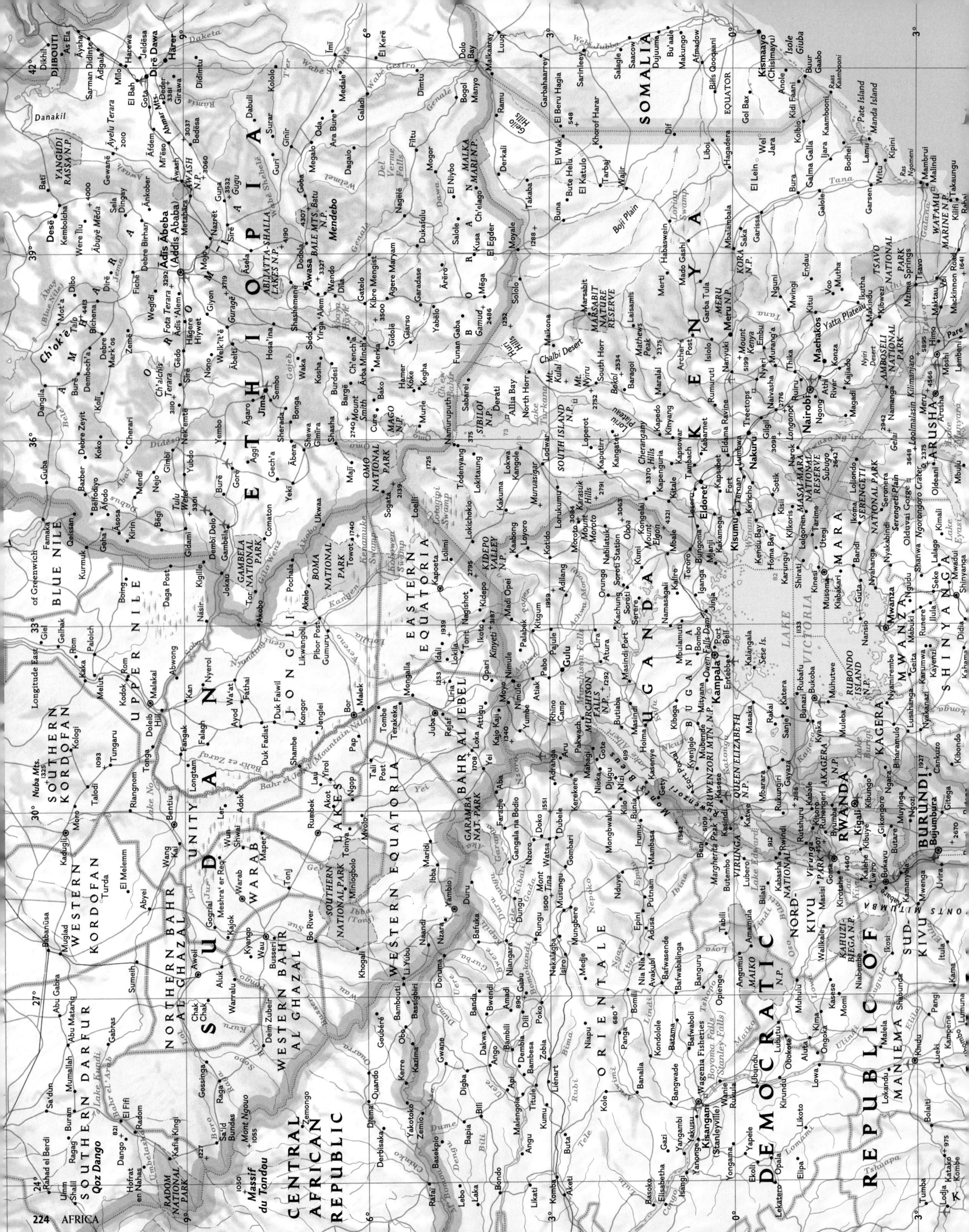

24°
27°
30°
33°
36°
39°
42°
Longitude East of Greenwich
Rahad el Berdi
Sa'dun
Babanūsa
Nuba Mts.
1325
SOUTHERN KORDOFAN
Giel
Famaka
Guba
Dangila
Ch'ok'ē
Abay (Blue Nile)
Desē
Batī
Danakil
Dikhil
DJIBOUTI
Umm Shalil
Ragag
Buram
Mumallah
Abu Gabra
Abu Matariq
Muglad
WESTERN KORDOFAN
Kadugli
Moro
Kologi
Gelhak
Rom
Kaka
Paloich
BLUE NILE
Qeissan
Kurmuk
Bazber
Debre Zeyit
Koko
Bele
Burē
Mot'a
Talo
4413
Dibo
Dembech'a
Bichena
Kolī
Debre Mark'os
Kembolcha
Were Ilu
Ābuyē Mēda
4000
YANGUDI RASSA N.P.
As Ela
Āysha
Sarman Didinte
Ādīgala
SOUTHERN DARFUR
Qoz Dango
Lake Kundi
Bahr el 'Arab
Gabras
Turda
Talodi
1093
Tungaru
Melut
Goha
Bēlfodiyo
Āfodo
Dirē
Jema
Sela Dingay
Gewanē
Āyelu Terara
2010
Mīlo
Harewa
Jeldēsa
Hofrat en Nahas
Dango
821
El Fifi
Radom
Umbelasha
Sumeih
El Melemm
Riangnom
Kodok
Boing
Āsosa
Kirin
Dabus
Mendī
Cherari
Zemē
Fichē
Debre Birhan
Ānkober
Āfdem
El Bah
Gota
Dirē Dawa
Abyei
UPPER NILE
Lake No
Tonga
Doleib Hill
Malakal
Nejo
Bēgī
Gīmbī
Wegīdī
Ch'alchīs Terara
3110
Fota Terara
3292
Ādīs 'Alem
Ādīs Ābeba (Addis Ababa)
Mī'ēso
Ahmar Mts.
Deder
3381
Harer
RADOM NATIONAL PARK
Kafia Kingi
NORTHERN BAHR AL GHAZAL
Wang Kai
Bentiu
Fangak
Abwong
Daga Post
Tulu Welel
3301
Gīdamī
Yubdo
Nek'emtē
Sīrē
Gēdo
Hāgere Hiywet
Metahāra
Āwash
AWASH N.P.
3037
Bedēsa
Girawa
Dīdīmtu
Dakata
9°
1227
Gossinga
Chak Chak
Aweil
UNITY
Longtam
Falagh
Kan
Nasir
Kigille
Dembī Dolo
Gambēla
Burē
Yembo
Nono
Welk'īt'ē
Ābeltī
Giyon
Gurage
3719
Mojo
Nazrēt
Sīrē
Guna
3532
Gugu
3060
Sa'id Bundas
Raga
Aluk
Gogrial
Meshra' er Req
Ler
Nyerol
Jokau
Gorē
1050
Massif du Tondou
Mont Ngouo
1055
Warralu
Kajok
Warab
Wun Shwai
Adok
Ayod
Wa'at
Fathai
Akobo
Tor
GAMBELA NATIONAL PARK
Gilo Wenz
Comaton
Aggi
Āgaro
Jīma
Sembo
Hosa'ina
Āsela
ABIJATTA-SHALLA LAKES N.P.
4190
Dabuli
Surar
Guri
Kololo
Deim Zubeir
Kyango
Wau
Busseri
WARAB
Maper
Duk Fadiat
Duk Faiwil
SUDAN
ETHIOPIA
WESTERN BAHR AL GHAZAL
Tonj
Shambe
Kongor
JONGLI
Likwangoli
Pochala
Gech'a
Yekī
Ābera
Sherada
Bonga
Gojeb
Waka
Shashemenē
Dodola
4307
Goba
BALE MTS. Batu N.P.
Gīnīr
Wabē Shebelē
CENTRAL AFRICAN REPUBLIC
Zemongo
Bo River
SOUTHERN NATIONAL PARK
Miniogbolo
Rumbek
Akot
Yirol
Lau
Jonglei
Akelo
Pibor Post
Gumuru
BOMA NATIONAL PARK
Ukwaa
Shewa Gīmīra
Kosha
Sodo
Āwasa
3327
Yirga 'Alem
Wendo
Dīla
Mendebo
Megalo
Oda
Ara Burē
Dagaio
Medalē
Īmī
LAKES
Toinya
Ngop
Mvolo
Bor
Malek
Pap
Veveno
Towot
1740
Kenamuke Swamp
Mountain Nile
Khogali
Djema
Ouando
Goubéré
Bambouti
Derbisaka
Tali Post
Tombe
Terakeka
Mongalla
Shasha
Majī
2740
Mount Smith
Burdesi
Bargē
Ch'ench'a
Ārba Minch'
Gatelo
Kibre Mengist
3500
Agere Maryam
Galadi
6°
El Kerē
WESTERN EQUATORIA
Obo
Kerre
Kazima
Yakotoko
Zemio
Bassigbiri
Li Yubu
Naandi
Nzara
Ibba
Maridi
Yambio
EASTERN EQUATORIA
Kapoeta
Sogata
2139
OMO NATIONAL PARK
Cure
Bako
MAGO N.P.
Merka
Gīdolē
Giarso
Hamer Koke
Kegha
Murle
Nagelē
Del Verme Falls
Fīltu
Dīmtu
Rafaï
Basekpio
Lebo
Laka
Bapia
Bili
Dengu
Digba
Gwane
Doruma
Duma
Uere
Juba
Rejaf
Liria
1253
Idali
1939
Lolimi
1725
Lotagipi Swamp
Loelli
Namuruputh
Yabēlo
Ārēro
Garadase
Dukafulu
Mogor
El Niybo
Dawa
Bogol Manyo
Dolo Bay
Bondo
Dakwa
Ango
Bwendi
Banda
Bafuka
Duru
GARAMBA NAT. PARK
BAHR AL JEBEL
1708
Loka
Yei
Lokila
Torit
Nagishot
2795
Ikoto
Kinyeti
3187
Kidepo
Lokichokio
Todenyang
Lokitaung
SIBILOI N.P.
375
Sabarei
Funan Gaba
Gamud
2486
Borana
Salole
Kusa
Mēga
Ch'elago
MALKA MARI N.P.
El Egder
Malkaaray
Luuq
Api
Bambili
Amadi
Dembia
Bambesa
Dili
890
Gabu
Niangara
Faradje
Aba
Gangala na Bodio
Kajo Kaji
1340
Attigu
Opari
Moyo
Nimule
Madi Opei
KIDEPO VALLEY N.P.
Kakuma
Lokwa Kangole
Kaabong
Loyoro
Derati
Allia Bay
North Horr
Huri Hills
1252
Sololo
Moyale
Derkali
Ramu
Takaba
Geilo Hills
Malengoia
Titule
Angu
Kumu
Zobia
Poko
Rungu
Dungu
Gada
Kibali
Nzoro
Doko
1551
Yumbe
Atiak
Palabek
Pabo
Kitgum
Pager
Muruasigar
Kotido
Lake Turkana
Chalbi Desert
Maikona
1288
Garbahaarrey
Likati
Komba
Aketi
Buta
Liénart
Nekalagba
Isiro
1500
Mont Tina
Watsa
Dubele
Adranga
Aru
Rhino Camp
Gulu
Pajule
1959
Adilang
Lorukumu
Lodwar
SOUTH ISLAND N.P.
Mt. Kulal
Buna
El Wak
El Beru Hagia
548
Bute Helu
El Katulo
Sarinleey
3°
Rubi
Tele
Bima
Mungbere
Musungu
Gombari
Kerekere
Pakwach
Mahagi
MURCHISON FALLS N.P.
Murchison Falls
Achwa (Moroto)
Moroto
3084
Karasuk Hills
Mount Moroto
Loperot
Mt. Nyiru
2752
South Horr
Marsabit
MARSABIT NATURE RESERVE
Niapu
Medje
Nepoko
ORIENTALE
Kole
680
Mongbwalu
Nioka
Djugu
Gote
1292
Atura
Lira
Orungo
Nabilatuk
2791
Kaputir
Loriu Plateau
Bokol
2534
Khorof Harar
Tarbaj
Wajir
Boji Plain
Salagle
Banalia
Panga
Bomili
Nduye
Kilo
Nizi
Butiaba
619
Masindi Port
Kachung
Soroti Station
3063
Kangatet
Baragoi
Laisamis
Basoko
Lindi
Nia Nia
Avakubi
Epini
Adusa
Putnam
Irumu
Mambasa
Bunia
Monts Bleus
Kasenye
Hoima
Masindi
UGANDA
Soroti
Serere
Kumi
Oboa
Kongelai
Mount Elgon
4321
Cherangany Hills
3370
Kapenguria
Kapedo
Kinyang
Maralal
Mathews Peak
2375
Merti
Habaswein
Lorian Swamp
SOMALIA
Saacow
Dujuuma
Bu'aale
Elisabetha
Gazi
Kondolole
Bafwasende
Batama
Bangwade
Bafwaboli
Bafwabalinga
Isangi
Yangambi
Yakusu
Yanonge
Kisangani (Stanleyville)
Wagenia Fisheries
Boyoma Falls (Stanley Falls)
Tshopo
Banguru
Opienge
Wanie Rukula
Gety
1542
Ruwenzori
Fort Portal
Kyenjojo
Kiboga
BUGANDA
Mbulamuti
Namasagali
Kaliro
Tororo
Mbale
Kitale
Kapsowar
Tambach
Archer's Post
Mado Gashi
KENYA
Dif
Makungo
Afmadow
Yongama
Tabili
Beni
5109
Margherita Peak
RUWENZORI MTN. N.P.
Kasese
Kasindi
Mubende
Mityana
Bombo
Owen Falls Dam
Kampala
Port Bell
Entebbe
Jinja
Iganga
Bungoma
Mjanji
Kakamega
Eldoret
Leseru
Kabarnet
Rumuruti
Isiolo
Garba Tula
MERU N.P.
Meru
Liboi
Bilis Qooqaani
Hagadera
EQUATOR
0°
Ekoli
Yapele
Ubundu
Angumu
MAIKO N.P.
Amamula
Butembo
VIRUNGA
Lubero
Lake Edward
Katwe
QUEEN ELIZABETH N.P.
Katonga
Masaka
Kalangala
Sese Is.
Kisumu
Fort Ternan
Kapsabet
Eldama Ravine
Lumbwa
Kericho
Winam
Nakuru
Treetops
Nanyuki
5199
Mount Kenya
KORA N.P.
Mbalambala
Saka
Garissa
El Lein
Gol Bax
Wel Jara
Kismaayo (Chisimayu)
DEMOCRATIC
Lekatero
Opala
Kirundu
Lubutu
Obokote
Bilati
Kabasha
Rwindi
NATIONAL
912
Mbarara
Rukungiri
Gayaza
Rakai
Sanje
Katera
Kendu Bay
Homa Bay
82
Karungu
Kisii
Sotik
Gilgil
3098
Naivasha
2776
Nyeri
Embu
Murang'a
Tana
Nguni
Mwingi
Anole
Kolbio
Kidi Faani
Isole Giuba
Buur Gaabo
Elipa
Likoto
Muhulu
Aluta
Lowa
Kima
Ongoka
Kasese
Momi
NORD-KIVU
Walikale
Masisi
Goma
Virunga PARK
4507
Kisoro
Rutshuru
2186
Kabale
Ruhengeri
AKAGERA N.P.
Byumba
Rubafu
Bukoba
Bunazi
Kyaka
LAKE VICTORIA
1133
Shirati
Kilkoris
Lolgorien
MASAI MARA NATIONAL RESERVE
Narok
Longonot
Ruiru
Thika
Nairobi
Ngong
Machakos
Kitui
Endau
Bura
Galma Galla
Ijara
Kaambooni
Raas Kaambooni
Kahuzi-Biega N.P.
Kirotshe
Niabembe
1460
RWANDA
Kigali
Kibungo
Muhutwe
Kinesi
Tarime
Utegi
Musoma
Kiabakari
MARA
Subugo
2642
Athi River
Konza
Yatta Plateau
Voo
Mutha
Galole
REPUBLIC OF
Lokandu
Malela
MANIEMA
Shabunda
Ikosi
Kalehe
Lwiro
Bukavu
Kibuye
Gikongoro
Butare
Ngara
Muleba
RUBONDO ISLAND N.P.
Lake Burigi
KAGERA
Biharamulo
Nansio
Guta
Baridi
Ikoma
Loliondo
SERENGETI NATIONAL PARK
Magadi
Kajiado
Nyiri Desert
Makindu
Ikutha
Kibwezi
TSAVO NATIONAL PARK
Bodhei
Lamu
Pate Island
Manda Island
Witu
Garsen
Kipini
Kindu
SUD-KIVU
Kamanyola
Kabare
Muyinga
Ngozi
Nyamirembe
Lusahanga
MWANZA
Mwanza
Nyahanga
Nyakabindi
Seronera
Serengeti Plain
Olduvai Gorge
Gelai
2942
Namanga
AMBOSELI NATIONAL PARK
Mzima Springs
Tsavo
Ras Ngomeni
Mambrui
Malindi
Tumba
Bolaiti
Pangi
Lueki
Kampene
Kama
Lumuna
Mwenga
Uvira
MITUMBA
Itula
BURUNDI
Bujumbura
1927
Cankuzo
Gitega
2670
Kibondo
Nyakanazi
Karumwa
Kayenzi
Mabuki
Ngudu
Runere
Ilula
Seke
Shanwa
Lalago
Ngorongoro Crater
3648
Loolmalasin
Kilimanjaro
2375
Meru
4566
Arusha
ARUSHA
5895
Himo
Moshi
Lembeni
Pare
Maktau
Voi
Mackinnon Road
1641
Galana
WATAMU MARINE N.P.
Kilifi
Takaungu
Rahai
SHINYANGA
Shinyanga
Mwadui
Kimali
Lake Eyasi
Oldeani
Mbulu
Lake Manyara
Kahama
Didia
Lodja
Katako-Kombe
975

CENTRAL RIFT VALLEY
ALBERS CONIC EQUAL-AREA PROJECTION
SCALE 1:8,000,000
0 KILOMETERS 120 160 200
0 MILES 40 80 120 160 200
INDIAN OCEAN
MOZAMBIQUE CHANNEL
TANZANIA
MOZAMBIQUE
MALAWI
ZAMBIA
ZIMBABWE
ANGOLA
NAMIBIA
BOTSWANA
Dar es Salaam
Dodoma
Lilongwe
Lusaka
Harare
Nampula
Beira
Blantyre
Lubumbashi (Élisabethville)
Quelimane
Livingstone

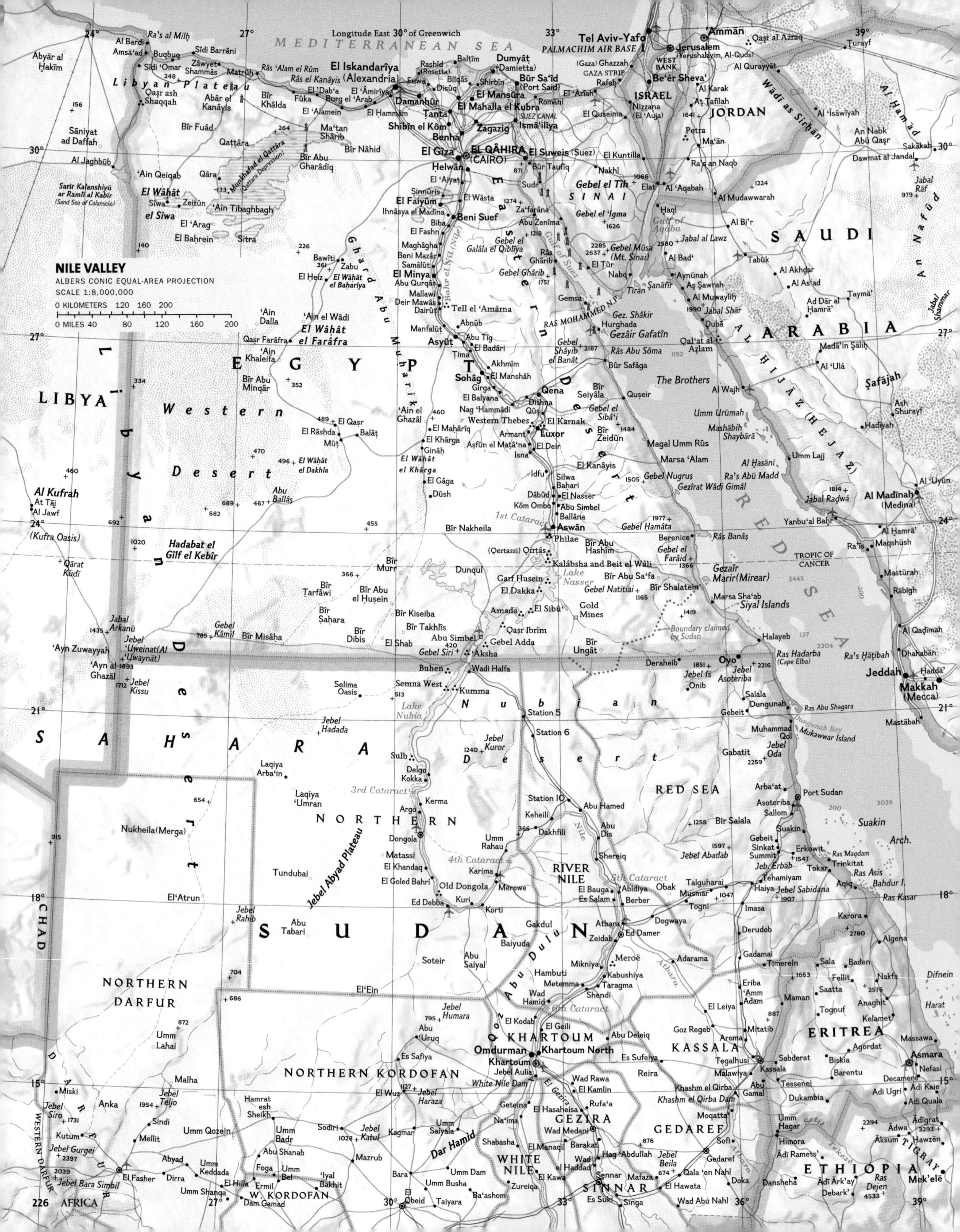
NILE VALLEY
ALBERS CONIC EQUAL-AREA PROJECTION
SCALE 1:8,000,000
0 KILOMETERS 120 160 200
0 MILES 40 80 120 160 200
Longitude East 30° of Greenwich
MEDITERRANEAN SEA
RED SEA
EGYPT
LIBYA
SUDAN
SAUDI ARABIA
JORDAN
ISRAEL
WEST BANK
GAZA STRIP
ERITREA
ETHIOPIA
CHAD
SAHARA
Libyan Plateau
Libyan Desert
Western Desert
Eastern Desert
Nubian Desert
SINAI
AL HIJAZ (HEJAZ)
TROPIC OF CANCER
El Iskandarîya (Alexandria)
El Qâhira (Cairo)
El Giza
Helwân
Bûr Sa'îd (Port Said)
El Suweis (Suez)
Ismâ'ilîya
Dumyât (Damietta)
Rashîd (Rosetta)
Tanta
Damanhûr
Zagazig
Benha
El Mansûra
El Mahalla el Kubra
Shibîn el Kôm
SUEZ CANAL
Munkhafad el Qattâra (Qattara Depression)
El Wâhât el Sîwa
Sîwa
Marsa Matrûh
El 'Alamein
Beni Suef
El Faiyûm
El Minya
Asyût
Sohâg
Qena
Luxor
El Karnak
Western Thebes
Isna
Idfu
Kôm Ombo
Aswân
1st Cataract
Philae
Lake Nasser
Abu Simbel
Wadi Halfa
Lake Nubia
El Wâhât el Farâfra
El Wâhât el Bahariya
El Wâhât el Dakhla
El Wâhât el Khârga
Hadabat el Gilf el Kebîr
Al Kufrah
Gebel Mûsa (Mt. Sinai)
Gulf of Suez
Gulf of Aqaba
Sharm el Sheikh
Hurghada
Bûr Safâga
Quseir
Marsa 'Alam
Berenice
Halayeb
Boundary claimed by Sudan
Tel Aviv-Yafo
Jerusalem
'Ammân
Be'ér Sheva'
Elat
Al 'Aqabah
Tabûk
Al Madînah (Medina)
Makkah (Mecca)
Jeddah
Yanbu' al Bahr
Port Sudan
Suakin
Tokar
NORTHERN
RED SEA
RIVER NILE
KHARTOUM
Khartoum
Omdurman
Khartoum North
KASSALA
Kassala
GEZIRA
GEDAREF
SINNAR
WHITE NILE
NORTHERN KORDOFAN
W. KORDOFAN
NORTHERN DARFUR
WESTERN DARFUR
DARFUR
Dongola
Kerma
3rd Cataract
4th Cataract
5th Cataract
6th Cataract
Karima
Merowe
Atbara
Ed Damer
Berber
Shendi
Meroë
Wad Medani
Sennar
El Obeid
El Fasher
Asmara
Mek'ele
TIGRAY
Jebel Abyad Plateau
Jebel Marra
Dar Hamid
Wadi Abu Dulu

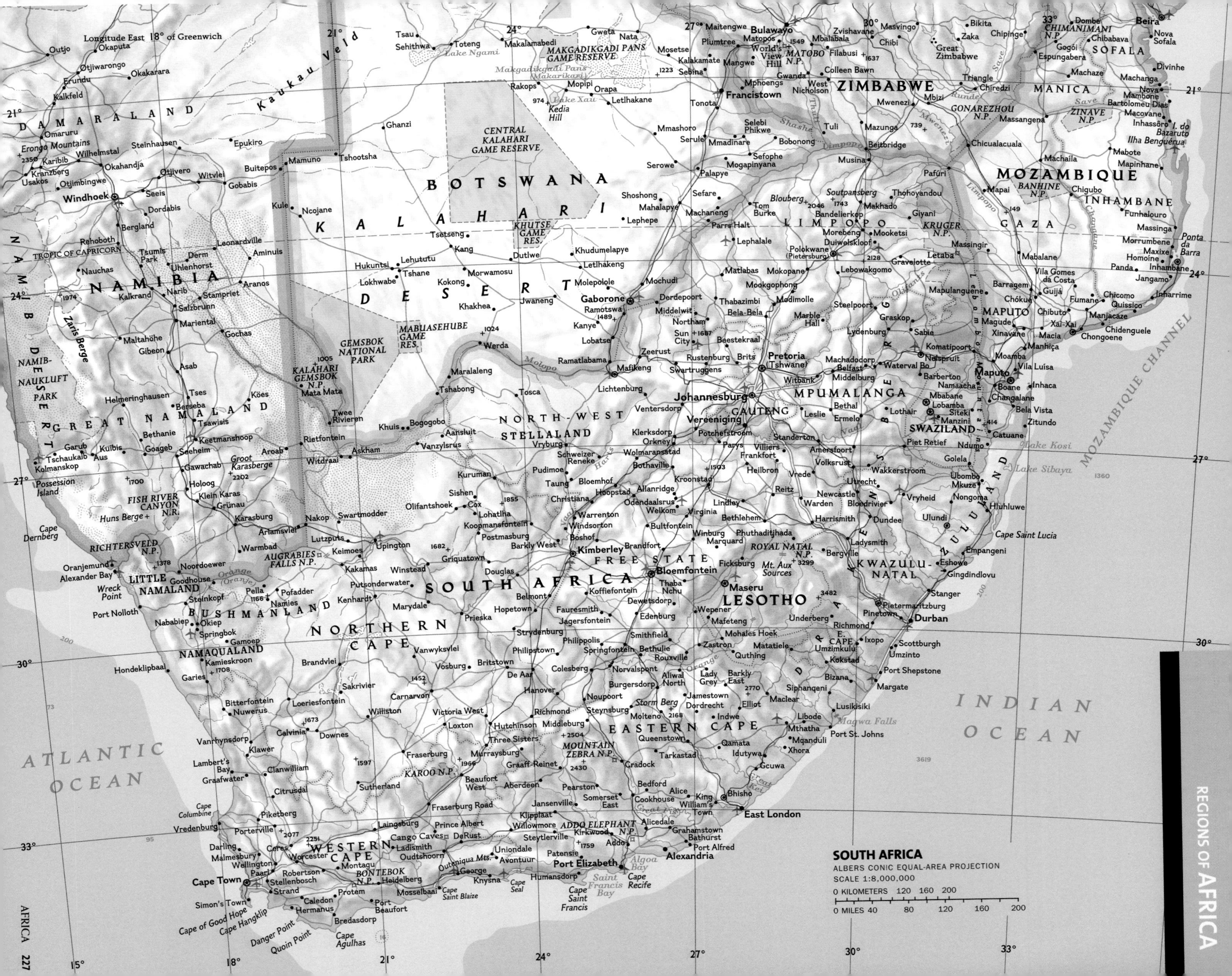
SOUTH AFRICA
ALBERS CONIC EQUAL-AREA PROJECTION
SCALE 1:8,000,000
0 KILOMETERS 120 160 200
0 MILES 40 80 120 160 200
INDIAN OCEAN
ATLANTIC OCEAN
MOZAMBIQUE CHANNEL
SOUTH AFRICA
BOTSWANA
NAMIBIA
ZIMBABWE
MOZAMBIQUE
LESOTHO
SWAZILAND
KALAHARI DESERT
NAMIB DESERT
GREAT NAMALAND
DAMARALAND
BUSHMANLAND
NAMAQUALAND
LITTLE NAMALAND
NORTHERN CAPE
WESTERN CAPE
EASTERN CAPE
FREE STATE
NORTH-WEST
GAUTENG
MPUMALANGA
LIMPOPO
KWAZULU-NATAL
ZULULAND
STELLALAND
MANICA
SOFALA
INHAMBANE
GAZA
MAPUTO
TROPIC OF CAPRICORN
Longitude East 18° of Greenwich
Johannesburg
Pretoria (Tshwane)
Cape Town
Durban
Port Elizabeth
East London
Bloemfontein
Kimberley
Maseru
Mbabane
Maputo
Gaborone
Windhoek
Bulawayo
Francistown
Beira
Upington
Mafikeng
Polokwane (Pietersburg)
Cape of Good Hope
Cape Agulhas
Orange
Limpopo
Molopo
Save
KRUGER N.P.
CENTRAL KALAHARI GAME RESERVE
GEMSBOK NATIONAL PARK
KALAHARI GEMSBOK N.P.
MABUASEHUBE GAME RES.
KHUTSE GAME RES.
MAKGADIKGADI PANS GAME RESERVE
NAMIB-NAUKLUFT PARK
FISH RIVER CANYON N.P.
RICHTERSVELD N.P.
AUGRABIES FALLS N.P.
KAROO N.P.
MOUNTAIN ZEBRA N.P.
ADDO ELEPHANT N.P.
ROYAL NATAL N.P.
BONTEBOK N.P.
GONAREZHOU N.P.
BANHINE N.P.
ZINAVE N.P.
CHIMANIMANI N.P.
MATOBO N.P.

Island nation and smallest, flattest continent, with a territory about the size of the United States, Australia has gone on a planetary walkabout since it broke away from the supercontinent of Gondwana about 65 million years ago. Isolated, dry, and scoured by erosion, Australia developed unique animals, notably marsupials such as kangaroos, and plants, such as more than 600 eucalyptus species. The land surface has been stable enough to preserve some of the world's oldest rocks and mineral deposits, dating to the original formation of Earth's crust. Precambrian fossils include stromatolites—photosynthetic bacteria that generated oxygen in the early atmosphere and whose descendants still grow mounded in shallow lagoons, such as in Shark Bay in western Australia. In contrast, New Zealand's two principal islands, about the size of Colorado, are younger and tell of a more violent geology that raised high volcanic mountains above deep fjords, leaving landscapes reminiscent of Europe's Alps, Norway's coast, and Scotland's moors. Both nations were first inhabited by seafarers, Australia as long as 50,000 years ago, New Zealand little more than a thousand. From the late 18th century to the early 20th, both were British colonies. Both have transformed themselves from commerce based on exports of beef and hides, lamb and wool, to fully integrated industrialized and service-oriented economies. Both have striven with varying success to accommodate aboriginal peoples, as well as recent immigrants—many from Vietnam and China and many of the Muslim faith—as part of a diverse, modern society. Oceania, roughly those islands of the southwest Pacific that include Polynesia, Micronesia, and Melanesia, was settled by indigenous expeditions sailing in multihulled vessels. These adventurers settled nearly every inhabitable Pacific island and perhaps made landfall as far distant as South America before Europeans appeared over the horizon in the 17th century. Today these islands are in various states of nationhood or dependency, prosperity or poverty, and often ignored if not outright exploited.

IMAGE BY ROBERT STACEY, WORLDSAT INTERNATIONAL INC.

ARAFURA SEA
CORAL SEA
TIMOR SEA
INDIAN OCEAN
TASMAN SEA
SOLOMON SEA
GULF OF CARPENTARIA
GREAT AUSTRALIAN BIGHT
BASS STRAIT
TORRES STRAIT
INDONESIA
TIMOR-LESTE (EAST TIMOR)
PAPUA NEW GUINEA
NEW GUINEA
TROBRIAND IS.
D'ENTRECASTEAUX IS.
LOUISIADE ARCHIPELAGO
AUSTRALIA
WESTERN AUSTRALIA
NORTHERN TERRITORY
QUEENSLAND
SOUTH AUSTRALIA
NEW SOUTH WALES
VICTORIA
TASMANIA
JERVIS BAY TERRITORY
Canberra, A.C.T.
GREAT DIVIDING RANGE
GREAT ARTESIAN BASIN
CENTRAL LOWLANDS
MURRAY RIVER BASIN
LAKE EYRE BASIN
WESTERN PLATEAU
GREAT SANDY DESERT
Gibson Desert
Tanami Desert
Simpson Desert
Sturt Stony Desert
Nullarbor Plain
Eucla Basin
Barkly Tableland
Kimberley Plateau
ARNHEM LAND
Cape York Peninsula
Eyre Peninsula
Darwin
Brisbane
Sydney
Melbourne
Adelaide
Perth
Hobart
Port Moresby
Dili
Surabaya
Lake Eyre
Lake Torrens
Lake Frome
Lake Gairdner
Lake Argyle
Uluru (Ayers Rock)
KataTjuta (Mt. Olga)
Mt. Kosciuszko
Highest point in Australia
Lowest point in Australia
Macdonnell Ranges
Musgrave Ranges
Hamersley Range
Flinders Ranges
Darling
Murray
Murrumbidgee
Lachlan
Macquarie
Great Barrier Reef
Kangaroo I.
King Island
Flinders I.
FURNEAUX GROUP
Groote Eylandt
Melville I.
Bathurst I.
Fraser Island
Lord Howe I.
Ball's Pyramid
Houtman Abrolhos
Shark Bay
Exmouth Gulf
Geographe Bay
Cape Leeuwin
Cheyne Bay
TROPIC OF CAPRICORN
Longitude East 130° of Greenwich
AZIMUTHAL EQUIDISTANT PROJECTION
SCALE 1:19,000,000
0 KILOMETERS 300 400 500
0 MILES 100 200 300 400 500

AUSTRALIA
WESTERN AUSTRALIA
NORTHERN TERRITORY
QUEENSLAND
SOUTH AUSTRALIA
NEW SOUTH WALES
VICTORIA
TASMANIA
JERVIS BAY TERRITORY
PAPUA NEW GUINEA
NEW GUINEA
INDONESIA
TIMOR-LESTE (EAST TIMOR)
CORAL SEA ISLANDS TERRITORY
SOLOMON SEA
CORAL SEA
TASMAN SEA
ARAFURA SEA
TIMOR SEA
INDIAN OCEAN
GREAT AUSTRALIAN BIGHT
GULF OF CARPENTARIA
BASS STRAIT
TORRES STRAIT
GREAT BARRIER REEF
GREAT SANDY DESERT
Gibson Desert
Great Victoria Desert
Tanami Desert
Simpson Desert
Nullarbor Plain
GREAT ARTESIAN BASIN
Barkly Tableland
Canberra
Sydney
Melbourne
Brisbane
Adelaide
Perth
Darwin
Hobart
Port Moresby
Dili
Cairns
Townsville
Alice Springs
Newcastle
Wollongong
Gold Coast
Geelong
Kalgoorlie
Broome
TROPIC OF CAPRICORN
Longitude East 130° of Greenwich
AZIMUTHAL EQUIDISTANT PROJECTION
SCALE 1:19,000,000
0 KILOMETERS 300 400 500
0 MILES 100 200 300 400 500

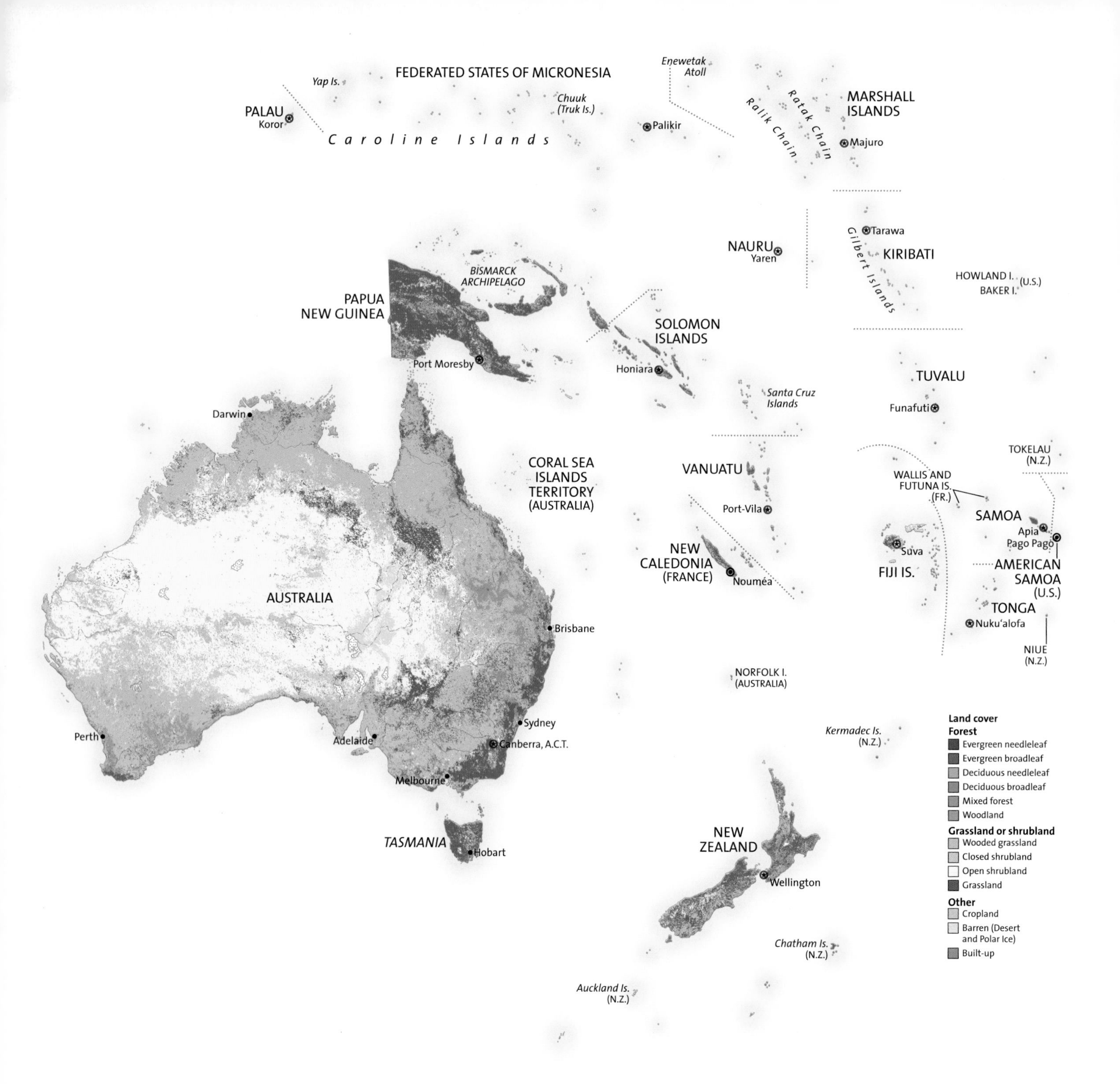

TEMPERATURE AND RAINFALL

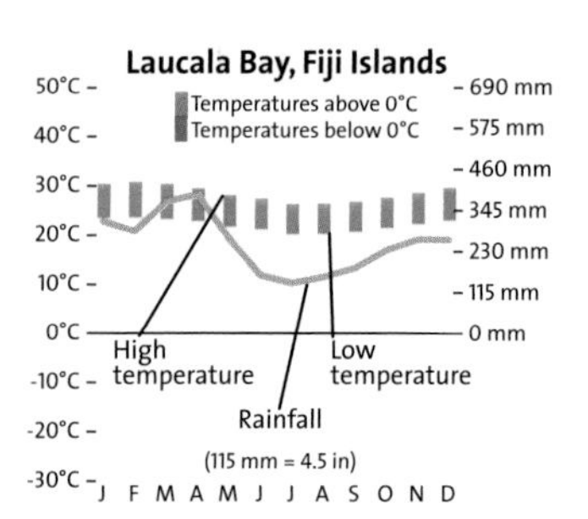

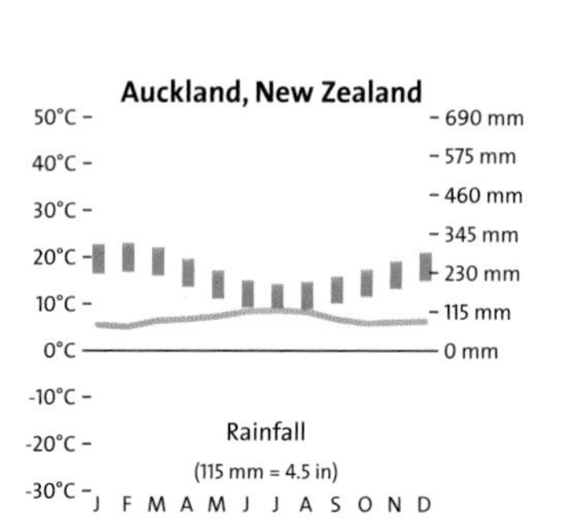

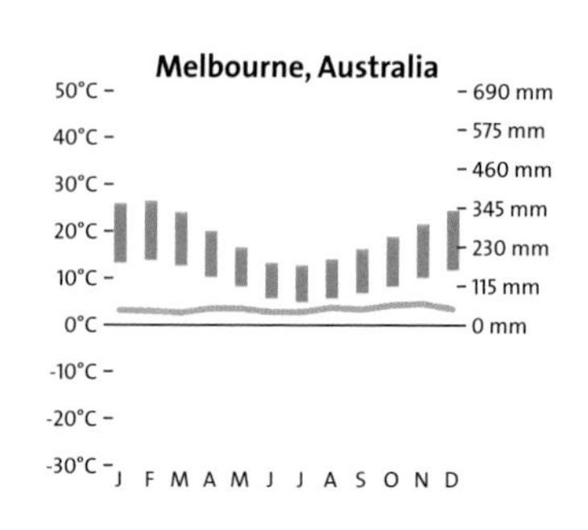

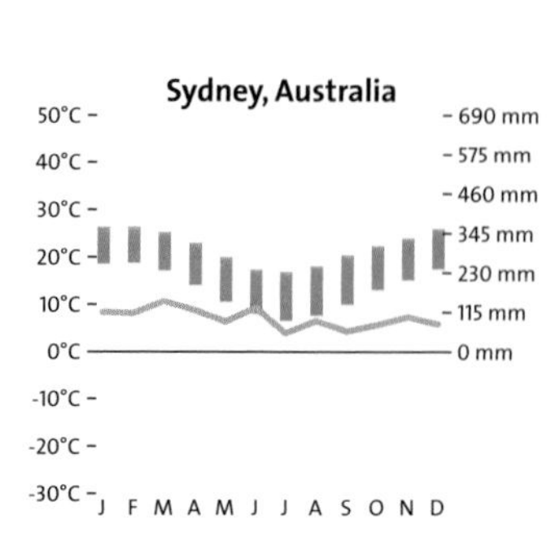

The entire extent of Oceania encompasses the islands of the Central and South Pacific, including Hawai'i, New Zealand, and Australia.

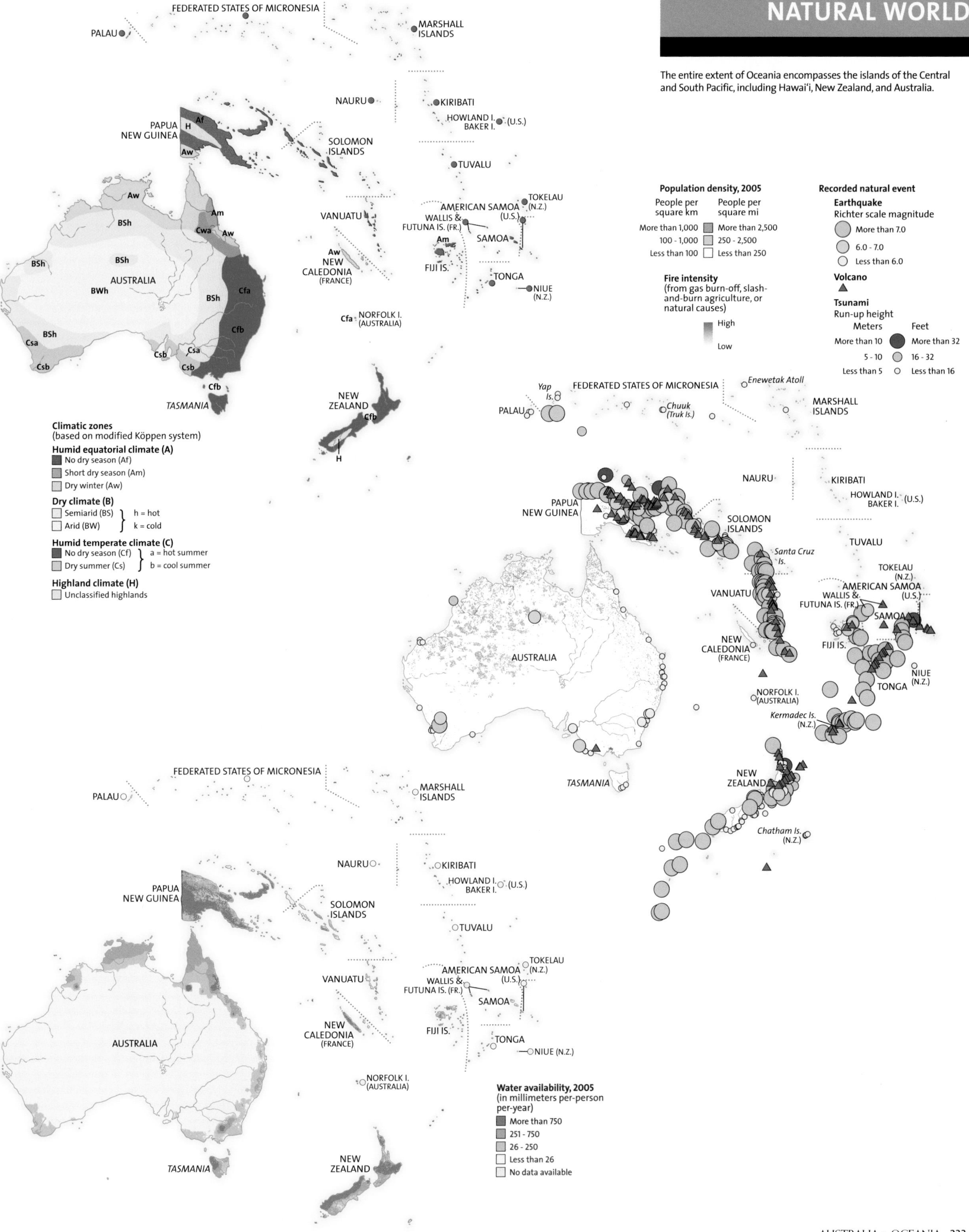
FEDERATED STATES OF MICRONESIA
PALAU
MARSHALL ISLANDS
NAURU
KIRIBATI
HOWLAND I.
BAKER I.
(U.S.)
PAPUA NEW GUINEA
SOLOMON ISLANDS
TUVALU
TOKELAU (N.Z.)
AMERICAN SAMOA (U.S.)
VANUATU
WALLIS & FUTUNA IS. (FR.)
SAMOA
NEW CALEDONIA (FRANCE)
FIJI IS.
TONGA
NIUE (N.Z.)
NORFOLK I. (AUSTRALIA)
AUSTRALIA
TASMANIA
NEW ZEALAND
Af
H
Aw
Am
Cwa
BSh
BWh
Cfa
Cfb
Csa
Csb
Climatic zones
(based on modified Köppen system)
Humid equatorial climate (A)
No dry season (Af)
Short dry season (Am)
Dry winter (Aw)
Dry climate (B)
Semiarid (BS)
Arid (BW)
h = hot
k = cold
Humid temperate climate (C)
No dry season (Cf)
Dry summer (Cs)
a = hot summer
b = cool summer
Highland climate (H)
Unclassified highlands
Population density, 2005
People per square km
People per square mi
More than 1,000
100 - 1,000
Less than 100
More than 2,500
250 - 2,500
Less than 250
Fire intensity
(from gas burn-off, slash-and-burn agriculture, or natural causes)
High
Low
Recorded natural event
Earthquake
Richter scale magnitude
More than 7.0
6.0 - 7.0
Less than 6.0
Volcano
Tsunami
Run-up height
Meters
Feet
More than 10
More than 32
5 - 10
16 - 32
Less than 5
Less than 16
Yap Is.
Chuuk (Truk Is.)
Enewetak Atoll
Santa Cruz Is.
Kermadec Is. (N.Z.)
Chatham Is. (N.Z.)
Water availability, 2005
(in millimeters per-person per-year)
More than 750
251 - 750
26 - 250
Less than 26
No data available

FEDERATED STATES OF MICRONESIA
Yap Is.
PALAU
Koror
Caroline Islands
Chuuk
(Truk Is.)
Enewetak
Atoll
Palikir
Ratak Chain
Ralik Chain
MARSHALL
ISLANDS
Majuro
Tarawa
Gilbert Islands
KIRIBATI
NAURU
Yaren
HOWLAND I.
BAKER I.
(U.S.)
BISMARCK
ARCHIPELAGO
PAPUA
NEW GUINEA
Port Moresby
SOLOMON
ISLANDS
Honiara
Santa Cruz
Islands
TUVALU
Funafuti
Darwin
CORAL SEA
ISLANDS
TERRITORY
(AUSTRALIA)
VANUATU
Port-Vila
TOKELAU
(N.Z.)
WALLIS AND
FUTUNA IS.
(FR.)
SAMOA
Apia
Pago Pago
AMERICAN
SAMOA
(U.S.)
NEW
CALEDONIA
(FRANCE)
Nouméa
Suva
FIJI IS.
TONGA
Nuku'alofa
NIUE
(N.Z.)
AUSTRALIA
Brisbane
NORFOLK I.
(AUSTRALIA)
Perth
Adelaide
Sydney
Canberra, A.C.T.
Kermadec Is.
(N.Z.)
Melbourne
TASMANIA
Hobart
NEW
ZEALAND
Wellington
Population density, 2005
People per square km
People per square mi
More than 195
More than 500
60 - 195
150 - 500
10 - 59
25 - 149
1 - 9
1 - 24
Less than 1
Less than 1
Chatham Is.
(N.Z.)
Auckland Is.
(N.Z.)

POPULATION PYRAMIDS

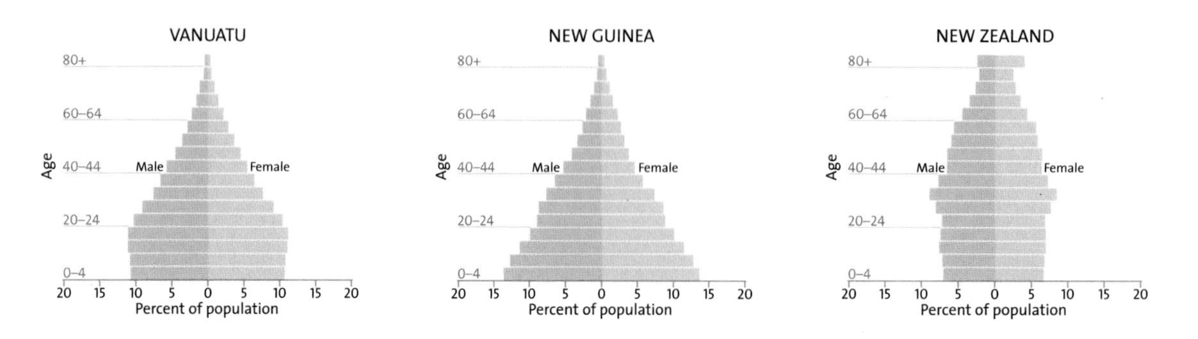
VANUATU
NEW GUINEA
NEW ZEALAND
80+
60–64
40–44
20–24
0–4
Age
Male
Female
20 15 10 5 0 5 10 15 20
Percent of population

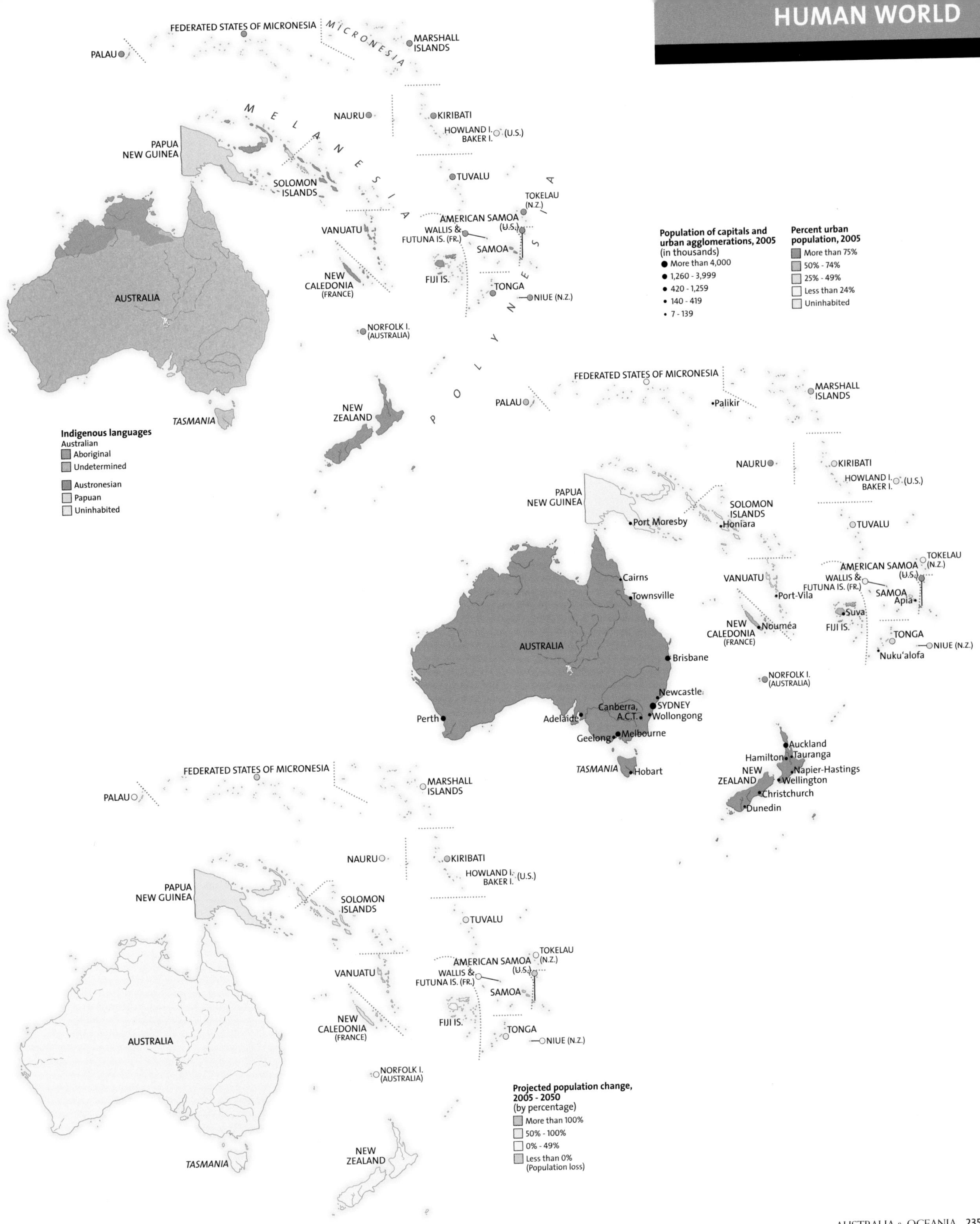

FEDERATED STATES OF MICRONESIA
MICRONESIA
MARSHALL ISLANDS
PALAU
MELANESIA
NAURU
KIRIBATI
HOWLAND I.
BAKER I.
(U.S.)
PAPUA NEW GUINEA
SOLOMON ISLANDS
TUVALU
TOKELAU (N.Z.)
AMERICAN SAMOA (U.S.)
VANUATU
WALLIS & FUTUNA IS. (FR.)
SAMOA
FIJI IS.
NEW CALEDONIA (FRANCE)
TONGA
NIUE (N.Z.)
AUSTRALIA
NORFOLK I. (AUSTRALIA)
POLYNESIA
NEW ZEALAND
TASMANIA
Indigenous languages
Australian
Aboriginal
Undetermined
Austronesian
Papuan
Uninhabited
Population of capitals and urban agglomerations, 2005 (in thousands)
More than 4,000
1,260 - 3,999
420 - 1,259
140 - 419
7 - 139
Percent urban population, 2005
More than 75%
50% - 74%
25% - 49%
Less than 24%
Uninhabited
Palikir
Port Moresby
Honiara
Cairns
Townsville
Port-Vila
Apia
Suva
Nouméa
Nuku'alofa
Brisbane
Newcastle
SYDNEY
Wollongong
Canberra, A.C.T.
Adelaide
Perth
Melbourne
Geelong
Hobart
Auckland
Hamilton
Tauranga
Napier-Hastings
Wellington
Christchurch
Dunedin
Projected population change, 2005 - 2050 (by percentage)
More than 100%
50% - 100%
0% - 49%
Less than 0% (Population loss)

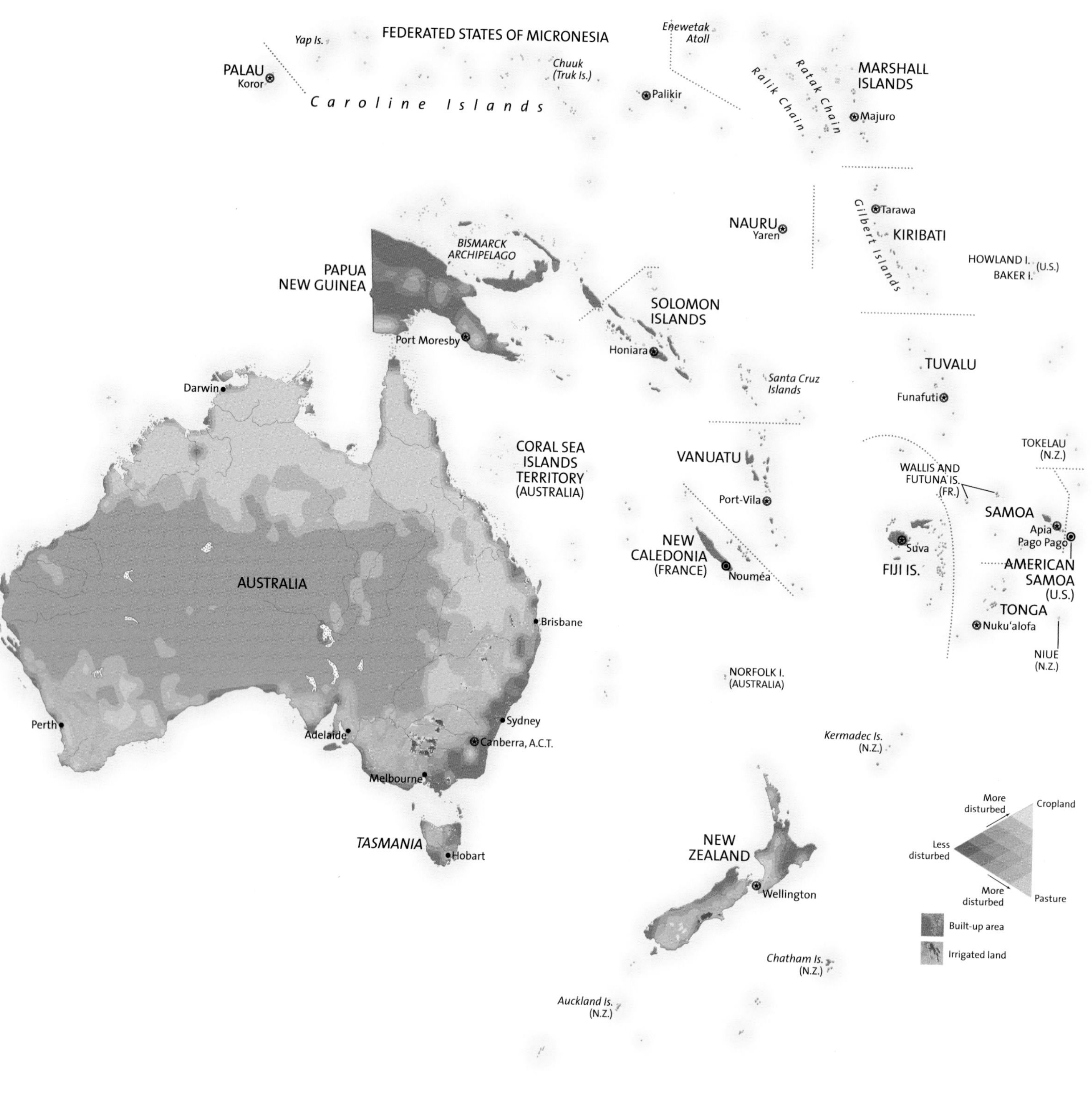

FEDERATED STATES OF MICRONESIA
Yap Is.
PALAU
Koror
Caroline Islands
Chuuk (Truk Is.)
Palikir
Enewetak Atoll
Ralik Chain
Ratak Chain
MARSHALL ISLANDS
Majuro
NAURU
Yaren
Tarawa
Gilbert Islands
KIRIBATI
HOWLAND I.
BAKER I.
(U.S.)
BISMARCK ARCHIPELAGO
PAPUA NEW GUINEA
Port Moresby
SOLOMON ISLANDS
Honiara
Santa Cruz Islands
TUVALU
Funafuti
Darwin
CORAL SEA ISLANDS TERRITORY (AUSTRALIA)
VANUATU
Port-Vila
TOKELAU (N.Z.)
WALLIS AND FUTUNA IS. (FR.)
SAMOA
Apia
Pago Pago
NEW CALEDONIA (FRANCE)
Nouméa
Suva
FIJI IS.
AMERICAN SAMOA (U.S.)
TONGA
Nuku'alofa
NIUE (N.Z.)
AUSTRALIA
Brisbane
NORFOLK I. (AUSTRALIA)
Perth
Adelaide
Sydney
Canberra, A.C.T.
Melbourne
Kermadec Is. (N.Z.)
TASMANIA
Hobart
NEW ZEALAND
Wellington
More disturbed
Cropland
Less disturbed
More disturbed
Pasture
Built-up area
Irrigated land
Chatham Is. (N.Z.)
Auckland Is. (N.Z.)

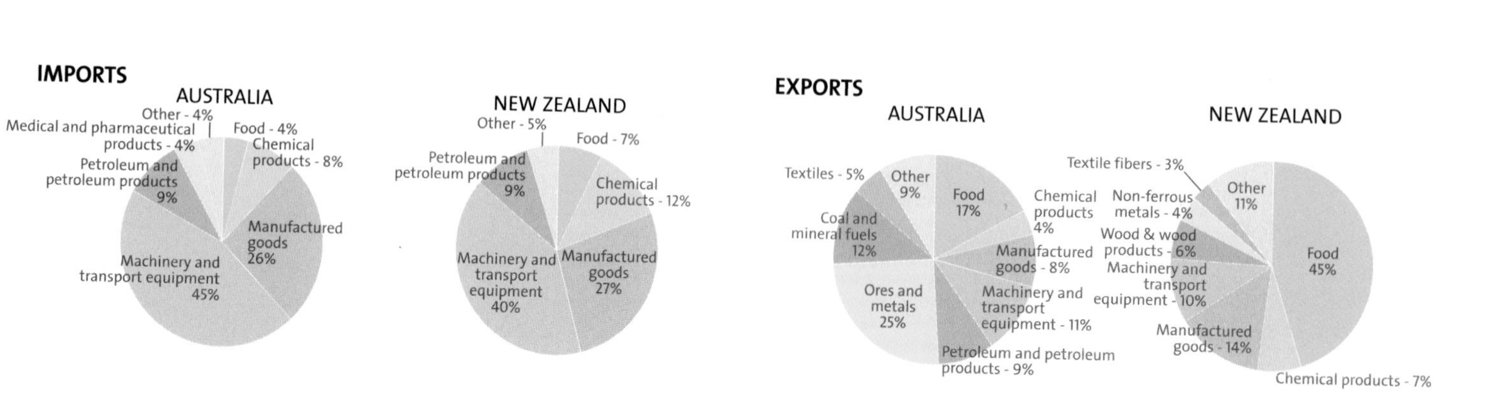

IMPORTS
AUSTRALIA
Other - 4%
Medical and pharmaceutical products - 4%
Food - 4%
Chemical products - 8%
Petroleum and petroleum products 9%
Manufactured goods 26%
Machinery and transport equipment 45%
NEW ZEALAND
Other - 5%
Food - 7%
Petroleum and petroleum products 9%
Chemical products - 12%
Machinery and transport equipment 40%
Manufactured goods 27%
EXPORTS
AUSTRALIA
Textiles - 5%
Other 9%
Food 17%
Chemical products 4%
Coal and mineral fuels 12%
Manufactured goods - 8%
Ores and metals 25%
Machinery and transport equipment - 11%
Petroleum and petroleum products - 9%
NEW ZEALAND
Textile fibers - 3%
Non-ferrous metals - 4%
Other 11%
Wood & wood products - 6%
Machinery and transport equipment - 10%
Food 45%
Manufactured goods - 14%
Chemical products - 7%

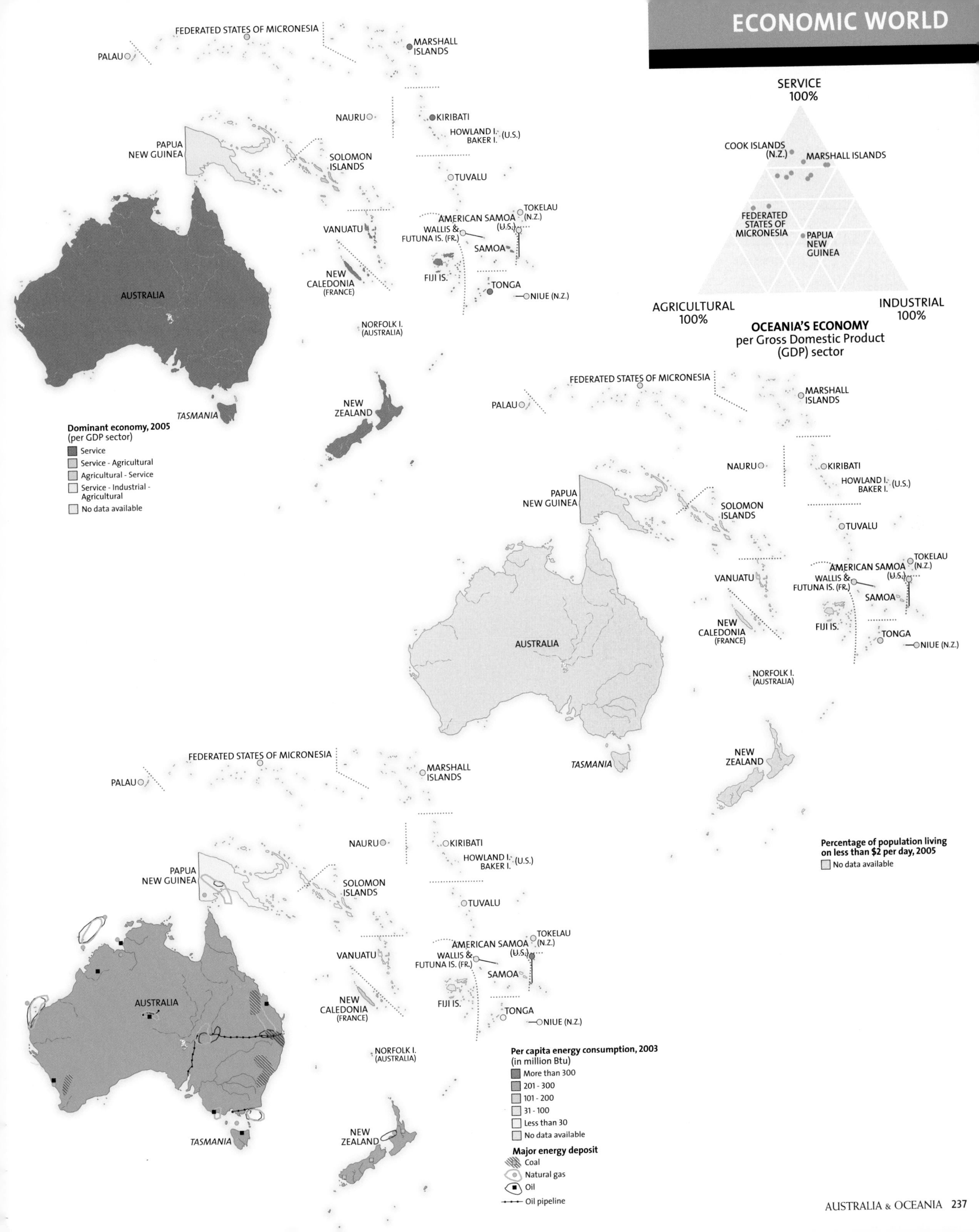

FEDERATED STATES OF MICRONESIA
PALAU
MARSHALL ISLANDS
NAURU
KIRIBATI
HOWLAND I.
BAKER I.
(U.S.)
PAPUA NEW GUINEA
SOLOMON ISLANDS
TUVALU
TOKELAU (N.Z.)
AMERICAN SAMOA (U.S.)
VANUATU
WALLIS & FUTUNA IS. (FR.)
SAMOA
NEW CALEDONIA (FRANCE)
FIJI IS.
TONGA
NIUE (N.Z.)
AUSTRALIA
NORFOLK I. (AUSTRALIA)
NEW ZEALAND
TASMANIA
Dominant economy, 2005
(per GDP sector)
Service
Service - Agricultural
Agricultural - Service
Service - Industrial - Agricultural
No data available
SERVICE 100%
COOK ISLANDS (N.Z.)
MARSHALL ISLANDS
FEDERATED STATES OF MICRONESIA
PAPUA NEW GUINEA
AGRICULTURAL 100%
INDUSTRIAL 100%
OCEANIA'S ECONOMY
per Gross Domestic Product (GDP) sector
Percentage of population living on less than $2 per day, 2005
No data available
Per capita energy consumption, 2003
(in million Btu)
More than 300
201 - 300
101 - 200
31 - 100
Less than 30
No data available
Major energy deposit
Coal
Natural gas
Oil
Oil pipeline

RUSSIA
MONGOLIA
GOBI
CHINA
NORTH KOREA
SOUTH KOREA
JAPAN
TAIWAN
HONG KONG
PHILIPPINES
VIETNAM
BRUNEI
MALAYSIA
INDONESIA
TIMOR-LESTE (EAST TIMOR)
PAPUA NEW GUINEA
AUSTRALIA
PALAU
FEDERATED STATES OF MICRONESIA
NORTHERN MARIANA ISLANDS U.S.
MARSHALL ISLANDS
NAURU
SOLOMON ISLANDS
VANUATU
NEW CALEDONIA France
FIJI ISLANDS
TUVALU
GILBERT ISLANDS
MICRONESIA
MELANESIA
NORTH
SEA OF OKHOTSK
SEA OF JAPAN (EAST SEA)
YELLOW SEA
EAST CHINA SEA
PHILIPPINE SEA
SOUTH CHINA SEA
Sulu Sea
Celebes Sea
Molucca Sea
Java Sea
Banda Sea
Flores Sea
Bali Sea
Timor Sea
Arafura Sea
Gulf of Carpentaria
Coral Sea
Solomon Sea
Bismarck Sea
INDIAN OCEAN
ULAANBAATAR
BEIJING (PEKING)
TIANJIN
SHENYANG
SHANGHAI
WUHAN
CHONGQING
GUANGZHOU (CANTON)
SEOUL
P'yŏngyang
TŌKYŌ
Yokohama
Nagoya
Ōsaka
Kōbe
Kyōto
Hiroshima
Fukuoka
Kitakyūshū
Sapporo
Vladivostok
Harbin
Changchun
Dalian
Manila
Quezon City
Ho Chi Minh City (Saigon)
Da Nang
Hanoi
JAKARTA
Bandung
Surabaya
Darwin
Cairns
Townsville
Port Moresby
T'aipei (Taibei)
Kaohsiung
Nanjing
Hangzhou
Ningbo
Fuzhou
Xi'an (Sian)
Zhengzhou
Nanning
Zhanjiang
Sakhalin
Kamchatka
KURIL ISLANDS (KURIL'SKIYE OSTROVA)
HOKKAIDŌ
HONSHŪ
KYŪSHŪ
Ryukyu Islands (Nansei Shotō)
Bonin Islands (Ogasawara Guntō)
Volcano Islands (Kazan Rettō) Japan
Minami Tori Shima (Marcus) Japan
Wake Island U.S.
Guam U.S.
CAROLINE ISLANDS
Admiralty Islands
BISMARCK ARCHIPELAGO
New Ireland
New Britain
Bougainville
Guadalcanal
Santa Cruz Islands
GREAT DIVIDING RANGE
Great Sandy Desert
Great Barrier Reef
Lesser Sunda Islands
BORNEO
SULAWESI
LUZON
MINDANAO
HAINAN
EQUATOR
Longitude East 160° of Greenwich
110° 120° 130° 140° 150° 160° 170°
50° 40° 20° 10° 0° 10° 20°

SEA
Islands of Four Mountains
2149
Unalaska
Fox Islands
Andreanof Is.
ALEUTIAN ISLANDS
United States
170°
160°
150°
140°
130°
Queen Charlotte Islands
Hecate Strait
4016
Mt. Waddington
CANADA
Calgary
Swift Current
Kamloops
Kelowna
Medicine Hat
50°
Vancouver
Lethbridge
Vancouver Island
2220
Havre
Victoria
Missouri
Spokane
Tacoma
Seattle
Great Falls
Olympia
4392
Mt. Rainier
Helena
Missoula
Billings
2550
Mt. St. Helens
Walla Walla
Butte
3566
Portland
Salem
Snake
Borah Peak
Worland
Redmond
3859
Boise
Eugene
Idaho Falls
Coos Bay
2665
Medford
UNITED STATES
Klamath Falls
4317
Alturas
Great Salt Lake
Mt. Shasta
Eureka
Salt Lake City
Provo
Lassen Pk.
3187
4687
Cape Mendocino
Reno
40°
Ely
Carson City
COAST MOUNTAINS
SIERRA NEVADA
ROCKY MOUNTAINS
Sacramento
Oakland
Colorado
San Francisco
San Jose
PACIFIC OCEAN
Fresno
4418
Mt. Whitney
86
Las Vegas
Bakersfield
Flagstaff
Santa Barbara
Albuquerque
Riverside
Los Angeles
Phoenix
Long Beach
San Diego
Mexicali
Tucson
Tijuana
Douglas
3444
Nogales
BAJA CALIFORNIA
Gulf of California
SIERRA MADRE OCCIDENTAL
30°
Hermosillo
Midway Islands
I. de Guadeloupe
Mexico
Guaymas
Pearl and Hermes Atoll
Punta Eugenia
MEXICO
Gardner Pinnacles
La Purísima
Los Mochis
HAWAIIAN ISLANDS
United States
TROPIC OF CANCER
La Paz
Cabo San Lucas
5121
Kaua'i
O'ahu
Islas Marías
Moloka'i
Honolulu
Maui
Islas Revillagigedo
Mexico
20°
Mauna Kea
4205
Hawai'i
Johnston Atoll
U.S.
POLYNESIA
5037
Clipperton
Fr.
10°
3091
Kingman Reef
Palmyra Atoll U.S.
5529
Teraina (Washington I.)
Tabuaeran (Fanning I.)
LINE ISLANDS
Kiritimati (Christmas I.)
3
Kiribati
5121
Howland Island
U.S.
Baker Island
EQUATOR
0°
Jarvis Island
U.S.
SOUTH PACIFIC OCEAN
5121
PHOENIX ISLANDS
KIRIBATI
4526
TOKELAU N.Z.
MARQUESAS ISLANDS
Ua Huka
Hiva Oa
10°
Pukapuka Atoll (Danger Islands)
2
AMERICAN SAMOA
U.S.
SAMOA
Savai'i
Apia
Pago Pago
Manua I.
5
Îles Wallis
Fr.
Tutuila
4
SAMOA ISLANDS
COOK ISLANDS
TUAMOTU ARCHIPELAGO
Manihi
Rangiroa
Bora Bora
Huahine
Raiatea
7
Papeete
Tahiti
SOCIETY ISLANDS
FRENCH POLYNESIA
France
Lau Group
TONGA ISLANDS
New Zealand
Niue
Ha'apai Group
Hervey Islands
Groupe Actéon
20°
TONGA
Nuku'alofa
Tongatapu Group
9
6
Rarotonga
Îles Duc de Gloucester
AUSTRAL ISLANDS (TUBUAI IS.)
Îles Gambier
110°
Longitude West 160° of Greenwich
120°
MERCATOR PROJECTION
SCALE 1:35,000,000
0 KILOMETERS 600 800 1000
0 MILES 200 400 600 800 1000
13
Red circled numbers are reference keys to larger scale maps on pages 241-243.

NEW ZEALAND
ALBERS CONIC EQUAL-AREA PROJECTION
SCALE 1:5,750,000
0 KILOMETERS 100 150
0 MILES 50 100 150
TASMAN SEA
PACIFIC OCEAN
NORTH ISLAND
SOUTH ISLAND
NEW ZEALAND
Cape Reinga
North Cape
Te Hapua
Te Kao
Cape Karikari
Ninety Mile Beach
Mangonui
Kaeo
Cape Brett
Ahipara
Mangamuka
Paihia
Opua
Pawarenga
Moerewa
Panguru
Rawene
Kawakawa
Whakapara
Waimamaku
Pakotai
Hikurangi
Donnellys Crossing
Kamo
Kaihu
Whangarei
Waiotira
Marsden Point
Te Kopuru
Waipu
Maungaturoto
Port Fitzroy
Ruawai
Paparoa
Great Barrier I.
Wellsford
Leigh
Cape Colville
Tryphena
Head North
Matakana
East Coast Bays
Hauraki Gulf
Colville
Helensville
Coromandel
Waitemata
Whitianga
Auckland
Howick
COROMANDEL PEN.
Manukau
Papakura
Tairua
Pukekohe
Thames
Pokeno
Tuakau
Waitakaruru
Te Kauwhata
Paeroa
Waihi
Huntly
Te Aroha
Pukemiro
Waitoa
Mount Maunganui
Bay of Plenty
Cape Runaway
Hicks Bay
Ngaruawahia
Raglan
Hamilton
Te Puke
Maketu
Te Araroa
Te Kaha
East Cape
Cambridge
Matata
Hikurangi
Tikitiki
Kawhia
Putaruru
Whakatane
Ruatoria
Otorohanga
Rotorua
Te Teko
Opotiki
Torere
Waitomo Caves
Tokoroa
Mt. Tarawera
Te Puia Springs
Tokomaru Bay
Te Kuiti
Hangatiki
Motu
Arowhana
Atiamuri
TE UREWERA N.P.
Moutohora
Matawai
Tolaga Bay
Benneydale
Te Karaka
Ormond
L. Taupo
Ruatahuna
Minginui
Patutahi
Awakino
Ongarue
Gisborne
Mokau
Whangara
Okahukura
Taupo
Ruakituri
Taringamotu
Waitahanui
Waitara
Uruti
Taumarunui
Tuai
Whakapunake
New Plymouth
Kakahi
Turangi
Oakura
Urenui
National Park
Tarawera
Raupunga
Frasertown
Lepperton
Mt. Ngauruhoe
Wairoa
EGMONT N.P.
WHANGANUI N.P.
Te Pohue
Putorino
Mahia Pen.
Rahotu
Mt. Ruapehu
Tutira
(Mt. Egmont) Mt. Taranaki
Toko
TONGARIRO N.P.
Kaweka
Hawke Bay
Opunake
Eltham
Raetihi
Eskdale
Napier
Manaia
Hawera
Waiouru
Taradale
Cape Kidnappers
Alton
Kakatahi
Taihape
Pakipaki
Kakaramea
Waverley
Utiku
Waimarama
Waitotara
Mangaweka
Kai Iwi
Wanganui
Waipawa
Pukehou
Castlecliff
Takapau
Rata
Omakere
Marton
Waipukurau
Bulls
Feilding
Palmerston North
Porangahau
Foxton
Taumatawhakatangihangakoauauotamateapokaiwhenuakitanatahu
Pongaroa
Cape Turnagain
Levin
Shannon
Otaki
Ohau
Alfredton
Akitio
Waikanae
Mauriceville
Mitre
Tinui
Carterton
Castlepoint
Porirua
Lower Hutt
Greytown
Wellington
Martinborough
Mount Ross
Cape Palliser
COOK STRAIT
Cape Farewell
Pakawau
Rockville
D'Urville I.
Collingwood
ABEL TASMAN N.P.
Takaka
French Pass
Mt. Stokes
KAHURANGI NATIONAL PARK
Riwaka
Tasman Bay
Karamea
Tasman
Picton
Tapawera
Stoke
Havelock
Blenheim
Seddonville
Mt. Owen
Tadmor
Granity
Wairau
Waimangaroa
Hector
Owen River
Valley
Seddon
Cape Campbell
Cape Foulwind
Westport
Murchison
Tapuaenuku
Charleston
Ward
Mt. Uriah
Cronadun
Molesworth
Kekerengu
PAPAROA N.P.
Reefton
NELSON LAKES N.P.
Barrytown
Maruia
Clarence
Rapahoe
Ikamatua
Manakau
Hanmer Springs
Greymouth
Ngahere
Lewis Pass
Kaikoura
Dobson
Arahura
Moana
Rotherham
Waiau
Oaro
Kumara
Culverden
Parnassus
Hokitika
Otira
ARTHUR'S PASS N.P.
Hawarden
Cheviot
Kowhitirangi
Domett
Ross
Arthur's Pass
Omihi
Scargill
Waipara
Harihari
Amberley
Franz Josef Glacier
Whataroa
Springfield
Oxford
Pegasus Bay
WESTLAND N.P. (TAI POUTINI)
Lake Coleridge
Rangiora
Fox Glacier
Belfast
Hororata
Christchurch
(Mt. Cook) Aoraki
Methven
Rolleston
Lyttelton
AORAKI (MT. COOK) N.P.
Lincoln
BANKS PEN.
Rakaia
Akaroa
Mayfield
Ashburton
Haast
Lake Tekapo
Hinds
Jackson Head
Jackson Bay
Lake Pukaki
Fairlie
Geraldine
Canterbury Bight
MT. ASPIRING N.P.
Pleasant Point
Orari
Temuka
Awarua Bay
Twizel
Cave
Timaru
Lake McKerrow
Mt. Aspiring
Omarama
Mount Tutoko
Otematata
Saint Andrews
Waimate
Makikihi
Hakataramea
Milford Sound
Coronet Pk.
Tarras
Kurow
Studholme Junction
Glenorchy
Arrowtown
Morven
George Sound
Duntroon
Glenavy
FIORDLAND
Cromwell
Enfield
Queenstown
Omakau
Totara
Oamaru
The Remarkables
Clyde
Ranfurly
Maheno
Kakanui
Lake Te Anau
Kingston
Herbert
Hampden
NATIONAL PARK
Coal Creek
Earnscleugh
Hyde
Te Anau
Palmerston
Athol
Waikouaiti
L. Manapouri
Karitane
Manapouri
Roxburgh
Ettrick
Waitati
Mossburn
Seacliff
Port Chalmers
Dusky Sound
Edievale
Mosgiel
Dunedin
Kelso
Allanton
Green Island
Dipton
Lawrence
Riversdale
Tapanui
Waihola
Waipahi
Milton
Orawia
Winton
Gore
Balclutha
Otautau
Browns
Clinton
Kaitangata
Puysegur Point
Thornbury
Wakikiwi
Invercargill
Owaka
Tahakopa
FOVEAUX STRAIT
Otatara
Bluff
Tiwai Point
Waikawa
Mt. Anglem
Oban
STEWART ISLAND
Mason Bay
RAKIURA NATIONAL PARK
Mt. Allen
Mernoo Bank
Longitude East 174° of Greenwich
168°
171°
174°
177°
180°
165°
36°
39°
42°
45°

Polynesia

FUNAFUTI
TUVALU
0 KILOMETERS 8
0 STATUTE MILES 8

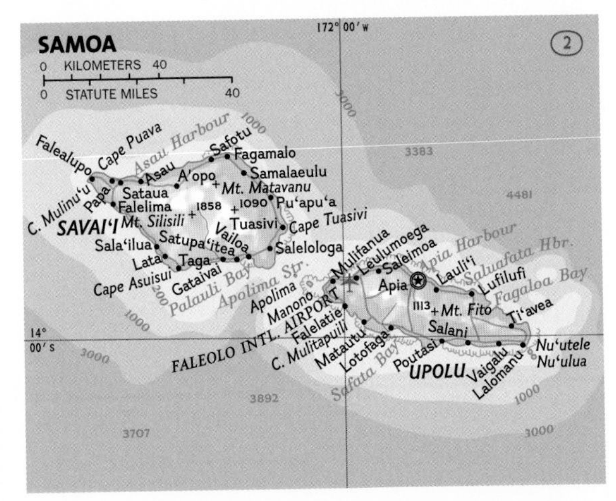

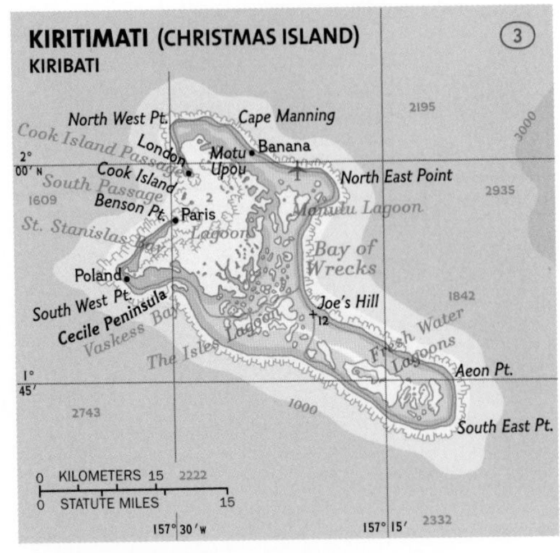

TUTUILA
United States
0 KILOMETERS 8
0 STATUTE MILES 8

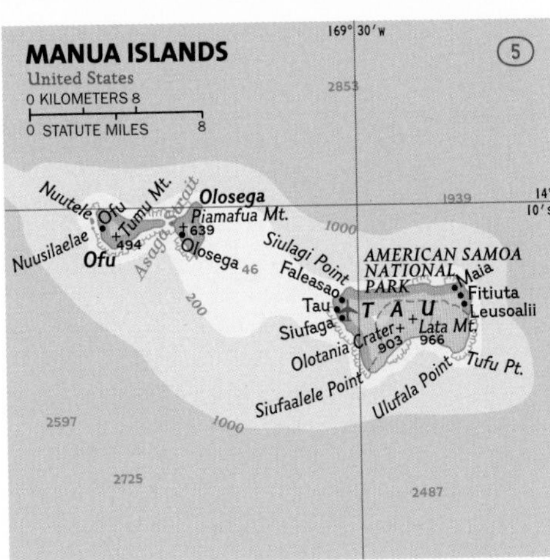

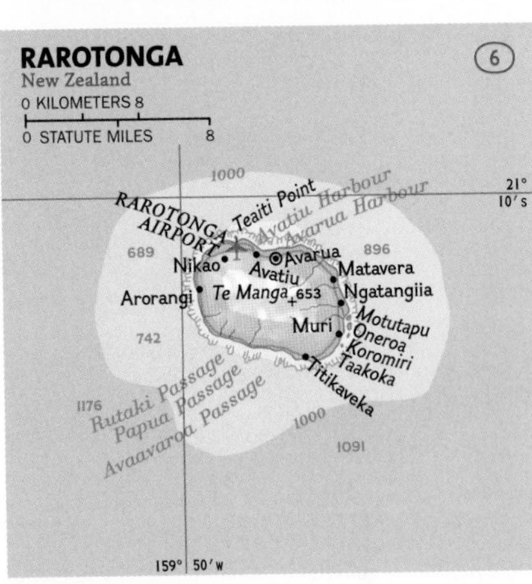

TAHITI AND MOOREA
France
0 KILOMETERS 15
0 STATUTE MILES 15

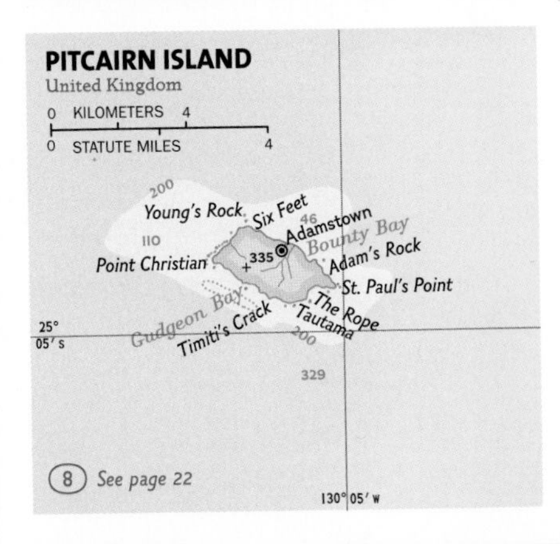

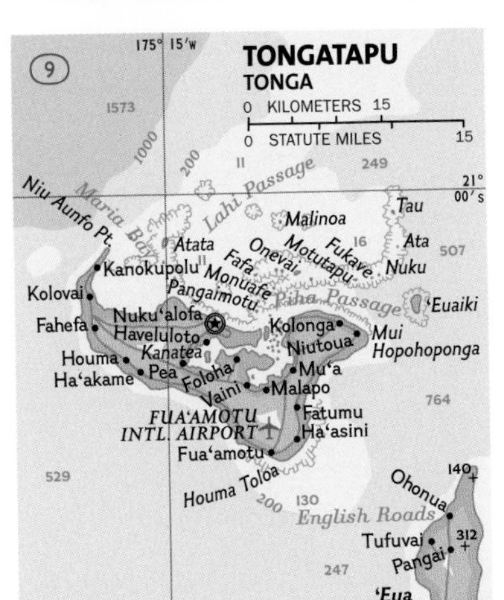

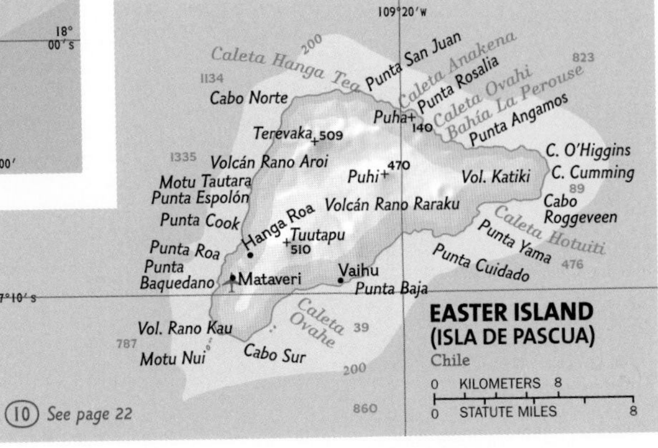

Micronesia

SAIPAN
United States
0 KILOMETERS 6
0 STATUTE MILES 6

Puntan Sabaneta
Marpi Point
Puntan Magpi
Puntan Lagua Lichan
Pta. I Maddock
103
San Roque
279
15° 15 N
Mañagaha I.
Tanapag
Bahia Fañunchuluyan
Puetton Tanapag
Puntan Muchot
Capital Hill
Saipan Harbor
Garapan
Puntan Gloria
Lagunan Garapan
471
Okso' Takpochao
San Jose
Susupe
Hagoi Susupe
Puntan Laula Katan
Chalan Kanoa
89
San Vicente
Puntan Hagman
Bahia Laulau
Puntan Agingan
San Antonio
Puntan Dandan
SAIPAN INTL. AIRPORT
Puntan Opyan
Unai Obyan
Puntan I Naftan
Saipan Channel
TINIAN
145° 45′ E
594
494
988
22
200
1000
1518
490
(11)

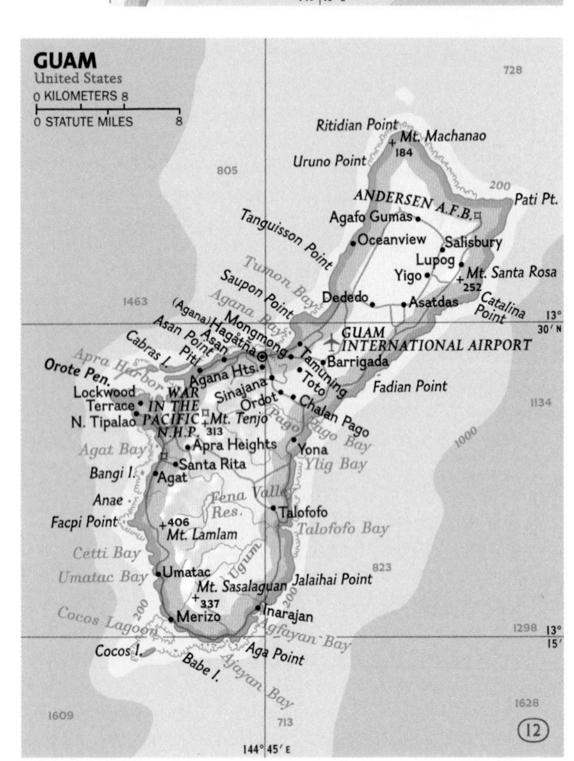

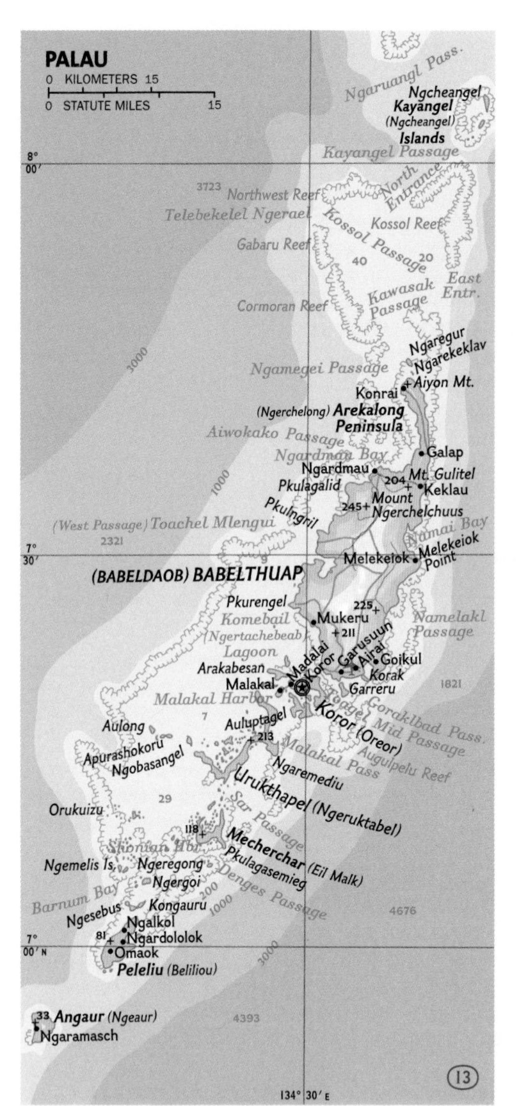

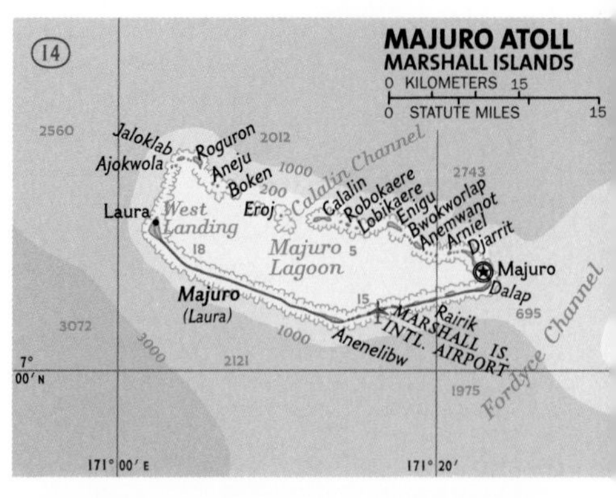

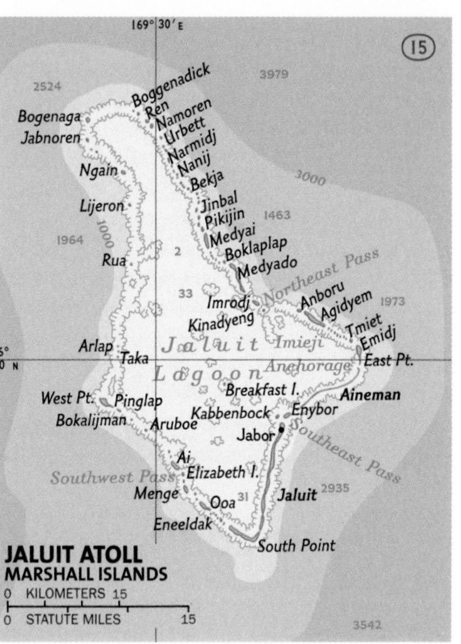

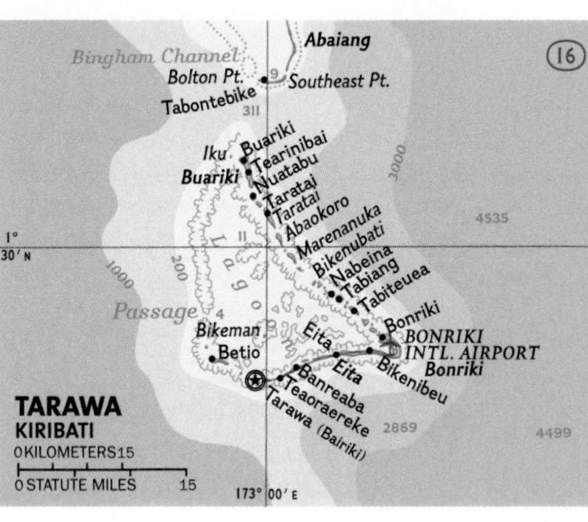

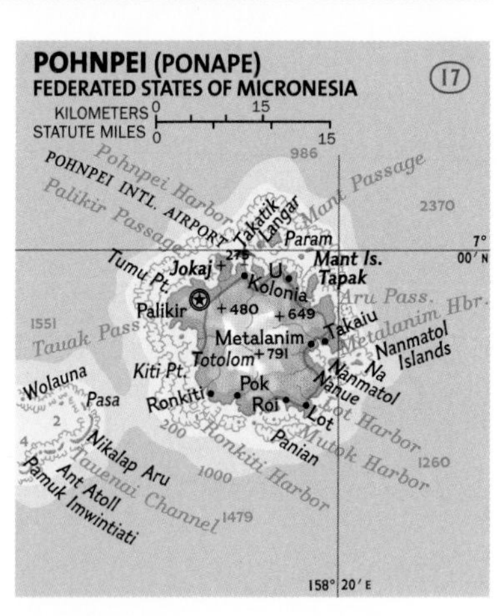

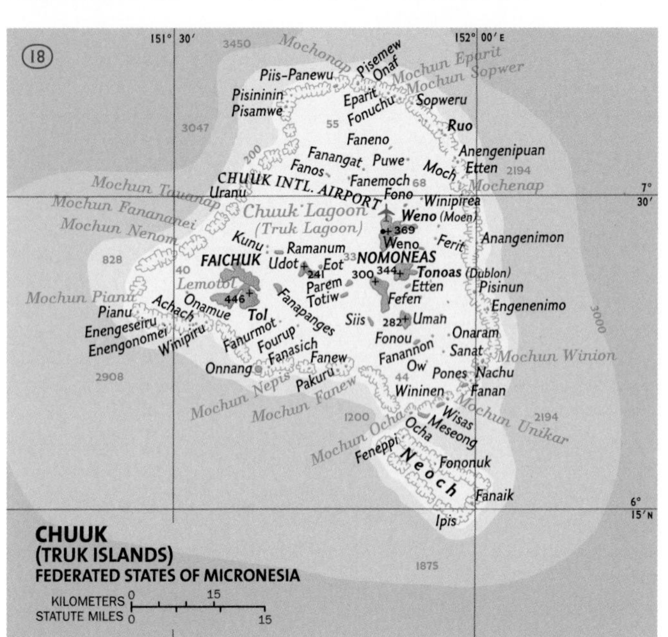

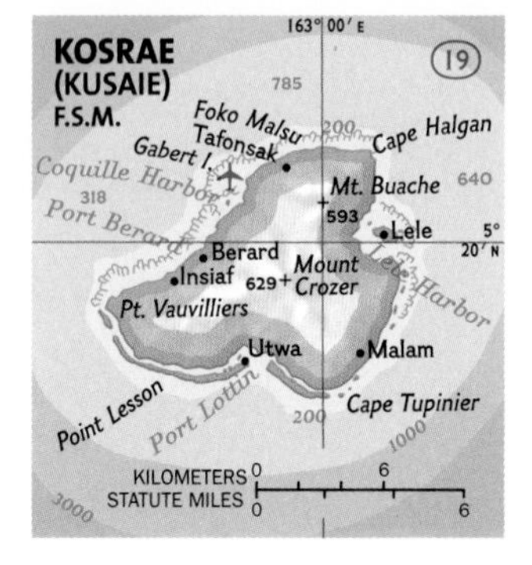

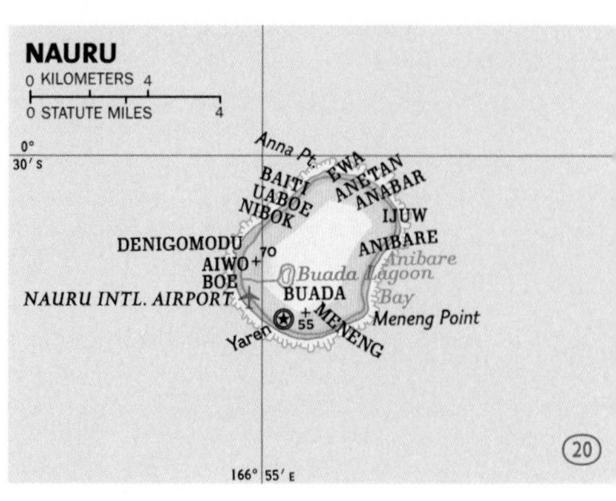

Melanesia

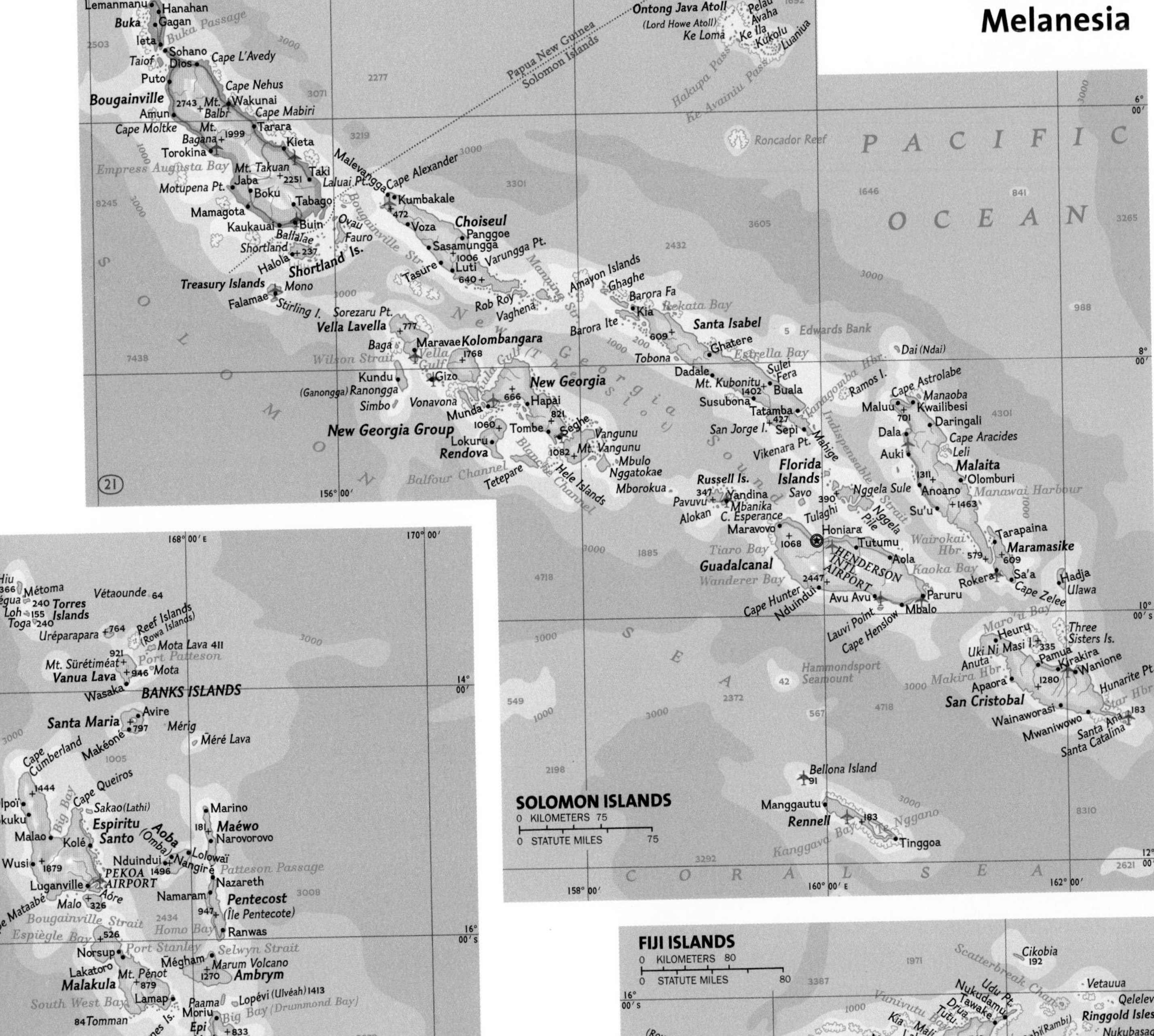
SOLOMON ISLANDS
0 KILOMETERS 75
0 STATUTE MILES 75
PACIFIC OCEAN
SOLOMON SEA
CORAL SEA
Papua New Guinea
Solomon Islands
Pinipel
Green Islands
Nissan
Jangain
Yovo
Kilinailau Is.
Veharnu
Tauu Is.
Nukumanu Is.
Nogu Dabu
Ontong Java Atoll
(Lord Howe Atoll)
Ke Loma
Pelau
Avaha
Ke Ila
Kukolu
Luaniua
Hakupa Pass
Ke Avainiu Pass
Roncador Reef
Cape Hanpan
Lemanmanu
Hanahan
Buka
Gagan
Buka Passage
Ieta
Sohano
Taiof
Dios
Cape L'Avedy
Puto
Cape Nehus
Bougainville
Wakunai
Mt. Balbi
Cape Mabiri
Amun
Cape Moltke
Tarara
Mt. Bagana
Torokina
Kieta
Empress Augusta Bay
Mt. Takuan
Jaba
Taki
Motupena Pt.
Boku
Laluai Pt.
Tabago
Mamagota
Kaukauai
Buin
Ballalae
Shortland
Halola
Shortland Is.
Ovau
Fauro
Treasury Islands
Mono
Falamae
Stirling I.
Malevangga
Cape Alexander
Kumbakale
Voza
Choiseul
Panggoe
Sasamungga
Luti
Tasure
Varungga Pt.
Bougainville Strait
Manning Strait
Rob Roy
Vaghena
Amayon Islands
Ghaghe
Barora Fa
Barora Ite
Kia
Rekata Bay
Santa Isabel
Edwards Bank
Sorezaru Pt.
Vella Lavella
Baga
Maravae
Kolombangara
Wilson Strait
Vella Gulf
Kundu
Gizo
(Ganongga) Ranongga
Simbo
Vonavona
New Georgia
Munda
Hapai
New Georgia Group
Lokuru
Rendova
Tombe
Seghe
Vangunu
Mt. Vangunu
Mbulo
Ngatokae
Mborokua
Tetepare
Blanche Channel
Hele Islands
Balfour Channel
Ghatere
Estrella Bay
Tobona
Dadale
Mt. Kubonitu
Sulei
Fera
Buala
Susubona
Tatamba
San Jorge I.
Sepi
Vikenara Pt.
Mahige
Tanagomba Hbr.
Ramos I.
Indispensable Strait
Russell Is.
Pavuvu
Yandina
Mbanika
Alokan
C. Esperance
Florida Islands
Savo
Tulaghi
Nggela Sule
Nggela Pile
Maravovo
Honiara
Tutumu
HENDERSON INTL. AIRPORT
Tiaro Bay
Guadalcanal
Wanderer Bay
Aola
Cape Hunter
Nduindui
Avu Avu
Paruru
Lauvi Point
Cape Henslow
Mbalo
Dai (Ndai)
Cape Astrolabe
Manaoba
Kwailibesi
Maluu
Dala
Daringali
Cape Aracides
Leli
Auki
Malaita
Olomburi
Manawai Harbour
Anoano
Su'u
Wairokai Hbr.
Tarapaina
Maramasike
Kaoka Bay
Rokera
Sa'a
Cape Zelee
Hadja
Ulawa
Maro'u Bay
Heuru
Three Sisters Is.
Uki Ni Masi I.
Pamua
Kirakira
Wanione
Anuta
Makira Hbr.
Apaora
Hunarite Pt.
San Cristobal
Star Hbr.
Wainaworasi
Mwaniwowo
Santa Ana
Santa Catalina
Hammondsport Seamount
Bellona Island
Manggautu
Rennell
Nggano
Kanggava Bay
Tinggoa
VANUATU
0 KILOMETERS 80
0 STATUTE MILES 80
Hiu
Métoma
Tégua
Torres Islands
Loh
Toga
Vétaounde
Uréparapara
Reef Islands
(Rowa Islands)
Mota Lava
Port Patteson
Mt. Sûrétiméat
Vanua Lava
Mota
Wasaka
BANKS ISLANDS
Santa Maria
Avire
Mérig
Makéone
Méré Lava
Cape Cumberland
Cape Queiros
Olpoï
Nokuku
Big Bay
Sakao (Lathi)
Marino
Espiritu Santo
Aoba (Omba)
Maéwo
Malao
Kolé
Narovorovo
Wusi
Nduindui
Lolowaï
Nangire
PEKOA AIRPORT
Luganville
Patteson Passage
Nazareth
Malo
Aore
Namaram
Pentecost
(Île Pentecote)
Cape Mataabé
Bougainville Strait
Espiègle Bay
Homo Bay
Ranwas
Port Stanley
Selwyn Strait
Norsup
Mégham
Marum Volcano
Lakatoro
Mt. Pénot
Ambrym
Malakula
Lamap
South West Bay
Paama
Lopévi (Ulvéah)
Big Bay (Drummond Bay)
Tomman
Moriu
Epi
Maskelynes Is.
Votlo
Laïka
Shepherd Islands
Tongoa (Kuwaé)
Tongariki
Émaé
Makura
(Matah) Mataso
Monument (Étarik)
Nguna
Moso
Émao
Lélépa
Éfaté (Île Vaté)
Devil's Pt.
BAUERFIELD AIRPORT
Mélé Bay
Port-Vila
Mt. Santop
Potnarvin
Cook Bay
Dillon's Bay
Erromango
Pilbarra Point
Lowital
Aniwa
Tanna
Waïsisi Bay
Futuna
Waïsisi
Isangel
Yasur Volcano
Mt. Tukosméra
Port Patrick
Anatom
(Kéamu)
Anelghowhat
Anelghowhat Bay

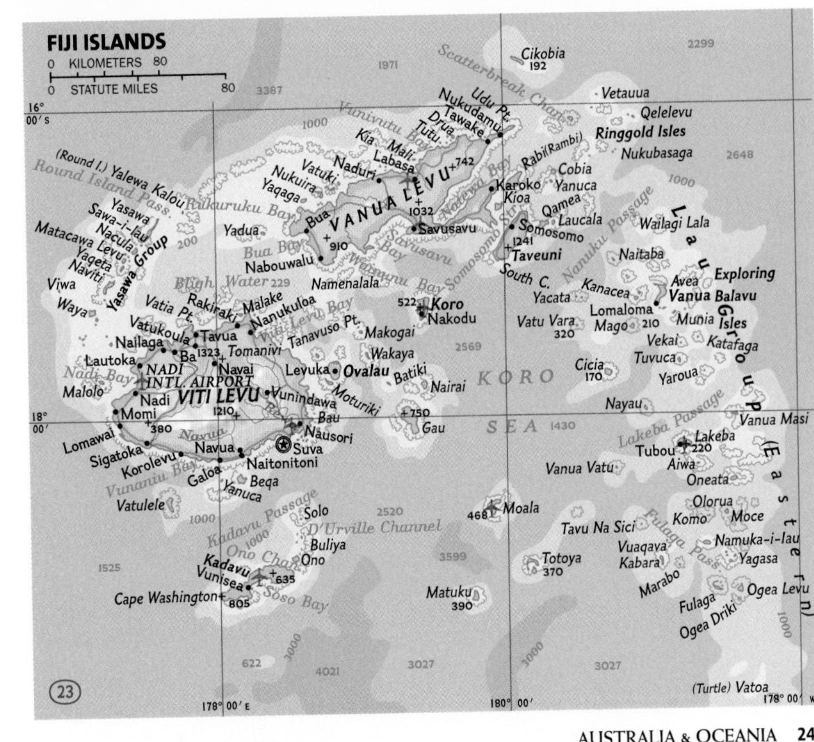
FIJI ISLANDS
0 KILOMETERS 80
0 STATUTE MILES 80
Cikobia
Scatterbreak Channel
Vetauua
Udu Pt.
Nukudamu
Qelelevu
Tawake
Drua
Tutu
Ringgold Isles
Vanuavutu Bay
Kia
Mali
Labasa
Nukubasaga
(Round I.) Yalewa Kalou
Round Island Pass.
Naduri
Rabi (Rambi)
Vatuki
Nukuira
Yaqaga
Karoko
Cobia
Yanuca
Kioa
Yasawa
Sawa-i-lau
Nacula
Yasawa Group
Matacawa Levu
Yageta
Naviti
Bua
VANUA LEVU
Savusavu
Qamea
Laucala
Somosomo
Taveuni
Wailagi Lala
Yadua
Bua Bay
Nabouwalu
Savusavu Bay
Somosomo Str.
Naitaba
Lau Group (Eastern)
Exploring Isles
Viwa
Waya
Bligh Water
Namenalala
South C.
Nanuku Passage
Kanacea
Yacata
Avea
Vanua Balavu
Munia
Vatia Pt.
Rakiraki
Malake
Nanukuloa
Koro
Nakodu
Vatu Vara
Lomaloma
Mago
Katafaga
Vekai
Tuvuca
Vatukoula
Tavua
Tanavuso Pt.
Makogai
Wakaya
Nailaga
Ba
Tomanivi
Lautoka
NADI INTL. AIRPORT
Navai
Levuka
Ovalau
Batiki
Nairai
KORO SEA
Cicia
Yaroua
Nayau
Nadi Bay
Malolo
Nadi
VITI LEVU
Vunindawa
Moturiki
Momi
Bau
Nausori
Gau
Lakeba Passage
Vanua Masi
Lakeba
Tubou
Lomawai
Sigatoka
Navua
Suva
Korolevu
Naitonitoni
Vanua Vatu
Aiwa
Oneata
Vunaniu Bay
Galoa
Yanuca
Beqa
Olorua
Komo
Moce
Vatulele
Solo
D'Urville Channel
Moala
Tavu Na Sici
Namuka-i-lau
Kadavu Passage
Ono Channel
Buliya
Ono
Vuaqava
Kabara
Yagasa
Kadavu
Vunisea
Totoya
Marabo
Ogea Levu
Cape Washington
Soso Bay
Matuku
Fulaga
Ogea Driki
Fulaga Pass
(Turtle) Vatoa

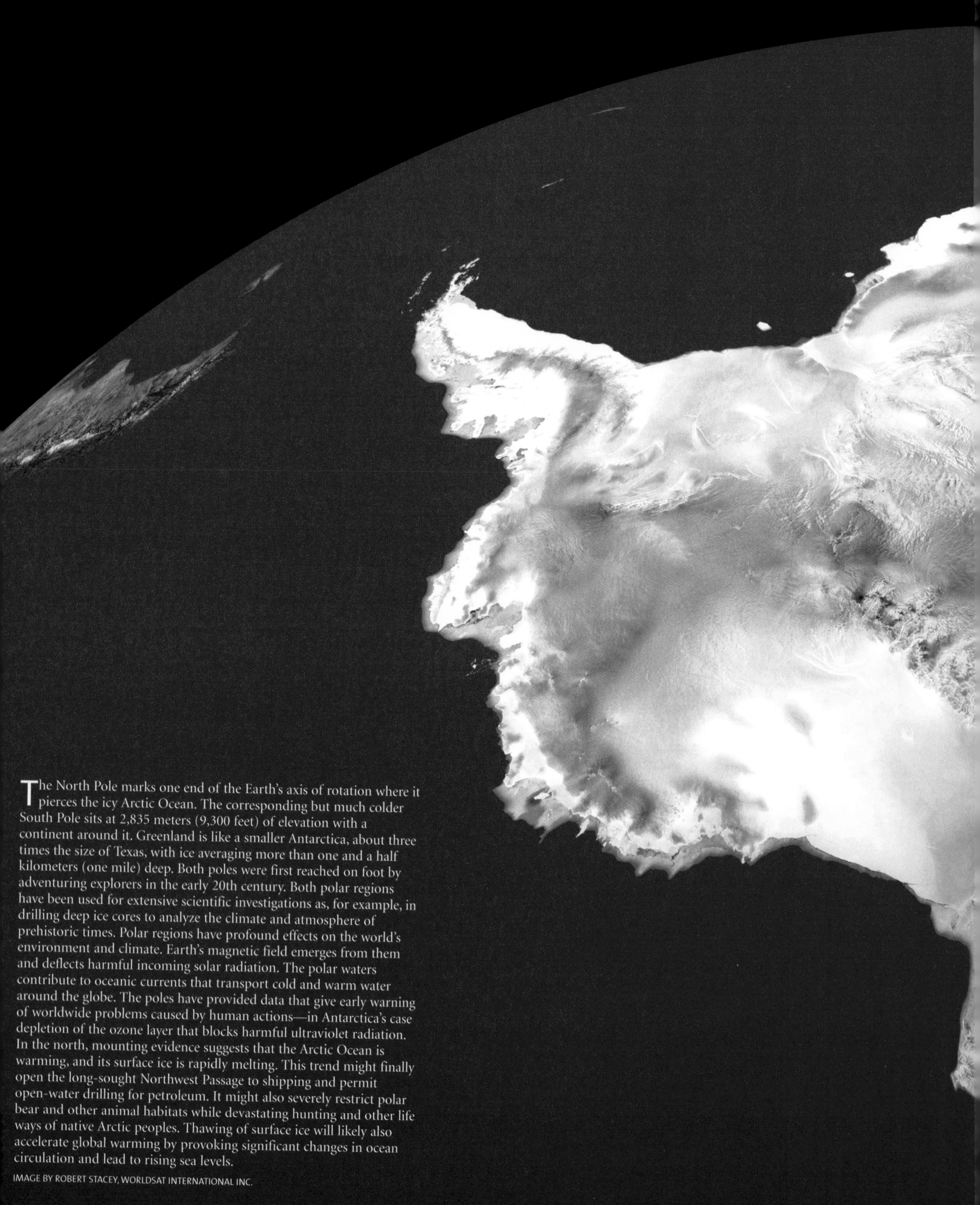

The North Pole marks one end of the Earth's axis of rotation where it pierces the icy Arctic Ocean. The corresponding but much colder South Pole sits at 2,835 meters (9,300 feet) of elevation with a continent around it. Greenland is like a smaller Antarctica, about three times the size of Texas, with ice averaging more than one and a half kilometers (one mile) deep. Both poles were first reached on foot by adventuring explorers in the early 20th century. Both polar regions have been used for extensive scientific investigations as, for example, in drilling deep ice cores to analyze the climate and atmosphere of prehistoric times. Polar regions have profound effects on the world's environment and climate. Earth's magnetic field emerges from them and deflects harmful incoming solar radiation. The polar waters contribute to oceanic currents that transport cold and warm water around the globe. The poles have provided data that give early warning of worldwide problems caused by human actions—in Antarctica's case depletion of the ozone layer that blocks harmful ultraviolet radiation. In the north, mounting evidence suggests that the Arctic Ocean is warming, and its surface ice is rapidly melting. This trend might finally open the long-sought Northwest Passage to shipping and permit open-water drilling for petroleum. It might also severely restrict polar bear and other animal habitats while devastating hunting and other life ways of native Arctic peoples. Thawing of surface ice will likely also accelerate global warming by provoking significant changes in ocean circulation and lead to rising sea levels.

IMAGE BY ROBERT STACEY, WORLDSAT INTERNATIONAL INC.

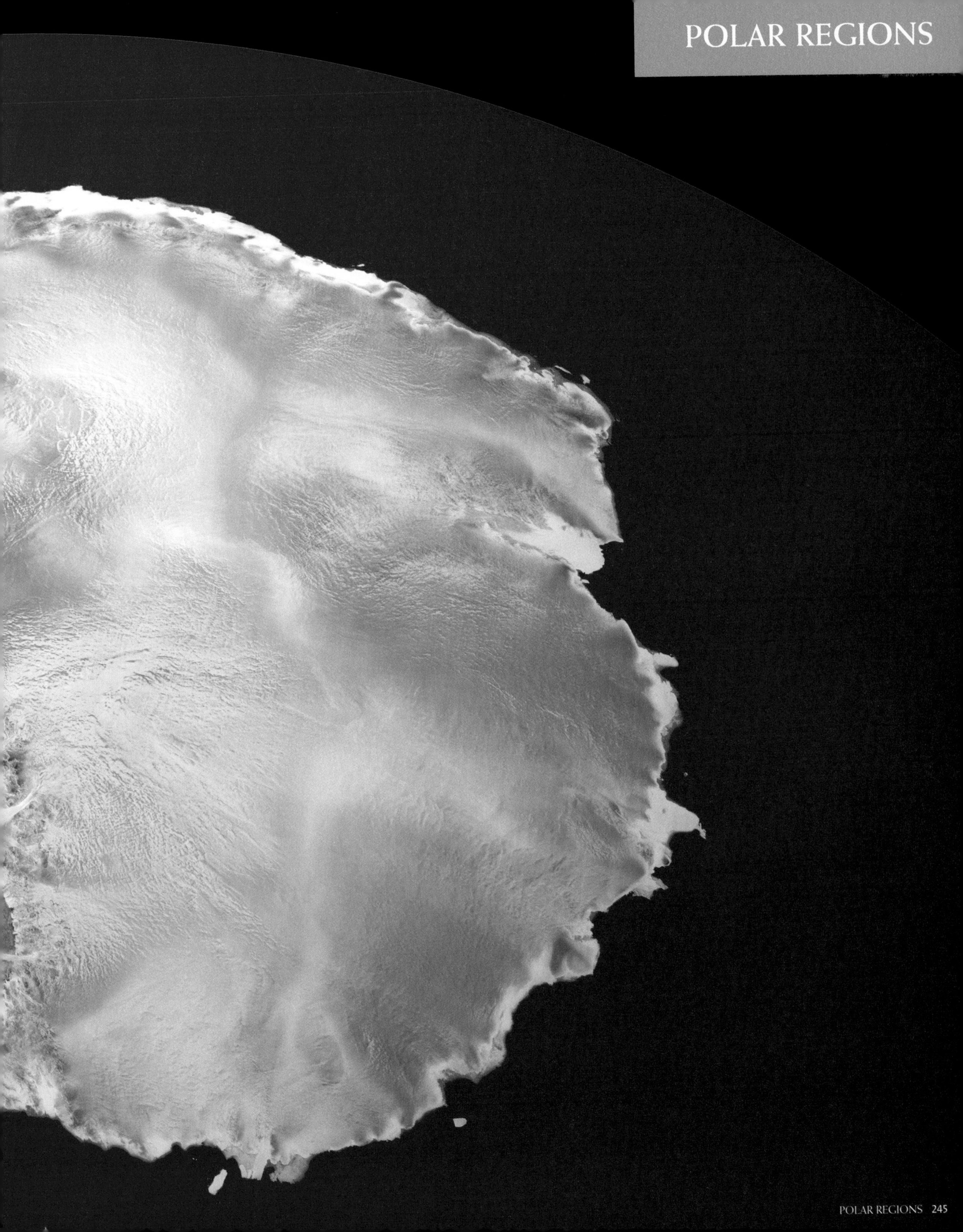

ICE
Pack ice responds to prevailing winds and oce
currents. Tabular icebergs up to 700 sq km i
area sometimes break away from the norther
edge of small ice shelves. These ice islands flo
slowly in erratic clockwise patterns around th
North American side of the Arctic Ocean,
completing full circuits in five to ten years, ur
they disintegrate or move into the Atlantic. Ea
year hundreds of much smaller bergs break of
calve - from the Greenland ice sheet and
Canada's glaciers and move southward into th
North Atlantic shipping lanes. After the sinki
of the Titanic in 1912, leading maritime natio
formed the International Ice Patrol to monito
icebergs and to study polar currents
and iceberg dynamics.
North Magnetic Pole
AZIMUTHAL EQUIDISTANT PROJECTION
SCALE 1:20,000,000
0 KILOMETERS 300 400 500
0 MILES 200 300 400 500
Longitude West 160° of Greenwich
Longitude West 10° of Greenwich
UNITED STATES
CANADA
ALASKA
COAST MOUNTAINS
ROCKY MOUNTAINS
BROOKS RANGE
NORTH SLOPE
Mackenzie Mountains
Selwyn Mountains
Ogilvie Mountains
BEAUFORT SEA
CHUKCHI SEA
HUDSON BAY
FOXE BASIN
HUDSON STRAIT
BAFFIN BAY
DAVIS STRAIT
DENMARK STRAIT
LINCOLN SEA
GULF OF ST. LAWRENCE
LABRADOR
QUEEN ELIZABETH ISLANDS
PARRY ISLANDS
SVERDRUP IS.
Victoria Island
Banks Island
Prince of Wales Island
Somerset Island
Devon Island
Ellesmere Island
Baffin Island
Southampton Island
Melville Island
Prince Patrick Island
Axel Heiberg Island
GREENLAND (KALAALLIT NUNAAT)
KNUD RASMUSSEN LAND
KONG FREDERIK VIII LAND
KONG CHRISTIAN X LAND
Peary Land
ARCTIC CIRCLE
ICELAND
Jan Mayen Nor.
NEWFOUNDLAND
ISLAND OF NEWFOUNDLAND
Great Slave Lake
Great Bear Lake
Lake Athabasca
Lake Winnipeg
Vancouver
Seattle
Calgary
Edmonton
Regina
Yellowknife
Whitehorse
Inuvik
Iqaluit
Nuuk (Godthåb)
Qaanaaq (Thule)
Akureyri
Ísafjörður
Mt. McKinley (Denali)
Mt. Logan
Mt. St. Elias
Gunnbjørn

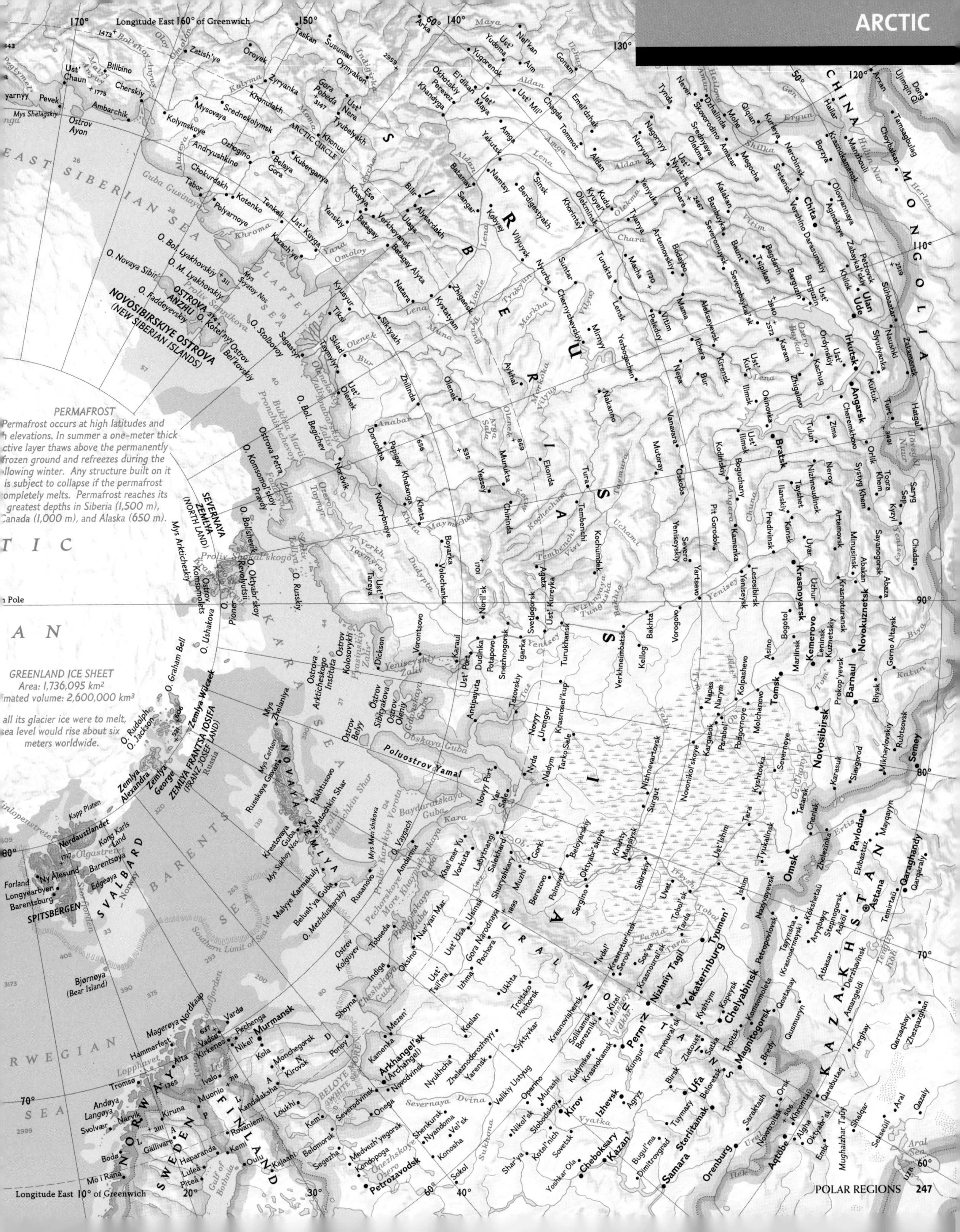
PERMAFROST
Permafrost occurs at high latitudes and
h elevations. In summer a one-meter thick
ctive layer thaws above the permanently
frozen ground and refreezes during the
ollowing winter. Any structure built on it
is subject to collapse if the permafrost
ompletely melts. Permafrost reaches its
greatest depths in Siberia (1,500 m),
Canada (1,000 m), and Alaska (650 m).
GREENLAND ICE SHEET
Area: 1,736,095 km²
mated volume: 2,600,000 km³
all its glacier ice were to melt,
sea level would rise about six
meters worldwide.
Longitude East 160° of Greenwich
Longitude East 10° of Greenwich
EAST SIBERIAN SEA
LAPTEV SEA
KARA SEA
BARENTS SEA
NORWEGIAN SEA
NOVOSIBIRSKIYE OSTROVA
(NEW SIBERIAN ISLANDS)
SEVERNAYA ZEMLYA
(NORTH LAND)
ZEMLYA FRANTSA IOSIFA
(FRANZ JOSEF LAND)
NOVAYA ZEMLYA
SVALBARD
SPITSBERGEN
Bjørnøya
(Bear Island)
SIBERIA
URAL MOUNTAINS
CHINA
MONGOLIA
KAZAKHSTAN
NORWAY
SWEDEN
FINLAND
ARCTIC CIRCLE
Poluostrov Yamal
Ozero Baykal
Murmansk
Arkhangel'sk
(Archangel)
Novosibirsk
Krasnoyarsk
Irkutsk
Yekaterinburg
Omsk
Astana
Chelyabinsk
Perm'
Kazan'
Samara
Ufa
Yakutsk
Bratsk
Noril'sk

ATLANTIC OCEAN
Scotia Sea
South Orkney Is.
Orcadas, Argentina
ANTARCTIC PENINSULA AREA STATIONS
Argentina
1 Jubany
Brazil
2 Comandante Ferraz
Chile
3 Escudero
4 General Bernardo O'Higgins
5 Presidente Eduardo Frei
China
6 Great Wall
Korea, South
7 King Sejong
Poland
8 Arctowski
Russia
9 Bellingshausen
Uruguay
10 Artigas
Research Stations: Year-round Other
Stanley
E. Falkland
W. Falkland
Weddell Island
Mt. Adam
Cape Meredith
FALKLAND ISLANDS (ISLAS MALVINAS) U.K.
Cabo San Juan
I. de los Estado (Staten Island)
I. GRANDE DE TIERRA DEL FUEGO
ARGENTINA
CHILE
Punta Dungeness
Punta de Arenas
I. Navarino
Cape Horn
Islas Wollaston
Mte. Italia
I. Londonderry
I. Stewart
Peninsula Brecknock
I. Carlos
I. Sta. Ines
Drake Passage
Elephant I.
Clarence I.
Antarctic Sound
Joinville I.
Esperanza, Argentina
Marambio, Argentina
Vega I.
Seymour I.
SOUTH SHETLAND IS.
King George I.
Chile, Capitán Arturo Prat
Livingston I.
ANTARCTIC PENINSULA
Larsen Inlet
GRAHAM LAND
Cape Disappointment
Cape Framnes
Churchill Pen.
Cape Alexander
Brabant I.
PALMER ARCH.
Anvers I.
Palmer, U.S.
Ukraine, Vernadsky
BISCOE IS.
Renaud I.
Cape Mascart
Adelaide I.
San Martín, Argentina
Rothera, United Kingdom
Eternity Range
Mt. Courtauld
Cape Jeremy
Mt. Stephenson
ALEXANDER I.
Rothschild I.
Charcot I.
Cape Byrd
Latady Island
Francis I.
Joerg Peninsula
Hearst I.
Ewing I.
C. Collier
C. Boggs
C. Dolleman I.
Steele I.
C. Bryant
Butler I.
Merz Peninsula
Cape Mackintosh
Kemp Peninsula
Cape Brooks
Cape Fiske
Cape Adams
C. Schlossbach
Nantucket Inlet
PALMER LAND
Mt. Ward
Mt. Vang
WEDDELL SEA
RONNE ICE SHELF
Korff Ice Rise
Henry Ice Rise
Gould Bay
Belgrano II, Argentina
Bertrab Nunatak
LUITPOLD COAST
FILCHNER ICE SHELF
BERKNER I.
McCarthy Inlet
Halley, United Kingdom
Brunt Ice Shelf
CAIRD COAST
COATS LAND
Lyddan I.
ICE SHELF
RIISER-LARSEN
Aboa, Finland
Seal Bay
Cape Norvegia
Maudheim, Sweden
Neumayer, Germany
PRINCESS MARTHA COAST
Heimefront Range
RITSCHER UPLAND
Mt. Absalom
Lewis Chain
TRANSANTARCTIC MOUNTAINS
PENSACOLA MOUNTAINS
Saratoga Table
Cordiner Peaks
Eklund Is.
DeAtley I.
Perce Point
Spaatz I.
Sweeney Mts.
Mt. Edward
Thomas Mts.
Mt. Becker
Zumberge Coast
Smyley I.
Case I.
Mt. Tuve
Fladerer Bay
Mendelssohn Inlet
Verdi Inlet
Schubert Inlet
BELLINGSHAUSEN SEA
Allison Pen.
Venable Ice Shelf
ELLSWORTH LAND
Anderson Massif
Hercules Inlet
Patriot Hill, Chile
Vinson Massif
4897 (16067 ft)
ELLSWORTH MOUNTAINS
Peter I I.
Lars Christensen Pk.
Dendtler I.
Farwell I.
Abbot Ice Shelf
Dustin I.
WEST ANTARCTICA
Hart Hills
King Peak
Havola Escarpment
HERCULES DOME
Mt. Woollard
Mt. Seelig
Ohio Range
Wisconsin Range
Mt. Howe
QUEEN MAUD MTS.
Harold Byrd Mts.
GOULD COAST
Tapley Mts.
THURSTON ISLAND
Murphy Inlet
Noville Pen.
Cape Davies
Cape Flying Fish
Cape Waite
Carpenter I.
Sherman I.
King Pen.
Canisteo Pen.
Pine Island Bay
Burke I.
WALGREEN COAST
HOLLICK-KENYON PLATEAU
MARIE BYRD LAND
Lowest known point in Antarctica
-2,555 m (18,383 ft)
ICE SHELVES
Large areas of floating glacier ice fringe the coast of Antarctica. The two largest ice shelves are the Ross Ice Shelf and the Ronne Ice Shelf, both separated by glacier ice that is grounded below sea level. Large tabular icebergs periodically calve from ice shelves.
AMUNDSEN SEA
Bear Pen.
Philbin Inlet
Toney Mt.
Mt. Frakes
BAKUTIS COAST
Mt. Waesche
Mt. Galla
Ramage Point
Carney I.
Siple I.
Mt. Siple
Dean I.
Getz Ice Shelf
Wrigley Gulf
Grant I.
Shepard I.
Schwob Pk.
HOBBS COAST
RUPPERT COAST
ROCKEFELLER PLATEAU
SIPLE COAST
SHIRASE COAST
Steers Head
Roosevelt Island
SAUNDERS COAST
Scott Nunataks
Guest Pen.
Driscoll I.
Newman I.
PACIFIC OCEAN
A SEA OF ICE
When winter comes, the ocean surface around Antarctica begins to freeze. Spreading over an average of 77,700 square kilometers (30,000 sq. miles) a day, the ring of sea ice eventually covers more than 18 million square kilometers (7 million sq. miles), an area larger than the continent itself. Reducing the ocean's absorption of atmospheric carbon dioxide and blocking ocean-atmosphere heat exchange, sea ice plays a role in shaping regional climate that in turn has impacts over much of the globe.
ANTARCTIC CONVERGENCE
About 1,600 km (990 mi) off-shore is the Antarctic Convergence, where cold waters meet warmer waters from the north, enclosing a distinct ecosystem sometimes called the Southern Ocean.
ANTARCTIC CIRCLE
Longitude West of Greenwich

WEIGHT OF THE ICE SHEET
The ice mass covering Antarctica is so heavy that it depresses the Earth's crust more than 914 meters (3,000 feet). Ice-free continental shelves actually tilt in toward the land, rather than sloping away toward the deep seafloor.
ICE DESERT
Although Antarctica stores some 72 percent of the world's fresh water as ice, precipitation on six million sq km (2.3 million sq mi) of the continents's interior averages less than five cm a year, similar to the amount of rainfall in the driest part of the Sahara.
CLIMATE
The southern polar region is substantially colder than its northern counterpart. The lofty ice sheet reflects as much as 90 percent of solar radiation back to space, whereas in the Arctic Ocean ice partly melts in summer and the dark waters absorb heat. The temperature difference between the equatorial and polar regions drives atmospheric circulation. Because the South Pole is colder than the North, winds are stronger in the Southern Hemisphere. The ice sheet contains a climate record that extends back at least 200,000 years at some locations. Ice cores preserve a record of past atmospheric composition, volcanic eruptions, and other environmental information.
THICKEST ICE
Echo-sounding from aircraft has identified an ice thickness of 4,776 m (15,670 ft). Bedrock was found at 2,341 m below sea level.
Coldest place on Earth: Average annual temperature -56.7°C (-70.1°F)
A record low temperature of minus 89.2°C (-128.6°F) was recorded here on July 21, 1983.
INDIAN OCEAN
ANTARCTIC CIRCLE
EAST ANTARCTICA
QUEEN MAUD LAND
PRINCESS ASTRID COAST
PRINCESS RAGNHILD COAST
ENDERBY LAND
MAC. ROBERTSON LAND
AMERICAN HIGHLAND
MAWSON COAST
INGRID CHRISTENSEN COAST
QUEEN MARY COAST
WILKES LAND
KNOX COAST
BUDD LAW DOME COAST
SABRINA COAST
BANZARE COAST
CLARIE COAST
ADÉLIE COAST
GEORGE V COAST
OATES COAST
PENNELL COAST
BORCHGREVINK COAST
SCOTT COAST
HILLARY COAST
SHACKLETON COAST
VICTORIA LAND
PRINCE ALBERT MOUNTAINS
TALOS DOME
DOME ARGUS
VALKYRIE DOME
SCHWABENLAND
Dome Fuji, Japan
South Geomagnetic Pole
Vostok, Russia
Dome Concordia, France and Italy
Maitri, India
Novolazarevskaya, Russia
Syowa, Japan
Molodezhnaya, Russia
Mawson, Australia
Zhongshan, China
Progress, Russia
Davis, Australia
Mirnyy, Russia
Casey, Australia
McMurdo, United States
Scott Base
Dumont d'Urville, France
Lützow-Holm Bay
Amery Ice Shelf
Prydz Bay
MacKenzie Bay
Barrier Bay
West Ice Shelf
Posadowsky Bay
DAVIS SEA
Farr Bay
Shackleton Ice Shelf
Moscow University Ice Shelf
Henry Bay
Maury Bay
Porpoise Bay
Murphy Bay
Prince Charles Mountains
Heard Island Austral.
Tange Promontory
Cape Close
Aagaard Islands
Cape Borle
Øygarden Group
Colbeck Arch.
Douglas Is.
Cape Fletcher
Gustav Bull Mts.
Point Williams
Cape Darnley
Vestfold Hills
Leskov I.
Mikhaylov I.
Cape Penck
Masson I.
Gillies Is.
Melba Peninsula
Highjump Archipelago
Mill Island
Bunger Hills
Cape Elliott
Bowman Island
Cape Peremennyy
Davis Is.
Windmill Is.
Cape Poinsett
Cape Waldron
Cape Mikhaylov
Cape Goodenough
Cape Spieden
Cape Mose
Cape Carr
Freeman Point
Cape Keltie
Cape Cesney
Rock X
Cape Robert
Point Alden
Way Arch.
Cape Wild
C. Freshfield
Cape Hudson
Cape Novosil'skiy
Archer Point
Cape Kinsey
Yermak Point
Cape Cheetham
Cape North
Lyall Is.
Adare Peninsula
Cape McCormick
Possession Is.
Mt. Northampton 2467
Cape Sibbald
Cape Washington
Mt. Melbourne 2732
Roberts Butte 2828
Mt. Minto 4165
Mt. Ford 2580
Mt. Joyce
Allan Hills
Mt. Erebus 3794
Ross I.
Cape Crozier
White I.
Minna Bluff
Mt. Lister 4025
Mt. Longhurst
Cape Murray
Wright Hill
Cape Kerr
Penny Point
Darley Hills
Cape Parr
Cape May
Mt. McClintock 3492
Mt. Albert
Mt. Christmas
Miller Range
Mt. Markham 4351
Coalsack Bluff
Filchner Mts.
Drygalski Mts.
Kurze Mts.
Vorposten Pk. 2200
Payer Mts.
Habermehl Pk.
Mt. Widerøe 3180
Isachsen Mt. 3425
Vørterkaka Nunatak 3630
Mt. Derom 2390
Queen Fabiola Mts. (Yamato Mts.)
Botnnuten 1460
Mt. Christensen
Nye Mts.
Scott Mts.
White I.
Sandercock Nunataks
Dismal Mts.
Conradi Pk. 1040
Rayner Pk. 1270
Fram Pk. 1781
Masson Range
Riddell Nunataks
Depot Peak
Mt. Macey 1960
Athos Range
Gillock I.
Reinbolt Hills
Mt. Strathcona 1380
Mt. Sandow 1445
Amundsen
Cape Dovers
AZIMUTHAL EQUIDISTANT PROJECTION
SCALE 1:18,000,000
0 KILOMETERS 300 400 500
0 MILES 100 200 300 400 500
*2005 South Magnetic Pole
Longitude East of Greenwich

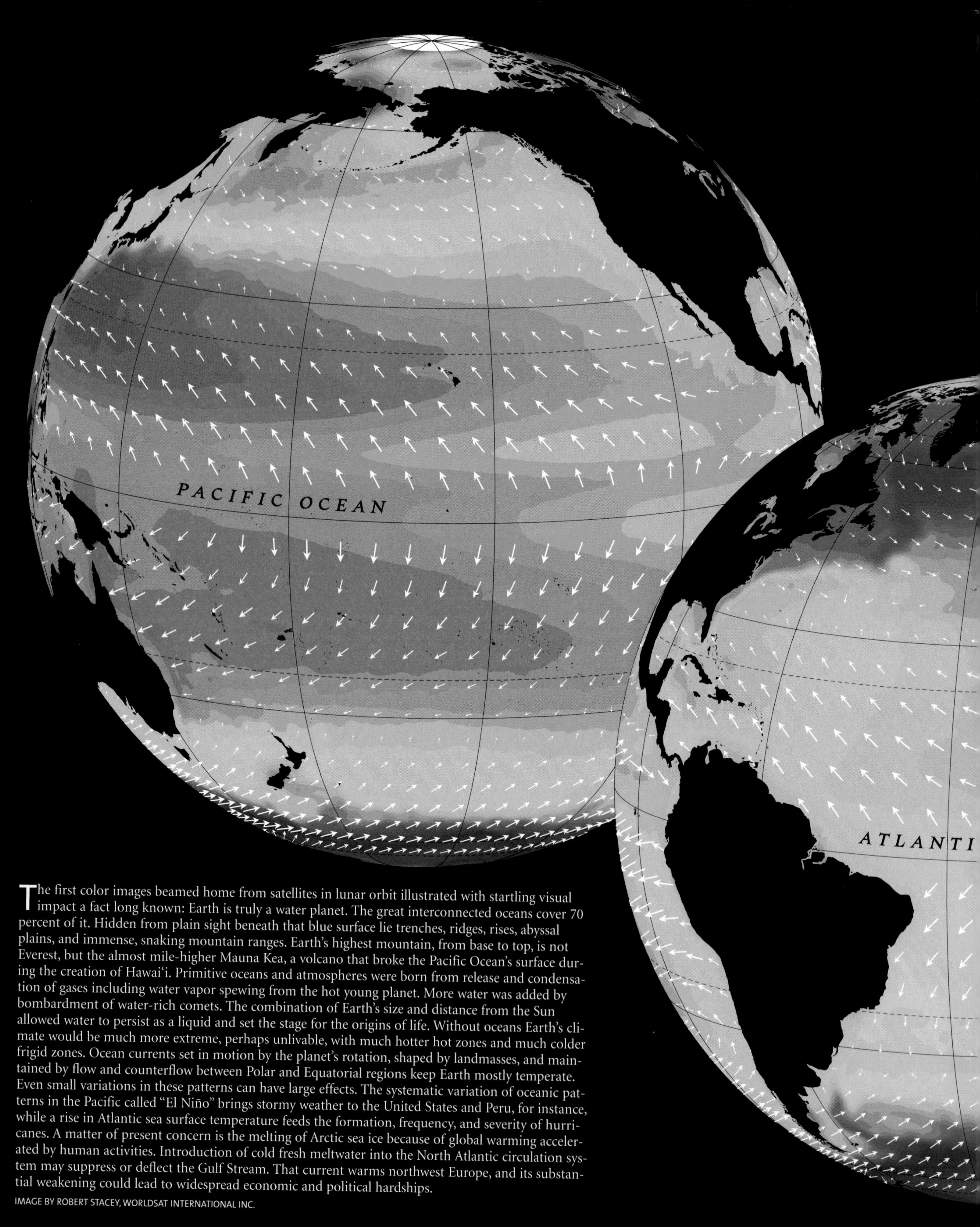

The first color images beamed home from satellites in lunar orbit illustrated with startling visual impact a fact long known: Earth is truly a water planet. The great interconnected oceans cover 70 percent of it. Hidden from plain sight beneath that blue surface lie trenches, ridges, rises, abyssal plains, and immense, snaking mountain ranges. Earth's highest mountain, from base to top, is not Everest, but the almost mile-higher Mauna Kea, a volcano that broke the Pacific Ocean's surface during the creation of Hawai'i. Primitive oceans and atmospheres were born from release and condensation of gases including water vapor spewing from the hot young planet. More water was added by bombardment of water-rich comets. The combination of Earth's size and distance from the Sun allowed water to persist as a liquid and set the stage for the origins of life. Without oceans Earth's climate would be much more extreme, perhaps unlivable, with much hotter hot zones and much colder frigid zones. Ocean currents set in motion by the planet's rotation, shaped by landmasses, and maintained by flow and counterflow between Polar and Equatorial regions keep Earth mostly temperate. Even small variations in these patterns can have large effects. The systematic variation of oceanic patterns in the Pacific called "El Niño" brings stormy weather to the United States and Peru, for instance, while a rise in Atlantic sea surface temperature feeds the formation, frequency, and severity of hurricanes. A matter of present concern is the melting of Arctic sea ice because of global warming accelerated by human activities. Introduction of cold fresh meltwater into the North Atlantic circulation system may suppress or deflect the Gulf Stream. That current warms northwest Europe, and its substantial weakening could lead to widespread economic and political hardships.

IMAGE BY ROBERT STACEY, WORLDSAT INTERNATIONAL INC.

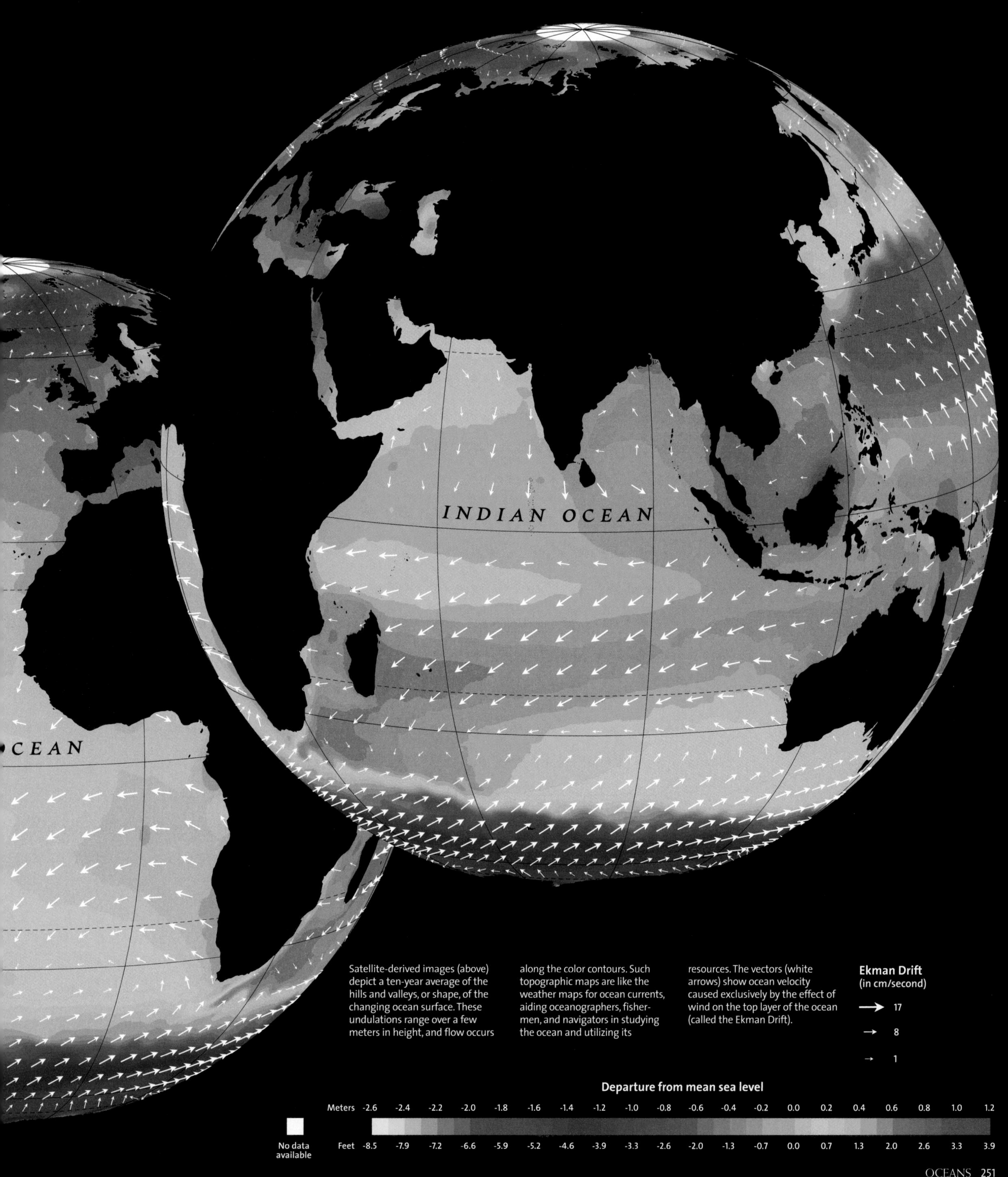

Satellite-derived images (above) depict a ten-year average of the hills and valleys, or shape, of the changing ocean surface. These undulations range over a few meters in height, and flow occurs along the color contours. Such topographic maps are like the weather maps for ocean currents, aiding oceanographers, fishermen, and navigators in studying the ocean and utilizing its resources. The vectors (white arrows) show ocean velocity caused exclusively by the effect of wind on the top layer of the ocean (called the Ekman Drift).

Ekman Drift
(in cm/second)

- 17
- 8
- 1

Departure from mean sea level

Meters	-2.6	-2.4	-2.2	-2.0	-1.8	-1.6	-1.4	-1.2	-1.0	-0.8	-0.6	-0.4	-0.2	0.0	0.2	0.4	0.6	0.8	1.0	1.2
Feet	-8.5	-7.9	-7.2	-6.6	-5.9	-5.2	-4.6	-3.9	-3.3	-2.6	-2.0	-1.3	-0.7	0.0	0.7	1.3	2.0	2.6	3.3	3.9

No data available

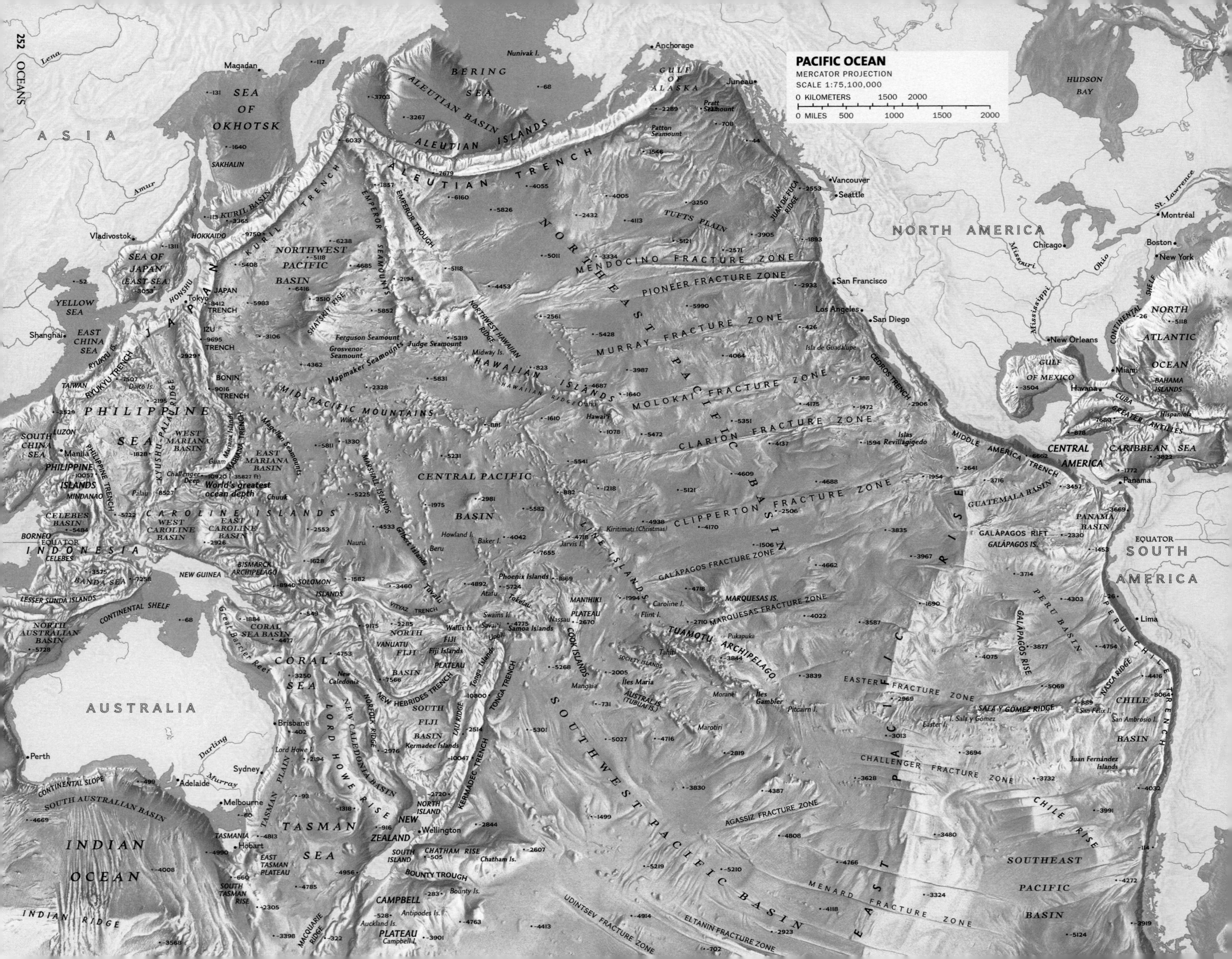
PACIFIC OCEAN
MERCATOR PROJECTION
SCALE 1:75,100,000
0 KILOMETERS 1500 2000
0 MILES 500 1000 1500 2000
NORTH AMERICA
SOUTH AMERICA
ASIA
AUSTRALIA
NORTH ATLANTIC OCEAN
INDIAN OCEAN
HUDSON BAY
GULF OF MEXICO
CARIBBEAN SEA
BERING SEA
SEA OF OKHOTSK
SEA OF JAPAN (EAST SEA)
YELLOW SEA
EAST CHINA SEA
SOUTH CHINA SEA
PHILIPPINE SEA
CORAL SEA
TASMAN SEA
GULF OF ALASKA
NORTHEAST PACIFIC BASIN
NORTHWEST PACIFIC BASIN
CENTRAL PACIFIC BASIN
SOUTHWEST PACIFIC BASIN
SOUTHEAST PACIFIC BASIN
PERU BASIN
CHILE BASIN
EAST PACIFIC RISE
ALEUTIAN TRENCH
ALEUTIAN ISLANDS
ALEUTIAN BASIN
KURIL TRENCH
JAPAN TRENCH
MARIANA TRENCH
World's greatest ocean depth
PHILIPPINE TRENCH
TONGA TRENCH
KERMADEC TRENCH
PERU-CHILE TRENCH
MIDDLE AMERICA TRENCH
HAWAIIAN ISLANDS
EMPEROR SEAMOUNTS
MID-PACIFIC MOUNTAINS
MENDOCINO FRACTURE ZONE
PIONEER FRACTURE ZONE
MURRAY FRACTURE ZONE
MOLOKAI FRACTURE ZONE
CLARION FRACTURE ZONE
CLIPPERTON FRACTURE ZONE
GALÁPAGOS RISE
TUAMOTU ARCHIPELAGO
LINE ISLANDS
COOK ISLANDS
CHALLENGER FRACTURE ZONE
MENARD FRACTURE ZONE
ELTANIN FRACTURE ZONE
UDINTSEV FRACTURE ZONE
CHILE RISE
LORD HOWE RISE
NEW CALEDONIA BASIN
CAMPBELL PLATEAU
NEW ZEALAND
INDONESIA
CAROLINE ISLANDS
MARSHALL ISLANDS
SOLOMON ISLANDS
FIJI
SOUTH AUSTRALIAN BASIN
INDIAN RIDGE
EQUATOR

ATLANTIC OCEAN
MERCATOR PROJECTION
SCALE 1:62,600,000
0 KILOMETERS 1200 1600
0 MILES 400 800 1200 1600
GREENLAND
FOXE BASIN
HUDSON BAY
DAVIS STRAIT
CONTINENTAL SHELF
Tasiilaq (Ammassalik)
Nuuk (Godthåb)
DENMARK STRAIT
ICELAND
Reykjavík
Surtsey
FAROE-ICELAND RIDGE
FAROE ISLANDS
Halten Bank
SCANDINAVIA
GULF OF BOTHNIA
Helsinki
Bergen
Oslo
Stockholm
BALTIC SEA
CONTINENTAL SLOPE
CONTINENTAL SHELF
NORTHWEST ATLANTIC MID-OCEAN CANYON
LABRADOR SEA
Eirik Ridge
IMARSSUAK SEACHANNEL
REYKJANES RIDGE
MAURY SEACHANNEL
WYVILLE THOMSON RIDGE
Rockall
Gloria Ridge
NORTH SEA
BRITISH ISLES
Dublin
Hamburg
CHARLIE-GIBBS FRACTURE ZONE
PORCUPINE PLAIN
CELTIC SEA
ENGLISH CHANNEL
EUROPE
NORTH AMERICA
St. Lawrence
Québec
Montréal
GULF OF ST. LAWRENCE
St. John's
Flemish Cap
Grand Banks of Newfoundland
Cape Breton Island
Halifax
Sable Island
Gulf of Maine
Boston
Chicago
New York
Laurentian Fan
MID-ATLANTIC RIDGE
BISCAY PLAIN
BAY OF BISCAY
Danube
Marseille
CORSICA
ADRIATIC SEA
Rome
SARDINIA
TYRRHENIAN SEA
BALEARIC IS.
MEDITERRANEAN SEA
SICILY
Athens
CRETE
Missouri
Ohio
Mississippi
SOHM PLAIN
New England Seamounts
Hudson Canyon
Cape Hatteras
Corner Seamounts
OCEANOGRAPHER FRACTURE ZONE
AZORES
Pico
Lisbon
Strait of Gibraltar
Algiers
Rabat
Tripoli
CONTINENTAL SHELF
Bermuda Islands
BERMUDA RISE
HATTERAS PLAIN
BLAKE PLATEAU
Blake-Bahama Ridge
MADEIRA ISLANDS
ATLANTIS FRACTURE ZONE
CANARY ISLANDS
New Orleans
GULF OF MEXICO
Miami
BAHAMA ISLANDS
NARES PLAIN
CAPE VERDE PLAIN
Mexico Basin
Campeche Bank
Havana
CUBA
Atlantic Ocean's deepest point
KANE FRACTURE ZONE
PUERTO RICO TRENCH
HISPANIOLA
-8605 (-28232 ft)
Cayman Trench
GREATER ANTILLES
AVES RIDGE
LESSER ANTILLES
CAPE VERDE ISLANDS
Nouakchott
AFRICA
Dakar
GAMBIA PLAIN
Niger
L. Chad
CENTRAL AMERICA
MIDDLE AMERICA TRENCH
Panama
Trinidad
VEMA FRACTURE ZONE
DEMERARA PLAIN
DOLDRUMS FRACTURE ZONE
Freetown
SIERRA LEONE RISE
Abidjan
Accra
Lagos
Georgetown
Amazon Fan
COCOS RIDGE
St. Peter and St. Paul Rocks
ROMANCHE FRACTURE ZONE
Bioko
São Tomé
Libreville
Congo
EQUATOR
GALÁPAGOS ISLANDS
CARNEGIE RIDGE
CONTINENTAL SHELF
CEARA PLAIN
CHAIN FRACTURE ZONE
Belém
Amazon
Fernando de Noronha
PERNAMBUCO PLAIN
Congo Canyon
ASCENSION FRACTURE ZONE
Luanda
SOUTH AMERICA
Lima
PERU-CHILE TRENCH
ANGOLA PLAIN
St. Helena
Zambezi
NASCA RIDGE
Trindade
Martin Vaz Islands
Vitória Seamount
Paraguay
Rio de Janeiro
São Paulo
Santos Plateau
WALVIS RIDGE
SOUTH PACIFIC OCEAN
San Félix Island
San Ambrosio Island
Orange
RIO GRANDE RISE
Juan Fernández Islands
Paraná
Buenos Aires
Montevideo
CAPE PLAIN
Cape of Good Hope
Cape Town
CHILE RISE
CONTINENTAL SHELF
CONTINENTAL SLOPE
CONTINENTAL RISE
Tristan da Cunha Group
Discovery Tablemount
Zapiola Ridge
Gulf of San Jorge
ARGENTINE PLAIN

INDIAN OCEAN
MERCATOR PROJECTION
SCALE 1:51,400,000
0 KILOMETERS 800 1200
0 MILES 400 800 1200
ASIA
INDIA
AFRICA
AUSTRALIA
INDONESIA
ARABIAN PENINSULA
JAPAN
NEW GUINEA
MADAGASCAR
SRI LANKA (CEYLON)
BORNEO
SUMATRA
JAVA
CELEBES
MINDANAO
LUZON
KYUSHU
MEDITERRANEAN SEA
RED SEA
PERSIAN GULF
GULF OF OMAN
GULF OF ADEN
ARABIAN SEA
BAY OF BENGAL
SOUTH CHINA SEA
EAST CHINA SEA
PHILIPPINE SEA
BANDA SEA
GREATER SUNDA ISLANDS
LESSER SUNDA ISLANDS
PHILIPPINE ISLANDS
RYUKYU ISLANDS
CELEBES BASIN
SULU BASIN
ANDAMAN BASIN
PHILIPPINE BASIN
WEST MARIANA BASIN
WEST CAROLINE BASIN
NORTH AUSTRALIAN BASIN
WHARTON BASIN
PERTH BASIN
SOUTH AUSTRALIAN BASIN
MID-INDIAN BASIN
ARABIAN BASIN
SOMALI BASIN
MASCARENE BASIN
MADAGASCAR BASIN
MASCARENE PLAIN
NATAL BASIN
CROZET BASIN
AGULHAS BASIN
NINETYEAST RIDGE
INVESTIGATOR RIDGE
BROKEN RIDGE
EAST INDIAMAN RIDGE
MID-INDIAN RIDGE
SOUTHEAST INDIAN RIDGE
SOUTHWEST INDIAN RIDGE
CARLSBERG RIDGE
KYUSHU-PALAU RIDGE
JAVA RIDGE
CHAGOS-LACCADIVE PLATEAU
MASCARENE PLATEAU
MADAGASCAR PLATEAU
MOZAMBIQUE PLATEAU
MOZAMBIQUE ESCARPMENT
AGULHAS PLATEAU
CROZET PLATEAU
KERGUELEN PLATEAU
NATURALISTE PLATEAU
CUVIER PLATEAU
WALLABY PLATEAU
EXMOUTH PLATEAU
OSBORN PLATEAU
OWEN FRACTURE ZONE
RODRIGUES FRACTURE ZONE
EGERIA FRACTURE ZONE
ATLANTIS II FRACTURE ZONE
INDOMED FRACTURE ZONE
PRINCE EDWARD FRACTURE ZONE
DIAMANTINA FRACTURE ZONE
JAVA TRENCH
PHILIPPINE TRENCH
RYUKYU TRENCH
PALAU TRENCH
YAP TRENCH
CHAGOS TRENCH
AMIRANTE TRENCH
MAURITIUS TRENCH
PALAWAN TROUGH
CONTINENTAL SHELF
CONTINENTAL SLOPE
Indian Ocean's deepest point
Mt. Everest + 8850 (29035 ft)
World's highest point
Dead Sea -416 (-1365ft)
World's lowest point
Ganges Fan
Indus Fan
Nikitin Seamount
COCO-DE-MER SEAMOUNTS
Error Tablemount
SUEZ CANAL
Alexandria
Ābādān
Karachi
Muscat
Aden
Djibouti
Mumbai (Bombay)
Chennai (Madras)
Kolkata (Calcutta)
Yangon (Rangoon)
Bangkok
Ho Chi Minh City (Saigon)
Singapore
Jakarta
Hong Kong
Shanghai
Manila
Darwin
Perth
Adelaide
Mogadishu
Mombasa
Dar es Salaam
Maputo
Durban
Socotra
Seychelles
Amirante Isles
Maldive Islands
Chagos Archipelago
Diego Garcia
Agalega Islands
Farquhar Group
Aldabra Is.
Comoro Islands
Zanzibar I.
Cargados Carajos Bank
Tromelin
Mauritius
Réunion
Rodrigues
Bassas da India
Europa
Walters Shoal
Amsterdam
St. Paul
Kerguelen Islands
Crozet Islands
Prince Edward Islands
Agulhas Bank
Andaman Islands
Nicobar Islands
Christmas I.
Paracel Islands
Hainan
Taiwan
Bali
Timor
Palau
Tigris
Euphrates
Indus
Ganges
Brahmaputra
Nile
Congo
Zambezi
Mekong
Yangtze
Lake Victoria
Lake Tanganyika
Lake Malawi
EQUATOR

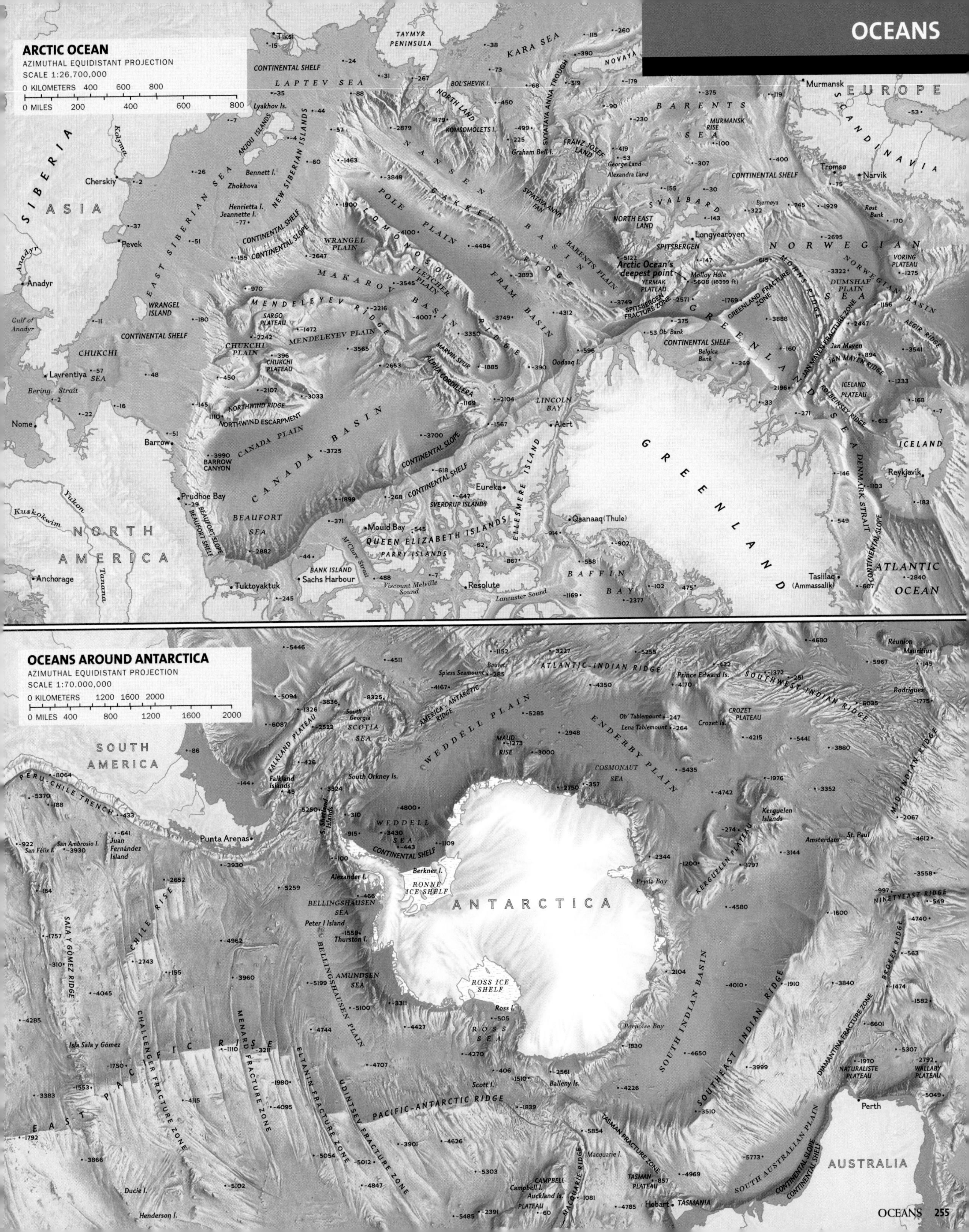
ARCTIC OCEAN
AZIMUTHAL EQUIDISTANT PROJECTION
SCALE 1:26,700,000
0 KILOMETERS 400 600 800
0 MILES 200 400 600 800
SIBERIA
ASIA
EAST SIBERIAN SEA
LAPTEV SEA
KARA SEA
TAYMYR PENINSULA
NEW SIBERIAN ISLANDS
ANJOU ISLANDS
NORTH LAND
BARENTS SEA
FRANZ JOSEF LAND
SVALBARD
SPITSBERGEN
NORTH EAST LAND
NANSEN BASIN
GAKKEL RIDGE
POLE PLAIN
LOMONOSOV RIDGE
FRAM BASIN
MAKAROV BASIN
MENDELEYEV RIDGE
MENDELEYEV PLAIN
WRANGEL PLAIN
WRANGEL ISLAND
CHUKCHI SEA
CHUKCHI PLAIN
CHUKCHI PLATEAU
NORTHWIND RIDGE
NORTHWIND ESCARPMENT
CANADA PLAIN
CANADA BASIN
ALPHA CORDILLERA
BEAUFORT SEA
BEAUFORT SHELF
BEAUFORT SLOPE
QUEEN ELIZABETH ISLANDS
PARRY ISLANDS
SVERDRUP ISLANDS
ELLESMERE ISLAND
LINCOLN BAY
BAFFIN BAY
GREENLAND
GREENLAND SEA
NORWEGIAN SEA
NORWEGIAN BASIN
ICELAND
ICELAND PLATEAU
JAN MAYEN RIDGE
DENMARK STRAIT
EUROPE
SCANDINAVIA
NORTH AMERICA
ATLANTIC OCEAN
Arctic Ocean's deepest point
Molloy Hole -5608 (18399 ft)
Murmansk
Tromsø
Narvik
Longyearbyen
Reykjavík
Tasiilaq (Ammassalik)
Qaanaaq (Thule)
Alert
Eureka
Resolute
Mould Bay
Sachs Harbour
Tuktoyaktuk
Prudhoe Bay
Barrow
Nome
Anchorage
Anadyr
Pevek
Cherskiy
Tiksi
Lavrentiya
OCEANS AROUND ANTARCTICA
AZIMUTHAL EQUIDISTANT PROJECTION
SCALE 1:70,000,000
0 KILOMETERS 400 1200 1600 2000
0 MILES 400 800 1200 1600 2000
SOUTH AMERICA
ANTARCTICA
AUSTRALIA
PERU-CHILE TRENCH
CHILE RISE
SALA Y GÓMEZ RIDGE
EAST PACIFIC RISE
CHALLENGER FRACTURE ZONE
MENARD FRACTURE ZONE
ELTANIN FRACTURE ZONE
UDINTSEV FRACTURE ZONE
PACIFIC-ANTARCTIC RIDGE
BELLINGSHAUSEN SEA
BELLINGSHAUSEN PLAIN
AMUNDSEN SEA
ROSS SEA
ROSS ICE SHELF
RONNE ICE SHELF
WEDDELL SEA
WEDDELL PLAIN
SCOTIA SEA
FALKLAND PLATEAU
AMERICA-ANTARCTIC RIDGE
ATLANTIC-INDIAN RIDGE
ENDERBY PLAIN
COSMONAUT SEA
MAUD RISE
CROZET PLATEAU
SOUTHWEST INDIAN RIDGE
MID-INDIAN RIDGE
KERGUELEN PLATEAU
NINETYEAST RIDGE
BROKEN RIDGE
SOUTH INDIAN BASIN
SOUTHEAST INDIAN RIDGE
DIAMANTINA FRACTURE ZONE
NATURALISTE PLATEAU
WALLABY PLATEAU
SOUTH AUSTRALIAN PLAIN
TASMAN FRACTURE ZONE
TASMAN PLATEAU
MACQUARIE RIDGE
CAMPBELL PLATEAU
TASMANIA
Perth
Hobart
Punta Arenas
Falkland Islands
South Georgia
South Orkney Is.
S. Shetland Islands
Kerguelen Islands
Prince Edward Is.
Crozet Is.
Réunion
Mauritius
Rodrigues
Amsterdam
St. Paul
Peter I Island
Thurston I.
Alexander I.
Berkner I.
Ross I.
Scott I.
Balleny Is.
Macquarie I.
Campbell I.
Auckland Is.
Bouvet
Spiess Seamount
Ob' Tablemount
Lena Tablemount
Prydz Bay
Porpoise Bay
Isla Sala y Gómez
San Félix I.
San Ambrosio I.
Juan Fernández Island
Ducie I.
Henderson I.

NATIONAL GEOGRAPHIC SOCIETY'S PLACE-NAMES POLICY

In keeping with the National Geographic Society's 118-year chartered purpose as a not-for-profit scientific and educational organization, the Society's cartographic policy is one of portraying de facto situations; that is, to portray to the best of our judgment a current reality. National Geographic strives to be apolitical, to consult multiple authoritative sources, and to make independent decisions based on extensive research. When there are conflicting or variant names, National Geographic does not purport to be the arbiter or determiner of a single name, but simply tries to provide the reader of the map sufficient information in which the reality of conflicting naming claims can be presented.

The Society's policy for naming geographic features is governed by a representative council of Society cartographers. This council meets frequently to assess available information about naming issues and, based on the best information and research available, seeks to make an independent judgment about future changes or clarifications on its maps, as well as to correct any errors. It is the policy of the Society to correct any errors as quickly as possible on the next published version of a particular map or Atlas.

Depending on the type of map (whether physical or political), the Society uses either conventional (English) or native spellings, or, where space permits, a combination of both. For example, when a commonly recognized form of a well-known place-name, such as Bombay, differs from the official national form – Mumbai—the conventional form is listed in parenthesis: Mumbai (Bombay). The Society does not follow any single source in making its naming determinations. Decisions regarding the naming assigned to geographic places, locations, bodies of water, and the like are checked against a number of external entities, including: the Board on Geographic Names; recognized reference books such as encyclopedias, dictionaries, geographical dictionaries, other atlases, independent academic texts and other similar sources; international bodies such as the United Nations, the European Community, and the like; as well as the policies of individual governmental entities. Names commonly recognized as alternatives or variants by such sources are often used on our maps. In such instances, the primary name is determined by using the form recognized by the de facto controlling country of the area, or by using the generally held conventional form of the name. On occasion where warranted and where space permits, explanatory notes stating the basis or context of a recognized variant naming are provided. Current examples of the application of this variant naming policy are: Falkland Islands (Islas Malvinas); Sea of Japan (East Sea).

National Geographic Maps frequently applies a secondary place-name in parenthesis ( ) after a recognized primary form of a place-name. This treatment is used even when the primary name is more widely recognized, provided that the variant name is used widely enough that National Geographic considers the inclusion of both to have real reference and educational value for the users of its products. Some instances of this use and examples are listed below.

Conventional Names
Used when the commonly recognized form (conventional) of a well-known place name differs from the official national form. The conventional form is listed in parenthesis. Conventional names are recognized as an official variant form for a place-name by multiple reference sources. On physical maps only the conventional form is generally used.

= Roma (Rome)
= Mumbai (Bombay)
= Ghazzah (Gaza)

If a feature crosses over multiple countries (usually a river), the official national form is labeled within that specific country with the conventional in parentheses. As the feature moves into another country, then that country's official form is used as the primary name.

= Dọnau (Danube)
= Duna (Danube)
= Dunaj (Danube)
= Dunărea (Danube)
= Dunav (Danube)
= Dunay (Danube)

Historic Names
Given same treatment as conventional names.
= İstanbul (Constantinople)
= Guangzhou (Canton)
= Ho Chi Minh City (Saigon)

Variant Names: Similar to conventional names, but are not necessarily officially recognized as an official variant. Often used by the media.

= Al Fallūjah (Fallujah)

Names with shared possession
When a name (usually a border mountain) is jointly controlled by more then one country and has multiple official names, the general rule is to list the conventional name first and then list the official names together in parentheses. Order of the secondary names can vary. The country that is the main subject of the map would be first. If both countries are the subject of the map, the names are listed in order of the country.

- Mount Everest (Sagarmāthā, Qomolangma): for a map of South Asia when Nepal is the map subject.
- Mount Everest (Qomolangma, Sagarmāthā): for a map of China or when both countries are the map subject.

Disputed Names
When a name has differing forms recognized by different countries. The primary name is determined by using the form recognized by the de facto controlling country of the area, or using the generally held conventional form of the name.

Cyprus
= Lefkosia (Nicosia, Lefkoşa)
= Ammochostos (Famagusta, Gazimagusa)
= Keryneia (Kyrenia, Girne)
Dokdo
= Dokdo (Takeshima, Liancourt Rocks)
Southern Kuril Islands
= Iturup (Etorofu)
= Kunashir (Kunashiri)
Other Features
= English Channel (La Manche)
= Falkland Islands (Islas Malvinas)
= Sea of Japan (East Sea)

Possession Labels
National Geographic Maps applies possession labels in red type to non-contiguous territorial areas (generally islands), identifying the country that has political control of it. Where an area is controlled by one country but is also claimed by another, a longer red note identifying the controlling country and the party claiming ownership is given in red type.

= Falkland Islands (Islas Malvinas)-United Kingdom
Administered by United Kingdom (claimed by Argentina)
= Paracel Islands-China
Administered by China (claimed by Vietnam)
= Senkaku Shotō (Diaoyu Islands)-Japan
Administered by Japan (claimed by China and Taiwan)

Map Notes
Where scale permits, explanatory notes, as those listed below, are added to our maps to explain the current political situation of disputed possessions or territories.

Abkhazia:
ABKHAZIA
Separatists defeated Georgian troops to gain control of this region in 1993-negotiations continue on resolving the conflict.

Cyprus:
DIVIDED CYPRUS
Cyprus was partitioned in 1974 following a coup backed by Greece and an invasion by Turkey. The island is composed of a Greek Cypriot south with an internationally recognized government and a Turkish Cypriot north (gray) with a government recognized only by Turkey. The UN patrols the dividing line and works toward reunification of the island.

Kashmir:
KASHMIR India and Pakistan both claim Kashmir-a disputed region of some 10 million people. India administers only the area south of the line of control; Pakistan controls northwestern Kashmir. China took eastern Kashmir from India in a 1962 war.

Kosovo:
KOSOVO
NATO ended ethnic fighting between Kosovo's Albanian majority and Serbian forces in 1999; Kosovo has been administered by the UN since that time.

Kuril Islands:
KURIL ISLANDS
The southern Kuril Islands of Iturup (Etorofu), Kunashir (Kunashiri), Shikotan, and the Habomai group were lost by Japan to the Soviet Union in 1945. Japan continues to claim these Russian-administered islands.

Nagorno-Karabakh:
NAGORNO-KARABAKH
Since a cease-fire in 1994 ethnic Armenians in Azerbaijan's Nagorno-Karabakh region have exercised autonomous control over the region. International mediation to resolve the conflict continues.

Somaliland:
SOMALILAND
In 1991 the Somali National Movement declared Somaliland an independent republic (in gray) with Hargeysa as the capital. It is not internationally recognized.

South Ossetia:
SOUTH OSSETIA
A 1992 cease-fire ended fighting between Ossetians and Georgians, but with no political settlement.

Taiwan:
TAIWAN (long form)
The People's Republic of China claims Taiwan as its 23rd province. Taiwan's government (Republic of China) maintains that there are two political entities. The Islands of Matsu, Pescadores, Pratas, and Quemoy are administered by Taiwan.

TAIWAN (short form)
The People's Republic of China claims Taiwan as its 23rd province. Taiwan's government (Republic of China) maintains that there are two political entities.

Transdniestria:
TRANSDNIESTRIA
Since the break-up of the Soviet Union, Ukrainian and Russian minorities have been struggling for independence from Moldova.

West Bank and Gaza:
WEST BANK & GAZA STRIP
Captured by Israel in the 1967 Six Day War, a 1993 peace agreement gives areas of the West Bank and Gaza limited Palestinian autonomy. The future for these autonomous areas and 3 million Palestinians is subject to Israeli-Palestinian negotiations.

Western Sahara:
WESTERN SAHARA
Western Sahara, formerly Spanish Sahara, was divided by Morocco and Mauritania in 1976. Morocco has administered the territory since Mauritania's withdrawal in August 1979. The United Nations does not recognize this annexation, and Western Sahara remains in dispute.

CONTINENT/Country	Capital	Language	Religion	Area sq km
NORTH AMERICA				
Antigua and Barbuda	Saint John's	English, local dialects	Anglican, other Protestant, Roman Catholic	442
Bahamas	Nassau	English, Creole	Baptist, Anglican, Roman Catholic	13,939
Barbados	Bridgetown	English	Protestant, Roman Catholic	430
Belize	Belmopan	English, Spanish, Mayan, Garifuna, Creole	Roman Catholic, Protestant	22,965
Canada	Ottawa	English, French	Roman Catholic, Protestant	9,984,670
Costa Rica	San José	Spanish, English	Roman Catholic, Evangelical	51,100
Cuba	La Habana (Havana)	Spanish	Roman Catholic, Protestant, Jehovah's Witness, Jewish, Santeria	110,860
Dominica	Roseau	English, French patios	Roman Catholic, Protestant	751
Dominican Republic	Santo Domingo	Spanish	Roman Catholic	48,442
El Salvador	San Salvador	Spanish, Nahua	Roman Catholic, Evangelical	21,041
Grenada	Saint George's	English, French patios	Roman Catholic, Anglican, other Protestant	344
Guatemala	Guatemala (Guatemala City)	Spanish, Amerindian languages	Roman Catholic, Protestant, indigenous Mayan beliefs	108,889
Haiti	Port-au-Prince	French, Creole	Roman Catholic, Protestant, Voodoo	27,750
Honduras	Tegucigalpa	Spanish, Amerindian dialects	Roman Catholic	112,492
Jamaica	Kingston	English, patois English	Protestant, Roman Catholic, other spiritual beliefs	10,991
Mexico	México (Mexico City)	Spanish, various Mayan, Nahuatl, and other indigenous languages	Roman Catholic, Protestant	1,964,375
Nicaragua	Managua	Spanish, English, indigenous languages	Roman Catholic, Protestant	130,000
Panama	Panamá (Panama City)	Spanish, English	Roman Catholic, Protestant	75,517
Saint Kitts and Nevis	Basseterre	English	Anglican, other Protestant	269
Saint Lucia	Castries	English, French patios	Roman Catholic, Protestant	616
Saint Vincent and the Grenadines	Kingstown	English, French patios	Anglican, Methodist, Roman Catholic, other Protestant	389
Trinidad and Tobago	Port-of-Spain	English, Hindi, French, Spanish	Roman Catholic, Hindu, Anglican, Muslim, Presbyterian	5,128
United States	Washington, D.C.	English, Spanish	Protestant, Roman Catholic, Jewish	9,826,630
NORTH AMERICA: TERRITORIES AND AREAS OF SPECIAL STATUS				
Denmark				
Greenland	Nuuk (Godthåb)	Greenlandic (East Inuit), Danish, English	Evangelical Lutheran	2,166,086
France				
Guadeloupe	Basse-Terre	French, Creole patios	Roman Catholic, Hindu, pagan African	1,706
Martinique	Fort-de-France	French, Creole patios	Roman Catholic, Protestant	1,101
Saint-Pierre and Miquelon	St.-Pierre	French	Roman Catholic	241
Netherlands				
Aruba	Oranjestad	Dutch, Papiamento, English, Spanish	Roman Catholic, Protestant	193
Netherlands Antilles	Willemstad, Curaçao	Dutch, Papiamento, English, Spanish	Roman Catholic, Protestant	809
United Kingdom				
Anguilla	The Valley	English	Anglican, Methodist	96
Bermuda	Hamilton	English, Portuguese	Protestant, Anglican, Roman Catholic	53
British Virgin Islands	Road Town	English	Methodist, Anglican	153
Cayman Islands	George Town	English	Protestant, Roman Catholic	262
Montserrat	Plymouth (abandoned)	English	Anglican, Methodist, Roman Catholic	102
Turks and Caicos Islands	Cockburn Town	English	Baptist, Anglican, Methodist	430
United States				
Navassa Island	Administered from Washington, D.C.	- - -	- - -	5
Puerto Rico	San Juan	Spanish, English	Roman Catholic, Protestant	9,084
Virgin Islands	Charlotte Amalie	English, Spanish, Creole	Protestant, Roman Catholic	386
SOUTH AMERICA				
Argentina	Buenos Aires	Spanish, English, Italian, German, French	Roman Catholic	2,780,400
Bolivia	La Paz (Administrative) Sucre (Constitutional)	Spanish, Quechua, Aymara	Roman Catholic	1,098,581
Brazil	Brasília	Portuguese, Spanish, English, French	Roman Catholic	8,547,403
Chile	Santiago	Spanish	Roman Catholic, Protestant	756,096
Colombia	Bogotá	Spanish	Roman Catholic	1,141,748
Ecuador	Quito	Spanish, Quechua	Roman Catholic	283,560
Guyana	Georgetown	English, Amerindian dialects, Creole, Hindi, Urdu	Christian, Hindu, Muslim	214,969
Paraguay	Asunción	Spanish, Guaraní	Roman Catholic	406,752
Peru	Lima	Spanish, Quechua, Aymara	Roman Catholic	1,285,216
Suriname	Paramaribo	Dutch, English, Sranang Tongo (Taki-Taki), Hindustani, Javanese	Hindu, Protestant (Moravian), Roman Catholic, Muslim	163,265
Uruguay	Montevideo	Spanish, Portunol, Brazilero	Roman Catholic	176,215
Venezuela	Caracas	Spanish, indigenous dialects	Roman Catholic	912,050
SOUTH AMERICA: TERRITORIES AND AREAS OF SPECIAL STATUS				
France				
French Guiana	Cayenne	French	Roman Catholic	86,504
United Kingdom				
Falkland Islands	Stanley	English	Anglican, Roman Catholic	12,173
EUROPE				
Albania	Tiranë (Tirana)	Albanian, Greek	Muslim, Albanian Orthodox, Roman Catholic	28,748
Andorra	Andorra la Vella	Catalan, French, Castilian (Spanish)	Roman Catholic	468
Austria	Wien (Vienna)	German	Roman Catholic, Protestant	83,858
Belarus	Minsk	Belarusian, Russian	Eastern Othodox, Roman Catholic, Protestant, Jewish, Muslim	207,595
Belgium	Bruxelles (Brussels)	Dutch, French, German	Roman Catholic, Protestant	30,528
Bosnia and Herzegovina	Sarajevo	Croatian, Serbian, Bosnian	Muslim, Orthodox, Roman Catholic	51,129
Bulgaria	Sofiya (Sofia)	Bulgarian	Bulgarian Orthodox, Muslim	110,994
Croatia	Zagreb	Croatian	Roman Catholic, Orthodox	56,542
Cyprus	Lefkosia (Lefkosa, Nicosia)	Greek, Turkish, English	Greek Orthodox, Muslim	9,251
Czech Republic	Praha (Prague)	Czech	Roman Catholic, Protestant, atheist	78,866
Denmark	København (Copenhagen)	Danish, Faroese, Greenlandic	Evangelical Lutheran	43,098
Estonia	Tallinn	Estonian, Russian, Ukrainian	Evangelical Lutheran, Russian Orthodox, Eastern Orthodox	45,227
Finland	Helsinki (Helsingfors)	Finnish, Swedish	Evangelical Lutheran	338,145
France	Paris	French	Roman Catholic	543,965
Germany	Berlin	German	Protestant, Roman Catholic	357,022
Greece	Athína (Athens)	Greek	Greek Orthodox	131,957
Hungary	Budapest	Hungarian	Roman Catholic, Calvinist, Lutheran	93,030
Iceland	Reykjavík	Icelandic, English, Nordic languages, German	Evangelical Lutheran	103,000
Ireland	Baile Átha Cliath (Dublin)	English, Irish	Roman Catholic	70,273
Italy	Roma (Rome)	Italian, German, French, Slovene	Roman Catholic	301,333
Latvia	Riga	Latvian, Lithuanian, Russian	Lutheran, Roman Catholic, Russian Orthodox	64,589
Liechtenstein	Vaduz	German, Alemannic dialect	Roman Catholic, Protestant	160
Lithuania	Vilnius	Lithuanian, Polish, Russian	Roman Catholic, Lutheran, Russian Orthodox, Protestant	65,300
Luxembourg	Luxembourg	Luxembourgish, German, French	Roman Catholic	2,586
Macedonia	Skopje	Macedonian, Albanian, Turkish	Macedonian Orthodox, Muslim	25,713
Malta	Valletta	Maltese, English	Roman Catholic	316
Moldova	Chisinau	Moldovan, Russian, Gagauz	Eastern Orthodox	33,800
Monaco	Monaco	French, English, Italian, Monegasque	Roman Catholic	2
Montenegro (Mid-2006 Data)	Podgorica	Montenegrin, Serbian, Albanian	Orthodox, Muslim, Roman Catholic	13,812

rea (sq mi)	Population Mid-2005 (in 1,000s)	Projected pop. change 2005-2050	Pop density sq km (sq mi)	Urban pop.	Natural increase	Total fertility / infant mortality rate	Pop. <15 / >65	Life expectancy: Male/Female	HIV/AIDS Pop. 15-49 2003-04	CONTINENT / Country Formal Name
										NORTH AMERICA
(171)	80	0%	181 (468)	37%	1.39%	2.30 / 20.90	26.40% / 7.80%	69.00 / 73.80	---	Antigua and Barbuda
(5,382)	319	46%	23 (59)	89%	1.17%	2.20 / 12.70	29.60% / 5.20%	66.60 / 72.73	3.00%	Commonwealth of The Bahamas
(166)	258	-2%	600 (1,554)	50%	0.63%	1.80 / 13.20	21.80% / 11.80%	70.00 / 74.10	1.50%	Barbados
(8,867)	292	64%	13 (33)	49%	2.25%	3.30 / 31.00	36.30% / 4.10%	66.70 / 73.50	2.40%	Belize
,855,101)	32,225	14%	3 (8)	79%	0.30%	1.50 / 5.40	17.90% / 13.10%	77.20 / 82.10	0.30%	Canada
(19,730)	4,331	46%	85 (220)	59%	1.33%	2.00 / 9.25	30.00% / 5.60%	76.30 / 81.10	0.60%	Republic of Costa Rica
(42,803)	11,275	-2%	102 (263)	76%	0.44%	1.50 / 5.80	20.90% / 10.30%	75.29 / 79.09	0.10%	Republic of Cuba
(290)	70	17%	93 (241)	71%	0.80%	1.90 / 22.20	27.80% / 7.90%	71.20 / 77.20	---	Commonwealth of Dominica
(18,704)	8,862	50%	183 (474)	64%	1.70%	2.90 / 31.00	33.60% / 5.20%	66.40 / 69.30	1.70%	Dominican Republic
(8,124)	6,881	57%	327 (847)	59%	2.03%	3.00 / 24.60	32.90% / 5.00%	67.10 / 73.00	0.70%	Republic of El Salvador
(133)	101	-14%	294 (759)	39%	1.16%	2.10 / 17.40	35.00% / 7.80%	--- / ---	---	Grenada
(42,042)	12,701	120%	117 (302)	39%	2.79%	4.40 / 39.00	41.90% / 4.00%	63.01 / 68.87	1.10%	Republic of Guatemala
(10,714)	8,288	127%	299 (774)	36%	1.87%	4.70 / 80.30	41.80% / 3.40%	51.00 / 53.70	5.60%	Republic of Haiti
(43,433)	7,212	104%	64 (166)	47%	2.79%	4.10 / 32.00	41.40% / 3.80%	67.40 / 74.30	1.80%	Republic of Honduras
(4,244)	2,666	28%	243 (628)	52%	1.29%	2.30 / 24.40	30.70% / 7.20%	71.80 / 75.20	1.20%	Jamaica
758,449)	107,029	30%	54 (141)	75%	1.85%	2.60 / 24.90	30.60% / 4.80%	73.10 / 77.60	0.30%	United Mexican States
(50,193)	5,774	88%	44 (115)	59%	2.70%	3.80 / 35.50	41.90% / 3.10%	65.65 / 70.36	0.20%	Republic of Nicaragua
(29,157)	3,232	55%	43 (111)	62%	1.76%	2.70 / 20.64	29.30% / 5.60%	72.25 / 77.36	0.90%	Republic of Panama
(104)	48	33%	178 (462)	33%	0.98%	2.30 / 16.70	28.00% / 8.30%	67.58 / 71.65	---	Federation of Saint Kitts and Nevis
(238)	163	44%	265 (685)	30%	0.99%	2.20 / 14.20	30.40% / 7.40%	72.00 / 76.70	---	Saint Lucia
(150)	111	-12%	285 (740)	55%	1.13%	2.10 / 18.10	30.40% / 6.30%	70.30 / 73.70	---	Saint Vincent and the Grenadines
(1,980)	1,305	-6%	254 (659)	74%	0.65%	1.60 / 18.60	21.20% / 6.60%	67.31 / 73.73	3.20%	Republic of Trinidad and Tobago
,794,083)	296,483	42%	30 (78)	79%	0.58%	2.00 / 6.60	20.90% / 12.40%	74.80 / 80.10	0.60%	United States of America
										NORTH AMERICA: TERRITORIES AND AREAS OF SPECIAL STATUS
836,086)	57	0%	0.03 (0.07)	83%	0.85%	2.40 / 8.90	25.90% / 5.40%	64.10 / 69.50	---	Overseas Region of Denmark
(658)	450*	5%	264 (684)	100%	1.04%	2.20 / 6.40	23.10% / 8.90%	74.50 / 81.10	---	French Overseas Department
(425)	397	10%	361 (934)	95%	0.66%	2.00 / 7.50	23.10% / 10.10%	75.20 / 81.70	---	French Overseas Department
(93)	7	-14%	29 (75)	89%	0.25%	--- 0	19.90% / 11.48%	--- / ---	---	French Overseas Territorial Collectivity
(75)	97	13%	503 (1,293)	47%	0.70%	2.00 / 2.60	21.00% / 10.60%	75.30 / 82.20	---	Overseas Region of the Netherlands
(312)	187	35%	231 (605)	69%	0.78%	2.20 / 8.80	23.40% / 9.60%	72.10 / 78.70	---	Overseas Region of the Netherlands
(37)	13	23%	135 (351)	100%	0.61%	1.70 / 14.40	28.00% / 8.00%	77.90 / 78.02	---	British Overseas Territory
(21)	62	2%	1,170 (2,952)	100%	0.67%	2.10 / 0	19.40% / 11.30%	75.20 / 79.30	---	British Overseas Territory
(59)	22	55%	144 (373)	61%	1.05%	2.00 / 17.86	25.61% / 4.91%	70.20 / 78.60	---	British Overseas Territory
(101)	44	105%	168 (436)	100%	1.18%	2.20 / 8.00	22.00% / 7.10%	76.70 / 81.80	---	British Overseas Territory
(39)	5	0%	49 (128)	13%	-0.30%	--- / ---	22.70% / 16.43%	--- / ---	---	British Overseas Territory
(166)	21	100%	49 (127)	45%	1.98%	3.20 / 16.90	32.50% / 3.70%	72.30 / 76.80	---	British Overseas Territory
(2)	0	---	--- ---	---	---	--- ---	--- ---	--- ---	---	Territory of the United States
(3,507)	3,912	-4%	431 (1,115)	94%	0.65%	1.80 / 9.80	22.20% / 12.20%	72.90 / 80.70	---	Self-Governing Commonwealth in Association with the United States
(149)	109	-6%	282 (732)	93%	0.93%	2.30 / 3.10	24.40% / 9.70%	74.90 / 82.70	---	Territory of the United States
										SOUTH AMERICA
,073,518)	38,592	39%	14 (36)	89%	1.06%	2.40 / 16.80	27.20% / 9.90%	70.60 / 78.10	0.70%	Argentine Republic
424,164)	8,922	62%	8 (21)	63%	2.11%	3.85 / 54.00	37.10% / 4.30%	61.80 / 65.99	0.10%	Republic of Bolivia
,300,169)	184,184	41%	22 (56)	81%	1.41%	2.40 / 27.00	28.90% / 5.80%	67.60 / 75.20	0.70%	Federative Republic of Brazil
291,930)	16,136	27%	21 (55)	87%	1.03%	2.05 / 7.80	24.20% / 7.20%	72.99 / 79.04	0.30%	Republic of Chile
440,831)	46,039	44%	40 (104)	75%	1.68%	2.60 / 25.60	31.70% / 4.90%	69.17 / 75.32	0.70%	Republic of Colombia
109,483)	13,032	56%	46 (119)	61%	2.12%	3.30 / 29.00	33.23% / 6.69%	71.30 / 77.00	0.30%	Republic of Ecuador
(83,000)	751	-35%	3 (9)	36%	1.28%	2.30 / 49.00	28.40% / 4.80%	59.81 / 65.86	2.50%	Co-operative Republic of Guyana
157,048)	6,158	67%	15 (39)	54%	1.73%	2.90 / 37.00	32.30% / 4.40%	68.60 / 73.12	0.50%	Republic of Paraguay
496,224)	27,947	53%	22 (56)	73%	1.61%	2.70 / 33.00	32.20% / 5.20%	67.34 / 72.42	0.50%	Republic of Peru
(63,037)	447	-4%	3 (7)	74%	1.42%	2.60 / 26.00	29.10% / 5.80%	65.75 / 72.51	1.70%	Republic of Suriname
(68,037)	3,419	23%	19 (50)	93%	0.59%	2.20 / 15.00	23.80% / 13.30%	71.29 / 79.20	0.30%	Oriental Republic of Uruguay
352,144)	26,749	57%	29 (76)	87%	1.80%	2.70 / 19.58	30.70% / 4.60%	69.90 / 75.81	0.70%	Bolivarian Republic of Venezuela
										SOUTH AMERICA: TERRITORIES AND AREAS OF SPECIAL STATUS
(33,400)	195	91%	2 (6)	75%	2.63%	3.90 / 12.40	35.00% / 3.80%	71.70 / 79.20	---	French Overseas Department
(4,700)	3	3%	0.25 (0.64)	79%	0.55%	--- / ---	--- / ---	--- / ---	---	British Overseas Territory
										EUROPE
(11,100)	3,170	13%	110 (286)	42%	0.93%	2.00 / 8.40	27.29% / 8.10%	71.70 / 76.40	---	Republic of Albania
(181)	74	-3%	158 (409)	92%	0.71%	1.30 / 3.86	14.90% / 12.60%	--- / ---	---	Principality of Andorra
(32,378)	8,151	0%	97 (252)	54%	0.05%	1.40 / 4.50	16.30% / 15.49%	75.90 / 81.60	0.30%	Republic of Austria
(80,153)	9,776	-13%	47 (122)	72%	-0.55%	1.20 / 7.70	16.20% / 14.30%	62.70 / 74.70	---	Republic of Belarus
(11,787)	10,458	5%	343 (887)	97%	0.05%	1.60 / 4.40	17.40% / 17.02%	75.58 / 81.69	0.20%	Kingdom of Belgium
(19,741)	3,840	-19%	75 (195)	43%	0.09%	1.20 / 7.60	18.30% / 12.20%	71.30 / 76.70	< 0.05%	Bosnia and Herzegovina
(42,855)	7,741	-34%	70 (181)	70%	-0.52%	1.30 / 11.60	14.20% / 17.10%	68.70 / 75.60	< 0.05%	Republic of Bulgaria
(21,831)	4,438	-14%	78 (203)	56%	-0.29%	1.30 / 6.30	16.60% / 16.30%	71.20 / 78.30	< 0.05%	Republic of Croatia
(3,572)	965	12%	104 (270)	65%	0.40%	1.60 / 6.20	20.49% / 10.90%	74.80 / 79.10	---	Republic of Cyprus
(30,450)	10,212	-8%	129 (335)	77%	-0.09%	1.20 / 3.70	15.20% / 13.90%	72.03 / 78.51	0.10%	Czech Republic
(16,640)	5,418	1%	126 (326)	72%	0.16%	1.80 / 4.39	18.90% / 14.90%	74.89 / 79.48	0.20%	Kingdom of Denmark
(17,462)	1,345	-23%	30 (77)	69%	-0.28%	1.50 / 7.00	15.97% / 16.18%	66.04 / 76.90	1.10%	Republic of Estonia
130,558)	5,246	1%	16 (40)	62%	0.19%	1.80 / 3.10	17.50% / 15.90%	75.30 / 82.30	0.10%	Republic of Finland
210,026)	60,742	5%	112 (289)	76%	0.43%	1.90 / 3.90	18.57% / 16.40%	76.70 / 83.80	0.40%	French Republic
137,847)	82,490	-9%	231 (598)	88%	-0.14%	1.30 / 4.32	14.70% / 18.00%	75.59 / 81.34	0.10%	Federal Republic of Germany
(50,949)	11,100	-4%	84 (218)	60%	0.01%	1.30 / 5.10	14.60% / 17.50%	76.40 / 81.10	0.20%	Hellenic Republic
(35,919)	10,086	-12%	108 (281)	65%	-0.37%	1.30 / 6.60	15.60% / 15.50%	68.29 / 76.53	0.10%	Republic of Hungary
(39,769)	295	21%	3 (7)	94%	0.83%	2.00 / 2.40	22.60% / 11.80%	78.70 / 82.50	0.20%	Republic of Iceland
(27,133)	4,125	14%	59 (152)	60%	0.83%	2.00 / 4.78	20.85% / 11.15%	75.10 / 80.30	0.10%	Republic of Ireland
116,345)	58,742	-11%	195 (505)	90%	0.04%	1.30 / 4.80	14.20% / 19.20%	76.80 / 82.50	0.50%	Italian Republic
(24,938)	2,300	-23%	36 (92)	68%	-0.50%	1.30 / 9.40	15.40% / 16.20%	65.90 / 76.90	0.60%	Republic of Latvia
(62)	35	26%	219 (565)	21%	0.39%	1.30 / 2.90	18.00% / 10.80%	78.70 / 82.10	---	Principality of Liechtenstein
(25,212)	3,415	-16%	52 (135)	67%	-0.31%	1.30 / 7.90	17.70% / 15.00%	66.48 / 77.85	0.10%	Republic of Lithuania
(998)	457	41%	177 (458)	91%	0.41%	1.60 / 3.85	18.80% / 14.10%	74.90 / 81.50	0.20%	Grand Duchy of Luxembourg
(9,928)	2,039	-2%	79 (205)	59%	0.44%	1.50 / 11.30	20.40% / 10.80%	70.80 / 75.70	< 0.05%	Republic of Macedonia
(122)	405	-10%	1,282 (3,320)	91%	0.21%	1.50 / 7.20	18.20% / 13.00%	75.78 / 80.48	0.20%	Republic of Malta
(13,050)	4,206	-21%	124 (322)	45%	-0.18%	1.20 / 14.40	19.80% / 9.90%	64.50 / 71.60	0.20%	Republic of Moldova
(1)	33	67%	16,500 (33,000)	100%	0.64%	--- / ---	13.23% / 22.43%	--- / ---	---	Principality of Monaco
(5,333)	600	-4%	43 (113)	---	0.30%	1.70 / 8.00	21.00% / 12.00%	--- / ---	---	Republic of Montenegro

CONTINENT/Country	Capital	Language	Religion	Area sq
Netherlands	Amsterdam	Dutch, Frisian	Roman Catholic, Protestant, Muslim	41,52
Norway	Oslo	Norwegian	Evangelical Lutheran	323,7
Poland	Warszawa (Warsaw)	Polish	Roman Catholic	312,6
Portugal	Lisboa (Lisbon)	Portuguese, Mirandese	Roman Catholic	92,34
Romania	Bucuresti (Bucharest)	Romanian, Hungarian, German	Eastern Orthodox, Protestant, Catholic	238,3
Russia	Moskva (Moscow)	Russian	Russian Orthodox, Muslim, other	17,075,
San Marino	San Marino	Italian	Roman Catholic	61
Serbia (Mid -2006 Data)	Belgrade	Serbian, Hungarian, Bosnian, Albanian	Orthodox, Muslim, Roman Catholic, Protestant	88,36
Slovakia	Bratislava (Pressburg)	Slovak, Hungarian	Roman Catholic, atheist, Protestant	49,03
Slovenia	Ljubljana	Slovenian, Serbo-Croatian	Roman Catholic, other	20,27
Spain	Madrid	Castilian Spanish, Catalan, Galician, Basque	Roman Catholic	505,9
Sweden	Stockholm	Swedish	Lutheran, Roman Catholic	449,9
Switzerland	Bern	German, French, Romanisch	Roman Catholic, Protestant	41,28
Ukraine	Kyiv (Kiev)	Ukrainian, Russian, Romanian, Polish, Hungarian	Ukrainian Orthodox, Ukrainian Catholic (Uniate), Protestant, Jewish	603,7
United Kingdom	London	English, Welsh, Scottish form of Gaelic	Anglican, Roman Catholic, other Protestant, Muslim	242,9
Vatican City	Vatican City	Italian, Latin, French	Roman Catholic	0.4
EUROPE: TERRITORIES AND AREAS OF SPECIAL STATUS				
Denmark				
Faroe Islands	Tórshavn	Faroese, Danish	Evangelical Lutheran	1,39
Norway				
Svalbard	Longyearbyen	Norwegian, Russian	Evangelical Lutheran, Russian Orthodox	62,04
United Kingdom				
Channel Islands (Guernsey and Jersey)	Saint Peter Port, Guernsey Saint Helier, Jersey	English, French, Norman French dialect	Anglican, Roman Catholic, Baptist	194
Gibraltar	Gibraltar	English, Spanish, Italian, Portuguese	Roman Catholic, Church of England	7
Isle of Man	Douglas	English, Manx Gaelic	Anglican, Roman Catholic, Methodist, Baptist	572
ASIA				
Afghanistan	Kabol (Kabul)	Pashtu, Afghan Persian (Dari), Uzbek, Turkmen, 30 minor languages	Sunni and Shiite Muslim	652,0
Armenia	Yerevan	Armenian, Russian	Armenian Apostolic	29,74
Azerbaijan	Baku	Azerbaijani, Russian, Armenian	Muslim, Russian Orthodox, Armenian Orthodox	86,60
Bahrain	Al Manamah (Manama)	Arabic, English, Farsi, Urdu	Shiite and Sunni Muslim	717
Bangladesh	Dhaka	Bangla (Bengali), English	Muslim, Hindu	147,5
Bhutan	Thimphu	Dzonkha, Tibetan and Nepali dialects	Lamaistic Buddhist, Hindu	46,50
Brunei	Bandar Seri Begawan	Malay, English, Chinese	Muslim, Buddhist, Christian, indigenous beliefs	5,76
Cambodia	Phnom Penh	Khmer, French, English	Theravada Buddhist	181,0
China	Beijing (Peking)	Chinese (Mandarin), Cantonese, other dialects and minority languages	Toist, Buddhist, Muslim	9,596,
Georgia	T'bilisi (Tiflis)	Georgian, Russian, Armenian, Azeri	Georgian Orthodox, Muslim, Russian Orthodox	69,70
India	New Delhi	Hindi, English, 14 other official languages	Hindu, Muslim, Christian, Sikh, Buddhist, Jain, Parsi	3,287,
Indonesia	Jakarta	Bahasa Indonesia, English, Dutch, Javanese, and other local dialects	Muslim, Protestant, Roman Catholic, Hindu, Buddhist	1,922,
Iran	Tehran	Persian, Turkic, Kurdish, various local dialects	Shiite and Sunni Muslim	1,648,
Iraq	Baghdad	Arabic, Kurdish, Assyrian, Armenian	Shiite and Sunni Muslim	437,0
Israel	Jerusalem (Yerushalayim, Al-Quds)	Hebrew, Arabic, English	Jewish, Muslim, Christian	22,14
Japan	Tokyo	Japanese	Shinto, Buddhist	377,8
Jordan	Amman	Arabic, English	Sunni Muslim, Christian	89,34
Kazakhstan	Astana	Kazakh (Qazaq), Russian	Muslim, Russian Orthodox	2,717,
Korea, North	Pyongyang	Korean	Buddhist, Confucianist	120,5
Korea, South	Seoul	Korean, English widely taught	Christian, Buddhist	99,25
Kuwait	Kuwait City	Arabic, English	Sunni and Shiite Muslim, Christian, Hindu, Parsi	17,81
Kyrgyzstan	Bishkek	Kyrgyz, Russian	Muslim, Russian Orthodox	199,9
Laos	Viangchan (Vientiane)	Lao, French, English, varous ethnic languages	Buddhist, Animist, other	236,8
Lebanon	Beyrouth (Beirut)	Arabic, French, English, Armenian	Muslim, Christian	10,45
Malaysia	Kuala Lumpur	Bahasa Melayu, English, Chinese /regional dialects, indigenous languages	Muslim, Buddhist, Daoist, Hindu, Christian, Sikh, Shamanist	329,8
Maldives	Maale (Male)	Maldivian Dhivehi, (dialect of Sinhala), English	Sunni Muslim	298
Mongolia	Ulaanbaatar (Ulan Bator)	Khalkha Mongol, Turkic, Russian	Tibetan Buddhist, Lamaism	1,564,
Myanmar (Burma)	Yangon (Rangoon)	Burmese, minor languages	Buddhist, Christian, Muslim	676,5
Nepal	Kathmandu	Nepali, English, many other languages and dialects	Hindu, Buddhist, Muslim	147,1
Oman	Masqat (Muscat)	Arabic, English, Baluchi, Urdu, Indian dialects	Ibadhi Muslim, Sunni Muslim, Shiite Muslim, Hindu	309,5
Pakistan	Islamabad	Punjabi, Sindhi, Siraiki, Pashtu, Urdu, English	Sunni and Shiite Muslim, Christian, Hindu	796,0
Philippines	Manila	Filipino (based on Tagalog), English, and 8 major dialects	Roman Catholic, Protestant, Muslim, Buddhist	300,0
Qatar	Ad Dawhah (Doha)	Arabic, English	Muslim	11,52
Saudi Arabia	Ar Riyad (Riyadh)	Arabic	Muslim	1,960,
Singapore	Singapore	Chinese, Malay, Tamil, English	Buddhist, Muslim, Christian, Hindu, Sikh, Taoist, Confucianist	660
Sri Lanka	Colombo	Sinhala, Tamil, English	Buddhist, Hindu, Christian, Muslim	65,52
Syria	Dimashq (Damascus)	Arabic, Kurdish, Armenian, Aramaic, Circassian, French, English	Sunni, Alawite, Druze and other Muslim sects, Christian	185,1
Tajikistan	Dushanbe	Tajik, Russian	Sunni and Shiite Muslim	143,1
Thailand	Krung Thep (Bangkok)	Thai, English, ethnic and regional dialects	Buddhist, Muslim	513,1
Timor-Leste (East Timor)	Dili	Tetum, Portuguese, Bahasa, Indonesian, English	Christian (mostly Roman Catholic)	14,60
Turkey	Ankara (Angora)	Turkish, Kurdish, Arabic, Armenian, Greek	Muslim (mostly Sunni)	779,4
Turkmenistan	Asgabat (Ashgabat)	Turkmen, Russian, Uzbek	Muslim, Eastern Orthodox	488,1
United Arab Emirates	Abu Zaby (Abu Dhabi)	Arabic, Persian, English, Hindi, Urdu	Sunni and Shiite Muslim, Christian, Hindu,	77,70
Uzbekistan	Toshkent (Tashkent)	Uzbek, Russian, Tajik	Muslim, Eastern Orthodox	447,4
Vietnam	Hanoi	Vietnamese, English, French, Chinese, Khmer, local languages	Buddhist, Hoa Hao, Cao Dai, Christian, indigenous beliefs, Muslim	331,1
Yemen	Sana (Sanaa)	Arabic	Sunni and Shiite Muslim	536,8
ASIA: TERRITORIES AND AREAS OF SPECIAL STATUS				
China				
Hong Kong	- - -	Chinese (Cantonese), English	Local religions, Christian	1092
Macau	- - -	Portuguese, Chinese (Cantonese)	Buddhist, Roman Catholic	25
Taiwan	T'aipei (Taipei)	Mandarin Chinese, Taiwanese	Mixture of Buddhist, Confucian, and Taoist; Christian	35,98
Israel - Palestinian Areas	- - -	Arabic, Hebrew, English	Muslim (mostly Sunni), Jewish, Christian	- - -
Gaza Strip	- - -	Arabic, Hebrew, English	Muslim (mostly Sunni), Jewish	365
West Bank	- - -	Arabic, Hebrew, English	Muslim (mostly Sunni), Jewish, Christian	5,65
United Kingdom				
British Indian Ocean Territory	Administered from London	English	- - -	44
AFRICA				
Algeria	Alger (Algiers)	Arabic, French, Berber dialects	Sunni Muslim	2,381,7
Angola	Luanda	Portuguese, Bantu	Indigenous beliefs, Roman Catholic, Protestant	1,246,
Benin	Cotonou (Administrative) Porto-Novo (Constitutional)	French, Fon, Yoruba, tribal languages	Indigenous beliefs, Christian, Muslim	112,6
Botswana	Gaborone	English, Setswana	Indigenous beliefs, Christian	581,7
Burkina Faso	Ouagadougou	French, native African languages	Muslim, indigenous beliefs, Christian	274,2
Burundi	Bujumbura	Kirundi, French, Swahili	Roman Catholic, indigenous beliefs, Muslim, Protestant	27,83
Cameroon	Yaoundé	French, English, 24 major African language groups	Indigenous beliefs, Christian, Muslim	475,4
Cape Verde	Praia	Portuguese, Crioulo (Kriolu)	Roman Catholic, Protestant	4,03
Central African Republic	Bangui	French, Sangho, Arabic, tribal languages	Indigenous beliefs, Protestant, Roman Catholic, Muslim	622,9
Chad	N'Djamena	French, Arabic, Sara, Sango, more than 120 different languages and dialects	Muslim, Christian, animist	1,284,

Area (sq mi)	Population Mid-2005 (in 1,000s)	Projected pop. change 2005-2050	Pop density sq km (sq mi)	Urban pop.	Natural increase	Total fertility / infant mortality rate	Pop. <15 / >65	Life expectancy: Male / Female	HIV/AIDS Pop. 15-49 2003-04	CONTINENT / Country Formal Name
(16,034)	16,296	4%	392 (1,016)	62%	0.35%	1.70 / 4.14	18.55% / 13.80%	76.20 / 80.80	0.20%	Kingdom of the Netherlands
(125,004)	4,620	21%	14 (37)	78%	0.34%	1.80 / 3.20	19.70% / 14.70%	77.50 / 82.33	0.10%	Kingdom of Norway
(120,728)	38,163	-15%	122 (316)	62%	0.02%	1.20 / 6.75	17.20% / 12.96%	70.52 / 78.90	0.10%	Republic of Poland
(35,655)	10,576	-12%	115 (297)	53%	0.04%	1.40 / 4.10	15.70% / 16.80%	74.00 / 80.57	0.40%	Portuguese Republic
(92,043)	21,612	-29%	91 (235)	53%	-0.19%	1.30 / 16.70	16.40% / 14.40%	67.50 / 74.80	< 0.05%	Romania
(6,592,850)	143,025	-23%	8 (22)	73%	-0.55%	1.40 / 12.40	15.70% / 13.40%	58.80 / 72.00	1.10%	Russian Federation
(24)	30	0%	492 (1,250)	84%	0.33%	1.20 / 6.70	15.00% / 16.00%	77.80 / 84.20	---	Republic of San Marino
(34,116)	9,500	-10%	107 (278)	---	0.10%	1.80 / 10.0	19.00% / 15.00%	--- / ---	---	Republic of Serbia
(18,932)	5,382	-12%	110 (284)	56%	0.01%	1.20 / 7.80	17.60% / 11.60%	69.80 / 77.80	< 0.05%	Slovak Republic
(7,827)	1,998	-5%	99 (255)	51%	-0.10%	1.20 / 4.00	14.47% / 15.20%	73.20 / 80.70	< 0.05%	Republic of Slovenia
(195,363)	43,484	1%	86 (223)	76%	0.13%	1.30 / 3.57	14.50% / 16.80%	76.90 / 83.60	0.70%	Kingdom of Spain
(173,732)	9,029	18%	20 (52)	84%	0.11%	1.70 / 3.10	17.57% / 17.25%	78.35 / 82.68	0.10%	Kingdom of Sweden
(15,940)	7,446	-4%	180 (467)	68%	0.17%	1.40 / 4.30	16.20% / 15.80%	77.90 / 83.00	0.40%	Swiss Confederation
(233,090)	47,110	-29%	78 (202)	68%	-0.70%	1.20 / 9.50	15.27% / 15.53%	62.64 / 74.06	1.40%	Ukraine
(93,788)	60,068	12%	247 (640)	89%	0.17%	1.70 / 5.20	18.34% / 15.97%	75.90 / 80.50	0.20%	United Kingdom of Great Britain and Northern Ireland
(0.2)	0.798	25%	1,995 (3,990)	100%	-0.90%	--- / ---	--- / ---	--- / ---	---	State of the Vatican City (The Holy See)
										EUROPE: TERRITORIES AND AREAS OF SPECIAL STATUS
(540)	50	16%	36 (93)	38%	0.70%	2.50 / 2.80	23.60% / 13.20%	77.00 / 81.00	---	Overseas Region of Denmark
(23,957)	3	-0.02%	.05 (.13)	---	-1.99%	--- ---	--- ---	--- ---	0.00%	Norwegian Dependency
(75)	149	15%	768 (1,987)	31%	0.23%	1.40 / 3.40	14.70% / 12.60%	75.54 / 80.33	---	British Crown Dependencies
(3)	29	-7%	4,143 (9,667)	100%	0.48%	--- / 5.50	--- / ---	--- / ---	---	British Overseas Territory
(221)	78	6%	136 (353)	52%	0.01%	1.60 / 3.30	17.80% / 16.70%	--- / ---	---	British Crown Dependency
										ASIA
(251,773)	29,929	174%	46 (119)	22%	2.56%	6.80 / 171.90	44.90% / 2.40%	41.40 / 41.80	---	Transitional Islamic State of Afghanistan
(11,484)	3,033	8%	102 (264)	65%	0.25%	1.40 / 36.10	22.31% / 10.78%	67.49 / 74.97	0.10%	Republic of Armenia
(33,436)	8,388	38%	97 (251)	51%	0.99%	2.00 / 9.80	26.40% / 6.80%	69.60 / 75.20	< 0.05%	Republic of Azerbaijan
(277)	731	58%	1,020 (2,639)	87%	1.81%	2.80 / 8.00	27.90% / 2.52%	73.10 / 74.80	0.20%	Kingdom of Bahrain
(56,977)	144,233	60%	977 (2,531)	23%	1.88%	3.00 / 65.00	34.66% / 3.38%	61.00 / 61.80	---	People's Republic of Bangladesh
(17,954)	970	108%	21 (54)	21%	2.55%	4.70 / 60.50	40.00% / 4.30%	61.65 / 64.74	---	Kingdom of Bhutan
(2,226)	363	62%	63 (163)	74%	1.88%	2.60 / 8.30	31.80% / 2.60%	71.70 / 76.60	< 0.05%	Negara Brunei Darussalam
(69,898)	13,329	85%	74 (191)	15%	2.18%	4.50 / 95.10	37.10% / 3.20%	52.13 / 59.62	2.60%	Kingdom of Cambodia
(3,705,405)	1,303,701	10%	136 (352)	37%	0.59%	1.60 / 27.20	21.50% / 7.60%	70.40 / 73.70	0.10%	People's Republic of China
(26,911)	4,501	-19%	65 (167)	52%	0.01%	1.40 / 24.80	18.60% / 13.30%	68.00 / 74.80	0.10%	Republic of Georgia
(1,269,221)	1,103,596	48%	336 (870)	28%	1.68%	3.00 / 60.00	35.90% / 4.43%	60.80 / 62.50	0.90%	Republic of India
(742,308)	221,932	39%	115 (299)	42%	1.56%	2.60 / 45.70	29.71% / 4.72%	66.44 / 70.44	0.10%	Republic of Indonesia
(636,296)	69,515	47%	42 (109)	67%	1.20%	2.10 / 32.10	29.70% / 4.30%	68.83 / 71.74	0.10%	Islamic Republic of Iran
(168,754)	28,807	121%	66 (171)	68%	2.72%	5.10 / 94.00	42.00% / 2.80%	57.30 / 60.40	< 0.05%	Republic of Iraq
(8,550)	7,105	55%	321 (831)	92%	1.55%	2.90 / 5.10	28.35% / 9.90%	77.50 / 81.50	0.10%	State of Israel
(145,902)	127,728	-21%	338 (875)	79%	0.08%	1.30 / 2.80	13.80% / 19.80%	78.36 / 85.33	< 0.05%	Japan
(34,495)	5,795	79%	65 (168)	79%	2.40%	3.70 / 22.10	36.90% / 3.00%	70.60 / 72.40	< 0.05%	Hashemite Kingdom of Jordan
(1,049,155)	15,079	-1%	6 (14)	57%	0.58%	2.00 / 61.00	27.20% / 7.50%	60.50 / 71.50	0.20%	Republic of Kazakhstan
(46,540)	22,912	15%	190 (492)	60%	0.92%	2.00 / 21.00	27.00% / 7.90%	68.70 / 74.20	---	Democratic People's Republic of Korea
(38,321)	48,294	-12%	487 (1,260)	80%	0.51%	1.20 / 5.10	19.10% / 9.10%	73.38 / 80.44	< 0.05%	Republic of Korea
(6,880)	2,589	172%	145 (376)	96%	1.73%	4.00 / 9.60	25.60% / 1.60%	76.70 / 78.50	---	State of Kuwait
(77,182)	5,172	60%	26 (67)	35%	1.34%	2.60 / 55.00	33.00% / 6.00%	64.50 / 72.20	0.10%	Kyrgyz Republic
(91,429)	5,924	96%	25 (65)	19%	2.33%	4.80 / 88.00	40.20% / 3.50%	53.25 / 55.75	0.10%	Lao People's Democratic Republic
(4,036)	3,779	31%	362 (936)	87%	1.58%	2.20 / 17.20	28.10% / 6.20%	71.90 / 75.10	0.10%	Lebanese Republic
(127,355)	26,121	80%	79 (205)	62%	2.09%	3.30 / 10.00	33.00% / 4.60%	70.40 / 76.20	0.40%	Malaysia
(115)	294	83%	987 (2,557)	27%	1.40%	2.80 / 18.00	36.10% / 4.20%	71.30 / 72.30	---	Republic of Maldives
(603,909)	2,646	46%	2 (4)	57%	1.55%	2.50 / 58.00	31.00% / 3.60%	61.90 / 65.90	< 0.05%	Mongolia
(261,218)	50,519	26%	75 (193)	29%	1.22%	2.70 / 75.00	29.30% / 4.60%	57.35 / 62.93	1.20%	Union of Myanmar
(56,827)	25,371	89%	172 (446)	14%	2.21%	3.70 / 64.40	38.50% / 3.50%	61.76 / 62.50	0.50%	Kingdom of Nepal
(119,500)	2,436	50%	8 (20)	76%	1.83%	3.40 / 16.20	32.82% / 2.78%	72.22 / 75.43	0.10%	Sultanate of Oman
(307,374)	162,420	82%	204 (528)	34%	2.41%	4.80 / 85.10	41.80% / 4.00%	60.90 / 62.60	0.10%	Islamic Republic of Pakistan
(115,831)	84,765	68%	283 (732)	48%	2.26%	3.50 / 29.00	35.49% / 3.94%	66.93 / 72.18	< 0.05%	Republic of the Philippines
(4,448)	768	44%	67 (173)	92%	1.79%	3.30 / 11.20	25.40% / 2.20%	69.40 / 72.10	---	State of Qatar
(756,985)	24,573	101%	13 (32)	86%	2.73%	4.50 / 23.00	37.20% / 2.70%	69.93 / 73.76	---	Kingdom of Saudi Arabia
(255)	4,296	21%	6,509 (16,847)	100%	0.53%	1.30 / 1.90	20.10% / 7.99%	77.40 / 81.30	0.20%	Republic of Singapore
(25,299)	19,722	14%	301 (780)	30%	1.30%	2.00 / 11.20	26.70% / 6.40%	70.70 / 75.40	< 0.05%	Democratic Socialist Republic of Sri Lanka
(71,498)	18,389	91%	99 (257)	50%	2.67%	3.70 / 22.30	37.10% / 3.20%	70.60 / 73.10	< 0.05%	Syrian Arab Republic
(55,251)	6,813	60%	48 (123)	27%	2.32%	4.10 / 89.00	40.00% / 4.00%	60.85 / 66.13	< 0.05%	Republic of Tajikistan
(198,115)	65,002	13%	127 (328)	31%	0.72%	1.70 / 20.00	22.80% / 7.30%	67.90 / 75.00	1.50%	Kingdom of Thailand
(5,640)	947	245%	65 (168)	8%	2.70%	6.40 / 94.00	41.30% / 2.80%	54.14 / 56.25	---	Democratic Republic of Timor-Leste
(300,948)	72,907	38%	94 (242)	65%	1.39%	2.40 / 38.30	29.30% / 5.60%	66.40 / 71.00	---	Republic of Turkey
(188,456)	5,240	40%	11 (28)	47%	1.56%	2.90 / 73.90	32.10% / 4.40%	58.24 / 66.74	< 0.05%	Turkmenistan
(30,000)	4,618	101%	59 (154)	78%	1.36%	2.50 / 7.90	25.30% / 0.97%	75.50 / 79.76	---	United Arab Emirates
(172,742)	26,444	45%	59 (153)	37%	1.59%	2.70 / 61.70	34.70% / 4.70%	63.32 / 69.72	0.10%	Republic of Uzbekistan
(127,844)	83,305	38%	252 (652)	26%	1.29%	2.20 / 18.00	29.20% / 6.50%	70.00 / 73.00	0.40%	Socialist Republic of Vietnam
(207,286)	20,727	243%	39 (100)	26%	3.30%	6.20 / 74.80	45.70% / 3.90%	58.80 / 62.50	0.10%	Republic of Yemen
										ASIA: TERRITORIES AND AREAS OF SPECIAL STATUS
(422)	6,921	27%	6,338 (16,400)	100%	0.17%	1.00 / 2.50	14.90% / 12.00%	78.60 / 84.60	0.10%	Special Administrative Region of China
(10)	474	13%	18,960 (47,400)	99%	0.39%	0.80 / 3.47	17.10% / 8.10%	--- / ---	---	Special Administrative Region of China
(13,891)	22,731	-13%	632 (1,636)	78%	0.36%	1.20 / 5.35	19.34% / 9.48%	73.35 / 79.05	---	
---	3,762	197%	625 (1,619)	57%	3.40%	5.60 / 20.70	45.50% / 3.10%	70.70 / 73.80	---	Areas of Special Status
(141)	---	---	--- ---	---	---	--- / ---	--- / ---	--- / ---	---	Area of Special Status
(2,183)	---	---	--- ---	---	---	--- / ---	--- / ---	--- / ---	---	Area of Special Status
(17)	---	---	--- ---	---	---	--- / ---	--- / ---	--- / ---	---	British Overseas Territory
										AFRICA
(919,595)	32,814	35%	14 (36)	49%	1.53%	2.40 / 31.60	30.70% / 5.20%	72.50 / 74.40	0.10%	People's Democratic Republic of Algeria
(481,354)	15,375	173%	12 (32)	33%	2.56%	6.80 / 139.00	45.60% / 2.40%	38.85 / 41.99	3.90%	Republic of Angola
(43,484)	8,439	162%	75 (194)	40%	2.92%	5.90 / 105.00	43.60% / 2.60%	52.97 / 54.52	1.90%	Republic of Benin
(224,607)	1,640	-14%	3 (7)	54%	-0.34%	3.10 / 56.80	39.40% / 3.80%	34.20 / 35.30	37.30%	Republic of Botswana
(105,869)	13,925	184%	51 (132)	17%	2.53%	6.20 / 81.00	46.00% / 2.90%	42.19 / 45.70	1.80%	Burkina Faso
(10,747)	7,795	193%	280 (725)	9%	2.84%	6.80 / 66.90	46.60% / 2.60%	48.70 / 49.80	6.00%	Republic of Burundi
(183,569)	16,380	88%	34 (89)	48%	2.26%	5.00 / 74.00	43.60% / 3.00%	47.10 / 49.00	5.50%	Republic of Cameroon
(1,558)	476	94%	118 (306)	53%	2.26%	4.00 / 31.00	41.90% / 6.20%	66.16 / 72.16	---	Republic of Cape Verde
(240,535)	4,238	53%	7 (18)	41%	1.74%	4.90 / 94.10	43.20% / 4.20%	43.20 / 44.40	13.50%	Central African Republic
(495,755)	9,657	206%	8 (19)	24%	2.72%	6.30 / 101.00	48.00% / 2.80%	45.00 / 48.40	4.80%	Republic of Chad

CONTINENT/Country	Capital	Language	Religion	Area sq
Comoros	Moroni	Arabic, French, Shikomoro	Sunni Muslim, Roman Catholic	1,86
Congo	Brazzaville	French, Lingala, Monokutuba	Christian, animist, Muslim	342,0
Congo, Dem. Rep. of the	Kinshasa (Léopoldville)	French, Lingala, Kingwana, Kikongo, Tshiluba	Roman Catholic, Protestant, Kimbanguist, Muslim, traditional	2,344,8
Côte d'Ivoire (Ivory Coast)	Abidjan (Administrative) Yamoussoukro (Legislative)	French, Dioula, 60 native dialects	Christian, Muslim, indigenous beliefs	322,4
Djibouti	Djibouti	French, Arabic, Somali, Afar	Muslim, Christian	23,20
Egypt	El Qâhira (Cairo)	Arabic, English, French	Sunni Muslim, Coptic Christian	1,002,0
Equatorial Guinea	Malabo	Spanish, French, pidgin English, Fang Bubi, Ibo	Roman Catholic, pagan practices	28,05
Eritrea	Asmara	Afar, Arabic, Tigre, Kunama, Tigrinya	Muslim, Coptic Christian, Roman Catholic, Protestant	121,14
Ethiopia	Adis Abeba (Addis Ababa)	Amharic, Tigrinya, Orominga, Guaraginga, Somali, Arabic	Muslim, Ethiopian Orthodox, animist	1,133,3
Gabon	Libreville	French, Fang, Myene, Nzebi, Bapounou/Eschira, Bandjabi	Christian, indigenous beliefs	267,66
Gambia	Banjul	English, Mandinka, Wolof, Fula	Muslim, Christian	11,29
Ghana	Accra	English, Akan, Moshi-Dagomba, Ewe, Ga	Christian, indigenous beliefs, Muslim	238,53
Guinea	Conakry	French, local languages	Muslim, Christian, indigenous beliefs	245,85
Guinea-Bissau	Bissau	Portuguese, Crioulo, African languages	Indigenous beliefs, Muslim, Christian	36,125
Kenya	Nairobi	English, Kiswahili, numerous indigenous languages	Protestant, Roman Catholic, indigenous beliefs, Muslim	580,36
Lesotho	Maseru	English, Sesotho, Zulu, Xhosa	Christian, indigenous beliefs	30,355
Liberia	Monrovia	English, 20 ethnic languages	Indigenous beliefs, Christian, Muslim	111,37
Libya	Tarabulus (Tripoli)	Arabic, Italian, English	Sunni Muslim	1,759,54
Madagascar	Antananarivo	French, Malagasy	Indigenous beliefs, Christian, Muslim	587,04
Malawi	Lilongwe	English, Chichewa	Protestant, Roman Catholic, Muslim	118,484
Mali	Bamako	French, Bambara, numerous African languages	Muslim, indigenous beliefs	1,240,19
Mauritania	Nouakchott	Hassaniya Arabic, Wolof, Pulaar, Soninke, French	Muslim	1,030,70
Mauritius	Port Louis	English, French, Creole, Hindi, Urdu, Hakka, Bhojpuri	Hindu, Christian, Muslim, Protestant	2,040
Morocco	Rabat	Arabic, Berber dialects, French	Muslim	710,850
Mozambique	Maputo	Portuguese, indigenous dialects	Indigenous beliefs, Christian, Muslim	799,380
Namibia	Windhoek	English, Afrikaans, German, indigenous languages	Christian, indigenous beliefs	824,292
Niger	Niamey	French, Hausa, Djerma	Muslim, indigenous beliefs, Christian	1,267,00
Nigeria	Abuja	English, Hausa, Yoruba, Igbo, Fulani	Muslim, Christian, indigenous beliefs	923,768
Rwanda	Kigali	Kinyarwanda, French, English, Kiswahili	Roman Catholic, Protestant, Adventist, Muslim	26,338
Sao Tome and Principe	SãoTomé	Portuguese	Roman Catholic, Evangelical, Protestant, Seventh-Day Adventist	1,001
Senegal	Dakar	French, Wolof, Pulaar Diola, Jola, Mandinka	Muslim, Christian	196,722
Seychelles	Victoria	English, French, Creole	Roman Catholic, Anglican	455
Sierra Leone	Freetown	English, Mende, Temne, Krio	Muslim, indigenous beliefs, Christian	71,740
Somalia	Muqdisho (Mogadishu)	Somali, Arabic, Italian, English	Sunni Muslim	637,657
South Africa	Pretoria(Tshwane)(Admin.) Bloemfontein (Judicial) Cape Town (Legislative)	Afrikaans, English, Ndebele, Pedi, Sotho, Swazi, Tsonga, Tswana, Venda, Xhosa,	Christian, indigenous beliefs, Muslim, Hindu	1,219,090
Sudan	Khartoum	Arabic, Nubian, Ta Bedawie, many local dialects	Sunni Muslim, indigenous beliefs, Christian	2,505,813
Swaziland	Mbabane (Administrative) Lobamba (Legislative and Royal)	English, siSwati	Indigenous beliefs, Roman Catholic, Muslim	17,363
Tanzania	Dar es Salaam (Administrative) Dodoma (Legislative)	Kiswahili, Kiungujo, English, Arabic, many local languages	Christian, Muslim, indigenous beliefs	945,087
Togo	Lomé	French, Ewe, Mina, Kabye, Dagomba	Indigenous beliefs, Christian, Muslim	56,785
Tunisia	Tunis	Arabic, French	Muslim	163,610
Uganda	Kampala	English, Ganda, Luganda, many local languages	Roman Catholic, Protestant, indigenous beliefs, Muslim	241,139
Zambia	Lusaka	English, indigenous languages	Christian, Muslim, Hindu	752,614
Zimbabwe	Harare	English, Shona, Sindebele	Syncretic (part Christian, part indigenous beliefs), Christian,	390,757
AFRICA: TERRITORIES AND AREAS OF SPECIAL STATUS				
France				
Mayotte	Mamoudzou	Mahorian, French	Muslim, Christian	374
Réunion	St.-Denis	French, Creole	Roman Catholic, Hindu, Muslim, Buddhist	2,507
Morocco				
Western Sahara	- - -	Hassaniya Arabic, Moroccan Arabic	Muslim	252,120
Norway				
Bouvet Island	Administered from Oslo	- - -	- - -	59
South Africa				
Prince Edward Islands	Administered from Bisho, Eastern Cape Province	- - -	- - -	335
United Kingdom				
Saint Helena	Jamestown	English	Anglican (majority)	411
AUSTRALIA & OCEANIA				
Australia	Canberra, A.T.C.	English, native languages	Protestant, Roman Catholic	7,692,024
Fiji Islands	Suva	English, Fijian, Hindustani	Christian, Hindu, Muslim	18,376
Kiribati	Tarawa	English, I-Kiribati	Roman Catholic, Protestant	811
Marshall Islands	Majuro	English, Marshallese, Japanese	Christian (mostly Protestant)	181
Micronesia	Palikir	English, Turkese, Pohnpeian, Yapese, Kosraean, Ulithian	Roman Catholic, Protestant	702
Nauru	Yaren	Nauruan, English	Protestant, Roman Catholic	21
New Zealand	Wellington	English, Maori	Protestant, Roman Catholic	270,534
Palau	Koror	English, Palauan, Japanese, 3 additional local languages	Roman Catholic, Protestant, Modekngei (indigenous)	489
Papua New Guinea	Port Moresby	715 indigenous languages	Protestant, indigenous beliefs, Roman Catholic	462,840
Samoa	Apia	Samoan, English	Christian	2,831
Solomon Islands	Honiara	Melanesian pidgin, 120 indigenous languages, English	Protestant, Roman Catholic, indigenous beliefs	28,370
Tonga	Nuku'alofa	Tongan, English	Christian	748
Tuvalu	Funafuti	Tuvaluan, English, Samoan	Church of Tuvalu (Congregationalist), Seventh-Day Adventist, Baha'i	26
Vanuatu	Port-Vila	English, French, more than 100 local languages	Protestant, Catholic, indigenous beliefs	12,190
AUSTRALIA & OCEANIA: TERRITORIES AND AREAS OF SPECIAL STATUS				
Australia				
Ashmore and Cartier Islands	Administered from Canberra, A.T.C.	- - -	- - -	5
Christmas Island	The Settlement	English, Chinese, Malay	Buddhist, Muslim, Christian	135
Cocos (Keeling) Islands	West Island	Malay (Cocos dialect), English	Sunni Muslim	14
Coral Sea Islands Territory	Administered from Canberra, A.T.C.	- - -	- - -	3
Norfolk Island	Kingston	English, Norfolk	Protestant, Roman Catholic	35
France				
Clipperton Island	- - -	- - -	- - -	7
French Polynesia	Papeete,Tahiti	French, Tahitian	Protestant, Roman Catholic	4,167
New Caledonia	Nouméa	French, 33 Melanesia-Polynesian dialects	Roman Catholic, Protestant	19,060
Wallis and Futuna	Matā'utu	French, Wallisian (indigenous Polynesian language)	Roman Catholic	161
New Zealand				
Cook Islands	Avarua	English, Maori	Christian	240
Niue	Alofi	Niuean, English	Ekalesia Niue (a Protestant Church)	263
Tokelau	Administered from Wellington	Tokelauan, English	Congregational Christian Church	12
United Kingdom				
Pitcairn Islands	Adamstown	English, Pitcairnese	Seventh-Day Adventist	47
United States				
American Samoa	Pago Pago	Samoan, English	Christian Congregationalist	233
Baker Island	Administered from Washington, D.C.	- - -	- - -	2
Guam	Hagåtña (Agana)	English, Chamorro, Japanese	Roman Catholic	561
Northern Mariana Islands	Saipan	English, Chamorro, Carolinian	Christian, traditional beliefs	464

Area (sq mi)	Population Mid-2005 (in 1,000s)	Projected pop. change 2005-2050	Pop density sq km (sq mi)	Urban pop.	Natural increase	Total fertility / infant mortality rate	Pop. <15 / >65	Life expectancy: Male / Female	HIV/AIDS Pop. 15-49 2003-04	CONTINENT / Country Formal Name
(719)	671	173%	360 (933)	33%	3.04%	5.40 / 96.30	42.70% / 2.90%	57.90 / 62.30	- - -	Union of the Comoros
(132,047)	3,999	243%	12 (30)	52%	3.09%	6.30 / 72.00	45.60% / 2.90%	50.62 / 53.09	4.90%	Republic of the Congo
(905,365)	60,764	201%	26 (67)	30%	3.06%	6.70 / 94.70	47.70% / 2.50%	49.00 / 51.80	4.20%	Democratic Republic of the Congo
(124,503)	18,154	87%	56 (146)	46%	2.23%	5.20 / 118.00	41.10% / 3.10%	45.80 / 47.80	7.00%	Republic of Côte d'Ivoire
(8,958)	793	95%	34 (89)	82%	1.85%	4.20 / 99.80	41.00% / 2.70%	51.08 / 53.84	2.90%	Republic of Djibouti
(386,874)	74,033	70%	74 (191)	43%	2.01%	3.20 / 37.00	36.30% / 4.50%	67.49 / 71.83	< 0.05%	Arab Republic of Egypt
(10,831)	504	127%	18 (47)	45%	2.29%	5.90 / 102.00	42.50% / 3.80%	43.45 / 45.55	- - -	Republic of Equatorial Guinea
(46,774)	4,670	118%	39 (100)	19%	2.62%	5.40 / 49.70	44.80% / 3.40%	56.10 / 59.00	2.70%	State of Eritrea
(437,600)	77,431	120%	68 (177)	15%	2.50%	5.90 / 100.00	43.78% / 2.98%	46.51 / 48.61	4.40%	Federal Democratic Republic of Ethiopia
(103,347)	1,384	65%	5 (13)	81%	2.11%	4.30 / 57.30	40.00% / 4.30%	55.29 / 57.57	8.10%	Gabonese Republic
(4,361)	1,595	155%	141 (366)	26%	2.79%	5.50 / 76.00	44.80% / 2.70%	51.30 / 55.00	1.20%	Republic of The Gambia
(92,100)	22,019	115%	92 (239)	44%	2.25%	4.50 / 64.00	40.20% / 3.30%	56.50 / 59.30	2.20%	Republic of Ghana
(94,926)	9,453	204%	38 (100)	33%	2.66%	5.90 / 94.20	44.40% / 3.10%	47.90 / 50.40	3.20%	Republic of Guinea
(13,948)	1,586	235%	44 (114)	32%	2.96%	7.10 / 120.00	45.80% / 3.00%	42.83 / 46.08	- - -	Republic of Guinea-Bissau
(224,081)	33,830	92%	58 (151)	36%	2.23%	4.90 / 77.00	42.60% / 2.30%	48.09 / 46.30	6.70%	Republic of Kenya
(11,720)	1,804	-29%	59 (154)	13%	-0.13%	3.50 / 92.10	37.80% / 4.90%	35.80 / 34.80	28.90%	Kingdom of Lesotho
(43,000)	3,283	224%	29 (76)	45%	2.90%	6.80 / 142.00	45.90% / 2.20%	40.97 / 43.46	5.90%	Republic of Liberia
(679,362)	5,766	88%	3 (8)	86%	2.39%	3.50 / 26.80	34.50% / 4.10%	73.90 / 78.30	0.30%	Great Socialist People's Libyan Arab Jamahiriya
(226,658)	17,308	141%	29 (76)	26%	2.74%	5.20 / 87.70	44.79% / 2.83%	52.50 / 56.80	1.70%	Republic of Madagascar
(45,747)	12,341	260%	104 (270)	14%	3.16%	6.50 / 99.60	46.40% / 2.90%	43.41 / 46.03	14.20%	Republic of Malawi
(478,841)	13,518	211%	11 (28)	30%	3.24%	7.10 / 133.00	47.00% / 2.70%	46.83 / 48.28	1.90%	Republic of Mali
(397,955)	3,069	144%	3 (8)	40%	2.73%	5.90 / 97.00	43.30% / 3.40%	49.90 / 53.10	0.60%	Islamic Republic of Mauritania
(788)	1,243	21%	609 (1,577)	42%	0.87%	1.90 / 14.40	24.90% / 6.50%	68.57 / 75.29	- - -	Republic of Mauritius
(274,461)	30,704	47%	43 (112)	57%	1.55%	2.50 / 40.40	30.40% / 4.85%	68.00 / 72.10	0.10%	Kingdom of Morocco
(308,642)	19,420	94%	24 (63)	32%	2.15%	5.50 / 119.00	44.20% / 2.70%	41.01 / 42.78	12.20%	Republic of Mozambique
(318,261)	2,031	-12%	2 (6)	33%	1.07%	4.20 / 50.70	39.50% / 3.50%	46.00 / 46.10	21.3%	Republic of Namibia
(489,191)	13,957	259%	11 (29)	21%	3.41%	8.00 / 153.00	48.10% / 1.90%	43.37 / 43.53	1.20%	Republic of Niger
(356,669)	131,530	96%	142 (369)	44%	2.38%	5.90 / 100.00	43.40% / 2.90%	43.39 / 44.44	5.40%	Federal Republic of Nigeria
(10,169)	8,722	101%	331 (858)	17%	2.27%	5.70 / 107.00	43.80% / 2.30%	41.87 / 45.26	5.10%	Republic of Rwanda
(386)	153	93%	153 (396)	38%	2.54%	4.10 / 82.00	38.40% / 4.20%	61.87 / 63.83	- - -	Democratic Republic of Sao Tome and Principe
(75,955)	11,658	98%	59 (153)	43%	2.57%	5.10 / 83.00	42.10% / 3.00%	54.35 / 56.76	0.80%	Republic of Senegal
(176)	81	11%	178 (460)	50%	1.00%	2.10 / 16.00	25.50% / 7.80%	66.17 / 76.10	- - -	Republic of Seychelles
(27,699)	5,525	150%	77 (199)	37%	2.27%	6.50 / 165.00	41.40% / 3.20%	38.72 / 41.58	- - -	Republic of Sierra Leone
(246,201)	8,592	197%	13 (35)	33%	2.88%	7.00 / 120.00	44.80% / 2.70%	45.70 / 49.00	- - -	Somalia
(470,693)	46,923	3%	38 (100)	53%	0.72%	2.80 / 43.00	32.90% / 4.00%	50.00 / 53.00	21.50%	Republic of South Africa
(967,500)	40,187	110%	16 (42)	36%	2.74%	5.20 / 67.14	44.20% / 2.20%	56.20 / 58.50	2.30%	Republic of the Sudan
(6,704)	1,138	-34%	66 (170)	25%	0.34%	3.90 / 74.80	42.70% / 3.20%	33.90 / 36.80	38.80%	Kingdom of Swaziland
(364,900)	36,481	96%	39 (100)	32%	2.44%	5.70 / 68.00	44.90% / 2.60%	43.20 / 45.00	7.00%	United Republic of Tanzania
(21,925)	6,145	120%	108 (280)	33%	2.72%	5.40 / 93.00	42.60% / 3.00%	52.26 / 56.20	4.10%	Togolese Republic
(63,170)	10,043	21%	61 (159)	65%	1.10%	2.10 / 21.10	26.70% / 6.80%	71.10 / 75.10	< 0.05%	Tunisian Republic
(93,104)	26,907	387%	112 (289)	12%	3.24%	6.90 / 88.40	50.50% / 2.30%	47.60 / 48.30	7.10%	Republic of Uganda
(290,586)	11,227	95%	15 (39)	35%	1.85%	5.70 / 95.00	44.80% / 2.90%	37.88 / 36.92	16.50%	Republic of Zambia
(150,872)	13,010	21%	33 (86)	34%	1.11%	3.80 / 62.00	39.60% / 3.40%	39.90 / 41.10	24.60%	Republic of Zimbabwe
										AFRICA: TERRITORIES AND AREAS OF SPECIAL STATUS
(144)	181	207%	484 (1,257)	28%	3.07%	5.60 / - - -	42.10% / 1.70%	57.80 / 62.00	- - -	French Overseas Territorial Collectivity
(968)	782	36%	312 (808)	89%	1.44%	2.50 / 6.10	27.30% / 7.20%	71.20 / 79.60	- - -	French Overseas Department
(97,344)	341	163%	1 (4)	93%	1.98%	3.90 / 53.00	34.30% / 3.30%	62.23 / 65.71	- - -	Area of Special Status
(23)	0	- - -	- - - - - -	- - -	- - -	- - - - - -	- - - - - -	- - - - - -	- - -	Territory of Norway
(129)	0	- - -	- - - - - -	- - -	- - -	- - - - - -	- - - - - -	- - - - - -	- - -	Territory of South Africa
(159)	6	- - -	15 (38)	35%	-0.10%	1.50 / 0	19.10% / 9.20%	74.10 / 80.00	- - -	British Overseas Territory
										AUSTRALIA & OCEANIA
(2,969,906)	20,351	29%	3 (7)	91%	0.61%	1.80 / 4.50	19.80% / 13.00%	77.80 / 82.80	0.10%	Commonwealth of Australia
(7,095)	842	11%	46 (119)	46%	1.47%	2.70 / 15.60	29.80% / 4.20%	65.65 / 70.04	0.10%	Republic of the Fiji Islands
(313)	92	128%	113 (294)	43%	1.80%	4.30 / 43.00	40.10% / 3.30%	58.20 / 67.30	- - -	Republic of Kiribati
(70)	59	75%	326 (843)	68%	3.01%	4.40 / 35.00	41.60% / 2.70%	66.60 / 70.40	- - -	Republic of the Marshall Islands
(271)	108	-10%	154 (399)	22%	2.14%	4.40 / 40	40.30% / 3.70%	66.50 / 67.00	- - -	Federated States of Micronesia
(8)	13	77%	619 (1,625)	100%	1.78%	3.70 / 12.10	41.00% / 1.60%	57.30 / 64.50	- - -	Republic of Nauru
(104,454)	4,107	23%	15 (39)	86%	0.73%	2.00 / 5.58	21.60% / 12.04%	76.30 / 81.10	0.10%	New Zealand
(189)	21	24%	43 (111)	70%	0.87%	2.10 / 15.40	23.90% / 5.40%	66.64 / 74.54	- - -	Republic of Palau
(178,703)	5,887	80%	13 (33)	13%	2.10%	4.10 / 71.00	40.10% / 2.30%	54.67 / 55.79	0.60%	Independent State of Papua New Guinea
(1,093)	188	-15%	66 (172)	22%	2.40%	4.30 / 17.80	40.70% / 4.47%	71.80 / 73.80	- - -	Independent State of Samoa
(10,954)	472	93%	17 (43)	16%	2.60%	4.50 / 66.00	40.10% / 3.20%	61.90 / 63.10	- - -	Solomon Islands
(289)	102	68%	136 (353)	33%	1.81%	3.10 / 19.00	39.49% / 5.20%	69.80 / 71.70	- - -	Kingdom of Tonga
(10)	10	80%	385 (1,000)	47%	1.72%	3.70 / 35.00	36.20% / 5.70%	61.70 / 65.10	- - -	Tuvalu
(4,707)	218	78%	18 (46)	21%	2.57%	4.20 / 34.00	41.70% / 3.30%	65.60 / 69.00	- - -	Republic of Vanuatu
										AUSTRALIA & OCEANIA: TERRITORIES AND AREAS OF SPECIAL STATUS
(2)	0	- - -	- - - - - -	- - -	- - -	- - - - - -	- - - - - -	- - - - - -	- - -	Australian External Territory
(52)	0.474	111%	4 (9)	- - -	- - -	- - - / - - -	- - - / - - -	- - - / - - -	- - -	Australian External Territory
(5)	0.632	58%	45 (126)	- - -	- - -	- - - / - - -	- - - / - - -	- - - / - - -	- - -	Australian External Territory
(1)	0	- - -								Australian External Territory
(14)	2	0%	57 (143)	80%	0.15%	- - - / 0	- - - / - - -	- - - / - - -	- - -	Australian External Territory
(3)	0	- - -	- - - - - -	- - -	- - -	- - - - - -	- - - - - -	- - - - - -	- - -	French Possession
(1,608)	255	40%	61 (159)	53%	1.32%	2.50 / 5.20	30.80% / 4.30%	66.90 / 68.16	- - -	French Overseas Territory
(7,359)	227	61%	12 (31)	71%	1.35%	2.40 / 8.60	29.40% / 6.30%	69.80 / 75.80	- - -	French Overseas Territory
(62)	15	33%	93 (242)	0%	1.35%	2.70 / 5.50	- - - / - - -	- - - / - - -	- - -	French Overseas Territory
(93)	13	23%	54 (140)	63%	1.52%	3.70 / 16.90	30.00% / 5.90%	68.40 / 71.50	- - -	Self-Governing in Free Association with New Zealand
(102)	1.617	24%	6 (16)	34%	1.07%	3.00 / 29.40	29.60% / 9.30%	69.80 / 71.20	- - -	Self-Governing in Free Association with New Zealand
(5)	1.538	30%	128 (308)	0%	2.40%	4.90 / 33.00	- - - / - - -	67.80 / 70.40	- - -	Territory of New Zealand
(18)	0.045	0%	1 (3)	- - -	- - -	- - - / - - -	26.40% / 15.00%	- - - / - - -	- - -	British Overseas Territory
(90)	63	-33%	270 (700)	89%	2.31%	3.90 / 15.40	38.70% / 3.30%	70.70 / 79.80	- - -	Territory of the United States
(1)	0	- - -	- - - - - -	- - -	- - -		- - - - - -	- - - - - -	- - -	Territory of the United States
(217)	169	45%	301 (779)	93%	1.59%	2.60 / 6.20	30.46% / 5.30%	75.50 / 80.40	- - -	Territory of the United States
(179)	80	79%	172 (447)	90%	1.52%	1.70 / 7.00	22.50% / 1.50%	70.70 / 79.80	- - -	Commonwealth in Political Union with the United States

CONTINENT/Country	GDP per capita in U.S. dollars Mid-2005 estimate	Services as % of GDP Sector 2003	Industry as % of GDP Sector 2003	Agriculture as % of GDP Sector 2003	Total estimated value of imports in million U.S. dollars 2005	Total estimated value of exports in million U.S. dollars 2005	% of population with access to electricity 2003
NORTH AMERICA							
Antigua and Barbuda	$11,000	76.8%	18.0%	4.0%	$735	$214	- - -
Bahamas	$20,200	90.0%	7.0%	3.0%	$5,806	$1,507	- - -
Barbados	$17,000	78.0%	16.0%	6.0%	$1,476	$209	- - -
Belize	$6,800	67.3%	15.0%	17.7%	$622	$350	- - -
Canada	$34,000	71.3%	26.4%	2.3%	$317,700	$364,800	- - -
Costa Rica	$11,100	62.5%	28.7%	8.8%	$9,690	$7,005	95.7%
Cuba	$3,500	67.9%	25.5%	6.6%	$6,916	$2,388	97.0%
Dominica	$5,500	58.0%	24.0%	18.0%	$234	$74	- - -
Dominican Republic	$7,000	58.1%	30.6%	11.2%	$9,747	$5,818	66.8%
El Salvador	$4,700	59.4%	32.1%	8.5%	$6,678	$3,586	70.8%
Grenada	$5,000	68.4%	23.9%	7.7%	$276	$40	- - -
Guatemala	$4,700	58.5%	19.3%	22.3%	$7,744	$3,940	66.7%
Haiti	$1,700	50.0&	20.0%	30.0%	$1,471	$391	34.0%
Honduras	$2,900	55.8%	30.7%	13.5%	$4,161	$1,726	54.5%
Jamaica	$4,400	65.0%	29.8%	5.2%	$4,144	$1,593	90.0%
Mexico	$10,000	69.6%	26.4%	4.0%	$223,700	$213,700	- - -
Nicaragua	$2,900	56.3%	25.7%	17.9%	$2,952	$1,550	48.0%
Panama	$7,200	76.2%	16.3%	7.5%	$8,734	$7,481	76.1%
Saint Kitts and Nevis	$8,800	68.7%	28.3%	3.0%	$405	$70	- - -
Saint Lucia	$5,400	76.6%	18.0%	5.4%	$410	$82	- - -
Saint Vincent and the Grenadines	$2,900	66.9%	24.4%	8.7%	$225	$37	- - -
Trinidad and Tobago	$16,700	50.0%	48.8%	1.2%	$6,011	$9,161	99.0%
United States	$41,800	79.4%	19.7%	0.9%	$1,727,000	$927,500	- - -
NORTH AMERICA: TERRITORIES AND AREAS OF SPECIAL STATUS							
Denmark							
Greenland	$20,000	- - -	- - -	- - -	$601	$480	- - -
France							
Guadeloupe	$7,900	68.0%	17.0%	15.0%	$1,700	$140	- - -
Martinique	$14,400	83.0%	11.0%	6.0%	$2,000	$250	- - -
Saint-Pierre and Miquelon	$7,000	- - -	- - -	- - -	$70	$7	- - -
Netherlands							
Aruba	$21,800	- - -	- - -	- - -	$875	$80	- - -
Netherlands Antilles	$16,000	84.0%	15.0%	1.0%	$4,383	$2,076	- - -
United Kingdom							
Anguilla	$7,500	78.0%	18.0%	4.0%	$81	$2.6	- - -
Bermuda	$69,900	89.0%	10.0%	1.0%	$8,078	$1,469	- - -
British Virgin Islands	$38,500	92.0%	6.2%	1.8%	$187	$25.3	- - -
Cayman Islands	$32,300	95.4%	3.2%	1.4%	$457	$1.2	- - -
Montserrat	$3,400	- - -	- - -	- - -	$17	$0.7	- - -
Turks and Caicos Islands	$11,500	- - -	- - -	- - -	$176	$169	- - -
United States							
Navassa Island	- - -	- - -	- - -	- - -	- - -	- - -	- - -
Puerto Rico	$18,600	56.0%	43.0%	1.0%	$29,100	$46,900	- - -
Virgin Islands	$14,500	80.0%	19.0%	1.0%	- - -	- - -	- - -
SOUTH AMERICA							
Argentina	$13,100	54.1%	34.8%	11.1%	$28,800	$40,000	94.6%
Bolivia	$2,900	55.1%	30.1%	14.9%	$1,845	$2,371	60.4%
Brazil	$8,400	75.1%	19.1%	5.8%	$78,020	$115,100	94.9%
Chile	$11,300	56.9%	34.3%	8.8%	$30,090	$38,030	99.0%
Colombia	$7,900	58.3%	29.4%	12.3%	$20,420	$23,060	81.0%
Ecuador	$4,300	63.6%	28.7%	7.7%	$8,436	$9,224	80.0%
Guyana	$4,600	41.8%	19.9%	38.3%	$682	$587.2	- - -
Paraguay	$4,900	48.5%	24.2%	27.2%	$3,832	$3,130	74.7%
Peru	$5,900	60.4%	29.3%	10.3%	$12,150	$15,950	73.0%
Suriname	$4,100	65.0%	22.0%	13.0%	$750	$881	- - -
Uruguay	$9,600	59.9%	27.3%	12.8%	$3,540	$3,550	98.0%
Venezuela	$6,100	54.4%	41.1%	4.5%	$24,630	$52,730	94.0%
SOUTH AMERICA: TERRITORIES AND AREAS OF SPECIAL STATUS							
France							
French Guiana	$8,300	- - -	- - -	- - -	$625	$155	- - -
United Kingdom							
Falkland Islands	$25,000	- - -	- - -	- - -	$90	$125	- - -
EUROPE							
Albania	$4,900	56.1%	19.2%	24.7%	$2,473	$708.8	- - -
Andorra	$24,000	- - -	- - -	- - -	$1,077	$58	- - -
Austria	$32,700	65.9%	31.7%	2.3%	$118,800	$122,500	- - -
Belarus	$6,900	60.1%	30.1%	9.8%	$16,940	$16,140	- - -
Belgium	$31,400	72.2%	26.5%	1.3%	$264,500	$269,600	- - -
Bosnia and Herzegovina	$6,800	53.0%	32.1%	14.9%	$6,800	$2,700	- - -
Bulgaria	$9,600	57.5%	30.7%	11.7%	$15,900	$11,670	- - -
Croatia	$11,600	61.5%	30.1%	8.4%	$18,930	$10,300	- - -
Cyprus	$21,600	76.0%	19.9%	4.1%	$5,552	$1,237	- - -
Czech Republic	$19,500	57.1%	39.4%	3.5%	$76,590	$78,370	- - -
Denmark	$34,600	71.5%	26.4%	2.1%	$74,690	$84,950	- - -
Estonia	$16,700	67.0%	28.5%	4.5%	$9,189	$7,439	- - -
Finland	$30,900	66.0%	30.5%	3.5%	$56,450	$67,880	- - -
France	$29,900	72.8%	24.5%	2.7%	$473,300	$443,400	- - -
Germany	$30,400	69.4%	29.4%	1.1%	$801,000	$1,016,000	- - -
Greece	$22,200	69.3%	23.8%	6.9%	$48,200	$18,540	- - -
Hungary	$16,300	65.3%	31.4%	3.3%	$64,830	$61,750	- - -
Iceland	$35,600	79.2%	9.6%	11.2%	$4,582	$3,215	- - -
Ireland	$41,000	49.0%	46.0%	5.0%	$65,470	$102,000	- - -
Italy	$29,200	69.5%	27.8%	2.6%	$369,200	$371,900	- - -
Latvia	$13,200	71.0%	24.4%	4.5%	$8,559	$5,749	- - -
Liechtenstein	$25,000	- - -	- - -	- - -	$917	$2,470	- - -
Lithuania	$13,700	59.0%	33.8%	7.3%	$13,330	$10,950	- - -
Luxembourg	$55,600	78.9%	20.5%	0.6%	$18,740	$13,390	- - -
Macedonia	$7,800	57.3%	30.4%	12.2%	$3,196	$2,047	- - -
Malta	$19,900	74.0%	23.0%	3.0%	$3,859	$2,744	- - -
Moldova	$1,800	52.8%	24.7%	22.5%	$2,230	$1,040	- - -
Monaco	$27,000	- - -	- - -	- - -	- - -	- - -	- - -
Montenegro	$3,800	- - -	- - -	- - -	- - -	- - -	- - -

Telephone mainlines per 1,000 people 2003	Arable & permanent cropland area 2003 sq km (sq mi)	Forested area as % of total land area 2000	Protected areas as % of total land area 2003	Average annual deforestation: % change 1990 - 2000 *(Negative number indicates an increase in forest area.)*	Carbon dioxide emissions : metric tonnes per capita 2000	CONTINENT / Country Formal Name
						NORTH AMERICA
---	100 (39)	21.4%	---	---	4.9	Antigua and Barbuda
415	120 (46)	51.5%	---	---	5.9	Commonwealth of The Bahamas
497	170 (66)	4.0%	---	---	4.4	Barbados
113	1,020 (394)	72.5%	---	---	3.1	Belize
629	521,150 (201,217)	33.6%	11.1%	0.0%	14.2	Canada
251	5,250 (2,027)	46.8%	23.0%	0.8%	1.4	Republic of Costa Rica
51	37,880 (14,626)	24.7%	69.1%	-1.3%	2.8	Republic of Cuba
304	210 (81)	61.3%	---	---	1.4	Commonwealth of Dominica
115	15,960 (6,162)	28.4%	51.9%	0.0%	3.0	Dominican Republic
116	9,100 (3,514)	14.4%	0.4%	4.6%	1.1	Republic of El Salvador
290	120 (46)	12.2%	---	---	2.1	Grenada
71	20,500 (7,915)	36.3%	20.0%	1.7%	0.9	Republic of Guatemala
17	11,000 (4,247)	3.8%	0.4%	5.7%	0.2	Republic of Haiti
48	14,280 (5,514)	41.5%	6.4%	1.0%	0.7	Republic of Honduras
170	2,840 (1,097)	31.3%	---	1.5%	4.2	Jamaica
158	273,000 (105,406)	33.7%	10.2%	1.1%	4.3	United Mexican States
37	21,610 (8,344)	42.7%	17.8%	3.0%	0.7	Republic of Nicaragua
122	6,950 (2,683)	57.7%	21.7%	1.6%	2.2	Republic of Panama
500	80 (31)	14.7%	---	---	---	Federation of Saint Kitts and Nevis
320	180 (69)	27.9%	---	---	---	Saint Lucia
234	140 (54)	27.4%	---	---	---	Saint Vincent and the Grenadines
250	1,220 (471)	44.1%	6.0%	0.8%	20.5	Republic of Trinidad and Tobago
621	1,755,000 (677,609)	33.1%	25.9%	-0.2%	19.8	United States of America
						NORTH AMERICA: TERRITORIES AND AREAS OF SPECIAL STATUS
---	------	---	---	---	---	Overseas Region of Denmark
---	250 (97)	47.2%	---	---	---	French Overseas Department
---	210 (81)	43.9%		---	---	French Overseas Department
---	30 (12)	13.0%	---	---	---	French Overseas Territorial Collectivity
---	20 (8)	2.2%		---	---	Overseas Region of the Netherlands
---	80 (31)	1.5%	---	---	---	Overseas Region of the Netherlands
---	------	71.4%	---	---	---	British Overseas Territory
---	10 (4)	20.0%	---	---	---	British Overseas Territory
---	40 (15)	24.4%	---	---	---	British Overseas Territory
---	10 (4)	48.4%	---	---	---	British Overseas Territory
---	20 (8)	35.0%	---	---	---	British Overseas Territory
---	10 (4)	80.0%	---	---	---	British Overseas Territory
---	------			---	---	Territory of the United States
346	830 (320)	46.0%	3.5%	0.2%	2.3	Self-Governing Commonwealth in Association with the United States
---	30 (12)	27.9%		---	---	Territory of the United States
						SOUTH AMERICA
219	289,000 (111,584)	12.1%	6.6%	0.8%	3.9	Argentine Republic
72	32,560 (12,571)	54.2%	13.4%	0.3%	1.3	Republic of Bolivia
223	666,000 (257,144)	57.2%	6.7%	0.4%	1.8	Federative Republic of Brazil
221	23,070 (8,907)	21.5%	18.9%	0.1%	3.9	Republic of Chile
179	38,500 (14,865)	58.5%	10.2%	0.4%	1.4	Republic of Colombia
122	29,850 (11,525)	39.2%	18.3%	1.2%	2.0	Republic of Ecuador
---	5,100 (1,969)	76.7%	---	---	2.1	Co-operative Republic of Guyana
46	31,360 (12,108)	46.5%	3.5%	0.5%	0.7	Republic of Paraguay
67	43,100 (16,641)	53.7%	6.1%	0.4%	1.1	Republic of Peru
152	680 (263)	94.7%	---	---	5.0	Republic of Suriname
---	14,120 (5,452)	8.6%	0.3%	-5.0%	1.6	Oriental Republic of Uruguay
111	34,000 (13,127)	54.1%	63.8%	0.4%	6.5	Bolivarian Republic of Venezuela
						SOUTH AMERICA: TERRITORIES AND AREAS OF SPECIAL STATUS
---	160 (62)	91.8%	---	---	---	French Overseas Department
---	------	0.0%	---	---	---	British Overseas Territory
						EUROPE
83	6,990 (2,699)	29.0%	3.8%	0.8%	0.9	Republic of Albania
438	10 (4)	35.6%	---	---	---	Principality of Andorra
481	14,620 (5,645)	46.7%	33.0%	-0.2%	7.6	Republic of Austria
311	56,810 (21,934)	38.0%	6.3%	-3.2%	5.9	Republic of Belarus
489	8,580 (3,313)	22.0%	2.6%	-0.2%	10.0	Kingdom of Belgium
245	11,010 (4,251)	43.1%	0.5%	0.0%	4.8	Bosnia and Herzegovina
380	35,340 (13,645)	32.8%	4.5%	-0.6%	5.3	Republic of Bulgaria
417	15,840 (6,116)	38.2%	7.5%	-0.1%	4.5	Republic of Croatia
572	1,400 (541)	18.9%	---	---	8.5	Republic of Cyprus
360	32,990 (12,738)	34.3%	16.1%	-0.0%	11.6	Czech Republic
669	22,740 (8,780)	11.8%	34.0%	-0.2%	8.4	Kingdom of Denmark
341	5,610 (2,166)	53.9%	11.8%	-0.6%	11.7	Republic of Estonia
492	22,180 (8,564)	73.9%	9.3%	-0.0%	10.3	Republic of Finland
566	195,730 (75,572)	28.3%	13.3%	-0.4%	6.2	French Republic
657	120,400 (46,487)	31.7%	31.9%	0.0%	9.6	Federal Republic of Germany
454	38,310 (14,792)	29.1%	3.6%	-0.9%	8.2	Hellenic Republic
349	48,040 (18,548)	21.5%	7.0%	-0.4%	5.4	Republic of Hungary
660	70 (27)	0.5%	---	---	7.7	Republic of Iceland
491	11,840 (4,571)	9.7%	1.7%	-3.0%	11.1	Republic of Ireland
484	106,970 (41,301)	33.9%	7.9%	-0.3%	7.4	Italian Republic
285	18,500 (7,143)	47.4%	13.4%	-0.4%	2.5	Republic of Latvia
583	40 (15)	43.1%	---	---	---	Principality of Liechtenstein
239	29,850 (11,525)	33.5%	10.3%	-0.2%	3.4	Republic of Lithuania
798	630 (243)	33.5%	---	---	19.4	Grand Duchy of Luxembourg
271	6,120 (2,363)	35.8%	7.1%	0.0%	5.5	Republic of Macedonia
521	110 (42)	1.1%	---	---	7.2	Republic of Malta
219	21,430 (8,274)	10.0%	1.4%	-0.2%	1.5	Republic of Moldova
1040	------	0.0%	---	---	---	Principality of Monaco
---	--- ---	---	---	---	---	Republic of Montenegro

CONTINENT/Country	GDP per capita in U.S. dollars Mid-2005 estimate	Services as % of GDP Sector 2003	Industry as % of GDP Sector 2003	Agriculture as % of GDP Sector 2003	Total estimated value of imports in million U.S. dollars 2005	Total estimated value of exports in million U.S. dollars 2005	% of population with access to electricity 2003
Netherlands	$30,500	73.1%	24.5%	2.4%	$326,600	$365,100	---
Norway	$42,300	61.0%	37.5%	1.5%	$58,120	$111,200	---
Poland	$13,300	66.1%	30.7%	3.1%	$95,670	$92,720	---
Portugal	$19,300	63.9%	30.2%	5.9%	$60,350	$38,800	---
Romania	$8,200	52.0%	36.1%	11.9%	$38,150	$27,720	---
Russia	$11,100	60.7%	34.2%	5.2%	$125,000	$245,000	---
San Marino	$34,600	---	---	---	---	---	---
Serbia	$4,400	---	---	---	---	---	---
Slovakia	$16,100	66.6%	29.7%	3.7%	$34,480	$32,390	---
Slovenia	$21,600	60.3%	36.9%	2.8%	$19,620	$18,530	---
Spain	$25,500	67.1%	29.6%	3.3%	$271,800	$194,300	---
Sweden	$29,800	70.3%	27.9%	1.8%	$104,400	$126,600	---
Switzerland	$32,300	64.5%	34.0%	1.5%	$135,000	$148,600	---
Ukraine	$7,200	45.6%	40.3%	14.1%	$37,180	$38,220	---
United Kingdom	$30,300	72.4%	26.6%	1.0%	$483,700	$372,700	---
Vatican City	---	---	---	---	---	---	---
EUROPE: TERRITORIES AND AREAS OF SPECIAL STATUS							
Denmark							
Faroe Islands	$22,000	62.0%	11.0%	27.0%	$639	$533	---
Norway							
Svalbard	---	---	---	---	---	---	---
United Kingdom							
Channel Islands	---	---	---	---	---	---	---
Gibraltar	$27,900	86.0%	13.0%	1.0%	$2,967	$271	---
Isle of Man	$28,500	---	---	---	---	---	---
ASIA							
Afghanistan	$800	20.0%	20.0%	60.0%	$3,870	$471	2.0%
Armenia	$4,500	37.3%	39.2%	23.5%	$1,500	$800	---
Azerbaijan	$4,800	31.1%	54.5%	14.3%	$4,656	$6,117	---
Bahrain	$23,000	58.3%	41.0%	0.7%	$7,830	$11,170	---
Bangladesh	$2,100	52.0%	26.3%	21.8%	$12,970	$9,372	20.4%
Bhutan	$1,400	27.3%	39.5%	33.2%	$196	$154	---
Brunei	$23,600	50.0%	45.0%	5.0%	$1,641	$4,514	---
Cambodia	$2,200	35.9%	29.7%	34.5%	$3,538	$2,663	15.8%
China	$6,800	33.1%	52.3%	14.6%	$631,800	$752,200	98.6%
Georgia	$3,300	54.1%	25.5%	20.5%	$2,500	$1,400	---
India	$3,300	51.2%	26.6%	22.2%	$113,100	$76,230	43.0%
Indonesia	$3,600	39.9%	43.6%	16.6%	$62,020	$83,640	53.4%
Iran	$8,300	47.6%	41.2%	11.3%	$42,500	$55,420	97.9%
Iraq	$3,400	27.8%	58.6%	13.6%	$19,570	$17,780	95.0%
Israel	$24,600	59.5%	37.7%	2.8%	$43,190	$40,140	100.0%
Japan	$31,500	74.0%	24.7%	1.3%	$451,100	$550,500	---
Jordan	$4,700	71.8%	26.0%	2.2%	$8,681	$4,226	95.0%
Kazakhstan	$8,200	53.9%	38.3%	7.8%	$17,510	$30,090	---
Korea, North	$1,700	56.3%	40.4%	3.3%	$2,819	$1,275	20.0%
Korea, South	$20,400	62.2%	34.6%	3.2%	$248,400	$277,600	---
Kuwait	$19,200	39.1%	60.5%	0.4%	$12,230	$44,430	100.0%
Kyrgyzstan	$2,100	38.4%	22.9%	38.7%	$937	$759	---
Laos	$1,900	25.5%	25.9%	48.6%	$541	$379	---
Lebanon	$6,200	67.7%	20.0%	12.2%	$8,855	$1,782	95.0%
Malaysia	$12,100	41.8%	48.5%	9.7%	$118,700	$147,100	96.9%
Maldives	$3,900	62.0%	18.0%	20.0%	$645	$123	---
Mongolia	$1,900	57.0%	14.9%	28.1%	$1,011	$852	90.0%
Myanmar (Burma)	$1,700	34.5%	8.9%	56.6%	$2,183	$2,514	5.0%
Nepal	$1,400	37.8%	21.6%	40.6%	$1,696	$626	15.4%
Oman	$13,200	3.1%	55.8%	41.1%	$8,709	$19,010	94.0%
Pakistan	$2,400	53.2%	23.5%	23.3%	$21,260	$14,850	52.9%
Philippines	$5,100	53.2%	32.3%	14.5%	$42,660	$41,250	87.4%
Qatar	$27,400	41.5%	58.2%	0.3%	$6,706	$24,900	---
Saudi Arabia	$12,800	40.3%	55.2%	4.5%	$44,930	$165,000	97.7%
Singapore	$28,100	65.0%	34.9%	0.1%	$187,500	$212,400	100.0%
Sri Lanka	$4,300	54.7%	26.3%	19.0%	$8,370	$6,442	62.0%
Syria	$3,900	48.0%	28.6%	23.5%	$5,973	$6,344	85.9%
Tajikistan	$1,200	56.4%	20.2%	23.4%	$1,250	$950	---
Thailand	$8,300	46.3%	44.0%	9.8%	$107,000	$105,800	82.1%
Timor-Leste (East Timor)	$400	57.4%	17.2%	25.4%	$202	$10	---
Turkey	$8,200	64.7%	21.9%	13.4%	$101,200	$72,490	---
Turkmenistan	$8,000	28.8%	42.7%	28.5%	$4,175	$4,700	---
United Arab Emirates	$43,400	37.5%	58.5%	4.0%	$60,150	4103,100	96.0%
Uzbekistan	$1,800	43.1%	21.7%	35.2%	$4,140	$5,360	---
Vietnam	$2,800	38.2%	40.0%	21.8%	$34,440	$31,340	75.8%
Yemen	$900	45.0%	40.0%	15.0%	$4,190	$6,387	50.0%
ASIA: TERRITORIES AND AREAS OF SPECIAL STATUS							
China							
Hong Kong	$32,900	88.0%	12.0%	0.0%	$291,600	$286,300	---
Macau	$22,000	92.7%	7.2%	0.1%	$3,478	$3,465	---
Taiwan	$27,600	67.4%	30.9%	1.7%	$172,900	$185,100	---
Israel - Palestinian Areas					$1,952	$270	---
Gaza Strip	$600	63.0%	28.0%	9.0%	---	---	---
West Bank	$1,100	63.0%	28.0%	9.0%	---	---	---
United Kingdom							
British Indian Ocean Territory	---	93.0%	2.0%	5.0%	---	---	---
AFRICA							
Algeria	$7,200	34.7%	55.1%	10.2%	$22,530	$49,590	98.0%
Angola	$3,200	26.6%	64.6%	8.8%	$8,165	$26,800	12.0%
Benin	$1,100	50%	14.4%	35.7%	$1,043	$827	22.0%
Botswana	$10,500	52.5%	45.2%	2.4%	$3,370	$3,680	22.0%
Burkina Faso	$1,300	50.1%	18.9%	31.0%	$992	$395	13.0%
Burundi	$700	32.0%	19.0%	49.0%	$200	$52	---
Cameroon	$2,400	39.1%	16.7%	44.2%	$2,514	$3,236	20.0%
Cape Verde	$6,200	73.4%	19.7%	6.8%	$500	$73	---
Central African Republic	$1,100	14.3%	24.9%	60.8%	$203	$131	---
Chad	$1,500	40.9%	13.5%	45.6%	$749,100	$3,016	---

Telephone mainlines per 1,000 people 2003	Arable & permanent cropland area 2003 sq km (sq mi)	Forested area as % of total land area 2000	Protected areas as % of total land area 2003	Average annual deforestation: % change 1990 - 2000 (Negative number indicates an increase in forest area.)	Carbon dioxide emissions : metric tonnes per capita 2000	CONTINENT / Country Formal Name
614	9,440 (3,645)	10.8%	14.2%	-0.3%	8.7	Kingdom of the Netherlands
713	8,730 (3,371)	30.7%	6.8%	-0.4%	11.1	Kingdom of Norway
319	129,010 (49,811)	30.0%	12.4%	-0.1%	7.8	Republic of Poland
411	23,110 (8,923)	41.3%	6.6%	-1.7%	5.8	Portuguese Republic
199	98,720 (38,116)	27.7%	4.7%	-0.2%	3.8	Romania
242	1,243,730 (480,207)	47.9%	7.8%	-0.0%	9.9	Russian Federation
763	10 (4)	1.6%	---	---	---	Republic of San Marino
---	--- ---	---	---	---	---	Republic of Serbia
241	15,640 (6,039)	40.1%	22.8%	-0.3%	6.6	Slovak Republic
407	2,020 (780)	62.8%	6.0%	-0.2%	7.3	Republic of Slovenia
434	187,150 (72,259)	35.9%	8.5%	-0.6%	7.0	Kingdom of Spain
736	26,720 (10,317)	66.9%	9.1%	-0.0%	5.3	Kingdom of Sweden
744	4,330 (1,672)	30.9%	30.0%	-0.4%	5.4	Swiss Confederation
216	333,870 (128,908)	16.5%	3.9%	-0.3%	6.9	Ukraine
591	57,080 (22,039)	11.8%	20.9%	-0.8%	9.6	United Kingdom of Great Britain and Northern Ireland
---	------	0.0%	---	---	---	State of the Vatican City (The Holy See)
						EUROPE: TERRITORIES AND AREAS OF SPECIAL STATUS
---	30 (12)	0.1%	---	---	---	Overseas Region of Denmark
---	------	---	---	---	---	Norwegian Dependency
---	------	4.1%	---	---	---	British Crown Dependencies
---	------	0.0%	---	---	---	British Overseas Territory
---	------	6.1%	---	---	---	British Crown Dependency
						ASIA
2	80,480 (31,074)	1.3%	0.3%	---	0.0	Transitional Islamic State of Afghanistan
148	5,600 (2,162)	10.0%	7.6%	-1.3%	1.1	Republic of Armenia
114	20,120 (7,768)	11.3%	6.1%	-1.3%	3.6	Republic of Azerbaijan
268	60 (23)	0.6%	---	---	29.1	Kingdom of Bahrain
5	84,190 (32,506)	6.7%	0.8%	-1.3%	0.2	People's Republic of Bangladesh
34	1,280 (494)	68.0%	---	---	0.5	Kingdom of Bhutan
256	170 (66)	52.8%	---	---	---	Negara Brunei Darussalam
3	38,070 (14,699)	59.2%	18.5%	0.6%	0.0	Kingdom of Cambodia
209	1,548,500 (597,879)	21.2%	7.8%	-0.9%	2.2	People's Republic of China
133	10,660 (4,116)	39.7%	2.3%	0.0%	1.2	Republic of Georgia
46	1,697,390 (655,366)	22.8%	5.2%	-0.1%	1.1	Republic of India
39	344,000 (132,819)	48.8%	20.6%	1.2%	1.3	Republic of Indonesia
220	182,480 (70,456)	6.8%	4.8%	0.0%	4.9	Islamic Republic of Iran
28	60,190 (23,239)	1.9%	0.0%	0.0%	3.3	Republic of Iraq
458	4,280 (1,653)	8.3%	15.8%	-4.9%	10.0	State of Israel
472	47,360 (18,286)	68.2%	6.8%	0.0%	9.3	Japan
114	4,000 (1,544)	0.9%	3.4%	0.0%	3.2	Hashemite Kingdom of Jordan
130	226,860 (87,591)	1.2%	2.7%	-2.2%	8.1	Republic of Kazakhstan
41	29,000 (11,197)	51.4%	2.6%	0.0%	8.5	Democratic People's Republic of Korea
538	18,460 (7,127)	63.5%	6.9%	0.1%	9.1	Republic of Korea
198	180 (69)	0.3%	1.5%	-5.2%	21.9	State of Kuwait
76	13,650 (5,270)	4.5%	12.5%	-2.6%	0.9	Kyrgyz Republic
12	10,310 (3,981)	69.9%	3.6%	0.4%	0.1	Lao People's Democratic Republic
199	3,130 (1,208)	13.3%	0.5%	0.3%	3.5	Lebanese Republic
182	75,850 (29,286)	63.6%	5.7%	1.2%	6.2	Malaysia
102	130 (50)	3.0%	---	---	1.8	Republic of Maldives
56	12,000 (4,633)	6.5%	11.5%	0.5%	3.1	Mongolia
7	109,810 (42,398)	49.0%	0.3%	1.4%	0.2	Union of Myanmar
16	24,900 (9,614)	25.4%	8.9%	1.8%	0.1	Kingdom of Nepal
84	800 (309)	3.1%	14.0%	0.0%	8.2	Sultanate of Oman
27	201,300 (77,722)	2.5%	4.9%	1.1%	0.8	Islamic Republic of Pakistan
41	107,000 (41,313)	24.0%	5.7%	1.4%	1.0	Republic of the Philippines
261	210 (81)	---	---	---	69.6	State of Qatar
155	37,980 (14,664)	1.3%	38.3%	0.0%	18.1	Kingdom of Saudi Arabia
450	20 (8)	3.4%	4.9%	0.0%	14.7	Republic of Singapore
49	19,160 (7,398)	29.9%	13.5%	1.6%	0.6	Democratic Socialist Republic of Sri Lanka
123	54,210 (20,931)	2.5%	---	0.0%	3.3	Syrian Arab Republic
37	10,570 (4,081)	2.9%	4.2%	-0.5%	0.6	Republic of Tajikistan
105	176,870 (68,290)	28.4%	13.9%	0.7%	3.3	Kingdom of Thailand
---	1,900 (734)	53.7%	---	---	---	Democratic Republic of Timor-Leste
268	260,130 (100,437)	13.2%	1.6%	-0.2%	3.3	Republic of Turkey
77	22,660 (8,749)	8.8%	4.2%	0.0%	7.5	Turkmenistan
281	2,540 (981)	3.7%	0.0%	-2.8%	18.1	United Arab Emirates
67	50,400 (19,460)	8.0%	2.0%	-0.2%	4.8	Republic of Uzbekistan
54	89,800 (34,672)	39.7%	3.7%	-0.5%	0.7	Socialist Republic of Vietnam
28	16,690 (6,444)	1.0%	---	1.8%	0.5	Republic of Yemen
						ASIA: TERRITORIES AND AREAS OF SPECIAL STATUS
559	--- ---	---	---	---	5.0	Special Administrative Region of China
---	--- ---	---	---	---	---	Special Administrative Region of China
---	------	---	---	---	---	
---	1,950 (753)	1.5%	---	---	---	Areas of Special Status
---	--- ---	---	---	---	---	Area of Special Status
---	--- ---	---	---	---	---	Area of Special Status
---	--- ---	---	---	---	---	British Overseas Territory
						AFRICA
69	82,150 (31,718)	1.0%	5.0%	-1.3%	2.9	People's Democratic Republic of Algeria
7	35,900 (13,861)	47.4%	6.6%	0.2%	0.5	Republic of Angola
9	29,170 (11,263)	21.3%	11.4%	2.3%	0.3	Republic of Benin
75	3,800 (1,467)	21.1%	18.5%	0.9%	2.3	Republic of Botswana
5	49,000 (18,919)	29.0%	11.5%	0.2%	0.1	Burkina Faso
3	13,550 (5,232)	5.9%	5.7%	9.0%	0.0	Republic of Burundi
7	71,600 (27,645)	45.6%	4.5%	0.9%	0.4	Republic of Cameroon
156	490 (189)	20.7%	---	---	0.3	Republic of Cape Verde
2	20,240 (7,815)	36.5%	8.7%	0.1%	0.1	Central African Republic
2	36,300 (14,016)	9.5%	9.1%	0.6%	0.0	Republic of Chad

CONTINENT/Country	GDP per capita in U.S. dollars Mid-2005 estimate	Services as % of GDP Sector 2003	Industry as % of GDP Sector 2003	Agriculture as % of GDP Sector 2003	Total estimated value of imports in million U.S. dollars 2005	Total estimated value of exports in million U.S. dollars 2005	% of population with access to electricity 2003
Comoros	$600	47.2%	11.9%	40.9%	$115	$34	---
Congo	$1,300	33.8%	60.1%	6.2%	$807	$2,209	20.9%
Congo, Dem. Rep. of the	$700	34.0%	11.0%	55.0%	$1,319	$1,108	6.7%
Côte d'Ivoire (Ivory Coast)	$1,600	55.2%	18.6%	26.2%	$4,759	$6,490	50.0%
Djibouti	$1,300	80.7%	15.8%	3.5%	$987	$250	---
Egypt	$3,900	49.8%	34%	16.1%	$24,100	$14,330	93.8%
Equatorial Guinea	$50,200	4.3%	88.9%	6.8%	$1,864	$6,727	---
Eritrea	$1,000	61.4%	24.7%	13.9%	$677	$33.6	17.0%
Ethiopia	$900	47.4%	10.7%	41.8%	$2,722	$612	4.7%
Gabon	$6,800	29.8%	62.1%	8.1%	$1,533	$5,813	31.0%
Gambia	$1,900	55.2%	14.6%	30.1%	$197	$140.3	---
Ghana	$2,500	39.3%	24.9%	35.8%	$4,273	$2,911	45.0%
Guinea	$2,000	39.0%	36.4%	24.6%	$680	$612	---
Guinea-Bissau	$800	17.9%	13.3%	68.7%	$176	$116	---
Kenya	$1,100	64.7%	19.6%	15.8%	$5,126	$3,173	7.9%
Lesotho	$2,500	39.8%	43.5%	16.6%	$1,166	$603	5.0%
Liberia	$1,000	17.7%	5.4%	76.9%	$4,839	$910	---
Libya	$11,400	45.6%	45.7%	8.7%	$10,820	$30,790	99.8%
Madagascar	$900	55.4%	15.4%	29.2%	$1,400	$951	8.0%
Malawi	$600	46.7%	14.9%	38.4%	$645	$364	5.0%
Mali	$1,200	35.5%	26.1%	38.4%	$1,858	$323	---
Mauritania	$2,200	50.8%	30.0%	19.3%	$1,124	$784	---
Mauritius	$13,100	63.3%	30.6%	6.1%	$2,507	$1,949	100.0%
Morocco	$4,200	53.6%	29.6%	16.8%	$18,150	$9,472	71.1%
Mozambique	$1,300	42.8%	31.2%	26.1%	$2,041	$1,690	7.2%
Namibia	$7,000	63.6%	25.6%	10.8%	$2,350	$2,040	34.0%
Niger	$900	43.4%	16.8%	39.9%	$588	$222	---
Nigeria	$1,400	24.2%	49.5%	26.4%	$25,950	$52,160	40.0%
Rwanda	$1,500	36.5%	21.9%	41.6%	$243	$98	---
Sao Tome and Principe	$1,200	68.4%	14.6%	17.0%	$38	$8	
Senegal	$1,800	62%	21.2%	16.8%	$2,405	$1,526	30.1%
Seychelles	$7,800	61.7%	35.1%	3.3%	$460	$312	---
Sierra Leone	$800	16.5%	30.8%	52.7%	$531	$185	---
Somalia	$600	25.0%	10.0%	65.0%	$576	$241	---
South Africa	$12,000	65.2%	31.0%	3.8%	$52,970	$50,910	66.1%
Sudan	$2,100	41.0%	20.3%	38.7%	$5,028	$6,989	30.0%
Swaziland	$5,000	36.2%	51.5%	12.2%	$2,149	$1,991	---
Tanzania	$700	38.6%	16.4%	45.0%	$2,391	$1,581	10.5%
Togo	$1,700	37.1%	22.2%	40.8%	$1,047	$768	9.0%
Tunisia	$8,300	59.8%	28.1%	12.1%	$12,860	$10,300	94.6%
Uganda	$1,800	46.4%	21.2%	32.4%	$1,608	$768	3.7%
Zambia	$900	50.2%	27%	22.8%	$1,934	$1,947	12.0%
Zimbabwe	$2,300	57.6%	24.3%	18.1%	$2,059	$1,644	39.7%
AFRICA: TERRITORIES AND AREAS OF SPECIAL STATUS							
France							
Mayotte	$2,600	---	---	---	$141	$3.44	---
Réunion	$6,200	73.0%	19.0%	8.0%	$2,500	$214	---
Morocco							
Western Sahara	---	---	---	---	---	---	---
Norway							
Bouvet Island	---	---	---	---	---	---	---
South Africa							
Prince Edward Islands	---	---	---	---	---	---	---
United Kingdom							
Saint Helena	$2,500	87.0%	10.0%	3.0%	$45	$19	---
AUSTRALIA & OCEANIA							
Australia	$31,900	71.2%	25.9%	2.9%	$119,600	$103,000	---
Fiji Islands	$6,000	56.8%	27.0%	16.2%	$1,235	$862	---
Kiribati	$800	74.9%	10.9%	14.2%	$62	$17	---
Marshall Islands	$2,300	70.0%	16.0%	14.0%	$54	$9	---
Micronesia	$3,900	46.0%	4.00%	50.0%	$149	$22	---
Nauru	$5,000	---	---	---	$20	$17	---
New Zealand	$25,200	68.0%	27.4%	4.6%	$24,570	$22,210	---
Palau	$5,800	---	---	---	$99	$18	---
Papua New Guinea	$2,600	35.2%	39.4%	25.7%	$1,651	$2,833	---
Samoa	$5,600	63.0%	23.0%	14.0%	$285	$94	---
Solomon Islands	$1,700	47.0%	11.0%	42.0%	$159	$171	---
Tonga	$2,300	56.4%	15.1%	28.5%	$122	$34	---
Tuvalu	$1,100	---	---	---	$31	$1	---
Vanuatu	$2,900	62.0%	12.0%	26.0%	$233	$205	---
AUSTRALIA & OCEANIA: TERRITORIES AND AREAS OF SPECIAL STATUS							
Australia							
Ashmore and Cartier Islands	---	---	---	---	---	---	---
Christmas Island	---	---	---	---	---	---	---
Cocos (Keeling) Islands	---	---	---	---	---	---	---
Coral Sea Islands Territory	---	---	---	---	---	---	---
Norfolk Island	---	---	---	---	$18	$1.5	---
France							
Clipperton Island	---	---	---	---			---
French Polynesia	$17,500	78.0%	18.0%	4.0%	$1,437	$385	---
New Caledonia	$15,000	65.0%	30.0%	5.0%	$1,636	$999	---
Wallis and Futuna	$3,800	---	---	---	$0.3	$0.25	---
New Zealand							
Cook Islands	$5,000	75.2%	7.8%	17.0%	$51	$9.1	---
Niue	$3,600	---	---	---	$2	$0.137	---
Tokelau	$1,000	---	---	---	$0.3	$0.098	---
United Kingdom							
Pitcairn Islands	---	81.0%	13.6%	5.4%	---	---	---
United States							
American Samoa	$5,800	---	---	---	$105	$10	---
Baker Island	---	---	---	---	---	---	---
Guam	$15,000	78.0%	15.0%	7.0%	$701	$45	---
Northern Mariana Islands	$12,500	---	---	---	---	---	---

Telephone mainlines per 1,000 people 2003	Arable & permanent cropland area 2003 sq km (sq mi)	Forested area as % of total land area 2000	Protected areas as % of total land area 2003	Average annual deforestation: % change 1990 - 2000 *(Negative number indicates an increase in forest area.)*	Carbon dioxide emissions : metric tonnes per capita 2000	CONTINENT / Country Formal Name
17	1,320 (510)	2.9%	- - -	- - -	0.1	Union of the Comoros
2	5,470 (2,112)	65.8%	6.5%	0.1%	0.5	Republic of the Congo
0	78,000 (30,116)	58.9%	5.0%	0.4%	0.1	Democratic Republic of the Congo
14	69,000 (26,641)	32.7%	6.0%	3.1%	0.7	Republic of Côte d'Ivoire
15	10 (4)	0.2%	- - -	- - -	0.6	Republic of Djibouti
127	34,240 (13,220)	0.1%	9.7%	-3.4%	2.2	Arab Republic of Egypt
18	2,300 (888)	58.2%	- - -	- - -	0.4	Republic of Equatorial Guinea
9	5,650 (2,181)	15.4%	4.3%	0.3%	0.1	State of Eritrea
6	117,690 (45,440)	11.9%	16.9%	0.8%	0.1	Federal Democratic Republic of Ethiopia
29	4,950 (1,911)	84.5%	0.7%	0.0%	2.8	Gabonese Republic
28	3,200 (1,236)	41.7%	2.3%	-1.0%	0.2	Republic of The Gambia
13	63,850 (24,653)	24.2%	5.6%	1.7%	0.3	Republic of Ghana
3	17,500 (6,757)	27.4%	0.7%	0.5%	0.2	Republic of Guinea
8	5,500 (2,124)	73.7%	- - -	0.9%	0.2	Republic of Guinea-Bissau
10	52,120 (20,124)	6.2%	8.0%	0.5%	0.3	Republic of Kenya
13	3,340 (1,290)	0.3%	0.2%	0.0%	- - -	Kingdom of Lesotho
- - -	6,020 (2,324)	32.7%	1.7%	2.0%	0.1	Republic of Liberia
136	21,500 (8,301)	0.1%	0.1%	-1.4%	10.9	Great Socialist People's Libyan Arab Jamahiriya
4	35,500 (13,707)	22.1%	4.3%	0.9%	0.1	Republic of Madagascar
8	25,900 (10,000)	36.2%	11.2%	2.4%	0.1	Republic of Malawi
5	47,000 (18,147)	10.3%	3.7%	0.7%	0.1	Republic of Mali
14	5,000 (1,931)	0.3%	1.7%	2.7%	1.2	Islamic Republic of Mauritania
285	1,060 (409)	18.2%	7.8%	0.6%	2.4	Republic of Mauritius
40	93,760 (36,201)	9.8%	0.7%	0.0%	1.3	Kingdom of Morocco
5	45,800 (17,683)	24.6%	8.4%	0.2%	0.1	Republic of Mozambique
66	8,200 (3,166)	9.3%	13.6%	0.9%	1.0	Republic of Namibia
2	145,000 (55,985)	1.0%	7.7%	3.7%	0.1	Republic of Niger
7	334,000 (128,958)	12.2%	3.3%	2.6%	0.3	Federal Republic of Nigeria
3	14,700 (5,676)	19.5%	6.2%	3.9%	0.1	Republic of Rwanda
46	550 (212)	28.4%	- - -	- - -	0.6	Democratic Republic of Sao Tome and Principe
22	25,070 (9,680)	45.0%	11.6%	0.7%	0.4	Republic of Senegal
256	70 (27)	88.9%	- - -	- - -	2.8	Republic of Seychelles
5	6,450 (2,490)	38.5%	2.1%	2.9%	0.1	Republic of Sierra Leone
10	10,710 (4,135)	11.4%	0.8%	1.0%	- - -	Somalia
107	157,120 (60,664)	7.6%	5.5%	0.1%	7.4	Republic of South Africa
27	174,200 (67,259)	28.4%	5.2%	1.4%	0.2	Republic of the Sudan
44	1,920 (741)	31.5%	3.5%	-1.2%	0.4	Kingdom of Swaziland
4	51,000 (19,691)	39.9%	29.8%	0.2%	0.1	United Republic of Tanzania
12	26,300 (10,154)	7.1%	7.9%	3.4%	0.4	Togolese Republic
118	49,300 (19,035)	6.8%	0.3%	-0.2%	1.9	Tunisian Republic
2	73,500 (28,379)	18.4%	24.6%	2.0%	0.1	Republic of Uganda
8	52,890 (20,421)	57.1%	31.9%	2.4%	0.2	Republic of Zambia
26	33,500 (12,934)	45.3%	12.1%	1.5%	1.2	Republic of Zimbabwe
						AFRICA: TERRITORIES AND AREAS OF SPECIAL STATUS
	- - - - - -	14.7%	- - -	- - -	- - -	French Overseas Territorial Collectivity
- - -	390 (151)	33.6%	- - -	- - -	- - -	French Overseas Department
- - -	50 (19)	3.8%	- - -	- - -	- - -	Area of Special Status
- - -	- - - - - -	- - -	- - -	- - -	- - -	Territory of Norway
- - -	- - - - - -	- - -	- - -	- - -	- - -	Territory of South Africa
- - -	40 (15)	6.5%	- - -	- - -	- - -	British Overseas Territory
						AUSTRALIA & OCEANIA
542	479,350 (185,078)	21.3%	13.4%	0.0%	18.0	Commonwealth of Australia
124	2,850 (1,100)	54.7%	- - -	- - -	0.9	Republic of the Fiji Islands
51	370 (143)	3.0%	- - -	- - -	0.3	Republic of Kiribati
83	100 (39)	- - -	- - -	- - -	- - -	Republic
103	360 (139)	90.6%	- - -	- - -	- - -	Federated
- - -	- - - - - -	0.0%	- - -	- - -	- - -	Republic of Nauru
448	33,720 (13,019)	31.0%	29.6%	-0.5%	8.3	New Zealand
- - -	60 (23)	87.6%	- - -	- - -	- - -	Republic of Palau
12	8,750 (3,378)	65.0%	2.3%	0.4%	0.5	Independent State
73	1,290 (498)	60.4%	- - -	- - -	0.8	Independent State of Samoa
13	770 (297)	77.6%	- - -	- - -	0.4	Solomon Islands
113	260 (100)	5.0%	- - -	- - -	1.2	Kingdom of Tonga
	20 (8)	33.3%	- - -	- - -	- - -	Tuvalu
31	1,050 (405)	36.1%	- - -	- - -	0.4	Republic of Vanuatu
						AUSTRALIA & OCEANIA: TERRITORIES AND AREAS OF SPECIAL STATUS
- - -	- - - - - -	- - -	- - -	- - -	- - -	Australian External Territory
- - -	- - - - - -	- - -	- - -	- - -	- - -	Australian External Territory
- - -	- - - - - -	- - -	- - -	- - -	- - -	Australian External Territory
- - -			- - -	- - -	- - -	Australian External Territory
- - -	- - - - - -	- - -	- - -	- - -	- - -	Australian External Territory
- - -	- - - - - -	- - -	- - -	- - -	- - -	French Possession
- - -	250 (97)	28.7%	- - -	- - -	- - -	French Overseas Territory
- - -	10 (4)	39.2%	- - -	- - -	- - -	French Overseas Territory
- - -	60 (23)	35.3%	- - -	- - -	- - -	French Overseas Territory
- - -	60 (23)	66.5%	- - -	- - -	- - -	Self-Governing in Free Association with New Zealand
- - -	70 (27)	54.2%	- - -	- - -	- - -	Self-Governing in Free Association with New Zealand
- - -	- - - - - -	0.0%	- - -	- - -	- - -	Territory of New Zealand
- - -	- - - - - -	83.3%	- - -	- - -	- - -	British Overseas Territory
- - -	50 (19)	89.4%	- - -	- - -	- - -	Territory of the United States
- - -	- - - - - -	- - -	- - -	- - -	- - -	Territory of the United States
- - -	120 (46)	47.1%	- - -	- - -	- - -	Territory of the United States
- - -	80 (31)	72.4%	- - -	- - -	- - -	Commonwealth in Political Union with the United States

GEOGRAPHIC COMPARISONS

THE EARTH

MASS: 5,974,000,000,000,000,000,000 metric tonnes
AREA: 510,066,000 sq km
LAND: 148,647,000 sq km (29.1%)
WATER: 361,419,000 sq km (70.9%)
POPULATION Mid-2005: 6,477,000,000

THE CONTINENTS

	AREA (SQ KM)	PERCENT OF EARTH'S LAND
Asia	44,579,000	30.0
Africa	30,065,000	20.2
North America	24,474,000	16.5
South America	17,819,000	12.0
Antarctica	13,209,000	8.9
Europe	9,938,000	6.7
Australia	7,687,000	5.2

HIGHEST POINT ON EACH CONTINENT

		METERS
1	Everest, Asia	8,850
2	Aconcagua, South America	6,960
3	McKinley (Denali), North America	6,194
4	Kilimanjaro, Africa	5,895
5	El'brus, Europe	5,642
6	Vinson Massif, Antarctica	4,897
7	Kosciuszko, Australia	2,228

LOWEST SURFACE POINT ON EACH CONTINENT

		METERS
1	Dead Sea, Asia	-416
2	Lake Assal, Africa	-156
3	Laguna del Carbón, South America	-105
4	Death Valley, North America	-86
5	Caspian Sea, Europe	-28
6	Lake Eyre, Australia	-16
7	Antarctica (ice covered)	-2,555

POPULATION OF EACH CONTINENT, Mid-2005

	POPULATION	PERCENT OF WORLD TOTAL
Asia	3,921,000,000	60.5
Africa	906,000,000	14.0
Europe	730,000,000	11.3
North America	515,000,000	7.9
South America	373,000,000	5.8
Australia	20,400,000	0.3
Islands of the Pacific	13,000,000	0.2

THE OCEANS

	AREA (SQ KM)	PERCENT OF EARTH'S WATER AREA
Pacific	169,479,000	46.8
Atlantic	91,526,400	25.3
Indian	74,694,800	20.6
Arctic	13,960,100	3.9

DEEPEST POINT IN EACH OCEAN

		METERS
1	Challenger Deep, Mariana Trench, Pacific	10,920
2	Puerto Rico Trench, Atlantic	8,605
3	Java Trench, Indian	7,125
4	Molloy Hole, Arctic	5,669

MAJOR SEAS

		AREA (SQ KM)	AVERAGE DEPTH (METERS)
1	Coral	4,183,510	2,471
2	South China	3,596,390	1,180
3	Caribbean	2,834,290	2,596
4	Bering	2,519,580	1,832
5	Mediterranean	2,469,100	1,572
6	Sea of Okhotsk	1,625,190	814
7	Gulf of Mexico	1,531,810	1,544
8	Norwegian	1,425,280	1,768
9	Greenland	1,157,850	1,443
10	Sea of Japan (East Sea)	1,008,260	1,647
11	Hudson Bay	1,005,510	119
12	East China Sea	785,986	374

LONGEST RIVERS

		LENGTH (KM)
1	Nile, Africa	6,825
2	Amazon, South America	6,437
3	Chang Jiang (Yangtze), Asia	6,380
4	Mississippi-Missouri, North America	5,971
5	Yenisey-Angara, Asia	5,536
6	Huang (Yellow), Asia	5,464
7	Ob-Irtysh, Asia	5,410
8	Amur, Asia	4,416
9	Lena, Asia	4,400
10	Congo, Africa	4,370
11	Mackenzie-Peace, North America	4,241
12	Mekong, Asia	4,184
13	Niger, Africa	4,170

METRIC CONVERSION TABLES

CONVERSION FROM METRIC MEASURES

SYMBOL	WHEN YOU KNOW	MULTIPLY BY	TO FIND	SYMBOL
		LENGTH		
cm	centimeters	0.393701	inches	in
m	meters	3.280840	feet	ft
m	meters	1.093613	yards	yd
km	kilometers	0.621371	miles	mi
		AREA		
cm^2	square centimeters	0.155000	square inches	in^2
m^2	square meters	10.76391	square feet	ft^2
m^2	square meters	1.195990	square yards	yd^2
km^2	square kilometers	0.386102	square miles	mi^2
ha	hectares	2.471054	acres	—
		MASS		
g	grams	0.035274	ounces	oz
kg	kilograms	2.204623	pounds	lb
t	metric tonnes	1.102311	short tons	—
		VOLUME		
mL	milliliters	0.061024	cubic inches	in^3
mL	milliliters	0.033814	liquid ounces	liq oz
L	liters	2.113376	pints	pt
L	liters	1.056688	quarts	qt
L	liters	0.264172	gallons	gal
m^3	cubic meters	35.31467	cubic feet	ft^3
m^3	cubic meters	1.307951	cubic yards	yd^3
		TEMPERATURE		
°C	degrees Celsius (centigrade)	9/5 & add 32	degrees Fahrenheit	°F

CONVERSION TO METRIC MEASURES

SYMBOL	WHEN YOU KNOW	MULTIPLY BY	TO FIND	SYMBOL
		LENGTH		
in	inches	2.54	centimeters	cm
ft	feet	0.3048	meters	m
yd	yards	0.9144	meters	m
mi	miles	1.609344	kilometers	km
		AREA		
in^2	square inches	6.4516	square centimeters	cm^2
ft^2	square feet	0.092903	square meters	m^2
yd^2	square yards	0.836127	square meters	m^2
mi^2	square miles	2.589988	square kilometers	km^2
—	acres	0.404686	hectares	ha
		MASS		
oz	ounces	28.349523	grams	g
lb	pounds	0.453592	kilograms	kg
—	short tons	0.907185	metric tonnes	t
		VOLUME		
in^3	cubic inches	16.387064	milliliters	mL
liq oz	liquid ounces	29.57353	milliliters	mL
pt	pints	0.473176	liters	L
qt	quarts	0.946353	liters	L
gal	gallons	3.785412	liters	L
ft^3	cubic feet	0.028317	cubic meters	m^3
yd^3	cubic yards	0.764555	cubic meters	m^3
		TEMPERATURE		
°F	degrees Fahrenheit	5/9 after subtracting 32	degrees Celsius (centigrade)	°C

URBAN AGGLOMERATIONS, 2005

(Population in thousands)

Tokyo	Japan	35,327
Mexico City	Mexico	19,013
New York-Newark	United States	18,498
Mumbai (Bombay)	India	18,336
São Paulo	Brazil	18,333
Delhi	India	15,334
Kolkata (Calcutta)	India	14,299
Buenos Aires	Argentina	13,349
Jakarta	Indonesia	13,194
Shanghai	China	12,665
Dhaka	Bangladesh	12,560
Los Angeles-Long Beach-Santa Ana,	United States	12,146
Karachi	Pakistan	11,819
Rio de Janeiro	Brazil	11,469
Osaka-Kōbe	Japan	11,286
Cairo	Egypt	11,146
Lagos	Nigeria	11,135
Beijing	China	10,849
Metro Manila	Philippines	10,677
Moscow	Russia	10,672
Paris	France	9,854
Istanbul	Turkey	9,760
Seoul	South Korea	9,592
Tianjin	China	9,346
Chicago	United States	8,711
Lima	Peru	8,180
London	United Kingdom	7,615
Bogotá	Colombia	7,594
Tehran	Iran	7,352
Hong Kong	China,	7,182
Chennai (Madras)	India	6,915
Bangkok	Thailand	6,604
Rhein-Ruhr North (Duisburg, Essen, Krefeld, Mülheim, Oberhausen, Bottrop, Gelsenkirchen, Bochum, Dortmund, Hagen, Hamm and Herne)	Germany	6,566
Bangalore	India	6,532
Lahore	Pakistan	6,373
Hyderabad	India	6,145
Wuhan	China	6,003
Baghdad	Iraq	5,910
Kinshasa	Dem. Rep. Congo	5,717
Santiago	Chile	5,623
Riyadh	Saudi Arabia	5,514
Miami	United States	5,380
Brasília	Brazil	5,341
Philadelphia	United States	5,325
Saint Petersburg	Russia	5,315
Belo Horizonte	Brazil	5,304
Ahmadabad	India	5,171
Madrid	Spain	5,145
Toronto	Canada	5,060
Ho Chi Minh City	Vietnam	5,030
Chongqing	China	4,975
Shenyang	China	4,916
Dallas-Fort Worth	United States	4,612
Khartoum	Sudan	4,495
Pune (Poona)	India	4,485
Barcelona	Spain	4,424
Sydney	Australia	4,388
Singapore	Singapore	4,372
Boston	United States	4,313
Atlanta	United States	4,284
Houston	United States	4,283
Washington, D.C.	United States	4,190
Chittagong	Bangladesh	4,171
Hanoi	Vietnam	4,147
Yangon (Rangoon)	Myanmar (Burma)	4,082
Bandung	Indonesia	4,020
Milan	Italy	4,007
Detroit	United States	3,980
Guadalajara	Mexico	3,881
Jeddah	Saudi Arabia	3,807
Porto Alegre	Brazil	3,795
Alexandria	Egypt	3,760
Casablanca	Morocco	3,743
Rhein-Main (Darmstadt, Frankfurt, Offenbach and Wiesbaden)	Germany	3,721
Surat	India	3,671
Melbourne	Australia	3,663
Ankara	Turkey	3,593
Recife	Brazil	3,527
Busan (Pusan)	South Korea	3,527
Monterrey	Mexico	3,517
Abidjan	Côte d'Ivoire (Ivory Coast)	3,516
Montréal	Canada	3,511
Chengdu	China	3,478
Phoenix-Mesa	United States	3,393
San Francisco-Oakland	United States	3,342
Salvador	Brazil	3,331
Berlin	Germany	3,328
Rhein-Ruhr Middle (Düsseldorf, Mönchengladbach, Remscheid, Solingen and Wuppertal)	Germany	3,325
Kabul	Afghanistan	3,288
Johannesburg	South Africa	3,288
Pyongyang	North Korea	3,284

Abbreviations

- A. *Arroio, Arroyo*
- A. Buryat *Agin Buryat*
- A.C.T. *Australian Capital Territory*
- A.F.B. *Air Force Base*
- A.F.S. *Air Force Station*
- A.R.B. *Air Reserve Base*
- Adm. *Administrative*
- Af. *Africa*
- Afghan. *Afghanistan*
- Ala. *Alabama*
- Alas. *Alaska*
- Alban. *Albania*
- Alg. *Algeria*
- Alta. *Alberta*
- Amer. *America-n*
- Amzns. *Amazonas*
- Anch. *Anchorage*
- And. & Nic. *Andaman and Nicobar Islands*
- And. Prad. *Andhra Pradesh*
- Antil. *Antilles*
- Arch. *Archipelago, Archipiélago*
- Arg. *Argentina*
- Ariz. *Arizona*
- Ark. *Arkansas*
- Arkh. *Arkhangel'sk*
- Arm. *Armenia*
- Arun. Prad. *Arunachal Pradesh*
- Astrak. *Astrakhan'*
- Atl. Oc. *Atlantic Ocean*
- Aust. *Austria*
- Austral. *Australia*
- Auton. *Autonomous*
- Azerb. *Azerbaijan*
- B. *Baai, Baía, Baie, Bahía, Bay, Buḩayrat*
- B. Aires *Buenos Aires*
- B.C. *British Columbia*
- B. Qazaq. *Batys Qazaqstan*
- Bashk. *Bashkortostan*
- Bayq. *Bayqongyr*
- Belg. *Belgium*
- Bol. *Bolivia*
- Bol. *Bol'sh-oy, -aya, -oye*
- Bosn. & Herzg. *Bosnia and Herzegovina*
- Br. *Branch*
- Braz. *Brazil*
- Bulg. *Bulgaria*
- Burya. *Buryatiya*
- C. *Cabo, Cap, Cape, Capo*
- C.H. *Court House*
- C.P. *Conservation Park*
- C.R. *Costa Rica*
- C.S.I. Terr. *Coral Sea Islands Territory*
- Cach. *Cachoeira*
- Calif. *California*
- Can. *Canada*
- Cap. *Capitán*
- Catam. *Catamarca*
- Cd. *Ciudad*
- Cen. Af. Rep. *Central African Republic*
- Cga. *Ciénaga*
- Chan. *Channel*
- Chand. *Chandigarh*
- Chap. *Chapada*
- Chech. *Chechnya*
- Chely. *Chelyabinsk*
- Chhat. *Chhattīsgarh*
- Chongq. *Chongqing Shi*
- Chuk. *Chukotskiy*
- Chuv. *Chuvashiya*
- Chyrv. *Chyrvony, -aya, -aye*
- Cmte. *Comandante*
- Cnel. *Coronel*
- Co.-s. *Cerro-s*
- Col. *Colombia*
- Colo. *Colorado*
- Conn. *Connecticut*
- Cord. *Cordillera*
- Corr. *Corrientes*
- Cr. *Creek, Crique*
- D. *Danau*
- D. & Diu *Daman and Diu*
- D. & Nagar *Dadra and Nagar Haveli*
- D.C. *District of Columbia*
- D.F. *Distrito Federal*
- Del. *Delaware*
- Dem. *Democratic*
- Den. *Denmark*
- Dist. *District, Distrito*
- Dom. Rep. *Dominican Republic*
- Dr. *Doctor*
- Dz. *Dzong*
- E. *East-ern*
- E. Ríos *Entre Ríos*
- E. Santo *Espírito Santo*
- Ea. *Estancia*
- Ecua. *Ecuador*
- El Salv. *El Salvador*
- Emb. *Embalse*
- Eng. *England*
- Ens. *Ensenada*
- Entr. *Entrance*
- Eq. *Equatorial*
- Est. *Estación*
- Est. *Estonia*
- Ét. *Étang*
- Eth. *Ethiopia*
- Eur. *Europe*
- Ez. *Ezers*
- F. *Fiume*
- F.S.M. *Federated States of Micronesia*
- Falk. Is. *Falkland Islands*
- Fd. *Fiord, Fiordo, Fjord*
- Fed. *Federal, Federation*
- Fin. *Finland*
- Fk. *Fork*
- Fla. *Florida*
- Fn. *Fortín*
- Fr. *France, French*
- Ft. *Fort*
- Fy. *Ferry*
- G. *Golfe, Golfo, Gulf*
- G. Altay *Gorno-Altay*
- G.R. *Game Reserve*
- Ga. *Georgia*
- Geb. *Gebergte, Gebirge*
- Gen. *General*
- Ger. *Germany*
- Gez. *Gezîra-t, Gezîret*
- Gezr. *Gezâir*
- Gl. *Glacier*
- Gob. *Gobernador*
- Gr. *Greece,*
- Gr. *Gross-er*
- Gral. *General*
- Gt. *Great-er*
- Guang. *Guangdong*
- H.K. *Hong Kong*
- Hbr. *Harbor, Harbour*
- Hdqrs. *Headquarters*
- Heilong. *Heilongjiang*
- Hi. Prad. *Himachal Pradesh*
- Hist. *Historic, -al*
- Hond. *Honduras*
- Hts. *Heights*
- Hung. *Hungary*
- Hwy. *Highway*
- I.H.S. *International Historic Site*
- I.-s. *Île-s, Ilha-s, Isla-s, Island-s, Isle, Isol-a, -e*
- Ice. *Iceland*
- Ig. *Igarapé*
- Igr. *Ingeniero*
- Ill. *Illinois*
- Ind. *Indiana*
- Ind. Oc. *Indian Ocean*
- Ingush. *Ingushetiya*
- Intl. *International*
- Ire. *Ireland*
- It. *Italy*
- J. *Järvi, Joki*
- J. & Kash. *Jammu and Kashmir*
- J.A.R. *Jewish Autonomous Region*
- Jab., Jeb. *Jabal, Jebel*
- Jam. *Jamaica*
- Jct. *Jonction, Junction*
- Jez. *Jezero, Jezioro*
- Jhark. *Jharkhand*
- K. *Kanal*
- K. Balka. *Kabardino-Balkariya*
- K. Cherk. *Karachayevo-Cherkesiya*
- K. Mansi *Khanty-Mansi*
- K. Permy. *Komi-Permyak*
- Kalin. *Kaliningrad*
- Kalmy. *Kalmykiya*
- Kamchat. *Kamchatka*
- Kans. *Kansas*
- Karna. *Karnataka*
- Kaz. *Kazakhstan*
- Kemer. *Kemerovo*
- Kep. *Kepulauan*
- Kh. *Khor*
- Khabar. *Khabarovsk*
- Khak. *Khakasiya*
- Khr. *Khrebet*
- Km. *Kilómetro*
- Kól. *Kólpos*
- Kör. *Körfez,-i*
- Koryak. *Koryakskiy*
- Kr. *Krasn-yy, -aya, -oye*
- Krasnod. *Krasnodar*
- Krasnoy. *Krasnoyarsk*
- Ky. *Kentucky*
- Kyrg. *Kyrgyzstan*
- L. *Lac, Lago, Lake, Límni, Loch, Lough*
- La. *Louisiana*
- Lag. *Laguna*
- Lakshad. *Lakshadweep*
- Latv. *Latvia*
- Ldg. *Landing*
- Leb. *Lebanon*
- Lib. *Libya*
- Liech. *Liechtenstein*
- Lith. *Lithuania*
- Lux. *Luxembourg*
- M. *Mal-yy, -aya, -oye*
- M.C.A.S. *Marine Corps Air Station*
- M. Gerais *Minas Gerais*
- M. Grosso *Mato Grosso*
- M. Grosso S. *Mato Grosso do Sul*
- M. Prad. *Madhya Pradesh*
- Maced. *Macedonia*
- Mahar. *Maharashtra*
- Mal. *Mal-y-y, -aya, -aye*
- Man. *Manitoba*
- Mangg. *Mangghystaū*
- Maran. *Maranhão*
- Mass. *Massachusetts*
- Md. *Maryland*
- Me. *Maine*
- Medit. Sea *Mediterranean Sea*
- Meghal. *Meghalaya*
- Mex. *Mexico*
- Mgne. *Montagne*
- Mich. *Michigan*
- Minn. *Minnesota*
- Miss. *Mississippi*
- Mo. *Missouri*
- Mold. *Moldova*
- Mon. *Monument*
- Mont. *Montana, Montenegro*
- Mor. *Morocco*
- Mord. *Mordoviya*
- Mt.-s. *Mont-s, Mount-ain-s*
- Mte.-s. *Monte-s*
- Mti., Mtii. *Munţi-i*
- Mun. *Municipal*
- Murm. *Murmansk*
- N. *North-ern*
- N.A.S. *Naval Air Station*
- N.B. *National Battlefield*
- N.B. *New Brunswick*
- N.B.P. *National Battlefield Park*
- N.B.S. *National Battlefield Site*
- N.C. *National Cemetery*
- N.C. *North Carolina*
- N.C.A. *National Conservation Area*
- N. Dak. *North Dakota*
- N.E. *North East*
- N.H. *New Hampshire*
- N.H.P. *National Historic, -al Park*
- N.H.S. *National Historic Site*
- N. Ire. *Northern Ireland*
- N.J. *New Jersey*
- N.L. *National Lakeshore*
- N.M. *National Monument*
- N.M.P. *National Military Park*
- N. Mem. *National Memorial*
- N. Mem. P. *National Memorial Park*
- N. Mex. *New Mexico*
- N. Mongol *Nei Mongol*
- N.P. *National Park*
- N.R. *Nature Reserve*
- N.R.A. *National Recreation Area*
- N.S. *Nova Scotia, National Seashore*
- N.S.R. *National Scenic Riverway*
- N.S.R.A. *National Seashore Recreational Area*
- N.S.T. *National Scenic Trail*
- N.S.W. *New South Wales*
- N.T. *Northern Territory*
- N.T.C. *Naval Training Center*
- N.T.S. *Naval Training Station*
- N.V.M. *National Volcanic Monument*
- N.W.T. *Northwest Territories*
- N.Y. *New York*
- N.Z. *New Zealand*
- Nat. Mem. *National Memorial*
- Nat. Mon. *National Monument*
- Nat. Park *National Park*
- Nebr. *Nebraska*
- Neth. *Netherlands*
- Nev. *Nevada, Nevado*
- Nfld. & Lab. *Newfoundland and Labrador*
- Nicar. *Nicaragua*
- Niz. Nov. *Nizhniy Novgorod*
- Nizh. *Nizhn-iy, -yaya, -eye*
- Nor. *Norway*
- Nov. *Nov-yy, -aya, -aye, -oye*
- Novg. *Novgorod*
- Novo. *Novosibirsk*
- Nr. *Nørre*
- O. *Ostrov, Oued*
- Oc. *Ocean*
- Of. *Oficina*
- Okla. *Oklahoma*
- Ong. Qazaq. *Ongtüstik Qazaqstan*
- Ont. *Ontario*
- Ør. *Øster*
- Oreg. *Oregon*
- Orenb. *Orenburg*
- Oz. *Ozero*
- P. *Paso, Pass, Passo*
- P.E.I. *Prince Edward Island*
- P.N.G. *Papua New Guinea*
- P.R. *Puerto Rico*
- Pa. *Pennsylvania*
- Pac. Oc. *Pacific Ocean*
- Pak. *Pakistan*
- Pan. *Panama*
- Pant. *Pantano*
- Parag. *Paraguay*
- Parq. Nac. *Parque Nacional*
- Pass. *Passage*
- Peg. *Pegunungan*
- Pen. *Peninsula, Péninsule*
- Per. *Pereval*
- Pern. *Pernambuco*
- Pivd. *Pivdennyy*
- Pk. *Peak*
- Pl. *Planina*
- Plat. *Plateau*
- Pol. *Poland*
- Pol. *Poluostrov*
- Pondi. *Pondicherry*
- Por. *Porog*
- Port. *Portugal*
- Pres. *Presidente*
- Prov. *Province, Provincial*
- Pt.-e. *Point-e*
- Pta. *Ponta, Punta*
- Pto. *Puerto*
- Q. *Quebrada*
- Qarag. *Qaraghandy*
- Qnsld. *Queensland*
- Que. *Quebec*
- Qyzyl. *Qyzylorda*
- R. *Rio, River, Rivière*
- R. Gr. Norte *Rio Grande do Norte*
- R. Gr. Sul *Rio Grande do Sul*
- R.I. *Rhode Island*
- R. Jan. *Rio de Janeiro*
- R. Negro *Río Negro*
- Ra.-s. *Range-s*
- Raja. *Rajasthan*
- Reg. *Region*
- Rep. *Republic*
- Res. *Reservoir, Reserve, Reservatório*
- Rk. *Rock*
- Rom. *Romania*
- Russ. *Russia*
- S. *South-ern*
- S.A.R. *Special Administrative Region*
- S. Aust. *South Australia*
- S.C. *South Carolina*
- S. Dak. *South Dakota*
- S. Estero *Santiago del Estero*
- S. Paulo *São Paulo*
- S.W. *Southwest*
- Sa.-s. *Serra, Sierra-s*
- Sal. *Salar, Salina*
- Sask. *Saskatchewan*
- Scot. *Scotland*
- Sd. *Sound*
- Sel. *Selat*
- Ser. *Serranía*
- Serb. *Serbia*
- Sev. *Severn-yy, -aya, -oye*
- Sev. Oset. *Severnaya Osetiya-Alaniya*
- Sgt. *Sargento*
- Shand. *Shandong*
- Shy. Qazaq. *Shyghys Qazaqstan*
- Sk. *Shankou*
- Slov. *Slovenia*
- Solt. Qazaq. *Soltüstik Qazaqstan*
- Sp. *Spain, Spanish*
- Spr.-s. *Spring-s*
- Sq. *Square*
- Sr. *Sønder*
- St.-e. *Saint-e, Sankt, Sint*
- St. Peter. *Saint Petersburg*
- Sta., Sto. *Santa, Station, Santo*
- Sta. Cata. *Santa Catarina*
- Sta. Cruz. *Santa Cruz*
- Stavr. *Stavropol'*
- Str.-s. *Straat, Strait-s*
- Sv. *Svyat-oy, -aya, -oye*
- Sverd. *Sverdlovsk*
- Sw. *Sweden*
- Switz. *Switzerland*
- Syr. *Syria*
- T. Fuego *Tierra del Fuego*
- T. Nadu *Tamil Nadu*
- Taj. *Tajikistan*
- Tartar. *Tartarstan*
- Tas. *Tasmania*
- Tel. *Teluk*
- Tenn. *Tennessee*
- Terr. *Territory*
- Tex. *Texas*
- Tg. *Tanjung*
- Thai. *Thailand*
- Tocant. *Tocantins*
- Trin. *Trinidad*
- Tun. *Tunisia*
- Turk. *Turkey*
- Turkm. *Turkmenistan*
- U.A.E. *United Arab Emirates*
- U.K. *United Kingdom*
- U. O. Buryat *Ust' Ordynskiy Buryat*
- U. Prad. *Uttar Pradesh*
- U.S. *United States*
- Udmur. *Udmurtiya*
- Uj. *Ujung*
- Ukr. *Ukraine*
- Ulyan. *Ul'yanovsk*
- Uru. *Uruguay*
- Uttar. *Uttaranchal*
- Uzb. *Uzbekistan*
- Va. *Virginia*
- Val. *Valle*
- Vdkhr. *Vodokhranilishche*
- Vdskh. *Vodoskhovyshche*
- Venez. *Venezuela*
- Verkh. *Verkhn-iy, -yaya, -eye*
- Vic. *Victoria*
- Vol. *Volcán, Volcano*
- Volg. *Volgograd*
- Voz. *Vozyera, -yero, -yera*
- Vozv. *Vozvyshennost'*
- Vr. *Vester*
- Vt. *Vermont*
- Vyal. *Vyaliki, -ikaya, -ikaye*
- W. *Wadi, Wādī, Webi*
- W. *West-ern*
- W. Aust. *Western Australia*
- W. Bengal *West Bengal*
- W.H. *Water Hole*
- W. Va. *West Virginia*
- Wash. *Washington*
- Wis. *Wisconsin*
- Wyo. *Wyoming*
- Y. Nenets *Yemal-Nenets*
- Yar. *Yarymadasy*
- Yaro. *Yaroslavl'*
- Yu. *Yuzhn-yy, -aya, -oye*
- Zakh. *Zakhod-ni, -nyaya, -nye*
- Zal. *Zaliv*
- Zap. *Zapadn-yy, -aya, -oye*
- Zimb. *Zimbabwe*

Foreign Terms

- Aaglet *well*
- Aain *spring*
- Aauinat *spring*
- Āb *river, water*
- Ache *stream*
- Açude *reservoir*
- Ada,-si *island*
- Adrar *mountain-s, plateau*
- Aguada *dry lake bed*
- Aguelt *water hole, well*
- 'Ain, Aïn *spring, well*
- Aïoun-et *spring-s, well*
- Aivi *mountain*
- Akra, Akrotírio *cape, promontory*
- Alb *mountain, ridge*
- Alföld *plain*
- Alin' *mountain range*
- Alpe-n *mountain-s*
- Altiplanicie *high-plain, plateau*
- Alto *hill-s, mountain-s, ridge*
- Älv-en *river*
- Āmba *hill, mountain*
- Anou *well*
- Anse *bay, inlet*
- Ao *bay, cove, estuary*
- Ap *cape, point*
- Archipel, Archipiélago *archipelago*
- Arcipelago, Arkhipelag *archipelago*
- Arquipélago *archipelago*
- Arrecife-s *reef-s*
- Arroio, Arroyo *brook, gully, rivulet, stream*
- Ås *ridge*
- Ava *channel*
- Aylagy *gulf*
- 'Ayn *spring, well*

- Ba *intermittent stream,river*
- Baai *bay, cove, lagoon*
- Bāb *gate, strait*
- Badia *bay*
- Bælt *strait*
- Bagh *bay*
- Bahar *drainage basin*
- Bahía *bay*
- Bahr, Baḩr *bay, lake, river, sea, wadi*
- Baía, Baie *bay*
- Bajo-s *shoal-s*
- Ban *village*
- Bañado-s *flooded area, swamp-s*
- Banc, Banco-s *bank-s, sandbank-s, shoal-s*
- Bandao *peninsula*
- Baño-s *hot spring-s, spa*
- Baraj-ı *dam, reservoir*
- Barra *bar, sandbank*
- Barrage, Barragem *dam, lake, reservoir*
- Barranca *gorge, ravine*
- Bazar *marketplace*
- Ben, Benin *mountain*
- Belt *strait*
- Bereg *bank, coast, shore*
- Berg-e *mountain-s*
- Bil *lake*
- Biq'at *plain, valley*
- Bir, Bîr, Bi'r *spring, well*
- Birket *lake, pool, swamp*
- Bjerg-e *mountain-s, range*
- Boca, Bocca *channel, river, mouth*
- Bocht *bay*
- Bodden *bay*
- Boğaz, -ı *strait*
- Bögeni *reservoir*
- Boka *gulf, mouth*
- Bol'sh-oy, -aya, -oye *big*
- Bolsón *inland basin*
- Boubairet *lagoon, lake*
- Bras *arm, branch of a stream*
- Braţ, -ul *arm, branch of a stream*
- Bre, -en *glacier, ice cap*
- Bredning *bay, broad water*
- Bruch *marsh*
- Bucht *bay*
- Bugt-en *bay*
- Buḩayrat, Buheirat *lagoon, lake,marsh*
- Bukhta, Bukta, Bukt-en *bay*
- Bulak, Bulaq *spring*
- Bum *hill, mountain*
- Burnu, Burun *cape, point*
- Busen *gulf*
- Buuraha *hill-s, mountain-s*
- Buyuk *big, large*

- Cabeza-s *head-s, summit-s*
- Cabo *cape*
- Cachoeira *rapids, waterfall*
- Cal *hill, peak*
- Caleta *cove, inlet*
- Campo-s *field-s, flat country*
- Canal *canal, channel, strait*
- Caño *channel, stream*
- Cao Nguyen *mountain, plateau*
- Cap, Capo *cape*
- Capitán *captain*
- Càrn *mountain*
- Castillo *castle, fort*
- Catarata-s *cataract-s, waterfall-s*
- Causse *upland*
- Çay *brook, stream*
- Cay-s, Cayo-s *island-s, key-s, shoal-s*
- Cerro-s *hill-s, peak-s*
- Chaîne, Chaînons *mountain chain, range*
- Chapada-s *plateau, upland-s*
- Chedo *archipelago*
- Chenal *river channel*
- Chersónisos *peninsula*
- Chhung *bay*
- Chi *lake*
- Chiang *bay*
- Chiao *cape, point, rock*
- Ch'ih *lake*
- Chink *escarpment*
- Chott *intermittent salt lake, salt marsh*
- Chou *island*
- Ch'ü *canal*
- Ch'üntao *archipelago, islands*
- Chute-s *cataract-s, waterfall-s*
- Chyrvony *red*
- Cima *mountain, peak, summit*
- Ciudad *city*
- Co *lake*
- Col *pass*
- Collina, Colline *hill, mountains*
- Con *island*
- Cordillera *mountain chain*
- Corno *mountain, peak*
- Coronel *colonel*
- Corredeira *cascade, rapids*
- Costa *coast*
- Côte *coast, slope*
- Coxilha, Cuchilla *range of low hills*
- Crique *creek, stream*
- Csatorna *canal, channel*
- Cul de Sac *bay, inlet*

- Da *great, greater*
- Daban *pass*
- Dağ, -ı, Dāgh *mountain*
- Dağlar, -ı *mountains*
- Dahr *cliff, mesa*
- Dake *mountain, peak*
- Dal-en *valley*
- Dala *steppe*
- Dan *cape, point*
- Danau *lake*
- Dao *island*
- Dar'ya *lake, river*
- Daryācheh *lake, marshy lake*
- Dasht *desert, plain*
- Dawan *pass*
- Dawḩat *bay, cove, inlet*
- Deniz, -i *sea*
- Dent-s *peak-s*
- Deo *pass*
- Desët *hummock, island, land-tied island*
- Desierto *desert*
- Détroit *channel, strait*
- Dhar *hills, ridge, tableland*
- Ding *mountain*
- Distrito *district*
- Djebel *mountain, range*
- Do *island-s, rock-s*
- Doi *hill, mountain*
- Dome *ice dome*
- Dong *village*
- Dooxo *floodplain*
- Dzong *castle, fortress*

- Eiland-en *island-s*
- Eilean *island*
- Ejland *island*
- Elv *river*
- Embalse *lake, reservoir*
- Emi *mountain, rock*
- Enseada, Ensenada *bay, cove*
- Ér *rivulet, stream*
- Erg *sand dune region*
- Est,e *east*
- Estación *railroad station*
- Estany *lagoon, lake*
- Estero *estuary, inlet, lagoon, marsh*
- Estrecho *strait*
- Étang *lake, pond*
- Eylandt *island*
- Ežeras *lake*
- Ezers *lake*

Falaise *cliff, escarpment*
Farvand-et *channel, sound*
Fell *mountain*
Feng *mount, peak*
Fiord-o *inlet, sound*
Fiume *river*
Fjäll-et *mountain*
Fjällen *mountains*
Fjärd-en *fjord*
Fjardar, Fjördur *fjord*
Fjeld *mountain*
Fjell-ene *mountain-s*
Fjöll *mountain-s*
Fjord-en *inlet, fjord*
Fleuve *river*
Fljót *large river*
Flói *bay, marshland*
Foci *river mouths*
Főcsatorna *principal canal*
Förde *fjord, gulf, inlet*
Forsen *rapids, waterfall*
Fortaleza *fort, fortress*
Fortín *fortified post*
Foss-en *waterfall*
Foum *pass, passage*
Foz *mouth of a river*
Fuerte *fort, fortress*
Fwafwate *waterfalls*

Gacan-ka *hill, peak*
Gal *pond, spring, waterhole, well*
Gang *harbor*
Gangri *peak, range*
Gaoyuan *plateau*
Garaet, Gara'et *lake, lake bed, salt lake*
Gardaneh *pass*
Garet *hill, mountain*
Gat *channel*
Gata *bay, inlet, lake*
Gattet *channel, strait*
Gaud *depression, saline tract*
Gave *mountain stream*
Gebel *mountain-s, range*
Gebergte *mountain range*
Gebirge *mountains, range*
Geçidi *mountain pass, passage*
Geçit *mountain pass, passage*
Gezâir *islands*
Gezîra-t, Gezîret *island, peninsula*
Ghats *mountain range*
Ghubb-at, -et *bay, gulf*
Giri *mountain*
Gjiri *bay*
Gletscher *glacier*
Gobernador *governor*
Gobi *desert*
Gol *river, stream*
Göl, -ü *lake*
Golets *mountain, peak*
Golf, -e, -o *gulf*
Gor-a, -y, Gór-a, -y *mountain,-s*
Got *point*
Gowd *depression*
Goz *sand ridge*
Gran, -de *great, large*
Gryada *mountains, ridge*
Guan *pass*
Guba *bay, gulf*
Guelta *well*
Guntō *archipelago*
Gunung *mountain*
Gura *mouth, passage*
Guyot *table mount*

Ḥadabat *plateau*
Haehyŏp *strait*
Haff *lagoon*
Hai *lake, sea*
Haihsia *strait*
Haixia *channel, strait*
Hakau *reef, rock*
Hakuchi *anchorage*
Halvø, Halvøy-a *peninsula*
Hama *beach*
Hamada, Ḩammādah *rocky desert*
Hamn *harbor, port*
Hāmūn, Hamun *depression, lake*
Hana *cape, point*
Hantō *peninsula*
Har *hill, mound, mountain*
Ḩarrat *lava field*
Hasi, Hassi *spring, well*
Hauteur *elevation, height*
Hav-et *sea*
Havn, Havre *harbor, port*
Hawr *lake, marsh*
Hāyk' *lake, reservoir*
Hegy, -ség *mountain, -s, range*
Heiau *temple*
Ho *canal, lake, river*
Hoek *hook, point*
Hög-en *high, hill*
Höhe, -n *height, high*
Høj *height, hill*
Holm, -e, Holmene *island-s, islet -s*
Holot *dunes*
Hon *island-s*
Hor-a, -y *mountain, -s*
Horn *horn, peak*
Houma *point*
Hoved *headland, peninsula, point*
Hraun *lava field*
Hsü *island*
Hu *lake, reservoir*
Huk *cape, point*
Hüyük *hill, mound*

Idehan *sand dunes*
Île-s, Ilha-s, Illa-s, Îlot-s *island-s, islet-s*
Îlet, Ilhéu-s *islet, -s*
Irhil *mountain-s*
'Irq *sand dune-s*
Isblink *glacier, ice field*
Is-en *glacier*
Isla-s, Islote *island-s, islet*
Isol-a, -e *island, -s*
Istmo *isthmus*
Iwa *island, islet, rock*

Jabal, Jebel *mountain-s, range*
Järv, -i, Jaure, Javrre *lake*
Jazā'ir, Jazīrat, Jazīreh *island-s*
Jehīl *lake*
Jezero, Jezioro *lake*
Jiang *river, stream*
Jiao *cape*
Jibal *hill, mountain, ridge*
Jima *island-s, rock-s*
Jøkel, Jökull *glacier, ice cap*
Joki, Jokka *river*
Jökulsá *river from a glacier*
Jūn *bay*

Kaap *cape*
Kafr *village*
Kaikyō *channel, strait*
Kaise *mountain*
Kaiwan *bay, gulf, sea*
Kanal *canal, channel*
Kangri *mountain, peak*
Kap, Kapp *cape*
Kavīr *salt desert*
Kefar *village*
Kënet' *lagoon, lake*
Kep *cape, point*
Kepulauan *archipelago, islands*
Khalīg, Khalīj *bay, gulf*
Khirb-at, -et *ancient site, ruins*
Khrebet *mountain range*
Kinh *canal*
Klint *bluff, cliff*
Kō *bay, cove, harbor*
Ko *island, lake*
Koh *island, mountain, range*
Köl-i *lake*
Kólpos *gulf*
Kong *mountain*
Körfez, -i *bay, gulf*
Kosa *spit of land*
Kou *estuary, river mouth*
Kowtal-e *pass*
Krasn-yy, -aya, -oye *red*
Kryazh *mountain range, ridge*
Kuala *estuary, river mouth*
Kuan *mountain pass*
Kūh, Kūhhā *mountain-s, range*
Kul', Kuli *lake*
Kum *sandy desert*
Kundo *archipelago*
Kuppe *hill-s, mountain-s*
Kust *coast, shore*
Kyst *coast*
Kyun *island*

La *pass*
Lac, Lac-ul, -us *lake*
Lae *cape, point*
Lago, -a *lagoon, lake*
Lagoen, Lagune *lagoon*
Laguna-s *lagoon-s, lake-s*
Laht *bay, gulf, harbor*
Laje *reef, rock ledge*
Laut *sea*
Lednik *glacier*
Leida *channel*
Lhari *mountain*
Li *village*
Liedao *archipelago, islands*
Liehtao *archipelago, islands*
Liman-ı *bay, estuary*
Límni *lake*
Ling *mountain-s, range*
Linn *pool, waterfall*
Lintasan *passage*
Liqen *lake*
Llano-s *plain-s*
Loch, Lough *lake, arm of the sea*
Loma-s *hill-s, knoll-s*

Mal *mountain, range*
Mal-yy, -aya, -oye *little, small*
Mamarr *pass, path*
Man *bay*
Mar, Mare *large lake, sea*
Marsa, Marsá *bay, inlet*
Masabb *mouth of river*
Massif *massif, mountain-s*
Mauna *mountain*
Mēda *plain*
Meer *lake, sea*
Melkosopochnik *undulating plain*
Mesa, Meseta *plateau, tableland*
Mierzeja *sandspit*
Minami *south*
Mios *island*
Misaki *cape, peninsula, point*
Mochun *passage*
Mong *town, village*
Mont-e, -i, -s *mount, -ain, -s*
Montagne, -s *mount, -ain, -s*
Montaña, -s *mountain, -s*
More *sea*
Morne *hill, peak*
Morro *bluff, headland, hill*
Motu, -s *islands*
Mouïet *well*
Mouillage *anchorage*
Muang *town, village*
Mui *cape, point*
Mull *headland, promontory*
Munkhafad *depression*
Munte *mountain*
Munţi-i *mountains*
Muong *town, village*
Mynydd *mountain*
Mys *cape*

Nacional *national*
Nada *gulf, sea*
Næs, Näs *cape, point*
Nafūd *area of dunes, desert*
Nagor'ye *mountain range, plateau*
Nahar, Nahr *river, stream*
Nakhon *town*
Namakzār *salt waste*
Ne *island, reef, rock-s*
Neem *cape, point, promontory*
Nes, Ness *peninsula, point*
Nevado-s *snow-capped mountain-s*
Nez *cape, promontory*
Ni *village*
Nísi, Nísia, Nisís, Nísoi *island-s, islet-s*
Nisidhes *islets*
Nizhn-iy, -yaya, -eye *lower*
Nizmennost' *low country*
Noord *north*
Nord-re *north-ern*
Nørre *north-ern*
Nos *cape, nose, point*
Nosy *island, reef, rock*
Nov-yy, -aya, -oye *new*
Nudo *mountain*
Numa *lake*
Nunatak, -s, -ker *peak-s surrounded by ice cap*
Nur *lake, salt lake*
Nuruu *mountain range, ridge*
Nut-en *peak*
Nuur *lake*

O-n, Ø-er *island-s*
Oblast' *administrative division, province, region*
Oceanus *ocean*
Odde-n *cape, point*
Øer-ne *islands*
Oficina *nitrate plant (local usage in Chile)*
Oglat *group of wells*
Oguilet *well*
Ór-os, -i *mountain, -s*
Órmos *bay, port*
Ort *place, point*
Øst-er *east*
Ostrov, -a, Ostrv-o, -a *island, -s*
Otoci, Otok *islands, island*
Ouadi, Oued *river, watercourse*
Øy-a *island*
Øyane *islands*
Ozer-o, -a *lake, -s*

Pää *mountain, point*
Palus *marsh*
Pampa-s *grassy plain-s*
Pantà *lake, reservoir*
Pantanal *marsh, swamp*
Pao, P'ao *lake*
Parbat *mountain*
Parque *park*
Pas, -ul *pass*
Paso, Passo *pass*
Passe *channel, pass*
Pasul *pass*
Pedra *rock*
Pegunungan *mountain range*
Pellg *bay, bight*
Peña *cliff, rock*
Pendi *basin*
Penedo-s *rock-s*
Péninsule *peninsula*
Peñón *point, rock*
Pereval *mountain pass*
Pertuis *strait*
Peski *sands, sandy region*
Phnom *hill, mountain, range*
Phou *mountain range*
Phu *mountain*
Piana-o *plain*
Pic, Pik, Piz *peak*
Picacho *mountain, peak*
Pico-s *peak-s*
Pistyll *waterfall*
Piton-s *peak-s*
Pivdennyy *southern*
Plaja, Playa *beach, inlet, shore*
Planalto, Plato *plateau*
Planina *mountain, plateau*
Plassen *lake*
Ploskogor'ye *plateau, upland*
Pointe *point*
Polder *reclaimed land*
Poluostrov *peninsula*
Pongo *water gap*
Ponta, -l *cape, point*
Ponte *bridge*
Poolsaar *peninsula*
Portezuelo *pass*
Porto *port*
Poulo *island*
Praia *beach, seashore*
Presa *reservoir*
Presidente *president*
Presqu'île *peninsula*
Prokhod *pass*
Proliv *strait*
Promontorio *promontory*
Průsmyk *mountain pass*
Przylądek *cape*
Puerto *bay, pass, port*
Pulao *island-s*
Pulau, Pulo *island*
Puncak *peak, summit, top*
Punt, Punta, -n *point, -s*
Pun *peak*
Pu'u *hill, mountain*
Puy *peak*

Qā' *depression, marsh, mud flat*
Qal'at *fort*
Qal'eh *castle, fort*
Qanâ *canal*
Qārat *hill-s, mountain-s*
Qaşr *castle, fort, hill*
Qila *fort*
Qiryat *settlement, suburb*
Qolleh *peak*
Qooriga *anchorage, bay*
Qoz *dunes, sand ridge*
Qu *canal*
Quebrada *ravine, stream*
Qullai *peak, summit*
Qum-y *desert, sand*
Qundao *archipelago, islands*
Qurayyāt *hills*

Raas *cape, point*
Rabt *hill*
Rada *roadstead*
Rade *anchorage, roadstead*
Rags *point*
Ramat *hill, mountain*
Rand *ridge of hills*
Rann *swamp*
Raqaba *wadi, watercourse*
Ras, Râs, Ra's *cape*
Ravnina *plain*
Récif-s *reef-s*
Regreg *marsh*
Represa *reservoir*
Reservatório *reservoir*
Reshten *hill, mountain*
Restinga *barrier, sand area*
Rettō *chain of islands*
Ri *mountain range, village*
Ría *estuary*
Ribeirão *stream*
Río, Rio *river*
Rivière *river*
Roca-s *cliff, rock-s*
Roche-r, -s *rock-s*
Rosh *mountain, point*
Rt *cape, point*
Rubha *headland*
Rupes *scarp*

Saar *island*
Saari, Sari *island*
Sabkha-t, Sabkhet *lagoon, marsh, salt lake*
Sagar *lake, sea*
Sahara, Şaḩrā' *desert*
Sahl *plain*
Saki *cape, point*
Salar *salt flat*
Salina *salt pan*
Salin-as, -es *salt flat-s, salt marsh-es*
Salto *waterfall*
Sammyaku *mountain range*
San *hill, mountain*
San, -ta, -to *saint*
Sandur *sandy area*
Sankt *saint*
Sanmaek *mountain range*
São *saint*
Sarīr *gravel desert*
Sasso *mountain, stone*
Savane *savanna*
Scoglio *reef, rock*
Se *reef, rock-s, shoal-s*
Sebjet *salt lake, salt marsh*
Sebkha *salt lake, salt marsh*
Sebkhet *lagoon, salt lake*
See *lake, sea*
Selat *strait*
Selkä *lake, ridge*
Semenanjung *peninsula*
Sen *mountain*
Seno *bay, gulf*
Serra, Serranía *range of hills or mountains*
Severn-yy, -aya, -oye *northern*
Sgùrr *peak*
Sha *island, shoal*
Sha'īb *ravine, watercourse*
Shamo *desert*
Shan *island-s, mountain-s, range*
Shankou *mountain pass*
Shanmo *mountain range*
Sharm *cove, creek, harbor*
Shatt, Shaţţ *large river*
Shi *administrative division, municipality*
Shima *island-s, rock-s*
Shō *island, reef, rock*
Shotō *archipelago*
Shott *intermittent salt lake*
Shuiku *reservoir*
Shuitao *channel*
Shyghanaghy *bay, gulf*
Sierra *mountain range*
Silsilesi *mountain chain, ridge*
Sint *saint*
Sinus *bay, sea*
Sjö-n *lake*
Skarv-et *barren mountain*
Skerry *rock*
Slieve *mountain*
Sø *lake*
Sønder, Søndre *south-ern*
Sopka *conical mountain, volcano*
Sor *lake, salt lake*
Sør, Sör *south-ern*
Sory *salt lake, salt marsh*
Spitz-e *peak, point, top*
Sredn-iy, -yaya, -eye *central, middle*
Stagno *lake, pond*
Stantsiya *station*
Stausee *reservoir*
Stenón *channel, strait*
Step'-i *steppe-s*
Štít *summit, top*
Stor-e *big, great*
Straat *strait*
Straum-en *current-s*
Strelka *spit of land*
Stretet, Stretto *strait*
Su *reef, river, rock, stream*
Sudo *channel, strait*
Suidō *channel, strait*
Şummān *rocky desert*
Sund *sound, strait*
Sunden *channel, inlet, sound*
Svyat-oy, -aya, -oye *holy, saint*
Sziget *island*

Tagh *mountain-s*
Tall *hill, mound*
T'an *lake*
Tanezrouft *desert*
Tang *plain, steppe*
Tangi *peninsula, point*
Tanjong, Tanjung *cape, point*
Tao *island-s*
Tarso *hill-s, mountain-s*
Tassili *plateau, upland*
Tau *mountain-s, range*
Taūy *hills, mountains*
Tchabal *mountain-s*
Tel-l *hill, mound*
Telok, Teluk *bay*
Tepe, -si *hill, peak*
Tepuí *mesa, mountain*
Terara *hill, mountain, peak*
Testa *bluff, head*
Thale *lake*
Thang *plain, steppe*
Tien *lake*
Tierra *land, region*
Ting *hill, mountain*
Tir'at *canal*
Tō *lake, pool*
To, Tō *island-s, rock-s*
Tonle *lake*
Tope *hill, mountain, peak*
Top-pen *peak-s*
Träsk *bog, lake*
Tso *lake*
Tsui *cape, point*
Tübegi *peninsula*
Tulu *hill, mountain*
Tunturi-t *hill-s, mountain-s*

Uad *wadi, watercourse*
Udde-m *point*
Ujong, Ujung *cape, point*
Umi *bay, lagoon, lake*
Ura *bay, inlet, lake*
'Urūq *dune area*
Uul, Uula *mountain, range*
'Uyûn *springs*

Vaara *mountain*
Vaart *canal*
Vær *fishing station*
Vaïn *channel, strait*
Valle, Vallée *valley, wadi*
Vallen *waterfall*
Valli *lagoon, lake*
Vallis *valley*
Vanua *land*
Varre *mountain*
Vatn, Vatten, Vatnet *lake, water*
Veld *grassland, plain*
Verkhn-iy, -yaya, -eye *higher, upper*
Vesi *lake, water*
Vest-er *west*
Via *road*
Vidda *plateau*
Vig, Vík, Vik, -en *bay, cove*
Vinh *bay, gulf*
Vodokhranilishche *reservoir*
Vodoskhovyshche *reservoir*
Volcan, Volcán *volcano*
Vostochn-yy, -aya, -oye *eastern*
Vötn *stream*
Vozvyshennost' *plateau, upland*
Vozyera *lake-s*
Vrchovina *mountains*
Vrch-y *mountain-s*
Vrh *hill, mountain*
Vrŭkh *mountain*
Vyaliki *big, large*
Vysočina *highland*

Wabē *stream*
Wadi, Wâdi, Wādī *valley, watercourse*
Wâhât, Wāḩat *oasis*
Wald *forest, wood*
Wan *bay, gulf*
Water *harbor*
Webi *stream*
Wiek *cove, inlet*

Xia *gorge, strait*
Xiao *lesser, little*

Yanchi *salt lake*
Yang *ocean*
Yarımadası *peninsula*
Yazovir *reservoir*
Yŏlto *island group*
Yoma *mountain range*
Yü *island*
Yumco *lake*
Yunhe *canal*
Yuzhn-yy, -aya, -oye *southern*

Zaki *cape, point*
Zaliv *bay, gulf*
Zan *mountain, ridge*
Zangbo *river, stream*
Zapadn-yy, -aya, -oye *western*
Zatoka *bay, gulf*
Zee *bay, sea*
Zemlya *land*
Zhotasy *mountains*

A

150 Mile House, *Can.* 52°7′ N, 121°57′ W **108**
19 de Abril, *Uru.* 34°23′ S, 54°5′ W **139**
23 August, *Rom.* 43°55′ N, 28°35′ E **156**
25 de Mayo, *Arg.* 35°26′ S, 60°12′ W **139**
26 Baky Komissary, *Azerb.* 39°18′ N, 49°10′ E **195**
2nd Cataract, fall(s), *Sudan* 21°54′ N, 30°50′ E **226**
31 de Janeiro, *Angola* 6°53′ S, 15°18′ E **218**
31 de Março, Pico, peak, *Braz.* 0°48′ N, 65°60′ W **136**
3rd Cataract, fall(s), *Sudan* 19°55′ N, 29°47′ E **226**
6th Cataract, fall(s), *Sudan* 16°29′ N, 32°36′ E **182**
9 de Julio, *Arg.* 35°26′ S, 60°54′ W **139**
A Coruña, *Sp.* 43°21′ N, 8°27′ W **150**
Aa, river, *Ger.* 52°26′ N, 7°28′ E **163**
Aachen, *Ger.* 50°46′ N, 6°5′ E **167**
Aagaard Islands, *Indian Ocean* 65°36′ S, 52°31′ E **248**
Aalsmeer, *Neth.* 52°15′ N, 4°45′ E **163**
Aalst, *Belg.* 50°56′ N, 4°2′ E **163**
Aalten, *Neth.* 51°55′ N, 6°34′ E **167**
Äänekoski, *Fin.* 62°36′ N, 25°41′ E **152**
Aansluit, *S. Af.* 26°46′ S, 22°30′ E **227**
Aapajärvi, *Fin.* 67°13′ N, 27°16′ E **152**
Aarau, *Switz.* 47°22′ N, 8°1′ E **156**
Aare, river, *Switz.* 47°6′ N, 7°20′ E **165**
Aarschot, *Belg.* 50°58′ N, 4°49′ E **167**
Aasiaat (Egedesminde), *Den.* 68°45′ N, 52°53′ W **106**
Aavasaksa, *Fin.* 66°23′ N, 23°42′ E **152**
Aba, *Dem. Rep. of the Congo* 3°51′ N, 30°17′ E **224**
Aba, *Nig.* 5°9′ N, 7°23′ E **222**
Abā as Sa'ūd, *Saudi Arabia* 17°27′ N, 44°8′ E **182**
Abacaxis, river, *Braz.* 5°29′ S, 58°39′ W **130**
Abaclia, *Mold.* 46°22′ N, 28°55′ E **156**
Abaco Island, *Bahamas* 26°0′ N, 77°0′ W **118**
Abaco Islands, *North Atlantic Ocean* 27°0′ N, 77°0′ W **118**
Abadab, Jebel, peak, *Sudan* 18°52′ N, 35°52′ E **182**
Ābādān, *Iran* 30°20′ N, 48°21′ E **180**
Ābādeh, *Iran* 31°6′ N, 52°39′ E **180**
Abádszalók, *Hung.* 47°29′ N, 20°35′ E **168**
Abaeté, *Braz.* 19°9′ S, 45°25′ W **138**
Abaetetuba, *Braz.* 1°45′ S, 48°54′ W **130**
Abag Qi (Xin Hot), *China* 44°1′ N, 114°56′ E **198**
Abaí, *Parag.* 26°1′ S, 55°53′ W **139**
Abaji, *Nig.* 8°28′ N, 6°55′ E **222**
Abajo Mountains, *Utah, U.S.* 37°57′ N, 109°50′ W **90**
Abajo Peak, *Utah, U.S.* 37°49′ N, 109°31′ W **92**
Abak, *Nig.* 4°57′ N, 7°47′ E **222**
Abakaliki, *Nig.* 6°17′ N, 8°5′ E **222**
Abakan, *Russ.* 53°42′ N, 91°25′ E **184**
Abakan, river, *Russ.* 52°22′ N, 89°24′ E **184**
Abala, *Congo* 1°19′ S, 15°34′ E **218**
Abala, spring, *Niger* 14°56′ N, 3°27′ E **222**
Abalak, *Niger* 15°19′ N, 6°11′ E **222**
Abalemma, spring, *Alg.* 20°57′ N, 5°55′ E **222**
Abalemma, spring, *Niger* 16°18′ N, 7°49′ E **222**
Abalessa, *Alg.* 22°55′ N, 4°49′ E **214**
Abancay, *Peru* 13°40′ S, 72°52′ W **137**
Abapó, *Bol.* 18°52′ S, 63°30′ W **137**
Ābār al Hazīm, spring, *Jordan* 31°35′ N, 37°13′ E **194**
Abâr el Kanâyis, spring, *Egypt* 31°0′ N, 26°47′ E **180**
Abarán, *Sp.* 38°12′ N, 1°24′ W **164**
Abarqū, *Iran* 31°6′ N, 53°19′ E **180**
Abasān, *Gaza Strip* 31°18′ N, 34°21′ E **194**
Abashiri, *Japan* 43°53′ N, 144°8′ E **190**
Abasolo, *Mex.* 27°10′ N, 101°26′ W **96**
Abasolo, *Mex.* 25°18′ N, 104°41′ W **114**
Abasolo, *Mex.* 24°2′ N, 98°23′ W **114**
Abast'umani, *Ga.* 41°45′ N, 42°48′ E **195**
Abatskiy, *Russ.* 56°15′ N, 70°27′ E **184**
Abau, *P.N.G.* 10°10′ S, 148°43′ E **192**
Abava, river, *Latv.* 57°6′ N, 22°18′ E **166**
Abay, *Kaz.* 41°18′ N, 68°51′ E **197**
Ābay (Blue Nile), river, *Eth.* 11°15′ N, 38°15′ E **224**
Ābaya Hāyk', lake, *Eth.* 6°24′ N, 37°45′ E **224**
Abaza, *Russ.* 52°42′ N, 90°7′ E **184**
Abba, *Cen. Af. Rep.* 5°18′ N, 15°9′ E **218**
Abbaye, Point, *Mich., U.S.* 46°59′ N, 88°13′ W **94**
Abbeville, *Ala., U.S.* 31°33′ N, 85°15′ W **96**
Abbeville, *Fr.* 50°5′ N, 1°49′ E **163**
Abbeville, *La., U.S.* 29°57′ N, 92°8′ W **103**
Abbey, *Can.* 50°43′ N, 108°46′ W **90**
Abbotsford, *Can.* 49°2′ N, 122°17′ W **100**
Abbotsford, *Wis., U.S.* 44°57′ N, 90°19′ W **110**
Abbotsford, site, *U.K.* 55°34′ N, 2°51′ W **150**
Abbottabad, *Pak.* 34°7′ N, 73°14′ E **186**
'Abda (Eboda), ruin(s), *Israel* 30°47′ N, 34°43′ E **194**
Abdelmalek Ramdan, *Alg.* 36°6′ N, 0°15′ E **150**
Abdera, ruin(s), *Gr.* 40°55′ N, 24°52′ E **156**
Abdi, *Chad* 12°40′ N, 21°18′ E **216**
Abdulino, *Russ.* 53°38′ N, 53°43′ E **154**
Ab-e Istadeh-ye Moqor, lake, *Afghan.* 32°25′ N, 66°51′ E **186**
Ab-e Vakhan (Oxus), river, *Afghan.* 37°8′ N, 72°26′ E **186**
Abéché, *Chad* 13°48′ N, 20°49′ E **216**
Ābeltī, *Eth.* 8°9′ N, 37°32′ E **224**
Abelvær, *Nor.* 64°44′ N, 11°14′ E **152**
Abenab, *Namibia* 19°19′ S, 18°7′ E **220**
Abengourou, *Côte d'Ivoire* 6°41′ N, 3°30′ W **222**
Abenójar, *Sp.* 38°52′ N, 4°22′ W **164**
Abeokuta, *Nig.* 7°12′ N, 3°22′ E **222**
Ābera, *Eth.* 7°12′ N, 35°57′ E **224**
Aberaeron, *U.K.* 52°13′ N, 4°15′ W **162**
Abercorn see Mbala, *Zambia* 8°53′ S, 31°23′ E **224**
Aberdare, *U.K.* 51°42′ N, 3°26′ W **162**
Aberdeen, *Idaho, U.S.* 42°57′ N, 112°50′ W **90**
Aberdeen, *Md., U.S.* 39°30′ N, 76°11′ W **94**
Aberdeen, *Miss., U.S.* 33°49′ N, 88°33′ W **96**
Aberdeen, *N.C., U.S.* 35°7′ N, 79°26′ W **96**
Aberdeen, *Ohio, U.S.* 38°39′ N, 83°45′ W **102**
Aberdeen, *S. Af.* 32°29′ S, 24°4′ E **227**
Aberdeen, *S. Dak., U.S.* 45°26′ N, 98°30′ W **90**
Aberdeen, *U.K.* 57°8′ N, 2°8′ W **150**
Aberdeen, *Wash., U.S.* 46°58′ N, 123°50′ W **100**
Aberdeen Lake, lake, *Can.* 64°17′ N, 101°1′ W **106**
Aberdyfi, *U.K.* 52°32′ N, 4°2′ W **162**
Aberedw, *U.K.* 52°6′ N, 3°20′ W **162**
Abergavenny, *U.K.* 51°49′ N, 3°1′ W **162**
Abergele, *U.K.* 53°17′ N, 3°35′ W **162**
Abersychan, *U.K.* 51°44′ N, 3°3′ W **162**
Abert, Lake, *Oreg., U.S.* 42°42′ N, 120°35′ W **82**
Abertawe see Swansea, *U.K.* 51°37′ N, 3°57′ W **162**
Abertillery, *U.K.* 51°43′ N, 3°8′ W **162**
Aberystwyth, *U.K.* 52°25′ N, 4°4′ W **162**
Abez', *Russ.* 66°28′ N, 61°49′ E **169**
Abhā, *Saudi Arabia* 18°11′ N, 42°30′ E **182**
Ābhē Bid Hāyk', lake, *Eth.* 11°2′ N, 40°54′ E **216**
Abibe, Serranía de, *Col.* 7°44′ N, 76°42′ W **136**
'Abidiya, *Sudan* 18°12′ N, 33°59′ E **182**
Abidjan, *Côte d'Ivoire* 5°20′ N, 4°12′ W **222**
Abijatta-Shalla Lakes National Park, *Eth.* 7°16′ N, 37°53′ E **224**
Abilene, *Kans., U.S.* 38°53′ N, 97°12′ W **90**
Abilene, *Tex., U.S.* 32°26′ N, 99°44′ W **92**
Abingdon, *Mo., U.S.* 40°47′ N, 90°24′ W **94**
Abingdon, *U.K.* 51°40′ N, 1°18′ W **162**
Abingdon, *Va., U.S.* 36°42′ N, 81°59′ W **96**
Abington, *Conn., U.S.* 41°51′ N, 72°1′ W **104**
Abiquiu, *N. Mex., U.S.* 36°11′ N, 106°19′ W **92**
Abisko, *Nor.* 68°20′ N, 18°47′ E **152**
Abita Springs, *La., U.S.* 30°28′ N, 90°2′ W **103**
Abitau, river, *Can.* 60°23′ N, 108°5′ W **108**
Abitibi, Lake, *Can.* 48°36′ N, 80°21′ W **110**
Ābīy Ādī, *Eth.* 13°34′ N, 38°59′ E **182**
Abja Paluoja, *Est.* 58°6′ N, 25°20′ E **166**
Abkhazia, special sovereignty, *Ga.* 42°59′ N, 41°14′ E **195**
Abnūb, *Egypt* 27°18′ N, 31°8′ E **180**
Åbo see Turku, *Fin.* 60°27′ N, 22°15′ E **166**
Aboa, station, *Antarctica* 73°4′ S, 13°21′ W **248**
Aboabo, *Philippines* 9°9′ N, 118°7′ E **203**
Abohar, *India* 30°9′ N, 74°11′ E **186**
Aboisso, *Côte d'Ivoire* 5°25′ N, 3°15′ W **222**
Abomey, *Benin* 7°13′ N, 1°57′ E **222**
Abondance, *Fr.* 46°16′ N, 6°44′ E **167**
Abong Mbang, *Cameroon* 3°59′ N, 13°12′ E **218**
Abongabong, peak, *Indonesia* 4°14′ N, 96°41′ E **196**
Abony, *Hung.* 47°11′ N, 20°1′ E **168**
Aborlan, *Philippines* 9°27′ N, 118°33′ E **203**
Abou Deïa, *Chad* 11°27′ N, 19°18′ E **216**
Abou Goulem, *Chad* 13°35′ N, 21°39′ E **216**
Abra Pampa, *Arg.* 22°42′ S, 65°44′ W **137**
Abrantes, *Port.* 39°29′ N, 8°16′ W **214**
Abreojos, Punta, *Mex.* 26°44′ N, 114°58′ W **112**
Abreschviller, *Fr.* 48°38′ N, 7°5′ E **163**
Abreú, *Dom. Rep.* 19°41′ N, 69°59′ W **116**
Abreuvoir Timg'aouine, spring, *Alg.* 21°40′ N, 4°29′ E **222**
Abriès, *Fr.* 44°48′ N, 6°54′ E **167**
Abrolhos, Arquipélago dos, *South Atlantic Ocean* 18°35′ S, 39°25′ W **132**
Abruka Saar, island, *Est.* 58°0′ N, 22°32′ E **166**
Abruzzi, adm. division, *It.* 41°59′ N, 13°13′ E **156**
Abruzzi, Mount, *Can.* 50°26′ N, 115°13′ W **90**
Absalom, Mount, *Antarctica* 80°26′ S, 26°24′ W **248**
Absaroka Range, *Wyo., U.S.* 44°17′ N, 110°13′ W **90**
Absarokee, *Mont., U.S.* 45°29′ N, 109°26′ W **90**
Abu, *Japan* 34°28′ N, 131°28′ E **200**
Abū al Abyaḑ, island, *U.A.E.* 24°17′ N, 53°46′ E **182**
Abū 'Alī, island, *Saudi Arabia* 27°21′ N, 49°32′ E **180**
Abu 'Aweigîla, *Egypt* 30°50′ N, 34°6′ E **194**
Abu Ballâş, peak, *Egypt* 24°27′ N, 27°33′ E **226**
Abū Dālī, *Syr.* 34°40′ N, 36°53′ E **194**
Abu Deleiq, *Sudan* 15°50′ N, 33°45′ E **182**
Abu Dhabi see Abū Ẓaby, *U.A.E.* 24°25′ N, 54°14′ E **196**
Abu Dis, *Sudan* 19°5′ N, 33°38′ E **182**
Abu Dulu, Qoz, *Sudan* 15°50′ N, 31°47′ E **182**
Abu Gabra, *Sudan* 11°4′ N, 26°43′ E **224**
Abu Gamal, *Sudan* 15°6′ N, 36°24′ E **182**
Abu Gubeiha, *Sudan* 11°26′ N, 31°17′ E **218**
Abu Hamed, *Sudan* 19°31′ N, 33°19′ E **182**
Abu Hashim, *Sudan* 12°59′ N, 34°21′ E **182**
Abū Kamāl, *Syr.* 34°27′ N, 40°54′ E **180**
Abu Mataríq, *Sudan* 10°56′ N, 26°14′ E **224**
Abū Mūsā, island, *Iran* 25°55′ N, 54°49′ E **180**
Abū Nā'im, spring, *Lib.* 28°57′ N, 18°46′ E **216**
Abu Qurqâş, *Egypt* 27°58′ N, 30°47′ E **180**
Abu Road, *India* 24°28′ N, 72°47′ E **186**
Abu Safah, oil field, *Saudi Arabia* 27°5′ N, 50°39′ E **196**
Abu Saiyal, spring, *Sudan* 17°16′ N, 31°12′ E **182**
Abu Shagara, Ras, *Sudan* 21°6′ N, 37°15′ E **182**
Abu Shanab, *Sudan* 13°55′ N, 27°43′ E **226**
Abu Simbel, *Egypt* 24°25′ N, 33°0′ E **182**
Abu Simbel, site, *Egypt* 22°19′ N, 31°29′ E **182**
Abū Sōma, Râs, *Egypt* 26°31′ N, 34°1′ E **180**
Abu Sufyan, *Sudan* 11°55′ N, 26°21′ E **216**
Abu Şuweir, *Egypt* 30°32′ N, 32°4′ E **194**
Abu Tabari, spring, *Sudan* 17°30′ N, 28°29′ E **226**
Abu Tîg, *Egypt* 27°3′ N, 31°14′ E **180**
Abu 'Uruq, *Sudan* 15°53′ N, 30°25′ E **226**
Abu Zabad, *Sudan* 12°20′ N, 29°13′ E **216**
Abū Ẓaby (Abu Dhabi), *U.A.E.* 24°25′ N, 54°14′ E **196**
Abu Zenîma, *Egypt* 29°2′ N, 33°6′ E **180**
Abuja, *Nig.* 9°4′ N, 7°2′ E **222**
Abulug, *Philippines* 18°25′ N, 121°26′ E **203**
Abumombazi, *Dem. Rep. of the Congo* 3°32′ N, 22°2′ E **218**
Abunã, *Braz.* 9°42′ S, 65°22′ W **137**
Abunã, river, *South America* 10°24′ S, 67°6′ W **137**
Ābūr, *Jordan* 30°48′ N, 35°42′ E **194**
Aburatsu, *Japan* 31°34′ N, 131°23′ E **201**
Ābuyē Mēda, peak, *Eth.* 10°30′ N, 39°43′ E **224**
Abwong, *Sudan* 9°5′ N, 32°9′ E **224**
Abyad, *Sudan* 13°44′ N, 26°29′ E **226**
Abyad Plateau, Jebel, *Sudan* 19°0′ N, 26°57′ E **226**
Abyār al Ḩakīm, spring, *Lib.* 31°35′ N, 23°27′ E **180**
Åbybro, *Den.* 57°8′ N, 9°43′ E **150**
Abyei, *Sudan* 9°34′ N, 28°26′ E **224**
Abyek, *Iran* 36°1′ N, 50°36′ E **180**
Açailândia, *Braz.* 4°57′ S, 47°42′ W **130**
Acala, *Mex.* 16°34′ N, 92°49′ W **115**
Acámbaro, *Mex.* 20°0′ N, 100°43′ W **114**
Acancéh, *Mex.* 20°47′ N, 89°27′ W **116**
Acandí, *Col.* 8°31′ N, 77°19′ W **136**
Acaponeta, *Mex.* 22°29′ N, 105°22′ W **114**
Acaponeta, river, *Mex.* 23°39′ N, 105°17′ W **114**
Acapulco, *Mex.* 16°51′ N, 99°55′ W **112**
Acaraí, Serra, *Guyana* 1°50′ N, 57°38′ W **130**
Acaraú, *Braz.* 2°55′ S, 40°7′ W **132**
Acarí, *Peru* 15°28′ S, 74°35′ W **137**
Acari, river, *Braz.* 5°32′ S, 60°5′ W **130**
Acari, river, *Peru* 15°19′ S, 74°37′ W **137**
Acaricuara, *Col.* 0°36′ N, 70°22′ W **136**
Acarigua, *Venez.* 9°34′ N, 69°13′ W **136**
Acatenango, Volcán de, *Guatemala* 14°28′ N, 90°58′ W **115**
Acatlán, *Mex.* 18°11′ N, 98°5′ W **114**
Acayucan, *Mex.* 17°56′ N, 94°55′ W **114**
Accomac, *Va., U.S.* 37°42′ N, 75°41′ W **94**
Accous, *Fr.* 42°58′ N, 0°35′ E **164**
Accra, *Ghana* 5°34′ N, 0°22′ E **222**
Accrington, *U.K.* 53°45′ N, 2°23′ W **162**
Aceguá, *Braz.* 31°52′ S, 54°12′ W **139**
Achacachi, *Bol.* 16°8′ S, 68°43′ W **137**
Achaguas, *Venez.* 7°47′ N, 68°16′ W **136**
Achahoish, *U.K.* 55°56′ N, 5°34′ W **150**
Achalpur, *India* 21°17′ N, 77°30′ E **188**
Achar, *Uru.* 32°25′ S, 56°10′ W **139**
Achegour, spring, *Niger* 19°4′ N, 11°45′ E **222**
Acheng, *China* 45°32′ N, 126°55′ E **198**
Achénouma, *Niger* 19°14′ N, 12°57′ E **216**
Acheux, *Fr.* 50°4′ N, 2°33′ E **163**
Achikulak, *Russ.* 44°31′ N, 44°47′ E **158**
Achinsk, *Russ.* 56°16′ N, 90°41′ E **169**
Achisu, *Russ.* 42°37′ N, 47°45′ E **195**
Achit, *Russ.* 56°48′ N, 57°56′ E **154**
Achna, *Northern Cyprus* 35°2′ N, 33°46′ E **194**
Acht, Hohe, peak, *Ger.* 50°22′ N, 6°58′ E **167**
Achuyevo, *Russ.* 45°44′ N, 37°43′ E **156**
Achwa (Moroto), river, *Uganda* 2°14′ N, 32°58′ E **224**
Achwa, river, *Uganda* 3°31′ N, 32°12′ E **224**
Acıgöl, lake, *Turk.* 37°49′ N, 29°43′ E **156**
Acıpayam, *Turk.* 37°25′ N, 29°20′ E **156**
Acîş, *Rom.* 47°30′ N, 22°48′ E **168**
Ackerman, *Miss., U.S.* 33°17′ N, 89°11′ W **103**
Ackley, *Iowa, U.S.* 42°32′ N, 93°3′ W **94**
Acklins and Crooked Islands, adm. division, *Bahamas* 22°52′ N, 74°50′ W **116**
Acklins Island, *Bahamas* 22°22′ N, 75°3′ W **116**
Acle, *U.K.* 52°38′ N, 1°32′ E **163**
Acobamba, *Peru* 12°53′ S, 74°33′ W **137**
Acoma Pueblo, site, *N. Mex., U.S.* 34°54′ N, 107°40′ W **92**
Acomayo, *Peru* 13°56′ S, 71°41′ W **137**
Acona, *Miss., U.S.* 33°15′ N, 90°2′ W **103**
Aconcagua, Cerro, *Arg.* 32°33′ S, 69°57′ W **134**
Aconchi, *Mex.* 29°49′ N, 110°14′ W **92**
Aconi, Point, *Can.* 46°21′ N, 60°50′ W **111**
Acora, *Peru* 16°1′ S, 69°46′ W **137**
Açores see Azores, islands, *Port.* 39°29′ N, 27°35′ W **207**
Acoyapa, *Nicar.* 11°55′ N, 85°9′ W **115**
Acqui Terme, *It.* 44°41′ N, 8°28′ E **167**
Acrae, ruin(s), *It.* 37°1′ N, 14°47′ E **156**
Acre, adm. division, *Braz.* 9°34′ S, 70°21′ W **137**
Acre, river, *Braz.* 10°24′ S, 68°2′ W **137**
Acre see 'Akko, *Israel* 32°55′ N, 35°4′ E **194**
Ács, *Hung.* 47°41′ N, 18°2′ E **156**
Actéon, Groupe, islands, *South Pacific Ocean* 21°2′ S, 137°14′ W **238**
Actium, ruin(s), *Gr.* 38°55′ N, 20°39′ E **156**
Acton, *Calif., U.S.* 34°28′ N, 118°13′ W **101**
Acton, *Me., U.S.* 43°31′ N, 70°55′ W **104**
Actopan, *Mex.* 20°15′ N, 98°56′ W **114**
Açuã, river, *Braz.* 7°39′ S, 64°12′ W **130**
Acuitzio, *Mex.* 19°29′ N, 101°21′ W **114**
Acurauá, river, *Braz.* 8°44′ S, 71°25′ W **130**
Açurizal, *Braz.* 15°11′ S, 56°24′ W **132**
Acworth, *N.H., U.S.* 43°12′ N, 72°18′ W **104**
Ad Dahnā', *Saudi Arabia* 26°39′ N, 46°15′ E **196**
Ad Dakhla, *Western Sahara* 23°42′ N, 15°58′ W **214**
Aḑ Ḑāli', *Yemen* 13°41′ N, 44°44′ E **182**
Ad Dammām, *Saudi Arabia* 26°23′ N, 50°5′ E **196**
Ad Dār al Ḩamrā', *Saudi Arabia* 27°21′ N, 37°41′ E **180**
Ad Dawādimī, *Saudi Arabia* 24°29′ N, 44°23′ E **182**
Ad Dawḩah (Doha), *Qatar* 25°13′ N, 51°25′ E **196**
Ad Dibdibah, region, *Asia* 28°10′ N, 46°32′ E **180**
Ad Dilam, *Saudi Arabia* 23°57′ N, 47°13′ E **196**
Ad Dīwānīyah, *Iraq* 31°59′ N, 44°51′ E **180**
Ad Durūz, Jabal, peak, *Syr.* 32°39′ N, 36°41′ E **194**
Ada, *Ghana* 5°46′ N, 0°34′ E **222**
Ada, *Minn., U.S.* 47°16′ N, 96°32′ W **90**
Ada, *Ohio, U.S.* 40°45′ N, 83°50′ W **102**
Ada, *Okla., U.S.* 34°45′ N, 96°40′ W **92**
Ada, *Serb. and Mont.* 45°48′ N, 20°7′ E **168**
Adâfer el Abiod, region, *Africa* 18°47′ N, 10°37′ W **222**
Adailo, *Eritrea* 14°26′ N, 40°50′ E **182**
Adair, Bahía de, *Mex.* 31°22′ N, 114°33′ W **80**
Adair, Cape, *Can.* 71°24′ N, 71°5′ W **106**
Adak, *Nor.* 65°20′ N, 18°34′ E **152**
Adak, island, *Alas., U.S.* 51°18′ N, 176°44′ W **160**
Adaleh, spring, *Eth.* 7°27′ N, 46°22′ E **218**
Adam, *Oman* 22°23′ N, 57°30′ E **182**
Adam, Mount, *U.K.* 51°37′ S, 60°5′ W **134**
Adam Peak, *Nev., U.S.* 41°9′ N, 117°24′ W **90**
Adamantina, *Braz.* 21°41′ S, 51°5′ W **138**
Adamello, peak, *It.* 46°9′ N, 10°27′ E **167**
Adamovka, *Russ.* 51°32′ N, 59°53′ E **154**
Adams, *Mass., U.S.* 42°36′ N, 73°8′ W **104**
Adams, *Minn., U.S.* 43°33′ N, 92°43′ W **94**
Adams, *Wis., U.S.* 43°56′ N, 89°49′ W **94**
Adams, Cape, *Antarctica* 75°10′ S, 61°57′ W **248**
Adams Lake, *Can.* 51°15′ N, 120°1′ W **90**
Adams, Mount, *Wash., U.S.* 46°11′ N, 121°33′ W **100**
Adams Mountain, *Mass., U.S.* 42°40′ N, 72°55′ W **104**
Adam's Peak, *Sri Lanka* 6°46′ N, 80°24′ E **188**
Adams Point, *Mich., U.S.* 45°24′ N, 83°41′ W **94**
Adamstown, *Pitcairn Is., U.K.* 25°0′ S, 130°0′ W **241**
Adamsville, *Tenn., U.S.* 35°13′ N, 88°23′ W **96**
Adamuz, *Sp.* 38°1′ N, 4°32′ W **164**
'Adan (Aden), *Yemen* 12°46′ N, 44°59′ E **182**
'Adan aş Şughrá, *Yemen* 12°35′ N, 44°1′ E **182**
Adana, *Turk.* 36°59′ N, 35°18′ E **156**
Adapazarı, *Turk.* 40°46′ N, 30°25′ E **156**
Adar Doutchi, region, *Africa* 14°33′ N, 5°50′ E **222**
Adarama, *Sudan* 17°3′ N, 34°54′ E **182**
Adare Peninsula, *Antarctica* 71°10′ S, 175°59′ E **248**
Addington, *Okla., U.S.* 34°13′ N, 97°58′ W **92**
Addis, *La., U.S.* 30°19′ N, 91°17′ W **103**
Addis Ababa see Ādīs Ābeba, *Eth.* 8°58′ N, 38°34′ E **224**
Addison, *Vt., U.S.* 44°5′ N, 73°19′ W **104**
Addo, *S. Af.* 33°34′ S, 25°42′ E **227**
Addo Elephant National Park, *S. Af.* 33°31′ S, 25°41′ E **227**
Addu Atoll, *Maldives* 0°54′ N, 72°39′ E **188**
Addy, *Wash., U.S.* 48°20′ N, 117°50′ W **90**
Adel, *Ga., U.S.* 31°7′ N, 83°26′ W **96**
Adel, *Oreg., U.S.* 42°11′ N, 119°54′ W **90**
Adelaide, *Austral.* 34°59′ S, 138°14′ E **230**
Adelaide Island, *Antarctica* 66°56′ S, 72°20′ W **248**
Adelaide Peninsula, *Can.* 67°53′ N, 97°8′ W **106**
Adelanto, *Calif., U.S.* 34°35′ N, 117°26′ W **101**
Adélfi, islands, *Aegean Sea* 36°26′ N, 26°40′ E **156**
Adelia María, *Arg.* 33°39′ S, 64°2′ W **139**
Adélie Coast, *Antarctica* 66°59′ S, 145°40′ E **248**
Adelunga Toghi, peak, *Uzb.* 42°7′ N, 70°59′ E **197**
Ademuz, *Sp.* 40°3′ N, 1°18′ W **164**
Aden, Gulf of 12°29′ N, 45°45′ E **173**
Aden see 'Adan, *Yemen* 12°46′ N, 44°59′ E **182**
Adenau, *Ger.* 50°23′ N, 6°57′ E **163**
Aderbissinat, *Niger* 15°39′ N, 7°53′ E **222**
Aderg, peak, *Mauritania* 21°24′ N, 11°58′ W **222**
Adh Dhayd, *U.A.E.* 25°16′ N, 55°48′ E **196**
Adhoi, *India* 23°23′ N, 70°29′ E **186**
Ādī Ārk'ay, *Eth.* 13°29′ N, 37°55′ E **182**
Adi Kaie, *Eritrea* 14°47′ N, 39°22′ E **182**
Adi Quala, *Eritrea* 14°38′ N, 38°49′ E **182**
Ādī Ramets', *Eth.* 13°49′ N, 37°22′ E **182**
Adi Ugri, *Eritrea* 14°52′ N, 38°50′ E **182**
Adiaké, *Côte d'Ivoire* 5°12′ N, 3°20′ W **214**
Adie Inlet, *Antarctica* 66°40′ S, 63°15′ W **248**
Ādīgala, *Eth.* 10°23′ N, 42°17′ E **224**
Adige, river, *It.* 45°11′ N, 11°20′ E **167**
Adigeni, *Ga.* 41°41′ N, 42°42′ E **195**
Ādīgrat, *Eth.* 14°16′ N, 39°26′ E **182**
Adilabad, *India* 19°40′ N, 78°33′ E **188**
Adilang, *Uganda* 2°42′ N, 33°28′ E **224**
Adin, *Calif., U.S.* 41°11′ N, 120°58′ W **90**
Adīrī, *Lib.* 27°32′ N, 13°13′ E **216**
Adirondack Mountains, *N.Y., U.S.* 43°57′ N, 76°16′ W **106**
Ādīs Ābeba (Addis Ababa), *Eth.* 8°58′ N, 38°34′ E **224**
Ādīs 'Alem, *Eth.* 9°2′ N, 38°21′ E **224**
Adıyaman, *Turk.* 37°45′ N, 38°16′ E **180**
Adjud, *Rom.* 46°5′ N, 27°10′ E **156**
Adlavik Islands, *North Atlantic Ocean* 54°39′ N, 62°27′ W **106**
Adler, *Russ.* 43°28′ N, 40°0′ E **195**
Admiralty Island, *Alas., U.S.* 57°30′ N, 133°39′ W **106**
Admiralty Islands, *Bismarck Sea* 3°32′ S, 145°14′ E **192**
Ado, *Nig.* 6°37′ N, 2°55′ E **222**
Ado Ekiti, *Nig.* 7°38′ N, 5°13′ E **222**
Adobe Flat, *Nev., U.S.* 40°2′ N, 119°8′ W **90**
Adok, *Sudan* 8°7′ N, 30°17′ E **224**
Adolfo López Mateos, *Mex.* 28°26′ N, 107°23′ W **92**
Adolfo López Mateos, Presa, lake, *Mex.* 25°10′ N, 108°53′ W **81**
Adoni, *India* 15°38′ N, 77°16′ E **188**
Adony, *Hung.* 47°6′ N, 18°51′ E **168**
Adorf, *Ger.* 50°19′ N, 12°15′ E **152**
Adour, river, *Fr.* 43°24′ N, 1°10′ W **214**
Adra, *Sp.* 36°44′ N, 3°1′ W **164**
Adranga, *Dem. Rep. of the Congo* 2°53′ N, 30°25′ E **224**
Adrar, *Alg.* 27°55′ N, 0°18′ E **214**
Adrar, region, *Mauritania* 20°22′ N, 14°7′ W **222**
Adraskan, *Afghan.* 33°38′ N, 62°18′ E **186**
Adré, *Chad* 13°26′ N, 22°12′ E **216**
Adria, *It.* 45°4′ N, 12°1′ E **167**
Adrian, *Mich., U.S.* 41°52′ N, 84°2′ W **102**
Adrian, *Minn., U.S.* 43°36′ N, 95°56′ W **90**
Adrian, *Tex., U.S.* 35°15′ N, 102°40′ W **92**
Adrianople see Edirne, *Turk.* 41°39′ N, 26°34′ E **156**
Adriatic Sea 41°51′ N, 17°3′ E **156**
Adun Gol, *China* 42°4′ N, 107°56′ E **198**
Adusa, *Dem. Rep. of the Congo* 1°24′ N, 28°4′ E **224**
Ādwa, *Eth.* 14°9′ N, 38°52′ E **182**
Adwick le Street, *U.K.* 53°33′ N, 1°12′ W **162**
Adycha, river, *Russ.* 66°53′ N, 135°23′ E **160**
Adygeya, adm. division, *Russ.* 44°59′ N, 40°1′ E **158**
Adzopé, *Côte d'Ivoire* 6°3′ N, 3°52′ W **222**
Adz'vavom, *Russ.* 66°36′ N, 59°17′ E **169**
Aegae, ruin(s), *Gr.* 38°8′ N, 22°13′ E **156**
Aegean Sea 36°34′ N, 23°7′ E **156**
Aegir Ridge, *Norwegian Sea* 65°42′ N, 4°7′ W **255**
Aegna, island, *Est.* 59°37′ N, 24°35′ E **166**
Aegviidu, *Est.* 59°15′ N, 25°35′ E **166**
Afadé, *Cameroon* 12°15′ N, 14°39′ E **216**
Afam, *Nig.* 4°45′ N, 7°23′ E **222**
Afándou, *Gr.* 36°17′ N, 28°10′ E **156**
Afar, region, *Africa* 12°59′ N, 40°4′ E **182**
Āfdem, *Eth.* 9°27′ N, 41°0′ E **224**
Affollé, *Mauritania* 16°21′ N, 11°11′ W **222**
Afghanistan 34°0′ N, 66°0′ E **186**
Afgooye, *Somalia* 2°5′ N, 45°8′ E **218**
Afgooye Caddo, *Somalia* 3°12′ N, 45°33′ E **218**
'Afīf, *Saudi Arabia* 23°53′ N, 42°56′ E **182**
Afikpo, *Nig.* 5°55′ N, 7°55′ E **222**
Afiq, *Israel* 32°46′ N, 35°42′ E **194**
Åfjord, *Nor.* 63°57′ N, 10°14′ E **152**
Aflou, *Alg.* 34°6′ N, 2°5′ E **214**
Afmadow, *Somalia* 0°28′ N, 42°4′ E **224**
Āfodo, *Eth.* 10°13′ N, 34°47′ E **224**
Afognak Island, *Alas., U.S.* 57°51′ N, 151°54′ W **98**
Afonso Cláudio, *Braz.* 20°6′ S, 41°10′ W **138**
Afqā, *Leb.* 34°4′ N, 35°53′ E **194**
Africa 1°0′ N, 17°0′ E **207**
Afşin, *Turk.* 38°14′ N, 36°53′ E **156**
Afton, *Okla., U.S.* 36°41′ N, 94°58′ W **94**
Afton, *Wyo., U.S.* 42°42′ N, 110°55′ W **82**
Afuá, *Braz.* 0°10′ N, 50°23′ W **130**
'Afula, *Israel* 32°36′ N, 35°17′ E **194**
Afyon, *Turk.* 38°44′ N, 30°31′ E **156**
Agadem, *Niger* 16°49′ N, 13°17′ E **216**
Agadez, *Niger* 16°59′ N, 7°58′ E **222**
Agadir, *Mor.* 30°25′ N, 9°37′ W **214**
Agaie, *Nig.* 8°59′ N, 6°18′ E **222**
Agalega Islands, *Indian Ocean* 12°45′ S, 55°37′ E **173**
Agamenticus, Mount, *Me., U.S.* 43°13′ N, 70°44′ W **104**
Agamor, spring, *Mali* 17°16′ N, 3°178′ E **222**
Agana see Hagåtña, *Guam, U.S.* 13°0′ N, 145°0′ E **242**
Agapa, *Russ.* 71°43′ N, 89°24′ E **173**
Agapovka, *Russ.* 53°20′ N, 59°12′ E **154**
Agar, *India* 23°43′ N, 76°3′ E **197**
Āgaro, *Eth.* 7°49′ N, 36°37′ E **224**
Agartala, *India* 23°47′ N, 91°18′ E **197**
Agaruut, *Mongolia* 43°18′ N, 109°26′ E **198**
Agassiz Fracture Zone, *South Pacific Ocean* 39°32′ S, 131°55′ W **252**
Agata, *Russ.* 66°51′ N, 93°40′ E **169**
Agata, Ozero, lake, *Russ.* 67°14′ N, 92°22′ E **169**
Agate, *Colo., U.S.* 39°27′ N, 103°57′ W **90**
Agats, *Indonesia* 5°34′ S, 138°4′ E **192**
Agattu, island, *Alas., U.S.* 52°17′ N, 171°43′ E **160**
Agawam, *Mass., U.S.* 42°3′ N, 72°37′ W **104**
Agbaja, *Nig.* 7°58′ N, 6°38′ E **222**
Agboville, *Côte d'Ivoire* 5°51′ N, 4°12′ W **222**
Ağdam, *Azerb.* 39°59′ N, 46°54′ E **195**
Agde, *Fr.* 43°19′ N, 3°27′ E **164**
Agde, Cap d', *Fr.* 43°11′ N, 3°30′ E **165**
Agdz, *Mor.* 30°41′ N, 6°29′ W **214**
Agematsu, *Japan* 35°47′ N, 137°43′ E **201**
Agen, *Fr.* 44°14′ N, 0°36′ E **214**
Àger, *Sp.* 41°59′ N, 0°46′ E **164**
Agere Maryam, *Eth.* 5°37′ N, 38°16′ E **224**
Agger, river, *Ger.* 50°55′ N, 7°20′ E **167**
Aggi, *Eth.* 7°55′ N, 35°38′ E **224**
Āghā Jārī, *Iran* 30°43′ N, 49°53′ E **180**
Aghaylas, *Western Sahara* 22°28′ N, 14°23′ W **214**
Aghdash, *Azerb.* 40°39′ N, 47°28′ E **195**
Aghireşu, *Rom.* 46°51′ N, 23°14′ E **168**
Aghjabädi, *Azerb.* 40°2′ N, 47°28′ E **195**
Aghsu, *Azerb.* 40°34′ N, 48°25′ E **195**
Aghwinit, *Western Sahara* 22°11′ N, 13°10′ W **214**
Agia Napa, *Cyprus* 34°59′ N, 33°59′ E **194**
Agiabampo, Estero de 26°15′ N, 110°30′ W **80**
Agimont, *Belg.* 50°9′ N, 4°45′ E **163**
Agin Buryat, adm. division, *Russ.* 51°4′ N, 114°22′ E **190**
Aginskoye, *Russ.* 51°6′ N, 114°30′ E **190**
Ágio Óros (Mount Athos), region, *Europe* 40°14′ N, 23°2′ E **156**
Ágióros, *Europe* 40°8′ N, 24°3′ E **156**
Ágios Nikólaos, *Gr.* 35°12′ N, 25°40′ E **180**
Agios Sergios, *Northern Cyprus* 35°11′ N, 33°52′ E **194**
Aglat Jrayfiya, spring, *Western Sahara* 25°1′ N, 14°18′ W **214**
Agliano, *It.* 44°47′ N, 8°13′ E **167**
Agmar, *Mauritania* 25°18′ N, 10°48′ W **214**
Agnes, Mount, *Austral.* 26°55′ S, 128°44′ E **230**
Agnibilékrou, *Côte d'Ivoire* 7°5′ N, 3°12′ W **222**
Agnières, *Fr.* 44°41′ N, 5°53′ E **150**
Agno, river, *Philippines* 16°6′ N, 120°49′ E **203**
Agön, island, *Sw.* 61°29′ N, 17°17′ E **166**
Agoncillo, *Sp.* 42°25′ N, 2°18′ W **164**
Agordat, *Eritrea* 15°32′ N, 37°53′ E **182**
Agordo, *It.* 46°17′ N, 12°2′ E **167**
Agostinho, *Braz.* 9°58′ S, 68°33′ W **137**
Agoua, *Benin* 8°17′ N, 1°57′ E **222**
Agouénit, *Mauritania* 16°41′ N, 7°34′ W **222**
Agouma, *Gabon* 1°35′ S, 10°11′ E **218**
Agous-n-Ehsel, spring, *Mali* 16°20′ N, 1°44′ E **222**
Agout, river, *Fr.* 43°44′ N, 1°47′ E **165**
Agra, *India* 27°9′ N, 77°59′ E **197**
Agrakhanskiy Poluostrov, *Russ.* 43°41′ N, 47°7′ E **195**
Agramunt, *Sp.* 41°46′ N, 1°6′ E **164**
Agraouri, spring, *Niger* 18°16′ N, 14°14′ E **222**
Agreda, *Sp.* 41°50′ N, 1°55′ W **164**

ğrı Dağı (Ararat, Mount), Turk. 39°42' N, 44°15' E 195
ğrı (Karaköse), Turk. 39°43' N, 43°3' E 195
grichay, river, Azerb. 41°18' N, 46°42' E 195
gricola, Miss., U.S. 30°47' N, 88°30' W 103
grigento, It. 37°18' N, 13°34' E 216
grihan, island, U.S. 18°37' N, 144°36' E 192
grinio, Gr. 38°35' N, 21°22' E 143
gryz, Russ. 56°30' N, 53°2' E 154
ğstafa, Azerb. 41°6' N, 45°26' E 195
gua Brava, Laguna, lake, Mex. 22°8' N, 105°49' W 114
Agua Clara, Braz. 20°25' S, 52°56' W 138
Agua Nueva, Mex. 25°5' N, 101°7' W 114
Água Preta, river, Braz. 1°58' S, 64°53' W 130
Agua Prieta, Mex. 31°18' N, 109°34' W 92
Agua Tibia Mountain, Calif., U.S. 33°24' N, 117°1' W 101
Agua Verde, Mex. 22°55' N, 105°58' W 114
Aguachica, Col. 8°19' N, 73°38' W 136
Aguaclara, Col. 4°43' N, 73°2' W 136
Aguadas, Col. 5°35' N, 75°26' W 136
Agualeguas, Mex. 26°18' N, 99°33' W 114
Aguanga, Calif., U.S. 33°26' N, 116°52' W 101
Aguapeí, Braz. 16°12' S, 59°41' W 132
Aguapeí, Serra do, peak, Braz. 16°5' S, 59°29' W 132
Aguarey, Arg. 22°13' S, 63°51' W 137
Aguarico, river, Ecua. 0°18' N, 76°27' W 136
Aguaro-Guariquito National Park, Venez. 8°21' N, 66°34' W 136
Aguas Blancas, Chile 24°11' S, 69°54' W 132
Aguas Dulces, Uru. 34°20' S, 53°50' W 139
Águas Formosas, Braz. 17°5' S, 40°59' W 138
Aguas Negras, Peru 0°27' N, 75°23' W 136
Aguascalientes, Mex. 21°50' N, 102°23' W 114
Aguascalientes, adm. division, Mex. 21°45' N, 102°53' W 114
Aguelal, spring, Niger 18°44' N, 8°6' E 222
Aguelhok, Mali 19°27' N, 0°50' E 222
Agueraktem, spring, Mauritania 23°11' N, 6°24' W 214
Aguié, Niger 13°28' N, 7°33' E 222
Aguilâl Faye, spring, Mauritania 18°27' N, 14°47' W 222
Aguilar, Colo., U.S. 37°24' N, 104°40' W 92
Aguilar de Campoo, Sp. 42°46' N, 4°16' W 150
Águilas, Sp. 37°24' N, 1°36' W 164
Aguililla, Mex. 18°44' N, 102°45' W 114
Aguja, Cabo de la, Col. 11°20' N, 75°3' W 116
Aguja, Punta, Peru 5°43' S, 82°17' W 130
Agujita, Mex. 27°52' N, 101°10' W 92
Āgula'i, Eth. 13°40' N, 39°36' E 182
Agulhas Basin, Indian Ocean 46°55' S, 24°17' E 254
Agulhas, Cape, S. Af. 35°7' S, 20°3' E 227
Agulhas Plateau, Indian Ocean 39°48' S, 26°43' E 254
Agustín Codazzi, Col. 10°2' N, 73°16' W 136
Aha Hills, Botswana 19°49' S, 20°57' E 220
Ahaggar (Hoggar), Alg. 21°56' N, 4°32' E 222
Ahaggar National Park, Alg. 23°5' N, 4°38' E 214
Ahar, Iran 38°30' N, 47°3' E 195
Ahaus, Ger. 52°4' N, 7°0' E 163
Ahelleguen, spring, Alg. 25°36' N, 7°2' E 214
Ahipara, N.Z. 35°11' S, 173°10' E 240
Ahlainen, Fin. 61°40' N, 21°36' E 166
Ahlat, Turk. 38°43' N, 42°26' E 195
Ahlatlıbel, ruin(s), Turk. 39°48' N, 32°38' E 156
Ahlen, Ger. 51°46' N, 7°54' E 167
Ahmadabad, India 23°1' N, 72°36' E 186
Ahmadi, oil field, Kuwait 29°2' N, 48°1' E 196
Ahmadpur East, Pak. 29°9' N, 71°16' E 186
Ahmar Mountains, Eth. 9°9' N, 40°49' E 224
Ahmeyine, spring, Mauritania 20°53' N, 14°28' W 222
Ahnet, region, Africa 25°8' N, 2°58' E 214
Ahoada, Nig. 5°6' N, 6°37' E 222
Ahome, Mex. 25°53' N, 109°10' W 112
Ahoskie, N.C., U.S. 36°17' N, 77°1' W 96
Ahram, Iran 28°51' N, 51°20' E 196
Ahrensburg, Ger. 53°40' N, 10°13' E 152
Ähtäri, Fin. 62°32' N, 24°4' E 152
Ahtme, Est. 59°17' N, 27°27' E 166
Ahua 'Umi Heiau, site, Hawai'i, U.S. 19°37' N, 155°50' W 99
Ahuacatlán, Mex. 21°2' N, 104°30' W 114
Ahuachapán, El Salv. 13°56' N, 89°52' W 115
Ahualulco, Mex. 20°41' N, 103°59' W 114
Ahvāz (Ahwāz), Iran 31°19' N, 48°41' E 180
Ahvenanmaa see Åland, island, Fin. 60°26' N, 19°33' E 166
Ahwahnee, Calif., U.S. 37°22' N, 119°44' W 100
Aḩwar, Yemen 13°32' N, 46°42' E 182
Ahwāz see Ahvāz, Iran 31°19' N, 48°41' E 180
Ai Qurayyāt, Saudi Arabia 31°19' N, 37°20' E 180
Aiari, river, Braz. 1°15' N, 69°5' W 136
Aichi, adm. division, Japan 35°3' N, 136°54' E 201
Aigialousa, Northern Cyprus 35°32' N, 34°11' E 194
Aigle, Switz. 46°20' N, 6°58' E 167
Aigle, Lac à l', lake, Can. 51°12' N, 65°54' W 111
Aigoual, Mont, peak, Fr. 44°7' N, 3°32' E 165
Aiguá, Uru. 34°14' S, 54°44' W 139
Aiguebelle, Fr. 45°32' N, 6°18' E 167
Aigües, Sp. 38°29' N, 0°22' E 164
Aiguilles, Fr. 44°47' N, 6°51' E 167
Aijiekebey, China 37°11' N, 75°22' E 184
Aikawa, Japan 38°2' N, 138°15' E 201
Aiken, S.C., U.S. 33°33' N, 81°44' W 96
Aileach, Grianan of, peak, Ire. 55°0' N, 7°33' W 150
Ailet Jridani, Tun. 35°6' N, 10°1' E 156
Ailigandí, Pan. 9°13' N, 78°2' W 115
Ailigas, peak, Fin. 69°25' N, 25°49' E 152
Ailly-sur-Noye, Fr. 49°45' N, 2°20' E 163
Aim, Russ. 58°49' N, 134°4' E 160
Aimorés, Braz. 19°29' S, 41°5' W 138
Aimorés, Serra dos, Braz. 18°14' S, 41°22' W 132
'Aïn Azaz, spring, Alg. 27°5' N, 3°30' E 214
Aïn Ben Tili, Mauritania 25°57' N, 9°34' W 214
Aïn Cheikr, spring, Alg. 22°9' N, 9°535' E 222
'Ain Dalla, spring, Egypt 27°18' N, 27°19' E 180
'Aïn Deheb, Alg. 34°51' N, 1°31' E 214
Aïn Djasser, Alg. 35°53' N, 6°17' E 150
'Aïn el Berd, Alg. 35°20' N, 0°31' E 150
'Ain el Ghazâl, spring, Egypt 25°47' N, 30°31' E 180
'Aïn el Hadjel, Alg. 35°36' N, 3°55' E 214
'Ain el Qideirât (Kadesh-Barnea), spring, Egypt 30°39' N, 34°25' E 194
'Ain el Wâdi, spring, Egypt 27°22' N, 28°12' E 180
'Ain Khaleifa, spring, Egypt 26°44' N, 27°46' E 180
'Aïn M'lila, Alg. 36°0' N, 6°34' E 150
'Aïn Oussera, Alg. 35°26' N, 2°55' E 150
'Ain Qeiqab, spring, Egypt 29°35' N, 24°56' E 180
Ain, river, Fr. 45°52' N, 5°17' E 165
'Aïn Sefra, Alg. 32°50' N, 0°39' E 143
'Aïn Sefra, Alg. 32°47' N, 0°37' E 214
'Aïn Souf, spring, Alg. 28°6' N, 2°14' E 214
'Aïn Taïba, spring, Alg. 30°18' N, 5°49' E 214
'Aïn Temouchent, Alg. 35°17' N, 1°9' W 150
'Ain Tibaghbagh, spring, Egypt 29°6' N, 26°24' E 180
'Aïn Tidjoubar, spring, Alg. 27°46' N, 1°22' E 214
'Aïn Tiguift, spring, Alg. 26°12' N, 3°38' E 214
Ain Zalah, oil field, Iraq 36°44' N, 42°24' E 195
Aïna, river, Congo 1°30' N, 13°14' E 218
Ainaži, Latv. 57°51' N, 24°20' E 166
Aínos National Park, Gr. 38°8' N, 20°34' E 156
Aínsa, Sp. 42°25' N, 0°7' E 164
Ainsworth, Nebr., U.S. 42°31' N, 99°53' W 90
Aipe, Col. 3°13' N, 75°18' W 136
Aiquile, Bol. 18°12' S, 65°13' W 137
Aïr (Aïr Massif), region, Africa 17°26' N, 6°28' E 222
Air Force Island, Can. 67°34' N, 76°15' W 106
Aïr Massif see Aïr, region, Africa 17°26' N, 6°28' E 222
Airaines, Fr. 49°57' N, 1°55' E 163
Airbangis, Indonesia 0°14' N, 99°22' E 196
Airdrie, Can. 51°18' N, 114°2' W 90
Aire, Fr. 50°38' N, 2°24' E 163
Aire, river, Fr. 49°3' N, 5°9' E 163
Airiselkä, Fin. 66°16' N, 23°56' E 152
Airolo, Switz. 46°32' N, 8°36' E 167
Aisén del General Carlos Ibáñez del Campo, adm. division, Chile 48°43' S, 77°8' W 134
Aishalton, Guyana 2°28' N, 59°9' W 130
Aisne, river, Fr. 49°22' N, 2°54' E 163
Aïssa, Djebel, peak, Alg. 32°52' N, 0°38' E 214
Aït Baha, Mor. 30°3' N, 9°10' W 214
Aït Ourir, Mor. 31°36' N, 7°43' W 214
Aitape, P.N.G. 3°14' S, 142°19' E 238
Aitkin, Minn., U.S. 46°30' N, 93°43' W 94
Aitona, Sp. 41°29' N, 0°27' E 164
Aiviekste, river, Latv. 56°47' N, 26°29' E 166
Aix, Mount, Wash., U.S. 46°46' N, 121°17' W 100
Aix-en-Othe, Fr. 48°13' N, 3°45' E 163
Aix-en-Provence, Fr. 43°31' N, 5°26' E 150
Aizawl, India 23°39' N, 92°42' E 197
Aizpute, Latv. 56°42' N, 21°36' E 166
Aizuwakamatsu, Japan 37°29' N, 139°54' E 201
'Ajab Shīr, Iran 37°28' N, 45°54' E 195
Ajaccio, Fr. 41°55' N, 8°41' E 156
Ajajú, river, Col. 0°59' N, 73°20' W 136
Ajalpan, Mex. 18°21' N, 97°16' W 114
Ajax Peak, Mont., U.S. 45°18' N, 113°49' W 90
Ajdābiyā, Lib. 30°44' N, 20°15' E 216
Ajir, region, Africa 18°0' N, 6°22' E 222
Ajka, Hung. 47°5' N, 17°34' E 168
'Ajlūn, Jordan 32°20' N, 35°44' E 194
'Ajmān, U.A.E. 25°26' N, 55°28' E 196
Ajmer, India 26°27' N, 74°38' E 186
Ajo, Ariz., U.S. 32°22' N, 112°51' W 92
Ajo, Mount, Ariz., U.S. 32°0' N, 112°45' W 92
Ajuana, river, Braz. 1°1' S, 65°40' W 136
Ajuchitlán, Mex. 18°7' N, 100°31' W 114
Ajuy, Philippines 11°11' N, 122°59' E 203
Ak Dağlar, peak, Turk. 36°30' N, 29°29' E 156
Ak Dovurak, Russ. 51°7' N, 90°31' E 184
Aka, Mali 15°25' N, 4°12' W 222
Aka, river, Dem. Rep. of the Congo 4°3' N, 29°25' E 224
Akadomari, Japan 37°53' N, 138°25' E 201
Akagera National Park, Rwanda 1°48' S, 30°38' E 224
Akagi, Japan 34°59' N, 132°43' E 201
Akaki, Cyprus 35°7' N, 33°7' E 194
Akal, oil field, Mex. 19°26' N, 92°7' W 115
Akalkot, India 17°31' N, 76°11' E 188
Akanthou, Northern Cyprus 35°21' N, 33°44' E 194
Akaroa, N.Z. 43°50' S, 172°58' E 240
Akasaki, Japan 35°28' N, 133°40' E 201
Akashi, Japan 34°40' N, 134°59' E 201
Akaska, S. Dak., U.S. 45°19' N, 100°8' W 90
Akbulak, Russ. 51°1' N, 55°38' E 158
Akçaabat, Turk. 41°1' N, 39°31' E 195
Akçadağ, Turk. 38°17' N, 37°57' E 180
Akçakışla, Turk. 39°31' N, 36°19' E 156
Akçakoca, Turk. 41°4' N, 31°8' E 156
Akçay, Turk. 39°35' N, 26°50' E 156
Akçay, Turk. 36°35' N, 29°43' E 156
Akchâr, region, Africa 20°12' N, 15°6' W 222
Akdağ, peak, Turk. 38°29' N, 26°25' E 156
Akdağ, peak, Turk. 36°47' N, 32°8' E 156
Akdağmadeni, Turk. 39°39' N, 35°54' E 156
Akdepe, Turkm. 42°3' N, 59°23' E 180
Akelo, Sudan 6°55' N, 33°38' E 224
Akera, river, Azerb. 39°28' N, 46°37' E 195
Åkernes, Nor. 58°44' N, 7°29' E 152
Akespe, Kaz. 46°48' N, 60°32' E 184
Aketi, Dem. Rep. of the Congo 2°45' N, 23°46' E 224
Akhalts'ikhe, Ga. 41°39' N, 42°57' E 195
Akhisar, Turk. 38°54' N, 27°50' E 156
Akhmeta, Ga. 42°1' N, 45°17' E 195
Akhmîm, Egypt 26°38' N, 31°42' E 180
Akhta, Arm. 40°28' N, 44°45' E 195
Akhtopol, Bulg. 42°7' N, 27°54' E 156
Akhtuba, river, Russ. 47°55' N, 46°29' E 158
Akhtubinsk, Russ. 48°17' N, 46°10' E 158
Aki, Japan 33°30' N, 133°54' E 201
Akie, river, Can. 57°15' N, 124°59' W 108
Akimiski Island, Can. 53°8' N, 84°10' W 106
Akita, Japan 39°48' N, 140°10' E 190
Akitio, N.Z. 40°37' S, 176°23' E 240
Akjoujt, Mauritania 19°43' N, 14°24' W 222
Akka, Mor. 29°24' N, 8°15' W 214
Akkala, Uzb. 43°40' N, 59°32' E 207
Akkaraipattu, Sri Lanka 7°14' N, 81°52' E 188
Akkarvik, Nor. 70°3' N, 20°30' E 152
'Akko (Acre), Israel 32°55' N, 35°4' E 194
Akkuş, Turk. 40°48' N, 36°59' E 156
Aklavik, Can. 68°13' N, 135°6' W 98
Aklera, India 24°24' N, 76°34' E 197
Akmenė, Lith. 56°15' N, 22°41' E 166
Akmeqit, China 37°7' N, 77°0' E 184
Aknīste, Latv. 56°8' N, 25°46' E 166
Akō, Japan 34°45' N, 134°22' E 201
Akobo, Sudan 7°45' N, 33°0' E 224
Ākobo, river, Africa 7°0' N, 34°13' E 224
Akokane, Niger 18°43' N, 7°9' E 222
Akola, India 20°41' N, 77°1' E 188
Akom, Cameroon 2°50' N, 10°34' E 218
Akonolinga, Cameroon 3°50' N, 12°15' E 218
Akor, Mali 14°52' N, 6°59' W 222
Akosombo, Ghana 6°20' N, 2°119' E 222
Akosombo Dam, Ghana 6°1' N, 0°14' E 222
Akot, India 21°6' N, 77°5' E 188
Akot, Sudan 6°31' N, 30°4' E 224
Akpatok Island, Can. 60°24' N, 72°3' W 106
Akqi, China 40°56' N, 78°33' E 184
Akrabat, Turkm. 35°29' N, 61°45' E 186
'Akramah, ruin(s), Lib. 31°59' N, 23°31' E 180
Akranes, Ice. 64°21' N, 21°60' W 143
Akreidil, spring, Mauritania 18°29' N, 15°39' W 222
Akron, Ala., U.S. 32°52' N, 87°44' W 103
Akron, Colo., U.S. 40°9' N, 103°13' W 90
Akron, Ind., U.S. 41°1' N, 86°1' W 102
Akron, Iowa, U.S. 42°48' N, 96°34' W 90
Akron, Mich., U.S. 43°33' N, 83°31' W 102
Akron, Ohio, U.S. 41°5' N, 81°31' W 102
Akrotiri, Cyprus 34°35' N, 32°56' E 194
Akrotírio Apolitáres, Gr. 35°50' N, 23°21' E 156
Akrotírio Dafnoúdi, Gr. 38°28' N, 19°38' E 156
Akrotírio Doukáto, Gr. 38°35' N, 19°40' E 156
Akrotírio Gérakas, Gr. 36°46' N, 23°7' E 156
Akrotírio Ginas, Gr. 36°4' N, 28°5' E 156
Akrotírio Griá, Gr. 37°49' N, 24°58' E 156
Akrotírio Hélatros, Gr. 35°12' N, 27°2' E 156
Akrotírio Kafiéas, Gr. 38°9' N, 24°37' E 156
Akrotírio Kapélo, Gr. 36°4' N, 23°4' E 156
Akrotírio Katomíi, Gr. 36°50' N, 24°36' E 156
Akrotírio Keáli, Gr. 35°49' N, 22°34' E 156
Akrotírio Kilopas, Gr. 37°3' N, 23°37' E 156
Akrotírio Korakas, Gr. 39°23' N, 25°29' E 156
Akrotírio Maléas, Gr. 36°22' N, 23°13' E 156
Akrotírio Mestá, Gr. 38°15' N, 25°6' E 156
Akrotírio Moúnda, Gr. 37°59' N, 19°56' E 156
Akrotírio Pláka, Gr. 35°4' N, 26°19' E 156
Akrotírio Spánda, Gr. 35°41' N, 23°46' E 156
Akrotírio Spathí, Gr. 36°16' N, 22°58' E 156
Akrotírio Stavrí, Gr. 37°13' N, 24°54' E 156
Akrotírio Stenó, Gr. 37°42' N, 24°58' E 156
Akrotírio Ténaro (Matapás, Taenarum), Gr. 36°13' N, 21°38' E 156
Aksaray, Turk. 38°21' N, 34°1' E 156
Aksarka, Russ. 66°29' N, 67°47' E 169
Aksay, China 39°25' N, 94°14' E 188
Aksay, Russ. 47°58' N, 39°52' E 158
Aksayqin Hu, lake, China 35°8' N, 78°55' E 188
Akşehir, Turk. 38°20' N, 31°25' E 156
Akşehir Gölü, lake, Turk. 38°32' N, 31°9' E 156
Akseki, Turk. 37°2' N, 31°47' E 156
'Aksha, ruin(s), Egypt 22°4' N, 31°12' E 182
Ak-Shyyrak, Kyrg. 41°54' N, 78°43' E 184
Aksu, China 41°9' N, 80°15' E 184
Aksu, Kaz. 42°34' N, 52°43' E 158
Aksu, river, China 40°58' N, 80°24' E 184
Aksū, river, Kaz. 45°44' N, 79°0' E 184
Āksum, Eth. 14°7' N, 38°41' E 182
Aktag, peak, China 36°43' N, 84°36' E 184
Aktash, Russ. 50°21' N, 87°48' E 184
Ak-Tektir, Kyrg. 42°12' N, 72°26' E 197
Akto, China 39°8' N, 75°54' E 184
Aktogay, Kaz. 48°51' N, 60°6' E 158
Aktsyabrski, Belarus 52°36' N, 28°58' E 152
Akujärvi, Fin. 68°40' N, 27°42' E 152
Akula, Dem. Rep. of the Congo 2°20' N, 20°15' E 218
Akune, Japan 32°1' N, 130°13' E 201
Akure, Nig. 7°18' N, 5°11' E 222
Akureyri, Ice. 65°41' N, 18°16' W 246
Akuse, Ghana 6°4' N, 9°535' E 222
Akwatia, Ghana 6°0' N, 0°48' E 214
Akyaka, Turk. 40°45' N, 43°32' E 195
Āl 'Ābis, Saudi Arabia 18°1' N, 43°9' E 182
Al 'Adam, Lib. 31°53' N, 23°57' E 180
Al Aḩmadī, Kuwait 29°3' N, 48°4' E 180
Al Akhḑar, Saudi Arabia 28°3' N, 37°7' E 180
Al' Amādīyah, Iraq 37°7' N, 43°29' E 180
Al' Amārah, Iraq 31°53' N, 47°9' E 180
Al 'Ammārīyah, Iraq 37°6' N, 43°22' E 195
Al 'Ānāt, Syr. 32°20' N, 36°48' E 194
Al 'Aqabah, Jordan 29°34' N, 35°4' E 180
Al 'Aqīq, Saudi Arabia 20°40' N, 41°22' E 182
Al 'Arīḑah, Leb. 34°38' N, 35°59' E 194
Al Arţāwīyah, Saudi Arabia 26°29' N, 45°23' E 180
Al As'ad, Saudi Arabia 27°50' N, 37°22' E 180
Al Ashkharah, Oman 21°52' N, 59°32' E 182
Al 'Athāmīn, peak, Iraq 30°20' N, 43°33' E 180
Al 'Ayn, U.A.E. 24°10' N, 55°38' E 196
Al 'Ayzarīyah, Israel 31°45' N, 35°15' E 194
Al Bad', Saudi Arabia 28°26' N, 35°4' E 180
Al Badī', Saudi Arabia 22°5' N, 46°30' E 207
Al Bāḩah, Saudi Arabia 20°3' N, 41°33' E 182
Al Baḩrah, spring, Kuwait 29°35' N, 47°59' E 196
Al Bardī, Lib. 31°46' N, 25°3' E 180
Al Basīt, Ra's, Syr. 35°50' N, 35°50' E 156
Al Başrah, Iraq 30°29' N, 47°49' E 180
Al Bayād, Saudi Arabia 23°42' N, 47°48' E 196
Al Biqā' (Bekaa Valley), region, Leb. 33°43' N, 35°51' E 194
Al Bi'r, Saudi Arabia 28°51' N, 36°15' E 180
Al Bir Lahlou, Western Sahara 26°23' N, 9°32' W 214
Al Bīrah, West Bank 31°53' N, 35°12' E 194
Al Birk, Saudi Arabia 18°8' N, 41°36' E 182
Al Birkah, Lib. 24°50' N, 10°8' E 216
Al Bunduq, oil field, U.A.E. 25°2' N, 52°25' E 196
Al Burayj, Gaza Strip 31°25' N, 34°24' E 194
Al Buraymī, Oman 24°11' N, 55°49' E 196
Al Burjayn, Tun. 35°40' N, 10°35' E 156
Al Dafyānah, Jordan 32°18' N, 36°38' E 194
Al Fallūjah (Falljuh), Iraq 33°19' N, 43°46' E 180
Al Farciya, Western Sahara 27°8' N, 9°52' W 214
Al Fāw, Iraq 29°59' N, 48°28' E 196
Al Fayḑah, Saudi Arabia 25°15' N, 44°25' E 182
Al Fujayrah, U.A.E. 25°10' N, 56°18' E 196
Al Fuqahā', Lib. 27°50' N, 16°20' E 216
Al Furāt (Euphrates), river, Syr. 35°43' N, 39°21' E 180
Al Furāt, river, Iraq 32°7' N, 44°56' E 180
Al Ghārīyah, Syr. 32°23' N, 36°39' E 194
Al Ghayḑah, Yemen 16°12' N, 52°14' E 182
Al Ghayḑah, Yemen 14°55' N, 49°58' E 182
Al Ghayl, Saudi Arabia 22°33' N, 46°18' E 182
Al Ghayl, Yemen 16°3' N, 44°48' E 182
Al Ghazālah, Saudi Arabia 26°42' N, 41°22' E 180
Al Ghuwayr, Jordan 31°8' N, 35°45' E 194
Al Ḩaddār, Saudi Arabia 21°56' N, 45°58' E 182
Al Ḩadīdah, Saudi Arabia 21°32' N, 50°30' E 182
Al Ḩadīthah, Iraq 34°8' N, 42°27' E 180
Al Haggounia, Western Sahara 27°25' N, 12°26' W 214
Al Ḩallānīyah, island, Oman 17°35' N, 55°22' E 182
Al Ḩamād, Saudi Arabia 31°17' N, 37°38' E 180
Al Ḩamīdīyah, Syr. 34°42' N, 35°56' E 194
Al Ḩammār, Hawr, lake, Iraq 30°49' N, 46°38' E 180
Al Ḩamrā', Lib. 29°39' N, 12°0' E 216
Al Ḩamrā', Saudi Arabia 23°55' N, 38°51' E 182
Al Ḩamūd, Jordan 31°17' N, 35°47' E 194
Al Ḩanākīyah, Saudi Arabia 24°50' N, 40°29' E 182
Al Ḩaqw, Saudi Arabia 17°33' N, 42°40' E 182
Al Ḩarīq, Saudi Arabia 23°35' N, 46°33' E 196
Al Harūj al Aswad, Lib. 28°27' N, 17°15' E 216
Al Ḩasakah, Syr. 36°31' N, 40°46' E 195
Al Ḩasānī, island, Saudi Arabia 25°1' N, 36°30' E 182
Al Ḩawīyah, Saudi Arabia 21°26' N, 40°31' E 182
Al Ḩawrah, Yemen 13°51' N, 47°33' E 182
Al Ḩayy, Iraq 32°9' N, 46°5' E 180
Al Hījānah, Syr. 33°21' N, 36°32' E 194
Al Ḩijāz (Hejaz), region, Saudi Arabia 26°54' N, 36°41' E 180
Al Ḩillah, Iraq 32°27' N, 44°26' E 180
Al Ḩillah (Hauta), Saudi Arabia 23°28' N, 46°52' E 196
Al Ḩimā, spring, Saudi Arabia 18°13' N, 44°30' E 182
Al Ḩişn, Jordan 32°28' N, 35°53' E 194
Al Hoceima, Mor. 35°14' N, 3°57' W 150
Al Ḩudaydah, Yemen 14°48' N, 42°56' E 182
Al Hufūf (Hofuf), Saudi Arabia 25°21' N, 49°34' E 196
Al Ḩulwah, Saudi Arabia 23°23' N, 46°49' E 182
Al Ḩunayy, Saudi Arabia 24°58' N, 48°46' E 196
Al Hūwah, Saudi Arabia 23°0' N, 45°48' E 182
Al Ikhwān (The Brothers), islands, Yemen 11°24' N, 52°52' E 182
Al 'Irqah, Yemen 13°40' N, 47°19' E 182
Al 'Īsāwīyah, Saudi Arabia 30°41' N, 38°1' E 180
Al Jabalash Sharqī (Anti-Lebanon), Leb. 34°5' N, 36°21' E 194
Al Jaghbūb, Lib. 29°45' N, 24°30' E 180
Al Jawf, Lib. 24°10' N, 23°16' E 216
Al Jawf, Saudi Arabia 29°54' N, 39°51' E 143
Al Jazīrah, spring, Lib. 25°43' N, 21°7' E 216
Al Jehrā, Kuwait 29°21' N, 47°40' E 196
Al Jīb, West Bank 31°50' N, 35°10' E 194
Al Jifāra, Tun. 32°1' N, 11°10' E 214
Al Jīzah, Jordan 31°41' N, 35°57' E 194
Al Jubayl, Saudi Arabia 26°59' N, 49°39' E 196
Al Jubaylah, Saudi Arabia 24°52' N, 46°28' E 196
Al Jumaylīyah, Qatar 25°36' N, 51°7' E 196
Al Jumaymah, spring, Saudi Arabia 29°41' N, 43°37' E 180
Al Junaynah, Saudi Arabia 20°15' N, 42°50' E 182
Al Kahfah, Saudi Arabia 27°2' N, 43°3' E 180
Al Karak, Jordan 31°10' N, 35°42' E 194
Al Kawm, Syr. 35°12' N, 38°51' E 180
Al Khābūrah, Oman 23°54' N, 57°7' E 196
Al Khalīl (Hebron), West Bank 31°31' N, 35°6' E 194
Al Kharfah, Saudi Arabia 22°11' N, 46°41' E 182
Al Kharj, Saudi Arabia 24°10' N, 47°20' E 196
Al Khāşirah, Saudi Arabia 23°29' N, 43°44' E 182
Al Khawr, Qatar 25°41' N, 51°30' E 196
Al Khīrān, Kuwait 28°36' N, 48°21' E 196
Al Khiyam, Leb. 33°19' N, 35°36' E 194
Al Khubar, Saudi Arabia 26°13' N, 50°8' E 196
Al Khufayfīyah, Saudi Arabia 24°54' N, 44°44' E 182
Al Khums, Lib. 32°42' N, 14°16' E 216
Al Khunn, Saudi Arabia 23°16' N, 49°15' E 182
Al Khuraybah, Yemen 15°7' N, 48°20' E 182
Al Khurmah, Saudi Arabia 21°51' N, 42°3' E 182
Al Kifl, Iraq 32°16' N, 44°24' E 180
Al Kūfah (Kufah), Iraq 32°5' N, 44°27' E 186
Al Kufrah (Kufra Oasis), Lib. 24°20' N, 23°44' E 226
Al Kūt, Iraq 32°34' N, 45°49' E 180
Al Kuwayt (Kuwait), Kuwait 29°20' N, 47°52' E 196
Al La'bān, Jordan 30°54' N, 35°42' E 194
Al Labwah, Leb. 34°11' N, 36°21' E 194
Al Lādhiqīyah (Latakia), Syr. 35°31' N, 35°47' E 194
Al Lajā, Syr. 32°53' N, 36°19' E 194
Al Lawz, Jabal, peak, Saudi Arabia 28°38' N, 35°13' E 180
Al Lidām, Saudi Arabia 20°27' N, 44°48' E 182
Al Līth, Saudi Arabia 20°8' N, 40°18' E 182
Al Luḩayyah, Yemen 15°41' N, 42°42' E 182
Al Luwaymī, Saudi Arabia 27°54' N, 42°12' E 180
Al Ma'ānīyah, spring, Iraq 30°42' N, 42°57' E 180
Al Madīnah (Medina), Saudi Arabia 24°26' N, 39°34' E 182
Al Madwar, Jordan 32°17' N, 35°59' E 194
Al Mafraq, Jordan 32°20' N, 36°12' E 194
Al Mahbas, Western Sahara 27°27' N, 9°2' W 214
Al Maḩrūqah, Lib. 27°29' N, 14°0' E 216
Al Majma'ah, Saudi Arabia 25°52' N, 45°23' E 182
Al Malāqī, spring, Lib. 26°53' N, 16°49' E 216
Al Mālikīyah, Syr. 37°11' N, 42°4' E 195
Al Manāmah (Manama), Bahrain 26°10' N, 50°27' E 196
Al Manzil, Jordan 31°3' N, 36°0' E 194
Al Marj (Barce), Lib. 32°30' N, 20°53' E 216
Al Mashrafah, Syr. 34°50' N, 36°52' E 194
Al Mawşil (Mosul), Iraq 36°20' N, 43°0' E 195
Al Mayādīn, Syr. 35°0' N, 40°24' E 180
Al Mayyāh, Saudi Arabia 27°50' N, 42°49' E 180
Al Mazra'ah, Jordan 31°17' N, 35°32' E 194
Al Mazzah, Syr. 33°30' N, 36°14' E 194
Al Mintirib, Oman 22°24' N, 58°49' E 182
Al Minyah, Leb. 34°28' N, 35°56' E 194
Al Mismīyah, Syr. 33°7' N, 36°23' E 194
Al Mubarraz, Saudi Arabia 25°27' N, 49°35' E 196
Al Mudawwarah, Jordan 29°23' N, 36°2' E 180
Al Mughayrā', U.A.E. 24°3' N, 53°31' E 196
Al Mukallā, Yemen 14°33' N, 49°6' E 182
Al Mukhā, Yemen 13°20' N, 43°14' E 182
Al Musayyib, Iraq 32°47' N, 44°21' E 180
Al Mushannaf, Syr. 32°44' N, 36°46' E 194
Al Muwaqqar, ruin(s), Jordan 31°48' N, 36°2' E 194
Al Muwayh, Saudi Arabia 22°43' N, 41°37' E 182
Al Muwayliḩ, Saudi Arabia 27°41' N, 35°28' E 180
Al Qābil, Oman 23°52' N, 55°51' E 196
Al Qaḑīmah, Saudi Arabia 22°19' N, 39°8' E 182
Al Qadmūs, Syr. 35°5' N, 36°9' E 194
Al Qā'im, Iraq 34°17' N, 41°11' E 180
Al Qa'īyah, Saudi Arabia 24°19' N, 43°32' E 182
Al Qā'īyah, spring, Saudi Arabia 26°28' N, 45°33' E 196
Al Qāmishlī, Syr. 37°2' N, 41°16' E 195
Al Qārah, Yemen 13°41' N, 45°15' E 182
Al Qaryah ash Sharqīyah, Lib. 30°23' N, 13°33' E 216
Al Qaryatayn, Syr. 34°10' N, 37°17' E 180
Al Qaşr, Jordan 31°18' N, 35°44' E 194
Al Qaţīf, Saudi Arabia 26°32' N, 49°59' E 196
Al Qaţrānah, Jordan 31°14' N, 36°1' E 194
Al Qaţrūn, Lib. 24°53' N, 14°29' E 216
Al Qawārishah, Lib. 32°1' N, 20°5' E 216
Al Qaws, site, Lib. 30°26' N, 18°21' E 216
Al Qayşūmah, Saudi Arabia 28°18' N, 46°9' E 196
Al Qunayţirah (Quneitra), Syr. 33°7' N, 35°49' E 194
Al Qunfudhah, Saudi Arabia 19°6' N, 41°7' E 182
Al Quraynī, spring, Saudi Arabia 21°51' N, 53°48' E 182
Al Qurayyah, Syr. 32°32' N, 36°35' E 194
Al Qurnah, Iraq 30°55' N, 47°22' E 180
Al Quşayr, Syr. 34°30' N, 36°34' E 194
Al Quşūrīyah, Saudi Arabia 23°43' N, 44°37' E 182
Al Quţayfah, Syr. 33°43' N, 36°35' E 194
Al Quway'īyah, Saudi Arabia 24°2' N, 45°15' E 182
Al 'Ubaylah, Saudi Arabia 21°58' N, 50°56' E 182
Al 'Udaysah, Leb. 33°15' N, 35°32' E 194
Al 'Ulá, Saudi Arabia 26°36' N, 37°51' E 180
Al 'Uqaylah, Lib. 30°13' N, 19°11' E 216
Al 'Uqayr, Saudi Arabia 25°38' N, 50°8' E 196
Al 'Uwaynāt see 'Uweinat, Jebel, peak, Sudan 21°51' N, 24°58' E 226
Al 'Uwaynāt (Serdeles), Lib. 25°47' N, 10°33' E 216
Al 'Uwaynid, Saudi Arabia 24°54' N, 45°48' E 182
Al 'Uwayqīlah, Saudi Arabia 30°18' N, 42°12' E 180
Al 'Uyūn, Saudi Arabia 26°30' N, 43°40' E 180
Al 'Uyūn, Saudi Arabia 24°33' N, 39°33' E 182
Al 'Uzayr, Iraq 31°19' N, 47°23' E 180
Al Wābirīyah, spring, Lib. 27°24' N, 18°5' E 216
Al Wafra, Kuwait 28°35' N, 47°57' E 196
Al Wajh, Saudi Arabia 26°15' N, 36°27' E 180
Al Wakrah, Qatar 25°6' N, 51°35' E 196
Al Wannān, Saudi Arabia 26°53' N, 48°26' E 196
Al Waqbah, spring, Saudi Arabia 28°52' N, 45°26' E 196
Al Warī'ah, Saudi Arabia 27°47' N, 47°32' E 196
Al Yādūdah, Jordan 31°50' N, 35°54' E 194
Ala, It. 45°45' N, 11°0' E 167
Alà, Monti di, It. 40°33' N, 8°47' E 156
Ala-Archa National Park, site, Kyrg. 42°35' N, 74°19' E 197
Alabama, adm. division, Ala., U.S. 31°51' N, 88°21' W 96
Alabama, river, Ala., U.S. 31°12' N, 87°54' W 103
Alabaster, Ala., U.S. 33°14' N, 86°49' W 96
Alaca, Turk. 40°8' N, 34°50' E 156
Alaca Dağ, peak, Turk. 37°28' N, 32°4' E 156
Alacahöyük, ruin(s), Turk. 40°13' N, 34°37' E 156
Alaçam, Turk. 41°35' N, 35°36' E 156
Alachua, Fla., U.S. 29°47' N, 82°30' W 105
Alacón, Sp. 41°1' N, 0°43' E 164
Aladağ, peak, Turk. 37°42' N, 35°5' E 156
Aladağ, peak, Turk. 37°56' N, 32°0' E 156
Ālagē, Āmba, peak, Eth. 12°57' N, 39°23' E 182
Alagir, Russ. 43°3' N, 44°14' E 195
Alagna Valsesia, It. 45°51' N, 7°56' E 167
Alagoas, adm. division, Braz. 9°35' S, 37°52' W 132
Alagoinhas, Braz. 12°10' S, 38°24' W 132
Alagón, Sp. 41°45' N, 1°8' W 164
Alai Mountains, Kyrg. 39°53' N, 72°4' E 184

Alaior, *Sp.* 39°55′ N, 4°8′ E 164
Alajärvi, *Fin.* 62°59′ N, 23°46′ E 152
Alajärvi, *Fin.* 64°58′ N, 28°45′ E 152
Alajuela, *C.R.* 10°0′ N, 84°12′ W 115
Alakanuk, *Alas., U.S.* 62°34′ N, 164°50′ W 98
Alakoko Fishpond, site, *Hawai'i, U.S.* 21°56′ N, 159°25′ W 99
Alaköl, lake, *Kaz.* 46°20′ N, 81°30′ E 184
Alakurtti, *Russ.* 66°58′ N, 30°24′ E 152
Alalakh, ruin(s), *Turk.* 36°11′ N, 36°16′ E 156
Alalaú, river, *Braz.* 0°23′ N, 60°19′ W 130
'Alam el Rûm, Râs, *Egypt* 31°25′ N, 27°18′ E 226
Alama, *Cen. Af. Rep.* 5°29′ N, 21°51′ E 218
Alamagan, island, *U.S.* 17°32′ N, 144°34′ E 192
Alameda, *Calif., U.S.* 37°46′ N, 122°17′ W 100
Alameda, *Can.* 49°15′ N, 102°19′ W 90
Alameda, *N. Mex., U.S.* 35°10′ N, 106°38′ W 92
Alameda, *Sp.* 37°13′ N, 4°40′ W 164
Alamedilla, *Sp.* 37°36′ N, 3°15′ W 164
Alamillo, *Sp.* 38°39′ N, 4°47′ W 164
Alamitos, Sierra de los, peak, *Mex.* 26°19′ N, 102°22′ W 114
Alamo, *Ind., U.S.* 39°58′ N, 87°4′ W 102
Álamo, *Mex.* 20°54′ N, 97°41′ W 114
Alamo, *Tenn., U.S.* 35°48′ N, 89°6′ W 96
Alamo Lake, *Ariz., U.S.* 34°18′ N, 113°36′ W 101
Alamo, river, *Calif., U.S.* 32°55′ N, 115°31′ W 101
Álamo, river, *Mex.* 26°31′ N, 99°57′ W 114
Alamogordo, *N. Mex., U.S.* 32°54′ N, 105°57′ W 92
Álamos, *Mex.* 29°12′ N, 110°8′ W 92
Álamos, river, *Mex.* 26°56′ N, 109°8′ W 80
Alanäs, *Nor.* 64°8′ N, 15°39′ E 152
Åland (Ahvenanmaa), island, *Fin.* 60°26′ N, 19°33′ E 166
Alanís, *Sp.* 38°2′ N, 5°44′ W 164
Alanta, *Lith.* 55°21′ N, 25°17′ E 166
Alantika Mountains, *Cameroon* 8°35′ N, 12°15′ E 216
Alanya (Coracesium), *Turk.* 36°31′ N, 32°1′ E 180
Alapayevsk, *Russ.* 57°50′ N, 61°38′ E 154
Alappuzha see Alleppey, *India* 9°29′ N, 76°20′ E 188
Alaquines, *Mex.* 22°6′ N, 99°36′ W 114
Alarcón, *Sp.* 39°32′ N, 2°5′ W 164
Alas Purwo National Park, *Indonesia* 8°40′ S, 114°4′ E 238
Alas, river, *Indonesia* 3°22′ N, 97°44′ E 196
Alaşehir, *Turk.* 38°21′ N, 28°31′ E 156
Alaska, adm. division, *Alas., U.S.* 64°46′ N, 156°29′ W 98
Alaska, Gulf of 57°56′ N, 149°1′ W 98
Alaska Highway, *Can.* 57°34′ N, 122°49′ W 108
Alaska Peninsula, *North America* 58°0′ N, 157°11′ W 98
Alaska Range, *North America* 62°13′ N, 153°16′ W 98
Alassio, *It.* 44°0′ N, 8°10′ E 167
Alasuolijärvi, lake, *Fin.* 66°17′ N, 27°9′ E 152
Älät, *Azerb.* 39°56′ N, 49°23′ E 195
Alatoz, *Sp.* 39°5′ N, 1°22′ W 164
Alatyr', *Russ.* 54°47′ N, 46°37′ E 154
Alava, Cape, *Wash., U.S.* 48°4′ N, 124°53′ W 100
Alaverdi, *Arm.* 41°6′ N, 44°38′ E 195
Alāyat Samā'il, *Oman* 23°14′ N, 58°3′ E 182
Alazeya, river, *Russ.* 70°55′ N, 153°45′ E 160
Alba, *It.* 44°41′ N, 8°2′ E 167
Alba, *Tex., U.S.* 32°46′ N, 95°38′ W 103
Alba, adm. division, *Rom.* 46°13′ N, 22°59′ E 156
Alba, Foum el, pass, *Mali* 20°40′ N, 3°37′ W 222
Alba Iulia, *Rom.* 46°3′ N, 23°35′ E 168
Albac, *Rom.* 46°27′ N, 22°58′ E 168
Albacete, *Sp.* 38°58′ N, 1°51′ W 164
Albalá del Caudillo, *Sp.* 39°14′ N, 6°11′ W 164
Albalate del Arzobispo, *Sp.* 41°7′ N, 0°31′ E 164
Albanel, Lac, lake, *Can.* 50°52′ N, 74°31′ W 106
Albania 40°43′ N, 19°44′ E 156
Albano, *Braz.* 2°29′ S, 57°32′ W 130
Albany, *Ga., U.S.* 31°34′ N, 84°10′ W 96
Albany, *Ind., U.S.* 40°18′ N, 85°14′ W 102
Albany, *Ky., U.S.* 36°40′ N, 85°8′ W 96
Albany, *La., U.S.* 30°29′ N, 90°35′ W 103
Albany, *Mo., U.S.* 40°13′ N, 94°19′ W 94
Albany, *N.Y., U.S.* 42°38′ N, 73°50′ W 104
Albany, *Ohio, U.S.* 39°13′ N, 82°13′ W 102
Albany, *Oreg., U.S.* 44°36′ N, 123°6′ W 90
Albany, *Tex., U.S.* 32°43′ N, 99°18′ W 92
Albany, *Wis., U.S.* 42°42′ N, 89°26′ W 102
Albany Island, *Can.* 52°20′ N, 82°53′ W 81
Albany, river, *Can.* 51°8′ N, 89°34′ W 110
Albares, *Sp.* 40°17′ N, 2°60′ W 164
Albarracín, *Sp.* 40°24′ N, 1°28′ W 164
Albemarle Sound 35°57′ N, 77°15′ W 80
Albenga, *It.* 44°3′ N, 8°13′ E 167
Albens, *Fr.* 45°46′ N, 5°56′ E 150
Alberdi, *Parag.* 26°12′ S, 58°4′ W 139
Alberese, *It.* 42°40′ N, 11°5′ E 156
Alberic, *Sp.* 39°6′ N, 0°31′ E 164
Alberni Inlet 48°57′ N, 124°47′ W 100
Albert, *Fr.* 50°0′ N, 2°39′ E 163
Albert Icefield, *Can.* 50°49′ N, 118°18′ W 90
Albert Kanaal, canal, *Belg.* 51°8′ N, 4°47′ E 163
Albert Lea, *Minn., U.S.* 43°37′ N, 93°23′ W 94
Albert Markham, Mount, *Antarctica* 81°20′ S, 159°13′ E 248
Albert, Mount, *Can.* 53°31′ N, 66°47′ W 111
Alberta, *Ala., U.S.* 32°13′ N, 87°25′ W 103
Alberta, adm. division, *Can.* 54°43′ N, 116°17′ W 108
Alberti, *Arg.* 35°1′ S, 60°18′ W 139
Albertirsa, *Hung.* 47°14′ N, 19°37′ E 168
Alberton, *Mont., U.S.* 46°59′ N, 114°29′ W 90
Albertville, *Ala., U.S.* 34°15′ N, 86°12′ W 96
Albi, *Fr.* 43°54′ N, 2°9′ E 150
Albia, *Iowa, U.S.* 41°1′ N, 92°47′ W 94
Albin, *Wyo., U.S.* 41°25′ N, 104°6′ W 90
Albina, *Suriname* 5°31′ N, 54°6′ W 130
Albina, Ponta, *Angola* 15°56′ S, 11°11′ E 220
Albinia, *It.* 42°31′ N, 11°13′ E 156
Albino, *It.* 45°46′ N, 9°47′ E 167
Al'bino, *Russ.* 59°22′ N, 83°4′ E 169
Albion, *Mich., U.S.* 42°14′ N, 84°45′ W 102
Albion, *Nebr., U.S.* 41°39′ N, 98°1′ W 90
Albion, *N.Y., U.S.* 43°14′ N, 78°13′ W 110
Albisola Marina, *It.* 44°19′ N, 8°30′ E 167
Albocácer, *Sp.* 40°21′ N, 0°2′ E 164
Alborán, Isla de, island, *Sp.* 35°57′ N, 3°17′ W 164
Alboran Sea 35°34′ N, 4°26′ W 150
Alborea, *Sp.* 39°15′ N, 1°23′ W 164
Ålborg, *Den.* 57°1′ N, 9°55′ E 150
Ålborg Bugt 56°51′ N, 9°52′ E 152
Alborz, oil field, *Iran* 34°39′ N, 51°0′ E 180
Alborz, Reshteh-ye (Elburz Mountains), *Iran* 36°43′ N, 49°25′ E 195
Albota de Jos, *Mold.* 45°56′ N, 28°29′ E 158
Albox, *Sp.* 37°23′ N, 2°10′ W 164
Albreda, *Can.* 52°37′ N, 119°10′ W 108
Albuquerque, *N. Mex., U.S.* 35°5′ N, 106°39′ W 92
Albury, *Austral.* 36°4′ S, 146°57′ E 231
Alby, *Nor.* 62°29′ N, 15°27′ E 152
Alca, *Peru* 15°10′ S, 72°46′ W 137
Alcácer do Sal, *Port.* 38°21′ N, 8°31′ W 150
Alcadozo, *Sp.* 38°38′ N, 1°59′ W 164
Alcalá de Chivert, *Sp.* 40°17′ N, 0°12′ E 164
Alcalá de Henares, *Sp.* 40°28′ N, 3°22′ W 164
Alcalá de los Gazules, *Sp.* 36°27′ N, 5°44′ W 150
Alcalá la Real, *Sp.* 37°28′ N, 3°56′ W 164
Alcalde, Punta, *Chile* 28°34′ S, 72°35′ W 134
Alcamo, *It.* 37°59′ N, 12°58′ E 156
Alcanar, *Sp.* 40°32′ N, 0°28′ E 164
Alcañiz, *Sp.* 41°1′ N, 0°7′ E 164
Alcántara, *Sp.* 39°42′ N, 6°53′ W 150
Alcantara Lake, *Can.* 60°55′ N, 109°3′ W 108
Alcantara Launch Center, spaceport, *Braz.* 2°18′ S, 44°32′ W 132
Alcantarilla, *Sp.* 37°58′ N, 1°14′ W 164
Alcaraz, *Sp.* 38°39′ N, 2°29′ W 164
Alcarràs, *Sp.* 41°33′ N, 0°30′ E 164
Alcaudete, *Sp.* 37°35′ N, 4°5′ W 164
Alcázar de San Juan, *Sp.* 39°23′ N, 3°13′ W 164
Alchevs'k, *Ukr.* 48°27′ N, 38°44′ E 158
Alcoa, *Tenn., U.S.* 35°47′ N, 83°58′ W 96
Alcoak, Cerro, peak, *Bol.* 22°26′ S, 66°54′ W 137
Alcocer, *Sp.* 40°28′ N, 2°36′ W 150
Alcoi see Alcoy, *Sp.* 38°41′ N, 0°29′ E 164
Alcolea, *Sp.* 37°55′ N, 4°41′ W 164
Alcolea del Pinar, *Sp.* 41°1′ N, 2°29′ W 164
Alconbury, *U.K.* 52°21′ N, 0°16′ E 162
Alcorcón, *Sp.* 40°19′ N, 3°51′ W 150
Alcorisa, *Sp.* 40°52′ N, 0°24′ E 164
Alcorta, *Arg.* 33°33′ S, 61°8′ W 139
Alcoutim, *Port.* 37°27′ N, 7°31′ W 150
Alcoy (Alcoi), *Sp.* 38°41′ N, 0°29′ E 164
Alcubierre, Sierra de, *Sp.* 41°42′ N, 0°44′ E 164
Alcúdia, *Sp.* 39°50′ N, 3°7′ E 164
Alcudia, Sierra de, *Sp.* 38°38′ N, 4°49′ W 164
Aldabra Islands, *Indian Ocean* 9°54′ S, 45°17′ E 218
Aldama, *Mex.* 28°49′ N, 105°56′ W 92
Aldama, *Mex.* 22°53′ N, 98°5′ W 114
Aldan, *Russ.* 58°39′ N, 125°29′ E 160
Aldan, river, *Russ.* 58°50′ N, 130°46′ E 160
Aldaz, Mount, *Antarctica* 75°57′ S, 123°51′ W 248
Aldbrough, *U.K.* 53°49′ N, 0°7′ E 162
Aldea Moret, *Sp.* 39°26′ N, 6°24′ W 164
Aldeburgh, *U.K.* 52°9′ N, 1°35′ E 163
Alden, Point, *Antarctica* 66°56′ S, 142°24′ E 248
Alder Dam, *Wash., U.S.* 46°48′ N, 122°26′ W 100
Alder Peak, *Calif., U.S.* 35°52′ N, 121°25′ W 100
Aldershot, *U.K.* 51°14′ N, 0°46′ E 162
Aldora, *Ga., U.S.* 33°2′ N, 84°12′ W 96
Aledo, *Mo., U.S.* 41°12′ N, 90°45′ W 94
Aleg, *Mauritania* 17°3′ N, 13°57′ W 222
Alegranza, island, *Sp.* 29°27′ N, 14°36′ W 214
Alegre, *Braz.* 20°48′ S, 41°35′ W 138
Alegre, *Braz.* 18°18′ S, 47°7′ W 138
Alegre, river, *Braz.* 15°11′ S, 59°48′ W 132
Alegres Mountain, *N. Mex., U.S.* 34°9′ N, 108°16′ W 92
Alegrete, *Braz.* 29°49′ S, 55°50′ W 139
Alejandra, *Arg.* 29°53′ S, 59°50′ W 139
Alejandro Roca, *Arg.* 33°26′ S, 63°43′ W 139
Alejo Ledesma, *Arg.* 33°37′ S, 62°37′ W 139
Alekhovshchina, *Russ.* 60°25′ N, 33°54′ E 154
Aleksandro Nevskiy, *Russ.* 53°26′ N, 40°12′ E 154
Aleksandrov, *Russ.* 56°23′ N, 38°42′ E 154
Aleksandrov Gay, *Russ.* 50°9′ N, 48°35′ E 158
Aleksandrovac, *Serb. and Mont.* 43°27′ N, 21°2′ E 168
Aleksandrovka, *Russ.* 52°40′ N, 54°25′ E 154
Aleksandrovsk, *Russ.* 59°10′ N, 57°36′ E 154
Aleksandrovsk Sakhalinskiy, *Russ.* 50°47′ N, 142°22′ E 190
Aleksandrovskoye, *Russ.* 56°47′ N, 85°37′ E 169
Alekseyevka, *Russ.* 52°18′ N, 48°3′ E 158
Alekseyevka, *Russ.* 50°40′ N, 38°41′ E 158
Alekseyevka, *Russ.* 52°35′ N, 51°15′ E 154
Alekseyevsk, *Russ.* 57°49′ N, 108°40′ E 160
Aleksin, *Russ.* 54°30′ N, 37°10′ E 154
Aleksinac, *Serb. and Mont.* 43°32′ N, 21°42′ E 168
Além Paraíba, *Braz.* 21°54′ S, 42°44′ W 138
Alemania, *Arg.* 25°37′ S, 65°38′ W 134
Alenquer, *Braz.* 1°59′ S, 54°49′ W 130
'Alenuihāhā Channel, *Hawai'i, U.S.* 20°17′ N, 156°24′ W 99
Alépé, *Côte d'Ivoire* 5°30′ N, 3°42′ W 222
Aleppo see Ḥalab, *Syr.* 36°11′ N, 37°9′ E 156
Aléria, *Fr.* 42°5′ N, 9°32′ E 156
Alert, *Can.* 82°29′ N, 61°46′ W 246
Alert Bay, *Can.* 50°31′ N, 126°50′ W 90
Alerta, *Peru* 10°46′ S, 71°50′ W 137
Alès, *Fr.* 44°7′ N, 4°4′ E 214
Aleşd, *Rom.* 47°4′ N, 22°23′ E 168
Alessandria, *It.* 44°54′ N, 8°37′ E 167
Ålesund, *Nor.* 62°27′ N, 6°2′ E 160
Alet, *Fr.* 42°59′ N, 2°14′ E 164
Aleutian Basin, *Bering Sea* 56°6′ N, 179°52′ E 252
Aleutian Islands, *Bering Sea* 54°5′ N, 164°2′ W 98
Aleutian Range, *North America* 56°36′ N, 158°49′ W 98
Aleutian Trench, *North Pacific Ocean* 49°58′ N, 174°26′ W 252
Alevina, Mys, *Russ.* 58°36′ N, 148°19′ E 160
Alexander, *N. Dak., U.S.* 47°49′ N, 103°40′ W 90
Alexander Archipelago, *North Pacific Ocean* 56°25′ N, 135°30′ W 98
Alexander Bay, *S. Af.* 28°43′ S, 16°27′ E 207
Alexander, Cape, *Antarctica* 67°21′ S, 61°14′ W 248
Alexander City, *Ala., U.S.* 32°56′ N, 85°57′ W 112
Alexander Island, *Wash., U.S.* 47°44′ N, 124°42′ W 100
Alexander, Mount, *Austral.* 22°39′ S, 115°23′ E 230
Alexandra Falls, *Can.* 60°42′ N, 116°54′ W 108
Alexandra Land, *Russ.* 81°0′ N, 47°0′ E 255
Alexandra, Zemlya, islands, *Zemlya Alexandra* 80°31′ N, 33°19′ E 160
Alexandria, *Can.* 52°38′ N, 122°27′ W 108
Alexandria, *Can.* 45°19′ N, 74°39′ W 94
Alexandria, *Ind., U.S.* 40°16′ N, 85°41′ W 102
Alexandria, *Ky., U.S.* 38°57′ N, 84°24′ W 102
Alexandria, *La., U.S.* 31°17′ N, 92°28′ W 103
Alexandria, *Minn., U.S.* 45°52′ N, 95°23′ W 90
Alexandria, *N.H., U.S.* 43°36′ N, 71°48′ W 104
Alexandria, *Rom.* 43°59′ N, 25°20′ E 156
Alexandria, *S. Af.* 33°39′ S, 26°24′ E 227
Alexandria, *S. Dak., U.S.* 43°37′ N, 97°46′ W 90
Alexandria, *Va., U.S.* 38°48′ N, 77°4′ W 94
Alexandria Bay, *N.Y., U.S.* 44°19′ N, 75°55′ W 94
Alexandria see El Iskandarîya, *Egypt* 31°10′ N, 29°55′ E 180
Alexandrium, ruin(s), *West Bank* 32°4′ N, 35°26′ E 194
Alexandroúpoli, *Gr.* 40°52′ N, 25°52′ E 180
Alexis Creek, *Can.* 52°5′ N, 123°19′ W 108
Alexis, river, *Can.* 52°28′ N, 57°29′ W 111
Aley, *Leb.* 33°48′ N, 35°36′ E 194
Aleysk, *Russ.* 52°32′ N, 82°53′ E 184
Aleza Lake, *Can.* 54°6′ N, 122°4′ W 108
Alfambra, *Sp.* 40°32′ N, 1°2′ W 164
Alfândega da Fé, *Port.* 41°20′ N, 6°59′ W 150
Alfaro, *Sp.* 42°10′ N, 1°45′ W 164
Alfenas, *Braz.* 21°28′ S, 45°56′ W 138
Alföld, *Hung.* 46°44′ N, 20°4′ E 168
Alfonsine, *It.* 44°29′ N, 12°2′ E 167
Alford, *U.K.* 53°15′ N, 0°11′ E 162
Alfred, *Me., U.S.* 43°28′ N, 70°44′ W 104
Alfred, Mount, *Can.* 50°10′ N, 124°4′ W 100
Alfredo M. Terrazas, *Mex.* 21°26′ N, 98°52′ W 114
Alfredton, *N.Z.* 40°41′ S, 175°53′ E 240
Alfreton, *U.K.* 53°6′ N, 1°24′ W 162
Alfta, *Nor.* 61°19′ N, 16°0′ E 152
Algarrobal, *Arg.* 25°29′ S, 64°1′ W 134
Algeciras, *Sp.* 36°7′ N, 5°28′ W 164
Algemesí, *Sp.* 39°11′ N, 0°26′ E 150
Algena, *Eritrea* 17°15′ N, 38°30′ E 182
Alger, *Mich., U.S.* 44°7′ N, 84°7′ W 102
Alger (Algiers), *Alg.* 36°44′ N, 2°56′ E 150
Alger, Mount, *Can.* 56°55′ N, 130°4′ W 108
Algeria 28°10′ N, 1°37′ W 214
Algha, *Kaz.* 49°57′ N, 57°20′ E 158
Alghabas, *Kaz.* 50°39′ N, 52°4′ E 158
Alghero, *It.* 40°33′ N, 8°19′ E 156
Algiers see Alger, *Alg.* 36°44′ N, 2°56′ E 150
Alginet, *Sp.* 39°16′ N, 0°29′ E 164
Algoa Bay 33°54′ S, 25°43′ E 227
Algodones, *Mex.* 32°42′ N, 114°45′ W 101
Algoma, *Wis., U.S.* 44°35′ N, 87°28′ W 94
Algona, *Iowa, U.S.* 43°3′ N, 94°14′ W 94
Algonac, *Mich., U.S.* 42°36′ N, 82°33′ W 102
Algonquin Park, *Can.* 45°32′ N, 78°35′ W 94
Algorta, *Uru.* 32°26′ S, 57°24′ W 139
Algy o, *Hung.* 46°19′ N, 20°13′ E 168
Alhama de Granada, *Sp.* 37°0′ N, 3°59′ W 164
Alhama de Murcia, *Sp.* 37°50′ N, 1°27′ W 164
Alhambra, *Sp.* 38°53′ N, 3°4′ W 164
Alhaurín el Grande, *Sp.* 36°38′ N, 4°42′ W 164
Alhuampa, *Arg.* 27°7′ S, 62°35′ W 139
Äli Bayramlı, *Azerb.* 39°56′ N, 48°54′ E 195
'Ali Sabīḥ, *Djibouti* 11°7′ N, 42°43′ E 218
Alía, *Sp.* 39°26′ N, 5°13′ W 164
Aliabad, *Iran* 28°33′ N, 55°47′ E 196
Aliaga, *Sp.* 40°40′ N, 0°42′ E 164
Alibunar, *Serb. and Mont.* 45°5′ N, 20°58′ E 168
Alicante, *Sp.* 38°20′ N, 0°30′ E 164
Alice, *S. Af.* 32°47′ S, 26°51′ E 227
Alice, *Tex., U.S.* 27°43′ N, 98°4′ W 92
Alice Arm, *Can.* 55°28′ N, 129°33′ W 108
Alice Creek, river, *Can.* 58°22′ N, 113°21′ W 108
Alice, Punta, *It.* 39°18′ N, 17°11′ E 156
Alice Town, *Bahamas* 25°43′ N, 79°17′ W 105
Alicedale, *S. Af.* 33°18′ S, 26°2′ E 227
Aliceville, *Ala., U.S.* 33°7′ N, 88°9′ W 103
Alicia, *Philippines* 7°33′ N, 122°57′ E 203
Alida, *Can.* 49°22′ N, 101°51′ W 90
Alida, peak, *Gr.* 39°6′ N, 21°11′ E 156
Alif, oil field, *Yemen* 15°45′ N, 46°7′ E 182
Aligarh, *India* 27°52′ N, 78°4′ E 197
Alijos, Rocas, islands, *North Pacific Ocean* 25°9′ N, 116°16′ W 112
'Ālika Cone, peak, *Hawai'i, U.S.* 19°15′ N, 155°47′ W 99
Alima, river, *Congo* 1°21′ S, 15°44′ E 218
Alimodian, *Philippines* 10°50′ N, 122°24′ E 203
Alindao, *Cen. Af. Rep.* 5°3′ N, 21°14′ E 218
Alingsås, *Nor.* 57°55′ N, 12°33′ E 152
Alins, *Sp.* 42°32′ N, 1°18′ E 164
Alinskoye, *Russ.* 63°19′ N, 87°36′ E 169
Alipur, *Pak.* 29°24′ N, 70°54′ E 186
Aliquippa, *Pa., U.S.* 40°37′ N, 80°15′ W 94
Alişar Hüyük (Alishar), ruin(s), *Turk.* 39°34′ N, 35°7′ E 156
Aliseda, *Sp.* 39°25′ N, 6°43′ W 164
Alishar see Alişar Hüyük, ruin(s), *Turk.* 39°34′ N, 35°7′ E 156
Alittjåkko, peak, *Nor.* 67°53′ N, 17°20′ E 152
Alivéri, *Gr.* 38°24′ N, 24°2′ E 156
Aliwal North, *S. Af.* 30°43′ S, 26°42′ E 227
Alix, *Can.* 52°22′ N, 113°11′ W 108
Alkmaar, *Neth.* 52°37′ N, 4°43′ E 163
Alla, *Russ.* 54°43′ N, 110°49′ E 173
Allada, *Benin* 6°45′ N, 2°9′ E 222
Allagash Falls, *Me., U.S.* 46°45′ N, 70°14′ W 94
Allagash Lake, lake, *Me., U.S.* 46°16′ N, 69°59′ W 94
Allahabad, *India* 25°26′ N, 81°49′ E 197
Allahabad, *Pak.* 28°55′ N, 70°53′ E 186
Allahüekber Dağı, peak, *Turk.* 40°33′ N, 42°28′ E 195
Allakaket, *Alas., U.S.* 66°30′ N, 152°26′ W 106
Allan Creek, river, *Can.* 60°20′ N, 130°53′ W 108
Allan Hills, *Antarctica* 76°41′ S, 158°26′ E 248
Allan Mountain, *Idaho, U.S.* 45°34′ N, 114°7′ W 90
Allan Water, *Can.* 50°14′ N, 90°12′ W 94
Allanmyo, *Myanmar* 19°23′ N, 95°12′ E 202
Allanridge, *S. Af.* 27°48′ S, 26°38′ E 227
Allanton, *N.Z.* 45°57′ S, 170°16′ E 240
Allegan, *Mich., U.S.* 42°31′ N, 85°51′ W 102
Alleghe, *It.* 46°25′ N, 12°1′ E 167
Allegheny Mountains, *North America* 37°1′ N, 82°33′ W 96
Allegheny Mountains, *W. Va., U.S.* 39°57′ N, 78°49′ W 106
Allen, *Philippines* 12°31′ N, 124°18′ E 203
Allen, Mount, *N.Z.* 47°8′ S, 167°43′ E 240
Allen, Punta, *Mex.* 19°51′ N, 88°7′ W 115
Allendale, *S.C., U.S.* 33°0′ N, 81°19′ W 96
Allendale Town, *U.K.* 54°53′ N, 2°16′ W 162
Allende, *Mex.* 28°19′ N, 100°51′ W 92
Allende, *Mex.* 25°18′ N, 99°60′ W 114
Allendorf, *Ger.* 50°40′ N, 8°47′ E 167
Allensworth, *Calif., U.S.* 35°51′ N, 119°24′ W 100
Allentown, *Pa., U.S.* 40°35′ N, 75°30′ W 94
Allentsteig, *Aust.* 48°41′ N, 15°20′ E 156
Alleppey (Alappuzha), *India* 9°29′ N, 76°20′ E 188
Allerton, *Ill., U.S.* 39°54′ N, 87°56′ W 102
Allgäuer Alpen, *Ger.* 47°27′ N, 9°48′ E 156
Allia Bay, site, *Kenya* 3°38′ N, 36°16′ E 224
Alliance, *Can.* 52°25′ N, 111°47′ W 108
Alliance, *Nebr., U.S.* 42°5′ N, 102°53′ W 90
Alliance, *Ohio, U.S.* 40°54′ N, 81°7′ W 102
Allier, river, *Fr.* 44°53′ N, 3°36′ E 165
Allison Peninsula, *Antarctica* 73°1′ S, 85°31′ W 248
Alliston, *Can.* 44°8′ N, 79°51′ W 94
Allo, *Sp.* 42°34′ N, 2°2′ W 164
Allos, *Fr.* 44°14′ N, 6°37′ E 167
Alluvial City, *La., U.S.* 29°49′ N, 89°43′ W 103
Allyn, *Wash., U.S.* 47°22′ N, 122°50′ W 100
Alma, *Can.* 48°30′ N, 71°40′ W 94
Alma, *Ga., U.S.* 31°31′ N, 82°28′ W 96
Alma, *Kans., U.S.* 38°59′ N, 96°18′ W 90
Alma, *Mich., U.S.* 43°22′ N, 84°40′ W 102
Alma, *Nebr., U.S.* 40°5′ N, 99°23′ W 90
Alma Peak, *Can.* 56°43′ N, 127°38′ W 108
Almacelles, *Sp.* 41°43′ N, 0°26′ E 164
Almadén, *Sp.* 38°46′ N, 4°51′ W 164
Almagro, *Sp.* 38°52′ N, 3°42′ W 164
Almami, *Mali* 14°55′ N, 5°2′ W 222
Almansa, *Sp.* 38°51′ N, 1°6′ W 164
Almanza, *Sp.* 42°38′ N, 5°4′ W 150
Almanzor, peak, *Sp.* 40°13′ N, 5°23′ W 150
Almas, *Braz.* 11°35′ S, 47°9′ W 130
Almaş, *Rom.* 46°56′ N, 23°8′ E 168
Almaş, Munţii, *Rom.* 44°42′ N, 22°4′ E 168
Almas, river, *Braz.* 15°8′ S, 49°18′ W 138
Almassora, *Sp.* 39°57′ N, 4°237′ W 150
Almaty, *Kaz.* 43°15′ N, 76°57′ E 184
Almaty, adm. division, *Kaz.* 44°42′ N, 75°55′ E 184
Almazán, *Sp.* 41°28′ N, 2°32′ W 164
Almaznoe, *Kaz.* 50°13′ N, 54°14′ E 158
Almeirim, *Braz.* 1°31′ S, 52°36′ W 130
Almelo, *Neth.* 52°20′ N, 6°39′ E 163
Almena, *Kans., U.S.* 39°53′ N, 99°43′ W 90
Almenar, *Sp.* 41°46′ N, 0°34′ E 164
Almenara, *Braz.* 16°11′ S, 40°45′ W 138
Almenara, peak, *Sp.* 38°32′ N, 2°29′ W 164
Almendra, *Sp.* 41°34′ N, 5°54′ W 150
Almendralejo, *Sp.* 38°41′ N, 6°25′ W 164
Almere, *Neth.* 52°20′ N, 5°9′ E 163
Almería, *Sp.* 36°49′ N, 2°28′ W 164
Al'met'yevsk, *Russ.* 54°51′ N, 52°17′ E 154
Almina, Punta, *Sp.* 35°53′ N, 5°17′ W 164
Almo, *Idaho, U.S.* 42°6′ N, 113°38′ W 92
Almonaster la Real, *Sp.* 37°51′ N, 6°48′ W 164
Almond Mountain, *Can.* 49°17′ N, 118°42′ W 90
Almont, *Mich., U.S.* 42°55′ N, 83°4′ W 102
Almonte, *Can.* 45°13′ N, 76°11′ W 94
Almonte, *Sp.* 37°15′ N, 6°31′ W 164
Almonte, river, *Sp.* 39°32′ N, 6°18′ W 164
Almoradí, *Sp.* 38°6′ N, 0°48′ E 164
Almudévar, *Sp.* 42°2′ N, 0°36′ E 164
Almuñécar, *Sp.* 36°43′ N, 3°41′ W 164
Almunge, *Sw.* 59°52′ N, 18°0′ E 166
Almuradiel, *Sp.* 38°30′ N, 3°30′ W 164
Almus, *Turk.* 40°22′ N, 36°53′ E 156
Almvik, *Nor.* 57°49′ N, 16°27′ E 152
Alnif, *Mor.* 31°8′ N, 5°12′ W 214
Aloja, *Latv.* 57°45′ N, 24°52′ E 166
Alonsa, *Can.* 50°48′ N, 98°59′ W 90
Alor, island, *Indonesia* 8°9′ S, 124°15′ E 192
Alor Setar, *Malaysia* 6°4′ N, 100°24′ E 196
Álora, *Sp.* 36°49′ N, 4°43′ W 164
Alot, *India* 23°45′ N, 75°31′ E 197
Aloysius, Mount, *Austral.* 26°3′ S, 128°22′ E 230
Alpachiri, *Arg.* 37°25′ S, 63°44′ W 139
Alpaugh, *Calif., U.S.* 35°53′ N, 119°30′ W 100
Alpedrinha, *Port.* 40°5′ N, 7°29′ W 150
Alpena, *Mich., U.S.* 45°3′ N, 83°28′ W 94
Alpera, *Sp.* 38°56′ N, 1°14′ W 164
Alpercatas, Serra das, *Braz.* 6°24′ S, 46°9′ W 130
Alpha Cordillera, *Arctic Ocean* 85°33′ N, 120°28′ W 255
Alpine, *Ariz., U.S.* 33°50′ N, 109°7′ W 92
Alpine, *Calif., U.S.* 32°50′ N, 116°47′ W 101
Alpine, *Tex., U.S.* 30°20′ N, 103°40′ W 92
Alps, *Europe* 44°14′ N, 6°2′ E 165
Al-Quds see Jerusalem, *Israel* 31°46′ N, 35°9′ E 194
Alsace, adm. division, *Fr.* 47°41′ N, 7°21′ E 150
Alsace, region, *Europe* 48°41′ N, 7°17′ E 163
Alsask, *Can.* 51°23′ N, 109°59′ W 90
Alsdorf, *Ger.* 50°52′ N, 6°10′ E 167
Alsea, river, *Oreg., U.S.* 44°18′ N, 124°1′ W 90
Alsfeld, *Ger.* 50°45′ N, 9°16′ E 167
Alstahaug, *Nor.* 65°53′ N, 12°23′ E 152
Alstead, *N.H., U.S.* 43°8′ N, 72°22′ W 104
Alston, *U.K.* 54°48′ N, 2°26′ W 162
Alsunga, *Latv.* 56°58′ N, 21°32′ E 166
Alta, *Iowa, U.S.* 42°39′ N, 95°19′ W 90
Alta, *Nor.* 69°56′ N, 23°12′ E 152
Alta Coloma, peak, *Sp.* 37°34′ N, 3°36′ W 164
Alta Sierra, *Calif., U.S.* 35°43′ N, 118°34′ W 101
Altagracia, *Venez.* 10°43′ N, 71°32′ W 136
Altagracia de Orituco, *Venez.* 9°51′ N, 66°25′ W 136
Altamachi, *Bol.* 16°54′ S, 66°23′ W 137
Altamachi, river, *Bol.* 16°4′ S, 66°58′ W 137
Altamaha, river, *Ga., U.S.* 31°52′ N, 82°32′ W 80
Altamira, *Braz.* 1°38′ N, 67°12′ W 136
Altamira, *Braz.* 3°13′ S, 52°16′ W 130
Altamira, *Chile* 25°48′ S, 69°53′ W 132
Altamira, *Col.* 2°4′ N, 75°50′ W 136
Altamira, *C.R.* 10°29′ N, 84°22′ W 116
Altamira, *Mex.* 22°23′ N, 97°56′ W 114
Altamont, *Ill., U.S.* 39°3′ N, 88°45′ W 102
Altamont, *N.Y., U.S.* 42°42′ N, 74°3′ W 104
Altamura, Isla de, island, *Mex.* 24°52′ N, 109°26′ W 112
Altan Xiret see Ejin Horo Qi, *China* 39°33′ N, 109°44′ E 198
Altano, Capo, *It.* 39°15′ N, 7°47′ E 156
Altar, *Mex.* 30°43′ N, 111°51′ W 92
Altar, Desierto de, *Mex.* 32°29′ N, 114°39′ W 101
Altares, *Mex.* 28°50′ N, 103°22′ W 92
Altata, *Mex.* 24°37′ N, 107°56′ W 112
Altaville, *Calif., U.S.* 38°5′ N, 120°34′ W 100
Altavista, *Va., U.S.* 37°6′ N, 79°18′ W 96
Altay, *China* 47°53′ N, 88°12′ E 184
Altay, *Mongolia* 46°18′ N, 96°16′ E 190
Altay, *Russ.* 60°18′ N, 68°55′ E 169
Altay, adm. division, *Russ.* 52°16′ N, 81°43′ E 184
Altay Mountains, *Asia* 53°12′ N, 81°13′ E 184
Altayskiy, *Russ.* 51°57′ N, 85°25′ E 184
Altdorf, *Ger.* 48°33′ N, 12°6′ E 152
Altdorf, *Switz.* 46°52′ N, 8°38′ E 167
Altea, *Sp.* 38°35′ N, 4°237′ W 164
Altena, *Ger.* 51°16′ N, 7°39′ E 167
Altenberge, *Ger.* 52°2′ N, 7°28′ E 167
Altenbruch, *Ger.* 53°48′ N, 8°46′ E 163
Altenkirchen, *Ger.* 50°41′ N, 7°39′ E 167
Alter do Chão, *Braz.* 2°30′ S, 55°2′ W 130
Altıağac, *Azerb.* 40°52′ N, 48°57′ E 195
Altınekin, *Turk.* 38°17′ N, 32°52′ E 156
Altıntaş, *Turk.* 39°4′ N, 30°7′ E 156
Altınyayla, *Turk.* 36°59′ N, 29°32′ E 156
Altiplano, *Bol.–Peru* 18°49′ S, 68°8′ W 137
Altkirch, *Fr.* 47°37′ N, 7°13′ E 150
Alto, *La., U.S.* 32°20′ N, 91°52′ W 103
Alto, *Tex., U.S.* 31°38′ N, 95°5′ W 103
Alto Araguaia, *Braz.* 17°22′ S, 53°17′ W 138
Alto, Cerro, peak, *Tex., U.S.* 31°54′ N, 106°1′ W 92
Alto Chicapa, *Angola* 10°54′ S, 19°12′ E 220
Alto Garças, *Braz.* 16°58′ S, 53°32′ W 132
Alto Ligonha, *Mozambique* 15°32′ S, 38°17′ E 224
Alto Molócuè, *Mozambique* 15°37′ S, 37°42′ E 224
Alto Paraguai, *Braz.* 14°36′ S, 56°36′ W 132
Alto Paraíso de Goias, *Braz.* 14°8′ S, 47°31′ W 138
Alto Paraná, *Braz.* 23°6′ S, 52°30′ W 138
Alto Parnaíba, *Braz.* 9°7′ S, 45°59′ W 132
Alto Purús, river, *Peru* 10°46′ S, 71°45′ W 137
Alto Río Senguerr, *Arg.* 45°3′ S, 70°50′ W 134
Alto Sucuriú, *Braz.* 19°17′ S, 52°50′ W 138
Alto Uruguai, *Braz.* 27°22′ S, 54°9′ W 139
Alto Yuruá, river, *Braz.* 9°10′ S, 72°49′ W 137
Alton, *Calif., U.S.* 40°33′ N, 124°9′ W 90
Alton, *Iowa, U.S.* 42°57′ N, 96°2′ W 90
Alton, *Mo., U.S.* 38°53′ N, 90°11′ W 94
Alton, *N.H., U.S.* 43°27′ N, 71°14′ W 104
Alton, *N.Z.* 39°40′ S, 174°25′ E 240
Alton, *U.K.* 51°8′ N, 0°59′ E 162
Alton Bay, *N.H., U.S.* 43°28′ N, 71°16′ W 104
Alton, oil field, *Austral.* 27°55′ S, 149°8′ E 230
Altona, *Can.* 49°7′ N, 97°34′ W 90
Altona, *Ger.* 53°33′ N, 9°58′ E 150
Altoona, *Wis., U.S.* 44°47′ N, 91°26′ W 94
Altotonga, *Mex.* 19°45′ N, 97°15′ W 114
Altrincham, *U.K.* 53°23′ N, 2°21′ W 162
Altun Ha, ruin(s), *Belize* 17°45′ N, 88°29′ W 115
Altunhisar, *Turk.* 37°59′ N, 34°21′ E 156
Alturas, *Calif., U.S.* 41°29′ N, 120°34′ W 90
Altus, *Okla., U.S.* 34°37′ N, 99°20′ W 92
Aluk, *Sudan* 8°23′ N, 27°29′ E 224
Alūksne, *Latv.* 57°25′ N, 27°0′ E 166
Aluniş, *Rom.* 46°53′ N, 24°50′ E 156
Alunite, *Nev., U.S.* 35°58′ N, 114°55′ W 101
Alupka, *Ukr.* 44°25′ N, 34°0′ E 156
Alushta, *Ukr.* 44°40′ N, 34°20′ E 156
Alustante, *Sp.* 40°36′ N, 1°40′ W 164
Aluta, *Dem. Rep. of the Congo* 1°16′ S, 26°17′ E 224
Alva, *Okla., U.S.* 36°47′ N, 98°40′ W 92
Alvajärvi, *Fin.* 63°26′ N, 25°21′ E 152
Alvarado, *Mex.* 18°45′ N, 95°45′ W 114
Alvarado, *Tex., U.S.* 32°24′ N, 97°11′ W 96
Alvarães, *Braz.* 3°15′ S, 64°56′ W 130
Álvaro Obregón, Presa, lake, *Mex.* 28°1′ N, 111°16′ W 81
Alvdal, *Nor.* 62°5′ N, 10°39′ E 152
Alvear, *Arg.* 29°4′ S, 56°33′ W 139
Alvin, *Ill., U.S.* 40°18′ N, 87°36′ W 102
Alvin, *Tex., U.S.* 29°24′ N, 95°14′ W 103
Alvinston, *Can.* 42°49′ N, 81°51′ W 102
Alvito, *Port.* 38°14′ N, 7°60′ W 150
Alvkarleby, *Sw.* 60°32′ N, 17°22′ E 166
Alvorada, *Braz.* 12°33′ S, 49°9′ W 130
Alvord, *Tex., U.S.* 33°21′ N, 97°42′ W 92
Alvord Desert, *Oreg., U.S.* 42°35′ N, 118°19′ W 90
Älvros, *Nor.* 62°3′ N, 14°37′ E 152
Älvsbyn, *Nor.* 65°40′ N, 20°58′ E 152
Alwar, *India* 27°33′ N, 76°36′ E 197

lxa Zuoqi, *China* 38°51' N, 105°44' E **198**
lyangula, *Austral.* 13°52' S, 136°30' E **173**
lysardakh, *Russ.* 65°53' N, 131°29' E **160**
lytus, *Lith.* 54°23' N, 24°1' E **166**
lyzia, ruin(s), *Gr.* 38°40' N, 20°49' E **156**
lzada, *Mont., U.S.* 45°0' N, 104°24' W **90**
lzenau, *Ger.* 50°5' N, 9°3' E **167**
lzira, *Sp.* 39°7' N, 0°29' E **214**
m Dam, *Chad* 12°45' N, 20°28' E **216**
m Djéména, *Chad* 13°6' N, 17°19' E **216**
m Djeress, spring, *Chad* 16°7' N, 22°54' E **226**
m Khoumi, *Chad* 12°48' N, 19°43' E **216**
m Léiouna, *Chad* 12°47' N, 21°49' E **216**
m Timan, *Chad* 11°0' N, 20°18' E **216**
m Zoer, *Chad* 14°11' N, 21°22' E **216**
macayacu National Park, *Col.* 3°48' S, 70°34' W **136**
mada Gaza, *Cen. Af. Rep.* 4°45' N, 15°10' E **218**
mada, ruin(s), *Egypt* 22°41' N, 32°11' E **182**
madi, *Dem. Rep. of the Congo* 3°37' N, 26°45' E **224**
madi, *Sudan* 5°30' N, 30°21' E **218**
madjuak Lake, *Can.* 64°49' N, 73°51' W **106**
madora, *Port.* 38°45' N, 9°15' W **150**
magansett, *N.Y., U.S.* 40°58' N, 72°10' W **104**
magi, *Japan* 33°24' N, 130°39' E **201**
maiur-Maia, *Sp.* 43°11' N, 1°28' W **164**
mål, *Nor.* 59°2' N, 12°38' E **152**
mal, oil field, *Lib.* 29°23' N, 21°3' E **216**
malfi, *Col.* 6°57' N, 75°5' W **136**
malyk, *Russ.* 57°31' N, 116°39' E **173**
mamapare, *Indonesia* 4°47' S, 136°38' E **238**
mambaí, *Braz.* 23°6' S, 55°16' W **134**
mambaí, river, *Braz.* 22°48' S, 54°50' W **132**
mambaí, Serra de, *Braz.* 23°18' S, 55°51' W **132**
mami Ō Shima, island, *Japan* 28°23' N, 129°46' E **190**
mamula, *Dem. Rep. of the Congo* 0°19' N, 27°46' E **224**
manda, *Ohio, U.S.* 39°38' N, 82°45' W **102**
manda Park, *Wash., U.S.* 47°25' N, 123°53' W **100**
mangeldi, *Kaz.* 50°11' N, 65°13' E **184**
maniú, river, *Braz.* 1°19' S, 67°42' W **136**
manos Dağları, *Turk.* 36°14' N, 36°0' E **156**
mantea, *It.* 39°9' N, 16°4' E **156**
mapá, *Braz.* 10°19' S, 69°28' W **137**
mapá, *Braz.* 2°2' N, 50°50' W **130**
mapá, adm. division, *Braz.* 1°12' N, 53°2' W **130**
marante, *Braz.* 6°17' S, 42°51' W **132**
mardalay, *Mongolia* 46°7' N, 106°22' E **198**
margosa, *Braz.* 13°1' S, 39°38' W **138**
margosa Desert, *Nev., U.S.* 36°47' N, 116°46' W **101**
margosa Range, *Calif., U.S.* 36°17' N, 116°48' W **101**
margosa Valley, *Nev., U.S.* 36°38' N, 116°25' W **101**
marillo, *Tex., U.S.* 35°10' N, 101°51' W **92**
markantak, *India* 22°40' N, 81°46' E **197**
maro, Monte, peak, *It.* 42°4' N, 14°1' E **156**
marpur, *India* 23°30' N, 91°37' E **197**
marwara, *India* 22°19' N, 79°10' E **197**
masa, *Mich., U.S.* 46°14' N, 88°27' W **94**
masia see Amasya, *Turk.* 40°40' N, 35°50' E **156**
masine, *Western Sahara* 25°48' N, 13°20' W **214**
masra, *Turk.* 41°44' N, 32°24' E **156**
masya (Amasia), *Turk.* 40°40' N, 35°50' E **156**
matari, *Braz.* 3°16' S, 58°55' W **130**
mataurá, *Braz.* 3°32' S, 68°4' W **136**
matepec, *Mex.* 18°38' N, 100°9' W **114**
mathous, ruin(s), *Cyprus* 34°42' N, 33°5' E **194**
matlán de Cañas, *Mex.* 20°49' N, 104°27' W **114**
mavon Islands, *Solomon Sea* 7°0' S, 158°0' E **242**
may, *Belg.* 50°33' N, 5°18' E **167**
mazar, *Russ.* 53°50' N, 120°55' E **190**
mazon Fan, *North Atlantic Ocean* 5°17' N, 46°22' W **253**
mazon see Amazonas, river, *Braz.* 3°8' S, 55°59' W **123**
mazonas, adm. division, *Braz.* 5°31' S, 65°36' W **130**
mazonas (Amazon), river, *Braz.* 3°8' S, 55°59' W **123**
mazonas see Solimões, river, *Braz.* 2°50' S, 66°35' W **123**
mazônia National Park, *Braz.* 4°19' S, 57°15' W **130**
mb, *Pak.* 34°14' N, 72°48' E **186**
mba Gīyorgīs, *Eth.* 12°41' N, 37°37' E **218**
mba Maryam, *Eth.* 11°23' N, 39°16' E **182**
mbala, *India* 30°21' N, 76°50' E **197**
mbalangoda, *Sri Lanka* 6°16' N, 80°4' E **188**
mbalantota, *Sri Lanka* 6°7' N, 81°4' E **188**
mbarchik, *Russ.* 69°33' N, 162°14' E **160**
mbato, *Ecua.* 1°21' S, 78°48' W **130**
mbato Boeny, *Madagascar* 16°27' S, 46°44' E **220**
mbatolampy, *Madagascar* 19°24' S, 47°27' E **220**
mbatondrazaka, *Madagascar* 17°60' S, 48°24' E **207**
mbazac, *Fr.* 45°57' N, 1°23' E **150**
mbelau, island, *Indonesia* 4°17' S, 127°15' E **192**
mbergris Cay, island, *Belize* 17°58' N, 87°52' W **115**
mbergris Cays, islands, *North Atlantic Ocean* 21°19' N, 72°57' W **116**
mberley, *Can.* 44°1' N, 81°42' W **102**
mberley, *N.Z.* 43°10' S, 172°44' E **240**
mberley, *U.K.* 50°54' N, 0°32' E **162**
mbidédi, *Mali* 14°34' N, 11°50' W **222**
mbikapur, *India* 23°7' N, 83°12' E **197**
mbilobe, *Madagascar* 13°13' S, 49°2' E **220**
mbla, *Est.* 59°10' N, 25°48' E **166**
mbler, *Alas., U.S.* 67°5' N, 157°52' W **98**
mbleside, *U.K.* 54°25' N, 2°58' W **162**
mbleteuse, *Fr.* 50°48' N, 1°36' E **163**
mbo, *Peru* 10°11' S, 76°10' W **130**
mboasary, *Madagascar* 25°4' S, 46°26' E **220**
mbodifotatra, *Madagascar* 16°58' S, 49°51' E **220**
Ambohimahasoa, *Madagascar* 21°6' S, 47°13' E **220**
Ambohimanga Atsimo, *Madagascar* 20°53' S, 47°36' E **220**
Amboise, *Fr.* 47°24' N, 0°58' E **150**
Amboiva, *Angola* 11°34' S, 14°44' E **220**
Ambolauri, *Ga.* 42°28' N, 43°9' E **195**
Ambon, *Indonesia* 3°41' S, 128°3' E **192**
Amboró National Park, *Bol.* 17°42' S, 64°48' W **137**
Amborompotsy, *Madagascar* 20°35' S, 46°14' E **220**
Amboseli National Park, *Kenya* 2°50' S, 37°15' E **224**
Amboy, *Ill., U.S.* 41°42' N, 89°20' W **102**
Amboy Crater, *Calif., U.S.* 34°31' N, 115°48' W **101**
Ambre, Cap d', *Madagascar* 12°1' S, 49°15' E **220**
Ambre, Montagne d', peak, *Madagascar* 12°41' S, 48°58' E **220**
Ambriz, *Angola* 7°51' S, 13°6' E **218**
Ambrogio, *It.* 44°55' N, 11°55' E **167**
Ambrósio, *Braz.* 2°53' S, 68°19' W **136**
Amburan Burnu, *Azerb.* 40°36' N, 49°49' E **195**
Amchitka, island, *Alas., U.S.* 51°7' N, 177°20' E **160**
Amderma, *Russ.* 69°42' N, 61°41' E **169**
Amdillis, spring, *Mali* 18°24' N, 0°17' E **222**
Ameca, *Mex.* 20°33' N, 104°3' W **114**
Ameca, river, *Mex.* 20°55' N, 105°12' W **114**
Ameghino, *Arg.* 34°51' S, 62°28' W **139**
Ameland, island, *Neth.* 53°28' N, 5°37' E **163**
Amelia, *La., U.S.* 29°40' N, 91°7' W **103**
Amenia, *N.Y., U.S.* 41°50' N, 73°34' W **104**
America-Antarctic Ridge, *South Atlantic Ocean* 59°11' S, 12°30' W **255**
American Highland, *Antarctica* 74°55' S, 76°3' E **248**
American, river, *Wash., U.S.* 46°53' N, 121°26' W **100**
American Samoa, *United States* 14°0' S, 171°0' W **238**
Americus, *Ga., U.S.* 32°3' N, 84°15' W **112**
Amersfoort, *S. Af.* 27°2' S, 29°51' E **227**
Amery, *Wis., U.S.* 45°18' N, 92°23' W **94**
Amery Ice Shelf, *Antarctica* 71°16' S, 69°44' E **248**
Ames, *Iowa, U.S.* 42°0' N, 93°37' W **94**
Amesbury, *Mass., U.S.* 42°50' N, 70°57' W **104**
Amesbury, *U.K.* 51°10' N, 1°47' W **162**
Amga, *Russ.* 61°1' N, 131°52' E **160**
Amga, river, *Russ.* 59°34' N, 126°34' E **160**
Amgu, *Russ.* 45°56' N, 137°30' E **190**
Amguema, river, *Russ.* 67°26' N, 178°38' W **98**
Amguid, *Alg.* 26°26' N, 5°23' E **214**
Amhara, region, *Africa* 12°12' N, 36°11' E **182**
Amherst, *Can.* 45°49' N, 64°13' W **111**
Amherst, *N.H., U.S.* 42°51' N, 71°38' W **104**
Amherst, *N.Y., U.S.* 42°58' N, 78°50' W **94**
Amherst, *Ohio, U.S.* 41°23' N, 82°14' W **102**
Amherst, *Tex., U.S.* 33°59' N, 102°23' W **92**
Amherst, *Va., U.S.* 37°34' N, 79°4' W **96**
Amherstburg, *Can.* 42°5' N, 83°6' W **102**
Amhovichy, *Belarus* 53°6' N, 27°50' E **158**
Amiata, Monte, peak, *It.* 42°53' N, 11°32' E **156**
Amidon, *N. Dak., U.S.* 46°27' N, 103°19' W **90**
Amiens, *Fr.* 49°52' N, 2°18' E **163**
Amili, *India* 28°23' N, 95°50' E **188**
Amino, *Japan* 35°39' N, 135°1' E **201**
Aminuis, *Namibia* 23°43' S, 19°18' E **227**
Amiot Islands, *South Pacific Ocean* 67°26' S, 74°9' W **248**
Amioun, *Leb.* 34°17' N, 35°48' E **194**
Amirante Isles, *Indian Ocean* 4°41' S, 51°23' E **173**
Amirante Trench, *Indian Ocean* 9°12' S, 53°16' E **254**
Amisk Lake, lake, *Can.* 54°33' N, 102°35' W **108**
Amisk, river, *Can.* 54°40' N, 112°29' W **108**
Amistad National Recreation Area, *Tex., U.S.* 29°32' N, 101°42' W **96**
Amistad Reservoir, lake, *Tex., U.S.* 29°33' N, 101°44' W **92**
Amisus see Samsun, *Turk.* 41°17' N, 36°20' E **158**
Amite, *La., U.S.* 30°42' N, 90°31' W **103**
Amity, *Ark., U.S.* 34°14' N, 93°28' W **96**
Amla, *India* 21°56' N, 78°9' E **197**
Åmli, *Nor.* 58°45' N, 8°29' E **152**
Amlia, island, *Alas., U.S.* 52°10' N, 173°59' W **160**
'Amm Adam, *Sudan* 16°21' N, 36°4' E **182**
'Ammān (Philadelphia), *Jordan* 31°56' N, 35°53' E **194**
Ammanford, *U.K.* 51°47' N, 3°60' W **162**
Ammänsaari, *Fin.* 64°50' N, 28°52' E **152**
Ammarfjället, peak, *Nor.* 66°4' N, 15°30' E **152**
Ammarnäs, *Nor.* 65°57' N, 16°10' E **152**
Ammeloe, *Ger.* 52°4' N, 6°47' E **167**
Ammochostos (Famagusta, Gazimagusa), *Northern Cyprus* 35°7' N, 33°56' E **194**
Amo, *Ind., U.S.* 39°41' N, 86°37' W **102**
'Āmol, *Iran* 36°36' N, 52°17' E **180**
Amolar, *Braz.* 18°1' S, 57°31' W **132**
Amos, *Can.* 48°34' N, 78°8' W **94**
Amot, *Mor.* 27°57' N, 10°6' W **214**
Åmot, *Nor.* 59°36' N, 7°57' E **152**
Åmotfors, *Nor.* 59°47' N, 12°24' E **152**
Amoúdia, peak, *Gr.* 37°31' N, 25°56' E **156**
Amoy see Xiamen, *China* 24°25' N, 118°6' E **198**
Ampani, *India* 19°34' N, 82°36' E **188**
Ampanihy, *Madagascar* 24°39' S, 44°42' E **220**
Amparafaravola, *Madagascar* 17°36' S, 48°13' E **220**
Amparihy Est, *Madagascar* 23°58' S, 47°22' E **220**
Amparo, *Braz.* 22°42' S, 46°47' W **138**
Ampato, Nevado, peak, *Peru* 15°52' S, 71°55' W **137**
Ampere, *Braz.* 25°57' S, 53°30' W **139**
Ampezzo, *It.* 46°23' N, 12°47' E **167**
Amphiareion, ruin(s), *Gr.* 38°17' N, 23°43' E **156**
Amphitrite Point, *Can.* 48°43' N, 125°48' W **90**
Amposta, *Sp.* 40°42' N, 0°34' E **164**
Ampthill, *U.K.* 52°1' N, 0°30' E **162**
Amqui, *Can.* 48°27' N, 67°27' W **94**
'Amrān, *Yemen* 15°40' N, 43°57' E **182**
Amravati, *India* 20°56' N, 77°46' E **188**
Amreli, *India* 21°36' N, 71°12' E **186**
'Amrīt (Marathus), ruin(s), *Syr.* 34°50' N, 35°52' E **194**
'Amrīt, ruin(s), *Syr.* 34°48' N, 35°49' E **156**
Amritsar, *India* 31°39' N, 74°52' E **186**
Amroha, *India* 28°54' N, 78°28' E **188**
Amsā'ad, *Lib.* 31°37' N, 25°2' E **180**
'Amshīt, *Leb.* 34°9' N, 35°38' E **194**
Amsterdam, *Neth.* 52°22' N, 4°50' E **163**
Amsterdam, *N.Y., U.S.* 42°56' N, 74°12' W **104**
Amsterdam, island, *Fr.* 37°45' S, 78°0' E **254**
Amstetten, *Aust.* 48°7' N, 14°51' E **152**
Amston, *Conn., U.S.* 41°37' N, 72°21' W **104**
Amu Darya, river, *Uzb.* 41°1' N, 61°42' E **184**
Amuay, *Venez.* 11°51' N, 70°4' W **123**
'Āmūdah, *Syr.* 37°6' N, 40°57' E **195**
Amukta, island, *Alas., U.S.* 52°4' N, 171°7' W **160**
Amuku Mountains, *Guyana* 2°4' N, 58°12' W **130**
Amundsen Gulf 70°20' N, 123°56' W **98**
Amundsen, Mount, *Antarctica* 67°13' S, 101°28' E **248**
Amundsen Sea 73°41' S, 105°21' W **248**
Amundsen-Scott South Pole, station, *Antarctica* 89°59' S, 164°21' W **248**
Amur, adm. division, *Russ.* 53°36' N, 124°46' E **190**
Amur, river, *Russ.* 51°18' N, 138°37' E **190**
Amurang, *Indonesia* 1°13' N, 124°28' E **192**
Amurrio, *Sp.* 43°2' N, 3°1' W **164**
Amusco, *Sp.* 42°10' N, 4°28' W **150**
Amvrosiyivka, *Ukr.* 47°44' N, 38°26' E **158**
Amydery'a, *Turkm.* 37°56' N, 65°18' E **197**
An, *Myanmar* 19°46' N, 94°7' E **202**
An Khe, *Vietnam* 13°58' N, 108°40' E **202**
An Nabī Shīt, *Leb.* 33°52' N, 36°6' E **194**
An Nabk, *Syr.* 34°1' N, 36°44' E **194**
An Nabk Abū Qaşr, spring, *Saudi Arabia* 30°18' N, 38°41' E **180**
An Nafūd, *Saudi Arabia* 28°35' N, 39°18' E **180**
An Najaf (Najaf), *Iraq* 31°58' N, 44°19' E **180**
An Namatah, *Jordan* 30°48' N, 35°32' E **194**
An Nashshāsh, *U.A.E.* 23°1' N, 54°3' E **182**
An Nāşirīyah, *Syr.* 33°52' N, 36°48' E **194**
An Nāşirīyah (Nasiriyah), *Iraq* 31°5' N, 46°11' E **180**
An Nawfalīyah, *Lib.* 30°41' N, 17°49' E **143**
An Nimāş, *Saudi Arabia* 19°2' N, 42°9' E **182**
An Nu'ayrīyah, *Saudi Arabia* 27°28' N, 48°27' E **196**
An Pass, *Myanmar* 19°59' N, 94°17' E **202**
An Phuoc, *Vietnam* 11°36' N, 108°54' E **202**
An Uaimh see Navan, *Ire.* 53°38' N, 6°42' W **150**
Ana María, Cayos, islands, *Caribbean Sea* 21°11' N, 79°29' W **116**
Anabar, river, *Russ.* 70°31' N, 114°9' E **160**
Anabarskiy Zaliv 73°25' N, 108°6' E **160**
Anacapa Islands, *North Pacific Ocean* 34°4' N, 119°29' W **100**
Anaco, *Venez.* 9°26' N, 64°30' W **116**
Anacoco, *La., U.S.* 31°14' N, 93°21' W **103**
Anaconda, *Mont., U.S.* 46°7' N, 112°58' W **90**
Anaconda Range, *Mont., U.S.* 45°49' N, 113°46' W **90**
Anacortes, *Wash., U.S.* 48°28' N, 122°38' W **100**
Anactorium, ruin(s), *Gr.* 38°55' N, 20°45' E **156**
Anadyr', *Russ.* 64°38' N, 177°6' E **160**
Anadyr, Gulf of see Anadyrskiy Zaliv 66°48' N, 179°18' W **160**
Anadyr', river, *Russ.* 66°42' N, 169°30' E **160**
Anadyrskiy Zaliv (Anadyr, Gulf of) 66°48' N, 179°18' W **160**
Anáfi, *Gr.* 36°20' N, 25°46' E **156**
Anáfi, island, *Gr.* 36°24' N, 25°52' E **180**
Anagé, *Braz.* 14°45' S, 41°10' W **138**
Anaghit, *Eritrea* 16°20' N, 38°35' E **182**
'Ānah, *Iraq* 34°25' N, 41°58' E **180**
Anaheim, *Calif., U.S.* 33°50' N, 117°56' W **101**
Anahim Lake, *Can.* 52°28' N, 125°20' W **108**
Anahola, *Hawai'i, U.S.* 22°8' N, 159°19' W **99**
Anáhuac, *Mex.* 27°13' N, 100°9' W **96**
Anáhuac, *Mex.* 24°27' N, 101°31' W **114**
Anahuac, *Tex., U.S.* 29°45' N, 94°41' W **103**
Anai Mudi, peak, *India* 10°8' N, 76°55' E **188**
Anaï, spring, *Alg.* 24°9' N, 11°27' E **214**
Anajás, *Braz.* 0°60' N, 49°58' W **130**
Anak, *N. Korea* 38°29' N, 125°29' E **200**
Anaktuvuk Pass, *Alas., U.S.* 68°11' N, 151°54' W **98**
Analalava, *Madagascar* 14°38' S, 47°47' E **220**
Analavelona, peak, *Madagascar* 22°36' S, 44°2' E **220**
Anamã, *Braz.* 3°33' S, 61°30' W **130**
Anambas, Kepulauan, islands, *South China Sea* 2°41' N, 105°43' E **196**
Anamizu, *Japan* 37°13' N, 136°54' E **201**
Anamoose, *N. Dak., U.S.* 47°51' N, 100°15' W **90**
Anamosa, *Iowa, U.S.* 42°6' N, 91°17' W **94**
Anamu, river, *Braz.* 0°42' N, 56°51' W **130**
Anamur, *Turk.* 36°5' N, 32°51' E **156**
Anamur Burnu, *Azerb.* 36°2' N, 32°4' E **156**
Anan, *Japan* 33°52' N, 134°37' E **201**
Ananchichi, *Belarus* 52°31' N, 27°39' E **152**
Anand, *India* 22°33' N, 73°0' E **186**
Anan'yiv, *Ukr.* 47°43' N, 29°58' E **156**
Anapa, *Russ.* 44°54' N, 37°23' E **156**
Anápolis, *Braz.* 16°21' S, 48°59' W **138**
Anār, *Iran* 30°51' N, 55°18' E **180**
Anārak, *Iran* 33°20' N, 53°43' E **180**
Ånäset, *Nor.* 64°14' N, 21°2' E **152**
Anastasia Island, *Fla., U.S.* 29°52' N, 81°16' W **105**
Anatahan, island, *U.S.* 16°12' N, 144°27' E **192**
Anatolia (Asia Minor), region, *Asia* 38°39' N, 30°18' E **180**
Anatolikí Makedonia Kai Thráki, adm. division, *Gr.* 41°5' N, 15°57' E **156**
Anatone, *Wash., U.S.* 46°7' N, 117°9' W **90**
Añatuya, *Arg.* 28°28' S, 62°49' W **139**
Anauá, river, *Braz.* 0°60' N, 60°9' W **130**
Anaurilândia, *Braz.* 22°2' S, 52°48' W **138**
Añavieja, *Sp.* 41°51' N, 1°56' W **164**
Anavilhanas, Arquipélago das, *South America* 3°13' S, 62°22' W **130**
Anbyŏn, *N. Korea* 39°2' N, 127°31' E **200**
Ancares, Sierra de, *Sp.* 42°54' N, 7°7' W **150**
Ancash, adm. division, *Peru* 9°4' S, 78°36' W **130**
Ancasti, Sierra de, *Arg.* 28°4' S, 65°55' W **132**
Anchieta, *Braz.* 20°51' S, 40°44' W **138**
Anchorage, *Alas., U.S.* 61°5' N, 149°53' W **98**
Anchorena, *Arg.* 35°40' S, 65°23' W **134**
Anclitas, Cayo, island, *Cuba* 20°30' N, 79°14' W **116**
Ancona, *It.* 43°36' N, 13°30' E **167**
Ancram, *N.Y., U.S.* 42°2' N, 73°40' W **104**
Ancuabe, *Mozambique* 13°2' S, 39°54' E **224**
Ancud, *Chile* 41°59' S, 73°55' W **123**
Ancud, Golfo de 42°13' S, 73°45' W **134**
Ancy-le-Franc, *Fr.* 47°46' N, 4°9' E **150**
Anda, *China* 46°22' N, 125°24' E **198**
Andacollo, *Arg.* 37°13' S, 70°40' W **134**
Andahuaylas, *Peru* 13°41' S, 73°24' W **137**
Andalgalá, *Arg.* 27°36' S, 66°19' W **132**
Åndalsnes, *Nor.* 62°33' N, 7°42' E **152**
Andalusia, *Ala., U.S.* 31°18' N, 86°28' W **96**
Andalusia, adm. division, *Sp.* 37°27' N, 4°53' W **164**
Andaman and Nicobar Islands, *India* 11°25' N, 92°50' E **192**
Andaman Basin, *Andaman Sea* 9°56' N, 95°4' E **254**
Andaman Islands, *Andaman Sea* 12°47' N, 94°43' E **202**
Andaman Sea 15°15' N, 94°7' E **188**
Andapa, *Madagascar* 14°39' S, 49°40' E **220**
Andara, *Namibia* 18°3' S, 21°32' E **220**
Andaraí, *Braz.* 12°49' S, 41°21' W **138**
Andavaka, Cap, *Madagascar* 25°40' S, 46°43' E **220**
Andeg, *Russ.* 67°55' N, 53°10' E **169**
Andelot-Blancheville, *Fr.* 48°14' N, 5°17' E **163**
Andenne, *Belg.* 50°29' N, 5°5' E **167**
Andéranboukane, *Mali* 15°27' N, 3°2' E **222**
Andermatt, *Switz.* 46°38' N, 8°36' E **167**
Andernach, *Ger.* 50°26' N, 7°23' E **167**
Anderson, *Calif., U.S.* 40°26' N, 122°19' W **90**
Anderson, *Ind., U.S.* 40°5' N, 85°41' W **102**
Anderson, *Mo., U.S.* 36°38' N, 94°27' W **96**
Anderson, *S.C., U.S.* 34°29' N, 82°40' W **96**
Anderson Dome, *Antarctica* 72°28' S, 87°2' W **248**
Anderson Massif, *Antarctica* 78°56' S, 82°12' W **248**
Anderson Ranch Dam, *Idaho, U.S.* 43°28' N, 115°37' W **90**
Anderson, river, *Can.* 68°35' N, 127°50' W **98**
Andersson Island, *Antarctica* 63°39' S, 59°14' W **134**
Andes, Cordillera de los, mountains, *South America* 9°47' S, 74°52' W **136**
Andhra Pradesh, adm. division, *India* 16°19' N, 79°37' E **188**
Andijon, *Uzb.* 40°46' N, 72°21' E **197**
Andikíra, *Gr.* 38°22' N, 22°36' E **156**
Andikíthira, island, *Gr.* 35°48' N, 22°23' E **180**
Andilálou, ruin(s), *Gr.* 41°29' N, 24°9' E **156**
Andilamena, *Madagascar* 17°2' S, 48°33' E **220**
Andir, river, *China* 36°34' N, 84°8' E **184**
Andirá, *Braz.* 3°45' S, 66°17' W **136**
Andırın, *Turk.* 37°34' N, 36°21' E **156**
Andirlangar, *China* 37°37' N, 83°47' E **184**
Andkhvoy, *Afghan.* 36°55' N, 65°8' E **186**
Andoany (Hell-Ville), *Madagascar* 13°24' S, 48°17' E **207**
Andoas, *Peru* 2°57' S, 76°25' W **136**
Andomskiy Pogost, *Russ.* 61°14' N, 36°39' E **154**
Andong, *S. Korea* 36°33' N, 128°43' E **200**
Andorra La Vella, *Andorra* 42°29' N, 1°26' E **164**
Andorra 42°29' N, 1°26' E **164**
Andover, *Me., U.S.* 44°37' N, 70°46' W **94**
Andover, *N.H., U.S.* 43°26' N, 71°50' W **104**
Andover, *U.K.* 51°12' N, 1°30' W **162**
Andovoranto, *Madagascar* 18°57' S, 49°5' E **220**
Andøya, island, *Nor.* 69°24' N, 14°6' E **160**
Andradina, *Braz.* 20°56' S, 51°24' W **138**
Andreapol', *Russ.* 56°39' N, 32°18' E **154**
Andreba, *Madagascar* 17°40' S, 48°33' E **220**
Andrew, *Can.* 53°52' N, 112°20' W **108**
Andrews, *Ind., U.S.* 40°50' N, 85°37' W **102**
Andrews, *S.C., U.S.* 33°26' N, 79°34' W **96**
Andrews, *Tex., U.S.* 32°18' N, 102°33' W **92**
Andreyevka, *Russ.* 52°20' N, 51°50' E **158**
Andrijevica, *Serb. and Mont.* 42°43' N, 19°47' E **168**
Androka, *Madagascar* 25°1' S, 44°7' E **220**
Ándros, island, *Gr.* 37°54' N, 24°57' E **180**
Androscoggin, river, *Me., U.S.* 44°23' N, 71°6' W **104**
Andryushino, *Russ.* 59°17' N, 62°59' E **154**
Andryushkino, *Russ.* 69°9' N, 154°31' E **160**
Andújar, *Sp.* 38°2' N, 4°3' W **164**
Andulo, *Angola* 11°31' S, 16°41' E **220**
Aneby, *Nor.* 57°49' N, 14°46' E **152**
Anefis I-n-Darane, *Mali* 18°2' N, 0°37' E **222**
Anegada, island, *U.K.* 18°43' N, 65°1' W **116**
Anegada, Punta, *Pan.* 7°14' N, 81°48' W **115**
Añelo, Cuenca del, *Arg.* 37°56' S, 69°57' W **134**
Anenii Noi, *Mold.* 46°52' N, 29°13' E **156**
Aneroid, *Can.* 49°42' N, 107°18' W **90**
Anet, *Fr.* 48°51' N, 1°26' E **163**
Aneta, *N. Dak., U.S.* 47°39' N, 97°60' W **90**
Aneto, peak, *Sp.* 42°37' N, 0°36' E **164**
Aney, *Niger* 19°27' N, 12°54' E **216**
Anfah, *Leb.* 34°21' N, 35°44' E **194**
Angamos, Punta, *Chile* 23°1' S, 71°22' W **132**
Angang, *S. Korea* 35°58' N, 129°15' E **200**
Angangueo, *Mex.* 19°36' N, 100°17' W **114**
Ang'angxi, *China* 47°7' N, 123°48' E **198**
Angara, river, *Russ.* 58°38' N, 98°21' E **246**
Angarsk, *Russ.* 52°43' N, 103°32' E **190**
Angaur (Ngeaur), island, *Palau* 7°0' N, 134°0' E **242**
Ånge, *Nor.* 62°31' N, 15°37' E **152**
Ángel de la Guarda, Isla, island, *Mex.* 29°35' N, 113°31' W **112**
Angel Falls, *Venez.* 4°34' N, 63°39' W **123**
Angeles, *Philippines* 15°8' N, 120°35' E **203**
Angélica, *Arg.* 31°33' S, 61°32' W **139**
Angelina, river, *Tex., U.S.* 31°30' N, 94°50' W **103**
Angels Camp, *Calif., U.S.* 38°4' N, 120°33' W **100**
Angermünde, *Ger.* 53°1' N, 14°0' E **152**
Angers, *Fr.* 47°28' N, 0°33' E **150**
Angerville, *Fr.* 48°18' N, 1°59' E **163**
Angical, *Braz.* 11°60' S, 44°40' W **132**
Angie, *La., U.S.* 30°57' N, 89°49' W **103**
Angkor, ruin(s), *Cambodia* 13°28' N, 103°45' E **202**
Angle Inlet, *Minn., U.S.* 49°18' N, 95°7' W **90**
Anglem, Mount, *N.Z.* 46°46' S, 167°48' E **240**
Anglès, *Sp.* 41°56' N, 2°38' E **164**
Angleton, *Tex., U.S.* 29°9' N, 95°26' W **103**
Anglure, *Fr.* 48°35' N, 3°48' E **163**
Ango, *Dem. Rep. of the Congo* 3°58' N, 25°52' E **224**
Angoche, *Mozambique* 16°12' S, 39°57' E **224**
Angohrān, *Iran* 26°33' N, 57°50' E **196**
Angol, *Chile* 37°49' S, 72°43' W **134**
Angola 12°18' S, 17°4' E **220**
Angola, *Ind., U.S.* 41°38' N, 84°60' W **102**
Angola, *La., U.S.* 30°56' N, 91°34' W **103**
Angola, *N.Y., U.S.* 42°38' N, 79°3' W **94**
Angola Plain, *South Atlantic Ocean* 15°4' S, 3°22' E **253**
Angora see Ankara, *Turk.* 39°55' N, 32°43' E **156**
Angostura, *Col.* 0°28' N, 72°30' W **136**
Angostura, *Mex.* 25°21' N, 108°10' W **112**
Angostura, Presa de la, *Mex.* 30°32' N, 109°47' W **92**
Angoulême, *Fr.* 45°39' N, 0°10' E **150**
Angouma, *Gabon* 1°11' N, 12°19' E **218**
Angoumois, region, *Europe* 45°50' N, 0°49' E **165**
Angra dos Reis, *Braz.* 23°2' S, 44°20' W **138**
Angren, *Uzb.* 41°1' N, 70°14' E **197**
Angtassom, *Cambodia* 11°1' N, 104°39' E **202**
Angu, *Dem. Rep. of the Congo* 3°27' N, 24°26' E **224**
Angüés, *Sp.* 42°6' N, 0°9' E **164**
Anguil, *Arg.* 36°31' S, 64°2' W **139**
Anguilla, *U.K.* 18°48' N, 69°45' W **116**
Anguilla Cays, *North Atlantic Ocean* 23°19' N, 79°28' W **116**
Anguille, Cape, *Can.* 47°49' N, 60°20' W **111**
Angumu, *Dem. Rep. of the Congo* 0°7' N, 27°39' E **224**
Anguo, *China* 38°26' N, 115°21' E **198**
Angutikha, *Russ.* 65°58' N, 87°24' E **169**
Angvik, *Nor.* 62°53' N, 8°3' E **152**
Anhua, *China* 28°23' N, 111°3' E **198**
Anhui, adm. division, *China* 31°34' N, 117°12' E **198**
Aniak, *Alas., U.S.* 61°24' N, 159°45' W **98**
Anicuns, *Braz.* 16°32' S, 49°58' W **138**
Anie, Pic d', peak, *Fr.* 42°55' N, 0°45' E **164**
Anikhovka, *Russ.* 51°29' N, 60°15' E **154**
Animas, *N. Mex., U.S.* 31°57' N, 108°47' W **92**
Animas Peak, *N. Mex., U.S.* 31°33' N, 108°50' W **92**
Ánimas, Punta de las, *Mex.* 28°44' N, 114°7' W **112**
Anin, *Myanmar* 15°41' N, 97°46' E **202**
Aniñón, *Sp.* 41°26' N, 1°43' W **164**
Anipemza, *Arm.* 40°26' N, 43°36' E **195**
Anishinabi Lake, lake, *Can.* 50°26' N, 94°1' W **90**
Anita, *Chile* 20°29' S, 69°51' W **137**
Anita, *Pa., U.S.* 40°59' N, 78°59' W **94**
Aniva, Mys, *Russ.* 45°46' N, 142°25' E **190**
Anivorano, *Madagascar* 18°47' S, 48°58' E **220**
Anixab, *Namibia* 20°58' S, 14°46' E **220**
Anjalankoski, *Fin.* 60°41' N, 26°51' E **166**
Anjosvarden, peak, *Nor.* 61°24' N, 14°7' E **152**
Anjou Islands, *East Siberian Sea* 74°45' N, 144°8' E **255**
Anjou, region, *Europe* 47°39' N, 1°10' W **150**
Anju, *N. Korea* 39°35' N, 125°44' E **198**
Anka, spring, *Sudan* 14°37' N, 24°51' E **226**
Ankang, *China* 32°36' N, 109°3' E **198**
Ankara (Angora), *Turk.* 39°55' N, 32°43' E **156**
Ankaramena, *Madagascar* 21°58' S, 46°39' E **220**
Ankarede, *Nor.* 64°49' N, 14°12' E **152**
Ankasakasa, *Madagascar* 16°22' S, 44°50' E **220**
Ankazoabo, *Madagascar* 22°15' S, 44°28' E **220**
Ankazobe, *Madagascar* 18°20' S, 47°8' E **220**
Anklam, *Ger.* 53°51' N, 13°41' E **152**
Ānkober, *Eth.* 9°31' N, 39°42' E **224**
Ankofa, peak, *Madagascar* 16°23' S, 48°27' E **220**
Ankoro, *Dem. Rep. of the Congo* 6°48' S, 26°52' E **224**
Ankpa, *Nig.* 7°21' N, 7°36' E **222**
Anlong, *China* 25°0' N, 105°26' E **198**
Anlu, *China* 31°14' N, 113°42' E **198**
Ann Arbor, *Mich., U.S.* 42°15' N, 83°46' W **102**
Ann, Cape, *Mass., U.S.* 42°36' N, 70°36' W **104**
Anna, *Mo., U.S.* 37°27' N, 89°14' W **96**
Anna Paulowna, *Neth.* 52°52' N, 4°50' E **163**
Annaba (Bône), *Alg.* 36°53' N, 7°45' E **156**
Annai, *Guyana* 3°55' N, 59°7' W **130**
Annan, *U.K.* 54°59' N, 3°16' W **150**
Annapolis, *Md., U.S.* 38°58' N, 76°37' W **94**
Annapolis Royal, *Can.* 44°43' N, 65°31' W **111**
Annecy, *Fr.* 45°54' N, 6°7' E **167**
Annecy, Lac d', lake, *Fr.* 45°52' N, 6°0' E **165**
Annemasse, *Fr.* 46°11' N, 6°14' E **167**
Annenkov Island, *U.K.* 54°35' S, 38°57' W **134**
Annenskiy Most, *Russ.* 60°44' N, 37°6' E **154**
Annette, *Alas., U.S.* 55°2' N, 131°38' W **108**
Anniston, *Ala., U.S.* 33°38' N, 85°50' W **96**
Annobón, island, *Equatorial Guinea* 1°32' S, 4°43' E **214**
Annweiler, *Ger.* 49°11' N, 7°56' E **163**
Año Nuevo, Point, *Calif., U.S.* 37°10' N, 122°33' W **100**
Anoka, *Minn., U.S.* 45°10' N, 93°22' W **94**
Anole, *Somalia* 0°54' N, 41°57' E **224**
Anori, *Braz.* 3°49' S, 61°42' W **130**

Anotaie, river, *Braz.* 3°23' N, 52°15' W **130**
Ânou Mellene, spring, *Mali* 17°27' N, 0°32' E **222**
Ânou Mellene, spring, *Mali* 18°0' N, 3°58' E **222**
Anou Meniet, spring, *Alg.* 24°59' N, 4°19' E **214**
Anou-I-n-Ouzzal, spring, *Alg.* 20°40' N, 2°27' E **222**
Anoumaba, *Côte d'Ivoire* 6°14' N, 4°32' W **222**
Anping, *China* 41°9' N, 123°28' E **200**
Anpu, *China* 21°25' N, 110°2' E **198**
Anqing, *China* 30°36' N, 116°59' E **198**
Anren, *China* 26°42' N, 113°17' E **198**
Anröchte, *Ger.* 51°33' N, 8°19' E **167**
Ans, *Belg.* 50°40' N, 5°29' E **167**
Ansai, *China* 36°53' N, 109°21' E **198**
Ansan, *S. Korea* 37°18' N, 126°52' E **198**
Ansbach, *Ger.* 49°18' N, 10°33' E **152**
Anse-à-Foleur, *Haiti* 19°53' N, 72°38' W **116**
Anse-à-Galets, *Haiti* 18°50' N, 72°53' W **116**
Anselmo, *Nebr., U.S.* 41°36' N, 99°53' W **90**
Anseong, *S. Korea* 37°0' N, 127°16' E **200**
Anse-Rouge, *Haiti* 19°39' N, 73°3' W **116**
Anshan, *China* 41°7' N, 122°59' E **200**
Anshun, *China* 26°16' N, 105°54' E **198**
Ansina, *Uru.* 31°54' S, 55°29' W **139**
Ansley, *Nebr., U.S.* 41°16' N, 99°23' W **92**
Anson, *Me., U.S.* 44°47' N, 69°55' W **94**
Anson, *Tex., U.S.* 32°44' N, 99°54' W **92**
Ansongo, *Mali* 15°39' N, 0°28' E **222**
Ansonia, *Conn., U.S.* 41°20' N, 73°5' W **104**
Ansonia, *Ohio, U.S.* 40°12' N, 84°39' W **102**
Ansonville, *Can.* 48°45' N, 80°42' W **94**
Anta, *Peru* 13°29' S, 72°9' W **137**
Antabamba, *Peru* 14°24' S, 72°53' W **137**
Antakya, *Turk.* 36°10' N, 36°6' E **143**
Antalaha, *Madagascar* 15°1' S, 50°13' E **207**
Antalya, *Turk.* 36°52' N, 30°43' E **156**
Antalya Körfezi 36°30' N, 30°36' E **180**
Antanambe, *Madagascar* 16°27' S, 49°48' E **220**
Antananarivo, *Madagascar* 18°59' S, 47°21' E **220**
Antanifotsy, *Madagascar* 19°40' S, 47°20' E **220**
Antarctic Sound 62°24' S, 58°49' W **248**
Antarctica 81°0' S, 0°0' E **248**
Antarctica 71°33' S, 29°36' E **248**
Antas, river, *Braz.* 28°48' S, 51°2' W **139**
Antelope, *Oreg., U.S.* 44°53' N, 120°44' W **90**
Antelope Lake, lake, *Can.* 50°13' N, 108°54' W **90**
Antelope Peak, *Nev., U.S.* 39°23' N, 116°33' W **90**
Antelope Point, peak, *Mont., U.S.* 45°45' N, 109°11' W **90**
Antelope Range, *Nev., U.S.* 39°3' N, 116°34' W **90**
Antelope Valley, *Calif., U.S.* 34°47' N, 118°27' W **101**
Antequera, *Parag.* 24°5' S, 57°12' W **132**
Antequera, *Sp.* 37°1' N, 4°34' W **164**
Anterselva, *It.* 46°52' N, 12°5' E **167**
Anthony, *Fla., U.S.* 29°17' N, 82°7' W **105**
Anthony, *Kans., U.S.* 37°8' N, 98°2' W **92**
Anthony, *N. Mex., U.S.* 32°1' N, 106°38' W **112**
Anti Atlas, mountains, *Mor.* 30°17' N, 8°12' W **214**
Antibes, Cap d', *Fr.* 43°28' N, 7°8' E **165**
Anticosti, Île d', island, *Can.* 48°50' N, 63°33' W **81**
Antifer, Cap d', *Fr.* 49°39' N, 0°14' E **150**
Antigo, *Wis., U.S.* 45°8' N, 89°9' W **94**
Antigonish, *Can.* 45°36' N, 61°60' W **111**
Antigua and Barbuda 17°0' N, 62°0' W **116**
Antigua, island, *Antigua and Barbuda* 17°5' N, 61°41' W **116**
Antiguo Morelos, *Mex.* 22°32' N, 99°6' W **114**
Anti-Lebanon see Al Jabalash Sharqī, *Leb.* 34°5' N, 36°21' E **194**
Antilla, *Cuba* 20°51' N, 75°44' W **116**
Anti-m-Misaou, spring, *Alg.* 21°57' N, 3°4' E **222**
Antimony, *Utah, U.S.* 38°6' N, 111°59' W **92**
Antioch, *Calif., U.S.* 38°0' N, 121°50' W **100**
Antioch, *Ill., U.S.* 42°28' N, 88°6' W **102**
Antioch see Hatay, *Turk.* 36°12' N, 36°8' E **156**
Antioquia, *Col.* 6°34' N, 75°51' W **136**
Antioquia, adm. division, *Col.* 6°56' N, 76°39' W **136**
Antipatris, ruin(s), *Israel* 32°5' N, 34°54' E **194**
Antipayuta, *Russ.* 69°4' N, 76°54' E **169**
Antisana, peak, *Ecua.* 0°31' N, 78°23' W **136**
Antler Peak, *Nev., U.S.* 40°35' N, 117°13' W **90**
Antlers, *Okla., U.S.* 34°12' N, 95°37' W **96**
Antofagasta, *Chile* 23°40' S, 70°25' W **132**
Antofagasta, adm. division, *Chile* 22°1' S, 70°14' W **137**
Antofagasta de la Sierra, *Arg.* 26°5' S, 67°22' W **132**
Antón, *Pan.* 8°24' N, 80°16' W **115**
Anton, *Tex., U.S.* 33°48' N, 102°11' W **92**
Anton Chico, *N. Mex., U.S.* 35°11' N, 105°10' W **92**
Antón Lizardo, Punta, *Mex.* 18°49' N, 95°58' W **114**
Antonibe, *Madagascar* 15°8' S, 47°25' E **220**
Antonina, *Braz.* 25°27' S, 48°43' W **138**
Antoniny, *Ukr.* 49°48' N, 26°53' E **152**
Antonio Prado, *Braz.* 28°53' S, 51°16' W **139**
Antonito, *Colo., U.S.* 37°3' N, 106°1' W **92**
Antonovo, *Kaz.* 49°21' N, 51°45' E **158**
Antons, Lac des, lake, *Can.* 52°49' N, 74°20' W **111**
Antopal', *Belarus* 52°12' N, 24°45' E **152**
Antrim Mountains, *U.K.* 54°52' N, 6°38' W **150**
Antropovo, *Russ.* 58°24' N, 43°6' E **154**
Antsirabe, *Madagascar* 19°53' S, 47°7' E **207**
Antsirabe, *Madagascar* 13°60' S, 49°58' E **220**
Antsiraňana, *Madagascar* 12°26' S, 49°16' E **220**
Antsla, *Est.* 57°48' N, 26°31' E **166**
Antsohihy, *Madagascar* 14°53' S, 47°59' E **220**
Anttila, *Fin.* 65°7' N, 29°48' E **154**
Anttila, *Fin.* 61°2' N, 26°49' E **166**
Anttis, *Nor.* 67°16' N, 22°48' E **152**
Anttola, *Fin.* 61°34' N, 27°35' E **166**
Antu, *China* 42°32' N, 128°18' E **200**
Antubia, *Ghana* 6°18' N, 2°51' W **222**
Antufash, Jazīrat, island, *Yemen* 15°45' N, 42°17' E **182**
Antwerp, *Ohio, U.S.* 41°9' N, 84°44' W **102**
Antwerpen (Antwerp), *Belg.* 51°13' N, 4°24' E **167**
Anuppur, *India* 23°7' N, 81°42' E **197**
Anupshahr, *India* 28°20' N, 78°15' E **197**
Anuradhapura, *Sri Lanka* 8°22' N, 80°22' E **188**
Anvers Island, *Antarctica* 64°36' S, 66°3' W **134**
Anvik, *Alas., U.S.* 62°30' N, 160°23' W **98**
Anxi, *China* 25°5' N, 118°13' E **198**
Anxi, *China* 40°31' N, 95°47' E **188**
Anxiang, *China* 29°24' N, 112°12' E **198**
Anxin, *China* 38°57' N, 115°54' E **198**
Anyang, *China* 36°5' N, 114°19' E **198**
Anyang, *S. Korea* 37°22' N, 126°54' E **200**
Anyi, *China* 28°49' N, 115°28' E **198**
Anyi, *China* 35°5' N, 111°4' E **198**
Anykščiai, *Lith.* 55°32' N, 25°8' E **166**
Anyou, *China* 18°11' N, 109°34' E **198**
Anyuan, *China* 25°6' N, 115°24' E **198**
Anyue, *China* 30°5' N, 105°22' E **198**
Anza, *Calif., U.S.* 33°33' N, 116°42' W **101**
Anzá, *Col.* 6°18' N, 75°54' W **136**
Anze, *China* 36°8' N, 112°10' E **198**
Anzhero Sudzhensk, *Russ.* 56°3' N, 86°8' E **169**
Anzhu, Ostrova, islands, *Ostrov Kotel'nyy;Ostrov Faddeyevskiy* 75°26' N, 135°19' E **160**
Anzio, *It.* 41°26' N, 12°37' E **156**
Anzoátegui, adm. division, *Venez.* 8°48' N, 64°48' W **116**
Aohan Qi, *China* 42°17' N, 119°55' E **198**
Aoiz, *Sp.* 42°47' N, 1°21' W **164**
Aokas, *Alg.* 36°38' N, 5°14' E **150**
Aomori, *Japan* 40°51' N, 140°48' E **190**
Aoraki (Cook, Mount), *N.Z.* 43°45' S, 170°4' E **240**
Aosta, *It.* 45°44' N, 7°19' E **167**
Aouchich, spring, *Mauritania* 22°4' N, 12°4' W **222**
Aouderas, *Niger* 17°38' N, 8°25' E **222**
Aougoundou, Lac, lake, *Mali* 15°47' N, 5°12' W **222**
'Aouinet Bel Egrâ, spring, *Alg.* 26°52' N, 6°53' W **214**
Aoukâr, plain, *Mali* 23°48' N, 5°5' W **214**
Aoukâr, region, *Africa* 17°48' N, 10°56' W **222**
Aoulef, *Alg.* 26°59' N, 1°5' E **214**
Aoya, *Japan* 35°29' N, 133°58' E **201**
Aozi, *Chad* 21°3' N, 18°40' E **216**
Aozou, *Chad* 21°49' N, 17°26' E **216**
Ap Iwan, Cerro, peak, *Chile* 46°13' S, 71°59' W **134**
Apa, river, *South America* 22°10' S, 57°17' W **132**
Apache, *Okla., U.S.* 34°52' N, 98°22' W **96**
Apache Mountain, *N. Mex., U.S.* 33°55' N, 108°41' W **92**
Apache Mountains, *Tex., U.S.* 31°9' N, 104°30' W **92**
Apahida, *Rom.* 46°48' N, 23°46' E **156**
Apalachicola, *Fla., U.S.* 29°43' N, 84°60' W **96**
Apam, *Ghana* 5°19' N, 0°47' E **222**
Apamea, ruin(s), *Syr.* 35°24' N, 36°21' E **194**
Apaporis, river, *Col.* 0°17' N, 71°46' W **136**
Aparecida do Taboado, *Braz.* 20°5' S, 51°8' W **138**
Aparri, *Philippines* 18°18' N, 121°40' E **203**
Apateu, *Rom.* 46°37' N, 21°46' E **168**
Apatin, *Serb. and Mont.* 45°39' N, 18°58' E **168**
Apatity, *Russ.* 67°34' N, 33°19' E **152**
Apatzingán, *Mex.* 19°5' N, 102°22' W **114**
Apaxtla, *Mex.* 18°8' N, 99°53' W **114**
Ape, *Latv.* 57°31' N, 26°43' E **166**
Apeldoorn, *Neth.* 52°13' N, 5°57' E **163**
Apen, *Ger.* 53°13' N, 7°50' E **163**
Apere, *Bol.* 12°7' S, 66°17' W **137**
Apere, river, *Bol.* 15°6' S, 66°7' W **137**
Aphaea, ruin(s), *Gr.* 37°44' N, 23°26' E **156**
Api, *Dem. Rep. of the Congo* 3°41' N, 25°28' E **224**
Apia, *Samoa* 14°0' S, 172°0' W **241**
Apiacá, river, *Braz.* 9°19' S, 57°6' W **130**
Apiacás, Serra dos, *Braz.* 9°38' S, 57°21' W **130**
Apiaí, *Braz.* 24°38' S, 48°58' W **138**
Apiaú, Serra do, *Braz.* 2°53' N, 61°48' W **130**
Apidiá, river, *Braz.* 12°33' S, 61°11' W **130**
Apizaco, *Mex.* 19°23' N, 98°11' W **114**
Aplao, *Peru* 16°6' S, 72°31' W **137**
Apo, Mount, *Philippines* 6°59' N, 125°11' E **203**
Apodaca, *Mex.* 25°46' N, 100°12' W **114**
Apodi, Chapada do, *Braz.* 5°8' S, 38°11' W **132**
Apollonia, ruin(s), *Alban.* 40°41' N, 19°21' E **156**
Apollonia see Sozopol, *Bulg.* 42°25' N, 27°42' E **156**
Apollonia see Sūsah, *Lib.* 32°52' N, 21°59' E **143**
Apolo, *Bol.* 14°41' S, 68°31' W **137**
Apopka, *Fla., U.S.* 28°40' N, 81°31' W **105**
Apopka, Lake, *Fla., U.S.* 28°38' N, 81°44' W **105**
Aporé, *Braz.* 18°57' S, 52°3' W **138**
Aporé, river, *Braz.* 19°9' S, 51°35' W **138**
Apostle Islands, *Lake Superior* 47°6' N, 90°53' W **94**
Apóstoles, *Arg.* 27°55' S, 55°44' W **139**
Apostolos Andreas, Cape, *Northern Cyprus* 35°34' N, 34°34' E **194**
Apostolos Andreas Monastery, site, *Northern Cyprus* 35°40' N, 34°32' E **194**
Apoteri, *Guyana* 4°0' N, 58°34' W **130**
Apozol, *Mex.* 21°28' N, 103°7' W **114**
Appalachian Mountains, *North America* 47°54' N, 68°40' W **82**
Appennini, mountains, *Europe* 44°37' N, 8°30' E **167**
Appiano, *It.* 46°27' N, 11°15' E **167**
Apple Springs, *Tex., U.S.* 31°12' N, 94°59' W **103**
Apple Valley, *Calif., U.S.* 34°30' N, 117°12' W **101**
Appleby, *U.K.* 54°34' N, 2°29' W **162**
Appleton, *Wis., U.S.* 44°16' N, 88°25' W **94**
Appleton City, *Mo., U.S.* 38°10' N, 94°2' W **94**
Apriķi, *Latv.* 56°49' N, 21°31' E **166**
Apsheron Yarymadasy, *Azerb.* 40°21' N, 49°19' E **180**
Apsheronsk, *Russ.* 44°26' N, 39°48' E **180**
Aptera, ruin(s), *Gr.* 35°26' N, 24°1' E **156**
Aptos, *Calif., U.S.* 36°59' N, 121°53' W **100**
Apuane, Alpi, *It.* 43°57' N, 10°17' E **167**
Apucarana, *Braz.* 23°36' S, 51°31' W **138**
Apuí, *Braz.* 1°11' N, 69°14' W **136**
Apuka, *Russ.* 60°35' N, 169°28' E **160**
Apulia, adm. division, *It.* 41°1' N, 15°35' E **156**
Apure, adm. division, *Venez.* 7°4' N, 70°6' W **136**
Apurímac, adm. division, *Peru* 13°58' S, 73°41' W **137**
Apurímac, river, *Peru* 13°27' S, 73°16' W **137**
Apurito, *Venez.* 7°55' N, 68°28' W **136**
Apuseni, Munţii, *Rom.* 46°38' N, 22°39' E **168**
Aq Kopruk, *Afghan.* 36°4' N, 66°54' E **186**
Aqaba, Gulf of 28°52' N, 34°11' E **180**
Aqadyr, *Kaz.* 48°13' N, 72°52' E **184**
Aqchan, *Afghan.* 36°57' N, 66°14' E **186**
Aqiq, *Sudan* 18°9' N, 38°7' E **182**
Aqköl, *Kaz.* 46°40' N, 49°6' E **158**
Aqköl, *Kaz.* 43°24' N, 70°46' E **184**
Aqköl, *Kaz.* 45°0' N, 75°39' E **184**
Aqköl, *Kaz.* 52°0' N, 70°59' E **184**
Aqmola, adm. division, *Kaz.* 51°31' N, 68°23' E **184**
Aqqikkol Hu, lake, *China* 37°10' N, 87°39' E **188**
Aqqystaū, *Kaz.* 47°14' N, 51°4' E **158**
'Aqrah, *Iraq* 36°45' N, 43°47' E **195**
Aqsay, *Kaz.* 51°10' N, 52°58' E **158**
Aqshataū, *Kaz.* 49°25' N, 54°45' E **158**
Aqshataū, *Kaz.* 47°58' N, 73°59' E **184**
Aqsū, *Kaz.* 52°27' N, 71°58' E **184**
Aqsū, *Kaz.* 42°25' N, 69°50' E **197**
Aqsūat, *Kaz.* 47°47' N, 82°49' E **184**
Aqsū-Ayuly, *Kaz.* 48°45' N, 73°42' E **184**
Aqsūgek, *Kaz.* 44°37' N, 74°28' E **184**
Aqtaū, *Kaz.* 43°38' N, 51°14' E **195**
Aqtaysay, *Kaz.* 49°40' N, 54°1' E **158**
Aqtöbe, *Kaz.* 50°15' N, 57°12' E **158**
Aqtöbe, adm. division, *Kaz.* 48°43' N, 56°0' E **158**
Aqtoghay, *Kaz.* 48°12' N, 75°2' E **184**
Aqtoghay, *Kaz.* 46°55' N, 79°39' E **184**
Aquarius Mountains, *Ariz., U.S.* 35°1' N, 113°36' W **101**
Aquidauana, *Braz.* 20°29' S, 55°48' W **134**
Aquileia, *It.* 45°46' N, 13°21' E **167**
Aquiles Serdán, *Mex.* 28°35' N, 105°55' W **92**
Aquitaine, adm. division, *Fr.* 44°10' N, 1°18' W **150**
Aqyrab, *Kaz.* 50°35' N, 55°8' E **158**
Aqzhal, *Kaz.* 49°13' N, 81°23' E **184**
Aqzhar, *Kaz.* 47°35' N, 83°45' E **184**
Aqzhayyq, *Kaz.* 50°50' N, 51°17' E **158**
Ar Horqin Qi (Tianshan), *China* 43°55' N, 120°7' E **198**
Ar Rabbah, *Jordan* 31°16' N, 35°44' E **194**
Ar Rafīd, *Syr.* 32°57' N, 35°53' E **194**
Ar Ramādī, *Iraq* 33°23' N, 43°14' E **180**
Ar Ramthā, *Jordan* 32°33' N, 36°0' E **194**
Ar Raqqah, *Syr.* 35°54' N, 39°2' E **180**
Ar Rashādīyah, *Jordan* 30°42' N, 35°37' E **194**
Ar Rass, *Saudi Arabia* 25°50' N, 43°28' E **182**
Ar Rastan (Arethusa), *Syr.* 34°55' N, 36°44' E **194**
Ar Rawḑah, *Saudi Arabia* 21°12' N, 42°47' E **182**
Ar Riyāḑ (Riyadh), *Saudi Arabia* 24°35' N, 46°35' E **186**
Ar Riyān, *Yemen* 14°40' N, 49°21' E **182**
Ar Rub' al Khālī (Empty Quarter), *Saudi Arabia* 24°33' N, 54°53' E **196**
Ar Rummān, *Jordan* 32°9' N, 35°49' E **194**
Ar Ruşayfah, *Jordan* 32°1' N, 36°2' E **194**
Ar Rustāq, *Oman* 23°23' N, 57°24' E **182**
Ar Ruţbah, *Iraq* 33°3' N, 40°14' E **180**
Ara, *India* 25°32' N, 84°37' E **197**
Ara Bure, *Eth.* 6°31' N, 41°17' E **224**
'Arab al Mulk, *Syr.* 35°16' N, 35°55' E **194**
'Arabah, Wādī al, *Israel-Jordan* 30°23' N, 35°1' E **194**
Arabian Basin, *Arabian Sea* 10°36' N, 65°57' E **254**
Arabian Gulf see Persian Gulf 26°40' N, 51°30' E **180**
Arabian Sea 13°38' N, 58°38' E **173**
Araç, *Turk.* 41°15' N, 33°19' E **156**
Araç, river, *Turk.* 41°9' N, 32°58' E **158**
Aracaju, *Braz.* 10°54' S, 37°5' W **132**
Aracati, *Braz.* 4°35' S, 37°43' W **132**
Aracatu, *Braz.* 14°27' S, 41°29' W **138**
Araçatuba, *Braz.* 21°11' S, 50°27' W **138**
Aracena, *Sp.* 37°53' N, 6°35' W **164**
Aracena, Sierra de, *Sp.* 37°58' N, 6°51' W **164**
Aracruz, *Braz.* 19°51' S, 40°19' W **132**
Araçuaí, *Braz.* 16°52' S, 42°4' W **138**
Araçuaí, river, *Braz.* 17°50' S, 42°60' W **138**
'Arad, *Israel* 31°14' N, 35°12' E **194**
Arad, *Rom.* 46°11' N, 21°19' E **168**
Arad, adm. division, *Rom.* 46°9' N, 21°5' E **156**
Arada, *Chad* 15°1' N, 20°39' E **216**
Araden, ruin(s), *Gr.* 35°12' N, 23°57' E **156**
Aradu Nou, *Rom.* 46°9' N, 21°20' E **168**
Arafali, *Eritrea* 15°1' N, 39°42' E **182**
Arafura Sea 9°12' S, 134°22' E **192**
Araga, spring, *Niger* 17°25' N, 11°36' E **222**
Aragarças, *Braz.* 15°58' S, 52°14' W **138**
Aragats, peak, *Arm.* 40°30' N, 44°8' E **195**
Arago, Cape, *Oreg., U.S.* 43°20' N, 124°41' W **90**
Aragon, adm. division, *Sp.* 41°26' N, 1°15' W **164**
Aragua, adm. division, *Venez.* 10°3' N, 67°40' W **136**
Aragua de Barcelona, *Venez.* 9°29' N, 64°52' W **116**
Araguacema, *Braz.* 8°50' S, 49°37' W **130**
Araguaçu, *Braz.* 12°52' S, 49°56' W **138**
Araguaia National Park, *Braz.* 11°14' S, 50°56' W **130**
Araguaia, river, *Braz.* 15°22' S, 51°48' W **132**
Araguaina, *Braz.* 7°12' S, 48°16' W **130**
Araguao, Boca 9°11' N, 61°20' W **116**
Araguapiche, Punta, *Venez.* 9°21' N, 60°53' W **116**
Araguari, *Braz.* 18°40' S, 48°15' W **138**
Araguari, river, *Braz.* 18°56' S, 48°13' W **138**
Araguatins, *Braz.* 5°39' S, 48°8' W **130**
Arahal, *Sp.* 37°15' N, 5°34' W **164**
Arahura, *N.Z.* 42°42' S, 171°4' E **240**
Arai, *Japan* 37°0' N, 138°14' E **201**
Araia, *Sp.* 42°52' N, 2°19' W **164**
Arak, *Alg.* 25°18' N, 3°44' E **214**
Arāk, *Iran* 34°6' N, 49°42' E **180**
Araka, spring, *Niger* 18°54' N, 15°24' E **216**
Arakamchechen, Ostrov, island, *Russ.* 64°44' N, 172°1' W **98**
Arakan Yoma, *Myanmar* 19°6' N, 94°18' E **202**
Aral, *China* 38°8' N, 90°43' E **188**
Aral, *China* 40°40' N, 81°28' E **184**
Aral, *Kaz.* 46°54' N, 61°36' E **184**
Aral Mangy Qaraqumy, *Kaz.* 47°11' N, 61°51' E **184**
Aral Sea, lake 45°32' N, 58°10' E **160**
Aralqi, *China* 39°27' N, 87°44' E **188**
Aralqum, *Kaz.* 44°8' N, 58°11' E **180**
Aralsor Köli, lake, *Kaz.* 49°0' N, 48°1' E **158**
Araltobe, *Kaz.* 50°31' N, 60°6' E **158**
Aramac, *Austral.* 22°60' S, 145°16' E **231**
Aramberri, *Mex.* 24°4' N, 99°50' W **114**
Aramits, *Fr.* 43°6' N, 0°44' E **164**
Arampampa, *Bol.* 17°60' S, 65°58' W **137**
Ārān, *Iran* 34°9' N, 51°30' E **180**
Aran Islands, *Celtic Sea* 53°12' N, 10°30' W **150**
Aranda de Duero, *Sp.* 41°40' N, 3°44' W **164**
Arandas, *Mex.* 20°41' N, 102°22' W **114**
Arani, *Bol.* 17°38' S, 65°41' W **137**
Aranjuez, *Sp.* 40°1' N, 3°36' W **164**
Aranos, *Namibia* 24°5' S, 19°7' E **227**
Aransas Pass, *Tex., U.S.* 27°53' N, 97°9' W **96**
Arantes, river, *Braz.* 19°25' S, 50°20' W **138**
Arantur, *Russ.* 60°59' N, 63°37' E **169**
Aranyaprathet, *Thai.* 13°44' N, 102°31' E **202**
Arao, *Japan* 32°57' N, 130°26' E **201**
Araouane, *Mali* 18°53' N, 3°34' W **222**
Arapa, Laguna, lake, *Peru* 15°11' S, 70°11' W **137**
Arapaho, *Okla., U.S.* 35°33' N, 98°58' W **96**
Arapey, *Uru.* 30°57' S, 57°33' W **139**
Arapiraca, *Braz.* 9°45' S, 36°42' W **132**
Arapkir, *Turk.* 39°1' N, 38°31' E **180**
Arapongas, *Braz.* 23°26' S, 51°28' W **138**
Araracuara, *Col.* 0°29' N, 72°17' W **136**
Araranguá, *Braz.* 28°58' S, 49°29' W **138**
Araraquara, *Braz.* 21°48' S, 48°12' W **138**
Araras, *Braz.* 9°5' S, 68°6' W **137**
Araras, *Braz.* 6°13' S, 54°34' W **130**
Araras, *Braz.* 22°22' S, 47°23' W **138**
Ararat, *Arm.* 39°50' N, 44°40' E **195**
Ararat, Mount see Ağrı Dağı, *Turk.* 39°39' N, 44°12' E **180**
Ararat, Mount see Ağrı Dağı, peak, *Turk.* 39°42' N, 44°15' E **195**
Arari, *Braz.* 3°28' S, 44°46' W **132**
Araria, *India* 26°5' N, 87°27' E **197**
Araripe, Chapada do, *Braz.* 7°34' S, 40°28' W **132**
Araruama, *Braz.* 22°52' S, 42°22' W **138**
Aras (Araxes), river, *Asia* 40°0' N, 42°18' E **195**
Arataca, *Braz.* 15°18' S, 39°24' W **138**
Aratane, spring, *Mauritania* 18°24' N, 8°33' W **222**
Arataú, river, *Braz.* 3°14' S, 50°37' W **130**
Arauã, river, *Braz.* 4°14' S, 64°51' W **130**
Arauca, *Col.* 7°0' N, 70°47' W **136**
Arauca, adm. division, *Col.* 6°39' N, 71°44' W **136**
Arauca, river, *Venez.* 7°27' N, 67°58' W **136**
Araucanía, La, adm. division, *Chile* 39°21' S, 73°44' W **134**
Araucária, *Braz.* 25°36' S, 49°24' W **138**
Arauquita, *Col.* 6°58' N, 71°22' W **136**
Arawa, *P.N.G.* 6°14' S, 155°31' E **238**
Araxá, *Braz.* 19°36' S, 46°56' W **138**
Araxes see Aras, river, *Turk.* 40°0' N, 42°18' E **195**
Arayit Dağı, peak, *Turk.* 39°17' N, 31°39' E **156**
Ārba Minch', *Eth.* 5°59' N, 37°37' E **224**
Arba'at, *Sudan* 19°46' N, 36°57' E **182**
Arbazh, *Russ.* 57°41' N, 48°24' E **154**
Arbela see Irbid, *Jordan* 32°32' N, 35°51' E **194**
Arbīl, *Iraq* 36°10' N, 43°59' E **180**
Arboledas, *Arg.* 36°51' S, 61°28' W **139**
Arborea, *It.* 39°46' N, 8°34' E **156**
Arborfield, *Can.* 53°6' N, 103°40' W **108**
Arborg, *Can.* 50°53' N, 97°13' W **90**
Arbrå, *Nor.* 61°29' N, 16°19' E **152**
Arbre du Ténéré, site, *Niger* 17°44' N, 10°5' E **222**
Arbroath, *U.K.* 56°33' N, 2°38' W **150**
Arc, *Fr.* 47°27' N, 5°33' E **150**
Arc Dome, peak, *Nev., U.S.* 38°49' N, 117°26' W **90**
Arc, river, *Fr.* 45°23' N, 6°17' E **165**
Arcachon, *Fr.* 44°36' N, 1°15' W **214**
Arcadia, *Fla., U.S.* 27°13' N, 81°52' W **105**
Arcadia, *Ind., U.S.* 40°10' N, 86°1' W **102**
Arcadia, *La., U.S.* 32°31' N, 92°56' W **103**
Arcadia, *Mich., U.S.* 44°29' N, 86°14' W **94**
Arcadia, *Peru* 1°3' S, 75°18' W **136**
Arcadia, *Wis., U.S.* 44°15' N, 91°29' W **94**
Arcanum, *Ohio, U.S.* 39°59' N, 84°32' W **102**
Arcas, Cayos, islands, *Gulf of Mexico* 20°19' N, 92°6' W **115**
Arcata, *Calif., U.S.* 40°52' N, 124°6' W **90**
Arcelia, *Mex.* 18°16' N, 100°16' W **114**
Archangel see Arkhangel'sk, *Russ.* 64°35' N, 40°37' E **154**
Archar, *Bulg.* 43°48' N, 22°54' E **168**
Archbold, *Ohio, U.S.* 41°30' N, 84°18' W **102**
Archeï, spring, *Chad* 16°53' N, 21°44' E **216**
Archena, *Sp.* 38°6' N, 1°19' W **164**
Archer, *Fla., U.S.* 29°32' N, 82°32' W **105**
Archer Bay 13°40' S, 141°24' E **230**
Archer Bend National Park, *Austral.* 13°35' S, 141°56' E **238**
Archer City, *Tex., U.S.* 33°34' N, 98°38' W **92**
Archer Point, *Antarctica* 68°54' S, 161°17' E **248**
Archer, river, *Austral.* 13°39' S, 141°16' E **231**
Archer's Post, *Kenya* 0°36' N, 37°40' E **224**
Archerwill, *Can.* 52°25' N, 103°52' W **108**
Archidona, *Sp.* 37°5' N, 4°24' W **164**
Archipiélago de Colón see Galápagos Islands, *Ecuador* 0°13' N, 92°2' W **130**
Archipiélago Los Roques National Park, *Caribbean Sea* 11°50' N, 67°27' W **136**
Archman, *Turkm.* 38°33' N, 57°9' E **180**
Arci, Monte, peak, *It.* 39°46' N, 8°41' E **156**
Arcis, *Fr.* 48°32' N, 4°8' E **163**
Arco, *Idaho, U.S.* 43°38' N, 113°18' W **90**
Arco, *It.* 45°55' N, 10°52' E **167**
Arco, Paso del, pass, *Arg.* 38°47' S, 71°6' W **134**
Arcola, *Ill., U.S.* 39°41' N, 88°19' W **102**
Arcola, *Miss., U.S.* 33°14' N, 90°53' W **103**
Arcos, *Braz.* 20°17' S, 45°34' W **138**
Arcos de Jalón, *Sp.* 41°12' N, 2°17' W **150**
Arcoverde, *Braz.* 8°24' S, 37°1' W **132**
Arctic Bay, *Can.* 73°3' N, 85°6' W **73**
Arctic Ocean 79°19' N, 170°44' W **246**
Arctic Red, river, *Can.* 66°40' N, 132°38' W **98**
Arctic Village, *Alas., U.S.* 68°6' N, 145°32' W **98**
Arctowski, station, *Antarctica* 62°12' S, 58°12' W **134**
Arda, river, *Bulg.* 41°30' N, 25°42' E **156**
Ardabīl, *Iran* 38°15' N, 48°18' E **195**
Ardahan, *Turk.* 41°5' N, 42°40' E **195**
Ardakān, *Iran* 32°14' N, 54°3' E **180**
Ardakān, *Iran* 30°14' N, 51°59' E **196**
Årdal, *Nor.* 61°14' N, 7°43' E **152**
Årdal, *Nor.* 59°8' N, 6°11' E **152**
Ardales, *Sp.* 36°51' N, 4°51' W **164**
Ardanuç, *Turk.* 41°9' N, 42°2' E **195**
Ardaşşawwān, *Jordan* 30°58' N, 36°46' E **194**
Ardatov, *Russ.* 54°48' N, 46°19' E **154**
Ardencaple Fjord 74°46' N, 25°23' W **246**
Ardestān, *Iran* 33°20' N, 52°25' E **180**
Ardmore, *Okla., U.S.* 34°9' N, 97°7' W **92**
Ardmore, *S. Dak., U.S.* 43°1' N, 103°40' W **90**
Ardres, *Fr.* 50°51' N, 1°58' E **163**
Ards Peninsula, *U.K.* 54°21' N, 6°3' W **150**
Ardud, *Rom.* 47°38' N, 22°53' E **168**
Ardvrach Castle, site, *U.K.* 58°9' N, 5°6' W **150**
Ardvule, Rubha, *U.K.* 57°15' N, 8°1' W **150**
Åre, *Nor.* 63°24' N, 13°3' E **152**
Arena, Point, *U.S.* 38°47' N, 124°3' W **90**
Arenápolis, *Braz.* 14°28' S, 56°53' W **132**
Arenas, Punta de, *Arg.* 53°3' S, 68°13' W **134**
Arendal, *Nor.* 58°27' N, 8°43' E **152**
Arendsee, *Ger.* 52°53' N, 11°30' E **152**
Arenys de Mar, *Sp.* 41°34' N, 2°33' E **164**
Arenzano, *It.* 44°23' N, 8°41' E **167**
Arequipa, *Peru* 16°24' S, 71°35' W **137**
Arequipa, adm. division, *Peru* 16°8' S, 73°31' W **137**
Ārēro, *Eth.* 4°43' N, 38°48' E **224**
Arês, *Braz.* 6°14' S, 35°8' W **132**
Åreskutan, peak, *Nor.* 63°26' N, 12°55' E **152**
Arethusa see Ar Rastan, *Syr.* 34°55' N, 36°44' E **194**
Arévalo, *Sp.* 41°3' N, 4°44' W **150**
Arezzaf, spring, *Mali* 18°5' N, 1°47' W **222**
Arezzo, *It.* 43°27' N, 11°52' E **156**
Arga Sala, river, *Russ.* 67°51' N, 107°46' E **160**
Argaman, *West Bank* 32°8' N, 35°30' E **194**
Argamasilla de Alba, *Sp.* 39°7' N, 3°7' W **164**
Argamasilla de Calatrava, *Sp.* 38°44' N, 4°5' W **164**
Argan, *China* 40°6' N, 88°17' E **188**
Argatay, *Mongolia* 45°33' N, 108°4' E **198**
Argelès, *Fr.* 42°32' N, 3°0' E **164**
Argens, river, *Fr.* 43°25' N, 6°3' E **165**
Argenta, *It.* 44°36' N, 11°49' E **167**
Argentario, Monte, peak, *It.* 42°23' N, 11°5' E **156**
Argentera, peak, *It.* 44°10' N, 7°17' E **165**
Argenteuil, *Fr.* 48°55' N, 2°13' E **163**
Argentina 35°22' S, 67°13' W **134**
Argentine Plain, *South Atlantic Ocean* 46°42' S, 48°15' W **253**
Argentré, *Fr.* 48°3' N, 0°34' E **150**
Argeş, adm. division, *Rom.* 44°57' N, 24°28' E **156**
Arghandab Dam, *Afghan.* 32°2' N, 65°50' E **186**
Argo, *Sudan* 19°30' N, 30°27' E **226**
Argolas, *Braz.* 20°26' S, 40°25' W **138**
Argonaut Mountain, *Can.* 51°49' N, 118°25' W **90**
Argonne, *Fr.* 49°43' N, 4°51' E **167**
Árgos, *Gr.* 37°35' N, 22°41' E **180**
Argos, *Ind., U.S.* 41°13' N, 86°14' W **102**
Argoub, *Western Sahara* 23°35' N, 15°51' W **214**
Arguello, Point, *Calif., U.S.* 34°30' N, 120°49' W **100**
Arguin, Cap d', *Mauritania* 20°25' N, 16°42' W **214**
Argungu, *Nig.* 12°43' N, 4°31' E **222**
Argus, *Calif., U.S.* 35°44' N, 117°25' W **101**
Argus, Dome, *Antarctica* 79°52' S, 74°47' E **248**
Argus Range, *Calif., U.S.* 36°0' N, 117°34' W **101**
Arguut, *Mongolia* 45°28' N, 102°18' E **190**
Argyle, *Mich., U.S.* 43°33' N, 82°56' W **102**
Argyle, *Minn., U.S.* 48°18' N, 96°51' W **90**
Argyle, *N.Y., U.S.* 43°14' N, 73°31' W **104**
Argyle, Lake, *Austral.* 16°12' S, 128°11' E **230**
Arhebeb, spring, *Mali* 21°5' N, 0°8' E **222**
Arhrîjît, *Mauritania* 18°21' N, 9°15' W **222**
Århus, *Den.* 56°9' N, 10°11' E **150**
Ari Atoll, *Maldives* 3°33' N, 72°22' E **188**
Ariamsvlei, *Namibia* 28°7' S, 19°50' E **227**
Ariana, *Tun.* 36°51' N, 10°11' E **156**
Arias, *Arg.* 33°39' S, 62°23' W **139**
Aribinda, *Burkina Faso* 14°14' N, 0°52' E **222**
Arica, *Chile* 18°34' S, 70°20' W **137**
Arica, *Col.* 2°9' S, 71°46' W **136**
Arica, *Peru* 1°39' S, 75°12' W **136**
Arid, Mount, *Austral.* 34°1' S, 122°58' E **230**
Arida, *Japan* 34°4' N, 135°7' E **201**
Aridal, *Western Sahara* 25°59' N, 13°48' W **214**
Arīḩā, *Syr.* 35°48' N, 36°35' E **156**
Arīḩā (Jericho), *West Bank* 31°51' N, 35°27' E **194**
Arija, *Sp.* 42°57' N, 3°59' W **164**
Arikaree, river, *Colo., U.S.* 39°48' N, 102°40' W **90**
Arimã, *Braz.* 5°47' S, 63°42' W **130**
Arinos, *Braz.* 15°54' S, 46°4' W **138**
Arinos, river, *Braz.* 10°28' S, 58°34' W **132**
Ariogala, *Lith.* 55°15' N, 23°29' E **166**
Aripao, *Venez.* 7°19' N, 65°4' W **130**
Ariporo, river, *Col.* 5°57' N, 71°13' W **136**
Aripuanã, *Braz.* 9°59' S, 59°28' W **130**
Aripuanã, river, *Braz.* 7°52' S, 60°35' W **130**
Aripuanã, river, *Braz.* 11°15' S, 59°41' W **130**

Ariquemes, Braz. 9°57' S, 63°6' W 130
Arismendi, Venez. 8°29' N, 68°22' W 136
Arista, Mex. 22°37' N, 100°51' W 114
Aristizábal, Cabo, Arg. 45°23' S, 66°29' W 134
Arivechi, Mex. 28°54' N, 109°10' W 92
Ariza, Sp. 41°18' N, 2°4' W 164
Arizona, adm. division, Ariz., U.S. 34°22' N, 112°38' W 92
Arizpe, Mex. 30°19' N, 110°12' W 92
Arjona, Col. 10°16' N, 75°22' W 136
Ark, The, peak, Antarctica 80°43' S, 26°3' W 248
Arka, Russ. 60°10' N, 142°13' E 160
Arkadak, Russ. 51°53' N, 43°35' E 158
Arkadelphia, Ark., U.S. 34°6' N, 93°5' W 96
Arkansas, adm. division, Ark., U.S. 35°4' N, 93°21' W 96
Arkansas City, Kans., U.S. 37°2' N, 97°3' W 92
Arkansas, river, Okla., U.S. 35°13' N, 95°34' W 80
Arkanū, Jabal, peak, Lib. 22°16' N, 24°40' E 226
Arkhangel'sk, Russ. 64°32' N, 40°54' E 160
Arkhangel'sk, adm. division, Russ. 63°2' N, 38°58' E 154
Arkhangel'sk (Archangel), Russ. 64°35' N, 40°37' E 154
Arkhangel'skoye, Russ. 44°34' N, 44°3' E 158
Arkhangel'skoye, Russ. 51°28' N, 40°52' E 158
Arklow, Ire. 52°47' N, 6°10' W 150
Arkona, Kap, Ger. 54°42' N, 13°34' E 152
Arkösund, Nor. 58°28' N, 16°53' E 152
Arkticheskiy, Mys, Russ. 81°1' N, 79°59' E 160
Arkticheskogo Instituta, Ostrova, island, Russ. 75°29' N, 77°0' E 160
Arkul', Russ. 57°19' N, 50°9' E 154
Arlanzón, Sp. 42°18' N, 3°27' W 164
Arles, Fr. 43°41' N, 4°40' E 214
Arlington, Ga., U.S. 31°25' N, 84°43' W 96
Arlington, Ill., U.S. 41°28' N, 89°15' W 102
Arlington, Mass., U.S. 42°24' N, 71°10' W 104
Arlington, N.Y., U.S. 41°41' N, 73°54' W 104
Arlington, Oreg., U.S. 45°42' N, 120°12' W 90
Arlington, S. Dak., U.S. 44°20' N, 97°9' W 94
Arlington, Tex., U.S. 32°43' N, 97°7' W 92
Arlington, Vt., U.S. 43°4' N, 73°10' W 104
Arlington, Wash., U.S. 48°10' N, 122°7' W 100
Arlit, Niger 18°50' N, 7°14' E 222
Arlon, Belg. 49°40' N, 5°48' E 163
Arly, river, Fr. 45°44' N, 6°31' E 165
Arma, Kans., U.S. 37°31' N, 94°42' W 94
Armada, Mich., U.S. 42°50' N, 82°53' W 102
Armadale Castle, site, U.K. 57°2' N, 6°1' W 150
Armadillo, Mex. 22°13' N, 100°40' W 114
Armant, Egypt 25°36' N, 32°27' E 182
Armavir, Arm. 40°9' N, 44°2' E 195
Armavir, Russ. 44°59' N, 41°6' E 158
Armenia 40°14' N, 44°43' E 195
Armenia, Col. 4°28' N, 75°45' W 136
Armenia Mountain, Pa., U.S. 41°44' N, 76°60' W 94
Armeniş, Rom. 45°13' N, 22°18' E 168
Armentières, Fr. 50°40' N, 2°53' E 163
Armeria, Mex. 18°55' N, 103°60' W 114
Armero, Col. 4°57' N, 74°55' W 136
Armijo, N. Mex., U.S. 35°2' N, 106°41' W 92
Armilla, Sp. 37°8' N, 3°38' W 164
Armit, Can. 52°49' N, 101°47' W 108
Armizonskoye, Russ. 55°56' N, 67°39' E 184
Armona, Calif., U.S. 36°19' N, 119°43' W 100
Armour, S. Dak., U.S. 43°18' N, 98°21' W 90
Armstrong, Arg. 32°49' S, 61°35' W 139
Armstrong, Can. 50°18' N, 89°2' W 110
Armstrong, Can. 50°26' N, 119°12' W 90
Armutcuk, Turk. 41°20' N, 31°31' E 156
Armyans'k, Ukr. 46°5' N, 33°41' E 156
Arnaoutis, Cape, Cyprus 35°5' N, 32°4' E 194
Arnaud, Can. 49°14' N, 97°6' W 90
Arnaudville, La., U.S. 30°23' N, 91°57' W 103
Arnbach, Aust. 46°44' N, 12°23' E 167
Årnes, Nor. 60°7' N, 11°28' E 152
Arnett, Okla., U.S. 36°7' N, 99°46' W 92
Arnhem, Neth. 51°59' N, 5°54' E 167
Arnhem Land, region, Australia 11°54' S, 131°40' E 192
Arnold, Calif., U.S. 38°15' N, 120°22' W 100
Arnold, Nebr., U.S. 41°25' N, 100°12' W 90
Arnold, river, Austral. 14°50' S, 133°57' E 230
Arnolds Park, Iowa, U.S. 43°21' N, 95°8' W 90
Arnoldstein, Aust. 46°33' N, 13°42' E 167
Arnot, Can. 55°45' N, 96°45' W 108
Arnsberg, Ger. 51°23' N, 8°4' E 167
Arnstein, Ger. 49°58' N, 9°58' E 167
Aroa, Venez. 10°25' N, 68°54' W 136
Aroab, Namibia 26°50' S, 19°43' E 227
Aroánia, Óri, peak, Gr. 37°57' N, 22°8' E 156
Arock, Oreg., U.S. 42°55' N, 117°31' W 90
Arolsen, Ger. 51°23' N, 9°1' E 167
Aroma, Sudan 15°46' N, 36°8' E 182
Aroma Park, Ill., U.S. 41°4' N, 87°48' W 102
Aron, India 25°57' N, 77°54' E 197
Arona, It. 45°45' N, 8°32' E 167
Arosa, Switz. 46°46' N, 9°38' E 167
Ærøskøbing, Den. 54°53' N, 10°24' E 150
Arowhana, peak, N.Z. 38°8' S, 177°45' E 240
Arp, Tex., U.S. 32°13' N, 95°4' W 103
Arpa, river, Asia 40°28' N, 43°31' E 195
Arpaçay, Turk. 40°52' N, 43°19' E 195
Arpajon, Fr. 48°35' N, 2°14' E 163
Arqalyq, Kaz. 50°13' N, 66°54' E 184
Arque, Bol. 17°51' S, 66°22' W 137
Arques, Fr. 50°44' N, 2°18' E 150
Arquia, Col. 7°58' N, 77°7' W 136
'Arrābah, West Bank 32°24' N, 35°11' E 194
Arraias, Braz. 12°56' S, 46°58' W 130
Arras, Alban. 41°45' N, 20°18' E 168
Arras, Fr. 50°17' N, 2°47' E 163
Arreau, Fr. 42°54' N, 0°20' E 164
Arrecifes, Arg. 34°4' S, 60°7' W 139
Arrée, Montagnes d', Fr. 48°29' N, 4°12' W 150
Arriate, Sp. 36°47' N, 5°9' W 164
Arris, Alg. 35°12' N, 6°17' E 150
Arroio dos Ratos, Braz. 30°6' S, 51°44' W 139
Arroio Grande, Braz. 32°12' S, 53°7' W 139
Arrojado, river, Braz. 13°40' S, 45°16' W 138
Arrou, Fr. 48°6' N, 1°7' E 163
Arroux, river, Fr. 46°45' N, 4°8' E 165
Arrowhead, river, Can. 60°18' N, 123°11' W 108
Arrowsmith, Ill., U.S. 40°26' N, 88°38' W 102
Arrowtown, N.Z. 44°57' S, 168°51' E 240
Arrowwood, Can. 50°44' N, 113°10' W 90
Arroyito, Arg. 31°27' S, 63°4' W 139
Arroyo de la Luz, Sp. 39°28' N, 6°36' W 164
Arroyo Grande, Calif., U.S. 35°8' N, 120°35' W 100
Arroyo Hondo, N. Mex., U.S. 36°31' N, 105°40' W 92
Arroyo Verde see Puerto Lobos, Arg. 42°2' S, 65°5' W 134
Arroyos y Esteros, Parag. 25°5' S, 57°7' W 132
Arrufó, Arg. 30°13' S, 61°44' W 139
Ars-en-Ré, Fr. 46°12' N, 1°33' W 150
Arshaly, Kaz. 50°49' N, 72°11' E 184
Arshaty, Kaz. 49°17' N, 86°36' E 184
Arsiero, It. 45°48' N, 11°20' E 167
Arsikere, India 13°20' N, 76°14' E 188
Arsk, Russ. 56°7' N, 49°54' E 154
Arsuk, Den. 61°13' N, 48°8' W 106
Artashat, Arm. 39°58' N, 44°32' E 195
Arteaga, Mex. 25°25' N, 100°52' W 114
Arteaga, Mex. 18°24' N, 102°16' W 114
Artem, Russ. 43°26' N, 132°21' E 190
Artemisa, Cuba 22°49' N, 82°46' W 116
Artemivs'k, Ukr. 48°35' N, 37°57' E 158
Artemovsk, Russ. 54°24' N, 93°22' E 190
Artemovskiy, Russ. 58°19' N, 114°40' E 160
Artemovskiy, Russ. 57°22' N, 61°47' E 154
Artenay, Fr. 48°4' N, 1°51' E 150
Artesa de Segre, Sp. 41°53' N, 1°3' E 164
Artesia, Miss., U.S. 33°23' N, 88°38' W 103
Artesia, N. Mex., U.S. 32°50' N, 104°25' W 92
Artesian, S. Dak., U.S. 43°59' N, 97°57' W 90
Arthez, Fr. 43°28' N, 0°37' E 150
Arthog, U.K. 52°42' N, 4°1' W 162
Arthonnay, Fr. 47°55' N, 4°13' E 150
Arthur, Ill., U.S. 39°42' N, 88°28' W 102
Arthur, Nebr., U.S. 41°33' N, 101°42' W 90
Arthur, Lac, lake, Can. 51°6' N, 62°48' W 111
Arthur's Pass, N.Z. 42°57' S, 171°33' E 240
Arti, Russ. 56°25' N, 58°37' E 154
Artigas, Uru. 30°24' S, 56°31' W 139
Artigas, station, Antarctica 61°59' S, 58°38' W 134
Art'ik, Arm. 40°37' N, 43°57' E 195
Artix, Fr. 43°24' N, 0°33' E 150
Artois, region, Europe 50°17' N, 1°58' E 163
Artova, Turk. 40°2' N, 36°16' E 156
Artrutx, Cabo d', Sp. 39°56' N, 3°27' E 150
Artux, China 39°45' N, 76°6' E 184
Artvin, Turk. 41°11' N, 41°49' E 195
Artyom, Azerb. 40°28' N, 50°19' E 195
Aru, Dem. Rep. of the Congo 2°48' N, 30°50' E 224
Aru, Kepulauan, islands, Arafura Sea 6°8' S, 133°44' E 192
Arua, Dem. Rep. of the Congo 3°4' N, 30°56' E 207
Aruajá, Braz. 4°60' S, 66°51' W 130
Aruanã, Braz. 14°58' S, 51°8' W 138
Aruba, island, Netherlands 13°0' N, 70°0' W 118
Arun Qi, China 48°8' N, 123°34' E 198
Arunachal Pradesh, adm. division, India 28°39' N, 94°2' E 188
Arundel, U.K. 50°51' N, 0°34' E 162
Arusha, Tanzania 3°22' S, 36°42' E 224
Arusha, adm. division, Tanzania 4°7' S, 35°4' E 218
Aruwimi, river, Dem. Rep. of the Congo 1°37' N, 25°21' E 224
Arvada, Colo., U.S. 39°47' N, 105°6' W 90
Arvayheer, Mongolia 46°12' N, 102°50' E 198
Arve, river, Fr. 46°3' N, 6°36' E 167
Arvi, India 20°59' N, 78°13' E 188
Arviat, Can. 61°5' N, 94°10' W 106
Arvika, Nor. 59°39' N, 12°36' E 152
Arvin, Calif., U.S. 35°12' N, 118°50' W 101
Arvon, Mount, Mich., U.S. 46°44' N, 88°14' W 94
Arxan, China 47°12' N, 119°55' E 198
Ary, Russ. 72°50' N, 122°37' E 173
Arya Köli, lake, Kaz. 45°55' N, 66°3' E 184
Aryqbayq, Kaz. 52°55' N, 68°12' E 184
Arys, Kaz. 42°25' N, 68°47' E 197
Arys, river, Kaz. 42°32' N, 69°1' E 197
Arzamas, Russ. 55°21' N, 43°55' E 154
Aržano, Croatia 43°35' N, 16°58' E 168
Arzew, Alg. 35°50' N, 0°19' E 150
Arzgir, Russ. 45°21' N, 44°10' E 158
Arzni, Arm. 40°19' N, 44°36' E 195
As Ela, Djibouti 10°59' N, 42°12' E 224
As Sabkhah, Syr. 35°46' N, 39°19' E 180
Aş Şāfī, Jordan 31°1' N, 35°27' E 194
As Salmān, Iraq 30°30' N, 44°32' E 180
As Salţ, Jordan 32°2' N, 35°43' E 194
As Salwá, Saudi Arabia 24°41' N, 50°48' E 196
As Samāwah (Samawah), Iraq 31°15' N, 45°15' E 180
As Sanām, Saudi Arabia 23°34' N, 51°7' E 196
Aş Şanamayn, Syr. 33°4' N, 36°11' E 194
Aş Şaqlabīyah, Syr. 35°21' N, 36°22' E 194
Aş Şarafand, Leb. 33°27' N, 35°17' E 194
As Sarfaia, spring, Lib. 23°38' N, 17°11' E 216
Aş Şawrah, Saudi Arabia 27°52' N, 35°22' E 180
As Sīb, Oman 23°41' N, 58°11' E 196
As Sidr, Lib. 30°39' N, 18°18' E 216
As Sidr, Saudi Arabia 23°24' N, 39°44' E 182
As Sikr, spring, Iraq 30°44' N, 43°44' E 180
As Sirḩān, Wādī, Jordan 31°9' N, 36°42' E 180
Aş Şufuq, spring, U.A.E. 23°43' N, 51°48' E 196
As Sulaymānīyah, Iraq 35°33' N, 45°25' E 180
As Sulaymānīyah, Saudi Arabia 24°6' N, 47°16' E 196
As Sulaymī, Saudi Arabia 26°15' N, 41°23' E 182
As Sulayyil, Saudi Arabia 20°27' N, 45°34' E 182
As Sulţān, Lib. 31°6' N, 17°7' E 216
Aş Şurrah, Yemen 13°56' N, 46°11' E 182
As Suwāqah, Jordan 31°21' N, 36°6' E 194
Aş Şuwār, Syr. 35°31' N, 40°38' E 180
As Suwaydā', Syr. 32°42' N, 36°34' E 194
As Suwayḩ, Oman 22°6' N, 59°41' E 182
Asa, river, Dem. Rep. of the Congo 4°55' N, 25°15' E 224
Asab, Namibia 25°27' S, 17°54' E 227
Asab, oil field, U.A.E. 23°12' N, 54°8' E 182
Asadābād, Gardaneh-ye, pass, Iran 34°48' N, 48°10' E 180
Asahi, river, Japan 35°0' N, 133°47' E 201
Asahikawa, Japan 43°50' N, 142°36' E 190
Āsalē, Eth. 14°12' N, 40°18' E 182
Asansol, India 23°40' N, 86°59' E 197
Åsarna, Nor. 62°39' N, 14°20' E 152
Āsayita, Eth. 11°31' N, 41°25' E 182
Asbest, Russ. 57°2' N, 61°28' E 154
Asbestos, Can. 45°45' N, 71°57' W 94
Ascención, Bol. 15°43' S, 63°8' W 132
Ascensión, Mex. 24°18' N, 99°55' W 114
Ascensión, Mex. 31°5' N, 107°60' W 92
Ascensión, Bahía de la 19°30' N, 88°2' W 115
Ascension Fracture Zone, South Atlantic Ocean 6°36' S, 11°59' W 253
Aschaffenburg, Ger. 49°58' N, 9°9' E 167
Ascheberg, Ger. 51°48' N, 7°36' E 167
Aschendorf, Ger. 53°3' N, 7°19' E 163
Ascira, Somalia 10°19' N, 50°56' E 216
Ascó, Sp. 41°10' N, 0°33' E 164
Ascot, U.K. 51°24' N, 0°40' E 162
Ascotán, Chile 21°45' S, 68°19' W 137
Ascutney, Vt., U.S. 43°24' N, 72°25' W 104
Åseda, Nor. 57°10' N, 15°20' E 152
Asedjrad, Alg. 24°55' N, 1°0' E 214
Āsela, Eth. 7°51' N, 39°2' E 224
Åsele, Nor. 64°9' N, 17°19' E 152
Åseral, Nor. 58°36' N, 7°25' E 152
Asfeld, Fr. 49°27' N, 4°7' E 163
Aşfūn el Maţā'na, Egypt 25°25' N, 32°28' E 226
Aşgabat (Ashgabat), Turkm. 37°54' N, 58°14' E 180
Ash Fork, Ariz., U.S. 35°11' N, 112°29' W 82
Ash Grove, Mo., U.S. 37°18' N, 93°34' W 94
Ash Mountain, Can. 59°16' N, 130°38' W 108
Ash, river, Can. 50°27' N, 84°56' W 94
Ash Shabakah, Iraq 30°48' N, 43°36' E 180
Ash Sha'rā', Saudi Arabia 24°15' N, 44°11' E 182
Ash Sharawrah, Saudi Arabia 17°54' N, 47°26' E 182
Ash Sharqāţ, Iraq 35°26' N, 43°15' E 180
Ash Shaţrah, Iraq 31°25' N, 46°6' E 180
Ash Shawbak, Jordan 30°31' N, 35°33' E 194
Ash Shaykh Badr, Syr. 34°59' N, 36°4' E 194
Ash Shiḩr, Yemen 14°45' N, 49°33' E 182
Ash Shināfīyah, Iraq 31°37' N, 44°39' E 180
Ash Shişar, Oman 18°15' N, 53°39' E 182
Ash Shumlūl, Saudi Arabia 26°29' N, 47°22' E 196
Ash Shuqayq, Saudi Arabia 17°42' N, 42°4' E 182
Ash Shurayf, Saudi Arabia 25°42' N, 39°12' E 182
Ash Shuwayfāt, Leb. 33°48' N, 35°30' E 194
Ash Shuwayrif, Lib. 29°58' N, 14°12' E 216
Asha, Russ. 55°3' N, 57°18' E 154
Ashbourne, U.K. 53°0' N, 1°45' W 162
Ashburn, Ga., U.S. 31°42' N, 83°39' W 96
Ashburnham, Mass., U.S. 42°37' N, 71°55' W 104
Ashburton, N.Z. 43°55' S, 171°47' E 240
Ashby, Mass., U.S. 42°40' N, 71°50' W 104
Ashby de la Zouch, U.K. 52°44' N, 1°29' W 162
Ashchy Köl, lake, Kaz. 45°11' N, 67°38' E 184
Ashcroft, Can. 50°43' N, 121°15' W 90
Ashdod, Israel 31°47' N, 34°39' E 194
Ashdown, Ark., U.S. 33°40' N, 94°8' W 96
Ashdown Forest, region, Europe 50°57' N, 0°12' E 162
Ashern, Can. 51°11' N, 98°21' W 90
Asherton, Tex., U.S. 28°26' N, 99°45' W 92
Ashfield, Mass., U.S. 42°31' N, 72°48' W 104
Ashford, U.K. 51°9' N, 0°52' E 162
Ashford, Wash., U.S. 46°44' N, 122°2' W 100
Ashgabat see Aşgabat, Turkm. 37°54' N, 58°14' E 180
Ashikaga, Japan 36°20' N, 139°27' E 201
Ashikita, Japan 32°18' N, 130°30' E 201
Ashizuri Misaki, Japan 32°36' N, 133°0' E 201
Ashkadar, river, Russ. 53°2' N, 55°16' E 154
Ashkelon, ruin(s), Israel 31°39' N, 34°30' E 194
Ashkum, Ill., U.S. 40°51' N, 87°57' W 102
Ashland, Kans., U.S. 37°11' N, 99°47' W 92
Ashland, Ky., U.S. 38°27' N, 82°39' W 102
Ashland, La., U.S. 32°7' N, 93°6' W 103
Ashland, Me., U.S. 46°37' N, 68°25' W 94
Ashland, Mont., U.S. 45°34' N, 106°16' W 90
Ashland, Nebr., U.S. 41°1' N, 96°21' W 94
Ashland, N.H., U.S. 43°41' N, 71°38' W 104
Ashland, Ohio, U.S. 40°52' N, 82°18' W 102
Ashland, Pa., U.S. 40°46' N, 76°22' W 110
Ashland, Va., U.S. 37°45' N, 77°29' W 94
Ashland, Wis., U.S. 46°35' N, 90°53' W 94
Ashland, Mount, Oreg., U.S. 42°5' N, 122°48' W 90
Ashley, Ind., U.S. 41°30' N, 85°5' W 102
Ashley, N. Dak., U.S. 46°0' N, 99°24' W 94
Ashley, Ohio, U.S. 40°23' N, 82°57' W 102
Ashmont, Can. 54°7' N, 111°35' W 108
Ashmore Islands, Indian Ocean 12°34' S, 122°16' E 231
Ashmyany, Belarus 54°26' N, 25°55' E 166
Ashoknagar, India 24°32' N, 77°44' E 197
Ashqelon, Israel 31°40' N, 34°34' E 194
Ashtabula, Ohio, U.S. 41°51' N, 80°48' W 102
Ashtabula, Lake, N. Dak., U.S. 47°10' N, 98°38' W 90
Ashton, Idaho, U.S. 44°4' N, 111°27' W 90
Ashton, Ill., U.S. 41°51' N, 89°14' W 102
Ashton, Mich., U.S. 43°58' N, 85°30' W 102
Ashton, R.I., U.S. 41°56' N, 71°26' W 104
Ashton under Lyne, U.K. 53°29' N, 2°6' W 162
Ashuanipi, Can. 52°45' N, 66°6' W 111
Ashuanipi Lake, Can. 52°31' N, 66°34' W 111
Ashuapmushuan, Lac, lake, Can. 49°10' N, 74°40' W 94
Ashville, Can. 51°10' N, 100°18' W 90
Ashville, Ohio, U.S. 39°43' N, 82°57' W 102
Ashyrymy, Bichänäk, Arm. 39°33' N, 45°7' E 195
'Āşī (Orontes), river, Syr. 35°40' N, 36°21' E 194
Asia 3°0' N, 103°0' E 173
Asia, Kepulauan, islands, North Pacific Ocean 1°12' N, 129°17' E 192
Asia Minor see Anatolia, region, Asia 38°39' N, 30°18' E 180
Asiago, It. 45°52' N, 11°30' E 167
Asika, India 19°38' N, 84°38' E 188
Asikkala, Fin. 61°11' N, 25°28' E 166
Asilah, Mor. 35°28' N, 6°2' W 150
Asillo, Peru 14°50' S, 70°21' W 137
Asinara, Isola, island, It. 41°4' N, 7°5' E 214
Asino, Russ. 56°59' N, 86°9' E 169
Asipovichy, Belarus 53°17' N, 28°45' E 152
Asis, Ras, Sudan 18°17' N, 37°36' E 182
Ask, Nor. 60°28' N, 5°10' E 152
Aşkale, Turk. 39°56' N, 40°41' E 195
Askaniya Nova, Ukr. 46°27' N, 33°53' E 156
Asker, Nor. 59°50' N, 10°26' E 152
Askham, S. Af. 27°2' S, 20°51' E 227
Askī Mawşil, Iraq 36°31' N, 42°37' E 195
Åskilje, Nor. 64°53' N, 17°51' E 152
Askino, Russ. 56°6' N, 56°35' E 154
Askiz, Russ. 53°10' N, 90°33' E 184
Askole, Pak. 35°40' N, 75°50' E 188
Askrigg, U.K. 54°18' N, 2°5' W 162
Askvoll, Nor. 61°21' N, 5°4' E 152
Asler, spring, Mali 18°53' N, 0°9' E 222
Asmar, Afghan. 35°2' N, 71°27' E 186
Asmara, Eritrea 15°16' N, 38°48' E 182
Åsnes, Nor. 60°36' N, 11°57' E 152
Asni, Mor. 31°14' N, 8°1' W 214
Aso, peak, Japan 32°51' N, 131°3' E 201
Asola, It. 45°13' N, 10°25' E 167
Asopus, ruin(s), Gr. 36°41' N, 22°45' E 156
Āsosa, Eth. 10°2' N, 34°29' E 224
Asoteriba, Sudan 19°31' N, 37°5' E 182
Asoteriba, Jebel, peak, Sudan 21°49' N, 36°24' E 182
Aspang, Aust. 47°33' N, 16°3' E 168
Aspatria, U.K. 54°46' N, 3°20' W 162
Aspeå, Nor. 63°22' N, 17°36' E 152
Aspen, Colo., U.S. 39°11' N, 106°50' W 92
Aspen Butte, peak, Oreg., U.S. 42°18' N, 122°11' W 90
Aspen Range, Idaho, U.S. 42°42' N, 111°34' W 90
Aspermont, Tex., U.S. 33°6' N, 100°14' W 92
Aspiring, Mount, N.Z. 44°25' S, 168°39' E 240
Asprókavos, Ákra, Gr. 39°21' N, 19°35' E 156
Aspromonte, It. 38°1' N, 15°50' E 156
Aspy Bay 46°53' N, 60°50' W 111
Asquith, Can. 52°8' N, 107°13' W 90
Assa, Mor. 28°37' N, 9°24' W 214
Assab, Eritrea 12°59' N, 42°41' E 182
'Assâba, Mauritania 16°36' N, 12°26' W 222
Aşşafā, Syr. 33°13' N, 36°48' E 194
Assaikio, Nig. 8°34' N, 8°53' E 222
Assala, Congo 2°18' S, 14°28' E 218
Assam, adm. division, India 26°28' N, 90°56' E 188
Assaouas, spring, Niger 16°53' N, 7°24' E 222
Assateague Island National Seashore, Va., U.S. 38°4' N, 75°9' W 94
Assean Lake, lake, Can. 56°7' N, 97°7' W 108
Assebroek, Belg. 51°10' N, 3°16' E 163
Assen, Neth. 52°59' N, 6°33' E 163
Assiniboia, Can. 49°37' N, 105°60' W 90
Assiniboine, Mount, Can. 50°51' N, 115°44' W 90
Assiniboine, river, Can. 49°21' N, 99°32' W 80
Assinica, Lac, lake, Can. 50°30' N, 75°45' W 110
Assiou (Azéo), spring, Alg. 21°6' N, 7°35' E 222
Assis, Braz. 22°40' S, 50°28' W 138
Asslar, Ger. 50°35' N, 8°26' E 167
Assodé, Niger 18°29' N, 8°35' E 222
Assok-Ngoum, Gabon 1°45' N, 11°35' E 218
Assos, ruin(s), Turk. 39°29' N, 26°15' E 156
Assoul, Mor. 32°2' N, 5°17' W 214
Assumption, Ill., U.S. 39°30' N, 89°2' W 102
Assumption Island, Seychelles 9°51' S, 46°7' E 218
Astana, Kaz. 51°7' N, 71°14' E 184
Astara, Azerb. 38°28' N, 48°50' E 195
Āstārā, Iran 38°25' N, 48°48' E 195
Asten, Neth. 51°24' N, 5°44' E 167
Asti, It. 44°54' N, 8°12' E 167
Astillero, Peru 13°24' S, 69°38' W 137
Astillero, Cerro del, peak, Mex. 20°16' N, 99°39' W 114
Asto, Mont, peak, Fr. 42°34' N, 9°8' E 156
Astola Island, Pak. 24°57' N, 63°54' E 182
Astorga, Sp. 42°26' N, 6°4' W 150
Astoria, Oreg., U.S. 46°10' N, 123°48' W 100
Astove Island, Seychelles 10°29' S, 47°53' E 220
Astrakhan', Russ. 46°19' N, 48°4' E 158
Astrakhan', adm. division, Russ. 47°9' N, 46°39' E 158
Åsträsk, Nor. 64°35' N, 19°57' E 152
Astravyets, Belarus 54°36' N, 25°57' E 166
Astryna, Belarus 53°44' N, 24°34' E 154
Asturias, adm. division, Sp. 43°24' N, 7°1' W 150
Asunción, Bol. 11°49' S, 67°52' W 137
Asunción, Parag. 25°19' S, 57°49' W 132
Asunción, Punta, Arg. 39°7' S, 60°30' W 139
Åsunden, lake, Nor. 57°53' N, 15°25' E 152
Asūne, Latv. 56°0' N, 27°37' E 166
Åsvær, island, Nor. 66°16' N, 11°14' E 152
Asvyeya, Belarus 56°1' N, 28°5' E 166
Asvyeyskaye, Vozyera, lake, Belarus 56°1' N, 27°32' E 166
Aswân, Egypt 24°4' N, 32°54' E 182
Asyûţ, Egypt 27°8' N, 31°5' E 180
Aszód, Hung. 47°39' N, 19°28' E 168
Aţ Ţafīlah, Jordan 30°50' N, 35°36' E 194
Aţ Ţā'if, Saudi Arabia 21°15' N, 40°24' E 182
At Tāj, Lib. 24°17' N, 23°15' E 216
At Tall, Syr. 33°35' N, 36°18' E 194
Aţ Ţayyibah, Jordan 31°3' N, 35°36' E 194
At Turbah, Yemen 12°45' N, 43°29' E 182
Aţ Ţuwayyah, spring, Saudi Arabia 27°41' N, 40°50' E 180
Ataa, Den. 69°46' N, 51°1' W 106
Atacama, adm. division, Chile 27°6' S, 70°45' W 132
Atacama, Desierto de, Chile 25°53' S, 70°11' W 132
Atacuari, river, Peru 3°25' S, 71°16' W 136
Atafu, island, N.Z. 8°29' S, 172°40' W 252
Atakora, Chaîne de l', Benin 10°7' N, 1°12' E 222
Atakpamé, Togo 7°33' N, 1°8' E 222
Atalaia do Norte, Braz. 4°19' S, 70°7' W 130
Atalaya, Peru 10°44' S, 73°48' W 137
Ataléia, Braz. 18°4' S, 41°7' W 138
Atami, Japan 35°4' N, 139°3' E 201
Atammik, Den. 64°51' N, 52°9' W 106
Atamyrat, Turkm. 37°52' N, 65°11' E 160
Atamyrat (Kerki), Turkm. 37°49' N, 65°10' E 197
Atar, Mauritania 20°31' N, 13°3' W 222
Atarfe, Sp. 37°13' N, 3°41' W 164
Atascadero, Calif., U.S. 35°29' N, 120°41' W 100
Atašiene, Latv. 56°32' N, 26°21' E 166
Atasta, ruin(s), Mex. 18°37' N, 92°14' W 115
Atasū, Kaz. 48°40' N, 71°39' E 184
Atauro, island, Indonesia 8°31' S, 125°42' E 192
Atáviros, peak, Gr. 36°11' N, 27°47' E 156
Atbara, Sudan 17°42' N, 34°3' E 182
Atbara, river, Sudan 14°10' N, 35°57' E 226
Atbasar, Kaz. 51°48' N, 68°22' E 184
At-Bashy, Kyrg. 41°7' N, 75°47' E 184
Atchafalaya Bay 29°27' N, 91°38' W 103
Atchison, Kans., U.S. 39°32' N, 95°8' W 94
Atea, Sp. 41°9' N, 1°33' W 164
Ateca, Sp. 41°19' N, 1°49' W 164
Ath, Belg. 50°37' N, 3°47' E 163
Ath Thumāmah, spring, Saudi Arabia 27°41' N, 45°0' E 180
Athabasca, Can. 54°41' N, 113°15' W 108
Athabasca, Lake, Can. 59°8' N, 109°58' W 108
Athabasca, Mount, Can. 52°10' N, 117°17' W 108
Athabasca, oil field, Can. 56°54' N, 111°38' W 108
Athabasca, river, Can. 53°26' N, 117°6' W 106
Athamánon, peak, Gr. 39°31' N, 21°7' E 156
Athenry, Ire. 53°17' N, 8°46' W 150
Athens, Ala., U.S. 34°48' N, 86°58' W 96
Athens, Ga., U.S. 33°57' N, 83°24' W 96
Athens, Ill., U.S. 39°57' N, 89°44' W 102
Athens, La., U.S. 32°38' N, 93°2' W 103
Athens, N.Y., U.S. 42°15' N, 73°50' W 104
Athens, Ohio, U.S. 39°19' N, 82°6' W 102
Athens, Pa., U.S. 41°57' N, 76°32' W 110
Athens, Tenn., U.S. 35°26' N, 84°36' W 96
Athens, Tex., U.S. 32°11' N, 95°51' W 96
Athens see Athína, Gr. 37°58' N, 23°36' E 156
Atherley, Can. 44°35' N, 79°21' W 110
Athi River, Kenya 1°28' S, 36°59' E 224
Athi, river, Kenya 2°31' S, 38°21' E 224
Athienou, Northern Cyprus 35°4' N, 33°32' E 194
Athína (Athens), Gr. 37°58' N, 23°36' E 156
Athlone, Ire. 53°25' N, 7°58' W 150
Athna, Cyprus 35°2' N, 33°47' E 156
Athol, Mass., U.S. 42°35' N, 72°14' W 104
Athol, N.Z. 45°30' S, 168°35' E 240
Atholl, Kap, Den. 76°6' N, 73°24' W 106
Atholville, Can. 47°58' N, 66°44' W 94
Áthos, Mount see Ágio Óros, peak, Gr. 40°8' N, 24°15' E 156
Athos, Mount see Ágio Óros, region, Gr. 40°14' N, 23°2' E 156
Athos Range, Antarctica 70°15' S, 61°18' E 248
Ati, Chad 13°15' N, 18°22' E 216
Ati Ardébé, Chad 12°45' N, 17°41' E 216
Atiak, Uganda 3°14' N, 32°7' E 224
Atiamuri, N.Z. 38°26' S, 176°1' E 240
Atico, Peru 16°12' S, 73°38' W 137
Atienza, Sp. 41°11' N, 2°52' W 164
Atik Lake, Can. 55°16' N, 96°19' W 108
Atikameg, Can. 55°54' N, 115°41' W 108
Atikameg Lake, Can. 53°57' N, 100°58' W 108
Atikameg, river, Can. 51°45' N, 83°34' W 110
Atiki, adm. division, Gr. 37°26' N, 23°14' E 156
Atikokan, Can. 48°44' N, 91°37' W 94
Atikonak Lake, Can. 52°30' N, 65°11' W 111
Atikwa Lake, lake, Can. 49°27' N, 93°56' W 90
Atiquipa, Peru 15°50' S, 74°22' W 137
Atka, Alas., U.S. 52°10' N, 174°12' W 160
Atka, Russ. 60°51' N, 151°50' E 160
Atka, island, Alas., U.S. 51°38' N, 175°35' W 160
Atkarsk, Russ. 51°53' N, 45°2' E 158
Atkinson, Nebr., U.S. 42°30' N, 98°59' W 90
Atkinson, N.H., U.S. 42°50' N, 71°10' W 104
Atkinson Lake, Can. 55°57' N, 95°34' W 108
Atkinson Point, Can. 69°54' N, 134°2' W 98
Atlacomulco, Mex. 19°47' N, 99°55' W 114
Atlanta, Ga., U.S. 33°44' N, 84°29' W 96
Atlanta, Ill., U.S. 40°15' N, 89°14' W 102
Atlanta, Mich., U.S. 45°0' N, 84°9' W 94
Atlanta, Tex., U.S. 33°6' N, 94°10' W 103
Atlantic, Iowa, U.S. 41°22' N, 95°1' W 94
Atlantic Beach, Fla., U.S. 30°19' N, 81°25' W 96
Atlantic Beach, N.C., U.S. 34°42' N, 76°46' W 96
Atlantic Ocean 38°49' N, 72°7' W 253
Atlantic-Indian Ridge, Indian Ocean 53°30' S, 21°10' E 255
Atlántico, adm. division, Col. 10°25' N, 75°5' W 136
Atlántida, Uru. 34°46' S, 55°43' W 139
Atlantis Fracture Zone, North Atlantic Ocean 29°7' N, 40°8' W 253
Atlantis II Fracture Zone, Indian Ocean 34°58' S, 57°3' E 254
Atlas Mountains, Africa 35°53' N, 0°28' E 164
Atlas Saharien, mountains, Alg. 35°5' N, 3°42' E 150
Atlin, Can. 59°35' N, 133°44' W 108
'Atlit, Israel 32°41' N, 34°56' E 194
Atlixco, Mex. 18°51' N, 98°27' W 114
Atmakur, India 14°39' N, 79°38' E 188
Atmakur, India 18°44' N, 78°35' E 188
Atmautluak, Alas., U.S. 60°49' N, 162°33' W 98
Atmore, Ala., U.S. 31°0' N, 87°30' W 103

Atna Peak, Can. 53°55′ N, 128°10′ W 108
Atocha, Bol. 20°60′ S, 66°20′ W 137
Atoka, N. Mex., U.S. 32°46′ N, 104°24′ W 92
Atoka, Okla., U.S. 34°21′ N, 96°7′ W 96
Atokila, spring, Mali 22°46′ N, 5°56′ W 214
Atome, Angola 11°54′ S, 14°37′ E 220
Atotonilco, Mex. 24°14′ N, 102°50′ W 114
Atotonilco el Alto, Mex. 20°32′ N, 102°32′ W 114
Atoyac, Mex. 20°0′ N, 103°33′ W 114
Atoyac, river, Mex. 17°58′ N, 98°42′ W 114
Atqasuk, Alas., U.S. 70°28′ N, 157°34′ W 98
Atrak, river, Iran 37°20′ N, 57°36′ E 180
Atrato, river, Col. 7°29′ N, 77°11′ W 136
Atsumi, Japan 38°38′ N, 139°37′ E 201
Atsumi, Japan 34°37′ N, 137°7′ E 201
Attachie, Can. 56°12′ N, 121°28′ W 108
Attalla, Ala., U.S. 34°0′ N, 86°6′ W 96
Attapu, Laos 14°48′ N, 106°46′ E 202
Attawapiskat, Can. 52°58′ N, 82°31′ W 106
Attawapiskat, river, Can. 52°3′ N, 87°31′ W 110
Attendorn, Ger. 51°7′ N, 7°54′ E 167
Attica, Ind., U.S. 40°16′ N, 87°15′ W 102
Attica, Kans., U.S. 37°13′ N, 98°14′ W 92
Attica, Ohio, U.S. 41°3′ N, 82°54′ W 102
Attigny, Fr. 49°27′ N, 4°34′ E 163
Attigu, Sudan 4°1′ N, 31°43′ E 224
Attingal, India 8°40′ N, 76°48′ E 188
Attleboro, Mass., U.S. 41°56′ N, 71°17′ W 104
Attleborough, U.K. 52°30′ N, 1°1′ E 162
Attoyac, river, Tex., U.S. 31°37′ N, 94°21′ W 103
Attu, Den. 67°55′ N, 53°39′ W 106
Attu, island, Alas., U.S. 52°47′ N, 171°26′ E 160
Attur, India 11°35′ N, 78°36′ E 188
Attwood Lake, Can. 51°11′ N, 89°9′ W 110
Atuel, river, Arg. 35°38′ S, 67°47′ W 134
Atura, Uganda 2°7′ N, 32°23′ E 224
Atwater, Calif., U.S. 37°21′ N, 120°37′ W 100
Atwood, Kans., U.S. 39°47′ N, 101°4′ W 90
Atwood see Crooked Island, Bahamas 22°39′ N, 76°43′ W 81
Atyashevo, Russ. 54°37′ N, 46°10′ E 154
Atyraū, Kaz. 47°6′ N, 51°53′ E 158
Atyrau, adm. division, Kaz. 47°28′ N, 50°45′ E 158
Atzinging Lake, lake, Can. 60°9′ N, 103°50′ W 108
Au Fer, Point, La., U.S. 29°11′ N, 91°28′ W 103
Au Gres, Mich., U.S. 44°3′ N, 83°42′ W 102
Au Gres, Point, Mich., U.S. 43°51′ N, 83°51′ W 102
Au Sable, Mich., U.S. 44°25′ N, 83°21′ W 94
Au Sable Forks, N.Y., U.S. 44°25′ N, 73°41′ W 104
Au Sable Point, Mich., U.S. 46°21′ N, 86°10′ W 110
Au Sable Point, Mich., U.S. 44°19′ N, 83°40′ W 110
Au Sable, river, Mich., U.S. 44°41′ N, 84°44′ W 80
Auas Mountains, Namibia 22°40′ S, 17°6′ E 227
Aubarede Point, Philippines 17°17′ N, 122°28′ E 203
Aúbe, Mozambique 16°22′ S, 39°46′ E 224
Aube, river, Fr. 48°18′ N, 4°35′ E 163
Aubenton, Fr. 49°49′ N, 4°12′ E 163
Auberry, Calif., U.S. 37°4′ N, 119°30′ W 100
Aubin, Fr. 44°31′ N, 2°13′ E 150
Aubrac, Monts d', Fr. 44°47′ N, 2°47′ E 165
Aubrey Cliffs, Ariz., U.S. 35°51′ N, 113°14′ W 92
Aubrey Falls, Can. 46°54′ N, 83°14′ W 94
Aubry Lake, Can. 67°31′ N, 127°14′ W 98
Auburn, Ala., U.S. 32°36′ N, 85°29′ W 96
Auburn, Calif., U.S. 38°53′ N, 121°6′ W 90
Auburn, Ill., U.S. 39°34′ N, 89°44′ W 102
Auburn, Ind., U.S. 41°21′ N, 85°4′ W 102
Auburn, Me., U.S. 44°5′ N, 70°15′ W 104
Auburn, Mich., U.S. 43°36′ N, 84°5′ W 102
Auburn, Miss., U.S. 31°20′ N, 90°37′ W 103
Auburn, Mo., U.S. 39°34′ N, 89°44′ W 94
Auburn, Nebr., U.S. 40°22′ N, 95°51′ W 90
Auburn, N.H., U.S. 43°0′ N, 71°21′ W 104
Auburn, N.Y., U.S. 42°55′ N, 76°34′ W 94
Auburn, Wash., U.S. 47°17′ N, 122°15′ W 100
Auburn Range, Austral. 25°28′ S, 150°9′ E 230
Auburndale, Fla., U.S. 28°4′ N, 81°48′ W 105
Aucanquilcha, peak, Chile 21°15′ S, 68°34′ W 137
Aucará, Peru 14°18′ S, 74°5′ W 137
Auce, Latv. 56°28′ N, 22°52′ E 166
Auch, Fr. 43°38′ N, 0°34′ E 150
Auchi, Nig. 7°6′ N, 6°13′ E 222
Auckland, N.Z. 36°53′ S, 174°48′ E 240
Aude, river, Fr. 42°54′ N, 2°12′ E 165
Auden, Can. 50°14′ N, 87°52′ W 94
Auderville, Fr. 49°42′ N, 1°57′ W 150
Audoin, Lac, lake, Can. 46°46′ N, 79°8′ W 94
Audubon, Iowa, U.S. 41°41′ N, 94°55′ W 94
Audun-le-Roman, Fr. 49°22′ N, 5°51′ E 163
Aūezov, Kaz. 49°42′ N, 81°30′ E 184
Auffay, Fr. 49°43′ N, 1°6′ E 163
Aughty Mountains, Slieve, Ire. 52°54′ N, 9°21′ W 150
Augrabies Falls National Park, S. Af. 28°38′ S, 20°6′ E 227
Augsburg, Ger. 48°22′ N, 10°53′ E 152
Augusta, Austral. 34°16′ S, 115°10′ E 231
Augusta, Ga., U.S. 33°28′ N, 81°58′ W 96
Augusta, Kans., U.S. 37°39′ N, 96°59′ W 92
Augusta, Ky., U.S. 38°45′ N, 84°1′ W 102
Augusta, Me., U.S. 44°18′ N, 69°49′ W 104
Augusta, Mont., U.S. 47°28′ N, 112°24′ W 90
Augusta, Tex., U.S. 31°30′ N, 95°19′ W 103
Augusta, Wis., U.S. 44°40′ N, 91°7′ W 94
Augusta, Mount, Can. 60°16′ N, 140°39′ W 98
Augusta Victoria, Chile 24°7′ S, 69°25′ W 132
Augusto Lima, Braz. 18°7′ S, 44°18′ W 138
Augustów, Pol. 53°51′ N, 22°58′ E 166
Augustus Island, Austral. 15°21′ S, 122°46′ E 230
Augustus, Mount, Austral. 24°23′ S, 116°37′ E 230
Auk, oil field, North Sea 56°23′ N, 1°57′ E 150
Auke Bay, Alas., U.S. 58°24′ N, 134°41′ W 108
Aukra, Nor. 62°46′ N, 6°54′ E 152
Aukštaitija National Park, Lith. 55°22′ N, 25°37′ E 166
Aul, India 20°40′ N, 86°39′ E 188
Āūlīeköl, Kaz. 52°22′ N, 64°5′ E 184
Aulis, ruin(s), Gr. 38°24′ N, 23°30′ E 156
Aulla, It. 44°12′ N, 9°59′ E 167
Aulneau Peninsula, Can. 49°22′ N, 94°42′ W 90
Ault, Fr. 50°5′ N, 1°27′ E 163
Aultbea, U.K. 57°50′ N, 5°35′ W 150
Aulus-les-Bains, Fr. 42°46′ N, 1°20′ E 164
Aumale, Fr. 49°45′ N, 1°45′ E 163
Auna, Nig. 10°10′ N, 4°42′ E 222
Auneau, Fr. 48°27′ N, 1°45′ E 163
Auneuil, Fr. 49°22′ N, 1°59′ E 163
Auno, Nig. 11°51′ N, 12°55′ E 216
Aups, Fr. 43°37′ N, 6°12′ E 150
Aur, island, Malaysia 2°20′ N, 104°22′ E 196
Aura, Fin. 60°36′ N, 22°32′ E 166
Aura, river, Nor. 62°19′ N, 8°10′ E 152
Auraiya, India 26°26′ N, 79°29′ E 197
Aurdal, Nor. 60°54′ N, 9°25′ E 152
Aure, Nor. 63°15′ N, 8°34′ E 152
Aurich, Ger. 53°28′ N, 7°28′ E 163
Aurillac, Fr. 44°54′ N, 2°27′ E 150
Aurisina, It. 45°45′ N, 13°40′ E 167
Auritz (Burguete), Sp. 42°59′ N, 1°21′ W 164
Auronzo di Cadore, It. 46°32′ N, 12°26′ E 167
Aurora, Can. 43°59′ N, 79°28′ W 110
Aurora, Ill., U.S. 41°45′ N, 88°18′ W 102
Aurora, Ind., U.S. 39°2′ N, 84°56′ W 102
Aurora, Minn., U.S. 47°31′ N, 92°16′ W 94
Aurora, Mo., U.S. 41°45′ N, 88°18′ W 94
Aurora, Mo., U.S. 36°57′ N, 93°43′ W 96
Aurora, Nebr., U.S. 40°51′ N, 98°1′ W 90
Aurora, Ohio, U.S. 41°18′ N, 81°21′ W 102
Aurukun, Austral. 13°9′ S, 141°46′ E 238
Aus, Namibia 26°41′ S, 16°16′ E 227
Austevoll, Nor. 60°5′ N, 5°13′ E 152
Austin, Ind., U.S. 38°45′ N, 85°48′ W 102
Austin, Minn., U.S. 43°39′ N, 92°60′ W 94
Austin, Nev., U.S. 39°30′ N, 117°5′ W 90
Austin, Pa., U.S. 41°37′ N, 78°5′ W 94
Austin, Tex., U.S. 30°14′ N, 97°50′ W 92
Austral Islands (Tubuai Islands), South Pacific Ocean 21°30′ S, 152°33′ W 238
Australia 24°25′ S, 128°31′ E 231
Australia 22°0′ S, 133°0′ E 231
Australian, Can. 52°43′ N, 122°26′ W 108
Australian Alps, Austral. 37°20′ S, 145°56′ E 230
Australian Capital Territory, adm. division, Austral. 35°42′ S, 148°21′ E 231
Austråt, Nor. 63°41′ N, 9°45′ E 152
Austria 48°27′ N, 14°52′ E 152
Autazes, Braz. 3°38′ S, 59°8′ W 130
Auterive, Fr. 43°19′ N, 1°27′ E 164
Authon-du-Perche, Fr. 48°11′ N, 0°53′ E 163
Autlán, Mex. 19°46′ N, 104°22′ W 114
Auve, Fr. 49°2′ N, 4°41′ E 163
Auvergne, adm. division, Fr. 45°9′ N, 2°15′ E 150
Auvergne, region, Europe 44°55′ N, 2°13′ E 165
Auvillar, Fr. 44°3′ N, 0°53′ E 150
Aux Sources, Mont, peak, Lesotho 28°56′ S, 28°42′ E 227
Auxerre, Fr. 47°47′ N, 3°33′ E 150
Auxonne, Fr. 47°11′ N, 5°23′ E 156
Auyán Tepuí, peak, Venez. 5°48′ N, 62°42′ W 130
Auyuittuq National Park, Can. 67°30′ N, 66°0′ W 106
Ava, Mo., U.S. 36°57′ N, 92°39′ W 96
Avakubi, Dem. Rep. of the Congo 1°21′ N, 27°39′ E 224
Avala, peak, Serb. and Mont. 44°42′ N, 20°29′ E 168
Avallon, Fr. 47°28′ N, 3°54′ E 150
Avalon, Calif., U.S. 33°19′ N, 118°20′ W 101
Avalon Peninsula, Can. 47°20′ N, 53°50′ W 111
Avaré, Braz. 23°6′ S, 48°57′ W 138
Avarua, New Zealand 21°0′ S, 160°0′ W 241
Avawatz Mountains, Calif., U.S. 35°36′ N, 116°30′ W 101
Avawatz Pass, Calif., U.S. 35°31′ N, 116°27′ W 101
Avay, Kaz. 49°34′ N, 72°52′ E 184
Avebury, site, U.K. 51°26′ N, 1°53′ W 162
Aveiro, Braz. 3°37′ S, 55°23′ W 130
Aveiro, Port. 40°37′ N, 8°42′ W 214
Aveiro, Port. 40°38′ N, 8°40′ W 150
Aveiro, adm. division, Port. 40°37′ N, 8°58′ W 150
Avellaneda, Arg. 34°42′ S, 58°20′ W 139
Avenal, Calif., U.S. 36°0′ N, 120°9′ W 100
Averías, Arg. 28°45′ S, 62°28′ W 139
Aversa, It. 40°59′ N, 14°12′ E 156
Avery, Calif., U.S. 38°12′ N, 120°23′ W 100
Avery Island, La., U.S. 29°52′ N, 91°56′ W 103
Aves, Islas de, islands, Caribbean Sea 12°7′ N, 67°29′ W 116
Aves Ridge, Caribbean Sea 15°1′ N, 63°37′ W 253
Avesnes, Fr. 50°7′ N, 3°55′ E 163
Avesta, Nor. 60°7′ N, 16°7′ E 152
Aveyron, river, Fr. 44°22′ N, 2°7′ E 165
Avia Terai, Arg. 26°41′ S, 60°46′ W 139
Aviano, It. 46°4′ N, 12°34′ E 167
Avignon, Fr. 43°57′ N, 4°50′ E 214
Ávila, Sp. 40°39′ N, 4°42′ W 150
Avila Beach, Calif., U.S. 35°11′ N, 120°44′ W 100
Ávila, Sierra de, Sp. 40°30′ N, 5°33′ W 150
Avilla, Ind., U.S. 41°21′ N, 85°15′ W 102
Avinger, Tex., U.S. 32°53′ N, 94°35′ W 103
Avinurme, Est. 58°58′ N, 26°53′ E 166
Avize, Fr. 48°57′ N, 4°0′ E 163
Avoca, Ind., U.S. 38°54′ N, 86°34′ W 102
Avoca, Iowa, U.S. 41°26′ N, 95°21′ W 90
Avola, It. 36°54′ N, 15°7′ E 156
Avon, Mass., U.S. 42°7′ N, 71°3′ W 104
Avon, N.C., U.S. 35°21′ N, 75°31′ W 96
Avon Park, Fla., U.S. 27°36′ N, 81°30′ W 105
Avon, river, U.K. 51°27′ N, 2°43′ W 162
Avonlea, Can. 50°0′ N, 105°5′ W 90
Avonmouth, U.K. 51°30′ N, 2°42′ W 162
Avontuur, S. Af. 33°44′ S, 23°11′ E 227
Avraga, Mongolia 47°13′ N, 109°10′ E 198
Avre, river, Fr. 48°41′ N, 0°53′ E 163
Avsa, Gora, peak, Russ. 63°18′ N, 93°27′ E 169
Avtovac, Bosn. and Herzg. 43°8′ N, 18°33′ E 168
Awakino, N.Z. 38°42′ S, 174°39′ E 240
Awali, oil field, Bahrain 25°55′ N, 50°29′ E 196
Āwarē, Eth. 8°13′ N, 44°5′ E 218
Awarua Bay 44°22′ S, 167°39′ E 240
Āwasa, Eth. 6°57′ N, 38°26′ E 224
Āwash, Eth. 8°59′ N, 40°10′ E 224
Āwash National Park, Eth. 8°43′ N, 39°27′ E 224
Awash, river, Eth. 9°38′ N, 40°17′ E 224
Awaso, Ghana 6°13′ N, 2°16′ W 222
Awat, China 40°38′ N, 80°22′ E 184
Awbārī (Ubari), Lib. 26°37′ N, 12°45′ E 216
Awdheegle, Somalia 1°57′ N, 44°50′ E 218
Awe, Nig. 8°9′ N, 9°7′ E 222
Aweil, Sudan 8°46′ N, 27°22′ E 224
Awfist, Western Sahara 25°45′ N, 14°38′ W 214
Awgu, Nig. 6°4′ N, 7°26′ E 222
Awio, P.N.G. 6°13′ S, 150°6′ E 192
Awjilah, Lib. 29°9′ N, 21°14′ E 216
Awka, Nig. 6°12′ N, 7°3′ E 222
Awsard, Western Sahara 22°39′ N, 14°19′ W 214
Awwalī, river, Leb. 33°35′ N, 35°23′ E 194
Axat, Fr. 42°48′ N, 2°12′ E 164
Axbridge, U.K. 51°16′ N, 2°49′ W 162
Axel Heiberg Island, Can. 80°42′ N, 95°47′ W 246
Axim, Ghana 4°53′ N, 2°14′ W 222
Axinim, Braz. 4°2′ S, 59°25′ W 130
Axmarsbruk, Nor. 61°3′ N, 17°4′ E 152
Axminster, U.K. 50°46′ N, 2°59′ W 162
Axochiapan, Mex. 18°28′ N, 98°45′ W 114
Axos, ruin(s), Gr. 35°17′ N, 24°44′ E 156
Axtell, Nebr., U.S. 40°28′ N, 99°8′ W 90
Ay, Fr. 49°3′ N, 4°0′ E 163
Ay, Kaz. 47°29′ N, 80°35′ E 184
Aya Bentih, Eth. 8°0′ N, 46°36′ E 218
Ayabe, Japan 35°16′ N, 135°15′ E 201
Ayacucho, Arg. 37°9′ S, 58°32′ W 139
Ayacucho, Bol. 17°54′ S, 63°24′ W 137
Ayacucho, Col. 8°35′ N, 73°34′ W 136
Ayacucho, Peru 13°11′ S, 74°15′ W 137
Ayacucho, adm. division, Peru 14°1′ S, 74°38′ W 137
Ayad, oil field, Yemen 15°11′ N, 46°58′ E 182
Ayakkum Hu, lake, China 37°38′ N, 88°29′ E 188
Ayaköz, Kaz. 47°57′ N, 80°22′ E 184
Ayaköz, river, Kaz. 46°55′ N, 79°28′ E 184
Ayamonte, Sp. 37°12′ N, 7°24′ W 150
Ayan, Russ. 56°27′ N, 137°54′ E 160
Ayancık, Turk. 41°56′ N, 34°33′ E 156
Ayanganna Mountain, Guyana 5°16′ N, 60°5′ W 130
Ayangba, Nig. 7°29′ N, 7°8′ E 222
Ayanka, Russ. 63°46′ N, 166°45′ E 160
Ayapel, Col. 8°19′ N, 75°9′ W 136
Ayapel, Serranía de, Col. 7°14′ N, 75°53′ W 136
Ayaş, Turk. 40°1′ N, 32°20′ E 156
Ayaviri, Peru 14°54′ S, 70°34′ W 137
Aybak, Afghan. 36°13′ N, 68°5′ E 186
Aydar Kŏl, lake, Uzb. 40°52′ N, 66°59′ E 197
Ayde, Lac, lake, Can. 52°17′ N, 73°52′ W 111
Aydın, Turk. 37°51′ N, 27°48′ E 156
Aydıncık, Turk. 36°8′ N, 33°19′ E 156
Aydyrlinskiy, Russ. 52°3′ N, 59°50′ E 154
Aye, Nig. 6°40′ N, 4°43′ E 222
Āyelu Terara, peak, Eth. 10°3′ N, 40°37′ E 224
Ayer, Mass., U.S. 42°33′ N, 71°36′ W 104
Ayerbe, Sp. 42°16′ N, 0°41′ E 164
Ayers Rock see Uluru, peak, Austral. 25°23′ S, 130°52′ E 230
Ayersville, Ohio, U.S. 41°13′ N, 84°17′ W 102
Ayeyarwady (Irrawady), river, Myanmar 21°54′ N, 95°42′ W 202
Āykel, Eth. 12°30′ N, 37°3′ E 182
Aykhal, Russ. 65°55′ N, 111°24′ E 160
Aykino, Russ. 62°12′ N, 49°58′ E 154
Aylesbury, U.K. 51°48′ N, 0°49′ E 162
Ayllón, Sp. 41°24′ N, 3°22′ W 164
Aylmer, Can. 42°46′ N, 80°58′ W 102
Aylmer Lake, lake, Can. 63°39′ N, 108°52′ W 106
Aylmer, Mount, Can. 51°19′ N, 115°31′ W 90
Aylsham, U.K. 52°47′ N, 1°15′ E 162
'Ayn al Ghazāl, spring, Lib. 21°50′ N, 24°52′ E 226
'Ayn Dīwār, Syr. 37°16′ N, 42°9′ E 195
'Ayn Sīdī Muḥammad, spring, Lib. 29°5′ N, 20°12′ E 216
'Ayn Sifnī, Iraq 36°42′ N, 43°14′ E 195
'Ayn Wabrah, spring, Saudi Arabia 27°25′ N, 47°20′ E 196
'Ayn Zuwayyah, spring, Lib. 21°54′ N, 24°48′ E 226
Ayna, Peru 12°43′ S, 73°53′ W 137
Ayna, Sp. 38°32′ N, 2°4′ W 164
Ayni, Taj. 39°22′ N, 68°31′ E 197
'Aynūnah, Saudi Arabia 28°6′ N, 35°10′ E 180
Ayod, Sudan 8°3′ N, 31°22′ E 224
Ayon, Ostrov, island, Russ. 70°5′ N, 164°44′ E 160
Ayora, Sp. 39°3′ N, 1°4′ W 164
Ayorou, Niger 14°40′ N, 0°54′ E 222
Ayos, Cameroon 3°57′ N, 12°31′ E 218
'Ayoûn 'Abd el Mâlek, spring, Mauritania 24°55′ N, 7°28′ W 214
'Ayoûnel el 'Atroûs, Mauritania 16°40′ N, 9°35′ W 222
Aypolovo, Russ. 58°46′ N, 76°43′ E 169
Ayr, Austral. 19°33′ S, 147°24′ E 231
Ayr, U.K. 55°27′ N, 4°38′ W 150
'Ayrah, Syr. 32°36′ N, 36°32′ E 194
Ayrancı, Turk. 37°21′ N, 33°39′ E 156
Ayribaba, Gora, peak, Turkm. 37°46′ N, 66°28′ E 197
Āysha, Eth. 10°42′ N, 42°35′ E 224
Āyteke Bī, Kaz. 45°52′ N, 62°8′ E 184
Aytos, Bulg. 42°42′ N, 27°15′ E 156
Ayu, Kepulauan, islands, North Pacific Ocean 0°41′ N, 128°54′ E 192
Ayutla, Mex. 20°7′ N, 104°22′ W 114
Ayutthaya, Thai. 14°21′ N, 100°32′ E 202
Ayvaj, Taj. 36°59′ N, 68°0′ E 186
Ayvalık, Turk. 39°17′ N, 26°43′ E 180
Aywaille, Belg. 50°28′ N, 5°40′ E 167
Az Zabadānī, Syr. 33°43′ N, 36°6′ E 194
Az̧ Z̧āhirīyah, West Bank 31°24′ N, 34°57′ E 194
Az̧ Z̧ahrān (Dhahran), Saudi Arabia 26°15′ N, 50°1′ E 196
Az Zarqā', Jordan 32°3′ N, 36°5′ E 194
Az Zarqā', Jordan 32°3′ N, 36°7′ E 180
Az Zawr, Kuwait 28°43′ N, 48°23′ E 196
Az Zibār, Iraq 36°53′ N, 43°58′ E 195
Az Zilfī, Saudi Arabia 26°17′ N, 44°49′ E 182
Az Zubayr, Iraq 30°20′ N, 47°42′ E 180
Āzād Shahr, Iran 37°11′ N, 55°19′ E 180
Azamgarh, India 26°4′ N, 83°10′ E 197
Azángaro, Peru 14°56′ S, 70°14′ W 137
Azanja, Serb. and Mont. 44°25′ N, 20°53′ E 168
Azaouâd, region, Africa 17°57′ N, 3°35′ W 222
Azaouagh, region, Africa 16°29′ N, 3°46′ E 222
Azapa, Chile 18°35′ S, 70°14′ W 137
Azapol'ye, Russ. 65°17′ N, 45°11′ E 154
Azara, Nig. 8°20′ N, 9°12′ E 222
Āzārān, Iran 37°30′ N, 47°3′ E 195
Azare, Nig. 11°41′ N, 10°10′ E 222
A'zāz, Syr. 36°35′ N, 37°2′ E 156
Azdavay, Turk. 41°39′ N, 33°16′ E 156
Azefal, Mauritania 20°51′ N, 15°9′ W 222
Azeffoun, Alg. 36°53′ N, 4°25′ E 150
Azélik, Niger 17°34′ N, 6°45′ E 222
Azéo see Assiou, spring, Alg. 21°6′ N, 7°35′ E 222
Azerbaijan 40°19′ N, 46°58′ E 195
Azero, river, Bol. 19°42′ S, 64°7′ W 137
Azerraf, spring, Mali 19°28′ N, 2°29′ E 222
Azigui, spring, Mali 16°38′ N, 2°36′ E 222
Azigzane, spring, Mali 22°20′ N, 3°18′ W 222
Azilal, Mor. 31°58′ N, 6°33′ W 214
Azlat, spring, Mauritania 16°49′ N, 14°5′ W 222
Aznakayevo, Russ. 54°52′ N, 53°8′ E 154
Aznalcóllar, Sp. 37°30′ N, 6°16′ W 164
Azores (Açores), islands, Port. 39°29′ N, 27°35′ W 207
Azov, Russ. 47°4′ N, 39°25′ E 158
Azov, Sea of 45°58′ N, 35°0′ E 160
Azovy, Russ. 64°50′ N, 65°11′ E 169
Azraq ash Shīshān, Jordan 31°49′ N, 36°48′ E 194
Azrou, Mor. 33°30′ N, 5°14′ W 214
Azua, Dom. Rep. 18°28′ N, 70°43′ W 116
Azuaga, Sp. 38°15′ N, 5°42′ W 164
Azuara, Sp. 41°15′ N, 0°53′ E 164
Azucena, Arg. 37°33′ S, 59°21′ W 139
Azuer, river, Sp. 38°55′ N, 3°26′ W 164
Azuero, Península de, Pan. 7°36′ N, 80°51′ W 115
Azufre Norte, Paso del, pass, Arg. 31°16′ S, 70°34′ W 134
Azul, Arg. 36°46′ S, 59°50′ W 139
Azul, river, Mex. 17°9′ N, 99°9′ W 114
Azurduy, Bol. 19°60′ S, 64°28′ W 137
Azure Lake, lake, Can. 52°22′ N, 120°23′ W 108

B

Ba Dong, Vietnam 9°40′ N, 106°33′ E 202
Ba Ria, Vietnam 10°29′ N, 107°10′ E 202
Ba, river, Vietnam 13°25′ N, 108°29′ E 202
Baabda, Leb. 33°50′ N, 35°31′ E 194
Baalbeck, Leb. 34°0′ N, 36°12′ E 194
Baarle Hertog, Belg. 51°26′ N, 4°55′ E 167
Baarn, Neth. 52°12′ N, 5°16′ E 163
Ba'ashom, Sudan 13°25′ N, 31°22′ E 226
Bab, oil field, U.A.E. 23°52′ N, 53°43′ E 196
Bab Ozero, lake, Russ. 68°19′ N, 33°38′ E 152
Baba Burnu, Turk. 39°30′ N, 25°37′ E 156
Baba Dağ, peak, Turk. 36°29′ N, 29°6′ E 156
Baba, peak, Bulg. 42°45′ N, 23°54′ E 156
Babadag, Rom. 44°53′ N, 28°43′ E 156
Babadag, peak, Azerb. 41°0′ N, 48°15′ E 195
Babadaykhan, Turkm. 37°53′ N, 60°21′ E 180
Babaeski, Turk. 41°25′ N, 27°4′ E 156
Babak, Philippines 7°9′ N, 125°43′ E 203
Babana, Nig. 10°27′ N, 3°49′ E 222
Babanūsa, Sudan 11°15′ N, 27°46′ E 224
Babar, island, Indonesia 8°21′ S, 129°10′ E 192
Babati, Tanzania 4°12′ S, 35°44′ E 224
Babayevo, Russ. 59°23′ N, 35°59′ E 154
Babayurt, Russ. 43°34′ N, 46°44′ E 195
Babb, Mont., U.S. 48°51′ N, 113°28′ W 90
B'abdāt, Leb. 33°53′ N, 35°40′ E 194
Babel, Mont de, peak, Can. 51°25′ N, 68°49′ W 111
Babeldaob see Babelthuap, island, Palau 8°0′ N, 135°0′ E 242
Babelthuap (Babeldaob), island, Palau 8°0′ N, 135°0′ E 242
Baberu, India 25°34′ N, 80°44′ E 197
Babi, island, Indonesia 2°3′ N, 96°40′ E 196
Babia Góra, peak, Slovakia 49°33′ N, 19°28′ E 152
Babian, river, China 23°31′ N, 101°16′ E 202
Babilafuente, Sp. 40°58′ N, 5°27′ W 150
Babin Nos, peak, Bulg. 43°41′ N, 22°22′ E 168
Babine, Can. 55°19′ N, 126°36′ W 108
Babine, river, Can. 55°41′ N, 127°32′ W 108
Babino Polje, Croatia 42°43′ N, 17°31′ E 168
Bābol, Iran 36°35′ N, 52°43′ E 180
Babonã, river, Braz. 6°16′ S, 67°4′ W 130
Baboquivari Peak, Ariz., U.S. 31°45′ N, 111°39′ W 92
Babruysk, Belarus 53°5′ N, 29°17′ E 152
Babson Park, Fla., U.S. 27°50′ N, 81°31′ W 105
Babuna, Maced. 41°30′ N, 21°24′ E 168
Babusar Pass, Pak. 35°8′ N, 74°2′ E 186
Babushkina, Russ. 59°44′ N, 43°11′ E 154
Babušnica, Serb. and Mont. 43°4′ N, 22°25′ E 168
Babuyan Channel 18°34′ N, 121°27′ E 203
Babuyan, island, Philippines 19°34′ N, 122°1′ E 198
Babuyan Islands, South China Sea 19°8′ N, 121°56′ E 203
Babylon, N.Y., U.S. 40°41′ N, 73°19′ W 104
Babylon, ruin(s), Iraq 32°30′ N, 44°16′ E 180
Bač, Serb. and Mont. 45°22′ N, 19°15′ E 168
Bac Can, Vietnam 22°9′ N, 105°50′ E 198
Bac Giang, Vietnam 21°16′ N, 106°13′ E 198
Bac Lieu, Vietnam 9°18′ N, 105°42′ E 202
Bac Ninh, Vietnam 21°11′ N, 106°2′ E 198
Bacaadweyne, Somalia 7°10′ N, 47°34′ E 218
Bacabal, Braz. 4°15′ S, 44°53′ W 132
Bacadéhuachi, Mex. 29°41′ N, 109°9′ W 92
Bacajá, river, Braz. 3°51′ S, 51°48′ W 130
Bacan, island, Indonesia 0°38′ N, 126°26′ E 192
Bacanora, Mex. 28°58′ N, 109°24′ W 92
Bacarra, Philippines 18°16′ N, 120°37′ E 203
Bacău, Rom. 46°33′ N, 26°55′ E 156
Bacău, adm. division, Rom. 46°13′ N, 26°17′ E 156
Baccarat, Fr. 48°27′ N, 6°45′ E 163
Bæccegelhalde, peak, Nor. 69°31′ N, 21°45′ E 152
Baceno, It. 46°16′ N, 8°18′ E 167
Bacerac, Mex. 30°20′ N, 108°58′ W 92
Băceşti, Rom. 46°50′ N, 27°14′ E 156
Bačevci, Serb. and Mont. 44°11′ N, 19°55′ E 168
Bach, Mich., U.S. 43°40′ N, 83°21′ W 102
Bach Long Vi, Dao (Nightingale Island), Vietnam 19°46′ N, 107°30′ E 198
Bach Ma National Park, Vietnam 16°12′ N, 108°7′ E 202
Bach, Mynydd, peak, U.K. 52°17′ N, 4°4′ W 162
Bacharach, Ger. 50°3′ N, 7°44′ E 167
Bachelor, Mount, Oreg., U.S. 43°57′ N, 121°47′ W 90
Bachiniva, Mex. 28°46′ N, 107°15′ W 92
Bachu, China 39°44′ N, 78°34′ E 184
Baciuty, Pol. 53°3′ N, 22°58′ E 152
Back, river, Can. 64°47′ N, 105°2′ W 106
Bačka Palanka, Serb. and Mont. 45°14′ N, 19°23′ E 168
Bačka, region, Europe 45°44′ N, 18°55′ E 168
Bačka Topola, Serb. and Mont. 45°48′ N, 19°38′ E 168
Backbone Mountain, Md., U.S. 39°12′ N, 79°34′ W 94
Backbone Ranges, Can. 61°28′ N, 124°16′ W 108
Backe, Nor. 63°49′ N, 16°22′ E 152
Bäckefors, Nor. 58°49′ N, 12°8′ E 152
Bačko Gradište, Serb. and Mont. 45°32′ N, 20°1′ E 168
Bačko Petrovo Selo, Serb. and Mont. 45°42′ N, 20°4′ E 168
Bacnotan, Philippines 16°44′ N, 120°20′ E 203
Baco, Mount, Philippines 12°49′ N, 121°6′ E 203
Bacoachi, Mex. 30°38′ N, 109°59′ W 92
Bacolod, Philippines 10°39′ N, 122°57′ E 203
Bácsalmás, Hung. 46°7′ N, 19°20′ E 168
Bács-Kiskun, adm. division, Hung. 46°31′ N, 19°2′ E 156
Bad Axe, Mich., U.S. 43°47′ N, 82°60′ W 102
Bad Bentheim, Ger. 52°18′ N, 7°10′ E 163
Bad Bergzabern, Ger. 49°6′ N, 7°59′ E 163
Bad Brückenau, Ger. 50°18′ N, 9°47′ E 167
Bad Camberg, Ger. 50°18′ N, 8°16′ E 167
Bad Driburg, Ger. 51°44′ N, 9°0′ E 167
Bad Ems, Ger. 50°20′ N, 7°42′ E 167
Bad Godesberg, Ger. 50°41′ N, 7°9′ E 167
Bad Hersfeld, Ger. 50°51′ N, 9°42′ E 167
Bad Homburg, Ger. 50°14′ N, 8°36′ E 167
Bad Honnef, Ger. 50°38′ N, 7°13′ E 167
Bad Hönningen, Ger. 50°30′ N, 7°19′ E 167
Bad Iburg, Ger. 52°9′ N, 8°2′ E 163
Bad Ischl, Aust. 47°42′ N, 13°38′ E 156
Bad Karlshafen, Ger. 51°38′ N, 9°29′ E 167
Bad Kissingen, Ger. 50°11′ N, 10°4′ E 167
Bad Kreuznach, Ger. 49°50′ N, 7°52′ E 167
Bad Laasphe, Ger. 50°55′ N, 8°24′ E 167
Bad Lauterberg, Ger. 51°37′ N, 10°26′ E 167
Bad Marienberg, Ger. 50°38′ N, 7°56′ E 167
Bad Nauheim, Ger. 50°21′ N, 8°43′ E 167
Bad Neuenahr-Ahrweiler, Ger. 50°33′ N, 7°7′ E 167
Bad Neustadt, Ger. 50°19′ N, 10°11′ E 167
Bad Orb, Ger. 50°13′ N, 9°21′ E 167
Bad, river, S. Dak., U.S. 43°58′ N, 101°7′ W 90
Bad Salzig, Ger. 50°12′ N, 7°37′ E 167
Bad Soden-Salmünster, Ger. 50°16′ N, 9°21′ E 167
Bad Sooden-Allendorf, Ger. 51°16′ N, 9°58′ E 167
Bad Vilbel, Ger. 50°11′ N, 8°44′ E 167
Bad Vöslau, Aust. 47°58′ N, 16°12′ E 168
Bad Waldsee, Ger. 47°55′ N, 9°45′ E 152
Bad Wildungen, Ger. 51°6′ N, 9°7′ E 167
Badacsony, peak, Hung. 46°47′ N, 17°26′ E 168
Badagri, Nig. 6°29′ N, 2°55′ E 222
Badajoz, Sp. 38°51′ N, 6°58′ W 150
Badalona, Sp. 41°26′ N, 2°14′ E 164
Badalucco, It. 43°55′ N, 7°51′ E 167
Badam, Kaz. 42°22′ N, 69°13′ E 197
Badamsha, Kaz. 50°33′ N, 58°16′ E 158
Badanah, Saudi Arabia 30°58′ N, 40°57′ E 180
Badaohe, China 43°11′ N, 126°32′ E 200
Baddeck, Can. 46°6′ N, 60°46′ W 111
Baddo, river, Pak. 28°5′ N, 64°35′ E 182
Baden, Aust. 48°0′ N, 16°14′ E 168
Baden, Eritrea 16°53′ N, 37°54′ E 182
Baden, Ger. 53°0′ N, 9°6′ E 150
Baden, Switz. 47°27′ N, 8°18′ E 150
Baden-Württemberg, adm. division, Ger. 47°47′ N, 7°43′ E 165
Badger, Minn., U.S. 48°45′ N, 96°3′ W 90
Badger Creek, river, Mont., U.S. 48°4′ N, 113°13′ W 108
Badia Polesine, It. 45°5′ N, 11°28′ E 167
Badiar National Park, Guinea 12°23′ N, 13°51′ W 222
Badin, Pak. 24°39′ N, 68°48′ E 186
Badjoki, Dem. Rep. of the Congo 2°53′ N, 22°21′ E 218
Badjoudé (Dompago), Benin 9°42′ N, 1°23′ E 222
Badlands, N. Dak., U.S. 47°2′ N, 104°19′ W 90
Badlands National Park, S. Dak., U.S. 43°15′ N, 102°43′ W 90
Badnjevac, Serb. and Mont. 44°7′ N, 20°58′ E 168

Badogo, Mali 11°3′ N, 8°13′ W 222
Badong, China 30°58′ N, 110°23′ E 198
Badoumbé, Mali 13°41′ N, 10°15′ W 222
Badreïna, spring, Mauritania 17°47′ N, 11°6′ W 222
Baduein, Eth. 6°30′ N, 43°22′ E 218
Badupi, Myanmar 21°37′ N, 93°24′ E 188
Badvel, India 14°44′ N, 79°5′ E 188
Bad'ya, Russ. 60°29′ N, 53°22′ E 154
Baena, Sp. 37°37′ N, 4°21′ W 164
Baengnyeongdo, island, S. Korea 37°50′ N, 123°23′ E 198
Baeza, Sp. 37°59′ N, 3°28′ W 164
Bafang, Cameroon 5°8′ N, 10°10′ E 222
Bafarara, Mali 15°23′ N, 11°29′ W 222
Baffin Bay 73°51′ N, 73°33′ W 106
Bafia, Cameroon 4°42′ N, 11°14′ E 222
Bafing, river, Guinea 12°23′ N, 10°13′ W 222
Bafoulabé, Mali 13°49′ N, 10°52′ W 222
Bafousam, Cameroon 5°27′ N, 10°23′ E 222
Bāfq, Iran 31°32′ N, 55°22′ E 180
Bafra, Turk. 41°33′ N, 35°54′ E 156
Bafra Burnu, Turk. 41°45′ N, 35°24′ E 156
Bāft, Iran 29°16′ N, 56°39′ E 196
Bafuka, Dem. Rep. of the Congo 4°9′ N, 27°52′ E 224
Bafwabalinga, Dem. Rep. of the Congo 0°54′ N, 27°1′ E 224
Bafwaboli, Dem. Rep. of the Congo 0°42′ N, 26°7′ E 224
Bafwasende, Dem. Rep. of the Congo 1°8′ N, 27°11′ E 224
Bagabag, island, P.N.G. 4°48′ S, 146°17′ E 192
Bagadó, Col. 5°22′ N, 76°28′ W 136
Bagalkot, India 16°10′ N, 75°42′ E 188
Bagam, spring, Niger 15°40′ N, 6°34′ E 222
Bagamoyo, Tanzania 6°23′ S, 38°55′ E 224
Bagan, Russ. 54°3′ N, 77°45′ E 184
Bagan Datoh, Malaysia 3°58′ N, 100°47′ E 196
Bagan Serai, Malaysia 5°1′ N, 100°31′ E 196
Bagana, Nig. 7°58′ N, 7°34′ E 222
Baganga, Philippines 7°37′ N, 126°33′ E 203
Bagansiapiapi, Indonesia 2°12′ N, 100°49′ E 196
Bagan'yuvom, Russ. 66°5′ N, 58°2′ E 154
Bagaroua, Niger 14°30′ N, 4°25′ E 222
Bagata, Dem. Rep. of the Congo 3°49′ S, 17°56′ E 218
Bagatogo, Côte d'Ivoire 8°42′ N, 6°42′ W 222
Bagdad, Ariz., U.S. 34°34′ N, 113°12′ W 92
Bagdad, Fla., U.S. 30°35′ N, 87°2′ W 96
Bagdarin, Russ. 54°28′ N, 113°39′ E 190
Bagé, Braz. 31°21′ S, 54°8′ W 139
Bågede, Nor. 64°21′ N, 14°48′ E 152
Baggs, Wyo., U.S. 41°2′ N, 107°40′ W 90
Baghdād, Iraq 33°21′ N, 44°23′ E 180
Bagheria, It. 38°4′ N, 13°30′ E 156
Bāghīn, Iran 30°9′ N, 56°51′ E 196
Baghlan, Afghan. 36°11′ N, 68°48′ E 186
Baghran Khowleh, Afghan. 32°57′ N, 64°58′ E 186
Bağırpaşa Dağı, peak, Turk. 39°28′ N, 40°2′ E 195
Bağışlı, Turk. 37°51′ N, 44°0′ E 195
Bagley, Minn., U.S. 47°30′ N, 95°25′ W 90
Bagni del Masino, It. 46°15′ N, 9°35′ E 167
Bagno di Romagna, It. 43°50′ N, 11°56′ E 167
Bagnols-les-Bains, Fr. 44°31′ N, 3°40′ E 150
Bagnone, It. 44°19′ N, 9°59′ E 167
Bago, Myanmar 17°20′ N, 96°29′ E 202
Bagodar, India 24°4′ N, 85°49′ E 197
Bagoé, river, Mali 11°44′ N, 6°22′ W 222
Bagot, Mount, Can. 59°20′ N, 135°8′ W 108
Bagrationovsk, Russ. 54°22′ N, 20°31′ E 166
Bagrax see Bohu, China 41°56′ N, 86°40′ E 184
Bagrdan, Serb. and Mont. 44°4′ N, 21°9′ E 168
Baguia, Timor-Leste 8°33′ S, 126°39′ E 238
Baguio, Philippines 16°23′ N, 120°34′ E 203
Baguio Point, Philippines 17°31′ N, 122°11′ E 203
Bagzane, Monts, Niger 17°49′ N, 8°37′ E 222
Bahabón de Esgueva, Sp. 41°51′ N, 3°44′ W 164
Bahama Islands, North Atlantic Ocean 23°51′ N, 76°7′ W 253
Bahamas 26°0′ N, 77°0′ W 118
Baharak, Afghan. 37°0′ N, 70°52′ E 186
Baharampur, India 24°3′ N, 88°16′ E 188
Baḥarîya, El Wâḥât el, Egypt 27°49′ N, 28°21′ E 180
Bahau, Malaysia 2°50′ N, 102°24′ E 196
Bahawalnagar, Pak. 30°2′ N, 73°16′ E 186
Bahawalpur, Pak. 29°24′ N, 71°40′ E 186
Bahçe, Turk. 37°14′ N, 36°35′ E 156
Bahçesaray, Turk. 38°4′ N, 42°47′ E 195
Bahdanaw, Belarus 54°10′ N, 26°8′ E 166
Bahdur Island, Sudan 17°59′ N, 37°52′ E 182
Bäherden, Turkm. 38°22′ N, 57°10′ E 160
Bahi, Tanzania 5°57′ S, 35°19′ E 224
Bahia, adm. division, Braz. 13°49′ S, 42°23′ W 138
Bahía Blanca, Arg. 38°43′ S, 62°17′ W 139
Bahía de Caráquez, Ecua. 0°42′ N, 80°19′ W 130
Bahía de Loreto National Park, Mex. 25°52′ N, 111°32′ W 238
Bahía de los Ángeles, Mex. 28°56′ N, 113°37′ W 92
Bahía, Islas de la, islands, Isla de Roatán 16°27′ N, 87°19′ W 115
Bahía Kino, Mex. 28°49′ N, 111°55′ W 92
Bahía Laura, Arg. 48°22′ S, 66°30′ W 134
Bahia see Salvador, Braz. 12°59′ S, 38°28′ W 132
Bahía Solano (Puerto Mutis), Col. 6°12′ N, 77°25′ W 136
Bahía Tortugas, Mex. 27°41′ N, 114°52′ W 112
Bahir Dar, Eth. 11°31′ N, 37°21′ E 182
Bahlah, Oman 22°57′ N, 57°15′ E 182
Bahr el 'Arab, river, Sudan 10°4′ N, 25°6′ E 224
Bahr ez Zaraf, river, Sudan 7°42′ N, 30°43′ E 224
Bahr Kéita (Doka), river, Chad 9°8′ N, 18°38′ E 218
Bahr Salamat, river, Chad 10°17′ N, 19°27′ E 216
Bahrah, oil field, Kuwait 29°39′ N, 47°49′ E 196
Bahraich, India 27°32′ N, 81°36′ E 197
Bahrain 26°0′ N, 51°0′ E 196
Bahrain, Gulf of 25°31′ N, 50°13′ E 196
Bāhū Kalāt, Iran 25°44′ N, 61°25′ E 182
Bahuaja-Sonene National Park, Peru 13°28′ S, 69°24′ W 137
Bai Bung, Mui, Vietnam 8°15′ N, 104°19′ E 202
Baia, Rom. 44°43′ N, 28°40′ E 156
Baia de Aramă, Rom. 44°59′ N, 22°49′ E 168
Baia de Arieş, Rom. 46°21′ N, 23°16′ E 168
Baia dos Tigres, Angola 16°38′ S, 11°40′ E 220
Baia Mare, Rom. 47°39′ N, 23°36′ E 168
Baïbokoum, Chad 7°40′ N, 15°42′ E 218
Baicheng, China 45°35′ N, 122°50′ E 198
Baicheng, China 41°46′ N, 81°51′ E 184
Baidoa see Baydhabo, Somalia 3°5′ N, 43°41′ E 218
Baie-Comeau, Can. 49°13′ N, 68°10′ W 111
Baie-du-Poste see Mistassini, Can. 50°24′ N, 73°50′ W 110
Baie-Johan-Beetz, Can. 50°17′ N, 62°49′ W 111
Baie-Sainte-Catherine, Can. 48°6′ N, 69°44′ W 94
Baie-Sainte-Claire, site, Can. 49°52′ N, 64°35′ W 111
Baie-Saint-Paul, Can. 47°26′ N, 70°31′ W 94
Baihar, India 22°7′ N, 80°33′ E 197
Baihe, China 42°22′ N, 128°7′ E 198
Ba'ījī, Iraq 34°54′ N, 43°27′ E 180
Baijnath, India 29°57′ N, 79°37′ E 188
Baikal, Lake, Russ. 52°49′ N, 106°59′ E 238
Baikha, Russ. 64°54′ N, 88°0′ E 169
Baikonur Cosmodrome, spaceport, Kaz. 46°6′ N, 63°9′ E 184
Baile Átha Cliath see Dublin, Ire. 53°18′ N, 6°26′ W 150
Băile Herculane, Rom. 44°54′ N, 22°26′ E 168
Bailén, Sp. 38°5′ N, 3°46′ W 164
Bailey Island, Me., U.S. 43°43′ N, 69°60′ W 104
Bailingmiao see Darhan Muminggan Lianheqi, China 41°41′ N, 110°23′ E 198
Bailique, Braz. 1°0′ N, 50°3′ W 130
Bailique, Ilha, island, Braz. 1°4′ N, 49°56′ W 130
Bailleul, Fr. 50°43′ N, 2°44′ E 163
Baillie Islands, Beaufort Sea 70°39′ N, 129°39′ W 98
Baillieu Peak, Antarctica 67°57′ S, 60°27′ E 248
Bailong, river, China 33°26′ N, 104°17′ E 198
Bailundo, Angola 12°13′ S, 15°51′ E 220
Bainang, China 29°13′ N, 89°15′ E 197
Bainbridge, Ga., U.S. 30°53′ N, 84°34′ W 96
Bainbridge, Ind., U.S. 39°45′ N, 86°49′ W 102
Bainbridge, Ohio, U.S. 39°13′ N, 83°16′ W 102
Bainbridge Island, Wash., U.S. 47°37′ N, 122°32′ W 100
Baingoin, China 31°37′ N, 89°51′ E 188
Bainville, Mont., U.S. 48°7′ N, 104°15′ W 90
Baiona, Sp. 42°6′ N, 8°53′ W 150
Baiquan, China 47°37′ N, 126°4′ E 198
Bā'ir, Jordan 30°45′ N, 36°40′ E 194
Bairab Co, lake, China 34°55′ N, 82°29′ E 188
Baird, Miss., U.S. 33°23′ N, 90°36′ W 103
Baird, Tex., U.S. 32°23′ N, 99°24′ W 92
Baird Inlet 60°44′ N, 164°34′ W 98
Baird, Mount, Idaho, U.S. 43°21′ N, 111°11′ W 90
Baird Mountains, Alas., U.S. 67°24′ N, 161°29′ W 98
Bairiki see Tarawa, Kiribati 1°15′ N, 169°58′ E 242
Bairin Youqi, China 43°30′ N, 118°40′ E 198
Bairin Zuoqi, China 43°59′ N, 119°24′ E 198
Bairoil, Wyo., U.S. 42°15′ N, 107°33′ W 90
Baisha, China 29°31′ N, 119°15′ E 198
Baishan, China 42°38′ N, 127°12′ E 200
Baiso, It. 44°29′ N, 10°37′ E 167
Baitadi, Nepal 29°34′ N, 80°26′ E 197
Baixo Guandu, Braz. 19°32′ S, 40°59′ W 138
Baiyin, China 36°34′ N, 104°15′ E 198
Baiyuda, spring, Sudan 17°29′ N, 32°8′ E 182
Baja, Hung. 46°10′ N, 18°57′ E 168
Baja California, region, North America 31°27′ N, 115°59′ W 92
Baja California, adm. division, Mex. 30°0′ N, 115°0′ W 112
Baja California Sur, adm. division, Mex. 26°3′ N, 112°13′ W 112
Baja, Punta, Mex. 28°17′ N, 111°59′ W 92
Baja, Punta, Mex. 29°59′ N, 115°58′ W 92
Bajag, India 22°42′ N, 81°21′ E 197
Baján, Mex. 26°32′ N, 101°15′ W 114
Bājgīrān, Iran 37°37′ N, 58°24′ E 180
Bajiazi, China 42°41′ N, 129°9′ E 200
Bājil, Yemen 14°58′ N, 43°15′ E 182
Bajina Bašta, Serb. and Mont. 43°58′ N, 19°35′ E 168
Bajitpur, Bangladesh 24°9′ N, 90°54′ E 197
Bajmok, Serb. and Mont. 45°57′ N, 19°24′ E 168
Bajo Baudó, Col. 4°57′ N, 77°22′ W 136
Bajoga, Nig. 10°52′ N, 11°17′ E 222
Bajovo Polje, Serb. and Mont. 43°0′ N, 18°53′ E 168
Bajram Curri, Alban. 42°21′ N, 20°3′ E 168
Bajzë, Alban. 42°16′ N, 19°26′ E 168
Bak, Hung. 46°43′ N, 16°51′ E 168
Bakaba, Chad 7°43′ N, 16°54′ E 218
Bakal, Russ. 54°59′ N, 58°51′ E 154
Bakala, Cen. Af. Rep. 6°9′ N, 20°21′ E 218
Bakałarzewo, Pol. 54°5′ N, 22°38′ E 166
Bakaly, Russ. 55°11′ N, 53°50′ E 154
Bakanas, Kaz. 44°49′ N, 76°17′ E 184
Bakaoré, Chad 15°17′ N, 21°47′ E 216
Bakchar, Russ. 56°59′ N, 82°4′ E 169
Bakel, Senegal 14°53′ N, 12°31′ W 222
Baker, Calif., U.S. 35°16′ N, 116°5′ W 101
Baker, La., U.S. 30°35′ N, 91°10′ W 103
Baker, Mont., U.S. 46°20′ N, 104°18′ W 90
Baker, Nev., U.S. 39°0′ N, 114°8′ W 92
Baker, Oreg., U.S. 44°46′ N, 117°52′ W 90
Baker Foreland, Can. 62°46′ N, 90°36′ W 106
Baker Island, U.S. 0°13′ N, 176°37′ W 238
Baker Lake, Can. 62°18′ N, 99°20′ W 106
Baker Lake, Can. 64°19′ N, 96°7′ W 73
Baker Lake, Wash., U.S. 48°42′ N, 121°52′ W 100
Baker, Mount, Wash., U.S. 48°46′ N, 121°51′ W 100
Bakersfield, Calif., U.S. 35°22′ N, 119°1′ W 101
Bakewell, U.K. 53°12′ N, 1°41′ W 162
Bakhanay, Russ. 66°16′ N, 123°37′ E 173
Bakhchysaray, Ukr. 44°45′ N, 33°51′ E 156
Bakhma Dam, Iraq 36°31′ N, 44°10′ E 195
Bakhmach, Ukr. 51°11′ N, 32°48′ E 158
Bakhta, Russ. 62°19′ N, 89°10′ E 160
Bakhta, river, Russ. 63°43′ N, 90°2′ E 169
Bakhtegān, Daryācheh-ye, lake, Iran 29°21′ N, 53°32′ E 196
Bakı (Baku), Azerb. 40°23′ N, 49°44′ E 195
Baki, spring, Chad 16°58′ N, 21°10′ E 216
Bakin Birji, Niger 14°10′ N, 8°52′ E 222
Bakırdağı, Turk. 38°12′ N, 35°47′ E 156
Bako, Côte d'Ivoire 9°7′ N, 7°36′ W 222
Bako, Eth. 5°50′ N, 36°37′ E 224
Bakony, Hung. 47°17′ N, 17°23′ E 168
Bakouma, Cen. Af. Rep. 5°42′ N, 22°50′ E 218
Bakoye, river, Africa 12°50′ N, 9°26′ W 222
Bakr Uzyak, Russ. 52°59′ N, 58°36′ E 154
Baktalórántháza, Hung. 48°0′ N, 22°3′ E 168
Baku see Bakı, Azerb. 40°23′ N, 49°44′ E 195
Bakundi, Nig. 8°1′ N, 10°45′ E 222
Bakungan, Indonesia 2°58′ N, 97°29′ E 196
Bakuriani, Ga. 41°44′ N, 43°31′ E 195
Bakutis Coast, Antarctica 74°60′ S, 115°49′ W 248
Bakwanga see Mbuji-Mayi, Dem. Rep. of the Congo 6°10′ S, 23°36′ E 224
Bala, Senegal 14°1′ N, 13°11′ W 222
Bâlâ, Turk. 39°32′ N, 33°7′ E 156
Bala, U.K. 52°54′ N, 3°37′ W 162
Balabac, Philippines 8°1′ N, 117°2′ E 203
Balabac, island, Philippines 7°49′ N, 115°56′ E 192
Balabac Strait 7°38′ N, 116°33′ E 203
Bălăciţa, Rom. 44°23′ N, 23°7′ E 168
Balaena Islands, Indian Ocean 65°59′ S, 112°14′ E 248
Balaghat, India 21°49′ N, 80°13′ E 197
Balaguer, Sp. 41°47′ N, 0°46′ E 164
Balaka, Malawi 14°54′ S, 34°56′ E 224
Balakän, Azerb. 41°43′ N, 46°25′ E 195
Balakété, Cen. Af. Rep. 6°54′ N, 19°57′ E 218
Balakhna, Russ. 56°25′ N, 43°37′ E 154
Balaki, Guinea 12°12′ N, 11°52′ W 222
Balaklava, Ukr. 44°30′ N, 33°34′ E 158
Balakliya, Ukr. 49°29′ N, 36°52′ E 158
Balakovo, Russ. 52°0′ N, 47°50′ E 158
Balama, Mozambique 13°15′ S, 38°38′ E 224
Balancán, Mex. 17°47′ N, 91°34′ W 115
Balangir, India 20°42′ N, 83°28′ E 188
Balanikha, Russ. 65°56′ N, 43°19′ E 154
Balao, Ecua. 3°2′ S, 79°48′ W 130
Balashivka, Ukr. 50°59′ N, 26°57′ E 152
Balashov, Russ. 51°29′ N, 43°10′ E 158
Balástya, Hung. 46°25′ N, 20°1′ E 168
Balâţ, Egypt 25°33′ N, 29°14′ E 226
Balatina, Mold. 47°41′ N, 27°20′ E 158
Balatonföldvár, Hung. 46°50′ N, 17°51′ E 168
Balatonfüred, Hung. 46°57′ N, 17°53′ E 168
Balavé, Burkina Faso 12°23′ N, 4°11′ W 222
Balazote, Sp. 38°53′ N, 2°9′ W 164
Balbina, Represa da, dam, Braz. 1°25′ S, 60°25′ W 130
Balcad, Somalia 2°18′ N, 45°26′ E 218
Balcarce, Arg. 37°51′ S, 58°17′ W 139
Balcarres, Can. 50°47′ N, 103°33′ W 90
Balchik, Bulg. 43°26′ N, 28°11′ E 156
Balclutha, N.Z. 46°15′ S, 169°42′ E 240
Bald Butte, peak, Oreg., U.S. 43°40′ N, 119°27′ W 90
Bald Eagle Mountain, Pa., U.S. 40°59′ N, 77°48′ W 94
Bald Knob, Ark., U.S. 35°17′ N, 91°35′ W 96
Bald Mountain, peak, Calif., U.S. 40°54′ N, 121°11′ W 90
Bald Mountain, peak, Can. 54°5′ N, 61°29′ W 111
Bald Mountain, peak, Idaho, U.S. 44°20′ N, 114°26′ W 90
Bald Mountain, peak, Nev., U.S. 38°34′ N, 117°8′ W 90
Bald Mountain, peak, Oreg., U.S. 44°33′ N, 117°60′ W 90
Bald Mountain, peak, Vt., U.S. 44°45′ N, 72°5′ W 94
Baldhill Dam, N. Dak., U.S. 47°19′ N, 98°45′ W 82
Baldock Lake, Can. 56°32′ N, 98°25′ W 108
Baldone, Latv. 56°44′ N, 24°23′ E 166
Baldwin, La., U.S. 29°49′ N, 91°33′ W 103
Baldwin, Mich., U.S. 43°53′ N, 85°52′ W 102
Baldwinville, Mass., U.S. 42°36′ N, 72°5′ W 104
Baldwyn, Miss., U.S. 34°30′ N, 88°38′ W 96
Baldy Mountain, peak, Can. 51°28′ N, 120°6′ W 90
Baldy Mountain, peak, Can. 51°27′ N, 100°49′ W 90
Baldy Mountain, peak, Can. 49°8′ N, 119°20′ W 90
Baldy Mountain, peak, Mont., U.S. 45°20′ N, 113°7′ W 90
Baldy Peak, Ariz., U.S. 33°53′ N, 109°37′ W 92
Bale Mountains National Park, Eth. 6°33′ N, 38°57′ E 224
Balearic Islands, Sp. 40°4′ N, 3°1′ E 164
Balearic Sea 40°47′ N, 1°23′ E 150
Baleia, Ponta da, Braz. 17°40′ S, 39°9′ W 132
Baleine, Rivière à la, river, Can. 57°24′ N, 67°59′ W 106
Balen, Belg. 51°9′ N, 5°9′ E 167
Baler, Philippines 15°46′ N, 121°32′ E 203
Balerma, Sp. 36°43′ N, 2°54′ W 164
Baleshwar, India 21°29′ N, 86°53′ E 188
Baley, Russ. 51°36′ N, 116°35′ E 238
Baléya, Mali 12°16′ N, 9°58′ W 222
Baleyara, Niger 13°56′ N, 2°50′ E 222
Balezino, Russ. 57°57′ N, 53°5′ E 154
Balguntay, China 42°46′ N, 86°18′ E 184
Balḥāf, Yemen 14°1′ N, 48°10′ E 182
Balḥo, Djibouti 12°2′ N, 42°12′ E 182
Bali, India 25°13′ N, 73°16′ E 186
Bali, island, Indonesia 9°21′ S, 114°38′ E 192
Bali Sea 7°47′ S, 114°55′ E 192
Baliangao, Philippines 8°40′ N, 123°37′ E 203
Balige, Indonesia 2°21′ N, 99°3′ E 196
Balık Göl, lake, Turk. 41°34′ N, 35°44′ E 156
Balıkesir, Turk. 39°38′ N, 27°51′ E 156
Balikpapan, Indonesia 1°12′ S, 116°46′ E 192
Baling, Malaysia 5°40′ N, 100°54′ E 196
Balinţ, Rom. 45°49′ N, 21°51′ E 168
Balintang Channel 19°44′ N, 121°25′ E 203
Balipara, India 26°48′ N, 92°43′ E 188
Baliza, Braz. 16°14′ S, 52°25′ W 138
Balkan Mountians, Bulg. 43°16′ N, 22°39′ E 168
Balkanabat (Nebitdag), Turkm. 39°31′ N, 54°21′ E 180
Balkány, Hung. 47°46′ N, 21°49′ E 168
Balkany, Russ. 53°29′ N, 59°34′ E 154
Balkashīno, Kaz. 52°27′ N, 68°40′ E 184
Balkh, Afghan. 36°46′ N, 66°58′ E 186
Balkhash, Lake, Kaz. 46°0′ N, 69°44′ E 173
Ball Lake, lake, Can. 50°13′ N, 94°17′ W 90
Ballâna, Egypt 24°17′ N, 32°58′ E 182
Ballantine, Mont., U.S. 45°55′ N, 108°9′ W 90
Ballarat, Austral. 37°34′ S, 143°55′ E 231
Ballé, Mali 15°21′ N, 8°36′ W 222
Ballenas, Canal de 29°14′ N, 113°60′ W 92
Balleny Islands, South Pacific Ocean 66°21′ S, 162°20′ E 255
Balleza, Mex. 26°57′ N, 106°22′ W 112
Ballinger, Tex., U.S. 31°43′ N, 99°57′ W 92
Ballobar, Sp. 41°36′ N, 0°11′ E 164
Ball's Pyramid, island, Austral. 32°15′ S, 157°57′ E 230
Ballstad, Nor. 68°4′ N, 13°28′ E 152
Ballston Spa, N.Y., U.S. 43°0′ N, 73°52′ W 104
Balmaceda, Chile 45°59′ S, 71°48′ W 123
Balmertown, Can. 51°3′ N, 93°45′ W 90
Balmoral Castle, site, U.K. 57°0′ N, 3°20′ W 150
Balmorhea, Tex., U.S. 30°57′ N, 103°45′ W 92
Balnearia, Arg. 30°60′ S, 62°40′ W 139
Balneario de los Novillos see I, Mex. 29°22′ N, 101°19′ W 112
Balod, India 20°44′ N, 81°12′ E 188
Balombo, Angola 12°22′ S, 14°47′ E 220
Balonne, river, Austral. 28°41′ S, 147°59′ E 230
Balotra, India 25°51′ N, 72°14′ E 186
Balqash, Kaz. 46°52′ N, 74°58′ E 184
Balqash Köli, lake, Kaz. 45°35′ N, 73°9′ E 190
Balş, Rom. 44°22′ N, 24°4′ E 156
Balsas, Braz. 7°32′ S, 46°3′ W 130
Balsas, Mex. 17°59′ N, 99°46′ W 114
Balsas, river, Braz. 8°24′ S, 46°19′ W 130
Balsas, river, Braz. 10°47′ S, 47°39′ W 130
Balsas, river, Mex. 18°29′ N, 100°56′ W 114
Balta, N. Dak., U.S. 48°9′ N, 100°3′ W 90
Balta, Rom. 44°52′ N, 22°39′ E 168
Balta, Ukr. 47°55′ N, 29°38′ E 156
Balta Albă, Rom. 45°18′ N, 27°16′ E 156
Baltasar Brum, Uru. 30°43′ S, 57°20′ W 139
Bălţi, Mold. 47°45′ N, 27°57′ E 152
Baltic Sea 59°13′ N, 17°48′ E 152
Balṭîm, Egypt 31°34′ N, 31°4′ E 180
Baltimore, Md., U.S. 39°17′ N, 76°38′ W 94
Baltimore, Ohio, U.S. 39°50′ N, 82°36′ W 102
Baltit, Pak. 36°19′ N, 74°41′ E 186
Baltiysk, Russ. 54°39′ N, 19°54′ E 166
Baltrum, island, Ger. 53°41′ N, 7°26′ E 163
Balumbal, Eth. 8°33′ N, 45°10′ E 218
Balurghat, India 25°12′ N, 88°47′ E 197
Balvi, Latv. 57°6′ N, 27°14′ E 166
Balya, Turk. 39°43′ N, 27°34′ E 156
Balykcha, Russ. 51°18′ N, 87°43′ E 184
Balykchy, Kyrg. 42°26′ N, 76°10′ E 184
Balyksa, Russ. 53°23′ N, 89°8′ E 184
Balyqshy, Kaz. 47°2′ N, 51°52′ E 158
Balzola, It. 45°11′ N, 8°24′ E 167
Bam, Iran 29°2′ N, 58°23′ E 196
Bam Co, lake, China 31°29′ N, 90°37′ E 188
Bama, Nig. 11°32′ N, 13°41′ E 216
Bamako, Mali 12°37′ N, 8°10′ W 222
Bamba, Mali 17°2′ N, 1°26′ W 222
Bambafouga, Guinea 10°11′ N, 11°53′ W 222
Bambamarca, Peru 6°35′ S, 78°34′ W 130
Bambara, Chad 8°54′ N, 18°34′ E 218
Bambara, Mali 13°25′ N, 4°11′ W 222
Bambari, Cen. Af. Rep. 5°45′ N, 20°39′ E 218
Bambesa, Dem. Rep. of the Congo 3°24′ N, 25°43′ E 224
Bambey, Senegal 14°44′ N, 16°19′ W 222
Bambili, Dem. Rep. of the Congo 3°36′ N, 26°7′ E 224
Bambinga, Dem. Rep. of the Congo 3°45′ S, 18°51′ E 218
Bambio, Cen. Af. Rep. 3°59′ N, 16°58′ E 218
Bambouti, Cen. Af. Rep. 5°23′ N, 27°11′ E 224
Bambuí, Braz. 20°2′ S, 45°57′ W 138
Bambuyka, Russ. 55°46′ N, 115°33′ E 190
Bamenda, Cameroon 5°53′ N, 10°9′ E 222
Bamfield, Can. 48°47′ N, 125°8′ W 100
Bamian, Afghan. 34°51′ N, 67°51′ E 186
Bamingui, Cen. Af. Rep. 7°30′ N, 20°12′ E 218
Bampton, U.K. 51°44′ N, 1°33′ W 162
Bampton, U.K. 50°59′ N, 3°29′ W 162
Bamy, Turkm. 38°43′ N, 56°49′ E 180
Ban Bang Hin, Thai. 9°32′ N, 98°35′ E 202
Ban Don, Vietnam 12°54′ N, 107°47′ E 202
Ban Don, Ao 9°17′ N, 99°0′ E 202
Ban Don see Surat Thani, Thai. 9°7′ N, 99°20′ E 202
Ban Dong, Thai. 19°33′ N, 100°57′ E 202
Ban Hinboun, Laos 17°37′ N, 104°37′ E 202
Ban Khai, Thai. 12°47′ N, 101°20′ E 202
Ban Nam-Om, Laos 20°43′ N, 101°4′ E 202
Ban Napè, Laos 18°19′ N, 105°6′ E 202
Ban Phai, Thai. 16°6′ N, 102°41′ E 202
Ban Sanam Chai, Thai. 7°34′ N, 100°25′ E 196
Ban Taphan, Laos 15°56′ N, 105°25′ E 202
Ban Xénô, Laos 16°41′ N, 105°0′ E 202
Bañados de Otuquis, marsh, Braz. 20°54′ S, 60°29′ W 132
Bañados del Izozog, marsh, Bol. 18°55′ S, 62°31′ W 132
Banak, Nor. 70°2′ N, 25°1′ E 152
Banalia, Dem. Rep. of the Congo 1°33′ N, 25°25′ E 224
Banam, Cambodia 11°19′ N, 105°16′ E 202
Banamba, Mali 13°34′ N, 7°26′ W 222
Banana Islands, North Atlantic Ocean 7°56′ N, 13°50′ W 222
Bananfara, Guinea 11°19′ N, 8°56′ W 222
Bananga, India 6°56′ N, 93°58′ E 188
Banankoro, Guinea 9°10′ N, 9°18′ W 222
Banaras see Varanasi, India 25°18′ N, 82°57′ E 197
Banâs, Râs, Egypt 23°52′ N, 35°49′ E 182
Banas, river, India 25°15′ N, 74°2′ E 186
Banatsko Novo Selo, Serb. and Mont. 44°59′ N, 20°46′ E 168
Banaz, Turk. 38°44′ N, 29°45′ E 156
Banbalah, Tun. 35°42′ N, 10°48′ E 156
Banbān, Saudi Arabia 24°58′ N, 46°36′ E 196
Banbar, China 31°4′ N, 94°46′ E 188
Banbury, U.K. 52°3′ N, 1°21′ W 162
Banco, Punta, C.R. 8°17′ N, 83°54′ W 115
Bancroft, Can. 45°3′ N, 77°52′ W 94
Bancroft, Iowa, U.S. 43°17′ N, 94°14′ W 94
Bancroft, Mich., U.S. 42°51′ N, 84°4′ W 102
Banda, Dem. Rep. of the Congo 4°8′ N, 27°4′ E 224
Banda, India 24°3′ N, 78°57′ E 197
Banda, India 25°27′ N, 80°19′ E 197
Banda Aceh, Indonesia 5°30′ N, 95°20′ E 196
Banda, Kepulauan, islands, Banda Sea 5°8′ S, 129°26′ E 192
Banda Nkwanta, Ghana 8°22′ N, 2°8′ W 222
Banda, Pointe, Gabon 3°46′ S, 10°57′ E 218
Banda Sea 5°42′ S, 127°27′ E 254
Banda Sea 5°13′ S, 123°58′ E 173
Bandai-Asahi National Park, Japan 38°17′ N, 139°38′ E 201
Bandajuma, Sierra Leone 7°35′ N, 11°39′ W 222
Bandān, Iran 31°23′ N, 60°42′ E 186
Bandar Lampung, Indonesia 5°28′ S, 105°7′ E 192
Bandar Murcaayo, Somalia 11°36′ N, 50°26′ E 182
Bandar see Machilipatnam, India 16°11′ N, 81°10′ E 188
Bandar Seri Begawan, Brunei 4°52′ N, 114°50′ E 203
Bandarban, Bangladesh 22°12′ N, 92°11′ E 188
Bandarbeyla, Somalia 9°25′ N, 50°48′ E 216
Bandar-e 'Abbās, Iran 27°11′ N, 56°13′ E 196
Bandar-e Anzalī, Iran 37°30′ N, 49°20′ E 195
Bandar-e Būshehr, Iran 28°54′ N, 50°52′ E 196
Bandar-e Chārak, Iran 26°46′ N, 54°17′ E 196
Bandar-e Deylam, Iran 30°2′ N, 50°13′ E 196
Bandar-e Khoemir, Iran 26°57′ N, 55°34′ E 196
Bandar-e Khomeynī, Iran 30°27′ N, 49°3′ E 180
Bandar-e Lengeh, Iran 26°37′ N, 54°54′ E 196
Bandar-e Māh Shahr, Iran 30°38′ N, 49°12′ E 180
Bandar-e Maqām, Iran 26°58′ N, 53°29′ E 196
Bandar-e Rīg, Iran 29°29′ N, 50°39′ E 196
Bandar-e Torkaman, Iran 36°54′ N, 54°3′ E 180
Bandau, Malaysia 6°33′ N, 116°46′ E 203
Bandeira, peak, Braz. 20°30′ S, 41°53′ W 138
Bandeirante, Braz. 13°43′ S, 50°51′ W 138
Bandéko, Congo 1°56′ N, 17°27′ E 218
Bandelierkop, S. Af. 23°21′ S, 29°49′ E 227
Bandera, Arg. 28°52′ S, 62°17′ W 139
Bandera, Tex., U.S. 29°43′ N, 99°5′ W 92
Bandiagara, Mali 14°20′ N, 3°38′ W 222
Bandikui, India 27°2′ N, 76°35′ E 197
Bandırma, Turk. 40°19′ N, 27°57′ E 156
Bandon, Oreg., U.S. 43°6′ N, 124°24′ W 90
Bändovan Burnu, Azerb. 39°34′ N, 49°20′ E 195
Bandundu, Dem. Rep. of the Congo 3°24′ S, 17°23′ E 218
Bandundu, adm. division, Dem. Rep. of the Congo 4°38′ S, 16°30′ E 218
Bandung, Indonesia 7°1′ S, 107°32′ E 192
Băneasa, Rom. 45°57′ N, 27°55′ E 156
Bañeres, Sp. 38°43′ N, 0°40′ E 164
Banes, Cuba 20°58′ N, 75°44′ W 116
Banff, Can. 51°11′ N, 115°33′ W 108
Banff National Park, Can. 51°29′ N, 116°37′ W 238
Banfora, Burkina Faso 10°38′ N, 4°47′ W 222
Bang Mun Nak, Thai. 16°1′ N, 100°21′ E 202
Bang Saphan, Thai. 11°14′ N, 99°31′ E 202
Bangalore, India 12°59′ N, 77°35′ E 188
Bangar, Philippines 16°54′ N, 120°25′ E 203
Bangassou, Cen. Af. Rep. 4°38′ N, 22°48′ E 207
Banggai, Kepulauan, islands, Banda Sea 2°42′ S, 123°39′ E 192
Banggi, island, Malaysia 7°2′ N, 117°21′ E 192
Banghāzī (Benghazi), Lib. 32°6′ N, 20°4′ E 216
Banghiang, river, Laos 16°17′ N, 105°14′ E 202
Bangka, island, Indonesia 2°24′ S, 106°18′ E 192
Bangkaru, island, Indonesia 1°52′ N, 97°4′ E 196
Bangkinang, Indonesia 0°21′ N, 101°1′ E 196
Bangkok see Krung Thep, Thai. 13°44′ N, 100°24′ E 202
Bangladesh 24°0′ N, 90°0′ E 188
Bangor, Me., U.S. 44°48′ N, 68°47′ W 111
Bangor, Mich., U.S. 42°18′ N, 86°7′ W 102
Bangor, U.K. 53°13′ N, 4°7′ W 162
Bangs, Tex., U.S. 31°41′ N, 99°8′ W 92
Bangs, Mount, Ariz., U.S. 36°46′ N, 113°54′ W 101
Bangu, Dem. Rep. of the Congo 9°5′ S, 23°43′ E 224
Bangué, Cameroon 3°12′ N, 15°9′ E 218
Bangued, Philippines 17°37′ N, 120°38′ E 203
Bangui, Cen. Af. Rep. 4°21′ N, 18°22′ E 218
Bangui, Congo 2°28′ N, 17°16′ E 218
Bangui, Philippines 18°32′ N, 120°46′ E 203
Banguru, Dem. Rep. of the Congo 0°28′ N, 27°6′ E 224
Bangwade, Dem. Rep. of the Congo 1°0′ N, 25°14′ E 224
Banh, Burkina Faso 14°4′ N, 2°27′ W 222
Banhine National Park, Mozambique 22°54′ S, 32°6′ E 227
Bani, Cen. Af. Rep. 7°7′ N, 22°54′ E 218
Baní, Dom. Rep. 18°16′ N, 70°20′ W 116
Bani, Jebel, Mor. 29°44′ N, 7°57′ W 214

Bani, river, Mali 13°31' N, 4°52' W 222
Banī Sharfā, Saudi Arabia 19°38' N, 41°30' E 182
Banī Walīd, Lib. 31°46' N, 14°0' E 216
Bania, Cen. Af. Rep. 4°6' N, 16°6' E 218
Bania, Côte d'Ivoire 9°0' N, 3°10' W 222
Banihal Pass, India 33°30' N, 75°12' E 186
Banikoara, Benin 11°19' N, 2°27' E 222
Baniou, Alg. 35°24' N, 4°20' E 150
Bāniyās, Syr. 35°11' N, 35°57' E 194
Banja, Serb. and Mont. 43°33' N, 19°33' E 168
Banja Koviljača, Serb. and Mont. 44°30' N, 19°9' E 168
Banja Luka, Bosn. and Herzg. 44°46' N, 17°10' E 168
Banjarmasin, Indonesia 3°24' S, 114°29' E 192
Banjska, Serb. and Mont. 42°58' N, 20°47' E 168
Banjul, Gambia 13°23' N, 16°38' W 222
Bankä, Azerb. 39°25' N, 49°15' E 195
Bankas, Mali 14°4' N, 3°33' W 222
Banket, Zimb. 17°25' S, 30°24' E 224
Bankilare, Niger 14°27' N, 0°44' E 222
Bankim, Cameroon 6°4' N, 11°29' E 222
Bankor, Mali 16°51' N, 3°47' W 222
Banks Island, Can. 53°3' N, 130°60' W 98
Banks Island, Can. 73°31' N, 129°47' W 106
Banks Islands, Coral Sea 14°34' S, 168°7' E 238
Banks Peninsula, N.Z. 43°50' S, 172°37' E 240
Bankura, India 23°12' N, 87°4' E 197
Bankya, Bulg. 42°42' N, 23°8' E 168
Bannalec, Fr. 47°55' N, 3°42' W 150
Banner, Wyo., U.S. 44°36' N, 106°52' W 90
Banning, Calif., U.S. 33°56' N, 116°54' W 101
Bannock Peak, Idaho, U.S. 42°36' N, 112°46' W 90
Bannock Range, Idaho, U.S. 42°34' N, 112°36' W 90
Bannu, Pak. 32°57' N, 70°38' E 186
Banova Jaruga, Croatia 45°26' N, 16°55' E 168
Banovići, Bosn. and Herzg. 44°24' N, 18°28' E 168
Banow, Afghan. 35°36' N, 69°20' E 186
Bánréve, Slovakia 48°18' N, 20°21' E 156
Bansang, Gambia 13°25' N, 14°41' W 222
Banská Bystrica, Slovakia 48°44' N, 19°8' E 152
Banskobystrický, adm. division, Slovakia 48°28' N, 18°34' E 152
Bantaeng, Indonesia 5°31' S, 119°52' E 192
Bantala, Ghana 9°51' N, 1°49' W 222
Bantam, Conn., U.S. 41°43' N, 73°14' W 104
Banyak, Kepulauan, islands, Indian Ocean 1°45' N, 96°30' E 196
Banyas, Israel 33°14' N, 35°41' E 194
Banyo, Cameroon 6°42' N, 11°48' E 218
Banyos, Cap de, Sp. 39°51' N, 3°36' E 164
Banyuwangi, Indonesia 8°10' S, 114°21' E 192
Banzare Coast, Antarctica 68°40' S, 129°50' E 248
Bao Bilia, spring, Chad 16°27' N, 22°56' E 226
Bao Flala, Mali 12°12' N, 6°35' W 222
Bao Ha, Vietnam 22°13' N, 104°20' E 202
Bao Lac, Vietnam 22°58' N, 105°39' E 198
Baode, China 38°57' N, 111°2' E 198
Baoding, China 38°51' N, 115°28' E 198
Baofeng, China 33°52' N, 113°5' E 198
Baogarada, Chad 12°9' N, 16°19' E 216
Baoji, China 34°25' N, 107°9' E 198
Baojing, China 28°41' N, 109°41' E 198
Baoro, Cen. Af. Rep. 5°39' N, 15°57' E 218
Baoshan, China 25°8' N, 99°8' E 190
Baoting, China 18°36' N, 109°39' E 198
Baotou, China 40°36' N, 110°0' E 198
Baoulé, Mali 12°56' N, 8°36' W 222
Baoulé, river, Mali 13°57' N, 9°27' W 222
Baoying, China 33°16' N, 119°22' E 198
Bapaume, Fr. 50°5' N, 2°50' E 163
Bapia, Dem. Rep. of the Congo 4°24' N, 24°57' E 224
Baqên, China 31°54' N, 93°59' E 188
Baqty, Kaz. 46°41' N, 82°48' E 184
Ba'qūbah, Iraq 33°43' N, 44°40' E 180
Bar, Serb. and Mont. 42°5' N, 19°5' E 168
Bar, Ukr. 49°4' N, 27°44' E 152
Bărăganul, Rom. 44°15' N, 26°55' E 156
Bar Harbor, Me., U.S. 44°23' N, 68°12' W 82
Bar Mills, Me., U.S. 43°36' N, 70°33' W 104
Bara, Sudan 13°41' N, 30°20' E 226
Bara Banki, India 26°54' N, 81°11' E 197
Bara Simbil, Jebel, peak, Sudan 13°27' N, 24°10' E 226
Baraawe, Somalia 1°3' N, 44°2' E 218
Barabinsk, Russ. 55°17' N, 78°23' E 184
Baraboo, Wis., U.S. 43°28' N, 89°44' W 94
Baraboo, river, Wis., U.S. 43°30' N, 90°5' W 102
Baraboulé, Burkina Faso 14°13' N, 1°52' W 222
Baracoa, Cuba 20°20' N, 74°30' W 116
Baradá, river, Syr. 33°36' N, 36°1' E 194
Baradero, Arg. 33°51' S, 59°30' W 139
Baraga, Mich., U.S. 46°47' N, 88°31' W 94
Baragoi, Kenya 1°44' N, 36°47' E 224
Barahona, Dom. Rep. 18°11' N, 71°5' W 116
Barakat, Sudan 14°13' N, 33°35' E 182
Baram, river, Malaysia 3°55' N, 113°58' E 192
Baramandougou, Mali 13°37' N, 4°38' W 222
Baramula, India 34°10' N, 74°23' E 186
Baran', Belarus 54°29' N, 28°40' E 166
Baran, India 25°5' N, 76°31' E 197
Baranama, Guinea 10°11' N, 8°46' W 222
Baranavichy, Belarus 53°6' N, 26°1' E 152
Baranoa, Col. 10°47' N, 74°57' W 136
Baranof Island, Alas., U.S. 56°3' N, 135°55' W 98
Baranovka, Russ. 49°55' N, 46°2' E 158
Baranya, adm. division, Hung. 45°55' N, 17°41' E 156
Barão de Grajaú, Braz. 6°43' S, 43°3' W 132
Barão de Melgaço, Braz. 16°15' S, 55°57' W 132
Barassoli, spring, Eritrea 13°36' N, 42°5' E 182
Barat Daya, Kepulauan, islands, Banda Sea 6°36' S, 126°45' E 192
Barataria, La., U.S. 29°43' N, 90°8' W 103
Barataria Bay 29°22' N, 90°11' W 103
Barbacena, Braz. 21°13' S, 43°46' W 138
Barbacoas, Col. 1°38' N, 78°13' W 136
Barbadillo, Sp. 40°55' N, 5°52' W 150
Barbadillo del Mercado, Sp. 42°2' N, 3°22' W 164
Barbados 13°0' N, 60°0' W 116
Barbaria, Cap de, Sp. 38°19' N, 1°24' E 150
Barbas, Cap, Western Sahara 21°56' N, 16°47' W 214
Barbastro, Sp. 42°2' N, 0°7' E 164
Barbate, Sp. 36°11' N, 5°57' W 164
Barbazan, Fr. 43°2' N, 0°36' E 164
Bārbele, Latv. 56°26' N, 24°35' E 166
Barberton, Ohio, U.S. 41°0' N, 81°37' W 110
Barberton, S. Af. 25°50' S, 31°0' E 227
Barberville, Fla., U.S. 29°11' N, 81°26' W 105
Barbosa, Col. 5°56' N, 73°39' W 136
Barbourville, Ky., U.S. 36°52' N, 83°54' W 96
Barbuda, island, Antigua and Barbuda 17°45' N, 61°51' W 116
Barcarrota, Sp. 38°31' N, 6°52' W 164
Barce see Al Marj, Lib. 32°30' N, 20°53' E 216
Barcelona, Sp. 41°23' N, 2°10' E 164
Barcelona, Venez. 10°5' N, 64°44' W 136
Barcelonnette, Fr. 44°23' N, 6°38' E 167
Barcelos, Braz. 0°60' N, 62°58' W 130
Barco, N.C., U.S. 36°23' N, 75°60' W 96
Barcs, Hung. 45°57' N, 17°28' E 168
Barczewo, Pol. 53°50' N, 20°40' E 166
Bard, Calif., U.S. 32°47' N, 114°34' W 101
Bärdä, Azerb. 40°23' N, 47°6' E 195
Barda, Russ. 56°56' N, 55°39' E 154
Barda Hills, India 21°50' N, 69°41' E 186
Bardaale, Somalia 7°0' N, 47°54' E 218
Bardaï, Chad 21°20' N, 17°1' E 216
Bardas Blancas, Arg. 35°52' S, 69°50' W 134
Bardawīl, Sabkhet el 31°7' N, 33°2' E 194
Barddhaman, India 23°13' N, 87°52' E 197
Bardoli, India 21°8' N, 73°7' E 186
Bardon Hill, peak, U.K. 52°42' N, 1°21' W 162
Bardonecchia, It. 45°5' N, 6°42' E 167
Bardstown, Ky., U.S. 37°47' N, 85°29' W 94
Bardwell, Ky., U.S. 36°51' N, 89°1' W 96
Bare Mountain, Nev., U.S. 36°50' N, 116°43' W 101
Barèges, Fr. 42°53' N, 6°357' E 164
Bareilly, India 28°20' N, 79°24' E 197
Barents Plain, Arctic Ocean 83°46' N, 15°37' E 255
Barents Sea 71°12' N, 27°58' E 152
Barentsburg, Nor. 77°58' N, 14°33' E 160
Barentsøya, island, Nor. 78°41' N, 22°17' E 246
Barentu, Eritrea 15°6' N, 37°35' E 182
Barevo, Bosn. and Herzg. 44°25' N, 17°14' E 168
Barfleur, Pointe de, Fr. 49°39' N, 1°54' W 150
Barga, China 30°52' N, 81°19' E 197
Barga, It. 44°5' N, 10°29' E 167
Bargaal, Somalia 11°13' N, 51°3' E 216
Bargarh, India 21°19' N, 83°35' E 188
Bargē, Eth. 6°13' N, 36°53' E 224
Bârgo, peak, Nor. 66°16' N, 18°7' E 152
Barguzin, Russ. 53°41' N, 109°32' E 190
Barham, Mount, Can. 59°44' N, 133°36' W 98
Barharwa, India 24°51' N, 87°47' E 197
Barhi, India 24°14' N, 85°23' E 197
Barhi, India 23°56' N, 80°51' E 197
Bari, Dem. Rep. of the Congo 3°22' N, 19°24' E 218
Bari, India 26°37' N, 77°36' E 197
Bari, It. 41°7' N, 16°51' E 156
Baridi, Tanzania 1°60' S, 33°55' E 224
Barika, Alg. 35°21' N, 5°22' E 150
Barikowt, Afghan. 35°17' N, 71°32' E 186
Baril Lake, Can. 58°45' N, 111°57' W 108
Barīm (Perim), island, Yemen 12°36' N, 42°32' E 182
Barinas, Venez. 8°38' N, 70°15' W 136
Barinas, adm. division, Venez. 8°23' N, 70°58' W 136
Baringa, Dem. Rep. of the Congo 0°42' N, 20°53' E 218
Baripada, India 21°57' N, 86°43' E 197
Bariri, Braz. 22°5' S, 48°41' W 138
Bârîs, Egypt 24°40' N, 30°30' E 182
Barisal, Bangladesh 22°42' N, 90°17' E 197
Barisan, Pegunungan, Indonesia 1°4' S, 100°23' E 196
Barito, river, Indonesia 2°13' S, 114°39' E 192
Baritú National Park, Arg. 22°25' S, 64°46' W 137
Bark Lake, Can. 46°50' N, 82°54' W 94
Bark Point, Wis., U.S. 46°40' N, 91°13' W 94
Barkā', Oman 23°40' N, 57°54' E 196
Barkald, Nor. 61°59' N, 10°54' E 152
Barkley, Lake, Ky., U.S. 36°20' N, 88°40' W 81
Barkley Sound 48°50' N, 125°50' W 108
Barkly East, S. Af. 30°58' S, 27°33' E 227
Barkly Tableland, Austral. 19°43' S, 136°41' E 230
Barkly West, S. Af. 28°33' S, 24°31' E 227
Barkol, China 43°31' N, 92°51' E 190
Barksdale, Tex., U.S. 29°44' N, 100°2' W 92
Barksdale Air Force Base, La., U.S. 32°27' N, 93°42' W 103
Barla Dağı, peak, Turk. 38°2' N, 30°37' E 156
Bar-le-Duc, Fr. 48°46' N, 5°10' E 163
Barlee Range Nature Reserve, Austral. 23°21' S, 115°39' E 238
Barlow Pass, Oreg., U.S. 45°16' N, 121°42' W 90
Barmer, India 25°43' N, 71°23' E 186
Barmou, Niger 15°8' N, 5°27' E 222
Barmouth, U.K. 52°43' N, 4°3' W 162
Barnard, Vt., U.S. 43°43' N, 72°38' W 104
Barnaul, Russ. 53°23' N, 83°48' E 184
Barnegat, N.J., U.S. 39°45' N, 74°14' W 94
Barnegat Light, N.J., U.S. 39°44' N, 74°7' W 94
Barnes Ice Cap, Can. 68°46' N, 73°57' W 106
Barnes Sound 25°13' N, 80°35' W 105
Barnesville, Minn., U.S. 46°37' N, 96°26' W 90
Barnesville, Ohio, U.S. 39°58' N, 81°11' W 102
Barnet, Vt., U.S. 44°17' N, 72°4' W 104
Barnhart, Tex., U.S. 31°6' N, 101°10' W 92
Barnoldswick, U.K. 53°55' N, 2°12' W 162
Barnsley, U.K. 53°32' N, 1°28' W 162
Barnstaple, U.K. 51°5' N, 4°3' W 162
Barnum, Minn., U.S. 46°29' N, 92°44' W 94
Baro, Nig. 8°33' N, 6°22' E 222
Barons, Can. 49°59' N, 113°5' W 90
Barouéli, Mali 13°4' N, 6°50' W 222
Barpeta, India 26°19' N, 90°57' E 197
Barques, Pointe aux, Mich., U.S. 44°4' N, 82°55' W 102
Barquisimeto, Venez. 10°0' N, 69°19' W 136
Barr, Fr. 48°24' N, 7°26' E 163
Barra, Braz. 11°6' S, 43°11' W 132
Barra da Estiva, Braz. 13°39' S, 41°20' W 138
Barra de Navidad, Mex. 19°12' N, 104°43' W 114
Barra de São João, Braz. 22°34' S, 41°60' W 138
Barra del Tordo, Mex. 23°0' N, 97°47' W 114
Barra do Bugres, Braz. 15°4' S, 57°13' W 132
Barra do Corda, Braz. 5°33' S, 45°15' W 132
Barra do Cuanza, Angola 9°18' S, 13°7' E 220
Barra do Dande, Angola 8°29' S, 13°21' E 218
Barra do Garças, Braz. 15°53' S, 52°16' W 138
Barra do Piraí, Braz. 22°30' S, 43°46' W 138
Barra do Quaraí, Uru. 30°15' S, 57°34' W 139
Barra do São Manuel, Braz. 7°19' S, 58°2' W 130
Barra Head, U.K. 56°38' N, 8°2' W 150
Barra Mansa, Braz. 10°58' S, 43°8' W 123
Barra Mansa, Braz. 22°34' S, 44°9' W 138
Barra Patuca, Hond. 15°48' N, 84°18' W 115
Barra, Ponta da, Mozambique 23°42' S, 35°29' E 227
Barracão do Barreto, Braz. 8°50' S, 58°25' W 130
Barrage Daniel-Johnson, dam, Can. 50°23' N, 69°12' W 111
Barrage Gouin, dam, Can. 48°7' N, 74°5' W 94
Barragem, Mozambique 24°24' S, 32°53' E 227
Barrancabermeja, Col. 7°3' N, 73°50' W 136
Barrancas, Venez. 8°43' N, 62°14' W 116
Barranco Branco, Braz. 19°35' S, 56°8' W 132
Barranco Branco, Braz. 21°7' S, 57°51' W 134
Barrancos de Guadalupe, Mex. 29°57' N, 104°45' W 92
Barranqueras, Arg. 27°30' S, 58°57' W 139
Barranquilla, Col. 10°57' N, 74°50' W 136
Barras, Braz. 4°17' S, 42°19' W 132
Barras, Col. 1°46' S, 73°13' W 136
Barraute, Can. 48°26' N, 77°40' W 94
Barrax, Sp. 39°2' N, 2°13' W 164
Barre, Mass., U.S. 42°25' N, 72°7' W 104
Barre, Vt., U.S. 44°12' N, 72°31' W 104
Barreiras, Braz. 12°10' S, 44°58' W 132
Barreirinha, Braz. 2°49' S, 57°5' W 130
Barreiro, Port. 38°36' N, 9°8' W 214
Barrême, Fr. 43°57' N, 6°21' E 167
Barren Island, U.S. 52°44' N, 60°8' W 134
Barretos, Braz. 20°35' S, 48°36' W 138
Barrhead, Can. 54°8' N, 114°25' W 108
Barrie, Can. 44°23' N, 79°42' W 94
Barrier Bay 67°42' S, 78°28' E 248
Barrier Range, Austral. 31°5' S, 140°54' E 230
Barriles, ruin(s), Pan. 8°42' N, 82°50' W 115
Barrington, Ill., U.S. 42°9' N, 88°8' W 102
Barrington, N.H., U.S. 43°13' N, 71°3' W 104
Barrington, R.I., U.S. 41°44' N, 71°19' W 104
Barro Alto, Braz. 15°6' S, 48°58' W 138
Barrocão, Braz. 16°24' S, 43°16' W 138
Barron, Wis., U.S. 45°23' N, 91°52' W 94
Barrow, Alas., U.S. 71°8' N, 156°35' W 98
Barrow Canyon, Arctic Ocean 72°4' N, 151°21' W 255
Barrow Creek, Austral. 21°33' S, 133°54' E 231
Barrow in Furness, U.K. 54°7' N, 3°13' W 162
Barrow Island, Austral. 20°51' S, 114°19' E 230
Barrow, Point, Alas., U.S. 71°40' N, 155°42' W 246
Barrow Strait 74°8' N, 97°17' W 106
Barrows, Can. 52°49' N, 101°27' W 108
Barry, U.K. 51°23' N, 3°17' W 162
Barry, Lac, lake, Can. 48°59' N, 75°59' W 94
Barry's Bay, Can. 45°28' N, 77°41' W 94
Barryton, Mich., U.S. 43°44' N, 85°9' W 102
Barrytown, N.Z. 42°15' S, 171°20' E 240
Barshatas, Kaz. 48°4' N, 78°32' E 184
Barshyn, Kaz. 49°37' N, 69°30' E 184
Barsi, India 18°14' N, 75°41' E 188
Barstow, Calif., U.S. 34°53' N, 117°2' W 101
Bar-sur-Aube, Fr. 48°13' N, 4°43' E 163
Bārta, Latv. 56°21' N, 21°18' E 166
Bārta, river, Latv. 56°18' N, 21°2' E 166
Barter Island, Alas., U.S. 70°11' N, 145°51' W 106
Barthelemy Pass, Laos 19°31' N, 104°1' E 202
Bartica, Guyana 6°19' N, 58°41' W 130
Bartın, Turk. 41°38' N, 32°20' E 156
Bartlesville, Okla., U.S. 36°43' N, 95°59' W 96
Bartlett, Nebr., U.S. 41°51' N, 98°33' W 90
Bartlett, N.H., U.S. 44°4' N, 71°18' W 104
Bartlett, Tex., U.S. 30°46' N, 97°26' W 92
Bartolomeu Dias, Mozambique 21°12' S, 35°6' E 227
Barton, N. Dak., U.S. 48°29' N, 100°12' W 94
Barton upon Humber, U.K. 53°40' N, 0°27' E 162
Bartoszyce, Pol. 54°14' N, 20°48' E 166
Bartow, Fla., U.S. 27°50' N, 81°51' W 112
Bartow, Ger. 53°49' N, 13°20' E 152
Barú, Volcán, Pan. 8°47' N, 82°41' W 115
Barus, Indonesia 2°3' N, 98°22' E 196
Baruth, Ger. 52°4' N, 13°29' E 152
Baruun Urt, Mongolia 46°40' N, 113°16' E 198
Baruunharaa, Mongolia 48°58' N, 106°3' E 198
Baruunsuu, Mongolia 43°45' N, 105°31' E 198
Barvinkove, Ukr. 48°56' N, 37°6' E 158
Barysaw, Belarus 54°13' N, 28°29' E 166
Barysh, Russ. 53°39' N, 47°13' E 154
Barzas, Russ. 55°45' N, 86°29' E 169
Bāsa'īdū, Iran 26°37' N, 55°17' E 196
Basail, Arg. 27°51' S, 59°18' W 139
Basal, Pak. 33°32' N, 72°19' E 186
Basankusu, Dem. Rep. of the Congo 1°7' N, 19°50' E 207
Basargech'ar, Arm. 40°12' N, 45°42' E 195
Basaseachic, Mex. 28°10' N, 108°11' W 92
Basavilbaso, Arg. 32°23' S, 58°51' W 139
Basco, Philippines 20°25' N, 121°58' E 203
Bas-Congo, adm. division, Dem. Rep. of the Congo 5°10' S, 13°44' E 218
Bascuñán, Cabo, Chile 28°48' S, 72°52' W 134
Basekpio, Dem. Rep. of the Congo 4°45' N, 24°38' E 224
Basel, Switz. 47°33' N, 7°35' E 150
Basey, Philippines 11°18' N, 125°3' E 203
Bashaw, Can. 52°35' N, 112°59' W 108
Bashi, Ala., U.S. 31°57' N, 87°51' W 103
Bashi Channel 21°28' N, 120°30' E 198
Bashkortostan, adm. division, Russ. 54°0' N, 55°48' E 154
Basilan, island, Philippines 6°14' N, 122°25' E 192
Basile, La., U.S. 30°28' N, 92°37' W 103
Basiliano, It. 46°1' N, 13°5' E 167
Basilicata, adm. division, It. 40°59' N, 15°38' E 156
Basilio, Braz. 31°53' S, 53°2' W 139
Basin, Wyo., U.S. 44°21' N, 108°3' W 90
Basin Harbor, Vt., U.S. 44°11' N, 73°22' W 104
Basinger, Fla., U.S. 27°23' N, 81°2' W 105
Basingstoke, U.K. 51°16' N, 1°6' W 162
Basirhat, India 22°40' N, 88°48' E 197
Baška, Croatia 44°58' N, 14°44' E 156
Başkale, Turk. 38°2' N, 43°56' E 195
Baskin, La., U.S. 32°14' N, 91°44' W 103
Baskomutan National Park, Turk. 38°51' N, 30°15' E 156
Baslow, U.K. 53°15' N, 1°37' W 162
Basoda, India 23°51' N, 77°56' E 197
Basoko, Dem. Rep. of the Congo 1°17' N, 23°35' E 224
Basongo, Dem. Rep. of the Congo 4°23' S, 20°22' E 218
Basque Country, adm. division, Sp. 43°10' N, 3°2' W 164
Basra see Al Başrah, Iraq 30°30' N, 47°48' E 207
Bass Islands, Lake Erie 41°36' N, 82°60' W 102
Bass Lake, Calif., U.S. 37°20' N, 119°34' W 100
Bass Strait 39°32' S, 143°59' E 231
Bassae, ruin(s), Gr. 37°25' N, 21°42' E 156
Bassano, Can. 50°47' N, 112°29' W 90
Bassano del Grappa, It. 45°46' N, 11°44' E 167
Bassar, Togo 9°14' N, 0°46' E 222
Bassas da India, adm. division, Fr. 21°15' S, 39°13' E 220
Basse Santa Su, Gambia 13°17' N, 14°15' W 222
Basse-Normandie, adm. division, Fr. 49°7' N, 1°9' W 150
Basse-Terre, Fr. 16°0' N, 61°44' W 116
Basseterre, Saint Kitts and Nevis 17°0' N, 63°0' W 118
Basse-Terre, island, Fr. 16°10' N, 62°34' W 116
Bassett, Nebr., U.S. 42°33' N, 99°33' W 90
Bassfield, Miss., U.S. 31°28' N, 89°45' W 103
Bassigbiri, Cen. Af. Rep. 5°18' N, 26°54' E 224
Bassikounou, Mauritania 15°52' N, 5°58' W 222
Bastak, Iran 27°11' N, 54°25' E 196
Bastar, India 19°14' N, 81°58' E 188
Bastevarre, peak, Nor. 68°57' N, 22°12' E 152
Basti, India 26°46' N, 82°44' E 197
Bastia, Fr. 42°40' N, 9°23' E 214
Bastimentos, Isla, island, Pan. 9°23' N, 82°9' W 115
Bastrop, La., U.S. 32°46' N, 91°55' W 103
Bastrop, Tex., U.S. 30°6' N, 97°19' W 92
Bastuträsk, Nor. 64°46' N, 20°1' E 152
Bastyn', Belarus 52°23' N, 26°44' E 152
Basuo see Dongfang, China 19°3' N, 108°38' E 198
Bat Yam, Israel 32°1' N, 34°44' E 194
Bata, Equatorial Guinea 2°1' N, 9°47' E 207
Bata, Rom. 46°1' N, 22°2' E 168
Batac, Philippines 18°4' N, 120°33' E 203
Batagay, Russ. 67°42' N, 134°52' E 160
Batagay Alyta, Russ. 67°47' N, 130°22' E 160
Batajnica, Serb. and Mont. 44°53' N, 20°17' E 168
Batala, India 31°47' N, 75°13' E 186
Batam, island, Indonesia 0°53' N, 103°40' E 196
Batama, Dem. Rep. of the Congo 0°53' N, 26°35' E 224
Batamay, Russ. 63°30' N, 129°24' E 160
Batamorghab, Afghan. 35°37' N, 63°20' E 186
Batan, island, Philippines 20°30' N, 122°3' E 198
Batan Islands, Philippine Sea 20°36' N, 122°2' E 203
Batang, China 30°6' N, 98°58' E 190
Batang Ai National Park, Malaysia 1°14' N, 111°42' E 238
Batang Berjuntai, Malaysia 3°22' N, 101°25' E 196
Batanga, Gabon 0°19' N, 9°21' E 218
Batangafo, Cen. Af. Rep. 7°15' N, 18°18' E 218
Batangas, Philippines 13°48' N, 121°2' E 203
Batangtoru, Indonesia 1°30' N, 99°4' E 196
Batara, Cen. Af. Rep. 5°50' N, 16°8' E 218
Bátaszék, Hung. 46°11' N, 18°42' E 168
Batatais, Braz. 20°55' S, 47°36' W 138
Batavia, N.Y., U.S. 42°59' N, 78°11' W 94
Bataysk, Russ. 47°6' N, 39°46' E 156
Batchawana Bay, Can. 46°56' N, 84°36' W 94
Batchawana Mountain, Can. 47°5' N, 84°29' W 94
Batesville, Ark., U.S. 35°45' N, 91°42' W 96
Batesville, Miss., U.S. 34°17' N, 89°57' W 96
Batesville, Tex., U.S. 28°56' N, 99°38' W 92
Batetskaya, Russ. 58°38' N, 30°22' E 166
Bath, Me., U.S. 43°54' N, 69°50' W 104
Bath, N.H., U.S. 44°9' N, 71°58' W 104
Bath, N.Y., U.S. 42°20' N, 77°20' W 94
Bath, U.K. 51°23' N, 2°23' W 162
Bathurst, Can. 47°32' N, 65°44' W 106
Bathurst, S. Af. 33°32' S, 26°48' E 227
Bathurst, Cape, Can. 70°19' N, 130°47' W 98
Bathurst Inlet 67°37' N, 110°60' W 106
Bathurst Inlet, Can. 66°24' N, 107°24' W 73
Bathurst Island, Austral. 12°5' S, 128°51' E 230
Bathurst Island, Can. 74°41' N, 102°4' W 106
Batī, Eth. 11°12' N, 40°1' E 224
Batié, Burkina Faso 9°54' N, 2°58' W 222
Batina, Croatia 45°49' N, 18°48' E 168
Batista, Serra da, Braz. 6°40' S, 41°49' W 132
Batkanu, Sierra Leone 9°3' N, 12°25' W 222
Batlava, Serb. and Mont. 42°50' N, 21°14' E 168
Batley, U.K. 53°43' N, 1°38' W 162
Batman, Turk. 37°53' N, 41°10' E 195
Batna, Alg. 35°31' N, 6°8' E 150
Batoche National Historic Site, Can. 52°42' N, 106°10' W 108
Batočina, Serb. and Mont. 44°9' N, 21°3' E 168
Baton Rouge, La., U.S. 30°25' N, 91°13' W 103
Batopilas, Mex. 27°1' N, 107°45' W 112
Batouri, Cameroon 4°25' N, 14°20' E 218
Batovi see Tamitatoala, river, Braz. 14°11' S, 53°58' W 132
Batrina, Croatia 45°11' N, 17°39' E 168
Bătrîna, Rom. 45°48' N, 22°35' E 168
Batroun, Leb. 34°16' N, 35°40' E 194
Batsí, Gr. 37°51' N, 24°46' E 156
Batson, Tex., U.S. 30°13' N, 94°37' W 103
Battambang, Cambodia 13°7' N, 103°11' E 202
Battenberg, Ger. 51°0' N, 8°39' E 167
Batticaloa, Sri Lanka 7°44' N, 81°43' E 188
Battle, U.K. 50°54' N, 0°29' E 162
Battle Creek, Mich., U.S. 42°18' N, 85°12' W 102
Battle Creek, river, Mont., U.S. 49°3' N, 109°29' W 108
Battle Ground, Ind., U.S. 40°30' N, 86°50' W 102
Battle Ground, Wash., U.S. 45°46' N, 122°33' W 100
Battle Harbour, Can. 52°15' N, 55°38' W 111
Battle Mountain, Nev., U.S. 40°43' N, 117°19' W 90
Battle, river, Can. 52°17' N, 112°10' W 80
Battleford, Can. 52°43' N, 108°20' W 108
Battonya, Hung. 46°17' N, 21°2' E 168
Batu, Kepulauan, islands, Tanahmasa 5°297' N, 98°10' E 196
Batu Pahat, Malaysia 1°52' N, 102°56' E 196
Batu, peak, Eth. 6°53' N, 39°39' E 224
Bat'umi, Ga. 41°38' N, 41°38' E 195
Batupanjang, Indonesia 1°45' N, 101°33' E 196
Baturaja, Indonesia 4°10' S, 104°9' E 192
Baturino, Russ. 57°42' N, 85°17' E 169
Baturité, Braz. 4°20' S, 38°54' W 132
Baturité, Serra de, Braz. 4°45' S, 39°36' W 132
Batys Qazaqstan, adm. division, Kaz. 49°52' N, 49°51' E 158
Bau, Sudan 11°22' N, 34°6' E 216
Baú, river, Braz. 6°41' S, 52°57' W 130
Baubau, Indonesia 5°36' S, 122°41' E 192
Bauchi, Nig. 10°19' N, 9°50' E 222
Baudeau, Lac, lake, Can. 51°37' N, 73°44' W 110
Baudette, Minn., U.S. 48°41' N, 94°39' W 90
Baudó, Col. 5°1' N, 77°7' W 136
Baudó, Serranía de, Col. 5°31' N, 78°6' W 115
Bauges, Fr. 45°34' N, 5°59' E 165
Bauld, Cape, Can. 51°40' N, 55°58' W 111
Baunatal, Ger. 51°15' N, 9°26' E 167
Baunei, It. 40°2' N, 9°39' E 156
Baunt, Russ. 55°20' N, 113°12' E 190
Baure, Nig. 12°50' N, 8°44' E 222
Baures, Bol. 13°39' S, 63°36' W 137
Baures, river, Bol. 12°43' S, 64°5' W 137
Bauru, Braz. 22°21' S, 49°5' W 138
Baús, Braz. 18°27' S, 52°60' W 138
Bauska, Latv. 56°24' N, 24°11' E 166
Bautino, Kaz. 44°33' N, 50°16' E 158
Bauya, Sierra Leone 8°10' N, 12°37' W 222
Baŭyrzhan Momyshuly, Kaz. 42°37' N, 70°45' E 197
Bavanište, Serb. and Mont. 44°48' N, 20°52' E 168
Bavaria, adm. division, Ger. 49°12' N, 11°22' E 167
Bavay, Fr. 50°16' N, 3°48' E 163
Bavícora, Mex. 29°43' N, 110°11' W 92
Bavispe, river, Mex. 30°27' N, 109°6' W 92
Bavly, Russ. 54°21' N, 53°24' E 154
Bawītī, Egypt 28°21' N, 28°50' E 180
Bawku, Ghana 11°3' N, 0°16' E 222
Bawlake, Myanmar 19°11' N, 97°17' E 202
Bawlf, Can. 52°54' N, 112°28' W 108
Bawmi, Myanmar 17°20' N, 94°36' E 202
Bawtry, U.K. 53°26' N, 1°1' W 162
Baxaya, peak, Somalia 11°17' N, 49°35' E 218
Baxdo, Somalia 5°48' N, 47°17' E 218
Baxley, Ga., U.S. 31°46' N, 82°22' W 96
Baxoi, China 30°2' N, 96°57' E 188
Baxter, Minn., U.S. 46°21' N, 94°18' W 94
Baxter Peak, Colo., U.S. 39°39' N, 107°24' W 90
Baxterville, Miss., U.S. 31°4' N, 89°37' W 103
Bay City, Mich., U.S. 43°35' N, 83°53' W 102
Bay City, Tex., U.S. 28°58' N, 95°58' W 96
Bay City, Wis., U.S. 44°35' N, 92°27' W 94
Bay de Verde, Can. 48°6' N, 52°54' W 111
Bay Minette, Ala., U.S. 30°51' N, 87°46' W 103
Bay Port, Mich., U.S. 43°50' N, 83°23' W 102
Bay Roberts, Can. 47°35' N, 53°16' W 111
Bay Saint Louis, Miss., U.S. 30°18' N, 89°20' W 103
Bay Shore, N.Y., U.S. 40°43' N, 73°16' W 104
Bay Springs, Miss., U.S. 31°58' N, 89°17' W 103
Baya, Dem. Rep. of the Congo 2°31' N, 20°17' E 218
Bay'ah, Oman 25°45' N, 56°18' E 196
Bayamo, Cuba 20°21' N, 76°38' W 115
Bayan, China 46°3' N, 127°25' E 198
Bayan, Mongolia 47°11' N, 107°33' E 198
Bayan, Mongolia 48°27' N, 111°0' E 198
Bayan Har Shan, China 34°35' N, 95°13' E 188
Bayan Har Shankou, pass, China 34°10' N, 97°41' E 188
Bayan Huxu see Horqin Youyi Zhongqi, China 45°5' N, 121°25' E 198
Bayan Mod, China 40°45' N, 104°31' E 198
Bayan Obo, China 41°46' N, 109°58' E 198
Bayan Ovoo, Mongolia 47°49' N, 112°4' E 198
Bayan Uul, Mongolia 49°5' N, 112°45' E 198
Bayana, India 26°53' N, 77°14' E 197
Bayanaūyl, Kaz. 50°45' N, 75°42' E 184
Bayanhongor, Mongolia 46°37' N, 100°8' E 190
Bayano, Lago, lake, Pan. 9°0' N, 78°60' W 116
Bayan-Ölgiy, adm. division, Mongolia 48°37' N, 89°55' E 184
Bayan-Ovoo, Mongolia 48°57' N, 111°25' E 198
Bayard, Nebr., U.S. 41°45' N, 103°21' W 92

Bayard, *N. Mex., U.S.* 32°44' N, 108°8' W **92**
Bayasgalant, *Mongolia* 46°57' N, 112°2' E **198**
Bayat, *Turk.* 38°58' N, 30°55' E **156**
Bayawan, *Philippines* 9°23' N, 122°48' E **203**
Baybay, *Philippines* 10°40' N, 124°50' E **203**
Bayboro, *N.C., U.S.* 35°9' N, 76°47' W **96**
Bayburt, *Turk.* 40°16' N, 40°14' E **195**
Baydhabo (Baidoa), *Somalia* 3°5' N, 43°41' E **218**
Bayerischer Wald, *Ger.* 48°59' N, 12°19' E **152**
Bayfield, *Can.* 43°32' N, 81°41' W **102**
Bayfield, *Wis., U.S.* 46°49' N, 90°50' W **94**
Bayghanïn, *Kaz.* 48°42' N, 55°53' E **158**
Bayḩān al Qişāb, *Yemen* 14°49' N, 45°46' E **182**
Baykal, Ozero, lake, *Russ.* 53°48' N, 103°44' E **190**
Baykalovo, *Russ.* 57°26' N, 63°42' E **154**
Baykalovo, *Russ.* 57°45' N, 67°40' E **169**
Baykan, *Turk.* 38°8' N, 41°47' E **195**
Baykurt, *China* 39°56' N, 75°32' E **184**
Bayliss, Mount, *Antarctica* 73°30' S, 62°4' E **248**
Baymak, *Russ.* 52°38' N, 58°11' E **154**
Baynū, *Leb.* 34°32' N, 36°10' E **194**
Bayombong, *Philippines* 16°29' N, 121°8' E **203**
Bayon, *Fr.* 48°28' N, 6°19' E **163**
Bayonet Point, *Fla., U.S.* 28°19' N, 82°43' W **105**
Bayonne, *Fr.* 43°29' N, 1°30' W **164**
Bayonne, *N.J., U.S.* 40°40' N, 74°8' W **104**
Bayou La Batre, *Ala., U.S.* 30°23' N, 88°16' W **103**
Bayou Macon, river, *La., U.S.* 32°6' N, 91°32' W **103**
Bayovar, *Peru* 5°47' S, 81°4' W **130**
Bayport, *Minn., U.S.* 45°0' N, 92°48' W **94**
Bayqongyr, *Kaz.* 47°47' N, 66°0' E **184**
Bayqongyr, adm. division, *Kaz.* 46°3' N, 62°27' E **184**
Bayramaly, *Turkm.* 37°36' N, 62°10' E **184**
Bayramiç, *Turk.* 39°48' N, 26°35' E **156**
Bayreuth, *Ger.* 49°56' N, 11°34' E **152**
Bays, Lake of, *Can.* 45°15' N, 79°35' W **94**
Bayshint, *Mongolia* 49°40' N, 90°20' E **184**
Bayshonas, *Kaz.* 47°18' N, 53°0' E **158**
Bayt al Faqīh, *Yemen* 14°29' N, 43°16' E **182**
Bayt Lahiyah, *Gaza Strip* 31°33' N, 34°30' E **194**
Bayt Laḩm (Bethlehem), *West Bank* 31°41' N, 35°12' E **194**
Baytīn, *West Bank* 31°55' N, 35°14' E **194**
Baytown, *Tex., U.S.* 29°43' N, 94°58' W **103**
Bayville, *N.Y., U.S.* 40°54' N, 73°34' W **104**
Bayyrqum, *Kaz.* 41°54' N, 68°5' E **184**
Bayzo, *Niger* 13°52' N, 4°45' E **222**
Baza, *Sp.* 37°29' N, 2°48' W **164**
Baza'i Gonbad, *Afghan.* 37°13' N, 74°5' E **186**
Bazar-Kurgan, *Kyrg.* 41°1' N, 72°46' E **197**
Bazarnyy Karabulak, *Russ.* 52°15' N, 46°27' E **158**
Bazarsholan, *Kaz.* 48°58' N, 51°55' E **158**
Bazartöbe, *Kaz.* 49°23' N, 51°53' E **158**
Bazaruto, Ilha do, island, *Mozambique* 21°44' S, 34°29' E **227**
Bazber, *Eth.* 10°36' N, 35°7' E **224**
Bazhong, *China* 31°53' N, 106°39' E **198**
Baziaş, *Rom.* 44°48' N, 21°22' E **168**
Bazin, river, *Can.* 47°29' N, 74°60' W **94**
Bazkovskaya, *Russ.* 49°33' N, 41°35' E **158**
Bazmān, Kūh-e, peak, *Iran* 27°51' N, 60°2' E **182**
Bazzano, *It.* 44°30' N, 11°4' E **167**
Bcharre, *Leb.* 34°14' N, 36°0' E **194**
Be, Nosy, island, *Madagascar* 13°24' S, 47°23' E **220**
Beach, *N. Dak., U.S.* 46°53' N, 104°1' W **90**
Beach Haven, *N.J., U.S.* 39°33' N, 74°16' W **94**
Beacon, *N.Y., U.S.* 41°29' N, 73°59' W **104**
Beaconsfield, *U.K.* 51°36' N, 0°39' E **162**
Beade, *Sp.* 42°19' N, 8°10' W **150**
Beale Air Force Base, *Calif., U.S.* 39°8' N, 121°30' W **90**
Beale, Cape, *Can.* 48°37' N, 125°31' W **90**
Beaminster, *U.K.* 50°48' N, 2°44' W **162**
Beampingaratra, peak, *Madagascar* 24°36' S, 46°39' E **220**
Bear Bay 75°23' N, 88°10' W **106**
Bear Creek, river, *Colo., U.S.* 37°26' N, 102°48' W **80**
Bear Island see Bjørnøya, *Nor.* 73°46' N, 15°27' E **160**
Bear Islands see Medvezh'i Ostrova, islands, *East Siberian Sea* 71°5' N, 151°1' E **160**
Bear Lake, *Can.* 55°2' N, 96°49' W **108**
Bear Lake, *Can.* 56°6' N, 127°4' W **108**
Bear Lake, *Mich., U.S.* 44°24' N, 86°9' W **94**
Bear Lodge Mountains, *Wyo., U.S.* 44°39' N, 104°42' W **90**
Bear Peninsula, *Antarctica* 74°18' S, 106°40' W **248**
Bear River, *Utah, U.S.* 41°37' N, 112°8' W **90**
Bear, river, *Idaho, U.S.* 42°27' N, 111°48' W **90**
Bear River Range, *Utah, U.S.* 41°18' N, 111°34' W **90**
Beardmore, *Can.* 49°37' N, 87°57' W **94**
Beardstown, *Mo., U.S.* 40°0' N, 90°25' W **94**
Béarn, region, *Europe* 42°57' N, 0°52' E **164**
Bears Paw Mountains, *Mont., U.S.* 48°18' N, 109°52' W **90**
Beas, *Sp.* 37°25' N, 6°48' W **164**
Beas de Segura, *Sp.* 38°14' N, 2°52' W **164**
Beasain, *Sp.* 43°2' N, 2°13' W **164**
Beata, Cabo, *Dom. Rep.* 17°30' N, 71°22' W **116**
Beata, Isla, island, *Dom. Rep.* 17°16' N, 71°33' W **116**
Beatrice, *Nebr., U.S.* 40°15' N, 96°45' W **90**
Beatton River, *Can.* 57°22' N, 121°27' W **108**
Beatton, river, *Can.* 57°18' N, 121°27' W **108**
Beatty, *Nev., U.S.* 36°54' N, 116°47' W **101**
Beattyville, *Can.* 48°51' N, 77°10' W **94**
Beatys Butte, peak, *Oreg., U.S.* 42°23' N, 119°25' W **90**
Beaucamps, *Fr.* 49°49' N, 1°47' E **163**
Beauceville, *Can.* 46°13' N, 70°46' W **111**
Beauchêne Island, *U.K.* 52°56' S, 61°53' W **134**
Beaufort, *Malaysia* 5°22' N, 115°46' E **203**
Beaufort, *S.C., U.S.* 32°24' N, 80°53' W **112**
Beaufort Marine Corps Air Station, *S.C., U.S.* 32°29' N, 80°48' W **96**
Beaufort Sea 69°54' N, 141°54' W **106**
Beaufort Sea 72°45' N, 137°20' W **255**
Beaufort see Belfort, ruin(s), *Leb.* 33°19' N, 35°30' E **194**
Beaufort Shelf, *Beaufort Sea* 70°4' N, 142°6' W **255**
Beaufort Slope, *Beaufort Sea* 70°37' N, 141°34' W **255**
Beaufort West, *S. Af.* 32°21' S, 22°35' E **227**
Beaugency, *Fr.* 47°47' N, 1°37' E **150**
Beaumaris, *U.K.* 53°15' N, 4°5' W **162**
Beaumetz-lès-Loges, *Fr.* 50°13' N, 2°38' E **163**
Beaumont, *Belg.* 50°14' N, 4°14' E **163**
Beaumont, *Calif., U.S.* 33°56' N, 116°59' W **101**
Beaumont, *Fr.* 49°8' N, 2°16' E **163**
Beaumont, *Miss., U.S.* 31°8' N, 88°54' W **103**
Beaumont, *Tex., U.S.* 30°4' N, 94°7' W **103**
Beaumont-le-Roger, *Fr.* 49°5' N, 0°47' E **163**
Beaupré, *Can.* 47°2' N, 70°54' W **94**
Beauraing, *Belg.* 50°6' N, 4°56' E **167**
Beauregard, *Miss., U.S.* 31°43' N, 90°24' W **103**
Beausejour, *Can.* 50°3' N, 96°31' W **108**
Beauvais, *Fr.* 49°26' N, 2°5' E **163**
Beauval, *Can.* 55°9' N, 107°39' W **108**
Beauval, *Fr.* 50°5' N, 2°20' E **163**
Beauvezer, *Fr.* 44°8' N, 6°34' E **167**
Beaver, *Alas., U.S.* 66°14' N, 147°28' W **98**
Beaver, *Ohio, U.S.* 39°1' N, 82°49' W **102**
Beaver, *Okla., U.S.* 36°47' N, 100°32' W **96**
Beaver, *Oreg., U.S.* 45°16' N, 123°50' W **90**
Beaver, *Pa., U.S.* 40°41' N, 80°19' W **94**
Beaver, *Utah, U.S.* 38°16' N, 112°38' W **90**
Beaver, *Wash., U.S.* 48°2' N, 124°20' W **100**
Beaver Bay, *Minn., U.S.* 47°14' N, 91°20' W **94**
Beaver City, *Nebr., U.S.* 40°7' N, 99°50' W **90**
Beaver Creek, *Can.* 62°24' N, 140°52' W **98**
Beaver Dam, *Ky., U.S.* 37°24' N, 86°53' W **96**
Beaver Dam, *Wis., U.S.* 43°27' N, 88°50' W **102**
Beaver Falls, *Pa., U.S.* 40°44' N, 80°20' W **94**
Beaver Hill Lake, *Can.* 54°14' N, 95°24' W **108**
Beaver Island, *Mich., U.S.* 45°20' N, 85°49' W **81**
Beaver Lake, *N. Dak., U.S.* 46°20' N, 100°7' W **90**
Beaver, river, *Can.* 60°29' N, 126°29' W **108**
Beaver, river, *Can.* 54°40' N, 112°3' W **108**
Beaver, river, *Can.* 53°43' N, 61°38' W **111**
Beaverdell, *Can.* 49°25' N, 119°4' W **90**
Beaverhead Mountains, *Mont., U.S.* 45°36' N, 113°50' W **90**
Beaverlodge, *Can.* 55°12' N, 119°27' W **108**
Beaverton, *Can.* 44°25' N, 79°9' W **94**
Beaverton, *Mich., U.S.* 43°51' N, 84°30' W **102**
Beawar, *India* 26°4' N, 74°18' E **186**
Bebedouro, *Braz.* 20°57' S, 48°30' W **138**
Bebeji, *Nig.* 11°39' N, 8°16' E **222**
Bebington, *U.K.* 53°22' N, 2°60' W **162**
Béboto, *Chad* 8°17' N, 16°55' E **218**
Bebra, *Ger.* 50°58' N, 9°46' E **167**
Becán, ruin(s), *Mex.* 18°33' N, 89°39' W **115**
Bécancour, *Can.* 46°21' N, 72°25' W **94**
Beccles, *U.K.* 52°26' N, 1°33' E **163**
Bečej, *Serb. and Mont.* 45°37' N, 20°2' E **168**
Béchar, *Alg.* 31°39' N, 2°13' W **214**
Becharof Lake, *Alas., U.S.* 58°4' N, 159°33' W **106**
Bechater, *Tun.* 37°18' N, 9°45' E **156**
Bechem, *Ghana* 7°7' N, 2°3' W **222**
Bechetu, *Rom.* 43°46' N, 23°57' E **156**
Becker, Mount, *Antarctica* 75°9' S, 72°53' W **248**
Becket, *Mass., U.S.* 42°19' N, 73°6' W **104**
Beckley, *W. Va., U.S.* 37°46' N, 81°12' W **94**
Beckum, *Ger.* 51°45' N, 8°1' E **167**
Beckville, *Tex., U.S.* 32°14' N, 94°28' W **103**
Beckwourth Pass, *Calif., U.S.* 39°47' N, 120°8' W **90**
Beda, oil field, *Lib.* 28°14' N, 18°44' E **216**
Bedale, *U.K.* 54°17' N, 1°36' W **162**
Beddgelert, *U.K.* 53°0' N, 4°6' W **162**
Beddouza, Cap, *Mor.* 32°37' N, 10°38' W **214**
Bedēsa, *Eth.* 8°51' N, 40°45' E **224**
Bedford, *Can.* 44°43' N, 63°41' W **111**
Bedford, *Ind., U.S.* 38°52' N, 86°29' W **102**
Bedford, *Iowa, U.S.* 40°39' N, 94°43' W **94**
Bedford, *N.H., U.S.* 42°56' N, 71°32' W **104**
Bedford, *Pa., U.S.* 40°0' N, 78°31' W **94**
Bedford, *S. Af.* 32°41' S, 26°4' E **227**
Bedford, *U.K.* 52°8' N, 0°28' E **162**
Bedi, *India* 22°32' N, 70°0' E **186**
Bednesti, *Can.* 53°51' N, 123°8' W **108**
Bednodem'yanovsk, *Russ.* 53°53' N, 43°10' E **154**
Bedonia, *It.* 44°30' N, 9°38' E **167**
Bédouaram, *Niger* 15°44' N, 13°8' E **216**
Bedous, *Fr.* 43°0' N, 0°36' E **164**
Bee Ridge, *Fla., U.S.* 27°18' N, 82°27' W **105**
Beebe, *Ark., U.S.* 35°3' N, 91°53' W **96**
Beebe River, *N.H., U.S.* 43°49' N, 71°40' W **104**
Beech Grove, *Ind., U.S.* 39°43' N, 86°5' W **102**
Beecher City, *Ill., U.S.* 39°10' N, 88°47' W **102**
Beechy, *Can.* 50°53' N, 107°25' W **90**
Beer, *Somalia* 9°21' N, 45°48' E **216**
Be'ér 'ada, spring, *Israel* 30°19' N, 34°54' E **194**
Be'ér Ḩafir, spring, *Israel* 30°43' N, 34°35' E **194**
Be'ér Sheva, *Israel* 31°13' N, 34°50' E **180**
Be'ér Sheva' (Beersheba), *Israel* 31°14' N, 34°47' E **194**
Beerberg, Grosser, peak, *Ger.* 50°38' N, 10°38' E **152**
Beersheba see Be'ér Sheva', *Israel* 31°14' N, 34°47' E **194**
Beestekraal, *S. Af.* 25°24' S, 27°35' E **227**
Beeston, *U.K.* 52°55' N, 1°14' W **162**
Beetz, Lac, lake, *Can.* 50°30' N, 63°11' W **111**
Beeville, *Tex., U.S.* 28°23' N, 97°45' W **92**
Befale, *Dem. Rep. of the Congo* 0°26' N, 20°58' E **218**
Befandriana, *Madagascar* 15°15' S, 48°35' E **220**
Befandriana Atsimo, *Madagascar* 22°7' S, 43°51' E **220**
Befori, *Dem. Rep. of the Congo* 0°9' N, 22°17' E **218**
Befotaka, *Madagascar* 23°48' S, 47°1' E **220**
Bega, river, *Rom.* 45°51' N, 21°56' E **168**
Begaly, *Kaz.* 49°55' N, 55°17' E **158**
Begejski Kanal, canal, *Serb. and Mont.* 45°31' N, 20°28' E **168**
Bēgī, *Eth.* 9°20' N, 34°32' E **224**
Begonte, *Sp.* 43°8' N, 7°42' W **150**
Béguégué, *Chad* 8°53' N, 18°52' E **218**
Begunitsy, *Russ.* 59°33' N, 29°16' E **152**
Behagle see Laï, *Chad* 9°23' N, 16°20' E **216**
Béhague, Pointe, *Fr.* 4°43' N, 51°56' W **130**
Behan, *Can.* 55°14' N, 111°28' W **108**
Behara, *Madagascar* 24°57' S, 46°25' E **220**
Behbehān, *Iran* 30°34' N, 50°15' E **180**
Behm Canal 55°45' N, 132°3' W **108**
Beho, *Belg.* 50°14' N, 5°58' E **167**
Behring Point, *Bahamas* 24°30' N, 77°46' W **96**
Behshahr, *Iran* 36°43' N, 53°33' E **180**
Bei'an, *China* 48°16' N, 126°32' E **198**
Beiarn, *Nor.* 67°0' N, 14°35' E **152**
Beida, river, *China* 39°9' N, 97°39' E **188**
Beigang, *China* 42°23' N, 127°28' E **200**
Beihai, *China* 21°26' N, 109°8' E **198**
Beijing, adm. division, *China* 40°32' N, 116°8' E **198**
Beijing (Peking), *China* 39°52' N, 116°9' E **198**
Beila, Jebel, peak, *Sudan* 13°41' N, 34°46' E **182**
Beilen, *Neth.* 52°51' N, 6°31' E **163**
Beiliu, *China* 22°42' N, 110°19' E **198**
Beilrode, *Ger.* 51°33' N, 13°4' E **152**
Beilu, river, *China* 34°47' N, 93°23' E **188**
Beilul, *Eritrea* 13°9' N, 42°22' E **182**
Beinn Bhreagh, site, *Can.* 46°4' N, 60°48' W **111**
Beipiao, *China* 41°52' N, 120°47' E **198**
Beira, *Mozambique* 19°50' S, 34°53' E **224**
Beirut see Beyrouth, *Leb.* 33°53' N, 35°26' E **194**
Beitbridge, *Zimb.* 22°10' S, 29°58' E **227**
Beitun, *China* 47°19' N, 87°48' E **184**
Beiuş, *Rom.* 46°40' N, 22°23' E **168**
Beizhen, *China* 41°37' N, 121°50' E **198**
Beja, *Port.* 38°1' N, 7°52' W **150**
Beja, *Tun.* 36°43' N, 9°11' E **156**
Beja, adm. division, *Port.* 37°41' N, 8°36' W **150**
Bejaïa (Bougie), *Alg.* 36°46' N, 5°2' E **150**
Béjar, *Sp.* 40°23' N, 5°47' W **150**
Bek, river, *Cameroon* 3°1' N, 14°23' E **218**
Bekaa Valley see Al Biqā', region, *Leb.* 33°43' N, 35°51' E **194**
Bekaie, *Dem. Rep. of the Congo* 2°29' S, 18°17' E **218**
Bekdash see Karabogaz, *Turkm.* 41°32' N, 52°35' E **158**
Békés, *Hung.* 46°46' N, 21°8' E **168**
Békés, adm. division, *Hung.* 46°50' N, 20°45' E **156**
Békéscsaba, *Hung.* 46°40' N, 21°5' E **168**
Bekily, *Madagascar* 24°11' S, 45°17' E **220**
Bekobod, *Uzb.* 40°12' N, 69°15' E **197**
Bekodoka, *Madagascar* 17°1' S, 45°7' E **220**
Bekoropoka-Antongo, *Madagascar* 21°27' S, 43°32' E **220**
Bekwai, *Ghana* 6°29' N, 1°34' W **222**
Bela, *India* 25°53' N, 81°58' E **197**
Bela, *Pak.* 26°14' N, 66°20' E **186**
Bela Crkva, *Serb. and Mont.* 44°53' N, 21°26' E **168**
Bela Vista, *Mozambique* 26°18' S, 32°40' E **227**
Bela Vista de Goiás, *Braz.* 17°1' S, 48°59' W **138**
Bela-Bela (Warmbaths), *S. Af.* 24°55' S, 28°16' E **227**
Bélabo, *Cameroon* 4°49' N, 13°16' E **218**
Belalcázar, *Sp.* 38°34' N, 5°10' W **164**
Bélanger, river, *Can.* 53°14' N, 97°28' W **108**
Belarus 53°57' N, 27°35' E **154**
Belasica, *Gr.* 41°23' N, 23°1' E **168**
Belawan, *Indonesia* 3°46' N, 98°42' E **196**
Belaya Glina, *Russ.* 46°5' N, 40°52' E **158**
Belaya Gora, *Russ.* 68°8' N, 146°6' E **160**
Belaya Kalitva, *Russ.* 48°10' N, 40°50' E **158**
Belaya Kholunitsa, *Russ.* 58°50' N, 50°52' E **154**
Belaya, peak, *Eth.* 11°23' N, 36°4' E **182**
Belaya, river, *Russ.* 52°52' N, 56°57' E **154**
Belcaire, *Fr.* 42°48' N, 1°56' E **164**
Belcher, *La., U.S.* 32°44' N, 93°51' W **103**
Belcher Channel 76°55' N, 100°16' W **106**
Belcher Islands, *Hudson Bay* 56°1' N, 80°5' W **106**
Belcheragh, *Afghan.* 35°46' N, 65°13' E **186**
Belchertown, *Mass., U.S.* 42°16' N, 72°25' W **104**
Belchite, *Sp.* 41°17' N, 0°46' E **164**
Belding, *Mich., U.S.* 43°6' N, 85°14' W **102**
Belebey, *Russ.* 54°6' N, 54°12' E **154**
Belecke, *Ger.* 51°28' N, 8°20' E **167**
Beled, *Hung.* 47°27' N, 17°5' E **168**
Beledweyne, *Somalia* 4°43' N, 45°10' E **218**
Belej, *Croatia* 44°47' N, 14°24' E **156**
Belém, *Braz.* 1°24' S, 48°28' W **130**
Belén, *Arg.* 27°39' S, 67°3' W **134**
Belén, *Chile* 18°30' S, 69°34' W **137**
Belén, *Col.* 1°25' N, 75°57' W **136**
Belen, *N. Mex., U.S.* 34°39' N, 106°46' W **92**
Belén, *Parag.* 23°29' S, 57°18' W **132**
Belén, *Uru.* 30°49' S, 57°45' W **139**
Beles, river, *Eth.* 11°1' N, 36°15' E **182**
Bélesta, *Fr.* 42°54' N, 1°54' E **164**
Belev, *Russ.* 53°47' N, 36°5' E **154**
Beleza, river, *Braz.* 10°11' S, 51°13' W **132**
Belfair, *Wash., U.S.* 47°26' N, 122°49' W **100**
Belfast, *Me., U.S.* 44°25' N, 69°2' W **94**
Belfast, *N.Z.* 43°28' S, 172°36' E **240**
Belfast, *S. Af.* 25°42' S, 30°2' E **227**
Belfast, *U.K.* 54°34' N, 6°5' W **150**
Belfield, *N. Dak., U.S.* 46°52' N, 103°13' W **90**
Bēlfodiyo, *Eth.* 10°29' N, 34°48' E **224**
Belford, *U.K.* 55°35' N, 1°50' W **150**
Belfort, *Fr.* 47°38' N, 6°50' E **150**
Belfort (Beaufort), ruin(s), *Leb.* 33°19' N, 35°30' E **194**
Belgaum, *India* 15°49' N, 74°31' E **188**
Belgica Bank, *Greenland Sea* 78°11' N, 13°45' W **255**
Belgioioso, *It.* 45°9' N, 9°19' E **167**
Belgium 50°41' N, 4°16' E **163**
Belgorod, *Russ.* 50°37' N, 36°32' E **158**
Belgorod, adm. division, *Russ.* 50°59' N, 36°52' E **158**
Belgrade, *Me., U.S.* 44°26' N, 69°51' W **104**
Belgrade, *Mont., U.S.* 45°45' N, 111°11' W **90**
Belgrade see Beograd, *Serb.* 44°47' N, 20°24' E **168**
Belgrano II, station, *Antarctica* 77°55' S, 34°4' W **248**
Belhaven, *N.C., U.S.* 35°33' N, 76°38' W **96**
Belhedan, oil field, *Lib.* 27°53' N, 19°10' E **216**
Beli, *Nig.* 7°49' N, 10°58' E **222**
Beli Manastir, *Croatia* 45°44' N, 18°36' E **168**
Beli Potok, *Serb. and Mont.* 43°30' N, 22°4' E **168**
Belica, *Alban.* 41°14' N, 20°23' E **156**
Belica, *Croatia* 46°25' N, 16°31' E **168**
Belidzhi, *Russ.* 41°50' N, 48°28' E **195**
Beliliou see Peleliu, island, *Palau* 7°0' N, 134°15' E **242**
Belinskiy, *Russ.* 52°57' N, 43°23' E **154**
Beliş, *Rom.* 46°39' N, 23°2' E **168**
Belitung (Billiton), island, *Indonesia* 3°41' S, 107°3' E **192**
Beliu, *Rom.* 46°29' N, 21°59' E **168**
Belize 16°58' N, 89°1' W **115**
Belize City, *Belize* 17°30' N, 88°13' W **115**
Beljanica, *Serb. and Mont.* 44°10' N, 21°30' E **168**
Bel'kovskiy, Ostrov, island, *Russ.* 75°28' N, 126°33' E **160**
Bell Lake, lake, *Can.* 49°47' N, 91°13' W **94**
Bell Peninsula, *Can.* 63°28' N, 84°36' W **106**
Bell, river, *Can.* 49°40' N, 77°37' W **94**
Bell Rock, *Can.* 60°0' N, 112°5' W **108**
Bell Ville, *Arg.* 32°40' S, 62°38' W **139**
Bella Bella, *Can.* 52°8' N, 128°3' W **108**
Bella Flor, *Bol.* 11°8' S, 67°49' W **137**
Bella Unión, *Uru.* 30°17' S, 57°37' W **139**
Bella Vista, *Arg.* 28°31' S, 59°2' W **132**
Bella Vista, *Braz.* 22°8' S, 56°24' W **132**
Bellac, *Fr.* 46°6' N, 1°3' E **150**
Bellagio, *It.* 45°58' N, 9°14' E **167**
Bellaire, *Mich., U.S.* 44°58' N, 85°12' W **94**
Bellaire, *Tex., U.S.* 29°41' N, 95°29' W **96**
Bellamy, *Ala., U.S.* 32°26' N, 88°9' W **103**
Bellary, *India* 15°8' N, 76°53' E **188**
Bellavista, *Peru* 5°33' S, 78°43' W **130**
Bellavista, *Peru* 1°35' S, 75°33' W **136**
Belle Fourche, *S. Dak., U.S.* 44°38' N, 103°52' W **82**
Belle Fourche, river, *Wyo., U.S.* 43°45' N, 105°45' W **80**
Belle Glade, *Fla., U.S.* 26°40' N, 80°41' W **105**
Belle Isle, island, *Can.* 52°4' N, 55°26' W **106**
Belle Isle, Strait of 51°28' N, 56°49' W **111**
Belle Plaine, *Iowa, U.S.* 41°53' N, 92°17' W **94**
Belle Plaine, *Minn., U.S.* 44°36' N, 93°46' W **94**
Belle Yella, *Liberia* 7°13' N, 10°2' W **222**
Belledonne, Chaîne de, *Fr.* 45°10' N, 5°50' E **165**
Bellefontaine, *Ohio, U.S.* 40°21' N, 83°45' W **102**
Bellefonte, *Pa., U.S.* 40°53' N, 77°47' W **94**
Bellenden Ker National Park, *Austral.* 17°25' S, 145°31' E **238**
Belleoram, *Can.* 47°30' N, 55°25' W **111**
Belleview, *Fla., U.S.* 29°3' N, 82°3' W **105**
Belleville, *Can.* 44°9' N, 77°22' W **94**
Belleville, *Fr.* 46°5' N, 4°43' E **150**
Belleville, *Ill., U.S.* 38°30' N, 89°58' W **102**
Belleville, *Kans., U.S.* 39°48' N, 97°38' W **90**
Belleville, *Mo., U.S.* 38°30' N, 89°58' W **94**
Belleville, *Wis., U.S.* 42°50' N, 89°32' W **102**
Bellevue, *Congo* 2°5' N, 13°51' E **218**
Bellevue, *Idaho, U.S.* 43°28' N, 114°16' W **90**
Bellevue, *Iowa, U.S.* 42°15' N, 90°26' W **94**
Bellevue, *Mich., U.S.* 42°27' N, 85°1' W **102**
Bellevue, *Nebr., U.S.* 41°8' N, 95°54' W **90**
Bellevue, *Ohio, U.S.* 41°16' N, 82°50' W **102**
Bellevue, *Tex., U.S.* 33°36' N, 98°1' W **96**
Bellevue, *Wash., U.S.* 47°35' N, 122°13' W **100**
Bellflower, *Ill., U.S.* 40°19' N, 88°32' W **102**
Bellinger, Lac, lake, *Can.* 51°10' N, 74°60' W **110**
Bellingham, *Wash., U.S.* 48°46' N, 122°29' W **100**
Bellingrath Gardens, site, *Ala., U.S.* 30°24' N, 88°11' W **103**
Bellingshausen Plain, *South Pacific Ocean* 65°21' S, 112°43' W **255**
Bellingshausen Sea 70°32' S, 88°38' W **248**
Bellingshausen, station, *Antarctica* 62°17' S, 58°44' W **248**
Bellinzona, *Switz.* 46°11' N, 9°1' E **167**
Bellmore, *Ind., U.S.* 39°45' N, 87°6' W **102**
Bello, *Col.* 6°20' N, 75°35' W **136**
Bello Islands, Monte, *Indian Ocean* 20°10' S, 113°11' E **230**
Bellona Island, *Solomon Islands* 11°0' S, 160°0' E **242**
Bellows Falls, *Vt., U.S.* 43°7' N, 72°28' W **104**
Bellpat, *Pak.* 29°1' N, 68°5' E **186**
Belluno, *It.* 46°8' N, 12°12' E **167**
Bellville, *Ohio, U.S.* 40°36' N, 82°31' W **102**
Bellville, *Tex., U.S.* 29°55' N, 96°16' W **96**
Bellvís, *Sp.* 41°39' N, 0°49' E **164**
Bellwood, *La., U.S.* 31°29' N, 93°12' W **103**
Belmar, *N.J., U.S.* 40°10' N, 74°2' W **94**
Bélmez, *Sp.* 38°15' N, 5°12' W **164**
Belmond, *Iowa, U.S.* 42°49' N, 93°36' W **94**
Belmont, *N.H., U.S.* 43°26' N, 71°29' W **104**
Belmont, *S. Af.* 29°27' S, 24°20' E **227**
Belmont, *Vt., U.S.* 43°24' N, 72°50' W **104**
Belmonte, *Braz.* 15°56' S, 38°56' W **132**
Belmonte, *Sp.* 39°33' N, 2°43' W **150**
Belmopan, *Belize* 17°10' N, 88°56' W **115**
Belo, *Madagascar* 20°48' S, 44°1' E **220**
Belo Horizonte, *Braz.* 19°55' S, 43°55' W **138**
Belo Horizonte, *Braz.* 5°18' S, 52°56' W **130**
Beloci, *Mold.* 47°52' N, 28°56' E **156**
Belogorsk, *Russ.* 51°2' N, 128°27' E **190**
Belogorsk, *Russ.* 54°59' N, 88°33' E **169**
Belogorskīy, *Kaz.* 49°26' N, 83°9' E **184**
Beloha, *Madagascar* 25°9' S, 45°2' E **220**
Beloit, *Kans., U.S.* 39°27' N, 98°7' W **90**
Beloit, *Wis., U.S.* 42°31' N, 89°2' W **102**
Beloljin, *Serb. and Mont.* 43°13' N, 21°23' E **168**
Belomorsk, *Russ.* 64°28' N, 34°38' E **154**
Belonia, *India* 23°12' N, 91°28' E **197**
Belorado, *Sp.* 42°24' N, 3°12' W **164**
Belorechensk, *Russ.* 44°46' N, 39°52' E **158**
Beloretsk, *Russ.* 53°58' N, 58°23' E **154**
Beloshchel'ye, *Russ.* 64°56' N, 46°48' E **154**
Belot'i, *Ga.* 42°17' N, 44°7' E **195**
Belo-Tsiribihina, *Madagascar* 19°41' S, 44°31' E **220**
Belovo, *Russ.* 54°22' N, 86°22' E **184**
Beloyarskiy, *Russ.* 63°42' N, 66°58' E **169**
Beloye More (White Sea) 63°17' N, 35°24' E **160**
Beloye Ozero, lake, *Russ.* 59°33' N, 37°43' E **154**
Belozersk, *Russ.* 59°57' N, 37°50' E **154**
Belpre, *Ohio, U.S.* 39°16' N, 81°35' W **102**
Belt, *Mont., U.S.* 47°22' N, 110°56' W **90**
Belterra, *Braz.* 2°38' S, 54°59' W **130**
Belton, *S.C., U.S.* 34°30' N, 82°31' W **96**
Belton, *Tex., U.S.* 31°2' N, 97°27' W **92**
Belukha, Gora, peak, *Russ.* 49°46' N, 86°31' E **184**
Belush'ya Guba, *Russ.* 71°28' N, 52°29' E **160**
Belush'ye, *Russ.* 66°52' N, 47°37' E **154**
Belušić, *Serb. and Mont.* 43°47' N, 21°8' E **168**
Belvidere, *Ill., U.S.* 42°14' N, 88°51' W **102**
Belvidere, *S. Dak., U.S.* 43°49' N, 101°17' W **90**
Belvidere Mountain, *Vt., U.S.* 44°45' N, 72°39' W **94**
Belvoir, *U.K.* 52°53' N, 0°48' E **162**
Belyayevka, *Russ.* 51°23' N, 56°23' E **158**
Belyy, *Russ.* 55°48' N, 33°1' E **154**
Belyy, Ostrov, island, *Russ.* 73°28' N, 65°53' E **160**
Belyy, Ostrov, island, *Russ.* 73°26' N, 70°30' E **160**
Belyy Yar, *Russ.* 58°25' N, 85°8' E **169**
Belz, *Ukr.* 50°23' N, 24°1' E **152**
Belzoni, *Miss., U.S.* 33°9' N, 90°31' W **103**
Bemaraha, *Madagascar* 20°44' S, 44°42' E **220**
Bembe, *Angola* 7°2' S, 14°18' E **218**
Bembéréké, *Benin* 10°12' N, 2°40' E **222**
Bement, *Ill., U.S.* 39°54' N, 88°34' W **102**
Bemetara, *India* 21°44' N, 81°31' E **188**
Bemidji, *Minn., U.S.* 47°28' N, 94°55' W **90**
Bemis, *Tenn., U.S.* 35°33' N, 88°49' W **96**
Ben Gardane, *Tun.* 33°9' N, 11°12' E **214**
Ben Lomond, *Calif., U.S.* 37°5' N, 122°6' W **100**
Ben S'Rour, *Alg.* 35°3' N, 4°34' E **150**
Ben Zohra, spring, *Alg.* 28°37' N, 3°50' W **214**
Bena Dibele, *Dem. Rep. of the Congo* 4°8' S, 22°48' E **218**
Bena Makima, *Dem. Rep. of the Congo* 5°2' S, 21°7' E **218**
Benabarre, *Sp.* 42°6' N, 0°28' E **164**
Benalup, *Sp.* 36°21' N, 5°50' W **164**
Benamaurel, *Sp.* 37°35' N, 2°41' W **164**
Benamejí, *Sp.* 37°16' N, 4°33' W **164**
Benasque, *Sp.* 42°35' N, 0°32' E **164**
Bénat, Cap, *Fr.* 43°1' N, 6°11' E **165**
Benavente, *Sp.* 42°0' N, 5°43' W **150**
Benavides, *Tex., U.S.* 27°35' N, 98°24' W **92**
Benbow, *Calif., U.S.* 40°3' N, 123°47' W **90**
Benbulbin, peak, *Ire.* 54°20' N, 8°36' W **150**
Bende, *Nig.* 5°35' N, 7°38' E **222**
Bender, *Mold.* 46°48' N, 29°28' E **156**
Bendorf, *Ger.* 50°25' N, 7°34' E **167**
Bēne, *Latv.* 56°28' N, 23°1' E **166**
Bené Beraq, *Israel* 32°5' N, 34°50' E **194**
Benedito Leite, *Braz.* 7°13' S, 44°36' W **132**
Bénéna, *Mali* 13°7' N, 4°24' W **222**
Benenitra, *Madagascar* 23°24' S, 45°3' E **220**
Beneraird, peak, *U.K.* 55°3' N, 5°2' W **150**
Bénestroff, *Fr.* 48°54' N, 6°45' E **163**
Benfeld, *Fr.* 48°22' N, 7°34' E **163**
Bengal, adm. division, *India* 21°51' N, 88°25' E **197**
Bengal, Bay of 13°12' N, 85°28' E **188**
Bengbu, *China* 32°53' N, 117°21' E **198**
Benghazi see Banghāzī, *Lib.* 32°6' N, 20°4' E **216**
Bengkalis, *Indonesia* 1°30' N, 102°7' E **196**
Bengkalis, island, *Indonesia* 1°38' N, 102°5' E **196**
Bengkayang, *Indonesia* 0°51' N, 109°27' E **196**
Bengkulu, *Indonesia* 3°49' S, 102°18' E **192**
Bengo, adm. division, *Angola* 8°8' S, 13°15' E **220**
Bengough, *Can.* 49°23' N, 105°8' W **90**
Benguela, *Angola* 12°38' S, 13°23' E **220**
Benguela, adm. division, *Angola* 13°17' S, 12°57' E **220**
Benguérua, Ilha, island, *Mozambique* 22°11' S, 34°56' E **227**
Benha, *Egypt* 30°25' N, 31°12' E **180**
Beni, *Dem. Rep. of the Congo* 0°24' N, 29°26' E **224**
Beni Abbes, *Alg.* 30°8' N, 2°10' W **214**
Beni, adm. division, *Bol.* 13°40' S, 65°45' W **137**
Beni Mazâr, *Egypt* 28°27' N, 30°46' E **180**
Beni Mellal, *Mor.* 32°24' N, 6°22' W **214**
Beni, river, *Bol.* 12°25' S, 66°55' W **137**
Beni Saf, *Alg.* 35°17' N, 1°23' W **150**
Beni Suef, *Egypt* 29°4' N, 31°3' E **180**
Beni Tajit, *Mor.* 32°21' N, 3°28' W **214**
Benicarló, *Sp.* 40°24' N, 0°25' E **164**
Benicasim, *Sp.* 40°3' N, 7°416' E **164**
Benicia, *Calif., U.S.* 38°3' N, 122°10' W **100**
Benidorm, *Sp.* 38°31' N, 0°8' E **164**
Benifaió, *Sp.* 39°16' N, 0°26' E **164**
Benin 10°4' N, 1°52' E **214**
Benin, Bight of 4°25' N, 1°49' E **222**
Benin City, *Nig.* 6°23' N, 5°38' E **222**
Benissa, *Sp.* 38°42' N, 5°297' E **164**
Benito, *Can.* 51°54' N, 101°33' W **108**
Benito Juárez, *Mex.* 17°49' N, 92°33' W **115**
Benito Juárez National Park see 2, *Mex.* 17°15' N, 96°46' W **112**
Benjamin, *Tex., U.S.* 33°34' N, 99°48' W **92**
Benjamin Constant, *Braz.* 4°25' S, 70°4' W **132**
Benjamin Hill, *Mex.* 30°11' N, 111°8' W **92**
Benkelman, *Nebr., U.S.* 40°3' N, 101°33' W **90**
Benld, *Ill., U.S.* 39°5' N, 89°49' W **102**

Bennane Head, U.K. 55°10′ N, 5°15′ W 150
Bennett, Can. 59°51′ N, 134°56′ W 108
Bennett Island, Russ. 77°0′ N, 149°0′ E 255
Bennett Lake, lake, Can. 53°23′ N, 96°35′ W 108
Benneydale, N.Z. 38°31′ S, 175°20′ E 240
Bennington, N.H., U.S. 43°0′ N, 71°56′ W 104
Bennington, Vt., U.S. 42°52′ N, 73°12′ W 104
Bénnsané, Guinea 11°26′ N, 14°1′ W 222
Benom, peak, Malaysia 3°50′ N, 102°0′ E 196
Benoud, Alg. 32°20′ N, 0°15′ E 214
Benoy, Chad 8°57′ N, 16°20′ E 216
Bensberg, Ger. 50°58′ N, 7°8′ E 167
Benson, Ariz., U.S. 31°57′ N, 110°20′ W 112
Benson, Minn., U.S. 45°18′ N, 95°37′ W 90
Benson, N.C., U.S. 35°22′ N, 78°34′ W 96
Benson, Vt., U.S. 43°42′ N, 73°19′ W 104
Bent Jbail, Leb. 33°7′ N, 35°25′ E 194
Benta, Malaysia 4°1′ N, 101°58′ E 196
Bentiaba, Angola 14°18′ S, 12°22′ E 220
Bentinck Island, Austral. 17°25′ S, 137°54′ E 230
Bentinck, island, Myanmar 11°30′ N, 97°26′ E 202
Bentinck Point, Can. 46°26′ N, 61°17′ W 111
Bentiu, Sudan 9°9′ N, 29°47′ E 224
Bentley, Mich., U.S. 43°56′ N, 84°9′ W 102
Bento Gonçalves, Braz. 29°10′ S, 51°30′ W 139
Benton, Ark., U.S. 34°32′ N, 92°36′ W 96
Benton, Ky., U.S. 36°51′ N, 88°21′ W 94
Benton, La., U.S. 32°40′ N, 93°45′ W 103
Benton, Me., U.S. 44°34′ N, 69°34′ W 94
Benton, Miss., U.S. 32°48′ N, 90°16′ W 103
Benton, N.H., U.S. 44°5′ N, 71°55′ W 104
Benton Harbor, Mich., U.S. 42°6′ N, 86°27′ W 102
Bentong, Malaysia 3°34′ N, 101°55′ E 196
Bentonia, Miss., U.S. 32°37′ N, 90°23′ W 103
Bentonville, Ark., U.S. 36°21′ N, 94°13′ W 94
Benty, Guinea 9°8′ N, 13°13′ W 222
Benue, river, Nig. 8°0′ N, 7°50′ E 222
Benwee Head, Ire. 54°21′ N, 10°10′ W 150
Benxi, China 41°16′ N, 123°47′ E 200
Benzdorp, Suriname 3°42′ N, 54°7′ W 130
Benzú, Mor. 35°54′ N, 5°23′ W 150
Beo, Indonesia 4°15′ N, 126°52′ E 192
Beočin, Serb. and Mont. 45°11′ N, 19°44′ E 168
Beograd (Belgrade), Serb. 44°47′ N, 20°24′ E 168
Beohari, India 24°2′ N, 81°22′ E 197
Beolgyo, S. Korea 34°48′ N, 127°21′ E 200
Beowawe, Nev., U.S. 40°35′ N, 116°30′ W 90
Beppu, Japan 36°7′ N, 133°4′ E 201
Beppu, Japan 33°16′ N, 131°29′ E 201
Bequia, island, Saint Vincent and The Grenadines 13°0′ N, 61°11′ W 116
Bera Ndjoko, Congo 3°15′ N, 16°58′ E 218
Berau, Teluk 2°35′ S, 131°10′ E 192
Berber, Sudan 18°0′ N, 34°2′ E 182
Berbérati, Cen. Af. Rep. 4°18′ N, 15°47′ E 218
Berceda, Sp. 43°4′ N, 3°27′ W 164
Berceto, It. 44°30′ N, 9°59′ E 167
Berck, Fr. 50°25′ N, 1°35′ E 163
Berdigestyakh, Russ. 62°8′ N, 127°5′ E 160
Berdoba, Chad 16°0′ N, 22°53′ E 216
Berdsk, Russ. 54°46′ N, 83°11′ E 184
Berdún, Sp. 42°36′ N, 0°52′ E 164
Berdyans'k, Ukr. 46°46′ N, 36°46′ E 156
Berdyaush, Russ. 55°11′ N, 59°12′ E 154
Berdychiv, Ukr. 49°53′ N, 28°41′ E 152
Berdyuzh'ye, Russ. 55°48′ N, 68°20′ E 184
Berea, Ky., U.S. 37°33′ N, 84°18′ W 96
Berea, Ohio, U.S. 41°21′ N, 81°51′ W 102
Bérébi, Côte d'Ivoire 4°40′ N, 7°2′ W 222
Bereeda, Somalia 11°44′ N, 51°3′ E 182
Bereku, Tanzania 4°27′ S, 35°46′ E 224
Berekum, Ghana 7°29′ N, 2°35′ W 222
Beremend, Hung. 45°46′ N, 18°25′ E 168
Beren, Liman, lake, Russ. 46°52′ N, 44°37′ E 158
Berenda, Calif., U.S. 37°2′ N, 120°10′ W 100
Berenice, Egypt 23°54′ N, 35°25′ E 182
Berens River, Can. 52°21′ N, 96°59′ W 82
Berens, river, Can. 51°49′ N, 93°43′ W 110
Berens, river, Can. 52°5′ N, 96°53′ W 80
Berestechko, Ukr. 50°20′ N, 25°6′ E 158
Bereşti, Rom. 46°5′ N, 27°51′ E 156
Berettyó, river, Rom. 47°15′ N, 21°39′ E 168
Berettyóújfalu, Hung. 47°14′ N, 21°32′ E 168
Berevo, Madagascar 19°46′ S, 44°58′ E 220
Berezivka, Ukr. 47°16′ N, 30°54′ E 156
Bereznik, Russ. 62°49′ N, 42°49′ E 154
Berezniki, Russ. 59°24′ N, 56°48′ E 154
Berezovka, Russ. 57°38′ N, 57°22′ E 154
Berezovka, Russ. 59°20′ N, 82°47′ E 169
Berezovka, Russ. 65°0′ N, 56°38′ E 154
Berezovo, Russ. 63°58′ N, 65°5′ E 169
Berezovskaya, Russ. 50°14′ N, 43°59′ E 158
Berezovskiy, Russ. 55°34′ N, 86°18′ E 169
Berga, Nor. 57°14′ N, 16°0′ E 152
Berga, Sp. 42°6′ N, 1°50′ E 164
Bergama, Turk. 39°4′ N, 27°11′ E 180
Bergamo, It. 45°42′ N, 9°39′ E 167
Bergedorf, Ger. 53°29′ N, 10°12′ E 150
Bergen, Ger. 54°25′ N, 13°26′ E 152
Bergen, Nor. 60°23′ N, 5°19′ E 152
Bergen aan Zee, Neth. 52°40′ N, 4°38′ E 163
Bergen op Zoom, Neth. 51°29′ N, 4°17′ E 163
Bergerac, Fr. 44°51′ N, 0°28′ E 150
Bergersen, Mount, Antarctica 72°6′ S, 25°32′ E 248
Bergheim, Ger. 50°57′ N, 6°39′ E 167
Bergisch Gladbach, Ger. 50°59′ N, 7°7′ E 167
Bergkamen, Ger. 51°37′ N, 7°39′ E 167
Bergland, Namibia 22°60′ S, 17°5′ E 227
Bergö, Fin. 62°56′ N, 21°9′ E 152
Bergsfjord, Nor. 70°15′ N, 21°49′ E 152
Bergshamra, Sw. 59°37′ N, 18°35′ E 166
Bergsjö, Nor. 61°58′ N, 17°1′ E 152
Berguent, Mor. 34°1′ N, 1°60′ W 214
Bergues, Fr. 50°57′ N, 2°26′ E 163
Bergum, Neth. 53°11′ N, 5°58′ E 163
Bergville, S. Af. 28°44′ S, 29°20′ E 227
Berh, Mongolia 47°44′ N, 111°8′ E 198
Berhala, Selat 0°50′ N, 103°54′ E 196
Berikei, oil field, Russ. 42°20′ N, 47°58′ E 195
Bering Sea 65°53′ N, 166°10′ W 246
Bering Strait 65°53′ N, 168°36′ W 255
Beringil, Sudan 12°8′ N, 25°43′ E 216
Beringovskiy, Russ. 63°8′ N, 179°6′ E 160
Berja, Sp. 36°50′ N, 2°57′ W 164
Berkåk, Nor. 62°49′ N, 10°1′ E 152
Berkeley, Calif., U.S. 37°52′ N, 122°16′ W 100
Berkner Island, Antarctica 78°9′ S, 43°53′ W 248
Berkovići, Bosn. and Herzg. 43°4′ N, 18°10′ E 168
Berkshire, Mass., U.S. 42°30′ N, 73°12′ W 104
Berkshires, The, Mass., U.S. 42°27′ N, 73°8′ W 104
Berland, river, Can. 53°40′ N, 118°10′ W 108
Berlikum, Neth. 53°14′ N, 5°38′ E 163
Berlin, Ger. 52°29′ N, 13°14′ E 152
Berlin, Md., U.S. 38°19′ N, 75°14′ W 94
Berlin, N.H., U.S. 44°28′ N, 71°12′ W 104
Berlin, N.Y., U.S. 42°41′ N, 73°23′ W 104
Berlin, Wis., U.S. 43°57′ N, 88°56′ W 94
Berlin, Mount, Antarctica 75°56′ S, 135°13′ W 248
Bermeja, Punta, Arg. 41°21′ S, 63°11′ W 134
Bermeja, Sierra, Sp. 36°33′ N, 5°16′ W 164
Bermejillo, Mex. 25°52′ N, 103°39′ W 114
Bermejo, river, Arg. 25°37′ S, 60°8′ W 134
Bermeo, Sp. 43°23′ N, 2°45′ W 164
Bermuda Islands, U.K. 32°0′ N, 65°0′ W 118
Bermuda Rise, North Atlantic Ocean 32°2′ N, 64°35′ W 253
Bern, Switz. 46°55′ N, 7°21′ E 165
Bernalillo, N. Mex., U.S. 35°17′ N, 106°34′ W 82
Bernard Lake, lake, Can. 45°41′ N, 79°50′ W 110
Bernardo de Irigoyen, Arg. 32°11′ S, 61°8′ W 139
Bernardo de Irigoyen, Arg. 26°15′ S, 53°41′ W 139
Bernardston, Mass., U.S. 42°40′ N, 72°34′ W 104
Bernasconi, Arg. 37°57′ S, 63°42′ W 139
Bernay, Fr. 49°5′ N, 0°35′ E 150
Berne, Ind., U.S. 40°38′ N, 84°57′ W 102
Berner Alpen, Switz. 46°20′ N, 6°59′ E 165
Berneval, Fr. 49°57′ N, 1°10′ E 163
Bernice, La., U.S. 32°48′ N, 92°40′ W 103
Bernie, Mo., U.S. 36°40′ N, 89°58′ W 96
Bernier Bay 70°59′ N, 90°44′ W 106
Bernier Island, Austral. 24°41′ S, 111°44′ E 230
Bernina Pass, Switz. 46°26′ N, 10°0′ E 167
Bernina, Piz, peak, Switz. 46°23′ N, 9°52′ E 167
Bernkastel-Kues, Ger. 49°55′ N, 7°5′ E 167
Bernterode, Ger. 51°24′ N, 10°29′ E 167
Bero, river, Angola 15°3′ S, 12°9′ E 220
Berón de Astrada, Arg. 27°33′ S, 57°32′ W 139
Beroroha, Madagascar 21°37′ S, 45°9′ E 220
Béroubouay, Benin 10°32′ N, 2°41′ E 222
Beroun, Czech Rep. 49°58′ N, 14°4′ E 152
Berovo, Maced. 41°43′ N, 22°52′ E 168
Berri, oil field, Saudi Arabia 27°5′ N, 49°29′ E 196
Berriane, Alg. 32°51′ N, 3°45′ E 214
Berrien Springs, Mich., U.S. 41°56′ N, 86°21′ W 102
Berrouaghia, Alg. 36°7′ N, 2°54′ E 150
Berry, Ky., U.S. 38°30′ N, 84°23′ W 102
Berry Creek, river, Can. 51°34′ N, 111°39′ W 90
Berry Islands, Atlantic Ocean 25°23′ N, 77°42′ W 96
Berry, region, Europe 46°51′ N, 1°18′ E 165
Berryville, Ark., U.S. 36°21′ N, 93°35′ W 96
Berseba, Namibia 25°60′ S, 17°46′ E 227
Bersenbrück, Ger. 52°33′ N, 7°57′ E 163
Bershad', Ukr. 48°24′ N, 29°38′ E 156
Bertam, Malaysia 5°11′ N, 102°1′ E 196
Berthierville, Can. 46°5′ N, 73°11′ W 110
Berthold, N. Dak., U.S. 48°18′ N, 101°45′ W 90
Berthoud, Colo., U.S. 40°18′ N, 105°6′ W 90
Berthoud Pass, Colo., U.S. 39°47′ N, 105°47′ W 90
Bertincourt, Fr. 50°4′ N, 2°56′ E 163
Bertoua, Cameroon 4°32′ N, 13°40′ E 218
Bertrab Nunatak, peak, Antarctica 78°26′ S, 36°22′ W 248
Bertrand, Nebr., U.S. 40°31′ N, 99°39′ W 92
Bertwell, Can. 52°35′ N, 102°36′ W 108
Beru, island, Kiribati 1°12′ S, 175°57′ E 252
Beruniy, Uzb. 41°43′ N, 60°43′ E 180
Beruri, Braz. 3°53′ S, 61°23′ W 130
Berutti, Arg. 35°50′ S, 62°29′ W 139
Berveni, Rom. 47°45′ N, 22°28′ E 168
Berwick, La., U.S. 29°41′ N, 91°15′ W 103
Berwick, Me., U.S. 43°16′ N, 70°52′ W 104
Berwick upon Tweed, U.K. 55°45′ N, 2°1′ W 150
Berwyn, Can. 56°9′ N, 117°44′ W 108
Berwyn, U.K. 52°51′ N, 3°26′ W 162
Beryslav, Ukr. 46°53′ N, 33°19′ E 156
Bērzaune, Latv. 56°48′ N, 26°2′ E 166
Bērze, river, Latv. 56°37′ N, 23°18′ E 166
Berzosilla, Sp. 42°46′ N, 4°3′ W 164
Berzovia, Rom. 45°25′ N, 21°36′ E 168
Besançon, Fr. 47°14′ N, 6°1′ E 150
Beserah, Malaysia 3°54′ N, 103°20′ E 196
Beshanq, Uzb. 40°25′ N, 70°33′ E 197
Beshkent, Uzb. 38°47′ N, 65°37′ E 197
Beşiri, Turk. 37°54′ N, 41°20′ E 195
Beška, Serb. and Mont. 45°7′ N, 20°4′ E 168
Besko, Pol. 49°34′ N, 21°56′ E 152
Besköl, Kaz. 54°45′ N, 69°4′ E 184
Beslan, Russ. 43°9′ N, 44°32′ E 195
Beslet, peak, Bulg. 41°47′ N, 23°48′ E 156
Besna Kobila, peak, Serb. and Mont. 42°31′ N, 22°11′ E 168
Besnard Lake, lake, Can. 55°25′ N, 106°33′ W 108
Besni Fok, Serb. and Mont. 44°58′ N, 20°24′ E 168
Beşparmak Dağı, peak, Turk. 37°29′ N, 27°30′ E 156
Bessaker, Nor. 64°14′ N, 10°20′ E 152
Bessemer, Ala., U.S. 33°23′ N, 86°56′ W 96
Bestöbe, Kaz. 52°29′ N, 73°8′ E 184
Bestuzhevo, Russ. 61°37′ N, 44°1′ E 154
Bet Guvrin, Israel 31°36′ N, 34°53′ E 194
Bét ha Shitta, Israel 32°33′ N, 35°26′ E 194
Bét She'an (Beth-shan), Israel 32°29′ N, 35°30′ E 194
Bét She'arim, ruin(s), Israel 32°41′ N, 35°5′ E 194
Bét Shemesh, Israel 31°44′ N, 34°59′ E 194
Betafo, Madagascar 19°52′ S, 46°51′ E 220
Betamba, Dem. Rep. of the Congo 2°16′ S, 21°25′ E 218
Betanty (Faux Cap), Madagascar 25°34′ S, 45°31′ E 220
Betanzos, Bol. 19°33′ S, 65°23′ W 137
Betanzos, Sp. 43°15′ N, 8°14′ W 150
Bétaré Oya, Cameroon 5°31′ N, 14°5′ E 218
Betbeder, Peninsula, Arg. 44°43′ S, 65°19′ W 134
Bete Hor, Eth. 11°33′ N, 38°58′ E 182
Bétera, Sp. 39°35′ N, 0°28′ E 164
Bétérou, Benin 9°12′ N, 2°13′ E 222
Bethal, S. Af. 26°26′ S, 29°25′ E 227
Bethanie, Namibia 26°31′ S, 17°9′ E 227
Bethany, Ill., U.S. 39°38′ N, 88°45′ W 102
Bethany, Mo., U.S. 40°15′ N, 94°1′ W 94
Bethany Beach, Del., U.S. 38°31′ N, 75°4′ W 94
Bethel, Alas., U.S. 60°45′ N, 161°52′ W 98
Bethel, Conn., U.S. 41°22′ N, 73°25′ W 104
Bethel, Ohio, U.S. 38°57′ N, 84°5′ W 102
Bethel, Vt., U.S. 43°49′ N, 72°38′ W 104
Bethesda, U.K. 53°11′ N, 4°3′ W 162
Bethlehem, N.H., U.S. 44°16′ N, 71°42′ W 104
Bethlehem, S. Af. 28°16′ S, 28°15′ E 227
Bethlehem see Bayt Laḥm, West Bank 31°41′ N, 35°12′ E 194
Bethpage, N.Y., U.S. 40°44′ N, 73°30′ W 104
Beth-shan see Bét She'an, Israel 32°29′ N, 35°30′ E 194
Bethulie, S. Af. 30°27′ S, 25°59′ E 227
Béthune, Fr. 50°31′ N, 2°38′ E 163
Betijoque, Venez. 9°22′ N, 70°44′ W 136
Betioky, Madagascar 23°43′ S, 44°19′ E 220
Betong, Thai. 5°47′ N, 101°4′ E 196
Bétou, Congo 3°5′ N, 18°30′ E 218
Betpaqdala, Asia 45°34′ N, 64°32′ E 184
Betroka, Madagascar 23°13′ S, 46°8′ E 220
Betsiamites, Can. 48°56′ N, 68°39′ W 94
Betsiamites, river, Can. 49°24′ N, 69°51′ W 94
Bettendorf, Iowa, U.S. 41°33′ N, 90°30′ W 94
Bettie, Tex., U.S. 32°48′ N, 94°58′ W 103
Bettioua, Alg. 35°47′ N, 0°16′ E 150
Bettola, It. 44°46′ N, 9°36′ E 167
Bettsville, Ohio, U.S. 41°14′ N, 83°13′ W 102
Bettul, India 21°55′ N, 77°54′ E 197
Betws-y-Coed, U.K. 53°5′ N, 3°48′ W 162
Betzdorf, Ger. 50°47′ N, 7°52′ E 167
Béu, Angola 6°14′ S, 15°27′ E 218
Beuil, Fr. 44°5′ N, 6°57′ E 167
Beulah, Colo., U.S. 38°5′ N, 104°60′ W 90
Beulah, N. Dak., U.S. 47°15′ N, 101°48′ W 90
Beurfou, spring, Chad 15°54′ N, 14°58′ E 216
Beverley, U.K. 53°50′ N, 0°26′ E 162
Beverley Head, Can. 49°11′ N, 59°4′ W 111
Beverly, Mass., U.S. 42°32′ N, 70°53′ W 104
Beverly, Ohio, U.S. 39°32′ N, 81°38′ W 102
Beverly Hills, Fla., U.S. 28°56′ N, 82°27′ W 105
Beverungen, Ger. 51°40′ N, 9°22′ E 167
Beverwijk, Neth. 52°30′ N, 4°37′ E 163
Bewdley, U.K. 52°21′ N, 2°20′ W 162
Bex, Switz. 46°15′ N, 7°0′ E 167
Bexhill, U.K. 50°50′ N, 0°28′ E 162
Bey da ğları, Turk. 36°36′ N, 29°46′ E 156
Bey Dağı, peak, Turk. 39°41′ N, 37°47′ E 156
Bey Dağı, peak, Turk. 38°16′ N, 35°59′ E 156
Beycesultan, ruin(s), Turk. 38°14′ N, 29°33′ E 156
Beyla, Guinea 8°39′ N, 8°39′ W 222
Beyneu, Kaz. 45°18′ N, 55°13′ E 158
Beypazarı, Turk. 40°9′ N, 31°54′ E 156
Beyra, Somalia 6°55′ N, 47°25′ E 218
Beyrouth (Beirut), Leb. 33°53′ N, 35°26′ E 194
Beyşehir, Turk. 37°41′ N, 31°44′ E 156
Beyşehir Gölü, lake, Turk. 37°43′ N, 31°9′ E 180
Beysug, river, Russ. 45°53′ N, 39°3′ E 156
Beytüşşebap, Turk. 37°33′ N, 43°3′ E 195
Bezdan, Serb. and Mont. 45°50′ N, 18°55′ E 168
Bezerra, river, Braz. 13°14′ S, 47°29′ W 138
Bezhanitsy, Russ. 56°57′ N, 29°52′ E 166
Bezhetsk, Russ. 57°44′ N, 36°44′ E 154
Béziers, Fr. 43°20′ N, 3°13′ E 164
Bhadarwah, India 32°57′ N, 75°45′ E 186
Bhadra, India 29°7′ N, 75°10′ E 186
Bhadrakh, India 21°5′ N, 86°31′ E 188
Bhadravati, India 13°52′ N, 75°44′ E 188
Bhagalpur, India 25°13′ N, 87°0′ E 197
Bhairahawa, Nepal 27°32′ N, 83°23′ E 197
Bhakkar, Pak. 31°37′ N, 71°7′ E 186
Bhaktapur, Nepal 27°41′ N, 85°26′ E 197
Bhamo, Myanmar 24°17′ N, 97°16′ E 190
Bhandara, India 21°2′ N, 79°38′ E 190
Bhanpura, India 24°31′ N, 75°46′ E 197
Bharatpur, India 27°13′ N, 77°28′ E 197
Bharatpur, India 23°46′ N, 81°47′ E 197
Bharthana, India 26°43′ N, 79°14′ E 197
Bharuch, India 21°42′ N, 72°57′ E 186
Bhatapara, India 21°44′ N, 81°56′ E 188
Bhatinda, India 30°13′ N, 74°57′ E 186
Bhatkal, India 14°0′ N, 74°32′ E 188
Bhatpara, India 22°51′ N, 88°25′ E 197
Bhavnagar, India 21°46′ N, 72°7′ E 186
Bheigeir, Beinn, peak, U.K. 55°43′ N, 6°12′ W 150
Bhera, Pak. 32°27′ N, 72°58′ E 186
Bhikangaon, India 21°53′ N, 75°58′ E 197
Bhilai, India 21°13′ N, 81°21′ E 188
Bhilsa see Vidisha, India 23°32′ N, 77°51′ E 197
Bhind, India 26°32′ N, 78°46′ E 197
Bhinmal, India 24°59′ N, 72°16′ E 186
Bhisho, S. Af. 32°49′ S, 27°31′ E 227
Bhiwani, India 28°46′ N, 76°9′ E 197
Bhojpur, Nepal 27°9′ N, 87°4′ E 197
Bhopal, India 23°16′ N, 77°25′ E 197
Bhubaneshwar, India 20°17′ N, 85°48′ E 188
Bhumibol Dam, Thai. 17°9′ N, 98°57′ E 202
Bhusawal, India 21°2′ N, 75°46′ E 188
Bhutan 27°24′ N, 89°54′ E 188
Bia, Monts, Dem. Rep. of the Congo 9°32′ S, 26°9′ E 224
Biá, river, Braz. 3°24′ S, 67°24′ W 136
Bia, river, Ghana 6°27′ N, 2°49′ W 222
Biak, Indonesia 1°4′ S, 136°1′ E 192
Biak, island, Indonesia 0°45′ N, 135°57′ E 192
Biała Góra, peak, Pol. 50°15′ N, 23°16′ E 152
Biała Podlaska, Pol. 52°2′ N, 23°6′ E 158
Białogard, Pol. 54°0′ N, 15°59′ E 152
Białowieża, Pol. 52°2′ N, 23°6′ E 152
Biały Bór, Pol. 53°54′ N, 16°49′ E 152
Białystok, Pol. 53°8′ N, 23°9′ E 152
Bianco, It. 38°6′ N, 16°8′ E 156
Biankouma, Côte d'Ivoire 7°38′ N, 7°36′ W 222
Biaora, India 23°56′ N, 76°55′ E 197
Biar, Sp. 38°37′ N, 0°46′ E 164
Biar Zahr, spring, Tun. 31°29′ N, 10°6′ E 214
Bīārjomand, Iran 36°2′ N, 55°57′ E 180
Biarritz, Fr. 43°25′ N, 1°39′ W 214
Bias, Fr. 44°8′ N, 1°15′ W 150
Biasca, Switz. 46°21′ N, 8°58′ E 167
Biaza, Russ. 56°34′ N, 78°18′ E 169
Biba, Burkina Faso 12°49′ N, 2°59′ W 222
Biba, Egypt 28°55′ N, 30°57′ E 180
Bibai, Japan 43°18′ N, 141°52′ E 190
Bibala, Angola 14°44′ S, 13°18′ E 220
Bibémi, Cameroon 9°18′ N, 13°52′ E 216
Bibiani, Ghana 6°28′ N, 2°18′ W 222
Bibile, Sri Lanka 7°9′ N, 81°15′ E 188
Bibione, It. 45°38′ N, 13°1′ E 167
Bibury, U.K. 51°45′ N, 1°50′ W 162
Bicaj, Alban. 41°59′ N, 20°25′ E 168
Bicas, Braz. 21°43′ S, 43°6′ W 138
Bicaz, Rom. 46°54′ N, 26°4′ E 156
Bicester, U.K. 51°53′ N, 1°9′ W 162
Biche, Lac la, lake, Can. 54°53′ N, 112°30′ W 108
Bichena, Eth. 10°23′ N, 38°14′ E 224
Bichi, Nig. 12°12′ N, 8°13′ E 222
Bichvint'a, Ga. 43°9′ N, 40°20′ E 195
Bickerdike, Can. 53°32′ N, 116°39′ W 108
Bickerton Island, Austral. 13°39′ S, 134°25′ E 230
Bicknell, Ind., U.S. 38°46′ N, 87°18′ W 102
Bicknell, Utah, U.S. 38°20′ N, 111°33′ W 90
Bicske, Hung. 47°28′ N, 18°39′ E 168
Bida, Nig. 9°3′ N, 5°59′ E 222
Bidar, India 17°54′ N, 77°32′ E 188
Bidarray, Fr. 43°16′ N, 1°21′ W 164
Biddeford, Me., U.S. 43°29′ N, 70°28′ W 104
Bidwell, Mount, Calif., U.S. 41°57′ N, 120°15′ W 90
Bié, adm. division, Angola 12°56′ S, 16°44′ E 220
Bié Plateau, Angola 11°41′ S, 15°45′ E 220
Biele Karpaty, Czech Rep. 49°5′ N, 17°49′ E 152
Bieler See, lake, Switz. 47°5′ N, 7°4′ E 165
Biella, It. 45°34′ N, 8°2′ E 167
Bielsa, Sp. 42°37′ N, 0°13′ E 164
Bielsk, Pol. 52°39′ N, 19°48′ E 152
Bielsk Podlaski, Pol. 52°46′ N, 23°10′ E 152
Bielsko-Biała, Pol. 49°49′ N, 19°2′ E 152
Bien Hoa, Vietnam 10°58′ N, 106°49′ E 202
Bienvenida, Sp. 38°18′ N, 6°13′ W 164
Bienville, Lac, lake, Can. 54°59′ N, 74°39′ W 106
Biescas, Sp. 42°37′ N, 0°19′ E 164
Bieżuń, Pol. 52°57′ N, 19°52′ E 152
Bifoum, Gabon 0°20′ N, 10°24′ E 218
Big Baldy Mountain, Mont., U.S. 46°56′ N, 110°41′ W 90
Big Baldy, peak, Idaho, U.S. 44°45′ N, 115°18′ W 90
Big Bay, Mich., U.S. 46°48′ N, 87°44′ W 94
Big Bear Lake, Calif., U.S. 34°14′ N, 116°57′ W 101
Big Beaver House, Can. 52°55′ N, 89°52′ W 82
Big Belt Mountains, Mont., U.S. 46°58′ N, 111°39′ W 90
Big Bend National Park, Tex., U.S. 29°9′ N, 103°44′ W 72
Big Black, river, Miss., U.S. 32°43′ N, 90°14′ W 103
Big Blue, river, Nebr., U.S. 41°1′ N, 97°55′ W 80
Big Bog, marsh, Minn., U.S. 48°18′ N, 94°29′ W 90
Big Creek, Calif., U.S. 37°12′ N, 119°15′ W 100
Big Cypress National Preserve, Fla., U.S. 26°5′ N, 81°11′ W 105
Big Cypress Swamp, marsh, Fla., U.S. 26°1′ N, 81°12′ W 105
Big Delta, Alas., U.S. 64°1′ N, 145°49′ W 98
Big Elk Mountain, Idaho, U.S. 43°12′ N, 111°21′ W 90
Big Falls, Minn., U.S. 48°9′ N, 93°50′ W 90
Big Fork, river, Minn., U.S. 48°4′ N, 93°60′ W 90
Big Horn Peak, Ariz., U.S. 33°36′ N, 113°13′ W 92
Big Interior Mountain, Can. 49°27′ N, 125°36′ W 90
Big Lake, Minn., U.S. 45°18′ N, 93°45′ W 94
Big Lake, Tex., U.S. 31°11′ N, 101°28′ W 92
Big Lake Ranch, Can. 52°23′ N, 121°52′ W 108
Big Lookout Mountain, Oreg., U.S. 44°35′ N, 117°23′ W 90
Big Maria Mountains, Calif., U.S. 33°54′ N, 114°56′ W 101
Big Mountain, Nev., U.S. 41°16′ N, 119°9′ W 90
Big Pine, Calif., U.S. 37°10′ N, 118°19′ W 101
Big Pine Key, Fla., U.S. 24°39′ N, 81°22′ W 105
Big Pine Mountain, Calif., U.S. 34°41′ N, 119°42′ W 100
Big Piney, Wyo., U.S. 42°32′ N, 110°6′ W 90
Big Piskwanish Point, Can. 51°44′ N, 80°27′ W 110
Big Port Walter, Alas., U.S. 56°23′ N, 134°45′ W 108
Big Rapids, Mich., U.S. 43°42′ N, 85°30′ W 102
Big River, Can. 53°50′ N, 107°1′ W 108
Big, river, Mo., U.S. 38°16′ N, 90°40′ W 80
Big Sable Point, Mich., U.S. 44°2′ N, 86°40′ W 102
Big Salmon, river, Can. 61°46′ N, 134°30′ W 98
Big Sand Lake, Can. 57°33′ N, 100°35′ W 108
Big Sandy, Mont., U.S. 48°9′ N, 110°6′ W 90
Big Sandy, Tex., U.S. 32°34′ N, 95°7′ W 103
Big Sandy Lake, lake, Can. 54°22′ N, 104°45′ W 108
Big Sandy Reservoir, Wyo., U.S. 42°17′ N, 109°49′ W 90
Big Sioux, river, S. Dak., U.S. 45°17′ N, 97°38′ W 80
Big Smoky Valley, Nev., U.S. 38°13′ N, 117°46′ W 90
Big Snowy Mountains, Mont., U.S. 46°51′ N, 109°39′ W 90
Big Southern Butte, Idaho, U.S. 43°23′ N, 113°6′ W 90
Big Spring, Tex., U.S. 32°13′ N, 101°28′ W 92
Big Springs, Nebr., U.S. 41°3′ N, 102°6′ W 90
Big Squaw Mountain, Me., U.S. 45°28′ N, 69°48′ W 94
Big Stone City, S. Dak., U.S. 45°16′ N, 96°30′ W 90
Big Sur, Calif., U.S. 36°16′ N, 121°49′ W 100
Big Thicket National Preserve, Tex., U.S. 30°26′ N, 94°41′ W 103
Big Timber, Mont., U.S. 45°48′ N, 109°58′ W 90
Big Trout Lake, Can. 53°51′ N, 92°1′ W 106
Big Trout Lake, Can. 53°43′ N, 89°55′ W 106
Big Valley, Can. 52°2′ N, 112°46′ W 90
Big Valley Mountains, Calif., U.S. 41°10′ N, 121°33′ W 90
Big Wells, Tex., U.S. 28°33′ N, 99°35′ W 92
Big White Mountain, Can. 49°43′ N, 119°2′ W 90
Big Wood Cay, island, Bahamas 24°25′ N, 77°40′ W 116
Biga, Turk. 40°13′ N, 27°12′ E 156
Bigadiç, Turk. 39°23′ N, 28°7′ E 156
Bigelow Mountain, Me., U.S. 45°8′ N, 70°22′ W 94
Bigfork, Minn., U.S. 47°42′ N, 93°40′ W 90
Bigfork, Mont., U.S. 48°2′ N, 114°7′ W 90
Biggar, Can. 52°3′ N, 107°59′ W 90
Bigge Island, Austral. 14°3′ S, 124°2′ E 230
Biggeluobbal, Nor. 69°22′ N, 23°22′ E 152
Biggleswade, U.K. 52°4′ N, 0°16′ E 162
Biggs, Calif., U.S. 39°24′ N, 121°43′ W 90
Bighorn Mountains, Wyo., U.S. 43°48′ N, 107°26′ W 90
Bignasco, Switz. 46°21′ N, 8°36′ E 167
Bigniba, river, Can. 49°2′ N, 77°43′ W 94
Bignona, Senegal 12°48′ N, 16°10′ W 222
Bigobo, Dem. Rep. of the Congo 5°27′ S, 27°34′ E 224
Bigstick Lake, Can. 50°16′ N, 109°40′ W 90
Bigstone Lake, lake, Can. 53°36′ N, 96°20′ W 108
Bigstone, river, Can. 55°28′ N, 95°12′ W 108
Bihać, Bosn. and Herzg. 44°49′ N, 15°53′ E 168
Bihar, adm. division, India 25°9′ N, 84°25′ E 188
Bihar Sharif, India 25°10′ N, 85°30′ E 197
Biharamulo, Tanzania 2°40′ S, 31°21′ E 224
Biharkeresztes, Hung. 47°7′ N, 21°42′ E 168
Bihor, adm. division, Rom. 46°51′ N, 21°40′ E 156
Bihor, Munţii, Rom. 46°42′ N, 22°25′ E 168
Bihosava, Belarus 55°50′ N, 27°42′ E 166
Biikzhal, Kaz. 46°51′ N, 54°48′ E 158
Bijagós, Arquipélago dos, North Atlantic Ocean 10°37′ N, 16°42′ W 222
Bijapur, India 18°46′ N, 80°49′ E 188
Bijapur, India 16°49′ N, 75°42′ E 188
Bījār, Iran 35°50′ N, 47°32′ E 180
Bijauri, Nepal 28°5′ N, 82°28′ E 197
Bijawar, India 24°37′ N, 79°30′ E 197
Bijeljina, Bosn. and Herzg. 44°45′ N, 19°14′ E 168
Bijelo Polje, Serb. and Mont. 43°1′ N, 19°44′ E 168
Bijie, China 27°18′ N, 105°19′ E 198
Bikaner, India 28°1′ N, 73°20′ E 186
Bikava, Latv. 56°44′ N, 27°2′ E 166
Bikin, Russ. 46°53′ N, 134°22′ E 190
Bikita, Zimb. 20°6′ S, 31°37′ E 227
Bīkkū Bīttī, peak, Lib. 22°8′ N, 19°11′ E 216
Bikoro, Dem. Rep. of the Congo 0°45′ N, 18°6′ E 218
Bikovo, Serb. and Mont. 46°0′ N, 19°45′ E 168
Bila, river, China 49°9′ N, 122°19′ E 198
Bila, Tanjung, Indonesia 1°8′ N, 108°39′ E 196
Bila Tserkva, Ukr. 49°47′ N, 30°14′ E 158
Biläcäri, Azerb. 40°27′ N, 49°47′ E 195
Bilād Banī Bū 'Alī, Oman 22°4′ N, 59°18′ E 182
Bilanga, Burkina Faso 12°32′ N, 5°296′ W 222
Bilaspur, India 22°4′ N, 82°8′ E 197
Biläsuvar, Azerb. 39°26′ N, 48°31′ E 195
Bilati, Dem. Rep. of the Congo 0°36′ N, 28°47′ E 224
Bilati, river, Dem. Rep. of the Congo 0°53′ N, 28°12′ E 224
Bilbao, Sp. 43°14′ N, 2°58′ W 150
Bile, Ukr. 51°38′ N, 26°4′ E 152
Bileća, Bosn. and Herzg. 42°52′ N, 18°24′ E 168
Bilecik, Turk. 40°9′ N, 29°58′ E 156
Bilhorod-Dnistrovs'kyy, Ukr. 46°11′ N, 30°17′ E 156
Bili, Dem. Rep. of the Congo 4°7′ N, 25°3′ E 224
Bili, river, Dem. Rep. of the Congo 4°4′ N, 24°28′ E 224
Bilibino, Russ. 67°54′ N, 166°13′ E 160
Bilican Dağları, peak, Turk. 38°56′ N, 42°6′ E 195
Bilimora, India 20°46′ N, 72°56′ E 188
Bilin, Myanmar 17°14′ N, 97°12′ E 202
Bilir, Russ. 65°29′ N, 131°52′ E 160
Bilis Qooqaani, Somalia 0°15′ N, 41°36′ E 224
Bilje, Croatia 45°35′ N, 18°45′ E 168
Bill, Wyo., U.S. 43°12′ N, 105°16′ W 90
Bill Williams, river, Ariz., U.S. 34°18′ N, 113°54′ W 101
Billerbeck, Ger. 51°58′ N, 7°17′ E 167
Billerica, Mass., U.S. 42°33′ N, 71°17′ W 104
Billingham, U.K. 54°35′ N, 1°17′ W 162
Billings, Mont., U.S. 45°46′ N, 108°31′ W 90
Billings, Okla., U.S. 36°30′ N, 97°25′ W 92
Billiton see Belitung, island, Indonesia 3°41′ S, 107°3′ E 192
Bilma, Niger 18°42′ N, 12°54′ E 216
Bilma, Grand Erg de, Niger 18°42′ N, 13°31′ E 216
Bilo Gora, Croatia 45°48′ N, 16°57′ E 168
Bilohirs'k, Ukr. 45°5′ N, 34°31′ E 156
Bilohir'ya, Ukr. 50°0′ N, 26°24′ E 152
Bilohorodka, Ukr. 49°59′ N, 26°38′ E 158
Biloli, India 18°45′ N, 77°44′ E 188
Bilopillya, Ukr. 51°7′ N, 34°20′ E 158

Biloxi, *Miss., U.S.* 30°23′ N, 88°55′ W **103**
Bilqās, *Egypt* 31°13′ N, 31°21′ E **180**
Bil'shivtsi, *Ukr.* 49°9′ N, 24°46′ E **152**
Biltine, *Chad* 14°30′ N, 20°55′ E **216**
Bilto, *Nor.* 69°28′ N, 21°36′ E **152**
Bilüü, *Mongolia* 48°58′ N, 89°21′ E **184**
Bilwaskarma, *Nicar.* 14°45′ N, 83°52′ W **115**
Bilzen, *Belg.* 50°52′ N, 5°30′ E **167**
Bima, river, *Dem. Rep. of the Congo* 3°3′ N, 25°44′ E **224**
Bimbila, *Ghana* 8°49′ N, 5°297′ E **222**
Bimini, adm. division, *Bahamas* 25°43′ N, 79°27′ W **96**
Bimini Islands, *North Atlantic Ocean* 25°45′ N, 79°5′ W **116**
Bin Ghunaymah, Jabal, *Lib.* 24°45′ N, 15°21′ E **216**
Bina, *India* 24°10′ N, 78°12′ E **197**
Binaced, *Sp.* 41°49′ N, 0°12′ E **164**
Binasco, *It.* 45°19′ N, 9°5′ E **167**
Binche, *Belg.* 50°24′ N, 4°9′ E **163**
Bindura, *Zimb.* 17°20′ S, 31°19′ E **224**
Binford, *N. Dak., U.S.* 47°32′ N, 98°23′ W **90**
Binga, *Zimb.* 17°37′ S, 27°20′ E **224**
Bingen, *Wash., U.S.* 45°42′ N, 121°28′ W **100**
Binger, *Okla., U.S.* 35°17′ N, 98°22′ W **92**
BingerbrÜck, *Ger.* 49°57′ N, 7°52′ E **167**
Bingham, *Me., U.S.* 45°2′ N, 69°53′ W **111**
Binghamton, *N.Y., U.S.* 42°6′ N, 75°54′ W **110**
Bingkor, *Malaysia* 5°25′ N, 116°11′ E **203**
Bingley, *U.K.* 53°51′ N, 1°50′ W **162**
Bingöl, *Turk.* 38°52′ N, 40°29′ E **195**
Bingöl Dağları, peak, *Turk.* 39°19′ N, 41°24′ E **195**
Binh Khe, *Vietnam* 13°59′ N, 108°48′ E **202**
Binh Son, *Vietnam* 15°19′ N, 108°44′ E **202**
Binhai, *China* 34°2′ N, 119°51′ E **198**
Binham, *U.K.* 52°55′ N, 0°57′ E **162**
Bini Erdi, spring, *Chad* 20°9′ N, 18°1′ E **216**
Binjai, *Indonesia* 3°51′ N, 108°13′ E **196**
Binjai, *Indonesia* 3°38′ N, 98°29′ E **196**
Binna, Raas, *Somalia* 11°10′ N, 51°10′ E **216**
Binongko, island, *Indonesia* 6°16′ S, 122°51′ E **192**
Bintan, island, *Indonesia* 1°16′ N, 104°33′ E **196**
Bintuan, *Philippines* 12°2′ N, 120°2′ E **203**
Bintulu, *Malaysia* 3°11′ N, 113°2′ E **192**
Binxian, *China* 45°44′ N, 127°29′ E **198**
Binxian, *China* 35°2′ N, 108°3′ E **198**
Binyamina, *Israel* 32°30′ N, 34°56′ E **194**
Binyang, *China* 23°9′ N, 108°46′ E **198**
Binza, *Dem. Rep. of the Congo* 4°30′ S, 15°10′ E **218**
Binzhou, *China* 37°23′ N, 118°4′ E **198**
Bio Addo, *Somalia* 8°10′ N, 49°47′ E **216**
Bio-Bio, adm. division, *Chile* 37°12′ S, 73°8′ W **134**
Bioč, peak, *Serb. and Mont.* 43°12′ N, 18°43′ E **168**
Bioče, *Serb. and Mont.* 42°30′ N, 19°20′ E **168**
Bioko, island, *Equatorial Guinea* 3°20′ N, 8°35′ E **253**
Bioko, region, *Africa* 3°13′ N, 8°14′ E **218**
Biokovo, peak, *Croatia* 43°18′ N, 17°0′ E **168**
Biola, *Calif., U.S.* 36°48′ N, 120°2′ W **100**
Bíópio, *Angola* 12°26′ S, 13°45′ E **220**
Bioska, *Serb. and Mont.* 43°52′ N, 19°39′ E **168**
Biota, *Sp.* 42°16′ N, 1°12′ W **164**
Bipindi, *Cameroon* 3°14′ N, 10°24′ E **218**
Bir, *India* 18°59′ N, 75°46′ E **188**
Bîr Abu el Ḥuṣein, spring, *Egypt* 22°52′ N, 29°54′ E **182**
Bîr Abu Gharâdiq, spring, *Egypt* 30°5′ N, 28°2′ E **180**
Bîr Abu Hashîm, spring, *Egypt* 23°41′ N, 34°3′ E **182**
Bîr Abu Minqâr, spring, *Egypt* 26°29′ N, 27°35′ E **180**
Bîr Abu Sa'fa, spring, *Egypt* 23°14′ N, 34°48′ E **182**
Bi'r adh Dhakar, spring, *Lib.* 25°42′ N, 22°42′ E **226**
Bi'r al Ma'rūf, spring, *Lib.* 25°6′ N, 18°31′ E **216**
Bi'r al Qāf, spring, *Lib.* 28°16′ N, 15°22′ E **216**
Bi'r al Qarḑī, spring, *Yemen* 15°35′ N, 47°18′ E **182**
Bi'r 'Allāq, spring, *Lib.* 31°7′ N, 11°54′ E **214**
Bir Anzarane, *Western Sahara* 23°51′ N, 14°33′ W **214**
Bir Bel Guerdâne, spring, *Mauritania* 25°23′ N, 10°31′ W **214**
Bir Beressof, spring, *Alg.* 32°33′ N, 7°56′ E **214**
Bi'r Bin Ghanīyah, spring, *Lib.* 31°10′ N, 21°52′ E **226**
Bi'r Bū Ḩawsh, spring, *Lib.* 25°29′ N, 22°4′ E **216**
Bi'r Bū Zurayyiq, spring, *Lib.* 25°34′ N, 22°15′ E **226**
Bir Chali, spring, *Mali* 22°58′ N, 4°60′ W **214**
Bîr Dibis, spring, *Egypt* 22°11′ N, 29°29′ E **226**
Bir ed Deheb, spring, *Alg.* 25°8′ N, 1°58′ W **214**
Bîr el 'Abd, *Egypt* 31°0′ N, 32°59′ E **194**
Bir el Hadjaj, spring, *Alg.* 26°26′ N, 1°26′ W **214**
Bîr el Ḥamma, *Egypt* 30°37′ N, 33°32′ E **194**
Bîr el Kaseiba, spring, *Egypt* 30°59′ N, 33°17′ E **194**
Bir el Khzaïm, spring, *Mauritania* 24°28′ N, 7°50′ W **214**
Bir el Ksaïb, spring, *Mali* 21°16′ N, 5°38′ W **222**
Bîr el Maqeibra, spring, *Egypt* 30°52′ N, 32°50′ E **194**
Bîr el Qandîl, spring, *Egypt* 30°58′ N, 33°7′ E **194**
Bîr el Roghwi, spring, *Egypt* 30°46′ N, 33°26′ E **194**
Bi'r Fardān, spring, *Saudi Arabia* 22°4′ N, 48°38′ E **182**
Bîr Fuâd, spring, *Egypt* 30°25′ N, 26°27′ E **180**
Bi'r Ghawdah, spring, *Saudi Arabia* 23°0′ N, 44°17′ E **182**
Bîr Gifgâfa, *Egypt* 30°26′ N, 33°11′ E **194**
Bîr Ḥasana, *Egypt* 30°27′ N, 33°47′ E **194**
Bîr Ḥibeiṭa, spring, *Egypt* 30°27′ N, 32°25′ E **194**
Bir Igueni, spring, *Mauritania* 20°27′ N, 14°55′ W **222**
Bi'r Juraybī'āt, spring, *Iraq* 29°10′ N, 45°30′ E **196**
Bîr Khâlda, spring, *Egypt* 30°48′ N, 27°14′ E **180**
Bîr Kiseiba, spring, *Egypt* 22°40′ N, 29°55′ E **182**
Bîr Lahfân, *Egypt* 31°0′ N, 33°51′ E **194**
Bir Lahmar, *Western Sahara* 26°4′ N, 11°4′ W **214**
Bir Lahrache, spring, *Alg.* 32°0′ N, 8°13′ E **214**
Bir Lemouissat, spring, *Mauritania* 25°3′ N, 10°33′ W **214**
Bîr Madkûr, spring, *Egypt* 30°42′ N, 32°31′ E **194**
Bîr Misâḥa, spring, *Egypt* 22°11′ N, 27°56′ E **226**
Bir Mogreïn (Fort Trinquet), *Mauritania* 25°13′ N, 11°37′ W **214**
Bîr Murr, spring, *Egypt* 23°21′ N, 30°4′ E **182**
Bîr Nâhid, spring, *Egypt* 30°14′ N, 28°53′ E **180**
Bîr Nakheila, spring, *Egypt* 23°59′ N, 30°51′ E **182**
Bi'r Nāşirah, spring, *Lib.* 30°18′ N, 11°23′ E **214**
Bir Ould Brini, spring, *Alg.* 25°24′ N, 1°50′ W **214**
Bir Ounâne, spring, *Mali* 21°26′ N, 3°53′ W **222**
Bîr Qaṭia, spring, *Egypt* 30°57′ N, 32°44′ E **194**
Bir Rhorrafa, spring, *Alg.* 32°20′ N, 8°4′ E **214**
Bir Romane, spring, *Tun.* 32°32′ N, 8°21′ E **214**
Bîr Ṣahara, spring, *Egypt* 22°50′ N, 28°34′ E **226**
Bîr Salala, spring, *Sudan* 19°24′ N, 35°38′ E **182**
Bîr Seiyâla, spring, *Egypt* 26°7′ N, 33°54′ E **180**
Bîr Shalatein, spring, *Egypt* 23°3′ N, 35°35′ E **182**
Bîr Takhlîs, spring, *Egypt* 22°24′ N, 30°7′ E **182**
Bîr Ṭarfâwi, spring, *Egypt* 22°56′ N, 28°51′ E **226**
Bi'r Tārsīn, spring, *Lib.* 31°41′ N, 13°23′ E **216**
Bir Tinkardad, spring, *Western Sahara* 23°57′ N, 12°58′ W **214**
B'ir Tlakshin, oil field, *Lib.* 30°55′ N, 11°53′ E **143**
Bîr Ungât, spring, *Egypt* 22°6′ N, 33°44′ E **182**
Bi'r Uoigh, spring, *Lib.* 23°7′ N, 17°20′ E **216**
Bi'r Zalṭan, spring, *Lib.* 28°27′ N, 19°44′ E **216**
Bîr Zeidûn, spring, *Egypt* 25°42′ N, 33°42′ E **180**
Bir Zîrî, spring, *Mauritania* 21°32′ N, 10°47′ W **222**
Bir Zreïgat, spring, *Mauritania* 22°28′ N, 8°54′ W **222**
Birāk, *Lib.* 27°34′ N, 14°14′ E **216**
Birao, *Cen. Af. Rep.* 10°16′ N, 22°47′ E **218**
Biratnagar, *Nepal* 26°28′ N, 87°16′ E **197**
Birch Creek, *Alas., U.S.* 66°16′ N, 145°51′ W **98**
Birch Hills, *Can.* 52°59′ N, 105°27′ W **108**
Birch Lake, *Can.* 51°21′ N, 92°57′ W **110**
Birch Mountains, *Can.* 57°34′ N, 113°37′ W **108**
Birch River, *Can.* 52°23′ N, 101°8′ W **108**
Birch, river, *Can.* 58°17′ N, 113°56′ W **108**
Birchiş, *Rom.* 45°58′ N, 22°10′ E **168**
Birchwood, *Alas., U.S.* 61°25′ N, 149°25′ W **98**
Bird, *Can.* 56°29′ N, 94°15′ W **108**
Bird City, *Kans., U.S.* 39°45′ N, 101°31′ W **90**
Bird Island, *Minn., U.S.* 44°45′ N, 94°55′ W **94**
Bird, river, *Can.* 50°34′ N, 95°11′ W **90**
Bireun, *Indonesia* 5°11′ N, 96°41′ E **196**
Birganj, *Nepal* 27°1′ N, 84°54′ E **197**
Biri, river, *Sudan* 7°40′ N, 26°4′ E **224**
Biria, river, *Venez.* 1°14′ N, 66°34′ W **136**
Birigui, *Braz.* 21°16′ S, 50°20′ W **138**
Birilyussy, *Russ.* 57°9′ N, 90°39′ E **169**
Bīrīn, *Syr.* 35°0′ N, 36°39′ E **194**
Birine, *Alg.* 35°38′ N, 3°13′ E **150**
Birini, *Cen. Af. Rep.* 7°50′ N, 22°26′ E **218**
Bīrjand, *Iran* 32°55′ N, 59°17′ E **180**
Birkenfeld, *Ger.* 49°38′ N, 7°10′ E **163**
Birkenfeld, *Oreg., U.S.* 45°58′ N, 123°19′ W **100**
Birkenhead, *U.K.* 53°24′ N, 3°2′ W **162**
Birkfeld, *Aust.* 47°20′ N, 15°41′ E **168**
Bîrlad, *Rom.* 46°13′ N, 27°40′ E **156**
Birlik, *Kaz.* 44°3′ N, 73°33′ E **184**
Birmingham, *Ala., U.S.* 33°30′ N, 86°49′ W **96**
Birmingham, *U.K.* 52°28′ N, 1°53′ W **162**
Birmitrapur, *India* 22°22′ N, 84°43′ E **197**
Birni, *Benin* 10°1′ N, 1°30′ E **222**
Birni Ngaouré, *Niger* 13°6′ N, 2°55′ E **222**
Birni Nkonni, *Niger* 13°47′ N, 5°15′ E **222**
Birnie, *Can.* 50°27′ N, 99°27′ W **90**
Birnin Gwari, *Nig.* 10°59′ N, 6°47′ E **222**
Birnin Kebbi, *Nig.* 12°26′ N, 4°12′ E **222**
Birniwa, *Nig.* 12°48′ N, 10°15′ E **222**
Birobidzhan, *Russ.* 48°54′ N, 133°0′ E **190**
Birong, *Philippines* 9°24′ N, 118°9′ E **203**
Birou, *Mali* 15°4′ N, 9°56′ W **222**
Birougou, Monts, peak, *Gabon* 1°55′ S, 12°9′ E **218**
Birrie, river, *Austral.* 29°22′ S, 146°48′ E **230**
Birshoghyr, *Kaz.* 48°24′ N, 58°43′ E **158**
Birsk, *Russ.* 55°26′ N, 55°36′ E **154**
Birštonas, *Lith.* 54°36′ N, 24°0′ E **166**
Birtin, *Rom.* 46°58′ N, 22°32′ E **168**
Birtle, *Can.* 50°26′ N, 101°4′ W **90**
Biru, *China* 31°32′ N, 93°47′ E **188**
Biryakovo, *Russ.* 59°33′ N, 41°29′ E **154**
Biržai, *Lith.* 56°11′ N, 24°44′ E **166**
Bîrzava, *Rom.* 46°6′ N, 21°59′ E **168**
Bîrzava, river, *Rom.* 45°16′ N, 20°56′ E **168**
Bisaccia, *It.* 41°1′ N, 15°22′ E **156**
Bisbee, *Ariz., U.S.* 31°27′ N, 109°54′ W **92**
Bisbee, *N. Dak., U.S.* 48°36′ N, 99°24′ W **90**
Biscarrués, *Sp.* 42°13′ N, 0°45′ E **164**
Biscay, Bay of 43°48′ N, 7°35′ W **143**
Biscay Plain, *North Atlantic Ocean* 45°12′ N, 8°17′ W **253**
Biscayne Bay 25°34′ N, 80°28′ W **105**
Biscayne, Key, island, *Fla., U.S.* 25°42′ N, 80°10′ W **105**
Biscayne National Park, *Atlantic Ocean* 25°34′ N, 80°7′ W **105**
Bischleben, *Ger.* 50°56′ N, 10°58′ E **152**
Bischofsheim, *Ger.* 50°24′ N, 10°0′ E **167**
Bischwiller, *Fr.* 48°46′ N, 7°50′ E **163**
Biscotasing, *Can.* 47°18′ N, 82°7′ W **94**
Biser, *Bulg.* 41°53′ N, 25°57′ E **156**
Biserovo, *Russ.* 59°4′ N, 53°24′ E **154**
Bisert', *Russ.* 56°52′ N, 59°4′ E **154**
Biševo, island, *Croatia* 42°53′ N, 15°57′ E **168**
Bishkek, *Kyrg.* 42°50′ N, 74°26′ E **184**
Bishop, *Tex., U.S.* 27°34′ N, 97°48′ W **96**
Bishop Auckland, *U.K.* 54°40′ N, 1°42′ W **162**
Bishop Creek Reservoir, lake, *Nev., U.S.* 41°13′ N, 115°34′ W **90**
Bishops and Clerks, islands, *St George's Channel* 51°42′ N, 6°54′ W **150**
Bishop's Castle, *U.K.* 52°28′ N, 2°59′ W **162**
Bishop's Falls, *Can.* 49°1′ N, 55°31′ W **111**
Bishop's Stortford, *U.K.* 51°51′ N, 0°8′ E **162**
Biskia, *Eritrea* 15°28′ N, 37°30′ E **182**
Biskintā, *Leb.* 33°56′ N, 35°48′ E **194**
Biskra, *Alg.* 34°50′ N, 5°44′ E **214**
Bislig, *Philippines* 8°13′ N, 126°16′ E **203**
Bismarck, *Ill., U.S.* 40°15′ N, 87°36′ W **102**
Bismarck, *N. Dak., U.S.* 46°46′ N, 100°54′ W **90**
Bismarck Archipelago, *Bismarck Sea* 1°32′ S, 145°44′ E **192**
Bismarck Range, *P.N.G.* 5°1′ S, 144°9′ E **192**
Bismarck Sea 4°3′ S, 145°12′ E **192**
Bismil, *Turk.* 37°52′ N, 40°42′ E **195**
Bison, *S. Dak., U.S.* 45°31′ N, 102°28′ W **90**
Bison Lake, *Can.* 57°13′ N, 116°28′ W **108**
Bison Peak, *Colo., U.S.* 39°13′ N, 105°34′ W **90**
Bissameuttack, *India* 19°30′ N, 83°30′ E **188**
Bissau, *Guinea-Bissau* 11°49′ N, 15°45′ W **222**
Bissett, *Can.* 51°0′ N, 95°41′ W **90**
Bissiga, *Burkina Faso* 12°41′ N, 1°14′ W **222**
Bissikrima, *Guinea* 10°53′ N, 10°59′ W **222**
Bistcho Lake, *Can.* 59°49′ N, 119°18′ W **108**
Bistrica, *Serb. and Mont.* 43°28′ N, 19°41′ E **168**
Bistriţa-Năsăud, adm. division, *Rom.* 47°20′ N, 24°9′ E **156**
Bistriţa, *Rom.* 47°9′ N, 24°29′ E **156**
Bistriţei, Munţii, *Rom.* 47°14′ N, 25°3′ E **156**
Biswan, *India* 27°29′ N, 81°0′ E **197**
Bita, river, *Col.* 5°39′ N, 69°8′ W **136**
Bitburg, *Ger.* 49°58′ N, 6°31′ E **167**
Bitche, *Fr.* 49°3′ N, 7°26′ E **163**
Bitely, *Mich., U.S.* 43°44′ N, 85°52′ W **102**
Bitkin, *Chad* 11°58′ N, 18°18′ E **216**
Bitlis, *Turk.* 38°21′ N, 42°3′ E **195**
Bitola, *Maced.* 41°1′ N, 21°23′ E **180**
Bitter Root Range, *North America* 47°31′ N, 116°18′ W **90**
Bitterfeld, *Ger.* 51°37′ N, 12°18′ E **152**
Bitterfontein, *S. Af.* 31°3′ S, 18°14′ E **227**
Bitterroot Range, *Idaho, U.S.* 47°46′ N, 116°27′ W **80**
Bitumount, *Can.* 57°22′ N, 111°36′ W **108**
Biu, *Nig.* 10°36′ N, 12°12′ E **216**
Bivolu, peak, *Rom.* 47°13′ N, 25°51′ E **156**
Bixad, *Rom.* 47°55′ N, 23°22′ E **168**
Bixby, *Okla., U.S.* 35°54′ N, 95°54′ W **96**
Biya, river, *Russ.* 51°16′ N, 87°47′ E **190**
Biyang, *China* 32°44′ N, 113°23′ E **198**
Biysk, *Russ.* 52°35′ N, 85°13′ E **184**
Bizana, *S. Af.* 30°53′ S, 29°52′ E **227**
Bizerte, *Tun.* 37°17′ N, 9°51′ E **156**
Bjärnum, *Nor.* 56°18′ N, 13°42′ E **152**
Bjelolasica, peak, *Croatia* 45°15′ N, 14°53′ E **156**
Bjelovar, *Croatia* 45°53′ N, 16°49′ E **168**
Björbo, *Nor.* 60°24′ N, 14°44′ E **152**
Björkholmen, *Nor.* 66°47′ N, 19°6′ E **152**
Björkö, island, *Sw.* 59°54′ N, 19°3′ E **166**
Björköby, *Fin.* 63°19′ N, 21°20′ E **152**
Björksele, *Nor.* 64°59′ N, 18°33′ E **152**
Björna, *Nor.* 63°32′ N, 18°35′ E **152**
Björneborg see Pori, *Fin.* 61°26′ N, 21°44′ E **166**
Bjørnøya (Bear Island), *Nor.* 73°46′ N, 15°27′ E **160**
Bjørnskinn, *Nor.* 68°59′ N, 15°41′ E **152**
Bjuröklubb, *Nor.* 64°28′ N, 21°35′ E **152**
Bjuv, *Nor.* 56°6′ N, 12°52′ E **152**
Bla, *Mali* 13°0′ N, 5°49′ W **222**
Blace, *Serb. and Mont.* 43°17′ N, 21°17′ E **168**
Blache, Lac de La, lake, *Can.* 50°5′ N, 69°53′ W **111**
Black Bay 48°37′ N, 89°19′ W **80**
Black Bay Peninsula, *Can.* 48°34′ N, 88°43′ W **94**
Black Bear Bay 53°15′ N, 56°36′ W **111**
Black Birch Lake, *Can.* 56°48′ N, 108°45′ W **108**
Black Butte, peak, *Calif., U.S.* 39°42′ N, 122°57′ W **90**
Black Butte, peak, *Mont., U.S.* 44°52′ N, 111°55′ W **90**
Black Creek, *Can.* 52°18′ N, 121°8′ W **108**
Black Creek, river, *Miss., U.S.* 31°0′ N, 88°58′ W **103**
Black Diamond, *Can.* 50°41′ N, 114°14′ W **90**
Black Diamond, *Wash., U.S.* 47°17′ N, 121°60′ W **100**
Black Fox Mountain, *Calif., U.S.* 41°20′ N, 121°59′ W **90**
Black Hills, *S. Dak., U.S.* 43°30′ N, 103°50′ W **90**
Black Island, *Antarctica* 78°21′ S, 166°54′ E **248**
Black Lake, *Can.* 59°5′ N, 105°42′ W **108**
Black Lake, lake, *Can.* 59°13′ N, 105°39′ W **108**
Black Lassic, peak, *Calif., U.S.* 40°19′ N, 123°39′ W **90**
Black Mesa, *Ariz., U.S.* 35°57′ N, 111°8′ W **80**
Black Mountain, *Colo., U.S.* 40°46′ N, 107°27′ W **90**
Black Mountain, *Ky., U.S.* 36°53′ N, 82°58′ W **96**
Black Mountain, *Va., U.S.* 36°52′ N, 83°2′ W **80**
Black Mountains, *Ariz., U.S.* 34°56′ N, 114°28′ W **101**
Black Mountains, *Calif., U.S.* 36°10′ N, 116°46′ W **101**
Black Mountains, *U.K.* 52°4′ N, 3°9′ W **162**
Black Peak, *Ariz., U.S.* 34°6′ N, 114°15′ W **101**
Black Peak, *N. Mex., U.S.* 32°54′ N, 108°14′ W **92**
Black Pine Peak, *Idaho, U.S.* 42°8′ N, 113°12′ W **90**
Black Range, *N. Mex., U.S.* 33°29′ N, 108°42′ W **112**
Black, river, *Ark., U.S.* 35°51′ N, 91°15′ W **80**
Black River Falls, *Wis., U.S.* 44°17′ N, 90°52′ W **94**
Black, river, *La., U.S.* 31°35′ N, 91°54′ W **103**
Black, river, *Minn., U.S.* 48°25′ N, 94°20′ W **90**
Black, river, *N.Y., U.S.* 44°3′ N, 75°54′ W **80**
Black Rock Desert, *Nev., U.S.* 40°50′ N, 119°26′ W **90**
Black Rock Range, *Nev., U.S.* 41°25′ N, 119°9′ W **90**
Black Sea 43°19′ N, 33°22′ E **158**
Black see Da, river, *Vietnam* 21°11′ N, 104°8′ E **202**
Black Volta, river, *Ghana* 8°33′ N, 2°3′ W **222**
Black Volta see Mouhoun, river, *Burkina Faso* 11°43′ N, 4°30′ W **222**
Black Warrior, river, *Ala., U.S.* 34°6′ N, 88°13′ W **80**
Blackall, *Austral.* 24°26′ S, 145°31′ E **231**
Blackburn, *U.K.* 53°45′ N, 2°30′ W **162**
Blackburn, Mount, *Alas., U.S.* 61°36′ N, 143°37′ W **98**
Blackdown Hills, *U.K.* 50°56′ N, 3°7′ W **162**
Blackduck, *Minn., U.S.* 47°42′ N, 94°33′ W **90**
Blackfoot, *Idaho, U.S.* 43°11′ N, 112°20′ W **90**
Blackfoot Mountains, *Idaho, U.S.* 42°58′ N, 111°45′ W **90**
Blackie, *Can.* 50°37′ N, 113°37′ W **108**
Blackmoor Vale, *U.K.* 50°57′ N, 2°24′ W **162**
Blackpool, *U.K.* 53°49′ N, 3°3′ W **162**
Blacksburg, *Va., U.S.* 37°13′ N, 80°26′ W **96**
Blackstone, *Mass., U.S.* 42°0′ N, 71°33′ W **104**
Blackstone, river, *Can.* 61°10′ N, 123°2′ W **108**
Blackville, *Can.* 46°44′ N, 65°51′ W **94**
Blackwell, *Okla., U.S.* 36°47′ N, 97°17′ W **92**
Blackwell, *Tex., U.S.* 32°3′ N, 100°19′ W **92**
Blaenau Ffestiniog, *U.K.* 52°59′ N, 3°55′ W **162**
Blåfjellhatten, peak, *Nor.* 64°47′ N, 13°15′ E **152**
Blagaj, *Bosn. and Herzg.* 44°3′ N, 17°11′ E **168**
Blagodarnyy, *Russ.* 45°3′ N, 43°20′ E **158**
Blagoevgrad, *Bulg.* 42°1′ N, 23°6′ E **168**
Blagoevgrad, adm. division, *Bulg.* 41°27′ N, 23°5′ E **168**
Blagopoluchiya, Zaliv 75°8′ N, 58°41′ E **160**
Blagoveshchenka, *Russ.* 52°49′ N, 79°55′ E **184**
Blagoveshchensk, *Russ.* 50°22′ N, 127°32′ E **198**
Blagoveshchenskoye, *Russ.* 61°28′ N, 42°36′ E **154**
Blagoyevo, *Russ.* 63°25′ N, 47°57′ E **154**
Blaiken, *Nor.* 65°15′ N, 16°49′ E **152**
Blaine, *Wash., U.S.* 48°58′ N, 122°44′ W **100**
Blainville-sur-l'Eau, *Fr.* 48°32′ N, 6°24′ E **163**
Blair, *Nebr., U.S.* 41°31′ N, 96°8′ W **90**
Blaj, *Rom.* 46°10′ N, 23°57′ E **156**
Blake Plateau, *North Atlantic Ocean* 29°56′ N, 78°19′ W **253**
Blake Point, *Mich., U.S.* 47°58′ N, 88°28′ W **110**
Blake-Bahama Ridge, *North Atlantic Ocean* 29°6′ N, 73°10′ W **253**
Blakeney, *U.K.* 52°57′ N, 1°1′ E **162**
Blakeney, *U.K.* 51°45′ N, 2°29′ W **162**
Blakiston, Mount, *Can.* 49°4′ N, 114°8′ W **90**
Blâmont, *Fr.* 48°34′ N, 6°50′ E **163**
Blanc, Cap, *Sp.* 39°9′ N, 2°28′ E **150**
Blanc, Cap, *Western Sahara* 20°59′ N, 17°36′ W **222**
Blanc, Mont, peak, *Fr.-It.* 45°50′ N, 6°49′ E **150**
Blanc, Réservoir, lake, *Can.* 47°46′ N, 73°19′ W **94**
Blanca, *Bahía* 39°3′ S, 62°43′ W **139**
Blanca Peak, *Sierra, N. Mex., U.S.* 33°21′ N, 105°52′ W **92**
Blanca, Sierra, peak, *Tex., U.S.* 31°13′ N, 105°30′ W **92**
Blanchard, *La., U.S.* 32°34′ N, 93°55′ W **103**
Blanchard, *Mich., U.S.* 43°30′ N, 85°5′ W **102**
Blanchard, *Okla., U.S.* 35°7′ N, 97°40′ W **92**
Blanchardville, *Wis., U.S.* 42°47′ N, 89°52′ W **102**
Blanchester, *Ohio, U.S.* 39°17′ N, 83°59′ W **102**
Blanchland, *U.K.* 54°51′ N, 2°4′ W **162**
Blanco, *Tex., U.S.* 30°5′ N, 98°25′ W **92**
Blanco, *Bahía* 29°0′ N, 115°4′ W **92**
Blanco, *Cabo, C.R.* 9°31′ N, 85°55′ W **115**
Blanco, *Cape, Oreg., U.S.* 42°39′ N, 124°56′ W **90**
Blanco, Lago, lake, *Arg.* 45°56′ S, 71°8′ W **134**
Blanco, Punta, *Mex.* 29°6′ N, 115°5′ W **92**
Blanco, river, *Arg.* 29°28′ S, 69°10′ W **134**
Blanco, river, *Bol.* 14°47′ S, 63°37′ W **137**
Blandford Forum, *U.K.* 50°51′ N, 2°10′ W **162**
Blanding, *Utah, U.S.* 37°37′ N, 109°29′ W **92**
Blanes, *Sp.* 41°41′ N, 2°48′ E **164**
Blangy, *Fr.* 49°54′ N, 1°37′ E **163**
Blankenberge, *Belg.* 51°18′ N, 3°7′ E **163**
Blankenheim, *Ger.* 50°26′ N, 6°39′ E **167**
Blanquilla, La, island, *Venez.* 11°59′ N, 64°58′ W **116**
Blantyre, *Malawi* 15°52′ S, 35°2′ E **224**
Blasket Islands, *Atlantic Ocean* 51°59′ N, 11°30′ W **150**
Błaszki, *Pol.* 51°39′ N, 18°27′ E **152**
Blatec, *Maced.* 41°49′ N, 22°35′ E **168**
Blato, *Croatia* 42°55′ N, 16°46′ E **168**
Blattnicksele, *Nor.* 65°18′ N, 17°38′ E **152**
Bléneau, *Fr.* 47°42′ N, 2°56′ E **150**
Blenheim, *Can.* 42°20′ N, 81°60′ W **102**
Blenheim, *N.Z.* 41°32′ S, 173°55′ E **240**
Blenheim Palace, site, *U.K.* 51°49′ N, 1°23′ W **162**
Bletchley, *U.K.* 51°59′ N, 0°45′ E **162**
Bleue, *Indonesia* 5°0′ N, 96°13′ E **196**
Bleus, Monts, *Dem. Rep. of the Congo* 1°8′ N, 29°35′ E **224**
Blexen, *Ger.* 53°31′ N, 8°33′ E **163**
Blida, *Alg.* 36°27′ N, 2°49′ E **150**
Blind River, *Can.* 46°11′ N, 82°58′ W **94**
Blinisht, *Alban.* 41°52′ N, 19°59′ E **168**
Blissfield, *Mich., U.S.* 41°49′ N, 83°51′ W **102**
Blitta, *Togo* 8°20′ N, 0°58′ E **222**
Block Island, *R.I., U.S.* 41°12′ N, 71°43′ W **104**
Bloedrivier, *S. Af.* 27°56′ S, 30°32′ E **227**
Bloemfontein, *S. Af.* 29°9′ S, 26°3′ E **227**
Bloemhof, *S. Af.* 27°40′ S, 25°34′ E **227**
Blois, *Fr.* 47°35′ N, 1°20′ E **150**
Blönduós, *Ice.* 65°39′ N, 20°21′ W **246**
Bloodvein, river, *Can.* 51°25′ N, 96°32′ W **108**
Bloody Mountain, *Calif., U.S.* 37°32′ N, 118°60′ W **92**
Bloody Run Hills, *Nev., U.S.* 41°6′ N, 117°59′ W **90**
Bloomburg, *Tex., U.S.* 33°8′ N, 94°4′ W **103**
Bloomer, *Wis., U.S.* 45°6′ N, 91°29′ W **94**
Bloomfield, *Conn., U.S.* 41°49′ N, 72°44′ W **104**
Bloomfield, *Iowa, U.S.* 40°44′ N, 92°25′ W **94**
Bloomfield, *Nebr., U.S.* 42°33′ N, 97°39′ W **90**
Bloomfield, *N. Mex., U.S.* 36°42′ N, 107°59′ W **92**
Bloomfield Hills, *Mich., U.S.* 42°35′ N, 83°16′ W **102**
Bloomingburg, *Ohio, U.S.* 39°35′ N, 83°24′ W **102**
Bloomingdale, *N.Y., U.S.* 44°24′ N, 74°6′ W **104**
Bloomington, *Ill., U.S.* 40°28′ N, 88°59′ W **102**
Bloomington, *Ind., U.S.* 39°10′ N, 86°32′ W **102**
Bloomington, *Tex., U.S.* 28°38′ N, 96°54′ W **96**
Bloomsburg, *Pa., U.S.* 40°59′ N, 76°28′ W **94**
Bloomville, *Ohio, U.S.* 41°2′ N, 83°1′ W **102**
Blouberg, peak, *S. Af.* 23°5′ S, 28°52′ E **227**
Blount Nunatak, peak, *Antarctica* 83°20′ S, 52°56′ W **248**
Blue Bell Knoll, peak, *Utah, U.S.* 38°8′ N, 111°34′ W **90**
Blue Diamond, *Nev., U.S.* 36°2′ N, 115°25′ W **101**
Blue Hill, *Nebr., U.S.* 40°18′ N, 98°27′ W **90**
Blue Hill Bay 44°6′ N, 68°45′ W **111**
Blue Lagoon National Park, *Zambia* 15°36′ S, 26°55′ E **224**
Blue Lake, *Calif., U.S.* 40°53′ N, 123°60′ W **90**
Blue Mound, *Ill., U.S.* 39°41′ N, 89°8′ W **102**
Blue Mountain, *Pa., U.S.* 40°30′ N, 76°43′ W **94**
Blue Mountain Pass, *Oreg., U.S.* 42°18′ N, 117°50′ W **90**
Blue Mountain, peak, *Ark., U.S.* 34°38′ N, 94°8′ W **96**
Blue Mountain, peak, *Calif., U.S.* 41°49′ N, 120°57′ W **90**
Blue Mountain, peak, *Nev., U.S.* 40°58′ N, 118°10′ W **90**
Blue Mountain, peak, *Oreg., U.S.* 42°19′ N, 117°58′ W **90**
Blue Mountains, *Oreg., U.S.* 45°14′ N, 118°33′ W **90**
Blue Nile, adm. division, *Sudan* 11°18′ N, 33°10′ E **182**
Blue Nile see Ābay, river, *Eth.* 11°15′ N, 38°15′ E **224**
Blue Rapids, *Kans., U.S.* 39°40′ N, 96°40′ W **94**
Blue Ridge, *Can.* 54°8′ N, 115°24′ W **108**
Blue Ridge, *Ga., U.S.* 34°50′ N, 84°19′ W **96**
Blue Ridge, mountains, *North America* 36°39′ N, 80°30′ W **96**
Blue River, *Can.* 52°6′ N, 119°19′ W **108**
Blue, river, *Can.* 59°23′ N, 129°53′ W **108**
Blue Springs, *Nebr., U.S.* 40°7′ N, 96°41′ W **92**
Blue Stack Mountains, *Ire.* 54°44′ N, 8°11′ W **150**
Bluefields, *Nicar.* 12°1′ N, 83°47′ W **116**
Bluenose Lake, *Can.* 68°21′ N, 120°48′ W **98**
Bluff, *Alas., U.S.* 64°43′ N, 147°13′ W **98**
Bluff, *N.Z.* 46°37′ S, 168°20′ E **240**
Bluff, *Utah, U.S.* 37°16′ N, 109°33′ W **92**
Bluff, *Cape, Can.* 52°49′ N, 56°38′ W **111**
Bluff Knoll, peak, *Austral.* 34°26′ S, 118°1′ E **230**
Bluffton, *Ind., U.S.* 40°44′ N, 85°10′ W **102**
Bluffton, *Ohio, U.S.* 40°53′ N, 83°53′ W **102**
Bluffy Lake, lake, *Can.* 50°46′ N, 93°23′ W **90**
Blumenau, *Braz.* 26°57′ S, 49°3′ W **138**
Blumenthal, *Ger.* 53°11′ N, 8°34′ E **163**
Blunt, *S. Dak., U.S.* 44°30′ N, 99°59′ W **90**
Blustry Mountain, *Can.* 50°36′ N, 121°48′ W **90**
Bly, *Oreg., U.S.* 42°24′ N, 121°3′ W **90**
Blyth, *Can.* 43°44′ N, 81°25′ W **102**
Blyth, *U.K.* 53°22′ N, 1°4′ W **162**
Blyth Range, *Austral.* 26°54′ S, 129°8′ E **230**
Blythe, *Calif., U.S.* 33°36′ N, 114°36′ W **101**
Blytheville, *Ark., U.S.* 35°55′ N, 89°56′ W **82**
Bø, *Nor.* 59°24′ N, 9°1′ E **152**
Bø, *Nor.* 61°8′ N, 5°18′ E **152**
Bø, *Nor.* 68°36′ N, 14°34′ E **152**
Bo, *Sierra Leone* 7°58′ N, 11°44′ W **222**
Bo Duc, *Vietnam* 11°59′ N, 106°48′ E **202**
Bo River, *Sudan* 6°50′ N, 27°54′ E **224**
Boa Nova, *Braz.* 14°25′ S, 40°11′ W **138**
Boa Vista, *Braz.* 2°50′ N, 60°43′ W **130**
Boac, *Philippines* 13°28′ N, 121°52′ E **203**
Boali, *Cen. Af. Rep.* 4°47′ N, 18°6′ E **218**
Boane, *Mozambique* 25°58′ S, 32°19′ E **227**
Boang, island, *P.N.G.* 3°20′ S, 153°22′ E **192**
Boario Terme, *It.* 45°54′ N, 10°9′ E **167**
Boatswain, Baie 51°47′ N, 79°34′ W **110**
Boaz, *Ala., U.S.* 34°11′ N, 86°10′ W **96**
Boba, *Hung.* 47°10′ N, 17°11′ E **168**
Bobai, *China* 22°16′ N, 110°1′ E **198**
Bobbio, *It.* 44°45′ N, 9°22′ E **167**
Böblingen, *Ger.* 48°40′ N, 9°0′ E **152**
Bobo Dioulasso, *Burkina Faso* 11°11′ N, 4°18′ W **222**
Bobonaza, river, *Ecua.* 2°7′ S, 76°57′ W **136**
Bobonong, *Botswana* 21°60′ S, 28°25′ E **227**
Bobota, *Rom.* 47°22′ N, 22°48′ E **168**
Bobovdol, *Bulg.* 42°22′ N, 23°0′ E **168**
Boboye, *Niger* 13°0′ N, 2°47′ E **222**
Bobrov, *Russ.* 51°7′ N, 40°1′ E **158**
Bobures, *Venez.* 9°14′ N, 71°11′ W **136**
Boby, peak, *Madagascar* 22°13′ S, 46°48′ E **220**
Boca del Rio, *Mex.* 25°18′ N, 108°32′ W **112**
Boca do Acre, *Braz.* 8°48′ S, 67°24′ W **130**
Boca do Curuquetê, *Braz.* 8°23′ S, 65°43′ W **130**
Boca do Jari, *Braz.* 1°7′ S, 51°58′ W **130**
Boca Grande, *Fla., U.S.* 26°45′ N, 82°15′ W **105**
Boca Mavaca, *Venez.* 2°30′ N, 65°15′ W **136**
Boca Raton, *Fla., U.S.* 26°22′ N, 80°7′ W **105**
Bocaiúva, *Braz.* 17°9′ S, 43°47′ W **138**
Bocay, *Nicar.* 14°19′ N, 85°8′ W **115**
Bocay, river, *Nicar.* 13°34′ N, 85°23′ W **115**
Boceguillas, *Sp.* 41°20′ N, 3°38′ W **164**
Bocheykovo, *Belarus* 55°1′ N, 29°9′ E **166**
Bocholt, *Ger.* 51°50′ N, 6°37′ E **167**
Bochum, *Ger.* 51°29′ N, 7°12′ E **167**
Bockhorn, *Ger.* 53°23′ N, 8°1′ E **163**
Bockum-Hövel, *Ger.* 51°41′ N, 7°44′ E **167**
Bocón, river, *Col.* 3°4′ N, 68°58′ W **136**
Boçoroca, *Braz.* 28°42′ S, 54°57′ W **139**
Bocşa, *Rom.* 45°22′ N, 21°43′ E **168**
Boda, *Cen. Af. Rep.* 4°21′ N, 17°26′ E **218**
Böda, *Sw.* 57°15′ N, 17°1′ E **152**
Bodaybo, *Russ.* 57°59′ N, 114°13′ E **160**
Boddam, *U.K.* 57°27′ N, 1°48′ W **150**
Bodden Town, *U.K.* 19°18′ N, 81°15′ W **115**
Bode, river, *Ger.* 51°55′ N, 11°15′ E **152**

Bode Sadu, Nig. 8°54' N, 4°47' E 222
Bodega Head, Calif., U.S. 38°17' N, 123°21' W 90
Boden, Nor. 65°49' N, 21°40' E 152
Bodfish, Calif., U.S. 35°35' N, 118°30' W 101
Bodhei, Kenya 1°51' S, 40°46' E 224
Bodiam, U.K. 51°0' N, 0°33' E 162
Bodle, Eth. 5°3' N, 42°51' E 218
Bodmin Moor, U.K. 50°30' N, 5°4' W 150
Bodø, Nor. 67°16' N, 14°41' E 160
Bodocó, Braz. 7°48' S, 39°56' W 132
Bodoquena, Serra da, Braz. 20°23' S, 56°53' W 132
Bodrum, Turk. 37°2' N, 27°24' E 156
Boeae, ruin(s), Gr. 36°30' N, 22°58' E 156
Boende, Dem. Rep. of the Congo 0°15' N, 20°50' E 218
Boerne, Tex., U.S. 29°47' N, 98°45' W 92
Boeuf, river, La., U.S. 32°15' N, 92°17' W 80
Boffa, Guinea 10°11' N, 14°6' W 222
Bofosso, Guinea 8°38' N, 9°43' W 222
Bogachiel, river, Wash., U.S. 47°52' N, 124°20' W 100
Bogalusa, La., U.S. 30°45' N, 89°52' W 103
Bogan, river, Austral. 30°31' S, 147°4' E 230
Bogandé, Burkina Faso 12°56' N, 0°9' E 222
Bogangolo, Cen. Af. Rep. 5°34' N, 18°18' E 218
Bogani Nani Wartabone National Park, Indonesia 0°23' N, 123°11' E 238
Bogarra, Sp. 38°34' N, 2°13' W 164
Bogart, Mount, Can. 50°55' N, 115°20' W 90
Bogatić, Serb. and Mont. 44°50' N, 19°29' E 168
Bogatka, Russ. 63°16' N, 44°13' E 154
Bogazi, Northern Cyprus 35°19' N, 33°57' E 194
Boğazkale, Turk. 40°1' N, 34°35' E 156
Boğazlıyan, Turk. 39°10' N, 35°15' E 156
Bogcang, river, China 31°38' N, 85°48' E 188
Bogda Feng, peak, China 43°51' N, 88°12' E 184
Bogdan, peak, Bulg. 42°35' N, 24°23' E 156
Bogdanovich, Russ. 56°47' N, 62°2' E 154
Bogdanovka, Ga. 41°16' N, 43°34' E 195
Bogdanovka, Russ. 52°10' N, 52°33' E 158
Bögen, Kaz. 46°12' N, 61°16' E 184
Bogetići, Serb. and Mont. 42°40' N, 18°58' E 168
Boggeragh Mountains, Ire. 52°0' N, 9°3' W 150
Boggola, Mount, Austral. 23°49' S, 117°26' E 230
Boggs, Cape, Antarctica 70°39' S, 63°52' W 248
Boghar, Alg. 35°54' N, 2°43' E 150
Boglárlelle, Hung. 46°45' N, 17°40' E 168
Bognor Regis, U.K. 50°47' N, 0°40' E 162
Bogo, Philippines 11°3' N, 124°0' E 203
Bogogobo, Botswana 26°37' S, 21°54' E 227
Bogojevo, Serb. and Mont. 45°31' N, 19°8' E 168
Bogol Manyo, Eth. 4°29' N, 41°30' E 224
Bogomila, Maced. 41°35' N, 21°27' E 168
Bogoroditsk, Russ. 53°45' N, 38°7' E 154
Bogorodsk, Russ. 62°16' N, 52°36' E 154
Bogorodskoye, Russ. 52°24' N, 140°35' E 190
Bogorodskoye, Russ. 57°48' N, 50°50' E 154
Bogotá, Col. 4°36' N, 74°13' W 136
Bogotol, Russ. 56°13' N, 89°39' E 169
Bogou, Togo 10°38' N, 0°9' E 222
Bogovina, Serb. and Mont. 43°53' N, 21°55' E 168
Bogra, Bangladesh 24°49' N, 89°21' E 197
Boguchany, Russ. 58°17' N, 97°27' E 160
Boguchar, Russ. 49°59' N, 40°33' E 158
Bogué, Mauritania 16°35' N, 14°19' W 222
Bogue Chitto, Miss., U.S. 31°26' N, 90°27' W 103
Bogue Chitto, river, La., U.S. 30°48' N, 90°14' W 103
Bogushevsk, Belarus 54°51' N, 30°17' E 152
Bogutovac, Serb. and Mont. 43°38' N, 20°32' E 168
Bohain, Fr. 49°59' N, 3°26' E 163
Bohe, China 21°31' N, 111°9' E 198
Bohicon, Benin 7°13' N, 2°3' E 222
Böhmer Wald, Ger. 49°28' N, 12°14' E 152
Bohodukhiv, Ukr. 50°11' N, 35°32' E 158
Bohol, island, Philippines 9°7' N, 123°42' E 192
Bohol Sea 8°50' N, 123°36' E 192
Böhönye, Hung. 46°23' N, 17°23' E 168
Böhöt, Mongolia 45°8' N, 108°10' E 198
Bohu (Bagrax), China 41°56' N, 86°40' E 184
Boi, Nig. 9°34' N, 9°29' E 222
Boiaçu, Braz. 0°28' N, 61°48' W 130
Boila, Mozambique 16°10' S, 39°50' E 224
Boim, Braz. 3°4' S, 55°16' W 130
Boing, Sudan 9°55' N, 33°45' E 224
Boinso, Ghana 5°31' N, 2°44' W 222
Boipeba, Ilha de, island, Braz. 14°3' S, 39°38' W 132
Bois Blanc Island, Mich., U.S. 45°25' N, 84°20' W 81
Bois, river, Braz. 18°11' S, 50°8' W 138
Boise, Idaho, U.S. 43°36' N, 116°20' W 90
Boise City, Okla., U.S. 36°42' N, 102°31' W 92
Boissevain, Can. 49°14' N, 100°4' W 90
Bojeador, Cape, Philippines 18°30' N, 120°11' E 203
Boji Plain, Kenya 1°41' N, 39°35' E 224
Bojnūrd, Iran 37°28' N, 57°18' E 180
Bojo, island, Indonesia 0°36' N, 98°30' E 196
Bojuru, Braz. 31°38' S, 51°31' W 139
Boka, Serb. and Mont. 45°21' N, 20°50' E 156
Bo'ka, Uzb. 40°49' N, 69°12' E 197
Bokada, Dem. Rep. of the Congo 4°8' N, 19°21' E 218
Bokalia, spring, Chad 17°24' N, 19°14' E 216
Bokani, Nig. 9°25' N, 5°10' E 222
Bokatola, Dem. Rep. of the Congo 0°36' N, 18°44' E 218
Boké, Guinea 10°55' N, 14°18' W 222
Bokito, Cameroon 4°29' N, 10°58' E 222
Bokol, peak, Kenya 1°46' N, 36°58' E 224
Bökönbaev, Kyrg. 42°7' N, 77°7' E 184
Bokongo, Dem. Rep. of the Congo 3°21' N, 20°56' E 218
Bokoro, Chad 12°21' N, 17°3' E 216
Bokote, Dem. Rep. of the Congo 0°7' N, 20°5' E 218
Bokovskaya, Russ. 49°14' N, 41°45' E 158
Bokpyinn, Myanmar 11°15' N, 98°45' E 202
Boksitogorsk, Russ. 59°28' N, 33°51' E 154
Bokungu, Dem. Rep. of the Congo 0°45' N, 22°27' E 218
Bokurdak, Turkm. 38°47' N, 58°29' E 180
Bol, Chad 13°33' N, 14°44' E 216
Bol, Croatia 43°15' N, 16°39' E 168
Bolaiti, Dem. Rep. of the Congo 3°16' S, 24°51' E 224
Bolama, Guinea-Bissau 11°35' N, 15°31' W 222
Bolan Pass, Pak. 29°43' N, 67°33' E 186
Bolaños, river, Mex. 21°18' N, 103°53' W 114
Bolderāja, Latv. 57°1' N, 24°1' E 166
Boldeşti, oil field, Rom. 45°2' N, 25°57' E 156
Bole, China 44°49' N, 82°9' E 184
Bole, Ghana 9°2' N, 2°32' W 222
Boleko, Dem. Rep. of the Congo 1°31' S, 19°50' E 218
Bolesławiec, Pol. 51°15' N, 15°35' E 152
Boleszkowice, Pol. 52°42' N, 14°33' E 152
Bolgatanga, Ghana 10°45' N, 0°53' E 222
Bolhrad, Ukr. 45°41' N, 28°38' E 156
Boliden, Nor. 64°52' N, 20°20' E 152
Boligee, Ala., U.S. 32°45' N, 88°3' W 103
Bolinao, Cape, Philippines 16°20' N, 119°24' E 203
Bolívar, Bol. 12°9' S, 67°21' W 137
Bolívar, Col. 1°48' N, 76°60' W 136
Bolivar, Mo., U.S. 37°36' N, 93°24' W 96
Bolívar, Peru 7°16' S, 77°50' W 130
Bolivar, Tenn., U.S. 35°14' N, 88°59' W 96
Bolívar, adm. division, Col. 9°45' N, 75°9' W 115
Bolívar, adm. division, Venez. 6°10' N, 64°34' W 136
Bolívar, Cerro, peak, Venez. 7°20' N, 63°34' W 130
Bolivar, Mount, Oreg., U.S. 42°46' N, 123°55' W 90
Bolívar, Pico, peak, Venez. 8°33' N, 71°7' W 136
Bolivia 16°4' S, 66°43' W 132
Bolivia, Cuba 22°4' N, 78°18' W 116
Boljevac, Serb. and Mont. 43°50' N, 21°58' E 168
Boljevci, Serb. and Mont. 44°43' N, 20°12' E 168
Bolkhov, Russ. 53°26' N, 36°1' E 154
Bollendorf, Ger. 49°51' N, 6°21' E 167
Bollnäs, Nor. 61°20' N, 16°22' E 152
Bollstabruk, Nor. 62°59' N, 17°39' E 152
Bolluk Gölü, lake, Turk. 38°27' N, 32°29' E 156
Bolullos Par del Condado, Sp. 37°20' N, 6°33' W 164
Bolnisi, Ga. 41°25' N, 44°32' E 195
Bolobo, Dem. Rep. of the Congo 2°12' S, 16°16' E 218
Bologna, It. 44°29' N, 11°20' E 167
Bologne, Fr. 48°11' N, 5°8' E 163
Bolognesi, Peru 10°3' S, 73°60' W 137
Bologoye, Russ. 57°52' N, 34°4' E 154
Bolomba, Dem. Rep. of the Congo 0°30' N, 19°9' E 218
Bolona, Côte d'Ivoire 10°18' N, 6°26' W 222
Bolong, Chad 12°3' N, 17°46' E 216
Bolotnoye, Russ. 55°38' N, 84°26' E 169
Bolotovskoye, Russ. 58°31' N, 62°26' E 154
Bolpebra, Bol. 10°59' S, 69°34' W 137
Bol'shakovo, Russ. 54°51' N, 21°38' E 166
Bol'shaya Bicha, Russ. 57°56' N, 70°36' E 169
Bol'shaya Chernigovka, Russ. 52°7' N, 50°52' E 158
Bol'shaya Glushitsa, Russ. 52°24' N, 50°28' E 158
Bol'shaya Kheta, river, Russ. 68°22' N, 82°43' E 169
Bol'shaya Pyssa, Russ. 64°11' N, 48°44' E 154
Bol'shaya Tovra, Russ. 64°5' N, 41°41' E 154
Bol'shaya Ucha, Russ. 56°36' N, 52°7' E 154
Bol'shaya Vladimīrovka, Kaz. 50°53' N, 79°29' E 184
Bol'sheretsk, Russ. 52°20' N, 156°22' E 238
Bol'shevik Island, Russ. 79°0' N, 102°0' E 255
Bol'shezemel'skaya Tundra, region, Europe 66°30' N, 52°39' E 154
Bol'shiye Kozly, Russ. 65°18' N, 39°45' E 154
Bol'shiye Sluditsy, Russ. 59°16' N, 30°28' E 166
Bol'shiye Tarkhany, Russ. 54°42' N, 48°34' E 154
Bol'shoy Anyuy, river, Russ. 68°20' N, 161°41' E 160
Bol'shoy Begichev, Ostrov, island, Russ. 73°50' N, 113°22' E 160
Bol'shoy Begichev, Ostrov, island, Russ. 74°38' N, 106°27' E 160
Bol'shoy Chirk, Russ. 63°54' N, 47°7' E 154
Bol'shoy Ental', Russ. 60°54' N, 49°40' E 154
Bol'shoy Lyakhovskiy, Ostrov, island, Russ. 72°34' N, 143°33' E 160
Bol'shoy Porog, Russ. 65°35' N, 90°11' E 169
Bol'shoy Sabsk, Russ. 59°8' N, 29°2' E 166
Bol'shoy Shantar, Ostrov, island, Russ. 55°15' N, 136°51' E 160
Bol'shoy Tyuters, Ostrov, island, Russ. 59°48' N, 27°15' E 166
Bolsover, U.K. 53°13' N, 1°18' W 162
Bolsward, Neth. 53°4' N, 5°30' E 163
Bolt Head, U.K. 50°14' N, 3°49' W 150
Boltaña, Sp. 42°26' N, 6°356' E 164
Bolton, U.K. 53°34' N, 2°27' W 162
Bolton, Vt., U.S. 44°22' N, 72°53' W 104
Bolton Abbey, site, U.K. 53°59' N, 1°57' W 162
Bolton Lake, lake, Can. 54°10' N, 96°19' W 108
Bolton Landing, N.Y., U.S. 43°33' N, 73°41' W 104
Bolu, Turk. 40°43' N, 31°36' E 156
Boluo, China 23°7' N, 114°16' E 198
Bolvadin, Turk. 38°43' N, 31°2' E 156
Bóly, Hung. 45°57' N, 18°31' E 168
Bom Comércio, Braz. 9°46' S, 65°56' W 137
Bom Despacho, Braz. 19°44' S, 45°16' W 138
Bom Destino, Braz. 9°46' S, 67°32' W 137
Bom Jesus, Braz. 28°39' S, 50°24' W 138
Bom Jesus, Braz. 9°4' S, 44°23' W 132
Bom Jesus da Gurguéia, Serra, Braz. 8°41' S, 43°40' W 132
Bom Jesus da Lapa, Braz. 13°18' S, 43°25' W 138
Bom Jesus do Itabapoana, Braz. 21°11' S, 41°41' W 138
Bom Retiro, Braz. 27°49' S, 49°30' W 138
Boma, Angola 5°58' S, 13°6' E 207
Boma National Park, Sudan 6°33' N, 33°45' E 224
Bomana, Dem. Rep. of the Congo 1°25' N, 18°25' E 218
Bomassa, Congo 2°23' N, 16°10' E 218
Bombay see Mumbai, India 18°57' N, 72°49' E 188
Bombo, Uganda 0°32' N, 32°30' E 224
Bomdila, India 27°18' N, 92°25' E 188
Bomi (Bowo), China 29°53' N, 95°40' E 188
Bomili, Dem. Rep. of the Congo 1°42' N, 27°5' E 224
Bomokandi, river, Dem. Rep. of the Congo 3°15' N, 27°9' E 224
Bomongo, Dem. Rep. of the Congo 1°26' N, 18°19' E 218
Bomotu, Dem. Rep. of the Congo 3°46' N, 19°1' E 218
Bomu, oil field, Nig. 4°37' N, 7°14' E 222
Bomu, river, Africa 5°3' N, 23°57' E 206
Bon Secour, Ala., U.S. 30°18' N, 87°44' W 103
Bon Wier, Tex., U.S. 30°44' N, 93°39' W 103
Bonāb, Iran 37°19' N, 46°10' E 195
Bonaire, island, Netherlands 12°0' N, 68°0' W 118
Bonampak, ruin(s), Mex. 16°39' N, 91°8' W 115
Bonandolok, Indonesia 1°51' N, 98°49' E 196
Bonanza, Nicar. 14°0' N, 84°35' W 115
Bonanza, Oreg., U.S. 42°13' N, 121°26' W 90
Bonanza, Sp. 36°48' N, 6°21' W 164
Bonanza, Utah, U.S. 40°0' N, 109°10' W 90
Bonaparte Archipelago, Indian Ocean 13°15' S, 122°48' E 230
Bonaparte Lake, Can. 51°17' N, 121°3' W 90
Bonaparte, Mount, Wash., U.S. 48°45' N, 119°13' W 90
Boñar, Sp. 42°50' N, 5°20' W 150
Bonaventure, Can. 48°9' N, 65°35' W 82
Bonavista, Can. 48°38' N, 53°7' W 111
Bonavista, Cape, Can. 48°43' N, 53°16' W 111
Bond, Miss., U.S. 30°53' N, 89°9' W 103
Bondari, Russ. 56°9' N, 28°20' E 166
Bondary, Russ. 52°58' N, 41°53' E 154
Bondeno, It. 44°54' N, 11°23' E 167
Bondo, Dem. Rep. of the Congo 3°49' N, 23°48' E 224
Bondoukou, Côte d'Ivoire 8°3' N, 2°49' W 222
Bondyug, Russ. 60°30' N, 55°58' E 154
Bone Creek, river, Can. 49°50' N, 109°24' W 90
Bône see Annaba, Alg. 36°53' N, 7°45' E 156
Bone, Teluk 4°59' S, 120°30' E 192
Bonesteel, S. Dak., U.S. 43°4' N, 98°58' W 90
Bonete, Sp. 38°52' N, 1°21' W 164
Bonete, Cerro, peak, Arg. 27°54' S, 68°55' W 132
Bonfinópolis de Minas, Braz. 16°33' S, 45°60' W 138
Bong Son, Vietnam 14°27' N, 109°0' E 202
Bonga, Eth. 7°12' N, 36°16' E 224
Bongandanga, Dem. Rep. of the Congo 1°29' N, 21°1' E 218
Bongao, Philippines 5°3' N, 119°44' E 203
Bongo, Dem. Rep. of the Congo 2°59' N, 20°1' E 218
Bongo, Dem. Rep. of the Congo 1°48' S, 17°39' E 218
Bongo, Gabon 2°9' S, 10°15' E 218
Bongolava, Madagascar 18°36' S, 45°27' E 220
Bongor, Chad 10°18' N, 15°23' E 216
Bongouanou, Côte d'Ivoire 6°35' N, 4°14' W 222
Bongoul, river, Cen. Af. Rep. 9°2' N, 21°9' E 218
Bonham, Tex., U.S. 33°34' N, 96°11' W 96
Bonifacio, Fr. 41°23' N, 9°11' E 156
Bonin Islands (Ogasawara Guntō), North Pacific Ocean 27°46' N, 140°2' E 190
Bonin Trench, North Pacific Ocean 23°46' N, 143°57' E 252
Bonita, La., U.S. 32°54' N, 91°41' W 103
Bonita Springs, Fla., U.S. 26°20' N, 81°47' W 105
Bonito, Braz. 21°9' S, 56°28' W 132
Bonito, peak, Hond. 15°35' N, 86°58' W 115
Bonkoukou, Niger 14°2' N, 3°10' E 222
Bonn, Ger. 50°44' N, 7°5' E 167
Bonne Terre, Mo., U.S. 37°55' N, 90°34' W 96
Bonner, Mont., U.S. 46°51' N, 113°48' W 90
Bonners Ferry, Idaho, U.S. 48°40' N, 116°21' W 90
Bonnet, Fr. 46°19' N, 1°54' E 150
Bonnet Plume, river, Can. 65°34' N, 134°14' W 98
Bonneval, Fr. 48°10' N, 1°24' E 163
Bonneville Salt Flats, Utah, U.S. 40°39' N, 114°12' W 90
Bonnie Rock, Austral. 30°34' S, 118°22' E 231
Bonny, Fr. 47°33' N, 2°50' E 150
Bonny, Nig. 4°26' N, 7°9' E 222
Bonny Reservoir, lake, Colo., U.S. 39°34' N, 102°37' W 90
Bonnyville, Can. 54°15' N, 110°43' W 108
Bonobono, Philippines 8°43' N, 117°36' E 203
Bonokoski Lake, lake, Can. 59°39' N, 104°7' W 108
Bonpland, Arg. 29°49' S, 57°27' W 139
Bonsall, Calif., U.S. 33°17' N, 117°15' W 101
Bonsecours, Baie 49°26' N, 64°20' W 111
Bontang, Indonesia 0°11' N, 117°21' E 192
Bontebok National Park, S. Af. 34°5' S, 20°21' E 227
Bonthe, Sierra Leone 7°32' N, 12°33' W 222
Bontoc, Philippines 17°6' N, 120°57' E 203
Bonvouloir Islands, Solomon Sea 10°6' S, 151°55' E 230
Bonyhád, Hung. 46°16' N, 18°31' E 168
Booker, Tex., U.S. 36°26' N, 100°33' W 96
Booker T. Washington National Monument, Va., U.S. 37°5' N, 79°48' W 96
Boola, Guinea 8°18' N, 8°43' W 222
Boomer, W. Va., U.S. 38°9' N, 81°18' W 94
Boone, Colo., U.S. 38°14' N, 104°16' W 90
Boone, Iowa, U.S. 42°3' N, 93°54' W 94
Boone, N.C., U.S. 36°13' N, 81°41' W 96
Booneville, Ark., U.S. 35°7' N, 93°56' W 96
Boonville, Ind., U.S. 38°2' N, 87°16' W 96
Boonville, N.Y., U.S. 43°28' N, 75°21' W 94
Boorama, Somalia 9°54' N, 43°6' E 216
Booroondara, Mount, Austral. 31°6' S, 145°5' E 230
Boothbay Harbor, Me., U.S. 43°51' N, 69°38' W 104
Boothia, Gulf of 70°9' N, 92°10' W 106
Boothia Peninsula, Can. 70°5' N, 95°32' W 106
Boothville, La., U.S. 29°19' N, 89°25' W 103
Booué, Gabon 4°237' S, 11°52' E 218
Bopolu, Liberia 6°58' N, 10°30' W 222
Boppard, Ger. 50°13' N, 7°35' E 167
Boqueirão, Serra do, Braz. 11°10' S, 43°60' W 132
Boquerón, Cuba 19°58' N, 75°7' W 116
Boquilla, Presa de la, lake, Mex. 27°34' N, 106°8' W 81
Boquillas del Carmen, Mex. 29°8' N, 102°60' W 92
Bor, Russ. 56°21' N, 44°9' E 154
Bor, Serb. and Mont. 44°5' N, 22°6' E 168
Bor, Sudan 6°17' N, 31°39' E 207
Bor, Sudan 6°11' N, 31°32' E 224
Bor, Turk. 37°53' N, 34°31' E 156
Borah Peak, Idaho, U.S. 44°7' N, 113°51' W 90
Boralday, Kaz. 43°20' N, 76°51' E 184
Boran, Kaz. 48°0' N, 85°14' E 184
Boran, region, Africa 3°11' N, 38°18' E 224
Borås, Nor. 57°43' N, 12°56' E 152
Borau, Sp. 42°39' N, 0°36' E 150
Borāzjān, Iran 29°14' N, 51°12' E 196
Borba, Braz. 4°24' S, 59°36' W 130
Borbon, Philippines 10°49' N, 124°1' E 203
Borborema, Planalto da, Braz. 7°28' S, 38°3' W 132
Borchgrevink Coast, Antarctica 73°11' S, 178°45' W 248
Borçka, Turk. 41°22' N, 41°40' E 195
Bordeaux, Fr. 44°51' N, 0°36' E 150
Borden Island, Can. 79°8' N, 110°41' W 246
Borden Peninsula, Can. 72°43' N, 89°38' W 106
Bordertown, Austral. 36°18' S, 140°47' E 231
Bordj bou Arreridj, Alg. 36°3' N, 4°45' E 150
Bordj Bou Rerhda, Alg. 36°8' N, 5°22' E 150
Bordj Flye Sainte Marie, Alg. 27°16' N, 2°59' W 214
Bordj le Prieur, Alg. 21°20' N, 0°53' E 222
Bordj Messouda, Alg. 30°13' N, 9°24' E 216
Bordj Omar Driss, Alg. 28°6' N, 6°49' E 214
Bordj Welvert, Alg. 35°39' N, 3°52' E 150
Boré, Mali 15°7' N, 3°30' W 222
Boreas Nunatak, peak, Antarctica 71°27' S, 4°34' W 248
Borènta, Mali 15°49' N, 1°19' W 222
Borgå see Porvoo, Fin. 60°23' N, 25°40' E 166
Borgafjäll, Nor. 64°48' N, 15°1' E 152
Børgefjell, Nor. 65°12' N, 13°15' E 152
Børgefjell National Park, Nor. 65°12' N, 14°27' E 152
Borgentreich, Ger. 51°34' N, 9°15' E 167
Borger, Neth. 52°55' N, 6°47' E 163
Borger, Tex., U.S. 35°38' N, 101°24' W 92
Borgholm, Sw. 56°51' N, 16°37' E 152
Borghorst, Ger. 52°7' N, 7°24' E 167
Borgne, Lake 30°1' N, 89°42' W 103
Borgo, It. 46°3' N, 11°27' E 167
Borgo San Dalmazzo, It. 44°19' N, 7°29' E 167
Borgo San Lorenzo, It. 43°57' N, 11°22' E 167
Borgo Val di Taro, It. 44°29' N, 9°46' E 167
Borgomanero, It. 45°42' N, 8°29' E 167
Borgosesia, It. 45°43' N, 8°17' E 167
Borgou, region, Africa 10°9' N, 2°49' E 222
Borgsjö, Nor. 64°11' N, 17°48' E 152
Borgvattnet, Nor. 63°25' N, 15°49' E 154
Borhoyn Tal, Mongolia 43°44' N, 111°47' E 198
Bori, Benin 9°45' N, 2°25' E 222
Borikhan, Laos 18°36' N, 103°42' E 202
Börili, Kaz. 51°24' N, 52°44' E 158
Borisoglebsk, Russ. 51°21' N, 42°3' E 158
Borisovo Sudskoye, Russ. 59°52' N, 36°1' E 154
Boriziny (Port-Bergé), Madagascar 15°35' S, 47°43' E 220
Borj el Kessira, Tun. 32°14' N, 10°2' E 214
Borja, Peru 4°21' S, 77°36' W 130
Borja, Sp. 41°48' N, 1°33' W 164
Borjomi, Ga. 41°50' N, 43°22' E 180
Borkavichy, Belarus 55°39' N, 28°18' E 166
Borken, Ger. 51°50' N, 6°52' E 167
Borken, Ger. 51°3' N, 9°17' E 167
Borkou, region, Africa 19°13' N, 15°50' E 216
Borkovskaya, Russ. 65°10' N, 49°27' E 154
Borkum, Ger. 53°35' N, 6°40' E 163
Borkum, island, Ger. 53°36' N, 6°25' E 163
Borland, Mount, Antarctica 74°20' S, 67°18' E 248
Borlänge, Nor. 60°28' N, 15°23' E 152
Borle, Cape, Antarctica 65°54' S, 55°17' E 248
Borleşti, Rom. 47°40' N, 23°19' E 168
Borlova, Rom. 45°22' N, 22°23' E 168
Bormio, It. 46°28' N, 10°21' E 167
Borneo (Kalimantan), island, Indonesia 4°28' S, 111°26' E 192
Bornheim, Ger. 50°46' N, 6°59' E 167
Bornholm, island, Den. 55°18' N, 14°51' E 143
Borno, It. 45°57' N, 10°11' E 167
Bornos, Sp. 36°48' N, 5°45' W 164
Boro, Mali 12°54' N, 9°24' W 222
Boro, river, Sudan 8°28' N, 24°43' E 224
Borodūlikha, Kaz. 50°44' N, 80°49' E 184
Borokoro, Guinea 9°30' N, 10°23' W 222
Boromo, Burkina Faso 11°45' N, 2°57' W 222
Boron, Calif., U.S. 35°0' N, 117°40' W 101
Borotou, Côte d'Ivoire 8°41' N, 7°29' W 222
Boroughbridge, U.K. 54°6' N, 1°24' W 162
Borove, Ukr. 51°38' N, 25°51' E 152
Borovichi, Russ. 57°57' N, 29°39' E 166
Borovichi, Russ. 58°22' N, 33°57' E 154
Borovlyanka, Russ. 52°38' N, 84°33' E 184
Borovo, Croatia 45°24' N, 18°57' E 168
Borovsk, Russ. 55°9' N, 36°31' E 154
Borovskoy, Kaz. 53°47' N, 64°10' E 184
Borovtsi, Bulg. 43°18' N, 23°9' E 168
Borrego Springs, Calif., U.S. 33°15' N, 116°23' W 101
Borroloola, Austral. 16°7' S, 136°17' E 238
Borş, Rom. 47°6' N, 21°48' E 168
Borsod-Abaúj-Zemplén, adm. division, Hung. 48°17' N, 20°26' E 152
Borūjen, Iran 31°59' N, 51°20' E 180
Borūjerd, Iran 33°54' N, 48°44' E 180
Boryeong, S. Korea 36°21' N, 126°36' E 200
Borzna, Ukr. 51°13' N, 32°25' E 158
Börzsöny, Hung. 47°52' N, 18°43' E 168
Borzya, Russ. 50°25' N, 116°39' E 190
Bosanska Dubica, Bosn. and Herzg. 45°10' N, 16°48' E 168
Bosanska Krupa, Bosn. and Herzg. 44°52' N, 16°9' E 168
Bosanski Brod, Bosn. and Herzg. 45°7' N, 18°1' E 168
Bosanski Novi, Bosn. and Herzg. 45°2' N, 16°22' E 168
Bosanski Petrovac, Bosn. and Herzg. 44°32' N, 16°21' E 168
Bosansko Grahovo, Bosn. and Herzg. 44°9' N, 16°20' E 168
B osárkány, Hung. 47°41' N, 17°17' E 168
Bosbury, U.K. 52°4' N, 2°27' W 162
Bosco Chiesanuova, It. 45°36' N, 11°1' E 167
Bose, China 23°54' N, 106°32' E 198
Boseong, S. Korea 34°43' N, 127°6' E 200
Boshof, S. Af. 28°33' S, 25°13' E 227
Boshrūyeh, Iran 33°52' N, 57°28' E 180
Bosilegrad, Serb. and Mont. 42°30' N, 22°29' E 168
Bosnia and Herzegovina 44°0' N, 18°0' E 156
Bošnjaci, Croatia 45°1' N, 18°45' E 168
Bosobele, Dem. Rep. of the Congo 1°11' N, 18°12' E 218
Bosobolo, Dem. Rep. of the Congo 4°13' N, 19°54' E 218
Bosques Petrificados Natural Monument, Arg. 47°43' S, 68°17' W 134
Bossangoa, Cen. Af. Rep. 6°28' N, 17°25' E 218
Bossé Bangou, Niger 13°21' N, 1°16' E 222
Bossembélé, Cen. Af. Rep. 5°13' N, 17°37' E 218
Bossier City, La., U.S. 32°30' N, 93°43' W 103
Bosso, Niger 13°44' N, 13°17' E 216
Bossòst, Sp. 42°46' N, 0°40' E 164
Bost see Lashkar Gah, Afghan. 31°35' N, 64°22' E 186
Bosten Hu, lake, China 41°57' N, 86°51' E 184
Boston, Mass., U.S. 42°20' N, 71°6' W 104
Boston, U.K. 52°59' N, 0°1' E 162
Boston Bar, Can. 49°51' N, 121°25' W 100
Boston Mountains, Ark., U.S. 35°44' N, 94°18' W 96
Bostonnais, Grand lac, lake, Can. 47°51' N, 73°8' W 94
Bosut, river, Croatia 45°12' N, 18°57' E 168
Boswell, Ind., U.S. 40°30' N, 87°23' W 102
Boswell, Okla., U.S. 34°0' N, 95°52' W 96
Bosworth, battle, U.K. 52°35' N, 1°27' W 162
Bot, Sp. 41°0' N, 0°22' E 164
Botesdale, U.K. 52°20' N, 1°0' E 162
Botev, peak, Bulg. 42°42' N, 24°50' E 156
Botevgrad, Bulg. 42°51' N, 23°44' E 180
Bothaville, S. Af. 27°22' S, 26°36' E 227
Bothnia, Gulf of 61°26' N, 17°58' E 152
Bothwell, Can. 42°37' N, 81°51' W 102
Botkins, Ohio, U.S. 40°27' N, 84°11' W 102
Botnnuten, peak, Antarctica 70°22' S, 37°37' E 248
BotoЕani, adm. division, Rom. 47°54' N, 26°10' E 156
Botoşani, Rom. 47°43' N, 26°38' E 152
Botsford, Conn., U.S. 41°22' N, 73°16' W 104
Botsmark, Nor. 64°15' N, 20°14' E 152
Botswana 22°36' S, 24°16' E 220
Bottineau, N. Dak., U.S. 48°48' N, 100°29' W 90
Bottrop, Ger. 51°31' N, 6°56' E 167
Botucatu, Braz. 22°54' S, 48°28' W 138
Botum Sakor National Park, Cambodia 10°53' N, 102°34' E 202
Botwood, Can. 49°8' N, 55°23' W 111
Bou Akba, spring, Alg. 28°48' N, 7°45' W 214
Bou Ali, Alg. 27°11' N, 0°12' E 214
Bou Arfa, Mor. 32°35' N, 1°56' W 214
Boû Djébéha, Mali 18°31' N, 2°46' W 222
Bou Hadjar, Alg. 36°30' N, 8°6' E 156
Bou Izakarn, Mor. 29°11' N, 9°44' W 214
Bou Naga, spring, Mauritania 19°0' N, 13°13' W 222
Boû Rjeïmât, Mauritania 19°3' N, 15°8' W 222
Bou Saâda, Alg. 35°11' N, 4°10' E 214
Bou Thadi, Tun. 35°5' N, 10°14' E 216
Boû Zérîbé, spring, Mauritania 16°13' N, 5°25' W 222
Bouaflé, Côte d'Ivoire 6°56' N, 5°43' W 222
Bouaké, Côte d'Ivoire 7°37' N, 5°3' W 222
Bouala, Cen. Af. Rep. 6°18' N, 15°35' E 218
Bouali, Gabon 3°7' S, 11°30' E 218
Bouar, Cen. Af. Rep. 5°53' N, 15°34' E 218
Boubout, spring, Alg. 27°30' N, 4°34' W 214
Bouca, Cen. Af. Rep. 6°29' N, 18°18' E 218
Boucau, Fr. 43°31' N, 1°30' W 150
Bouchier, Lac, lake, Can. 50°2' N, 78°23' W 110
Boucle Du Baoulé National Park, Mali 13°39' N, 9°25' W 222
Boudenib, Mor. 32°1' N, 3°36' W 214
Boudjellil, Alg. 36°19' N, 4°20' E 150
Bouga, Chad 8°8' N, 15°34' E 218
Bougainville, Cape, Austral. 13°49' S, 126°3' E 231
Bougainville, island, P.N.G. 5°54' S, 153°10' E 192
Bougar'oûn, Cap, Alg. 37°7' N, 6°26' E 150
Boughzoul, Alg. 35°44' N, 2°50' E 150
Bougie see Bejaïa, Alg. 36°46' N, 5°2' E 150
Bougouni, Mali 11°26' N, 7°30' W 222
Bouilly, Fr. 48°10' N, 4°0' E 163
Bouira, Alg. 36°21' N, 3°54' E 150
Boujad, Mor. 32°50' N, 6°25' W 214
Boujdour, Western Sahara 26°8' N, 14°29' W 214

Boujdour, Cap, *Western Sahara* 26°7′ N, 16°1′ W **214**
Boukombé, *Benin* 10°11′ N, 1°6′ E **222**
Boukoula, *Cameroon* 10°9′ N, 13°29′ E **216**
Boukra, *Western Sahara* 26°22′ N, 12°53′ W **214**
Boula, *Mali* 15°4′ N, 8°27′ W **222**
Boulder, *Colo., U.S.* 40°2′ N, 105°17′ W **90**
Boulder, *Mont., U.S.* 46°13′ N, 112°7′ W **90**
Boulder City, *Nev., U.S.* 35°55′ N, 114°50′ W **82**
Boulder Creek, *Calif., U.S.* 37°7′ N, 122°9′ W **100**
Boulder Peak, *Calif., U.S.* 41°34′ N, 123°11′ W **90**
Boulogne, *Fr.* 43°17′ N, 0°37′ E **164**
Boulogne-sur-Mer, *Fr.* 50°44′ N, 1°36′ E **163**
Boulouli, *Mali* 15°36′ N, 9°20′ W **222**
Boulsa, *Burkina Faso* 12°39′ N, 0°37′ E **222**
Boultoum, *Niger* 14°41′ N, 10°18′ E **222**
Boumdeït, spring, *Mauritania* 17°27′ N, 11°22′ W **222**
Boumerdas, *Alg.* 36°45′ N, 3°29′ E **150**
Boun Nua, *Laos* 21°40′ N, 101°54′ E **202**
Boun Tai, *Laos* 21°25′ N, 101°58′ E **202**
Bouna, *Côte d'Ivoire* 9°16′ N, 2°60′ W **222**
Boundary, *Can.* 49°0′ N, 109°22′ W **90**
Boundary Bald Mountain, *Me., U.S.* 45°45′ N, 70°18′ W **94**
Boundary Peak, *Nev., U.S.* 37°50′ N, 118°26′ W **90**
Boundiali, *Côte d'Ivoire* 9°31′ N, 6°29′ W **222**
Boundji, *Congo* 1°2′ S, 15°22′ E **218**
Bountiful Islands, *Gulf of Carpentaria* 17°3′ S, 140°1′ E **230**
Bounty Trough, *South Pacific Ocean* 47°2′ S, 178°29′ W **252**
Bourbon, *Ind., U.S.* 41°17′ N, 86°7′ W **102**
Bourbonnais, *Ill., U.S.* 41°9′ N, 87°54′ W **102**
Bourbonnais, region, *Europe* 46°45′ N, 2°23′ E **165**
Bourbourg, *Fr.* 50°56′ N, 2°12′ E **163**
Bouré Siké, spring, *Mali* 15°50′ N, 5°18′ W **222**
Bourem, *Mali* 16°58′ N, 0°20′ E **222**
Bouressa, *Mali* 19°58′ N, 2°13′ E **222**
Bourg, *La., U.S.* 29°33′ N, 90°38′ W **103**
Bourges, *Fr.* 47°4′ N, 2°24′ E **150**
Bourg-Madame, *Fr.* 42°25′ N, 1°56′ E **164**
Bourgneuf, *Fr.* 47°2′ N, 1°57′ W **150**
Bourgogne, adm. division, *Fr.* 47°19′ N, 2°55′ E **150**
Bourke, *Austral.* 30°8′ S, 145°56′ E **231**
Bourlier, *Alg.* 35°23′ N, 1°38′ E **150**
Bourne, *U.K.* 52°46′ N, 0°22′ E **162**
Bournemouth, *U.K.* 50°43′ N, 1°54′ W **162**
Bouroum, *Burkina Faso* 13°38′ N, 0°39′ E **222**
Bourscheid, *Lux.* 49°53′ N, 6°4′ E **167**
Bourtoutou, *Chad* 11°14′ N, 22°50′ E **218**
Bouse, *Ariz., U.S.* 33°56′ N, 114°1′ W **101**
Boussens, *Fr.* 43°10′ N, 0°57′ E **164**
Bousso, *Chad* 10°32′ N, 16°43′ E **216**
Bouszibé Aneyda, spring, *Mali* 16°14′ N, 5°16′ W **222**
Boutilimit, *Mauritania* 17°32′ N, 14°44′ W **222**
Bouvet Island, *Norway* 54°28′ S, 3°23′ E **255**
Bouza, *Niger* 14°22′ N, 5°55′ E **222**
Bovec, *Slov.* 46°20′ N, 13°34′ E **167**
Bovenden, *Ger.* 51°35′ N, 9°56′ E **167**
Boves, *Fr.* 49°49′ N, 2°22′ E **163**
Bovill, *Idaho, U.S.* 46°50′ N, 116°24′ W **90**
Bovina, *Tex., U.S.* 34°30′ N, 102°53′ W **92**
Bovril, *Arg.* 31°19′ S, 59°25′ W **139**
Bow, *N.H., U.S.* 43°9′ N, 71°33′ W **104**
Bow Island, *Can.* 49°51′ N, 111°23′ W **90**
Bow, river, *Can.* 51°6′ N, 114°34′ W **90**
Bowbells, *N. Dak., U.S.* 48°48′ N, 102°15′ W **90**
Bowdle, *S. Dak., U.S.* 45°26′ N, 99°41′ W **90**
Bowdoin Canyon, *Can.* 53°34′ N, 65°28′ W **111**
Bowen, *Austral.* 19°60′ S, 148°15′ E **231**
Bowen Island, *Can.* 49°22′ N, 123°21′ W **100**
Bowes, *U.K.* 54°31′ N, 2°1′ W **162**
Bowie, *Ariz., U.S.* 32°19′ N, 109°28′ W **92**
Bowie, *Tex., U.S.* 33°32′ N, 97°51′ W **92**
Bowling Green, *Fla., U.S.* 27°38′ N, 81°49′ W **105**
Bowling Green, *Ind., U.S.* 39°22′ N, 87°1′ W **102**
Bowling Green, *Ky., U.S.* 36°59′ N, 86°27′ W **96**
Bowling Green, *Ohio, U.S.* 41°22′ N, 83°39′ W **102**
Bowling Green, *Va., U.S.* 38°2′ N, 77°21′ W **94**
Bowling Green Bay National Park, *Austral.* 19°34′ S, 146°39′ E **238**
Bowman, *N. Dak., U.S.* 46°10′ N, 103°26′ W **90**
Bowman Bay 65°33′ N, 77°12′ W **106**
Bowman Island, *Antarctica* 64°34′ S, 104°9′ E **248**
Bowman, Mount, *Can.* 51°11′ N, 121°52′ W **90**
Bowness, *U.K.* 54°21′ N, 2°55′ W **162**
Bowo see Bomi, *China* 29°53′ N, 95°40′ E **188**
Bowser, *Can.* 49°25′ N, 124°41′ W **100**
Bowser Lake, *Can.* 56°24′ N, 129°52′ W **108**
Bowsman, *Can.* 52°14′ N, 101°13′ W **108**
Bowwood, *Zambia* 17°7′ S, 26°16′ E **224**
Boxing, *China* 37°9′ N, 118°7′ E **198**
Boxtel, *Neth.* 51°35′ N, 5°19′ E **167**
Boyabat, *Turk.* 41°27′ N, 34°45′ E **156**
Boyacá, adm. division, *Col.* 5°17′ N, 73°33′ W **136**
Boyang, *China* 29°0′ N, 116°38′ E **198**
Boyarka, *Russ.* 70°43′ N, 97°24′ E **160**
Boyce, *La., U.S.* 31°22′ N, 92°40′ W **103**
Boyd, *Can.* 55°53′ N, 96°27′ W **108**
Boyd Lake, *Can.* 61°22′ N, 104°4′ W **108**
Boyer, river, *Can.* 57°54′ N, 117°43′ W **108**
Boyes Hot Springs, *Calif., U.S.* 38°19′ N, 122°29′ W **100**
Boykétté, *Cen. Af. Rep.* 5°24′ N, 20°49′ E **218**
Boyle, *Can.* 54°35′ N, 112°48′ W **108**
Boyle, *Ire.* 53°58′ N, 8°20′ W **150**
Boyne City, *Mich., U.S.* 45°12′ N, 85°1′ W **94**
Boynitsa, *Bulg.* 43°57′ N, 22°31′ E **168**
Boynton Beach, *Fla., U.S.* 26°32′ N, 80°5′ W **105**
Boyoma Falls, *Dem. Rep. of the Congo* 1°23′ N, 21°41′ E **206**
Boyoma Falls (Stanley Falls), *Dem. Rep. of the Congo* 0°14′ N, 25°9′ E **224**
Boyson, *Uzb.* 38°12′ N, 67°12′ E **197**
Boyuibe, *Bol.* 20°28′ S, 63°16′ W **137**
Boz Burun, *Turk.* 40°32′ N, 28°50′ E **156**
Boz Dağ, peak, *Turk.* 37°18′ N, 29°7′ E **156**
Bozalan Burun, *Turk.* 38°12′ N, 26°27′ E **156**
Bozashchy Tübegi, *Kaz.* 45°9′ N, 51°36′ E **158**
Bozburun, *Turk.* 36°41′ N, 28°4′ E **156**
Bozburun Daği, peak, *Turk.* 37°16′ N, 31°0′ E **156**
Bozdoğan, *Turk.* 37°39′ N, 28°18′ E **156**
Bozeman, *Mont., U.S.* 45°38′ N, 111°3′ W **90**
Bozene, *Dem. Rep. of the Congo* 2°58′ N, 19°13′ E **218**
Boževac, *Serb. and Mont.* 44°32′ N, 21°23′ E **168**
Bozhou, *China* 33°49′ N, 115°44′ E **198**
Božica, *Serb. and Mont.* 42°36′ N, 22°24′ E **168**
Bozkır, *Turk.* 37°11′ N, 32°13′ E **156**
Bozkurt, *Turk.* 41°58′ N, 34°1′ E **158**
Bozoum, *Cen. Af. Rep.* 6°15′ N, 16°23′ E **218**
Bozoy, *Kaz.* 46°10′ N, 58°45′ E **158**
Bozüyük, *Turk.* 39°55′ N, 30°1′ E **156**
Bozzolo, *It.* 45°5′ N, 10°28′ E **167**
Bra, *It.* 44°41′ N, 7°51′ E **167**
Brabant Island, *Antarctica* 64°4′ S, 64°38′ W **134**
Brabant Lake, *Can.* 56°0′ N, 104°18′ W **108**
Brač, island, *Croatia* 43°15′ N, 16°54′ E **168**
Bracebridge, *Can.* 45°2′ N, 79°20′ W **94**
Bräcke, *Nor.* 62°45′ N, 15°26′ E **152**
Bracken Lake, lake, *Can.* 53°35′ N, 100°14′ W **108**
Brackendale, *Can.* 49°45′ N, 123°8′ W **100**
Brackettville, *Tex., U.S.* 29°18′ N, 100°25′ W **92**
Brackley, *U.K.* 52°2′ N, 1°9′ W **162**
Bracknell, *U.K.* 51°22′ N, 0°46′ E **162**
Brackwede, *Ger.* 51°59′ N, 8°29′ E **167**
Brad, *Rom.* 46°7′ N, 22°49′ E **168**
Bradenton, *Fla., U.S.* 27°29′ N, 82°35′ W **105**
Bradenton Beach, *Fla., U.S.* 27°28′ N, 82°41′ W **105**
Bradford, *Ill., U.S.* 41°10′ N, 89°41′ W **102**
Bradford, *Ohio, U.S.* 40°7′ N, 84°26′ W **102**
Bradford, *Pa., U.S.* 41°57′ N, 78°40′ W **94**
Bradford, *U.K.* 53°47′ N, 1°46′ W **162**
Bradford, *Vt., U.S.* 43°59′ N, 72°9′ W **104**
Bradford on Avon, *U.K.* 51°21′ N, 2°15′ W **162**
Bradley, *Ark., U.S.* 33°5′ N, 93°41′ W **103**
Bradley, *Calif., U.S.* 35°52′ N, 120°49′ W **100**
Bradley, *Ill., U.S.* 41°9′ N, 87°51′ W **102**
Bradley, *S. Dak., U.S.* 45°4′ N, 97°40′ W **90**
Bradley Junction, *Fla., U.S.* 27°47′ N, 81°59′ W **105**
Bradninch, *U.K.* 50°49′ N, 3°26′ W **162**
Brador, Collines de, peak, *Can.* 51°33′ N, 57°18′ W **111**
Bradwell on Sea, *U.K.* 51°43′ N, 0°54′ E **162**
Brady, *Nebr., U.S.* 41°2′ N, 100°21′ W **90**
Brady, *Tex., U.S.* 31°7′ N, 99°20′ W **92**
BraĔov, adm. division, *Rom.* 45°42′ N, 24°42′ E **156**
Braeside, *Can.* 45°27′ N, 76°26′ W **94**
Braga, *Port.* 41°32′ N, 8°27′ W **150**
Braga, adm. division, *Port.* 41°24′ N, 8°40′ W **150**
Bragado, *Arg.* 35°7′ S, 60°30′ W **139**
Bragança, *Braz.* 1°4′ S, 46°48′ W **130**
Bragança, *Port.* 41°46′ N, 6°48′ W **214**
Bragança, *Port.* 41°49′ N, 6°47′ W **150**
Bragança, adm. division, *Port.* 41°28′ N, 7°16′ W **150**
Braham, *Minn., U.S.* 45°42′ N, 93°10′ W **94**
Brahestad see Raahe, *Fin.* 64°41′ N, 24°27′ E **152**
Brahmapur, *India* 19°19′ N, 84°47′ E **188**
Brahmaputra, river, *India* 26°18′ N, 92°11′ E **190**
Brăila, *Rom.* 45°16′ N, 27°57′ E **156**
Brăila, adm. division, *Rom.* 44°57′ N, 27°19′ E **156**
Braine, *Fr.* 49°20′ N, 3°30′ E **163**
Braine l'Alleud, *Belg.* 50°41′ N, 4°21′ E **163**
Brainerd, *Minn., U.S.* 46°20′ N, 94°11′ W **90**
Braintree, *Mass., U.S.* 42°12′ N, 71°1′ W **104**
Braintree, *U.K.* 51°53′ N, 0°32′ E **162**
Brakel, *Ger.* 51°43′ N, 9°11′ E **167**
Bräkne-Hoby, *Nor.* 56°14′ N, 15°8′ E **152**
Bralorne, *Can.* 50°47′ N, 122°48′ W **90**
Bramber, *U.K.* 50°51′ N, 0°18′ E **162**
Brampton, *Can.* 43°41′ N, 79°46′ W **94**
Bramsche, *Ger.* 52°24′ N, 7°58′ E **163**
Branchville, *S.C., U.S.* 33°14′ N, 80°49′ W **96**
Branco, river, *Braz.* 13°41′ S, 60°24′ W **130**
Brandberg, peak, *Namibia* 21°10′ S, 14°27′ E **220**
Brandbu, *Nor.* 60°24′ N, 10°31′ E **152**
Brandenburg, adm. division, *Ger.* 52°36′ N, 12°16′ E **152**
Brandfort, *S. Af.* 28°43′ S, 26°25′ E **227**
Brändö, *Fin.* 60°24′ N, 21°2′ E **166**
Brandon, *Can.* 49°49′ N, 99°57′ W **90**
Brandon, *Fla., U.S.* 27°57′ N, 82°16′ W **105**
Brandon, *Miss., U.S.* 32°15′ N, 89°60′ W **103**
Brandon, *U.K.* 52°26′ N, 0°37′ E **162**
Brandon, *Vt., U.S.* 43°47′ N, 73°7′ W **104**
Brandon, *Wis., U.S.* 43°43′ N, 88°47′ W **102**
Brandon Mountain, *Ire.* 52°13′ N, 10°20′ W **150**
Brandsen, *Arg.* 35°9′ S, 58°16′ W **139**
Brandvlei, *S. Af.* 30°26′ S, 20°26′ E **227**
Brandy Peak, *Oreg., U.S.* 42°35′ N, 123°58′ W **90**
Branford, *Conn., U.S.* 41°16′ N, 72°50′ W **104**
Branford, *Fla., U.S.* 29°58′ N, 82°56′ W **96**
Braniewo, *Pol.* 54°21′ N, 19°48′ E **166**
Brankovina, *Serb. and Mont.* 44°21′ N, 19°52′ E **168**
Bransfield Island, *Antarctica* 63°28′ S, 58°57′ W **134**
Branson, *Mo., U.S.* 36°38′ N, 93°14′ W **96**
Brant, *N.Y., U.S.* 42°34′ N, 79°2′ W **110**
Brant Lake, *N.Y., U.S.* 43°40′ N, 73°45′ W **104**
Brantford, *Can.* 43°7′ N, 80°16′ W **110**
Bras Coupé, Lac du, lake, *Can.* 49°33′ N, 75°43′ W **94**
Bras d'Or Lake, *Can.* 45°55′ N, 61°18′ W **111**
Brasil, Planalto Do, *South America* 17°41′ S, 44°49′ W **138**
Brasiléia, *Braz.* 10°57′ S, 68°44′ W **137**
Brasília, *Braz.* 15°49′ S, 47°60′ W **138**
Brasília de Minas, *Braz.* 16°13′ S, 44°28′ W **138**
Brasília Legal, *Braz.* 3°52′ S, 55°39′ W **130**
Braslaw, *Belarus* 55°38′ N, 27°3′ E **166**
Brașov, *Rom.* 45°38′ N, 25°35′ E **156**
Brass, *Nig.* 4°17′ N, 6°15′ E **222**
Brasschaat, *Belg.* 51°17′ N, 4°28′ E **167**
Brasstown Bald, peak, *Ga., U.S.* 34°51′ N, 83°53′ W **96**
Bratan, peak, *Bulg.* 42°29′ N, 25°4′ E **156**
Bratca, *Rom.* 46°54′ N, 22°39′ E **168**
Bratislava (Pressburg), *Slovakia* 48°7′ N, 16°57′ E **152**
Bratislavský, adm. division, *Slovakia* 47°40′ N, 10°52′ E **156**
Bratiya, peak, *Bulg.* 42°34′ N, 24°5′ E **156**
Bratsk, *Russ.* 56°24′ N, 101°23′ E **160**
Brattleboro, *Vt., U.S.* 42°50′ N, 72°34′ W **104**
Bratunac, *Bosn. and Herzg.* 44°12′ N, 19°20′ E **168**
Brauron, ruin(s), *Gr.* 37°54′ N, 23°52′ E **156**
Braux, *Fr.* 49°50′ N, 4°45′ E **163**
Brawley, *Calif., U.S.* 32°59′ N, 115°33′ W **101**
Bray, *Fr.* 49°56′ N, 2°42′ E **163**
Brazeau, Mount, *Can.* 52°31′ N, 117°27′ W **108**
Brazeau, river, *Can.* 52°46′ N, 116°22′ W **108**
Brazeau see Nordegg, *Can.* 52°28′ N, 116°7′ W **108**
Brazil 10°11′ S, 55°28′ W **132**
Brazil, *Ind., U.S.* 39°31′ N, 87°7′ W **102**
Brazoria, *Tex., U.S.* 29°2′ N, 95°34′ W **96**
Brazos Peak, *N. Mex., U.S.* 36°48′ N, 106°30′ W **92**
Brazzaville, *Congo* 4°13′ S, 15°0′ E **218**
Brčko, *Bosn. and Herzg.* 44°52′ N, 18°47′ E **168**
Brea, *Calif., U.S.* 33°55′ N, 117°55′ W **101**
Brea, Cerros de la, *Peru* 4°32′ S, 80°56′ W **130**
Breakenridge, Mount, *Can.* 49°42′ N, 121°58′ W **100**
Breaux Bridge, *La., U.S.* 30°15′ N, 91°55′ W **103**
Breaza, *Rom.* 45°11′ N, 25°38′ E **158**
Breckenridge, *Mich., U.S.* 43°23′ N, 84°29′ W **102**
Breckenridge, *Minn., U.S.* 46°14′ N, 96°35′ W **90**
Breckenridge, *Tex., U.S.* 32°45′ N, 98°55′ W **112**
Brecknock, Peninsula, *Chile* 54°36′ S, 74°29′ W **134**
Břeclav, *Czech Rep.* 48°45′ N, 16°53′ E **152**
Brecon, *U.K.* 51°56′ N, 3°23′ W **162**
Brecon Beacons, peak, *U.K.* 51°53′ N, 3°28′ W **162**
Breda, *Neth.* 51°34′ N, 4°45′ E **167**
Bredasdorp, *S. Af.* 34°32′ S, 20°2′ E **227**
Bredbyn, *Nor.* 63°26′ N, 18°6′ E **152**
Bredene, *Belg.* 51°13′ N, 2°57′ E **150**
Bredon Hill, *U.K.* 52°3′ N, 2°5′ W **162**
Bredy, *Russ.* 52°25′ N, 60°17′ E **154**
Breezewood, *Pa., U.S.* 39°59′ N, 78°15′ W **94**
Bregovo, *Bulg.* 44°9′ N, 22°38′ E **168**
Breil-sur-Roya, *Fr.* 43°56′ N, 7°29′ E **167**
Breitenworbis, *Ger.* 51°25′ N, 10°25′ E **167**
Breitungen, *Ger.* 50°45′ N, 10°18′ E **167**
Brejo, *Braz.* 3°41′ S, 42°50′ W **132**
Brejolândia, *Braz.* 12°30′ S, 43°58′ W **132**
Brekovica, *Bosn. and Herzg.* 44°51′ N, 15°51′ E **168**
Breloh, *Ger.* 53°1′ N, 10°5′ E **150**
Bremangerpollen, *Nor.* 61°51′ N, 4°58′ E **152**
Bremen, *Ga., U.S.* 33°41′ N, 85°8′ W **96**
Bremen, *Ger.* 53°5′ N, 8°47′ E **163**
Bremen, *Ind., U.S.* 41°26′ N, 86°9′ W **102**
Bremen, *Ohio, U.S.* 39°41′ N, 82°26′ W **102**
Bremen, adm. division, *Ger.* 53°4′ N, 8°27′ E **150**
Bremer Bay 34°47′ S, 119°6′ E **230**
Bremerhaven, *Ger.* 53°32′ N, 8°36′ E **150**
Bremerton, *Wash., U.S.* 47°32′ N, 122°40′ W **100**
Bremnes, *Nor.* 59°46′ N, 5°9′ E **152**
Bremsnes, *Nor.* 63°4′ N, 7°39′ E **152**
Brenes, *Sp.* 37°32′ N, 5°53′ W **164**
Brenham, *Tex., U.S.* 30°9′ N, 96°24′ W **96**
Brenner Pass, *It.* 47°0′ N, 11°30′ E **167**
Breno, *It.* 45°57′ N, 10°18′ E **167**
Brenton Bay 11°34′ S, 130°45′ E **230**
Brentwood, *Calif., U.S.* 37°55′ N, 121°43′ W **100**
Brentwood, *N.Y., U.S.* 40°47′ N, 73°14′ W **104**
Brentwood, *U.K.* 51°37′ N, 0°17′ E **162**
Brescia, *It.* 45°32′ N, 10°13′ E **167**
Breskens, *Neth.* 51°23′ N, 3°33′ E **163**
Bresles, *Fr.* 49°24′ N, 2°15′ E **163**
Bressanone, *It.* 46°44′ N, 11°38′ E **167**
Brest, *Belarus* 52°5′ N, 23°41′ E **152**
Brest, *Fr.* 48°23′ N, 4°30′ W **150**
Brest, *Pol.* 52°4′ N, 23°42′ E **160**
Brestovac, *Serb. and Mont.* 43°9′ N, 21°52′ E **168**
Bretagne, adm. division, *Fr.* 48°10′ N, 4°8′ W **150**
Breteuil, *Fr.* 49°37′ N, 2°17′ E **163**
Breteuil, *Fr.* 48°49′ N, 0°54′ E **163**
Breton, *Can.* 53°5′ N, 114°29′ W **108**
Breton, Cape, *Can.* 45°56′ N, 59°46′ W **111**
Bretón, Cayo, island, *Cuba* 21°7′ N, 80°16′ W **116**
Breton Island, Cape, *Can.* 45°19′ N, 63°50′ W **81**
Breton Sound 29°28′ N, 89°22′ W **103**
Brett, Cape, *N.Z.* 35°11′ S, 174°16′ E **240**
Breu, river, *Braz.* 3°45′ S, 66°39′ W **136**
Breu, river, *South America* 9°25′ S, 72°31′ W **137**
Breueh, island, *Indonesia* 5°47′ N, 94°35′ E **196**
Breuil-Cervinia, *It.* 45°56′ N, 7°38′ E **167**
Breves, *Braz.* 1°39′ S, 50°31′ W **130**
Brevik, *Nor.* 59°3′ N, 9°41′ E **152**
Brevoort Island, *Can.* 63°4′ N, 63°59′ W **106**
Brevoort Lake, lake, *Mich., U.S.* 45°58′ N, 85°25′ W **110**
Brew, Mount, *Can.* 50°34′ N, 122°2′ W **90**
Brewer, *Me., U.S.* 44°47′ N, 68°46′ W **94**
Brewerville, *Liberia* 6°20′ N, 10°47′ W **222**
Brewster, *Kans., U.S.* 39°22′ N, 101°24′ W **90**
Brewster, *Mass., U.S.* 41°45′ N, 70°5′ W **104**
Brewster, *Nebr., U.S.* 41°54′ N, 99°52′ W **90**
Brewster, *N.Y., U.S.* 41°23′ N, 73°39′ W **104**
Brewster, *Ohio, U.S.* 40°42′ N, 81°36′ W **102**
Brewster, *Wash., U.S.* 48°5′ N, 119°49′ W **90**
Brewster, Mount, *Antarctica* 72°54′ S, 169°59′ E **248**
Brewton, *Ala., U.S.* 31°6′ N, 87°4′ W **96**
Breza, *Bosn. and Herzg.* 44°1′ N, 18°15′ E **168**
Brezičani, *Bosn. and Herzg.* 45°0′ N, 16°40′ E **168**
Brezina, *Alg.* 33°7′ N, 1°14′ E **214**
Brezno, *Slovakia* 48°48′ N, 19°39′ E **156**
Brezolles, *Fr.* 48°41′ N, 1°4′ E **163**
Brezovo Polje, *Bosn. and Herzg.* 44°50′ N, 18°57′ E **168**
Bria, *Cen. Af. Rep.* 6°29′ N, 22°2′ E **218**
Brian Head, peak, *Utah, U.S.* 37°40′ N, 112°54′ W **92**
Briançon, *Fr.* 44°53′ N, 6°38′ E **167**
Briare, *Fr.* 47°38′ N, 2°43′ E **150**
Bribie Island, *Austral.* 27°17′ S, 151°4′ E **230**
Bridge City, *Tex., U.S.* 30°0′ N, 93°52′ W **103**
Bridgehampton, *N.Y., U.S.* 40°56′ N, 72°19′ W **104**
Bridgend, *U.K.* 51°30′ N, 3°34′ W **162**
Bridgeport, *Ala., U.S.* 34°56′ N, 85°43′ W **96**
Bridgeport, *Calif., U.S.* 38°15′ N, 119°16′ W **100**
Bridgeport, *Conn., U.S.* 41°10′ N, 73°12′ W **104**
Bridgeport, *Nebr., U.S.* 41°39′ N, 103°8′ W **90**
Bridgeport, *Tex., U.S.* 33°11′ N, 97°45′ W **92**
Bridgeport, Lake, *Tex., U.S.* 33°17′ N, 98°40′ W **81**
Bridger Peak, *Wyo., U.S.* 41°10′ N, 107°7′ W **90**
Bridgeton, *N.C., U.S.* 35°7′ N, 77°2′ W **96**
Bridgetown, *Barbados* 13°3′ N, 59°43′ W **116**
Bridgetown, *Ohio, U.S.* 39°8′ N, 84°39′ W **102**
Bridgewater, *Can.* 44°22′ N, 64°33′ W **111**
Bridgewater, *Mass., U.S.* 41°59′ N, 70°59′ W **104**
Bridgnorth, *U.K.* 52°31′ N, 2°26′ W **162**
Bridgton, *Me., U.S.* 44°3′ N, 70°43′ W **104**
Bridgwater, *U.K.* 51°7′ N, 3°1′ W **162**
Bridlington, *U.K.* 54°4′ N, 0°14′ E **162**
Bridport, *Vt., U.S.* 43°58′ N, 73°20′ W **104**
Brienne-le-Château, *Fr.* 48°23′ N, 4°31′ E **163**
Brienz, *Switz.* 46°45′ N, 8°0′ E **167**
Brienzer See, lake, *Switz.* 46°41′ N, 7°42′ E **167**
Brig, *Switz.* 46°20′ N, 8°0′ E **167**
Brigantine, *N.J., U.S.* 39°23′ N, 74°24′ W **94**
Brigden, *Can.* 42°48′ N, 82°18′ W **102**
Brigg, *U.K.* 53°32′ N, 0°29′ E **162**
Brigham City, *Utah, U.S.* 41°30′ N, 111°60′ W **90**
Brighouse, *U.K.* 53°42′ N, 1°47′ W **162**
Brightlingsea, *U.K.* 51°48′ N, 1°1′ E **162**
Brighton, *Can.* 44°1′ N, 77°43′ W **110**
Brighton, *Colo., U.S.* 39°58′ N, 104°49′ W **90**
Brighton, *Mich., U.S.* 42°30′ N, 83°47′ W **102**
Brighton, *U.K.* 50°50′ N, 0°9′ E **162**
Brijuni Otoci (Brioni Islands), *Gulf of Venice* 44°51′ N, 13°23′ E **167**
Brikama, *Gambia* 13°17′ N, 16°33′ W **222**
Brilon, *Ger.* 51°24′ N, 8°32′ E **167**
Brimfield, *Ill., U.S.* 40°49′ N, 89°54′ W **102**
Brinkburn Priory, site, *U.K.* 55°16′ N, 1°55′ W **150**
Brinkley, *Ark., U.S.* 34°51′ N, 91°12′ W **96**
Brinnon, *Wash., U.S.* 47°39′ N, 122°55′ W **100**
Brion, Île, island, *Can.* 47°28′ N, 61°18′ W **81**
Brioni Islands see Brijuni Otoci, *Gulf of Venice* 44°51′ N, 13°23′ E **167**
Brioude, *Fr.* 45°17′ N, 3°21′ E **150**
Briouze, *Fr.* 48°41′ N, 0°23′ E **150**
Brisbane, *Austral.* 27°28′ S, 152°53′ E **230**
Bristol, *Conn., U.S.* 41°40′ N, 72°56′ W **104**
Bristol, *Ind., U.S.* 41°42′ N, 85°50′ W **102**
Bristol, *N.H., U.S.* 43°35′ N, 71°45′ W **104**
Bristol, *R.I., U.S.* 41°40′ N, 71°17′ W **104**
Bristol, *S. Dak., U.S.* 45°19′ N, 97°47′ W **90**
Bristol, *Tenn., U.S.* 36°35′ N, 82°12′ W **96**
Bristol, *U.K.* 51°26′ N, 2°35′ W **162**
Bristol, *Vt., U.S.* 44°8′ N, 73°5′ W **104**
Bristol Bay 56°13′ N, 160°33′ W **106**
Bristol Channel 51°25′ N, 4°42′ W **150**
Bristol Mountains, *Calif., U.S.* 34°58′ N, 116°11′ W **101**
Bristow, *Okla., U.S.* 35°47′ N, 96°23′ W **94**
Britannia Beach, *Can.* 49°36′ N, 123°12′ W **100**
British Channel 80°37′ N, 47°37′ E **160**
British Columbia, adm. division, *Can.* 54°39′ N, 126°22′ W **106**
British Indian Ocean Territory, *United Kingdom* 7°0′ S, 72°0′ E **188**
British Mountains, *Can.* 69°15′ N, 141°7′ W **98**
British Virgin Islands, *United Kingdom* 18°31′ N, 64°41′ W **116**
Brits, *S. Af.* 25°40′ S, 27°46′ E **227**
Britstown, *S. Af.* 30°36′ S, 23°31′ E **227**
Britt, *Can.* 45°47′ N, 80°32′ W **94**
Britt, *Iowa, U.S.* 43°4′ N, 93°47′ W **94**
Britton, *S. Dak., U.S.* 45°46′ N, 97°46′ W **94**
Brive, *Fr.* 45°8′ N, 1°31′ E **150**
Briviesca, *Sp.* 42°32′ N, 3°21′ W **150**
Brnaze, *Croatia* 43°40′ N, 16°39′ E **168**
Brno, *Czech Rep.* 49°11′ N, 16°37′ E **152**
Broadback, river, *Can.* 51°13′ N, 78°42′ W **110**
Broaddus, *Tex., U.S.* 31°17′ N, 94°17′ W **103**
Broadstairs, *U.K.* 51°21′ N, 1°25′ E **163**
Broadus, *Mont., U.S.* 45°25′ N, 105°26′ W **90**
Broadview, *Can.* 50°22′ N, 102°35′ W **108**
Broadwater, *Nebr., U.S.* 41°36′ N, 102°52′ W **90**
Brocēni, *Latv.* 56°41′ N, 22°33′ E **166**
Brochet, *Can.* 57°54′ N, 101°39′ W **108**
Brochet, Lac au, lake, *Can.* 49°40′ N, 70°15′ W **94**
Brochet, Lac, lake, *Can.* 58°38′ N, 101°52′ W **108**
Brock Island, *Can.* 78°23′ N, 115°4′ W **246**
Brock, river, *Can.* 50°5′ N, 75°5′ W **110**
Brocken, peak, *Ger.* 51°47′ N, 10°30′ E **152**
Brockport, *N.Y., U.S.* 43°12′ N, 77°58′ W **94**
Brockport, *Pa., U.S.* 41°15′ N, 78°45′ W **94**
Brockton, *Mass., U.S.* 42°4′ N, 71°2′ W **104**
Brockville, *Can.* 44°36′ N, 75°42′ W **110**
Brockway, *Mont., U.S.* 47°16′ N, 105°46′ W **90**
Brockway, *Pa., U.S.* 41°14′ N, 78°48′ W **94**
Brocton, *Ill., U.S.* 39°43′ N, 87°56′ W **102**
Brod, *Maced.* 41°31′ N, 21°12′ E **168**
Brodarevo, *Serb. and Mont.* 43°13′ N, 19°42′ E **168**
Brodec, *Maced.* 41°46′ N, 20°41′ E **168**
Brodeur Peninsula, *Can.* 71°43′ N, 89°33′ W **106**
Brodhead, *Wis., U.S.* 42°37′ N, 89°23′ W **102**
Brodica, *Serb. and Mont.* 44°29′ N, 21°49′ E **168**
Brodick, *U.K.* 55°34′ N, 5°9′ W **150**
Brodilovo, *Bulg.* 42°5′ N, 27°51′ E **156**
Brodnytsya, *Ukr.* 51°45′ N, 26°16′ E **152**
Brodokalmak, *Russ.* 55°33′ N, 61°59′ E **154**
Brody, *Ukr.* 50°4′ N, 25°8′ E **152**
Brogan, *Oreg., U.S.* 44°14′ N, 117°32′ W **90**
Broken Arrow, *Okla., U.S.* 36°2′ N, 95°47′ W **96**
Broken Bow, *Nebr., U.S.* 41°24′ N, 99°39′ W **90**
Broken Bow, *Okla., U.S.* 34°1′ N, 94°45′ W **96**
Broken Bow Lake, lake, *Okla., U.S.* 34°10′ N, 94°57′ W **96**
Broken Hill see Kabwe, *Zambia* 14°29′ S, 28°25′ E **224**
Broken Ridge, *Indian Ocean* 31°50′ S, 95°31′ E **254**
Brokind, *Nor.* 58°12′ N, 15°40′ E **152**
Brokopondo, *Suriname* 5°4′ N, 55°2′ W **130**
Bromarv, *Fin.* 59°58′ N, 23°0′ E **166**
Bromley Mountain, *Vt., U.S.* 43°13′ N, 72°58′ W **104**
Bromyard, *U.K.* 52°10′ N, 2°31′ W **162**
Brønderslev, *Den.* 57°15′ N, 9°56′ E **150**
Broni, *It.* 45°4′ N, 9°15′ E **167**
Brønnøysund, *Nor.* 65°26′ N, 12°12′ E **152**
Bronson, *Fla., U.S.* 29°26′ N, 82°40′ W **105**
Bronson, *Tex., U.S.* 31°19′ N, 94°1′ W **103**
Bronte, *Tex., U.S.* 31°52′ N, 100°18′ W **92**
Bronyts'ka Huta, *Ukr.* 50°54′ N, 27°18′ E **152**
Brook, *Ind., U.S.* 40°51′ N, 87°22′ W **102**
Brookeland, *Tex., U.S.* 31°7′ N, 93°59′ W **103**
Brooker, *Fla., U.S.* 29°53′ N, 82°21′ W **105**
Brooke's Point, *Philippines* 8°48′ N, 117°50′ E **203**
Brookfield, *Conn., U.S.* 41°28′ N, 73°25′ W **104**
Brookfield, *Mo., U.S.* 39°46′ N, 93°3′ W **94**
Brookfield, *Wis., U.S.* 43°4′ N, 88°7′ W **102**
Brookhaven, *Miss., U.S.* 31°34′ N, 90°26′ W **103**
Brookhaven National Laboratory, *N.Y., U.S.* 40°52′ N, 72°54′ W **104**
Brookings, *Oreg., U.S.* 42°3′ N, 124°16′ W **82**
Brookline, *Mass., U.S.* 42°19′ N, 71°8′ W **104**
Brooklyn, *Conn., U.S.* 41°47′ N, 71°58′ W **104**
Brooklyn, *Ind., U.S.* 39°32′ N, 86°24′ W **102**
Brooklyn, *Mich., U.S.* 42°5′ N, 84°15′ W **102**
Brooklyn, *Miss., U.S.* 31°2′ N, 89°10′ W **103**
Brookmere, *Can.* 49°48′ N, 120°51′ W **100**
Brookport, *Mo., U.S.* 37°7′ N, 88°37′ W **96**
Brooks, *Can.* 50°33′ N, 111°55′ W **90**
Brooks Bay 50°11′ N, 128°1′ W **108**
Brooks Brook, *Can.* 60°25′ N, 133°10′ W **108**
Brooks, Cape, *Antarctica* 73°53′ S, 60°24′ W **248**
Brooks Range, *Alas., U.S.* 67°30′ N, 153°45′ W **106**
Brookston, *Ind., U.S.* 40°35′ N, 86°52′ W **102**
Brooksville, *Fla., U.S.* 28°34′ N, 82°24′ W **105**
Brooksville, *Ky., U.S.* 38°39′ N, 84°5′ W **102**
Brooksville, *Miss., U.S.* 33°12′ N, 88°35′ W **103**
Brookville, *Ind., U.S.* 39°25′ N, 85°1′ W **102**
Brookville, *Pa., U.S.* 41°9′ N, 79°5′ W **94**
Brookville Lake, *Ind., U.S.* 39°31′ N, 85°11′ W **102**
Brookwood, *Ala., U.S.* 33°16′ N, 87°19′ W **103**
Broome, *Austral.* 17°58′ S, 122°20′ E **238**
Broqueles, Punta, *Col.* 9°13′ N, 76°36′ W **136**
Brøstrud, *Nor.* 60°18′ N, 8°30′ E **152**
Brothers, The, islands, *North Atlantic Ocean* 21°50′ N, 75°43′ W **116**
Brothers, The, islands, *Red Sea* 26°35′ N, 34°31′ E **180**
Brou, *Fr.* 48°12′ N, 1°10′ E **163**
Brough, *U.K.* 54°31′ N, 2°19′ W **162**
Broughton in Furness, *U.K.* 54°17′ N, 3°13′ W **162**
Broughton Island see Qikiqtarjuaq, *Can.* 67°30′ N, 63°52′ W **73**
Broulkou, spring, *Chad* 16°39′ N, 18°11′ E **216**
Brouwershaven, *Neth.* 51°43′ N, 3°53′ E **163**
Brovary, *Ukr.* 50°30′ N, 30°52′ E **158**
Browerville, *Minn., U.S.* 46°4′ N, 94°53′ W **90**
Brown City, *Mich., U.S.* 43°13′ N, 82°59′ W **102**
Brown Willy, peak, *U.K.* 50°34′ N, 4°41′ W **150**
Browne Bay 72°57′ N, 100°30′ W **106**
Brownfield, *Me., U.S.* 43°56′ N, 70°56′ W **104**
Brownfield, *Tex., U.S.* 33°9′ N, 102°17′ W **92**
Brownhills, *U.K.* 52°39′ N, 1°56′ W **162**
Browning, *Mont., U.S.* 48°31′ N, 113°2′ W **90**
Browns, *Ala., U.S.* 32°26′ N, 87°22′ W **103**
Browns, *N.Z.* 46°10′ S, 168°25′ E **240**
Brown's Cay, island, *Bahamas* 25°19′ N, 79°26′ W **105**
Browns Town, *Jam.* 18°23′ N, 77°23′ W **115**
Browns Valley, *Minn., U.S.* 45°35′ N, 96°50′ W **90**
Brownsboro, *Tex., U.S.* 32°17′ N, 95°37′ W **103**
Brownson Islands, *Amundsen Sea* 73°56′ S, 104°11′ W **248**
Brownstown, *Ind., U.S.* 38°53′ N, 86°3′ W **102**
Brownsville, *Tenn., U.S.* 35°34′ N, 89°16′ W **96**
Brownsville, *Tex., U.S.* 25°57′ N, 97°28′ W **114**
Brownsville, *Vt., U.S.* 43°28′ N, 72°29′ W **104**
Brownsweg, *Suriname* 4°59′ N, 55°11′ W **130**
Brownwood, *Tex., U.S.* 31°41′ N, 98°58′ W **92**
Brownwood, Lake, *Tex., U.S.* 31°52′ N, 99°50′ W **81**
Brsečine, *Croatia* 42°43′ N, 17°57′ E **168**
Bru, *Nor.* 61°32′ N, 5°12′ E **152**
Bruce Mines, *Can.* 46°18′ N, 83°48′ W **94**
Bruce, Mount, *Austral.* 22°39′ S, 117°57′ E **230**
Bruce Peninsula, *North America* 44°50′ N, 81°23′ W **110**
Bruck, *Aust.* 48°1′ N, 16°47′ E **168**
Brugg, *Switz.* 47°28′ N, 8°13′ E **156**
Brugge, *Belg.* 51°12′ N, 3°13′ E **163**
Brüggen, *Ger.* 51°14′ N, 6°10′ E **167**
Brühl, *Ger.* 50°49′ N, 6°53′ E **167**
Bruini, *India* 29°10′ N, 96°8′ E **188**
Brûlé, Lac, lake, *Can.* 46°54′ N, 77°32′ W **94**
Brumado, *Braz.* 14°15′ S, 41°38′ W **138**
Brumath, *Fr.* 48°44′ N, 7°41′ E **163**
Brundidge, *Ala., U.S.* 31°42′ N, 85°49′ W **96**
Bruneau, *Idaho, U.S.* 42°53′ N, 115°48′ W **90**
Bruneau, river, *Idaho, U.S.* 42°57′ N, 115°48′ W **90**
Brunei 5°0′ N, 115°0′ E **192**
Brunico, *It.* 46°47′ N, 11°56′ E **167**
Bruno, *Can.* 52°15′ N, 105°32′ W **108**
Bruno, *It.* 44°46′ N, 8°26′ E **167**
Brunson, *S.C., U.S.* 32°55′ N, 81°12′ W **96**
Brunssum, *Neth.* 50°57′ N, 5°58′ E **167**

Brunswick, *Ga., U.S.* 31°8′ N, 81°30′ W **96**
Brunswick, *Me., U.S.* 43°54′ N, 69°59′ W **104**
Brunswick, *Ohio, U.S.* 41°13′ N, 81°51′ W **102**
Brunswick Lake, lake, *Can.* 48°56′ N, 83°57′ W **94**
Brunswick Naval Air Station, *Me., U.S.* 43°53′ N, 69°58′ W **104**
Brunswick, Península de, *Chile* 53°26′ S, 73°18′ W **134**
Brunt Ice Shelf, *Antarctica* 76°2′ S, 31°32′ W **248**
Brus, *Serb. and Mont.* 43°22′ N, 21°1′ E **168**
Brus Laguna, *Hond.* 15°44′ N, 84°32′ W **115**
Brusartsi, *Bulg.* 43°39′ N, 23°4′ E **168**
Brush, *Colo., U.S.* 40°15′ N, 103°38′ W **90**
Brusnik, *Serb. and Mont.* 44°6′ N, 22°27′ E **168**
Brusovo, *Russ.* 60°30′ N, 87°24′ E **169**
Brusque, *Braz.* 27°6′ S, 48°55′ W **138**
Brussels Capital, adm. division, *Belg.* 50°53′ N, 3°56′ E **150**
Brussels see Bruxelles, *Belg.* 50°50′ N, 4°17′ E **163**
Brusturi, *Rom.* 47°9′ N, 22°16′ E **168**
Brusy, *Pol.* 53°53′ N, 17°43′ E **152**
Bruxelles (Brussels), *Belg.* 50°50′ N, 4°17′ E **163**
Bruyères, *Fr.* 48°12′ N, 6°42′ E **163**
Bruzgi, *Belarus* 53°34′ N, 23°42′ E **152**
Bruzual, *Venez.* 8°1′ N, 69°21′ W **136**
Bryan, *Ohio, U.S.* 41°27′ N, 84°33′ W **102**
Bryan, *Tex., U.S.* 30°39′ N, 96°22′ W **96**
Bryansk, *Russ.* 53°12′ N, 34°25′ E **154**
Bryansk, *Russ.* 44°19′ N, 46°58′ E **158**
Bryansk, adm. division, *Russ.* 52°59′ N, 32°4′ E **154**
Bryant, *Ark., U.S.* 34°34′ N, 92°30′ W **96**
Bryant, *Fla., U.S.* 26°49′ N, 80°35′ W **105**
Bryant, *S. Dak., U.S.* 44°33′ N, 97°30′ W **90**
Bryant, Cape, *Antarctica* 71°34′ S, 60°10′ W **248**
Bryant Pond, *Me., U.S.* 44°22′ N, 70°39′ W **104**
Bryce Canyon National Park, *Utah, U.S.* 37°22′ N, 112°11′ W **92**
Bryceland, *La., U.S.* 32°27′ N, 92°59′ W **103**
Brykalansk, *Russ.* 65°28′ N, 54°14′ E **154**
Bryne, *Nor.* 58°44′ N, 5°38′ E **152**
Bryson City, *N.C., U.S.* 35°25′ N, 83°26′ W **96**
Bryukhovetskaya, *Russ.* 45°50′ N, 38°56′ E **156**
Brza Palanka, *Serb. and Mont.* 44°28′ N, 22°25′ E **168**
Brzeg, *Pol.* 50°50′ N, 17°28′ E **152**
Bu Hasa, oil field, *U.A.E.* 23°27′ N, 53°7′ E **182**
Bū Sunbul, Jabal, peak, *Lib.* 23°8′ N, 22°12′ E **216**
Bua, river, *Malawi* 13°43′ S, 33°25′ E **224**
Bua Yai, *Thai.* 15°35′ N, 102°24′ E **202**
Bu'aale, *Somalia* 1°1′ N, 42°38′ E **224**
Buan, *S. Korea* 35°43′ N, 126°45′ E **200**
Buatan, *Indonesia* 0°44′ N, 101°47′ E **196**
Buatyrma, river, *Kaz.* 49°39′ N, 84°23′ E **184**
Bu'ayrāt al Ḩasūn, *Lib.* 31°23′ N, 15°41′ E **216**
Buba, *Guinea-Bissau* 11°34′ N, 15°2′ W **222**
Buberos, *Sp.* 41°38′ N, 2°12′ W **164**
Būbīyān, island, *Kuwait* 29°40′ N, 48°23′ E **180**
Bucak, *Turk.* 37°26′ N, 30°36′ E **180**
Bucakkışla, *Turk.* 36°56′ N, 33°1′ E **156**
Bucaramanga, *Col.* 7°7′ N, 73°6′ W **136**
Buccaneer Archipelago, *Indian Ocean* 15°46′ S, 122°50′ E **230**
Buchach, *Ukr.* 49°2′ N, 25°24′ E **152**
Buchan Gulf 71°43′ N, 76°50′ W **106**
Buchanan, *Liberia* 5°49′ N, 10°3′ W **222**
Buchanan, *Mich., U.S.* 41°48′ N, 86°22′ W **102**
Buchanan Bay 78°53′ N, 82°59′ W **246**
Buchanan, Lake, *Tex., U.S.* 30°47′ N, 98°54′ W **92**
Buchans, *Can.* 48°48′ N, 56°52′ W **111**
Buchardo, *Arg.* 34°44′ S, 63°26′ W **139**
Bucharest see București, *Rom.* 44°27′ N, 25°57′ E **156**
Buchon, Point, *U.S.* 35°10′ N, 121°14′ W **100**
Buchy, *Fr.* 49°34′ N, 1°21′ E **163**
Buciumi, *Rom.* 47°2′ N, 23°3′ E **168**
Buck Point, *Can.* 52°52′ N, 132°58′ W **108**
Buckatunna, *Miss., U.S.* 31°33′ N, 88°32′ W **103**
Buckeye Lake, *Ohio, U.S.* 39°55′ N, 82°30′ W **102**
Buckfield, *Me., U.S.* 44°16′ N, 70°23′ W **104**
Buckingham, *Can.* 45°35′ N, 75°24′ W **94**
Buckingham, *U.K.* 51°59′ N, 0°60′ E **162**
Buckley, *Ill., U.S.* 40°35′ N, 88°3′ W **102**
Buckley, *Wash., U.S.* 47°8′ N, 122°2′ W **100**
Bucklin, *Kans., U.S.* 37°32′ N, 99°39′ W **90**
Buckner, *Ark., U.S.* 33°21′ N, 93°27′ W **103**
Buckner, *Mo., U.S.* 37°58′ N, 89°1′ W **96**
Bucks, *Ala., U.S.* 31°0′ N, 88°1′ W **103**
Buckskin Mountains, *Ariz., U.S.* 34°7′ N, 114°4′ W **101**
Bucksport, *Me., U.S.* 44°34′ N, 68°48′ W **111**
Buco Zau, *Angola* 4°44′ S, 12°30′ E **218**
Bucoda, *Wash., U.S.* 46°47′ N, 122°53′ W **100**
Bucovăț, *Mold.* 47°11′ N, 28°28′ E **158**
București, adm. division, *Rom.* 44°32′ N, 25°44′ E **156**
București (Bucharest), *Rom.* 44°27′ N, 25°57′ E **156**
Bucyrus, *Ohio, U.S.* 40°47′ N, 82°58′ W **102**
Bud, *Nor.* 62°54′ N, 6°55′ E **152**
Bud Bud, *Somalia* 4°12′ N, 46°30′ E **218**
Buda, *Tex., U.S.* 30°3′ N, 97°50′ W **92**
Buda, *Ukr.* 51°14′ N, 27°16′ E **152**
Budac, peak, *Rom.* 47°5′ N, 25°35′ E **156**
Budăi, *Mold.* 45°51′ N, 28°28′ E **156**
Budalin, *Myanmar* 22°24′ N, 95°8′ E **202**
Budanovci, *Serb. and Mont.* 44°53′ N, 19°51′ E **168**
Budapest, *Hung.* 47°28′ N, 19°1′ E **168**
Budapest, adm. division, *Hung.* 47°25′ N, 18°44′ E **156**
Budaun, *India* 28°1′ N, 79°8′ E **197**
Budd Coast, *Antarctica* 67°41′ S, 114°55′ E **248**
Bude, *Miss., U.S.* 31°27′ N, 90°51′ W **103**
Budennovsk, *Russ.* 44°44′ N, 44°2′ E **158**
Budennovskaya, *Russ.* 46°51′ N, 41°33′ E **158**
Budevo, *Serb. and Mont.* 43°7′ N, 20°3′ E **168**
Büdingen, *Ger.* 50°17′ N, 9°7′ E **167**
Budogoshch', *Russ.* 59°18′ N, 32°30′ E **154**
Budrio, *It.* 44°32′ N, 11°33′ E **167**
Budva, *Serb. and Mont.* 42°16′ N, 18°50′ E **168**
Buech, river, *Fr.* 44°28′ N, 5°39′ E **165**
Bueil, Lac, lake, *Can.* 50°46′ N, 74°38′ W **110**
Buellton, *Calif., U.S.* 34°37′ N, 120°13′ W **100**
Buen Tiempo, Cabo, *Arg.* 51°29′ S, 68°57′ W **134**
Buena Vista, *Bol.* 17°29′ S, 63°39′ W **137**
Buena Vista, *Venez.* 6°11′ N, 68°34′ W **136**
Buena Vista, *Va., U.S.* 37°44′ N, 79°22′ W **96**
Buenaventura, *Col.* 3°49′ N, 77°4′ W **136**
Buenaventura, *Mex.* 29°50′ N, 107°30′ W **92**
Buenavista, *Mex.* 23°37′ N, 109°39′ W **112**
Buenavista, *Philippines* 9°0′ N, 125°25′ E **203**
Buenópolis, *Braz.* 17°53′ S, 44°12′ W **138**
Buenos Aires, *Arg.* 34°37′ S, 58°34′ W **139**
Buenos Aires, *Col.* 3°13′ S, 70°2′ W **136**
Buenos Aires, adm. division, *Arg.* 36°12′ S, 61°3′ W **139**
Buenos Aires, Punta, *Arg.* 42°12′ S, 66°20′ W **134**
Buey, Cabeza de, peak, *Sp.* 38°37′ N, 3°15′ W **164**
Buffalo, *Minn., U.S.* 45°9′ N, 93°53′ W **94**
Buffalo, *Mo., U.S.* 37°37′ N, 93°5′ W **96**
Buffalo, *N.Y., U.S.* 42°53′ N, 78°54′ W **94**
Buffalo, *Ohio, U.S.* 39°55′ N, 81°29′ W **102**
Buffalo, *Okla., U.S.* 36°48′ N, 99°38′ W **92**
Buffalo, *S. Dak., U.S.* 45°34′ N, 103°34′ W **90**
Buffalo, *Tex., U.S.* 31°27′ N, 96°4′ W **96**
Buffalo, *W. Va., U.S.* 38°36′ N, 81°60′ W **102**
Buffalo, *Wyo., U.S.* 44°20′ N, 106°42′ W **90**
Buffalo Head Prairie, *Can.* 58°2′ N, 116°21′ W **108**
Buffalo Hump, peak, *Idaho, U.S.* 45°35′ N, 115°46′ W **90**
Buffalo Lake, *Can.* 60°18′ N, 115°54′ W **108**
Buffalo Mountain, *Nev., U.S.* 40°12′ N, 118°13′ W **90**
Buffalo Narrows, *Can.* 55°52′ N, 108°30′ W **108**
Buffalo, river, *Can.* 59°23′ N, 114°33′ W **108**
Buford, *Ga., U.S.* 34°6′ N, 84°1′ W **96**
Bug, peninsula, *Ger.* 54°30′ N, 13°11′ E **152**
Buga, *Col.* 3°54′ N, 76°21′ W **136**
Buganda, region, *Africa* 1°2′ N, 31°15′ E **224**
Bugdayly, *Turkm.* 38°24′ N, 54°23′ E **180**
Bugge Islands, *Bellingshausen Sea* 69°2′ S, 69°44′ W **248**
Bugojno, *Bosn. and Herzg.* 44°2′ N, 17°26′ E **168**
Bugrino, *Russ.* 68°48′ N, 49°11′ E **169**
Bugt, *China* 48°44′ N, 121°57′ E **198**
Buguey, *Philippines* 18°16′ N, 121°49′ E **203**
Bugul'ma, *Russ.* 54°33′ N, 52°52′ E **154**
Buguruslan, *Russ.* 53°38′ N, 52°26′ E **154**
Buhăești, *Rom.* 46°46′ N, 27°33′ E **156**
Buḩayrat al'Utaybah, lake, *Syr.* 33°30′ N, 36°22′ E **194**
Buhen, ruin(s), *Sudan* 21°46′ N, 30°51′ E **182**
Buhera, *Zimb.* 19°21′ S, 31°26′ E **224**
Buhl, *Idaho, U.S.* 42°37′ N, 114°46′ W **90**
Buhl, *Minn., U.S.* 47°29′ N, 92°48′ W **110**
Buhuşi, *Rom.* 46°43′ N, 26°41′ E **158**
Bui National Park, *Ghana* 8°39′ N, 3°8′ W **222**
Builth Wells, *U.K.* 52°8′ N, 3°24′ W **162**
Buinsk, *Russ.* 54°58′ N, 48°17′ E **154**
Buitepos, *Namibia* 22°17′ S, 19°56′ E **227**
Bujalance, *Sp.* 37°53′ N, 4°23′ W **164**
Bujanovac, *Serb. and Mont.* 42°28′ N, 21°46′ E **168**
Bujaraloz, *Sp.* 41°29′ N, 0°10′ E **164**
Bujumbura, *Burundi* 3°25′ S, 29°11′ E **224**
Bük, *Hung.* 47°22′ N, 16°46′ E **168**
Buk, *Pol.* 52°21′ N, 16°31′ E **152**
Buka, island, *P.N.G.* 5°15′ S, 153°51′ E **192**
Bukachivtsi, *Ukr.* 49°14′ N, 24°30′ E **152**
Bukadaban Feng, peak, *China* 36°12′ N, 90°26′ E **188**
Bukama, *Dem. Rep. of the Congo* 9°15′ S, 25°50′ E **224**
Bukanik, Maja, peak, *Alban.* 41°0′ N, 20°10′ E **156**
Bukavu, *Dem. Rep. of the Congo* 2°32′ S, 28°48′ E **224**
Bukcha, *Belarus* 51°45′ N, 27°38′ E **152**
Bukene, *Tanzania* 4°15′ S, 32°52′ E **224**
Bukhara see Buxoro, *Uzb.* 39°47′ N, 64°25′ E **197**
Bukit Baka-Bukit Raya National Park, *Indonesia* 0°53′ N, 112°3′ E **238**
Bukit Tawau National Park, *Malaysia* 4°28′ N, 117°35′ E **238**
Bukit Tigah Puluh National Park, *Indonesia* 0°58′ N, 102°38′ E **196**
Bukittinggi, *Indonesia* 0°17′ N, 100°22′ E **196**
Bükk, *Hung.* 47°58′ N, 20°23′ E **168**
Bükkösd, *Hung.* 46°6′ N, 17°59′ E **168**
Bukmuiža, *Latv.* 56°10′ N, 27°40′ E **166**
Bukoba, *Tanzania* 1°22′ S, 31°47′ E **224**
Bukowiec, *Pol.* 52°16′ N, 16°14′ E **152**
Bukukun, *Russ.* 49°24′ N, 111°9′ E **198**
Bukwiuni, *Nig.* 12°5′ N, 5°26′ E **222**
Bula, *Indonesia* 3°5′ S, 130°24′ E **192**
Bula, *Nig.* 10°1′ N, 9°36′ E **222**
Bülach, *Switz.* 47°31′ N, 8°32′ E **150**
Bulacle, *Somalia* 5°20′ N, 46°32′ E **218**
Bülaevo, *Kaz.* 54°55′ N, 70°26′ E **184**
Bulag, *Mongolia* 48°12′ N, 108°30′ E **198**
Bulan, *Ky., U.S.* 37°17′ N, 83°10′ W **96**
Bulan, *Philippines* 12°42′ N, 123°53′ E **203**
Bulanash, *Russ.* 57°17′ N, 61°59′ E **154**
Bulancak, *Turk.* 40°57′ N, 38°12′ E **156**
Bulandshahr, *India* 28°24′ N, 77°52′ E **197**
Bulanık, *Turk.* 39°5′ N, 42°14′ E **195**
Bulawayo, *Zimb.* 20°9′ S, 28°36′ E **227**
Buldan, *Turk.* 38°2′ N, 28°49′ E **156**
Bulgan, *Mongolia* 48°49′ N, 103°38′ E **198**
Bulgan, *Mongolia* 44°6′ N, 103°34′ E **198**
Bulgan, adm. division, *Mongolia* 48°20′ N, 102°20′ E **198**
Bulgar, *Russ.* 54°59′ N, 49°17′ E **154**
Bulgaria 42°38′ N, 24°1′ E **156**
Bulgnéville, *Fr.* 48°12′ N, 5°49′ E **163**
Bulilyan, Cape, *Philippines* 8°21′ N, 116°45′ E **203**
Bull Mountains, *Mont., U.S.* 46°9′ N, 108°41′ W **90**
Bulla Régia, ruin(s), *Tun.* 36°33′ N, 8°38′ E **156**
Bullard, *Tex., U.S.* 32°7′ N, 95°19′ W **103**
Bullas, *Sp.* 38°2′ N, 1°41′ W **164**
Bullaxaar, *Somalia* 10°20′ N, 44°22′ E **216**
Bulle, *Switz.* 46°37′ N, 7°3′ E **167**
Bullhead City, *Ariz., U.S.* 35°8′ N, 114°34′ W **101**
Bullion Mountains, *Calif., U.S.* 34°28′ N, 116°14′ W **101**
Bullmoose Mountain, *Can.* 55°0′ N, 121°39′ W **108**
Bulls, *N.Z.* 40°11′ S, 175°23′ E **240**
Bulls Head, peak, *Can.* 49°36′ N, 110°55′ W **90**
Bully Choop Mountain, *Calif., U.S.* 40°32′ N, 122°52′ W **90**
Bultfontein, *S. Af.* 28°20′ S, 26°8′ E **227**
Buluan, *Philippines* 6°43′ N, 124°47′ E **203**
Bulukumba, *Indonesia* 5°34′ S, 120°3′ E **192**
Bulungkol, *China* 38°40′ N, 74°55′ E **184**
Bulungu, *Dem. Rep. of the Congo* 4°35′ S, 18°33′ E **218**
Bulung'ur, *Uzb.* 39°45′ N, 67°15′ E **197**
Bum La, pass, *China* 27°49′ N, 91°54′ E **197**
Bumba, *Dem. Rep. of the Congo* 6°56′ S, 19°16′ E **218**
Bumba, *Dem. Rep. of the Congo* 2°11′ N, 22°25′ E **218**
Bumbah, Khalīj al 32°18′ N, 22°3′ E **216**
Bumbat, *Mongolia* 46°29′ N, 104°3′ E **198**
Bumbuli, *Dem. Rep. of the Congo* 3°25′ S, 20°29′ E **218**
Buna, *Bosn. and Herzg.* 43°14′ N, 17°49′ E **168**
Buna, *Dem. Rep. of the Congo* 3°18′ S, 18°56′ E **218**
Buna, *Kenya* 2°44′ N, 39°31′ E **224**
Buna, *Tex., U.S.* 30°24′ N, 93°58′ W **103**
Bunazi, *Tanzania* 1°15′ S, 31°25′ E **224**
Bunbury, *Austral.* 33°21′ S, 115°40′ E **231**
Bunde, *Ger.* 53°10′ N, 7°17′ E **163**
Bundi, *India* 25°25′ N, 75°38′ E **197**
Bundoran, *Ire.* 54°27′ N, 8°18′ W **150**
Bundyur, *Russ.* 57°33′ N, 81°58′ E **169**
Bunga, *Nig.* 11°2′ N, 9°40′ E **222**
Bungay, *U.K.* 52°27′ N, 1°26′ E **163**
Bunger Hills, *Antarctica* 65°28′ S, 101°11′ E **248**
Bungle Bungle Range, site, *Austral.* 17°26′ S, 128°18′ E **230**
Bungo, *Angola* 7°28′ S, 15°22′ E **218**
Bungo Suidō 33°1′ N, 132°0′ E **201**
Bungoma, *Kenya* 0°32′ N, 34°34′ E **224**
Bungotakada, *Japan* 33°33′ N, 131°26′ E **201**
Bunia, *Dem. Rep. of the Congo* 1°31′ N, 30°11′ E **224**
Bunker, *Mo., U.S.* 37°27′ N, 91°13′ W **94**
Bunker Group, islands, *Coral Sea* 23°51′ S, 152°40′ E **230**
Bunker Hill, *Ind., U.S.* 40°38′ N, 86°6′ W **102**
Bunker Hill, *Nev., U.S.* 39°15′ N, 117°13′ W **90**
Bunkerville, *Nev., U.S.* 36°46′ N, 114°8′ W **101**
Bunkeya, *Dem. Rep. of the Congo* 10°25′ S, 26°56′ E **224**
Bunkie, *La., U.S.* 30°56′ N, 92°11′ W **103**
Bunnell, *Fla., U.S.* 29°27′ N, 81°17′ W **105**
Bunnell Mountain, peak, *N.H., U.S.* 44°46′ N, 71°34′ W **94**
Buñol, *Sp.* 39°25′ N, 0°48′ E **164**
Bünyan, *Turk.* 38°50′ N, 35°51′ E **156**
Bunza, *Nig.* 12°4′ N, 3°59′ E **222**
Bunzoqa, *Sudan* 12°28′ N, 34°13′ E **182**
Buol, *Indonesia* 1°7′ N, 121°19′ E **192**
Buon Me Thuot, *Vietnam* 12°41′ N, 108°2′ E **202**
Buor Khaya, Mys, *Russ.* 71°47′ N, 131°9′ E **172**
Buq'ata, *Israel* 33°12′ N, 35°46′ E **194**
Buqayq, *Saudi Arabia* 25°56′ N, 49°40′ E **196**
Buqbuq, *Egypt* 31°31′ N, 25°33′ E **226**
Bur, *Russ.* 58°48′ N, 107°4′ E **160**
Bûr Fu'ad, *Egypt* 31°14′ N, 32°19′ E **194**
Bur, river, *Russ.* 70°58′ N, 120°22′ E **160**
Bûr Safâga, *Egypt* 26°44′ N, 33°54′ E **180**
Bûr Sa'îd (Port Said), *Egypt* 31°15′ N, 32°18′ E **194**
Bûr Taufiq, *Egypt* 29°56′ N, 32°30′ E **180**
Bura, *Kenya* 1°6′ S, 39°58′ E **224**
Buraan, *Somalia* 10°10′ N, 48°43′ E **216**
Buram, *Sudan* 10°50′ N, 25°11′ E **224**
Buranhém, river, *Braz.* 16°30′ S, 40°4′ W **138**
Burannoye, *Russ.* 50°59′ N, 54°29′ E **158**
Burao (Burco), *Somalia* 9°34′ N, 45°36′ E **207**
Burāq, *Syr.* 33°10′ N, 36°29′ E **194**
Buras, *La., U.S.* 29°20′ N, 89°32′ W **103**
Buratai, *Nig.* 10°54′ N, 12°4′ E **216**
Buraydah, *Saudi Arabia* 26°21′ N, 44°0′ E **180**
Burbach, *Ger.* 50°44′ N, 8°4′ E **163**
Burbank, *Calif., U.S.* 34°10′ N, 118°18′ W **101**
Burco see Burao, *Somalia* 9°34′ N, 45°36′ E **207**
Burdalyk, *Turkm.* 38°24′ N, 64°22′ E **197**
Burden, Mount, *Can.* 56°9′ N, 123°33′ W **108**
Burdesi, *Eth.* 6°32′ N, 37°13′ E **224**
Burditt Lake, lake, *Can.* 48°53′ N, 94°13′ W **90**
Burdur, *Turk.* 37°42′ N, 30°17′ E **156**
Burduy, *Russ.* 65°39′ N, 48°5′ E **154**
Burē, *Eth.* 8°18′ N, 35°7′ E **224**
Burē, *Eth.* 10°42′ N, 37°3′ E **224**
Bure, river, *U.K.* 52°50′ N, 1°9′ E **162**
Büren, *Ger.* 51°32′ N, 8°33′ E **167**
Bürenhayrhan, *Mongolia* 46°13′ N, 91°34′ E **190**
Burford, *U.K.* 51°48′ N, 1°38′ W **162**
Burg, *Ger.* 54°26′ N, 11°12′ E **152**
Burg, *Ger.* 53°59′ N, 9°16′ E **152**
Burg el 'Arab, *Egypt* 30°54′ N, 29°30′ E **180**
Burgan, oil field, *Kuwait* 28°53′ N, 47°51′ E **196**
Burgas, *Bulg.* 42°30′ N, 27°28′ E **156**
Burgas, adm. division, *Bulg.* 42°44′ N, 26°44′ E **156**
Burgaw, *N.C., U.S.* 34°33′ N, 77°56′ W **96**
Burgdorf, *Switz.* 47°2′ N, 7°37′ E **150**
Burgersdorp, *S. Af.* 30°60′ S, 26°17′ E **227**
Burgess Hill, *U.K.* 50°57′ N, 0°9′ E **162**
Burgess, Mount, *Can.* 66°4′ N, 139°58′ W **98**
Burgos, *Mex.* 24°55′ N, 98°47′ W **114**
Burgos, *Sp.* 42°18′ N, 3°43′ W **164**
Burgsinn, *Ger.* 50°8′ N, 9°38′ E **167**
Burgsvik, *Sw.* 57°2′ N, 18°16′ E **166**
Burguete see Auritz, *Sp.* 42°59′ N, 1°21′ W **164**
Burgui, *Sp.* 42°43′ N, 1°2′ W **164**
Burgundy, region, *Europe* 47°10′ N, 4°11′ E **165**
Burhaniye, *Turk.* 39°30′ N, 26°57′ E **156**
Burhanpur, *India* 21°18′ N, 76°12′ E **188**
Burhave, *Ger.* 53°34′ N, 8°22′ E **163**
Buribay, *Russ.* 51°57′ N, 58°11′ E **154**
Burica, Punta, *C.R.* 7°56′ N, 83°32′ W **115**
Burigi, Lake, *Tanzania* 2°5′ S, 30°45′ E **224**
Burin, *Can.* 47°2′ N, 55°10′ W **111**
Buritis, *Braz.* 15°38′ S, 46°27′ W **138**
Burkburnett, *Tex., U.S.* 34°4′ N, 98°34′ W **92**
Burke, *S. Dak., U.S.* 43°9′ N, 99°18′ W **90**
Burke, *Tex., U.S.* 31°13′ N, 94°47′ W **103**
Burke Island, *Antarctica* 72°57′ S, 105°21′ W **248**
Burketown, *Austral.* 17°46′ S, 139°40′ E **238**
Burkett, Mount, *Can.* 57°9′ N, 132°27′ W **108**
Burkeville, *Tex., U.S.* 30°58′ N, 93°40′ W **103**
Burkina Faso 12°40′ N, 1°39′ W **214**
Burk's Falls, *Can.* 45°37′ N, 79°24′ W **94**
Burla, *Russ.* 53°16′ N, 78°23′ E **184**
Burleson, *Tex., U.S.* 32°32′ N, 97°19′ W **96**
Burlingame, *Kans., U.S.* 38°43′ N, 95°50′ W **90**
Burlington, *Can.* 43°19′ N, 79°47′ W **94**
Burlington, *Colo., U.S.* 39°17′ N, 102°16′ W **90**
Burlington, *N.J., U.S.* 40°3′ N, 74°52′ W **94**
Burlington, *Vt., U.S.* 44°28′ N, 73°13′ W **104**
Burlington, *Wash., U.S.* 48°28′ N, 122°20′ W **100**
Burlington, *Wis., U.S.* 42°40′ N, 88°17′ W **102**
Burma see Myanmar 21°5′ N, 95°9′ E **192**
Burmantovo, *Russ.* 61°17′ N, 60°29′ E **154**
Burnaby, *Can.* 49°16′ N, 122°57′ W **100**
Burnet, *Tex., U.S.* 30°44′ N, 98°13′ W **96**
Burnett Bay 73°53′ N, 127°36′ W **106**
Burnett Lake, lake, *Can.* 59°1′ N, 102°51′ W **108**
Burney, *Calif., U.S.* 40°53′ N, 121°40′ W **90**
Burney Mountain, *Calif., U.S.* 40°47′ N, 121°43′ W **90**
Burnham Market, *U.K.* 52°56′ N, 0°44′ E **162**
Burnham on Crouch, *U.K.* 51°37′ N, 0°49′ E **162**
Burnham on Sea, *U.K.* 51°14′ N, 2°59′ W **162**
Burnie, *Austral.* 41°3′ S, 145°55′ E **231**
Burnley, *U.K.* 53°47′ N, 2°14′ W **162**
Burnmouth, *U.K.* 55°50′ N, 2°5′ W **150**
Burns, *Miss., U.S.* 32°6′ N, 89°33′ W **103**
Burns, *Oreg., U.S.* 43°35′ N, 119°4′ W **90**
Burns, *Wyo., U.S.* 41°11′ N, 104°22′ W **90**
Burns Lake, *Can.* 54°13′ N, 125°46′ W **108**
Burnt Peak, *Calif., U.S.* 34°40′ N, 118°38′ W **101**
Burnt, river, *Oreg., U.S.* 44°33′ N, 118°8′ W **80**
Burqin, *China* 47°44′ N, 86°53′ E **184**
Burr, Mount, *Austral.* 37°40′ S, 140°15′ E **230**
Burra, *Nig.* 11°1′ N, 8°59′ E **222**
Burrel, *Alban.* 41°36′ N, 20°0′ E **168**
Burren, region, *Europe* 52°59′ N, 9°22′ W **150**
Burriana, *Sp.* 39°54′ N, 6°356′ W **164**
Burrinjuck Reservoir, lake, *Austral.* 34°54′ S, 147°35′ E **230**
Burro Peak, *N. Mex., U.S.* 32°34′ N, 108°30′ W **92**
Burro, Serranías del, *Mex.* 29°31′ N, 102°42′ W **112**
Burrow Head, *U.K.* 54°42′ N, 4°22′ W **150**
Burrton, *Kans., U.S.* 38°1′ N, 97°41′ W **90**
Burrwood, *La., U.S.* 28°58′ N, 89°23′ W **103**
Bursa, *Turk.* 40°12′ N, 29°2′ E **156**
Burscheid, *Ger.* 51°5′ N, 7°6′ E **167**
Bursey, Mount, *Antarctica* 75°54′ S, 131°52′ W **248**
Burt Lake, lake, *Mich., U.S.* 45°25′ N, 84°58′ W **94**
Burtnieku Ezers, lake, *Latv.* 57°45′ N, 24°55′ E **166**
Burton, *Mich., U.S.* 42°57′ N, 83°36′ W **102**
Burton, *Nebr., U.S.* 42°53′ N, 99°36′ W **90**
Burton Agnes, *U.K.* 54°2′ N, 0°20′ E **162**
Burton upon Trent, *U.K.* 52°48′ N, 1°39′ W **162**
Buru, island, *Indonesia* 3°2′ S, 126°2′ E **192**
Burûn, Râs, *Egypt* 31°13′ N, 32°58′ E **194**
Burun Shibertuy, Gora, peak, *Russ.* 49°36′ N, 109°46′ E **198**
Burundi 3°0′ S, 30°0′ E **224**
Bururi, *Burundi* 3°57′ S, 29°38′ E **224**
Burutu, *Nig.* 5°23′ N, 5°31′ E **222**
Burwash Landing, *Can.* 61°26′ N, 139°1′ W **98**
Burwell, *Nebr., U.S.* 41°45′ N, 99°9′ W **90**
Bury Saint Edmunds, *U.K.* 52°14′ N, 0°42′ E **162**
Buryatiya, adm. division, *Russ.* 53°21′ N, 108°28′ E **160**
Bürylbaytal, *Kaz.* 44°52′ N, 74°3′ E **184**
Burzil Pass, *Pak.* 34°52′ N, 75°4′ E **186**
Busan (Pusan), *S. Korea* 35°6′ N, 129°3′ E **200**
Busanga, *Dem. Rep. of the Congo* 10°13′ S, 25°19′ E **224**
Busanga Swamp, marsh, *Zambia* 14°24′ S, 25°16′ E **224**
Busangu, *Dem. Rep. of the Congo* 8°32′ S, 25°27′ E **224**
Buşayrā, *Jordan* 30°44′ N, 35°36′ E **194**
Busca, *It.* 44°31′ N, 7°28′ E **167**
Buseck, *Ger.* 50°36′ N, 8°47′ E **167**
Bushgan, oil field, *Iran* 28°56′ N, 51°53′ E **196**
Bushmanland, region, *Africa* 29°42′ S, 19°4′ E **227**
Bushnell, *Fla., U.S.* 28°40′ N, 82°7′ W **105**
Bushnell, *Mo., U.S.* 40°32′ N, 90°31′ W **94**
Bushnell, *Nebr., U.S.* 41°13′ N, 103°54′ W **90**
Bushtricë, *Alban.* 41°52′ N, 20°25′ E **168**
Businga, *Dem. Rep. of the Congo* 3°17′ N, 20°56′ E **218**
Busira, river, *Dem. Rep. of the Congo* 0°26′ N, 19°3′ E **218**
Buslē, *Eth.* 5°23′ N, 44°20′ E **218**
Busovača, *Bosn. and Herzg.* 44°6′ N, 17°51′ E **168**
Buşrá al Ḩarīrī, *Syr.* 32°50′ N, 36°20′ E **194**
Buşrá ash Shām, *Syr.* 32°31′ N, 36°28′ E **194**
Busseri, *Sudan* 7°31′ N, 27°57′ E **224**
Busseri, river, *Sudan* 6°38′ N, 26°33′ E **224**
Bussoleno, *It.* 45°8′ N, 7°8′ E **167**
Bussum, *Neth.* 52°16′ N, 5°9′ E **163**
Bustamante, *Mex.* 26°30′ N, 100°32′ W **114**
Bustard Islands, *North America* 45°37′ N, 81°16′ W **94**
Bustarviejo, *Sp.* 40°51′ N, 3°42′ W **164**
Buştenari, oil field, *Rom.* 45°7′ N, 25°44′ E **156**
Bustillos, Laguna, lake, *Mex.* 28°34′ N, 107°21′ W **92**
Busto, Cabo, *Sp.* 43°34′ N, 6°28′ W **150**
Buston, *Taj.* 40°30′ N, 69°17′ E **197**
Busu Mandji, *Dem. Rep. of the Congo* 2°51′ N, 21°15′ E **218**
Busu-Djanoa, *Dem. Rep. of the Congo* 1°39′ N, 21°20′ E **218**
Busuulu, *Dem. Rep. of the Congo* 0°49′ N, 20°44′ E **218**
But e Koritës, peak, *Alban.* 40°45′ N, 20°47′ E **156**
Buta, *Dem. Rep. of the Congo* 2°44′ N, 24°44′ E **224**
Butare, *Rwanda* 2°37′ S, 29°42′ E **224**
Bute Helu, *Kenya* 2°40′ N, 39°51′ E **224**
Bute Inlet 50°34′ N, 125°22′ W **90**
Butembo, *Dem. Rep. of the Congo* 0°6′ N, 29°15′ E **224**
Buteni, *Rom.* 46°20′ N, 22°8′ E **168**
Buthidaung, *Myanmar* 20°54′ N, 92°28′ E **188**
Butiá, *Braz.* 30°8′ S, 51°56′ W **139**
Butiaba, *Uganda* 1°47′ N, 31°19′ E **224**
Butler, *Ala., U.S.* 32°5′ N, 88°13′ W **103**
Butler, *Ga., U.S.* 32°33′ N, 84°14′ W **96**
Butler, *Ky., U.S.* 38°46′ N, 84°22′ W **102**
Butler, *Mo., U.S.* 38°14′ N, 94°20′ W **94**
Butler, *Ohio, U.S.* 40°34′ N, 82°26′ W **102**
Butler, *Pa., U.S.* 40°51′ N, 79°54′ W **94**
Butler Island, *Antarctica* 72°6′ S, 60°8′ W **248**
Butlēri, *Latv.* 57°3′ N, 25°49′ E **166**
Butlerville, *Ind., U.S.* 39°1′ N, 85°31′ W **102**
Buţmah, oil field, *Iraq* 36°40′ N, 42°36′ E **195**
Buton, island, *Indonesia* 4°47′ S, 123°16′ E **192**
Butte, *Mont., U.S.* 45°59′ N, 112°32′ W **82**
Butte, *Nebr., U.S.* 42°53′ N, 98°52′ W **90**
Butte Mountains, *Nev., U.S.* 39°43′ N, 115°26′ W **90**
Butterwick, *U.K.* 52°58′ N, 7°416′ E **162**
Butterworth, *Malaysia* 5°24′ N, 100°23′ E **196**
Buttes, Sierra, peak, *Calif., U.S.* 39°34′ N, 120°44′ W **90**
Buttle Lake, lake, *Can.* 49°33′ N, 125°56′ W **90**
Button Islands, *Labrador Sea* 60°23′ N, 64°18′ W **106**
Buttonwillow, *Calif., U.S.* 35°24′ N, 119°30′ W **100**
Butuan, *Philippines* 8°59′ N, 125°32′ E **203**
Buturlinovka, *Russ.* 50°50′ N, 40°36′ E **158**
Butwal, *Nepal* 27°41′ N, 83°30′ E **197**
Butyaalo, *Somalia* 11°26′ N, 49°57′ E **216**
Butzbach, *Ger.* 50°26′ N, 8°40′ E **167**
Buuhoodle, *Somalia* 8°14′ N, 46°22′ E **218**
Buulobarde, *Somalia* 3°48′ N, 45°37′ E **218**
Buur Gaabo, *Somalia* 1°13′ S, 41°51′ E **224**
Buurhakaba, *Somalia* 2°45′ N, 44°7′ E **218**
Buwayḑān, *Syr.* 33°11′ N, 36°26′ E **194**
Buxar, *India* 25°32′ N, 83°56′ E **197**
Buxoro (Bukhara), *Uzb.* 39°47′ N, 64°25′ E **197**
Buxton, *Guyana* 6°39′ N, 58°3′ W **130**
Buxton, *Me., U.S.* 43°38′ N, 70°32′ W **104**
Buxton, *N.C., U.S.* 35°16′ N, 75°34′ W **96**
Buxton, *U.K.* 53°15′ N, 1°55′ W **162**
Buy, *Russ.* 58°29′ N, 41°36′ E **154**
Buyant, *Mongolia* 46°12′ N, 110°49′ E **198**
Buyant Ovoo, *Mongolia* 44°56′ N, 107°12′ E **198**
Buyant-Uhaa see Saynshand, *Mongolia* 44°51′ N, 110°9′ E **190**
Buynaksk, *Russ.* 42°48′ N, 47°7′ E **195**
Buyo, *Côte d'Ivoire* 6°11′ N, 7°1′ W **222**
Buyr Nuur, lake, *Mongolia* 47°49′ N, 117°29′ E **198**
Buyun Shan, peak, *China* 40°4′ N, 122°41′ E **200**
Buzancy, *Fr.* 49°25′ N, 4°57′ E **163**
Buzău, adm. division, *Rom.* 45°26′ N, 26°10′ E **156**
Buzău, Pasul, pass, *Rom.* 45°35′ N, 26°9′ E **156**
Buzaymah, *Lib.* 24°55′ N, 22°1′ E **216**
Buzlove, *Ukr.* 48°19′ N, 22°23′ E **152**
Büzmey'in, *Turkm.* 38°1′ N, 58°16′ E **180**
Buzul Daği, peak, *Turk.* 37°27′ N, 43°50′ E **195**
Buzuluk, *Russ.* 52°46′ N, 52°13′ E **154**
Buzzards Bay, *Mass., U.S.* 41°44′ N, 70°38′ W **104**
Bwendi, *Dem. Rep. of the Congo* 4°1′ N, 26°42′ E **224**
Bwere, river, *Dem. Rep. of the Congo* 3°44′ N, 27°19′ E **224**
Byahoml', *Belarus* 54°43′ N, 28°3′ E **166**
Byala, *Bulg.* 43°28′ N, 25°44′ E **156**
Byala, *Bulg.* 42°52′ N, 27°53′ E **156**
Byalynichy, *Belarus* 54°0′ N, 29°43′ E **166**
Byam Channel 75°15′ N, 109°24′ W **106**
Byam Martin, Cape, *Can.* 73°20′ N, 77°1′ W **106**
Byam Martin Island, *Can.* 74°29′ N, 104°57′ W **106**
Byarezina, river, *Belarus* 53°24′ N, 29°5′ E **152**
Byarezina, river, *Belarus* 54°13′ N, 26°34′ E **166**
Byaroza, *Belarus* 52°31′ N, 24°58′ E **152**
Byblos see Jbail, *Leb.* 34°7′ N, 35°39′ E **194**
Bychikha, *Belarus* 55°40′ N, 30°3′ E **166**
Bydalen, *Nor.* 63°5′ N, 13°45′ E **152**
Bydgoszcz, *Pol.* 53°8′ N, 18°1′ E **152**
Byer, *Ohio, U.S.* 39°9′ N, 82°38′ W **102**
Byerazino, *Belarus* 53°53′ N, 29°1′ E **166**
Byers, *Colo., U.S.* 39°42′ N, 104°14′ W **90**
Byesville, *Ohio, U.S.* 39°57′ N, 81°33′ W **102**
Bygdeå, *Nor.* 64°3′ N, 20°51′ E **152**
Bygstad, *Nor.* 61°22′ N, 5°41′ E **152**
Bykhaw, *Belarus* 53°30′ N, 30°18′ E **154**
Bykovo, *Russ.* 49°37′ N, 45°21′ E **158**
Bykovskiy, *Russ.* 71°43′ N, 129°19′ E **160**
Bylas, *Ariz., U.S.* 33°7′ N, 110°7′ W **92**
Bylot Island, *Can.* 73°51′ N, 81°13′ W **106**
Bylot, island, *Can.* 72°49′ N, 75°55′ W **106**
Byng Inlet, *Can.* 45°44′ N, 80°33′ W **94**
Bynguano Range, *Austral.* 31°8′ S, 142°42′ E **230**
Byram, *Miss., U.S.* 32°10′ N, 90°16′ W **103**
Byrd, Cape, *Antarctica* 69°52′ S, 79°21′ W **248**
Byrd, Lac, lake, *Can.* 47°1′ N, 77°12′ W **110**

Byron, Calif., U.S. 37°51' N, 121°39' W 100
Byron, Ill., U.S. 42°7' N, 89°16' W 102
Byron, Cape, Austral. 28°38' S, 153°45' E 230
Byron, Isla, island, Chile 47°44' S, 76°33' W 134
Byrum, Den. 57°14' N, 10°59' E 150
Byske, Nor. 64°57' N, 21°10' E 152
Bytów, Pol. 54°9' N, 17°29' E 152
Byumba, Rwanda 1°39' S, 30°2' E 224
Bzip'i, river, Europe 43°22' N, 40°37' E 195

C

Ca Mau, Vietnam 9°12' N, 105°7' E 202
Ca Na, Vietnam 11°22' N, 108°51' E 202
Ca Na, Mui, Vietnam 10°56' N, 109°0' E 202
Ca, river, Vietnam 19°12' N, 104°44' E 202
C.A. Rosetti, Rom. 45°17' N, 29°33' E 156
Caaguazú, Parag. 25°27' S, 56°1' W 132
Caamaño Sound 52°48' N, 129°56' W 108
Caapucú, Parag. 26°15' S, 57°11' W 139
Caatinga, Braz. 17°8' S, 45°58' W 138
Caazapá, Parag. 26°9' S, 56°23' W 139
Cabaiguán, Cuba 22°5' N, 79°31' W 116
Caballococha, Peru 3°58' S, 70°30' W 130
Caballos Mesteños, Llano de los, Mex. 28°36' N, 104°37' W 112
Cabana, Peru 8°25' S, 78°1' W 130
Cabanaconde, Peru 15°40' S, 71°58' W 137
Cabanatuan, Philippines 15°28' N, 120°58' E 203
Cabañeros National Park, Sp. 39°14' N, 4°33' W 164
Cabanes, Sp. 40°9' N, 4°238' E 164
Cabano, Can. 47°39' N, 68°55' W 94
Cabedelo, Braz. 7°4' S, 34°52' W 132
Cabery, Ill., U.S. 40°59' N, 88°13' W 102
Cabeza de Lagarto, Punta, Peru 10°15' S, 80°8' W 130
Cabeza de Pava, Col. 2°47' N, 69°13' W 136
Cabeza del Buey, Sp. 38°43' N, 5°14' W 164
Cabezas, Bol. 18°49' S, 63°26' W 137
Cabildo, Arg. 38°30' S, 61°57' W 139
Cabimas, Venez. 10°24' N, 71°29' W 136
Cabinda, Angola 5°35' S, 12°10' E 218
Cabinet Mountains, Mont., U.S. 48°20' N, 116°13' W 90
Cabiri, Angola 8°53' S, 13°40' E 220
Cable, Wis., U.S. 46°12' N, 91°17' W 94
Cabo Blanco, Arg. 47°12' S, 65°47' W 134
Cabo Delgado, adm. division, Mozambique 12°22' S, 38°34' E 220
Cabo Frio, Braz. 22°51' S, 42°1' W 138
Cabo Gracias a Dios, Nicar. 14°58' N, 83°14' W 115
Cabo Raso, Arg. 44°21' S, 65°17' W 134
Cabo San Lucas, Mex. 22°51' N, 109°56' W 112
Cabonga, Réservoir, lake, Can. 47°6' N, 78°13' W 81
Cabonga, Réservoir, lake, Can. 47°14' N, 78°10' W 106
Cabool, Mo., U.S. 37°6' N, 92°6' W 96
Caborca, Mex. 30°42' N, 112°11' W 92
Cabot, Vt., U.S. 44°23' N, 72°20' W 104
Cabot Head, Can. 45°15' N, 81°17' W 94
Cabot, Mount, N.H., U.S. 44°29' N, 71°26' W 104
Cabra de Santo Cristo, Sp. 37°42' N, 3°16' W 164
Cabral, Dom. Rep. 18°14' N, 71°12' W 116
Cabrera Baja, Sierra de la, Sp. 42°3' N, 7°8' W 150
Cabrera, island, Sp. 38°52' N, 2°54' E 214
Cabri, Can. 50°37' N, 108°28' W 90
Cabri Lake, lake, Can. 51°4' N, 110°5' W 90
Cabriel, river, Sp. 39°23' N, 1°27' W 164
Cabrillo National Monument, Calif., U.S. 32°40' N, 117°17' W 101
Cabrobó, Braz. 8°31' S, 39°21' W 132
Cabrón, Cabo, Dom. Rep. 19°22' N, 69°11' W 116
Cabruta, Venez. 7°40' N, 66°16' W 136
Cabugao, Philippines 17°49' N, 120°27' E 203
Cabure, Venez. 11°9' N, 69°38' W 136
Cabuyaro, Col. 4°16' N, 72°48' W 136
Caçador, Braz. 26°47' S, 50°60' W 139
Cacahuamilpa, Mex. 18°40' N, 99°33' W 114
Cacahuatepec, Mex. 16°34' N, 98°11' W 112
Cacahuatique, peak, El Salv. 13°45' N, 88°20' W 115
Čačak, Serb. and Mont. 43°52' N, 20°20' E 168
Cacalotán, Mex. 23°4' N, 105°50' W 114
Cacaoui, Lac, lake, Can. 50°52' N, 67°26' W 111
Caçapava do Sul, Braz. 30°30' S, 53°30' W 139
Caccia, Capo, It. 40°34' N, 7°24' E 156
Cacequi, Braz. 29°55' S, 54°51' W 139
Cáceres, Braz. 16°7' S, 57°39' W 132
Cáceres, Col. 7°35' N, 75°19' W 136
Cáceres, Sp. 39°28' N, 6°23' W 164
Cachari, Arg. 36°23' S, 59°31' W 139
Cache Bay, Can. 46°22' N, 79°59' W 94
Cache Peak, Idaho, U.S. 42°11' N, 113°43' W 90
Cacheu, Guinea-Bissau 12°14' N, 16°7' W 222
Cachi, Arg. 25°5' S, 66°11' W 134
Cachimbo, Braz. 9°19' S, 54°51' W 130
Cachimbo, Serra do, Braz. 7°52' S, 56°39' W 130
Cachingues, Angola 13°7' S, 16°43' E 220
Cachisca, Lac, lake, Can. 50°24' N, 75°36' W 110
Cachoeira, Braz. 14°23' S, 55°34' W 132
Cachoeira Alta, Braz. 18°51' S, 50°56' W 138
Cachoeira do Sul, Braz. 30°2' S, 52°56' W 139
Cachoeira Ipadu, fall(s), Braz. 0°15' N, 67°20' W 136
Cachoeira Ipanoré, fall(s), Braz. 0°13' N, 68°29' W 136
Cachoeiro do Itapemirim, Braz. 20°54' S, 41°9' W 138
Cachos, Punta, Chile 27°41' S, 72°17' W 134
Cachuela Esperanza, Bol. 10°36' S, 65°34' W 137
Cacine, Guinea-Bissau 11°6' N, 15°2' W 222
Cacolo, Angola 10°11' S, 19°13' E 207
Caconda, Angola 13°44' S, 15°4' E 220
Cacongo, Angola 5°15' S, 12°7' E 218
Cactus, Tex., U.S. 36°0' N, 101°59' W 92
Cactus Flat, Nev., U.S. 37°52' N, 116°55' W 90
Cactus Range, Nev., U.S. 37°54' N, 117°6' W 90
Caçu, Braz. 18°35' S, 51°12' W 138
Caculé, Braz. 14°34' S, 42°12' W 138
Cacuri, Venez. 4°48' N, 65°20' W 136
Cacuso, Angola 9°27' S, 15°44' E 218
Cadaadley, Somalia 9°44' N, 44°40' E 218
Cadair Idris, peak, U.K. 52°41' N, 3°57' W 162
Cadale, Somalia 2°44' N, 46°27' E 218
Cadaqués, Sp. 42°16' N, 3°16' E 164
Čadavica, Croatia 45°45' N, 17°50' E 168
Caddo, Okla., U.S. 34°6' N, 96°16' W 96
Caddo Lake, Tex., U.S. 32°44' N, 94°30' W 81
Cade, La., U.S. 30°2' N, 91°54' W 103
Cadereyta, Mex. 25°34' N, 99°59' W 114
Cadí, Serra del, Sp. 42°16' N, 1°28' E 164
Cadillac, Can. 49°43' N, 107°45' W 90
Cadillac Mountain, Me., U.S. 44°20' N, 68°19' W 94
Çadır Dağı, peak, Turk. 38°12' N, 43°3' E 195
Cadiz, Ky., U.S. 36°52' N, 87°50' W 96
Cadiz, Ohio, U.S. 40°15' N, 80°60' W 102
Cadiz, Philippines 10°56' N, 123°16' E 203
Cádiz, Sp. 36°31' N, 6°18' W 164
Cadomin, Can. 53°0' N, 117°20' W 108
Cady Mountains, Calif., U.S. 34°57' N, 116°20' W 101
Caen, Fr. 49°11' N, 0°22' E 150
Caerdydd see Cardiff, U.K. 51°28' N, 3°12' W 162
Caerlaverock Castle, site, U.K. 54°58' N, 3°38' W 150
Caerleon, U.K. 51°36' N, 2°57' W 162
Caernarfon, U.K. 53°9' N, 4°14' W 162
Caerphilly, U.K. 51°35' N, 3°13' W 162
Caesarea, ruin(s), Israel 32°29' N, 34°51' E 194
Caeté, Braz. 19°54' S, 43°35' W 138
Caeté, river, Braz. 9°29' S, 69°35' W 130
Caetité, Braz. 14°5' S, 42°31' W 138
Cafayate, Arg. 26°4' S, 65°58' W 132
Cafuini, river, Braz. 1°12' N, 58°27' W 130
Cagayan de Oro, Philippines 8°31' N, 124°36' E 203
Cagayan Islands, Sulu Sea 9°6' N, 121°20' E 203
Cagayan, river, Philippines 18°5' N, 121°37' E 203
Cagayan Sulu Island, Philippines 6°52' N, 118°36' E 192
Cagliari, It. 39°13' N, 9°6' E 156
Cagnano Varano, It. 41°49' N, 15°46' E 156
Caguán, river, Col. 1°9' N, 74°44' W 136
Cahama, Angola 16°15' S, 14°12' E 220
Cahora Bassa, Mozambique 15°38' S, 32°46' E 224
Cahora Bassa Dam, Mozambique 15°46' S, 32°3' E 224
Cahore Point, Ire. 52°34' N, 6°9' W 150
Cahors, Fr. 44°31' N, 1°18' E 214
Cahuinari National Park, Col. 1°18' S, 71°54' W 136
Cahuinari, river, Col. 1°22' S, 71°29' W 136
Cahuita National Park, C.R. 9°42' N, 82°55' W 115
Cahul, Mold. 45°54' N, 28°10' E 156
Cai Bau, Vietnam 21°8' N, 107°28' E 198
Caia, Mozambique 17°49' S, 35°18' E 224
Caiabis, Serra dos, Braz. 12°29' S, 56°51' W 130
Caianda, Angola 11°4' S, 23°30' E 224
Caiapó, river, Braz. 16°33' S, 51°17' W 138
Caiapó, Serra do, Braz. 17°38' S, 53°25' W 132
Caiaponia, Braz. 16°59' S, 51°49' W 138
Caibarién, Cuba 22°29' N, 79°28' W 116
Caicara, Venez. 7°36' N, 66°10' W 136
Caicó, Braz. 6°30' S, 37°7' W 132
Caicos Islands, North Atlantic Ocean 21°25' N, 71°58' W 116
Caijiapo, China 34°19' N, 107°33' E 198
Cailloma, Peru 15°13' S, 71°45' W 137
Caimito, Col. 8°49' N, 75°8' W 136
Cainde, Angola 15°34' S, 13°20' E 220
Cains, river, Can. 46°20' N, 66°23' W 94
Cainsville, Mo., U.S. 40°25' N, 93°46' W 94
Caird Coast, Antarctica 76°29' S, 32°29' W 248
Cairngorm Mountains, U.K. 57°3' N, 4°35' W 150
Cairns, Austral. 16°56' S, 145°45' E 231
Cairnwell Pass, U.K. 56°52' N, 3°25' W 150
Cairo, Ga., U.S. 30°52' N, 84°13' W 96
Cairo, Mo., U.S. 37°0' N, 89°10' W 96
Cairo, N.Y., U.S. 42°17' N, 74°1' W 104
Cairo Montenotte, It. 44°23' N, 8°16' E 167
Cairo see El Qâhira, Egypt 30°3' N, 31°8' E 180
Caistor, U.K. 53°29' N, 0°19' E 162
Caithness, Ord of, peak, U.K. 58°8' N, 3°41' W 150
Caitou, Angola 14°31' S, 13°4' E 220
Caiundo, Angola 15°44' S, 17°26' E 220
Caiza, Bol. 20°4' S, 65°45' W 137
Caiza see Villa Ingavi, Bol. 21°47' S, 63°33' W 137
Cajamarca, Peru 7°8' S, 78°32' W 130
Cajamarca, adm. division, Peru 4°58' S, 79°20' W 130
Cajatambo, Peru 10°30' S, 77°1' W 130
Cajàzeiras, Braz. 6°54' S, 38°32' W 132
Cajniče, Bosn. and Herzg. 43°33' N, 19°4' E 168
Cajon Pass, Calif., U.S. 34°20' N, 117°27' W 101
Caju, Ilha do, island, Braz. 2°56' S, 42°35' W 132
Çakırgöl Dağı, peak, Turk. 40°33' N, 39°38' E 195
Çakmak, Turk. 39°10' N, 31°52' E 156
Çakmak Dağı, peak, Turk. 39°45' N, 42°9' E 195
Çal, Turk. 38°4' N, 29°23' E 156
Cal Madow, Buuraha, peak, Somalia 10°56' N, 48°7' E 218
Cala, Sp. 37°57' N, 6°19' W 164
Cala Rajada, Sp. 39°41' N, 3°27' E 150
Cala see Doğruyol, Turk. 41°3' N, 43°20' E 195
Calabar, Nig. 4°57' N, 8°20' E 222
Calabozo, Venez. 8°55' N, 67°28' W 136
Calabria, adm. division, It. 39°5' N, 16°5' E 156
Calaburras, Punta de, Sp. 36°20' N, 4°39' W 164
Calacoto, Bol. 17°22' S, 68°43' W 137
Calaf, Sp. 41°43' N, 1°30' E 164
Calafat, Rom. 43°59' N, 22°56' E 168
Calahorra, Sp. 42°18' N, 1°58' W 164
Calais, Fr. 50°57' N, 1°51' E 163
Calais, Me., U.S. 45°10' N, 67°17' W 94
Calakmul, ruin(s), Mex. 18°4' N, 89°57' W 115
Calalaste, Sierra de, Arg. 25°16' S, 67°50' W 132
Calalzo, It. 46°27' N, 12°21' E 167
Calama, Braz. 8°3' S, 62°51' W 130
Calama, Chile 22°28' S, 68°58' W 137
Calamar, Col. 10°13' N, 74°58' W 136
Calamar, Col. 1°57' N, 72°34' W 136
Calamarca, Bol. 16°59' S, 68°8' W 137
Calamian Group, islands, Sulu Sea 11°37' N, 119°18' E 203
Calamocha, Sp. 40°54' N, 1°18' W 164
Calamonte, Sp. 38°53' N, 6°23' W 164
Calamus, river, Nebr., U.S. 42°18' N, 100°3' W 90
Calañas, Sp. 37°39' N, 6°54' W 150
Calanda, Sp. 40°55' N, 0°15' E 164
Calandula, Angola 9°6' S, 15°58' E 218
Calang, Indonesia 4°39' N, 95°35' E 196
Calanscio, oil field, Lib. 28°1' N, 21°18' E 216
Calapan, Philippines 13°24' N, 121°10' E 203
Călăraşi, adm. division, Rom. 44°23' N, 26°25' E 156
Călăraşi, Mold. 47°16' N, 28°18' E 156
Călăraşi, Rom. 44°11' N, 27°19' E 156
Calasparra, Sp. 38°13' N, 1°43' W 164
Calatayud, Sp. 41°21' N, 1°40' W 164
Călăţele, Rom. 46°45' N, 23°1' E 168
Calatorao, Sp. 41°31' N, 1°21' W 164
Calavà, Capo, It. 38°12' N, 14°19' E 156
Calayan, island, Philippines 19°26' N, 120°55' E 198
Calbayog, Philippines 12°4' N, 124°35' E 203
Calbiga, Philippines 11°37' N, 125°1' E 203
Calca, Peru 13°19' S, 71°59' W 137
Calcanhar, Ponta do, Braz. 5°8' S, 35°29' W 132
Calcasieu Lake, La., U.S. 29°52' N, 93°33' W 103
Calcasieu, river, La., U.S. 30°22' N, 93°8' W 103
Calceta, Venez. 7°4' N, 62°30' W 130
Calchaqui, Arg. 29°50' S, 60°18' W 139
Calcutta see Kolkata, India 22°33' N, 88°21' E 197
Caldas, adm. division, Col. 5°10' N, 75°51' W 136
Caldas da Rainha, Port. 39°23' N, 9°9' W 150
Caldas Novas, Braz. 17°48' S, 48°40' W 138
Caldbeck, U.K. 54°45' N, 3°3' W 162
Caldera, Chile 27°6' S, 70°52' W 132
Calderitas, Mex. 18°34' N, 88°17' W 115
Caldes de Malavella, Sp. 41°50' N, 2°49' E 164
Çaldıran, Turk. 39°6' N, 43°50' E 195
Caldonazzo, It. 45°59' N, 11°14' E 167
Caldron Snout, lake, U.K. 54°40' N, 2°32' W 162
Caldwell, Idaho, U.S. 43°39' N, 116°40' W 82
Caldwell, Kans., U.S. 37°0' N, 97°37' W 92
Caldwell, Ohio, U.S. 39°44' N, 81°31' W 102
Caldwell, Tex., U.S. 30°31' N, 96°42' W 96
Caledon, S. Af. 34°13' S, 19°26' E 227
Caledonia, Minn., U.S. 43°38' N, 91°29' W 94
Calella, Sp. 41°36' N, 2°39' E 164
Caleta Buena, Chile 19°53' S, 70°10' W 137
Caleta Pabellón de Pica, Chile 20°56' S, 70°10' W 137
Calexico, Calif., U.S. 32°40' N, 115°30' W 101
Calf, The, peak, U.K. 54°22' N, 2°33' W 162
Calgary, Can. 51°3' N, 114°5' W 90
Calhoun Falls, S.C., U.S. 34°5' N, 82°36' W 96
Cali, Col. 3°24' N, 76°33' W 136
Calico Peak, Nev., U.S. 41°49' N, 117°22' W 90
Calico Rock, Ark., U.S. 36°6' N, 92°10' W 96
Caliente, Calif., U.S. 35°18' N, 118°38' W 101
Caliente, Nev., U.S. 37°35' N, 114°30' W 82
Caliente Range, Calif., U.S. 35°0' N, 119°45' W 100
California, Mo., U.S. 38°37' N, 92°33' W 94
California, adm. division, Calif., U.S. 36°52' N, 120°58' W 92
California City, Calif., U.S. 35°7' N, 117°59' W 101
California Coastal National Monument, Pacific Ocean 37°19' N, 122°49' W 100
California, Golfo de 30°47' N, 114°31' W 112
California, Gulf of 31°12' N, 114°47' W 73
California Hot Springs, Calif., U.S. 35°53' N, 118°41' W 101
California Spaceport, Calif., U.S. 34°35' N, 120°39' W 100
California Valley, Calif., U.S. 35°19' N, 120°1' W 100
Càlig, Sp. 40°26' N, 0°20' E 164
Calilegua, Arg. 23°45' S, 64°46' W 132
Cälilabad, Azerb. 39°12' N, 48°28' E 195
Călimani, Munţii, Rom. 47°0' N, 24°32' E 156
Calion, Ark., U.S. 33°18' N, 92°33' W 103
Calipatria, Calif., U.S. 33°7' N, 115°31' W 101
Calispell Peak, Wash., U.S. 48°24' N, 117°36' W 90
Calkini, Mex. 20°23' N, 90°4' W 115
Callaghan, Mount, Nev., U.S. 39°42' N, 117°2' W 90
Callamura, spring, Austral. 27°39' S, 140°53' E 230
Callander, Can. 46°13' N, 79°22' W 94
Callao, Peru 12°4' S, 77°9' W 130
Callaway, Nebr., U.S. 41°15' N, 99°55' W 90
Calling Lake, Can. 55°8' N, 113°47' W 108
Calling Lake, Can. 55°15' N, 113°12' W 108
Callirhoe, ruin(s), Jordan 31°35' N, 35°32' E 194
Calmar, Can. 53°15' N, 113°49' W 108
Calnali, Mex. 20°52' N, 98°35' W 114
Calne, U.K. 51°25' N, 2°1' W 162
Calonga, Angola 16°1' S, 15°13' E 220
Caloosahatchee, canal, Fla., U.S. 26°45' N, 81°29' W 105
Calotmul, Mex. 21°0' N, 88°12' W 112
Caloto, Col. 3°3' N, 76°24' W 136
Calpe, Sp. 38°38' N, 4°238' E 164
Calpulalpan de Méndez, Mex. 17°19' N, 96°25' W 114
Çaltı Burnu, Turk. 41°17' N, 37°0' E 156
Caluango, Angola 8°21' S, 19°36' E 218
Calulo, Angola 9°60' S, 14°54' E 220
Calunda, Angola 12°8' S, 23°33' E 220
Caluso, It. 45°18' N, 7°52' E 167
Caluula, Somalia 11°52' N, 50°43' E 182
Calvados Chain, islands, Solomon Sea 11°41' S, 150°22' E 192
Calvert, Ala., U.S. 31°9' N, 87°60' W 103
Calvert, Tex., U.S. 30°57' N, 96°40' W 96
Calvin, La., U.S. 31°56' N, 92°47' W 103
Calvinia, S. Af. 31°28' S, 19°46' E 227
Calwa, Calif., U.S. 36°42' N, 119°45' W 100
Calydon, ruin(s), Gr. 38°21' N, 21°25' E 156
Çam Burnu, Turk. 41°9' N, 37°45' E 156
Cam Pha, Vietnam 21°2' N, 107°18' E 198
Cam Ranh, Vietnam 11°53' N, 109°14' E 202
Cam Ranh, Vung 11°37' N, 109°3' E 202
Cam Xuyen, Vietnam 18°15' N, 106°2' E 198
Camabatela, Angola 8°11' S, 15°22' E 218
Camacan, Braz. 15°26' S, 39°29' W 138
Camachigama, Lac, lake, Can. 47°48' N, 77°5' W 94
Camacho, Mex. 24°25' N, 102°22' W 114
Camacupa, Angola 12°2' S, 17°28' E 220
Camaguán, Venez. 8°6' N, 67°34' W 136
Camagüey, Cuba 21°23' N, 77°54' W 116
Camagüey, adm. division, Cuba 21°27' N, 78°32' W 116
Camagüey, Archipiélago de, North Atlantic Ocean 22°40' N, 78°24' W 116
Camaleão, Ilha, island, Braz. 0°8' N, 48°50' W 130
Camaná, Peru 16°38' S, 72°43' W 137
Camanche Reservoir, lake, Calif., U.S. 38°13' N, 121°8' W 100
Camanongue, Angola 11°26' S, 20°11' E 220
Camapuã, Braz. 19°32' S, 54°6' W 132
Camaquã, Braz. 30°52' S, 51°51' W 139
Camaquã, river, Braz. 31°3' S, 53°4' W 139
Camăr, Rom. 47°17' N, 22°38' E 168
Camarat, Cap, Fr. 43°7' N, 6°40' E 165
Çamardı, Turk. 37°50' N, 34°58' E 156
Camargo, Bol. 20°40' S, 65°16' W 137
Camargo, Okla., U.S. 36°0' N, 99°18' W 92
Camargue, Île de la, islands, Golfe Dulion 43°28' N, 4°23' E 167
Camarón, Cabo, Hond. 15°59' N, 84°60' W 115
Camarones, Arg. 44°46' S, 65°45' W 134
Camarones, Chile 19°3' S, 69°56' W 137
Camas, Sp. 37°24' N, 6°3' W 164
Camas, Wash., U.S. 45°34' N, 122°26' W 90
Camas Valley, Oreg., U.S. 43°1' N, 123°41' W 90
Camatindi, Bol. 20°60' S, 63°31' W 137
Cambeak, point, U.K. 50°45' N, 5°11' W 150
Camblaya, river, Bol. 20°57' S, 65°16' W 137
Cambodia 12°37' N, 103°48' E 192
Cambona, Mozambique 11°47' S, 36°33' E 224
Camborne, U.K. 50°13' N, 5°19' W 150
Cambrai, Fr. 50°9' N, 3°15' E 163
Cambria, Calif., U.S. 35°34' N, 121°7' W 100
Cambria Icefield, Can. 55°51' N, 129°25' W 108
Cambrian Mountains, U.K. 52°2' N, 3°33' W 162
Cambridge, Idaho, U.S. 44°34' N, 116°41' W 90
Cambridge, Nebr., U.S. 40°16' N, 100°11' W 90
Cambridge, N.Z. 37°54' S, 175°29' E 240
Cambridge, Ohio, U.S. 40°1' N, 81°35' W 102
Cambridge, U.K. 52°11' N, 0°9' E 162
Cambridge Bay, Can. 69°6' N, 105°2' W 106
Cambridge City, Ind., U.S. 39°48' N, 85°11' W 102
Cambridge Gulf 15°11' S, 127°52' E 230
Cambrils de Mar, Sp. 41°4' N, 1°3' E 164
Cambulo, Angola 7°44' S, 21°14' E 218
Cambundi-Catembo, Angola 10°4' S, 17°31' E 220
Cambutal, Cerro, peak, Pan. 7°18' N, 80°38' W 115
Camden, Ala., U.S. 31°59' N, 87°17' W 96
Camden, Ark., U.S. 33°33' N, 92°51' W 96
Camden, Ind., U.S. 40°36' N, 86°32' W 102
Camden, Me., U.S. 44°13' N, 69°4' W 94
Camden, Miss., U.S. 32°46' N, 89°51' W 103
Camden, N.J., U.S. 39°56' N, 75°8' W 94
Camden, N.Y., U.S. 43°20' N, 75°46' W 94
Camden, N.C., U.S. 36°19' N, 76°11' W 96
Camden, Tex., U.S. 30°53' N, 94°45' W 103
Camden Bay 69°56' N, 147°43' W 98
Camdenton, Mo., U.S. 37°59' N, 92°44' W 94
Camelgooda Hill, Austral. 18°31' S, 123°43' E 230
Çameli, Turk. 37°4' N, 29°19' E 156
Camels Hump, peak, Austral. 23°51' S, 131°27' E 230
Camels Hump, peak, Vt., U.S. 44°18' N, 72°55' W 104
Camenca, Mold. 48°2' N, 28°44' E 156
Cameron, Ariz., U.S. 35°51' N, 111°25' W 92
Cameron, La., U.S. 29°47' N, 93°20' W 103
Cameron, Tex., U.S. 30°50' N, 96°58' W 96
Cameron Falls, Can. 49°8' N, 88°19' W 94
Cameron Lake, lake, Can. 48°59' N, 84°45' W 110
Cameroon 4°33' N, 11°3' E 218
Cameroon Mountain, Cameroon 4°15' N, 9°4' E 222
Cametá, Braz. 2°14' S, 49°31' W 130
Camiguin, island, Philippines 18°49' N, 122°1' E 198
Camilla, Ga., U.S. 31°13' N, 84°13' W 96
Camiña, Chile 19°18' S, 69°27' W 137
Caminha, Port. 41°52' N, 8°51' W 150
Camiranga, Braz. 1°51' S, 46°18' W 130
Camiri, Bol. 20°7' S, 63°34' W 137
Camirus, ruin(s), Gr. 36°18' N, 27°48' E 156
Camisea, Peru 11°43' S, 73°2' W 137
Camisea, river, Peru 11°57' S, 72°59' W 137
Camissombo, Angola 8°11' S, 20°40' E 218
Camocim, Braz. 2°57' S, 40°52' W 132
Camooweal, Austral. 19°56' S, 138°8' E 231
Camopi, Fr. 3°11' N, 52°20' W 130
Camopi, river, Braz. 2°28' N, 53°20' W 130
Camorta Island, India 7°38' N, 93°39' E 188
Camoruco, Col. 6°27' N, 70°31' W 136
Camousitchouane, Lac, lake, Can. 51°2' N, 76°24' W 110
Camp Crook, S. Dak., U.S. 45°32' N, 103°60' W 90
Camp David, site, Md., U.S. 39°39' N, 77°32' W 94
Camp Douglas, Wis., U.S. 43°54' N, 90°16' W 102
Camp Nelson, Calif., U.S. 36°9' N, 118°38' W 101
Camp Pendleton Marine Corps Base, Calif., U.S. 33°20' N, 117°29' W 101
Camp Point, Mo., U.S. 40°1' N, 91°4' W 94
Camp Wood, Tex., U.S. 29°39' N, 100°1' W 92
Campagne-lès-Hesdin, Fr. 50°23' N, 1°52' E 163
Campamento, Col. 4°30' N, 70°24' W 136
Campana, Arg. 34°11' S, 58°56' W 139
Campana, Isla, island, Chile 48°13' S, 77°9' W 134
Campanario, Sp. 38°51' N, 5°37' W 164
Campania, adm. division, It. 41°12' N, 13°54' E 156
Campbell, Calif., U.S. 37°17' N, 121°57' W 100
Campbell, Cape, N.Z. 41°44' S, 174°12' E 240
Campbell Hill, Ohio, U.S. 40°21' N, 83°45' W 102
Campbell Island, N.Z. 52°37' S, 169°0' E 252
Campbell Plateau, South Pacific Ocean 50°28' S, 171°45' E 252
Campbell River, Can. 50°1' N, 125°15' W 90
Campbell's Bay, Can. 45°43' N, 76°36' W 94
Campbellsburg, Ind., U.S. 38°38' N, 86°16' W 102
Campbellsburg, Ky., U.S. 38°30' N, 85°13' W 102
Campbellsville, Ky., U.S. 37°19' N, 85°21' W 96
Campbellton, Can. 47°58' N, 66°41' W 94
Campeche, Mex. 19°48' N, 90°40' W 115
Campeche, adm. division, Mex. 18°56' N, 91°2' W 112
Campeche Bank, Gulf of Mexico 21°58' N, 90°5' W 253
Camperville, Can. 52°1' N, 100°12' W 108
Campidano, It. 39°44' N, 8°33' E 156
Campina Grande, Braz. 7°11' S, 35°53' W 123
Campina Verde, Braz. 19°33' S, 49°29' W 138
Campinas, Braz. 22°56' S, 47°5' W 138
Campo, Calif., U.S. 32°36' N, 116°29' W 101
Campo, Colo., U.S. 37°6' N, 102°35' W 92
Campo, Mozambique 17°46' S, 36°22' E 224
Campo, Sp. 42°24' N, 0°24' E 164
Campo Belo, Braz. 20°53' S, 45°15' W 138
Campo Corral, Col. 5°3' N, 70°43' W 136
Campo de Criptana, Sp. 39°24' N, 3°7' W 164
Campo Durán, oil field, Arg. 22°15' S, 63°46' W 137
Campo Erê, Braz. 26°24' S, 53°1' W 139
Campo Esperanza, Parag. 22°19' S, 59°38' W 132
Campo Florido, Braz. 19°48' S, 48°36' W 138
Campo Gallo, Arg. 26°35' S, 62°50' W 139
Campo Grande, Braz. 20°28' S, 54°36' W 132
Campo Largo, Arg. 26°47' S, 60°51' W 139
Campo Largo, Braz. 25°30' S, 49°34' W 138
Campo Maior, Braz. 4°52' S, 42°13' W 132
Campo Mourão, Braz. 24°4' S, 52°24' W 138
Campo, Punta, Equatorial Guinea 2°18' N, 9°14' E 218
Campo Troco, Col. 4°52' N, 68°9' W 136
Campoalegre, Col. 2°41' N, 75°21' W 136
Campobasso, It. 41°34' N, 14°39' E 156
Campobello, S.C., U.S. 35°6' N, 82°10' W 96
Campodolcino, It. 46°24' N, 9°20' E 167
Campos, Braz. 21°48' S, 41°23' W 138
Campos Altos, Braz. 19°43' S, 46°12' W 138
Campos Belos, Braz. 13°4' S, 46°55' W 138
Campos Novos, Braz. 27°25' S, 51°14' W 139
Campos, Punta, Mex. 18°53' N, 104°40' W 114
Camposampiero, It. 45°34' N, 11°55' E 167
Camprodon, Sp. 42°17' N, 2°22' E 164
Campti, La., U.S. 31°52' N, 93°7' W 103
Campton, N.H., U.S. 43°51' N, 71°39' W 104
Campuya, Peru 1°46' S, 73°31' W 136
Camrose, Can. 53°0' N, 112°51' W 108
Camsell Portage, Can. 59°37' N, 109°14' W 108
Camucuio, Angola 14°8' S, 13°17' E 220
Çan, Turk. 40°1' N, 27°1' E 156
Can Tho, Vietnam 10°2' N, 105°44' E 202
Cana Brava, Braz. 17°22' S, 45°52' W 138
Canaan, Conn., U.S. 42°1' N, 73°20' W 104
Canaan, N.H., U.S. 43°39' N, 72°1' W 104
Canaan, Trinidad and Tobago 11°8' N, 60°49' W 116
Canada 58°59' N, 99°52' W 106
Canada Basin, Arctic Ocean 77°38' N, 139°23' W 255
Canada Bay 50°40' N, 56°41' W 111
Cañada de Gómez, Arg. 32°50' S, 61°21' W 139
Cañada Honda, Arg. 31°59' S, 68°33' W 134
Cañada Ombú, Arg. 28°19' S, 60°2' W 139
Canada Plain, Arctic Ocean 76°14' N, 148°23' W 255
Cañada Seca, Arg. 34°25' S, 62°57' W 139
Canadian, Tex., U.S. 35°53' N, 100°24' W 92
Canadian, river, Oklahoma-Texas, U.S. 35°22' N, 103°1' W 92
Çanakkale, Turk. 40°9' N, 26°23' E 156
Çanakkale Boğazı (Dardanelles), Turk. 40°9' N, 24°58' E 157
Canal du Midi, Fr. 43°33' N, 1°32' E 165
Canal du Rhône au Rhin, Fr. 47°35' N, 6°53' E 165
Canal Flats, Can. 50°9' N, 115°48' W 90
Canal Point, Fla., U.S. 26°51' N, 80°38' W 105
Canale, It. 44°48' N, 7°59' E 167
Canals, Arg. 33°35' S, 62°50' W 139
Canals, Sp. 38°57' N, 0°35' E 150
Canalul Bega, Rom. 45°39' N, 21°1' E 168
Canamari, Braz. 10°10' S, 69°16' W 137
Cañamero, Sp. 39°22' N, 5°23' W 164
Cananea, Mex. 30°57' N, 110°19' W 92
Cananéia, Braz. 25°1' S, 47°58' W 138
Canapiare, Cerro, peak, Col. 2°38' N, 68°32' W 136
Canárias, Ilha das, island, Braz. 2°42' S, 41°53' W 132
Canarias, Islas see Canary Islands, North Atlantic Ocean 28°47' N, 16°41' W 214

Canarreos, Archipiélago de los, Caribbean Sea 21°39' N, 82°40' W 116
Canary Islands (Canarias, Islas), North Atlantic Ocean 28°47' N, 16°41' W 214
Cañas, C.R. 10°26' N, 85°7' W 115
Canastota, N.Y., U.S. 43°4' N, 75°46' W 94
Canatiba, Braz. 13°6' S, 42°51' W 138
Canatlán, Mex. 24°30' N, 104°46' W 114
Cañaveral, Sp. 39°47' N, 6°24' W 150
Canaveral, Cape (Kennedy, Cape), Fla., U.S. 28°24' N, 80°34' W 105
Canaveral National Seashore, Fla., U.S. 28°37' N, 80°47' W 105
Cañaveras, Sp. 40°20' N, 2°25' W 164
Canavieiras, Braz. 15°41' S, 38°58' W 132
Canberra, Austral. 35°22' S, 148°43' E 230
Canby, Calif., U.S. 41°26' N, 120°54' W 90
Canby, Minn., U.S. 44°42' N, 96°18' W 90
Cancún, Mex. 21°6' N, 86°52' W 116
Cancún, Isla, island, Mex. 21°12' N, 86°56' W 116
Çandarli, Turk. 38°56' N, 26°56' E 156
Candeias, Braz. 12°41' S, 38°31' W 132
Candela, Mex. 26°50' N, 100°41' W 96
Candelaria, Arg. 27°29' S, 55°45' W 139
Candelaria, Tex., U.S. 30°7' N, 104°41' W 92
Candelaria, Punta, Sp. 43°43' N, 8°29' W 150
Candelaria, river, Bol. 16°39' S, 59°48' W 132
Candelaria, river, Mex. 18°21' N, 91°35' W 116
Candia, N.H., U.S. 43°4' N, 71°17' W 104
Candia see Iráklio, Gr. 35°19' N, 25°7' E 156
Cándido Aguilar, Mex. 25°33' N, 98°3' W 114
Cândido Sales, Braz. 15°36' S, 41°14' W 138
Candle Lake, Can. 53°45' N, 105°46' W 108
Candle Lake, Can. 53°44' N, 105°17' W 108
Cando, Can. 52°22' N, 108°13' W 108
Cando, N. Dak., U.S. 48°28' N, 99°13' W 90
Candon, Philippines 17°12' N, 120°26' E 203
Canea see Haniá, Gr. 35°25' N, 23°59' E 180
Canelas, Mex. 25°4' N, 106°31' W 114
Canelli, It. 44°44' N, 8°17' E 167
Canelones, Uru. 34°32' S, 56°16' W 139
Canelos, Ecua. 1°39' S, 77°47' W 136
Cañete, Sp. 40°2' N, 1°40' W 164
Cañete see San Vicente de Cañete, Peru 13°5' S, 76°23' W 130
Canet-Plage, Fr. 42°42' N, 2°59' E 164
Caney, Kans., U.S. 37°0' N, 95°56' W 96
Canfield, Ark., U.S. 33°9' N, 93°39' W 103
Canfranc, Sp. 42°42' N, 0°32' E 164
Cangallo, Peru 13°39' S, 74°5' W 137
Cangamba, Angola 13°43' S, 19°50' E 220
Cangandala, Angola 9°46' S, 16°32' E 220
Cangas del Narcea, Sp. 43°9' N, 6°34' W 150
Cango Caves, site, S. Af. 33°22' S, 22°9' E 227
Cangola, Angola 7°60' S, 15°53' E 218
Cangombe, Angola 14°25' S, 19°56' E 220
Canguaretama, Braz. 6°23' S, 35°9' W 132
Canguçu, Braz. 31°24' S, 52°40' W 139
Cangumbe, Angola 12°1' S, 19°9' E 220
Cangwu, China 23°25' N, 111°13' E 198
Cangyuan, China 23°8' N, 99°15' E 202
Cangzhou, China 38°15' N, 116°55' E 198
Cani Islands, Mediterranean Sea 37°26' N, 9°40' E 156
Caniapiscau, Réservoir, lake, Can. 54°37' N, 72°3' W 106
Caniapiscau, river, Can. 58°9' N, 70°2' W 106
Canicattì, It. 37°22' N, 13°50' E 156
Caniles, Sp. 37°25' N, 2°43' W 164
Canim Lake, Can. 51°47' N, 120°55' W 90
Canindé, Braz. 2°35' S, 46°31' W 130
Canindé, Braz. 4°25' S, 39°22' W 132
Canipaan, Philippines 8°34' N, 117°15' E 203
Canisp, peak, U.K. 58°6' N, 5°10' W 150
Canisteo, N.Y., U.S. 42°15' N, 77°38' W 94
Canisteo Peninsula, Antarctica 73°45' S, 96°42' W 248
Cañitas, Mex. 23°35' N, 102°45' W 112
Canjáyar, Sp. 37°0' N, 2°46' W 164
Cankhor, spring, Somalia 10°39' N, 46°11' E 216
Çankırı, Turk. 40°35' N, 33°35' E 156
Cankuzo, Burundi 3°16' S, 30°32' E 224
Canmore, Can. 51°6' N, 115°21' W 90
Cannae, ruin(s), It. 41°16' N, 16°2' E 156
Cannes, Fr. 43°34' N, 6°58' E 214
Canning Hill, Austral. 28°52' S, 117°36' E 230
Cannobio, It. 46°3' N, 8°40' E 167
Cannock, U.K. 52°41' N, 2°2' W 162
Cannon Beach, Oreg., U.S. 45°52' N, 123°57' W 100
Cannonball, river, N. Dak., U.S. 46°7' N, 102°27' W 80
Caño Chiquito, Col. 5°45' N, 71°29' W 136
Canoas, Braz. 29°54' S, 51°11' W 139
Canoas, Punta, Mex. 29°13' N, 115°27' W 92
Canoas, river, Braz. 27°43' S, 49°58' W 138
Canobie Lake, N.H., U.S. 42°48' N, 71°15' W 104
Canoe Lake, Can. 55°4' N, 108°19' W 108
Canoe Lake, lake, Can. 55°10' N, 108°39' W 108
Canoinhas, Braz. 26°10' S, 50°20' W 138
Cañon City, Colo., U.S. 38°27' N, 105°15' W 90
Canoochee, river, Ga., U.S. 32°45' N, 82°25' W 80
Canora, Can. 51°38' N, 102°27' W 90
Canouan, island, Saint Vincent and The Grenadines 12°34' N, 61°18' W 116
Canso, Can. 45°19' N, 60°60' W 111
Canso, Strait of 45°16' N, 62°42' W 106
Cantabria, adm. division, Sp. 43°13' N, 4°9' W 164
Cantabria, Sierra de, Sp. 42°34' N, 2°38' W 164
Cantábrica, Cordillera, Europe 42°32' N, 3°58' W 164
Cantavieja, Sp. 40°31' N, 0°25' E 164
Cantavir, Serb. and Mont. 45°55' N, 19°45' E 168
Canterbury, N.H., U.S. 43°20' N, 71°34' W 104
Canterbury, U.K. 51°16' N, 1°3' E 162
Cantil, Calif., U.S. 35°18' N, 117°59' W 101
Canto do Buriti, Braz. 8°7' S, 42°57' W 132
Canton, Ga., U.S. 34°13' N, 84°29' W 96
Canton, Ill., U.S. 40°32' N, 90°2' W 102
Canton, Me., U.S. 44°26' N, 70°20' W 104
Canton, Mass., U.S. 42°9' N, 71°10' W 104
Canton, Miss., U.S. 32°36' N, 90°3' W 103
Canton, Mo., U.S. 40°32' N, 92°2' W 94
Canton, Mo., U.S. 40°7' N, 91°32' W 94
Canton, N.Y., U.S. 44°35' N, 75°11' W 110
Canton, N.C., U.S. 35°32' N, 82°50' W 96
Canton, Ohio, U.S. 40°47' N, 81°22' W 102
Canton, Okla., U.S. 36°1' N, 98°36' W 92
Canton, Pa., U.S. 41°38' N, 76°52' W 110
Canton, S. Dak., U.S. 43°16' N, 96°36' W 90
Canton Lake, Okla., U.S. 36°2' N, 99°34' W 81
Canton see Guangzhou, China 23°6' N, 113°17' E 198
Cantù, It. 45°43' N, 9°7' E 167
Cantua Creek, Calif., U.S. 36°30' N, 120°20' W 100
Cantwell, Alas., U.S. 63°17' N, 149°2' W 106
Canudos, Braz. 7°18' S, 58°10' W 130
Cañuelas, Arg. 35°4' S, 58°47' W 139
Canumã, Braz. 6°11' S, 60°13' W 130
Canumã, Braz. 4°3' S, 59°5' W 130
Canutama, Braz. 6°35' S, 64°25' W 130
Canutillo, Mex. 26°21' N, 105°23' W 114
Canyon, Can. 60°52' N, 136°58' W 98
Canyon, Tex., U.S. 34°57' N, 101°56' W 92
Canzar, Angola 7°36' S, 21°34' E 218
Cao Bang, Vietnam 22°40' N, 106°15' E 198
Cao Lanh, Vietnam 10°27' N, 105°37' E 202
Caombo, Angola 8°44' S, 16°31' E 218
Caorle, It. 45°35' N, 12°53' E 167
Caoshi, China 42°17' N, 125°14' E 200
Caotibi, Grand lac, lake, Can. 50°38' N, 68°20' W 111
Caoxian, China 34°49' N, 115°31' E 198
Cap Barbas, Western Sahara 22°17' N, 16°40' W 214
Capac, Mich., U.S. 42°59' N, 82°55' W 102
Capachica, Peru 15°42' S, 69°49' W 137
Cap-à-Foux, Haiti 19°44' N, 74°14' W 116
Capaia, Angola 8°28' S, 20°12' E 218
Capana, Braz. 1°55' S, 68°59' W 136
Capanaparo, river, Venez. 6°42' N, 69°54' W 136
Capannori, It. 43°50' N, 10°34' E 167
Capão Alto, Braz. 27°57' S, 50°32' W 138
Caparro, Cerro, peak, Braz. 1°54' N, 68°11' W 136
Capatárida, Venez. 11°10' N, 70°39' W 136
Cap-de-la-Madeleine, Can. 46°22' N, 72°32' W 94
Capdepera, Sp. 39°41' N, 3°25' E 150
Cape Barren Island, Austral. 40°47' S, 148°31' E 230
Cape Canaveral, Fla., U.S. 28°24' N, 80°37' W 105
Cape Charles, Va., U.S. 37°14' N, 76°1' W 82
Cape Coast, Ghana 5°10' N, 1°17' W 222
Cape Cod National Seashore, Mass., U.S. 42°5' N, 70°11' W 104
Cape Coral, Fla., U.S. 26°33' N, 81°57' W 105
Cape Dorset, Can. 64°11' N, 76°41' W 106
Cape Elizabeth, Me., U.S. 43°34' N, 70°13' W 104
Cape May, N.J., U.S. 38°56' N, 74°56' W 94
Cape Melville National Park, Austral. 14°20' S, 144°10' E 238
Cape Neddick, Me., U.S. 43°11' N, 70°38' W 104
Cape Parry, Can. 70°8' N, 124°37' W 98
Cape Pole, Alas., U.S. 55°57' N, 133°47' W 108
Cape Range National Park, Austral. 22°22' S, 113°34' E 238
Cape Tormentine, Can. 46°7' N, 63°47' W 111
Cape Town, S. Af. 33°57' S, 18°15' E 227
Cape Tribulation National Park, Austral. 16°10' S, 145°5' E 238
Cape Verde 15°0' N, 24°0' W
Cape Verde Islands, North Atlantic Ocean 16°0' N, 24°11' W 253
Cape Verde Plain, North Atlantic Ocean 25°19' N, 23°53' W 253
Cape Vincent, N.Y., U.S. 44°7' N, 76°21' W 94
Cape Yakataga, Alas., U.S. 60°2' N, 142°25' W 98
Capel Curig, U.K. 53°6' N, 3°55' W 162
Capella, Sp. 42°11' N, 0°23' E 164
Capembe, river, Angola 16°21' S, 20°13' E 220
Capenda-Camulemba, Angola 9°25' S, 18°32' E 218
Capendu, Fr. 43°11' N, 2°32' E 150
Capernaum, ruin(s), Israel 32°53' N, 35°32' E 194
Cap-Haïtien, Haiti 19°44' N, 72°16' W 116
Capibara, Venez. 2°33' N, 66°19' W 136
Capim, river, Braz. 2°56' S, 47°51' W 130
Capinópolis, Braz. 18°46' S, 49°39' W 138
Capinota, Bol. 17°48' S, 66°14' W 137
Capistrano Beach, Calif., U.S. 33°28' N, 117°41' W 101
Capital District, adm. division, Col. 3°45' N, 74°24' W 136
Capitan, N. Mex., U.S. 33°32' N, 105°34' W 92
Capitán Aracena, Isla, island, Chile 54°24' S, 73°8' W 134
Capitán Arturo Prat, station, Antarctica 62°38' S, 59°39' W 134
Capitán Bezada, Peru 2°54' S, 77°7' W 136
Capitán Pablo Lagerenza, Parag. 19°58' S, 60°48' W 132
Capitão Poço, Braz. 1°42' S, 46°57' W 130
Capitol Hill, Northern Mariana Islands, U.S. 15°0' N, 146°0' E 242
Caplani, Mold. 46°22' N, 29°52' E 156
Capo di Ponte, It. 46°2' N, 10°19' E 167
Capolo, Angola 10°27' S, 14°5' E 220
Capraia, island, It. 43°6' N, 9°39' E 214
Capraia Isola, It. 43°3' N, 9°50' E 156
Caprara, Punta, It. 41°8' N, 7°41' E 156
Capreol, Can. 46°42' N, 80°55' W 94
Capricorn Group, islands, Coral Sea 23°7' S, 150°57' E 230
Caprivi Game Park, Namibia 18°7' S, 21°48' E 220
Caprivi Strip, region, Africa 17°60' S, 23°28' E 224
Caprock Escarpment, North America 32°55' N, 101°38' W 92
Captain Cook Monument, Hawai'i, U.S. 19°28' N, 155°59' W 99
Captain Cook's Landing, site, Hawai'i, U.S. 21°57' N, 159°44' W 99
Captiva, Fla., U.S. 26°31' N, 82°11' W 105
Captiva Island, Fla., U.S. 26°32' N, 82°30' W 105
Capulin, N. Mex., U.S. 36°43' N, 103°60' W 92
Capulin Volcano National Monument, N. Mex., U.S. 36°46' N, 104°3' W 92
Capunda, Angola 10°35' S, 17°22' E 220
Căpuş, Rom. 46°47' N, 23°18' E 168
Caquetá, adm. division, Col. 0°33' N, 74°33' W 136
Caquetá, river, Col. 0°59' N, 73°44' W 123
Car Nicobar, island, India 9°5' N, 91°37' E 188
Carabinani, river, Braz. 2°50' S, 62°44' W 132
Caracal, Rom. 44°7' N, 24°21' E 156
Caracaraí, Braz. 1°50' N, 61°10' W 130
Caracas, Venez. 10°25' N, 67°2' W 136
Caracol, Braz. 9°15' S, 43°22' W 132
Caracoles, Punta, Pan. 7°37' N, 78°60' W 115
Caracolí, Col. 10°4' N, 73°47' W 136
Caraş-Severin, adm. division, Rom. 45°8' N, 21°34' E 156
Caraga, Philippines 7°23' N, 126°32' E 203
Caraglio, It. 44°25' N, 7°26' E 167
Caraí, Braz. 17°12' S, 41°44' W 138
Carajari, river, Braz. 4°60' S, 54°20' W 130
Carajás, Serra dos, Braz. 5°42' S, 52°12' W 130
Caramulo, Serra do, Port. 40°25' N, 8°47' W 150
Caranavi, Bol. 15°51' S, 67°37' W 137
Carandayti, Bol. 20°46' S, 63°6' W 137
Carangola, Braz. 20°45' S, 42°3' W 138
Caransebeş, Rom. 45°25' N, 22°14' E 168
Caraparaná, river, Col. 0°35' N, 74°2' W 136
Carapari, Bol. 21°48' S, 63°47' W 137
Caraquet, Can. 47°46' N, 64°57' W 94
Caraşova, Rom. 45°12' N, 21°51' E 168
Caratasca, Laguna de 15°14' N, 84°16' W 115
Caratinga, Braz. 19°49' S, 42°9' W 138
Carauari, Braz. 4°55' S, 66°56' W 130
Caraúbas, Braz. 5°49' S, 37°34' W 132
Carauna see Grande, Serra, peak, Braz. 2°34' N, 60°46' W 130
Caravaca de la Cruz, Sp. 38°6' N, 1°52' W 164
Caravelas, Braz. 17°42' S, 39°15' W 132
Caràzinho, Braz. 28°18' S, 52°48' W 139
Carberry, Can. 49°52' N, 99°22' W 90
Carbó, Mex. 29°40' N, 110°58' W 92
Carbon, Can. 51°31' N, 113°10' W 90
Carbón, Laguna del, Arg. 49°35' S, 68°21' W 122
Carbonado, Wash., U.S. 47°4' N, 122°3' W 100
Carbonara, Capo, It. 38°54' N, 9°33' E 214
Carbondale, Mo., U.S. 37°43' N, 89°12' W 96
Carbondale, Pa., U.S. 41°33' N, 75°31' W 94
Carboneras, Sp. 36°59' N, 1°54' W 164
Carboneras de Guadazaón, Sp. 39°53' N, 1°50' W 164
Carbonia, It. 39°10' N, 8°25' E 214
Carbonville, Utah, U.S. 39°37' N, 110°51' W 92
Cărbunari, Rom. 44°50' N, 21°44' E 168
Carcaixent, Sp. 39°6' N, 0°27' E 164
Carcajou, Can. 57°47' N, 117°5' W 108
Carcajou, river, Can. 64°17' N, 128°22' W 98
Carcans, Fr. 45°4' N, 1°4' W 150
Carcaraña, Arg. 32°53' S, 61°7' W 139
Carcasse, Cap, Haiti 18°16' N, 75°14' W 115
Carcassonne, Fr. 43°12' N, 2°20' E 164
Carcastillo, Sp. 42°22' N, 1°27' W 164
Carche, peak, Sp. 38°24' N, 1°12' W 164
Carcross, Can. 60°12' N, 134°42' W 108
Card Sound 25°18' N, 80°29' W 105
Cardeña, Sp. 38°16' N, 4°21' W 164
Cárdenas, Cuba 23°2' N, 81°14' W 112
Cárdenas, Mex. 21°57' N, 99°40' W 114
Cardenete, Sp. 39°46' N, 1°42' W 150
Cardiff, U.K. 51°30' N, 3°55' W 143
Cardiff by the Sea, Calif., U.S. 33°1' N, 117°18' W 101
Cardiff (Caerdydd), U.K. 51°28' N, 3°12' W 162
Cardigan Bay 52°3' N, 4°51' W 150
Cardinal, Can. 44°47' N, 75°25' W 94
Cardington, Ohio, U.S. 40°29' N, 82°53' W 102
Cardona, Sp. 41°55' N, 1°39' E 164
Cardona, Uru. 33°54' S, 57°22' W 139
Cardston, Can. 49°11' N, 113°18' W 90
Careen Lake, lake, Can. 56°56' N, 108°43' W 108
Carei, Rom. 47°41' N, 22°29' E 168
Careiro, Braz. 3°13' S, 59°47' W 130
Carencro, La., U.S. 30°18' N, 92°4' W 103
Carentan, Fr. 49°19' N, 1°16' W 150
Caretta, W. Va., U.S. 37°19' N, 81°41' W 96
Carevdar, Croatia 46°4' N, 16°40' E 168
Carey, Ohio, U.S. 40°56' N, 83°22' W 102
Careysburg, Liberia 6°18' N, 10°33' W 222
Cargados Carajos Bank, Indian Ocean 16°17' S, 59°38' E 254
Cargèse, Fr. 42°8' N, 8°37' E 156
Carhué, Arg. 37°10' S, 62°44' W 139
Cariacica, Braz. 20°15' S, 40°24' W 138
Cariati, It. 39°29' N, 16°57' E 156
Caribana, Punta, Col. 8°35' N, 77°9' W 136
Caribbean Sea 15°24' N, 75°30' W 116
Caribou, Me., U.S. 46°51' N, 68°2' W 94
Caribou Lake, Can. 59°23' N, 96°38' W 108
Caribou Lake, lake, Can. 50°26' N, 89°31' W 110
Caribou Range, Idaho, U.S. 43°26' N, 111°33' W 90
Carigara, Philippines 11°17' N, 124°40' E 203
Carignan, Fr. 49°38' N, 5°10' E 163
Carignano, It. 44°54' N, 7°40' E 167
Cariñena, Sp. 41°20' N, 1°13' W 164
Carinhanha, Braz. 14°16' S, 43°53' W 138
Carinhanha, river, Braz. 14°59' S, 45°40' W 138
Carinthia, region, Europe 46°51' N, 12°53' E 167
Caripare, Braz. 11°33' S, 45°4' W 130
Caripito, Venez. 10°6' N, 63°6' W 116
Caritianas, Braz. 9°27' S, 63°6' W 130
Carlet, Sp. 39°12' N, 0°32' E 164
Carleton, Can. 48°6' N, 66°8' W 94
Carleton, Mich., U.S. 42°3' N, 83°23' W 102
Carleton, Mount, Can. 47°21' N, 66°58' W 94
Carleton Place, Can. 45°7' N, 76°8' W 94
Carleton, Pointe, Can. 49°45' N, 62°57' W 111
Carlin, Nev., U.S. 40°42' N, 116°7' W 92
Carlinville, Ill., U.S. 39°16' N, 89°53' W 102
Carlisle, U.K. 54°53' N, 2°56' W 162
Carlos Casares, Arg. 35°36' S, 61°21' W 139
Carlos Chagas, Braz. 17°42' S, 40°48' W 138
Carlos, Isla, island, Chile 54°11' S, 74°54' W 134
Carlos Tejedor, Arg. 35°22' S, 62°26' W 139
Carlow, Ire. 52°50' N, 6°56' W 150
Carlsbad, Calif., U.S. 33°9' N, 117°21' W 101
Carlsbad, N. Mex., U.S. 32°25' N, 104°14' W 92
Carlsbad, Tex., U.S. 31°34' N, 100°37' W 92
Carlsbad Caverns National Park, N. Mex., U.S. 31°52' N, 105°45' W 112
Carlsberg Ridge, Arabian Sea 5°2' N, 62°6' E 254
Carlsborg, Wash., U.S. 48°4' N, 123°11' W 100
Carlsen, Mys, Russ. 76°38' N, 69°32' E 160
Carlton, Minn., U.S. 46°39' N, 92°27' W 94
Carlyle, Can. 49°37' N, 102°17' W 90
Carlyle, Ill., U.S. 38°36' N, 89°22' W 102
Carlyle Lake, Ill., U.S. 38°40' N, 89°30' W 102
Carmacks, Can. 62°8' N, 136°13' W 98
Carmagnola, It. 44°50' N, 7°43' E 167
Carman, Can. 49°28' N, 98°1' W 90
Carmanah Point, Can. 48°32' N, 124°54' W 100
Carmangay, Can. 50°7' N, 113°7' W 90
Carmanovo, Mold. 47°15' N, 29°30' E 156
Carmarthen, U.K. 51°51' N, 4°19' W 162
Carmel, Ind., U.S. 39°58' N, 86°7' W 102
Carmel, N.Y., U.S. 41°24' N, 73°41' W 104
Carmel Head, U.K. 53°24' N, 4°56' W 150
Carmel Highlands, Calif., U.S. 36°30' N, 121°57' W 100
Carmel, Mount, Calif., U.S. 36°22' N, 121°51' W 100
Carmel, Mount, Israel 32°43' N, 35°1' E 194
Carmel, ruin(s), West Bank 31°24' N, 35°6' E 194
Carmel-by-the-Sea, Calif., U.S. 36°33' N, 121°56' W 100
Carmelita, Guatemala 17°29' N, 90°11' W 115
Carmelo, Uru. 33°58' S, 58°13' W 139
Carmen, Bol. 11°39' S, 67°51' W 137
Carmen, Okla., U.S. 36°34' N, 98°28' W 92
Carmen, Philippines 7°24' N, 125°42' E 203
Carmen, Uru. 33°15' S, 56°2' W 139
Carmen de Areco, Arg. 34°23' S, 59°50' W 139
Carmen de Bolívar, Col. 9°41' N, 75°8' W 136
Carmén del Paraná, Parag. 27°13' S, 56°9' W 139
Carmen, Isla del, island, Mex. 18°22' N, 91°42' W 115
Carmen, Isla, island, Mex. 25°50' N, 111°7' W 112
Carmen, river, Mex. 29°57' N, 107°3' W 80
Carmen, Sierra del, Mex. 29°11' N, 102°46' W 112
Carmi, Mo., U.S. 38°4' N, 88°11' W 94
Carmo do Paranaíba, Braz. 19°4' S, 46°21' W 138
Carmona, Sp. 37°28' N, 5°39' W 164
Carnarvon, S. Af. 30°57' S, 22°6' E 227
Carnduff, Can. 49°9' N, 101°51' W 90
Carnegie, Okla., U.S. 35°4' N, 98°37' W 92
Carnegie Ridge, South Pacific Ocean 1°29' S, 86°58' W 253
Carney Island, Antarctica 73°20' S, 120°12' W 248
Carnforth, U.K. 54°7' N, 2°46' W 162
Carnic Alps, Aust. 46°31' N, 12°32' E 167
Carno, U.K. 52°33' N, 3°32' W 162
Carnot, Cen. Af. Rep. 4°55' N, 15°51' E 218
Caro, Mich., U.S. 43°28' N, 83°23' W 102
Carol City, Fla., U.S. 25°57' N, 80°16' W 105
Carolina, Braz. 7°19' S, 47°28' W 130
Carolina, P.R., U.S. 18°0' N, 66°0' W 118
Carolina Beach, N.C., U.S. 34°2' N, 77°55' W 96
Caroline, Can. 52°5' N, 114°46' W 90
Caroline Island, Kiribati 9°49' S, 150°9' W 252
Caroline Islands, North Pacific Ocean 4°49' N, 141°18' E 192
Carora, Venez. 10°11' N, 70°5' W 136
Carouge, Switz. 46°10' N, 6°8' E 167
Carp, Nev., U.S. 37°6' N, 114°31' W 101
Carp Lake, lake, Can. 54°43' N, 123°45' W 108
Carpathian Mountains, Ukr. 48°52' N, 24°24' E 160
Carpatho-Ukraine, region, Europe 48°2' N, 22°41' E 168
Carpentaria, Gulf of 12°17' S, 138°12' E 231
Carpenter, Miss., U.S. 32°1' N, 90°42' W 103
Carpenter Island, Antarctica 72°49' S, 95°35' W 248
Carpenter Lake, lake, Can. 50°52' N, 123°11' W 90
Carpi, It. 44°46' N, 10°51' E 167
Carpignano Sesia, It. 45°32' N, 8°24' E 167
Carpinteria, Calif., U.S. 34°24' N, 119°32' W 101
Carpio, N. Dak., U.S. 48°25' N, 101°45' W 90
Carr, Cape, Antarctica 66°21' S, 133°24' E 248
Carr Pond Mountain, Me., U.S. 46°44' N, 68°48' W 94
Carrabelle, Fla., U.S. 29°50' N, 84°40' W 96
Carrantuohill, peak, Ire. 51°58' N, 9°51' W 150
Carrara, It. 44°4' N, 10°5' E 167
Carrasco, Cerro, peak, Chile 20°58' S, 70°11' W 137
Carrasco Ichilo National Park, Bol. 17°13' S, 65°59' W 137
Carrascosa del Campo, Sp. 40°2' N, 2°45' W 164
Carregal do Sal, Port. 40°25' N, 8°1' W 150
Carreto, Pan. 8°45' N, 77°36' W 136
Carriacou, island, Grenada 12°20' N, 62°7' W 116
Carrick on Shannon, Ire. 53°57' N, 8°6' W 150
Carriere, Miss., U.S. 30°37' N, 89°39' W 103
Carrière, Lac, lake, Can. 47°12' N, 77°43' W 110
Carrigan, Mount, N.H., U.S. 44°5' N, 71°29' W 104
Carrilobo, Arg. 31°55' S, 63°7' W 139
Carrington, N. Dak., U.S. 47°25' N, 99°8' W 90
Carrión de Calatrava, Sp. 39°1' N, 3°49' W 164
Carrizal, Col. 11°59' N, 72°11' W 136
Carrizal, Mex. 30°34' N, 106°40' W 92
Carrizal Bajo, Chile 28°6' S, 71°10' W 134
Carrizal, river, Mex. 23°24' N, 98°12' W 114
Carrizo Plain, Calif., U.S. 35°17' N, 119°60' W 100
Carrizo Plain National Monument, Calif., U.S. 35°4' N, 120°8' W 100
Carrizozo, N. Mex., U.S. 33°38' N, 105°52' W 92
Carro, peak, Sp. 39°8' N, 2°27' W 164
Carroll, Iowa, U.S. 42°2' N, 94°52' W 94
Carrollton, Ala., U.S. 33°16' N, 88°6' W 103
Carrollton, Ga., U.S. 33°33' N, 85°5' W 96
Carrollton, Ky., U.S. 38°39' N, 85°10' W 102
Carrollton, Mich., U.S. 43°27' N, 83°56' W 102
Carrollton, Miss., U.S. 33°28' N, 89°56' W 103
Carrollton, Mo., U.S. 39°21' N, 93°30' W 94
Carrollton, Mo., U.S. 39°17' N, 90°25' W 94
Carrollton, Ohio, U.S. 40°33' N, 81°5' W 102
Carrollton, Tex., U.S. 32°57' N, 96°54' W 92
Carrot River, Can. 53°16' N, 103°36' W 108
Carrot, river, Can. 53°5' N, 103°26' W 108
Carrowmore, ruin(s), Ire. 54°13' N, 8°41' W 150
Carrù, It. 44°28' N, 7°52' E 167
Çarşamba, Turk. 41°12' N, 36°44' E 180
Carson, Miss., U.S. 31°31' N, 89°47' W 103
Carson, N. Dak., U.S. 46°25' N, 101°34' W 90
Carson, Wash., U.S. 45°42' N, 121°50' W 100
Carson City, Mich., U.S. 43°10' N, 84°51' W 102
Carson City, Nev., U.S. 39°9' N, 119°52' W 90
Carson Pass, Calif., U.S. 38°42' N, 119°59' W 90
Carsonville, Mich., U.S. 43°25' N, 82°40' W 102
Carstairs, Can. 51°35' N, 114°6' W 90
Carswell Lake, Can. 58°40' N, 109°48' W 108
Cartagena, Col. 10°25' N, 75°32' W 136
Cartagena, Sp. 37°36' N, 0°59' E 164
Cartago, Calif., U.S. 36°19' N, 118°2' W 101
Cartago, C.R. 9°51' N, 83°54' W 115
Carter, Wis., U.S. 45°22' N, 88°38' W 110
Carter, Mount, Austral. 13°5' S, 143°5' E 230
Cartersville, Ga., U.S. 34°9' N, 84°48' W 96
Carterton, N.Z. 41°3' S, 175°32' E 240
Carthage, Ind., U.S. 39°43' N, 85°34' W 102
Carthage, Miss., U.S. 32°42' N, 89°32' W 103
Carthage, Mo., U.S. 37°9' N, 94°18' W 96
Carthage, Mo., U.S. 40°24' N, 91°9' W 94
Carthage, N.Y., U.S. 43°58' N, 75°37' W 110
Carthage, S. Dak., U.S. 44°9' N, 97°45' W 90
Carthage, Tenn., U.S. 36°16' N, 85°57' W 96
Carthage, Tex., U.S. 32°9' N, 94°21' W 103
Carthage, ruin(s), Tun. 36°50' N, 10°12' E 156
Cartmel, U.K. 54°12' N, 2°58' W 162
Cartwright, Can. 53°41' N, 57°2' W 106
Caruaru, Braz. 8°15' S, 35°60' W 132
Carumas, Peru 16°51' S, 70°42' W 137
Carvalho, Braz. 2°19' S, 51°29' W 130
Carville, La., U.S. 30°12' N, 91°7' W 103
Carvoeiro, Braz. 1°30' S, 61°58' W 130
Carvoeiro, Cabo, Port. 39°10' N, 9°53' W 150
Cary, Ill., U.S. 42°12' N, 88°16' W 102
Cary, Miss., U.S. 32°47' N, 90°56' W 103
Cary, Mo., U.S. 42°12' N, 88°16' W 102
Casa Grande, Ariz., U.S. 32°51' N, 111°46' W 112
Casablanca, Mor. 33°36' N, 7°37' W 214
Casale Monferrato, It. 45°8' N, 8°27' E 167
Casalmaggiore, It. 44°59' N, 10°25' E 167
Casalpusterlengo, It. 45°10' N, 9°38' E 167
Casamance, river, Senegal 12°37' N, 15°8' W 222
Casanare, adm. division, Col. 5°33' N, 72°17' W 136
Casares, Nicar. 11°38' N, 86°20' W 115
Casares, Sp. 36°26' N, 5°16' W 164
Casas, Mex. 23°41' N, 98°44' W 114
Casas de Juan Núñez, Sp. 39°5' N, 1°34' W 164
Casas de Ves, Sp. 39°14' N, 1°19' W 164
Casas Grandes, Mex. 30°23' N, 107°59' W 92
Casas Ibáñez, Sp. 39°16' N, 1°28' W 164
Casca, Braz. 28°39' S, 51°60' W 139
Cascada de Basaseachic National Park (6), Mex. 28°7' N, 108°17' W 112
Cascade, Idaho, U.S. 44°30' N, 116°3' W 90
Cascade, Mont., U.S. 47°14' N, 111°43' W 90
Cascade Head, Oreg., U.S. 44°52' N, 123°58' W 90
Cascade Range, North America 49°29' N, 121°25' W 100
Cascais, Port. 38°42' N, 9°25' W 150
Cascalho Rico, Braz. 18°33' S, 47°54' W 138
Cascas, Senegal 16°22' N, 14°11' W 222
Cascavel, Braz. 24°56' S, 53°24' W 138
Cascavel, Braz. 4°10' S, 38°16' W 132
Casco, Me., U.S. 44°0' N, 70°32' W 104
Casco Bay 43°42' N, 70°51' W 80
Case Island, Antarctica 73°37' S, 81°22' W 248
Caseda, Sp. 42°31' N, 1°22' W 164
Cases Velles de Formentor, site, Sp. 39°54' N, 3°6' E 164
Caseville, Mich., U.S. 43°55' N, 83°17' W 102
Casey, Ill., U.S. 39°17' N, 87°60' W 102
Casey, station, Antarctica 66°12' S, 110°52' E 248
Casigua, Venez. 8°42' N, 72°35' W 136
Casiguran, Philippines 16°17' N, 122°9' E 203
Casilda, Arg. 33°3' S, 61°9' W 139
Casiquiare, river, Venez. 2°27' N, 66°40' W 136
Casma, Peru 9°28' S, 78°18' W 130
Casmalia, Calif., U.S. 34°50' N, 120°33' W 100
Caspar, Calif., U.S. 39°21' N, 123°49' W 90
Caspe, Sp. 41°14' N, 3°177' W 164
Casper, Wyo., U.S. 42°50' N, 106°19' W 90
Caspian Depression, Kaz. 43°48' N, 46°17' E 195
Caspian Sea 38°26' N, 49°1' E 160
Caspiana, La., U.S. 32°16' N, 93°36' W 103
Cass, W. Va., U.S. 38°24' N, 79°56' W 94
Cass City, Mich., U.S. 43°35' N, 83°10' W 102
Cass Lake, Minn., U.S. 47°21' N, 94°38' W 90
Cass, river, Mich., U.S. 43°28' N, 83°16' W 102
Cassai, Angola 10°31' S, 21°59' E 220
Cassai, river, Angola 11°13' S, 20°20' E 220
Cassamba, Angola 13°7' S, 20°20' E 220
Cassel, Fr. 50°48' N, 2°28' E 163
Casselberry, Fla., U.S. 28°40' N, 81°22' W 105
Casselton, N. Dak., U.S. 46°53' N, 97°14' W 90
Cássia, Braz. 20°34' S, 46°58' W 138
Cassiar, Can. 59°17' N, 129°50' W 108
Cassiar Mountains, Can. 58°18' N, 129°24' W 108
Cassidy, Can. 49°2' N, 123°52' W 100

Cassilândia, *Braz.* 19°7′ S, 51°48′ W **138**
Cassinga, *Angola* 15°9′ S, 16°5′ E **220**
Cassino, *Braz.* 32°10′ S, 52°13′ W **139**
Cassiporé, Cabo, *Braz.* 3°46′ N, 51°3′ W **130**
Cassou, *Burkina Faso* 11°34′ N, 2°5′ W **222**
Cassumbe, *Angola* 11°6′ S, 16°41′ E **220**
Cassville, *Mo., U.S.* 36°40′ N, 93°53′ W **94**
Cassville, *Wis., U.S.* 42°42′ N, 90°59′ W **94**
Castaic, *Calif., U.S.* 34°30′ N, 118°38′ W **101**
Castalla, *Sp.* 38°35′ N, 0°41′ E **164**
Castanhal, *Braz.* 1°18′ S, 47°58′ W **130**
Castaño Nuevo, *Arg.* 31°2′ S, 69°36′ W **134**
Castaños, *Mex.* 26°46′ N, 101°27′ W **96**
Casteggio, *It.* 45°0′ N, 9°7′ E **167**
Castel Bolognese, *It.* 44°19′ N, 11°46′ E **167**
Castel San Giovanni, *It.* 45°3′ N, 9°26′ E **167**
Castelfranco Veneto, *It.* 45°40′ N, 11°55′ E **156**
Castelli, *Arg.* 36°6′ S, 57°49′ W **139**
Castelló de la Plana, *Sp.* 39°58′ N, 2°118′ W **164**
Castellote, *Sp.* 40°47′ N, 0°20′ E **164**
Castelnovo ne' Monti, *It.* 44°25′ N, 10°23′ E **167**
Castelo Branco, *Port.* 39°49′ N, 7°31′ W **150**
Castelo Branco, adm. division, *Port.* 39°50′ N, 7°58′ W **150**
Casterton, *U.K.* 54°12′ N, 2°34′ W **162**
Castets, *Fr.* 43°53′ N, 1°10′ W **150**
Castiglione delle Stiviere, *It.* 45°22′ N, 10°29′ E **167**
Castile and Leon, adm. division, *Sp.* 41°56′ N, 3°33′ W **164**
Castile La Mancha, adm. division, *Sp.* 40°28′ N, 2°58′ W **164**
Castilla, Playa de, *Sp.* 37°3′ N, 6°45′ W **164**
Castillo de San Marcos National Monument, *Fla., U.S.* 29°53′ N, 81°22′ W **105**
Castillo de Teayo, ruin(s), *Mex.* 20°39′ N, 97°45′ W **114**
Castillo, Pampa del, *Arg.* 46°18′ S, 68°44′ W **134**
Castillos, *Uru.* 34°14′ S, 53°53′ W **139**
Castle Acre, *U.K.* 52°42′ N, 0°41′ E **162**
Castle Dale, *Utah, U.S.* 39°12′ N, 111°1′ W **90**
Castle Hedingham, *U.K.* 51°59′ N, 0°36′ E **162**
Castle Mountain, peak, *Alas., U.S.* 56°51′ N, 132°16′ W **108**
Castle Mountain, peak, *Calif., U.S.* 35°56′ N, 120°23′ W **100**
Castle Mountain, peak, *Can.* 51°19′ N, 115°60′ W **90**
Castle Mountain, peak, *Tex., U.S.* 31°15′ N, 102°22′ W **92**
Castle Peak, *Colo., U.S.* 38°59′ N, 106°57′ W **90**
Castle Peak, *Idaho, U.S.* 44°1′ N, 114°40′ W **90**
Castle Rising, *U.K.* 52°47′ N, 0°29′ E **162**
Castle Rock, *Colo., U.S.* 39°22′ N, 104°52′ W **90**
Castle Rock, *Wash., U.S.* 46°16′ N, 122°54′ W **100**
Castle Rock, peak, *Oreg., U.S.* 44°0′ N, 118°16′ W **90**
astle Sinclair, site, *U.K.* 58°26′ N, 3°12′ W **150**
astlebar, *Ire.* 53°51′ N, 9°19′ W **150**
astlebay, *U.K.* 56°57′ N, 7°29′ W **150**
astlecliff, *N.Z.* 39°57′ S, 174°58′ E **240**
astleford, *U.K.* 53°43′ N, 1°21′ W **162**
astlegar, *Can.* 49°18′ N, 117°41′ W **90**
astlepoint, *N.Z.* 40°55′ S, 176°12′ E **240**
astleton, *U.K.* 54°27′ N, 0°57′ E **162**
astleton, *Vt., U.S.* 43°36′ N, 73°11′ W **104**
Castleton-on-Hudson, *N.Y., U.S.* 42°31′ N, 73°46′ W **104**
Castlewood, *S. Dak., U.S.* 44°42′ N, 97°3′ W **90**
astor, *Can.* 52°12′ N, 111°55′ W **90**
astor, *La., U.S.* 32°14′ N, 93°10′ W **103**
astries, *Saint Lucia* 13°59′ N, 61°8′ W **116**
astril, *Sp.* 37°47′ N, 2°46′ W **164**
astro, *Braz.* 24°46′ S, 50°1′ W **138**
astro, *Chile* 42°27′ S, 73°51′ W **134**
astronuño, *Sp.* 41°22′ N, 5°17′ W **150**
astropol, *Sp.* 43°30′ N, 7°2′ W **150**
astroville, *Calif., U.S.* 36°46′ N, 121°45′ W **100**
astuera, *Sp.* 38°43′ N, 5°34′ W **164**
asula, *Mozambique* 15°23′ S, 33°37′ E **224**
asummit Lake, *Can.* 51°28′ N, 92°22′ W **110**
at, *Turk.* 39°37′ N, 41°1′ E **195**
at Island, *Bahamas* 24°30′ N, 75°28′ W **116**
at Island, *Miss., U.S.* 30°7′ N, 89°7′ W **103**
at Lake, *Can.* 51°43′ N, 91°48′ W **110**
at Tien National Park, *Vietnam* 11°20′ N, 106°58′ E **202**
atacaos, *Peru* 5°11′ S, 80°44′ W **130**
ataguases, *Braz.* 21°23′ S, 42°40′ W **138**
atahoula Lake, *La., U.S.* 31°25′ N, 92°27′ W **103**
ataingan, *Philippines* 12°1′ N, 123°58′ E **203**
atak, *Turk.* 38°0′ N, 43°2′ E **195**
atalão, *Braz.* 18°12′ S, 47°57′ W **138**
atalina, *Chile* 25°14′ S, 69°47′ W **132**
atalina, Punta, *Chile* 52°44′ S, 68°43′ W **134**
atalonia, adm. division, *Sp.* 41°46′ N, 1°7′ E **164**
atamarca, *Arg.* 28°30′ S, 65°47′ W **132**
atamarca, adm. division, *Arg.* 28°47′ S, 68°39′ W **134**
atán Lil, *Arg.* 39°43′ S, 70°37′ W **134**
atandica, *Mozambique* 18°4′ S, 33°10′ E **220**
atanduanes, island, *Philippines* 13°52′ N, 124°26′ E **192**
atanduva, *Braz.* 21°6′ S, 48°58′ W **138**
atania, *It.* 37°30′ N, 15°4′ E **156**
atania, Piana di, *It.* 37°17′ N, 14°26′ E **156**
atanzaro, *It.* 38°53′ N, 16°35′ E **156**
atarina, *Tex., U.S.* 28°20′ N, 99°37′ W **92**
atarman, *Philippines* 12°29′ N, 124°38′ E **203**
atarroja, *Sp.* 39°24′ N, 0°24′ E **164**
atatumbo-Barí National Park, *Col.* 9°0′ N, 73°30′ W **136**
atauara, *Braz.* 3°19′ S, 56°26′ W **130**
ataviña, *Mex.* 29°45′ N, 114°49′ W **92**
atawba Island, *Ohio, U.S.* 41°34′ N, 82°50′ W **102**
atbalogan, *Philippines* 11°46′ N, 124°55′ E **203**
ateel, *Philippines* 7°51′ N, 126°25′ E **203**
atemaco, *Mex.* 18°25′ N, 95°7′ W **114**
atete, *Angola* 9°8′ S, 13°40′ E **218**
atete, river, *Braz.* 6°22′ S, 54°14′ W **130**
Cathedral Mountain, *Tex., U.S.* 30°8′ N, 103°43′ W **92**
Catherine, *Ala., U.S.* 32°10′ N, 87°29′ W **103**
Catheys Valley, *Calif., U.S.* 37°25′ N, 120°8′ W **100**
Cathlamet, *Wash., U.S.* 46°11′ N, 123°22′ W **100**
Catinaccio, peak, *It.* 46°28′ N, 11°36′ E **167**
Catió, *Guinea-Bissau* 11°16′ N, 15°15′ W **222**
Catirina, Punta, peak, *It.* 40°28′ N, 9°27′ E **156**
Catlow Valley, *Oreg., U.S.* 42°45′ N, 119°7′ W **90**
Catnip Mountain, *Nev., U.S.* 41°50′ N, 119°28′ W **90**
Catoche, Cabo, *Mex.* 21°28′ N, 87°10′ W **116**
Catoctin Mountain, *Md., U.S.* 39°50′ N, 77°35′ W **94**
Catoctin Mountain Park, *Md., U.S.* 39°37′ N, 77°33′ W **94**
Catorce, *Mex.* 23°39′ N, 100°53′ W **114**
Catota, *Angola* 14°2′ S, 17°23′ E **220**
Catria, Monte, peak, *It.* 43°26′ N, 12°37′ E **156**
Catriló, *Arg.* 36°25′ S, 63°27′ W **139**
Catskill, *N.Y., U.S.* 42°13′ N, 73°53′ W **104**
Catskill Mountains, *N.Y., U.S.* 42°26′ N, 74°10′ W **104**
Catterick, *U.K.* 54°22′ N, 1°38′ W **162**
Cattolica, *It.* 43°58′ N, 12°44′ E **167**
Catuane, *Mozambique* 26°44′ S, 32°15′ E **227**
Catur, *Mozambique* 13°45′ S, 35°37′ E **224**
Cau Giat, *Vietnam* 19°9′ N, 105°38′ E **202**
Cauaburi, river, *Braz.* 4°238′ N, 66°19′ W **136**
Cauayan, *Philippines* 9°58′ N, 122°36′ E **203**
Cauca, adm. division, *Col.* 2°29′ N, 77°31′ W **136**
Cauca, river, *Col.* 6°18′ N, 75°46′ W **136**
Caucaia, *Braz.* 3°44′ S, 38°40′ W **132**
Caucasia, *Col.* 7°57′ N, 75°14′ W **136**
Caucasus Mountains, *Asia-Europe* 42°3′ N, 44°7′ E **158**
Caucete, *Arg.* 31°40′ S, 68°18′ W **134**
Cauchon Lake, *Can.* 55°28′ N, 97°4′ W **108**
Caudéran, *Fr.* 44°51′ N, 0°38′ E **150**
Caudete, *Sp.* 38°42′ N, 0°59′ E **164**
Caudry, *Fr.* 50°7′ N, 3°23′ E **163**
Caungula, *Angola* 8°27′ S, 18°38′ E **218**
Cauquenes, *Chile* 35°59′ S, 72°21′ W **134**
Caura, river, *Venez.* 6°56′ N, 64°51′ W **130**
Caurés, river, *Braz.* 1°16′ S, 63°17′ W **130**
Cauro, *Fr.* 41°54′ N, 8°54′ E **156**
Causapscal, *Can.* 48°20′ N, 67°13′ W **94**
Căuseni, *Mold.* 46°37′ N, 29°23′ E **156**
Cautário, river, *Braz.* 11°47′ S, 63°55′ W **137**
Caution, Cape, *Can.* 50°58′ N, 128°14′ W **108**
Cauto, river, *Cuba* 20°39′ N, 76°41′ W **116**
Cavalaire, *Fr.* 43°10′ N, 6°30′ E **150**
Cavalcante, *Braz.* 13°48′ S, 47°31′ W **138**
Cavalese, *It.* 46°17′ N, 11°27′ E **167**
Cavalier, *N. Dak., U.S.* 48°45′ N, 97°39′ W **90**
Cavalla, river, *Africa* 6°18′ N, 7°56′ W **222**
Cavalleria, Cap de, *Sp.* 40°3′ N, 3°48′ E **164**
Cavallermaggiore, *It.* 44°42′ N, 7°41′ E **167**
Cavallo Pass, *U.S.* 28°17′ N, 96°20′ W **96**
Cavally, river, *Côte d'Ivoire* 6°19′ N, 8°14′ W **222**
Cavan, *Ire.* 53°58′ N, 7°22′ W **150**
Cavarzere, *It.* 45°7′ N, 12°4′ E **167**
Cave, *N.Z.* 44°19′ S, 170°59′ E **240**
Cave Creek, *Ariz., U.S.* 33°49′ N, 111°56′ W **92**
Cave Mountain, *Calif., U.S.* 35°3′ N, 116°22′ W **101**
Cave Point, *U.S.* 44°45′ N, 87°9′ W **94**
Cavendish, *Vt., U.S.* 43°23′ N, 72°37′ W **104**
Caviana, Ilha, island, *Braz.* 0°22′ N, 49°54′ W **130**
Cavignac, *Fr.* 45°5′ N, 0°24′ E **150**
Cavinas, *Bol.* 12°34′ S, 66°50′ W **137**
Cavite, *Philippines* 14°29′ N, 120°53′ E **203**
Cavo, Monte, peak, *It.* 41°44′ N, 12°37′ E **156**
Cavour, *It.* 44°46′ N, 7°23′ E **167**
Cavtat (Epidaurum), *Croatia* 42°34′ N, 18°13′ E **168**
Çavuş Burnu, *Turk.* 36°19′ N, 30°32′ E **156**
Çavuşçu Gölü, lake, *Turk.* 38°25′ N, 31°35′ E **156**
Cawker City, *Kans., U.S.* 39°29′ N, 98°27′ W **92**
Cawood, *U.K.* 53°50′ N, 1°8′ W **162**
Cawston, *U.K.* 52°45′ N, 1°9′ E **162**
Caxambu, *Braz.* 21°60′ S, 44°56′ W **138**
Caxias, *Braz.* 4°29′ S, 71°26′ W **130**
Caxias, *Braz.* 4°47′ S, 43°19′ W **132**
Caxias do Sul, *Braz.* 29°11′ S, 51°10′ W **139**
Caxito, *Angola* 8°35′ S, 13°41′ E **218**
Çay, *Turk.* 38°35′ N, 31°1′ E **156**
Cayacal, Punta, *Mex.* 17°44′ N, 102°12′ W **114**
Çaycuma, *Turk.* 41°25′ N, 32°2′ E **156**
Çayeli, *Turk.* 41°5′ N, 40°43′ E **195**
Cayenne, *Fr. Guiana, Fr.* 4°58′ N, 52°19′ W **130**
Cayeux-sur-Mer, *Fr.* 50°10′ N, 1°30′ E **163**
Cayey, *U.S.* 18°7′ N, 66°11′ W **116**
Çayıralan, *Turk.* 39°18′ N, 35°38′ E **156**
Cayman Trench, *Caribbean Sea* 17°52′ N, 80°50′ W **253**
Caynaba, *Somalia* 8°56′ N, 46°25′ E **216**
Cayo Agua, Isla, island, *Pan.* 9°2′ N, 81°60′ W **115**
Cayucos, *Calif., U.S.* 35°27′ N, 120°55′ W **100**
Cayuga, *Ind., U.S.* 39°56′ N, 87°28′ W **102**
Cayuga Lake, *N.Y., U.S.* 42°41′ N, 77°13′ W **94**
Cazage, *Angola* 11°3′ S, 20°44′ E **220**
Cazalla de la Sierra, *Sp.* 37°55′ N, 5°47′ W **164**
Cazères, *Fr.* 43°12′ N, 1°3′ E **164**
Cazombo, *Angola* 11°55′ S, 22°58′ E **220**
Cazones, river, *Mex.* 20°14′ N, 98°10′ W **114**
Cazorla, *Sp.* 37°54′ N, 3°2′ W **164**
Cazorla, *Venez.* 8°0′ N, 66°60′ W **136**
Ceadîr-Lunga, *Mold.* 46°2′ N, 28°50′ E **156**
Ceará, adm. division, *Braz.* 5°20′ S, 40°29′ W **132**
Ceará Mirim, *Braz.* 5°38′ S, 35°26′ W **132**
Ceara Plain, *South Atlantic Ocean* 0°23′ N, 37°43′ W **253**
Cébaco, Isla de, island, *Pan.* 7°22′ N, 81°30′ W **115**
Ceballos, *Mex.* 26°31′ N, 104°9′ W **114**
Cebollar, *Arg.* 29°6′ S, 66°32′ W **134**
Cebollatí, *Uru.* 33°17′ S, 53°51′ W **139**
Céboruco, Volcán, *Mex.* 21°7′ N, 104°32′ W **114**
Cebu, *Philippines* 10°20′ N, 123°54′ E **203**
Cebu, island, *Philippines* 11°11′ N, 123°27′ E **192**
Cece, *Hung.* 46°45′ N, 18°38′ E **168**
Cecil Lake, *Can.* 56°17′ N, 120°35′ W **108**
Cecil Rhodes, Mount, *Austral.* 25°28′ S, 121°15′ E **230**
Cecina, *It.* 43°18′ N, 10°31′ E **156**
Cedar Creek Peak, *Idaho, U.S.* 42°26′ N, 113°8′ W **90**
Cedar Creek Reservoir, lake, *Tex., U.S.* 32°20′ N, 96°47′ W **96**
Cedar Falls, *Iowa, U.S.* 42°30′ N, 92°28′ W **94**
Cedar Grove, *Calif., U.S.* 36°48′ N, 118°41′ W **101**
Cedar Grove, *Wis., U.S.* 43°34′ N, 87°49′ W **102**
Cedar Key, *Fla., U.S.* 29°8′ N, 83°3′ W **105**
Cedar Lake, *Can.* 53°1′ N, 101°7′ W **81**
Cedar Lake, *Can.* 50°7′ N, 93°38′ W **90**
Cedar Lake, *Ind., U.S.* 41°20′ N, 87°28′ W **102**
Cedar Lake, lake, *Can.* 45°58′ N, 78°50′ W **94**
Cedar Mountains, *Utah, U.S.* 40°35′ N, 113°9′ W **90**
Cedar Pass, *Calif., U.S.* 41°33′ N, 120°17′ W **90**
Cedar Pass, *S. Dak., U.S.* 43°45′ N, 101°56′ W **90**
Cedar Rapids, *Iowa, U.S.* 41°57′ N, 91°39′ W **94**
Cedar Ridge, *Calif., U.S.* 39°11′ N, 121°2′ W **90**
Cedar, river, *Iowa, U.S.* 42°9′ N, 92°21′ W **80**
Cedar Vale, *Kans., U.S.* 37°4′ N, 96°30′ W **92**
Cedarburg, *Wis., U.S.* 43°17′ N, 87°59′ W **102**
Cedars of Lebanon, site, *Leb.* 34°14′ N, 36°2′ E **194**
Cedarvale, *Can.* 55°0′ N, 128°19′ W **108**
Cedarville, *Calif., U.S.* 41°31′ N, 120°11′ W **90**
Cedral, *Mex.* 23°47′ N, 100°43′ W **114**
Cedros, *Mex.* 24°39′ N, 101°48′ W **114**
Cedros, Isla, island, *Mex.* 27°56′ N, 115°10′ W **112**
Cedros Trench, *North Pacific Ocean* 24°2′ N, 112°32′ W **252**
Ceek, *Somalia* 8°55′ N, 45°19′ E **216**
Ceel Afweyn, *Somalia* 9°52′ N, 47°15′ E **216**
Ceel Buur, *Somalia* 4°44′ N, 46°35′ E **218**
Ceel Dhaab, *Somalia* 8°49′ N, 46°34′ E **216**
Ceel Huur, *Somalia* 5°0′ N, 48°20′ E **218**
Ceeldheere, *Somalia* 3°52′ N, 47°13′ E **218**
Ceepeecee, *Can.* 49°53′ N, 126°44′ W **90**
Ceerigaabo (Erigavo), *Somalia* 10°34′ N, 47°24′ E **218**
Cefa, *Rom.* 46°54′ N, 21°42′ E **168**
Cegléd, *Hung.* 47°10′ N, 19°49′ E **168**
Cehegín, *Sp.* 38°5′ N, 1°48′ W **164**
Ceheng, *China* 24°58′ N, 105°49′ E **198**
Cehotina, river, *Europe* 43°30′ N, 18°48′ E **168**
Cehu Silvaniei, *Rom.* 47°24′ N, 23°12′ E **168**
Ceiba Grande, ruin(s), *Mex.* 17°22′ N, 93°51′ W **115**
Ceica, *Rom.* 46°51′ N, 22°10′ E **168**
Cejal, *Col.* 2°42′ N, 67°55′ W **136**
Cejolao, *Arg.* 27°28′ S, 62°20′ W **139**
Çekerek, *Turk.* 40°5′ N, 35°29′ E **156**
Çekerek, river, *Turk.* 40°25′ N, 35°18′ E **156**
Celarain, Punta, *Mex.* 20°10′ N, 86°59′ W **115**
Celaya, *Mex.* 20°30′ N, 100°49′ W **114**
Celebes Basin, *Celebes Sea* 3°27′ N, 121°47′ E **254**
Celebes Sea 3°49′ N, 119°35′ E **192**
Celebes see Sulawesi, island, *Indonesia* 0°39′ N, 123°14′ E **192**
Çeleken, *Turkm.* 39°26′ N, 53°8′ E **180**
Čelić, *Bosn. and Herzg.* 44°43′ N, 18°47′ E **168**
Celina, *Ohio, U.S.* 40°32′ N, 84°35′ W **102**
Celje, *Slov.* 46°14′ N, 15°14′ E **156**
Cella, *Sp.* 40°27′ N, 1°18′ W **164**
Cellar Head, *U.K.* 58°25′ N, 6°8′ W **150**
Celldömölk, *Hung.* 47°15′ N, 17°10′ E **168**
Celle, *Ger.* 52°36′ N, 10°5′ E **150**
Celtic Sea 50°32′ N, 8°3′ W **150**
Cement, *Okla., U.S.* 34°54′ N, 98°8′ W **92**
Cemerno, *Serb. and Mont.* 43°38′ N, 20°13′ E **168**
Çemişgezek, *Turk.* 39°4′ N, 38°54′ E **195**
Cempoala see Zempoala, ruin(s), *Mex.* 19°23′ N, 96°28′ W **114**
Cenchreae, ruin(s), *Gr.* 37°53′ N, 22°55′ E **156**
Cencia see Ch'encha, *Eth.* 6°15′ N, 37°38′ E **224**
Cenderawasih, Teluk 2°60′ S, 133°34′ E **192**
Cenicero, *Sp.* 42°28′ N, 2°39′ W **164**
Centenario, *Mex.* 18°39′ N, 90°17′ W **115**
Centennial Mountains, *Idaho, U.S.* 44°29′ N, 112°28′ W **90**
Center, *Colo., U.S.* 37°44′ N, 106°6′ W **92**
Center, *N. Dak., U.S.* 47°5′ N, 101°17′ W **90**
Center, *Tex., U.S.* 31°46′ N, 94°11′ W **103**
Center Barnstead, *N.H., U.S.* 43°20′ N, 71°17′ W **104**
Center Conway, *N.H., U.S.* 43°59′ N, 71°4′ W **104**
Center Harbor, *N.H., U.S.* 43°42′ N, 71°28′ W **104**
Center Hill, *Fla., U.S.* 28°38′ N, 81°60′ W **105**
Center Lovell, *Me., U.S.* 44°10′ N, 70°54′ W **104**
Center Moriches, *N.Y., U.S.* 40°48′ N, 72°48′ W **104**
Center Ossipee, *N.H., U.S.* 43°45′ N, 71°10′ W **104**
Center Peak, *Calif., U.S.* 36°12′ N, 120°40′ W **100**
Center Point, *Tex., U.S.* 29°54′ N, 99°2′ W **92**
Centerburg, *Ohio, U.S.* 40°17′ N, 82°41′ W **102**
Centerfield, *Utah, U.S.* 39°7′ N, 111°48′ W **92**
Centerville, *Calif., U.S.* 36°43′ N, 119°30′ W **100**
Centerville, *Iowa, U.S.* 40°43′ N, 92°53′ W **94**
Centerville, *Mass., U.S.* 41°38′ N, 70°22′ W **104**
Centerville, *S. Dak., U.S.* 43°5′ N, 96°58′ W **94**
Centerville, *Tex., U.S.* 31°14′ N, 95°58′ W **96**
Centerville, *Utah, U.S.* 40°55′ N, 111°52′ W **90**
Centinela, Picacho del, peak, *Mex.* 29°3′ N, 102°42′ W **92**
Cento, *It.* 44°43′ N, 11°17′ E **167**
Central, *Alas., U.S.* 65°33′ N, 144°52′ W **98**
Central, *Ariz., U.S.* 32°52′ N, 109°47′ W **92**
Central, adm. division, *Mongolia* 46°58′ N, 105°11′ E **198**
Central African Republic 7°1′ N, 21°10′ E **218**
Central Butte, *Can.* 50°48′ N, 106°32′ W **90**
Central City, *Ill., U.S.* 38°32′ N, 89°8′ W **102**
Central City, *Ky., U.S.* 37°17′ N, 87°7′ W **96**
Central City, *Nebr., U.S.* 41°6′ N, 98°1′ W **92**
Central City, *S. Dak., U.S.* 44°22′ N, 103°46′ W **90**
Central, Cordillera, *Dom. Rep.* 19°16′ N, 71°38′ W **116**
Central, Cordillera, *Peru* 6°52′ S, 77°30′ W **130**
Central Islip, *N.Y., U.S.* 40°47′ N, 73°12′ W **104**
Central Kalahari Game Reserve, *Botswana* 22°34′ S, 23°16′ E **227**
Central, Massif, *Europe* 44°5′ N, 1°58′ E **214**
Central Mount Wedge, peak, *Austral.* 22°57′ S, 131°37′ E **230**
Central Pacific Basin, *North Pacific Ocean* 7°5′ N, 176°34′ W **252**
Central Range, *P.N.G.* 5°6′ S, 141°26′ E **192**
Centralia, *Ill., U.S.* 38°31′ N, 89°8′ W **102**
Centralia, *Mo., U.S.* 39°11′ N, 92°8′ W **94**
Centralia, *Wash., U.S.* 46°41′ N, 122°58′ W **100**
Centre, *Ala., U.S.* 34°8′ N, 85°41′ W **96**
Centre, adm. division, *Fr.* 47°39′ N, 0°50′ E **150**
Centre de Marcoule, site, *Fr.* 44°8′ N, 4°40′ E **165**
Centre Island, *Austral.* 16°25′ S, 136°48′ E **230**
Centreville, *Mich., U.S.* 41°54′ N, 85°31′ W **102**
Centreville, *Miss., U.S.* 31°4′ N, 91°4′ W **103**
Cenxi, *China* 22°56′ N, 111°1′ E **198**
Çepan, *Alban.* 40°25′ N, 20°15′ E **156**
Cephalonia see Kefaloniá, adm. division, *Gr.* 38°22′ N, 20°3′ E **156**
Cepin, *Croatia* 45°30′ N, 18°32′ E **168**
Ceprano, *It.* 41°32′ N, 13°31′ E **156**
Cer, peak, *Serb. and Mont.* 44°35′ N, 19°27′ E **168**
Ceram, island, *Indonesia* 3°48′ S, 129°2′ E **192**
Ceram Sea 2°26′ S, 128°3′ E **192**
Cerbat Mountains, *Ariz., U.S.* 35°29′ N, 114°7′ W **101**
Cerbatana, Serranía de la, *Venez.* 6°31′ N, 66°45′ W **130**
Cerbère, *Fr.* 42°26′ N, 3°8′ E **164**
Cerbicales, Îles, islands, *Tyrrhenian Sea* 41°24′ N, 9°24′ E **156**
Cère, river, *Fr.* 44°50′ N, 2°21′ E **165**
Cerea, *It.* 45°12′ N, 11°12′ E **167**
Cereal, *Can.* 51°26′ N, 110°48′ W **90**
Cereales, *Arg.* 36°52′ S, 63°51′ W **139**
Ceres, *Arg.* 29°53′ S, 61°57′ W **139**
Ceres, *Braz.* 15°21′ S, 49°37′ W **138**
Ceres, *Calif., U.S.* 37°35′ N, 120°58′ W **100**
Ceres, *S. Af.* 33°21′ S, 19°18′ E **227**
Cerf Island, *Seychelles* 9°36′ S, 49°54′ E **218**
Cerigo see Kíthira, island, *Gr.* 36°17′ N, 23°3′ E **180**
Cermei, *Rom.* 46°33′ N, 21°50′ E **168**
Çermik, *Turk.* 38°8′ N, 39°27′ E **195**
Cerna, *Croatia* 45°11′ N, 18°41′ E **168**
Cerne Abbas, *U.K.* 50°48′ N, 2°29′ W **162**
Cernik, *Croatia* 45°17′ N, 17°23′ E **168**
Cerovljani, *Bosn. and Herzg.* 45°3′ N, 17°14′ E **168**
Cerralvo, *Mex.* 26°5′ N, 99°37′ W **114**
Cerralvo, Isla, island, *Mex.* 23°58′ N, 109°49′ W **112**
Cerrillos, ruin(s), *Mex.* 18°33′ N, 92°10′ W **115**
Cerritos, *Mex.* 22°24′ N, 100°16′ W **114**
Cerro Azul, *Mex.* 21°12′ N, 97°44′ W **114**
Cerro Azul, *Peru* 13°2′ S, 76°31′ W **130**
Cerro Chato, *Uru.* 33°5′ S, 55°10′ W **139**
Cerro de Garnica National Park, *Mex.* 19°39′ N, 101°5′ W **112**
Cerro de la Estrella National Park (8), *Mex.* 19°11′ N, 99°10′ W **112**
Cerro de las Mesas, ruin(s), *Mex.* 18°41′ N, 96°7′ W **114**
Cerro de Pasco, *Peru* 10°42′ S, 76°16′ W **130**
Cerro Gordo, *Ill., U.S.* 39°52′ N, 88°44′ W **102**
Cerro Jáua, Meseta del, *Venez.* 5°36′ N, 65°51′ W **136**
Cerrón, peak, *Venez.* 10°17′ N, 70°44′ W **136**
Cervales, peak, *Sp.* 39°32′ N, 5°21′ W **164**
Cervera, *Sp.* 41°39′ N, 1°16′ E **164**
Cervia, *It.* 44°15′ N, 12°19′ E **167**
Cervià, *Sp.* 41°26′ N, 0°51′ E **164**
Cervignano, *It.* 45°49′ N, 13°19′ E **167**
Cervo, *Sp.* 43°39′ N, 7°26′ W **150**
Cesana Torinese, *It.* 44°57′ N, 6°49′ E **167**
César, adm. division, *Col.* 9°23′ N, 73°54′ W **136**
Cesena, *It.* 44°8′ N, 12°14′ E **167**
Cesenatico, *It.* 44°11′ N, 12°24′ E **167**
Cesiomaggiore, *It.* 46°5′ N, 11°58′ E **167**
Cēsis, *Latv.* 57°17′ N, 25°15′ E **166**
České Budějovice, *Czech Rep.* 48°59′ N, 14°27′ E **152**
Český Les, *Czech Rep.* 49°28′ N, 12°41′ E **152**
Çeşme, *Turk.* 38°16′ N, 26°18′ E **156**
Cesney, Cape, *Antarctica* 66°10′ S, 136°15′ E **248**
Cess, river, *Liberia* 5°40′ N, 8°58′ W **222**
Cessnock, *Austral.* 32°48′ S, 151°22′ E **231**
Cesvaine, *Latv.* 56°57′ N, 26°18′ E **166**
Cetate, *Rom.* 44°6′ N, 23°4′ E **168**
Cetina, *Sp.* 41°16′ N, 1°59′ W **164**
Cetinje, *Serb. and Mont.* 42°23′ N, 18°54′ E **168**
Ceuta, *Sp.* 35°53′ N, 5°20′ W **150**
Cévennes, region, *Europe* 45°7′ N, 4°13′ E **165**
Cevio, *Switz.* 46°19′ N, 8°35′ E **167**
Ceyhan, *Turk.* 37°1′ N, 35°49′ E **156**
Ceyhan, river, *Turk.* 37°21′ N, 36°16′ E **180**
Ceylanpınar, *Turk.* 36°50′ N, 40°5′ E **195**
Ceylon, *Can.* 49°27′ N, 104°36′ W **90**
Chaadayevka, *Russ.* 53°8′ N, 45°58′ E **154**
Chābahār, *Iran* 25°18′ N, 60°39′ E **182**
Chaboullié, Lac, lake, *Can.* 50°52′ N, 78°32′ W **110**
Chac, oil field, *Mex.* 19°14′ N, 92°33′ W **115**
Chacabuco, *Arg.* 34°40′ S, 60°28′ W **139**
Chacalluta, *Chile* 18°25′ S, 70°20′ W **137**
Chacarilla, *Chile* 20°39′ S, 69°8′ W **137**
Chachani, Nevado, peak, *Peru* 16°14′ S, 71°35′ W **137**
Chachapoyas, *Peru* 6°9′ S, 77°51′ W **130**
Chachersk, *Belarus* 52°50′ N, 30°57′ E **154**
Chachoengsao, *Thai.* 13°43′ N, 101°4′ E **202**
Chachora, *India* 24°10′ N, 77°0′ E **197**
Chachro, *Pak.* 25°7′ N, 70°17′ E **186**
Chaco, adm. division, *Arg.* 27°11′ S, 60°49′ W **139**
Chaco Culture National Historic Park, *N. Mex., U.S.* 36°6′ N, 108°26′ W **92**
Chaco National Park, *Arg.* 26°54′ S, 59°45′ W **139**
Chacon, Cape, *Alas., U.S.* 54°29′ N, 132°5′ W **108**
Chad 15°25′ N, 17°21′ E **216**
Chad Basain National Park, *Nig.* 12°10′ N, 13°45′ E **218**
Chad, Lake, *Chad* 13°48′ N, 13°22′ E **216**
Chadan, *Russ.* 51°19′ N, 91°41′ E **184**
Chadron, *Nebr., U.S.* 42°49′ N, 102°60′ W **90**
Chadwick, *Mo., U.S.* 36°55′ N, 93°3′ W **96**
Chaedong, *N. Korea* 39°28′ N, 126°12′ E **200**
Chaeronea, ruin(s), *Gr.* 38°28′ N, 22°43′ E **156**
Chaeryŏng, *N. Korea* 38°24′ N, 125°38′ E **200**
Chafarinas, Islas, islands, *Alboran Sea* 35°13′ N, 2°52′ W **150**
Chafe, *Nig.* 11°54′ N, 6°55′ E **222**
Chaffee, *Mo., U.S.* 37°10′ N, 89°40′ W **96**
Chafurray, *Col.* 3°9′ N, 73°16′ W **136**
Chagai, *Pak.* 29°19′ N, 64°43′ E **182**
Chagda, *Russ.* 58°44′ N, 130°49′ E **160**
Chagdo Kangri, peak, *China* 34°10′ N, 84°4′ E **188**
Chaghcharan, *Afghan.* 34°28′ N, 65°13′ E **186**
Chagoda, *Russ.* 59°7′ N, 35°18′ E **154**
Chagos Archipelago (Oil Islands), *Indian Ocean* 6°42′ S, 71°25′ E **188**
Chagos Trench, *Indian Ocean* 10°25′ S, 72°50′ E **254**
Chagos-Laccadive Plateau, *Arabian Sea* 2°17′ N, 72°13′ E **254**
Chaguaramas, *Venez.* 9°20′ N, 66°17′ W **136**
Chagyl, *Turkm.* 40°49′ N, 55°17′ E **158**
Chahar Borj, *Afghan.* 34°20′ N, 62°12′ E **186**
Chahbounia, *Alg.* 35°31′ N, 2°36′ E **150**
Chah-e Ab, *Afghan.* 37°25′ N, 69°50′ E **186**
Ch'aho, *N. Korea* 40°12′ N, 128°41′ E **200**
Chaibasa, *India* 22°32′ N, 85°49′ E **197**
Chaïmane, spring, *Mauritania* 21°4′ N, 13°6′ W **222**
Chain Fracture Zone, *South Atlantic Ocean* 1°56′ S, 16°17′ W **253**
Chai-Nat, *Thai.* 15°14′ N, 100°10′ E **202**
Chaira, Laguna, lake, *Col.* 1°13′ N, 75°21′ W **136**
Chaitén, *Chile* 42°54′ S, 72°45′ W **134**
Chaiya, *Thai.* 9°23′ N, 99°10′ E **202**
Chajarí, *Arg.* 30°44′ S, 57°57′ W **139**
Chak Chak, *Sudan* 8°36′ N, 26°57′ E **224**
Chakar, river, *Pak.* 29°24′ N, 68°7′ E **186**
Chakaran, *Afghan.* 36°54′ N, 71°9′ E **186**
Chakaria, *Bangladesh* 21°47′ N, 92°4′ E **188**
Chake Chake, *Tanzania* 5°12′ S, 39°46′ E **218**
Chakhansur, *Afghan.* 31°10′ N, 62°6′ E **186**
Chakia, *India* 25°2′ N, 83°11′ E **188**
Chakkarat, *Thai.* 15°2′ N, 102°25′ E **202**
Chakmak-Suu, *Kyrg.* 41°59′ N, 71°26′ E **197**
Chakola, *Russ.* 64°17′ N, 44°14′ E **154**
Chakradharpur, *India* 22°41′ N, 85°38′ E **197**
Chakrata, *India* 30°42′ N, 77°53′ E **197**
Chakwal, *Pak.* 32°55′ N, 72°53′ E **186**
Chala, *Peru* 15°54′ S, 74°16′ W **137**
Chala, *Tanzania* 7°37′ S, 31°17′ E **224**
Chalabesa, *Zambia* 11°23′ S, 30°59′ E **224**
Chalatenango, *El Salv.* 14°1′ N, 88°55′ W **115**
Chalaua, *Mozambique* 16°5′ S, 39°13′ E **224**
Chalbi Desert, *Kenya* 3°33′ N, 36°48′ E **224**
Chalchihuites, *Mex.* 23°27′ N, 103°54′ W **114**
Ch'alchīs Terara, peak, *Eth.* 9°6′ N, 36°37′ E **224**
Chalengkou, *China* 38°1′ N, 93°55′ E **188**
Chaleur Bay 47°51′ N, 65°60′ W **111**
Chalhuanca, *Peru* 14°19′ S, 73°15′ W **137**
Chaling, *China* 26°51′ N, 113°31′ E **198**
Chalkyitsik, *Alas., U.S.* 66°38′ N, 143°44′ W **98**
Challacollo, *Chile* 20°59′ S, 69°24′ W **137**
Challans, *Fr.* 46°51′ N, 1°54′ W **150**
Challapata, *Bol.* 18°55′ S, 66°45′ W **137**
Challenger Deep, *North Pacific Ocean* 10°16′ N, 142°13′ E **252**
Challenger Fracture Zone, *South Pacific Ocean* 33°32′ S, 105°50′ W **252**
Challenger Point, peak, *Colo., U.S.* 37°57′ N, 105°40′ W **90**
Challis, *Idaho, U.S.* 44°30′ N, 114°14′ W **90**
Chālmeh, *Iran* 39°29′ N, 48°3′ E **195**
Chalon, *Fr.* 46°47′ N, 4°50′ E **150**
Châlons-sur-Marne, *Fr.* 48°57′ N, 4°22′ E **163**
Chaloyuk, *Turkm.* 37°26′ N, 54°13′ E **180**
Chālūs, *Iran* 36°41′ N, 51°19′ E **180**
Cham, *Ger.* 49°12′ N, 12°40′ E **152**
Chama, *Ghana* 8°49′ N, 0°58′ E **222**
Chama, *N. Mex., U.S.* 36°53′ N, 106°36′ W **92**
Chamah, peak, *Malaysia* 5°12′ N, 101°29′ E **196**
Chaman, *Pak.* 30°53′ N, 66°33′ E **186**
Chaman Bid, *Iran* 37°28′ N, 56°39′ E **180**
Chamba, *Nepal* 32°34′ N, 76°9′ E **188**
Chamba, *Tanzania* 11°32′ S, 37°1′ E **224**
Chambak, *Cambodia* 11°14′ N, 104°47′ E **202**
Chambeaux, Lac, lake, *Can.* 53°39′ N, 69°17′ W **111**
Chamberlain, *S. Dak., U.S.* 43°47′ N, 99°19′ W **90**
Chamberlain Lake, *Me., U.S.* 46°8′ N, 70°3′ W **94**
Chambers, *Ariz., U.S.* 35°12′ N, 109°26′ W **92**
Chambeshi, river, *Zambia* 11°2′ S, 31°11′ E **224**
Chambira, river, *Peru* 3°58′ S, 75°57′ W **130**
Chambishi, *Zambia* 12°40′ S, 28°4′ E **224**
Chambless, *Calif., U.S.* 34°33′ N, 115°33′ W **101**
Chambley, *Fr.* 49°3′ N, 5°53′ E **163**
Chambord, *Can.* 48°24′ N, 72°4′ W **94**
Chame, Punta, *Pan.* 8°32′ N, 79°41′ W **115**
Chamela, *Mex.* 19°32′ N, 105°5′ W **114**
Chamical, *Arg.* 30°23′ S, 66°19′ W **134**
Chamiss Bay, *Can.* 50°5′ N, 127°20′ W **90**
Chamizal National Memorial, *Tex., U.S.* 31°44′ N, 106°30′ W **92**
Chamonix, *Fr.* 45°55′ N, 6°51′ E **167**
Champa, *India* 22°2′ N, 82°40′ E **197**
Champagne, region, *Europe* 49°46′ N, 4°21′ E **167**
Champagne-Ardenne, adm. division, *Fr.* 48°18′ N, 3°36′ E **150**
Champaign, *Ill., U.S.* 40°6′ N, 88°15′ W **102**
Champasak, *Laos* 14°56′ N, 105°50′ E **202**
Champion, *Can.* 50°14′ N, 113°10′ W **90**

Champion, Ohio, U.S. 41°18' N, 80°51' W 102
Champlain, N.Y., U.S. 44°59' N, 73°28' W 94
Champotón, Mex. 19°21' N, 90°44' W 115
Champotón, river, Mex. 19°29' N, 90°38' W 115
Chamzinka, Russ. 54°25' N, 45°48' E 154
Chanac, Fr. 44°27' N, 3°20' E 150
Chañaral, Chile 26°23' S, 70°39' W 132
Chanārān, Iran 36°39' N, 59°5' E 180
Chanaro, Cerro, peak, Venez. 5°28' N, 63°60' W 130
Chancamayo, Peru 12°36' S, 72°26' W 137
Chancay, Peru 11°34' S, 77°17' W 130
Chanco, Chile 35°44' S, 72°34' W 134
Chandalar, river, Alas., U.S. 66°56' N, 149°16' W 98
Chandausi, India 28°26' N, 78°46' E 197
Chandeleur Islands, Gulf of Mexico 29°39' N, 88°48' W 103
Chandeleur Sound 29°48' N, 89°15' W 103
Chandigarh, India 30°43' N, 76°51' E 197
Chandigarh, adm. division, India 30°45' N, 76°18' E 188
Chandler, Ariz., U.S. 33°18' N, 111°50' W 92
Chandler, Can. 48°20' N, 64°40' W 111
Chandler, Okla., U.S. 35°40' N, 96°52' W 92
Chandler, Mount, Antarctica 75°19' S, 73°25' W 248
Chandless, river, Braz. 10°2' S, 70°12' W 137
Chandpur, Bangladesh 23°13' N, 90°41' E 197
Chandpur, India 29°7' N, 78°15' E 197
Chandrapur, India 20°3' N, 79°17' E 190
Chang, Ko, island, Thai. 11°52' N, 101°42' E 202
Chang La, pass, India 34°2' N, 77°55' E 188
Changalane, Mozambique 26°14' S, 32°14' E 227
Changane, river, Mozambique 24°3' S, 34°3' E 227
Changara, Mozambique 16°50' S, 33°16' E 224
Changbai, China 41°27' N, 128°12' E 200
Changchun, China 43°52' N, 125°16' E 198
Changde, China 29°5' N, 111°43' E 198
Ch'angdo, N. Korea 38°31' N, 127°40' E 200
Changhua, Taiwan 23°59' N, 120°31' E 198
Changhŭng, N. Korea 40°24' N, 128°20' E 200
Changji, China 44°3' N, 87°19' E 184
Changjiang (Shiliu), China 19°13' N, 109°2' E 198
Changjin, N. Korea 40°21' N, 127°15' E 200
Changjin Reservoir, lake, N. Korea 40°29' N, 126°46' E 200
Changjin, river, N. Korea 40°55' N, 127°15' E 200
Changle, China 25°58' N, 119°33' E 198
Changli, China 39°43' N, 119°11' E 198
Changling, China 44°16' N, 124°1' E 198
Changma, China 39°52' N, 96°43' E 188
Changmar, China 34°27' N, 79°57' E 188
Changni, S. Korea 37°19' N, 128°31' E 200
Changning, China 26°23' N, 112°24' E 198
Changping, China 40°12' N, 116°13' E 198
Changsha, China 28°13' N, 113°1' E 198
Changshou, China 29°51' N, 107°4' E 198
Changshu, China 31°36' N, 120°40' E 198
Changting, China 25°50' N, 116°16' E 198
Changtu, China 42°43' N, 124°8' E 200
Changwon, S. Korea 35°16' N, 128°45' E 200
Changxi, China 31°48' N, 105°59' E 198
Changxing Dao, island, China 39°29' N, 120°1' E 198
Changyŏn, N. Korea 38°14' N, 125°5' E 200
Changzheng, China 36°41' N, 105°2' E 198
Changzhi, China 36°10' N, 113°6' E 198
Changzhou, China 31°50' N, 120°0' E 198
Channapatna, India 12°40' N, 77°11' E 188
Channel Country, Austral. 25°2' S, 138°35' E 230
Channel Islands, adm. division, U.K. 49°26' N, 2°48' W 150
Channel Islands National Park, Calif., U.S. 34°5' N, 120°34' W 101
Channel-Port aux Basques, Can. 47°34' N, 59°9' W 111
Chanthaburi, Thai. 12°36' N, 102°9' E 202
Chantilly, Fr. 49°11' N, 2°28' E 163
Chantrey Inlet 67°23' N, 98°31' W 106
Chanute, Kans., U.S. 37°39' N, 95°28' W 94
Chany, Russ. 55°16' N, 76°54' E 184
Chany, Ozero, lake, Russ. 54°57' N, 76°49' E 184
Chany, Ozero, lake, Russ. 54°39' N, 75°46' E 160
Chaor, river, China 47°14' N, 121°38' E 198
Chaoyang, China 41°35' N, 120°24' E 198
Chaoyang, China 23°13' N, 116°33' E 198
Chaoyang see Huinan, China 42°42' N, 126°4' E 200
Chaoyangchuan, China 42°51' N, 129°19' E 200
Chaozhou, China 23°37' N, 116°33' E 198
Chapada dos Guimarães, Braz. 15°25' S, 55°47' W 132
Chapada Dos Veadeiros National Park, Braz. 14°10' S, 47°50' W 138
Chapadinha, Braz. 3°46' S, 43°20' W 132
Chapaev, Kaz. 50°11' N, 51°8' E 158
Chapais, Can. 49°48' N, 74°54' W 94
Chapala, Mex. 20°18' N, 103°12' W 112
Chapala, Lago de, lake, Mex. 20°2' N, 103°30' W 114
Chapare, river, Bol. 16°21' S, 65°2' W 137
Chaparral, Col. 3°41' N, 75°26' W 136
Chapayevsk, Russ. 52°58' N, 49°48' E 154
Chapeau, Can. 45°55' N, 77°4' W 94
Chapeauroux, Fr. 44°49' N, 3°44' E 150
Chapimarca, Peru 13°59' S, 73°3' W 137
Chapleau, Can. 47°49' N, 83°24' W 94
Chaplin Lake, Can. 50°13' N, 107°8' W 108
Chapman, Ala., U.S. 31°40' N, 86°43' W 96
Chapman, Kans., U.S. 38°57' N, 97°2' W 90
Chapman, Mount, Antarctica 82°25' S, 104°25' W 248
Chapman, Mount, Can. 51°56' N, 118°24' W 90
Chapoma, Russ. 66°8' N, 38°44' E 154
Chappaquiddick Island, Mass., U.S. 41°23' N, 70°27' W 104
Chappell, Nebr., U.S. 41°4' N, 102°28' W 90
Chaput Hughes, Can. 48°8' N, 80°4' W 94
Chaqui, Bol. 19°35' S, 65°28' W 137
Char, Mauritania 21°32' N, 12°50' W 222
Chara, Russ. 56°48' N, 118°10' E 160
Chara, river, Russ. 59°0' N, 118°31' E 160
Charadai, Arg. 27°37' S, 59°54' W 139
Charagua, Bol. 19°48' S, 63°18' W 137
Charalá, Col. 6°15' N, 73°7' W 136
Charambirá, Punta, Col. 4°8' N, 78°10' W 136
Charaña, Bol. 17°40' S, 69°27' W 137
Charanwala, India 27°51' N, 72°11' E 186
Charata, Arg. 27°13' S, 61°12' W 139
Charay, Mex. 26°0' N, 108°50' W 112
Charcoal Lake, Can. 58°44' N, 103°14' W 108
Charcot Bay 63°49' S, 61°4' W 134
Charcot Island, Antarctica 70°11' S, 79°50' W 248
Chard, Can. 55°50' N, 110°54' W 108
Chard, U.K. 50°52' N, 2°58' W 162
Charenton, La., U.S. 29°52' N, 91°32' W 103
Chari, river, Africa 13°9' N, 14°33' E 216
Charikar, Afghan. 35°1' N, 69°10' E 186
Chariton, Iowa, U.S. 41°1' N, 93°19' W 94
Chariton, river, Mo., U.S. 40°44' N, 93°9' W 80
Charity, Guyana 7°21' N, 58°37' W 130
Charity Island, Mich., U.S. 43°59' N, 83°25' W 102
Chärjew see Türkmenabat, Turkm. 39°4' N, 63°35' E 184
Charkayuvom, Russ. 65°48' N, 54°51' E 154
Charlemont, Mass., U.S. 42°37' N, 72°53' W 104
Charleroi, Belg. 50°25' N, 4°26' E 167
Charles, Cape, Va., U.S. 37°1' N, 75°57' W 96
Charles Fuhr, Arg. 50°13' S, 71°53' W 134
Charles Island, Can. 62°36' N, 77°12' W 106
Charles Lake, lake, Can. 59°45' N, 111°12' W 108
Charles Mound, Ill., U.S. 42°28' N, 90°17' W 102
Charles, Mount, Austral. 27°46' S, 117°13' E 230
Charlesbourg, Can. 46°51' N, 71°17' W 94
Charleston, Ill., U.S. 39°29' N, 88°11' W 102
Charleston, N.Z. 41°56' S, 171°27' E 240
Charleston, S.C., U.S. 32°47' N, 79°57' W 96
Charleston, W. Va., U.S. 38°19' N, 81°43' W 94
Charleston Peak, Nev., U.S. 36°15' N, 115°45' W 101
Charlestown, N.H., U.S. 43°13' N, 72°26' W 104
Charleville-Mézières, Fr. 49°46' N, 4°43' E 163
Charlevoix, Mich., U.S. 45°18' N, 85°16' W 94
Charlie Lake, Can. 56°15' N, 120°59' W 108
Charlie-Gibbs Fracture Zone, North Atlantic Ocean 51°53' N, 33°3' W 253
Charlotte, Mich., U.S. 42°33' N, 84°51' W 102
Charlotte, N.C., U.S. 35°12' N, 80°51' W 96
Charlotte, Tex., U.S. 28°51' N, 98°43' W 96
Charlotte, Vt., U.S. 44°18' N, 73°16' W 104
Charlotte Amalie, Virgin Islands, U.S. 18°0' N, 65°0' W 118
Charlotte Harbor 26°42' N, 83°11' W 80
Charlotte Harbor, Fla., U.S. 26°58' N, 82°4' W 105
Charlotte Lake, lake, Can. 52°6' N, 125°48' W 108
Charlottetown, Can. 46°13' N, 63°16' W 111
Charlotteville, Trinidad and Tobago 11°16' N, 60°33' W 116
Charlton City, Mass., U.S. 42°8' N, 71°60' W 104
Charlton Island, Can. 52°5' N, 80°29' W 81
Charly, Fr. 48°58' N, 3°16' E 163
Charmes, Fr. 48°21' N, 6°17' E 163
Charny, Can. 46°43' N, 71°16' W 94
Charouine, Alg. 29°2' N, 0°15' E 214
Charron Lake, lake, Can. 52°39' N, 95°47' W 108
Charters Towers, Austral. 20°7' S, 146°17' E 231
Chartres, Fr. 48°27' N, 1°27' E 163
Charyshskoye, Russ. 51°26' N, 83°43' E 184
Chascomús, Arg. 35°34' S, 58°1' W 139
Chase, Alas., U.S. 62°27' N, 150°6' W 98
Chase, Can. 50°49' N, 119°40' W 90
Chase, Mich., U.S. 43°53' N, 85°38' W 102
Chase City, Va., U.S. 36°47' N, 78°28' W 96
Chase, Mount, Me., U.S. 46°5' N, 68°34' W 94
Chase Mountain, Can. 56°32' N, 125°22' W 108
Chasel'ka, Russ. 65°7' N, 81°26' E 169
Chashniki, Belarus 54°51' N, 29°13' E 166
Chaska, Minn., U.S. 44°46' N, 93°38' W 94
Chasŏng, N. Korea 41°26' N, 126°38' E 200
Chasovo, Russ. 62°2' N, 50°40' E 154
Chassahowitzka, Fla., U.S. 28°41' N, 82°35' W 105
Chastyye, Russ. 57°16' N, 55°4' E 154
Chataignier, La., U.S. 30°32' N, 92°20' W 103
Chatawa, Miss., U.S. 31°2' N, 90°29' W 103
Châteaumeillant, Fr. 46°34' N, 2°11' E 150
Châteauneuf-en-Thymerais, Fr. 48°34' N, 1°14' E 163
Château-Porcien, Fr. 49°32' N, 4°14' E 163
Châteauroux, Fr. 46°49' N, 1°41' E 150
Château-Salins, Fr. 48°49' N, 6°30' E 163
Châteauvert, Lac, lake, Can. 47°34' N, 74°36' W 110
Chateh, Can. 58°41' N, 118°48' W 108
Châtel, Fr. 46°16' N, 6°49' E 167
Châtelet, Belg. 50°24' N, 4°32' E 167
Châtellerault, Fr. 46°48' N, 0°31' E 150
Châtel-Saint-Denis, Switz. 46°33' N, 6°55' E 167
Châtel-sur-Moselle, Fr. 48°18' N, 6°24' E 163
Châtenois, Fr. 48°17' N, 5°49' E 163
Chatfield, Minn., U.S. 43°50' N, 92°12' W 110
Chatham, Can. 47°1' N, 65°28' W 94
Chatham, Can. 42°23' N, 82°11' W 102
Chatham, Ill., U.S. 39°39' N, 89°42' W 102
Chatham, La., U.S. 32°18' N, 92°29' W 103
Chatham, Mass., U.S. 41°40' N, 69°58' W 104
Chatham, Miss., U.S. 33°4' N, 91°7' W 103
Chatham, Mo., U.S. 39°39' N, 89°42' W 94
Chatham, N.H., U.S. 44°9' N, 71°1' W 104
Chatham, N.Y., U.S. 42°21' N, 73°37' W 104
Chatham, U.K. 51°21' N, 0°30' E 162
Chatham, Va., U.S. 36°48' N, 79°25' W 96
Chatham, Isla, island, Chile 51°9' S, 74°8' W 134
Chatham Rise, South Pacific Ocean 43°29' S, 178°25' W 252
Châtillon, Fr. 49°6' N, 3°46' E 163
Chatom, Ala., U.S. 31°27' N, 88°15' W 103
Chatra, India 24°11' N, 84°51' E 197
Chatsu, India 26°35' N, 75°57' E 197
Chatsworth, Ill., U.S. 40°45' N, 88°19' W 102
Chattahoochee, Fla., U.S. 30°40' N, 84°54' W 112
Chattahoochee, river, U.S. 32°4' N, 85°8' W 80
Chattanooga, Tenn., U.S. 35°1' N, 85°19' W 96
Chattaroy, W. Va., U.S. 37°42' N, 82°18' W 96
Chatteris, U.K. 52°27' N, 5°297' E 162
Chatyr-Tash, Kyrg. 40°54' N, 76°26' E 184
Chau Doc, Vietnam 10°41' N, 105°7' E 202
Chauk, Myanmar 20°53' N, 94°50' E 202
Chaullay, Peru 13°1' S, 72°39' W 137
Chaulnes, Fr. 49°48' N, 2°47' E 163
Chaumont, Fr. 48°6' N, 5°8' E 150
Chaumont-en-Vexin, Fr. 49°16' N, 1°53' E 163
Chaumu, India 27°10' N, 75°42' E 197
Chauncey, Ohio, U.S. 39°24' N, 82°8' W 102
Chaunskaya Guba 69°10' N, 165°0' E 160
Chauny, Fr. 49°36' N, 3°14' E 163
Chauvin, Can. 52°41' N, 110°9' W 108
Chauvin, La., U.S. 29°26' N, 90°36' W 103
Chavan'ga, Russ. 66°8' N, 37°40' E 154
Chaves, Braz. 0°24' N, 49°48' W 123
Chaves, Port. 41°44' N, 7°30' W 150
Chaveslândia, Braz. 18°58' S, 50°36' W 138
Cháviva, Col. 4°18' N, 72°18' W 136
Chavuma, Zambia 13°5' S, 22°43' E 220
Chavusy, Belarus 53°46' N, 31°0' E 154
Chawang, Thai. 8°26' N, 99°31' E 202
Chayanta, Bol. 18°28' S, 66°28' W 137
Chaykovskiy, Russ. 56°48' N, 54°9' E 154
Cheadle, U.K. 52°59' N, 1°60' W 162
Cheaha Mountain, Ala., U.S. 33°27' N, 85°53' W 96
Cheapside, Va., U.S. 37°12' N, 75°59' W 96
Cheb, Czech Rep. 50°4' N, 12°22' E 152
Chebanse, Ill., U.S. 41°0' N, 87°55' W 102
Chebarkul', Russ. 55°0' N, 60°19' E 154
Chebeague Island, Me., U.S. 43°44' N, 70°8' W 104
Cheboksary, Russ. 56°5' N, 47°11' E 154
Cheboygan, Mich., U.S. 45°38' N, 84°30' W 94
Chebsara, Russ. 59°10' N, 38°49' E 154
Checa, Sp. 40°34' N, 1°47' W 164
Chech, Erg, Alg. 23°26' N, 4°20' W 206
Chechnya, adm. division, Russ. 43°33' N, 44°59' E 158
Checotah, Okla., U.S. 35°27' N, 95°32' W 96
Cheddar, U.K. 51°16' N, 2°47' W 162
Cheduba Island, Myanmar 18°29' N, 92°36' E 188
Chedworth, U.K. 51°48' N, 1°55' W 162
Cheecham, Can. 56°16' N, 110°53' W 108
Cheepash, river, Can. 50°42' N, 82°33' W 110
Cheepay, river, Can. 51°7' N, 83°35' W 110
Cheetham, Cape, Antarctica 69°54' S, 167°30' E 248
Chefornak, Alas., U.S. 60°12' N, 164°14' W 98
Chegdomyn, Russ. 51°6' N, 133°12' E 238
Chegga, spring, Mauritania 25°22' N, 5°47' W 214
Chegutu, Zimb. 18°9' S, 30°10' E 224
Chehalis, Wash., U.S. 46°39' N, 122°58' W 100
Chehalis, river, Wash., U.S. 46°59' N, 123°25' W 100
Chehar Borjak, Afghan. 30°17' N, 62°7' E 186
Cheïkria, spring, Alg. 25°29' N, 5°28' W 214
Cheju see Jeju, S. Korea 33°29' N, 126°32' E 200
Chela, Serra da, Angola 16°7' S, 12°39' E 220
Ch'elago, Eth. 9°4' N, 40°3' E 224
Chelak, Uzb. 39°58' N, 66°51' E 197
Chelan, Wash., U.S. 47°50' N, 120°1' W 90
Chelan Falls, Wash., U.S. 47°47' N, 119°59' W 108
Chelem, Mex. 21°15' N, 89°44' W 116
Chelforó, Arg. 39°6' S, 66°31' W 134
Chellal, Alg. 35°30' N, 4°23' E 150
Chełm, Pol. 51°7' N, 23°27' E 152
Chełmża, Pol. 53°21' N, 18°26' E 152
Chelmsford, Mass., U.S. 42°35' N, 71°22' W 104
Chelmsford, U.K. 51°44' N, 0°29' E 162
Chelmuzhi, Russ. 62°32' N, 35°43' E 154
Chelsea, Mich., U.S. 42°18' N, 84°2' W 102
Chelsea, Okla., U.S. 36°31' N, 95°26' W 96
Chelsea, Vt., U.S. 43°59' N, 72°27' W 104
Cheltenham, U.K. 51°53' N, 2°5' W 162
Chelva, Sp. 39°44' N, 0°60' E 150
Chelyabinsk, Russ. 55°9' N, 61°25' E 154
Chelyabinsk, adm. division, Russ. 53°58' N, 59°14' E 154
Chelyuskin, Mys, Russ. 76°44' N, 103°34' E 172
Chemaïa, Mor. 32°5' N, 8°40' W 214
Chemba, Mozambique 17°11' S, 34°50' E 224
Chemehuevi Peak, Calif., U.S. 34°32' N, 114°36' W 101
Chémery, Fr. 49°35' N, 4°50' E 163
Chemnitz, Ger. 50°48' N, 12°55' E 160
Chemtou, ruin(s), Tun. 36°28' N, 8°29' E 156
Chemult, Oreg., U.S. 43°13' N, 121°48' W 90
Chen Barag Qi, China 49°17' N, 119°24' E 198
Chenab, river, Pak. 31°18' N, 72°22' E 186
Chenachane, Alg. 26°3' N, 4°14' W 214
Chenango Bridge, N.Y., U.S. 42°10' N, 75°53' W 94
Ch'ench'a (Cencia), Eth. 6°15' N, 37°38' E 224
Chénérailles, Fr. 46°7' N, 2°10' E 150
Cheney, Wash., U.S. 47°28' N, 117°36' W 90
Cheneyville, La., U.S. 30°59' N, 92°18' W 103
Chengbu, China 26°22' N, 110°19' E 198
Chengchow see Zhengzhou, China 34°46' N, 113°36' E 198
Chengde, China 41°0' N, 117°55' E 198
Chengdu, China 30°43' N, 104°2' E 198
Chengele, India 28°47' N, 96°17' E 188
Chenggu, China 33°8' N, 107°19' E 198
Chenghai, China 23°29' N, 116°48' E 198
Chengkou, China 31°54' N, 108°39' E 198
Ch'engkung, Taiwan 23°8' N, 121°24' E 198
Chengshan Jiao, China 37°24' N, 122°45' E 198
Chengxian, China 33°44' N, 105°40' E 198
Chennai (Madras), India 13°5' N, 80°16' E 188
Chenoa, Ill., U.S. 40°44' N, 88°43' W 102
Chenxi, China 28°2' N, 110°12' E 198
Chenxiangtun, China 41°33' N, 123°29' E 200
Chenzhou, China 25°48' N, 113°2' E 198
Cheo Reo, Vietnam 13°23' N, 108°25' E 202
Cheom Ksan, Cambodia 14°16' N, 104°56' E 202
Cheonan, S. Korea 36°47' N, 127°8' E 200
Cheongeong, S. Korea 36°26' N, 129°6' E 200
Cheongju, S. Korea 36°37' N, 127°30' E 200
Cheongyang, S. Korea 36°26' N, 126°48' E 200
Cheorwon, S. Korea 38°14' N, 127°13' E 200
Chepachet, R.I., U.S. 41°54' N, 71°41' W 104
Chepes, Arg. 31°20' S, 66°35' W 134
Chepstow, U.K. 51°38' N, 2°41' W 162
Cheptsa, river, Russ. 58°8' N, 52°54' E 154
Cher, river, Fr. 46°54' N, 2°17' E 165
Cherán, Mex. 19°40' N, 101°57' W 114
Cherangany Hills, Kenya 1°32' N, 35°1' E 224
Cherari, Eth. 9°55' N, 35°52' E 224
Cheraw, S.C., U.S. 34°40' N, 79°55' W 96
Cherchell, Alg. 36°35' N, 2°12' E 150
Cherdyn', Russ. 60°24' N, 56°25' E 154
Cheremkhovo, Russ. 53°16' N, 102°55' E 190
Cheremukhovo, Russ. 60°21' N, 59°59' E 154
Cherepanovo, Russ. 54°14' N, 83°29' E 184
Chereponi, Ghana 10°7' N, 0°17' E 222
Cherepovets, Russ. 59°7' N, 37°55' E 154
Cherevkovo, Russ. 61°46' N, 45°17' E 154
Chereya, Belarus 54°36' N, 29°20' E 166
Chéri, Niger 13°25' N, 11°21' E 222
Cheriton, Va., U.S. 37°17' N, 75°58' W 96
Cherkasy, Ukr. 49°26' N, 32°3' E 158
Cherkessk, Russ. 44°14' N, 42°3' E 158
Cherla, India 18°4' N, 80°50' E 188
Cherlak, Russ. 54°9' N, 74°53' E 184
Chermenino, Russ. 59°2' N, 43°59' E 154
Chermoz, Russ. 58°46' N, 56°5' E 154
Chern', Russ. 53°25' N, 36°57' E 154
Chernaya Kholunitsa, Russ. 58°52' N, 51°46' E 154
Chernevichi, Belarus 54°1' N, 28°49' E 166
Chernevo, Russ. 58°39' N, 28°12' E 166
Cherni Vrŭkh, peak, Bulg. 42°32' N, 23°12' E 156
Chernihiv, Ukr. 51°27' N, 31°20' E 158
Chernivtsi, Ukr. 48°17' N, 25°57' E 152
Chernoborskaya, Russ. 65°8' N, 53°38' E 154
Chernofski, Alas., U.S. 53°22' N, 167°34' W 98
Chernogorsk, Russ. 53°49' N, 91°16' E 184
Chernorechenskiy, Russ. 60°42' N, 52°15' E 154
Chernovka, Russ. 54°12' N, 80°5' E 184
Chernushka, Russ. 56°30' N, 56°1' E 154
Chernyakhovsk, Russ. 54°36' N, 21°49' E 152
Chernyanka, Russ. 50°55' N, 37°48' E 158
Chernyshevskiy, Russ. 62°52' N, 112°40' E 160
Chernyy Otrog, Russ. 51°51' N, 56°0' E 158
Chernyy Yar, Russ. 48°2' N, 46°4' E 158
Cherokee, Okla., U.S. 36°44' N, 98°21' W 92
Cherokee Sound, Bahamas 26°16' N, 77°3' W 96
Cherokees, Lake O' The, Okla., U.S. 36°42' N, 95°40' W 80
Cherrapunji, India 25°15' N, 91°42' E 197
Cherry Creek Range, Nev., U.S. 39°59' N, 115°6' W 90
Cherry Creek, river, S. Dak., U.S. 44°42' N, 102°31' W 90
Cherskaya, Russ. 57°39' N, 28°17' E 166
Cherskiy, Russ. 68°39' N, 161°29' E 160
Cherskogo, Khrebet, Russ. 66°20' N, 138°20' E 160
Chersonesus, ruin(s), Gr. 35°18' N, 25°17' E 156
Chertkovo, Russ. 49°27' N, 40°8' E 158
Cherva, Russ. 62°16' N, 48°41' E 154
Chervonohrad, Ukr. 50°22' N, 24°15' E 152
Chervyanka, Russ. 57°39' N, 99°28' E 160
Cherykaw, Belarus 53°32' N, 31°23' E 154
Chesaning, Mich., U.S. 43°10' N, 84°7' W 102
Chesapeake, Va., U.S. 36°49' N, 76°17' W 96
Chesapeake, W. Va., U.S. 38°12' N, 81°34' W 94
Chesham, U.K. 51°42' N, 0°38' E 162
Cheshire, Conn., U.S. 41°29' N, 72°54' W 104
Cheshire, Mass., U.S. 42°33' N, 73°10' W 104
Cheshskaya Guba 67°9' N, 44°36' E 169
Cheshunt, U.K. 51°41' N, 0°3' E 162
Cheslatta Lake, lake, Can. 53°38' N, 125°40' W 108
Chesley, Can. 44°17' N, 81°6' W 110
Chesma, Russ. 53°51' N, 60°32' E 154
Cheste, Sp. 39°29' N, 0°42' E 164
Chester, Mo., U.S. 37°54' N, 89°49' W 96
Chester, Mont., U.S. 48°28' N, 110°59' W 90
Chester, N.H., U.S. 42°57' N, 71°16' W 104
Chester, S.C., U.S. 34°42' N, 81°13' W 96
Chester, U.K. 53°12' N, 2°51' W 162
Chester, Vt., U.S. 43°15' N, 72°36' W 104
Chester le Street, U.K. 54°51' N, 1°36' W 162
Chesterfield, Ind., U.S. 40°6' N, 85°36' W 102
Chesterfield, U.K. 53°14' N, 1°27' W 162
Chesterfield, Îles, islands, Coral Sea 18°54' S, 154°49' E 238
Chesterfield Inlet, Can. 63°19' N, 90°50' W 106
Chesterhill, Ohio, U.S. 39°28' N, 81°51' W 102
Chesterton Range, Austral. 26°17' S, 147°27' E 230
Chestertown, N.Y., U.S. 43°38' N, 73°49' W 104
Chestnut Ridge, Pa., U.S. 40°29' N, 79°22' W 94
Chetamale, India 10°44' N, 92°41' E 188
Chete Safari Area, Zimb. 17°30' S, 27°12' E 224
Chetek, Wis., U.S. 45°18' N, 91°40' W 94
Chéticamp, Can. 46°36' N, 61°1' W 111
Chetumal, Mex. 18°30' N, 88°27' W 115
Chetwynd, Can. 55°41' N, 121°39' W 108
Chevillon, Fr. 48°31' N, 5°7' E 163
Cheviot, N.Z. 42°50' S, 173°16' E 240
Cheviot Hills, U.K. 55°10' N, 2°47' W 150
Cheviot, The, peak, U.K. 55°27' N, 2°16' W 150
Ch'ew Bahir, lake, Eth. 4°40' N, 36°40' E 224
Chewelah, Wash., U.S. 48°15' N, 117°45' W 90
Chewore Safari Area, Zimb. 15°58' S, 29°52' E 224
Cheyenne, Okla., U.S. 35°35' N, 99°40' W 92
Cheyenne, Wyo., U.S. 41°6' N, 104°55' W 90
Cheyenne, river, S. Dak., U.S. 44°24' N, 102°2' W 90
Cheyenne, river, Wyo., U.S. 42°53' N, 104°36' W 80
Cheyenne Wells, Colo., U.S. 38°48' N, 102°21' W 90
Chezacut, Can. 52°25' N, 124°2' W 108
Chhad Bet, site, Pak. 24°13' N, 69°54' E 186
Chhapra, India 25°46' N, 84°43' E 197
Chhatarpur, India 24°54' N, 79°35' E 197
Chhattīsgarh, adm. division, India 19°11' N, 81°20' E 188
Chhep, Cambodia 13°46' N, 105°27' E 202
Chhindwara, India 22°4' N, 78°56' E 197
Chhlong, Cambodia 12°14' N, 105°57' E 202
Chhukha, Bhutan 27°10' N, 89°30' E 197
Chi, river, Thai. 15°56' N, 102°18' E 202
Chia, Sp. 42°31' N, 0°27' E 164
Chiai, Taiwan 23°28' N, 120°25' E 198
Chiang Dao, Thai. 19°23' N, 98°57' E 202
Chiang Khan, Thai. 17°53' N, 101°37' E 202
Chiang Mai, Thai. 18°48' N, 98°58' E 202
Chiang Rai, Thai. 19°55' N, 99°48' E 202
Chiang Saen, Laos 20°18' N, 100°3' E 202
Chiange, Angola 15°43' S, 13°54' E 220
Chiapa, Chile 19°33' S, 69°14' W 137
Chiapas, adm. division, Mex. 16°28' N, 93°24' W 112
Chiari, It. 45°32' N, 9°54' E 167
Chiasso, Switz. 45°51' N, 9°1' E 167
Chiat'aisi, Ga. 42°14' N, 43°17' E 195
Chiautla, Mex. 18°15' N, 98°36' W 114
Chiavari, It. 44°19' N, 9°20' E 167
Chiavenna, It. 46°19' N, 9°23' E 167
Chiba, Japan 35°34' N, 140°9' E 201
Chiba, adm. division, Japan 35°44' N, 139°54' E 201
Chibabava, Mozambique 20°17' S, 33°41' E 227
Chibi, Zimb. 20°19' S, 30°29' E 227
Chibia, Angola 15°14' S, 13°40' E 220
Chibougamau, Can. 49°54' N, 74°22' W 94
Chibougamau, Lac, lake, Can. 49°49' N, 75°44' W 81
Chibuto, Mozambique 24°42' S, 33°34' E 227
Chibwe, Zambia 14°12' S, 28°29' E 224
Chic Chocs Mountains, Can. 48°42' N, 67°1' W 94
Chicago, Ill., U.S. 41°51' N, 87°37' W 102
Chicamba, Angola 4°59' S, 12°2' E 218
Chichagof, Alas., U.S. 57°41' N, 136°8' W 108
Chichagof Island, Alas., U.S. 58°3' N, 138°7' W 98
Chichaoua, Mor. 31°31' N, 8°47' W 214
Chichas, Cordillera de, Bol. 20°47' S, 66°25' W 132
Chiché, river, Braz. 8°54' S, 54°6' W 130
Chichén Itzá, ruin(s), Mex. 20°40' N, 88°42' W 115
Chichester, N.H., U.S. 43°14' N, 71°25' W 104
Chichester, U.K. 50°50' N, 0°47' E 162
Chichi Jima Rettō, islands, Philippine Sea 26°41' N, 142°19' E 190
Chichibu, Japan 35°58' N, 139°6' E 201
Chichibu-Tama National Park, Japan 35°50' N, 138°11' E 201
Chichihualco, Mex. 17°40' N, 99°41' W 114
Chichiriviche, Venez. 10°56' N, 68°17' W 136
Chickaloon, Alas., U.S. 61°48' N, 148°28' W 98
Chickasaw, Ala., U.S. 30°45' N, 88°3' W 103
Chickasha, Okla., U.S. 35°2' N, 97°57' W 92
Chiclana de la Frontera, Sp. 36°25' N, 6°9' W 164
Chiclayo, Peru 6°44' S, 79°51' W 130
Chico, Calif., U.S. 39°43' N, 121°51' W 90
Chico, river, Arg. 48°23' S, 71°58' W 134
Chico, river, Arg. 45°2' S, 67°5' W 134
Chicomo, Mozambique 24°31' S, 34°9' E 227
Chicontepec, Mex. 20°57' N, 98°10' W 114
Chicopee, Ga., U.S. 34°14' N, 83°51' W 96
Chicopee, Mass., U.S. 42°8' N, 72°37' W 104
Chicot Island, La., U.S. 29°39' N, 89°22' W 103
Chicoutai, Point, Can. 50°5' N, 61°8' W 111
Chicoutimi, Can. 48°14' N, 70°58' W 106
Chicoutimi-Nord, Can. 48°26' N, 71°6' W 94
Chicualacuala, Mozambique 22°4' S, 31°43' E 227
Chicuma, Angola 13°26' S, 14°49' E 220
Chidenguele, Mozambique 24°54' S, 34°10' E 227
Chiefland, Fla., U.S. 29°28' N, 82°51' W 105
Chiengi, Zambia 8°41' S, 29°10' E 224
Chietla, Mex. 18°29' N, 98°34' W 114
Chifeng, China 42°15' N, 118°59' E 198
Chifre, Serra do, Braz. 17°46' S, 42°41' W 132
Chifungwe, Lake, Zambia 11°37' S, 29°6' E 224
Chignahuapan, Mex. 19°48' N, 98°2' W 114
Chignecto Bay 45°35' N, 64°44' W 111
Chignecto, Cape, Can. 45°15' N, 65°39' W 111
Chignik, Alas., U.S. 56°8' N, 158°13' W 106
Chiguana, Bol. 21°7' S, 67°58' W 137
Chiguaza, Ecua. 2°2' S, 77°52' W 136
Chigubo, Mozambique 22°49' S, 33°30' E 227
Chihertey, Mongolia 48°15' N, 89°30' E 184
Chihuahua, Mex. 28°35' N, 106°9' W 92
Chihuahua, adm. division, Mex. 29°0' N, 107°42' W 92
Chikalda, India 21°24' N, 77°19' E 188
Chikhachevo, Russ. 57°17' N, 29°55' E 166
Chikhli, India 20°21' N, 76°16' E 188
Chikwawa, Malawi 16°6' S, 34°45' E 224
Chilac, Mex. 18°18' N, 97°22' W 114
Chilako, river, Can. 53°31' N, 124°10' W 108
Chilanga, Malawi 13°14' S, 33°31' E 224
Chilapa, Mex. 17°34' N, 99°10' W 114
Chilas, Pak. 35°23' N, 74°7' E 186
Chilcotin, river, Can. 52°52' N, 124°49' W 108
Childersburg, Ala., U.S. 33°16' N, 86°22' W 96
Childress, Tex., U.S. 34°24' N, 100°13' W 92
Chile 36°9' S, 71°58' W 134
Chile Chico, Chile 46°31' S, 71°48' W 134
Chile Rise, South Pacific Ocean 40°45' S, 87°42' W 253
Chilecito, Arg. 29°11' S, 67°30' W 134
Chililabombwe, Zambia 12°23' S, 27°49' E 224
Chilko, river, Can. 51°45' N, 124°9' W 108
Chilkoot Pass, Can. 59°40' N, 135°15' W 108
Chillán, Chile 36°36' S, 72°7' W 123
Chillar, Arg. 37°20' S, 59°58' W 139
Chillicothe, Ill., U.S. 40°54' N, 89°31' W 102
Chillicothe, Mo., U.S. 39°47' N, 93°33' W 94

Chillicothe, *Ohio, U.S.* 39°19′ N, 82°59′ W **102**
Chillicothe, *Tex., U.S.* 34°14′ N, 99°30′ W **92**
Chilliwack, *Can.* 49°9′ N, 121°57′ W **100**
Chilliwack Lake, *Can.* 49°2′ N, 121°43′ W **100**
Chilliwack, river, *Can.* 49°5′ N, 121°53′ W **100**
Chilmark, *Mass., U.S.* 41°20′ N, 70°45′ W **104**
Chilo, *India* 27°26′ N, 73°32′ E **186**
Chiloé, Isla Grande de, island, *Chile* 42°1′ S, 76°28′ W **134**
Chilonga, *Zambia* 12°2′ S, 31°20′ E **224**
Chiloquin, *Oreg., U.S.* 42°35′ N, 121°52′ W **90**
Chilpancingo, *Mex.* 17°31′ N, 99°34′ W **114**
Chil′tal′d, Gora, peak, *Russ.* 68°17′ N, 30°50′ E **152**
Chiltern Hills, *U.K.* 51°46′ N, 0°55′ E **162**
Chilton, *Wis., U.S.* 44°1′ N, 88°11′ W **102**
Chiluage, *Angola* 9°30′ S, 21°46′ E **218**
Chilumba (Deep Bay), *Malawi* 10°24′ S, 34°13′ E **224**
Chilung (Keelung), *Taiwan* 25°6′ N, 121°45′ E **198**
Chilwa, Lake, *Malawi* 15°22′ S, 35°26′ E **224**
Chim Berkaouane, *Niger* 15°8′ N, 3°37′ E **222**
Chimacum, *Wash., U.S.* 48°0′ N, 122°46′ W **100**
Chimaltenango, *Guatemala* 14°39′ N, 90°49′ W **115**
Chimaltitan, *Mex.* 21°48′ N, 103°46′ W **114**
Chimán, *Pan.* 8°42′ N, 78°37′ W **115**
Chimanimani, *Zimb.* 19°50′ S, 32°51′ E **224**
Chimanimani National Park, *Zimb.* 19°55′ S, 33°12′ E **224**
Chimay, *Belg.* 50°2′ N, 4°19′ E **163**
Chimbote, *Peru* 9°5′ S, 78°35′ W **130**
Chimboy, *Uzb.* 42°55′ N, 59°47′ E **180**
Chimney Reservoir, *Nev., U.S.* 41°42′ N, 116°53′ W **90**
Chimney Rock, site, *N.C., U.S.* 35°24′ N, 82°22′ W **96**
Chimoio, *Mozambique* 19°8′ S, 33°31′ E **224**
China 33°31′ N, 97°47′ E **190**
China, *Mex.* 25°41′ N, 99°13′ W **114**
China, *Tex., U.S.* 30°2′ N, 94°21′ W **103**
China Lake, *Calif., U.S.* 35°39′ N, 117°40′ W **101**
China Mountain, peak, *Calif., U.S.* 41°21′ N, 122°40′ W **90**
Chinandega, *Nicar.* 12°36′ N, 87°7′ W **115**
Chinati Mountains, *Tex., U.S.* 29°46′ N, 104°36′ W **92**
Chinati Peak, *Tex., U.S.* 29°54′ N, 104°32′ W **92**
Chinchaga, river, *Can.* 57°11′ N, 119°35′ W **108**
Chincheros, *Peru* 13°34′ S, 73°44′ W **137**
Chinchilla de Monte Aragón, *Sp.* 38°54′ N, 1°45′ W **164**
Chinchón, *Sp.* 40°8′ N, 3°26′ W **164**
Chincoteague, *Va., U.S.* 37°55′ N, 75°22′ W **94**
Chincoteague Bay 37°58′ N, 76°35′ W **80**
Chinde, *Mozambique* 18°36′ S, 36°26′ E **224**
Chindu, *China* 33°21′ N, 97°4′ E **188**
Chindwin, river, *Myanmar* 25°37′ N, 95°16′ E **190**
Chinese Camp, *Calif., U.S.* 37°51′ N, 120°27′ W **100**
Chingola, *Zambia* 12°36′ S, 27°49′ E **224**
Chingpu, *Taiwan* 23°28′ N, 121°28′ E **198**
Chinguetti, *Mauritania* 20°27′ N, 12°23′ W **222**
Chinhoyi, *Zimb.* 17°23′ S, 30°11′ E **224**
Chiniot, *Pak.* 31°41′ N, 72°57′ E **186**
Chinipas, *Mex.* 27°23′ N, 108°32′ W **112**
Chinko, river, *Cen. Af. Rep.* 5°4′ N, 24°12′ E **224**
Chinle, *Ariz., U.S.* 36°8′ N, 109°33′ W **92**
Chino, *Japan* 35°58′ N, 138°11′ E **201**
Chino Valley, *Ariz., U.S.* 34°44′ N, 112°27′ W **92**
Chinobampo, *Mex.* 26°18′ N, 108°29′ W **112**
Chinon, *Fr.* 47°10′ N, 0°14′ E **150**
Chinook, *Mont., U.S.* 48°34′ N, 109°14′ W **90**
Chinook, *Wash., U.S.* 46°16′ N, 123°56′ W **100**
Chinsali, *Zambia* 10°35′ S, 32°2′ E **224**
Chinsong, *N. Korea* 41°24′ N, 126°50′ E **200**
Chinteche, *Malawi* 11°52′ S, 34°8′ E **224**
Chiôco, *Mozambique* 16°26′ S, 32°50′ E **224**
Chioggia, *It.* 45°12′ N, 12°14′ E **167**
Chipata, *Zambia* 13°39′ S, 32°38′ E **224**
Chipchase Castle, site, *U.K.* 55°4′ N, 2°18′ W **150**
Chiperceni, *Mold.* 47°30′ N, 28°50′ E **156**
Chipewyan Lake, *Can.* 56°54′ N, 113°30′ W **108**
Chipili, *Zambia* 10°46′ S, 29°3′ E **224**
Chipinge, *Zimb.* 20°11′ S, 32°36′ E **227**
Chipiona, *Sp.* 36°43′ N, 6°26′ W **164**
Chipley, *Fla., U.S.* 30°46′ N, 85°33′ W **96**
Chipman Lake, lake, *Can.* 49°58′ N, 86°42′ W **94**
Chipoka, *Malawi* 13°57′ S, 34°30′ E **224**
Chippenham, *U.K.* 51°28′ N, 2°8′ W **162**
Chippewa, river, *Mich., U.S.* 43°37′ N, 85°6′ W **102**
Chipping Campden, *U.K.* 52°2′ N, 1°48′ W **162**
Chipping Norton, *U.K.* 51°56′ N, 1°33′ W **162**
Chipping Sodbury, *U.K.* 51°32′ N, 2°24′ W **162**
Chiquihuitlán, *Mex.* 17°56′ N, 96°50′ W **114**
Chiquilá, *Mex.* 21°26′ N, 87°18′ W **116**
Chiquimula, *Guatemala* 14°49′ N, 89°35′ W **116**
Chiquimulilla, *Guatemala* 14°5′ N, 90°25′ W **116**
Chiquinquirá, *Col.* 5°37′ N, 73°50′ W **136**
Chiradzulu, *Malawi* 15°41′ S, 35°13′ E **224**
Chirala, *India* 15°49′ N, 80°21′ E **188**
Chiramba, *Mozambique* 16°58′ S, 34°39′ E **224**
Chiran, *Japan* 31°20′ N, 130°27′ E **201**
Chirchiq, *Uzb.* 41°29′ N, 69°34′ E **197**
Chirchirri, *Somalia* 4°43′ N, 44°43′ E **218**
Chiredzi, *Zimb.* 21°8′ S, 31°48′ E **227**
Chireno, *Tex., U.S.* 31°29′ N, 94°21′ W **103**
Chirfa, *Niger* 20°55′ N, 12°19′ E **222**
Chiribiquete National Park, *Col.* 0°11′ N, 72°51′ W **136**
Chiribiquete, Sierra de, *Col.* 1°3′ N, 73°33′ W **136**
Chiricahua Peak, *Ariz., U.S.* 31°50′ N, 109°20′ W **92**
Chiriguaná, *Col.* 9°20′ N, 73°38′ W **136**
Chirikof Island, *Alas., U.S.* 55°35′ N, 157°15′ W **98**
Chirinda, *Russ.* 67°23′ N, 100°23′ E **169**
Chirk, *U.K.* 52°56′ N, 3°2′ W **162**
Chirnogeni, *Rom.* 43°54′ N, 28°13′ E **158**
Chiromo, *Malawi* 16°33′ S, 35°7′ E **224**
Chiroqchi, *Uzb.* 39°3′ N, 66°36′ E **197**
Chirpan, *Bulg.* 42°12′ N, 25°19′ E **156**
Chirripó, Cerro, peak, *C.R.* 9°29′ N, 83°34′ W **115**
Chirripó, river, *C.R.* 10°13′ N, 83°45′ W **116**
Chirundu, *Zambia* 16°2′ S, 28°48′ E **224**
Chisamba, *Zambia* 14°60′ S, 28°22′ E **224**
Chisasibi, *Can.* 53°45′ N, 79°1′ W **106**
Ch′ishan, *Taiwan* 22°56′ N, 120°29′ E **198**
Chishmy, *Russ.* 54°35′ N, 55°21′ E **154**
Chisholm, *Can.* 54°54′ N, 114°8′ W **108**
Chisholm, *Me., U.S.* 44°29′ N, 70°13′ W **104**
Chishui, *China* 28°34′ N, 105°41′ E **198**
Chisimayu see Kismaayo, *Somalia* 0°27′ N, 42°35′ E **224**
Chişineu Criş, *Rom.* 46°32′ N, 21°32′ E **168**
Chişinău, *Mold.* 47°0′ N, 28°41′ E **156**
Chisos Mountains, *Tex., U.S.* 29°10′ N, 103°26′ W **92**
Chistochina, *Alas., U.S.* 62°35′ N, 144°40′ W **98**
Chistoozernoye, *Russ.* 54°40′ N, 76°39′ E **184**
Chistopel′e, *Kaz.* 52°32′ N, 67°15′ E **184**
Chistopol′, *Russ.* 55°19′ N, 50°31′ E **154**
Chita, *Col.* 6°11′ N, 72°30′ W **136**
Chita, *Russ.* 52°8′ N, 113°31′ E **190**
Chitado, *Angola* 17°18′ S, 13°55′ E **220**
Chitambo, *Zambia* 12°57′ S, 30°38′ E **224**
Chitato, *Angola* 7°20′ S, 20°47′ E **218**
Chitek Lake, lake, *Can.* 52°23′ N, 99°49′ W **108**
Chitembo, *Angola* 13°33′ S, 16°43′ E **220**
Chitimba, *Malawi* 10°33′ S, 34°10′ E **224**
Chitipa (Fort Hill), *Malawi* 9°43′ S, 33°14′ E **224**
Chitokoloki, *Zambia* 13°50′ S, 23°14′ E **220**
Chitose, *Japan* 42°47′ N, 141°49′ E **238**
Chitradurga, *India* 14°13′ N, 76°24′ E **188**
Chitral, *Pak.* 35°50′ N, 71°47′ E **186**
Chitré, *Pan.* 7°59′ N, 80°26′ W **115**
Chittagong, *Bangladesh* 22°19′ N, 91°50′ E **197**
Chittoor, *India* 13°13′ N, 79°6′ E **188**
Chitungwiza, *Zimb.* 17°58′ S, 31°3′ E **224**
Chiuchiu, *Chile* 22°21′ S, 68°42′ W **137**
Chiumbe, river, *Angola* 8°47′ S, 21°10′ E **220**
Chiume, *Angola* 15°3′ S, 21°12′ E **220**
Chiúre, *Mozambique* 13°24′ S, 39°58′ E **224**
Chiusa, *It.* 46°38′ N, 11°32′ E **167**
Chiusaforte, *It.* 46°24′ N, 13°18′ E **167**
Chiuta, Lago, lake, *Mozambique* 14°50′ S, 35°36′ E **224**
Chiva, *Sp.* 39°28′ N, 0°43′ E **150**
Chivapuri, river, *Venez.* 6°28′ N, 66°48′ W **136**
Chivasso, *It.* 45°12′ N, 7°52′ E **167**
Chivay, *Peru* 15°40′ S, 71°35′ W **137**
Chive, *Bol.* 12°23′ S, 68°37′ W **137**
Chivhu, *Zimb.* 19°2′ S, 30°52′ E **224**
Chivilcoy, *Arg.* 34°56′ S, 60°3′ W **139**
Chiwanda, *Tanzania* 11°21′ S, 34°58′ E **224**
Chiwefwe, *Zambia* 13°40′ S, 29°27′ E **224**
Chizdia, *Rom.* 45°56′ N, 21°45′ E **168**
Chizha, *Russ.* 67°8′ N, 44°18′ E **169**
Chizu, *Japan* 35°14′ N, 134°12′ E **201**
Chkalov, *Kaz.* 53°37′ N, 70°25′ E **184**
Chlef, *Alg.* 36°9′ N, 1°19′ E **150**
Chloride, *Ariz., U.S.* 35°24′ N, 114°12′ W **101**
Cho La, pass, *China* 31°55′ N, 98°43′ E **188**
Choate, *Can.* 49°27′ N, 121°26′ W **100**
Chocaya, *Bol.* 20°57′ S, 66°23′ W **137**
Chocó, adm. division, *Col.* 5°57′ N, 77°21′ W **136**
Chocontá, *Col.* 5°7′ N, 73°39′ W **136**
Chocorua, *N.H., U.S.* 43°52′ N, 71°14′ W **104**
Chocorua, Mount, *N.H., U.S.* 43°57′ N, 71°18′ W **104**
Choctawhatchee Bay 30°15′ N, 86°29′ W **80**
Chodzież, *Pol.* 52°59′ N, 16°55′ E **152**
Choele Choel, *Arg.* 39°17′ S, 65°40′ W **134**
Choggar, spring, *Mauritania* 17°20′ N, 13°47′ W **222**
Chogyuryong Sanmaek, *N. Korea* 40°18′ N, 126°6′ E **200**
Choique Mahuida, Sierra, *Arg.* 38°24′ S, 67°41′ W **134**
Choirokoitia, *Cyprus* 34°47′ N, 33°20′ E **194**
Choiseul, island, *Solomon Islands* 7°0′ S, 157°0′ E **242**
Choisy, *Fr.* 48°46′ N, 2°24′ E **163**
Choix, *Mex.* 26°42′ N, 108°22′ W **112**
Chojna, *Pol.* 52°57′ N, 14°26′ E **152**
Chojnice, *Pol.* 53°41′ N, 17°33′ E **152**
Ch′ok′ē, *Eth.* 11°7′ N, 36°46′ E **182**
Chokoloskee, *Fla., U.S.* 25°48′ N, 81°22′ W **105**
Chokoyan, *Chad* 13°20′ N, 21°13′ E **216**
Chókué, *Mozambique* 24°31′ S, 32°58′ E **227**
Chokurdakh, *Russ.* 70°36′ N, 148°1′ E **160**
Cholovo, *Russ.* 58°57′ N, 30°26′ E **166**
Cholpon-Ata, *Kyrg.* 42°37′ N, 76°59′ E **184**
Ch′ŏlsan, *N. Korea* 39°45′ N, 124°38′ E **200**
Choluteca, *Hond.* 13°17′ N, 87°11′ W **115**
Choma, *Zambia* 16°49′ S, 26°57′ E **224**
Chon Buri, *Thai.* 13°25′ N, 101°1′ E **202**
Chonchi, *Chile* 42°38′ S, 73°49′ W **134**
Chŏnch′ŏn, *N. Korea* 40°39′ N, 126°28′ E **200**
Chone, *Ecua.* 0°48′ N, 80°4′ W **130**
Chong Kal, *Cambodia* 13°58′ N, 103°34′ E **202**
Chong′an, *China* 27°43′ N, 118°2′ E **198**
Ch′ongch′ŏn, river, *N. Korea* 39°45′ N, 125°51′ E **200**
Ch′ŏngdan, *N. Korea* 37°57′ N, 125°54′ E **200**
Ch′ŏngjin, *N. Korea* 41°45′ N, 129°44′ E **200**
Ch′ŏngjŏng, *N. Korea* 39°40′ N, 125°22′ E **200**
Chŏngju, *N. Korea* 39°40′ N, 125°12′ E **200**
Chongming, *China* 31°39′ N, 121°27′ E **198**
Chongming Dao, island, *China* 31°22′ N, 121°54′ E **198**
Chongoene, *Mozambique* 24°60′ S, 33°48′ E **227**
Chongoroi, *Angola* 13°36′ S, 13°58′ E **220**
Chŏngp′yŏng, *N. Korea* 39°46′ N, 127°23′ E **200**
Chongqing, *China* 29°32′ N, 106°28′ E **198**
Chongqing Shi, adm. division, *China* 31°28′ N, 108°25′ E **198**
Ch′ŏngsŏng, *N. Korea* 40°21′ N, 124°51′ E **200**
Chongsŏng, *N. Korea* 42°45′ N, 129°49′ E **200**
Chongxin, *China* 35°20′ N, 107°2′ E **198**
Chongyi, *China* 25°40′ N, 114°17′ E **198**
Chongzuo, *China* 22°22′ N, 107°24′ E **190**
Ch′ŏnnae, *N. Korea* 39°22′ N, 127°11′ E **200**
Chonogol, *Mongolia* 45°52′ N, 115°23′ E **198**
Chonos, Archipiélago de los, *South Pacific Ocean* 44°53′ S, 74°46′ W **134**
Chop, *Ukr.* 48°25′ N, 22°10′ E **152**
Chopim, river, *Braz.* 26°16′ S, 52°11′ W **139**
Chorges, *Fr.* 44°32′ N, 6°16′ E **167**
Chorley, *U.K.* 53°39′ N, 2°38′ W **162**
Chornobyl′, *Ukr.* 51°16′ N, 30°15′ E **158**
Chornomors′ke, *Ukr.* 45°29′ N, 32°43′ E **156**
Chornyy Ostriv, *Ukr.* 49°28′ N, 26°46′ E **152**
Chorotis, *Arg.* 27°53′ S, 61°24′ W **139**
Ch′osan, *N. Korea* 40°48′ N, 125°46′ E **200**
Chōshi, *Japan* 35°44′ N, 140°49′ E **201**
Chosica, *Peru* 11°54′ S, 76°45′ W **130**
Choszczno, *Pol.* 53°10′ N, 15°25′ E **152**
Choteau, *Mont., U.S.* 47°47′ N, 112°10′ W **90**
Choudrant, *La., U.S.* 32°29′ N, 92°32′ W **103**
Chouikhia, spring, *Alg.* 27°52′ N, 4°16′ W **214**
Chouzé, *Fr.* 47°14′ N, 0°7′ E **150**
Chowchilla, *Calif., U.S.* 37°6′ N, 120°17′ W **100**
Choybalsan, *Mongolia* 48°4′ N, 114°31′ E **198**
Choyr, *Mongolia* 46°14′ N, 108°44′ E **198**
Chrea National Park, *Alg.* 36°39′ N, 3°55′ E **150**
Christchurch, *N.Z.* 43°33′ S, 172°37′ E **240**
Christensen, Mount, *Antarctica* 68°2′ S, 47°46′ E **248**
Christiana, *S. Af.* 27°55′ S, 25°9′ E **227**
Christianshåb see Qasigiannguit, *Den.* 68°47′ N, 51°7′ W **106**
Christiansted, *U.S.* 17°45′ N, 64°43′ W **116**
Christie Lake, lake, *Can.* 56°52′ N, 97°30′ W **108**
Christie, Mount, *Can.* 62°56′ N, 129°59′ W **98**
Christina Falls, *Can.* 56°38′ N, 123°27′ W **108**
Christmas, *Fla., U.S.* 28°32′ N, 81°1′ W **105**
Christmas Island see Kiritimati, *Kiribati* 2°0′ N, 157°24′ W **241**
Christmas Lake Valley, *Oreg., U.S.* 43°19′ N, 120°39′ W **90**
Christmas, Mount, *Antarctica* 81°50′ S, 163°14′ E **248**
Christopher Lake, *Can.* 53°33′ N, 105°45′ W **108**
Christoval, *Tex., U.S.* 31°11′ N, 100°29′ W **92**
Chu, river, *Laos* 20°3′ N, 104°38′ E **202**
Chuacús, Sierra de, *Guatemala* 15°13′ N, 91°12′ W **115**
Chualar, *Calif., U.S.* 36°34′ N, 121°32′ W **100**
Chubb Crater see Cratère du Nouveau-Québec, *Can.* 61°19′ N, 73°41′ W **106**
Chubu Sangaku National Park, *Japan* 36°22′ N, 137°26′ E **201**
Chubut, adm. division, *Arg.* 43°44′ S, 70°18′ W **134**
Chubut, river, *Arg.* 42°36′ S, 69°41′ W **134**
Chuchi Lake, *Can.* 55°5′ N, 124°57′ W **108**
Chuckwalla Mountains, *Calif., U.S.* 33°37′ N, 115°29′ W **101**
Chudovo, *Russ.* 59°6′ N, 31°44′ E **152**
Chudz′yavr, *Russ.* 68°17′ N, 34°19′ E **152**
Chugach Mountains, *Alas., U.S.* 60°40′ N, 144°17′ W **98**
Chuginadak, island, *Alas., U.S.* 52°52′ N, 172°34′ W **160**
Chugwater, *Wyo., U.S.* 41°46′ N, 104°49′ W **90**
Chuhuyiv, *Ukr.* 49°52′ N, 36°43′ E **158**
Chukai, *Malaysia* 4°15′ N, 103°25′ E **196**
Chukchi Plain, *Arctic Ocean* 76°29′ N, 169°2′ W **255**
Chukchi Plateau, *Arctic Ocean* 78°6′ N, 163°16′ W **255**
Chukchi Sea 70°53′ N, 178°53′ W **173**
Chukhloma, *Russ.* 58°45′ N, 42°46′ E **154**
Chukotskiy, adm. division, *Russ.* 66°20′ N, 170°50′ E **160**
Chukotskiy, Mys, *Russ.* 64°15′ N, 173°3′ W **98**
Chukotskiy Poluostrov, *Russ.* 66°33′ N, 176°46′ W **98**
Chukotskoye Nagor′ye, *Russ.* 64°32′ N, 176°36′ E **73**
Chula Vista, *Calif., U.S.* 32°38′ N, 117°6′ W **101**
Chulkovo, *Russ.* 62°44′ N, 88°22′ E **169**
Chul′man, *Russ.* 56°53′ N, 124°50′ E **173**
Chulmleigh, *U.K.* 50°55′ N, 3°52′ W **162**
Chulo, *Chile* 27°19′ S, 70°13′ W **132**
Chulumani, *Bol.* 16°23′ S, 67°30′ W **137**
Chulym, *Russ.* 55°7′ N, 80°52′ E **184**
Chulym, river, *Russ.* 57°26′ N, 88°13′ E **169**
Chuma, *Bol.* 15°23′ S, 68°56′ W **137**
Chumakovo, *Russ.* 55°39′ N, 79°10′ E **184**
Chumerna, peak, *Bulg.* 42°46′ N, 25°53′ E **156**
Chumikan, *Russ.* 54°35′ N, 135°12′ E **190**
Chumphon, *Thai.* 10°29′ N, 99°11′ E **202**
Chumphon Buri, *Thai.* 15°21′ N, 103°14′ E **202**
Chumpi, *Peru* 15°7′ S, 73°45′ W **137**
Chuna, river, *Russ.* 57°48′ N, 95°37′ E **160**
Chun′an, *China* 29°37′ N, 119°9′ E **198**
Chuncheon, *S. Korea* 37°52′ N, 127°44′ E **200**
Chundikkulam, *Sri Lanka* 9°27′ N, 80°36′ E **188**
Chunga, *Zambia* 15°3′ S, 25°58′ E **224**
Chunghwa, *N. Korea* 38°52′ N, 125°48′ E **200**
Chungju, *S. Korea* 36°57′ N, 127°56′ E **200**
Chungli, *Taiwan* 24°51′ N, 121°8′ E **198**
Chŭngsan, *N. Korea* 39°5′ N, 125°22′ E **200**
Chunhua, *China* 34°48′ N, 108°36′ E **198**
Chunian, *Pak.* 30°57′ N, 73°57′ E **186**
Chunky, *Miss., U.S.* 32°18′ N, 88°55′ W **103**
Chupa, *Russ.* 66°16′ N, 33°2′ E **152**
Chuprovo, *Russ.* 64°14′ N, 46°32′ E **154**
Chuquibamba, *Peru* 15°53′ S, 72°41′ W **137**
Chuquibambilla, *Peru* 14°8′ S, 72°43′ W **137**
Chuquicamata, *Chile* 22°19′ S, 68°58′ W **137**
Chuquisaca, adm. division, *Bol.* 19°60′ S, 65°2′ W **137**
Chuquito, *Peru* 15°56′ S, 69°54′ W **137**
Chur, *Switz.* 46°51′ N, 9°31′ E **167**
Church Point, *La., U.S.* 30°22′ N, 92°14′ W **103**
Church Stretton, *U.K.* 52°32′ N, 2°49′ W **162**
Churchill, *Can.* 58°45′ N, 94°9′ W **73**
Churchill, Cape, *Can.* 58°48′ N, 93°13′ W **108**
Churchill Falls, *Can.* 53°31′ N, 64°1′ W **111**
Churchill, Mount, *Alas., U.S.* 61°24′ N, 141°56′ W **98**
Churchill, Mount, *Can.* 49°58′ N, 123°52′ W **100**
Churchill Peak, *Can.* 58°12′ N, 125°20′ W **108**
Churchill Peninsula, *Antarctica* 66°54′ S, 60°58′ W **248**
Churchill, river, *Can.* 57°44′ N, 95°11′ W **108**
Churchill, river, *Can.* 55°7′ N, 105°1′ W **72**
Churchill Rocket Research Range, *Can.* 58°39′ N, 94°6′ W **108**
Churki, *India* 23°50′ N, 83°10′ E **197**
Churkino, *Russ.* 64°3′ N, 44°17′ E **154**
Churuguara, *Venez.* 10°49′ N, 69°33′ W **136**
Chushul, *India* 33°34′ N, 78°38′ E **188**
Chuska Mountains, *N. Mex., U.S.* 36°20′ N, 109°6′ W **92**
Chusovoy, *Russ.* 58°17′ N, 57°51′ E **154**
Chusovskoy, *Russ.* 61°10′ N, 56°31′ E **154**
Chust, *Uzb.* 41°0′ N, 71°13′ E **197**
Chute Island, fall(s), *Can.* 52°5′ N, 78°59′ W **110**
Chute-des-Passes, *Can.* 49°52′ N, 71°17′ W **94**
Chutine, river, *Can.* 57°57′ N, 132°47′ W **108**
Chuuk (Truk Islands), *F.S.M.* 7°44′ N, 152°5′ E **242**
Chuvashiya, adm. division, *Russ.* 55°39′ N, 46°9′ E **154**
Chyrvonaya Slabada, *Belarus* 52°49′ N, 27°10′ E **154**
Ciacova, *Rom.* 45°30′ N, 21°7′ E **168**
Cianorte, *Braz.* 23°41′ S, 52°42′ W **138**
Ciasna, *Pol.* 50°45′ N, 18°36′ E **152**
Cibecue, *Ariz., U.S.* 34°2′ N, 110°28′ W **92**
Cibinului, Munţii, *Rom.* 45°33′ N, 23°16′ E **156**
Cibola, *Ariz., U.S.* 33°18′ N, 114°40′ W **101**
Cibolo, *Tex., U.S.* 29°32′ N, 98°14′ W **96**
Çiçekdağı, *Turk.* 39°36′ N, 34°24′ E **156**
Cicero, *Ill., U.S.* 41°49′ N, 87°46′ W **102**
Ćićevac, *Serb. and Mont.* 43°42′ N, 21°27′ E **168**
Cicuco, oil field, *Col.* 9°13′ N, 74°36′ W **136**
Cide, *Turk.* 41°53′ N, 33°0′ E **156**
Ciechanów, *Pol.* 52°52′ N, 20°37′ E **152**
Ciego de Ávila, *Cuba* 21°51′ N, 78°46′ W **116**
Ciego de Ávila, adm. division, *Cuba* 21°59′ N, 78°60′ W **116**
Ciempozuelos, *Sp.* 40°9′ N, 3°38′ W **164**
Ciénaga, *Col.* 10°59′ N, 74°14′ W **136**
Ciénaga de Oro, *Col.* 8°52′ N, 75°38′ W **136**
Cienagas de Catatumbo National Park, *Venez.* 9°19′ N, 72°17′ W **136**
Cienfuegos, *Cuba* 22°10′ N, 80°27′ W **116**
Cienfuegos, adm. division, *Cuba* 22°17′ N, 80°54′ W **116**
ierp-Gaud, *Fr.* 42°54′ N, 0°38′ E **164**
Cíes, Illas, islands, *North Atlantic Ocean* 42°5′ N, 9°35′ W **150**
Cieza, *Sp.* 38°14′ N, 1°25′ W **164**
Cifuentes, *Sp.* 40°46′ N, 2°37′ W **164**
Cihanbeyli, *Turk.* 38°39′ N, 32°54′ E **156**
Cihuatlán, *Mex.* 19°13′ N, 104°36′ W **114**
Ciiradhame, *Somalia* 10°25′ N, 49°23′ E **216**
Çikës, Maja e, peak, *Alban.* 40°11′ N, 19°33′ E **156**
Cilacap, *Indonesia* 7°39′ S, 108°54′ E **192**
Çıldır, *Turk.* 41°7′ N, 43°7′ E **195**
Cilibia, *Rom.* 45°3′ N, 27°2′ E **156**
Cilician Gates, pass, *Turk.* 37°16′ N, 34°47′ E **156**
Cilnicu, *Rom.* 44°57′ N, 23°5′ E **168**
Cim, *Bosn. and Herzg.* 43°22′ N, 17°45′ E **168**
Cima, *Calif., U.S.* 35°14′ N, 115°31′ W **101**
Cimadle, spring, *Somalia* 5°14′ N, 47°1′ E **218**
Cimarron, *Kans., U.S.* 37°48′ N, 100°21′ W **90**
Cimişlia, *Mold.* 46°31′ N, 28°48′ E **158**
Cimolais, *It.* 46°17′ N, 12°26′ E **167**
Cimone, Monte, peak, *It.* 44°11′ N, 10°40′ E **167**
Cîmpeni, *Rom.* 46°22′ N, 23°4′ E **168**
Çınar, *Turk.* 37°43′ N, 40°27′ E **195**
Cinaruco, river, *Venez.* 6°31′ N, 68°40′ W **136**
Cinaruco-Capanaparo National Park, *Venez.* 6°35′ N, 67°42′ W **136**
Cincar, peak, *Bosn. and Herzg.* 43°53′ N, 17°0′ E **168**
Cincinnati, *Ohio, U.S.* 39°6′ N, 84°32′ W **102**
Cinco Balas, Cayos, islands, *Caribbean Sea* 20°49′ N, 80°20′ W **116**
Cîndrelu, peak, *Rom.* 45°34′ N, 23°44′ E **156**
Çine, *Turk.* 37°36′ N, 28°1′ E **156**
Cinema, *Can.* 53°10′ N, 122°31′ W **108**
Ciney, *Belg.* 50°18′ N, 5°5′ E **167**
Cinnabar Mountain, *Idaho, U.S.* 42°58′ N, 116°45′ W **90**
Cintegabelle, *Fr.* 43°17′ N, 1°31′ E **164**
Cinto, Monte, peak, *Fr.* 42°22′ N, 8°52′ E **156**
Cintruénigo, *Sp.* 42°4′ N, 1°47′ W **164**
Ciovîrnăşani, *Rom.* 44°45′ N, 22°52′ E **168**
ipoal, *Braz.* 1°40′ S, 55°29′ W **130**
Circeo, Monte, peak, *It.* 41°13′ N, 12°59′ E **156**
Çırçır, *Turk.* 40°1′ N, 36°49′ E **156**
Circle, *Alas., U.S.* 65°43′ N, 144°18′ W **98**
Circle, *Mont., U.S.* 47°23′ N, 105°37′ W **90**
Circle Hot Springs, *Alas., U.S.* 65°29′ N, 144°39′ W **98**
Circleville, *Ohio, U.S.* 39°35′ N, 82°56′ W **102**
Cirebon, *Indonesia* 6°47′ S, 108°25′ E **192**
Cirencester, *U.K.* 51°42′ N, 1°58′ W **162**
Cireşu, *Rom.* 44°49′ N, 22°33′ E **168**
Ciria, *Sp.* 41°36′ N, 1°58′ W **164**
Ciriè, *It.* 45°13′ N, 7°36′ E **167**
Ciriquiri, river, *Braz.* 7°52′ S, 65°33′ W **132**
Cisco, *Ill., U.S.* 40°0′ N, 88°43′ W **102**
Cisco, *Tex., U.S.* 32°22′ N, 98°59′ W **92**
Cisco, *Utah, U.S.* 38°58′ N, 109°19′ W **90**
Cislău, *Rom.* 45°14′ N, 26°22′ E **156**
Cisne, *Ill., U.S.* 38°30′ N, 88°26′ W **102**
Cisneros, *Col.* 6°33′ N, 75°5′ W **136**
Cissna Park, *Ill., U.S.* 40°33′ N, 87°54′ W **102**
Cistern Point, *Bahamas* 23°39′ N, 77°37′ W **96**
Citaré, river, *Braz.* 1°40′ N, 55°32′ W **130**
Citra, *Fla., U.S.* 29°24′ N, 82°8′ W **105**
Citronelle, *Ala., U.S.* 31°4′ N, 88°14′ W **103**
Citrusdal, *S. Af.* 32°32′ S, 19°1′ E **227**
Cittadella, *It.* 45°39′ N, 11°46′ E **167**
City of Refuge National Historical Park see Pu′uhonua O Hōnaunau National Historical Park, *Hawai′i, U.S.* 19°24′ N, 155°57′ W **99**
City Trenton, *Mo., U.S.* 40°3′ N, 93°37′ W **94**
Ciuc, Munţii, *Rom.* 46°20′ N, 25°49′ E **156**
Ciucaş, peak, *Rom.* 45°30′ N, 25°53′ E **156**
Ciucea, *Rom.* 46°57′ N, 22°51′ E **168**
Ciudad Acuña, *Mex.* 29°17′ N, 100°57′ W **92**
Ciudad Altamirano, *Mex.* 18°20′ N, 100°41′ W **114**
Ciudad Bolívar, *Venez.* 8°4′ N, 63°34′ W **116**
Ciudad Bolivia, *Venez.* 8°19′ N, 70°36′ W **136**
Ciudad Camargo, *Mex.* 27°40′ N, 105°11′ W **112**
Ciudad Constitución, *Mex.* 25°0′ N, 111°43′ W **112**
Ciudad Cortés, *C.R.* 8°58′ N, 83°33′ W **115**
Ciudad de La Habana, adm. division, *Cuba* 23°6′ N, 82°47′ W **116**
Ciudad del Maíz, *Mex.* 22°22′ N, 99°37′ W **114**
Ciudad Guayana, *Venez.* 8°23′ N, 62°36′ W **130**
Ciudad Guerrero, *Mex.* 28°31′ N, 107°31′ W **92**
Ciudad Guzmán, *Mex.* 19°41′ N, 103°29′ W **114**
Ciudad Hidalgo, *Mex.* 14°41′ N, 92°11′ W **115**
Ciudad Hidalgo, *Mex.* 19°41′ N, 100°33′ W **114**
Ciudad Juárez, *Mex.* 31°41′ N, 106°30′ W **92**
Ciudad Lerdo, *Mex.* 25°31′ N, 103°30′ W **114**
Ciudad Madero, *Mex.* 22°15′ N, 97°49′ W **114**
Ciudad Mante, *Mex.* 22°44′ N, 98°58′ W **114**
Ciudad Mendoza, *Mex.* 18°46′ N, 97°12′ W **114**
Ciudad Obregón, *Mex.* 27°28′ N, 109°57′ W **112**
Ciudad Ojeda, *Venez.* 10°12′ N, 71°21′ W **136**
Ciudad Piar, *Venez.* 7°24′ N, 63°19′ W **130**
Ciudad Real, *Sp.* 38°58′ N, 3°56′ W **164**
Ciudad Sandino, *Cuba* 22°5′ N, 84°10′ W **116**
Ciudad Valles, *Mex.* 21°58′ N, 98°60′ W **114**
Ciudad Victoria, *Mex.* 23°42′ N, 99°12′ W **114**
Ciumeghiu, *Rom.* 46°44′ N, 21°36′ E **168**
Ciutadella de Menorca, *Sp.* 39°59′ N, 3°50′ E **164**
Civa Burnu, *Turk.* 41°23′ N, 36°28′ E **156**
Civitanova Marche, *It.* 43°18′ N, 13°43′ E **156**
Civitavecchia, *It.* 42°5′ N, 11°47′ E **156**
Çivril, *Turk.* 38°18′ N, 29°43′ E **156**
Cixian, *China* 36°22′ N, 114°24′ E **198**
Cizer, *Rom.* 47°4′ N, 22°53′ E **168**
Cizre, *Turk.* 37°19′ N, 42°8′ E **195**
Clach Leathad, peak, *U.K.* 56°35′ N, 4°58′ W **150**
Clacton on Sea, *U.K.* 51°47′ N, 1°8′ E **162**
Claiborne, *Ala., U.S.* 31°32′ N, 87°31′ W **103**
Clairmont, *Can.* 55°15′ N, 118°48′ W **108**
Claise, river, *Fr.* 46°47′ N, 0°46′ E **150**
Clallam Bay, *Wash., U.S.* 48°13′ N, 124°16′ W **100**
Clam Lake, *Wis., U.S.* 46°10′ N, 90°55′ W **94**
Clan Alpine Mountains, *Nev., U.S.* 39°27′ N, 118°20′ W **90**
Clanton, *Ala., U.S.* 32°50′ N, 86°38′ W **96**
Clanwilliam, *S. Af.* 32°10′ S, 18°54′ E **227**
Clapham, *U.K.* 54°7′ N, 2°24′ W **162**
Clara, *Miss., U.S.* 31°35′ N, 88°42′ W **103**
Clara, island, *Myanmar* 10°45′ N, 97°39′ E **202**
Clara, Punta, *Arg.* 44°11′ S, 65°11′ W **134**
Claraz, *Arg.* 37°53′ S, 59°18′ W **139**
Clare, *Mich., U.S.* 43°48′ N, 84°46′ W **102**
Claremont, *N.H., U.S.* 43°22′ N, 72°21′ W **104**
Claremore, *Okla., U.S.* 36°17′ N, 95°37′ W **96**
Clarence, *N.Z.* 42°9′ S, 173°54′ E **240**
Clarence Island, *Antarctica* 61°30′ S, 54°3′ W **134**
Clarendon, *Ark., U.S.* 34°40′ N, 91°19′ W **96**
Clarendon, *Tex., U.S.* 34°56′ N, 100°54′ W **92**
Clarendon, *Vt., U.S.* 43°31′ N, 72°59′ W **104**
Clarenville, *Can.* 48°9′ N, 53°59′ W **111**
Claresholm, *Can.* 50°1′ N, 113°35′ W **90**
Clarie Coast, *Antarctica* 67°48′ S, 136°42′ E **248**
Clarinda, *Iowa, U.S.* 40°43′ N, 95°3′ W **94**
Clarines, *Venez.* 10°0′ N, 65°10′ W **136**
Clarion, *Iowa, U.S.* 42°42′ N, 93°44′ W **94**
Clarion, *Pa., U.S.* 41°12′ N, 79°23′ W **94**
Clarion Fracture Zone, *North Pacific Ocean* 17°0′ N, 130°47′ W **252**
Clarión, Isla, island, *Mex.* 18°27′ N, 115°40′ W **112**
Clark, *S. Dak., U.S.* 44°52′ N, 97°45′ W **90**
Clark Fork, *Idaho, U.S.* 48°8′ N, 116°11′ W **108**
Clark, Mount, peak, *Can.* 64°21′ N, 124°7′ W **98**
Clark Mountain, *Calif., U.S.* 35°31′ N, 115°37′ W **101**
Clark Peak, *Colo., U.S.* 40°35′ N, 105°60′ W **90**
Clark, Point, *Can.* 44°4′ N, 81°54′ W **102**
Clarkdale, *Ariz., U.S.* 34°46′ N, 112°3′ W **92**
Clarke City, *Can.* 50°10′ N, 66°37′ W **111**
Clarke Island, *Austral.* 41°8′ S, 147°50′ E **230**
Clarke Range, *Austral.* 20°29′ S, 147°39′ E **230**
Clarks, *La., U.S.* 32°0′ N, 92°9′ W **103**
Clark′s Harbour, *Can.* 43°22′ N, 65°36′ W **82**
Clarks Hill Lake, *Ga., U.S.* 33°51′ N, 82°55′ W **112**
Clarksburg, *W. Va., U.S.* 39°16′ N, 80°22′ W **94**
Clarksdale, *Miss., U.S.* 34°11′ N, 90°34′ W **96**
Clarkson, *Nebr., U.S.* 41°41′ N, 97°8′ W **90**
Clarksville, *Mich., U.S.* 42°49′ N, 85°15′ W **102**
Clarksville, *Tenn., U.S.* 36°31′ N, 87°21′ W **96**
Clarksville, *Tex., U.S.* 33°36′ N, 95°4′ W **96**
Claro, river, *Braz.* 15°56′ S, 51°12′ W **138**
Claro, river, *Braz.* 18°8′ S, 51°41′ W **138**
Clary, *Fr.* 50°4′ N, 3°24′ E **163**
Clatskanie, *Oreg., U.S.* 46°5′ N, 123°13′ W **100**
Claude, *Tex., U.S.* 35°6′ N, 101°22′ W **92**
Claveria, *Philippines* 18°36′ N, 121°5′ E **203**
Clavering Ø, island, *Den.* 73°50′ N, 19°47′ W **246**
Clawson, *Utah, U.S.* 39°8′ N, 111°6′ W **90**
Claxton, *Ga., U.S.* 32°9′ N, 81°55′ W **96**
Clay, *Ky., U.S.* 37°28′ N, 87°50′ W **96**
Clay Center, *Kans., U.S.* 39°21′ N, 97°8′ W **90**
Clay City, *Ill., U.S.* 38°40′ N, 88°22′ W **102**
Clay City, *Ind., U.S.* 39°16′ N, 87°7′ W **102**
Claymore, oil field, *U.K.* 58°26′ N, 0°26′ E **150**
Clayoquot Sound 49°13′ N, 126°37′ W **90**
Clayton, *Ala., U.S.* 31°52′ N, 85°27′ W **96**
Clayton, *Ind., U.S.* 39°40′ N, 86°32′ W **102**
Clayton, *La., U.S.* 31°42′ N, 91°34′ W **103**
Clayton, *N. Mex., U.S.* 36°26′ N, 103°11′ W **92**
Clayton, *N.Y., U.S.* 44°13′ N, 76°5′ W **94**
Clayton, *Okla., U.S.* 34°33′ N, 95°21′ W **96**
Clayton Lake, *Me., U.S.* 46°36′ N, 69°34′ W **94**
Cle Elum, *Wash., U.S.* 47°11′ N, 120°58′ W **100**
Clear, *Alas., U.S.* 64°26′ N, 148°30′ W **73**
Clear, Cape, *Ire.* 51°14′ N, 9°28′ W **150**
Clear Hills, *Can.* 56°29′ N, 119°50′ W **108**
Clear Lake, *S. Dak., U.S.* 44°44′ N, 96°42′ W **90**
Clear Lake, *Wash., U.S.* 48°27′ N, 122°14′ W **100**
Clear Lake, *Wis., U.S.* 45°14′ N, 92°17′ W **110**

Clear Lake Reservoir, Calif., U.S. 41°45′ N, 122°46′ W 81
Clearfield, Utah, U.S. 41°6′ N, 112°2′ W 90
Clearmont, Wyo., U.S. 44°36′ N, 106°23′ W 90
Clearwater, Fla., U.S. 27°57′ N, 82°47′ W 105
Clearwater, Wash., U.S. 47°34′ N, 124°16′ W 100
Clearwater Lake, lake, Can. 52°15′ N, 120°43′ W 108
Clearwater Lake, lake, Can. 54°4′ N, 101°37′ W 108
Clearwater Mountains, Idaho, U.S. 45°47′ N, 116°18′ W 90
Clearwater, river, Can. 51°58′ N, 115°52′ W 90
Clearwater, river, Can. 56°41′ N, 111°1′ W 108
Cleburne, Tex., U.S. 32°20′ N, 97°23′ W 92
Clee Hills, U.K. 52°27′ N, 2°39′ W 162
Cleethorpes, U.K. 53°32′ N, 4°237′ W 162
Clemence Massif, Antarctica 72°14′ S, 68°11′ E 248
Clendenin, W. Va., U.S. 38°28′ N, 81°21′ W 102
Cleopatra Needle, peak, Philippines 10°8′ N, 118°55′ E 203
Clermont, Fla., U.S. 28°32′ N, 81°46′ W 105
Clermont, Fr. 49°22′ N, 2°24′ E 163
Clermont-en-Argonne, Fr. 49°6′ N, 5°3′ E 163
Clermont-Ferrand, Fr. 45°46′ N, 3°5′ E 150
Cles, It. 46°22′ N, 11°2′ E 167
Clevedon, U.K. 51°26′ N, 2°51′ W 162
Cleveland, Miss., U.S. 33°45′ N, 90°47′ W 112
Cleveland, Ohio, U.S. 41°29′ N, 81°40′ W 102
Cleveland, Okla., U.S. 36°17′ N, 96°28′ W 96
Cleveland, Tex., U.S. 30°20′ N, 95°5′ W 103
Cleveland, Wis., U.S. 43°54′ N, 87°45′ W 102
Cleveland Heights, Ohio, U.S. 41°29′ N, 81°34′ W 102
Cleveland Hills, U.K. 54°24′ N, 1°7′ W 162
Cleveland, Mount, Mont., U.S. 48°53′ N, 113°56′ W 90
Clevelândia, Braz. 26°23′ S, 52°24′ W 139
Cleveleys, U.K. 53°52′ N, 3°2′ W 162
Clewiston, Fla., U.S. 26°45′ N, 80°56′ W 105
Cliff, N. Mex., U.S. 32°57′ N, 108°36′ W 92
Cliff Palace, site, Colo., U.S. 37°8′ N, 108°32′ W 92
Clifford, Can. 43°57′ N, 80°58′ W 102
Clifton, Ariz., U.S. 33°3′ N, 109°18′ W 112
Clifton, Ill., U.S. 40°55′ N, 87°56′ W 102
Clifton, Kans., U.S. 39°33′ N, 97°17′ W 90
Clifton, N.J., U.S. 40°52′ N, 74°10′ W 104
Clifton, Tex., U.S. 31°45′ N, 97°35′ W 92
Clifton Forge, Va., U.S. 37°48′ N, 79°50′ W 94
Clifton Park, N.Y., U.S. 42°51′ N, 73°47′ W 104
Climax, Can. 49°11′ N, 108°23′ W 90
Climax, Mich., U.S. 42°13′ N, 85°20′ W 102
Clinch Mountain, Va., U.S. 36°44′ N, 82°30′ W 96
Clinch, river, Va., U.S. 36°20′ N, 83°2′ W 80
Clingmans Dome, Tenn., U.S. 35°33′ N, 83°36′ W 96
Clint, Tex., U.S. 31°34′ N, 106°13′ W 92
Clinton, Ala., U.S. 32°54′ N, 87°59′ W 103
Clinton, Can. 51°6′ N, 121°35′ W 90
Clinton, Can. 43°36′ N, 81°33′ W 102
Clinton, Conn., U.S. 41°16′ N, 72°32′ W 104
Clinton, Ill., U.S. 40°9′ N, 88°58′ W 102
Clinton, Ind., U.S. 39°38′ N, 87°25′ W 94
Clinton, Iowa, U.S. 41°50′ N, 90°12′ W 102
Clinton, Ky., U.S. 36°40′ N, 88°58′ W 96
Clinton, La., U.S. 30°51′ N, 91°2′ W 103
Clinton, Mass., U.S. 42°24′ N, 71°42′ W 104
Clinton, Mich., U.S. 42°3′ N, 83°57′ W 102
Clinton, Miss., U.S. 32°19′ N, 90°20′ W 103
Clinton, Mo., U.S. 40°9′ N, 88°58′ W 94
Clinton, Mo., U.S. 38°21′ N, 93°46′ W 94
Clinton, N.Z. 46°14′ S, 169°22′ E 240
Clinton, Okla., U.S. 35°29′ N, 98°59′ W 96
Clinton, Wash., U.S. 47°57′ N, 122°23′ W 100
Clinton, Wis., U.S. 42°33′ N, 88°52′ W 102
Clio, Mich., U.S. 43°10′ N, 83°44′ W 102
Clion, Fr. 46°56′ N, 1°13′ E 150
Clipper Mountains, Calif., U.S. 34°44′ N, 115°26′ W 101
Clipperton Fracture Zone, North Pacific Ocean 6°22′ N, 126°9′ W 252
Clisham, peak, U.K. 57°56′ N, 6°56′ W 150
Clisson, Fr. 47°5′ N, 1°17′ W 150
Clitheroe, U.K. 53°52′ N, 2°23′ W 162
Clitor, ruin(s), Gr. 37°51′ N, 21°56′ E 156
Cliza, Bol. 17°38′ S, 65°49′ W 137
Clodomira, Arg. 27°34′ S, 64°10′ W 132
Clonakilty, Ire. 51°36′ N, 8°54′ W 150
Cloncurry, Austral. 20°38′ S, 140°31′ E 238
Clonmel, Ire. 52°22′ N, 7°42′ W 150
Clo-oose, Can. 48°39′ N, 124°49′ W 100
Clopotiva, Rom. 45°29′ N, 22°51′ E 168
Cloppenburg, Ger. 52°49′ N, 8°3′ E 163
Cloquet, Minn., U.S. 46°42′ N, 92°29′ W 94
Close, Cape, Antarctica 65°52′ S, 49°26′ E 248
Close Lake, lake, Can. 57°52′ N, 105°22′ W 108
Cloud Peak, Wyo., U.S. 44°20′ N, 107°15′ W 90
Cloutierville, La., U.S. 31°32′ N, 92°56′ W 103
Clova, Can. 48°7′ N, 75°22′ W 94
Cloverdale, Oreg., U.S. 45°11′ N, 123°57′ W 90
Clovis, Calif., U.S. 36°49′ N, 119°43′ W 100
Cluff Lake Mine, site, Can. 58°16′ N, 109°42′ W 108
Cluj, adm. division, Rom. 47°1′ N, 23°32′ E 156
Cluj-Napoca, Rom. 46°45′ N, 23°38′ E 168
Clun, U.K. 52°25′ N, 3°1′ W 162
Cluny, Fr. 46°26′ N, 4°38′ E 150
Cluny Castle, site, U.K. 57°10′ N, 2°38′ W 150
Cluny Castle, site, U.K. 57°1′ N, 4°20′ W 150
Cluses, Fr. 46°3′ N, 6°34′ E 167
Clusone, It. 45°53′ N, 9°57′ E 167
Clute, Tex., U.S. 29°0′ N, 95°24′ W 103
Clydach Vale, U.K. 51°38′ N, 3°30′ W 162
Clyde, Can. 54°8′ N, 113°38′ W 108
Clyde, Kans., U.S. 39°34′ N, 97°25′ W 90
Clyde, N.Z. 45°11′ S, 169°19′ E 240
Clyde, Ohio, U.S. 41°18′ N, 82°58′ W 102
Clyde, Tex., U.S. 32°24′ N, 99°30′ W 92
Clyde River, Can. 70°28′ N, 68°35′ W 106
Ćmielów, Pol. 50°52′ N, 21°31′ E 152
Cnalwa, Western Sahara 24°51′ N, 13°55′ W 214
Cnoc Moy, peak, U.K. 55°21′ N, 5°53′ W 150
Cnossus (Knosós), ruin(s), Gr. 35°16′ N, 25°4′ E 156
Coachella, Calif., U.S. 33°41′ N, 116°11′ W 101
Coacoachou, Lac, lake, Can. 50°20′ N, 60°58′ W 111
Coahoma, Tex., U.S. 32°17′ N, 101°19′ W 92
Coahuayana, Mex. 18°42′ N, 103°42′ W 114
Coahuila, adm. division, Mex. 25°38′ N, 102°51′ W 114
Coal City, Ill., U.S. 41°16′ N, 88°17′ W 102
Coal Creek, Colo., U.S. 38°21′ N, 105°9′ W 92
Coal Creek, N.Z. 45°30′ S, 169°17′ E 240
Coal River, Can. 59°39′ N, 126°54′ W 108
Coal, river, Can. 60°59′ N, 127°40′ W 108
Coala, Burkina Faso 13°24′ N, 0°8′ E 222
Coalane, Mozambique 17°50′ S, 36°58′ E 224
Coalcomán, Mex. 18°46′ N, 103°9′ W 114
Coaldale, Can. 49°43′ N, 112°37′ W 90
Coaldale, Nev., U.S. 38°2′ N, 117°54′ W 90
Coalgate, Okla., U.S. 34°30′ N, 96°13′ W 96
Coalinga, Calif., U.S. 36°8′ N, 120°23′ W 100
Coalsack Bluff, peak, Antarctica 84°10′ S, 164°12′ E 248
Coalspur, Can. 53°10′ N, 117°3′ W 108
Coalton, Ohio, U.S. 39°6′ N, 82°37′ W 102
Coalville, U.K. 52°43′ N, 1°23′ W 162
Coaraci, Braz. 14°38′ S, 39°34′ W 138
Coarsegold, Calif., U.S. 37°15′ N, 119°43′ W 100
Coasa, Peru 14°9′ S, 70°1′ W 137
Coast Mountains, North America 50°29′ N, 123°30′ W 90
Coast Ranges, North America 35°42′ N, 120°54′ W 100
Coats Island, Can. 62°25′ N, 86°9′ W 106
Coats Land, region, Antarctica 77°21′ S, 31°9′ W 248
Coatzacoalcos, Mex. 18°7′ N, 94°26′ W 114
Cobá, ruin(s), Mex. 20°32′ N, 87°45′ W 115
Cobadin, Rom. 44°3′ N, 28°13′ E 156
Cobalt, Can. 47°23′ N, 79°40′ W 94
Cobán, Guatemala 15°30′ N, 90°21′ W 115
Cobble Hill, Can. 48°40′ N, 123°38′ W 100
Cobden, Mo., U.S. 37°31′ N, 89°15′ W 96
Cobequid Bay 45°15′ N, 63°36′ W 111
Cobh, Ire. 51°58′ N, 8°7′ W 143
Cobham, river, Can. 52°55′ N, 95°12′ W 108
Cobija, Bol. 11°1′ S, 68°46′ W 137
Cobija, Punta, Chile 22°49′ S, 70°20′ W 137
Cobol, Alas., U.S. 57°30′ N, 135°52′ W 108
Cobos, Mex. 20°54′ N, 97°22′ W 114
Cobourg, Can. 43°57′ N, 78°11′ W 94
Cobourg Peninsula, Austral. 11°33′ S, 131°12′ E 192
Cobre, Barranca de, Mex. 27°14′ N, 108°19′ W 112
Cóbuè, Mozambique 12°9′ S, 34°47′ E 224
Coburg Island, Can. 75°37′ N, 78°52′ W 106
Coburn Mountain, Me., U.S. 45°27′ N, 70°13′ W 94
Coca, river, Ecua. 8°474′ S, 77°17′ W 136
Cocachacra, Peru 17°9′ S, 71°45′ W 137
Cocalinho, Braz. 14°21′ S, 51°3′ W 138
Cocanada see Kakinada, India 16°59′ N, 82°15′ E 188
Cocentaina, Sp. 38°44′ N, 0°27′ E 164
Cochabamba, Bol. 17°25′ S, 66°4′ W 137
Cochabamba, adm. division, Bol. 17°21′ S, 66°50′ W 137
Coche, Isla, island, Venez. 10°35′ N, 64°7′ W 116
Cochem, Ger. 50°8′ N, 7°8′ E 167
Cochetopa Hills, Colo., U.S. 38°19′ N, 106°38′ W 90
Cochin, India 9°50′ N, 76°24′ E 173
Cochinoca, Arg. 22°44′ S, 65°55′ W 137
Cochise Head, peak, Ariz., U.S. 32°2′ N, 109°21′ W 92
Cochrane, Can. 51°12′ N, 114°28′ W 90
Cochrane, Can. 49°4′ N, 81°3′ W 94
Cochrane, Chile 47°12′ S, 72°34′ W 134
Cochrane, river, Can. 57°55′ N, 101°12′ W 108
Cockburn Town, Bahamas 21°26′ N, 71°9′ W 116
Cockermouth, U.K. 54°40′ N, 3°21′ W 162
Coco, Cayo, island, Cuba 22°29′ N, 78°16′ W 116
Coco, Isla del, island, C.R. 5°31′ N, 87°1′ W 115
Coco, river, North America 14°43′ N, 83°44′ W 115
Cocoa, Fla., U.S. 28°22′ N, 80°45′ W 105
Cocoa Beach, Fla., U.S. 28°19′ N, 80°37′ W 105
Cocobeach, Gabon 0°59′ N, 9°36′ E 218
Coco-de-Mer Seamounts, Indian Ocean 0°41′ N, 55°21′ E 254
Coconino Plateau, Ariz., U.S. 35°28′ N, 112°21′ W 92
Cócorit, Mex. 27°33′ N, 109°58′ W 112
Cocos, Braz. 14°9′ S, 44°33′ W 138
Cocos Ridge, North Pacific Ocean 5°28′ N, 84°55′ W 253
Cocula, Mex. 18°13′ N, 99°39′ W 114
Cocula, Mex. 20°21′ N, 103°51′ W 114
Cocxá, river, Braz. 14°48′ S, 44°60′ W 138
Cod Bay, Cape 41°48′ N, 70°19′ W 104
Cod, Cape, U.S. 41°36′ N, 70°38′ W 104
Cod Island, Can. 57°41′ N, 61°35′ W 106
Coda Cavallo, Capo, It. 40°49′ N, 9°44′ E 156
Codajás, Braz. 3°50′ S, 62°4′ W 130
Codigoro, It. 44°50′ N, 12°6′ E 167
Codó, Braz. 4°30′ S, 43°53′ W 132
Codogno, It. 45°9′ N, 9°41′ E 167
Codpa, Chile 18°51′ S, 69°47′ W 137
Codrington, Mount, Antarctica 66°22′ S, 52°35′ E 248
Codroipo, It. 45°57′ N, 12°59′ E 167
Codru, Munţii, Rom. 46°22′ N, 22°20′ E 168
Cody, Nebr., U.S. 42°55′ N, 101°15′ W 90
Cody, Wyo., U.S. 44°30′ N, 109°3′ W 90
Coelho Neto, Braz. 4°18′ S, 43°3′ W 132
Coen, Austral. 13°58′ S, 143°12′ E 238
Coen, river, Austral. 13°29′ S, 142°21′ E 230
Coesfeld, Ger. 51°57′ N, 7°9′ E 167
Coeur d'Alene, Idaho, U.S. 47°39′ N, 116°47′ W 82
Coevorden, Neth. 52°40′ N, 6°43′ E 163
Coffeen, Ill., U.S. 39°6′ N, 89°24′ W 102
Coffeeville, Ala., U.S. 31°44′ N, 88°5′ W 103
Cofre de Perote (Nauhcampatépetl), peak, Mex. 19°27′ N, 97°13′ W 114
Cofrentes, Sp. 39°13′ N, 1°5′ W 164
Cogealac, Rom. 44°33′ N, 28°32′ E 156
Coglar Buttes, peak, Oreg., U.S. 42°40′ N, 120°29′ W 90
Cogoleto, It. 44°23′ N, 8°39′ E 156
Cogollos, Sp. 42°11′ N, 3°42′ W 164
Cogolludo, Sp. 40°56′ N, 3°5′ W 164
Cohagen, Mont., U.S. 47°2′ N, 106°38′ W 90
Cohasset, Mass., U.S. 42°14′ N, 70°49′ W 104
Cohay, Miss., U.S. 31°55′ N, 89°36′ W 103
Cohoes, N.Y., U.S. 42°46′ N, 73°44′ W 104
Coiba, Isla de, island, Pan. 7°41′ N, 81°59′ W 115
Coihaique, Chile 45°30′ S, 72°4′ W 134
Coila, Miss., U.S. 33°22′ N, 89°57′ W 103
Coimbatore, India 11°1′ N, 76°55′ E 188
Coimbra, Port. 40°12′ N, 8°26′ W 150
Coimbra, adm. division, Port. 40°6′ N, 8°53′ W 150
Coín, Sp. 36°38′ N, 4°46′ W 164
Coin, Île du, island, U.K. 5°53′ S, 71°36′ E 188
Coipasa, Lago de, lake, Bol. 19°15′ S, 68°35′ W 137
Cojata, Peru 15°5′ S, 69°23′ W 137
Cojedes, adm. division, Venez. 9°19′ N, 68°47′ W 136
Cojedes, river, Venez. 9°21′ N, 68°59′ W 136
Cojimíes, Boca de 0°10′ N, 80°30′ W 130
Cojocna, Rom. 46°45′ N, 23°50′ E 156
Cojutepeque, El Salv. 13°43′ N, 88°58′ W 115
Cokato, Minn., U.S. 45°3′ N, 94°12′ W 90
Cokeville, Wyo., U.S. 42°5′ N, 110°56′ W 90
Coki, Senegal 15°31′ N, 15°59′ W 222
Colatina, Braz. 19°37′ S, 40°40′ W 138
Cölbe, Ger. 50°51′ N, 8°46′ E 167
Colbeck Archipelago, islands, Indian Ocean 66°50′ S, 61°31′ E 248
Colborne, Can. 44°0′ N, 77°53′ W 94
Colby, Kans., U.S. 39°23′ N, 101°4′ W 90
Colby, Wis., U.S. 44°54′ N, 90°19′ W 94
Colchester, Conn., U.S. 41°34′ N, 72°20′ W 104
Colchester, U.K. 51°53′ N, 0°53′ E 162
Colchester, Vt., U.S. 44°32′ N, 73°9′ W 104
Cold Lake, Can. 55°7′ N, 101°8′ W 108
Cold Lake, Can. 54°26′ N, 110°12′ W 108
Cold Spring, Minn., U.S. 45°26′ N, 94°27′ W 90
Coldspring, Tex., U.S. 30°34′ N, 95°8′ W 103
Coldwater, Kans., U.S. 37°15′ N, 99°20′ W 96
Coldwater, Mich., U.S. 41°56′ N, 84°60′ W 102
Coldwater, Ohio, U.S. 40°28′ N, 84°37′ W 102
Coleman, Fla., U.S. 28°47′ N, 82°5′ W 105
Coleman, Mich., U.S. 43°45′ N, 84°35′ W 102
Coleman, Tex., U.S. 31°48′ N, 99°26′ W 92
Coleraine, Can. 45°57′ N, 71°22′ W 111
Coles, Miss., U.S. 31°15′ N, 91°1′ W 103
Coles, Punta, Peru 17°53′ S, 71°41′ W 137
Colesberg, S. Af. 30°42′ S, 25°4′ E 227
Coleville, Can. 51°44′ N, 109°15′ W 90
Colfax, Calif., U.S. 39°6′ N, 120°58′ W 90
Colfax, Ill., U.S. 40°33′ N, 88°37′ W 102
Colfax, Iowa, U.S. 41°39′ N, 93°14′ W 94
Colfax, La., U.S. 31°30′ N, 92°43′ W 103
Colfax, Wash., U.S. 46°51′ N, 117°23′ W 90
Colico, It. 46°8′ N, 9°22′ E 167
Colima, Mex. 19°12′ N, 103°46′ W 114
Colima, adm. division, Mex. 18°57′ N, 104°8′ W 114
Colima, Nevado de, peak, Mex. 19°32′ N, 103°40′ W 114
Colin Lake, lake, Can. 59°31′ N, 110°38′ W 108
Colinas, Braz. 6°5′ S, 44°15′ W 132
Colinton, Can. 54°37′ N, 113°16′ W 108
Collaguasi, Chile 20°60′ S, 68°45′ W 137
Colleen Bawn, Zimb. 20°57′ S, 29°12′ E 227
Colleymount, Can. 54°2′ N, 126°11′ W 108
Collie, Austral. 33°20′ S, 116°11′ E 231
Collier Bay 16°14′ S, 122°5′ E 238
Collier, Cape, Antarctica 70°14′ S, 60°48′ W 248
Colliers Point, U.K. 19°15′ N, 81°4′ W 115
Collierville, Tenn., U.S. 35°2′ N, 89°40′ W 96
Collingwood, Can. 44°29′ N, 80°12′ W 94
Collingwood, N.Z. 40°44′ S, 172°40′ E 240
Collins, Can. 50°17′ N, 89°27′ W 94
Collins, Miss., U.S. 31°39′ N, 89°33′ W 103
Collinson Peninsula, Can. 69°51′ N, 101°10′ W 106
Collinston, La., U.S. 32°40′ N, 91°52′ W 103
Collinsville, Conn., U.S. 41°48′ N, 72°55′ W 104
Collinsville, Ill., U.S. 38°39′ N, 89°59′ W 102
Collinsville, Va., U.S. 36°43′ N, 79°56′ W 94
Collipulli, Chile 37°58′ S, 72°29′ W 134
Colmar, Fr. 48°4′ N, 7°21′ E 150
Colmena, Arg. 28°43′ S, 60°8′ W 139
Colmenar, Sp. 36°54′ N, 4°21′ W 164
Colmenar Viejo, Sp. 40°38′ N, 3°46′ W 164
Colmesneil, Tex., U.S. 30°53′ N, 94°25′ W 103
Colne, U.K. 53°51′ N, 2°10′ W 162
Cologne see Köln, Ger. 50°56′ N, 6°57′ E 167
Coloma, Mich., U.S. 42°10′ N, 86°17′ W 102
Coloma, Wis., U.S. 44°1′ N, 89°31′ W 102
Colombey-les-Belles, Fr. 48°31′ N, 5°53′ E 163
Colombey-les-Deux-Églises, Fr. 48°13′ N, 4°52′ E 163
Colombia 3°30′ N, 74°40′ W 130
Colombia, Braz. 20°12′ S, 48°41′ W 138
Colombo, Sri Lanka 6°51′ N, 79°38′ E 188
Colón, Arg. 32°14′ S, 58°8′ W 139
Colón, Arg. 33°55′ S, 61°4′ W 139
Colón, Cuba 22°43′ N, 80°54′ W 116
Colon, Mich., U.S. 41°56′ N, 85°19′ W 102
Colón, Pan. 9°22′ N, 79°54′ W 115
Colón, Venez. 2°7′ N, 67°7′ W 136
Colón, Isla, island, Pan. 9°4′ N, 82°35′ W 115
Colonet, Mex. 31°0′ N, 116°14′ W 92
Colonia 25 de Mayo, Arg. 37°50′ S, 67°42′ W 134
Colonia Dora, Arg. 28°36′ S, 62°58′ W 139
Colonia Elisa, Arg. 26°55′ S, 59°31′ W 139
Colonia Montefiore, Arg. 29°41′ S, 61°51′ W 139
Colonia Morelos, Mex. 30°48′ N, 109°12′ W 92
Colonia Penal del Sepa, Peru 10°51′ S, 73°15′ W 137
Colophon, ruin(s), Turk. 38°4′ N, 27°2′ E 156
Colorada, Laguna, lake, Arg. 44°50′ S, 68°60′ W 134
Colorada, Laguna, lake, Bol. 22°12′ S, 68°5′ W 137
Coloradas, Lomas, Arg. 43°26′ S, 67°31′ W 134
Colorado, adm. division, Colo., U.S. 38°49′ N, 106°40′ W 92
Colorado City, Tex., U.S. 32°23′ N, 100°52′ W 96
Colorado Desert, Calif., U.S. 33°8′ N, 116°5′ W 101
Colorado Plateau, North America 36°28′ N, 113°46′ W 101
Colorado, river, Arg. 39°27′ S, 63°4′ W 139
Colorado, river, Braz. 13°1′ S, 62°22′ W 132
Colorado, river, Mex.-U.S. 36°51′ N, 109°48′ W 238
Colorado Springs, Colo., U.S. 38°49′ N, 104°49′ W 90
Colorno, It. 44°55′ N, 10°21′ E 167
Colotepec, Mex. 15°52′ N, 96°57′ W 112
Colotlán, Mex. 22°6′ N, 103°15′ W 114
Colotlán, river, Mex. 22°1′ N, 103°44′ W 114
Colquechaca, Bol. 18°43′ S, 66°3′ W 137
Colquemarca, Peru 14°20′ S, 72°3′ W 137
Colquiri, Bol. 17°27′ S, 67°10′ W 137
Colquitt, Ga., U.S. 31°9′ N, 84°43′ W 96
Colrain, Mass., U.S. 42°40′ N, 72°42′ W 104
Colstrip, Mont., U.S. 45°52′ N, 106°39′ W 90
Columbia, Calif., U.S. 38°2′ N, 120°25′ W 100
Columbia, Ky., U.S. 37°5′ N, 85°18′ W 96
Columbia, La., U.S. 32°4′ N, 92°5′ W 103
Columbia, Miss., U.S. 31°15′ N, 89°51′ W 103
Columbia, Mo., U.S. 38°56′ N, 92°20′ W 94
Columbia, N.C., U.S. 35°54′ N, 76°16′ W 96
Columbia, S.C., U.S. 33°58′ N, 81°6′ W 96
Columbia, Tenn., U.S. 35°36′ N, 87°2′ W 96
Columbia, Cape, Can. 82°47′ N, 87°54′ W 246
Columbia City, Oreg., U.S. 45°52′ N, 122°50′ W 100
Columbia Lake, Can. 50°11′ N, 116°15′ W 108
Columbia, Mount, Can. 52°7′ N, 117°34′ W 108
Columbia Mountains, Can. 51°18′ N, 119°5′ W 80
Columbine, Cape, S. Af. 32°46′ S, 17°14′ E 227
Columbretes, Islas, islands, Balearic Sea 39°48′ N, 0°44′ E 164
Columbus, Ga., U.S. 32°27′ N, 84°59′ W 96
Columbus, Ind., U.S. 39°12′ N, 85°54′ W 102
Columbus, Miss., U.S. 33°28′ N, 88°25′ W 96
Columbus, Mont., U.S. 45°38′ N, 109°14′ W 90
Columbus, Nebr., U.S. 41°25′ N, 97°22′ W 90
Columbus, N. Mex., U.S. 31°49′ N, 107°38′ W 92
Columbus, N. Dak., U.S. 48°52′ N, 102°47′ W 90
Columbus, Ohio, U.S. 39°57′ N, 83°4′ W 102
Columbus, Tex., U.S. 29°41′ N, 96°32′ W 96
Columbus, Wis., U.S. 43°20′ N, 89°2′ W 102
Columbus Grove, Ohio, U.S. 40°54′ N, 84°4′ W 102
Columbus Monument, site, Bahamas 24°4′ N, 74°33′ W 116
Colupo, Cerro, peak, Chile 22°27′ S, 70°5′ W 137
Colville, N.Z. 36°40′ S, 175°29′ E 240
Colville, Wash., U.S. 48°32′ N, 117°54′ W 90
Colville, Cape, N.Z. 36°28′ S, 175°4′ E 240
Colville Lake, Can. 67°11′ N, 127°42′ W 98
Colville Lake, Can. 67°8′ N, 126°23′ W 98
Colville, river, Alas., U.S. 68°56′ N, 154°2′ W 98
Colwyn Bay, U.K. 53°17′ N, 3°43′ W 162
Comacchio, It. 44°42′ N, 12°11′ E 167
Comai, China 28°26′ N, 91°30′ E 197
Comala, Mex. 19°19′ N, 103°46′ W 114
Comallo, Arg. 40°60′ S, 70°15′ W 134
Coman, Mount, Antarctica 73°52′ S, 64°56′ W 248
Comanche, Okla., U.S. 34°21′ N, 97°57′ W 92
Comanche, Tex., U.S. 31°53′ N, 98°36′ W 92
Comandante Ferraz, station, Antarctica 62°2′ S, 58°22′ W 134
Comandante Fontana, Arg. 25°22′ S, 59°39′ W 132
Comandante N. Otamendi, Arg. 38°8′ S, 57°51′ W 139
Comarapa, Bol. 17°56′ S, 64°34′ W 137
Comaton, Eth. 7°39′ N, 34°23′ E 224
Comayagua, Hond. 14°27′ N, 87°37′ W 115
Combe Martin, U.K. 51°12′ N, 4°1′ W 162
Comber, Can. 42°14′ N, 82°33′ W 102
Comblain, Belg. 50°29′ N, 5°34′ E 167
Combs, Ky., U.S. 37°16′ N, 83°14′ W 96
Comendador, Dom. Rep. 18°53′ N, 71°41′ W 116
Comercinho, Braz. 16°18′ S, 41°50′ W 138
Comfort, Tex., U.S. 29°57′ N, 98°55′ W 92
Comilla, Bangladesh 23°24′ N, 91°6′ E 197
Comino, Capo, It. 40°27′ N, 9°51′ E 156
Comitán, Mex. 16°15′ N, 92°8′ W 115
Comloşu Mare, Rom. 45°52′ N, 20°38′ E 168
Commander Islands see Komandorskiye Ostrova, Bering Sea 53°42′ N, 162°31′ E 160
Commerce, Okla., U.S. 36°55′ N, 94°53′ W 96
Commercy, Fr. 48°45′ N, 5°34′ E 163
Commissaires, Lac des, lake, Can. 48°6′ N, 73°11′ W 111
Committee Bay 68°41′ N, 89°55′ W 106
Communism Peak see Ismoili Somoni, Qullai, Taj. 39°3′ N, 72°1′ E 197
Como, It. 45°48′ N, 9°5′ E 167
Como, Miss., U.S. 34°30′ N, 89°56′ W 96
Como, Tex., U.S. 33°3′ N, 95°28′ W 103
Como Bluff Fossil Beds, site, Wyo., U.S. 41°51′ N, 106°8′ W 90
Como, Lago di, lake, It. 46°3′ N, 9°1′ E 167
Como, Mount, Nev., U.S. 39°0′ N, 119°34′ W 90
Comodoro Rivadavia, Arg. 45°49′ S, 67°32′ W 134
Comoé National Park, Côte d'Ivoire 9°10′ N, 3°55′ W 222
Comorişte, Rom. 45°11′ N, 21°33′ E 168
Comoros 12°0′ S, 43°0′ E 220
Comoros, islands, Mozambique Channel 11°7′ S, 41°17′ E 207
Comox, Can. 49°40′ N, 124°54′ W 100
Compiègne, Fr. 49°24′ N, 2°49′ E 163
Compostela, Mex. 21°14′ N, 104°55′ W 114
Compostela, Philippines 7°42′ N, 126°3′ E 203
Comrat, Mold. 46°17′ N, 28°39′ E 156
Comstock, Mich., U.S. 42°17′ N, 85°30′ W 102
Comstock Park, Mich., U.S. 43°2′ N, 85°41′ W 102
Comunidad, Venez. 2°22′ N, 67°12′ W 136
Con Cuong, Vietnam 19°2′ N, 104°53′ E 202
Con Son, Vietnam 8°43′ N, 106°38′ E 202
Cona, China 27°58′ N, 91°56′ E 197
Cona Niyeu, Arg. 41°46′ S, 67°13′ W 134
Conakry, Guinea 9°29′ N, 13°52′ W 222
Conambo, river, Ecua. 1°50′ S, 76°55′ W 136
Concarneau, Fr. 47°52′ N, 3°56′ W 150
Conceição, Braz. 7°31′ S, 38°25′ W 132
Conceição da Barra, Braz. 18°37′ S, 39°45′ W 138
Conceição das Alagoas, Braz. 19°56′ S, 48°24′ W 138
Conceição do Araguaia, Braz. 8°16′ S, 49°20′ W 130
Conceição do Maú, Braz. 3°35′ N, 59°52′ W 130
Concepción, Arg. 28°23′ S, 57°54′ W 139
Concepción, Arg. 27°23′ S, 65°36′ W 132
Concepción, Bol. 16°17′ S, 62°4′ W 132
Concepción, Bol. 11°31′ S, 66°32′ W 137
Concepción, Chile 36°49′ S, 73°3′ W 134
Concepción, Col. 0°5′ N, 75°38′ W 136
Concepción, Parag. 23°21′ S, 57°26′ W 134
Concepción de la Sierra, Arg. 27°58′ S, 55°30′ W 139
Concepción del Oro, Mex. 24°35′ N, 101°26′ W 114
Concepción del Uruguay, Arg. 32°30′ S, 58°13′ W 139
Concepción, Laguna, lake, Bol. 14°23′ S, 63°39′ W 132
Concepción, Punta, Mex. 26°55′ N, 111°50′ W 112
Conception Bay 24°7′ S, 14°14′ E 220
Conception Bay South, Can. 47°31′ N, 52°58′ W 111
Conception Island, Bahamas 23°44′ N, 75°16′ W 116
Conception, Point, Calif., U.S. 34°23′ N, 120°43′ W 100
Conchas Dam, N. Mex., U.S. 35°22′ N, 104°10′ W 92
Conchas Lake, N. Mex., U.S. 35°25′ N, 104°49′ W 81
Conches, Fr. 48°57′ N, 0°56′ E 163
Conchi, Chile 22°1′ S, 68°40′ W 137
Concho, Ariz., U.S. 34°29′ N, 109°36′ W 92
Concho, river, Tex., U.S. 31°11′ N, 100°33′ W 80
Conchos, Mex. 27°56′ N, 105°18′ W 92
Conchos, river, Mex. 29°7′ N, 105°10′ W 92
Conchos, river, Mex. 24°57′ N, 98°56′ W 114
Conchy-les-Pots, Fr. 49°34′ N, 2°41′ E 163
Concord, Calif., U.S. 37°58′ N, 122°3′ W 100
Concord, N.H., U.S. 43°11′ N, 71°35′ W 104
Concord, N.C., U.S. 35°21′ N, 80°36′ W 82
Concordia, Arg. 31°21′ S, 58°1′ W 139
Concórdia, Braz. 27°14′ S, 52°2′ W 139
Concordia, Mex. 25°46′ N, 103°7′ W 114
Concordia, Mex. 23°17′ N, 106°4′ W 114
Concordia, Peru 4°32′ S, 74°46′ W 130
Concordia, station, Antarctica 75°3′ S, 123°12′ E 248
Concrete, Wash., U.S. 48°31′ N, 121°46′ W 100
Condar, Col. 1°34′ S, 72°2′ W 136
Conde, Braz. 11°50′ S, 37°37′ W 132
Conde, S. Dak., U.S. 45°8′ N, 98°7′ W 90
Condeúba, Braz. 14°56′ S, 41°58′ W 138
Condon, Oreg., U.S. 45°13′ N, 120°11′ W 90
Condoroma, Peru 15°17′ S, 71°3′ W 137
Cone Peak, Calif., U.S. 36°2′ N, 121°33′ W 100
Conecuh, river, Ala., U.S. 31°7′ N, 87°4′ W 80
Conegliano, It. 45°52′ N, 12°16′ E 167
Conejos, Colo., U.S. 37°5′ N, 106°1′ W 92
Conero, Monte, peak, It. 43°32′ N, 13°31′ E 156
Coneto de Comonfort, Mex. 24°57′ N, 104°46′ W 114
Coney Island, N.Y., U.S. 40°34′ N, 73°59′ W 104
Conflict Group, islands, Solomon Sea 11°5′ S, 149°10′ E 230
Confusion Range, Utah, U.S. 39°21′ N, 113°58′ W 90
Confuso, river, Parag. 24°34′ S, 59°10′ W 134
Congaree National Park, S.C., U.S. 33°48′ N, 80°47′ W 97
Congaz, Mold. 46°7′ N, 28°36′ E 156
Conghua, China 23°31′ N, 113°33′ E 198
Congjiang, China 25°41′ N, 108°52′ E 198
Congleton, U.K. 53°9′ N, 2°13′ W 162
Congo 2°118′ S, 15°13′ E 218
Congo Canyon, Gulf of Guinea 6°12′ S, 10°30′ E 253
Congo, Democratic Republic of the 2°26′ S, 5°7′ E 218
Congo see Lualaba, river, Dem. Rep. of the Congo 5°35′ S, 27°7′ E 224
Congress, Ariz., U.S. 34°9′ N, 112°51′ W 92
Conibear Lake, Can. 59°35′ N, 114°3′ W 108
Conie, river, Fr. 48°7′ N, 1°25′ E 163
Conil de la Frontera, Sp. 36°16′ N, 6°6′ W 164
Coniston, Can. 46°29′ N, 80°51′ W 94
Coniston, U.K. 54°21′ N, 3°5′ W 162
Conklin, Can. 55°36′ N, 111°9′ W 108
Connantre, Fr. 48°43′ N, 3°56′ E 163
Connecticut, adm. division, Conn., U.S. 41°38′ N, 73°9′ W 104
Connecticut, river, U.S. 42°37′ N, 72°43′ W 80
Connell, Mount, Can. 49°16′ N, 115°43′ W 90
Connerré, Fr. 48°3′ N, 0°29′ E 150
Connersville, Ind., U.S. 39°38′ N, 85°9′ W 102
Conness, Mount, Calif., U.S. 37°57′ N, 119°22′ W 100
Connoire Bay 47°34′ N, 58°5′ W 111
Connor, Mount, Austral. 25°31′ S, 131°43′ E 230
Connor, Mount, Austral. 14°36′ S, 125°53′ E 230
Connors Pass, Nev., U.S. 39°2′ N, 114°39′ W 90
Cononaco, Ecua. 1°35′ S, 75°38′ W 136
Cononaco, river, Ecua. 1°17′ S, 76°17′ W 136

Conorochite, river, Venez. 2°33' N, 67°23' W 136
Conover, N.C., U.S. 35°42' N, 81°13' W 96
Conques, Sp. 42°6' N, 1°1' E 164
Conquista, Bol. 11°26' S, 67°11' W 137
Conquista, Sp. 38°24' N, 4°30' W 150
Conrad, Mont., U.S. 48°9' N, 111°55' W 90
Conradi Peak, Antarctica 66°12' S, 54°14' E 248
Conroe, Tex., U.S. 30°17' N, 95°27' W 103
Conroe, Lake, Tex., U.S. 30°18' N, 95°53' W 96
Conselheiro Lafaiete, Braz. 20°40' S, 43°48' W 138
Conselheiro Pena, Braz. 19°13' S, 41°28' W 138
Conselice, It. 44°31' N, 11°48' E 167
Consett, U.K. 54°50' N, 1°51' W 162
Consort, Can. 52°2' N, 110°47' W 90
Constância dos Baetas, Braz. 6°13' S, 62°17' W 130
Constanţa, adm. division, Rom. 44°3' N, 27°29' E 156
Constanţa, Rom. 44°10' N, 28°38' E 156
Constantina, Sp. 37°52' N, 5°38' W 164
Constantine, Mich., U.S. 41°48' N, 85°39' W 102
Constantinople see İstanbul, Turk. 41°1' N, 28°55' E 156
Constitución, Uru. 31°5' S, 57°49' W 139
Constitución de 1857, park, Mex. 31°57' N, 116°16' W 238
Consuegra, Sp. 39°27' N, 3°37' W 164
Consul, Can. 49°17' N, 109°31' W 90
Contact, Nev., U.S. 41°46' N, 114°46' W 90
Contai, India 21°49' N, 87°45' E 197
Contamana, Peru 7°22' S, 75°2' W 130
Contas, river, Braz. 13°57' S, 40°34' W 138
Continental, Ohio, U.S. 41°5' N, 84°17' W 102
Contoocook, N.H., U.S. 43°12' N, 71°43' W 104
Contramaestre, Cuba 21°11' N, 77°56' W 116
Contrexéville, Fr. 48°10' N, 5°53' E 163
Contria, Braz. 18°10' S, 44°33' W 138
Control Dam, Can. 50°23' N, 88°27' W 110
Control Dam, Can. 49°6' N, 87°29' W 110
Contwoyto Lake, Can. 65°29' N, 112°11' W 106
Convención, Col. 8°28' N, 73°23' W 136
Convent, La., U.S. 30°0' N, 90°50' W 103
Converse, Ind., U.S. 40°34' N, 85°53' W 102
Converse, La., U.S. 31°46' N, 93°42' W 103
Convoy, Ohio, U.S. 40°54' N, 84°42' W 102
Conway, Ark., U.S. 35°4' N, 92°27' W 96
Conway, Mass., U.S. 42°30' N, 72°43' W 104
Conway, N.H., U.S. 43°58' N, 71°8' W 104
Conway, S.C., U.S. 33°49' N, 79°4' W 96
Conway, Wash., U.S. 48°19' N, 122°21' W 100
Conway Range National Park, Austral. 20°30' S, 148°29' E 238
Conway Springs, Kans., U.S. 37°22' N, 97°39' W 90
Conwy, U.K. 53°17' N, 3°50' W 162
Cook, Minn., U.S. 47°50' N, 92°41' W 94
Cook, Cape, Can. 49°54' N, 128°17' W 90
Cook Inlet 58°41' N, 154°24' W 73
Cook Islands, N.Z. 13°19' S, 163°15' W 238
Cook, Mount see Aoraki, N.Z. 43°45' S, 170°4' E 240
Cook Strait 40°32' S, 173°31' E 240
Cookes Peak, N. Mex., U.S. 32°31' N, 107°48' W 92
Cookeville, Tenn., U.S. 36°9' N, 85°31' W 96
Cookhouse, S. Af. 32°46' S, 25°48' E 227
Cooktown, Austral. 15°34' S, 145°15' E 238
Coolidge, Ariz., U.S. 32°58' N, 111°33' W 82
Coolville, Ohio, U.S. 39°11' N, 81°48' W 102
Cooma, Austral. 36°14' S, 149°10' E 231
Cooper, Tex., U.S. 33°21' N, 95°42' W 103
Cooper, Mount, Can. 50°10' N, 117°18' W 90
Cooper's Town, Bahamas 26°51' N, 77°31' W 96
Cooperstown, N.Y., U.S. 42°41' N, 74°57' W 94
Cooperstown, N. Dak., U.S. 47°24' N, 98°9' W 90
Coor de Wandy, peak, Austral. 25°46' S, 115°58' E 230
Coorong, The 36°3' S, 138°4' E 230
Coos Bay, Oreg., U.S. 43°22' N, 124°17' W 82
Coosa, river, Ala., U.S. 33°46' N, 85°51' W 112
Copacabana, Bol. 16°13' S, 69°3' W 137
Copake, N.Y., U.S. 42°5' N, 73°34' W 104
Copalis Beach, Wash., U.S. 47°5' N, 124°10' W 100
Copalis Crossing, Wash., U.S. 47°5' N, 124°4' W 100
Copan, Okla., U.S. 36°52' N, 95°56' W 96
Cope, Colo., U.S. 39°39' N, 102°51' W 90
Cope, Cabo, Sp. 37°18' N, 1°29' W 164
Copenhagen see København, Den. 55°40' N, 12°23' E 152
Copero, Sp. 37°18' N, 6°1' W 164
Copetonas, Arg. 38°42' S, 60°27' W 139
Copiague, N.Y., U.S. 40°40' N, 73°24' W 104
Copiapó, Chile 27°21' S, 70°21' W 132
Coporito, Venez. 8°53' N, 61°60' W 116
Copp Lake, Can. 60°9' N, 115°13' W 108
Copper Butte, peak, Wash., U.S. 48°41' N, 118°34' W 90
Copper Harbor, Mich., U.S. 47°28' N, 87°55' W 110
Copper Mountain, Nev., U.S. 41°45' N, 115°36' W 90
Copper Nunataks, Antarctica 73°41' S, 68°29' W 248
Copper River, Can. 54°30' N, 128°30' W 108
Copperas Cove, Tex., U.S. 31°6' N, 97°54' W 92
Coppolani, Mauritania 18°20' N, 16°4' W 222
Copulhue, Paso de, pass, Chile 37°34' S, 71°9' W 134
Coqên, China 31°14' N, 85°12' E 188
Coquilhatville see Mbandaka, Dem. Rep. of the Congo 2°119' N, 18°17' E 218
Coquille Point, Oreg., U.S. 43°7' N, 124°44' W 90
Coquimatlán, Mex. 19°12' N, 103°48' W 114
Coquimbo, Chile 29°59' S, 71°23' W 134
Coquimbo, adm. division, Chile 32°2' S, 71°15' W 134
Corabia, Rom. 43°47' N, 24°30' E 156
Coração de Jesus, Braz. 16°43' S, 44°23' W 138
Coracesium see Alanya, Turk. 36°31' N, 32°1' E 180
Coracora, Peru 15°2' S, 73°48' W 137
Coral, Can. 50°12' N, 81°43' W 94
Coral Gables, Fla., U.S. 25°44' N, 80°17' W 105
Coral Harbour, Can. 64°9' N, 83°16' W 106
Coral Sea 28°58' S, 154°59' E 231
Coral Sea Basin, Coral Sea 13°56' S, 151°11' E 252
Coral Sea Islands, adm. division, Austral. 18°0' S, 148°0' E 231
Coral Springs, Fla., U.S. 26°17' N, 80°13' W 105
Coranzuli, Arg. 23°2' S, 66°27' W 137
Corbeil Point, Can. 46°52' N, 84°58' W 94
Corbett National Park, India 29°34' N, 78°41' E 197
Corbie, Fr. 49°54' N, 2°30' E 163
Corbières, Fr. 43°6' N, 2°18' E 165
Corbin, Ky., U.S. 36°56' N, 84°6' W 96
Corbu, Mold. 48°15' N, 27°35' E 152
Corby, U.K. 52°29' N, 0°41' E 162
Corcaigh see Cork, Ire. 51°54' N, 8°28' W 150
Corcoran, Calif., U.S. 36°6' N, 119°35' W 100
Corcovado National Park, C.R. 8°25' N, 83°24' W 115
Cordele, Ga., U.S. 31°57' N, 83°47' W 96
Cordell, Okla., U.S. 35°16' N, 98°60' W 92
Cordillera de Los Picachos National Park, Col. 2°44' N, 75°5' W 136
Cordiner Peaks, Antarctica 82°2' S, 68°40' W 248
Córdoba, Arg. 31°23' S, 64°10' W 139
Córdoba, Mex. 18°51' N, 96°56' W 114
Córdoba, Mex. 26°15' N, 103°26' W 114
Córdoba, Sp. 37°53' N, 4°47' W 164
Córdoba, Sp. 37°54' N, 4°48' W 214
Córdoba, adm. division, Arg. 32°19' S, 63°57' W 139
Córdoba, adm. division, Col. 8°22' N, 76°13' W 136
Córdoba, Sierras de, Arg. 32°56' S, 65°9' W 134
Cordova, Ala., U.S. 33°45' N, 87°11' W 96
Cordova, Alas., U.S. 60°25' N, 145°42' W 98
Cordova Bay 54°48' N, 132°49' W 108
Corduente, Sp. 40°50' N, 1°59' W 164
Corella, Sp. 42°6' N, 1°47' W 164
Coreses, Sp. 41°33' N, 5°38' W 150
Corey Peak, Nev., U.S. 38°26' N, 118°52' W 90
Corfu see Kérkira, island, Gr. 39°10' N, 16°33' E 143
Corguinho, Braz. 19°51' S, 54°54' W 132
Coria, Sp. 39°58' N, 6°34' W 150
Coria del Río, Sp. 37°16' N, 6°5' W 164
Coribe, Braz. 13°51' S, 44°29' W 138
Coringa Islets, Coral Sea 17°26' S, 148°17' E 230
Corinth, Miss., U.S. 34°54' N, 88°31' W 96
Corinth, N.Y., U.S. 43°14' N, 73°51' W 104
Corinto, Braz. 18°22' S, 44°31' W 138
Coripata, Bol. 16°19' S, 67°35' W 137
Corisco, island, Equatorial Guinea 0°58' N, 8°40' E 218
Cork (Corcaigh), Ire. 51°54' N, 8°28' W 150
Corkscrew Swamp Sanctuary, site, Fla., U.S. 26°22' N, 81°40' W 105
Çorlu, Turk. 41°9' N, 27°47' E 156
Cormack Lake, Can. 60°56' N, 122°28' W 108
Cormòns, It. 45°57' N, 13°29' E 167
Cormoran, Pointe au, Can. 48°59' N, 61°56' W 111
Cormorant, Can. 54°13' N, 100°37' W 108
Cornelia, Ga., U.S. 34°30' N, 83°32' W 96
Cornélio Procópio, Braz. 23°9' S, 50°43' W 138
Cornell, Ill., U.S. 40°58' N, 88°44' W 102
Cornell, Wis., U.S. 45°10' N, 91°9' W 94
Corner Brook, Can. 48°57' N, 57°58' W 111
Corner Seamounts, North Atlantic Ocean 35°31' N, 51°30' W 253
Corning, Ark., U.S. 36°24' N, 90°36' W 96
Corning, Calif., U.S. 39°55' N, 122°12' W 92
Corning, Iowa, U.S. 40°58' N, 94°46' W 94
Corning, N.Y., U.S. 42°8' N, 77°5' W 94
Cornish, Mount, Austral. 20°16' S, 126°16' E 230
Cornwall, Can. 45°1' N, 74°47' W 110
Cornwall, Conn., U.S. 41°50' N, 73°20' W 104
Cornwallis Island, Can. 74°24' N, 100°42' W 106
Coro, Venez. 11°23' N, 69°41' W 136
Coro, Golfete de 11°28' N, 70°9' W 136
Coroaci, Braz. 18°37' S, 42°18' W 138
Corocoro, Bol. 17°16' S, 68°30' W 137
Coroico, Bol. 16°11' S, 67°49' W 137
Coromandel, Braz. 18°28' S, 47°13' W 138
Coromandel, N.Z. 36°47' S, 175°30' E 240
Coromandel Peninsula, N.Z. 36°59' S, 175°18' E 240
Corona, Calif., U.S. 33°52' N, 117°35' W 101
Corona, N. Mex., U.S. 34°15' N, 105°35' W 92
Coronado, Calif., U.S. 32°41' N, 117°11' W 101
Coronado, Bahía de 8°50' N, 84°21' W 115
Coronados, Islas, islands, Pacific Ocean 32°27' N, 117°47' W 101
Coronation, Can. 52°5' N, 111°28' W 90
Coronation Gulf 67°43' N, 113°4' W 106
Coronation Island, Antarctica 60°32' S, 45°25' W 134
Coronation Islands, Indian Ocean 15°22' S, 125°6' E 230
Coronda, Arg. 31°59' S, 60°54' W 139
Coronel Bogado, Parag. 27°10' S, 56°16' W 139
Coronel Dorrego, Arg. 38°44' S, 61°17' W 139
Coronel du Graty, Arg. 27°41' S, 60°57' W 139
Coronel Fabriciano, Braz. 19°31' S, 42°34' W 138
Coronel Oviedo, Parag. 25°25' S, 56°28' W 132
Coronel Portillo, Peru 3°20' S, 76°36' W 136
Coronel Pringles, Arg. 37°58' S, 61°24' W 139
Coronel Suárez, Arg. 37°28' S, 61°59' W 139
Coronel Vidal, Arg. 37°27' S, 57°46' W 139
Coronet Peak, N.Z. 44°56' S, 168°39' E 240
Coronie see Totness, Suriname 5°49' N, 56°18' W 130
Coropceni, Rom. 46°55' N, 27°49' E 156
Coropuna, Nevado, peak, Peru 15°32' S, 72°47' W 137
Corozal, Col. 9°18' N, 75°18' W 136
Corozo Pando, Venez. 8°29' N, 67°35' W 136
Corporaque, Peru 14°50' S, 71°33' W 137
Corpus Christi, Tex., U.S. 27°46' N, 97°25' W 96
Corque, Bol. 18°21' S, 67°43' W 137
Corral, Chile 39°54' S, 73°28' W 134
Corral de Almaguer, Sp. 39°45' N, 3°10' W 164
Corral de Bustos, Arg. 33°17' S, 62°10' W 139
Corrales, N. Mex., U.S. 35°14' N, 106°37' W 92
Corralillo, Cuba 22°59' N, 80°35' W 116
Corrane, Mozambique 15°29' S, 39°39' E 224
Correggio, It. 44°46' N, 10°46' E 167
Corrente, river, Braz. 18°30' S, 52°3' W 138
Corrente, river, Braz. 13°20' S, 44°8' W 138
Corrente, river, Braz. 14°24' S, 46°59' W 138
Correntes, river, Braz. 17°32' S, 55°5' W 132
Correntina, Braz. 13°23' S, 44°42' W 138
Correntina see Éguas, river, Braz. 13°42' S, 45°43' W 138
Corrientes, Arg. 27°29' S, 58°48' W 139
Corrientes, adm. division, Arg. 28°39' S, 58°48' W 139
Corrientes, Cabo, Col. 5°19' N, 78°9' W 136
Corrientes, Cabo, Mex. 20°17' N, 106°42' W 112
Corrientes, river, Arg. 29°44' S, 59°19' W 139
Corrientes, river, Peru 3°2' S, 75°44' W 136
Corrigan, Tex., U.S. 30°59' N, 94°50' W 103
Corriverton, Guyana 5°49' N, 57°11' W 130
Corrubedo, Cabo, Sp. 42°25' N, 9°40' W 150
Corse, adm. division, Fr. 42°20' N, 8°39' E 156
Corse, Cap, Fr. 43°2' N, 8°54' E 156
Corsham, U.K. 51°25' N, 2°11' W 162
Corsica, S. Dak., U.S. 43°24' N, 98°25' W 90
Corsica, island, Fr. 41°40' N, 6°21' E 143
Corsicana, Tex., U.S. 32°4' N, 96°28' W 96
Cort Adelaer, Kap, Den. 61°51' N, 42°1' W 106
Cortazar, Mex. 20°27' N, 100°58' W 114
Corte, Fr. 42°18' N, 9°9' E 156
Cortemaggiore, It. 44°59' N, 9°55' E 167
Cortes de la Frontera, Sp. 36°36' N, 5°21' W 164
Cortes Island, Can. 50°4' N, 124°52' W 100
Cortez, Colo., U.S. 37°20' N, 108°36' W 92
Cortez Mountains, Nev., U.S. 40°20' N, 116°34' W 90
Cortina d'Ampezzo, It. 46°32' N, 12°8' E 167
Cortland, N.Y., U.S. 42°35' N, 76°12' W 94
Coruche, Port. 38°57' N, 8°33' W 150
Çoruh, river, Turk. 40°21' N, 40°41' E 195
Çorum, Turk. 40°33' N, 34°57' E 156
Corumbá, Braz. 19°1' S, 57°42' W 132
Corumbá de Goiás, Braz. 15°59' S, 48°50' W 138
Corumbá, river, Braz. 18°4' S, 48°36' W 138
Corumbaíba, Braz. 18°12' S, 48°37' W 138
Corunna, Can. 42°53' N, 82°27' W 102
Corunna, Mich., U.S. 42°57' N, 84°8' W 102
Corvallis, Mont., U.S. 46°17' N, 114°7' W 90
Corvallis, Oreg., U.S. 44°33' N, 123°16' W 90
Corvette, Lac de la, lake, Can. 53°24' N, 74°31' W 111
Corwen, U.K. 52°58' N, 3°22' W 162
Corydon, Iowa, U.S. 40°45' N, 93°19' W 94
Corzu, Rom. 44°27' N, 23°10' E 168
Corzuela, Arg. 26°57' S, 60°59' W 139
Cosalá, Mex. 24°23' N, 106°42' W 114
Cosamaloapan, Mex. 18°22' N, 95°48' W 114
Coşava, Rom. 45°51' N, 22°18' E 168
Coscomatepec, Mex. 19°2' N, 97°3' W 114
Cosenza, It. 39°17' N, 16°15' E 156
Coshocton, Ohio, U.S. 40°15' N, 81°51' W 102
Cosigüina, Punta, Nicar. 12°51' N, 88°44' W 115
Cosio, Mex. 22°21' N, 102°18' W 114
Cosmoledo Group, islands, Indian Ocean 9°18' S, 46°45' E 218
Cosmonaut Sea 62°48' S, 40°53' E 255
Cosmopolis, Wash., U.S. 46°56' N, 123°47' W 100
Cosñipata, Peru 13°2' S, 71°14' W 137
Coso Range, Calif., U.S. 36°9' N, 117°44' W 101
Cosoleacaque, Mex. 18°1' N, 94°38' W 112
Cossato, It. 45°34' N, 8°11' E 167
Cosson, river, Fr. 47°39' N, 1°34' E 165
Cossonay, Switz. 46°36' N, 6°31' E 167
Costa Marques, Braz. 12°30' S, 64°14' W 137
Costa Mesa, Calif., U.S. 33°39' N, 117°55' W 101
Costa Rica 10°0' N, 84°0' W 115
Costa Rica, Bol. 11°15' S, 68°16' W 137
Costa Rica, Mex. 31°19' N, 112°37' W 92
Costigan Lake, Can. 56°54' N, 106°39' W 108
Coswig, Ger. 51°52' N, 12°27' E 152
Cotabambas, Peru 13°47' S, 72°22' W 137
Cotabato, Philippines 7°14' N, 124°13' E 203
Cotagaita, Bol. 20°50' S, 65°43' W 137
Cotahuasi, Peru 15°16' S, 72°55' W 137
Cotati, Calif., U.S. 38°19' N, 122°43' W 100
Côte d'Ivoire (Ivory Coast) 7°26' N, 6°9' W 214
Côte d'Or, Fr. 46°59' N, 4°33' E 165
Cotentin, Fr. 49°29' N, 1°52' W 150
Côtes-de-Fer, Haiti 18°12' N, 72°60' W 116
Cotija, Mex. 19°47' N, 102°43' W 114
Cotonou, Benin 6°23' N, 2°15' E 222
Cotopaxi National Park, Ecua. 0°40' N, 78°44' W 130
Cotopaxi, peak, Ecua. 0°47' N, 78°43' W 130
Cotorro, Cuba 23°3' N, 82°16' W 116
Cotswold Hills, U.K. 51°58' N, 1°59' W 162
Cottage Grove, Oreg., U.S. 43°47' N, 123°3' W 90
Cottageville, W. Va., U.S. 38°51' N, 81°50' W 102
Cottbus, Ger. 51°45' N, 14°19' E 152
Cotter, Ark., U.S. 36°15' N, 92°33' W 96
Cottian Alps, It. 45°16' N, 6°59' E 165
Cottica, Suriname 3°40' N, 54°5' W 123
Cottingham, U.K. 53°46' N, 0°26' E 162
Cotton Valley, La., U.S. 32°48' N, 93°25' W 103
Cottonport, La., U.S. 30°57' N, 92°3' W 103
Cottonwood, Calif., U.S. 40°23' N, 122°18' W 90
Cottonwood Mountains, Calif., U.S. 36°41' N, 117°26' W 101
Cottonwood Pass, Calif., U.S. 35°46' N, 120°14' W 100
Cottonwood Pass, Calif., U.S. 33°43' N, 115°50' W 101
Cotulla, Tex., U.S. 28°26' N, 99°14' W 92
Coucy-Auffrique, Fr. 49°31' N, 3°18' E 163
Cougar, Wash., U.S. 46°3' N, 122°18' W 100
Cougar Peak, Oreg., U.S. 42°18' N, 120°44' W 90
Couiza, Fr. 42°56' N, 2°14' E 164
Coulee Dam, Wash., U.S. 47°57' N, 118°57' W 90
Coulman Island, Antarctica 73°28' S, 175°10' E 248
Coulmiers, Alg. 36°8' N, 6°7' E 150
Coulommiers, Fr. 48°49' N, 3°4' E 163
Coulonge, river, Can. 46°54' N, 77°24' W 94
Coulterville, Calif., U.S. 37°42' N, 120°13' W 100
Council, Alas., U.S. 64°53' N, 163°41' W 98
Council, Idaho, U.S. 44°43' N, 116°26' W 90
Council Grove, Kans., U.S. 38°38' N, 96°30' W 92
Council Mountain, Idaho, U.S. 44°41' N, 116°22' W 90
Coupé, Cap see Ouest, Pointe de l', Fr. 46°48' N, 56°60' W 111
Coupeville, Wash., U.S. 48°11' N, 122°41' W 100
Courcellete Peak, Can. 50°16' N, 114°54' W 90
Couronne, Cap, Fr. 43°14' N, 5°0' E 165
Coursan, Fr. 43°13' N, 3°1' E 164
Courtauld, Mount, Antarctica 70°19' S, 68°3' W 248
Courtenay, Can. 49°40' N, 124°60' W 100
Courtisols, Fr. 48°58' N, 4°29' E 163
Courtland, Calif., U.S. 38°19' N, 121°34' W 100
Courtright, Can. 42°48' N, 82°28' W 94
Coushatta, La., U.S. 31°59' N, 93°20' W 103
Couterne, Fr. 48°31' N, 0°26' E 150
Couto Magalhães, Braz. 8°20' S, 49°17' W 130
Coutts, Can. 49°0' N, 111°59' W 90
Covadonga, site, Sp. 43°18' N, 5°8' W 150
Covarrubias, Sp. 42°3' N, 3°32' W 164
Covăsinţ, Rom. 46°11' N, 21°38' E 168
Covasna, adm. division, Rom. 45°55' N, 25°36' E 156
Cove, Oreg., U.S. 45°17' N, 117°49' W 90
Covendo, Bol. 15°53' S, 67°6' W 137
Coventry, Conn., U.S. 41°46' N, 72°19' W 104
Coventry, U.K. 52°24' N, 1°31' W 162
Coventry Lake, Can. 61°7' N, 107°1' W 108
Covert, Mich., U.S. 42°17' N, 86°16' W 102
Coves del Drac, site, Sp. 39°31' N, 3°15' E 150
Covilhã, Port. 40°15' N, 7°34' W 214
Covington, Ga., U.S. 33°35' N, 83°54' W 112
Covington, Ind., U.S. 40°7' N, 87°24' W 102
Covington, Ky., U.S. 39°3' N, 84°32' W 102
Covington, La., U.S. 30°28' N, 90°7' W 103
Covington, Ohio, U.S. 40°7' N, 84°21' W 102
Covington, Okla., U.S. 36°17' N, 97°35' W 92
Covington, Tenn., U.S. 35°33' N, 89°40' W 96
Covington, Va., U.S. 37°47' N, 79°60' W 96
Cowan, Can. 52°1' N, 100°39' W 108
Cowan Lake, lake, Can. 53°58' N, 107°43' W 108
Cowan, Mount, Mont., U.S. 45°22' N, 110°32' W 90
Cowansville, Can. 45°12' N, 72°45' W 94
Cowbridge, U.K. 51°27' N, 3°27' W 162
Cowden, Ill., U.S. 39°15' N, 88°52' W 102
Cowes, Austral. 50°45' N, 1°18' W 150
Coweta, Okla., U.S. 35°55' N, 95°39' W 96
Cowhorn Mountain, Oreg., U.S. 43°22' N, 122°8' W 90
Cowley, Can. 49°34' N, 114°5' W 90
Cowley, Wyo., U.S. 44°52' N, 108°29' W 90
Cox, S. Af. 27°56' S, 22°51' E 227
Coxcatlán, Mex. 18°16' N, 97°11' W 114
Coxcomb Mountains, Calif., U.S. 34°19' N, 115°34' W 101
Coxilha, Braz. 28°6' S, 52°18' W 139
Coxim, Braz. 18°28' S, 54°46' W 132
Coxim, river, Braz. 18°46' S, 54°28' W 132
Coxipi, Lac, lake, Can. 51°30' N, 58°47' W 111
Coxipi, river, Can. 52°9' N, 58°34' W 111
Coxsackie, N.Y., U.S. 42°20' N, 73°50' W 104
Coxwold, U.K. 54°11' N, 1°11' W 162
Coyah, Guinea 9°41' N, 13°25' W 222
Coyotitán, Mex. 23°45' N, 106°37' W 112
Cozad, Nebr., U.S. 40°50' N, 99°60' W 90
Cozón, Cerro, peak, Mex. 31°13' N, 112°39' W 92
Cozumel, Isla, island, Mex. 20°25' N, 86°45' W 115
Cradock, S. Af. 32°12' S, 25°36' E 227
Craig, Alas., U.S. 55°28' N, 133°9' W 108
Craig, Colo., U.S. 40°31' N, 107°34' W 90
Crail, U.K. 56°15' N, 2°38' W 150
Craiova, Rom. 44°19' N, 23°48' E 156
Cranberry Isles, Atlantic Ocean 43°58' N, 68°17' W 94
Cranberry Portage, Can. 54°35' N, 101°24' W 108
Cranbrook, Can. 49°30' N, 115°45' W 90
Cranbrook, U.K. 51°5' N, 0°32' E 162
Crane, Ind., U.S. 38°53' N, 86°54' W 102
Crane, Oreg., U.S. 43°24' N, 118°35' W 90
Crane, Tex., U.S. 31°22' N, 102°21' W 92
Crane Beach, Mass., U.S. 42°40' N, 70°45' W 104
Crane Lake, Minn., U.S. 48°14' N, 92°31' W 94
Crane Lake, lake, Can. 50°1' N, 109°28' W 90
Crane Mountain, Oreg., U.S. 42°3' N, 120°19' W 90
Cranii, ruin(s), Gr. 38°10' N, 20°24' E 156
Cranwell, U.K. 53°2' N, 0°28' E 162
Craon, Fr. 47°50' N, 0°57' E 150
Craonne, Fr. 49°26' N, 3°46' E 163
Crary Ice Rise, islands, South Pacific Ocean 82°38' S, 174°28' W 248
Craryville, N.Y., U.S. 42°9' N, 73°37' W 104
Crasna, Rom. 46°30' N, 27°50' E 156
Crasna, Rom. 47°9' N, 22°54' E 168
Crasna, river, Rom. 47°35' N, 22°44' E 168
Crasnencoe, Mold. 47°50' N, 29°8' E 156
Crater Mountain, Calif., U.S. 40°37' N, 121°8' W 90
Crater Peak, Calif., U.S. 40°41' N, 121°42' W 90
Cratère du Nouveau-Québec (Chubb Crater), Can. 61°19' N, 73°41' W 106
Crateús, Braz. 5°16' S, 40°26' W 123
Crato, Braz. 7°15' S, 39°27' W 132
Crato, Braz. 7°28' S, 63°6' W 130
Cravari, river, Braz. 12°28' S, 58°10' W 132
Cravo Norte, Col. 6°19' N, 70°12' W 136
Cravo Norte, river, Col. 6°32' N, 71°37' W 136
Cravo Sur, river, Col. 4°59' N, 72°3' W 136
Crawford, Miss., U.S. 33°16' N, 88°37' W 103
Crawford, Nebr., U.S. 42°40' N, 103°25' W 90
Crawford Notch, pass, N.H., U.S. 44°11' N, 71°25' W 104
Crawfordsville, Ind., U.S. 40°1' N, 86°54' W 102
Crawley, U.K. 51°7' N, 0°12' E 162
Crayke, U.K. 54°7' N, 1°9' W 162
Crazy Mountains, Mont., U.S. 46°17' N, 110°29' W 90
Crazy Peak, Mont., U.S. 45°58' N, 110°22' W 90
Crean Lake, lake, Can. 54°6' N, 106°26' W 108
Crécy, Fr. 49°42' N, 3°37' E 163
Crécy-en-Ponthieu, Fr. 50°14' N, 1°52' E 163
Crécy-la-Chapelle, Fr. 48°51' N, 2°54' E 163
Crediton, U.K. 50°47' N, 3°39' W 162
Cree Lake, Can. 57°20' N, 106°52' W 108
Cree Lake, Can. 57°24' N, 106°51' W 106
Cree, river, Can. 57°38' N, 105°55' W 106
Creede, Colo., U.S. 37°51' N, 106°56' W 92
Creek Butte, Rock, peak, Oreg., U.S. 44°47' N, 118°11' W 90
Creil, Fr. 49°15' N, 2°28' E 163
Crema, It. 45°21' N, 9°40' E 167
Cremona, It. 45°7' N, 10°1' E 156
Crepaja, Serb. and Mont. 45°0' N, 20°38' E 168
Crépeau, Lac, lake, Can. 53°53' N, 71°13' W 111
Crepori, river, Braz. 6°54' S, 56°32' W 130
Crépy, Fr. 49°35' N, 3°30' E 163
Crépy-en-Valois, Fr. 49°14' N, 2°52' E 163
Cresbard, S. Dak., U.S. 45°9' N, 98°58' W 90
Crescent, Okla., U.S. 35°55' N, 97°36' W 92
Crescent City, Calif., U.S. 41°44' N, 124°8' W 106
Crescent City, Fla., U.S. 29°26' N, 81°32' W 105
Crescent Junction, Utah, U.S. 38°57' N, 109°49' W 92
Crescent, Lake, Wash., U.S. 48°3' N, 123°59' W 100
Crescent Spur, Can. 53°33' N, 120°43' W 108
Cresco, Iowa, U.S. 43°22' N, 92°7' W 94
Crespo, Arg. 32°2' S, 60°19' W 139
Crestline, Calif., U.S. 34°15' N, 117°17' W 101
Crestline, Ohio, U.S. 40°46' N, 82°45' W 102
Creston, Calif., U.S. 35°32' N, 120°32' W 100
Creston, Can. 49°5' N, 116°32' W 90
Creston, Iowa, U.S. 41°2' N, 94°22' W 94
Crestview, Fla., U.S. 30°45' N, 86°34' W 96
Creswell, Oreg., U.S. 43°54' N, 123°2' W 90
Creswell Bay 72°20' N, 93°54' W 106
Cretas, Sp. 40°55' N, 0°13' E 164
Crete, Nebr., U.S. 40°36' N, 96°57' W 90
Crete see Kriti, island, Gr. 35°36' N, 24°6' E 180
Crete, Sea of 35°24' N, 22°56' E 156
Creus, Cap de, Sp. 42°8' N, 3°19' E 164
Creuzburg, Ger. 51°3' N, 10°14' E 167
Crèvecour, Fr. 49°36' N, 2°4' E 163
Crevillente, Sp. 38°14' N, 0°49' E 164
Crewe, U.K. 53°5' N, 2°26' W 162
Crewe, Va., U.S. 37°10' N, 78°7' W 96
Crewkerne, U.K. 50°53' N, 2°48' W 162
Criciúma, Braz. 28°42' S, 49°21' W 138
Crickhowell, U.K. 51°51' N, 3°7' W 162
Cridersville, Ohio, U.S. 40°39' N, 84°9' W 102
Criel-sur-Mer, Fr. 50°0' N, 1°18' E 163
Criffell, peak, U.K. 54°55' N, 3°43' W 150
Crillon, Mount, Alas., U.S. 58°37' N, 137°13' W 108
Crimea, region, Europe 45°25' N, 33°20' E 156
Crinan, U.K. 56°4' N, 5°34' W 150
Cripple Creek, Colo., U.S. 38°44' N, 105°11' W 90
Crishy Swash, Bahamas 26°47' N, 78°51' W 105
Cristal, Monts de, Gabon 0°31' N, 9°45' E 218
Cristalândia, Braz. 10°36' S, 49°12' W 130
Cristalina, Braz. 16°48' S, 47°39' W 138
Cristalino, river, Braz. 13°56' S, 51°11' W 138
Cristo Mountains, N. Mex., U.S. 38°3' N, 105°42' W 90
Crişul Alb, river, Rom. 46°38' N, 21°22' E 168
Criuleni, Mold. 47°12' N, 29°10' E 156
Crixás, Braz. 14°29' S, 49°59' W 138
Crixás Açu, river, Braz. 14°45' S, 49°49' W 138
Crixás Mirim, river, Braz. 13°57' S, 50°43' W 138
Crljivica, Bosn. and Herzg. 44°25' N, 16°23' E 168
Crna Gora, Serb. and Mont. 42°20' N, 21°23' E 168
Crnajka, Serb. and Mont. 44°17' N, 22°9' E 168
Crnča, Serb. and Mont. 44°17' N, 19°16' E 168
Crni Lug, Bosn. and Herzg. 44°4' N, 16°35' E 168
Crnoljeva Planina, Serb. and Mont. 42°29' N, 20°43' E 168
Croatia 45°46' N, 16°12' E 156
Crocker Hill, Austral. 24°55' S, 135°24' E 230
Crocker Range National Park, Malaysia 5°32' N, 115°22' E 203
Crocker Range National Park, Malaysia 5°35' N, 115°49' E 238
Crockett, Tex., U.S. 31°17' N, 95°27' W 103
Crocodile Islands, Arafura Sea 12°30' S, 133°42' E 230
Crofton, Nebr., U.S. 42°42' N, 97°31' W 90
Croisette, Cap, Fr. 43°8' N, 5°6' E 165
Croisic, Pointe du, Fr. 47°1' N, 2°58' W 150
Croix, Pointe à la, Can. 49°11' N, 67°49' W 111
Croker Bay 74°14' N, 84°17' W 106
Croker Island, Austral. 11°6' S, 132°40' E 192
Crombie, Mount, Austral. 26°43' S, 130°36' E 230
Cromer, U.K. 52°55' N, 1°17' E 162
Cromwell, N.Z. 45°4' S, 169°12' E 240
Cronadun, N.Z. 42°3' S, 171°52' E 240
Cronin, Mount, Can. 54°55' N, 126°59' W 108
Crook, Colo., U.S. 40°51' N, 102°49' W 90
Crook, U.K. 54°43' N, 1°46' W 162
Crooked Island (Atwood), Bahamas 22°39' N, 76°43' W 81
Crooked River, Can. 52°50' N, 103°47' W 108
Crooked, river, Can. 54°46' N, 122°49' W 108
Crookston, Minn., U.S. 47°46' N, 96°38' W 82
Crooksville, Ohio, U.S. 39°45' N, 82°6' W 102

Crosby, Miss., U.S. 31°15' N, 91°4' W 103
Crosby, N. Dak., U.S. 48°53' N, 103°18' W 90
Crosby, Tex., U.S. 29°54' N, 95°4' W 103
Crosby, U.K. 53°29' N, 3°1' W 162
Crosbyton, Tex., U.S. 33°38' N, 101°15' W 92
Cross, Cape, Namibia 22°13' S, 13°26' E 220
Cross City, Fla., U.S. 29°37' N, 83°9' W 105
Cross Creek, Can. 46°18' N, 66°43' W 94
Cross Fell, peak, U.K. 54°42' N, 2°32' W 162
Cross Hands, U.K. 51°47' N, 4°5' W 162
Cross Lake, Can. 54°37' N, 97°46' W 108
Cross Lake, lake, Can. 46°52' N, 80°17' W 94
Cross Plains, Tex., U.S. 32°7' N, 99°10' W 96
Cross River National Park, Nig. 5°28' N, 7°48' E 222
Crossett, Ark., U.S. 33°7' N, 91°59' W 103
Crossfield, Can. 51°26' N, 114°2' W 90
Crossing Rocks, Bahamas 26°7' N, 77°14' W 96
Crossman Peak, Ariz., U.S. 34°32' N, 114°14' W 101
Croswell, Mich., U.S. 43°16' N, 82°36' W 102
Crothersville, Ind., U.S. 38°47' N, 85°50' W 102
Crotone, It. 39°4' N, 17°7' E 156
Croton-on-Hudson, N.Y., U.S. 41°11' N, 73°54' W 104
Crouy-sur-Ourcq, Fr. 49°4' N, 3°4' E 163
Crow Agency, Mont., U.S. 45°35' N, 107°27' W 90
Crow Peak, Mont., U.S. 46°15' N, 111°59' W 90
Crow, river, Can. 60°16' N, 125°47' W 108
Crowell, Tex., U.S. 33°57' N, 99°44' W 92
Crowland, U.K. 52°40' N, 0°9' E 162
Crowle, U.K. 53°36' N, 0°51' E 162
Crowley, La., U.S. 30°11' N, 92°23' W 103
Crowleys Ridge, Ark., U.S. 36°2' N, 90°38' W 96
Crown City, Ohio, U.S. 38°35' N, 82°18' W 102
Crown Point, Ind., U.S. 41°24' N, 87°21' W 102
Crown Point, N.Y., U.S. 43°56' N, 73°27' W 104
Crownpoint, N. Mex., U.S. 35°40' N, 108°9' W 92
Crows Landing, Calif., U.S. 37°23' N, 121°6' W 100
Crowsnest Mountain, Can. 49°41' N, 114°40' W 90
Crowsnest Pass, Can. 49°36' N, 114°26' W 90
Croydon, Austral. 18°12' S, 142°14' E 231
Croydon, U.K. 51°22' N, 9°534' W 162
Crozet Basin, Indian Ocean 40°18' S, 59°51' E 254
Crozet Islands, Indian Ocean 46°18' S, 51°8' E 254
Crozet Plateau, Indian Ocean 45°27' S, 50°24' E 254
Crozier, Cape, Antarctica 77°1' S, 179°30' E 248
Crucero, Peru 14°22' S, 70°1' W 137
Cruces, Cuba 22°20' N, 80°16' W 116
Cruces, Punta, Col. 6°28' N, 77°32' W 136
Cruger, Miss., U.S. 33°17' N, 90°14' W 103
Cruillas, Mex. 24°44' N, 98°31' W 114
Cruta, river, Hond. 14°52' N, 83°45' W 115
Cruz Alta, Arg. 33°1' S, 61°48' W 139
Cruz Alta, Braz. 28°40' S, 53°36' W 139
Cruz, Cabo, Cuba 19°51' N, 78°25' W 115
Cruz del Eje, Arg. 30°46' S, 64°48' W 134
Cruz Grande, Chile 29°27' S, 71°19' W 134
Cruzeiro, Braz. 22°38' S, 44°58' W 138
Cruzeiro do Oeste, Braz. 23°45' S, 53°3' W 138
Cruzeiro do Sul, Braz. 7°40' S, 72°42' W 132
Crvenka, Serb. and Mont. 45°37' N, 19°27' E 168
Cry Lake, Can. 58°47' N, 129°13' W 108
Crysdale, Mount, Can. 55°53' N, 123°33' W 108
Crystal, Me., U.S. 46°0' N, 68°23' W 111
Crystal Bay 28°51' N, 82°49' W 105
Crystal City, Can. 49°8' N, 98°58' W 90
Crystal City, Tex., U.S. 28°41' N, 99°50' W 92
Crystal Falls, Mich., U.S. 46°5' N, 88°20' W 94
Crystal Lake, Ill., U.S. 42°14' N, 88°19' W 102
Crystal River, Fla., U.S. 28°54' N, 82°36' W 105
Crystal Springs, Miss., U.S. 31°59' N, 90°21' W 103
Csákvár, Hung. 47°24' N, 18°28' E 168
Csanytelek, Hung. 46°36' N, 20°7' E 168
Csenger, Hung. 47°51' N, 22°41' E 168
Csepel-sziget, Hung. 47°7' N, 18°57' E 168
Cserhát, Hung. 47°51' N, 19°8' E 168
Csesztreg, Hung. 46°42' N, 16°31' E 168
Csongrád, Hung. 46°42' N, 20°8' E 168
Csongrád, adm. division, Hung. 46°12' N, 19°42' E 156
Csorna, Hung. 47°35' N, 17°16' E 156
Csorvás, Hung. 46°38' N, 20°49' E 168
Csóványos, peak, Hung. 47°55' N, 18°56' E 168
Csurgó, Hung. 46°15' N, 17°6' E 168
Cuale, Angola 8°24' S, 16°10' E 220
Cuamba, Mozambique 14°50' S, 36°33' E 224
Cuando Cubango, adm. division, Angola 17°53' S, 19°15' E 220
Cuando, river, Angola 15°31' S, 21°12' E 220
Cuangar, Angola 17°35' S, 18°39' E 220
Cuango, Angola 6°17' S, 16°39' E 218
Cuango, Angola 9°10' S, 18°2' E 218
Cuanza Norte, adm. division, Angola 8°42' S, 14°20' E 218
Cuanza Sul, adm. division, Angola 10°29' S, 13°38' E 220
Cuaró, Uru. 31°55' S, 55°11' W 139
Cuaró, Uru. 30°37' S, 56°55' W 139
Cuatir, river, Angola 17°10' S, 18°18' E 220
Cuatro Ciénegas, Mex. 26°59' N, 102°6' W 82
Cuatro Ojos, Bol. 16°52' S, 63°38' W 137
Cuauhtémoc, Mex. 19°19' N, 103°36' W 114
Cuauhtémoc, Mex. 28°24' N, 106°52' W 112
Cuautepec, Mex. 20°1' N, 98°17' W 114
Cuautitlán, Mex. 19°26' N, 104°24' W 114
Cuautla, Mex. 18°47' N, 98°56' W 114
Cub Hills, peak, Can. 54°13' N, 104°49' W 108
Cuba 21°4' N, 77°43' W 116
Cuba, Ala., U.S. 32°26' N, 88°23' W 103
Cuba, Port. 38°9' N, 7°55' W 150
Cubabi, Cerro, peak, Mex. 31°42' N, 112°54' W 92
Cubagua, Isla, island, Venez. 10°41' N, 64°50' W 116
Çubuk, Turk. 40°14' N, 33°2' E 156
Cuchi, Angola 14°41' S, 16°54' E 220
Cuchillo Parado, Mex. 29°27' N, 104°52' W 92
Cuchivero, river, Venez. 6°28' N, 65°56' W 136
Cuchumatanes, Sierra los, Guatemala 15°39' N, 91°48' W 115
Cucui, Braz. 1°7' N, 66°49' W 136
Cucumbi, Angola 10°17' S, 19°3' E 220
Cucurpé, Mex. 30°20' N, 110°43' W 92
Cúcuta, Col. 7°54' N, 72°30' W 136
Cudahy, Wis., U.S. 42°57' N, 87°52' W 102
Cuddalore, India 11°44' N, 79°45' E 188
Cuddapah, India 14°27' N, 78°51' E 188
Cuduyari, river, Col. 1°24' N, 70°41' W 136
Cudworth, Can. 52°29' N, 105°45' W 108
Cuéllar, Sp. 41°23' N, 4°19' W 150
Cuello, ruin(s), Belize 18°3' N, 88°45' W 115
Cuenca, Ecua. 2°58' S, 79°3' W 130
Cuenca, Sp. 40°4' N, 2°8' W 164
Cuenca, Serranía de, Sp. 39°38' N, 1°55' W 164
Cuencamé, Mex. 24°51' N, 103°43' W 114
Cuernavaca, Mex. 18°52' N, 99°18' W 114
Cuero, Tex., U.S. 29°4' N, 97°18' W 96
Cuervo, N. Mex., U.S. 35°2' N, 104°24' W 92
Cuervos, Mex. 32°37' N, 114°52' W 101
Cuetzalan, Mex. 20°2' N, 97°31' W 114
Cuevas, Cerro, peak, Mex. 29°10' N, 111°29' W 92
Cuevas de Altamira, site, Sp. 43°22' N, 4°10' W 164
Cuevas de Vinromà, Sp. 40°18' N, 0°6' E 164
Cuevita, Col. 5°28' N, 77°27' W 136
Cuevitas, Chile 23°26' S, 69°60' W 134
Cuevo, Bol. 20°27' S, 63°33' W 137
Cugir, Rom. 45°49' N, 23°21' E 168
Cuiabá, Braz. 15°33' S, 56°7' W 132
Cuiabá, river, Braz. 17°6' S, 56°39' W 132
Cuiari, Braz. 1°28' N, 68°11' W 136
Cuicatlán, Mex. 17°49' N, 96°58' W 114
Cuilcagh, peak, U.K. 54°11' N, 7°55' W 150
Cuillin Hills, U.K. 57°14' N, 6°18' W 150
Cuilo, Angola 7°42' S, 19°23' E 218
Cuiluan, China 47°42' N, 128°42' E 198
Cuima, Angola 13°18' S, 15°38' E 220
Cuio, Angola 12°60' S, 12°58' E 220
Cuito Cuanavale, Angola 15°9' S, 19°8' E 220
Cuito, river, Angola 14°7' S, 18°39' E 220
Cuitzeo, Mex. 19°57' N, 101°8' W 114
Cuiuni, river, Braz. 1°19' S, 64°10' W 130
Cuizăuca, Mold. 47°36' N, 28°49' E 156
Cujmir, Rom. 44°13' N, 22°56' E 168
Çukurca, Turk. 37°14' N, 43°30' E 195
Cùl Mór, peak, U.K. 58°2' N, 5°13' W 150
Culasi, Philippines 11°25' N, 122°5' E 203
Culbertson, Nebr., U.S. 40°13' N, 100°51' W 90
Culebra, Col. 6°6' N, 69°25' W 136
Culebra, island, P.R., U.S. 18°0' N, 65°0' W 118
Culebra, Sierra de la, Sp. 41°47' N, 6°49' W 150
Culfa, Azerb. 38°58' N, 45°38' E 195
Culgoa, river, Austral. 29°14' S, 147°34' E 230
Culiacán, Mex. 24°44' N, 107°34' W 112
Culiacán, Cerro, peak, Mex. 20°18' N, 101°3' W 114
Culion, Philippines 11°53' N, 119°59' E 203
Culiseu, river, Braz. 13°23' S, 53°44' W 130
Cúllar-Baza, Sp. 37°34' N, 2°34' W 164
Cullera, Sp. 39°9' N, 0°16' E 164
Cullman, Ala., U.S. 34°12' N, 86°54' W 112
Culloden Moor, battle, U.K. 57°26' N, 4°17' W 150
Cullom, Ill., U.S. 40°52' N, 88°16' W 102
Cullompton, U.K. 50°51' N, 3°24' W 162
Culuene, river, Braz. 15°7' S, 54°17' W 132
Culver, Ind., U.S. 41°12' N, 86°26' W 102
Culverden, N.Z. 42°48' S, 172°50' E 240
Cumaná, Venez. 10°26' N, 64°11' W 116
Cumari, Braz. 18°18' S, 48°11' W 138
Cumaria, Peru 9°54' S, 73°56' W 137
Cumberland, Md., U.S. 39°39' N, 78°46' W 94
Cumberland, Wis., U.S. 45°31' N, 92°1' W 110
Cumberland House, Can. 53°56' N, 102°17' W 108
Cumberland Island, Ga., U.S. 30°47' N, 81°23' W 112
Cumberland Island National Seashore, Ga., U.S. 30°38' N, 81°26' W 96
Cumberland Islands, Coral Sea 20°47' S, 149°43' E 230
Cumberland, Lake, Ky., U.S. 36°52' N, 85°35' W 94
Cumberland Peninsula, Can. 66°44' N, 73°46' W 106
Cumberland Plateau, North America 34°11' N, 87°21' W 96
Cumberland Point, Mich., U.S. 47°38' N, 89°17' W 110
Cumberland Sound 64°31' N, 72°15' W 73
Cumbrera, Cerro, peak, Chile 48°6' S, 72°55' W 134
Cumbres de Majalca National Park see 11, Mex. 28°57' N, 106°43' W 112
Cumbres del Ajusco National Park see 10, Mex. 19°12' N, 99°24' W 112
Cumbrian Mountains, U.K. 54°43' N, 3°25' W 162
Cumming, Mount, Antarctica 76°35' S, 125°8' W 248
Cummins Peak, Oreg., U.S. 44°12' N, 124°4' W 90
Cúmpas, Mex. 29°58' N, 109°47' W 92
Çumra, Turk. 37°33' N, 32°47' E 156
Cumshewa Head, Can. 53°4' N, 131°42' W 108
Cumuruxatiba, Braz. 17°6' S, 39°12' W 132
Cunani, Braz. 2°53' N, 51°8' W 130
Cunaré, Col. 0°51' N, 72°35' W 136
Cunaviche, Venez. 7°19' N, 67°27' W 136
Cunco, Chile 38°55' S, 72°1' W 134
Cundinamarca, adm. division, Col. 4°8' N, 74°27' W 136
Cunene, adm. division, Angola 17°30' S, 15°28' E 220
Cunene, river, Angola 14°3' S, 15°29' E 220
Cuneo, It. 44°22' N, 7°32' E 167
Cuney, Tex., U.S. 32°1' N, 95°25' W 103
Cunhinga, Angola 12°15' S, 16°46' E 220
Cunjamba, Angola 15°23' S, 20°4' E 220
Cunningham, Tex., U.S. 33°24' N, 95°22' W 103
Cunningham Landing, Can. 60°4' N, 112°8' W 108
Cunningham Mountain, Ariz., U.S. 33°33' N, 114°23' W 101
Cuokkarassa, peak, Nor. 69°57' N, 24°22' E 152
Cuorgnè, It. 45°23' N, 7°38' E 167
Cupar, U.K. 56°19' N, 3°1' W 150
Cupcini, Mold. 48°4' N, 27°21' E 152
Cupica, Col. 6°44' N, 77°32' W 136
Cúpula, Pico, peak, Mex. 24°45' N, 110°50' W 112
Curaçá, Braz. 9°1' S, 39°52' W 132
Curaçao, island, Neth. Antilles 12°0' N, 69°0' W 118
Curaguara de Carangas, Bol. 17°57' S, 68°23' W 137
Curale, Eth. 7°38' N, 44°21' E 218
Curanilahue, Chile 37°28' S, 73°25' W 134
Curanja, river, Peru 10°6' S, 71°39' W 137
Curaray, river, Ecua.-Peru 1°24' S, 77°1' W 136
Curare, Venez. 12°2' N, 66°29' W 136
Curcubăta, peak, Rom. 46°27' N, 22°37' E 168
Cure, Eth. 5°47' N, 36°28' E 224
Curiapo, Venez. 8°33' N, 61°2' W 116
Curichi, Bol. 18°43' S, 63°17' W 137
Curicó, Chile 34°57' S, 71°15' W 134
Curicuriari, river, Braz. 0°32' N, 68°34' W 136
Curicuriari, Serra, peak, Braz. 0°22' N, 66°57' W 136
Curiplaya, Col. 0°16' N, 74°52' W 136
Curitiba, Braz. 25°25' S, 49°18' W 138
Curium, ruin(s), Cyprus 34°40' N, 32°50' E 194
Curley Cut Cays, North Atlantic Ocean 23°20' N, 78°3' W 116
Currais Novos, Braz. 6°17' S, 36°32' W 132
Curralinho, Braz. 1°47' S, 49°50' W 130
Currant Mountain, Nev., U.S. 38°53' N, 115°30' W 90
Currant, pass, Colo., U.S. 38°51' N, 105°39' W 90
Curraun Peninsula, Ire. 53°50' N, 10°32' W 150
Currie Lake, lake, Can. 57°45' N, 98°3' W 108
Curtici, Rom. 46°21' N, 21°18' E 168
Curtis, Nebr., U.S. 40°38' N, 100°31' W 90
Curtis Group, islands, Bass Strait 39°55' S, 144°45' E 231
Curtis Island, Austral. 24°5' S, 150°2' E 230
Curuá, Braz. 2°25' S, 54°4' W 130
Curuá, Ilha, island, Braz. 0°52' N, 50°57' W 130
Curuá, river, Braz. 0°27' N, 54°52' W 130
Curuaés, river, Braz. 7°58' S, 54°33' W 130
Curuçá, river, South America 5°12' S, 71°29' W 132
Curug, Serb. and Mont. 45°28' N, 20°3' E 168
Curupaiti, Braz. 3°25' S, 68°53' W 136
Curupira, Serra, Braz. 1°36' N, 64°19' W 130
Cururu, river, Braz. 8°4' S, 57°21' W 130
Cururupu, Braz. 1°47' S, 44°54' W 132
Curutú, Cerro, peak, Venez. 4°16' N, 63°45' W 130
Curuzú Cuatiá, Arg. 29°46' S, 58°3' W 139
Curvelo, Braz. 18°45' S, 44°27' W 138
Cusapín, Pan. 9°10' N, 81°53' W 115
Cusárare, Mex. 27°33' N, 107°33' W 82
Cusco, Peru 13°33' S, 71°57' W 137
Cusco, adm. division, Peru 13°5' S, 72°47' W 137
Cushing, Okla., U.S. 35°58' N, 96°45' W 96
Cushing, Tex., U.S. 31°48' N, 94°50' W 103
Cushing, Mount, Can. 57°36' N, 126°57' W 108
Cushman, Lake, Wash., U.S. 47°29' N, 123°26' W 100
Cusiana, river, Col. 4°44' N, 72°25' W 136
Cusihuiriachic, Mex. 28°14' N, 106°51' W 92
Cusset, Fr. 46°8' N, 3°27' E 150
Cusson, Pointe, Can. 60°11' N, 77°35' W 106
Custer, Mich., U.S. 43°56' N, 86°13' W 102
Custer, Mont., U.S. 46°7' N, 107°33' W 90
Custer, Wash., U.S. 48°54' N, 122°39' W 100
Cut Bank, Mont., U.S. 48°37' N, 112°20' W 90
Cut Beaver Lake, Can. 53°47' N, 103°9' W 108
Cut Knife, Can. 52°45' N, 109°1' W 108
Cut Off, La., U.S. 29°32' N, 90°22' W 103
Cutbank, river, Can. 54°21' N, 119°20' W 108
Cutchogue, N.Y., U.S. 41°0' N, 72°30' W 104
Cutler, Calif., U.S. 36°31' N, 119°18' W 100
Cutler Ridge, Fla., U.S. 25°33' N, 80°22' W 105
Cutlerville, Mich., U.S. 42°49' N, 85°40' W 102
Cuttack, India 20°25' N, 85°52' E 188
Cuttingsville, Vt., U.S. 43°29' N, 72°53' W 104
Cuttyhunk, Mass., U.S. 41°25' N, 70°57' W 104
Cuttyhunk Island, Mass., U.S. 41°25' N, 71°15' W 104
Cutzamala, Mex. 18°26' N, 100°36' W 114
Cuveşdia, Rom. 45°57' N, 21°42' E 168
Cuvier Plateau, Indian Ocean 24°32' S, 108°34' E 254
Cuxhaven, Ger. 53°51' N, 8°42' E 150
Cuya, Chile 19°12' S, 70°12' W 137
Cuyahoga Falls, Ohio, U.S. 41°9' N, 81°29' W 102
Cuyama, Calif., U.S. 34°56' N, 119°38' W 100
Cuyapo, Philippines 15°47' N, 120°39' E 203
Cuyuna Range, Minn., U.S. 46°24' N, 93°60' W 90
Cuyuni, river, Guyana 6°50' N, 60°6' W 130
Cvrsnica, Bosn. and Herzg. 43°31' N, 17°25' E 168
Cwmbran, U.K. 51°38' N, 3°1' W 162
Cybur, Miss., U.S. 30°36' N, 89°46' W 103
Cyclades see Kilkádes, islands, Mediterranean Sea 36°31' N, 24°28' E 156
Cygnet Lake, lake, Can. 56°45' N, 95°21' W 108
Cynthiana, Ky., U.S. 38°23' N, 84°17' W 94
Cypress Hills, Can. 49°34' N, 110°46' W 108
Cypress Lake, Can. 49°29' N, 109°47' W 90
Cyprus 35°2' N, 33°17' E 194
Cyrenaica, region, Africa 26°14' N, 24°46' E 180
Cyrene see Shaḩḩāt, Lib. 32°50' N, 21°50' E 216
Cyrus Field Bay 62°29' N, 66°6' W 106
Czech Republic 49°41' N, 14°5' E 152
Czempiń, Pol. 52°8' N, 16°46' E 152
Czeremcha, Pol. 52°31' N, 23°18' E 154
Czersk, Pol. 53°47' N, 17°58' E 152
Czerwin, Pol. 52°55' N, 21°44' E 152
Częstochowa, Pol. 50°48' N, 19°6' E 152
Czyżewo, Pol. 52°48' N, 22°17' E 152

D

Da (Black), river, Vietnam 21°11' N, 104°8' E 202
Da Lat, Vietnam 11°56' N, 108°26' E 202
Da Nang, Vietnam 16°2' N, 108°12' E 202
Da Qaidam, China 37°52' N, 95°25' E 188
Daaden, Ger. 50°43' N, 7°58' E 167
Da'an, China 45°28' N, 124°20' E 198
Dabaga, Tanzania 8°5' S, 35°55' E 224
Ḑab'ah, Jordan 31°35' N, 36°2' E 194
Dabajuro, Venez. 11°2' N, 70°42' W 136
Dabakala, Côte d'Ivoire 8°21' N, 4°27' W 222
Dabas, Hung. 47°10' N, 19°20' E 168
Dabat, Eth. 12°58' N, 37°42' E 182
Dabatou, Guinea 11°49' N, 10°41' W 222
Dabeiba, Col. 7°2' N, 76°17' W 136
Dabhoi, India 22°5' N, 73°27' E 186
Dabilja, Maced. 41°27' N, 22°42' E 168
Daboji, China 42°57' N, 126°51' E 200
Dabola, Guinea 10°44' N, 11°9' W 222
Daborow, Somalia 6°21' N, 48°43' E 218
Dabou, Côte d'Ivoire 5°19' N, 4°23' W 222
Daboya, Ghana 9°31' N, 1°26' W 222
Dabqig see Uxin Qi, China 38°24' N, 108°59' E 198
Dabsan Hu, lake, China 37°1' N, 94°22' E 188
Dâbûd, Egypt 24°34' N, 32°55' E 182
Dabuli, Eth. 7°48' N, 41°8' E 224
Dabus, river, Eth. 9°44' N, 34°54' E 224
Dabwali, India 29°57' N, 74°45' E 186
Dac To, Vietnam 14°43' N, 107°47' E 202
Dachang, China 24°50' N, 107°31' E 198
Dachigam National Park, India 34°9' N, 74°57' E 186
Daday, Turk. 41°30' N, 33°26' E 156
Daḍḍa'to, Djibouti 12°20' N, 42°46' E 182
Dade City, Fla., U.S. 28°21' N, 82°12' W 105
Dadhar, Pak. 29°30' N, 67°41' E 186
Dadianzi, China 42°52' N, 128°17' E 200
Dadiya, Nig. 9°36' N, 11°26' E 222
Ḑadnah, U.A.E. 25°32' N, 56°16' E 196
Dadu, Pak. 26°43' N, 67°50' E 186
Daegu (Taegu), S. Korea 35°51' N, 128°37' E 200
Daejeon (Taejŏn), S. Korea 36°18' N, 127°27' E 200
Dăeni, Rom. 44°50' N, 28°6' E 156
Daet, Philippines 14°7' N, 122°56' E 203
Dafang, China 27°8' N, 105°33' E 198
Dafeng, China 33°15' N, 120°29' E 198
Dafoe, Can. 51°44' N, 104°31' W 90
Dafoe Lake, lake, Can. 55°38' N, 96°50' W 108
Dafoe, river, Can. 55°44' N, 95°16' W 108
Daga Medo, Eth. 7°57' N, 42°59' E 218
Daga Post, Sudan 9°11' N, 33°57' E 224
Dagaio, Eth. 6°10' N, 40°42' E 224
Dagana, Senegal 16°30' N, 15°33' W 222
Dagda, Latv. 56°5' N, 27°30' E 166
Dagestan, adm. division, Russ. 42°34' N, 46°10' E 195
Dagestanskiye Ogni, Russ. 42°4' N, 48°17' E 195
Daggett, Calif., U.S. 34°51' N, 116°54' W 101
Daggett, Mich., U.S. 45°27' N, 87°36' W 94
Dagö see Hiiumaa, island, Est. 58°49' N, 21°20' E 166
Dagongcha, China 39°44' N, 96°6' E 188
Dagujiazi, China 42°18' N, 123°24' E 200
Dagupan, Philippines 16°2' N, 120°19' E 203
Dagzê, China 29°40' N, 91°19' E 197
Dahaneh-ye Ghowri, Afghan. 35°54' N, 68°33' E 186
Dahlak Archipelago, Red Sea 16°13' N, 39°29' E 182
Dahlak Kebir, island, Eritrea 15°28' N, 39°33' E 182
Dahmouni, Alg. 35°24' N, 1°28' E 150
Dahn, Ger. 49°8' N, 7°46' E 163
Dahod, India 22°48' N, 74°15' E 188
Dahongliutan, China 36°0' N, 79°19' E 188
Dahra, Senegal 15°22' N, 15°29' W 222
Dahra, oil field, Lib. 29°27' N, 17°37' E 216
Dahuofang Shuiku, lake, China 41°55' N, 123°58' E 200
Daḩy, Nafūd ad, Saudi Arabia 21°51' N, 45°20' E 182
Daïet Abeidi, spring, Mali 21°42' N, 5°43' W 222
Daigo, Japan 36°45' N, 140°20' E 201
Dailekh, Nepal 28°50' N, 81°44' E 197
Daimiel, Sp. 39°3' N, 3°38' W 164
Daingerfield, Tex., U.S. 33°1' N, 94°44' W 103
Dainkog, China 32°30' N, 97°52' E 188
Daintree River National Park, Austral. 16°21' S, 144°50' E 238
Daiō, Japan 34°17' N, 136°53' E 201
Dair, Jebel ed, peak, Sudan 12°27' N, 30°36' E 218
Daireaux, Arg. 36°37' S, 61°42' W 139
Dairen see Dalian, China 38°56' N, 121°33' E 198
Dairût, Egypt 27°35' N, 30°47' E 180
Daisen-Oki National Park, Japan 35°16' N, 133°3' E 201
Daisetta, Tex., U.S. 30°6' N, 94°39' W 103
Daitō, Japan 35°18' N, 132°58' E 201
Daitō Islands, Philippine Sea 24°48' N, 129°27' E 190
Daixian, China 39°3' N, 112°55' E 198
Dajarra, Austral. 21°41' S, 139°34' E 231
Dajt, Mal, peak, Alban. 41°21' N, 19°50' E 156
Dajt National Park, Alban. 41°20' N, 19°52' E 156
Dakar, Senegal 14°39' N, 17°13' W 222
Daketa, river, Eth. 8°52' N, 42°24' E 224
Dakhfili, Sudan 19°15' N, 32°32' E 182
Dakhla, El Wâḥât el, Egypt 25°35' N, 28°10' E 180
Dakingari, Nig. 11°38' N, 4°4' E 222
Dakoank, India 7°4' N, 93°45' E 188
Dakoro, Niger 14°35' N, 6°48' E 222
Ðakovica, Serb. and Mont. 42°23' N, 20°26' E 168
Ðakovo, Croatia 45°18' N, 18°24' E 168
Dákura, Nicar. 14°22' N, 83°14' W 115
Dakwa, Dem. Rep. of the Congo 3°59' N, 26°29' E 224
Dala, Angola 11°5' S, 20°14' E 220
Dalaba, Guinea 10°41' N, 12°18' W 222
Dalai Nur, lake, China 43°13' N, 116°7' E 198
Dalandzadgad, Mongolia 43°33' N, 104°23' E 198
Dalane, region, Europe 58°31' N, 6°0' E 150
Dalarö, Sw. 59°8' N, 18°23' E 166
Dalbandin, Pak. 28°55' N, 64°27' E 182
Dalbosjön, lake, Nor. 58°41' N, 12°30' E 152
Dale, Nor. 60°35' N, 5°47' E 152
Dale, Nor. 61°27' N, 7°25' E 152
Dale Country, region, Europe 53°35' N, 1°46' W 162
Dale Hollow Lake, U.S. 36°33' N, 86°33' W 82
Dalen, Nor. 59°27' N, 7°58' E 152
Dalet, Myanmar 19°59' N, 93°57' E 188
Daleville, Miss., U.S. 32°33' N, 88°41' W 103
Dalfors, Nor. 61°12' N, 15°24' E 152
Dalgaranga Hill, Austral. 27°54' S, 116°54' E 230
Dalhart, Tex., U.S. 36°3' N, 102°32' W 92
Dalhousie, Cape, Can. 70°7' N, 132°37' W 98
Dali, China 34°50' N, 109°57' E 198
Dali, China 25°40' N, 99°58' E 190
Dali, Cyprus 35°1' N, 33°25' E 194
Dalian (Dairen), China 38°56' N, 121°33' E 198
Dalias, Sp. 36°49' N, 2°52' W 164
Dalidag, peak, Azerb. 39°54' N, 46°0' E 195
Dalizi, China 41°44' N, 126°48' E 200
Dalj, Croatia 45°29' N, 18°57' E 168
Dall Island, Alas., U.S. 54°35' N, 135°26' W 106
Dall, river, Can. 58°41' N, 127°56' W 108
Dallas, Oreg., U.S. 44°54' N, 123°21' W 82
Dallas, Tex., U.S. 32°46' N, 96°48' W 92
Dallas Naval Air Station, Tex., U.S. 32°41' N, 96°60' W 92
Dalmā, island, U.A.E. 24°34' N, 51°58' E 182
Dalmas, Lac, lake, Can. 53°27' N, 72°16' W 111
Dalmatia, region, Adriatic Sea 42°51' N, 17°2' E 168
Dal'negorsk, Russ. 44°34' N, 135°35' E 238
Dal'nerechensk, Russ. 45°53' N, 133°51' E 190
Daloa, Côte d'Ivoire 6°48' N, 6°27' W 222
Dalol, Eth. 14°8' N, 40°15' E 182
Dalqān, spring, Saudi Arabia 24°17' N, 45°32' E 182
Dalsbruk (Taalintehdas), Fin. 60°1' N, 22°31' E 166
Daltenganj, India 24°1' N, 84°8' E 197
Dalton, Ga., U.S. 34°45' N, 84°57' W 96
Dalton, Mass., U.S. 42°28' N, 73°10' W 104
Dalton, Nebr., U.S. 41°24' N, 102°59' W 90
Dalton, Wis., U.S. 43°38' N, 89°12' W 102
Dalton in Furness, U.K. 54°9' N, 3°11' W 162
Dalton, Kap, Den. 69°11' N, 24°2' W 246
Dalum, Ger. 52°35' N, 7°13' E 163
Dalupiri, island, Philippines 19°10' N, 120°43' E 198
Dalwallinu, Austral. 30°16' S, 116°41' E 231
Daly City, Calif., U.S. 37°42' N, 122°29' W 100
Daly Lake, lake, Can. 56°26' N, 106°4' W 108
Daly, river, Austral. 13°35' S, 130°35' E 231
Daly River Wildlife Sanctuary, Austral. 13°42' S, 129°44' E 238
Daly Waters, Austral. 16°15' S, 133°20' E 231
Dam Doi, Vietnam 9°2' N, 105°10' E 202
Dam Gamad, Sudan 13°14' N, 27°26' E 226
Damagarim, region, Africa 14°13' N, 7°35' E 222
Daman and Diu, adm. division, India 20°18' N, 71°51' E 188
Daman (Damão), India 20°25' N, 72°52' E 186
Damanava, Belarus 52°49' N, 25°30' E 152
Damane, spring, Mauritania 19°20' N, 14°33' W 222
Damanhûr, Egypt 31°1' N, 30°22' E 180
Damão see Daman, India 20°25' N, 72°52' E 186
Damar, island, Indonesia 7°28' S, 127°44' E 192
Damara, Cen. Af. Rep. 4°57' N, 18°43' E 218
Damaraland, region, Africa 21°4' S, 15°26' E 227
Damas Cays, North Atlantic Ocean 23°23' N, 80°1' W 116
Damasak, Nig. 13°8' N, 12°33' E 216
Damascus see Dimashq, Syr. 33°30' N, 36°14' E 194
Damaturu, Nig. 11°44' N, 11°55' E 222
Damāvand, Qolleh-ye, peak, Iran 35°58' N, 52°0' E 180
Damba, Angola 6°41' S, 15°7' E 218
Dambarta, Nig. 12°26' N, 8°31' E 222
Damboa, Nig. 11°10' N, 12°49' E 216
Damergou, region, Africa 14°49' N, 9°0' E 222
Dāmghān, Iran 36°11' N, 54°19' E 180
Damietta see Dumyāţ, Egypt 31°25' N, 31°49' E 180
Daming, China 36°15' N, 115°8' E 198
Damingzhen, China 42°32' N, 123°40' E 200
Damīr Qābū, Syr. 36°57' N, 41°52' E 195
Dāmiyā, Jordan 32°6' N, 35°33' E 194
Dammarie, Fr. 48°20' N, 1°29' E 163
Dammartin-en-Goële, Fr. 49°2' N, 2°40' E 163
Damme, Ger. 52°31' N, 8°12' E 163
Damnjane, Serb. and Mont. 42°17' N, 20°31' E 168
Damongo, Ghana 9°4' N, 1°49' W 222
Damour, Leb. 33°43' N, 35°27' E 194
Damous, Alg. 36°32' N, 1°43' E 150
Dampier, Austral. 20°40' S, 116°43' E 231
Dampier Archipelago, Indian Ocean 20°18' S, 117°11' E 230
Dampier Land, Austral. 17°35' S, 122°12' E 230
Dampierre, Fr. 48°32' N, 4°21' E 163
Damqawt, Yemen 16°35' N, 52°49' E 182
Damsarkhū, Syr. 35°32' N, 35°46' E 194
Damvillers, Fr. 49°20' N, 5°23' E 163

Damxung, *China* 30°35′ N, 91°9′ E **197**
Damyang, *S. Korea* 35°18′ N, 126°59′ E **200**
Dan, *Israel* 33°13′ N, 35°38′ E **194**
Dan Gulbi, *Nig.* 11°35′ N, 6°16′ E **222**
Dan, river, *N.C., U.S.* 36°35′ N, 79°20′ W **80**
Dana, *Ind., U.S.* 39°48′ N, 87°30′ W **102**
Dānā, *Jordan* 30°40′ N, 35°36′ E **194**
Dana, Mount, *Calif., U.S.* 37°53′ N, 119°16′ W **100**
Dana Point, *Calif., U.S.* 33°28′ N, 117°43′ W **101**
Danané, *Côte d'Ivoire* 7°8′ N, 8°9′ W **222**
Danbury, *Conn., U.S.* 41°23′ N, 73°28′ W **104**
Danbury, *Iowa, U.S.* 42°13′ N, 95°44′ W **90**
Danbury, *N.H., U.S.* 43°31′ N, 71°53′ W **104**
Danbury, *Tex., U.S.* 29°13′ N, 95°21′ W **103**
Danby, *Vt., U.S.* 43°20′ N, 72°60′ W **104**
Dancheng, *China* 33°37′ N, 115°14′ E **198**
Danco Coast, *Antarctica* 64°6′ S, 61°55′ W **134**
Dandéla, *Guinea* 10°55′ N, 8°24′ W **222**
Dandeldhura, *Nepal* 29°16′ N, 80°34′ E **197**
Dandong, *China* 40°10′ N, 124°24′ E **200**
Dandurand, Lac, lake, *Can.* 47°8′ N, 75°9′ W **94**
Dane, *Can.* 48°5′ N, 80°1′ W **94**
Danfa, *Mali* 14°9′ N, 7°30′ W **222**
Danfeng, *China* 33°42′ N, 110°24′ E **198**
Danfina, *Mali* 11°2′ N, 7°9′ W **222**
Danforth Hills, *Colo., U.S.* 40°20′ N, 108°25′ W **90**
Danforth, *Me., U.S.* 45°39′ N, 67°52′ W **94**
Dangara, *Taj.* 38°15′ N, 69°16′ E **197**
Dangchang, *China* 33°55′ N, 104°25′ E **198**
Dange, *Angola* 7°58′ S, 15°1′ E **218**
Danger Islands, *Weddell Sea* 63°57′ S, 54°20′ W **134**
Danger Islands see Pukapuka Atoll, *South Pacific Ocean* 10°35′ S, 167°12′ W **238**
Danger Point, *S. Af.* 34°53′ S, 19°1′ E **227**
Dangé-Saint-Romain, *Fr.* 46°56′ N, 0°37′ E **150**
Dangila, *Eth.* 11°15′ N, 36°52′ E **182**
Dangjin Shankou, pass, *China* 39°17′ N, 94°15′ E **188**
Dango, *Sudan* 9°58′ N, 24°43′ E **224**
Dango, Qoz, *Sudan* 10°29′ N, 24°11′ E **224**
Dangrek Range, *Thai.* 14°34′ N, 103°21′ E **202**
Dangriga, *Belize* 16°57′ N, 88°15′ W **115**
Dangshan, *China* 34°27′ N, 116°21′ E **198**
Dangtu, *China* 31°34′ N, 118°28′ E **198**
Danguya, *Cen. Af. Rep.* 6°27′ N, 22°41′ E **218**
Daniel, *Wyo., U.S.* 42°52′ N, 110°4′ W **90**
Daniel, oil field, *Arg.* 52°17′ S, 68°54′ W **134**
Daniel's Harbour, *Can.* 50°14′ N, 57°35′ W **111**
Danilov, *Russ.* 58°11′ N, 40°8′ E **154**
Danilovgrad, *Serb. and Mont.* 42°32′ N, 19°7′ E **168**
Danilovka, *Russ.* 64°42′ N, 57°47′ E **154**
Danjiangkou, *China* 32°34′ N, 111°31′ E **198**
Ḑank, *Oman* 23°32′ N, 56°17′ E **196**
Dankov, *Russ.* 53°14′ N, 39°1′ E **154**
Danlí, *Hond.* 14°1′ N, 86°31′ W **112**
Danmark Havn, *Den.* 76°46′ N, 18°35′ W **246**
Dannemora, *N.Y., U.S.* 44°42′ N, 73°44′ W **94**
Dañoso, Cabo, *Arg.* 49°2′ S, 67°13′ W **134**
Dansheha, *Eth.* 13°30′ N, 36°54′ E **182**
Dansville, *N.Y., U.S.* 42°33′ N, 77°43′ W **94**
Danu, *Mold.* 47°51′ N, 27°30′ E **152**
Danube, river, *Europe* 44°29′ N, 21°15′ E **143**
Danvers, *Ill., U.S.* 40°30′ N, 89°11′ W **102**
Danvers, *Mass., U.S.* 42°33′ N, 70°57′ W **104**
Danville, *Ill., U.S.* 40°9′ N, 87°37′ W **102**
Danville, *Ind., U.S.* 39°45′ N, 86°32′ W **102**
Danville, *Ky., U.S.* 37°38′ N, 84°46′ W **94**
Danville, *N.H., U.S.* 42°54′ N, 71°8′ W **104**
Danville, *Ohio, U.S.* 40°26′ N, 82°16′ W **102**
Danville, *Va., U.S.* 36°34′ N, 79°25′ W **96**
Danxian (Nada), *China* 19°28′ N, 109°34′ E **198**
Danzhai, *China* 26°11′ N, 107°47′ E **198**
Dao, *Philippines* 10°30′ N, 121°57′ E **203**
Dao Timmi, *Niger* 20°33′ N, 13°31′ E **216**
Daoxian, *China* 25°32′ N, 111°34′ E **198**
Daozhen, *China* 28°52′ N, 107°40′ E **198**
Dapa, *Philippines* 9°47′ N, 126°3′ E **203**
Dapaong, *Togo* 10°50′ N, 0°11′ E **222**
Dapchi, *Nig.* 12°29′ N, 11°31′ E **222**
Daphne, *Ala., U.S.* 30°35′ N, 87°54′ W **103**
Dapp, *Can.* 54°20′ N, 113°56′ W **108**
Dapuchaihe, *China* 42°50′ N, 128°1′ E **200**
Daqing, *China* 46°33′ N, 125°6′ E **198**
Daqqaq, *Sudan* 12°57′ N, 26°53′ E **216**
Dār B'ishtār, *Leb.* 34°15′ N, 35°47′ E **194**
Dar es Salaam, *Tanzania* 6°49′ S, 39°6′ E **224**
Dar et Toubia, *Tun.* 35°19′ N, 10°12′ E **156**
Dar Rounga, region, *Africa* 10°24′ N, 23°37′ E **224**
Dar'ā (Edrei), *Syr.* 32°37′ N, 36°6′ E **194**
Dārāb, *Iran* 28°45′ N, 54°33′ E **196**
Daraban, *Pak.* 31°42′ N, 70°22′ E **186**
Daraina, *Madagascar* 13°17′ S, 49°38′ E **220**
Darakhiv, *Ukr.* 49°21′ N, 25°33′ E **152**
Darakht-e Yahya, *Pak.* 31°48′ N, 68°10′ E **186**
Darány, *Hung.* 45°59′ N, 17°34′ E **168**
Ðaravica, peak, *Serb. and Mont.* 42°31′ N, 20°5′ E **168**
Darâw, *Egypt* 24°22′ N, 32°54′ E **182**
Darazo, *Nig.* 10°58′ N, 10°25′ E **222**
Darbandi Khan Dam, *Iraq* 34°44′ N, 45°3′ E **180**
Darbėnai, *Lith.* 56°1′ N, 21°12′ E **166**
Darbhanga, *India* 26°10′ N, 85°53′ E **197**
D'Arcole Islands, *Indian Ocean* 14°60′ S, 122°41′ E **230**
Darda, *Croatia* 45°37′ N, 18°40′ E **168**
Dardanelle, *Ark., U.S.* 35°12′ N, 93°10′ W **96**
Dardanelle, *Calif., U.S.* 38°20′ N, 119°52′ W **100**
Dardanelles see Çanakkale Boğazı, *Turk.* 40°9′ N, 24°58′ E **157**
Darende, *Turk.* 38°33′ N, 37°28′ E **156**
Darero, river, *Somalia* 9°15′ N, 47°47′ E **218**
Darfur, region, *Africa* 11°6′ N, 23°28′ E **224**
Darganata, *Turkm.* 40°27′ N, 62°9′ E **180**
Dargaz, *Iran* 37°27′ N, 59°6′ E **180**
Dargeçit, *Turk.* 37°33′ N, 41°46′ E **195**
Dargol, *Niger* 13°54′ N, 1°12′ E **222**
Darhan, *Mongolia* 46°43′ N, 109°15′ E **198**
Darhan, *Mongolia* 49°31′ N, 105°58′ E **198**
Darhan Muminggan Lianheqi (Bailingmiao), *China* 41°41′ N, 110°23′ E **198**
Darhan-Uul, adm. division, *Mongolia* 49°29′ N, 105°55′ E **198**
Darien, *Conn., U.S.* 41°4′ N, 73°28′ W **104**
Darien, *Ga., U.S.* 31°21′ N, 81°27′ W **96**
Darién National Park, *Pan.* 7°23′ N, 77°60′ W **136**
Darién, Serranía del, *Pan.* 8°31′ N, 77°58′ W **136**
Darjiling, *India* 26°58′ N, 88°14′ E **197**
Dark Canyon, *Utah, U.S.* 37°48′ N, 109°60′ W **92**
Darley Hills, *Antarctica* 80°41′ S, 172°40′ E **248**
Darling, *S. Af.* 33°22′ S, 18°19′ E **227**
Darling Downs, *Austral.* 27°20′ S, 149°55′ E **230**
Darling, river, *Austral.* 31°16′ S, 144°40′ E **230**
Darlington, *U.K.* 54°31′ N, 1°34′ W **162**
Darlington, *Wis., U.S.* 42°40′ N, 90°6′ W **102**
Darmstadt, *Ger.* 49°52′ N, 8°38′ E **167**
Darnah (Derna), *Lib.* 32°44′ N, 22°38′ E **216**
Darney, *Fr.* 48°5′ N, 6°1′ E **150**
Darnley Bay 69°23′ N, 124°25′ W **106**
Daroca, *Sp.* 41°6′ N, 1°25′ W **164**
Daroot-Korgon, *Kyrg.* 39°32′ N, 72°3′ E **197**
Daror, *Eth.* 8°12′ N, 44°30′ E **218**
Darou Khoudos, *Senegal* 15°7′ N, 16°40′ W **222**
Darovskoy, *Russ.* 58°43′ N, 47°56′ E **154**
Darregueira, *Arg.* 37°45′ S, 63°9′ W **139**
Darreh Gaz, *Iran* 37°26′ N, 59°4′ E **180**
Darrington, *Wash., U.S.* 48°13′ N, 121°38′ W **100**
Darrouzett, *Tex., U.S.* 36°25′ N, 100°21′ W **92**
Darss, *Europe* 54°18′ N, 12°27′ E **152**
Dartmoor, region, *Europe* 50°45′ N, 4°7′ W **162**
Dartmouth, *Can.* 44°40′ N, 63°35′ W **111**
Dartmouth, *Mass., U.S.* 41°34′ N, 71°1′ W **104**
Daru, *P.N.G.* 9°9′ S, 143°11′ E **192**
Daruvar, *Croatia* 45°35′ N, 17°12′ E **168**
Darvaza, *Turkm.* 40°5′ N, 58°30′ E **180**
Darvel Bay 4°50′ N, 117°51′ E **203**
Darwen, *U.K.* 53°42′ N, 2°28′ W **162**
Darwendale, *Zimb.* 17°45′ S, 30°32′ E **224**
Darwin, *Austral.* 12°30′ S, 130°37′ E **230**
Darwin, *Calif., U.S.* 36°15′ N, 117°37′ W **101**
Darwin, Isla, island, *Ecua.* 1°8′ N, 92°28′ W **130**
Darwin, Mount, *Calif., U.S.* 37°10′ N, 118°43′ W **101**
Darya Khan, *Pak.* 31°47′ N, 71°11′ E **186**
Dārzīn, *Iran* 29°6′ N, 58°8′ E **196**
Das, *Pak.* 35°6′ N, 75°5′ E **186**
D'Asagny National Park, *Côte d'Ivoire* 5°11′ N, 4°56′ W **222**
Dasburg, *Ger.* 50°2′ N, 6°8′ E **167**
Dashbalbar, *Mongolia* 49°31′ N, 114°22′ E **198**
Dashkäsän, *Azerb.* 40°30′ N, 46°3′ E **195**
Dashkuduk, *Turkm.* 40°37′ N, 52°53′ E **158**
Dasht, river, *Pak.* 25°37′ N, 61°59′ E **182**
Dasht-e Navar, marsh, *Afghan.* 33°40′ N, 67°7′ E **186**
Daşköpri, *Turkm.* 36°18′ N, 62°36′ E **186**
Daşoguz, *Turkm.* 41°51′ N, 59°58′ E **180**
Dassel, *Ger.* 51°47′ N, 9°40′ E **167**
Datça, *Turk.* 36°44′ N, 27°39′ E **156**
Dateland, *Ariz., U.S.* 32°47′ N, 113°32′ W **101**
Datia, *India* 25°38′ N, 78°26′ E **197**
Datian, *China* 25°40′ N, 117°51′ E **198**
Datong, *China* 40°7′ N, 113°14′ E **198**
Datteln, *Ger.* 51°39′ N, 7°20′ E **167**
Datu Piang, *Philippines* 7°2′ N, 124°28′ E **203**
Datu, Tanjong, *Malaysia* 2°8′ N, 109°23′ E **196**
Datuk, island, *Indonesia* 0°12′ N, 108°14′ E **196**
Daud Khel, *Pak.* 32°52′ N, 71°40′ E **186**
Daudnagar, *India* 25°0′ N, 84°23′ E **197**
Daugaard-Jensen Land, *Den.* 80°8′ N, 63°33′ W **246**
Daugai, *Lith.* 54°22′ N, 24°20′ E **166**
Daugava, river, *Latv.* 56°17′ N, 26°13′ E **166**
Daugava, river, *Latv.* 56°46′ N, 24°10′ E **166**
Daugavpils, *Latv.* 55°51′ N, 26°30′ E **166**
Dauli, *Somalia* 8°48′ N, 50°26′ E **216**
Daun, *Ger.* 50°11′ N, 6°49′ E **167**
D'Aunay Bugt 68°49′ N, 28°49′ W **246**
Daung Kyun, island, *Myanmar* 12°6′ N, 98°7′ E **202**
Dauphin, *Can.* 51°8′ N, 100°3′ W **90**
Dauphin Island, *Ala., U.S.* 30°6′ N, 88°18′ W **103**
Dauphin Lake, *Can.* 51°16′ N, 100°32′ W **81**
Dauphin, Péninsule du, *Can.* 51°18′ N, 72°54′ W **110**
Dauphiné, region, *Europe* 44°22′ N, 4°50′ E **165**
Däväçi, *Azerb.* 41°11′ N, 48°59′ E **195**
Davangere, *India* 14°27′ N, 75°55′ E **188**
Davant, *La., U.S.* 29°36′ N, 89°53′ W **103**
Davao, *Philippines* 7°7′ N, 125°36′ E **203**
Dāvar Panāh, *Iran* 27°18′ N, 62°21′ E **182**
Davegoriale, *Somalia* 8°43′ N, 44°52′ E **218**
Davenport, *Calif., U.S.* 37°0′ N, 122°12′ W **100**
Davenport, *Fla., U.S.* 28°9′ N, 81°37′ W **105**
Davenport, *Iowa, U.S.* 41°32′ N, 90°37′ W **110**
Davenport, Mount, *Austral.* 22°28′ S, 130°38′ E **230**
Daventry, *U.K.* 52°15′ N, 1°10′ W **162**
David, *Pan.* 8°22′ N, 82°19′ W **123**
Davidson, *Can.* 51°16′ N, 105°60′ W **90**
Davie, *Fla., U.S.* 26°3′ N, 80°15′ W **105**
Davies, Cape, *Antarctica* 71°35′ S, 100°20′ W **248**
Davis, *Calif., U.S.* 38°32′ N, 121°46′ W **90**
Davis, *Okla., U.S.* 34°29′ N, 97°7′ W **92**
Davis Dam, *Ariz., U.S.* 35°10′ N, 114°34′ W **101**
Davis Dam, *Nev., U.S.* 35°12′ N, 114°37′ W **101**
Davis Inlet, *Can.* 55°53′ N, 60°48′ W **106**
Davis Islands, *Indian Ocean* 66°35′ S, 108°0′ E **248**
Davis, Mount, *Pa., U.S.* 39°46′ N, 79°16′ W **94**
Davis Mountains, *Tex., U.S.* 30°44′ N, 104°13′ W **92**
Davis Sea 66°31′ S, 89°40′ E **248**
Davis, station, *Antarctica* 68°30′ S, 78°25′ E **248**
Davis Strait 70°31′ N, 60°40′ W **73**
Davison, *Mich., U.S.* 43°1′ N, 83°30′ W **102**
Davlekanovo, *Russ.* 54°14′ N, 54°58′ E **154**
Davlos, *Northern Cyprus* 35°24′ N, 33°54′ E **194**
Davor, *Croatia* 45°7′ N, 17°29′ E **168**
Davos, *Switz.* 46°47′ N, 9°47′ E **167**
Davy Lake, *Can.* 58°51′ N, 108°49′ W **108**
Dawa, river, *Eth.* 4°42′ N, 39°44′ E **224**
Dawadawa, *Ghana* 8°21′ N, 1°35′ W **222**
Dawei, *Myanmar* 14°5′ N, 98°13′ E **202**
Dawhinava, *Belarus* 54°39′ N, 27°26′ E **166**
Dawkah, *Oman* 18°41′ N, 53°58′ E **182**
Dawmat al Jandal, *Saudi Arabia* 29°47′ N, 39°53′ E **180**
Dawna Range, *Myanmar* 16°49′ N, 98°1′ E **202**
Dawqah, *Saudi Arabia* 19°35′ N, 40°55′ E **182**
Dawra, *Western Sahara* 27°27′ N, 12°60′ W **214**
Dawros Head, *Ire.* 54°48′ N, 8°57′ W **150**
Dawson, *Can.* 64°5′ N, 139°18′ W **98**
Dawson, *Ga., U.S.* 31°45′ N, 84°27′ W **96**
Dawson, *Minn., U.S.* 44°55′ N, 96°4′ W **90**
Dawson, *N. Dak., U.S.* 46°51′ N, 99°46′ W **90**
Dawson, *Tex., U.S.* 31°52′ N, 96°41′ W **96**
Dawson Bay 52°50′ N, 101°22′ W **108**
Dawson Creek, *Can.* 55°44′ N, 120°16′ W **108**
Dawson, Isla, island, *Chile* 54°10′ S, 70°9′ W **134**
Dawson, Mount, *Can.* 51°8′ N, 117°32′ W **90**
Dawson Springs, *Ky., U.S.* 37°9′ N, 87°41′ W **96**
Dawu, *China* 31°30′ N, 114°4′ E **198**
Dawukou see Shizuishan, *China* 39°4′ N, 106°25′ E **198**
Dawwah, *Oman* 20°39′ N, 58°53′ E **182**
Dax, *Fr.* 43°42′ N, 1°3′ W **150**
Daxian, *China* 31°15′ N, 107°24′ E **198**
Daxing, *China* 39°44′ N, 116°19′ E **198**
Dayang, river, *China* 40°15′ N, 123°18′ E **200**
Dayet el Khadra, spring, *Alg.* 27°25′ N, 8°30′ W **214**
Daying, *China* 42°8′ N, 127°17′ E **200**
Daylight Pass, *Calif., U.S.* 36°46′ N, 116°57′ W **101**
Daymán, river, *Uru.* 31°34′ S, 57°40′ W **139**
Dayong, *China* 29°8′ N, 110°35′ E **198**
Dayr Abū Sa'īd, *Jordan* 32°29′ N, 35°41′ E **194**
Dayr al Aḩmar, *Leb.* 34°7′ N, 36°7′ E **194**
Dayr al Balaḩ, *Gaza Strip* 31°25′ N, 34°21′ E **194**
Dayr 'Aţīyah, *Syr.* 34°5′ N, 36°46′ E **194**
Dayr az Zawr, *Syr.* 35°19′ N, 40°5′ E **180**
Daysland, *Can.* 52°51′ N, 112°17′ W **108**
Dayton, *Nev., U.S.* 39°15′ N, 119°37′ W **90**
Dayton, *Ohio, U.S.* 39°44′ N, 84°11′ W **102**
Dayton, *Tenn., U.S.* 35°29′ N, 85°1′ W **96**
Dayton, *Tex., U.S.* 30°1′ N, 94°54′ W **103**
Dayton, *Wash., U.S.* 46°18′ N, 117°58′ W **82**
Dayton, *Wyo., U.S.* 44°50′ N, 107°16′ W **90**
Daytona Beach, *Fla., U.S.* 29°13′ N, 81°3′ W **105**
Dayu, *China* 25°24′ N, 114°19′ E **198**
Dayville, *Conn., U.S.* 41°50′ N, 71°54′ W **104**
Dazhu, *China* 30°46′ N, 107°15′ E **198**
Dazkırı, *Turk.* 37°54′ N, 29°51′ E **156**
Dazu, *China* 29°46′ N, 105°44′ E **198**
Dchira, *Western Sahara* 27°1′ N, 13°3′ W **214**
De Aar, *S. Af.* 30°39′ S, 23°59′ E **227**
De Beque, *Colo., U.S.* 39°20′ N, 108°13′ W **90**
De Berry, *Tex., U.S.* 32°17′ N, 94°11′ W **103**
De Cocksdorp, *Neth.* 53°9′ N, 4°51′ E **163**
De Forest, *Wis., U.S.* 43°15′ N, 89°21′ W **102**
De Graff, *Ohio, U.S.* 40°18′ N, 83°55′ W **102**
De Kalb, *Miss., U.S.* 32°44′ N, 88°39′ W **103**
De Kalb, *Tex., U.S.* 33°30′ N, 94°38′ W **96**
De Kastri, *Russ.* 51°38′ N, 140°35′ E **190**
De la Garma, *Arg.* 37°58′ S, 60°25′ W **139**
De Land, *Fla., U.S.* 29°1′ N, 81°19′ W **105**
De Land, *Ill., U.S.* 40°6′ N, 88°39′ W **102**
De Leon Springs, *Fla., U.S.* 29°6′ N, 81°22′ W **105**
De Long Mountains, *Alas., U.S.* 68°7′ N, 164°15′ W **98**
De Long, Ostrova, islands, *East Siberian Sea* 75°48′ N, 158°9′ E **160**
De Queen, *Ark., U.S.* 34°0′ N, 94°21′ W **96**
De Quincy, *La., U.S.* 30°26′ N, 93°27′ W **103**
De Ridder, *La., U.S.* 30°49′ N, 93°18′ W **103**
De Smet, *S. Dak., U.S.* 44°22′ N, 97°35′ W **90**
De Soto, *Miss., U.S.* 31°58′ N, 88°43′ W **103**
De Soto, *Mo., U.S.* 38°7′ N, 90°34′ W **94**
De Soto, *Wis., U.S.* 43°25′ N, 91°12′ W **94**
De Tour Village, *Mich., U.S.* 45°59′ N, 83°55′ W **94**
De Witt, *Ark., U.S.* 34°16′ N, 91°21′ W **96**
De Witt, *Iowa, U.S.* 41°49′ N, 90°32′ W **94**
Dead Horse Point, site, *Utah, U.S.* 38°30′ N, 109°47′ W **90**
Dead Indian Peak, *Wyo., U.S.* 44°35′ N, 109°42′ W **90**
Dead Mountains, *Calif., U.S.* 35°6′ N, 114°50′ W **101**
Dead Sea, lake, *Jordan* 31°28′ N, 35°24′ E **194**
Deadmans Cay, *Bahamas* 23°7′ N, 75°4′ W **116**
Deadman's Cays, *North Atlantic Ocean* 24°6′ N, 80°37′ W **116**
Deadmen Valley, *Can.* 61°2′ N, 124°23′ W **108**
Deadwood, *Can.* 56°44′ N, 117°30′ W **108**
Deadwood, *S. Dak., U.S.* 44°22′ N, 103°42′ W **82**
Deadwood Lake, *Can.* 59°0′ N, 129°12′ W **108**
Deadwood Reservoir, *Idaho, U.S.* 44°19′ N, 116°4′ W **90**
Deakin, *Austral.* 30°46′ S, 128°57′ E **231**
Deal, *U.K.* 51°13′ N, 1°23′ E **163**
De'an, *China* 29°18′ N, 115°45′ E **198**
Dean Channel 52°33′ N, 127°44′ W **108**
Deán Funes, *Arg.* 30°25′ S, 64°21′ W **134**
Dean Island, *Antarctica* 74°22′ S, 126°8′ W **248**
Dean, river, *Can.* 52°53′ N, 126°11′ W **108**
Dearborn, *Mich., U.S.* 42°18′ N, 83°13′ W **102**
Dearg, Beinn, peak, *U.K.* 56°51′ N, 3°60′ W **150**
Dearg, Beinn, peak, *U.K.* 57°45′ N, 5°3′ W **150**
Dease Arm 66°42′ N, 120°16′ W **98**
Dease Inlet 70°56′ N, 156°54′ W **98**
Dease Lake, *Can.* 58°27′ N, 130°4′ W **108**
Dease, river, *Can.* 58°54′ N, 130°11′ W **108**
Dease Strait 69°0′ N, 106°42′ W **246**
Death Valley, *Calif., U.S.* 36°27′ N, 116°53′ W **101**
Death Valley Junction, *Calif., U.S.* 36°17′ N, 116°26′ W **101**
Death Valley National Park (Devils Hole), *Nev., U.S.* 36°25′ N, 116°19′ W **101**
Deatley Island, *Antarctica* 73°45′ S, 73°41′ W **248**
Debao, *China* 23°16′ N, 106°34′ E **198**
Debar, *Maced.* 41°31′ N, 20°32′ E **168**
Debark', *Eth.* 13°12′ N, 37°51′ E **182**
Debary, *Fla., U.S.* 28°53′ N, 81°19′ W **105**
Debden, *Can.* 53°31′ N, 106°52′ W **108**
Debdou, *Mor.* 34°0′ N, 3°2′ W **214**
Dębek, *Pol.* 54°48′ N, 18°5′ E **152**
Debelica, *Serb. and Mont.* 43°39′ N, 22°15′ E **168**
Debenham, *U.K.* 52°13′ N, 1°10′ E **162**
Débéré, *Mali* 15°5′ N, 3°1′ W **222**
Debikut, *India* 25°21′ N, 88°32′ E **197**
Debin, *Russ.* 62°18′ N, 150°29′ E **160**
Debir, ruin(s), *Israel* 31°27′ N, 34°51′ E **194**
Dęblin, *Pol.* 51°33′ N, 21°50′ E **152**
Débo, Lake, *Mali* 15°13′ N, 4°26′ W **222**
Debrc, *Serb. and Mont.* 44°36′ N, 19°53′ E **168**
Debre Birhan, *Eth.* 9°39′ N, 39°31′ E **224**
Debre Mark'os, *Eth.* 10°19′ N, 37°42′ E **224**
Debre Tabor, *Eth.* 11°50′ N, 38°0′ E **182**
Debre Zebīt, *Eth.* 11°48′ N, 38°35′ E **182**
Debre Zeyit, *Eth.* 10°36′ N, 35°42′ E **224**
Debrecen, *Hung.* 47°31′ N, 21°38′ E **168**
Debrzno, *Pol.* 53°32′ N, 17°14′ E **152**
Decamere, *Eritrea* 15°4′ N, 39°4′ E **182**
Dečani, *Serb. and Mont.* 42°31′ N, 20°18′ E **168**
Decatur, *Ill., U.S.* 39°50′ N, 88°57′ W **102**
Decatur, *Ind., U.S.* 40°49′ N, 84°56′ W **102**
Decatur, *Mich., U.S.* 42°6′ N, 85°58′ W **102**
Decatur, *Miss., U.S.* 32°25′ N, 89°7′ W **103**
Decatur, *Mo., U.S.* 39°50′ N, 88°57′ W **94**
Decatur, *Tex., U.S.* 33°13′ N, 97°35′ W **92**
Deception Island, *Antarctica* 63°16′ S, 60°43′ W **134**
Dechu, *India* 26°47′ N, 72°19′ E **186**
Deckerville, *Mich., U.S.* 43°31′ N, 82°44′ W **102**
Decorah, *Iowa, U.S.* 43°17′ N, 91°48′ W **94**
Deddington, *U.K.* 51°58′ N, 1°20′ W **162**
Dededo, *Guam, U.S.* 14°0′ N, 147°0′ E **242**
Dedegöl Dağı, peak, *Turk.* 37°37′ N, 31°12′ E **156**
Deder, *Eth.* 9°17′ N, 41°26′ E **224**
Dedham, *Mass., U.S.* 42°14′ N, 71°11′ W **104**
Dedino, *Maced.* 41°34′ N, 22°25′ E **168**
Dédougou, *Burkina Faso* 12°27′ N, 3°28′ W **222**
Dedovichi, *Russ.* 57°32′ N, 30°0′ E **166**
Dedu, *China* 48°30′ N, 126°9′ E **198**
Dedza, *Malawi* 14°23′ S, 34°16′ E **224**
Dee, river, *Ire.* 53°51′ N, 6°42′ W **150**
Dee, river, *U.K.* 53°5′ N, 2°53′ W **162**
Deep Bay 61°13′ N, 117°11′ W **108**
Deep Bay see Chilumba, *Malawi* 10°24′ S, 34°13′ E **224**
Deep Crater, *Calif., U.S.* 41°26′ N, 121°38′ W **90**
Deep Creek, *Bahamas* 24°49′ N, 76°17′ W **96**
Deep Creek Peak, *Idaho, U.S.* 42°28′ N, 112°43′ W **90**
Deep Creek Range, *Utah, U.S.* 39°36′ N, 114°20′ W **90**
Deep River, *Can.* 46°6′ N, 77°31′ W **94**
Deep River, *Conn., U.S.* 41°23′ N, 72°27′ W **104**
Deer Creek, *Ill., U.S.* 40°37′ N, 89°20′ W **102**
Deer Lake, *Can.* 52°40′ N, 94°59′ W **81**
Deer Lake, *Can.* 49°1′ N, 58°2′ W **111**
Deer Lodge, *Mont., U.S.* 46°23′ N, 112°44′ W **90**
Deer Park, *Ala., U.S.* 31°12′ N, 88°19′ W **103**
Deer River, *Minn., U.S.* 47°19′ N, 93°49′ W **94**
Deer, river, *Can.* 57°36′ N, 94°32′ W **108**
Deer Trail, *Colo., U.S.* 39°36′ N, 104°3′ W **90**
Deerfield, *Ill., U.S.* 42°10′ N, 87°52′ W **102**
Deerfield, *Mass., U.S.* 42°31′ N, 72°37′ W **104**
Deerfield, *N.H., U.S.* 43°8′ N, 71°14′ W **104**
Deerfield Beach, *Fla., U.S.* 26°18′ N, 80°7′ W **105**
Deerhurst, *U.K.* 51°57′ N, 2°11′ W **162**
Deering, *Alas., U.S.* 65°54′ N, 162°50′ W **98**
Deeth, *Nev., U.S.* 41°4′ N, 115°17′ W **90**
Defa, oil field, *Lib.* 27°45′ N, 19°46′ E **216**
Defensores del Chaco National Park, *Parag.* 20°12′ S, 62°1′ W **132**
Defiance, *Ohio, U.S.* 41°15′ N, 84°23′ W **102**
Défirou, spring, *Niger* 20°33′ N, 15°3′ E **216**
Dég, *Hung.* 46°51′ N, 18°27′ E **168**
Degana, *India* 26°53′ N, 74°19′ E **186**
Deganya, *Israel* 32°41′ N, 35°34′ E **194**
Dêgê, *China* 31°51′ N, 98°37′ E **190**
Degeh Bur, *Eth.* 8°10′ N, 43°30′ E **218**
Degelen, peak, *Kaz.* 49°52′ N, 77°51′ E **184**
Degerby, *Fin.* 60°4′ N, 24°9′ E **166**
Degerfors, *Nor.* 59°14′ N, 14°22′ E **152**
Degerhamn, *Sw.* 56°21′ N, 16°23′ E **152**
Dego, *It.* 44°26′ N, 8°19′ E **167**
Deh Bīd, *Iran* 30°36′ N, 53°11′ E **180**
Deh Khavak, *Afghan.* 35°39′ N, 69°55′ E **186**
Deh Mollā, *Iran* 30°33′ N, 49°38′ E **186**
Deh Shu, *Afghan.* 30°23′ N, 63°19′ E **186**
Dehgam, *India* 23°9′ N, 72°48′ E **186**
Dehibat, *Tun.* 32°2′ N, 10°41′ E **214**
Dehqonobod, *Uzb.* 38°21′ N, 66°30′ E **197**
Dehra Dun, *India* 30°20′ N, 78°2′ E **197**
Dehui, *China* 44°30′ N, 125°40′ E **198**
Dein Zubeir, *Sudan* 7°42′ N, 26°13′ E **224**
Deinze, *Belg.* 50°58′ N, 3°31′ E **163**
Deir Mawâs, *Egypt* 27°40′ N, 30°46′ E **180**
Dej, *Rom.* 47°8′ N, 23°55′ E **156**
Dejë, Mal, peak, *Alban.* 41°41′ N, 20°7′ E **168**
Dejen, Ras, peak, *Eth.* 13°11′ N, 38°19′ E **182**
Dejiang, *China* 28°16′ N, 108°6′ E **198**
Dekalb, *Ill., U.S.* 41°55′ N, 88°44′ W **102**
Dekese, *Dem. Rep. of the Congo* 3°29′ S, 21°24′ E **218**
Dekhisor, *Taj.* 39°27′ N, 69°32′ E **197**
Dekina, *Nig.* 7°38′ N, 7°0′ E **222**
Dekle Beach, *Fla., U.S.* 29°51′ N, 83°37′ W **105**
Dekoa, *Cen. Af. Rep.* 6°14′ N, 19°3′ E **218**
Del Rio, *Tex., U.S.* 29°21′ N, 100°55′ W **112**
Del Verme Falls, *Eth.* 5°9′ N, 40°15′ E **224**
Delacroix, *La., U.S.* 29°45′ N, 89°48′ W **103**
Delamar Mountains, *Nev., U.S.* 37°8′ N, 114°58′ W **101**
Delami, *Sudan* 11°50′ N, 30°28′ E **218**
Delano, *Calif., U.S.* 35°46′ N, 119°14′ W **100**
Delano Peak, *Utah, U.S.* 38°21′ N, 112°26′ W **90**
Delanson, *N.Y., U.S.* 42°44′ N, 74°12′ W **104**
Delaram, *Afghan.* 32°14′ N, 63°26′ E **186**
Delareyville, *S. Af.* 26°42′ S, 25°25′ E **220**
Delavan, *Ill., U.S.* 40°21′ N, 89°33′ W **102**
Delaware, *Ohio, U.S.* 40°17′ N, 83°5′ W **102**
Delaware, adm. division, *Del., U.S.* 39°36′ N, 75°46′ W **94**
Delaware Bay 38°16′ N, 76°18′ W **94**
Delaware Mountains, *Tex., U.S.* 31°54′ N, 104°55′ W **92**
Delbrück, *Ger.* 51°45′ N, 8°32′ E **167**
Delcambre, *La., U.S.* 29°56′ N, 91°60′ W **103**
Delčevo, *Maced.* 41°57′ N, 22°46′ E **168**
Delémont, *Switz.* 47°22′ N, 7°19′ E **156**
Delesseps Lake, *Can.* 50°41′ N, 91°15′ W **110**
Delft, *Neth.* 52°1′ N, 4°21′ E **163**
Delfzijl, *Neth.* 53°20′ N, 6°55′ E **163**
Delgada, Point, *Calif., U.S.* 39°51′ N, 124°30′ W **90**
Delgado, Cabo, *Mozambique* 10°43′ S, 40°42′ E **224**
Delgerhet, *Mongolia* 45°50′ N, 110°29′ E **198**
Delgo, *Sudan* 20°6′ N, 30°36′ E **226**
Delhi, *Calif., U.S.* 37°25′ N, 120°47′ W **100**
Delhi, *India* 28°41′ N, 77°10′ E **197**
Delhi, *La., U.S.* 32°26′ N, 91°30′ W **103**
Delhi, *N.Y., U.S.* 42°16′ N, 74°56′ W **94**
Delhi, adm. division, *India* 28°37′ N, 76°44′ E **188**
Deli Jovan, *Serb. and Mont.* 44°21′ N, 22°12′ E **168**
Delia, *Can.* 51°39′ N, 112°23′ W **90**
Délices, *Fr.* 4°43′ N, 53°47′ W **130**
Delicias, *Mex.* 28°9′ N, 105°29′ W **92**
Deligrad, *Serb. and Mont.* 43°36′ N, 21°35′ E **168**
Delījān, *Iran* 34°0′ N, 50°40′ E **180**
Deliktaş, *Turk.* 39°19′ N, 37°12′ E **156**
Délı̨ne, *Can.* 65°13′ N, 123°26′ W **98**
Delingha, *China* 37°22′ N, 97°29′ E **188**
Delisle, *Can.* 51°55′ N, 107°8′ W **90**
Delisle, *Can.* 48°37′ N, 71°42′ W **94**
Delium, battle, *Gr.* 38°19′ N, 23°32′ E **156**
Dell, *U.K.* 58°28′ N, 6°20′ W **150**
Dell Rapids, *S. Dak., U.S.* 43°48′ N, 96°43′ W **90**
Delle, *Fr.* 47°30′ N, 6°59′ E **150**
Dellenbaugh, Mount, *Ariz., U.S.* 36°6′ N, 113°34′ W **101**
Dellys, *Alg.* 36°54′ N, 3°54′ E **150**
Delmar, *Md., U.S.* 38°27′ N, 75°35′ W **94**
Delmar, *N.Y., U.S.* 42°37′ N, 73°51′ W **104**
Deloraine, *Can.* 49°11′ N, 100°30′ W **90**
Delos, ruin(s), *Gr.* 37°22′ N, 25°10′ E **156**
Delphi, ruin(s), *Gr.* 38°28′ N, 22°24′ E **156**
Delphos, *Ohio, U.S.* 40°50′ N, 84°21′ W **102**
Delray Beach, *Fla., U.S.* 26°28′ N, 80°6′ W **105**
Delta, *Colo., U.S.* 38°44′ N, 108°4′ W **90**
Delta, *La., U.S.* 32°18′ N, 90°56′ W **103**
Delta, *Utah, U.S.* 39°20′ N, 112°34′ W **90**
Delta Amacuro, adm. division, *Venez.* 8°57′ N, 61°48′ W **130**
Delta du Saloum National Park, *Senegal* 13°39′ N, 16°27′ W **222**
Deltona, *Fla., U.S.* 28°53′ N, 81°15′ W **105**
Dema, river, *Russ.* 54°28′ N, 55°29′ E **154**
Demanda, Sierra de la, *Sp.* 42°19′ N, 3°14′ W **164**
Demange-aux-Eaux, *Fr.* 48°34′ N, 5°27′ E **163**
Demarcation Point, *Can.* 69°34′ N, 143°59′ W **98**
Demba, *Dem. Rep. of the Congo* 5°30′ S, 22°13′ E **218**
Dembech'a, *Eth.* 10°31′ N, 37°28′ E **224**
Dembī Dolo, *Eth.* 8°31′ N, 34°47′ E **224**
Dembia, *Dem. Rep. of the Congo* 3°29′ N, 25°51′ E **224**
Demerara Plain, *North Atlantic Ocean* 9°25′ N, 48°41′ W **253**
Demetrias, ruin(s), *Gr.* 39°20′ N, 22°52′ E **156**
Demidov, *Russ.* 55°14′ N, 31°31′ E **154**
Demidovo, *Russ.* 56°45′ N, 29°33′ E **166**
Deming, *N. Mex., U.S.* 32°15′ N, 107°45′ W **92**
Deming, *Wash., U.S.* 48°49′ N, 122°13′ W **100**
Demini, river, *Braz.* 1°24′ N, 63°13′ W **130**
Demirci, *Turk.* 39°3′ N, 28°38′ E **156**
Demirköprü Barajı, dam, *Turk.* 38°48′ N, 28°0′ E **156**
Demirtaş, *Turk.* 36°25′ N, 32°10′ E **156**
Demiti, river, *Braz.* 0°51′ N, 67°4′ W **136**
Demmitt, *Can.* 55°25′ N, 119°55′ W **108**
Democratic Republic of the Congo 1°57′ S, 17°24′ E **218**
Demon, *Ghana* 9°29′ N, 0°11′ E **222**
Demonte, *It.* 44°18′ N, 7°17′ E **167**
Demopolis, *Ala., U.S.* 32°32′ N, 87°50′ W **103**
Demotte, *Ind., U.S.* 41°11′ N, 87°13′ W **102**
Demşuş, *Rom.* 45°34′ N, 22°48′ E **168**
Demta, *Indonesia* 2°23′ S, 140°10′ E **192**
Dem'yanka, river, *Russ.* 58°52′ N, 71°21′ E **169**
Demyansk, *Russ.* 57°37′ N, 32°28′ E **154**
Dem'yanskoye, *Russ.* 59°32′ N, 69°25′ E **169**
Demydivka, *Ukr.* 50°24′ N, 25°20′ E **152**
Den Burg, *Neth.* 53°3′ N, 4°46′ E **163**
Den Chai, *Thai.* 17°59′ N, 100°3′ E **202**
Den Helder, *Neth.* 52°57′ N, 4°45′ E **163**
Den Oever, *Neth.* 52°55′ N, 5°1′ E **163**
Denain, *Fr.* 50°19′ N, 3°23′ E **163**
Denair, *Calif., U.S.* 37°31′ N, 120°49′ W **100**
Denakil, region, *Africa* 12°35′ N, 40°8′ E **182**
Denali see Mckinley, Mount, *Alas., U.S.* 62°54′ N, 151°17′ W **98**
Denan, *Eth.* 6°27′ N, 43°29′ E **218**
Denare Beach, *Can.* 54°40′ N, 102°4′ W **108**
Denbigh, *U.K.* 53°11′ N, 3°24′ W **162**
Dendtler Island, *Antarctica* 72°46′ S, 90°30′ W **248**
Denekamp, *Neth.* 52°23′ N, 7°0′ E **163**
Deng Deng, *Cameroon* 5°8′ N, 13°28′ E **218**
Dengkou, *China* 40°18′ N, 106°54′ E **198**
Dêngqên, *China* 31°33′ N, 95°35′ E **188**
Dengu, river, *Dem. Rep. of the Congo* 4°30′ N, 24°14′ E **224**
Dengzhou, *China* 32°39′ N, 112°5′ E **198**
Denham Springs, *La., U.S.* 30°28′ N, 90°58′ W **96**
Denholm, *Can.* 52°39′ N, 108°2′ W **108**
Dénia, *Sp.* 38°49′ N, 0°535′ E **164**
Deniliquin, *Austral.* 35°31′ S, 144°55′ E **231**
Denio, *Nev., U.S.* 41°59′ N, 118°39′ W **90**
Denis, *Gabon* 0°17′ N, 9°22′ E **218**
Denison, *Iowa, U.S.* 41°59′ N, 95°21′ W **90**

Denison, *Tex., U.S.* 33°44′ N, 96°32′ W **96**
Denisovka, *Russ.* 66°14′ N, 55°19′ E **154**
Denisovskaya, *Russ.* 60°18′ N, 41°34′ E **154**
Denizli, *Turk.* 37°45′ N, 29°5′ E **156**
Denman Island, *Can.* 49°32′ N, 124°49′ W **100**
Denmark 56°12′ N, 8°45′ E **152**
Denmark, *Me., U.S.* 43°58′ N, 70°49′ W **104**
Denmark, *S.C., U.S.* 33°18′ N, 81°9′ W **96**
Denmark Strait 64°13′ N, 38°21′ W **246**
Dennis, *Mass., U.S.* 41°44′ N, 70°12′ W **104**
Dennison, *Ohio, U.S.* 40°23′ N, 81°20′ W **102**
Denow, *Uzb.* 38°17′ N, 67°54′ E **197**
Denpasar, *Indonesia* 8°44′ S, 115°1′ E **192**
Denso, *Mali* 10°27′ N, 8°5′ W **222**
Denton, *Md., U.S.* 38°52′ N, 75°50′ W **94**
Denton, *Tex., U.S.* 33°12′ N, 97°8′ W **92**
D'Entrecasteaux Islands, *Solomon Sea* 9°50′ S, 151°24′ E **231**
Denver, *Colo., U.S.* 39°43′ N, 105°6′ W **90**
Denver, *Ind., U.S.* 40°51′ N, 86°5′ W **102**
Denver City, *Tex., U.S.* 32°56′ N, 102°50′ W **92**
Denzil, *Can.* 52°13′ N, 109°38′ W **108**
Deoband, *India* 29°40′ N, 77°41′ E **197**
Deobhog, *India* 19°56′ N, 82°39′ E **188**
Deoghar, *India* 24°27′ N, 86°42′ E **197**
Deoria, *India* 26°29′ N, 83°47′ E **197**
Departure Bay, *Can.* 49°11′ N, 123°58′ W **100**
Deposit, *N.Y., U.S.* 42°3′ N, 75°26′ W **110**
Depot Harbour, *Can.* 45°18′ N, 80°5′ W **94**
Depot Peak, *Antarctica* 69°6′ S, 64°14′ E **248**
Deputatskiy, *Russ.* 69°16′ N, 139°52′ E **173**
Deqing, *China* 30°33′ N, 120°4′ E **198**
Deqing, *China* 23°10′ N, 111°46′ E **198**
Dera Ghazi Khan, *Pak.* 30°3′ N, 70°41′ E **186**
Dera Ismail Khan, *Pak.* 31°47′ N, 70°55′ E **186**
Deraheib, *Sudan* 21°55′ N, 35°8′ E **182**
Derati, spring, *Kenya* 3°47′ N, 36°23′ E **224**
Derbent, *Russ.* 42°0′ N, 48°20′ E **195**
Derbisaka, *Cen. Af. Rep.* 5°43′ N, 24°52′ E **224**
Derby, *Austral.* 17°23′ S, 123°43′ E **238**
Derby, *Conn., U.S.* 41°19′ N, 73°6′ W **104**
Derby, *Kans., U.S.* 37°31′ N, 97°16′ W **90**
Derby, *Miss., U.S.* 30°45′ N, 89°35′ W **103**
Derby, *U.K.* 52°55′ N, 1°29′ W **162**
Derby Acres, *Calif., U.S.* 35°15′ N, 119°37′ W **101**
Derdara, *Mor.* 35°7′ N, 5°18′ W **150**
Derdepoort, *S. Af.* 24°41′ S, 26°21′ E **227**
Derecske, *Hung.* 47°21′ N, 21°34′ E **168**
Dérégoué, *Burkina Faso* 10°46′ N, 4°9′ W **222**
Dereisa, *Sudan* 12°43′ N, 22°47′ E **216**
Derevyansk, *Russ.* 61°44′ N, 53°23′ E **154**
Dergachi, *Russ.* 51°12′ N, 48°48′ E **158**
Derhachi, *Ukr.* 50°7′ N, 36°7′ E **158**
Derik, *Turk.* 37°20′ N, 40°19′ E **195**
Derkali, *Kenya* 3°47′ N, 40°16′ E **224**
Derm, *Namibia* 23°40′ S, 18°13′ E **227**
Dermbach, *Ger.* 50°42′ N, 10°6′ E **167**
Dermott, *Ark., U.S.* 33°30′ N, 91°27′ W **96**
Derna see Darnah, *Lib.* 32°44′ N, 22°38′ E **216**
Dernberg, Cape, *Namibia* 27°44′ S, 15°33′ E **227**
Dernieres, Isles, *Gulf of Mexico* 29°3′ N, 90°55′ W **103**
Derom, Mount, *Antarctica* 71°36′ S, 35°22′ E **248**
Derri, *Somalia* 4°21′ N, 46°38′ E **218**
Derry, *La., U.S.* 31°30′ N, 92°58′ W **103**
Derry, *N.H., U.S.* 42°52′ N, 71°20′ W **104**
Derudeb, *Sudan* 17°29′ N, 36°4′ E **182**
Derust, *S. Af.* 33°27′ S, 22°32′ E **227**
Derval, *Fr.* 47°39′ N, 1°41′ W **150**
Derventa, *Bosn. and Herzg.* 44°58′ N, 17°53′ E **168**
Derwent, *Can.* 53°38′ N, 110°58′ W **108**
Derwent, river, *U.K.* 54°11′ N, 0°44′ E **162**
Derwent Water, lake, *U.K.* 54°33′ N, 3°22′ W **162**
Deryneia, *Northern Cyprus* 35°3′ N, 33°57′ E **194**
Derzhavino, *Russ.* 53°14′ N, 52°19′ E **154**
Derzhavīnsk, *Kaz.* 51°6′ N, 66°18′ E **184**
Des Allemands, *La., U.S.* 29°50′ N, 90°29′ W **103**
Des Moines, *Iowa, U.S.* 41°33′ N, 93°40′ W **94**
Des Moines, *N. Mex., U.S.* 36°44′ N, 103°50′ W **92**
Des Moines, river, *Iowa, U.S.* 43°26′ N, 95°10′ W **80**
Des Plaines, *Ill., U.S.* 42°2′ N, 87°54′ W **102**
Desa, *Rom.* 43°53′ N, 23°1′ E **168**
Desaguadero, *Peru* 16°39′ S, 69°5′ W **137**
Desatoya Mountains, *Nev., U.S.* 39°31′ N, 117°53′ W **90**
Desbiens, *Can.* 48°24′ N, 71°57′ W **94**
Descalvado, *Braz.* 21°57′ S, 47°38′ W **138**
Descanso, *Calif., U.S.* 32°51′ N, 116°37′ W **101**
Deschutes, river, *Oreg., U.S.* 44°13′ N, 121°5′ W **80**
Desē, *Eth.* 11°5′ N, 39°36′ E **224**
Deseada, *Chile* 22°53′ S, 69°51′ W **137**
Deseado, river, *Arg.* 46°54′ S, 69°39′ W **134**
Desemboque, *Mex.* 30°34′ N, 113°3′ W **92**
Desengaño, Punta, *Arg.* 49°15′ S, 67°33′ W **134**
Deseret, *Utah, U.S.* 39°16′ N, 112°39′ W **90**
Deseret Peak, *Utah, U.S.* 40°26′ N, 112°41′ W **90**
Deseronto, *Can.* 44°12′ N, 77°3′ W **94**
Desert Center, *Calif., U.S.* 33°43′ N, 115°25′ W **101**
Desert Hot Springs, *Calif., U.S.* 33°57′ N, 116°31′ W **101**
Desert Island, Mount, *Me., U.S.* 43°48′ N, 68°16′ W **81**
Désert, Lac, lake, *Can.* 46°34′ N, 76°44′ W **94**
Desert National Park, *India* 26°16′ N, 70°18′ E **186**
Desert Peak, *Utah, U.S.* 41°10′ N, 113°26′ W **90**
Desert Range, *Nev., U.S.* 36°51′ N, 115°27′ W **101**
Desert Shores, *Calif., U.S.* 33°24′ N, 116°3′ W **101**
Desert Valley, *Nev., U.S.* 41°12′ N, 118°30′ W **90**
Desertas, Ilhas, islands, *North Atlantic Ocean* 33°17′ N, 17°23′ W **214**
Deserters Peak, *Can.* 56°56′ N, 124°60′ W **108**
Deshler, *Nebr., U.S.* 40°6′ N, 97°45′ W **90**
Deshler, *Ohio, U.S.* 41°12′ N, 83°54′ W **102**
Deshnoke, *India* 27°48′ N, 73°21′ E **186**
Desierto del Carmen National Park see 13, *Mex.* 18°52′ N, 99°38′ W **112**
Désirade, La, island, *Fr.* 16°15′ N, 60°59′ W **116**
Deskenatlata Lake, *Can.* 60°55′ N, 113°9′ W **108**
Desloge, *Mo., U.S.* 37°51′ N, 90°31′ W **94**
Desmarais, Point, *Can.* 60°50′ N, 117°6′ W **108**
Desmaraisville, *Can.* 49°30′ N, 76°12′ W **94**
Desmochado, *Parag.* 27°7′ S, 58°5′ W **139**
Desna, *Russ.* 54°20′ N, 32°53′ E **154**
Desna, river, *Ukr.* 51°6′ N, 31°7′ E **158**
Desnogorsk, *Russ.* 54°8′ N, 33°13′ E **154**
Desnudez, Punta, *Arg.* 38°59′ S, 59°37′ W **139**
Desolación, Isla, island, *Chile* 53°2′ S, 76°38′ W **134**
Desolation Canyon, *Utah, U.S.* 39°42′ N, 110°18′ W **90**
Desordem, Serra da, *Braz.* 3°15′ S, 46°60′ W **130**
Despotovac, *Serb. and Mont.* 44°5′ N, 21°25′ E **168**
Desroches, islands, *Indian Ocean* 6°36′ S, 51°11′ E **218**
Dessalines, *Haiti* 19°17′ N, 72°32′ W **116**
Dessau, *Ger.* 51°50′ N, 12°15′ E **152**
Destruction Island, *Wash., U.S.* 47°34′ N, 124°36′ W **100**
Destruction, Mount, *Austral.* 24°35′ S, 127°45′ E **230**
Desvres, *Fr.* 50°39′ N, 1°50′ E **163**
Deta, *Rom.* 45°24′ N, 21°13′ E **168**
Dete, *Zimb.* 18°38′ S, 26°50′ E **224**
Detour, Point, *U.S.* 45°27′ N, 86°34′ W **94**
Detroit, *Me., U.S.* 44°47′ N, 69°19′ W **94**
Detroit, *Mich., U.S.* 42°20′ N, 83°3′ W **102**
Dettelbach, *Ger.* 49°47′ N, 10°8′ E **167**
Deurne, *Neth.* 51°28′ N, 5°46′ E **167**
Deux Balé National Park, *Burkina Faso* 11°34′ N, 3°2′ W **222**
Deux Décharges, Lac aux, lake, *Can.* 51°58′ N, 71°19′ W **111**
Deva, *Rom.* 45°53′ N, 22°55′ E **168**
Devarkonda, *India* 16°41′ N, 78°57′ E **188**
Dévaványa, *Hung.* 47°1′ N, 20°58′ E **168**
Deveci Dağı, peak, *Turk.* 40°5′ N, 35°51′ E **156**
Devecser, *Hung.* 47°5′ N, 17°26′ E **168**
Develi, *Turk.* 38°22′ N, 35°31′ E **156**
Deventer, *Neth.* 52°15′ N, 6°8′ E **163**
Devenyns, Lac, lake, *Can.* 47°3′ N, 74°25′ W **94**
Devers, *Tex., U.S.* 30°0′ N, 94°36′ W **103**
Devgarh, *India* 25°30′ N, 73°59′ E **186**
Devi, river, *India* 20°33′ N, 85°53′ E **188**
Devil's Bridge, *U.K.* 52°21′ N, 3°51′ W **162**
Devils Cataract see Raudal Yupurari, fall(s), *Col.* 0°58′ N, 71°28′ W **136**
Devils Gate, pass, *Calif., U.S.* 38°21′ N, 119°23′ W **100**
Devils Hole see Death Valley National Park, *Nev., U.S.* 36°25′ N, 116°19′ W **101**
Devils Lake, *N. Dak., U.S.* 48°5′ N, 98°52′ W **90**
Devils Paw, mountain, *Can.-U.S.* 58°42′ N, 134°2′ W **108**
Devils Playground, *Calif., U.S.* 35°1′ N, 115°54′ W **101**
Devils Postpile National Monument, *Calif., U.S.* 37°36′ N, 119°11′ W **92**
Devils, river, *Tex., U.S.* 29°58′ N, 101°18′ W **92**
Devilsbit Mountain, *Ire.* 52°48′ N, 8°1′ W **150**
Devine, *Tex., U.S.* 29°7′ N, 98°55′ W **96**
Devine, Mount, *Ariz., U.S.* 32°7′ N, 111°52′ W **92**
Devizes, *U.K.* 51°21′ N, 1°60′ W **162**
Devli, *India* 25°45′ N, 75°23′ E **197**
Devola, *Ohio, U.S.* 39°27′ N, 81°28′ W **102**
Devon Island, *Can.* 75°13′ N, 79°17′ W **106**
Devoto, *Arg.* 31°27′ S, 62°19′ W **139**
Devrek, *Turk.* 41°13′ N, 31°54′ E **156**
Devrekâni, *Turk.* 41°36′ N, 33°49′ E **156**
Đevrske, *Croatia* 43°56′ N, 15°50′ E **156**
Dewa, Ujung, *Indonesia* 2°58′ N, 95°46′ E **196**
Dewar, *Okla., U.S.* 35°26′ N, 95°57′ W **96**
Dewas, *India* 22°58′ N, 76°3′ E **197**
Dewetsdorp, *S. Af.* 29°37′ S, 26°36′ E **227**
Dewey, *Okla., U.S.* 36°46′ N, 95°57′ W **96**
Dewey Lake, *Ky., U.S.* 37°27′ N, 83°21′ W **81**
Deweyville, *Tex., U.S.* 30°16′ N, 93°45′ W **103**
Dewitt, *Mich., U.S.* 42°50′ N, 84°34′ W **102**
Dewsbury, *U.K.* 53°41′ N, 1°38′ W **162**
Dexter, *Me., U.S.* 45°1′ N, 69°18′ W **94**
Dexter, *Mich., U.S.* 42°19′ N, 83°54′ W **102**
Dexter, *Mo., U.S.* 36°47′ N, 89°57′ W **96**
Deyhūk, *Iran* 33°16′ N, 57°31′ E **180**
Deyyer, *Iran* 27°49′ N, 51°56′ E **196**
Dez, river, *Iran* 33°0′ N, 48°44′ E **180**
Dezfūl, *Iran* 32°23′ N, 48°23′ E **180**
Dezhneva, Mys (East Cape), *Russ.* 65°45′ N, 169°46′ W **98**
Dezhou, *China* 37°28′ N, 116°18′ E **198**
Dgūqara, *Kaz.* 46°1′ N, 55°58′ E **158**
Dhahabān, *Saudi Arabia* 21°56′ N, 39°5′ E **182**
Dhahran see Az̧ Z̧ahrān, *Saudi Arabia* 26°15′ N, 50°1′ E **196**
Dhaka, *Bangladesh* 23°38′ N, 90°17′ E **197**
Dhamār, *Yemen* 14°30′ N, 44°27′ E **182**
Dhanbad, *India* 23°47′ N, 86°24′ E **197**
Dhandhuka, *India* 22°16′ N, 71°58′ E **186**
Dhangadhi, *Nepal* 28°40′ N, 80°39′ E **197**
D'Hanis, *Tex., U.S.* 29°19′ N, 99°16′ W **92**
Dhankuta, *Nepal* 26°57′ N, 87°19′ E **197**
Dhanora, *India* 20°15′ N, 80°20′ E **188**
Dharan, *Nepal* 26°45′ N, 87°11′ E **197**
Dharmjaygarh, *India* 22°29′ N, 83°13′ E **197**
Dhasan, river, *India* 24°11′ N, 78°46′ E **197**
Dhāt Ra's, *Jordan* 30°59′ N, 35°44′ E **194**
Dhaulagiri, peak, *Nepal* 28°41′ N, 83°29′ E **197**
Dhebar Lake, *India* 24°16′ N, 73°41′ E **186**
Dhërmi, *Alban.* 40°9′ N, 19°38′ E **156**
Dhībān (Dibon), *Jordan* 31°29′ N, 35°46′ E **194**
Dhone, *India* 15°24′ N, 77°52′ E **188**
Dhorain, Beinn, peak, *U.K.* 58°6′ N, 3°57′ W **150**
Dhule, *India* 20°52′ N, 74°45′ E **188**
Dhupgarh, peak, *India* 22°25′ N, 78°19′ E **197**
Dhuusamarreeb (Dusa Marreb), *Somalia* 5°31′ N, 46°24′ E **218**
Di Linh, *Vietnam* 11°35′ N, 108°4′ E **202**
Dia, *Mali* 14°53′ N, 3°17′ W **222**
Diablo, Cerro, peak, *Tex., U.S.* 31°51′ N, 105°28′ W **92**
Diablo, El Picacho del, peak, *Mex.* 30°56′ N, 115°27′ W **92**
Diablo, Mount, *Calif., U.S.* 37°52′ N, 121°57′ W **100**
Diablo Peak, *Oreg., U.S.* 42°57′ N, 120°40′ W **90**
Diablo Range, *Calif., U.S.* 37°13′ N, 121°39′ W **100**
Diablo, Sierra, *Tex., U.S.* 31°3′ N, 104°60′ W **92**
Diadé, *Mauritania* 16°15′ N, 7°33′ W **222**
Diafarabé, *Mali* 14°11′ N, 4°60′ W **222**
Diala, *Mali* 14°13′ N, 10°10′ W **222**
Dialafara, *Mali* 13°28′ N, 11°25′ W **222**
Dialakoto, *Senegal* 13°18′ N, 13°20′ W **222**
Diamante, *Arg.* 32°3′ S, 60°34′ W **139**
Diamantina, *Braz.* 18°16′ S, 43°35′ W **138**
Diamantina, Chapada, *Braz.* 12°50′ S, 42°58′ W **138**
Diamantina Fracture Zone, *Indian Ocean* 36°3′ S, 105°25′ E **254**
Diamantino, *Braz.* 16°32′ S, 53°14′ W **138**
Diamantino, *Braz.* 14°28′ S, 56°29′ W **132**
Diamond Craters, *Oreg., U.S.* 43°8′ N, 119°2′ W **90**
Diamond Harbour, *India* 22°11′ N, 88°12′ E **197**
Diamond Head, peak, *Hawai'i, U.S.* 21°14′ N, 157°51′ W **99**
Diamond Island, *Myanmar* 15°35′ N, 94°16′ E **202**
Diamond Mountains, *Calif., U.S.* 40°7′ N, 120°34′ W **90**
Diamond Mountains, *Nev., U.S.* 39°43′ N, 116°5′ W **90**
Diamond Peak, *Colo., U.S.* 40°56′ N, 108°57′ W **90**
Diamond Peak, *Oreg., U.S.* 43°30′ N, 122°14′ W **90**
Diamond Peak, *Wash., U.S.* 46°5′ N, 117°38′ W **90**
Diamond Point, *N.Y., U.S.* 43°28′ N, 73°43′ W **104**
Diamond Valley, *Nev., U.S.* 39°56′ N, 116°12′ W **90**
Diamondville, *Wyo., U.S.* 41°45′ N, 110°32′ W **90**
Diamou, *Mali* 14°6′ N, 11°17′ W **222**
Diana, *Tex., U.S.* 32°41′ N, 94°46′ W **103**
Dianbai, *China* 21°32′ N, 110°59′ E **198**
Diandioumé, *Mali* 15°27′ N, 9°21′ W **222**
Dianguina, *Mauritania* 15°19′ N, 10°56′ W **222**
Dianjiang, *China* 30°18′ N, 107°23′ E **198**
Diano d'Alba, *It.* 44°38′ N, 8°2′ E **167**
Diapaga, *Burkina Faso* 12°4′ N, 1°46′ E **222**
Diar el Hadj Hassan, *Tun.* 35°17′ N, 11°3′ E **156**
Diarville, *Fr.* 48°22′ N, 6°7′ E **163**
Diavolo, Mount, *India* 12°41′ N, 92°54′ E **188**
Dībā al Ḩişn, *U.A.E.* 25°38′ N, 56°12′ E **196**
Dibaya, *Dem. Rep. of the Congo* 6°34′ S, 22°55′ E **218**
Dibaya Lubue, *Dem. Rep. of the Congo* 4°14′ S, 19°50′ E **218**
Dibbis, *Sudan* 12°33′ N, 24°12′ E **216**
Dibella, spring, *Niger* 17°23′ N, 13°13′ E **222**
Dibo, *Eth.* 10°46′ N, 38°19′ E **224**
Diboll, *Tex., U.S.* 31°9′ N, 94°48′ W **103**
Dibon see Dhībān, *Jordan* 31°29′ N, 35°46′ E **194**
Dibrugarh, *India* 27°27′ N, 94°56′ E **188**
Dibulla, *Col.* 11°14′ N, 73°20′ W **136**
Dickens, *Tex., U.S.* 33°35′ N, 100°51′ W **92**
Dickey Peak, *Idaho, U.S.* 44°13′ N, 113°57′ W **90**
Dickinson, *Tex., U.S.* 29°26′ N, 95°3′ W **103**
Dickson, *Russ.* 73°19′ N, 81°0′ E **160**
Dickson, *Tenn., U.S.* 36°4′ N, 87°23′ W **96**
Dicle, *Turk.* 38°22′ N, 40°5′ E **195**
Dicle see Tigris, river, *Turk.* 37°41′ N, 41°7′ E **195**
Dicomano, *It.* 43°54′ N, 11°31′ E **167**
Didbiran, *Russ.* 52°4′ N, 139°13′ E **190**
Didcot, *U.K.* 51°36′ N, 1°15′ W **162**
Dider, *Alg.* 25°12′ N, 8°26′ E **214**
Dīdēsa, river, *Eth.* 9°31′ N, 35°52′ E **224**
Didhav, *Eth.* 12°35′ N, 40°54′ E **182**
Didi Abuli, Mt'a, peak, *Ga.* 41°26′ N, 43°35′ E **195**
Didia, *Tanzania* 3°50′ S, 33°3′ E **224**
Didiéni, *Mali* 13°54′ N, 8°5′ W **222**
Dīdīmtu, *Eth.* 8°45′ N, 42°9′ E **224**
Didoko, *Côte d'Ivoire* 5°58′ N, 5°19′ W **222**
Didsbury, *Can.* 51°41′ N, 114°8′ W **90**
Didwana, *India* 27°23′ N, 74°35′ E **186**
Diébougou, *Burkina Faso* 10°57′ N, 3°16′ W **222**
Diecke, *Guinea* 7°19′ N, 8°59′ W **222**
Diefenbaker, Lake, *Can.* 51°15′ N, 107°39′ W **90**
Diego de Almagro, *Chile* 26°23′ S, 70°5′ W **134**
Diego de Almagro, Isla, island, *Chile* 51°19′ S, 78°10′ W **134**
Diego Garcia, island, *U.K.* 7°53′ S, 72°18′ E **188**
Diego Garcia, island, *U.K.* 7°17′ S, 72°25′ E **254**
Diekirch, *Lux.* 49°52′ N, 6°9′ E **167**
Diélé, *Congo* 1°56′ S, 14°37′ E **218**
Diéma, *Mali* 14°35′ N, 9°12′ W **222**
Diemel, river, *Ger.* 51°30′ N, 9°24′ E **167**
Dien Bien, *Vietnam* 21°21′ N, 103°0′ E **202**
Dien Chou, *Vietnam* 18°59′ N, 105°35′ E **202**
Dien Khanh, *Vietnam* 12°14′ N, 109°6′ E **202**
Diepholz, *Ger.* 52°36′ N, 8°22′ E **150**
Dieppe, *Fr.* 49°54′ N, 1°3′ E **163**
Dieppe Lake, lake, *Can.* 61°37′ N, 116°55′ W **108**
Dierdorf, *Ger.* 50°32′ N, 7°39′ E **163**
Dieren, *Neth.* 52°3′ N, 6°5′ E **167**
Diest, *Belg.* 50°59′ N, 5°2′ E **167**
Dieterich, *Ill., U.S.* 39°3′ N, 88°24′ W **102**
Dieulouard, *Fr.* 48°50′ N, 6°4′ E **163**
Dieuze, *Fr.* 48°49′ N, 6°43′ E **163**
Dieveniškės, *Lith.* 54°12′ N, 25°37′ E **166**
Diez, *Ger.* 50°22′ N, 8°0′ E **167**
Dif, *Kenya* 0°55′ N, 40°55′ E **224**
Diffa, *Niger* 13°21′ N, 12°37′ E **216**
Differdange, *Lux.* 49°32′ N, 5°53′ E **163**
Difnein, island, *Eritrea* 16°29′ N, 38°48′ E **182**
Digba, *Dem. Rep. of the Congo* 4°20′ N, 25°47′ E **224**
Digboi, *India* 27°23′ N, 95°38′ E **188**
Digby, *Can.* 44°37′ N, 65°46′ W **111**
Dighton, *Kans., U.S.* 38°29′ N, 100°28′ W **90**
Dighton, *Mass., U.S.* 41°48′ N, 71°8′ W **104**
Dighton, *Mich., U.S.* 44°5′ N, 85°21′ W **102**
Digne, *Fr.* 44°5′ N, 6°14′ E **167**
Digny, *Fr.* 48°32′ N, 1°8′ E **163**
Digor, *Turk.* 40°22′ N, 43°24′ E **195**
Digos, *Philippines* 6°47′ N, 125°20′ E **203**
Digri, *Pak.* 25°10′ N, 69°7′ E **186**
Digul, river, *Indonesia* 7°13′ S, 139°20′ E **192**
Digya National Park, *Ghana* 7°10′ N, 0°48′ E **222**
Dihōk, *Iraq* 36°52′ N, 42°52′ E **195**
Diinsoor, *Somalia* 2°25′ N, 42°57′ E **218**
Dijlah see Tigris, river, *Iraq* 32°8′ N, 46°36′ E **180**
Dijon, *Fr.* 47°19′ N, 5°2′ E **150**
Dik, *Chad* 9°57′ N, 17°30′ E **216**
Dika, Mys, *Russ.* 75°37′ N, 114°26′ E **172**
Dikhil, *Djibouti* 11°12′ N, 42°22′ E **224**
Dikili, *Turk.* 39°2′ N, 26°53′ E **156**
Diksmuide, *Belg.* 51°2′ N, 2°51′ E **163**
Dikwa, *Nig.* 12°3′ N, 13°56′ E **216**
Dīla, *Eth.* 6°28′ N, 38°8′ E **224**
Dildarde Burnu, *Turk.* 36°26′ N, 31°17′ E **156**
Dili, *Dem. Rep. of the Congo* 3°25′ N, 26°44′ E **224**
Dili, *Timor-Leste* 8°47′ S, 125°17′ E **230**
Dilijan, *Arm.* 40°44′ N, 44°50′ E **195**
Dilj Planina, *Croatia* 45°16′ N, 17°52′ E **168**
Dillenburg, *Ger.* 50°44′ N, 8°16′ E **167**
Dilley, *Tex., U.S.* 28°39′ N, 99°10′ W **92**
Dilling, *Sudan* 12°1′ N, 29°40′ E **216**
Dillingen, *Ger.* 49°21′ N, 6°44′ E **163**
Dillingham, *Alas., U.S.* 58°57′ N, 158°36′ W **73**
Dillon, *Can.* 55°54′ N, 108°55′ W **108**
Dillon, *Mont., U.S.* 45°11′ N, 112°38′ W **90**
Dillon, *S.C., U.S.* 34°25′ N, 79°23′ W **96**
Dillon, river, *Can.* 55°31′ N, 110°13′ W **108**
Dillsboro, *Ind., U.S.* 39°0′ N, 85°3′ W **102**
Dilolo, *Dem. Rep. of the Congo* 10°44′ S, 22°22′ E **220**
Dilworth, *Minn., U.S.* 46°51′ N, 96°41′ W **90**
Dima, *Dem. Rep. of the Congo* 3°19′ S, 17°24′ E **218**
Dimapur, *India* 25°52′ N, 93°47′ E **188**
Dimas, *Mex.* 23°40′ N, 106°47′ W **114**
Dimashq (Damascus), *Syr.* 33°30′ N, 36°14′ E **194**
Dimbelenge, *Dem. Rep. of the Congo* 5°32′ S, 23°3′ E **218**
Dimbokro, *Côte d'Ivoire* 6°34′ N, 4°42′ W **222**
Dimitrovgrad, *Bulg.* 42°3′ N, 25°35′ E **156**
Dimitrovgrad, *Russ.* 54°15′ N, 49°34′ E **154**
Dimitrovgrad, *Serb. and Mont.* 43°0′ N, 22°46′ E **168**
Dimmitt, *Tex., U.S.* 34°31′ N, 102°19′ W **92**
Dimock, *S. Dak., U.S.* 43°26′ N, 97°59′ W **90**
Dimona, *Israel* 31°3′ N, 35°0′ E **194**
Dīmtu, *Eth.* 5°8′ N, 41°57′ E **224**
Dinajpur, *Bangladesh* 25°36′ N, 88°36′ E **197**
Dinan, *Fr.* 48°27′ N, 2°4′ W **150**
Dinant, *Belg.* 50°16′ N, 4°55′ E **167**
Dinar, *Turk.* 38°3′ N, 30°10′ E **156**
Dīnār, Kūh-e, peak, *Iran* 30°45′ N, 51°30′ E **180**
Dinara, *Bosn. and Herzg.* 43°50′ N, 16°33′ E **168**
Dinas Mawddwy, *U.K.* 52°42′ N, 3°42′ W **162**
Dinde, *Angola* 14°14′ S, 13°41′ E **220**
Dinder National Park, *Sudan* 12°32′ N, 35°8′ E **182**
Dinder, river, *Sudan* 12°26′ N, 35°4′ E **182**
Dinga, *Dem. Rep. of the Congo* 5°17′ S, 16°39′ E **218**
Ding'an, *China* 19°39′ N, 110°19′ E **198**
Dingbian, *China* 37°36′ N, 107°36′ E **198**
Dinggyê, *China* 28°26′ N, 87°46′ E **197**
Dingnan, *China* 24°44′ N, 115°0′ E **198**
Dingtao, *China* 35°3′ N, 115°36′ E **198**
Dinguiraye, *Guinea* 11°17′ N, 10°44′ W **222**
Dingxi, *China* 35°33′ N, 104°32′ E **198**
Dingxiang, *China* 38°28′ N, 112°58′ E **198**
Dingxing, *China* 39°17′ N, 115°49′ E **198**
Dingzhou, *China* 38°31′ N, 114°59′ E **198**
Dingzi Gang 36°21′ N, 120°50′ E **198**
Dinkey Creek, *Calif., U.S.* 37°5′ N, 119°11′ W **101**
Dinklage, *Ger.* 52°39′ N, 8°8′ E **163**
Dinorwic, *Can.* 49°41′ N, 92°30′ W **94**
Dinorwic Lake, lake, *Can.* 49°31′ N, 93°7′ W **94**
Dinosaur, *Colo., U.S.* 40°14′ N, 109°1′ W **90**
Dinslaken, *Ger.* 51°33′ N, 6°44′ E **167**
Dinuba, *Calif., U.S.* 36°32′ N, 119°24′ W **100**
Dioïla, *Mali* 12°29′ N, 6°48′ W **222**
Dioka, *Mali* 14°54′ N, 10°7′ W **222**
Diona, spring, *Chad* 17°52′ N, 22°37′ E **216**
Diongoï, *Mali* 14°53′ N, 9°35′ W **222**
Dionisio Cerqueira, *Arg.* 26°17′ S, 53°37′ W **139**
Diorbivol, *Senegal* 16°5′ N, 13°48′ W **222**
Dios, Cayos de, *Caribbean Sea* 21°16′ N, 81°16′ W **116**
Diosig, *Rom.* 47°17′ N, 22°1′ E **168**
Diouloulou, *Senegal* 13°1′ N, 16°31′ W **222**
Dioumdiouréré, *Mali* 14°51′ N, 1°60′ W **222**
Dioundiou, *Niger* 12°35′ N, 3°30′ E **222**
Dioura, *Mali* 14°52′ N, 5°15′ W **222**
Diourbel, *Senegal* 14°39′ N, 16°7′ W **222**
Diphu Pass, *India* 28°14′ N, 97°21′ E **188**
Diplo, *Pak.* 24°28′ N, 69°36′ E **186**
Dipolog, *Philippines* 8°36′ N, 123°21′ E **203**
Dipton, *N.Z.* 45°55′ S, 168°23′ E **240**
Dir, *Pak.* 35°11′ N, 71°53′ E **186**
Dira, Djebel, peak, *Alg.* 36°4′ N, 3°34′ E **150**
Dirdal, *Nor.* 58°49′ N, 6°9′ E **152**
Dirē, *Eth.* 10°9′ N, 38°41′ E **224**
Diré, *Mali* 16°17′ N, 3°24′ W **222**
Dirē Dawa, *Eth.* 9°34′ N, 41°51′ E **224**
Dírfis, Óros, *Gr.* 38°32′ N, 23°38′ E **156**
Dirico, *Angola* 17°56′ S, 20°43′ E **220**
Dirj, *Lib.* 30°9′ N, 10°26′ E **214**
Dirk Hartog Island, *Austral.* 26°19′ S, 110°56′ E **230**
Dirkou, *Niger* 19°4′ N, 12°50′ E **216**
Dirra, *Sudan* 13°35′ N, 26°5′ E **226**
Dirranbandi, *Austral.* 28°36′ S, 148°19′ E **231**
Disa, *India* 24°15′ N, 72°11′ E **186**
Disappointment, Cape, *Wash., U.S.* 46°13′ N, 124°26′ W **100**
Disaster Bay 37°41′ S, 149°37′ E **231**
Discovery Bay 38°20′ S, 139°30′ E **230**
Discovery Tablemount, *South Atlantic Ocean* 42°9′ S, 0°31′ E **253**
Disentis, *Switz.* 46°42′ N, 8°50′ E **167**
Dishna, *Egypt* 26°10′ N, 32°25′ E **180**
Disko see Qeqertarsuaq, island, *Den.* 69°31′ N, 62°11′ W **106**
Dismal Mountains, *Antarctica* 68°45′ S, 53°53′ E **248**
Dismal, river, *Nebr., U.S.* 41°45′ N, 101°4′ W **90**
Dispur, *India* 26°6′ N, 91°44′ E **197**
Disraëli, *Can.* 45°53′ N, 71°21′ W **94**
Diss, *U.K.* 52°22′ N, 1°6′ E **162**
Disteghil Sar, peak, *Pak.* 36°16′ N, 75°4′ E **186**
District, Lake, region, *Europe* 54°15′ N, 3°22′ W **162**
District of Columbia, adm. division, *D.C., U.S.* 38°55′ N, 77°12′ W **94**
District, Peak, region, *Europe* 53°17′ N, 1°57′ W **162**
Distrito Federal, adm. division, *Braz.* 15°42′ S, 48°13′ W **138**
Distrito Federal, adm. division, *Mex.* 19°9′ N, 99°21′ W **114**
Disūq, *Egypt* 31°7′ N, 30°39′ E **180**
Ditaranto, Golfo 39°48′ N, 16°53′ E **156**
Ditinn, *Guinea* 10°53′ N, 12°13′ W **222**
Diu, *India* 20°41′ N, 70°56′ E **188**
Dium, ruin(s), *Gr.* 40°9′ N, 22°23′ E **156**
Dīvāndarreh, *Iran* 36°0′ N, 46°58′ E **180**
Divénié, *Congo* 2°39′ S, 12°3′ E **218**
Divernon, *Ill., U.S.* 39°32′ N, 89°41′ W **102**
Divinhe, *Mozambique* 20°42′ S, 34°48′ E **227**
Divinópolis, *Braz.* 20°10′ S, 44°55′ W **138**
Divisadero Barrancas, *Mex.* 27°32′ N, 107°48′ W **112**
Diviso, *Col.* 1°22′ N, 78°27′ W **136**
Divisor, Serra do, *Braz.* 8°10′ S, 73°52′ W **130**
Divjakë, *Alban.* 40°59′ N, 19°31′ E **156**
Divnoye, *Russ.* 45°52′ N, 43°10′ E **158**
Divo, *Côte d'Ivoire* 5°47′ N, 5°21′ W **222**
Divonne, *Fr.* 46°21′ N, 6°8′ E **167**
Divriği, *Turk.* 39°20′ N, 38°7′ E **180**
Diwal Qol, *Afghan.* 34°20′ N, 67°57′ E **186**
Diwana, *Pak.* 26°5′ N, 67°19′ E **186**
Dixfield, *Me., U.S.* 44°31′ N, 70°27′ W **104**
Dixie Butte, peak, *Oreg., U.S.* 44°34′ N, 118°42′ W **90**
Dixon, *Calif., U.S.* 38°26′ N, 121°50′ W **90**
Dixon, *Ill., U.S.* 41°49′ N, 89°29′ W **102**
Dixon, *Ky., U.S.* 37°30′ N, 87°42′ W **94**
Dixon, *Mo., U.S.* 37°58′ N, 92°6′ W **94**
Dixon, *Mont., U.S.* 47°17′ N, 114°20′ W **90**
Dixon Entrance 54°17′ N, 133°50′ W **108**
Dixons Mills, *Ala., U.S.* 32°3′ N, 87°48′ W **103**
Dixonville, *Can.* 56°32′ N, 117°41′ W **108**
Diyadin, *Turk.* 39°32′ N, 43°41′ E **195**
Diyālá, river, *Iraq* 34°20′ N, 45°5′ E **186**
Diyarbakır, *Turk.* 37°54′ N, 40°17′ E **195**
Diz, *Pak.* 26°36′ N, 63°27′ E **182**
Dizy, *Fr.* 49°3′ N, 3°57′ E **163**
Dja, river, *Cameroon* 3°14′ N, 12°30′ E **218**
Dja, river, *Cameroon* 3°1′ N, 14°6′ E **218**
Djado, *Niger* 21°1′ N, 12°18′ E **222**
Djado, Plateau du, *Niger* 21°41′ N, 11°25′ E **222**
Djako, *Cen. Af. Rep.* 8°18′ N, 22°29′ E **218**
Djamaa, *Alg.* 33°31′ N, 5°57′ E **214**
Djambala, *Congo* 2°32′ S, 14°45′ E **218**
Djanet, *Alg.* 24°23′ N, 9°22′ E **207**
Djaul, island, *P.N.G.* 3°10′ S, 150°7′ E **192**
Djebel Onk, *Alg.* 34°41′ N, 8°2′ E **214**
Djédaa, *Chad* 13°31′ N, 18°36′ E **216**
Djelfa, *Alg.* 34°41′ N, 3°15′ E **214**
Djéli Mahé, *Mali* 15°25′ N, 10°37′ W **222**
Djema, *Cen. Af. Rep.* 5°58′ N, 25°18′ E **224**
Djember, *Chad* 10°26′ N, 17°50′ E **216**
Djeniene bou Rezg, *Alg.* 32°23′ N, 0°47′ E **214**
Djénné, *Mali* 13°55′ N, 4°35′ W **222**
Djenoun, Garet el, peak, *Alg.* 25°2′ N, 5°17′ E **214**
Djérem, river, *Cameroon* 5°58′ N, 12°41′ E **218**
Djéroual, *Chad* 14°29′ N, 18°32′ E **216**
Dji, river, *Cen. Af. Rep.* 6°48′ N, 22°28′ E **218**
Djibasso, *Burkina Faso* 13°8′ N, 4°10′ W **222**
Djibo, *Burkina Faso* 14°5′ N, 1°39′ W **222**
Djibouti 12°0′ N, 43°0′ E **216**
Djibouti, *Djibouti* 11°29′ N, 43°0′ E **182**
Djidja, *Benin* 7°25′ N, 1°50′ E **222**
Djiénié, *Mali* 12°12′ N, 7°17′ W **222**
Djilbé, *Cameroon* 11°54′ N, 14°39′ E **216**
Djirkjik, spring, *Chad* 16°53′ N, 20°39′ E **216**
Djohong, *Cameroon* 6°47′ N, 14°42′ E **218**
Djokupunda, *Dem. Rep. of the Congo* 5°28′ S, 20°58′ E **218**
Djolu, *Dem. Rep. of the Congo* 0°35′ N, 22°26′ E **218**
Djougou, *Benin* 9°42′ N, 1°41′ E **222**
Djouho Battinga, *Cen. Af. Rep.* 6°37′ N, 20°30′ E **218**
Djoum, *Cameroon* 2°44′ N, 12°40′ E **218**
Djugu, *Dem. Rep. of the Congo* 1°53′ N, 30°30′ E **224**
Djupvik, *Nor.* 69°44′ N, 20°31′ E **152**
D'Lo, *Miss., U.S.* 31°58′ N, 89°55′ W **103**
Dmitriyev L'govskiy, *Russ.* 52°6′ N, 35°7′ E **158**
Dmitrov, *Russ.* 56°20′ N, 37°33′ E **154**
Dmitrovsk Orlovskiy, *Russ.* 52°26′ N, 35°10′ E **158**
Dnipropetrovs'k, *Ukr.* 48°28′ N, 34°59′ E **156**
Dno, *Russ.* 57°48′ N, 30°0′ E **166**
Dnyapro, river, *Belarus* 53°18′ N, 30°37′ E **154**
Do Ab-e Mikh-e Zarrin, *Afghan.* 35°19′ N, 67°59′ E **186**
Do, Lac, lake, *Mali* 15°52′ N, 3°2′ W **222**
Do, river, *China* 34°15′ N, 97°2′ E **188**
Doa, *Mozambique* 16°42′ S, 34°44′ E **224**
Doba, *Chad* 8°39′ N, 16°51′ E **218**
Dobane, *Cen. Af. Rep.* 6°24′ N, 24°39′ E **218**
Dobbiaco, *It.* 46°44′ N, 12°13′ E **167**
Dobele, *Latv.* 56°37′ N, 23°15′ E **166**
Dobie Lake, lake, *Can.* 51°26′ N, 91°24′ W **110**
Dobie, river, *Can.* 51°29′ N, 90°58′ W **110**
Dobiegniew, *Pol.* 52°57′ N, 15°46′ E **152**
Dobo, *Indonesia* 5°48′ S, 134°9′ E **192**

Doboj, Bosn. and Herzg. 44°44′ N, 18°3′ E 168
Dobra, Rom. 45°54′ N, 22°35′ E 168
Dobra, Serb. and Mont. 44°37′ N, 21°54′ E 168
Dobreşti, Rom. 46°50′ N, 22°18′ E 168
Dobrich, Bulg. 43°34′ N, 27°50′ E 156
Dobrich, adm. division, Bulg. 43°38′ N, 27°14′ E 156
Dobrinka, Russ. 50°48′ N, 41°44′ E 158
Dobrino, Maced. 41°48′ N, 21°36′ E 168
Dobro Polje, Bosn. and Herzg. 43°34′ N, 18°29′ E 168
Döbrököz, Hung. 46°25′ N, 18°13′ E 168
Dobroselica, Serb. and Mont. 43°37′ N, 19°42′ E 168
Dobruchi, Russ. 58°52′ N, 27°53′ E 166
Dobrush, Belarus 52°26′ N, 31°21′ E 158
Dobryanka, Russ. 58°28′ N, 56°21′ E 154
Dobryszyce, Pol. 51°7′ N, 19°25′ E 152
Dobson, N.Z. 42°29′ S, 171°19′ E 240
Docampadó, Ensenada 4°34′ N, 77°43′ W 136
Doce, river, Braz. 19°3′ S, 41°42′ W 138
Doce, river, Braz. 17°46′ S, 51°40′ W 138
Dock Junction, Ga., U.S. 31°11′ N, 81°31′ W 96
Docksta, Nor. 63°2′ N, 18°20′ E 152
Doclin, Rom. 45°18′ N, 21°39′ E 168
Doctor Arroyo, Mex. 23°39′ N, 100°10′ W 114
Doctor Coss, Mex. 25°53′ N, 99°10′ W 114
Doctor González, Mex. 25°50′ N, 99°56′ W 114
Doctor Pedro P. Peña, Parag. 22°27′ S, 62°20′ W 132
Doctor Petru Groza, Rom. 46°32′ N, 22°29′ E 168
Doda, Lac, lake, Can. 49°20′ N, 75°39′ W 110
Doddridge, Ark., U.S. 33°5′ N, 93°55′ W 103
Dodecanese see Dodekánissa, islands, Aegean Sea 35°59′ N, 26°31′ E 180
Dodekánissa (Dodecanese), islands, Aegean Sea 35°26′ N, 27°28′ E 156
Dodge City, Kans., U.S. 37°45′ N, 100°2′ W 90
Dodge Lake, Can. 59°45′ N, 106°15′ W 108
Dodgeville, Wis., U.S. 42°57′ N, 90°8′ W 102
Dodman Point, U.K. 50°3′ N, 4°45′ W 150
Dodola, Eth. 6°57′ N, 39°9′ E 224
Dodoma, Tanzania 6°10′ S, 35°35′ E 224
Dodoma, adm. division, Tanzania 6°43′ S, 35°14′ E 218
Dodona, ruin(s), Gr. 39°31′ N, 20°39′ E 156
Dodsland, Can. 51°49′ N, 108°50′ W 90
Dodson, La., U.S. 32°3′ N, 92°40′ W 103
Dodson, Mont., U.S. 48°23′ N, 108°15′ W 90
Doe Castle, site, Ire. 55°6′ N, 7°60′ W 150
Doe River, Can. 55°59′ N, 120°7′ W 108
Doerun, Ga., U.S. 31°18′ N, 83°55′ W 96
Doesburg, Neth. 52°0′ N, 6°10′ E 167
Doetinchem, Neth. 51°57′ N, 6°18′ E 167
Dog Creek, Can. 51°37′ N, 122°14′ W 90
Dog Lake, Can. 48°48′ N, 89°57′ W 94
Dog Lake, Can. 48°15′ N, 84°26′ W 94
Dog Lake, lake, Can. 50°58′ N, 98°49′ W 90
Dog Rocks, islands, North Atlantic Ocean 24°5′ N, 79°48′ W 116
Dogai Coring, lake, China 34°25′ N, 88°11′ E 188
Dogface Lake, Can. 60°17′ N, 119°34′ W 108
Dogondoutchi, Niger 13°38′ N, 4°0′ E 222
Doğruyol (Cala), Turk. 41°3′ N, 43°20′ E 195
Doğubayazıt, Turk. 39°30′ N, 44°8′ E 195
Dogwaya, Sudan 17°48′ N, 34°33′ E 182
Doha see Ad Dawḩah, Qatar 25°13′ N, 51°25′ E 196
Dohoukota, Cen. Af. Rep. 6°1′ N, 17°27′ E 218
Doig, river, Can. 56°50′ N, 120°6′ W 108
Doilungdêqên, China 29°49′ N, 90°44′ E 197
Dois Irmãos, Serra, Braz. 8°27′ S, 41°26′ W 132
Doka, Sudan 13°27′ N, 35°45′ E 182
Doka see Bahr Kéita, river, Chad 9°8′ N, 18°38′ E 218
Dokan Dam, Iraq 36°1′ N, 44°37′ E 180
Dokka, Nor. 60°49′ N, 10°3′ E 152
Dokkara, Alg. 35°49′ N, 4°25′ E 150
Dokkum, Neth. 53°19′ N, 6°0′ E 163
Doko, Dem. Rep. of the Congo 3°6′ N, 29°34′ E 224
Dokshytsy, Belarus 54°53′ N, 27°45′ E 166
Dokŭchaev, Kaz. 51°40′ N, 64°13′ E 184
Dokuchayevs'k, Ukr. 47°42′ N, 37°37′ E 156
Dolak, island, Indonesia 8°43′ S, 136°42′ E 192
Dolan Springs, Ariz., U.S. 35°35′ N, 114°16′ W 101
Doland, S. Dak., U.S. 44°52′ N, 98°7′ W 90
Dolbeau, Can. 48°49′ N, 72°18′ W 82
Dolbeau-Mistassini, Can. 48°53′ N, 72°11′ W 94
Doldrums Fracture Zone, North Atlantic Ocean 8°41′ N, 33°42′ W 253
Dole, Fr. 47°5′ N, 5°28′ E 150
Doleib Hill, Sudan 9°20′ N, 31°38′ E 224
Dolgoshchel'ye, Russ. 66°3′ N, 43°29′ E 154
Dolhasca, Rom. 47°24′ N, 26°36′ E 156
Doli, Croatia 42°48′ N, 17°48′ E 168
Dolina, Ukr. 48°56′ N, 24°1′ E 152
Dolinsk, Russ. 47°19′ N, 142°44′ E 190
Dolj, adm. division, Rom. 44°2′ N, 23°6′ E 156
Dollard 53°15′ N, 7°1′ E 163
Dolleman Island, Antarctica 70°41′ S, 60°17′ W 248
Dolly Cays, North Atlantic Ocean 23°28′ N, 77°16′ W 116
Dolní Dvořiště, Czech Rep. 48°39′ N, 14°27′ E 152
Dolnośląskie, adm. division, Pol. 51°10′ N, 15°2′ E 152
Dolo, It. 45°25′ N, 12°3′ E 156
Dolo Bay, Eth. 4°10′ N, 42°6′ E 224
Dolomites, It. 46°44′ N, 11°41′ E 167
Doloon, Mongolia 44°25′ N, 105°18′ E 198
Dolores, Arg. 36°17′ S, 57°41′ W 139
Dolores, Colo., U.S. 37°28′ N, 108°30′ W 92
Dolores, Uru. 33°33′ S, 58°9′ W 139
Dolores Hidalgo, Mex. 21°8′ N, 100°57′ W 114
Dolphin and Union Strait 69°9′ N, 118°43′ W 98
Dolphin, Cape, U.K. 51°11′ S, 60°16′ W 134
Dolsan, S. Korea 34°37′ N, 127°45′ E 200
Dolzhanskaya, Russ. 46°38′ N, 37°45′ E 156
Dolzhitsy, Russ. 58°29′ N, 29°5′ E 166
Dolzhok, Ukr. 48°39′ N, 26°30′ E 156
Dom Joaquim, Braz. 18°58′ S, 43°19′ W 138
Dom, peak, Switz. 46°6′ N, 7°49′ E 165
Dom Pedrito, Braz. 30°60′ S, 54°41′ W 139
Dom Pedro, Braz. 4°60′ S, 44°28′ W 132
Domagaya Lake, Can. 51°53′ N, 65°7′ W 111
Domaniç, Turk. 39°47′ N, 29°35′ E 156
Domanovići, Bosn. and Herzg. 43°7′ N, 17°46′ E 168
Domar, China 33°49′ N, 80°14′ E 188
Domart, Fr. 50°4′ N, 2°7′ E 163
Domaşnea, Rom. 45°5′ N, 22°19′ E 168
Dombarovskiy, Russ. 50°45′ N, 59°31′ E 158
Dombe, Mozambique 19°60′ S, 33°23′ E 224
Dombóvár, Hung. 46°22′ N, 18°7′ E 168
Domburg, Neth. 51°33′ N, 3°29′ E 163
Dome, Ariz., U.S. 32°44′ N, 114°22′ W 101
Dome Circe, region, Antarctica 72°58′ S, 129°17′ E 248
Dome Creek, Can. 53°41′ N, 121°2′ W 108
Dome Fuji, station, Antarctica 77°27′ S, 39°56′ E 248
Dome Mountain, peak, Can. 53°16′ N, 60°38′ W 111
Dome Peak, Can. 61°28′ N, 127°6′ W 98
Dome Peak, Wyo., U.S. 44°33′ N, 107°29′ W 90
Dome Peak, Castle, Ariz., U.S. 33°4′ N, 114°11′ W 101
Dôme, Puy de, peak, Fr. 45°45′ N, 2°55′ E 165
Dome Rock Mountains, Ariz., U.S. 33°37′ N, 114°31′ W 101
Domett, N.Z. 42°53′ S, 173°14′ E 240
Domingo M. Irala, Parag. 25°56′ S, 54°36′ W 139
Dominica 15°25′ N, 61°20′ W 116
Dominican Republic 18°55′ N, 70°60′ W 116
Dominion, Cape, Can. 66°9′ N, 77°33′ W 106
Dominion Lake, Can. 52°40′ N, 62°28′ W 111
Dömitz, Ger. 53°8′ N, 11°15′ E 152
Dommary-Baroncourt, Fr. 49°17′ N, 5°41′ E 163
Domo, Eth. 7°49′ N, 46°55′ E 218
Domodossola, It. 46°7′ N, 8°16′ E 167
Dompago see Badjoudé, Benin 9°42′ N, 1°23′ E 222
Domrémy, Fr. 48°26′ N, 5°40′ E 163
Dömsöd, Hung. 47°5′ N, 19°1′ E 168
Domuyo, Volcán, Arg. 36°38′ S, 70°34′ W 134
Don Benito, Sp. 38°57′ N, 5°52′ W 164
Don Pedro Reservoir, lake, Calif., U.S. 37°43′ N, 120°34′ W 100
Don Peninsula, Can. 52°27′ N, 128°10′ W 108
Dôn, river, Laos 15°43′ N, 105°56′ E 202
Don, river, Russ. 52°0′ N, 39°2′ E 160
Donadeu, Arg. 26°41′ S, 62°42′ W 139
Donald Landing, Can. 54°29′ N, 125°41′ W 108
Donalda, Can. 52°35′ N, 112°34′ W 108
Donaldson, Minn., U.S. 48°33′ N, 96°55′ W 90
Donaldsonville, La., U.S. 30°4′ N, 90°60′ W 103
Donau, river, Ger. 47°48′ N, 8°25′ E 150
Donauwörth, Ger. 48°43′ N, 10°46′ E 152
Doncaster, U.K. 53°31′ N, 1°9′ W 162
Dondo, Angola 9°41′ S, 14°26′ E 218
Dondo, Mozambique 19°39′ S, 34°43′ E 224
Donets' Kryazh, Ukr. 47°29′ N, 36°35′ E 156
Donets'k, Ukr. 47°57′ N, 37°47′ E 156
Dong Hoi, Vietnam 17°29′ N, 106°36′ E 202
Dong Taijnar Hu, lake, China 37°27′ N, 92°46′ E 188
Dong Ujimqin Qi, China 45°31′ N, 116°57′ E 198
Donga, Nig. 7°41′ N, 10°6′ E 222
Dong-Alysh, Kyrg. 42°17′ N, 74°46′ E 184
Dong'an, China 26°24′ N, 111°13′ E 198
Dongara, Austral. 29°14′ S, 114°57′ E 231
Dongbei (Manchuria), region, Asia 40°34′ N, 122°39′ E 200
Dongfang (Basuo), China 19°3′ N, 108°38′ E 198
Dongfeng, China 42°41′ N, 125°25′ E 200
Donggala, Indonesia 0°37′ N, 119°45′ E 192
Donggou, China 39°53′ N, 124°8′ E 200
Dongguan, China 23°2′ N, 113°44′ E 190
Dongguang, China 37°53′ N, 116°32′ E 198
Donghae, S. Korea 37°33′ N, 129°7′ E 200
Dônghén, Laos 16°43′ N, 105°16′ E 202
Donglan, China 24°28′ N, 107°20′ E 198
Dongo, Angola 14°38′ S, 15°39′ E 220
Dongo, Dem. Rep. of the Congo 2°40′ N, 18°27′ E 218
Dongola, Sudan 19°9′ N, 30°28′ E 182
Dongou, Congo 2°2′ N, 18°3′ E 218
Dongping, China 35°49′ N, 116°22′ E 198
Dongping, China 21°42′ N, 112°15′ E 198
Dongqiao, China 31°58′ N, 90°38′ E 188
Dongshan, China 23°37′ N, 117°23′ E 198
Dongsheng, China 39°51′ N, 109°59′ E 198
Dongtai, China 32°52′ N, 120°17′ E 198
Dongting Hu, lake, China 28°54′ N, 111°45′ E 198
Dongwe, river, Zambia 13°52′ S, 24°59′ E 224
Dongxiang, China 28°12′ N, 116°33′ E 198
Dongxing, China 21°33′ N, 107°59′ E 198
Dongyztaŭ, Kaz. 46°38′ N, 57°37′ E 158
Dongzhen, China 38°59′ N, 103°40′ E 198
Donington, U.K. 52°54′ N, 0°12′ E 162
Doniphan, Mo., U.S. 36°36′ N, 90°49′ W 96
Donji Kamengrad, Bosn. and Herzg. 44°47′ N, 16°33′ E 168
Donji Miholjac, Croatia 45°44′ N, 18°9′ E 168
Donji Tovarnik, Serb. and Mont. 44°48′ N, 19°56′ E 168
Donji Vakuf, Bosn. and Herzg. 44°9′ N, 17°24′ E 168
Donkese, Dem. Rep. of the Congo 1°33′ S, 18°28′ E 218
Donnacona, Can. 46°40′ N, 71°45′ W 94
Donnelly, Can. 55°43′ N, 117°8′ W 108
Donnelly Peak, Nev., U.S. 41°5′ N, 119°21′ W 90
Donnellys Crossing, N.Z. 35°43′ S, 173°36′ E 240
Donner, La., U.S. 29°41′ N, 90°57′ W 103
Donner Pass, Calif., U.S. 39°18′ N, 120°20′ W 90
Donnersberg, peak, Ger. 49°36′ N, 7°52′ E 163
Donostia-San Sebastián, Sp. 43°17′ N, 2°1′ W 164
Donovan, Ill., U.S. 40°52′ N, 87°37′ W 102
Donzère, Fr. 44°26′ N, 4°43′ E 150
Doon, river, U.K. 55°23′ N, 4°51′ W 150
Doone Valley, site, U.K. 51°11′ N, 3°47′ W 162
Doonerak, Mount, Alas., U.S. 67°55′ N, 150°54′ W 98
Door Peninsula, Wis., U.S. 44°29′ N, 87°41′ W 94
Door Point, La., U.S. 30°2′ N, 88°52′ W 103
Dora, Ala., U.S. 33°43′ N, 87°6′ W 96
Dora, N. Mex., U.S. 33°55′ N, 103°20′ W 92
Dora Riparia, river, It. 45°6′ N, 6°50′ E 165
Doran Lake, Can. 61°13′ N, 108°32′ W 108
Dorbod, China 46°54′ N, 124°27′ E 198
Đorđe Petrov, Maced. 42°1′ N, 21°21′ E 168
Dorchester, U.K. 50°42′ N, 2°27′ W 162
Dorchester, U.K. 51°38′ N, 1°10′ W 162
Dorchester, Cape, Can. 65°29′ N, 81°58′ W 246
Dordabis, Namibia 22°52′ S, 17°34′ E 227
Dordives, Fr. 48°8′ N, 2°45′ E 163
Dordogne, river, Fr. 44°52′ N, 1°31′ E 165
Dordrecht, Neth. 51°47′ N, 4°40′ E 167
Dordrecht, S. Af. 31°24′ S, 27°0′ E 227
Doré Lake, Can. 54°36′ N, 107°21′ W 108
Dores do Indaiá, Braz. 19°27′ S, 45°37′ W 138
Dorfen, Ger. 48°16′ N, 12°9′ E 152
Dorfmark, Ger. 52°54′ N, 9°47′ E 150
Dori, Burkina Faso 14°1′ N, 0°3′ E 222
Dorintosh, Can. 54°21′ N, 108°38′ W 108
Dorking, U.K. 51°14′ N, 0°20′ E 162
Dormaa Ahenkro, Ghana 7°17′ N, 2°53′ W 222
Dormagen, Ger. 51°5′ N, 6°49′ E 167
Dormans, Fr. 49°4′ N, 3°39′ E 163
Dorneşti, Rom. 47°52′ N, 26°0′ E 152
Dorno Djoutougé, Chad 12°29′ N, 22°15′ E 216
Doro, Mali 16°1′ N, 1°5′ W 222
Dorog, Hung. 47°42′ N, 18°43′ E 168
Dorogobuzh, Russ. 54°52′ N, 33°22′ E 154
Dorogorskoye, Russ. 65°39′ N, 44°27′ E 154
Dorohoi, Rom. 47°56′ N, 26°22′ E 152
Dorora, spring, Chad 17°57′ N, 18°41′ E 216
Dorotea, Nor. 64°16′ N, 16°22′ E 152
Dorris, Calif., U.S. 41°57′ N, 121°56′ W 90
Dorset, Vt., U.S. 43°15′ N, 73°7′ W 104
Dorsten, Ger. 51°39′ N, 6°57′ E 167
Dortmund, Ger. 51°30′ N, 7°27′ E 167
Dörtyol, Turk. 36°50′ N, 36°12′ E 156
Doruma, Dem. Rep. of the Congo 4°42′ N, 27°39′ E 224
Doruokha, Russ. 72°6′ N, 113°30′ E 160
Dörverden, Ger. 52°50′ N, 9°14′ E 152
Dos Bahías, Cabo, Arg. 45°7′ S, 65°30′ W 134
Dos Hermanas, Sp. 37°17′ N, 5°56′ W 164
Dos Lagunas, Guatemala 17°43′ N, 89°38′ W 115
Dos Lagunas Biotope, Guatemala 17°35′ N, 90°14′ W 115
Dos Palos, Calif., U.S. 36°58′ N, 120°38′ W 100
Dos Pozos, Arg. 43°53′ S, 65°25′ W 134
Doso, Côte d'Ivoire 4°45′ N, 6°50′ W 222
Dosso, Niger 13°2′ N, 3°11′ E 222
Dossor, Kaz. 47°31′ N, 52°59′ E 158
Do'stlik, Uzb. 40°33′ N, 68°1′ E 197
Dostlux, Turkm. 37°43′ N, 65°22′ E 197
Dostyq, Kaz. 45°14′ N, 82°29′ E 184
Dot Lake, Alas., U.S. 63°41′ N, 144°9′ W 98
Dothan, Ala., U.S. 31°13′ N, 85°23′ W 96
Dothan, ruin(s), West Bank 32°23′ N, 35°12′ E 194
Dotnuva, Lith. 55°22′ N, 23°51′ E 166
Doty, Wash., U.S. 46°36′ N, 123°17′ W 100
Douai, Fr. 50°21′ N, 3°4′ E 163
Douako, Guinea 9°43′ N, 10°11′ W 222
Douala, Cameroon 4°5′ N, 9°42′ E 222
Douaouir, Mali 20°8′ N, 2°59′ W 222
Douar Sadok, Tun. 35°56′ N, 9°43′ E 156
Douara, spring, Mauritania 17°36′ N, 12°47′ W 222
Douarnenez, Fr. 48°4′ N, 4°20′ W 150
Double Mountain, Calif., U.S. 35°1′ N, 118°32′ W 101
Doubs, river, Switz. 47°19′ N, 6°48′ E 165
Doucette, Tex., U.S. 30°48′ N, 94°26′ W 103
Doudeville, Fr. 49°42′ N, 0°46′ E 163
Doué, Côte d'Ivoire 7°42′ N, 7°39′ W 222
Douentza, Mali 14°58′ N, 2°59′ W 222
Douglas, Ariz., U.S. 31°21′ N, 109°35′ W 112
Douglas, Ga., U.S. 31°29′ N, 82°52′ W 96
Douglas, Mich., U.S. 42°37′ N, 86°12′ W 102
Douglas, S. Af. 29°5′ S, 23°46′ E 227
Douglas, U.K. 54°9′ N, 4°29′ W 162
Douglas, Wyo., U.S. 42°45′ N, 105°23′ W 90
Douglas Islands, Indian Ocean 67°21′ S, 63°31′ E 248
Douglas Lake, Tenn., U.S. 35°59′ N, 84°3′ W 81
Douglas Pass, Colo., U.S. 39°36′ N, 108°49′ W 90
Douglass, Kans., U.S. 37°29′ N, 97°1′ W 92
Douglass, Tex., U.S. 31°39′ N, 94°53′ W 103
Douglassville, Tex., U.S. 33°11′ N, 94°21′ W 103
Doukoula, Cameroon 10°7′ N, 14°56′ E 218
Doulevant-le-Château, Fr. 48°22′ N, 4°55′ E 163
Doullens, Fr. 50°9′ N, 2°20′ E 163
Doulus Head, Ire. 51°58′ N, 10°38′ W 150
Douma, Leb. 34°12′ N, 35°50′ E 194
Doumé, Cameroon 4°15′ N, 13°27′ E 218
Douna, Mali 14°44′ N, 1°43′ W 222
Doura, Mali 13°16′ N, 5°58′ W 222
Dourada, Serra, Braz. 12°47′ S, 48°59′ W 130
Dourados, Braz. 22°15′ S, 54°50′ W 132
Dourados, river, Braz. 22°23′ S, 55°26′ W 132
Dourbali, Chad 11°48′ N, 15°52′ E 218
Dourdan, Fr. 48°31′ N, 2°1′ E 163
Douro, river, Port. 40°43′ N, 8°23′ W 143
Douvaine, Fr. 46°18′ N, 6°18′ E 167
Douz, Tun. 33°28′ N, 9°0′ E 216
Dove Bugt 76°15′ N, 26°60′ W 73
Dove, river, U.K. 53°8′ N, 1°52′ W 162
Dover, Del., U.S. 39°7′ N, 75°38′ W 94
Dover, Fla., U.S. 27°59′ N, 82°12′ W 105
Dover, N.H., U.S. 43°12′ N, 70°53′ W 104
Dover, Ohio, U.S. 40°31′ N, 81°28′ W 102
Dover, U.K. 51°7′ N, 1°17′ E 163
Dover Air Force Base, Del., U.S. 39°7′ N, 75°33′ W 94
Dover, Strait of 50°52′ N, 0°56′ E 162
Dover-Foxcroft, Me., U.S. 45°11′ N, 69°14′ W 94
Dovers, Cape, Antarctica 67°10′ S, 97°16′ E 248
Dovrefjell, Nor. 62°5′ N, 9°20′ E 152
Dow Gonbadān, Iran 30°20′ N, 50°46′ E 196
Dow Polān, Iran 31°54′ N, 50°43′ E 180
Dow Rūd, Iran 33°29′ N, 49°8′ E 180
Dowa, Malawi 13°38′ S, 33°56′ E 224
Dowagiac, Mich., U.S. 41°59′ N, 86°7′ W 102
Dowi, Tanjung, Indonesia 1°30′ N, 97°0′ E 196
Dowlat Yar, Afghan. 34°31′ N, 65°49′ E 186
Dowlatabad, Afghan. 36°25′ N, 64°56′ E 186
Dowlatābād, Iran 28°17′ N, 56°41′ E 196
Dowling Lake, Can. 51°42′ N, 112°39′ W 108
Downes, S. Af. 31°30′ S, 19°56′ E 227
Downey, Calif., U.S. 33°56′ N, 118°9′ W 101
Downham Market, U.K. 52°36′ N, 0°22′ E 162
Downs, Kans., U.S. 39°29′ N, 98°34′ W 90
Downs Mountain, Wyo., U.S. 43°17′ N, 109°45′ W 90
Dowshi, Afghan. 35°36′ N, 68°44′ E 186
Doyang, S. Korea 34°32′ N, 127°10′ E 200
Doyline, La., U.S. 32°31′ N, 93°25′ W 103
Dozois, Réservoir, lake, Can. 47°19′ N, 77°56′ W 94
Drâa, Cap, Mor. 28°47′ N, 11°53′ W 214
Drâa, Hamada du, Alg. 28°59′ N, 7°8′ W 214
Draç, Alban. 41°33′ N, 19°30′ E 168
Dracena, Braz. 21°29′ S, 51°30′ W 138
Drachten, Neth. 53°6′ N, 6°6′ E 163
Dracut, Mass., U.S. 42°40′ N, 71°19′ W 104
Dragaš, Serb. and Mont. 42°3′ N, 20°38′ E 168
Draginac, Serb. and Mont. 44°31′ N, 19°25′ E 168
Dragočaj, Bosn. and Herzg. 44°51′ N, 17°8′ E 168
Dragočava, Bosn. and Herzg. 43°28′ N, 18°49′ E 168
Dragoevo, Maced. 41°40′ N, 22°7′ E 168
Dragovishtitsa, Bulg. 42°21′ N, 22°39′ E 168
Dragsfjärd, Fin. 60°4′ N, 22°30′ E 166
Drake, N. Dak., U.S. 47°53′ N, 100°24′ W 90
Drake Peak, Oreg., U.S. 42°17′ N, 120°14′ W 90
Drakensberg, Africa 24°47′ S, 30°24′ E 227
Dráma, Gr. 41°10′ N, 24°17′ E 180
Drammen, Nor. 59°43′ N, 10°11′ E 152
Dran, Vietnam 11°52′ N, 108°37′ E 202
Drangedal, Nor. 59°6′ N, 9°1′ E 152
Dranov, Lacul, lake, Rom. 44°50′ N, 28°48′ E 156
Dransfeld, Ger. 51°29′ N, 9°45′ E 167
Dras, India 34°26′ N, 75°46′ E 186
Drava, river, Croatia 46°19′ N, 16°42′ E 168
Drávaszabolcs, Hung. 45°48′ N, 18°12′ E 168
Drawsko, Pol. 52°51′ N, 16°3′ E 152
Drayton, Can. 43°44′ N, 80°41′ W 102
Drayton, N. Dak., U.S. 48°32′ N, 97°12′ W 94
Drayton Plains, Mich., U.S. 42°40′ N, 83°22′ W 102
Drayton Valley, Can. 53°12′ N, 114°60′ W 108
Drebkau, Ger. 51°39′ N, 14°12′ E 152
Dreieich, Ger. 50°1′ N, 8°40′ E 167
Dreistelzberg, peak, Ger. 50°16′ N, 9°44′ E 167
Dren, Bulg. 42°25′ N, 23°9′ E 168
Drenovci, Croatia 44°54′ N, 18°54′ E 168
Dresden, Can. 42°34′ N, 82°10′ W 102
Dresden, Ger. 51°2′ N, 13°44′ E 152
Dresden, Ohio, U.S. 40°6′ N, 82°1′ W 102
Dretun', Belarus 55°41′ N, 29°10′ E 166
Dreux, Fr. 48°44′ N, 1°21′ E 163
Drevsjø, Nor. 61°52′ N, 12°2′ E 152
Drezdenko, Pol. 52°50′ N, 15°50′ E 152
Drežnik, Serb. and Mont. 43°46′ N, 19°53′ E 168
Driftwood, river, Can. 55°55′ N, 126°59′ W 108
Drin, river, Alban. 42°11′ N, 19°51′ E 168
Drinjača, Bosn. and Herzg. 44°18′ N, 19°9′ E 168
Drinkwater Pass, Oreg., U.S. 43°46′ N, 118°17′ W 90
Driscoll Island, Antarctica 75°59′ S, 145°33′ W 248
Driskill Mountain, La., U.S. 32°24′ N, 92°56′ W 103
Drlače, Serb. and Mont. 44°8′ N, 19°29′ E 168
Drniš, Croatia 43°51′ N, 16°8′ E 168
Drobeta-Turnu Severin, Rom. 44°37′ N, 22°38′ E 168
Drochia, Mold. 48°2′ N, 27°48′ E 156
Droitwich, U.K. 52°15′ N, 2°9′ W 162
Dronero, It. 44°28′ N, 7°22′ E 167
Dronten, Neth. 52°30′ N, 5°43′ E 163
Droué, Fr. 48°2′ N, 1°5′ E 150
Drowning, river, Can. 50°31′ N, 86°4′ W 110
Droyssig, Ger. 51°2′ N, 12°1′ E 152
Drozdyn', Ukr. 51°38′ N, 27°14′ E 152
Drūkšių Ežeras, lake, Lith. 55°37′ N, 26°8′ E 166
Drum Castle, site, U.K. 57°4′ N, 2°27′ W 150
Drumheller, Can. 51°28′ N, 112°43′ W 90
Drumlanrig Castle, site, U.K. 55°16′ N, 3°55′ W 150
Drummond, Mont., U.S. 46°38′ N, 113°9′ W 90
Drummond Island, Mich., U.S. 45°53′ N, 85°45′ W 81
Drummond Range, Austral. 23°59′ S, 146°26′ E 230
Drummondville, Can. 45°51′ N, 72°31′ W 94
Drumochter Pass, U.K. 56°51′ N, 4°14′ W 150
Drumright, Okla., U.S. 35°57′ N, 96°36′ W 92
Druya, Belarus 55°45′ N, 27°26′ E 166
Druzhba, Ukr. 52°2′ N, 34°3′ E 158
Druzhnaya Gorka, Russ. 59°16′ N, 30°6′ E 166
Drvar, Bosn. and Herzg. 44°21′ N, 16°22′ E 168
Dry Bay 59°1′ N, 138°60′ W 98
Dry Creek, La., U.S. 30°39′ N, 93°4′ W 103
Dry Falls, site, Wash., U.S. 47°33′ N, 119°27′ W 90
Dry Lake, Nev., U.S. 36°27′ N, 114°51′ W 101
Dry Mills, Me., U.S. 43°55′ N, 70°22′ W 104
Dry Prong, La., U.S. 31°33′ N, 92°32′ W 103
Dry Ridge, Ky., U.S. 38°40′ N, 84°36′ W 102
Dry Tortugas, islands, Gulf of Mexico 24°40′ N, 83°1′ W 105
Dry Tortugas National Park, Fla., U.S. 24°38′ N, 82°54′ W 105
Dryanovo, Bulg. 42°58′ N, 25°28′ E 156
Dryberry Lake, Can. 49°34′ N, 94°22′ W 90
Drybrough, Can. 56°32′ N, 101°15′ W 108
Dryden, Can. 49°47′ N, 92°50′ W 94
Dryden, Mich., U.S. 42°55′ N, 83°8′ W 102
Dryden, Tex., U.S. 30°2′ N, 102°7′ W 92
Dryden Flight Research Center, Calif., U.S. 34°59′ N, 117°56′ W 101
Drygalski Island, Antarctica 64°59′ S, 92°17′ E 248
Drygalski Mountains, Antarctica 71°37′ S, 10°5′ E 248
Drysa, river, Belarus 55°44′ N, 28°54′ E 166
Drysdale River National Park, Austral. 15°7′ S, 126°34′ E 238
Drysvyaty, Vozyera, lake, Belarus 55°34′ N, 26°38′ E 166
Dschang, Cameroon 5°24′ N, 10°4′ E 222
Du Bois, Pa., U.S. 41°7′ N, 78°46′ W 94
Du Pont, Wash., U.S. 47°5′ N, 122°34′ W 100
Du Quoin, Mo., U.S. 38°0′ N, 89°14′ W 96
Dua, river, Dem. Rep. of the Congo 2°54′ N, 21°59′ E 218
Duart Castle, site, U.K. 56°25′ N, 5°45′ W 150
Duarte, Pico, peak, Dom. Rep. 19°0′ N, 71°3′ W 116
Dub, Pol. 50°39′ N, 23°34′ E 158
Ḑubā, Saudi Arabia 27°21′ N, 35°43′ E 180
Dubac, Croatia 42°37′ N, 18°9′ E 168
Dubach, La., U.S. 32°40′ N, 92°40′ W 103
Dubai see Dubayy, U.A.E. 25°13′ N, 55°17′ E 196
Dubăsari, Mold. 47°15′ N, 29°10′ E 158
Dubawnt Lake, Can. 63°2′ N, 103°52′ W 106
Dubawnt, river, Can. 60°44′ N, 106°19′ W 108
Dubayy (Dubai), U.A.E. 25°13′ N, 55°17′ E 196
Dubele, Dem. Rep. of the Congo 2°52′ N, 29°33′ E 224
Dubeninki, Pol. 54°17′ N, 22°32′ E 166
Dubenskiy, Russ. 51°28′ N, 56°35′ E 158
Dubica, Croatia 45°11′ N, 16°48′ E 168
Dubičiai, Lith. 54°1′ N, 24°44′ E 166
Dubinskaya, Kaz. 43°43′ N, 80°12′ E 184
Dubivtsi, Ukr. 49°4′ N, 24°46′ E 152
Dublán, Mex. 30°27′ N, 107°55′ W 92
Dublin, Ga., U.S. 32°31′ N, 82°55′ W 96
Dublin, Ind., U.S. 39°48′ N, 85°13′ W 102
Dublin, N.H., U.S. 42°54′ N, 72°5′ W 104
Dublin, Tex., U.S. 32°5′ N, 98°21′ W 92
Dublin (Baile Átha Cliath), Ire. 53°18′ N, 6°26′ W 150
Dubna, Russ. 56°43′ N, 37°12′ E 154
Dubois, Idaho, U.S. 44°9′ N, 112°13′ W 90
Dubois, Wyo., U.S. 43°32′ N, 109°37′ W 90
Dubose, Can. 54°16′ N, 128°40′ W 108
Duboštica, Bosn. and Herzg. 44°14′ N, 18°20′ E 168
Dubove, Ukr. 51°14′ N, 24°40′ E 152
Dubovka, Russ. 49°2′ N, 44°42′ E 158
Dubrava, Croatia 45°49′ N, 16°3′ E 168
Dubrave, Bosn. and Herzg. 44°48′ N, 18°33′ E 168
Dubravica, Serb. and Mont. 44°41′ N, 21°5′ E 168
Dubréka, Guinea 9°47′ N, 13°34′ W 222
Dubrovka, Russ. 56°22′ N, 28°39′ E 166
Dubrovnik (Ragusa), Croatia 42°38′ N, 18°5′ E 168
Dubrovnoye, Russ. 57°54′ N, 69°29′ E 169
Dubrovytsya, Ukr. 51°33′ N, 26°32′ E 152
Dubrowna, Belarus 54°36′ N, 30°49′ E 154
Dubuque, Iowa, U.S. 42°30′ N, 90°40′ W 94
Duc Tho, Vietnam 18°30′ N, 105°35′ E 202
Duchesne, Utah, U.S. 40°10′ N, 110°24′ W 90
Ducie Island, U.K. 24°38′ S, 124°48′ W 255
Duck Bay, Can. 52°8′ N, 100°10′ W 108
Duck Hill, Miss., U.S. 33°35′ N, 89°43′ W 96
Duck Lake, Can. 52°48′ N, 106°13′ W 108
Duck, river, Tenn., U.S. 35°41′ N, 86°60′ W 80
Duckbill Point, Can. 50°30′ N, 56°13′ W 111
Ducktown, Tenn., U.S. 35°2′ N, 84°23′ W 96
Ducor, Calif., U.S. 35°53′ N, 119°3′ W 101
Duda, river, Col. 2°58′ N, 74°15′ W 136
Dudelange, Lux. 49°28′ N, 6°4′ E 163
Duderstadt, Ger. 51°31′ N, 10°14′ E 167
Dudhi, India 24°12′ N, 83°13′ E 197
Dudhnai, India 25°58′ N, 90°45′ E 197
Dudinka, Russ. 69°25′ N, 86°24′ E 169
Dudley, Mass., U.S. 42°2′ N, 71°56′ W 104
Dudley, U.K. 52°30′ N, 2°6′ W 162
Dudleyville, Ariz., U.S. 32°56′ N, 110°44′ W 92
Dudo, Somalia 9°16′ N, 50°11′ E 216
Dudub, Eth. 6°54′ N, 46°44′ E 218
Dudypta, river, Russ. 71°10′ N, 91°51′ E 160
Duékoué, Côte d'Ivoire 6°39′ N, 7°20′ W 222
Dueodde, Den. 54°53′ N, 14°30′ E 152
Duero, river, Sp. 41°17′ N, 2°56′ W 214
Dufek Coast, Antarctica 84°41′ S, 154°15′ W 248
Dufek Massif, peak, Antarctica 82°41′ S, 54°13′ W 248
Duff Islands, South Pacific Ocean 9°30′ S, 167°28′ E 238
Dugo Selo, Croatia 45°48′ N, 16°13′ E 168
Dugulle, spring, Somalia 2°14′ N, 44°30′ E 218
Dugway, Utah, U.S. 40°13′ N, 112°45′ W 90
Duida-Marahuaca National Park, Venez. 3°36′ N, 65°58′ W 136
Duisburg, Ger. 51°25′ N, 6°45′ E 167
Duitama, Col. 5°49′ N, 73°3′ W 136
Duiwelskloof, S. Af. 23°42′ S, 30°9′ E 227
Dujuuma, Somalia 1°10′ N, 42°34′ E 224
Duk Fadiat, Sudan 7°42′ N, 31°25′ E 224
Duk Faiwil, Sudan 7°30′ N, 31°26′ E 224
Dukafulu, Eth. 5°7′ N, 39°7′ E 224
Dukambia, Eritrea 14°44′ N, 37°29′ E 182
Dukhān, Qatar 25°20′ N, 50°47′ E 196
Dukku, Nig. 10°47′ N, 10°46′ E 222
Dūkštas, Lith. 55°31′ N, 26°18′ E 166
Dula, Dem. Rep. of the Congo 4°41′ N, 20°17′ E 218
Dulan, China 36°19′ N, 98°8′ E 188
Dulce, river, Arg. 29°58′ S, 62°44′ W 139
Dulion, Golfe 43°2′ N, 3°49′ E 150
Dülmen, Ger. 51°50′ N, 7°16′ E 167
Dulovka, Russ. 57°30′ N, 28°20′ E 166
Duluth, Minn., U.S. 46°47′ N, 92°8′ W 94
Dulverton, U.K. 51°2′ N, 3°33′ W 162
Dūmā, Syr. 33°34′ N, 36°24′ E 194
Duma, river, Dem. Rep. of the Congo 4°32′ N, 26°35′ E 224

Dumaguete, *Philippines* 9°18′ N, 123°14′ E 203
Dumai, *Indonesia* 1°41′ N, 101°27′ E 196
Dumaran, island, *Philippines* 10°19′ N, 119°57′ E 192
Dumas, *Ark., U.S.* 33°52′ N, 91°30′ W 96
Dumas, *Tex., U.S.* 35°50′ N, 101°59′ W 92
Dumas, Peninsula, *Chile* 55°4′ S, 68°22′ W 134
Dumayr, *Syr.* 33°38′ N, 36°41′ E 194
Dume, river, *Dem. Rep. of the Congo* 5°3′ N, 24°48′ E 224
Dumfries, *U.K.* 55°4′ N, 3°36′ W 150
Dumka, *India* 24°14′ N, 87°15′ E 197
Dummett, Mount, *Antarctica* 73°16′ S, 63°25′ E 248
Dumoine, Lac, lake, *Can.* 46°51′ N, 78°28′ W 94
Dumont d'Urville, station, *Antarctica* 66°39′ S, 139°39′ E 248
Dümpelfeld, *Ger.* 50°26′ N, 6°57′ E 167
Dumra, *India* 26°33′ N, 85°30′ E 197
Dumshaf Plain, *Norwegian Sea* 69°58′ N, 1°51′ E 255
Dumyâṭ (Damietta), *Egypt* 31°25′ N, 31°49′ E 180
Dun, *Fr.* 49°23′ N, 5°12′ E 163
Dun Aengus, ruin(s), *Ire.* 53°7′ N, 9°55′ W 150
Dún Dealgan see Dundalk, *Ire.* 53°59′ N, 6°24′ W 150
Duna, river, *Europe* 47°44′ N, 17°37′ E 168
Dunaff Head, *Ire.* 55°17′ N, 7°53′ W 150
Dunaharaszti, *Hung.* 47°21′ N, 19°6′ E 168
Dunakeszi, *Hung.* 47°37′ N, 19°9′ E 168
Dunapataj, *Hung.* 46°38′ N, 19°0′ E 168
Dunărea, river, *Europe* 43°42′ N, 22°49′ E 180
Dunaszekcs o, *Hung.* 46°4′ N, 18°44′ E 168
Dunaújváros, *Hung.* 46°58′ N, 18°55′ E 168
Dunavecse, *Hung.* 46°54′ N, 18°58′ E 168
Dunay, *Russ.* 42°53′ N, 132°20′ E 200
Dunayivtsi, *Ukr.* 48°52′ N, 26°51′ E 152
Dunbar, *W. Va., U.S.* 38°21′ N, 81°45′ W 94
Dunblane, *Can.* 51°12′ N, 106°55′ W 90
Duncan, *Ariz., U.S.* 32°42′ N, 109°6′ W 92
Duncan, *Can.* 48°46′ N, 123°41′ W 100
Duncan, *Okla., U.S.* 34°28′ N, 97°58′ W 96
Duncan Passage 10°58′ N, 91°46′ E 188
Dundaga, *Latv.* 57°30′ N, 22°19′ E 166
Dundalk (Dún Dealgan), *Ire.* 53°59′ N, 6°24′ W 150
Dundas, *Ill., U.S.* 38°50′ N, 88°6′ W 102
Dundas Islands, *North Pacific Ocean* 54°35′ N, 130°38′ W 98
Dundas Peninsula, *Can.* 74°29′ N, 116°39′ W 106
Dundbürd, *Mongolia* 47°57′ N, 111°29′ E 198
Dundee, *Fla., U.S.* 28°1′ N, 81°38′ W 105
Dundee, *Mich., U.S.* 41°57′ N, 83°39′ W 102
Dundee, *S. Af.* 28°10′ S, 30°9′ E 227
Dundee, *U.K.* 56°36′ N, 3°10′ W 143
Dundee Island, *Antarctica* 63°49′ S, 58°1′ W 134
Dundo, *Angola* 7°24′ S, 20°47′ E 218
Dundrennan, *U.K.* 54°49′ N, 3°57′ W 162
Dundret, peak, *Nor.* 67°5′ N, 20°23′ E 152
Dund-Urt, *Mongolia* 47°56′ N, 106°12′ E 198
Dund-Us see Hovd, *Mongolia* 48°2′ N, 91°40′ E 190
Dune Sandy Hook, *Can.* 47°11′ N, 61°45′ W 111
Dunedin, *Fla., U.S.* 28°1′ N, 82°46′ W 105
Dunedin, *N.Z.* 45°52′ S, 170°28′ E 240
Dunedin, river, *Can.* 58°56′ N, 124°29′ W 108
Dunes City, *Oreg., U.S.* 43°52′ N, 124°8′ W 90
Dunfermline, *U.K.* 56°4′ N, 3°28′ W 150
Dungannon, *Can.* 43°50′ N, 81°37′ W 102
Dungarpur, *India* 23°50′ N, 73°43′ E 186
Dungas, *Niger* 13°4′ N, 9°19′ E 222
Dungeness, *U.K.* 50°54′ N, 0°58′ E 162
Dungeness, Punta, *Arg.* 52°31′ S, 68°22′ W 134
Dungu, *Dem. Rep. of the Congo* 3°33′ N, 28°34′ E 224
Dungu, river, *Dem. Rep. of the Congo* 3°40′ N, 28°34′ E 224
Dungunab, *Sudan* 21°5′ N, 37°4′ E 182
Dunhua, *China* 43°23′ N, 128°7′ E 198
Dunhuang, *China* 40°10′ N, 94°42′ E 188
Dunilavichy, *Belarus* 55°4′ N, 27°13′ E 166
Dunk Island, *Austral.* 18°2′ S, 146°15′ E 230
Dunkassa, *Benin* 10°19′ N, 3°7′ E 222
Dunkerque (Dunkirk), *Fr.* 51°1′ N, 2°21′ E 163
Dunkery Beacon, peak, *U.K.* 51°9′ N, 3°37′ W 162
Dunkirk, *Ind., U.S.* 40°22′ N, 85°12′ W 94
Dunkirk, *N.Y., U.S.* 42°28′ N, 79°21′ W 94
Dunkirk, river, *Can.* 57°8′ N, 113°2′ W 108
Dunkirk see Dunkerque, *Fr.* 51°1′ N, 2°21′ E 163
Dunkur, *Eth.* 11°54′ N, 35°56′ E 182
Dunkwa, *Ghana* 5°56′ N, 1°48′ W 222
Dunlap, *Iowa, U.S.* 41°50′ N, 95°35′ W 90
Dunlop, *Can.* 54°44′ N, 98°51′ W 108
Dunluce Castle, site, *U.K.* 55°11′ N, 6°41′ W 150
Dunmore Town, *Bahamas* 25°30′ N, 76°38′ W 96
Dunn, *N.C., U.S.* 35°18′ N, 78°37′ W 96
Dunnellon, *Fla., U.S.* 29°3′ N, 82°28′ W 105
Dunning, *Nebr., U.S.* 41°48′ N, 100°7′ W 90
Dunnottar Castle, site, *U.K.* 56°55′ N, 2°19′ W 150
Dunqul, spring, *Egypt* 23°23′ N, 31°39′ E 182
Dunrobin Castle, site, *U.K.* 57°58′ N, 4°5′ W 150
Dunseith, *N. Dak., U.S.* 48°47′ N, 100°4′ W 90
Dunsmuir, *Calif., U.S.* 41°12′ N, 122°18′ W 92
Dunstable, *U.K.* 51°53′ N, 0°32′ E 162
Dunstanburgh Castle, site, *U.K.* 55°28′ N, 1°42′ W 150
Dunster, *Can.* 53°6′ N, 119°53′ W 108
Dunster, *U.K.* 51°11′ N, 3°26′ W 162
Dunte, *Latv.* 57°25′ N, 24°25′ E 166
Duntroon, *N.Z.* 44°53′ S, 170°38′ E 240
Dunvegan, *Can.* 55°57′ N, 118°37′ W 108
Dunvegan Lake, *Can.* 60°10′ N, 107°45′ W 108
Duolun, *China* 42°10′ N, 116°30′ E 198
Duparquet, Lac, lake, *Can.* 48°27′ N, 79°52′ W 110
Dupont, *Ind., U.S.* 38°53′ N, 85°31′ W 102
Dupree, *S. Dak., U.S.* 45°2′ N, 101°37′ W 90
Dupuyer, *Mont., U.S.* 48°9′ N, 112°31′ W 90
Duqm, *Oman* 19°37′ N, 57°41′ E 182
Duque de Caxias, *Braz.* 22°44′ S, 43°18′ W 138
Duque de York, Isla, island, *Chile* 50°51′ S, 77°57′ W 134
Dur Sharrukin, ruin(s), *Iraq* 36°30′ N, 43°3′ E 195
Durack Range, *Austral.* 16°42′ S, 127°6′ E 230
Durance, river, *Fr.* 43°50′ N, 5°55′ E 165
Durance, river, *Fr.* 44°41′ N, 6°35′ E 165
Durand, *Ill., U.S.* 42°25′ N, 89°21′ W 102
Durand, *Mich., U.S.* 42°53′ N, 83°59′ W 102
Durand, *Wis., U.S.* 44°37′ N, 91°58′ W 94
Duranes, peak, *Sp.* 38°50′ N, 4°42′ W 164
Durango, *Colo., U.S.* 37°15′ N, 107°52′ W 92
Durango, *Mex.* 24°0′ N, 104°43′ W 114
Durango, adm. division, *Mex.* 24°46′ N, 105°26′ W 114
Durant, *Miss., U.S.* 33°3′ N, 89°52′ W 103
Durant, *Okla., U.S.* 33°58′ N, 96°23′ W 96
Duraykīsh, *Syr.* 34°54′ N, 36°7′ E 194
Durazno, *Uru.* 33°22′ S, 56°30′ W 139
Durban, *S. Af.* 29°52′ S, 30°57′ E 227
Durbe, *Latv.* 56°35′ N, 21°22′ E 166
Durbuy, *Belg.* 50°21′ N, 5°25′ E 167
Dúrcal, *Sp.* 36°59′ N, 3°34′ W 164
Đurđevac, *Croatia* 46°2′ N, 17°4′ E 168
Đurđevik, *Bosn. and Herzg.* 44°26′ N, 18°38′ E 168
Durduri, *Somalia* 11°14′ N, 48°35′ E 216
Düren, *Ger.* 50°48′ N, 6°29′ E 167
Durham, *Can.* 44°9′ N, 80°49′ W 102
Durham, *Conn., U.S.* 41°28′ N, 72°41′ W 104
Durham, *N.H., U.S.* 43°8′ N, 70°57′ W 104
Durham, *N.C., U.S.* 35°58′ N, 78°55′ W 96
Durham, *U.K.* 54°47′ N, 1°35′ W 162
Duri, oil field, *Indonesia* 1°22′ N, 101°5′ E 196
Durlston Head, *U.K.* 50°23′ N, 1°57′ W 150
Durmā, *Saudi Arabia* 24°35′ N, 46°7′ E 182
Durmitor, mountains, *Serb. and Mont.* 43°10′ N, 18°54′ E 168
Durmitor National Park, *Europe* 43°10′ N, 19°21′ E 168
Durov Dag, oil field, *Azerb.* 39°30′ N, 49°4′ E 195
Dursley, *U.K.* 51°40′ N, 2°21′ W 162
Dursunbey, *Turk.* 39°36′ N, 28°37′ E 156
Duru, *Dem. Rep. of the Congo* 4°15′ N, 28°49′ E 224
Duru, river, *Dem. Rep. of the Congo* 3°39′ N, 28°11′ E 224
Dūruḩ, *Iran* 32°17′ N, 60°33′ E 180
D'Urville Island, *Antarctica* 62°60′ S, 57°29′ W 134
Durwalē, *Eth.* 8°47′ N, 43°4′ E 218
Dusa Marreb see Dhuusamarreeb, *Somalia* 5°31′ N, 46°24′ E 218
Duşak, *Turkm.* 37°12′ N, 60°2′ E 180
Dusetos, *Lith.* 55°44′ N, 25°52′ E 166
Dusey, river, *Can.* 51°10′ N, 87°15′ W 110
Dûsh, *Egypt* 24°34′ N, 30°37′ E 182
Dushan, *China* 25°48′ N, 107°31′ E 198
Dushanbe, *Taj.* 38°34′ N, 68°40′ E 197
Dushanzi (Maytag), *China* 44°17′ N, 84°53′ E 184
Dushet'i, *Ga.* 42°3′ N, 44°41′ E 195
Dūskotna, *Bulg.* 42°52′ N, 27°11′ E 156
Dusky Sound 45°49′ S, 165°58′ E 240
Duson, *La., U.S.* 30°13′ N, 92°11′ W 103
Düsseldorf, *Ger.* 51°14′ N, 6°47′ E 167
Dustin Island, *Antarctica* 71°52′ S, 94°44′ W 248
Dutch John, *Utah, U.S.* 40°55′ N, 109°24′ W 90
Dutch Mountain, *Utah, U.S.* 40°12′ N, 113°55′ W 90
Dutlwe, *Botswana* 23°56′ S, 23°50′ E 227
Dutovo, *Russ.* 63°49′ N, 56°42′ E 154
Dutse, *Nig.* 11°43′ N, 9°19′ E 222
Dutsin Ma, *Nig.* 12°27′ N, 7°29′ E 222
Dutton, *Can.* 42°38′ N, 81°30′ W 102
Dutton, Mount, *Utah, U.S.* 38°0′ N, 112°17′ W 90
Duvan, *Russ.* 55°42′ N, 57°51′ E 154
Duvergé, *Dom. Rep.* 18°22′ N, 71°33′ W 116
Duvno, *Bosn. and Herzg.* 43°43′ N, 17°13′ E 168
Duwayhin, Khawr 24°14′ N, 51°0′ E 196
Duxbury, *Mass., U.S.* 42°2′ N, 70°41′ W 104
Duxford, *U.K.* 52°5′ N, 0°9′ E 162
Duy Xuyen, *Vietnam* 15°53′ N, 108°15′ E 202
Duyun, *China* 26°16′ N, 107°34′ E 198
Duz Dag, oil field, *Azerb.* 39°22′ N, 49°6′ E 195
Düzce, *Turk.* 40°50′ N, 31°10′ E 156
Dvarets, *Belarus* 53°24′ N, 25°35′ E 152
Dvina, river, *Russ.* 61°15′ N, 46°22′ E 160
Dvinskaya Guba 64°31′ N, 38°23′ E 143
Dvinskoy, *Russ.* 62°11′ N, 45°8′ E 154
Dvor, *Croatia* 45°3′ N, 16°22′ E 168
Dvukh Pilotov, Kosa, *Russ.* 68°5′ N, 178°33′ E 98
Dwarfie Stane, ruin(s), *U.K.* 58°51′ N, 3°28′ W 150
Dwarka, *India* 22°15′ N, 68°59′ E 186
Dwight, *Ill., U.S.* 41°5′ N, 88°25′ W 102
Dwikozy, *Pol.* 50°43′ N, 21°48′ E 152
Dyalakoro, *Mali* 12°3′ N, 7°51′ W 222
Dyat'kovo, *Russ.* 53°32′ N, 34°21′ E 154
Dyce, *Can.* 54°21′ N, 100°11′ W 108
Dyer, Cape, *Can.* 66°20′ N, 61°26′ W 106
Dyero, *Mali* 12°50′ N, 6°30′ W 222
Dyersburg, *Tenn., U.S.* 36°2′ N, 89°23′ W 96
Dymchurch, *U.K.* 51°1′ N, 1°0′ E 162
Dyment, *Can.* 49°37′ N, 92°20′ W 94
Dyrøy, *Nor.* 69°3′ N, 17°30′ E 152
Dytiki Eláda, adm. division, *Gr.* 38°2′ N, 21°22′ E 156
Dytiki Makedonía, adm. division, *Gr.* 40°26′ N, 21°7′ E 156
Dyupkun, Ozero, lake, *Russ.* 67°58′ N, 96°30′ E 169
Dyurtyuli, *Russ.* 55°28′ N, 54°55′ E 154
Dzanga-Ndoki National Park, *Cen. Af. Rep.* 2°30′ N, 15°16′ E 218
Dzavhan, river, *Mongolia* 47°49′ N, 93°37′ E 190
Dzerzhinsk, *Russ.* 56°14′ N, 43°31′ E 154
Dzerzhīnskoe, *Kaz.* 45°48′ N, 81°4′ E 184
Dzhagdy, Khrebet, *Russ.* 53°42′ N, 130°43′ E 190
Dzhalinda, *Russ.* 53°35′ N, 123°57′ E 190
Dzhankoy, *Ukr.* 45°41′ N, 34°20′ E 156
Dzhugdzhur, Khrebet, *Russ.* 57°47′ N, 136°52′ E 160
Działdowo, *Pol.* 53°13′ N, 20°10′ E 152
Dzibalchén, *Mex.* 19°27′ N, 89°45′ W 115
Dzibilchaltún, ruin(s), *Mex.* 21°5′ N, 89°42′ W 116
Džigolj, *Serb. and Mont.* 43°20′ N, 21°35′ E 168
Dzilam de Bravo, *Mex.* 21°22′ N, 88°55′ W 116
Dzioua, *Alg.* 33°14′ N, 5°16′ E 214
Dzisna, *Belarus* 55°34′ N, 28°9′ E 166
Dzisna, river, *Belarus* 55°26′ N, 27°41′ E 166
Dzivin, *Belarus* 51°56′ N, 24°35′ E 152
Dzodze, *Ghana* 6°14′ N, 0°57′ E 222
Dzogsool, *Mongolia* 46°47′ N, 107°7′ E 198
Dzonot Carretero, *Mex.* 21°24′ N, 87°53′ W 116
Dzotol, *Mongolia* 45°52′ N, 115°5′ E 198
Dzuiché, *Mex.* 19°53′ N, 88°51′ W 115
Dzūkija National Park, *Lith.* 53°56′ N, 24°10′ E 166
Džūkste, *Latv.* 56°47′ N, 23°13′ E 166
Dzungarian Basin, *China* 45°51′ N, 82°34′ E 172
Dzungarian Gate, *Kaz.* 44°59′ N, 73°45′ E 172
Dzüünbayan, *Mongolia* 44°30′ N, 110°7′ E 198
Dzüünbulag, *Mongolia* 47°8′ N, 115°40′ E 198
Dzüünharaa, *Mongolia* 48°55′ N, 106°28′ E 198
Dzuunmod, *Mongolia* 47°41′ N, 107°0′ E 198
Dzvina Zakh, river, *Belarus* 55°34′ N, 28°34′ E 166
Dzyalyatsichy, *Belarus* 53°46′ N, 25°59′ E 158

E

Eabamet Lake, *Can.* 51°31′ N, 89°14′ W 81
Eads, *Colo., U.S.* 38°28′ N, 102°48′ W 90
Eagle, *Alas., U.S.* 64°43′ N, 141°21′ W 98
Eagle, *Colo., U.S.* 39°38′ N, 106°49′ W 90
Eagle Butte, *S. Dak., U.S.* 44°56′ N, 101°15′ W 90
Eagle Cap, peak, *Oreg., U.S.* 45°8′ N, 117°23′ W 90
Eagle Crags, peak, *Calif., U.S.* 35°23′ N, 117°6′ W 101
Eagle Creek, river, *Can.* 52°12′ N, 109°23′ W 80
Eagle Grove, *Iowa, U.S.* 42°39′ N, 93°53′ W 94
Eagle Islands, *Indian Ocean* 6°13′ S, 69°38′ E 188
Eagle Lake, *Calif., U.S.* 40°34′ N, 121°33′ W 81
Eagle Lake, *Can.* 49°32′ N, 93°29′ W 110
Eagle Lake, *Fla., U.S.* 27°58′ N, 81°47′ W 105
Eagle Mountain, *Minn., U.S.* 47°52′ N, 90°40′ W 94
Eagle Mountains, *Calif., U.S.* 33°50′ N, 115°41′ W 101
Eagle Peak, *Calif., U.S.* 41°16′ N, 120°18′ W 90
Eagle Peak, *Calif., U.S.* 38°10′ N, 119°27′ W 100
Eagle Peak, *Mont., U.S.* 47°14′ N, 115°28′ W 90
Eagle Peak, *N. Mex., U.S.* 33°39′ N, 108°38′ W 92
Eagle Peak, *Tex., U.S.* 30°53′ N, 105°9′ W 92
Eagle River, *Mich., U.S.* 47°24′ N, 88°18′ W 94
Eagle, river, *Can.* 52°46′ N, 58°44′ W 111
Eaglesham, *Can.* 55°46′ N, 117°54′ W 108
Eagletail Mountains, *Ariz., U.S.* 33°40′ N, 113°43′ W 101
Ear Falls, *Can.* 50°38′ N, 93°14′ W 90
Earl Park, *Ind., U.S.* 40°40′ N, 87°24′ W 102
Earlimart, *Calif., U.S.* 35°52′ N, 119°17′ W 100
Earlington, *Ky., U.S.* 37°15′ N, 87°31′ W 96
Earlton, *Can.* 47°42′ N, 79°49′ W 94
Earlville, *Ill., U.S.* 41°34′ N, 88°56′ W 102
Earnscleugh, *N.Z.* 45°14′ S, 169°18′ E 240
Earp, *Calif., U.S.* 34°9′ N, 114°19′ W 101
Earth, *Tex., U.S.* 34°12′ N, 102°25′ W 92
Easingwold, *U.K.* 54°7′ N, 1°11′ W 162
Easley, *S.C., U.S.* 34°49′ N, 82°37′ W 96
East Anglia, region, *Europe* 52°26′ N, 0°22′ E 162
East Anglian Heights, *U.K.* 52°23′ N, 0°27′ E 162
East Angus, *Can.* 45°28′ N, 71°40′ W 94
East Antarctica, region, *Antarctica* 75°20′ S, 113°12′ E 248
East Arlington, *Vt., U.S.* 43°3′ N, 73°9′ W 104
East Aurora, *N.Y., U.S.* 42°45′ N, 78°38′ W 94
East Barnet, *Vt., U.S.* 44°19′ N, 72°3′ W 104
East Barre, *Vt., U.S.* 44°9′ N, 72°28′ W 104
East Base, station, *Antarctica* 68°4′ S, 67°16′ W 248
East Bay 28°57′ N, 89°18′ W 103
East Bay 29°31′ N, 94°43′ W 103
East Bergholt, *U.K.* 51°58′ N, 1°1′ E 162
East Beskids, *Pol.* 49°28′ N, 20°46′ E 152
East Brewton, *Ala., U.S.* 31°4′ N, 87°3′ W 96
East Bridgewater, *Mass., U.S.* 42°1′ N, 70°58′ W 104
East Burke, *Vt., U.S.* 44°35′ N, 71°57′ W 104
East Butte, peak, *Idaho, U.S.* 43°29′ N, 112°44′ W 90
East Butte, peak, *Mont., U.S.* 48°50′ N, 111°14′ W 90
East Caicos, island, *U.K.* 21°45′ N, 71°27′ W 116
East Cape, *N.Z.* 37°42′ S, 178°33′ E 240
East Cape see Dezhneva, Mys, *Russ.* 65°45′ N, 169°46′ W 98
East Caroline Basin, *North Pacific Ocean* 2°2′ N, 146°50′ E 252
East Chicago, *Ind., U.S.* 41°37′ N, 87°26′ W 102
East China Sea 30°53′ N, 125°13′ E 190
East Coast Bays, *N.Z.* 36°45′ S, 174°45′ E 240
East Corinth, *Vt., U.S.* 44°3′ N, 72°14′ W 104
East Cote Blanche Bay 29°31′ N, 91°39′ W 103
East Coulee, *Can.* 51°22′ N, 112°31′ W 90
East Dereham, *U.K.* 52°40′ N, 0°56′ E 162
East Dubuque, *Mo., U.S.* 42°29′ N, 90°37′ W 94
East Fairview, *N. Dak., U.S.* 47°50′ N, 104°2′ W 108
East Falkland, island, *Falk. Is., U.K.* 51°14′ S, 58°25′ W 134
East Freetown, *Mass., U.S.* 41°45′ N, 70°58′ W 104
East Frisian Islands, *North Sea* 53°46′ N, 7°12′ E 163
East Glacier Park, *Mont., U.S.* 48°25′ N, 113°14′ W 90
East Govç, adm. division, *Mongolia* 44°17′ N, 108°52′ E 198
East Grand Forks, *Minn., U.S.* 47°55′ N, 97°2′ W 108
East Greenbush, *N.Y., U.S.* 42°34′ N, 73°43′ W 104
East Greenwich, *R.I., U.S.* 41°39′ N, 71°28′ W 104
East Grinstead, *U.K.* 51°7′ N, 1°58′ W 162
East Hampton, *N.Y., U.S.* 40°57′ N, 72°12′ W 104
East Hardwick, *Vt., U.S.* 44°30′ N, 72°19′ W 104
East Hartford, *Conn., U.S.* 41°45′ N, 72°39′ W 104
East Hartland, *Conn., U.S.* 41°59′ N, 72°55′ W 104
East Hebron, *N.H., U.S.* 43°41′ N, 71°47′ W 104
East Isaac, island, *Bahamas* 25°51′ N, 78°53′ W 105
East Jordan, *Mich., U.S.* 45°9′ N, 85°7′ W 94
East Lake, *Mich., U.S.* 44°14′ N, 86°17′ W 102
East Lansing, *Mich., U.S.* 42°44′ N, 84°28′ W 102
East Las Vegas, *Nev., U.S.* 36°5′ N, 115°3′ W 101
East Lempster, *N.H., U.S.* 43°13′ N, 72°11′ W 104
East London, *S. Af.* 32°59′ S, 27°52′ E 227
East Machias, *Me., U.S.* 44°44′ N, 67°25′ W 94
East Mariana Basin, *North Pacific Ocean* 12°38′ N, 151°56′ E 252
East Marion, *N.Y., U.S.* 41°7′ N, 72°21′ W 104
East Montpelier, *Vt., U.S.* 44°16′ N, 72°30′ W 104
East Mountain, *Oreg., U.S.* 44°59′ N, 122°14′ W 90
East Mountain, *Vt., U.S.* 44°38′ N, 71°51′ W 94
East Naples, *Fla., U.S.* 26°6′ N, 81°46′ W 105
East Pacific Rise, *South Pacific Ocean* 25°9′ S, 113°45′ W 252
East Palatka, *Fla., U.S.* 29°38′ N, 81°36′ W 105
East Pepperell, *Mass., U.S.* 42°39′ N, 71°35′ W 104
East Pine, *Can.* 55°42′ N, 121°12′ W 108
East Point, *Can.* 44°2′ N, 60°9′ W 111
East Point, *Can.* 51°21′ N, 80°2′ W 110
East Point, *Can.* 46°29′ N, 62°3′ W 111
East Prairie, *Mo., U.S.* 36°46′ N, 89°23′ W 94
East Providence, *R.I., U.S.* 41°49′ N, 71°23′ W 104
East Quogue, *N.Y., U.S.* 40°50′ N, 72°36′ W 104
East Range, *Nev., U.S.* 40°40′ N, 118°1′ W 90
East Retford, *U.K.* 53°19′ N, 0°57′ E 162
East Ridge, *Tenn., U.S.* 34°59′ N, 85°14′ W 96
East Saint Johnsbury, *Vt., U.S.* 44°26′ N, 71°58′ W 104
East Saint Louis, *Mo., U.S.* 38°36′ N, 90°8′ W 94
East Sea see Japan, Sea of 39°9′ N, 128°12′ E 200
East Sebago, *Me., U.S.* 43°50′ N, 70°39′ W 104
East Siberian Sea 72°23′ N, 162°36′ E 246
East Springfield, *Pa., U.S.* 41°57′ N, 80°25′ W 94
East Stoneham, *Me., U.S.* 44°15′ N, 70°50′ W 104
East Sullivan, *N.H., U.S.* 42°59′ N, 72°13′ W 104
East Tasman Plateau, *Tasman Sea* 43°59′ S, 150°40′ E 252
East Tavaputs Plateau, *Utah, U.S.* 39°28′ N, 110°1′ W 90
East Templeton, *Mass., U.S.* 42°33′ N, 72°3′ W 104
East Thetford, *Vt., U.S.* 43°48′ N, 72°12′ W 104
East Timor see Timor-Leste 9°37′ S, 126°32′ E 192
East Topsham, *Vt., U.S.* 44°7′ N, 72°15′ W 104
East Troy, *Wis., U.S.* 42°47′ N, 88°24′ W 102
East Wallingford, *Vt., U.S.* 43°26′ N, 72°54′ W 104
Eastbourne, *U.K.* 50°46′ N, 0°16′ E 162
Eastend, *Can.* 49°29′ N, 108°50′ W 90
Easter Fracture Zone, *South Pacific Ocean* 22°42′ S, 111°2′ W 252
Easter Group, islands, *Indian Ocean* 28°53′ S, 111°18′ E 230
Easter Island (Pascua, Isla de), *Chile* 27°0′ S, 109°0′ W 241
Eastern, adm. division, *Mongolia* 47°33′ N, 114°13′ E 198
Eastern Cape, adm. division, *S. Af.* 31°43′ S, 25°38′ E 227
Eastern Cape, adm. division, *S. Af.* 30°10′ S, 29°10′ E 227
Eastern Desert, *Africa* 30°44′ N, 32°4′ E 194
Eastern Equatoria, adm. division, *Sudan* 5°14′ N, 32°41′ E 218
Eastern Ghats, *Asia* 20°12′ N, 83°44′ E 188
Eastern Group, islands, *Great Australian Bight* 34°17′ S, 124°9′ E 230
Eastern Point, *Mass., U.S.* 42°31′ N, 70°41′ W 104
Easterville, *Can.* 53°3′ N, 99°40′ W 108
Eastford, *Conn., U.S.* 41°53′ N, 72°5′ W 104
Eastham, *Mass., U.S.* 41°50′ N, 69°59′ W 104
Easthampton, *Mass., U.S.* 42°15′ N, 72°41′ W 104
Eastlake, *Ohio, U.S.* 41°38′ N, 81°27′ W 102
Eastleigh, *U.K.* 50°58′ N, 1°22′ W 162
Eastmain, *Can.* 52°10′ N, 78°33′ W 106
Eastmain, river, *Can.* 51°58′ N, 73°51′ W 110
Eastmain Un, Réservoir de, lake, *Can.* 51°56′ N, 77°4′ W 110
Eastman, *Ga., U.S.* 32°11′ N, 83°11′ W 96
Easton, *Calif., U.S.* 36°38′ N, 119°48′ W 100
Easton, *Conn., U.S.* 41°14′ N, 73°19′ W 104
Easton, *Ill., U.S.* 40°13′ N, 89°51′ W 102
Easton, *Md., U.S.* 38°46′ N, 76°4′ W 94
Easton, *Pa., U.S.* 40°41′ N, 75°14′ W 94
Easton, *Wash., U.S.* 47°12′ N, 121°12′ W 100
Eastpoint, *Fla., U.S.* 29°45′ N, 84°52′ W 96
Eastport, *Me., U.S.* 44°54′ N, 66°60′ W 94
Eastport, *N.Y., U.S.* 40°49′ N, 72°44′ W 104
Eastsound, *Wash., U.S.* 48°41′ N, 122°55′ W 100
Eaton, *Colo., U.S.* 40°31′ N, 104°44′ W 90
Eaton, *Ohio, U.S.* 39°44′ N, 84°38′ W 102
Eaton Rapids, *Mich., U.S.* 42°31′ N, 84°40′ W 102
Eatonia, *Can.* 51°13′ N, 109°23′ W 90
Eatonton, *Ga., U.S.* 33°18′ N, 83°24′ W 96
Eatonville, *Wash., U.S.* 46°50′ N, 122°17′ W 100
Eau Claire, *Wis., U.S.* 44°48′ N, 91°29′ W 94
Eau Claire, Lac à l', lake, *Can.* 55°52′ N, 76°46′ W 106
Eau Froide, Lac à l', lake, *Can.* 50°49′ N, 73°17′ W 110
Eau Jaune, Lac à l', lake, *Can.* 49°39′ N, 75°29′ W 94
Eauripik Atoll, *F.S.M.* 6°41′ N, 140°4′ E 192
Eauze, *Fr.* 43°51′ N, 0°5′ E 150
Eaval, peak, *U.K.* 57°30′ N, 7°16′ W 150
Ébano, *Mex.* 22°11′ N, 98°23′ W 114
Ebbetts Pass, *Calif., U.S.* 38°33′ N, 119°49′ W 100
Ebbw Vale, *U.K.* 51°46′ N, 3°13′ W 162
Ebenezer, *Miss., U.S.* 32°57′ N, 90°6′ W 103
Ebeyti, *Kaz.* 48°9′ N, 55°24′ E 158
Ebino, *Japan* 32°3′ N, 130°49′ E 201
Ebinur Hu, lake, *China* 44°41′ N, 82°37′ E 184
Eboda see 'Abda, ruin(s), *Israel* 30°47′ N, 34°43′ E 194
Ebola, river, *Dem. Rep. of the Congo* 3°31′ N, 21°25′ E 218
Ebolowa, *Cameroon* 2°57′ N, 11°7′ E 218
Ebro, Embalse del, lake, *Sp.* 43°2′ N, 4°7′ W 164
Ebro, river, *Sp.* 42°42′ N, 3°23′ W 164
Ebruchorr, Gora, *Russ.* 67°43′ N, 31°55′ E 152
Ecbatana see Hamadān, *Iran* 34°48′ N, 48°27′ E 180
Eccleshall, *U.K.* 52°50′ N, 2°15′ W 162
Eceabat, *Turk.* 40°11′ N, 26°19′ E 156
Echallens, *Switz.* 46°38′ N, 6°38′ E 167
Echarate, *Peru* 12°46′ S, 72°35′ W 137
Echizen Misaki, *Japan* 35°53′ N, 135°42′ E 201
Echkill-Tash, *Kyrg.* 42°20′ N, 79°25′ E 184
Echo Bay, *Can.* 66°5′ N, 117°54′ W 106
Echo Bay, *Can.* 46°29′ N, 84°4′ W 94
Echo Cliffs, *Ariz., U.S.* 36°28′ N, 111°36′ W 92
Echo Summit, pass, *Calif., U.S.* 38°48′ N, 120°3′ W 90
Echternach, *Lux.* 49°48′ N, 6°25′ E 167
Echuca, *Austral.* 36°8′ S, 144°48′ E 231
Écija, *Sp.* 37°32′ N, 5°5′ W 164
Eckerö, *Fin.* 60°12′ N, 19°36′ E 166
Écommoy, *Fr.* 47°49′ N, 0°16′ E 150
Ecoporanga, *Braz.* 18°25′ S, 40°53′ W 138
Écorce, Lac de l', lake, *Can.* 47°0′ N, 77°17′ W 94
Ecrins National Park, *Fr.* 44°44′ N, 6°21′ E 167
Ecuador 1°33′ S, 78°58′ W 130
Ecueillé, *Fr.* 47°4′ N, 1°20′ E 150
Ed, *Nor.* 58°54′ N, 11°54′ E 152
Ed Da'ein, *Sudan* 11°25′ N, 26°7′ E 216
Ed Damazin, *Sudan* 11°49′ N, 34°18′ E 182
Ed Damer, *Sudan* 17°31′ N, 34°0′ E 182
Ed Debba, *Sudan* 18°0′ N, 30°57′ E 226
Ed Dueim, *Sudan* 13°56′ N, 32°18′ E 182
Edam, *Can.* 53°11′ N, 108°45′ W 108
Edberg, *Can.* 52°46′ N, 112°47′ W 108
Edd, *Eritrea* 13°55′ N, 41°36′ E 182
Eddiceton, *Miss., U.S.* 31°30′ N, 90°48′ W 103
Eddontenajon, *Can.* 57°47′ N, 129°56′ W 108
Eddy, Mount, *Calif., U.S.* 41°18′ N, 122°35′ W 90
Eddystone Rocks, islands, *English Channel* 50°15′ N, 5°13′ W 150
Eddyville, *Ky., U.S.* 37°5′ N, 88°6′ W 96
Ede, *Neth.* 52°2′ N, 5°39′ E 167
Edéa, *Cameroon* 3°47′ N, 10°9′ E 222
Edehon Lake, *Can.* 60°25′ N, 97°45′ W 108
Eden, *Can.* 42°46′ N, 80°44′ W 102
Eden, *Miss., U.S.* 32°58′ N, 90°21′ W 103
Eden, *N.C., U.S.* 36°30′ N, 79°47′ W 96
Eden, *Tex., U.S.* 31°11′ N, 99°51′ W 92
Eden, *Wyo., U.S.* 42°3′ N, 109°26′ W 90
Eden, river, *U.K.* 54°47′ N, 2°49′ W 162
Edenburg, *S. Af.* 29°46′ S, 25°55′ E 227
Edenton, *N.C., U.S.* 36°3′ N, 76°38′ W 96
Edessa see Şanlıurfa, *Turk.* 37°6′ N, 38°45′ E 180
Edewecht, *Ger.* 53°7′ N, 7°59′ E 163
Edgar, *Nebr., U.S.* 40°21′ N, 97°59′ W 90
Edgecomb, *Me., U.S.* 43°57′ N, 69°38′ W 104
Edgeley, *N. Dak., U.S.* 46°20′ N, 98°44′ W 90
Edgell Island, *Can.* 61°45′ N, 64°46′ W 106
Edgemont, *S. Dak., U.S.* 43°18′ N, 103°49′ W 90
Edgeøya, island, *Nor.* 77°32′ N, 25°31′ E 160
Edgerly, *La., U.S.* 30°13′ N, 93°31′ W 103
Edgerton, *Can.* 52°43′ N, 110°27′ W 108
Edgerton, *Minn., U.S.* 43°51′ N, 96°8′ W 90
Edgerton, *Wis., U.S.* 42°49′ N, 89°5′ W 110
Edgerton, *Wyo., U.S.* 43°24′ N, 106°13′ W 90
Edgewater, *Fla., U.S.* 28°58′ N, 80°54′ W 105
Edgewood, *Ill., U.S.* 38°55′ N, 88°40′ W 102
Edgeworthstown see Mostrim, *Ire.* 53°41′ N, 7°38′ W 150
Edievale, *N.Z.* 45°48′ S, 169°23′ E 240
Edigueri, spring, *Chad* 19°54′ N, 15°54′ E 216
Edina, *Mo., U.S.* 40°9′ N, 92°10′ W 94
Edinburg, *Miss., U.S.* 32°47′ N, 89°21′ W 103
Edinburgh, *Ind., U.S.* 39°21′ N, 85°58′ W 102
Edinburgh, *U.K.* 55°55′ N, 3°22′ W 150
Edirne (Adrianople), *Turk.* 41°39′ N, 26°34′ E 156
Edison, *Calif., U.S.* 35°21′ N, 118°53′ W 101
Edison, *Ga., U.S.* 31°32′ N, 84°44′ W 96
Edison, *N.J., U.S.* 40°30′ N, 74°26′ W 94
Edison, *Wash., U.S.* 48°32′ N, 122°27′ W 100
Edith Cavell, Mount, *Can.* 52°39′ N, 118°8′ W 108
Edith, Mount, *Mont., U.S.* 46°23′ N, 111°15′ W 90
Edjeleh, oil field, *Alg.* 27°49′ N, 9°44′ E 214
Edmond, *Okla., U.S.* 35°37′ N, 97°29′ W 96
Edmonds, *Wash., U.S.* 47°47′ N, 122°22′ W 100
Edmonton, *Can.* 53°33′ N, 113°39′ W 108
Edmore, *Mich., U.S.* 43°24′ N, 85°3′ W 102
Edmore, *N. Dak., U.S.* 48°23′ N, 98°28′ W 90
Edmundston, *Can.* 47°22′ N, 68°19′ W 94
Edna, *Tex., U.S.* 28°58′ N, 96°38′ W 96
Edna Bay, *Alas., U.S.* 55°57′ N, 133°40′ W 108
Edolo, *It.* 46°11′ N, 10°20′ E 167

Edough, Djebel, Alg. 36°57′ N, 6°55′ E 150
Edøy, Nor. 63°19′ N, 8°2′ E 152
Edrei see Dar'ā, Syr. 32°37′ N, 36°6′ E 194
Edremit, Turk. 39°34′ N, 27°0′ E 156
Edrengiyn Nuruu, Mongolia 44°49′ N, 97°6′ E 190
Edson, Can. 53°35′ N, 116°27′ W 108
Edsvalla, Nor. 59°26′ N, 13°8′ E 152
Eduardo Castex, Arg. 35°54′ S, 64°18′ W 134
Edward, Mount, Antarctica 75°6′ S, 70°29′ W 248
Edwards, Calif., U.S. 34°56′ N, 117°56′ W 101
Edwards, Miss., U.S. 32°18′ N, 90°36′ W 103
Edwards Air Force Base, Calif., U.S. 34°54′ N, 117°56′ W 101
Edwards Plateau, Tex., U.S. 30°39′ N, 101°4′ W 92
Edwardsport, Ind., U.S. 38°48′ N, 87°16′ W 102
Edwardsville, Ill., U.S. 38°48′ N, 89°58′ W 102
Edziza, Mount, Can. 57°41′ N, 130°45′ W 108
Edzná, ruin(s), Mex. 19°33′ N, 90°23′ W 115
Eede, Neth. 51°15′ N, 3°27′ E 163
Eeklo, Belg. 51°11′ N, 3°33′ E 163
Eel, river, Ind., U.S. 39°21′ N, 87°6′ W 102
Effie, La., U.S. 31°11′ N, 92°10′ W 103
Effingham, Ill., U.S. 39°6′ N, 88°32′ W 102
Eflâni, Turk. 41°25′ N, 32°57′ E 156
Eg, Mongolia 48°49′ N, 110°5′ E 198
Egadi, Isole, islands, Tyrrhenian Sea 37°48′ N, 11°13′ E 156
Egalah, Adrar, peak, Niger 18°9′ N, 8°32′ E 222
Egan Range, Nev., U.S. 39°49′ N, 115°8′ W 90
Eganville, Can. 45°32′ N, 77°6′ W 94
Egedesminde see Aasiaat, Den. 68°45′ N, 52°53′ W 106
Egenolf Lake, Can. 59°2′ N, 100°32′ W 108
Eger, Hung. 47°53′ N, 20°22′ E 168
Egeria Fracture Zone, Indian Ocean 19°30′ S, 68°2′ E 254
Egersund, Nor. 58°26′ N, 6°0′ E 150
Egerton, Mount, Austral. 24°50′ S, 117°30′ E 230
Egg Lake, Can. 54°58′ N, 106°50′ W 108
Egg, river, Can. 59°58′ N, 95°33′ W 108
Eggan, Nig. 8°39′ N, 6°13′ E 222
Eggebek, Ger. 54°38′ N, 9°22′ E 150
Eggenburg, Aust. 48°38′ N, 15°49′ E 152
Éghezée, Belg. 50°35′ N, 4°53′ E 167
Eğil, Turk. 38°15′ N, 40°5′ E 195
Egindibulaq, Kaz. 49°49′ N, 76°26′ E 184
Egindiköl, Kaz. 51°3′ N, 69°31′ E 184
Égio, Gr. 38°12′ N, 22°6′ E 180
Eglinton Island, Can. 75°24′ N, 126°46′ W 106
Eglon, ruin(s), Israel 31°31′ N, 34°41′ E 194
Egmont Islands, Indian Ocean 7°21′ S, 70°31′ E 188
Egmont, Mount see Taranaki, Mount, peak, N.Z. 39°20′ S, 173°58′ E 240
Egremont, U.K. 54°28′ N, 3°32′ W 162
Eğridir, Turk. 37°50′ N, 30°49′ E 156
Eğridir Gölü, lake, Turk. 38°5′ N, 30°11′ E 180
Eğrigöz Dağı, peak, Turk. 39°23′ N, 29°2′ E 156
Éguas (Correntina), river, Braz. 13°42′ S, 45°43′ W 138
Egvekinot, Russ. 66°17′ N, 179°1′ W 160
Egyek, Hung. 47°38′ N, 20°52′ E 168
Egypt 26°46′ N, 27°58′ E 216
Ehime, adm. division, Japan 33°37′ N, 132°38′ E 201
Ehingen, Ger. 48°16′ N, 9°44′ E 152
Ehrang, Ger. 49°48′ N, 6°41′ E 167
Ehrenberg, Ger. 50°30′ N, 9°59′ E 167
Ei, Japan 31°12′ N, 130°30′ E 201
Eide, Nor. 62°53′ N, 7°26′ E 152
Eiderdamm, Ger. 54°14′ N, 7°58′ E 150
Eidsbugarden, Nor. 61°22′ N, 8°15′ E 152
Eidskog, Nor. 60°1′ N, 12°6′ E 152
Eidsvoll, Nor. 60°19′ N, 11°12′ E 152
Eifel, region, Europe 50°38′ N, 6°3′ E 167
Eige, Càrn, peak, U.K. 57°16′ N, 5°13′ W 150
Eigerøy, region, North Sea 58°25′ N, 5°35′ E 150
Eight Degree Channel 7°30′ N, 71°39′ E 188
Eight Mile Rock, Bahamas 26°31′ N, 78°47′ W 105
Eighty Mile Beach, Austral. 20°6′ S, 119°49′ E 231
Eil Malk see Mecherchar, island, Palau 7°7′ N, 134°22′ E 242
Eilendorf, Ger. 50°46′ N, 6°10′ E 167
Eiler Rasmussen, Cape, Den. 81°2′ N, 11°2′ W 246
Eiler Rasmussen, Kap, Den. 82°38′ N, 19°35′ W 246
Eilerts de Haan Gebergte, Suriname 2°50′ N, 56°17′ W 130
Eina, Nor. 60°38′ N, 10°35′ E 152
Eindhoven, Neth. 51°26′ N, 5°28′ E 167
Eion, ruin(s), Gr. 40°46′ N, 23°46′ E 156
Eirik Ridge, North Atlantic Ocean 57°47′ N, 44°35′ W 253
Eirunepé, Braz. 6°40′ S, 69°55′ W 130
Eisenach, Ger. 50°58′ N, 10°19′ E 167
Eisenstadt, Aust. 47°50′ N, 16°31′ E 168
Eišiškės, Lith. 54°10′ N, 24°58′ E 166
Eitorf, Ger. 50°45′ N, 7°27′ E 167
Eivissa, Sp. 38°53′ N, 1°25′ E 150
Eixe, Sierra do, Sp. 42°16′ N, 7°23′ W 150
Ejea de los Caballeros, Sp. 42°7′ N, 1°10′ W 164
Ejeda, Madagascar 24°20′ S, 44°30′ E 220
Ejin Horo Qi (Altan Xiret), China 39°33′ N, 109°44′ E 198
Ejin Qi, China 42°1′ N, 101°30′ E 190
Ejouj, spring, Mauritania 17°1′ N, 9°23′ W 222
Ejura, Ghana 7°25′ N, 1°24′ W 222
Ekalaka, Mont., U.S. 45°52′ N, 104°34′ W 90
Ekenäs (Tammisaari), Fin. 59°58′ N, 23°26′ E 166
Ekerem, Turkm. 38°5′ N, 53°50′ E 180
Ekeren, Belg. 51°16′ N, 4°25′ E 163
Eket, Nig. 4°39′ N, 7°56′ E 222
Ekibastuz, Kaz. 51°44′ N, 75°19′ E 184
Ekkerøy, Nor. 70°4′ N, 30°8′ E 152
Eklund Islands, Bellingshausen Sea 73°25′ S, 70°57′ W 248
Ekoli, Dem. Rep. of the Congo 0°25′ N, 24°16′ E 224
Ekombe, Dem. Rep. of the Congo 1°8′ N, 21°32′ E 218
Ekonda, Russ. 66°5′ N, 103°55′ E 160
Ekrafane, Niger 15°21′ N, 3°43′ E 222
Ekukola, Dem. Rep. of the Congo 0°30′ N, 18°53′ E 218
Ekwan, river, Can. 53°36′ N, 84°16′ W 106
Ekwendeni, Malawi 11°23′ S, 33°48′ E 224
El Abiadh, Ras, Tun. 37°16′ N, 9°8′ E 156
Ēl Ābrēd, Eth. 5°30′ N, 45°14′ E 218
El Adeb Larache, oil field, Alg. 27°23′ N, 8°44′ E 214
El Agreb, oil field, Alg. 30°37′ N, 5°30′ E 214
El Aïoun, Mor. 34°35′ N, 2°29′ W 214
El 'Aiyat, Egypt 29°37′ N, 31°12′ E 180
El 'Alamein, Egypt 30°49′ N, 28°52′ E 180
El Álamo, Mex. 31°32′ N, 116°1′ W 92
El 'Âmirîya, Egypt 31°1′ N, 29°48′ E 180
El Angel, Ecua. 0°36′ N, 78°7′ W 136
El 'Arag, spring, Egypt 28°53′ N, 26°27′ E 180
El Aricha, Alg. 34°13′ N, 1°16′ W 214
El 'Arîsh (Rhinocolura), Egypt 31°6′ N, 33°46′ E 194
El Arneb, spring, Mali 16°19′ N, 4°55′ W 222
El Atimine, spring, Alg. 28°51′ N, 3°9′ W 214
El Badâri, Egypt 27°1′ N, 31°23′ E 180
El Bagre, Col. 7°36′ N, 74°47′ W 136
El Bah, Eth. 9°44′ N, 41°47′ E 224
El Bahrein, spring, Egypt 28°41′ N, 26°30′ E 180
El Ballâh, Egypt 30°45′ N, 32°17′ E 194
El Ballestero, Sp. 38°50′ N, 2°28′ W 164
El Balyana, Egypt 26°14′ N, 31°55′ E 180
El Banco, Col. 9°1′ N, 73°58′ W 136
El Bauga, Sudan 18°13′ N, 33°52′ E 182
El Baúl, Venez. 8°56′ N, 68°20′ W 136
El Bayadh, Alg. 33°42′ N, 1°0′ E 214
El Béoua, spring, Mali 15°6′ N, 6°25′ W 222
El Berié, spring, Mauritania 16°11′ N, 9°57′ W 222
El Beru Hagia, Somalia 2°47′ N, 41°3′ E 224
El Beyed, spring, Mauritania 16°55′ N, 10°3′ W 222
El Bher, spring, Mauritania 15°59′ N, 8°42′ W 222
El Biar, Alg. 36°44′ N, 3°1′ E 150
El Bonillo, Sp. 38°57′ N, 2°33′ W 164
El Borma, oil field, Tun. 31°36′ N, 9°9′ E 214
El Bosque, Sp. 36°45′ N, 5°31′ W 164
El Burgo de Osma, Sp. 41°35′ N, 3°4′ W 164
El Cabo de Gata, Sp. 36°46′ N, 2°15′ W 164
El Caburé, Arg. 26°2′ S, 62°21′ W 139
El Caín, Arg. 41°37′ S, 68°16′ W 134
El Calafate (Lago Argentino), Arg. 50°26′ S, 72°13′ W 123
El Callao, Venez. 7°22′ N, 61°49′ W 130
El Calvario, Venez. 9°0′ N, 66°59′ W 136
El Campello, Sp. 38°25′ N, 0°24′ E 164
El Campillo de la Jara, Sp. 39°35′ N, 5°3′ W 164
El Campo, Tex., U.S. 29°11′ N, 96°17′ W 96
El Cap, Egypt 30°56′ N, 32°17′ E 194
El Capitan, peak, Mont., U.S. 45°59′ N, 114°29′ W 90
El Carmen, Arg. 24°24′ S, 65°18′ W 132
El Carmen, Bol. 18°49′ S, 58°35′ W 132
El Carmen, Bol. 13°60′ S, 63°41′ W 137
El Carmen, Col. 5°55′ N, 76°14′ W 136
El Carmen, Venez. 1°15′ N, 66°50′ W 136
El Carpio, Sp. 37°56′ N, 4°31′ W 164
El Castillo de Las Concepción, Nicar. 10°58′ N, 84°24′ W 115
El Ceibo, Guatemala 17°16′ N, 90°55′ W 115
El Centro, Calif., U.S. 32°47′ N, 115°34′ W 101
El Chichón, peak, Mex. 17°21′ N, 93°23′ W 115
El Chico, Mex. 20°8′ N, 98°54′ W 112
El Choro, Bol. 18°24′ S, 67°9′ W 137
El Cimaterio, Mex. 20°29′ N, 100°27′ W 112
El Claro, Mex. 30°28′ N, 111°11′ W 92
El Cocuy, Col. 6°24′ N, 72°28′ W 136
El Cocuy National Park, Col. 6°35′ N, 72°43′ W 136
El Cogoi, Arg. 24°48′ S, 59°12′ W 132
El Colorado, Arg. 26°18′ S, 59°23′ W 139
El Corcovado, Arg. 43°30′ S, 71°32′ W 134
El Cuyo, Mex. 21°32′ N, 87°42′ W 116
El 'Dab'a, Egypt 31°1′ N, 28°23′ E 180
El Dakka, ruin(s), Egypt 23°4′ N, 32°32′ E 182
El Deir, Egypt 25°19′ N, 32°33′ E 182
El Descanso, Mex. 32°12′ N, 116°54′ W 92
El Desemboque, Mex. 29°33′ N, 112°26′ W 92
El Desmonte, Arg. 22°42′ S, 62°17′ W 132
El Djouf, Mauritania 19°53′ N, 10°5′ W 222
El Dorado, Ark., U.S. 33°11′ N, 92°41′ W 103
El Dorado, Kans., U.S. 37°47′ N, 96°52′ W 92
El Dorado, Venez. 6°43′ N, 61°36′ W 130
El Dorado Springs, Mo., U.S. 37°51′ N, 94°2′ W 94
El Egder, spring, Eth. 3°51′ N, 38°54′ E 224
El Eglab, region, Africa 25°45′ N, 5°58′ W 214
El Encanto, Col. 1°38′ S, 73°14′ W 136
El Esfuerzo, Mex. 25°23′ N, 103°15′ W 114
El Faiyûm, Egypt 29°16′ N, 30°48′ E 180
El Faráid, Gebel, peak, Egypt 23°31′ N, 35°19′ E 182
El Fasher, Sudan 13°37′ N, 25°19′ E 226
El Fashn, Egypt 28°48′ N, 30°50′ E 180
El Fifi, Sudan 10°3′ N, 25°1′ E 224
El Fuerte, Mex. 23°49′ N, 103°8′ W 114
El Fula, Sudan 11°46′ N, 28°20′ E 216
El Gâga, Egypt 24°48′ N, 30°30′ E 226
El Gallego, Mex. 29°48′ N, 106°23′ W 92
El Galpón, Arg. 25°24′ S, 64°39′ W 134
El Gassi, oil field, Alg. 30°53′ N, 5°37′ E 214
El Geili, Sudan 16°0′ N, 32°37′ E 182
El Gezira, region, Africa 14°22′ N, 32°15′ E 182
El Ghobena, Tun. 35°29′ N, 9°38′ E 156
El Gîza, Egypt 30°1′ N, 31°8′ E 180
El Golea, Alg. 30°33′ N, 2°43′ E 207
El Goled Bahri, Sudan 18°27′ N, 30°40′ E 226
El Golfo de Santa Clara, Mex. 31°41′ N, 114°32′ W 92
El Grau, Sp. 38°59′ N, 0°10′ E 164
El Grau de Castelló, Sp. 39°58′ N, 1°60′ E 164
El Grullo, Mex. 19°48′ N, 104°14′ W 114
El Guapo, Venez. 10°8′ N, 66°2′ W 136
El Hadjira, Alg. 32°37′ N, 5°31′ E 214
El Hajeb, Mor. 33°41′ N, 5°25′ W 214
El Hamma, Tun. 33°55′ N, 9°48′ E 216
El Hammâm, Egypt 30°51′ N, 29°19′ E 180
El Hank, region, Africa 24°58′ N, 6°26′ W 214
El Haouaria, Tun. 37°3′ N, 11°0′ E 156
El Haraïg, Tun. 35°47′ N, 9°13′ E 156
El Harrach, Alg. 36°48′ N, 3°9′ E 214
El Hasaheisa, Sudan 14°41′ N, 33°17′ E 182
El Hawata, Sudan 13°24′ N, 34°36′ E 182
El Heiz, Egypt 28°2′ N, 28°37′ E 180
El Hiaïda, Mor. 35°5′ N, 6°11′ W 150
El Higo, Mex. 21°45′ N, 98°27′ W 114
El Hilla, Sudan 13°24′ N, 27°5′ E 226
El Hobra, Alg. 32°10′ N, 4°43′ E 214
El Homeur, Alg. 29°52′ N, 1°36′ E 214
El Huariche, Mex. 24°49′ N, 103°9′ W 114
El Iskandarîya (Alexandria), Egypt 31°10′ N, 29°55′ E 180
El Jabha (Puerto Capaz), Mor. 35°12′ N, 4°40′ W 150
El Jadida (Mazagan), Mor. 33°15′ N, 8°33′ W 214
El Jardín, Sp. 38°48′ N, 2°19′ W 164
El Jebelein, Sudan 12°34′ N, 32°52′ E 182
El Jemm, Tun. 35°18′ N, 10°43′ E 156
El Kanâyis, spring, Egypt 25°0′ N, 33°16′ E 182
El Karaba, Sudan 18°29′ N, 33°44′ E 182
El Karnak, ruin(s), Egypt 25°44′ N, 32°37′ E 182
El Katulo, spring, Kenya 2°26′ N, 40°35′ E 224
El Kawa, Sudan 13°42′ N, 32°31′ E 182
El Kef, Tun. 36°11′ N, 8°42′ E 156
El Kelaa des Srarhna, Mor. 32°5′ N, 7°25′ W 214
Ēl Kerē, Eth. 5°48′ N, 42°9′ E 224
El Khandaq, Sudan 18°36′ N, 30°34′ E 226
El Khârga, Egypt 25°28′ N, 30°29′ E 182
El Kharrouba, Tun. 35°23′ N, 9°59′ E 156
El Khnâchîch, Mali 21°6′ N, 5°26′ W 222
El Kodab, Sudan 16°12′ N, 32°30′ E 182
El Koin, Sudan 19°18′ N, 30°33′ E 216
El Kseïbat, Alg. 27°58′ N, 0°30′ E 214
El Kseur, Alg. 36°40′ N, 4°51′ E 150
El Ksiba, Mor. 32°38′ N, 6°3′ W 214
El Kuntilla, Egypt 29°58′ N, 34°41′ E 180
El Lagowa, Sudan 11°25′ N, 29°8′ E 216
El Lein, spring, Kenya 0°26′ N, 40°30′ E 224
El Leiya, Sudan 16°15′ N, 35°26′ E 182
El Limón, Mex. 22°48′ N, 99°1′ W 114
El Lucero, Mex. 25°56′ N, 103°26′ W 114
El Macao, Dom. Rep. 18°45′ N, 68°31′ W 116
El Mahalla el Kubra, Egypt 30°59′ N, 31°8′ E 226
El Maḥâriq, Egypt 25°39′ N, 30°36′ E 226
El Mahfoura, spring, Alg. 32°34′ N, 2°12′ E 214
El Maitén, Arg. 42°3′ S, 71°11′ W 134
El Maïz, Alg. 28°25′ N, 0°15′ E 214
El Malpais National Monument, N. Mex., U.S. 34°36′ N, 110°21′ W 92
El Manaqil, Sudan 14°12′ N, 33°0′ E 182
El Mango, Venez. 1°54′ N, 66°33′ W 136
El Manshâh, Egypt 26°29′ N, 31°42′ E 180
El Mansour, Alg. 27°38′ N, 0°19′ E 214
El Manṣûra, Egypt 30°58′ N, 31°24′ E 180
El Maqḍaba, spring, Egypt 30°53′ N, 34°0′ E 194
El Mazâr, Egypt 31°1′ N, 33°23′ E 194
El Medda, Mauritania 19°56′ N, 13°20′ W 222
El Meghaïer, Alg. 33°56′ N, 5°54′ E 214
El Melemm, Sudan 9°55′ N, 28°43′ E 224
El Messir, spring, Chad 15°43′ N, 16°59′ E 216
El Mhabes, spring, Mauritania 23°43′ N, 8°53′ W 214
El Milagro, Arg. 31°1′ S, 65°59′ W 134
El Milhas, spring, Mauritania 25°25′ N, 6°55′ W 214
El Milia, Alg. 36°48′ N, 6°16′ E 150
El Mina, Leb. 34°27′ N, 35°49′ E 194
El Mîna, Leb. 34°27′ N, 35°49′ E 194
El Minya, Egypt 28°7′ N, 30°41′ E 180
El Mirador, ruin(s), Guatemala 17°43′ N, 90°3′ W 115
El Mirage, Ariz., U.S. 33°37′ N, 112°19′ W 92
El Moale, spring, Sudan 10°20′ N, 23°46′ E 224
El Moïnane, spring, Mauritania 19°10′ N, 11°29′ W 222
El Morro National Monument, N. Mex., U.S. 35°1′ N, 108°26′ W 92
El Moueïla, Mauritania 21°38′ N, 10°36′ W 222
El Mouilha, spring, Mali 16°40′ N, 5°6′ W 222
El Mraïti, spring, Mali 19°12′ N, 2°19′ W 222
El Mrâyer, spring, Mauritania 21°28′ N, 8°12′ W 222
El Mreïti, spring, Mauritania 23°29′ N, 7°56′ W 214
El Mreyyé, region, Africa 18°48′ N, 8°16′ W 222
El Mughâzî, Gaza Strip 31°23′ N, 34°22′ E 194
El Mulato, Mex. 29°22′ N, 104°11′ W 92
El Mzereb, spring, Mali 24°46′ N, 6°23′ W 214
El Nasser, Egypt 24°34′ N, 33°2′ E 182
El Nayar, Mex. 23°55′ N, 104°41′ W 114
El Nido, Philippines 11°10′ N, 119°24′ E 203
El Niybo, Eth. 4°31′ N, 39°54′ E 224
El Obeid, Sudan 13°8′ N, 30°11′ E 226
El Oro, Mex. 19°46′ N, 100°8′ W 114
El Oualadji, Mali 16°13′ N, 3°28′ W 214
El Palmito, Mex. 25°35′ N, 104°59′ W 114
El Pao, Venez. 8°1′ N, 62°38′ W 130
El Pao, Venez. 8°46′ N, 64°39′ W 116
El Paso, Ill., U.S. 40°43′ N, 89°1′ W 102
El Paso, Tex., U.S. 31°45′ N, 106°29′ W 92
El Paso Mountains, Calif., U.S. 35°23′ N, 117°59′ W 101
El Payo, Sp. 40°18′ N, 6°45′ W 150
El Perelló, Sp. 40°52′ N, 0°43′ E 164
El Perú, Venez. 7°18′ N, 61°50′ W 130
El Pescadero, Mex. 23°20′ N, 110°11′ W 112
El Picazo, Sp. 39°26′ N, 2°7′ W 164
El Piñal, Venez. 7°26′ N, 68°41′ W 136
El Plomo, Mex. 31°14′ N, 112°4′ W 92
El Pobo de Dueñas, Sp. 40°45′ N, 1°39′ W 164
El Portal, Calif., U.S. 37°41′ N, 119°48′ W 100
El Portezuelo, Arg. 46°2′ S, 71°38′ W 134
El Porvenir, Col. 4°42′ N, 71°23′ W 136
El Porvenir, Pan. 9°34′ N, 78°59′ W 115
El Porvenir, Venez. 6°56′ N, 68°43′ W 136
El Potosi, Mex. 24°50′ N, 100°20′ W 114
El Potosi National Park, Mex. 21°58′ N, 100°4′ W 112
El Pozo, Mex. 30°55′ N, 109°16′ W 92
El Pozo, Mex. 24°54′ N, 107°15′ W 112
El Progreso, Hond. 15°21′ N, 87°48′ W 115
El Pueblito, Mex. 29°5′ N, 105°8′ W 92
El Puente, Bol. 21°14′ S, 65°19′ W 137
El Qâhira (Cairo), Egypt 30°3′ N, 31°8′ E 180
El Qanṭara, Egypt 30°51′ N, 32°19′ E 194
El Qaṣr, Egypt 25°42′ N, 28°50′ E 180
El Quṣeima, Egypt 30°39′ N, 34°22′ E 194
El Râshda, Egypt 25°33′ N, 28°54′ E 226
El Real, Pan. 8°6′ N, 77°45′ W 115
El Reno, Okla., U.S. 35°30′ N, 97°57′ W 92
El Rhaïlassiya Oumm Amoura, spring, Mauritania 16°26′ N, 9°24′ W 222
El Rio, Calif., U.S. 34°14′ N, 119°11′ W 101
El Rito, N. Mex., U.S. 36°21′ N, 106°12′ W 92
El Roble, Mex. 23°13′ N, 106°14′ W 114
El Ronquillo, Sp. 37°43′ N, 6°11′ W 164
El Rosario, Mex. 30°4′ N, 115°46′ W 92
El Ruâfa, spring, Egypt 30°49′ N, 34°7′ E 194
El Rubio, Sp. 37°21′ N, 4°60′ W 164
El Rucio, Mex. 23°23′ N, 102°4′ W 114
El Rusbayo, Mex. 31°1′ N, 109°15′ W 92
El Sabinal National Park, Mex. 26°3′ N, 99°47′ W 112
El Salado, Mex. 24°15′ N, 100°51′ W 114
El Salto, Mex. 20°31′ N, 103°11′ W 114
El Salto, Mex. 23°44′ N, 105°22′ W 114
El Salvador 14°0′ N, 89°0′ W 115
El Salvador, Mex. 24°28′ N, 100°53′ W 114
El Samán de Apure, Venez. 7°52′ N, 68°43′ W 136
El Sauz, Mex. 29°0′ N, 106°15′ W 92
El Sauzal, Mex. 31°53′ N, 116°41′ W 92
El Seco, Mex. 19°6′ N, 97°39′ W 114
El Shab, spring, Egypt 22°18′ N, 29°45′ E 226
El Sibû', ruin(s), Egypt 22°44′ N, 32°22′ E 182
El Soberbio, Arg. 27°21′ S, 54°15′ W 139
El Socorro, Venez. 8°59′ N, 65°45′ W 136
El Sombrero, Venez. 9°23′ N, 67°4′ W 136
El Sueco, Mex. 29°51′ N, 106°23′ W 92
El Suweis (Suez), Egypt 30°1′ N, 32°26′ E 180
El Tajín, ruin(s), Mex. 20°24′ N, 97°28′ W 114
El Tama National Park, Venez. 7°10′ N, 72°14′ W 136
El Tecuan, Mex. 19°21′ N, 104°58′ W 114
El Teleno, peak, Sp. 42°19′ N, 6°28′ W 150
El Tell el Ahmar, Egypt 30°53′ N, 32°24′ E 194
El Tigre, Col. 6°45′ N, 71°46′ W 136
El Tîna, Egypt 31°2′ N, 32°17′ E 194
El Toboso, Sp. 39°31′ N, 3°2′ W 164
El Tocuyo, Venez. 9°45′ N, 69°49′ W 136
El Tomatal, Mex. 28°26′ N, 114°6′ W 92
El Toro, peak, Sp. 39°58′ N, 4°5′ E 164
El Trébol, Arg. 32°13′ S, 61°42′ W 139
El Triunfo, Pirámide, peak, Arg. 25°45′ S, 61°51′ W 132
El Tuito, Mex. 20°19′ N, 105°25′ W 114
El Tuparro National Park, Col. 5°10′ N, 68°60′ W 136
El Ṭûr, Egypt 28°14′ N, 33°37′ E 180
El Turbio, Arg. 51°42′ S, 72°8′ W 134
El Valle, Col. 6°5′ N, 77°26′ W 136
El Veladero National Park, Mex. 16°53′ N, 99°60′ W 112
El Vendrell, Sp. 41°13′ N, 1°32′ E 164
El Vergel, Mex. 26°26′ N, 106°24′ W 114
El Wak, Kenya 2°44′ N, 40°53′ E 224
El Walamo, Mex. 23°6′ N, 106°13′ W 114
El Wasifîya, Egypt 30°33′ N, 32°8′ E 194
El Wâsṭa, Egypt 29°20′ N, 31°10′ E 180
El Wuz, Sudan 15°1′ N, 30°12′ E 226
El Yagual, Venez. 7°29′ N, 68°26′ W 136
El Zape, Mex. 25°46′ N, 105°45′ W 114
Elaho, river, Can. 50°14′ N, 123°38′ W 100
Elaia, Cape, Northern Cyprus 35°16′ N, 34°4′ E 194
Elan', Russ. 57°38′ N, 63°38′ E 154
Elat, Israel 29°35′ N, 34°59′ E 180
Elato Atoll, F.S.M. 6°59′ N, 145°34′ E 192
El'Atrun, spring, Sudan 18°6′ N, 26°36′ E 226
El'Auja see Nizzana, Israel 30°52′ N, 34°25′ E 194
Elâzığ, Turk. 38°39′ N, 39°12′ E 195
Elba, Ala., U.S. 31°24′ N, 86°4′ W 96
Elba, Cape see Hadarba, Ras, Egypt 21°49′ N, 36°55′ E 182
Elba, island, It. 42°54′ N, 9°57′ E 214
Elbe, Wash., U.S. 46°45′ N, 122°12′ W 100
Elbe, river, Ger. 53°7′ N, 10°4′ E 143
Elbert, Mount, Colo., U.S. 39°6′ N, 106°31′ W 90
Elberta, Mich., U.S. 44°35′ N, 86°13′ W 94
Elbeuf, Fr. 49°17′ N, 1°0′ E 163
Elbistan, Turk. 38°11′ N, 37°10′ E 156
Elbląg, Pol. 54°9′ N, 19°25′ E 166
Elbow, Can. 51°8′ N, 106°38′ W 90
Elbow Cays, North Atlantic Ocean 23°56′ N, 81°24′ W 116
Elbow Lake, Minn., U.S. 45°59′ N, 95°59′ W 90
El'brus, peak, Russ. 43°18′ N, 42°24′ E 195
Elburg, Neth. 52°26′ N, 5°49′ E 163
Elburz, Iran 36°26′ N, 52°39′ E 207
Elburz Mountains see Alborz, Reshteh-ye, Iran 36°43′ N, 49°25′ E 195
Elche de la Sierra, Sp. 38°26′ N, 2°3′ W 164
Elche (Elx), Sp. 38°15′ N, 0°42′ E 164
Elcho Island, Austral. 11°51′ S, 135°35′ E 192
Elda, Sp. 38°28′ N, 0°49′ E 150
Eldama Ravine, Kenya 4°238′ N, 35°43′ E 224
El'dikan, Russ. 60°48′ N, 135°14′ E 160
Eldon, Iowa, U.S. 40°55′ N, 92°13′ W 94
Eldon, Mo., U.S. 38°19′ N, 92°35′ W 94
Eldorado, Arg. 26°29′ S, 54°42′ W 139
Eldorado, Mex. 24°18′ N, 107°23′ W 112
Eldorado, Mo., U.S. 37°47′ N, 88°26′ W 96
Eldorado, Okla., U.S. 34°26′ N, 99°39′ W 96
Eldorado, Tex., U.S. 30°51′ N, 100°36′ W 92
Eldorado Mountains, Nev., U.S. 35°49′ N, 114°58′ W 101
Eldorado Pass, Oreg., U.S. 44°20′ N, 118°7′ W 90
Eldorado Paulista, Braz. 24°35′ S, 48°9′ W 138
Eldoret, Kenya 0°28′ N, 35°18′ E 224
Electra, Tex., U.S. 34°0′ N, 98°55′ W 92
Electric Mills, Miss., U.S. 32°44′ N, 88°28′ W 103
Electric Peak, Mont., U.S. 44°59′ N, 110°56′ W 90
El'Ein, spring, Sudan 16°34′ N, 29°17′ E 226
Eleja, Latv. 56°24′ N, 23°41′ E 166
Elek, Hung. 46°32′ N, 21°14′ E 168
Elektrostal', Russ. 55°45′ N, 38°30′ E 154
Elephant Island, Antarctica 61°4′ S, 55°14′ W 134
Elephant Mountain, Tex., U.S. 29°59′ N, 103°36′ W 92
Elephant Point, U.S. 66°15′ N, 161°24′ W 98
Eleşkirt, Turk. 39°47′ N, 42°39′ E 195
Eleuthera Island, Bahamas 25°12′ N, 76°7′ W 116
Eleutherae, ruin(s), Gr. 38°10′ N, 23°17′ E 156
Eleutherna, ruin(s), Gr. 35°18′ N, 24°34′ E 156
Elfers, Fla., U.S. 28°13′ N, 82°42′ W 105
Elfin Cove, U.S. 58°11′ N, 136°20′ W 98
Elfrida, Ariz., U.S. 31°41′ N, 109°40′ W 92
Elgå, Nor. 62°9′ N, 11°56′ E 152
Elgin, Ill., U.S. 42°2′ N, 88°16′ W 102
Elgin, Nebr., U.S. 41°57′ N, 98°6′ W 90
Elgin, N. Dak., U.S. 46°23′ N, 101°52′ W 90
Elgin, Oreg., U.S. 45°33′ N, 117°56′ W 90
Elgin, Tex., U.S. 30°20′ N, 97°22′ W 92
El'ginskiy, Russ. 64°42′ N, 142°12′ E 173
Elgon, Mount, Uganda 1°4′ N, 34°29′ E 224
Elgoras, Gora, peak, Russ. 68°5′ N, 31°24′ E 152
Elias Garcia, Angola 9°3′ S, 20°14′ E 218
Elida, N. Mex., U.S. 33°56′ N, 103°40′ W 92
Elida, Ohio, U.S. 40°46′ N, 84°12′ W 102
Eliki Gounda, Niger 15°3′ N, 8°36′ E 222
Elikónas (Helicon), peak, Gr. 38°17′ N, 22°47′ E 156
Elila, river, Dem. Rep. of the Congo 3°26′ S, 27°52′ E 224
Elila, river, Dem. Rep. of the Congo 2°55′ S, 26°23′ E 224
Eliot, Me., U.S. 43°9′ N, 70°48′ W 104
Elipa, Dem. Rep. of the Congo 1°4′ S, 24°19′ E 224
Elis, ruin(s), Gr. 37°52′ N, 21°18′ E 156
Elisabetha, Dem. Rep. of the Congo 1°5′ N, 23°36′ E 224
Élisabethville see Lubumbashi, Dem. Rep. of the Congo 11°43′ S, 27°26′ E 224
Elisenvaara, Russ. 61°23′ N, 29°45′ E 166
Eliseu Martins, Braz. 8°11′ S, 43°43′ W 132
Elista, Russ. 46°16′ N, 44°9′ E 158
Elizabeth, La., U.S. 30°51′ N, 92°48′ W 103
Elizabeth, Miss., U.S. 33°24′ N, 90°53′ W 103
Elizabeth, N.J., U.S. 40°39′ N, 74°14′ W 94
Elizabeth, W. Va., U.S. 39°3′ N, 81°25′ W 102
Elizabeth City, N.C., U.S. 36°18′ N, 76°16′ W 96
Elizabeth Falls, Can. 59°20′ N, 105°49′ W 108
Elizabeth Islands, Atlantic Ocean 41°21′ N, 71°2′ W 104
Elizabeth Mountain, Utah, U.S. 40°57′ N, 110°48′ W 90
Elizabethton, Tenn., U.S. 36°20′ N, 82°14′ W 96
Elizabethtown, Ind., U.S. 39°7′ N, 85°49′ W 102
Elizabethtown, Ky., U.S. 37°40′ N, 85°52′ W 96
Elizabethtown, Mo., U.S. 37°27′ N, 88°18′ W 96
Elizabethtown, N.Y., U.S. 44°13′ N, 73°37′ W 104
Elizondo, Sp. 43°8′ N, 1°31′ W 150
Ełk, Pol. 53°50′ N, 22°21′ E 152
Elk, Calif., U.S. 39°8′ N, 123°43′ W 90
Elk City, Okla., U.S. 35°23′ N, 99°26′ W 92
Elk Creek, river, S. Dak., U.S. 44°13′ N, 102°53′ W 90
Elk Grove, Calif., U.S. 38°24′ N, 121°23′ W 100
Elk Hills, Calif., U.S. 35°20′ N, 119°31′ W 100
Elk Island National Park, Can. 53°32′ N, 113°12′ W 238
Elk Lake, Can. 47°43′ N, 80°21′ W 94
Elk Lake, Mich., U.S. 44°47′ N, 85°37′ W 94
Elk Mountain, Wyo., U.S. 41°37′ N, 106°36′ W 90
Elk Peak, Mont., U.S. 46°25′ N, 110°50′ W 90
Elk Point, Can. 53°53′ N, 110°55′ W 108
Elk Point, S. Dak., U.S. 42°39′ N, 96°41′ W 90
Elk River, Idaho, U.S. 46°45′ N, 116°13′ W 90
Elk River, Minn., U.S. 45°17′ N, 93°34′ W 94
Elk, river, Can. 49°23′ N, 114°53′ W 108
Elk, river, Colo., U.S. 40°34′ N, 106°58′ W 90
Elk, river, W. Va., U.S. 38°22′ N, 80°55′ W 80
Elkhart, Ind., U.S. 41°40′ N, 85°59′ W 82
Elkhart, Kans., U.S. 37°0′ N, 101°54′ W 92
Elkhart, Tex., U.S. 31°36′ N, 95°35′ W 103
Elkhart Lake, Wis., U.S. 43°49′ N, 88°1′ W 102
Elkhead Mountains, Colo., U.S. 40°40′ N, 107°46′ W 90
Elkhorn, Can. 49°59′ N, 101°15′ W 90
Elkhorn, Wis., U.S. 42°40′ N, 88°33′ W 102
Elkhorn City, Ky., U.S. 37°18′ N, 82°22′ W 94
Elkhorn Mountain, Can. 49°47′ N, 125°55′ W 90
Elkhorn, river, Nebr., U.S. 42°21′ N, 99°26′ W 80
Elkhovo, Bulg. 42°10′ N, 26°34′ E 158
Elkin, N.C., U.S. 36°14′ N, 80°53′ W 96
Elkins, N. Mex., U.S. 33°41′ N, 104°4′ W 92
Elkins, W. Va., U.S. 38°55′ N, 79°51′ W 94
Elkland, Pa., U.S. 41°59′ N, 77°20′ W 94
Elko, Can. 49°18′ N, 115°7′ W 90
Elko, Nev., U.S. 40°53′ N, 115°51′ W 106
Elkton, Fla., U.S. 29°46′ N, 81°27′ W 105
Elkton, Ky., U.S. 36°48′ N, 87°10′ W 96
Elkton, Md., U.S. 39°36′ N, 75°51′ W 94
Elkton, Mich., U.S. 43°48′ N, 83°11′ W 102
Elkview, W. Va., U.S. 38°26′ N, 81°30′ W 102
Ellef Ringnes Island, Can. 77°11′ N, 103°31′ W 106
Elleh Creek, river, Can. 58°32′ N, 122°26′ W 108
Ellen, Mount, Utah, U.S. 38°5′ N, 110°53′ W 90
Ellenboro, W. Va., U.S. 39°16′ N, 81°4′ W 102
Ellendale, N. Dak., U.S. 46°0′ N, 98°32′ W 90
Ellensburg, Wash., U.S. 46°58′ N, 120°35′ W 90
Ellenton, Fla., U.S. 27°32′ N, 82°30′ W 105
Ellesmere Island, Can. 76°28′ N, 77°40′ W 106
Ellesmere Port, U.K. 53°17′ N, 2°54′ W 162
Ellettsville, Ind., U.S. 39°13′ N, 86°38′ W 102
Ellila, spring, Chad 16°42′ N, 20°20′ E 216

Ellington, Conn., U.S. 41°53′ N, 72°29′ W 104
Ellinwood, Kans., U.S. 38°20′ N, 98°35′ W 82
Elliot, S. Af. 31°21′ S, 27°49′ E 227
Elliot Lake, Can. 46°23′ N, 82°40′ W 110
Elliott, Cape, Antarctica 65°39′ S, 106°26′ E 248
Elliott Lake, Can. 61°1′ N, 100°2′ W 108
Ellis, Idaho, U.S. 44°41′ N, 114°2′ W 90
Ellis, Kans., U.S. 38°55′ N, 99°34′ W 90
Ellis, Mount, Mont., U.S. 45°32′ N, 111°1′ W 90
Ellisburg, N.Y., U.S. 43°43′ N, 76°9′ W 110
Ellisland, site, U.K. 55°6′ N, 3°46′ W 150
Ellisras see Lephalale, S. Af. 23°40′ S, 27°42′ E 227
Elliston, Austral. 33°40′ S, 134°54′ E 231
Ellisville, Miss., U.S. 31°35′ N, 89°13′ W 103
Ełk, Pol. 53°50′ N, 22°20′ E 152
Ellore see Eluru, India 16°46′ N, 81°7′ E 188
Ells, river, Can. 56°59′ N, 112°21′ W 108
Ellsworth, Kans., U.S. 38°43′ N, 98°14′ W 90
Ellsworth, Me., U.S. 44°31′ N, 68°24′ W 82
Ellsworth Land, region, Antarctica 73°44′ S, 96°14′ W 248
Ellsworth, Mount, Utah, U.S. 37°44′ N, 110°42′ W 92
Ellsworth Mountains, Antarctica 76°23′ S, 90°19′ W 248
Elm Creek, Nebr., U.S. 40°42′ N, 99°23′ W 90
Elma, Wash., U.S. 47°0′ N, 123°24′ W 100
Elmadağı, Turk. 39°55′ N, 33°14′ E 156
Elmalı, Turk. 36°43′ N, 29°55′ E 156
Elmer City, Wash., U.S. 47°59′ N, 118°56′ W 90
Elmira, N.Y., U.S. 42°5′ N, 76°50′ W 94
Elmo, Wyo., U.S. 41°53′ N, 106°31′ W 90
Elmsta, Sw. 59°58′ N, 18°42′ E 166
Elmwood, Ill., U.S. 40°45′ N, 89°58′ W 102
Elnora, Ind., U.S. 38°52′ N, 87°5′ W 102
Elortondo, Arg. 33°43′ S, 61°38′ W 139
Elorza, Venez. 7°1′ N, 69°31′ W 136
Elos, ruin(s), Gr. 36°47′ N, 22°40′ E 156
Elota, Mex. 23°56′ N, 106°42′ W 114
Eloy, Ariz., U.S. 32°44′ N, 111°34′ W 112
Eloy Alfaro, Ecua. 2°16′ S, 79°51′ W 130
Elrose, Can. 51°12′ N, 108°4′ W 90
Elroy, Wis., U.S. 43°44′ N, 90°17′ W 102
Elsa, Tex., U.S. 26°17′ N, 97°59′ W 114
Elsas, Can. 48°32′ N, 82°55′ W 94
Elsberry, Mo., U.S. 39°9′ N, 90°47′ W 94
Elsdorf, Ger. 53°14′ N, 9°22′ E 152
Elsen Nur, lake, China 35°14′ N, 91°46′ E 188
Elsie, Mich., U.S. 43°4′ N, 84°24′ W 102
Elst, Neth. 51°55′ N, 5°50′ E 167
Elstow, U.K. 52°7′ N, 0°28′ E 162
Eltanin Fracture Zone, South Pacific Ocean 52°39′ S, 138°6′ W 252
Elten, Ger. 51°51′ N, 6°10′ E 167
Eltham, N.Z. 39°27′ S, 174°18′ E 240
Elton, La., U.S. 30°28′ N, 92°42′ W 103
El'ton, Russ. 49°9′ N, 46°47′ E 158
Eltopia, Wash., U.S. 46°26′ N, 119°1′ W 90
Eltville, Ger. 50°1′ N, 8°6′ E 167
Eluru (Ellore), India 16°46′ N, 81°7′ E 188
Elva, Est. 58°10′ N, 26°22′ E 166
Elvas, Port. 38°52′ N, 7°10′ W 150
Elvenes, Nor. 69°40′ N, 30°8′ E 152
Elvins, Mo., U.S. 37°49′ N, 90°33′ W 96
Elwell, Lake, Mont., U.S. 48°20′ N, 111°36′ W 90
Elwood, Ill., U.S. 41°24′ N, 88°7′ W 102
Elwood, Ind., U.S. 40°16′ N, 85°50′ W 102
Elwood, Kans., U.S. 39°43′ N, 94°53′ W 94
Elwood, Nebr., U.S. 40°34′ N, 99°52′ W 90
Elx see Elche, Sp. 38°15′ N, 0°42′ E 164
Ely, Minn., U.S. 47°53′ N, 91°53′ W 94
Ely, Nev., U.S. 39°17′ N, 114°48′ W 238
Ely, U.K. 52°23′ N, 0°15′ E 162
Ely, Isle of, U.K. 52°24′ N, 0°11′ E 162
Elyria, Ohio, U.S. 41°21′ N, 82°5′ W 102
Elyrus, ruin(s), Gr. 35°15′ N, 23°42′ E 156
Emådalen, Nor. 61°19′ N, 14°42′ E 152
Emajõgi, river, Est. 58°24′ N, 26°7′ E 166
Emām Taqī, Iran 35°59′ N, 59°23′ E 180
Emas National Park, Braz. 18°19′ S, 53°5′ W 138
Embarí, river, Braz. 0°48′ N, 66°60′ W 136
Embarras Portage, Can. 58°24′ N, 111°26′ W 108
Embi, Kaz. 48°50′ N, 58°6′ E 158
Embira, river, Braz. 9°17′ S, 70°51′ W 137
Embu, Kenya 0°33′ N, 37°27′ E 224
Emden, Ger. 53°21′ N, 7°12′ E 163
Emel'dzhak, Russ. 58°19′ N, 126°40′ E 160
Emerald Island, Can. 76°42′ N, 113°8′ W 106
Emero, river, Bol. 13°38′ S, 68°3′ W 137
Emerson, Ark., U.S. 33°5′ N, 93°12′ W 103
Emerson, Can. 49°0′ N, 97°11′ W 90
Emerson Peak, Calif., U.S. 41°13′ N, 120°15′ W 90
Emery, Utah, U.S. 38°55′ N, 111°14′ W 90
Emery Mills, Me., U.S. 43°30′ N, 70°51′ W 104
Emet, Turk. 39°21′ N, 29°14′ E 156
Emgayet, oil field, Lib. 28°57′ N, 12°45′ E 143
Emigrant Pass, Nev., U.S. 40°40′ N, 116°14′ W 90
Emigrant Peak, Mont., U.S. 45°14′ N, 110°47′ W 90
Emilia-Romagna, adm. division, It. 44°40′ N, 10°18′ E 167
Emilius, Mount, It. 45°39′ N, 7°24′ E 165
Emily, Minn., U.S. 46°43′ N, 93°58′ W 94
Emily, Mount, Oreg., U.S. 45°24′ N, 118°11′ W 90
Emin, China 46°29′ N, 83°38′ E 184
Emin, river, China 46°24′ N, 83°0′ E 184
Emin, river, Kaz. 46°16′ N, 81°53′ E 184
Emir Dağları, peak, Turk. 38°50′ N, 31°9′ E 156
Emirdağ, Turk. 39°0′ N, 31°6′ E 156
Emisou, Tarso, peak, Chad 21°23′ N, 18°32′ E 216
Emlichheim, Ger. 52°36′ N, 6°51′ E 163
Emma, Mount, Ariz., U.S. 36°15′ N, 113°14′ W 92
Emmaboda, Nor. 56°37′ N, 15°31′ E 152
Emmaste, Est. 58°43′ N, 22°33′ E 166
Emmaus, Pa., U.S. 40°31′ N, 75°30′ W 94
Emmeloord, Neth. 52°42′ N, 5°44′ E 163
Emmen, Neth. 52°47′ N, 6°53′ E 163
Emmen, Switz. 47°3′ N, 8°18′ E 150
Emmerich, Ger. 51°49′ N, 6°15′ E 167
Emmetsburg, Iowa, U.S. 43°5′ N, 94°41′ W 90
Emmett, Idaho, U.S. 43°51′ N, 116°30′ W 90
Emmonak, Alas., U.S. 62°42′ N, 164°42′ W 98
Emmons, Mount, Utah, U.S. 40°41′ N, 110°23′ W 90
Emo, Can. 48°38′ N, 93°50′ W 90
Emory Peak, Tex., U.S. 29°12′ N, 103°21′ W 92
Empangeni, S. Af. 28°44′ S, 31°51′ E 227
Empedrado, Arg. 27°55′ S, 58°48′ W 139
Emperor Seamounts, North Pacific Ocean 43°13′ N, 170°0′ E 252
Emperor Trough, North Pacific Ocean 44°20′ N, 174°43′ E 252
Empire, La., U.S. 29°22′ N, 89°36′ W 103
Empire, Mich., U.S. 44°48′ N, 86°3′ W 94
Empoli, It. 43°43′ N, 10°57′ E 156
Emporia, Kans., U.S. 38°23′ N, 96°11′ W 90
Emporia, Va., U.S. 36°41′ N, 77°32′ W 96
Emporio, ruin(s), Gr. 38°11′ N, 25°55′ E 156
Emporium, Pa., U.S. 41°30′ N, 78°15′ W 94
Empress, Can. 50°57′ N, 110°1′ W 90
Empty Quarter see Ar Rub' al Khālī, Saudi Arabia 18°28′ N, 46°3′ E 182
Ems, river, Ger. 52°1′ N, 7°43′ E 167
Emsdetten, Ger. 52°10′ N, 7°32′ E 163
En Amakane, spring, Mali 16°35′ N, 0°59′ E 222
'En Boqeq, Israel 31°11′ N, 35°21′ E 194
'En Gedi, Israel 31°27′ N, 35°22′ E 194
'En Gev, Israel 32°46′ N, 35°38′ E 194
En Nahud, Sudan 12°40′ N, 28°26′ E 226
'En Yahav, Israel 30°37′ N, 35°11′ E 194
Ena, Japan 35°25′ N, 137°24′ E 201
Ena Lake, Can. 59°57′ N, 108°27′ W 108
Enånger, Nor. 61°32′ N, 16°58′ E 152
Encantadas, Serra das, Braz. 30°51′ S, 53°28′ W 139
Encantado, Cerro, peak, Mex. 27°2′ N, 112°38′ W 112
Encanto, Cape, Philippines 15°29′ N, 121°37′ E 203
Encarnación, Parag. 27°20′ S, 55°50′ W 139
Encarnación de Díaz, Mex. 21°30′ N, 102°15′ W 114
Enchi, Ghana 5°49′ N, 2°50′ W 222
Encinal, Tex., U.S. 28°2′ N, 99°21′ W 92
Encinillas, Mex. 29°13′ N, 106°17′ W 92
Encinillas, Laguna de, lake, Mex. 29°24′ N, 107°45′ W 81
Encinitas, Calif., U.S. 33°2′ N, 117°18′ W 101
Encino, Tex., U.S. 26°56′ N, 98°8′ W 96
Encontrados, Venez. 9°2′ N, 72°15′ W 136
Encruzilhada, Braz. 15°33′ S, 40°55′ W 138
Encruzilhada do Sul, Braz. 30°33′ S, 52°34′ W 139
Endako, Can. 54°5′ N, 125°1′ W 108
Endau, Kenya 1°19′ S, 38°34′ E 224
Endeavour, Can. 52°10′ N, 102°40′ W 108
Enderby, Can. 50°33′ N, 119°9′ W 90
Enderby Land, region, Antarctica 69°55′ S, 39°37′ E 248
Enderby Plain, Indian Ocean 58°55′ S, 44°16′ E 255
Enderlin, N. Dak., U.S. 46°36′ N, 97°37′ W 90
Endicott Mountains, Alas., U.S. 67°34′ N, 155°1′ W 98
Endr od, Hung. 46°56′ N, 20°46′ E 168
Endwell, N.Y., U.S. 42°6′ N, 76°1′ W 94
Energetik, Russ. 51°44′ N, 58°56′ E 154
Enez, Turk. 40°42′ N, 26°3′ E 156
Enfer, Pointe d', Fr. 14°17′ N, 61°38′ W 116
Enfida, Tun. 36°7′ N, 10°23′ E 156
Enfield, Conn., U.S. 41°57′ N, 72°36′ W 104
Enfield, N.Z. 45°3′ S, 170°50′ E 240
Enfield, U.K. 51°39′ N, 7°415′ W 162
Enfield Center, N.H., U.S. 43°35′ N, 72°7′ W 104
Engaño, Cabo, Dom. Rep. 18°35′ N, 68°15′ W 116
'En-Gedi, ruin(s), Israel 31°27′ N, 35°21′ E 194
Engelberg, Switz. 46°48′ N, 8°24′ E 167
Engelhard, N.C., U.S. 35°31′ N, 76°1′ W 96
Engels, Russ. 51°25′ N, 46°9′ E 158
Engemann Lake, Can. 57°49′ N, 107°49′ W 108
Engen, Can. 54°1′ N, 124°17′ W 108
Engerdal, Nor. 61°45′ N, 11°56′ E 152
Engershand, Mongolia 47°44′ N, 107°21′ E 198
Enggano, island, Indonesia 5°46′ S, 101°5′ E 192
Enghien, Belg. 50°41′ N, 4°2′ E 163
Engizek Dağı, Turk. 37°46′ N, 36°29′ E 156
England, adm. division, U.K. 52°25′ N, 2°59′ W 143
Englehart, Can. 47°50′ N, 79°52′ W 94
Englewood, Fla., U.S. 26°58′ N, 82°21′ W 105
Englewood, Kans., U.S. 37°1′ N, 99°60′ W 92
Englewood, Ohio, U.S. 39°52′ N, 84°19′ W 102
English Channel (La Manche) 49°57′ N, 3°16′ W 150
English River, Can. 49°13′ N, 90°58′ W 94
English, river, Can. 50°30′ N, 95°13′ W 80
English, river, Can. 49°50′ N, 92°1′ W 94
Engure, Latv. 57°8′ N, 23°12′ E 166
Engures Ezers, lake, Latv. 57°14′ N, 22°50′ E 166
Enid, Okla., U.S. 36°22′ N, 97°52′ W 92
Enid, Mount, Austral. 21°46′ S, 116°12′ E 230
Enilda, Can. 55°24′ N, 116°18′ W 108
Enken, Mys, Russ. 56°57′ N, 139°57′ E 172
Enkirch, Ger. 49°58′ N, 7°8′ E 167
Enköping, Nor. 59°37′ N, 17°3′ E 152
Enmelen, Russ. 65°1′ N, 175°51′ W 98
Enna, It. 37°34′ N, 14°16′ E 156
Ennadai, Can. 61°7′ N, 100°52′ W 108
Ennadai Lake, Can. 60°42′ N, 102°23′ W 108
Ennigerloh, Ger. 51°49′ N, 8°0′ E 167
Enning, S. Dak., U.S. 44°33′ N, 102°34′ W 90
Ennis, Ire. 52°50′ N, 8°60′ W 150
Ennis, Tex., U.S. 32°18′ N, 96°38′ W 96
Enniskillen, U.K. 54°20′ N, 7°38′ W 150
Enns, Aust. 48°13′ N, 14°28′ E 156
Eno, Fin. 62°45′ N, 30°8′ E 154
Eno, river, Japan 34°33′ N, 132°40′ E 201
Enonkoski, Fin. 62°4′ N, 28°55′ E 152
Enontekiö, Fin. 68°23′ N, 23°35′ E 152
Énos, Óros, peak, Gr. 38°7′ N, 20°35′ E 156
Enrique Urien, Arg. 27°33′ S, 60°37′ W 139
Enschede, Neth. 52°13′ N, 6°53′ E 163
Ensenada, Mex. 31°51′ N, 116°38′ W 92
Enshi, China 30°14′ N, 109°24′ E 198
Entebbe, Uganda 6°357′ N, 32°27′ E 224
Enterprise, Ala., U.S. 31°18′ N, 85°51′ W 96
Enterprise, Can. 60°40′ N, 116°4′ W 108
Enterprise, Miss., U.S. 32°10′ N, 88°48′ W 103
Enterprise, Utah, U.S. 37°34′ N, 113°43′ W 92
Entinas, Punta, Sp. 36°31′ N, 2°44′ W 150
Entrada, Punta, Arg. 50°22′ S, 68°28′ W 134
Entrance, Can. 53°21′ N, 117°42′ W 108
Entraunes, Fr. 44°10′ N, 6°45′ E 167
Entre Ríos, Bol. 21°33′ S, 64°13′ W 137
Entre Ríos, adm. division, Arg. 31°43′ S, 59°58′ W 139
Entre-Rios, Mozambique 14°58′ S, 37°24′ E 224
Entwistle, Can. 53°33′ N, 114°56′ W 108
Enugu, Nig. 6°26′ N, 7°29′ E 222
Enumclaw, Wash., U.S. 47°10′ N, 121°59′ W 100
Enurmino, Russ. 66°55′ N, 171°46′ W 98
Envigado, Col. 6°8′ N, 75°37′ W 130
Envira, Braz. 7°23′ S, 70°14′ W 130
Enyellé, Congo 2°51′ N, 18°4′ E 218
Enying, Hung. 46°56′ N, 18°15′ E 168
Enzan, Japan 35°41′ N, 138°44′ E 201
Eola, La., U.S. 30°53′ N, 92°14′ W 103
Eolie see Lipari, Isole, islands, Mediterranean Sea 38°39′ N, 13°46′ E 156
Eonyang, S. Korea 35°33′ N, 129°10′ E 200
Epe, Neth. 52°21′ N, 5°58′ E 163
Epembe, spring, Namibia 17°35′ S, 13°34′ E 220
Epéna, Congo 1°23′ N, 17°27′ E 218
Épernay, Fr. 49°2′ N, 3°56′ E 163
Épernon, Fr. 48°35′ N, 1°40′ E 163
Epes, Ala., U.S. 32°41′ N, 88°8′ W 103
Ephesus, ruin(s), Turk. 37°55′ N, 27°12′ E 156
Ephraim, Utah, U.S. 39°21′ N, 111°35′ W 90
Ephrata, Wash., U.S. 47°18′ N, 119°34′ W 90
Epidaurum see Cavtat, Croatia 42°34′ N, 18°13′ E 168
Epidaurus Limerás, ruin(s), Gr. 36°43′ N, 22°56′ E 156
Épila, Sp. 41°37′ N, 1°17′ W 164
Épinal, Fr. 48°10′ N, 6°26′ E 163
Epini, Dem. Rep. of the Congo 1°26′ N, 28°21′ E 224
Epirus, region, Europe 40°27′ N, 19°28′ E 156
Episkopi, Cyprus 34°40′ N, 32°54′ E 194
Epping Forest, U.K. 51°38′ N, 2°119′ E 162
Epps, La., U.S. 32°35′ N, 91°29′ W 103
Epsom, U.K. 51°20′ N, 0°17′ E 162
Epu Pel, Arg. 37°36′ S, 64°16′ W 139
Epukiro, Namibia 21°45′ S, 19°8′ E 227
Epulu, river, Dem. Rep. of the Congo 1°29′ N, 28°42′ E 224
Equator, adm. division, Dem. Rep. of the Congo 9°535′ N, 18°55′ E 218
Equatorial Channel 0°14′ N, 72°8′ E 188
Equatorial Guinea 1°38′ N, 10°28′ E 218
Er Rachidia, Mor. 31°58′ N, 4°21′ W 143
Er Rahad, Sudan 12°43′ N, 30°36′ E 216
Er Rif, Mor. 35°15′ N, 5°28′ W 150
Er Roseires, Sudan 11°52′ N, 34°24′ E 182
Er Rout Sanihida, spring, Niger 21°53′ N, 11°52′ E 222
Eraclea, It. 45°34′ N, 12°40′ E 167
Erath, La., U.S. 29°56′ N, 92°2′ W 103
Erbaa, Turk. 40°40′ N, 36°34′ E 156
Erbab, Jebel, peak, Sudan 18°40′ N, 36°59′ E 182
Erçek, Turk. 38°37′ N, 43°34′ E 195
Erçek Gölü, lake, Turk. 38°39′ N, 43°23′ E 195
Erciş, Turk. 38°59′ N, 43°18′ E 195
Erciyeş Dağı, peak, Turk. 38°30′ N, 35°22′ E 156
Ercsi, Hung. 47°14′ N, 18°53′ E 168
Érd, Hung. 47°22′ N, 18°55′ E 168
Erdao, river, China 42°44′ N, 127°38′ E 200
Erdaobaihe, China 42°26′ N, 128°7′ E 200
Erdébé, Plateau d', Chad 17°17′ N, 21°23′ E 216
Erdek, Turk. 40°24′ N, 27°45′ E 156
Erdemli, Turk. 36°36′ N, 34°18′ E 156
Erdenet, Mongolia 48°57′ N, 104°17′ E 198
Erdut, Croatia 45°31′ N, 19°2′ E 168
Erebus, Mount, Antarctica 77°26′ S, 167°55′ E 248
Erechim, Braz. 27°39′ S, 52°18′ W 139
Ereğli, Turk. 41°17′ N, 31°25′ E 156
Ereğli, Turk. 37°29′ N, 34°2′ E 156
Erego, Mozambique 16°3′ S, 37°11′ E 224
Erei, Monti, It. 37°23′ N, 14°3′ E 156
Eremiya, Bulg. 42°12′ N, 22°50′ E 168
Erenhot, China 43°39′ N, 111°57′ E 198
Eresus, ruin(s), Gr. 39°7′ N, 25°50′ E 156
Erétria, ruin(s), Gr. 38°23′ N, 23°42′ E 156
Ereymentaū, Kaz. 51°41′ N, 73°22′ E 184
Erfoud, Mor. 31°29′ N, 4°15′ W 214
Erft, river, Ger. 51°2′ N, 6°29′ E 167
Erftstadt, Ger. 50°47′ N, 6°44′ E 167
Erfurt, Ger. 50°59′ N, 11°2′ E 152
'Erg Chech, Alg. 25°13′ N, 3°16′ W 214
'Erg el Ahmar, Mali 24°14′ N, 4°55′ W 214
'Erg Iguidi, Alg. 24°15′ N, 8°24′ W 214
'Erg I-n-Sâkâne, Mali 20°43′ N, 0°54′ E 222
Ergani, Turk. 38°17′ N, 39°45′ E 195
Ergel, Mongolia 43°13′ N, 109°8′ E 198
Ērgļi, Latv. 56°53′ N, 25°39′ E 166
Erg-n-Ataram, Alg. 23°45′ N, 1°6′ E 214
Ergun, river, Asia 50°18′ N, 119°1′ E 190
Eriba, Sudan 16°37′ N, 36°3′ E 182
Éric, Lac, lake, Can. 51°50′ N, 65°59′ W 111
Erice, It. 38°2′ N, 12°35′ E 156
Erick, Okla., U.S. 35°11′ N, 99°53′ W 92
Erickson, Can. 50°30′ N, 99°54′ W 90
Erie, Ill., U.S. 41°38′ N, 90°5′ W 102
Erie, Pa., U.S. 42°6′ N, 80°5′ W 94
Erie, Lake 42°11′ N, 83°6′ W 73
Erieau, Can. 42°15′ N, 81°56′ W 102
Erigavo see Ceerigaabo, Somalia 10°34′ N, 47°24′ E 218
Eriksdale, Can. 50°51′ N, 98°6′ W 90
Erímanthos, Óros, peak, Gr. 37°58′ N, 21°45′ E 156
Erimi, Cyprus 34°40′ N, 32°55′ E 194
Eritrea 15°32′ N, 37°35′ E 182
Erits, river, Kaz. 51°34′ N, 77°33′ E 184
Erkelenz, Ger. 51°4′ N, 6°19′ E 167
Erkilet, Turk. 38°48′ N, 35°27′ E 156
Erkner, Ger. 52°24′ N, 13°45′ E 152
Erkowit, Sudan 18°45′ N, 37°3′ E 182
Erla, Sp. 42°6′ N, 0°57′ E 164
Erlangen, Ger. 49°35′ N, 11°0′ E 152
Ermelo, S. Af. 26°32′ S, 29°58′ E 227
Ermenek, Turk. 36°36′ N, 32°55′ E 156
Ermidas-Sado, Port. 37°59′ N, 8°25′ W 150
Ermil, Sudan 13°33′ N, 27°38′ E 226
Ermoúpoli, Gr. 37°26′ N, 24°56′ E 156
Ernakulam, India 9°59′ N, 76°17′ E 188
Erndtebrück, Ger. 50°59′ N, 8°15′ E 167
Ernstberg, peak, Ger. 50°13′ N, 6°44′ E 167
Eromanga, Austral. 26°39′ S, 143°17′ E 231
Erongo Mountains, Namibia 21°44′ S, 15°27′ E 227
Eros, La., U.S. 32°22′ N, 92°25′ W 103
Eroug, spring, Mali 18°20′ N, 2°4′ W 222
Erpengdianzi, China 41°10′ N, 125°33′ E 200
Er-Remla, Tun. 34°46′ N, 11°14′ E 156
Errigal Mountain, Ire. 55°0′ N, 8°13′ W 150
Error Tablemount, Arabian Sea 9°58′ N, 56°3′ E 254
Erskine, Minn., U.S. 47°38′ N, 96°2′ W 90
Erstein, Fr. 48°25′ N, 7°39′ E 163
Ertai, China 46°8′ N, 90°7′ E 190
Ertis, Kaz. 53°19′ N, 75°27′ E 184
Ertis, river, Kaz. 54°12′ N, 74°56′ E 160
Ertix, river, China 48°2′ N, 85°34′ E 184
Eruh, Turk. 37°44′ N, 42°9′ E 195
Erundu, Namibia 20°41′ S, 16°23′ E 227
Erval, Braz. 32°2′ S, 53°27′ W 139
Ervenik, Croatia 44°5′ N, 15°55′ E 168
Erwin, N.C., U.S. 35°19′ N, 78°42′ W 96
Erwitte, Ger. 51°36′ N, 8°21′ E 167
Erzgebirge, Czech Rep. 50°18′ N, 12°34′ E 152
Erzin, Russ. 50°14′ N, 95°18′ E 190
Erzincan, Turk. 39°44′ N, 39°28′ E 195
Erzurum, Turk. 39°54′ N, 41°17′ E 195
Es Bordes, Sp. 42°43′ N, 0°42′ E 164
Es Mercadal, Sp. 39°59′ N, 4°4′ E 150
Es Safiya, Sudan 15°31′ N, 30°6′ E 226
Es Salam, Sudan 18°5′ N, 33°53′ E 182
Es Sufeiya, Sudan 15°27′ N, 34°40′ E 182
Esa, river, Belarus 54°43′ N, 28°30′ E 166
Esbjerg, Den. 55°27′ N, 8°36′ E 160
Esbo see Espoo, Fin. 60°11′ N, 24°34′ E 166
Escalante, Utah, U.S. 37°46′ N, 111°37′ W 92
Escanaba, Mich., U.S. 45°48′ N, 87°7′ W 106
Escárcega, Mex. 18°36′ N, 90°46′ W 115
Escatawpa, river, Ala., U.S. 30°27′ N, 88°27′ W 103
Escatrón, Sp. 41°16′ N, 0°20′ E 164
Eschenburg, Ger. 50°48′ N, 8°20′ E 167
Eschweiler, Ger. 50°48′ N, 6°15′ E 167
Escobedo, Mex. 27°11′ N, 101°22′ W 96
Escondido, Calif., U.S. 33°7′ N, 117°6′ W 101
Escudero, station, Antarctica 62°5′ S, 58°48′ W 134
Escudilla Mountain, Ariz., U.S. 33°56′ N, 109°11′ W 92
Escuela de Caza de Morón, Sp. 37°9′ N, 5°37′ W 164
Escuinapa, Mex. 22°50′ N, 105°47′ W 114
Escuintla, Guatemala 14°16′ N, 90°47′ W 115
Escuintla, Mex. 15°18′ N, 92°40′ W 115
Escuminac, Point, Can. 47°6′ N, 64°49′ W 111
Ese Khayya, Russ. 67°28′ N, 134°38′ E 160
Eséka, Cameroon 3°41′ N, 10°47′ E 222
Esenguly, Turkm. 37°27′ N, 53°57′ E 180
Esens, Ger. 53°39′ N, 7°36′ E 163
Eşfahān (Isfahan), Iran 32°40′ N, 51°38′ E 180
Esfandak, Iran 27°5′ N, 62°51′ E 182
Eshkamesh, Afghan. 36°27′ N, 69°16′ E 186
Eshkashem, Taj. 36°44′ N, 71°34′ E 186
Eshowe, S. Af. 28°54′ S, 31°24′ E 227
Esiama, Ghana 4°58′ N, 2°21′ W 222
Esik, Kaz. 43°21′ N, 77°25′ E 184
Esil, Kaz. 51°57′ N, 66°27′ E 184
Esil, river, Kaz. 53°18′ N, 66°55′ E 184
Esimi, Gr. 41°1′ N, 25°57′ E 156
Esira, Madagascar 24°21′ S, 46°47′ E 220
Esk, river, U.K. 55°14′ N, 3°17′ W 150
Esk, river, U.K. 54°28′ N, 0°54′ E 162
Eskdale, N.Z. 39°25′ S, 176°49′ E 240
Eskene, Kaz. 47°20′ N, 52°52′ E 158
Esker, Can. 54°0′ N, 66°33′ W 106
Eskimo Point, Can. 58°49′ N, 94°20′ W 108
Eskipazar, Turk. 40°58′ N, 32°32′ E 156
Eskişehir, Turk. 39°46′ N, 30°31′ E 156
Eslāmābād, Iran 34°9′ N, 46°32′ E 180
Eşler Dağı, peak, Turk. 37°39′ N, 29°12′ E 156
Eşme, Turk. 38°24′ N, 28°57′ E 156
Esmeralda, river, Bol. 13°28′ S, 67°59′ W 137
Esmeraldas, Ecua. 0°55′ N, 79°48′ W 130
Esmoraca, Bol. 21°41′ S, 66°19′ W 137
Esnagi Lake, Can. 48°40′ N, 84°49′ W 94
Espa, Nor. 60°34′ N, 11°16′ E 152
Espada, Punta, Col. 12°4′ N, 71°8′ W 136
Espakeh, Iran 26°46′ N, 60°12′ E 182
Espanola, Can. 46°15′ N, 81°46′ W 94
Espanola, N. Mex., U.S. 35°59′ N, 106°6′ W 92
Esparza, C.R. 9°58′ N, 84°40′ W 116
Esperanza, Arg. 31°27′ S, 60°54′ W 139
Esperanza, Arg. 51°5′ S, 70°38′ W 134
Esperanza, Peru 9°49′ S, 70°44′ W 137
Esperanza Inlet 49°45′ N, 127°40′ W 90
Esperanza, station, Antarctica 63°34′ S, 57°4′ W 248
Espichel, Cabo, Port. 38°11′ N, 9°37′ W 150
Espiel, Sp. 38°11′ N, 5°1′ W 164
Espigão Mestre, Braz. 14°41′ S, 46°14′ W 138
Espinal, Bol. 17°13′ S, 58°28′ W 132
Espinar see Yauri, Peru 14°51′ S, 71°24′ W 137
Espinazo, Mex. 26°16′ N, 101°6′ W 114
Espino, Venez. 8°32′ N, 66°1′ W 136
Espinosa, Braz. 14°59′ S, 42°50′ W 138
Espírito Santo, adm. division, Braz. 19°55′ S, 41°11′ W 138
Espírito Santo see Vila Velha, Braz. 20°25′ S, 40°21′ W 138
Espiritu, Philippines 17°59′ N, 120°39′ E 203
Espita, Mex. 21°0′ N, 88°20′ W 116
Espoo (Esbo), Fin. 60°11′ N, 24°34′ E 166
Esposende, Port. 41°31′ N, 8°48′ W 150
Espuña, peak, Sp. 37°51′ N, 1°37′ W 164
Espungabera, Mozambique 20°30′ S, 32°47′ E 227
Espy, Pa., U.S. 41°0′ N, 76°25′ W 110
Esqueda, Mex. 30°41′ N, 109°35′ W 92
Esquel, Arg. 42°58′ S, 71°19′ W 123
Esquimalt, Can. 48°25′ N, 123°24′ W 100
Esquina, Arg. 29°60′ S, 59°33′ W 139
Essaouira, Mor. 31°35′ N, 9°39′ W 143
Essé, Cameroon 4°6′ N, 11°50′ E 218
Essen, Belg. 51°27′ N, 4°29′ E 167
Essen, Ger. 51°27′ N, 7°0′ E 167
Essen, Ger. 52°44′ N, 7°56′ E 163
Essendon, Mount, Austral. 25°2′ S, 120°18′ E 230
Essex, Calif., U.S. 34°44′ N, 115°15′ W 101
Essex, Conn., U.S. 41°21′ N, 72°24′ W 104
Essex, Mass., U.S. 42°37′ N, 70°48′ W 104
Essex, N.Y., U.S. 44°18′ N, 73°23′ W 104
Essex Junction, Vt., U.S. 44°29′ N, 73°7′ W 104
Essexville, Mich., U.S. 43°36′ N, 83°50′ W 102
Esson, Gabon 1°14′ N, 11°34′ E 218
Essoûk, Mali 18°46′ N, 1°5′ E 222
Est, Cap, Madagascar 15°13′ S, 50°28′ E 220
Est, Pointe de l', Can. 49°5′ N, 61°39′ W 111
Estacado, Llano, North America 34°53′ N, 103°50′ W 92
Estados, Isla de los (Staten Island), Arg. 55°28′ S, 64°48′ W 134
Eşţahbānāt, Iran 29°5′ N, 54°3′ E 196
Estância, Braz. 11°15′ S, 37°28′ W 132
Estancia Rojas Silva, Parag. 22°33′ S, 59°5′ W 132
Estancias, peak, Sp. 37°34′ N, 2°6′ W 164
Estavayer-le-Lac, Switz. 46°50′ N, 6°51′ E 167
Estcourt, S. Af. 29°2′ S, 29°51′ E 220
Este, It. 45°14′ N, 11°39′ E 167
Estelí, Nicar. 13°5′ N, 86°21′ W 115
Estella (Lizarra), Sp. 42°39′ N, 2°2′ W 164
Estelline, S. Dak., U.S. 44°33′ N, 96°55′ W 90
Estelline, Tex., U.S. 34°31′ N, 100°27′ W 92
Estepa, Sp. 37°17′ N, 4°54′ W 164
Estepona, Sp. 36°25′ N, 5°9′ W 164
Estérel, Fr. 43°28′ N, 6°35′ E 165
Esterfeld, Ger. 52°41′ N, 7°15′ E 163
Esterhazy, Can. 50°38′ N, 102°8′ W 90
Esternay, Fr. 48°43′ N, 3°32′ E 163
Estero, Point, Calif., U.S. 35°23′ N, 121°7′ W 100
Esteros del Iberá, marsh, Arg. 28°15′ S, 58°7′ W 139
Esterwegen, Ger. 52°59′ N, 7°37′ E 163
Estes Park, Colo., U.S. 40°22′ N, 105°32′ W 90
Estevan, Can. 49°7′ N, 103°2′ W 90
Estherville, Iowa, U.S. 43°23′ N, 94°49′ W 94
Estherwood, La., U.S. 30°10′ N, 92°28′ W 103
Estill, S.C., U.S. 32°45′ N, 81°15′ W 96
Estissac, Fr. 48°15′ N, 3°48′ E 163
Eston, Can. 51°9′ N, 108°45′ W 90
Estonia 58°38′ N, 25°30′ E 166
Estreito, Braz. 31°49′ S, 51°45′ W 139
Estreito, Serra do, Braz. 10°32′ S, 43°49′ W 132
Estrêla do Norte, Braz. 13°50′ S, 49°6′ W 138
Estrela, Serra da, Port. 39°59′ N, 8°2′ W 150
Estrella, peak, Sp. 38°23′ N, 3°39′ W 164
Estrella, Punta, Mex. 30°55′ N, 114°43′ W 92
Estrondo, Serra do, Braz. 9°16′ S, 49°36′ W 130
Etah, site, Den. 78°18′ N, 73°12′ W 246
Étain, Fr. 49°12′ N, 5°38′ E 163
Etajima, Japan 34°13′ N, 132°29′ E 201
Etal Atoll, F.S.M. 5°46′ N, 154°5′ E 192
Étampes, Fr. 48°25′ N, 2°9′ E 163
Étaples, Fr. 50°31′ N, 1°38′ E 163
Etawah, India 26°45′ N, 79°0′ E 197
Etawney Lake, Can. 57°50′ N, 97°31′ W 108
Etéké, Gabon 1°30′ S, 11°33′ E 218
Eternity Range, Antarctica 69°10′ S, 68°24′ W 248
Ethel, Miss., U.S. 33°6′ N, 89°28′ W 103
Ethel, Wash., U.S. 46°30′ N, 122°45′ W 100
Ethel, W. Va., U.S. 37°51′ N, 81°55′ W 94
Ethelbert, Can. 51°31′ N, 100°25′ W 90
Ethelsville, Ala., U.S. 33°23′ N, 88°12′ W 103
Ethiopia 8°36′ N, 37°8′ E 218
Etna, Wyo., U.S. 43°2′ N, 110°60′ W 90
Etna, peak, It. 37°44′ N, 14°54′ E 156
Etne, Nor. 59°39′ N, 5°55′ E 152
Etoile, Dem. Rep. of the Congo 11°38′ S, 27°31′ E 224
Etoile, Tex., U.S. 31°21′ N, 94°27′ W 103
Etoka, Dem. Rep. of the Congo 0°8′ N, 23°17′ E 218
Etosha National Park, Namibia 18°57′ S, 14°47′ E 220
Etoumbi, Congo 4°237′ S, 14°54′ E 218
Etowah, Tenn., U.S. 35°19′ N, 84°32′ W 96
Étrépagny, Fr. 49°18′ N, 1°37′ E 163
Ettenheim, Ger. 48°14′ N, 7°47′ E 163
Ettersberg, Grosser, peak, Ger. 51°0′ N, 11°10′ E 152
Ettrick, N.Z. 45°39′ S, 169°21′ E 240
Etulia, Mold. 45°32′ N, 28°27′ E 156
Etxarri-Aranatz, Sp. 42°55′ N, 2°3′ W 164
Etzatlán, Mex. 20°46′ N, 104°7′ W 114
Eu, Fr. 50°2′ N, 1°24′ E 163
Euca, Braz. 2°38′ N, 50°54′ W 130
Eucla Motel, Austral. 31°39′ S, 128°51′ E 231
Euclid, Ohio, U.S. 41°34′ N, 81°31′ W 102
Eudora, Ark., U.S. 33°5′ N, 91°16′ W 103
Eufaula, Ala., U.S. 31°53′ N, 85°9′ W 96
Eufaula, Okla., U.S. 35°15′ N, 95°34′ W 96
Eufaula Lake, Okla., U.S. 34°58′ N, 96°6′ W 96
Eugene, Oreg., U.S. 44°2′ N, 123°7′ W 90
Eugenia, Punta, Mex. 27°43′ N, 116°17′ W 112
Eumseong, S. Korea 36°55′ N, 127°42′ E 200
Eungella National Park, Austral. 21°4′ S, 148°14′ E 238
Eunice, La., U.S. 30°28′ N, 92°25′ W 103
Eunice, N. Mex., U.S. 32°26′ N, 103°9′ W 92
Eupen, Belg. 50°37′ N, 6°2′ E 167
Euphrates, river, Syr. 35°33′ N, 40°3′ E 207

Euphrates see Al Furāt, river, *Syr.* 35°43' N, 39°21' E **180**
Eura, *Fin.* 61°6' N, 22°9' E **166**
Eurajoki, *Fin.* 61°12' N, 21°42' E **166**
Eure, river, *Fr.* 49°1' N, 1°24' E **163**
Eureka, *Calif., U.S.* 40°46' N, 124°10' W **90**
Eureka, *Can.* 80°2' N, 85°43' W **246**
Eureka, *Ill., U.S.* 40°42' N, 89°17' W **102**
Eureka, *Kans., U.S.* 37°48' N, 96°18' W **90**
Eureka, *Mont., U.S.* 48°52' N, 115°3' W **90**
Eureka, *Nev., U.S.* 39°31' N, 115°59' W **90**
Eureka, *S. Dak., U.S.* 45°46' N, 99°39' W **90**
Eureka, *Utah, U.S.* 39°56' N, 112°6' W **90**
Eureka Springs, *Ark., U.S.* 36°23' N, 93°45' W **94**
Eureka Valley, *Calif., U.S.* 37°12' N, 117°54' W **101**
Europa, Île, *Fr.* 22°44' S, 39°43' E **220**
Europa, Picos de, peak, *Sp.* 43°10' N, 4°55' W **150**
Europa Point, *U.K.* 35°58' N, 5°14' W **164**
Europe 41°0' N, 28°0' E **143**
Euskirchen, *Ger.* 50°39' N, 6°47' E **167**
Eustis, *Fla., U.S.* 28°51' N, 81°41' W **105**
Eutaw, *Ala., U.S.* 32°49' N, 87°54' W **103**
Eutin, *Ger.* 54°8' N, 10°37' E **152**
Eutsuk Lake, *Can.* 53°11' N, 127°16' W **108**
Evadale, *Tex., U.S.* 30°20' N, 94°4' W **103**
Evangelistas, Grupo, islands, *South Pacific Ocean* 52°34' S, 78°23' W **134**
Evans, *Colo., U.S.* 40°23' N, 104°43' W **90**
Evans, *La., U.S.* 30°58' N, 93°31' W **103**
Evans, Lac, lake, *Can.* 50°46' N, 77°28' W **110**
Evans, Mount, *Can.* 49°32' N, 116°23' W **90**
Evans, Mount, *Colo., U.S.* 39°34' N, 105°42' W **90**
Evans, Mount, *Mont., U.S.* 46°2' N, 113°18' W **90**
Evans Notch, pass, *Me., U.S.* 44°18' N, 70°60' W **104**
Evansburg, *Can.* 53°35' N, 115°2' W **108**
Evanston, *Ill., U.S.* 42°2' N, 87°41' W **102**
Evanston, *Wyo., U.S.* 41°17' N, 110°60' W **90**
Evansville, *Ind., U.S.* 37°58' N, 87°33' W **96**
Evansville, *Wis., U.S.* 42°47' N, 89°18' W **102**
Evansville, *Wyo., U.S.* 42°51' N, 106°15' W **90**
Evart, *Mich., U.S.* 43°54' N, 85°17' W **102**
Evelyn, *Can.* 54°53' N, 127°19' W **108**
Even Yehuda, *Israel* 32°15' N, 34°52' E **194**
Evenk, adm. division, *Russ.* 65°19' N, 91°42' E **169**
Evensk, *Russ.* 61°57' N, 159°17' E **173**
Everest, Mount (Qomolangma, Sagarmāthā), *China-Nepal* 28°0' N, 86°53' E **197**
Everett, *Wash., U.S.* 47°58' N, 122°11' W **100**
Everglades City, *Fla., U.S.* 25°51' N, 81°24' W **105**
Everglades National Park, *Fla., U.S.* 25°24' N, 80°54' W **105**
Evergreen, *Ala., U.S.* 31°26' N, 86°57' W **96**
Everson, *Wash., U.S.* 48°54' N, 122°20' W **100**
Evesham, *U.K.* 52°6' N, 1°57' W **162**
Évia, island, *Gr.* 38°45' N, 23°36' E **180**
Évian, *Fr.* 46°23' N, 6°35' E **167**
Evje, *Nor.* 58°34' N, 7°49' E **152**
Évora, *Port.* 38°33' N, 7°55' W **150**
Évora, adm. division, *Port.* 38°40' N, 8°25' W **150**
Évreux, *Fr.* 49°1' N, 1°9' E **163**
Évron, *Fr.* 48°9' N, 0°25' E **150**
Evrychou, *Cyprus* 35°2' N, 32°55' E **194**
Ewaso Ng'iro, river, *Kenya* 1°16' S, 35°51' E **224**
Ewenkizu Zizhiqi, *China* 49°4' N, 119°40' E **198**
Ewing, *Nebr., U.S.* 42°14' N, 98°21' W **90**
Ewing Island, *Antarctica* 69°46' S, 60°60' W **248**
Ewo, *Congo* 0°51' N, 14°48' E **218**
Exaltación, *Bol.* 13°18' S, 65°18' W **137**
Excelsior Mountains, *Nev., U.S.* 38°17' N, 118°39' W **90**
Exeter, *Calif., U.S.* 36°18' N, 119°9' W **101**
Exeter, *Can.* 43°21' N, 81°29' W **102**
Exeter, *Mo., U.S.* 36°40' N, 93°56' W **96**
Exeter, *N.H., U.S.* 42°58' N, 70°58' W **104**
Exeter, *R.I., U.S.* 41°34' N, 71°33' W **104**
Exeter, *U.K.* 50°43' N, 3°31' W **162**
Exeter Sound 66°3' N, 64°29' W **106**
Exford, *U.K.* 51°7' N, 3°38' W **162**
Exmoor, region, *Europe* 51°8' N, 3°55' W **162**
Exmouth, *Austral.* 22°5' S, 114°3' E **238**
Exmouth Gulf 22°8' S, 113°3' E **230**
Exmouth, Peninsula, *Chile* 49°22' S, 75°30' W **134**
Exmouth Plateau, *Indian Ocean* 19°26' S, 112°55' E **254**
Expedition Range, *Austral.* 24°34' S, 148°33' E **230**
Experiment, *Ga., U.S.* 33°15' N, 84°17' W **96**
Extremadura, adm. division, *Sp.* 38°59' N, 6°46' W **164**
Exuma, adm. division, *Bahamas* 23°39' N, 76°4' W **96**
Exuma Sound 24°7' N, 76°20' W **96**
Eyasi, Lake, *Tanzania* 3°38' S, 34°46' E **224**
Eye, *U.K.* 52°19' N, 1°8' E **162**
Eye Peninsula, *U.K.* 58°12' N, 6°42' W **150**
Eyl, *Somalia* 7°56' N, 49°49' E **218**
Eyrarbakki, *Ice.* 63°54' N, 21°6' W **143**
Eyre Peninsula, *Austral.* 33°21' S, 135°33' E **230**
Eyumojok, *Cameroon* 5°46' N, 8°56' E **222**
Ezeriş, *Rom.* 45°24' N, 21°52' E **168**
Ezeru, peak, *Rom.* 45°27' N, 24°51' E **156**
Ezine, *Turk.* 39°46' N, 26°19' E **156**

F

Fabala, *Guinea* 9°43' N, 9°6' W **222**
Fabara, *Sp.* 41°9' N, 0°10' E **164**
Faber Lake, *Can.* 63°42' N, 116°6' W **246**
Facatativá, *Col.* 4°48' N, 74°22' W **130**
Facha, oil field, *Lib.* 29°21' N, 17°3' E **216**
Fachi, *Niger* 18°5' N, 11°33' E **222**
Facho, Pico do, peak, *Port.* 32°55' N, 16°30' W **214**
Facinas, *Sp.* 36°8' N, 5°43' W **164**
Facture, *Fr.* 44°38' N, 0°59' E **150**
Fada, *Chad* 17°11' N, 21°34' E **216**
Fada N'Gourma, *Burkina Faso* 12°3' N, 0°19' E **222**
Fadd, *Hung.* 46°27' N, 18°49' E **168**
Faddeya, Zaliv 76°57' N, 110°31' E **246**
Faddeyevskiy, Ostrov, island, *Russ.* 76°12' N, 127°53' E **160**
Fadhili, oil field, *Saudi Arabia* 26°54' N, 49°6' E **196**
Fadiffolu Atoll, *Maldives* 5°18' N, 72°47' E **188**
Faenza, *It.* 44°17' N, 11°51' E **167**
Fafa, *Mali* 15°17' N, 0°42' E **222**
Făgăraş, Munţii, *Rom.* 45°29' N, 24°10' E **156**
Fågelsjö, *Nor.* 61°47' N, 14°39' E **152**
Fagersta, *Nor.* 59°59' N, 15°45' E **152**
Făget, *Rom.* 45°50' N, 22°11' E **168**
Făget, Munţii, *Rom.* 47°36' N, 23°0' E **168**
Faggo, *Nig.* 11°25' N, 9°57' E **222**
Fagnières, *Fr.* 48°57' N, 4°20' E **163**
Fahala, island, *Maldives* 2°24' N, 73°19' E **188**
Fahraj, *Iran* 28°56' N, 58°50' E **196**
Fahud, oil field, *Oman* 22°11' N, 56°26' E **182**
Faichuk, island, *Federated States of Micronesia* 7°0' N, 152°0' E **242**
Fair Haven, *Vt., U.S.* 43°35' N, 73°17' W **104**
Fair Oaks, *Ind., U.S.* 41°4' N, 87°16' W **102**
Fairbanks, *Alas., U.S.* 64°49' N, 147°39' W **106**
Fairbanks, *Me., U.S.* 44°42' N, 70°11' W **111**
Fairbury, *Mo., U.S.* 40°44' N, 88°31' W **94**
Fairbury, *Nebr., U.S.* 40°7' N, 97°11' W **92**
Fairfax, *Okla., U.S.* 36°33' N, 96°43' W **94**
Fairfax, *S.C., U.S.* 32°57' N, 81°15' W **96**
Fairfield, *Ala., U.S.* 33°29' N, 86°53' W **96**
Fairfield, *Calif., U.S.* 38°14' N, 122°3' W **100**
Fairfield, *Conn., U.S.* 41°8' N, 73°16' W **104**
Fairfield, *Fla., U.S.* 29°21' N, 82°16' W **105**
Fairfield, *Idaho, U.S.* 43°21' N, 114°48' W **90**
Fairfield, *Mo., U.S.* 38°22' N, 88°22' W **94**
Fairfield, *Mont., U.S.* 47°36' N, 111°59' W **90**
Fairfield, *Ohio, U.S.* 39°19' N, 84°35' W **102**
Fairfield, *Tex., U.S.* 31°42' N, 96°9' W **96**
Fairhaven, *Mass., U.S.* 41°38' N, 70°55' W **104**
Fairhope, *Ala., U.S.* 30°30' N, 87°54' W **103**
Fairlawn, *Va., U.S.* 37°8' N, 80°36' W **94**
Fairlee, *Vt., U.S.* 43°54' N, 72°10' W **104**
Fairlie, *N.Z.* 44°7' S, 170°49' E **240**
Fairlight, *Can.* 49°53' N, 101°40' W **90**
Fairmead, *Calif., U.S.* 37°4' N, 120°12' W **100**
Fairmont, *Minn., U.S.* 43°38' N, 94°27' W **94**
Fairmont, *W. Va., U.S.* 39°29' N, 80°11' W **94**
Fairmount, *Ind., U.S.* 40°24' N, 85°39' W **102**
Fairport, *Mich., U.S.* 45°37' N, 86°39' W **94**
Fairport Harbor, *Ohio, U.S.* 41°43' N, 81°16' W **102**
Fairview, *Can.* 56°4' N, 118°25' W **108**
Fairview, *Ill., U.S.* 40°37' N, 90°10' W **102**
Fairview, *Okla., U.S.* 36°15' N, 98°29' W **92**
Fairview, *Pa., U.S.* 42°1' N, 80°16' W **94**
Fairview, *Tenn., U.S.* 35°58' N, 87°7' W **96**
Fairview Park, *Ind., U.S.* 39°40' N, 87°25' W **102**
Fairview Peak, *Oreg., U.S.* 43°34' N, 122°44' W **90**
Fairweather, Cape, *Antarctica* 64°57' S, 60°47' W **134**
Fairweather, Mount, *Alas., U.S.* 58°54' N, 137°43' W **98**
Faisalabad, *Pak.* 31°24' N, 73°0' E **186**
Faith, *S. Dak., U.S.* 45°0' N, 102°4' W **90**
Faizabad, *India* 26°46' N, 82°6' E **197**
Fakel, *Russ.* 57°36' N, 53°6' E **154**
Fakenham, *U.K.* 52°49' N, 0°51' E **162**
Fakfak, *Indonesia* 2°54' S, 132°11' E **192**
Fakiya, *Bulg.* 42°11' N, 27°4' E **156**
Fakse Bugt 55°4' N, 11°41' E **152**
Faku, *China* 42°31' N, 123°27' E **200**
Falagh, *Sudan* 8°35' N, 31°5' E **224**
Falakró, Óros, *Gr.* 41°12' N, 23°39' E **156**
Falam, *Myanmar* 22°50' N, 93°39' E **188**
Falces, *Sp.* 42°23' N, 1°49' W **164**
Fălciu, *Rom.* 46°17' N, 28°7' E **156**
Falcón, adm. division, *Venez.* 10°54' N, 70°36' W **136**
Falcon, Cape, *Oreg., U.S.* 45°45' N, 123°58' W **100**
Falcon Lake, *Mex.* 26°52' N, 99°39' W **112**
Falcone, Capo del, *It.* 40°57' N, 7°19' E **156**
Falconer, *N.Y., U.S.* 42°7' N, 79°14' W **110**
Faléa, *Mali* 12°17' N, 11°18' W **222**
Falémé, river, *Africa* 13°52' N, 12°10' W **222**
Falenki, *Russ.* 58°22' N, 51°45' E **154**
Făleşti, *Mold.* 47°34' N, 27°42' E **156**
Falfurrias, *Tex., U.S.* 27°11' N, 98°8' W **96**
Falher, *Can.* 55°44' N, 117°14' W **108**
Falkenberg, *Nor.* 56°54' N, 12°29' E **152**
Falkirk, *U.K.* 55°59' N, 3°48' W **150**
Falkland Islands (Islas Malvinas), *Falk. Is., U.K.* 52°18' S, 62°14' W **134**
Falkland Plateau, *South Atlantic Ocean* 51°7' S, 49°25' W **255**
Falköping, *Nor.* 58°9' N, 13°33' E **152**
Fallbrook, *Calif., U.S.* 33°23' N, 117°16' W **101**
Fallon, *Nev., U.S.* 39°28' N, 118°48' W **90**
Falls City, *Nebr., U.S.* 40°2' N, 95°36' W **90**
Fallujah see Al Fallūjah, *Iraq* 33°19' N, 43°46' E **180**
Falmey, *Niger* 12°40' N, 2°47' E **222**
Falmouth, *Ky., U.S.* 38°39' N, 84°20' W **102**
Falmouth, *Mass., U.S.* 41°33' N, 70°38' W **104**
Falmouth, *Va., U.S.* 38°19' N, 77°29' W **94**
Falou, *Mali* 14°36' N, 7°56' W **222**
Falsa, Bahia 39°20' S, 62°29' W **139**
False Point, *India* 20°17' N, 86°50' E **188**
Falset, *Sp.* 41°8' N, 0°48' E **164**
Falso, Cabo, *Hond.* 15°15' N, 83°23' W **115**
Falso, Cabo, *Mex.* 22°43' N, 110°51' W **112**
Falun, *Nor.* 60°34' N, 15°35' E **152**
Famagusta see Ammochostos, *Northern Cyprus* 35°7' N, 33°56' E **194**
Famaka, *Sudan* 11°18' N, 34°43' E **182**
Famana, *Mali* 11°51' N, 7°51' W **222**
Fan, river, *Alban.* 41°47' N, 19°44' E **168**
Fana, *Mali* 12°47' N, 6°60' W **222**
Fana, *Nor.* 60°13' N, 5°23' E **152**
Fanchang, *China* 31°6' N, 118°12' E **198**
Fandriana, *Madagascar* 20°14' S, 47°22' E **220**
Fang, *Thai.* 19°57' N, 99°11' E **202**
Fangak, *Sudan* 9°2' N, 30°55' E **224**
Fangcheng, *China* 21°48' N, 108°21' E **198**
Fangcheng, *China* 33°17' N, 113°4' E **198**
Fangshan, *China* 37°50' N, 111°16' E **198**
Fanjeaux, *Fr.* 43°11' N, 2°1' E **164**
Fanny Bay, *Can.* 49°31' N, 124°51' W **100**
Fano, *It.* 43°49' N, 13°1' E **167**
Fanshan, *China* 27°22' N, 120°27' E **198**
Fanshi, *China* 39°13' N, 113°18' E **198**
Fanūdah, *Saudi Arabia* 25°25' N, 40°36' E **182**
Fanxian, *China* 35°53' N, 115°25' E **198**
Far Mountain, *Can.* 52°45' N, 125°25' W **108**
Farabana, *Guinea* 9°53' N, 9°8' W **222**
Faradje, *Dem. Rep. of the Congo* 3°43' N, 29°42' E **224**
Farafangana, *Madagascar* 22°50' S, 47°50' E **220**
Farâfra, El Wâhât el, *Egypt* 27°18' N, 28°17' E **180**
Farah, *Afghan.* 32°25' N, 62°10' E **186**
Farah, river, *Afghan.* 31°54' N, 61°33' E **186**
Farallon Islands, *Pacific Ocean* 37°28' N, 123°10' W **90**
Farallones de Cali National Park, *Col.* 2°54' N, 76°60' W **136**
Faranah, *Guinea* 10°2' N, 10°45' W **222**
Faraulep Atoll, *F.S.M.* 8°56' N, 141°38' E **192**
Fareham, *U.K.* 50°51' N, 1°11' W **162**
Farewell, *Alas., U.S.* 62°22' N, 153°57' W **98**
Farewell, Cape, *N.Z.* 40°31' S, 172°44' E **240**
Fargo, *N. Dak., U.S.* 46°49' N, 97°1' W **73**
Farg'ona, *Uzb.* 40°23' N, 71°47' E **197**
Fari, *Mali* 12°10' N, 10°41' W **222**
Faribault, *Minn., U.S.* 44°16' N, 93°17' W **94**
Faridpur, *Bangladesh* 23°33' N, 89°51' E **197**
Farim, *Guinea-Bissau* 12°30' N, 15°13' W **222**
Farīmān, *Iran* 35°44' N, 59°53' E **180**
Farina, *Ill., U.S.* 38°49' N, 88°47' W **102**
Færingehavn see Kangerluarsoruseq, *Den.* 63°43' N, 51°21' W **106**
Farinha, river, *Braz.* 6°52' S, 47°29' W **130**
Farkhar, *Afghan.* 36°40' N, 69°50' E **186**
Farkhor, *Taj.* 37°29' N, 69°22' E **184**
Farkovo, *Russ.* 65°36' N, 86°58' E **169**
Farkwa, *Tanzania* 5°23' S, 35°35' E **224**
Farmer City, *Ill., U.S.* 40°14' N, 88°39' W **102**
Farmersburg, *Ind., U.S.* 39°15' N, 87°22' W **102**
Farmersville, *Calif., U.S.* 36°18' N, 119°13' W **101**
Farmerville, *La., U.S.* 32°45' N, 92°25' W **103**
Farmingdale, *Me., U.S.* 44°14' N, 69°47' W **104**
Farmington, *Ill., U.S.* 40°41' N, 90°1' W **102**
Farmington, *N.H., U.S.* 43°23' N, 71°4' W **104**
Farmington, *N. Mex., U.S.* 36°44' N, 108°10' W **82**
Farmington, *Utah, U.S.* 40°58' N, 111°52' W **90**
Farmville, *Va., U.S.* 37°17' N, 78°25' W **94**
Farnborough, *U.K.* 51°16' N, 0°45' E **162**
Farne Islands, *North Sea* 55°40' N, 1°35' W **150**
Farnham, *U.K.* 51°12' N, 0°48' E **162**
Farnham, Mount, *Can.* 50°28' N, 116°35' W **90**
Faro, *Braz.* 2°10' S, 56°45' W **130**
Faro, *Can.* 62°15' N, 133°24' W **98**
Faro, *Port.* 37°2' N, 7°60' W **214**
Faro, *Port.* 37°1' N, 7°57' W **150**
Faro, adm. division, *Port.* 37°6' N, 8°50' W **150**
Fårö, island, *Sw.* 57°59' N, 19°16' E **166**
Faro, Punta, *Col.* 11°7' N, 75°4' W **136**
Faro, river, *Cameroon* 8°17' N, 12°55' E **218**
Faro, Sierra do, *Sp.* 42°18' N, 8°5' W **150**
Faroe Islands (Føroyar), *North Atlantic Ocean* 62°34' N, 11°40' W **143**
Faroe-Iceland Ridge, *North Atlantic Ocean* 63°30' N, 10°2' W **253**
Fårösund, *Sw.* 57°50' N, 19°2' E **166**
Farquhar Group, islands, *Indian Ocean* 9°52' S, 50°31' E **218**
Farr Bay 66°23' S, 96°0' E **248**
Farrāshband, *Iran* 28°49' N, 52°5' E **196**
Farrel, Isla, island, *Chile* 51°2' S, 75°51' W **134**
Farsi, *Afghan.* 33°44' N, 63°15' E **186**
Farsø, *Den.* 56°46' N, 9°20' E **152**
Farsund, *Nor.* 58°5' N, 6°46' E **150**
Fartura, *Braz.* 23°23' S, 49°32' W **138**
Farwell, *Mich., U.S.* 43°50' N, 84°51' W **102**
Farwell, *Tex., U.S.* 34°22' N, 103°2' W **92**
Farwell Island, *Antarctica* 72°15' S, 88°28' W **248**
Fasā, *Iran* 28°53' N, 53°44' E **196**
Fashven, peak, *U.K.* 58°32' N, 5°1' W **150**
Fastiv, *Ukr.* 50°3' N, 29°59' E **158**
Fatala, river, *Guinea* 10°42' N, 13°45' W **222**
Fatehabad, *India* 29°30' N, 75°28' E **197**
Fatehgarh, *India* 27°22' N, 79°33' E **197**
Fatehpur, *India* 27°59' N, 74°59' E **186**
Fatehpur, *India* 25°54' N, 80°49' E **197**
Fatehpur Sikri, *India* 27°5' N, 77°40' E **197**
Fatezh, *Russ.* 52°3' N, 35°49' E **158**
Fathai, *Sudan* 8°2' N, 31°45' E **224**
Father, Lac, lake, *Can.* 49°20' N, 75°52' W **94**
Fátima, *Port.* 39°36' N, 8°40' W **150**
Fatsa, *Turk.* 41°0' N, 37°29' E **158**
Faucille, Col de la, pass, *Fr.* 46°21' N, 6°0' E **167**
Faucilles, Monts, *Fr.* 48°17' N, 5°51' E **163**
Faulkton, *S. Dak., U.S.* 45°0' N, 99°9' W **90**
Faulquemont, *Fr.* 49°2' N, 6°36' E **163**
Fauresmith, *S. Af.* 29°44' S, 25°17' E **227**
Fauro, island, *Solomon Islands* 7°0' S, 156°0' E **242**
Fauske, *Nor.* 67°16' N, 15°22' E **152**
Faust, *Can.* 55°18' N, 115°40' W **108**
Faux Cap see Betanty, *Madagascar* 25°34' S, 45°31' E **220**
Fåvang, *Nor.* 61°25' N, 10°13' E **152**
Faverges, *Fr.* 45°44' N, 6°17' E **150**
Faversham, *U.K.* 51°18' N, 0°53' E **162**
Fawcett, *Can.* 54°32' N, 114°6' W **108**
Faya-Largeau, *Chad* 17°54' N, 19°6' E **216**
Fayd, *Saudi Arabia* 27°8' N, 42°38' E **180**
Fayette, *Ala., U.S.* 33°41' N, 87°50' W **96**
Fayette, *Me., U.S.* 44°24' N, 70°3' W **104**
Fayette, *Miss., U.S.* 31°41' N, 91°3' W **103**
Fayette, *Mo., U.S.* 39°8' N, 92°41' W **94**
Fayette, *Ohio, U.S.* 41°39' N, 84°20' W **102**
Fayette, *Utah, U.S.* 39°13' N, 111°50' W **90**
Fayetteville, *Ark., U.S.* 36°3' N, 94°10' W **94**
Faynān, ruin(s), *Jordan* 30°37' N, 35°27' E **194**
Fayón, *Sp.* 41°14' N, 0°19' E **164**
Faysh Khābūr, *Iraq* 37°4' N, 42°17' E **195**
Fazao-Malfakassa National Park, *Togo* 8°39' N, 0°14' E **222**
Fazilka, *India* 30°24' N, 74°3' E **186**
Fazran, oil field, *Saudi Arabia* 26°2' N, 49°0' E **196**
Fdérik (Fort Gouraud), *Mauritania* 22°41' N, 12°43' W **214**
Fear, Cape, *N.C., U.S.* 33°45' N, 77°57' W **96**
Fear, Cape, *N.C., U.S.* 34°47' N, 78°50' W **80**
Feather River Canyon, *Calif., U.S.* 39°50' N, 121°36' W **90**
Fedala see Mohammedia, *Mor.* 33°43' N, 7°22' W **214**
Federación, *Arg.* 30°59' S, 57°54' W **139**
Federal, *Arg.* 30°55' S, 58°45' W **139**
Federally Administered Tribal Areas, adm. division, *Pak.* 32°7' N, 69°33' E **186**
Fedje, *Nor.* 60°46' N, 4°41' E **152**
Fedorovka, *Kaz.* 53°38' N, 62°42' E **184**
Fedorovka, *Kaz.* 51°10' N, 51°59' E **158**
Fedorovka, *Russ.* 53°10' N, 55°12' E **154**
Feeding Hills, *Mass., U.S.* 42°3' N, 72°41' W **104**
Fegen, lake, *Nor.* 57°10' N, 12°51' E **152**
Feia, Lagoa, lake, *Braz.* 22°1' S, 41°34' W **138**
Feijó, *Braz.* 8°10' S, 70°23' W **130**
Feilding, *N.Z.* 40°13' S, 175°33' E **240**
Feira de Santana, *Braz.* 12°16' S, 38°59' W **132**
Feixi, *China* 31°42' N, 117°8' E **198**
Fejér, adm. division, *Hung.* 46°57' N, 18°15' E **156**
Feke, *Turk.* 37°51' N, 35°56' E **156**
Feklistova, Ostrov, island, *Russ.* 55°7' N, 134°15' E **160**
Felanitx, *Sp.* 39°27' N, 3°9' E **150**
Felchville, *Vt., U.S.* 43°27' N, 72°33' W **104**
Feldbach, *Aust.* 46°56' N, 15°53' E **168**
Feldberg, peak, *Ger.* 47°51' N, 7°57' E **165**
Felicity, *Ohio, U.S.* 38°50' N, 84°6' W **102**
Felidu Atoll, *Maldives* 3°10' N, 73°1' E **188**
Felipe Carrillo Puerto, *Mex.* 24°17' N, 104°1' W **114**
Felipe Carrillo Puerto, *Mex.* 19°34' N, 88°4' W **115**
Felixlândia, *Braz.* 18°46' S, 44°54' W **138**
Felixstowe, *U.K.* 51°57' N, 1°20' E **163**
Felizzano, *It.* 44°54' N, 8°26' E **167**
Fellit, *Eritrea* 16°39' N, 38°0' E **182**
Fellows, *Calif., U.S.* 35°10' N, 119°34' W **100**
Fellsmere, *Fla., U.S.* 27°46' N, 80°36' W **105**
Felsenthal, *Ark., U.S.* 33°2' N, 92°10' W **103**
Fels ocsatár, *Hung.* 47°12' N, 16°27' E **168**
Felton, *Calif., U.S.* 37°3' N, 122°6' W **100**
Feltre, *It.* 46°0' N, 11°53' E **167**
Femund, lake, *Nor.* 62°4' N, 11°19' E **152**
Fen, river, *China* 36°45' N, 111°35' E **198**
Fenelon Falls, *Can.* 44°31' N, 78°43' W **94**
Fengari, peak, *Gr.* 40°27' N, 25°29' E **156**
Fengcheng, *China* 28°10' N, 115°43' E **198**
Fengcheng, *China* 40°26' N, 124°3' E **200**
Fengdu, *China* 29°47' N, 107°44' E **198**
Fenggang, *China* 27°58' N, 107°44' E **198**
Fenghuang, *China* 27°54' N, 109°37' E **198**
Fengjie, *China* 31°5' N, 109°34' E **198**
Fengkai, *China* 23°27' N, 111°33' E **198**
Fenglin, *Taiwan* 23°43' N, 121°24' E **198**
Fengning, *China* 41°9' N, 116°35' E **198**
Fengshan, *China* 24°30' N, 107°1' E **198**
Fengxian, *China* 33°52' N, 106°37' E **198**
Fengzhen, *China* 40°26' N, 113°7' E **198**
Fennville, *Mich., U.S.* 42°34' N, 86°6' W **102**
Feno, Cap de, *Fr.* 41°19' N, 8°29' E **156**
Feno, Capo di, *Fr.* 41°58' N, 7°55' E **156**
Fenoarivo, *Madagascar* 18°27' S, 46°32' E **220**
Fenoarivo Atsinanana, *Madagascar* 17°25' S, 49°23' E **220**
Fenton, *La., U.S.* 30°21' N, 92°57' W **103**
Fenxi, *China* 36°38' N, 111°31' E **198**
Fenyang, *China* 37°15' N, 111°46' E **198**
Feodosiya, *Ukr.* 45°2' N, 35°18' E **156**
Ferdows, *Iran* 33°58' N, 58°10' E **180**
Fère-Champenoise, *Fr.* 48°45' N, 3°59' E **163**
Féres, *Gr.* 40°53' N, 26°10' E **156**
Fērfēr, *Eth.* 5°4' N, 45°10' E **218**
Fergana Valley, *Asia* 40°38' N, 70°26' E **197**
Fergus Falls, *Minn., U.S.* 46°16' N, 96°5' W **90**
Ferguson, *Ky., U.S.* 37°3' N, 84°36' W **96**
Ferguson Lake, *Ariz., U.S.* 33°2' N, 114°39' W **101**
Ferguson, Mount, *Nev., U.S.* 38°38' N, 118°15' W **90**
Ferguson Seamount, *North Pacific Ocean* 30°46' N, 172°25' E **252**
Fergusson Island, *P.N.G.* 9°19' S, 150°40' E **192**
Feria, *Sp.* 38°30' N, 6°34' W **164**
Feriana, *Tun.* 34°56' N, 8°34' E **156**
Feridu, island, *Maldives* 3°46' N, 72°0' E **188**
Ferkéssédougou, *Côte d'Ivoire* 9°34' N, 5°13' W **222**
Fern Grotto, site, *Hawai'i, U.S.* 22°1' N, 159°24' W **99**
Fernández Leal, *Mex.* 30°49' N, 108°16' W **92**
Fernandina Beach, *Fla., U.S.* 30°39' N, 81°28' W **96**
Fernandina, Isla, island, *Ecua.* 0°39' N, 92°41' W **130**
Fernando de Noronha, Arquipélago de, *South Atlantic Ocean* 3°19' S, 33°15' W **132**
Fernandópolis, *Braz.* 20°17' S, 50°15' W **138**
Fernán-Núñez, *Sp.* 37°40' N, 4°45' W **164**
Fernão Dias, *Braz.* 16°23' S, 44°30' W **138**
Fernão Veloso, Baía de 14°30' S, 39°50' E **224**
Ferndale, *Calif., U.S.* 40°34' N, 124°17' W **92**
Ferndale, *Wash., U.S.* 48°50' N, 122°36' W **100**
Fernie, *Can.* 49°30' N, 115°3' W **90**
Fernley, *Nev., U.S.* 39°36' N, 119°17' W **90**
Ferns, *Ire.* 52°35' N, 6°30' W **150**
Fernwood, *Miss., U.S.* 31°10' N, 90°28' W **103**
Ferolle Point, *Can.* 51°0' N, 57°53' W **111**
Ferrara, *It.* 44°50' N, 11°37' E **167**
Ferrara, Mount, *Antarctica* 82°18' S, 42°54' W **248**
Ferrat, Cap, *Alg.* 35°54' N, 0°22' E **164**
Ferreira Gomes, *Braz.* 0°49' N, 51°7' W **130**
Ferrelo, Cape, *Oreg., U.S.* 41°56' N, 124°44' W **90**
Ferret, Cap, *Fr.* 44°38' N, 1°35' W **150**
Ferriday, *La., U.S.* 31°37' N, 91°34' W **103**
Ferris Mountains, *Wyo., U.S.* 42°21' N, 107°23' W **90**
Ferrisburg, *Vt., U.S.* 44°12' N, 73°15' W **104**
Ferro, river, *Braz.* 12°60' S, 55°5' W **130**
Ferro see Hierro, island, *Sp.* 27°25' N, 17°55' W **214**
Ferrol, *Sp.* 43°30' N, 8°17' W **214**
Ferron, *Utah, U.S.* 39°5' N, 111°7' W **90**
Ferros, *Braz.* 19°16' S, 43°3' W **138**
Ferryland, *Can.* 47°1' N, 52°54' W **111**
Ferrysburg, *Mich., U.S.* 43°5' N, 86°12' W **102**
Ferryville see Menzel Bourguiba, *Tun.* 37°9' N, 9°47' E **156**
Fertile, *Minn., U.S.* 47°31' N, 96°18' W **90**
Fès (Fez), *Mor.* 34°6' N, 4°60' W **214**
Feshi, *Dem. Rep. of the Congo* 6°8' S, 18°6' E **218**
Fessenden, *N. Dak., U.S.* 47°37' N, 99°38' W **90**
Fet, *Nor.* 59°55' N, 11°10' E **152**
Fété Bowé, *Senegal* 14°55' N, 13°33' W **222**
Feteşti, *Rom.* 44°22' N, 27°49' E **156**
Fethiye, *Turk.* 36°34' N, 29°9' E **180**
Feuet, spring, *Lib.* 24°57' N, 10°2' E **214**
Feuilles, Rivière aux, river, *Can.* 58°19' N, 73°4' W **106**
Feurs, *Fr.* 45°44' N, 4°13' E **150**
Fevral'sk, *Russ.* 52°30' N, 131°24' E **190**
Feyzabad, *Afghan.* 37°8' N, 70°35' E **186**
Fez see Fès, *Mor.* 34°6' N, 4°60' W **214**
Fezzan, region, *Africa* 29°39' N, 9°56' E **214**
Fezzane, spring, *Niger* 21°53' N, 14°29' E **222**
Ffestiniog, *U.K.* 52°57' N, 3°55' W **162**
Fhada, Beinn, peak, *U.K.* 57°12' N, 5°23' W **150**
Fian, *Ghana* 10°22' N, 2°30' W **222**
Fianarantsoa, *Madagascar* 21°34' S, 47°3' E **207**
Fianga, *Chad* 9°54' N, 15°6' E **216**
Fibiş, *Rom.* 45°58' N, 21°25' E **168**
Fichē, *Eth.* 9°48' N, 38°42' E **224**
Fichtelgebirge, *Ger.* 50°3' N, 11°20' E **152**
Ficksburg, *S. Af.* 28°52' S, 27°51' E **227**
Fidenza, *It.* 44°51' N, 10°4' E **167**
Fidler Lake, *Can.* 57°10' N, 97°26' W **108**
Field Island, *Austral.* 12°15' S, 131°20' E **230**
Field Naval Air Station, *Fla., U.S.* 30°43' N, 87°5' W **96**
Fields Peak, *Oreg., U.S.* 44°18' N, 119°20' W **90**
Fier, *Alban.* 40°43' N, 19°32' E **156**
Fier, river, *Fr.* 45°54' N, 5°55' E **165**
Fiesole, *It.* 43°48' N, 11°17' E **156**
Fiesso, *It.* 44°58' N, 11°36' E **167**
Fife Lake, *Can.* 49°11' N, 106°19' W **90**
Fife Lake, *Mich., U.S.* 44°34' N, 85°21' W **94**
Fife Ness, *U.K.* 56°17' N, 2°34' W **150**
Fifield, *Wis., U.S.* 45°52' N, 90°26' W **94**
Figari, Capo, *It.* 41°1' N, 9°38' E **156**
Figeac, *Fr.* 44°36' N, 2°2' E **150**
Figols, *Sp.* 42°10' N, 1°49' E **150**
Figueira da Foz, *Port.* 40°8' N, 8°53' W **150**
Figueirão, *Braz.* 18°44' S, 53°41' W **132**
Figueres, *Sp.* 42°15' N, 2°57' E **164**
Figuig, *Mor.* 32°7' N, 1°13' W **214**
Figuil, *Cameroon* 9°44' N, 13°56' E **216**
Fihaonana, *Madagascar* 18°36' S, 47°13' E **220**
Fiji Islands 18°0' N, 178°0' E **242**
Fiji Plateau, *South Pacific Ocean* 17°4' S, 179°39' E **252**
Fika, *Nig.* 11°17' N, 11°17' E **222**
Filabres, Sierra de los, *Sp.* 37°12' N, 2°32' W **164**
Filabusi, *Zimb.* 20°31' S, 29°17' E **227**
Filadelfia, *Bol.* 11°24' S, 68°49' W **137**
Filadélfia, *Braz.* 7°22' S, 47°32' W **130**
Filadelfia, *Parag.* 22°19' S, 60°4' W **132**
Fil'akovo, *Slovakia* 48°15' N, 19°50' E **152**
Filattiera, *It.* 44°19' N, 9°56' E **167**
Filchner Mountains, *Antarctica* 72°42' S, 4°23' E **248**
File Axe, Lac, lake, *Can.* 50°15' N, 74°7' W **110**
File Lake, *Can.* 54°50' N, 100°42' W **108**
Filer, *Idaho, U.S.* 42°34' N, 114°37' W **90**
Filer City, *Mich., U.S.* 44°12' N, 86°18' W **102**
Filey, *U.K.* 54°12' N, 0°18' E **162**
Filia, *Gr.* 39°15' N, 26°8' E **156**
Filiaşi, *Rom.* 44°33' N, 23°31' E **156**
Filimon Sîrbu, *Rom.* 45°5' N, 27°15' E **156**
Filingué, *Niger* 14°23' N, 3°17' E **222**
Filipów, *Pol.* 54°10' N, 22°36' E **152**
Filisur, *Switz.* 46°40' N, 9°40' E **167**
Fillmore, *Calif., U.S.* 34°24' N, 118°55' W **101**
Fillmore, *Utah, U.S.* 38°57' N, 112°19' W **90**
Fils, Lac du, lake, *Can.* 46°38' N, 78°36' W **94**
Filton, *U.K.* 51°30' N, 2°35' W **162**
Filtu, *Eth.* 5°8' N, 40°39' E **224**
Filyos, river, *Turk.* 41°28' N, 31°53' E **180**
Fimbul Ice Shelf, *Antarctica* 70°45' S, 0°21' E **248**
Finale Emilia, *It.* 44°50' N, 11°17' E **167**
Fiñana, *Sp.* 37°9' N, 2°51' W **164**
Finarwa, *Eth.* 13°4' N, 38°59' E **182**
Fındıklı, *Turk.* 41°16' N, 41°7' E **195**
Findlay, *Ill., U.S.* 39°31' N, 88°45' W **102**
Findlay, *Ohio, U.S.* 41°1' N, 83°38' W **102**
Findlay, Mount, *Can.* 50°4' N, 116°35' W **90**
Fingoè, *Mozambique* 15°12' S, 31°51' E **224**
Finike, *Turk.* 36°17' N, 30°7' E **156**
Finiq, *Alban.* 39°54' N, 20°3' E **156**
Finke, *Austral.* 25°37' S, 134°36' E **231**
Finland 63°28' N, 25°46' E **152**
Finland, *Minn., U.S.* 47°24' N, 91°16' W **94**

Finland, Gulf of 60°11' N, 25°58' E 152
Finlay, river, Can. 57°38' N, 126°26' W 108
Finley, Calif., U.S. 39°0' N, 122°53' W 90
Finley, N. Dak., U.S. 47°29' N, 97°51' W 90
Finmoore, Can. 53°56' N, 123°37' W 108
Finne, region, Europe 51°7' N, 11°16' E 152
Finnentrop, Ger. 51°11' N, 7°58' E 167
Finnmarks-vidda, Nor. 69°2' N, 22°6' E 152
Finnskog, Nor. 60°42' N, 12°22' E 152
Finnsnes, Nor. 69°14' N, 18°0' E 152
Finse, Nor. 60°36' N, 7°23' E 152
Finspång, Nor. 58°41' N, 15°44' E 152
Finsteraarhorn, peak, Switz. 46°32' N, 8°5' E 167
Finström, Fin. 60°15' N, 19°54' E 166
Fiordland National Park, N.Z. 44°60' S, 165°54' E 240
Fîrdea, Rom. 45°45' N, 22°10' E 168
Fire Island National Seashore, Atlantic Ocean 40°35' N, 73°26' W 104
Firebag, river, Can. 57°27' N, 110°59' W 108
Firedrake Lake, Can. 61°15' N, 105°31' W 108
Firenze (Florence), It. 43°47' N, 11°14' E 167
Firenzuola, It. 44°7' N, 11°22' E 167
Firmat, Arg. 33°28' S, 61°30' W 139
Firozabad, India 27°7' N, 78°22' E 197
Firozpur, India 30°57' N, 74°38' E 186
First Sugar Mill, site, Hawai'i, U.S. 21°53' N, 159°30' W 90
Fīrūzābād, Iran 28°48' N, 52°38' E 196
Fīrūzkūh, Iran 35°46' N, 52°44' E 180
Fish Camp, Calif., U.S. 37°28' N, 119°39' W 100
Fish Cove Point, Can. 54°4' N, 57°19' W 111
Fish Haven, Idaho, U.S. 42°3' N, 111°24' W 92
Fish River Canyon Nature Reserve, Namibia 28°4' S, 17°32' E 227
Fisher, Ill., U.S. 40°18' N, 88°21' W 102
Fisher, La., U.S. 31°28' N, 93°29' W 103
Fisher Branch, Can. 51°5' N, 97°38' W 90
Fisher Strait 62°55' N, 84°37' W 106
Fishers Island, N.Y., U.S. 41°15' N, 72°12' W 104
Fishers Peak, Colo., U.S. 37°4' N, 104°33' W 92
Fishing Lake, Can. 52°8' N, 95°50' W 108
Fiskdale, Mass., U.S. 42°6' N, 72°8' W 104
Fiske, Cape, Antarctica 74°15' S, 60°22' W 248
Fiskenæsset see Qeqertarsuatsiaat, Den. 63°6' N, 50°43' W 106
Fismes, Fr. 49°18' N, 3°41' E 163
Fisterra, Cabo, Sp. 42°51' N, 9°43' W 150
Fitchburg, Mass., U.S. 42°34' N, 71°48' W 104
Fitchville, Conn., U.S. 41°33' N, 72°9' W 104
Fitero, Sp. 42°3' N, 1°52' W 164
Fitri, Lac, lake, Chad 12°53' N, 16°54' E 216
Fitz Roy, Monte, peak, Arg. 49°18' S, 73°23' W 134
Fitzcarrald, Peru 11°48' S, 72°22' W 137
Fitzgerald, Can. 59°51' N, 111°41' W 108
Fitzgerald, Ga., U.S. 31°42' N, 83°15' W 96
Fitzpatrick, Can. 47°28' N, 72°46' W 94
Fitzroy Crossing, Austral. 18°15' S, 125°32' E 238
Fiume see Rijeka, Croatia 45°20' N, 14°26' E 156
Fiumicino, It. 41°46' N, 12°13' E 156
Fivizzano, It. 44°14' N, 10°8' E 167
Fizi, Dem. Rep. of the Congo 4°21' S, 28°54' E 224
Fjällåsen, Nor. 67°30' N, 20°4' E 152
Flå, Nor. 63°11' N, 10°19' E 152
Fladerer Bay 73°19' S, 84°19' W 248
Fladungen, Ger. 50°31' N, 10°7' E 167
Flagler, Colo., U.S. 39°17' N, 103°4' W 90
Flagler Beach, Fla., U.S. 29°28' N, 81°9' W 105
Flagstaff, Ariz., U.S. 35°19' N, 111°35' W 238
Flåm, Nor. 60°50' N, 7°7' E 152
Flamand, Lac, lake, Can. 47°40' N, 73°50' W 94
Flamborough, U.K. 54°6' N, 0°7' E 162
Flamborough Head, U.K. 54°6' N, 8°475' W 162
Flamenco, Isla, island, Arg. 40°29' S, 62°7' W 134
Flamingo, Fla., U.S. 25°8' N, 80°56' W 105
Flamingo Point, Bahamas 24°43' N, 76°15' W 96
Flanagan, Ill., U.S. 40°52' N, 88°52' W 102
Flandreau, S. Dak., U.S. 44°1' N, 96°37' W 90
Flannan Isles, Atlantic Ocean 58°7' N, 8°10' W 150
Flat, Alas., U.S. 62°20' N, 158°7' W 98
Flat River, Mo., U.S. 37°50' N, 90°31' W 96
Flat, river, Mich., U.S. 43°16' N, 85°17' W 102
Flat Rock, Ill., U.S. 38°54' N, 87°40' W 102
Flat Top Mountain, Va., U.S. 37°25' N, 79°39' W 96
Flatbush, Can. 54°41' N, 114°9' W 108
Flateland, Nor. 59°16' N, 7°29' E 152
Flathead Lake, Mont., U.S. 47°49' N, 114°45' W 90
Flathead Range, Mont., U.S. 48°18' N, 114°3' W 90
Flattery, Cape, Wash., U.S. 48°22' N, 124°53' W 100
Flavigny-sur-Ozerain, Fr. 47°30' N, 4°31' E 150
Flavy-le-Martel, Fr. 49°42' N, 3°12' E 163
Flaxton, N. Dak., U.S. 48°53' N, 102°24' W 90
Fleeton, Va., U.S. 37°48' N, 76°17' W 94
Fleetwood, U.K. 53°55' N, 3°1' W 162
Flekkefjord, Nor. 58°13' N, 6°40' E 160
Flemingsburg, Ky., U.S. 38°24' N, 83°45' W 94
Flemish Cap, North Atlantic Ocean 47°7' N, 44°36' W 253
Flen, Nor. 59°3' N, 16°33' E 152
Flensburg, Ger. 54°47' N, 9°25' E 152
Flers, Fr. 48°44' N, 0°35' E 150
Flesberg, Nor. 59°51' N, 9°25' E 152
Fletcher, Cape, Antarctica 67°38' S, 61°20' E 248
Fletcher Lake, Can. 58°11' N, 94°18' W 108
Fletcher Plain, Arctic Ocean 86°43' N, 162°1' E 255
Flett Lake, Can. 60°27' N, 104°25' W 108
Fleurance, Fr. 43°50' N, 0°39' E 150
Fleurier, Switz. 46°54' N, 6°35' E 167
Flevoland, adm. division, Neth. 52°18' N, 4°50' E 150
Flieden, Ger. 50°25' N, 9°35' E 167
Flims, Switz. 46°50' N, 9°18' E 167
Flin Flon, Can. 54°47' N, 101°52' W 108
Flinders Entrance 9°52' S, 143°32' E 230
Flinders Group, islands, Coral Sea 14°38' S, 144°11' E 230
Flinders Island, Austral. 40°15' S, 146°5' E 230
Flinders Island, Austral. 33°35' S, 132°48' E 230
Flinders Passage 19°4' S, 147°16' E 230
Flinders Ranges, Austral. 30°14' S, 138°14' E 230
Flint, Mich., U.S. 43°0' N, 83°41' W 102
Flint, U.K. 53°14' N, 3°8' W 162
Flint Creek Range, Mont., U.S. 46°20' N, 113°15' W 90
Flint Hills, Kans., U.S. 38°28' N, 96°36' W 90
Flint Island, Kiribati 11°27' S, 151°51' W 252
Flint Lake, Can. 49°50' N, 86°11' W 94
Flint, river, Ala., U.S. 35°3' N, 86°30' W 96
Flint, river, Ga., U.S. 30°58' N, 84°31' W 112
Flix, Sp. 41°12' N, 0°32' E 164
Flixecourt, Fr. 50°0' N, 2°5' E 163
Flize, Fr. 49°41' N, 4°47' E 163
Flodden, battle, U.K. 55°37' N, 2°21' W 150
Flomaton, Ala., U.S. 30°59' N, 87°17' W 96
Floodwood, Minn., U.S. 46°55' N, 92°57' W 94
Flor de Agosto, Peru 2°24' S, 73°8' W 136
Flora, Ill., U.S. 38°39' N, 88°29' W 102
Flora, Ind., U.S. 40°32' N, 86°31' W 102
Flora, Miss., U.S. 32°31' N, 90°19' W 103
Flora, Mo., U.S. 38°39' N, 88°29' W 94
Flora, Oreg., U.S. 45°53' N, 117°20' W 90
Floral City, Fla., U.S. 28°45' N, 82°18' W 105
Florange, Fr. 49°20' N, 6°8' E 163
Florence, Ala., U.S. 34°48' N, 87°43' W 112
Florence, Ariz., U.S. 33°1' N, 111°23' W 92
Florence, Colo., U.S. 38°23' N, 105°7' W 90
Florence, Kans., U.S. 38°13' N, 96°56' W 90
Florence, Ky., U.S. 38°59' N, 84°37' W 102
Florence, Miss., U.S. 32°9' N, 90°7' W 103
Florence, Oreg., U.S. 43°58' N, 124°6' W 90
Florence, S.C., U.S. 34°11' N, 79°47' W 96
Florence, Vt., U.S. 43°42' N, 73°5' W 104
Florence, Wis., U.S. 45°55' N, 88°15' W 94
Florence Peak, Calif., U.S. 36°24' N, 118°36' W 101
Florence see Firenze, It. 43°47' N, 11°14' E 167
Florencia, Col. 1°37' N, 75°38' W 136
Florennes, Belg. 50°15' N, 4°36' E 167
Florenville, Belg. 49°41' N, 5°19' E 163
Flores, Braz. 7°53' S, 37°59' W 132
Flores, Guatemala 16°57' N, 89°53' W 116
Flores, island, Indonesia 9°22' S, 120°40' E 192
Flores Sea 7°54' S, 118°8' E 192
Florescência, Braz. 9°39' S, 68°45' W 137
Floriano, Braz. 6°49' S, 43°3' W 132
Florianópolis, Braz. 27°35' S, 48°30' W 138
Florida, Bol. 18°32' S, 63°31' W 137
Florida, N. Mex., U.S. 34°5' N, 106°54' W 92
Florida, Uru. 34°6' S, 56°14' W 139
Florida, adm. division, Fla., U.S. 26°39' N, 82°22' W 96
Florida Bay 24°55' N, 80°49' W 116
Florida Bay 25°4' N, 80°55' W 105
Florida City, Fla., U.S. 25°26' N, 80°30' W 105
Florida Islands, Solomon Sea 9°0' S, 160°0' E 242
Florida Keys, Atlantic Ocean 24°52' N, 80°55' W 105
Florida Negra, Arg. 48°18' S, 67°21' W 134
Florida Ridge, Fla., U.S. 27°34' N, 80°22' W 105
Florida, Straits of 25°7' N, 79°48' W 105
Florida's Turnpike, Fla., U.S. 27°49' N, 81°4' W 105
Florido, river, Mex. 26°41' N, 105°4' W 80
Florien, La., U.S. 31°25' N, 93°29' W 103
Florissant, Mo., U.S. 38°47' N, 90°20' W 94
Florø, Nor. 61°33' N, 5°1' E 160
Flötningen, Nor. 61°51' N, 12°12' E 152
Flower Garden Banks National Marine Sanctuary, Gulf of Mexico 28°1' N, 94°27' W 103
Flower's Cove, Can. 51°18' N, 56°43' W 111
Floyd, La., U.S. 32°39' N, 91°25' W 103
Floyd, N. Mex., U.S. 34°12' N, 103°35' W 92
Floyd, Mount, Ariz., U.S. 35°22' N, 112°47' W 92
Floyd, river, Iowa, U.S. 42°21' N, 96°36' W 80
Floydada, Tex., U.S. 33°58' N, 101°20' W 92
Flumet, Fr. 45°49' N, 6°30' E 167
Flushing, Mich., U.S. 43°4' N, 83°50' W 102
Flushing, Ohio, U.S. 40°8' N, 81°3' W 102
Flushing see Vlissingen, Neth. 51°27' N, 3°34' E 163
Fly Lake, oil field, Austral. 27°35' S, 139°26' E 230
Flying Fish, Cape, Antarctica 71°55' S, 102°43' W 248
Foam Lake, Can. 51°39' N, 103°32' W 90
Foča, Bosn. and Herzg. 43°29' N, 18°46' E 168
Fochi, spring, Chad 18°57' N, 15°56' E 216
Focşani, Rom. 45°42' N, 27°10' E 143
Foga, Sudan 13°37' N, 27°59' E 226
Fogang, China 23°48' N, 113°32' E 198
Foggaret el Arab, Alg. 27°11' N, 2°48' E 214
Foggia, It. 41°29' N, 15°33' E 143
Föglö, Fin. 60°0' N, 20°25' E 166
Fogo Island, Can. 49°43' N, 53°60' W 106
Foinaven, peak, U.K. 58°23' N, 4°60' W 150
Foix, Fr. 42°57' N, 1°37' E 164
Foix, region, Europe 42°58' N, 1°22' E 165
Fojnica, Bosn. and Herzg. 43°56' N, 17°53' E 168
Fokino, Russ. 53°23' N, 34°26' E 154
Fokku, Nig. 11°41' N, 4°29' E 222
Földeák, Hung. 46°20' N, 20°30' E 168
Folégandros, island, Gr. 36°28' N, 24°13' E 180
Foley, Ala., U.S. 30°24' N, 87°41' W 103
Foley, Minn., U.S. 45°38' N, 93°56' W 94
Foley Island, Can. 68°24' N, 77°53' W 106
Foleyet, Can. 48°14' N, 82°26' W 94
Foligno, It. 42°56' N, 12°43' E 156
Folkestone, U.K. 51°5' N, 1°10' E 163
Folkingham, U.K. 52°53' N, 0°24' E 162
Follett, Tex., U.S. 36°25' N, 100°8' W 92
Föllinge, Nor. 63°39' N, 14°37' E 152
Follonica, It. 42°55' N, 10°45' E 156
Folsom, Calif., U.S. 38°40' N, 121°11' W 90
Folsom, La., U.S. 30°38' N, 90°12' W 103
Folteşti, Rom. 45°44' N, 28°2' E 158
Fond du Lac, Wis., U.S. 43°47' N, 88°26' W 102
Fond-du-Lac, Can. 59°19' N, 107°11' W 108
Fonelas, Sp. 37°24' N, 3°11' W 164
Fongafale see Funafuti, Tuvalu 9°0' S, 179°0' E 241
Fongen, peak, Nor. 63°9' N, 11°30' E 152
Fonseca, Col. 10°52' N, 72°52' W 136
Fonseca, Golfo de 13°9' N, 88°27' W 112
Fontaine Lake, Can. 59°38' N, 107°7' W 108
Fontainebleau, Fr. 48°23' N, 2°42' E 163
Fontana, Calif., U.S. 34°5' N, 117°27' W 101
Fontas, Can. 58°17' N, 121°44' W 108
Fontas, river, Can. 58°10' N, 121°53' W 108
Fonte Boa, Braz. 2°33' S, 66°6' W 136
Fonteneau, Lac, lake, Can. 51°54' N, 62°11' W 111
Fonyód, Hung. 46°43' N, 17°32' E 168
Foothills, Can. 53°3' N, 116°49' W 108
Foping, China 33°32' N, 108°1' E 198
Foppolo, It. 46°3' N, 9°44' E 167
Forbes, Mount, Austral. 23°44' S, 130°22' E 230
Forbes, Mount, Can. 51°51' N, 117°3' W 90
Forcados, Nig. 5°23' N, 5°26' E 222
Ford, U.K. 56°10' N, 5°27' W 150
Ford City, Calif., U.S. 35°9' N, 119°29' W 100
Ford City, Pa., U.S. 40°45' N, 79°32' W 94
Ford, Mount, Antarctica 70°50' S, 163°28' E 248
Førde, Nor. 61°26' N, 5°51' E 152
Fordingbridge, U.K. 50°55' N, 1°48' W 162
Fordyce, Ark., U.S. 33°47' N, 92°24' W 96
Fore, Nor. 66°55' N, 13°38' E 152
Forécariah, Guinea 9°24' N, 13°7' W 222
Forel, Mont, peak, Den. 66°56' N, 37°16' W 106
Foreman, Ark., U.S. 33°42' N, 94°25' W 96
Foremost, Can. 49°28' N, 111°27' W 90
Forest, Can. 43°4' N, 81°60' W 102
Forest, Miss., U.S. 32°21' N, 89°30' W 112
Forest, Ohio, U.S. 40°47' N, 83°31' W 102
Forest City, Iowa, U.S. 43°14' N, 93°39' W 94
Forest Dale, Vt., U.S. 43°49' N, 73°4' W 104
Forest Grove, Oreg., U.S. 45°30' N, 123°7' W 90
Forest Hill, La., U.S. 31°1' N, 92°33' W 103
Forest Park, Ohio, U.S. 39°16' N, 84°30' W 102
Forester Pass, Calif., U.S. 36°42' N, 118°23' W 101
Forestville, Can. 48°44' N, 69°5' W 94
Forestville, Mich., U.S. 43°39' N, 82°37' W 102
Forez, Monts du, Fr. 45°55' N, 3°30' E 165
Forgan, Okla., U.S. 36°53' N, 100°32' W 92
Forges-les-Eaux, Fr. 49°36' N, 1°32' E 163
Forillon National Park, Can. 48°51' N, 63°58' W 111
Forks, Wash., U.S. 47°55' N, 124°24' W 100
Forlì, It. 44°13' N, 12°1' E 167
Forlimpopoli, It. 44°11' N, 12°6' E 167
Forman, N. Dak., U.S. 46°5' N, 97°39' W 90
Formentera, island, Sp. 38°27' N, 1°37' E 214
Formentor, Cap de, Sp. 40°5' N, 3°19' E 164
Formerie, Fr. 49°38' N, 1°44' E 163
Formiga, Braz. 20°30' S, 45°26' W 138
Formosa, Arg. 26°11' S, 58°11' W 139
Formosa, Braz. 15°34' S, 47°20' W 138
Formosa, adm. division, Arg. 26°6' S, 59°40' W 139
Formosa do Rio Prêto, Braz. 11°3' S, 45°13' W 130
Formosa, island, Guinea-Bissau 11°37' N, 16°30' W 222
Formosa, Serra, Braz. 12°8' S, 55°27' W 130
Formoso, Braz. 14°60' S, 46°15' W 138
Formoso, Braz. 13°38' S, 48°55' W 138
Formoso, river, Braz. 12°45' S, 49°34' W 138
Formoso, river, Braz. 14°27' S, 45°28' W 138
Forno di Zoldo, It. 46°20' N, 12°9' E 167
Fornovo di Taro, It. 44°40' N, 10°5' E 167
Føroyar see Faroe Islands, North Atlantic Ocean 62°34' N, 11°40' W 143
Forozan, oil field, Kuwait 28°44' N, 49°43' E 196
Forrest, Ill., U.S. 40°44' N, 88°25' W 102
Forrest City, Ark., U.S. 34°59' N, 90°48' W 96
Forrest Lake, Can. 57°31' N, 109°57' W 108
Forreston, Ill., U.S. 42°7' N, 89°35' W 102
Fors, Nor. 62°59' N, 16°41' E 152
Forsand, Nor. 58°53' N, 6°7' E 152
Forsayth, Austral. 18°35' S, 143°34' E 231
Forsby, Fin. 60°30' N, 25°57' E 166
Forse, Nor. 63°8' N, 17°0' E 154
Forsmark, Nor. 65°29' N, 15°49' E 152
Forsnäs, Nor. 66°14' N, 18°37' E 152
Forssa, Fin. 60°49' N, 23°37' E 166
Forst, Ger. 51°44' N, 14°38' E 152
Forsyth, Mo., U.S. 36°40' N, 93°7' W 96
Forsyth, Mont., U.S. 46°14' N, 106°40' W 90
Forsyth Island, Austral. 16°59' S, 137°1' E 230
Forsyth Lake, Can. 59°31' N, 107°59' W 108
Fort Abbas, Pak. 29°13' N, 72°54' E 186
Fort Adams, Miss., U.S. 31°4' N, 91°34' W 103
Fort Albany, Can. 52°13' N, 81°39' W 110
Fort Assiniboine, Can. 54°21' N, 114°47' W 108
Fort Atkinson, Wis., U.S. 42°55' N, 88°51' W 102
Fort Belvoir, Va., U.S. 38°40' N, 77°13' W 94
Fort Benjamin Harrison, Ind., U.S. 39°51' N, 86°4' W 102
Fort Benning, Ga., U.S. 32°19' N, 85°2' W 96
Fort Benton, Mont., U.S. 47°48' N, 110°40' W 90
Fort Black, Can. 55°24' N, 107°45' W 108
Fort Bragg, Calif., U.S. 39°26' N, 123°49' W 90
Fort Caroline National Memorial, Fla., U.S. 30°20' N, 81°34' W 96
Fort Chipewyan, Can. 58°43' N, 111°7' W 108
Fort Clatsop National Memorial, Oreg., U.S. 46°6' N, 123°55' W 100
Fort Collins, Colo., U.S. 40°34' N, 105°6' W 90
Fort Collinson, site, Can. 71°36' N, 118°5' W 106
Fort Conger, site, Can. 81°49' N, 65°5' W 246
Fort Defiance, Ariz., U.S. 35°43' N, 109°6' W 82
Fort Deposit, Ala., U.S. 31°59' N, 86°34' W 96
Fort Detrick, Md., U.S. 39°25' N, 77°31' W 94
Fort Devens, Mass., U.S. 42°31' N, 71°38' W 104
Fort Dick, Calif., U.S. 41°51' N, 124°10' W 90
Fort Dodge, Iowa, U.S. 42°29' N, 94°11' W 94
Fort Dorval, Péninsule du, Can. 50°56' N, 73°21' W 111
Fort Edward, N.Y., U.S. 43°15' N, 73°36' W 104
Fort Frances, Can. 48°40' N, 93°33' W 106
Fort Fraser, Can. 54°3' N, 124°31' W 108
Fort Gay, W. Va., U.S. 38°6' N, 82°37' W 94
Fort Gibson, Okla., U.S. 35°46' N, 95°15' W 96
Fort Good Hope, Can. 66°14' N, 128°29' W 106
Fort Gordon, Ga., U.S. 33°22' N, 82°16' W 96
Fort Gouraud see Fdérik, Mauritania 22°41' N, 12°43' W 214
Fort Hall, Idaho, U.S. 43°3' N, 112°26' W 90
Fort Hill see Chitipa, Malawi 9°43' S, 33°14' E 224
Fort Hope, Can. 51°33' N, 88°1' W 110
Fort Irwin, Calif., U.S. 35°15' N, 116°42' W 101
Fort Kent, Me., U.S. 47°15' N, 68°35' W 111
Fort Laramie, Wyo., U.S. 42°12' N, 104°31' W 90
Fort Laramie National Historic Site, Wyo., U.S. 42°10' N, 104°38' W 90
Fort Lauderdale, Fla., U.S. 26°7' N, 80°10' W 105
Fort Lewis, Wash., U.S. 47°2' N, 122°36' W 100
Fort Liard, Can. 60°14' N, 123°26' W 108
Fort Lupton, Colo., U.S. 40°4' N, 104°49' W 90
Fort Mackay, Can. 57°12' N, 111°42' W 108
Fort Macleod, Can. 49°42' N, 113°24' W 90
Fort Madison, Iowa, U.S. 40°38' N, 91°20' W 94
Fort Matanzas National Monument, Fla., U.S. 29°43' N, 81°19' W 105
Fort Mckinley, Ohio, U.S. 39°47' N, 84°16' W 102
Fort Mcmurray, Can. 56°40' N, 111°23' W 108
Fort Mcpherson, Can. 67°27' N, 134°44' W 98
Fort Mill, S.C., U.S. 35°0' N, 80°56' W 96
Fort Miribel, Alg. 29°26' N, 3°1' E 214
Fort Morgan, Ala., U.S. 30°13' N, 88°3' W 103
Fort Morgan, Colo., U.S. 40°15' N, 103°49' W 90
Fort Motylinski see Tarhaouhaout, Alg. 22°38' N, 5°55' E 214
Fort Myers, Fla., U.S. 26°38' N, 81°52' W 105
Fort Myers Beach, Fla., U.S. 26°27' N, 81°57' W 105
Fort Necessity National Battlefield, Pa., U.S. 39°47' N, 79°42' W 94
Fort Nelson, Can. 58°42' N, 122°42' W 106
Fort Nelson, river, Can. 59°20' N, 123°45' W 108
Fort Niagara, site, N.Y., U.S. 43°14' N, 79°8' W 94
Fort Ogden, Fla., U.S. 27°5' N, 81°57' W 105
Fort Payne, Ala., U.S. 34°25' N, 85°44' W 96
Fort Peck, Mont., U.S. 47°59' N, 106°28' W 90
Fort Peck Dam, Mont., U.S. 47°43' N, 106°34' W 90
Fort Peck Lake, Mont., U.S. 47°40' N, 107°29' W 90
Fort Pierce, Fla., U.S. 27°26' N, 80°20' W 105
Fort Pierre, S. Dak., U.S. 44°21' N, 100°23' W 90
Fort Pierre Bordes see Ti-n-Zaouâtene, Alg. 19°58' N, 2°57' E 222
Fort Polk, La., U.S. 31°0' N, 93°15' W 103
Fort Portal, Uganda 0°38' N, 30°16' E 224
Fort Prince of Wales National Historical Park, Can. 58°44' N, 94°24' W 108
Fort Providence, Can. 61°24' N, 117°36' W 108
Fort Qu' Appelle, Can. 50°43' N, 103°50' W 90
Fort Quitman, site, Tex., U.S. 31°3' N, 105°40' W 92
Fort Recovery, Ohio, U.S. 40°23' N, 84°46' W 102
Fort Resolution, Can. 61°10' N, 113°39' W 108
Fort Ritchie, Md., U.S. 39°41' N, 77°35' W 94
Fort Rock, Oreg., U.S. 43°20' N, 121°4' W 90
Fort Saint, Tun. 30°16' N, 9°36' E 214
Fort Saint James, Can. 54°25' N, 124°12' W 108
Fort Saint John, Can. 56°13' N, 120°52' W 108
Fort Sam Houston, Tex., U.S. 29°26' N, 98°31' W 92
Fort Saskatchewan, Can. 53°41' N, 113°14' W 108
Fort Scott, Kans., U.S. 37°48' N, 94°42' W 96
Fort Severn, Can. 56°0' N, 87°42' W 106
Fort Shafter, Hawai'i, U.S. 21°19' N, 157°56' W 99
Fort Shawnee, Ohio, U.S. 40°40' N, 84°8' W 102
Fort Shevchenko, Kaz. 44°30' N, 50°16' E 158
Fort Sill, Okla., U.S. 34°38' N, 98°29' W 92
Fort Simcoe, site, Wash., U.S. 46°18' N, 120°57' W 90
Fort Simpson, Can. 61°49' N, 121°23' W 106
Fort Smith, Ark., U.S. 35°20' N, 94°25' W 96
Fort Smith, Can. 60°2' N, 112°11' W 106
Fort St. John, Can. 56°13' N, 120°53' W 246
Fort Stockton, Tex., U.S. 30°52' N, 102°53' W 92
Fort Sumner, N. Mex., U.S. 34°28' N, 104°14' W 92
Fort Supply, Okla., U.S. 36°33' N, 99°34' W 92
Fort Supply Lake, Okla., U.S. 36°21' N, 100°49' W 81
Fort Ternan, Kenya 0°13' N, 35°22' E 224
Fort Thompson, S. Dak., U.S. 44°4' N, 99°28' W 90
Fort Trinquet see Bir Mogreïn, Mauritania 25°13' N, 11°37' W 214
Fort Union National Monument, N. Mex., U.S. 35°53' N, 105°6' W 92
Fort Valley, Ga., U.S. 32°32' N, 83°53' W 96
Fort Vermilion, Can. 58°22' N, 115°58' W 108
Fort Wayne, Ind., U.S. 41°3' N, 85°8' W 102
Fort White, Fla., U.S. 29°55' N, 82°43' W 105
Fort Worth, Tex., U.S. 32°43' N, 97°19' W 92
Fort Yates, N. Dak., U.S. 46°4' N, 100°40' W 90
Fort Yukon, Alas., U.S. 66°32' N, 145°5' W 106
Fortaleza, Bol. 12°6' S, 66°51' W 137
Fortaleza, Bol. 9°49' S, 65°30' W 137
Fortaleza, Braz. 3°46' S, 38°32' W 132
Fort-Coulonge, Can. 45°50' N, 76°44' W 94
Fort-de-France, Fr. 14°36' N, 61°4' W 116
Forteau, Can. 51°26' N, 56°59' W 111
Fortezza, It. 46°47' N, 11°35' E 167
Fortim, Braz. 4°30' S, 37°49' W 132
Fortín, Mex. 18°54' N, 97°1' W 114
Fortín Carlos A. López, Parag. 21°19' S, 59°42' W 132
Fortín General Díaz, Parag. 23°31' S, 60°35' W 132
Fortín Infante Rivarola, Parag. 21°38' S, 62°25' W 132
Fortín Madrejón, Parag. 20°37' S, 59°52' W 132
Fortín Presidente Ayala, Parag. 23°29' S, 59°43' W 132
Fortín Suárez Arana, Bol. 18°39' S, 60°9' W 132
Fortín Teniente Américo Picco, Parag. 19°39' S, 59°47' W 132
Fortress Mountain, Wyo., U.S. 44°18' N, 109°53' W 90
Fortress of Louisbourg National Historic Site, Can. 45°52' N, 60°7' W 111
Fortun, Nor. 61°30' N, 7°39' E 152
Fortuna, N. Dak., U.S. 48°53' N, 103°47' W 90
Fortune Island see Long Cay, Bahamas 22°35' N, 76°5' W 116
Fortville, Ind., U.S. 39°55' N, 85°51' W 102
Forūr, island, Iran 26°8' N, 54°22' E 180
Foshan, China 23°3' N, 113°6' E 198
Fosheim Peninsula, Can. 79°5' N, 90°14' W 246
Fosna, Nor. 63°36' N, 9°53' E 152
Fosnes, Nor. 64°39' N, 11°17' E 152
Foso, Ghana 5°42' N, 1°18' W 222
Fossacesia, It. 42°14' N, 14°28' E 156
Fossano, It. 44°33' N, 7°42' E 167
Fossil, Oreg., U.S. 44°59' N, 120°13' W 82
Fosston, Minn., U.S. 47°33' N, 95°47' W 90
Foster, Austral. 38°38' S, 146°11' E 231
Foster Bugt 72°24' N, 28°4' W 73
Foster Center, R.I., U.S. 41°47' N, 71°44' W 104
Foster, Mount, Can. 59°45' N, 135°37' W 108
Foster Peak, Can. 51°3' N, 116°15' W 90
Foster, river, Can. 56°21' N, 105°54' W 108
Fostoria, Ohio, U.S. 41°9' N, 83°24' W 102
Fota Terara, peak, Eth. 9°8' N, 38°24' E 224
Fotokol, Cameroon 12°26' N, 14°16' E 216
Fouke, Ark., U.S. 33°15' N, 93°54' W 103
Foulweather, Cape, Oreg., U.S. 44°47' N, 124°44' W 90
Foulwind, Cape, N.Z. 41°48' S, 171°0' E 240
Foum Tataouine, Tun. 32°57' N, 10°26' E 216
Foum Zguid, Mor. 30°6' N, 6°55' W 214
Foumban, Cameroon 5°42' N, 10°52' E 222
Fountain, Colo., U.S. 38°41' N, 104°42' W 92
Fountain, Mich., U.S. 44°3' N, 86°11' W 102
Fountain City, Ind., U.S. 39°57' N, 84°55' W 102
Fountain City, Wis., U.S. 44°8' N, 91°42' W 110
Fountain Hill, Ark., U.S. 33°20' N, 91°52' W 103
Four Corners Monument, U.S. 36°59' N, 109°6' W 92
Four, spring, Mauritania 16°3' N, 8°50' W 222
Fourcroy, Cape, Austral. 11°36' S, 128°59' E 230
Fourmies, Fr. 50°1' N, 4°2' E 163
Foúrni, Gr. 37°34' N, 26°29' E 156
Fournier, Lac, lake, Can. 51°28' N, 65°60' W 111
Fouta Djallon, region, Africa 12°3' N, 12°50' W 222
Fowler, Calif., U.S. 36°38' N, 119°42' W 100
Fowler, Colo., U.S. 38°7' N, 104°2' W 90
Fowler, Ind., U.S. 40°36' N, 87°19' W 102
Fowler, Kans., U.S. 37°22' N, 100°12' W 92
Fowler, Mich., U.S. 42°59' N, 84°45' W 102
Fowlers Bay 32°11' S, 131°19' E 230
Fowlerville, Mich., U.S. 42°39' N, 84°4' W 102
Fox Creek, Can. 54°23' N, 116°48' W 108
Fox Glacier, N.Z. 43°30' S, 170°0' E 240
Fox Islands, Anadyrskiy Zaliv 52°57' N, 168°37' W 98
Fox Lake, Can. 58°26' N, 114°31' W 108
Fox Lake, Wis., U.S. 43°32' N, 88°54' W 102
Fox Mountain, Nev., U.S. 41°0' N, 119°39' W 90
Fox Point, Wis., U.S. 43°9' N, 87°54' W 102
Fox, river, Can. 55°57' N, 93°55' W 108
Fox, river, Wis., U.S. 43°56' N, 89°2' W 102
Fox Valley, Can. 50°28' N, 109°29' W 90
Foxboro, Mass., U.S. 42°3' N, 71°16' W 104
Foxe Basin 67°2' N, 80°27' W 106
Foxe Channel 64°14' N, 82°12' W 106
Foxe Peninsula, Can. 64°50' N, 80°3' W 106
Foxton, N.Z. 40°29' S, 175°19' E 240
Foxworth, Miss., U.S. 31°13' N, 89°53' W 103
Foyé, Guinea 11°17' N, 13°31' W 222
Foyn Coast, Antarctica 66°58' S, 64°23' W 248
Foz do Breu, Braz. 9°22' S, 72°45' W 137
Foz do Cunene, Angola 17°13' S, 11°46' E 220
Foz do Jamari, Braz. 8°29' S, 63°30' W 130
Foz do Jordão, Braz. 9°21' S, 71°58' W 137
Foz do Jutaí, Braz. 2°46' S, 66°57' W 136
Foz do Mamoriá, Braz. 2°26' S, 66°38' W 136
Foz do Tarauacá, Braz. 6°46' S, 69°47' W 130
Frącki, Pol. 53°58' N, 23°17' E 166
Fraga, Sp. 41°31' N, 0°21' E 164
Fraile Muerto, Uru. 32°30' S, 54°34' W 139
Frailes, Cordillera de los, Bol. 19°24' S, 67°12' W 132
Frailes, Sierra de los, Mex. 24°9' N, 105°60' W 112
Fraize, Fr. 48°11' N, 7°0' E 163
Frakes, Mount, Antarctica 76°45' S, 117°2' W 248
Fram Basin, Arctic Ocean 88°9' N, 0°36' E 255
Fram Peak, Antarctica 68°4' S, 58°9' E 248
Framingham, Mass., U.S. 42°16' N, 71°26' W 104
Frammersbach, Ger. 50°3' N, 9°28' E 167
Framnes, Cape, Antarctica 65°54' S, 60°39' W 134
Franca, Braz. 20°35' S, 47°24' W 138
France 47°30' N, 1°48' E 150
France, Île de, island, Den. 77°37' N, 16°49' W 246
Francés, Cabo, Cuba 21°54' N, 83°58' W 116
Frances Lake, Can. 61°24' N, 130°41' W 98
Francés, Punta, Cuba 21°32' N, 83°58' W 116
Frances, river, Can. 60°17' N, 129°2' W 108
Francés Viejo, Cabo, Dom. Rep. 19°44' N, 69°57' W 116
Francesville, Ind., U.S. 40°59' N, 86°53' W 102
Franceville, Gabon 1°43' S, 13°32' E 218
Franche-Comté, adm. division, Fr. 47°13' N, 5°31' E 150
Francis Case, Lake, S. Dak., U.S. 43°7' N, 100°51' W 90
Francis E. Warren Air Force Base, Wyo., U.S. 41°10' N, 104°58' W 90
Francis Island, Antarctica 67°45' S, 64°16' W 248

rancisco de Orellana, Peru 3°23' S, 72°50' W 136
rancisco I. Madero, Mex. 24°24' N, 104°20' W 114
rancistown, Botswana 21°14' S, 27°30' E 227
rançois, Lacs à, lake, Can. 51°41' N, 66°11' W 111
rançois Lake, Can. 54°3' N, 125°46' W 108
ranconia, N.H., U.S. 44°13' N, 71°45' W 104
ranconia Notch, pass, N.H., U.S. 44°9' N, 71°41' W 104
ranconia, region, Europe 49°54' N, 8°2' E 167
rancs Peak, Wyo., U.S. 43°55' N, 109°25' W 90
raneker, Neth. 53°11' N, 5°31' E 163
rankenberg, Ger. 51°3' N, 8°48' E 167
rankenhöhe, Ger. 49°12' N, 9°48' E 152
rankenmuth, Mich., U.S. 43°20' N, 83°44' W 102
Frankenwald, Ger. 50°16' N, 11°7' E 152
Frankfort, Ind., U.S. 40°16' N, 86°32' W 102
Frankfort, Kans., U.S. 39°41' N, 96°25' W 90
Frankfort, Ky., U.S. 38°10' N, 84°57' W 94
Frankfort, Mich., U.S. 44°38' N, 86°14' W 94
Frankfort, Ohio, U.S. 39°24' N, 83°11' W 102
Frankfort, S. Af. 27°16' S, 28°28' E 227
Frankfurt am Main, Ger. 50°6' N, 8°40' E 167
Fränkische Alb, Ger. 49°33' N, 11°12' E 152
Franklin, Ala., U.S. 31°42' N, 87°24' W 103
Franklin, Ariz., U.S. 32°39' N, 109°3' W 92
Franklin, Idaho, U.S. 42°1' N, 111°47' W 90
Franklin, Ind., U.S. 39°28' N, 86°3' W 102
Franklin, La., U.S. 29°47' N, 91°31' W 103
Franklin, Mass., U.S. 42°4' N, 71°25' W 104
Franklin, Nebr., U.S. 40°4' N, 98°58' W 90
Franklin, N.H., U.S. 43°26' N, 71°39' W 94
Franklin, Ohio, U.S. 39°32' N, 84°18' W 102
Franklin, Tenn., U.S. 35°54' N, 86°52' W 96
Franklin, Va., U.S. 36°40' N, 76°56' W 96
Franklin, Wis., U.S. 42°52' N, 88°1' W 102
Franklin Bay 69°42' N, 122°26' W 246
Franklin Grove, Ill., U.S. 41°50' N, 89°18' W 102
Franklin Lake, Can. 59°17' N, 104°2' W 108
Franklin Mountains, Can. 65°17' N, 125°31' W 98
Franklin Strait 71°15' N, 100°8' W 106
Franklinton, La., U.S. 30°50' N, 90°10' W 103
Franklinville, N.Y., U.S. 42°20' N, 78°28' W 94
Frankston, Tex., U.S. 32°2' N, 95°31' W 103
Fransfontein, Namibia 20°14' S, 14°59' E 220
Franske Øer, islands, Greenland Sea 78°16' N, 17°28' W 246
Fränsta, Nor. 62°29' N, 16°11' E 152
Franz, Can. 48°28' N, 84°24' W 94
Franz Josef Glacier, N.Z. 43°24' S, 170°12' E 240
Franz Josef Land, Barents Sea 80°39' N, 63°19' E 255
Frasca, Capo della, It. 39°41' N, 7°36' E 156
Fraser Island, Austral. 25°59' S, 153°16' E 230
Fraser, river, Can. 53°23' N, 122°46' W 108
Fraser, river, Can. 51°30' N, 122°24' W 90
Fraser, river, Can. 49°20' N, 121°40' W 100
Fraser, river, Can. 53°51' N, 121°49' W 108
Fraserburg, S. Af. 31°55' S, 21°31' E 227
Fraserburg Road, S. Af. 32°48' S, 21°57' E 227
Fraserdale, Can. 49°51' N, 81°38' W 94
Frasertown, N.Z. 38°59' S, 177°26' E 240
Fray Bentos, Uru. 33°10' S, 58°15' W 139
Fray Jorge National Park, Chile 30°42' S, 71°48' W 134
Frazee, Minn., U.S. 46°42' N, 95°43' W 90
Frazer Lake, Can. 49°13' N, 88°56' W 94
Frazier, Mount, Antarctica 77°45' S, 154°7' W 248
Frazier Mountain, Calif., U.S. 34°46' N, 119°1' W 101
Frazier Park, Calif., U.S. 34°50' N, 118°58' W 101
Frechen, Ger. 50°54' N, 6°48' E 167
Fredericia, Den. 55°33' N, 9°43' E 150
Frederick, Md., U.S. 39°23' N, 77°25' W 82
Frederick, Okla., U.S. 34°21' N, 99°1' W 92
Frederick, S. Dak., U.S. 45°49' N, 98°33' W 90
Frederick Sound 56°54' N, 133°26' W 108
Fredericksburg, Tex., U.S. 30°15' N, 98°52' W 92
Fredericksburg and Spotsylvania National Military Park, Va., U.S. 38°14' N, 77°34' W 94
Fredericktown, Ohio, U.S. 40°28' N, 82°32' W 102
Fredericton, Can. 45°55' N, 66°48' W 94
Frederikshåb see Paamiut, Den. 62°4' N, 49°33' W 106
Frederikshavn, Den. 57°25' N, 10°29' E 150
Fredonia, Ariz., U.S. 36°56' N, 112°31' W 92
Fredonia, Kans., U.S. 37°30' N, 95°50' W 96
Fredonia, N.Y., U.S. 42°26' N, 79°21' W 94
Fredonia, Wis., U.S. 43°27' N, 87°57' W 102
Fredonyer Pass, Calif., U.S. 40°22' N, 120°52' W 90
Fredonyer Peak, Calif., U.S. 40°40' N, 120°42' W 90
Fredrikstad, Nor. 59°13' N, 10°56' E 152
Free State, adm. division, S. Af. 29°23' S, 26°36' E 220
Freedom, N.H., U.S. 43°48' N, 71°3' W 104
Freedom, Okla., U.S. 36°45' N, 99°7' W 92
Freels, Cape, Can. 49°9' N, 53°27' W 111
Freeman Point, Antarctica 65°49' S, 132°15' E 248
Freeport, Bahamas 26°31' N, 78°41' W 105
Freeport, Ill., U.S. 42°17' N, 89°37' W 102
Freeport, Me., U.S. 43°51' N, 70°7' W 94
Freeport, Mo., U.S. 42°17' N, 89°37' W 94
Freeport, N.Y., U.S. 40°39' N, 73°35' W 104
Freeport, Tex., U.S. 28°55' N, 95°22' W 103
Freer, Tex., U.S. 27°51' N, 98°38' W 92
Freesoil, Mich., U.S. 44°6' N, 86°13' W 102
Freetown, Ind., U.S. 38°58' N, 86°7' W 102
Freetown, Sierra Leone 8°24' N, 13°21' W 222
Freezeout Mountain, Oreg., U.S. 43°36' N, 117°40' W 90
Fregenal de la Sierra, Sp. 38°10' N, 6°40' W 164
Freguesia do Andirá, Braz. 2°55' S, 56°60' W 130
Fréhel, Cap, Fr. 48°29' N, 2°40' W 150
Freiburg, Ger. 48°0' N, 7°51' E 152
Freienohl, Ger. 51°22' N, 8°9' E 167
Freila, Sp. 37°31' N, 2°54' W 164
Freising, Ger. 48°24' N, 11°44' E 156
Freistadt, Aust. 48°30' N, 14°29' E 152
Fremont, Calif., U.S. 37°33' N, 121°59' W 100
Fremont, Ind., U.S. 41°43' N, 84°56' W 102
Fremont, Mich., U.S. 43°26' N, 85°57' W 102
Fremont, Nebr., U.S. 41°24' N, 96°30' W 90
Fremont, Ohio, U.S. 41°20' N, 83°8' W 102
Fremont Mountains, Oreg., U.S. 42°49' N, 121°27' W 90
Fremont Peak, Calif., U.S. 36°46' N, 121°35' W 100
Fremont Peak, Wyo., U.S. 43°6' N, 109°42' W 90
Fremont, river, Utah, U.S. 38°17' N, 111°42' W 80
French Camp, Miss., U.S. 33°16' N, 89°24' W 103
French Cays see Plana Cays, North Atlantic Ocean 22°41' N, 73°33' W 116
French Guiana, Fr. 3°47' N, 53°56' W 130
French Lick, Ind., U.S. 38°32' N, 86°37' W 102
French Pass, N.Z. 40°59' S, 173°50' E 240
French Polynesia, Fr. 15°4' S, 145°29' W 238
French River, Can. 46°1' N, 80°35' W 94
French Settlement, La., U.S. 30°17' N, 90°49' W 103
Frenchman Butte, Can. 53°35' N, 109°38' W 108
Frenchman Flat, Nev., U.S. 36°47' N, 115°59' W 101
Frenchman, river, Can. 49°30' N, 108°41' W 90
Frenchville, Me., U.S. 47°16' N, 68°23' W 94
Freren, Ger. 52°29' N, 7°33' E 163
Fresco, Côte d'Ivoire 5°5' N, 5°32' W 222
Freshfield, Cape, Antarctica 68°29' S, 150°37' E 248
Freshfield Icefield, Can. 51°43' N, 117°41' W 90
Fresnillo, Mex. 23°9' N, 102°53' W 114
Fresno, Calif., U.S. 36°44' N, 119°48' W 100
Fresno Reservoir, lake, Mont., U.S. 48°43' N, 110°51' W 90
Fresno Slough, river, Calif., U.S. 36°28' N, 120°4' W 101
Fresnoy-le-Grand, Fr. 49°56' N, 3°25' E 163
Freudenberg, Ger. 50°53' N, 7°53' E 167
Frévent, Fr. 50°16' N, 2°17' E 163
Freyre, Arg. 31°10' S, 62°6' W 139
Fria, Guinea 10°22' N, 13°36' W 222
Fria, Cape, Namibia 18°27' S, 12°4' E 220
Friant, Calif., U.S. 36°59' N, 119°43' W 100
Frías, Arg. 28°39' S, 65°7' W 132
Fribourg, Switz. 46°48' N, 7°8' E 167
Friday Creek, river, Can. 49°44' N, 82°59' W 94
Friday Harbour, Wash., U.S. 48°31' N, 123°2' W 100
Fridtjof Nansen, Mount, Antarctica 85°17' S, 165°5' W 248
Friedberg, Aust. 47°26' N, 16°3' E 168
Friedberg, Ger. 50°19' N, 8°45' E 167
Friedland, Ger. 51°25' N, 9°55' E 167
Frielendorf, Ger. 50°58' N, 9°20' E 167
Friend, Nebr., U.S. 40°38' N, 97°18' W 90
Friendship, Wis., U.S. 43°58' N, 89°49' W 102
Friguiagbé, Guinea 9°57' N, 12°58' W 222
Frinton on Sea, U.K. 51°50' N, 1°15' E 162
Friona, Tex., U.S. 34°37' N, 102°43' W 92
Frisco, Colo., U.S. 39°33' N, 106°6' W 90
Frisco City, Ala., U.S. 31°25' N, 87°24' W 103
Frisco Peak, Utah, U.S. 38°30' N, 113°21' W 90
Frissell, Mount, Conn., U.S. 42°2' N, 73°30' W 104
Fritzlar, Ger. 51°8' N, 9°17' E 167
Friuli-Venezia Giulia, adm. division, It. 46°11' N, 12°48' E 167
Froan, islands, Norwegian Sea 64°11' N, 8°31' E 152
Frobisher Bay 62°26' N, 67°19' W 246
Frobisher Lake, Can. 56°36' N, 109°20' W 108
Frog Lake, Can. 53°50' N, 110°42' W 108
Frog, river, Can. 58°16' N, 127°1' W 108
Frohavet 63°59' N, 8°38' E 152
Frolovo, Russ. 49°45' N, 43°41' E 158
Fromberg, Mont., U.S. 45°22' N, 108°55' W 90
Frombork, Pol. 54°20' N, 19°40' E 166
Frome, U.K. 51°13' N, 2°20' W 162
Fromenteau, Lac, lake, Can. 51°24' N, 74°5' W 111
Front Range, North America 39°3' N, 105°43' W 90
Front Royal, Va., U.S. 38°55' N, 78°13' W 94
Fronteiras, Braz. 7°6' S, 40°37' W 132
Frontenac, Kans., U.S. 37°26' N, 94°41' W 94
Frontera, Arg. 31°31' S, 62°1' W 139
Frontera, Mex. 18°31' N, 92°39' W 115
Frontera, Mex. 26°56' N, 101°28' W 112
Frontera, Punta, Mex. 18°38' N, 93°30' W 115
Fronteras, Mex. 30°56' N, 109°33' W 92
Frontier, Wyo., U.S. 41°50' N, 110°33' W 90
Frontignan, Fr. 43°27' N, 3°44' E 164
Frostburg, Md., U.S. 39°39' N, 78°56' W 94
Frostproof, Fla., U.S. 27°44' N, 81°32' W 105
Frotet, Lac, lake, Can. 50°38' N, 75°16' W 110
Frövi, Nor. 59°27' N, 15°20' E 152
Fruita, Colo., U.S. 39°9' N, 108°44' W 90
Fruitdale, Ala., U.S. 31°19' N, 88°24' W 103
Fruitport, Mich., U.S. 43°7' N, 86°10' W 102
Fruitville, Fla., U.S. 27°21' N, 82°27' W 105
Fruška Gora, Serb. and Mont. 45°10' N, 19°19' E 168
Frutal, Braz. 20°3' S, 48°55' W 138
Frutigen, Switz. 46°36' N, 7°38' E 167
Fryeburg, Me., U.S. 44°0' N, 70°59' W 104
Fu, river, China 28°10' N, 116°2' E 198
Fua Mulaku, island, Maldives 0°27' N, 73°24' E 188
Fu'an, China 27°11' N, 119°40' E 198
Fubo, Angola 5°28' S, 12°23' E 218
Fucecchio, It. 43°44' N, 10°48' E 167
Fuchs Dome, peak, Antarctica 80°38' S, 29°4' W 248
Fuchū, Japan 34°35' N, 133°14' E 201
Fudong, China 42°34' N, 129°12' E 200
Fuego Mountain, Oreg., U.S. 42°37' N, 121°32' W 90
Fuente, Mex. 28°38' N, 100°33' W 92
Fuente de Cantos, Sp. 38°14' N, 6°19' W 164
Fuente el Fresno, Sp. 39°13' N, 3°47' W 164
Fuente Obejuna, Sp. 38°15' N, 5°26' W 164
Fuente-Álamo, Sp. 38°41' N, 1°26' W 164
Fuenterrebollo, Sp. 41°17' N, 3°56' W 164
Fuentes de Andalucía, Sp. 37°28' N, 5°22' W 164
Fuentes de Ebro, Sp. 41°30' N, 0°40' E 164
Fuentes-Claras, Sp. 40°51' N, 1°19' W 164
Fuerteventura, island, Sp. 28°46' N, 15°30' W 214
Fuga, island, Philippines 18°56' N, 121°27' E 198
Fugou, China 34°1' N, 114°24' E 198
Fugu, China 39°3' N, 111°2' E 198
Fuhai, China 47°8' N, 87°28' E 184
Fuji, peak, Japan 35°20' N, 138°41' E 201
Fujian, adm. division, China 25°27' N, 116°57' E 198
Fujieda, Japan 34°52' N, 138°15' E 201
Fuji-Hakone-Izu National Park, Japan 34°42' N, 138°36' E 201
Fujisawa, Japan 35°19' N, 139°30' E 201
Fujiyoshida, Japan 35°27' N, 138°48' E 201
Fûka, Egypt 31°3' N, 27°55' E 180
Fukang, China 44°8' N, 87°55' E 184
Fukuchiyama, Japan 35°15' N, 135°6' E 201
Fukui, Japan 36°3' N, 136°14' E 201
Fukui, adm. division, Japan 35°49' N, 136°3' E 201
Fukuoka, Japan 33°35' N, 130°24' E 200
Fukuoka, adm. division, Japan 33°29' N, 130°11' E 201
Fukushima, Japan 37°45' N, 140°26' E 201
Fukushima, adm. division, Japan 37°20' N, 139°16' E 201
Fukushima, Mount, Antarctica 71°18' S, 35°0' E 248
Fukuyama, Japan 34°29' N, 133°22' E 201
Fulacunda, Guinea-Bissau 11°46' N, 15°11' W 222
Fulbourn, U.K. 52°10' N, 0°13' E 162
Fulda, Ger. 50°33' N, 9°41' E 167
Fulda, Minn., U.S. 43°51' N, 95°36' W 90
Fulda, river, Ger. 51°12' N, 9°28' E 167
Fulford Harbour, Can. 48°45' N, 123°27' W 100
Fuling, China 29°40' N, 107°19' E 198
Fullerton, Calif., U.S. 33°52' N, 117°56' W 101
Fullerton, Nebr., U.S. 41°21' N, 97°59' W 90
Fülöpszállás, Hung. 46°49' N, 19°14' E 168
Fulton, Ala., U.S. 31°47' N, 87°43' W 103
Fulton, Ill., U.S. 41°51' N, 90°9' W 102
Fulton, Ky., U.S. 36°31' N, 88°52' W 96
Fulton, Miss., U.S. 34°15' N, 88°24' W 96
Fulton, Mo., U.S. 38°50' N, 91°58' W 94
Fulton, N.Y., U.S. 43°19' N, 76°25' W 110
Fulufjället, peak, Nor. 61°34' N, 12°29' E 152
Fūman, Iran 37°14' N, 49°18' E 195
Fumane, Mozambique 24°27' S, 33°58' E 227
Fumel, Fr. 44°28' N, 0°56' E 150
Funabashi, Japan 35°41' N, 140°0' E 201
Funafuti, Tuvalu 8°42' S, 178°24' E 238
Funafuti (Fongafale), Tuvalu 9°0' S, 179°0' E 241
Funafuti, island, Tuvalu 9°0' S, 179°0' E 241
Funan, China 32°38' N, 115°35' E 198
Funan Gaba, Eth. 4°22' N, 37°59' E 224
Funan see Fushun, China 41°44' N, 123°53' E 200
Funan see Fusui, China 22°37' N, 107°54' E 198
Funäsdalen, Nor. 62°32' N, 12°29' E 152
Funauke, Japan 24°14' N, 123°43' E 198
Funchal, Port. 32°34' N, 17°9' W 207
Fundación, Col. 10°32' N, 74°12' W 136
Fundão, Port. 40°8' N, 7°31' W 150
Fundong, Cameroon 6°14' N, 10°10' E 222
Fundy, Bay of 45°6' N, 66°10' W 111
Fundy National Park, Can. 45°26' N, 65°42' W 111
Funeral Mountains, Calif., U.S. 36°44' N, 116°53' W 101
Funeral Peak, Calif., U.S. 36°5' N, 116°40' W 101
Funhalouro, Mozambique 23°2' S, 34°24' E 227
Funing, China 23°35' N, 105°37' E 198
Funtua, Nig. 11°29' N, 7°19' E 222
Fuping, China 34°47' N, 109°9' E 198
Fuqing, China 25°43' N, 119°23' E 198
Fuquan, China 26°44' N, 107°30' E 198
Furancungo, Mozambique 14°55' S, 33°37' E 224
Furawiya, spring, Sudan 15°20' N, 23°41' E 226
Furillen, island, Sw. 57°41' N, 19°2' E 166
Furmanov, Russ. 57°16' N, 41°5' E 154
Furnas Dam, Braz. 20°50' S, 46°15' W 132
Furneaux Group, islands, Flinders Island 39°48' S, 148°30' E 230
Furnes see Veurne, Belg. 51°4' N, 2°40' E 150
Furqlus, Syr. 34°36' N, 37°4' E 194
Fürstenau, Ger. 52°31' N, 7°41' E 163
Fürstenfeld, Aust. 47°3' N, 16°5' E 168
Fürth, Ger. 49°27' N, 10°59' E 152
Furudal, Nor. 61°10' N, 15°8' E 152
Furukawa, Japan 38°35' N, 140°57' E 201
Furukawa, Japan 36°14' N, 137°11' E 201
Furusund, Sw. 59°40' N, 18°52' E 166
Furuvik, Nor. 60°38' N, 17°17' E 152
Fuscaldo, It. 39°25' N, 16°2' E 156
Fuse, Japan 36°19' N, 133°21' E 201
Fushan, China 37°30' N, 121°13' E 198
Fushimi Lake, Can. 49°47' N, 84°21' W 94
Fushun, China 29°13' N, 104°56' E 198
Fushun (Funan), China 41°44' N, 123°53' E 200
Fusio, Switz. 46°27' N, 8°38' E 167
Fusong, China 42°16' N, 127°18' E 200
Fusui (Funan), China 22°37' N, 107°54' E 198
Futaleufú, Chile 43°12' S, 71°55' W 134
Fuveau, Fr. 43°26' N, 5°33' E 150
Fuwa, Egypt 31°12' N, 30°32' E 180
Fuxian, China 36°0' N, 109°20' E 198
Fuxin, China 42°4' N, 121°39' E 198
Fuya, Japan 38°30' N, 139°32' E 201
Fuyang, China 32°52' N, 115°46' E 198
Fuyang, river, China 37°46' N, 115°57' E 198
Fuyu, China 45°12' N, 124°53' E 198
Fuyu, China 47°46' N, 124°28' E 198
Fuyun, China 47°3' N, 89°25' E 184
Füzesabony, Hung. 47°45' N, 20°26' E 168
Fuzhou, China 26°8' N, 119°20' E 198
Füzuli, Azerb. 39°34' N, 47°6' E 195
Fylingdales Moor, site, U.K. 54°21' N, 0°38' E 162

G

Ga, Ghana 9°47' N, 2°30' W 222
Gaal Goble, Somalia 9°50' N, 49°50' E 216
Gaalkacyo (Galcaio), Somalia 6°44' N, 47°29' E 218
Gabakly, Turkm. 39°48' N, 62°31' E 180
Gabarus, Cape, Can. 45°41' N, 60°43' W 111
Gabasawa, Nig. 12°9' N, 8°54' E 222
Gabatit, spring, Sudan 20°28' N, 35°49' E 182
Gabbac, Raas, Somalia 7°37' N, 50°3' E 218
Gabbs, Nev., U.S. 38°52' N, 117°57' W 90
Gabbs Valley, Nev., U.S. 38°54' N, 118°18' W 90
Gabbs Valley Range, Nev., U.S. 38°37' N, 118°15' W 90
Gabela, Angola 10°50' S, 14°21' E 220
Gabela, Bosn. and Herzg. 43°3' N, 17°39' E 168
Gabes, Tun. 33°53' N, 10°4' E 214
Gabes, Gulf of 34°9' N, 9°36' E 156
Gabilan Range, Calif., U.S. 36°41' N, 121°36' W 100
Gabon 0°41' N, 11°20' E 218
Gaborone, Botswana 24°42' S, 25°45' E 227
Gabras, Sudan 10°16' N, 26°15' E 224
Gabriel, Lac, lake, Can. 49°15' N, 74°57' W 94
Gabriel Vera, Bol. 19°15' S, 65°54' W 137
Gabriels, N.Y., U.S. 44°25' N, 74°12' W 104
Gabro, Eth. 6°16' N, 43°14' E 218
Gabrovo, Bulg. 42°52' N, 25°17' E 156
Gabrovo, adm. division, Bulg. 42°54' N, 24°51' E 156
Gabu, Dem. Rep. of the Congo 3°22' N, 27°2' E 224
Gach Sārān, oil field, Iran 30°12' N, 50°51' E 196
Gackle, N. Dak., U.S. 46°35' N, 99°9' W 90
Gacko, Bosn. and Herzg. 43°10' N, 18°31' E 168
Gada, river, Dem. Rep. of the Congo 3°21' N, 28°30' E 224
Gädäbäy, Azerb. 40°34' N, 45°48' E 195
Gadamai, Sudan 17°5' N, 36°4' E 182
Gadarwara, India 22°53' N, 78°46' E 197
Gadifuri, island, Maldives 2°25' N, 72°1' E 188
Gádor, Sierra de, Sp. 36°55' N, 3°1' W 164
Gádoros, Hung. 46°40' N, 20°36' E 168
Gadra Road, India 25°44' N, 70°38' E 186
Gadrut, Azerb. 39°30' N, 47°0' E 195
Gadsden, Ariz., U.S. 32°32' N, 114°46' W 101
Gadzi, Cen. Af. Rep. 4°46' N, 16°41' E 218
Găeşti, Rom. 44°44' N, 25°18' E 156
Gafatîn, Gezâir, islands, Red Sea 26°59' N, 34°2' E 180
Gaferut, island, F.S.M. 9°22' N, 144°22' E 192
Gafsa, Tun. 34°24' N, 8°48' E 156
Gagal, Chad 9°1' N, 15°9' E 216
Gagarin, Russ. 55°32' N, 35°1' E 154
Gagetown, Mich., U.S. 43°38' N, 83°15' W 102
Gagino, Russ. 55°13' N, 45°6' E 154
Gagliano del Capo, It. 39°50' N, 18°21' E 156
Gagnoa, Côte d'Ivoire 6°2' N, 5°56' W 222
Gagra, Ga. 43°21' N, 40°15' E 195
Gagshor, Russ. 60°47' N, 50°11' E 154
Gahnpa, Liberia 7°5' N, 8°60' W 222
Gaibandha, Bangladesh 25°18' N, 89°29' E 197
Gaillefontaine, Fr. 49°39' N, 1°35' E 163
Gaillimh see Galway, Ire. 53°16' N, 9°3' W 150
Gaillon, Fr. 49°9' N, 1°18' E 163
Gaimán, Arg. 43°15' S, 65°30' W 134
Gainesville, Ala., U.S. 32°47' N, 88°10' W 103
Gainesville, Fla., U.S. 29°38' N, 82°20' W 105
Gainesville, Ga., U.S. 34°17' N, 83°50' W 96
Gainesville, Mo., U.S. 36°35' N, 92°26' W 96
Gainesville, Tex., U.S. 33°35' N, 97°8' W 92
Gainsborough, Can. 49°10' N, 101°27' W 90
Gainsborough, U.K. 53°24' N, 0°47' E 162
Gaissane, region, Europe 69°47' N, 26°1' E 152
Gaixian, China 40°24' N, 122°24' E 198
Gajdobra, Serb. and Mont. 45°20' N, 19°27' E 168
Gajiram, Nig. 12°32' N, 13°12' E 216
Gakdul, spring, Sudan 17°36' N, 32°51' E 182
Gakkel Ridge, Arctic Ocean 86°39' N, 68°19' E 255
Gakona, Alas., U.S. 62°16' N, 145°16' W 98
Gakuch, Pak. 36°9' N, 73°45' E 186
Gal Tardo, Somalia 3°34' N, 46°0' E 218
Galadi, Eth. 5°57' N, 41°34' E 224
Galadi, Nig. 13°0' N, 6°24' E 222
Galahad, Can. 52°31' N, 111°57' W 108
Galaţi, adm. division, Rom. 45°48' N, 27°19' E 156
Galâla el Qiblîya, Gebel el, peak, Egypt 28°46' N, 32°22' E 180
Galán, Cerro, peak, Arg. 25°57' S, 66°60' W 132
Galana, river, Kenya 3°12' S, 39°14' E 224
Galaosiyo, Uzb. 39°52' N, 64°29' E 197
Galápagos Fracture Zone, South Pacific Ocean 3°38' S, 139°34' W 252
Galápagos Islands (Archipiélago de Colón), Ecuador 0°13' N, 92°2' W 130
Galápagos Rift, North Pacific Ocean 1°22' N, 94°53' W 252
Galápagos Rise, South Pacific Ocean 15°51' S, 94°41' W 252
Galateia, Northern Cyprus 35°25' N, 34°4' E 194
Galaţi, Rom. 45°27' N, 28°3' E 156
Galatxo, Punta del, Sp. 40°24' N, 0°32' E 164
Galax, Va., U.S. 36°40' N, 80°56' W 96
Galcaio see Gaalkacyo, Somalia 6°44' N, 47°29' E 218
Galdhøpiggen, peak, Nor. 61°37' N, 8°9' E 152
Galé, Mali 12°37' N, 9°30' W 222
Galeana, Mex. 30°6' N, 107°38' W 92
Galeana, Mex. 24°49' N, 100°4' W 114
Galegu, Sudan 12°33' N, 35°1' E 182
Galena, Alas., U.S. 64°37' N, 156°56' W 98
Galena, Kans., U.S. 37°3' N, 94°39' W 96
Galena, Mo., U.S. 42°24' N, 90°26' W 94
Galena Peak, Idaho, U.S. 43°52' N, 114°40' W 90
Galera, Sp. 37°43' N, 2°33' W 164
Galera Point, Trinidad and Tobago 10°50' N, 61°24' W 116
Galera, Punta, Chile 40°4' S, 75°3' W 134
Galera, Punta, Ecua. 0°48' N, 81°14' W 130
Galera, river, Braz. 14°22' S, 60°3' W 132
Galesburg, Mich., U.S. 42°17' N, 85°25' W 102
Galesburg, Mo., U.S. 40°57' N, 90°22' W 94
Galeton, Can. 51°8' N, 80°56' W 110
Galeton, Pa., U.S. 41°44' N, 77°39' W 94
Galgate, U.K. 53°59' N, 2°48' W 162
Gali, Ga. 42°36' N, 41°43' E 195
Galiano Island, Can. 48°56' N, 123°26' W 100
Galich, Russ. 58°20' N, 42°24' E 154
Galicia, adm. division, Sp. 42°36' N, 8°44' W 150
Galičnik, Maced. 41°35' N, 20°39' E 168
Galim, Cameroon 7°3' N, 12°27' E 218
Galinoporni, Northern Cyprus 35°31' N, 34°18' E 194
Galio, Liberia 5°42' N, 7°34' W 222
Galion, Ohio, U.S. 40°42' N, 82°48' W 102
Galkino, Kaz. 52°20' N, 78°13' E 184
Galla, Mount, Antarctica 75°49' S, 125°18' W 248
Gallanito, Nor. 68°53' N, 22°50' E 152
G'allaorol, Uzb. 40°0' N, 67°34' E 197
Gallarate, It. 45°39' N, 8°47' E 167
Gallardon, Fr. 48°31' N, 1°41' E 163
Gallatin, Mo., U.S. 39°54' N, 93°58' W 94
Gallatin, Tenn., U.S. 36°23' N, 86°27' W 96
Gallatin Peak, Mont., U.S. 45°20' N, 111°26' W 90
Gallatin Range, Mont., U.S. 45°24' N, 111°13' W 90
Galle, Sri Lanka 6°8' N, 80°11' E 173
Gallegos, Cabo, Chile 46°30' S, 77°9' W 134
Gallegos, river, Arg. 51°60' S, 72°10' W 134
Galliano, La., U.S. 29°26' N, 90°18' W 103
Galliate, It. 45°28' N, 8°40' E 167
Gallinas, Punta, Col. 12°27' N, 71°42' W 136
Gallipoli, It. 40°3' N, 17°59' E 156
Gallipoli see Gelibolu, Turk. 40°25' N, 26°38' E 156
Gällivare, Nor. 67°8' N, 20°39' E 152
Gallman, Miss., U.S. 31°55' N, 90°24' W 103
Gällö, Nor. 62°55' N, 15°11' E 152
Gallo, Capo, It. 38°15' N, 12°42' E 156
Gallo Mountains, N. Mex., U.S. 34°1' N, 108°39' W 92
Gallo, river, Sp. 40°43' N, 2°3' W 150
Gallup, N. Mex., U.S. 35°30' N, 108°44' W 92
Gallur, Sp. 41°51' N, 1°19' W 164
Galma Galla, spring, Kenya 1°14' S, 40°49' E 224
Galole, Kenya 1°27' S, 40°0' E 224
Galt, Calif., U.S. 38°14' N, 121°19' W 100
Galtat Zemmour, Western Sahara 25°9' N, 12°24' W 214
Galten, Nor. 70°42' N, 22°44' E 152
Galtymore, peak, Ire. 52°21' N, 8°19' W 150
Galu, Dem. Rep. of the Congo 11°22' S, 26°37' E 224
Galula, Tanzania 8°38' S, 33°2' E 224
Galva, Ill., U.S. 41°9' N, 90°3' W 102
Galveston, Tex., U.S. 29°16' N, 94°49' W 103
Galveston Bay 29°22' N, 95°48' W 80
Galveston Island, Tex., U.S. 29°4' N, 94°58' W 103
Gálvez, Arg. 32°3' S, 61°13' W 139
Galwa, Nepal 29°39' N, 81°53' E 197
Galway (Gaillimh), Ire. 53°16' N, 9°3' W 150
Gam, river, Vietnam 22°5' N, 105°11' E 202
Gamba, China 28°16' N, 88°31' E 197
Gamba, Gabon 2°43' S, 10°0' E 218
Gambaga, Ghana 10°32' N, 0°27' E 222
Gambēla, Eth. 8°14' N, 34°35' E 224
Gambela National Park, Eth. 7°42' N, 33°59' E 224
Gambell, Alas., U.S. 63°40' N, 171°50' W 98
Gambia 13°23' N, 16°0' W 214
Gambia, river, Gambia 13°59' N, 28°49' W 222
Gambia Plain, North Atlantic Ocean 12°33' N, 27°53' W 253
Gambie, river, Senegal 12°54' N, 13°7' W 222
Gambier, Ohio, U.S. 40°22' N, 82°23' W 102
Gambier, Îles, islands, South Pacific Ocean 22°42' S, 138°12' W 238
Gambier Island, Can. 49°32' N, 123°36' W 100
Gambier Islands, Great Australian Bight 35°21' S, 136°39' E 230
Gamboma, Congo 1°54' S, 15°51' E 218
Gamboula, Cen. Af. Rep. 4°10' N, 15°12' E 218
Gamdou, Niger 13°27' N, 10°3' E 222
Gamlakarleby see Kokkola, Fin. 63°49' N, 23°5' E 152
Gamleby, Nor. 57°54' N, 16°23' E 152
Gamma, oil field, Azerb. 39°43' N, 49°19' E 195
Gammelstad, Nor. 65°37' N, 22°1' E 152
Gamoep, S. Af. 29°55' S, 18°23' E 227
Gamova, Mys, Russ. 42°24' N, 131°12' E 200
Gamph, Slieve (Ox Mountains, The), Ire. 54°2' N, 9°28' W 150
Gampo, S. Korea 35°47' N, 129°32' E 200
Gamsby, river, Can. 53°5' N, 127°21' W 108
Gamud, peak, Eth. 4°1' N, 38°3' E 224
Gamyshlyja, Turkm. 38°21' N, 54°0' E 180
Gan, Fr. 43°14' N, 0°23' E 164
Gan Gan, Arg. 42°29' S, 68°11' W 134
Gan, island, Maldives 0°2' N, 73°22' E 188
Gan, river, China 26°29' N, 114°32' E 198
Gan, river, China 49°20' N, 124°41' E 198
Ganado, Ariz., U.S. 35°42' N, 109°32' W 92
Ganado, Tex., U.S. 29°2' N, 96°31' W 96
Ganāveh, Iran 29°36' N, 50°29' E 196
Gäncä, Azerb. 40°41' N, 46°20' E 195
Gandajika, Dem. Rep. of the Congo 6°46' S, 23°58' E 224
Gander, Can. 48°56' N, 54°29' W 106
Gander, river, Can. 48°55' N, 54°53' W 111
Gandhidham, India 23°5' N, 70°8' E 186
Gandhinagar, India 23°19' N, 72°38' E 186
Gandi, Nig. 12°55' N, 5°48' E 222
Gandía, Sp. 38°57' N, 0°11' E 164

Gandino, It. 45°49′ N, 9°54′ E 167
Gandole, Nig. 8°24′ N, 11°37′ E 222
Gandu, Braz. 13°46′ S, 39°30′ W 138
Gang, island, Maldives 1°34′ N, 73°29′ E 188
Ganga (Ganges), river, India 26°9′ N, 81°17′ E 190
Gangala na Bodio, Dem. Rep. of the Congo 3°38′ N, 29°9′ E 224
Ganganagar, India 29°56′ N, 73°54′ E 186
Gangdaba, Tchabal, Cameroon 7°23′ N, 11°49′ E 218
Gangdisê Shan, China 30°58′ N, 83°13′ E 197
Gangelt, Ger. 50°59′ N, 5°59′ E 167
Ganges Fan, Bay of Bengal 14°34′ N, 84°35′ E 254
Ganges, river, India 25°40′ N, 81°12′ E 197
Ganges see Ganga, river, India 26°9′ N, 81°17′ E 190
Ganggyeong, S. Korea 36°9′ N, 127°3′ E 200
Ganghwa, S. Korea 37°44′ N, 126°29′ E 200
Gangi, It. 37°47′ N, 14°12′ E 156
Gangjin, S. Korea 34°37′ N, 126°47′ E 200
Gangneung, S. Korea 37°45′ N, 128°53′ E 200
Gangtok, India 27°23′ N, 88°35′ E 197
Gangu, China 34°43′ N, 105°18′ E 198
Ganhe, China 50°43′ N, 123°14′ E 238
Gania, Guinea 11°1′ N, 10°21′ W 222
Ganjam, India 19°25′ N, 85°3′ E 188
Gannan, China 47°53′ N, 123°31′ E 198
Gannat, Fr. 46°5′ N, 3°12′ E 150
Gannett Peak, Wyo., U.S. 43°10′ N, 109°45′ W 90
Ganongga see Ranongga, island, Solomon Islands 8°5′ S, 156°30′ E 242
Ganquan, China 36°19′ N, 109°25′ E 198
Ganseong, S. Korea 38°22′ N, 128°27′ E 200
Gansu, adm. division, China 38°17′ N, 101°53′ E 188
Gantgaw, Myanmar 22°12′ N, 94°9′ E 188
Ganwo, Nig. 11°11′ N, 4°37′ E 222
Ganyushkino, Kaz. 46°36′ N, 49°16′ E 158
Ganzhou, China 25°56′ N, 114°57′ E 198
Gao, Mali 16°16′ N, 1°59′ W 222
Gaolan, China 36°22′ N, 103°56′ E 198
Gaoping, China 35°46′ N, 112°53′ E 198
Gaoua, Burkina Faso 10°19′ N, 3°12′ W 222
Gaoual, Guinea 11°46′ N, 13°16′ W 222
Gaoyang, China 38°42′ N, 115°49′ E 198
Gaoyou Hu, lake, China 32°42′ N, 118°40′ E 198
Gap, Fr. 44°32′ N, 6°4′ E 150
Gapan, Philippines 15°19′ N, 120°56′ E 203
Gapyeong, S. Korea 37°49′ N, 127°31′ E 200
Gar, China 32°11′ N, 79°57′ E 188
Gara, Hung. 46°1′ N, 19°3′ E 168
Garabogaz Aylagy, lake, Turkm. 41°4′ N, 51°40′ E 160
Garabogazköl, Turkm. 41°2′ N, 52°55′ E 158
Garacad, Somalia 6°55′ N, 49°23′ E 218
Garachiné, Pan. 8°3′ N, 78°23′ W 115
Garadag, Somalia 9°26′ N, 46°55′ E 216
Garadase, Eth. 5°4′ N, 38°9′ E 224
Garagum, Turkm. 37°50′ N, 63°24′ E 197
Garamba National Park, Dem. Rep. of the Congo 4°27′ N, 28°50′ E 224
Garamba, river, Dem. Rep. of the Congo 3°44′ N, 29°17′ E 224
Garanhuns, Braz. 8°52′ S, 36°31′ W 132
Garapuava, Braz. 16°6′ S, 46°37′ W 138
Garavuti, Taj. 37°31′ N, 68°25′ E 184
Garawe, Liberia 4°37′ N, 7°53′ W 222
Garba Tula, Kenya 0°29′ N, 38°32′ E 224
Garbahaarrey, Somalia 3°7′ N, 42°11′ E 224
Garberville, Calif., U.S. 40°6′ N, 123°48′ W 82
Garbyang, India 30°9′ N, 80°49′ E 197
Garça, Braz. 22°14′ S, 49°43′ W 138
Garças, river, Braz. 8°40′ S, 40°29′ W 132
García de la Cadena, Mex. 21°9′ N, 103°28′ W 114
Garcias, Braz. 20°36′ S, 52°14′ W 138
Garden City, Kans., U.S. 37°58′ N, 100°53′ W 90
Garden City, N.Y., U.S. 40°43′ N, 73°38′ W 104
Garden Creek, Can. 58°43′ N, 113°56′ W 108
Garden Lake, Can. 49°28′ N, 90°15′ W 94
Garden of the Gods, site, Hawai'i, U.S. 20°52′ N, 157°2′ W 99
Garden Peninsula, Mich., U.S. 45°49′ N, 86°42′ W 94
Garden, river, Can. 46°37′ N, 84°5′ W 94
Gardiner, Me., U.S. 44°12′ N, 69°47′ W 104
Gardiner, Mont., U.S. 45°2′ N, 110°42′ W 90
Gardiner, Oreg., U.S. 43°43′ N, 124°6′ W 90
Gardiner Dam, Can. 51°2′ N, 107°12′ W 90
Gardiner, Mount, Austral. 22°15′ S, 132°27′ E 230
Gardiners Island, N.Y., U.S. 41°4′ N, 72°5′ W 104
Gardiz, Afghan. 33°35′ N, 69°12′ E 186
Gardner, Ill., U.S. 41°11′ N, 88°18′ W 102
Gardner, Mass., U.S. 42°34′ N, 71°60′ W 104
Gardner Canal 53°19′ N, 128°44′ W 108
Gardner Pinnacles, Hawai'i, U.S. 24°57′ N, 169°23′ W 99
Gárdony, Hung. 47°12′ N, 18°38′ E 168
Gares see Puente la Reina, Sp. 42°39′ N, 1°49′ W 164
Garešnica, Croatia 45°33′ N, 16°56′ E 168
Garf Ḥusein, ruin(s), Egypt 23°12′ N, 32°42′ E 182
Garfield Mountain, Mont., U.S. 44°29′ N, 112°40′ W 90
Garfield Peak, Wyo., U.S. 42°42′ N, 107°21′ W 90
Gargan, Mont, peak, Fr. 45°36′ N, 1°37′ E 165
Gargano, Promontorio del, It. 41°45′ N, 15°55′ E 168
Gargano, Testa del, It. 41°48′ N, 16°12′ E 168
Gargantua, Cape, Can. 47°34′ N, 85°38′ W 94
Gargouna, Mali 15°59′ N, 0°14′ E 222
Gargždai, Lith. 55°43′ N, 21°23′ E 166
Garhakota, India 23°45′ N, 79°10′ E 197
Gari, Russ. 59°26′ N, 62°21′ E 154
Garibaldi, Braz. 29°16′ S, 51°32′ W 139
Garibaldi, Can. 49°57′ N, 123°9′ W 100
Garibaldi, Mount, Can. 49°49′ N, 123°2′ W 100
Garibaldi, Paso, pass, Arg. 54°35′ S, 67°38′ W 134
Garies, S. Af. 30°34′ S, 17°58′ E 227
Garissa, Kenya 0°30′ N, 39°39′ E 224
Garitz, Ger. 50°11′ N, 10°2′ E 167
Garko, Nig. 11°37′ N, 8°48′ E 222
Garland, Ark., U.S. 33°20′ N, 93°44′ W 103
Garland, Tex., U.S. 32°52′ N, 96°39′ W 96
Garlasco, It. 45°11′ N, 8°54′ E 167
Garliava, Lith. 54°49′ N, 23°51′ E 166
Garlin, Fr. 43°33′ N, 0°17′ E 150
Garmsār, Iran 35°13′ N, 52°15′ E 180
Garner, Iowa, U.S. 43°5′ N, 93°35′ W 94
Garnet Range, Mont., U.S. 46°51′ N, 113°35′ W 90
Garnett, Kans., U.S. 38°15′ N, 95°14′ W 94
Garonne, river, Fr. 44°36′ N, 0°60′ E 143
Garopaba, Braz. 28°4′ S, 48°40′ W 138
Garou, Lac, lake, Mali 16°2′ N, 3°4′ W 222
Garoua, Cameroon 9°18′ N, 13°22′ E 216
Garoua, Niger 13°53′ N, 13°9′ E 216
Garoua Boulaï, Cameroon 5°48′ N, 14°34′ E 218
Garré, Arg. 36°34′ S, 62°35′ W 139
Garrett, Ind., U.S. 41°20′ N, 85°9′ W 102
Garrettsville, Ohio, U.S. 41°16′ N, 81°6′ W 102
Garrison, Ky., U.S. 38°35′ N, 83°10′ W 102
Garrison, N. Dak., U.S. 47°38′ N, 101°26′ W 90
Garrison, Tex., U.S. 31°49′ N, 94°30′ W 103
Garrison, Utah, U.S. 38°55′ N, 114°2′ W 92
Garrucha, Sp. 37°10′ N, 1°50′ W 164
Garruchos, Braz. 28°16′ S, 55°41′ W 139
Garry Lake, Can. 65°58′ N, 102°24′ W 106
Garrygala, Turkm. 38°27′ N, 56°17′ E 180
Garsen, Kenya 2°18′ S, 40°5′ E 224
Garsila, Sudan 12°21′ N, 23°7′ E 216
Garson Lake, Can. 56°14′ N, 110°41′ W 108
Garssen, Ger. 52°39′ N, 10°7′ E 150
Garstang, U.K. 53°54′ N, 2°47′ W 162
Gartow, Ger. 53°1′ N, 11°27′ E 152
Garub, Namibia 26°38′ S, 16°5′ E 227
Garvão, Port. 37°42′ N, 8°21′ W 150
Garwa, India 24°9′ N, 83°48′ E 197
Gary, Ind., U.S. 41°34′ N, 87°22′ W 102
Gary, Tex., U.S. 32°1′ N, 94°23′ W 103
Garyarsa, China 31°36′ N, 80°31′ E 188
Garyville, La., U.S. 30°3′ N, 90°37′ W 103
Garza, Arg. 28°10′ S, 63°34′ W 139
Garzan, oil field, Turk. 37°53′ N, 41°38′ E 195
Garzê, China 31°42′ N, 99°51′ E 190
Garzón, Col. 2°11′ N, 75°40′ W 136
Garzón, Uru. 34°37′ S, 54°34′ W 139
Gas, Kans., U.S. 37°53′ N, 95°21′ W 94
Gas City, Ind., U.S. 40°28′ N, 85°37′ W 102
Gasa, Bhutan 27°54′ N, 89°35′ E 197
Gascony, region, Europe 42°47′ N, 1°18′ E 165
Gascueña, Sp. 40°17′ N, 2°31′ W 164
Gåsefjord 69°54′ N, 29°46′ W 246
Gåseland, Den. 70°12′ N, 32°55′ W 246
Gashagar, Nig. 13°20′ N, 12°46′ E 216
Gashaka, Nig. 7°19′ N, 11°29′ E 222
Gashua, Nig. 12°52′ N, 11°5′ E 222
Gąski, Pol. 53°56′ N, 22°25′ E 166
Gąsocin, Pol. 52°43′ N, 20°41′ E 152
Gasparilla Island, Fla., U.S. 26°43′ N, 82°25′ W 105
Gaspé, Cap, Can. 48°41′ N, 64°8′ W 111
Gaspé Peninsula, Can. 48°18′ N, 67°57′ W 80
Gass Peak, Nev., U.S. 36°22′ N, 115°14′ W 101
Gassol, Nig. 8°31′ N, 10°29′ E 222
Gassville, Ark., U.S. 36°16′ N, 92°30′ W 96
Gastilovtsy, Belarus 53°44′ N, 24°57′ E 152
Gaston, N.C., U.S. 36°30′ N, 77°39′ W 96
Gaston, Lake, Va., U.S. 36°30′ N, 78°23′ W 96
Gastonia, N.C., U.S. 35°15′ N, 81°12′ W 96
Gastre, Arg. 42°19′ S, 69°18′ W 134
Gåsvær, islands, Norwegian Sea 66°1′ N, 10°55′ E 152
Gata, Cabo de, Sp. 36°32′ N, 2°12′ W 164
Gata, Cape, Cyprus 34°29′ N, 32°59′ E 194
Gata de Gorgos, Sp. 38°45′ N, 9°535′ E 164
Gata, Sierra de, Sp. 40°8′ N, 6°50′ W 150
Gataga, river, Can. 58°25′ N, 126°18′ W 108
Gătaia, Rom. 45°26′ N, 21°26′ E 168
Gatchina, Russ. 59°32′ N, 30°5′ E 152
Gate, Okla., U.S. 36°49′ N, 100°2′ W 92
Gate City, Va., U.S. 36°38′ N, 82°36′ W 96
Gatelo, Eth. 5°59′ N, 38°11′ E 224
Gates of the Rocky Mountains, pass, Mont., U.S. 46°51′ N, 111°56′ W 90
Gateshead, U.K. 54°56′ N, 1°37′ W 150
Gateway, Colo., U.S. 38°42′ N, 108°58′ W 90
Gatico, Chile 22°32′ S, 70°17′ W 137
Gâtine, Hauteurs de, Fr. 47°1′ N, 1°14′ W 150
Gatineau, Can. 45°28′ N, 75°40′ W 82
Gatineau, river, Can. 45°55′ N, 76°8′ W 94
Gaṭrūyeh, Iran 29°13′ N, 54°40′ E 196
Gattinara, It. 45°37′ N, 8°21′ E 167
Gatwick, U.K. 51°8′ N, 0°10′ E 162
Gaucín, Sp. 36°30′ N, 5°20′ W 164
Gauer Lake, Can. 57°1′ N, 98°6′ W 108
Gauja, river, Latv. 57°13′ N, 24°50′ E 166
Gaujiena, Latv. 57°30′ N, 26°23′ E 166
Gaurė, Lith. 55°14′ N, 22°28′ E 166
Gausta, peak, Nor. 59°50′ N, 8°31′ E 152
Gauteng, adm. division, S. Af. 26°24′ S, 27°21′ E 227
Gauya National Park, Latv. 57°19′ N, 24°42′ E 166
Gavà, Sp. 41°17′ N, 2°1′ E 164
Gaväter, Iran 25°7′ N, 61°29′ E 182
Gāvbandī, Iran 27°8′ N, 53°5′ E 196
Gávdos, island, Gr. 34°37′ N, 23°48′ E 180
Gavião, Port. 39°26′ N, 7°57′ W 150
Gavião, river, Braz. 14°42′ S, 40°60′ W 138
Gaviota, Calif., U.S. 34°28′ N, 120°14′ W 100
Gaviotas, Col. 4°26′ N, 70°47′ W 136
Gavirate, It. 45°51′ N, 8°42′ E 167
Gävle, Sw. 60°40′ N, 16°57′ E 160
Gavrilov Yam, Russ. 57°16′ N, 39°51′ E 154
Gavrilovo, Russ. 69°12′ N, 35°51′ E 152
Gávrovon, peak, Gr. 39°8′ N, 21°15′ E 156
Gavry, Russ. 56°54′ N, 27°52′ E 166
Gawachab, Namibia 27°4′ S, 17°50′ E 227
Gawler, Austral. 34°35′ S, 138°45′ E 231
Gawler Ranges, Austral. 32°9′ S, 135°22′ E 230
Gay, Russ. 51°25′ N, 58°25′ E 158
Gay Head, Mass., U.S. 41°17′ N, 70°55′ W 104
Gaya, India 24°48′ N, 84°59′ E 197
Gaya, Nig. 11°51′ N, 9°1′ E 222
Gaya, Niger 11°55′ N, 3°26′ E 222
Gayaza, Uganda 0°50′ N, 30°47′ E 224
Gaylor Mountain, Ark., U.S. 35°43′ N, 94°11′ W 96
Gaylord, Mich., U.S. 45°1′ N, 84°41′ W 94
Gaylord, Minn., U.S. 44°32′ N, 94°15′ W 90
Gayny, Russ. 60°19′ N, 54°19′ E 154
Gaza, adm. division, Mozambique 23°14′ S, 31°51′ E 220
Gaza see Ghazzah, Gaza Strip 31°29′ N, 34°28′ E 194
Gaza Strip, special sovereignity 31°21′ N, 33°57′ E 194
Gazak, Iran 27°37′ N, 59°57′ E 182
G'azalkent, Uzb. 41°33′ N, 69°44′ E 197
Gazamni, Niger 14°20′ N, 10°31′ E 222
Gazanjyk, Turkm. 39°10′ N, 55°47′ E 180
Gazaoua, Niger 13°35′ N, 7°55′ E 222
Gazelle Peninsula, P.N.G. 4°33′ S, 151°15′ E 192
Gazi, Dem. Rep. of the Congo 1°3′ N, 24°28′ E 224
Gazi, Kenya 4°25′ S, 39°29′ E 224
Gaziantep, Turk. 37°2′ N, 37°25′ E 180
Gazimagusa see Ammochostos, Northern Cyprus 35°7′ N, 33°56′ E 194
Gazipaşa, Turk. 36°17′ N, 32°18′ E 156
Gazli, Uzb. 40°8′ N, 63°28′ E 197
Gazojak, Turkm. 41°10′ N, 61°22′ E 180
Gazū, Kūh-e, peak, Iran 28°16′ N, 61°30′ E 182
Gbadolite, Dem. Rep. of the Congo 4°18′ N, 21°3′ E 218
Gbarnga, Liberia 6°51′ N, 9°33′ W 222
Gberia Fotombu, Sierra Leone 9°51′ N, 11°12′ W 222
Gboko, Nig. 7°19′ N, 8°57′ E 222
Gcuwa, S. Af. 32°21′ S, 28°7′ E 227
Gdańsk, Pol. 54°21′ N, 18°38′ E 166
Gdanskaya Guba 71°3′ N, 74°49′ E 160
Gdov, Russ. 58°44′ N, 27°48′ E 166
Gdynia, Pol. 54°29′ N, 18°31′ E 166
Gearhart, Oreg., U.S. 46°1′ N, 123°54′ W 100
Gearhart Mountain, Oreg., U.S. 42°30′ N, 120°57′ W 90
Gêba, river, Senegal 12°38′ N, 14°29′ W 222
Gebe, island, Indonesia 0°6′ N, 129°13′ E 192
Gebeit, Sudan 18°57′ N, 36°46′ E 182
Gebeit, Sudan 21°4′ N, 36°19′ E 182
Gebel Adda, ruin(s), Egypt 22°12′ N, 31°32′ E 182
Gebiley, Somalia 9°38′ N, 43°36′ E 216
Gebra, Ger. 51°25′ N, 10°37′ E 152
Gebze, Turk. 40°48′ N, 29°26′ E 156
Gech'a, Eth. 7°26′ N, 35°21′ E 224
Gedaref, Sudan 14°0′ N, 35°24′ E 182
Gedaref, adm. division, Sudan 14°5′ N, 34°13′ E 182
Geddes, S. Dak., U.S. 43°14′ N, 98°42′ W 90
Gedern, Ger. 50°25′ N, 9°12′ E 167
Gedid Ras el Fil, Sudan 12°41′ N, 25°43′ E 216
Gediz, Turk. 39°3′ N, 29°24′ E 156
Gedlegubē, Eth. 6°50′ N, 45°2′ E 218
Gēdo, Eth. 8°58′ N, 37°26′ E 224
Gèdre, Fr. 42°48′ N, 0°1′ E 164
Gedser, Den. 54°35′ N, 11°56′ E 152
Geel, Belg. 51°9′ N, 4°58′ E 167
Geelong, Austral. 38°11′ S, 144°23′ E 231
Geelvink Channel 28°34′ S, 112°19′ E 230
Geeste, Ger. 52°36′ N, 7°16′ E 163
Geeveston, Austral. 43°5′ S, 146°56′ E 231
Ge'gyai, China 32°29′ N, 80°58′ E 188
Geidam, Nig. 12°53′ N, 11°56′ E 222
Geikie, river, Can. 57°28′ N, 104°9′ W 108
Geilenkirchen, Ger. 50°58′ N, 6°7′ E 167
Geilo Hills, Kenya 3°12′ N, 40°49′ E 224
Geisa, Ger. 50°43′ N, 9°56′ E 167
Geisenheim, Ger. 49°58′ N, 7°57′ E 167
Geita, Tanzania 2°56′ S, 32°9′ E 224
Gejiu, China 23°18′ N, 103°6′ E 202
Gel, river, Sudan 6°59′ N, 29°3′ E 224
Gela, It. 37°4′ N, 14°14′ E 156
Geladaintong, peak, China 33°6′ N, 90°38′ E 188
Geladī, Eth. 6°57′ N, 46°28′ E 218
Gelahun, Liberia 7°43′ N, 10°28′ W 222
Gelai, peak, Tanzania 2°37′ S, 36°2′ E 224
Gelasa, Selat 3°8′ S, 106°41′ E 192
Geldermalsen, Neth. 51°53′ N, 5°16′ E 167
Geldern, Ger. 51°29′ N, 6°20′ E 167
Geldrop, Neth. 51°25′ N, 5°33′ E 167
Geleen, Neth. 50°58′ N, 5°49′ E 167
Gelendzhik, Russ. 44°34′ N, 38°6′ E 156
Gélengdeng, Chad 10°54′ N, 15°31′ E 216
Gelgaudiškis, Lith. 55°4′ N, 22°57′ E 166
Gelhak, Sudan 11°3′ N, 32°40′ E 182
Gelibolu (Gallipoli), Turk. 40°25′ N, 26°38′ E 156
Gellinsoor, Somalia 6°20′ N, 46°42′ E 218
Gelnhausen, Ger. 50°12′ N, 9°11′ E 167
Gelse, Hung. 46°35′ N, 16°59′ E 168
Gelsenkirchen, Ger. 51°30′ N, 7°5′ E 167
Gemas, Malaysia 2°37′ N, 102°36′ E 196
Gembloux, Belg. 50°34′ N, 4°41′ E 167
Gemena, Dem. Rep. of the Congo 3°12′ N, 19°54′ E 207
Gemerek, Turk. 39°10′ N, 36°3′ E 156
Gemert, Neth. 51°33′ N, 5°40′ E 167
Gemlik, Turk. 40°25′ N, 29°9′ E 156
Gemona del Friuli, It. 46°16′ N, 13°8′ E 167
Gemsa, Egypt 27°40′ N, 33°33′ E 180
Gemsbok National Park, Botswana 25°25′ S, 20°49′ E 227
Gemünden, Ger. 50°58′ N, 8°57′ E 167
Gen, river, China 50°24′ N, 121°3′ E 190
Genalē, river, Eth. 4°55′ N, 41°17′ E 224
Genalē, river, Eth. 6°8′ N, 39°1′ E 224
Genç, Turk. 38°44′ N, 40°32′ E 195
Geneina, Sudan 13°20′ N, 22°29′ E 216
General Alvear, Arg. 36°3′ S, 60°3′ W 139
General Alvear, Arg. 34°57′ S, 67°41′ W 134
General Arenales, Arg. 34°18′ S, 61°17′ W 139
General Artigas, Parag. 26°51′ S, 56°13′ W 139
General Belgrano, Arg. 35°45′ S, 58°30′ W 139
General Bernardo O'Higgins, station, Antarctica 63°26′ S, 57°47′ W 134
General Bravo, Mex. 25°47′ N, 99°10′ W 114
General Cabrera, Arg. 32°49′ S, 63°52′ W 139
General Cepeda, Mex. 25°21′ N, 101°29′ W 114
General Conesa, Arg. 36°29′ S, 57°19′ W 139
General D. Cerri, Arg. 38°44′ S, 62°24′ W 139
General Enrique Martínez, Uru. 33°13′ S, 53°51′ W 139
General Eugenio A. Garay, Parag. 20°33′ S, 62°10′ W 134
General Galarza, Arg. 32°43′ S, 59°22′ W 139
General Galeana, Mex. 25°27′ N, 105°13′ W 114
General Güemes, Arg. 24°40′ S, 65°4′ W 132
General Guido, Arg. 36°38′ S, 57°46′ W 139
General José de San Martín, Arg. 26°33′ S, 59°21′ W 139
General Juan Madariaga, Arg. 36°60′ S, 57°7′ W 139
General La Madrid, Arg. 37°15′ S, 61°17′ W 139
General Lavalle, Arg. 36°25′ S, 56°56′ W 139
General Leonidas Plaza Gutiérrez, Ecua. 3°4′ S, 78°25′ W 136
General Levalle, Arg. 34°3′ S, 63°53′ W 134
General Lorenzo Vintter, Arg. 40°44′ S, 64°28′ W 134
General Macarthur, Philippines 11°16′ N, 125°33′ E 203
General Paz, Arg. 35°31′ S, 58°20′ W 139
General Paz, Arg. 27°45′ S, 57°38′ W 139
General Pico, Arg. 35°39′ S, 63°44′ W 139
General Pinedo, Arg. 27°19′ S, 61°18′ W 139
General Pinto, Arg. 34°46′ S, 61°52′ W 139
General Pirán, Arg. 37°17′ S, 57°49′ W 139
General Saavedra, Bol. 17°15′ S, 63°14′ W 137
General San Martín, Arg. 38°2′ S, 63°34′ W 139
General San Martín, Arg. 34°33′ S, 58°33′ W 139
General San Martín, Arg. 44°5′ S, 70°28′ W 134
General Santos, Philippines 6°9′ N, 125°13′ E 203
General Terán, Mex. 25°15′ N, 99°42′ W 114
General Treviño, Mex. 26°12′ N, 99°29′ W 114
General Trías, Mex. 28°19′ N, 106°23′ W 92
General Viamonte, Arg. 34°59′ S, 61°4′ W 139
General Villegas, Arg. 35°1′ S, 63°1′ W 139
Genesee, Idaho, U.S. 46°32′ N, 116°57′ W 90
Genesee, river, N.Y., U.S. 42°15′ N, 78°17′ W 80
Geneseo, Ill., U.S. 41°27′ N, 90°10′ W 102
Geneseo, N.Y., U.S. 42°47′ N, 77°50′ W 94
Geneva, Ala., U.S. 31°1′ N, 85°53′ W 96
Geneva, Ill., U.S. 41°52′ N, 88°19′ W 102
Geneva, Nebr., U.S. 40°30′ N, 97°37′ W 94
Geneva, N.Y., U.S. 42°52′ N, 76°59′ W 94
Geneva, Ohio, U.S. 41°47′ N, 80°58′ W 102
Genève, Switz. 46°11′ N, 6°9′ E 167
Gengma, China 23°33′ N, 99°22′ E 202
Geni, river, Sudan 7°22′ N, 32°53′ E 224
Genk, Belg. 50°56′ N, 5°30′ E 167
Gennargentu, Monti del, It. 39°48′ N, 8°39′ E 156
Genoa, Ill., U.S. 42°4′ N, 88°42′ W 102
Genoa, Nebr., U.S. 41°26′ N, 97°45′ W 90
Genoa, Ohio, U.S. 41°30′ N, 83°21′ W 102
Genoa see Genova, It. 44°24′ N, 8°57′ E 167
Génolhac, Fr. 44°21′ N, 3°56′ E 150
Génoto, Senegal 13°35′ N, 13°53′ W 222
Genova (Genoa), It. 44°24′ N, 8°57′ E 167
Genova, Golfo di 44°4′ N, 7°33′ E 150
Gent, Belg. 51°3′ N, 3°44′ E 163
Genthin, Ger. 52°24′ N, 12°9′ E 152
Genyem, Indonesia 2°33′ S, 140°9′ E 192
Geoagiu, Rom. 45°55′ N, 23°12′ E 168
Geochang, S. Korea 35°41′ N, 127°55′ E 200
Geographical Society Ø, island, Den. 72°30′ N, 21°29′ W 246
Geoje, S. Korea 34°51′ N, 128°37′ E 200
George, S. Af. 33°58′ S, 22°26′ E 227
George, Lake, Fla., U.S. 29°15′ N, 81°41′ W 105
George, Lake, N.Y., U.S. 43°36′ N, 74°9′ W 81
George, river, Can. 57°32′ N, 66°1′ W 106
George Sound 44°59′ S, 167°7′ E 240
George Town, Malaysia 5°25′ N, 100°17′ E 196
George Town, U.K. 19°18′ N, 81°24′ W 115
George Town, United Kingdom 19°0′ N, 81°0′ W 118
George V Coast, Antarctica 69°8′ S, 153°28′ E 248
George Washington Birthplace National Monument, Va., U.S. 38°10′ N, 76°60′ W 94
George West, Tex., U.S. 28°19′ N, 98°7′ W 92
George, Zemlya, island, Russ. 79°13′ N, 47°22′ E 160
Georgetown, Austral. 18°17′ S, 143°32′ E 238
Georgetown, Fla., U.S. 29°23′ N, 81°38′ W 105
Georgetown, Gambia 13°29′ N, 14°48′ W 222
Georgetown, Guyana 6°40′ N, 58°21′ W 130
Georgetown, Ill., U.S. 39°58′ N, 87°38′ W 102
Georgetown, La., U.S. 31°45′ N, 92°23′ W 103
Georgetown, Me., U.S. 43°48′ N, 69°46′ W 104
Georgetown, Miss., U.S. 31°52′ N, 90°11′ W 103
Georgetown, Ohio, U.S. 38°51′ N, 83°54′ W 102
Georgetown, S.C., U.S. 33°22′ N, 79°19′ W 96
Georgetown, Tex., U.S. 30°37′ N, 97°40′ W 92
Georgia 42°0′ N, 44°0′ E 195
Georgia, adm. division, Ga., U.S. 32°40′ N, 84°11′ W 96
Georgia, Strait of 49°53′ N, 124°58′ W 90
Georgian Bay 45°4′ N, 81°13′ W 80
Georgīevka, Kaz. 49°19′ N, 81°33′ E 184
Georgiyevsk, Russ. 44°9′ N, 43°28′ E 158
Georgiyevskoye, Russ. 58°41′ N, 45°6′ E 154
Gera, Ger. 50°53′ N, 12°5′ E 152
Geraardsbergen, Belg. 50°47′ N, 3°54′ E 163
Geral de Goiás, Serra, Braz. 12°46′ S, 46°59′ W 130
Geral, Serra, Braz. 25°36′ S, 51°43′ W 132
Geraldine, Mont., U.S. 47°34′ N, 110°17′ W 90
Geraldine, N.Z. 44°6′ S, 171°14′ E 240
Geraldton, Can. 49°44′ N, 86°57′ W 94
Gerar, ruin(s), Israel 31°21′ N, 34°33′ E 194
Gerasa see Jarash, Jordan 32°17′ N, 35°53′ E 194
Gerbéviller, Fr. 48°30′ N, 6°30′ E 163
Gercüş, Turk. 37°33′ N, 41°25′ E 195
Gerdine, Mount, Alas., U.S. 61°25′ N, 152°42′ W 98
Gerede, Turk. 40°48′ N, 32°11′ E 156
Gereshk, Afghan. 31°48′ N, 64°34′ E 186
Gérgal, Sp. 37°6′ N, 2°33′ W 164
Gerik, Malaysia 5°25′ N, 101°6′ E 196
Gering, Nebr., U.S. 41°49′ N, 103°40′ W 90
Gerlachovský Štít, peak, Slovakia 49°8′ N, 20°3′ E 152
Germain, Grand lac, lake, Can. 51°11′ N, 67°11′ W 111
Germaine, Lac, lake, Can. 52°59′ N, 68°16′ W 111
Germânia, Braz. 10°36′ S, 70°5′ W 137
Germania Land, Den. 76°52′ N, 17°54′ W 246
Germansen Landing, Can. 55°43′ N, 124°43′ W 108
Germantown, Ill., U.S. 38°32′ N, 89°32′ W 102
Germantown, N.Y., U.S. 42°8′ N, 73°54′ W 104
Germantown, Tenn., U.S. 35°4′ N, 89°49′ W 96
Germany 51°17′ N, 7°48′ E 150
Germfask, Mich., U.S. 46°16′ N, 85°56′ W 110
Germī, Iran 39°3′ N, 48°6′ E 195
Gernsbach, Ger. 48°45′ N, 8°19′ E 152
Gerolakkos, Cyprus 35°10′ N, 33°15′ E 194
Gerolstein, Ger. 50°13′ N, 6°40′ E 163
Gerrard, Can. 50°30′ N, 117°18′ W 90
Gersfeld, Ger. 50°27′ N, 9°55′ E 167
Gerstungen, Ger. 50°58′ N, 10°3′ E 167
Gêrzê, China 32°29′ N, 84°3′ E 188
Gerze, Turk. 41°48′ N, 35°11′ E 156
Gescher, Ger. 51°57′ N, 7°0′ E 167
Geseke, Ger. 51°38′ N, 8°29′ E 167
Geser, Indonesia 3°57′ S, 130°51′ E 192
Geta, Fin. 60°21′ N, 19°50′ E 166
Getafe, Sp. 40°18′ N, 3°44′ W 164
Geteina, Sudan 14°49′ N, 32°23′ E 182
Gettysburg, S. Dak., U.S. 44°59′ N, 99°59′ W 90
Getúlio Vargas, Braz. 27°54′ S, 52°13′ W 139
Gety, Dem. Rep. of the Congo 1°11′ N, 30°11′ E 224
Geumpang, Indonesia 4°56′ N, 96°6′ E 196
Geumsan, S. Korea 36°5′ N, 127°29′ E 200
Gevaş, Turk. 38°16′ N, 43°4′ E 195
Gevelsberg, Ger. 51°18′ N, 7°20′ E 163
Gewanē, Eth. 10°7′ N, 40°36′ E 224
Gex, Fr. 46°19′ N, 6°3′ E 167
Geylegphug, Bhutan 26°49′ N, 90°37′ E 197
Geyve, Turk. 40°30′ N, 30°19′ E 156
Gézenti, Chad 21°39′ N, 18°19′ E 216
Gezer, ruin(s), Israel 31°51′ N, 34°52′ E 194
Gezira, adm. division, Sudan 14°32′ N, 32°33′ E 182
Ghaba North, oil field, Oman 21°24′ N, 57°15′ E 182
Ghabāghib, Syr. 33°11′ N, 36°12′ E 194
Ghabeish, Sudan 12°9′ N, 27°18′ E 216
Ghadāmis (Ghadames), Lib. 30°7′ N, 9°28′ E 214
Ghaddūwah, Lib. 26°27′ N, 14°18′ E 216
Ghagghar, river, India 29°40′ N, 75°1′ E 197
Ghana 7°51′ N, 1°42′ W 214
Ghanzi, Botswana 21°41′ S, 21°44′ E 227
Gharbi Island, Tun. 34°27′ N, 10°39′ E 214
Ghardaïa, Alg. 32°17′ N, 3°34′ E 207
Ghârib, Gebel, peak, Egypt 28°6′ N, 32°47′ E 180
Gharm, Taj. 39°4′ N, 70°25′ E 197
Gharo, Pak. 24°44′ N, 67°37′ E 186
Gharyān, Lib. 32°9′ N, 13°0′ E 216
Ghāt, Lib. 24°57′ N, 10°10′ E 214
Ghatampur, India 26°9′ N, 80°9′ E 188
Ghawar Oil Field, Saudi Arabia 25°5′ N, 49°15′ E 196
Ghaziabad, India 28°40′ N, 77°25′ E 197
Ghazipur, India 25°35′ N, 83°34′ E 197
Ghazīr, Leb. 34°1′ N, 35°40′ E 194
Ghazni, Afghan. 33°34′ N, 68°33′ E 186
Ghazzah (Gaza), Gaza Strip 31°29′ N, 34°28′ E 194
Ghelar, Rom. 45°42′ N, 22°47′ E 168
Ghent, Ky., U.S. 38°43′ N, 85°3′ W 102
Ghent, N.Y., U.S. 42°19′ N, 73°38′ W 104
Ghilarza, It. 40°8′ N, 8°50′ E 156
Ghilvaci, Rom. 47°41′ N, 22°41′ E 168
Ghisonaccia, Fr. 42°0′ N, 9°25′ E 156
Ghlo, Beinn a', peak, U.K. 56°49′ N, 3°48′ W 150
Ghost River, Can. 50°9′ N, 91°27′ W 94
Ghoumrassen, Tun. 33°1′ N, 10°15′ E 214
Ghraiba, Tun. 34°31′ N, 10°12′ E 156
Ghunthur, Syr. 34°23′ N, 37°8′ E 194
Ghurian, Afghan. 34°27′ N, 61°30′ E 186
Gia Nghia, Vietnam 12°15′ N, 107°37′ E 202
Gia Rai, Vietnam 9°13′ N, 105°28′ E 202
Gialo, oil field, Lib. 28°30′ N, 21°21′ E 216
Giant Forest, Calif., U.S. 36°34′ N, 118°47′ W 101
Giant's Ring, ruin(s), U.K. 54°31′ N, 6°5′ W 150
Giarso, Eth. 5°14′ N, 37°33′ E 224
Gibara, Cuba 21°7′ N, 76°11′ W 116
Gibbon, Nebr., U.S. 40°44′ N, 98°51′ W 90
Gibbs Island, Antarctica 61°44′ S, 55°25′ W 134
Gibeah, ruin(s), Israel 31°48′ N, 35°11′ E 194
Gibeon, Namibia 25°8′ S, 17°46′ E 227
Gibraltar, adm. division, U.K. 36°7′ N, 5°35′ W 164
Gibraltar, Strait of 36°2′ N, 6°40′ W 150
Gibsland, La., U.S. 32°31′ N, 93°3′ W 96
Gibson City, Ill., U.S. 40°27′ N, 88°22′ W 102
Gibson Desert, Austral. 23°7′ S, 121°58′ E 230
Gibsonburg, Ohio, U.S. 41°22′ N, 83°19′ W 102
Gibsons, Can. 49°24′ N, 123°31′ W 100
Gibsonton, Fla., U.S. 27°50′ N, 82°22′ W 105
Gīdamī, Eth. 8°56′ N, 34°33′ E 224
Giddalur, India 15°22′ N, 78°56′ E 188
Giddings, Tex., U.S. 30°10′ N, 96°56′ W 96
Gīdolē, Eth. 5°37′ N, 37°27′ E 224
Giel, Sudan 11°20′ N, 32°44′ E 182
Gien, Fr. 47°41′ N, 2°38′ E 150
Giera, Rom. 45°25′ N, 20°59′ E 168
Giessen, Ger. 50°34′ N, 8°39′ E 167
Gieten, Neth. 53°0′ N, 6°45′ E 163
Giffard, Lac, lake, Can. 51°7′ N, 77°25′ W 110
Gifford, Fla., U.S. 27°40′ N, 80°25′ W 105
Gifford, river, Can. 70°40′ N, 84°39′ W 106
Gift Lake, Can. 55°53′ N, 115°54′ W 108
Gifu, Japan 35°24′ N, 136°46′ E 201

Gifu, adm. division, Japan 35°48' N, 136°49' E 201
Gig Harbor, Wash., U.S. 47°18' N, 122°36' W 100
Gigant, Russ. 46°30' N, 41°14' E 158
Giganta, Sierra de la, Mex. 25°57' N, 111°37' W 112
Gijón, Sp. 43°30' N, 5°42' W 150
Gikongoro, Rwanda 2°31' S, 29°33' E 224
Gila, N. Mex., U.S. 32°57' N, 108°34' W 92
Gila Bend, Ariz., U.S. 32°56' N, 112°43' W 92
Gila Bend Mountains, Ariz., U.S. 33°24' N, 113°42' W 101
Gila Cliff Dwellings National Monument, N. Mex., U.S. 33°13' N, 108°21' W 92
Gila Mountains, Ariz., U.S. 33°9' N, 109°59' W 92
Gila, river, Ariz., U.S. 33°12' N, 110°9' W 80
Gilbâna, Egypt 30°55' N, 32°28' E 194
Gilbert, La., U.S. 32°3' N, 91°40' W 103
Gilbert, Minn., U.S. 47°29' N, 92°29' W 94
Gilbert Islands, North Pacific Ocean 0°46' N, 173°11' E 238
Gilbert, Islas, Drake Passage 55°7' S, 73°15' W 134
Gilbert, Mount, Can. 50°51' N, 124°21' W 90
Gilbert Peak, Utah, U.S. 40°47' N, 110°25' W 90
Gilbert Peak, Wash., U.S. 46°27' N, 121°26' W 100
Gilbert Plains, Can. 51°7' N, 100°30' W 90
Gilbertville, Mass., U.S. 42°18' N, 72°13' W 104
Gilbués, Braz. 9°51' S, 45°23' W 130
Gildeskål, Nor. 67°3' N, 14°2' E 152
Gildford, Mont., U.S. 48°33' N, 110°17' W 90
Gilead, Me., U.S. 44°23' N, 70°59' W 104
Giles Meteorological Station, site, Austral. 25°7' S, 128°4' E 230
Giles, Mount, Antarctica 75°2' S, 137°1' W 248
Gilford, N.H., U.S. 43°32' N, 71°25' W 104
Gilgal, West Bank 31°58' N, 35°26' E 194
Gilgil, Kenya 0°30' N, 36°19' E 224
Gilgit, Pak. 35°52' N, 74°19' E 186
Giljeva Planina, Serb. and Mont. 43°3' N, 19°50' E 168
Gillam, Can. 56°20' N, 94°44' W 108
Gilleleje, Den. 56°6' N, 12°18' E 152
Gillespie, Ill., U.S. 39°7' N, 89°50' W 102
Gillett, Ark., U.S. 34°5' N, 91°23' W 96
Gillette, Wyo., U.S. 44°16' N, 105°30' W 90
Gilliam, Mo., U.S. 39°14' N, 92°60' W 94
Gillies Islands, Davis Sea 66°37' S, 98°44' E 248
Gillingham, U.K. 51°22' N, 0°32' E 162
Gills Range, Nev., U.S. 38°43' N, 118°40' W 90
Gillock Island, Antarctica 70°22' S, 72°12' E 248
Gills Rock, Wis., U.S. 45°16' N, 87°1' W 94
Gilman, Ill., U.S. 40°45' N, 87°60' W 102
Gilman, Vt., U.S. 44°24' N, 71°44' W 104
Gilmer, Tex., U.S. 32°43' N, 94°58' W 103
Gilo Wenz, river, Eth. 7°40' N, 33°38' E 224
Gilroy, Calif., U.S. 37°0' N, 121°35' W 100
Gimbī, Eth. 9°8' N, 35°49' E 224
Gimcheon, S. Korea 36°5' N, 128°8' E 200
Gimhae, S. Korea 35°12' N, 128°54' E 200
Gimhwa, S. Korea 38°17' N, 127°28' E 200
Gimje, S. Korea 35°48' N, 126°54' E 200
Gimli, Can. 50°37' N, 97°2' W 90
Gimo, Sw. 60°10' N, 18°8' E 166
Ginâh, Egypt 25°21' N, 30°28' E 226
Gingindlovu, S. Af. 29°2' S, 31°32' E 227
Gingoog, Philippines 8°48' N, 125°7' E 203
Ginir, Eth. 7°12' N, 40°43' E 224
Ginostra, It. 38°47' N, 15°11' E 156
Giohar see Jawhar, Somalia 2°47' N, 45°34' E 218
Gióna, Óros, peak, Gr. 38°38' N, 22°10' E 156
Giovinazzo, It. 41°11' N, 16°40' E 156
Gipka, Latv. 57°34' N, 22°36' E 166
Gir National Park, India 21°15' N, 70°30' E 186
Girard, Ill., U.S. 39°26' N, 89°47' W 102
Girard, Kans., U.S. 37°28' N, 94°50' W 94
Girard, Ohio, U.S. 41°9' N, 80°42' W 94
Girardot, Col. 4°19' N, 74°48' W 136
Girawa, Eth. 9°7' N, 41°51' E 224
Girbanat, Sudan 12°0' N, 33°9' E 182
Girbou, Rom. 47°10' N, 23°24' E 168
Girbovi, Rom. 44°48' N, 26°45' E 156
Giresun, Turk. 40°55' N, 38°22' E 158
Girga, Egypt 26°19' N, 31°49' E 180
Giridih, India 24°9' N, 86°19' E 197
Girla Mare, Rom. 44°12' N, 22°46' E 168
Girlişte, Rom. 45°10' N, 21°48' E 168
Girne see Keryneia, Northern Cyprus 35°20' N, 33°18' E 194
Giroc, Rom. 45°42' N, 21°15' E 168
Girolata, Fr. 42°21' N, 8°37' E 156
Girona, Sp. 41°58' N, 2°50' E 164
Giruliai, Lith. 55°46' N, 21°6' E 166
Girvas, Russ. 62°28' N, 33°44' E 154
Gisborne, N.Z. 38°40' S, 178°0' E 240
Giscome, Can. 54°3' N, 122°23' W 108
Gisors, Fr. 49°16' N, 1°45' E 163
Gisselberg, Ger. 50°45' N, 8°44' E 167
Gitega, Burundi 3°27' S, 29°55' E 224
Giuba, Isole, islands, Indian Ocean 0°45' N, 41°29' E 224
Giulianova, It. 42°44' N, 13°56' E 156
Giuncarico, It. 42°55' N, 10°58' E 156
Giurgeni, Rom. 44°44' N, 27°51' E 158
Giurgiu, Rom. 43°53' N, 25°56' E 156
Giurgiu, adm. division, Rom. 44°8' N, 25°43' E 156
Give, Den. 55°49' N, 9°13' E 150
Givet, Fr. 50°7' N, 4°48' E 167
Giyani, S. Af. 23°17' S, 30°44' E 227
Giyon, Eth. 8°34' N, 38°1' E 224
Gizab, Afghan. 33°27' N, 66°0' E 186
Gizhiga, Russ. 62°2' N, 160°11' E 160
Gizhduvan, Uzb. 40°6' N, 64°42' E 197
Giżycko, Pol. 54°1' N, 21°45' E 166
Gjalicë e Lumës, Mal, peak, Alban. 42°0' N, 20°25' E 168
Gjegjan, Alban. 41°56' N, 20°0' E 168
Gjelsvik Mountains, Antarctica 72°8' S, 4°59' W 248
Gjerstad, Nor. 58°52' N, 9°0' E 152
Gjinar, Alban. 41°2' N, 20°12' E 156
Gjoa Haven, Can. 68°36' N, 95°60' W 106
Gjøvdal, Nor. 58°51' N, 8°17' E 152
Gjuhëzës, Kepi i, Alban. 40°27' N, 18°34' E 156
Gjuvikfjell, peak, Nor. 59°57' N, 7°55' E 152
Gkreko, Cape, Cyprus 34°53' N, 33°55' E 194
Gla, ruin(s), Gr. 38°23' N, 23°10' E 156
Glace Bay, Can. 46°11' N, 59°58' W 111
Glacier, Wash., U.S. 48°52' N, 121°58' W 100
Glacier Bay 58°40' N, 136°50' W 108
Glacier Bay National Park and Preserve, Alas., U.S. 58°40' N, 137°23' W 73
Glacier Peak, Wash., U.S. 48°5' N, 121°10' W 100
Glacier Strait 75°57' N, 80°39' W 106
Gladstone, Can. 50°13' N, 98°58' W 90
Gladstone, Mich., U.S. 45°50' N, 87°2' W 94
Gladstone, Oreg., U.S. 45°23' N, 122°37' W 90
Gladwin, Mich., U.S. 43°58' N, 84°29' W 102
Gladys Lake, Can. 59°52' N, 133°39' W 108
Glamoč, Bosn. and Herzg. 44°2' N, 16°50' E 168
Glan, Philippines 5°50' N, 125°11' E 203
Glandore, Ire. 51°34' N, 9°7' W 150
Glandorf, Ger. 52°4' N, 8°0' E 163
Glarus, Switz. 47°2' N, 9°2' E 156
Glas, Lac du, lake, Can. 51°49' N, 75°47' W 110
Glasco, Kans., U.S. 39°20' N, 97°51' W 90
Glasco, N.Y., U.S. 42°1' N, 73°58' W 104
Glasford, Ill., U.S. 40°33' N, 89°48' W 102
Glasgow, Ky., U.S. 37°0' N, 85°55' W 96
Glasgow, Mont., U.S. 48°11' N, 106°39' W 90
Glasgow, U.K. 55°51' N, 4°27' W 143
Glaslyn, Can. 53°21' N, 108°22' W 108
Glass Buttes, peak, Oreg., U.S. 43°32' N, 120°10' W 90
Glass Mountain, Calif., U.S. 37°45' N, 118°47' W 90
Glass Mountain, Calif., U.S. 41°35' N, 121°35' W 90
Glass Mountains, Tex., U.S. 30°30' N, 103°11' W 92
Glastonbury, Conn., U.S. 41°42' N, 72°37' W 104
Glastonbury, U.K. 51°8' N, 2°43' W 162
Glavičice, Bosn. and Herzg. 44°35' N, 19°12' E 168
Glazachevo, Russ. 57°12' N, 30°13' E 166
Glazov, Russ. 58°6' N, 52°43' E 154
Gleichberg, Grosser, peak, Ger. 50°22' N, 10°29' E 152
Gleichen, Can. 50°52' N, 113°4' W 90
Gleisdorf, Aust. 47°6' N, 15°42' E 168
Glen, N.H., U.S. 44°6' N, 71°11' W 104
Glen Allan, Miss., U.S. 33°0' N, 91°2' W 103
Glen Arbor, Mich., U.S. 44°53' N, 85°59' W 94
Glen Cove, N.Y., U.S. 40°52' N, 73°38' W 104
Glen Park, N.Y., U.S. 44°0' N, 75°58' W 94
Glen, river, U.K. 52°47' N, 0°34' E 162
Glen Rose, Tex., U.S. 32°14' N, 97°45' W 92
Glen Ullin, N. Dak., U.S. 46°47' N, 101°51' W 90
Glenada, Oreg., U.S. 43°56' N, 124°6' W 90
Glenavy, N.Z. 44°54' S, 171°5' E 240
Glenboro, Can. 49°32' N, 99°18' W 90
Glencliff, N.H., U.S. 43°58' N, 71°54' W 104
Glencoe, Can. 42°44' N, 81°42' W 102
Glencoe, Minn., U.S. 44°45' N, 94°10' W 94
Glendale, Ariz., U.S. 33°32' N, 112°10' W 92
Glendale, Calif., U.S. 34°8' N, 118°16' W 101
Glendive, Mont., U.S. 47°4' N, 104°44' W 90
Glendo, Wyo., U.S. 42°29' N, 105°1' W 90
Glendon, Can. 54°14' N, 111°10' W 108
Glenfield, U.K. 52°38' N, 1°14' W 162
Glenmora, La., U.S. 30°57' N, 92°36' W 103
Glenn, Mount, Ariz., U.S. 31°56' N, 110°3' W 92
Glenns Ferry, Idaho, U.S. 42°58' N, 115°19' W 90
Glennville, Calif., U.S. 35°44' N, 118°43' W 101
Glennville, Ga., U.S. 31°55' N, 81°56' W 96
Glenora, Can. 57°52' N, 131°26' W 108
Glenorchy, N.Z. 44°52' S, 168°26' E 240
Glenrock, Wyo., U.S. 42°51' N, 105°53' W 90
Glens Falls, N.Y., U.S. 43°18' N, 73°39' W 104
Glenwood, Minn., U.S. 45°38' N, 95°24' W 94
Glenwood, N. Mex., U.S. 33°18' N, 108°52' W 92
Glenwood, Oreg., U.S. 45°38' N, 123°16' W 100
Glenwood, Va., U.S. 36°35' N, 79°23' W 96
Glenwood, Wash., U.S. 46°0' N, 121°18' W 100
Glenwood, W. Va., U.S. 38°34' N, 82°12' W 102
Glidden, Wis., U.S. 46°8' N, 90°36' W 94
Glina, Croatia 45°20' N, 16°6' E 168
Glíthion, Gr. 36°43' N, 22°32' E 216
Glittertind, peak, Nor. 61°38' N, 8°24' E 152
Gliwice, Pol. 50°17' N, 18°38' E 152
Głogów, Pol. 51°39' N, 16°5' E 152
Głomno, Pol. 54°18' N, 20°44' E 152
Globe, Ariz., U.S. 33°24' N, 110°47' W 92
Gloggnitz, Aust. 47°40' N, 15°56' E 168
Glommersträsk, Nor. 65°14' N, 19°40' E 152
Glorenza, It. 46°40' N, 10°33' E 167
Glória, Braz. 9°13' S, 38°20' W 132
Gloria Ridge, North Atlantic Ocean 54°34' N, 45°3' W 253
Glorieuses, Îles, islands, Indian Ocean 11°10' S, 47°2' E 220
Glorioso Islands, Indian Ocean 11°19' S, 44°49' E 207
Gloster, Miss., U.S. 31°11' N, 91°2' W 103
Gloucester, Can. 45°24' N, 75°35' W 94
Gloucester, Mass., U.S. 42°36' N, 70°40' W 104
Gloucester, U.K. 51°51' N, 2°14' W 162
Gloucester, Ohio, U.S. 39°29' N, 82°4' W 102
Glubokiy, Russ. 46°58' N, 42°38' E 158
Glubokiy, Russ. 48°32' N, 40°20' E 158
Glubokoe, Kaz. 50°8' N, 82°18' E 184
Glubokoye, Russ. 56°38' N, 28°59' E 166
Glusk, Belarus 52°52' N, 28°47' E 152
Glyncorrwg, U.K. 51°41' N, 3°37' W 162
Glyndon, Minn., U.S. 46°52' N, 96°37' W 94
Gmelinka, Russ. 50°21' N, 46°52' E 158
Gmünd, Aust. 48°45' N, 14°58' E 152
Gmunden, Aust. 47°55' N, 13°47' E 156
Gnadenhutten, Ohio, U.S. 40°20' N, 81°25' W 102
Gnarp, Nor. 62°4' N, 17°12' E 152
Gnas, Aust. 46°52' N, 15°51' E 168
Gnesta, Nor. 59°2' N, 17°18' E 152
Gnetalovo, Russ. 56°52' N, 29°37' E 166
Gnjilane, Serb. and Mont. 42°27' N, 21°27' E 168
Go Cong, Vietnam 10°22' N, 106°41' E 202
Goa, adm. division, India 14°59' N, 74°13' E 188
Goageb, Namibia 26°45' S, 17°12' E 227
Goalpara, India 26°7' N, 90°34' E 197
Goaso, Ghana 6°49' N, 2°32' W 222
Goat Mountain, Mont., U.S. 47°17' N, 113°26' W 90
Goat, river, Can. 49°10' N, 116°12' W 90
Goathland, U.K. 54°24' N, 0°44' E 162
Goba, Eth. 6°58' N, 39°55' E 224
Gobabis, Namibia 22°27' S, 18°58' E 227
Gobernador Crespo, Arg. 30°21' S, 60°24' W 139
Gobernador Duval, Arg. 38°42' S, 66°26' W 134
Gobernador Gregores, Arg. 48°45' S, 70°16' W 134
Gobernador Ingeniero Valentín Virasoro, Arg. 28°3' S, 56°3' W 139
Gobi, Asia 41°49' N, 103°50' E 198
Gobles, Mich., U.S. 42°20' N, 85°52' W 102
Gobō, Japan 33°53' N, 135°9' E 201
Goch, Ger. 51°40' N, 6°10' E 167
Gochang, S. Korea 35°26' N, 126°42' E 200
Gochas, Namibia 24°51' S, 18°44' E 227
Godalming, U.K. 51°11' N, 0°37' E 162
Godbout, Can. 49°19' N, 67°38' W 82
Godda, India 24°49' N, 87°13' E 197
Goddard, Can. 56°50' N, 135°19' W 108
Godeanu, peak, Rom. 45°16' N, 22°38' E 168
Godech, Bulg. 43°0' N, 23°4' E 168
Godere, Eth. 5°2' N, 43°59' E 218
Goderich, Can. 43°43' N, 81°42' W 102
Godfrey, Mo., U.S. 38°57' N, 90°12' W 94
Godfrey Tank, spring, Austral. 20°15' S, 126°34' E 230
Godhavn see Qeqertarsuaq, Den. 69°15' N, 53°30' W 106
Godhra, India 22°46' N, 73°35' E 186
Gödöllő, Hung. 47°35' N, 19°21' E 168
Gods Lake, Can. 54°38' N, 94°12' W 108
Gods, river, Can. 55°18' N, 93°23' W 108
Godthåb see Nuuk, Greenland, Den. 64°14' N, 51°38' W 106
Godwin Austen see K2, peak, Pak. 35°51' N, 76°25' E 186
Godzikowice, Pol. 50°54' N, 17°19' E 152
Goéland, Lac au, lake, Can. 49°36' N, 78°10' W 81
Goélands, Lac aux, lake, Can. 55°13' N, 66°38' W 106
Goes, Neth. 51°30' N, 3°52' E 163
Goffstown, N.H., U.S. 43°1' N, 71°37' W 104
Gog Magog Hills, U.K. 52°4' N, 0°10' E 162
Gogama, Can. 47°40' N, 81°43' W 94
Gogebic Range, Mich., U.S. 46°32' N, 90°10' W 94
Göggingen, Ger. 48°20' N, 10°52' E 152
Gogland, island, Russ. 60°6' N, 26°43' E 166
Gogói, Mozambique 20°19' S, 33°8' E 227
Gogounou, Benin 10°46' N, 2°47' E 222
Gogrial, Sudan 8°29' N, 28°7' E 224
Goha, Eth. 10°19' N, 34°33' E 224
Gohad, India 26°24' N, 78°26' E 197
Goheung, S. Korea 34°35' N, 127°18' E 200
Goiandira, Braz. 18°10' S, 48°7' W 138
Goianésia, Braz. 15°22' S, 49°9' W 138
Goiânia, Braz. 16°43' S, 49°17' W 138
Goianinha, Braz. 6°17' S, 35°11' W 132
Goiás, Braz. 15°55' S, 50°6' W 138
Goiás, adm. division, Braz. 16°18' S, 50°32' W 138
Goiatuba, Braz. 18°5' S, 49°24' W 138
Goio Erê, Braz. 24°12' S, 53°3' W 138
Goioxim, Braz. 25°13' S, 52°2' W 138
Goito, It. 45°15' N, 10°40' E 167
Gojeb, river, Eth. 7°10' N, 36°58' E 224
Gök, river, Turk. 41°38' N, 34°30' E 156
Goka, Japan 36°18' N, 139°43' E 201
Gokase, river, Japan 32°38' N, 131°16' E 201
Gökçeada, island, Turk. 39°55' N, 25°30' E 180
Gökdepe, Turkm. 38°9' N, 57°58' E 180
Göksu, river, Turk. 37°3' N, 32°40' E 156
Göksu, river, Turk. 37°56' N, 36°21' E 156
Göksun, Turk. 38°2' N, 36°29' E 156
Gokwe, Zimb. 18°13' S, 28°57' E 224
Gol, Nor. 60°42' N, 8°53' E 152
Gol Bax, Somalia 0°19' N, 41°36' E 224
Golaghat, India 26°34' N, 93°55' E 188
Golan Heights, region, Asia 32°56' N, 35°38' E 194
Gölbaşı, Turk. 39°47' N, 32°48' E 156
Golconda, Nev., U.S. 40°57' N, 117°30' W 90
Gölcük, Turk. 40°43' N, 29°48' E 158
Gold Bar, Wash., U.S. 47°50' N, 121°41' W 100
Gold Beach, Oreg., U.S. 42°24' N, 124°26' W 82
Gold Coast, Austral. 27°58' S, 153°23' E 231
Gold Coast, region, Africa 5°10' N, 2°17' W 222
Gold Hill, Nev., U.S. 39°17' N, 119°40' W 92
Gold Mines, site, Egypt 22°37' N, 33°13' E 182
Gold Rock, Can. 49°27' N, 92°42' W 90
Gołdap, Pol. 54°17' N, 22°17' E 154
Golden, Can. 51°18' N, 116°58' W 108
Golden Hinde, peak, Can. 49°38' N, 125°50' W 90
Golden Meadow, La., U.S. 29°22' N, 90°17' W 103
Goldendale, Wash., U.S. 45°48' N, 120°49' W 90
Goldfield, Iowa, U.S. 42°43' N, 93°55' W 94
Goldfield, Nev., U.S. 37°40' N, 117°14' W 82
Goldonna, La., U.S. 32°0' N, 92°55' W 103
Goldpines, Can. 50°39' N, 93°11' W 90
Goldsboro, N.C., U.S. 35°23' N, 78°1' W 96
Goldsmith, Tex., U.S. 31°57' N, 102°37' W 92
Goldsmith Channel 73°5' N, 111°1' W 106
Goldthwaite, Tex., U.S. 31°26' N, 98°34' W 92
Göle, Turk. 40°47' N, 42°35' E 195
Golela, Swaziland 27°16' S, 31°55' E 227
Goleta, Calif., U.S. 34°26' N, 119°51' W 100
Golfito, C.R. 8°39' N, 83°11' W 115
Goliad, Tex., U.S. 28°39' N, 97°23' W 96
Gölköy, Turk. 40°42' N, 37°37' E 156
Golmud, China 36°19' N, 94°52' E 190
Golmud, river, China 35°44' N, 95°6' E 188
Golondrina, Arg. 28°32' S, 60°4' W 139
Gölören, Turk. 37°52' N, 33°51' E 156
Golovin, Alas., U.S. 64°27' N, 162°59' W 98
Golpāyegān, Iran 33°28' N, 50°14' E 180
Gölpazarı, Turk. 40°16' N, 30°18' E 158
Golran, Afghan. 35°7' N, 61°41' E 186
Golubac, Serb. and Mont. 44°38' N, 21°37' E 168
Golubovci, Serb. and Mont. 42°21' N, 19°13' E 168
Golūboyka, Kaz. 53°7' N, 74°12' E 184
Golyam Perelik, peak, Bulg. 41°35' N, 24°29' E 156
Golyshmanovo, Russ. 56°22' N, 68°24' E 184
Goma, Dem. Rep. of the Congo 1°41' S, 29°11' E 224
Gómara, Sp. 41°36' N, 2°14' W 164
Gombari, Dem. Rep. of the Congo 2°43' N, 29°5' E 224
Gombe, Nig. 10°15' N, 11°7' E 222
Gombe National Park, Tanzania 4°47' S, 29°34' E 224
Gomera, island, Sp. 28°6' N, 18°13' W 214
Gómez Farías, Mex. 24°56' N, 101°2' W 114
Gómez Palacio, Mex. 25°34' N, 103°31' W 114
Gomīshān, Iran 37°4' N, 53°59' E 180
Gomo, China 33°57' N, 85°19' E 188
Gomo Co, lake, China 34°1' N, 84°47' E 188
Gomoh, India 23°51' N, 86°9' E 197
Gomotartsi, Bulg. 44°4' N, 22°58' E 168
Gomphi, ruin(s), Gr. 39°24' N, 21°30' E 156
Gonam, Russ. 57°15' N, 130°53' E 160
Gonarezhou National Park, Zimb. 21°50' S, 31°35' E 227
Gonâve, Île de la, island, Haiti 19°1' N, 74°5' W 116
Gonbad-e Kāvūs, Iran 37°22' N, 55°18' E 180
Gonda, India 27°7' N, 81°58' E 197
Gondal, India 21°57' N, 70°47' E 186
Gonder, Eth. 12°34' N, 37°25' E 182
Gondey, Chad 9°4' N, 19°21' E 218
Gondia, India 21°27' N, 80°10' E 188
Gondola, Mozambique 19°10' S, 33°38' E 224
Gondrecourt, Fr. 48°30' N, 5°31' E 163
Gönen, Turk. 40°6' N, 27°38' E 156
Gong'an, China 30°1' N, 112°11' E 198
Gongbo'gyamda, China 29°55' N, 93°0' E 190
Gongcheng, China 24°52' N, 110°45' E 198
Gongga Shan, peak, China 29°38' N, 101°36' E 190
Gonggar, China 29°17' N, 90°48' E 197
Gongju, S. Korea 36°25' N, 127°9' E 200
Gonglee, Liberia 5°43' N, 9°27' W 222
Gongliu, China 43°25' N, 82°18' E 184
Gongola, river, Nig. 11°5' N, 11°29' E 222
Gongoúe, Gabon 0°33' N, 9°15' E 218
Gongxi, China 27°38' N, 115°51' E 198
Gongzhuling, China 43°30' N, 124°52' E 198
Goniądz, Pol. 53°28' N, 22°43' E 158
Gonja, Tanzania 4°21' S, 38°5' E 224
Gonjo, China 30°52' N, 98°16' E 188
Gōno, river, Japan 34°53' N, 132°27' E 201
Gōnoura, Japan 33°44' N, 129°41' E 201
Gonzales, Calif., U.S. 36°30' N, 121°28' W 100
Gonzales, La., U.S. 30°13' N, 90°56' W 103
Gonzales, Tex., U.S. 29°29' N, 97°27' W 96
González, Mex. 22°48' N, 98°26' W 114
González Chaves, Arg. 38°4' S, 60°6' W 139
González Moreno, Arg. 35°32' S, 63°20' W 139
Good Hope, Cape of, S. Af. 34°13' S, 18°30' E 253
Good Hope, Cape of, S. Af. 34°33' S, 12°22' E 206
Good Hope Mountain, Can. 51°9' N, 124°15' W 90
Good Pine, La., U.S. 31°40' N, 92°11' W 103
Goodenough, Cape, Antarctica 65°58' S, 126°13' E 248
Goodenough Island, P.N.G. 9°15' S, 149°59' E 192
Goodenough, Mount, Can. 67°56' N, 135°41' W 98
Goodhouse, S. Af. 28°57' S, 18°14' E 227
Gooding, Idaho, U.S. 42°57' N, 114°43' W 90
Goodland, Fla., U.S. 25°55' N, 81°41' W 105
Goodland, Ind., U.S. 40°45' N, 87°18' W 102
Goodland, Kans., U.S. 39°20' N, 101°42' W 82
Goodman, Miss., U.S. 32°56' N, 89°56' W 103
Goodman, Wis., U.S. 45°37' N, 88°22' W 94
Goodnews Bay, Alas., U.S. 59°8' N, 161°31' W 106
Goodrich, Tex., U.S. 30°35' N, 94°57' W 103
Goodridge, Minn., U.S. 48°8' N, 95°50' W 90
Goodsir, Mount, Can. 51°11' N, 116°28' W 90
Goodsoil, Can. 54°22' N, 109°15' W 108
Goodsprings, Nev., U.S. 35°49' N, 115°27' W 101
Goodwell, Okla., U.S. 36°34' N, 101°39' W 92
Goole, U.K. 53°42' N, 0°54' E 162
Goondiwindi, Austral. 28°30' S, 150°21' E 231
Goonhilly Downs, site, U.K. 50°0' N, 5°18' W 150
Goor, Neth. 52°14' N, 6°35' E 163
Goose, Lac, lake, Can. 53°3' N, 74°38' W 111
Goose Lake, Calif., U.S. 41°58' N, 121°18' W 81
Goose Lake, Can. 51°43' N, 107°47' W 90
Goose, river, Can. 54°54' N, 117°3' W 108
Goose Rocks Beach, Me., U.S. 43°24' N, 70°25' W 104
Goosenest, peak, Calif., U.S. 41°42' N, 122°19' W 90
Gooseprairie, Wash., U.S. 46°53' N, 121°17' W 100
Gooty, India 15°6' N, 77°40' E 188
Gop, India 22°3' N, 69°54' E 186
Gor, Sp. 37°21' N, 2°58' W 164
Gorakhpur, India 26°43' N, 83°21' E 197
Goranci, Bosn. and Herzg. 43°25' N, 17°43' E 168
Goransko, Serb. and Mont. 43°7' N, 18°50' E 168
Goražde, Bosn. and Herzg. 43°40' N, 18°58' E 168
Gorbukova, Russ. 59°31' N, 89°33' E 169
Gorda, Punta, Calif., U.S. 40°5' N, 124°41' W 90
Gorda, Punta, Nicar. 14°13' N, 84°2' W 115
Gördalen, Nor. 61°35' N, 12°28' E 152
Gordion, ruin(s), Turk. 39°35' N, 31°52' E 156
Gordo, Ala., U.S. 33°17' N, 87°54' W 103
Gordon, Nebr., U.S. 42°47' N, 102°13' W 90
Gordon, Wis., U.S. 46°13' N, 91°49' W 94
Gordon Horne Peak, Can. 51°47' N, 118°55' W 90
Gordon Lake, Can. 56°23' N, 111°4' W 108
Gordondale, Can. 55°50' N, 119°34' W 108
Gordon's, Bahamas 22°52' N, 74°52' W 116
Goré, Chad 7°54' N, 16°38' E 218
Gorē, Eth. 8°10' N, 35°31' E 224
Gore, N.Z. 46°7' S, 168°56' E 240
Gore Bay, Can. 45°55' N, 82°29' W 94
Gore Mountain, Vt., U.S. 44°54' N, 71°53' W 94
Gore Range, Colo., U.S. 40°5' N, 106°44' W 90
Gorecki, Mount, Antarctica 83°23' S, 59°14' W 248
Goree, Tex., U.S. 33°27' N, 99°32' W 92
Görele, Turk. 41°2' N, 38°59' E 158
Gorey, Ire. 49°11' N, 2°3' W 150
Gorgān, Iran 36°50' N, 54°25' E 180
Gorgonta, Arg. 33°48' S, 66°45' W 134
Gorgora, Eth. 12°13' N, 37°17' E 182
Gorgova, Rom. 45°10' N, 29°10' E 156
Gorguz, Mex. 28°53' N, 111°10' W 92
Gorham, Me., U.S. 43°40' N, 70°27' W 104
Gori, Ga. 41°57' N, 44°8' E 195
Gori Rit, Somalia 8°0' N, 48°8' E 218
Gorinchem, Neth. 51°49' N, 4°59' E 167
Goris, Arm. 39°30' N, 46°20' E 195
Gorizia, It. 45°56' N, 13°36' E 167
Gorj, adm. division, Rom. 44°42' N, 23°8' E 156
Gorjani, Croatia 45°23' N, 18°21' E 168
Gorkha, Nepal 28°2' N, 84°40' E 197
Gorki, Russ. 65°4' N, 65°29' E 169
Gorleston, U.K. 52°34' N, 1°42' E 163
Görlitz, Ger. 51°8' N, 14°58' E 152
Gorman, Calif., U.S. 34°45' N, 118°49' W 101
Gorman, Tex., U.S. 32°12' N, 98°41' W 92
Gornja Tuzla, Bosn. and Herzg. 44°34' N, 18°44' E 168
Gornji Muć, Croatia 43°41' N, 16°25' E 168
Gornji Streoc, Serb. and Mont. 42°35' N, 20°18' E 168
Gornji Vakuf (Uskoplje), Bosn. and Herzg. 43°55' N, 17°33' E 168
Gorno Altaysk, Russ. 51°57' N, 86°2' E 184
Gorno-Altay, adm. division, Russ. 50°43' N, 85°39' E 184
Gornozavodsk, Russ. 46°32' N, 141°52' E 190
Gornyak, Russ. 51°0' N, 81°30' E 184
Gornyatskiy, Russ. 67°31' N, 64°13' E 169
Gornyy, Russ. 51°43' N, 48°36' E 158
Gornyy Balykley, Russ. 49°35' N, 45°0' E 158
Goro, river, Cen. Af. Rep. 9°13' N, 21°36' E 218
Gorodets, Russ. 58°30' N, 29°47' E 166
Gorodets, Russ. 56°37' N, 43°35' E 154
Gorodishche, Russ. 53°16' N, 45°45' E 154
Gorodishche, Russ. 58°14' N, 29°53' E 166
Gorodovikovsk, Russ. 46°4' N, 41°48' E 158
Gorom Gorom, Burkina Faso 14°27' N, 0°15' E 222
Gorong, Kepulauan, islands, Banda Sea 4°39' S, 130°39' E 192
Gorongosa National Park, Mozambique 19°13' S, 34°35' E 224
Gorongosa, Serra da, peak, Mozambique 18°27' S, 34°0' E 224
Gorontalo, Indonesia 0°38' N, 123°2' E 192
Gortyn, ruin(s), Gr. 35°3' N, 24°50' E 156
Gorutuba, river, Braz. 15°10' S, 43°32' W 138
Goryachiy Klyuch, Russ. 44°37' N, 39°6' E 156
Gorzów Wielkopolski, Pol. 52°44' N, 15°15' E 152
Górzyca, Pol. 52°29' N, 14°40' E 152
Goschen Strait 10°40' S, 150°46' E 192
Gosen, Japan 37°43' N, 139°10' E 201
Goseong, S. Korea 34°58' N, 128°19' E 200
Gosford, Austral. 33°23' S, 151°20' E 231
Gosforth, U.K. 54°25' N, 3°26' W 162
Goshen, Calif., U.S. 36°21' N, 119°26' W 100
Goshen, N.H., U.S. 43°18' N, 72°9' W 104
Goshen, Utah, U.S. 39°56' N, 111°54' W 90
Goshute Mountains, Nev., U.S. 40°27' N, 114°29' W 90
Gospić, Croatia 44°32' N, 15°21' E 156
Gosport, Ind., U.S. 39°20' N, 86°40' W 102
Goss, Miss., U.S. 31°20' N, 89°54' W 103
Gosselies, Belg. 50°28' N, 4°26' E 167
Gossinga, Sudan 8°38' N, 25°57' E 224
Gostilje, Serb. and Mont. 43°39' N, 19°50' E 168
Gostiņi, Latv. 56°36' N, 25°46' E 166
Gostivar, Maced. 41°47' N, 20°54' E 168
Gota, Eth. 9°31' N, 41°21' E 224
Götaland, region, Europe 58°8' N, 10°51' E 150
Gote, Dem. Rep. of the Congo 2°12' N, 30°48' E 224
Göteborg, Nor. 57°41' N, 11°57' E 152
Gotha, Ger. 50°57' N, 10°42' E 152
Gothenburg, Nebr., U.S. 40°56' N, 100°11' W 92
Gothèye, Niger 13°49' N, 1°31' E 222
Gotland, island, Sw. 57°33' N, 18°49' E 166
Gotska Sandön, island, Sw. 58°24' N, 19°12' E 166
Gotska Sandön National Park, Sw. 58°12' N, 19°28' E 166
Gōtsu, Japan 35°0' N, 132°13' E 200
Göttingen, Ger. 51°32' N, 9°55' E 167
Goubéré, Cen. Af. Rep. 5°50' N, 26°43' E 224
Gouda, Neth. 52°0' N, 4°42' E 167
Goudiry, Senegal 14°10' N, 12°45' W 222
Goudoumaria, Niger 13°43' N, 11°8' E 222
Gouéké, Guinea 7°57' N, 8°43' W 222
Gouin, Réservoir, lake, Can. 48°18' N, 76°31' W 106
Gouin, Réservoir, lake, Can. 48°18' N, 76°42' W 81
Goulais, river, Can. 46°44' N, 84°41' W 110
Goulburn, Austral. 34°46' S, 149°45' E 231
Goulburn Islands, Arafura Sea 11°36' S, 133°38' E 192
Gould, Ark., U.S. 33°58' N, 91°35' W 96
Gould Bay 77°46' S, 49°17' W 248
Gould Coast, Antarctica 84°15' S, 127°3' W 248
Gouldsboro, Me., U.S. 44°28' N, 68°3' W 111
Goulimine, Mor. 28°57' N, 10°5' W 143
Goulmima, Mor. 31°43' N, 4°57' W 214
Goumbou, Mali 14°58' N, 7°27' W 222
Gouméré, Côte d'Ivoire 7°55' N, 2°60' W 222
Gounarou, Benin 10°51' N, 2°49' E 222
Goundam, Mali 16°24' N, 3°41' W 222
Goundi, Chad 9°20' N, 17°21' E 216
Gounou Gaya, Chad 9°39' N, 15°28' E 216
Gouradi, spring, Chad 16°24' N, 17°11' E 216
Gouré, Niger 14°0' N, 10°15' E 222

Gouring, spring, Chad 18°44' N, 19°8' E 216
Gourlay Lake, Can. 48°51' N, 85°29' W 94
Gourma, region, Africa 12°15' N, 2°118' W 222
Gourma Rharous, Mali 16°52' N, 1°55' W 222
Gournay, Fr. 49°28' N, 1°43' E 163
Gournia, ruin(s), Gr. 35°5' N, 25°42' E 156
Gouro, Chad 19°32' N, 19°33' E 216
Gove, Kans., U.S. 38°58' N, 100°29' W 90
Govena, Mys, Russ. 59°34' N, 165°28' E 160
Govenlock, Can. 49°12' N, 109°47' W 90
Governador Valadares, Braz. 18°51' S, 41°55' W 138
Governor's Harbour, adm. division, Bahamas 25°18' N, 77°33' W 116
Govĭsümber, adm. division, Mongolia 46°22' N, 108°22' E 198
Gowanda, N.Y., U.S. 42°27' N, 78°57' W 94
Gowen, Okla., U.S. 34°51' N, 95°29' W 96
Gower Peninsula, U.K. 51°36' N, 4°6' W 162
Gowganda, Can. 47°38' N, 80°45' W 110
Gowmal Kalay, Afghan. 32°28' N, 69°0' E 186
Goya, Arg. 29°10' S, 59°16' W 139
Göyçay, Azerb. 40°38' N, 47°44' E 195
Goyeau, Pointe, Can. 51°37' N, 78°58' W 110
Goyelle, Lac, lake, Can. 50°43' N, 61°15' W 111
Göynük, Turk. 40°24' N, 30°48' E 156
Goz Beïda, Chad 12°13' N, 21°25' E 216
Goz Pass, Can. 64°31' N, 132°24' W 98
Goz Regeb, Sudan 16°1' N, 35°34' E 182
Gozo, island, Malta 36°4' N, 13°38' E 216
Graaff-Reinet, S. Af. 32°17' S, 24°27' E 227
Graafwater, S. Af. 32°9' S, 18°34' E 227
Grabo, Côte d'Ivoire 4°55' N, 7°30' W 214
Grabovac, Serb. and Mont. 44°35' N, 20°5' E 168
Gračanica, Bosn. and Herzg. 44°42' N, 18°17' E 168
Grace, Mount, Mass., U.S. 42°41' N, 72°23' W 104
Gracefield, Can. 46°6' N, 76°3' W 94
Graceville, Minn., U.S. 45°33' N, 96°28' W 90
Grachevka, Russ. 52°54' N, 52°54' E 158
Gracias a Dios, Cabo, Nicar. 14°51' N, 83°10' W 115
Gradac, Serb. and Mont. 43°22' N, 19°9' E 168
Gradačac, Bosn. and Herzg. 44°53' N, 18°25' E 168
Gradaús, Braz. 7°41' S, 51°11' W 130
Gradaús, Serra dos, Braz. 8°20' S, 50°60' W 130
Gradisca d'Isonzo, It. 45°54' N, 13°30' E 167
Gradište, Croatia 45°8' N, 18°42' E 168
Grado, It. 45°41' N, 13°23' E 167
Gradsko, Maced. 41°34' N, 21°57' E 168
Gräfenhainichen, Ger. 51°44' N, 12°27' E 152
Grafing, Ger. 48°2' N, 11°58' E 152
Graford, Tex., U.S. 32°55' N, 98°15' W 92
Grafton, N. Dak., U.S. 48°23' N, 97°27' W 90
Grafton, Vt., U.S. 43°10' N, 72°37' W 104
Grafton, W. Va., U.S. 39°20' N, 80°2' W 94
Grafton, Wis., U.S. 43°18' N, 87°58' W 102
Grafton, Mount, Nev., U.S. 38°40' N, 114°50' W 90
Grafton Notch, pass, Me., U.S. 44°35' N, 70°56' W 104
Graham, Can. 49°15' N, 90°34' W 94
Graham, Tex., U.S. 33°5' N, 98°34' W 92
Graham Bell, Ostrov, island, Russ. 81°26' N, 63°57' E 160
Graham Island, Can. 54°11' N, 133°54' W 98
Graham Lake, Can. 56°30' N, 115°16' W 108
Graham, Mount, Ariz., U.S. 32°41' N, 109°56' W 92
Graham, river, Can. 56°23' N, 123°5' W 108
Grahamstown, S. Af. 33°18' S, 26°29' E 227
Grahovo, Serb. and Mont. 42°38' N, 18°40' E 168
Graian Alps, It. 45°31' N, 6°43' E 165
Grain Coast, region, Africa 5°23' N, 9°22' W 222
Grajal de Campos, Sp. 42°18' N, 5°3' W 150
Grajaú, river, Braz. 5°19' S, 46°2' W 130
Gramada, Bulg. 43°50' N, 22°39' E 168
Gramado, Braz. 29°20' S, 50°50' W 139
Gramercy, La., U.S. 30°3' N, 90°42' W 103
Grámos, Óros, Gr. 40°11' N, 20°38' E 156
Grampian Mountains, U.K. 56°38' N, 5°6' W 150
Gran, Nor. 60°21' N, 10°34' E 152
Gran Bajo de San Julián, Arg. 49°23' S, 70°59' W 134
Gran Canaria, island, Sp. 27°21' N, 15°22' W 214
Gran Chaco, region, Parag. 21°5' S, 61°33' W 134
Gran Morelos, Mex. 28°14' N, 106°33' W 92
Gran Pajonal, region, South America 10°40' S, 74°28' W 130
Gran Paradiso, peak, It. 45°31' N, 7°13' E 165
Gran Sabana, La, Venez. 5°4' N, 62°25' W 130
Gran Sasso d'Italia, It. 42°24' N, 13°13' E 156
Gran Tarajal, Sp. 28°14' N, 14°3' W 214
Granada, Col. 3°31' N, 73°44' W 136
Granada, Colo., U.S. 38°3' N, 102°19' W 90
Granada, Nicar. 11°55' N, 85°59' W 115
Granada, Sp. 37°13' N, 3°39' W 143
Granada, Sp. 37°11' N, 3°36' W 164
Granadero Gatica, Arg. 26°52' S, 62°42' W 139
Granados, Mex. 29°51' N, 109°21' W 92
Granbori, Suriname 3°48' N, 54°54' W 130
Granbury, Tex., U.S. 32°26' N, 97°46' W 92
Granby, Colo., U.S. 40°4' N, 105°56' W 90
Granby, Mass., U.S. 42°15' N, 72°31' W 104
Granby, Vt., U.S. 44°34' N, 71°46' W 104
Grand Bahama, island, Bahamas 27°0' N, 78°0' W 118
Grand Bank, Can. 47°4' N, 55°48' W 111
Grand Banks of Newfoundland, North Atlantic Ocean 45°14' N, 52°41' W 253
Grand Bend, Can. 43°18' N, 81°44' W 102
Grand Blanc, Mich., U.S. 42°55' N, 83°37' W 102
Grand Cane, La., U.S. 32°4' N, 93°49' W 103
Grand Canyon, Ariz., U.S. 35°46' N, 113°37' W 101
Grand Canyon National Park, Ariz., U.S. 35°50' N, 114°11' W 101
Grand Cayman, island, U.K. 19°0' N, 81°0' W 118
Grand Centre, Can. 54°23' N, 110°14' W 108
Grand Cess, Liberia 4°40' N, 8°11' W 214
Grand Chenier, La., U.S. 29°45' N, 92°58' W 103
Grand Coteau, La., U.S. 30°24' N, 92°2' W 103
Grand Coulee, Wash., U.S. 47°48' N, 119°24' W 90
Grand Coulee, Wash., U.S. 47°55' N, 119°1' W 90
Grand Falls, Can. 47°1' N, 67°47' W 94
Grand Falls-Windsor, Can. 48°53' N, 55°42' W 106
Grand Forks, Can. 49°1' N, 118°28' W 108
Grand Forks, N. Dak., U.S. 47°53' N, 97°3' W 90
Grand Forks Air Force Base, N. Dak., U.S. 47°56' N, 97°31' W 90
Grand Haven, Mich., U.S. 43°2' N, 86°14' W 102
Grand Island, Nebr., U.S. 40°54' N, 98°22' W 90
Grand Isle, La., U.S. 29°15' N, 89°60' W 103
Grand Junction, Colo., U.S. 39°4' N, 108°34' W 90
Grand Junction, Mich., U.S. 42°23' N, 86°4' W 102
Grand Lake, Can. 46°3' N, 66°25' W 94
Grand Lake, La., U.S. 29°46' N, 91°28' W 103
Grand Lake, La., U.S. 30°10' N, 93°16' W 103
Grand Ledge, Mich., U.S. 42°44' N, 84°46' W 102
Grand Manan Island, island, Can. 44°42' N, 66°47' W 111
Grand Marais, Can. 50°31' N, 96°34' W 90
Grand Marais, Mich., U.S. 46°39' N, 85°60' W 94
Grand Marais, Minn., U.S. 47°45' N, 90°23' W 94
Grand Mesa, Colo., U.S. 38°57' N, 108°22' W 90
Grand Popo, Benin 6°17' N, 1°51' E 222
Grand Portage, Minn., U.S. 47°57' N, 89°45' W 82
Grand Portal Point, Mich., U.S. 46°14' N, 86°30' W 94
Grand Prairie, Tex., U.S. 32°43' N, 96°58' W 92
Grand Rapids, Can. 53°10' N, 99°20' W 108
Grand Rapids, Mich., U.S. 42°56' N, 85°40' W 102
Grand Rapids, Minn., U.S. 47°13' N, 93°32' W 90
Grand Ridge, Ill., U.S. 41°14' N, 88°50' W 102
Grand, river, Mich., U.S. 42°57' N, 85°46' W 80
Grand, river, Mo., U.S. 40°15' N, 94°24' W 80
Grand, river, S. Dak., U.S. 45°40' N, 101°46' W 90
Grand Saline, Tex., U.S. 32°39' N, 95°43' W 96
Grand Santi, Fr. 4°20' N, 54°23' W 130
Grand Teton, peak, Wyo., U.S. 43°42' N, 110°53' W 90
Grand Traverse Bay 44°59' N, 85°60' W 110
Grandas, Sp. 43°12' N, 6°54' W 150
Grand-Bassam, Côte d'Ivoire 5°13' N, 3°46' W 222
Grande, Bahía 51°3' S, 70°13' W 134
Grande, Baía, lake, Bol. 15°28' S, 60°41' W 132
Grande Cache, Can. 53°53' N, 119°10' W 108
Grande Cayemite, island, Haiti 18°33' N, 73°42' W 116
Grande, Cayo, island, Cuba 20°40' N, 79°37' W 116
Grande, Cayo, island, Venez. 11°32' N, 66°37' W 116
Grande, Corno, peak, It. 42°27' N, 13°29' E 156
Grande, Cuchilla, Uru. 33°58' S, 56°15' W 139
Grande de Lípez, river, Bol. 21°60' S, 67°21' W 137
Grande Prairie, Can. 55°10' N, 118°49' W 108
Grande, Punta, Chile 25°7' S, 70°31' W 132
Grande, river, Braz. 20°30' S, 48°51' W 138
Grande, river, Braz. 13°5' S, 45°35' W 138
Grande, river, Can. 48°40' N, 65°15' W 111
Grande, Serra, Braz. 10°11' S, 61°36' W 130
Grande, Serra (Carauna), peak, Braz. 2°34' N, 60°46' W 130
Grande Sertão Veredas National Park, Braz. 15°32' S, 46°6' W 138
Grande, Sierra, Mex. 29°42' N, 105°8' W 112
Grande-Terre, island, Fr. 16°32' N, 61°28' W 116
Grandfalls, Tex., U.S. 31°19' N, 102°51' W 92
Grandfather Mountain, N.C., U.S. 36°5' N, 81°54' W 96
Grandfield, Okla., U.S. 34°12' N, 98°41' W 92
Grand-Fort-Philippe, Fr. 50°59' N, 2°5' E 163
Grand-Lahou, Côte d'Ivoire 5°8' N, 5°2' W 222
Grand-Mère, Can. 46°36' N, 72°43' W 94
Grandpré, Fr. 49°20' N, 4°51' E 163
Grandview, Can. 51°9' N, 100°43' W 90
Grandview, Wash., U.S. 46°14' N, 119°55' W 90
Grandvilliers, Fr. 49°39' N, 1°56' E 163
Grañén, Sp. 41°56' N, 0°22' E 164
Grange, U.K. 54°10' N, 2°56' W 162
Granger, Ind., U.S. 41°44' N, 86°7' W 102
Granger, Tex., U.S. 30°41' N, 97°27' W 92
Granger, Wyo., U.S. 41°36' N, 109°58' W 90
Granges, Fr. 48°8' N, 6°47' E 163
Grangeville, Idaho, U.S. 45°53' N, 116°7' W 82
Granisle, Can. 54°54' N, 126°18' W 108
Granite, Okla., U.S. 34°56' N, 99°24' W 92
Granite Falls, Minn., U.S. 44°46' N, 95°34' W 90
Granite Falls, Wash., U.S. 48°4' N, 121°58' W 100
Granite Mountain, Nev., U.S. 40°16' N, 117°54' W 90
Granite Mountains, Wyo., U.S. 42°44' N, 108°1' W 90
Granite Pass, Calif., U.S. 35°25' N, 116°35' W 101
Granite Peak, Mont., U.S. 45°8' N, 109°53' W 90
Granite Peak, Nev., U.S. 41°38' N, 117°41' W 90
Granite Peak, Nev., U.S. 40°46' N, 119°31' W 90
Granite Peak, Utah, U.S. 40°6' N, 113°20' W 90
Granite Range, Nev., U.S. 40°32' N, 108°57' W 90
Granity, N.Z. 41°40' S, 171°51' E 240
Granja, Braz. 3°9' S, 40°51' W 132
Granja de Torrehermosa, Sp. 38°18' N, 5°37' W 164
Grankulla (Kauniainen), Fin. 60°11' N, 24°43' E 152
Granma, Cuba 19°51' N, 77°33' W 116
Gränna, Nor. 58°1' N, 14°28' E 152
Grannd Erg Oriental, Alg. 33°50' N, 7°52' E 156
Gransee, Ger. 53°1' N, 13°8' E 152
Grant, Mich., U.S. 43°19' N, 85°49' W 102
Grant, Nebr., U.S. 40°50' N, 101°44' W 90
Grant City, Mo., U.S. 40°27' N, 94°25' W 94
Grant Island, Antarctica 73°36' S, 131°2' W 248
Grant, Mount, Nev., U.S. 38°33' N, 118°53' W 90
Grant Range, Nev., U.S. 38°35' N, 115°34' W 90
Grantham, N.H., U.S. 43°29' N, 72°8' W 104
Grantham, U.K. 52°54' N, 0°39' E 162
Grant-Kohrs Ranch National Historic Site, Mont., U.S. 46°22' N, 112°52' W 90
Grants, N. Mex., U.S. 35°8' N, 107°51' W 112
Grants Pass, Oreg., U.S. 42°26' N, 123°21' W 90
Grantsburg, Wis., U.S. 45°45' N, 92°41' W 110
Grantsville, W. Va., U.S. 38°55' N, 81°6' W 102
Grantville, Ga., U.S. 33°13' N, 84°51' W 96
Granum, Can. 49°52' N, 113°31' W 90
Granville, Fr. 48°50' N, 1°36' W 150
Granville, N. Dak., U.S. 48°14' N, 100°51' W 90
Granville, Vt., U.S. 43°58' N, 72°51' W 104
Granville, W. Va., U.S. 39°38' N, 79°60' W 94
Granville Lake, Can. 56°16' N, 101°37' W 108
Granvin, Nor. 60°34' N, 6°41' E 152
Grão Mogol, Braz. 16°35' S, 42°57' W 138
Grapeland, Tex., U.S. 31°28' N, 95°29' W 103
Grapevine Mountains, Calif., U.S. 36°56' N, 117°13' W 101
Grapevine Peak, Nev., U.S. 36°57' N, 117°11' W 101
Graphite Peak, Antarctica 85°15' S, 167°50' E 248
Grapska Donja, Bosn. and Herzg. 44°47' N, 18°4' E 168
Graskop, S. Af. 24°58' S, 30°50' E 227
Grasmere, U.K. 54°27' N, 3°1' W 162
Gräsö, island, Sw. 60°26' N, 18°25' E 166
Grass, river, Can. 55°6' N, 98°33' W 108
Grass Valley, Calif., U.S. 39°12' N, 121°5' W 90
Grasset, Lac, lake, Can. 49°55' N, 78°40' W 94
Grassington, U.K. 54°4' N, 1°59' W 162
Grassland, Can. 54°48' N, 112°42' W 108
Grasslands National Park, Can. 48°54' N, 107°60' W 90
Grassrange, Mont., U.S. 47°0' N, 108°48' W 90
Grassy Butte, N. Dak., U.S. 47°22' N, 103°17' W 90
Grassy Island Lake, Can. 51°51' N, 110°51' W 90
Grassy Key, island, Fla., U.S. 24°43' N, 80°55' W 105
Grassy Mountain, Oreg., U.S. 42°37' N, 117°25' W 90
Grästorp, Nor. 58°19' N, 12°39' E 152
Grates Point, Can. 48°11' N, 53°9' W 111
Graton, Calif., U.S. 38°26' N, 122°53' W 92
Gråträsk, Nor. 65°28' N, 19°45' E 152
Graus, Sp. 42°10' N, 0°19' E 164
Grave, Neth. 51°45' N, 5°43' E 167
Grave Peak, Idaho, U.S. 46°22' N, 114°49' W 90
Gravedona, It. 46°9' N, 9°17' E 167
Gravelbourg, Can. 49°52' N, 106°34' W 90
Gravelines, Fr. 50°59' N, 2°8' E 163
Gravelotte, S. Af. 23°56' S, 30°36' E 227
Gravenhurst, Can. 44°54' N, 79°22' W 94
Gravesend, U.K. 51°25' N, 0°21' E 162
Gravette, Ark., U.S. 36°23' N, 94°28' W 96
Gravvik, Nor. 64°59' N, 11°48' E 152
Gray, Me., U.S. 43°53' N, 70°20' W 104
Gray, Mount, Antarctica 74°53' S, 136°11' W 248
Grayland, Wash., U.S. 46°47' N, 124°6' W 100
Grayling, Alas., U.S. 62°57' N, 160°9' W 98
Grayling, Mich., U.S. 44°40' N, 84°43' W 94
Grays, U.K. 51°29' N, 0°20' E 162
Grays Harbor 46°49' N, 125°15' W 80
Grays Peak, Colo., U.S. 39°36' N, 105°54' W 90
Grayslake, Ill., U.S. 42°20' N, 88°3' W 102
Grayson, Ky., U.S. 38°19' N, 82°57' W 94
Grayson, La., U.S. 32°2' N, 92°7' W 103
Grayville, Mo., U.S. 38°14' N, 87°60' W 94
Grayvoron, Russ. 50°28' N, 35°39' E 158
Graz, Aust. 47°4' N, 15°26' E 156
Grazie, Monte le, peak, It. 42°10' N, 11°50' E 156
Grdelica, Serb. and Mont. 42°53' N, 22°4' E 168
Grea de Albarracin, Sp. 40°24' N, 1°22' W 164
Great Artesian Basin, Australia 22°45' S, 142°18' E 230
Great Australian Bight 37°7' S, 130°17' E 231
Great Badminton, U.K. 51°32' N, 2°17' W 162
Great Barrier Reef, Coral Sea 16°34' S, 147°16' E 252
Great Barrier Reef Marine Park, Coral Sea 19°12' S, 147°53' E 238
Great Barrington, Mass., U.S. 42°11' N, 73°23' W 104
Great Basalt Wall National Park, Austral. 20°7' S, 144°57' E 238
Great Basin, North America 36°22' N, 114°27' W 101
Great Basin National Park, Nev., U.S. 38°36' N, 114°29' W 90
Great Bear Lake, Can. 65°31' N, 121°54' W 106
Great Britain, island, U.K. 52°5' N, 1°42' W 143
Great Channel 6°12' N, 93°33' E 188
Great Corn Island see Maíz Grande, Isla del, Nicar. 11°44' N, 83°2' W 115
Great Crater, Israel 30°55' N, 34°59' E 194
Great Divide Basin, Wyo., U.S. 41°58' N, 108°11' W 90
Great Dividing Range, Australia 11°52' S, 142°8' E 192
Great Driffield, U.K. 54°0' N, 0°26' E 162
Great Exuma, island, Bahamas 23°23' N, 76°30' W 116
Great Falls, Can. 50°23' N, 96°4' W 90
Great Falls, Mont., U.S. 47°28' N, 111°18' W 90
Great Falls, S.C., U.S. 34°33' N, 80°54' W 96
Great Fish, river, S. Af. 33°1' S, 25°53' E 227
Great Guana Cay, island, Bahamas 23°53' N, 76°37' W 116
Great Harbour Cay, island, Bahamas 25°39' N, 77°45' W 81
Great Harbour Deep, Can. 50°22' N, 56°33' W 111
Great Inagua Island, Bahamas 21°14' N, 73°53' W 116
Great Indian Desert, India 26°55' N, 68°30' E 186
Great Isaac, island, Bahamas 26°0' N, 79°20' W 105
Great Island, peak, Can. 58°59' N, 96°42' W 108
Great Islets Harbour 51°7' N, 56°40' W 111
Great Kei, river, S. Af. 32°20' S, 27°54' E 227
Great Lakes Naval Training Center, Ill., U.S. 42°17' N, 87°54' W 102
Great Namaland, region, Africa 26°5' S, 14°59' E 227
Great Nicobar, island, India 6°29' N, 93°53' E 188
Great Orme's Head, U.K. 53°20' N, 3°60' W 162
Great Ouse, river, U.K. 52°36' N, 0°17' E 162
Great Pedro Bluff, Jam. 17°45' N, 78°41' W 115
Great Point, Mass., U.S. 41°23' N, 70°8' W 104
Great Pond, lake, Me., U.S. 44°29' N, 70°3' W 104
Great Ruaha, river, Tanzania 7°21' S, 35°14' E 224
Great Sacandaga Lake, N.Y., U.S. 43°17' N, 74°11' W 104
Great Salt Lake, Utah, U.S. 41°16' N, 113°26' W 106
Great Salt Lake Desert, Utah, U.S. 40°26' N, 113°47' W 90
Great Salt Plains Lake, Okla., U.S. 36°45' N, 99°5' W 81
Great Sandy Desert, Australia 20°22' S, 122°54' E 230
Great Sitkin, island, Alas., U.S. 52°12' N, 177°22' W 160
Great Slave Lake, Can. 61°13' N, 117°25' W 73
Great Smoky Mountains, N.C., U.S. 35°44' N, 83°34' W 96
Great Snow Mountain, Can. 57°25' N, 124°12' W 108
Great Victoria Desert, Austral. 28°18' S, 126°42' E 230
Great Wall, China 39°15' N, 110°33' E 198
Great Wall, station, Antarctica 62°21' S, 58°57' W 134
Great Yarmouth, U.K. 52°36' N, 1°42' E 163
Great Zab, river, Turk. 37°27' N, 43°41' E 195
Great Zab see Zāb al Kabīr, river, Iraq 36°32' N, 43°40' E 195
Great Zimbabwe, ruin(s), Zimb. 20°24' S, 30°58' E 227
Greater Antilles, Caribbean Sea 17°49' N, 73°28' W 116
Greater Khingan Range, China 52°0' N, 122°48' E 172
Grebbestad, Nor. 58°41' N, 11°15' E 152
Grebenau, Ger. 50°44' N, 9°27' E 167
Grebenstein, Ger. 51°27' N, 9°25' E 167
Gréboun, peak, Niger 19°55' N, 8°29' E 222
Greco, Monte, peak, It. 41°47' N, 13°54' E 156
Gredos, Sierra de, Sp. 40°16' N, 5°43' W 150
Greece 39°6' N, 21°44' E 156
Greeley, Colo., U.S. 40°25' N, 104°43' W 90
Greeley, Nebr., U.S. 41°32' N, 98°33' W 90
Green Bay 44°38' N, 87°59' W 94
Green Island, N.Z. 45°53' S, 170°24' E 240
Green Islands, South Pacific Ocean 3°45' S, 153°35' E 192
Green Islands, South Pacific Ocean 4°1' S, 154°11' E 238
Green Lake, Can. 54°18' N, 107°47' W 108
Green Lake, Wis., U.S. 43°49' N, 88°57' W 102
Green Mountains, Vt., U.S. 44°2' N, 72°60' W 104
Green Mountains, Wyo., U.S. 42°27' N, 107°57' W 90
Green River, Utah, U.S. 38°59' N, 110°10' W 92
Green River, Wyo., U.S. 41°32' N, 109°28' W 90
Green, river, Ky., U.S. 37°37' N, 87°33' W 94
Green, river, U.S. 39°51' N, 109°57' W 90
Greenacres, Calif., U.S. 35°23' N, 119°8' W 101
Greenbush, Minn., U.S. 48°40' N, 96°13' W 90
Greenbush Lake, Can. 50°55' N, 90°38' W 110
Greencastle, Ind., U.S. 39°38' N, 86°52' W 102
Greene, Me., U.S. 44°11' N, 70°8' W 104
Greeneville, Tenn., U.S. 36°9' N, 82°51' W 96
Greenfield, Calif., U.S. 36°19' N, 121°15' W 100
Greenfield, Ind., U.S. 39°47' N, 85°46' W 102
Greenfield, Iowa, U.S. 41°18' N, 94°27' W 94
Greenfield, Mo., U.S. 37°24' N, 93°51' W 96
Greenfield, N.H., U.S. 42°56' N, 71°53' W 104
Greenfield, N. Mex., U.S. 33°9' N, 104°21' W 92
Greenfield, Ohio, U.S. 39°21' N, 83°24' W 102
Greenhorn Mountain, Colo., U.S. 37°52' N, 105°6' W 90
Greenhorn Mountains, Calif., U.S. 35°41' N, 118°54' W 92
Greenland (Kalaallit Nunaat), Den. 67°11' N, 50°25' W 106
Greenland, N.H., U.S. 43°1' N, 70°51' W 104
Greenland Fracture Zone, Greenland Sea 74°53' N, 2°12' E 255
Greenland Sea 74°52' N, 4°29' E 160
Greenland Sea 68°26' N, 25°49' W 246
Greenland Sea 73°24' N, 12°53' W 255
Greenough, Mount, Alas., U.S. 69°6' N, 141°54' W 98
Greenport, N.Y., U.S. 41°6' N, 72°23' W 104
Greensboro, Ala., U.S. 32°42' N, 87°36' W 103
Greensboro, Ga., U.S. 33°33' N, 83°11' W 96
Greensboro, N.C., U.S. 36°3' N, 79°49' W 96
Greensboro Bend, Vt., U.S. 44°32' N, 72°16' W 104
Greensburg, Ind., U.S. 39°19' N, 85°29' W 102
Greensburg, Kans., U.S. 37°35' N, 99°18' W 92
Greensburg, La., U.S. 30°49' N, 90°41' W 103
Greensburg, Pa., U.S. 40°17' N, 79°34' W 94
Greentown, Ind., U.S. 40°28' N, 85°58' W 102
Greenup, Ill., U.S. 39°13' N, 88°10' W 102
Greenup, Ky., U.S. 38°33' N, 82°50' W 102
Greenview, Ill., U.S. 40°4' N, 89°45' W 102
Greenville, Ala., U.S. 31°49' N, 86°37' W 96
Greenville, Can. 55°3' N, 129°36' W 108
Greenville, Fla., U.S. 30°26' N, 83°38' W 96
Greenville, Ill., U.S. 38°53' N, 89°24' W 102
Greenville, Ky., U.S. 37°12' N, 87°11' W 94
Greenville, Liberia 5°0' N, 9°3' W 222
Greenville, Me., U.S. 45°27' N, 69°36' W 94
Greenville, Mich., U.S. 43°10' N, 85°16' W 102
Greenville, Miss., U.S. 33°23' N, 91°4' W 103
Greenville, N.H., U.S. 42°46' N, 71°50' W 104
Greenville, Ohio, U.S. 40°5' N, 84°38' W 102
Greenville, Pa., U.S. 41°24' N, 80°23' W 94
Greenville, S.C., U.S. 34°50' N, 82°25' W 96
Greenville, Tex., U.S. 33°6' N, 96°6' W 96
Greenwich, Conn., U.S. 41°1' N, 73°38' W 104
Greenwich, N.Y., U.S. 43°5' N, 73°31' W 104
Greenwich, Ohio, U.S. 41°1' N, 82°31' W 102
Greenwich, U.K. 51°27' N, 3°180' E 162
Greenwich Island, Antarctica 62°45' S, 59°27' W 134
Greenwood, Ark., U.S. 35°11' N, 94°16' W 96
Greenwood, Can. 49°5' N, 118°41' W 90
Greenwood, Ind., U.S. 39°37' N, 86°6' W 102
Greenwood, Me., U.S. 44°18' N, 70°39' W 104
Greenwood, Miss., U.S. 33°29' N, 90°11' W 96
Greenwood, S.C., U.S. 34°11' N, 82°11' W 112
Greenwood, Mount, Austral. 13°47' S, 129°52' E 230
Greer, Ariz., U.S. 34°1' N, 109°27' W 92
Greetsiel, Ger. 53°30' N, 7°5' E 163
Gregoire Lake, Can. 56°27' N, 111°36' W 108
Gregório, river, Braz. 7°39' S, 71°13' W 130
Gregory, S. Dak., U.S. 43°12' N, 99°27' W 90
Gregory National Park, Austral. 16°23' S, 129°58' E 238
Gregory Range, Austral. 18°43' S, 142°20' E 230
Greiffenberg, Ger. 53°5' N, 13°56' E 152
Greifswald, Ger. 54°6' N, 13°22' E 152
Gremikha, Russ. 68°0' N, 39°23' E 169
Gremyachinsk, Russ. 58°35' N, 57°52' E 154
Grenå, Den. 56°25' N, 10°51' E 150
Grenada 12°0' N, 62°0' W 116
Grenada, Calif., U.S. 41°39' N, 122°32' W 92
Grenada, Miss., U.S. 33°43' N, 89°49' W 96
Grenchen, Switz. 47°11' N, 7°22' E 150
Grenfell, Can. 50°24' N, 102°56' W 90
Grenoble, Fr. 45°11' N, 5°43' E 150
Grenora, N. Dak., U.S. 48°36' N, 103°57' W 90
Grenville, Can. 45°37' N, 74°37' W 94
Grenville Channel 53°42' N, 130°45' W 108
Grenville, Mount, Can. 50°58' N, 124°36' W 90
Grenville, Point, Wash., U.S. 47°13' N, 124°31' W 100
Gresford, U.K. 53°5' N, 2°59' W 162
Gressåmoen National Park, Nor. 64°18' N, 12°52' E 152
Gretna, La., U.S. 29°54' N, 90°4' W 103
Greven, Ger. 52°5' N, 7°37' E 163
Grevenbroich, Ger. 51°5' N, 6°35' E 167
Grevenmacher, Lux. 49°40' N, 6°25' E 163
Grevesmühlen, Ger. 53°51' N, 11°12' E 152
Grey Islands, Labrador Sea 50°26' N, 55°8' W 106
Grey Range, Austral. 28°39' S, 142°4' E 230
Greybull, Wyo., U.S. 44°28' N, 108°4' W 90
Greylock, Mount, Mass., U.S. 42°37' N, 73°12' W 104
Greymouth, N.Z. 42°30' S, 171°13' E 240
Greytown, N.Z. 41°6' S, 175°29' E 240
Grezzana, It. 45°30' N, 11°0' E 167
Griam More, Ben, peak, U.K. 58°18' N, 4°9' W 150
Gribanovskiy, Russ. 51°27' N, 41°53' E 158
Gribe, Mal, Alban. 40°15' N, 19°29' E 156
Grico, oil field, Venez. 8°55' N, 66°40' W 136
Gridino, Russ. 65°53' N, 34°28' E 152
Gridley, Ill., U.S. 40°44' N, 88°53' W 102
Grieskirchen, Aust. 48°13' N, 13°50' E 152
Griffin, Ga., U.S. 33°13' N, 84°16' W 96
Grigorevka, Kyrg. 42°44' N, 77°48' E 184
Grigoriopol, Mold. 47°9' N, 29°17' E 158
Grimari, Cen. Af. Rep. 5°43' N, 20°5' E 218
Grimsby, Can. 43°10' N, 79°34' W 94
Grimsby, U.K. 53°34' N, 0°5' E 162
Grimshaw, Can. 56°11' N, 117°37' W 108
Grimstad, Nor. 58°20' N, 8°34' E 150
Grindelwald, Switz. 46°37' N, 8°2' E 167
Grinnell, Iowa, U.S. 41°44' N, 92°43' W 94
Grinnell Peninsula, Can. 76°38' N, 95°22' W 106
Griñón, Sp. 40°12' N, 3°51' W 164
Grintavec, peak, Slov. 46°21' N, 14°28' E 156
Gripsholm, site, Nor. 59°14' N, 17°5' E 152
Griquatown, S. Af. 28°51' S, 23°15' E 227
Grise Fiord, Can. 76°21' N, 82°51' W 106
Grishkino, Russ. 57°57' N, 82°44' E 169
Grisslehamn, Sw. 60°4' N, 18°44' E 166
Griswoldville, Mass., U.S. 42°39' N, 72°43' W 104
Griva, Latv. 55°49' N, 26°31' E 166
Griva, Russ. 60°34' N, 50°55' E 154
Grizim, spring, Alg. 25°25' N, 3°4' W 214
Grizzly Bear Hills, Can. 55°35' N, 109°42' W 108
Grizzly Mountain, Can. 51°42' N, 120°20' W 90
Grmeic, Bosn. and Herzg. 44°21' N, 16°29' E 168
Grobiņa, Latv. 56°32' N, 21°9' E 166
Grocka, Serb. and Mont. 44°39' N, 20°42' E 168
Groenlo, Neth. 52°2' N, 6°36' E 167
Grombalia, Tun. 36°35' N, 10°31' E 214
Gromovo, Russ. 60°41' N, 30°16' E 166
Grong, Nor. 64°27' N, 12°20' E 152
Groningen, Neth. 53°12' N, 6°33' E 163
Gronlid, Can. 53°5' N, 104°28' W 108
Grønøy, Nor. 66°47' N, 13°25' E 152
Groom, Tex., U.S. 35°13' N, 101°5' W 92
Groot Karasberge, peak, Namibia 27°12' S, 18°37' E 227
Groote Eylandt, island, Austral. 14°27' S, 137°3' E 230
Grootfontein, Namibia 19°32' S, 18°7' E 220
Gros Mécatina, Cap du, Can. 50°38' N, 59°8' W 111
Gros Morne National Park, Can. 49°46' N, 58°30' W 111
Gros Morne, peak, Can. 49°34' N, 57°52' W 111
Gros Ventre, Wyo., U.S. 43°24' N, 111°16' W 80
Gros Ventre Range, Wyo., U.S. 43°28' N, 110°52' W 90
Grosio, It. 46°17' N, 10°14' E 167

Grosne, river, Fr. 46°32′ N, 4°38′ E 165
Grossa, Ponta, Braz. 1°14′ N, 49°54′ W 130
Grossa, Punta, Sp. 39°5′ N, 1°16′ E 150
Grossalmerode, Ger. 51°15′ N, 9°46′ E 167
Grossefehn, Ger. 53°24′ N, 7°36′ E 163
Grossenkneten, Ger. 52°56′ N, 8°16′ E 163
Grossenlüder, Ger. 50°36′ N, 9°32′ E 167
Grosseto, It. 42°45′ N, 11°5′ E 156
Grossglockner, peak, Aust. 47°4′ N, 12°37′ E 156
Gross-Umstadt, Ger. 49°52′ N, 8°54′ E 167
Grostenquin, Fr. 48°57′ N, 6°43′ E 163
Grosvenor Seamount, North Pacific Ocean 28°4′ N, 166°46′ E 252
Groton, Mass., U.S. 42°36′ N, 71°35′ W 104
Groton, S. Dak., U.S. 45°26′ N, 98°7′ W 90
Groton, Vt., U.S. 44°12′ N, 72°12′ W 104
Grøtøy, Nor. 67°49′ N, 14°42′ E 152
Grottammare, It. 42°59′ N, 13°51′ E 156
Grotte de Lascaux, site, Fr. 45°2′ N, 1°9′ E 165
Grouard, Can. 55°31′ N, 116°8′ W 108
Groundhog, river, Can. 49°22′ N, 82°15′ W 94
Grouse Creek, Utah, U.S. 41°42′ N, 113°54′ W 92
Grouse Creek Mountain, Idaho, U.S. 44°21′ N, 113°59′ W 90
Grouse Creek Mountains, Utah, U.S. 41°29′ N, 114°8′ W 90
Grovane, Nor. 58°17′ N, 7°58′ E 152
Grove Hill, Ala., U.S. 31°42′ N, 87°46′ W 103
Groveland, Calif., U.S. 37°49′ N, 120°15′ W 100
Groveland, Fla., U.S. 28°33′ N, 81°51′ W 105
Groveport, Ohio, U.S. 39°51′ N, 82°53′ W 102
Grover, Colo., U.S. 40°52′ N, 104°15′ W 90
Grover, Pa., U.S. 41°36′ N, 76°53′ W 94
Grover Beach, Calif., U.S. 35°7′ N, 120°38′ W 92
Groves, Tex., U.S. 29°55′ N, 93°56′ W 103
Groveton, N.H., U.S. 44°36′ N, 71°32′ W 94
Groveton, Tex., U.S. 31°2′ N, 95°7′ W 103
Growler Pass, Ariz., U.S. 32°10′ N, 112°55′ W 92
Groznyy, Russ. 43°18′ N, 45°39′ E 195
Grubišno Polje, Croatia 45°41′ N, 17°10′ E 168
Gruda, Croatia 42°30′ N, 18°22′ E 168
Grudopole, Belarus 52°53′ N, 25°42′ E 152
Grudovo, Bulg. 42°20′ N, 27°10′ E 156
Grue, Nor. 60°26′ N, 12°2′ E 152
Gruemirë, Alban. 42°9′ N, 19°31′ E 168
Gruesa, Punta, Chile 20°23′ S, 70°36′ W 137
Grulla, Tex., U.S. 26°17′ N, 98°39′ W 114
Grums, Nor. 59°21′ N, 13°4′ E 152
Grünau, Namibia 27°44′ S, 18°21′ E 227
Grünberg, Ger. 50°35′ N, 8°57′ E 167
Grundforsen, Nor. 61°17′ N, 12°52′ E 152
Gruver, Tex., U.S. 36°14′ N, 101°25′ W 92
Gruža, Serb. and Mont. 43°54′ N, 20°46′ E 168
Gryazi, Russ. 52°28′ N, 39°48′ E 158
Gryazovets, Russ. 58°52′ N, 40°14′ E 154
Grygla, Minn., U.S. 48°16′ N, 95°39′ W 90
Gryžliny, Pol. 53°37′ N, 20°20′ E 152
Gstaad, Switz. 46°27′ N, 7°18′ E 167
Gua Musang, Malaysia 4°52′ N, 101°58′ E 196
Guabito, Pan. 9°29′ N, 82°36′ W 115
Guaca, Col. 6°50′ N, 72°50′ W 136
Guacamaya, Col. 2°15′ N, 75°1′ W 136
Guachara, Venez. 7°16′ N, 68°23′ W 136
Guachochi, Mex. 26°50′ N, 107°5′ W 112
Guaçui, Braz. 20°49′ S, 41°44′ W 138
Guadalajara, Mex. 20°39′ N, 103°26′ W 114
Guadalajara, Sp. 40°36′ N, 3°10′ W 164
Guadalajara, Sp. 40°37′ N, 3°10′ W 214
Guadalcanal, Sp. 38°5′ N, 5°50′ W 164
Guadalcanal, island, Solomon Islands 10°0′ S, 160°0′ E 242
Guadalquivir, river, Sp. 37°52′ N, 6°2′ W 143
Guadalupe, Braz. 6°49′ S, 43°35′ W 132
Guadalupe, Calif., U.S. 34°57′ N, 120°35′ W 100
Guadalupe, Mex. 25°40′ N, 100°15′ W 114
Guadalupe, Mex. 32°1′ N, 116°40′ W 112
Guadalupe, Mex. 29°22′ N, 110°27′ W 92
Guadalupe, Mex. 22°44′ N, 102°29′ W 114
Guadalupe, Sp. 39°27′ N, 5°19′ W 164
Guadalupe Bravos, Mex. 31°22′ N, 106°7′ W 92
Guadalupe, Isla de, island, Fr. 28°27′ N, 118°49′ W 112
Guadalupe Mountains, N. Mex., U.S. 32°16′ N, 105°7′ W 92
Guadalupe Peak, Tex., U.S. 31°51′ N, 104°56′ W 92
Guadalupe, Sierra de, Sp. 39°15′ N, 5°52′ W 164
Guadarrama, Sierra de, Sp. 41°18′ N, 3°18′ W 164
Guadeloupe, islands, Fr. 16°23′ N, 61°59′ W 116
Guadiana, river, Sp. 38°15′ N, 7°35′ W 143
Guadix, Sp. 37°18′ N, 3°9′ W 164
Guafo, Isla, island, Chile 43°32′ S, 75°41′ W 134
Guaíba, Braz. 30°10′ S, 51°21′ W 139
Guaicuí, Braz. 17°12′ S, 44°51′ W 138
Guáimaro, Cuba 21°3′ N, 77°24′ W 116
Guainía, adm. division, Col. 2°47′ N, 69°53′ W 136
Guainía, river, Col. 2°8′ N, 69°29′ W 136
Guaíra, Braz. 24°7′ S, 54°15′ W 132
Guaitecas, Islas, islands, South Pacific Ocean 43°59′ S, 76°28′ W 134
Guajaba, Cayo, island, Cuba 21°51′ N, 77°26′ W 116
Guajará-Miram, Braz. 10°49′ S, 65°20′ W 137
Guajarraã, Braz. 7°46′ S, 66°57′ W 130
Guaje, Llano del, Mex. 27°50′ N, 103°43′ W 112
Guajira, adm. division, Col. 11°6′ N, 73°23′ W 136
Guajira, Peninsula de la, Col. 11°58′ N, 72°6′ W 136
Gualaca, Pan. 8°31′ N, 82°18′ W 115
Gualaguala, Punta, Chile 22°47′ S, 70°56′ W 137
Gualala, Calif., U.S. 38°46′ N, 123°32′ W 90
Gualán, Guatemala 15°7′ N, 89°24′ W 115
Gualeguay, Arg. 33°7′ S, 59°18′ W 139
Gualeguaychú, Arg. 33°3′ S, 58°29′ W 139
Gualicho, Gran Bajo del, Arg. 40°15′ S, 67°12′ W 134
Gualjaina, Arg. 42°42′ S, 70°33′ W 134
Guam, U.S. 13°18′ N, 144°15′ E 242
Guamareyes, Col. 0°30′ N, 73°1′ W 136
Guamblin, Isla, island, Chile 45°1′ S, 76°41′ W 134
Guaminí, Arg. 37°2′ S, 62°23′ W 139
Guamo, Col. 3°59′ N, 75°1′ W 136
Guamúchil, Mex. 25°27′ N, 108°5′ W 112
Guanabacoa, Cuba 23°7′ N, 82°18′ W 96
Guanabara, Braz. 10°41′ S, 70°8′ W 137
Guanaceví, Mex. 25°58′ N, 105°57′ W 114
Guanaco, Arg. 35°42′ S, 61°40′ W 139
Guanaco, Paso del, pass, Chile 36°1′ S, 70°23′ W 134
Guanaja, Isla de, island, Hond. 16°31′ N, 85°49′ W 115
Guanajuato, Mex. 20°58′ N, 101°20′ W 114
Guanajuato, adm. division, Mex. 21°2′ N, 101°49′ W 114
Guanambi, Braz. 14°14′ S, 42°46′ W 138
Guanare, Venez. 9°2′ N, 69°47′ W 136
Guanare, river, Venez. 8°44′ N, 69°30′ W 136
Guanay, Bol. 15°28′ S, 67°53′ W 137
Guandacol, Arg. 29°32′ S, 68°32′ W 134
Guangchang, China 26°50′ N, 116°11′ E 198
Guangdong, adm. division, China 23°48′ N, 112°55′ E 198
Guangfeng, China 28°27′ N, 118°13′ E 198
Guanghai, China 21°55′ N, 112°46′ E 198
Guangrao, China 37°6′ N, 118°25′ E 198
Guangshan, China 32°0′ N, 114°52′ E 198
Guangshui, China 31°37′ N, 114°3′ E 198
Guangxi, adm. division, China 23°49′ N, 107°53′ E 198
Guangyuan, China 32°23′ N, 105°52′ E 173
Guangzhou (Canton), China 23°6′ N, 113°17′ E 198
Guanhaes, Braz. 18°48′ S, 43°1′ W 138
Guanshui, China 40°52′ N, 124°33′ E 200
Guanta, Venez. 10°14′ N, 64°35′ W 116
Guantánamo, Cuba 20°8′ N, 75°14′ W 116
Guantánamo, adm. division, Cuba 20°8′ N, 75°31′ W 116
Guanyan, China 34°16′ N, 119°14′ E 198
Guanyang, China 25°29′ N, 111°6′ E 198
Guapé, Braz. 20°47′ S, 45°56′ W 138
Guapi, Col. 2°33′ N, 77°57′ W 136
Guaporé, Braz. 28°58′ S, 51°57′ W 139
Guaporé Iténez, river, South America 11°49′ S, 65°5′ W 137
Guaporé, river, Braz. 15°29′ S, 58°50′ W 132
Guaqui, Bol. 16°40′ S, 68°51′ W 137
Guará, river, Braz. 13°26′ S, 45°34′ W 132
Guara, Sierra de, Sp. 42°23′ N, 0°26′ E 164
Guarabira, Braz. 6°52′ S, 35°32′ W 132
Guaraci, Braz. 20°33′ S, 48°56′ W 138
Guarai, Braz. 8°59′ S, 48°13′ W 130
Guarapari, Braz. 20°41′ S, 40°31′ W 138
Guarapuava, Braz. 25°23′ S, 51°29′ W 138
Guaraqueçaba, Braz. 25°18′ S, 48°20′ W 138
Guaratinguetá, Braz. 22°51′ S, 45°10′ W 138
Guaratuba, Braz. 25°55′ S, 48°35′ W 138
Guarda, Port. 40°32′ N, 7°17′ W 150
Guarda, adm. division, Port. 40°43′ N, 7°34′ W 150
Guarda Mor, Braz. 17°48′ S, 47°7′ W 138
Guardatinajas, Venez. 9°1′ N, 67°38′ W 136
Guardia Escolta, Arg. 28°57′ S, 62°11′ W 139
Guaribe, river, Braz. 8°2′ S, 60°33′ W 130
Guárico, adm. division, Venez. 8°47′ N, 67°29′ W 136
Guarico, Punta, Cuba 20°40′ N, 74°44′ W 116
Guarromán, Sp. 38°10′ N, 3°41′ W 164
Guasave, Mex. 25°33′ N, 108°29′ W 82
Guascama, Punta, Col. 2°21′ N, 78°28′ W 136
Guasipati, Venez. 7°27′ N, 61°56′ W 130
Guastalla, It. 44°55′ N, 10°38′ E 167
Guatemala 15°4′ N, 91°3′ W 115
Guatemala, Guatemala 14°34′ N, 90°40′ W 115
Guatemala Basin, North Pacific Ocean 6°59′ N, 94°28′ W 252
Guateque, Col. 5°0′ N, 73°28′ W 136
Guatraché, Arg. 37°42′ S, 63°29′ W 139
Guaviare, adm. division, Col. 1°43′ N, 73°27′ W 136
Guaviare, river, Col. 3°12′ N, 70°17′ W 136
Guaxupé, Braz. 21°18′ S, 46°43′ W 138
Guayabal, Cuba 20°42′ N, 77°39′ W 116
Guayabal, Venez. 7°58′ N, 67°23′ W 136
Guayabero, river, Col. 2°13′ N, 73°43′ W 136
Guayalejo, river, Mex. 23°24′ N, 99°4′ W 114
Guayaquil, Ecua. 2°17′ S, 79°57′ W 130
Guaymas, Mex. 28°4′ N, 110°50′ W 238
Guaymas, Cerro, peak, Mex. 28°10′ N, 111°14′ W 92
Guaymas, Valle de, Mex. 28°16′ N, 110°51′ W 112
Guaynabo, P.R., U.S. 18°0′ N, 66°0′ W 118
Guba, Dem. Rep. of the Congo 10°38′ S, 26°24′ E 224
Guba, Eth. 11°14′ N, 35°18′ E 182
Guba Dolgaya, Russ. 70°17′ N, 58°45′ E 169
Gubakha, Russ. 58°50′ N, 57°34′ E 169
Guban, region, Africa 10°31′ N, 42°50′ E 216
Gubat, Philippines 12°55′ N, 124°7′ E 203
Gubdor, Russ. 60°13′ N, 56°34′ E 154
Guben, Pol. 51°57′ N, 14°41′ E 152
Gubio, Nig. 12°27′ N, 12°45′ E 216
Gubkin, Russ. 51°15′ N, 37°32′ E 158
Guča, Serb. and Mont. 43°46′ N, 20°12′ E 168
Gucheng, China 32°15′ N, 111°33′ E 198
Gudaut'a, Ga. 43°6′ N, 40°40′ E 195
Gudbrandsdalen, Nor. 61°58′ N, 9°10′ E 152
Guddu Barrage, dam, Pak. 28°31′ N, 69°35′ E 186
Gudensberg, Ger. 51°11′ N, 9°23′ E 167
Gudivada, India 16°23′ N, 81°1′ E 188
Gudžiūnai, Lith. 55°31′ N, 23°45′ E 166
Guéckédou, Guinea 8°33′ N, 10°9′ W 222
Guedon Dong, oil field, Indonesia 4°51′ N, 97°45′ E 196
Guelph, Can. 43°33′ N, 80°14′ W 94
Guelta Mouiri Idié, spring, Chad 23°3′ N, 15°14′ E 216
Guemar, Alg. 33°29′ N, 6°48′ E 214
Guéné, Benin 11°45′ N, 3°14′ E 222
Güeppí, Peru 0°8′ N, 75°13′ W 136
Güepsa, Col. 6°2′ N, 73°37′ W 136
Guer, Fr. 47°54′ N, 2°9′ W 150
Güer Aike, Arg. 51°36′ S, 69°37′ W 134
Guéra, Massif de, peak, Chad 11°55′ N, 18°5′ E 218
Guerara, Alg. 32°47′ N, 4°29′ E 214
Guercif, Mor. 34°16′ N, 3°19′ W 214
Guéréda, Chad 14°29′ N, 22°2′ E 216
Guernsey, island, U.K. 49°27′ N, 2°36′ W 150
Guernsey, Wyo., U.S. 42°16′ N, 104°43′ W 90
Guerrero, adm. division, Mex. 17°45′ N, 100°51′ W 114
Guerzim, Alg. 29°40′ N, 1°40′ W 214
Guest Peninsula, Antarctica 76°20′ S, 149°54′ W 248
Gueydan, La., U.S. 30°1′ N, 92°31′ W 103
Guézaoua, Niger 14°29′ N, 8°47′ E 222
Gugu, peak, Eth. 8°11′ N, 39°50′ E 224
Guguan, island, U.S. 17°22′ N, 146°1′ E 192
Gui, river, China 24°0′ N, 110°41′ E 198
Guia Lopes da Laguna, Braz. 21°28′ S, 56°2′ W 132
Guiborosso, Côte d'Ivoire 8°45′ N, 7°2′ W 222
Guichen Bay 37°15′ S, 138°16′ E 230
Guichi, China 30°40′ N, 117°27′ E 198
Güicho, Kyrg. 40°18′ N, 73°29′ E 197
Guidan Roumji, Niger 13°41′ N, 6°33′ E 222
Guide, China 35°52′ N, 101°36′ E 190
Guider, Cameroon 9°55′ N, 13°56′ E 218
Guidiguir, Niger 13°41′ N, 9°49′ E 222
Guidimouni, Niger 13°42′ N, 9°26′ E 222
Guiding, China 26°33′ N, 107°14′ E 198
Guidouma, Gabon 1°38′ S, 10°42′ E 218
Guienne, region, Europe 44°10′ N, 1°7′ E 165
Guiglo, Côte d'Ivoire 6°26′ N, 7°30′ W 222
Guijá, Mozambique 24°27′ S, 33°3′ E 227
Guildford, U.K. 51°14′ N, 0°36′ E 162
Guildhall, Vt., U.S. 44°34′ N, 71°35′ W 104
Guilford, Conn., U.S. 41°16′ N, 72°41′ W 104
Guilford, Me., U.S. 45°10′ N, 69°24′ W 94
Guilford, Vt., U.S. 42°48′ N, 72°35′ W 104
Guilin, China 25°17′ N, 110°13′ E 198
Guillaume-Delisle, Lac, lake, Can. 56°7′ N, 79°17′ W 106
Guillaumes, Fr. 44°5′ N, 6°51′ E 167
Guillestre, Fr. 44°39′ N, 6°38′ E 167
Guilvinec, Fr. 47°47′ N, 4°18′ W 150
Guimarães, Braz. 2°6′ S, 44°36′ W 132
Guimarães, Port. 41°26′ N, 8°20′ W 214
Guimi, spring, Mauritania 17°29′ N, 13°18′ W 222
Guin, Ala., U.S. 33°59′ N, 87°55′ W 96
Guindulman, Philippines 9°47′ N, 124°28′ E 203
Guinea 10°20′ N, 10°36′ W 214
Guinea, Gulf of 4°29′ N, 0°6′ E 222
Guinea-Bissau 12°7′ N, 15°13′ W 214
Güines, Cuba 22°50′ N, 82°3′ W 112
Guînes, Fr. 50°51′ N, 1°52′ E 163
Guinguinéo, Senegal 14°16′ N, 15°54′ W 222
Guiones, Punta, C.R. 9°51′ N, 86°34′ W 115
Guiping, China 23°21′ N, 110°1′ E 198
Guir, Hamada du, Alg. 31°41′ N, 3°42′ W 214
Guir, spring, Mali 18°52′ N, 2°51′ W 222
Guiratinga, Braz. 16°23′ S, 53°47′ W 132
Guisborough, U.K. 54°32′ N, 1°3′ W 162
Guise, Fr. 49°54′ N, 3°39′ E 163
Guita Koulouba, Cen. Af. Rep. 5°55′ N, 23°22′ E 218
Guitiriz, Sp. 43°9′ N, 7°57′ W 150
Guitri, Côte d'Ivoire 5°30′ N, 5°14′ W 222
Guiuan, Philippines 11°4′ N, 125°43′ E 203
Guixi, China 28°18′ N, 116°59′ E 198
Guixian, China 23°10′ N, 109°35′ E 198
Guiyang, China 26°36′ N, 106°41′ E 198
Guiyang, China 25°46′ N, 112°43′ E 198
Guizhou, adm. division, China 27°34′ N, 106°15′ E 198
Gujar Khan, Pak. 33°12′ N, 73°18′ E 186
Gujarat, adm. division, India 22°12′ N, 69°57′ E 188
Gujba, Nig. 11°29′ N, 11°52′ E 222
Gujranwala, Pak. 32°8′ N, 74°9′ E 186
Gujrat, Pak. 32°32′ N, 74°6′ E 186
Gulbarga, India 17°19′ N, 76°50′ E 188
Gulbene, Latv. 57°10′ N, 26°45′ E 166
Gulen, Nor. 60°59′ N, 5°5′ E 152
Gulf Hammock, Fla., U.S. 29°14′ N, 82°44′ W 105
Gulf Shores, Ala., U.S. 30°14′ N, 87°42′ W 103
Gulfport, Fla., U.S. 27°45′ N, 82°42′ W 105
Gulfport, Miss., U.S. 30°21′ N, 89°5′ W 103
Gulfport, Mo., U.S. 40°48′ N, 91°4′ W 94
Gulin, China 28°5′ N, 105°52′ E 198
Guling, China 29°36′ N, 115°52′ E 198
Guliston, Uzb. 40°29′ N, 68°47′ E 197
Guliya Shan, peak, China 49°48′ N, 122°21′ E 198
Gulkana, Alas., U.S. 62°18′ N, 145°20′ W 106
Gull Islands, Lake Superior 48°11′ N, 88°12′ W 94
Gull Lake, Can. 50°4′ N, 108°29′ W 90
Gull Lake, Can. 52°30′ N, 114°20′ W 108
Gull Lake, Can. 51°13′ N, 92°16′ W 110
Gull Lake, Mich., U.S. 42°24′ N, 85°30′ W 102
Gullion, Slieve, peak, U.K. 54°6′ N, 6°32′ W 150
Güllük, Turk. 37°13′ N, 27°35′ E 156
Gulma, Nig. 12°37′ N, 4°20′ E 222
Gülnar, Turk. 36°20′ N, 33°24′ E 156
Gülşehir, Turk. 38°44′ N, 34°37′ E 156
Gülshat, Kaz. 46°39′ N, 74°23′ E 184
Gulsvik, Nor. 60°22′ N, 9°36′ E 152
Gulu, Uganda 2°45′ N, 32°17′ E 224
Gulwe, Tanzania 6°26′ S, 36°23′ E 224
Gulyayevo, Russ. 64°30′ N, 40°33′ E 154
Guma see Pishan, China 37°39′ N, 78°22′ E 184
Gumal, river, Pak. 31°45′ N, 69°17′ E 186
Gumare, Botswana 19°21′ S, 22°11′ E 220
Gumban, Eth. 7°37′ N, 43°15′ E 218
Gumdag, Turkm. 39°16′ N, 54°35′ E 180
Gumel, Nig. 12°36′ N, 9°23′ E 222
Gumiel de Hizán, Sp. 41°46′ N, 3°42′ W 164
Gumla, India 23°2′ N, 84°33′ E 197
Gumma, adm. division, Japan 36°32′ N, 138°28′ E 201
Gummersbach, Ger. 51°1′ N, 7°33′ E 167
Gummi, Nig. 12°2′ N, 5°9′ E 222
Gumuru, Sudan 6°36′ N, 32°54′ E 224
Gümüşdere, Turk. 38°22′ N, 43°12′ E 195
Gümüşhane, Turk. 40°26′ N, 39°26′ E 195
Gümüşören, Turk. 38°14′ N, 35°37′ E 156
Gun Cay, island, Bahamas 25°33′ N, 79°29′ W 105
Guna, Eth. 8°17′ N, 39°51′ E 224
Guna, India 24°37′ N, 77°19′ E 197
Guna Terara, peak, Eth. 11°42′ N, 38°7′ E 182
Gundlupet, India 11°49′ N, 76°40′ E 188
Gungu, Dem. Rep. of the Congo 5°46′ S, 19°14′ E 218
Gunib, Russ. 42°20′ N, 46°52′ E 195
Gunisao Lake, Can. 53°30′ N, 96°43′ W 108
Gunnbjørn, peak, Den. 68°56′ N, 30°33′ W 246
Gunnbøjrn Fjeld, peak, Den. 68°41′ N, 30°44′ W 73
Gunnison, Utah, U.S. 39°9′ N, 111°48′ W 90
Gunsan, S. Korea 35°57′ N, 126°44′ E 200
Guntersville, Ala., U.S. 34°19′ N, 86°21′ W 112
Guntur, India 16°17′ N, 80°26′ E 190
Gunung Bentuang National Park, Indonesia 1°14′ N, 112°46′ E 238
Gunung Leuser National Park, Indonesia 3°50′ N, 96°48′ E 196
Gunung Lorentz National Park, Indonesia 4°32′ S, 137°12′ E 238
Gunung Mulu National Park, Malaysia 4°2′ N, 114°34′ E 238
Gunung Palung National Park, Indonesia 1°14′ S, 109°51′ E 238
Gunungsitoli, Indonesia 1°20′ N, 97°31′ E 196
Guoyang, China 33°29′ N, 116°11′ E 198
Gupis, Pak. 36°12′ N, 73°25′ E 186
Gura Văii, Rom. 44°40′ N, 22°33′ E 168
Guragē, peak, Eth. 8°14′ N, 38°17′ E 224
Gurahonț, Rom. 46°16′ N, 22°21′ E 168
Gurais, India 34°35′ N, 74°52′ E 186
Gurba, river, Dem. Rep. of the Congo 4°0′ N, 27°27′ E 224
Gurbis, peak, Nor. 68°57′ N, 24°55′ E 152
Gurdaspur, India 32°3′ N, 75°25′ E 186
Gurdon, Ark., U.S. 33°54′ N, 93°9′ W 96
Güre, Turk. 38°38′ N, 29°7′ E 156
Gurgaon, India 28°26′ N, 77°2′ E 197
Gurgei, Jebel, peak, Sudan 13°49′ N, 24°13′ E 226
Gurghiu, Munții, Rom. 46°52′ N, 24°42′ E 156
Gurha, India 25°9′ N, 71°39′ E 186
Gurī, Eth. 7°30′ N, 40°35′ E 224
Guri Dam, Venez. 7°24′ N, 63°16′ W 130
Guri i Topit, peak, Alban. 40°46′ N, 20°23′ E 156
Gurig National Park, Austral. 11°34′ S, 131°52′ E 238
Gurinhatã, Braz. 19°14′ S, 49°49′ W 138
Gurktaler Alpen, Aust. 46°50′ N, 13°31′ E 167
Gurnet Point, Mass., U.S. 42°0′ N, 70°37′ W 104
Gurrea del Gállego, Sp. 42°0′ N, 0°46′ E 164
Gürün, Turk. 38°42′ N, 37°15′ E 156
Gurupá, Braz. 1°27′ S, 51°38′ W 132
Gurupi, Braz. 11°47′ S, 49°6′ W 130
Gurupi, Cabo, Braz. 0°54′ N, 46°18′ W 130
Gurupi, river, Braz. 2°55′ S, 46°25′ W 130
Gurupi, Serra do, Braz. 5°4′ S, 48°1′ W 130
Guruve, Zimb. 16°40′ S, 30°42′ E 224
Gur'yevsk, Russ. 54°47′ N, 20°34′ E 166
Gur'yevsk, Russ. 54°17′ N, 86°4′ E 184
Gus' Khrustal'nyy, Russ. 55°35′ N, 40°39′ E 154
Gusau, Nig. 12°10′ N, 6°42′ E 222
Güsen, Ger. 52°21′ N, 11°59′ E 152
Gusev, Russ. 54°36′ N, 22°13′ E 166
Guşgy, Turkm. 35°18′ N, 62°25′ E 186
Guşgy, river, Turkm. 37°12′ N, 62°30′ E 186
Gushan, China 39°53′ N, 123°33′ E 200
Gushi, China 32°10′ N, 115°38′ E 198
Gusinaya, Guba 71°25′ N, 145°37′ E 160
Güssing, Aust. 47°2′ N, 16°19′ E 168
Gustav Bull Mountains, Antarctica 67°41′ S, 65°17′ E 248
Gustav Holm, Kap, Den. 66°28′ N, 34°2′ W 106
Gustavia, Fr. 17°53′ N, 62°51′ W 116
Gustavo Díaz Ordaz, Mex. 26°13′ N, 98°36′ W 114
Gustavus, Alas., U.S. 58°25′ N, 135°44′ W 108
Gustine, Calif., U.S. 37°15′ N, 121°2′ W 100
Guta, Tanzania 2°8′ S, 33°41′ E 224
Gutâiu, peak, Rom. 47°41′ N, 23°47′ E 156
Gutenstein, Aust. 47°53′ N, 15°53′ E 168
Gütersloh, Ger. 51°54′ N, 8°22′ E 167
Guthrie, Ky., U.S. 36°38′ N, 87°10′ W 96
Guthrie, Okla., U.S. 35°51′ N, 97°24′ W 96
Guthrie, Tex., U.S. 33°36′ N, 100°20′ W 92
Gutian, China 26°36′ N, 118°42′ E 198
Gutiérrez, Bol. 19°28′ S, 63°36′ W 137
Gutiérrez Zamora, Mex. 20°27′ N, 97°6′ W 114
Guttenberg, Iowa, U.S. 42°46′ N, 91°7′ W 94
Gutu, Zimb. 19°41′ S, 31°9′ E 224
Güvem, Turk. 40°35′ N, 32°40′ E 156
Guwahati, India 26°11′ N, 91°42′ E 197
Guyana 5°35′ N, 59°12′ W 130
Guyanais Space Center, Fr. 5°9′ N, 52°52′ W 130
Guyang, China 41°1′ N, 110°5′ E 198
Guymon, Okla., U.S. 36°40′ N, 101°30′ W 92
Guyuan, China 41°40′ N, 115°38′ E 198
Guyuan, China 35°59′ N, 106°14′ E 198
Güzeloluk, Turk. 36°45′ N, 34°5′ E 156
Güzelyurt, Turk. 38°15′ N, 34°22′ E 156
Guzhang, China 28°35′ N, 109°57′ E 198
Guzmán, Mex. 31°11′ N, 107°27′ W 92
G'uzor, Uzb. 38°36′ N, 66°15′ E 197
Gwa, Myanmar 17°36′ N, 94°36′ E 202
Gwadabawa, Nig. 13°21′ N, 5°12′ E 222
Gwadar, Pak. 25°8′ N, 62°23′ E 182
Gwagwada, Nig. 10°14′ N, 7°12′ E 222
Gwai, Zimb. 19°19′ S, 27°42′ E 224
Gwaii Haanas National Park Reserve and Haida Heritage Site, Can. 52°10′ N, 130°59′ W 108
Gwalangu, Dem. Rep. of the Congo 2°17′ N, 18°14′ E 218
Gwalior, India 26°14′ N, 78°8′ E 197
Gwanda, Zimb. 20°56′ S, 28°58′ E 227
Gwandu, Nig. 12°31′ N, 4°38′ E 222
Gwane, Dem. Rep. of the Congo 4°41′ N, 25°54′ E 224
Gwane, river, Dem. Rep. of the Congo 4°53′ N, 25°25′ E 218
Gwangju (Kwangju), S. Korea 35°8′ N, 126°56′ E 200
Gwangyang, S. Korea 34°56′ N, 127°36′ E 200
Gwardafuy, Cape, Somalia 11°38′ N, 51°18′ E 182
Gwayi River, Zimb. 18°37′ S, 27°11′ E 224
Gwayi, river, Zimb. 18°50′ S, 27°10′ E 224
Gwembe, Zambia 16°30′ S, 27°36′ E 224
Gweru, Zimb. 19°30′ S, 29°47′ E 224
Gweta, Botswana 20°10′ S, 25°15′ E 227
Gwinn, Mich., U.S. 46°17′ N, 87°27′ W 94
Gwinner, N. Dak., U.S. 46°13′ N, 97°41′ W 90
Gwoza, Nig. 11°7′ N, 13°43′ E 216
Gwydir, river, Austral. 29°22′ S, 148°51′ E 230
Gya La Pass, China 28°46′ N, 84°32′ E 197
Gyaca, China 29°7′ N, 92°30′ E 188
Gyamysh, peak, Azerb. 40°17′ N, 46°19′ E 195
Gyangzê, China 28°57′ N, 89°39′ E 197
Gyaring Hu, lake, China 34°55′ N, 96°23′ E 188
Gyarmat, Hung. 47°27′ N, 17°29′ E 168
Gyda, Russ. 70°50′ N, 78°36′ E 169
Gydanskiy Poluostrov, Russ. 69°23′ N, 74°30′ E 169
Gyêgu, China 33°1′ N, 96°54′ E 188
Gyékényes, Hung. 46°13′ N, 17°0′ E 168
Gyeongju (Kyŏngju), S. Korea 35°48′ N, 129°15′ E 200
Gyeongsan, S. Korea 35°47′ N, 128°46′ E 200
Gyirong (Zongga), China 28°59′ N, 85°16′ E 197
Gyldenløve Fjord 64°6′ N, 43°28′ W 106
Gylgen, Nor. 66°21′ N, 22°41′ E 152
Gympie, Austral. 26°9′ S, 152°41′ E 231
Gyōda, Japan 36°7′ N, 139°28′ E 201
Gyoga, S. Korea 37°28′ N, 127°59′ E 200
Gyoha, S. Korea 37°45′ N, 126°46′ E 200
Gyoma, Hung. 46°56′ N, 20°50′ E 168
Gyönk, Hung. 46°34′ N, 18°28′ E 168
Gyopáros, Hung. 46°34′ N, 20°38′ E 168
Győr, Hung. 47°39′ N, 17°39′ E 168
Győr-Moson-Sopron, adm. division, Hung. 47°29′ N, 16°47′ E 156
Gypsumville, Can. 51°46′ N, 98°39′ W 108
Gyueshevo, Bulg. 42°13′ N, 22°29′ E 168
Gyula, Hung. 46°39′ N, 21°17′ E 168
Gyumri, Arm. 40°46′ N, 43°50′ E 195
Gyzylarbat, Turkm. 38°58′ N, 56°14′ E 180
Gyzyletrek, Turkm. 37°41′ N, 54°44′ E 180
Gyzylgaya, Turkm. 40°36′ N, 55°27′ E 158
Gyzylsuw, Turkm. 39°46′ N, 53°1′ E 180

H

Ha Coi, Vietnam 21°27′ N, 107°43′ E 202
Ha Giang, Vietnam 22°48′ N, 104°59′ E 202
Ha On, Israel 32°43′ N, 35°37′ E 194
Ha Tien, Vietnam 10°26′ N, 104°27′ E 202
Ha Tinh, Vietnam 18°21′ N, 105°53′ E 202
Ha Trung, Vietnam 20°0′ N, 105°48′ E 198
Häädemeeste, Est. 58°4′ N, 24°28′ E 166
Haag, Aust. 48°5′ N, 14°35′ E 156
Haamstede, Neth. 51°42′ N, 3°44′ E 163
Ha'apai Group, islands, South Pacific Ocean 19°16′ S, 177°22′ W 238
Haapajärvi, Fin. 63°44′ N, 25°18′ E 152
Haapamäki, Fin. 62°14′ N, 24°24′ E 152
Haapasaari, Fin. 60°16′ N, 27°12′ E 166
Haapavesi, Fin. 64°7′ N, 25°19′ E 152
Haapsalu, Est. 58°55′ N, 23°30′ E 166
Haar, Ger. 48°6′ N, 11°44′ E 152
Haarlem, Neth. 52°23′ N, 4°37′ E 163
Haast, N.Z. 43°54′ S, 169°0′ E 240
Haaway, Somalia 1°7′ N, 43°45′ E 218
Hab, river, Pak. 25°7′ N, 66°55′ E 186
Habahe (Kaba), China 48°4′ N, 86°21′ E 184
Ḩabarūt, Oman 17°15′ N, 52°48′ E 182
Habaswein, Kenya 0°59′ N, 39°30′ E 224
Habay, Can. 58°51′ N, 118°47′ W 108
Ḩabbūsh, Leb. 33°25′ N, 35°28′ E 194
Habermehl Peak, Antarctica 71°54′ S, 6°7′ E 248
Habibas, Îles, islands, Mediterranean Sea 35°46′ N, 1°30′ W 150
Habiganj, Bangladesh 24°20′ N, 91°20′ E 197
Habomai Islands, North Pacific Ocean 42°31′ N, 145°36′ E 190
Ḩabshān, U.A.E. 23°51′ N, 53°37′ E 196
Hacha, Col. 7°420′ N, 75°31′ W 136
Hachenburg, Ger. 50°39′ N, 7°48′ E 167
Hachi, India 27°49′ N, 94°1′ E 188
Hachijō Jima, island, Japan 33°6′ N, 137°49′ E 190
Hachiman, Japan 35°44′ N, 136°57′ E 201
Hachinohe, Japan 40°26′ N, 141°30′ E 190
Hachiōji, Japan 35°38′ N, 139°20′ E 201
Hachita, N. Mex., U.S. 31°55′ N, 108°19′ W 92
Hacıbektaş, Turk. 38°56′ N, 34°34′ E 156
Hackås, Nor. 62°55′ N, 14°31′ E 152
Hackberry, Ariz., U.S. 35°21′ N, 113°44′ W 101
Hackberry, La., U.S. 29°59′ N, 93°21′ W 103
Hackness, U.K. 54°17′ N, 0°31′ E 162
Hadabat el Gilf el Kebîr, Egypt 24°6′ N, 25°40′ E 226
Hadada, Jebel, peak, Sudan 20°46′ N, 28°33′ E 226
Hadamar, Ger. 50°26′ N, 8°2′ E 167
Hadarba, Ras (Elba, Cape), Egypt 21°49′ N, 36°55′ E 182
Ḩaddā', Saudi Arabia 21°27′ N, 39°32′ E 182
Haddo House, site, U.K. 57°22′ N, 2°21′ W 150
Haddummati Atoll, Maldives 1°47′ N, 72°32′ E 188
Hadejia, Nig. 12°30′ N, 10°5′ E 222
Ḩadera, Israel 32°26′ N, 34°55′ E 194
Haderslev, Den. 55°15′ N, 9°29′ E 150
Hadīboh, Yemen 12°37′ N, 53°57′ E 182
Hadid, Cap, Mor. 31°45′ N, 10°42′ W 214
Ḩadīd, Jabal, peak, Lib. 20°21′ N, 22°11′ E 216
Hadilik, China 37°52′ N, 86°6′ E 184
Hadım, Turk. 36°59′ N, 32°26′ E 156
Hadīyah, Saudi Arabia 25°32′ N, 38°37′ E 182

Hadjadj, Alg. 36°5' N, 0°19' E 164
Hadleigh, U.K. 52°2' N, 0°56' E 162
Hadley, Mass., U.S. 42°19' N, 72°36' W 104
Hadley Bay 72°0' N, 110°44' W 106
Hadong, S. Korea 35°4' N, 127°46' E 200
Ḥaḍramawt, region, Asia 16°17' N, 49°26' E 182
Hadsten, Den. 56°19' N, 10°2' E 152
Hadsund, Den. 56°43' N, 10°7' E 150
Hadyach, Ukr. 50°20' N, 33°54' E 158
Haedo, Cuchilla de, Uru. 31°29' S, 56°45' W 139
Haeju, N. Korea 38°2' N, 125°42' E 200
Haeju-man 37°47' N, 125°42' E 200
Haemi, S. Korea 36°41' N, 126°33' E 200
Haenam, S. Korea 34°32' N, 126°37' E 200
Ḥafar al Bāṭin, Saudi Arabia 28°24' N, 46°0' E 180
Haffkrug, Ger. 54°3' N, 10°45' E 150
Hafford, Can. 52°44' N, 107°22' W 108
Hafik, Turk. 39°51' N, 37°23' E 156
Ḥafīt, Jabal, peak, U.A.E. 24°3' N, 55°41' E 196
Hafizabad, Pak. 32°3' N, 73°39' E 186
Haflong, India 25°10' N, 92°59' E 188
Haft Gel, Iran 31°28' N, 49°34' E 180
Hag 'Abdullah, Sudan 13°55' N, 33°34' E 182
Hagadera, Kenya 2°119' N, 40°23' E 224
Hagåtña (Agana), Guam, U.S. 13°0' N, 145°0' E 242
Hagemeister Island, Alas., U.S. 58°9' N, 161°42' W 98
Hagen, Ger. 51°22' N, 7°28' E 167
Hagen Fjord 81°30' N, 28°8' W 246
Hagenower Heide, Ger. 53°24' N, 11°13' E 150
Hagensborg, Can. 52°22' N, 126°33' W 108
Hägere Hiywet, Eth. 8°56' N, 37°54' E 224
Hagerhill, Ky., U.S. 37°46' N, 82°48' W 96
Hagerman, N. Mex., U.S. 33°6' N, 104°20' W 92
Hagerman Fossil Beds National Monument, Idaho, U.S. 42°47' N, 115°2' W 90
Hagfors, Nor. 60°2' N, 13°41' E 152
Häggenås, Nor. 63°23' N, 14°53' E 152
Häggsjön, Nor. 63°54' N, 14°11' E 152
Hagi, Japan 34°24' N, 131°25' E 200
Hagia Triada, ruin(s), Gr. 35°2' N, 24°41' E 156
Hags Head, Ire. 52°46' N, 9°50' W 150
Hague, N.Y., U.S. 43°44' N, 73°31' W 104
Hague, Cap de la, Fr. 49°41' N, 2°29' W 150
Haguenau, Fr. 48°48' N, 7°47' E 163
Haha Jima Rettō, islands, North Pacific Ocean 26°35' N, 139°20' E 190
Hahn, Ger. 50°31' N, 7°53' E 167
Hahót, Hung. 46°38' N, 16°54' E 168
Hai'an, China 32°32' N, 120°25' E 198
Haicheng, China 40°52' N, 122°44' E 200
Haidargarh, India 26°35' N, 81°20' E 197
Haifa, Israel 32°46' N, 35°0' E 180
Haifa see Ḥefa, Israel 32°47' N, 35°0' E 194
Haifeng, China 22°57' N, 115°20' E 198
Haig, Austral. 31°1' S, 126°4' E 231
Haiger, Ger. 50°44' N, 8°12' E 167
Haikang, China 20°50' N, 110°2' E 198
Haikou, China 20°1' N, 110°19' E 198
Ha'iku, Hawai'i, U.S. 20°55' N, 156°20' W 99
Ḥā'il, Saudi Arabia 27°30' N, 41°43' E 180
Hailar, China 49°9' N, 119°38' E 198
Hailar, river, China 49°32' N, 121°17' E 198
Hailesboro, N.Y., U.S. 44°17' N, 75°28' W 110
Haileybury, Can. 47°27' N, 79°38' W 94
Hailong, China 42°39' N, 125°50' E 200
Hails, China 41°25' N, 106°25' E 198
Hailun, China 47°28' N, 126°58' E 198
Hailuoto, Fin. 65°0' N, 24°42' E 152
Hainan, adm. division, China 19°22' N, 108°59' E 198
Hainan, island, China 19°47' N, 108°42' E 198
Haines, Alas., U.S. 59°14' N, 135°31' W 108
Haines City, Fla., U.S. 28°6' N, 81°38' W 105
Haines Junction, Can. 60°53' N, 137°27' W 98
Haiphong, Vietnam 20°52' N, 106°39' E 198
Haitan Dao, island, China 25°30' N, 119°55' E 198
Haiti 19°8' N, 72°17' W 116
Haiwee Reservoir, lake, Calif., U.S. 36°9' N, 118°6' W 101
Haiya, Sudan 18°17' N, 36°19' E 182
Haiyan, China 30°31' N, 120°52' E 198
Haiyuan, China 36°35' N, 105°36' E 198
Hajdú-Bihar, adm. division, Hung. 47°17' N, 21°10' E 156
Hajdúhadház, Hung. 47°40' N, 21°40' E 168
Hajdúnánás, Hung. 47°50' N, 21°26' E 168
Hajdúszoboszló, Hung. 47°26' N, 21°26' E 168
Haji Pir Pass, Pak. 33°55' N, 74°4' E 186
Hajinbu, S. Korea 37°37' N, 128°32' E 200
Ḥajjah, Yemen 15°40' N, 43°33' E 182
Ḥājjīābād, Iran 28°18' N, 55°50' E 196
Hajnówka, Pol. 52°44' N, 23°35' E 158
Hajós, Hung. 46°23' N, 19°7' E 168
Hakai Passage 51°41' N, 128°43' W 108
Hakanssonmonts, Dem. Rep. of the Congo 8°49' S, 25°38' E 224
Hakataramea, N.Z. 44°44' S, 170°31' E 240
Hakkâri, Turk. 37°33' N, 43°38' E 195
Hakkas, Nor. 66°54' N, 21°34' E 152
Hakken San, peak, Japan 34°10' N, 135°50' E 201
Hakodate, Japan 41°55' N, 140°33' E 190
Hakui, Japan 36°53' N, 136°47' E 201
Hakusan National Park, Japan 36°6' N, 136°33' E 201
Ḥalab (Aleppo), Syr. 36°11' N, 37°9' E 156
Ḥalab (Aleppo), Syr. 36°11' N, 37°9' E 180
Ḥalabjah, Iraq 35°10' N, 45°59' E 180
Halâl, Gebel el, Egypt 30°34' N, 33°53' E 194
Halali, Namibia 19°1' S, 16°30' E 220
Halastó, lake, Hung. 47°35' N, 20°48' E 156
Halayeb, Egypt 22°11' N, 36°35' E 182
Halba, Leb. 34°32' N, 36°4' E 194
Halba Desēt, island, Eritrea 12°43' N, 42°12' E 182
Halbturn, Aust. 47°52' N, 16°58' E 168
Ḥalbūn, Syr. 33°39' N, 36°14' E 194
Halcon, Mount, Philippines 13°15' N, 120°55' E 203
Halden, Nor. 59°6' N, 11°22' E 152
Haldia, India 22°3' N, 88°4' E 197
Haldwani, India 29°14' N, 79°30' E 197
Hale, Mich., U.S. 44°22' N, 83°49' W 110
Hale Eddy, N.Y., U.S. 42°0' N, 75°24' W 94
Haleakalā Observatories, site, Hawai'i, U.S. 20°41' N, 156°19' W 99
Haleki'i-Pihana Heiaus, site, Hawai'i, U.S. 20°54' N, 156°33' W 99
Halesowen, U.K. 52°27' N, 2°3' W 162
Halesworth, U.K. 52°20' N, 1°29' E 163
Haleyville, Ala., U.S. 34°13' N, 87°38' W 96
Half Assini, Ghana 5°4' N, 2°53' W 214
Half Moon Bay, Calif., U.S. 37°27' N, 122°27' W 100
Half Moon Cay Natural Monument Reserve, Belize 17°6' N, 87°41' W 115
Halfmoon Bay see Oban, N.Z. 46°55' S, 168°7' E 240
Halfway, Oreg., U.S. 44°51' N, 117°8' W 90
Halfway Point, Can. 51°40' N, 81°4' W 110
Halfway, river, Can. 56°52' N, 122°50' W 108
Haliartus, battle, Gr. 38°22' N, 22°56' E 156
Halibut, oil field, Austral. 38°33' S, 148°18' E 230
Halibut Point, Mass., U.S. 42°41' N, 70°39' W 104
Halicz, peak, Pol. 49°4' N, 22°40' E 152
Halifax, Can. 44°37' N, 63°43' W 111
Halifax, Mass., U.S. 41°59' N, 70°53' W 104
Halifax, N.C., U.S. 36°19' N, 77°37' W 96
Halifax, Va., U.S. 36°45' N, 78°56' W 96
Halkett, Cape, Alas., U.S. 70°44' N, 152°18' W 98
Halkida, Gr. 38°30' N, 23°37' E 180
Halkidiki, Gr. 40°35' N, 22°57' E 156
Halkirk, Can. 52°16' N, 112°10' W 108
Hall Beach, Can. 68°46' N, 81°21' W 73
Hall Islands, North Pacific Ocean 8°9' N, 152°10' E 192
Hall Peninsula, Can. 63°28' N, 66°19' W 106
Hall Summit, La., U.S. 32°9' N, 93°18' W 103
Hälla, Nor. 63°55' N, 17°16' E 152
Hallam Peak, Can. 52°10' N, 118°53' W 108
Hallandale, Fla., U.S. 25°59' N, 80°10' W 105
Halle, Belg. 50°44' N, 4°13' E 163
Halle, Ger. 52°3' N, 8°22' E 167
Halle, Ger. 51°27' N, 11°58' E 152
Hallenberg, Ger. 51°6' N, 8°36' E 150
Hallendorf, Ger. 52°9' N, 10°21' E 167
Hallettsville, Tex., U.S. 29°25' N, 96°56' W 96
Halley, station, Antarctica 75°38' S, 26°34' W 248
Hallgren, Mount, Antarctica 73°26' S, 3°58' W 248
Halliday, N. Dak., U.S. 47°19' N, 102°22' W 90
Halliday Lake, Can. 61°19' N, 109°42' W 108
Halligen, islands, North Sea 54°44' N, 7°33' E 152
Hallim, S. Korea 33°23' N, 126°15' E 198
Hallingdal, Nor. 60°26' N, 8°43' E 152
Hallingskarvet, peak, Nor. 60°35' N, 7°40' E 152
Halliste, river, Est. 58°27' N, 24°58' E 166
Hällnäs, Nor. 64°18' N, 19°37' E 152
Hallock, Minn., U.S. 48°45' N, 96°59' W 90
Halloran Springs, Calif., U.S. 35°21' N, 115°54' W 101
Hallowell, Me., U.S. 44°16' N, 69°49' W 104
Halls Creek, Austral. 18°17' S, 127°44' E 238
Hallschlag, Ger. 50°21' N, 6°27' E 167
Hallsville, Tex., U.S. 32°29' N, 94°35' W 103
Hălmagiu, Rom. 46°16' N, 22°38' E 168
Halmahera, island, Indonesia 1°32' N, 128°44' E 192
Halmeu, Rom. 47°58' N, 23°1' E 168
Halmstad, Sw. 56°42' N, 12°52' E 160
Hal'shany, Belarus 54°15' N, 26°1' E 166
Halstead, Kans., U.S. 37°59' N, 97°31' W 90
Halstead, U.K. 51°56' N, 0°39' E 162
Halten Bank, Norwegian Sea 65°1' N, 6°31' E 253
Haltern, Ger. 51°45' N, 7°10' E 167
Halulu Heiau, site, Hawai'i, U.S. 20°44' N, 157°1' W 99
Halus, ruin(s), Gr. 39°7' N, 22°45' E 156
Ḥaluza, Ḥolot, Israel 31°7' N, 34°16' E 194
Ham, Chad 10°1' N, 15°42' E 216
Ham, Fr. 49°44' N, 3°2' E 163
Hamada, Japan 34°53' N, 132°5' E 200
Hamadade Tinrhert, Alg.-Lib. 28°40' N, 6°46' E 214
Hamadān (Ecbatana), Iran 34°48' N, 48°27' E 180
Hamaguir, Alg. 30°51' N, 3°4' W 214
Ḥamāh (Hamath), Syr. 35°7' N, 36°45' E 194
Hamajima, Japan 34°18' N, 136°46' E 201
Hāmākua, region, Oceania 19°34' N, 155°33' W 99
Hamamatsu, Japan 34°42' N, 137°45' E 201
Haman, S. Korea 35°13' N, 128°25' E 200
Hamar, Nor. 60°47' N, 11°4' E 152
Hamarøy, Nor. 68°3' N, 15°38' E 152
Hamasaka, Japan 35°36' N, 134°27' E 201
Ḥamāta, Gebel, peak, Egypt 24°10' N, 34°56' E 182
Hamath see Ḥamāh, Syr. 35°7' N, 36°45' E 194
Hamburg, Ark., U.S. 33°12' N, 91°48' W 103
Hamburg, Ger. 53°33' N, 10°1' E 150
Hamburg, Iowa, U.S. 40°36' N, 95°39' W 90
Hamburg, N.Y., U.S. 42°43' N, 78°50' W 94
Hamburg, adm. division, Ger. 53°34' N, 9°31' E 150
Hambuti, spring, Sudan 16°50' N, 32°26' E 182
Hamchang, S. Korea 36°32' N, 128°11' E 200
Ḥamḍah, Saudi Arabia 18°57' N, 43°40' E 182
Ḥamḍānah, Saudi Arabia 19°57' N, 40°35' E 182
Hamden, Conn., U.S. 41°22' N, 72°55' W 104
Hamden, Ohio, U.S. 39°8' N, 82°32' W 102
Hämeenkyrö, Fin. 61°37' N, 23°8' E 166
Hämeenlinna, Fin. 61°0' N, 24°22' E 166
Hamelin Pool 26°29' S, 113°37' E 230
Hameln, Ger. 52°6' N, 9°22' E 150
Hamer Koke, Eth. 5°11' N, 36°46' E 224
Hamersley Range, Austral. 21°46' S, 116°17' E 230
Hamhŭng, N. Korea 39°53' N, 127°32' E 200
Hami, China 42°48' N, 93°23' E 190
Hamid, Dar, Sudan 13°44' N, 31°24' E 182
Hamilton, Ala., U.S. 34°8' N, 87°59' W 96
Hamilton, Bermuda Islands, U.K. 32°0' N, 65°0' W 118
Hamilton, Can. 43°14' N, 79°51' W 110
Hamilton, Mo., U.S. 39°43' N, 93°60' W 94
Hamilton, Mo., U.S. 40°23' N, 91°21' W 94
Hamilton, N.Y., U.S. 42°49' N, 75°33' W 94
Hamilton, N.Z. 37°48' S, 175°15' E 240
Hamilton, Ohio, U.S. 39°23' N, 84°33' W 102
Hamilton, Tex., U.S. 31°41' N, 98°7' W 92
Hamilton, U.K. 55°45' N, 4°3' W 150
Hamilton Inlet 54°3' N, 61°22' W 73
Hamilton, Mount, Antarctica 80°38' S, 159°7' E 248
Hamilton, Mount, Nev., U.S. 39°13' N, 115°37' W 90
Hamilton Sound 49°31' N, 55°5' W 111
Hamina, Fin. 60°34' N, 27°11' E 166
Hamiota, Can. 50°11' N, 100°36' W 90
Hamirpur, India 25°54' N, 80°9' E 197
Hamjun, N. Korea 39°32' N, 127°13' E 200
Hamlet, Ind., U.S. 41°22' N, 86°35' W 102
Hamlet, N.C., U.S. 34°52' N, 79°43' W 96
Hamlin, Me., U.S. 47°3' N, 67°49' W 111
Hamlin, N.Y., U.S. 43°18' N, 77°56' W 94
Hamlin, Tex., U.S. 32°52' N, 100°8' W 92
Hamm, Ger. 51°40' N, 7°48' E 167
Hammam Lif, Tun. 36°41' N, 10°19' E 214
Hammarland, Fin. 60°12' N, 19°43' E 154
Hammerdal, Nor. 63°35' N, 15°19' E 152
Hammeren, Den. 55°17' N, 14°49' E 152
Hammerfest, Nor. 70°37' N, 24°3' E 160
Hamminkeln, Ger. 51°43' N, 6°35' E 167
Hammond, Ill., U.S. 39°47' N, 88°36' W 102
Hammond, Ind., U.S. 41°35' N, 87°29' W 102
Hammond, La., U.S. 30°29' N, 90°27' W 103
Hammond, Mont., U.S. 45°11' N, 104°55' W 90
Hammond, Oreg., U.S. 46°10' N, 123°57' W 100
Hammonton, N.J., U.S. 39°37' N, 74°49' W 94
Hamningberg, Nor. 70°30' N, 30°36' E 152
Hamont, Belg. 51°14' N, 5°32' E 167
Hampden, N.Z. 45°21' S, 170°47' E 240
Hampton, Ark., U.S. 33°30' N, 92°29' W 96
Hampton, Fla., U.S. 29°51' N, 82°9' W 105
Hampton, Iowa, U.S. 42°44' N, 93°12' W 94
Hampton, N.H., U.S. 42°56' N, 70°50' W 104
Hampton, S.C., U.S. 32°51' N, 81°7' W 96
Hampton, Va., U.S. 37°1' N, 76°22' W 96
Hampton Bays, N.Y., U.S. 40°52' N, 72°32' W 104
Hampton Beach, N.H., U.S. 42°54' N, 70°50' W 104
Hampton Butte, peak, Oreg., U.S. 43°45' N, 120°22' W 90
Hampton, Mount, Antarctica 76°22' S, 125°11' W 248
Hampyeong, S. Korea 35°2' N, 126°30' E 200
Hamrånge, Nor. 60°55' N, 17°1' E 152
Hamrat esh Sheikh, Sudan 14°32' N, 27°57' E 226
Hamyang, S. Korea 35°30' N, 127°44' E 200
Han, Ghana 10°41' N, 2°28' W 222
Han Pijesak, Bosn. and Herzg. 44°4' N, 18°58' E 168
Han, river, China 23°54' N, 116°25' E 198
Han, river, China 32°44' N, 109°0' E 198
Han, river, S. Korea 37°33' N, 128°29' E 200
Han sur Lesse, Belg. 50°6' N, 5°12' E 167
Han Uul, Mongolia 47°58' N, 114°40' E 198
Hanamalo Point, U.S. 19°6' N, 156°15' W 99
Hanang, peak, Tanzania 4°28' S, 35°21' E 224
Hanau, Ger. 50°7' N, 8°55' E 167
Hancheng, China 35°30' N, 110°25' E 198
Hanchuan, China 30°36' N, 113°47' E 198
Hancock, Mich., U.S. 47°8' N, 88°36' W 94
Hancock, Minn., U.S. 45°28' N, 95°49' W 90
Hancock, Vt., U.S. 43°55' N, 72°52' W 104
Handa, Japan 34°52' N, 136°56' E 201
Handan, China 36°37' N, 114°27' E 198
Handen, Sw. 59°9' N, 18°9' E 166
Handies Peak, Colo., U.S. 37°53' N, 107°35' W 90
Haneti, Tanzania 5°29' S, 35°54' E 224
Hanford, Calif., U.S. 36°20' N, 119°40' W 100
Hangatiki, N.Z. 38°17' S, 175°9' E 240
Hanggin Houqi, China 40°51' N, 107°5' E 198
Hanggin Qi, China 39°51' N, 108°43' E 198
Hangklip, Cape, S. Af. 34°38' S, 18°11' E 227
Hangö (Hanko), Fin. 59°49' N, 22°57' E 166
Hangu, China 39°13' N, 117°43' E 198
Hangzhou, China 30°21' N, 120°13' E 198
Hanhöhiy, Mongolia 47°39' N, 112°7' E 198
Hani, Turk. 38°24' N, 40°24' E 195
Haniá (Canea), Gr. 35°25' N, 23°59' E 180
Ḥanīsh al Kabīr, island, Yemen 13°25' N, 42°45' E 182
Hankinson, N. Dak., U.S. 46°3' N, 96°55' W 90
Hanko see Hangö, Fin. 59°49' N, 22°57' E 166
Hanksville, Utah, U.S. 38°21' N, 110°42' W 90
Hanle, India 32°45' N, 78°57' E 188
Hanley, U.K. 53°1' N, 2°11' W 162
Hanmer Springs, N.Z. 42°32' S, 172°50' E 240
Hann, Mount, Austral. 15°55' S, 125°35' E 230
Hanna, Can. 51°39' N, 111°56' W 90
Hanna, Ind., U.S. 41°24' N, 86°47' W 102
Hanna, Wyo., U.S. 41°52' N, 106°33' W 90
Hannibal, Mo., U.S. 39°42' N, 91°23' W 94
Hannibal, Ohio, U.S. 39°39' N, 80°53' W 94
Hannover (Hanover), Ger. 52°22' N, 9°45' E 150
Hanoi, Vietnam 21°0' N, 105°40' E 198
Hanover, Can. 44°8' N, 80°60' W 102
Hanover, Conn., U.S. 41°38' N, 72°5' W 104
Hanover, Ill., U.S. 42°14' N, 90°16' W 102
Hanover, Ind., U.S. 38°42' N, 85°28' W 102
Hanover, Kans., U.S. 39°52' N, 96°53' W 90
Hanover, Mich., U.S. 42°5' N, 84°34' W 102
Hanover, N.H., U.S. 43°42' N, 72°18' W 104
Hanover, N. Mex., U.S. 32°48' N, 108°5' W 92
Hanover, Pa., U.S. 39°48' N, 76°59' W 94
Hanover, S. Af. 31°4' S, 24°26' E 227
Hanover, Isla, island, Chile 51°9' S, 76°32' W 134
Hanover see Hannover, Ger. 52°22' N, 9°45' E 150
Hanp'o, N. Korea 38°12' N, 126°29' E 200
Hansard, Can. 54°4' N, 121°55' W 108
Hansen, Idaho, U.S. 42°32' N, 114°18' W 90
Hansen Inlet 75°20' S, 67°43' W 248
Hansjö, Nor. 61°9' N, 14°34' E 152
Hantsavichy, Belarus 52°45' N, 26°26' E 152
Hanumangarh, India 29°36' N, 74°17' E 186
Hanuy, river, Mongolia 48°41' N, 102°6' E 198
Hanyang, China 30°32' N, 114°4' E 198
Hanyin, China 32°53' N, 108°31' E 198
Hanzhong, China 33°6' N, 107°3' E 198
Haparanda, Nor. 65°49' N, 24°5' E 152
Happisburgh, U.K. 52°49' N, 1°31' E 163
Happy, Tex., U.S. 34°43' N, 101°52' W 92
Happy Valley-Goose Bay, Can. 53°19' N, 60°22' W 106
Hapur, India 28°42' N, 77°47' E 197
Ḥaql, Saudi Arabia 29°13' N, 34°56' E 180
Har Ayrag, Mongolia 45°41' N, 109°15' E 198
Har Horin (Karakorum), ruin(s), Mongolia 47°14' N, 102°43' E 198
Ḥaraḍ, Saudi Arabia 24°7' N, 49°5' E 196
Haradnaya, Belarus 51°51' N, 26°30' E 152
Haradok, Belarus 55°28' N, 30°0' E 166
Harads, Nor. 66°4' N, 20°57' E 152
Haradzyeya, Belarus 53°18' N, 26°32' E 152
Haranomachi, Japan 37°38' N, 140°57' E 201
Harappa, ruin(s), Pak. 30°40' N, 72°45' E 186
Harare, Zimb. 17°53' S, 30°56' E 224
Harat, island, Eritrea 15°53' N, 39°5' E 182
Haraz, Chad 13°57' N, 19°25' E 216
Haraza, Jebel, peak, Sudan 15°3' N, 30°19' E 226
Harazé Mangueigne, Chad 9°54' N, 20°47' E 216
Harbin, China 45°43' N, 126°42' E 198
Harbor Beach, Mich., U.S. 43°50' N, 82°41' W 102
Harbour Breton, Can. 47°28' N, 55°50' W 111
Harcuvar Mountains, Ariz., U.S. 33°56' N, 113°45' W 101
Harda, India 22°22' N, 77°5' E 197
Hardangervidda, Nor. 60°13' N, 7°19' E 152
Hardenberg, Neth. 52°34' N, 6°38' E 163
Harderwijk, Neth. 52°20' N, 5°36' E 163
Hardin, Mo., U.S. 39°8' N, 90°39' W 94
Hardin, Mont., U.S. 45°43' N, 107°37' W 90
Hardin, Tex., U.S. 30°8' N, 94°44' W 103
Harding Lake, Can. 56°7' N, 98°59' W 108
Hardisty, Can. 52°39' N, 111°18' W 108
Hardman, Oreg., U.S. 45°10' N, 119°44' W 90
Hardwick, Mass., U.S. 42°20' N, 72°13' W 104
Hardwick, Vt., U.S. 44°29' N, 72°23' W 104
Hardwood Point, Mich., U.S. 43°54' N, 82°41' W 102
Hardy, Ark., U.S. 36°18' N, 91°29' W 96
Hardy, Peninsula, Chile 55°49' S, 67°37' W 248
Hardy, river, Mex. 32°26' N, 115°17' W 101
Hareid, Nor. 62°21' N, 6°0' E 152
Haren, Ger. 52°48' N, 7°14' E 163
Hārer, Eth. 9°15' N, 42°7' E 224
Harewa, Eth. 9°55' N, 42°1' E 224
Harg, Nor. 58°45' N, 16°56' E 152
Hargeysa, Somalia 9°29' N, 44°2' E 216
Harghita, adm. division, Rom. 46°25' N, 25°1' E 156
Harghita, Munții, Rom. 46°8' N, 25°13' E 156
Hargla, Est. 57°37' N, 26°22' E 166
Hargshamn, Nor. 60°9' N, 18°23' E 152
Hari, river, Indonesia 1°15' S, 101°51' E 196
Haría, Sp. 29°10' N, 13°29' W 214
Hariat, spring, Mali 16°10' N, 2°24' E 222
Haricha, Hamâda el, Mali 22°44' N, 3°50' W 214
Haridwar, India 29°58' N, 78°8' E 197
Harihari, N.Z. 43°11' S, 170°32' E 240
Harirud, river, Afghan. 34°35' N, 65°7' E 186
Harīrūd, river, Asia 35°46' N, 61°16' E 180
Hariyo, Somalia 5°1' N, 47°26' E 218
Harjavalta, Fin. 61°16' N, 22°6' E 166
Harkány, Hung. 45°51' N, 18°13' E 168
Harlan, Iowa, U.S. 41°38' N, 95°20' W 90
Harlandsville, Liberia 5°49' N, 9°58' W 222
Harlem, Mont., U.S. 48°31' N, 108°47' W 90
Harleston, U.K. 52°24' N, 1°17' E 162
Harlingen, Neth. 53°10' N, 5°25' E 163
Harlowton, Mont., U.S. 46°25' N, 109°49' W 82
Harmaliyah, oil field, Saudi Arabia 24°11' N, 49°37' E 196
Harmancık, Turk. 39°41' N, 29°7' E 156
Harmil, island, Eritrea 16°26' N, 40°13' E 182
Harmony, Minn., U.S. 43°33' N, 92°1' W 94
Harnai, India 17°51' N, 73°8' E 188
Harney Basin, Oreg., U.S. 43°35' N, 119°50' W 90
Harney, Lake, Fla., U.S. 28°44' N, 81°14' W 105
Harney Lake, Oreg., U.S. 43°13' N, 119°42' W 81
Harney Peak, S. Dak., U.S. 43°50' N, 103°37' W 90
Härnösand, Nor. 62°37' N, 17°54' E 152
Haro, Sp. 42°33' N, 2°52' W 164
Haro, Cabo, Mex. 27°44' N, 111°40' W 112
Harold Byrd Mountains, Antarctica 85°15' S, 138°26' W 248
Haro-Shiikh, Somalia 9°17' N, 44°48' E 218
Harpanahalli, India 14°49' N, 75°58' E 188
Harper, Liberia 4°32' N, 7°43' W 222
Harper Creek, river, Can. 58°0' N, 114°56' W 108
Harperville, Miss., U.S. 32°28' N, 89°30' W 103
Harpster, Ohio, U.S. 40°43' N, 83°14' W 102
Harput, Turk. 38°42' N, 39°13' E 195
Harqin, China 41°8' N, 119°45' E 198
Harqin Qi, China 41°56' N, 118°39' E 198
Harquahala Mountains, Ariz., U.S. 33°44' N, 115°23' W 112
Ḥarrah, Yemen 14°59' N, 50°18' E 182
Ḥarrākah, Syr. 34°43' N, 37°2' E 194
Harran, Nor. 64°34' N, 12°27' E 152
Harrell, Ark., U.S. 33°29' N, 92°25' W 103
Harricana, river, Can. 50°50' N, 79°33' W 80
Harriet, Mount, Austral. 26°36' S, 130°52' E 230
Harrington, U.K. 54°36' N, 3°35' W 162
Harrington, Wash., U.S. 47°27' N, 118°16' W 90
Harriott Lake, Can. 56°7' N, 103°22' W 108
Harris, Mount, Can. 59°12' N, 136°39' W 108
Harris Park, region, Europe 58°2' N, 6°56' W 150
Harrisburg, Ark., U.S. 35°33' N, 90°44' W 96
Harrisburg, Mo., U.S. 37°43' N, 88°32' W 94
Harrisburg, Nebr., U.S. 41°33' N, 103°46' W 90
Harrisburg, Oreg., U.S. 44°15' N, 123°9' W 90
Harrisburg, Pa., U.S. 40°14' N, 76°60' W 94
Harrislee, Ger. 54°48' N, 9°23' E 150
Harrismith, S. Af. 28°17' S, 29°7' E 227
Harrison, Ark., U.S. 36°13' N, 93°7' W 96
Harrison, Idaho, U.S. 47°26' N, 116°47' W 90
Harrison, Me., U.S. 44°6' N, 70°41' W 104
Harrison, Mich., U.S. 44°1' N, 84°48' W 102
Harrison, Nebr., U.S. 42°41' N, 103°54' W 90
Harrison Bay 70°18' N, 152°41' W 98
Harrison, Cape, Can. 54°48' N, 58°3' W 106
Harrison Hot Springs, Can. 49°17' N, 121°47' W 100
Harrison Lake, Can. 49°34' N, 122°16' W 100
Harrison Pass, Nev., U.S. 40°19' N, 115°31' W 90
Harrisonburg, La., U.S. 31°46' N, 91°50' W 103
Harrisonburg, Va., U.S. 38°26' N, 78°53' W 94
Harriston, Can. 43°53' N, 80°51' W 102
Harriston, Miss., U.S. 31°43' N, 91°1' W 103
Harrisville, Mich., U.S. 44°39' N, 83°19' W 94
Harrisville, R.I., U.S. 41°57' N, 71°41' W 104
Harrisville, W. Va., U.S. 39°12' N, 81°4' W 102
Harrodsburg, Ind., U.S. 39°0' N, 86°33' W 102
Harrogate, U.K. 53°59' N, 1°33' W 162
Harrow, Can. 42°2' N, 82°55' W 102
Harry S. Truman Reservoir, lake, Mo., U.S. 38°18' N, 94°56' W 81
Harsewinkel, Ger. 51°57' N, 8°13' E 167
Harşit, river, Turk. 40°42' N, 38°53' E 195
Harsud, India 22°5' N, 76°45' E 197
Hart, Mich., U.S. 43°41' N, 86°22' W 102
Hart, Tex., U.S. 34°23' N, 102°8' W 92
Hart Fell, peak, U.K. 55°23' N, 3°31' W 150
Hart Hills, Antarctica 84°21' S, 89°48' W 248
Hart Mountain, Oreg., U.S. 42°27' N, 119°49' W 90
Hart, river, Can. 64°56' N, 137°28' W 98
Harta, Hung. 46°42' N, 19°1' E 168
Hartberg, Aust. 47°16' N, 15°56' E 168
Hårteigen, peak, Nor. 60°10' N, 6°56' E 152
Hartford, Ala., U.S. 31°5' N, 85°42' W 96
Hartford, Conn., U.S. 41°45' N, 72°43' W 104
Hartford, Liberia 5°56' N, 10°2' W 222
Hartford, Me., U.S. 44°21' N, 70°21' W 104
Hartford, Mich., U.S. 42°11' N, 86°10' W 102
Hartford, S. Dak., U.S. 43°36' N, 96°57' W 90
Hartford, Vt., U.S. 43°39' N, 72°21' W 104
Hartford, Wis., U.S. 43°18' N, 88°23' W 102
Hartford City, Ind., U.S. 40°27' N, 85°22' W 102
Hartigan, Mount, Antarctica 76°48' S, 125°29' W 248
Hartland, Can. 46°16' N, 67°32' W 94
Hartland, U.K. 50°59' N, 4°29' W 150
Hartland, Vt., U.S. 43°32' N, 72°25' W 104
Hartlepool, U.K. 54°41' N, 1°13' W 162
Hartley, Iowa, U.S. 43°10' N, 95°29' W 94
Hartley, Tex., U.S. 35°51' N, 102°24' W 92
Hartney, Can. 49°28' N, 100°30' W 90
Hartola, Fin. 61°34' N, 26°0' E 166
Harts, river, S. Af. 27°24' S, 25°14' E 227
Hartselle, Ala., U.S. 34°25' N, 86°55' W 96
Hartshorne, Okla., U.S. 34°49' N, 95°33' W 96
Hartsville, Tenn., U.S. 36°23' N, 86°9' W 96
Hartville, Wyo., U.S. 42°19' N, 104°44' W 90
Harut, river, Afghan. 32°36' N, 61°27' E 186
Harūz-e Bālā, Iran 30°42' N, 57°6' E 180
Harvard, Ill., U.S. 42°24' N, 88°36' W 102
Harvard, Mass., U.S. 42°30' N, 71°35' W 104
Harvard, Nebr., U.S. 40°35' N, 98°6' W 94
Harvard, Mount, Colo., U.S. 38°54' N, 106°23' W 90
Harvey, Ill., U.S. 41°35' N, 87°39' W 102
Harvey, N. Dak., U.S. 47°45' N, 99°57' W 94
Harwell, U.K. 51°35' N, 1°18' W 162
Harwich, U.K. 51°56' N, 1°16' E 162
Harwich Port, Mass., U.S. 41°39' N, 70°5' W 104
Haryana, adm. division, India 29°11' N, 76°18' E 186
Harz, Ger. 51°44' N, 9°56' E 167
Hasan Dağı, peak, Turk. 38°6' N, 34°5' E 156
Ḥasan Langī, Iran 27°20' N, 56°51' E 196
Ḥāṣbayyā, Leb. 33°23' N, 35°41' E 194
Hasdo, river, India 23°2' N, 82°23' E 197
Haselünne, Ger. 52°40' N, 7°29' E 163
Hasenkamp, Arg. 31°29' S, 59°49' W 139
Hashaat, Mongolia 45°15' N, 104°48' E 198
Hashimoto, Japan 34°20' N, 135°37' E 201
Ḥāsik, Oman 17°25' N, 55°14' E 182
Haskell, Tex., U.S. 33°8' N, 99°44' W 92
Hasle, Den. 55°11' N, 14°42' E 152
Haslemere, U.K. 51°5' N, 0°43' E 162
Ḥaṣrūn, Leb. 34°14' N, 35°58' E 194
Hassberge, Ger. 50°16' N, 10°11' E 167
Hassela, Nor. 62°7' N, 16°39' E 152
Hasselt, Belg. 50°56' N, 5°19' E 167
Hassi Allal, spring, Alg. 31°19' N, 2°38' E 214
Hassi bel Guebbour, spring, Alg. 28°49' N, 6°28' E 214
Hassi Berkane, spring, Alg. 31°7' N, 4°30' E 214
Hassi bou Khechba, spring, Alg. 29°44' N, 5°41' E 214
Hassi bou Zid, Alg. 32°6' N, 1°42' E 214
Hassi Chefaïa, spring, Alg. 29°48' N, 4°21' W 214
Hassi Djafou, spring, Alg. 30°50' N, 3°36' E 214
Hassi el Abiod, spring, Alg. 31°48' N, 3°34' E 214
Hassi el Hadjar, spring, Alg. 31°28' N, 4°44' E 214
Hassi el Mislane, spring, Alg. 27°36' N, 9°50' E 214
Hassi el Motlah, spring, Mauritania 19°23' N, 12°46' W 222
Hassi Erg Sedra, spring, Alg. 30°4' N, 2°6' E 214
Hassi Fokra, spring, Alg. 30°12' N, 1°26' W 214
Hassi Fouini, spring, Mauritania 17°21' N, 7°28' W 222
Hassi Guern el Guessaa, spring, Alg. 31°9' N, 0°47' E 214
Hassi Habadra, spring, Alg. 26°32' N, 4°6' E 214

Hassi Imoulaye, spring, *Alg.* 29°54′ N, 9°10′ E **214**
Hassi I-n-Belrem, spring, *Alg.* 26°3′ N, 3°10′ E **214**
Hassi Inifel, *Alg.* 29°50′ N, 3°44′ E **214**
Hassi I-n-Sokki, spring, *Alg.* 28°34′ N, 3°45′ E **214**
Hassi Issaouane, spring, *Alg.* 27°0′ N, 8°44′ E **214**
Hassi Koussane, spring, *Alg.* 25°31′ N, 4°50′ E **214**
Hassi Larrocque, spring, *Alg.* 30°50′ N, 6°18′ E **214**
Hassi Mameche, *Alg.* 35°50′ N, 7°416′ E **164**
Hassi Marroket, spring, *Alg.* 30°13′ N, 2°57′ E **214**
Hassi Mdakane, spring, *Alg.* 28°27′ N, 2°20′ W **214**
Hassi Messaoud, oil field, *Alg.* 31°43′ N, 5°56′ E **214**
Hassi Moungar, spring, *Alg.* 27°35′ N, 3°6′ E **214**
Hassi Nechou, spring, *Alg.* 30°35′ N, 2°8′ E **214**
Hassi Ouchene, spring, *Alg.* 30°17′ N, 0°33′ E **214**
Hassi R'mel, *Alg.* 32°56′ N, 3°8′ E **214**
Hassi Sedjra Touila, spring, *Alg.* 30°5′ N, 4°6′ E **214**
Hassi Tabaloulet, spring, *Alg.* 29°5′ N, 3°1′ E **214**
Hassi Tabelbalet, spring, *Alg.* 27°20′ N, 6°54′ E **214**
Hassi Taïeb, spring, *Alg.* 32°5′ N, 6°8′ E **214**
Hassi Tanezrouft, spring, *Alg.* 28°28′ N, 6°37′ E **214**
Hassi Targant, spring, *Alg.* 28°20′ N, 8°33′ W **214**
Hassi Tartrat, spring, *Alg.* 30°6′ N, 6°32′ E **214**
Hassi Tiguentourine, spring, *Alg.* 26°51′ N, 2°43′ E **214**
Hassi Ti-n-Fouchaye, spring, *Alg.* 29°30′ N, 8°50′ E **214**
Hassi Touareg, spring, *Alg.* 30°33′ N, 6°26′ E **214**
Hassi Zegdou, spring, *Alg.* 29°49′ N, 4°44′ W **214**
Hassi Zirara, spring, *Alg.* 31°15′ N, 3°13′ E **214**
Hastings, *Fla., U.S.* 29°42′ N, 81°32′ W **105**
Hastings, *Mich., U.S.* 42°37′ N, 85°17′ W **102**
Hastings, *Minn., U.S.* 44°45′ N, 92°53′ W **82**
Hastings, *U.K.* 50°51′ N, 0°34′ E **162**
Hastings, battle, *U.K.* 50°53′ N, 0°24′ E **162**
Haswell, *Colo., U.S.* 38°26′ N, 103°10′ W **90**
Hat, Cape, *Can.* 50°4′ N, 56°4′ W **111**
Hat Yai, *Thai.* 6°59′ N, 100°29′ E **202**
Hatay (Antioch), *Turk.* 36°12′ N, 36°8′ E **156**
Hatch, *N. Mex., U.S.* 32°39′ N, 107°9′ W **92**
Hatchet Lake, *Can.* 58°37′ N, 104°4′ W **108**
Haţeg, *Rom.* 45°36′ N, 22°58′ E **168**
Hatfield, *Mass., U.S.* 42°21′ N, 72°37′ W **104**
Hatfield, *U.K.* 51°45′ N, 0°14′ E **162**
Hatgal, *Mongolia* 50°15′ N, 100°0′ E **190**
Hatherleigh, *U.K.* 50°49′ N, 4°4′ W **162**
Hathras, *India* 27°34′ N, 78°2′ E **197**
Hato Corozal, *Col.* 6°9′ N, 71°43′ W **136**
Hatsuki, *Belarus* 53°19′ N, 27°32′ E **152**
Hatta, *India* 24°7′ N, 79°37′ E **197**
Hatteras, *N.C., U.S.* 35°13′ N, 75°42′ W **96**
Hatteras, Cape, *N.C., U.S.* 35°10′ N, 75°31′ W **96**
Hatteras Plain, *North Atlantic Ocean* 29°2′ N, 69°36′ W **253**
Hattersheim, *Ger.* 50°3′ N, 8°28′ E **167**
Hattie, Lake, *Wyo., U.S.* 41°16′ N, 106°9′ W **90**
Hattiesburg, *Miss., U.S.* 31°18′ N, 89°18′ W **103**
Hatton, *N. Dak., U.S.* 47°37′ N, 97°29′ W **90**
Hattorf, *Ger.* 51°39′ N, 10°14′ E **167**
Hattstedt, *Ger.* 54°31′ N, 9°1′ E **150**
Hattula, *Fin.* 61°4′ N, 24°23′ E **166**
Hatvan, *Hung.* 47°40′ N, 19°42′ E **168**
Haugesund, *Nor.* 59°24′ N, 5°15′ E **152**
Hauho, *Fin.* 61°9′ N, 24°32′ E **166**
Haukivuori, *Fin.* 62°0′ N, 27°11′ E **166**
Hauklappi, *Fin.* 61°25′ N, 28°28′ E **166**
Haulover, *Nicar.* 12°18′ N, 83°42′ W **115**
Haultain Lake, *Can.* 56°46′ N, 106°57′ W **108**
Haultain, river, *Can.* 55°45′ N, 106°26′ W **108**
Haumonia, *Arg.* 27°28′ S, 60°12′ W **139**
Hauola Place of Refuge, site, *Hawai'i, U.S.* 22°1′ N, 159°23′ W **99**
Haus, *Nor.* 60°27′ N, 5°29′ E **152**
Hauser, *Oreg., U.S.* 43°30′ N, 124°14′ W **90**
Hausjärvi, *Fin.* 60°46′ N, 24°54′ E **166**
Hausruck, *Aust.* 48°7′ N, 13°11′ E **152**
Haut Atlas, *Mor.* 32°31′ N, 5°4′ W **214**
Hauta see Al Ḩillah, *Saudi Arabia* 23°28′ N, 46°52′ E **196**
Haute-Normandie, adm. division, *Fr.* 49°40′ N, 0°27′ E **150**
Hauterive, *Can.* 49°12′ N, 68°15′ W **94**
Hautmont, *Fr.* 50°14′ N, 3°54′ E **163**
Hauts Plateaux, *Alg.* 34°11′ N, 0°38′ E **214**
Havana, *Fla., U.S.* 30°36′ N, 84°25′ W **96**
Havana, *Ill., U.S.* 40°17′ N, 90°4′ W **102**
Havana see La Habana, *Cuba* 23°6′ N, 82°33′ W **116**
Havant, *U.K.* 50°51′ N, 0°59′ E **162**
Havasu, Lake, *Ariz., U.S.* 34°24′ N, 114°29′ W **101**
Havdhem, *Sw.* 57°9′ N, 18°19′ E **166**
Haveli, *Pak.* 30°26′ N, 73°43′ E **186**
Havelock, *Can.* 44°26′ N, 77°53′ W **94**
Havelock, *N.C., U.S.* 34°52′ N, 76°55′ W **96**
Havelock, *N.Z.* 41°19′ S, 173°45′ E **240**
Havelock Island, *India* 11°44′ N, 93°11′ E **188**
Haven, *Kans., U.S.* 37°53′ N, 97°48′ W **90**
Haverhill, *Mass., U.S.* 42°46′ N, 71°5′ W **104**
Haverhill, *N.H., U.S.* 44°1′ N, 72°5′ W **104**
Haverhill, *U.K.* 52°5′ N, 0°26′ E **162**
Haverö, *Nor.* 62°22′ N, 15°4′ E **152**
Häverödal, *Sw.* 60°1′ N, 18°34′ E **166**
Haviland, *Kans., U.S.* 37°36′ N, 99°7′ W **90**
Havirga, *Mongolia* 45°43′ N, 113°4′ E **198**
Havola Escarpment, *Antarctica* 84°34′ S, 95°24′ W **248**
Havøysund, *Nor.* 70°58′ N, 24°38′ E **152**
Havre, *Mont., U.S.* 48°31′ N, 109°40′ W **90**
Havre-Aubert, *Can.* 47°12′ N, 61°52′ W **111**
Havre-Saint-Pierre, *Can.* 50°14′ N, 63°37′ W **111**
Havza, *Turk.* 40°58′ N, 35°38′ E **156**
Hawai'i, adm. division, *Hawai'i, U.S.* 20°0′ N, 156°0′ W **99**
Hawai'i, island, *Hawai'i, U.S.* 19°33′ N, 154°52′ W **99**
Hawai'i Volcanoes National Park, *Hawai'i, U.S.* 18°57′ N, 156°9′ W **99**
Hawaiian Ridge, *North Pacific Ocean* 23°8′ N, 164°25′ W **252**
Ḩawār, island, *Qatar* 25°40′ N, 50°15′ E **182**
Hawarden, *Iowa, U.S.* 42°58′ N, 96°29′ W **90**
Hawarden, *N.Z.* 42°55′ S, 172°37′ E **240**
Hawarden, *U.K.* 53°11′ N, 3°2′ W **162**
Hawera, *N.Z.* 39°35′ S, 174°16′ E **240**
Hawes, *U.K.* 54°18′ N, 2°12′ W **162**
Hawesville, *Ky., U.S.* 37°53′ N, 86°45′ W **94**
Hawke Harbour, *Can.* 53°2′ N, 55°50′ W **111**
Hawkes, Mount, *Antarctica* 83°57′ S, 58°11′ W **248**
Hawkins, *Tex., U.S.* 32°35′ N, 95°12′ W **103**
Hawksbill, peak, *Va., U.S.* 38°32′ N, 78°29′ W **94**
Hawley, *Minn., U.S.* 46°52′ N, 96°19′ W **90**
Hawthorne, *Fla., U.S.* 29°35′ N, 82°6′ W **105**
Hawza, *Western Sahara* 27°9′ N, 11°3′ W **214**
Hawzēn, *Eth.* 13°57′ N, 39°26′ E **182**
Haxtun, *Colo., U.S.* 40°38′ N, 102°39′ W **90**
Hay, Mount, peak, *Can.* 59°12′ N, 137°38′ W **108**
Hay River, *Can.* 60°45′ N, 115°36′ W **106**
Hay, river, *Can.* 58°37′ N, 117°59′ W **246**
Hay, river, *Can.* 59°53′ N, 116°49′ W **108**
Hay, river, *Can.* 58°15′ N, 120°23′ W **108**
Hay Springs, *Nebr., U.S.* 42°40′ N, 102°42′ W **90**
Haya, *Sp.* 36°43′ N, 6°5′ W **164**
Hayang, *S. Korea* 35°53′ N, 128°49′ E **200**
Hayange, *Fr.* 49°20′ N, 6°2′ E **163**
Hayden, *Colo., U.S.* 40°29′ N, 107°14′ W **90**
Hayden Peak, *Utah, U.S.* 40°44′ N, 110°55′ W **90**
Haydenville, *Mass., U.S.* 42°22′ N, 72°42′ W **104**
Hayes, *La., U.S.* 30°5′ N, 92°56′ W **103**
Hayes, *S. Dak., U.S.* 44°21′ N, 101°3′ W **90**
Hayes Center, *Nebr., U.S.* 40°29′ N, 101°2′ W **90**
Hayes, Mount, *Alas., U.S.* 63°36′ N, 146°55′ W **98**
Hayes, river, *Can.* 55°8′ N, 94°7′ W **108**
Hayes, river, *Can.* 54°14′ N, 96°24′ W **108**
Hayes, river, *Can.* 56°43′ N, 92°38′ W **108**
Haylaastay, *Mongolia* 46°51′ N, 113°26′ E **198**
Haymā', *Oman* 19°55′ N, 56°23′ E **182**
Haymana, *Turk.* 39°26′ N, 32°30′ E **156**
Haynesville, *La., U.S.* 32°56′ N, 93°9′ W **103**
Hayneville, *Ala., U.S.* 32°10′ N, 86°35′ W **96**
Hayrabolu, *Turk.* 41°12′ N, 27°5′ E **156**
Hays, *Kans., U.S.* 38°51′ N, 99°20′ W **90**
Hays, *Mont., U.S.* 47°57′ N, 108°41′ W **90**
Haystack Mountain, *Can.* 50°18′ N, 88°41′ W **94**
Haysville, *Kans., U.S.* 37°33′ N, 97°23′ W **92**
Haysyn, *Ukr.* 48°48′ N, 29°35′ E **158**
Hayti, *Mo., U.S.* 36°14′ N, 89°45′ W **96**
Hayvoron, *Ukr.* 48°22′ N, 30°0′ E **156**
Hayward, *Calif., U.S.* 37°40′ N, 122°6′ W **100**
Hayward, *Wis., U.S.* 46°1′ N, 91°29′ W **94**
Haywards Heath, *U.K.* 50°59′ N, 0°7′ E **162**
Haywood, Mount, *Can.* 63°48′ N, 125°11′ W **98**
Hazar Gölü, lake, *Turk.* 38°53′ N, 38°57′ E **195**
Hazārān, Kūh-e, peak, *Iran* 29°29′ N, 57°13′ E **196**
Hazard, *Ky., U.S.* 37°15′ N, 83°11′ W **96**
Hazardville, *Conn., U.S.* 41°59′ N, 72°33′ W **104**
Hazareh Toghay, *Afghan.* 37°9′ N, 67°16′ E **186**
Hazaribag, *India* 23°52′ N, 85°18′ E **190**
Hazebrouck, *Fr.* 50°43′ N, 2°32′ E **163**
Hazelton, *Can.* 55°15′ N, 127°39′ W **108**
Hazelton, *N. Dak., U.S.* 46°28′ N, 100°17′ W **90**
Hazen, *Ark., U.S.* 34°45′ N, 91°35′ W **96**
Hazen, *Nev., U.S.* 39°33′ N, 119°4′ W **90**
Hazen, *N. Dak., U.S.* 47°17′ N, 101°39′ W **90**
Hazen Bay 60°52′ N, 167°10′ W **98**
Hazen Strait 77°9′ N, 106°1′ W **246**
Ḩazerim, *Israel* 31°14′ N, 34°41′ E **194**
Ḩazeva, *Israel* 30°48′ N, 35°14′ E **194**
Hazlehurst, *Miss., U.S.* 31°51′ N, 90°24′ W **103**
Hazleton, *Ind., U.S.* 38°28′ N, 87°33′ W **102**
Hazleton, *Pa., U.S.* 40°57′ N, 75°60′ W **94**
Hazor, ruin(s), *Israel* 33°1′ N, 35°31′ E **194**
Hazro, *Turk.* 38°14′ N, 40°47′ E **195**
Heacham, *U.K.* 52°54′ N, 0°29′ E **162**
Head, Mount, *Can.* 50°26′ N, 114°44′ W **90**
Headcorn, *U.K.* 51°10′ N, 0°37′ E **162**
Headley, Mount, *Mont., U.S.* 47°42′ N, 115°21′ W **90**
Healaval Beg, peak, *U.K.* 57°21′ N, 6°44′ W **150**
Healdsburg, *Calif., U.S.* 38°37′ N, 122°52′ W **90**
Healdton, *Okla., U.S.* 34°12′ N, 97°29′ W **96**
Healy, *Kans., U.S.* 38°35′ N, 100°38′ W **90**
Healy Peak, *Nev., U.S.* 39°40′ N, 117°54′ W **90**
Heard Island and McDonald Islands, *Australia* 53°0′ S, 74°0′ E **248**
Hearne, *Tex., U.S.* 30°52′ N, 96°35′ W **96**
Hearne Bay 60°12′ N, 99°60′ W **108**
Hearst, *Can.* 49°41′ N, 83°41′ W **94**
Hearst Island, *Antarctica* 69°27′ S, 61°32′ W **248**
Heart Mountain, *Wyo., U.S.* 44°37′ N, 109°12′ W **90**
Heart Peaks, *Can.* 58°35′ N, 132°6′ W **108**
Heart, river, *N. Dak., U.S.* 46°24′ N, 101°50′ W **80**
Heath, *Ohio, U.S.* 40°1′ N, 82°27′ W **94**
Heath, Pointe, *Can.* 49°8′ N, 62°26′ W **111**
Heath, river, *South America* 13°6′ S, 69°1′ W **137**
Heaval, peak, *U.K.* 56°57′ N, 7°34′ W **150**
Heavener, *Okla., U.S.* 34°51′ N, 94°37′ W **96**
Hebbronville, *Tex., U.S.* 27°17′ N, 98°40′ W **96**
Hebei, adm. division, *China* 40°36′ N, 115°19′ E **198**
Heber, *Ariz., U.S.* 34°25′ N, 110°35′ W **92**
Heber, *Calif., U.S.* 32°43′ N, 115°33′ W **101**
Heber City, *Utah, U.S.* 40°30′ N, 111°25′ W **90**
Hébert, Lac, lake, *Can.* 49°8′ N, 75°46′ W **94**
Hebi, *China* 35°57′ N, 114°9′ E **198**
Hebrides, islands, *North Atlantic Ocean* 57°39′ N, 11°49′ W **143**
Hebrides, islands, *North Atlantic Ocean* 58°20′ N, 12°32′ W **72**
Hebrides, Sea of the 56°42′ N, 7°40′ W **150**
Hebron, *Ill., U.S.* 42°27′ N, 88°27′ W **102**
Hebron, *Ind., U.S.* 41°18′ N, 87°12′ W **102**
Hebron, *Nebr., U.S.* 40°9′ N, 97°35′ W **90**
Hebron, *N.H., U.S.* 43°41′ N, 71°49′ W **104**
Hebron, *N. Dak., U.S.* 46°53′ N, 102°3′ W **90**
Hebron see Al Khalīl, *West Bank* 31°31′ N, 35°6′ E **194**
Hecate Strait 51°44′ N, 128°18′ W **106**
Hecelchakán, *Mex.* 20°10′ N, 90°9′ W **115**
Heceta Head, *Oreg., U.S.* 44°6′ N, 124°26′ W **90**
Hechi, *China* 24°39′ N, 108°1′ E **198**
Hecho, *Sp.* 42°43′ N, 0°45′ E **164**
Hechuan, *China* 30°1′ N, 106°12′ E **198**
Hecla, *Can.* 51°7′ N, 96°42′ W **90**
Hecla, *S. Dak., U.S.* 45°51′ N, 98°10′ W **90**
Hecla and Griper Bay 75°33′ N, 113°59′ W **106**
Hecla, Cape, *Can.* 82°56′ N, 67°3′ W **246**
Hécla, Lac, lake, *Can.* 52°33′ N, 72°28′ W **111**
Hector, *N.Z.* 41°38′ S, 171°54′ E **240**
Hector, Mount, *Can.* 51°34′ N, 116°19′ W **90**
Hédé, *Fr.* 48°17′ N, 1°48′ W **150**
Hede, *Nor.* 62°25′ N, 13°30′ E **152**
HedemÜnden, *Ger.* 51°23′ N, 9°46′ E **167**
Hedley, *Tex., U.S.* 34°50′ N, 100°40′ W **92**
Hedmark, region, *Europe* 60°57′ N, 10°38′ E **152**
Hedon, *U.K.* 53°43′ N, 0°12′ E **162**
Heemstede, *Neth.* 52°21′ N, 4°36′ E **163**
Heerde, *Neth.* 52°23′ N, 6°2′ E **163**
Heerlen, *Neth.* 50°52′ N, 5°58′ E **167**
Ḩefa (Haifa), *Israel* 32°47′ N, 35°0′ E **194**
Hefei, *China* 31°53′ N, 117°20′ E **198**
Hefeng, *China* 29°54′ N, 110°0′ E **198**
Hegang, *China* 47°29′ N, 130°15′ E **190**
Hegyeshalom, *Hung.* 47°55′ N, 17°10′ E **168**
Heiau o Kalalea, site, *Hawai'i, U.S.* 18°54′ N, 155°44′ W **99**
Heide, *Ger.* 54°12′ N, 9°6′ E **150**
Heidelberg, *Ger.* 49°24′ N, 8°40′ E **150**
Heidelberg, *Miss., U.S.* 31°52′ N, 88°59′ W **103**
Heidelberg, *S. Af.* 34°4′ S, 20°55′ E **227**
Heihe, *China* 50°9′ N, 127°24′ E **190**
Heilbron, *S. Af.* 27°19′ S, 27°56′ E **227**
Heilbronn, *Ger.* 49°8′ N, 9°13′ E **152**
Heiligenstadt, *Ger.* 51°22′ N, 10°8′ E **167**
Heilinzi, *China* 44°34′ N, 126°40′ E **198**
Heilongjiang, adm. division, *China* 46°58′ N, 128°21′ E **198**
Heimdal, *Nor.* 63°19′ N, 10°20′ E **152**
Heimefront Range, *Antarctica* 74°46′ S, 11°55′ W **248**
Heinävesi, *Fin.* 62°23′ N, 28°35′ E **152**
Heinola, *Fin.* 61°12′ N, 26°2′ E **166**
Heinsberg, *Ger.* 51°3′ N, 6°5′ E **167**
Heinsburg, *Can.* 53°46′ N, 110°32′ W **108**
Heishan, *China* 41°42′ N, 122°9′ E **198**
Hejaz see Al Ḩijāz, region, *Saudi Arabia* 26°54′ N, 36°41′ E **180**
Hejian, *China* 38°29′ N, 116°4′ E **198**
Hejiang, *China* 28°50′ N, 105°42′ E **198**
Hejing, *China* 42°18′ N, 86°30′ E **184**
Hekla, peak, *Ice.* 64°1′ N, 20°7′ W **143**
Hekou, *China* 22°34′ N, 103°57′ E **202**
Hel, *Pol.* 54°37′ N, 18°49′ E **166**
Helagsfjället, peak, *Nor.* 62°56′ N, 12°20′ E **152**
Helan Shan, peak, *China* 38°37′ N, 105°47′ E **198**
Hele Islands, *Solomon Sea* 9°0′ S, 158°0′ E **242**
Helechosa, *Sp.* 39°18′ N, 4°56′ W **164**
Helen Island, *Palau* 2°18′ N, 131°51′ E **192**
Helen Lake, *Can.* 49°3′ N, 88°38′ W **110**
Helen, Mount, *Nev., U.S.* 37°29′ N, 116°50′ W **92**
Helena, *Ark., U.S.* 34°31′ N, 90°39′ W **112**
Helena, *Ga., U.S.* 32°4′ N, 82°56′ W **96**
Helena, *Mont., U.S.* 46°33′ N, 112°10′ W **90**
Helena, *Okla., U.S.* 36°32′ N, 98°17′ W **96**
Helena, *S.C., U.S.* 34°16′ N, 81°39′ W **96**
Helengili, island, *Maldives* 4°18′ N, 73°41′ E **188**
Helensville, *N.Z.* 36°41′ S, 174°27′ E **240**
Helgøy, *Nor.* 70°6′ N, 19°23′ E **152**
Helicon see Elikónas, peak, *Gr.* 38°17′ N, 22°47′ E **156**
Hellberge, peak, *Ger.* 52°33′ N, 11°12′ E **152**
Hellemobotn, *Nor.* 67°49′ N, 16°31′ E **152**
Hellenthal, *Ger.* 50°28′ N, 6°25′ E **167**
Hellesylt, *Nor.* 62°4′ N, 6°52′ E **152**
Helligvær, islands, *Norwegian Sea* 67°27′ N, 12°27′ E **152**
Hellín, *Sp.* 38°30′ N, 1°42′ W **164**
Hells Canyon, *Oreg., U.S.* 45°30′ N, 116°43′ W **90**
Hells Gate, *Can.* 49°43′ N, 121°35′ W **100**
Hells Half Acre, site, *Wyo., U.S.* 43°1′ N, 107°9′ W **90**
Hell-Ville see Andoany, *Madagascar* 13°24′ S, 48°17′ E **207**
Helmand, river, *Afghan.* 30°13′ N, 62°36′ E **186**
Helmand, river, *Afghan.* 33°24′ N, 66°12′ E **186**
Helmeringhausen, *Namibia* 25°56′ S, 16°54′ E **227**
Helmond, *Neth.* 51°28′ N, 5°40′ E **167**
Helong, *China* 42°31′ N, 128°58′ E **200**
Helper, *Utah, U.S.* 39°40′ N, 110°51′ W **90**
Helsingborg, *Nor.* 56°3′ N, 12°43′ E **152**
Helsingfors see Helsinki, *Fin.* 60°9′ N, 24°48′ E **166**
Helsingør, *Den.* 56°1′ N, 12°34′ E **152**
Helsinki (Helsingfors), *Fin.* 60°9′ N, 24°48′ E **166**
Helska, Mierzeja, *Pol.* 54°45′ N, 18°32′ E **166**
Heltermaa, *Est.* 58°51′ N, 23°0′ E **166**
Helvecia, *Arg.* 31°6′ S, 60°8′ W **139**
Helvécia, *Hung.* 46°49′ N, 19°38′ E **168**
Helvellyn, peak, *U.K.* 54°30′ N, 3°3′ W **162**
Helvick Head, *Ire.* 51°53′ N, 7°31′ W **150**
Ḩelwân, *Egypt* 29°50′ N, 31°19′ E **182**
Hemet, *Calif., U.S.* 33°45′ N, 116°60′ W **101**
Heming Lake, *Can.* 54°56′ N, 101°7′ W **108**
Hemingford, *Nebr., U.S.* 42°19′ N, 103°8′ W **90**
Hemis National Park, *India* 33°48′ N, 77°22′ E **188**
Hemne, *Nor.* 63°15′ N, 9°5′ E **152**
Hemphill, *Tex., U.S.* 31°19′ N, 93°52′ W **103**
Hempstead, *N.Y., U.S.* 40°41′ N, 73°38′ W **104**
Hempstead, *Tex., U.S.* 30°4′ N, 96°5′ W **96**
Hemse, *Sw.* 57°13′ N, 18°22′ E **166**
Hemsedal, *Nor.* 60°52′ N, 8°33′ E **152**
Hemsedalsfjell, *Nor.* 60°56′ N, 7°9′ E **152**
Henan, adm. division, *China* 33°22′ N, 112°17′ E **198**
Hendek, *Turk.* 40°48′ N, 30°46′ E **158**
Henderson, *Ky., U.S.* 37°49′ N, 87°35′ W **96**
Henderson, *Nev., U.S.* 36°1′ N, 114°60′ W **101**
Henderson, *Tenn., U.S.* 35°25′ N, 88°38′ W **96**
Henderson, *Tex., U.S.* 32°8′ N, 94°48′ W **103**
Henderson, *W. Va., U.S.* 38°48′ N, 82°10′ W **102**
Henderson Island, *U.K.* 24°19′ S, 128°22′ W **255**
Hendersonville, *Tenn., U.S.* 36°18′ N, 86°37′ W **96**
Hendon, *Can.* 52°4′ N, 103°49′ W **108**
Hendrik Top, peak, *Suriname* 4°11′ N, 56°21′ W **130**
Hengām, island, *Iran* 26°28′ N, 55°51′ E **180**
Hengch'un, *Taiwan* 22°2′ N, 120°45′ E **198**
Hengshan, *China* 37°57′ N, 109°18′ E **198**
Hengshui, *China* 37°41′ N, 115°43′ E **198**
Hengxian, *China* 22°42′ N, 109°13′ E **198**
Hengyang, *China* 27°1′ N, 112°27′ E **190**
Henhoaha, *India* 6°48′ N, 93°54′ E **188**
Heniches'k, *Ukr.* 46°12′ N, 34°46′ E **156**
Hénin-Beaumont, *Fr.* 50°24′ N, 2°57′ E **163**
Henley on Thames, *U.K.* 51°32′ N, 0°55′ E **162**
Hennan, *Nor.* 62°2′ N, 15°52′ E **152**
Hennessey, *Okla., U.S.* 36°4′ N, 97°53′ W **92**
Henniker, *N.H., U.S.* 43°10′ N, 71°51′ W **104**
Henning, *Minn., U.S.* 46°18′ N, 95°28′ W **90**
Henrietta, *Tex., U.S.* 33°47′ N, 98°11′ W **92**
Henrietta Island, *Can.* 76°54′ N, 157°30′ E **255**
Henrietta Maria, Cape, *Can.* 55°5′ N, 82°20′ W **106**
Henrieville, *Utah, U.S.* 37°34′ N, 111°59′ W **92**
Henry, *Ill., U.S.* 41°6′ N, 89°23′ W **102**
Henry Bay 66°28′ S, 121°28′ E **248**
Henry, Cape, *Va., U.S.* 36°34′ N, 75°57′ W **80**
Henry Kater Peninsula, *Can.* 69°15′ N, 66°31′ W **106**
Henry Lawrence Island, *India* 11°59′ N, 93°14′ E **188**
Henry Mountains, *Utah, U.S.* 38°3′ N, 110°56′ W **90**
Henryetta, *Okla., U.S.* 35°25′ N, 95°59′ W **96**
Henryville, *Ind., U.S.* 38°32′ N, 85°45′ W **102**
Hensall, *Can.* 43°26′ N, 81°30′ W **102**
Henshaw, Lake, *Calif., U.S.* 33°15′ N, 116°53′ W **101**
Hentiy, *Mongolia* 48°5′ N, 109°50′ E **198**
Hentiy, adm. division, *Mongolia* 48°14′ N, 109°39′ E **198**
Hephaestia, ruin(s), *Gr.* 39°56′ N, 25°13′ E **156**
Heping, *China* 24°25′ N, 114°56′ E **198**
Heppner, *Oreg., U.S.* 45°20′ N, 119°34′ W **90**
Hepu, *China* 21°38′ N, 109°14′ E **198**
Heraea, ruin(s), *Gr.* 37°36′ N, 21°47′ E **156**
Herald Cays, *Coral Sea* 16°47′ S, 147°46′ E **230**
Herat, *Afghan.* 34°27′ N, 62°11′ E **186**
Herb Lake, *Can.* 54°46′ N, 99°46′ W **108**
Herbert, *Can.* 50°25′ N, 107°15′ W **90**
Herbert, *N.Z.* 45°14′ S, 170°48′ E **240**
Herbertabad, *India* 11°43′ N, 92°46′ E **188**
Herbertingen, *Ger.* 48°3′ N, 9°26′ E **156**
Herbolzheim, *Ger.* 48°13′ N, 7°45′ E **163**
Herborn, *Ger.* 50°40′ N, 8°18′ E **167**
Herbstein, *Ger.* 50°34′ N, 9°21′ E **167**
Herceg-Novi, *Serb. and Mont.* 42°27′ N, 18°31′ E **168**
Hercegszántó, *Hung.* 45°57′ N, 18°55′ E **168**
Herchmer, *Can.* 57°24′ N, 94°12′ W **108**
Hercules Dome, *Antarctica* 87°4′ S, 106°58′ W **248**
Hercules Inlet 80°22′ S, 80°16′ W **248**
Herdecke, *Ger.* 51°24′ N, 7°25′ E **167**
Herdorf, *Ger.* 50°46′ N, 7°57′ E **167**
Hereford, *Tex., U.S.* 34°47′ N, 102°24′ W **92**
Hereford, *U.K.* 52°3′ N, 2°43′ W **162**
Herefoss, *Nor.* 58°32′ N, 8°20′ E **152**
Hérémakono, *Guinea* 9°53′ N, 11°5′ W **222**
Herencia, *Sp.* 39°22′ N, 3°22′ W **164**
Herend, *Hung.* 47°7′ N, 17°46′ E **168**
Herentals, *Belg.* 51°10′ N, 4°49′ E **167**
Heringen, *Ger.* 50°53′ N, 10°0′ E **167**
Herington, *Kans., U.S.* 38°38′ N, 96°57′ W **90**
Herkimer, *N.Y., U.S.* 43°1′ N, 74°60′ W **94**
Herlen, river, *Mongolia* 46°56′ N, 110°48′ E **190**
Herlenbayan, *Mongolia* 48°20′ N, 114°11′ E **198**
Herleshausen, *Ger.* 51°0′ N, 10°8′ E **167**
Hermagor, *Aust.* 46°38′ N, 13°21′ E **167**
Herman, *Minn., U.S.* 45°47′ N, 96°10′ W **90**
Hermann, *Mo., U.S.* 38°41′ N, 91°26′ W **94**
Hermansville, *Mich., U.S.* 45°42′ N, 87°35′ W **110**
Hermanus, *S. Af.* 34°23′ S, 19°14′ E **227**
Hermanville, *Miss., U.S.* 31°57′ N, 90°51′ W **103**
Hermel, *Leb.* 34°23′ N, 36°23′ E **194**
Hermies, *Fr.* 50°5′ N, 3°2′ E **163**
Hermit Islands, *South Pacific Ocean* 2°1′ S, 144°22′ E **192**
Hermitage, *Ark., U.S.* 33°26′ N, 92°11′ W **103**
Hermitage Bay 47°32′ N, 56°47′ W **111**
Hermitage Castle, site, *U.K.* 55°14′ N, 2°55′ W **150**
Hermite, Isla, island, *Chile* 56°9′ S, 69°7′ W **134**
Hermleigh, *Tex., U.S.* 32°38′ N, 100°47′ W **96**
Hermon, Mount see Shaykh, Jabal ash, peak, *Leb.* 33°24′ N, 35°49′ E **194**
Hermon, Mount see Shaykh, Jabal ash, peak, *Leb.* 33°24′ N, 35°49′ E **194**
Hermosillo, *Mex.* 29°1′ N, 111°3′ W **92**
Hernández, *Mex.* 22°59′ N, 102°2′ W **114**
Hernani, *Sp.* 43°14′ N, 1°59′ W **164**
Herne, *Ger.* 51°32′ N, 7°13′ E **167**
Herne Bay, *U.K.* 51°22′ N, 1°7′ E **162**
Herning, *Den.* 56°7′ N, 8°56′ E **150**
Heron Bay, *Can.* 48°39′ N, 86°17′ W **94**
Herøy, *Nor.* 65°57′ N, 12°14′ E **152**
Herradura, *Arg.* 26°32′ S, 58°17′ W **139**
Herreid, *S. Dak., U.S.* 45°49′ N, 100°6′ W **90**
Herrera, *Arg.* 28°28′ S, 63°5′ W **139**
Herrera del Duque, *Sp.* 39°9′ N, 5°4′ W **164**
Herrero, Punta, *Mex.* 19°12′ N, 87°27′ W **115**
Herrick, *Ill., U.S.* 39°13′ N, 88°59′ W **102**
Herriot, *Can.* 56°23′ N, 101°17′ W **108**
Herrljunga, *Nor.* 58°3′ N, 12°58′ E **152**
Herschel Island, *Can.* 69°38′ N, 139°31′ W **98**
Herscher, *Ill., U.S.* 41°1′ N, 88°7′ W **102**
Hersey, *Mich., U.S.* 43°51′ N, 85°26′ W **102**
Hersilia, *Arg.* 29°59′ S, 61°52′ W **139**
Hérso, *Gr.* 41°6′ N, 22°47′ E **156**
Hersónissos Akrotírio, *Gr.* 35°31′ N, 23°35′ E **156**
Herstal, *Belg.* 50°40′ N, 5°37′ E **167**
Herstmonceux, *U.K.* 50°52′ N, 0°19′ E **162**
Hersvik, *Nor.* 61°11′ N, 4°54′ E **152**
Hertford, *N.C., U.S.* 36°11′ N, 76°30′ W **96**
Hertford, *U.K.* 51°47′ N, 8°474′ W **162**
Hervey Island, *South Pacific Ocean* 20°47′ S, 160°24′ W **238**
Herzberg, *Ger.* 51°38′ N, 10°20′ E **167**
Herzebrock-Clarholz, *Ger.* 51°53′ N, 8°14′ E **167**
Herzliyya, *Israel* 32°10′ N, 34°49′ E **194**
Hesdin, *Fr.* 50°21′ N, 2°2′ E **163**
Hesel, *Ger.* 53°18′ N, 7°35′ E **163**
Hesepe, *Ger.* 52°26′ N, 7°58′ E **163**
Heshui, *China* 35°49′ N, 108°2′ E **198**
Heskestad, *Nor.* 58°29′ N, 6°20′ E **152**
Hesperia, *Calif., U.S.* 34°25′ N, 117°19′ W **101**
Hesperia, *Mich., U.S.* 43°33′ N, 86°3′ W **102**
Hess, river, *Can.* 63°10′ N, 131°36′ W **98**
Hesse, adm. division, *Ger.* 50°52′ N, 8°9′ E **150**
Hessisch Lichtenau, *Ger.* 51°12′ N, 9°44′ E **167**
Hessmer, *La., U.S.* 31°2′ N, 92°8′ W **103**
Hetin, *Serb. and Mont.* 45°39′ N, 20°46′ E **168**
Hettinger, *N. Dak., U.S.* 46°0′ N, 102°39′ W **90**
Hetzerath, *Ger.* 49°52′ N, 6°49′ E **167**
Heunghae, *S. Korea* 36°6′ N, 129°23′ E **200**
Heusden, *Belg.* 51°2′ N, 5°17′ E **167**
Heves, *Hung.* 47°35′ N, 20°17′ E **168**
Heves, adm. division, *Hung.* 47°46′ N, 19°46′ E **156**
Hévíz, *Hung.* 46°46′ N, 17°11′ E **168**
Hexi, *China* 32°28′ N, 105°46′ E **198**
Hexian, *China* 24°23′ N, 111°33′ E **198**
Hexian, *China* 31°41′ N, 118°21′ E **198**
Hexigten Qi (Jingpeng), *China* 43°16′ N, 117°28′ E **198**
Heysham, *U.K.* 54°2′ N, 2°54′ W **162**
Heyuan, *China* 23°41′ N, 114°41′ E **198**
Heyworth, *Ill., U.S.* 40°18′ N, 88°59′ W **102**
Heze, *China* 35°14′ N, 115°24′ E **198**
Hi Vista, *Calif., U.S.* 34°44′ N, 117°48′ W **101**
Hialeah, *Fla., U.S.* 25°51′ N, 80°18′ W **105**
Hiawatha, *Kans., U.S.* 39°49′ N, 95°33′ W **90**
Hiawatha, *Utah, U.S.* 39°28′ N, 111°1′ W **90**
Hickam Air Force Base, *Hawai'i, U.S.* 21°18′ N, 157°60′ W **99**
Hickiwan, *Ariz., U.S.* 32°21′ N, 112°27′ W **92**
Hickman, Mount, *Can.* 57°15′ N, 131°14′ W **108**
Hickmann, *Arg.* 23°11′ S, 63°35′ W **132**
Hickory, *Miss., U.S.* 32°18′ N, 88°60′ W **103**
Hickory, *N.C., U.S.* 35°44′ N, 81°21′ W **96**
Hicks Bay, *N.Z.* 37°37′ S, 178°15′ E **240**
Hick's Cays, *Caribbean Sea* 17°45′ N, 87°57′ W **115**
Hickson Lake, *Can.* 56°15′ N, 104°57′ W **108**
Hicksville, *N.Y., U.S.* 40°46′ N, 73°32′ W **104**
Hicksville, *Ohio, U.S.* 41°16′ N, 84°46′ W **102**
Hico, *Tex., U.S.* 31°58′ N, 98°2′ W **92**
Hidalgo, *Mex.* 27°46′ N, 99°52′ W **96**
Hidalgo, *Mex.* 25°56′ N, 100°27′ W **114**
Hidalgo, *Mex.* 24°14′ N, 99°28′ W **114**
Hidalgo, adm. division, *Mex.* 20°15′ N, 99°40′ W **114**
Hidalgo del Parral, *Mex.* 26°56′ N, 105°41′ W **112**
Hiddensee, *Ger.* 54°34′ N, 13°6′ E **152**
Hididelli, *Eth.* 6°6′ N, 43°29′ E **218**
Hidrolândia, *Braz.* 16°60′ S, 49°15′ W **138**
Hiendelaencina, *Sp.* 41°4′ N, 2°60′ W **164**
Hierro (Ferro), island, *Sp.* 27°25′ N, 17°55′ W **214**
Higashisongi, *Japan* 33°3′ N, 129°55′ E **201**
Higganum, *Conn., U.S.* 41°29′ N, 72°34′ W **104**
Higgins, *Tex., U.S.* 36°5′ N, 100°2′ W **92**
Higginsville, *Mo., U.S.* 39°3′ N, 93°43′ W **94**
High Falls Reservoir, lake, *Wis., U.S.* 45°16′ N, 88°49′ W **94**
High Force, fall(s), *U.K.* 54°38′ N, 2°32′ W **162**
High Island, *Tex., U.S.* 29°33′ N, 94°25′ W **103**
High Level, *Can.* 58°31′ N, 117°7′ W **108**
High Plains, *North America* 45°37′ N, 105°5′ W **90**
High Point, *N.C., U.S.* 35°57′ N, 80°1′ W **96**
High Point, peak, *N.J., U.S.* 41°18′ N, 74°45′ W **94**
High Prairie, *Can.* 55°24′ N, 116°28′ W **108**
High River, *Can.* 50°31′ N, 113°48′ W **82**
High Rock, *Bahamas* 26°37′ N, 78°19′ W **96**
High Springs, *Fla., U.S.* 29°48′ N, 82°36′ W **105**
High Willhays, peak, *U.K.* 50°40′ N, 4°7′ W **150**
High Wycombe, *U.K.* 51°37′ N, 0°46′ E **162**
Highgate, *Can.* 42°29′ N, 81°49′ W **102**
Highjump Archipelago, *Antarctica* 66°18′ S, 104°58′ E **248**
Highland, *Ill., U.S.* 38°44′ N, 89°40′ W **102**
Highland, *N.Y., U.S.* 41°43′ N, 73°59′ W **104**
Highland Falls, *N.Y., U.S.* 41°21′ N, 73°60′ W **104**
Highland Park, *Ill., U.S.* 42°11′ N, 87°48′ W **102**
Highland Park, *Mich., U.S.* 42°23′ N, 83°6′ W **102**
Highland Peak, *Nev., U.S.* 37°52′ N, 114°40′ W **90**
Highland Rocks, *Austral.* 21°20′ S, 129°18′ E **230**
Highrock, *Can.* 55°51′ N, 100°24′ W **108**
Highrock Lake, *Can.* 57°3′ N, 106°22′ W **108**
Highrock Lake, *Can.* 55°59′ N, 100°21′ W **108**
Highway City, *Calif., U.S.* 36°48′ N, 119°54′ W **100**
Highwood Baldy, peak, *Mont., U.S.* 47°23′ N, 110°42′ W **90**
Higüero, Punta, *U.S.* 18°16′ N, 68°4′ W **116**

Higuerote, Venez. 10°29' N, 66°7' W 136
Higüey, Dom. Rep. 18°36' N, 68°44' W 116
Hiirola, Fin. 61°47' N, 27°16' E 166
Hiittinen see Hitis, Fin. 59°51' N, 22°29' E 166
Hiiumaa (Dagö), island, Est. 58°49' N, 21°20' E 166
Hijānah, Buḩayrat al, lake, Syr. 33°16' N, 36°21' E 194
Hikari, Japan 33°57' N, 131°56' E 200
Hikiau Heiau State Monument, site, Hawai'i, U.S. 19°28' N, 155°58' W 99
Hiko, Nev., U.S. 37°34' N, 115°15' W 92
Hikone, Japan 35°13' N, 136°14' E 201
Hikurangi, N.Z. 35°36' S, 174°17' E 240
Hikurangi, peak, N.Z. 37°57' S, 177°59' E 240
Hilalaya, Somalia 6°3' N, 49°1' E 218
Hilchenbach, Ger. 50°59' N, 8°5' E 167
Hilden, Ger. 51°10' N, 6°56' E 167
Hiliotaluwa, Indonesia 0°43' N, 97°50' E 196
Hilisimaetano, Indonesia 0°40' N, 97°44' E 196
Hill, N.H., U.S. 43°31' N, 71°43' W 104
Hill Air Force Base, Utah, U.S. 41°6' N, 112°4' W 90
Hill Bank, Belize 17°36' N, 88°45' W 115
Hill City, Kans., U.S. 39°21' N, 99°51' W 90
Hill City, Minn., U.S. 46°58' N, 93°36' W 90
Hill City, S. Dak., U.S. 43°55' N, 103°35' W 90
Hill Island Lake, Can. 60°32' N, 110°57' W 108
Hillary Coast, Antarctica 79°49' S, 171°48' E 248
Hilleknuten, peak, Nor. 58°58' N, 6°51' E 152
Hillers, Mount, Utah, U.S. 37°52' N, 110°46' W 92
Hillesøy, Nor. 69°35' N, 18°2' E 152
Hilliard, Ohio, U.S. 40°1' N, 83°9' W 102
Hillman, Mich., U.S. 45°4' N, 83°54' W 94
Hillsboro, Ill., U.S. 39°8' N, 89°29' W 102
Hillsboro, Kans., U.S. 38°20' N, 97°13' W 90
Hillsboro, Mo., U.S. 39°8' N, 89°29' W 94
Hillsboro, N.H., U.S. 43°6' N, 71°54' W 104
Hillsboro, N. Dak., U.S. 47°23' N, 97°4' W 90
Hillsboro, Ohio, U.S. 39°11' N, 83°37' W 102
Hillsboro, Tex., U.S. 32°0' N, 97°7' W 92
Hillsboro, Wis., U.S. 43°38' N, 90°21' W 102
Hillsboro Lower Village, N.H., U.S. 43°6' N, 71°57' W 104
Hillsborough, Grenada 12°26' N, 61°28' W 116
Hillsdale, Mich., U.S. 41°54' N, 84°40' W 102
Hillsville, Va., U.S. 36°45' N, 80°45' W 94
Hilo, Hawai'i, U.S. 19°43' N, 155°6' W 99
Hilo, region, Oceania 19°48' N, 155°25' W 99
Hilonghilong, Mount, Philippines 9°5' N, 125°37' E 203
Hilton Head Island, S.C., U.S. 32°12' N, 80°46' W 96
Hiltrup, Ger. 51°54' N, 7°38' E 167
Hilversum, Neth. 52°12' N, 5°10' E 163
Hima, Ky., U.S. 37°6' N, 83°48' W 96
Himachal Pradesh, adm. division, India 32°20' N, 75°58' E 188
Himalaya, Asia 32°53' N, 74°1' E 186
Himanka, Fin. 64°3' N, 23°38' E 152
Himatnagar, India 23°36' N, 72°58' E 186
Himeji, Japan 34°50' N, 134°41' E 201
Himi, Japan 36°51' N, 136°58' E 201
Himo, Tanzania 3°25' S, 37°33' E 224
Himora, Eth. 14°12' N, 36°36' E 182
Ḩimş, Syr. 34°43' N, 36°42' E 143
Ḩimş, Baḩrat, lake, Syr. 34°39' N, 36°29' E 194
Ḩimş (Homs), Syr. 34°43' N, 36°42' E 194
Hinatuan, Philippines 8°24' N, 126°16' E 203
Hinche, Haiti 19°8' N, 72°2' W 116
Hinchinbrook Island, Austral. 18°47' S, 143°13' E 231
Hinchinbrook Island National Park, Coral Sea 18°32' S, 145°55' E 238
Hinckley, Ill., U.S. 41°45' N, 88°39' W 102
Hinckley, Minn., U.S. 46°0' N, 92°58' W 94
Hinckley, U.K. 52°32' N, 1°23' W 162
Hinckley, Utah, U.S. 39°19' N, 112°40' W 90
Hindon, U.K. 51°5' N, 2°8' W 162
Hinds, N.Z. 44°1' S, 171°33' E 240
Hindubagh, Pak. 30°51' N, 67°45' E 186
Hindupur, India 13°50' N, 77°29' E 188
Hines, Oreg., U.S. 43°33' N, 119°5' W 90
Hines Creek, Can. 56°14' N, 118°36' W 108
Hinesburg, Vt., U.S. 44°19' N, 73°7' W 104
Hinesville, Ga., U.S. 31°50' N, 81°37' W 96
Hinganghat, India 20°31' N, 78°51' E 188
Hinggan Ling, Da, China 44°15' N, 118°1' E 198
Hingham, Mass., U.S. 42°14' N, 70°54' W 104
Hingol, river, Pak. 25°50' N, 65°26' E 182
Hınıs, Turk. 39°22' N, 41°43' E 195
Hinkley, Calif., U.S. 34°56' N, 117°13' W 101
Hinkley Point, site, U.K. 51°11' N, 3°4' W 162
Hinks, Mount, Antarctica 67°54' S, 65°45' E 248
Hinlopenstretet 79°46' N, 19°22' E 160
Hinnerjoki, Fin. 60°59' N, 21°57' E 166
Hinnøya, Norwegian Sea 68°37' N, 15°28' E 152
Hino, Japan 35°12' N, 133°25' E 201
Hinoba-an, Philippines 9°37' N, 122°29' E 203
Hinoemata, Japan 37°1' N, 139°22' E 201
Hinojosa del Duque, Sp. 38°29' N, 5°9' W 164
Hinomi Saki, Japan 35°25' N, 132°28' E 201
Hinsdale, N.H., U.S. 42°47' N, 72°30' W 104
Hinterweidenthal, Ger. 49°11' N, 7°44' E 163
Hinthada, Myanmar 17°38' N, 95°26' E 202
Hinton, Can. 53°24' N, 117°35' W 108
Hinton, Okla., U.S. 35°26' N, 98°22' W 96
Hinton, W. Va., U.S. 37°39' N, 80°54' W 96
Hınzır Burnu, Turk. 36°18' N, 35°2' E 156
Híos, Gr. 38°22' N, 26°6' E 180
Híos, island, Gr. 38°9' N, 25°31' E 180
Hippolytushoef, Neth. 52°54' N, 4°57' E 163
Hirado, Japan 33°22' N, 129°32' E 201
Hiram, Me., U.S. 43°52' N, 70°49' W 104
Hirata, Japan 35°23' N, 132°47' E 201
Hirfanlı Barajı, dam, Turk. 39°4' N, 33°36' E 156
Hirky, Ukr. 51°53' N, 25°16' E 154
Hirnyky, Ukr. 51°42' N, 24°27' E 152
Hirosaki, Japan 40°33' N, 140°25' E 190
Hiroshima, Japan 34°23' N, 132°27' E 200
Hiroshima, adm. division, Japan 34°32' N, 132°9' E 201
Hirson, Fr. 49°54' N, 4°4' E 163
Hîrşova, Rom. 44°41' N, 27°57' E 156
Hirtshals, Den. 57°34' N, 9°57' E 150
Hirvasvaara, Fin. 66°32' N, 28°34' E 152
Hirvensalmi, Fin. 61°37' N, 26°46' E 166
Hisar, India 29°7' N, 75°44' E 197
Hisarönü, Turk. 41°34' N, 32°2' E 156
Ḩişn al 'Abr, Yemen 16°8' N, 47°18' E 182
Ḩişn Tāqrifat, Lib. 29°12' N, 17°20' E 216
Hisor, Taj. 38°33' N, 68°33' E 197
Hispaniola, island, Caribbean Sea 18°54' N, 71°8' W 253
Hispaniola, island, Dom. Rep. 19°57' N, 70°50' W 116
Ḩisyah, Syr. 34°24' N, 36°45' E 194
Hīt, Iraq 33°37' N, 42°44' E 180
Hita, Japan 33°19' N, 130°56' E 201
Hitachi, Japan 36°35' N, 140°38' E 201
Hitachiōta, Japan 36°31' N, 140°32' E 201
Hitadu, island, Maldives 0°36' N, 72°17' E 188
Hitchcock, Tex., U.S. 29°20' N, 95°2' W 103
Hitchin, U.K. 51°57' N, 0°17' E 162
Hitis (Hiittinen), Fin. 59°51' N, 22°29' E 166
Hitoyoshi, Japan 32°13' N, 130°45' E 201
Hitra, Nor. 63°35' N, 8°42' E 152
Hitterdal, Minn., U.S. 46°56' N, 96°17' W 90
Hiuchi Nada 34°5' N, 133°12' E 201
Hiusta Meadow, Can. 58°4' N, 130°59' W 98
Hiver, Lac de l', lake, Can. 53°55' N, 72°38' W 111
Hiwannee, Miss., U.S. 31°47' N, 88°40' W 103
Hiwasa, Japan 33°44' N, 134°31' E 201
Hixon, Can. 53°26' N, 122°37' W 108
Hizan, Turk. 38°9' N, 42°24' E 195
Hjallerup, Den. 57°10' N, 10°8' E 152
Hjalmar Lake, Can. 61°30' N, 110°6' W 108
Hjartdal, Nor. 59°35' N, 8°39' E 152
Hjerkinn, Nor. 62°13' N, 9°35' E 152
Hjørring, Den. 57°26' N, 9°58' E 150
Hlaingbwe, Myanmar 17°8' N, 97°50' E 202
Hlohovec, Slovakia 48°25' N, 17°47' E 152
Hluhluwe, S. Af. 28°1' S, 32°16' E 227
Hlukhiv, Ukr. 51°38' N, 33°57' E 158
Hlyboka, Ukr. 48°4' N, 25°55' E 152
Hlybokaye, Belarus 55°9' N, 27°41' E 166
Ho, Ghana 6°36' N, 0°28' E 222
Ho Chi Minh City (Saigon), Vietnam 10°48' N, 106°40' E 202
Ho Xa, Vietnam 17°4' N, 107°2' E 202
Hoa Binh, Vietnam 20°52' N, 105°17' E 202
Hoachanas, Namibia 23°57' S, 18°4' E 220
Hoai An, Vietnam 14°23' N, 108°58' E 202
Hoare Bay 65°23' N, 64°55' W 106
Hoback Peak, Wyo., U.S. 43°4' N, 110°39' W 90
Hobart, Austral. 42°53' S, 146°56' E 230
Hobart, Okla., U.S. 35°0' N, 99°6' W 92
Hobbs, N. Mex., U.S. 32°41' N, 103°8' W 92
Hobbs Coast, Antarctica 75°18' S, 127°36' W 248
Hobe Sound, Fla., U.S. 27°3' N, 80°9' W 105
Hobo, Col. 2°33' N, 75°29' W 136
Hoboksar, China 46°47' N, 85°47' E 184
Hobot Xar see Xianghuang Qi, China 42°11' N, 113°53' E 198
Hobro, Den. 56°38' N, 9°46' E 150
Hobucken, N.C., U.S. 35°15' N, 76°35' W 96
Hoburgen, Sw. 56°52' N, 18°10' E 166
Hobyo, Somalia 5°22' N, 48°36' E 218
Höch'ŏn, N. Korea 40°38' N, 128°35' E 200
Hochschwab, Aust. 47°35' N, 14°46' E 156
Höchst, Ger. 49°48' N, 8°59' E 167
Hochstetter Forland, Den. 75°16' N, 18°24' W 246
Hodda, peak, Somalia 11°30' N, 50°32' E 182
Hoddesdon, U.K. 51°45' N, 2°118' W 162
Hodge, Calif., U.S. 34°49' N, 117°12' W 101
Hodge, La., U.S. 32°16' N, 92°44' W 103
Hodges Hill, peak, Can. 49°3' N, 55°59' W 111
Hodgeville, Can. 50°6' N, 106°58' W 90
Hodgson, Can. 51°12' N, 97°35' W 90
Hodh, region, Africa 16°35' N, 8°36' W 222
Hódmez ovásárhely, Hung. 46°25' N, 20°20' E 168
Hodonín, Czech Rep. 48°51' N, 17°8' E 152
Hödrögö, Mongolia 48°54' N, 96°51' E 173
Hoek van Holland, Neth. 51°58' N, 4°7' E 163
Hoeryŏng, N. Korea 42°28' N, 129°46' E 200
Hoeyang, N. Korea 38°41' N, 127°37' E 200
Hof, Ger. 50°18' N, 11°55' E 152
Hoffman, Minn., U.S. 45°48' N, 95°50' W 90
Hofgeismar, Ger. 51°30' N, 9°22' E 167
Hofheim, Ger. 50°5' N, 8°26' E 167
Höfn, Ice. 64°20' N, 15°13' W 143
Hofors, Nor. 60°32' N, 16°18' E 152
Hofra, oil field, Lib. 29°18' N, 17°43' E 216
Hofrat en Nahas, Sudan 9°41' N, 24°16' E 224
Hofstad, Nor. 64°12' N, 10°24' E 152
Hōfu, Japan 34°2' N, 131°34' E 200
Hofuf see Al Hufūf, Saudi Arabia 25°21' N, 49°34' E 196
Hogback Mountain, Mont., U.S. 44°52' N, 112°12' W 90
Hogback Mountain, Va., U.S. 38°45' N, 78°20' W 94
Högby, Sw. 57°10' N, 16°59' E 152
Högen, Nor. 58°54' N, 11°41' E 152
Hoggar see Ahaggar, Alg. 21°56' N, 4°32' E 222
Hogoro, Tanzania 5°54' S, 36°28' E 224
Högsby, Nor. 57°10' N, 16°1' E 152
Høgstegia, peak, Nor. 62°22' N, 10°0' E 152
Hogtinden, peak, Nor. 66°57' N, 14°24' E 152
Hogup Mountains, Utah, U.S. 41°26' N, 113°22' W 90
Hoh Xil Hu, lake, China 35°37' N, 90°47' E 188
Hohenau, Parag. 27°6' S, 55°42' W 139
Hohenlimburg, Ger. 51°20' N, 7°33' E 167
Hoher Dachstein, peak, Aust. 47°27' N, 13°30' E 156
Hohhot, China 40°51' N, 111°42' E 198
Hohoe, Ghana 7°10' N, 0°26' E 222
Hōhoku, Japan 34°19' N, 130°55' E 200
Höhr-Grenzhausen, Ger. 50°25' N, 7°40' E 167
Hoi An, Vietnam 15°54' N, 108°20' E 202
Hoima, Uganda 1°23' N, 31°21' E 224
Hoisington, Kans., U.S. 38°29' N, 98°47' W 92
Hok, Nor. 57°30' N, 14°15' E 152
Hokitika, N.Z. 42°44' S, 171°0' E 240
Hokkaidō, island, Japan 44°1' N, 139°29' E 190
Hokksund, Nor. 59°47' N, 9°54' E 152
Hokota, Japan 36°9' N, 140°30' E 201
Hōkūkano Heiau, site, Hawai'i, U.S. 21°3' N, 156°54' W 99
Hol, Nor. 60°34' N, 8°21' E 152
Hola Prystan', Ukr. 46°30' N, 32°30' E 156
Holanda, Bol. 11°50' S, 68°38' W 137
Holandsfjord, Nor. 66°43' N, 13°39' E 152
Holbeach, U.K. 52°47' N, 1°59' E 162
Holberg, Can. 50°39' N, 127°60' W 90
Holbox, Isla, island, Mex. 21°39' N, 87°14' W 116
Holbrook, Ariz., U.S. 34°54' N, 110°10' W 92
Holbrook, Idaho, U.S. 42°11' N, 112°39' W 92
Holbrook, Mass., U.S. 42°9' N, 71°1' W 104
Holcombe, Wis., U.S. 45°12' N, 91°7' W 94
Hold with Hope, Den. 73°19' N, 20°18' W 246
Holden, Can. 53°13' N, 112°13' W 108
Holden, Mass., U.S. 42°20' N, 71°52' W 104
Holden, Mo., U.S. 38°41' N, 93°59' W 94
Holden, Utah, U.S. 39°5' N, 112°16' W 90
Holdenville, Okla., U.S. 35°3' N, 96°24' W 96
Holdfast, Can. 50°57' N, 105°26' W 90
Holdrege, Nebr., U.S. 40°25' N, 99°23' W 90
Hole in the Ground, site, Oreg., U.S. 43°22' N, 121°16' W 90
Hole in the Mountain Peak, Nev., U.S. 40°56' N, 115°12' W 90
Holgate, Ohio, U.S. 41°13' N, 84°8' W 102
Holguín, Cuba 20°53' N, 76°15' W 115
Holguín, adm. division, Cuba 20°31' N, 75°55' W 116
Holinshead Lake, lake, Can. 49°38' N, 90°16' W 94
Holladay, Utah, U.S. 40°40' N, 111°48' W 90
Holland, Mich., U.S. 42°46' N, 86°6' W 102
Hollandale, Miss., U.S. 33°8' N, 90°54' W 103
Hollick-Kenyon Peninsula, Antarctica 69°3' S, 60°55' W 248
Hollick-Kenyon Plateau, Antarctica 78°34' S, 104°13' W 248
Hollis, Alas., U.S. 55°28' N, 132°45' W 108
Hollis, N.H., U.S. 42°44' N, 71°36' W 104
Hollis, Okla., U.S. 34°39' N, 99°55' W 92
Hollis Center, Me., U.S. 43°36' N, 70°36' W 104
Hollister, Calif., U.S. 36°50' N, 121°25' W 100
Hollister, Mo., U.S. 36°36' N, 93°13' W 96
Holliston, Mass., U.S. 42°12' N, 71°26' W 104
Holloman Air Force Base, N. Mex., U.S. 32°51' N, 106°9' W 92
Hollum, Neth. 53°26' N, 5°37' E 163
Holly, Colo., U.S. 38°2' N, 102°7' W 90
Holly, Mich., U.S. 42°46' N, 83°37' W 102
Holly Bluff, Miss., U.S. 32°48' N, 90°43' W 103
Holly Hill, Fla., U.S. 29°14' N, 81°3' W 105
Holly Ridge, N.C., U.S. 34°29' N, 77°34' W 96
Holly Springs, Miss., U.S. 34°42' N, 89°27' W 112
Hollywood, Calif., U.S. 34°6' N, 118°22' W 101
Hollywood, Fla., U.S. 26°1' N, 80°10' W 105
Holm Land, Den. 80°13' N, 19°10' W 246
Holman, Can. 70°42' N, 117°39' W 106
Holman, N. Mex., U.S. 36°2' N, 105°24' W 92
Hólmavík, Ice. 65°35' N, 21°53' W 73
Holmer, Lac, lake, Can. 54°2' N, 72°13' W 111
Holmes Lake, Can. 57°3' N, 97°17' W 108
Holmes, Mount, Wyo., U.S. 44°47' N, 110°55' W 90
Holmestrand, Nor. 59°29' N, 10°18' E 152
Holmfors, Nor. 65°13' N, 18°9' E 152
Holmudden, Sw. 57°52' N, 19°12' E 166
Holoby, Ukr. 51°5' N, 25°0' E 152
Holod, Rom. 46°47' N, 22°8' E 168
Holohit, Punta, Mex. 21°42' N, 89°4' W 116
Holoog, Namibia 27°23' S, 17°54' E 227
Holopaw, Fla., U.S. 28°8' N, 81°5' W 105
Holstebro, Den. 56°21' N, 8°36' E 150
Holstein, Can. 44°3' N, 80°46' W 102
Holstein, Iowa, U.S. 42°28' N, 95°33' W 94
Holsteinsborg see Sisimiut, Den. 66°56' N, 53°43' W 106
Holt, Ala., U.S. 33°13' N, 87°29' W 103
Holt, Mich., U.S. 42°37' N, 84°31' W 102
Holt, U.K. 52°54' N, 1°5' E 162
Holton, Kans., U.S. 39°26' N, 95°45' W 90
Holton, Mich., U.S. 43°24' N, 86°5' W 102
Holtorf, Ger. 52°41' N, 9°15' E 150
Holtville, Calif., U.S. 32°48' N, 115°23' W 101
Holtyre, Can. 48°28' N, 80°17' W 110
Holwerd, Neth. 53°21' N, 5°53' E 163
Holy Cross, Alas., U.S. 62°3' N, 159°60' W 98
Holyoke, Colo., U.S. 40°34' N, 102°18' W 90
Holyoke, Mass., U.S. 42°12' N, 72°37' W 104
Holywell, U.K. 53°16' N, 3°13' W 162
Holzminden, Ger. 51°48' N, 9°27' E 167
Homa Bay, Kenya 0°35' N, 34°29' E 224
Homberg, Ger. 51°2' N, 9°24' E 167
Hombori, Mali 15°16' N, 1°43' W 222
Homburg, Ger. 49°18' N, 7°19' E 163
Home Bay 68°36' N, 67°37' W 106
Homedale, Idaho, U.S. 43°37' N, 116°57' W 90
Homeland, Fla., U.S. 27°49' N, 81°49' W 105
Homeland, Ga., U.S. 30°50' N, 82°2' W 96
Homer, Alas., U.S. 59°37' N, 151°36' W 98
Homer, Ill., U.S. 40°2' N, 87°58' W 102
Homer, La., U.S. 32°46' N, 93°4' W 103
Homer, Mich., U.S. 42°8' N, 84°49' W 102
Homer, N.Y., U.S. 42°38' N, 76°12' W 94
Homerville, Ga., U.S. 31°1' N, 82°46' W 96
Homestead, Fla., U.S. 25°28' N, 80°30' W 105
Homewood, Miss., U.S. 32°14' N, 89°30' W 103
Hominy, Okla., U.S. 36°23' N, 96°24' W 92
Hommalinn, Myanmar 24°51' N, 94°54' E 188
Hommura, Japan 34°22' N, 139°16' E 201
Homnabad, India 17°45' N, 77°8' E 188
Homodji, spring, Niger 16°34' N, 13°40' E 222
Homoine, Mozambique 23°50' S, 35°9' E 227
Homoljske Planina, Serb. and Mont. 44°18' N, 21°36' E 168
Homosassa, Fla., U.S. 28°46' N, 82°36' W 105
Homosassa Springs, Fla., U.S. 28°48' N, 82°35' W 105
Homs, Syr. 34°32' N, 36°57' E 173
Homs see Ḩimş, Syr. 34°43' N, 36°42' E 194
Homyel', Belarus 52°25' N, 31°4' E 154
Hon Chong, Vietnam 10°10' N, 104°37' E 202
Hon Quan, Vietnam 11°41' N, 106°37' E 202
Honaz, Turk. 37°44' N, 29°15' E 156
Honda, Col. 5°10' N, 74°46' W 136
Honda, Bahía 12°19' N, 72°15' W 136
Hondeklipbaai, S. Af. 30°20' S, 17°16' E 227
Hondo, Can. 55°3' N, 114°3' W 108
Hondo, Japan 32°27' N, 130°10' E 201
Hondo, N. Mex., U.S. 33°23' N, 105°16' W 92
Hondo, Tex., U.S. 29°20' N, 99°8' W 96
Honduras 14°39' N, 87°51' W 115
Hønefoss, Nor. 60°9' N, 10°15' E 152
Honey Grove, Tex., U.S. 33°34' N, 95°55' W 96
Honey Island, Tex., U.S. 30°23' N, 94°27' W 103
Hong Gai, Vietnam 20°58' N, 107°5' E 198
Hong Kong, China 22°15' N, 114°10' E 198
Hong Kong (Xianggang), island, China 21°55' N, 114°15' E 198
Hong'an, China 31°17' N, 114°35' E 198
Hongcheon, S. Korea 37°42' N, 127°53' E 200
Honghe, China 23°18' N, 102°22' E 202
Honghu, China 29°51' N, 113°28' E 198
Hongjiang, China 27°3' N, 109°55' E 198
Hongliuyuan, China 41°3' N, 95°26' E 188
Hongnong, S. Korea 35°24' N, 126°34' E 200
Hongor, Mongolia 45°47' N, 112°43' E 198
Hongqiling, China 42°56' N, 126°24' E 200
Hongseong, S. Korea 36°35' N, 126°40' E 200
Hongshi, China 42°58' N, 127°7' E 200
Hongtong, China 36°16' N, 111°42' E 198
Hongū, Japan 33°50' N, 135°44' E 201
Hongwŏn, N. Korea 40°1' N, 127°58' E 200
Hongze Hu, lake, China 32°58' N, 117°53' E 198
Honiara, Solomon Islands 9°29' S, 159°10' E 238
Honiara, Solomon Islands 9°0' S, 160°0' E 242
Honiton, U.K. 50°47' N, 3°11' W 162
Honkajoki, Fin. 61°58' N, 22°13' E 166
Honkilahti, Fin. 60°56' N, 22°5' E 166
Hönö, Sw. 57°41' N, 11°39' E 152
Honokōhau, Hawai'i, U.S. 19°39' N, 156°2' W 99
Honolulu, Hawai'i, U.S. 21°17' N, 157°55' W 99
Honshū, island, Japan 35°3' N, 130°44' E 190
Hontoria del Pinar, Sp. 41°51' N, 3°10' W 164
Hood, Calif., U.S. 38°21' N, 121°32' W 100
Hood Bay, Alas., U.S. 57°23' N, 134°26' W 108
Hood Canal 48°6' N, 122°38' W 100
Hood, Mount, Oreg., U.S. 45°20' N, 121°48' W 90
Hood Point, P.N.G. 10°21' S, 146°34' E 192
Hood River, Oreg., U.S. 45°41' N, 121°33' W 100
Hoodsport, Wash., U.S. 47°22' N, 123°9' W 100
Hoogeveen, Neth. 52°44' N, 6°28' E 163
Hoogezand-Sappemeer, Neth. 53°9' N, 6°47' E 163
Hook Head, Ire. 51°55' N, 6°59' W 150
Hooker, Okla., U.S. 36°50' N, 101°14' W 92
Hooksett, N.H., U.S. 43°5' N, 71°28' W 104
Hoonah, Alas., U.S. 58°1' N, 135°23' W 98
Hooper Bay, Alas., U.S. 61°39' N, 166°2' W 73
Hooper, Cape, Can. 68°22' N, 66°48' W 106
Hoopeston, Ill., U.S. 40°28' N, 87°40' W 102
Hooppole, Ill., U.S. 41°31' N, 89°55' W 102
Hoopstad, S. Af. 27°50' S, 25°54' E 227
Höör, Nor. 55°56' N, 13°32' E 152
Hoorn, Neth. 52°38' N, 5°4' E 163
Hoosick Falls, N.Y., U.S. 42°54' N, 73°22' W 104
Hoover, Ala., U.S. 33°24' N, 86°50' W 96
Hoover Dam, Nev., U.S. 35°55' N, 114°54' W 101
Höövör, Mongolia 48°27' N, 113°23' E 198
Hopa, Turk. 41°25' N, 41°25' E 195
Hope, Ariz., U.S. 33°42' N, 113°43' W 101
Hope, Ark., U.S. 33°38' N, 93°36' W 96
Hope, Can. 49°21' N, 121°26' W 100
Hope, Ind., U.S. 39°17' N, 85°46' W 102
Hope, N. Dak., U.S. 47°18' N, 97°44' W 90
Hope, Ben, peak, U.K. 58°23' N, 4°43' W 150
Hope, Cape, Can. 68°55' N, 118°27' W 98
Hope Mills, N.C., U.S. 34°58' N, 78°58' W 96
Hope Point, Myanmar 15°5' N, 97°20' E 202
Hope Town, Bahamas 26°31' N, 76°58' W 96
Hope Valley, R.I., U.S. 41°30' N, 71°44' W 104
Hopedale, Can. 55°24' N, 60°19' W 106
Hopedale, Ill., U.S. 40°24' N, 89°25' W 102
Hopelchén, Mex. 19°44' N, 89°51' W 115
Hopeless, Mount, Austral. 29°41' S, 139°27' E 230
Hopen, Nor. 63°26' N, 8°0' E 152
Hopetoun, Austral. 33°55' S, 120°8' E 231
Hopetown, S. Af. 29°41' S, 24°4' E 227
Hopewell, Va., U.S. 37°17' N, 77°18' W 96
Hopewell Culture National Historic Park, Ohio, U.S. 39°21' N, 83°4' W 102
Hopewell Furnace National Historic Site, Pa., U.S. 40°10' N, 75°52' W 94
Hopewell Islands, Hudson Bay 58°28' N, 82°13' W 106
Hopi Buttes, Ariz., U.S. 35°29' N, 110°23' W 92
Hopkins, Mich., U.S. 42°36' N, 85°45' W 102
Hopkins, Mount, Ariz., U.S. 31°39' N, 110°57' W 92
Hopkinsville, Ky., U.S. 36°51' N, 87°29' W 96
Hopkinton, N.H., U.S. 43°11' N, 71°41' W 104
Hopseidet, Nor. 70°46' N, 27°42' E 152
Hopsten, Ger. 52°23' N, 7°36' E 163
Hoque, Angola 14°41' S, 13°49' E 220
Hoquiam, Wash., U.S. 46°58' N, 123°54' W 100
Hora, Polonyna Runa, peak, Ukr. 48°46' N, 22°44' E 152
Horace, Kans., U.S. 38°29' N, 101°49' W 90
Horasan, Turk. 40°5' N, 42°14' E 195
Horcajo de Santiago, Sp. 39°50' N, 2°60' W 164
Horche, Sp. 40°33' N, 3°4' W 164
Horgos, Serb. and Mont. 46°8' N, 19°58' E 168
Hörh Uul, peak, Mongolia 42°38' N, 105°16' E 198
Horicon, Wis., U.S. 43°26' N, 88°37' W 102
Horinger, China 40°22' N, 111°48' E 198
Horizonte, Braz. 9°41' S, 68°27' W 137
Horki, Belarus 54°17' N, 30°59' E 154
Horlivka, Ukr. 48°18' N, 38°1' E 158
Ḩormak, Iran 29°57' N, 60°55' E 182
Hormoz, island, Iran 26°53' N, 56°25' E 180
Hormuz, Strait of 26°20' N, 55°54' E 196
Horn, Ben, peak, U.K. 58°1' N, 4°9' W 150
Horn, Cape see Hornos, Cabo de, Chile 55°49' S, 66°59' W 134
Horn Island, Austral. 10°30' S, 141°38' E 230
Horn Island, Miss., U.S. 30°9' N, 88°44' W 103
Horn (North Cape), Ice. 66°30' N, 26°3' W 246
Horn, river, Can. 61°33' N, 117°58' W 108
Horn, The, peak, Austral. 36°53' S, 146°34' E 230
Hornachos, Sp. 38°33' N, 6°5' W 164
Hornachuelos, Sp. 37°50' N, 5°15' W 164
Hornavan, lake, Nor. 65°37' N, 17°40' E 152
Hornbeck, La., U.S. 31°19' N, 93°24' W 103
Hornbrook, Calif., U.S. 41°54' N, 122°34' W 90
Horncastle, U.K. 53°12' N, 0°7' E 162
Hornell, N.Y., U.S. 42°18' N, 77°41' W 94
Hornepayne, Can. 49°14' N, 84°47' W 94
Hornito, Cerro, peak, Pan. 8°41' N, 82°10' W 115
Hornos, Cabo de (Horn, Cape), Chile 55°49' S, 66°59' W 134
Hornsea, U.K. 53°54' N, 0°11' E 162
Hörnsjö, Nor. 63°48' N, 19°30' E 154
Hornslandet, Sw. 61°35' N, 17°29' E 166
Hornsund 76°46' N, 11°11' E 160
Hornu, Belg. 50°25' N, 3°48' E 163
Horodnya, Ukr. 51°51' N, 31°39' E 158
Horodnytsya, Ukr. 50°49' N, 27°18' E 158
Horodok, Ukr. 50°40' N, 26°7' E 152
Horodok, Ukr. 49°8' N, 26°32' E 152
Horodyshche, Ukr. 49°21' N, 31°31' E 158
Horokhiv, Ukr. 50°29' N, 24°45' E 152
Hororata, N.Z. 43°33' S, 171°58' E 240
Horqin Youyi Zhongqi (Bayan Huxu), China 45°5' N, 121°25' E 198
Horqin Zuoyi Houqi, China 42°58' N, 122°22' E 198
Horqin Zuoyi Zhongqi, China 44°7' N, 123°20' E 198
Horqueta, Parag. 23°19' S, 57°4' W 132
Horse Lake, Can. 51°35' N, 121°40' W 90
Horse, river, Can. 56°23' N, 112°24' W 108
Horsehead Lake, N. Dak., U.S. 46°58' N, 100°21' W 90
Horsens, Den. 55°51' N, 9°49' E 150
Horseshoe Beach, Fla., U.S. 29°27' N, 83°18' W 105
Horseshoe Bend, Idaho, U.S. 43°55' N, 116°11' W 90
Horseshoe Cove 29°23' N, 83°26' W 105
Horsham, Austral. 36°40' S, 142°10' E 231
Horsham, U.K. 51°3' N, 0°21' E 162
Horsvær, islands, Norwegian Sea 65°24' N, 10°32' E 152
Hort, Hung. 47°41' N, 19°48' E 168
Horten, Nor. 59°25' N, 10°28' E 152
Horton, Mich., U.S. 42°8' N, 84°31' W 102
Horton Lake, Can. 67°30' N, 124°4' W 98
Horton, river, Can. 69°0' N, 125°15' W 98
Horwood Lake, Can. 47°58' N, 82°55' W 94
Hosa'ina, Eth. 7°29' N, 37°51' E 224
Hösbach, Ger. 50°0' N, 9°12' E 167
Hosdrug, India 12°15' N, 75°8' E 188
Hosenofu, spring, Lib. 23°39' N, 20°58' E 216
Hoshab, Pak. 26°0' N, 63°56' E 182
Hoshiarpur, India 31°32' N, 75°58' E 188
Höshööt, Mongolia 48°5' N, 102°26' E 198
Hosmer, S. Dak., U.S. 45°34' N, 99°29' W 90
Hosororo, Guyana 8°11' N, 59°46' W 130
Hososhima, Japan 32°25' N, 131°39' E 201
Hospet, India 15°17' N, 76°23' E 188
Hossa, Fin. 65°26' N, 29°33' E 152
Hosszúpályi, Hung. 47°23' N, 21°43' E 168
Hoste, Isla, island, Chile 55°53' S, 70°2' W 248
Hot, Thai. 18°7' N, 98°33' E 202
Hot Creek Range, Nev., U.S. 38°10' N, 116°28' W 90
Hot Springs, Ark., U.S. 34°29' N, 93°5' W 112
Hot Springs, S. Dak., U.S. 43°26' N, 103°29' W 90
Hot Springs National Park, Ark., U.S. 34°29' N, 93°9' W 96
Hot Springs Peak, Calif., U.S. 40°20' N, 120°12' W 90
Hot Springs Peak, Nev., U.S. 41°21' N, 117°31' W 90
Hotaka, Japan 36°20' N, 137°53' E 201
Hotan, China 37°7' N, 79°51' E 184
Hotan, river, China 38°20' N, 80°51' E 184
Hotchkiss, Can. 57°4' N, 117°34' W 108
Hotchkiss, Colo., U.S. 38°48' N, 107°44' W 90
Hotchkiss, river, Can. 57°19' N, 118°33' W 108
Hotevilla, Ariz., U.S. 35°54' N, 110°41' W 92
Hottah Lake, Can. 65°19' N, 119°32' W 106
Hotte, Massif de la, Haiti 18°34' N, 74°30' W 115
Hottentot Bay 26°20' S, 14°43' E 220
Hotton, Belg. 50°15' N, 5°26' E 167
Houayxay, Laos 20°18' N, 100°27' E 202
Houdan, Fr. 48°47' N, 1°35' E 163
Houghton Lake, Mich., U.S. 44°15' N, 85°60' W 81
Houghton, Point, Mich., U.S. 47°41' N, 89°29' W 94
Houlton, Me., U.S. 46°7' N, 67°49' W 82
Houma, China 35°37' N, 111°21' E 198
Houma, La., U.S. 29°34' N, 90°44' W 103
Houndé, Burkina Faso 11°30' N, 3°33' W 222
Housatonic, Mass., U.S. 42°15' N, 73°23' W 104
House Range, Utah, U.S. 39°16' N, 113°32' W 90
House, river, Can. 55°51' N, 112°25' W 108
Houston, Can. 54°24' N, 126°40' W 108
Houston, Miss., U.S. 43°44' N, 91°35' W 94
Houston, Mo., U.S. 37°19' N, 91°56' W 96

Houston, *Tex., U.S.* 29°44′ N, 95°22′ W **103**
Houthalen, *Belg.* 51°2′ N, 5°22′ E **167**
Houtman Abrolhos, islands, *Indian Ocean* 28°8′ S, 110°9′ E **230**
Houtskär, *Fin.* 60°12′ N, 21°20′ E **166**
Hovd (Dund-Us), *Mongolia* 48°2′ N, 91°40′ E **190**
Hovden, *Nor.* 59°31′ N, 7°21′ E **152**
Hövelhof, *Ger.* 51°49′ N, 8°38′ E **167**
Hoven, *S. Dak., U.S.* 45°13′ N, 99°48′ W **90**
Hovenweep National Monument, *Utah, U.S.* 37°17′ N, 109°15′ W **92**
Hoverla, Hora, peak, *Ukr.* 48°7′ N, 24°24′ E **152**
Hoveyzeh, *Iran* 31°26′ N, 48°5′ E **180**
Hövsgöl, *Mongolia* 43°38′ N, 109°37′ E **198**
Hövsgöl Nuur, lake, *Mongolia* 50°48′ N, 98°47′ E **190**
Howard, *Kans., U.S.* 37°27′ N, 96°17′ W **90**
Howard, *S. Dak., U.S.* 43°59′ N, 97°34′ W **90**
Howard City, *Mich., U.S.* 43°23′ N, 85°28′ W **102**
Howard Island, *Austral.* 12°4′ S, 135°3′ E **230**
Howard Lake, *Can.* 62°45′ N, 107°53′ W **106**
Howe, *Ind., U.S.* 41°43′ N, 85°25′ W **102**
Howe, *Okla., U.S.* 34°55′ N, 94°39′ W **96**
Howe, *Tex., U.S.* 33°29′ N, 96°36′ W **96**
Howe, Cape, *Austral.* 38°13′ S, 149°59′ E **230**
Howe, Mount, *Antarctica* 87°17′ S, 145°9′ W **248**
Howe Sound 49°26′ N, 123°24′ W **108**
Howell, *Mich., U.S.* 42°35′ N, 83°56′ W **102**
Howells, *Nebr., U.S.* 41°42′ N, 97°1′ W **90**
Howick, *N.Z.* 36°55′ S, 174°56′ E **240**
Howland Island, *United States* 1°0′ N, 177°0′ W **238**
Howland, *Me., U.S.* 45°13′ N, 68°40′ W **94**
Howth, *Ire.* 53°22′ N, 6°4′ W **150**
Hoxie, *Ark., U.S.* 36°2′ N, 90°59′ W **96**
Hoxie, *Kans., U.S.* 39°20′ N, 100°27′ W **90**
Höxter, *Ger.* 51°46′ N, 9°23′ E **167**
Hoxud, *China* 42°13′ N, 86°58′ E **184**
Høyanger, *Nor.* 61°13′ N, 6°4′ E **152**
Hoyt Peak, *Utah, U.S.* 40°40′ N, 111°16′ W **90**
Hozat, *Turk.* 39°5′ N, 39°11′ E **195**
Hpa-an, *Myanmar* 16°54′ N, 97°39′ E **202**
Hradec Králové, *Czech Rep.* 50°13′ N, 15°51′ E **152**
Hrasnica, *Bosn. and Herzg.* 43°46′ N, 18°18′ E **168**
Hrastnik, *Slov.* 46°8′ N, 15°5′ E **156**
Hrazdan, *Arm.* 40°4′ N, 44°25′ E **195**
Hrazdan, river, *Arm.* 40°16′ N, 44°31′ E **195**
Hrodna, *Belarus* 53°40′ N, 23°50′ E **152**
Hrtkovci, *Serb. and Mont.* 44°52′ N, 19°46′ E **168**
Hrubieszów, *Pol.* 50°49′ N, 23°52′ E **152**
Hrvatska Kostajnica, *Croatia* 45°13′ N, 16°32′ E **168**
Hrymayliv, *Ukr.* 49°19′ N, 26°0′ E **158**
Hrynyava, *Ukr.* 47°58′ N, 24°52′ E **152**
Hsi-hseng, *Myanmar* 20°10′ N, 97°14′ E **202**
Hsinchu, *Taiwan* 24°47′ N, 120°57′ E **198**
Hsinying, *Taiwan* 23°18′ N, 120°17′ E **198**
Hsipaw, *Myanmar* 22°39′ N, 97°17′ E **202**
Hu, Har, lake, *China* 38°18′ N, 97°6′ E **188**
Hua Hin, *Thai.* 12°39′ N, 99°56′ E **202**
Huacaraje, *Bol.* 13°36′ S, 63°47′ W **137**
Huacaya, *Bol.* 20°44′ S, 63°42′ W **137**
Huachacalla, *Bol.* 18°48′ S, 68°16′ W **137**
Huachi, *Bol.* 14°16′ S, 63°34′ W **137**
Huachi, *China* 36°26′ N, 107°57′ E **198**
Huacho, *Peru* 11°9′ S, 77°36′ W **130**
Huade, *China* 41°53′ N, 114°1′ E **198**
Huadian, *China* 42°58′ N, 126°41′ E **200**
Huai Yang, *Thai.* 11°37′ N, 99°40′ E **202**
Huaibei, *China* 33°56′ N, 116°48′ E **198**
Huaibin, *China* 32°30′ N, 115°23′ E **198**
Huaiji, *China* 23°51′ N, 112°13′ E **198**
Huailai, *China* 40°25′ N, 115°29′ E **198**
Huainan, *China* 32°38′ N, 117°1′ E **198**
Huaining, *China* 30°23′ N, 116°35′ E **198**
Huairen, *China* 39°50′ N, 113°6′ E **198**
Huaitunas, Laguna, lake, *Bol.* 13°2′ S, 66°17′ W **137**
Huaiyin, *China* 33°33′ N, 119°2′ E **198**
Huajicori, *Mex.* 22°38′ N, 105°20′ W **114**
Huajimic, *Mex.* 21°40′ N, 104°19′ W **114**
Huajuapan de León, *Mex.* 17°48′ N, 97°47′ W **114**
Hualahuises, *Mex.* 24°53′ N, 99°41′ W **114**
Hualālai, peak, *Hawai'i, U.S.* 19°40′ N, 155°55′ W **99**
Hualapai Mountains, *Ariz., U.S.* 35°0′ N, 113°57′ W **101**
Hualfín, *Arg.* 27°13′ S, 66°48′ W **132**
Hualien, *Taiwan* 24°1′ N, 121°33′ E **198**
Huamachuco, *Peru* 7°49′ S, 78°3′ W **130**
Huamantla, *Mex.* 19°17′ N, 97°57′ W **114**
Huambo, *Angola* 12°49′ S, 15°45′ E **220**
Huambo, adm. division, *Angola* 13°1′ S, 15°14′ E **220**
Huancané, *Peru* 15°16′ S, 69°45′ W **137**
Huancavelica, *Peru* 12°48′ S, 74°59′ W **137**
Huancayo, *Peru* 12°5′ S, 75°12′ W **137**
Huanchaca, *Bol.* 20°23′ S, 66°42′ W **137**
Huanchaca, Serranía de, *Bol.* 14°6′ S, 61°17′ W **130**
Huang (Yellow), river, *China* 37°14′ N, 104°6′ E **198**
Huangchuan, *China* 32°8′ N, 115°0′ E **198**
Huanggang, *China* 30°30′ N, 114°51′ E **198**
Huanggangliang, peak, *China* 43°32′ N, 117°23′ E **198**
Huanghua, *China* 38°24′ N, 117°23′ E **198**
Huangling, *China* 35°35′ N, 109°15′ E **198**
Huangliu, *China* 18°28′ N, 108°47′ E **198**
Huangnihe, *China* 43°35′ N, 128°2′ E **198**
Huangquqiao, *China* 39°3′ N, 106°38′ E **198**
Huangshan, *China* 29°42′ N, 118°14′ E **198**
Huangshi, *China* 30°9′ N, 115°0′ E **198**
Huanguelén, *Arg.* 37°2′ S, 61°57′ W **139**
Huangxian, *China* 37°41′ N, 120°36′ E **198**
Huangyan, *China* 28°37′ N, 121°21′ E **198**
Huanjiang, *China* 24°48′ N, 108°14′ E **198**
Huanren, *China* 41°15′ N, 125°25′ E **200**
Huanta, *Peru* 12°57′ S, 74°15′ W **137**
Huantai, *China* 36°58′ N, 118°9′ E **198**
Huánuco, *Peru* 9°53′ S, 76°18′ W **130**
Huánuco, adm. division, *Peru* 9°41′ S, 74°46′ W **137**
Huanxian, *China* 36°34′ N, 107°21′ E **198**
Huara, *Chile* 19°59′ S, 69°50′ W **137**
Huaral, *Peru* 11°29′ S, 77°14′ W **130**
Huaraz, *Peru* 9°34′ S, 77°31′ W **130**
Huari, *Bol.* 19°1′ S, 66°47′ W **137**
Huari, *Peru* 13°56′ S, 69°20′ W **137**
Huarmey, *Peru* 10°4′ S, 78°10′ W **130**
Huarong, *China* 29°31′ N, 112°32′ E **198**
Huásabas, *Mex.* 29°54′ N, 109°21′ W **92**
Huasaga, *Peru* 3°41′ S, 76°25′ W **136**
Huascarán, Nevado, peak, *Peru* 9°10′ S, 77°44′ W **130**
Huasco, *Chile* 28°30′ S, 71°15′ W **134**
Huashulinzi, *China* 43°13′ N, 127°1′ E **200**
Huatabampo, *Mex.* 26°47′ N, 109°41′ W **112**
Huatusco, *Mex.* 19°7′ N, 96°57′ W **114**
Huauchinango, *Mex.* 20°10′ N, 98°4′ W **114**
Huaura, *Peru* 11°5′ S, 77°36′ W **130**
Huautla, *Mex.* 21°0′ N, 98°17′ W **114**
Huautla, *Mex.* 18°7′ N, 96°51′ W **114**
Huaxi, *China* 41°23′ N, 123°28′ E **200**
Huaxian, *China* 35°30′ N, 114°31′ E **198**
Huaynamota, river, *Mex.* 21°53′ N, 104°25′ W **114**
Huayuan, *China* 28°32′ N, 109°29′ E **198**
Huazhou, *China* 21°34′ N, 110°33′ E **198**
Hub, *Miss., U.S.* 31°9′ N, 89°45′ W **103**
Hubbard, *Tex., U.S.* 31°49′ N, 96°47′ W **96**
Hubbard Lake, *Mich., U.S.* 44°45′ N, 84°46′ W **82**
Hubbard, Mount, *Alas., U.S.* 60°15′ N, 139°17′ W **98**
Hubbardston, *Mass., U.S.* 42°28′ N, 72°1′ W **104**
Hubbardston, *Mich., U.S.* 43°5′ N, 84°50′ W **102**
Hubbart Point, *Can.* 59°24′ N, 94°46′ W **108**
Hubbell Trading Post National Historic Site, *Ariz., U.S.* 35°41′ N, 109°39′ W **92**
Hubei, adm. division, *China* 31°27′ N, 111°33′ E **198**
Huben, *Aust.* 46°55′ N, 12°35′ E **167**
Hubli, *India* 15°21′ N, 75°8′ E **188**
Hucknall, *U.K.* 53°2′ N, 1°12′ W **162**
Huddersfield, *U.K.* 53°39′ N, 1°47′ W **162**
Hudiksvall, *Nor.* 61°42′ N, 17°4′ E **152**
Hudson, *Can.* 50°5′ N, 92°12′ W **110**
Hudson, *Fla., U.S.* 28°21′ N, 82°42′ W **105**
Hudson, *Mich., U.S.* 41°50′ N, 84°23′ W **102**
Hudson, *N.H., U.S.* 42°45′ N, 71°27′ W **104**
Hudson, *N.Y., U.S.* 42°14′ N, 73°48′ W **104**
Hudson Bay 59°43′ N, 86°21′ W **253**
Hudson Bay 59°19′ N, 93°51′ W **108**
Hudson Bay, *Can.* 52°52′ N, 102°25′ W **108**
Hudson Canyon, *North Atlantic Ocean* 37°8′ N, 70°6′ W **253**
Hudson, Cape, *Antarctica* 67°60′ S, 156°56′ E **248**
Hudson Falls, *N.Y., U.S.* 43°18′ N, 73°36′ W **104**
Hudson, river, *N.Y., U.S.* 41°34′ N, 73°59′ W **104**
Hudson Strait 62°30′ N, 79°14′ W **106**
Hudson's Hope, *Can.* 56°2′ N, 121°57′ W **108**
Hudsonville, *Mich., U.S.* 42°51′ N, 85°52′ W **102**
Hudwin Lake, *Can.* 53°9′ N, 96°12′ W **108**
Hue, *Vietnam* 16°28′ N, 107°34′ E **202**
Huedin, *Rom.* 46°50′ N, 23°1′ E **168**
Huejúcar, *Mex.* 22°20′ N, 103°12′ W **114**
Huejuquilla, *Mex.* 22°37′ N, 103°54′ W **114**
Huejutla, *Mex.* 21°7′ N, 98°25′ W **114**
Huelma, *Sp.* 37°39′ N, 3°27′ W **164**
Huelva, *Sp.* 37°15′ N, 6°57′ W **150**
Huercal-Overa, *Sp.* 37°23′ N, 1°57′ W **164**
Huerta, Sierra de la, *Arg.* 31°43′ S, 68°11′ W **134**
Huertecillas, *Mex.* 24°3′ N, 101°9′ W **114**
Huesca, *Sp.* 42°7′ N, 0°25′ E **164**
Huéscar, *Sp.* 37°48′ N, 2°33′ W **164**
Hueso, Sierra del, *Mex.* 30°19′ N, 105°34′ W **112**
Huetamo, *Mex.* 18°35′ N, 100°53′ W **114**
Huete, *Sp.* 40°8′ N, 2°43′ W **164**
Huff, *N. Dak., U.S.* 46°36′ N, 100°41′ W **90**
Hughes, *Alas., U.S.* 65°53′ N, 154°17′ W **98**
Hughes, *Ark., U.S.* 34°56′ N, 90°29′ W **96**
Hughes Bay 64°31′ S, 62°6′ W **134**
Hughes Springs, *Tex., U.S.* 32°59′ N, 94°39′ W **103**
Hugo, *Colo., U.S.* 39°8′ N, 103°29′ W **90**
Hugo, *Okla., U.S.* 34°0′ N, 95°31′ W **96**
Hugo Lake, *Okla., U.S.* 34°3′ N, 95°44′ W **96**
Hugoton, *Kans., U.S.* 37°10′ N, 101°21′ W **92**
Hui, river, *China* 48°43′ N, 118°52′ E **198**
Hui'an, *China* 25°1′ N, 118°46′ E **198**
Huichang, *China* 25°30′ N, 115°37′ E **198**
Hŭich'ŏn, *N. Korea* 40°9′ N, 126°17′ E **200**
Huidong, *China* 22°54′ N, 114°43′ E **198**
Huifa, river, *China* 42°44′ N, 126°20′ E **200**
Huíla, *Angola* 15°6′ S, 13°29′ E **220**
Huíla, adm. division, *Angola* 15°5′ S, 13°52′ E **220**
Huila, adm. division, *Col.* 2°33′ N, 75°50′ W **136**
Huíla Plateau, *Angola* 16°12′ S, 14°36′ E **220**
Huilai, *China* 23°1′ N, 116°15′ E **198**
Huimin, *China* 37°29′ N, 117°28′ E **198**
Huinan (Chaoyang), *China* 42°42′ N, 126°4′ E **200**
Huinca Renancó, *Arg.* 34°51′ S, 64°21′ W **134**
Huining, *China* 35°43′ N, 105°2′ E **198**
Huisachal, *Mex.* 26°45′ N, 101°6′ W **96**
Huishui, *China* 26°9′ N, 106°36′ E **198**
Huitong, *China* 26°53′ N, 109°42′ E **198**
Huittinen, *Fin.* 61°9′ N, 22°41′ E **166**
Huitzuco, *Mex.* 18°16′ N, 99°20′ W **114**
Huixian, *China* 33°45′ N, 106°5′ E **198**
Huixtla, *Mex.* 15°8′ N, 92°30′ W **115**
Huize, *China* 26°20′ N, 103°17′ E **190**
Huizhou, *China* 22°59′ N, 114°21′ E **198**
Hujirt, *Mongolia* 46°35′ N, 104°36′ E **198**
Hujirt, *Mongolia* 46°58′ N, 102°44′ E **198**
Hukuntsi, *Botswana* 24°1′ S, 21°46′ E **227**
Hulan, *China* 46°2′ N, 126°39′ E **198**
Ḥulayfā', *Saudi Arabia* 25°55′ N, 40°46′ E **182**
Hulbert, *Mich., U.S.* 46°21′ N, 85°10′ W **94**
Hulin, *China* 45°57′ N, 133°10′ E **190**
Hull, *Can.* 45°26′ N, 75°44′ W **94**
Hull, *Mass., U.S.* 42°18′ N, 70°55′ W **104**
Hull, *Tex., U.S.* 30°8′ N, 94°39′ W **103**
Hull Mountain, *Calif., U.S.* 39°30′ N, 123°1′ W **90**
Hull, river, *U.K.* 53°51′ N, 0°24′ E **162**
Hullo, *Est.* 58°59′ N, 23°13′ E **166**
Hulls Cove, *Me., U.S.* 44°24′ N, 68°16′ W **94**
Hulne Priory, site, *U.K.* 55°25′ N, 1°51′ W **150**
Hulst, *Neth.* 51°17′ N, 4°3′ E **163**
Hulstay, *Mongolia* 48°29′ N, 114°52′ E **198**
Hultsfred, *Nor.* 57°29′ N, 15°48′ E **152**
Hulu, river, *China* 36°1′ N, 108°35′ E **198**
Hulun Nur, lake, *China* 48°59′ N, 116°20′ E **190**
Hulyaypole, *Ukr.* 47°38′ N, 36°15′ E **156**
Hum, *Bosn. and Herzg.* 42°43′ N, 18°10′ E **168**
Huma, *China* 51°40′ N, 126°45′ E **190**
Humahuaca, *Arg.* 23°11′ S, 65°19′ W **132**
Humaitá, *Braz.* 7°31′ S, 63°4′ W **130**
Humaneso de Mohernando, *Sp.* 40°48′ N, 3°10′ W **164**
Humansdorp, *S. Af.* 34°1′ S, 24°45′ E **227**
Ḥumar, *U.A.E.* 23°2′ N, 53°35′ E **182**
Humara, Jebel, peak, *Sudan* 16°10′ N, 30°45′ E **226**
Humaya, river, *Mex.* 25°9′ N, 106°59′ W **114**
Humbe, *Angola* 16°41′ S, 14°48′ E **207**
Humble, *Tex., U.S.* 29°58′ N, 95°15′ W **103**
Humboldt, *Ariz., U.S.* 34°30′ N, 112°13′ W **92**
Humboldt, *Can.* 52°11′ N, 105°8′ W **108**
Humboldt, *Kans., U.S.* 37°47′ N, 95°26′ W **96**
Humboldt, *Nebr., U.S.* 40°7′ N, 95°56′ W **90**
Humboldt, *Tenn., U.S.* 35°50′ N, 88°54′ W **96**
Humboldt Range, *Nev., U.S.* 40°23′ N, 118°25′ W **90**
Hume, *Calif., U.S.* 36°47′ N, 118°55′ W **101**
Hume, *Ill., U.S.* 39°47′ N, 87°52′ W **102**
Hume, river, *Can.* 66°4′ N, 130°13′ W **98**
Hūmedān, *Iran* 25°25′ N, 59°40′ E **182**
Humphreys, Mount, *Calif., U.S.* 37°15′ N, 118°46′ W **92**
Humphreys Peak, *Ariz., U.S.* 35°20′ N, 111°44′ W **92**
Humppila, *Fin.* 60°54′ N, 23°20′ E **166**
Humptulips, *Wash., U.S.* 47°13′ N, 123°58′ W **100**
Humu'ula Saddle, pass, *Hawai'i, U.S.* 19°41′ N, 155°30′ W **99**
Hūn, *Lib.* 29°10′ N, 15°53′ E **143**
Hun, river, *China* 41°20′ N, 125°43′ E **200**
Hun, river, *China* 41°52′ N, 123°44′ E **200**
Húnaflói 65°36′ N, 23°17′ W **143**
Hunan, adm. division, *China* 27°50′ N, 110°37′ E **198**
Hunchun, *China* 42°53′ N, 130°21′ E **200**
Hunedoara, adm. division, *Rom.* 46°7′ N, 22°35′ E **156**
Hünfeld, *Ger.* 50°40′ N, 9°46′ E **167**
Hungary 46°45′ N, 18°2′ E **156**
Hungen, *Ger.* 50°28′ N, 8°53′ E **167**
Hungerford, *U.K.* 51°24′ N, 1°31′ W **162**
Hŭngnam, *N. Korea* 39°51′ N, 127°38′ E **200**
Hŭngsu-ri, *N. Korea* 38°27′ N, 126°1′ E **200**
Hunjiang, *China* 41°51′ N, 126°23′ E **200**
Hunlen Falls, *Can.* 51°53′ N, 126°39′ W **108**
Hunmanby, *U.K.* 54°10′ N, 0°20′ E **162**
Huns Berge, peak, *Namibia* 27°48′ S, 17°3′ E **227**
Hunsrück, *Ger.* 50°3′ N, 7°14′ E **167**
Hunstanton, *U.K.* 52°56′ N, 0°29′ E **162**
Hunt, *Mongolia* 47°59′ N, 99°33′ E **190**
Hunt Mountain, *Wyo., U.S.* 44°42′ N, 107°50′ W **90**
Hunter, *N. Dak., U.S.* 47°11′ N, 97°15′ W **90**
Hunter Island, *Austral.* 40°16′ S, 144°40′ E **230**
Hunter Island, *Can.* 48°14′ N, 91°43′ W **94**
Hunter Islands, *Hunter Island* 40°42′ S, 142°25′ E **230**
Hunters Bay 19°36′ N, 93°5′ E **188**
Hunters Road, *Zimb.* 19°10′ S, 29°47′ E **224**
Huntingdon, *Can.* 45°5′ N, 74°11′ W **94**
Huntingdon, *Pa., U.S.* 40°29′ N, 78°1′ W **94**
Huntingdon, *Tenn., U.S.* 36°1′ N, 88°25′ W **96**
Huntingdon, *U.K.* 52°20′ N, 0°11′ E **162**
Huntington, *Ark., U.S.* 35°4′ N, 94°16′ W **96**
Huntington, *Ind., U.S.* 40°52′ N, 85°30′ W **102**
Huntington, *Mass., U.S.* 42°14′ N, 72°53′ W **104**
Huntington, *N.Y., U.S.* 40°52′ N, 73°26′ W **104**
Huntington, *Oreg., U.S.* 44°20′ N, 117°17′ W **90**
Huntington, *Tex., U.S.* 31°16′ N, 94°34′ W **103**
Huntington, *Utah, U.S.* 39°19′ N, 110°59′ W **90**
Huntington Beach, *Calif., U.S.* 33°40′ N, 118°2′ W **101**
Huntington Station, *N.Y., U.S.* 40°51′ N, 73°25′ W **104**
Huntly, *N.Z.* 37°34′ S, 175°9′ E **240**
Hunts Inlet, *Can.* 54°3′ N, 130°28′ W **108**
Huntsville, *Ala., U.S.* 34°43′ N, 86°36′ W **96**
Huntsville, *Ark., U.S.* 36°4′ N, 93°45′ W **96**
Huntsville, *Can.* 45°20′ N, 79°15′ W **94**
Huntsville, *Mo., U.S.* 39°26′ N, 92°32′ W **94**
Huntsville, *Tex., U.S.* 30°42′ N, 95°33′ W **103**
Huntsville, *Utah, U.S.* 41°15′ N, 111°46′ W **90**
Hunucmá, *Mex.* 20°59′ N, 89°54′ W **116**
Hunyuan, *China* 39°41′ N, 113°42′ E **198**
Huocheng, *China* 44°3′ N, 80°54′ E **184**
Huolin Gol, *China* 45°29′ N, 119°44′ E **198**
Huolin, river, *China* 44°43′ N, 121°47′ E **198**
Huolu, *China* 38°5′ N, 114°18′ E **198**
Huon Gulf 7°27′ S, 146°5′ E **238**
Huon Peninsula, *P.N.G.* 6°30′ S, 146°32′ E **192**
Huong Hoa, *Vietnam* 16°38′ N, 106°44′ E **202**
Huong Khe, *Vietnam* 18°14′ N, 105°41′ E **202**
Huoqiu, *China* 32°21′ N, 116°17′ E **198**
Huoshan, *China* 31°25′ N, 116°21′ E **198**
Huoxian, *China* 36°33′ N, 111°44′ E **198**
Hŭpkok, *N. Korea* 39°4′ N, 127°44′ E **200**
Hupo, *S. Korea* 36°41′ N, 129°28′ E **200**
Hurault, Lac, lake, *Can.* 54°16′ N, 71°12′ W **111**
Hurd, Cape, *Can.* 45°1′ N, 81°58′ W **110**
Hurdiyo, *Somalia* 10°33′ N, 51°7′ E **216**
Hure Qi, *China* 42°44′ N, 121°47′ E **198**
Hüremt, *Mongolia* 48°38′ N, 102°31′ E **198**
Hurghada, *Egypt* 27°14′ N, 33°47′ E **180**
Huri Hills, *Kenya* 3°31′ N, 37°24′ E **224**
Hurley, *Miss., U.S.* 30°38′ N, 88°28′ W **103**
Huron, *Calif., U.S.* 36°12′ N, 120°7′ W **100**
Huron, *Ind., U.S.* 38°42′ N, 86°40′ W **102**
Huron, *S. Dak., U.S.* 44°21′ N, 98°13′ W **90**
Huron Islands, *Lake Superior* 47°0′ N, 88°6′ W **94**
Huron, Lake 44°22′ N, 83°8′ W **106**
Huron, Lake 45°3′ N, 82°25′ W **110**
Huron, Lake 44°39′ N, 83°58′ W **73**
Huron, Lake 44°58′ N, 85°17′ W **73**
Huron Mountain, *Mich., U.S.* 46°52′ N, 87°52′ W **110**
Huron Mountains, *Mich., U.S.* 46°43′ N, 87°59′ W **94**
Hurricane, *Alas., U.S.* 62°58′ N, 149°39′ W **98**
Hurricane, *Utah, U.S.* 37°10′ N, 113°17′ W **92**
Hürth, *Ger.* 50°51′ N, 6°51′ E **167**
Hurup, *Den.* 56°43′ N, 8°24′ E **150**
Husainabad, *India* 24°31′ N, 84°0′ E **197**
Huşi, *Rom.* 46°40′ N, 28°4′ E **156**
Huslia, *Alas., U.S.* 65°40′ N, 156°25′ W **98**
Husøy, *Nor.* 61°1′ N, 4°40′ E **152**
Husum, *Ger.* 54°28′ N, 9°3′ E **150**
Husum, *Nor.* 63°19′ N, 19°10′ E **152**
Hutanopan, *Indonesia* 0°43′ N, 99°44′ E **196**
Hutch Mountain, *Ariz., U.S.* 34°48′ N, 111°28′ W **92**
Hutchinson, *Kans., U.S.* 38°2′ N, 97°55′ W **90**
Hutchinson, *Minn., U.S.* 44°51′ N, 94°24′ W **90**
Hutchinson, *S. Af.* 31°31′ S, 23°10′ E **227**
Hutchinson Island, *Fla., U.S.* 27°18′ N, 80°13′ W **105**
Huthi, *Myanmar* 16°11′ N, 98°49′ E **202**
Hutig, Ben, peak, *U.K.* 58°32′ N, 4°39′ W **150**
Hutovo, *Bosn. and Herzg.* 42°57′ N, 17°48′ E **168**
Hutsonville, *Ill., U.S.* 39°6′ N, 87°41′ W **102**
Huttig, *Ark., U.S.* 33°1′ N, 92°12′ W **103**
Hutton, *Can.* 53°58′ N, 121°38′ W **108**
Hutuo, river, *China* 38°12′ N, 115°9′ E **198**
Huuhkala, *Fin.* 61°28′ N, 28°15′ E **166**
Huvadu see Suvadiva Atoll, *Maldives* 0°39′ N, 72°35′ E **188**
Huwaisah, oil field, *Oman* 21°48′ N, 56°3′ E **182**
Huxford, *Ala., U.S.* 31°12′ N, 87°27′ W **103**
Huxian, *China* 34°5′ N, 108°35′ E **198**
Huy, *Belg.* 50°30′ N, 5°15′ E **167**
Hüyük, *Turk.* 37°57′ N, 31°36′ E **156**
Huzhou, *China* 30°49′ N, 120°12′ E **198**
Hvaler, islands, *Norwegian Sea* 58°57′ N, 11°11′ E **152**
Hvar, *Croatia* 43°10′ N, 16°26′ E **168**
Hvar (Pharus), island, *Croatia* 43°3′ N, 16°47′ E **168**
Hwadae, *N. Korea* 40°48′ N, 129°32′ E **200**
Hwajin, *N. Korea* 39°11′ N, 125°25′ E **200**
Hwange, *Zimb.* 18°24′ S, 26°30′ E **224**
Hwange National Park, *Zimb.* 19°17′ S, 26°23′ E **224**
Hwangju, *N. Korea* 38°39′ N, 125°48′ E **200**
Hwap'yŏng, *N. Korea* 41°15′ N, 126°53′ E **200**
Hwayang, *S. Korea* 35°38′ N, 128°46′ E **200**
Hyalite Peak, *Mont., U.S.* 45°21′ N, 111°1′ W **90**
Hyannis, *Mass., U.S.* 41°39′ N, 70°18′ W **104**
Hyannis, *Nebr., U.S.* 41°59′ N, 101°46′ W **90**
Hyannis Port, *Mass., U.S.* 41°37′ N, 70°19′ W **104**
Hyargas Nuur, lake, *Mongolia* 49°4′ N, 91°34′ E **190**
Hydaburg, *Alas., U.S.* 55°13′ N, 132°48′ W **108**
Hyde, *N.Z.* 45°19′ S, 170°15′ E **240**
Hyde Park, *N.Y., U.S.* 41°46′ N, 73°57′ W **104**
Hyde Park, *Vt., U.S.* 44°35′ N, 72°38′ W **104**
Hyden, *Austral.* 32°26′ S, 118°53′ E **231**
Hyder, *Alas., U.S.* 55°55′ N, 130°7′ W **108**
Hyderabad, *India* 17°19′ N, 78°28′ E **188**
Hyderabad, *Pak.* 25°24′ N, 68°24′ E **186**
Hydeville, *Vt., U.S.* 43°36′ N, 73°15′ W **104**
Hyeolli, *S. Korea* 37°57′ N, 128°21′ E **200**
Hyères, Îles d' (Les Îles d'Or), islands, *Mediterranean Sea* 42°57′ N, 6°33′ E **165**
Hyesan, *N. Korea* 41°23′ N, 128°12′ E **200**
Hyland Post, *Can.* 57°39′ N, 128°10′ W **108**
Hyland, river, *Can.* 60°11′ N, 128°3′ W **108**
Hyltebruk, *Nor.* 56°59′ N, 13°15′ E **152**
Hymera, *Ind., U.S.* 39°10′ N, 87°18′ W **102**
Hyndman Peak, *Idaho, U.S.* 43°44′ N, 114°13′ W **90**
Hynish, Ben, peak, *U.K.* 56°26′ N, 7°2′ W **150**
Hyōgo, adm. division, *Japan* 35°3′ N, 134°26′ E **201**
Hyrra Banda, *Cen. Af. Rep.* 5°56′ N, 22°4′ E **218**
Hyrynsalmi, *Fin.* 64°40′ N, 28°31′ E **154**
Hysham, *Mont., U.S.* 46°16′ N, 107°14′ W **90**
Hythe, *Can.* 55°19′ N, 119°35′ W **108**
Hythe, *U.K.* 51°4′ N, 1°4′ E **162**
Hyūga, *Japan* 32°25′ N, 131°36′ E **201**
Hyvinkää, *Fin.* 60°37′ N, 24°50′ E **166**

I

Ía, *Gr.* 36°27′ N, 25°23′ E **156**
Iá, river, *Braz.* 0°19′ N, 66°47′ W **136**
Iablaniţa, *Rom.* 44°56′ N, 22°18′ E **168**
Iaciara, *Braz.* 14°12′ S, 46°39′ W **138**
Iaco, river, *Braz.* 10°10′ S, 69°7′ W **137**
Iaçu, *Braz.* 12°46′ S, 40°16′ W **138**
Iaeger, *W. Va., U.S.* 37°27′ N, 81°49′ W **96**
Iakora, *Madagascar* 23°6′ S, 46°40′ E **220**
Ialomiţae, adm. division, *Rom.* 44°39′ N, 26°21′ E **156**
Ialysus see Triánda, *Gr.* 36°24′ N, 28°10′ E **156**
Ianca, *Rom.* 45°7′ N, 27°28′ E **158**
Iar Connaught, region, *Europe* 53°18′ N, 9°27′ W **150**
Iaşi, adm. division, *Rom.* 47°16′ N, 26°47′ E **156**
Iaşi, *Rom.* 47°9′ N, 27°37′ E **152**
Iauaretê, *Braz.* 0°34′ N, 69°14′ W **136**
Ib, *Russ.* 61°16′ N, 50°34′ E **154**
Ibadan, *Nig.* 7°26′ N, 3°54′ E **222**
Ibagué, *Col.* 4°23′ N, 75°15′ W **136**
Ibaiti, *Braz.* 23°50′ S, 50°14′ W **138**
Iballë, *Alban.* 42°11′ N, 19°59′ E **168**
Ibapah, *Utah, U.S.* 40°1′ N, 113°59′ W **90**
Ibapah Peak, *Utah, U.S.* 39°47′ N, 113°60′ W **90**
Ibar, river, *Serb. and Mont.* 43°35′ N, 20°32′ E **168**
Ibaraki, adm. division, *Japan* 36°17′ N, 140°0′ E **201**
Ibarra, *Ecua.* 0°19′ N, 78°16′ W **136**
Ibb, *Yemen* 13°59′ N, 44°10′ E **182**
Ibba, *Sudan* 4°49′ N, 29°7′ E **224**
Ibba (Tonj), river, *Sudan* 6°16′ N, 28°21′ E **224**
Ibbenbüren, *Ger.* 52°16′ N, 7°43′ E **150**
Iberá, Laguna, lake, *Arg.* 28°22′ S, 57°22′ W **139**
Iberia, *Peru* 11°23′ S, 69°36′ W **137**
Ibestad, *Nor.* 68°46′ N, 17°8′ E **152**
Ibeto, *Nig.* 10°28′ N, 5°7′ E **222**
Ibex Pass, *Calif., U.S.* 35°47′ N, 116°21′ W **101**
Ibi, *Nig.* 8°8′ N, 9°45′ E **222**
Ibi, *Sp.* 38°37′ N, 0°36′ E **164**
Ibiá, *Braz.* 19°31′ S, 46°33′ W **138**
Ibicaraí, *Braz.* 14°54′ S, 39°37′ W **138**
Ibicuí, *Braz.* 29°24′ S, 56°42′ W **139**
Ibicuy, *Arg.* 33°43′ S, 59°7′ W **139**
Ibina, river, *Dem. Rep. of the Congo* 0°57′ N, 28°35′ E **224**
Ibipetuba, *Braz.* 11°1′ S, 44°32′ W **132**
Ibiraba, *Braz.* 10°47′ S, 42°50′ W **132**
Ibirama, *Braz.* 27°5′ S, 49°30′ W **138**
Ibiranhém, *Braz.* 17°52′ S, 40°10′ W **138**
Ibitiara, *Braz.* 12°39′ S, 42°15′ W **132**
Ibiza (Iviza), island, *Sp.* 39°1′ N, 6°356′ W **214**
Iblei, Monti, *It.* 37°18′ N, 14°25′ E **156**
Ibo, *Mozambique* 12°21′ S, 40°38′ E **220**
Iboperenda, *Bol.* 19°4′ S, 62°38′ W **132**
Ibotirama, *Braz.* 12°11′ S, 43°13′ W **132**
Iboundji, Mont, peak, *Gabon* 1°11′ S, 11°41′ E **218**
Ibresi, *Russ.* 55°18′ N, 47°4′ E **154**
'Ibrī, *Oman* 23°10′ N, 56°29′ E **182**
Ibusuki, *Japan* 31°14′ N, 130°36′ E **201**
Ibwe Munyama, *Zambia* 16°10′ S, 28°31′ E **224**
Ica, *Peru* 14°6′ S, 75°48′ W **130**
Ica, adm. division, *Peru* 15°7′ S, 75°3′ W **137**
Ica, river, *Peru* 13°55′ S, 75°47′ W **130**
Içana, *Braz.* 0°19′ N, 67°23′ W **136**
Içana, river, *Braz.* 1°10′ N, 67°59′ W **136**
Icaño, *Arg.* 28°41′ S, 62°53′ W **139**
Icaria, ruin(s), *Gr.* 38°4′ N, 23°48′ E **156**
Ice Age National Scientific Reserve, *Wis., U.S.* 43°39′ N, 88°13′ W **102**
Ice Mountain, *Can.* 54°24′ N, 121°15′ W **108**
İçel (Mersin), *Turk.* 36°48′ N, 34°36′ E **156**
Iceland 65°21′ N, 25°52′ W **246**
Iceland Plateau, *Greenland Sea* 69°18′ N, 13°34′ W **255**
Icheon, *S. Korea* 37°16′ N, 127°26′ E **200**
Ichera, *Russ.* 58°36′ N, 109°37′ E **160**
Ichikawa, *Japan* 35°42′ N, 139°56′ E **201**
Ichilo, river, *Bol.* 16°58′ S, 64°44′ W **137**
Ichinomiya, *Japan* 35°17′ N, 136°48′ E **201**
Ichinskiy, *Russ.* 56°41′ N, 156°10′ E **160**
Ichnya, *Ukr.* 50°49′ N, 32°23′ E **158**
Ichoa, river, *Bol.* 15°55′ S, 65°34′ W **137**
Ich'ŏn, *N. Korea* 38°28′ N, 126°54′ E **200**
Ichuña, *Peru* 16°9′ S, 70°31′ W **137**
Icó, *Braz.* 6°27′ S, 38°51′ W **132**
Iconium see Konya, *Turk.* 37°51′ N, 32°29′ E **156**
Iconoclast Mountain, *Can.* 51°27′ N, 117°51′ W **90**
Icy Cape, *Alas., U.S.* 70°12′ N, 163°39′ W **98**
Ida, *La., U.S.* 32°59′ N, 93°54′ W **103**
Ida Grove, *Iowa, U.S.* 42°20′ N, 95°27′ W **94**
Idabel, *Okla., U.S.* 33°53′ N, 94°50′ W **96**
Idah, *Nig.* 7°7′ N, 6°43′ E **222**
Idaho, adm. division, *Idaho, U.S.* 44°25′ N, 114°53′ W **90**
Idaho City, *Idaho, U.S.* 43°49′ N, 115°49′ W **90**
Idaho Falls, *Idaho, U.S.* 43°29′ N, 112°2′ W **90**
Idali, *Sudan* 4°43′ N, 32°41′ E **224**
Idalou, *Tex., U.S.* 33°38′ N, 101°41′ W **96**
Idar-Oberstein, *Ger.* 49°42′ N, 7°19′ E **163**
Idawgaw, *Nig.* 6°54′ N, 2°56′ E **222**
Iday, spring, *Niger* 14°58′ N, 11°32′ E **222**
'Idd el Ghanam, *Sudan* 11°31′ N, 24°19′ E **216**
Iddo, *Nig.* 7°55′ N, 5°11′ E **214**
Idel', *Russ.* 64°12′ N, 34°5′ E **152**
Ideles, *Alg.* 23°48′ N, 5°55′ E **214**
Ider, river, *Mongolia* 48°32′ N, 98°4′ E **190**
Idermeg, *Mongolia* 47°36′ N, 111°22′ E **198**
Idfu, *Egypt* 24°58′ N, 32°47′ E **182**
Idi, *Indonesia* 4°59′ N, 97°43′ E **196**
Ídi, Óros (Psiloreítis), peak, *Gr.* 35°12′ N, 24°41′ E **156**
İdil, *Turk.* 37°20′ N, 41°54′ E **195**
Idiofa, *Dem. Rep. of the Congo* 5°2′ S, 19°36′ E **218**
Idle, river, *U.K.* 53°14′ N, 0°54′ E **162**
Idlewild, *Mich., U.S.* 43°53′ N, 85°46′ W **102**
Idlib, *Syr.* 35°56′ N, 36°36′ E **156**
Idria, *Calif., U.S.* 36°24′ N, 120°41′ W **100**
Idritsa, *Russ.* 56°18′ N, 28°51′ E **166**
Idro, *It.* 45°44′ N, 10°29′ E **167**
Idstein, *Ger.* 50°13′ N, 8°15′ E **167**
Idutywa, *S. Af.* 32°8′ S, 28°17′ E **227**
Idyllwild, *Calif., U.S.* 33°44′ N, 116°44′ W **101**
Iecava, *Latv.* 56°36′ N, 24°11′ E **166**
Iepê, *Braz.* 22°42′ S, 51°7′ W **138**
Ieper (Ypres), *Belg.* 50°50′ N, 2°53′ E **163**
Ierápetra, *Gr.* 35°3′ N, 25°43′ E **180**
Iernut, *Rom.* 46°28′ N, 24°12′ E **156**
Ifakara, *Tanzania* 8°8′ S, 36°39′ E **218**
Ifalik Atoll, *F.S.M.* 6°18′ N, 143°39′ E **192**
Ifanadiana, *Madagascar* 21°18′ S, 47°37′ E **220**
Ife, *Nig.* 7°30′ N, 4°33′ E **222**
Iferouâne, *Niger* 19°3′ N, 8°23′ E **222**
Iforas, Adrar des, *Mali* 18°56′ N, 9°535′ E **222**
Igal, *Hung.* 46°31′ N, 17°56′ E **168**
Igalukilo, *Tanzania* 6°1′ S, 30°41′ E **224**
Igalula, *Tanzania* 5°13′ S, 33°0′ E **224**
Igan, *Malaysia* 2°46′ N, 111°44′ E **192**

Iganga, Uganda 0°34' N, 33°27' E 224
Igarka, Russ. 67°23' N, 86°42' E 169
Iğdır, Turk. 39°55' N, 44°1' E 195
Igiugig, Alas., U.S. 59°18' N, 155°54' W 98
Igli, Alg. 30°27' N, 2°19' W 214
Iglino, Russ. 54°51' N, 56°23' E 154
Igloolik, Can. 69°13' N, 81°50' W 73
'Igma, Gebel el, Egypt 29°3' N, 33°9' E 180
Ignace, Can. 49°26' N, 91°40' W 94
Ignacio, Colo., U.S. 37°6' N, 107°38' W 92
Ignacio Allende, Mex. 24°27' N, 103°60' W 114
Ignalina, Lith. 55°20' N, 26°7' E 166
Ignatovka, Russ. 53°54' N, 47°43' E 154
İğneada, Turk. 41°52' N, 27°57' E 158
İğneada Burnu, Turk. 41°48' N, 28°3' E 156
Igoma, Tanzania 7°51' S, 33°20' E 224
Igombe, river, Tanzania 4°38' S, 32°1' E 224
Igra, Russ. 57°33' N, 53°11' E 154
Igrim, Russ. 63°9' N, 64°30' E 169
Iguala, Mex. 18°19' N, 99°32' W 114
Igualdade, Braz. 1°49' S, 68°29' W 136
Iguape, Braz. 24°41' S, 47°37' W 138
Iguatu, Braz. 6°23' S, 39°17' W 132
Iguazú Falls, South America 26°4' S, 54°13' W 123
Iguazú National Park, Braz. 25°46' S, 53°36' W 138
Iguéla, Gabon 1°58' S, 9°21' E 218
Iguidi, Erg, Alg. 24°5' N, 7°50' W 206
Igula, Tanzania 7°12' S, 34°40' E 224
Igumira, Tanzania 6°49' S, 33°17' E 224
Ihbulag, Mongolia 43°13' N, 107°12' E 198
Ihdin, Leb. 34°17' N, 35°57' E 194
Ihlow, Ger. 53°23' N, 7°26' E 163
Ihnâsya el Madîna, Egypt 29°6' N, 30°56' E 180
Ihosy, Madagascar 22°24' S, 46°9' E 220
Ihsuuj, Mongolia 48°10' N, 106°6' E 198
Ihugh, Nig. 6°58' N, 8°59' E 222
Ii, Fin. 65°18' N, 25°23' E 152
Iida, Japan 35°31' N, 137°50' E 201
Iida see Suzu, Japan 37°26' N, 137°15' E 201
Iijärvi, lake, Fin. 69°23' N, 27°17' E 152
Iisaku, Est. 59°5' N, 27°17' E 166
Iisalmi, Fin. 63°33' N, 27°8' E 152
Iisvesi, Fin. 62°38' N, 26°57' E 152
Iitto, Fin. 68°44' N, 21°24' E 152
Iittuarmiit, Den. 63°29' N, 41°18' W 106
Iiyama, Japan 36°51' N, 138°20' E 201
Iizaka, Japan 37°50' N, 140°25' E 201
Iizuka, Japan 33°37' N, 130°41' E 201
Ijara, Kenya 1°38' S, 40°30' E 224
Ijebu Ode, Nig. 6°54' N, 3°55' E 222
Ijevan, Arm. 40°53' N, 45°7' E 195
IJmuiden, Neth. 52°27' N, 4°35' E 163
IJsselmeer 52°47' N, 5°7' E 163
IJsselstein, Neth. 52°0' N, 5°2' E 167
Ijuí, Braz. 28°24' S, 53°56' W 139
Ik, river, Russ. 55°11' N, 53°18' E 154
Ikaalinen, Fin. 61°45' N, 23°2' E 166
Ikamatua, N.Z. 42°17' S, 171°43' E 240
Ikare, Nig. 7°32' N, 5°44' E 222
Ikaría, island, Gr. 37°41' N, 26°3' E 180
Ikast, Den. 56°8' N, 9°8' E 150
Ikela, Dem. Rep. of the Congo 1°5' S, 23°4' E 218
Ikélemba, Congo 1°15' N, 16°31' E 218
Ikeq 64°47' N, 41°4' W 106
Ikerasassuaq 59°54' N, 45°2' W 106
Ikervár, Hung. 47°12' N, 16°53' E 168
Iki, Mauna, peak, Hawai'i, U.S. 19°20' N, 155°25' W 99
İkizdere, Turk. 40°47' N, 40°30' E 195
Ikla, Est. 57°53' N, 24°21' E 166
Ikom, Nig. 5°57' N, 8°42' E 222
Ikoma, Tanzania 2°7' S, 34°37' E 224
Ikongo, Madagascar 21°51' S, 47°29' E 220
Ikorodu, Nig. 6°42' N, 3°29' E 222
Ikosi, Dem. Rep. of the Congo 2°38' S, 27°38' E 224
Ikoto, Sudan 4°3' N, 33°3' E 224
Ikoyi, Nig. 8°17' N, 4°9' E 222
Ikryanoye, Russ. 46°5' N, 47°43' E 158
Iksan, S. Korea 35°55' N, 126°58' E 200
Ikungi, Tanzania 5°6' S, 34°45' E 224
Ikuno, Japan 35°9' N, 134°47' E 201
Ikutha, Kenya 2°5' S, 38°11' E 224
Ila, Dem. Rep. of the Congo 2°56' S, 21°4' E 218
Ilaferh, spring, Alg. 21°41' N, 1°58' E 222
Ilagan, Philippines 17°7' N, 121°52' E 203
Īlām, Iran 33°38' N, 46°25' E 180
Ilan, Taiwan 24°44' N, 121°42' E 198
Ilandža, Serb. and Mont. 45°9' N, 20°55' E 168
Ilanskiy, Russ. 56°15' N, 96°7' E 160
Ilaro, Nig. 6°58' N, 3°1' E 222
Ilatane, spring, Niger 16°33' N, 4°36' E 222
Ilava, Slovakia 48°59' N, 18°15' E 152
Ilave, Peru 16°7' S, 69°40' W 137
Ilchester, U.K. 50°59' N, 2°40' W 162
Île de France, region, Europe 49°1' N, 1°33' E 163
Île d'Orléans, island, Can. 47°3' N, 72°9' W 81
Ile, river, Kaz. 43°54' N, 79°15' E 184
Île-à-la-Crosse, Can. 55°27' N, 107°55' W 108
Île-à-la-Crosse, Lac, lake, Can. 55°37' N, 108°36' W 108
Ilebo, Dem. Rep. of the Congo 4°20' S, 20°35' E 218
Île-De-France, adm. division, Fr. 48°43' N, 1°37' E 150
Ilek, Russ. 51°33' N, 53°27' E 158
Ilek, river, Russ. 50°58' N, 55°20' E 158
Ileksa, river, Russ. 63°6' N, 36°46' E 154
Iles, Lac des, lake, Can. 49°9' N, 90°7' W 94
Ilesha, Nig. 7°37' N, 4°44' E 222
Ilford, Can. 56°4' N, 95°38' W 108
Ilford, U.K. 51°33' N, 7°416' E 162
Ilgaz, Turk. 40°55' N, 33°37' E 156
Ilgın, Turk. 38°15' N, 31°55' E 156
Ilhéus, Braz. 14°49' S, 39°10' W 123
Ili, river, China 43°55' N, 80°49' E 184
Ilia, Rom. 45°57' N, 22°40' E 168
Iliamna Lake, Alas., U.S. 59°58' N, 157°10' W 106
Iliamna Volcano, Alas., U.S. 60°0' N, 153°15' W 98
Ilıca, Turk. 39°57' N, 41°6' E 195
Ilidža, Bosn. and Herzg. 43°48' N, 18°18' E 168
Iligan, Philippines 8°16' N, 124°15' E 203
Iligan Bay 8°14' N, 123°55' E 203
Iligan Point, Philippines 18°29' N, 122°15' E 203
'Ili'ili'ōpae Heiau, site, Hawai'i, U.S. 21°4' N, 156°52' W 99
Ilimsk, Russ. 56°46' N, 104°1' E 246
Ilīnka, Kaz. 49°55' N, 56°13' E 158
Ilinka, Russ. 55°23' N, 69°16' E 184
Ilinska Planina, Maced. 41°18' N, 20°31' E 156
Il'inskaya, Russ. 45°45' N, 40°40' E 158
Il'insko Podomskoye, Russ. 61°9' N, 48°2' E 154
'Īlio Point, U.S. 21°10' N, 157°33' W 99
Ilion, N.Y., U.S. 43°0' N, 75°3' W 110
Ilkal, India 15°58' N, 76°9' E 188
Ilkeston, U.K. 52°57' N, 1°19' W 162
Ill, river, Fr. 48°6' N, 7°28' E 163
Illampu, peak, Bol. 15°52' S, 68°41' W 137
Illana Bay 7°42' N, 123°18' E 203
Illbillee, Mount, Austral. 27°4' S, 132°15' E 230
Illéla, Niger 14°28' N, 5°14' E 222
Illescas, Mex. 23°12' N, 102°7' W 114
Illescas, Sp. 40°6' N, 3°51' W 164
Ille-sur-Têt, Fr. 42°40' N, 2°35' E 164
Illichivs'k, Ukr. 46°19' N, 30°35' E 156
Illiers, Fr. 48°17' N, 1°15' E 163
Illimani, peak, Bol. 16°40' S, 67°58' W 137
Illinois, adm. division, Ill., U.S. 40°33' N, 89°18' W 102
Illinois Peak, Mont., U.S. 46°59' N, 115°9' W 90
Illinois, river, Ark., U.S. 36°4' N, 94°51' W 96
Illiopolis, Ill., U.S. 39°50' N, 89°15' W 102
Illizi, Alg. 26°30' N, 8°18' E 207
Iłowo, Pol. 53°9' N, 20°17' E 152
Illmo, Mo., U.S. 37°13' N, 89°30' W 96
Íllora, Sp. 37°16' N, 3°53' W 164
Ilminster, U.K. 50°55' N, 2°54' W 162
Ilo, Peru 17°41' S, 71°21' W 137
Iloilo, Philippines 10°42' N, 122°32' E 203
Ilok, Croatia 45°12' N, 19°22' E 168
Ilomantsi, Fin. 62°38' N, 30°55' E 152
Ilonga, Tanzania 6°43' S, 37°3' E 224
Ilorin, Nig. 8°30' N, 4°33' E 222
Ilovlya, Russ. 49°18' N, 43°59' E 158
Ilpela, Paso de, pass, Arg. 40°10' S, 71°50' W 134
Il'pyrskiy, Russ. 60°1' N, 164°9' E 160
Ilu, Dem. Rep. of the Congo 4°1' N, 23°9' E 218
Ilūkste, Latv. 55°58' N, 26°16' E 166
Ilula, Tanzania 3°16' S, 33°19' E 224
Ilulissat (Jakobshavn), Den. 69°11' N, 50°60' W 106
Ilwaco, Wash., U.S. 46°17' N, 124°3' W 100
Il'ya, Belarus 54°25' N, 27°15' E 166
Ilych, river, Russ. 62°57' N, 58°40' E 154
Imabari, Japan 34°2' N, 133°0' E 201
Imabu, river, Braz. 1°60' N, 57°46' W 130
Imaichi, Japan 36°42' N, 139°41' E 201
Imajō, Japan 35°45' N, 136°11' E 201
Imanombo, Madagascar 24°25' S, 45°50' E 220
Imari, Japan 33°17' N, 129°52' E 201
Imarssuak Seachannel, North Atlantic Ocean 58°30' N, 38°40' W 253
Imasa, Sudan 17°58' N, 36°8' E 182
Imataca, Serranía de, Venez. 8°6' N, 62°19' W 116
Imatra, Fin. 61°9' N, 28°46' E 166
Imazu, Japan 35°22' N, 136°0' E 201
Imbert, Dom. Rep. 19°46' N, 70°50' W 116
Imbituba, Braz. 28°18' S, 48°42' W 138
Iménas, spring, Mali 16°21' N, 0°36' E 222
Imeni Stalina, Turkm. 39°9' N, 63°37' E 197
Imeri, Serra, Venez. 0°47' N, 66°22' W 130
Imese, Dem. Rep. of the Congo 2°2' N, 18°9' E 218
Īmī, Eth. 6°29' N, 42°12' E 224
Imi n 'Tanout, Mor. 31°10' N, 8°52' W 214
İmişli, Azerb. 39°51' N, 48°2' E 195
Imjin, river, N. Korea 38°44' N, 126°59' E 200
Imlay, Nev., U.S. 40°40' N, 118°10' W 92
Imlay City, Mich., U.S. 43°0' N, 83°4' W 102
Imlily, Western Sahara 23°16' N, 15°55' W 214
Immenhausen, Ger. 51°26' N, 9°29' E 167
Immenstadt, Ger. 47°33' N, 10°12' E 156
Immingham, U.K. 53°36' N, 0°14' E 162
Immokalee, Fla., U.S. 26°25' N, 81°25' W 105
Imnaha, Oreg., U.S. 45°33' N, 116°50' W 90
Imola, It. 44°21' N, 11°42' E 156
Imotski, Croatia 43°25' N, 17°12' E 168
Imperatriz, Braz. 5°18' S, 67°12' W 130
Imperatriz, Braz. 5°29' S, 47°28' W 130
Imperia, It. 43°53' N, 8°1' E 167
Imperial, Calif., U.S. 32°50' N, 115°35' W 101
Imperial, Can. 51°22' N, 105°28' W 90
Imperial, Nebr., U.S. 40°30' N, 101°39' W 90
Imperial, Peru 13°3' S, 76°20' W 130
Imperial Beach, Calif., U.S. 32°34' N, 117°8' W 101
Imperial Dam, Calif., U.S. 32°48' N, 114°37' W 101
Imperial Valley, Calif., U.S. 32°56' N, 115°52' W 101
Imphal, India 24°50' N, 93°55' E 188
Impiö, Fin. 65°57' N, 27°10' E 152
Impora, Bol. 21°28' S, 65°20' W 137
Imst, Aust. 47°14' N, 10°43' E 156
Imtān, Syr. 32°25' N, 36°48' E 194
Imuris, Mex. 30°48' N, 110°51' W 92
Imuruan Bay 10°33' N, 118°50' E 203
In Azar, spring, Lib. 28°56' N, 9°57' E 214
Ina, Japan 35°51' N, 137°57' E 201
Ina, river, Pol. 53°25' N, 14°44' E 152
I-n-abâlene, spring, Mali 18°53' N, 2°23' E 222
I-n-Abanrherit, spring, Niger 17°54' N, 6°2' E 222
Inaccessible Islands, Scotia Sea 60°37' S, 47°27' W 134
I-n-Afarag, Erg, Alg. 23°58' N, 2°5' E 214
Inagauan, Philippines 9°33' N, 118°37' E 203
Inagua, adm. division, Bahamas 20°59' N, 73°41' W 116
I-n-Ahmar, spring, Mauritania 17°18' N, 9°11' W 222
Inajá, Braz. 8°56' S, 37°47' W 132
I-n-Akhmed, spring, Mali 19°53' N, 0°54' E 222
I-n-Alchi, spring, Mali 17°39' N, 1°11' W 222
I-n-Aleï, spring, Mali 17°40' N, 2°34' W 222
I-n-Allarhene Guériguéri, spring, Niger 18°12' N, 6°18' E 222
Inambari, Peru 12°46' S, 69°41' W 137
I-n-Amenas, Alg. 28°3' N, 9°28' E 214
I-n-Amguel, Alg. 23°37' N, 5°9' E 214
Inami, Japan 36°32' N, 136°58' E 201
Inanwatan, Indonesia 2°6' S, 132°5' E 192
Iñapari, Peru 10°59' S, 69°39' W 137
Inari, Fin. 68°54' N, 27°0' E 152
Inari, Fin. 63°16' N, 30°58' E 154
Inari, lake, Fin. 68°54' N, 27°1' E 246
Inauini, river, Braz. 8°17' S, 68°19' W 132
Inawashiro, Japan 37°33' N, 140°6' E 201
I-n-Azaoua, spring, Alg. 25°43' N, 7°0' E 214
I-n-Azaoua, spring, Niger 20°52' N, 7°28' E 222
I-n-Belbel, Alg. 27°54' N, 1°8' E 214
I-n-Beriem, spring, Mali 19°24' N, 0°26' E 222
Inca de Oro, Chile 26°45' S, 69°56' W 132
Inca, Paso del, pass, Chile 28°43' S, 69°44' W 132
İnce Burun, Turk. 42°1' N, 34°14' E 156
İncekum Burnu, Turk. 36°16' N, 33°57' E 156
İncesu, Turk. 38°36' N, 35°11' E 156
Incheon (Inch'ŏn), S. Korea 37°27' N, 126°39' E 200
Inch'ŏn see Incheon, S. Korea 37°27' N, 126°39' E 200
Inchoun, Russ. 66°16' N, 170°14' W 98
Incudine, Monte, peak, Fr. 41°50' N, 9°8' E 156
Inčukalns, Latv. 57°5' N, 24°41' E 166
I-n-Dagouber, spring, Mali 22°13' N, 2°39' W 222
Indaiá, river, Braz. 19°9' S, 45°48' W 138
Indaial, Braz. 26°60' S, 49°16' W 138
Indaparapeo, Mex. 19°45' N, 100°58' W 114
Indaw, Myanmar 24°9' N, 96°6' E 188
Indawgyi Lake, Myanmar 25°1' N, 95°22' E 188
Indé, Mex. 25°51' N, 105°10' W 114
I-n-Délimane, Mali 15°52' N, 1°24' E 222
Independence, Calif., U.S. 36°48' N, 118°13' W 101
Independence, Iowa, U.S. 42°28' N, 91°53' W 94
Independence, Kans., U.S. 37°12' N, 95°43' W 94
Independence, La., U.S. 30°36' N, 90°30' W 103
Independence, Mo., U.S. 39°4' N, 94°26' W 94
Independence Mountains, Nev., U.S. 41°4' N, 116°25' W 90
Independence Rock, site, Wyo., U.S. 42°29' N, 107°11' W 90
Independencia, Bol. 17°2' S, 66°47' W 137
Independência, Braz. 5°26' S, 40°20' W 132
Independência, Braz. 2°53' S, 52°5' W 130
Independencia, Parag. 21°35' S, 62°9' W 132
Inder see Jalaid Qi, China 46°41' N, 122°53' E 198
Inderapura, Indonesia 2°4' S, 100°54' E 192
Index, Wash., U.S. 47°49' N, 121°34' W 100
Indi, India 17°9' N, 75°58' E 188
India 22°56' N, 77°2' E 188
India, Bassas da, islands, Mozambique Channel 21°15' S, 39°13' E 220
Indialantic, Fla., U.S. 28°5' N, 80°36' W 105
Indian Cabins, Can. 59°53' N, 117°3' W 108
Indian Harbour 45°1' N, 62°26' W 111
Indian Harbour, Can. 54°26' N, 57°13' W 111
Indian Head, Can. 50°31' N, 103°42' W 90
Indian Head, peak, Utah, U.S. 39°51' N, 110°59' W 90
Indian Lake, Can. 47°5' N, 82°30' W 94
Indian Ocean 26°43' S, 30°5' E 254
Indian Peak, Utah, U.S. 38°14' N, 113°57' W 90
Indian Peak, Wyo., U.S. 44°45' N, 109°56' W 90
Indian Springs, Nev., U.S. 36°34' N, 115°41' W 101
Indiana, adm. division, Ind., U.S. 40°10' N, 86°37' W 102
Indianapolis, Ind., U.S. 39°45' N, 86°13' W 102
Indianola, Iowa, U.S. 41°21' N, 93°33' W 94
Indianola, Miss., U.S. 33°26' N, 90°40' W 103
Indianola, Nebr., U.S. 40°13' N, 100°26' W 90
Indianópolis, Braz. 19°2' S, 47°58' W 138
Indiantown, Fla., U.S. 27°1' N, 80°29' W 105
Indiga, Russ. 67°40' N, 49°3' E 169
Indigirka, river, Russ. 63°22' N, 141°33' E 160
Indija, Serb. and Mont. 45°2' N, 20°5' E 168
Indio, Calif., U.S. 33°43' N, 116°14' W 101
Indio Rico, Arg. 38°20' S, 60°53' W 139
Índios, Braz. 27°46' S, 50°11' W 138
Índios, Cachoeira dos, fall(s), Braz. 0°18' N, 63°47' W 130
Indomed Fracture Zone, Indian Ocean 40°19' S, 45°6' E 254
Indonesia 2°19' S, 115°43' E 192
Indore, India 22°43' N, 75°50' E 197
Indostán, Col. 1°45' S, 72°13' W 136
Indra, Latv. 55°52' N, 27°34' E 166
Indravati National Park, India 19°13' N, 80°24' E 188
Indre, river, Fr. 46°59' N, 1°4' E 165
Indus Fan, Arabian Sea 19°1' N, 65°10' E 254
Indus, river, China 34°4' N, 77°38' E 190
Indus, river, Pak. 35°18' N, 74°13' E 186
Indwe, S. Af. 31°29' S, 27°19' E 227
I-n-Ebeggi, spring, Alg. 21°42' N, 6°36' E 222
İnebolu, Turk. 41°58' N, 33°44' E 156
I-n-Échaï, spring, Mali 20°2' N, 2°7' W 222
İnegöl, Turk. 40°4' N, 29°29' E 156
I-n-Eker, Alg. 24°1' N, 5°5' E 214
I-n-Emzel, spring, Mali 19°25' N, 0°46' E 222
Ineu, Rom. 46°25' N, 21°53' E 168
Ineu, peak, Rom. 47°30' N, 24°48' E 156
Inez, Ky., U.S. 37°51' N, 82°33' W 96
Inezgane, Mor. 30°21' N, 9°33' W 214
I-n-Ezzane, spring, Alg. 23°30' N, 11°12' E 214
Infieles, Punta, Chile 26°22' S, 71°29' W 132
Infiernillo, Mex. 18°17' N, 101°53' W 114
Infiernillo, Presa del, lake, Mex. 18°38' N, 102°2' W 114
Infiesto, Sp. 43°20' N, 5°24' W 150
Ingal, Niger 16°48' N, 6°55' E 222
Ingalls, Ark., U.S. 33°22' N, 92°10' W 103
Ingalls, Mich., U.S. 45°22' N, 87°36' W 94
Ingalls Lake, Can. 60°18' N, 105°31' W 108
Ingalls, Mount, Calif., U.S. 39°58' N, 120°43' W 90
Ingawa, Nig. 12°38' N, 8°2' E 222
Ingende, Dem. Rep. of the Congo 0°16' N, 18°54' E 218
Ingeniero Guillermo N. Juárez, Arg. 23°54' S, 61°53' W 132
Ingeniero Luiggi, Arg. 35°25' S, 64°27' W 134
Ingenika, river, Can. 56°43' N, 125°52' W 108
Ingersoll, Can. 43°2' N, 80°53' W 102
Ingettolgoy, Mongolia 49°24' N, 104°0' E 198
Ingichka, Uzb. 39°44' N, 66°0' E 197
Ingleborough, peak, U.K. 54°10' N, 2°25' W 162
Inglefield Land, Den. 78°46' N, 68°29' W 246
Ingleside, Tex., U.S. 27°51' N, 97°13' W 96
Inglewood, Calif., U.S. 33°58' N, 118°22' W 101
Inglis, Fla., U.S. 29°1' N, 82°40' W 105
Inglis Island, Austral. 12°16' S, 136°22' E 230
Ingololo, Dem. Rep. of the Congo 5°49' S, 16°49' E 218
Ingonish, Can. 46°41' N, 60°23' W 111
Ingraj Bazar, India 24°57' N, 88°8' E 197
Ingram, Tex., U.S. 30°4' N, 99°14' W 92
Ingrid Christensen Coast, Antarctica 72°60' S, 75°59' E 248
I-n-Guezzâm, spring, Alg. 19°34' N, 5°42' E 222
Ingushetiya, adm. division, Russ. 43°15' N, 44°35' E 195
Inhaca, Mozambique 25°58' S, 32°57' E 227
Inhambane, Mozambique 23°49' S, 35°25' E 227
Inhambane, adm. division, Mozambique 23°10' S, 34°36' E 220
Inhambupe, Braz. 11°46' S, 38°21' W 132
Inharrime, Mozambique 24°26' S, 35°0' E 227
Inhassôro, Mozambique 21°32' S, 35°7' E 227
Inhaúmas, Braz. 13°3' S, 44°39' W 138
I-n-Hihaou, Adrar, peak, Alg. 23°28' N, 2°26' E 214
Inhul, river, Ukr. 48°12' N, 32°11' E 156
Inhulets, river, Ukr. 47°53' N, 33°3' E 156
Inhumas, Braz. 16°22' S, 49°31' W 138
Iniesta, Sp. 39°26' N, 1°45' W 164
Inírida, river, Col. 2°13' N, 70°50' W 136
Inirida, river, Col. 3°9' N, 68°6' W 136
Inishturk, peak, Ire. 53°41' N, 10°13' W 150
I-n-Jakoh, spring, Mali 16°49' N, 2°17' E 222
Injune, Austral. 25°50' S, 148°32' E 231
Inkee, Fin. 65°44' N, 28°31' E 152
Inklin, river, Can. 58°46' N, 133°8' W 108
Inkster, Mich., U.S. 42°16' N, 83°20' W 102
Inle Lake, Myanmar 20°28' N, 96°31' E 202
Inn, river, Switz. 46°34' N, 10°2' E 167
Inner Mongolia, region, Asia 41°40' N, 103°25' E 198
Inner Pond, lake, Can. 50°6' N, 57°56' W 111
Innisfail, Austral. 17°33' S, 146°2' E 231
Innisfail, Can. 52°2' N, 113°57' W 90
Innoshima, Japan 34°18' N, 133°10' E 201
Ino, Japan 33°33' N, 133°25' E 201
Inocência, Braz. 19°47' S, 51°50' W 138
Inongo, Dem. Rep. of the Congo 1°58' S, 18°20' E 207
İnönü, Turk. 39°49' N, 30°7' E 156
Inostrantseva, Zaliv 76°16' N, 57°48' E 160
Inovo, Serb. and Mont. 43°23' N, 22°26' E 168
Inowrocław, Pol. 52°46' N, 18°15' E 152
Inquisivi, Bol. 17°1' S, 67°10' W 137
I-n-Rahr, Alg. 27°5' N, 1°54' E 214
I-n-Rhar, spring, Mali 18°17' N, 0°20' E 222
I-n-Salah, Alg. 27°13' N, 2°28' E 214
Insar, Russ. 53°50' N, 44°21' E 154
Inscription, Cape, Austral. 25°30' S, 111°26' E 230
Insein, Myanmar 16°57' N, 96°6' E 202
Inselsberg, Grosser, peak, Ger. 50°50' N, 10°25' E 167
Insjön, Nor. 60°40' N, 15°5' E 152
Insurgente José María Morelos y Pavón National Park see 23, Mex. 19°38' N, 101°11' W 112
Insurgente Miguel Hidalgo y Costilla National Park see 24, Mex. 19°14' N, 99°28' W 112
Inta, Russ. 66°1' N, 60°8' E 154
I-n-Tebezas, spring, Mali 17°49' N, 1°55' E 222
Intendente Alvear, Arg. 35°16' S, 63°38' W 139
International Falls, Minn., U.S. 48°34' N, 93°28' W 106
Interview Island, India 12°43' N, 91°37' E 188
Inthanon, Doi, peak, Thai. 18°35' N, 98°23' E 202
I-n-Tileit, spring, Mali 15°26' N, 0°25' E 222
Intiyaco, Arg. 28°39' S, 60°6' W 139
Intuto, Peru 3°34' S, 74°46' W 136
Inukjuak, Can. 58°28' N, 78°9' W 106
Inuvik, Can. 68°15' N, 133°59' W 106
Inuya, river, Peru 10°34' S, 72°53' W 137
Inuyama, Japan 35°21' N, 136°57' E 201
Invercargill, N.Z. 46°27' S, 168°22' E 240
Invermere, Can. 50°29' N, 116°2' W 108
Inverness, Can. 46°13' N, 61°19' W 111
Inverness, Fla., U.S. 28°50' N, 82°21' W 105
Inverness, Miss., U.S. 33°19' N, 90°36' W 103
Inverness, U.K. 57°27' N, 4°15' W 143
Investigator Group, islands, Great Australian Bight 34°18' S, 131°19' E 230
Investigator Ridge, Indian Ocean 11°21' S, 98°10' E 254
Inya, Russ. 50°29' N, 86°43' E 184
Inyati, Zimb. 19°42' S, 28°50' E 224
Inyo, Mount, Calif., U.S. 36°43' N, 118°2' W 101
Inyo Mountains, Calif., U.S. 37°11' N, 118°9' W 101
Inza, Russ. 53°49' N, 46°26' E 154
Inzana Lake, Can. 54°57' N, 124°56' W 108
Inzhavino, Russ. 52°19' N, 42°25' E 158
I-n-Ziza, spring, Alg. 23°32' N, 2°36' E 214
Ioánina, Gr. 39°40' N, 20°50' E 156
Ioaniş, Rom. 46°40' N, 22°18' E 168
Iola, Kans., U.S. 37°53' N, 95°24' W 96
Iona, Idaho, U.S. 43°32' N, 111°56' W 90
Iona National Park, Angola 17°9' S, 11°53' E 220
Ione, Calif., U.S. 38°20' N, 120°57' W 100
Ione, Nev., U.S. 38°57' N, 117°36' W 90
Ione, Oreg., U.S. 45°29' N, 119°50' W 90
Ione, Wash., U.S. 48°43' N, 117°26' W 108
Iongo, Angola 9°13' S, 17°44' E 218
Ionia, Mich., U.S. 42°58' N, 85°4' W 102
Ionian Sea 37°56' N, 17°35' E 156
Iónioi Nísoi, adm. division, Gr. 38°37' N, 20°34' E 156
Ionn N'yug Oayv, Gora, peak, Russ. 68°18' N, 28°48' E 152
Iori, river, Ga. 41°8' N, 46°0' E 195
Íos, island, Gr. 36°35' N, 25°24' E 180
Iota, La., U.S. 30°18' N, 92°30' W 103
Iouik, Mauritania 19°53' N, 16°18' W 222
Iowa, La., U.S. 30°12' N, 93°1' W 103
Iowa, adm. division, Iowa, U.S. 42°18' N, 93°59' W 94
Iowa City, Iowa, U.S. 41°39' N, 91°31' W 94
Iowa Falls, Iowa, U.S. 42°30' N, 93°15' W 94
Iowa, river, Iowa, U.S. 41°52' N, 92°57' W 80
Ipameri, Braz. 17°45' S, 48°12' W 138
Ipamu, Dem. Rep. of the Congo 4°10' S, 19°34' E 218
Ipanema, Braz. 19°54' S, 41°44' W 138
Iparia, Peru 9°19' S, 74°28' W 137
Ipatovo, Russ. 45°43' N, 42°44' E 158
Ipiales, Col. 0°50' N, 77°49' W 136
Ipiaú, Braz. 14°10' S, 39°42' W 138
Ipiķi, Latv. 57°59' N, 25°12' E 166
Ipiranga, Braz. 3°10' S, 66°6' W 136
Ipiranga, Braz. 3°1' S, 69°36' W 136
Ipiranga, Braz. 25°3' S, 50°36' W 138
Ípiros, adm. division, Gr. 39°40' N, 20°40' E 156
Ipitinga, river, Braz. 0°21' N, 53°53' W 130
Ipixuna, river, Braz. 7°7' S, 73°20' W 130
Ipoh, Malaysia 4°37' N, 101°3' E 196
Ipole, Tanzania 5°46' S, 32°45' E 224
Iporá, Braz. 16°28' S, 51°8' W 138
Ippy, Cen. Af. Rep. 6°15' N, 21°12' E 218
Ipsala, Turk. 40°55' N, 26°21' E 156
Ipsalio, Óros, peak, Gr. 40°42' N, 24°34' E 156
Ipswich, Mass., U.S. 42°40' N, 70°51' W 104
Ipswich, S. Dak., U.S. 45°25' N, 99°3' W 90
Ipswich, U.K. 52°3' N, 1°9' E 162
Ipu, Braz. 4°19' S, 40°44' W 132
Ipueiras, Braz. 4°33' S, 40°45' W 132
Ipun, Isla, island, Chile 44°31' S, 75°24' W 134
Ipupiara, Braz. 11°50' S, 42°38' W 132
Iput', river, Russ. 52°41' N, 31°48' E 154
Iqaluit, Can. 63°42' N, 69°1' W 106
Iqe, China 38°4' N, 95°0' E 188
Iqe, river, China 38°13' N, 95°23' E 188
Iquique, Chile 20°15' S, 70°10' W 137
Iquitos, Peru 3°48' S, 73°14' W 136
Iraan, Tex., U.S. 30°53' N, 101°53' W 92
Īrafshān, Iran 26°44' N, 61°57' E 182
Iraí, Braz. 27°13' S, 53°17' W 139
Iraiti, Braz. 0°12' N, 69°26' W 136
Iráklio (Candia), Gr. 35°19' N, 25°7' E 156
Iran 32°49' N, 52°32' E 180
Īrānshahr, Iran 27°12' N, 60°41' E 182
Irapuato, Mex. 20°39' N, 101°23' W 114
Iraq 32°28' N, 43°26' E 180
Irati, Braz. 25°28' S, 50°37' W 138
Irayel', Russ. 64°22' N, 55°6' E 154
Irazú, Volcán, C.R. 9°57' N, 83°55' W 115
Irazusta, Arg. 32°56' S, 58°55' W 139
Irbe Strait 57°43' N, 21°29' E 152
Irbid, Jordan 32°32' N, 35°51' E 180
Irbid (Arbela), Jordan 32°32' N, 35°51' E 194
Irbit, Russ. 57°40' N, 62°58' E 154
Irebu, Dem. Rep. of the Congo 0°39' N, 17°43' E 218
Irecê, Braz. 11°21' S, 41°54' W 132
Ireland 53°17' N, 8°19' W 150
Ireland, Mount, Oreg., U.S. 44°48' N, 118°25' W 90
Ireng, river, South America 4°26' N, 60°6' W 130
Iriba, Chad 15°6' N, 22°14' E 216
Irié, Guinea 8°14' N, 9°11' W 222
Irig, Serb. and Mont. 45°5' N, 19°51' E 168
Iriga, Philippines 13°25' N, 123°25' E 203
Iriklinskiy, Russ. 51°39' N, 58°38' E 154
Irimi, Indonesia 1°58' S, 133°11' E 192
Iringa, Tanzania 7°46' S, 35°42' E 224
Iringa, adm. division, Tanzania 9°28' S, 34°6' E 220
Iriomote, island, Japan 23°59' N, 122°47' E 190
Iriomote Jima, island, Japan 24°23' N, 123°23' E 198
Iriri Novo, river, Braz. 9°52' S, 53°23' W 130
Iriri, river, Braz. 7°21' S, 53°36' W 132
Irish Mountain, Oreg., U.S. 43°50' N, 122°3' W 90
Irish Sea 52°27' N, 5°55' W 150
Irkutsk, Russ. 52°24' N, 104°22' E 190
Irkutsk, adm. division, Russ. 57°13' N, 105°42' E 160
Irma, Can. 52°54' N, 111°14' W 108
Iro, Lac, lake, Chad 10°5' N, 18°58' E 216
Irō Zaki, Japan 34°28' N, 138°49' E 201
Iron Mountain, Oreg., U.S. 43°15' N, 119°32' W 90
Iron Mountain, Oreg., U.S. 42°40' N, 124°14' W 90
Iron Mountains, Calif., U.S. 34°13' N, 115°16' W 101
Iron Range, Austral. 12°51' S, 143°20' E 231
Iron Range National Park, Coral Sea 12°43' S, 143°0' E 238
Iron River, Mich., U.S. 46°5' N, 88°39' W 94
Iron River, Wis., U.S. 46°33' N, 91°25' W 94
Irons, Mich., U.S. 44°8' N, 85°55' W 102
Ironside Mountain, Oreg., U.S. 44°13' N, 118°14' W 90
Ironton, Minn., U.S. 46°27' N, 93°59' W 94
Ironton, Mo., U.S. 37°35' N, 90°38' W 96
Ironton, Ohio, U.S. 38°31' N, 82°40' W 94
Iroquois Falls, Can. 48°45' N, 80°41' W 94
Iroquois, river, Can. 68°9' N, 130°23' W 98
Iroquois, river, Ind., U.S. 40°49' N, 87°44' W 102
Írottk o, peak, Hung. 47°20' N, 16°25' E 168
Irpin', Ukr. 50°33' N, 30°22' E 158
Irrawady see Ayeyarwady, river, Myanmar 21°54' N, 95°42' E 202
Irrel, Ger. 49°50' N, 6°28' E 167
Irrua, Nig. 6°50' N, 6°13' E 222

Irshava, *Ukr.* 48°17′ N, 23°1′ E **152**
Irtysh, *Russ.* 54°27′ N, 74°28′ E **184**
Irtysh, river, *Russ.* 59°32′ N, 69°13′ E **169**
Irumu, *Dem. Rep. of the Congo* 1°28′ N, 29°49′ E **224**
Iruña see Pamplona, *Sp.* 42°47′ N, 1°40′ W **164**
Irupana, *Bol.* 16°27′ S, 67°25′ W **137**
Irurtzun, *Sp.* 42°54′ N, 1°50′ W **164**
Iruya, *Arg.* 22°41′ S, 65°13′ W **137**
Iruya, river, *Arg.* 22°37′ S, 65°13′ W **137**
Irvine, *Calif., U.S.* 33°41′ N, 117°49′ W **101**
Irvine, *Can.* 49°57′ N, 110°15′ W **90**
Irvine, *Ky., U.S.* 37°41′ N, 83°59′ W **96**
Irvine, *U.K.* 55°36′ N, 4°40′ W **150**
Irvines Landing, *Can.* 49°38′ N, 124°2′ W **100**
Is, *Russ.* 58°49′ N, 59°44′ E **154**
Is, Jebel, peak, *Sudan* 21°48′ N, 35°36′ E **182**
Isa, *Nig.* 13°11′ N, 6°21′ E **222**
Isa Khel, *Pak.* 32°41′ N, 71°20′ E **186**
Isaba, *Sp.* 42°51′ N, 0°55′ E **164**
Isabel, *S. Dak., U.S.* 45°22′ N, 101°27′ W **90**
Isabela, *Philippines* 6°41′ N, 121°56′ E **203**
Isabela, *Philippines* 10°11′ N, 122°57′ E **203**
Isabela, Cabo, *Dom. Rep.* 20°0′ N, 71°35′ W **116**
Isabela, Isla, island, *Ecua.* 1°17′ S, 92°8′ W **130**
Isabella, *Minn., U.S.* 47°36′ N, 91°23′ W **94**
Isabelle, Point, *Mich., U.S.* 47°8′ N, 87°56′ W **94**
Isaccea, *Rom.* 45°15′ N, 28°26′ E **156**
Isachsen, *Can.* 78°47′ N, 103°28′ W **246**
Isachsen Mount, *Antarctica* 72°18′ S, 26°0′ E **248**
Ísafjörður, *Ice.* 66°8′ N, 23°9′ W **246**
Isagarh, *India* 24°50′ N, 77°54′ E **197**
Isahaya, *Japan* 32°51′ N, 130°2′ E **201**
Isaka, *Tanzania* 3°54′ S, 32°55′ E **224**
Isaki, *Russ.* 56°39′ N, 28°35′ E **166**
Isalo, Massif de l', *Madagascar* 23°10′ S, 44°24′ E **220**
Isana, river, *Col.* 1°48′ N, 69°4′ W **136**
Isangano National Park, *Zambia* 11°21′ S, 30°2′ E **224**
Isangi, *Dem. Rep. of the Congo* 0°45′ N, 24°7′ E **224**
Isangila, *Dem. Rep. of the Congo* 5°18′ S, 13°33′ E **218**
Isanlu Makutu, *Nig.* 8°15′ N, 5°45′ E **222**
Isar, river, *Ger.* 48°35′ N, 12°46′ E **152**
Isarog, Mount, *Philippines* 13°40′ N, 123°16′ E **203**
Isbister, river, *Can.* 53°41′ N, 94°48′ W **108**
Íscar, *Sp.* 41°20′ N, 4°32′ W **150**
Iscayachi, *Bol.* 21°33′ S, 65°2′ W **137**
Ischia, *It.* 40°44′ N, 13°56′ E **156**
Isdu, island, *Maldives* 1°56′ N, 73°36′ E **188**
Ise, *Japan* 34°28′ N, 136°43′ E **201**
Ise Wan 34°39′ N, 136°34′ E **201**
Iseo, *It.* 45°39′ N, 10°2′ E **167**
Isère, Pointe, *Fr.* 5°48′ N, 53°50′ W **130**
Isère, river, *Fr.* 44°59′ N, 5°2′ E **165**
Isesaki, *Japan* 36°18′ N, 139°13′ E **201**
Ise-Shima National Park, *Japan* 34°19′ N, 136°29′ E **201**
Iset', river, *Russ.* 56°7′ N, 64°54′ E **184**
Iseyin, *Nig.* 8°1′ N, 3°37′ E **222**
Isfahan see Eşfahān, *Iran* 32°40′ N, 51°38′ E **180**
Isfara, *Taj.* 40°8′ N, 70°36′ E **197**
Ishëm, *Alban.* 41°32′ N, 19°34′ E **168**
Isheyevka, *Russ.* 54°25′ N, 48°23′ E **154**
Ishigaki, *Japan* 24°16′ N, 124°9′ E **198**
Ishigaki Shima, island, *Japan* 24°35′ N, 123°54′ E **198**
Ishikawa, *Japan* 37°8′ N, 140°27′ E **201**
Ishikawa, adm. division, *Japan* 36°16′ N, 136°18′ E **201**
Ishim, *Russ.* 56°8′ N, 69°36′ E **184**
Ishim, river, *Russ.* 56°1′ N, 70°27′ E **184**
Ishimbay, *Russ.* 53°28′ N, 56°4′ E **154**
Ishinomaki, *Japan* 38°33′ N, 141°5′ E **190**
Ishioka, *Japan* 36°10′ N, 140°17′ E **201**
Ishkuman, *Pak.* 36°30′ N, 73°47′ E **186**
Ishpatina Ridge, *Can.* 47°20′ N, 80°48′ W **94**
Ishpeming, *Mich., U.S.* 46°29′ N, 87°40′ W **110**
Ishtixon, *Uzb.* 40°0′ N, 66°33′ E **197**
Isiboro, river, *Bol.* 16°16′ S, 65°15′ W **137**
Isiboro Sécure National Park, *Bol.* 16°2′ S, 66°19′ W **137**
Isidora, *Col.* 6°7′ N, 68°31′ W **136**
Işık Dağı, peak, *Turk.* 40°40′ N, 32°40′ E **156**
Isikveren, *Turk.* 37°23′ N, 42°58′ E **195**
Isil'kul', *Russ.* 54°52′ N, 71°18′ E **184**
Isiolo, *Kenya* 0°18′ N, 37°36′ E **224**
Isiro (Paulis), *Dem. Rep. of the Congo* 2°43′ N, 27°39′ E **224**
İskenderun, *Turk.* 36°33′ N, 36°13′ E **180**
İskilip, *Turk.* 40°44′ N, 34°28′ E **156**
Iskitim, *Russ.* 54°39′ N, 83°17′ E **184**
Iskrets, *Bulg.* 42°59′ N, 23°14′ E **168**
Iskŭr, river, *Bulg.* 43°21′ N, 24°5′ E **156**
Iskushuban, *Somalia* 10°11′ N, 50°15′ E **216**
Iskut, river, *Can.* 57°9′ N, 130°34′ W **108**
Isla de Lobos, oil field, *Mex.* 21°20′ N, 97°12′ W **114**
Isla Guamblin National Park, site, *Chile* 44°51′ S, 75°19′ W **134**
Isla Isabel National Park, *Mex.* 21°51′ N, 106°1′ W **112**
Isla Mujeres, *Mex.* 21°17′ N, 86°50′ W **116**
Isla Verde, *Arg.* 33°15′ S, 62°24′ W **139**
Islamabad, *Pak.* 33°37′ N, 73°2′ E **186**
Islamkot, *Pak.* 24°43′ N, 70°11′ E **186**
Islamorada, *Fla., U.S.* 24°55′ N, 80°38′ W **105**
Island Falls, *Me., U.S.* 46°0′ N, 68°16′ W **94**
Island Grove, *Fla., U.S.* 29°27′ N, 82°8′ W **105**
Island Lake, *Can.* 53°51′ N, 94°42′ W **108**
Island Lake, *Can.* 53°58′ N, 95°7′ W **108**
Island Lake, *Minn., U.S.* 47°48′ N, 94°31′ W **90**
Island Park, *Idaho, U.S.* 44°25′ N, 111°22′ W **90**
Isle of Hope, *Ga., U.S.* 31°58′ N, 81°4′ W **96**
Isle Pierre, *Can.* 53°56′ N, 123°16′ W **108**
Isle, river, *Fr.* 45°30′ N, 1°3′ E **165**
Isleton, *Calif., U.S.* 38°9′ N, 121°37′ W **100**
Ismâ'ilîya, *Egypt* 30°35′ N, 32°15′ E **194**
Ismoili Somoni, Qullai (Communism Peak), *Taj.* 39°3′ N, 72°1′ E **197**
Isna, *Egypt* 25°16′ N, 32°29′ E **182**
Isoanala, *Madagascar* 23°48′ S, 45°46′ E **220**
Isojoki, *Fin.* 62°6′ N, 21°55′ E **152**
Isoka, *Zambia* 10°11′ S, 32°36′ E **224**
Isola, *Miss., U.S.* 33°14′ N, 90°36′ W **103**
Isola del Cantone, *It.* 44°39′ N, 8°57′ E **167**
Isola della Scala, *It.* 45°16′ N, 11°0′ E **167**
Isola delle Correnti, Capo, *It.* 36°32′ N, 15°5′ E **156**
Isola Peak, *Can.* 50°6′ N, 114°37′ W **90**
Isparta, *Turk.* 37°44′ N, 30°32′ E **156**
Ispica, *It.* 36°46′ N, 14°53′ E **156**
İspir, *Turk.* 40°29′ N, 41°0′ E **195**
Ispra, *It.* 45°49′ N, 8°36′ E **167**
Israel 31°0′ N, 34°41′ E **194**
Israelite Bay 33°48′ S, 122°33′ E **230**
Isratu, island, *Eritrea* 16°21′ N, 39°48′ E **182**
Issa, river, *Russ.* 56°18′ N, 28°20′ E **166**
Issano, *Guyana* 5°46′ N, 59°30′ W **130**
Issel, river, *Ger.* 51°47′ N, 6°29′ E **167**
Issia, *Côte d'Ivoire* 6°23′ N, 6°35′ W **222**
Issoudun, *Fr.* 46°56′ N, 1°59′ E **150**
Issus, battle, *Turk.* 36°53′ N, 36°4′ E **156**
Istállósko, peak, *Hung.* 48°2′ N, 20°22′ E **168**
İstanbul (Constantinople), *Turk.* 41°1′ N, 28°55′ E **156**
Istaravshan (Üroteppa), *Taj.* 39°53′ N, 69°0′ E **197**
Istmina, *Col.* 5°10′ N, 76°42′ W **136**
Isto, Mount, *Alas., U.S.* 69°5′ N, 144°8′ W **98**
Istok, *Serb. and Mont.* 42°46′ N, 20°29′ E **168**
Istokpoga, Lake, *Fla., U.S.* 27°24′ N, 81°25′ W **105**
Istres, *Fr.* 43°29′ N, 4°58′ E **150**
Istria, *Croatia* 45°16′ N, 13°33′ E **167**
Isulan, *Philippines* 6°37′ N, 124°37′ E **203**
Isyangulovo, *Russ.* 52°12′ N, 56°27′ E **154**
Itá, *Parag.* 25°31′ S, 57°21′ W **132**
Itabaiana, *Braz.* 10°37′ S, 37°22′ W **132**
Itabaianinha, *Braz.* 11°17′ S, 37°47′ W **132**
Itabapoana, *Braz.* 21°20′ S, 41°1′ W **138**
Itaberaba, *Braz.* 12°33′ S, 40°21′ W **132**
Itaberaí, *Braz.* 16°6′ S, 49°49′ W **138**
Itabira, *Braz.* 19°39′ S, 43°13′ W **138**
Itabirito, *Braz.* 20°21′ S, 43°48′ W **138**
Itabuna, *Braz.* 14°27′ S, 39°36′ W **123**
Itacaiúnas, river, *Braz.* 5°58′ S, 50°40′ W **130**
Itacajá, *Braz.* 8°22′ S, 47°46′ W **130**
Itacarambi, *Braz.* 15°8′ S, 44°9′ W **138**
Itacoatiara, *Braz.* 3°9′ S, 58°33′ W **130**
Itaeté, *Braz.* 13°1′ S, 41°1′ W **138**
Itaguari, river, *Braz.* 14°36′ S, 45°16′ W **138**
Itagüí, *Col.* 6°11′ N, 75°41′ W **136**
Itahuania, *Peru* 12°38′ S, 71°9′ W **137**
Itaí, *Braz.* 23°25′ S, 49°8′ W **138**
Itaituba, *Braz.* 4°15′ S, 56°1′ W **130**
Itajaí, *Braz.* 26°56′ S, 48°40′ W **138**
Itajimirim, *Braz.* 16°5′ S, 39°36′ W **138**
Itajubá, *Braz.* 22°24′ S, 45°30′ W **138**
Itaka, *Tanzania* 8°54′ S, 32°48′ E **224**
Italia, Monte, peak, *Chile* 54°48′ S, 69°21′ W **134**
Italy 42°58′ N, 11°46′ E **156**
Itamaraju, *Braz.* 17°11′ S, 39°33′ W **138**
Itamarandiba, *Braz.* 17°53′ S, 42°55′ W **138**
Itambacuri, *Braz.* 18°3′ S, 41°42′ W **138**
Itambé, *Braz.* 15°18′ S, 40°40′ W **138**
Itambé, Pico de, peak, *Braz.* 18°27′ S, 43°24′ W **138**
Itanagar, *India* 27°7′ N, 93°46′ E **188**
Itanhaém, *Braz.* 24°11′ S, 46°47′ W **138**
Itanhauã, river, *Braz.* 5°2′ S, 64°50′ W **130**
Itanhém, *Braz.* 17°9′ S, 40°20′ W **138**
Itany, river, *Suriname* 2°48′ N, 54°14′ W **130**
Itapaci, *Braz.* 14°60′ S, 49°37′ W **138**
Itapagipe, *Braz.* 19°56′ S, 49°22′ W **138**
Itaparanã, river, *Braz.* 7°28′ S, 63°50′ W **130**
Itaparica, Ilha de, island, *Braz.* 13°16′ S, 40°1′ W **132**
Itapebi, *Braz.* 15°58′ S, 39°33′ W **138**
Itapecerica, *Braz.* 20°31′ S, 45°8′ W **138**
Itapecuru Mirim, *Braz.* 3°25′ S, 44°22′ W **132**
Itapemirim, *Braz.* 21°5′ S, 40°52′ W **138**
Itaperina, Pointe, *Madagascar* 25°18′ S, 47°14′ E **220**
Itaperuna, *Braz.* 21°13′ S, 41°53′ W **138**
Itapetinga, *Braz.* 15°18′ S, 40°18′ W **138**
Itapetininga, *Braz.* 23°35′ S, 48°5′ W **138**
Itapeva, *Braz.* 23°58′ S, 48°53′ W **138**
Itapiranga, *Braz.* 27°9′ S, 53°44′ W **139**
Itápolis, *Braz.* 21°34′ S, 48°49′ W **138**
Itaporanga, *Braz.* 23°43′ S, 49°31′ W **138**
Itapuranga, *Braz.* 15°35′ S, 49°58′ W **138**
Itaqui, *Braz.* 29°11′ S, 56°36′ W **139**
Itararé, *Braz.* 24°7′ S, 49°19′ W **138**
Itararé, river, *Braz.* 24°16′ S, 49°13′ W **138**
Itarsi, *India* 22°37′ N, 77°46′ E **197**
Itarumã, *Braz.* 18°44′ S, 51°29′ W **138**
Itasca, *Tex., U.S.* 32°8′ N, 97°9′ W **92**
Itasca, Lake, *Minn., U.S.* 47°9′ N, 96°14′ W **82**
Itatá, river, *Braz.* 4°13′ S, 52°7′ W **132**
Itatí, *Arg.* 27°17′ S, 58°13′ W **139**
Itatupã, *Braz.* 0°36′ N, 51°14′ W **130**
Itaú, *Bol.* 21°41′ S, 63°55′ W **137**
Itaúba, *Braz.* 10°55′ S, 55°8′ W **123**
Itaúna, *Braz.* 20°5′ S, 44°34′ W **138**
Itaúna, *Braz.* 2°59′ S, 66°5′ W **136**
Itaúnas, *Braz.* 18°24′ S, 39°44′ W **138**
Itbayat, island, *Philippines* 20°44′ N, 121°21′ E **198**
Itende, *Tanzania* 6°44′ S, 34°23′ E **224**
Itezhi-Tezhi, Lake, *Zambia* 15°55′ S, 25°14′ E **224**
Ithaca, *Mich., U.S.* 43°16′ N, 84°37′ W **102**
Ithaca, *N.Y., U.S.* 42°26′ N, 76°31′ W **94**
Itigi, *Tanzania* 5°39′ S, 34°29′ E **224**
Itimbiri, river, *Dem. Rep. of the Congo* 2°20′ N, 23°1′ E **218**
Itinga, *Braz.* 16°36′ S, 41°50′ W **138**
Itiquines, *Col.* 0°38′ N, 73°15′ W **136**
Itiquira, *Braz.* 17°12′ S, 54°9′ W **132**
Itiquira, river, *Braz.* 17°15′ S, 56°29′ W **132**
Itiruçu, *Braz.* 13°30′ S, 40°10′ W **138**
Itiúba, Serra de, *Braz.* 10°6′ S, 40°31′ W **132**
Itō, *Japan* 34°57′ N, 139°5′ E **201**
Itobo, *Tanzania* 4°12′ S, 33°1′ E **224**
Itoigawa, *Japan* 37°2′ N, 137°51′ E **201**
Itoko, *Dem. Rep. of the Congo* 0°60′ N, 21°46′ E **218**
Iton, river, *Fr.* 49°7′ N, 1°7′ E **163**
Itonamas, river, *Bol.* 12°30′ S, 64°25′ W **137**
Itta Bena, *Miss., U.S.* 33°28′ N, 90°20′ W **103**
Ittoqqortoormiit (Scoresbysund), *Den.* 70°26′ N, 21°53′ W **246**
Itu, *Braz.* 23°17′ S, 47°21′ W **138**
Itu, river, *Braz.* 29°20′ S, 55°23′ W **139**
Ituaçu, *Braz.* 13°51′ S, 41°19′ W **138**
Ituí, river, *Braz.* 4°59′ S, 70°47′ W **130**
Ituiutaba, *Braz.* 19°1′ S, 49°31′ W **138**
Itula, *Dem. Rep. of the Congo* 3°32′ S, 27°49′ E **224**
Itumbiara, *Braz.* 18°28′ S, 49°15′ W **138**
Ituna, *Can.* 51°9′ N, 103°31′ W **90**
Ituni, *Guyana* 5°24′ N, 58°18′ W **130**
Itupiranga, *Braz.* 5°12′ S, 49°19′ W **130**
Iturama, *Braz.* 19°43′ S, 50°14′ W **138**
Iturbe, *Arg.* 22°60′ S, 65°21′ W **137**
Iturbe, *Parag.* 26°2′ S, 56°28′ W **139**
Iturbide, *Mex.* 24°42′ N, 99°54′ W **114**
Ituri, river, *Dem. Rep. of the Congo* 1°41′ N, 27°21′ E **224**
Iturup, island, *Russ.* 44°16′ N, 147°11′ E **190**
Ituverava, *Braz.* 20°21′ S, 47°50′ W **138**
Ituxi, river, *Braz.* 7°58′ S, 65°3′ W **130**
Ituzaingó, *Arg.* 27°37′ S, 56°40′ W **139**
Itzehoe, *Ger.* 53°55′ N, 9°31′ E **150**
Iuka, *Miss., U.S.* 34°47′ N, 88°12′ W **96**
Iul'tin, *Russ.* 67°49′ N, 178°46′ W **98**
Iulúti, *Mozambique* 15°53′ S, 39°2′ E **224**
Iúna, *Braz.* 20°22′ S, 41°35′ W **138**
Iutica, *Braz.* 1°4′ N, 69°31′ W **136**
Ivád, *Hung.* 48°1′ N, 20°4′ E **168**
Ivaí, river, *Braz.* 23°19′ S, 53°24′ W **138**
Ivaipora, *Braz.* 24°16′ S, 51°43′ W **138**
Ivalo, *Fin.* 68°37′ N, 27°33′ E **160**
Ivan Gorod, *Russ.* 59°21′ N, 28°12′ E **166**
Ivan Sedlo, *Bosn. and Herzg.* 43°46′ N, 18°2′ E **168**
Ivanava, *Belarus* 52°8′ N, 25°32′ E **152**
Ivanchina, *Russ.* 60°3′ N, 54°17′ E **154**
Ivanec, *Croatia* 46°13′ N, 16°8′ E **168**
Ivangrad, *Serb. and Mont.* 42°50′ N, 19°50′ E **168**
Ivanhoe, *Austral.* 32°53′ S, 144°17′ E **231**
Ivanhoe, *Calif., U.S.* 36°23′ N, 119°14′ W **100**
Ivanhoe Lake, *Can.* 60°23′ N, 107°8′ W **108**
Ivanhoe, river, *Can.* 48°19′ N, 82°29′ W **110**
Ivanić Grad, *Croatia* 45°41′ N, 16°24′ E **168**
Ivanjica, *Serb. and Mont.* 43°34′ N, 20°13′ E **168**
Ivanjska, *Bosn. and Herzg.* 44°55′ N, 17°4′ E **168**
Ivankovo, *Croatia* 45°16′ N, 18°39′ E **168**
Ivano-Frankivs'k, *Ukr.* 48°53′ N, 24°41′ E **152**
Ivanovo, *Russ.* 57°0′ N, 40°58′ E **154**
Ivanovo, adm. division, *Russ.* 56°55′ N, 41°55′ E **154**
Ivanpah, *Calif., U.S.* 35°19′ N, 115°20′ W **101**
Ivanteyevka, *Russ.* 52°15′ N, 49°8′ E **158**
Ivatsevichy, *Belarus* 52°43′ N, 25°22′ E **152**
Ivaylovgrad, *Bulg.* 41°31′ N, 26°6′ E **156**
Ivdel', *Russ.* 60°40′ N, 60°23′ E **154**
Ivi, Cap, *Alg.* 36°6′ N, 0°8′ E **164**
Ivinheima, *Braz.* 22°12′ S, 53°33′ W **138**
Iviza see Ibiza, island, *Sp.* 39°1′ N, 6°356′ W **214**
Ivo, *Bol.* 20°29′ S, 63°28′ W **137**
Ivohibe, *Madagascar* 22°29′ S, 46°53′ E **220**
Ivón, *Bol.* 11°10′ S, 66°9′ W **137**
Ivory Coast, region, *Africa* 5°58′ N, 5°7′ W **222**
Ivory Coast see Côte d'Ivoire 7°16′ N, 7°29′ W **214**
Ivoryton, *Conn., U.S.* 41°20′ N, 72°27′ W **104**
Ivrea, *It.* 45°29′ N, 7°52′ E **167**
Ivrognes, Pointe aux, *Can.* 49°42′ N, 65°31′ W **111**
Ivujivik, *Can.* 62°22′ N, 78°2′ W **106**
Ivyanyets, *Belarus* 53°52′ N, 26°44′ E **166**
Ivydale, *W. Va., U.S.* 38°32′ N, 81°3′ W **102**
Iwaki, *Japan* 36°58′ N, 140°52′ E **201**
Iwanuma, *Japan* 38°7′ N, 140°51′ E **201**
Iwembere Steppe, *Tanzania* 4°26′ S, 33°20′ E **224**
Iwo, *Nig.* 7°42′ N, 4°11′ E **222**
Iwŏn, *N. Korea* 40°20′ N, 128°39′ E **200**
Iwye, *Belarus* 53°55′ N, 25°45′ E **166**
Ixhuatán, *Mex.* 16°21′ N, 94°30′ W **112**
Ixiamas, *Bol.* 13°47′ S, 68°8′ W **137**
Ixopo, *S. Af.* 30°11′ S, 30°3′ E **227**
Ixpalino, *Mex.* 23°52′ N, 106°39′ W **114**
Ixtapa, *Mex.* 17°39′ N, 101°36′ W **114**
Ixtapa, Punta, *Mex.* 17°29′ N, 101°52′ W **114**
Ixtapan del Oro, *Mex.* 19°14′ N, 100°16′ W **114**
Ixtlán, *Mex.* 21°1′ N, 104°22′ W **114**
Ixtoc, oil field, *Mex.* 19°36′ N, 92°21′ W **115**
'Iyal Bakhit, *Sudan* 13°25′ N, 28°43′ E **226**
Iyo, *Japan* 33°44′ N, 132°42′ E **201**
Iyo Nada 33°29′ N, 131°49′ E **201**
Iyomishima, *Japan* 33°57′ N, 133°31′ E **201**
Izabal, Lago de, lake, *Guatemala* 15°22′ N, 89°53′ W **115**
Īzad Khvāst, *Iran* 31°31′ N, 52°5′ E **180**
Izamal, *Mex.* 20°55′ N, 89°2′ W **116**
Izapa, ruin(s), *Mex.* 14°53′ N, 92°17′ W **115**
Izberbash, *Russ.* 42°31′ N, 47°52′ E **195**
Izbica, *Pol.* 50°53′ N, 23°9′ E **152**
Izdeshkovo, *Russ.* 55°7′ N, 33°41′ E **154**
Izegem, *Belg.* 50°54′ N, 3°12′ E **163**
Izhevsk, *Russ.* 56°48′ N, 53°15′ E **154**
Izhma, *Russ.* 64°59′ N, 53°53′ E **154**
Izhma, river, *Russ.* 64°25′ N, 53°38′ E **154**
Izmayil, *Ukr.* 45°21′ N, 28°51′ E **156**
İzmir (Smyrna), *Turk.* 38°24′ N, 27°8′ E **156**
İzmit see Kocaeli, *Turk.* 40°47′ N, 29°46′ E **180**
Iznalloz, *Sp.* 37°24′ N, 3°32′ W **164**
İznik, *Turk.* 40°25′ N, 29°43′ E **156**
Izobil'nyy, *Russ.* 45°22′ N, 41°37′ E **158**
Izola, *Slov.* 45°32′ N, 13°39′ E **167**
Izra', *Syr.* 32°52′ N, 36°15′ E **194**
Izsák, *Hung.* 46°48′ N, 19°22′ E **168**
Izu Trench, *North Pacific Ocean* 30°26′ N, 142°40′ E **252**
Izuhara, *Japan* 34°12′ N, 129°17′ E **201**
Izumi, *Japan* 32°4′ N, 130°22′ E **201**
Izvor, *Bulg.* 42°26′ N, 22°53′ E **168**
Izvor, *Maced.* 41°33′ N, 21°41′ E **168**
Izvori, *Serb. and Mont.* 42°36′ N, 18°45′ E **168**
Izyaslav, *Ukr.* 50°5′ N, 26°49′ E **152**
Izyum, *Ukr.* 49°14′ N, 37°20′ E **158**

J

Jaab Lake, *Can.* 51°6′ N, 83°27′ W **110**
Jaala, *Fin.* 61°3′ N, 26°29′ E **166**
Jaalanka, *Fin.* 64°33′ N, 27°7′ E **152**
Jabal os Saraj, *Afghan.* 35°7′ N, 69°16′ E **186**
Jabal Zuqar, Jazīrat, island, *Yemen* 14°5′ N, 42°31′ E **182**
Jabalan Nuşayrīyah, *Syr.* 35°39′ N, 36°8′ E **194**
Jabalar Ruwāq, *Syr.* 33°42′ N, 36°57′ E **194**
Jabalón, river, *Sp.* 38°46′ N, 3°44′ W **164**
Jabalpur, *India* 23°8′ N, 79°57′ E **197**
Jābir, *Jordan* 32°30′ N, 36°12′ E **194**
Jabiru, *Austral.* 12°38′ S, 132°52′ E **238**
Jablah, *Syr.* 35°21′ N, 35°55′ E **194**
Jablanica, *Bosn. and Herzg.* 43°39′ N, 17°43′ E **168**
Jablanica, *Maced.* 41°26′ N, 20°21′ E **168**
Jabłonowo, *Pol.* 53°23′ N, 19°10′ E **152**
Jablunkovský Průsmyk, pass, *Slovakia* 49°29′ N, 18°46′ E **152**
Jaboticabal, *Braz.* 21°13′ S, 48°21′ W **138**
Jäbrayyl, *Azerb.* 39°24′ N, 47°1′ E **195**
Jabukovac, *Serb. and Mont.* 44°20′ N, 22°23′ E **168**
Jabung, Tanjung, *Indonesia* 1°15′ S, 104°23′ E **196**
Jaca, *Sp.* 42°33′ N, 0°34′ E **164**
Jacareacanga, *Braz.* 6°13′ S, 57°40′ W **123**
Jacareí, *Braz.* 23°17′ S, 45°55′ W **138**
Jacarèzinho, *Braz.* 23°10′ S, 49°58′ W **138**
Jacinto, *Braz.* 16°10′ S, 40°20′ W **138**
Jaciparaná, *Braz.* 9°19′ S, 64°25′ W **137**
Jackfish, river, *Can.* 59°31′ N, 113°37′ W **108**
Jackhead Harbour, *Can.* 51°51′ N, 97°19′ W **108**
Jackman, *Me., U.S.* 45°38′ N, 70°14′ W **82**
Jackpot, *Nev., U.S.* 41°59′ N, 114°40′ W **90**
Jacks Mountain, *Pa., U.S.* 40°46′ N, 77°40′ W **94**
Jacks Peak, *Utah, U.S.* 38°58′ N, 112°11′ W **90**
Jacksboro, *Tex., U.S.* 33°11′ N, 98°10′ W **92**
Jackson, *Ala., U.S.* 31°30′ N, 87°54′ W **103**
Jackson, *Calif., U.S.* 38°21′ N, 120°47′ W **100**
Jackson, *Ga., U.S.* 33°16′ N, 83°58′ W **96**
Jackson, *La., U.S.* 30°49′ N, 91°13′ W **103**
Jackson, *Mich., U.S.* 42°14′ N, 84°26′ W **102**
Jackson, *Minn., U.S.* 43°35′ N, 95°1′ W **94**
Jackson, *Miss., U.S.* 32°16′ N, 90°15′ W **103**
Jackson, *Mo., U.S.* 37°23′ N, 89°40′ W **94**
Jackson, *N.H., U.S.* 44°8′ N, 71°12′ W **104**
Jackson, *Ohio, U.S.* 39°2′ N, 82°38′ W **102**
Jackson, *S.C., U.S.* 33°18′ N, 81°48′ W **96**
Jackson, *Tenn., U.S.* 35°36′ N, 88°48′ W **96**
Jackson Bay, *N.Z.* 44°1′ S, 168°37′ E **240**
Jackson Field, oil field, *Austral.* 27°37′ S, 142°0′ E **230**
Jackson Head, *N.Z.* 43°58′ S, 168°36′ E **240**
Jackson, Mount, *Antarctica* 71°28′ S, 63°49′ W **248**
Jackson Mountains, *Nev., U.S.* 41°28′ N, 118°41′ W **90**
Jackson, Ostrov, island, *Russ.* 81°23′ N, 53°33′ E **160**
Jacksonville, *Ark., U.S.* 34°51′ N, 92°8′ W **96**
Jacksonville, *Fla., U.S.* 30°20′ N, 81°40′ W **96**
Jacksonville, *N.C., U.S.* 34°45′ N, 77°26′ W **96**
Jacksonville, *Oreg., U.S.* 42°18′ N, 122°59′ W **90**
Jacksonville, *Tex., U.S.* 31°56′ N, 95°16′ W **103**
Jacksonville Beach, *Fla., U.S.* 30°16′ N, 81°24′ W **96**
Jäckvik, *Nor.* 66°22′ N, 16°56′ E **152**
Jacmel, *Haiti* 18°15′ N, 72°31′ W **116**
Jacob Lake, *Ariz., U.S.* 36°42′ N, 112°12′ W **92**
Jacobabad, *Pak.* 28°17′ N, 68°29′ E **186**
Jacobina, *Braz.* 11°11′ S, 40°32′ W **132**
Jacona, *Mex.* 19°57′ N, 102°18′ W **114**
Jacques-Cartier, Mont, peak, *Can.* 48°57′ N, 66°2′ W **94**
Jacquet River, *Can.* 47°54′ N, 66°2′ W **94**
Jacuí, *Braz.* 21°2′ S, 46°45′ W **138**
Jacumba, *Calif., U.S.* 32°37′ N, 116°11′ W **101**
Jacupiranga, *Braz.* 24°42′ S, 48°3′ W **138**
J.A.D. Jensen Nunatakker, peak, *Den.* 62°50′ N, 49°7′ W **106**
Jada, *Nig.* 8°45′ N, 12°8′ E **218**
Jaddi, Ras, *Pak.* 25°2′ N, 63°0′ E **182**
Jade, *Ger.* 53°20′ N, 8°15′ E **163**
Jadraque, *Sp.* 40°55′ N, 2°56′ W **164**
Jādū, *Lib.* 31°59′ N, 12°1′ E **216**
Jaén, *Sp.* 37°46′ N, 3°48′ W **164**
Jaffna, *Sri Lanka* 9°33′ N, 80°8′ E **173**
Jagadhri, *India* 30°12′ N, 77°20′ E **197**
Jagdalpur, *India* 19°5′ N, 82°1′ E **188**
Jagersfontein, *S. Af.* 29°47′ S, 25°26′ E **227**
Jāghir Bāzār, *Syr.* 36°52′ N, 40°56′ E **195**
Jaghjagh, river, *Syr.* 36°35′ N, 41°11′ E **195**
Jagodina, *Serb. and Mont.* 43°58′ N, 21°14′ E **168**
Jaguaquara, *Braz.* 13°33′ S, 39°59′ W **138**
Jaguarão, *Braz.* 32°31′ S, 53°24′ W **139**
Jaguari, river, *Braz.* 29°45′ S, 54°40′ W **134**
Jaguariaíva, *Braz.* 24°18′ S, 49°43′ W **138**
Jahanabad, *India* 25°11′ N, 84°59′ E **197**
Jahorina, peak, *Bosn. and Herzg.* 43°42′ N, 18°30′ E **168**
Jahrom, *Iran* 28°33′ N, 53°34′ E **196**
Jaicós, *Braz.* 7°22′ S, 41°8′ W **132**
Jaigarh, *India* 17°17′ N, 73°13′ E **188**
Jailolo, *Indonesia* 1°4′ N, 127°25′ E **192**
Jaina, ruin(s), *Mex.* 20°11′ N, 90°39′ W **115**
Jaipur, *India* 26°54′ N, 75°49′ E **186**
Jaisalmer, *India* 26°55′ N, 70°58′ E **186**
Jajarkot, *Nepal* 28°41′ N, 82°11′ E **197**
Jājarm, *Iran* 36°56′ N, 56°24′ E **180**
Jajce, *Bosn. and Herzg.* 44°21′ N, 17°15′ E **168**
Jajiri, *Niger* 13°38′ N, 11°26′ E **222**
Jajpur Road, *India* 20°56′ N, 86°6′ E **188**
Ják, *Hung.* 47°8′ N, 16°34′ E **168**
Jakar, *Bhutan* 27°31′ N, 90°42′ E **197**
Jakarta, *Indonesia* 6°22′ S, 106°14′ E **238**
Jakes Corner, *Can.* 60°21′ N, 134°1′ W **98**
Jákfa, *Hung.* 47°18′ N, 16°58′ E **168**
Jakhal, *India* 29°47′ N, 75°49′ E **197**
Jakhau, *India* 23°13′ N, 68°43′ E **186**
Jakobshavn see Ilulissat, *Den.* 69°11′ N, 50°60′ W **106**
Jakobstad (Pietarsaari), *Fin.* 63°39′ N, 22°39′ E **152**
Jakupica, *Maced.* 41°43′ N, 21°22′ E **168**
Jal, *N. Mex., U.S.* 32°6′ N, 103°12′ W **92**
Jalaaqsi, *Somalia* 3°23′ N, 45°36′ E **218**
Jalaid Qi (Inder), *China* 46°41′ N, 122°53′ E **198**
Jalālābād, *Afghan.* 34°26′ N, 70°30′ E **186**
Jalal-Abad, *Kyrg.* 40°55′ N, 72°59′ E **197**
Jalán, river, *Hond.* 14°17′ N, 86°43′ W **115**
Jalapa, *Guatemala* 14°38′ N, 89°60′ W **115**
Jalapa, *Mex.* 17°43′ N, 92°49′ W **115**
Jalasjärvi, *Fin.* 62°29′ N, 22°45′ E **152**
Jalcocotán, *Mex.* 21°29′ N, 105°8′ W **114**
Jales, *Braz.* 20°12′ S, 50°36′ W **138**
Jalesar, *India* 27°25′ N, 78°19′ E **197**
Jaleswar, *India* 21°49′ N, 87°13′ E **197**
Jalgaon, *India* 21°1′ N, 75°33′ E **188**
Jalingo, *Nig.* 8°51′ N, 11°20′ E **222**
Jalisco, *Mex.* 21°26′ N, 104°53′ W **114**
Jalisco, adm. division, *Mex.* 20°33′ N, 104°13′ W **114**
Jalitah Island, *Tun.* 37°31′ N, 7°53′ E **214**
Jalkot, *Pak.* 35°17′ N, 73°23′ E **186**
Jalna, *India* 19°50′ N, 75°52′ E **188**
Jalor, *India* 25°19′ N, 72°38′ E **186**
Jalostotitlán, *Mex.* 21°10′ N, 102°29′ W **114**
Jałowka, *Pol.* 53°1′ N, 23°54′ E **154**
Jalpa, *Mex.* 18°10′ N, 93°5′ W **112**
Jalpa, *Mex.* 21°37′ N, 102°60′ W **114**
Jalpaiguri, *India* 26°26′ N, 88°40′ E **197**
Jalpan, *Mex.* 21°10′ N, 99°33′ W **114**
Jáltipan, *Mex.* 17°57′ N, 94°44′ W **114**
Jālū, *Lib.* 29°1′ N, 21°30′ E **216**
Jaluit Atoll, *Marshall Islands* 6°0′ N, 170°0′ E **242**
Jam, *Iran* 27°55′ N, 52°22′ E **196**
Jamaame, *Somalia* 2°119′ N, 42°46′ E **218**
Jamaica 18°0′ N, 78°0′ W **118**
Jämaja, *Est.* 58°0′ N, 22°3′ E **166**
Jamalpur, *Bangladesh* 24°53′ N, 89°54′ E **197**
Jaman Pass, *Taj.* 37°25′ N, 74°41′ E **197**
Jamanari, river, *Braz.* 2°26′ S, 69°13′ W **136**
Jamari, river, *Braz.* 8°52′ S, 63°30′ W **130**
Jambes, *Belg.* 50°27′ N, 4°53′ E **167**
Jambi, *Indonesia* 1°41′ S, 103°33′ E **192**
Jambur, oil field, *Iraq* 35°1′ N, 44°31′ E **180**
Jambusar, *India* 22°3′ N, 72°48′ E **186**
James Bay 52°12′ N, 81°23′ W **110**
James City, *Pa., U.S.* 41°36′ N, 78°50′ W **94**
James Lake, *Can.* 57°15′ N, 100°15′ W **108**
James, river, *Can.* 51°47′ N, 115°9′ W **90**
James, river, *N. Dak., U.S.* 46°39′ N, 98°34′ W **90**
James, river, *S. Dak., U.S.* 45°3′ N, 98°16′ W **94**
James, river, *Va., U.S.* 37°54′ N, 78°33′ W **94**
James Ross Island, *Antarctica* 64°13′ S, 57°4′ W **134**
Jameson Land, *Den.* 70°56′ N, 23°8′ W **246**
Jamesport, *N.Y., U.S.* 40°56′ N, 72°35′ W **104**
Jamestown, *Calif., U.S.* 37°56′ N, 120°26′ W **100**
Jamestown, *Ind., U.S.* 39°55′ N, 86°38′ W **102**
Jamestown, *N.Y., U.S.* 42°6′ N, 79°15′ W **94**
Jamestown, *N.C., U.S.* 35°59′ N, 79°57′ W **96**
Jamestown, *R.I., U.S.* 41°29′ N, 71°23′ W **104**
Jamestown, *S. Af.* 31°7′ S, 26°47′ E **227**
Jämijärvi, *Fin.* 61°48′ N, 22°40′ E **166**
Jamkhandi, *India* 16°30′ N, 75°16′ E **188**
Jammu, *India* 32°44′ N, 74°51′ E **186**
Jammu and Kashmir, adm. division, *India* 33°48′ N, 76°20′ E **188**
Jamnagar, *India* 22°26′ N, 70°4′ E **186**
Jamno, *Pol.* 54°14′ N, 16°11′ E **152**
Jampur, *Pak.* 29°33′ N, 70°35′ E **186**
Jämsä, *Fin.* 61°51′ N, 25°10′ E **166**
Jämsänkoski, *Fin.* 61°54′ N, 25°8′ E **166**
Jamshedpur, *India* 22°46′ N, 86°13′ E **197**
Jämtlands Sikås, *Nor.* 63°37′ N, 15°13′ E **152**
Jamui, *India* 24°54′ N, 86°12′ E **197**
Jan Mayen, island, *Nor.* 71°0′ N, 8°0′ W **246**
Jan Mayen Fracture Zone, *Norwegian Sea* 70°55′ N, 6°54′ W **255**
Jan Mayen Ridge, *Norwegian Sea* 69°26′ N, 8°15′ W **255**
Jana, oil field, *Saudi Arabia* 27°23′ N, 49°48′ E **196**
Janakkala, *Fin.* 60°53′ N, 24°33′ E **166**
Janakpur, *Nepal* 26°40′ N, 85°55′ E **197**
Janaúba, *Braz.* 15°47′ S, 43°20′ W **138**
Janaucu, Ilha, island, *Braz.* 0°27′ N, 51°15′ W **130**
Jandaq, *Iran* 34°2′ N, 54°28′ E **180**
Janesville, *Wis., U.S.* 42°42′ N, 88°60′ W **102**
Jangamo, *Mozambique* 24°4′ S, 35°18′ E **227**
Janghang, *S. Korea* 36°1′ N, 126°44′ E **200**
Jangheung, *S. Korea* 34°38′ N, 126°54′ E **200**
Janghowon, *S. Korea* 37°6′ N, 127°37′ E **200**
Jangpyeong, *S. Korea* 37°35′ N, 128°24′ E **200**
Jangseong, *S. Korea* 35°17′ N, 126°51′ E **200**
Janikowo, *Pol.* 52°45′ N, 18°7′ E **152**
Janīn, *West Bank* 32°27′ N, 35°18′ E **194**
Janja, *Bosn. and Herzg.* 44°40′ N, 19°16′ E **168**
Janjina, *Croatia* 42°54′ N, 17°25′ E **168**
Jannaale, *Somalia* 1°45′ N, 44°41′ E **218**
Janos, *Mex.* 30°51′ N, 108°10′ W **92**
Jánossomorja, *Hung.* 47°46′ N, 17°8′ E **168**
Jansen, *Colo., U.S.* 37°10′ N, 104°33′ W **92**
Jansenville, *S. Af.* 32°54′ S, 24°44′ E **227**

Januária, Braz. 15°27' S, 44°26' W 138
Janville, Fr. 48°11' N, 1°52' E 163
Jaora, India 23°37' N, 75°9' E 188
Japan 36°0' N, 137°35' E 190
Japan, Sea of (East Sea) 39°9' N, 128°12' E 200
Japan Trench, North Pacific Ocean 35°43' N, 143°30' E 252
Japurá, Braz. 1°52' S, 66°41' W 136
Jaqué, Pan. 7°30' N, 78°9' W 136
Jaquí, Peru 15°31' S, 74°27' W 137
Jarābulus, Syr. 36°47' N, 37°58' E 180
Jarafuel, Sp. 39°8' N, 1°5' W 164
Jaraguá, Braz. 15°49' S, 49°23' W 138
Jaraguá do Sul, Braz. 26°29' S, 49°3' W 138
Jaraicejo, Sp. 39°39' N, 5°49' W 150
Jarales, N. Mex., U.S. 34°36' N, 106°46' W 92
Jaramillo, Arg. 47°9' S, 67°8' W 134
Jarash (Gerasa), Jordan 32°17' N, 35°53' E 194
Jarauçu, river, Braz. 2°47' S, 53°6' W 130
Jaray, Sp. 41°41' N, 2°8' W 164
Jarbidge, Nev., U.S. 41°53' N, 115°25' W 90
Jarbidge, river, Idaho, U.S. 42°24' N, 115°39' W 90
Järbo, Nor. 60°41' N, 16°35' E 152
Jardim, Braz. 21°30' S, 56°5' W 132
Jardim do Seridó, Braz. 6°38' S, 36°47' W 132
Jardine River National Park, Austral. 11°20' S, 142°18' E 238
Jardinésia, Braz. 19°17' S, 48°44' W 138
Jæren, region, Europe 58°33' N, 5°32' E 150
Jargalant, Mongolia 46°57' N, 115°15' E 198
Jari, river, Braz. 1°49' N, 54°28' W 130
Jari, river, Braz. 0°15' N, 53°7' W 130
Jarkovac, Serb. and Mont. 45°16' N, 20°46' E 168
Jarny, Fr. 49°10' N, 5°53' E 163
Jarocin, Pol. 51°57' N, 17°30' E 152
Järpen, Nor. 63°21' N, 13°28' E 152
Jars, Plain of, Laos 19°24' N, 103°2' E 202
Jartai, China 39°45' N, 105°47' E 198
Jaru, Braz. 10°25' S, 62°30' W 130
Jaru, river, Braz. 10°38' S, 62°25' W 132
Jarud Qi, China 44°35' N, 120°55' E 198
Järva Jaani, Est. 59°0' N, 25°51' E 166
Järvakandi, Est. 58°46' N, 24°47' E 166
Järvenpää, Fin. 69°27' N, 28°47' E 152
Järvenpää, Fin. 60°27' N, 25°4' E 166
Jarvie, Can. 54°26' N, 113°59' W 108
Järvsö, Nor. 61°42' N, 16°6' E 152
Jarwa, India 27°38' N, 82°30' E 197
Jaša Tomić, Serb. and Mont. 45°27' N, 20°50' E 168
Jasdan, India 22°1' N, 71°12' E 186
Jasenjani, Bosn. and Herzg. 43°29' N, 17°49' E 168
Jasenovac, Croatia 45°16' N, 16°54' E 168
Jasenovo Polje, Serb. and Mont. 42°52' N, 18°58' E 168
Jashpurnagar, India 22°53' N, 84°8' E 197
Jasikan, Ghana 7°25' N, 0°28' E 222
Jašiūnai, Lith. 54°27' N, 25°18' E 166
Jāsk, Iran 25°40' N, 57°50' E 196
Jasło, Pol. 49°44' N, 21°28' E 152
Jasmund National Park, Ger. 54°32' N, 13°33' E 152
Jason Islands, South Atlantic Ocean 51°19' S, 63°21' W 134
Jasonville, Ind., U.S. 39°9' N, 87°12' W 102
Jasper, Ala., U.S. 33°48' N, 87°16' W 96
Jasper, Ark., U.S. 35°59' N, 93°13' W 96
Jasper, Can. 52°53' N, 118°8' W 106
Jasper, Fla., U.S. 30°30' N, 82°58' W 96
Jasper, Ga., U.S. 34°27' N, 84°26' W 96
Jasper, Mich., U.S. 41°47' N, 84°2' W 102
Jasper, Tex., U.S. 30°54' N, 93°60' W 103
Jasper National Park, Can. 53°16' N, 119°17' W 108
Jastarnia, Pol. 54°42' N, 18°38' E 166
Jastrebac, Serb. and Mont. 43°31' N, 21°5' E 168
Jastrebarsko, Croatia 45°39' N, 15°39' E 156
Jastrowie, Pol. 53°25' N, 16°49' E 152
Jászapáti, Hung. 47°30' N, 20°9' E 168
Jászberény, Hung. 47°29' N, 19°55' E 168
Jászfényszaru, Hung. 47°34' N, 19°44' E 168
Jász-Nagykún-Szolnok, adm. division, Hung. 47°26' N, 19°47' E 156
Jászszentandrás, Hung. 47°34' N, 20°10' E 168
Jataí, Braz. 17°54' S, 51°43' W 138
Jatapu, river, Braz. 0°49' N, 58°59' W 130
Jath, India 17°2' N, 75°11' E 188
Jati, Pak. 24°21' N, 68°16' E 186
Jatobá, river, Braz. 13°59' S, 54°21' W 130
Jatobal, Braz. 4°36' S, 49°45' W 130
Jau, Angola 15°16' S, 13°27' E 220
Jaú, Braz. 22°20' S, 48°36' W 138
Jaú National Park, Braz. 2°36' S, 62°56' W 130
Jaú, river, Braz. 2°36' S, 63°25' W 130
Jauaperi, river, Braz. 0°20' N, 61°1' W 130
Jaumave, Mex. 23°23' N, 99°23' W 114
Jaunciems, Latv. 57°2' N, 24°11' E 166
Jaungulbene, Latv. 57°3' N, 26°34' E 166
Jaunjelgava, Latv. 56°35' N, 25°4' E 166
Jaunpiebalga, Latv. 57°9' N, 26°1' E 166
Jaunpur, India 25°43' N, 82°40' E 197
Jauru, river, Braz. 15°53' S, 58°17' W 132
Jauru, river, Braz. 18°42' S, 54°12' W 132
Java, island, Indonesia 8°16' S, 109°10' E 192
Java Ridge, Indian Ocean 9°48' S, 112°28' E 254
Java Sea 4°53' S, 109°50' E 192
Java Trench, Indian Ocean 9°27' S, 106°13' E 254
Javari, river, South America 6°25' S, 73°12' W 130
Jávea (Xàbia), Sp. 38°47' N, 0°9' E 164
Javier, Isla, island, Chile 47°17' S, 75°35' W 134
Javor, Serb. and Mont. 43°27' N, 19°57' E 168
Jawan, oil field, Iraq 35°54' N, 42°51' E 180
Jawhar (Giohar), Somalia 2°47' N, 45°34' E 218
Jawi, Indonesia 0°48' N, 109°14' E 196
Jay, Me., U.S. 44°30' N, 70°14' W 104
Jay, N.Y., U.S. 44°22' N, 73°45' W 104
Jay, Okla., U.S. 36°24' N, 94°48' W 94
Jay Em, Wyo., U.S. 42°28' N, 104°22' W 90
Jay Peak, Vt., U.S. 44°54' N, 72°37' W 94
Jaya, Puncak, peak, Indonesia 4°1' S, 137°0' E 192
Jayanti, India 26°41' N, 89°32' E 197
Jayapura, Indonesia 2°39' S, 140°44' E 192
Jayrūd, Syr. 33°48' N, 36°44' E 194
Jayton, Tex., U.S. 33°14' N, 100°35' W 92
Jaz Mūrīān, Hāmūn-e, lake, Iran 27°27' N, 58°26' E 180
Jazā'ir az Zubayr, island, Yemen 14°58' N, 41°3' E 182
Jazā'ir Farasān, islands, Red Sea 17°8' N, 41°25' E 182
Jbail (Byblos), Leb. 34°7' N, 35°39' E 194
Jbinate, Mor. 35°7' N, 5°58' W 150
Jdiriya, Western Sahara 27°17' N, 10°27' W 214
Jean, Nev., U.S. 35°46' N, 115°20' W 101
Jean Lafitte National Historical Park and Preserve, La., U.S. 29°55' N, 90°2' W 103
Jean Marie River, Can. 61°31' N, 120°39' W 108
Jeannette Island, Russ. 76°39' N, 159°13' E 255
Jean-Rabel, Haiti 19°52' N, 73°12' W 116
Jebāl Bārez, Kūh-e, peak, Iran 28°46' N, 58°7' E 196
Jebarna, Tun. 34°49' N, 10°28' E 156
Jebba, Nig. 9°7' N, 4°48' E 222
Jebel, Rom. 45°34' N, 21°14' E 168
Jebel Aulia, Sudan 15°15' N, 32°30' E 182
Jebel, Bahr al, adm. division, Sudan 4°21' N, 30°14' E 224
Jebel, oil field, Lib. 28°32' N, 19°47' E 216
Jebibina, Tun. 36°7' N, 10°5' E 156
Jecheon, S. Korea 37°7' N, 128°13' E 200
Jeddah, Saudi Arabia 21°31' N, 39°12' E 182
Jędrzejów, Pol. 50°38' N, 20°19' E 152
Jef Jef el Kebir, peak, Chad 20°30' N, 21°13' E 216
Jefferson, Ala., U.S. 32°23' N, 87°54' W 103
Jefferson, N.H., U.S. 44°24' N, 71°29' W 104
Jefferson, N.Y., U.S. 42°28' N, 74°37' W 94
Jefferson, Tex., U.S. 32°46' N, 94°23' W 103
Jefferson, Wis., U.S. 43°0' N, 88°47' W 102
Jefferson City, Mo., U.S. 38°31' N, 92°17' W 94
Jefferson City, Tenn., U.S. 36°7' N, 83°30' W 96
Jefferson, Mount, Nev., U.S. 38°44' N, 117°1' W 90
Jefferson, Mount, Oreg., U.S. 44°39' N, 121°53' W 90
Jeffersonville, Ind., U.S. 38°17' N, 85°44' W 94
Jeffersonville, Ohio, U.S. 39°39' N, 83°33' W 102
Jega, Nig. 12°13' N, 4°23' E 222
Jeju (Cheju), S. Korea 33°29' N, 126°32' E 200
Jeju-Do, island, S. Korea 33°34' N, 125°54' E 198
Jēkabpils, Latv. 56°30' N, 25°53' E 166
Jelbart Ice Shelf, Antarctica 70°24' S, 6°22' W 248
Jeldēsa, Eth. 9°41' N, 42°9' E 224
Jelenia Góra, Pol. 50°53' N, 15°44' E 152
Jelgava, Latv. 56°38' N, 23°40' E 152
Jelgava (Mitau), Latv. 56°38' N, 23°40' E 166
Jellico, Tenn., U.S. 36°34' N, 84°8' W 96
Jellicoe, Can. 49°42' N, 87°32' W 94
Jelnica, Pol. 51°57' N, 22°40' E 154
Jelsa, Croatia 43°8' N, 16°41' E 168
Jema, river, Eth. 10°2' N, 38°32' E 224
Jemaja, island, Indonesia 3°7' N, 105°17' E 196
Jember, Indonesia 8°8' S, 113°41' E 238
Jemez Pueblo, N. Mex., U.S. 35°37' N, 106°43' W 92
Jeminay, China 47°29' N, 85°52' E 184
Jena, Fla., U.S. 29°39' N, 83°23' W 105
Jena, La., U.S. 31°40' N, 92°9' W 96
Jenaien, Tun. 31°44' N, 10°8' E 216
Jengish Chokusu see Pobedy Peak, China 42°2' N, 80°3' E 184
Jenkins, Ky., U.S. 37°10' N, 82°38' W 96
Jenner, peak, Ger. 47°32' N, 12°56' E 156
Jennie, Ark., U.S. 33°14' N, 91°17' W 103
Jennings, La., U.S. 30°12' N, 92°40' W 103
Jennings, river, Can. 59°29' N, 131°60' W 108
Jenpeg, Can. 54°30' N, 98°6' W 108
Jensen, Utah, U.S. 40°22' N, 109°20' W 90
Jensen Beach, Fla., U.S. 27°14' N, 80°14' W 105
Jenu, Indonesia 0°36' N, 109°50' E 196
Jeogu, S. Korea 34°44' N, 128°38' E 200
Jeongeup, S. Korea 35°33' N, 126°52' E 200
Jeongseon, S. Korea 37°23' N, 128°40' E 200
Jeonju, S. Korea 35°48' N, 127°9' E 200
Jequié, Braz. 13°50' S, 40°6' W 138
Jequitaí, Braz. 17°15' S, 44°30' W 138
Jequitaí, river, Braz. 17°22' S, 44°7' W 138
Jequitinhonha, Braz. 16°27' S, 41°3' W 138
Jerantut, Malaysia 3°57' N, 102°21' E 196
Jerba Island, Tun. 34°0' N, 10°25' E 214
Jeremoabo, Braz. 10°4' S, 38°21' W 132
Jeremy, Cape, Antarctica 69°14' S, 72°52' W 248
Jerez de García Salinas, Mex. 22°38' N, 103°1' W 114
Jerez de la Frontera, Sp. 36°41' N, 6°9' W 164
Jeréz de los Caballeros, Sp. 38°18' N, 6°47' W 164
Jerez, Punta, Mex. 22°53' N, 97°42' W 114
Jérica, Sp. 39°55' N, 0°34' E 164
Jericho, Vt., U.S. 44°30' N, 72°60' W 104
Jericho see Arīḩā, West Bank 31°51' N, 35°27' E 194
Jericó, Col. 5°46' N, 75°48' W 136
Jermyn, Pa., U.S. 41°31' N, 75°34' W 110
Jerome, Ariz., U.S. 34°45' N, 112°5' W 112
Jerome, Ark., U.S. 33°23' N, 91°28' W 103
Jersey, island, U.K. 49°13' N, 2°7' W 150
Jersey City, N.J., U.S. 40°43' N, 74°4' W 104
Jerseyside, Can. 47°15' N, 53°57' W 111
Jerseyville, Mo., U.S. 39°6' N, 90°20' W 94
Jerusalem (Yerushalayim, Al-Quds), Israel 31°46' N, 35°9' E 194
Jervis Bay Territory 35°11' S, 149°35' E 230
Jervis Inlet 50°0' N, 124°8' W 100
Jeseník, Czech Rep. 49°45' N, 17°9' E 152
Jessen, Ger. 51°47' N, 12°56' E 152
Jessnitz, Ger. 51°41' N, 12°17' E 152
Jessore, Bangladesh 23°9' N, 89°9' E 197
Jesup, Ga., U.S. 31°35' N, 81°54' W 96
Jesús Carranza, Mex. 17°26' N, 95°1' W 114
Jesús María, Arg. 30°60' S, 64°8' W 134
Jesús María, Mex. 21°58' N, 102°21' W 114
Jesús María, Boca de 24°30' N, 98°13' W 114
Jetait, Can. 56°3' N, 101°20' W 108
Jetmore, Kans., U.S. 38°5' N, 99°55' W 90
Jetpur, India 21°44' N, 70°36' E 186
Jeumont, Fr. 50°17' N, 4°5' E 163
Jeungpyeong, S. Korea 36°46' N, 127°34' E 200
Jever, Ger. 53°34' N, 7°54' E 163
Jewell, Iowa, U.S. 42°17' N, 93°38' W 94
Jewett, Ill., U.S. 39°11' N, 88°15' W 102
Jewett, Tex., U.S. 31°20' N, 96°8' W 96
Jewett City, Conn., U.S. 41°36' N, 71°60' W 104
Jewish Autonomous Region, Russ. 49°5' N, 131°14' E 160
Jeypore, India 18°55' N, 82°30' E 190
Jez. Kopań, lake, Pol. 54°37' N, 16°4' E 152
Jezercë, Maja, peak, Alban. 42°26' N, 19°46' E 168
Ježevica, Serb. and Mont. 43°56' N, 20°5' E 168
Jeżewo, Pol. 53°30' N, 18°28' E 152
Jezzine, Leb. 33°33' N, 35°34' E 194
J.F.K. International Airport, N.Y., U.S. 40°36' N, 73°57' W 94
Jhalawar, India 24°34' N, 76°10' E 197
Jhang Sadr, Pak. 31°15' N, 72°20' E 186
Jhansi, India 25°25' N, 78°32' E 197
Jharkhand, adm. division, India 23°44' N, 85°22' E 188
Jharsuguda, India 21°52' N, 84°3' E 188
Jhatpat, Pak. 28°25' N, 68°20' E 186
Jhelum, Pak. 32°54' N, 73°45' E 186
Jhelum, river, Pak. 32°16' N, 72°35' E 186
Jhunjhunun, India 28°6' N, 75°24' E 197
Jiahe, China 25°34' N, 112°19' E 198
Jiamusi, China 46°53' N, 130°18' E 190
Ji'an, China 27°8' N, 114°56' E 198
Ji'an, China 41°8' N, 126°10' E 200
Jianchang, China 40°50' N, 119°45' E 198
Jiang'an, China 28°38' N, 105°2' E 198
Jiangcheng, China 22°34' N, 101°50' E 202
Jianghua, China 24°55' N, 111°44' E 198
Jiangle, China 26°48' N, 117°25' E 198
Jiangling, China 30°23' N, 112°9' E 198
Jiangmen, China 22°33' N, 113°1' E 198
Jiangshan, China 28°45' N, 118°37' E 198
Jiangsu, adm. division, China 33°41' N, 118°13' E 198
Jiangxi, adm. division, China 27°28' N, 115°30' E 198
Jiangyou, China 31°47' N, 104°34' E 198
Jianli, China 29°50' N, 112°51' E 198
Jianning, China 26°50' N, 116°45' E 198
Jianping, China 41°23' N, 119°40' E 198
Jianshui, China 23°33' N, 102°46' E 202
Jianyang, China 27°18' N, 118°5' E 198
Jiaohe, China 43°44' N, 127°25' E 198
Jiaokou, China 36°58' N, 111°13' E 198
Jiaonan, China 35°53' N, 119°59' E 198
Jiaozhou, China 36°20' N, 120°3' E 198
Jiaozuo, China 35°12' N, 113°11' E 198
Jiashi, China 39°28' N, 76°37' E 184
Jiawang, China 34°28' N, 117°23' E 198
Jiaxian, China 38°3' N, 110°26' E 198
Jiaxing, China 30°44' N, 120°42' E 198
Jiayu, China 29°58' N, 113°57' E 198
Jiayuguan, China 39°50' N, 98°18' E 188
Jibal, oil field, Oman 22°14' N, 56°1' E 182
Jibóia, Braz. 1°13' N, 69°34' W 136
Jibou, Rom. 47°15' N, 23°17' E 168
Jicarón, Isla, island, Pan. 7°10' N, 82°31' W 115
Jicatuyo, river, Hond. 14°59' N, 88°43' W 116
Jičín, Czech Rep. 50°26' N, 15°21' E 152
Jidali, Somalia 10°40' N, 47°39' E 216
Jiddat al Ḩarāsīs, Oman 19°19' N, 55°56' E 182
Jieshou, China 33°21' N, 115°20' E 198
Jiexiu, China 37°1' N, 111°54' E 198
Jieyang, China 23°31' N, 116°17' E 198
Jieznas, Lith. 54°36' N, 24°10' E 166
Jigme Dorji National Park, Bhutan 27°52' N, 89°53' E 197
Jihlava, Czech Rep. 49°23' N, 15°35' E 152
Jihočeský, adm. division, Czech Rep. 49°4' N, 13°42' E 152
Jihomoravský, adm. division, Czech Rep. 48°53' N, 15°51' E 152
Jijel, Alg. 36°48' N, 5°45' E 150
Jijiga, Eth. 9°18' N, 42°44' E 218
Jilava, Rom. 44°21' N, 26°5' E 156
Jilib, Somalia 0°26' N, 42°48' E 218
Jilin, China 43°50' N, 126°35' E 198
Jilin, adm. division, China 43°43' N, 126°4' E 198
Jiloy, Azerb. 40°19' N, 50°34' E 195
Jīma, Eth. 7°37' N, 36°47' E 224
Jimbolia, Rom. 45°47' N, 20°43' E 168
Jimena de la Frontera, Sp. 36°26' N, 5°28' W 164
Jiménez, Mex. 27°6' N, 104°55' W 112
Jiménez, Mex. 29°2' N, 100°41' W 92
Jiménez del Teul, Mex. 23°8' N, 104°5' W 114
Jimo, China 36°26' N, 120°30' E 198
Jin, river, China 28°9' N, 114°59' E 198
Jinan, China 36°39' N, 116°58' E 198
Jinan, S. Korea 36°32' N, 129°3' E 200
Jinan, S. Korea 35°46' N, 127°26' E 200
Jincheng, China 35°30' N, 112°49' E 198
Jindo, S. Korea 34°26' N, 126°15' E 200
Jing see Jinghe, China 44°35' N, 82°58' E 184
Jingbian, China 37°35' N, 108°47' E 198
Jingde, China 30°18' N, 118°33' E 198
Jingdezhen, China 29°19' N, 117°16' E 198
Jinggu, China 23°30' N, 100°41' E 202
Jinghai, China 38°57' N, 117°3' E 198
Jinghe (Jing), China 44°35' N, 82°58' E 184
Jinghong, China 22°0' N, 100°45' E 202
Jingle, China 38°20' N, 111°57' E 198
Jingmen, China 31°0' N, 112°10' E 198
Jingpeng see Hexigten Qi, China 43°16' N, 117°28' E 198
Jingtai, China 37°9' N, 104°7' E 198
Jingxi, China 23°6' N, 106°27' E 198
Jingxian, China 26°35' N, 109°39' E 198
Jingxing, China 38°3' N, 113°58' E 198
Jingyu, China 42°23' N, 126°49' E 200
Jingyuan, China 36°32' N, 104°41' E 198
Jingyuan, China 35°27' N, 106°21' E 198
Jinhae, S. Korea 35°9' N, 128°40' E 200
Jinhua, China 29°11' N, 119°41' E 198
Jining, China 41°4' N, 113°5' E 198
Jining, China 35°23' N, 116°38' E 198
Jinja, Uganda 0°24' N, 33°12' E 224
Jinjiang, China 24°46' N, 118°35' E 198
Jinotega, Nicar. 13°5' N, 85°58' W 115
Jinping, China 26°43' N, 109°10' E 198
Jinping, China 22°48' N, 103°11' E 202
Jinsha, China 27°23' N, 106°13' E 198
Jinsha (Yangtze), river, China 25°47' N, 103°15' E 190
Jinshan, China 30°52' N, 121°6' E 198
Jinshi, China 29°39' N, 111°53' E 198
Jinta, China 39°59' N, 98°58' E 188
Jinxi, China 40°47' N, 120°54' E 198
Jinxiang, China 35°5' N, 116°21' E 198
Jinzhai, China 31°43' N, 115°47' E 198
Jinzhou, China 39°8' N, 121°47' E 198
Jinzhou, China 41°10' N, 121°10' E 198
Ji-Paraná (Rondonia), Braz. 10°53' S, 61°58' W 130
Jiquilpan, Mex. 19°59' N, 102°44' W 114
Jirgatol, Taj. 39°13' N, 71°13' E 197
Jirisan, peak, S. Korea 35°19' N, 127°42' E 200
Jīroft, Iran 28°41' N, 57°47' E 196
Jiruá, Braz. 28°5' S, 54°21' W 139
Jishou, China 28°15' N, 109°43' E 198
Jishui, China 27°15' N, 115°7' E 198
Jisr ash Shughūr, Syr. 35°48' N, 36°17' E 156
Jitra, Malaysia 6°15' N, 100°25' E 196
Jiu, river, Rom. 45°16' N, 23°19' E 168
Jiujiang, China 29°40' N, 115°57' E 198
Jiuquan Space Launch Center, China 40°42' N, 99°37' E 188
Jiutai, China 44°9' N, 125°48' E 198
Jiwani, Pak. 25°2' N, 61°48' E 182
Jixi, China 30°4' N, 118°38' E 198
Jixi, China 45°7' N, 130°54' E 190
Jixian, China 36°6' N, 110°40' E 198
Jixian, China 40°2' N, 117°21' E 198
Jiyuan, China 35°6' N, 112°32' E 198
Jīzān, Saudi Arabia 16°52' N, 42°35' E 182
Jizzax, Uzb. 40°6' N, 67°50' E 197
Joaçaba, Braz. 27°10' S, 51°32' W 139
Joaíma, Braz. 16°40' S, 41°4' W 138
Joal, Senegal 14°12' N, 16°37' W 222
João Monlevade, Braz. 19°52' S, 43°8' W 138
João Pessoa, Braz. 7°7' S, 34°53' W 132
João Pinheiro, Braz. 17°43' S, 46°12' W 138
Joaquim Távora, Braz. 23°29' S, 49°59' W 138
Joaquin, Tex., U.S. 31°57' N, 94°3' W 103
Joaquín V. González, Arg. 25°8' S, 64°9' W 132
Job Peak, Nev., U.S. 39°34' N, 118°20' W 90
Jōban, Japan 36°59' N, 140°49' E 201
Jochiwon, S. Korea 36°34' N, 127°17' E 200
Joconoxtle, Mex. 23°12' N, 104°26' W 114
Jocotepec, Mex. 20°17' N, 103°28' W 114
Jocotepec, Mex. 17°32' N, 95°57' W 114
Jodar, Sp. 37°50' N, 3°21' W 164
Jodhpur, India 26°15' N, 73°1' E 188
Jodoigne, Belg. 50°43' N, 4°51' E 167
Joensuu, Fin. 62°36' N, 29°43' E 152
Joerg Peninsula, Antarctica 68°21' S, 64°22' W 248
Joesjö, Nor. 65°43' N, 14°36' E 152
Jōetsu, Japan 37°8' N, 138°13' E 201
Joeuf, Fr. 49°13' N, 6°0' E 163
Joffre, Mount, Can. 50°31' N, 115°17' W 90
Jõgeva, Est. 58°44' N, 26°22' E 166
Johannesburg, Calif., U.S. 35°22' N, 117°39' W 101
Johannesburg, S. Af. 26°12' S, 28°2' E 227
John, Cape, Can. 45°49' N, 63°14' W 111
John Day, Oreg., U.S. 44°24' N, 118°58' W 90
John Day, river, Oreg., U.S. 45°7' N, 120°3' W 106
John D'Or Prairie, Can. 58°30' N, 115°8' W 108
John F. Kennedy Space Center, Fla., U.S. 28°30' N, 80°44' W 105
John Jay, Mount, Alas., U.S. 56°8' N, 130°36' W 108
John Long Mountains, Mont., U.S. 46°34' N, 113°48' W 90
John Muir National Historic Site, Calif., U.S. 37°59' N, 122°9' W 100
John o'Groats, site, U.K. 58°37' N, 3°11' W 150
Johnsburg, N.Y., U.S. 43°36' N, 73°60' W 104
Johnson, Kans., U.S. 37°33' N, 101°46' W 92
Johnson City, Tenn., U.S. 36°18' N, 82°22' W 96
Johnson City, Tex., U.S. 30°15' N, 98°25' W 92
Johnson, Pico de, peak, Mex. 29°7' N, 112°16' W 92
Johnson Space Center, Tex., U.S. 29°30' N, 95°8' W 103
Johnsonburg, Pa., U.S. 41°28' N, 78°40' W 94
Johnsondale, Calif., U.S. 35°58' N, 118°33' W 101
Johnsons Crossing, Can. 60°30' N, 133°18' W 108
Johnsons Pass, Utah, U.S. 40°19' N, 112°35' W 90
Johnsons Station, Miss., U.S. 31°20' N, 90°28' W 103
Johnston, R.I., U.S. 41°49' N, 71°30' W 104
Johnston Atoll, United States 17°0' N, 170°0' W 99
Johnston Falls, Zambia 10°39' S, 28°9' E 224
Johnston, Mount, Antarctica 71°37' S, 66°55' E 248
Johnstone Hill, Austral. 23°41' S, 129°48' E 230
Johnstown, N.Y., U.S. 43°0' N, 74°24' W 94
Johnstown, Ohio, U.S. 40°8' N, 82°41' W 102
Johor Bahru, Malaysia 1°30' N, 103°44' E 196
Johovac, Bosn. and Herzg. 44°50' N, 18°1' E 168
Jõhvi, Est. 59°21' N, 27°24' E 166
Joinville, Braz. 26°18' S, 48°50' W 138
Joinville, Fr. 48°26' N, 5°6' E 163
Joinville Island, Antarctica 63°11' S, 55°28' W 134
Jojutla, Mex. 18°35' N, 99°11' W 114
Jokau, Sudan 8°21' N, 33°50' E 224
Jokijärvi, Fin. 65°28' N, 28°35' E 152
Jokioinen, Fin. 60°47' N, 23°26' E 166
Jokkmokk, Nor. 66°36' N, 19°50' E 152
Joliet, Ill., U.S. 41°31' N, 88°4' W 102
Joliette, Can. 46°1' N, 73°27' W 94
Jolliet, Lac, lake, Can. 51°30' N, 77°25' W 110
Jolo, Philippines 6°3' N, 120°59' E 203
Jomboy, Uzb. 39°42' N, 67°4' E 197
Jomda, China 31°29' N, 98°11' E 188
Jomppala, Fin. 69°46' N, 26°58' E 152
Jomu (Tinde), Tanzania 3°53' S, 33°11' E 224
Jonathan Point, Belize 16°35' N, 88°18' W 115
Jonava, Lith. 55°5' N, 24°16' E 166
Jonesboro, Ark., U.S. 35°50' N, 90°42' W 96
Jonesboro, Ind., U.S. 40°28' N, 85°38' W 102
Jonesboro, La., U.S. 32°13' N, 92°43' W 103
Jonesboro, Mo., U.S. 37°26' N, 89°16' W 96
Jonesville, Ind., U.S. 39°5' N, 85°54' W 102
Jonesville, La., U.S. 31°36' N, 91°50' W 103
Jonesville, N.C., U.S. 36°13' N, 80°51' W 96
Jonesville, S.C., U.S. 34°49' N, 81°42' W 96
Jonglei, Sudan 6°48' N, 31°15' E 224
Jongli, adm. division, Sudan 7°18' N, 31°5' E 218
Joniškėlis, Lith. 56°2' N, 24°9' E 166
Joniškis, Lith. 56°13' N, 23°35' E 166
Jönköping, Nor. 57°45' N, 14°8' E 152
Jonquière, Can. 48°23' N, 71°14' W 94
Jonuta, Mex. 18°5' N, 92°9' W 115
Joplin, Mont., U.S. 48°31' N, 110°47' W 90
Jora, India 26°19' N, 77°48' E 197
Jordan 30°42' N, 36°5' E 180
Jordan, Ala., U.S. 31°29' N, 88°15' W 103
Jordan, Minn., U.S. 44°39' N, 93°38' W 94
Jordan, Mont., U.S. 47°18' N, 106°55' W 90
Jordan, river, Asia 32°0' N, 36°0' E 194
Jordânia, Braz. 15°56' S, 40°12' W 138
Jordet, Nor. 61°25' N, 12°8' E 152
Jorge Montt, Isla, island, Chile 51°22' S, 74°31' W 134
Jörn, Nor. 65°3' N, 20°1' E 152
Jornada del Muerto, N. Mex., U.S. 33°10' N, 106°46' W 112
Jørpeland, Nor. 59°1' N, 6°2' E 152
Jos, Nig. 9°53' N, 8°53' E 222
Jošanička Banja, Serb. and Mont. 43°23' N, 20°45' E 168
Jose Abad Santos, Philippines 5°55' N, 125°36' E 203
José Batlle y Ordóñez, Uru. 33°28' S, 55°10' W 139
José Enrique Rodó, Uru. 33°43' S, 57°31' W 139
José María, Col. 2°11' N, 68°5' W 136
Jose Panganiban, Philippines 14°17' N, 122°42' E 203
José Pedro Varela, Uru. 33°28' S, 54°32' W 139
Joseph, Oreg., U.S. 45°21' N, 117°14' W 90
Joseph Bonaparte Gulf 13°4' S, 127°7' E 231
Joseph City, Ariz., U.S. 34°57' N, 110°20' W 92
Joseph, Lac, lake, Can. 52°49' N, 65°47' W 111
Josephine, Mount, Antarctica 77°25' S, 151°60' W 248
Joshimath, India 30°30' N, 79°34' E 197
Joshua Tree, Calif., U.S. 34°8' N, 116°20' W 101
Joshua Tree National Park, Calif., U.S. 33°47' N, 115°60' W 101
Josipdol, Croatia 45°11' N, 15°17' E 156
Jøssund, Nor. 63°50' N, 9°47' E 152
Jotunheimen, Nor. 61°27' N, 7°38' E 152
Joulter Cays, Atlantic Ocean 25°15' N, 78°52' W 96
Jounie, Leb. 33°58' N, 35°37' E 194
Jourdanton, Tex., U.S. 28°53' N, 98°33' W 92
Joure, Neth. 52°58' N, 5°48' E 163
Joussard, Can. 55°22' N, 115°59' W 108
Joutsa, Fin. 61°44' N, 26°6' E 166
Joutseno, Fin. 61°5' N, 28°28' E 166
Jowai, India 25°24' N, 92°11' E 188
Joya, Mex. 26°27' N, 101°13' W 114
Joyce, Wash., U.S. 48°7' N, 123°44' W 100
Joyce, Mount, Antarctica 75°32' S, 161°28' E 248
Ju, river, China 31°26' N, 111°5' E 198
Juami, river, Braz. 2°13' S, 68°13' W 136
Juan Aldama, Mex. 24°15' N, 103°25' W 114
Juan Cousté, Arg. 38°55' S, 63°8' W 139
Juan de Fuca Ridge, North Pacific Ocean 46°49' N, 129°21' W 252
Juan de Fuca, Strait of 48°17' N, 124°1' W 90
Juan de Nova, Île, island, France 17°7' S, 41°34' E 224
Juan E. Barra, Arg. 37°50' S, 60°31' W 139
Juan Fernández, Archipiélago, South Pacific Ocean 33°15' S, 82°48' W 123
Juan Fernández Islands, South Pacific Ocean 33°38' S, 80°1' W 253
Juan José Castelli, Arg. 25°58' S, 60°37' W 139
Juan Lacaze, Uru. 34°25' S, 57°25' W 139
Juan N. Fernández, Arg. 38°1' S, 59°17' W 139
Juan Perez Sound 52°30' N, 132°27' W 108
Juan Stuven, Isla, island, Chile 47°57' S, 77°11' W 134
Juan Viego, Col. 3°24' N, 68°18' W 136
Juankoski, Fin. 63°3' N, 28°18' E 152
Juárez, Arg. 37°42' S, 59°49' W 139
Juárez, Mex. 30°19' N, 108°8' W 92
Juárez, Mex. 27°36' N, 100°44' W 96
Juárez, Sierra de, Mex. 31°47' N, 116°1' W 112
Juazeiro, Braz. 9°28' S, 40°32' W 132
Juazeiro do Norte, Braz. 7°13' S, 39°21' W 132
Juba, Sudan 4°50' N, 31°34' E 224
Juba, river, Somalia 1°26' N, 42°22' E 206
Jubany, station, Antarctica 62°18' S, 58°29' W 134
Jubayl, Leb. 34°6' N, 35°40' E 216
Jubb Jannīn, Leb. 33°37' N, 35°47' E 194
Jubbah, Saudi Arabia 28°0' N, 40°55' E 180
Jubilee Pass, Calif., U.S. 35°54' N, 116°36' W 101
Juby, Cap, Mor. 27°48' N, 13°57' W 214
Jucás, Braz. 6°31' S, 39°34' W 132
Juchitán, Mex. 16°26' N, 95°5' W 112
Juchitlán, Mex. 20°4' N, 104°7' W 114
Judas, Punta, C.R. 9°23' N, 85°5' W 115

Judayyidat ʻArʻar, Saudi Arabia 31°14′ N, 41°21′ E 180
Judge Howay, Mount, Can. 49°28′ N, 122°22′ W 100
Judge Seamount, North Pacific Ocean 29°13′ N, 173°8′ E 252
Judith Basin, Mont., U.S. 47°2′ N, 110°10′ W 90
Judith Gap, Mont., U.S. 46°39′ N, 109°46′ W 90
Judith Mountains, Mont., U.S. 47°7′ N, 109°16′ W 90
Judsonia, Ark., U.S. 35°16′ N, 91°39′ W 96
Jufari, river, Braz. 0°20′ N, 62°36′ W 130
Juhaym, spring, Iraq 29°37′ N, 45°23′ E 196
Juhor, Serb. and Mont. 43°53′ N, 20°59′ E 168
Juifang, Taiwan 25°5′ N, 121°51′ E 198
Juigalpa, Nicar. 12°6′ N, 85°23′ W 115
Juist, island, Ger. 53°40′ N, 6°44′ E 163
Juiz de Fora, Braz. 21°44′ S, 43°21′ W 138
Jujuy, adm. division, Arg. 22°42′ S, 66°40′ W 137
Jukbyeon, S. Korea 37°3′ N, 129°25′ E 200
Jukkasjärvi, Nor. 67°50′ N, 20°36′ E 152
Jukuniemi, Fin. 61°46′ N, 29°58′ E 166
Julaca, Bol. 20°57′ S, 67°33′ W 137
Juli, Peru 16°17′ S, 69°27′ W 137
Juliaca, Peru 15°31′ S, 70°8′ W 137
Julian, Calif., U.S. 33°4′ N, 116°37′ W 101
Julian Alps, Slov. 46°26′ N, 13°33′ E 167
Julian Peak, Can. 50°27′ N, 124°23′ W 90
Julianehåb see Qaqortoq, Den. 60°47′ N, 46°7′ W 106
Jülich, Ger. 50°55′ N, 6°21′ E 167
Julimes, Mex. 28°24′ N, 105°27′ W 92
Júlio de Castilhos, Braz. 29°15′ S, 53°42′ W 139
Jullundur, India 31°19′ N, 75°35′ E 186
Julpo, S. Korea 35°35′ N, 126°41′ E 200
Julu, China 37°13′ N, 115°0′ E 198
Julu Rayeu, oil field, Indonesia 4°58′ N, 97°36′ E 196
Juma, Uzb. 39°41′ N, 66°38′ E 197
Juma, river, Braz. 5°31′ S, 65°2′ W 132
Jumba, Somalia 0°18′ N, 42°38′ E 218
Jumbilla, Peru 5°49′ S, 77°47′ W 130
Jumbo Peak, Nev., U.S. 36°10′ N, 114°15′ W 101
Jumilla, Sp. 38°28′ N, 1°21′ W 164
Jumla, Nepal 29°17′ N, 82°12′ E 197
Jumunjin, S. Korea 37°53′ N, 128°49′ E 200
Junagadh, India 21°32′ N, 70°26′ E 186
Junan, China 35°13′ N, 118°52′ E 198
Junction, Tex., U.S. 30°28′ N, 99°46′ W 92
Junction, Utah, U.S. 38°14′ N, 112°13′ W 90
Junction City, Ark., U.S. 33°1′ N, 92°44′ W 103
Junction City, Kans., U.S. 39°0′ N, 96°51′ W 90
Jundiaí, Braz. 23°10′ S, 46°54′ W 138
Juneau, Alas., U.S. 58°19′ N, 134°31′ W 108
Juneau, Wis., U.S. 43°24′ N, 88°42′ W 102
Juneda, Sp. 41°32′ N, 0°48′ E 164
Jungar Qi, China 39°39′ N, 110°54′ E 198
Jungfrau, peak, Switz. 46°32′ N, 7°56′ E 167
Junggar Pendi, China 45°57′ N, 84°44′ E 184
Junín, Arg. 34°37′ S, 60°55′ W 139
Junín, Col. 1°19′ N, 78°17′ W 136
Junín, adm. division, Peru 11°26′ S, 74°42′ W 137
Junín de los Andes, Arg. 39°55′ S, 71°6′ W 134
Juniper Mountain, peak, Oreg., U.S. 42°55′ N, 120°1′ W 90
Juniper Peak, Nev., U.S. 39°46′ N, 119°17′ W 90
Junipero Serra Peak, Calif., U.S. 36°8′ N, 121°28′ W 100
Juniville, Fr. 49°23′ N, 4°22′ E 163
Junnar, India 19°12′ N, 73°53′ E 188
Juno Beach, Fla., U.S. 26°52′ N, 80°4′ W 105
Junosuando, Nor. 67°25′ N, 22°28′ E 152
Junsele, Nor. 63°41′ N, 16°56′ E 152
Juntura, Oreg., U.S. 43°44′ N, 118°5′ W 90
Juntusranta, Fin. 65°12′ N, 29°27′ E 152
Juodkrantė, Russ. 55°34′ N, 21°6′ E 166
Jupaguá, Braz. 11°50′ S, 44°20′ W 132
Jupiter, Fla., U.S. 26°56′ N, 80°6′ W 105
Jupiter, river, Can. 49°40′ N, 63°36′ W 111
Jupiter Well, spring, Austral. 22°59′ S, 126°42′ E 230
Juquiá, Braz. 24°19′ S, 47°37′ W 138
Jur, river, Sudan 8°34′ N, 28°35′ E 224
Jura Mountains, Switz. 46°58′ N, 6°23′ E 165
Jura, Paps of, mountain, U.K. 55°53′ N, 6°7′ W 150
Juradó, Col. 7°7′ N, 77°47′ W 136
Juramento, Braz. 16°50′ S, 43°36′ W 138
Juramento see Pasaje, river, Arg. 28°44′ S, 62°58′ W 139
Jurbarkas, Lith. 55°4′ N, 22°45′ E 166
Jurf ad Darāwīsh, Jordan 30°41′ N, 35°51′ E 194
Jurien Bay 30°46′ S, 114°35′ E 230
Jūrmala, Latv. 56°57′ N, 23°48′ E 166
Jūrmalciems, Latv. 56°18′ N, 21°0′ E 166
Jurmo, Fin. 59°49′ N, 21°34′ E 166
Juruá, Braz. 3°28′ S, 66°9′ W 136
Juruá, river, Braz. 3°1′ S, 66°9′ W 132
Jurumirim Dam, Braz. 23°24′ S, 49°18′ W 138
Juruti, Braz. 2°10′ S, 56°8′ W 130
Jussey, Fr. 47°49′ N, 5°53′ E 150
Justo Daract, Arg. 33°53′ S, 65°10′ W 134
Jutaí, Braz. 5°11′ S, 68°52′ W 130
Jutaí, Ilha Grande de, islands, South America 3°21′ S, 49°31′ W 130
Jutaí, river, Braz. 3°21′ S, 67°32′ W 136
Jutiapa, Guatemala 14°17′ N, 89°52′ W 115
Juticalpa, Hond. 14°43′ N, 86°12′ W 115
Jutland, Europe 55°35′ N, 8°29′ E 150
Juuru, Est. 59°2′ N, 24°56′ E 166
Juva, Fin. 61°53′ N, 27°47′ E 166
Juventino Rosas, Mex. 20°37′ N, 100°60′ W 114
Juventud, Isla de La, adm. division, Cuba 21°24′ N, 83°32′ W 116
Juxian, China 35°36′ N, 118°50′ E 198
Juxtlahuaca, Mex. 17°19′ N, 98°2′ W 114
Juye, China 35°22′ N, 116°6′ E 198
Jūymand, Iran 34°20′ N, 58°41′ E 180
Jūyom, Iran 28°5′ N, 53°49′ E 196
Juzennecourt, Fr. 48°10′ N, 4°58′ E 163
Jwaneng, Botswana 24°34′ S, 24°35′ E 227
Jyderup, Den. 55°39′ N, 11°24′ E 152
Jyrgalang, Kyrg. 42°38′ N, 78°58′ E 184
Jyväskylä, Fin. 62°12′ N, 25°42′ E 152

K

K2 (Qoghir, Godwin Austen), peak, Pak. 35°51′ N, 76°25′ E 186
Ka, river, Nig. 11°38′ N, 5°19′ E 222
Kaʻ Ū, region, Oceania 19°15′ N, 155°39′ W 99
Kaabong, Uganda 3°30′ N, 34°6′ E 224
Kaa-Iya National Park, Bol. 19°25′ S, 61°49′ W 132
Kaamanen, Fin. 69°6′ N, 27°12′ E 152
Kaambooni, Somalia 1°38′ S, 41°36′ E 224
Kaambooni, Raas, Somalia 1°36′ S, 40°53′ E 224
Kaaresuvanto, Fin. 68°27′ N, 22°27′ E 152
Kaba, Hung. 47°22′ N, 21°16′ E 168
Kaba see Habahe, China 48°4′ N, 86°21′ E 184
Kabaena, island, Indonesia 5°48′ S, 121°7′ E 192
Kabala, Sierra Leone 9°34′ N, 11°34′ W 222
Kabale, Uganda 1°19′ S, 29°59′ E 224
Kabalo, Dem. Rep. of the Congo 6°4′ S, 26°55′ E 224
Kabambare, Dem. Rep. of the Congo 4°44′ S, 27°38′ E 224
Kabanga, Zambia 17°30′ S, 26°47′ E 224
Kabangoué, Côte d'Ivoire 10°10′ N, 7°33′ W 222
Kabanjahe, Indonesia 3°8′ N, 98°29′ E 196
Kabara, Mali 16°40′ N, 2°60′ W 222
Kabardino-Balkariya, adm. division, Russ. 43°33′ N, 42°31′ E 195
Kabare, Dem. Rep. of the Congo 2°32′ S, 28°42′ E 224
Kabarnet, Kenya 0°28′ N, 35°45′ E 224
Kabasalan, Philippines 7°50′ N, 122°45′ E 203
Kabasha, Dem. Rep. of the Congo 0°43′ N, 29°12′ E 224
Kabba, Nig. 7°52′ N, 6°3′ E 222
Kåbdalis, Nor. 66°8′ N, 19°56′ E 152
Kabenung Lake, Can. 48°15′ N, 85°30′ W 94
Kabinakagami Lake, Can. 48°47′ N, 86°7′ W 81
Kabinda, Dem. Rep. of the Congo 6°11′ S, 24°27′ E 224
Kabīr, river, Asia 34°35′ N, 36°7′ E 194
Kabo, Cen. Af. Rep. 7°36′ N, 18°36′ E 218
Kabol (Kabul), Afghan. 34°34′ N, 69°2′ E 186
Kabompo, Zambia 13°37′ S, 24°10′ E 224
Kabompo, river, Zambia 13°34′ S, 24°16′ E 224
Kabongo, Dem. Rep. of the Congo 7°21′ S, 25°34′ E 224
Kabore-Tambi National Park, Burkina Faso 11°10′ N, 1°50′ W 222
Kabosa Island, Myanmar 12°51′ N, 97°24′ E 202
Kaboudia, Ras, Tun. 35°10′ N, 11°9′ E 156
Kabūd Gombad, Iran 37°1′ N, 59°48′ E 180
Kabugao, Philippines 18°3′ N, 121°8′ E 203
Kabul see Kabol, Afghan. 34°34′ N, 69°2′ E 186
Kabunda, Dem. Rep. of the Congo 12°29′ S, 29°20′ E 224
Kabushiya, Sudan 16°51′ N, 33°42′ E 182
Kabwe (Broken Hill), Zambia 14°29′ S, 28°25′ E 224
Kabylie, region, Africa 36°31′ N, 4°4′ E 150
Kać, Serb. and Mont. 45°18′ N, 19°56′ E 168
Kačanik, Serb. and Mont. 42°14′ N, 21°15′ E 168
Kachanovo, Russ. 57°27′ N, 27°46′ E 166
Kachia, Nig. 9°52′ N, 7°57′ E 222
Kachikau, Botswana 18°10′ S, 24°28′ E 224
Kachīry, Kaz. 53°4′ N, 76°7′ E 184
Kachkanar, Russ. 58°44′ N, 59°30′ E 154
Kachreti, Ga. 41°39′ N, 45°40′ E 195
Kachug, Russ. 54°3′ N, 105°59′ E 190
Kachung, Uganda 1°54′ N, 32°56′ E 224
Kaçkar Dağı, peak, Turk. 40°50′ N, 41°6′ E 195
Kada, spring, Chad 19°21′ N, 19°36′ E 216
Kadaingti, Myanmar 17°37′ N, 97°30′ E 202
Kadan Kyun, island, Myanmar 12°33′ N, 98°29′ E 202
Kadarkút, Hung. 46°14′ N, 17°37′ E 168
Kade, Ghana 6°6′ N, 0°52′ E 222
Kadé, Guinea 12°10′ N, 13°53′ W 222
Kadéï, river, Cen. Af. Rep. 3°48′ N, 15°32′ E 218
Kadesh, battle, Syr. 34°34′ N, 36°25′ E 194
Kadesh-Barnea see ʻAin el Qideirât, spring, Egypt 30°39′ N, 34°25′ E 194
Kadiana, Mali 10°44′ N, 6°31′ W 222
Kadıköy, Turk. 40°39′ N, 26°52′ E 158
Kadıköy, Turk. 40°58′ N, 29°2′ E 158
Kading, river, Laos 18°19′ N, 104°10′ E 202
Kadınhanı, Turk. 38°13′ N, 32°13′ E 156
Kadiolo, Mali 10°33′ N, 5°46′ W 222
Kadiria, Alg. 36°31′ N, 3°41′ E 150
Kadirli, Turk. 37°21′ N, 36°5′ E 156
Kadivka, Ukr. 48°31′ N, 38°36′ E 158
Kadnikov, Russ. 59°30′ N, 40°21′ E 154
Kado, Nig. 7°37′ N, 9°40′ E 222
Kadom, Russ. 54°32′ N, 42°30′ E 154
Kadoma, Zimb. 18°21′ S, 29°56′ E 224
Kadrifakovo, Maced. 41°48′ N, 22°3′ E 168
Kadugli, Sudan 10°57′ N, 29°40′ E 224
Kaduna, Nig. 10°30′ N, 7°24′ E 222
Kaduy, Russ. 59°10′ N, 37°12′ E 154
Kadyy, Russ. 57°47′ N, 43°10′ E 154
Kadzherom, Russ. 64°40′ N, 55°48′ E 154
Kaech'ŏn, N. Korea 39°42′ N, 125°52′ E 200
Kaédi, Mauritania 16°8′ N, 13°36′ W 222
Kaélé, Cameroon 10°6′ N, 14°26′ E 216
Kaʻena Point, Hawaiʻi, U.S. 21°34′ N, 158°40′ W 99
Kaeng Krachan National Park, Thai. 12°44′ N, 98°58′ E 202
Kaeo, N.Z. 35°6′ S, 173°47′ E 240
Kaʻeo, peak, Hawaiʻi, U.S. 21°53′ N, 160°12′ W 99
Kaesŏng, N. Korea 37°58′ N, 126°32′ E 200
Kafakumba, Dem. Rep. of the Congo 9°41′ S, 23°45′ E 224
Kafanchan, Nig. 9°36′ N, 8°18′ E 222
Kaffrine, Senegal 14°6′ N, 15°32′ W 222
Kafia Kingi, Sudan 9°15′ N, 24°24′ E 224
Kafin, Nig. 9°29′ N, 7°5′ E 222
Kåfjord, Nor. 69°56′ N, 23°0′ E 152
Kåfjord, Nor. 69°31′ N, 20°51′ E 152
Kafr Buhum, Syr. 35°3′ N, 36°41′ E 194
Kafu, river, Uganda 1°8′ N, 31°26′ E 224
Kafue, Zambia 15°47′ S, 28°10′ E 224
Kafue National Park, Zambia 14°52′ S, 25°40′ E 224
Kafue, river, Zambia 14°31′ S, 26°26′ E 224
Kafue, river, Zambia 15°41′ S, 26°27′ E 224
Kafufu, river, Tanzania 7°5′ S, 31°31′ E 224
Kafulwe, Zambia 8°60′ S, 29°1′ E 224
Kaga, Japan 36°18′ N, 136°17′ E 201
Kaga Bandoro, Cen. Af. Rep. 6°54′ N, 19°11′ E 218
Kagan, Pak. 34°45′ N, 73°34′ E 186
Kagawa, adm. division, Japan 34°11′ N, 133°41′ E 201
Kåge, Nor. 64°49′ N, 20°56′ E 152
Kagera, adm. division, Tanzania 2°38′ S, 30°33′ E 218
Kagera, river, Africa 1°8′ S, 30°42′ E 224
Kagianagami Lake, Can. 50°58′ N, 88°38′ W 110
Kağızman, Turk. 40°8′ N, 43°6′ E 195
Kagmar, Sudan 14°25′ N, 30°23′ E 226
Kagopal, Chad 8°15′ N, 16°26′ E 218
Kagoshima, Japan 31°34′ N, 130°32′ E 201
Kagoshima, adm. division, Japan 31°15′ N, 130°34′ E 201
Kagoshima Space Center, Japan 31°16′ N, 131°0′ E 201
Kaguyak, Alas., U.S. 56°51′ N, 153°51′ W 98
Kahama, Tanzania 3°49′ S, 32°35′ E 224
Kahan, Pak. 29°18′ N, 68°57′ E 186
Kahemba, Dem. Rep. of the Congo 7°20′ S, 18°59′ E 218
Kāhili, peak, Hawaiʻi, U.S. 21°58′ N, 159°33′ W 99
Kahler Asten, peak, Ger. 51°10′ N, 8°26′ E 167
Kahlotus, Wash., U.S. 46°37′ N, 118°33′ W 90
Kahntah, Can. 58°19′ N, 120°55′ W 108
Kahntah, river, Can. 57°50′ N, 120°51′ W 108
Kahnūj, Iran 27°54′ N, 57°45′ E 196
Kahoku, Japan 38°26′ N, 140°18′ E 201
Kahoʻolawe, island, Hawaiʻi, U.S. 20°21′ N, 157°18′ W 99
Kahperusvaara, peak, Fin. 69°8′ N, 21°1′ E 152
Kahramanmaraş, Turk. 37°35′ N, 36°55′ E 156
Kahtla, Est. 58°24′ N, 22°59′ E 166
Kahuku Point, Hawaiʻi, U.S. 21°44′ N, 158°21′ W 99
Kahurangi National Park, N.Z. 41°11′ S, 171°19′ E 240
Kahuzi-Biega National Park, Dem. Rep. of the Congo 1°60′ S, 27°14′ E 224
Kai Iwi, N.Z. 39°53′ S, 174°54′ E 240
Kai, Kepulauan, islands, Banda Sea 5°58′ S, 130°47′ E 192
Kaiama, Nig. 9°35′ N, 4°0′ E 222
Kaibara, Japan 35°7′ N, 135°3′ E 201
Kāʼid, spring, Iraq 32°2′ N, 40°57′ E 180
Kaifeng, China 34°48′ N, 114°19′ E 198
Kaifu, Japan 33°36′ N, 134°20′ E 201
Kaiholena, peak, Hawaiʻi, U.S. 19°10′ N, 155°38′ W 99
Kaihu, N.Z. 35°45′ S, 173°42′ E 240
Kaikoura, N.Z. 42°25′ S, 173°39′ E 240
Kailahun, Sierra Leone 8°14′ N, 10°35′ W 222
Kaili, China 26°34′ N, 107°59′ E 198
Kailu, China 43°39′ N, 121°16′ E 198
Kaimana, Indonesia 3°39′ S, 133°45′ E 192
Käina, Est. 58°49′ N, 22°46′ E 166
Kainan, Japan 34°9′ N, 135°13′ E 201
Kainji Dam, Nig. 9°40′ N, 4°19′ E 222
Kainji Lake National Park, Nig. 9°45′ N, 5°4′ E 222
Kainuunkylä, Fin. 66°13′ N, 23°47′ E 152
Kairala, Fin. 67°10′ N, 27°23′ E 152
Kaisersesch, Ger. 50°13′ N, 7°8′ E 167
Kaiserslautern, Ger. 49°26′ N, 7°45′ E 163
Kaishantun, China 42°42′ N, 129°44′ E 200
Kaišiadorys, Lith. 54°52′ N, 24°26′ E 166
Kaitangata, N.Z. 46°17′ S, 169°50′ E 240
Kaithal, India 29°47′ N, 76°25′ E 197
Kaʻiwaloa Heiau and Olowalu Petroglyphs, site, Hawaiʻi, U.S. 20°49′ N, 156°40′ W 99
Kaixian, China 31°11′ N, 108°20′ E 198
Kaiyang, China 27°4′ N, 107°0′ E 198
Kaiyuan, China 42°32′ N, 124°3′ E 200
Kaiyuan, China 23°40′ N, 103°9′ E 202
Kajaani, Fin. 64°12′ N, 27°39′ E 152
Kajaki, Afghan. 32°12′ N, 65°5′ E 186
Kajaki Dam, Afghan. 32°1′ N, 64°29′ E 186
Kajang, Malaysia 3°0′ N, 101°45′ E 196
Kajiado, Kenya 1°52′ S, 36°48′ E 224
Kajiki, Japan 31°43′ N, 130°40′ E 201
Kajo Kaji, Sudan 3°48′ N, 31°36′ E 224
Kajok, Sudan 8°16′ N, 27°58′ E 224
Kajuru, Nig. 10°19′ N, 7°38′ E 222
Kaka, Sudan 10°37′ N, 32°7′ E 224
Kaka, Turkm. 37°21′ N, 59°36′ E 180
Kakada, spring, Chad 16°8′ N, 15°29′ E 216
Kakadu National Park, Austral. 13°22′ S, 132°5′ E 238
Kakahi, N.Z. 38°59′ S, 175°21′ E 240
Kakamas, S. Af. 28°47′ S, 20°35′ E 227
Kakamega, Kenya 0°15′ N, 34°46′ E 224
Kakana, India 9°9′ N, 92°55′ E 188
Kakanj, Bosn. and Herzg. 44°9′ N, 18°5′ E 168
Kakanui, N.Z. 45°12′ S, 170°53′ E 240
Kakaramea, N.Z. 39°43′ S, 174°25′ E 240
Kakasszék, Hung. 46°32′ N, 20°36′ E 168
Kakata, Liberia 6°25′ N, 10°21′ W 222
Kakatahi, N.Z. 39°41′ S, 175°21′ E 240
Kake, Alas., U.S. 56°58′ N, 133°57′ W 108
Kake, Japan 34°36′ N, 132°20′ E 201
Kaketsa Mountain, Can. 58°10′ N, 131°59′ W 108
Kakhib, Russ. 42°23′ N, 46°36′ E 195
Kākhk, Iran 34°7′ N, 58°38′ E 180
Kakhovka, Ukr. 46°48′ N, 33°29′ E 156
Kakhovs'ke Vodoskhovyshche, lake, Ukr. 46°59′ N, 32°23′ E 156
Kakinada (Cocanada), India 16°59′ N, 82°15′ E 188
Kakisa, Can. 60°54′ N, 117°21′ W 108
Kakisa Lake, Can. 60°57′ N, 118°37′ W 108
Kakisa, river, Can. 60°44′ N, 119°16′ W 108
Kakogawa, Japan 34°46′ N, 134°51′ E 201
Kakshaal Range see Kök Shal Tau, Kyrg. 41°22′ N, 77°33′ E 184
Kakskerta, Fin. 60°20′ N, 22°13′ E 166
Kaktovik, Alas., U.S. 69°59′ N, 143°40′ W 98
Kakuda, Japan 37°58′ N, 140°45′ E 201
Kakuma, Kenya 3°40′ N, 34°50′ E 224
Kakwa, river, Can. 54°13′ N, 118°43′ W 108
Kál, Hung. 47°43′ N, 20°17′ E 168
Kala, Azerb. 40°27′ N, 50°10′ E 195
Kala, Tanzania 8°8′ S, 31°0′ E 224
Kalaallit Nunaat see Greenland, Den. 67°11′ N, 50°25′ W 106
Kalabagh, Pak. 32°59′ N, 71°35′ E 186
Kalabo, Zambia 14°59′ S, 22°40′ E 220
Kalâbsha and Beit el Wâli, ruin(s), Egypt 23°32′ N, 32°42′ E 182
Kalach, Russ. 50°25′ N, 40°58′ E 158
Kalach na Donu, Russ. 48°43′ N, 43°32′ E 158
Kalachinsk, Russ. 54°59′ N, 74°36′ E 184
Kalae (South Point), Hawaiʻi, U.S. 18°40′ N, 155°43′ W 99
Kalahari Desert, Africa 19°27′ S, 24°2′ E 224
Kalahari Gemsbok National Park, S. Af. 26°6′ S, 19°47′ E 227
Kalaikhum, Taj. 38°28′ N, 70°47′ E 197
Kalajoki, Fin. 64°12′ N, 23°55′ E 152
Kalakamate, Botswana 20°39′ S, 27°18′ E 227
Kalakan, Russ. 55°11′ N, 116°45′ E 190
Kalakepen, Indonesia 2°47′ N, 97°48′ E 196
Kalalua, peak, Hawaiʻi, U.S. 19°23′ N, 155°7′ W 99
Kalam, Pak. 35°31′ N, 72°36′ E 186
Kalama, Wash., U.S. 46°0′ N, 122°50′ W 100
Kalama, river, Wash., U.S. 46°1′ N, 122°45′ W 100
Kalamalka Lake, Can. 50°5′ N, 119°57′ W 108
Kalamáta, Gr. 37°2′ N, 22°7′ E 216
Kalamazoo, Mich., U.S. 42°17′ N, 85°36′ W 102
Kalambo Falls, Zambia 8°51′ S, 31°17′ E 224
Kalana, Mali 10°47′ N, 8°13′ W 222
Kalangala, Uganda 0°23′ N, 32°16′ E 224
Kalangali, Tanzania 6°6′ S, 33°55′ E 224
Kalanshiyū ar Ramlī al Kabīr, Sarīr (Sand Sea of Calanscio), Lib. 28°52′ N, 23°25′ E 180
Kalanshiyū, Sarīr, Lib. 26°35′ N, 20°7′ E 216
Kalao, island, Indonesia 7°27′ S, 119°55′ E 192
Kalaotoa, island, Indonesia 7°28′ S, 121°50′ E 192
Kälarne, Nor. 62°59′ N, 16°4′ E 152
Kalasin, Thai. 16°28′ N, 103°31′ E 202
Kalat, Pak. 29°2′ N, 66°33′ E 186
Kalaupapa National Historic Park, Hawaiʻi, U.S. 20°42′ N, 157°60′ W 99
Kalaus, river, Russ. 45°50′ N, 43°15′ E 158
Kalawao, site, Hawaiʻi, U.S. 21°10′ N, 156°60′ W 99
Kalayʼmor, Turkm. 35°41′ N, 62°33′ E 186
Kalay-wa, Myanmar 23°10′ N, 94°13′ E 202
Kalbā, U.A.E. 25°4′ N, 56°17′ E 196
Kälbäjär, Azerb. 40°8′ N, 46°1′ E 195
Kalbān, Oman 20°17′ N, 58°41′ E 182
Kaldrma, Bosn. and Herzg. 44°18′ N, 16°11′ E 168
Kale Burnu, Turk. 41°4′ N, 38°54′ E 195
Kale (Myra), Turk. 36°13′ N, 29°57′ E 156
Kalecik, Turk. 40°6′ N, 33°25′ E 156
Kalehe, Dem. Rep. of the Congo 2°7′ S, 28°50′ E 224
Kalemie, Dem. Rep. of the Congo 5°57′ S, 29°11′ E 224
Kalemyo, Myanmar 23°10′ N, 94°1′ E 202
Kalene Hill, Zambia 11°13′ S, 24°10′ E 224
Kalenyy, Kaz. 49°32′ N, 51°35′ E 158
Kalesija, Bosn. and Herzg. 44°27′ N, 18°55′ E 168
Kaletnik, Pol. 54°10′ N, 23°5′ E 152
Kalevala, Russ. 65°12′ N, 31°12′ E 152
Kaleybar, Iran 38°56′ N, 47°3′ E 195
Kalgachikha, Russ. 63°20′ N, 36°48′ E 154
Kalí Límni, peak, Gr. 35°34′ N, 27°4′ E 156
Kali Sindh, river, India 24°28′ N, 76°7′ E 197
Kaliakoúda, peak, Gr. 38°47′ N, 21°40′ E 156
Kaliakra, Nos, Bulg. 43°17′ N, 28°17′ E 156
Kalibo, Philippines 11°40′ N, 122°22′ E 203
Kalida, Ohio, U.S. 40°58′ N, 84°12′ W 102
Kalima, Dem. Rep. of the Congo 2°39′ S, 26°35′ E 218
Kalimantan see Borneo, island, Indonesia 4°28′ S, 111°26′ E 192
Kalimash, Alban. 42°5′ N, 20°18′ E 168
Kálimnos, Gr. 36°57′ N, 26°59′ E 156
Kalimpang, India 27°4′ N, 88°26′ E 197
Kaliningrad, Russ. 54°42′ N, 20°27′ E 166
Kaliningrad Oblast, adm. division, Russ. 54°47′ N, 20°9′ E 166
Kalinino, Arm. 41°7′ N, 44°15′ E 195
Kalinino, Russ. 45°9′ N, 39°1′ E 156
Kalinino, Russ. 57°18′ N, 56°23′ E 154
Kalininsk, Russ. 51°29′ N, 44°28′ E 158
Kalinivka, Ukr. 49°28′ N, 28°42′ E 152
Kalinkavichy, Belarus 52°5′ N, 29°26′ E 152
Kalino, Russ. 58°14′ N, 57°38′ E 154
Kalinovik, Bosn. and Herzg. 43°30′ N, 18°26′ E 168
Kaliro, Uganda 0°52′ N, 33°29′ E 224
Kalis, Somalia 8°23′ N, 49°3′ E 216
Kalispell, Mont., U.S. 48°12′ N, 114°21′ W 106
Kalisz, Pol. 51°45′ N, 18°5′ E 152
Kaliua, Tanzania 5°4′ S, 31°46′ E 224
Kalix, Nor. 65°51′ N, 23°7′ E 154
Kalixälven, river, Nor. 67°41′ N, 19°45′ E 152
Kalkan, Turk. 36°15′ N, 29°25′ E 156
Kalkar, Ger. 51°42′ N, 6°17′ E 167
Kalkaska, Mich., U.S. 44°43′ N, 85°11′ W 94
Kalkfeld, Namibia 20°55′ S, 16°12′ E 227
Kalkkinen, Fin. 61°17′ N, 25°41′ E 166
Kalkrand, Namibia 24°5′ S, 17°35′ E 227
Kallam, India 18°32′ N, 76°1′ E 188
Kallaste, Est. 58°38′ N, 27°7′ E 166
Kallithéa, Gr. 37°57′ N, 23°42′ E 156
Kałuszyn, Pol. 52°12′ N, 21°47′ E 152
Kallmet, Alban. 41°50′ N, 19°41′ E 168
Kallo, Fin. 67°25′ N, 24°27′ E 152
Kallunki, Fin. 66°38′ N, 28°54′ E 152
Kalmar, Nor. 56°39′ N, 16°20′ E 152
Kalmthout, Belg. 51°23′ N, 4°28′ E 167
Kalmykiya, adm. division, Russ. 46°7′ N, 43°37′ E 158
Kalnai, India 22°47′ N, 83°29′ E 197
Kalnik, peak, Croatia 46°7′ N, 16°26′ E 168
Kalo Chorio, Cyprus 34°50′ N, 33°2′ E 194
Kalocsa, Hung. 46°31′ N, 18°58′ E 168
Kaloko-Honokōhau National Historical Park, Hawaiʻi, U.S. 19°40′ N, 156°5′ W 99
Kaloli Point, U.S. 19°34′ N, 154°56′ W 99
Kalomo, Zambia 17°3′ S, 26°28′ E 224
Kalotina, Bulg. 42°59′ N, 22°51′ E 168
Kalpi, India 26°6′ N, 79°43′ E 197
Kalpin, China 40°34′ N, 78°54′ E 184
Kalsubai, peak, India 19°34′ N, 73°34′ E 188
Kaltag, Alas., U.S. 64°11′ N, 158°53′ W 98
Kaltay, Russ. 56°14′ N, 84°54′ E 169
Kalterherberg, Ger. 50°31′ N, 6°12′ E 167
Kaltungo, Nig. 9°48′ N, 11°18′ E 222
Kaluga, Russ. 54°34′ N, 36°20′ E 154
Kaluga, adm. division, Russ. 54°14′ N, 34°5′ E 154
Kalulushi, Zambia 12°52′ S, 28°5′ E 224
Kalundu, Zambia 10°17′ S, 29°22′ E 224
Kalungwishi, river, Zambia 9°40′ S, 29°0′ E 220
Kalush, Ukr. 49°0′ N, 24°21′ E 158
Kalvåg, Nor. 61°46′ N, 4°51′ E 152
Kalvarija, Lith. 54°26′ N, 23°11′ E 166
Kälviä, Fin. 63°51′ N, 23°24′ E 152
Kalvitsa, Fin. 61°53′ N, 27°15′ E 166
Kalvola, Fin. 61°5′ N, 24°7′ E 166
Kalwang, Aust. 47°26′ N, 14°46′ E 156
Kalweyn, Ghubbet, Somalia 11°7′ N, 46°28′ E 216
Kal'ya, Russ. 60°17′ N, 59°54′ E 154
Kalyan, India 19°14′ N, 73°8′ E 188
Kalyazin, Russ. 57°12′ N, 37°50′ E 154
Kám, Hung. 47°5′ N, 16°53′ E 168
Kam, river, Nig. 8°10′ N, 11°4′ E 222
Kama, Dem. Rep. of the Congo 3°38′ S, 27°7′ E 224
Kama, Myanmar 19°3′ N, 95°4′ E 202
Kama, Russ. 60°8′ N, 62°1′ E 154
Kama, river, Dem. Rep. of the Congo 3°30′ S, 26°55′ E 218
Kama, river, Russ. 60°10′ N, 55°25′ E 154
Kamae, Japan 32°47′ N, 131°55′ E 201
Kamaing, Myanmar 25°29′ N, 96°40′ E 188
Kamaishi, Japan 39°17′ N, 141°42′ E 190
Kamakou, peak, Hawaiʻi, U.S. 21°6′ N, 156°55′ W 99
Kamakura, Japan 35°18′ N, 139°34′ E 201
Kamalia, Pak. 30°45′ N, 72°38′ E 186
Kamalino, Hawaiʻi, U.S. 21°50′ N, 160°15′ W 99
Kamalu, Sierra Leone 9°22′ N, 12°17′ W 222
Kaman, India 27°38′ N, 77°14′ E 197
Kaman, Turk. 39°21′ N, 33°43′ E 156
Kamanjab, Namibia 19°40′ S, 14°49′ E 220
Kamanyola, Dem. Rep. of the Congo 2°47′ S, 28°57′ E 224
Kamapanda, Zambia 12°1′ S, 24°6′ E 224
Kamarān, island, Yemen 15°16′ N, 41°57′ E 182
Kamarod, Pak. 27°28′ N, 63°36′ E 186
Kamba, Nig. 11°51′ N, 3°40′ E 222
Kambarka, Russ. 56°16′ N, 54°17′ E 154
Kambaya, Guinea 10°40′ N, 13°1′ W 222
Kambia, Sierra Leone 9°5′ N, 12°56′ W 222
Kambja, Est. 58°12′ N, 26°41′ E 166
Kambove, Dem. Rep. of the Congo 10°51′ S, 26°36′ E 224
Kamchatka, adm. division, Russ. 43°39′ N, 145°30′ E 160
Kamchatka, Poluostrov, Asia 58°47′ N, 161°17′ E 160
Kamchatskiy Zaliv 55°17′ N, 159°46′ E 160
Kameda, Japan 37°52′ N, 139°7′ E 201
Kamehameha I Birthplace, site, Hawaiʻi, U.S. 20°14′ N, 155°56′ W 99
Kamen', Belarus 53°51′ N, 26°40′ E 166
Kamen, Ger. 51°35′ N, 7°39′ E 167
Kamen, Gora, peak, Russ. 69°6′ N, 95°4′ E 169
Kamenica, Bosn. and Herzg. 44°20′ N, 18°12′ E 168
Kamenka, Kaz. 51°5′ N, 50°16′ E 158
Kamenka, Russ. 65°53′ N, 44°0′ E 154
Kamenka, Russ. 58°29′ N, 95°34′ E 160
Kamenka, Russ. 53°9′ N, 44°5′ E 154
Kamenka, Russ. 65°52′ N, 43°51′ E 173
Kamen'na Obi, Russ. 53°44′ N, 81°27′ E 184
Kamennoe, Kaz. 44°55′ N, 54°47′ E 158
Kamennogorsk, Russ. 60°57′ N, 29°6′ E 166
Kamensk Shakhtinskiy, Russ. 48°16′ N, 40°16′ E 158
Kamensk Ural'skiy, Russ. 56°27′ N, 61°47′ E 154
Kamenskiy, Russ. 50°50′ N, 45°29′ E 158
Kamenskoye, Russ. 62°31′ N, 165°59′ E 160
Kameoka, Japan 35°0′ N, 135°34′ E 201
Kameur, river, Cen. Af. Rep. 9°42′ N, 21°14′ E 218
Kamiagata, Japan 34°38′ N, 129°24′ E 200
Kamieskroon, S. Af. 30°12′ S, 17°54′ E 227
Kamiji, Dem. Rep. of the Congo 6°37′ S, 23°16′ E 218
Kâmil, Gebel, peak, Egypt 22°15′ N, 26°33′ E 226
Kamina, Dem. Rep. of the Congo 8°45′ S, 24°58′ E 224
Kaministiquia, Can. 48°32′ N, 89°34′ W 94
Kaminoyama, Japan 38°9′ N, 140°15′ E 201
Kaminuriak Lake, Can. 63°4′ N, 97°47′ W 106
Kamioka, Japan 36°20′ N, 137°19′ E 201
Kamitsuki, Japan 34°6′ N, 139°32′ E 201
Kamitsushima, Japan 34°39′ N, 129°28′ E 200
Kamkhat Muḩaywir, peak, Jordan 31°7′ N, 36°28′ E 194
Kamloops, Can. 50°39′ N, 120°20′ W 82
Kammuri, peak, Japan 34°28′ N, 132°2′ E 200
Kamo, Arm. 40°22′ N, 45°5′ E 195
Kamo, Japan 37°39′ N, 139°3′ E 201

Kamo, Japan 38°46′ N, 139°44′ E 201
Kamo, N.Z. 35°42′ S, 174°18′ E 240
Kamoa Mountains, Guyana 1°32′ N, 60°5′ W 130
Kampala, Uganda 0°14′ N, 32°22′ E 224
Kampar, Malaysia 4°18′ N, 101°9′ E 196
Kampene, Dem. Rep. of the Congo 3°37′ S, 26°39′ E 224
Kamphaeng Phet, Thai. 16°28′ N, 99°28′ E 202
Kamp-Lintfort, Ger. 51°29′ N, 6°33′ E 167
Kampolombo, Lake, Zambia 11°49′ S, 28°59′ E 224
Kâmpóng Cham, Cambodia 11°59′ N, 105°25′ E 202
Kampong Kuala Besut, Malaysia 5°48′ N, 102°35′ E 196
Kampos, Cyprus 35°1′ N, 32°43′ E 194
Kampot, Cambodia 10°37′ N, 104°12′ E 202
Kampti, Burkina Faso 10°8′ N, 3°28′ W 222
Kamsack, Can. 51°34′ N, 101°56′ W 90
Kamsar, Guinea 10°39′ N, 14°35′ W 222
Kamskoye Vdkhr., lake, Russ. 58°48′ N, 56°38′ E 246
Kamskoye Vodokhranilishche, lake, Russ. 58°35′ N, 54°17′ E 154
Kamsuuma, Somalia 0°14′ N, 42°48′ E 218
Kámuk, Cerro, peak, C.R. 9°15′ N, 83°6′ W 115
Kam'yanka-Dniprovs'ka, Ukr. 47°28′ N, 34°24′ E 156
Kamyshin, Russ. 50°6′ N, 45°22′ E 158
Kamyshla, Russ. 54°7′ N, 52°9′ E 154
Kamyzyak, Russ. 46°5′ N, 48°6′ E 158
Kan, Sudan 8°57′ N, 31°47′ E 224
Kanab, Utah, U.S. 37°2′ N, 112°32′ W 82
Kanagawa, adm. division, Japan 35°20′ N, 139°2′ E 201
Kanak, river, Turk. 39°33′ N, 34°58′ E 156
Kanākir, Syr. 33°15′ N, 36°5′ E 194
Kanaktok Mountain, Alas., U.S. 67°48′ N, 160°12′ W 98
Kanal, Slov. 46°5′ N, 13°38′ E 167
Kanalla, India 6°53′ N, 93°52′ E 188
Kananga, Dem. Rep. of the Congo 5°54′ S, 22°25′ E 218
Kanash, Russ. 55°28′ N, 47°29′ E 154
Kanata, Can. 45°16′ N, 75°51′ W 82
Kanava, Russ. 61°5′ N, 55°4′ E 154
Kanāyis, Rās el, Egypt 31°16′ N, 27°50′ E 180
Kanazawa, Japan 36°33′ N, 136°40′ E 201
Kanbalu, Myanmar 23°11′ N, 95°31′ E 202
Kanchipuram, India 12°51′ N, 79°43′ E 188
Kanda Kanda, Dem. Rep. of the Congo 6°55′ S, 23°32′ E 218
Kandahar, Afghan. 31°36′ N, 65°43′ E 186
Kandalaksha, Russ. 67°9′ N, 32°24′ E 152
Kandalakshskiy Zaliv 66°18′ N, 29°7′ E 160
Kandale, Dem. Rep. of the Congo 6°2′ S, 19°23′ E 218
Kandang, Indonesia 3°6′ N, 97°18′ E 196
Kandangan, Indonesia 2°43′ S, 115°13′ E 192
Kandava, Latv. 57°2′ N, 22°44′ E 166
Kandel, Ger. 49°5′ N, 8°10′ E 152
Kandersteg, Switz. 46°29′ N, 7°40′ E 167
Kandhkot, Pak. 28°13′ N, 69°12′ E 186
Kandi, Benin 11°7′ N, 2°56′ E 222
Kandiaro, Pak. 27°6′ N, 68°15′ E 186
Kandıra, Turk. 41°4′ N, 30°8′ E 156
Kandla, India 23°12′ N, 70°25′ E 173
Kandrach, Pak. 25°29′ N, 65°27′ E 182
Kandreho, Madagascar 17°31′ S, 46°6′ E 220
Kandudu, island, Maldives 2°2′ N, 72°0′ E 188
Kandy, Sri Lanka 7°16′ N, 80°40′ E 188
Kane, Pa., U.S. 41°39′ N, 78°49′ W 94
Kāneʻākī Heiau, site, Hawaiʻi, U.S. 21°29′ N, 158°14′ W 99
Kāneiolouma Heiau, site, Hawaiʻi, U.S. 21°52′ N, 159°30′ W 99
Kanel, Senegal 15°29′ N, 13°14′ W 222
Kanepi, Est. 57°58′ N, 26°45′ E 166
Kanevskaya, Russ. 46°6′ N, 38°55′ E 156
Kang, Afghan. 31°7′ N, 61°55′ E 186
Kang, Botswana 23°41′ S, 22°48′ E 227
Kangaamiut, Den. 65°50′ N, 53°21′ W 106
Kangaatsiaq, Den. 68°18′ N, 53°25′ W 106
Kangaba, Mali 11°57′ N, 8°26′ W 222
Kangal, Turk. 39°13′ N, 37°22′ E 156
Kangān, Iran 25°49′ N, 57°28′ E 196
Kangān, Iran 27°51′ N, 52°7′ E 196
Kangar, Malaysia 6°25′ N, 100°12′ E 202
Kangaroo Island, Austral. 36°51′ S, 137°17′ E 230
Kangasala, Fin. 61°26′ N, 24°2′ E 166
Kangasniemi, Fin. 61°58′ N, 26°34′ E 166
Kangatet, Kenya 1°55′ N, 36°6′ E 224
Kangāvar, Iran 34°26′ N, 47°48′ E 180
Kangbao, China 41°51′ N, 114°36′ E 198
Kangdong, N. Korea 39°8′ N, 126°5′ E 200
Kangean, Kepulauan, islands, Java Sea 6°17′ S, 113°56′ E 192
Kangeeak Point, Can. 67°47′ N, 64°28′ W 106
Kangen, river, Sudan 6°35′ N, 33°17′ E 224
Kangerluarsoruseq (Færingehavn), Den. 63°43′ N, 51°21′ W 106
Kangerlussuaq 67°49′ N, 35°25′ W 246
Kangerlussuaq, Den. 67°4′ N, 50°50′ W 106
Kangersuatsiaq, Den. 72°16′ N, 55°39′ W 106
Kanggye, N. Korea 40°58′ N, 126°35′ E 200
Kangikajiip Agpalia, Den. 69°48′ N, 22°11′ W 246
Kangiqsualujjuaq, Can. 58°30′ N, 65°54′ W 106
Kangiqsujuaq, Can. 61°35′ N, 72°2′ W 106
Kangmar, China 28°36′ N, 89°41′ E 197
Kangmar, China 30°48′ N, 85°39′ E 197
Kangnyŏng, N. Korea 37°53′ N, 125°31′ E 200
Kango, Gabon 0°11′ N, 10°8′ E 218
Kangping, China 42°45′ N, 123°24′ E 200
Kangrinboqê Feng, peak, China 31°4′ N, 81°18′ E 197
Kangsang, N. Korea 40°6′ N, 128°23′ E 200
Kangsŏ, N. Korea 38°56′ N, 125°30′ E 200
Kangto, peak, China 27°40′ N, 92°10′ E 190
Kaniama, Dem. Rep. of the Congo 7°33′ S, 24°10′ E 224
Kaniet Islands, South Pacific Ocean 0°47′ N, 145°35′ E 192
Kanin Nos, Russ. 68°34′ N, 43°22′ E 169
Kanin Nos, Mys, Russ. 68°10′ N, 42°25′ E 169
Kanin, Poluostrov, Russ. 68°1′ N, 39°33′ E 169
Kanin, Poluostrov, Russ. 67°0′ N, 44°14′ E 160
Kanirom, Chad 14°26′ N, 13°45′ E 216
Kanish, ruin(s), Turk. 38°51′ N, 35°29′ E 156
Kaniv, Ukr. 49°43′ N, 31°30′ E 158
Kanjarkot, site, Pak. 24°15′ N, 69°5′ E 186
Kanjiža, Serb. and Mont. 46°4′ N, 20°3′ E 168
Kankaanpää, Fin. 61°47′ N, 22°23′ E 166
Kankakee, Ill., U.S. 41°7′ N, 87°52′ W 102
Kankan, Guinea 10°25′ N, 9°19′ W 222
Kankossa, Mauritania 15°54′ N, 11°32′ W 222
Kanmaw Kyun, island, Myanmar 11°33′ N, 98°32′ E 202
Kanmen, China 28°5′ N, 121°16′ E 198
Kannapolis, N.C., U.S. 35°29′ N, 80°38′ W 96
Kannauj, India 27°1′ N, 79°54′ E 197
Kannod, India 22°40′ N, 76°46′ E 197
Kannusuo, Russ. 65°8′ N, 31°54′ E 152
Kano, Nig. 11°59′ N, 8°30′ E 222
Kanonji, Japan 34°7′ N, 133°38′ E 201
Kanopolis, Kans., U.S. 38°41′ N, 98°10′ W 90
Kanorado, Kans., U.S. 39°20′ N, 102°2′ W 90
Kanosh, Utah, U.S. 38°48′ N, 112°26′ W 90
Kanoya, Japan 31°21′ N, 130°51′ E 201
Kanpur, India 26°25′ N, 80°19′ E 197
Kansanshi, Zambia 12°5′ S, 26°22′ E 224
Kansas, Ill., U.S. 39°32′ N, 87°56′ W 102
Kansas, adm. division, Kans., U.S. 38°7′ N, 100°3′ W 82
Kansas City, Mo., U.S. 39°4′ N, 94°33′ W 82
Kansas, river, Kans., U.S. 39°18′ N, 96°32′ W 80
Kansk, Russ. 56°6′ N, 95°41′ E 160
Kant, Kyrg. 42°52′ N, 74°55′ E 184
Kantang, Thai. 7°24′ N, 99°31′ E 196
Kantankufri, Ghana 7°49′ N, 2°118′ W 222
Kantara Castle, site, Northern Cyprus 35°23′ N, 33°53′ E 194
Kantchari, Burkina Faso 12°32′ N, 1°33′ E 222
Kanté, Togo 9°56′ N, 1°1′ E 222
Kantemirovka, Russ. 49°43′ N, 39°53′ E 158
Kanuma, Japan 36°33′ N, 139°45′ E 201
Kanyato, Tanzania 4°28′ S, 30°15′ E 224
Kanye, Botswana 24°60′ S, 25°19′ E 227
Kaohsiung, Taiwan 22°41′ N, 120°20′ E 198
Kaokoveld, Namibia 19°17′ S, 13°48′ E 220
Kaolack, Senegal 14°11′ N, 16°3′ W 222
Kaoma, Zambia 14°49′ S, 24°47′ E 224
Kaongeshi, river, Dem. Rep. of the Congo 7°48′ S, 22°22′ E 218
Kaouar, Niger 19°41′ N, 12°17′ E 222
Kap Farvel see Nunap Isua, Den. 59°20′ N, 43°43′ W 106
Kapa Moračka, peak, Serb. and Mont. 42°48′ N, 19°13′ E 168
Kapalala, Zambia 12°24′ S, 29°22′ E 224
Kapan, Arm. 39°11′ N, 46°23′ E 195
Kapanga, Dem. Rep. of the Congo 8°23′ S, 22°35′ E 218
Kapatu, Zambia 9°45′ S, 30°45′ E 224
Kapedo, Kenya 1°9′ N, 36°3′ E 224
Kapela, Croatia 44°50′ N, 15°10′ E 156
Kapellen, Belg. 51°20′ N, 4°25′ E 167
Kapenguria, Kenya 1°15′ N, 35°6′ E 224
Kapıdağı, peak, Turk. 40°26′ N, 27°43′ E 156
Kapikik Lake, Can. 51°30′ N, 92°24′ W 110
Kapili, river, Dem. Rep. of the Congo 3°45′ N, 27°51′ E 224
Kapingamarangi Atoll, North Pacific Ocean 0°43′ N, 152°44′ E 238
Kapiri Mposhi, Zambia 13°60′ S, 28°40′ E 224
Kapisillit, Den. 64°23′ N, 50°19′ W 106
Kapiskau, river, Can. 52°0′ N, 84°33′ W 110
Kapit, Malaysia 1°55′ N, 112°57′ E 192
Kaplan, La., U.S. 29°59′ N, 92°18′ W 96
Kaplice, Czech Rep. 48°44′ N, 14°28′ E 152
Kapoeta, Sudan 4°45′ N, 33°35′ E 224
Kapoho Crater, Hawaiʻi, U.S. 19°29′ N, 154°53′ W 99
Kapombo, Dem. Rep. of the Congo 10°39′ S, 23°27′ E 224
Kaposvár, Hung. 46°22′ N, 17°47′ E 168
Kappeln, Ger. 54°40′ N, 9°56′ E 150
Kappelshamn, Sw. 57°50′ N, 18°45′ E 166
Kapsabet, Kenya 0°10′ N, 35°8′ E 224
Kapsan, N. Korea 41°4′ N, 128°19′ E 200
Kapsowar, Kenya 0°57′ N, 35°35′ E 224
Kapterko, spring, Chad 16°50′ N, 23°12′ E 226
Kaptol, Croatia 45°25′ N, 17°42′ E 168
Kapuāiwa Coconut Grove, site, Hawaiʻi, U.S. 21°5′ N, 157°6′ W 99
Kapuas, river, Indonesia 0°28′ N, 110°18′ E 192
Kapulo, Dem. Rep. of the Congo 8°18′ S, 29°11′ E 224
Kapuskasing, Can. 49°24′ N, 82°24′ W 82
Kapustin Yar, Russ. 48°35′ N, 45°45′ E 158
Kaputirr, Kenya 2°3′ N, 35°27′ E 224
Kapuvár, Hung. 47°35′ N, 17°2′ E 168
Kapydzhik, peak, Arm. 39°9′ N, 45°59′ E 195
Kara Balta, Kyrg. 42°48′ N, 73°52′ E 184
Kara Burun, Turk. 36°40′ N, 31°40′ E 156
Kara Burun, Turk. 38°41′ N, 26°21′ E 156
Kara Dağ, peak, Turk. 37°40′ N, 43°33′ E 195
Kara Dağ, peak, Turk. 37°22′ N, 33°5′ E 156
Kara, river, Russ. 69°10′ N, 65°11′ E 246
Kara Sea 78°26′ N, 78°5′ E 160
Karabash, Russ. 55°27′ N, 60°19′ E 154
Karabekaul, Turkm. 38°25′ N, 64°13′ E 197
Karabiga, Turk. 40°24′ N, 27°16′ E 158
Karabogaz (Bekdash), Turkm. 41°32′ N, 52°35′ E 158
Karabudakhkent, Russ. 42°42′ N, 47°37′ E 195
Karabük, Turk. 41°12′ N, 32°36′ E 156
Karaburun, Alban. 40°21′ N, 19°4′ E 156
Karaca Dağ, peak, Turk. 37°40′ N, 39°50′ E 195
Karacabey, Turk. 40°12′ N, 28°20′ E 156
Karacadağ, Turk. 37°43′ N, 39°39′ E 195
Karacaköy, Turk. 41°24′ N, 28°21′ E 156
Karacasu, Turk. 37°43′ N, 28°35′ E 156
Karachala, Azerb. 39°48′ N, 48°56′ E 195
Karachayevo-Cherkesiya, adm. division, Russ. 43°42′ N, 40°40′ E 195
Karachayevsk, Russ. 43°46′ N, 41°55′ E 195
Karachev, Russ. 53°3′ N, 35°0′ E 154
Karachi, Pak. 24°49′ N, 67°2′ E 186
Karád, Hung. 46°40′ N, 17°50′ E 168
Karadag, Azerb. 40°17′ N, 49°34′ E 195
Karadžica, Maced. 41°54′ N, 21°14′ E 168
Karaga, Ghana 9°54′ N, 0°29′ E 222
Karaginskiy, Ostrov, island, Russ. 57°53′ N, 163°44′ E 160
Karagosh, Gora, peak, Russ. 51°41′ N, 89°17′ E 184
Karahallı, Turk. 38°19′ N, 29°31′ E 156
Karahüyük, Turk. 37°47′ N, 32°25′ E 156
Karaidel', Russ. 55°50′ N, 56°35′ E 154
Karaidel'skiy, Russ. 55°50′ N, 57°2′ E 154
Karaikal, India 10°56′ N, 79°48′ E 188
Karaisalı, Turk. 37°15′ N, 35°2′ E 156
Karaj, Iran 35°51′ N, 50°57′ E 186
Karakaralong, Kepulauan, islands, Philippine Sea 4°51′ N, 125°34′ E 203
Karakax, river, China 36°39′ N, 78°58′ E 184
Karakeçi, Turk. 37°26′ N, 39°27′ E 195
Karakoçan, Turk. 38°56′ N, 40°2′ E 195
Kara-Köl, Kyrg. 41°35′ N, 72°38′ E 197
Karakol, Kyrg. 42°27′ N, 78°17′ E 190
Kara-Koo, Kyrg. 42°13′ N, 76°36′ E 184
Karakoram Pass, China 35°32′ N, 77°52′ E 188
Karakoro, river, Mauritania 15°22′ N, 11°47′ W 222
Karakorum see Har Horin, ruin(s), Mongolia 47°14′ N, 102°43′ E 198
Karaköse see Ağrı, Turk. 39°43′ N, 43°3′ E 195
Karakul', Taj. 39°0′ N, 73°34′ E 197
Karakulino, Russ. 56°2′ N, 53°43′ E 154
Karakuwisa, Namibia 18°54′ S, 19°40′ E 220
Karam, Russ. 55°14′ N, 107°37′ E 190
Karaman, Turk. 37°10′ N, 33°12′ E 156
Karamay, China 45°30′ N, 84°51′ E 184
Karamea, N.Z. 41°16′ S, 172°8′ E 240
Karamiran, river, China 37°12′ N, 85°3′ E 188
Karamiran Shankou, pass, China 36°18′ N, 87°4′ E 188
Karamken, Russ. 60°25′ N, 151°27′ E 173
Karamyshevo, Russ. 57°45′ N, 28°41′ E 166
Karan, Serb. and Mont. 43°54′ N, 19°53′ E 168
Karan, oil field, Saudi Arabia 27°41′ N, 49°45′ E 196
Karapınar, Turk. 37°41′ N, 33°33′ E 156
Kara-Say, Kyrg. 41°34′ N, 77°57′ E 184
Karasburg, Namibia 28°1′ S, 18°42′ E 227
Karašica, river, Croatia 45°44′ N, 17°41′ E 156
Karasino, Russ. 66°46′ N, 86°56′ E 169
Karasu, Taj. 37°57′ N, 73°57′ E 197
Karasu, Turk. 41°6′ N, 30°39′ E 156
Karasu, river, Turk. 39°54′ N, 40°4′ E 195
Karasu, river, Turk. 38°46′ N, 43°37′ E 195
Karasuk, Russ. 53°42′ N, 78°4′ E 184
Karasuk Hills, Kenya 2°16′ N, 34°57′ E 224
Kara-Suu, Kyrg. 41°5′ N, 75°34′ E 184
Karataş, Turk. 36°34′ N, 35°22′ E 156
Karathuri, Myanmar 10°56′ N, 98°46′ E 202
Karatsu, Japan 33°26′ N, 129°57′ E 201
Karaul, Russ. 70°5′ N, 83°22′ E 169
Karauli, India 26°31′ N, 76°58′ E 197
Kara-Ünkür, Kyrg. 41°43′ N, 75°45′ E 184
Karavás, Gr. 36°20′ N, 22°57′ E 156
Karavónissia, islands, Aegean Sea 35°54′ N, 25°36′ E 156
Karavostasi, Northern Cyprus 35°8′ N, 32°49′ E 194
Karawa, Dem. Rep. of the Congo 3°14′ N, 20°17′ E 218
Karawanken, Aust. 46°31′ N, 13°54′ E 156
Karayazı, Turk. 39°40′ N, 42°8′ E 195
Karayün, Turk. 39°38′ N, 37°19′ E 156
Karbalā', Iraq 32°36′ N, 44°2′ E 180
Kårböle, Nor. 61°58′ N, 15°17′ E 152
Karcag, Hung. 47°18′ N, 20°54′ E 168
Kardašova Řečice, Czech Rep. 49°10′ N, 14°52′ E 152
Karditsa, Gr. 39°20′ N, 21°56′ E 180
Kardiva Channel 4°49′ N, 72°13′ E 188
Kärdla, Est. 58°59′ N, 22°42′ E 166
Kareliya, adm. division, Russ. 63°15′ N, 33°53′ E 154
Karel'skaya, Russ. 62°11′ N, 39°27′ E 154
Karem Shalom, Israel 31°13′ N, 34°16′ E 194
Karema, Tanzania 6°48′ S, 30°24′ E 224
Karera, India 25°28′ N, 78°10′ E 197
Karesuando, Nor. 68°26′ N, 22°26′ E 152
Karêt, region, Africa 23°35′ N, 9°38′ W 214
Kargānrūd, Iran 37°52′ N, 48°56′ E 195
Kargasok, Russ. 58°58′ N, 80°50′ E 169
Kargat, Russ. 55°10′ N, 80°21′ E 184
Kargı, Turk. 41°8′ N, 34°29′ E 156
Kargil, India 34°32′ N, 76°7′ E 186
Kargilik see Yecheng, China 37°52′ N, 77°31′ E 184
Kargopol', Russ. 61°30′ N, 38°53′ E 154
Karhula, Fin. 60°30′ N, 26°55′ E 166
Kari, Nig. 11°12′ N, 10°35′ E 222
Kariá, Gr. 39°59′ N, 22°23′ E 156
Kariá, Gr. 38°45′ N, 20°38′ E 156
Kariba, Zimb. 16°28′ S, 28°51′ E 224
Kariba, Lake, Zimb. 17°27′ S, 25°50′ E 207
Karibib, Namibia 21°56′ S, 15°52′ E 227
Karijini National Park, Austral. 22°48′ S, 117°59′ E 238
Karikari, Cape, N.Z. 34°49′ S, 173°25′ E 240
Karima, Sudan 18°30′ N, 31°50′ E 182
Karimata, Kepulauan, islands, Indian Ocean 1°31′ S, 106°26′ E 192
Karimganj, India 24°44′ N, 92°22′ E 188
Karimnagar, India 18°25′ N, 79°7′ E 188
Kariniemi, Fin. 65°36′ N, 27°56′ E 152
Karis (Karjaa), Fin. 60°4′ N, 23°39′ E 166
Karitane, N.Z. 45°39′ S, 170°38′ E 240
Kariya, Japan 34°57′ N, 137°0′ E 201
Karizak, Afghan. 32°26′ N, 61°28′ E 186
Karjaa see Karis, Fin. 60°4′ N, 23°39′ E 166
Karjala, Fin. 60°46′ N, 22°4′ E 166
Karkaar, Somalia 9°42′ N, 48°36′ E 216
Karkar, island, P.N.G. 4°49′ S, 145°4′ E 192
Karkas, Kūh-e, peak, Iran 33°26′ N, 51°41′ E 180
Karkkila, Fin. 60°31′ N, 24°7′ E 166
Karkku, Fin. 61°23′ N, 22°57′ E 166
Karkoj, Sudan 12°57′ N, 34°2′ E 182
Kärkölä, Fin. 60°54′ N, 25°14′ E 166
Karkūk (Kirkūk), Iraq 35°27′ N, 44°23′ E 180
Karlholm, Sw. 60°30′ N, 17°34′ E 166
Karlino, Pol. 54°2′ N, 15°53′ E 152
Karlıova, Turk. 39°16′ N, 41°0′ E 195
Karlovac, Croatia 45°28′ N, 15°33′ E 156
Karlovarský, adm. division, Czech Rep. 49°55′ N, 12°2′ E 152
Karlovka, Ukr. 49°29′ N, 35°9′ E 158
Karlovy Vary, Czech Rep. 50°13′ N, 12°52′ E 152
Karlsborg, Nor. 65°48′ N, 23°16′ E 152
Karlsborg, Nor. 58°31′ N, 14°29′ E 152
Karlskrona, Nor. 56°9′ N, 15°33′ E 152
Karlsøy, Nor. 70°0′ N, 19°54′ E 152
Karlsøyvær, islands, Norwegian Sea 67°35′ N, 12°59′ E 152
Karlsruhe, Ger. 49°0′ N, 8°24′ E 150
Karlstad, Minn., U.S. 48°33′ N, 96°33′ W 90
Karluk, Alas., U.S. 57°25′ N, 154°33′ W 98
Karma, Belarus 53°5′ N, 30°51′ E 154
Karmana, Uzb. 40°9′ N, 65°20′ E 197
Karmir Blur, ruin(s), Arm. 40°7′ N, 44°22′ E 195
Karnack, Tex., U.S. 32°39′ N, 94°10′ W 103
Karnal, India 29°41′ N, 77°1′ E 197
Karnataka, adm. division, India 13°56′ N, 74°36′ E 188
Karnes City, Tex., U.S. 28°52′ N, 97°54′ W 96
Karoi, Zimb. 16°50′ S, 29°39′ E 224
Karokh, Afghan. 34°33′ N, 62°30′ E 186
Kārokh, peak, Iraq 36°28′ N, 44°36′ E 195
Karonga, Malawi 9°55′ S, 33°54′ E 224
Karoo National Park, S. Af. 32°30′ S, 21°51′ E 227
Karor, Pak. 31°14′ N, 71°0′ E 186
Karora, Sudan 17°41′ N, 38°17′ E 182
Karou, Mali 15°6′ N, 0°37′ E 222
Karpasia Peninsula, Northern Cyprus 35°21′ N, 33°59′ E 194
Kárpathos, island, Gr. 35°15′ N, 27°9′ E 180
Karpinsk, Russ. 59°45′ N, 60°0′ E 154
Karpogory, Russ. 64°1′ N, 44°33′ E 154
Kärrgruvan, Nor. 60°4′ N, 15°56′ E 152
Kars, Turk. 40°34′ N, 43°10′ E 180
Kärsämäki, Fin. 63°58′ N, 25°44′ E 152
Kārsava, Latv. 56°47′ N, 27°40′ E 166
Karsiyang, India 26°49′ N, 88°17′ E 197
Karskiye Vorota, Proliv 70°38′ N, 59°23′ E 246
Karsun, Russ. 54°10′ N, 47°1′ E 154
Kartal, Turk. 40°54′ N, 29°10′ E 156
Kartaly, Russ. 53°5′ N, 60°35′ E 154
Kartayel', Russ. 64°29′ N, 53°12′ E 154
Karttula, Fin. 62°50′ N, 27°7′ E 152
Kartung, Senegal 13°6′ N, 16°39′ W 222
Karubwe, Zambia 15°8′ S, 28°22′ E 224
Karufa, Indonesia 3°47′ S, 133°17′ E 192
Karumwa, Tanzania 3°12′ S, 32°37′ E 224
Kārūn, river, Iran 30°44′ N, 48°16′ E 180
Karuna, Fin. 60°15′ N, 22°31′ E 166
Karungu, Kenya 0°51′ N, 34°12′ E 224
Karvio, Fin. 62°30′ N, 28°38′ E 152
Karwar, India 14°47′ N, 74°8′ E 188
Karwi, India 25°12′ N, 80°55′ E 197
Karyaí, Gr. 40°15′ N, 24°15′ E 156
Kar'yepol'ye, Russ. 65°34′ N, 43°42′ E 154
Karymkary, Russ. 62°4′ N, 67°38′ E 169
Kas, Sudan 12°30′ N, 24°19′ E 216
Kaş, Turk. 36°11′ N, 29°37′ E 156
Kas, river, Russ. 59°33′ N, 90°5′ E 169
Kas Saar, Est. 58°41′ N, 22°52′ E 166
Kasaan, Alas., U.S. 55°33′ N, 132°25′ W 108
Kasaba, Turk. 36°17′ N, 29°44′ E 156
Kasaba Bay, Zambia 8°35′ S, 30°43′ E 224
Kasai, river, Dem. Rep. of the Congo 6°48′ S, 20°59′ E 218
Kasaï-Occidental, adm. division, Dem. Rep. of the Congo 5°59′ S, 20°39′ E 218
Kasaï-Oriental, adm. division, Dem. Rep. of the Congo 4°17′ S, 23°24′ E 218
Kasaji, Dem. Rep. of the Congo 10°22′ S, 23°28′ E 224
Kasala, Fin. 61°57′ N, 21°21′ E 166
Kasama, Zambia 10°13′ S, 31°10′ E 224
Kasane, Botswana 17°51′ S, 25°5′ E 224
Kasanga, Tanzania 8°27′ S, 31°10′ E 224
Kasanka National Park, Zambia 12°48′ S, 29°40′ E 224
Kasar, Ras, Eritrea 17°50′ N, 38°34′ E 182
Kasaragod, India 12°31′ N, 75°1′ E 188
Kasari, river, Est. 58°44′ N, 23°54′ E 166
Kasba Lake, Can. 60°2′ N, 103°43′ W 106
Kaseda, Japan 31°23′ N, 130°20′ E 201
Kasempa, Zambia 13°29′ S, 25°48′ E 224
Kasenga, Dem. Rep. of the Congo 10°18′ S, 28°40′ E 224
Kasenye, Dem. Rep. of the Congo 1°23′ N, 30°26′ E 224
Kasese, Dem. Rep. of the Congo 1°37′ S, 27°13′ E 224
Kasese, Uganda 0°10′ N, 30°7′ E 224
Kasganj, India 27°48′ N, 78°39′ E 197
Kāshān, Iran 34°1′ N, 51°27′ E 180
Kashegelok, Alas., U.S. 60°50′ N, 157°48′ W 98
Kashi, China 39°31′ N, 75°59′ E 184
Kashima, Japan 33°6′ N, 130°5′ E 201
Kashin, Russ. 57°18′ N, 37°31′ E 154
Kashipur, India 29°11′ N, 78°57′ E 197
Kashira, Russ. 54°48′ N, 38°10′ E 154
Kashishibog Lake, Can. 49°47′ N, 90°36′ W 94
Kashitu, Zambia 13°44′ S, 28°38′ E 224
Kashiwazaki, Japan 37°21′ N, 138°33′ E 201
Kashkadar'ya, Uzb. 38°55′ N, 65°45′ E 197
Kashkarantsy, Russ. 66°21′ N, 35°55′ E 154
Kāshmar, Iran 35°13′ N, 58°28′ E 180
Kashmir, region, Asia 34°38′ N, 75°56′ E 188
Kashmor, Pak. 28°29′ N, 69°34′ E 186
Kashnjet, Alban. 41°54′ N, 19°48′ E 168
Kasimov, Russ. 54°55′ N, 41°26′ E 154
Kasindi, Dem. Rep. of the Congo 2°119′ N, 29°40′ E 224
Kaskaskia, river, Ill., U.S. 38°42′ N, 89°26′ W 80
Kaskö (Kaskinen), Fin. 62°22′ N, 21°12′ E 152
Kasli, Russ. 55°52′ N, 60°45′ E 154
Kaslo, Can. 49°54′ N, 116°56′ W 90
Kasmere Lake, Can. 59°35′ N, 101°38′ W 108
Kasongo, Dem. Rep. of the Congo 4°29′ S, 26°36′ E 224
Kasongo-Lunda, Dem. Rep. of the Congo 6°30′ S, 16°49′ E 220
Kaspiysk, Russ. 42°51′ N, 47°41′ E 195
Kaspiyskiy, Russ. 45°21′ N, 47°21′ E 158
Kasrik see Kırkgeçit, Turk. 38°7′ N, 43°27′ E 195
Kassala, Sudan 15°25′ N, 36°22′ E 182
Kassala, adm. division, Sudan 15°47′ N, 35°39′ E 182
Kassándra, Gr. 40°1′ N, 23°7′ E 156
Kassari, spring, Mauritania 15°50′ N, 7°54′ W 222
Kassaro, Mali 13°0′ N, 8°54′ W 222
Kassel, Ger. 51°19′ N, 9°29′ E 167
Kasserine see Qasserine, Tun. 35°9′ N, 8°51′ E 156
Kasson, Minn., U.S. 44°0′ N, 92°47′ W 94
Kássos, island, Gr. 35°11′ N, 26°48′ E 180
Kassouloua, spring, Niger 14°29′ N, 11°23′ E 222
Kastamonu, Turk. 41°23′ N, 33°45′ E 156
Kaštel Sućurac, Croatia 43°32′ N, 16°25′ E 168
Kastellaun, Ger. 50°3′ N, 7°25′ E 167
Kastornoye, Russ. 51°48′ N, 38°5′ E 158
Kastrossikiá, Gr. 39°6′ N, 20°38′ E 156
Kastsyukovichy, Belarus 53°19′ N, 32°5′ E 154
Kasulu, Tanzania 4°36′ S, 30°6′ E 224
Kasumkent, Russ. 41°40′ N, 48°11′ E 195
Kasungu, Malawi 13°4′ S, 33°28′ E 224
Kasungu National Park, Malawi 12°58′ S, 32°56′ E 224
Kasupe, Malawi 15°12′ S, 35°16′ E 224
Kasur, Pak. 31°9′ N, 74°26′ E 186
Kata Tjuta (Mount Olga), Austral. 25°21′ S, 130°31′ E 230
Kataba, Zambia 16°5′ S, 25°6′ E 224
Kataeregi, Nig. 9°20′ N, 6°18′ E 222
Katagum, Nig. 12°17′ N, 10°21′ E 222
Katahdin, Mount, Me., U.S. 45°53′ N, 69°1′ W 94
Katako Kombe, Dem. Rep. of the Congo 3°28′ S, 24°21′ E 224
Katal'ga, Russ. 59°8′ N, 76°50′ E 169
Katanda, Russ. 50°11′ N, 86°14′ E 184
Katanga, adm. division, Dem. Rep. of the Congo 8°40′ S, 23°51′ E 220
Katanning, Austral. 33°41′ S, 117°33′ E 231
Katav Ivanovsk, Russ. 54°45′ N, 58°10′ E 154
Katavi National Park, Tanzania 7°21′ S, 30°38′ E 224
Katavía, Gr. 35°57′ N, 27°46′ E 156
Katavivanovsk, Russ. 54°44′ N, 58°13′ E 184
Katchall Island, India 7°40′ N, 92°29′ E 188
Kate, Tanzania 7°50′ S, 31°8′ E 224
Katera, Uganda 0°55′ N, 31°37′ E 224
Katerini, Gr. 40°15′ N, 22°30′ E 156
Kates Needle, peak, Can. 57°2′ N, 132°14′ W 108
Katha, Myanmar 24°8′ N, 96°19′ E 188
Katherine, Austral. 14°29′ S, 132°20′ E 231
Kathleen, Mount, Austral. 23°56′ S, 135°13′ E 230
Kathmandu, Nepal 27°46′ N, 85°11′ E 197
Kati, Mali 12°44′ N, 8°4′ W 222
Katihar, India 25°30′ N, 87°33′ E 197
Katima Mulilo, Namibia 17°33′ S, 24°16′ E 224
Katimik Lake, Can. 52°51′ N, 99°52′ W 108
Katiola, Côte d'Ivoire 8°6′ N, 5°5′ W 222
Kätkäsuvanto, Fin. 68°7′ N, 23°20′ E 152
Katlanovo, Maced. 41°53′ N, 21°40′ E 168
Katmai, Mount, Alas., U.S. 58°10′ N, 155°14′ W 98
Katonah, N.Y., U.S. 41°14′ N, 73°42′ W 104
Katondwe, Zambia 15°15′ S, 30°12′ E 224
Katonga, river, Uganda 3°179′ N, 30°33′ E 224
Katowice, Pol. 50°15′ N, 19°1′ E 152
Katrancık Dağı, peak, Turk. 37°26′ N, 30°15′ E 156
Katrineholm, Nor. 59°0′ N, 16°8′ E 152
Katrovozh, Russ. 66°22′ N, 66°9′ E 169
Katsina, Nig. 13°0′ N, 7°38′ E 222
Katsina Ala, river, Nig. 7°51′ N, 8°33′ E 222
Katsumoto, Japan 33°50′ N, 129°42′ E 200
Katsuta, Japan 36°23′ N, 140°32′ E 201
Katsuura, Japan 35°9′ N, 140°18′ E 201
Katsuyama, Japan 35°5′ N, 133°40′ E 201
Katsuyama, Japan 36°4′ N, 136°31′ E 201
Kattankudi, Sri Lanka 7°34′ N, 81°48′ E 188
Kattaqoʻrgʻon, Uzb. 39°54′ N, 66°16′ E 197
Kattegat 55°53′ N, 10°43′ E 150
Katthammarsvik, Sw. 57°25′ N, 18°49′ E 166
Kattisavan, Nor. 64°46′ N, 18°8′ E 152
Kattskill Bay, N.Y., U.S. 43°28′ N, 73°38′ W 104
Katul, Jebel, peak, Sudan 14°13′ N, 29°19′ E 226
Katumbi, Zambia 10°49′ S, 33°30′ E 220
Katun', river, Russ. 51°28′ N, 86°4′ E 184
Katwa, India 23°34′ N, 88°6′ E 197
Katwe, Uganda 0°10′ N, 29°51′ E 224
Katwijk aan Zee, Neth. 52°12′ N, 4°25′ E 163
Kauaʻi, island, Hawaiʻi, U.S. 22°7′ N, 160°15′ W 99
Kauakaiakaola Heiau, site, Hawaiʻi, U.S. 19°37′ N, 156°1′ W 99
Kaub, Ger. 50°5′ N, 7°46′ E 163
Kaugama, Nig. 12°28′ N, 9°46′ E 222
Kauhajoki, Fin. 62°24′ N, 22°8′ E 154
Kauhako Crater, peak, Hawaiʻi, U.S. 21°11′ N, 157°1′ W 99
Kauhava, Fin. 63°5′ N, 23°2′ E 152
Kaukau Veld, Namibia 20°24′ S, 18°49′ E 227
Kaukonen, Fin. 67°29′ N, 24°52′ E 152
Kaʻula, island, Hawaiʻi, U.S. 21°27′ N, 160°43′ W 99
Kauliranta, Fin. 66°27′ N, 23°40′ E 152
Kaulu Paoa Heiau, site, Hawaiʻi, U.S. 22°12′ N, 159°38′ W 99
Kaunā Point, Hawaiʻi, U.S. 18°59′ N, 156°18′ W 99
Kaunas, Lith. 54°53′ N, 23°54′ E 162
Kaunata, Latv. 56°19′ N, 27°33′ E 166

Kaunatava, *Lith.* 55°58' N, 22°32' E 166
Kauniainen see Grankulla, *Fin.* 60°11' N, 24°43' E 152
Kaunolū, site, *Hawai'i, U.S.* 20°43' N, 156°60' W 99
Ka'ūpūlehu, site, *Hawai'i, U.S.* 19°49' N, 156°2' W 99
Kaura-Namoda, *Nig.* 12°36' N, 6°35' E 222
Kauru, *Nig.* 10°33' N, 8°11' E 222
Kavacha, *Russ.* 60°22' N, 169°55' E 160
Kavak, *Turk.* 41°4' N, 36°2' E 156
Kavála, *Gr.* 40°57' N, 24°24' E 180
Kavali, *India* 14°55' N, 79°59' E 188
Kavaratti, *India* 10°34' N, 72°38' E 188
Kavarna, *Bulg.* 43°26' N, 28°19' E 158
Kavarskas, *Lith.* 55°26' N, 24°55' E 166
Kavieng, *P.N.G.* 2°41' S, 150°59' E 238
Kavkaz, *Russ.* 45°22' N, 36°39' E 156
Kavungo, *Angola* 11°32' S, 23°2' E 220
Kawagoe, *Japan* 35°54' N, 139°29' E 201
Kawaihoa Point, *Hawai'i, U.S.* 21°42' N, 160°13' W 99
Kawakawa, *N.Z.* 35°25' S, 174°5' E 240
Kawambwa, *Zambia* 9°49' S, 29°5' E 224
Kawanishi, *Japan* 38°0' N, 140°3' E 201
Kawanoe, *Japan* 34°0' N, 133°35' E 201
Kawardha, *India* 22°1' N, 81°14' E 197
Kawasaki, *Japan* 35°30' N, 139°43' E 201
Kawashiri Misaki, *Japan* 34°23' N, 130°41' E 200
Kawaweogama Lake, *Can.* 50°9' N, 91°3' W 110
Kaweah, Mount, *Calif., U.S.* 36°31' N, 118°32' W 101
Kaweka, peak, *N.Z.* 39°20' S, 176°18' E 240
Kawela Place of Refuge, site, *Hawai'i, U.S.* 21°4' N, 157°1' W 99
Kawhia, *N.Z.* 38°4' S, 174°48' E 240
Kawich Peak, *Nev., U.S.* 37°56' N, 116°33' W 90
Kawich Range, *Nev., U.S.* 37°53' N, 116°38' W 90
Kawlinn, *Myanmar* 23°46' N, 95°41' E 202
Kawnipi Lake, *Can.* 48°27' N, 91°30' W 94
Kawthoung, *Myanmar* 9°59' N, 98°32' E 202
Kax, river, *China* 43°44' N, 84°4' E 184
Kay, *Russ.* 59°57' N, 53°1' E 154
Kaya, *Burkina Faso* 13°5' N, 1°6' W 222
Kayambi, *Zambia* 9°28' S, 31°59' E 224
Kayan-Mentarang National Park, *Indonesia* 2°38' N, 115°12' E 238
Kayapınar, *Turk.* 37°32' N, 41°12' E 195
Kayar, *Senegal* 14°55' N, 16°52' W 222
Kayasula, *Russ.* 44°17' N, 45°0' E 158
Kaycee, *Wyo., U.S.* 43°42' N, 106°39' W 90
Kayenzi, *Tanzania* 3°16' S, 32°37' E 224
Kayes, *Congo* 4°12' S, 13°10' E 218
Kayes, *Congo* 4°25' S, 11°39' E 218
Kayes, *Mali* 14°26' N, 11°28' W 222
Kaymaz, *Turk.* 39°31' N, 31°10' E 156
Kaynar, *Turk.* 38°53' N, 36°25' E 156
Käyrämo, *Fin.* 66°57' N, 26°17' E 152
Kaysatskoye, *Russ.* 49°43' N, 46°46' E 158
Kayser Gebergte, *Suriname* 3°5' N, 56°60' W 130
Kayseri, *Turk.* 38°41' N, 35°30' E 156
Kayyerhan, *Russ.* 69°12' N, 83°53' E 169
Kaz Dağı, peak, *Turk.* 39°41' N, 26°47' E 156
Kazachka, *Russ.* 51°27' N, 43°57' E 158
Kazach'ye, *Russ.* 70°40' N, 136°18' E 160
Kazakh Uplands, *Asia* 47°30' N, 69°46' E 184
Kazakhstan 48°18' N, 63°42' E 184
Kazan', *Russ.* 55°45' N, 49°9' E 154
Kazan Rettō see Volcano Islands, *Philippine Sea* 23°11' N, 139°38' E 190
Kazan, river, *Can.* 63°10' N, 98°16' W 72
Kazanlŭk, *Bulg.* 42°35' N, 25°24' E 180
Kazanskaya, *Russ.* 49°50' N, 41°9' E 158
Kazanskoye, *Russ.* 57°9' N, 49°9' E 154
Kazarman, *Kyrg.* 41°22' N, 74°3' E 197
Kazbek, peak, *Ga.* 42°40' N, 44°29' E 195
Kāzerūn, *Iran* 29°35' N, 51°37' E 196
Kazhim, *Russ.* 60°20' N, 51°36' E 154
Kazima, *Cen. Af. Rep.* 5°14' N, 26°13' E 224
Kazimoto, *Tanzania* 9°6' S, 36°50' E 224
Kazlų Rūda, *Lith.* 54°44' N, 23°26' E 166
Kaztalovka, *Kaz.* 49°45' N, 48°43' E 158
Kazumba, *Dem. Rep. of the Congo* 6°26' S, 21°59' E 218
Kazyany, *Belarus* 55°18' N, 26°51' E 166
Kazym Mys, *Russ.* 64°45' N, 65°52' E 169
Kazym, river, *Russ.* 63°54' N, 67°41' E 169
Ké Macina, *Mali* 14°1' N, 5°22' W 222
Kéa, *Gr.* 37°38' N, 24°20' E 156
Kéa, island, *Gr.* 37°28' N, 24°23' E 180
Kea, Mauna, peak, *Hawai'i, U.S.* 19°49' N, 155°31' W 99
Kea'au Ranch, site, *Hawai'i, U.S.* 19°37' N, 155°2' W 99
Keams Canyon, *Ariz., U.S.* 35°48' N, 110°12' W 92
Kearney, *Can.* 45°32' N, 79°13' W 94
Kearney, *Nebr., U.S.* 40°41' N, 99°5' W 90
Kearny, *Ariz., U.S.* 33°3' N, 110°54' W 92
Kearsarge, *Mich., U.S.* 47°16' N, 88°26' W 94
Keatchie, *La., U.S.* 32°9' N, 93°55' W 103
Keauhou Landing, site, *Hawai'i, U.S.* 19°16' N, 155°17' W 99
Kebbe, *Nig.* 12°4' N, 4°46' E 222
Kébémer, *Senegal* 15°24' N, 16°27' W 222
Kebili, *Tun.* 33°42' N, 8°59' E 214
Kebkabiya, *Sudan* 13°35' N, 24°5' E 216
Keble, peak, *Nor.* 67°21' N, 20°10' E 152
Kebnekaise, peak, *Nor.* 67°52' N, 18°23' E 152
K'ebrī Dehar, *Eth.* 6°46' N, 44°10' E 218
Kecel, *Hung.* 46°30' N, 19°16' E 168
Kechika, river, *Can.* 59°5' N, 127°25' W 108
Keçiborlu, *Turk.* 37°56' N, 30°18' E 156
Kecskemét, *Hung.* 46°54' N, 19°42' E 168
Kėdainiai, *Lith.* 55°17' N, 23°56' E 166
Kedarnath, *India* 30°44' N, 79°4' E 197
Kédédéssé, *Chad* 11°8' N, 16°44' E 216
Kedgwick, river, *Can.* 48°2' N, 68°7' W 94
Kedia Hill, *Botswana* 21°25' S, 24°28' E 227
Kediri, *Indonesia* 7°50' S, 111°54' E 192
Kédougou, *Senegal* 12°35' N, 12°13' W 222
Kedvavom, *Russ.* 64°13' N, 53°27' E 154
Keele Peak, *Can.* 63°23' N, 130°26' W 98
Keele, river, *Can.* 64°3' N, 127°57' W 98
Keeler, *Calif., U.S.* 36°29' N, 117°53' W 101
Keeler, *Mich., U.S.* 42°6' N, 86°9' W 102
Keeley Lake, *Can.* 54°51' N, 108°44' W 108
Keelung see Chilung, *Taiwan* 25°6' N, 121°45' E 198
Keen, Mount, *U.K.* 56°56' N, 3°5' W 150
Keene, *Calif., U.S.* 35°13' N, 118°35' W 101
Keene, *N.H., U.S.* 42°55' N, 72°17' W 104
Keene, *N.Y., U.S.* 44°15' N, 73°48' W 104
Keep R. National Park, *Austral.* 15°55' S, 128°49' E 238
Keeper Hill, *Ire.* 52°44' N, 8°21' W 150
Keeseville, *N.Y., U.S.* 44°30' N, 73°30' W 104
Keesler Air Force Base, *Miss., U.S.* 30°22' N, 88°60' W 103
Keetmanshoop, *Namibia* 26°35' S, 18°7' E 227
Keewatin, *Can.* 49°45' N, 94°32' W 90
Keezhik Lake, *Can.* 51°40' N, 89°8' W 110
Kefaloniá (Cephalonia), adm. division, *Gr.* 38°22' N, 20°3' E 156
Kefar 'Ezyon, *West Bank* 31°37' N, 35°5' E 194
Kefar Rosh ha Niqra, *Israel* 33°4' N, 35°6' E 194
Kefar Sava, *Israel* 32°10' N, 34°53' E 194
Kefar Yona, *Israel* 32°19' N, 34°56' E 194
Keffi, *Nig.* 8°51' N, 7°49' E 222
Keflavík, *Ice.* 63°58' N, 22°41' W 143
Keg River, *Can.* 57°43' N, 117°35' W 108
Kegaska, Lac, lake, *Can.* 50°17' N, 61°56' W 111
Kegen, *Kaz.* 43°1' N, 79°13' E 184
Kegha, *Eth.* 5°5' N, 36°48' E 224
Keheili, *Sudan* 19°24' N, 32°49' E 182
Kehlstein, peak, *Ger.* 47°35' N, 12°57' E 156
Kehra, *Est.* 59°19' N, 25°18' E 166
Keighley, *U.K.* 53°51' N, 1°55' W 162
Keikyä, *Fin.* 61°15' N, 22°42' E 166
Keila, *Est.* 59°17' N, 24°23' E 166
Keila, river, *Est.* 59°18' N, 24°28' E 166
Keimoes, *S. Af.* 28°40' S, 20°55' E 227
Keïta, *Niger* 14°40' N, 5°44' E 222
Keitele, lake, *Fin.* 62°56' N, 25°33' E 152
Keithley Creek, *Can.* 52°44' N, 121°26' W 108
Keithsburg, *Mo., U.S.* 41°5' N, 90°56' W 94
Keizer, *Oreg., U.S.* 44°59' N, 123°2' W 90
Kejimkujik National Park, *Can.* 43°42' N, 64°46' W 111
Kekerengu, *N.Z.* 41°60' S, 174°0' E 240
Kékes, peak, *Hung.* 47°51' N, 19°59' E 168
Kekurskiy, Mys, *Russ.* 69°55' N, 32°9' E 152
K'elafo, *Eth.* 5°35' N, 44°11' E 218
Kelai, island, *Maldives* 6°43' N, 73°12' E 188
Kélakam, *Niger* 13°32' N, 11°48' E 222
Kelamet, *Eritrea* 16°4' N, 38°41' E 182
Kelang, *Malaysia* 3°3' N, 101°26' E 196
Kelberg, *Ger.* 50°17' N, 6°55' E 167
Keld, *U.K.* 54°24' N, 2°11' W 162
Kelebia, *Hung.* 46°10' N, 19°37' E 168
Keleft, *Afghan.* 37°18' N, 66°15' E 186
Kelkit, *Turk.* 40°7' N, 39°26' E 195
Kelkit, river, *Turk.* 40°0' N, 38°38' E 180
Kellé, *Congo* 0°8' N, 14°31' E 218
Kéllé, *Niger* 14°15' N, 10°9' E 222
Kellen, *Ger.* 51°47' N, 6°9' E 167
Keller Lake, *Can.* 63°22' N, 119°60' W 246
Kellet, Cape, *Can.* 71°57' N, 130°22' W 106
Kellett Strait 75°40' N, 120°58' W 106
Kelleys Island, *Ohio, U.S.* 41°37' N, 82°40' W 102
Kelliher, *Can.* 51°15' N, 103°46' W 90
Kello, *Fin.* 65°6' N, 25°23' E 152
Kellog, *Russ.* 62°27' N, 86°21' E 169
Kellogora, *Russ.* 64°19' N, 32°14' E 152
Kellojärvi, lake, *Fin.* 64°13' N, 28°24' E 152
Kelly, *La., U.S.* 31°58' N, 92°11' W 103
Kelly Air Force Base, *Tex., U.S.* 29°19' N, 98°38' W 92
Kelmė, *Lith.* 55°38' N, 22°55' E 166
Kelmis, *Belg.* 50°42' N, 6°0' E 167
Kélo, *Chad* 9°18' N, 15°47' E 216
Kelottijärvi, *Fin.* 68°31' N, 22°1' E 152
Kelowna, *Can.* 49°51' N, 119°28' W 106
Kelsall, Mount, *Can.* 59°48' N, 136°28' W 108
Kelsey, *Can.* 56°2' N, 96°31' W 108
Kelsey Creek, river, *Can.* 57°47' N, 94°17' W 108
Kelso, *Calif., U.S.* 35°1' N, 115°39' W 101
Kelso, *N.Z.* 45°56' S, 169°16' E 240
Kelso, *Wash., U.S.* 46°8' N, 122°54' W 100
Keltie, Cape, *Antarctica* 65°44' S, 135°58' E 248
Keluang, *Malaysia* 2°3' N, 103°20' E 196
Kelvä, *Fin.* 63°3' N, 30°6' E 152
Kelvington, *Can.* 52°10' N, 103°31' W 108
Kelyexed, *Somalia* 8°45' N, 49°11' E 216
Kem', *Russ.* 64°59' N, 34°31' E 152
Kemah, *Turk.* 39°35' N, 39°2' E 195
Kemano, *Can.* 53°33' N, 127°56' W 108
Kemasik, *Malaysia* 4°26' N, 103°26' E 196
Kembé, *Cen. Af. Rep.* 4°35' N, 21°52' E 218
Kembolcha, *Eth.* 11°1' N, 39°46' E 224
Kemboma, *Gabon* 0°40' N, 13°31' E 218
Kemer, *Kaz.* 49°32' N, 54°58' E 158
Kemer, *Turk.* 40°24' N, 27°2' E 156
Kemer, *Turk.* 36°37' N, 29°19' E 156
Kemer, *Turk.* 36°34' N, 30°34' E 156
Ķemeri, *Latv.* 56°56' N, 23°28' E 166
Kemerovo, *Russ.* 55°17' N, 86°11' E 184
Kemeten, *Aust.* 47°14' N, 16°9' E 168
Kemi, *Fin.* 65°43' N, 24°49' E 160
Kemijärvi, *Fin.* 66°42' N, 27°23' E 152
Kemin, *Kyrg.* 42°47' N, 75°40' E 184
Kemiya, *Russ.* 54°39' N, 45°17' E 154
Kemmerer, *Wyo., U.S.* 41°48' N, 110°33' W 90
Kemp, Lake, *Tex., U.S.* 33°45' N, 99°23' W 92
Kemp Peninsula, *Antarctica* 73°32' S, 59°37' W 248
Kemparana, *Mali* 12°51' N, 4°57' W 222
Kempen, *Ger.* 51°22' N, 6°25' E 167
Kemps Bay, *Bahamas* 24°2' N, 77°34' W 96
Kemps Bay, adm. division, *Bahamas* 24°34' N, 78°20' W 116
Kenadsa, *Alg.* 31°34' N, 2°25' W 214
Kenai, *Alas., U.S.* 60°27' N, 151°19' W 98
Kenai Peninsula, *North America* 60°23' N, 150°43' W 98
Kenamu, river, *Can.* 52°45' N, 60°4' W 111
Kenamuke Swamp, marsh, *Sudan* 5°52' N, 33°30' E 224
Kenansville, *Fla., U.S.* 27°52' N, 80°60' W 105
Kenaston, *Can.* 51°31' N, 106°18' W 90
Kendal, *U.K.* 54°20' N, 2°43' W 162
Kendall, *Fla., U.S.* 25°41' N, 80°20' W 105
Kendall, Cape, *Can.* 63°48' N, 88°54' W 106
Kendallville, *Ind., U.S.* 41°26' N, 85°17' W 102
Kendari, *Indonesia* 3°55' S, 122°27' E 192
Kendikolu, island, *Maldives* 5°45' N, 73°26' E 188
Këndrevicës, Maja e, peak, *Alban.* 40°16' N, 19°45' E 156
Kendrick, *Idaho, U.S.* 46°36' N, 116°41' W 90
Kendu Bay, *Kenya* 0°25' N, 34°40' E 224
Kenedy, *Tex., U.S.* 28°48' N, 97°51' W 92
Kenema, *Sierra Leone* 7°49' N, 11°12' W 222
Kenga, *Russ.* 57°24' N, 81°5' E 169
Kenge, *Dem. Rep. of the Congo* 4°59' S, 17°2' E 218
Kèngkok, *Laos* 16°26' N, 105°11' E 202
Kengtung, *Myanmar* 21°18' N, 99°38' E 202
Kengyel, *Hung.* 47°5' N, 20°20' E 168
Kengzhaly, *Kaz.* 48°57' N, 56°13' E 158
Kenhardt, *S. Af.* 29°20' S, 21°9' E 227
Kéniéba, *Mali* 12°50' N, 11°15' W 222
Kenilworth, *U.K.* 52°20' N, 1°35' W 162
Kenitra (Port Lyautey), *Mor.* 34°17' N, 6°37' W 214
Kenli, *China* 37°36' N, 118°35' E 198
Kenmare, *N. Dak., U.S.* 48°39' N, 102°4' W 90
Kenna, *N. Mex., U.S.* 33°50' N, 103°47' W 92
Kennard, *Tex., U.S.* 31°20' N, 95°11' W 103
Kennebec, *S. Dak., U.S.* 43°54' N, 99°53' W 90
Kennebunk, *Me., U.S.* 43°23' N, 70°33' W 104
Kennebunk Beach, *Me., U.S.* 43°20' N, 70°31' W 104
Kennebunkport, *Me., U.S.* 43°21' N, 70°29' W 104
Kennedy, *Can.* 50°0' N, 102°22' W 90
Kennedy Bight 52°5' N, 56°24' W 111
Kennedy, Cape see Canaveral, Cape, *Fla., U.S.* 28°24' N, 80°34' W 105
Kennedy Channel 78°17' N, 71°33' W 246
Kennedy, Mount, *Can.* 60°18' N, 139°5' W 98
Kennett, *Mo., U.S.* 36°14' N, 90°3' W 96
Kenney, *Ill., U.S.* 40°5' N, 89°5' W 102
Kenney Dam, *Can.* 53°27' N, 125°23' W 108
Kenny, Mount, *Can.* 56°54' N, 123°58' W 108
Keno Hill, *Can.* 63°53' N, 135°25' W 106
Kenogami, river, *Can.* 50°5' N, 85°54' W 94
Kenogamissi Lake, *Can.* 48°13' N, 82°18' W 94
Kenora, *Can.* 49°47' N, 94°28' W 90
Kenosha, *Wis., U.S.* 42°36' N, 87°50' W 102
Kenova, *W. Va., U.S.* 38°23' N, 82°36' W 94
Kent, *Can.* 49°13' N, 121°46' W 100
Kent, *Conn., U.S.* 41°42' N, 73°29' W 104
Kent, *Ohio, U.S.* 41°8' N, 81°21' W 102
Kent, *Oreg., U.S.* 45°9' N, 120°42' W 90
Kent, *Tex., U.S.* 31°2' N, 104°13' W 92
Kent, *Wash., U.S.* 47°22' N, 122°15' W 100
Kent Group, islands, *Bass Strait* 39°20' S, 147°14' E 230
Kent Peninsula, *Can.* 68°39' N, 107°16' W 106
Kentaū, *Kaz.* 43°28' N, 68°26' E 184
Kentland, *Ind., U.S.* 40°45' N, 87°27' W 102
Kenton, *Ky., U.S.* 38°51' N, 84°28' W 102
Kenton, *Ohio, U.S.* 40°38' N, 83°36' W 102
Kentozero, *Russ.* 64°51' N, 31°8' E 152
Kentriki Makedonia, adm. division, *Gr.* 40°52' N, 21°59' E 156
Kents Hill, *Me., U.S.* 44°23' N, 70°1' W 104
Kentuck, *W. Va., U.S.* 38°38' N, 81°37' W 102
Kentucky, adm. division, *Ky., U.S.* 37°37' N, 86°20' W 94
Kentville, *Can.* 45°4' N, 64°31' W 111
Kentwood, *La., U.S.* 30°56' N, 90°31' W 103
Kentwood, *Mich., U.S.* 42°54' N, 85°35' W 102
Kenville, *Can.* 51°59' N, 101°20' W 108
Kenwood, *Ohio, U.S.* 39°11' N, 84°23' W 102
Kenya 0°37' N, 37°25' E 224
Kenya, Mount, *Kenya* 0°10' N, 37°14' E 224
Kenzingen, *Ger.* 48°11' N, 7°45' E 163
Keokuk, *Iowa, U.S.* 40°24' N, 91°28' W 82
Kep, *Cambodia* 10°30' N, 104°18' E 202
Kepa, *Russ.* 65°9' N, 32°9' E 152
Kepi, *Indonesia* 6°26' S, 139°11' E 192
Kepino, *Russ.* 65°24' N, 41°41' E 154
Kępno, *Pol.* 51°16' N, 17°59' E 152
Keppel Bay 23°35' S, 149°50' E 230
Kepsut, *Turk.* 39°40' N, 28°8' E 156
Keräla, *Fin.* 64°45' N, 28°46' E 152
Kerala, adm. division, *India* 10°0' N, 76°29' E 188
Keran, *India* 34°39' N, 73°59' E 186
Kéran National Park, *Togo* 9°51' N, 0°8' E 222
Kerava, *Fin.* 60°23' N, 25°3' E 166
Kerby, *Oreg., U.S.* 42°12' N, 123°38' W 90
Kerch, *Ukr.* 45°24' N, 36°29' E 156
Kerchel', *Russ.* 59°19' N, 64°43' E 154
Kerchem'ya, *Russ.* 61°26' N, 53°59' E 154
Kerchenskiy Proliv 45°5' N, 35°45' E 156
Kerchevskiy, *Russ.* 59°56' N, 56°16' E 154
Kerchouel, *Mali* 17°10' N, 0°15' E 222
Kerekere, *Dem. Rep. of the Congo* 2°37' N, 30°33' E 224
Kerempe Burnu, *Turk.* 42°2' N, 33°13' E 156
Keren, *Eritrea* 15°44' N, 38°27' E 182
Kerend-e Gharb, *Iran* 34°15' N, 46°14' E 180
Kerens, *Tex., U.S.* 32°6' N, 96°13' W 96
Keret', *Russ.* 66°17' N, 33°38' E 152
Kericho, *Kenya* 0°22' N, 35°16' E 224
Kerimäki, *Fin.* 61°54' N, 29°16' E 166
Kerinci, peak, *Indonesia* 1°45' S, 100°55' E 192
Keriske, *Russ.* 69°56' N, 132°21' E 173
Keriya, river, *China* 36°46' N, 81°26' E 184
Keriya see Yutian, *China* 36°55' N, 81°36' E 184
Keriya Shankou, pass, *China* 35°9' N, 81°33' E 188
Kerki, *Russ.* 63°43' N, 54°13' E 154
Kerki see Atamyrat, *Turkm.* 37°49' N, 65°10' E 197
Kerkiçi, *Turkm.* 37°52' N, 65°15' E 197
Kérkira, *Gr.* 39°37' N, 19°54' E 156
Kérkira (Corfu), island, *Gr.* 39°10' N, 19°53' E 143
Kerkour Nourene, Massif du, *Chad* 15°41' N, 21°0' E 216
Kerkrade, *Neth.* 50°52' N, 6°3' E 167
Kerma, *Sudan* 19°38' N, 30°28' E 226
Kerman, *Calif., U.S.* 36°43' N, 120°5' W 100
Kermänshäh, *Iran* 34°15' N, 47°0' E 180
Kermänshähän, *Iran* 31°16' N, 54°56' E 180
Kermit, *Tex., U.S.* 31°50' N, 103°5' W 92
Kermode, Mount, *Can.* 52°56' N, 131°58' W 108
Kern Canyon, *Calif., U.S.* 36°20' N, 118°26' W 101
Kern, river, *Calif., U.S.* 36°22' N, 118°28' W 101
Kernville, *Calif., U.S.* 35°45' N, 118°27' W 101
Keroh, *Malaysia* 5°41' N, 101°1' E 196
Kérouané, *Guinea* 9°17' N, 8°60' W 222
Kerpen, *Ger.* 50°51' N, 6°41' E 167
Kerr, Cape, *Antarctica* 80°4' S, 170°43' E 248
Kerre, *Cen. Af. Rep.* 5°21' N, 25°35' E 224
Kerrobert, *Can.* 51°56' N, 109°9' W 90
Kerrville, *Tex., U.S.* 30°1' N, 99°8' W 92
Kershaw, *S.C., U.S.* 34°32' N, 80°35' W 96
Kersilö, *Fin.* 67°34' N, 26°41' E 152
Kersley, *Can.* 52°47' N, 122°25' W 108
Kertamulia, *Indonesia* 0°20' N, 109°7' E 196
Kerulen, river, *Mongolia* 47°22' N, 111°2' E 198
Keryneia (Girne, Kyrenia), *Northern Cyprus* 35°20' N, 33°18' E 194
Keryneia Range, *Northern Cyprus* 35°16' N, 33°25' E 194
Kerzaz, *Alg.* 29°30' N, 1°24' W 214
Kesagami Lake, *Can.* 50°23' N, 80°52' W 94
Kesagami, river, *Can.* 50°27' N, 80°10' W 110
Kesälahti, *Fin.* 61°52' N, 29°48' E 166
Keşan, *Turk.* 40°49' N, 26°40' E 180
Keşap, *Turk.* 40°55' N, 38°29' E 158
Keshan, *China* 48°2' N, 125°50' E 198
Keşiş Dağı, peak, *Turk.* 39°47' N, 39°37' E 195
Keskal, *India* 20°3' N, 81°36' E 188
Kes'ma, *Russ.* 58°22' N, 37°7' E 154
Kessingland, *U.K.* 52°25' N, 1°42' E 163
Kesten'ga, *Russ.* 65°54' N, 31°51' E 152
Kestilä, *Fin.* 64°21' N, 26°14' E 152
Keswick, *U.K.* 54°35' N, 3°8' W 162
Keszthely, *Hung.* 46°45' N, 17°14' E 168
Ket', river, *Russ.* 58°33' N, 85°20' E 169
Keta, *Ghana* 5°54' N, 0°57' E 222
Ketapang, *Indonesia* 1°57' S, 109°59' E 192
Ketchikan, *Alas., U.S.* 55°22' N, 131°41' W 108
Ketchum Mountain, *Tex., U.S.* 31°19' N, 101°7' W 92
Kétegyháza, *Hung.* 46°33' N, 21°11' E 168
Keti Bandar, *Pak.* 24°4' N, 67°30' E 186
Kętrzyn, *Pol.* 54°4' N, 21°23' E 166
Kettering, *Ohio, U.S.* 39°40' N, 84°10' W 102
Kettering, *U.K.* 52°23' N, 0°43' E 162
Kettle Lake, *Can.* 47°0' N, 82°54' W 110
Kettle Rapids, fall(s), *Can.* 56°23' N, 94°37' W 108
Kettle River Range, *Wash., U.S.* 48°10' N, 118°29' W 90
Kettleman City, *Calif., U.S.* 36°0' N, 119°58' W 100
Keudepanga, *Indonesia* 4°33' N, 95°41' E 196
Keur Momar Sarr, *Senegal* 15°58' N, 16°1' W 222
Keuruu, *Fin.* 62°14' N, 24°38' E 152
Keuruunselkä, lake, *Fin.* 61°53' N, 23°10' E 152
Kevelaer, *Ger.* 51°34' N, 6°14' E 167
Kewanee, *Ala., U.S.* 32°25' N, 88°25' W 103
Kewanee, *Ill., U.S.* 41°14' N, 89°56' W 102
Kewanna, *Ind., U.S.* 41°0' N, 86°25' W 102
Kewaskum, *Wis., U.S.* 43°30' N, 88°15' W 102
Keweenaw Peninsula, *U.S.* 47°1' N, 88°60' W 94
Keweenaw Point, *Mich., U.S.* 47°26' N, 87°44' W 94
Key Colony Beach, *Fla., U.S.* 24°45' N, 80°58' W 105
Key Harbour, *Can.* 45°53' N, 80°43' W 94
Key Largo, *Fla., U.S.* 25°6' N, 80°27' W 105
Key West, *Fla., U.S.* 24°33' N, 81°48' W 105
Keya Paha, river, *S. Dak., U.S.* 43°11' N, 100°19' W 90
Keyano, *Can.* 53°50' N, 73°26' W 111
Keyes, *Okla., U.S.* 36°48' N, 102°15' W 92
Keyi, *China* 42°8' N, 82°40' E 184
Keynsham, *U.K.* 51°24' N, 2°30' W 162
Keys View, peak, *Calif., U.S.* 33°55' N, 116°15' W 101
Keyser, *W. Va., U.S.* 39°26' N, 78°59' W 94
Keystone, *W. Va., U.S.* 37°24' N, 81°27' W 94
Keystone Heights, *Fla., U.S.* 29°46' N, 82°3' W 105
Keystone Peak, *Ariz., U.S.* 31°52' N, 111°16' W 92
Kez, *Russ.* 57°53' N, 53°46' E 154
Kezar Falls, *Me., U.S.* 43°48' N, 70°54' W 104
Khabab, *Syr.* 33°1' N, 36°16' E 194
Khabarikha, *Russ.* 65°49' N, 52°20' E 154
Khabarovo, *Russ.* 69°35' N, 60°21' E 169
Khabarovsk, *Russ.* 48°30' N, 135°8' E 190
Khabarovsk, adm. division, *Russ.* 56°15' N, 135°49' E 160
Khabrat Umm al Ḩīrān, spring, *Kuwait* 29°25' N, 47°14' E 196
Khābūr, river, *Syr.* 36°11' N, 40°54' E 195
Khadyzhensk, *Russ.* 44°24' N, 39°31' E 158
Khagaria, *India* 25°30' N, 86°25' E 197
Khairpur, *Pak.* 27°30' N, 68°47' E 186
Khaishi, *Ga.* 42°58' N, 42°16' E 195
Khakasiya, adm. division, *Russ.* 53°22' N, 90°13' E 169
Khakhea, *Botswana* 24°44' S, 23°30' E 227
Khalasa, ruin(s), *Israel* 31°5' N, 34°35' E 194
Khalatse, *India* 34°21' N, 76°54' E 188
Khālid Ibn al Walīd, dam, *Asia* 32°36' N, 35°19' E 194
Khalilovo, *Russ.* 51°20' N, 58°4' E 158
Khalkhāl, *Iran* 37°39' N, 48°33' E 195
Khal'mer Yu, *Russ.* 67°56' N, 64°55' E 169
Khalturin, *Russ.* 58°32' N, 48°52' E 154
Khalūf, *Oman* 20°30' N, 58°2' E 182
Khalyasavey, *Russ.* 63°22' N, 78°26' E 169
Khambhaliya, *India* 22°12' N, 69°40' E 186
Khamīs Mushayţ, *Saudi Arabia* 18°17' N, 42°44' E 182
Khammam, *India* 17°14' N, 80°10' E 188
Khammouan, *Laos* 17°24' N, 104°49' E 202
Khamr, *Yemen* 15°59' N, 43°56' E 182
Khamsa, *Egypt* 30°26' N, 32°22' E 194
Khān Abū Shāmāt, *Syr.* 33°39' N, 36°53' E 194
Khān az Zābīb, *Jordan* 31°28' N, 36°5' E 194
Khān Shaykhūn, *Syr.* 35°26' N, 36°38' E 194
Khan Tängiri (Khan Tengri), peak, *Kyrg.* 42°11' N, 80°5' E 184
Khan Tengri see Khan Tängiri, peak, *Kyrg.* 42°11' N, 80°5' E 184
Khān Yūnis, *Gaza Strip* 31°20' N, 34°18' E 194
Khanabad, *Afghan.* 36°39' N, 69°9' E 186
Khanai, *Pak.* 30°29' N, 67°15' E 186
Khānaqīn, *Iraq* 34°21' N, 45°22' E 180
Khandwa, *India* 21°49' N, 76°21' E 197
Khandyga, *Russ.* 62°32' N, 135°34' E 160
Khanewal, *Pak.* 30°19' N, 71°57' E 186
Khangarh, *Pak.* 28°21' N, 71°43' E 186
Khanka, Ozero, lake, *Russ.* 45°12' N, 129°53' E 173
Khanlar, *Azerb.* 40°35' N, 46°20' E 195
Khanovey, *Russ.* 67°15' N, 63°36' E 169
Khanpur, *Pak.* 28°38' N, 70°39' E 186
Khansiir, Raas, *Somalia* 10°50' N, 44°43' E 216
Khantaū, *Kaz.* 44°12' N, 73°48' E 184
Khantayskoye, Ozero, lake, *Russ.* 68°13' N, 88°18' E 169
Khanty Mansiysk, *Russ.* 61°2' N, 69°10' E 169
Khanty-Mansi, adm. division, *Russ.* 62°2' N, 69°26' E 169
Khanymey, *Russ.* 63°47' N, 75°58' E 169
Khao Yai National Park, *Thai.* 14°17' N, 101°43' E 202
Khapalu, *Pak.* 35°8' N, 76°21' E 186
Khapcheranga, *Russ.* 49°41' N, 112°26' E 198
Kharabali, *Russ.* 47°23' N, 47°10' E 158
Kharagauli, *Ga.* 42°0' N, 43°7' E 195
Kharagpur, *India* 22°19' N, 87°19' E 197
Kharampur, *Russ.* 64°18' N, 78°12' E 169
Kharan, *Pak.* 28°36' N, 65°25' E 182
Kharānaq, *Iran* 32°20' N, 54°41' E 180
Kharasavey, Mys, *Russ.* 70°41' N, 64°10' E 169
Khārga, El Wâhât el, *Egypt* 25°41' N, 29°48' E 180
Khargon, *India* 21°47' N, 75°38' E 197
Khārk, island, *Iran* 29°4' N, 50°10' E 180
Kharkiv, *Ukr.* 49°59' N, 36°15' E 158
Kharlovka, *Russ.* 68°44' N, 37°15' E 152
Kharlu, *Russ.* 61°47' N, 30°53' E 152
Kharsān, *Syr.* 35°17' N, 37°2' E 194
Khartoum, *Sudan* 15°27' N, 32°23' E 182
Khartoum, adm. division, *Sudan* 15°48' N, 31°44' E 216
Khartoum North, *Sudan* 15°37' N, 32°34' E 226
Khaşab, *Oman* 26°10' N, 56°12' E 196
Khasan, *Russ.* 42°24' N, 130°41' E 200
Khasavyurt, *Russ.* 43°12' N, 46°34' E 195
Khash, *Afghan.* 31°31' N, 62°54' E 186
Khāsh, *Iran* 28°10' N, 61°11' E 182
Khash, river, *Afghan.* 32°42' N, 64°13' E 186
Khashm el Qirba, *Sudan* 14°55' N, 35°55' E 182
Khashm el Qirba Dam, *Sudan* 14°25' N, 34°49' E 182
Khashri, *Ga.* 41°57' N, 43°33' E 195
Khaskovo, *Bulg.* 41°56' N, 25°32' E 156
Khaskovo, adm. division, *Bulg.* 41°52' N, 25°17' E 156
Khatanga, *Russ.* 71°57' N, 102°45' E 160
Khātūnīyah, *Syr.* 36°23' N, 41°14' E 195
Khatyrka, *Russ.* 62°1' N, 174°56' E 160
Khaur, *Pak.* 33°16' N, 72°33' E 186
Khavda, *India* 23°51' N, 69°45' E 186
Khaydarkan, *Kyrg.* 39°56' N, 71°26' E 197
Khaypudyrskaya Guba 68°30' N, 59°0' E 160
Khayryuzovo, *Russ.* 56°58' N, 157°7' E 160
Khed Brahma, *India* 24°3' N, 73°2' E 186
Khemmarat, *Thai.* 16°2' N, 105°12' E 202
Kherson, *Ukr.* 46°40' N, 32°35' E 156
Kheta, *Russ.* 71°31' N, 99°56' E 160
Kheta, river, *Russ.* 71°30' N, 99°5' E 160
Khewra, *Pak.* 32°37' N, 73°4' E 186
Khibiny, *Russ.* 67°49' N, 33°16' E 152
Khiitola, *Russ.* 61°13' N, 29°40' E 166
Khilchipur, *India* 24°2' N, 76°34' E 197
Khilok, *Russ.* 51°30' N, 110°29' E 190
Khimki, *Russ.* 55°53' N, 37°26' E 154
Khirbat Ad Dayr, ruin(s), *Jordan* 31°32' N, 35°35' E 194
Khirbat al Ghazālah, *Syr.* 32°43' N, 36°12' E 194
Khirbat aş Şafrā', ruin(s), *Jordan* 31°37' N, 35°36' E 194
Khirbat as Samrā', ruin(s), *Jordan* 32°10' N, 36°8' E 194
Khirbat Qumrān, ruin(s), *West Bank* 31°43' N, 35°25' E 194
Khirbat Umm al Jimāl, ruin(s), *Jordan* 32°19' N, 36°20' E 194
Khiri Ratthanikhom, *Thai.* 9°2' N, 98°53' E 202
Khislavichi, *Russ.* 54°12' N, 32°10' E 154
Khiwa, *Uzb.* 41°23' N, 60°22' E 180
Khizy, *Azerb.* 40°54' N, 49°4' E 195
Khlevnoye, *Russ.* 52°12' N, 39°0' E 158
Khmel'nyts'kyy, *Ukr.* 49°24' N, 26°58' E 158
Khoai, Hon, island, *Vietnam* 8°9' N, 104°40' E 202
Khodoriv, *Ukr.* 49°23' N, 24°19' E 152
Khodzhatau, *Taj.* 39°11' N, 71°41' E 197
Khogali, *Sudan* 6°9' N, 27°46' E 224
Khok Kloi, *Thai.* 8°17' N, 98°17' E 202
Khokhol'skiy, *Russ.* 51°29' N, 38°42' E 158
Khokhropar, *Pak.* 25°42' N, 70°14' E 186
Kholm, *Afghan.* 36°42' N, 67°41' E 186
Kholm, *Russ.* 57°8' N, 31°12' E 154
Kholmogorskaya, *Russ.* 63°49' N, 40°40' E 154
Kholmogory, *Russ.* 64°13' N, 41°37' E 154
Kholmsk, *Russ.* 47°1' N, 142°5' E 190
Kholopenichi, *Belarus* 54°30' N, 29°1' E 166
Khomeyn, *Iran* 33°42' N, 50°6' E 180
Khomeynīshahr, *Iran* 32°44' N, 51°32' E 180

Khon Kaen, Thai. 16°29' N, 102°40' E 202
Không, Laos 14°9' N, 105°49' E 202
Khôngxédôn, Laos 15°37' N, 105°47' E 202
Khonsa, India 27°37' N, 93°50' E 188
Khonulakh, Russ. 66°20' N, 151°26' E 160
Khonuu, Russ. 66°30' N, 143°15' E 160
Khoper, river, Russ. 52°5' N, 43°18' E 158
Khoper, river, Russ. 50°14' N, 41°53' E 184
Khor, Russ. 48°0' N, 135°5' E 190
Khorāsān, region, Asia 34°30' N, 53°1' E 180
Khorat see Nakhon Ratchasima, Thai. 14°58' N, 102°7' E 202
Khorb el Ethel, spring, Alg. 28°34' N, 6°19' W 214
Khorintsy, Russ. 60°41' N, 121°20' E 160
Khorixas, Namibia 20°24' S, 14°55' E 220
Khorof Harar, Kenya 2°7' N, 40°42' E 224
Khorol, Ukr. 49°48' N, 33°12' E 158
Khoroûfa, spring, Mauritania 17°21' N, 15°49' W 222
Khorramābād, Iran 33°29' N, 48°19' E 180
Khorramshahr, Iran 30°29' N, 48°9' E 180
Khorugh, Taj. 37°29' N, 71°35' E 184
Khosheutovo, Russ. 47°0' N, 47°50' E 158
Khost, Afghan. 33°22' N, 69°58' E 186
Khost, Pak. 30°14' N, 67°38' E 186
Khotyn, Ukr. 48°30' N, 26°30' E 152
Khouribga, Mor. 32°56' N, 6°57' W 214
Khoyniki, Belarus 51°51' N, 30°4' E 158
Khrami, river, Ga. 41°31' N, 44°3' E 195
Khrenovoye, Russ. 51°8' N, 40°15' E 158
Khroma, river, Russ. 71°50' N, 144°2' E 160
Khromtaū, Kaz. 50°16' N, 58°27' E 158
Khuchni, Russ. 41°53' N, 47°55' E 195
Khudabad, Pak. 36°42' N, 74°53' E 186
Khudosey, river, Russ. 65°23' N, 82°18' E 169
Khudumelapye, Botswana 23°53' S, 24°53' E 227
Khuff, oil field, Lib. 28°8' N, 18°17' E 216
Khuis, Botswana 26°37' S, 21°49' E 227
Khujand, Taj. 40°15' N, 69°41' E 197
Khŭjayli, Uzb. 42°24' N, 59°27' E 180
Khulkhuta, Russ. 46°16' N, 46°21' E 158
Khulna, Bangladesh 22°48' N, 89°28' E 197
Khun Yuam, Thai. 18°53' N, 97°52' E 202
Khunjerab Pass, China 36°50' N, 75°26' E 184
Khunsar, Iran 33°14' N, 50°17' E 180
Khunti, India 23°6' N, 85°16' E 197
Khunzakh, Russ. 42°29' N, 46°42' E 195
Khurais, oil field, Saudi Arabia 25°10' N, 48°1' E 196
Khushab, Pak. 32°18' N, 72°24' E 186
Khutse Game Reserve, Botswana 23°43' S, 23°52' E 227
Khuwei, Sudan 13°3' N, 29°14' E 216
Khuzdar, Pak. 27°43' N, 66°34' E 186
Khvāf, Iran 34°36' N, 60°9' E 180
Khvalynsk, Russ. 52°28' N, 48°6' E 158
Khvor, Iran 33°49' N, 55°5' E 180
Khvormūj, Iran 28°35' N, 51°24' E 196
Khvorostyanka, Russ. 52°37' N, 49°0' E 158
Khvosh Asia, Afghan. 32°53' N, 62°14' E 186
Khvoy, Iran 38°34' N, 44°55' E 195
Khvoynaya, Russ. 58°51' N, 34°40' E 154
Khyber Pass, Pak. 34°6' N, 71°9' E 186
Kiabakari, Tanzania 1°48' S, 33°50' E 224
Kiamba, Philippines 6°2' N, 124°37' E 203
Kiambi, Dem. Rep. of the Congo 7°20' S, 28°0' E 224
Kiamichi Mountains, Okla., U.S. 34°30' N, 95°25' W 96
Kiang West National Park, Gambia 13°22' N, 15°58' W 222
Kianta, Fin. 65°7' N, 28°54' E 154
Kibali, river, Dem. Rep. of the Congo 3°29' N, 28°37' E 224
Kibangou, Congo 3°28' S, 12°18' E 218
Kibara, Monts, Dem. Rep. of the Congo 8°29' S, 26°39' E 224
Kibau, Tanzania 8°36' S, 35°18' E 224
Kibawe, Philippines 7°37' N, 124°59' E 203
Kibaya, Tanzania 5°19' S, 36°33' E 224
Kiberashi, Tanzania 5°20' S, 37°25' E 224
Kiberege, Tanzania 7°57' S, 36°54' E 224
Kibiti, Tanzania 7°41' S, 38°54' E 224
Kiboga, Uganda 0°53' N, 31°45' E 224
Kibombo, Dem. Rep. of the Congo 3°59' S, 25°53' E 224
Kibondo, Tanzania 3°37' S, 30°42' E 224
Kibre Mengist, Eth. 5°55' N, 38°58' E 224
Kibungo, Rwanda 2°12' S, 30°30' E 224
Kibuye, Rwanda 2°7' S, 29°20' E 224
Kibwesa, Tanzania 6°29' S, 29°56' E 224
Kibwezi, Kenya 2°27' S, 37°57' E 224
Kičevo, Maced. 41°31' N, 20°58' E 168
Kichi Kichi, spring, Chad 17°36' N, 17°18' E 216
Kichmengskiy Gorodok, Russ. 60°1' N, 45°52' E 154
Kidal, Mali 18°27' N, 1°23' E 222
Kidatu, Tanzania 7°43' S, 37°0' E 224
Kidderminster, U.K. 52°22' N, 2°15' W 162
Kidepo, Sudan 4°6' N, 33°14' E 224
Kidepo Valley National Park, Uganda 3°41' N, 33°22' E 224
Kidete, Tanzania 6°38' S, 36°45' E 224
Kidi Faani, Somalia 1°6' S, 41°46' E 224
Kidika, Tanzania 7°28' S, 36°30' E 224
Kidira, Senegal 14°26' N, 12°16' W 222
Kidnappers, Cape, N.Z. 39°41' S, 177°7' E 240
Kidodi, Tanzania 7°38' S, 37°3' E 224
Kidsgrove, U.K. 53°4' N, 2°16' W 162
Kiel, Ger. 54°20' N, 10°8' E 150
Kiel, Wis., U.S. 43°54' N, 88°3' W 102
Kielce, Pol. 50°52' N, 20°36' E 152
Kiémou, Côte d'Ivoire 9°3' N, 5°33' W 222
Kien Duc, Vietnam 12°19' N, 107°31' E 202
Kiéré, Burkina Faso 11°38' N, 3°31' W 222
Kiev see Kyiv, Ukr. 50°25' N, 30°29' E 158
Kīevka, Kaz. 50°16' N, 71°32' E 184
Kifaya, Guinea 12°10' N, 13°6' W 222
Kiffa, Mauritania 16°36' N, 11°26' W 222
Kifino Selo, Bosn. and Herzg. 43°16' N, 18°11' E 168
Kigali, Rwanda 2°3' S, 29°56' E 224
Kiğı, Turk. 39°18' N, 40°19' E 195
Kigille, Sudan 8°38' N, 34°1' E 224
Kigoma, Tanzania 4°54' S, 29°36' E 224
Kihelkonna, Est. 58°21' N, 22°2' E 166
Kihniö, Fin. 62°10' N, 23°10' E 152
Kihnu, island, Est. 58°8' N, 23°47' E 166
Kii Suidō 33°56' N, 134°39' E 201
Kiihtelysvaara, Fin. 62°29' N, 30°14' E 152
Kiikala, Fin. 60°27' N, 23°33' E 166
Kiistala, Fin. 67°51' N, 25°21' E 152
Kijevo, Croatia 43°58' N, 16°22' E 168
Kikiakki, Russ. 63°46' N, 82°42' E 169
Kikinda, Serb. and Mont. 45°49' N, 20°28' E 168
Kiknur, Russ. 57°19' N, 47°14' E 154
Kikombo, Tanzania 6°12' S, 35°58' E 224
Kikondja, Dem. Rep. of the Congo 8°12' S, 26°24' E 224
Kikori, river, P.N.G. 6°53' S, 143°4' E 192
Kikwit, Dem. Rep. of the Congo 5°6' S, 18°47' E 218
Kil, Nor. 59°31' N, 13°17' E 152
Kilafors, Nor. 61°14' N, 16°30' E 152
Kilakkarai, India 9°16' N, 78°46' E 188
Kilambé, peak, Nicar. 13°33' N, 85°47' W 115
Kilani, Cyprus 34°49' N, 32°51' E 156
Kilar, India 33°6' N, 76°24' E 188
Kilauea Lighthouse, site, U.S. 22°13' N, 159°27' W 94
Kilbaha, Ire. 52°33' N, 9°52' W 150
Kilbourne, Ill., U.S. 40°8' N, 90°1' W 102
Kilbourne, La., U.S. 32°59' N, 91°19' W 103
Kilbride, Can. 57°6' N, 7°22' W 150
Kilbuck Mountains, Alas., U.S. 60°3' N, 161°24' W 98
Kilchoman, U.K. 55°46' N, 6°27' W 150
Kil'din, Russ. 69°20' N, 34°20' E 152
Kilembe, Dem. Rep. of the Congo 5°48' S, 19°51' E 218
Kilgore, Nebr., U.S. 42°55' N, 100°57' W 90
Kilgore, Tex., U.S. 32°22' N, 94°53' W 103
Kılıçkaya, Turk. 40°42' N, 41°28' E 195
Kilifi, Kenya 3°37' S, 39°50' E 224
Kilimanjaro, peak, Tanzania 3°6' S, 37°17' E 224
Kılınç Tepesi, peak, Turk. 40°31' N, 38°4' E 156
Kilindoni, Tanzania 7°54' S, 39°40' E 224
Kilingi Nõmme, Est. 58°8' N, 24°57' E 166
Kilíni, Óros, peak, Gr. 37°55' N, 22°19' E 156
Kilinochchi, Sri Lanka 9°22' N, 80°23' E 188
Kilis, Turk. 36°44' N, 37°6' E 156
Kiliya, Ukr. 45°29' N, 29°15' E 156
Kilju, N. Korea 40°57' N, 129°22' E 200
Kilkádes (Cyclades), islands, Mediterranean Sea 36°31' N, 24°28' E 156
Kilkee, Ire. 52°40' N, 9°38' W 150
Kilkenny, Ire. 52°39' N, 7°16' W 150
Kilkoris, Kenya 1°1' S, 34°53' E 224
Killala, Ire. 54°12' N, 9°15' W 150
Killala Lake, Can. 49°2' N, 86°55' W 94
Killam, Can. 52°46' N, 111°51' W 108
Killarney, Can. 49°10' N, 99°40' W 108
Killarney, Can. 45°58' N, 81°29' W 94
Killdeer, N. Dak., U.S. 47°21' N, 102°46' W 90
Killdeer Mountains, N. Dak., U.S. 47°44' N, 102°59' W 90
Killeen, Tex., U.S. 31°6' N, 97°44' W 92
Killough, U.K. 54°14' N, 5°40' W 150
Killybegs, Ire. 54°37' N, 8°28' W 150
Kil'mez', Russ. 56°56' N, 51°8' E 154
Kilmichael, Miss., U.S. 33°25' N, 89°34' W 103
Kilo, Dem. Rep. of the Congo 1°48' N, 30°10' E 224
Kilómetro, Arg. 28°26' S, 60°3' W 139
Kilosa, Tanzania 6°47' S, 37°0' E 224
Kilpua, Fin. 64°20' N, 24°54' E 154
Kilvaxter, U.K. 57°38' N, 6°23' W 150
Kilwa, Dem. Rep. of the Congo 9°18' S, 28°19' E 224
Kilwa Kivinje, Tanzania 8°45' S, 39°23' E 224
Kilwa Masoko, Tanzania 8°56' S, 39°33' E 224
Kim, Chad 9°42' N, 15°57' E 216
Kim, Colo., U.S. 37°14' N, 103°21' W 92
Kima, Dem. Rep. of the Congo 1°27' S, 26°42' E 224
Kimali, Tanzania 3°28' S, 34°26' E 224
Kimasozero, Russ. 64°21' N, 31°11' E 152
Kimball, Nebr., U.S. 41°13' N, 103°41' W 90
Kimball, S. Dak., U.S. 43°43' N, 98°60' W 90
Kimball, Mount, Alas., U.S. 63°15' N, 144°51' W 98
Kimberley, Can. 49°40' N, 115°59' W 90
Kimberley, S. Af. 28°46' S, 24°47' E 227
Kimberley, region, Australia 18°35' S, 125°40' E 230
Kimbirila, Côte d'Ivoire 10°22' N, 7°32' W 222
Kimbolton, U.K. 52°17' N, 0°24' E 162
Kimboto, Congo 3°17' S, 14°1' E 218
Kimbrough, Ala., U.S. 32°1' N, 87°33' W 103
Kimch'aek (Sŏngjin), N. Korea 40°38' N, 129°11' E 200
Kiméria, Gr. 41°8' N, 24°56' E 156
Kimhwa (Kŭmsŏng), N. Korea 38°26' N, 127°36' E 200
Kimhyŏnggwŏn, N. Korea 40°47' N, 128°10' E 200
Kimi, Gr. 38°38' N, 24°6' E 156
Kimina, Gr. 40°37' N, 22°41' E 156
Kimito, Fin. 60°9' N, 22°42' E 166
Kimjŏngsuk (Sinp'a), N. Korea 41°24' N, 127°48' E 200
Kimmirut (Lake Harbor), Can. 62°52' N, 69°53' W 106
Kimovaara, Russ. 63°37' N, 31°1' E 152
Kimovsk, Russ. 53°56' N, 38°27' E 154
Kimpese, Dem. Rep. of the Congo 5°33' S, 14°22' E 218
Kimry, Russ. 56°53' N, 37°21' E 154
Kimsquit, Can. 52°50' N, 126°56' W 108
Kimvula, Dem. Rep. of the Congo 5°43' S, 15°57' E 218
Kinabalu Park, Malaysia 6°14' N, 116°1' E 203
Kinabalu, peak, Malaysia 6°6' N, 116°29' E 203
Kinaskan Lake, Can. 57°29' N, 131°2' W 108
Kincaid, Can. 49°38' N, 107°1' W 90
Kincaid, Ill., U.S. 39°34' N, 89°25' W 102
Kincardine, Can. 44°9' N, 81°37' W 102
Kincolith, Can. 55°2' N, 129°59' W 108
Kinda, Dem. Rep. of the Congo 9°19' S, 25°2' E 224
Kindakun Point, Can. 53°7' N, 132°60' W 108
Kindanba, Congo 3°45' S, 14°34' E 218
Kinde, Mich., U.S. 43°56' N, 82°60' W 102
Kinder, La., U.S. 30°28' N, 92°51' W 103
Kinder Scout, peak, U.K. 53°23' N, 1°54' W 162
Kinderhook, N.Y., U.S. 42°23' N, 73°43' W 104
Kindersley, Can. 51°29' N, 109°9' W 90
Kindia, Guinea 10°3' N, 12°54' W 222
Kindu, Dem. Rep. of the Congo 2°60' S, 25°54' E 224
Kinel', Russ. 53°14' N, 50°33' E 154
Kineo, Mount, Me., U.S. 45°41' N, 69°49' W 94
Kineshma, Russ. 57°24' N, 42°12' E 154
Kinesi, Tanzania 1°26' S, 33°54' E 224
King Arthur's Castle see Tintagel, site, U.K. 50°39' N, 4°49' W 150
King Christian Ix Land, Den. 71°9' N, 41°7' W 73
King City, Calif., U.S. 36°13' N, 121°9' W 100
King City, Mo., U.S. 40°2' N, 94°32' W 94
King Frederik Vi Coast, Den. 64°54' N, 50°21' W 73
King George Island, Antarctica 61°46' S, 61°4' W 248
King George Islands, Hudson Bay 57°39' N, 80°48' W 106
King George, Mount, Can. 50°35' N, 115°31' W 90
King Island, Alas., U.S. 65°14' N, 167°26' W 160
King Island, Austral. 39°58' S, 142°39' E 230
King Khalid Military City, site, Saudi Arabia 27°52' N, 45°27' E 180
King Lear Peak, Nev., U.S. 41°11' N, 118°39' W 90
King Leopold Ranges, Austral. 17°39' S, 125°3' E 230
King Mountain, Can. 58°17' N, 128°59' W 108
King Mountain, Oreg., U.S. 43°47' N, 118°57' W 90
King Mountain, Oreg., U.S. 42°40' N, 123°19' W 90
King Peak, Antarctica 85°20' S, 90°39' W 248
King Peak, Calif., U.S. 40°8' N, 124°12' W 90
King Peninsula, Antarctica 73°6' S, 98°45' W 248
King Salmon, Alas., U.S. 58°37' N, 156°48' W 98
King Sejong, station, Antarctica 62°8' S, 58°27' W 134
King William Island, Can. 69°57' N, 100°41' W 106
King William's Town, S. Af. 32°54' S, 27°22' E 227
Kingaroy, Austral. 26°33' S, 151°49' E 231
Kingcome Inlet, Can. 50°57' N, 126°14' W 90
Kingfish, oil field, Austral. 38°32' S, 147°57' E 230
Kingfisher, Okla., U.S. 35°49' N, 97°56' W 92
Kingisepp, Russ. 59°22' N, 28°38' E 166
Kingman, Ariz., U.S. 35°11' N, 114°4' W 101
Kingman, Kans., U.S. 37°38' N, 98°7' W 90
Kingri, Pak. 30°27' N, 69°52' E 186
Kings Canyon, Calif., U.S. 36°49' N, 119°2' W 101
Kings Canyon National Park, Calif., U.S. 36°55' N, 118°58' W 101
King's Cliffe, U.K. 52°33' N, 0°31' E 162
King's Lynn, U.K. 52°44' N, 0°24' E 162
Kings Mountain National Military Park, S.C., U.S. 35°8' N, 81°27' W 96
Kings Peak, Utah, U.S. 40°44' N, 110°27' W 90
Kings, river, Calif., U.S. 36°23' N, 119°40' W 100
Kingsburg, Calif., U.S. 36°31' N, 119°34' W 100
Kingsford Heights, Ind., U.S. 41°28' N, 86°42' W 102
Kingsnorth, U.K. 51°7' N, 0°51' E 162
Kingsport, Tenn., U.S. 36°31' N, 82°33' W 82
Kingston, Can. 44°14' N, 76°30' W 94
Kingston, Jam. 17°58' N, 76°55' W 115
Kingston, Mich., U.S. 43°24' N, 83°11' W 102
Kingston, N.Y., U.S. 41°55' N, 74°1' W 104
Kingston, N.Z. 45°21' S, 168°43' E 240
Kingston, Ohio, U.S. 39°28' N, 82°56' W 102
Kingston, Pa., U.S. 41°15' N, 75°55' W 94
Kingston, R.I., U.S. 41°28' N, 71°32' W 104
Kingston, Wash., U.S. 47°47' N, 122°31' W 100
Kingston Lake, Can. 58°55' N, 103°6' W 108
Kingston Peak, Calif., U.S. 35°42' N, 115°57' W 101
Kingston Range, Calif., U.S. 35°46' N, 115°60' W 101
Kingston South East, Austral. 36°52' S, 139°53' E 231
Kingston upon Hull, U.K. 53°44' N, 0°22' E 162
Kingston Upon Thames, U.K. 51°24' N, 0°18' E 162
Kingstown, Saint Vincent and The Grenadines 13°8' N, 61°20' W 116
Kingstree, S.C., U.S. 33°39' N, 79°50' W 96
Kingsville, Can. 42°1' N, 82°44' W 102
Kingsville, Tex., U.S. 27°30' N, 97°52' W 96
Kingungi, Dem. Rep. of the Congo 5°20' S, 17°57' E 218
Kiniama, Dem. Rep. of the Congo 11°32' S, 28°22' E 224
Kinistino, Can. 52°57' N, 105°3' W 108
Kinkala, Congo 4°22' S, 14°45' E 218
Kinloch Castle, site, U.K. 56°59' N, 6°23' W 150
Kinloch Lake, Can. 51°53' N, 91°31' W 110
Kinmen (Quemoy), island, China 24°23' N, 118°32' E 198
Kinmundy, Ill., U.S. 38°45' N, 88°51' W 102
Kinnaird Castle, site, U.K. 56°41' N, 2°43' W 150
Kinniyai, Sri Lanka 8°26' N, 81°12' E 188
Kinnula, Fin. 63°21' N, 24°56' E 152
Kino, river, Japan 34°16' N, 135°20' E 201
Kinoosao, Can. 57°5' N, 102°3' W 108
Kinosaki, Japan 35°36' N, 134°47' E 201
Kinosheo, river, Can. 51°22' N, 82°3' W 110
Kinsey, Cape, Antarctica 69°14' S, 162°35' E 248
Kinshasa, adm. division, Dem. Rep. of the Congo 4°58' S, 15°25' E 218
Kinshasa (Léopoldville), Dem. Rep. of the Congo 4°24' S, 15°6' E 218
Kinsley, Kans., U.S. 37°54' N, 99°25' W 90
Kinston, N.C., U.S. 35°16' N, 77°36' W 96
Kintai, Lith. 55°25' N, 21°17' E 166
Kintampo, Ghana 8°3' N, 1°43' W 222
Kintinian, Guinea 11°37' N, 9°22' W 222
Kintla Peak, Mont., U.S. 48°54' N, 114°15' W 90
Kintyre, U.K. 55°25' N, 5°34' W 150
Kinuso, Can. 55°20' N, 115°28' W 108
Kinyang, Kenya 0°56' N, 36°0' E 224
Kinyangiri, Tanzania 4°26' S, 34°36' E 224
Kinyeti, peak, Sudan 3°55' N, 32°52' E 224
Kiokluk Mountains, Alas., U.S. 61°29' N, 158°44' W 106
Kiomboi, Tanzania 4°17' S, 34°20' E 224
Kióni, Gr. 38°26' N, 20°41' E 156
Kiowa, Colo., U.S. 39°20' N, 104°28' W 90
Kiowa, Kans., U.S. 37°1' N, 98°30' W 92
Kiparissí, Gr. 36°57' N, 22°58' E 156
Kipawa, Lac, lake, Can. 46°47' N, 79°27' W 110
Kipembawe, Tanzania 7°42' S, 33°25' E 224
Kipengere Range, Tanzania 9°34' S, 34°15' E 224
Kipili, Tanzania 7°27' S, 30°36' E 224
Kipilingu, Dem. Rep. of the Congo 13°17' S, 29°1' E 224
Kipinä, Fin. 65°15' N, 26°27' E 152
Kipini, Kenya 2°32' S, 40°29' E 224
Kipiyevo, Russ. 65°40' N, 54°27' E 154
Kipling, Can. 50°6' N, 102°39' W 90
Kipushi, Dem. Rep. of the Congo 11°48' S, 27°14' E 224
Kipushia, Dem. Rep. of the Congo 13°1' S, 29°30' E 224
Kir, Alban. 42°14' N, 19°41' E 168
Kiraz, Turk. 38°14' N, 28°12' E 156
Kirbla, Est. 58°42' N, 23°55' E 166
Kirbymoorside, U.K. 54°16' N, 0°55' E 162
Kirbyville, Tex., U.S. 30°38' N, 93°54' W 103
Kirchberg, Ger. 49°56' N, 7°23' E 167
Kirchen, Ger. 50°48' N, 7°53' E 167
Kirchhain, Ger. 50°49' N, 8°55' E 167
Kirchheim, Ger. 50°50' N, 9°34' E 167
Kirchheimbolanden, Ger. 49°40' N, 8°0' E 163
Kirchhundem, Ger. 51°5' N, 8°4' E 167
Kirensk, Russ. 57°35' N, 107°50' E 160
Kiri, Dem. Rep. of the Congo 1°28' S, 18°59' E 218
Kiri, Mali 13°57' N, 2°60' W 222
Kiriaki, Gr. 41°17' N, 26°12' E 156
Kiribati 1°4' S, 172°37' E 238
Kiridh, Somalia 8°54' N, 46°11' E 216
Kırıkkale, Turk. 39°50' N, 33°30' E 156
Kirillov, Russ. 59°53' N, 38°21' E 154
Kirillovskoye, Russ. 60°27' N, 29°18' E 166
Kirin, Eth. 9°54' N, 34°22' E 224
Kirishi, Russ. 59°27' N, 32°6' E 154
Kirishima Yaku National Park, Japan 31°45' N, 130°52' E 201
Kiritimati (Christmas Island), Kiribati 2°0' N, 157°24' W 241
Kiriwina, island, P.N.G. 8°31' S, 149°58' E 192
Kırka, Turk. 39°17' N, 30°30' E 156
Kırkağaç, Turk. 39°5' N, 27°39' E 156
Kirkbride, U.K. 54°53' N, 3°12' W 162
Kirkby Lonsdale, U.K. 54°12' N, 2°36' W 162
Kirkby Stephen, U.K. 54°28' N, 2°22' W 162
Kirkcudbright, U.K. 54°49' N, 4°3' W 162
Kirkenes, Nor. 69°42' N, 30°20' E 160
Kırkgeçit (Kasrik), Turk. 38°7' N, 43°27' E 195
Kirkham, U.K. 53°47' N, 2°55' W 162
Kirkkola, Fin. 61°37' N, 26°0' E 166
Kirkkonummi see Kyrkslätt, Fin. 60°7' N, 24°26' E 166
Kirkland, Tex., U.S. 34°21' N, 100°5' W 92
Kirkland, Wash., U.S. 47°39' N, 122°12' W 100
Kirkland Lake, Can. 48°9' N, 79°60' W 82
Kırklar Dağı, peak, Turk. 40°33' N, 40°31' E 195
Kırklareli, Turk. 41°42' N, 27°13' E 180
Kirklin, Ind., U.S. 40°11' N, 86°21' W 102
Kirkoswald, U.K. 54°46' N, 2°41' W 162
Kirksville, Mo., U.S. 40°11' N, 92°34' W 94
Kirkūk see Karkūk, Iraq 35°27' N, 44°23' E 180
Kirkwall, U.K. 58°59' N, 3°3' W 143
Kirkwood, Mo., U.S. 38°34' N, 90°24' W 94
Kirkwood, S. Af. 33°23' S, 25°23' E 227
Kirn, Ger. 49°47' N, 7°27' E 167
Kirotshe, Dem. Rep. of the Congo 1°45' S, 28°57' E 224
Kirov, Russ. 54°0' N, 34°17' E 154
Kirov, Russ. 58°34' N, 49°38' E 154
Kirov, adm. division, Russ. 58°45' N, 48°49' E 154
Kirovgrad, Russ. 57°27' N, 60°5' E 154
Kirovo Chepetsk, Russ. 58°31' N, 50°7' E 154
Kirovohrad, Ukr. 48°30' N, 32°18' E 156
Kirovsk, Russ. 67°35' N, 33°43' E 152
Kirovskiy, Russ. 45°49' N, 48°11' E 158
Kirovskiy, Russ. 54°18' N, 155°43' E 173
Kirs, Russ. 59°19' N, 52°17' E 154
Kirs, peak, Azerb. 39°38' N, 46°41' E 195
Kirsanov, Russ. 52°40' N, 42°39' E 158
Kırşehir, Turk. 39°8' N, 34°10' E 143
Kirtachi, Niger 12°47' N, 2°29' E 222
Kirthar National Park, Pak. 25°37' N, 66°58' E 186
Kirton in Lindsey, U.K. 53°28' N, 0°36' E 162
Kirtshki, Ga. 42°32' N, 42°5' E 195
Kiruna, Sw. 68°0' N, 19°54' E 160
Kirundu, Dem. Rep. of the Congo 0°46' N, 25°38' E 224
Kirungu, Dem. Rep. of the Congo 7°6' S, 29°42' E 224
Kirya, Russ. 55°4' N, 46°54' E 154
Kiryū, Japan 36°24' N, 139°21' E 201
Kisaki, Tanzania 7°25' S, 37°42' E 224
Kisangani (Stanleyville), Dem. Rep. of the Congo 0°33' N, 25°16' E 224
Kisangire, Tanzania 7°21' S, 38°43' E 224
Kisaran, Indonesia 3°1' N, 99°37' E 196
Kisbér, Hung. 47°29' N, 18°2' E 168
Kiselevsk, Russ. 53°59' N, 86°44' E 184
Kiseljak, Bosn. and Herzg. 43°56' N, 18°4' E 168
Kisengwa, Dem. Rep. of the Congo 6°1' S, 25°50' E 224
Kishanganj, India 26°8' N, 87°55' E 197
Kishangarh, India 26°35' N, 74°53' E 188
Kishi, Nig. 9°3' N, 3°50' E 222
Kishiwada, Japan 34°26' N, 135°22' E 201
Kishkenekŏl, Kaz. 53°38' N, 72°21' E 184
Kishorganj, Bangladesh 24°21' N, 90°43' E 197
Kisigo, river, Tanzania 6°52' S, 35°8' E 224
Kisii, Kenya 0°43' N, 34°46' E 224
Kisiju, Tanzania 7°18' S, 39°19' E 224
Kısır Dağı, peak, Turk. 40°56' N, 43°1' E 195
Kiska, island, Alas., U.S. 51°31' N, 176°29' E 160
Kiskittogisu Lake, Can. 54°5' N, 99°6' W 108
Kisk orös, Hung. 46°37' N, 19°18' E 168
Kiskundorozsma, Hung. 46°16' N, 20°4' E 168
Kiskunhalas, Hung. 46°24' N, 19°29' E 168
Kiskunlacháza, Hung. 47°10' N, 19°2' E 168
Kiskunmajsa, Hung. 46°29' N, 19°45' E 168
Kislovodsk, Russ. 43°56' N, 42°46' E 158
Kismaayo (Chisimayu), Somalia 0°27' N, 42°35' E 224
Kiso, river, Japan 35°33' N, 137°31' E 201
Kisoro, Uganda 1°20' S, 29°40' E 224
Kispiox, Can. 55°23' N, 127°43' W 108
Kispiox, river, Can. 55°28' N, 128°38' W 108
Kissidougou, Guinea 9°10' N, 10°6' W 222
Kissimmee, Fla., U.S. 28°18' N, 81°25' W 105
Kissimmee, Lake, Fla., U.S. 27°54' N, 81°30' W 105
Kissimmee, river, Fla., U.S. 27°23' N, 81°10' W 105
Kississing Lake, Can. 55°14' N, 101°51' W 108
Kissu, Jebel, peak, Sudan 21°32' N, 25°3' E 226
Kistanje, Croatia 43°58' N, 15°56' E 168
Kistelek, Hung. 46°28' N, 19°58' E 168
Kisterenye, Hung. 48°1' N, 19°49' E 168
Kistrand, Nor. 70°26' N, 25°12' E 152
Kisújszállás, Hung. 47°12' N, 20°46' E 168
Kisumu, Kenya 0°8' S, 34°46' E 224
Kisvárda, Hung. 48°13' N, 22°5' E 156
Kiswere, Tanzania 9°27' S, 39°33' E 224
Kiszombor, Hung. 46°11' N, 20°26' E 168
Kit Carson, Colo., U.S. 38°45' N, 102°48' W 90
Kita, Mali 13°2' N, 9°30' W 222
Kitaibaraki, Japan 36°46' N, 140°43' E 201
Kitakata, Japan 37°39' N, 139°51' E 201
Kitakyūshū, Japan 33°52' N, 130°53' E 200
Kitale, Kenya 1°0' N, 34°58' E 224
Kitchener, Can. 43°26' N, 80°29' W 94
Kitchener Lake, Can. 56°59' N, 128°11' W 108
Kitchigama, river, Can. 50°58' N, 79°24' W 80
Kitee, Fin. 62°4' N, 30°6' E 152
Kitenda, Dem. Rep. of the Congo 6°49' S, 17°26' E 218
Kitgum, Uganda 3°14' N, 32°53' E 224
Kithairńas, Óros, peak, Gr. 38°10' N, 23°10' E 156
Kithira (Cerigo), island, Gr. 36°17' N, 23°3' E 180
Kithira, island, Gr. 36°22' N, 23°6' E 143
Kiti, Cape, Cyprus 34°44' N, 33°34' E 194
Kitimat, Can. 54°4' N, 128°42' W 108
Kitlope, river, Can. 53°14' N, 128°8' W 108
Kitob, Uzb. 39°8' N, 66°53' E 197
Kitombe, Dem. Rep. of the Congo 5°23' S, 18°57' E 218
Kitsa, Russ. 68°30' N, 33°11' E 152
Kitscoty, Can. 53°19' N, 110°20' W 108
Kitsuki, Japan 33°25' N, 131°36' E 201
Kittery, Me., U.S. 43°5' N, 70°45' W 104
Kittery Point, Me., U.S. 43°5' N, 70°42' W 104
Kittilä, Fin. 67°39' N, 24°51' E 152
Kittitas, Wash., U.S. 46°57' N, 120°26' W 90
Kitty Hawk, N.C., U.S. 36°2' N, 75°41' W 82
Kitui, Kenya 1°23' S, 38°1' E 224
Kitwanga, Can. 55°5' N, 128°4' W 108
Kitwe, Zambia 12°50' S, 28°11' E 224
Kitzbühel, Aust. 47°26' N, 12°23' E 156
Kitzbüheler Alpen, Aust. 47°22' N, 11°45' E 156
Kitzingen, Ger. 49°44' N, 10°8' E 152
Kiukainen, Fin. 61°12' N, 22°5' E 166
Kiuruvesi, Fin. 63°38' N, 26°34' E 154
Kiuyu, Ras, Tanzania 4°55' S, 39°53' E 224
Kivalina, Alas., U.S. 67°40' N, 164°30' W 98
Kivalo, Fin. 65°43' N, 25°0' E 152
Kivertsi, Ukr. 50°49' N, 25°26' E 152
Kivijärvi, Fin. 63°7' N, 25°5' E 152
Kivik, Nor. 55°40' N, 14°14' E 152
Kiviõli, Est. 59°20' N, 26°55' E 166
Kivivaara, Fin. 63°36' N, 30°10' E 152
Kivumba, Tanzania 4°38' S, 30°40' E 224
Kiwai, island, P.N.G. 8°51' S, 143°38' E 192
Kiwalik, U.S. 66°1' N, 161°55' W 98
Kiya, Russ. 67°36' N, 44°11' E 169
Kiyāt, Saudi Arabia 18°41' N, 41°26' E 182
Kıyıköy, Turk. 41°36' N, 28°5' E 156
Kiyiu Lake, Can. 51°35' N, 109°24' W 90
Kiyuk Lake, Can. 60°27' N, 100°55' W 108
Kizel, Russ. 59°0' N, 57°42' E 154
Kizema, Russ. 61°7' N, 44°56' E 154
Kızılcahamam, Turk. 40°27' N, 32°37' E 156
Kızılırmak, Turk. 40°21' N, 33°58' E 156
Kızılırmak, river, Turk. 40°33' N, 34°43' E 180
Kızılliman Burnu, Turk. 35°58' N, 32°26' E 156
Kizil'skoye, Russ. 52°43' N, 58°49' E 154
Kızıltepe, Turk. 37°11' N, 40°36' E 195
Kizimkazi, Ras, Tanzania 6°39' S, 39°0' E 224
Kizlyar, Russ. 43°49' N, 46°40' E 195
Kizlyarskiy Zaliv 44°24' N, 46°34' E 158
Kizner, Russ. 56°16' N, 51°34' E 154
Kizreka, Russ. 65°32' N, 31°54' E 152
Kjelvik, Nor. 70°58' N, 26°7' E 152
Kjøpsvik, Nor. 68°5' N, 16°21' E 152
Kjya, islands, Norwegian Sea 64°33' N, 9°43' E 152
Klabat, peak, Indonesia 1°34' N, 124°51' E 192
Kladanj, Bosn. and Herzg. 44°13' N, 18°40' E 168
Kladnica, Serb. and Mont. 43°22' N, 20°2' E 168
Klafeld, Ger. 50°55' N, 8°0' E 167
Klaipėda, Lith. 55°42' N, 21°10' E 166
Klamath, Calif., U.S. 41°31' N, 124°2' W 90

Klamath, Calif., U.S. 40°45′ N, 123°5′ W 90
Klamath Falls, Oreg., U.S. 42°13′ N, 121°46′ W 82
Klamath Mountains Mountains, Calif., U.S. 42°1′ N, 125°19′ W 80
Klamono, Indonesia 1°4′ S, 131°25′ E 192
Klarabro, Nor. 60°46′ N, 12°46′ E 152
Klawer, S. Af. 31°50′ S, 18°36′ E 227
Kle, Liberia 6°37′ N, 10°54′ W 222
Kleczkowski, Lac, lake, Can. 50°47′ N, 64°6′ W 111
Klein Karas, Namibia 27°35′ S, 18°3′ E 227
Klekovača, peak, Bosn. and Herzg. 44°25′ N, 16°27′ E 168
Kléla, Mali 11°43′ N, 5°40′ W 222
Klemtu, Can. 52°34′ N, 128°33′ W 108
Klenike, Serb. and Mont. 42°23′ N, 21°54′ E 168
Klenje, Serb. and Mont. 44°48′ N, 19°26′ E 168
Klerksdorp, S. Af. 26°53′ S, 26°39′ E 227
Klery Creek, Alas., U.S. 67°10′ N, 160°25′ W 98
Kleshchevo, Russ. 63°16′ N, 39°11′ E 154
Klesiv, Ukr. 51°18′ N, 26°52′ E 152
Kleszczele, Pol. 52°36′ N, 23°19′ E 154
Kletnya, Russ. 53°19′ N, 33°12′ E 154
Kletskiy, Russ. 49°18′ N, 43°3′ E 158
Klevan', Ukr. 50°44′ N, 25°57′ E 152
Kleve, Ger. 51°47′ N, 6°8′ E 167
Klibreck, Ben, peak, U.K. 58°13′ N, 4°31′ W 150
Kličevac, Serb. and Mont. 44°45′ N, 21°17′ E 168
Klichaw, Belarus 53°27′ N, 29°23′ E 152
Klickitat, Wash., U.S. 45°48′ N, 121°9′ W 100
Klickitat, river, Wash., U.S. 46°9′ N, 121°14′ W 100
Klimovsk, Russ. 55°17′ N, 37°28′ E 154
Klin, Russ. 56°20′ N, 36°42′ E 154
Klinaklini, river, Can. 51°15′ N, 125°47′ W 108
Klingenbach, Aust. 47°45′ N, 16°32′ E 168
Klingenberg, Ger. 49°45′ N, 9°12′ E 167
Klintehamn, Sw. 57°23′ N, 18°11′ E 166
Klintsovka, Russ. 51°40′ N, 49°15′ E 158
Klintsy, Russ. 52°44′ N, 32°14′ E 154
Klipplaat, S. Af. 32°60′ S, 24°19′ E 227
Klisura, Serb. and Mont. 42°45′ N, 22°23′ E 168
Ključ, Bosn. and Herzg. 44°32′ N, 16°45′ E 168
Kłodzko, Pol. 50°25′ N, 16°40′ E 152
Klomnice, Pol. 50°55′ N, 19°21′ E 152
Klos, Alban. 41°29′ N, 20°8′ E 168
Kloster, Ger. 54°35′ N, 13°7′ E 152
Klosters, Switz. 46°52′ N, 9°52′ E 167
Klövsjö, Nor. 62°31′ N, 14°8′ E 152
Klukshu, Can. 60°17′ N, 137°2′ W 98
Klukwan, Alas., U.S. 59°25′ N, 135°48′ W 108
Klyastitsa, Russ. 55°47′ N, 29°36′ E 166
Klyastitsy, Belarus 55°52′ N, 28°37′ E 166
Klyavlino, Russ. 54°15′ N, 52°2′ E 154
Klyetsk, Belarus 53°3′ N, 26°40′ E 154
Klyuchevoye, Russ. 60°26′ N, 28°44′ E 166
Klyuchi, Russ. 52°6′ N, 79°16′ E 184
Klyukvenka, Russ. 58°31′ N, 85°57′ E 169
Knaresborough, U.K. 54°1′ N, 1°28′ W 162
Knee Lake, Can. 55°9′ N, 94°45′ W 108
Knee Lake, Can. 55°50′ N, 107°20′ W 108
Kneippbyn, Sw. 57°35′ N, 18°13′ E 166
Knesebeck, Ger. 52°41′ N, 10°42′ E 150
Knife Delta 58°50′ N, 94°60′ W 108
Knife, river, N. Dak., U.S. 47°3′ N, 102°59′ W 80
Knighton, U.K. 52°19′ N, 3°3′ W 162
Knightsville, Ind., U.S. 39°31′ N, 87°5′ W 102
Knin, Croatia 44°2′ N, 16°11′ E 168
Knittelfeld, Aust. 47°14′ N, 14°48′ E 156
Knjaževac, Serb. and Mont. 43°33′ N, 22°15′ E 168
Knock Farril, ruin(s), U.K. 57°34′ N, 4°38′ W 150
Knockadoon Head, Ire. 51°40′ N, 7°53′ W 150
Knockboy, peak, Ire. 51°47′ N, 9°32′ W 150
Knockmealdown Mountains, Ire. 52°13′ N, 8°1′ W 150
Knokke-Heist, Belg. 51°20′ N, 3°18′ E 163
Knosós see Cnossus, ruin(s), Gr. 35°16′ N, 25°4′ E 156
Knottingley, U.K. 53°42′ N, 1°14′ W 162
Knox, Ind., U.S. 41°16′ N, 86°37′ W 102
Knox, Cape, Can. 53°59′ N, 133°31′ W 108
Knox City, Tex., U.S. 33°24′ N, 99°49′ W 92
Knox Coast, Antarctica 68°16′ S, 107°4′ E 248
Knoxville, Iowa, U.S. 41°18′ N, 93°5′ W 94
Knoxville, Tenn., U.S. 35°58′ N, 83°56′ W 96
Knucklas, U.K. 52°21′ N, 3°6′ W 162
Knud Rasmussen Land, region, Arctic Ocean 77°1′ N, 66°28′ W 106
Knüllwald, Ger. 51°0′ N, 9°28′ E 167
Knysna, S. Af. 34°1′ S, 23°3′ E 227
Kō Saki, Japan 33°58′ N, 129°1′ E 200
Koal, spring, Chad 14°26′ N, 16°26′ E 216
Koani, Tanzania 5°60′ S, 39°20′ E 218
Kobayashi, Japan 31°59′ N, 130°58′ E 201
Kōbe, Japan 34°41′ N, 135°9′ E 201
Kobelyaky, Ukr. 49°11′ N, 34°8′ E 158
København (Copenhagen), Den. 55°40′ N, 12°23′ E 152
Kobern-Gondorf, Ger. 50°18′ N, 7°27′ E 167
Kobi-ri, N. Korea 39°5′ N, 126°1′ E 200
Koblenz, Ger. 50°20′ N, 7°34′ E 167
K'obo, Eth. 12°7′ N, 39°37′ E 182
Kobowen Swamp, marsh, Sudan 5°23′ N, 33°14′ E 224
Kobozha, Russ. 58°48′ N, 35°0′ E 154
Kobroor, island, Indonesia 6°31′ S, 134°40′ E 192
Kobryn, Belarus 52°14′ N, 24°21′ E 152
Kobu, Azerb. 40°24′ N, 49°42′ E 195
Kobuk, Alas., U.S. 66°49′ N, 156°58′ W 98
Kobuk, river, Alas., U.S. 66°55′ N, 159°28′ W 98
K'obulet'i, Ga. 41°49′ N, 41°47′ E 195
Kobyay, Russ. 63°29′ N, 127°1′ E 160
Kocaeli (İzmit), Turk. 40°47′ N, 29°46′ E 180
Kočani, Maced. 41°55′ N, 22°24′ E 168
Koçbaşı Tepe, peak, Turk. 39°24′ N, 43°18′ E 195
Koceljevo, Serb. and Mont. 44°28′ N, 19°50′ E 168
Koch Bihar, India 26°18′ N, 89°23′ E 197
Koch Peak, Mont., U.S. 45°0′ N, 111°32′ W 90
Kochas, India 25°13′ N, 83°53′ E 188
Kochechum, river, Russ. 67°10′ N, 98°19′ E 160
Kochen'ga, Russ. 60°9′ N, 43°33′ E 154
Kocherinovo, Bulg. 42°5′ N, 23°4′ E 168
Kochevo, Russ. 59°36′ N, 54°20′ E 154
Kōchi, Japan 33°34′ N, 133°31′ E 201
Kōchi, adm. division, Japan 33°13′ N, 132°48′ E 201
Kochkor, Kyrg. 42°8′ N, 75°41′ E 184
Kochubey, Russ. 44°23′ N, 46°31′ E 158
Kochumdek, Russ. 64°24′ N, 93°11′ E 169
Kocie, Góry, Pol. 51°24′ N, 16°2′ E 152
Kock, Pol. 51°38′ N, 22°26′ E 152
Kocs, Hung. 47°35′ N, 18°11′ E 168
Kocsola, Hung. 46°31′ N, 18°10′ E 168
Kodesjärvi, Fin. 62°2′ N, 22°4′ E 166
Kodiak, Alas., U.S. 57°43′ N, 152°30′ W 98
Kodiak Island, Alas., U.S. 56°52′ N, 152°48′ W 98
Kodinar, India 20°46′ N, 70°42′ E 188
Kodino, Russ. 63°42′ N, 39°43′ E 154
Kodinskiy, Russ. 58°34′ N, 99°5′ E 160
Kodok, Sudan 9°55′ N, 32°7′ E 224
Kōes, Namibia 25°60′ S, 19°7′ E 227
Kofa Mountains, Ariz., U.S. 33°19′ N, 113°59′ W 101
Kofarnihon, Taj. 38°32′ N, 69°1′ E 197
Koffiefontein, S. Af. 29°25′ S, 25°0′ E 227
Kofili, Mali 15°15′ N, 8°46′ W 222
Koforidua, Ghana 6°6′ N, 0°16′ E 222
Kōfu, Japan 35°39′ N, 138°35′ E 201
Koga, Japan 36°11′ N, 139°44′ E 201
Køge Bugt 55°23′ N, 12°3′ E 152
Kogolym, Russ. 62°20′ N, 74°49′ E 169
Kogon, Uzb. 39°43′ N, 64°34′ E 197
Kogon, river, Guinea 11°26′ N, 14°29′ W 222
Kohala, region, Oceania 20°10′ N, 155°53′ W 99
Kohat, Pak. 33°34′ N, 71°29′ E 186
Kohila, Est. 59°9′ N, 24°43′ E 166
Kohima, India 25°43′ N, 94°9′ E 188
Kohler, Wis., U.S. 43°44′ N, 87°47′ W 102
Kohlu, Pak. 29°55′ N, 69°16′ E 186
Kohnieh, Cambodia 13°6′ N, 107°3′ E 202
Kohtla-Järve, Est. 59°22′ N, 27°14′ E 166
Kohunlich, ruin(s), Mex. 18°21′ N, 89°4′ W 115
Koide, Japan 37°13′ N, 138°58′ E 201
Koidern, Can. 61°57′ N, 140°33′ W 98
Koidu, Sierra Leone 8°38′ N, 10°59′ W 222
Koilani, Cyprus 34°49′ N, 32°51′ E 194
Koin, N. Korea 40°29′ N, 126°23′ E 200
Koivu, Fin. 66°9′ N, 25°11′ E 152
Kojā, river, Iran 25°30′ N, 61°18′ E 182
Kok, river, Asia 20°6′ N, 99°28′ E 202
Kök Shal Tau (Kakshaal Range), Kyrg. 41°22′ N, 77°33′ E 184
Kokanee Peak, Can. 49°42′ N, 117°14′ W 90
Kökar, Fin. 59°56′ N, 20°52′ E 166
Kokas, Indonesia 2°47′ S, 132°19′ E 192
Kök-Aygyr, Kyrg. 40°43′ N, 75°39′ E 184
Kōke'e Lodge, site, Hawai'i, U.S. 22°7′ N, 159°43′ W 99
Kokemäki, Fin. 61°13′ N, 22°16′ E 166
Kokenau, Indonesia 4°37′ S, 136°13′ E 192
Koķickŋy, adm. division, Slovakia 48°34′ N, 20°35′ E 152
Kokin Brod, Serb. and Mont. 43°29′ N, 19°49′ E 168
Kokka, Sudan 20°1′ N, 30°33′ E 226
Kokkina, Northern Cyprus 35°10′ N, 32°36′ E 194
Kokkola (Gamlakarleby), Fin. 63°49′ N, 23°5′ E 152
Koko, Eth. 10°20′ N, 36°3′ E 224
Koko, Nig. 11°26′ N, 4°31′ E 222
Koko Head, peak, Hawai'i, U.S. 21°14′ N, 157°44′ W 99
Kokomo, Ind., U.S. 40°29′ N, 86°8′ W 102
Kokomo, Miss., U.S. 31°11′ N, 90°1′ W 103
Kokong, Botswana 24°20′ S, 23°4′ E 227
Kokoro, Nig. 8°54′ N, 3°9′ E 222
Kökpekti, Kaz. 48°44′ N, 82°23′ E 184
Kokrines, Alas., U.S. 64°56′ N, 154°41′ W 98
Koksan, N. Korea 38°45′ N, 126°40′ E 200
Kökshetaū, Kaz. 53°17′ N, 69°25′ E 184
Koksovyy, Russ. 48°9′ N, 40°37′ E 158
Kokstad, S. Af. 30°35′ S, 29°25′ E 227
Köktal, Kaz. 44°6′ N, 79°47′ E 184
Köktöbe, Kaz. 51°37′ N, 77°23′ E 184
Kokubu, Japan 31°42′ N, 130°45′ E 201
Kola, Bosn. and Herzg. 44°42′ N, 17°4′ E 168
Kola, Russ. 68°49′ N, 33°14′ E 160
Kola Peninsula, Russ. 67°40′ N, 28°12′ E 172
Kolahun, Liberia 8°17′ N, 10°6′ W 222
Kolaka, Indonesia 4°2′ S, 121°30′ E 192
Kolar, India 13°9′ N, 78°8′ E 188
Kolari, Fin. 67°21′ N, 23°46′ E 152
Kolarovgrad see Shumen, Bulg. 43°16′ N, 26°55′ E 156
Kolárovo, Slovakia 47°54′ N, 17°59′ E 168
Kolåsen, Nor. 63°45′ N, 12°58′ E 152
Kolayat, India 27°50′ N, 72°57′ E 186
Kolbio, Kenya 1°11′ S, 41°7′ E 224
Kol'chugino, Russ. 56°18′ N, 39°18′ E 154
Kolda, Senegal 12°54′ N, 14°58′ W 222
Koldewey, Store, island, Den. 75°50′ N, 17°54′ W 246
Kolding, Den. 55°28′ N, 9°27′ E 150
Köldük, Kyrg. 39°56′ N, 73°30′ E 197
Kole, Dem. Rep. of the Congo 2°4′ N, 25°26′ E 224
Kole, Dem. Rep. of the Congo 3°33′ S, 22°27′ E 218
Kolé, Mali 12°6′ N, 8°21′ W 222
Koler, Nor. 65°28′ N, 20°27′ E 152
Kolezhma, Russ. 64°14′ N, 35°45′ E 154
Kolga Laht 59°28′ N, 25°13′ E 166
Kolguyev, Ostrov, island, Russ. 69°29′ N, 48°57′ E 169
Kolhapur, India 16°41′ N, 74°14′ E 188
Kolī, Eth. 10°19′ N, 36°45′ E 224
Koli, Fin. 63°6′ N, 29°45′ E 152
Koliganek, Alas., U.S. 59°45′ N, 157°20′ W 98
Kolik'yegan, Russ. 61°42′ N, 79°8′ E 169
Kolik'yegan, river, Russ. 61°31′ N, 79°14′ E 169
Kolimbiné, river, Mali 14°49′ N, 12°8′ W 222
Kolka, Latv. 57°43′ N, 22°32′ E 166
Kolkas Rags, Latv. 57°44′ N, 22°36′ E 166
Kolkata (Calcutta), India 22°33′ N, 88°21′ E 197
Kolky, Ukr. 51°5′ N, 25°39′ E 152
Kollegal, India 12°9′ N, 77°9′ E 188
Kollioura, Gabon 0°11′ N, 12°8′ E 218
Kolmanskop, Namibia 26°44′ S, 15°14′ E 227
Kolmogorovo, Russ. 59°14′ N, 91°15′ E 169
Köln (Cologne), Ger. 50°56′ N, 6°57′ E 167
Kolo, Niger 13°19′ N, 2°23′ E 222
Kołobrzeg, Pol. 54°9′ N, 15°33′ E 152
Kolodishchi, Belarus 53°56′ N, 27°46′ E 166
Kolodnya, Russ. 54°47′ N, 32°16′ E 154
Kologi, Sudan 10°51′ N, 31°0′ E 224
Kologriv, Russ. 58°49′ N, 44°22′ E 154
Kolokani, Mali 13°36′ N, 8°2′ W 222
Kololo, Eth. 7°27′ N, 42°0′ E 224
Kolomna, Russ. 55°4′ N, 38°41′ E 154
Kolomyya, Ukr. 48°31′ N, 25°2′ E 158
Kolosib, India 24°13′ N, 92°38′ E 188
Kolosovka, Russ. 56°31′ N, 73°37′ E 169
Kolosovykh, Ostrov, island, Russ. 74°9′ N, 87°14′ E 160
Kolozhno, Ozero, lake, Russ. 67°44′ N, 30°18′ E 152
Kolpakovskiy, Russ. 54°31′ N, 155°58′ E 160
Kolpashevo, Russ. 58°19′ N, 82°57′ E 169
Kolpino, Russ. 59°44′ N, 30°36′ E 166
Kolpny, Russ. 52°13′ N, 37°3′ E 158
Kol'skiy Poluostrov, Europe 67°17′ N, 38°11′ E 169
Koluszki, Pol. 51°44′ N, 19°48′ E 152
Kolva, river, Russ. 60°47′ N, 56°50′ E 154
Kolva, river, Russ. 66°19′ N, 56°53′ E 154
Kolvereid, Nor. 64°52′ N, 11°38′ E 152
Kolvitsa, Russ. 67°4′ N, 33°0′ E 152
Kolwezi, Dem. Rep. of the Congo 10°46′ S, 25°26′ E 224
Kolyma, river, Russ. 67°7′ N, 152°3′ E 160
Kolyma, river, Russ. 65°53′ N, 152°45′ E 172
Kolymskoye, Russ. 68°47′ N, 158°38′ E 160
Kolymskoye Nagor'ye, Russ. 61°35′ N, 155°21′ E 160
Kolyuchin, Ostrov, island, Russ. 67°21′ N, 174°33′ W 98
Kolyuchinskaya Guba 66°38′ N, 177°60′ W 98
Kolyvan', Russ. 51°19′ N, 82°42′ E 184
Kôm Dafana, ruin(s), Egypt 30°50′ N, 32°7′ E 194
Kôm Ombo, Egypt 24°27′ N, 32°55′ E 182
Kom, peak, Bulg. 43°9′ N, 23°1′ E 168
Komádi, Hung. 47°0′ N, 21°30′ E 168
Komagane, Japan 35°44′ N, 137°56′ E 201
Komagvær, Nor. 70°14′ N, 30°36′ E 152
Komandorskiye Ostrova (Commander Islands), Bering Sea 53°42′ N, 162°31′ E 160
Komarne, Ukr. 49°37′ N, 23°41′ E 152
Komárno, Slovakia 47°46′ N, 18°7′ E 168
Komárom, Hung. 47°44′ N, 18°7′ E 168
Komárom-Esztergom, adm. division, Hung. 47°45′ N, 17°55′ E 156
Komarovo, Russ. 59°33′ N, 50°18′ E 154
Komatipoort, S. Af. 25°26′ S, 31°56′ E 227
Komatsu, Japan 36°24′ N, 136°28′ E 201
Komatsushima, Japan 33°59′ N, 134°34′ E 201
Komba, Dem. Rep. of the Congo 2°52′ N, 24°3′ E 224
Komenotsu, Japan 32°6′ N, 130°20′ E 201
Komi, adm. division, Russ. 63°40′ N, 52°9′ E 154
Komi-Permyak, adm. division, Russ. 60°27′ N, 52°55′ E 169
Komiža, Croatia 43°2′ N, 16°5′ E 168
Komló, Hung. 46°10′ N, 18°16′ E 168
Komodo, island, Indonesia 9°13′ S, 119°17′ E 230
Komoé, river, Africa 9°15′ N, 4°13′ W 222
Komoé, river, Côte d'Ivoire 5°40′ N, 3°23′ W 222
Komoro, Japan 36°19′ N, 138°26′ E 201
Komotini, Gr. 41°7′ N, 25°24′ E 156
Komovi, peak, Serb. and Mont. 42°40′ N, 19°37′ E 168
Kompong Chhnang, Cambodia 12°15′ N, 104°39′ E 202
Kompong Som, Cambodia 10°38′ N, 103°32′ E 202
Kompong Speu, Cambodia 11°24′ N, 104°29′ E 202
Kompong Sralao, Cambodia 14°5′ N, 105°45′ E 202
Kompong Trach, Cambodia 10°34′ N, 104°27′ E 202
Komsa, Russ. 61°45′ N, 89°19′ E 169
Komses'yegan, Russ. 61°16′ N, 83°32′ E 169
Komsomol, Kaz. 47°26′ N, 53°40′ E 158
Komsomolets, Kaz. 53°47′ N, 62°3′ E 154
Komsomolets, Ostrov, island, Russ. 81°49′ N, 109°24′ E 246
Komsomolets Shyghanaghy 45°19′ N, 52°3′ E 158
Komsomol'sk, Russ. 57°2′ N, 40°16′ E 154
Komsomol'sk na Amure, Russ. 50°30′ N, 136°57′ E 190
Komsomol'skiy, Russ. 69°5′ N, 172°43′ E 173
Komsomol'skoe, Kaz. 50°26′ N, 60°27′ E 158
Komsomol'skoy Pravdy, Ostrova, islands, Laptev Sea 76°50′ N, 108°45′ E 160
Komsomol'skoye, Russ. 50°45′ N, 46°59′ E 158
Komu, Fin. 63°40′ N, 26°8′ E 152
Komusan, N. Korea 42°7′ N, 129°41′ E 200
Kon Tum, Vietnam 14°21′ N, 107°59′ E 202
Kona, Mali 14°56′ N, 3°55′ W 222
Kona, region, Oceania 19°25′ N, 155°54′ W 99
Konakovo, Russ. 56°40′ N, 36°47′ E 154
Konakpınar, Turk. 38°54′ N, 37°17′ E 156
Konarak, India 19°53′ N, 86°4′ E 188
Konawa, Okla., U.S. 34°56′ N, 96°44′ W 96
Konch, India 25°58′ N, 79°8′ E 197
Konda, river, Russ. 60°42′ N, 63°22′ E 169
Kondiás, Gr. 39°51′ N, 25°9′ E 156
Kondoa, Tanzania 4°55′ S, 35°48′ E 224
Kondol', Russ. 52°47′ N, 45°5′ E 158
Kondolole, Dem. Rep. of the Congo 1°20′ N, 26°0′ E 224
Kondopoga, Russ. 62°11′ N, 34°22′ E 154
Kondoz, Afghan. 36°47′ N, 68°54′ E 186
Kondrovo, Russ. 54°49′ N, 35°57′ E 154
Konduga, Nig. 11°38′ N, 13°25′ E 216
Kondukur, India 15°11′ N, 79°55′ E 188
Konergino, Russ. 65°57′ N, 178°47′ W 98
Konetsbor, Russ. 64°51′ N, 57°42′ E 154
Köneürgench, Turkm. 42°18′ N, 59°10′ E 180
Konevo, Russ. 62°6′ N, 39°19′ E 154
Konfara, Guinea 11°55′ N, 8°52′ W 222
Kong, Côte d'Ivoire 9°9′ N, 4°38′ W 222
Kong Christian Ix Land, Den. 68°38′ N, 33°55′ W 106
Kong Christian X Land, Den. 73°44′ N, 52°49′ W 246
Kong Frederik Vi Kyst, Den. 61°32′ N, 52°50′ W 106
Kong Frederik Viii Land, Den. 79°7′ N, 62°48′ W 246
Kong Karls Land, islands, Barents Sea 78°20′ N, 30°46′ E 160
Kong Kemul, peak, Indonesia 1°54′ N, 115°51′ E 192
Kong, Koh, island, Cambodia 11°20′ N, 102°19′ E 202
Kong, river, Laos 15°33′ N, 106°51′ E 202
Köngäs, Fin. 67°52′ N, 24°51′ E 152
Kongelai, Kenya 1°22′ N, 35°1′ E 224
Konginkangas, Fin. 62°45′ N, 25°44′ E 154
Konglu, Myanmar 27°17′ N, 97°56′ E 188
Kongolo, Dem. Rep. of the Congo 5°25′ S, 26°56′ E 224
Kongor, Sudan 7°8′ N, 31°21′ E 224
Kongsfjord, Nor. 70°41′ N, 29°20′ E 152
Kongsmoen, Nor. 64°52′ N, 12°25′ E 152
Kongur Shan, peak, China 38°36′ N, 75°14′ E 184
Kongwa, Tanzania 6°9′ S, 36°26′ E 224
Konibodom, Taj. 40°18′ N, 70°27′ E 197
Königswinter, Ger. 50°40′ N, 7°11′ E 167
Konin, Pol. 52°12′ N, 18°14′ E 152
Köniz, Switz. 46°54′ N, 7°25′ E 167
Konjic, Bosn. and Herzg. 43°38′ N, 17°58′ E 168
Konjuh, peak, Bosn. and Herzg. 44°17′ N, 18°30′ E 168
Konkouré, river, Guinea 10°17′ N, 13°31′ W 222
Konnur, India 16°10′ N, 74°44′ E 188
Konosha, Russ. 60°59′ N, 40°12′ E 154
Konotop, Ukr. 51°12′ N, 33°16′ E 158
Kon'ovo, Bulg. 42°32′ N, 26°10′ E 156
Konta, India 17°48′ N, 81°22′ E 188
Kontagora, Nig. 10°21′ N, 5°29′ E 222
Kontcha, Cameroon 7°54′ N, 12°13′ E 218
Kontiomäki, Fin. 64°20′ N, 28°4′ E 152
Konya (Iconium), Turk. 37°51′ N, 32°29′ E 156
Konz, Ger. 49°41′ N, 6°36′ E 163
Konza, Kenya 1°47′ S, 37°7′ E 224
Koocanusa, Lake, Can. 49°1′ N, 115°56′ W 108
Ko'oko'olau, peak, Hawai'i, U.S. 19°36′ N, 155°37′ W 99
Koopmansfontein, S. Af. 28°15′ S, 24°3′ E 227
Koosa, Est. 58°30′ N, 27°2′ E 166
Koostatak, Can. 51°25′ N, 97°22′ W 90
Kootenai, Idaho, U.S. 48°17′ N, 116°33′ W 108
Kootenay Lake, Can. 49°44′ N, 116°47′ W 108
Koou, Mauritania 15°54′ N, 12°47′ W 222
Kopaonik, mountains, Serb. and Mont. 42°57′ N, 20°52′ E 168
Kópasker, Ice. 66°21′ N, 16°31′ W 246
Köpbirlik, Kaz. 46°27′ N, 77°12′ E 184
Köpekkayası Burnu, Turk. 41°56′ N, 31°52′ E 156
Köpenick, Ger. 52°27′ N, 13°33′ E 152
Kopetdag Mountains, Iran 38°27′ N, 55°37′ E 180
Kopeysk, Russ. 55°5′ N, 61°36′ E 154
Köping, Nor. 59°29′ N, 15°58′ E 152
Kopište, island, Croatia 42°41′ N, 16°33′ E 168
Koplik, Alban. 42°12′ N, 19°26′ E 168
Koporskiy Zaliv 59°47′ N, 28°26′ E 166
Koppang, Nor. 61°33′ N, 11°3′ E 152
Kopparberg, Nor. 59°52′ N, 15°0′ E 152
Kopperå, Nor. 63°23′ N, 11°53′ E 152
Koprivnica, Croatia 46°10′ N, 16°50′ E 168
Kõpu, Est. 58°54′ N, 22°11′ E 166
Kop'ung, N. Korea 40°35′ N, 125°55′ E 200
Kopylovka, Russ. 58°39′ N, 82°19′ E 169
Kora National Park, Kenya 0°29′ N, 38°18′ E 224
Korab, Mal, Alban. 41°43′ N, 20°27′ E 168
K'orahē, Eth. 6°35′ N, 44°11′ E 218
Korba, India 22°22′ N, 82°44′ E 197
Korba, Tun. 36°35′ N, 10°51′ E 156
Korbach, Ger. 51°16′ N, 8°51′ E 167
Korbevac, Serb. and Mont. 42°34′ N, 22°2′ E 168
Korbol, Chad 10°1′ N, 17°42′ E 216
Korbovo, Serb. and Mont. 44°31′ N, 22°42′ E 168
Korçë, Alban. 40°37′ N, 20°47′ E 143
Korčula, Croatia 42°56′ N, 17°7′ E 156
Korčula, island, Croatia 42°52′ N, 16°25′ E 168
Korčulanski Kanal 42°59′ N, 16°23′ E 168
Korday, Kaz. 43°3′ N, 74°42′ E 184
Koré Mayroua, Niger 13°23′ N, 3°53′ E 222
Korea, North 40°12′ N, 126°16′ E 200
Korea, South 36°43′ N, 127°7′ E 200
Korea Strait (Tsushima Strait) 34°9′ N, 125°22′ E 190
Korem, Eth. 12°28′ N, 39°31′ E 182
Korenevo, Russ. 51°23′ N, 34°59′ E 158
Korenovsk, Russ. 45°31′ N, 39°27′ E 156
Korepino, Russ. 61°4′ N, 57°5′ E 154
Korets', Ukr. 50°37′ N, 27°7′ E 152
Korf, Russ. 60°20′ N, 165°42′ E 173
Korgon, Kyrg. 39°51′ N, 70°5′ E 197
Korhogo, Côte d'Ivoire 9°26′ N, 5°39′ W 222
Korinthiakós Kólpos 38°23′ N, 21°36′ E 156
Kórinthos, Gr. 37°52′ N, 22°55′ E 180
K oris Hegy, peak, Hung. 47°16′ N, 17°43′ E 168
Korita, Bosn. and Herzg. 43°2′ N, 18°29′ E 168
Kōriyama, Japan 37°23′ N, 140°22′ E 201
Korkino, Russ. 54°53′ N, 61°27′ E 154
Korkuteli, Turk. 37°4′ N, 30°12′ E 156
Korla, China 41°41′ N, 86°14′ E 184
Korliki, Russ. 61°30′ N, 82°27′ E 169
Kormakitis, Northern Cyprus 35°20′ N, 33°0′ E 194
Kormakitis, Cape, Northern Cyprus 35°22′ N, 32°42′ E 194
Körmend, Hung. 47°0′ N, 16°37′ E 168
Kornaka, Niger 14°8′ N, 6°55′ E 222
Kornilovo, Russ. 53°31′ N, 81°13′ E 184
Koro, Côte d'Ivoire 8°29′ N, 7°26′ W 222
Koro Kidinga, spring, Chad 16°58′ N, 16°56′ E 216
Korocha, Russ. 50°48′ N, 37°12′ E 158
Korogwe, Tanzania 5°8′ S, 38°29′ E 224
Koronadal, Philippines 6°21′ N, 124°46′ E 203
Koronga, Mali 15°21′ N, 7°37′ W 222
Koronga, Mont, peak, Togo 9°2′ N, 1°10′ E 222
Kóronos, Gr. 37°7′ N, 25°33′ E 156
Palau, Palau 7°10′ N, 133°47′ E 238
Körösladany, Hung. 46°58′ N, 21°4′ E 168
Korosozero, Russ. 63°41′ N, 35°21′ E 154
Korosten', Ukr. 50°55′ N, 28°45′ E 152
Korotoyak, Russ. 50°59′ N, 39°10′ E 158
Korpela, Russ. 66°14′ N, 30°1′ E 152
Korpilahti, Fin. 62°0′ N, 25°31′ E 166
Korpilombolo, Nor. 66°51′ N, 23°1′ E 152
Korpisalmi, Fin. 63°57′ N, 29°37′ E 152
Korpisel'kya, Russ. 62°19′ N, 30°58′ E 152
Korpo, Fin. 60°9′ N, 21°32′ E 166
Korsakov, Russ. 46°44′ N, 142°58′ E 190
Korshiv, Ukr. 48°37′ N, 24°59′ E 152
Korsnäs, Fin. 62°46′ N, 21°9′ E 152
Korsnes, Nor. 70°12′ N, 23°15′ E 152
Korsnes, Nor. 68°14′ N, 16°1′ E 152
Korsør, Den. 55°18′ N, 11°11′ E 152
Korsze, Pol. 54°9′ N, 21°8′ E 166
Korti, Sudan 18°1′ N, 31°35′ E 182
Kortkeros, Russ. 61°49′ N, 51°38′ E 154
Kortrijk, Belg. 50°49′ N, 3°17′ E 163
Korup National Park, Cameroon 5°10′ N, 9°15′ E 222
Korvatunturi, peak, Fin. 68°3′ N, 29°10′ E 152
Koryakskiy, Russia 60°0′ N, 165°0′ E 160
Koryakskoye Nagor'ye, Russ. 60°46′ N, 165°33′ E 160
Koryazhma, Russ. 61°16′ N, 47°15′ E 154
Korytnitsi, Belarus 53°52′ N, 29°26′ E 166
Kos, Gr. 36°53′ N, 27°17′ E 156
Kosa, Eth. 7°50′ N, 36°49′ E 218
Kosa, Russ. 59°57′ N, 55°1′ E 154
Kosan, N. Korea 38°50′ N, 127°25′ E 200
Kosaya Gora, Russ. 54°5′ N, 37°29′ E 154
Kosciusko, Miss., U.S. 33°2′ N, 89°35′ W 103
Kosciusko, Mount, Austral. 36°30′ S, 148°2′ E 230
Kose, Est. 59°10′ N, 25°7′ E 166
Koserow, Ger. 54°2′ N, 14°0′ E 152
Kosh Agach, Russ. 49°58′ N, 88°34′ E 184
Kosha, Eth. 6°43′ N, 37°18′ E 224
Kosharevo, Bulg. 42°40′ N, 22°46′ E 168
Kosh-Döbö, Kyrg. 41°2′ N, 74°6′ E 197
Koshino, Japan 36°2′ N, 136°1′ E 201
Koshk-e Kohneh, Afghan. 34°53′ N, 62°28′ E 186
Koshki, Russ. 54°14′ N, 50°22′ E 154
Koshoba, Turkm. 40°13′ N, 54°6′ E 158
Koshuya, Ukr. 48°3′ N, 25°24′ E 158
Kosi, Lake, S. Af. 26°59′ S, 32°26′ E 227
Košice, Slovakia 48°43′ N, 21°15′ E 152
Košický, adm. division, Slovakia 48°43′ N, 21°6′ E 156
Kosjerić, Serb. and Mont. 44°0′ N, 19°54′ E 168
Koskenpää, Fin. 62°3′ N, 25°6′ E 166
Koski, Fin. 61°0′ N, 25°7′ E 166
Koski, Fin. 60°38′ N, 23°6′ E 166
Koskolovo, Russ. 59°39′ N, 28°27′ E 166
Kos'kovo, Russ. 56°30′ N, 29°39′ E 166
Koskullskulle, Nor. 67°10′ N, 20°41′ E 152
Koslan, Russ. 63°33′ N, 48°45′ E 154
Kosma, river, Russ. 66°8′ N, 49°26′ E 154
Kosman, Bosn. and Herzg. 43°22′ N, 18°46′ E 168
Koson, Uzb. 39°3′ N, 65°36′ E 197
Kosŏng, N. Korea 38°45′ N, 128°11′ E 200
Kosonov, Uzb. 41°17′ N, 71°40′ E 197
Kosovo Polje, Serb. and Mont. 42°38′ N, 21°6′ E 168
Kosovo, region, Europe 42°38′ N, 20°10′ E 168
Kosovska Mitrovica, Serb. and Mont. 42°53′ N, 20°51′ E 168
Kosrae (Kusaie), island, F.S.M. 5°19′ N, 162°59′ E 242
Kosso, Côte d'Ivoire 5°4′ N, 5°46′ W 222
Kossou, Lac de, lake, Côte d'Ivoire 8°9′ N, 5°55′ W 222
Kosti, Sudan 13°7′ N, 32°37′ E 182
Kostin Shar, Proliv 71°7′ N, 47°6′ E 160
Kostinbrod, Bulg. 42°49′ N, 23°13′ E 168
Kostino, Russ. 65°16′ N, 88°12′ E 169
Kostomuksha, Russ. 64°36′ N, 30°36′ E 152
Kostopil', Ukr. 50°53′ N, 26°26′ E 152
Kostroma, Russ. 57°47′ N, 41°3′ E 154
Kostroma, adm. division, Russ. 57°52′ N, 41°34′ E 160
Kostrzyn, Pol. 52°35′ N, 14°39′ E 152
Kostyantynivka, Ukr. 48°34′ N, 37°40′ E 158
Kos'ya, Russ. 58°49′ N, 59°20′ E 154
Kosyń, Pol. 51°22′ N, 23°32′ E 152
Kos'yu, Russ. 65°38′ N, 58°57′ E 154
Kos'yu, river, Russ. 65°24′ N, 58°57′ E 154
Kos'yuvom, Russ. 66°16′ N, 59°47′ E 169
Koszalin, Pol. 54°11′ N, 16°10′ E 152
Kot Addu, Pak. 30°29′ N, 71°1′ E 186
Kot Kapura, India 30°35′ N, 74°52′ E 186
Kota, India 25°8′ N, 75°51′ E 197
Kota Baharu, Malaysia 6°8′ N, 102°16′ E 196
Kota Belud, Malaysia 6°23′ N, 116°23′ E 203
Kota Kinabalu, Malaysia 5°59′ N, 116°4′ E 203
Kota Tinggi, Malaysia 1°42′ N, 103°52′ E 196
Kotabaru, Indonesia 1°6′ S, 101°44′ E 196
Kotabaru, Indonesia 3°26′ S, 116°11′ E 192
Kotadabok, Indonesia 0°29′ N, 104°32′ E 196
Kotadaik, Indonesia 0°11′ N, 104°38′ E 196
Kotakoli, Dem. Rep. of the Congo 4°7′ N, 21°42′ E 218
Kotamobagu, Indonesia 0°49′ N, 124°13′ E 192
Kotapad, India 19°7′ N, 82°17′ E 188
Kotatengah, Indonesia 1°8′ N, 100°33′ E 196
Kotcho Lake, Can. 59°3′ N, 121°52′ W 108
Kotcho, river, Can. 58°45′ N, 121°5′ W 108
Kötegyán, Hung. 46°44′ N, 21°28′ E 168
Kotel'nich, Russ. 58°18′ N, 48°22′ E 154

Kotel'nikovo, Russ. 47°35' N, 43°2' E 158
Kotel'nyy, Russ. 75°53' N, 137°53' E 173
Kotel'nyy, Ostrov, island, Russ. 74°17' N, 131°48' E 160
Kotenko, Russ. 70°33' N, 147°13' E 160
Kothi, India 24°46' N, 80°47' E 197
Kothi, India 23°19' N, 82°4' E 197
Kotido, Uganda 2°57' N, 34°4' E 224
Kotka, Fin. 60°27' N, 26°55' E 166
Kotlas, Russ. 61°13' N, 46°42' E 154
Kotly, Russ. 59°34' N, 28°46' E 166
Kotonkoro, Nig. 10°59' N, 5°58' E 222
Kotor Varoš, Bosn. and Herzg. 44°37' N, 17°22' E 168
Kotoriba, Croatia 46°21' N, 16°48' E 168
Kotovsk, Russ. 52°33' N, 41°30' E 158
Kotovs'k, Ukr. 47°40' N, 29°35' E 156
Kotraža, Serb. and Mont. 43°41' N, 20°12' E 168
Kotri, Pak. 25°21' N, 68°17' E 186
Kötschach, Aust. 46°41' N, 13°0' E 167
Kotto, river, Cen. Af. Rep. 4°48' N, 21°58' E 218
Kotuy, river, Russ. 71°33' N, 99°52' E 172
Kotuy, river, Russ. 67°53' N, 99°10' E 169
Kotuykan, river, Russ. 70°38' N, 103°26' E 160
Kotzebue, Alas., U.S. 66°45' N, 162°31' W 98
Kotzebue Sound 66°23' N, 163°57' W 98
Koualé, Mali 11°24' N, 7°2' W 222
Kouandé, Benin 10°18' N, 1°40' E 222
Kouba Modounga, Chad 15°39' N, 18°16' E 216
Kouchibouguac National Park, Can. 46°46' N, 65°38' W 111
Koudougou, Burkina Faso 12°15' N, 2°24' W 222
Koufeï, spring, Niger 14°49' N, 13°24' E 222
Koukdjuak, Great Plain of the, Can. 65°48' N, 79°52' W 106
Kouki, Cen. Af. Rep. 7°7' N, 17°18' E 218
Kouklia, Cyprus 34°42' N, 32°34' E 194
Koukou Angarana, Chad 12°0' N, 21°46' E 216
Koúla, peak, Gr. 41°20' N, 24°41' E 156
Koulé, Guinea 7°58' N, 9°2' W 222
Koulen, Cambodia 13°48' N, 104°32' E 202
Koulikoro, Mali 12°54' N, 7°36' W 222
Koulochéra, peak, Gr. 36°48' N, 22°57' E 156
Koumameyong, Gabon 0°11' N, 11°47' E 218
Koumása, ruin(s), Gr. 34°57' N, 24°55' E 156
Koumbia, Burkina Faso 11°14' N, 3°43' W 222
Koumbia, Guinea 11°47' N, 13°34' W 222
Koumogo, Chad 8°40' N, 18°16' E 218
Koumra, Chad 8°53' N, 17°33' E 218
Kouna, Burkina Faso 13°27' N, 4°4' W 222
Koundé, Cen. Af. Rep. 6°0' N, 14°38' E 218
Koungheul, Senegal 13°58' N, 14°49' W 222
Koungouri, Chad 10°44' N, 18°56' E 216
Kounkané, Senegal 12°55' N, 14°8' W 222
Kountze, Tex., U.S. 30°21' N, 94°19' W 103
Koupéla, Burkina Faso 12°9' N, 0°22' E 222
Kourou, French Guiana, Fr. 5°11' N, 52°41' W 130
Kourouadi, spring, Chad 17°33' N, 18°48' E 216
Kourouba, Mali 13°21' N, 10°58' W 222
Kouroussa, Guinea 10°39' N, 9°54' W 222
Kousha, Leb. 34°18' N, 35°50' E 194
Koussa Arma, spring, Niger 16°8' N, 13°12' E 222
Koussanar, Senegal 13°52' N, 14°8' W 222
Kousséri, Cameroon 12°3' N, 14°59' E 216
Koussi, Emi, peak, Chad 19°45' N, 18°26' E 216
Koutiala, Mali 12°23' N, 5°28' W 222
Kouto, Côte d'Ivoire 9°53' N, 6°26' W 222
Koutouba, Côte d'Ivoire 8°41' N, 3°13' W 222
Koutous, region, Africa 14°20' N, 9°41' E 222
Kouvola, Fin. 60°51' N, 26°41' E 166
Kovačica, Serb. and Mont. 45°7' N, 20°37' E 168
Kovd Ozero, lake, Russ. 66°27' N, 31°8' E 154
Kovdor, Russ. 67°33' N, 30°24' E 152
Kovel', Ukr. 51°11' N, 24°42' E 152
Kovero, Fin. 62°31' N, 30°30' E 152
Kovesjoki, Fin. 61°54' N, 22°43' E 166
Kovic, Baie 61°15' N, 78°53' W 106
Kovilj, Serb. and Mont. 45°12' N, 20°1' E 168
Kovin, Serb. and Mont. 44°44' N, 20°57' E 168
Kovrov, Russ. 56°21' N, 41°24' E 154
Kowalów, Pol. 52°24' N, 14°46' E 152
Kowhitirangi, N.Z. 42°53' S, 171°1' E 240
Kowkcheh, river, Afghan. 37°3' N, 69°44' E 186
Kowŏn, N. Korea 39°26' N, 127°14' E 200
Köyceğiz, Turk. 36°57' N, 28°40' E 156
Koyda, Russ. 66°21' N, 42°33' E 154
Koygorodok, Russ. 60°28' N, 51°9' E 154
Koynas, Russ. 64°46' N, 47°26' E 154
Koyuk, Alas., U.S. 64°48' N, 161°14' W 98
Koyukuk, river, Alas., U.S. 65°51' N, 155°8' W 106
Koyukuk, river, Alas., U.S. 65°2' N, 156°36' W 98
Koyulhisar, Turk. 40°18' N, 37°49' E 156
Kozan, Turk. 37°26' N, 35°48' E 156
Kozáni, Gr. 40°18' N, 21°47' E 156
Kozarac, Bosn. and Herzg. 44°57' N, 16°51' E 168
Kozel'shchyna, Ukr. 49°16' N, 33°45' E 158
Kozel'sk, Russ. 54°0' N, 35°46' E 154
Kozhasay, Kaz. 48°15' N, 57°11' E 158
Kozhevnikovo, Russ. 56°14' N, 83°59' E 169
Kozhim, Russ. 65°44' N, 59°31' E 154
Kozhva, Russ. 65°4' N, 56°59' E 154
Kozhva, river, Russ. 64°32' N, 54°57' E 154
Kozjak, peak, Maced. 41°22' N, 21°37' E 156
Kozlu, Turk. 41°25' N, 31°44' E 156
Kozluk, Bosn. and Herzg. 44°30' N, 19°7' E 168
Kozluk, Turk. 38°11' N, 41°31' E 195
Koz'modem'yansk, Russ. 56°13' N, 46°43' E 154
Kozova, Ukr. 49°25' N, 25°9' E 152
Kožuf, Maced. 41°8' N, 22°4' E 156
Kozyatyn, Ukr. 49°45' N, 29°0' E 158
Kpalimé, Togo 6°55' N, 0°36' E 222
Kpandae, Ghana 8°26' N, 2°118' W 222
Kpandu, Ghana 6°59' N, 0°17' E 222
Kra, Isthmus of, Thai. 10°18' N, 98°8' E 192
Krabi, Thai. 8°4' N, 98°55' E 202
Kragerø, Nor. 58°52' N, 9°22' E 152
Kragujevac, Serb. and Mont. 44°0' N, 20°54' E 168
Krak des Chevaliers, site, Syr. 34°45' N, 36°17' E 194
Krakor, Cambodia 12°31' N, 104°10' E 202
Kraków, Pol. 50°3' N, 19°58' E 152
Kralanh, Cambodia 13°36' N, 103°24' E 202
Kraljevo, Serb. and Mont. 43°43' N, 20°41' E 168
Královéhradecký, adm. division, Czech Rep. 50°28' N, 16°1' E 153
Kramators'k, Ukr. 48°43' N, 37°27' E 158
Kramfors, Nor. 62°55' N, 17°47' E 152
Kramis, Cap, Alg. 36°19' N, 0°28' E 164
Kranzberg, Namibia 21°56' S, 15°43' E 227
Krapina, Croatia 46°9' N, 15°53' E 168
Krasavino, Russ. 60°57' N, 46°30' E 154
Krasino, Russ. 70°47' N, 54°21' E 173
Kraskino, Russ. 42°42' N, 130°46' E 200
Krāslava, Latv. 55°53' N, 27°10' E 166
Krasnaya Polyana, Russ. 43°41' N, 40°10' E 195
Krasnaye, Belarus 54°14' N, 27°3' E 166
Krasneno, Russ. 64°38' N, 174°49' E 160
Krasnoarmeysk, Russ. 48°30' N, 44°29' E 158
Krasnoarmeysk, Russ. 50°58' N, 45°40' E 158
Krasnoarmeyskaya, Russ. 45°22' N, 38°5' E 156
Krasnodar, Russ. 45°4' N, 39°0' E 156
Krasnodar, adm. division, Russ. 45°40' N, 38°18' E 160
Krasnodon, Ukr. 48°16' N, 39°40' E 158
Krasnogorodskoye, Russ. 56°51' N, 28°19' E 166
Krasnogorskoye, Russ. 52°17' N, 86°16' E 184
Krasnohrad, Ukr. 49°24' N, 35°25' E 158
Krasnokamensk, Russ. 50°8' N, 118°0' E 190
Krasnokamsk, Russ. 58°5' N, 55°45' E 154
Krasnolesnyy, Russ. 51°51' N, 39°30' E 158
Krasnoostrovskiy, Russ. 60°16' N, 28°39' E 166
Krasnoperekops'k, Ukr. 45°57' N, 33°47' E 156
Krasnopillya, Ukr. 50°43' N, 35°16' E 158
Krasnopol, Pol. 54°6' N, 23°12' E 166
Krasnosel'kup, Russ. 65°41' N, 82°35' E 169
Krasnosel'sk, Arm. 40°36' N, 45°19' E 195
Krasnoslobodsk, Russ. 48°40' N, 44°30' E 158
Krasnoturansk, Russ. 54°19' N, 91°31' E 190
Krasnotur'insk, Russ. 59°46' N, 60°15' E 154
Krasnoufimsk, Russ. 56°37' N, 57°47' E 154
Krasnoural'sk, Russ. 58°21' N, 60°6' E 154
Krasnousol'skiy, Russ. 53°56' N, 56°23' E 154
Krasnovishersk, Russ. 60°25' N, 57°9' E 154
Krasnoy Armii, Proliv 79°41' N, 91°44' E 160
Krasnoyarsk, Russ. 56°10' N, 92°39' E 160
Krasnoyarsk, adm. division, Russ. 62°17' N, 84°57' E 169
Krasnoyarskiy, Russ. 51°57' N, 59°52' E 154
Krasnoye, Belarus 52°42' N, 24°24' E 154
Krasnoye, Russ. 59°12' N, 47°51' E 154
Krasnoye, Russ. 51°37' N, 51°30' E 158
Krasnoye, Russ. 56°35' N, 29°21' E 166
Krasnozatonskiy, Russ. 61°42' N, 51°9' E 169
Krasnyy, Russ. 54°37' N, 31°30' E 154
Krasnyy Kholm, Russ. 58°2' N, 37°5' E 154
Krasnyy Kholm, Russ. 51°35' N, 54°10' E 158
Krasnyy Klyuch, Russ. 55°24' N, 56°43' E 154
Krasnyy Kut, Russ. 50°56' N, 46°54' E 158
Krasnyy Luch, Ukr. 48°8' N, 39°0' E 158
Krasnyy Lyman, Ukr. 49°1' N, 37°46' E 158
Krasnyy Steklovar, Russ. 56°15' N, 48°47' E 154
Krasnyy Sulin, Russ. 47°53' N, 40°5' E 158
Krasnyy Tekstil'shchik, Russ. 51°18' N, 45°45' E 158
Krasnyy Yar, Russ. 50°39' N, 44°43' E 158
Krasnyy Yar, Russ. 46°30' N, 48°22' E 158
Krasnyy Yar, Russ. 55°14' N, 72°51' E 184
Krasnyy Yar, Russ. 57°4' N, 84°38' E 169
Krasnyye Baki, Russ. 57°5' N, 45°12' E 154
Kratie, Cambodia 12°30' N, 106°3' E 202
Kratovo, Maced. 42°4' N, 22°11' E 168
Kraulshavn see Nuussuaq, Den. 74°9' N, 57°1' W 106
Krefeld, Ger. 51°19' N, 6°34' E 167
Kreïjé, spring, Mauritania 16°4' N, 8°32' W 222
Kremen, peak, Croatia 44°26' N, 15°51' E 168
Kremenchuk, Ukr. 49°7' N, 33°19' E 158
Kremenchuts'ke Vdskh., lake, Ukr. 49°32' N, 30°53' E 158
Kremenets', Ukr. 50°5' N, 25°45' E 152
Kremna, Bosn. and Herzg. 44°48' N, 17°39' E 168
Kremnica, Slovakia 48°41' N, 18°55' E 152
Krems, Aust. 48°24' N, 15°36' E 156
Kreševo, Bosn. and Herzg. 43°51' N, 18°3' E 168
Kress, Tex., U.S. 34°21' N, 101°46' W 92
Kresta, Zaliv 65°38' N, 178°8' E 160
Krestovaya Guba, Russ. 74°2' N, 55°18' E 246
Krestovka, Russ. 66°23' N, 52°29' E 154
Krestovskiy, Mys, Russ. 69°24' N, 143°33' E 172
Kresttsy, Russ. 58°13' N, 32°32' E 154
Kretinga, Lith. 55°52' N, 21°15' E 166
Kreuzberg, peak, Ger. 50°22' N, 9°57' E 167
Kreuztal, Ger. 50°57' N, 7°59' E 167
Krieglach, Aust. 47°32' N, 15°33' E 156
Krim, peak, Slov. 45°55' N, 14°23' E 156
Krims'ke Hory, Ukr. 44°50' N, 33°47' E 156
Kristiansand, Nor. 58°10' N, 7°47' E 160
Kristiansund, Nor. 63°5' N, 7°45' E 160
Kristiinankaupunki see Kristinestad, Fin. 62°15' N, 21°20' E 152
Kristineberg, Nor. 65°3' N, 18°34' E 152
Kristinehamn, Nor. 59°18' N, 14°4' E 152
Kristinestad (Kristiinankaupunki), Fin. 62°15' N, 21°20' E 152
Kriti (Crete), island, Gr. 35°36' N, 24°6' E 180
Kriva Palanka, Maced. 42°11' N, 22°20' E 168
Krivaja, river, Bosn. and Herzg. 44°15' N, 18°20' E 168
Krivelj, Serb. and Mont. 44°8' N, 22°6' E 168
Krivolak, Maced. 41°31' N, 22°5' E 168
Krivoy Porog, Russ. 65°2' N, 33°38' E 152
Križ, Croatia 45°39' N, 16°31' E 168
Križevci, Croatia 46°1' N, 16°32' E 168
Krnalovehradecky, adm. division, Czech Rep. 50°32' N, 14°58' E 152
Krnjeuša, Bosn. and Herzg. 44°41' N, 16°12' E 168
Krnov, Czech Rep. 50°5' N, 17°42' E 152
Krognes, Nor. 70°24' N, 30°46' E 152
Krokom, Nor. 63°19' N, 14°26' E 152
Krokstad, Nor. 66°27' N, 15°5' E 152
Krolevets', Ukr. 51°29' N, 33°28' E 158
Kromy, Russ. 52°39' N, 35°45' E 158
Kronoby (Kruunupyy), Fin. 63°43' N, 23°1' E 152
Kronprins Christian Land, Den. 80°7' N, 38°45' W 246
Kronprins Frederik Bjerge, Den. 67°31' N, 34°33' W 246
Kronshtadt, Russ. 59°59' N, 29°45' E 152
Kroonstad, S. Af. 27°40' S, 27°15' E 227
Kropotkin, Russ. 45°26' N, 40°29' E 158
Kroshin, Belarus 53°10' N, 26°10' E 152
Krosno, Pol. 49°39' N, 21°46' E 152
Kröv, Ger. 49°58' N, 7°4' E 167
Krrab, peak, Alban. 42°6' N, 19°56' E 168
Krrabë, peak, Alban. 41°12' N, 19°56' E 156
Krš, Serb. and Mont. 44°5' N, 21°59' E 168
Krško, Slov. 45°58' N, 15°27' E 156
Krstača, peak, Serb. and Mont. 42°57' N, 20°4' E 168
Kruger National Park, S. Af. 23°37' S, 31°8' E 227
Kruhlaye, Belarus 54°14' N, 29°51' E 166
Krui, Indonesia 5°11' S, 103°53' E 192
Krujë, Alban. 41°30' N, 19°47' E 168
Krumë, Alban. 42°11' N, 20°25' E 168
Krung Thep (Bangkok), Thai. 13°44' N, 100°24' E 202
Krupa, Bosn. and Herzg. 44°50' N, 16°10' E 168
Krupac, Serb. and Mont. 43°6' N, 22°41' E 168
Krupanj, Serb. and Mont. 44°22' N, 19°23' E 156
Krupište, Maced. 41°51' N, 22°14' E 168
Krupki, Belarus 54°20' N, 29°12' E 166
Krutaya, Russ. 63°2' N, 54°46' E 154
Krutets, Russ. 60°18' N, 39°24' E 154
Krutinka, Russ. 55°58' N, 71°35' E 184
Kruunupyy see Kronoby, Fin. 63°43' N, 23°1' E 152
Kruzof Island, Alas., U.S. 57°3' N, 137°39' W 98
Krychaw, Belarus 53°38' N, 31°44' E 154
Krylovskaya, Russ. 46°18' N, 39°57' E 158
Krymsk, Russ. 44°56' N, 37°55' E 156
Krynki, Pol. 53°16' N, 23°45' E 152
Kryvichy, Belarus 54°42' N, 27°16' E 166
Kryvyy Rih, Ukr. 47°56' N, 33°22' E 156
Ksabi, Alg. 29°6' N, 0°56' E 214
Ksabi, Mor. 32°55' N, 4°24' W 214
Ksar Chellala (Reïbell), Alg. 35°12' N, 2°19' E 150
Ksar el Barka, Mauritania 18°23' N, 12°16' W 222
Ksar el Boukhari, Alg. 35°54' N, 2°46' E 216
Ksar el Hirane, Alg. 33°47' N, 3°14' E 214
Ksar el Kebir, Mor. 35°1' N, 5°54' W 214
Ksar Torchane, Mauritania 20°41' N, 12°60' W 222
Kshwan Mountain, Can. 55°40' N, 129°51' W 108
Ktima, Cyprus 34°46' N, 32°24' E 194
Kuah, Malaysia 6°19' N, 99°51' E 196
Kuaidamao see Tonghua, China 41°41' N, 125°45' E 200
Kuala, Indonesia 2°58' N, 105°47' E 196
Kuala, Indonesia 3°35' N, 98°24' E 196
Kuala Berang, Malaysia 5°5' N, 103°1' E 196
Kuala Dungun, Malaysia 4°46' N, 103°24' E 196
Kuala Kelawang, Malaysia 2°58' N, 102°4' E 196
Kuala Kerai, Malaysia 5°32' N, 102°12' E 196
Kuala Kubu Baharu, Malaysia 3°34' N, 101°38' E 196
Kuala Lipis, Malaysia 4°12' N, 102°1' E 196
Kuala Lumpur, Malaysia 3°8' N, 101°32' E 196
Kuala Nerang, Malaysia 6°14' N, 100°36' E 196
Kuala Rompin, Malaysia 2°48' N, 103°27' E 196
Kuala Selangor, Malaysia 3°20' N, 101°16' E 196
Kuala Terengganu, Malaysia 5°18' N, 103°7' E 196
Kualakapuas, Indonesia 2°55' S, 114°14' E 192
Kualalangsa, Indonesia 4°32' N, 98°1' E 196
Kualatungkal, Indonesia 0°49' N, 103°29' E 196
Kuancheng, China 40°35' N, 118°31' E 198
Kuandian, China 40°43' N, 124°46' E 200
Kuanshan, Taiwan 23°1' N, 121°7' E 198
Kuantan, Malaysia 3°50' N, 103°19' E 196
Kubachi, Russ. 42°6' N, 47°40' E 195
Kuban', river, Russ. 45°4' N, 38°18' E 156
Kubaybāt, Syr. 35°11' N, 37°9' E 194
Kubbum, Sudan 11°47' N, 23°44' E 216
Kubenskoye, Russ. 59°24' N, 39°38' E 154
Kubenskoye, Ozero, lake, Russ. 59°41' N, 38°13' E 154
Kuberganya, Russ. 67°41' N, 144°18' E 160
Kubokawa, Japan 33°11' N, 133°7' E 201
Kučevo, Serb. and Mont. 44°29' N, 21°40' E 168
Kuchaman, India 27°8' N, 74°52' E 186
Kuchchaveli, Sri Lanka 8°48' N, 81°6' E 188
Kuchin Tundra, Gora, peak, Russ. 69°3' N, 30°57' E 152
Kuching, Malaysia 1°27' N, 110°24' E 192
Kuchva, river, Russ. 57°7' N, 27°57' E 166
Küçüksu, Turk. 38°25' N, 42°16' E 195
Kudamatsu, Japan 34°0' N, 131°53' E 201
Kudara, Taj. 38°28' N, 72°41' E 197
Kudat, Malaysia 6°56' N, 116°49' E 203
Kudever', Russ. 56°47' N, 29°26' E 166
Kudeyevskiy, Russ. 54°54' N, 56°45' E 154
Kūdī, Qārat, peak, Lib. 23°22' N, 23°45' E 226
Kudirkos Naumiestis, Lith. 54°47' N, 22°52' E 166
Kudremukh, peak, India 13°5' N, 75°8' E 188
Kudu Kyuyel', Russ. 59°23' N, 121°3' E 160
Kudus, Indonesia 6°51' S, 110°46' E 192
Kudymkar, Russ. 59°0' N, 54°43' E 154
Kufah see Al Kūfah, Iraq 32°5' N, 44°27' E 186
Kufra Oasis see Al Kufrah, Lib. 24°20' N, 23°44' E 226
Kugluktuk, Can. 67°48' N, 115°16' W 106
Kugul'ta, Russ. 45°21' N, 42°18' E 158
Kūhak, Iran 27°6' N, 63°14' E 182
Kuh-e Sangan, peak, Afghan. 33°30' N, 64°46' E 186
Kūhestak, Iran 26°49' N, 57°6' E 196
Kühlung, peak, Ger. 54°5' N, 11°40' E 152
Kuhmalahti, Fin. 61°29' N, 24°32' E 166
Kuhmo, Fin. 64°5' N, 29°28' E 152
Kuhmoinen, Fin. 61°33' N, 25°9' E 166
Kuhn Ø, island, Den. 74°29' N, 24°60' W 246
Kūhpāyeh, Iran 32°41' N, 52°28' E 180
Kui Buri, Thai. 12°4' N, 99°52' E 202
Kuibis, Namibia 26°42' S, 16°49' E 227
Kuikuina, Nicar. 13°28' N, 84°48' W 115
Kū'ilioloa Heiau, site, Hawai'i, U.S. 21°25' N, 158°14' W 99
Kuitan, China 23°4' N, 115°57' E 198
Kuito, Angola 12°25' S, 16°56' E 220
Kuivaniemi, Fin. 65°34' N, 25°11' E 152
Kuizhuang, China 40°3' N, 118°46' E 198
Kujang, N. Korea 39°52' N, 126°2' E 200
Kujawsko-Pomorskie, adm. division, Pol. 52°58' N, 17°33' E 152
Kukalaya, river, Nicar. 14°14' N, 84°13' W 115
Kūkaniloko, site, Hawai'i, U.S. 21°30' N, 158°6' W 99
Kukas, Russ. 66°25' N, 31°20' E 152
Kukës, Alban. 42°5' N, 20°24' E 168
Kukisvumchor, Russ. 67°39' N, 33°43' E 152
Kukmor, Russ. 56°11' N, 50°58' E 154
Kukuihaele, Hawai'i, U.S. 20°7' N, 155°35' W 99
Kukukus Lake, Can. 49°47' N, 92°11' W 110
Kukunjevac, Croatia 45°28' N, 17°6' E 168
Kula, Bulg. 43°53' N, 22°31' E 168
Kula, Serb. and Mont. 45°36' N, 19°33' E 168
Kula, Turk. 38°32' N, 28°38' E 156
Kulagīno, Kaz. 48°15' N, 51°31' E 158
Kulal, Mount, Kenya 2°40' N, 36°51' E 224
Kūlani, peak, Hawai'i, U.S. 19°30' N, 155°21' W 99
Kular, Russ. 70°37' N, 134°19' E 173
Kulata, Bulg. 41°23' N, 23°21' E 156
Kulautuva, Lith. 54°58' N, 23°38' E 166
Kuldīga, Latv. 56°57' N, 21°57' E 166
Kuldo, Can. 55°51' N, 127°54' W 108
Kule, Botswana 22°56' S, 20°6' E 227
Kulebaki, Russ. 55°24' N, 42°33' E 154
Kulen Vakuf, Bosn. and Herzg. 44°34' N, 16°5' E 168
Kuliki, Russ. 57°21' N, 79°0' E 169
Kulju, Fin. 61°22' N, 23°44' E 166
Kulkuduk, Uzb. 42°33' N, 63°17' E 197
Kullaa, Fin. 61°27' N, 22°8' E 166
Kullen, Sw. 56°21' N, 11°57' E 152
Kulli, Est. 58°21' N, 23°46' E 166
Kullorsuaq, Den. 74°37' N, 56°57' W 106
Küllstedt, Ger. 51°17' N, 10°16' E 167
Kulm, N. Dak., U.S. 46°17' N, 98°58' W 90
Kulma Pass, China 38°3' N, 74°50' E 197
Kŭlob, Taj. 37°53' N, 69°46' E 197
Kuloy, Russ. 60°59' N, 42°35' E 154
Kuloy, Russ. 65°1' N, 43°31' E 154
Kulp, Turk. 38°29' N, 41°2' E 195
Kultuk, Russ. 51°48' N, 103°53' E 190
Kulu, Turk. 39°4' N, 33°5' E 156
Kululli, Eritrea 14°22' N, 40°21' E 182
Kulunda, Russ. 52°32' N, 79°0' E 184
Kum, river, S. Korea 35°34' N, 127°29' E 200
Kuma, river, Russ. 44°53' N, 45°59' E 158
Kumagaya, Japan 36°9' N, 139°23' E 201
Kumak, Russ. 51°10' N, 60°10' E 158
Kumak, river, Russ. 51°16' N, 59°10' E 158
Kumaka, Guyana 3°53' N, 58°26' W 130
Kumamoto, Japan 32°48' N, 130°42' E 201
Kumamoto, adm. division, Japan 32°57' N, 130°25' E 201
Kumanica, Serb. and Mont. 43°27' N, 20°13' E 168
Kumano, Japan 33°53' N, 136°6' E 201
Kumano Nada 34°2' N, 136°23' E 201
Kumanovo, Maced. 42°7' N, 21°41' E 168
Kumara, N.Z. 42°40' S, 171°11' E 240
Kumasi, Ghana 6°44' N, 1°38' W 222
Kumba, Cameroon 4°37' N, 9°24' E 222
Kumbakonam, India 11°0' N, 79°21' E 188
Kumbher, Nepal 28°15' N, 81°25' E 197
Kumbo, Cameroon 6°9' N, 10°38' E 222
Kŭmch'ŏn, N. Korea 38°9' N, 126°28' E 200
Kumeny, Russ. 58°6' N, 49°55' E 154
Kumertau, Russ. 52°46' N, 55°46' E 154
Kŭmgang, N. Korea 38°36' N, 127°58' E 200
Kumi, Uganda 1°27' N, 33°54' E 224
Kumiva Peak, Nev., U.S. 40°23' N, 119°21' W 90
Kumkol, oil field, Kaz. 46°17' N, 65°22' E 184
Kumla, Nor. 59°7' N, 15°7' E 152
Kumlinge, Fin. 60°15' N, 20°47' E 166
Kumma, ruin(s), Sudan 21°30' N, 30°58' E 182
Kumo, Nig. 10°2' N, 11°8' E 222
Kumphawapi, Thai. 17°13' N, 102°54' E 202
Kumputunturi, peak, Fin. 67°41' N, 25°23' E 152
Kŭmsŏng see Kimhwa, N. Korea 38°26' N, 127°36' E 200
Kumta, India 14°24' N, 74°24' E 188
Kumu, Dem. Rep. of the Congo 3°2' N, 25°14' E 224
Kumukh, Russ. 42°6' N, 47°4' E 195
Kumzār, Oman 26°19' N, 56°23' E 196
Kunanaggi Well, spring, Austral. 23°24' S, 122°31' E 230
Kūnas Linchang, China 43°12' N, 84°40' E 184
Kunashak, Russ. 55°41' N, 61°27' E 154
Kunashir, island, Russ. 44°21' N, 144°17' E 190
Kunchha, Nepal 28°9' N, 84°21' E 197
Kunda, Est. 59°28' N, 26°29' E 166
Kundelungu National Park, Dem. Rep. of the Congo 10°41' S, 27°43' E 224
Kundi, Lake, Sudan 10°24' N, 24°45' E 224
Kundian, Pak. 32°28' N, 71°33' E 186
Kundozero, Russ. 66°19' N, 31°50' E 152
Kundur, island, Indonesia 0°30' N, 103°27' E 196
Kunene, river, Africa 17°33' S, 11°31' E 220
Kūnes, river, China 43°30' N, 82°59' E 184
Kungsbacka, Nor. 57°29' N, 12°6' E 152
Kungu, Dem. Rep. of the Congo 2°47' N, 19°10' E 218
Kungur, Russ. 57°26' N, 57°3' E 154
Kungutas, Tanzania 8°29' S, 33°16' E 224
Kungwe Mountain, Tanzania 6°12' S, 29°44' E 224
Kunlon, Myanmar 23°22' N, 98°36' E 202
Kunlun Mountains, Asia 33°11' N, 97°38' E 172
Kunlun Shankou, pass, China 35°37' N, 94°5' E 188
Kunlunshan, Asia 37°6' N, 84°45' E 184
Kunmadaras, Hung. 47°25' N, 20°48' E 168
Kunming, China 25°3' N, 102°41' E 190
Kunszentmárton, Hung. 46°49' N, 20°18' E 168
Kuntaur, Gambia 13°40' N, 14°52' W 222
Kununurra, Austral. 15°45' S, 128°45' E 238
Kunya, Nig. 12°13' N, 8°32' E 222
Kuoliovaara, Fin. 65°50' N, 28°49' E 152
Kuolismaa, Russ. 62°41' N, 31°36' E 154
Kuopio, Fin. 62°53' N, 27°38' E 154
Kuorboaivi, peak, Fin. 69°40' N, 27°34' E 152
Kuorevesi, Fin. 61°55' N, 24°38' E 166
Kuormakka, peak, Nor. 68°9' N, 21°42' E 152
Kuortane, Fin. 62°47' N, 23°30' E 152
Kuoutatjärro, peak, Nor. 68°36' N, 20°10' E 152
Kupa, river, Croatia 45°30' N, 15°48' E 168
Kupang, Indonesia 10°21' S, 123°32' E 192
Kupino, Russ. 54°21' N, 77°18' E 184
Kupiškis, Lith. 55°48' N, 24°59' E 166
Kupopolo Heiau, site, Hawai'i, U.S. 21°38' N, 158°7' W 99
Kupreanof, Alas., U.S. 56°50' N, 133°3' W 108
Kupres, Bosn. and Herzg. 43°58' N, 17°16' E 168
Kup"yans'k, Ukr. 49°43' N, 37°33' E 158
Kuqa, China 41°43' N, 83°3' E 184
Kur Dili, Azerb. 38°51' N, 49°9' E 195
Kür, river, Azerb. 40°12' N, 47°24' E 195
Kurakh, Russ. 41°33' N, 47°47' E 195
Kūrān Dap, Iran 26°4' N, 59°40' E 182
Kuranyets, Belarus 54°33' N, 26°58' E 166
Kurashiki, Japan 34°35' N, 133°46' E 201
Kurchatov, Kaz. 50°46' N, 78°28' E 184
Kürdämir, Azerb. 40°20' N, 48°10' E 195
Kurdoğlu Burnu, Turk. 36°31' N, 28°11' E 156
Kŭrdzhali, Bulg. 41°38' N, 25°21' E 156
Kŭrdzhali, adm. division, Bulg. 41°24' N, 25°11' E 156
Kure, Japan 34°14' N, 132°33' E 201
Küre, Turk. 41°48' N, 33°42' E 156
Kurenala, Fin. 65°21' N, 26°57' E 152
Kuressaare, Est. 58°15' N, 22°28' E 166
Kureyka, Russ. 66°16' N, 87°17' E 169
Kureyka, river, Russ. 67°53' N, 96°35' E 169
Kurgan, Russ. 55°30' N, 65°19' E 184
Kurgan, adm. division, Russ. 55°27' N, 63°22' E 169
Kurganinsk, Russ. 44°54' N, 40°30' E 158
Kurgolovo, Russ. 59°45' N, 28°5' E 166
Kuria Muria Islands, Persian Gulf 17°13' N, 55°40' E 182
Kurikka, Fin. 62°36' N, 22°20' E 152
Kuril Islands (Kuril'skiye Ostrova), Sea of Okhotsk 47°9' N, 148°32' E 190
Kurilovka, Russ. 50°42' N, 48°0' E 158
Kuril'skiye Ostrova see Kuril Islands, Sea of Okhotsk 47°9' N, 148°32' E 190
Kurkiyoki, Russ. 61°18' N, 29°54' E 166
Kurleya, Russ. 52°6' N, 119°8' E 190
Kurmuk, Sudan 10°35' N, 34°15' E 224
Kurobe, Japan 36°52' N, 137°26' E 201
Kuroiso, Japan 36°56' N, 140°3' E 201
Kuropta, Russ. 67°29' N, 30°50' E 152
Kuror, Jebel, peak, Sudan 20°29' N, 31°30' E 182
Kurow, N.Z. 44°45' S, 170°25' E 240
Kurów, Pol. 51°23' N, 22°10' E 152
Kursavka, Russ. 44°28' N, 42°32' E 158
Kuršėnai, Lith. 56°0' N, 22°56' E 166
Kurshim, Kaz. 48°46' N, 83°30' E 184
Kurshskaya Kosa, Russ. 55°11' N, 20°37' E 166
Kuršių Nerija National Park, Russ. 55°29' N, 20°37' E 166
Kursk, Russ. 51°43' N, 36°12' E 158
Kursk, adm. division, Russ. 51°39' N, 34°47' E 160
Kurskaya Kosa, Russ. 55°4' N, 20°28' E 166
Kursu, Fin. 66°45' N, 28°7' E 152
Kuršumlija, Serb. and Mont. 43°7' N, 21°16' E 168
Kurşunlu, Turk. 40°51' N, 33°15' E 156
Kurtalan, Turk. 37°55' N, 41°43' E 195
Kurtamysh, Russ. 54°53' N, 64°31' E 184
Kürten, Ger. 51°3' N, 7°16' E 163
Kurthwood, La., U.S. 31°18' N, 93°10' W 103
Kürti, Kaz. 43°56' N, 76°19' E 184
Kurtti, Fin. 65°28' N, 28°8' E 152
Kuru, Fin. 61°51' N, 23°39' E 166
Kuru, river, Sudan 7°58' N, 26°31' E 224
Kurulush, Kyrg. 41°39' N, 70°53' E 197
Kuruman, S. Af. 27°29' S, 23°25' E 227
Kurume, Japan 33°17' N, 130°31' E 201
Kurupukari, Guyana 4°40' N, 58°40' W 130
Kur'ya, Russ. 61°38' N, 57°13' E 154
Kur'ya, Russ. 51°36' N, 82°17' E 184
Kurze Mountains, Antarctica 72°38' S, 10°13' E 248
Kurzheksa, Russ. 61°25' N, 36°45' E 154
Kus Gölü, lake, Turk. 40°9' N, 27°46' E 156
Kusa, Eth. 4°11' N, 38°58' E 224
Kusa, Russ. 55°21' N, 59°30' E 154
Kusadak, Serb. and Mont. 44°24' N, 20°47' E 168
Kuşadası, Turk. 37°50' N, 27°14' E 156
Kusaie see Kosrae, island, F.S.M. 5°19' N, 162°59' E 242
Kushereka, Russ. 63°49' N, 37°9' E 154
Kusheriki, Nig. 10°32' N, 6°26' E 222
Kushikino, Japan 31°41' N, 130°18' E 201
Kushima, Japan 31°26' N, 131°14' E 201
Kushimoto, Japan 33°28' N, 135°46' E 201
Kushiro, Japan 43°6' N, 144°14' E 190
Kushkushara, Russ. 65°0' N, 40°19' E 154
Kushnarenkovo, Russ. 55°7' N, 55°24' E 154
Kushnīya, Israel 33°0' N, 35°48' E 194
Kushva, Russ. 58°18' N, 59°47' E 154
Kuskokwim Bay 59°21' N, 163°25' W 98
Kuskokwim Mountains, North America 61°20' N, 157°59' W 98
Kuskokwim, river, Alas., U.S. 60°24' N, 161°42' W 98
Kusŏng, N. Korea 39°58' N, 125°14' E 200
Kustavi, Fin. 60°33' N, 21°20' E 166
Kusur, Russ. 41°44' N, 46°57' E 195
Küt Barrage, dam, Iraq 32°23' N, 44°49' E 216
Kut, Ko, island, Thai. 11°30' N, 102°5' E 202
Kuta, Nig. 9°50' N, 6°44' E 222
Kutabuloh, Indonesia 3°28' N, 97°3' E 196
Kutacane, Indonesia 3°31' N, 97°47' E 196

ütahya, Turk. 39°26′ N, 29°58′ E 156
utai National Park, Indonesia 0°15′ N, 116°57′ E 238
ut'aisi, Ga. 42°13′ N, 42°40′ E 195
utanibong, Indonesia 3°56′ N, 96°20′ E 173
utcho Creek, river, Can. 58°35′ N, 128°59′ W 108
utina, Croatia 45°27′ N, 16°46′ E 168
utjevo, Croatia 45°24′ N, 17°52′ E 168
utno, Pol. 52°14′ N, 19°22′ E 152
utu, Dem. Rep. of the Congo 2°43′ S, 18°6′ E 218
utum, Sudan 14°9′ N, 24°40′ E 226
utuzovo, Russ. 54°46′ N, 22°48′ E 166
úty, Slovakia 48°37′ N, 17°1′ E 156
uujjuaq, Can. 58°5′ N, 68°38′ W 106
uujjuarapik, Can. 55°17′ N, 77°47′ W 106
uurne, Belg. 50°51′ N, 3°19′ E 163
uusamo, Fin. 65°58′ N, 29°8′ E 152
uusankoski, Fin. 60°53′ N, 26°36′ E 166
uusivaara, Fin. 66°39′ N, 27°0′ E 152
uusjärvi, Fin. 62°41′ N, 28°54′ E 154
uusjoki, Fin. 60°30′ N, 23°11′ E 166
uvandyk, Russ. 51°27′ N, 57°20′ E 158
uvango, Angola 14°32′ S, 16°15′ E 220
uvet, river, Russ. 69°3′ N, 176°7′ E 98
uvshinovo, Russ. 57°0′ N, 34°13′ E 154
uwait 29°39′ N, 47°15′ E 196
uwait see Al Kuwayt, Kuwait 29°20′ N, 47°52′ E 196
uwana, Japan 35°3′ N, 136°41′ E 201
uybishevskiy, Taj. 37°56′ N, 68°46′ E 197
uybyshev, Russ. 55°30′ N, 78°21′ E 184
uyeda, Russ. 56°27′ N, 55°31′ E 154
uytun, China 44°29′ N, 84°56′ E 184
uyuwini, river, Guyana 1°55′ N, 59°25′ W 130
uzey Anadolu Dağlarx, Turk. 40°38′ N, 36°33′ E 180
uz'movka, Russ. 62°21′ N, 92°9′ E 169
uznetsk, Russ. 53°5′ N, 46°37′ E 154
uźnica, Pol. 53°30′ N, 23°38′ E 152
uzomen', Russ. 66°17′ N, 36°44′ E 154
uzomen', Russ. 64°19′ N, 43°4′ E 154
valsund, Nor. 70°29′ N, 23°58′ E 152
vænangsbotn, Nor. 69°43′ N, 22°4′ E 152
varkeno, Russ. 52°5′ N, 59°41′ E 154
'vemo Azhara, Turk. 43°8′ N, 41°49′ E 158
vernes, Nor. 62°59′ N, 7°42′ E 152
vikkjokk, Nor. 66°56′ N, 17°44′ E 152
vikne, Nor. 62°34′ N, 10°19′ E 152
visvik, Nor. 63°3′ N, 7°58′ E 152
wa Mtoro, Tanzania 5°12′ S, 35°26′ E 224
wadacha, river, Can. 57°28′ N, 125°37′ W 108
wail (P'ungch'ŏn), N. Korea 38°25′ N, 125°1′ E 200
wajaffa Babur, Nig. 10°27′ N, 12°24′ E 218
waksan, N. Korea 39°40′ N, 125°4′ E 200
wale, Kenya 4°12′ S, 39°27′ E 224
wale Station, Nig. 5°48′ N, 6°21′ E 222
wali, Nig. 8°51′ N, 7°0′ E 222
wamouth, Dem. Rep. of the Congo 3°16′ S, 16°14′ E 218
wangju see Gwangju, S. Korea 35°8′ N, 126°56′ E 200
wania, Lake, Uganda 0°52′ N, 32°45′ E 224
wazulu-Natal, adm. division, S. Af. 29°6′ S, 29°21′ E 227
wekwe, Zimb. 18°56′ S, 29°47′ E 224
wenge, river, Dem. Rep. of the Congo 6°16′ S, 18°20′ E 218
wiambana, Nig. 11°5′ N, 6°33′ E 222
wikila, P.N.G. 9°48′ S, 147°39′ E 192
wilu, river, Dem. Rep. of the Congo 3°35′ S, 17°14′ E 218
wokullie Lake, Can. 59°14′ N, 121°43′ W 108
y Son, Vietnam 19°24′ N, 104°8′ E 202
yabé, Chad 9°28′ N, 18°55′ E 216
yaikkami, Myanmar 16°5′ N, 97°35′ E 202
yaikto, Myanmar 17°20′ N, 97°1′ E 202
yaka, Tanzania 1°20′ S, 31°24′ E 224
yakhta, Russ. 50°26′ N, 106°25′ E 173
yango, Sudan 7°54′ N, 27°39′ E 224
yaukkyi, Myanmar 18°21′ N, 96°46′ E 202
yaukme, Myanmar 22°32′ N, 97°3′ E 202
yaukphyu, Myanmar 19°23′ N, 93°29′ E 190
yaukse, Myanmar 21°36′ N, 96°8′ E 202
ybartai, Lith. 54°39′ N, 22°45′ E 166
ydz'ras'yu, Russ. 65°15′ N, 58°13′ E 154
yeintali, Myanmar 18°0′ N, 94°30′ E 202
yenjojo, Uganda 0°33′ N, 30°39′ E 224
yffhäuser, peak, Ger. 51°23′ N, 11°1′ E 152
yiv (Kiev), Ukr. 50°25′ N, 30°29′ E 158
yle, Can. 50°50′ N, 108°2′ W 90
yle, Tex., U.S. 29°57′ N, 97°53′ W 92
yll, river, Ger. 50°1′ N, 6°34′ E 167
yllburg, Ger. 50°2′ N, 6°35′ E 167
ymijoki, river, Fin. 60°51′ N, 26°28′ E 166
yŏngju see Gyeongju, S. Korea 35°48′ N, 129°15′ E 200
yŏngsŏng, N. Korea 41°35′ N, 129°36′ E 200
yōto, Japan 35°0′ N, 135°44′ E 201
yōto, adm. division, Japan 35°18′ N, 134°59′ E 201
yperounta, Cyprus 34°56′ N, 32°57′ E 194
yrenia see Keryneia, Northern Cyprus 35°20′ N, 33°18′ E 194
yrgyz Range, Kyrg. 42°53′ N, 71°46′ E 184
yrgyzstan 41°38′ N, 73°40′ E 184
yrkslätt (Kirkkonummi), Fin. 60°7′ N, 24°26′ E 166
yrö, Fin. 60°42′ N, 22°45′ E 166
yrösjärvi, lake, Fin. 61°39′ N, 22°50′ E 166
yrta, Russ. 64°4′ N, 57°40′ E 154
yrtym'ya, Russ. 59°1′ N, 63°38′ E 154
yshtovka, Russ. 56°35′ N, 76°34′ E 169
yshtym, Russ. 55°41′ N, 60°33′ E 154
ystatyam, Russ. 67°34′ N, 123°24′ E 160
ythrea, Northern Cyprus 35°14′ N, 33°28′ E 194
ytlym, Russ. 59°31′ N, 59°11′ E 154
ytömaki, Fin. 64°46′ N, 28°16′ E 154
yunchaung, Myanmar 15°32′ N, 98°15′ E 202
yunhla, Myanmar 23°19′ N, 95°13′ E 202
yuquot, Can. 50°2′ N, 127°22′ W 108
Kyūshū, island, Japan 31°5′ N, 128°47′ E 190
Kyustendil, Bulg. 42°16′ N, 22°41′ E 168
Kyustendil, adm. division, Bulg. 42°18′ N, 22°28′ E 168
Kyusyur, Russ. 70°37′ N, 127°39′ E 160
Kyyjärvi, Fin. 63°0′ N, 24°31′ E 154
Kyzkl-Oy, Kyrg. 42°15′ N, 73°50′ E 197
Kyzyl, Russ. 51°36′ N, 94°38′ E 190
Kyzyl-Adyr, Kyrg. 42°35′ N, 71°43′ E 197
Kyzyl-Korgon, Kyrg. 40°9′ N, 73°32′ E 197
Kyzyl-Kyya, Kyrg. 40°14′ N, 72°6′ E 197
Kyzyl-Suu, river, Taj. 39°5′ N, 70°52′ E 197

L

La Adela, Arg. 38°57′ S, 64°4′ W 139
La Albuera, Sp. 38°42′ N, 6°50′ W 164
La Algaba, Sp. 37°27′ N, 6°2′ W 164
La Almolda, Sp. 41°32′ N, 0°12′ E 164
La Antiqua, Mex. 19°20′ N, 96°21′ W 114
La Asunción, Venez. 11°3′ N, 63°52′ W 116
La Baie, Can. 48°18′ N, 70°54′ W 94
La Banda, Arg. 27°44′ S, 64°15′ W 132
La Barca, Mex. 20°17′ N, 102°34′ W 114
La Bardelière, Lac, lake, Can. 51°18′ N, 76°6′ W 110
La Barge, Wyo., U.S. 42°15′ N, 110°12′ W 92
La Barra, Nicar. 12°55′ N, 83°33′ W 115
La Baule-Escoublac, Fr. 47°17′ N, 2°25′ W 150
La Belle, Fla., U.S. 26°45′ N, 81°27′ W 105
La Biche, river, Can. 60°29′ N, 124°30′ W 108
La Bisbal d' Empordà, Sp. 41°57′ N, 3°3′ E 164
La Bonita, Ecua. 0°24′ N, 77°39′ W 136
La Brecha, Mex. 25°21′ N, 108°26′ W 82
La Calera, Chile 32°50′ S, 71°15′ W 134
La Campana, Mex. 26°8′ N, 103°31′ W 114
La Cañada de San Urbano, Sp. 36°49′ N, 2°24′ W 164
La Carlota, Arg. 33°27′ S, 63°16′ W 139
La Carlota, Philippines 10°24′ N, 122°54′ E 203
La Carlota, Sp. 37°40′ N, 4°56′ W 164
La Carolina, Sp. 38°16′ N, 3°37′ W 164
La Cautiva, Arg. 33°60′ S, 64°6′ W 139
La Cava, Sp. 40°42′ N, 0°44′ E 164
La Ceiba, Col. 3°32′ N, 67°51′ W 136
La Ceiba, Hond. 15°45′ N, 86°47′ W 115
La Ceiba, Venez. 9°28′ N, 71°5′ W 136
La Cesira, Arg. 33°59′ S, 62°58′ W 139
La Chambre, Fr. 45°21′ N, 6°17′ E 167
La Charité, Fr. 47°10′ N, 3°0′ E 150
La Chorrera, Col. 0°48′ N, 73°1′ W 136
La Chorrera, Pan. 8°54′ N, 79°46′ W 115
La Ciudad Encantada, site, Sp. 40°11′ N, 2°4′ W 164
La Colorada, Mex. 23°48′ N, 102°28′ W 114
La Colorada, Mex. 28°46′ N, 110°33′ W 92
La Concepción, Venez. 10°27′ N, 71°44′ W 136
La Condamine-Châtelard, Fr. 44°27′ N, 6°43′ E 167
La Conner, Wash., U.S. 48°22′ N, 122°29′ W 100
La Copelina, Arg. 37°18′ S, 67°37′ W 134
La Coronilla, Uru. 33°53′ S, 53°34′ W 139
La Crete, Can. 58°12′ N, 116°21′ W 108
La Crosse, Ind., U.S. 41°18′ N, 86°54′ W 102
La Crosse, Kans., U.S. 38°31′ N, 99°20′ W 92
La Crosse, Va., U.S. 36°41′ N, 78°6′ W 96
La Crosse, Wash., U.S. 46°47′ N, 117°54′ W 90
La Crosse, Wis., U.S. 43°48′ N, 91°15′ W 110
La Cruz, Arg. 29°10′ S, 56°41′ W 139
La Cruz, C.R. 11°4′ N, 85°38′ W 115
La Cruz, Mex. 23°52′ N, 106°54′ W 114
La Cuesta, Mex. 28°43′ N, 102°29′ W 92
La Cygne, Kans., U.S. 38°19′ N, 94°45′ W 94
La Dorada, Col. 5°26′ N, 74°42′ W 136
La Esmeralda, Venez. 3°10′ N, 65°32′ W 136
La Esperanza, Cuba 22°45′ N, 83°45′ W 116
La Esperanza, Hond. 14°19′ N, 88°8′ W 115
La Fère, Fr. 49°39′ N, 3°21′ E 163
La Ferté-Gaucher, Fr. 48°47′ N, 3°17′ E 163
La Ferté-Macé, Fr. 48°35′ N, 0°22′ E 150
La Ferté-sous-Jouarre, Fr. 48°56′ N, 3°7′ E 163
La Feuillie, Fr. 49°27′ N, 1°30′ E 163
La Follette, Tenn., U.S. 36°22′ N, 84°8′ W 96
La Font de la Figuera, Sp. 38°48′ N, 0°53′ E 164
La Fontaine, Ind., U.S. 40°39′ N, 85°43′ W 102
La Fuente de San Esteban, Sp. 40°48′ N, 6°15′ W 150
La Gallareta, Arg. 29°31′ S, 60°25′ W 139
La Gineta, Sp. 39°6′ N, 1°60′ W 164
La Glace, Can. 55°23′ N, 119°8′ W 108
La Gloria, Col. 8°38′ N, 73°47′ W 136
La Gorce Peak, peak, Antarctica 77°31′ S, 152°20′ W 248
La Grande, Oreg., U.S. 45°18′ N, 118°5′ W 90
La Grande Deux, Réservoir de , lake, Can. 54°11′ N, 75°50′ W 106
La Grange, Ga., U.S. 33°1′ N, 85°2′ W 112
La Grange, Ky., U.S. 38°24′ N, 85°23′ W 94
La Grange, Mo., U.S. 40°1′ N, 91°31′ W 94
La Grange, N.C., U.S. 35°18′ N, 77°48′ W 96
La Grange, Tex., U.S. 29°53′ N, 96°52′ W 96
La Grange, Wyo., U.S. 41°38′ N, 104°10′ W 90
La Grave, Fr. 45°2′ N, 6°18′ E 167
La Gruta, Arg. 26°50′ S, 53°43′ W 139
La Guaira, Venez. 10°34′ N, 66°56′ W 136
La Guardia, Arg. 29°33′ S, 65°27′ W 134
La Guardia, Sp. 39°47′ N, 3°29′ W 164
La Habana, adm. division, Cuba 22°44′ N, 82°55′ W 116
La Habana (Havana), Cuba 23°6′ N, 82°33′ W 116
La Honda, Calif., U.S. 37°19′ N, 122°17′ W 100
La Huacana, Mex. 18°56′ N, 101°48′ W 114
La Jagua, Col. 9°33′ N, 73°23′ W 136
La Jagua, Col. 2°25′ N, 72°37′ W 136
La Jana, Sp. 40°31′ N, 0°15′ E 164
La Jara, Colo., U.S. 37°16′ N, 105°58′ W 92
La Javie, Fr. 44°10′ N, 6°20′ E 167
La Jolla, Calif., U.S. 32°50′ N, 117°17′ W 101
La Junta, Colo., U.S. 37°58′ N, 103°33′ W 90
La Leonesa, Arg. 27°3′ S, 58°42′ W 139
La Libertad, Ecua. 2°19′ S, 80°53′ W 130
La Libertad, Guatemala 16°47′ N, 90°8′ W 115
La Libertad, Mex. 29°55′ N, 112°41′ W 92
La Libertad, Nicar. 12°12′ N, 85°10′ W 115
La Libertad, adm. division, Peru 8°1′ S, 79°16′ W 130
La Ligua, Chile 32°28′ S, 71°17′ W 134
La Lima, Hond. 15°23′ N, 87°55′ W 115
La Loche, Can. 56°28′ N, 109°25′ W 108
La Loupe, Fr. 48°28′ N, 1°0′ E 163
La Louvière, Belg. 50°28′ N, 4°11′ E 163
La Madrid, Arg. 27°39′ S, 65°16′ W 132
La Malbaie, Can. 47°38′ N, 70°11′ W 94
La Malinche National Park, Mex. 19°6′ N, 98°21′ W 72
La Manche see English Channel 49°57′ N, 3°16′ W 150
La Maroma, Arg. 35°13′ S, 66°18′ W 134
La Marque, Tex., U.S. 29°21′ N, 94°58′ W 103
La Mauricie National Park, Can. 46°56′ N, 75°19′ W 94
La Merced, Peru 11°5′ S, 75°21′ W 130
La Mesa, Calif., U.S. 32°46′ N, 117°2′ W 101
La Mesa, N. Mex., U.S. 32°7′ N, 106°43′ W 92
La Misa, Mex. 28°24′ N, 110°32′ W 92
La Moille, Ill., U.S. 41°31′ N, 89°17′ W 102
La Mothe-Saint-Héraye, Fr. 46°21′ N, 0°8′ E 150
La Mugrosa, Col. 6°44′ N, 73°43′ W 136
La Noria, Mex. 23°27′ N, 106°21′ W 114
La Oroya, Peru 11°32′ S, 75°58′ W 130
La Paca, Sp. 37°52′ N, 1°51′ W 164
La Palma, Pan. 8°22′ N, 78°9′ W 136
La Palma, island, Sp. 28°27′ N, 18°53′ W 214
La Paloma, Uru. 34°39′ S, 54°11′ W 139
La Pampa, adm. division, Arg. 37°3′ S, 67°55′ W 134
La Para, Arg. 30°54′ S, 63°2′ W 139
La Paya National Park, Col. 0°15′ N, 75°53′ W 136
La Paz, Arg. 30°43′ S, 59°36′ W 139
La Paz, Arg. 33°29′ S, 67°32′ W 134
La Paz, Bol. 16°33′ S, 68°16′ W 137
La Paz, Ind., U.S. 41°27′ N, 86°19′ W 102
La Paz, Mex. 24°7′ N, 110°26′ W 112
La Paz, Mex. 23°38′ N, 100°43′ W 114
La Paz, adm. division, Bol. 15°11′ S, 68°59′ W 137
La Pedrera, Col. 1°21′ S, 69°42′ W 136
La Peraleja, Sp. 40°14′ N, 2°33′ W 164
La Perla, Mex. 28°13′ N, 104°36′ W 92
La Pérouse, Can. 55°12′ N, 97°59′ W 108
La Pesca, Mex. 23°47′ N, 97°47′ W 114
La Piedad de Cabadas, Mex. 20°19′ N, 102°2′ W 114
La Pine, Oreg., U.S. 43°39′ N, 121°31′ W 90
La Pintada, Pan. 8°37′ N, 80°25′ W 116
La Pita, ruin(s), Pan. 8°5′ N, 81°15′ W 115
La Place, La., U.S. 30°3′ N, 90°28′ W 103
La Placita, Mex. 18°34′ N, 103°39′ W 114
La Plant, S. Dak., U.S. 45°8′ N, 100°41′ W 90
La Plata, Arg. 34°55′ S, 57°58′ W 139
La Plata, Col. 2°23′ N, 75°57′ W 136
La Plata, Mo., U.S. 40°1′ N, 92°29′ W 94
La Pocatière, Can. 47°20′ N, 70°2′ W 94
La Pointe, Wis., U.S. 46°46′ N, 90°47′ W 94
La Porte, Ind., U.S. 41°36′ N, 86°43′ W 102
La Porte, Tex., U.S. 29°38′ N, 95°1′ W 103
La Porte City, Iowa, U.S. 42°16′ N, 92°11′ W 94
La Presa, Mex. 32°27′ N, 116°56′ W 101
La Pryor, Tex., U.S. 28°55′ N, 99°50′ W 92
La Puebla de Híjar, Sp. 41°12′ N, 0°27′ E 164
La Puebla de Valverde, Sp. 40°12′ N, 0°56′ E 164
La Puerta de Segura, Sp. 38°21′ N, 2°44′ W 164
La Purísima, Mex. 26°9′ N, 112°5′ W 112
La Push, Wash., U.S. 47°53′ N, 124°37′ W 100
La Quemada, ruin(s), Mex. 22°26′ N, 102°55′ W 114
La Quiaca, Arg. 22°11′ S, 65°35′ W 137
La Quinta, Calif., U.S. 33°41′ N, 116°19′ W 101
La Rambla, Sp. 37°37′ N, 4°45′ W 164
La Reale, It. 41°3′ N, 8°18′ E 156
La Réole, Fr. 44°34′ N, 5°296′ W 150
La Rioja, Arg. 29°25′ S, 66°49′ W 132
La Rioja, adm. division, Arg. 28°4′ S, 68°58′ W 132
La Rioja, adm. division, Sp. 42°10′ N, 3°5′ W 150
La Roca de la Sierra, Sp. 39°6′ N, 6°42′ W 164
La Roche, Belg. 50°10′ N, 5°33′ E 167
La Roche, Fr. 46°4′ N, 6°18′ E 167
La Rochelle, Fr. 46°7′ N, 1°11′ W 143
La Roda, Sp. 39°12′ N, 2°10′ W 164
La Romaine, Can. 50°13′ N, 60°40′ W 111
La Ronge, Can. 55°7′ N, 105°18′ W 108
La Rubia, Arg. 30°5′ S, 61°48′ W 139
La Rue, Ohio, U.S. 40°34′ N, 83°23′ W 102
La Rumorosa, Mex. 32°33′ N, 116°3′ W 101
La Sabana, Arg. 27°51′ S, 59°58′ W 139
La Sal, Utah, U.S. 38°18′ N, 109°14′ W 90
La Salceda, Sp. 41°2′ N, 3°54′ W 164
La Salle, Ill., U.S. 41°19′ N, 89°6′ W 102
La Sarre, Can. 48°48′ N, 79°13′ W 94
La Saulce, Fr. 44°25′ N, 5°59′ E 150
La Scie, Can. 49°57′ N, 55°36′ W 111
La Selva Beach, Calif., U.S. 36°56′ N, 121°52′ W 100
La Selva del Camp, Sp. 41°12′ N, 1°7′ E 164
La Sènia, Sp. 40°37′ N, 0°17′ E 164
La Serena, Chile 29°56′ S, 71°17′ W 134
La Solana, Sp. 38°56′ N, 3°15′ W 164
La Soledad, Mex. 24°44′ N, 104°55′ W 114
La Solita, Venez. 9°9′ N, 71°49′ W 136
La Souterraine, Fr. 46°14′ N, 1°28′ E 150
La Spezia, It. 44°6′ N, 9°49′ E 167
La Suze, Fr. 47°53′ N, 1°59′ E 150
La Tagua, Col. 0°5′ N, 74°40′ W 136
La Teste, Fr. 44°38′ N, 1°10′ W 150
La Tigra National Park, Hond. 14°11′ N, 87°13′ W 115
La Trinidad, Nicar. 12°56′ N, 86°13′ W 116
La Tuque, Can. 47°25′ N, 72°47′ W 94
La Unión, Bol. 15°20′ S, 61°7′ W 132
La Unión, Chile 40°16′ S, 73°7′ W 134
La Unión, Col. 1°31′ N, 77°10′ W 136
La Unión, Mex. 17°56′ N, 101°48′ W 114
La Unión, Sp. 37°37′ N, 0°54′ E 164
La Unión, Sp. 37°37′ N, 0°55′ E 214
La Unión, Venez. 8°14′ N, 67°47′ W 136
La Unión Morales, Mex. 24°32′ N, 98°59′ W 114
La Urbana, Venez. 7°7′ N, 66°55′ W 136
La Vanoise National Park, Fr. 45°21′ N, 6°49′ E 167
La Vela de Coro, Venez. 11°24′ N, 69°34′ W 136
La Venta, ruin(s), Mex. 18°2′ N, 94°10′ W 112
La Ventana, Mex. 22°59′ N, 100°14′ W 114
La Ventosa, Sp. 40°11′ N, 2°26′ W 164
La Ventura, Mex. 24°36′ N, 100°54′ W 114
La Vereda, Sp. 41°0′ N, 3°21′ W 164
La Verkin, Utah, U.S. 37°12′ N, 113°16′ W 92
La Veta, Colo., U.S. 37°29′ N, 105°1′ W 92
La Victoria, Venez. 7°17′ N, 70°5′ W 136
La Villa Joiosa see Villajoyosa, Sp. 38°29′ N, 0°14′ E 164
La Yarada, Peru 18°18′ S, 70°30′ W 137
La Yesca, Mex. 21°17′ N, 104°2′ W 114
La Yunta, Sp. 40°53′ N, 1°41′ W 164
Laanila, Fin. 68°24′ N, 27°22′ E 152
Laas Dawaco, Somalia 10°25′ N, 49°3′ E 216
Laayoune, Africa 27°6′ N, 13°12′ W 214
Laayoune, Alg. 35°41′ N, 2°0′ E 150
Labadaad, Somalia 0°30′ N, 42°45′ E 218
Labardén, Arg. 36°57′ S, 58°5′ W 139
Labbezanga, Mali 14°58′ N, 0°42′ E 222
Labé, Guinea 11°19′ N, 12°18′ W 222
Labelle, Can. 46°17′ N, 74°45′ W 94
Labenne, Fr. 43°35′ N, 1°28′ W 150
Laberge, Lake, Can. 61°12′ N, 136°23′ W 98
Labinsk, Russ. 44°40′ N, 40°39′ E 158
Labis, Malaysia 2°24′ N, 103°2′ E 196
Laborde, Arg. 33°10′ S, 62°51′ W 139
Laborovaya, Russ. 67°38′ N, 67°46′ E 169
Labouchere, Mount, peak, Austral. 25°16′ S, 118°5′ E 230
Laboulaye, Arg. 34°7′ S, 63°24′ W 139
Labrador City, Can. 52°57′ N, 67°3′ W 106
Labrador, region, Can. 52°2′ N, 63°21′ W 111
Labrador Sea 55°27′ N, 57°22′ W 106
Lábrea, Braz. 7°17′ S, 64°50′ W 130
Labuha, Indonesia 0°35′ N, 127°27′ E 192
Labuhanbatu, Indonesia 2°14′ N, 100°14′ E 196
Labuhanbilik, Indonesia 2°33′ N, 100°10′ E 196
Labutta, Myanmar 16°10′ N, 94°45′ E 202
Labyrinth Lake, Can. 60°40′ N, 107°11′ W 108
Labytnangi, Russ. 66°38′ N, 66°28′ E 169
Lac du Bonnet, Can. 50°14′ N, 96°5′ W 90
Lac du Flambeau, Wis., U.S. 45°58′ N, 89°53′ W 94
Lac La Biche, Can. 54°46′ N, 111°60′ W 108
Lac Seul, Can. 50°20′ N, 92°17′ W 110
Lac-Allard, Can. 50°32′ N, 63°27′ W 111
Lacanau, Fr. 44°58′ N, 1°6′ W 150
Lacanau-Océan, Fr. 45°0′ N, 1°13′ W 150
Lacantun, river, Mex. 16°10′ N, 91°26′ W 115
Laćarak, Serb. and Mont. 45°0′ N, 19°34′ E 168
Lacaune, Monts de, peak, Fr. 43°40′ N, 2°41′ E 165
Lac-au-Saumon, Can. 48°24′ N, 67°21′ W 94
Lac-Bouchette, Can. 48°16′ N, 72°10′ W 94
Lacepede Islands, Indian Ocean 17°3′ S, 120°1′ E 230
Lacerdónia, Mozambique 18°6′ S, 35°33′ E 224
Lacey, Wash., U.S. 47°0′ N, 122°48′ W 100
Lache, Lac La, lake, Can. 56°29′ N, 110°17′ W 108
Lachish, ruin(s), Israel 31°33′ N, 34°47′ E 194
Lachyn, Azerb. 39°38′ N, 46°33′ E 195
Lac-Mégantic, Can. 45°34′ N, 70°54′ W 94
Lacombe, La., U.S. 30°18′ N, 89°57′ W 103
Lacon, Ill., U.S. 41°0′ N, 89°24′ W 102
Laconia, N.H., U.S. 43°31′ N, 71°29′ W 104
Lacoochee, Fla., U.S. 28°27′ N, 82°11′ W 105
Lacq, Fr. 43°25′ N, 0°39′ E 164
Lacuy, Peninsula, Chile 41°46′ S, 75°37′ W 134
Ladainha, Braz. 17°39′ S, 41°45′ W 138
Ladd, Ill., U.S. 41°22′ N, 89°13′ W 102
Lâdik, Turk. 40°54′ N, 35°55′ E 156
Ladismith, S. Af. 33°29′ S, 21°13′ E 227
Ladispoli, It. 41°57′ N, 12°4′ E 156
Ladoga, Lake see Ladozhskoye Ozero, lake, Russ. 61°10′ N, 31°29′ E 154
Ladozhskoye Ozero see Ladozhskoye Ozero, lake, Russ. 61°10′ N, 31°29′ E 154
Ladushkin, Russ. 54°33′ N, 20°10′ E 166
Ladva, Russ. 61°20′ N, 34°43′ E 154
Ladva Vetka, Russ. 61°18′ N, 34°32′ E 154
Lady Evelyn Falls, Can. 60°38′ N, 117°43′ W 108
Lady Grey, S. Af. 30°42′ S, 27°12′ E 227
Ladysmith, Can. 48°58′ N, 123°49′ W 100
Ladysmith, S. Af. 28°32′ S, 29°46′ E 227
Ladysmith, Wis., U.S. 45°28′ N, 91°7′ W 94
Lae, P.N.G. 6°47′ S, 146°52′ E 238
Laem Ngop, Thai. 12°12′ N, 102°25′ E 202
Laer, Ger. 52°3′ N, 7°22′ E 163
Lafayette, Ala., U.S. 32°53′ N, 85°25′ W 96
Lafayette, Ga., U.S. 34°41′ N, 85°16′ W 96
Lafayette, Ind., U.S. 40°25′ N, 86°52′ W 102
Lafayette, La., U.S. 30°12′ N, 92°2′ W 103
Lafayette, Tenn., U.S. 36°31′ N, 86°2′ W 94
Lafayette, Mount, peak, N.H., U.S. 44°9′ N, 71°41′ W 104
Lafia, Nig. 8°28′ N, 8°29′ E 222
Lafiagi, Nig. 8°53′ N, 5°18′ E 222
Lafitte, La., U.S. 29°39′ N, 90°6′ W 103
Lafleche, Can. 49°41′ N, 106°34′ W 90
Lafou, Guinea 11°35′ N, 12°30′ W 222
Laful, India 7°9′ N, 93°55′ E 188
Laganya, Ghana 9°9′ N, 3°179′ E 222
Lagartera, Sp. 39°53′ N, 5°13′ W 150
Lagarto, Braz. 10°54′ S, 37°41′ W 132
Laghouat, Alg. 33°50′ N, 2°52′ E 214
Lagny, Fr. 48°52′ N, 2°42′ E 163
Lago Agrio, Ecua. 5°297′ N, 76°47′ W 136
Lago Argentino see El Calafate, Arg. 50°26′ S, 72°13′ W 123
Lago de Camécuaro National Park, Mex. 19°40′ N, 102°37′ W 112
Lago de Nicaragua, lake, Nicar. 11°30′ N, 85°30′ W 116
Lagoa da Prata, Braz. 20°4′ S, 45°32′ W 138
Lagoa do Peixe National Park, Braz. 31°0′ S, 50°42′ W 139
Lagoa Vermelha, Braz. 28°14′ S, 51°30′ W 139
Lagodekhi, Ga. 41°49′ N, 46°16′ E 195
Lagolândia, Braz. 15°38′ S, 49°4′ W 138
Lagos, Nig. 6°30′ N, 3°22′ E 222
Lagos, Port. 37°5′ N, 8°41′ W 150
Lagos de Moreno, Mex. 21°21′ N, 101°57′ W 114
Lagosa, Tanzania 5°59′ S, 29°50′ E 224
Lagrange, Austral. 18°42′ S, 121°47′ E 231
Lagrange, Ind., U.S. 41°37′ N, 85°25′ W 102
Lagrange Bay 18°46′ S, 120°26′ E 230
Lagro, Ind., U.S. 40°49′ N, 85°44′ W 102
Laguna, Braz. 28°30′ S, 48°47′ W 138
Laguna, N. Mex., U.S. 35°2′ N, 107°24′ W 92
Laguna Beach, Calif., U.S. 33°33′ N, 117°49′ W 101
Laguna Blanca, Arg. 25°8′ S, 58°16′ W 132
Laguna Blanca National Park, Arg. 38°60′ S, 70°46′ W 134
Laguna Dam, Calif., U.S. 32°52′ N, 114°33′ W 101
Laguna de Chautengo, Mex. 16°39′ N, 99°4′ W 112
Laguna de la Restinga National Park, Caribbean Sea 10°59′ N, 64°13′ W 116
Laguna del Laja National Park, Chile 37°32′ S, 71°28′ W 134
Laguna Grande, Arg. 49°30′ S, 70°17′ W 134
Laguna Mountains, Calif., U.S. 32°56′ N, 116°32′ W 101
Laguna Paiva, Arg. 31°18′ S, 60°38′ W 139
Laguna San Rafael National Park, Chile 47°28′ S, 74°37′ W 122
Laguna Yema, Arg. 24°15′ S, 61°15′ W 132
Lagunas, Chile 20°59′ S, 69°41′ W 137
Lagunas, Peru 5°15′ S, 75°41′ W 130
Lagunas de Chacahua National Park, Mex. 15°54′ N, 97°59′ W 72
Lagunas de Montebello National Park see 29, Mex. 16°3′ N, 91°50′ W 115
Lagunas de Zempoala National Park, Mex. 18°59′ N, 99°24′ W 112
Lagunilla, Sp. 40°18′ N, 5°58′ W 150
Lagunillas, Bol. 19°42′ S, 63°46′ W 137
Lagunillas, Venez. 10°7′ N, 71°16′ W 136
Lagunitos, Peru 4°35′ S, 81°17′ W 130
Lagwira, Africa 20°53′ N, 17°5′ W 222
Laha, China 48°14′ N, 124°40′ E 198
Lahad Datu, Malaysia 5°4′ N, 118°19′ E 203
Lahainaluna High School, site, Hawai'i, U.S. 20°52′ N, 156°43′ W 99
Lahar, India 26°11′ N, 78°56′ E 197
Lahat, Indonesia 3°50′ S, 103°26′ E 192
Lahemaa National Park, Est. 59°33′ N, 26°3′ E 166
Lahewa, Indonesia 1°24′ N, 97°8′ E 196
Lahıc, Azerb. 40°50′ N, 48°22′ E 195
Laḩij, Yemen 13°3′ N, 44°52′ E 182
Lāhījān, Iran 37°14′ N, 50°4′ E 195
Lahn, river, Ger. 50°54′ N, 8°27′ E 167
Lahnstein, Ger. 50°18′ N, 7°36′ E 167
Lahore, Pak. 31°35′ N, 74°18′ E 186
Lahoysk, Belarus 54°12′ N, 27°50′ E 166
Lahr, Ger. 48°20′ N, 7°51′ E 163
Lahti, Fin. 60°58′ N, 25°38′ E 166
Laï (Behagle), Chad 9°23′ N, 16°20′ E 216
Lai Chau, Vietnam 22°3′ N, 103°11′ E 202
Laibin, China 23°45′ N, 109°14′ E 198
Laifeng, China 29°32′ N, 109°22′ E 198
L'Aigle, Fr. 48°45′ N, 0°38′ E 150
Laihia, Fin. 62°57′ N, 22°0′ E 154
Lai-hka, Myanmar 21°17′ N, 97°40′ E 202
Laingsburg, Mich., U.S. 42°52′ N, 84°22′ W 102
Laingsburg, S. Af. 33°10′ S, 20°54′ E 227
Laird Hill, Tex., U.S. 32°20′ N, 94°55′ W 103
Lais, Indonesia 3°31′ S, 102°0′ E 192
Laisamis, Kenya 1°35′ N, 37°49′ E 224
Laisvall, Nor. 66°5′ N, 17°9′ E 152
Laitila, Fin. 60°51′ N, 21°42′ E 166
Laiwu, China 36°12′ N, 117°40′ E 198
Laiyang, China 37°0′ N, 120°39′ E 198
Laja, river, Mex. 21°17′ N, 100°58′ W 114
Laje, Braz. 5°35′ S, 56°51′ W 130
Lajeado, Braz. 29°23′ S, 51°57′ W 139
Lajes, Braz. 14°2′ S, 48°10′ W 138
Lajes, Braz. 27°51′ S, 50°21′ W 138
Lajitas, Tex., U.S. 29°15′ N, 103°47′ W 92
Lajkovac, Serb. and Mont. 44°22′ N, 20°9′ E 168
Lajosmizse, Hung. 47°1′ N, 19°34′ E 168
Laka, Dem. Rep. of the Congo 4°11′ N, 23°37′ E 224
Lakamané, Mali 14°31′ N, 9°53′ W 222
Lakaträsk, Nor. 66°17′ N, 21°7′ E 152
Lake, Mich., U.S. 43°51′ N, 85°1′ W 102
Lake, Miss., U.S. 32°19′ N, 89°19′ W 103
Lake Andes, S. Dak., U.S. 43°8′ N, 98°33′ W 90
Lake Arrowhead, Calif., U.S. 34°14′ N, 117°12′ W 101
Lake Arthur, La., U.S. 30°4′ N, 92°41′ W 103
Lake Arthur, N. Mex., U.S. 32°59′ N, 104°23′ W 92
Lake Charles, La., U.S. 30°12′ N, 93°13′ W 103
Lake Chelan National Recreation Area, Wash., U.S. 48°18′ N, 121°30′ W 100
Lake City, Colo., U.S. 38°2′ N, 107°20′ W 92
Lake City, Fla., U.S. 30°9′ N, 82°37′ W 112
Lake City, Iowa, U.S. 42°15′ N, 94°44′ W 94
Lake City, Mich., U.S. 44°20′ N, 85°13′ W 94
Lake City, Minn., U.S. 44°25′ N, 92°18′ W 94
Lake City, S.C., U.S. 33°51′ N, 79°46′ W 96
Lake Coleridge, N.Z. 43°23′ S, 171°32′ E 240
Lake Cowichan, Can. 48°48′ N, 124°3′ W 100
Lake Crystal, Minn., U.S. 44°5′ N, 94°13′ W 94
Lake Delton, Wis., U.S. 43°35′ N, 89°47′ W 102
Lake Elsinore, Calif., U.S. 33°40′ N, 117°21′ W 101

Lake Forest, *Ill., U.S.* 42°14′ N, 87°50′ W **102**
Lake Geneva, *Wis., U.S.* 42°35′ N, 88°27′ W **102**
Lake George, *Mich., U.S.* 43°58′ N, 84°57′ W **102**
Lake George, *N.Y., U.S.* 43°25′ N, 73°44′ W **104**
Lake Harbor, *Fla., U.S.* 26°40′ N, 80°48′ W **105**
Lake Harbor see Kimmirut, *Can.* 62°52′ N, 69°53′ W **106**
Lake Havasu City, *Ariz., U.S.* 34°29′ N, 114°20′ W **101**
Lake Helen, *Fla., U.S.* 28°58′ N, 81°14′ W **105**
Lake Hughes, *Calif., U.S.* 34°40′ N, 118°28′ W **101**
Lake Isabella, *Calif., U.S.* 35°38′ N, 118°29′ W **101**
Lake Jackson, *Tex., U.S.* 29°1′ N, 95°26′ W **103**
Lake Louise, *Can.* 51°26′ N, 116°8′ W **90**
Lake Luzerne, *N.Y., U.S.* 43°18′ N, 73°51′ W **104**
Lake Mburo National Park, *Uganda* 0°48′ N, 30°36′ E **206**
Lake Mead National Recreation Area, *Nev., U.S.* 36°1′ N, 114°39′ W **101**
Lake Mills, *Iowa, U.S.* 43°23′ N, 93°33′ W **94**
Lake Mills, *Wis., U.S.* 43°5′ N, 88°55′ W **102**
Lake Minchumina, *Alas., U.S.* 63°45′ N, 152°22′ W **98**
Lake Monroe, *Fla., U.S.* 28°49′ N, 81°19′ W **105**
Lake Nakuru National Park, *Kenya* 0°29′ N, 35°43′ E **206**
Lake Odessa, *Mich., U.S.* 42°46′ N, 85°8′ W **102**
Lake Orion, *Mich., U.S.* 42°46′ N, 83°15′ W **102**
Lake Park, *Fla., U.S.* 26°48′ N, 80°5′ W **105**
Lake Placid, *Fla., U.S.* 27°17′ N, 81°22′ W **105**
Lake Placid, *N.Y., U.S.* 44°16′ N, 73°60′ W **104**
Lake Preston, *S. Dak., U.S.* 44°20′ N, 97°24′ W **90**
Lake Providence, *La., U.S.* 32°47′ N, 91°11′ W **103**
Lake Pukaki, *N.Z.* 44°12′ S, 170°7′ E **240**
Lake Tekapo, *N.Z.* 44°2′ S, 170°30′ E **240**
Lake Traverse, *Can.* 45°56′ N, 78°5′ W **94**
Lake Village, *Ark., U.S.* 33°18′ N, 91°18′ W **103**
Lake Wales, *Fla., U.S.* 27°54′ N, 81°35′ W **105**
Lake Worth, *Fla., U.S.* 26°37′ N, 80°5′ W **105**
Lakefield, *Can.* 44°25′ N, 78°15′ W **94**
Lakefield National Park, *Austral.* 15°18′ S, 143°57′ E **238**
Lakeland, *Fla., U.S.* 28°2′ N, 81°58′ W **105**
Lakeland, *Ga., U.S.* 31°2′ N, 83°5′ W **96**
Lakelse Lake, *Can.* 54°22′ N, 128°32′ W **108**
Lakeport, *Mich., U.S.* 43°6′ N, 82°30′ W **102**
Lakes, adm. division, *Sudan* 6°24′ N, 29°29′ E **224**
Lakeside, *Calif., U.S.* 32°51′ N, 116°56′ W **101**
Lakeside, *Nebr., U.S.* 42°3′ N, 102°26′ W **90**
Lakeside, *Ohio, U.S.* 41°31′ N, 82°45′ W **102**
Lakeside, *Oreg., U.S.* 43°34′ N, 124°11′ W **90**
Lakeview, *Mich., U.S.* 43°26′ N, 85°17′ W **102**
Lakeview, *Ohio, U.S.* 40°28′ N, 83°56′ W **102**
Lakeville, *Conn., U.S.* 41°58′ N, 73°27′ W **104**
Lakeville, *Minn., U.S.* 44°38′ N, 93°15′ W **94**
Lakewood, *Colo., U.S.* 39°43′ N, 105°5′ W **90**
Lakewood, *Ohio, U.S.* 41°27′ N, 81°51′ W **82**
Lakhdenpokh'ya, *Russ.* 61°30′ N, 30°10′ E **166**
Lakhimpur, *India* 27°54′ N, 80°46′ E **197**
Lakhnadon, *India* 22°36′ N, 79°37′ E **197**
Lakhpat, *India* 23°48′ N, 68°47′ E **186**
Lakhva, *Belarus* 52°12′ N, 27°7′ E **152**
Laki, *Gr.* 37°7′ N, 26°52′ E **156**
Lakin, *Kans., U.S.* 37°56′ N, 101°17′ W **90**
Lákmos, Óri, peak, *Gr.* 39°40′ N, 21°2′ E **156**
Lakota, *Côte d'Ivoire* 5°47′ N, 5°40′ W **222**
Lakota, *N. Dak., U.S.* 48°1′ N, 98°22′ W **90**
Laksely, *Nor.* 70°2′ N, 24°56′ E **152**
Lakshadweep, islands, *Persian Gulf* 10°16′ N, 72°31′ E **188**
Laktaši, *Bosn. and Herzg.* 44°54′ N, 17°18′ E **168**
Lalago, *Tanzania* 3°25′ S, 33°56′ E **224**
Lalapansi, *Zimb.* 19°22′ S, 30°10′ E **224**
Lalaua, *Mozambique* 14°24′ S, 38°16′ E **224**
Lāleh Zār, Kūh-e, peak, *Iran* 29°23′ N, 56°45′ E **196**
Lalibela, *Eth.* 12°1′ N, 39°2′ E **182**
Lalinde, *Fr.* 44°50′ N, 0°44′ E **150**
Lalitpur, *India* 24°42′ N, 78°24′ E **197**
Lalitpur (Patan), *Nepal* 27°36′ N, 85°22′ E **197**
Laloche, river, *Can.* 61°36′ N, 112°26′ W **108**
Lal'sk, *Russ.* 60°45′ N, 47°36′ E **154**
Lalsot, *India* 26°32′ N, 76°21′ E **197**
Lama, Ozero, lake, *Russ.* 69°34′ N, 89°20′ E **169**
Lamag, *Malaysia* 5°30′ N, 117°48′ E **203**
Lamaing, *Myanmar* 15°29′ N, 97°50′ E **202**
Lama-Kara, *Togo* 9°36′ N, 1°11′ E **222**
Lamar, *Colo., U.S.* 38°4′ N, 102°37′ W **90**
Lamar, *Mo., U.S.* 37°28′ N, 94°16′ W **96**
Lamas, *Peru* 6°26′ S, 76°35′ W **130**
Lamas, *Turk.* 36°34′ N, 34°14′ E **156**
Lambach, *Aust.* 48°5′ N, 13°52′ E **156**
Lambaréné, *Gabon* 0°44′ N, 10°11′ E **218**
Lambasa, *Fiji Islands* 16°18′ S, 179°25′ E **238**
Lambayeque, *Peru* 6°39′ S, 79°56′ W **130**
Lambayeque, adm. division, *Peru* 5°30′ S, 80°27′ W **130**
Lamberhurst, *U.K.* 51°5′ N, 0°23′ E **162**
Lambert Land, *Norske Øer* 78°56′ N, 27°17′ W **246**
Lambert's Bay, *S. Af.* 32°5′ S, 18°18′ E **227**
Lambertville, *Mich., U.S.* 41°45′ N, 83°38′ W **102**
Lambourn, *U.K.* 51°30′ N, 1°33′ W **162**
Lambrecht, *Ger.* 49°22′ N, 8°4′ E **163**
Lambton, *Can.* 45°49′ N, 71°6′ W **111**
Lambton, Cape, *Can.* 70°53′ N, 127°37′ W **106**
Lamé, *Chad* 9°15′ N, 14°33′ E **216**
Lame Deer, *Mont., U.S.* 45°35′ N, 106°41′ W **90**
Lamesa, *Tex., U.S.* 32°43′ N, 101°57′ W **92**
L'Ametlla de Mar, *Sp.* 40°53′ N, 0°47′ E **164**
Lamia, *Gr.* 38°54′ N, 22°26′ E **156**
Lamitan, *Philippines* 6°40′ N, 122°7′ E **203**
Lamjaybir, *Africa* 25°21′ N, 14°48′ W **214**
Lammeulo, *Indonesia* 5°15′ N, 95°53′ E **196**
Lammhult, *Nor.* 57°9′ N, 14°34′ E **152**
Lammi, *Fin.* 61°4′ N, 25°0′ E **166**
Lamoille, *Nev., U.S.* 40°44′ N, 115°28′ W **90**
Lamoille, river, *Vt., U.S.* 44°41′ N, 73°18′ W **110**
Lamon Bay 14°26′ N, 122°0′ E **203**
Lamoni, *Iowa, U.S.* 40°37′ N, 93°56′ W **94**
Lamont, *Calif., U.S.* 35°16′ N, 118°56′ W **101**
Lamont, *Can.* 53°45′ N, 112°47′ W **108**
Lamont, *Wyo., U.S.* 42°12′ N, 107°29′ W **90**
Lamotrek Atoll 6°36′ N, 147°0′ E **192**
Lamoure, *N. Dak., U.S.* 46°20′ N, 98°18′ W **90**
Lampa, *Peru* 15°24′ S, 70°21′ W **137**
Lampang, *Thai.* 18°17′ N, 99°31′ E **202**
Lampasas, *Tex., U.S.* 31°3′ N, 98°11′ W **92**
Lampaul, *Fr.* 48°27′ N, 5°6′ W **150**
Lampazos, *Mex.* 27°1′ N, 100°31′ W **96**
Lampedusa, island, *It.* 35°22′ N, 11°14′ E **216**
Lampeter, *U.K.* 52°6′ N, 4°4′ W **162**
Lamphun, *Thai.* 18°36′ N, 99°3′ E **202**
L'Ampolla, *Sp.* 40°48′ N, 0°40′ E **164**
Lampozhnya, *Russ.* 65°42′ N, 44°20′ E **154**
Lamskoye, *Russ.* 52°55′ N, 38°2′ E **154**
Lamu, *Kenya* 2°16′ S, 40°50′ E **224**
Lāmu, *Myanmar* 19°12′ N, 94°12′ E **202**
Lan', river, *Belarus* 52°45′ N, 27°4′ E **154**
Lan Yü, island, *Taiwan* 22°6′ N, 121°35′ E **198**
Lana, *It.* 46°36′ N, 11°8′ E **167**
Lana, river, *Mex.* 17°27′ N, 95°38′ W **114**
Lāna'i, island, *Hawai'i, U.S.* 20°35′ N, 157°29′ W **99**
Lanaja, *Sp.* 41°45′ N, 0°19′ E **164**
Lanao, Lake, *Philippines* 7°53′ N, 123°54′ E **203**
Lanark, *Ill., U.S.* 42°6′ N, 89°50′ W **102**
Lanbi Kyun, island, *Myanmar* 10°38′ N, 98°18′ E **202**
Lancang, *China* 22°33′ N, 99°56′ E **202**
Lancang (Mekong), river, *China* 32°3′ N, 97°14′ E **190**
Lancaster, *Calif., U.S.* 34°41′ N, 118°9′ W **101**
Lancaster, *Mo., U.S.* 40°31′ N, 92°31′ W **94**
Lancaster, *N.H., U.S.* 44°29′ N, 71°35′ W **104**
Lancaster, *N.Y., U.S.* 42°53′ N, 78°40′ W **94**
Lancaster, *Ohio, U.S.* 39°43′ N, 82°36′ W **102**
Lancaster, *S.C., U.S.* 34°42′ N, 80°47′ W **96**
Lancaster, *U.K.* 54°2′ N, 2°48′ W **162**
Lancaster, *Wis., U.S.* 42°50′ N, 90°42′ W **110**
Lancaster Sound 73°38′ N, 94°47′ W **72**
Lance Creek, *Wyo., U.S.* 43°1′ N, 104°38′ W **90**
Land Between the Lakes, *Ky., U.S.* 37°1′ N, 87°60′ W **80**
Land O'Lakes, *Fla., U.S.* 28°12′ N, 82°28′ W **105**
Landau, *Ger.* 51°21′ N, 9°5′ E **167**
Landay, *Afghan.* 30°29′ N, 63°47′ E **186**
Landeck, *Aust.* 47°8′ N, 10°34′ E **156**
Lander, *Wyo., U.S.* 42°50′ N, 108°44′ W **90**
Landers, *Calif., U.S.* 34°16′ N, 116°25′ W **101**
Landeryd, *Nor.* 57°5′ N, 13°15′ E **152**
Landeta, *Arg.* 32°1′ S, 62°2′ W **139**
Landete, *Sp.* 39°54′ N, 1°23′ W **164**
Landfall Island, *India* 13°40′ N, 92°0′ E **188**
Landis, *Can.* 52°12′ N, 108°28′ W **108**
Landis, *N.C., U.S.* 35°32′ N, 80°37′ W **96**
Landrecies, *Fr.* 50°7′ N, 3°42′ E **163**
Landrum, *S.C., U.S.* 35°10′ N, 82°12′ W **96**
Lands End, *Can.* 76°47′ N, 123°5′ W **246**
Land's End, *U.K.* 50°0′ N, 6°1′ W **150**
Lane Mountain, peak, *Calif., U.S.* 35°4′ N, 116°59′ W **101**
Lanercost Priory, site, *U.K.* 54°57′ N, 2°49′ W **150**
Lanesboro, *Pa., U.S.* 41°57′ N, 75°35′ W **110**
Lanesborough, *Mass., U.S.* 42°30′ N, 73°14′ W **104**
Lanett, *Ala., U.S.* 32°51′ N, 85°12′ W **96**
Laneville, *Tex., U.S.* 31°57′ N, 94°48′ W **103**
Lang Son, *Vietnam* 21°51′ N, 106°44′ E **198**
Lang Suan, *Thai.* 9°55′ N, 99°5′ E **202**
Langå, *Den.* 56°24′ N, 9°51′ E **150**
La'nga Co, lake, *China* 30°37′ N, 80°48′ E **197**
Langa de Duero, *Sp.* 41°36′ N, 3°24′ W **164**
Langanes, *Ice.* 66°23′ N, 14°29′ W **246**
Langao, *China* 32°16′ N, 108°55′ E **198**
Langar, *Uzb.* 40°26′ N, 65°59′ E **197**
Langarūd, *Iran* 37°10′ N, 50°9′ E **195**
Långban, *Nor.* 59°51′ N, 14°15′ E **152**
Langdon, *N. Dak., U.S.* 48°44′ N, 98°24′ W **90**
Längelmäki, *Fin.* 61°41′ N, 24°41′ E **166**
Langen, *Ger.* 49°59′ N, 8°40′ E **167**
Langenau, *Ger.* 48°29′ N, 10°6′ E **152**
Langenburg, *Can.* 50°50′ N, 101°43′ W **90**
Langfang, *China* 39°33′ N, 116°38′ E **198**
Langfjordnes, *Nor.* 70°42′ N, 28°4′ E **152**
Långflon, *Nor.* 61°2′ N, 12°32′ E **152**
Langford, *S. Dak., U.S.* 45°35′ N, 97°51′ W **90**
Langham, *Can.* 52°21′ N, 106°56′ W **108**
Langhirano, *It.* 44°36′ N, 10°14′ E **167**
Langjökull, glacier, *Ice.* 64°48′ N, 29°24′ W **72**
Langkawi, island, *Malaysia* 6°14′ N, 99°5′ E **196**
Langley, *Can.* 49°5′ N, 122°39′ W **100**
Langley, *Wash., U.S.* 48°1′ N, 122°26′ W **100**
Langley Air Force Base, *Va., U.S.* 37°4′ N, 76°26′ W **94**
Langley, Mount, peak, *Calif., U.S.* 36°31′ N, 118°17′ W **101**
Langlois, *Oreg., U.S.* 42°55′ N, 124°27′ W **90**
Langøya, island, *Nor.* 68°55′ N, 11°48′ E **246**
Langport, *U.K.* 51°2′ N, 2°49′ W **162**
Langres, Plateau de, *Fr.* 47°41′ N, 4°44′ E **165**
Langsa, *Indonesia* 4°29′ N, 97°57′ E **196**
Långsele, *Nor.* 64°33′ N, 15°51′ E **154**
Långsele, *Nor.* 63°9′ N, 17°2′ E **152**
Langtou, *China* 40°1′ N, 124°19′ E **200**
Långtrask, *Nor.* 65°21′ N, 20°17′ E **152**
Langtry, *Tex., U.S.* 29°47′ N, 101°35′ W **92**
Langu, *Thai.* 6°52′ N, 99°46′ E **196**
Languedoc-Roussillon, adm. division, *Fr.* 42°36′ N, 2°13′ E **150**
Languedog, region, *Fr.* 44°39′ N, 3°3′ E **165**
Langwarden, *Ger.* 53°36′ N, 8°19′ E **163**
Langzhong, *China* 31°40′ N, 105°51′ E **190**
Laniel, *Can.* 47°3′ N, 79°15′ W **94**
Lanigan, *Can.* 51°51′ N, 105°3′ W **90**
Lanín National Park, *Arg.* 40°54′ S, 71°5′ W **134**
Lanjarón, *Sp.* 36°55′ N, 3°29′ W **164**
Länkäran, *Azerb.* 38°44′ N, 48°49′ E **195**
Lankio, *Côte d'Ivoire* 9°51′ N, 3°26′ W **222**
Lankoveri, *Nig.* 9°1′ N, 11°22′ E **222**
Lanlacuni Bajo, *Peru* 13°33′ S, 70°25′ W **137**
Lannemezan, *Fr.* 43°7′ N, 0°22′ E **164**
Lansdale, *Pa., U.S.* 40°13′ N, 75°18′ W **94**
Lansdowne House, *Can.* 52°11′ N, 87°55′ W **82**
L'Anse, *Mich., U.S.* 46°45′ N, 88°27′ W **94**
L'Anse aux Meadows, *Can.* 51°36′ N, 55°32′ W **111**
Lansing, *Ill., U.S.* 41°33′ N, 87°32′ W **102**
Lansing, *Iowa, U.S.* 43°21′ N, 91°14′ W **94**
Lansing, *Mich., U.S.* 42°42′ N, 84°36′ W **102**
Lanta Yai, Ko, island, *Thai.* 7°20′ N, 98°23′ E **196**
Lantana, *Fla., U.S.* 26°34′ N, 80°5′ W **105**
Lantewa, *Nig.* 12°15′ N, 11°46′ E **222**
Lantz, *Sp.* 42°59′ N, 1°38′ W **164**
Lanús, *Arg.* 34°46′ S, 58°24′ W **139**
Lanuza, *Philippines* 9°15′ N, 126°3′ E **203**
Lanxian, *China* 38°16′ N, 111°36′ E **198**
Lanz Peak, *Antarctica* 77°18′ S, 87°11′ W **248**
Lanzai, *Nig.* 11°20′ N, 10°49′ E **222**
Lanzarote, island, *Sp.* 29°6′ N, 14°51′ W **214**
Lanzhou, *China* 36°3′ N, 103°44′ E **198**
Lao Cai, *China* 22°29′ N, 104°1′ E **202**
Laoag, *Philippines* 18°12′ N, 120°38′ E **198**
Laocheng, *China* 42°37′ N, 124°5′ E **200**
Laohekou, *China* 32°22′ N, 111°40′ E **198**
Laon, *Fr.* 49°33′ N, 3°37′ E **163**
Laona, *Wis., U.S.* 45°34′ N, 88°40′ W **94**
Laos 19°46′ N, 102°26′ E **202**
Laoshan, *China* 36°13′ N, 120°25′ E **198**
Laotougou, *China* 42°55′ N, 129°8′ E **200**
Laouni, spring, *Alg.* 20°30′ N, 5°44′ E **222**
Lapa, *Braz.* 25°46′ S, 49°43′ W **138**
Lapai, *Nig.* 9°0′ N, 6°43′ E **222**
Lapeer, *Mich., U.S.* 43°2′ N, 83°18′ W **102**
Lapinlahti, *Fin.* 63°21′ N, 27°22′ E **152**
Lapithos 35°20′ N, 33°9′ E **194**
Lapovo, *Serb. and Mont.* 44°10′ N, 21°3′ E **156**
Lappa, ruin(s), *Gr.* 35°16′ N, 24°15′ E **156**
Lappfjärd (Lapväärtti), *Fin.* 62°13′ N, 21°29′ E **152**
Laprida, *Arg.* 37°35′ S, 60°48′ W **139**
Lâpseki, *Turk.* 40°20′ N, 26°39′ E **156**
Laptev Sea 72°2′ N, 139°4′ E **246**
Lapua, *Fin.* 62°57′ N, 22°59′ E **152**
Lăpuş, Munţii, *Rom.* 47°26′ N, 23°26′ E **168**
Lăpuşna, *Mold.* 46°52′ N, 28°25′ E **156**
Lapväärtti see Lappfjärd, *Fin.* 62°13′ N, 21°29′ E **152**
Łapy, *Pol.* 52°59′ N, 22°51′ E **152**
Laqiya Arba'in, *Sudan* 20°2′ N, 28°2′ E **226**
Laqiya 'Umran, spring, *Sudan* 19°52′ N, 28°10′ E **226**
L'Aquila, *It.* 42°21′ N, 13°23′ E **156**
Lār, *Iran* 27°38′ N, 54°16′ E **196**
Lara, *Gabon* 0°19′ N, 11°22′ E **218**
Lara, adm. division, *Venez.* 9°56′ N, 70°30′ W **136**
Larabanga, *Ghana* 9°13′ N, 1°52′ W **222**
Laracha, *Sp.* 43°15′ N, 8°35′ W **150**
Larache, *Mor.* 35°11′ N, 6°10′ W **150**
Lārak, island, *Iran* 26°43′ N, 56°24′ E **180**
Laramate, *Peru* 14°18′ S, 74°51′ W **137**
Laramie, *Wyo., U.S.* 41°19′ N, 105°34′ W **90**
Laramie Mountains, *Wyo., U.S.* 42°32′ N, 106°11′ W **90**
Laramie Peak, *Wyo., U.S.* 42°15′ N, 105°31′ W **90**
Laranjeiras do Sul, *Braz.* 25°27′ S, 52°27′ W **138**
Larat, *Indonesia* 7°15′ S, 131°43′ E **192**
Larb Creek, river, *Mont., U.S.* 48°15′ N, 107°43′ W **90**
Lärbro, *Sw.* 57°47′ N, 18°47′ E **166**
Larche, *Fr.* 44°27′ N, 6°50′ E **167**
Larde, *Mozambique* 16°27′ S, 39°42′ E **224**
Larder Lake, *Can.* 48°6′ N, 79°43′ W **94**
Laredo, *Sp.* 43°23′ N, 3°27′ W **150**
Laredo, *Tex., U.S.* 27°31′ N, 99°28′ W **73**
Laredo Sound 52°24′ N, 129°26′ W **108**
Largepike Lake, *Can.* 60°5′ N, 111°15′ W **108**
Largo, *Fla., U.S.* 27°55′ N, 82°46′ W **105**
Largo, Cayo, island, *Cuba* 21°45′ N, 81°42′ W **116**
Laribosière, Lac, lake, *Can.* 53°38′ N, 72°24′ W **111**
Larimore, *N. Dak., U.S.* 47°52′ N, 97°39′ W **90**
Larioja, adm. division, *Sp.* 42°11′ N, 3°3′ W **164**
Lárisa, *Gr.* 39°38′ N, 22°24′ E **156**
Lark Pass 15°11′ S, 144°46′ E **230**
Larkana, *Pak.* 27°32′ N, 68°13′ E **186**
Larnaka, *Cyprus* 34°55′ N, 33°38′ E **194**
Larned, *Kans., U.S.* 38°10′ N, 99°6′ W **92**
Laro, *Burkina Faso* 11°17′ N, 2°51′ W **222**
Laro, *Cameroon* 8°15′ N, 12°16′ E **218**
Larose, *La., U.S.* 29°34′ N, 90°23′ W **103**
Lars Christensen Peak, *Antarctica* 68°47′ S, 90°5′ W **248**
Larsen Inlet 64°52′ S, 60°11′ W **248**
Larsen, Mount, peak, *Antarctica* 74°44′ S, 162°27′ E **248**
Larsen Sound 70°15′ N, 101°52′ W **106**
Larsmont, *Minn., U.S.* 46°58′ N, 91°46′ W **94**
Larvik, *Nor.* 59°3′ N, 10°2′ E **152**
Larzac, Causse du, *Fr.* 43°53′ N, 3°1′ E **165**
Las Alpujarras, *Sp.* 36°44′ N, 3°26′ W **164**
Las Animas, *Colo., U.S.* 38°3′ N, 103°14′ W **90**
Las Arrias, *Arg.* 30°22′ S, 63°38′ W **139**
Las Avispas, *Arg.* 29°51′ S, 61°18′ W **139**
Las Bonitas, *Venez.* 7°48′ N, 65°42′ W **136**
Las Breñas, *Arg.* 27°5′ S, 61°6′ W **139**
Las Cabezas de San Juan, *Sp.* 36°58′ N, 5°57′ W **164**
Las Cruces, *Mex.* 29°25′ N, 107°23′ W **92**
Las Cruces, *N. Mex., U.S.* 32°17′ N, 106°48′ W **112**
Las Esperanzas, *Mex.* 27°44′ N, 101°21′ W **92**
Las Flores, *Arg.* 36°2′ S, 59°9′ W **139**
Las Garzas, *Arg.* 28°49′ S, 59°32′ W **139**
Las Heras, *Arg.* 46°31′ S, 68°55′ W **134**
Las Herreras, *Mex.* 25°7′ N, 105°30′ W **114**
Las Juntas, *Col.* 2°4′ N, 72°14′ W **136**
Las Lajitas, *Venez.* 6°54′ N, 65°42′ W **136**
Las Lomitas, *Arg.* 24°43′ S, 60°36′ W **132**
Las Mercedes, *Venez.* 9°6′ N, 66°24′ W **136**
Las Minas, peak, *Hond.* 14°32′ N, 88°44′ W **115**
Las Palmas, *Sp.* 28°4′ N, 15°29′ W **214**
Las Palmeras, *Arg.* 30°35′ S, 61°39′ W **139**
Las Peñas, *Mex.* 18°3′ N, 102°30′ W **114**
Las Piedras, *Bol.* 11°2′ S, 66°12′ W **130**
Las Piedras, *Uru.* 34°42′ S, 56°12′ W **139**
Las Plumas, *Arg.* 43°39′ S, 67°16′ W **134**
Las Tablas, *Pan.* 7°47′ N, 80°17′ W **115**
Las Tinajas, *Arg.* 27°30′ S, 62°51′ W **139**
Las Toscas, *Arg.* 28°20′ S, 59°16′ W **139**
Las Tres Vírgenes, Volcán, peak, *Mex.* 27°26′ N, 112°43′ W **112**
Las Trincheras, *Mex.* 30°21′ N, 111°33′ W **92**
Las Tunas, *Cuba* 20°57′ N, 76°59′ W **115**
Las Tunas, island, *Cuba* 20°23′ N, 77°42′ W **116**
Las Varas, *Mex.* 28°7′ N, 105°21′ W **92**
Las Varas, *Mex.* 29°28′ N, 108°2′ W **92**
Las Varas, *Mex.* 21°11′ N, 105°10′ W **114**
Las Varillas, *Arg.* 31°54′ S, 62°43′ W **139**
Las Vegas, *Nev., U.S.* 36°9′ N, 115°10′ W **101**
Las Vegas, *N. Mex., U.S.* 35°35′ N, 105°13′ W **92**
Las Vegas Valley, *Nev., U.S.* 36°21′ N, 115°27′ W **101**
Las Vigas, *Mex.* 19°36′ N, 97°6′ W **114**
Las Yaras, *Peru* 17°54′ S, 70°33′ W **137**
Las Zorras, Punta, *Peru* 10°32′ S, 79°30′ W **130**
Lasalle, *Can.* 45°25′ N, 73°39′ W **94**
Lascano, *Uru.* 33°42′ S, 54°13′ W **139**
Lasengmiao, *China* 39°19′ N, 106°54′ E **198**
Lashburn, *Can.* 53°7′ N, 109°36′ W **108**
Lāsh-e Joveyn, *Afghan.* 31°40′ N, 61°42′ E **186**
Lashio, *Myanmar* 22°51′ N, 97°42′ E **190**
Lashkar, *India* 26°10′ N, 78°7′ E **197**
Lashkar Gah (Bost), *Afghan.* 31°35′ N, 64°22′ E **186**
Lasia, island, *Indonesia* 2°12′ N, 96°36′ E **196**
Lāsjerd, *Iran* 35°22′ N, 53°0′ E **180**
Łaskarzew, *Pol.* 51°46′ N, 21°38′ E **152**
Laško, *Slov.* 46°9′ N, 15°14′ E **156**
Laskowice, *Pol.* 53°29′ N, 18°26′ E **152**
Läsna, *Est.* 59°25′ N, 25°53′ E **166**
Lassen Peak, *Calif., U.S.* 40°28′ N, 121°36′ W **90**
L'Assomption, *Can.* 45°49′ N, 73°27′ W **94**
Last Chance Range, *Calif., U.S.* 37°9′ N, 117°46′ W **101**
Last Mountain Lake, *Can.* 51°17′ N, 107°2′ W **80**
Last Mountain, peak, *Can.* 60°45′ N, 126°47′ W **108**
Lastoursville, *Gabon* 0°52′ N, 12°39′ E **218**
Lastovo, *Croatia* 42°45′ N, 16°53′ E **168**
Lastovski Kanal 42°45′ N, 16°39′ E **168**
Latady Island, *Antarctica* 70°55′ S, 81°57′ W **248**
Latakia see Al Lādhiqīyah, *Syr.* 35°31′ N, 35°47′ E **194**
Latehar, *India* 23°45′ N, 84°31′ E **197**
Latexo, *Tex., U.S.* 31°22′ N, 95°29′ W **103**
Latham Island, *Tanzania* 7°9′ S, 40°1′ E **224**
Lathrop, *Calif., U.S.* 37°49′ N, 121°17′ W **100**
Latina, *It.* 41°28′ N, 12°52′ E **156**
Latisana, *It.* 45°46′ N, 12°59′ E **167**
Lato, ruin(s), *Gr.* 35°9′ N, 25°32′ E **156**
Laton, *Calif., U.S.* 36°26′ N, 119°43′ W **100**
Latouma, spring, *Niger* 22°12′ N, 14°47′ E **216**
Latrobe, Mount, peak, *Austral.* 39°2′ S, 146°10′ E **230**
Latta, *S.C., U.S.* 34°19′ N, 79°27′ W **96**
Latur, *India* 18°23′ N, 76°33′ E **188**
Latvia 56°59′ N, 25°20′ E **166**
Latvozero, *Russ.* 64°49′ N, 29°54′ E **152**
Lau, *Nig.* 9°10′ N, 11°18′ E **222**
Lau, *Sudan* 6°44′ N, 30°25′ E **224**
Lau Group, islands, *South Pacific Ocean* 16°60′ S, 178°20′ W **238**
Lau Ridge, *South Pacific Ocean* 27°20′ S, 178°35′ W **252**
Lauca National Park, *Chile* 18°11′ S, 69°43′ W **137**
Lauca, river, *Bol.* 18°29′ S, 68°50′ W **137**
Laudal, *Nor.* 58°14′ N, 7°28′ E **152**
Lauderdale, *Miss., U.S.* 32°28′ N, 88°32′ W **103**
Lauderdale Lakes, *Fla., U.S.* 26°10′ N, 80°12′ W **105**
Ļaudona, *Latv.* 56°43′ N, 26°10′ E **166**
Lauenburg, *Ger.* 53°22′ N, 10°34′ E **152**
Lauenförde, *Ger.* 51°39′ N, 9°24′ E **167**
Laufen, *Switz.* 47°25′ N, 7°29′ E **150**
Laughlan Islands, *Solomon Sea* 9°41′ S, 152°47′ E **192**
Laughlin, *Nev., U.S.* 35°11′ N, 114°36′ W **101**
Laughlin Peak, *N. Mex., U.S.* 36°38′ N, 104°17′ W **92**
Laujar de Andarax, *Sp.* 36°59′ N, 2°54′ W **164**
Laukuva, *Lith.* 55°37′ N, 22°15′ E **166**
Laurel, *Del., U.S.* 38°32′ N, 75°35′ W **94**
Laurel, *Ind., U.S.* 39°30′ N, 85°11′ W **102**
Laurel, *Miss., U.S.* 31°41′ N, 89°7′ W **103**
Laurel, *Mont., U.S.* 45°39′ N, 108°46′ W **90**
Laurel, *Nebr., U.S.* 42°24′ N, 97°6′ W **90**
Laurel Hill, *Pa., U.S.* 39°57′ N, 79°23′ W **94**
Laurens, *Iowa, U.S.* 42°50′ N, 94°53′ W **90**
Laurens, *S.C., U.S.* 34°29′ N, 82°2′ W **96**
Laurentian Fan, *North Atlantic Ocean* 41°51′ N, 56°17′ W **253**
Laurentian Valley, *Can.* 46°1′ N, 77°28′ W **110**
Lauria, *It.* 40°2′ N, 15°49′ E **156**
Laurie Island, *Antarctica* 61°15′ S, 44°38′ W **134**
Laurie River, *Can.* 56°14′ N, 101°1′ W **108**
Laurinburg, *N.C., U.S.* 34°45′ N, 79°29′ W **96**
Lauritsala, *Fin.* 61°2′ N, 28°14′ E **166**
Lausanne, *Switz.* 46°32′ N, 6°39′ E **150**
Laut, island, *Indonesia* 4°49′ N, 107°51′ E **196**
Laut, island, *Indonesia* 4°6′ S, 116°19′ E **192**
Laut Kecil, Kepulauan, islands, *Java Sea* 4°59′ S, 116°1′ E **192**
Lautaro, Volcán, peak, *Chile* 49°3′ S, 73°43′ W **134**
Lautem, *Timor-Leste* 8°30′ S, 126°56′ E **192**
Lauterbach, *Ger.* 50°38′ N, 9°24′ E **167**
Lava Beds National Monument, *Calif., U.S.* 41°28′ N, 122°46′ W **80**
Lava Cast Forest, site, *Oreg., U.S.* 43°47′ N, 121°22′ W **90**
Lava River Cave, site, *Oreg., U.S.* 43°52′ N, 121°27′ W **90**
Laval, *Can.* 45°36′ N, 73°46′ W **94**
Laval, *Fr.* 48°2′ N, 0°54′ E **143**
Lavalle, *Arg.* 29°2′ S, 59°12′ W **139**
Lavalleja, *Uru.* 31°5′ S, 57°2′ W **139**
Lavangen, *Nor.* 68°46′ N, 17°48′ E **152**
Lavassaare, *Est.* 58°30′ N, 24°20′ E **166**
Laveaga Peak, *Calif., U.S.* 36°52′ N, 121°14′ W **100**
Lavelanet, *Fr.* 42°55′ N, 1°49′ E **164**
Lavenham, *U.K.* 52°6′ N, 0°47′ E **162**
Laverne, *Okla., U.S.* 36°41′ N, 99°54′ W **92**
Lavia, *Fin.* 61°34′ N, 22°35′ E **166**
Lavina, *Mont., U.S.* 46°17′ N, 108°57′ W **90**
Lavis, *It.* 46°9′ N, 11°6′ E **167**
Lavoisier Island, *Antarctica* 66°11′ S, 67°28′ W **248**
Lavos, *Port.* 40°5′ N, 8°51′ W **150**
Lavras, *Braz.* 21°15′ S, 44°60′ W **138**
Lavras da Mangabeira, *Braz.* 6°44′ S, 38°59′ W **132**
Lavras do Sul, *Braz.* 30°51′ S, 53°55′ W **139**
Lavrentiya, *Russ.* 65°37′ N, 171°9′ W **98**
Lavushi Manda National Park, *Zambia* 12°46′ S, 30°57′ E **224**
Law Dome, *Antarctica* 67°27′ S, 114°17′ E **248**
Lawabiskau, river, *Can.* 51°21′ N, 81°25′ W **110**
Lawagamau Lake, *Can.* 49°47′ N, 80°49′ W **94**
Lawers, Ben, peak, *U.K.* 56°32′ N, 4°19′ W **150**
Lawford Lake, *Can.* 54°25′ N, 97°14′ W **108**
Lawnhill, *Can.* 53°25′ N, 131°60′ W **108**
Lawqah, *Saudi Arabia* 29°46′ N, 42°47′ E **180**
Lawra, *Ghana* 10°38′ N, 2°54′ W **222**
Lawrence, *Ind., U.S.* 39°49′ N, 86°1′ W **102**
Lawrence, *Kans., U.S.* 38°56′ N, 95°14′ W **94**
Lawrence, *Mass., U.S.* 42°42′ N, 71°11′ W **104**
Lawrence, *Miss., U.S.* 32°18′ N, 89°13′ W **103**
Lawrence, *N.Z.* 45°55′ S, 169°39′ E **240**
Lawrenceburg, *Ind., U.S.* 39°5′ N, 84°52′ W **94**
Lawrenceburg, *Tenn., U.S.* 35°14′ N, 87°19′ W **96**
Lawrenceville, *Ill., U.S.* 38°43′ N, 87°41′ W **102**
Lawyet el Lagâma, spring, *Egypt* 30°47′ N, 33°26′ E **194**
Laxå, *Nor.* 58°58′ N, 14°36′ E **152**
Laxong Co, lake, *China* 34°18′ N, 84°18′ E **188**
Layda, *Russ.* 71°30′ N, 83°1′ E **173**
Laydasalma, *Russ.* 65°57′ N, 30°55′ E **152**
Laysan Island, *Hawai'i, U.S.* 25°26′ N, 171°52′ W **99**
Layshi, *Myanmar* 25°27′ N, 94°54′ E **188**
Laytamak, *Russ.* 58°26′ N, 67°26′ E **169**
Layton, *Utah, U.S.* 41°3′ N, 111°57′ W **90**
Lazarev, *Russ.* 52°13′ N, 141°17′ E **238**
Lazareva, *Russ.* 57°36′ N, 107°47′ E **173**
Lazarevac, *Serb. and Mont.* 44°23′ N, 20°15′ E **168**
Lazarevskoye, *Russ.* 43°56′ N, 39°18′ E **158**
Lázaro Cárdenas, *Mex.* 18°55′ N, 88°16′ W **115**
Lázaro Cárdenas, *Mex.* 17°59′ N, 102°13′ W **114**
Lázaro Cardenas, Presa, lake, *Mex.* 25°31′ N, 106°28′ W **80**
Lazdijai, *Lith.* 54°14′ N, 23°30′ E **166**
Lazio, adm. division, *It.* 41°57′ N, 12°5′ E **156**
Lbera, Serra de l', *Sp.* 42°23′ N, 2°32′ E **164**
Le Barcarès, *Fr.* 42°47′ N, 3°0′ E **164**
Le Bic, *Can.* 48°21′ N, 68°42′ W **94**
Le Bugue, *Fr.* 44°55′ N, 0°55′ E **150**
Le Cateau, *Fr.* 50°5′ N, 3°33′ E **163**
Le Catelet, *Fr.* 49°59′ N, 3°15′ E **163**
Le Châtelet-en-Brie, *Fr.* 48°29′ N, 2°47′ E **163**
Le Chesne, *Fr.* 49°31′ N, 4°46′ E **163**
Le Cocq, Lac, lake, *Can.* 52°16′ N, 68°32′ W **111**
Le Conquet, *Fr.* 48°21′ N, 4°47′ W **150**
Le Crotoy, *Fr.* 50°13′ N, 1°39′ E **163**
Le Gros Cap, *Can.* 47°8′ N, 62°50′ W **111**
Le Guelta, *Alg.* 36°20′ N, 0°50′ E **164**
Le Havre, *Fr.* 49°29′ N, 0°6′ E **150**
Le Madonie, *It.* 37°46′ N, 13°33′ E **156**
Le Mans, *Fr.* 48°0′ N, 0°11′ E **150**
Le Mars, *Iowa, U.S.* 42°46′ N, 96°11′ W **94**
Le Mont-Saint-Michel, *Fr.* 48°37′ N, 1°31′ W **150**
Le Moyen, *La., U.S.* 30°46′ N, 92°3′ W **103**
Le Perthus, *Fr.* 42°28′ N, 2°51′ E **164**
Le Petit-Quevilly, *Fr.* 49°24′ N, 1°2′ E **163**
Le Puy, *Fr.* 45°2′ N, 3°53′ E **150**
Le Quesnoy, *Fr.* 50°14′ N, 3°38′ E **163**
Le Rageois, Lac, lake, *Can.* 53°16′ N, 69°31′ W **111**
Le Roy, *Ill., U.S.* 40°20′ N, 88°46′ W **102**
Le Roy, *Mich., U.S.* 44°2′ N, 85°27′ W **102**
Le Roy, *N.Y., U.S.* 42°58′ N, 77°60′ W **94**
Le Thuy, *Vietnam* 17°14′ N, 106°52′ E **202**
Le Touquet-Paris-Plage, *Fr.* 50°31′ N, 1°35′ E **163**
Le Tréport, *Fr.* 50°3′ N, 1°21′ E **163**
Le Veneur, Île, *Can.* 51°36′ N, 74°11′ W **110**
Le Verdon-sur-Mer, *Fr.* 45°32′ N, 1°6′ W **150**
Le Vigan, *Fr.* 43°59′ N, 3°34′ E **150**
Leach, *Cambodia* 12°20′ N, 103°44′ E **202**
Leach Lake Mountain, peak, *Calif., U.S.* 39°54′ N, 123°10′ W **90**
Lead, *S. Dak., U.S.* 44°20′ N, 103°47′ W **82**
Lead Mountain, peak, *Me., U.S.* 44°51′ N, 68°12′ W **94**
Leadenham, *U.K.* 53°3′ N, 0°36′ E **162**
Leader, *Can.* 50°53′ N, 109°32′ W **90**
Leadore, *Idaho, U.S.* 44°39′ N, 113°22′ W **90**
Leadville, *Colo., U.S.* 39°14′ N, 106°17′ W **90**
Leaf Rapids, *Can.* 56°28′ N, 100°3′ W **108**
Leaf, river, *Miss., U.S.* 31°17′ N, 89°14′ W **103**
League, Slieve, peak, *Ire.* 54°38′ N, 8°49′ W **150**
Leakesville, *Miss., U.S.* 31°7′ N, 88°33′ W **103**
Leakey, *Tex., U.S.* 29°42′ N, 99°46′ W **92**
Lealui, *Zambia* 15°13′ S, 23°2′ E **220**
Leamington, *Can.* 42°3′ N, 82°36′ W **102**
Leamington, *U.K.* 52°17′ N, 1°33′ W **162**
Leandro N. Alem, *Arg.* 27°36′ S, 55°20′ W **139**
Leaota, peak, *Rom.* 45°18′ N, 25°13′ E **156**
Learned, *Miss., U.S.* 32°10′ N, 90°34′ W **103**
Leatherman Peak, *Idaho, U.S.* 44°4′ N, 113°48′ W **90**
Leavenworth, *Kans., U.S.* 39°17′ N, 94°56′ W **94**
Leavitt Bay 57°10′ N, 107°38′ W **108**
Leavitt Peak, *Calif., U.S.* 38°16′ N, 119°42′ W **100**
Łeba, *Pol.* 54°45′ N, 17°34′ E **152**
Lebach, *Ger.* 49°25′ N, 6°54′ E **163**
Lebak, *Philippines* 6°33′ N, 124°3′ E **203**
Leban, *Wash., U.S.* 46°33′ N, 123°33′ W **100**
Lebane, *Serb. and Mont.* 42°55′ N, 21°44′ E **168**

Lebango, Congo 0°15′ N, 14°51′ E 218
Lebanon, Ind., U.S. 40°2′ N, 86°28′ W 102
Lebanon, Kans., U.S. 39°48′ N, 98°33′ W 90
Lebanon, Ky., U.S. 37°34′ N, 85°15′ W 96
Lebanon, Leb. 34°27′ N, 36°5′ E 194
Lebanon 34°0′ N, 35°51′ E 194
Lebanon, Mo., U.S. 37°40′ N, 92°40′ W 96
Lebanon, N.H., U.S. 43°38′ N, 72°15′ W 104
Lebanon, Ohio, U.S. 39°25′ N, 84°12′ W 102
Lebanon, Oreg., U.S. 44°31′ N, 122°55′ W 90
Lebanon, Tenn., U.S. 36°11′ N, 86°18′ W 82
Lebec, Calif., U.S. 34°50′ N, 118°53′ W 101
Lebed', Russ. 62°1′ N, 89°15′ E 169
Lebedyan', Russ. 52°59′ N, 39°2′ E 154
Lebedyn, Ukr. 50°34′ N, 34°26′ E 158
Leben, ruin(s), Gr. 34°55′ N, 24°49′ E 156
Lebo, Dem. Rep. of the Congo 4°28′ N, 23°55′ E 218
Lebombo Mountains, S. Af. 24°10′ S, 31°21′ E 227
Lebon Régis, Braz. 26°56′ S, 50°45′ W 139
Lebork, Pol. 54°31′ N, 17°45′ E 152
Lebowakgomo, S. Af. 24°12′ S, 29°31′ E 227
Lebrija, Sp. 36°55′ N, 6°5′ W 164
Lebu, Chile 37°39′ S, 73°40′ W 134
Lecce, It. 40°20′ N, 18°10′ E 156
Lecco, It. 45°51′ N, 9°23′ E 167
Lece, Serb. and Mont. 42°53′ N, 21°32′ E 168
Lechang, China 25°8′ N, 113°23′ E 198
Lecompte, La., U.S. 31°4′ N, 92°25′ W 103
Léconi, Gabon 1°37′ S, 14°15′ E 218
Léconi, river, Gabon 1°5′ S, 13°17′ E 218
Ledaña, Sp. 39°21′ N, 1°43′ W 164
Ledbury, U.K. 52°2′ N, 2°26′ W 162
Ledo, India 27°19′ N, 95°48′ E 188
Ledo, Indonesia 1°3′ N, 109°34′ E 196
Ledo, Cabo, Angola 9°46′ S, 12°47′ E 218
Ledong, China 18°41′ N, 109°6′ E 198
Leduc, Can. 53°15′ N, 113°33′ W 108
Lee, Mass., U.S. 42°18′ N, 73°15′ W 104
Lee, Nev., U.S. 40°34′ N, 115°36′ W 90
Leech Lake, Minn., U.S. 47°9′ N, 94°56′ W 90
Leedey, Okla., U.S. 35°50′ N, 99°21′ W 92
Leeds, Ala., U.S. 33°32′ N, 86°33′ W 96
Leeds, N. Dak., U.S. 48°16′ N, 99°28′ W 90
Leeds, U.K. 53°48′ N, 1°33′ W 162
Leeds, Utah, U.S. 37°13′ N, 113°21′ W 92
Leek, Neth. 53°10′ N, 6°23′ E 163
Leek, U.K. 53°6′ N, 2°2′ W 162
Leek Spring Hill, peak, Calif., U.S. 38°36′ N, 120°22′ W 90
Leer, Ger. 53°13′ N, 7°27′ E 163
Leesburg, Fla., U.S. 28°48′ N, 81°54′ W 105
Leesburg, Ohio, U.S. 39°20′ N, 83°33′ W 102
Leesburg, Va., U.S. 39°6′ N, 77°34′ W 94
Leeste, Ger. 52°59′ N, 8°48′ E 163
Leesville, La., U.S. 31°7′ N, 93°17′ W 103
Leesville, S.C., U.S. 33°54′ N, 81°31′ W 96
Leeuwarden, Neth. 53°11′ N, 5°46′ E 163
Leeuwin, Cape, Austral. 34°51′ S, 113°51′ E 230
Leeville, La., U.S. 29°15′ N, 90°13′ W 103
Leeward Islands, Caribbean Sea 15°40′ N, 61°42′ W 116
Léfini Faunal Reserve, Congo 2°51′ S, 15°5′ E 206
Lefka 35°6′ N, 32°51′ E 194
Lefká Óri, Gr. 35°15′ N, 23°47′ E 156
Lefkonoiko 35°15′ N, 33°43′ E 194
Lefkoşa see Lefkosia, Cyprus 35°9′ N, 33°18′ E 194
Lefkosia (Nicosia, Lefkoşa), Cyprus 35°9′ N, 33°18′ E 194
Leftrook Lake, Can. 56°2′ N, 99°9′ W 108
Legal, Can. 53°56′ N, 113°35′ W 108
Légaré, Lac, lake, Can. 46°56′ N, 74°25′ W 110
Legat, Mauritania 16°45′ N, 14°52′ W 222
Legazpi, Philippines 13°8′ N, 123°43′ E 203
Legden, Ger. 52°1′ N, 7°6′ E 167
Legges Tor, peak, Austral. 41°34′ S, 147°31′ E 230
Leggett, Tex., U.S. 30°48′ N, 94°52′ W 103
Leghorn see Livorno, It. 43°33′ N, 10°19′ E 156
Legnano, It. 45°35′ N, 8°53′ E 167
Legnica, Pol. 51°12′ N, 16°9′ E 152
Leh, India 34°9′ N, 77°33′ E 190
Lehi, Utah, U.S. 40°23′ N, 111°51′ W 90
Lehigh Acres, Fla., U.S. 26°36′ N, 81°38′ W 105
Lehliu, Rom. 44°29′ N, 26°48′ E 158
Lehman Caves, site, Nev., U.S. 39°0′ N, 114°18′ W 90
Lehr, N. Dak., U.S. 46°16′ N, 99°23′ W 90
Lehtimäki, Fin. 62°45′ N, 23°51′ E 154
Lehututu, Botswana 23°57′ S, 21°52′ E 227
Leiah, Pak. 30°54′ N, 70°59′ E 186
Leicester, Mass., U.S. 42°14′ N, 71°55′ W 104
Leicester, U.K. 52°37′ N, 1°8′ W 162
Leiden, Neth. 52°9′ N, 4°29′ E 163
Leie, river, Belg. 50°57′ N, 3°24′ E 163
Leigh, N.Z. 36°19′ S, 174°47′ E 240
Leigh, U.K. 53°30′ N, 2°31′ W 162
Leighton Buzzard, U.K. 51°55′ N, 0°39′ E 162
Leikanger, Nor. 61°11′ N, 6°46′ E 152
Leiktho, Myanmar 19°14′ N, 96°33′ E 202
Leippe, Ger. 51°24′ N, 14°4′ E 152
Leipsic, Ohio, U.S. 41°5′ N, 83°59′ W 102
Leipzig, Ger. 51°19′ N, 12°22′ E 152
Leirbotn, Nor. 70°6′ N, 23°23′ E 152
Leiria, Port. 39°44′ N, 8°50′ W 150
Leiria, adm. division, Port. 39°53′ N, 8°54′ W 150
Leirpollen, Nor. 70°25′ N, 28°28′ E 152
Leishan, China 26°24′ N, 108°0′ E 198
Leisler, Mount, peak, Austral. 23°21′ S, 129°4′ E 230
Leismer, Can. 55°44′ N, 111°3′ W 108
Leiston, U.K. 52°12′ N, 1°34′ E 163
Leitchfield, Ky., U.S. 37°28′ N, 86°18′ W 96
Leitza, Sp. 43°4′ N, 1°55′ W 164
Leivonmäki, Fin. 61°54′ N, 26°4′ E 166
Leiway, Myanmar 19°38′ N, 96°4′ E 202
Leiyang, China 26°28′ N, 112°51′ E 198
Leizhou Wan 20°35′ N, 110°18′ E 198
Leka, Nor. 65°4′ N, 11°42′ E 152
Lekatero, Dem. Rep. of the Congo 0°41′ N, 23°57′ E 224
Lekbibaj, Alban. 42°18′ N, 19°55′ E 168
Lekemt see Nek'emtē, Eth. 9°2′ N, 36°33′ E 224
Lekhovskoye, Russ. 62°43′ N, 42°50′ E 154
Lekhwair, oil field, Oman 22°41′ N, 55°26′ E 182
Lekmartovskaya, Russ. 60°49′ N, 56°9′ E 154
Léko, Mali 13°36′ N, 9°3′ W 222
Lekshmozero, Russ. 61°46′ N, 38°5′ E 154
Leksula, Indonesia 3°46′ S, 126°30′ E 192
Lekunberri, Sp. 43°0′ N, 1°54′ W 164
Leland, Miss., U.S. 33°22′ N, 90°55′ W 103
Lel'chytsy, Belarus 51°45′ N, 28°22′ E 152
Lelić, Serb. and Mont. 44°13′ N, 19°49′ E 168
Lely Gebergte, Suriname 4°17′ N, 55°41′ W 130
Lelystad, Neth. 52°30′ N, 5°24′ E 163
Lema, Nig. 12°56′ N, 4°14′ E 222
Lembach, Fr. 48°59′ N, 7°47′ E 163
Lembé, Cameroon 4°16′ N, 12°19′ E 218
Lembeck, Ger. 51°45′ N, 6°59′ E 167
Lembeni, Tanzania 3°46′ S, 37°37′ E 224
Lemberg, Fr. 49°0′ N, 7°22′ E 163
Leme, Braz. 22°10′ S, 47°25′ W 138
Lemei Rock, peak, Wash., U.S. 46°0′ N, 121°49′ W 100
Lemesos (Limassol), Cyprus 34°40′ N, 33°1′ E 194
Lemhi Range, Idaho, U.S. 44°45′ N, 113°59′ W 90
Lemieux Islands, Davis Strait 63°50′ N, 63°57′ W 106
Lemitar, N. Mex., U.S. 34°10′ N, 106°55′ W 92
Lemmer, Neth. 52°51′ N, 5°42′ E 163
Lemmon, S. Dak., U.S. 45°54′ N, 102°9′ W 90
Lemmon, Mount, peak, Ariz., U.S. 32°25′ N, 110°51′ W 92
Lemoïlé, Mauritania 16°10′ N, 7°12′ W 222
Lemon Grove, Calif., U.S. 32°44′ N, 117°3′ W 101
Lemoncove, Calif., U.S. 36°23′ N, 119°2′ W 101
Lemont, Ill., U.S. 41°38′ N, 88°1′ W 102
Lemoore, Calif., U.S. 36°18′ N, 119°48′ W 100
Lempäälä, Fin. 61°18′ N, 23°44′ E 166
Lempster, N.H., U.S. 43°14′ N, 72°13′ W 104
Lemsid, Africa 26°31′ N, 13°49′ W 214
Lemtybozh, Russ. 63°51′ N, 57°2′ E 154
Lemva, river, Russ. 65°28′ N, 61°4′ E 154
Lemvig, Den. 56°32′ N, 8°17′ E 150
Lem'yu, Russ. 64°17′ N, 54°59′ E 154
Lem'yu, river, Russ. 64°15′ N, 55°12′ E 154
Lena, Ill., U.S. 42°22′ N, 89°49′ W 102
Lena, La., U.S. 31°26′ N, 92°47′ W 103
Lena, Miss., U.S. 32°34′ N, 89°37′ W 103
Lena, Mount, peak, Utah, U.S. 40°45′ N, 109°29′ W 90
Lena, river, Russ. 69°16′ N, 124°52′ E 172
Lena Tablemount, Indian Ocean 53°10′ S, 44°34′ E 255
Lenart, Slov. 46°35′ N, 15°50′ E 168
Lençóis, Braz. 12°34′ S, 41°24′ W 132
Lençóis Maranhenses National Park, Braz. 2°37′ S, 43°24′ W 122
Lendery, Russ. 63°24′ N, 31°12′ E 152
Lenger, Kaz. 42°10′ N, 69°50′ E 197
Lengerich, Ger. 52°11′ N, 7°52′ E 163
Lenghu, China 38°48′ N, 93°23′ E 188
Lengua de Vaca, Punta, Chile 30°20′ S, 73°37′ W 134
Lengwe National Park, Malawi 16°30′ S, 33°58′ E 224
Lengyeltóti, Hung. 46°39′ N, 17°38′ E 168
Lenhovda, Nor. 56°59′ N, 15°14′ E 152
Lenin Peak, Kyrg. 39°21′ N, 72°46′ E 197
Leningrad see Sankt-Peterburg, Russ. 59°55′ N, 30°17′ E 166
Leningradskaya, Russ. 46°21′ N, 39°23′ E 156
Leningradskiy, Russ. 69°19′ N, 178°23′ E 98
Lenīngradskoe, Kaz. 53°33′ N, 71°31′ E 184
Lenino, Belarus 53°2′ N, 27°13′ E 152
Leninogorsk, Russ. 54°37′ N, 52°32′ E 154
Lenīnogorsk see Ridder, Kaz. 50°21′ N, 83°32′ E 184
Leninpol', Kyrg. 42°28′ N, 71°58′ E 197
Leninsk, Russ. 48°42′ N, 45°12′ E 158
Leninsk Kuznetskiy, Russ. 54°39′ N, 86°18′ E 184
Leninsk see Baykonur, Kaz. 45°50′ N, 63°18′ E 173
Lenīnskīy, Kaz. 52°14′ N, 76°46′ E 184
Leninskiy, Russ. 56°32′ N, 46°3′ E 154
Lenīnskoe, Kaz. 49°5′ N, 49°59′ E 158
Lenīnskoe, Kaz. 50°45′ N, 57°53′ E 158
Leninskoye, Russ. 58°18′ N, 47°7′ E 154
Lenk, Switz. 46°27′ N, 7°28′ E 167
Lennox, S. Dak., U.S. 43°19′ N, 96°54′ W 94
Lenoir, N.C., U.S. 35°54′ N, 81°33′ W 96
Lenoir City, Tenn., U.S. 35°48′ N, 84°16′ W 96
Lenora, Kans., U.S. 39°37′ N, 99°60′ W 90
Lenox, Mass., U.S. 42°21′ N, 73°18′ W 104
Lenox Dale, Mass., U.S. 42°19′ N, 73°16′ W 104
Lens, Fr. 50°25′ N, 2°49′ E 163
Lensk, Russ. 60°44′ N, 114°42′ E 160
Lenskoye, Russ. 58°10′ N, 63°7′ E 154
Lentekhi, Ga. 42°46′ N, 42°43′ E 195
Lenti, Hung. 46°37′ N, 16°32′ E 168
Lentiira, Fin. 64°22′ N, 29°47′ E 152
Lentini, It. 37°16′ N, 15°3′ E 216
Lentvaris, Lith. 54°38′ N, 25°3′ E 166
Lenwood, Calif., U.S. 34°52′ N, 117°8′ W 101
Léo, Burkina Faso 11°5′ N, 2°7′ W 222
Leo, Ind., U.S. 41°13′ N, 85°1′ W 102
Leoben, Aust. 47°22′ N, 15°6′ E 156
Leocadio Paz, Arg. 26°9′ S, 65°19′ W 132
Leola, S. Dak., U.S. 45°42′ N, 98°58′ W 90
Leominster, Mass., U.S. 42°31′ N, 71°46′ W 104
Leominster, U.K. 52°13′ N, 2°44′ W 162
Leon, Iowa, U.S. 40°43′ N, 93°45′ W 94
León, Mex. 21°5′ N, 101°43′ W 112
León, Nicar. 12°25′ N, 86°53′ W 115
León, Sp. 42°36′ N, 5°35′ W 150
León, Sp. 42°34′ N, 5°37′ W 214
León, Cerro, peak, Parag. 20°21′ S, 60°29′ W 132
León, Montes de, Sp. 42°22′ N, 6°30′ W 150
León, Punta, Arg. 50°36′ S, 68°56′ W 134
Leon, river, Tex., U.S. 31°36′ N, 97°52′ W 112
Leona, oil field, Venez. 8°57′ N, 63°57′ W 116
Leonard, Tex., U.S. 33°22′ N, 96°15′ W 96
Leonardville, Namibia 23°31′ S, 18°43′ E 227
Leonarisso 35°28′ N, 34°8′ E 194
Leonding, Aust. 48°16′ N, 14°14′ E 152
Leones, Isla, island, Pan. 7°38′ N, 81°35′ W 115
Leopoldina, Braz. 21°33′ S, 42°40′ W 138
Leopoldo de Bulhões, Braz. 16°39′ S, 48°47′ W 138
Leopoldsburg, Belg. 51°7′ N, 5°16′ E 167
Léopoldville see Kinshasa, Dem. Rep. of the Congo 4°24′ S, 15°6′ E 218
Leoti, Kans., U.S. 38°29′ N, 101°22′ W 90
Leoville, Can. 53°38′ N, 107°31′ W 108
Lepanto, Ark., U.S. 35°36′ N, 90°21′ W 96
Lephalale (Ellisras), S. Af. 23°40′ S, 27°42′ E 227
Lephepe, Botswana 23°19′ S, 25°47′ E 227
Leping, China 28°58′ N, 117°3′ E 198
L'Épiphanie, Can. 45°51′ N, 73°29′ W 94
Lepontine Alps, Switz. 46°17′ N, 8°24′ E 167
Lepperton, N.Z. 39°6′ S, 174°13′ E 240
Lepsény, Hung. 46°59′ N, 18°14′ E 168
Lepsi, Kaz. 46°14′ N, 78°54′ E 184
Lepsi, river, Kaz. 45°59′ N, 79°47′ E 184
Ler, Sudan 8°18′ N, 30°5′ E 224
Léraba, Côte d'Ivoire 10°7′ N, 5°6′ W 222
Léraba, river, Africa 9°55′ N, 5°6′ W 222
Lerdo de Tejada, Mex. 18°37′ N, 95°30′ W 114
Léré, Chad 9°38′ N, 14°14′ E 216
Léré, Mali 15°42′ N, 4°57′ W 222
Lerici, It. 44°4′ N, 9°55′ E 167
Lérida, Col. 0°8′ N, 70°44′ W 136
Lerik, Azerb. 38°45′ N, 48°23′ E 195
Lerín, Sp. 42°28′ N, 1°58′ W 164
Lérins, Îles de, islands, Mediterranean Sea 43°21′ N, 7°0′ E 165
Lerma, Sp. 42°0′ N, 3°45′ W 164
Lerma, river, Mex. 20°23′ N, 102°10′ W 114
Lerna, Ill., U.S. 39°24′ N, 88°17′ W 102
Lerna, ruin(s), Gr. 37°33′ N, 22°36′ E 156
Lérouville, Fr. 48°47′ N, 5°31′ E 163
Leroy, Ala., U.S. 31°30′ N, 87°59′ W 103
Leroy, Can. 52°1′ N, 104°45′ W 90
Leroy, Kans., U.S. 38°3′ N, 95°38′ W 94
Lerwick, U.K. 60°11′ N, 1°17′ W 143
Leş, Rom. 46°57′ N, 21°51′ E 168
Les, Sp. 42°48′ N, 0°41′ E 164
Les Andelys, Fr. 49°14′ N, 1°25′ E 163
Les Borges Blanques, Sp. 41°31′ N, 0°50′ E 164
Les Cabannes, Fr. 42°47′ N, 1°40′ E 164
Les Cayes, Haiti 18°14′ N, 73°46′ W 116
Les Escoumins, Can. 48°20′ N, 69°26′ W 94
Les Essarts, Fr. 46°46′ N, 1°15′ W 150
Les Landes, region, Fr. 43°32′ N, 1°26′ W 164
Les Sables-d'Olonne, Fr. 46°29′ N, 1°47′ W 150
Les Salines, Tun. 36°4′ N, 8°57′ E 156
L'Escala, Sp. 42°7′ N, 3°6′ E 164
Lescar, Fr. 43°19′ N, 0°26′ E 164
Leseru, Kenya 0°34′ N, 35°10′ E 224
Leshan, China 29°22′ N, 103°49′ E 190
Leshukonskoye, Russ. 64°53′ N, 45°37′ E 154
Lesja, Nor. 62°7′ N, 8°49′ E 152
Leskov Island, Antarctica 66°30′ S, 82°12′ E 248
Leskovac, Serb. and Mont. 42°59′ N, 21°58′ E 168
Leslie, Ark., U.S. 35°48′ N, 92°34′ W 96
Leslie, Mich., U.S. 42°26′ N, 84°26′ W 102
Leslie, S. Af. 26°25′ S, 28°54′ E 227
Lesmont, Fr. 48°25′ N, 4°24′ E 163
Leśnica, Serb. and Mont. 44°39′ N, 19°18′ E 168
Lesnoy, Russ. 59°50′ N, 52°8′ E 154
Lesnoye, Russ. 58°16′ N, 35°32′ E 154
Lesogorskiy, Russ. 61°1′ N, 28°56′ E 166
Lesosibirsk, Russ. 58°2′ N, 92°33′ E 160
Lesotho 29°27′ S, 28°14′ E 227
Lesovo, Bulg. 41°59′ N, 26°35′ E 158
Lesozavodsk, Russ. 45°27′ N, 133°20′ E 190
Lesozavodskiy, Russ. 66°43′ N, 32°52′ E 152
L'Espluga de Francolí, Sp. 41°23′ N, 1°3′ E 164
Lessebo, Nor. 56°45′ N, 15°15′ E 152
Lesser Antilles, North Atlantic Ocean 11°25′ N, 62°26′ W 116
Lesser Caucasus, Arm. 40°7′ N, 45°47′ E 180
Lesser Slave Lake, Can. 55°12′ N, 117°10′ W 106
Lesser Sunda Islands, Indian Ocean 10°13′ S, 121°5′ E 238
Lester, Wash., U.S. 47°12′ N, 121°30′ W 100
Lestijärvi, Fin. 63°30′ N, 24°36′ E 152
Lésvos, island, Gr. 38°50′ N, 26°5′ E 180
Leszno, Pol. 51°49′ N, 16°35′ E 152
Letaba, site, S. Af. 23°52′ S, 31°30′ E 227
Létavértes, Hung. 47°23′ N, 21°53′ E 168
Letchworth, U.K. 51°58′ N, 0°14′ E 162
Letea, Rom. 45°18′ N, 29°30′ E 156
Lethbridge, Can. 49°40′ N, 112°49′ W 82
Lethem, Guyana 3°19′ N, 59°48′ W 130
Leticia, Col. 4°8′ S, 69°59′ W 136
Leting, China 39°24′ N, 118°57′ E 198
Letka, Russ. 59°35′ N, 49°24′ E 154
Letlhakane, Botswana 21°25′ S, 25°34′ E 227
Letlhakeng, Botswana 24°6′ S, 25°2′ E 227
Letnerechenskiy, Russ. 64°19′ N, 34°12′ E 152
Letniy Navolok, Russ. 65°8′ N, 36°57′ E 154
Letnyaya Stavka, Russ. 45°22′ N, 43°16′ E 158
Letnyaya Zolotitsa, Russ. 64°58′ N, 36°42′ E 154
Letsôk-aw Kyun, island, Myanmar 11°20′ N, 98°15′ E 202
Lette, Ger. 51°54′ N, 7°11′ E 167
Letur, Sp. 38°22′ N, 2°5′ W 164
Léua, Angola 11°39′ S, 20°24′ E 220
Leucadia, Calif., U.S. 33°4′ N, 117°19′ W 101
Leucate, Fr. 42°54′ N, 3°0′ E 164
Leucayec, Isla, island, Chile 43°55′ S, 73°41′ W 134
Leuk, Switz. 46°20′ N, 7°37′ E 167
Leuna, Ger. 51°19′ N, 12°1′ E 152
Leuser, peak, Indonesia 3°45′ N, 97°5′ E 196
Leuven, Belg. 50°52′ N, 4°41′ E 167
Leuze, Belg. 50°35′ N, 3°37′ E 163
Lev Tolstoy, Russ. 53°11′ N, 39°23′ E 154
Levajok, Nor. 69°54′ N, 26°24′ E 152
Levanger, Nor. 63°44′ N, 11°17′ E 152
Levant, Kans., U.S. 39°23′ N, 101°13′ W 90
Levant, Île du, island, Fr. 43°3′ N, 6°30′ E 165
Levanto, It. 44°10′ N, 9°37′ E 167
Levaya Khetta, river, Russ. 64°9′ N, 71°21′ E 169
Levelland, Tex., U.S. 33°34′ N, 102°23′ W 92
Levens, Fr. 43°51′ N, 7°12′ E 167
Leveque, Cape, Austral. 16°19′ S, 121°59′ E 230
Lever, river, Braz. 11°3′ S, 50°17′ W 130
Leverkusen, Ger. 51°0′ N, 6°59′ E 167
Levico, It. 46°1′ N, 11°18′ E 167
Levídi, Gr. 37°41′ N, 22°17′ E 156
Levikha, Russ. 57°36′ N, 59°52′ E 154
Levin, N.Z. 40°39′ S, 175°17′ E 240
Lévis, Can. 46°47′ N, 71°11′ W 94
Levittown, Pa., U.S. 40°8′ N, 74°51′ W 94
Levokumskoye, Russ. 44°48′ N, 44°38′ E 158
Lévrier, Baie du 20°6′ N, 16°46′ W 222
Lėvuo, river, Lith. 55°49′ N, 24°28′ E 166
Lewellen, Nebr., U.S. 41°19′ N, 102°10′ W 90
Lewes, U.K. 50°52′ N, 2°120′ E 162
Lewis, Ind., U.S. 39°15′ N, 87°16′ W 102
Lewis, Kans., U.S. 37°56′ N, 99°16′ W 92
Lewis, N.Y., U.S. 44°16′ N, 73°35′ W 104
Lewis and Clark Range, Mont., U.S. 48°1′ N, 113°19′ W 90
Lewis Chain 80°2′ S, 29°5′ W 248
Lewis Hills, peak, Can. 48°48′ N, 58°35′ W 111
Lewis, Isle of, island, U.K. 58°31′ N, 8°23′ W 142
Lewis, Mount, peak, Nev., U.S. 40°23′ N, 116°57′ W 90
Lewis Pass, N.Z. 42°26′ S, 172°23′ E 240
Lewis, river, Wash., U.S. 46°7′ N, 121°50′ W 100
Lewiston, Me., U.S. 44°6′ N, 70°13′ W 104
Lewistown, Ill., U.S. 40°23′ N, 90°9′ W 102
Lewistown, Pa., U.S. 40°35′ N, 77°36′ W 94
Lewisville, Ark., U.S. 33°21′ N, 93°35′ W 96
Lexington, Ky., U.S. 38°1′ N, 84°30′ W 94
Lexington, Mich., U.S. 43°16′ N, 82°32′ W 102
Lexington, Miss., U.S. 33°5′ N, 90°3′ W 103
Lexington, Mo., U.S. 39°10′ N, 93°52′ W 94
Lexington, Nebr., U.S. 40°45′ N, 99°45′ W 92
Lexington, N.C., U.S. 35°48′ N, 80°16′ W 96
Lexington, Ohio, U.S. 40°40′ N, 82°35′ W 102
Lexington, Oreg., U.S. 45°26′ N, 119°41′ W 90
Lexington Park, Md., U.S. 38°14′ N, 76°28′ W 82
Leyburn, U.K. 54°18′ N, 1°50′ W 162
Leye, China 24°47′ N, 106°25′ E 198
Leyte, island, Philippines 10°16′ N, 125°21′ E 192
Leżajsk, Pol. 50°14′ N, 22°25′ E 152
Lezha, Russ. 58°56′ N, 40°49′ E 154
Lezhë, Alban. 41°47′ N, 19°39′ E 168
Lezhi, China 30°15′ N, 105°5′ E 198
Lezuza, Sp. 38°56′ N, 2°21′ W 164
L'gov, Russ. 51°41′ N, 35°16′ E 158
Lhari, China 30°50′ N, 93°22′ E 188
Lhasa, China 29°46′ N, 91°3′ E 197
Lhasa, river, China 29°20′ N, 90°55′ E 197
Lhazhong, China 32°2′ N, 86°46′ E 188
L'Hillil, Alg. 35°43′ N, 0°22′ E 150
Lhokseumawe, Indonesia 5°10′ N, 97°5′ E 196
Lhorong, China 30°44′ N, 95°51′ E 188
L'Hospitalet, Fr. 42°35′ N, 1°47′ E 164
L'Hospitalet de Llobregat, Sp. 41°21′ N, 2°6′ E 164
Lhozhag, China 28°19′ N, 90°50′ E 197
Lhünzê, China 28°26′ N, 92°27′ E 197
Lhünzhub, China 30°10′ N, 91°13′ E 197
Li, river, China 29°23′ N, 110°55′ E 198
Li Yubu, Sudan 5°23′ N, 27°17′ E 224
Lian, river, China 24°28′ N, 112°44′ E 198
Liancheng, China 25°40′ N, 116°44′ E 198
Liancourt, Fr. 49°19′ N, 2°28′ E 163
Lianga, Philippines 8°40′ N, 126°5′ E 203
Liangcheng, China 40°31′ N, 112°30′ E 198
Liangdang, China 33°54′ N, 106°19′ E 198
Liangjiangkou, China 42°38′ N, 128°2′ E 200
Liangping, China 30°37′ N, 107°47′ E 198
Liangshui, China 40°58′ N, 125°51′ E 200
Lianjiang, China 26°15′ N, 119°33′ E 198
Lianjiang, China 21°36′ N, 110°14′ E 198
Lianping, China 24°21′ N, 114°27′ E 198
Lianshan, China 24°31′ N, 112°6′ E 198
Lianxian, China 24°45′ N, 112°24′ E 198
Lianyun, China 34°41′ N, 119°23′ E 198
Lianyungang (Xinpu), China 34°38′ N, 119°14′ E 198
Liao, river, China 42°7′ N, 123°29′ E 200
Liaocheng, China 36°25′ N, 115°53′ E 198
Liaodong Wan 40°21′ N, 120°30′ E 198
Liaoning, adm. division, China 41°19′ N, 123°22′ E 200
Liaoyang, China 41°17′ N, 123°10′ E 200
Liaoyuan, China 42°54′ N, 125°8′ E 200
Liaozhong, China 41°31′ N, 122°41′ E 200
Liard Island, Antarctica 66°36′ S, 67°58′ W 248
Liard River, Can. 59°24′ N, 126°6′ W 108
Liard, river, Can. 60°45′ N, 123°3′ W 106
Liathach, peak, U.K. 57°32′ N, 5°34′ W 150
Libanga, Dem. Rep. of the Congo 0°21′ N, 18°43′ E 218
Libby, Mont., U.S. 48°22′ N, 115°34′ W 90
Libby Dam, Mont., U.S. 48°8′ N, 115°34′ W 90
Libenge, Dem. Rep. of the Congo 3°35′ N, 18°41′ E 218
Liberal, Kans., U.S. 37°1′ N, 100°56′ W 92
Liberdade, river, Braz. 8°19′ S, 71°53′ W 130
Liberdade, river, Braz. 11°14′ S, 52°11′ W 130
Liberec, Czech Rep. 50°45′ N, 15°2′ E 152
Liberecký, adm. division, Czech Rep. 50°47′ N, 15°7′ E 152
Liberia, C.R. 10°38′ N, 85°27′ W 115
Liberia 6°38′ N, 10°19′ W 214
Libertad, Venez. 9°18′ N, 68°35′ W 136
Libertad, Venez. 8°20′ N, 69°37′ W 136
Libertador General Bernardo O'Higgins, adm. division, Chile 34°44′ S, 72°20′ W 134
Liberty, Ind., U.S. 39°37′ N, 84°56′ W 102
Liberty, Miss., U.S. 31°8′ N, 90°48′ W 103
Liberty, N.Y., U.S. 41°47′ N, 74°45′ W 94
Liberty, Tex., U.S. 30°2′ N, 94°47′ W 103
Libni, Gebel, peak, Egypt 30°43′ N, 33°48′ E 194
Libo, China 25°24′ N, 107°50′ E 198
Libode, S. Af. 31°34′ S, 29°1′ E 227
Liboi, Kenya 0°17′ N, 40°49′ E 224
Libourne, Fr. 44°55′ N, 0°14′ E 150
Libral Well, spring, Austral. 22°8′ S, 125°29′ E 230
Libreville, Gabon 0°20′ N, 9°18′ E 218
Libya 26°52′ N, 15°56′ E 216
Libyan Desert, Lib. 26°27′ N, 24°26′ E 180
Libyan Plateau, Egypt 30°0′ N, 25°33′ E 180
Licantén, Chile 34°58′ S, 72°1′ W 134
Lice, Turk. 38°27′ N, 40°39′ E 195
Lich, Ger. 50°31′ N, 8°49′ E 167
Lichfield, U.K. 52°40′ N, 1°50′ W 162
Lichinga, Mozambique 13°20′ S, 35°13′ E 224
Lichtenburg, S. Af. 26°11′ S, 26°8′ E 227
Lichuan, China 30°18′ N, 108°55′ E 198
Lichuan, China 27°22′ N, 116°51′ E 198
Licking, Mo., U.S. 37°29′ N, 91°51′ W 96
Licosa, Punta, It. 40°8′ N, 14°25′ E 156
Licungo, river, Mozambique 17°5′ S, 37°3′ E 224
Lida, Belarus 53°52′ N, 25°18′ E 166
Liddon Gulf 74°53′ N, 117°12′ W 106
Liden, Nor. 62°41′ N, 16°48′ E 152
Lidgerwood, N. Dak., U.S. 46°3′ N, 97°10′ W 90
Lidhult, Nor. 56°50′ N, 13°25′ E 152
Lidice, Czech Rep. 50°7′ N, 14°10′ E 152
Lidingö, Sw. 59°21′ N, 18°9′ E 166
Lidköping, Nor. 58°29′ N, 13°7′ E 152
Lido, It. 45°25′ N, 12°22′ E 167
Lido, Niger 12°51′ N, 3°36′ E 222
Lido di Jesolo, It. 45°30′ N, 12°38′ E 167
Liebig, Mount, peak, Austral. 23°21′ S, 131°16′ E 230
Liechtenstein 47°6′ N, 9°26′ E 156
Liège, Belg. 50°38′ N, 5°33′ E 167
Liège Island, Antarctica 64°7′ S, 61°45′ W 134
Liége, river, Can. 56°55′ N, 114°1′ W 108
Lieksa, Fin. 63°17′ N, 29°59′ E 152
Lielvārde, Latv. 56°42′ N, 24°51′ E 166
Liénart, Dem. Rep. of the Congo 3°0′ N, 25°36′ E 224
Lienz, Aust. 46°49′ N, 12°44′ E 167
Liepāja, Latv. 56°31′ N, 21°1′ E 166
Liepājas Ezers, lake, Latv. 56°25′ N, 20°37′ E 166
Liepna, Latv. 57°19′ N, 27°28′ E 166
Lier, Belg. 51°8′ N, 4°33′ E 167
Lierneux, Belg. 50°16′ N, 5°47′ E 167
Lieşti, Rom. 45°37′ N, 27°32′ E 156
Liétor, Sp. 38°32′ N, 1°57′ W 164
Liévin, Fr. 50°24′ N, 2°46′ E 163
Lifford, Ire. 54°49′ N, 7°31′ W 150
Liftāyā, Syr. 34°39′ N, 36°27′ E 194
Ligao, Philippines 13°14′ N, 123°31′ E 203
Līgatne, Latv. 57°10′ N, 25°1′ E 166
Lighthouse Point, Fla., U.S. 29°47′ N, 84°30′ W 96
Lighthouse Point, Fla., U.S. 26°16′ N, 80°6′ W 105
Ligneuville, Belg. 50°22′ N, 6°3′ E 167
Ligny-en-Barrois, Fr. 48°41′ N, 5°19′ E 163
Liguria, adm. division, It. 44°26′ N, 8°24′ E 167
Ligurian Sea 43°49′ N, 8°37′ E 167
Lihir Group, islands, South Pacific Ocean 2°55′ S, 152°47′ E 192
Lihula, Est. 58°41′ N, 23°47′ E 166
Lijeva Rijeka, Europe 42°38′ N, 19°29′ E 168
Likasi, Dem. Rep. of the Congo 10°60′ S, 26°44′ E 224
Likati, Dem. Rep. of the Congo 3°19′ N, 23°56′ E 224
Likati, river, Dem. Rep. of the Congo 3°23′ N, 22°32′ E 218
Likely, Can. 52°36′ N, 121°34′ W 108
Likely Mountain, peak, Calif., U.S. 41°8′ N, 120°40′ W 90
Likėnai, Lith. 56°12′ N, 24°37′ E 166
Likeo, Óros, peak, Gr. 37°26′ N, 21°53′ E 156
Likhoslavl', Russ. 57°5′ N, 35°30′ E 154
Likódimo, Óros, peak, Gr. 36°55′ N, 21°47′ E 156
Likoma Islands, Malawi 11°51′ S, 34°22′ E 224
Likoto, Dem. Rep. of the Congo 1°12′ S, 24°50′ E 224
Likwangoli, Sudan 6°59′ N, 33°2′ E 224
Lilbourn, Mo., U.S. 36°35′ N, 89°36′ W 94
L'Île-Rousse, Fr. 42°38′ N, 8°56′ E 156
Lilian, Point, peak, Austral. 27°43′ S, 125°51′ E 230
Liling, China 27°41′ N, 113°27′ E 198
Liljendal, Fin. 60°34′ N, 26°3′ E 166
Lille, Fr. 50°37′ N, 3°4′ E 163
Lillers, Fr. 50°34′ N, 2°28′ E 163
Lillesand, Nor. 58°15′ N, 8°21′ E 150
Lillhamra, Nor. 61°39′ N, 14°47′ E 152
Lillhärdal, Nor. 61°50′ N, 14°2′ E 152
Lillie, La., U.S. 32°55′ N, 92°40′ W 103
Lillooet, Can. 50°42′ N, 121°57′ W 108
Lillooet Lake, Can. 50°16′ N, 122°51′ W 108
Lilo Viejo, Arg. 26°56′ S, 62°58′ W 139
Lilongwe, Malawi 13°59′ S, 33°39′ E 224
Liloy, Philippines 8°8′ N, 122°40′ E 203
Lima, Arg. 34°3′ S, 59°10′ W 139
Lima, Mont., U.S. 44°38′ N, 112°36′ W 90
Lima, Ohio, U.S. 40°44′ N, 84°7′ W 102
Lima, Parag. 23°54′ S, 56°28′ W 132
Lima, Peru 12°9′ S, 77°12′ W 130
Lima, adm. division, Peru 11°45′ S, 77°10′ W 130
Lima Duarte, Braz. 21°52′ S, 43°51′ W 138
Lima, river, Port. 41°43′ N, 8°47′ W 150
Limal, Bol. 22°28′ S, 64°33′ W 137
Liman, Russ. 45°44′ N, 47°10′ E 158
Limas, Indonesia 0°13′ N, 104°31′ E 196
Limassol see Lemesos, Cyprus 34°40′ N, 33°1′ E 194
Limaumanis, Indonesia 1°37′ N, 109°19′ E 196
Limay Mahuida, Arg. 37°11′ S, 66°40′ W 134
Limbani, Peru 14°11′ S, 69°43′ W 137
Limbara, Monte, peak, It. 40°50′ N, 9°4′ E 156
Limbaži, Latv. 57°30′ N, 24°41′ E 166
Limbe, Cameroon 4°4′ N, 9°10′ E 222
Limbe, Malawi 15°59′ S, 35°4′ E 224
Limbourg, Belg. 50°37′ N, 5°56′ E 167
Limbung, Indonesia 0°13′ N, 109°48′ E 196
Limburg, Ger. 50°23′ N, 8°3′ E 167
Lime Village, Alas., U.S. 61°21′ N, 155°30′ W 98
Limedsforsen, Nor. 60°54′ N, 13°21′ E 152

Limeira, *Braz.* 22°34′ S, 47°26′ W 138
Limena, *It.* 45°29′ N, 11°49′ E 167
Limerick, *Can.* 49°38′ N, 106°16′ W 90
Limerick, *Me., U.S.* 43°41′ N, 70°48′ W 104
Limerick (Luimneach), *Ire.* 52°39′ N, 8°37′ W 150
Limestone, *Me., U.S.* 46°53′ N, 67°50′ W 82
Limestone Point, *Can.* 53°31′ N, 98°23′ W 108
Limestone, river, *Can.* 56°38′ N, 94°48′ W 108
Limington, *Me., U.S.* 43°43′ N, 70°43′ W 104
Liminka, *Fin.* 64°48′ N, 25°21′ E 152
Limmared, *Nor.* 57°32′ N, 13°21′ E 152
Límnos, island, *Gr.* 39°42′ N, 25°22′ E 180
Limoges, *Fr.* 45°50′ N, 1°15′ E 150
Limon, *Colo., U.S.* 39°16′ N, 103°41′ W 90
Limone Piemonte, *It.* 44°12′ N, 7°34′ E 167
Limoquije, *Bol.* 15°28′ S, 64°49′ W 137
Limousin, adm. division, *Fr.* 45°39′ N, 1°16′ E 165
Limousin, region, *Fr.* 45°39′ N, 1°5′ E 165
Limpias, *Sp.* 43°21′ N, 3°26′ W 164
Limpopo, adm. division, *S. Af.* 23°30′ S, 28°24′ E 227
Limpopo, river, *Africa* 22°10′ S, 29°16′ E 227
Līnah, *Saudi Arabia* 28°45′ N, 43°47′ E 180
Linakhamari, *Russ.* 69°38′ N, 31°20′ E 152
Lin'an, *China* 30°15′ N, 119°44′ E 198
Linares, *Mex.* 24°50′ N, 99°35′ W 114
Linares, *Sp.* 38°5′ N, 3°42′ W 214
Linares, *Sp.* 38°5′ N, 3°37′ W 164
Linaro, Capo, *It.* 41°57′ N, 11°18′ E 156
Linas, Monte, peak, *It.* 39°26′ N, 8°32′ E 156
Lincang, *China* 23°51′ N, 99°58′ E 202
Linchuan, *China* 27°58′ N, 116°18′ E 198
Linck Nunataks, *Antarctica* 83°20′ S, 104°39′ W 248
Lincoln, *Arg.* 34°53′ S, 61°30′ W 139
Lincoln, *Calif., U.S.* 38°53′ N, 121°19′ W 90
Lincoln, *Ill., U.S.* 40°8′ N, 89°22′ W 102
Lincoln, *Kans., U.S.* 39°1′ N, 98°10′ W 90
Lincoln, *Mich., U.S.* 44°40′ N, 83°26′ W 94
Lincoln, *Mo., U.S.* 40°8′ N, 89°22′ W 94
Lincoln, *Nebr., U.S.* 40°46′ N, 96°49′ W 90
Lincoln, *N.H., U.S.* 44°2′ N, 71°41′ W 104
Lincoln, *N. Mex., U.S.* 33°28′ N, 105°23′ W 92
Lincoln, *N.Z.* 43°40′ S, 172°28′ E 240
Lincoln, *S. Dak., U.S.* 40°39′ N, 97°21′ W 72
Lincoln, *U.K.* 53°13′ N, 0°33′ E 162
Lincoln, *Vt., U.S.* 44°6′ N, 72°60′ W 104
Lincoln Bay 83°25′ N, 56°35′ W 255
Lincoln Boyhood National Monument, *Ind., U.S.* 38°5′ N, 87°4′ W 96
Lincoln City, *Oreg., U.S.* 44°57′ N, 124°1′ W 90
Lincoln Heights, *U.K.* 53°24′ N, 0°40′ E 162
Lincoln Park, *Colo., U.S.* 38°25′ N, 105°13′ W 92
Lincoln Park, *Mich., U.S.* 42°14′ N, 83°11′ W 102
Lincoln Sea 81°13′ N, 60°27′ W 246
Lincoln's New Salem, site, *Ill., U.S.* 39°57′ N, 89°55′ W 102
Lincolnton, *Ga., U.S.* 33°46′ N, 82°29′ W 96
Lind, *Wash., U.S.* 46°58′ N, 118°37′ W 90
Linda, *Calif., U.S.* 39°7′ N, 121°35′ W 90
Lindale, *Tex., U.S.* 32°30′ N, 95°24′ W 103
Linde, river, *Russ.* 66°15′ N, 120°13′ E 160
Linden, *Ala., U.S.* 32°18′ N, 87°49′ W 103
Linden, *Calif., U.S.* 38°1′ N, 121°6′ W 100
Linden, *Guyana* 6°1′ N, 58°21′ W 130
Linden, *Ind., U.S.* 40°11′ N, 86°54′ W 102
Linden, *Mich., U.S.* 42°47′ N, 83°47′ W 102
Linden, *Tex., U.S.* 33°0′ N, 94°23′ W 103
Lindenhurst, *N.Y., U.S.* 40°40′ N, 73°22′ W 104
Lindenow Fjord 60°10′ N, 43°49′ W 106
Lindesberg, *Nor.* 59°35′ N, 15°14′ E 152
Lindesnes, *Nor.* 57°55′ N, 6°21′ E 150
Lindi, *Tanzania* 9°57′ S, 39°38′ E 224
Lindi, adm. division, *Tanzania* 9°36′ S, 37°48′ E 224
Lindi, river, *Dem. Rep. of the Congo* 0°23′ N, 28°1′ E 224
Lindian, *China* 47°11′ N, 124°54′ E 198
Lindley, *S. Af.* 27°56′ S, 27°52′ E 227
Lindsay, *Calif., U.S.* 36°12′ N, 119°6′ W 101
Lindsay, *Can.* 44°21′ N, 78°43′ W 94
Lindsay, *Mont., U.S.* 47°12′ N, 105°10′ W 90
Lindsay, *Okla., U.S.* 34°48′ N, 97°36′ W 92
Lindsborg, *Kans., U.S.* 38°33′ N, 97°41′ W 90
Lindsey Islands, *Amundsen Sea* 73°24′ S, 103°46′ W 248
Linevo, *Russ.* 54°29′ N, 83°25′ E 184
Linfen, *China* 36°6′ N, 111°35′ E 198
Lingao, *China* 19°56′ N, 109°40′ E 198
Lingayen, *Philippines* 15°59′ N, 120°12′ E 203
Lingbao, *China* 34°32′ N, 110°50′ E 198
Lingbi, *China* 33°33′ N, 117°31′ E 198
Lingbo, *Nor.* 61°2′ N, 16°39′ E 152
Lingchuan, *China* 25°31′ N, 110°21′ E 198
Lingen, *Ger.* 52°31′ N, 7°19′ E 163
Lingga, island, *Indonesia* 0°41′ N, 105°0′ E 192
Lingga, Kepulauan, islands, *South China Sea* 0°19′ N, 105°1′ E 196
Lingig, *Philippines* 8°5′ N, 126°24′ E 203
Lingle, *Wyo., U.S.* 42°8′ N, 104°21′ W 90
Lingomo, *Dem. Rep. of the Congo* 0°37′ N, 22°2′ E 218
Lingshan, *China* 22°25′ N, 109°14′ E 198
Lingshui, *China* 18°27′ N, 109°59′ E 198
Lingtai, *China* 35°4′ N, 107°33′ E 198
Linguère, *Senegal* 15°25′ N, 15°8′ W 222
Lingui, *China* 25°11′ N, 110°11′ E 198
Lingwu, *China* 38°6′ N, 106°18′ E 198
Lingxian, *China* 26°30′ N, 113°45′ E 198
Lingyuan, *China* 41°18′ N, 119°26′ E 198
Lingyun, *China* 24°16′ N, 106°33′ E 198
Linhai, *China* 28°49′ N, 121°11′ E 198
Linhares, *Braz.* 19°24′ S, 40°3′ W 138
Linhe, *China* 40°44′ N, 107°22′ E 198
Linjiang, *China* 41°48′ N, 126°55′ E 200
Linkmenys, *Lith.* 55°19′ N, 25°57′ E 166
Linköping, *Nor.* 58°23′ N, 15°35′ E 152
Linkuva, *Lith.* 56°4′ N, 23°57′ E 166
Linn, *Tex., U.S.* 26°34′ N, 98°7′ W 114
Linova, *Belarus* 52°27′ N, 24°30′ E 152
Linqing, *China* 36°50′ N, 115°43′ E 198
Linquan, *China* 33°4′ N, 115°15′ E 198
Linru, *China* 34°10′ N, 112°53′ E 198
Lins, *Braz.* 21°41′ S, 49°46′ W 138
Linsell, *Nor.* 62°8′ N, 13°53′ E 152
Linshui, *China* 30°20′ N, 106°54′ E 198
Lintang, *Malaysia* 5°20′ N, 118°28′ E 203
Linthal, *Switz.* 46°55′ N, 9°0′ E 167
Linton, *Ind., U.S.* 39°1′ N, 87°10′ W 102
Linton, *N. Dak., U.S.* 46°15′ N, 100°14′ W 90
Lintong, *China* 34°22′ N, 109°16′ E 198
Linwood, *Mich., U.S.* 43°44′ N, 83°58′ W 102
Linxi, *China* 39°44′ N, 118°29′ E 198
Linxi, *China* 43°36′ N, 118°2′ E 198
Linxia, *China* 35°29′ N, 103°1′ E 190
Linxian, *China* 37°57′ N, 110°53′ E 198
Linyi, *China* 35°3′ N, 118°20′ E 198
Linyi, *China* 37°8′ N, 116°52′ E 198
Linz, *Aust.* 48°16′ N, 14°18′ E 152
Linz, *Ger.* 50°33′ N, 7°17′ E 167
Lioma, *Mozambique* 15°12′ S, 36°49′ E 224
Lion, Golfe du 42°17′ N, 3°17′ E 142
Lion's Head, *Can.* 44°58′ N, 81°13′ W 94
Liot Point, *Can.* 73°12′ N, 128°57′ W 106
Liouesso, *Congo* 1°2′ N, 15°42′ E 218
Lipa, *Philippines* 13°57′ N, 121°9′ E 203
Lipari, Isole (Eolie), islands, *It.* 38°39′ N, 13°46′ E 156
Lipcani, *Mold.* 48°16′ N, 26°47′ E 152
Lipce, *Pol.* 51°53′ N, 19°57′ E 152
Lipetsk, *Russ.* 52°37′ N, 39°28′ E 154
Lipetsk, adm. division, *Russ.* 53°14′ N, 38°42′ E 154
Lípez, Cordillera de, *Bol.* 21°42′ S, 66°59′ W 132
Lipiany, *Pol.* 53°0′ N, 14°58′ E 152
Lipik, *Croatia* 45°25′ N, 17°9′ E 168
Liping, *China* 26°13′ N, 109°7′ E 198
Lipljan, *Europe* 42°31′ N, 21°8′ E 168
Lipnica, *Pol.* 53°59′ N, 17°25′ E 152
Lipník, *Czech Rep.* 49°31′ N, 17°35′ E 152
Lipnishki, *Belarus* 54°0′ N, 25°36′ E 166
Lipova, *Rom.* 46°5′ N, 21°43′ E 168
Lipovac, *Croatia* 45°3′ N, 19°4′ E 168
Lippe, river, *Ger.* 51°37′ N, 8°5′ E 167
Lippstadt, *Ger.* 51°39′ N, 8°21′ E 167
Lipscomb, *Tex., U.S.* 36°12′ N, 100°16′ W 92
Lipsí, *Gr.* 37°18′ N, 26°46′ E 156
Lipsko, *Pol.* 51°9′ N, 21°39′ E 152
Lipton, *Can.* 50°54′ N, 103°53′ W 90
Liptovský Mikuláš, *Slovakia* 49°4′ N, 19°39′ E 152
Lipu, *China* 24°30′ N, 110°23′ E 198
Lipu Lekh Pass, *China* 30°14′ N, 81°2′ E 197
Lipumba, *Tanzania* 10°51′ S, 35°3′ E 224
Lira, *Uganda* 2°13′ N, 32°54′ E 224
Liranga, *Congo* 0°41′ N, 17°30′ E 218
Lircay, *Peru* 13°1′ S, 74°43′ W 137
Liria, *Sudan* 4°36′ N, 32°4′ E 224
Lirik, oil field, *Indonesia* 0°13′ N, 102°8′ E 196
Lirik Ukul, oil field, *Indonesia* 5°296′ S, 101°48′ E 192
Lisa, *Europe* 43°9′ N, 19°33′ E 168
Lisakovsk, *Kaz.* 52°32′ N, 62°31′ E 184
Lisala, *Dem. Rep. of the Congo* 2°10′ N, 21°28′ E 218
Lisboa (Lisbon), *Port.* 38°42′ N, 9°17′ W 150
Lisbon, *Ill., U.S.* 41°28′ N, 88°30′ W 102
Lisbon, *La., U.S.* 32°47′ N, 92°53′ W 103
Lisbon, *Me., U.S.* 44°1′ N, 70°7′ W 104
Lisbon, *N. Dak., U.S.* 46°26′ N, 97°41′ W 90
Lisboa, adm. division, *Port.* 38°57′ N, 9°25′ W 150
Lisbon Falls, *Me., U.S.* 44°0′ N, 70°4′ W 104
Lisbon see Lisboa, *Port.* 38°42′ N, 9°17′ W 150
Lisburne, Cape, *Alas., U.S.* 69°21′ N, 163°16′ W 246
Lishu, *China* 43°22′ N, 124°20′ E 198
Lishui, *China* 28°29′ N, 119°54′ E 198
Lisieux, *Fr.* 49°8′ N, 0°14′ E 150
Lisino-Korpus, *Russ.* 59°25′ N, 30°41′ E 166
Lisitsa, river, *Russ.* 58°59′ N, 85°2′ E 169
Liski, *Rom.* 46°14′ N, 26°44′ E 156
Liski, *Russ.* 51°1′ N, 39°30′ E 158
L'Isle-Verte, *Can.* 47°59′ N, 69°21′ W 94
Lisman, *Ala., U.S.* 32°11′ N, 88°17′ W 103
Lisok, pass, *Ukr.* 48°47′ N, 23°8′ E 152
Lissa see Vis, island, *Croatia* 42°57′ N, 16°5′ E 168
Lister, Mount, peak, *Antarctica* 77°58′ S, 163°35′ E 248
Listerlandet, *Nor.* 55°55′ N, 14°45′ E 152
Listowel, *Can.* 43°43′ N, 80°57′ W 102
Lit, *Nor.* 63°19′ N, 14°47′ E 152
Litang, *China* 23°9′ N, 109°7′ E 198
Līţānī, river, *Leb.* 33°20′ N, 35°14′ E 194
Litani, river, *Suriname* 2°12′ N, 54°24′ W 130
Litberg, peak, *Ger.* 53°23′ N, 9°31′ E 150
Litchfield, *Conn., U.S.* 41°44′ N, 73°12′ W 104
Litchfield, *Ill., U.S.* 39°10′ N, 89°39′ W 102
Litchfield, *Mich., U.S.* 42°2′ N, 84°46′ W 102
Litchfield, *Minn., U.S.* 45°7′ N, 94°33′ W 90
Litchfield, *Mo., U.S.* 39°10′ N, 89°39′ W 94
Litchfield National Park, *Austral.* 13°22′ S, 130°32′ E 238
Liteni, *Rom.* 47°30′ N, 26°30′ E 156
Lithuania 55°20′ N, 23°34′ E 166
Litija, *Slov.* 46°3′ N, 14°49′ E 156
Little Abaco, island, *Bahamas* 26°52′ N, 77°44′ W 118
Little Abitibi Lake, *Can.* 49°21′ N, 81°12′ W 94
Little Abitibi, river, *Can.* 50°30′ N, 81°35′ W 94
Little America (historic), site, *Antarctica* 78°27′ S, 162°60′ W 248
Little Andaman, island, *India* 10°2′ N, 91°45′ E 188
Little Beaver, river, *Can.* 57°34′ N, 97°4′ W 108
Little Belt Mountains, *Mont., U.S.* 46°43′ N, 110°43′ W 90
Little Bighorn, river, *Mont., U.S.* 46°3′ N, 108°23′ W 80
Little Blue, river, *Nebr., U.S.* 40°31′ N, 98°31′ W 90
Little Buffalo, *Can.* 56°27′ N, 116°10′ W 108
Little Buffalo, river, *Can.* 60°48′ N, 113°36′ W 108
Little Cadotte, river, *Can.* 56°34′ N, 117°5′ W 108
Little Cayman, island, *Little Cayman* 19°23′ N, 80°33′ W 115
Little Creek Peak, *Utah, U.S.* 37°51′ N, 112°40′ W 92
Little Current, *Can.* 45°57′ N, 81°57′ W 94
Little Current, river, *Can.* 50°31′ N, 86°53′ W 110
Little Duck Lake, *Can.* 59°23′ N, 98°26′ W 108
Little Exuma, island, *Bahamas* 23°9′ N, 75°51′ W 116
Little Falls, *Minn., U.S.* 45°57′ N, 94°22′ W 90
Little Falls, *N.Y., U.S.* 43°2′ N, 74°53′ W 110
Little Gombi, *Nig.* 10°9′ N, 12°46′ E 216
Little Grand Rapids, *Can.* 52°2′ N, 95°27′ W 108
Little Inagua Island, *Bahamas* 21°36′ N, 73°21′ W 116
Little Isaac, island, *Bahamas* 25°56′ N, 78°59′ W 105
Little Juniper Mountain, peak, *Oreg., U.S.* 43°8′ N, 119°55′ W 90
Little Lake, *Calif., U.S.* 35°56′ N, 117°55′ W 101
Little Lake, *Mich., U.S.* 46°18′ N, 87°21′ W 110
Little Longlac, *Can.* 49°41′ N, 86°57′ W 94
Little Namaland, region, *S. Af.* 28°17′ S, 16°49′ E 227
Little Nicobar, island, *India* 7°21′ N, 92°20′ E 188
Little River, *Calif., U.S.* 39°16′ N, 123°47′ W 90
Little, river, *La., U.S.* 31°35′ N, 92°27′ W 103
Little, river, *Okla., U.S.* 34°9′ N, 95°7′ W 112
Little Rock, *Ark., U.S.* 34°40′ N, 92°24′ W 96
Little Rocky Mountains, *Mont., U.S.* 47°56′ N, 108°26′ W 90
Little Sable Point, *Mich., U.S.* 43°37′ N, 86°41′ W 102
Little Saint Bernard Pass, *It.* 45°41′ N, 6°54′ E 167
Little San Bernardino Mountains, *Calif., U.S.* 34°0′ N, 116°19′ W 101
Little San Salvador, island, *Bahamas* 24°26′ N, 77°1′ W 116
Little Seal, river, *Can.* 59°3′ N, 95°41′ W 108
Little Sioux, river, *Iowa, U.S.* 41°43′ N, 96°20′ W 80
Little Sitkin, island, *Alas., U.S.* 52°9′ N, 178°28′ E 160
Little Smoky, *Can.* 54°43′ N, 117°7′ W 108
Little Smoky, river, *Can.* 54°4′ N, 117°46′ W 108
Little Suamico, *Wis., U.S.* 44°42′ N, 88°1′ W 94
Little White Mountain, peak, *Can.* 49°40′ N, 119°26′ W 90
Littlefield, *Ariz., U.S.* 36°52′ N, 113°56′ W 101
Littlefield, *Tex., U.S.* 33°55′ N, 102°20′ W 92
Littlefork, *Minn., U.S.* 48°21′ N, 93°32′ W 94
Littlehampton, *U.K.* 50°48′ N, 0°32′ E 162
Littleton, *Colo., U.S.* 39°35′ N, 105°2′ W 90
Littleton, *Mass., U.S.* 42°32′ N, 71°32′ W 104
Littleton, *N.H., U.S.* 44°18′ N, 71°47′ W 104
Litva, *Bosn. and Herzg.* 44°24′ N, 18°31′ E 168
Lityn, *Ukr.* 49°18′ N, 28°13′ E 152
Liu, river, *China* 42°25′ N, 125°40′ E 200
Liu, river, *China* 42°13′ N, 122°39′ E 200
Liuba, *China* 33°37′ N, 106°53′ E 198
Liucheng, *China* 24°39′ N, 109°16′ E 198
Liudaogou, *China* 41°33′ N, 127°12′ E 200
Liuhe, *China* 42°16′ N, 125°45′ E 200
Liuli, *Tanzania* 11°5′ S, 34°40′ E 224
Liúpo, *Mozambique* 15°36′ S, 39°59′ E 224
Liuwa Plain, *Zambia* 14°33′ S, 22°27′ E 220
Liuwa Plain National Park, *Zambia* 14°41′ S, 22°14′ E 206
Liuzhou, *China* 24°18′ N, 109°23′ E 198
Livada, *Rom.* 47°52′ N, 23°6′ E 168
Līvāni, *Latv.* 56°20′ N, 26°10′ E 166
Live Oak, *Fla., U.S.* 30°16′ N, 82°59′ W 96
Live Oak Springs, *Calif., U.S.* 32°41′ N, 116°22′ W 101
Lively Island, *Lively Island* 52°14′ S, 58°23′ W 134
Livermore, *Calif., U.S.* 37°40′ N, 121°47′ W 100
Livermore, *Ky., U.S.* 37°29′ N, 87°9′ W 96
Livermore Falls, *Me., U.S.* 44°28′ N, 70°12′ W 104
Livermore, Mount, peak, *Tex., U.S.* 30°35′ N, 104°14′ W 92
Liverpool, *Can.* 44°1′ N, 64°44′ W 111
Liverpool, *N.Y., U.S.* 43°6′ N, 76°14′ W 110
Liverpool, *U.K.* 53°24′ N, 2°59′ W 162
Liverpool Bay 70°0′ N, 130°43′ W 98
Liverpool Land 70°41′ N, 21°27′ W 246
Livingston, *Ala., U.S.* 32°35′ N, 88°12′ W 103
Livingston, *Calif., U.S.* 37°23′ N, 120°43′ W 100
Livingston, *Guatemala* 15°49′ N, 88°49′ W 115
Livingston, *Ill., U.S.* 38°58′ N, 89°47′ W 102
Livingston, *La., U.S.* 30°29′ N, 90°46′ W 103
Livingston, *Mont., U.S.* 45°39′ N, 110°33′ W 90
Livingston, *Tenn., U.S.* 36°22′ N, 85°19′ W 96
Livingston, *Tex., U.S.* 30°41′ N, 94°56′ W 103
Livingston Island, *Antarctica* 62°59′ S, 60°12′ W 134
Livingstone, *Zambia* 17°50′ S, 25°50′ E 224
Livingstone Lake, *Can.* 58°33′ N, 108°4′ W 108
Livingstone Memorial, site, *Zambia* 12°21′ S, 30°13′ E 224
Livingstonia, *Malawi* 10°38′ S, 34°8′ E 224
Livno, *Bosn. and Herzg.* 43°49′ N, 17°1′ E 168
Livny, *Russ.* 52°24′ N, 37°32′ E 158
Livo, *Fin.* 65°32′ N, 26°56′ E 152
Livonia, *Mich., U.S.* 42°22′ N, 83°23′ W 102
Livorno (Leghorn), *It.* 43°33′ N, 10°19′ E 156
Livramento do Brumado, *Braz.* 13°38′ S, 41°53′ W 138
Livron, *Fr.* 44°46′ N, 4°50′ E 150
Liwale, *Tanzania* 9°46′ S, 38°0′ E 224
Liwonde, *Malawi* 15°7′ S, 35°13′ E 224
Lixian, *China* 29°40′ N, 111°44′ E 198
Lixian, *China* 34°13′ N, 105°6′ E 198
Lizard Head Peak, *Wyo., U.S.* 42°47′ N, 109°17′ W 90
Lizard Islands, *Lake Superior* 47°8′ N, 85°17′ W 94
Lizard Point, *U.K.* 49°44′ N, 5°17′ W 150
Lizarra see Estella, *Sp.* 42°39′ N, 2°2′ W 164
Ljig, *Serb. and Mont.* 44°13′ N, 20°14′ E 168
Ljubija, *Bosn. and Herzg.* 44°56′ N, 16°36′ E 168
Ljubinje, *Bosn. and Herzg.* 42°57′ N, 18°5′ E 168
Ljubiš, *Serb. and Mont.* 43°36′ N, 19°51′ E 168
Ljubišnja, peak, *Europe* 43°18′ N, 19°3′ E 168
Ljubljana, *Slov.* 46°2′ N, 14°21′ E 156
Ljuboten, peak, *Europe* 42°11′ N, 21°4′ E 168
Ljubovija, *Serb. and Mont.* 44°12′ N, 19°22′ E 168
Ljubuski, *Bosn. and Herzg.* 43°11′ N, 17°33′ E 168
Ljugarn, *Sw.* 57°20′ N, 18°40′ E 166
Ljungby, *Nor.* 56°50′ N, 13°54′ E 152
Ljusdal, *Nor.* 61°49′ N, 16°6′ E 152
Ljusterö, island, *Sw.* 59°31′ N, 18°45′ E 166
Ljutomer, *Slov.* 46°31′ N, 16°10′ E 168
Llaima, Volcán, peak, *Chile* 38°44′ S, 71°52′ W 134
Llajta Mauca, *Arg.* 28°11′ S, 63°6′ W 139
Llallagua, *Bol.* 18°25′ S, 66°42′ W 137
Llanbedr, *U.K.* 52°48′ N, 4°5′ W 162
Llanbister, *U.K.* 52°20′ N, 3°18′ W 162
Llançà, *Sp.* 42°21′ N, 3°9′ E 164
Llancanelo, Laguna, lake, *Arg.* 35°37′ S, 70°31′ W 134
Llanddewi Brefi, *U.K.* 52°10′ N, 3°57′ W 162
Llandeilo, *U.K.* 51°53′ N, 3°59′ W 162
Llandovery, *U.K.* 51°59′ N, 3°47′ W 162
Llandrindod Wells, *U.K.* 52°14′ N, 3°23′ W 162
Llanelltyd, *U.K.* 52°45′ N, 3°54′ W 162
Llanenddwyn, *U.K.* 52°47′ N, 4°5′ W 162
Llanfair Caereinion, *U.K.* 52°38′ N, 3°19′ W 162
Llanfyllin, *U.K.* 52°45′ N, 3°15′ W 162
Llangadog, *U.K.* 51°55′ N, 3°52′ W 162
Llanganates National Park, *Ecua.* 1°28′ S, 78°12′ W 136
Llangefni, *U.K.* 53°15′ N, 4°18′ W 162
Llangeitho, *U.K.* 52°12′ N, 4°1′ W 162
Llangollen, *U.K.* 52°57′ N, 3°10′ W 162
Llangorse, *U.K.* 51°56′ N, 3°15′ W 162
Llanidan, *U.K.* 53°13′ N, 4°13′ W 162
Llanidloes, *U.K.* 52°25′ N, 3°32′ W 162
Llanilar, *U.K.* 52°20′ N, 4°1′ W 162
Llanllugan, *U.K.* 52°36′ N, 3°23′ W 162
Llano, *Tex., U.S.* 30°44′ N, 98°40′ W 92
Llanrwst, *U.K.* 53°8′ N, 3°46′ W 162
Llanuwchllyn, *U.K.* 52°51′ N, 3°40′ W 162
Llanwrtyd Wells, *U.K.* 52°6′ N, 3°38′ W 162
Llavorsí, *Sp.* 42°29′ N, 1°10′ E 164
Lleida, *Sp.* 41°37′ N, 0°37′ E 164
Llera, *Mex.* 23°18′ N, 99°1′ W 114
Llerena, *Sp.* 38°14′ N, 6°2′ W 164
Lleyn Peninsula, *U.K.* 52°55′ N, 4°14′ W 162
Llica, *Bol.* 19°52′ S, 68°16′ W 137
Llimiana, *Sp.* 42°5′ N, 0°54′ E 164
Łapy, *Pol.* 53°0′ N, 23°0′ E 152
Łaskarzew, *Pol.* 52°0′ N, 22°0′ E 152
Łeba, *Pol.* 55°0′ N, 18°0′ E 152
Łochów, *Pol.* 52°0′ N, 22°0′ E 152
Łódź, *Pol.* 52°0′ N, 20°0′ E 152
Łódźkie, adm. division, *Pol.* 51°0′ N, 19°0′ E 152
Łomża, *Pol.* 53°0′ N, 22°0′ E 152
Łoniów, *Pol.* 52°0′ N, 22°0′ E 152
Łowicz, *Pol.* 52°0′ N, 20°0′ E 152
Łuków, *Pol.* 52°0′ N, 22°0′ E 152
Llodio, *Sp.* 43°7′ N, 2°59′ W 164
Lloret de Mar, *Sp.* 41°42′ N, 2°51′ E 164
Llorona, Punta, *C.R.* 8°41′ N, 84°26′ W 115
Lloyd, Cape 60°36′ S, 54°60′ W 248
Lloyd George, Mount, peak, *Can.* 57°52′ N, 125°10′ W 108
Lloyd Lake, *Can.* 57°20′ N, 109°27′ W 108
Lloydminster, *Can.* 53°16′ N, 109°59′ W 108
Llullaillaco National Park, *Chile* 24°58′ S, 69°4′ W 122
Llullaillaco, Volcán, peak, *Chile* 24°46′ S, 68°42′ W 132
Lluta, *Peru* 16°4′ S, 72°3′ W 137
Llyswen, *U.K.* 52°1′ N, 3°16′ W 162
Lo, river, *China* 22°54′ N, 104°33′ E 202
Loa, *Utah, U.S.* 38°23′ N, 111°38′ W 90
Loa, Mauna, peak, *Hawaiʻi, U.S.* 19°28′ N, 155°40′ W 99
Loa, river, *Chile* 22°37′ S, 69°18′ W 137
Loanda, *Braz.* 22°58′ S, 53°14′ W 138
Loange, river, *Dem. Rep. of the Congo* 4°20′ S, 20°8′ E 218
Loango, *Congo* 4°42′ S, 11°47′ E 218
Loano, *It.* 44°7′ N, 8°16′ E 167
Loarre, *Sp.* 42°18′ N, 0°37′ E 164
Lobamba, *Swaziland* 26°28′ S, 31°3′ E 227
Loban, *Russ.* 65°43′ N, 45°28′ E 154
Lobatse, *Botswana* 25°15′ S, 25°35′ E 227
Lobería, *Arg.* 42°7′ S, 63°48′ W 134
Lobería, *Arg.* 38°11′ S, 58°47′ W 139
Lobito, *Angola* 12°26′ S, 13°32′ E 220
Lobitos, *Peru* 4°21′ S, 81°17′ W 130
Lobo, river, *Côte d'Ivoire* 6°27′ N, 6°42′ W 222
Lobok, *Belarus* 55°51′ N, 30°2′ E 166
Lobos, *Arg.* 35°9′ S, 59°8′ W 139
Lobos, Cabo, *Chile* 19°1′ S, 70°43′ W 137
Lobos, Cabo, *Mex.* 29°43′ N, 113°4′ W 92
Lobos, Cayo 18°17′ N, 87°26′ W 115
Lobos de Afuera, Islas, islands, *South Pacific Ocean* 7°20′ S, 81°52′ W 130
Lobos de Tierra, Isla, island, *Peru* 6°23′ S, 82°43′ W 130
Lobos, Estero de 27°17′ N, 111°33′ W 80
Lobos, Isla, island, *Mex.* 27°26′ N, 111°21′ W 112
Lobos, Point, *U.S.* 36°22′ N, 122°16′ W 92
Lobos, Punta, *Chile* 21°13′ S, 70°29′ W 137
Lobster Point, *Can.* 51°13′ N, 55°36′ W 111
Lobva, *Russ.* 59°14′ N, 60°31′ E 154
Loc Binh, *Vietnam* 21°46′ N, 106°55′ E 198
Loc Ninh, *Vietnam* 11°50′ N, 106°36′ E 202
Locarno, *Switz.* 46°11′ N, 8°46′ E 167
Lochem, *Neth.* 52°8′ N, 6°24′ E 163
Lochinvar National Park, *Zambia* 16°3′ S, 26°49′ E 224
Łochów, *Pol.* 52°31′ N, 21°42′ E 152
Lock Haven, *Pa., U.S.* 41°7′ N, 77°27′ W 94
Lockbourne, *Ohio, U.S.* 39°47′ N, 82°58′ W 102
Locke Mills, *Me., U.S.* 44°24′ N, 70°43′ W 104
Lockeford, *Calif., U.S.* 38°9′ N, 121°10′ W 100
Lockhart, *Ala., U.S.* 31°1′ N, 86°21′ W 96
Lockhart, *Tex., U.S.* 29°51′ N, 97°40′ W 92
Lockney, *Tex., U.S.* 34°5′ N, 101°26′ W 92
Lockport, *Ill., U.S.* 41°35′ N, 88°3′ W 102
Lockport, *La., U.S.* 29°37′ N, 90°32′ W 103
Lockwood, *Calif., U.S.* 35°56′ N, 121°6′ W 100
Loco Mountain, peak, *Mont., U.S.* 46°11′ N, 110°24′ W 90
Locri, *It.* 38°15′ N, 16°15′ E 156
Locumba, *Peru* 17°37′ S, 70°47′ W 137
Lod (Lydda), *Israel* 31°56′ N, 34°53′ E 194
Loda, *Ill., U.S.* 40°31′ N, 88°4′ W 102
Lodalskåpa, peak, *Nor.* 61°46′ N, 7°4′ E 152
Lodeyka, *Russ.* 60°41′ N, 45°45′ E 154
Lodeynoye Pole, *Russ.* 60°42′ N, 33°34′ E 154
Lodge Creek, river, *Can.* 49°32′ N, 110°34′ W 90
Lodge Grass, *Mont., U.S.* 45°17′ N, 107°23′ W 90
Lodge, Mount, peak, *Can.* 59°3′ N, 137°34′ W 108
Lodgepole, *Nebr., U.S.* 41°9′ N, 102°40′ W 92
Lodhran, *Pak.* 29°35′ N, 71°38′ E 186
Lodi, *Calif., U.S.* 38°7′ N, 121°18′ W 100
Lodi, *It.* 45°18′ N, 9°29′ E 167
Lodi, *Wis., U.S.* 43°19′ N, 89°31′ W 102
Lodja, *Dem. Rep. of the Congo* 3°31′ S, 23°32′ E 224
Lodore, Canyon of, *Colo., U.S.* 40°18′ N, 109°1′ W 90
Lodosa, *Sp.* 42°25′ N, 2°5′ W 164
Lodwar, *Kenya* 3°4′ N, 35°35′ E 224
Łódź, *Pol.* 51°44′ N, 19°27′ E 152
Łodzkie, adm. division, *Pol.* 51°30′ N, 18°23′ E 152
Loei, *Thai.* 17°32′ N, 101°32′ E 202
Loelli, spring, *Sudan* 5°6′ N, 34°41′ E 224
Loen, *Nor.* 61°53′ N, 6°51′ E 152
Loengo, *Dem. Rep. of the Congo* 4°50′ S, 26°30′ E 224
Loera, river, *Mex.* 26°39′ N, 107°32′ W 80
Loeriesfontein, *S. Af.* 30°57′ S, 19°27′ E 227
Lofgren Peninsula 72°44′ S, 91°41′ W 248
Lofoten, islands, *Norwegian Sea* 67°57′ N, 12°59′ E 152
Lofthouse, *U.K.* 54°8′ N, 1°49′ W 162
Loftus, *U.K.* 54°33′ N, 0°53′ E 162
Log, *Russ.* 49°28′ N, 43°49′ E 158
Log Lane Village, *Colo., U.S.* 40°15′ N, 103°52′ W 90
Loga, *Niger* 13°33′ N, 3°21′ E 222
Logan, *Iowa, U.S.* 41°38′ N, 95°48′ W 90
Logan, *Kans., U.S.* 39°39′ N, 99°34′ W 90
Logan, *N. Mex., U.S.* 35°21′ N, 103°25′ W 92
Logan, *Ohio, U.S.* 39°32′ N, 82°24′ W 102
Logan, *Utah, U.S.* 41°44′ N, 111°48′ W 82
Logan, Mount, peak, *Ariz., U.S.* 36°20′ N, 113°16′ W 92
Logan, Mount, peak, *Can.* 60°37′ N, 140°32′ W 98
Logan, Mount, peak, *Can.* 48°52′ N, 66°44′ W 111
Logan, Mount, peak, *Wash., U.S.* 48°31′ N, 120°59′ W 100
Logan Pass, *Mont., U.S.* 48°41′ N, 113°42′ W 90
Logandale, *Nev., U.S.* 36°35′ N, 114°30′ W 101
Logăneşti, *Mold.* 46°55′ N, 28°32′ E 158
Logansport, *Ind., U.S.* 40°44′ N, 86°21′ W 102
Logansport, *La., U.S.* 31°57′ N, 94°1′ W 103
Logashkino, *Russ.* 70°49′ N, 153°44′ E 173
Loge, river, *Angola* 7°44′ S, 13°12′ E 220
Logone Birni, *Cameroon* 11°46′ N, 15°2′ E 216
Logoniégué, *Burkina Faso* 9°54′ N, 4°33′ W 222
Logoualé, *Côte d'Ivoire* 7°3′ N, 7°33′ W 222
Logroño, *Sp.* 42°26′ N, 2°27′ W 164
Logrosán, *Sp.* 39°20′ N, 5°30′ W 164
Løgstør, *Den.* 56°56′ N, 9°14′ E 150
Loharano, *Madagascar* 21°45′ S, 48°9′ E 220
Lohardaga, *India* 23°24′ N, 84°41′ E 197
Loharghat, *India* 25°57′ N, 91°26′ E 197
Loharu, *India* 28°26′ N, 75°49′ E 197
Lohatlha, *S. Af.* 28°3′ S, 23°2′ E 227
Lohikoski, *Fin.* 61°36′ N, 28°42′ E 166
Lohiniva, *Fin.* 67°9′ N, 24°58′ E 152
Lohja (Lojo), *Fin.* 60°14′ N, 24°1′ E 166
Lôho, *Côte d'Ivoire* 8°38′ N, 5°9′ W 222
Lohr, *Ger.* 49°59′ N, 9°33′ E 167
Lohusuu, *Est.* 58°55′ N, 27°0′ E 166
Loi Mwe, *Myanmar* 21°9′ N, 99°46′ E 202
Loi, Phou, peak, *Laos* 20°17′ N, 103°5′ E 202
Loiano, *It.* 44°16′ N, 11°18′ E 167
Loikaw, *Myanmar* 19°42′ N, 97°10′ E 202
Loile, river, *Dem. Rep. of the Congo* 1°11′ S, 20°17′ E 218
Loimaa, *Fin.* 60°49′ N, 23°1′ E 166
Loir, river, *Fr.* 48°13′ N, 1°17′ E 163
Loire, river, *Fr.* 46°26′ N, 3°56′ E 165
Loire, river, *Fr.* 46°48′ N, 1°52′ W 142
Loire, river, *Fr.* 45°9′ N, 3°58′ E 165
Loire, river, *Fr.* 48°16′ N, 2°37′ E 165
Loja, *Ecua.* 4°1′ S, 79°13′ W 130
Loja, *Sp.* 37°9′ N, 4°9′ W 164
Lojo see Lohja, *Fin.* 60°14′ N, 24°1′ E 166
Loka, *Sudan* 4°15′ N, 30°57′ E 224
Lokachi, *Ukr.* 50°44′ N, 24°38′ E 152
Lokalahti, *Fin.* 60°40′ N, 21°28′ E 166
Lokandu, *Dem. Rep. of the Congo* 2°34′ S, 25°45′ E 224
Lokchim, river, *Russ.* 61°36′ N, 51°43′ E 154
Lokeren, *Belg.* 51°5′ N, 4°0′ E 163
Lokhwabe, *Botswana* 24°9′ S, 21°50′ E 227
Lokichokio, *Kenya* 4°13′ N, 34°20′ E 224
Lokila, *Sudan* 4°38′ N, 32°26′ E 224
Lokitaung, *Kenya* 4°12′ N, 35°45′ E 224
Lokka, *Fin.* 67°47′ N, 27°40′ E 152
Løkken, *Nor.* 63°5′ N, 9°42′ E 152
Loknya, *Russ.* 56°50′ N, 30°10′ E 166
Lokoja, *Nig.* 7°45′ N, 6°41′ E 222
Lokolama, *Dem. Rep. of the Congo* 2°36′ S, 19°51′ E 218
Lokolenge, *Dem. Rep. of the Congo* 1°9′ N, 22°36′ E 218
Lokomo, *Cameroon* 2°52′ N, 15°17′ E 218
Lökösháza, *Hung.* 46°25′ N, 21°14′ E 168
Lokossa, *Benin* 6°39′ N, 1°40′ E 222
Loks Land, island, *Can.* 62°9′ N, 64°30′ W 106

Loksa, *Est.* 59°33′ N, 25°45′ E **166**
Lokwa Kangole, *Kenya* 3°26′ N, 35°50′ E **224**
Lol, river, *Sudan* 8°56′ N, 26°15′ E **224**
Lol, river, *Sudan* 8°48′ N, 28°36′ E **224**
Loleta, *Calif., U.S.* 40°38′ N, 124°14′ W **90**
Lolgorien, *Kenya* 1°14′ S, 34°48′ E **224**
Lolimi, *Sudan* 4°34′ N, 34°2′ E **224**
Loliondo, *Tanzania* 2°3′ S, 35°39′ E **224**
Lollar, *Ger.* 50°38′ N, 8°43′ E **167**
Lolo, Mount, peak, *Can.* 50°48′ N, 120°12′ W **90**
Lolo Pass, *Idaho, U.S.* 46°37′ N, 114°36′ W **90**
Lolobau, island, *P.N.G.* 4°51′ S, 150°14′ E **192**
Lolowau, *Indonesia* 0°57′ N, 97°33′ E **196**
Lom, *Bulg.* 43°49′ N, 23°13′ E **168**
Lom, *Nor.* 61°50′ N, 8°31′ E **152**
Lom Sak, *Thai.* 16°47′ N, 101°7′ E **202**
Loma Mountains, *Sierra Leone* 9°5′ N, 11°27′ W **222**
Lomami, river, *Dem. Rep. of the Congo* 0°47′ N, 24°17′ E **224**
Lomami, river, *Dem. Rep. of the Congo* 4°35′ S, 24°49′ E **224**
Lomami, river, *Dem. Rep. of the Congo* 7°19′ S, 25°26′ E **224**
Lomas del Real, *Mex.* 22°30′ N, 97°55′ W **114**
Lombarda, Serra, *Braz.* 3°17′ N, 51°55′ W **130**
Lombardy, adm. division, *It.* 45°33′ N, 9°3′ E **167**
Lombez, *Fr.* 43°28′ N, 0°52′ E **164**
Lomblen, island, *Indonesia* 8°58′ S, 123°36′ E **192**
Lombok, island, *Indonesia* 9°26′ S, 115°17′ E **192**
Lomé, *Togo* 6°10′ N, 1°7′ E **222**
Lomela, *Dem. Rep. of the Congo* 2°19′ S, 23°17′ E **218**
Lomela, river, *Dem. Rep. of the Congo* 0°35′ N, 21°5′ E **218**
Lometa, *Tex., U.S.* 31°12′ N, 98°24′ W **92**
Lomié, *Cameroon* 3°21′ N, 13°37′ E **218**
Lomira, *Wis., U.S.* 43°35′ N, 88°27′ W **102**
Lommel, *Belg.* 51°13′ N, 5°18′ E **167**
Lomond, Ben, peak, *U.K.* 56°10′ N, 4°44′ W **150**
Lomonosov, *Russ.* 59°51′ N, 29°42′ E **166**
Lomonosov Ridge, *Arctic Ocean* 88°59′ N, 116°17′ W **255**
Lomovoye, *Russ.* 64°2′ N, 40°38′ E **154**
Lomphat, *Cambodia* 13°39′ N, 106°57′ E **202**
Lompoc, *Calif., U.S.* 34°39′ N, 120°28′ W **100**
Łomża, *Pol.* 53°10′ N, 22°5′ E **152**
Lon, Hon, island, *Vietnam* 12°32′ N, 109°26′ E **202**
Lonauli, *India* 18°43′ N, 73°24′ E **188**
Londinières, *Fr.* 49°50′ N, 1°24′ E **163**
London, *Can.* 42°59′ N, 81°13′ W **102**
London, *Ohio, U.S.* 39°52′ N, 83°27′ W **102**
London, *U.K.* 51°31′ N, 0°9′ E **162**
Londonderry, *U.K.* 54°58′ N, 7°16′ W **143**
Londonderry, *Vt., U.S.* 43°13′ N, 72°49′ W **104**
Londonderry, Isla, island, *Chile* 55°33′ S, 72°31′ W **248**
Londres, *Arg.* 27°43′ S, 67°9′ W **132**
Londrina, *Braz.* 23°18′ S, 51°11′ W **138**
Lone Pine, *Calif., U.S.* 36°36′ N, 118°5′ W **101**
Lone Star, *Tex., U.S.* 32°55′ N, 94°44′ W **103**
Lonely Bay 61°39′ N, 115°31′ W **108**
Lonepine, *Mont., U.S.* 47°40′ N, 114°40′ W **90**
Long Barn, *Calif., U.S.* 38°5′ N, 120°9′ W **100**
Long Bay Cays, islands, *North Atlantic Ocean* 23°49′ N, 76°60′ W **116**
Long Beach, *Calif., U.S.* 33°46′ N, 118°12′ W **101**
Long Beach, *Miss., U.S.* 30°20′ N, 89°10′ W **103**
Long Beach, *N.Y., U.S.* 40°35′ N, 73°40′ W **104**
Long Beach, *Wash., U.S.* 46°20′ N, 124°3′ W **100**
Long Branch, *N.J., U.S.* 40°18′ N, 74°1′ W **94**
Long Branch, *Tex., U.S.* 32°4′ N, 94°35′ W **103**
Long Cay (Fortune Island), *Bahamas* 22°35′ N, 76°5′ W **116**
Long Creek, *Oreg., U.S.* 44°41′ N, 119°7′ W **90**
Long Creek, river, *North America* 49°3′ N, 103°40′ W **90**
Long Eaton, *U.K.* 52°53′ N, 1°17′ W **162**
Long Island, *Austral.* 22°4′ S, 148°43′ E **230**
Long Island, *Bahamas* 23°4′ N, 74°52′ W **116**
Long Island, *Can.* 54°23′ N, 81°10′ W **106**
Long Island, *Can.* 44°20′ N, 67°13′ W **80**
Long Island, *N.Y., U.S.* 40°38′ N, 73°14′ W **104**
Long Island, *P.N.G.* 5°35′ S, 146°13′ E **192**
Long Island Sound 41°5′ N, 73°6′ W **104**
Long Key, island, *Fla., U.S.* 24°47′ N, 80°49′ W **105**
Long Lake, *Can.* 49°20′ N, 87°26′ W **110**
Long Meg, ruin(s), *U.K.* 54°43′ N, 2°42′ W **162**
Long Melford, *U.K.* 52°4′ N, 0°43′ E **162**
Long Point, *Can.* 42°30′ N, 80°6′ W **94**
Long Point, *Can.* 54°13′ N, 58°6′ W **111**
Long Point, *Can.* 48°45′ N, 59°26′ W **111**
Long Point, *Can.* 53°2′ N, 98°26′ W **108**
Long Pond, lake, *Mass., U.S.* 41°47′ N, 71°5′ W **104**
Long Prairie, *Minn., U.S.* 45°57′ N, 94°52′ W **90**
Long Sutton, *U.K.* 52°46′ N, 0°7′ E **162**
Long Xuyen, *Vietnam* 10°19′ N, 105°18′ E **192**
Longa, *Angola* 14°43′ S, 18°30′ E **220**
Longa, Proliv 70°18′ N, 174°28′ E **160**
Long'an, *China* 23°7′ N, 107°39′ E **198**
Longares, *Sp.* 41°23′ N, 1°10′ W **164**
Longarone, *It.* 46°16′ N, 12°17′ E **167**
Longboat Key, *Fla., U.S.* 27°26′ N, 82°40′ W **105**
Longbranch, *Wash., U.S.* 47°11′ N, 122°46′ W **100**
Longchuan, *China* 24°4′ N, 115°17′ E **198**
Longde, *China* 35°37′ N, 106°6′ E **198**
Longfellow Mountains, *Me., U.S.* 44°27′ N, 71°10′ W **104**
Longford, *Ire.* 53°43′ N, 7°49′ W **150**
Longhai, *China* 24°19′ N, 117°51′ E **198**
Longhua, *China* 41°21′ N, 117°47′ E **198**
Longhurst, *N.C., U.S.* 36°25′ N, 78°59′ W **96**
Longhurst, Mount, peak, *Antarctica* 79°19′ S, 158°10′ E **248**
Longjiang, *China* 47°23′ N, 123°13′ E **198**
Longjing see Yanji, *China* 42°46′ N, 129°24′ E **200**
Longju, *India* 28°38′ N, 93°31′ E **188**
Longkou, *China* 37°42′ N, 120°25′ E **198**
Longlac, *Can.* 49°47′ N, 86°32′ W **110**
Longleaf, *La., U.S.* 30°59′ N, 92°34′ W **103**
Longli, *China* 26°30′ N, 106°57′ E **198**
Longlin, *China* 24°47′ N, 105°19′ E **198**
Longmeadow, *Mass., U.S.* 42°3′ N, 72°35′ W **104**
Longmen, *China* 23°43′ N, 114°15′ E **198**
Longmont, *Colo., U.S.* 40°10′ N, 105°2′ W **106**
Longnan, *China* 24°49′ N, 114°49′ E **198**
Longobucco, *It.* 39°27′ N, 16°37′ E **156**
Longonot, peak, *Kenya* 0°54′ N, 36°22′ E **224**
Longquan, *China* 28°6′ N, 119°7′ E **198**
Longrais, Lac, lake, *Can.* 54°10′ N, 68°48′ W **111**
Longs Peak, *Colo., U.S.* 40°14′ N, 105°41′ W **90**
Longshan, *China* 29°28′ N, 109°28′ E **198**
Longstreet, *La., U.S.* 32°4′ N, 93°57′ W **103**
Longtam, *Sudan* 8°55′ N, 30°44′ E **224**
Longueuil, *Can.* 45°31′ N, 73°30′ W **94**
Longuyon, *Fr.* 49°26′ N, 5°35′ E **163**
Longview, *N.C., U.S.* 35°44′ N, 81°23′ W **96**
Longview, *Tex., U.S.* 32°29′ N, 94°44′ W **103**
Longview, *Wash., U.S.* 46°7′ N, 122°57′ W **100**
Longville, *La., U.S.* 30°35′ N, 93°15′ W **103**
Longwy, *Fr.* 49°31′ N, 5°45′ E **163**
Longxi, *China* 35°1′ N, 104°36′ E **198**
Longxian, *China* 34°53′ N, 106°48′ E **198**
Longyan, *China* 25°4′ N, 117°0′ E **198**
Longyearbyen, *Nor.* 78°10′ N, 15°34′ E **160**
Long"yugan, *Russ.* 64°54′ N, 71°25′ E **169**
Longzhen, *China* 48°41′ N, 126°49′ E **198**
Longzhou, *China* 22°23′ N, 106°48′ E **198**
Löningen, *Ger.* 52°44′ N, 7°45′ E **163**
Łoniów, *Pol.* 50°32′ N, 21°31′ E **152**
Lonjica, *Croatia* 45°50′ N, 16°20′ E **168**
Lonkala, *Dem. Rep. of the Congo* 4°38′ S, 23°15′ E **218**
Lonquimay, *Arg.* 36°30′ S, 63°37′ W **139**
Lønsdal, *Nor.* 66°44′ N, 15°25′ E **152**
Lons-le-Saunier, *Fr.* 46°40′ N, 5°32′ E **150**
Loogootee, *Ind., U.S.* 38°40′ N, 86°54′ W **102**
Lookeba, *Okla., U.S.* 35°20′ N, 98°22′ W **92**
Lookout, Cape, *Alas., U.S.* 54°54′ N, 133°53′ W **108**
Lookout, Cape, *Antarctica* 62°6′ S, 55°18′ W **248**
Lookout, Cape, *N.C., U.S.* 34°30′ N, 76°32′ W **96**
Lookout, Cape, *U.S.* 45°8′ N, 124°26′ W **90**
Lookout Mountain, peak, *Can.* 53°35′ N, 64°13′ W **111**
Lookout Mountain, peak, *N. Mex., U.S.* 35°12′ N, 108°21′ W **92**
Lookout Mountain, peak, *Oreg., U.S.* 45°19′ N, 121°37′ W **90**
Lookout, Point, *Mich., U.S.* 44°3′ N, 83°35′ W **102**
Loolmalasin, peak, *Tanzania* 3°3′ S, 35°45′ E **224**
Loon Lake, *Can.* 54°2′ N, 109°9′ W **108**
Loon Lake, *N.Y., U.S.* 44°32′ N, 74°4′ W **104**
Loon, Pointe, *Can.* 51°52′ N, 78°39′ W **110**
Loon, river, *Can.* 56°33′ N, 115°24′ W **108**
Lop, *China* 37°6′ N, 80°6′ E **184**
Lop Buri, *Thai.* 14°49′ N, 100°36′ E **202**
Lop Nur, lake, *China* 40°35′ N, 89°42′ E **188**
Lopare, *Bosn. and Herzg.* 44°38′ N, 18°48′ E **168**
Lopatin, *Russ.* 43°50′ N, 47°40′ E **195**
Lopatino, *Russ.* 52°36′ N, 45°49′ E **158**
Lopatka, Mys, *Russ.* 51°8′ N, 156°37′ E **160**
Lopatyn, *Ukr.* 50°11′ N, 24°48′ E **152**
Lope Reserve, *Gabon* 0°38′ N, 11°20′ E **206**
Lopera, *Sp.* 37°57′ N, 4°13′ W **164**
Loperot, *Kenya* 2°17′ N, 35°51′ E **224**
Lopez, *Wash., U.S.* 48°30′ N, 122°54′ W **100**
López Collada, *Mex.* 31°40′ N, 113°59′ W **92**
Lopez Lake, *Calif., U.S.* 35°12′ N, 120°34′ W **101**
Lopez Point, *Calif., U.S.* 35°57′ N, 121°42′ W **100**
Lopi, *Congo* 2°55′ N, 16°39′ E **218**
Loppa, *Nor.* 70°19′ N, 21°26′ E **152**
Lopphavet 70°9′ N, 18°9′ E **160**
Loppi, *Fin.* 60°41′ N, 24°24′ E **166**
Lopshen'ga, *Russ.* 64°59′ N, 37°25′ E **154**
Lopud, island, *Croatia* 42°37′ N, 17°49′ E **168**
Lopydino, *Russ.* 61°8′ N, 52°8′ E **154**
Lora del Rio, *Sp.* 37°39′ N, 5°33′ W **164**
Lorain, *Ohio, U.S.* 41°26′ N, 82°11′ W **102**
Loralai, *Pak.* 30°21′ N, 68°39′ E **186**
Lorca, *Sp.* 37°40′ N, 1°42′ W **164**
Lorch, *Ger.* 50°2′ N, 7°48′ E **167**
Lord Howe Island, *Austral.* 31°31′ S, 156°53′ E **230**
Lord Howe Rise, *Tasman Sea* 33°48′ S, 163°25′ E **252**
Lord Loughborough, island, *Myanmar* 10°28′ N, 96°37′ E **202**
Lord Mayor Bay 69°41′ N, 94°10′ W **106**
Lord, river, *Can.* 50°52′ N, 123°36′ W **90**
Lordsburg, *N. Mex., U.S.* 32°21′ N, 108°42′ W **92**
Lore Lindu National Park, *Indonesia* 1°40′ S, 119°48′ E **238**
Loreauville, *La., U.S.* 30°2′ N, 91°45′ W **103**
Lorena, *Braz.* 22°46′ S, 45°6′ W **138**
Lorengau, *P.N.G.* 2°6′ S, 147°14′ E **192**
Lorenzo, *Idaho, U.S.* 43°43′ N, 111°53′ W **90**
Lorenzo, *Tex., U.S.* 33°38′ N, 101°32′ W **92**
Lorenzo Geyres, *Uru.* 32°2′ S, 57°51′ W **139**
Loreo, *It.* 45°3′ N, 12°10′ E **167**
Loreto, *Bol.* 15°16′ S, 64°39′ W **137**
Loreto, *Braz.* 7°5′ S, 45°9′ W **132**
Loreto, *Ecua.* 0°44′ N, 77°21′ W **136**
Loreto, *Mex.* 22°16′ N, 101°58′ W **114**
Loreto, *Philippines* 10°22′ N, 125°35′ E **203**
Loreto, adm. division, *Peru* 3°3′ S, 74°42′ W **136**
Loretto, *Tenn., U.S.* 35°3′ N, 87°26′ W **96**
Lorian Swamp, marsh, *Kenya* 0°52′ N, 39°6′ E **224**
Lorica, *Col.* 9°14′ N, 75°50′ W **136**
L orinci, *Hung.* 47°44′ N, 19°41′ E **168**
Loriol, *Fr.* 44°45′ N, 4°49′ E **150**
Loris, *S.C., U.S.* 34°3′ N, 78°54′ W **96**
Loriu Plateau, *Kenya* 1°51′ N, 36°13′ E **224**
Lorman, *Miss., U.S.* 31°48′ N, 91°3′ W **103**
Lormi, *India* 22°17′ N, 81°40′ E **197**
Lornel, Pointe de, *Fr.* 50°34′ N, 1°24′ E **163**
Loro, *Col.* 2°11′ N, 69°33′ W **136**
Lorraine, adm. division, *Fr.* 48°37′ N, 5°1′ E **150**
Lorraine, region, *Fr.* 49°50′ N, 4°47′ E **167**
Lorukumu, *Kenya* 2°50′ N, 35°12′ E **224**
Lorup, *Ger.* 52°55′ N, 7°38′ E **163**
Los, *Nor.* 61°43′ N, 15°8′ E **152**
Los Alamos, *Calif., U.S.* 34°44′ N, 120°18′ W **100**
Los Alamos, *N. Mex., U.S.* 35°52′ N, 106°19′ W **92**
Los Alerces National Park, *Arg.* 42°54′ S, 72°10′ W **122**
Los Altos, *Calif., U.S.* 37°21′ N, 122°9′ W **100**
Los Amores, *Arg.* 28°6′ S, 59°60′ W **139**
Los Angeles, *Calif., U.S.* 34°3′ N, 118°16′ W **101**
Los Ángeles, *Chile* 37°28′ S, 72°22′ W **134**
Los Banos, *Calif., U.S.* 37°3′ N, 120°52′ W **100**
Los Barrios, *Sp.* 36°11′ N, 5°30′ W **164**
Los Blancos, *Arg.* 23°34′ S, 62°38′ W **132**
Los Dolores, *Sp.* 37°38′ N, 1°1′ W **150**
Los Frentones, *Arg.* 26°24′ S, 61°27′ W **139**
Los Glaciares National Park, *Arg.* 50°6′ S, 73°33′ W **122**
Los Hermanos, islands, *Caribbean Sea* 11°55′ N, 64°25′ W **116**
Los, Îles de, islands, *North Atlantic Ocean* 9°5′ N, 13°56′ W **222**
Los Juríes, *Arg.* 28°27′ S, 62°7′ W **139**
Los Katios National Park, *Col.* 7°35′ N, 77°6′ W **136**
Los Lagos, adm. division, *Chile* 41°7′ S, 73°59′ W **134**
Los Lavaderos, *Mex.* 23°27′ N, 98°3′ W **114**
Los Loros, *Chile* 27°51′ S, 70°10′ W **132**
Los Mármoles National Park, *Mex.* 20°47′ N, 99°35′ W **72**
Los Mochis, *Mex.* 25°45′ N, 108°60′ W **112**
Los Monjes, Islas, islands, *Caribbean Sea* 12°0′ N, 71°6′ W **116**
Los Monos, ruin(s), *Mex.* 18°9′ N, 100°30′ W **114**
Los Ojos, *N. Mex., U.S.* 36°43′ N, 106°34′ W **92**
Los Olivos, *Calif., U.S.* 34°40′ N, 120°8′ W **100**
Los Organos, *Mex.* 23°43′ N, 103°51′ W **114**
Los Osos, *Calif., U.S.* 35°18′ N, 120°51′ W **100**
Los Palacios, *Cuba* 22°35′ N, 83°15′ W **116**
Los Pirpintos, *Arg.* 26°10′ S, 62°4′ W **139**
Los Remedios, *Mex.* 24°34′ N, 106°25′ W **114**
Los Remedios National Park, *Mex.* 19°28′ N, 99°23′ W **112**
Los Reyes, *Mex.* 19°34′ N, 102°29′ W **114**
Los Reyes Islands, *South Pacific Ocean* 1°51′ S, 147°45′ E **192**
Los Roques, Islas, islands, *Caribbean Sea* 12°4′ N, 66°32′ W **116**
Los Santos de Maimona, *Sp.* 38°27′ N, 6°24′ W **164**
Los Telares, *Arg.* 29°1′ S, 63°27′ W **139**
Los Teques, *Venez.* 10°21′ N, 67°3′ W **136**
Los Vilos, *Chile* 31°55′ S, 71°31′ W **134**
Los Yébenes, *Sp.* 39°34′ N, 3°53′ W **164**
Losada, river, *Col.* 2°19′ N, 74°30′ W **136**
Losap Atoll 6°37′ N, 153°19′ E **192**
Losha, *Belarus* 53°26′ N, 27°23′ E **152**
Łosice, *Pol.* 52°11′ N, 22°43′ E **158**
Losinoborskaya, *Russ.* 58°24′ N, 89°23′ E **169**
Łośki, *Pol.* 53°55′ N, 23°24′ E **166**
Lost Hills, *Calif., U.S.* 35°36′ N, 119°42′ W **100**
Lost River Range, *Idaho, U.S.* 44°20′ N, 113°53′ W **90**
Lost Springs, *Wyo., U.S.* 42°45′ N, 104°57′ W **90**
Lost Trail Pass, *Mont., U.S.* 45°39′ N, 113°57′ W **90**
Lost World Caverns, site, *W. Va., U.S.* 37°49′ N, 80°32′ W **96**
Lostmans River, *Fla., U.S.* 25°25′ N, 81°21′ W **105**
Lot, river, *Fr.* 44°28′ N, 3°3′ E **165**
Lota, *Chile* 37°8′ S, 73°9′ W **134**
Lotagipi Swamp, marsh, *Kenya* 4°51′ N, 34°29′ E **224**
Lothair, *S. Af.* 26°24′ S, 30°25′ E **227**
Lotilla, river, *Sudan* 5°40′ N, 32°46′ E **224**
Lotmozero, *Russ.* 68°7′ N, 30°11′ E **152**
Loto, *Dem. Rep. of the Congo* 2°50′ S, 22°29′ E **218**
Lott, *Tex., U.S.* 31°11′ N, 97°2′ W **96**
Lotte, *Ger.* 52°16′ N, 7°56′ E **163**
Lou, island, *P.N.G.* 2°42′ S, 146°53′ E **192**
Louangphrabang, *Laos* 19°51′ N, 102°6′ E **202**
Louann, *Ark., U.S.* 33°22′ N, 92°48′ W **103**
Loubet Coast, *Antarctica* 67°22′ S, 66°45′ W **248**
Loudon, *Malawi* 12°9′ S, 33°27′ E **224**
Loudon, *N.H., U.S.* 43°17′ N, 71°28′ W **104**
Loudonville, *Ohio, U.S.* 40°37′ N, 82°14′ W **102**
Loue, river, *Fr.* 47°1′ N, 5°29′ E **165**
Loufan, *China* 38°3′ N, 111°46′ E **198**
Louga, *Côte d'Ivoire* 5°4′ N, 6°14′ W **222**
Louga, *Senegal* 15°37′ N, 16°14′ W **222**
Louge, *Arg.* 36°54′ S, 61°39′ W **139**
Loughborough, *U.K.* 52°46′ N, 1°13′ W **162**
Lougheed Island, *Can.* 76°50′ N, 107°36′ W **106**
Louin, *Miss., U.S.* 32°3′ N, 89°16′ W **103**
Louis Trichardt see Makhado, *S. Af.* 23°3′ S, 29°53′ E **227**
Louis Ussing, Kap 67°2′ N, 33°5′ W **246**
Louisa, *Ky., U.S.* 38°5′ N, 82°37′ W **94**
Louisburg, *N.C., U.S.* 36°6′ N, 78°18′ W **96**
Louise, *Miss., U.S.* 32°58′ N, 90°36′ W **103**
Louise Falls, *Can.* 60°15′ N, 116°34′ W **108**
Louisiade Archipelago, islands, *Solomon Sea* 12°43′ S, 154°40′ E **238**
Louisiade Archipelago, islands, *Solomon Sea* 12°7′ S, 149°11′ E **192**
Louisiana, *Mo., U.S.* 39°26′ N, 91°4′ W **94**
Louisiana, adm. division, *La., U.S.* 31°7′ N, 93°7′ W **103**
Louisiana Point, *La., U.S.* 29°43′ N, 93°52′ W **103**
Louisville, *Ill., U.S.* 38°45′ N, 88°30′ W **102**
Louisville, *Ky., U.S.* 38°14′ N, 85°46′ W **94**
Louisville, *Miss., U.S.* 33°6′ N, 89°3′ W **103**
Louisville, *Ohio, U.S.* 40°49′ N, 81°16′ W **102**
Louis-Xiv, Pointe, *Can.* 54°27′ N, 79°40′ W **106**
Loukhi, *Russ.* 66°4′ N, 33°0′ E **152**
Loukouo, *Congo* 3°37′ S, 14°39′ E **218**
Loulan Yiji, ruin(s), *China* 40°25′ N, 89°43′ E **188**
Loulay, *Fr.* 46°2′ N, 0°32′ E **150**
Loulouni, *Mali* 10°54′ N, 5°38′ W **222**
Loum, *Cameroon* 4°41′ N, 9°46′ E **222**
Lount Lake, *Can.* 50°6′ N, 94°40′ W **90**
Louny, *Czech Rep.* 50°20′ N, 13°47′ E **152**
Loup City, *Nebr., U.S.* 41°15′ N, 98°59′ W **90**
Loup, river, *Nebr., U.S.* 41°14′ N, 97°58′ W **90**
Lourdes, *Fr.* 43°6′ N, 4°237′ W **164**
Lourdes-de-Blanc-Sablon, *Can.* 51°26′ N, 57°17′ W **106**
Louth, *U.K.* 53°21′ N, 3°179′ W **162**
Louviers, *Fr.* 49°12′ N, 1°9′ E **163**
Louza, *Tun.* 35°3′ N, 10°58′ E **156**
Lov Ozero, lake, *Russ.* 67°55′ N, 35°28′ E **152**
Lövånger, *Nor.* 64°21′ N, 21°17′ E **152**
Lovat', river, *Russ.* 57°29′ N, 31°34′ E **154**
Lövberga, *Nor.* 63°57′ N, 15°49′ E **152**
Lovea, *Cambodia* 13°21′ N, 102°55′ E **202**
Lovech, *Bulg.* 43°8′ N, 24°42′ E **156**
Lovech, adm. division, *Bulg.* 42°53′ N, 24°11′ E **156**
Lovelady, *Tex., U.S.* 31°6′ N, 95°27′ W **103**
Loveland Pass, *Colo., U.S.* 39°39′ N, 105°52′ W **90**
Lovell, *Me., U.S.* 44°7′ N, 70°55′ W **104**
Lovell, *Wyo., U.S.* 44°49′ N, 108°24′ W **90**
Lovelock, *Nev., U.S.* 40°11′ N, 118°29′ W **90**
Lovere, *It.* 45°49′ N, 10°4′ E **167**
Loverna, *Can.* 51°40′ N, 109°58′ W **90**
Loves Park, *Ill., U.S.* 42°18′ N, 89°4′ W **102**
Loviisa see Lovisa, *Fin.* 60°26′ N, 26°12′ E **166**
Loving, *N. Mex., U.S.* 32°17′ N, 104°6′ W **92**
Lovington, *N. Mex., U.S.* 32°56′ N, 103°21′ W **92**
Lovisa (Loviisa), *Fin.* 60°26′ N, 26°12′ E **166**
Lovlya, *Russ.* 59°55′ N, 49°22′ E **154**
Löv o, *Hung.* 47°29′ N, 16°47′ E **168**
Lovozero, *Russ.* 68°0′ N, 35°2′ E **152**
Lovran, *Croatia* 45°17′ N, 14°15′ E **156**
Lovreč, *Croatia* 43°29′ N, 16°58′ E **168**
Lovrin, *Rom.* 45°58′ N, 20°47′ E **168**
Lóvua, *Angola* 11°38′ S, 23°41′ E **220**
Lóvua, *Angola* 7°19′ S, 20°10′ E **218**
Low Bush River, *Can.* 48°56′ N, 80°10′ W **94**
Low, Cape, *Can.* 62°51′ N, 87°4′ W **106**
Low Island, *Antarctica* 63°21′ S, 61°57′ W **134**
Lowa, *Dem. Rep. of the Congo* 1°25′ S, 25°50′ E **224**
Lowa, river, *Dem. Rep. of the Congo* 1°23′ S, 26°55′ E **224**
Lowell, *Ind., U.S.* 41°16′ N, 87°25′ W **102**
Lowell, *Mass., U.S.* 42°38′ N, 71°20′ W **104**
Lowell, *Mich., U.S.* 42°56′ N, 85°21′ W **102**
Lower Arrow Lake, *Can.* 49°29′ N, 118°56′ W **90**
Lower Hutt, *N.Z.* 41°13′ S, 174°57′ E **240**
Lower Matecumbe Key, island, *Fla., U.S.* 24°50′ N, 80°42′ W **105**
Lower Post, *Can.* 59°57′ N, 128°27′ W **108**
Lower Red Lake, *Minn., U.S.* 48°0′ N, 95°35′ W **94**
Lower Saxony, adm. division, *Ger.* 51°47′ N, 9°27′ E **167**
Lower Zambezi National Park, *Zambia* 15°25′ S, 28°48′ E **224**
Lowestoft, *U.K.* 52°28′ N, 1°43′ E **163**
Łowicz, *Pol.* 52°5′ N, 19°54′ E **152**
Lowland, *N.C., U.S.* 35°18′ N, 76°36′ W **96**
Lowry, *Minn., U.S.* 45°41′ N, 95°32′ W **90**
Lowry, Îles, islands, *Indian Ocean* 12°35′ S, 49°42′ E **220**
Lowville, *N.Y., U.S.* 43°47′ N, 75°30′ W **110**
Loxley, *Ala., U.S.* 30°36′ N, 87°45′ W **103**
Loxton, *S. Af.* 31°30′ S, 22°19′ E **227**
Loya, river, *Dem. Rep. of the Congo* 8°475′ N, 27°45′ E **224**
Loyal, Ben, peak, *U.K.* 58°23′ N, 4°33′ W **150**
Loyall, *Ky., U.S.* 36°50′ N, 83°21′ W **96**
Loyalty Islands 20°7′ S, 166°47′ E **238**
Loyew, *Belarus* 51°55′ N, 30°53′ E **158**
Loyola, Punta, *Arg.* 51°48′ S, 68°54′ W **134**
Loyoro, *Uganda* 3°19′ N, 34°13′ E **224**
Lozenets, *Bulg.* 42°12′ N, 27°48′ E **156**
Loznica, *Serb. and Mont.* 44°31′ N, 19°12′ E **168**
Lozova, *Ukr.* 48°54′ N, 36°19′ E **158**
Lozovik, *Serb. and Mont.* 44°28′ N, 21°4′ E **168**
Loz'va, river, *Russ.* 61°47′ N, 59°54′ E **154**
Lü Tao, island, *Taiwan* 22°30′ N, 121°31′ E **198**
Lua Dekere, river, *Dem. Rep. of the Congo* 3°53′ N, 19°30′ E **218**
Lua, river, *Dem. Rep. of the Congo* 2°49′ N, 18°31′ E **218**
Luabo, *Mozambique* 18°24′ S, 36°8′ E **224**
Luacano, *Angola* 11°11′ S, 21°39′ E **220**
Luaha-sibuha, *Indonesia* 0°30′ N, 98°27′ E **196**
Luahiwa Petroglyphs, site, *Hawai'i, U.S.* 20°47′ N, 156°57′ W **99**
Lualaba (Congo), river, *Dem. Rep. of the Congo* 5°35′ S, 27°7′ E **224**
Luama, river, *Dem. Rep. of the Congo* 4°41′ S, 27°17′ E **224**
Luambe National Park, *Zambia* 12°37′ S, 31°37′ E **224**
Luampa, river, *Zambia* 15°16′ S, 24°38′ E **224**
Lu'an, *China* 31°44′ N, 116°31′ E **198**
Luan, river, *China* 41°27′ N, 117°5′ E **198**
Luanda, *Angola* 8°54′ S, 13°3′ E **218**
Luanda, adm. division, *Angola* 9°17′ S, 12°39′ E **218**
Luando, *Angola* 11°43′ S, 18°33′ E **220**
Luando Integral Nature Reserve, *Angola* 11°24′ S, 16°28′ E **220**
Luang, Thale, lake, *Thai.* 7°24′ N, 99°51′ E **196**
Luangundo, river, *Angola* 16°17′ S, 19°35′ E **220**
Luangwa, *Zambia* 15°37′ S, 30°20′ E **224**
Luangwa, river, *Zambia* 12°14′ S, 32°10′ E **224**
Luanping, *China* 40°54′ N, 117°18′ E **198**
Luanshya, *Zambia* 13°8′ S, 28°22′ E **224**
Luanxian, *China* 39°46′ N, 118°41′ E **198**
Luanza, *Dem. Rep. of the Congo* 8°42′ S, 28°39′ E **224**
Luarca, *Sp.* 43°31′ N, 6°34′ W **150**
Luashi, *Dem. Rep. of the Congo* 10°56′ S, 23°34′ E **224**
Luau, *Angola* 10°44′ S, 22°14′ E **220**
Lubaantun, ruin(s), *Belize* 16°15′ N, 89°7′ W **115**
Lubamiti, *Dem. Rep. of the Congo* 2°32′ S, 17°46′ E **218**
Lubāna, *Latv.* 56°53′ N, 26°42′ E **166**
Lubānas Ezers, lake, *Latv.* 56°45′ N, 26°36′ E **166**
Lubanda, *Dem. Rep. of the Congo* 5°13′ S, 26°38′ E **224**
Lubango, *Angola* 14°57′ S, 13°28′ E **220**
Lubao, *Dem. Rep. of the Congo* 5°20′ S, 25°43′ E **224**
Lubba Gerih, spring, *Somalia* 10°21′ N, 44°38′ E **216**
Lübben, *Ger.* 51°56′ N, 13°53′ E **152**
Lubbock, *Tex., U.S.* 33°32′ N, 101°50′ W **92**
Lubec, *Me., U.S.* 44°50′ N, 66°60′ W **94**
Lübeck, *Ger.* 53°51′ N, 10°42′ E **152**
Lubefu, *Dem. Rep. of the Congo* 4°44′ S, 24°24′ E **224**
Lubelskie, adm. division, *Pol.* 51°2′ N, 21°49′ E **152**
Lübenka, *Kaz.* 50°27′ N, 54°6′ E **158**
Lubero, *Dem. Rep. of the Congo* 0°12′ N, 29°11′ E **224**
Lubéron, Montagne du, *Fr.* 43°42′ N, 5°16′ E **165**
Lubi, river, *Dem. Rep. of the Congo* 5°49′ S, 23°28′ E **224**
Lubicon Lake, *Can.* 56°22′ N, 116°23′ W **108**
Lubilash, river, *Dem. Rep. of the Congo* 8°21′ S, 24°7′ E **224**
Lubine, Île, island, *U.K.* 6°46′ S, 70°20′ E **188**
Lublin, *Pol.* 51°15′ N, 22°33′ E **152**
Lubliniec, *Pol.* 50°40′ N, 18°41′ E **152**
Lubnica, *Serb. and Mont.* 43°51′ N, 22°12′ E **168**
Lubny, *Ukr.* 50°1′ N, 32°56′ E **158**
Lubongola, *Dem. Rep. of the Congo* 2°39′ S, 27°52′ E **218**
Lubosalma, *Russ.* 63°4′ N, 31°45′ E **152**
Lubuagan, *Philippines* 17°21′ N, 121°10′ E **203**
Lubudi, *Dem. Rep. of the Congo* 9°58′ S, 25°58′ E **224**
Lubudi, river, *Dem. Rep. of the Congo* 9°52′ S, 24°52′ E **224**
Lubukbertubung, *Indonesia* 5°297′ N, 102°6′ E **196**
Lubuksikaping, *Indonesia* 0°8′ N, 100°10′ E **196**
Lubumbashi (Élisabethville), *Dem. Rep. of the Congo* 11°43′ S, 27°26′ E **224**
Lubuskie, adm. division, *Pol.* 51°47′ N, 14°40′ E **152**
Lubutu, *Dem. Rep. of the Congo* 0°45′ N, 26°32′ E **224**
Lubwe, *Zambia* 11°5′ S, 29°34′ E **224**
Luc, Pointe à, *Can.* 49°44′ N, 67°4′ W **111**
Lucala, river, *Angola* 9°26′ S, 15°21′ E **220**
Lucan, *Can.* 43°10′ N, 81°24′ W **102**
Lucanas, *Peru* 14°39′ S, 74°15′ W **137**
Lucania, Mount, peak, *Can.* 60°59′ N, 140°39′ W **98**
Lucapa, *Angola* 8°40′ S, 20°57′ E **218**
Lucas, *Braz.* 13°7′ S, 55°57′ W **130**
Lucas, *Kans., U.S.* 39°1′ N, 98°33′ W **90**
Lucaya, *Bahamas* 26°31′ N, 78°39′ W **105**
Lucca, *It.* 43°50′ N, 10°30′ E **167**
Lucedale, *Miss., U.S.* 30°53′ N, 88°36′ W **103**
Lucena, *Philippines* 13°56′ N, 121°36′ E **203**
Lucena, *Sp.* 37°24′ N, 4°30′ W **164**
Lucena del Cid, *Sp.* 40°8′ N, 0°17′ E **164**
Lučenec, *Slovakia* 48°19′ N, 19°41′ E **152**
Lucerne, *Can.* 52°51′ N, 118°33′ W **108**
Lucerne Valley, *Calif., U.S.* 34°27′ N, 116°58′ W **101**
Lucero, *Mex.* 30°48′ N, 106°31′ W **92**
Luceville, *Can.* 48°30′ N, 68°21′ W **111**
Lüchow, *Ger.* 52°58′ N, 11°9′ E **152**
Luchuan, *China* 22°22′ N, 110°15′ E **198**
Luchulingo, river, *Mozambique* 12°21′ S, 35°30′ E **224**
Lüchun, *China* 23°1′ N, 102°16′ E **202**
Lučice, *Croatia* 43°49′ N, 15°17′ E **156**
Lucie, Lac, lake, *Can.* 50°22′ N, 78°55′ W **94**
Lucie, river, *Suriname* 3°37′ N, 57°29′ W **130**
Lucira, *Angola* 13°55′ S, 12°31′ E **220**
Lucknow, *Can.* 43°57′ N, 81°31′ W **102**
Lucknow, *India* 26°47′ N, 80°53′ E **197**
Lucky Boy Pass, *Nev., U.S.* 38°26′ N, 118°47′ W **90**
Luçon, *Fr.* 46°27′ N, 1°11′ W **150**
Lucunga, *Angola* 6°51′ S, 14°35′ E **218**
Lucusse, *Angola* 12°34′ S, 20°48′ E **220**
Ludborough, *U.K.* 53°26′ N, 4°237′ W **162**
Ludbreg, *Croatia* 46°15′ N, 16°36′ E **168**
Lüdenscheid, *Ger.* 51°13′ N, 7°37′ E **167**
Lüderitz, *Namibia* 26°41′ S, 15°12′ E **220**
Ludgershall, *U.K.* 51°14′ N, 1°39′ W **162**
Ludhiana, *India* 30°53′ N, 75°53′ E **186**
Lüdinghausen, *Ger.* 51°46′ N, 7°26′ E **167**
Ludington, *Mich., U.S.* 43°56′ N, 86°26′ W **102**
Ludlow, *Calif., U.S.* 34°43′ N, 116°11′ W **101**
Ludlow, *Ill., U.S.* 40°23′ N, 88°7′ W **102**
Ludlow, *Mass., U.S.* 42°9′ N, 72°29′ W **104**
Ludlow, *U.K.* 52°21′ N, 2°44′ W **162**
Ludlow, *Vt., U.S.* 43°23′ N, 72°43′ W **104**
Ludogorsko Plato, *Bulg.* 43°26′ N, 26°11′ E **156**
Ludwigsfelde, *Ger.* 52°18′ N, 13°15′ E **152**
Ludwigshafen, *Ger.* 49°28′ N, 8°26′ E **150**
Ludza, *Latv.* 56°32′ N, 27°43′ E **166**
Luebo, *Dem. Rep. of the Congo* 5°21′ S, 21°26′ E **218**
Lueki, *Dem. Rep. of the Congo* 3°26′ S, 25°49′ E **224**
Luembe, river, *Dem. Rep. of the Congo* 6°50′ S, 24°24′ E **224**
Luena, *Angola* 11°48′ S, 19°55′ E **220**
Luena, *Dem. Rep. of the Congo* 9°27′ S, 25°44′ E **224**
Luena, *Zambia* 10°37′ S, 30°11′ E **224**
Luena Flats, *Zambia* 14°33′ S, 23°29′ E **224**
Luena, river, *Angola-Zambia* 12°19′ S, 21°31′ E **220**
Lueo, river, *Dem. Rep. of the Congo* 9°33′ S, 23°43′ E **224**
Luepa, *Venez.* 5°52′ N, 61°27′ W **123**
Luesia, *Sp.* 42°22′ N, 1°1′ W **164**
Lufeng, *China* 22°54′ N, 115°38′ E **198**
Lufico, *Angola* 6°24′ S, 13°21′ E **218**

Lufira, river, *Dem. Rep. of the Congo* 9°40′ S, 27°14′ E **224**
Lufkin, *Tex., U.S.* 31°19′ N, 94°43′ W **103**
Lufu, *Dem. Rep. of the Congo* 5°41′ S, 13°52′ E **218**
Luga, *Russ.* 58°42′ N, 29°49′ E **166**
Lugano, *Switz.* 46°0′ N, 8°57′ E **167**
Lugg, river, *U.K.* 52°16′ N, 2°57′ W **162**
Lugnaquillia, peak, *Ire.* 52°57′ N, 6°34′ W **150**
Lugo, *It.* 44°24′ N, 11°54′ E **167**
Lugo, *Sp.* 43°0′ N, 7°34′ W **150**
Lugoj, *Rom.* 45°42′ N, 21°54′ E **168**
Lugones, *Arg.* 28°21′ S, 63°19′ W **139**
Lugovaya Proleyka, *Russ.* 49°19′ N, 45°4′ E **158**
Lugovoy, *Russ.* 59°40′ N, 65°56′ E **169**
Lūgovoy see Qulan, *Kaz.* 42°54′ N, 72°44′ E **184**
Lugulu, river, *Dem. Rep. of the Congo* 2°18′ S, 26°54′ E **224**
Luguruka, *Tanzania* 9°59′ S, 36°39′ E **224**
Luhanka, *Fin.* 61°47′ N, 25°39′ E **166**
Luhans'k, *Ukr.* 48°32′ N, 39°14′ E **158**
Lui, Ben, peak, *U.K.* 56°22′ N, 4°55′ W **150**
Lui, river, *Zambia* 15°50′ S, 23°27′ E **224**
Luiana, *Angola* 17°23′ S, 23°0′ E **220**
Luiana, river, *Angola* 17°22′ S, 22°1′ E **220**
Luilu, river, *Dem. Rep. of the Congo* 7°2′ S, 23°27′ E **224**
Luimneach see Limerick, *Ire.* 52°39′ N, 8°37′ W **150**
Luino, *It.* 46°0′ N, 8°45′ E **167**
Luis Gonzaga, *Mex.* 29°48′ N, 114°28′ W **92**
Luis Moya, *Mex.* 22°25′ N, 102°16′ W **114**
Luishia, *Dem. Rep. of the Congo* 11°12′ S, 27°1′ E **224**
Luisiana, *Peru* 12°43′ S, 73°44′ W **137**
Luitpold Coast, *Antarctica* 77°40′ S, 35°8′ W **248**
Luiza, *Dem. Rep. of the Congo* 7°13′ S, 22°25′ E **218**
Luizi, river, *Dem. Rep. of the Congo* 6°4′ S, 27°33′ E **224**
Luján, *Arg.* 34°36′ S, 59°6′ W **139**
Luka, *Bosn. and Herzg.* 43°25′ N, 18°7′ E **168**
Lukafu, *Dem. Rep. of the Congo* 10°29′ S, 27°29′ E **224**
Lukanga Swamp, marsh, *Zambia* 14°27′ S, 27°19′ E **224**
Lukashi, river, *Dem. Rep. of the Congo* 6°7′ S, 24°45′ E **224**
Lukavac, *Bosn. and Herzg.* 44°34′ N, 18°31′ E **168**
Luke, *Maced.* 42°19′ N, 22°16′ E **168**
Luke, *Serb. and Mont.* 43°36′ N, 20°16′ E **168**
Luke Air Force Base, *Ariz., U.S.* 33°32′ N, 112°26′ W **92**
Luke, Mount, peak, *Austral.* 27°16′ S, 116°39′ E **230**
Lukenie, river, *Dem. Rep. of the Congo* 3°33′ S, 22°5′ E **218**
Lukeville, *Ariz., U.S.* 31°53′ N, 112°48′ W **92**
Lukolela, *Dem. Rep. of the Congo* 1°10′ S, 17°10′ E **218**
Lukovë, *Alban.* 39°59′ N, 19°54′ E **156**
Łuków, *Pol.* 51°55′ N, 22°21′ E **152**
Lukoyanov, *Russ.* 55°1′ N, 44°33′ E **154**
Łukta, *Pol.* 53°47′ N, 20°5′ E **166**
Lukuga, river, *Dem. Rep. of the Congo* 5°59′ S, 27°21′ E **224**
Lukula, *Dem. Rep. of the Congo* 5°26′ S, 12°53′ E **218**
Lukuledi, *Tanzania* 10°35′ S, 38°48′ E **224**
Lukulu, *Zambia* 14°23′ S, 23°15′ E **220**
Lukunor Atoll 5°17′ N, 153°45′ E **192**
Lukup, *Indonesia* 4°25′ N, 97°29′ E **196**
Lukusuzi National Park, *Zambia* 13°8′ S, 32°20′ E **224**
Luleå, *Nor.* 65°35′ N, 22°9′ E **152**
Lüleburgaz, *Turk.* 41°24′ N, 27°21′ E **158**
Lules, *Arg.* 26°60′ S, 65°22′ W **132**
Luling, *Tex., U.S.* 29°39′ N, 97°39′ W **92**
Lulonga, *Dem. Rep. of the Congo* 0°32′ N, 18°24′ E **218**
Lulu, river, *Dem. Rep. of the Congo* 1°35′ N, 23°48′ E **224**
Lulua, river, *Dem. Rep. of the Congo* 8°22′ S, 22°45′ E **218**
Lumajangdong Co, lake, *China* 34°0′ N, 80°21′ E **188**
Lümanda, *Est.* 58°17′ N, 22°2′ E **166**
Lumbala Kaquengue, *Angola* 12°41′ S, 22°38′ E **220**
Lumbala N'guimbo, *Angola* 14°8′ S, 21°24′ E **220**
Lumberton, *Miss., U.S.* 30°59′ N, 89°28′ W **103**
Lumberton, *N.C., U.S.* 34°37′ N, 79°1′ W **96**
Lumbo, *Mozambique* 15°4′ S, 40°38′ E **224**
Lumbovka, *Russ.* 67°39′ N, 40°33′ E **169**
Lumbreras, *Sp.* 42°5′ N, 2°37′ W **164**
Lumbres, *Fr.* 50°42′ N, 2°7′ E **163**
Lumbwa, *Kenya* 0°10′ N, 35°30′ E **224**
Lumding, *India* 25°44′ N, 93°8′ E **188**
Lumeje, *Angola* 11°35′ S, 20°48′ E **220**
Lumholtz National Park, *Austral.* 18°27′ S, 145°30′ E **238**
Lumivaara, peak, *Nor.* 67°32′ N, 22°51′ E **152**
Lumparland, *Fin.* 60°5′ N, 20°15′ E **166**
Lumuna, *Dem. Rep. of the Congo* 3°50′ S, 26°29′ E **224**
Lumut, *Malaysia* 4°12′ N, 100°36′ E **196**
Lun, *Croatia* 44°41′ N, 14°45′ E **156**
Lün, *Mongolia* 47°24′ N, 102°54′ E **198**
Lün, *Mongolia* 47°49′ N, 105°17′ E **198**
Luna, *N. Mex., U.S.* 33°48′ N, 108°57′ W **92**
Lunar Crater, *Nev., U.S.* 38°23′ N, 115°60′ W **90**
Lunavada, *India* 23°7′ N, 73°36′ E **186**
Lund, *Can.* 49°59′ N, 124°45′ W **100**
Lund, *Nev., U.S.* 38°51′ N, 115°1′ W **90**
Lunda Norte, adm. division, *Angola* 8°37′ S, 18°34′ E **218**
Lunda Sul, adm. division, *Angola* 9°13′ S, 20°41′ E **218**
Lundar, *Can.* 50°41′ N, 98°3′ W **90**
Lundazi, *Zambia* 12°16′ S, 33°13′ E **224**
Lunde, *Nor.* 62°51′ N, 17°47′ E **152**
Lundu, *Malaysia* 1°42′ N, 109°51′ E **196**
Lune, river, *U.K.* 54°13′ N, 2°37′ W **162**
Lüneburger Heide, region, *Ger.* 53°2′ N, 9°31′ E **150**
Lunel, *Fr.* 43°40′ N, 4°7′ E **150**
Lünen, *Ger.* 51°37′ N, 7°32′ E **163**
Lunenburg, *Can.* 44°21′ N, 64°20′ W **111**
Lunenburg, *Mass., U.S.* 42°35′ N, 71°44′ W **104**
Lunenburg, *Vt., U.S.* 44°27′ N, 71°42′ W **104**
Lunéville, *Fr.* 48°35′ N, 6°30′ E **163**
Lunga, river, *Zambia* 13°1′ S, 26°36′ E **224**
Lungdo, *China* 33°54′ N, 82°10′ E **188**
Lunggar, *China* 31°8′ N, 84°1′ E **188**
Lungi, *Sierra Leone* 8°40′ N, 13°14′ W **222**
Lunglei, *India* 22°52′ N, 92°42′ E **188**
Luni, *India* 26°1′ N, 73°0′ E **186**
Luni, river, *India* 25°3′ N, 71°49′ E **186**
Lunino, *Russ.* 53°36′ N, 45°15′ E **154**
Luninyets, *Belarus* 52°14′ N, 26°47′ E **152**
Lunkaransar, *India* 28°29′ N, 73°45′ E **186**
Lunsar, *Sierra Leone* 8°41′ N, 12°34′ W **222**
Lunsemfwa, river, *Zambia* 15°3′ S, 29°20′ E **224**
Luntai, *China* 41°44′ N, 84°17′ E **184**
Lunyama, *Dem. Rep. of the Congo* 7°49′ S, 28°20′ E **224**
Lunz, *Aust.* 47°51′ N, 15°1′ E **156**
Luo, river, *China* 36°39′ N, 108°16′ E **198**
Luo, river, *China* 34°16′ N, 111°45′ E **198**
Luocheng, *China* 24°46′ N, 108°53′ E **198**
Luodian, *China* 25°24′ N, 106°45′ E **198**
Luoding, *China* 22°42′ N, 111°35′ E **198**
Luohe, *China* 33°37′ N, 114°4′ E **198**
Luonan, *China* 34°5′ N, 110°10′ E **198**
Luopioinen, *Fin.* 61°22′ N, 24°37′ E **166**
Luoshan, *China* 32°13′ N, 114°34′ E **198**
Luoyang, *China* 34°41′ N, 112°25′ E **198**
Luoyuan, *China* 26°32′ N, 119°33′ E **198**
Luozi, *Dem. Rep. of the Congo* 4°56′ S, 14°4′ E **218**
Lupa Market, *Tanzania* 8°42′ S, 33°16′ E **224**
Lupane, *Zimb.* 18°56′ S, 27°45′ E **224**
Lupeni, *Rom.* 45°20′ N, 23°15′ E **168**
Lupilichi, *Mozambique* 11°46′ S, 35°15′ E **224**
Lupin, *Can.* 65°41′ N, 111°19′ W **106**
Lupiñén, *Sp.* 42°9′ N, 0°34′ E **164**
Lupire, *Angola* 14°38′ S, 19°28′ E **220**
Lupon, *Philippines* 6°55′ N, 126°1′ E **203**
Luputa, *Dem. Rep. of the Congo* 7°6′ S, 23°40′ E **224**
Lupweji, river, *Dem. Rep. of the Congo* 10°26′ S, 24°13′ E **224**
Luque, *Sp.* 37°33′ N, 4°17′ W **164**
Luråsen, peak, *Nor.* 62°1′ N, 16°32′ E **152**
Lure, *Fr.* 47°41′ N, 6°29′ E **150**
Luremo, *Angola* 8°33′ S, 17°52′ E **218**
Luribay, *Bol.* 17°8′ S, 67°43′ W **137**
Lúrio, *Mozambique* 13°35′ S, 40°33′ E **224**
Lúrio, river, *Mozambique* 14°19′ S, 38°43′ E **224**
Luro, *Arg.* 36°38′ S, 62°9′ W **139**
Lurøy, *Nor.* 66°25′ N, 12°51′ E **152**
Lusahanga, *Tanzania* 2°54′ S, 31°14′ E **224**
Lusaka, *Zambia* 15°26′ S, 28°10′ E **224**
Lusambo, *Dem. Rep. of the Congo* 4°58′ S, 23°25′ E **224**
Lusanga, *Dem. Rep. of the Congo* 4°50′ S, 18°39′ E **218**
Lušci Palanka, *Bosn. and Herzg.* 44°44′ N, 16°25′ E **168**
Luseland, *Can.* 52°5′ N, 109°23′ W **90**
Lusenga Plain National Park, *Zambia* 9°45′ S, 29°1′ E **224**
Lushi, *China* 34°4′ N, 111°0′ E **198**
Lushiko, river, *Angola* 6°26′ S, 19°26′ E **218**
Lushoto, *Tanzania* 4°48′ S, 38°19′ E **224**
Lüshun (Port Arthur), *China* 38°52′ N, 121°16′ E **198**
Lusigny, *Fr.* 48°15′ N, 4°15′ E **163**
Lusikisiki, *S. Af.* 31°22′ S, 29°33′ E **227**
Lusk, *Wyo., U.S.* 42°45′ N, 104°27′ W **90**
Lussanvira, *Braz.* 20°43′ S, 51°9′ W **138**
Lustenau, *Aust.* 47°25′ N, 9°39′ E **156**
Lūt, Dasht-e, *Iran* 31°50′ N, 56°19′ E **160**
Lūţak, *Iran* 30°41′ N, 61°27′ E **186**
Lutcher, *La., U.S.* 30°2′ N, 90°44′ W **103**
Lutembo, *Angola* 13°29′ S, 21°17′ E **220**
Luther, *Mich., U.S.* 44°2′ N, 85°42′ W **102**
Luton, *U.K.* 51°52′ N, 0°26′ E **162**
Lutriņi, *Latv.* 56°44′ N, 22°23′ E **166**
Lutry, *Pol.* 54°0′ N, 20°53′ E **166**
Lutsen, *Minn., U.S.* 47°39′ N, 90°42′ W **94**
Lutshima, river, *Dem. Rep. of the Congo* 6°29′ S, 18°21′ E **218**
Luts'k, *Ukr.* 50°44′ N, 25°18′ E **152**
Lutterworth, *U.K.* 52°26′ N, 1°13′ W **162**
Lutuai, *Angola* 12°42′ S, 20°7′ E **220**
Lututów, *Pol.* 51°22′ N, 18°27′ E **152**
Lützow-Holm Bay 69°52′ S, 35°52′ E **248**
Lutzputs, *S. Af.* 28°24′ S, 20°43′ E **227**
Luuk, *Philippines* 5°58′ N, 121°19′ E **203**
Luuq, *Somalia* 3°48′ N, 42°34′ E **224**
Luverne, *Ala., U.S.* 31°42′ N, 86°16′ W **96**
Luverne, *Minn., U.S.* 43°37′ N, 96°13′ W **90**
Luvia, *Fin.* 61°21′ N, 21°35′ E **166**
Luvidjo, river, *Dem. Rep. of the Congo* 7°7′ S, 26°25′ E **224**
Luvo, *Angola* 5°52′ S, 14°4′ E **218**
Luvos, *Nor.* 66°38′ N, 18°51′ E **152**
Luvozero, *Russ.* 64°26′ N, 30°40′ E **152**
Luvua, river, *Dem. Rep. of the Congo* 6°44′ S, 26°58′ E **224**
Luvuei, *Angola* 13°6′ S, 21°12′ E **220**
Luwegu, river, *Tanzania* 9°40′ S, 36°30′ E **224**
Luwingu, *Zambia* 10°15′ S, 29°53′ E **224**
Luwuk, *Indonesia* 0°58′ N, 122°46′ E **192**
Luxembourg, *Lux.* 49°46′ N, 6°1′ E **163**
Luxembourg 49°43′ N, 5°50′ E **163**
Luxeuil, *Fr.* 47°49′ N, 6°23′ E **150**
Luxi, *China* 24°25′ N, 98°38′ E **190**
Luxi, *China* 28°18′ N, 110°9′ E **198**
Luxor, *Egypt* 25°40′ N, 32°38′ E **182**
Luyi, *China* 33°52′ N, 115°26′ E **198**
Luz, *Braz.* 19°48′ S, 45°42′ W **138**
Luz Range, *Antarctica* 72°22′ S, 4°40′ E **248**
Luza, *Russ.* 60°40′ N, 47°18′ E **154**
Luza, river, *Russ.* 60°20′ N, 48°39′ E **154**
Luzaga, *Sp.* 40°57′ N, 2°27′ W **164**
Luzaide (Valcarlos), *Fr.* 43°5′ N, 1°19′ W **164**
Lužane, *Europe* 42°47′ N, 21°10′ E **168**
Luzhai, *China* 24°23′ N, 109°43′ E **198**
Luzhi, *China* 26°19′ N, 105°16′ E **198**
Luzhma, *Russ.* 63°29′ N, 30°33′ E **152**
Luzhou, *China* 28°54′ N, 105°22′ E **198**
Luziânia, *Braz.* 16°18′ S, 47°58′ W **138**
Luzon, island, *Philippines* 17°39′ N, 122°18′ E **190**
Luzon Strait 19°39′ N, 119°44′ E **238**
L'viv, *Ukr.* 49°50′ N, 24°2′ E **152**
L'vovka, *Russ.* 57°9′ N, 78°48′ E **169**
Lwiro, *Dem. Rep. of the Congo* 2°17′ S, 28°43′ E **224**
Lyady, *Russ.* 58°36′ N, 28°46′ E **166**
Lyakhov Islands, *East Siberian Sea* 73°46′ N, 140°46′ E **255**
Lyaki, *Azerb.* 40°33′ N, 47°24′ E **195**
Lyall Islands, *South Pacific Ocean* 70°47′ S, 166°57′ E **248**
Lyall, Mount, peak, *Can.* 50°4′ N, 114°47′ W **90**
Lyamtsa, *Russ.* 64°32′ N, 36°54′ E **154**
Lyasnaya, *Belarus* 52°59′ N, 25°50′ E **154**
Lychkovo, *Russ.* 57°53′ N, 32°25′ E **154**
Lycksele, *Nor.* 64°35′ N, 18°39′ E **152**
Lycosura, ruin(s), *Gr.* 37°22′ N, 21°56′ E **156**
Lydd, *U.K.* 50°56′ N, 0°55′ E **162**
Lydda see Lod, *Israel* 31°56′ N, 34°53′ E **194**
Lyddal, *Can.* 55°0′ N, 98°25′ W **108**
Lyddan Island, *Antarctica* 73°46′ S, 25°33′ W **248**
Lydenburg, *S. Af.* 25°6′ S, 30°25′ E **227**
Lydney, *U.K.* 51°43′ N, 2°32′ W **162**
Lyduvėnai, *Lith.* 55°30′ N, 23°2′ E **166**
Lyell Brown, Mount, peak, *Austral.* 23°24′ S, 130°9′ E **230**
Lyell, Mount, peak, *Calif., U.S.* 37°43′ N, 119°20′ W **100**
Lyepyel', *Belarus* 54°51′ N, 28°40′ E **166**
Lyford, *Tex., U.S.* 26°23′ N, 97°47′ W **96**
Lyle, *Oreg., U.S.* 45°40′ N, 121°18′ W **100**
Lyman, *Miss., U.S.* 30°29′ N, 89°7′ W **103**
Lyman, *Utah, U.S.* 38°23′ N, 111°35′ W **92**
Lyman, *Wash., U.S.* 48°31′ N, 122°4′ W **100**
Lyman, *Wyo., U.S.* 41°21′ N, 110°18′ W **90**
Lymbel'karamo, *Russ.* 63°50′ N, 83°47′ E **169**
Lynch, *Nebr., U.S.* 42°49′ N, 98°29′ W **90**
Lynch Station, *Va., U.S.* 37°8′ N, 79°19′ W **96**
Lynchburg, *Ohio, U.S.* 39°14′ N, 83°47′ W **102**
Lynden, *Wash., U.S.* 48°57′ N, 122°27′ W **100**
Lyndhurst, *U.K.* 50°52′ N, 1°34′ W **162**
Lyndon, *Ill., U.S.* 41°42′ N, 89°57′ W **102**
Lyndon, *Vt., U.S.* 44°30′ N, 72°2′ W **104**
Lyndonville, *Vt., U.S.* 44°31′ N, 72°1′ W **104**
Lynn, *Ind., U.S.* 40°3′ N, 84°57′ W **102**
Lynn, *Mass., U.S.* 42°27′ N, 70°58′ W **104**
Lynn Canal 58°40′ N, 135°29′ W **108**
Lynn Lake, *Can.* 56°48′ N, 101°3′ W **106**
Lynton, *U.K.* 51°13′ N, 3°49′ W **162**
Lyntupy, *Belarus* 55°4′ N, 26°20′ E **166**
Lyon, *Miss., U.S.* 34°12′ N, 90°33′ W **96**
Lyon, Cape, *Can.* 69°41′ N, 122°54′ W **98**
Lyonnais, region, *Fr.* 45°53′ N, 3°45′ E **165**
Lyons, *Kans., U.S.* 38°20′ N, 98°13′ W **90**
Lyons, *Nebr., U.S.* 41°54′ N, 96°29′ W **90**
Lyons, *N.Y., U.S.* 43°3′ N, 76°60′ W **110**
Lyons, *Ohio, U.S.* 41°41′ N, 84°4′ W **102**
Lyons, *Tex., U.S.* 30°23′ N, 96°34′ W **96**
Lyozna, *Belarus* 55°3′ N, 30°53′ E **154**
Lys, river, *Fr.* 50°34′ N, 2°9′ E **163**
Lysekil, *Nor.* 58°17′ N, 11°26′ E **152**
Lysi 35°5′ N, 33°41′ E **194**
Łysica, *Pol.* 54°22′ N, 19°24′ E **166**
Lys'va, *Russ.* 58°6′ N, 57°49′ E **154**
Lysychans'k, *Ukr.* 48°51′ N, 38°27′ E **158**
Lytham Saint Anne's, *U.K.* 53°45′ N, 2°60′ W **162**
Lytle, *Tex., U.S.* 29°11′ N, 98°49′ W **96**
Lyttelton, *N.Z.* 43°36′ S, 172°43′ E **240**
Lytton, *Can.* 50°14′ N, 121°33′ W **108**
Lyttus, ruin(s), *Gr.* 35°10′ N, 25°16′ E **156**
Lyuban', *Russ.* 59°21′ N, 31°17′ E **152**
Lyubcha, *Belarus* 53°44′ N, 26°4′ E **154**
Lyubeshiv, *Ukr.* 51°46′ N, 25°30′ E **152**
Lyubim, *Russ.* 58°21′ N, 40°44′ E **154**
Lyubytino, *Russ.* 58°48′ N, 33°28′ E **154**
Lyubytiv, *Ukr.* 51°7′ N, 24°50′ E **152**
Lyudinovo, *Russ.* 53°48′ N, 34°28′ E **154**
Lyushcha, *Belarus* 52°25′ N, 26°41′ E **152**
Lyzha, river, *Russ.* 65°44′ N, 55°56′ E **154**

M

M' Bomou, river, *Africa* 4°36′ N, 23°30′ E **224**
Ma, river, *Asia* 20°38′ N, 104°57′ E **202**
Maafer, *Alg.* 35°51′ N, 5°21′ E **150**
Maale (Male), *Maldives* 4°9′ N, 73°15′ E **188**
Ma'āmīr, *Iraq* 30°2′ N, 48°24′ E **196**
Ma'ān, *Jordan* 30°10′ N, 35°44′ E **180**
Maaninka, *Fin.* 66°26′ N, 28°26′ E **154**
Maanīt, *Mongolia* 48°16′ N, 103°27′ E **198**
Maanselkä, *Fin.* 67°46′ N, 27°51′ E **152**
Ma'anshan, *China* 31°41′ N, 118°32′ E **198**
Maardu, *Est.* 59°27′ N, 25°0′ E **166**
Maarestunturit, peak, *Fin.* 68°44′ N, 25°31′ E **152**
Maarianhamina see Mariehamn, *Fin.* 60°5′ N, 19°55′ E **166**
Ma'arrat an Nu'mān, *Syr.* 35°39′ N, 36°41′ E **194**
Maas, river, *Neth.* 51°46′ N, 5°19′ E **167**
Maaseik, *Belg.* 51°6′ N, 5°46′ E **167**
Maastricht, *Neth.* 50°51′ N, 5°43′ E **167**
Mababe Depression, *Botswana* 18°50′ S, 23°43′ E **224**
Mabalane, *Mozambique* 23°48′ S, 32°39′ E **227**
Ma'bar, *Yemen* 14°47′ N, 44°18′ E **182**
Mabaruma, *Guyana* 8°12′ N, 59°43′ W **116**
Mabel Lake, *Can.* 50°37′ N, 118°59′ W **90**
Mabélé, *Cameroon* 6°0′ N, 13°58′ E **218**
Mabenga, *Dem. Rep. of the Congo* 3°40′ S, 18°38′ E **218**
Mabirou, *Congo* 1°8′ S, 15°45′ E **218**
Mablethorpe, *U.K.* 53°19′ N, 0°15′ E **162**
Mabote, *Mozambique* 22°2′ S, 34°8′ E **227**
Mabroûk, spring, *Mali* 19°29′ N, 1°15′ W **222**
Mabroûk, spring, *Mauritania* 17°58′ N, 12°20′ W **222**
Mabrous, spring, *Niger* 21°17′ N, 13°34′ E **222**
Mabruk, oil field, *Lib.* 29°45′ N, 17°7′ E **216**
Mabuasehube Game Reserve, *Botswana* 25°21′ S, 21°41′ E **227**
Mabuki, *Tanzania* 2°59′ S, 33°10′ E **224**
Mac. Robertson Land, region, *Antarctica* 72°44′ S, 59°21′ E **248**
Macachín, *Arg.* 37°10′ S, 63°41′ W **134**
Macaé, *Braz.* 22°23′ S, 41°50′ W **138**
Macaíba, *Braz.* 5°50′ S, 35°21′ W **132**
Macaloge, *Mozambique* 12°29′ S, 35°26′ E **224**
Macalpine Lake, *Can.* 66°32′ N, 105°59′ W **106**
Maçambara, *Braz.* 29°7′ S, 56°4′ W **139**
Macapá, *Braz.* 7°416′ N, 51°5′ W **130**
Macapá, *Braz.* 9°31′ S, 67°30′ W **137**
Macará, *Ecua.* 4°16′ S, 79°59′ W **130**
Macaranay, *Col.* 0°55′ N, 72°10′ W **136**
Macarani, *Braz.* 15°36′ S, 40°27′ W **138**
Macareo, river, *Venez.* 9°9′ N, 61°55′ W **116**
Macas, *Ecua.* 2°23′ S, 78°10′ W **136**
Macau, *Braz.* 5°9′ S, 36°36′ W **132**
Macau, *China* 22°10′ N, 113°31′ E **198**
Macauã, river, *Braz.* 10°14′ S, 69°54′ W **137**
Macaúba, *Braz.* 10°33′ S, 50°32′ W **130**
Macaúbas, *Braz.* 13°1′ S, 42°42′ W **138**
Macbride Head, *East Falkland* 51°29′ S, 57°44′ W **134**
Macclenny, *Fla., U.S.* 30°16′ N, 82°7′ W **96**
Macclesfield, *U.K.* 53°15′ N, 2°8′ W **162**
Macdiarmid, *Can.* 49°27′ N, 88°6′ W **94**
Macdill Air Force Base, *Fla., U.S.* 27°50′ N, 82°30′ W **105**
Macdonnell Ranges, *Austral.* 23°31′ S, 131°40′ E **230**
Macdui, Ben, peak, *U.K.* 57°3′ N, 3°46′ W **150**
Macedonia 41°38′ N, 21°37′ E **168**
Maceió, *Braz.* 9°36′ S, 35°42′ W **132**
Macenta, *Guinea* 8°30′ N, 9°28′ W **222**
Macerata, *It.* 43°18′ N, 13°26′ E **156**
Macey, Mount, peak, *Antarctica* 69°58′ S, 64°49′ E **248**
Macgillycuddy's Reeks, *Ire.* 51°43′ N, 10°50′ W **150**
Macgregor, *Can.* 49°58′ N, 98°46′ W **90**
Macha, *Russ.* 59°47′ N, 117°28′ E **160**
Machacalis, *Braz.* 17°3′ S, 40°47′ W **138**
Machacamarca, *Bol.* 18°12′ S, 67°5′ W **137**
Machado, *Braz.* 21°40′ S, 45°54′ W **138**
Machadodorp, *S. Af.* 25°43′ S, 30°11′ E **227**
Machaerus, ruin(s), *Jordan* 31°33′ N, 35°36′ E **194**
Machaíla, *Mozambique* 22°17′ S, 32°57′ E **227**
Machakos, *Kenya* 1°32′ S, 37°15′ E **224**
Machala, *Ecua.* 3°23′ S, 79°56′ W **130**
Machalilla National Park, *Ecua.* 1°42′ S, 80°55′ W **122**
Machaneng, *Botswana* 23°9′ S, 27°26′ E **227**
Machanga, *Mozambique* 20°56′ S, 34°55′ E **227**
Machareti, *Bol.* 20°49′ S, 63°31′ W **137**
Machault, *Fr.* 49°22′ N, 4°30′ E **163**
Machawaian Lake, *Can.* 51°50′ N, 88°56′ W **110**
Machaze, *Mozambique* 20°53′ S, 33°22′ E **227**
Macheke, *Zimb.* 18°10′ S, 31°45′ E **224**
Macheng, *China* 31°12′ N, 114°58′ E **198**
Machero, peak, *Sp.* 39°19′ N, 4°22′ W **164**
Machesney Park, *Ill., U.S.* 42°20′ N, 89°4′ W **102**
Machghara, *Leb.* 33°31′ N, 35°38′ E **194**
Machias, *Me., U.S.* 44°43′ N, 67°28′ W **94**
Machiasport, *Me., U.S.* 44°41′ N, 67°25′ W **94**
Machilipatnam (Bandar), *India* 16°11′ N, 81°10′ E **188**
Machipongo, *Va., U.S.* 37°24′ N, 75°54′ W **94**
Machiques, *Venez.* 10°1′ N, 72°34′ W **136**
Machu Picchu, ruin(s), *Peru* 13°11′ S, 72°40′ W **137**
Machupo, river, *Bol.* 13°10′ S, 64°44′ W **137**
Machynlleth, *U.K.* 52°34′ N, 3°50′ W **162**
Macia, *Mozambique* 25°1′ S, 33°7′ E **227**
Macintyre, river, *Austral.* 28°52′ S, 148°46′ E **230**
Macizo de la Maladeta, *Sp.* 42°29′ N, 0°38′ E **164**
Mack, *Colo., U.S.* 39°13′ N, 108°53′ W **90**
Mack Lake, *Can.* 58°1′ N, 95°56′ W **108**
Maçka, *Turk.* 40°49′ N, 39°37′ E **195**
Mackay, *Austral.* 21°15′ S, 149°7′ E **238**
Mackay, *Idaho, U.S.* 43°54′ N, 113°37′ W **90**
Mackay, river, *Can.* 56°45′ N, 112°13′ W **108**
Mackenzie, *Can.* 55°21′ N, 123°3′ W **108**
Mackenzie Bay 68°47′ N, 136°30′ W **98**
Mackenzie Bay 68°37′ S, 67°9′ E **248**
Mackenzie King Island, *Can.* 77°32′ N, 109°35′ W **106**
Mackenzie Mountains, *Can.* 63°16′ N, 128°53′ W **108**
Mackenzie, river, *Can.* 62°28′ N, 123°8′ W **106**
Mackinaw City, *Mich., U.S.* 45°46′ N, 84°44′ W **94**
Mackinnon, Cap, *Can.* 50°25′ N, 59°23′ W **111**
Mackinnon Road, *Kenya* 3°44′ S, 39°2′ E **224**
Mackintosh, Cape, *Antarctica* 72°59′ S, 59°28′ W **248**
Macklin, *Can.* 52°20′ N, 109°58′ W **108**
Mačkovci, *Slov.* 46°47′ N, 16°10′ E **168**
Macksville, *Kans., U.S.* 37°57′ N, 98°58′ W **90**
Maclear, *S. Af.* 31°6′ S, 28°19′ E **227**
Maclovio Herrera, *Mex.* 28°58′ N, 105°7′ W **92**
Maco, *Philippines* 7°24′ N, 125°49′ E **203**
Macocola, *Angola* 6°60′ S, 16°7′ E **218**
Macomb, *Mo., U.S.* 40°27′ N, 90°41′ W **94**
Macomer, *It.* 40°16′ N, 8°46′ E **156**
Macomia, *Mozambique* 12°12′ S, 40°8′ E **224**
Macon, *Ga., U.S.* 32°48′ N, 83°38′ W **96**
Macon, *Ill., U.S.* 39°42′ N, 88°60′ W **102**
Macon, *Miss., U.S.* 33°5′ N, 88°33′ W **103**
Macon, *Mo., U.S.* 39°43′ N, 92°28′ W **94**
Macondo, *Angola* 12°38′ S, 23°46′ E **224**
Macossa, *Mozambique* 17°55′ S, 33°55′ E **224**
Macoun Lake, *Can.* 56°29′ N, 104°24′ W **108**
Macovane, *Mozambique* 21°28′ S, 35°1′ E **227**
Macquarie Island, *Austral.* 54°55′ S, 158°31′ E **255**
Macquarie Ridge, *South Pacific Ocean* 52°33′ S, 160°15′ E **252**
Macrae, *Can.* 60°37′ N, 134°56′ W **108**
Macswyne's Gun, site, *Ire.* 55°10′ N, 8°7′ W **150**
Macuapanim, Ilhas, islands, *Braz.* 3°8′ S, 66°19′ W **130**
Macujer, *Col.* 0°23′ N, 73°7′ W **136**
Macurijes, Punta, *Cuba* 20°56′ N, 79°8′ W **116**
Macuro, *Venez.* 10°41′ N, 61°54′ W **116**
Macururé, *Braz.* 9°13′ S, 39°5′ W **132**
Macusani, *Peru* 14°4′ S, 70°27′ W **137**
Macuze, *Mozambique* 17°44′ S, 37°13′ E **224**
Ma'dabā, *Jordan* 31°42′ N, 35°47′ E **194**
Madaba, *Tanzania* 8°38′ S, 37°45′ E **224**
Madadi, *Chad* 18°29′ N, 20°43′ E **216**
Madagascar 18°5′ S, 45°32′ E **220**
Madagascar Basin, *Indian Ocean* 27°1′ S, 55°8′ E **254**
Madagascar Plateau, *Indian Ocean* 30°16′ S, 46°6′ E **254**
Madā'in Şāliḩ, *Saudi Arabia* 26°47′ N, 37°55′ E **180**
Madaket, *Mass., U.S.* 41°15′ N, 70°12′ W **104**
Madama, *Niger* 21°56′ N, 13°40′ E **216**
Madang, *P.N.G.* 5°15′ S, 145°43′ E **238**
Madaoua, *Niger* 14°5′ N, 5°55′ E **222**
Madara, *Bulg.* 43°15′ N, 27°5′ E **156**
Madaras, *Hung.* 46°2′ N, 19°16′ E **168**
Madaripur, *Bangladesh* 23°11′ N, 90°11′ E **197**
Madarounfa, *Niger* 13°19′ N, 7°4′ E **222**
Madau, island, *P.N.G.* 8°54′ S, 152°10′ E **192**
Madaure, ruin(s), *Alg.* 36°3′ N, 7°48′ E **156**
Madaw, *Turkm.* 38°11′ N, 54°42′ E **180**
Madayar, *Myanmar* 22°13′ N, 96°4′ E **202**
Maddock, *N. Dak., U.S.* 47°56′ N, 99°32′ W **90**
Madeira Islands, *Portugal* 33°23′ N, 18°12′ W **214**
Madeira, river, *Braz.* 5°30′ S, 60°51′ W **122**
Madeirinha, river, *Braz.* 9°56′ S, 61°3′ W **130**
Madeleine, Îles de la, island, *Can.* 47°31′ N, 63°44′ W **106**
Madelia, *Minn., U.S.* 44°2′ N, 94°25′ W **90**
Maden, *Turk.* 38°22′ N, 39°40′ E **195**
Madera, *Calif., U.S.* 36°57′ N, 120°4′ W **100**
Madera, *Mex.* 29°11′ N, 108°10′ W **92**
Madgaon, *India* 15°16′ N, 73°59′ E **188**
Madhya Pradesh, adm. division, *India* 23°57′ N, 78°8′ E **197**
Madi Opei, *Uganda* 3°35′ N, 33°4′ E **224**
Madibira, *Tanzania* 8°16′ S, 34°47′ E **224**
Madida, *China* 42°57′ N, 130°47′ E **200**
Madidi, *Bol.* 13°21′ S, 68°37′ W **137**
Madidi National Park, *Bol.* 14°46′ S, 68°6′ W **137**
Madidi, river, *Bol.* 12°38′ S, 67°26′ W **137**
Madill, *Okla., U.S.* 34°4′ N, 96°45′ W **92**
Madimba, *Dem. Rep. of the Congo* 5°1′ S, 15°8′ E **218**
Madina, *Mali* 13°24′ N, 8°52′ W **222**
Madina do Boé, *Guinea-Bissau* 11°46′ N, 14°14′ W **222**
Madīnat ash Sha'b, *Yemen* 12°52′ N, 44°52′ E **18**[illegible]
Madingo, *Congo* 4°6′ S, 11°21′ E **218**
Madingou, *Congo* 4°12′ S, 13°31′ E **218**
Madira, *Nig.* 12°38′ N, 6°29′ E **222**
Madirovalo, *Madagascar* 16°26′ S, 46°31′ E **220**
Madison, *Fla., U.S.* 30°26′ N, 83°25′ W **96**
Madison, *Ga., U.S.* 33°34′ N, 83°28′ W **96**
Madison, *Ind., U.S.* 38°44′ N, 85°23′ W **102**
Madison, *Kans., U.S.* 38°6′ N, 96°9′ W **90**
Madison, *Me., U.S.* 44°47′ N, 69°53′ W **94**
Madison, *Miss., U.S.* 32°27′ N, 90°8′ W **103**
Madison, *Nebr., U.S.* 41°48′ N, 97°28′ W **90**
Madison, *N.H., U.S.* 43°53′ N, 71°10′ W **104**
Madison, *Ohio, U.S.* 41°45′ N, 81°3′ W **102**
Madison, *S. Dak., U.S.* 43°59′ N, 97°8′ W **90**
Madison, *W. Va., U.S.* 38°3′ N, 81°50′ W **94**
Madison, *Wis., U.S.* 43°4′ N, 89°27′ W **102**
Madison Heights, *Va., U.S.* 37°25′ N, 79°8′ W **94**
Madison Range, *Mont., U.S.* 45°12′ N, 111°48′ W **90**
Madisonville, *Ky., U.S.* 37°19′ N, 87°31′ W **94**
Madisonville, *La., U.S.* 30°23′ N, 90°10′ W **103**
Madisonville, *Tex., U.S.* 30°55′ N, 95°55′ W **96**
Madjori, *Burkina Faso* 11°27′ N, 1°12′ E **222**
Madley, *U.K.* 52°2′ N, 2°52′ W **162**
Madley, Mount, peak, *Austral.* 24°37′ S, 123°41′ E **230**
Mado Gashi, *Kenya* 0°41′ N, 39°11′ E **224**
Madoc, *Can.* 44°29′ N, 77°29′ W **94**
Madocsa, *Hung.* 46°41′ N, 18°56′ E **168**
Madoi, *China* 34°54′ N, 98°10′ E **188**
Madona, *Latv.* 56°50′ N, 26°12′ E **166**
Madras, *Oreg., U.S.* 44°37′ N, 121°8′ W **90**
Madras see Chennai, *India* 13°5′ N, 80°16′ E **188**
Madrasat Lukk, *Lib.* 32°0′ N, 24°43′ E **180**
Madre de Dios, *Peru* 12°39′ S, 70°8′ W **137**
Madre de Dios, adm. division, *Peru* 12°9′ S, 71°9′ W **137**
Madre de Dios, Isla, island, *Chile* 50°5′ S, 77°46′ W **134**
Madre de Dios, river, *Bol.* 11°52′ S, 68°3′ W **137**
Madre de Dios, river, *Peru* 12°32′ S, 70°34′ W **13**[illegible]
Madre del Sur, Sierra, *Mex.* 18°15′ N, 101°45′ W **114**
Madre, Laguna 25°6′ N, 97°56′ W **114**
Madre Mountain, peak, *N. Mex., U.S.* 34°17′ N, 107°58′ W **92**
Madre, Sierra, *Guatemala* 15°44′ N, 93°15′ W **115**
Madre, Sierra, *Philippines* 16°12′ N, 121°14′ E **203**

Madre, Sierra, Wyo., U.S. 41°4′ N, 106°60′ W 90
Madrid, Sp. 40°24′ N, 3°47′ W 164
Madrid, adm. division, Sp. 40°20′ N, 3°58′ W 164
Madrid, Punta, Chile 19°2′ S, 70°21′ W 137
Madridejos, Sp. 39°28′ N, 3°34′ W 164
Madrigalejo, Sp. 39°7′ N, 5°38′ W 164
Madrona, Sierra, Sp. 38°28′ N, 4°17′ W 164
Madsen, Can. 50°57′ N, 93°55′ W 90
Madura, island, Indonesia 6°59′ S, 113°19′ E 192
Madurai, India 9°54′ N, 78°4′ E 188
Maduru Oya National Park, Sri Lanka 7°25′ N, 80°46′ E 172
Madzha, Russ. 61°53′ N, 51°32′ E 154
Mae Chaem, Thai. 18°29′ N, 98°22′ E 202
Mae Hong Son, Thai. 19°18′ N, 97°56′ E 202
Mae Ping National Park, Thai. 17°23′ N, 98°20′ E 202
Mae Rim, Thai. 18°55′ N, 98°56′ E 202
Mae Sariang, Thai. 18°10′ N, 97°55′ E 202
Mae Sot, Thai. 16°42′ N, 98°31′ E 202
Mae Suai, Thai. 19°48′ N, 99°32′ E 202
Maebashi, Japan 36°23′ N, 139°4′ E 201
Maella, Sp. 41°7′ N, 0°7′ E 164
Maentwrog, U.K. 52°56′ N, 3°59′ W 162
Maeruş, Rom. 45°54′ N, 25°32′ E 156
Maesteg, U.K. 51°36′ N, 3°39′ W 162
Maestra, Sierra, Cuba 20°12′ N, 76°53′ W 115
Maevatanana, Madagascar 16°60′ S, 46°51′ E 220
Mafaza, Sudan 13°35′ N, 34°32′ E 182
Mafeking, Can. 52°41′ N, 101°9′ W 108
Mafeteng, Lesotho 29°50′ S, 27°14′ E 227
Mafia Island, Tanzania 8°11′ S, 39°52′ E 224
Mafikeng, S. Af. 25°51′ S, 25°36′ E 227
Mafra, Braz. 26°9′ S, 49°50′ W 138
Magadan, Russ. 59°36′ N, 150°33′ E 160
Magadan, adm. division, Russ. 61°8′ N, 149°18′ E 160
Magadi, Kenya 1°53′ S, 36°21′ E 224
Magal Umm Rûs, spring, Egypt 25°28′ N, 34°35′ E 180
Magallanes, Estecho de (Magellan, Strait of), Chile 52°41′ S, 72°22′ W 122
Magallanes, Philippines 12°49′ N, 123°51′ E 203
Magallanes Y Antártica Chilena, adm. division, Chile 49°4′ S, 76°47′ W 134
Magangué, Col. 9°13′ N, 74°47′ W 130
Magaria, Niger 12°57′ N, 8°54′ E 222
Magazine Mountain, peak, Ark., U.S. 35°7′ N, 93°43′ W 96
Magdagachi, Russ. 53°29′ N, 125°48′ E 190
Magdalena, Arg. 35°4′ S, 57°33′ W 139
Magdalena, Bol. 13°21′ S, 64°11′ W 137
Magdalena, Mex. 20°54′ N, 103°58′ W 114
Magdalena, Mex. 30°37′ N, 110°59′ W 92
Magdalena, N. Mex., U.S. 34°6′ N, 107°15′ W 92
Magdalena, adm. division, Col. 10°33′ N, 74°45′ W 136
Magdalena, Bahía 24°32′ N, 112°50′ W 112
Magdalena, Isla, island, Mex. 25°20′ N, 113°13′ W 112
Magdalena, Llano de la, Mex. 24°13′ N, 111°25′ W 112
Magdalena, river, Mex. 30°32′ N, 112°42′ W 92
Magdeburg, Ger. 52°7′ N, 11°37′ E 152
Magdelaine Cays, islands, Coral Sea 17°5′ S, 150°25′ E 230
Magee, Miss., U.S. 31°52′ N, 89°42′ W 103
Magee Island, U.K. 54°45′ N, 6°12′ W 150
Magellan Seamounts, North Pacific Ocean 15°24′ N, 154°39′ E 252
Magellan, Strait of 52°41′ S, 72°44′ W 122
Magenta, It. 45°27′ N, 8°53′ E 167
Magerøya, island, Nor. 71°11′ N, 21°17′ E 160
Maggie Mountain, peak, Calif., U.S. 36°16′ N, 118°39′ W 101
Maggiorasca, Monte, peak, It. 44°32′ N, 9°27′ E 167
Maghâgha, Egypt 28°38′ N, 30°48′ E 182
Maghama, Mauritania 15°30′ N, 12°55′ W 222
Magid, oil field, Lib. 28°15′ N, 22°8′ E 216
Magilligan Point, U.K. 54°58′ N, 6°57′ W 150
Magina, peak, Sp. 37°43′ N, 3°29′ W 164
Magione, It. 43°8′ N, 12°12′ E 156
Magistral, Mex. 25°57′ N, 105°21′ W 114
Maglaj, Bosn. and Herzg. 44°33′ N, 18°5′ E 168
Maglie, It. 40°7′ N, 18°17′ E 156
Magnetic Island National Park, Austral. 19°14′ S, 146°30′ E 238
Magnitka, Russ. 55°20′ N, 59°44′ E 154
Magnitogorsk, Russ. 53°26′ N, 59°8′ E 154
Magnolia, Ark., U.S. 33°15′ N, 93°15′ W 103
Magnolia, Ill., U.S. 41°6′ N, 89°12′ W 102
Magnolia, Miss., U.S. 31°7′ N, 90°29′ W 103
Magnor, Nor. 59°57′ N, 12°11′ E 152
Mago National Park, Eth. 5°21′ N, 35°30′ E 224
Magog, Can. 45°15′ N, 72°9′ W 111
Magosal, Mex. 21°37′ N, 97°59′ W 114
Magpie, Can. 50°19′ N, 64°30′ W 111
Magpie, river, Can. 50°54′ N, 64°47′ W 111
Magrath, Can. 49°25′ N, 112°52′ W 90
Magruder Mountain, peak, Nev., U.S. 37°24′ N, 117°38′ W 92
Maguan, China 22°59′ N, 104°23′ E 202
Maguari, Cabo, Braz. 0°28′ N, 49°15′ W 130
Maguarichic, Mex. 27°51′ N, 107°58′ W 112
Magude, Mozambique 24°60′ S, 32°37′ E 227
Magué, Mozambique 15°51′ S, 31°43′ E 224
Maguire, Mount, peak, Antarctica 74°5′ S, 66°32′ E 248
Magumeri, Nig. 12°6′ N, 12°50′ E 216
Magwa Falls, S. Af. 31°14′ S, 28°52′ E 227
Magwa, oil field, Kuwait 29°3′ N, 47°52′ E 196
Magway, Myanmar 20°9′ N, 94°57′ E 202
Mahābād, Iran 36°45′ N, 45°41′ E 195
Mahabo, Madagascar 20°21′ S, 44°38′ E 220
Mahagi, Dem. Rep. of the Congo 2°15′ N, 30°59′ E 224
Mahajanga, Madagascar 15°42′ S, 46°20′ E 220
Mahalapye, Botswana 23°4′ S, 26°46′ E 227
Mahale Mountain National Park, Tanzania 6°26′ S, 29°29′ E 224
Maḩallāt, Iran 33°56′ N, 50°24′ E 180
Mahanadi, river, India 20°55′ N, 84°19′ E 190
Mahanoro, Madagascar 19°52′ S, 48°46′ E 220
Mahanoy City, Pa., U.S. 40°48′ N, 76°9′ W 94
Mahao, China 43°11′ N, 128°2′ E 200
Maharajganj, India 27°7′ N, 83°32′ E 197
Maharashtra, adm. division, India 19°35′ N, 73°17′ E 188
Mahasthan, ruin(s), Bangladesh 24°54′ N, 89°13′ E 197
Mahavelona, Madagascar 17°40′ S, 49°28′ E 220
Mahbubnagar, India 16°43′ N, 77°57′ E 188
Mahd adh Dhahab, Saudi Arabia 23°26′ N, 40°53′ E 182
Mahdere Maryam, Eth. 11°41′ N, 37°53′ E 182
Mahdia, Guyana 5°14′ N, 59°16′ W 130
Mahdia, Tun. 35°31′ N, 11°1′ E 156
Mahendra Giri, peak, India 18°58′ N, 84°11′ E 188
Mahenge, Tanzania 8°39′ S, 36°42′ E 224
Maheno, N.Z. 45°12′ S, 170°49′ E 240
Mahesana, India 23°33′ N, 72°24′ E 186
Maheshwar, India 22°11′ N, 75°34′ E 197
Mahewa, India 24°23′ N, 80°10′ E 197
Mahi, river, India 23°6′ N, 73°41′ E 186
Mahia Peninsula, N.Z. 39°7′ S, 177°45′ E 240
Mahilyow, Belarus 53°57′ N, 30°21′ E 154
Mahim, India 19°39′ N, 72°45′ E 188
Mahin, Nig. 6°16′ N, 4°45′ E 222
Mahires, Tun. 34°34′ N, 10°31′ E 156
Mahlberg, Ger. 48°17′ N, 7°48′ E 163
Mahmudiye, Turk. 39°30′ N, 30°58′ E 156
Mahnomen, Minn., U.S. 47°18′ N, 95°58′ W 90
Maho, Sri Lanka 7°50′ N, 80°17′ E 188
Mahoba, India 25°17′ N, 79°51′ E 197
Mahogany Hills, Nev., U.S. 39°26′ N, 116°21′ W 90
Mahogany Mountain, peak, Oreg., U.S. 43°13′ N, 117°21′ W 90
Mahomet, Ill., U.S. 40°10′ N, 88°24′ W 102
Mahón, Sp. 39°54′ N, 4°14′ E 143
Mahopac, N.Y., U.S. 41°22′ N, 73°44′ W 104
Mahora, Sp. 39°12′ N, 1°44′ W 164
Mahuta, Tanzania 10°52′ S, 39°25′ E 224
Mahuva, India 21°4′ N, 71°45′ E 188
Maials, Sp. 41°22′ N, 0°30′ E 164
Maicao, Col. 11°21′ N, 72°15′ W 136
Maicasagi, Lac, lake, Can. 49°53′ N, 77°19′ W 94
Maicasagi, river, Can. 49°59′ N, 76°54′ W 110
Maiden Castle, ruin(s), U.K. 50°40′ N, 2°37′ W 150
Maidenhead, U.K. 51°31′ N, 0°44′ E 162
Maidstone, Can. 53°5′ N, 109°17′ W 108
Maidstone, U.K. 51°16′ N, 0°31′ E 162
Maiduguri, Nig. 11°51′ N, 13°9′ E 216
Maigualida, Sierra, Venez. 5°34′ N, 65°28′ W 130
Maihar, India 24°15′ N, 80°44′ E 197
Maiko National Park, Dem. Rep. of the Congo 0°35′ N, 27°15′ E 224
Maiko, river, Dem. Rep. of the Congo 0°20′ N, 26°51′ E 224
Maikona, Kenya 2°53′ N, 37°30′ E 224
Mailsi, Pak. 29°48′ N, 72°11′ E 186
Main Centre, Can. 50°35′ N, 107°22′ W 90
Main Channel 45°19′ N, 82°17′ W 110
Main Pass 29°20′ N, 89°20′ W 103
Main, river, Ger. 49°59′ N, 10°12′ E 167
Maine, adm. division, Me., U.S. 45°16′ N, 69°59′ W 94
Maine, Gulf of 43°8′ N, 67°56′ W 253
Maine, Gulf of 44°10′ N, 69°15′ W 94
Maine, region, Fr. 48°25′ N, 0°48′ E 163
Maïné Soroa, Niger 13°14′ N, 12°3′ E 222
Maingkwan, Myanmar 26°20′ N, 96°35′ E 188
Mainit, Lake, Philippines 9°25′ N, 125°15′ E 203
Mainland, island, U.K. 59°44′ N, 0°54′ E 142
Mainling, China 29°12′ N, 94°6′ E 188
Mainpuri, India 27°12′ N, 79°1′ E 197
Maintal, Ger. 50°9′ N, 8°49′ E 167
Maintenon, Fr. 48°34′ N, 1°34′ E 163
Maintirano, Madagascar 18°4′ S, 44°1′ E 220
Mainz, Ger. 49°59′ N, 8°15′ E 167
Maipo, Paso de, pass, Chile 34°15′ S, 69°52′ W 134
Maipú, Arg. 36°52′ S, 57°53′ W 139
Maipures, Col. 5°8′ N, 67°51′ W 136
Maisí, Punta de, Cuba 20°14′ N, 74°6′ W 116
Maiskhal, island, Bangladesh 21°23′ N, 90°54′ E 188
Maisou Island, Mich., U.S. 43°46′ N, 83°45′ W 102
Maisse, Fr. 48°23′ N, 2°22′ E 163
Maitengwe, Botswana 20°8′ S, 27°10′ E 227
Maitri, India, station, Antarctica 70°37′ S, 11°36′ E 248
Maíz Grande, Isla del (Great Corn Island), Nicar. 11°44′ N, 83°2′ W 115
Maizhokunggar, China 29°52′ N, 91°45′ E 197
Maizières, Fr. 49°12′ N, 6°9′ E 163
Maizuru, Japan 35°24′ N, 135°19′ E 201
Majagual, Col. 8°33′ N, 74°37′ W 136
Majahual, Mex. 18°45′ N, 87°45′ W 115
Majdal Shams, Israel 33°16′ N, 35°46′ E 194
Majdanpek, Serb. and Mont. 44°24′ N, 21°56′ E 168
Majene, Indonesia 3°29′ S, 118°54′ E 192
Majevica, Bosn. and Herzg. 44°42′ N, 18°31′ E 168
Majī, Eth. 6°12′ N, 35°37′ E 224
Majorca see Mallorca, island, Sp. 39°38′ N, 2°37′ E 150
Majske Poljane, Croatia 45°19′ N, 16°8′ E 168
Majuro, Marshall Islands 7°5′ N, 171°22′ E 242
Majuro Atoll, Marshall Islands 7°7′ N, 171°10′ E 242
Mak, Ko, island, Thai. 11°40′ N, 101°58′ E 202
Maka, Senegal 13°40′ N, 14°20′ W 222
Makabana, Congo 3°30′ S, 12°36′ E 218
Makaha, Zimb. 17°20′ S, 32°34′ E 224
Makalamabedi, Botswana 20°20′ S, 23°48′ E 227
Makaleha Mountains, peak, Hawai'i, U.S. 22°6′ N, 159°28′ W 99
Makalu, peak, Nepal 27°52′ N, 87°2′ E 197
Makalu-Barun National Park, Nepal 27°29′ N, 86°21′ E 197
Makandja, Dem. Rep. of the Congo 0°46′ N, 23°14′ E 218
Makanya, Tanzania 4°22′ S, 37°49′ E 224
Makanza, Dem. Rep. of the Congo 1°35′ N, 19°4′ E 218
Makarfi, Nig. 11°19′ N, 7°53′ E 222
Makari, Cameroon 12°36′ N, 14°29′ E 216
Makarikha, Russ. 66°13′ N, 58°23′ E 169
Makarov, Russ. 48°34′ N, 142°40′ E 190
Makarov Basin, Arctic Ocean 87°7′ N, 170°10′ W 255
Makarska, Croatia 43°17′ N, 17°1′ E 168
Makar'yev, Russ. 57°53′ N, 43°46′ E 154
Makassar see Ujungpandang, Indonesia 5°11′ S, 119°25′ E 192
Makassar Strait 1°31′ S, 117°0′ E 192
Makeni, Sierra Leone 8°54′ N, 12°4′ W 222
Maketu, N.Z. 37°48′ S, 176°26′ E 240
Makgadikgadi Pans Game Reserve, Botswana 20°54′ S, 24°49′ E 227
Makhachkala, Russ. 42°55′ N, 47°35′ E 195
Makhad, Pak. 33°8′ N, 71°46′ E 186
Makhado (Louis Trichardt), S. Af. 23°3′ S, 29°53′ E 227
Makhambet, Kaz. 47°40′ N, 51°33′ E 158
Makhana, Senegal 16°8′ N, 16°26′ W 222
Makhfar al Buşayyah, Iraq 30°6′ N, 46°5′ E 196
Makhnovka, Russ. 57°25′ N, 29°20′ E 166
Makikihi, N.Z. 44°39′ S, 171°8′ E 240
Makindu, Kenya 2°19′ S, 37°49′ E 224
Makīnsk, Kaz. 52°39′ N, 70°25′ E 184
Makiyivka, Ukr. 48°2′ N, 37°59′ E 158
Makkah (Mecca), Saudi Arabia 21°24′ N, 39°49′ E 182
Makkovik, Can. 54°59′ N, 59°10′ W 106
Makó, Hung. 46°13′ N, 20°29′ E 168
Mako, Senegal 12°53′ N, 12°24′ W 222
Makoino, Madagascar 16°21′ S, 48°11′ E 220
Makok, Gabon 1°59′ S, 9°36′ E 218
Makokibatan Lake, Can. 51°14′ N, 88°52′ W 80
Makokou, Gabon 0°31′ N, 12°48′ E 218
Mākole'ā Point, Hawai'i, U.S. 19°47′ N, 156°31′ W 99
Makoli, Zambia 17°28′ S, 26°3′ E 224
Makongolosi, Tanzania 8°25′ S, 33°10′ E 224
Makrai, India 22°6′ N, 77°6′ E 197
Makrana, India 27°1′ N, 74°43′ E 186
Maksatikha, Russ. 57°44′ N, 35°52′ E 154
Maksimkin Yar, Russ. 58°42′ N, 86°50′ E 169
Maktau, Kenya 3°27′ S, 38°6′ E 224
Mākū, Iran 39°20′ N, 44°31′ E 195
Makumbako, Tanzania 8°50′ S, 34°49′ E 224
Makung, Taiwan 23°31′ N, 119°34′ E 198
Makungo, Somalia 0°48′ N, 42°33′ E 224
Makunudu Atoll, Maldives 5°26′ N, 67°51′ E 172
Makurazaki, Japan 31°15′ N, 130°18′ E 201
Makurdi, Nig. 7°41′ N, 8°33′ E 222
Makushin Volcano, peak, Alas., U.S. 53°51′ N, 167°3′ W 98
Makushino, Russ. 55°12′ N, 67°14′ E 184
Mal, Mauritania 16°59′ N, 13°25′ W 222
Malá, Sp. 37°6′ N, 3°43′ W 164
Mala, Punta, Pan. 7°24′ N, 79°59′ W 115
Mala Vyska, Ukr. 48°39′ N, 31°39′ E 158
Malabang, Philippines 7°39′ N, 124°6′ E 203
Malabo, Equatorial Guinea 3°45′ N, 8°40′ E 222
Malabuñgan, Philippines 9°2′ N, 117°40′ E 203
Malacca, Malaysia 2°13′ N, 102°16′ E 196
Malacca, Strait of 6°12′ N, 97°6′ E 196
Malad City, Idaho, U.S. 42°11′ N, 112°14′ W 82
Maladzyechna, Belarus 54°18′ N, 26°50′ E 166
Málaga, Calif., U.S. 36°40′ N, 119°45′ W 100
Málaga, Col. 6°41′ N, 72°45′ W 136
Málaga, N. Mex., U.S. 32°13′ N, 104°4′ W 92
Málaga, Sp. 36°42′ N, 4°27′ W 164
Málaga, Sp. 36°45′ N, 4°28′ W 214
Malagarasi, Tanzania 5°6′ S, 30°51′ E 224
Malagón, Sp. 39°10′ N, 3°51′ W 164
Malaita, island, Solomon Islands 9°0′ S, 161°0′ E 242
Malakal, Sudan 9°32′ N, 31°45′ E 224
Malakoff, Tex., U.S. 32°9′ N, 96°1′ W 96
Malalbergo, It. 44°44′ N, 11°32′ E 167
Malampaya Sound 10°55′ N, 118°41′ E 203
Malang, Indonesia 8°2′ S, 112°27′ E 192
Malangali, Tanzania 8°35′ S, 34°52′ E 224
Malangen, Nor. 69°23′ N, 18°37′ E 152
Malanje, Angola 9°34′ S, 16°13′ E 218
Malanje, adm. division, Angola 8°41′ S, 15°42′ E 218
Malanville, Benin 11°51′ N, 3°23′ E 222
Malargüe, Arg. 35°27′ S, 69°36′ W 134
Malartic, Can. 48°8′ N, 78°9′ W 94
Malaryta, Belarus 51°46′ N, 24°2′ E 154
Malaspina Glacier, Alas., U.S. 59°14′ N, 143°10′ W 106
Malatya, Turk. 38°20′ N, 38°17′ E 180
Malavate, South America 3°16′ N, 54°6′ W 130
Malawi 13°0′ S, 34°0′ E 224
Malawiya, Sudan 15°13′ N, 36°12′ E 182
Malay Peninsula, Malaysia 7°4′ N, 99°57′ E 196
Malaya Vishera, Russ. 58°48′ N, 32°20′ E 154
Malayagiri, peak, India 21°21′ N, 85°8′ E 188
Malaybalay, Philippines 8°12′ N, 125°8′ E 203
Malāyer, Iran 34°17′ N, 48°51′ E 180
Malaysia 2°20′ N, 112°47′ E 192
Malazgirt, Turk. 39°8′ N, 42°30′ E 195
Malbaza, Niger 13°58′ N, 5°39′ E 222
Malbork, Pol. 54°1′ N, 19°2′ E 166
Malbrán, Arg. 29°21′ S, 62°27′ W 139
Mal'chevskaya, Russ. 49°2′ N, 40°21′ E 158
Malden, Ill., U.S. 41°25′ N, 89°22′ W 102
Malden, Mo., U.S. 36°33′ N, 89°58′ W 94
Maldive Islands, Arabian Sea 1°14′ N, 72°26′ E 188
Maldives, Maldives 2°12′ N, 74°34′ E 188
Maldon, U.K. 51°43′ N, 0°39′ E 162
Maldonado, Uru. 34°53′ S, 54°59′ W 139
Maldonado, Punta, Mex. 15°32′ N, 103°13′ W 72
Malè, It. 46°20′ N, 10°55′ E 167
Male Atoll, Maldives 4°29′ N, 73°0′ E 188
Malé Karpaty, Slovakia 48°25′ N, 17°3′ E 152
Male see Maale, Maldives 4°9′ N, 73°15′ E 188
Malegaon, India 20°33′ N, 74°33′ E 188
Maléha, Guinea 11°50′ N, 9°44′ W 222
Malek, Sudan 6°2′ N, 31°38′ E 224
Malela, Dem. Rep. of the Congo 2°26′ S, 26°7′ E 224
Malela, Dem. Rep. of the Congo 4°23′ S, 26°8′ E 224
Malemba-Nkulu, Dem. Rep. of the Congo 8°1′ S, 26°46′ E 224
Malembé, Congo 3°5′ S, 12°2′ E 218
Malengoia, Dem. Rep. of the Congo 3°26′ N, 25°24′ E 224
Maler Kotla, India 30°31′ N, 75°55′ E 197
Maleševske Planina, Maced. 41°38′ N, 22°40′ E 168
Malesherbes, Fr. 48°16′ N, 2°23′ E 163
Maleza, Col. 4°22′ N, 69°25′ W 136
Malfa, It. 38°34′ N, 14°49′ E 156
Malgobek, Russ. 43°30′ N, 44°33′ E 195
Malgrat de Mar, Sp. 41°38′ N, 2°44′ E 164
Malha, spring, Sudan 15°4′ N, 26°9′ E 226
Malhada, Braz. 14°20′ S, 43°48′ W 138
Malhão, Serra do, Port. 37°24′ N, 8°28′ W 150
Malheur Cave, site, Oreg., U.S. 43°13′ N, 118°28′ W 90
Mali, Guinea 12°6′ N, 12°20′ W 222
Mali 18°26′ N, 1°60′ W 214
Mali Drvenik, island, Croatia 43°20′ N, 15°55′ E 168
Mali Kyun, island, Myanmar 13°17′ N, 98°7′ E 202
Mali Lošinj, Croatia 44°32′ N, 14°27′ E 156
Mali, river, Myanmar 25°18′ N, 97°11′ E 188
Malibu, Calif., U.S. 34°2′ N, 118°43′ W 101
Målilla, Nor. 57°22′ N, 15°48′ E 152
Malimba, Monts, Dem. Rep. of the Congo 7°41′ S, 29°8′ E 224
Malinau, Indonesia 3°41′ N, 116°30′ E 192
Malindi, Kenya 3°13′ S, 40°6′ E 224
Malinyi, Tanzania 8°57′ S, 35°59′ E 224
Malipo, China 23°5′ N, 104°42′ E 202
Mališevo, Europe 42°32′ N, 20°43′ E 168
Maljen, Serb. and Mont. 44°9′ N, 19°56′ E 168
Malka Mari National Park, Kenya 3°54′ N, 40°5′ E 224
Malkaaray, Somalia 3°54′ N, 41°53′ E 224
Malkara, Turk. 40°53′ N, 26°53′ E 156
Malki, Russ. 53°31′ N, 157°39′ E 160
Małkinia Górna, Pol. 53°0′ N, 22°0′ E 152
Malko Tŭrnovo, Bulg. 41°59′ N, 27°31′ E 156
Mal'kovichi, Belarus 52°31′ N, 26°35′ E 152
Mallāḩ, Syr. 32°30′ N, 36°50′ E 194
Mallaoua, Niger 13°2′ N, 9°36′ E 222
Mallawi, Egypt 27°46′ N, 30°46′ E 180
Mallén, Sp. 41°52′ N, 1°26′ W 164
Malles Venosta, It. 46°42′ N, 10°33′ E 167
Mallet, Braz. 25°55′ S, 50°52′ W 139
Malletts Bay, Vt., U.S. 44°32′ N, 73°14′ W 104
Mallorca (Majorca), island, Sp. 39°38′ N, 2°37′ E 150
Mallory Swamp, marsh, Fla., U.S. 29°42′ N, 83°17′ W 105
Malm, Nor. 64°4′ N, 11°12′ E 152
Malmédy, Belg. 50°26′ N, 6°1′ E 167
Malmesbury, S. Af. 33°28′ S, 18°41′ E 227
Malmesbury, U.K. 51°35′ N, 2°6′ W 162
Malmö, Nor. 55°35′ N, 12°59′ E 152
Malmstrom Air Force Base, Mont., U.S. 47°28′ N, 111°16′ W 90
Maloarkhangel'sk, Russ. 52°21′ N, 36°30′ E 158
Maloca, Braz. 0°42′ N, 55°58′ W 130
Maloca, Braz. 10°49′ S, 70°9′ W 137
Maloca de Índios, Braz. 11°42′ S, 58°16′ W 130
Maloca Timbé, Braz. 3°3′ S, 47°45′ W 130
Maloja, Switz. 46°26′ N, 9°42′ E 167
Malole, Zambia 10°8′ S, 31°33′ E 224
Malo-les-Bains, Fr. 51°1′ N, 2°25′ E 163
Malolos, Philippines 14°49′ N, 120°47′ E 203
Malombe, Lake, Malawi 14°40′ S, 34°54′ E 224
Malone, N.Y., U.S. 44°50′ N, 74°19′ W 94
Malone, Wash., U.S. 46°56′ N, 123°20′ W 100
Malonga, Dem. Rep. of the Congo 10°26′ S, 23°9′ E 220
Malongwe, Tanzania 5°24′ S, 33°39′ E 224
Małopolskie, adm. division, Pol. 52°41′ N, 22°0′ E 152
Malorad, Bulg. 43°29′ N, 23°40′ E 156
Maloshuyka, Russ. 63°44′ N, 37°28′ E 154
Malouin, river, Can. 50°9′ N, 79°11′ W 110
Mal'ovitsa, peak, Bulg. 42°9′ N, 23°16′ E 156
Måløy, Nor. 61°56′ N, 5°6′ E 152
Maloyaz, Russ. 55°13′ N, 58°11′ E 154
Malpas, U.K. 53°1′ N, 2°46′ W 162
Malpeque Bay 46°28′ N, 64°26′ W 111
Malpura, India 26°16′ N, 75°23′ E 197
Malta 35°56′ N, 14°26′ E 156
Malta, Idaho, U.S. 42°19′ N, 113°23′ W 90
Malta, Ill., U.S. 41°55′ N, 88°52′ W 102
Malta, Latv. 56°19′ N, 27°8′ E 166
Malta, Malta 35°56′ N, 14°26′ E 156
Malta, Mont., U.S. 48°20′ N, 107°53′ W 90
Malta, Ohio, U.S. 39°38′ N, 81°53′ W 102
Malta Channel 36°15′ N, 14°16′ E 156
Malta, river, Latv. 56°26′ N, 26°47′ E 166
Maltahöhe, Namibia 24°50′ S, 16°56′ E 227
Maltby, U.K. 53°25′ N, 1°13′ W 162
Maltese Islands, Malta 35°30′ N, 14°3′ E 156
Malton, U.K. 54°8′ N, 0°48′ E 162
Ma'lūlā, Syr. 33°50′ N, 36°32′ E 194
Malumfashi, Nig. 11°46′ N, 7°37′ E 222
Malvan, India 16°4′ N, 73°29′ E 188
Malvern, Ark., U.S. 34°20′ N, 92°50′ W 96
Malvern, Iowa, U.S. 41°0′ N, 95°35′ W 90
Malvern, U.K. 52°6′ N, 2°20′ W 162
Malvinas, Islas see Falkland Islands, Falk. Is., U.K. 53°40′ S, 58°56′ W 134
Malybay, Kaz. 43°30′ N, 78°30′ E 184
Malyn, Ukr. 50°47′ N, 29°23′ E 158
Malyns'k, Ukr. 51°4′ N, 26°32′ E 152
Malyy Anyuy, river, Russ. 67°32′ N, 168°13′ E 246
Malyy Atlym, Russ. 62°19′ N, 67°4′ E 169
Malyy Lyakhovskiy, Ostrov, island, Russ. 74°11′ N, 150°36′ E 246
Malyy, Ostrov, island, Russ. 60°3′ N, 28°0′ E 166
Malyy Tyuters, Ostrov, island, Russ. 59°37′ N, 26°44′ E 166
Malyye Derbety, Russ. 47°56′ N, 44°34′ E 158
Malyye Karmakuly, Russ. 72°15′ N, 52°58′ E 160
Mama, Russ. 58°17′ N, 112°55′ E 160
Mamadysh, Russ. 55°42′ N, 51°16′ E 154
Maman, Sudan 16°20′ N, 36°46′ E 182
Mambajao, Philippines 9°15′ N, 124°44′ E 203
Mambali, Tanzania 4°33′ S, 32°40′ E 224
Mambasa, Dem. Rep. of the Congo 1°19′ N, 29°3′ E 224
Mamboya, Tanzania 6°15′ S, 37°9′ E 224
Mambrui, Kenya 3°7′ S, 40°8′ E 224
Mamburao, Philippines 13°15′ N, 120°36′ E 203
Mamfé, Cameroon 5°43′ N, 9°17′ E 222
Mamiña, Chile 20°3′ S, 69°15′ W 137
Maminas, Alban. 41°23′ N, 19°36′ E 156
Mammamattawa, Can. 50°27′ N, 84°23′ W 94
Mammoth Cave National Park, Ky., U.S. 37°17′ N, 88°6′ W 80
Mamonovo, Russ. 54°27′ N, 19°54′ E 166
Mamoré, river, Bol. 13°52′ S, 65°11′ W 137
Mamori, Lago, lake, Braz. 3°39′ S, 60°46′ W 130
Mamoriá, river, Braz. 7°16′ S, 67°19′ W 130
Mamou, Guinea 10°23′ N, 12°7′ W 222
Mamou, La., U.S. 30°37′ N, 92°26′ W 103
Mampikony, Madagascar 16°5′ S, 47°39′ E 220
Mampong, Ghana 7°5′ N, 1°26′ W 222
Mamshit, ruin(s), Israel 31°0′ N, 35°1′ E 194
Mamuju, Indonesia 2°43′ S, 118°47′ E 192
Mamuno, Botswana 22°11′ S, 20°2′ E 227
Mamuras, Alban. 41°35′ N, 19°40′ E 168
Man, Côte d'Ivoire 7°18′ N, 7°34′ W 222
Man Aung, Myanmar 18°51′ N, 93°46′ E 188
Man, Isle of 54°17′ N, 4°55′ W 150
Man of War Point, Can. 54°25′ N, 58°25′ W 111
Man, river, China 42°10′ N, 127°23′ E 200
Mānā, Hawai'i, U.S. 22°2′ N, 159°47′ W 99
Mana, South America 5°40′ N, 53°50′ W 130
Mana La, pass, India 31°4′ N, 79°25′ E 197
Mana Pools National Park, Zimb. 16°11′ S, 28°55′ E 224
Manacacías, river, Col. 3°42′ N, 72°26′ W 136
Manacapuru, Braz. 3°19′ S, 60°36′ W 130
Manacor, Sp. 39°34′ N, 3°11′ E 214
Manado, Indonesia 1°30′ N, 124°42′ E 192
Managua, Nicar. 12°3′ N, 86°24′ W 115
Managua, Lago de, lake, Nicar. 12°14′ N, 87°5′ W 116
Manaia, N.Z. 39°34′ S, 174°7′ E 240
Manakara, Madagascar 22°15′ S, 48°2′ E 207
Manakau, peak, N.Z. 42°15′ S, 173°32′ E 240
Manākhah, Yemen 15°2′ N, 43°44′ E 182
Manam, island, P.N.G. 4°16′ S, 145°8′ E 192
Manama see Al Manāmah, Bahrain 26°10′ N, 50°27′ E 196
Manambolo, river, Madagascar 19°6′ S, 43°47′ E 220
Manankoro, Mali 10°30′ N, 7°27′ W 222
Manantenina, Madagascar 24°20′ S, 47°20′ E 220
Manantiales, Chile 52°46′ S, 69°16′ W 123
Manapouri, N.Z. 45°36′ S, 167°39′ E 240
Manapouri, Lake, N.Z. 45°31′ S, 166°52′ E 240
Manas, China 44°16′ N, 86°16′ E 184
Manas Hu, lake, China 45°38′ N, 85°18′ E 184
Manassa, Colo., U.S. 37°9′ N, 105°57′ W 92
Manassas National Battlefield Park, Va., U.S. 38°48′ N, 77°37′ W 94
Manatee, river, Fla., U.S. 27°25′ N, 82°11′ W 105
Manaus, Braz. 3°5′ S, 60°1′ W 130
Manavgat, Turk. 36°45′ N, 31°26′ E 180
Manay, Philippines 7°14′ N, 126°32′ E 203
Manbazar, India 23°4′ N, 86°39′ E 197
Mancha Real, Sp. 37°47′ N, 3°37′ W 164
Manchester, Conn., U.S. 41°46′ N, 72°32′ W 104
Manchester, Iowa, U.S. 42°29′ N, 91°28′ W 94
Manchester, Ky., U.S. 37°9′ N, 83°47′ W 96
Manchester, Me., U.S. 44°19′ N, 69°52′ W 104
Manchester, Mich., U.S. 42°9′ N, 84°2′ W 102
Manchester, N.H., U.S. 42°58′ N, 71°28′ W 104
Manchester, Ohio, U.S. 40°55′ N, 81°34′ W 102
Manchester, Tenn., U.S. 35°28′ N, 86°5′ W 96
Manchester, U.K. 53°28′ N, 2°16′ W 162
Manchester, Vt., U.S. 43°9′ N, 73°5′ W 104
Manchester Center, Vt., U.S. 43°10′ N, 73°4′ W 104
Manchester Lake, Can. 61°24′ N, 108°30′ W 108
Manchuria see Dongbei, region 40°34′ N, 122°39′ E 200
Mancos, Colo., U.S. 37°20′ N, 108°18′ W 92
Mand, Pak. 26°1′ N, 62°7′ E 182
Mand, river, Iran 28°19′ N, 51°45′ E 196
Manda, Tanzania 7°58′ S, 32°26′ E 224
Manda, Tanzania 10°29′ S, 34°35′ E 224
Manda Island, Kenya 2°24′ S, 40°58′ E 224
Manda National Park, Chad 9°9′ N, 17°26′ E 216
Mandab, Bāb al 12°28′ N, 42°51′ E 182
Mandabe, Madagascar 21°3′ S, 44°54′ E 220
Mandaguari, Braz. 23°31′ S, 51°49′ W 138
Mandal, Mongolia 48°26′ N, 106°42′ E 198
Mandal, Nor. 58°1′ N, 7°30′ E 150
Mandala, Puncak, peak, Indonesia 4°42′ S, 140°2′ E 192
Mandalay, Myanmar 21°58′ N, 96°7′ E 202
Mandalgovĭ, Mongolia 45°47′ N, 106°16′ E 198
Mandalī, Iraq 33°45′ N, 45°31′ E 180
Mandan, N. Dak., U.S. 46°49′ N, 100°54′ W 90
Mandara Mountains, Cameroon 9°18′ N, 12°57′ E 216
Mandau, river, Indonesia 1°7′ N, 101°17′ E 196
Mandel, Afghan. 33°19′ N, 61°52′ E 186
Mandera, Tanzania 6°10′ S, 38°23′ E 224
Manderfield, Utah, U.S. 38°21′ N, 112°39′ W 90
Manderscheid, Ger. 50°5′ N, 6°48′ E 167
Mandeville, La., U.S. 30°21′ N, 90°5′ W 103
Mandi, Nepal 31°41′ N, 76°56′ E 188
Mandiana, Guinea 10°40′ N, 8°42′ W 222
Mandie, Mozambique 16°30′ S, 33°33′ E 224

Mandimba, *Mozambique* 14°22' S, 35°40' E **224**
Mandjafa, *Chad* 11°13' N, 15°26' E **216**
Mandla, *India* 22°38' N, 80°22' E **197**
Mandor, *Indonesia* 0°19' N, 109°18' E **196**
Mandoto, *Madagascar* 19°38' S, 46°19' E **220**
Mandráki, *Gr.* 36°36' N, 27°8' E **156**
Mandu, island, *Maldives* 3°19' N, 72°0' E **188**
Mandvi, *India* 22°50' N, 69°21' E **186**
Manevichi, *Ukr.* 51°17' N, 25°31' E **152**
Manfalût, *Egypt* 27°19' N, 30°52' E **180**
Manfredonia, Golfo di 41°29' N, 15°9' E **156**
Manga, *Braz.* 14°49' S, 43°58' W **138**
Manga, *Burkina Faso* 11°40' N, 1°6' W **222**
Manga, *Mozambique* 19°46' S, 34°55' E **224**
Manga, region, *Niger* 14°17' N, 11°19' E **222**
Mangabeiras, Chapada das, *Braz.* 9°35' S, 46°50' W **130**
Mangai, *Dem. Rep. of the Congo* 4°4' S, 19°29' E **218**
Mangaia, island, *N.Z.* 21°52' S, 157°57' W **252**
Mangaïzé, *Niger* 14°54' N, 2°6' E **222**
Mangalia, *Rom.* 43°49' N, 28°32' E **156**
Mangalmé, *Chad* 12°24' N, 19°37' E **216**
Mangalore, *India* 12°52' N, 74°52' E **188**
Mangamuka, *N.Z.* 35°13' S, 173°31' E **240**
Mangando, *Angola* 8°4' S, 17°6' E **218**
Mangawan, *India* 24°42' N, 81°31' E **197**
Mangaweka, *N.Z.* 39°50' S, 175°46' E **240**
Mangeigne, *Chad* 10°31' N, 21°16' E **216**
Mangghystau, adm. division, *Kaz.* 43°56' N, 51°44' E **158**
Mangghyystaū, *Kaz.* 43°40' N, 51°17' E **158**
Mangham, *La., U.S.* 32°18' N, 91°47' W **103**
Mangkalihat, Tanjung, *Indonesia* 0°49' N, 117°56' E **192**
Manglares, Cabo, *Col.* 1°33' N, 80°27' W **130**
Mangnai, *China* 37°50' N, 91°45' E **188**
Mangnai Zhen, *China* 38°25' N, 90°17' E **188**
Mango, *Togo* 10°22' N, 0°25' E **222**
Mangoche, *Malawi* 14°29' S, 35°19' E **224**
Mangoky, river, *Madagascar* 22°3' S, 44°28' E **220**
Mangole, island, *Indonesia* 1°43' S, 125°43' E **192**
Mangonui, *N.Z.* 35°2' S, 173°31' E **240**
Mangqystaū Shyghanaghy 44°28' N, 50°41' E **158**
Mangrol, *India* 21°7' N, 70°7' E **188**
Mangrove Cay, island, *Bahamas* 26°55' N, 78°46' W **105**
Mangueira, Lagoa, lake, *Braz.* 32°60' S, 53°19' W **139**
Manguéni, Plateau de, *Niger* 23°9' N, 12°2' E **216**
Manguinho, Ponta do, *Braz.* 11°5' S, 36°25' W **132**
Mangum, *Okla., U.S.* 34°51' N, 99°31' W **92**
Mangunça, Ilha, island, *Braz.* 1°36' S, 44°38' W **132**
Mangut, *Russ.* 49°38' N, 112°38' E **198**
Mangwe, *Zimb.* 20°41' S, 28°2' E **227**
Manhattan, *Ill., U.S.* 41°24' N, 87°59' W **102**
Manhattan, *Kans., U.S.* 39°10' N, 96°34' W **90**
Manhattan, *Nev., U.S.* 38°32' N, 117°5' W **90**
Manhiça, *Mozambique* 25°21' S, 32°49' E **227**
Manhuaçu, *Braz.* 20°19' S, 41°60' W **138**
Maní, *Col.* 4°50' N, 72°18' W **136**
Mania, river, *Madagascar* 19°58' S, 45°19' E **220**
Maniamba, *Mozambique* 12°47' S, 34°58' E **224**
Manic Trois, Réservoir, lake, *Can.* 50°11' N, 70°32' W **80**
Manica, *Mozambique* 18°57' S, 32°54' E **224**
Manica, adm. division, *Mozambique* 18°9' S, 32°59' E **224**
Maniçaué Miçu, river, *Braz.* 11°35' S, 55°7' W **132**
Manicoré, river, *Braz.* 6°45' S, 61°2' W **130**
Manicouagan, Petit lac, lake, *Can.* 51°49' N, 68°45' W **111**
Manicouagan, Pointe, *Can.* 49°1' N, 68°18' W **111**
Manicouagan, Réservoir, lake, *Can.* 51°39' N, 69°10' W **111**
Manicouagan, Réservoir, lake, *Can.* 51°19' N, 70°56' W **106**
Maniema, adm. division, *Dem. Rep. of the Congo* 3°18' S, 25°0' E **218**
Manīfah, *Saudi Arabia* 27°28' N, 48°59' E **196**
Manigotagan, *Can.* 51°6' N, 96°16' W **90**
Manihiki Plateau, *South Pacific Ocean* 10°15' S, 159°44' W **252**
Maniitsoq (Sukkertoppen) 65°26' N, 52°60' W **106**
Manikpur, *India* 25°1' N, 81°6' E **197**
Manila, *Ark., U.S.* 35°52' N, 90°11' W **96**
Manila, *Philippines* 14°33' N, 120°53' E **203**
Manilaid, island, *Est.* 58°10' N, 24°9' E **166**
Manily, *Russ.* 62°34' N, 165°18' E **173**
Manipur, adm. division, *India* 24°32' N, 93°6' E **188**
Manisa, *Turk.* 38°34' N, 27°24' E **180**
Manistee, *Mich., U.S.* 44°13' N, 86°20' W **102**
Manistee, river, *Mich., U.S.* 44°1' N, 86°6' W **82**
Manistique, *Mich., U.S.* 45°58' N, 86°15' W **94**
Manitoba, adm. division, *Can.* 50°5' N, 99°36' W **90**
Manitoba, Lake, *Can.* 50°18' N, 98°55' W **90**
Manitou, *Can.* 49°14' N, 98°32' W **90**
Manitou Beach, *Mich., U.S.* 41°57' N, 84°19' W **102**
Manitou Islands, *Lake Michigan* 44°29' N, 86°12' W **80**
Manitou, Lac, lake, *Can.* 50°47' N, 65°38' W **111**
Manitou Lake, *Can.* 52°43' N, 110°13' W **108**
Manitoulin Island, *Can.* 45°15' N, 83°28' W **80**
Manitouwadge, *Can.* 49°8' N, 85°47' W **94**
Manitowik Lake, *Can.* 48°8' N, 84°60' W **94**
Manitowoc, *Wis., U.S.* 44°4' N, 87°41' W **102**
Maniwaki, *Can.* 46°21' N, 75°58' W **94**
Manizales, *Col.* 5°1' N, 75°32' W **136**
Manjā, *Jordan* 31°44' N, 35°51' E **194**
Manja, *Madagascar* 21°30' S, 44°22' E **207**
Manjacaze, *Mozambique* 24°41' S, 33°53' E **227**
Mankato, *Kans., U.S.* 39°46' N, 98°14' W **90**
Mankato, *Minn., U.S.* 44°8' N, 94°1' W **94**
Mankera, *Pak.* 31°22' N, 71°29' E **186**
Mankim, *Cameroon* 5°0' N, 12°1' E **218**
Mankono, *Côte d'Ivoire* 8°1' N, 6°12' W **222**
Manley Hot Springs, *Alas., U.S.* 64°59' N, 150°36' W **98**
Manlleu, *Sp.* 42°0' N, 2°16' E **164**
Manly, *Iowa, U.S.* 43°15' N, 93°12' W **94**
Mann Ranges, *Austral.* 25°59' S, 128°46' E **230**
Manna, *Indonesia* 4°27' S, 102°51' E **192**
Mannar, *Sri Lanka* 8°58' N, 79°53' E **188**
Mannar, Gulf of 7°42' N, 78°20' E **188**
Mannheim, *Ger.* 49°29' N, 8°27' E **152**
Manning, *Can.* 56°54' N, 117°37' W **108**
Manning, *Iowa, U.S.* 41°53' N, 95°5' W **94**
Manning, *N. Dak., U.S.* 47°12' N, 102°47' W **90**
Manning, *S.C., U.S.* 33°40' N, 80°13' W **96**
Manningtree, *U.K.* 51°56' N, 1°3' E **162**
Mannsville, *N.Y., U.S.* 43°42' N, 76°4' W **94**
Mannu, Capo, *It.* 40°1' N, 7°43' E **156**
Mannville, *Can.* 53°20' N, 111°11' W **108**
Mano, *Sierra Leone* 8°2' N, 12°4' W **222**
Mano, river, *Liberia* 7°14' N, 10°57' W **222**
Manoa, *Bol.* 9°45' S, 65°27' W **137**
Manoharpur, *India* 22°21' N, 85°13' E **197**
Manokotak, *Alas., U.S.* 58°58' N, 159°3' W **98**
Manokwari, *Indonesia* 0°50' N, 133°55' E **192**
Manombo, *Madagascar* 22°54' S, 43°24' E **220**
Manomet, *Mass., U.S.* 41°55' N, 70°34' W **104**
Manomet Point, *Mass., U.S.* 41°55' N, 70°33' W **104**
Manono, *Dem. Rep. of the Congo* 7°18' S, 27°23' E **224**
Manoron, *Myanmar* 11°37' N, 98°59' E **202**
Manouane, *Can.* 47°14' N, 74°24' W **94**
Manouane, Lac, lake, *Can.* 47°33' N, 74°43' W **94**
Manouane, Lac, lake, *Can.* 50°32' N, 71°22' W **111**
Manouba, *Tun.* 36°47' N, 10°5' E **156**
Manovo, river, *Cen. Af. Rep.* 9°7' N, 20°15' E **218**
Manovo-Gounda-Saint Floris National Park, *Cen. Af. Rep.* 9°23' N, 20°58' E **206**
Manp'o, *N. Korea* 41°10' N, 126°19' E **200**
Manpur, *India* 23°16' N, 83°35' E **197**
Manresa, *Sp.* 41°43' N, 1°46' E **214**
Mansa, *Zambia* 11°12' S, 28°53' E **224**
Mansa Konko, *Gambia* 13°26' N, 15°30' W **222**
Mansabá, *Guinea-Bissau* 12°18' N, 15°11' W **222**
Mansalar see Musala, island, *Indonesia* 1°31' N, 97°47' E **196**
Mansehra, *Pak.* 34°19' N, 73°15' E **186**
Mansel Island, *Can.* 61°4' N, 80°49' W **106**
Manseriche, Pongo de, *Peru* 4°16' S, 78°36' W **130**
Mansfield, *Ill., U.S.* 40°11' N, 88°31' W **102**
Mansfield, *La., U.S.* 32°1' N, 93°44' W **103**
Mansfield, *Mass., U.S.* 42°1' N, 71°14' W **104**
Mansfield, *Mo., U.S.* 37°5' N, 92°35' W **96**
Mansfield, *Ohio, U.S.* 40°44' N, 82°30' W **102**
Mansfield, *Pa., U.S.* 41°46' N, 77°5' W **82**
Mansfield, *U.K.* 53°8' N, 1°12' W **162**
Mansfield Center, *Conn., U.S.* 41°45' N, 72°12' W **104**
Mansfield, Mount, peak, *Vt., U.S.* 44°32' N, 72°51' W **104**
Manso (Rio das Mortes), river, *Braz.* 15°20' S, 53°1' W **138**
Manson, *Iowa, U.S.* 42°30' N, 94°33' W **94**
Manson Creek, *Can.* 55°38' N, 124°31' W **108**
Mansourah, *Alg.* 36°4' N, 4°28' E **150**
Manta, *Ecua.* 1°4' S, 80°31' W **130**
Mantakari, *Niger* 13°52' N, 3°59' E **222**
Mantaro, river, *Peru* 11°55' S, 74°47' W **137**
Manteca, *Calif., U.S.* 37°47' N, 121°13' W **100**
Mantecal, *Venez.* 7°33' N, 69°8' W **136**
Mantena, *Braz.* 18°51' S, 40°59' W **138**
Manteno, *Ill., U.S.* 41°14' N, 87°50' W **102**
Manteo, *N.C., U.S.* 35°54' N, 75°42' W **96**
Mantes-la-Jolie, *Fr.* 48°59' N, 1°42' E **163**
Manti, *Utah, U.S.* 39°15' N, 111°38' W **90**
Mantinea 362 B.C., battle, *Gr.* 37°36' N, 22°17' E **156**
Manto, *Hond.* 14°55' N, 86°20' W **115**
Manton, *Mich., U.S.* 44°24' N, 85°25' W **94**
Mantova, *It.* 45°8' N, 10°47' E **167**
Mäntsälä, *Fin.* 60°37' N, 25°18' E **166**
Mänttä, *Fin.* 62°0' N, 24°36' E **166**
Mantua, *Cuba* 22°17' N, 84°18' W **116**
Manturovo, *Russ.* 58°20' N, 44°47' E **154**
Mäntyharju, *Fin.* 61°22' N, 26°48' E **166**
Mäntyluoto, *Fin.* 61°34' N, 21°28' E **166**
Manú, *Peru* 12°17' S, 70°55' W **137**
Manu National Park, *Peru* 12°19' S, 71°54' W **137**
Manu see Mapiri, river, *Bol.* 10°40' S, 66°53' W **137**
Manua Islands, *South Pacific Ocean* 14°14' S, 169°35' W **241**
Manuel Alves, river, *Braz.* 11°53' S, 48°4' W **130**
Manuel Benavides, *Mex.* 29°5' N, 103°55' W **92**
Manuel J. Cobo, *Arg.* 35°53' S, 57°54' W **139**
Manuel Ribas, *Braz.* 24°34' S, 51°40' W **138**
Manuel Vitorino, *Braz.* 14°12' S, 40°16' W **138**
Manuelzinho, *Braz.* 7°24' S, 54°54' W **130**
Manukan, *Philippines* 8°32' N, 123°5' E **203**
Manukau, *N.Z.* 37°3' S, 174°54' E **240**
Manupari, river, *Bol.* 12°36' S, 67°42' W **137**
Manuripi, river, *Bol.* 11°42' S, 68°35' W **137**
Manus, island, *P.N.G.* 2°27' S, 145°40' E **192**
Manusela National Park, *Indonesia* 3°14' S, 129°4' E **238**
Manvers, Port 56°47' N, 63°21' W **246**
Manville, *R.I., U.S.* 41°58' N, 71°29' W **104**
Many, *La., U.S.* 31°33' N, 93°29' W **103**
Many Farms, *Ariz., U.S.* 36°21' N, 109°37' W **92**
Manyara, Lake, *Tanzania* 3°37' S, 35°16' E **224**
Manyberries, *Can.* 49°24' N, 110°42' W **90**
Manyinga, river, *Africa* 12°17' S, 24°1' E **220**
Manyoni, *Tanzania* 5°42' S, 34°49' E **224**
Manzala, Buheirat el, lake, *Egypt* 31°12' N, 32°3' E **194**
Manzanares, *Sp.* 38°59' N, 3°27' W **214**
Manzanera, *Sp.* 40°3' N, 0°50' E **164**
Manzanillo, *Mex.* 19°2' N, 104°18' W **114**
Manzanita, *Oreg., U.S.* 45°42' N, 123°56' W **100**
Manzano Peak, *N. Mex., U.S.* 34°34' N, 106°31' W **92**
Manzanola, *Colo., U.S.* 38°6' N, 103°52' W **92**
Manzhouli, *China* 49°34' N, 117°26' E **198**
Manzini, *Swaziland* 26°31' S, 31°20' E **227**
Mao, *Chad* 14°6' N, 15°17' E **216**
Mao, *Dom. Rep.* 19°34' N, 71°5' W **116**
Maoke, Pegunungan, *Indonesia* 4°23' S, 135°14' E **192**
Maoming, *China* 21°40' N, 110°50' E **198**
Maoudass, *Mauritania* 15°33' N, 10°55' W **222**
Mapai, *Mozambique* 22°49' S, 32°1' E **227**
Mapam Yumco, lake, *China* 30°45' N, 80°50' E **197**
Mapanza, *Zambia* 16°17' S, 26°55' E **224**
Maper, *Sudan* 7°42' N, 29°38' E **224**
Mapia, Kepulauan, islands, *North Pacific Ocean* 0°52' N, 134°31' E **192**
Mapimí, *Mex.* 25°47' N, 103°52' W **114**
Mapimí, Bolsón de, *Mex.* 26°47' N, 104°34' W **112**
Mapinhane, *Mozambique* 22°19' S, 35°2' E **227**
Mapiri, *Bol.* 15°13' S, 68°11' W **137**
Mapiri (Manu), river, *Bol.* 10°40' S, 66°53' W **137**
Mapiripán, river, *Col.* 3°10' N, 71°37' W **136**
Mapiripana, *Col.* 2°39' N, 70°58' W **136**
Maple Creek, *Can.* 49°53' N, 109°28' W **90**
Maple Ridge, *Can.* 49°13' N, 122°36' W **100**
Maple, river, *Mich., U.S.* 43°3' N, 84°41' W **102**
Maple Valley, *Wash., U.S.* 47°23' N, 122°3' W **100**
Mapleton, *Iowa, U.S.* 42°8' N, 95°47' W **90**
Mapleville, *R.I., U.S.* 41°56' N, 71°40' W **104**
Mapmaker Seamounts, *North Pacific Ocean* 26°45' N, 166°56' E **252**
Mapuera, river, *Braz.* 1°6' S, 58°10' W **130**
Mapulanguene, *Mozambique* 24°29' S, 32°7' E **227**
Maputo, *Mozambique* 25°55' S, 32°27' E **227**
Maputo, adm. division, *Mozambique* 25°22' S, 32°6' E **227**
Maqanshy, *Kaz.* 46°45' N, 82°9' E **184**
Maqat, *Kaz.* 47°38' N, 53°21' E **158**
Maqdam, Ras, *Sudan* 18°48' N, 36°58' E **182**
Maqên Gangri, peak, *China* 34°24' N, 99°22' E **190**
Maqnā, *Saudi Arabia* 28°22' N, 34°45' E **180**
Maqshūsh, *Saudi Arabia* 23°36' N, 38°41' E **182**
Maquela do Zombo, *Angola* 6°3' S, 15°4' E **218**
Maquinchao, *Arg.* 41°14' S, 68°43' W **134**
Maquoketa, *Iowa, U.S.* 42°3' N, 90°41' W **94**
Mar Chiquita, Laguna, lake, *Arg.* 30°34' S, 62°57' W **139**
Mar de Ajó, *Arg.* 36°42' S, 56°43' W **139**
Mar del Plata, *Arg.* 37°59' S, 57°36' W **139**
Mar, Serra do, *Braz.* 27°45' S, 48°59' W **132**
Mara, *Guyana* 5°57' N, 57°37' W **130**
Mara, *India* 28°10' N, 94°6' E **188**
Mara, adm. division, *Tanzania* 1°45' S, 33°47' E **224**
Mara, oil field, *Venez.* 10°49' N, 71°58' W **136**
Mara Rosa, *Braz.* 13°57' S, 49°10' W **138**
Maraã, *Braz.* 1°50' S, 65°26' W **136**
Marabá, *Braz.* 5°24' S, 49°9' W **130**
Marabitanas, *Braz.* 0°56' N, 66°54' W **136**
Maracá, Ilha de, island, *Braz.* 2°3' N, 50°17' W **130**
Maracaibo, *Venez.* 10°41' N, 71°41' W **136**
Maracaibo, Lago de, *Venez.* 9°20' N, 74°22' W **73**
Maracaju, *Braz.* 21°39' S, 55°9' W **132**
Maracaju, Serra de, *Braz.-Parag.* 19°12' S, 55°27' W **132**
Maracanã, *Braz.* 0°47' N, 47°27' W **130**
Maracás, *Braz.* 13°26' S, 40°29' W **138**
Maracay, *Venez.* 10°12' N, 67°38' W **136**
Marādah, *Lib.* 29°14' N, 19°12' E **216**
Maradi, *Niger* 13°30' N, 7°7' E **222**
Marāgheh, *Iran* 37°26' N, 46°15' E **195**
Maragogipe, *Braz.* 12°48' S, 38°57' W **132**
Marahoué National Park, *Côte d'Ivoire* 7°5' N, 6°41' W **222**
Marahuaca, Cerro, peak, *Venez.* 3°32' N, 65°30' W **136**
Marajó, Ilha de, *South America* 0°41' N, 50°31' W **123**
Maralal, *Kenya* 1°4' N, 36°42' E **224**
Maralaleng, *Botswana* 25°49' S, 22°40' E **227**
Marali, *Cen. Af. Rep.* 6°0' N, 18°23' E **218**
Maralinga, *Austral.* 30°7' S, 131°24' E **231**
Maramasike, island, *Solomon Islands* 9°35' S, 161°30' E **242**
Marambio, station, *Antarctica* 64°17' S, 56°44' W **134**
Maramureş, adm. division, *Rom.* 47°36' N, 23°20' E **156**
Maramureşului, Munţii, *Rom.* 47°57' N, 24°19' E **152**
Maran, *Malaysia* 3°36' N, 102°45' E **196**
Marana, *Ariz., U.S.* 32°26' N, 111°13' W **92**
Maranchón, *Sp.* 41°2' N, 2°13' W **164**
Marand, *Iran* 38°29' N, 45°43' E **195**
Mărăndeni, *Mold.* 47°39' N, 27°51' E **152**
Marang, *Malaysia* 5°12' N, 103°12' E **196**
Maranguape, *Braz.* 3°53' S, 38°41' W **132**
Maranhão, adm. division, *Braz.* 5°35' S, 47°22' W **130**
Marañón, river, *Peru* 5°34' S, 76°27' W **122**
Marão, Serra do, *Port.* 41°6' N, 8°31' W **150**
Mararaba, *Cameroon* 5°37' N, 13°47' E **218**
Marargiu, Capo, *It.* 40°17' N, 7°38' E **156**
Marari, *Braz.* 5°45' S, 67°45' W **130**
Mărăşeşti, *Rom.* 45°52' N, 27°13' E **156**
Marathon 490 B.C., battle, *Gr.* 38°6' N, 23°51' E **156**
Marathon, *Can.* 48°43' N, 86°22' W **94**
Marathon, *Fla., U.S.* 24°42' N, 81°5' W **105**
Marathon, *Tex., U.S.* 30°11' N, 103°15' W **92**
Marathus see 'Amrīt, ruin(s), *Syr.* 34°50' N, 35°52' E **194**
Maratua, island, *Indonesia* 2°16' N, 118°39' E **192**
Marau, *Braz.* 28°32' S, 52°13' W **139**
Marauá, *Braz.* 3°26' S, 66°23' W **136**
Marauiá, river, *Braz.* 0°28' N, 65°22' W **136**
Maravatío, *Mex.* 19°52' N, 100°27' W **114**
Marāveh Tappeh, *Iran* 37°54' N, 55°55' E **180**
Marawi, *Philippines* 8°5' N, 124°19' E **203**
Maraza, *Azerb.* 40°33' N, 48°55' E **195**
Marbella, *Sp.* 36°30' N, 4°53' W **164**
Marble, *Minn., U.S.* 47°18' N, 93°18' W **94**
Marble Bar, *Austral.* 21°10' S, 119°45' E **231**
Marble Canyon, *Ariz., U.S.* 36°32' N, 112°1' W **92**
Marble Falls, *Tex., U.S.* 30°33' N, 98°16' W **92**
Marble Hall, *S. Af.* 24°59' S, 29°16' E **227**
Marble Mountains, *Calif., U.S.* 34°42' N, 115°35' W **101**
Marblehead, *Mass., U.S.* 42°30' N, 70°52' W **104**
Marblemount, *Wash., U.S.* 48°31' N, 121°28' W **100**
Marbleton, *Wyo., U.S.* 42°34' N, 110°5' W **90**
Mårbu, *Nor.* 60°11' N, 8°10' E **152**
Marburg, *Ger.* 50°48' N, 8°46' E **167**
Marca, Ponta da, *Angola* 16°36' S, 11°3' E **220**
Marcali, *Hung.* 46°34' N, 17°24' E **168**
Marcapata, *Peru* 13°34' S, 70°54' W **137**
Marcaria, *It.* 45°7' N, 10°32' E **167**
Marcelin, *Can.* 52°56' N, 106°47' W **108**
Marceline, *Mo., U.S.* 39°42' N, 92°56' W **94**
Marcelino, *Braz.* 1°48' S, 66°25' W **136**
Marcelino Ramos, *Braz.* 27°30' S, 51°57' W **139**
Marcellus, *Mich., U.S.* 42°1' N, 85°48' W **102**
March, *U.K.* 52°33' N, 8°475' E **162**
March Air Force Base, *Calif., U.S.* 33°53' N, 117°17' W **101**
Marchamalo, *Sp.* 40°39' N, 3°12' W **164**
Marchand, *Can.* 49°26' N, 96°22' W **90**
Marche, *Belg.* 50°13' N, 5°20' E **167**
Marche, region, *Fr.* 46°21' N, 1°10' E **165**
Marchena, *Sp.* 37°19' N, 5°26' W **164**
Marches, adm. division, *It.* 43°44' N, 12°22' E **156**
Marchinbar Island, *Austral.* 11°17' S, 134°53' E **192**
Marck, *Fr.* 50°56' N, 1°55' E **163**
Marco, *Fla., U.S.* 25°57' N, 81°43' W **105**
Marcola, *Oreg., U.S.* 44°9' N, 122°53' W **90**
Marcos Juárez, *Arg.* 32°42' S, 62°5' W **139**
Marcus, *Wash., U.S.* 48°39' N, 118°4' W **90**
Marcy, Mount, peak, *N.Y., U.S.* 44°6' N, 73°57' W **104**
Mardan, *Pak.* 34°11' N, 72°6' E **188**
Mardin, *Turk.* 37°19' N, 40°46' E **195**
Mære, *Nor.* 63°55' N, 11°23' E **152**
Mare, Muntele, peak, *Rom.* 46°29' N, 23°11' E **168**
Marechal Taumaturgo, *Braz.* 8°58' S, 72°48' W **137**
Mareer, *Somalia* 1°35' N, 44°26' E **218**
Marengo, *Can.* 51°29' N, 109°47' W **90**
Marengo, *Ill., U.S.* 42°14' N, 88°37' W **102**
Marennes, *Fr.* 45°50' N, 1°8' W **150**
Mareshah, ruin(s), *Israel* 31°34' N, 34°50' E **194**
Marevo, *Russ.* 57°17' N, 32°6' E **154**
Marfa, *Tex., U.S.* 30°17' N, 104°2' W **92**
Marfa, Massif de, *Chad* 13°2' N, 20°4' E **216**
Marfino, *Russ.* 46°23' N, 48°44' E **158**
Margai Caka, lake, *China* 35°6' N, 86°25' E **188**
Margaret Lake, *Can.* 58°53' N, 116°9' W **108**
Margaret, Mount, peak, *Austral.* 22°3' S, 117°39' E **230**
Margarita, *Arg.* 29°39' S, 60°13' W **139**
Margarita, Isla de, island, *Venez.* 10°47' N, 63°53' W **116**
Margat (Marghab), ruin(s), *Syr.* 35°9' N, 35°55' E **194**
Margat, ruin(s), *Syr.* 35°7' N, 35°52' E **156**
Margate, *S. Af.* 30°52' S, 30°20' E **227**
Margento, *Col.* 8°2' N, 74°56' W **136**
Margeride, Monts de la, *Fr.* 45°6' N, 3°1' E **165**
Marghab see Margat, ruin(s), *Syr.* 35°9' N, 35°55' E **194**
Margherita Peak, *Dem. Rep. of the Congo* 0°19' N, 29°46' E **224**
Marghita, *Rom.* 47°20' N, 22°21' E **168**
Margie, *Can.* 55°24' N, 111°23' W **108**
Marg'ilon, *Uzb.* 40°27' N, 71°44' E **197**
Mărgineni, oil field, *Rom.* 44°56' N, 25°40' E **156**
Margita, *Serb. and Mont.* 45°12' N, 21°12' E **168**
Margog Caka, lake, *China* 33°47' N, 86°6' E **188**
Margosatubig, *Philippines* 7°36' N, 123°11' E **203**
Marguerite, *Can.* 52°30' N, 122°25' W **108**
Marhanets', *Ukr.* 47°37' N, 34°44' E **156**
María, *Sp.* 37°42' N, 2°9' W **164**
María Elena, *Chile* 22°20' S, 69°43' W **137**
Maria Island, *Austral.* 14°45' S, 135°43' E **230**
María Madre, Isla, island, *Mex.* 21°39' N, 108°7' W **112**
María, peak, *Sp.* 37°40' N, 2°15' W **164**
María Teresa, *Arg.* 34°3' S, 61°55' W **139**
Mariakani, *Kenya* 3°54' S, 39°28' E **224**
Mariana Lake, *Can.* 55°59' N, 112°2' W **108**
Mariana Trench, *North Pacific Ocean* 16°4' N, 148°3' E **252**
Marianao, *Cuba* 23°3' N, 82°29' W **116**
Marianna, *Ark., U.S.* 34°46' N, 90°47' W **96**
Marianna, *Fla., U.S.* 30°46' N, 85°14' W **96**
Mariannelund, *Nor.* 57°37' N, 15°32' E **152**
Marías, Islas, islands, *Mex.* 21°3' N, 107°18' W **112**
Marias Pass, *Mont., U.S.* 48°18' N, 113°20' W **90**
Ma'rib, *Yemen* 15°32' N, 45°19' E **182**
Maribo, *Den.* 54°47' N, 11°29' E **152**
Maribor, *Slov.* 46°32' N, 15°39' E **156**
Maricopa, *Ariz., U.S.* 33°3' N, 112°3' W **92**
Maricopa, *Calif., U.S.* 35°3' N, 119°25' W **100**
Maridi, *Sudan* 4°56' N, 29°30' E **224**
Marie Byrd Land, region, *Antarctica* 76°41' S, 109°34' W **248**
Marié, river, *Braz.* 0°50' N, 67°36' W **136**
Marie-Galante, island, *Fr.* 15°48' N, 61°11' W **116**
Mariehamn (Maarianhamina), *Fin.* 60°5' N, 19°55' E **166**
Marienbourg, *Belg.* 50°5' N, 4°30' E **163**
Marienhafe, *Ger.* 53°31' N, 7°17' E **163**
Mariental, *Namibia* 24°38' S, 17°57' E **227**
Mariestad, *Nor.* 58°42' N, 13°49' E **152**
Marietta, *Ga., U.S.* 33°57' N, 84°34' W **96**
Marietta, *Ohio, U.S.* 39°25' N, 81°27' W **102**
Marietta, *Okla., U.S.* 33°55' N, 97°6' W **92**
Marietta, *Wash., U.S.* 48°47' N, 122°34' W **100**
Marigny, *Fr.* 49°5' N, 1°15' W **150**
Marii Pronchishchevoy, Bukhta 75°46' N, 120°4' E **246**
Mariinsk, *Russ.* 56°13' N, 87°45' E **169**
Marijampolė, *Lith.* 54°33' N, 23°19' E **166**
Marilândia do Sul, *Braz.* 23°47' S, 51°18' W **138**
Marília, *Braz.* 22°15' S, 49°59' W **138**
Marilla, *Can.* 53°42' N, 125°50' W **108**
Marimba, *Angola* 8°25' S, 17°1' E **218**
Marina, *Calif., U.S.* 36°41' N, 121°47' W **100**
Marina di Carrara, *It.* 44°2' N, 10°1' E **167**
Marina di Ravenna, *It.* 44°28' N, 12°15' E **167**
Marine City, *Mich., U.S.* 42°41' N, 82°31' W **102**
Marineland, *Fla., U.S.* 29°39' N, 81°14' W **105**
Marinette, *Wis., U.S.* 45°4' N, 87°38' W **94**
Maringá, *Braz.* 23°25' S, 51°60' W **138**
Maringouin, *La., U.S.* 30°28' N, 91°32' W **103**
Maringuè, *Mozambique* 17°60' S, 34°23' E **224**
Mar'ino, *Russ.* 51°12' N, 36°43' E **158**
Mar'insko, *Russ.* 58°47' N, 28°32' E **166**
Marinuma, *Col.* 2°15' N, 69°22' W **136**
Marion, *Ala., U.S.* 32°37' N, 87°20' W **103**
Marion, *Ark., U.S.* 35°12' N, 90°13' W **96**
Marion, *Ind., U.S.* 40°33' N, 85°41' W **102**
Marion, *Iowa, U.S.* 42°1' N, 91°36' W **94**
Marion, *Kans., U.S.* 38°20' N, 97°2' W **90**
Marion, *La., U.S.* 32°53' N, 92°15' W **103**
Marion, *Mass., U.S.* 41°41' N, 70°47' W **104**
Marion, *Mich., U.S.* 44°6' N, 85°8' W **102**
Marion, *Miss., U.S.* 32°24' N, 88°39' W **103**
Marion, *Mo., U.S.* 37°43' N, 88°55' W **94**
Marion, *Ohio, U.S.* 40°34' N, 83°8' W **102**
Marion, *S.C., U.S.* 34°10' N, 79°24' W **96**
Marion, *S. Dak., U.S.* 43°24' N, 97°16' W **90**
Marion, *Va., U.S.* 36°50' N, 81°32' W **94**
Marion Nunataks 69°34' S, 79°8' W **248**
Marionville, *Mo., U.S.* 36°59' N, 93°38' W **96**
Maripa, *Venez.* 7°21' N, 65°8' W **136**
Mariposa, *Calif., U.S.* 37°29' N, 119°59' W **100**
Marir, Gezaîr (Mirear), islands, *Egypt* 23°5' N, 35°51' E **182**
Mariscal Estigarribia, *Parag.* 22°2' S, 60°37' W **132**
Maristova, *Nor.* 61°6' N, 8°1' E **152**
Maritime Alps, *Fr.* 44°2' N, 6°45' E **165**
Maritime Territory, adm. division, *Russ.* 45°20' N, 135°8' E **190**
Mariupol', *Ukr.* 47°5' N, 37°28' E **156**
Mariusa National Park, *Venez.* 9°23' N, 61°33' W **116**
Marīvān, *Iran* 35°31' N, 46°11' E **180**
Mariy-El, adm. division, *Russ.* 56°19' N, 46°11' E **154**
Mariyets, *Russ.* 56°30' N, 49°53' E **154**
Marj 'Uyūn, *Leb.* 33°21' N, 35°35' E **194**
Märjamaa, *Est.* 58°54' N, 24°23' E **166**
Marjonbuloq, *Uzb.* 39°59' N, 67°21' E **197**
Marka see Merca, *Somalia* 1°41' N, 44°53' E **207**
Markala, *Mali* 13°40' N, 6°4' W **222**
Markansu, *Taj.* 39°19' N, 73°21' E **197**
Markapur, *India* 15°42' N, 79°17' E **188**
Markaryd, *Nor.* 56°28' N, 13°35' E **152**
Markdale, *Can.* 44°18' N, 80°39' W **110**
Markelsdorfer Huk, *Kattegat* 54°37' N, 10°49' E **152**
Markesan, *Wis., U.S.* 43°42' N, 88°59' W **102**
Market Drayton, *U.K.* 52°53' N, 2°30' W **162**
Market Harborough, *U.K.* 52°28' N, 0°55' E **162**
Market Rasen, *U.K.* 53°22' N, 0°21' E **162**
Market Weighton, *U.K.* 53°51' N, 0°41' E **162**
Markha, river, *Russ.* 64°57' N, 116°6' E **160**
Markham, *Can.* 43°51' N, 79°17' W **94**
Markham Bay 63°24' N, 74°18' W **106**
Markham, Mount, peak, *Antarctica* 82°47' S, 162°59' E **248**
Markit, *China* 38°57' N, 77°37' E **184**
Markkina, *Fin.* 68°29' N, 22°16' E **152**
Markle, *Ind., U.S.* 40°49' N, 85°20' W **102**
Markounda, *Cen. Af. Rep.* 7°33' N, 16°57' E **218**
Markovac, *Serb. and Mont.* 44°13' N, 21°5' E **168**
Markovo, *Russ.* 64°41' N, 170°4' E **160**
Marks Butte, peak, *Colo., U.S.* 40°48' N, 102°36' W **90**
Marksville, *La., U.S.* 31°6' N, 92°5' W **103**
Markušica, *Croatia* 45°22' N, 18°41' E **168**
Marl, *Ger.* 51°39' N, 7°6' E **167**
Marlboro, *Vt., U.S.* 42°51' N, 72°44' W **104**
Marlborough, *N.H., U.S.* 42°53' N, 72°13' W **104**
Marlborough, *U.K.* 51°24' N, 1°44' W **162**
Marle, *Fr.* 49°44' N, 3°47' E **163**
Marles, *Fr.* 50°30' N, 2°30' E **150**
Marlette, *Mich., U.S.* 43°19' N, 83°5' W **102**
Marlin, *Tex., U.S.* 31°17' N, 96°53' W **96**
Marlin, oil field, *Bass Strait* 38°17' S, 148°12' E **230**
Marlow, *N.H., U.S.* 43°6' N, 72°13' W **104**
Marlow, *Okla., U.S.* 34°38' N, 97°58' W **92**
Marlow, *U.K.* 51°34' N, 0°47' E **162**
Marmagao, *India* 15°23' N, 73°48' E **173**
Marmara Denizi, *Turkey* 40°37' N, 27°43' E **156**
Marmaris, *Turk.* 36°51' N, 28°14' E **156**
Marmarth, *N. Dak., U.S.* 46°16' N, 103°54' W **90**
Marmolada, peak, *It.* 46°26' N, 11°47' E **167**
Marmolejo, *Sp.* 38°2' N, 4°11' W **164**
Marmul, oil field, *Oman* 18°10' N, 55°23' E **182**
Marne, river, *Fr.* 48°49' N, 2°37' E **163**
Maroa, *Ill., U.S.* 40°1' N, 88°57' W **102**
Maroa, *Venez.* 2°45' N, 67°33' W **136**
Maroantsetra, *Madagascar* 15°25' S, 49°41' E **220**
Marol, *Pak.* 34°45' N, 76°16' E **186**
Marolambo, *Madagascar* 20°4' S, 48°8' E **220**
Maromandia, *Madagascar* 14°9' S, 48°5' E **220**
Maromokotro, peak, *Madagascar* 14°4' S, 48°50' E **220**
Marondera, *Zimb.* 18°14' S, 31°30' E **224**
Marone, *It.* 45°44' N, 10°5' E **167**
Marónia, *Gr.* 40°54' N, 25°31' E **156**
Maronne, river, *Fr.* 45°1' N, 1°59' E **165**
Maros, *Indonesia* 4°58' S, 119°32' E **192**
Marotandrano, *Madagascar* 16°11' S, 48°48' E **220**

Marotiri, island, *Fr.* 27°49′ S, 143°42′ W **252**
Maroua, *Cameroon* 10°36′ N, 14°20′ E **216**
Marouini, river, *South America* 2°10′ N, 53°57′ W **130**
Marovoay, *Madagascar* 16°8′ S, 46°39′ E **220**
Marqaköl, lake, *Kaz.* 48°42′ N, 85°14′ E **184**
Marquard, *S. Af.* 28°41′ S, 27°23′ E **227**
Marquesas Fracture Zone, *South Pacific Ocean* 10°40′ S, 131°47′ W **252**
Marquesas Islands, *South Pacific Ocean* 11°28′ S, 141°48′ W **238**
Marquesas Keys, islands, *Gulf of Mexico* 24°26′ N, 82°20′ W **105**
Marquette, *Mich., U.S.* 46°32′ N, 87°24′ W **94**
Marquette, Lac, lake, *Can.* 48°54′ N, 74°33′ W **94**
Marquise, *Fr.* 50°49′ N, 1°42′ E **163**
Marra, Jebel, peak, *Sudan* 12°50′ N, 23°50′ E **206**
Marrakech, *Mor.* 31°39′ N, 8°1′ W **214**
Marrasjärvi, *Fin.* 66°53′ N, 25°6′ E **152**
Marrecas, Serra das, *Braz.* 9°33′ S, 41°40′ W **132**
Marromeu, *Mozambique* 18°19′ S, 35°55′ E **224**
Marrupa, *Mozambique* 13°12′ S, 37°30′ E **224**
Mars Hill, peak, *Me., U.S.* 46°30′ N, 67°54′ W **94**
Marsá al 'Uwayjā', *Lib.* 30°54′ N, 17°51′ E **216**
Marsa 'Alam, spring, *Egypt* 25°4′ N, 34°51′ E **182**
Marsa Fatma, *Eritrea* 14°51′ N, 40°20′ E **182**
Marsa Sha'ab, *Egypt* 22°49′ N, 35°45′ E **182**
Marsabit, *Kenya* 2°18′ N, 38°0′ E **224**
Marsabit Nature Reserve, *Kenya* 1°54′ N, 37°47′ E **224**
Marsala, *It.* 37°48′ N, 12°26′ E **156**
Marsberg, *Ger.* 51°27′ N, 8°52′ E **167**
Marsden Point, *N.Z.* 35°53′ S, 174°28′ E **240**
Marseillan, *Fr.* 43°21′ N, 3°30′ E **164**
Marseille, *Fr.* 43°17′ N, 5°22′ E **150**
Marsfjället, peak, *Nor.* 65°5′ N, 15°13′ E **152**
Marsh Island, *La., U.S.* 29°24′ N, 92°2′ W **103**
Marsh Pass, *Ariz., U.S.* 36°38′ N, 110°25′ W **92**
Marsh Peak, *Utah, U.S.* 40°41′ N, 109°54′ W **90**
Marsh Point, *Can.* 57°5′ N, 92°20′ W **108**
Marshall, *Alas., U.S.* 61°52′ N, 162°4′ W **98**
Marshall, *Ark., U.S.* 35°53′ N, 92°39′ W **96**
Marshall, *Ill., U.S.* 39°23′ N, 87°41′ W **102**
Marshall, *Liberia* 6°4′ N, 10°23′ W **222**
Marshall, *Mich., U.S.* 42°16′ N, 84°57′ W **102**
Marshall, *Minn., U.S.* 44°26′ N, 95°48′ W **90**
Marshall, *Mo., U.S.* 39°6′ N, 93°16′ W **82**
Marshall, *Tex., U.S.* 32°32′ N, 94°23′ W **103**
Marshall Bennett Islands, *Solomon Sea* 8°46′ S, 152°2′ E **230**
Marshall Islands, *Marshall Islands* 9°2′ N, 170°3′ E **238**
Marshalltown, *Iowa, U.S.* 42°4′ N, 92°53′ W **82**
Marshfield, *Mo., U.S.* 37°19′ N, 92°54′ W **94**
Marshfield, *Vt., U.S.* 44°21′ N, 72°22′ W **104**
Marshfield, *Wis., U.S.* 44°39′ N, 90°11′ W **94**
Marsland, *Nebr., U.S.* 42°26′ N, 103°18′ W **90**
Mars-la-Tour, *Fr.* 49°6′ N, 5°53′ E **163**
Marston Moor, battle, *U.K.* 53°58′ N, 1°16′ W **162**
Marstrand, *Sw.* 57°53′ N, 11°33′ E **150**
Marsyaty, *Russ.* 60°4′ N, 60°25′ E **154**
Mart, *Tex., U.S.* 31°31′ N, 96°49′ W **96**
Martaban, *Myanmar* 16°34′ N, 97°35′ E **202**
Martaban, Gulf of 15°50′ N, 96°1′ E **192**
Martap, *Cameroon* 6°50′ N, 13°3′ E **218**
Martapura, *Indonesia* 3°30′ S, 114°45′ E **192**
Marte R. Gómez, Presa, lake, *Mex.* 26°12′ N, 100°24′ W **80**
Martem'yanovskaya, *Russ.* 61°58′ N, 39°11′ E **154**
Marten Mountain, peak, *Can.* 55°28′ N, 114°50′ W **108**
Martés, peak, *Sp.* 39°18′ N, 0°60′ E **164**
Martf u, *Hung.* 47°0′ N, 20°17′ E **168**
Martha's Vineyard, island, *Mass., U.S.* 41°14′ N, 70°47′ W **104**
Marthaville, *La., U.S.* 31°43′ N, 93°25′ W **103**
Martigny, *Switz.* 46°6′ N, 7°3′ E **167**
Martigues, *Fr.* 43°23′ N, 5°3′ E **150**
Martil, *Mor.* 35°37′ N, 5°17′ W **150**
Martin, *Mich., U.S.* 42°32′ N, 85°39′ W **102**
Martin, *S. Dak., U.S.* 43°10′ N, 101°44′ W **90**
Martin, Lake, *Ala., U.S.* 32°51′ N, 86°22′ W **80**
Martin, river, *Can.* 61°31′ N, 122°26′ W **108**
Martin Vaz Islands, *South Atlantic Ocean* 20°29′ S, 28°57′ W **253**
Martinborough, *N.Z.* 41°15′ S, 175°29′ E **240**
Martinez, *Calif., U.S.* 38°1′ N, 122°9′ W **100**
Martinez, *Ga., U.S.* 33°30′ N, 82°6′ W **96**
Martinez Lake, *Ariz., U.S.* 32°58′ N, 114°28′ W **101**
Martinique, *Fr.* 14°26′ N, 61°27′ W **116**
Martinique Passage 15°1′ N, 62°3′ W **116**
Martinsburg, *N.Y., U.S.* 43°35′ N, 75°29′ W **94**
Martinsville, *Ill., U.S.* 39°19′ N, 87°53′ W **102**
Martinsville, *Ind., U.S.* 39°25′ N, 86°26′ W **102**
Martinsville, *Va., U.S.* 36°40′ N, 79°53′ W **96**
Martna, *Est.* 58°50′ N, 23°47′ E **166**
Marton, *N.Z.* 40°6′ S, 175°24′ E **240**
Martorell, *Sp.* 41°27′ N, 1°54′ E **164**
Martos, *Sp.* 37°43′ N, 3°59′ W **164**
Martti, *Fin.* 67°28′ N, 28°21′ E **152**
Martuni, *Arm.* 40°8′ N, 45°16′ E **195**
Martuni, *Azerb.* 39°48′ N, 47°5′ E **195**
Martyn, Mount, peak, *Antarctica* 69°19′ S, 157°39′ E **248**
Ma'ruf, *Afghan.* 31°29′ N, 67°3′ E **186**
Maruia, *N.Z.* 42°12′ S, 172°14′ E **240**
Marumori, *Japan* 37°55′ N, 140°46′ E **201**
Marungu, *Dem. Rep. of the Congo* 8°10′ S, 29°36′ E **224**
Maruoka, *Japan* 36°8′ N, 136°16′ E **201**
Marv Dasht, *Iran* 29°55′ N, 52°56′ E **196**
Marvin Spur, *Arctic Ocean* 86°15′ N, 118°55′ W **255**
Marvine, Mount, peak, *Utah, U.S.* 38°39′ N, 111°42′ W **90**
Marwar, *India* 25°43′ N, 73°37′ E **186**
Marx, *Russ.* 51°36′ N, 46°42′ E **158**
Mary, *Turkm.* 37°36′ N, 61°50′ E **180**
Mary, river, *Austral.* 25°36′ S, 152°13′ E **230**
Mar'yanovka, *Russ.* 54°55′ N, 72°44′ E **184**
Marydale, *S. Af.* 29°28′ S, 22°7′ E **227**
Maryland, adm. division, *Md., U.S.* 39°33′ N, 77°50′ W **94**
Maryport, *U.K.* 54°42′ N, 3°30′ W **162**
Mary's Harbour, *Can.* 52°24′ N, 55°58′ W **73**
Marystown, *Can.* 47°10′ N, 55°9′ W **111**
Marysvale, *Utah, U.S.* 38°26′ N, 112°13′ W **90**
Marysville, *Calif., U.S.* 39°9′ N, 121°37′ W **92**
Marysville, *Can.* 45°58′ N, 66°37′ W **94**
Marysville, *Kans., U.S.* 39°49′ N, 96°39′ W **92**
Marysville, *Mich., U.S.* 42°53′ N, 82°30′ W **102**
Marysville, *Ohio, U.S.* 40°13′ N, 83°22′ W **102**
Marysville, *Wash., U.S.* 48°2′ N, 122°11′ W **100**
Maryville, *Mo., U.S.* 40°20′ N, 94°53′ W **82**
Maryville, *Tenn., U.S.* 35°45′ N, 83°58′ W **96**
Marzafal, *Mali* 17°56′ N, 0°59′ E **222**
Marzo, Cabo, *Col.* 6°41′ N, 78°6′ W **136**
Marzūq, *Lib.* 25°55′ N, 13°53′ E **216**
Mas de las Matas, *Sp.* 40°51′ N, 0°15′ E **164**
Masada, ruin(s), *Israel* 31°18′ N, 35°19′ E **194**
Masai Mara National Reserve, *Kenya* 1°27′ S, 35°5′ E **224**
Masai Steppe, *Tanzania* 5°43′ S, 37°1′ E **224**
Masaka, *Uganda* 0°22′ N, 31°43′ E **224**
Masalasef, *Chad* 11°45′ N, 17°10′ E **216**
Masallı, *Azerb.* 39°1′ N, 48°39′ E **195**
Masalembu, Kepulauan, islands, *Java Sea* 5°56′ S, 113°19′ E **192**
Masan, *S. Korea* 35°11′ N, 128°33′ E **200**
Masasi, *Tanzania* 10°43′ S, 38°47′ E **224**
Masaví, *Bol.* 19°24′ S, 63°18′ W **137**
Masaya, *Nicar.* 11°57′ N, 86°6′ W **115**
Masayama, *Sierra Leone* 8°14′ N, 10°49′ W **222**
Masbate, *Philippines* 12°20′ N, 123°36′ E **203**
Masbate, island, *Philippines* 11°55′ N, 122°11′ E **192**
Mascara, *Alg.* 35°23′ N, 0°7′ E **150**
Mascarene Basin, *Indian Ocean* 13°57′ S, 55°8′ E **254**
Mascarene Plain, *Indian Ocean* 21°15′ S, 51°32′ E **254**
Mascart, Cape, *Antarctica* 66°35′ S, 71°50′ W **248**
Mascota, *Mex.* 20°31′ N, 104°48′ W **114**
Mascoutah, *Ill., U.S.* 38°28′ N, 89°47′ W **102**
Masein, *Myanmar* 23°22′ N, 94°21′ E **202**
Maseru, *Lesotho* 29°19′ S, 27°24′ E **227**
Masfjorden, *Nor.* 60°47′ N, 5°19′ E **152**
Mash'abbé Sade, *Israel* 30°59′ N, 34°46′ E **194**
Mashābih, island, *Saudi Arabia* 25°35′ N, 35°47′ E **182**
Masham, *U.K.* 54°13′ N, 1°40′ W **162**
Mashan, *China* 23°40′ N, 108°10′ E **198**
Mashhad, *Iran* 36°19′ N, 59°35′ E **180**
Mashigina, Guba 74°4′ N, 47°51′ E **160**
Mashkai, river, *Pak.* 26°44′ N, 65°14′ E **182**
Mashuray, *Afghan.* 32°8′ N, 68°20′ E **186**
Masi, *Nor.* 69°26′ N, 23°38′ E **152**
Masindi, *Uganda* 1°38′ N, 31°42′ E **224**
Masindi Port, *Uganda* 1°39′ N, 32°4′ E **224**
Masinloc, *Philippines* 15°34′ N, 119°58′ E **203**
Maṣīrah, Jazīrat (Masira), island, *Oman* 20°43′ N, 58°55′ E **182**
Masisea, *Peru* 8°40′ S, 74°21′ W **130**
Masisi, *Dem. Rep. of the Congo* 1°24′ S, 28°47′ E **224**
Māsiyah, Tall al, peak, *Syr.* 32°47′ N, 36°39′ E **194**
Masjed Soleymān, *Iran* 31°54′ N, 49°20′ E **180**
Maska, *Nig.* 11°17′ N, 7°19′ E **222**
Maskan, Raas, *Somalia* 11°9′ N, 43°34′ E **216**
Maskūtān, *Iran* 26°51′ N, 59°53′ E **182**
Maslen Nos, *Bulg.* 42°20′ N, 27°46′ E **156**
Maslovare, *Bosn. and Herzg.* 44°33′ N, 17°31′ E **168**
Maslovo, *Russ.* 60°9′ N, 60°31′ E **154**
Masoala, Presqu'île de, *Madagascar* 16°16′ S, 50°11′ E **220**
Masoller, *Uru.* 31°7′ S, 55°59′ W **139**
Masomeloka, *Madagascar* 20°17′ S, 48°37′ E **220**
Mason, *Ill., U.S.* 38°57′ N, 88°38′ W **102**
Mason, *Mich., U.S.* 42°34′ N, 84°26′ W **102**
Mason, *Ohio, U.S.* 39°21′ N, 84°19′ W **102**
Mason, *Tex., U.S.* 30°43′ N, 99°13′ W **92**
Mason Bay 47°3′ S, 167°36′ E **240**
Mason City, *Ill., U.S.* 40°12′ N, 89°42′ W **102**
Mason City, *Iowa, U.S.* 43°7′ N, 93°12′ W **94**
Masqaṭ (Muscat), *Oman* 23°30′ N, 58°32′ E **196**
Massa, *Congo* 3°46′ S, 15°27′ E **218**
Massa, *It.* 44°1′ N, 10°8′ E **167**
Massa Lombarda, *It.* 44°26′ N, 11°49′ E **167**
Massachusetts, adm. division, *Mass., U.S.* 42°14′ N, 72°39′ W **104**
Massachusetts Bay 42°11′ N, 70°43′ W **104**
Massafra, *It.* 40°35′ N, 17°7′ E **156**
Massaguet, *Chad* 12°31′ N, 15°25′ E **216**
Massakory, *Chad* 13°0′ N, 15°42′ E **216**
Massangena, *Mozambique* 21°33′ S, 33°2′ E **227**
Massat, *Fr.* 42°52′ N, 1°20′ E **164**
Massava, *Russ.* 60°38′ N, 62°5′ E **154**
Massawa, *Eritrea* 15°37′ N, 39°23′ E **182**
Massenya, *Chad* 11°27′ N, 16°9′ E **216**
Masset, *Can.* 53°59′ N, 132°2′ W **98**
Masseube, *Fr.* 43°25′ N, 0°33′ E **164**
Massillon, *Ohio, U.S.* 40°47′ N, 81°31′ W **102**
Massinga, *Mozambique* 23°16′ S, 35°20′ E **227**
Massingir, *Mozambique* 23°47′ S, 32°7′ E **227**
Masson Island, *Antarctica* 66°3′ S, 96°8′ E **248**
Masson Range, *Antarctica* 68°32′ S, 59°23′ E **248**
Mastābah, *Saudi Arabia* 20°49′ N, 39°26′ E **182**
Maştağa, *Azerb.* 40°33′ N, 49°59′ E **195**
Mastic Beach, *N.Y., U.S.* 40°45′ N, 72°51′ W **104**
Mastic Point, *Bahamas* 25°4′ N, 77°60′ W **96**
Mastuj, *Pak.* 36°15′ N, 72°33′ E **186**
Mastūrah, *Saudi Arabia* 23°7′ N, 38°51′ E **182**
Masty, *Belarus* 53°25′ N, 24°33′ E **152**
Masuda, *Japan* 34°39′ N, 131°51′ E **200**
Masuria, region, *Pol.* 54°12′ N, 19°41′ E **166**
Masvingo, *Zimb.* 20°6′ S, 30°47′ E **227**
Maşyāf, *Syr.* 35°3′ N, 36°20′ E **194**
Mat, river, *Alban.* 41°38′ N, 19°38′ E **168**
Mata, *Dem. Rep. of the Congo* 7°55′ S, 21°56′ E **218**
Mata Mata, *S. Af.* 25°50′ S, 20°3′ E **227**
Mata Ortiz, *Mex.* 30°7′ N, 108°4′ W **92**
Matachewan, *Can.* 47°56′ N, 80°38′ W **94**
Matachic, *Mex.* 28°50′ N, 107°44′ W **92**
Matadi, *Dem. Rep. of the Congo* 5°49′ S, 13°27′ E **218**
Matador, *Tex., U.S.* 33°59′ N, 100°50′ W **92**
Matagalpa, *Nicar.* 12°54′ N, 85°54′ W **115**
Matagami, *Can.* 49°47′ N, 77°39′ W **94**
Matagami, Lac, lake, *Can.* 50°0′ N, 78°4′ W **94**
Matagorda, *Tex., U.S.* 28°41′ N, 95°58′ W **96**
Matagorda Bay 28°28′ N, 97°19′ W **80**
Matagorda Peninsula, *Tex., U.S.* 28°31′ N, 96°26′ W **96**
Matak, island, *Indonesia* 3°25′ N, 106°17′ E **196**
Matakana, *N.Z.* 36°23′ S, 174°42′ E **240**
Matala, *Angola* 14°47′ S, 14°59′ E **220**
Matala, ruin(s), *Gr.* 34°58′ N, 24°39′ E **156**
Matam, *Senegal* 15°39′ N, 13°21′ W **222**
Matameye, *Niger* 13°23′ N, 8°26′ E **222**
Matamoros, *Mex.* 18°34′ N, 98°29′ W **114**
Matamoros, *Mex.* 25°31′ N, 103°15′ W **114**
Matamoros, *Mex.* 25°53′ N, 97°31′ W **114**
Ma'ṭan al Ḥusayyāt, spring, *Lib.* 30°21′ N, 20°33′ E **216**
Ma'ṭan as Sarra, spring, *Lib.* 21°35′ N, 21°52′ E **216**
Ma'ṭan Bishrah, spring, *Lib.* 23°0′ N, 22°41′ E **226**
Ma'ṭan Shārib, spring, *Egypt* 30°16′ N, 28°26′ E **180**
Matandu, river, *Tanzania* 8°52′ S, 38°38′ E **224**
Matane, *Can.* 48°49′ N, 67°33′ W **94**
Matanzas, *Cuba* 23°4′ N, 81°36′ W **96**
Matanzas, adm. division, *Cuba* 22°59′ N, 81°44′ W **116**
Matanzas, island, *Cuba* 22°5′ N, 82°46′ W **116**
Matão, Serra do, *Braz.* 9°38′ S, 51°31′ W **130**
Mataojo, *Uru.* 31°11′ S, 56°23′ W **139**
Matapás see Akrotírio Ténaro, *Gr.* 36°13′ N, 21°38′ E **156**
Matapi, *Suriname* 4°59′ N, 57°21′ W **130**
Mataporquera, *Sp.* 42°52′ N, 4°11′ W **150**
Matapwa, *Tanzania* 9°42′ S, 39°24′ E **224**
Matara, *Sri Lanka* 5°58′ N, 80°32′ E **188**
Mataram, *Indonesia* 8°36′ S, 116°6′ E **192**
Matarani, *Peru* 16°60′ S, 72°7′ W **137**
Matarka, *Mor.* 33°21′ N, 2°42′ W **214**
Mataró, *Sp.* 41°32′ N, 2°26′ E **164**
Matassi, spring, *Sudan* 18°49′ N, 29°47′ E **226**
Mätäsvaara, *Fin.* 63°25′ N, 29°32′ E **152**
Matata, *N.Z.* 37°55′ S, 176°46′ E **240**
Matatiele, *S. Af.* 30°22′ S, 28°46′ E **227**
Matauá, river, *Braz.* 6°15′ S, 60°59′ W **130**
Matawai, *N.Z.* 38°22′ S, 177°33′ E **240**
Matay, *Kaz.* 45°31′ N, 57°6′ E **158**
Matay, *Kaz.* 45°52′ N, 78°41′ E **184**
Mateguá, *Bol.* 13°3′ S, 62°49′ W **130**
Matehuala, *Mex.* 23°37′ N, 100°39′ W **96**
Matemo, Ilha, island, *Mozambique* 12°11′ S, 40°39′ E **224**
Matera, *It.* 40°39′ N, 16°36′ E **156**
Matese, *It.* 41°26′ N, 14°7′ E **156**
Mátészalka, *Hung.* 47°56′ N, 22°21′ E **168**
Matetsi, *Zimb.* 18°19′ S, 25°56′ E **224**
Matfors, *Nor.* 62°20′ N, 17°0′ E **152**
Matguia, *Tun.* 34°40′ N, 10°20′ E **156**
Mather, *Calif., U.S.* 37°52′ N, 119°52′ W **100**
Mather, Mount, peak, *Antarctica* 73°32′ S, 60°30′ E **248**
Matheson, *Can.* 48°32′ N, 80°29′ W **94**
Matheson Island, *Can.* 51°43′ N, 96°57′ W **108**
Mathews, *Va., U.S.* 37°25′ N, 76°20′ W **96**
Mathews Peak, *Kenya* 1°13′ N, 37°14′ E **224**
Mathis, *Tex., U.S.* 28°5′ N, 97°49′ W **92**
Mathura, *India* 27°27′ N, 77°38′ E **197**
Mati, *Philippines* 6°59′ N, 126°12′ E **203**
Matiakoali, *Burkina Faso* 12°21′ N, 1°3′ E **222**
Matias Cardoso, *Braz.* 14°56′ S, 43°55′ W **138**
Matin, *India* 22°46′ N, 82°25′ E **197**
Matkasel'kya, *Russ.* 61°57′ N, 30°30′ E **152**
Matlabas, *S. Af.* 24°15′ S, 27°30′ E **227**
Matli, *Pak.* 25°4′ N, 68°47′ E **186**
Matlock, *U.K.* 53°8′ N, 1°33′ W **162**
Mato, *Dem. Rep. of the Congo* 8°1′ S, 24°54′ E **224**
Mato, Cerro, peak, *Venez.* 7°12′ N, 65°23′ W **136**
Mato Grosso, *Braz.* 15°1′ S, 59°57′ W **132**
Mato Grosso, adm. division, *Braz.* 14°29′ S, 52°39′ W **138**
Mato Grosso do Sul, adm. division, *Braz.* 20°12′ S, 53°26′ W **138**
Mato Grosso, Planalto do, *South America* 14°13′ S, 58°51′ W **123**
Mato Verde, *Braz.* 15°25′ S, 42°55′ W **138**
Matobo National Park, *Zimb.* 20°38′ S, 28°11′ E **206**
Matochkin Shar, *Russ.* 73°21′ N, 56°33′ E **160**
Matochkin Shar, Proliv 72°52′ N, 49°46′ E **160**
Matoio, *Angola* 7°28′ S, 14°37′ E **220**
Matola, *Malawi* 13°39′ S, 34°55′ E **224**
Matombo, *Tanzania* 7°2′ S, 37°47′ E **224**
Matope, *Malawi* 15°21′ S, 34°58′ E **224**
Matopos, *Zimb.* 20°25′ S, 28°28′ E **227**
Matos, river, *Bol.* 14°30′ S, 65°60′ W **137**
Matosinhos, *Port.* 41°10′ N, 8°43′ W **150**
Mátra, *Hung.* 47°47′ N, 19°43′ E **168**
Matraca, *Col.* 3°1′ N, 69°7′ W **136**
Mátrafüred, *Hung.* 47°48′ N, 19°58′ E **168**
Maṭraḥ, *Oman* 23°36′ N, 58°32′ E **182**
Maṭrūḥ, *Egypt* 31°20′ N, 27°12′ E **180**
Matsena, *Nig.* 13°8′ N, 10°3′ E **222**
Matsu Tao (Matsu), island, *China* 26°16′ N, 120°3′ E **198**
Matsubase, *Japan* 32°37′ N, 130°41′ E **201**
Matsue, *Japan* 35°27′ N, 133°3′ E **201**
Matsumoto, *Japan* 36°13′ N, 137°59′ E **201**
Matsunaga, *Japan* 34°27′ N, 133°16′ E **201**
Matsusaka, *Japan* 34°33′ N, 136°33′ E **201**
Matsushiro, *Japan* 36°34′ N, 138°13′ E **201**
Matsutō, *Japan* 36°30′ N, 136°33′ E **201**
Matsuura, *Japan* 33°20′ N, 129°42′ E **201**
Matsuyama, *Japan* 33°49′ N, 132°46′ E **201**
Mattagami Lake, lake, *Can.* 47°47′ N, 82°6′ W **110**
Mattagami, river, *Can.* 50°10′ N, 82°17′ W **110**
Mattapoisett, *Mass., U.S.* 41°39′ N, 70°50′ W **104**
Mattawa, *Can.* 46°18′ N, 78°41′ W **94**
Matterhorn Peak, *Calif., U.S.* 38°5′ N, 119°25′ W **100**
Matterhorn, peak, *Nev., U.S.* 41°48′ N, 115°28′ W **90**
Matterhorn, peak, *Switz.* 45°59′ N, 7°37′ E **165**
Mattersburg, *Aust.* 47°43′ N, 16°24′ E **168**
Matthews Peak, *Ariz., U.S.* 36°21′ N, 109°13′ W **92**
Matthew's Ridge, *Guyana* 7°27′ N, 60°6′ W **130**
Mattili, *India* 18°32′ N, 82°13′ E **188**
Mattinata, *It.* 41°42′ N, 16°2′ E **156**
Mattituck, *N.Y., U.S.* 40°59′ N, 72°32′ W **104**
Mattoon, *Ill., U.S.* 39°29′ N, 88°22′ W **102**
Matugama, *Sri Lanka* 6°30′ N, 80°7′ E **188**
Matunuck, *R.I., U.S.* 41°22′ N, 71°33′ W **104**
Maturango Peak, *Calif., U.S.* 36°7′ N, 117°35′ W **92**
Maturín, *Venez.* 9°42′ N, 63°12′ W **116**
Matusadona National Park, *Zimb.* 17°10′ S, 28°4′ E **224**
Matveyevka, *Russ.* 53°29′ N, 53°35′ E **154**
Matxitxako, Cabo, *Sp.* 43°19′ N, 2°48′ W **164**
Matyl'ka, *Russ.* 63°20′ N, 85°34′ E **169**
Matzen, oil field, *Aust.* 48°21′ N, 16°35′ E **152**
Mau, *India* 25°54′ N, 83°31′ E **197**
Mau Ranipur, *India* 25°13′ N, 79°8′ E **197**
Mauá, *Mozambique* 13°52′ S, 37°10′ E **224**
Maubeuge, *Fr.* 50°16′ N, 3°58′ E **163**
Ma-ubin, *Myanmar* 16°43′ N, 95°36′ E **202**
Maubourguet, *Fr.* 43°27′ N, 3°178′ E **164**
Maud, *Tex., U.S.* 33°19′ N, 94°22′ W **103**
Maud Rise, *South Atlantic Ocean* 65°26′ S, 4°0′ E **255**
Maude, Cape, *Antarctica* 82°34′ S, 179°24′ E **248**
Maudheim, Sweden, station, *Antarctica* 71°4′ S, 10°46′ W **248**
Maués, *Braz.* 3°23′ S, 57°43′ W **130**
Maués, river, *Braz.* 4°23′ S, 57°25′ W **130**
Maug Islands, *Maug Islands* 20°2′ N, 145°20′ E **192**
Mauganj, *India* 24°42′ N, 81°52′ E **197**
Maugerville, *Can.* 45°53′ N, 66°28′ W **94**
Maui, island, *Hawai'i, U.S.* 20°39′ N, 156°2′ W **99**
Maukme, *Myanmar* 20°13′ N, 97°42′ E **202**
Maule, adm. division, *Chile* 35°44′ S, 72°37′ W **134**
Mauléon, *Fr.* 43°12′ N, 0°53′ E **164**
Maullín, *Chile* 41°38′ S, 73°37′ W **134**
Maumakeogh, peak, *Ire.* 54°15′ N, 9°36′ W **150**
Maumee, *Ohio, U.S.* 41°33′ N, 83°40′ W **102**
Maumelle, Lake, *Ark., U.S.* 34°50′ N, 93°1′ W **96**
Maumere, *Indonesia* 8°47′ S, 122°13′ E **192**
Maun, *Botswana* 19°59′ S, 23°23′ E **220**
Mauna Kea Observatories, site, *Hawai'i, U.S.* 19°49′ N, 155°32′ W **99**
Mauna Loa Observatory, site, *Hawai'i, U.S.* 19°31′ N, 155°38′ W **99**
Maungaturoto, *N.Z.* 36°7′ S, 174°21′ E **240**
Maungdaw, *Myanmar* 20°52′ N, 92°22′ E **188**
Maungmagan Islands, *Andaman Sea* 13°58′ N, 97°13′ E **202**
Maunoir, Lac, lake, *Can.* 67°36′ N, 118°28′ W **246**
Maurepas, Lake, *La., U.S.* 30°11′ N, 90°56′ W **96**
Maurepas, Lake, *La., U.S.* 30°14′ N, 90°46′ W **103**
Maures, Monts des, *Fr.* 43°19′ N, 5°52′ E **165**
Maurice, *La., U.S.* 30°5′ N, 92°8′ W **103**
Mauriceville, *N.Z.* 40°47′ S, 175°42′ E **240**
Mauriceville, *Tex., U.S.* 30°10′ N, 93°53′ W **103**
Mauritania 20°5′ N, 14°29′ W **214**
Mauritius 20°18′ S, 57°35′ E **254**
Mauritius Trench, *Indian Ocean* 22°23′ S, 56°10′ E **254**
Maurs, *Fr.* 44°42′ N, 2°11′ E **150**
Maury Bay 66°27′ S, 127°0′ E **248**
Maury Mountains, peak, *Oreg., U.S.* 44°1′ N, 120°27′ W **90**
Maury Seachannel, *North Atlantic Ocean* 56°23′ N, 24°27′ W **253**
Mauston, *Wis., U.S.* 43°46′ N, 90°4′ W **102**
Mauthen, *Aust.* 46°39′ N, 13°0′ E **167**
Mavago, *Mozambique* 12°27′ S, 36°13′ E **224**
Maverick, *Ariz., U.S.* 33°44′ N, 109°33′ W **92**
Mavinga, *Angola* 15°47′ S, 20°11′ E **207**
Mavonde, *Mozambique* 18°33′ S, 33°3′ E **224**
Mavroli, *Cyprus* 35°3′ N, 32°27′ E **194**
Mavrovo, *Maced.* 41°40′ N, 20°45′ E **168**
Mavrovo National Park, *Maced.* 41°13′ N, 20°50′ E **180**
Mavrovouni Mine, site, *Cyprus* 35°5′ N, 32°47′ E **194**
Mavrovoúni, peak, *Gr.* 39°26′ N, 22°31′ E **156**
Mawlá Maṭar, *Yemen* 14°48′ N, 48°38′ E **182**
Mawlamyine, *Myanmar* 16°24′ N, 97°41′ E **192**
Mawlite, *Myanmar* 23°36′ N, 94°19′ E **202**
Mawlu, *Myanmar* 24°26′ N, 96°13′ E **188**
Mawqaq, *Saudi Arabia* 27°25′ N, 41°9′ E **180**
Mawshij, *Yemen* 13°43′ N, 43°19′ E **182**
Mawson, Australia, station, *Antarctica* 67°38′ S, 63°5′ E **248**
Mawson, Cape, *Antarctica* 70°29′ S, 77°38′ W **248**
Mawson Coast, *Antarctica* 67°50′ S, 61°7′ E **248**
Max, *N. Dak., U.S.* 47°48′ N, 101°19′ W **90**
Maxaas, *Somalia* 4°23′ N, 46°8′ E **218**
Maxcanú, *Mex.* 20°33′ N, 89°60′ W **115**
Maxhamish Lake, *Can.* 59°48′ N, 124°19′ W **108**
Maxixe, *Mozambique* 23°45′ S, 35°18′ E **227**
Maxton, *N.C., U.S.* 34°43′ N, 79°22′ W **96**
Maxwell, *N. Mex., U.S.* 36°31′ N, 104°34′ W **92**
Maxwell Bay 74°19′ N, 89°56′ W **106**
Maxwelton House, site, *U.K.* 55°11′ N, 3°57′ W **150**
May, Cape 81°35′ S, 173°55′ E **248**
May Point, Cape, *N.J., U.S.* 38°38′ N, 75°1′ W **94**
Maya, island, *Indonesia* 1°39′ S, 109°16′ E **192**
Maya, Mesa de, *Colo., U.S.* 37°1′ N, 103°46′ W **92**
Maya Mountains, *Belize* 16°41′ N, 89°8′ W **115**
Maya, river, *Russ.* 55°23′ N, 132°42′ E **160**
Maya, river, *Russ.* 58°9′ N, 137°20′ E **160**
Mayabandar, *India* 12°52′ N, 92°59′ E **188**
Mayaguana, adm. division, *Bahamas* 22°15′ N, 73°18′ W **116**
Mayaguana Island, *Bahamas* 22°31′ N, 73°18′ W **116**
Mayagüez, *P.R., U.S.* 18°11′ N, 67°10′ W **116**
Mayahi, *Niger* 13°52′ N, 7°31′ E **222**
Mayāmey, *Iran* 36°30′ N, 55°46′ E **180**
Mayang, *China* 27°54′ N, 109°48′ E **198**
Mayapán, ruin(s), *Mex.* 20°35′ N, 89°35′ W **115**
Mayarí, *Cuba* 20°40′ N, 75°42′ W **116**
Maybeury, *W. Va., U.S.* 37°21′ N, 81°23′ W **96**
Maych'ew, *Eth.* 12°47′ N, 39°32′ E **182**
Mayda, *Russ.* 66°20′ N, 41°53′ E **154**
Maydān Ikbiz, *Syr.* 36°48′ N, 36°39′ E **156**
Maydelle, *Tex., U.S.* 31°46′ N, 95°18′ W **103**
Maydh, *Somalia* 10°53′ N, 47°4′ E **216**
Maydh, island, *Somalia* 11°21′ N, 46°49′ E **216**
Maydī, *Yemen* 16°18′ N, 42°52′ E **182**
Mayen, *Ger.* 50°19′ N, 7°13′ E **167**
Mayersville, *Miss., U.S.* 32°52′ N, 91°3′ W **103**
Mayerthorpe, *Can.* 53°56′ N, 115°11′ W **108**
Mayevo, *Russ.* 56°22′ N, 29°51′ E **166**
Mayfa'ah, *Yemen* 14°19′ N, 47°31′ E **182**
Mayfield, *Ky., U.S.* 36°44′ N, 88°40′ W **82**
Mayfield, *N.Z.* 43°51′ S, 171°25′ E **240**
Mayfield Peak, *Idaho, U.S.* 44°29′ N, 114°50′ W **90**
Mayhill, *N. Mex., U.S.* 32°53′ N, 105°29′ W **92**
Maykop, *Russ.* 44°38′ N, 40°3′ E **156**
Maymecha, river, *Russ.* 71°36′ N, 97°42′ E **160**
Maymont, *Can.* 52°32′ N, 107°42′ W **108**
Maynooth, *Can.* 45°14′ N, 77°57′ W **94**
Mayo, *Can.* 63°32′ N, 136°2′ W **246**
Mayo, Cerro, peak, *Chile* 50°22′ S, 73°40′ W **134**
Mayo Darlé, *Cameroon* 6°25′ N, 11°32′ E **222**
Mayo Faran, *Nig.* 8°56′ N, 12°5′ E **216**
Mayo Mayo, *Bol.* 12°19′ S, 65°12′ W **137**
Mayo Ndaga, *Nig.* 6°52′ N, 11°25′ E **222**
Mayodan, *N.C., U.S.* 36°24′ N, 79°59′ W **96**
Mayon Volcano, peak, *Philippines* 13°14′ N, 123°36′ E **203**
Mayor Buratovich, *Arg.* 39°17′ S, 62°37′ W **139**
Mayotte 12°58′ S, 44°34′ E **220**
Mayotte, Île de, island, *Fr.* 12°33′ S, 45°6′ E **220**
Mayqayyn, *Kaz.* 51°28′ N, 75°47′ E **184**
Mayraira Point, *Philippines* 18°39′ N, 120°38′ E **203**
Maysk, *Russ.* 57°47′ N, 77°10′ E **169**
Maysville, *Ky., U.S.* 38°37′ N, 83°45′ W **102**
Maysville, *Mo., U.S.* 39°52′ N, 94°22′ W **94**
Maytag see Dushanzi, *China* 44°17′ N, 84°53′ E **184**
Mayum La, pass, *China* 30°34′ N, 82°31′ E **197**
Mayumba, *Gabon* 3°29′ S, 10°40′ E **218**
Mayville, *Mich., U.S.* 43°19′ N, 83°20′ W **102**
Mayville, *N. Dak., U.S.* 47°28′ N, 97°20′ W **90**
Mayville, *Wis., U.S.* 43°28′ N, 88°34′ W **102**
Maywood, *Ill., U.S.* 41°52′ N, 87°50′ W **102**
Maza, *Arg.* 36°49′ S, 63°20′ W **139**
Mazabuka, *Zambia* 15°53′ S, 27°45′ E **224**
Mazagan see El Jadida, *Mor.* 33°15′ N, 8°33′ W **214**
Mazagão, *Braz.* 0°8′ N, 51°18′ W **130**
Mazalij, oil field, *Saudi Arabia* 24°24′ N, 48°26′ E **196**
Mazamet, *Fr.* 43°28′ N, 2°22′ E **164**
Mazán, *Peru* 3°29′ S, 73°9′ W **136**
Mazán, river, *Peru* 3°10′ S, 73°49′ W **136**
Mazapil, *Mex.* 24°37′ N, 101°34′ W **114**
Mazar-e Sharif, *Afghan.* 36°42′ N, 67°9′ E **186**
Mazarredo, *Arg.* 47°5′ S, 66°41′ W **134**
Mazarrón, *Sp.* 37°35′ N, 1°19′ W **164**
Mazatenango, *Guatemala* 14°30′ N, 91°30′ W **115**
Mazatlán, *Mex.* 23°12′ N, 106°24′ W **114**
Mazatlán, *Mex.* 29°1′ N, 110°10′ W **92**
Mazatzal Mountains, *Ariz., U.S.* 34°11′ N, 111°34′ W **92**
Mazée, *Belg.* 50°6′ N, 4°40′ E **167**
Mažeikiai, *Lith.* 56°19′ N, 22°20′ E **166**
Mazgirt, *Turk.* 39°1′ N, 39°36′ E **195**
Mazıdağı, *Turk.* 37°30′ N, 40°32′ E **195**
Mazīnān, *Iran* 36°22′ N, 56°43′ E **180**
Mazirbe, *Latv.* 57°38′ N, 22°10′ E **166**
Mazo Cruz, *Peru* 16°47′ S, 69°44′ W **137**
Mazomanie, *Wis., U.S.* 43°9′ N, 89°48′ W **102**
Mazong Shan, peak, *China* 41°27′ N, 96°25′ E **172**
Mazowe, *Zimb.* 17°31′ S, 30°59′ E **224**
Mazowieckie, adm. division, *Pol.* 52°21′ N, 19°23′ E **152**
Mazrag, oil field, *Oman* 18°17′ N, 55°30′ E **182**
Mazrub, *Sudan* 13°52′ N, 29°19′ E **226**
Mazsalaca, *Latv.* 57°51′ N, 25°2′ E **166**
Mazunga, *Zimb.* 21°44′ S, 29°53′ E **227**
Mazyr, *Belarus* 52°0′ N, 29°21′ E **152**
Mbabane, *Swaziland* 26°19′ S, 30°58′ E **227**
Mbahiakro, *Côte d'Ivoire* 7°24′ N, 4°21′ W **222**
Mbaïki, *Cen. Af. Rep.* 3°55′ N, 18°2′ E **218**
Mbala, *Cen. Af. Rep.* 7°47′ N, 20°49′ E **218**
Mbala (Abercorn), *Zambia* 8°53′ S, 31°23′ E **224**
Mbalabala, *Zimb.* 20°28′ S, 29°1′ E **227**
Mbalambala, *Kenya* 4°237′ S, 39°4′ E **224**
Mbale, *Uganda* 1°1′ N, 34°7′ E **224**
Mbalmayo, *Cameroon* 3°30′ N, 11°31′ E **222**
Mbamba Bay, *Tanzania* 11°15′ S, 34°50′ E **224**
Mbandaka (Coquilhatville), *Dem. Rep. of the Congo* 2°119′ N, 18°17′ E **218**
Mbandjok, *Cameroon* 4°21′ N, 11°50′ E **218**
Mbang, Monts, *Cameroon* 7°11′ N, 13°29′ E **218**
Mbanga, *Cameroon* 4°30′ N, 9°33′ E **222**
Mbanika, island, *Solomon Islands* 9°5′ S, 159°11′ E **242**
M'banza Congo, *Angola* 6°17′ S, 14°14′ E **218**

Mbanza-Ngungu, Dem. Rep. of the Congo 5°18' S, 14°49' E 218
Mbarangandu, river, Tanzania 10°4' S, 36°47' E 224
Mbarara, Uganda 0°37' N, 30°40' E 224
Mbari, river, Cen. Af. Rep. 4°56' N, 22°52' E 218
Mbé, Cameroon 7°43' N, 13°31' E 218
Mbé, Congo 3°20' S, 15°52' E 218
Mbegera, Tanzania 9°34' S, 34°58' E 224
Mbengwi, Cameroon 6°2' N, 10°2' E 222
Mbeya, Tanzania 8°54' S, 33°29' E 224
Mbeya, adm. division, Tanzania 8°32' S, 32°46' E 224
M'Binda, Congo 2°10' S, 12°52' E 218
Mbitao, Cameroon 7°13' N, 15°14' E 218
Mbizi, Zimb. 21°24' S, 31°1' E 227
Mbogo, Tanzania 7°25' S, 33°26' E 224
Mboi, Dem. Rep. of the Congo 6°57' S, 21°53' E 218
Mbomo, Congo 0°22' N, 14°42' E 218
Mborokua, island, Solomon Islands 9°2' S, 158°45' E 242
Mbour, Senegal 14°25' N, 16°43' W 222
Mbout, Mauritania 16°1' N, 12°38' W 222
Mbrés, Cen. Af. Rep. 6°36' N, 19°48' E 218
Mbuji-Mayi (Bakwanga), Dem. Rep. of the Congo 6°10' S, 23°36' E 224
Mbulamuti, Uganda 0°47' N, 33°2' E 224
Mbulo, island, Solomon Islands 8°45' S, 158°19' E 242
Mbulu, Tanzania 3°49' S, 35°33' E 224
Mburucuyá, Arg. 28°2' S, 58°13' W 139
Mcadam, Can. 45°35' N, 67°19' W 94
Mcafee Peak, Nev., U.S. 41°30' N, 116°4' W 90
Mcalester, Okla., U.S. 34°54' N, 95°46' W 96
Mcallen, Tex., U.S. 26°10' N, 98°13' W 112
Mcarthur, Ohio, U.S. 39°13' N, 82°29' W 102
Mcbain, Mich., U.S. 44°11' N, 85°13' W 102
Mcbride, Can. 53°17' N, 120°12' W 108
Mccall, Idaho, U.S. 44°53' N, 116°6' W 90
Mccamey, Tex., U.S. 31°7' N, 102°12' W 92
Mccann Lake, Can. 61°13' N, 107°4' W 108
Mccarran International Airport, Nev., U.S. 36°2' N, 115°14' W 101
Mccarthy, Alas., U.S. 61°25' N, 142°56' W 98
Mccarthy Inlet 78°49' S, 51°2' W 248
Mcchord Air Force Base, Wash., U.S. 47°7' N, 122°32' W 100
Mccleary, Wash., U.S. 47°2' N, 123°16' W 100
Mcclellanville, S.C., U.S. 33°5' N, 79°28' W 96
Mcclintock, Mount, peak, Antarctica 80°10' S, 158°39' E 248
Mcclure, Lake, Calif., U.S. 37°35' N, 120°23' W 100
Mccomb, Miss., U.S. 31°13' N, 90°27' W 103
Mccomb, Ohio, U.S. 41°6' N, 83°46' W 102
Mcconaughy, Lake, Nebr., U.S. 41°13' N, 103°23' W 80
Mcconnell Air Force Base, Kans., U.S. 37°35' N, 97°20' W 90
Mcconnelsville, Ohio, U.S. 39°38' N, 81°51' W 102
Mccook, Nebr., U.S. 40°11' N, 100°39' W 90
Mccool, Miss., U.S. 33°11' N, 89°20' W 103
Mccormick, Cape, Antarctica 71°28' S, 176°52' E 248
Mccoy, Mount, peak, Antarctica 75°46' S, 140°8' W 248
Mccoy Mountains, Calif., U.S. 33°45' N, 114°52' W 101
Mccrea Lake, Can. 50°49' N, 90°44' W 110
Mccreary, Can. 50°47' N, 99°30' W 90
Mccullough, Ala., U.S. 31°9' N, 87°31' W 103
Mccullough Range, Nev., U.S. 35°31' N, 115°17' W 101
Mccusker Lake, Can. 51°42' N, 95°38' W 108
Mcdame, Can. 59°12' N, 129°14' W 108
Mcdills, spring, Austral. 25°50' S, 135°15' E 230
Mcdonald, Kans., U.S. 39°46' N, 101°22' W 90
Mcdonald, Miss., U.S. 32°39' N, 89°8' W 103
Mcdonald Peak, Calif., U.S. 40°55' N, 120°30' W 90
Mcevoy, Mount, peak, Can. 56°45' N, 128°25' W 108
Mcfarland, Calif., U.S. 35°40' N, 119°15' W 100
Mcfarland, Kans., U.S. 39°2' N, 96°15' W 90
Mcfarland, Wis., U.S. 43°0' N, 89°18' W 102
Mcgehee, Ark., U.S. 33°36' N, 91°23' W 96
Mcgill, Nev., U.S. 39°24' N, 114°47' W 90
Mcgrath, Alas., U.S. 63°4' N, 155°28' W 73
Mcgregor, Tex., U.S. 31°25' N, 97°24' W 92
Mcgregor Lake, Can. 50°26' N, 113°32' W 90
Mcgregor, river, Can. 54°14' N, 121°26' W 108
Mcguire Air Force Base, N.J., U.S. 39°59' N, 74°41' W 94
Mcguire, Mount, peak, Idaho, U.S. 45°9' N, 114°41' W 90
Mchenry, Ky., U.S. 37°22' N, 86°55' W 96
Mchenry, Miss., U.S. 30°41' N, 89°7' W 103
Mcherrah, region, Alg. 26°45' N, 5°3' W 214
Mchinja, Tanzania 9°46' S, 39°41' E 224
Mchinji, Malawi 13°48' S, 32°54' E 224
Mcindoe Falls, Vt., U.S. 44°15' N, 72°5' W 104
Mcinnes Lake, Can. 52°8' N, 95°4' W 80
Mcintosh, Fla., U.S. 29°26' N, 82°15' W 105
Mcintosh, Minn., U.S. 47°36' N, 95°55' W 90
Mcintosh, S. Dak., U.S. 45°54' N, 101°22' W 90
Mcivor, river, Can. 57°53' N, 112°1' W 108
Mckay Lake, Can. 49°33' N, 86°52' W 94
Mckay Lake, Can. 53°45' N, 65°58' W 111
Mckay, Mount, peak, Can. 48°19' N, 89°22' W 94
Mckeesport, Pa., U.S. 40°20' N, 79°49' W 82
Mckelvey, Mount, peak, Antarctica 85°26' S, 87°27' W 248
Mckenzie Island, Can. 51°4' N, 93°49' W 82
Mckenzie Pass, Oreg., U.S. 44°14' N, 121°48' W 90
Mckerrow, Can. 46°16' N, 81°45' W 94
Mckerrow, Lake, N.Z. 44°30' S, 167°28' E 240
Mckinley, Mount (Denali), peak, Alas., U.S. 62°54' N, 151°17' W 98
Mckinley Peak, Antarctica 77°46' S, 147°15' W 248
Mckinney, Tex., U.S. 33°12' N, 96°39' W 112
Mckinnon, Wyo., U.S. 41°2' N, 109°56' W 90
Mckittrick, Calif., U.S. 35°18' N, 119°38' W 100
Mclain, Miss., U.S. 31°4' N, 88°49' W 103
Mclaughlin, S. Dak., U.S. 45°47' N, 100°50' W 90
Mclaurin, Miss., U.S. 31°9' N, 89°12' W 103
Mclean, Ill., U.S. 40°18' N, 89°11' W 102
Mclean, Tex., U.S. 35°12' N, 100°36' W 92
Mclean Mountain, peak, Me., U.S. 47°6' N, 68°57' W 94
Mcleansboro, Mo., U.S. 38°5' N, 88°32' W 94
Mclennan, Can. 55°41' N, 116°55' W 108
Mcleod, Tex., U.S. 32°55' N, 94°6' W 103
Mcleod Bay 62°35' N, 110°40' W 106
Mcleod Lake, Can. 54°59' N, 123°2' W 108
Mcleod Valley, Can. 53°44' N, 116°1' W 108
M'Clintock Channel 70°55' N, 106°28' W 72
Mcloughlin, Mount, peak, Oreg., U.S. 42°27' N, 122°24' W 90
M'Clure Strait 74°40' N, 118°17' W 255
Mcmechen, W. Va., U.S. 39°58' N, 80°45' W 94
Mcminnville, Tenn., U.S. 35°41' N, 85°46' W 96
Mcmurdo, U.S., station, Antarctica 77°48' S, 166°8' E 248
Mcnary, Ariz., U.S. 34°3' N, 109°51' W 92
Mcneil, Ark., U.S. 33°20' N, 93°13' W 103
Mcneill, Miss., U.S. 30°39' N, 89°38' W 103
Mcphadyen, river, Can. 53°57' N, 67°39' W 111
Mcpherson, Kans., U.S. 38°21' N, 97°41' W 90
Mcrae, Ark., U.S. 35°5' N, 91°49' W 96
Mcrae, Ga., U.S. 32°3' N, 82°54' W 96
Mctaggart Lake, Can. 58°2' N, 108°60' W 108
Mctavish Lake, Can. 55°54' N, 105°52' W 108
Mcveigh, Can. 56°42' N, 101°15' W 108
Mcvicar Arm 64°55' N, 122°55' W 106
Mcville, N. Dak., U.S. 47°44' N, 98°12' W 90
Mdandu, Tanzania 9°9' S, 34°41' E 224
Mdennah, region, Mali 24°19' N, 6°3' W 214
Mdiq, Mor. 35°40' N, 5°20' W 150
Mead, Lake, Nev., U.S. 36°26' N, 114°32' W 101
Meade, Kans., U.S. 37°17' N, 100°21' W 92
Meade Peak, Idaho, U.S. 42°29' N, 111°19' W 90
Meade, river, Alas., U.S. 69°34' N, 156°47' W 98
Meadow Lake, Can. 54°8' N, 108°26' W 108
Meadow Valley Wash, river, Nev., U.S. 36°53' N, 114°44' W 101
Meadows, Idaho, U.S. 44°56' N, 116°15' W 90
Meadows, N.H., U.S. 44°21' N, 71°29' W 104
Meadville, Miss., U.S. 31°27' N, 90°54' W 103
Meadville, Pa., U.S. 41°38' N, 80°9' W 94
Meander River, Can. 59°2' N, 117°41' W 108
Meares, Cape, Oreg., U.S. 45°20' N, 124°24' W 90
Mears, Mich., U.S. 43°40' N, 86°25' W 102
Meath Park, Can. 53°26' N, 105°25' W 108
Meaux, Fr. 48°57' N, 2°53' E 163
Mebane, N.C., U.S. 36°5' N, 79°17' W 96
Mecanhelas, Mozambique 15°11' S, 35°53' E 224
Mecca, Calif., U.S. 33°34' N, 116°6' W 101
Mecca see Makkah, Saudi Arabia 21°24' N, 39°49' E 182
Mechanic Falls, Me., U.S. 44°6' N, 70°25' W 104
Mechanicville, N.Y., U.S. 42°54' N, 73°43' W 104
Mechelen, Belg. 51°1' N, 4°29' E 167
Mechems, region, Alg. 27°0' N, 8°15' W 214
Mecheraa Asfa, Alg. 35°22' N, 1°4' E 150
Mecherchar (Eil Malk), island, Palau 7°7' N, 134°22' E 242
Mecheria, Alg. 33°33' N, 0°17' E 214
Mechernich, Ger. 50°35' N, 6°39' E 167
Mechetinskaya, Russ. 46°43' N, 40°26' E 158
Mechta Gara, Alg. 36°15' N, 5°25' E 150
Mechtat el Hiout, Alg. 36°33' N, 6°40' E 150
Mecitözü, Turk. 40°31' N, 35°17' E 156
Mecklenburg-Western Pomerania, adm. division, Ger. 53°47' N, 12°32' E 152
Meconta, Mozambique 14°58' S, 39°54' E 224
Mecosta, Mich., U.S. 43°37' N, 85°14' W 102
Mecsek, Hung. 46°15' N, 17°37' E 168
Mecubúri, Mozambique 14°41' S, 38°55' E 224
Mecúfi, Mozambique 13°22' S, 40°33' E 224
Mecula, Mozambique 12°6' S, 37°42' E 224
Medak, India 18°4' N, 78°15' E 188
Médala, Mauritania 15°31' N, 5°38' W 222
Medale, Eth. 6°23' N, 41°54' E 224
Medan, Indonesia 3°35' N, 98°40' E 196
Médanos, Arg. 33°26' S, 59°4' W 139
Médanos, Arg. 38°51' S, 62°42' W 139
Médanos de Coro National Park, Venez. 11°34' N, 70°3' W 122
Medanosa, Punta, Arg. 48°17' S, 65°58' W 134
Medaryville, Ind., U.S. 41°3' N, 86°54' W 102
Médéa, Alg. 36°15' N, 2°45' E 150
Medebach, Ger. 51°11' N, 8°42' E 167
Medeiros Neto, Braz. 17°22' S, 40°15' W 138
Medellín, Col. 6°13' N, 75°34' W 136
Medemblik, Neth. 52°46' N, 5°6' E 163
Medena Selišta, Bosn. and Herzg. 44°7' N, 16°47' E 168
Medenine, Tun. 33°21' N, 10°28' E 214
Meder, Eritrea 14°41' N, 40°42' E 182
Mederdra, Mauritania 16°56' N, 15°42' W 222
Medes, Les, islands, Sp. 42°5' N, 3°8' E 164
Medford, Mass., U.S. 42°25' N, 71°7' W 104
Medford, Okla., U.S. 36°47' N, 97°43' W 92
Medford, Oreg., U.S. 42°21' N, 122°50' W 106
Medford, Wis., U.S. 45°8' N, 90°20' W 94
Medgidia, Rom. 44°14' N, 28°16' E 156
Mediaş, Rom. 46°10' N, 24°20' E 156
Medical Lake, Wash., U.S. 47°33' N, 117°42' W 90
Medicina, It. 44°29' N, 11°36' E 167
Medicine Bow, Wyo., U.S. 41°54' N, 106°13' W 92
Medicine Bow Mountains, Wyo., U.S. 41°44' N, 106°32' W 90
Medicine Bow Peak, Wyo., U.S. 41°21' N, 106°23' W 90
Medicine Hat, Can. 50°2' N, 110°43' W 82
Medicine Lake, Mont., U.S. 48°23' N, 105°1' W 90
Medicine Lodge, Kans., U.S. 37°16' N, 98°37' W 90
Medicine Rocks, site, Mont., U.S. 45°56' N, 104°38' W 90
Medina, Braz. 16°13' S, 41°33' W 138
Medina, Col. 4°30' N, 73°21' W 136
Medina, N.Y., U.S. 43°12' N, 78°25' W 110
Medina, N. Dak., U.S. 46°53' N, 99°20' W 90
Medina, Ohio, U.S. 41°7' N, 81°52' W 102
Medina, Tex., U.S. 29°47' N, 99°15' W 92
Medina de Pomar, Sp. 42°53' N, 3°29' W 164
Medina de Rioseco, Sp. 41°51' N, 5°7' W 214
Medina del Campo, Sp. 41°18' N, 4°55' W 150
Médina Gadaoundou, Guinea 11°51' N, 11°36' W 222
Medina see Al Madīnah, Saudi Arabia 24°26' N, 39°34' E 182
Medina Sidonia, Sp. 36°28' N, 5°58' W 164
Medinaceli, Sp. 41°9' N, 2°27' W 164
Médine, Mali 14°22' N, 11°24' W 222
Medinipur, India 22°27' N, 87°20' E 197
Mediodia, Col. 1°51' S, 72°9' W 136
Mediterranean Sea 34°7' N, 16°42' E 143
Medje, Dem. Rep. of the Congo 2°24' N, 27°16' E 224
Medjerda, Monts de la, Tun. 36°40' N, 8°6' E 156
Medkovets, Bulg. 43°37' N, 23°10' E 168
Medley, Can. 54°25' N, 110°16' W 108
Mednogorsk, Russ. 51°24' N, 57°34' E 158
Médoc, region, Fr. 44°43' N, 1°16' W 150
Mêdog, China 29°19' N, 95°24' E 188
Medstead, Can. 53°17' N, 108°5' W 108
Međurječje, Europe 42°43' N, 19°22' E 168
Međuvođe, Bosn. and Herzg. 45°6' N, 16°46' E 168
Medveda, Serb. and Mont. 42°50' N, 21°35' E 168
Medveditsa, river, Russ. 49°40' N, 43°1' E 184
Medvedok, Russ. 57°25' N, 50°10' E 154
Medvezh'i Ostrova (Bear Islands), East Siberian Sea 71°5' N, 151°1' E 160
Medvezh'yegorsk, Russ. 62°54' N, 34°28' E 154
Medway, Mass., U.S. 42°8' N, 71°25' W 104
Medzhybizh, Ukr. 49°26' N, 27°26' E 152
Meehaus, Mount, peak, Can. 58°0' N, 130°41' W 108
Meeker, Colo., U.S. 40°2' N, 107°56' W 90
Meelpaeg Reservoir, lake, Can. 48°15' N, 57°26' W 111
Meerut, India 28°59' N, 77°40' E 197
Meerzorg, Suriname 5°47' N, 55°9' W 130
Meeteetse, Wyo., U.S. 44°8' N, 108°51' W 90
Mefjell Mount, peak, Antarctica 72°10' S, 24°38' E 248
Mēga, Eth. 4°1' N, 38°17' E 224
Megalo, Eth. 6°52' N, 40°47' E 224
Megargel, Ala., U.S. 31°22' N, 87°25' W 103
Meghalaya, adm. division, India 25°20' N, 89°54' E 197
Meghri, Arm. 38°53' N, 46°13' E 195
Megiddo, Israel 32°34' N, 35°10' E 194
Megiddo, Tel, peak, Israel 32°34' N, 35°8' E 194
Megion, Russ. 61°1' N, 76°19' E 169
Mégiscane, Lac, lake, Can. 48°37' N, 76°28' W 94
Megler, Wash., U.S. 46°14' N, 123°51' W 100
Mehar, Pak. 27°13' N, 67°50' E 186
Meharry, Mount, peak, Austral. 22°59' S, 118°24' E 230
Meharry, Mount, peak, Austral. 23°10' S, 118°10' E 238
Mehedinţi, adm. division, Rom. 44°49' N, 22°16' E 156
Mehedinţi, Munţii, Rom. 44°51' N, 22°25' E 168
Mehola, West Bank 32°20' N, 35°31' E 194
Mehrīz, Iran 31°32' N, 54°35' E 180
Meia Ponte, river, Braz. 18°4' S, 49°32' W 138
Meiganga, Cameroon 6°28' N, 14°17' E 218
Meighen Island, Can. 79°58' N, 102°32' W 246
Meigs, Ga., U.S. 31°3' N, 84°6' W 96
Meihekou, China 42°31' N, 125°37' E 200
Meikle Says Law, peak, U.K. 55°49' N, 2°47' W 150
Meiners Oaks, Calif., U.S. 34°27' N, 119°17' W 100
Meiningen, Ger. 50°34' N, 10°24' E 167
Meira, Sp. 43°12' N, 7°19' W 150
Meiringen, Switz. 46°43' N, 8°11' E 167
Meister, river, Can. 60°20' N, 131°12' W 108
Meizhou, China 24°19' N, 116°4' E 198
Meja, India 25°9' N, 82°6' E 197
Mejillones, Chile 23°8' S, 70°30' W 132
Mékambo, Gabon 0°59' N, 13°53' E 218
Mek'elē, Eth. 13°29' N, 39°25' E 182
Mekhel'ta, Russ. 42°44' N, 46°30' E 195
Mekhtar, Pak. 30°29' N, 69°24' E 186
Mékinac, Lac, lake, Can. 47°1' N, 73°13' W 110
Meknassy, Tun. 34°32' N, 9°36' E 156
Meko, Nig. 7°28' N, 2°50' E 222
Mekong see Lancang, river, China 32°3' N, 97°14' E 190
Mekoryuk, Alas., U.S. 60°17' N, 166°21' W 98
Mel, It. 46°3' N, 12°4' E 167
Melalap, Malaysia 5°15' N, 116°0' E 203
Melanesia, islands, Coral Sea 7°19' S, 149°12' E 192
Melaque, Mex. 19°14' N, 104°43' W 114
Melba Peninsula 65°39' S, 98°7' E 248
Melbourne, Austral. 37°51' S, 144°38' E 230
Melbourne, Fla., U.S. 28°6' N, 80°40' W 105
Melbourne Beach, Fla., U.S. 28°4' N, 80°35' W 105
Melbourne, Mount, peak, Antarctica 74°22' S, 165°18' E 248
Melbu, Nor. 68°29' N, 14°49' E 152
Melchett Lake, Can. 50°42' N, 87°36' W 110
Melchior Islands, Weddell Sea 64°16' S, 65°56' W 134
Melchor, Isla, island, Chile 45°15' S, 75°39' W 134
Melchor Ocampo, Mex. 24°48' N, 101°39' W 114
Meldola, It. 44°6' N, 12°2' E 167
Meldorf, Ger. 54°5' N, 9°4' E 150
Meldrum Creek, Can. 52°6' N, 122°22' W 108
Mele, Capo, It. 43°53' N, 8°10' E 167
Melegnano, It. 45°20' N, 9°18' E 167
Melenci, Serb. and Mont. 45°30' N, 20°19' E 168
Melenki, Russ. 55°19' N, 41°40' E 154
Meleski, Est. 58°24' N, 26°5' E 166
Meletsk, Russ. 57°28' N, 90°20' E 169
Meleuz, Russ. 52°58' N, 55°53' E 154
Melfi, Chad 11°3' N, 17°58' E 216
Melfi, It. 40°59' N, 15°39' E 156
Melfort, Can. 52°51' N, 104°37' W 108
Melilla, Sp. 35°15' N, 2°58' W 214
Melinka, Chile 43°52' S, 73°49' W 134
Melita, Can. 49°17' N, 100°58' W 90
Melita see Mljet, island, Croatia 42°37' N, 17°23' E 168
Melito di Porto Salvo, It. 37°55' N, 15°47' E 156
Melitopol', Ukr. 46°50' N, 35°19' E 156
Melksham, U.K. 51°21' N, 2°9' W 162
Mellakou, Alg. 35°15' N, 1°14' E 150
Mellansel, Nor. 63°25' N, 18°20' E 152
Mellen, Wis., U.S. 46°19' N, 90°41' W 94
Mellerud, Nor. 58°42' N, 12°26' E 152
Mellifont Abbey, site, Ire. 53°43' N, 6°32' W 150
Mellit, Sudan 14°6' N, 25°34' E 226
Mellrichstadt, Ger. 50°26' N, 10°17' E 167
Mellum, island, Ger. 53°39' N, 8°10' E 163
Melmerby, U.K. 54°43' N, 2°37' W 162
Melo, Arg. 34°20' S, 63°27' W 139
Melo, Uru. 32°20' S, 54°13' W 139
Meloco, Mozambique 13°31' S, 39°15' E 224
Melos, ruin(s), Aegean Sea 36°42' N, 24°20' E 156
Melouprey, Cambodia 13°49' N, 105°16' E 202
Melrose, Fla., U.S. 29°41' N, 82°3' W 105
Melrose, La., U.S. 31°36' N, 92°59' W 103
Melrose, Mass., U.S. 42°27' N, 71°4' W 104
Melrose, Minn., U.S. 45°38' N, 94°50' W 90
Melrose, N. Mex., U.S. 34°26' N, 103°38' W 92
Melsungen, Ger. 51°7' N, 9°32' E 167
Meltaus, Fin. 66°54' N, 25°20' E 152
Melton Constable, U.K. 52°51' N, 1°2' E 162
Melton Mowbray, U.K. 52°46' N, 0°53' E 162
Melun, Fr. 48°31' N, 2°39' E 163
Melut, Sudan 10°27' N, 32°12' E 224
Melville, Can. 50°55' N, 102°51' W 90
Melville, La., U.S. 30°41' N, 91°46' W 103
Melville, Cape, Austral. 14°8' S, 144°30' E 230
Melville Hills, Can. 69°17' N, 122°25' W 106
Melville Island, Austral. 11°9' S, 131°5' E 192
Melville Island, Can. 74°39' N, 109°22' W 106
Melville Peninsula, Can. 67°59' N, 85°41' W 106
Melville Sound 68°17' N, 103°42' W 246
Melvin, Ill., U.S. 40°33' N, 88°15' W 102
Melvin, Ky., U.S. 37°21' N, 82°42' W 96
Melvin, Tex., U.S. 31°10' N, 99°35' W 92
Melvin Lake, Can. 57°7' N, 100°46' W 108
Melvin, river, Can. 59°0' N, 117°27' W 108
Melvin Village, N.H., U.S. 43°41' N, 71°19' W 104
Mélykút, Hung. 46°12' N, 19°23' E 168
Mêmar Co, lake, China 34°13' N, 81°36' E 188
Memba, Mozambique 14°13' S, 40°31' E 224
Mēmele, river, Europe 56°21' N, 24°9' E 166
Mempawah, Indonesia 0°24' N, 108°57' E 196
Memphis, Mo., U.S. 40°27' N, 92°11' W 94
Memphis, Tenn., U.S. 35°8' N, 90°2' W 96
Memphis, Tex., U.S. 34°42' N, 100°33' W 92
Memphis, site, Egypt 29°51' N, 31°5' E 180
Mena, Ark., U.S. 34°33' N, 94°16' W 96
Mena, Ukr. 51°29' N, 32°13' E 158
Menahga, Minn., U.S. 46°43' N, 95°7' W 90
Ménaka, Mali 15°52' N, 2°25' E 222
Ménalo, Óros, peak, Gr. 37°38' N, 22°12' E 156
Menands, N.Y., U.S. 42°41' N, 73°45' W 104
Menard, Tex., U.S. 30°55' N, 99°47' W 92
Menard Fracture Zone, South Pacific Ocean 49°46' S, 113°56' W 252
Menasha, Wis., U.S. 44°12' N, 88°27' W 102
Menawashei, Sudan 12°41' N, 24°57' E 216
Mende, Fr. 44°30' N, 3°29' E 150
Mende, ruin(s), Gr. 39°58' N, 23°20' E 156
Mendebo, Eth. 6°21' N, 38°52' E 224
Mendeleyev Plain, Arctic Ocean 81°8' N, 167°15' W 255
Mendeleyev Ridge, Arctic Ocean 83°35' N, 172°10' W 255
Mendeleyevsk, Russ. 55°54' N, 52°24' E 154
Mendelssohn Inlet 71°19' S, 77°46' W 248
Menden, Ger. 51°26' N, 7°47' E 167
Méndez, Ecua. 2°47' S, 78°23' W 136
Méndez, Mex. 25°7' N, 98°35' W 114
Mendī, Eth. 9°46' N, 35°4' E 224
Mendip Hills, U.K. 51°9' N, 2°41' W 162
Mendocino, Cape, Calif., U.S. 40°25' N, 124°58' W 90
Mendocino Fracture Zone, North Pacific Ocean 40°1' N, 144°6' W 252
Mendol, island, Indonesia 0°23' N, 103°14' E 196
Mendon, Ohio, U.S. 40°39' N, 84°31' W 102
Mendota, Calif., U.S. 36°45' N, 120°24' W 100
Mendota, Ill., U.S. 41°32' N, 89°7' W 102
Mendoza, Arg. 32°52' S, 68°54' W 134
Mendoza, adm. division, Arg. 34°30' S, 70°3' W 134
Mendung, Indonesia 0°33' N, 103°11' E 196
Mene de Mauroa, Venez. 10°43' N, 70°58' W 136
Mene Grande, Venez. 9°50' N, 70°55' W 136
Menemen, Turk. 38°32' N, 27°2' E 180
Menemsha, Mass., U.S. 41°21' N, 70°46' W 104
Menen, Belg. 50°47' N, 3°7' E 163
Mengcheng, China 33°15' N, 116°32' E 198
Mengen, Ger. 48°3' N, 9°19' E 152
Mengen, Turk. 40°56' N, 32°10' E 156
Mengene Dağı, peak, Turk. 38°13' N, 43°56' E 195
Mengeringhausen, Ger. 51°22' N, 8°58' E 167
Menghai, China 21°58' N, 100°26' E 202
Mengibar, Sp. 37°58' N, 3°48' W 164
Mengla, China 21°29' N, 101°30' E 202
Menglian, China 22°21' N, 99°32' E 202
Mengoub, Mor. 32°20' N, 2°20' W 214
Mengzi, China 23°22' N, 103°23' E 202
Menindee, Austral. 32°19' S, 142°28' E 231
Menindee Lake, Austral. 32°16' S, 141°18' E 230
Menkere, Russ. 67°52' N, 123°17' E 173
Menlo, Wash., U.S. 46°35' N, 123°40' W 100
Menno, S. Dak., U.S. 43°12' N, 97°35' W 90
Menominee, river, U.S. 46°11' N, 88°37' W 80
Menomonie, Wis., U.S. 44°51' N, 91°55' W 94
Menongue, Angola 14°39' S, 17°39' E 220
Menorca, island, Sp. 39°29' N, 4°14' E 142
Menorca (Minorca), island, Sp. 39°47' N, 3°33' E 164
Menouarar, Alg. 31°12' N, 2°16' W 214
Men'shikova, Mys, Russ. 70°24' N, 56°10' E 169
Mentasta Lake, Alas., U.S. 62°56' N, 143°52' W 98
Mentawai, Kepulauan, islands, Indian Ocean 1°1' S, 97°24' E 196
Mentekab, Malaysia 3°29' N, 102°20' E 196
Mentès, spring, Niger 16°58' N, 4°17' E 222
Mentmore, N. Mex., U.S. 35°30' N, 108°50' W 92
Mentor, Ohio, U.S. 41°39' N, 81°20' W 102
Menyapa, peak, Indonesia 1°6' N, 115°48' E 192
Menza, Russ. 49°21' N, 108°51' E 198
Menzel Bourguiba (Ferryville), Tun. 37°9' N, 9°47' E 156
Menzel Chaker, Tun. 34°59' N, 10°22' E 156
Menzelinsk, Russ. 55°40' N, 53°8' E 154
Menzies, Austral. 29°42' S, 121°0' E 231
Menzies, Mount, peak, Antarctica 73°29' S, 61°23' E 248
Menzies, Mount, peak, Can. 50°12' N, 125°35' W 90
Me'ona, Israel 33°0' N, 35°15' E 194
Meota, Can. 53°2' N, 108°28' W 108
Meppel, Neth. 52°41' N, 6°10' E 163
Meppen, Ger. 52°42' N, 7°18' E 163
Mequens, river, Braz. 12°56' S, 62°11' W 132
Mequinenza, Sp. 41°21' N, 0°17' E 164
Mer Rouge, La., U.S. 32°45' N, 91°48' W 103
Meråker, Nor. 63°25' N, 11°43' E 152
Merakert, Asia 40°12' N, 46°47' E 195
Merano, It. 46°40' N, 11°8' E 167
Merauke, Indonesia 8°36' S, 140°31' E 192
Merca (Marka), Somalia 1°41' N, 44°53' E 207
Mercaderes, Col. 1°47' N, 77°14' W 136
Mercan Dağları, peak, Turk. 39°32' N, 39°28' E 195
Mercato Saraceno, It. 43°57' N, 12°10' E 167
Merced, Calif., U.S. 37°18' N, 120°29' W 100
Merced Peak, Calif., U.S. 37°37' N, 119°27' W 100
Mercedes, Arg. 34°42' S, 59°25' W 139
Mercedes, Arg. 29°12' S, 58°3' W 139
Mercedes, Tex., U.S. 26°10' N, 97°55' W 114
Mercedes, Uru. 33°17' S, 57°59' W 139
Merćez, Serb. and Mont. 43°13' N, 21°4' E 168
Mercoal, Can. 53°8' N, 117°7' W 108
Mercury, Nev., U.S. 36°39' N, 115°60' W 101
Mercy Bay 73°58' N, 119°36' W 106
Mercy, Cape, Can. 64°47' N, 63°27' W 106
Meredith, N.H., U.S. 43°38' N, 71°31' W 104
Meredith, Cape, West Falkland 52°28' S, 63°10' W 248
Meredith Center, N.H., U.S. 43°36' N, 71°33' W 104
Mereeg, Somalia 3°44' N, 47°20' E 218
Mereer-Gur, Somalia 5°46' N, 46°31' E 218
Merefa, Ukr. 49°47' N, 36°9' E 158
Méréville, Fr. 48°19' N, 2°4' E 163
Merga see Nukheila, spring, Sudan 19°3' N, 26°20' E 226
Mergenevo, Kaz. 49°57' N, 51°15' E 158
Mergui Archipelago, islands, Andaman Sea 11°3' N, 97°30' E 202
Méri, Cameroon 10°51' N, 14°6' E 218
Meriç, Turk. 41°10' N, 26°24' E 158
Meriç, river, Turk. 41°3' N, 26°22' E 180
Mérida, Mex. 20°56' N, 89°44' W 116
Mérida, Sp. 38°54' N, 6°24' W 214
Mérida, Sp. 38°54' N, 6°20' W 164
Mérida, Venez. 8°36' N, 71°10' W 136
Mérida, adm. division, Venez. 8°18' N, 71°50' W 136
Mérida, Cordillera de, Venez. 9°41' N, 69°46' W 136
Meriden, Conn., U.S. 41°32' N, 72°48' W 104
Meriden, N.H., U.S. 43°32' N, 72°16' W 104
Meridian, Miss., U.S. 32°21' N, 88°42' W 103
Meridian, Tex., U.S. 31°54' N, 97°39' W 92
Merijärvi, Fin. 64°17' N, 24°25' E 152
Merikarvia, Fin. 61°50' N, 21°29' E 166
Měřín, Czech Rep. 49°24' N, 15°52' E 152
Merinaghène, ruin(s), Senegal 16°1' N, 16°6' W 222
Merino Jarpa, Isla, island, Chile 47°44' S, 74°20' W 134
Merirumã, Braz. 1°7' N, 54°37' W 130
Merivälja, Est. 59°29' N, 24°48' E 166
Meriwether Lewis Monument, Tenn., U.S. 35°31' N, 87°33' W 96
Merka, Eth. 5°52' N, 37°6' E 224
Merke, Kaz. 42°51' N, 73°9' E 184
Merkinė, Lith. 54°10' N, 24°12' E 166
Merkoya, Mali 13°56' N, 8°13' W 222
Merksplas, Belg. 51°20' N, 4°51' E 167
Merkushino, Russ. 58°48' N, 61°32' E 154
Merkys, river, Lith. 54°21' N, 24°46' E 166
Merlimont, Fr. 50°27' N, 1°36' E 163
Merlin, Can. 42°14' N, 82°14' W 102
Mermentau, La., U.S. 30°10' N, 92°36' W 103
Meroë, ruin(s), Sudan 17°3' N, 33°45' E 182
Meron, Israel 32°59' N, 35°26' E 194
Merouana, Alg. 35°37' N, 5°54' E 150
Merowe, Sudan 18°23' N, 31°49' E 182
Merrill, Miss., U.S. 30°57' N, 88°43' W 103
Merrill, Wis., U.S. 45°10' N, 89°41' W 94
Merrillville, Ind., U.S. 41°28' N, 87°21' W 102
Merrimack, N.H., U.S. 42°51' N, 71°31' W 104
Merriman, Nebr., U.S. 42°55' N, 101°42' W 90
Merritt, Can. 50°5' N, 120°46' W 108
Merritt Island, Fla., U.S. 28°21' N, 80°42' W 105
Merritt Pass, Ariz., U.S. 34°5' N, 112°59' W 92

Merryville, La., U.S. 30°44′ N, 93°33′ W 103
Mers el Kebir, Alg. 35°43′ N, 0°43′ E 150
Mersey, river, U.K. 53°22′ N, 2°58′ W 162
Mersin see İçel, Turk. 36°48′ N, 34°36′ E 156
Mersing, Malaysia 2°25′ N, 103°49′ E 196
Mērsrags, Latv. 57°20′ N, 23°6′ E 166
Merta Road, India 26°43′ N, 73°55′ E 186
Mertert, Lux. 49°42′ N, 6°30′ E 163
Merthyr Tydfil, U.K. 51°45′ N, 3°22′ W 162
Merti, Kenya 1°1′ N, 38°40′ E 224
Mértola, Port. 37°38′ N, 7°41′ W 150
Mertzon, Tex., U.S. 31°15′ N, 100°50′ W 92
Méru, Fr. 49°14′ N, 2°8′ E 163
Meru, Kenya 1°60′ N, 37°40′ E 224
Meru National Park, Kenya 2°119′ N, 38°27′ E 224
Meru, peak, Tanzania 3°15′ S, 36°41′ E 224
Merville, Fr. 50°38′ N, 2°38′ E 163
Méry, Fr. 48°30′ N, 3°53′ E 163
Merz Peninsula 72°30′ S, 59°28′ W 248
Merzifon, Turk. 40°52′ N, 35°28′ E 156
Merzig, Ger. 49°26′ N, 6°38′ E 163
Mesa, Ariz., U.S. 33°25′ N, 111°49′ W 92
Mesa Verde National Park, Colo., U.S. 37°21′ N, 111°23′ W 80
Mesaaroole, spring, Somalia 3°20′ N, 45°2′ E 218
Mesabi Range, Minn., U.S. 47°26′ N, 93°37′ W 90
Mesach Mellet, Lib. 25°30′ N, 11°3′ E 216
Mésaconane, Pointe, Can. 51°31′ N, 79°28′ W 110
Mesagne, It. 40°33′ N, 17°50′ E 156
Mesai, river, Col. 6°357′ N, 72°43′ W 136
Mesará, Gr. 35°0′ N, 24°48′ E 156
Mescalero, N. Mex., U.S. 33°8′ N, 105°46′ W 92
Meschede, Ger. 51°20′ N, 8°16′ E 167
Mescit Dağı, peak, Turk. 40°22′ N, 41°8′ E 195
Meselefors, Nor. 64°25′ N, 16°50′ E 152
Mesemvria see Nesebŭr, Bulg. 42°39′ N, 27°44′ E 156
Meshchovsk, Russ. 54°18′ N, 35°18′ E 158
Meshkān, Iran 36°37′ N, 58°7′ E 180
Meshra' er Req, Sudan 8°24′ N, 29°15′ E 224
Mesići, Bosn. and Herzg. 43°44′ N, 18°59′ E 168
Mesier, Canal 48°31′ S, 75°10′ W 134
Mesilinka, river, Can. 56°26′ N, 126°8′ W 108
Mesilla, N. Mex., U.S. 32°16′ N, 106°49′ W 92
Meškuičiai, Lith. 56°4′ N, 23°26′ E 166
Mesola, It. 44°55′ N, 12°13′ E 167
Mesomikenda Lake, Can. 47°34′ N, 82°41′ W 110
Mesopotamia, region, Iraq 35°1′ N, 40°11′ E 180
Mesplet, Lac, lake, Can. 48°45′ N, 76°18′ W 94
Mesquite, Nev., U.S. 36°48′ N, 114°4′ W 101
Mesquite, Tex., U.S. 32°45′ N, 96°36′ W 96
Mesra, Alg. 35°50′ N, 0°10′ E 164
Messaad, Alg. 34°12′ N, 3°31′ E 214
Messalo, river, Mozambique 12°3′ S, 39°41′ E 224
Messdar, oil field, Alg. 31°1′ N, 6°35′ E 214
Messeïed, Mor. 27°57′ N, 10°51′ W 214
Messene, ruin(s), Gr. 37°9′ N, 21°49′ E 156
Messina, It. 38°11′ N, 15°31′ E 156
Messina see Musina, S. Af. 22°21′ S, 30°1′ E 227
Messoyakha, Russ. 69°12′ N, 82°44′ E 169
Mestanza, Sp. 38°34′ N, 4°4′ W 164
Mesteacăn, Rom. 47°22′ N, 23°32′ E 168
Mestia, Ga. 43°2′ N, 42°43′ E 195
Mestre, It. 45°29′ N, 12°14′ E 167
Meszah Peak, Can. 58°29′ N, 131°34′ W 108
Meta, adm. division, Col. 3°26′ N, 73°20′ W 136
Meta Incognita Peninsula, Can. 62°38′ N, 68°39′ W 106
Meta Lake, Can. 50°28′ N, 87°42′ W 110
Meta, river, Col. 5°22′ N, 70°30′ W 136
Metahāra, Eth. 8°51′ N, 39°55′ E 224
Metairie, La., U.S. 29°58′ N, 90°9′ W 103
Metalici, Munţii, Rom. 46°2′ N, 22°43′ E 168
Metaline Falls, Wash., U.S. 48°51′ N, 117°21′ W 90
Metallifere, Colline, It. 43°8′ N, 10°24′ E 156
Metamora, Ill., U.S. 40°47′ N, 89°22′ W 102
Metán, Arg. 25°31′ S, 64°58′ W 134
Metangula, Mozambique 12°40′ S, 34°50′ E 224
Métascouac, Lac, lake, Can. 47°43′ N, 72°23′ W 94
Metchosin, Can. 48°22′ N, 123°33′ W 100
Metema, Eth. 12°55′ N, 36°11′ E 182
Metemma, Sudan 16°43′ N, 33°20′ E 182
Meteor Crater, Ariz., U.S. 35°1′ N, 111°1′ W 92
Meteora, ruin(s), Gr. 39°43′ N, 21°30′ E 156
Methánon, Gr. 37°34′ N, 23°5′ E 156
Methone, ruin(s), Gr. 40°25′ N, 22°29′ E 156
Methuen, Mass., U.S. 42°43′ N, 71°13′ W 104
Methven, N.Z. 43°40′ S, 171°39′ E 240
Metileo, Arg. 35°47′ S, 63°56′ W 139
Metković, Croatia 43°1′ N, 17°37′ E 168
Metlakatla, Alas., U.S. 55°6′ N, 131°37′ W 108
Metlaoui, Tun. 34°18′ N, 8°26′ E 156
Metlili Chaamba, Alg. 32°20′ N, 3°40′ E 214
Metovnica, Serb. and Mont. 43°57′ N, 22°9′ E 168
Metropolis, Mo., U.S. 37°9′ N, 88°43′ W 96
Mettingen, Ger. 52°19′ N, 7°46′ E 163
Mettlach, Ger. 49°29′ N, 6°36′ E 163
Mettler, Calif., U.S. 35°3′ N, 118°58′ W 101
Mettmann, Ger. 51°16′ N, 6°57′ E 167
Mettur Dam, India 11°47′ N, 77°49′ E 188
Metuge, Mozambique 13°1′ S, 40°24′ E 224
Metulla, Israel 33°15′ N, 35°34′ E 194
Metz, Fr. 49°6′ N, 6°9′ E 163
Meuaú, river, Braz. 1°23′ S, 66°42′ W 136
Meulaboh, Indonesia 4°12′ N, 96°5′ E 196
Meung, Fr. 47°49′ N, 1°41′ E 150
Meureudu, Indonesia 5°15′ N, 96°10′ E 196
Meurthe, river, Fr. 48°26′ N, 6°41′ E 163
Meuse, river, Belg. 50°28′ N, 4°55′ E 167
Mexborough, U.K. 53°29′ N, 1°17′ W 162
Mexcaltitán, Mex. 21°54′ N, 105°30′ W 114
Mexia, Tex., U.S. 31°39′ N, 96°29′ W 96
Mexiana, Ilha, island, Braz. 0°8′ N, 49°32′ W 130
Mexicali, Mex. 32°38′ N, 115°32′ W 101
Mexican Hat, Utah, U.S. 37°9′ N, 109°52′ W 92
Mexicanos, Laguna de los, lake, Mex. 28°10′ N, 107°54′ W 81
México, Mex. 19°23′ N, 99°13′ W 114
Mexico 21°24′ N, 102°50′ W 112
Mexico, Mo., U.S. 39°9′ N, 91°54′ W 94
México, adm. division, Mex. 19°21′ N, 100°13′ W 114
Mexico Basin, Gulf of Mexico 24°13′ N, 92°2′ W 253
Mexico, Gulf of 25°10′ N, 89°8′ W 253
Mexico, Gulf of 24°35′ N, 91°4′ W 112
Meydan Khvolah, Afghan. 33°34′ N, 69°54′ E 186
Meyers Chuck, Alas., U.S. 55°44′ N, 132°16′ W 108
Meymac, Fr. 45°32′ N, 2°8′ E 150
Meymaneh, Afghan. 35°55′ N, 64°48′ E 186
Mezcala, Mex. 17°53′ N, 99°39′ W 114
Mezdra, Bulg. 43°9′ N, 23°43′ E 156
Mèze, Fr. 43°26′ N, 3°35′ E 164
Mezen′, Russ. 65°51′ N, 44°18′ E 154
Mezen′, river, Russ. 64°14′ N, 49°8′ E 154
Mézenc, Mont, peak, Fr. 44°52′ N, 4°7′ E 165
Meżenin, Pol. 53°5′ N, 22°28′ E 152
Mezenskaya Guba 66°33′ N, 43°17′ E 154
Mezeş, Munţii, Rom. 47°9′ N, 22°55′ E 168
Mezhdurechensk, Russ. 63°8′ N, 48°37′ E 154
Mezhdurechensk, Russ. 59°30′ N, 66°2′ E 169
Mezhdusharskiy, Ostrov, island, Russ. 70°47′ N, 53°44′ E 246
Mezhdusharskiy, Ostrov, island, Russ. 70°34′ N, 47°7′ E 160
Meziad, Rom. 46°45′ N, 22°25′ E 168
Mezőberény, Hung. 46°49′ N, 21°1′ E 168
Mezőfalva, Hung. 46°55′ N, 18°47′ E 168
Mezőhegyes, Hung. 46°19′ N, 20°49′ E 168
Mezőkeresztes, Hung. 47°49′ N, 20°42′ E 168
Mezőkövesd, Hung. 47°47′ N, 20°34′ E 168
Mezőtúr, Hung. 47°0′ N, 20°37′ E 168
Mezquital, Mex. 23°26′ N, 104°21′ W 114
Mezquitic, Mex. 22°22′ N, 103°44′ W 114
Mezzolombardo, It. 46°12′ N, 11°5′ E 167
Mfouati, Congo 4°24′ S, 13°47′ E 218
Mgera, Tanzania 5°25′ S, 37°34′ E 224
Mgeta, Tanzania 8°16′ S, 36°2′ E 224
Mglin, Russ. 53°2′ N, 32°52′ E 158
M'goun, Irhil, peak, Mor. 31°29′ N, 6°35′ W 214
Mhangura, Zimb. 16°52′ S, 30°8′ E 224
Mholach, Beinn, peak 58°14′ N, 6°37′ W 150
Mhòr, Beinn, peak 57°14′ N, 7°23′ W 150
Mhow, India 22°32′ N, 75°45′ E 197
Miahuatlán, Mex. 18°31′ N, 97°25′ W 114
Miajadas, Sp. 39°8′ N, 5°55′ W 164
Miami, Ariz., U.S. 33°23′ N, 110°53′ W 112
Miami, Fla., U.S. 25°48′ N, 80°13′ W 105
Miami, Okla., U.S. 36°52′ N, 94°53′ W 82
Miami, Tex., U.S. 35°40′ N, 100°38′ W 92
Miami Beach, Fla., U.S. 25°47′ N, 80°10′ W 105
Miami, river, Ohio, U.S. 39°16′ N, 84°50′ W 80
Mīānābād, Iran 37°2′ N, 57°28′ E 180
Mianchi, China 34°45′ N, 111°49′ E 198
Mīāndoāb, Iran 37°1′ N, 46°2′ E 195
Mianduhe, China 49°7′ N, 120°58′ E 198
Mīāneh, Iran 37°26′ N, 47°42′ E 195
Mianwali, Pak. 32°35′ N, 71°36′ E 186
Mianxian, China 33°9′ N, 106°41′ E 198
Mianyang, China 31°25′ N, 104°39′ E 198
Miaoli, Taiwan 24°33′ N, 120°47′ E 198
Miarinarivo, Madagascar 16°37′ S, 48°14′ E 220
Miarinarivo, Madagascar 18°60′ S, 46°54′ E 220
Miass, Russ. 54°59′ N, 60°7′ E 154
Miass, river, Russ. 55°21′ N, 61°22′ E 154
Miastkowo, Pol. 53°9′ N, 21°49′ E 152
Mica, Cerro de la, peak, Chile 21°42′ S, 70°2′ W 137
Mica Creek, Can. 52°2′ N, 118°34′ W 108
Micanopy, Fla., U.S. 29°30′ N, 82°17′ W 105
Micay, Col. 3°0′ N, 77°38′ W 136
Michaichmon', Russ. 64°13′ N, 50°4′ E 154
Michaud, Point 45°27′ N, 60°44′ W 111
Michel, Can. 55°59′ N, 109°8′ W 108
Michel Peak, Can. 53°32′ N, 126°35′ W 108
Michelson, Mount, peak, Alas., U.S. 69°10′ N, 144°39′ W 98
Michigamme Reservoir, Mich., U.S. 46°7′ N, 89°1′ W 110
Michigan, adm. division, Mich., U.S. 42°56′ N, 84°53′ W 102
Michigan Center, Mich., U.S. 42°13′ N, 84°19′ W 102
Michigan City, Ind., U.S. 41°42′ N, 86°54′ W 102
Michigan, Lake 42°44′ N, 87°43′ W 110
Michipicoten, Can. 47°57′ N, 84°54′ W 94
Michipicoten Island, Can. 47°31′ N, 87°15′ W 80
Michipicoten River, Can. 47°56′ N, 84°50′ W 94
Michoacán, adm. division, Mex. 19°9′ N, 102°33′ W 114
Michurinsk, Russ. 52°53′ N, 40°24′ E 154
Michurinskoye, Russ. 60°35′ N, 29°48′ E 166
Mico, river, Nicar. 11°55′ N, 84°38′ W 115
Miconje, Angola 4°28′ S, 12°50′ E 218
Micronesia, Federated States of 8°0′ N, 147°0′ E 192
Micronesia, islands, North Pacific Ocean 15°29′ N, 140°15′ E 190
Micui, Braz. 0°29′ N, 69°5′ W 136
Midai, island, Indonesia 3°4′ N, 107°25′ E 196
Mid-Atlantic Ridge, North Atlantic Ocean 3°49′ N, 31°17′ W 253
Middelburg, Neth. 51°29′ N, 3°37′ E 163
Middelburg, S. Af. 25°48′ S, 29°27′ E 227
Middelfart, Den. 55°29′ N, 9°44′ E 150
Middelkerke, Belg. 51°10′ N, 2°48′ E 163
Middelwit, S. Af. 24°52′ S, 27°2′ E 227
Middenmeer, Neth. 52°48′ N, 4°59′ E 163
Middle America Trench, North Pacific Ocean 11°50′ N, 89°38′ W 253
Middle Andaman, island, India 12°25′ N, 91°5′ E 188
Middle Bight 24°6′ N, 78°41′ W 96
Middle Butte, peak, Idaho, U.S. 43°28′ N, 112°49′ W 90
Middle Foster Lake, Can. 56°34′ N, 106°19′ W 108
Middle Govç, adm. division, Mongolia 45°3′ N, 104°54′ E 198
Middle Loup, river, Nebr., U.S. 42°8′ N, 101°26′ W 80
Middle River, Minn., U.S. 48°23′ N, 96°12′ W 90
Middle, river, Iowa, U.S. 41°11′ N, 94°15′ W 94
Middleboro, Mass., U.S. 41°53′ N, 70°55′ W 104
Middlebourne, W. Va., U.S. 39°29′ N, 80°55′ W 102
Middleburg, S. Af. 31°31′ S, 24°58′ E 227
Middlebury, Ind., U.S. 41°39′ N, 85°43′ W 102
Middlebury, Vt., U.S. 44°0′ N, 73°10′ W 104
Middleport, Ohio, U.S. 38°59′ N, 82°4′ W 94
Middlesboro, Ky., U.S. 36°36′ N, 83°43′ W 96
Middlesbrough, U.K. 54°33′ N, 1°15′ W 162
Middlesex, Vt., U.S. 44°17′ N, 72°41′ W 104
Middleton, Idaho, U.S. 43°42′ N, 116°38′ W 90
Middleton, Mass., U.S. 42°35′ N, 71°1′ W 104
Middleton, U.K. 53°33′ N, 2°12′ W 162
Middleton, Wis., U.S. 43°6′ N, 89°30′ W 102
Middleton in Teesdale, U.K. 54°38′ N, 2°6′ W 162
Middletown, Conn., U.S. 41°33′ N, 72°40′ W 104
Middletown, Ill., U.S. 40°5′ N, 89°35′ W 102
Middletown, Ind., U.S. 40°3′ N, 85°32′ W 102
Middletown, N.Y., U.S. 41°26′ N, 74°26′ W 94
Middletown, Ohio, U.S. 39°29′ N, 84°25′ W 82
Middletown, R.I., U.S. 41°31′ N, 71°18′ W 104
Middletown Springs, Vt., U.S. 43°29′ N, 73°8′ W 104
Middleville, Mich., U.S. 42°41′ N, 85°28′ W 102
Midhurst, U.K. 50°58′ N, 0°44′ E 162
Mid-Indian Basin, Indian Ocean 8°1′ S, 79°3′ E 254
Mid-Indian Ridge, Indian Ocean 13°41′ S, 66°4′ E 254
Midi-Pyrénées, adm. division, Fr. 43°57′ N, 0°59′ E 150
Midland, Can. 44°44′ N, 79°53′ W 94
Midland, Mich., U.S. 43°36′ N, 84°14′ W 102
Midland, Tex., U.S. 31°58′ N, 102°3′ W 92
Midlothian, Tex., U.S. 32°29′ N, 96°60′ W 96
Midnight, Miss., U.S. 33°1′ N, 90°35′ W 103
Midongy Atsimo, Madagascar 23°35′ S, 47°2′ E 220
Mid-Pacific Mountains, North Pacific Ocean 19°40′ N, 164°22′ E 252
Midpines, Calif., U.S. 37°32′ N, 119°56′ W 100
Midu, island, Maldives 0°41′ N, 73°11′ E 188
Midway, Utah, U.S. 40°30′ N, 111°28′ W 92
Midway Islands, North Pacific Ocean 28°27′ N, 177°29′ W 99
Midwest, Wyo., U.S. 43°24′ N, 106°16′ W 90
Midwest City, Okla., U.S. 35°25′ N, 97°22′ W 92
Midyat, Turk. 37°24′ N, 41°26′ E 195
Midžor, peak, Serb. and Mont. 43°23′ N, 22°38′ E 168
Mie, adm. division, Japan 34°30′ N, 136°11′ E 201
Miechów, Pol. 50°22′ N, 20°1′ E 152
Międzyrzec Podlaski, Pol. 51°58′ N, 22°45′ E 152
Międzyzdroje, Pol. 53°55′ N, 14°27′ E 152
Miehikkälä, Fin. 60°40′ N, 27°40′ E 166
Miélan, Fr. 43°26′ N, 0°18′ E 164
Mielec, Pol. 50°16′ N, 21°26′ E 152
Mier, Mex. 26°27′ N, 99°9′ W 114
Mier y Noriega, Mex. 23°24′ N, 100°6′ W 114
Miercurea Ciuc, Rom. 46°22′ N, 25°48′ E 156
Mieres, Sp. 43°14′ N, 5°46′ W 150
Mieslahti, Fin. 64°23′ N, 27°57′ E 152
Mī'ēso, Eth. 9°12′ N, 40°47′ E 224
Mifol, Alban. 40°36′ N, 19°28′ E 156
Migang Shan, peak, China 35°30′ N, 106°7′ E 198
Migdal, Israel 32°50′ N, 35°30′ E 194
Migole, Tanzania 7°5′ S, 35°52′ E 224
Miguel Alemán, Presa, lake, Mex. 18°15′ N, 96°49′ W 114
Miguel Auza, Mex. 24°16′ N, 103°28′ W 114
Miguel Calmon, Braz. 11°27′ S, 40°37′ W 132
Miguelturra, Sp. 38°57′ N, 3°53′ W 164
Migues, Uru. 34°29′ S, 55°38′ W 139
Migyaunglaung, Myanmar 14°41′ N, 98°9′ E 202
Mihai Viteazu, Rom. 44°37′ N, 28°39′ E 156
Mihailovca, Mold. 46°32′ N, 28°56′ E 156
Mihalţ, Rom. 46°9′ N, 23°44′ E 156
Mihara, Japan 34°24′ N, 133°5′ E 201
Miharu, Japan 37°26′ N, 140°29′ E 201
Mihla, Ger. 51°4′ N, 10°19′ E 167
Mijas, Sp. 36°35′ N, 4°39′ W 150
Mijdaḥah, Yemen 14°2′ N, 48°27′ E 182
Mijek, Africa 23°34′ N, 12°56′ W 214
Mikashevichy, Belarus 52°12′ N, 27°27′ E 154
Mikese, Tanzania 6°42′ S, 37°56′ E 224
Mikhanavichy, Belarus 53°46′ N, 27°43′ E 152
Mikhaylov, Russ. 54°13′ N, 38°59′ E 154
Mikhaylov, Cape 67°4′ S, 118°8′ E 248
Mikhaylov Island, Antarctica 67°19′ S, 86°6′ E 248
Mikhaylova, Russ. 75°2′ N, 87°8′ E 173
Mikhaylovka, Russ. 50°3′ N, 43°12′ E 158
Mikhaylovskiy, Russ. 51°47′ N, 79°32′ E 190
Mikhaylovskoye, Russ. 57°3′ N, 28°53′ E 166
Mikindani, Tanzania 10°18′ S, 40°4′ E 224
Mikkeli, Fin. 61°40′ N, 27°13′ E 166
Mikkolya, Russ. 65°13′ N, 31°40′ E 152
Mikkwa, river, Can. 57°56′ N, 115°14′ W 108
Mikniya, Sudan 16°59′ N, 33°39′ E 226
Mikumi, Tanzania 7°26′ S, 36°58′ E 220
Mikumi National Park, Tanzania 7°14′ S, 36°41′ E 224
Mikun', Russ. 62°21′ N, 50°12′ E 154
Mikuni, Japan 36°12′ N, 136°10′ E 201
Milaca, Minn., U.S. 45°44′ N, 93°38′ W 94
Miladummadulu Atoll, Maldives 6°13′ N, 73°12′ E 188
Milam, Tex., U.S. 31°24′ N, 93°51′ W 103
Milan, Ind., U.S. 39°7′ N, 85°8′ W 102
Milan, Mich., U.S. 42°5′ N, 83°41′ W 102
Milan, Mo., U.S. 41°26′ N, 90°35′ W 94
Milan, Mo., U.S. 40°11′ N, 93°6′ W 94
Milan, N.H., U.S. 44°34′ N, 71°12′ W 104
Milan see Milano, It. 45°27′ N, 9°10′ E 167
Milando, Angola 8°51′ S, 17°32′ E 218
Milange, Mozambique 16°7′ S, 35°46′ E 224
Milano (Milan), It. 45°27′ N, 9°10′ E 167
Milâs, Turk. 37°17′ N, 27°45′ E 156
Milbank, S. Dak., U.S. 45°12′ N, 96°40′ W 90
Milbridge, Me., U.S. 44°31′ N, 67°54′ W 94
Mildenhall, U.K. 52°20′ N, 0°30′ E 162
Mildmay, Can. 44°2′ N, 81°7′ W 102
Milejewo, Pol. 54°13′ N, 19°33′ E 166
Miles, Tex., U.S. 31°34′ N, 100°11′ W 92
Miles City, Mont., U.S. 46°23′ N, 105°51′ W 90
Milestone, Can. 49°59′ N, 104°31′ W 90
Miletto, Monte, peak, It. 41°26′ N, 14°17′ E 156
Miletus, ruin(s), Turk. 37°29′ N, 27°10′ E 156
Milford, Conn., U.S. 41°13′ N, 73°4′ W 104
Milford, Ill., U.S. 40°37′ N, 87°42′ W 102
Milford, Ind., U.S. 41°24′ N, 85°51′ W 102
Milford, Iowa, U.S. 43°19′ N, 95°9′ W 90
Milford, Me., U.S. 44°56′ N, 68°38′ W 94
Milford, Nebr., U.S. 40°45′ N, 97°5′ W 90
Milford, N.H., U.S. 42°49′ N, 71°40′ W 104
Milford, Utah, U.S. 38°23′ N, 113°1′ W 90
Milford Sound, N.Z. 44°40′ S, 167°56′ E 240
Miliana, Alg. 36°18′ N, 2°13′ E 150
Milk River, Can. 49°8′ N, 112°5′ W 90
Milk, river, Mont., U.S. 48°55′ N, 110°39′ W 90
Milk River Ridge, Can. 48°57′ N, 112°24′ W 90
Mil'kovo, Russ. 54°49′ N, 158°55′ E 160
Mill Island, Antarctica 65°5′ S, 102°22′ E 248
Mill Island, Can. 63°40′ N, 79°52′ W 106
Mill Valley, Calif., U.S. 37°54′ N, 122°34′ W 100
Millau, Fr. 44°6′ N, 3°3′ E 150
Millbrook, N.Y., U.S. 41°46′ N, 73°43′ W 104
Mille Lacs, Lac des, lake, Can. 48°44′ N, 91°27′ W 94
Milledgeville, Ga., U.S. 33°4′ N, 83°12′ W 112
Millen, Ga., U.S. 32°47′ N, 81°56′ W 96
Miller, Mount, peak, Antarctica 83°18′ S, 167°27′ E 248
Miller Peak, Ariz., U.S. 31°23′ N, 110°21′ W 92
Miller Range, Antarctica 82°19′ S, 158°47′ E 248
Millerovo, Russ. 48°54′ N, 40°25′ E 158
Millers Ferry, Ala., U.S. 32°6′ N, 87°22′ W 103
Millersburg, Ind., U.S. 41°31′ N, 85°42′ W 102
Millersburg, Ohio, U.S. 40°32′ N, 81°54′ W 102
Millerton, N.Y., U.S. 41°57′ N, 73°32′ W 104
Millesimo, It. 44°22′ N, 8°14′ E 167
Millevaches, Plateau de, Fr. 45°18′ N, 1°29′ E 165
Milligan Creek, river, Can. 56°43′ N, 121°25′ W 108
Millington, Mich., U.S. 43°16′ N, 83°31′ W 102
Millington, Tenn., U.S. 35°19′ N, 89°54′ W 96
Millinocket, Me., U.S. 45°39′ N, 68°43′ W 111
Millom, U.K. 54°12′ N, 3°16′ W 162
Millry, Ala., U.S. 31°38′ N, 88°18′ W 103
Mills, Wyo., U.S. 42°50′ N, 106°22′ W 90
Millstream-Chichester National Park, Austral. 21°30′ S, 117°1′ E 238
Millville, Mass., U.S. 42°1′ N, 71°35′ W 104
Millville, N.J., U.S. 39°23′ N, 75°3′ W 94
Millwater, Can. 54°35′ N, 101°36′ W 108
Millwood Lake, Ark., U.S. 33°43′ N, 94°23′ W 96
Milly, Fr. 48°23′ N, 2°28′ E 163
Milmarcos, Sp. 41°4′ N, 1°52′ W 164
Milna, Croatia 43°19′ N, 16°26′ E 168
Milnor, N. Dak., U.S. 46°14′ N, 97°28′ W 94
Milo, Eth. 10°0′ N, 42°2′ E 224
Milo, Tanzania 9°55′ S, 34°38′ E 224
Milo, river, Guinea 10°11′ N, 9°32′ W 222
Miločer, Europe 42°16′ N, 18°53′ E 168
Mílos, island, Gr. 36°37′ N, 23°49′ E 180
Milot, Alban. 41°40′ N, 19°43′ E 168
Milparinka, Austral. 29°45′ S, 141°55′ E 231
Milpitas, Calif., U.S. 37°26′ N, 121°55′ W 100
Milroy, Ind., U.S. 39°29′ N, 85°28′ W 102
Milton, Fla., U.S. 30°38′ N, 87°2′ W 96
Milton, Ky., U.S. 38°42′ N, 85°23′ W 102
Milton, Mass., U.S. 42°15′ N, 71°5′ W 104
Milton, N.H., U.S. 43°24′ N, 70°60′ W 104
Milton, N.Z. 46°8′ S, 169°56′ E 240
Milton, Pa., U.S. 41°1′ N, 76°51′ W 94
Milton, Wash., U.S. 47°13′ N, 122°19′ W 100
Milton, Wis., U.S. 42°46′ N, 88°57′ W 102
Milton Ernest, U.K. 52°11′ N, 0°31′ E 162
Milton Keynes, U.K. 52°1′ N, 0°46′ E 162
Milton Lake, Can. 59°27′ N, 104°22′ W 108
Milton Mills, N.H., U.S. 43°30′ N, 70°59′ W 104
Miltonvale, Kans., U.S. 39°19′ N, 97°28′ W 92
Milverton, Can. 43°33′ N, 80°55′ W 102
Milverton, U.K. 51°1′ N, 3°15′ W 162
Milwaukee, Wis., U.S. 43°1′ N, 87°56′ W 102
Milyutinka, Kaz. 51°58′ N, 61°3′ E 154
Milyutino, Russ. 58°21′ N, 29°38′ E 166
Mimizan-Plage, Fr. 44°13′ N, 1°19′ W 150
Mimongo, Gabon 1°40′ S, 11°39′ E 218
Mimot, Cambodia 11°49′ N, 106°11′ E 202
Mims, Fla., U.S. 28°40′ N, 80°52′ W 105
Min, river, China 26°20′ N, 118°32′ E 198
Min, river, China 29°27′ N, 104°1′ E 190
Mina, Nev., U.S. 38°23′ N, 118°8′ W 90
Mīnā' al Faḥl, Oman 23°34′ N, 58°24′ E 196
Mina Bazar, Pak. 31°3′ N, 69°18′ E 186
Mīnā' Jabal 'Alī, U.A.E. 25°1′ N, 55°6′ E 196
Mīnāb, Iran 27°5′ N, 57°4′ E 196
Minabe, Japan 33°46′ N, 135°19′ E 201
Minagish, oil field, Kuwait 28°59′ N, 47°28′ E 196
Minago, river, Can. 54°2′ N, 99°40′ W 108
Minakami, Japan 36°45′ N, 138°57′ E 201
Minaki, Can. 49°58′ N, 94°41′ W 90
Minamata, Japan 32°11′ N, 130°24′ E 201
Minami Alps National Park, Japan 35°25′ N, 138°3′ E 201
Minas, Cuba 21°28′ N, 77°37′ W 116
Minas, Uru. 34°23′ S, 55°14′ W 139
Minas de Corrales, Uru. 31°35′ S, 55°31′ W 139
Minas Gerais, adm. division, Braz. 18°58′ S, 47°16′ W 138
Minas Novas, Braz. 17°13′ S, 42°36′ W 138
Minas, oil field, Indonesia 0°49′ N, 101°19′ E 196
Minas, Sierra de las, Guatemala 15°10′ N, 90°16′ W 115
Minatitlán, Mex. 17°58′ N, 94°33′ W 114
Minbu, Myanmar 20°11′ N, 94°50′ E 202
Minch, The, channel 58°2′ N, 6°8′ W 150
Minchinmávida, Volcán, peak, Chile 42°48′ S, 72°36′ W 134
Minco, Okla., U.S. 35°17′ N, 97°56′ W 92
Mindanao, island, Philippines 5°26′ N, 123°17′ E 192
Minden, La., U.S. 32°36′ N, 93°17′ W 103
Minden, Nebr., U.S. 40°29′ N, 98°58′ W 90
Minden City, Mich., U.S. 43°40′ N, 82°47′ W 102
Mindif, Cameroon 10°24′ N, 14°27′ E 216
Mindon, Myanmar 19°20′ N, 94°44′ E 202
Mindoro, island, Philippines 12°31′ N, 119°20′ E 192
Mindszent, Hung. 46°32′ N, 20°12′ E 168
Mindyak, Russ. 54°3′ N, 58°47′ E 154
Mine, Japan 34°27′ N, 129°20′ E 200
Mine, Japan 34°8′ N, 131°13′ E 200
Mine Centre, Can. 48°46′ N, 92°37′ W 94
Minehead, U.K. 51°12′ N, 3°28′ W 162
Mineiros, Braz. 17°36′ S, 52°34′ W 138
Mineola, Tex., U.S. 32°39′ N, 95°30′ W 103
Mineral, Wash., U.S. 46°41′ N, 122°12′ W 100
Mineral King, Calif., U.S. 36°27′ N, 118°36′ W 101
Mineral Point, Wis., U.S. 42°51′ N, 90°10′ W 102
Mineral Wells, Tex., U.S. 32°47′ N, 98°7′ W 92
Mineral'nyye Vody, Russ. 44°13′ N, 43°10′ E 158
Minersville, Utah, U.S. 38°12′ N, 112°55′ W 92
Minerva, N.Y., U.S. 43°46′ N, 73°60′ W 104
Minerva, Ohio, U.S. 40°43′ N, 81°7′ W 102
Minetto, N.Y., U.S. 43°23′ N, 76°30′ W 94
Mineville, N.Y., U.S. 44°5′ N, 73°32′ W 104
Mineyama, Japan 35°36′ N, 135°3′ E 201
Minfeng, China 37°5′ N, 82°38′ E 184
Mingäçevir, Azerb. 40°46′ N, 47°3′ E 195
Mingäçevir Reservoir, Azerb. 41°2′ N, 46°18′ E 195
Mingan, Can. 50°18′ N, 64°2′ W 111
Mingin, Myanmar 22°51′ N, 94°24′ E 202
Minginui, N.Z. 38°41′ S, 176°45′ E 240
Ming-Kush, Kyrg. 41°38′ N, 74°18′ E 197
Minglanilla, Sp. 39°31′ N, 1°37′ W 164
Mingoyo, Tanzania 10°6′ S, 39°35′ E 224
Mingteke, China 37°6′ N, 74°59′ E 186
Mingteke Pass, China 37°2′ N, 74°44′ E 184
Mingyuegou, China 43°7′ N, 128°54′ E 200
Minhla, Myanmar 17°59′ N, 95°41′ E 202
Minićevo, Serb. and Mont. 43°41′ N, 22°17′ E 168
Minicoy Island, India 7°59′ N, 72°19′ E 188
Minidoka, Idaho, U.S. 42°45′ N, 113°30′ W 90
Minidoka Internment National Monument, Idaho, U.S. 42°40′ N, 114°27′ W 90
Minier, Ill., U.S. 40°25′ N, 89°20′ W 102
Minimarg, Pak. 34°46′ N, 75°3′ E 186
Miñimiñi, Chile 19°14′ S, 69°42′ W 137
Miniogbolo, Sudan 6°20′ N, 28°44′ E 224
Minipi Lake, Can. 52°21′ N, 60°55′ W 111
Ministra, peak, Sp. 41°6′ N, 2°32′ W 164
Ministro João Alberto, Braz. 14°39′ S, 52°23′ W 138
Minitonas, Can. 52°5′ N, 101°3′ W 108
Min'kovo, Russ. 59°30′ N, 44°7′ E 154
Minna, Nig. 9°36′ N, 6°33′ E 222
Minna Bluff 78°41′ S, 176°42′ E 248
Minneapolis, Kans., U.S. 39°6′ N, 97°43′ W 90
Minneapolis, Minn., U.S. 44°56′ N, 93°17′ W 94
Minnedosa, Can. 50°15′ N, 99°55′ W 82
Minneola, Kans., U.S. 37°26′ N, 100°2′ W 92
Minneota, Minn., U.S. 44°32′ N, 95°60′ W 90
Minnesota, adm. division, Minn., U.S. 46°13′ N, 95°54′ W 94
Minnesota, river, Minn., U.S. 44°56′ N, 95°41′ W 80
Minnewaukan, N. Dak., U.S. 48°3′ N, 99°16′ W 90
Minnitaki Lake, Can. 49°55′ N, 92°40′ W 110
Mino, Japan 35°31′ N, 136°56′ E 201
Minokamo, Japan 35°25′ N, 137°0′ E 201
Minonk, Mo., U.S. 40°53′ N, 89°3′ W 110
Minorca see Menorca, island, Sp. 39°47′ N, 3°33′ E 164
Minot, N. Dak., U.S. 48°12′ N, 101°20′ W 90
Minqin, China 38°46′ N, 103°4′ E 190
Minsen, Ger. 53°42′ N, 7°58′ E 163
Minsk, Belarus 53°52′ N, 27°26′ E 166
Minster, Ohio, U.S. 40°23′ N, 84°23′ W 102
Minta, Cameroon 4°33′ N, 12°48′ E 218
Minto, Can. 62°37′ N, 136°47′ W 98
Minto, N. Dak., U.S. 48°16′ N, 97°24′ W 90
Minto Inlet 71°5′ N, 120°37′ W 106
Minto, Lac, lake, Can. 57°22′ N, 75°53′ W 106
Minto, Mount, peak, Antarctica 71°48′ S, 170°19′ E 248
Minton, Can. 49°9′ N, 104°35′ W 90
Minusinsk, Russ. 53°42′ N, 91°46′ E 190
Minuteman Missle National Historic Site, S. Dak., U.S. 43°51′ N, 102°2′ W 90
Minvoul, Gabon 2°8′ N, 12°8′ E 218
Minwakh, Yemen 16°51′ N, 48°4′ E 182
Minxian, China 34°22′ N, 104°0′ E 173
Min'yar, Russ. 55°7′ N, 57°31′ E 154
Mio, Mich., U.S. 44°38′ N, 84°8′ W 94
Mionica, Bosn. and Herzg. 44°51′ N, 18°29′ E 168
Mionica, Serb. and Mont. 44°14′ N, 20°5′ E 168
Miquelon, Can. 49°25′ N, 76°26′ W 94
Miquihuana, Mex. 23°33′ N, 99°46′ W 114
Mir, Niger 14°3′ N, 11°58′ E 222
Mira, It. 45°26′ N, 12°6′ E 167
Mirabela, Braz. 16°18′ S, 44°12′ W 138
Miracema, Braz. 21°26′ S, 42°13′ W 138
Miracema do Norte, Braz. 9°34′ S, 48°28′ W 130
Miracle Hot Springs, Calif., U.S. 35°34′ N, 118°33′ W 101
Mirador, Braz. 6°23′ S, 44°25′ W 132
Miraflores, Col. 1°16′ N, 72°5′ W 136
Miragoâne, Haiti 18°26′ N, 73°7′ W 116
Miraj, India 16°50′ N, 74°39′ E 188
Miram Shah, Pak. 32°57′ N, 70°10′ E 186
Miramar, Arg. 30°55′ S, 62°39′ W 139
Miramar, Arg. 38°16′ S, 57°51′ W 139
Miramar, Fla., U.S. 25°59′ N, 80°13′ W 105
Miramar Naval Air Station, Calif., U.S. 32°52′ N, 117°10′ W 101
Miramas, Fr. 43°34′ N, 5°0′ E 150

Miramonte, Calif., U.S. 36°42′ N, 119°4′ W 101
Miran, China 39°16′ N, 88°51′ E 188
Miranda, Braz. 20°14′ S, 56°22′ W 132
Miranda, adm. division, Venez. 10°18′ N, 66°47′ W 136
Miranda de Ebro, Sp. 42°41′ N, 2°58′ W 164
Mirande, Fr. 43°30′ N, 0°23′ E 164
Mirandola, It. 44°52′ N, 11°3′ E 167
Mirandópolis, Braz. 21°7′ S, 51°8′ W 138
Mirapinima, Braz. 2°14′ S, 61°10′ W 130
Miras, Alban. 40°30′ N, 20°54′ E 156
Mirăs, Europe 42°28′ N, 21°12′ E 168
Mirasaka, Japan 34°46′ N, 132°57′ E 201
Mirassol, Braz. 20°51′ S, 49°31′ W 138
Miravalles, Volcán, peak, C.R. 10°43′ N, 85°15′ W 115
Mirbashir, Azerb. 40°20′ N, 46°55′ E 195
Mirbāţ, Oman 16°58′ N, 54°45′ E 182
Mirear see Marir, Gezaîr, islands, Egypt 23°5′ N, 35°51′ E 182
Mirik see Timiris, Cap, Mauritania 19°28′ N, 16°53′ W 222
Mirim, Lagoa, lake, Braz. 32°41′ S, 53°9′ W 139
Mirimire, Venez. 11°7′ N, 68°45′ W 136
Mirína, Gr. 39°52′ N, 25°4′ E 156
Miringa, Nig. 10°45′ N, 12°9′ E 216
Miriti, Col. 0°25′ N, 71°9′ W 136
Miriti Paraná, river, Col. 9°534′ S, 71°31′ W 136
Miritinitsy, Russ. 56°38′ N, 29°50′ E 166
Mīrjāveh, Iran 28°57′ N, 61°24′ E 182
Mirnyy, Russ. 62°27′ N, 113°27′ E 160
Mirnyy, Russia, station, Antarctica 66°41′ S, 93°5′ E 248
Miroč, Serb. and Mont. 44°26′ N, 22°14′ E 168
Mirond Lake, Can. 55°4′ N, 103°18′ W 108
Miros, Pol. 53°21′ N, 16°6′ E 152
Miroševce, Serb. and Mont. 42°51′ N, 21°50′ E 168
Mirpur, Pak. 33°10′ N, 73°48′ E 186
Mirpur Batoro, Pak. 24°43′ N, 68°18′ E 186
Mirpur Khas, Pak. 25°33′ N, 69°3′ E 186
Mirria, Niger 13°42′ N, 9°6′ E 222
Mirror, Can. 52°27′ N, 113°7′ W 108
Mirror Lake, N.H., U.S. 43°37′ N, 71°17′ W 104
Mirsaale, Somalia 5°57′ N, 47°57′ E 218
Mirsíni, Gr. 37°55′ N, 21°14′ E 156
Miruro, Mozambique 15°19′ S, 30°24′ E 224
Miryang, S. Korea 35°29′ N, 128°45′ E 200
Mirzaani, oil field, Ga. 41°21′ N, 46°7′ E 195
Mirzapur, India 25°6′ N, 82°33′ E 197
Misa, river, Latv. 56°38′ N, 23°50′ E 166
Misaki, Japan 33°23′ N, 132°7′ E 201
Misantla, Mex. 19°55′ N, 96°51′ W 114
Misaw Lake, Can. 59°51′ N, 102°59′ W 108
Misekumaw Lake, Can. 59°4′ N, 104°30′ W 108
Miseno, Capo, It. 40°49′ N, 13°26′ E 156
Mish Mountains, Slieve, peak, Ire. 52°11′ N, 9°55′ W 150
Misha, India 7°59′ N, 93°28′ E 188
Mishahua, river, Peru 11°24′ S, 72°40′ W 137
Mishawaka, Ind., U.S. 41°38′ N, 86°11′ W 102
Misheguk Mountain, peak, Alas., U.S. 68°13′ N, 161°20′ W 98
Mishkino, Russ. 55°35′ N, 55°56′ E 154
Misi, Fin. 66°36′ N, 26°40′ E 152
Misima, island, P.N.G. 10°40′ S, 152°54′ E 192
Misión San José Estero, Parag. 23°44′ S, 60°60′ W 132
Misiones, adm. division, Arg. 27°5′ S, 55°22′ W 139
Misiones, Sierra de, Arg. 26°48′ S, 54°11′ W 139
Miskah, Saudi Arabia 24°48′ N, 42°56′ E 182
Miski, Sudan 14°50′ N, 24°11′ E 226
Miskitos, Cayos, islands, Caribbean Sea 14°20′ N, 82°37′ W 115
Miskolc, Hung. 48°6′ N, 20°48′ E 168
Mislea, oil field, Rom. 44°48′ N, 25°15′ E 156
Misool, island, Indonesia 1°57′ S, 130°29′ E 192
Misquah Hills, peak, Minn., U.S. 47°56′ N, 90°35′ W 94
Mişrātah, Lib. 32°22′ N, 15°5′ E 216
Misséni, Mali 10°20′ N, 6°5′ W 222
Missinaibi Lake, Can. 48°22′ N, 84°24′ W 94
Missinaibi, river, Can. 49°18′ N, 83°33′ W 80
Missinaibi, river, Can. 50°14′ N, 82°43′ W 110
Missinipe, Can. 55°34′ N, 104°45′ W 108
Mission, S. Dak., U.S. 43°17′ N, 100°40′ W 90
Mission Range, Mont., U.S. 47°32′ N, 114°11′ W 90
Mission Viejo, Calif., U.S. 33°35′ N, 117°40′ W 101
Missira, Senegal 13°6′ N, 11°43′ W 222
Missisa Lake, Can. 52°14′ N, 85°45′ W 110
Missisicabi, river, Can. 51°12′ N, 79°38′ W 110
Mississauga, Can. 43°35′ N, 79°40′ W 94
Mississippi, adm. division, Miss., U.S. 32°33′ N, 90°59′ W 96
Mississippi River Delta, La., U.S. 29°43′ N, 90°1′ W 103
Mississippi, river, U.S. 42°45′ N, 91°52′ W 80
Mississippi State, Miss., U.S. 33°24′ N, 88°47′ W 103
Misso, Est. 57°36′ N, 27°12′ E 166
Missoula, Mont., U.S. 46°51′ N, 113°60′ W 82
Missour, Mor. 33°8′ N, 3°60′ W 214
Missouri, adm. division, Mo., U.S. 38°21′ N, 93°28′ W 94
Missouri, river, U.S. 40°32′ N, 96°8′ W 80
Mistaken Point, Can. 46°30′ N, 53°60′ W 111
Mistaouac, Lac, lake, Can. 49°23′ N, 79°19′ W 94
Mistassibi, river, Can. 50°31′ N, 72°8′ W 110
Mistassini, Can. 48°54′ N, 72°13′ W 82
Mistassini (Baie-du-Poste), Can. 50°24′ N, 73°50′ W 110
Mistassini, Lac, lake, Can. 50°44′ N, 74°60′ W 80
Mistassini, river, Can. 49°53′ N, 72°58′ W 94
Mistastin Lake, lake, Can. 55°57′ N, 67°21′ W 246
Mistatim, Can. 52°51′ N, 103°24′ W 108
Misti, Volcan, peak, Peru 16°21′ S, 71°27′ W 137
Mistinikon Lake, Can. 47°51′ N, 81°27′ W 94
Misty Fiords National Monument, Alas., U.S. 55°47′ N, 131°10′ W 108
Misty Lake, Can. 58°51′ N, 102°11′ W 108
Misumi, Japan 34°46′ N, 131°58′ E 200
Mita, Punta de, Mex. 20°33′ N, 105°46′ W 114
Mitai, Japan 32°42′ N, 131°18′ E 201
Mitatib, Sudan 15°55′ N, 36°7′ E 182
Mitau see Jelgava, Latv. 56°38′ N, 23°40′ E 166
Mitchell, Austral. 26°31′ S, 147°57′ E 231
Mitchell, Can. 43°26′ N, 81°11′ W 102
Mitchell, Ind., U.S. 38°43′ N, 86°28′ W 102
Mitchell, Nebr., U.S. 41°56′ N, 103°49′ W 90
Mitchell, S. Dak., U.S. 43°41′ N, 98°2′ W 90
Mitchell and Alice Rivers National Park, Austral. 15°34′ S, 141°46′ E 238
Mitchell, Mount, peak, N.C., U.S. 35°45′ N, 82°21′ W 96
Mitchell Peak, Antarctica 76°16′ S, 146°43′ W 248
Mitchell Peak, Ariz., U.S. 33°12′ N, 109°26′ W 92
Mitchell, river, Austral. 16°17′ S, 142°32′ E 231
Mitchinamécus, Réservoir, lake, Can. 47°8′ N, 75°9′ W 94
Mitilíni (Mytilene), Gr. 39°6′ N, 26°33′ E 156
Mito, Japan 36°21′ N, 140°27′ E 201
Mitō, Japan 34°12′ N, 131°22′ E 200
Mitre, peak, N.Z. 40°50′ S, 175°24′ E 240
Mitre, Peninsula, Arg. 54°44′ S, 67°9′ W 134
Mitrofanovskaya, Russ. 63°14′ N, 56°7′ E 154
Mitsero, Cyprus 35°2′ N, 33°7′ E 194
Mitsikéli, Óros, Gr. 39°50′ N, 20°17′ E 156
Mitsinjo, Madagascar 16°1′ S, 45°52′ E 220
Mitsio, Nosy, island, Madagascar 12°60′ S, 47°23′ E 220
Mitskevichi, Belarus 53°16′ N, 25°45′ E 152
Mitsuke, Japan 37°31′ N, 138°55′ E 201
Mitsushima, Japan 34°16′ N, 129°18′ E 201
Mitú, Col. 1°5′ N, 70°4′ W 136
Mitumba, Monts, Dem. Rep. of the Congo 3°49′ S, 28°12′ E 224
Mitumba Mountains, Dem. Rep. of the Congo 10°42′ S, 26°15′ E 206
Mitumba Mountains, Dem. Rep. of the Congo 8°5′ S, 27°22′ E 224
Mitwaba, Dem. Rep. of the Congo 8°35′ S, 27°18′ E 224
Mityana, Uganda 0°23′ N, 32°4′ E 224
Mityayevo, Russ. 60°17′ N, 61°3′ E 154
Miura, Japan 35°8′ N, 139°38′ E 201
Mi-Wuk Village, Calif., U.S. 38°3′ N, 120°13′ W 100
Mixian, China 34°29′ N, 113°26′ E 198
Mixteco, river, Mex. 17°57′ N, 98°16′ W 114
Miya, river, Japan 34°20′ N, 136°17′ E 201
Miyagi, adm. division, Japan 38°3′ N, 140°25′ E 201
Miyajima, Japan 34°17′ N, 132°19′ E 201
Miyako, island, Japan 24°25′ N, 125°29′ E 190
Miyako Jima, island, Japan 24°55′ N, 124°58′ E 198
Miyakonojō, Japan 31°43′ N, 131°4′ E 201
Miyaly, Kaz. 48°51′ N, 53°54′ E 158
Miyanojō, Japan 31°53′ N, 130°27′ E 201
Miyazaki, Japan 31°55′ N, 131°25′ E 201
Miyazaki, adm. division, Japan 32°2′ N, 130°52′ E 201
Miyazu, Japan 35°30′ N, 135°11′ E 201
Miyory, Belarus 55°38′ N, 27°37′ E 166
Miyoshi, Japan 34°49′ N, 132°51′ E 201
Miyun, China 40°25′ N, 116°51′ E 198
Mizdah, Lib. 31°28′ N, 12°55′ E 216
Mize, Miss., U.S. 31°52′ N, 89°33′ W 103
Mizen Head, Ire. 51°15′ N, 9°51′ W 150
Mizhevichy, Belarus 52°58′ N, 25°5′ E 154
Mizhi, China 37°47′ N, 110°16′ E 198
Miziya, Bulg. 43°40′ N, 23°52′ E 156
Mizo Hills, India 23°31′ N, 92°24′ E 188
Mizpé Ramon, Israel 30°36′ N, 34°48′ E 194
Mizpe Shalem, West Bank 31°35′ N, 35°23′ E 194
Mizque, Bol. 17°55′ S, 65°22′ W 137
Mizzen Topsail, peak, Can. 49°3′ N, 56°44′ W 111
Mjällom, Nor. 62°58′ N, 18°26′ E 152
Mjanji, Uganda 0°14′ N, 33°58′ E 224
Mjölby, Nor. 58°18′ N, 15°8′ E 152
Mkalama, Tanzania 4°8′ S, 34°35′ E 224
Mkangira, Tanzania 8°57′ S, 37°27′ E 224
Mkhi, Russ. 58°59′ N, 29°54′ E 166
Mkoani, Tanzania 5°22′ S, 39°39′ E 224
Mkobela, Tanzania 10°56′ S, 38°5′ E 224
Mkokotoni, Tanzania 5°52′ S, 39°18′ E 218
Mkomazi, Tanzania 4°36′ S, 38°4′ E 224
Mkumbi, Ras, Tanzania 7°53′ S, 39°55′ E 224
Mkunde, Tanzania 7°50′ S, 31°25′ E 224
Mkushi, Zambia 13°38′ S, 29°23′ E 224
Mkuze, S. Af. 27°35′ S, 32°6′ E 227
Mladenovac, Serb. and Mont. 44°26′ N, 20°41′ E 168
M'Lefaat, ruin(s), Iraq 36°17′ N, 43°21′ E 195
Mléhas, spring, Mauritania 22°38′ N, 6°60′ W 214
Mlini, Croatia 42°37′ N, 18°12′ E 168
Mlinište, Bosn. and Herzg. 44°14′ N, 16°49′ E 168
Mljet (Melita), island, Croatia 42°37′ N, 17°23′ E 168
Mljet National Park, Croatia 42°45′ N, 17°27′ E 168
Mława, Pol. 53°6′ N, 20°21′ E 152
Mloa, Tanzania 7°40′ S, 35°23′ E 224
Mmabatho, Botswana 25°42′ S, 25°39′ E 207
Mmadinare, Botswana 21°59′ S, 27°43′ E 227
Mmashoro, Botswana 21°56′ S, 26°22′ E 227
Mnero, Tanzania 10°10′ S, 38°40′ E 224
Mo, Nor. 59°28′ N, 7°48′ E 152
Mo Duc, Vietnam 14°54′ N, 108°55′ E 202
Mo i Rana, Nor. 66°15′ N, 14°22′ E 160
Moa, Cuba 20°41′ N, 74°58′ W 116
Moa, island, Indonesia 8°19′ S, 128°7′ E 192
Moa, river, Sierra Leone 7°53′ N, 11°2′ W 222
Moab, Utah, U.S. 38°34′ N, 109°32′ W 90
Moabi, Gabon 2°25′ S, 11°0′ E 218
Moaco, river, Braz. 8°21′ S, 69°28′ W 130
Moamba, Mozambique 25°35′ S, 32°17′ E 227
Moana, N.Z. 42°35′ S, 171°28′ E 240
Moanda, Gabon 1°35′ S, 13°8′ E 218
Moapa, Nev., U.S. 36°39′ N, 114°38′ W 101
Moar Lake, Can. 52°0′ N, 95°21′ W 108
Moatize, Mozambique 16°10′ S, 33°42′ E 224
Moba, Dem. Rep. of the Congo 7°6′ S, 29°46′ E 224
Mobaye, Cen. Af. Rep. 4°23′ N, 21°12′ E 218
Mobeetie, Tex., U.S. 35°29′ N, 100°26′ W 92
Mobenzélé, Congo 0°54′ N, 17°49′ E 218
Moberly, Mo., U.S. 39°24′ N, 92°26′ W 94
Mobile, Ala., U.S. 30°41′ N, 88°4′ W 103
Mobile Bay 30°25′ N, 88°46′ W 80
Mobile Point, Ala., U.S. 30°7′ N, 88°6′ W 103
Mobile, river, Ala., U.S. 30°59′ N, 88°3′ W 103
Mobridge, S. Dak., U.S. 45°32′ N, 100°27′ W 90
Mocajuba, Braz. 2°37′ S, 49°29′ W 130
Moçambique, Mozambique 15°6′ S, 40°41′ E 224
Moçamedes Reserve, Angola 15°41′ S, 12°2′ E 206
Moccasin, Calif., U.S. 37°47′ N, 120°19′ W 100
Mocejón, Sp. 39°56′ N, 3°55′ W 164
Mocha, Isla, island, Chile 38°32′ S, 74°51′ W 134
Mochigase, Japan 35°19′ N, 134°11′ E 201
Mochima National Park, Caribbean Sea 10°17′ N, 64°47′ W 122
Mochudi, Botswana 24°24′ S, 26°6′ E 227
Mocímboa da Praia, Mozambique 11°23′ S, 40°20′ E 224
Mocímboa do Rovuma, Mozambique 11°19′ S, 39°22′ E 224
Möckmühl, Ger. 49°19′ N, 9°21′ E 152
Moclips, Wash., U.S. 47°12′ N, 124°12′ W 100
Mocó, river, Braz. 2°9′ S, 67°22′ W 136
Mocoa, Col. 1°8′ N, 76°39′ W 136
Mococa, Braz. 21°27′ S, 47°2′ W 138
Moctezuma, Mex. 30°10′ N, 106°28′ W 92
Moctezuma, Mex. 22°44′ N, 101°6′ W 114
Moctezuma, Mex. 29°48′ N, 109°43′ W 92
Moctezuma, river, Mex. 20°38′ N, 99°26′ W 114
Mocuba, Mozambique 16°52′ S, 36°59′ E 224
Mocupe, Peru 6°60′ S, 79°39′ W 130
Modane, Fr. 45°11′ N, 6°39′ E 167
Model, Colo., U.S. 37°22′ N, 104°16′ W 92
Modesto, Calif., U.S. 37°38′ N, 120°60′ W 100
Modica, It. 36°51′ N, 14°45′ E 156
Modigliana, It. 44°9′ N, 11°47′ E 167
Modimolle (Nylstroom), S. Af. 24°44′ S, 28°24′ E 227
Modjamboli, Dem. Rep. of the Congo 2°25′ N, 22°8′ E 218
Modjigo, region, Niger 17°6′ N, 12°37′ E 216
Modriča, Bosn. and Herzg. 44°57′ N, 18°17′ E 168
Moebase, Mozambique 17°7′ S, 38°41′ E 224
Moenkopi, Ariz., U.S. 36°6′ N, 111°13′ W 92
Moerbeke, Dem. Rep. of the Congo 5°31′ S, 14°41′ E 218
Moerdijk, Neth. 51°41′ N, 4°37′ E 167
Moerewa, N.Z. 35°24′ S, 174°0′ E 240
Moffet Inlet 71°59′ N, 87°20′ W 106
Mogadishu see Muqdisho, Somalia 1°58′ N, 45°10′ E 218
Mogadouro, Port. 41°20′ N, 6°44′ W 150
Mogalo, Dem. Rep. of the Congo 3°12′ N, 19°5′ E 218
Mogandia, Congo 0°39′ N, 17°10′ E 218
Mogapinyana, Botswana 22°20′ S, 27°34′ E 227
Mogaung, Myanmar 25°17′ N, 96°59′ E 188
Mogen, Nor. 60°1′ N, 7°56′ E 152
Mogi, Japan 32°42′ N, 129°54′ E 201
Mogi Mirim, Braz. 22°26′ S, 46°57′ W 138
Mogilno, Pol. 52°39′ N, 17°58′ E 152
Mogincual, Mozambique 15°32′ S, 40°25′ E 224
Mogocha, Russ. 53°46′ N, 119°43′ E 190
Mogok, Myanmar 22°55′ N, 96°30′ E 202
Mogollon Mountains, N. Mex., U.S. 33°13′ N, 108°44′ W 92
Mogollon Rim, Ariz., U.S. 34°15′ N, 110°40′ W 92
Mogor, Eth. 4°49′ N, 40°18′ E 224
Mogotes, Punta, Arg. 38°15′ S, 57°34′ W 139
Mohales Hoek, Lesotho 30°11′ S, 27°29′ E 227
Mohall, N. Dak., U.S. 48°45′ N, 101°32′ W 90
Mohammadia, Alg. 35°35′ N, 7°416′ E 150
Mohammedia (Fedala), Mor. 33°43′ N, 7°22′ W 214
Mohave, Lake, Ariz., U.S. 35°21′ N, 114°49′ W 101
Mohave Mountains, Ariz., U.S. 34°35′ N, 114°20′ W 101
Mohawk, N.Y., U.S. 43°0′ N, 75°1′ W 94
Mohawk Mountains, Ariz., U.S. 32°39′ N, 113°46′ W 101
Mohawk, river, N.Y., U.S. 42°46′ N, 75°21′ W 80
Mohe, Russ. 53°24′ N, 122°17′ E 190
Moheda, Nor. 57°0′ N, 14°34′ E 152
Mohegan, Conn., U.S. 41°28′ N, 72°6′ W 104
Mohenjo Daro, ruin(s), Pak. 27°17′ N, 68°1′ E 186
Mohican, Cape, Alas., U.S. 60°7′ N, 169°41′ W 98
Möhkö, Fin. 62°35′ N, 31°14′ E 152
Mohn Basin, Antarctica 86°24′ S, 162°33′ W 248
Mohns Ridge, Norwegian Sea 72°37′ N, 3°17′ E 255
Mohnyin, Myanmar 24°45′ N, 96°23′ E 188
Moho, Peru 15°24′ S, 69°29′ W 137
Mohon Peak, Ariz., U.S. 34°55′ N, 113°22′ W 92
Mohoro, Tanzania 8°7′ S, 39°8′ E 224
Mohyliv-Podil's'kyy, Ukr. 48°28′ N, 27°52′ E 152
Moi, Nor. 58°26′ N, 6°31′ E 150
Moià, Sp. 41°49′ N, 2°5′ E 164
Mo-i-Rana, Nor. 66°13′ N, 14°11′ E 173
Mõisaküla, Est. 58°4′ N, 25°10′ E 166
Moisés Ville, Arg. 30°44′ S, 61°29′ W 139
Moisie, Can. 50°11′ N, 66°7′ W 111
Moissac, Fr. 44°6′ N, 1°5′ E 150
Moïssala, Chad 8°18′ N, 17°45′ E 218
Möja, island, Sw. 59°26′ N, 18°54′ E 166
Mojácar, Sp. 37°7′ N, 1°51′ W 164
Mojave, Calif., U.S. 35°3′ N, 118°11′ W 101
Mojave Desert, Calif., U.S. 34°34′ N, 116°28′ W 101
Mojave Nature Preserve, Calif., U.S. 35°4′ N, 115°40′ W 101
Mojave River Wash, Calif., U.S. 35°5′ N, 116°15′ W 101
Moji, China 38°56′ N, 74°37′ E 184
Mojiang, China 23°33′ N, 101°32′ E 202
Mojkovac, Europe 42°57′ N, 19°35′ E 168
Mojo, Bol. 21°50′ S, 65°37′ W 137
Mojo, Eth. 8°35′ N, 39°6′ E 224
Mojocoya, Bol. 18°44′ S, 64°41′ W 137
Mojos, Bol. 14°33′ S, 68°55′ W 137
Moju, river, Braz. 2°50′ S, 48°56′ W 130
Mokambo, Dem. Rep. of the Congo 12°28′ S, 28°20′ E 224
Mokau, N.Z. 38°44′ S, 174°38′ E 240
Mokelumne Hill, Calif., U.S. 38°17′ N, 120°43′ W 100
Mokelumne Peak, Calif., U.S. 38°31′ N, 120°11′ W 90
Mokhcha, Russ. 64°59′ N, 53°41′ E 154
Mokhtar, Alg. 36°17′ N, 6°18′ E 150
Moknine, Tun. 35°36′ N, 10°52′ E 156
Mokolo, Cameroon 10°44′ N, 13°48′ E 216
Mokopane (Potgietersrus), S. Af. 24°9′ S, 28°59′ E 227
Mokpo, S. Korea 34°48′ N, 126°23′ E 200
Mokra Gora, Europe 42°45′ N, 20°6′ E 168
Mokraya Ol'khovka, Russ. 50°26′ N, 44°56′ E 158
Mokrin, Serb. and Mont. 45°54′ N, 20°25′ E 168
Mokro Polje, Croatia 44°5′ N, 16°1′ E 168
Mokrous, Russ. 51°12′ N, 47°31′ E 158
Mol, Belg. 51°10′ N, 5°7′ E 167
Mol, Serb. and Mont. 45°45′ N, 20°7′ E 168
Molaly, Kaz. 45°26′ N, 78°21′ E 184
Molango, Mex. 20°46′ N, 98°44′ W 114
Molanosa, Can. 54°29′ N, 105°33′ W 108
Molas, Punta, Mex. 20°36′ N, 86°43′ W 115
Molatón, peak, Sp. 38°58′ N, 1°26′ W 164
Molchanovo, Russ. 57°31′ N, 83°46′ E 169
Mold, U.K. 53°9′ N, 3°8′ W 162
Molde, Nor. 62°44′ N, 7°8′ E 152
Moldova 47°17′ N, 28°27′ E 156
Moldoveanu, peak, Rom. 45°35′ N, 24°39′ E 156
Mole National Park, Ghana 9°20′ N, 2°18′ W 222
Molepolole, Botswana 24°27′ S, 25°30′ E 227
Molesworth, N.Z. 42°5′ S, 173°16′ E 240
Molėtai, Lith. 55°13′ N, 25°27′ E 166
Molihong Shan, peak, China 42°8′ N, 124°38′ E 200
Molina de Aragón, Sp. 40°50′ N, 1°54′ W 164
Molina de Segura, Sp. 38°3′ N, 1°14′ W 164
Moline, Kans., U.S. 37°20′ N, 96°19′ W 90
Moline, Mo., U.S. 41°30′ N, 90°28′ W 94
Molinella, It. 44°36′ N, 11°39′ E 167
Molino de Flores Netzahualcóyotl National Park, Mex. 19°27′ N, 98°55′ W 112
Moliro, Dem. Rep. of the Congo 8°14′ S, 30°30′ E 224
Molise, adm. division, It. 41°39′ N, 14°13′ E 156
Möllbrücke, Aust. 46°50′ N, 13°21′ E 167
Mollendo, Peru 17°2′ S, 72°2′ W 137
Moller, Port 55°48′ N, 161°42′ W 98
Mollerussa, Sp. 41°37′ N, 0°53′ E 164
Mölln, Ger. 53°37′ N, 10°41′ E 152
Molló, Sp. 42°20′ N, 2°23′ E 150
Molloy Hole, Greenland Sea 78°52′ N, 4°58′ E 255
Mölndal, Nor. 57°40′ N, 12°3′ E 152
Molochans'k, Ukr. 47°10′ N, 35°34′ E 156
Molodezhnaya, Russia, station, Antarctica 67°50′ S, 46°8′ E 248
Molodezhnyy, Kaz. 50°38′ N, 73°29′ E 184
Molodi, Russ. 58°1′ N, 28°43′ E 166
Molodo, Mali 14°15′ N, 6°3′ W 222
Molokai Fracture Zone, North Pacific Ocean 22°54′ N, 136°36′ W 252
Moloka'i, island, Hawai'i, U.S. 21°13′ N, 156°60′ W 99
Molsheim, Fr. 48°32′ N, 7°29′ E 163
Molson, Wash., U.S. 48°58′ N, 119°12′ W 90
Molson Lake, Can. 54°13′ N, 97°12′ W 108
Molteno, S. Af. 31°24′ S, 26°21′ E 227
Molu, island, Indonesia 6°58′ S, 131°32′ E 192
Molucca Sea 1°32′ N, 125°12′ E 192
Molula, Dem. Rep. of the Congo 5°59′ S, 29°4′ E 224
Molunat, Croatia 42°27′ N, 18°25′ E 168
Molveno, It. 46°9′ N, 10°57′ E 167
Moma, Dem. Rep. of the Congo 1°37′ S, 23°55′ E 218
Moma, Mozambique 16°41′ S, 39°14′ E 224
Moma, river, Russ. 65°47′ N, 143°26′ E 160
Momax, Mex. 21°54′ N, 103°19′ W 114
Mombasa, Kenya 4°3′ S, 39°38′ E 224
Mombetsu, Japan 44°24′ N, 142°58′ E 190
Mombo, Tanzania 4°54′ S, 38°18′ E 224
Mombongo, Dem. Rep. of the Congo 1°37′ N, 23°4′ E 218
Momence, Ill., U.S. 41°9′ N, 87°40′ W 102
Momi, Dem. Rep. of the Congo 1°45′ S, 27°0′ E 224
Mommark, Den. 54°56′ N, 10°1′ E 150
Momotombo, Volcán, peak, Nicar. 12°24′ N, 86°35′ W 115
Mompono, Dem. Rep. of the Congo 0°6′ N, 21°49′ E 218
Mon, Myanmar 18°33′ N, 96°35′ E 202
Mona, Isla, island, Isla Mona 17°55′ N, 68°6′ W 116
Mona Quimbundo, Angola 9°55′ S, 19°57′ E 220
Monaco 43°44′ N, 7°24′ E 167
Monadhliath Mountains, U.K. 57°9′ N, 5°11′ W 150
Monadnock Mountain, peak, N.H., U.S. 42°51′ N, 72°9′ W 104
Monagas, adm. division, Venez. 9°24′ N, 63°48′ W 116
Monaghan, Ire. 54°13′ N, 6°58′ W 150
Monahans, Tex., U.S. 31°34′ N, 102°53′ W 92
Monapo, Mozambique 14°55′ S, 40°20′ E 224
Monarch Pass, Colo., U.S. 38°29′ N, 106°20′ W 90
Monasterio de Piedra, site, Sp. 41°11′ N, 1°50′ W 164
Monasterio de Yuste, site, Sp. 40°6′ N, 5°48′ W 150
Moncalieri, It. 44°59′ N, 7°41′ E 167
Monchegorsk, Russ. 67°55′ N, 32°56′ E 152
Mönchengladbach, Ger. 51°11′ N, 6°26′ E 167
Monchique, Serra de, Port. 37°19′ N, 9°15′ W 150
Monchon, Guinea 10°26′ N, 14°30′ W 222
Moncks Corner, S.C., U.S. 33°11′ N, 80°2′ W 96
Monckton, Mount, peak, Can. 59°40′ N, 128°50′ W 108
Monclar, Col. 4°237′ S, 75°8′ W 136
Monclova, Mex. 18°3′ N, 90°52′ W 115
Monclova, Mex. 26°54′ N, 101°26′ W 96
Moncouche, Lac, lake, Can. 48°43′ N, 71°22′ W 94
Moncton, Can. 46°5′ N, 64°48′ W 111
Mondego, Cabo, Port. 40°12′ N, 9°25′ W 150
Mondéjar, Sp. 40°19′ N, 3°6′ W 164
Mondo, Chad 13°47′ N, 15°33′ E 216
Mondo, Tanzania 4°57′ S, 35°56′ E 224
Mondolfo, It. 43°45′ N, 13°6′ E 167
Mondonac, Lac, lake, Can. 47°22′ N, 74°31′ W 94
Mondovì, It. 44°23′ N, 7°50′ E 167
Moneasa, Rom. 46°26′ N, 22°18′ E 168
Monee, Ill., U.S. 41°24′ N, 87°44′ W 102
Monein, Fr. 43°19′ N, 0°35′ E 164
Monesterio, Sp. 38°5′ N, 6°16′ W 164
Monestir de Montserrat, site, Sp. 41°35′ N, 1°47′ E 164
Monett, Mo., U.S. 36°53′ N, 93°56′ W 96
Monforte, Sp. 42°30′ N, 7°35′ W 214
Mong Cai, Vietnam 21°31′ N, 107°55′ E 198
Möng Hsu, Myanmar 21°54′ N, 98°20′ E 202
Möng Küng, Myanmar 21°35′ N, 97°35′ E 202
Möng Kyawt, Myanmar 19°58′ N, 98°44′ E 202
Möng Maü, Myanmar 19°44′ N, 97°57′ E 202
Möng Nawng, Myanmar 21°40′ N, 98°6′ E 202
Möng Pai, Myanmar 19°44′ N, 97°1′ E 202
Möng Pan, Myanmar 20°19′ N, 98°19′ E 202
Möng Tung, Myanmar 22°1′ N, 97°42′ E 202
Möng Yai, Myanmar 22°24′ N, 98°0′ E 202
Monga, Dem. Rep. of the Congo 4°6′ N, 22°54′ E 218
Monga, Tanzania 9°9′ S, 37°55′ E 224
Mongala, river, Dem. Rep. of the Congo 1°51′ N, 19°46′ E 218
Mongalla, Sudan 5°13′ N, 31°51′ E 224
Mongana, Dem. Rep. of the Congo 2°1′ N, 21°40′ E 218
Mongar, Bhutan 27°16′ N, 91°8′ E 197
Mongbwalu, Dem. Rep. of the Congo 1°55′ N, 30°2′ E 224
Monggŭmp'o, N. Korea 38°9′ N, 124°46′ E 200
Mongmeik, Myanmar 23°4′ N, 96°36′ E 202
Mongo, Chad 12°11′ N, 18°40′ E 216
Mongolia 47°41′ N, 99°29′ E 190
Mongororo, Chad 11°59′ N, 22°30′ E 216
Mongoumba, Cen. Af. Rep. 3°40′ N, 18°32′ E 218
Mongstad, Nor. 60°47′ N, 5°2′ E 152
Mongton, Myanmar 20°21′ N, 98°52′ E 202
Mongu, Zambia 15°18′ S, 23°14′ E 207
Moni, Cyprus 34°43′ N, 33°11′ E 194
Moní Agíou, site, Gr. 40°13′ N, 24°8′ E 156
Moní Megístis Lávras, site, Gr. 40°9′ N, 24°19′ E 156
Moní Vatopedíou, site, Gr. 40°18′ N, 24°8′ E 156
Monigotes, Arg. 30°28′ S, 61°37′ W 139
Mõniste, Est. 57°34′ N, 26°32′ E 166
Monitor Peak, Nev., U.S. 38°48′ N, 116°40′ W 90
Monitor Range, Nev., U.S. 38°33′ N, 116°46′ W 90
Monkey Bay, Malawi 14°3′ S, 34°51′ E 224
Monkey Point see Mono, Punta, Nicar. 11°24′ N, 83°39′ W 115
Monkey River Town, Belize 16°20′ N, 88°33′ W 115
Monkman Pass, Can. 54°31′ N, 121°15′ W 108
Monkoto, Dem. Rep. of the Congo 1°36′ S, 20°40′ E 218
Monmouth, Mo., U.S. 40°54′ N, 90°39′ W 94
Monmouth, U.K. 51°49′ N, 2°43′ W 162
Monmouth Mountain, peak, Can. 50°59′ N, 123°51′ W 90
Mono Craters, Calif., U.S. 37°52′ N, 119°2′ W 100
Mono, Punta (Monkey Point), Nicar. 11°24′ N, 83°39′ W 115
Monolith, Calif., U.S. 35°7′ N, 118°24′ W 101
Monomoy Island, Mass., U.S. 41°31′ N, 69°59′ W 104
Monomoy Point, Mass., U.S. 41°29′ N, 70°7′ W 104
Monon, Ind., U.S. 40°51′ N, 86°53′ W 102
Monona, Wis., U.S. 43°3′ N, 89°20′ W 102
Monopoli, It. 40°56′ N, 17°17′ E 156
Monou, Chad 16°23′ N, 22°10′ E 216
Monóvar, Sp. 38°26′ N, 0°51′ E 164
Moñoz, Peru 2°6′ S, 73°58′ W 136
Monreal del Campo, Sp. 40°46′ N, 1°22′ W 164
Monroe, Conn., U.S. 41°19′ N, 73°13′ W 104
Monroe, Ga., U.S. 33°46′ N, 83°43′ W 96
Monroe, La., U.S. 32°29′ N, 92°7′ W 103
Monroe, Mich., U.S. 41°53′ N, 83°25′ W 102
Monroe, N.C., U.S. 34°59′ N, 80°33′ W 96
Monroe, Ohio, U.S. 39°26′ N, 84°22′ W 102
Monroe, Utah, U.S. 38°38′ N, 112°7′ W 92
Monroe, Wash., U.S. 47°51′ N, 121°59′ W 100
Monroe, Wis., U.S. 42°35′ N, 89°38′ W 102
Monroe Bridge, Mass., U.S. 42°43′ N, 72°57′ W 104
Monroe City, Mo., U.S. 39°37′ N, 91°45′ W 94
Monroe City, Tex., U.S. 29°46′ N, 94°35′ W 103
Monroe Lake, Ind., U.S. 39°5′ N, 86°33′ W 102
Monroeville, Ala., U.S. 31°31′ N, 87°19′ W 96
Monroeville, Ind., U.S. 40°57′ N, 84°52′ W 102
Monroeville, Ohio, U.S. 41°14′ N, 82°43′ W 102
Monrovia, Ind., U.S. 39°34′ N, 86°29′ W 102
Monrovia, Liberia 6°12′ N, 10°51′ W 222
Mons, Belg. 50°26′ N, 3°56′ E 163
Møns Klint, Kattegat 54°45′ N, 12°43′ E 152
Monschau, Ger. 50°33′ N, 6°14′ E 167
Monselice, It. 45°14′ N, 11°45′ E 167
Monserrato, It. 39°15′ N, 9°8′ E 156

Monson, Mass., U.S. 42°5′ N, 72°20′ W 104
Mönsterås, Nor. 57°2′ N, 16°24′ E 152
Mont Belvieu, Tex., U.S. 29°50′ N, 94°54′ W 103
Mont Cenis, Col du, pass, Fr. 45°16′ N, 6°53′ E 167
Mont D'Iberville see Caubvick, Mount, peak, Can. 58°48′ N, 64°6′ W 72
Mont Fouari Reserve, Congo 2°49′ S, 11°15′ E 206
Montabaur, Ger. 50°25′ N, 7°49′ E 167
Montacute, U.K. 50°57′ N, 2°43′ W 162
Montagnac, Fr. 43°29′ N, 3°28′ E 164
Montagnais Point, Can. 53°34′ N, 60°3′ W 111
Montagnana, It. 45°13′ N, 11°27′ E 167
Montagne D'Ambre National Park, Madagascar 12°41′ S, 49°4′ E 220
Montagnes, Lac des, lake, Can. 51°37′ N, 76°47′ W 110
Montagu, S. Af. 33°46′ S, 20°9′ E 227
Montague, Mass., U.S. 42°31′ N, 72°33′ W 104
Montague, Mich., U.S. 43°24′ N, 86°22′ W 102
Montague Island, Alas., U.S. 59°35′ N, 147°39′ W 98
Montague Lake, Can. 49°29′ N, 106°16′ W 90
Montalbán, Sp. 40°50′ N, 0°50′ E 164
Montalbo, Sp. 39°52′ N, 2°41′ W 164
Montana, Bulg. 43°25′ N, 23°13′ E 168
Montana, adm. division, Bulg. 43°26′ N, 22°50′ E 168
Montana, adm. division, Mont., U.S. 47°8′ N, 111°6′ W 90
Montaña, La, Braz. 6°34′ S, 74°22′ W 130
Montanha, Braz. 18°9′ S, 40°23′ W 138
Montargis, Fr. 47°59′ N, 2°44′ E 150
Montataire, Fr. 49°15′ N, 2°26′ E 163
Montauban, Fr. 44°0′ N, 1°20′ E 214
Montauk, N.Y., U.S. 41°2′ N, 71°57′ W 104
Montauk Point, N.Y., U.S. 41°4′ N, 71°52′ W 104
Montblanc, Sp. 41°21′ N, 1°9′ E 164
Montcornet, Fr. 49°41′ N, 4°1′ E 163
Mont-de-Marsan, Fr. 43°52′ N, 0°33′ E 214
Montdidier, Fr. 49°38′ N, 2°34′ E 163
Monte Albán, ruin(s), Mex. 17°1′ N, 96°51′ W 114
Monte Alegre, Braz. 1°60′ S, 54°7′ W 130
Monte Alegre de Goiás, Braz. 13°17′ S, 47°10′ W 138
Monte Alegre de Minas, Braz. 18°53′ S, 48°54′ W 138
Monte Alto, ruin(s), Guatemala 14°8′ N, 91°3′ W 115
Monte Azul, Braz. 15°10′ S, 42°55′ W 138
Monte Buey, Arg. 32°54′ S, 62°29′ W 139
Monte Carlo, Monaco 43°43′ N, 7°24′ E 167
Monte Carmelo, Braz. 18°45′ S, 47°31′ W 138
Monte Caseros, Uru. 30°15′ S, 57°41′ W 139
Monte Cristi, Dom. Rep. 19°51′ N, 71°39′ W 116
Monte Dinero, Arg. 52°19′ S, 68°29′ W 134
Monte Escobedo, Mex. 22°17′ N, 103°33′ W 114
Monte Maíz, Arg. 33°14′ S, 62°35′ W 139
Monte Nievas, Arg. 35°52′ S, 64°7′ W 139
Monte Pascoal National Park, Braz. 16°43′ S, 39°39′ W 138
Monte Quemado, Arg. 25°50′ S, 62°52′ W 139
Monte Roraima National Park, Braz. 4°34′ N, 60°52′ W 130
Monte Santu, Capo di, It. 40°7′ N, 9°44′ E 156
Monte Vista, Colo., U.S. 37°34′ N, 106°9′ W 92
Monteagle, Mount, peak, Antarctica 73°38′ S, 166°1′ E 248
Monteagudo, Bol. 19°49′ S, 63°59′ W 137
Montebello, Can. 45°39′ N, 74°57′ W 94
Montebelluna, It. 45°46′ N, 12°1′ E 167
Montecarlo, Arg. 26°41′ S, 54°48′ W 139
Montecatini Terme, It. 43°53′ N, 10°47′ E 167
Montecchio Maggiore, It. 45°31′ N, 11°25′ E 167
Montecito, Calif., U.S. 34°25′ N, 119°40′ W 100
Montecristi, Ecua. 1°10′ S, 80°31′ W 130
Montecristo, island, It. 42°7′ N, 9°35′ E 214
Montecristo National Park, El Salv. 14°20′ N, 89°28′ W 115
Montegiordano Marina, It. 40°3′ N, 16°33′ E 156
Montego Bay, Jam. 18°29′ N, 77°56′ W 115
Montejicar, Sp. 37°35′ N, 3°30′ W 164
Montelíbano, Col. 8°2′ N, 75°27′ W 136
Montélimar, Fr. 44°33′ N, 4°45′ E 150
Montello, Nev., U.S. 41°15′ N, 114°12′ W 90
Montello, Wis., U.S. 43°47′ N, 89°20′ W 102
Montemayor, Meseta de, Arg. 44°60′ S, 66°39′ W 134
Montemorelos, Mex. 25°11′ N, 99°48′ W 96
Montemuro, peak, Port. 40°57′ N, 8°4′ W 150
Montenegro 42°48′ N, 18°40′ E 168
Montepuez, Mozambique 13°8′ S, 39°8′ E 224
Monterado, Indonesia 0°47′ N, 109°7′ E 196
Montereau, Fr. 48°23′ N, 2°56′ E 163
Monterey, Calif., U.S. 36°35′ N, 121°55′ W 100
Monterey, Mass., U.S. 42°10′ N, 73°14′ W 104
Monterey, Tenn., U.S. 36°8′ N, 85°16′ W 96
Monterey Bay National Marine Sanctuary, Pacific Ocean 36°45′ N, 122°6′ W 100
Montería, Col. 8°44′ N, 75°53′ W 136
Montero, Bol. 17°23′ S, 63°17′ W 137
Monterrey, Col. 4°53′ N, 72°56′ W 136
Monterrey, Mex. 25°39′ N, 100°24′ W 114
Montes Claros, Braz. 16°45′ S, 43°52′ W 138
Montesano, Wash., U.S. 46°58′ N, 123°36′ W 100
Montese, It. 44°15′ N, 10°55′ E 167
Montets, Col des, pass, Fr. 45°59′ N, 6°54′ E 167
Montevallo, Ala., U.S. 33°5′ N, 86°53′ W 96
Montevideo, Minn., U.S. 44°56′ N, 95°43′ W 90
Montevideo, Uru. 34°55′ S, 56°19′ W 139
Montezuma, Ga., U.S. 32°17′ N, 84°2′ W 96
Montezuma, Iowa, U.S. 41°34′ N, 92°31′ W 94
Montezuma, Kans., U.S. 37°35′ N, 100°28′ W 90
Montezuma Castle National Monument, Ariz., U.S. 34°36′ N, 111°53′ W 92
Montezuma Creek, Utah, U.S. 37°16′ N, 109°20′ W 92
Montfaucon, Fr. 49°15′ N, 5°7′ E 163
Montfort, Fr. 48°8′ N, 1°58′ W 150
Montfort, ruin(s), Israel 33°1′ N, 35°10′ E 194
Montgomery, Ala., U.S. 32°20′ N, 86°24′ W 96
Montgomery, La., U.S. 31°39′ N, 92°54′ W 103
Montgomery, Mich., U.S. 41°46′ N, 84°48′ W 102
Montgomery, U.K. 52°33′ N, 3°9′ W 162
Montgomery Pass, Nev., U.S. 37°59′ N, 118°20′ W 90
Monthermé, Fr. 49°52′ N, 4°44′ E 163
Monthey, Switz. 46°15′ N, 6°56′ E 167
Monticelli d'Ongina, It. 45°5′ N, 9°56′ E 167
Monticello, Ark., U.S. 33°36′ N, 91°49′ W 112
Monticello, Fla., U.S. 30°32′ N, 83°51′ W 96
Monticello, Ind., U.S. 40°44′ N, 86°46′ W 102
Monticello, Iowa, U.S. 42°13′ N, 91°12′ W 110
Monticello, Ky., U.S. 36°50′ N, 84°52′ W 96
Monticello, Minn., U.S. 45°16′ N, 93°49′ W 94
Monticello, Miss., U.S. 31°33′ N, 90°7′ W 103
Monticello, Mo., U.S. 40°0′ N, 88°34′ W 94
Monticello, N. Mex., U.S. 33°24′ N, 107°27′ W 92
Monticello, N.Y., U.S. 41°38′ N, 74°42′ W 110
Monticello, Utah, U.S. 37°51′ N, 109°20′ W 92
Monticello, Wis., U.S. 42°44′ N, 89°35′ W 102
Monticello, site, Va., U.S. 37°59′ N, 78°32′ W 94
Montichiari, It. 45°24′ N, 10°23′ E 167
Montigny, Fr. 49°5′ N, 6°9′ E 163
Montijo, Port. 38°42′ N, 8°59′ W 150
Montijo, Sp. 38°53′ N, 6°37′ W 164
Montilla, Sp. 37°35′ N, 4°39′ W 164
Montividiu, Braz. 17°29′ S, 51°14′ W 138
Mont-Joli, Can. 48°34′ N, 68°11′ W 94
Mont-Laurier, Can. 46°31′ N, 75°34′ W 106
Mont-Laurier, Can. 46°33′ N, 75°31′ W 94
Mont-Louis, Can. 49°13′ N, 65°45′ W 111
Mont-Louis, Fr. 42°30′ N, 2°5′ E 164
Montmagny, Can. 46°57′ N, 70°36′ W 94
Montmartre, Can. 50°14′ N, 103°27′ W 90
Montmédy, Fr. 49°31′ N, 5°20′ E 163
Montmirail, Fr. 48°52′ N, 3°32′ E 163
Montmort-Lucy, Fr. 48°55′ N, 3°47′ E 163
Monto, Austral. 24°51′ S, 151°6′ E 231
Montoro, Sp. 38°0′ N, 4°23′ W 164
Montour Falls, N.Y., U.S. 42°20′ N, 76°50′ W 94
Montpelier, Idaho, U.S. 42°18′ N, 111°19′ W 82
Montpelier, Ind., U.S. 40°32′ N, 85°18′ W 102
Montpelier, Ohio, U.S. 41°34′ N, 84°36′ W 102
Montpelier, Vt., U.S. 44°14′ N, 72°37′ W 104
Montpellier, Fr. 43°36′ N, 3°52′ E 164
Montréal, Can. 45°30′ N, 73°36′ W 94
Montreal, Wis., U.S. 46°25′ N, 90°16′ W 110
Montreal Lake, Can. 54°3′ N, 105°51′ W 108
Montreal Lake, Can. 54°19′ N, 106°9′ W 108
Montreal Point, Can. 53°23′ N, 97°57′ W 108
Montreux, Switz. 46°26′ N, 6°56′ E 167
Montrichard, Fr. 47°20′ N, 1°11′ E 150
Montrose, Ark., U.S. 33°17′ N, 91°30′ W 103
Montrose, Colo., U.S. 38°28′ N, 107°53′ W 90
Montrose, Iowa, U.S. 40°31′ N, 91°25′ W 94
Montrose, Mich., U.S. 43°9′ N, 83°53′ W 102
Montrose, Miss., U.S. 32°7′ N, 89°13′ W 103
Montrose, U.K. 56°43′ N, 2°28′ W 150
Montrose, oil field, North Sea 57°22′ N, 1°19′ E 150
Monts des Nementcha, Alg. 35°7′ N, 5°41′ E 150
Monts, Pointe des, Can. 49°22′ N, 67°43′ W 94
Montsec, Serra del, Sp. 42°2′ N, 0°51′ E 164
Montserrat, U.K. 16°40′ N, 62°43′ W 116
Montserrat, island, Montserrat 16°49′ N, 62°11′ W 116
Montsûrs, Fr. 48°7′ N, 0°34′ E 150
Monturque, Sp. 37°28′ N, 4°36′ W 164
Monument Beach, Mass., U.S. 41°43′ N, 70°37′ W 104
Monument Butte, peak, Wyo., U.S. 42°12′ N, 110°2′ W 90
Monument Valley, Ariz., U.S. 37°3′ N, 110°8′ W 92
Monumental Buttes, peak, Idaho, U.S. 47°0′ N, 115°53′ W 90
Monveda, Dem. Rep. of the Congo 2°55′ N, 21°34′ E 218
Monywa, Myanmar 22°9′ N, 95°9′ E 202
Monywar, Myanmar 22°9′ N, 95°8′ E 190
Monza, It. 45°35′ N, 9°15′ E 167
Monze, Zambia 16°16′ S, 27°28′ E 224
Monzón, Sp. 41°54′ N, 0°11′ E 164
Moodus, Conn., U.S. 41°30′ N, 72°27′ W 104
Moody, Me., U.S. 43°16′ N, 70°37′ W 104
Moody, Tex., U.S. 31°18′ N, 97°21′ W 92
Moody Point, Antarctica 63°23′ S, 55°6′ W 134
Moogooloo Hill, peak, Austral. 23°39′ S, 114°31′ E 230
Mooketsi, S. Af. 23°34′ S, 30°4′ E 227
Mookgophong (Naboomspruit), S. Af. 24°31′ S, 28°44′ E 227
Moonie, oil field, Austral. 27°47′ S, 150°7′ E 230
Moorcroft, Wyo., U.S. 44°14′ N, 104°57′ W 90
Moore, Okla., U.S. 35°18′ N, 97°28′ W 92
Moore, Tex., U.S. 29°2′ N, 99°1′ W 96
Moore Haven, Fla., U.S. 26°50′ N, 81°6′ W 105
Moore, Mount, peak, Antarctica 80°18′ S, 96°46′ W 248
Moorea, island, France 17°35′ S, 149°50′ W 241
Mooreland, Okla., U.S. 36°25′ N, 99°12′ W 96
Moore's Island, Bahamas 26°8′ N, 78°13′ W 116
Mooresville, Ind., U.S. 39°36′ N, 86°22′ W 102
Mooresville, N.C., U.S. 35°35′ N, 80°49′ W 96
Moorfoot Hills, U.K. 55°42′ N, 3°33′ W 150
Moorhead, Minn., U.S. 46°52′ N, 96°45′ W 82
Moorpark, Calif., U.S. 34°17′ N, 118°54′ W 101
Moorrinya National Park, Austral. 21°27′ S, 144°33′ E 238
Moors, The, U.K. 54°56′ N, 4°58′ W 150
Moose Factory, Can. 51°15′ N, 80°37′ W 110
Moose Jaw, Can. 50°24′ N, 105°33′ W 90
Moose Jaw, river, Can. 50°10′ N, 105°12′ W 90
Moose Lake, Can. 53°39′ N, 100°21′ W 108
Moose Lake, Minn., U.S. 46°27′ N, 92°46′ W 94
Moose Mountain, peak, Can. 49°47′ N, 102°40′ W 90
Moose River, Can. 50°47′ N, 81°18′ W 110
Moose River, Me., U.S. 45°39′ N, 70°16′ W 111
Moosehead Lake, Me., U.S. 45°29′ N, 70°57′ W 80
Moosehorn, Can. 51°17′ N, 98°26′ W 90
Moosomin, Can. 50°9′ N, 101°41′ W 90
Moosonee, Can. 51°17′ N, 80°41′ W 82
Moosup, Conn., U.S. 41°43′ N, 71°53′ W 104
Mopeia Velha, Mozambique 17°59′ S, 35°43′ E 224
Mopipi, Botswana 21°11′ S, 24°52′ E 227
Mopti, Mali 14°30′ N, 4°11′ W 222
Moqatta', Sudan 14°38′ N, 35°51′ E 182
Moqor, Afghan. 32°51′ N, 67°50′ E 186
Moquegua, Peru 17°14′ S, 70°56′ W 137
Moquegua, adm. division, Peru 16°48′ S, 71°18′ W 137
Mór, Hung. 47°22′ N, 18°13′ E 168
Mor Dağı, peak, Turk. 37°45′ N, 44°12′ E 195
Mor, Glen, U.K. 56°59′ N, 4°49′ W 150
Mora, Cameroon 11°2′ N, 14°10′ E 216
Mora, Minn., U.S. 45°52′ N, 93°18′ W 94
Mora, N. Mex., U.S. 35°57′ N, 105°19′ W 92
Mora, Nor. 60°58′ N, 14°31′ E 152
Mora, Port. 38°55′ N, 8°10′ W 150
Móra d'Ebre, Sp. 41°5′ N, 0°36′ E 164
Morach, Belarus 52°50′ N, 26°50′ E 152
Moradabad, India 28°48′ N, 78°45′ E 197
Morąg, Pol. 53°54′ N, 19°56′ E 166
Moraine Point, Can. 61°20′ N, 115°40′ W 108
Morakovo, Europe 42°41′ N, 19°11′ E 168
Morales, Col. 2°44′ N, 76°41′ W 136
Morales, Laguna de 23°38′ N, 97°43′ W 114
Moramoria, Guinea 10°12′ N, 9°39′ W 222
Morane, island, Fr. 23°6′ S, 137°9′ W 252
Morant Cays, islands, Caribbean Sea 17°1′ N, 76°7′ W 115
Morant Point, Jam. 17°56′ N, 76°8′ W 115
Morata de Jiloca, Sp. 41°14′ N, 1°36′ W 164
Moratalla, Sp. 38°11′ N, 1°53′ W 164
Moravskoslezský, adm. division, Czech Rep. 49°54′ N, 16°50′ E 152
Morawhanna, Guyana 8°16′ N, 59°41′ W 116
Moray Firth 57°28′ N, 4°34′ W 142
Moraya, Bol. 21°44′ S, 65°32′ W 137
Morbach, Ger. 49°48′ N, 7°6′ E 167
Morbegno, It. 46°8′ N, 9°33′ E 167
Morbi, India 22°48′ N, 70°49′ E 186
Morcenx, Fr. 44°1′ N, 0°56′ E 150
Morden, Can. 49°10′ N, 98°7′ W 90
Mordino, Russ. 61°21′ N, 51°56′ E 154
Mordoviya, adm. division, Russ. 54°19′ N, 42°53′ E 154
Mordovo, Russ. 52°2′ N, 40°39′ E 158
Mordyyakha, Russ. 70°19′ N, 67°29′ E 169
More Assynt, Ben, peak, U.K. 58°7′ N, 4°58′ W 150
More, Ben, peak, U.K. 56°22′ N, 4°39′ W 150
More Coigach, Ben, peak, U.K. 57°58′ N, 5°20′ W 150
Moreau, river, S. Dak., U.S. 45°2′ N, 102°50′ W 90
Moreauville, La., U.S. 31°0′ N, 91°60′ W 103
Morebeng (Soekmekaar), S. Af. 23°30′ S, 29°56′ E 227
Morecambe, U.K. 54°3′ N, 2°52′ W 162
Morecambe Bay 54°4′ N, 3°11′ W 162
Morehead, Ky., U.S. 38°10′ N, 83°27′ W 94
Morehead City, N.C., U.S. 34°43′ N, 76°43′ W 82
Morehouse, Mo., U.S. 36°49′ N, 89°40′ W 94
Morelia, Col. 1°30′ N, 75°51′ W 136
Morelia, Mex. 19°39′ N, 101°15′ W 114
Morella, Sp. 40°36′ N, 9°534′ W 164
Morelos, Mex. 22°50′ N, 102°38′ W 114
Morelos, Mex. 28°23′ N, 100°53′ W 92
Morelos, adm. division, Mex. 18°38′ N, 99°28′ W 114
Moremi Game Reserve, Botswana 19°20′ S, 23°29′ E 224
Morena, India 26°29′ N, 78°0′ E 197
Morena, Sierra, Sp. 38°19′ N, 5°6′ W 164
Morenci, Ariz., U.S. 33°5′ N, 109°22′ W 92
Morenci, Mich., U.S. 41°42′ N, 84°13′ W 102
Moreni, oil field, Rom. 45°0′ N, 25°36′ E 156
Moreno, Bol. 11°7′ S, 66°13′ W 137
Moreno, Cerro, peak, Chile 23°32′ S, 70°46′ W 132
Moreno Valley, Calif., U.S. 33°55′ N, 117°11′ W 101
Moresby Island, Can. 52°51′ N, 134°23′ W 98
Moresby Islands, Indian Ocean 5°3′ S, 70°55′ E 188
Moret, Fr. 48°21′ N, 2°48′ E 163
Moreton Island, Austral. 27°10′ S, 153°32′ E 230
Morey Peak, Nev., U.S. 38°37′ N, 116°22′ W 90
Morez, Fr. 46°31′ N, 6°1′ E 167
Morfou 35°11′ N, 32°58′ E 194
Morgam Viibus, peak, Fin. 68°37′ N, 25°47′ E 152
Morgan City, La., U.S. 29°41′ N, 91°12′ W 103
Morgan Hill, Calif., U.S. 37°7′ N, 121°40′ W 100
Morganfield, Ky., U.S. 37°40′ N, 87°55′ W 96
Morganito, Venez. 5°2′ N, 67°42′ W 136
Morgantina, ruin(s), It. 37°23′ N, 14°18′ E 156
Morganza, La., U.S. 30°44′ N, 91°37′ W 103
Morges, Switz. 46°30′ N, 6°30′ E 167
Morghab, river, Afghan. 35°10′ N, 64°35′ E 186
Morhange, Fr. 48°55′ N, 6°38′ E 163
Morhiban, Lac de, lake, Can. 51°51′ N, 63°21′ W 111
Mori, It. 45°51′ N, 10°58′ E 167
Moriah, Mount, peak, Nev., U.S. 39°15′ N, 114°17′ W 90
Moriarty, N. Mex., U.S. 34°59′ N, 106°3′ W 92
Morice Lake, Can. 53°59′ N, 128°1′ W 108
Moricetown, Can. 55°1′ N, 127°24′ W 108
Moriki, Nig. 12°52′ N, 6°29′ E 222
Morin Dawa (Nirji), China 48°27′ N, 124°30′ E 198
Morino, Russ. 57°51′ N, 30°23′ E 166
Morinville, Can. 53°47′ N, 113°39′ W 108
Morioka, Japan 39°40′ N, 141°0′ E 190
Moriri, Tso, lake, India 32°55′ N, 77°53′ E 188
Morkoka, river, Russ. 65°55′ N, 109°43′ E 160
Morlaas, Fr. 43°20′ N, 0°15′ E 164
Morley, Mich., U.S. 43°29′ N, 85°27′ W 102
Morley, U.K. 53°44′ N, 1°36′ W 162
Mormon Mountain, peak, Idaho, U.S. 44°59′ N, 114°58′ W 90
Mormon Mountains, Nev., U.S. 36°54′ N, 114°34′ W 101
Mormon Peak, Nev., U.S. 36°58′ N, 114°33′ W 101
Mormon Temple, site, Hawai'i, U.S. 21°38′ N, 157°59′ W 99
Morning, Mount, peak, Antarctica 78°25′ S, 164°24′ E 248
Mornington, Isla, island, Chile 49°52′ S, 77°35′ W 134
Mornington Island, Austral. 16°11′ S, 138°32′ E 230
Moro, Pak. 26°42′ N, 68°1′ E 186
Moro, Sudan 10°48′ N, 30°5′ E 224
Moro Gulf 6°56′ N, 123°4′ E 203
Moro, Punta del, Sp. 36°31′ N, 2°60′ W 164
Moro, river, Africa 7°22′ N, 10°46′ W 222
Morobe, P.N.G. 7°48′ S, 147°41′ E 192
Morocco, Ind., U.S. 40°56′ N, 87°28′ W 102
Morocco 32°22′ N, 6°40′ W 214
Morogoro, Tanzania 6°47′ S, 37°43′ E 224
Morogoro, adm. division, Tanzania 8°10′ S, 36°22′ E 224
Morolaba, Burkina Faso 11°54′ N, 5°2′ W 222
Moroleón, Mex. 20°6′ N, 101°14′ W 114
Morombe, Madagascar 21°53′ S, 43°32′ E 207
Mörön, Mongolia 47°22′ N, 110°15′ E 198
Mörön, Mongolia 49°39′ N, 100°9′ E 190
Morón de Almazán, Sp. 41°24′ N, 2°26′ W 164
Morón de la Frontera, Sp. 37°7′ N, 5°28′ W 164
Morona, river, Peru 2°60′ S, 77°44′ W 136
Morondo, Côte d'Ivoire 8°57′ N, 6°46′ W 222
Morongo Valley, Calif., U.S. 34°2′ N, 116°36′ W 101
Moroni, Comoros 11°49′ S, 43°11′ E 220
Morotai, island, Indonesia 2°6′ N, 128°37′ E 192
Moroto, Uganda 2°29′ N, 34°39′ E 224
Moroto, Mount, peak, Uganda 2°29′ N, 34°38′ E 224
Moroto see Achwa, river, Uganda 2°14′ N, 32°58′ E 224
Morozovsk, Russ. 48°18′ N, 41°45′ E 158
Morpará, Braz. 11°36′ S, 43°16′ W 132
Morral, Ohio, U.S. 40°40′ N, 83°12′ W 102
Morrill, Nebr., U.S. 41°57′ N, 103°57′ W 90
Morrinhos, Braz. 17°46′ S, 49°8′ W 138
Morrinhos, Braz. 3°16′ S, 40°9′ W 132
Morris, Can. 49°19′ N, 97°23′ W 90
Morris, Conn., U.S. 41°40′ N, 73°12′ W 104
Morris, Ill., U.S. 41°21′ N, 88°26′ W 102
Morris, Minn., U.S. 45°34′ N, 95°56′ W 90
Morris, Mo., U.S. 41°21′ N, 88°26′ W 94
Morris, Okla., U.S. 35°35′ N, 95°51′ W 96
Morris Jesup, Kap 82°56′ N, 53°20′ W 246
Morris, Mount, peak, Austral. 26°11′ S, 130°52′ E 230
Morrisburg, Can. 44°54′ N, 75°12′ W 94
Morrison, Ill., U.S. 41°47′ N, 89°58′ W 102
Morrisonville, Ill., U.S. 39°24′ N, 89°28′ W 102
Morristown, Ind., U.S. 39°39′ N, 85°41′ W 102
Morristown, N.Y., U.S. 44°34′ N, 75°40′ W 94
Morristown, S. Dak., U.S. 45°55′ N, 101°44′ W 90
Morristown National Historical Park, N.J., U.S. 40°44′ N, 74°38′ W 94
Morrisville, Pa., U.S. 39°53′ N, 80°10′ W 94
Morrisville, Vt., U.S. 44°33′ N, 72°36′ W 104
Morro, Braz. 16°1′ S, 44°44′ W 138
Morro Agudo, Braz. 20°44′ S, 48°6′ W 138
Morro Bay, Calif., U.S. 35°22′ N, 120°52′ W 100
Morro de Puercos, Punta, Pan. 7°12′ N, 80°22′ W 115
Morro, Punta, Chile 27°6′ S, 71°35′ W 132
Morrocoy National Park, Venez. 10°52′ N, 68°23′ W 136
Morros, Braz. 2°54′ S, 44°2′ W 132
Morrow, Sierra, La., U.S. 30°49′ N, 92°6′ W 103
Morrumbala, Mozambique 17°19′ S, 35°35′ E 224
Morrumbene, Mozambique 23°35′ S, 35°18′ E 227
Morse, Can. 50°25′ N, 107°4′ W 90
Morse, La., U.S. 30°6′ N, 92°31′ W 103
Morshansk, Russ. 53°25′ N, 41°42′ E 154
Morskaya Masel'ga, Russ. 63°5′ N, 34°57′ E 154
Morson, Can. 49°5′ N, 94°19′ W 90
Morsott, Alg. 35°40′ N, 8°0′ E 156
Mortara, It. 45°14′ N, 8°43′ E 167
Morteros, Arg. 30°43′ S, 61°59′ W 139
Mortka, Russ. 59°14′ N, 66°8′ E 169
Mortlach, Can. 50°26′ N, 106°5′ W 90
Mortlock Islands, North Pacific Ocean 4°53′ N, 151°50′ E 192
Morton, Ill., U.S. 40°35′ N, 89°27′ W 102
Morton, Miss., U.S. 32°19′ N, 89°39′ W 103
Morton, Tex., U.S. 33°42′ N, 102°46′ W 92
Morton, Wash., U.S. 46°31′ N, 122°17′ W 100
Morton, Islas, islands, South Pacific Ocean 55°53′ S, 69°42′ W 134
Morton Pass, Wyo., U.S. 41°40′ N, 105°31′ W 90
Mortyq, Kaz. 50°45′ N, 56°28′ E 158
Morvan, Monts du, Fr. 46°51′ N, 3°43′ E 165
Morven, N.Z. 44°51′ S, 171°6′ E 240
Morven, peak, U.K. 58°12′ N, 3°49′ W 150
Morven, peak, U.K. 57°6′ N, 3°9′ W 150
Morvern, U.K. 56°36′ N, 6°2′ W 150
Morwamosu, Botswana 24°4′ S, 23°1′ E 227
Morzine, Fr. 46°10′ N, 6°41′ E 167
Mosal'sk, Russ. 54°29′ N, 34°59′ E 154
Moscow, Idaho, U.S. 46°42′ N, 117°1′ W 90
Moscow, Tex., U.S. 30°54′ N, 94°50′ W 103
Moscow, Vt., U.S. 44°26′ N, 72°44′ W 104
Moskva, adm. division, Russ. 55°26′ N, 36°31′ E 154
Moscow Canal, Russ. 56°28′ N, 37°14′ E 154
Moscow see Moskva, Russ. 55°44′ N, 37°29′ E 154
Moscow University Ice Shelf, Antarctica 67°17′ S, 124°55′ E 248
Mose, Cape, Antarctica 66°28′ S, 130°6′ E 248
Mosėdis, Lith. 56°9′ N, 21°33′ E 166
Moselle, Miss., U.S. 31°29′ N, 89°17′ W 103
Moselle, river, Fr. 49°2′ N, 6°4′ E 163
Moses Coulee, Wash., U.S. 47°37′ N, 119°54′ W 90
Moses Lake, Wash., U.S. 47°6′ N, 119°17′ W 90
Moses, Mount, peak, Nev., U.S. 40°8′ N, 117°30′ W 90
Mosetse, Botswana 20°39′ S, 26°36′ E 227
Mosgiel, N.Z. 45°53′ S, 170°20′ E 240
Mosha, Russ. 61°44′ N, 40°51′ E 154
Mosha, river, Russ. 61°35′ N, 40°57′ E 154
Moshchnyy, Ostrov, island, Russ. 60°3′ N, 27°18′ E 166
Moshi, Tanzania 3°23′ S, 37°21′ E 224
Mosinee, Wis., U.S. 44°47′ N, 89°43′ W 94
Mosi-Oa-Tunya National Park, Zambia 17°59′ S, 25°53′ E 224
Mosjøen, Nor. 65°48′ N, 13°12′ E 160
Moskal'vo, Russ. 53°23′ N, 142°18′ E 160
Moskosel, Nor. 65°51′ N, 19°27′ E 152
Moskva, Taj. 37°36′ N, 69°37′ E 184
Moskva (Moscow), Russ. 55°44′ N, 37°29′ E 154
Moskva, river, Russ. 55°33′ N, 36°39′ E 154
Mosonmagyaróvár, Hung. 47°51′ N, 17°17′ E 168
Mosonszolhok, Hung. 47°50′ N, 17°11′ E 168
Mosquera, Col. 2°29′ N, 78°25′ W 130
Mosquero, N. Mex., U.S. 35°45′ N, 103°58′ W 82
Mosquito Lagoon, lake, Fla., U.S. 28°46′ N, 80°60′ W 105
Mosquito, Ponta do, Braz. 4°14′ N, 51°24′ W 130
Moss, Nor. 59°26′ N, 10°42′ E 152
Moss Agate Hill, peak, Wyo., U.S. 42°38′ N, 105°46′ W 90
Moss Point, Miss., U.S. 30°23′ N, 88°30′ W 103
Mossaka, Congo 1°16′ S, 16°46′ E 218
Mossbank, Can. 49°56′ N, 105°59′ W 90
Mossburn, N.Z. 45°42′ S, 168°14′ E 240
Mossel Bay see Mosselbaai, S. Af. 34°11′ S, 22°4′ E 227
Mosselbaai (Mossel Bay), S. Af. 34°11′ S, 22°4′ E 227
Mossendjo, Congo 2°56′ S, 12°41′ E 218
Mossi, region, Burkina Faso 12°5′ N, 2°36′ W 222
Mossoró, Braz. 5°12′ S, 37°22′ W 132
Mossuril, Mozambique 14°59′ S, 40°42′ E 224
Mossy, river, Can. 54°1′ N, 103°28′ W 108
Mossyrock, Wash., U.S. 46°30′ N, 122°29′ W 100
Most, Czech Rep. 50°31′ N, 13°38′ E 152
Mostaganem, Alg. 35°55′ N, 9°535′ E 150
Mostar, Bosn. and Herzg. 43°20′ N, 17°47′ E 168
Mostardas, Braz. 31°5′ S, 50°57′ W 139
Moster, Nor. 59°43′ N, 5°20′ E 152
Moštica, Maced. 42°3′ N, 22°35′ E 168
Mosting, Kap 63°52′ N, 40°54′ W 106
Mostoos Hills, Can. 54°59′ N, 109°21′ W 108
Mostrim (Edgeworthstown), Ire. 53°41′ N, 7°38′ W 150
Mosul see Al Mawşil, Iraq 36°20′ N, 43°0′ E 195
Mot'a, Eth. 11°3′ N, 37°51′ E 224
Mota del Cuervo, Sp. 39°29′ N, 2°52′ W 164
Motacucito, Bol. 17°37′ S, 61°27′ W 132
Motal', Belarus 52°18′ N, 25°37′ E 152
Mother Lode, region, Calif., U.S. 37°38′ N, 120°36′ W 100
Motihari, India 26°38′ N, 84°54′ E 197
Motike, Bosn. and Herzg. 44°48′ N, 17°7′ E 168
Motilla del Palancar, Sp. 39°33′ N, 1°56′ W 164
Motomiya, Japan 37°31′ N, 140°23′ E 201
Motril, Sp. 36°44′ N, 3°32′ W 164
Motru, Rom. 44°45′ N, 23°1′ E 168
Mott, N. Dak., U.S. 46°22′ N, 102°19′ W 90
Motu, N.Z. 38°17′ S, 177°34′ E 240
Motupe, Peru 6°5′ S, 79°45′ W 130
Mouali, Congo 0°15′ N, 15°33′ E 218
Mouchoir Passage 21°6′ N, 71°34′ W 116
Moudjéria, Mauritania 17°52′ N, 12°24′ W 222
Moudon, Switz. 46°41′ N, 6°48′ E 167
Mouhijärvi, Fin. 61°30′ N, 22°59′ E 166
Mouhoun (Black Volta), river, Burkina Faso 11°43′ N, 4°30′ W 222
Mouiat el Behima, spring, Alg. 32°55′ N, 6°48′ E 214
Mouila, Gabon 1°52′ S, 11°3′ E 218
Mouilah, spring, Alg. 26°6′ N, 0°39′ E 214
Mouit, Mauritania 16°34′ N, 13°10′ W 222
Mould Bay, Can. 76°21′ N, 119°15′ W 106
Mouling National Park, India 28°31′ N, 94°46′ E 188
Moulins, Fr. 46°34′ N, 3°19′ E 150
Moulouya, Oued, river, Mor. 32°0′ N, 3°54′ W 142
Moulton, Ala., U.S. 34°28′ N, 87°17′ W 96
Moulton, Mount, peak, Antarctica 75°58′ S, 134°21′ W 248
Moultrie, Ga., U.S. 31°10′ N, 83°48′ W 96
Moultrie, Lake, S.C., U.S. 33°17′ N, 80°40′ W 80
Mounana, Gabon 1°25′ S, 13°6′ E 218
Mound City, Mo., U.S. 37°5′ N, 89°10′ W 94
Mound City, Mo., U.S. 40°7′ N, 95°14′ W 94
Moundou, Chad 8°35′ N, 16°4′ E 218
Mounds, Mo., U.S. 37°6′ N, 89°12′ W 96
Moundville, Ala., U.S. 32°59′ N, 87°38′ W 103
Moung Tong, Vietnam 22°10′ N, 102°35′ E 202
Mounlapamôk, Laos 14°20′ N, 105°51′ E 202
Mount Airy, N.C., U.S. 36°28′ N, 80°37′ W 96
Mount Ayr, Iowa, U.S. 40°42′ N, 94°15′ W 94
Mount Baldy, Calif., U.S. 34°14′ N, 117°40′ W 101
Mount Brydges, Can. 42°53′ N, 81°29′ W 102
Mount Calvary, Wis., U.S. 43°49′ N, 88°15′ W 102
Mount Carroll, Ill., U.S. 42°5′ N, 89°59′ W 102
Mount Ch' Ilbo National Park, N. Korea 41°2′ N, 129°26′ E 200
Mount Charleston, Nev., U.S. 36°15′ N, 115°40′ W 101
Mount Clemens, Mich., U.S. 42°35′ N, 82°54′ W 94
Mount Cook, N.Z. 43°45′ S, 170°4′ E 240
Mount Cook see Aoraki, peak, N.Z. 43°37′ S, 170°7′ E 240
Mount Currie, Can. 50°20′ N, 122°42′ W 100
Mount Darwin, Zimb. 16°48′ S, 31°35′ E 224
Mount Dora, Fla., U.S. 28°48′ N, 81°38′ W 105
Mount Edgecumbe, Hecate Strait 56°59′ N, 135°21′ W 98

Mount Enterprise, *Tex., U.S.* 31°54′ N, 94°41′ W 103
Mount Erie, *Ill., U.S.* 38°30′ N, 88°14′ W 102
Mount Gilead, *Ohio, U.S.* 40°32′ N, 82°50′ W 102
Mount Grace Priory, site, *U.K.* 54°22′ N, 1°21′ W 162
Mount Hermon, *La., U.S.* 30°57′ N, 90°18′ W 103
Mount Holly, *Ark., U.S.* 33°17′ N, 92°57′ W 103
Mount Hope, *W. Va., U.S.* 37°53′ N, 81°11′ W 94
Mount Isa, *Austral.* 20°45′ S, 139°33′ E 238
Mount Kenya National Park, *Kenya* 0°14′ N, 36°59′ E 206
Mount Kisco, *N.Y., U.S.* 41°11′ N, 73°44′ W 104
Mount Kŭmgang National Park, *N. Korea* 38°32′ N, 128°4′ E 200
Mount Kuwol National Park, *N. Korea* 38°30′ N, 125°15′ E 200
Mount Laguna, *Calif., U.S.* 32°52′ N, 116°26′ W 101
Mount Maunganui, *N.Z.* 37°41′ S, 176°12′ E 240
Mount Morgan, *Austral.* 23°39′ S, 150°23′ E 231
Mount Morris, *Ill., U.S.* 42°2′ N, 89°26′ W 102
Mount Morris, *Mich., U.S.* 43°6′ N, 83°41′ W 102
Mount Morris, *Mo., U.S.* 42°2′ N, 89°26′ W 110
Mount Olive, *Ill., U.S.* 39°3′ N, 89°43′ W 102
Mount Olive, *Miss., U.S.* 31°45′ N, 89°39′ W 103
Mount Olivet, *Ky., U.S.* 38°31′ N, 84°2′ W 102
Mount Orab, *Ohio, U.S.* 39°0′ N, 83°55′ W 102
Mount Pleasant, *Mich., U.S.* 43°35′ N, 84°46′ W 94
Mount Pleasant, *S.C., U.S.* 32°47′ N, 79°53′ W 96
Mount Pleasant, *Tex., U.S.* 33°8′ N, 94°60′ W 103
Mount Pulaski, *Ill., U.S.* 40°0′ N, 89°17′ W 102
Mount Rainier National Park, *Wash., U.S.* 46°54′ N, 121°49′ W 100
Mount Revelstoke National Park, *Can.* 51°4′ N, 118°24′ W 238
Mount Robson, *Can.* 52°59′ N, 119°16′ W 108
Mount Saint Helens National Volcanic Monument, *Wash., U.S.* 46°17′ N, 122°35′ W 100
Mount Sangbe National Park, *Côte d'Ivoire* 7°45′ N, 8°1′ W 222
Mount Sangbe National Park, *Côte d'Ivoire* 7°49′ N, 7°37′ W 206
Mount Shasta, *Calif., U.S.* 41°18′ N, 122°20′ W 90
Mount Somers, *N.Z.* 43°42′ S, 171°24′ E 240
Mount Sterling, *Ohio, U.S.* 39°42′ N, 83°16′ W 102
Mount Stewart, site, *U.K.* 54°32′ N, 5°41′ W 150
Mount Sunapee, *N.H., U.S.* 43°20′ N, 72°5′ W 104
Mount Vernon, *Ala., U.S.* 31°5′ N, 87°60′ W 103
Mount Vernon, *Ky., U.S.* 37°20′ N, 84°21′ W 96
Mount Vernon, *N.Y., U.S.* 40°54′ N, 73°51′ W 104
Mount Vernon, *Ohio, U.S.* 40°23′ N, 82°28′ W 102
Mount Vernon, *Tex., U.S.* 33°10′ N, 95°14′ W 103
Mount Vernon, *Wash., U.S.* 48°24′ N, 122°20′ W 100
Mount Vernon, site, *Va., U.S.* 38°42′ N, 77°10′ W 94
Mountain Center, *Calif., U.S.* 33°41′ N, 116°44′ W 101
Mountain City, *Nev., U.S.* 41°50′ N, 115°58′ W 90
Mountain City, *Tenn., U.S.* 36°28′ N, 81°49′ W 94
Mountain Grove, *Mo., U.S.* 37°7′ N, 92°16′ W 96
Mountain Home, *Ark., U.S.* 36°19′ N, 92°23′ W 96
Mountain Home, *Idaho, U.S.* 43°9′ N, 115°43′ W 82
Mountain Home Air Force Base, *Idaho, U.S.* 43°2′ N, 115°59′ W 90
Mountain Lake, *Minn., U.S.* 43°55′ N, 94°56′ W 94
Mountain Park, *Okla., U.S.* 34°41′ N, 98°57′ W 92
Mountain Pass, *Calif., U.S.* 35°28′ N, 115°35′ W 101
Mountain Point, *Alas., U.S.* 55°20′ N, 131°35′ W 108
Mountain, river, *Can.* 65°41′ N, 129°37′ W 98
Mountain View, *Mo., U.S.* 36°59′ N, 91°42′ W 96
Mountain View, *Wyo., U.S.* 41°17′ N, 110°20′ W 92
Mountain Zebra National Park, *S. Af.* 32°12′ S, 25°23′ E 227
Mountainair, *N. Mex., U.S.* 34°31′ N, 106°14′ W 92
Mountjoy, *Can.* 48°29′ N, 81°23′ W 94
Moupitou, *Congo* 2°26′ S, 11°57′ E 218
Moura, *Braz.* 1°31′ S, 61°40′ W 130
Moura, *Chad* 13°47′ N, 21°11′ E 216
Mourão, *Port.* 38°22′ N, 7°21′ W 150
Mourdi, Dépression du, *Chad* 18°1′ N, 20°25′ E 216
Mourdiah, *Mali* 14°27′ N, 7°28′ W 222
Mourmelon-le-Grand, *Fr.* 49°8′ N, 4°21′ E 163
Mourne Mountains, *U.K.* 54°4′ N, 6°49′ W 150
Mouscron, *Belg.* 50°44′ N, 3°14′ E 163
Moussoro, *Chad* 13°39′ N, 16°31′ E 216
Mouthe, *Fr.* 46°43′ N, 6°10′ E 167
Moutier, *Switz.* 47°17′ N, 7°21′ E 150
Moutohora, *N.Z.* 38°19′ S, 177°33′ E 240
Mouy, *Fr.* 49°18′ N, 2°19′ E 163
Mouzarak, *Chad* 13°19′ N, 15°58′ E 216
Mouzay, *Fr.* 49°28′ N, 5°12′ E 163
Mouzon, *Fr.* 49°36′ N, 5°3′ E 163
Mowchadz', *Belarus* 53°18′ N, 25°41′ E 152
Moweaqua, *Ill., U.S.* 39°36′ N, 89°1′ W 102
Moxico, adm. division, *Angola* 12°22′ S, 23°22′ E 224
Moÿ, *Fr.* 49°43′ N, 3°21′ E 163
Moyahua, *Mex.* 21°14′ N, 103°9′ W 114
Moyale, *Kenya* 3°28′ N, 39°3′ E 224
Moyamba, *Sierra Leone* 8°8′ N, 12°27′ W 222
Moyen Atlas, *Mor.* 33°3′ N, 5°20′ W 214
Moyie, river, *Idaho, U.S.* 49°2′ N, 116°14′ W 90
Moyo, *Uganda* 3°39′ N, 31°44′ E 224
Moyo, island, *Indonesia* 8°18′ S, 116°47′ E 192
Moyobamba, *Peru* 6°1′ S, 76°59′ W 130
Moyto, *Chad* 12°35′ N, 16°35′ E 216
Moyu, *China* 37°16′ N, 79°42′ E 184
Moyynqum, *Kaz.* 44°16′ N, 72°55′ E 184
Moyynqum, *Kaz.* 43°38′ N, 71°25′ E 184
Moyynty, *Kaz.* 47°11′ N, 73°22′ E 184
Mozambique 17°30′ S, 33°5′ E 220
Mozambique 23°32′ S, 33°38′ E 206
Mozambique Channel 17°57′ S, 38°34′ E 224
Mozambique Escarpment, *Indian Ocean* 35°57′ S, 35°12′ E 254
Mozambique Plateau, *Indian Ocean* 30°54′ S, 36°3′ E 254
Mozarlândia, *Braz.* 14°47′ S, 50°44′ W 138
Mozdok, *Russ.* 43°43′ N, 44°35′ E 195
Mozdūrān, *Iran* 36°10′ N, 60°30′ E 180
Mozhaysk, *Russ.* 55°29′ N, 36°3′ E 154
Mozhga, *Russ.* 56°25′ N, 52°17′ E 154
Mozuli, *Russ.* 56°34′ N, 28°11′ E 166
Mpala, *Dem. Rep. of the Congo* 6°46′ S, 29°32′ E 224
Mpanda, *Tanzania* 6°21′ S, 31°1′ E 224
Mpandamatenga, *Botswana* 18°39′ S, 25°41′ E 224
Mphoengs, *Zimb.* 21°11′ S, 27°51′ E 227
Mpika, *Zambia* 11°49′ S, 31°24′ E 224
Mpoko, river, *Cen. Af. Rep.* 6°1′ N, 17°30′ E 218
Mporokoso, *Zambia* 9°23′ S, 30°7′ E 224
Mpouya, *Congo* 2°37′ S, 16°8′ E 218
Mpui, *Tanzania* 8°20′ S, 31°50′ E 224
Mpulungu, *Zambia* 8°48′ S, 31°6′ E 224
Mpumalanga, adm. division, *S. Af.* 26°16′ S, 28°35′ E 227
Mpwapwa, *Tanzania* 6°19′ S, 36°28′ E 224
Mqanduli, *S. Af.* 31°50′ S, 28°45′ E 227
Mrągowo, *Pol.* 53°51′ N, 21°16′ E 166
Mrakovo, *Russ.* 52°43′ N, 56°29′ E 154
Mrkojević, Zaliv 42°0′ N, 18°51′ E 168
Msaken, *Tun.* 35°43′ N, 10°34′ E 156
M'sila, *Alg.* 35°41′ N, 4°33′ E 150
Msoro, *Zambia* 13°39′ S, 31°53′ E 224
Msta, river, *Russ.* 58°34′ N, 31°50′ E 154
Mstizh, *Belarus* 54°34′ N, 28°9′ E 166
Mstsislaw, *Belarus* 54°1′ N, 31°43′ E 154
Mtama, *Tanzania* 10°18′ S, 39°20′ E 224
Mtouf, spring, *Mauritania* 19°27′ N, 11°24′ W 222
Mtsensk, *Russ.* 53°15′ N, 36°39′ E 154
Mts'khet'a, *Ga.* 41°51′ N, 44°42′ E 195
Mtwara, *Tanzania* 10°20′ S, 40°11′ E 224
Mtwara, adm. division, *Tanzania* 10°52′ S, 38°25′ E 224
Mu, river, *Myanmar* 22°22′ N, 95°24′ E 202
Muaguide, *Mozambique* 12°31′ S, 40°5′ E 224
Mualama, *Mozambique* 16°54′ S, 38°19′ E 224
Muaná, *Braz.* 1°31′ S, 49°14′ W 130
Muang Bèng, *Laos* 20°24′ N, 101°47′ E 202
Muang Gnômmarat, *Laos* 17°37′ N, 105°10′ E 202
Muang Ham, *Laos* 20°21′ N, 103°59′ E 202
Muang Kao, *Laos* 14°55′ N, 106°53′ E 202
Muang Khamkeut, *Laos* 18°15′ N, 104°43′ E 202
Muang La, *Laos* 20°53′ N, 102°7′ E 202
Muang Namo, *Laos* 21°4′ N, 101°49′ E 202
Muang Ngoy, *Laos* 20°44′ N, 102°41′ E 202
Muang Paklay, *Laos* 18°13′ N, 101°23′ E 202
Muang Paktha, *Laos* 20°8′ N, 100°37′ E 202
Muang Sing, *Laos* 21°12′ N, 101°8′ E 202
Muang Souy, *Laos* 19°33′ N, 102°55′ E 202
Muang Va, *Laos* 21°54′ N, 102°19′ E 202
Muang Xai, *Laos* 20°45′ N, 101°58′ E 202
Muang Xon, *Laos* 20°28′ N, 103°16′ E 202
Muar, *Malaysia* 2°4′ N, 102°34′ E 196
Muara, *Indonesia* 0°39′ N, 100°58′ E 196
Muaraenim, *Indonesia* 3°36′ S, 103°36′ E 192
Muarakumpe, *Indonesia* 1°22′ S, 104°1′ E 196
Muarasabak, *Indonesia* 1°8′ S, 103°49′ E 196
Muarasipongi, *Indonesia* 0°38′ N, 99°53′ E 196
Muaratewe, *Indonesia* 0°54′ N, 114°42′ E 192
Muari, Ras, *Pak.* 24°48′ N, 66°18′ E 186
Muatua, *Mozambique* 15°46′ S, 39°45′ E 224
Mubarras, oil field, *Persian Gulf* 24°23′ N, 53°38′ E 196
Mubende, *Uganda* 0°32′ N, 31°23′ E 224
Mubi, *Nig.* 10°15′ N, 13°17′ E 216
Muborak, *Uzb.* 39°11′ N, 65°19′ E 197
Mubur, island, *Indonesia* 3°27′ N, 105°51′ E 196
Mucacata, *Mozambique* 13°25′ S, 39°46′ E 224
Mucajá, *Braz.* 3°58′ S, 57°32′ W 130
Mucajaí, river, *Braz.* 2°49′ N, 62°49′ W 130
Mucajaí, Serra do, *Braz.* 2°3′ N, 62°21′ W 130
Much Wenlock, *U.K.* 52°36′ N, 2°34′ W 162
Muchea, *Austral.* 31°35′ S, 115°59′ E 231
Muchinga Mountains, *Zambia* 10°53′ S, 31°40′ E 224
Muchkapskiy, *Russ.* 51°51′ N, 42°27′ E 158
Muckish Mountain, peak, *Ire.* 55°5′ N, 8°7′ W 150
Mucojo, *Mozambique* 12°4′ S, 40°29′ E 224
Muconda, *Angola* 10°37′ S, 21°19′ E 220
Mucubela, *Mozambique* 16°54′ S, 37°50′ E 224
Mucucuaú, river, *Braz.* 0°29′ N, 61°23′ W 130
Mucuim, river, *Braz.* 7°13′ S, 64°31′ W 130
Mucur, *Turk.* 39°3′ N, 34°22′ E 156
Mucuri, *Braz.* 18°5′ S, 39°36′ W 138
Mucuri, river, *Braz.* 17°26′ S, 41°23′ W 138
Mucurici, *Braz.* 18°5′ S, 40°37′ W 138
Mucusso, *Angola* 17°58′ S, 21°25′ E 220
Mud Lake, *S. Dak., U.S.* 45°43′ N, 98°32′ W 90
Mudanjiang, *China* 44°41′ N, 129°43′ E 190
Muddy Peak, *Nev., U.S.* 36°17′ N, 114°45′ W 101
Muddy, river, *Nev., U.S.* 36°39′ N, 114°32′ W 101
Mudersbach, *Ger.* 50°49′ N, 7°56′ E 167
Mudjatik, river, *Can.* 56°18′ N, 107°33′ W 108
Mudon, *Myanmar* 16°15′ N, 97°43′ E 202
Mudurnu, *Turk.* 40°28′ N, 31°12′ E 156
Mudvær, islands, *Norwegian Sea* 65°41′ N, 10°17′ E 152
Mud'yuga, *Russ.* 63°47′ N, 39°17′ E 154
Muecate, *Mozambique* 14°52′ S, 39°39′ E 224
Mueda, *Mozambique* 11°39′ S, 39°34′ E 224
Muembe, *Mozambique* 13°6′ S, 35°39′ E 224
Muen, peak, *Nor.* 61°42′ N, 10°3′ E 152
Muertos Cays, islands, *North Atlantic Ocean* 24°10′ N, 80°51′ W 82
Mufulira, *Zambia* 12°35′ S, 28°14′ E 220
Mug, river, *China* 34°8′ N, 93°6′ E 188
Muga, peak, *Sp.* 41°59′ N, 6°55′ W 150
Muganly, *Azerb.* 41°28′ N, 46°29′ E 195
Mugeba, *Mozambique* 16°35′ S, 37°14′ E 224
Mughalzhar Taūy, *Kaz.* 47°23′ N, 56°0′ E 184
Mugharet el Wad, ruin(s), *Israel* 32°38′ N, 34°56′ E 194
Mughayyir, *Jordan* 31°24′ N, 35°46′ E 194
Mugi, *Japan* 33°40′ N, 134°25′ E 201
Mugila, Monts, *Dem. Rep. of the Congo* 7°35′ S, 28°49′ E 224
Muğla, *Turk.* 37°12′ N, 28°20′ E 156
Muglad, *Sudan* 11°3′ N, 27°43′ E 224
Mugodzharskaya, *Kaz.* 48°37′ N, 58°25′ E 158
Mugu, *Nepal* 29°46′ N, 82°37′ E 197
Muhagiriya, *Sudan* 11°56′ N, 25°34′ E 216
Muhamdi, *India* 27°57′ N, 80°12′ E 197
Muhammad Qol, *Sudan* 20°52′ N, 37°6′ E 182
Muḩammad, Râs, *Egypt* 27°30′ N, 34°16′ E 180
Muḩayy, *Jordan* 30°59′ N, 35°50′ E 194
Muhembo, *Botswana* 18°18′ S, 21°45′ E 220
Muheza, *Tanzania* 5°10′ S, 38°47′ E 224
Mühlhausen, *Ger.* 51°12′ N, 10°27′ E 167
Mühlheim, *Ger.* 50°7′ N, 8°50′ E 167
Muhos, *Fin.* 64°46′ N, 25°58′ E 152
Muḩradah, *Syr.* 35°15′ N, 36°34′ E 194
Muhu, *Est.* 58°35′ N, 23°13′ E 166
Muhu, island, *Est.* 58°39′ N, 23°20′ E 166
Muhu Väin 58°55′ N, 22°51′ E 166
Muhulu, *Dem. Rep. of the Congo* 1°4′ S, 27°13′ E 224
Muhutwe, *Tanzania* 1°35′ S, 31°43′ E 224
Muié, *Angola* 14°26′ S, 20°35′ E 220
Muikamachi, *Japan* 37°3′ N, 138°52′ E 201
Muir Woods National Monument, *Calif., U.S.* 37°52′ N, 122°37′ W 100
Muiron Islands, *Indian Ocean* 21°36′ S, 111°35′ E 230
Muisne, *Ecua.* 0°35′ N, 80°1′ W 130
Muite, *Mozambique* 14°3′ S, 39°3′ E 224
Mujejärvi, *Fin.* 63°47′ N, 29°26′ E 152
Mujimbeji, *Zambia* 12°11′ S, 24°55′ E 224
Muju, *S. Korea* 36°0′ N, 127°40′ E 200
Mukacheve, *Ukr.* 48°25′ N, 22°43′ E 152
Mukawwar Island, *Sudan* 20°42′ N, 37°16′ E 182
Mukdahan, *Thai.* 16°33′ N, 104°41′ E 202
Mukhayzināt, Jibāl al, peak, *Jordan* 31°55′ N, 36°31′ E 194
Mukhomornoye, *Russ.* 66°21′ N, 173°19′ E 173
Mukhtadir, *Azerb.* 41°41′ N, 48°43′ E 195
Mukhtolovo, *Russ.* 55°25′ N, 43°14′ E 154
Mukilteo, *Wash., U.S.* 47°55′ N, 122°17′ W 100
Muko Jima Rettō, islands, *Philippine Sea* 27°36′ N, 142°16′ E 190
Mukry, *Turkm.* 37°36′ N, 65°45′ E 184
Muktiköl, *Kaz.* 51°50′ N, 60°52′ E 154
Muktinath, *Nepal* 28°48′ N, 83°54′ E 197
Mukutawa, river, *Can.* 53°3′ N, 97°29′ W 108
Mukwonago, *Wis., U.S.* 42°52′ N, 88°20′ W 102
Mul, *India* 20°3′ N, 79°40′ E 188
Mula, *Sp.* 38°2′ N, 1°29′ W 164
Muladu, island, *Maldives* 6°38′ N, 72°7′ E 188
Mulaku Atoll, *Persian Gulf* 2°38′ N, 72°47′ E 188
Mulan, *China* 45°59′ N, 128°4′ E 198
Mulanay, *Philippines* 13°32′ N, 122°26′ E 203
Mulanje Mountains, *Malawi* 15°60′ S, 35°30′ E 224
Mulatos, *Col.* 8°38′ N, 76°42′ W 136
Mulatos, *Mex.* 28°37′ N, 108°51′ W 92
Mulberry, *Fla., U.S.* 27°54′ N, 81°58′ W 105
Mulberry, *Ind., U.S.* 40°20′ N, 86°40′ W 102
Mulberry, *Kans., U.S.* 37°32′ N, 94°38′ W 96
Mulberry Grove, *Ill., U.S.* 38°55′ N, 89°16′ W 102
Muldraugh, *Ky., U.S.* 37°56′ N, 85°59′ W 96
Muleba, *Tanzania* 1°53′ S, 31°39′ E 224
Mulegé, *Mex.* 26°52′ N, 112°4′ W 112
Muleshoe, *Tex., U.S.* 34°12′ N, 102°44′ W 92
Mulhacén, peak, *Sp.* 37°2′ N, 3°21′ W 164
Mülheim, *Ger.* 51°25′ N, 6°52′ E 167
Muligudje, *Mozambique* 16°31′ S, 38°54′ E 224
Mulkonbar, spring, *Austral.* 27°45′ S, 140°45′ E 230
Mull, Ross of 56°13′ N, 6°46′ W 150
Mullaittivu, *Sri Lanka* 9°14′ N, 80°51′ E 188
Mullen, *Nebr., U.S.* 42°2′ N, 101°3′ W 90
Mullens, *W. Va., U.S.* 37°34′ N, 81°24′ W 96
Mullet Key, island, *Fla., U.S.* 27°34′ N, 82°51′ W 105
Mullet Peninsula, *Atlantic Ocean* 54°8′ N, 10°41′ W 150
Mullewa, *Austral.* 28°31′ S, 115°33′ E 231
Mullikkulam, *Sri Lanka* 8°36′ N, 79°57′ E 188
Mullingar, *Ire.* 53°31′ N, 7°21′ W 150
Mullsjö, *Nor.* 57°54′ N, 13°53′ E 152
Mulobezi, *Zambia* 16°50′ S, 25°11′ E 224
Mulondo, *Angola* 15°39′ S, 15°13′ E 220
Multan, *Pak.* 30°10′ N, 71°28′ E 186
Multé, *Mex.* 17°40′ N, 91°27′ W 115
Mulumbe Mountains, *Dem. Rep. of the Congo* 8°27′ S, 27°53′ E 224
Mulym'ya, *Russ.* 60°34′ N, 64°53′ E 169
Muma, *Dem. Rep. of the Congo* 3°28′ N, 23°17′ E 218
Mumallah, *Sudan* 10°49′ N, 25°30′ E 224
Mumbai (Bombay), *India* 18°57′ N, 72°49′ E 188
Mumbué, *Angola* 13°55′ S, 17°12′ E 220
Mumbwa, *Zambia* 14°59′ S, 27°2′ E 224
Mumra, *Russ.* 45°44′ N, 47°43′ E 158
Mumu, *Sudan* 12°7′ N, 23°42′ E 216
Mun, river, *Thai.* 15°9′ N, 103°28′ E 202
Muna, *Mex.* 20°28′ N, 89°44′ W 115
Muna, island, *Indonesia* 5°9′ S, 121°36′ E 192
Muna, river, *Russ.* 67°48′ N, 119°54′ E 160
München (Munich), *Ger.* 48°8′ N, 11°34′ E 152
Muncho Lake, *Can.* 58°55′ N, 125°47′ W 108
Munch'ŏn, *N. Korea* 39°17′ N, 127°16′ E 200
Munch'ŏn-ŭp, *N. Korea* 39°13′ N, 127°20′ E 200
Muncie, *Ind., U.S.* 40°10′ N, 85°23′ W 102
Muncy, *Pa., U.S.* 41°12′ N, 76°48′ W 94
Muncy Valley, *Pa., U.S.* 41°20′ N, 76°36′ W 94
Mundare, *Can.* 53°34′ N, 112°20′ W 108
Munday, *Tex., U.S.* 33°25′ N, 99°38′ W 92
Mundemba, *Cameroon* 4°53′ N, 8°50′ E 222
Münden, *Ger.* 51°24′ N, 9°40′ E 167
Mundesley, *U.K.* 52°52′ N, 1°25′ E 163
Mundeung-ni, *S. Korea* 38°19′ N, 127°58′ E 200
Mundra, *India* 22°50′ N, 69°44′ E 186
Mundybash, *Russ.* 53°13′ N, 87°24′ E 184
Munenga, *Angola* 10°2′ S, 14°38′ E 220
Munera, *Sp.* 39°2′ N, 2°29′ W 164
Mungári, *Mozambique* 17°12′ S, 33°32′ E 224
Mungbere, *Dem. Rep. of the Congo* 2°38′ N, 28°25′ E 224
Mungeli, *India* 22°4′ N, 81°39′ E 197
Munger, *India* 25°21′ N, 86°29′ E 197
Munger, *Mich., U.S.* 43°30′ N, 83°46′ W 102
Mungia, *Sp.* 43°20′ N, 2°51′ W 164
Mungret, *Ire.* 52°37′ N, 8°42′ W 150
Munguba, *Braz.* 0°58′ N, 52°25′ W 130
Munguy, *Russ.* 70°22′ N, 83°51′ E 169
Mungyeong, *S. Korea* 36°42′ N, 128°6′ E 200
Munhamade, *Mozambique* 16°37′ S, 36°58′ E 224
Munich see München, *Ger.* 48°8′ N, 11°34′ E 152
Munising, *Mich., U.S.* 46°24′ N, 86°41′ W 94
Muniz Freire, *Braz.* 20°28′ S, 41°26′ W 138
Munk, *Can.* 55°59′ N, 95°59′ W 108
Munkedal, *Nor.* 58°27′ N, 11°38′ E 152
Munkelv, *Nor.* 69°38′ N, 29°27′ E 152
Munkfors, *Nor.* 59°51′ N, 13°32′ E 152
Munksund, *Nor.* 65°17′ N, 21°29′ E 152
Münnerstadt, *Ger.* 50°15′ N, 10°10′ E 167
Muñoz Gamero, Peninsula, *Chile* 52°9′ S, 74°21′ W 134
Munroe Lake, *Can.* 59°6′ N, 99°12′ W 108
Munsan, *S. Korea* 37°51′ N, 126°48′ E 200
Münsingen, *Switz.* 46°52′ N, 7°34′ E 167
Munsonville, *N.H., U.S.* 43°0′ N, 72°9′ W 104
Münster, *Ger.* 51°57′ N, 7°38′ E 167
Munsungan Lake, *Me., U.S.* 46°20′ N, 69°36′ W 94
Muntok, *Indonesia* 2°3′ S, 105°11′ E 192
Munzur Vadisi National Park, *Turk.* 39°15′ N, 39°24′ E 195
Muodoslompolo, *Nor.* 67°56′ N, 23°19′ E 152
Muong Te, *Vietnam* 22°24′ N, 102°48′ E 202
Muonio, *Fin.* 67°54′ N, 24°4′ E 160
Mupa National Park, *Angola* 15°34′ S, 14°45′ E 220
Muping, *China* 37°24′ N, 121°37′ E 198
Muqakoori, *Somalia* 4°2′ N, 46°5′ E 218
Muqdisho (Mogadishu), *Somalia* 1°58′ N, 45°10′ E 218
Muqyr, *Kaz.* 48°3′ N, 54°27′ E 158
Mur, river, *Europe* 47°2′ N, 13°30′ E 156
Mura, river, *Europe* 46°39′ N, 16°2′ E 168
Muradiye, *Turk.* 38°59′ N, 43°44′ E 195
Murakami, *Japan* 38°13′ N, 139°30′ E 201
Murakeresztúr, *Hung.* 46°21′ N, 16°53′ E 168
Muramvya, *Burundi* 3°16′ S, 29°35′ E 218
Murang'a, *Kenya* 0°44′ N, 37°10′ E 224
Murashi, *Russ.* 59°22′ N, 48°59′ E 154
Murat Dağı, peak, *Turk.* 38°54′ N, 29°40′ E 156
Murat, river, *Turk.* 39°41′ N, 43°11′ E 195
Muratlı, *Turk.* 41°9′ N, 27°28′ E 158
Muravera, *It.* 39°25′ N, 9°35′ E 156
Murayama, *Japan* 38°29′ N, 140°23′ E 201
Murazzano, *It.* 44°28′ N, 8°1′ E 167
Mūrcheh Khvort, *Iran* 33°4′ N, 51°30′ E 180
Murchison, *N.Z.* 41°50′ S, 172°20′ E 240
Murchison Falls, *Uganda* 2°25′ N, 31°41′ E 224
Murchison Falls National Park, *Uganda* 2°0′ N, 31°26′ E 224
Murchison, Mount, peak, *Antarctica* 73°22′ S, 166°55′ E 248
Murchison, Mount, peak, *Austral.* 26°49′ S, 116°14′ E 230
Murcia, *Sp.* 37°58′ N, 1°8′ W 164
Murcia, adm. division, *Sp.* 37°51′ N, 1°52′ W 164
Murdo, *S. Dak., U.S.* 43°53′ N, 100°43′ W 90
Murdochville, *Can.* 48°57′ N, 65°32′ W 111
Mureş, adm. division, *Rom.* 46°20′ N, 24°2′ E 156
Mureş, river, *Rom.* 46°7′ N, 21°3′ E 168
Muret, *Fr.* 43°27′ N, 1°19′ E 164
Murewa, *Zimb.* 17°41′ S, 31°46′ E 224
Murfreesboro, *Ark., U.S.* 34°2′ N, 93°41′ W 96
Murfreesboro, *N.C., U.S.* 36°26′ N, 77°7′ W 96
Murfreesboro, *Tenn., U.S.* 35°50′ N, 86°23′ W 96
Murgab, *Taj.* 38°42′ N, 73°30′ E 197
Murgenella Wildlife Sanctuary, *Austral.* 11°48′ S, 132°31′ E 238
Murghob, *Taj.* 38°12′ N, 74°3′ E 197
Murghob, river, *Taj.* 38°7′ N, 73°26′ E 197
Murguz, peak, *Arm.* 40°43′ N, 45°12′ E 195
Muri, *China* 38°9′ N, 99°6′ E 188
Muri, *India* 23°22′ N, 85°50′ E 197
Muri, *Nig.* 9°12′ N, 10°52′ E 222
Muriaé, *Braz.* 21°8′ S, 42°22′ W 138
Muriege, *Angola* 9°56′ S, 21°13′ E 220
Murilo Atoll 8°38′ N, 153°0′ E 192
Murino, *Europe* 42°39′ N, 19°53′ E 168
Muritiba, *Braz.* 12°39′ S, 39°2′ W 132
Murjek, *Nor.* 66°28′ N, 20°50′ E 152
Murle, *Eth.* 5°5′ N, 36°12′ E 224
Murmansk, *Russ.* 68°58′ N, 33°3′ E 152
Murmansk, adm. division, *Russ.* 67°31′ N, 36°54′ E 169
Murmansk Rise, *Barents Sea* 74°41′ N, 37°39′ E 255
Murmino, *Russ.* 54°37′ N, 40°0′ E 154
Murnei, *Sudan* 12°55′ N, 22°48′ E 218
Muro, Capo di, *Fr.* 41°39′ N, 7°59′ E 156
Murom, *Russ.* 55°33′ N, 42°3′ E 154
Muromtsevo, *Russ.* 56°20′ N, 75°15′ E 169
Muroran, *Japan* 42°26′ N, 140°52′ E 190
Muroto, *Japan* 33°18′ N, 134°9′ E 201
Muroto Zaki, *Japan* 33°9′ N, 134°11′ E 201
Murphy, *Idaho, U.S.* 43°13′ N, 116°34′ W 90
Murphy Bay 67°28′ S, 149°3′ E 248
Murphy Inlet 71°42′ S, 96°56′ W 248
Murphy, Mount, peak, *Antarctica* 75°17′ S, 110°10′ W 248
Murphys, *Calif., U.S.* 38°7′ N, 120°29′ W 100
Murphysboro, *Mo., U.S.* 37°45′ N, 89°21′ W 96
Murra, *Nicar.* 13°42′ N, 85°60′ W 115
Murray, *Ky., U.S.* 36°37′ N, 88°17′ W 96
Murray, Cape 79°16′ S, 171°16′ E 248
Murray Fracture Zone, *North Pacific Ocean* 30°51′ N, 143°25′ W 252
Murray Head, *Can.* 45°53′ N, 62°30′ W 111
Murray Islands, *Coral Sea* 10°20′ S, 144°2′ E 192
Murray, Mount, peak, *Can.* 60°52′ N, 128°58′ W 108
Murray, river, *Can.* 54°50′ N, 121°21′ W 108
Murraysburg, *S. Af.* 31°58′ S, 23°44′ E 227
Murree, *Pak.* 33°53′ N, 73°28′ E 186
Murrells Inlet, *S.C., U.S.* 33°32′ N, 79°3′ W 96
Murro di Porco, Capo, *It.* 36°54′ N, 15°20′ E 156
Murrumbidgee, river, *Austral.* 34°41′ S, 143°38′ E 230
Murrupula, *Mozambique* 15°28′ S, 38°47′ E 224
Murska Sobota, *Slov.* 46°39′ N, 16°9′ E 168
Mursko Središće, *Croatia* 46°30′ N, 16°25′ E 168
Murtovaara, *Fin.* 65°40′ N, 29°20′ E 152
Muru, river, *Braz.* 9°9′ S, 71°27′ W 137
Muruasigar, peak, *Kenya* 3°6′ N, 34°51′ E 224
Murukta, *Russ.* 67°49′ N, 102°25′ E 160
Muruntau, *Uzb.* 41°27′ N, 64°41′ E 197
Murwara, *India* 23°49′ N, 80°23′ E 197
Murygino, *Russ.* 58°44′ N, 49°31′ E 154
Muş, *Turk.* 38°44′ N, 41°31′ E 195
Mus Khaya, Gora, peak, *Russ.* 62°18′ N, 140°8′ E 172
Musa, *Dem. Rep. of the Congo* 2°36′ N, 19°20′ E 218
Musa Ālī Terara, peak, *Eth.* 12°22′ N, 42°15′ E 182
Musa Dağ, peak, *Turk.* 36°9′ N, 35°50′ E 156
Mûsa, Gebel (Sinai, Mount), peak, *Egypt* 28°30′ N, 33°54′ E 226
Mūša, river, *Lith.* 56°18′ N, 24°7′ E 166
Musala (Mansalar), island, *Indonesia* 1°31′ N, 97°47′ E 196
Musala, peak, *Bulg.* 42°10′ N, 23°31′ E 156
Musan, *N. Korea* 42°15′ N, 129°15′ E 200
Musawa, *Nig.* 12°7′ N, 7°38′ E 222
Musaymīr, *Yemen* 13°25′ N, 44°36′ E 182
Muscat see Masqaţ, *Oman* 23°30′ N, 58°32′ E 196
Muscatine, *Iowa, U.S.* 41°25′ N, 91°4′ W 94
Müsch, *Ger.* 50°23′ N, 6°49′ E 167
Muse, *Okla., U.S.* 34°38′ N, 94°46′ W 96
Musgrave Land, *Can.* 53°56′ N, 56°12′ W 111
Musgrave, Port 12°9′ S, 141°2′ E 230
Musgrave Ranges, *Austral.* 25°59′ S, 131°49′ E 230
Mushandike Sanctuary, *Zimb.* 20°13′ S, 30°18′ E 206
Mushâsh el Sirr, spring, *Egypt* 30°37′ N, 33°46′ E 194
Mushenge, *Dem. Rep. of the Congo* 4°29′ S, 21°18′ E 218
Mushie, *Dem. Rep. of the Congo* 3°2′ S, 16°51′ E 218
Mushorah, oil field, *Iraq* 36°55′ N, 42°14′ E 195
Mushu, island, *P.N.G.* 3°39′ S, 142°39′ E 192
Music Mountains, peak, *Ariz., U.S.* 35°31′ N, 113°43′ W 101
Musina (Messina), *S. Af.* 22°21′ S, 30°1′ E 227
Musiri, *India* 10°58′ N, 78°29′ E 188
Muskeg, river, *Can.* 60°16′ N, 123°9′ W 108
Muskeget Channel 41°19′ N, 70°29′ W 104
Muskeget Island, *Mass., U.S.* 41°19′ N, 70°18′ W 104
Muskegon, *Mich., U.S.* 43°13′ N, 86°16′ W 102
Muskegon Heights, *Mich., U.S.* 43°11′ N, 86°15′ W 102
Muskegon, river, *Mich., U.S.* 43°50′ N, 85°18′ W 102
Muskogee, *Okla., U.S.* 35°44′ N, 95°22′ W 96
Muskwa, *Can.* 58°45′ N, 122°43′ W 108
Muskwa, river, *Can.* 56°8′ N, 114°38′ W 108
Musmar, *Sudan* 18°11′ N, 35°35′ E 182
Musoma, *Tanzania* 1°31′ S, 33°49′ E 224
Musquaro, Lac, lake, *Can.* 50°29′ N, 61°41′ W 111
Mussau, island, *P.N.G.* 1°31′ S, 149°47′ E 192
Mussau Islands, *P.N.G.* 1°17′ S, 149°36′ E 192
Musselshell, *Mont., U.S.* 46°28′ N, 108°6′ W 90
Musselshell, river, *Mont., U.S.* 46°38′ N, 109°57′ W 90
Mussende, *Angola* 10°33′ S, 16°2′ E 220
Mussuma, *Angola* 14°17′ S, 21°57′ E 220
Mustafakemalpaşa, *Turk.* 40°4′ N, 28°23′ E 180
Mustahīl, *Eth.* 5°14′ N, 44°42′ E 218
Mustang, *Nepal* 29°12′ N, 83°58′ E 197
Mustayevo, *Russ.* 51°47′ N, 53°27′ E 158
Mustio see Svarta, *Fin.* 60°8′ N, 23°51′ E 166
Mustjala, *Est.* 58°27′ N, 22°14′ E 166
Mustla, *Est.* 58°13′ N, 25°50′ E 166
Mustvee, *Est.* 58°50′ N, 26°53′ E 166
Musudan, *N. Korea* 40°46′ N, 129°44′ E 200
Musún, Cerro, peak, *Nicar.* 12°58′ N, 85°18′ W 115
Musungu, *Dem. Rep. of the Congo* 2°45′ N, 28°22′ E 224
Muswabik, river, *Can.* 51°56′ N, 85°31′ W 110
Mûṭ, *Egypt* 25°28′ N, 28°57′ E 226
Mut, *Turk.* 36°38′ N, 33°26′ E 156
Mutá, Ponta do, *Braz.* 14°23′ S, 38°50′ W 132
Mu'tah, *Jordan* 31°5′ N, 35°41′ E 194
Mutalahti, *Fin.* 62°25′ N, 31°4′ E 152
Mutanda, *Zambia* 12°23′ S, 26°14′ E 224
Mutarara, *Mozambique* 17°27′ S, 35°8′ E 224
Mutare, *Zimb.* 18°58′ S, 32°39′ E 224
Mutatá, *Col.* 7°16′ N, 76°32′ W 136
Mutha, *Kenya* 1°49′ S, 38°24′ E 224
Muting, *Indonesia* 7°21′ S, 140°14′ E 192
Mutki, *Turk.* 38°24′ N, 41°54′ E 195
Mutnyy Materik, *Russ.* 65°55′ N, 55°0′ E 154
Mutoko, *Zimb.* 17°26′ S, 32°13′ E 224
Mutombo Mukulu, *Dem. Rep. of the Congo* 7°58′ S, 23°59′ E 224
Mutoray, *Russ.* 61°27′ N, 100°26′ E 160

Mutriba, oil field, Kuwait 29°46' N, 47°14' E 196
Mutshatsha, Dem. Rep. of the Congo 10°40' S, 24°26' E 224
Mutumbo, Angola 13°15' S, 17°18' E 220
Mutumparaná, Braz. 9°40' S, 64°60' W 137
Mutunópolis, Braz. 13°41' S, 49°17' W 138
Muurla, Fin. 60°20' N, 23°14' E 166
Muuruvesi, Fin. 63°0' N, 28°10' E 152
Muxía, Sp. 43°5' N, 9°14' W 150
Muyinga, Burundi 2°52' S, 30°19' E 224
Mŭynoq, Uzb. 43°49' N, 58°56' E 160
Muyumba, Dem. Rep. of the Congo 7°15' S, 27°1' E 224
Muzaffarabad, Pak. 34°23' N, 73°33' E 186
Muzaffargarh, Pak. 30°4' N, 71°12' E 186
Muzaffarnagar, India 29°29' N, 77°40' E 197
Muzaffarpur, India 26°5' N, 85°23' E 197
Muzhi, Russ. 65°21' N, 64°36' E 169
Muzon, Cape, Alas., U.S. 54°29' N, 132°42' W 108
Múzquiz, Mex. 27°52' N, 101°31' W 92
Muztag, peak, China 36°24' N, 87°20' E 188
Muztag, peak, China 35°59' N, 80°10' E 188
Muztagata, peak, China 38°17' N, 75°2' E 184
Muztagh Pass, China 35°53' N, 76°12' E 186
Mvadhi-Ousyé, Gabon 1°12' N, 13°11' E 218
Mvolo, Sudan 6°3' N, 29°55' E 224
Mvomero, Tanzania 6°17' S, 37°26' E 224
Mvouti, Congo 4°16' S, 12°26' E 218
Mvuma, Zimb. 19°19' S, 30°29' E 224
Mwadingusha, Dem. Rep. of the Congo 10°45' S, 27°10' E 224
Mwadui, Tanzania 3°35' S, 33°39' E 224
Mwakete, Tanzania 9°20' S, 34°14' E 224
Mwali, island, Comoros 12°34' S, 43°15' E 220
Mwami, Zimb. 16°41' S, 29°46' E 224
Mwanza, Dem. Rep. of the Congo 7°51' S, 26°39' E 224
Mwanza, Tanzania 2°32' S, 32°55' E 224
Mwanza, adm. division, Tanzania 2°57' S, 31°56' E 224
Mwatate, Kenya 3°32' S, 38°21' E 218
Mwaya, Tanzania 9°32' S, 33°55' E 224
Mweelrea, peak, Ire. 53°36' N, 9°56' W 150
Mweka, Dem. Rep. of the Congo 4°52' S, 21°31' E 218
Mwene-Ditu, Dem. Rep. of the Congo 7°1' S, 23°24' E 224
Mwenezi, Zimb. 21°25' S, 30°45' E 227
Mwenezi, river, Zimb. 21°45' S, 31°8' E 227
Mwenga, Dem. Rep. of the Congo 3°4' S, 28°26' E 224
Mwenzo, Zambia 9°21' S, 32°41' E 224
Mweru, Lake, Dem. Rep. of the Congo 9°16' S, 26°39' E 207
Mweru Wantipa National Park, Zambia 9°9' S, 29°20' E 224
Mwimba, Dem. Rep. of the Congo 9°12' S, 22°46' E 218
Mwingi, Kenya 0°57' N, 38°4' E 224
Mwinilunga, Zambia 11°44' S, 24°25' E 224
Mwitikira, Tanzania 6°30' S, 35°39' E 224
Mwombezhi, river, Zambia 12°41' S, 25°43' E 224
My Tho, Vietnam 10°21' N, 106°21' E 202
Myadzyel, Belarus 54°51' N, 26°56' E 166
Myakit, Russ. 61°29' N, 151°59' E 160
Myakka City, Fla., U.S. 27°21' N, 82°9' W 105
Myakka, river, Fla., U.S. 27°13' N, 82°22' W 105
Myaksa, Russ. 58°52' N, 38°15' E 154
Myanaung, Myanmar 18°20' N, 95°13' E 202
Myanmar (Burma) 21°5' N, 95°9' E 192
Myeik, Myanmar 12°35' N, 98°38' E 192
Myingyan, Myanmar 21°28' N, 95°25' E 202
Myitkyinā, Myanmar 25°29' N, 97°20' E 190
Myitta, Myanmar 14°10' N, 98°30' E 202
Myken, islands, Norwegian Sea 66°43' N, 11°26' E 152
Mykhaylivka, Ukr. 47°14' N, 35°15' E 156
Mykolayiv, Ukr. 49°31' N, 23°57' E 158
Mykolayiv, Ukr. 46°59' N, 32°2' E 156
Myla, Russ. 65°25' N, 50°42' E 154
Mylius Erichsen Land 80°43' N, 42°2' W 246
Myllykoski, Fin. 60°46' N, 26°46' E 166
Mymensingh, Bangladesh 24°53' N, 90°40' E 197
Mynämäki, Fin. 60°40' N, 21°56' E 166
Mynbulak, Uzb. 42°12' N, 62°55' E 180
Myohaung, Myanmar 20°38' N, 93°10' E 188
Myohyang Sanmaek, N. Korea 39°58' N, 126°24' E 200
Myōkō, Japan 36°55' N, 138°12' E 201
Myoungmya, Myanmar 16°34' N, 94°55' E 202
Myra see Kale, Turk. 36°13' N, 29°57' E 156
Mýrdalsjökull, glacier, Ice. 63°11' N, 18°33' W 142
Myrhorod, Ukr. 49°57' N, 33°31' E 158
Myrskylä, Fin. 60°39' N, 25°48' E 166
Myrtle Beach, S.C., U.S. 33°39' N, 78°54' W 82
Myrtle Creek, Oreg., U.S. 43°1' N, 123°17' W 90
Myrtle Point, Oreg., U.S. 43°3' N, 124°8' W 90
Mys Kamennyy, Russ. 68°29' N, 73°26' E 169
Mys Shmidta, Russ. 68°54' N, 179°31' W 98
Mys Zhelaniya, Russ. 76°50' N, 68°29' E 160
Mysen, Nor. 59°34' N, 11°19' E 152
Myshkino, Russ. 57°46' N, 38°26' E 154
Myślice, Pol. 53°54' N, 19°30' E 166
Mysovaya, Russ. 67°44' N, 155°59' E 160
Mystic, Conn., U.S. 41°21' N, 71°58' W 104
Mystic, Iowa, U.S. 40°46' N, 92°57' W 94
Mysy, Russ. 60°36' N, 54°4' E 154
Mytilene see Mitilíni, Gr. 39°6' N, 26°33' E 156
Myton, Utah, U.S. 40°11' N, 110°3' W 90
Myyeldino, Russ. 61°48' N, 54°46' E 154
Mzima Springs, Kenya 2°59' S, 38°4' E 224
Mzimba, Malawi 11°52' S, 33°32' E 224
Mzuzu, Malawi 11°27' S, 33°54' E 224

N

Nā'ālehu, Hawai'i, U.S. 19°3' N, 155°36' W 99
Naama, Alg. 33°16' N, 0°21' E 214
Naandi, Sudan 4°58' N, 27°49' E 224
Naantali, Fin. 60°28' N, 22°2' E 166
Naas, Ire. 53°12' N, 6°40' W 150
Nabā, Jabal (Nebo, Mount), peak, Jordan 31°45' N, 35°43' E 194
Nababiep, S. Af. 29°36' S, 17°47' E 227
Nabas, Philippines 11°49' N, 122°6' E 203
Naberera, Tanzania 4°12' S, 36°56' E 224
Naberezhnyye Chelny, Russ. 55°40' N, 52°22' E 154
Nabeul, Tun. 36°27' N, 10°44' E 156
Nabilatuk, Uganda 2°3' N, 34°35' E 224
Nabire, Indonesia 3°21' S, 135°28' E 238
Nablus see Nābulus, West Bank 32°12' N, 35°17' E 194
Naboomspruit see Mookgophong, S. Af. 24°31' S, 28°44' E 227
Nabordo, Nig. 10°11' N, 9°25' E 222
Naborton, La., U.S. 32°1' N, 93°35' W 103
Nabq, Egypt 28°7' N, 34°23' E 180
Nābulus (Nablus), West Bank 32°12' N, 35°17' E 194
Nabúri, Mozambique 16°57' S, 39°0' E 224
Nacala, Mozambique 14°33' S, 40°43' E 224
Nacaome, Hond. 13°31' N, 87°29' W 115
Nacaroa, Mozambique 14°18' S, 39°49' E 224
Nacebe, Bol. 10°58' S, 67°27' W 137
Naches, Wash., U.S. 46°42' N, 120°42' W 90
Nachikatsuura, Japan 33°35' N, 135°54' E 201
Nachingwea, Tanzania 10°25' S, 38°46' E 224
Nachna, India 27°31' N, 71°44' E 186
Náchod, Czech Rep. 50°24' N, 16°10' E 152
Nachuge, India 10°44' N, 92°31' E 188
Nacimiento, Mex. 28°3' N, 101°45' W 92
Nacimiento, Lake, Calif., U.S. 35°44' N, 121°17' W 100
Naciria, Alg. 36°44' N, 3°50' E 150
Nacka, Sw. 59°17' N, 18°7' E 166
Nackhörn 54°18' N, 7°50' E 152
Naco, Mex. 31°17' N, 109°58' W 92
Nacogdoches, Tex., U.S. 31°34' N, 94°39' W 103
Nácori Chico, Mex. 29°39' N, 109°5' W 92
Nacozari, river, Mex. 29°23' N, 109°44' W 80
Nacozari Viejo, Mex. 30°21' N, 109°39' W 92
Ñacunday, Parag. 26°4' S, 54°35' W 139
Nada see Danxian, China 19°28' N, 109°34' E 198
Nadale, island, Maldives 0°16' N, 72°12' E 188
Nadanbo, China 43°9' N, 125°27' E 200
Nadap, Hung. 47°15' N, 18°36' E 168
Nadiad, India 22°41' N, 72°51' E 186
Nădlac, Rom. 46°10' N, 20°47' E 168
Nădrag, Rom. 45°40' N, 22°13' E 168
Nadu, adm. division, India 11°19' N, 79°30' E 188
Nádudvar, Hung. 47°25' N, 21°9' E 168
Nadvoitsy, Russ. 63°53' N, 34°13' E 152
Nadym, Russ. 65°35' N, 72°33' E 169
Nadym, river, Russ. 63°43' N, 72°30' E 169
Nafūsah, Jabal, Lib. 31°17' N, 10°13' E 214
Nafada, Nig. 11°2' N, 11°19' E 222
Nafana, Côte d'Ivoire 9°11' N, 4°48' W 222
Naft Khaneh Naft-e-Shāh, oil field, Iraq 34°6' N, 45°18' E 180
Naft-e Safīd, oil field, Iran 31°41' N, 49°12' E 180
Nafuce, Nig. 12°19' N, 6°30' E 222
Nag, Pak. 27°21' N, 65°4' E 186
Nag 'Hammâdi, Egypt 26°3' N, 32°9' E 180
Naga, Philippines 13°38' N, 123°10' E 203
Naga Hills, Myanmar 25°34' N, 94°35' E 188
Nagagami Lake, Can. 49°21' N, 85°32' W 94
Nagagami, river, Can. 49°45' N, 84°34' W 94
Nagagamisis Lake, Can. 49°27' N, 85°16' W 94
Nagahama, Japan 35°22' N, 136°16' E 201
Nagahama, Japan 33°36' N, 132°29' E 201
Nagai, Japan 38°6' N, 140°1' E 201
Nagano, Japan 36°40' N, 138°12' E 201
Nagano, adm. division, Japan 35°59' N, 137°38' E 201
Naganuma, Japan 37°17' N, 140°12' E 201
Nagaoka, Japan 37°26' N, 138°51' E 201
Nagar, India 32°5' N, 77°13' E 188
Nagar Parkar, Pak. 24°23' N, 70°47' E 186
Nagarzê, China 28°58' N, 90°21' E 197
Nagas Point, Can. 52°1' N, 131°45' W 108
Nagasaki, Japan 32°45' N, 129°52' E 201
Nagasaki, adm. division, Japan 32°47' N, 129°50' E 201
Nagashima, Japan 34°12' N, 136°20' E 201
Nagato, Japan 34°21' N, 131°11' E 200
Nagaur, India 27°10' N, 73°45' E 186
Nagda, India 23°26' N, 75°27' E 197
Nagēlē, Eth. 5°20' N, 39°36' E 224
Nagercoil, India 8°10' N, 77°25' E 188
Nagina, India 29°26' N, 78°24' E 197
Nagishot, Sudan 4°15' N, 33°33' E 224
Nagorno-Karabakh 39°45' N, 46°34' E 195
Nagornyy, Russ. 55°58' N, 124°54' E 160
Nagorsk, Russ. 59°19' N, 50°49' E 154
Nagoya, Japan 35°8' N, 136°55' E 201
Nagpur, India 21°8' N, 79°5' E 197
Nagqu, China 31°27' N, 92°0' E 188
Nagyatád, Hung. 46°13' N, 17°22' E 168
Nagybajom, Hung. 46°23' N, 17°30' E 168
Nagybátony, Hung. 47°58' N, 19°49' E 168
Nagycenk, Hung. 47°36' N, 16°41' E 168
Nagydorog, Hung. 46°37' N, 18°39' E 168
Nagykereki, Hung. 47°11' N, 21°47' E 168
Nagyk oros, Hung. 47°1' N, 19°46' E 168
Nagymányok, Hung. 46°16' N, 18°28' E 168
Nagyszénás, Hung. 46°41' N, 20°40' E 168
Naha, Japan 26°13' N, 127°38' E 190
Nahal Hever, ruin(s), Israel 31°25' N, 35°17' E 194
Naḥal 'Oz, Israel 31°27' N, 34°29' E 194
Nahanni Butte, Can. 61°2' N, 123°23' W 108
Nahanni National Park Reserve, Can. 61°8' N, 125°57' W 108
Nahant, Mass., U.S. 42°25' N, 70°55' W 104
Nahari, Japan 33°25' N, 134°1' E 201
Nahariyya, Israel 33°0' N, 35°5' E 194
Nahāvand, Iran 34°12' N, 48°21' E 180
Nahlin, river, Can. 58°48' N, 131°26' W 108
Nahrin, Afghan. 36°2' N, 69°8' E 186
Nahuel Huapí National Park, Arg. 41°4' S, 71°53' W 122
Naicam, Can. 52°25' N, 104°29' W 108
Naij Gol, river, China 35°52' N, 92°56' E 188
Nailsworth, U.K. 51°41' N, 2°13' W 162
Na'ima, Sudan 14°36' N, 32°15' E 182
Naiman Qi, China 42°48' N, 120°38' E 198
Nain, Can. 56°29' N, 61°49' W 106
Nā'īn, Iran 32°50' N, 53°7' E 180
Nainpur, India 22°25' N, 80°7' E 197
Nainwa, India 25°47' N, 75°53' E 197
Nairn, La., U.S. 29°25' N, 89°37' W 103
Nairn, U.K. 57°35' N, 3°53' W 150
Nairobi, Kenya 1°20' S, 36°39' E 224
Nairobi National Park, Kenya 1°28' S, 36°31' E 206
Nairôto, Mozambique 12°24' S, 39°6' E 224
Nais Saar, island, Est. 59°32' N, 23°57' E 166
Naivasha, Kenya 0°45' N, 36°27' E 224
Naj Tunich, site, Guatemala 16°18' N, 89°22' W 115
Najaf see An Najaf, Iraq 31°58' N, 44°19' E 180
Najafābād, Iran 32°38' N, 51°25' E 180
Najd, region, Saudi Arabia 26°8' N, 42°8' E 182
Najin (Rajin), N. Korea 42°15' N, 130°19' E 200
Najrān, Saudi Arabia 17°44' N, 44°27' E 182
Naju, S. Korea 35°0' N, 126°44' E 200
Naka, river, Japan 33°44' N, 134°17' E 201
Nakajō, Japan 38°3' N, 139°24' E 201
Nakaminato, Japan 36°20' N, 140°36' E 201
Nakamura, Japan 32°58' N, 132°55' E 201
Nakanno, Russ. 62°57' N, 108°15' E 160
Nakano, Japan 36°44' N, 138°22' E 201
Nakanojō, Japan 36°35' N, 138°50' E 201
Nakatosa, Japan 33°18' N, 133°12' E 201
Nakatsu, Japan 33°35' N, 131°12' E 201
Nakatsugawa, Japan 35°28' N, 137°31' E 201
Nakfa, Eritrea 16°38' N, 38°25' E 182
Nakhl, Egypt 29°52' N, 33°47' E 180
Nakhodka, Russ. 67°40' N, 77°44' E 169
Nakhodka, Russ. 42°51' N, 132°48' E 190
Nakhon Nayok, Thai. 14°13' N, 101°12' E 202
Nakhon Phanom, Thai. 17°23' N, 104°44' E 202
Nakhon Ratchasima (Khorat), Thai. 14°58' N, 102°7' E 202
Nakhon Sawan, Thai. 15°41' N, 100°5' E 202
Nakhon Si Thammarat, Thai. 8°26' N, 99°57' E 202
Nakina, Can. 50°11' N, 86°38' W 82
Nakina, river, Can. 58°51' N, 133°3' W 108
Näkkälä, Fin. 68°36' N, 23°31' E 152
Naknek, Alas., U.S. 58°41' N, 157°5' W 98
Nako, Burkina Faso 10°39' N, 3°3' W 222
Nakonde, Zambia 9°23' S, 32°45' E 224
Nakop, Namibia 28°6' S, 19°59' E 227
Nakovo, Serb. and Mont. 45°52' N, 20°32' E 168
Nakuru, Kenya 0°18' N, 36°5' E 224
Nakusp, Can. 50°14' N, 117°49' W 90
Nal'chik, Russ. 43°30' N, 43°38' E 195
Nallıhan, Turk. 40°11' N, 31°21' E 156
Nālūt, Lib. 31°54' N, 10°58' E 214
Nam Can, Vietnam 8°48' N, 105°1' E 202
Nam Co, lake, China 30°45' N, 89°50' E 188
Nam Dinh, Vietnam 20°26' N, 106°8' E 198
Nam Nao National Park, Thai. 16°25' N, 101°24' E 202
Nam Ngum Dam, Laos 18°42' N, 102°29' E 202
Nam Phong Dam, Thai. 16°34' N, 102°8' E 202
Nam Phung Dam, Thai. 16°49' N, 102°59' E 202
Nam, river, S. Korea 35°17' N, 128°16' E 200
Nam Tok, Thai. 14°23' N, 98°57' E 202
Namaacha, Mozambique 25°57' S, 32°1' E 227
Namacunde, Angola 17°19' S, 15°49' E 220
Namacurra, Mozambique 17°29' S, 37°2' E 224
Namanga, Kenya 2°33' S, 36°49' E 224
Namangan, Uzb. 40°59' N, 71°38' E 197
Namanyere, Tanzania 7°31' S, 31°2' E 224
Namapa, Mozambique 13°44' S, 39°51' E 224
Namaponda, Mozambique 15°51' S, 39°53' E 224
Namaqualand, region, S. Af. 30°11' S, 17°12' E 227
Namarrói, Mozambique 15°58' S, 36°49' E 224
Namasagali, Uganda 0°59' N, 32°58' E 224
Namatanai, P.N.G. 3°41' S, 152°25' E 238
Nambinda, Tanzania 9°37' S, 37°37' E 224
Nambu, Japan 35°16' N, 138°26' E 201
Namdae, river, N. Korea 41°8' N, 129°4' E 200
Namdapha National Park, India 27°30' N, 96°34' E 188
Nameigos Lake, Can. 48°45' N, 85°12' W 94
Namerikawa, Japan 36°45' N, 137°19' E 201
Nametil, Mozambique 15°44' S, 39°24' E 224
Namgia, India 31°46' N, 78°41' E 188
Namib Desert, Angola 15°54' S, 12°10' E 220
Namibe, Angola 15°14' S, 12°10' E 220
Namibe, adm. division, Angola 16°24' S, 11°50' E 220
Namibia 21°53' S, 15°16' E 220
Namib-Naukluft Park, Namibia 25°49' S, 15°21' E 227
Namies, S. Af. 29°17' S, 19°11' E 227
Namīn, Iran 38°29' N, 48°30' E 195
Namiquipa, Mex. 29°14' N, 107°25' W 92
Namjagbarwa Feng, peak, China 29°37' N, 94°55' E 188
Namji, S. Korea 35°23' N, 128°29' E 200
Namlea, Indonesia 3°16' S, 127°1' E 192
Namling, China 29°42' N, 89°3' E 197
Namoi, river, Austral. 30°32' S, 147°10' E 231
Nāmolokama Mountain, peak, Hawai'i, U.S. 22°7' N, 159°33' W 99
Namoluk Atoll 5°35' N, 150°28' E 192
Namonuito Atoll, North Pacific Ocean 8°43' N, 149°21' E 192
Nampa, Can. 56°3' N, 117°9' W 108
Nampa, Idaho, U.S. 43°32' N, 116°34' W 82
Nampala, Mali 15°15' N, 5°34' W 222
Namp'o, N. Korea 38°43' N, 125°25' E 200
Nampō Shotō, islands, North Pacific Ocean 30°47' N, 138°20' E 190
Nampula, Mozambique 15°8' S, 39°17' E 224
Nampula, adm. division, Mozambique 14°60' S, 37°41' E 224
Namsos, Nor. 64°29' N, 11°41' E 160
Namsskogan, Nor. 64°55' N, 13°12' E 152
Namtsy, Russ. 62°41' N, 129°32' E 160
Namtu, Myanmar 23°1' N, 97°27' E 202
Namu, Can. 51°50' N, 127°49' W 108
Namuli, peak, Mozambique 15°26' S, 36°59' E 224
Namuno, Mozambique 13°31' S, 38°52' E 224
Namur, Belg. 50°28' N, 4°51' E 167
Namur Lake, Can. 57°18' N, 113°21' W 108
Namuruputh, Kenya 4°31' N, 35°54' E 224
Namutoni, Namibia 18°51' S, 16°57' E 220
Namwala, Zambia 15°46' S, 26°25' E 224
Namwon, S. Korea 35°23' N, 127°23' E 200
Namyang, N. Korea 40°44' N, 129°17' E 200
Nan, Thai. 18°48' N, 100°45' E 202
Nan Hulsan Hu, lake, China 36°42' N, 94°42' E 188
Nan, river, Thai. 18°37' N, 100°46' E 202
Nana Kru, Liberia 4°52' N, 8°45' W 222
Nana, river, Cen. Af. Rep. 5°48' N, 15°21' E 218
Nanaimo, Can. 49°9' N, 123°57' W 100
Nanam, N. Korea 41°41' N, 129°39' E 200
Nan'an, China 24°55' N, 118°22' E 198
Nanao, Japan 37°2' N, 136°56' E 201
Nanbu, China 31°20' N, 106°0' E 198
Nanchang, China 28°41' N, 115°54' E 198
Nancheng, China 27°33' N, 116°37' E 198
Nanchong, China 30°49' N, 106°2' E 198
Nanchuan, China 29°11' N, 107°3' E 198
Ñancorainza, Bol. 20°41' S, 63°28' W 137
Nancy, Fr. 48°41' N, 6°11' E 163
Nanda Devi, peak, India 30°22' N, 79°52' E 197
Nandan, China 24°57' N, 107°30' E 198
Nanded, India 19°11' N, 77°19' E 188
Nanfen, China 41°8' N, 123°48' E 200
Nanfeng, China 27°13' N, 116°25' E 198
Nanga Parbat, peak, Pak. 35°13' N, 74°28' E 186
Nangade, Mozambique 11°6' S, 39°43' E 224
Nangapinoh, Indonesia 0°21' N, 111°38' E 192
Nangin, Myanmar 10°32' N, 98°29' E 202
Nangis, Fr. 48°33' N, 3°0' E 163
Nangnim, N. Korea 40°57' N, 127°8' E 200
Nangong, China 37°18' N, 115°23' E 198
Nangqên, China 32°15' N, 96°28' E 188
Nangtud, Mount, peak, Philippines 11°16' N, 122°6' E 203
Nangxian, China 29°5' N, 93°6' E 188
Nanika Lake, lake, Can. 53°45' N, 128°5' W 108
Nanjiang, China 32°24' N, 106°46' E 198
Nanjing, China 32°5' N, 118°48' E 198
Nanjing, China 24°22' N, 117°16' E 198
Nankang, China 25°39' N, 114°41' E 198
Nankoku, Japan 33°34' N, 133°38' E 201
Nanle, China 36°3' N, 115°11' E 198
Nanning, China 22°49' N, 108°19' E 198
Nanortalik 60°13' N, 45°14' W 106
Nanpara, India 27°50' N, 81°30' E 197
Nanping, China 42°18' N, 129°12' E 200
Nanping, China 26°37' N, 118°4' E 198
Nanri Dao, island, China 24°53' N, 119°22' E 198
Nansan Dao, island, China 21°1' N, 110°37' E 198
Nansei Shotō see Ryukyu Islands, East China Sea 25°0' N, 125°56' E 190
Nansen Basin, Arctic Ocean 85°0' N, 78°46' E 255
Nansen Land 82°0' N, 43°58' W 246
Nansen Sound 80°31' N, 104°17' W 72
Nansio, Tanzania 2°7' S, 33°4' E 224
Nantais, Lac, lake, Can. 61°33' N, 76°5' W 246
Nantes, Fr. 47°12' N, 1°36' W 150
Nanteuil-le-Haudouin, Fr. 49°8' N, 2°48' E 163
Nanticoke, Can. 42°46' N, 80°11' W 94
Nanticoke, Pa., U.S. 41°11' N, 76°1' W 110
Nanton, Can. 50°20' N, 113°47' W 108
Nantong, China 32°2' N, 120°54' E 198
Nantucket, Mass., U.S. 41°16' N, 70°7' W 104
Nantucket Inlet 74°39' S, 66°32' W 248
Nantucket Island, Mass., U.S. 41°24' N, 70°2' W 104
Nantucket Sound 41°26' N, 70°19' W 104
Nantulo, Mozambique 12°30' S, 39°1' E 224
Nantwich, U.K. 53°3' N, 2°31' W 162
Nanuque, Braz. 17°49' S, 40°21' W 138
Nanusa, Kepulauan, islands, Philippine Sea 4°57' N, 126°54' E 203
Nanxi, China 28°51' N, 104°56' E 198
Nanxian, China 29°23' N, 112°23' E 198
Nanxiong, China 25°6' N, 114°15' E 198
Nanyang, China 33°1' N, 112°34' E 198
Nanyuki, Kenya 1°58' S, 37°4' E 224
Nanzhang, China 31°47' N, 111°50' E 198
Nanzhila, Zambia 16°6' S, 26°1' E 224
Nao, Cabo de La, Sp. 38°30' N, 0°10' E 214
Naococane, Lac, lake, Can. 52°47' N, 71°20' W 111
Naozhou Dao, island, China 20°51' N, 110°39' E 198
Napa, Calif., U.S. 38°18' N, 122°19' W 100
Napá, Mozambique 13°17' S, 39°3' E 224
Napaimiut, Alas., U.S. 61°32' N, 158°41' W 98
Napaleofú, Arg. 37°38' S, 58°46' W 139
Napalkovo, Russ. 70°3' N, 73°54' E 169
Napanee, Can. 44°14' N, 76°59' W 82
Napas, Russ. 59°48' N, 81°57' E 169
Napasoq 65°4' N, 52°21' W 106
Napenay, Arg. 26°44' S, 60°38' W 139
Naperville, Ill., U.S. 41°46' N, 88°9' W 102
Napier, N.Z. 39°30' S, 176°54' E 240
Napier Bay 11°54' S, 131°12' E 231
Naples, Fla., U.S. 26°9' N, 81°48' W 105
Naples, Me., U.S. 43°57' N, 70°37' W 104
Naples, Tex., U.S. 33°11' N, 94°41' W 103
Naples see Napoli, It. 40°51' N, 14°15' E 156
Napo, China 23°21' N, 105°50' E 198
Napo, river, Ecua. 1°14' S, 77°33' W 136
Napo, river, Peru 2°38' S, 74°29' W 122
Napoleon, N. Dak., U.S. 46°29' N, 99°47' W 90
Napoleon, Ohio, U.S. 41°22' N, 84°8' W 102
Napoleonville, La., U.S. 29°55' N, 91°3' W 103
Napoli (Naples), It. 40°51' N, 14°15' E 156
Nappanee, Ind., U.S. 41°26' N, 86°1' W 102
Nāpu'ukūlua, peak, Hawai'i, U.S. 19°42' N, 155°40' W 99
Naqoura, Leb. 33°7' N, 35°8' E 194
Nara, Japan 34°42' N, 135°50' E 201
Nara, Mali 15°10' N, 7°18' W 222
Nara, adm. division, Japan 34°17' N, 135°40' E 201
Nara, river, Pak. 24°46' N, 69°35' E 186
Nara Visa, N. Mex., U.S. 35°36' N, 103°6' W 92
Narach, Belarus 54°55' N, 26°41' E 166
Narach, Vozyera, lake, Belarus 54°52' N, 26°17' E 166
Na'rān, Israel 33°2' N, 35°42' E 194
Naranbulag, Mongolia 49°14' N, 113°19' E 198
Narang, Afghan. 34°44' N, 70°57' E 186
Narasannapeta, India 18°24' N, 84°5' E 188
Narasapur, India 16°27' N, 81°40' E 188
Narathiwat, Thai. 6°26' N, 101°49' E 196
Narayanganj, Bangladesh 23°26' N, 90°40' E 197
Nærbø, Nor. 58°40' N, 5°38' E 152
Narbonne, Fr. 43°10' N, 2°59' E 164
Narcondam Island, India 13°28' N, 94°19' E 188
Nardīn, Iran 37°0' N, 55°57' E 180
Naré, Arg. 30°58' S, 60°28' W 139
Nares Land 81°45' N, 45°60' W 72
Nares Plain, North Atlantic Ocean 22°43' N, 63°8' W 253
Narib, Namibia 24°12' S, 17°46' E 227
Naricual, Venez. 10°2' N, 64°37' W 116
Narimanabad, Azerb. 38°51' N, 48°50' E 195
Narin, river, China 36°20' N, 92°32' E 188
Nariño, adm. division, Col. 1°27' N, 78°30' W 136
Narlı, Turk. 37°25' N, 37°8' E 156
Narmada, river, India 22°56' N, 78°26' E 197
Narodnaya, Gora, peak, Russ. 65°6' N, 59°49' E 154
Narok, Kenya 1°6' S, 35°50' E 224
Narowlya, Belarus 51°44' N, 29°38' E 158
Nærøy, Nor. 64°48' N, 11°16' E 152
Närpiö see Närpes, Fin. 62°27' N, 21°18' E 152
Narragansett Pier, R.I., U.S. 41°25' N, 71°28' W 104
Narran Lake, lake, Austral. 29°60' S, 146°18' E 230
Narrogin, Austral. 32°56' S, 117°11' E 231
Narsaq 60°59' N, 45°60' W 246
Narsarsuaq 61°10' N, 45°21' W 106
Narsimhapur, India 22°56' N, 79°12' E 197
Narsinghgarh, India 23°41' N, 77°5' E 197
Narsipatnam, India 17°39' N, 82°37' E 188
Nart, Mongolia 49°8' N, 105°27' E 198
Narta, Croatia 45°49' N, 16°47' E 168
Narthákі, Óros, peak, Gr. 39°12' N, 22°20' E 156
Nartkala, Russ. 43°32' N, 43°53' E 195
Naruko, Japan 38°45' N, 140°43' E 201
Naruto, Japan 34°10' N, 134°34' E 201
Narva, Est. 59°21' N, 28°8' E 154
Narva Jõesuu, Est. 59°26' N, 28°1' E 166
Narvacan, Philippines 17°26' N, 120°28' E 203
Narvik, Nor. 68°16' N, 17°45' E 160
Narvskoye Vodokhranilishche, lake, Russ. 59°17' N, 27°33' E 166
Narwana, India 29°36' N, 76°8' E 197
Nar'yan Mar, Russ. 67°43' N, 53°6' E 169
Narym, Russ. 58°57' N, 81°41' E 169
Naryn, Kyrg. 41°24' N, 76°2' E 184
Naryn Khuduk, Russ. 45°26' N, 46°32' E 158
Naryn Qum, Kaz. 48°1' N, 47°52' E 184
Naryn, river, Kyrg. 41°47' N, 73°27' E 197
Narynqol, Kaz. 42°41' N, 80°11' E 184
Naryshkino, Russ. 52°55' N, 35°46' E 154
Näs, Nor. 62°57' N, 14°33' E 152
Nasa, peak, Nor. 66°28' N, 15°13' E 152
Nasarawa, Nig. 8°29' N, 7°41' E 222
Nasca, Peru 14°53' S, 74°58' W 137
Nasca Ridge, South Pacific Ocean 20°50' S, 79°49' W 253
Naseby 1645, battle, U.K. 52°23' N, 0°59' E 162
Naselle, Wash., U.S. 46°20' N, 123°49' W 100
Nash, Tex., U.S. 33°25' N, 94°9' W 103
Nashua, Iowa, U.S. 42°56' N, 92°33' W 94
Nashua, Mont., U.S. 48°8' N, 106°24' W 90
Nashville, Ark., U.S. 33°54' N, 93°51' W 96
Nashville, Ga., U.S. 31°11' N, 83°15' W 96
Nashville, Ind., U.S. 39°12' N, 86°15' W 102
Nashville, Mich., U.S. 42°35' N, 85°5' W 102
Nashville, Mo., U.S. 38°20' N, 89°23' W 94
Nashville, Tenn., U.S. 36°7' N, 86°54' W 96
Nashwaaksis, Can. 45°58' N, 66°42' W 94
Našice, Croatia 45°29' N, 18°5' E 168
Näsijärvi, lake, Fin. 61°42' N, 23°24' E 166
Nasik, India 19°59' N, 73°46' E 188
Nasir, Sudan 8°36' N, 33°4' E 224
Nasirabad, India 26°16' N, 74°44' E 186
Nasiriyah see An Nāṣirīyah, Iraq 31°5' N, 46°11' E 180
Naskaupi, river, Can. 54°6' N, 62°58' W 111
Nasri, spring, Mauritania 19°49' N, 15°52' W 222
Nass, river, Can. 56°14' N, 128°29' W 108
Nassau, Bahamas 25°4' N, 77°23' W 118
Nassau, Ger. 50°19' N, 7°48' E 167
Nassau, N.Y., U.S. 42°30' N, 73°37' W 104
Nassau, island, American Samoa, U.S. 11°34' S, 165°33' W 252
Nassawadox, Va., U.S. 37°28' N, 75°52' W 96
Nasser, Lake, Egypt 23°18' N, 32°21' E 182
Nassian, Côte d'Ivoire 8°29' N, 3°29' W 222
Nässjö, Nor. 57°38' N, 14°41' E 152
Nastapoka Islands, islands, Hudson Bay 57°26' N, 76°40' W 106
Nastätten, Ger. 50°12' N, 7°51' E 167
Næstved, Den. 55°13' N, 11°45' E 152
Nasukoin Mountain, peak, Mont., U.S. 48°46' N, 114°39' W 90
Nasva, Russ. 56°34' N, 30°13' E 166

Näsviken, Nor. 61°43' N, 16°49' E 152
Naszály, peak, Hung. 47°50' N, 19°8' E 168
Nat, river, Can. 48°49' N, 82°8' W 94
Nata, Botswana 20°15' S, 26°5' E 227
Natá, Pan. 8°20' N, 80°31' W 115
Nata, river, Botswana 19°53' S, 26°31' E 224
Natal, Braz. 5°49' S, 35°12' W 132
Natal, Braz. 6°60' S, 60°19' W 130
Natal, Indonesia 0°36' N, 99°7' E 196
Natal Basin, Indian Ocean 29°34' S, 40°22' E 254
Natal'inskiy, Russ. 61°13' N, 172°5' E 160
Naṭanz, Iran 33°31' N, 51°55' E 180
Natara, Russ. 68°19' N, 124°1' E 160
Natashquan, Can. 50°11' N, 61°48' W 106
Natashquan, Pointe de, Can. 49°58' N, 61°45' W 111
Natashquan, river, Can. 52°21' N, 63°26' W 111
Natchitoches, La., U.S. 31°45' N, 93°5' W 103
Natera, Mex. 22°39' N, 102°7' W 114
Natick, Mass., U.S. 42°17' N, 71°21' W 104
Natih, oil field, Oman 22°22' N, 56°41' E 182
Nation, river, Can. 55°12' N, 124°23' W 108
National, Wash., U.S. 46°45' N, 122°4' W 100
National Bison Range, site, Mont., U.S. 47°18' N, 114°20' W 90
National City, Calif., U.S. 32°40' N, 117°7' W 101
National Park, N.Z. 39°13' S, 175°23' E 240
Natitiai, Gebel, peak, Egypt 23°2' N, 34°20' E 182
Natividade, Braz. 11°41' S, 47°48' W 130
Natkyizin, Myanmar 14°55' N, 97°57' E 202
Natogami Lake, lake, Can. 50°11' N, 81°5' W 94
Natoma, Kans., U.S. 39°11' N, 99°2' W 90
Nator, Bangladesh 24°20' N, 88°54' E 197
Nattavaara, Nor. 66°44' N, 20°54' E 152
Natuna Besar, island, Indonesia 3°37' N, 108°21' E 196
Natuna Besar, Kepulauan, islands, Indonesia 4°7' N, 107°49' E 196
Natuna Selatan, Kepulauan, islands, South China Sea 2°45' N, 107°49' E 196
Naturaliste, Cape, Austral. 33°25' S, 113°28' E 230
Naturaliste Plateau, Indian Ocean 34°20' S, 112°15' E 254
Naturita, Colo., U.S. 38°12' N, 108°34' W 90
Naturno, It. 46°40' N, 10°59' E 167
Naubinway, Mich., U.S. 46°5' N, 85°28' W 94
Nauchas, Namibia 23°41' S, 16°20' E 227
Naufrage, Pointe au, Can. 49°52' N, 63°31' W 111
Naugatuck, Conn., U.S. 41°29' N, 73°4' W 104
Nauhcampatépetl see Cofre de Perote, peak, Mex. 19°27' N, 97°13' W 114
Naujoji Vilnia, Lith. 54°42' N, 25°24' E 166
Naulila, Angola 17°12' S, 14°40' E 220
Naumburg, Ger. 51°8' N, 11°48' E 152
Naumburg, Ger. 51°14' N, 9°10' E 167
Naunak, Russ. 58°58' N, 80°11' E 169
Naungpale, Myanmar 19°32' N, 97°6' E 202
Nā'ūr, Jordan 31°52' N, 35°49' E 194
Naurskaya, Russ. 43°33' N, 45°21' E 195
Nauru 0°32' N, 166°55' E 242
Naushahra, India 33°9' N, 74°13' E 186
Naushki, Russ. 50°33' N, 106°15' E 190
Naushon Island, Mass., U.S. 41°31' N, 70°45' W 104
Nauta, Peru 4°29' S, 73°37' W 130
Nautla, Mex. 20°9' N, 96°47' W 114
Nautla, river, Mex. 20°7' N, 97°14' W 114
Nautsi, Russ. 68°58' N, 29°0' E 152
Nauvoo, Mo., U.S. 40°32' N, 91°23' W 94
Nava, Mex. 28°24' N, 100°46' W 92
Navabelitsa, Belarus 52°22' N, 31°8' E 158
Navadwip, India 23°22' N, 88°18' E 197
Navahrudak, Belarus 53°36' N, 25°50' E 152
Naval, Sp. 42°11' N, 0°9' E 164
Naval Submarine Base, Conn., U.S. 41°24' N, 72°7' W 104
Navalvillar de Pelea, Sp. 39°5' N, 5°28' W 164
Navan (An Uaimh), Ire. 53°38' N, 6°42' W 150
Navapolatsk, Belarus 55°30' N, 28°35' E 152
Navarin, Mys, Russ. 62°4' N, 179°6' E 160
Navarino, Isla, island, Chile 55°25' S, 67°12' W 134
Navarra, adm. division, Sp. 42°41' N, 2°13' W 164
Navarrenx, Fr. 43°20' N, 0°47' E 164
Navarro, Peru 6°20' S, 75°47' W 130
Navàs, Sp. 41°54' N, 1°52' E 164
Navasota, Tex., U.S. 30°22' N, 96°5' W 96
Navassa Island, U.S. 18°25' N, 75°2' W 116
Navayel'nya, Belarus 53°29' N, 25°32' E 152
Nave, It. 45°35' N, 10°16' E 167
Navesti, river, Est. 58°31' N, 25°1' E 166
Navia, Arg. 34°46' S, 66°35' W 134
Navidad, Chile 34°1' S, 71°51' W 134
Navlakhi, India 22°55' N, 70°31' E 186
Navlya, Russ. 52°48' N, 34°32' E 154
Navoiy, Uzb. 40°6' N, 65°22' E 197
Navojoa, Mex. 27°4' N, 109°27' W 112
Navrongo, Ghana 10°53' N, 1°8' W 222
Navsari, India 20°56' N, 72°57' E 186
Nawa, Japan 35°29' N, 133°30' E 201
Nawá, Syr. 32°53' N, 36°3' E 194
Nawabganj, Bangladesh 24°30' N, 88°18' E 197
Nawabganj, India 26°55' N, 81°14' E 197
Nawabshah, Pak. 26°15' N, 68°25' E 186
Nawada, India 24°51' N, 85°31' E 197
Nawah, Afghan. 32°19' N, 67°52' E 186
Nawalgarh, India 27°49' N, 75°16' E 197
Nawapara, India 20°49' N, 82°32' E 188
Naworth Castle, site, U.K. 54°56' N, 2°48' W 150
Naxçıvan, Azerb. 39°12' N, 45°23' E 195
Naxçıvan, adm. division, Azerb. 39°23' N, 45°1' E 195
Naxi, China 28°47' N, 105°27' E 198
Náxos, island, Gr. 37°10' N, 25°35' E 180
Naxos, ruin(s), It. 37°48' N, 15°9' E 156
Nay, Fr. 43°10' N, 0°16' E 164
Nāy Band, Iran 32°27' N, 57°41' E 186
Nāy Band, Iran 27°22' N, 52°37' E 196
Nay, Mui, Vietnam 12°52' N, 109°29' E 202
Naya, Col. 3°10' N, 77°22' W 136
Nayar, Mex. 22°15' N, 104°31' W 114
Nayarit, Mex. 32°20' N, 115°20' W 92
Nayarit, adm. division, Mex. 21°46' N, 105°30' W 114
Nayba, Russ. 70°43' N, 130°46' E 173
Nazaré, Port. 39°34' N, 9°5' W 150
Nazareno, Mex. 25°24' N, 103°26' W 114
Nazareth, Ky., U.S. 37°50' N, 85°29' W 96
Nazareth see Nazerat, Israel 32°42' N, 35°18' E 194
Nazas, Mex. 25°14' N, 104°7' W 114
Nazas, river, Mex. 25°8' N, 104°32' W 114
Naze, The, U.K. 51°52' N, 1°11' E 162
Nazerat (Nazareth), Israel 32°42' N, 35°18' E 194
Nāzīk, Iran 38°59' N, 45°0' E 195
Nazik Gölü, lake, Turk. 38°50' N, 42°6' E 195
Nazilli, Turk. 37°55' N, 28°20' E 156
Nazimiye, Turk. 39°10' N, 39°48' E 195
Nazimovo, Russ. 59°30' N, 90°52' E 169
Nazino, Russ. 60°8' N, 78°55' E 169
Nazir Hat, Bangladesh 22°35' N, 91°46' E 197
Naziya, Russ. 59°49' N, 31°35' E 152
Nazko, Can. 52°59' N, 123°39' W 108
Nazko, river, Can. 52°54' N, 123°47' W 108
Nazrēt, Eth. 8°31' N, 39°14' E 224
Nazyvayevsk, Russ. 55°33' N, 71°24' E 184
Nchelenge, Zambia 9°21' S, 28°48' E 224
Ncheu, Malawi 14°50' S, 34°40' E 224
Ncojane, Botswana 23°4' S, 20°14' E 227
Ndala, Tanzania 4°45' S, 33°15' E 224
N'dalatando, Angola 9°18' S, 14°54' E 218
Ndali, Benin 9°50' N, 2°46' E 222
Ndande, Senegal 15°17' N, 16°28' W 222
Ndélé, Cen. Af. Rep. 8°23' N, 20°37' E 218
Ndikiniméki, Cameroon 4°41' N, 10°49' E 222
N'Djamena, Chad 12°5' N, 14°53' E 218
Ndjolé, Gabon 0°11' N, 10°41' E 218
Ndola, Zambia 13°1' S, 28°39' E 224
Ndop, Cameroon 5°57' N, 10°23' E 222
Ndu, Dem. Rep. of the Congo 4°39' N, 22°49' E 218
Ndumbwe, Tanzania 10°15' S, 39°56' E 224
Ndumo, S. Af. 26°56' S, 32°14' E 227
Nduye, Dem. Rep. of the Congo 1°47' N, 28°59' E 224
Né, river, Fr. 45°27' N, 0°21' E 150
Neah Bay, Wash., U.S. 48°20' N, 124°39' W 100
Neamţ, adm. division, Rom. 47°4' N, 25°44' E 156
Near Islands, Bering Sea 53°10' N, 170°29' E 160
Nebbou, Burkina Faso 11°19' N, 1°55' W 222
Nebdino, Russ. 64°11' N, 48°4' E 154
Nebel, Ger. 54°39' N, 8°22' E 152
Nebelhorn, peak, Ger. 47°23' N, 10°15' E 156
Nebitdag see Balkanabat, Turkm. 39°31' N, 54°21' E 180
Neblina, Pico da, peak, Venez. 0°44' N, 66°8' W 136
Nebo, La., U.S. 31°34' N, 92°9' W 103
Nebo, Mount, peak, Utah, U.S. 39°47' N, 111°50' W 90
Nebo, Mount see Nabā, Jabal, peak, Jordan 31°45' N, 35°43' E 194
Nebolchi, Russ. 59°6' N, 33°25' E 154
Nebraska, adm. division, Nebr., U.S. 41°15' N, 101°2' W 90
Nebraska City, Nebr., U.S. 40°40' N, 95°52' W 94
Nebrodi, Monti, It. 37°55' N, 14°11' E 156
Necedah, Wis., U.S. 44°1' N, 90°5' W 102
Neches, Tex., U.S. 31°50' N, 95°30' W 103
Neches, river, Tex., U.S. 31°38' N, 95°16' W 103
Nechí, Col. 8°4' N, 74°49' W 136
Nechí, river, Col. 7°14' N, 75°17' W 136
Nechiou, Tun. 34°19' N, 8°58' E 156
Nechisar National Park, Eth. 5°50' N, 37°30' E 206
Necochea, Arg. 38°33' S, 58°48' W 139
Necoclí, Col. 8°27' N, 76°46' W 136
Necuto, Angola 4°54' S, 12°36' E 218
Nederrijn, river, Neth. 51°55' N, 5°14' E 167
Nêdong, China 29°13' N, 91°44' E 197
Nedvědice, Czech Rep. 49°26' N, 16°19' E 152
Needle Mountain, peak, Wyo., U.S. 44°2' N, 109°42' W 90
Needles, Calif., U.S. 34°50' N, 114°38' W 101
Needles, The, peak, Calif., U.S. 36°6' N, 118°32' W 101
Neenah, Wis., U.S. 44°9' N, 88°29' W 102
Neenoshe Reservoir, lake, Colo., U.S. 38°20' N, 103°2' W 90
Neepawa, Can. 50°16' N, 99°29' W 90
Neermoor, Ger. 53°18' N, 7°26' E 163
Neerpelt, Belg. 51°13' N, 5°25' E 167
Nefasi, Eritrea 15°15' N, 39°3' E 182
Nefedova, Russ. 58°49' N, 72°38' E 169
Nefta, Tun. 33°52' N, 7°53' E 214
Neftçala, Azerb. 39°23' N, 49°14' E 195
Neftegorsk, Russ. 44°19' N, 39°40' E 158
Neftekamsk, Russ. 56°4' N, 54°32' E 154
Neftekumsk, Russ. 44°43' N, 45°5' E 158
Nefteyugansk, Russ. 61°3' N, 72°41' E 169
Nega Nega, Zambia 15°52' S, 28°0' E 220
Negage, Angola 7°47' S, 15°16' E 218
Negaunee, Mich., U.S. 46°30' N, 87°36' W 94
Negev, region, Israel 30°27' N, 34°30' E 194
Negoiul, peak, Rom. 45°34' N, 24°28' E 156
Negola, Angola 14°10' S, 14°28' E 220
Negomano, Mozambique 11°25' S, 38°31' E 224
Negombo, Sri Lanka 7°13' N, 79°53' E 188
Negotin, Serb. and Mont. 44°13' N, 22°31' E 168
Negotka, Russ. 59°41' N, 80°40' E 169
Negra, Cordillera, Peru 9°45' S, 78°20' W 130
Negra, Laguna, lake, Uru. 34°7' S, 54°12' W 139
Negra, Loma, peak, Sp. 42°3' N, 1°25' W 164
Negra, Punta, Peru 5°56' S, 82°20' W 130
Negra, Serra, Braz. 6°46' S, 47°5' W 130
Negra, Serrania, Bol. 13°39' S, 61°23' W 132
Negreiros, Chile 19°53' S, 69°53' W 137
Negreşti-Oaş, Rom. 47°52' N, 23°25' E 168
Negría, Col. 4°43' N, 76°55' W 136
Negrillos, Bol. 18°50' S, 68°40' W 137
Negrine, Alg. 34°27' N, 7°30' E 214
Negro Mountain, Md., U.S. 39°41' N, 79°27' W 94
Negro, Río, adm. division, Arg. 39°34' S, 64°37' W 139
Negro, river, Arg. 39°44' S, 65°18' W 134
Negro, river, Bol. 14°45' S, 62°49' W 132
Negro, river, Bol. 10°26' S, 65°45' W 137
Negro, river, Braz. 5°22' S, 71°33' W 130
Negro, river, Braz. 0°23' N, 64°46' W 123
Negro, river, Braz. 19°21' S, 57°26' W 132
Negro, river, Guatemala 15°21' N, 91°12' W 115
Negro, river, Parag. 24°5' S, 59°11' W 132
Negro, river, Uru. 32°14' S, 54°53' W 139
Negros, island, Philippines 9°1' N, 121°30' E 192
Negru Vodă, Rom. 43°49' N, 28°12' E 156
Nehalem, Oreg., U.S. 45°42' N, 123°54' W 100
Nehalem, river, Oreg., U.S. 45°45' N, 123°41' W 100
Nehbandān, Iran 31°31' N, 60°4' E 180
Nehe, China 48°30' N, 124°54' E 198
Neheim-HÜsten, Ger. 51°26' N, 7°59' E 167
Nei Mongol, adm. division, China 42°32' N, 114°22' E 198
Neiba, Dom. Rep. 18°27' N, 71°26' W 116
Neihart, Mont., U.S. 46°54' N, 110°45' W 90
Neijiang, China 29°35' N, 105°2' E 198
Neilburg, Can. 52°51' N, 109°37' W 108
Neillsville, Wis., U.S. 44°32' N, 90°35' W 94
Neiqiu, China 37°18' N, 114°31' E 198
Neiva, Col. 2°55' N, 75°17' W 136
Nejanilini Lake, Can. 59°38' N, 98°13' W 108
Nejo, Eth. 9°27' N, 35°28' E 224
Nekalagba, Dem. Rep. of the Congo 2°49' N, 27°57' E 224
Nékaounié, Côte d'Ivoire 5°6' N, 7°27' W 222
Nek'emtē (Lekemt), Eth. 9°2' N, 36°33' E 224
Nekhayevskiy, Russ. 50°23' N, 41°38' E 158
Nekonda, India 17°46' N, 79°47' E 188
Nekoosa, Wis., U.S. 44°18' N, 89°55' W 110
Neksø, Den. 55°3' N, 15°7' E 152
Nelas, Port. 40°31' N, 7°53' W 150
Nelaug, Nor. 58°39' N, 8°38' E 152
Nelidovo, Russ. 56°13' N, 32°55' E 154
Neligh, Nebr., U.S. 42°6' N, 98°2' W 90
Nel'kan, Russ. 57°47' N, 135°57' E 160
Nellimo, Fin. 68°49' N, 28°15' E 152
Nellis Air Force Base, Nev., U.S. 36°13' N, 115°5' W 101
Nellore, India 14°24' N, 79°56' E 188
Nelson, Can. 49°28' N, 117°18' W 90
Nelson, Nebr., U.S. 40°11' N, 98°5' W 90
Nelson, Nev., U.S. 35°42' N, 114°50' W 101
Nelson, Pa., U.S. 41°58' N, 77°14' W 94
Nelson, U.K. 53°50' N, 2°12' W 162
Nelson Forks, Can. 59°30' N, 123°55' W 108
Nelson House, Can. 55°48' N, 98°54' W 108
Nelson Island, Antarctica 62°35' S, 59°3' W 134
Nelson Lagoon, Bristol Bay 55°59' N, 161°14' W 98
Nelson Lake, lake, Wis., U.S. 46°2' N, 91°51' W 94
Nelson Reservoir, lake, Mont., U.S. 48°28' N, 108°15' W 90
Nelson, river, Can. 56°7' N, 95°20' W 106
Nelsons Island, U.K. 5°38' S, 72°12' E 188
Nelsonville, Ohio, U.S. 39°27' N, 82°15' W 102
Nelspruit, S. Af. 25°30' S, 31°0' E 227
Nem, river, Russ. 61°20' N, 55°54' E 154
Néma, Mauritania 16°36' N, 7°13' W 222
Nema, Russ. 57°31' N, 50°35' E 154
Neman, Russ. 55°1' N, 22°1' E 166
Nembe, Nig. 4°33' N, 6°25' E 222
Nemeiben Lake, Can. 55°16' N, 106°14' W 108
Nemenčinė, Lith. 54°51' N, 25°28' E 166
Nementcha, Monts des, Alg. 34°57' N, 5°55' E 214
Nëmerçkë, Mal, Alban. 40°9' N, 19°57' E 156
Nemila, Bosn. and Herzg. 44°18' N, 17°53' E 168
Nemiscau, Can. 51°23' N, 76°60' W 82
Nemor, river, China 48°24' N, 125°22' E 198
Nemours, Fr. 48°15' N, 2°41' E 163
Nemrut Gölü, lake, Turk. 38°36' N, 42°1' E 195
Nemunas, river, Lith. 54°11' N, 24°4' E 166
Nen, river, China 47°45' N, 124°13' E 198
Nene, river, U.K. 52°21' N, 0°36' E 162
Nenets, adm. division, Russ. 66°30' N, 45°3' E 169
Nenjiang, China 49°11' N, 125°14' E 198
Neno, Malawi 15°26' S, 34°38' E 224
Neodesha, Kans., U.S. 37°24' N, 95°41' W 96
Neoga, Ill., U.S. 39°18' N, 88°27' W 102
Neosho, Mo., U.S. 36°51' N, 94°22' W 96
Neosho, river, Kans., U.S. 38°3' N, 95°56' W 80
Ne'ot ha Kikkar, Israel 30°55' N, 35°21' E 194
Nepa, Russ. 59°19' N, 108°22' E 160
Nepal 28°11' N, 83°31' E 188
Nepalganj, Nepal 28°6' N, 81°40' E 197
Nepean, Can. 45°20' N, 75°44' W 94
Nephi, Utah, U.S. 39°42' N, 111°49' W 92
Nephin, peak, Ire. 54°0' N, 9°29' W 150
Nepoko, river, Dem. Rep. of the Congo 2°15' N, 28°25' E 224
Neponset, Ill., U.S. 41°18' N, 89°47' W 102
Neptune, N.J., U.S. 40°12' N, 74°4' W 94
Neptune Islands, islands, Great Australian Bight 35°42' S, 133°49' E 230
Nerău, Rom. 45°58' N, 20°32' E 168
Nerchinsk, Russ. 52°0' N, 116°30' E 190
Nerdva, Russ. 58°44' N, 55°5' E 154
Nerekhta, Russ. 57°25' N, 40°32' E 154
Nereta, Latv. 56°12' N, 25°19' E 166
Neretva, river, Bosn. and Herzg. 43°33' N, 18°5' E 168
Nerezine, Croatia 44°40' N, 14°23' E 156
Neriquinha, Angola 15°54' S, 21°37' E 220
Neris, river, Lith. 55°2' N, 24°18' E 166
Nerja, Sp. 36°44' N, 3°53' W 164
Nérondes, Fr. 46°59' N, 2°48' E 150
Neroy, Russ. 54°31' N, 97°40' E 190
Neroyka, Gora, peak, Russ. 64°35' N, 59°18' E 154
Nerva, Sp. 37°41' N, 6°34' W 164
Neryungri, Russ. 56°43' N, 124°31' E 160
Nes, Neth. 53°26' N, 5°47' E 163
Nes, Nor. 60°33' N, 9°56' E 152
Nes', Russ. 66°37' N, 44°48' E 154
Nesbyen, Nor. 60°33' N, 9°7' E 152
Nesebŭr (Mesemvria), Bulg. 42°39' N, 27°44' E 156
Neshkan, Russ. 67°0' N, 172°56' W 98
Neshkoro, Wis., U.S. 43°56' N, 89°14' W 102
Neskaupstadur, Ice. 65°7' N, 13°46' W 143
Nesle, Fr. 49°45' N, 2°54' E 163
Nesna, Nor. 66°11' N, 13°0' E 152
Nespelem, Wash., U.S. 48°9' N, 118°59' W 90
Ness City, Kans., U.S. 38°27' N, 99°55' W 90
Nesseby, Nor. 70°9' N, 28°51' E 152
Nesselrode, Mount, peak, Can. 58°57' N, 134°28' W 108
Nestaocano, river, Can. 49°33' N, 73°34' W 94
Nesterov, Russ. 54°38' N, 22°34' E 166
Nestokhoríou, ruin(s), Gr. 41°18' N, 24°6' E 156
Nestor Falls, Can. 49°5' N, 93°55' W 90
Netanya, Israel 32°19' N, 34°51' E 194
Netherlands 52°20' N, 5°27' E 163
Netherlands Antilles 18°1' N, 63°57' W 116
Netla, Can. 60°59' N, 123°18' W 108
Nett Lake, Minn., U.S. 48°4' N, 93°30' W 94
Nettancourt, Fr. 48°53' N, 4°55' E 163
Nettetal, Ger. 51°18' N, 6°11' E 167
Nettichi, river, Can. 51°35' N, 81°41' W 110
Nettilling Lake, Can. 67°30' N, 71°20' W 246
Netzahualcóyotl, Mex. 19°21' N, 99°3' W 114
Neu Kaliss, Ger. 53°9' N, 11°19' E 152
Neuchâtel, Switz. 46°59' N, 6°55' E 150
Neuenhaus, Ger. 52°30' N, 6°58' E 163
Neuenkirchen, Ger. 53°14' N, 8°31' E 163
Neuerburg, Ger. 50°0' N, 6°18' E 167
Neufahrn, Ger. 48°44' N, 12°10' E 152
Neufchâtel, Fr. 49°26' N, 4°1' E 163
Neufchâtel, Fr. 49°43' N, 1°26' E 163
Neugablonz, Ger. 47°55' N, 10°38' E 152
Neuhaus, Ger. 50°31' N, 11°8' E 152
Neuhof, Ger. 50°27' N, 9°37' E 167
Neuillé-Pont-Pierre, Fr. 47°32' N, 0°32' E 150
Neuilly-Saint-Front, Fr. 49°9' N, 3°14' E 163
Neu-Isenburg, Ger. 50°2' N, 8°41' E 167
Neukirchen, Ger. 50°52' N, 9°22' E 167
Neumagen-Dhron, Ger. 49°51' N, 6°54' E 167
Neumarkt, Aust. 47°4' N, 14°25' E 156
Neumarkt, Aust. 48°16' N, 13°43' E 152
Neumayer, Germany, station, Antarctica 70°36' S, 8°23' W 248
Neumünster, Ger. 54°4' N, 9°59' E 152
Neun, river, Laos 20°4' N, 103°52' E 202
Neunkirchen, Aust. 47°42' N, 16°4' E 168
Neunkirchen, Ger. 49°19' N, 7°10' E 163
Neuquén, Arg. 38°57' S, 68°6' W 134
Neuquén, adm. division, Arg. 39°6' S, 71°18' W 134
Neureut, Ger. 49°2' N, 8°22' E 163
Neuse River, N.C., U.S. 35°26' N, 78°9' W 80
Neusiedl, Aust. 47°57' N, 16°50' E 168
Neuss, Ger. 51°11' N, 6°42' E 167
Neuvic, Fr. 45°5' N, 0°28' E 150
Neuville, Fr. 45°52' N, 4°51' E 150
Neuville-lès-Dieppe, Fr. 49°55' N, 1°6' E 163
Neuwied, Ger. 50°25' N, 7°27' E 167
Nevada, Iowa, U.S. 41°59' N, 93°27' W 94
Nevada, Mo., U.S. 37°49' N, 94°21' W 96
Nevada, adm. division, Nev., U.S. 39°15' N, 117°48' W 92
Nevada, Sierra, Calif., U.S. 37°27' N, 119°49' W 100
Nevada, Sierra, Sp. 36°53' N, 3°49' W 164
Nevado de Toluca National Park, Mex. 19°1' N, 100°9' W 72
Neve, Serra da, peak, Angola 13°55' S, 13°27' E 220
Nevel', Russ. 56°1' N, 30°0' E 166
Nevel'sk, Russ. 46°42' N, 141°59' E 190
Never, Russ. 53°56' N, 124°27' E 190
Nevers, Fr. 46°59' N, 3°9' E 150
Neves, Braz. 22°49' S, 43°2' W 138
Nevesinje, Bosn. and Herzg. 43°15' N, 18°5' E 168
Nevėžis, river, Lith. 55°26' N, 24°7' E 166
Nevinnomyssk, Russ. 44°39' N, 42°1' E 158
Nevis, Ben, peak, U.K. 56°46' N, 5°7' W 150
Nevis, island, Saint Kitts and Nevis 17°8' N, 62°35' W 118
Nevşehir, Turk. 38°35' N, 34°41' E 156
Nev'yansk, Russ. 57°32' N, 60°13' E 154
New Aiyansh, Can. 55°14' N, 129°4' W 108
New Albany, Ind., U.S. 38°17' N, 85°49' W 94
New Albany, Miss., U.S. 34°28' N, 89°4' W 112
New Amsterdam, Guyana 6°12' N, 57°30' W 130
New Augusta, Miss., U.S. 31°11' N, 89°1' W 103
New Baltimore, Mich., U.S. 42°39' N, 82°44' W 102
New Baltimore, N.Y., U.S. 42°26' N, 73°48' W 104
New Bedford, Mass., U.S. 41°38' N, 70°57' W 104
New Berlin, Wis., U.S. 42°59' N, 88°7' W 102
New Bern, N.C., U.S. 35°6' N, 77°5' W 96
New Boston, N.H., U.S. 42°57' N, 71°42' W 104
New Boston, Ohio, U.S. 38°45' N, 82°54' W 94
New Boston, Tex., U.S. 33°27' N, 94°27' W 103
New Braunfels, Tex., U.S. 29°41' N, 98°7' W 92
New Bremen, Ohio, U.S. 40°25' N, 84°23' W 102
New Britain, Conn., U.S. 41°39' N, 72°47' W 104
New Britain, island, P.N.G. 6°33' S, 151°20' E 192
New Brunswick, N.J., U.S. 40°27' N, 74°29' W 82
New Brunswick, adm. division, Can. 46°41' N, 66°53' W 94
New Buckenham, U.K. 52°28' N, 1°4' E 162
New Buffalo, Mich., U.S. 41°47' N, 86°44' W 102
New Caledonia Basin, South Pacific Ocean 30°55' S, 165°34' E 252
New Caledonia, island, Fr. 21°22' S, 165°30' E 252
New Canaan, Conn., U.S. 41°8' N, 73°30' W 104
New Caney, Tex., U.S. 30°7' N, 95°13' W 103
New Carlisle, Can. 48°0' N, 65°21' W 94
New Castle, Ind., U.S. 39°55' N, 85°22' W 102
New Castle, Pa., U.S. 41°0' N, 80°21' W 94
New City, N.Y., U.S. 41°8' N, 73°60' W 104
New Concord, Ohio, U.S. 39°59' N, 81°44' W [illegible]
New Cuyama, Calif., U.S. 34°56' N, 119°42' W 100
New Delhi, India 28°33' N, 77°3' E 197
New Denver, Can. 49°59' N, 117°23' W 90
New Durham, N.H., U.S. 43°25' N, 71°11' W 104
New England, N. Dak., U.S. 46°32' N, 102°52' W 90
New England Range, Austral. 30°48' S, 150°30' E 230
New England Seamounts, North Atlantic Ocean 38°16' N, 62°9' W 253
New Fairfield, Conn., U.S. 41°26' N, 73°30' W 104
New Forest, region, U.K. 50°47' N, 1°45' W 162
New Georgia Group, islands, Solomon Sea 8°5' S, 157°19' E 242
New Georgia, island, Solomon Islands 8°20' S, 157°40' E 242
New Georgia Sound (The Slot) 8°11' S, 158°30' E 242
New Glasgow, Can. 45°34' N, 62°40' W 111
New Gloucester, Me., U.S. 43°57' N, 70°17' W 104
New Goshen, Ind., U.S. 39°34' N, 87°28' W 102
New Guinea, island, Indonesia 4°27' S, 131°42' E 192
New Guni, Nig. 9°43' N, 6°56' E 222
New Hamburg, Can. 43°22' N, 80°41' W 102
New Hampshire, adm. division, N.H., U.S. 43°31' N, 71°50' W 104
New Hampton, N.H., U.S. 43°36' N, 71°40' W 104
New Hanover, island, P.N.G. 3°8' S, 149°5' E 192
New Harbor, Me., U.S. 43°52' N, 69°30' W 111
New Hartford, Conn., U.S. 41°52' N, 72°59' W 104
New Haven, Conn., U.S. 41°18' N, 72°56' W 104
New Haven, Ind., U.S. 41°3' N, 85°1' W 102
New Haven, N.Y., U.S. 43°28' N, 76°19' W 94
New Haven, Vt., U.S. 44°7' N, 73°10' W 104
New Hebrides Trench, South Pacific Ocean 23°47' S, 172°15' E 252
New Hebron, Miss., U.S. 31°43' N, 89°59' W 103
New Holstein, Wis., U.S. 43°56' N, 88°6' W 102
New Iberia, La., U.S. 29°58' N, 91°49' W 103
New Ipswich, N.H., U.S. 42°45' N, 71°52' W 104
New Ireland, island, P.N.G. 3°27' S, 149°43' E 192
New Island, New Island 51°50' S, 62°10' W 134
New Jersey, adm. division, N.J., U.S. 41°2' N, 74°51' W 94
New Lebanon, N.Y., U.S. 42°27' N, 73°25' W 104
New Lenox, Ill., U.S. 41°29' N, 87°58' W 102
New Lexington, Ohio, U.S. 39°41' N, 82°12' W 102
New Lisbon, Wis., U.S. 43°51' N, 90°11' W 102
New Liskeard, Can. 47°30' N, 79°41' W 94
New London, Conn., U.S. 41°20' N, 72°7' W 104
New London, N.H., U.S. 43°24' N, 71°59' W 104
New London, Ohio, U.S. 41°4' N, 82°24' W 102
New London, Tex., U.S. 32°14' N, 94°57' W 103
New London, Wis., U.S. 44°23' N, 88°46' W 110
New Madrid, Mo., U.S. 36°35' N, 89°31' W 96
New Market, Ind., U.S. 39°57' N, 86°56' W 102
New Matamoras, Ohio, U.S. 39°31' N, 81°4' W 102
New Meadows, Idaho, U.S. 44°57' N, 116°16' W 90
New Mexico, adm. division, N. Mex., U.S. 34°43' N, 106°25' W 92
New Miami, Ohio, U.S. 39°25' N, 84°32' W 102
New Milford, Conn., U.S. 41°34' N, 73°25' W 104
New Orleans, La., U.S. 29°56' N, 90°5' W 103
New Osnaburgh, Can. 51°12' N, 90°12' W 110
New Paltz, N.Y., U.S. 41°44' N, 74°5' W 104
New Paris, Ohio, U.S. 39°51' N, 84°47' W 102
New Philadelphia, Ohio, U.S. 40°28' N, 81°26' W 102
New Plymouth, Idaho, U.S. 43°57' N, 116°50' W 90
New Plymouth, N.Z. 39°6' S, 174°6' E 240
New Point, Ind., U.S. 39°17' N, 85°20' W 102
New Port Richey, Fla., U.S. 28°15' N, 82°43' W 105
New Prague, Minn., U.S. 44°31' N, 93°36' W 94
New Providence, island, Bahamas 25°1' N, 77°26' W 118
New Radnor, U.K. 52°14' N, 3°9' W 162
New Richmond, Can. 48°10' N, 65°53' W 94
New Richmond, Ohio, U.S. 38°56' N, 84°16' W 102
New Richmond, Wis., U.S. 45°7' N, 92°33' W 94
New, river, Calif., U.S. 33°5' N, 115°43' W 101
New, river, W. Va., U.S. 37°51' N, 81°3' W 94
New Roads, La., U.S. 30°41' N, 91°27' W 103
New Rochelle, N.Y., U.S. 40°55' N, 73°48' W 104
New Rockford, N. Dak., U.S. 47°39' N, 99°10' W 90
New Romney, U.K. 50°59' N, 0°56' E 162
New Salem, Mass., U.S. 42°30' N, 72°20' W 104
New Salem, N. Dak., U.S. 46°49' N, 101°27' W 90
New Schwabenland, region, Antarctica 73°46' S, 13°38' W 248
New Shoreham, R.I., U.S. 41°10' N, 71°34' W 104
New Siberian Islands see Novosi Birskiye Ostrova, Russ. 76°14' N, 142°6' E 160
New Smyrna Beach, Fla., U.S. 29°0' N, 80°56' W 105
New South Wales, adm. division, Austral. 32°28' S, 147°11' E 231
New Summerfield, Tex., U.S. 31°57' N, 95°5' W 103
New Town, N. Dak., U.S. 47°57' N, 102°30' W 90
New Ulm, Minn., U.S. 44°18' N, 94°29' W 90
New Washington, Ind., U.S. 38°33' N, 85°33' W 102

ew Waterford, *Can.* 46°14' N, 60°6' W **111**
ew Waverly, *Tex., U.S.* 30°31' N, 95°29' W **103**
ew Willard, *Tex., U.S.* 30°46' N, 94°53' W **103**
ew Windsor, *N.Y., U.S.* 41°28' N, 74°1' W **104**
ew York, *N.Y., U.S.* 40°43' N, 74°1' W **104**
ew York, adm. division, *N.Y., U.S.* 42°56' N, 76°33' W **94**
ew York Mountains, *Calif., U.S.* 35°22' N, 115°20' W **101**
ew York Mountains, *Calif., U.S.* 35°22' N, 115°26' W **80**
ew Zealand 42°2' S, 173°5' E **240**
ewala, *Tanzania* 10°58' S, 39°16' E **224**
ewark, *Ark., U.S.* 35°41' N, 91°26' W **96**
ewark, *Ill., U.S.* 41°32' N, 88°35' W **102**
ewark, *N.J., U.S.* 40°43' N, 74°12' W **94**
ewark, *N.Y., U.S.* 43°2' N, 77°6' W **94**
ewark, *Ohio, U.S.* 40°3' N, 82°25' W **102**
ewark, *U.K.* 53°4' N, 0°49' E **162**
ewaygo, *Mich., U.S.* 43°24' N, 85°48' W **102**
ewbald, *U.K.* 53°49' N, 0°38' E **162**
ewbern, *Ala., U.S.* 32°35' N, 87°32' W **103**
ewbern, *Tenn., U.S.* 36°6' N, 89°17' W **96**
ewberry, *Fla., U.S.* 29°38' N, 82°37' W **105**
ewberry, *Mich., U.S.* 46°21' N, 85°31' W **94**
ewberry Springs, *Calif., U.S.* 34°49' N, 116°42' W **101**
ewbrook, *Can.* 54°18' N, 112°58' W **108**
ewburgh, *N.Y., U.S.* 41°30' N, 74°2' W **104**
ewbury, *U.K.* 51°23' N, 1°20' W **162**
ewbury, *Vt., U.S.* 44°4' N, 72°4' W **104**
ewburyport, *Mass., U.S.* 42°48' N, 70°53' W **104**
ewcastle, *Can.* 47°0' N, 65°35' W **94**
ewcastle, *S. Af.* 27°46' S, 29°55' E **227**
ewcastle, *Tex., U.S.* 33°10' N, 98°44' W **92**
ewcastle, *U.K.* 54°12' N, 5°55' W **150**
ewcastle, *U.K.* 54°58' N, 1°38' W **162**
ewcastle, *Wyo., U.S.* 43°49' N, 104°12' W **90**
ewcastle Bay 10°58' S, 141°25' E **230**
ewcastle under Lyme, *U.K.* 53°0' N, 2°15' W **162**
ewcastle Waters, *Austral.* 17°23' S, 133°23' E **231**
ewcomb, *N.Y., U.S.* 43°57' N, 74°11' W **104**
ewcomb, *Tenn., U.S.* 36°32' N, 84°10' W **96**
ewcomerstown, *Ohio, U.S.* 40°16' N, 81°36' W **102**
ewell, *Ark., U.S.* 33°8' N, 92°45' W **103**
ewell, *S. Dak., U.S.* 44°42' N, 103°25' W **90**
ewell, Lake, *Can.* 50°19' N, 112°29' W **90**
ewellton, *La., U.S.* 32°3' N, 91°16' W **103**
ewenham, Cape, *Alas., U.S.* 58°18' N, 162°19' W **106**
ewenham, Cape, *Alas., U.S.* 58°38' N, 164°32' W **98**
ewfields, *N.H., U.S.* 43°2' N, 70°57' W **104**
ewfoundland and Labrador, adm. division, *Can.* 48°5' N, 58°29' W **111**
ewfoundland, Island of, *Can.* 48°58' N, 53°21' W **106**
ewgrange Mound, ruin(s), *Ire.* 53°40' N, 6°36' W **150**
ewhalem, *Wash., U.S.* 48°40' N, 121°17' W **100**
ewhalen, *Alas., U.S.* 59°39' N, 155°1' W **98**
ewhaven, *U.K.* 50°47' N, 4°238' E **162**
ewington, *Conn., U.S.* 41°41' N, 72°44' W **104**
ewkirk, *N. Mex., U.S.* 35°4' N, 104°16' W **92**
ewkirk, *Okla., U.S.* 36°52' N, 97°3' W **92**
ewllano, *La., U.S.* 31°5' N, 93°17' W **103**
ewman, *Calif., U.S.* 37°18' N, 121°3' W **100**
ewman, *Ill., U.S.* 39°47' N, 87°60' W **102**
ewman Island, island, *Antarctica* 75°13' S, 146°2' W **248**
ewman, Mount, peak, *Austral.* 23°17' S, 119°19' E **230**
ewmarket, *Can.* 44°2' N, 79°28' W **94**
ewmarket, *N.H., U.S.* 43°4' N, 70°57' W **104**
ewmarket, *U.K.* 52°14' N, 0°24' E **162**
ewnan, *Ga., U.S.* 33°22' N, 84°48' W **112**
ewport, *Ark., U.S.* 35°34' N, 91°18' W **82**
ewport, *Ind., U.S.* 39°51' N, 87°25' W **102**
ewport, *Mich., U.S.* 41°59' N, 83°18' W **102**
ewport, *N.H., U.S.* 43°22' N, 72°11' W **104**
ewport, *Oreg., U.S.* 44°38' N, 124°5' W **82**
ewport, *R.I., U.S.* 41°29' N, 71°19' W **104**
ewport, *Tenn., U.S.* 35°57' N, 83°12' W **96**
ewport, *U.K.* 50°41' N, 1°18' W **162**
ewport, *U.K.* 51°35' N, 2°60' W **162**
ewport, *U.K.* 52°45' N, 2°23' W **162**
ewport, *Vt., U.S.* 44°56' N, 72°13' W **82**
ewport, *Wash., U.S.* 48°10' N, 117°4' W **108**
ewport Beach, *Calif., U.S.* 33°38' N, 117°57' W **101**
ewport News, *Va., U.S.* 36°58' N, 76°26' W **94**
ewport Pagnell, *U.K.* 52°4' N, 0°44' E **162**
ewry, *Me., U.S.* 44°29' N, 70°48' W **104**
ewry, *S.C., U.S.* 34°43' N, 82°56' W **96**
ewsome, *Tex., U.S.* 32°57' N, 95°8' W **103**
ewtok, *Alas., U.S.* 60°57' N, 164°37' W **98**
ewton, *Ill., U.S.* 38°58' N, 88°11' W **102**
ewton, *Iowa, U.S.* 41°41' N, 93°3' W **94**
ewton, *Kans., U.S.* 38°2' N, 97°21' W **90**
ewton, *Mass., U.S.* 42°19' N, 71°15' W **104**
ewton, *Miss., U.S.* 32°18' N, 89°9' W **103**
ewton, *Mo., U.S.* 38°58' N, 88°11' W **94**
ewton, *Tex., U.S.* 30°49' N, 93°46' W **103**
ewton Falls, *Ohio, U.S.* 41°10' N, 80°58' W **102**
ewtown, *Conn., U.S.* 41°24' N, 73°19' W **104**
ewtown, *U.K.* 52°30' N, 3°18' W **162**
ew-Wes-Valley, *Can.* 49°9' N, 53°35' W **111**
expa, river, *Mex.* 18°7' N, 102°40' W **114**
eya, *Russ.* 58°17' N, 43°52' E **154**
eyrīz, *Iran* 29°12' N, 54°18' E **196**
eyshābūr, *Iran* 36°12' N, 58°51' E **180**
eyto, Ozero, lake, *Russ.* 69°51' N, 68°36' E **169**
eyvo Shaytanskiy, *Russ.* 57°46' N, 61°14' E **154**
ez Perce Pass, *Mont., U.S.* 45°42' N, 114°31' W **90**
ezperce, *Idaho, U.S.* 46°13' N, 116°14' W **90**
'Gabé, *Congo* 3°14' S, 16°8' E **218**
gahere, *N.Z.* 42°25' S, 171°27' E **240**
Ngambé, *Cameroon* 4°15' N, 10°39' E **222**
Ngamda, *China* 31°5' N, 96°37' E **188**
Ngamring, *China* 29°17' N, 87°11' E **197**
Ngangla Ringco, lake, *China* 31°40' N, 82°35' E **188**
Nganglong Kangri, peak, *China* 32°50' N, 80°41' E **188**
Ngangzê Co, lake, *China* 30°56' N, 86°20' E **197**
N'Gao, *Congo* 2°30' S, 15°45' E **218**
Ngao, *Thai.* 18°46' N, 99°57' E **202**
Ngaoundal, *Cameroon* 6°26' N, 13°25' E **218**
Ngaoundéré, *Cameroon* 7°16' N, 13°34' E **218**
Ngaputaw, *Myanmar* 16°31' N, 94°42' E **188**
Ngara, *Tanzania* 2°31' S, 30°39' E **224**
Ngaruawahia, *N.Z.* 37°43' S, 175°10' E **240**
Ngauruhoe, Mount, peak, *N.Z.* 39°12' S, 175°32' E **240**
Ngayu, river, *Dem. Rep. of the Congo* 1°53' N, 27°25' E **224**
Ngcheangel, island, *Palau* 8°4' N, 134°43' E **242**
Ngeaur see Angaur, island, *Palau* 7°0' N, 134°0' E **242**
Ngerengere, *Tanzania* 6°42' S, 38°7' E **224**
Ngeruktabel see Urukthapel, island, *Palau* 7°13' N, 134°24' E **242**
Nggatokae, island, *Solomon Islands* 8°45' S, 158°10' E **242**
Nghia Lo, *Vietnam* 21°37' N, 104°28' E **202**
Ngoïla, *Cameroon* 2°45' N, 14°0' E **218**
Ngoko, *Congo* 0°35' N, 15°21' E **218**
Ngola Shankou, pass, *China* 35°30' N, 99°28' E **188**
Ngomba, *Tanzania* 8°25' S, 32°54' E **224**
Ngomeni, Ras, *Kenya* 2°59' S, 40°14' E **224**
Ngong, *Kenya* 1°23' S, 36°40' E **224**
Ngop, *Sudan* 6°13' N, 30°10' E **224**
Ngoqumaima, *China* 32°30' N, 86°51' E **188**
Ngorno-Karabakh, special sovereignty, *Asia* 39°59' N, 46°23' E **195**
Ngorongoro Crater, peak, *Tanzania* 3°15' S, 35°31' E **224**
Ngoto, *Cen. Af. Rep.* 4°4' N, 17°18' E **218**
Ngouo, Mont, peak, *Cen. Af. Rep.* 7°55' N, 24°32' E **224**
Ngouri, *Chad* 13°39' N, 15°23' E **216**
Ngourti, *Niger* 15°19' N, 13°11' E **216**
Ngoywa, *Tanzania* 5°55' S, 32°47' E **224**
Ngozi, *Burundi* 2°56' S, 29°47' E **224**
Ngudu, *Tanzania* 2°56' S, 33°21' E **224**
Nguigmi, *Niger* 14°17' N, 13°6' E **216**
Ngukurr, *Austral.* 14°44' S, 134°46' E **238**
Ngulu Atoll, *F.S.M.* 8°42' N, 134°55' E **192**
Ngum, river, *Laos* 18°47' N, 102°47' E **202**
N'gungo, *Angola* 11°47' S, 14°9' E **220**
Nguni, *Kenya* 0°49' N, 38°17' E **224**
Nguru, *Nig.* 12°53' N, 10°28' E **222**
Ngurumahija, *Tanzania* 10°18' S, 37°57' E **224**
Nha Trang, *Vietnam* 12°15' N, 109°10' E **202**
Nhamundá, *Braz.* 2°13' S, 56°44' W **130**
Nhamundá, river, *Braz.* 1°33' S, 57°60' W **132**
Nhecolândia, *Braz.* 19°15' S, 57°1' W **132**
Nho Quan, *Vietnam* 20°20' N, 105°45' E **202**
Nhulunbuy, *Austral.* 12°18' S, 136°48' E **238**
Nia Nia, *Dem. Rep. of the Congo* 1°29' N, 27°40' E **224**
Niabembe, *Dem. Rep. of the Congo* 2°11' S, 27°40' E **224**
Niadi, *Dem. Rep. of the Congo* 4°25' S, 18°50' E **218**
Niafounké, *Mali* 15°56' N, 4°1' W **222**
Niagassola, *Guinea* 12°20' N, 9°8' W **222**
Niamey, *Niger* 13°29' N, 2°0' E **222**
Niandan Koro, *Guinea* 11°6' N, 9°14' W **222**
Niangara, *Dem. Rep. of the Congo* 3°41' N, 27°53' E **224**
Niangay, Lac, lake, *Mali* 15°54' N, 3°22' W **222**
Niangoloko, *Burkina Faso* 10°17' N, 4°56' W **222**
Niantic, *Conn., U.S.* 41°19' N, 72°12' W **104**
Niantic, *Ill., U.S.* 39°50' N, 89°10' W **102**
Nianzishan, *China* 47°33' N, 122°54' E **198**
Niapidou, *Côte d'Ivoire* 5°18' N, 6°3' W **222**
Niapu, *Dem. Rep. of the Congo* 2°24' N, 26°32' E **224**
Niari, river, *Congo* 3°33' S, 12°45' E **218**
Nias, island, *Indonesia* 0°26' N, 97°33' E **196**
Niassa, adm. division, *Mozambique* 12°52' S, 35°24' E **224**
Niaza, spring, *Mauritania* 18°13' N, 10°60' W **222**
Nīca, *Latv.* 56°21' N, 21°1' E **166**
Nicaragua 12°38' N, 85°49' W **115**
Nicaragua, Lago de, *Nicar.* 11°30' N, 85°30' W **116**
Nice, *Fr.* 43°42' N, 7°15' E **167**
Nichihara, *Japan* 34°31' N, 131°51' E **201**
Nichinan, *Japan* 31°36' N, 131°21' E **201**
Nicholasville, *Ky., U.S.* 37°52' N, 84°34' W **96**
Nicholls' Town, *Bahamas* 25°7' N, 78°2' W **96**
Nichollstown and Berry Islands, adm. division, *Bahamas* 25°47' N, 78°22' W **96**
Nicholson, *Can.* 47°58' N, 83°46' W **94**
Nickel Centre, *Can.* 46°33' N, 80°52' W **94**
Nickelsdorf, *Aust.* 47°56' N, 17°4' E **168**
Nickerson, *Kans., U.S.* 38°8' N, 98°6' W **90**
Nickol Bay 20°40' S, 115°56' E **230**
Nicobar Islands, *Andaman Sea* 8°59' N, 93°39' E **192**
Nicolás Bravo, *Mex.* 24°21' N, 104°44' W **114**
Nicolet, *Can.* 46°13' N, 72°37' W **94**
Nicopolis, ruin(s), *Gr.* 38°59' N, 20°37' E **156**
Nicopolis see Suşehri, *Turk.* 40°8' N, 38°5' E **180**
Nicosia see Lefkosia, *Cyprus* 35°9' N, 33°18' E **194**
Nicotera, *It.* 38°34' N, 15°55' E **156**
Nicoya, *C.R.* 10°8' N, 85°26' W **115**
Nicuadala, *Mozambique* 17°38' S, 36°48' E **224**
Nida, *Russ.* 55°19' N, 21°2' E **166**
Nidda, *Ger.* 50°24' N, 9°1' E **167**
Niddatal, *Ger.* 50°17' N, 8°48' E **167**
Nidder, river, *Ger.* 50°22' N, 9°3' E **167**
Nidže, *Maced.* 41°1' N, 21°41' E **156**
Nidzh, *Azerb.* 40°57' N, 47°39' E **195**
Niebla, *Sp.* 37°21' N, 6°42' W **164**
Niechorze, *Pol.* 54°5' N, 15°4' E **152**
Nied, river, *Fr.* 49°5' N, 6°20' E **163**
Nieddu, Monte, peak, *It.* 40°44' N, 9°30' E **156**
Niederaula, *Ger.* 50°48' N, 9°35' E **167**
Niederbronn, *Fr.* 48°57' N, 7°38' E **163**
Niedere Tauern, *Aust.* 47°11' N, 13°24' E **156**
Niedoradz, *Pol.* 51°52' N, 15°40' E **152**
Niéjirane, spring, *Mauritania* 17°32' N, 9°51' W **222**
Niem, *Cen. Af. Rep.* 6°5' N, 15°15' E **218**
Niemba, *Dem. Rep. of the Congo* 5°59' S, 28°24' E **224**
Niéna, *Mali* 11°26' N, 6°21' W **222**
Niers, river, *Ger.* 51°41' N, 5°58' E **167**
Nierstein, *Ger.* 49°52' N, 8°20' E **167**
Nieuw Amsterdam, *Suriname* 5°50' N, 55°6' W **130**
Nieuwe Pekela, *Neth.* 53°4' N, 6°56' E **163**
Nieuwpoort, *Belg.* 51°7' N, 2°44' E **163**
Nieves, *Bol.* 14°5' S, 65°54' W **137**
Nieves, *Mex.* 24°0' N, 103°2' W **114**
Nif, *Indonesia* 3°19' S, 130°34' E **192**
Niğde, *Turk.* 37°58' N, 34°42' E **180**
Niger 17°56' N, 8°41' E **216**
Niger Delta, *Nig.* 5°29' N, 6°7' E **222**
Niger, river, *Africa* 5°54' N, 6°33' E **222**
Nigeria 9°25' N, 6°46' E **218**
Nightingale Island see Bach Long Vi, Dao, *Vietnam* 19°46' N, 107°30' E **198**
Nihonmatsu, *Japan* 37°35' N, 140°26' E **201**
Niigata, *Japan* 37°55' N, 139°5' E **201**
Niigata, adm. division, *Japan* 37°27' N, 138°42' E **201**
Niihama, *Japan* 33°56' N, 133°17' E **201**
Ni'ihau, island, *Hawai'i, U.S.* 21°36' N, 160°11' W **99**
Niimi, *Japan* 35°0' N, 133°28' E **201**
Niitsu, *Japan* 37°47' N, 139°8' E **201**
Níjar, *Sp.* 36°57' N, 2°13' W **164**
Nijmegen, *Neth.* 51°50' N, 5°51' E **167**
Nīk Pey, *Iran* 36°52' N, 48°12' E **195**
Nikel', *Russ.* 69°24' N, 30°10' E **152**
Nikiniki, *Indonesia* 9°49' S, 124°28' E **192**
Nikiski, *Gulf of Alaska* 60°43' N, 151°18' W **98**
Nikitin Seamount, *Indian Ocean* 3°48' S, 82°58' E **254**
Nikki, *Benin* 9°56' N, 3°9' E **222**
Nikkō, *Japan* 36°43' N, 139°37' E **201**
Nikkō National Park, *Japan* 37°3' N, 139°40' E **201**
Nikolai, *Alas., U.S.* 63°0' N, 154°11' W **98**
Nikolayevo, *Russ.* 58°15' N, 29°28' E **166**
Nikolayevsk, *Russ.* 50°3' N, 45°33' E **158**
Nikolayevsk na Amure, *Russ.* 53°14' N, 140°36' E **190**
Nikolo Berezovka, *Russ.* 56°6' N, 54°18' E **154**
Nikol'sk, *Russ.* 53°41' N, 46°7' E **154**
Nikol'sk, *Russ.* 59°30' N, 45°32' E **154**
Nikol'skoye, *Russ.* 52°4' N, 55°42' E **154**
Nikol'skoye, *Russ.* 47°43' N, 46°21' E **158**
Nikol'skoye, *Russ.* 55°13' N, 165°54' E **160**
Nikonga, river, *Tanzania* 4°2' S, 31°30' E **224**
Nikopol', *Ukr.* 47°34' N, 34°24' E **156**
Niksar, *Turk.* 40°35' N, 36°57' E **156**
Nīkshahr, *Iran* 26°13' N, 60°13' E **182**
Nikšić, *Europe* 42°46' N, 18°56' E **168**
Nikulino, *Russ.* 60°21' N, 90°1' E **169**
Niland, *Calif., U.S.* 33°14' N, 115°32' W **101**
Nilandu Atoll, *Maldives* 2°56' N, 72°16' E **188**
Nilandu, island, *Maldives* 0°27' N, 73°24' E **188**
Nile, river, *Africa* 27°17' N, 31°18' E **206**
Niles, *Mich., U.S.* 41°48' N, 86°15' W **102**
Niles, *Ohio, U.S.* 41°10' N, 80°45' W **94**
Nili, *Alg.* 33°24' N, 3°2' E **214**
Nilka, *China* 43°47' N, 82°38' E **184**
Nilsen, Mount, peak, *Antarctica* 77°54' S, 154°11' W **248**
Nilsen Plateau, *Antarctica* 86°27' S, 180°0' E **248**
Nilsiä, *Fin.* 63°12' N, 28°0' E **152**
Nimach, *India* 24°27' N, 74°51' E **188**
Nimba Mountains, *Guinea* 8°22' N, 9°5' W **222**
Nimbahera, *India* 24°38' N, 74°40' E **188**
Nimberra Well, spring, *Austral.* 23°6' S, 123°18' E **230**
Nîmes, *Fr.* 43°49' N, 4°22' E **214**
Nimfai, *Gr.* 39°45' N, 19°47' E **156**
Nimule, *Sudan* 3°34' N, 32°5' E **224**
Nin, *Croatia* 44°14' N, 15°9' E **156**
Ninayeri, *Nicar.* 14°27' N, 83°18' W **115**
Ninda, *Angola* 14°54' S, 21°25' E **220**
Nine Degree Channel 8°40' N, 71°55' E **188**
Ninemile Peak, *Nev., U.S.* 39°8' N, 116°20' W **90**
Ninety East Ridge, *Indian Ocean* 8°11' S, 88°50' E **254**
Ninety Mile Beach, *N.Z.* 35°3' S, 172°43' E **240**
Nineveh, ruin(s), *Iraq* 36°21' N, 42°59' E **195**
Ninfas, Punta, *Arg.* 43°10' S, 64°20' W **134**
Ning'an, *China* 44°20' N, 129°32' E **190**
Ningbo, *China* 29°54' N, 121°29' E **198**
Ningcheng, *China* 41°34' N, 119°20' E **198**
Ningde, *China* 26°40' N, 119°31' E **198**
Ningdu, *China* 26°26' N, 115°55' E **198**
Ningguo, *China* 30°34' N, 119°1' E **198**
Ningi, *Nig.* 11°3' N, 9°32' E **222**
Ningming, *China* 22°5' N, 107°1' E **198**
Ningshan, *China* 33°20' N, 108°19' E **198**
Ningwu, *China* 39°0' N, 112°13' E **198**
Ningxia, adm. division, *China* 36°46' N, 105°17' E **198**
Ningyuan, *China* 25°36' N, 111°56' E **198**
Ninh Binh, *Vietnam* 20°14' N, 105°56' E **198**
Ninh Hoa, *Vietnam* 12°30' N, 109°8' E **202**
Ninigo Group, islands, *South Pacific Ocean* 0°49' N, 142°30' E **192**
Ninigo Islands, islands, *South Pacific Ocean* 1°10' S, 142°49' E **192**
Ninilchik, *Gulf of Alaska* 60°3' N, 151°39' W **98**
Nioaque, *Braz.* 21°9' S, 55°50' W **132**
Niobrara, river, *Nebr., U.S.* 42°37' N, 102°2' W **90**
Nioka, *Dem. Rep. of the Congo* 2°8' N, 30°39' E **224**
Nioki, *Dem. Rep. of the Congo* 2°44' S, 17°38' E **218**
Niokolo-Koba National Park, *Senegal* 13°2' N, 13°30' W **222**
Niono, *Mali* 14°16' N, 5°60' W **222**
Nioro du Sahel, *Mali* 15°14' N, 9°38' W **222**
Niort, *Fr.* 46°19' N, 0°28' E **150**
Niout, spring, *Mauritania* 16°3' N, 6°52' W **222**
Nipa, oil field, *Venez.* 9°6' N, 64°8' W **116**
Nipani, *India* 16°24' N, 74°23' E **188**
Nipawin, *Can.* 53°21' N, 104°1' W **108**
Nipigon, *Can.* 49°1' N, 88°16' W **94**
Nipigon Bay 48°50' N, 89°13' W **80**
Nipigon, Lake, *Can.* 50°12' N, 88°35' W **94**
Nipin, river, *Can.* 55°24' N, 109°25' W **108**
Nipissing, Lake, *Can.* 46°21' N, 80°13' W **80**
Nipomo, *Calif., U.S.* 35°2' N, 120°29' W **100**
Nipple, The, peak, *Can.* 49°56' N, 121°38' W **100**
Nipton, *Calif., U.S.* 35°27' N, 115°17' W **101**
Niquelândia, *Braz.* 14°33' S, 48°30' W **138**
Niquero, *Cuba* 20°2' N, 77°34' W **115**
Nīr, *Iran* 38°3' N, 47°59' E **195**
Nir Yizhaq, *Israel* 31°14' N, 34°21' E **194**
Nir'am, *Israel* 31°30' N, 34°34' E **194**
Nirasaki, *Japan* 35°41' N, 138°27' E **201**
Ñire Có, *Arg.* 36°60' S, 68°28' W **134**
Nirji see Morin Dawa, *China* 48°27' N, 124°30' E **198**
Nirmal, *India* 19°6' N, 78°20' E **188**
Nirmali, *India* 26°18' N, 86°34' E **197**
Niš, *Serb. and Mont.* 43°18' N, 21°54' E **168**
Nişāb, *Saudi Arabia* 29°8' N, 44°44' E **180**
Nişāb, *Yemen* 14°31' N, 46°33' E **182**
Nišava, river, *Serb. and Mont.* 43°18' N, 22°7' E **168**
Nishi Nasuno, *Japan* 36°52' N, 139°58' E **201**
Nishikō, *Japan* 32°36' N, 130°27' E **201**
Nishinomiya, *Japan* 34°44' N, 135°18' E **201**
Nishio, *Japan* 34°50' N, 137°4' E **201**
Nishiwaki, *Japan* 34°58' N, 134°57' E **201**
Nishtūn, *Yemen* 15°48' N, 52°10' E **182**
Niska, *Fin.* 64°35' N, 26°33' E **152**
Niskayuna, *N.Y., U.S.* 42°45' N, 73°51' W **104**
Nissedal, *Nor.* 59°9' N, 8°30' E **152**
Nissi, *Est.* 59°4' N, 24°17' E **166**
Nissilä, *Fin.* 63°56' N, 26°48' E **152**
Nisswa, *Minn., U.S.* 46°30' N, 94°18' W **90**
Niţā', *Saudi Arabia* 27°10' N, 48°23' E **196**
Nītaure, *Latv.* 57°3' N, 25°7' E **166**
Nitchequon, *Can.* 53°12' N, 70°53' W **111**
Niterói, *Braz.* 22°56' S, 43°3' W **138**
Nitmiluk National Park, *Austral.* 14°16' S, 132°7' E **238**
Nitra, *Slovakia* 48°18' N, 18°6' E **168**
Nitransky, adm. division, *Slovakia* 48°10' N, 17°51' E **152**
Nitro, *W. Va., U.S.* 38°25' N, 81°51' W **94**
Nitsa, river, *Russ.* 57°45' N, 63°3' E **154**
Niue, island, *N.Z.* 18°58' S, 169°55' W **238**
Niut, peak, *Indonesia* 0°59' N, 109°50' E **196**
Niutou Shan, island, *China* 28°54' N, 121°49' E **198**
Niuxintai, *China* 41°20' N, 123°55' E **200**
Niva, *Fin.* 65°9' N, 28°21' E **152**
Niva, *Russ.* 61°36' N, 30°14' E **166**
Nivala, *Fin.* 63°54' N, 24°55' E **152**
Nivelles, *Belg.* 50°35' N, 4°19' E **163**
Nivernais, region, *Fr.* 47°30' N, 3°17' E **165**
Nivshera, *Russ.* 62°24' N, 53°1' E **154**
Nixon, *Tex., U.S.* 29°15' N, 97°45' W **92**
Nizamabad, *India* 18°40' N, 78°5' E **188**
Nizamghat, *India* 28°14' N, 95°43' E **188**
Nizao, *Dom. Rep.* 18°14' N, 70°13' W **116**
Nizhnekamsk, *Russ.* 55°33' N, 51°53' E **154**
Nizhneshadrino, *Russ.* 59°53' N, 90°38' E **169**
Nizhneudinsk, *Russ.* 54°53' N, 99°14' E **190**
Nizhnevartovsk, *Russ.* 60°54' N, 76°35' E **169**
Nizhniy Baskunchak, *Russ.* 48°11' N, 46°42' E **158**
Nizhniy Lomov, *Russ.* 53°30' N, 43°40' E **154**
Nizhniy Novgorod, *Russ.* 56°15' N, 44°0' E **154**
Nizhniy Novgorod, adm. division, *Russ.* 56°0' N, 43°9' E **154**
Nizhniy Tagil, *Russ.* 57°56' N, 59°59' E **154**
Nizhniy Ufaley, *Russ.* 55°56' N, 60°3' E **154**
Nizhniye Nikulyasy, *Russ.* 60°27' N, 30°44' E **152**
Nizhniye Sergi, *Russ.* 56°40' N, 59°16' E **154**
Nizhnyaya Mgla, *Russ.* 66°29' N, 44°27' E **154**
Nizhnyaya Omra, *Russ.* 62°46' N, 55°51' E **154**
Nizhnyaya Pesha, *Russ.* 66°46' N, 47°38' E **154**
Nizhnyaya Salda, *Russ.* 58°5' N, 60°44' E **154**
Nizhnyaya Tunguska, river, *Russ.* 64°30' N, 90°34' E **169**
Nizhnyaya Tura, *Russ.* 58°41' N, 59°49' E **154**
Nizhnyaya Voch', *Russ.* 61°12' N, 54°11' E **154**
Nizhyn, *Ukr.* 51°2' N, 31°53' E **158**
Nizi, *Dem. Rep. of the Congo* 1°44' N, 30°17' E **224**
Nizip, *Turk.* 36°58' N, 37°50' E **180**
Nízke Tatry, *Slovakia* 48°51' N, 19°24' E **152**
Nizwá, *Oman* 22°55' N, 57°31' E **182**
Nizza Monferrato, *It.* 44°46' N, 8°21' E **167**
Nizzana (El'Auja), *Israel* 30°52' N, 34°25' E **194**
Njazidja, island, *Comoros* 11°46' S, 43°35' E **220**
Njegoš, peak, *Europe* 42°54' N, 18°43' E **168**
Njegoševo, *Serb. and Mont.* 45°45' N, 19°44' E **168**
Njombe, *Tanzania* 9°22' S, 34°45' E **224**
Njombe, river, *Tanzania* 7°22' S, 34°8' E **224**
Njunnesvarre, peak, *Nor.* 68°45' N, 19°17' E **152**
Njurunda, *Nor.* 62°14' N, 17°20' E **152**
Nkambe, *Cameroon* 6°29' N, 10°43' E **222**
Nkawkaw, *Ghana* 6°33' N, 0°46' E **222**
Nkayi, *Zimb.* 19°3' S, 28°55' E **224**
Nkhata Bay, *Malawi* 11°35' S, 34°17' E **224**
Nkhotakota, *Malawi* 12°56' S, 34°15' E **224**
Nkhunga, *Malawi* 12°29' S, 34°3' E **224**
Nkongsamba, *Cameroon* 4°53' N, 9°56' E **222**
Nkoul, *Cameroon* 3°30' N, 13°33' E **218**
Nkululu, river, *Tanzania* 6°19' S, 32°39' E **224**
Nkurenkuru, *Namibia* 17°39' S, 18°36' E **220**
Nkusi, river, *Uganda* 1°8' N, 30°56' E **224**
No, Lake, *Sudan* 9°22' N, 30°7' E **224**
Noamundi, *India* 22°11' N, 85°31' E **197**
Noarvas, peak, *Nor.* 68°47' N, 24°35' E **152**
Noatak, *Alas., U.S.* 67°29' N, 163°5' W **98**
Noatak, river, *Alas., U.S.* 68°4' N, 159°51' W **98**
Nobeoka, *Japan* 32°35' N, 131°39' E **201**
Noble, *Ill., U.S.* 38°41' N, 88°14' W **102**
Noble, *La., U.S.* 31°40' N, 93°42' W **103**
Noblesville, *Ind., U.S.* 40°2' N, 85°60' W **102**
Nobska Point, *Mass., U.S.* 41°28' N, 70°40' W **104**
Nocatee, *Fla., U.S.* 27°10' N, 81°53' W **105**
Noce, river, *It.* 46°16' N, 10°59' E **167**
Noceto, *It.* 44°48' N, 10°10' E **167**
Nochistlán, *Mex.* 21°20' N, 102°52' W **114**
Nochixtlán, *Mex.* 17°26' N, 97°14' W **114**
Nocona, *Tex., U.S.* 33°46' N, 97°42' W **92**
Nodales, Bahía de los 48°5' S, 67°43' W **134**
Nodaway, river, *Iowa, U.S.* 40°1' N, 95°9' W **80**
Noel Kempff Mercado National Park, *Bol.* 14°31' S, 62°11' W **132**
Noel, Mount, peak, *Can.* 50°43' N, 122°56' W **90**
Noelville, *Can.* 46°7' N, 80°26' W **94**
Nofre, Peña, peak, *Sp.* 42°0' N, 7°26' W **150**
Nogales, *Ariz., U.S.* 31°21' N, 110°57' W **112**
Nogáles, *Mex.* 31°17' N, 110°57' W **92**
Nogara, *It.* 45°10' N, 11°3' E **167**
Nōgata, *Japan* 33°43' N, 130°42' E **200**
Nogayskaya Step', *Russ.* 44°29' N, 46°3' E **180**
Nogayty, *Kaz.* 45°17' N, 55°55' E **158**
Nogent-le-Roi, *Fr.* 48°38' N, 1°32' E **163**
Nogent-le-Rotrou, *Fr.* 48°19' N, 0°49' E **163**
Nogent-sur-Seine, *Fr.* 48°29' N, 3°30' E **163**
Noginsk, *Russ.* 64°25' N, 91°16' E **169**
Nogliki, *Russ.* 51°47' N, 143°4' E **190**
Nógrád, adm. division, *Hung.* 47°58' N, 19°1' E **156**
Nohar, *India* 29°11' N, 74°47' E **186**
Nohfelden, *Ger.* 49°34' N, 7°8' E **163**
Nohona o Hae, peak, *Hawai'i, U.S.* 19°54' N, 155°44' W **99**
Noia, *Sp.* 42°47' N, 8°55' W **150**
Noir, Isla, island, *Chile* 54°23' S, 74°10' W **134**
Noire, Montagne, peak, *Fr.* 43°25' N, 2°25' E **165**
Noire, river, *Can.* 46°46' N, 77°41' W **94**
Noires, Montagnes, *Fr.* 48°2' N, 4°9' W **150**
Nojima Zaki, *Japan* 34°45' N, 139°53' E **201**
Nok Kundi, *Pak.* 28°49' N, 62°47' E **182**
Nokaneng, *Botswana* 19°41' S, 22°11' E **220**
Nokara, *Mali* 15°10' N, 2°24' W **222**
Nokia, *Fin.* 61°28' N, 23°31' E **166**
Nokola, *Russ.* 61°10' N, 38°51' E **154**
Nokomis, *Can.* 51°30' N, 105°2' W **90**
Nokomis, *Ill., U.S.* 39°17' N, 89°17' W **102**
Nokou, *Chad* 14°35' N, 14°45' E **216**
Nola, *Cen. Af. Rep.* 3°42' N, 16°5' E **218**
Noli, *It.* 44°12' N, 8°25' E **167**
Nolinsk, *Russ.* 57°33' N, 49°57' E **154**
Noma Misaki, *Japan* 31°16' N, 129°55' E **201**
Nomans Land, island, *Mass., U.S.* 41°11' N, 70°52' W **104**
Nomansland Point, *Can.* 52°1' N, 81°2' W **110**
Nombre de Dios, *Mex.* 23°49' N, 104°14' W **114**
Nombre de Dios, *Mex.* 28°42' N, 106°7' W **92**
Nome, *Alas., U.S.* 64°25' N, 165°28' W **98**
Nome, *Tex., U.S.* 30°1' N, 94°26' W **103**
Nome Lake, *Can.* 59°38' N, 131°35' W **108**
Nomgon, *Mongolia* 42°52' N, 104°53' E **198**
Nomhon, *China* 36°22' N, 96°26' E **188**
Nomhon, river, *China* 36°31' N, 96°27' E **188**
Nomo Saki, *Japan* 32°28' N, 129°35' E **201**
Nomoneas, island, *F.S.M.* 7°25' N, 151°52' E **242**
Nomwin Atoll, *F.S.M.* 9°13' N, 150°41' E **192**
Nonancourt, *Fr.* 48°46' N, 1°12' E **163**
Nonburg, *Russ.* 65°33' N, 50°32' E **154**
Nondalton, *Alas., U.S.* 59°56' N, 154°60' W **98**
Nong Khai, *Thai.* 17°52' N, 102°44' E **202**
Nong'an, *China* 44°27' N, 125°11' E **198**
Nongoma, *S. Af.* 27°54' S, 31°37' E **227**
Nongpoh, *India* 25°51' N, 91°51' E **197**
Nono, *Eth.* 8°30' N, 37°22' E **224**
Nonoava, *Mex.* 27°28' N, 106°44' W **112**
Nonsan, *S. Korea* 36°11' N, 127°6' E **200**
Nonthaburi, *Thai.* 13°53' N, 100°31' E **202**
Noonan, *N. Dak., U.S.* 48°52' N, 103°1' W **108**
Noord Beveland, *Neth.* 51°33' N, 3°42' E **163**
Noordoewer, *Namibia* 28°44' S, 17°37' E **227**
Noormarkku, *Fin.* 61°35' N, 21°51' E **166**
Nootka, *Can.* 49°37' N, 126°39' W **90**
Nopah Range, *Calif., U.S.* 36°4' N, 116°10' W **101**
Nóqui, *Angola* 5°55' S, 13°28' E **218**
Nora, *Ill., U.S.* 42°26' N, 89°57' W **102**
Nora, *Nor.* 59°30' N, 14°59' E **152**
Nora, island, *Eritrea* 16°4' N, 39°43' E **182**
Nora, ruin(s), *It.* 38°59' N, 8°55' E **156**
Norak, *Taj.* 38°23' N, 69°21' E **197**
Norberg, *Nor.* 60°3' N, 15°54' E **152**
Norco, *La., U.S.* 29°59' N, 90°25' W **103**
Nord 81°43' N, 17°32' W **246**
Nord Frøya, *Nor.* 63°45' N, 8°47' E **152**
Nord, Petit lac du, lake, *Can.* 50°46' N, 67°57' W **111**
Nordaustlandet, island, *Nor.* 80°34' N, 5°48' E **160**
Norddalsfjord, *Nor.* 61°39' N, 5°22' E **152**
Norddeich, *Ger.* 53°37' N, 7°10' E **163**
Nordegg (Brazeau), *Can.* 52°28' N, 116°7' W **108**
Norden, *Ger.* 53°36' N, 7°11' E **163**
Norderney, *Ger.* 53°42' N, 7°9' E **163**
Nordfold, *Nor.* 67°45' N, 15°11' E **152**
Nordhordland, region, *North Sea* 60°50' N, 4°39' E **152**
Nordhorn, *Ger.* 52°26' N, 7°3' E **163**
Nordkapp (North Cape), *Nor.* 71°6' N, 25°55' E **152**
Nordkinnhalvøya, *Nor.* 70°45' N, 26°37' E **152**
Nord-Kivu, adm. division, *Dem. Rep. of the Congo* 0°10' N, 28°8' E **224**
Nordli, *Nor.* 64°28' N, 13°36' E **152**
Nordmaling, *Nor.* 63°33' N, 19°30' E **152**

Nordøstrundingen 80°22' N, 30°36' W 72
Nordøyan, islands, Norwegian Sea 64°47' N, 9°13' E 152
Nordøyane, islands, Nor. 62°38' N, 4°46' E 152
Nordoyar, islands, Norwegian Sea 62°30' N, 9°12' W 72
Nord-Pas-De-Calais, adm. division, Fr. 50°24' N, 1°57' E 150
Nordreisa, Nor. 69°46' N, 21°2' E 152
Nordvik, Nor. 66°7' N, 12°31' E 152
Nordvik, Russ. 73°59' N, 111°16' E 160
Norfolk, Conn., U.S. 41°59' N, 73°12' W 104
Norfolk, Nebr., U.S. 42°0' N, 97°26' W 90
Norfolk, Va., U.S. 36°51' N, 76°17' W 96
Norfolk Island, Australia 29°0' S, 168°0' E
Norfolk Ridge, South Pacific Ocean 27°44' S, 167°48' E 252
Norfork Lake, Ark., U.S. 36°16' N, 93°15' W 80
Nori, Russ. 66°11' N, 72°31' E 169
Noril'sk, Russ. 69°20' N, 88°8' E 169
Normal, Ill., U.S. 40°30' N, 88°59' W 102
Norman, Okla., U.S. 35°11' N, 97°27' W 92
Norman Wells, Can. 65°18' N, 126°44' W 98
Normanby Island, P.N.G. 9°58' S, 151°19' E 192
Normandin, Can. 48°49' N, 72°31' W 94
Normandy, Tex., U.S. 28°53' N, 100°35' W 96
Normandy, region, Fr. 48°57' N, 0°46' E 163
Normanton, Austral. 17°46' S, 141°10' E 238
Normétal, Can. 49°0' N, 79°23' W 94
Norphlet, Ark., U.S. 33°17' N, 92°40' W 103
Ñorquincó, Arg. 41°50' S, 70°51' W 134
Norra Storfjället, peak, Nor. 65°51' N, 15°10' E 152
Norrby, Nor. 64°25' N, 15°37' E 152
Nørresundby, Den. 57°3' N, 9°55' E 150
Norrfors, Nor. 63°46' N, 18°59' E 152
Norrhult, Nor. 57°7' N, 15°9' E 152
Norris Lake, lake, Tenn., U.S. 36°18' N, 84°3' W 94
Norrköping, Nor. 58°33' N, 16°9' E 152
Norrland, region, Sw. 61°29' N, 17°15' E 166
Norrtälje, Sw. 59°45' N, 18°39' E 166
Norseman, Austral. 32°12' S, 121°47' E 231
Norske Øer, islands, Norske Øer 78°33' N, 16°48' W 246
Norte, adm. division, Braz. 4°51' S, 37°14' W 132
Norte, Cabo, Braz. 1°44' N, 49°56' W 130
Norte, Cayo 18°50' N, 87°32' W 115
Norte de Santander, adm. division, Col. 8°18' N, 73°17' W 136
Norte, Punta, Arg. 36°18' S, 56°43' W 139
Norte, Punta, Arg. 50°51' S, 69°6' W 134
Norte, Serra do, Braz. 10°18' S, 59°11' W 130
Nortelândia, Braz. 14°29' S, 56°48' W 132
Nörten-Hardenberg, Ger. 51°37' N, 9°57' E 167
North Adams, Mass., U.S. 42°41' N, 73°7' W 104
North Albanian Alps, Alban. 42°31' N, 19°47' E 168
North America 25°0' N, 112°0' W 73
North Amherst, Mass., U.S. 42°24' N, 72°32' W 104
North Andaman, island, India 13°28' N, 91°39' E 188
North Andover, Mass., U.S. 42°41' N, 71°9' W 104
North Anson, Me., U.S. 44°51' N, 69°55' W 94
North Atlantic Ocean 20°33' N, 74°33' W 253
North Augusta, S.C., U.S. 33°30' N, 81°59' W 96
North Aulatsivik Island, Can. 59°49' N, 63°58' W 106
North Australian Basin, Indian Ocean 14°56' S, 117°17' E 254
North Baldy, peak, Wash., U.S. 48°31' N, 117°14' W 90
North Baltimore, Ohio, U.S. 41°10' N, 83°40' W 102
North Barrule, peak 54°16' N, 4°29' W 150
North Battleford, Can. 52°47' N, 108°19' W 108
North Bay, Can. 46°18' N, 79°27' W 94
North Belcher Islands, islands, Hudson Bay 56°39' N, 83°25' W 106
North Bend, Can. 49°52' N, 121°27' W 100
North Bend, Wash., U.S. 47°28' N, 121°47' W 100
North Bennington, Vt., U.S. 42°55' N, 73°15' W 104
North Berwick, Me., U.S. 43°18' N, 70°44' W 104
North Bimini, island, Bahamas 25°46' N, 79°29' W 105
North Bonneville, Wash., U.S. 45°38' N, 121°58' W 100
North Boston, N.Y., U.S. 42°40' N, 78°48' W 110
North Bradley, Mich., U.S. 43°41' N, 84°29' W 102
North Branch, Mich., U.S. 43°13' N, 83°9' W 102
North Branch, Minn., U.S. 45°30' N, 92°59' W 94
North Branford, Conn., U.S. 41°19' N, 72°47' W 104
North Bridgton, Me., U.S. 44°6' N, 70°43' W 104
North Caicos, island, North Caicos 22°1' N, 72°1' W 80
North Canton, Ohio, U.S. 40°52' N, 81°24' W 102
North, Cape, Antarctica 70°15' S, 169°9' E 248
North, Cape, Can. 47°2' N, 60°54' W 111
North Cape, Can. 46°59' N, 64°47' W 111
North Cape, N.Z. 34°24' S, 172°51' E 240
North Cape May, N.J., U.S. 38°58' N, 74°58' W 94
North Cape see Horn, Ice. 66°30' N, 26°3' W 246
North Cape see Nordkapp, Nor. 71°10' N, 25°50' E 152
North Carolina, adm. division, N.C., U.S. 35°44' N, 80°14' W 96
North Carver, Mass., U.S. 41°55' N, 70°49' W 104
North Cascades National Park, Wash., U.S. 48°34' N, 121°27' W 100
North Cat Cay, island, Bahamas 25°32' N, 79°16' W 105
North Channel 45°49' N, 83°42' W 80
North Channel 54°35' N, 5°17' W 150
North Clarendon, Vt., U.S. 43°34' N, 72°59' W 104
North College Hill, Ohio, U.S. 39°12' N, 84°34' W 102
North Conway, N.H., U.S. 44°2' N, 71°8' W 104
North Cowichan, Can. 48°51' N, 123°42' W 100
North Creek, N.Y., U.S. 43°41' N, 73°60' W 104
North Dakota, adm. division, N. Dak., U.S. 47°45' N, 101°21' W 90
North Dartmouth, Mass., U.S. 41°37' N, 70°60' W 104
North Downs, region, U.K. 51°8' N, 0°49' E 162
North Eagle Butte, S. Dak., U.S. 44°59' N, 101°15' W 90
North East Land, island, Nor. 79°53' N, 23°37' E 255
North Edgecomb, Me., U.S. 43°59' N, 69°39' W 104
North Edwards, Calif., U.S. 35°2' N, 117°50' W 101
North Egremont, Mass., U.S. 42°11' N, 73°27' W 104
North Fiji Basin, South Pacific Ocean 17°30' S, 173°11' E 252
North Fond du Lac, Wis., U.S. 43°48' N, 88°30' W 102
North Foreland, Drake Passage 61°14' S, 61°24' W 248
North Foreland, U.K. 51°22' N, 1°25' E 163
North Fork, Calif., U.S. 37°13' N, 119°32' W 100
North Fork, river, Kans., U.S. 39°29' N, 100°4' W 90
North Fort Myers, Fla., U.S. 26°40' N, 81°53' W 105
North Fryeburg, Me., U.S. 44°7' N, 70°59' W 104
North Grosvenor Dale, Conn., U.S. 41°58' N, 71°55' W 104
North Hampton, N.H., U.S. 42°58' N, 70°51' W 104
North Hartland, Vt., U.S. 43°35' N, 72°22' W 104
North Haven, N.Y., U.S. 41°1' N, 72°19' W 104
North Head, Can. 53°43' N, 56°24' W 111
North Head, N.Z. 36°36' S, 173°49' E 240
North Hodge, La., U.S. 32°18' N, 92°43' W 96
North Holland, adm. division, Neth. 53°6' N, 4°6' E 150
North Horr, Kenya 3°18' N, 37°4' E 224
North Hudson, N.Y., U.S. 43°57' N, 73°44' W 104
North Industry, Ohio, U.S. 40°44' N, 81°22' W 102
North Island, Austral. 15°27' S, 136°40' E 230
North Jay, Me., U.S. 44°32' N, 70°15' W 104
North Judson, Ind., U.S. 41°12' N, 86°46' W 102
North Kingstown (Wickford), R.I., U.S. 41°34' N, 71°28' W 104
North Knife Lake, Can. 58°2' N, 97°42' W 108
North La Veta Pass, Colo., U.S. 37°36' N, 105°13' W 90
North Land see Severnaya Zemlya, islands, Russ. 80°22' N, 102°0' E 160
North Las Vegas, Nev., U.S. 36°11' N, 115°9' W 101
North Liberty, Ind., U.S. 41°31' N, 86°26' W 102
North Little Rock, Ark., U.S. 34°47' N, 92°16' W 82
North Loup, river, Nebr., U.S. 42°25' N, 101°5' W 80
North Luangwa National Park, Zambia 11°43' S, 32°2' E 224
North Mamm Peak, Colo., U.S. 39°22' N, 107°57' W 90
North Manchester, Ind., U.S. 40°59' N, 85°46' W 102
North Miami, Fla., U.S. 25°54' N, 80°12' W 105
North Montpelier, Vt., U.S. 44°17' N, 72°28' W 104
North Moose Lake, Can. 54°10' N, 100°33' W 108
North Muskegon, Mich., U.S. 43°15' N, 86°17' W 102
North Myrtle Beach, S.C., U.S. 33°48' N, 78°42' W 96
North Naples, Fla., U.S. 26°13' N, 81°48' W 105
North Negril Point, Jam. 18°23' N, 79°33' W 116
North Orange, Mass., U.S. 42°37' N, 72°17' W 104
North Oxford, Mass., U.S. 42°9' N, 71°53' W 104
North Pacific Ocean 22°12' N, 118°57' W 252
North Palisade, peak, Calif., U.S. 37°5' N, 118°34' W 101
North Palmetto Point, Bahamas 25°10' N, 76°10' W 96
North Pass, Colo., U.S. 38°11' N, 106°35' W 90
North Peak, Nev., U.S. 40°39' N, 117°13' W 90
North Pine, Can. 56°24' N, 120°48' W 108
North Platte, Nebr., U.S. 41°10' N, 100°44' W 106
North Platte, river, Wyo., U.S. 42°50' N, 105°34' W 106
North Point, Mich., U.S. 44°49' N, 83°16' W 94
North Port, Fla., U.S. 27°4' N, 82°15' W 105
North Powder, Oreg., U.S. 45°1' N, 117°56' W 90
North Pownal, Vt., U.S. 42°47' N, 73°16' W 104
North Rhine-Westphalia, adm. division, Ger. 51°18' N, 6°44' E 167
North River, Can. 59°0' N, 94°54' W 73
North, river, Can. 53°53' N, 58°14' W 111
North, river, Wash., U.S. 46°48' N, 123°42' W 100
North Salem, N.H., U.S. 42°50' N, 71°15' W 104
North Saskatchewan, river, Can. 52°15' N, 116°35' W 108
North Scituate, Mass., U.S. 42°13' N, 70°48' W 104
North Sea 55°38' N, 2°30' E 150
North Sentinel Island, India 11°29' N, 91°2' E 188
North Shapleigh, Me., U.S. 43°36' N, 70°54' W 104
North Shore, Calif., U.S. 33°31' N, 115°56' W 101
North Shoshone Peak, Nev., U.S. 39°8' N, 117°34' W 90
North Slope, Alas., U.S. 69°31' N, 155°32' W 98
North Springfield, Pa., U.S. 41°59' N, 80°27' W 94
North Springfield, Vt., U.S. 43°19' N, 72°32' W 104
North Star, Can. 56°51' N, 117°39' W 108
North Stradbroke Island, Austral. 28°5' S, 150°57' E 230
North Tawton, U.K. 50°48' N, 3°54' W 162
North Thetford, Vt., U.S. 43°50' N, 72°12' W 104
North Truro, Mass., U.S. 42°2' N, 70°6' W 104
North Turner, Me., U.S. 44°20' N, 70°15' W 104
North Vancouver, Can. 49°19' N, 123°3' W 100
North Vassalboro, Me., U.S. 44°29' N, 69°38' W 104
North Vernon, Ind., U.S. 39°0' N, 85°38' W 102
North Wabasca Lake, Can. 56°2' N, 114°57' W 108
North Walpole, N.H., U.S. 43°8' N, 72°27' W 104
North Walsham, U.K. 52°49' N, 1°22' E 163
North Warren, Pa., U.S. 41°52' N, 79°10' W 110
North Waterford, Me., U.S. 44°13' N, 70°46' W 104
North Webster, Ind., U.S. 41°19' N, 85°42' W 102
North West Cape, Austral. 21°48' S, 114°19' E 230
North West Point, Can. 53°25' N, 60°2' W 111
North West River, Can. 53°34' N, 60°8' W 111
North West Rocks, islands, Caribbean Sea 14°31' N, 80°34' W 115
North Wildwood, N.J., U.S. 39°0' N, 74°48' W 94
North Yolla Bolly Mountains, peak, Calif., U.S. 40°11' N, 123°4' W 90
North York Moors, U.K. 54°20' N, 1°2' W 162
Northallerton, U.K. 54°20' N, 1°27' W 162
Northam, Austral. 31°41' S, 116°41' E 231
Northam, S. Af. 24°58' S, 27°15' E 227
Northampton, Mass., U.S. 42°18' N, 72°38' W 104
Northampton, U.K. 52°14' N, 0°54' E 162
Northampton, Mount, peak, Antarctica 72°37' S, 169°35' E 248
Northbluff Point, Can. 51°27' N, 80°24' W 110
Northeast Cape, Alas., U.S. 63°5' N, 167°44' W 160
Northeast Pacific Basin, North Pacific Ocean 26°5' N, 145°35' W 252
Northeast Point, Bahamas 22°48' N, 74°14' W 80
Northeast Point, Can. 51°54' N, 55°18' W 111
Northeast Point, Jam. 18°12' N, 76°20' W 115
Northeim, Ger. 51°42' N, 9°59' E 167
Northern, adm. division, Sudan 20°14' N, 31°0' E 182
Northern Areas, adm. division, Pak. 35°38' N, 73°27' E 186
Northern Bahr Al Ghazal, adm. division, Sudan 9°11' N, 26°10' E 224
Northern Cape, adm. division, S. Af. 30°2' S, 19°39' E 227
Northern Cay, island, Belize 17°21' N, 87°29' W 116
Northern Cyprus, special sovereignty 35°16' N, 32°56' E 194
Northern Darfur, adm. division, Sudan 16°39' N, 23°59' E 226
Northern Head, Can. 46°4' N, 59°46' W 111
Northern Ireland, adm. division, U.K. 54°35' N, 7°41' W 150
Northern Mariana Islands, U.S. 20°7' N, 141°10' E 192
Northern Sierra Madre National Park, Philippines 16°48' N, 121°37' E 203
Northern Territory, adm. division, Austral. 19°14' S, 130°35' E 231
Northfield, Minn., U.S. 44°26' N, 93°8' W 94
Northfield, N.H., U.S. 43°25' N, 71°36' W 104
Northfield, Vt., U.S. 44°8' N, 72°40' W 104
Northfield Falls, Vt., U.S. 44°9' N, 72°39' W 104
Northford, Conn., U.S. 41°23' N, 72°48' W 104
Northport, Ala., U.S. 33°13' N, 87°35' W 103
Northport, Nebr., U.S. 41°41' N, 103°6' W 92
Northport, Wash., U.S. 48°53' N, 117°48' W 90
Northridge, Ohio, U.S. 39°59' N, 83°46' W 102
Northumberland, N.H., U.S. 44°33' N, 71°34' W 104
Northumberland Islands, Coral Sea 22°8' S, 150°56' E 230
Northville, N.Y., U.S. 43°13' N, 74°11' W 104
Northway, Alas., U.S. 62°51' N, 141°59' W 98
North-West, adm. division, S. Af. 26°44' S, 24°15' E 227
Northwest Angle, Minn., U.S. 49°4' N, 95°20' W 90
Northwest Atlantic Mid-Ocean Canyon, North Atlantic Ocean 52°31' N, 45°36' W 253
North-West Frontier, adm. division, Pak. 34°28' N, 71°45' E 186
Northwest Hawaiian Ridge, North Pacific Ocean 31°13' N, 173°59' W 252
Northwest Miscou Point, Can. 48°11' N, 65°14' W 94
Northwest Pacific Basin, North Pacific Ocean 39°52' N, 157°39' E 252
Northwest Passages 70°33' N, 125°19' W 72
Northwest Territories, adm. division, Can. 60°25' N, 115°14' W 108
Northwestern Hawaiian Islands, North Pacific Ocean 23°42' N, 165°44' W 99
Northwich, U.K. 53°15' N, 2°31' W 162
Northwind Escarpment, Arctic Ocean 75°55' N, 153°20' W 255
Northwind Ridge, Arctic Ocean 76°13' N, 156°12' W 255
Northwood, N.H., U.S. 43°11' N, 71°10' W 104
Northwood, N. Dak., U.S. 47°43' N, 97°35' W 90
Northwood, Ohio, U.S. 41°35' N, 83°27' W 102
Norton, Kans., U.S. 39°49' N, 99°54' W 90
Norton, Va., U.S. 36°55' N, 82°39' W 94
Norton, Zimb. 17°56' S, 30°40' E 224
Norton Bay 64°20' N, 162°6' W 98
Norton Shores, Mich., U.S. 43°9' N, 86°16' W 102
Norton Sound 63°37' N, 165°6' W 98
Norvalspont, S. Af. 30°38' S, 25°24' E 227
Norvegia, Cape, Antarctica 71°16' S, 18°23' W 248
Norwalk, Calif., U.S. 33°55' N, 118°4' W 101
Norwalk, Conn., U.S. 41°7' N, 73°25' W 104
Norwalk, Ohio, U.S. 41°13' N, 82°37' W 102
Norway, Me., U.S. 44°12' N, 70°33' W 104
Norway, Mich., U.S. 45°47' N, 87°55' W 94
Norway 63°25' N, 10°58' E 152
Norway House, Can. 53°56' N, 97°52' W 108
Norwegian Basin, Norwegian Sea 68°1' N, 1°43' E 255
Norwegian Sea 68°1' N, 5°35' E 152
Norwich, Conn., U.S. 41°31' N, 72°5' W 104
Norwich, N.Y., U.S. 42°31' N, 75°33' W 94
Norwich, U.K. 52°37' N, 1°16' E 162
Norwich, Vt., U.S. 43°42' N, 72°19' W 104
Norwood, Colo., U.S. 38°7' N, 108°17' W 90
Norwood, La., U.S. 30°57' N, 91°7' W 103
Norwood, Mass., U.S. 42°11' N, 71°13' W 104
Norwood, Ohio, U.S. 39°9' N, 84°27' W 94
Noshul', Russ. 60°8' N, 49°35' E 154
Nosivka, Ukr. 50°54' N, 31°38' E 158
Nosok, Russ. 70°8' N, 82°12' E 169
Nosovshchina, Russ. 62°57' N, 37°3' E 154
Noşratābād, Iran 29°51' N, 59°56' E 180
Nosy-Varika, Madagascar 20°33' S, 48°31' E 220
Noszlop, Hung. 47°10' N, 17°26' E 168
Not Ozero, lake, Russ. 66°26' N, 30°49' E 152
Notch Peak, Utah, U.S. 39°7' N, 113°29' W 90
Notikewin, Can. 56°58' N, 117°38' W 108
Notikewin, river, Can. 56°55' N, 119°2' W 108
Nótio Egéo, adm. division, Gr. 37°12' N, 25°30' E 156
Nötö, Fin. 59°57' N, 21°45' E 166
Noto, It. 36°53' N, 15°4' E 156
Noto, Japan 37°19' N, 137°8' E 201
Notodden, Nor. 59°33' N, 9°17' E 152
Notre Dame Bay 49°29' N, 55°32' W 111
Notre Dame de Lourdes, Can. 49°31' N, 98°34' W 90
Notre-Dame-du-Nord, Can. 47°36' N, 79°29' W 94
Notsé, Togo 6°57' N, 1°9' E 222
Nottaway, river, Can. 51°13' N, 78°54' W 80
Nottingham, N.H., U.S. 43°6' N, 71°7' W 104
Nottingham, U.K. 52°57' N, 1°9' W 162
Nottingham Island, Can. 63°12' N, 82°17' W 106
Nottuln, Ger. 51°55' N, 7°21' E 167
Nouabalé-Ndoki National Park, Congo 2°47' N, 16°11' E 206
Nouadhibou (Port Étienne), Mauritania 20°56' N, 17°2' W 222
Nouakchott, Mauritania 18°6' N, 16°11' W 222
Nouamrhar, Mauritania 19°22' N, 16°32' W 222
Nouaoudar, Mauritania 16°46' N, 7°18' W 222
Nouart, Fr. 49°26' N, 5°3' E 163
Nouasser, Mor. 33°22' N, 7°39' W 214
Nouméa, New Caledonia, Fr. 22°11' S, 166°42' E 238
Nouna, Burkina Faso 12°43' N, 3°53' W 222
Noupoort, S. Af. 31°10' S, 24°55' E 227
Nourounba, Mali 12°31' N, 9°8' W 222
Nousu, Fin. 67°10' N, 28°36' E 152
Nouzonville, Fr. 49°47' N, 4°44' E 163
Nova América, Braz. 15°3' S, 49°60' W 138
Nova Andradina, Braz. 22°15' S, 53°21' W 138
Nova Esperança, Braz. 23°10' S, 52°17' W 138
Nova Esperança, Braz. 16°34' S, 43°56' W 138
Nova Friburgo, Braz. 22°18' S, 42°31' W 138
Nova Gorica, Slov. 45°57' N, 13°38' E 167
Nova Gradiška, Croatia 45°15' N, 17°22' E 168
Nova Granada, Braz. 20°32' S, 49°21' W 138
Nova Iguaçu, Braz. 22°45' S, 43°28' W 138
Nova Kakhovka, Ukr. 46°45' N, 33°17' E 156
Nova Kapela, Croatia 45°12' N, 17°36' E 168
Nova Kasaba, Bosn. and Herzg. 44°13' N, 19°7' E 168
Nova Lamego, Guinea-Bissau 12°17' N, 14°16' W 222
Nova Lima, Braz. 19°58' S, 43°51' W 138
Nova Mambone, Mozambique 21°1' S, 34°57' E 227
Nova Nabúri, Mozambique 16°50' S, 38°55' E 224
Nova Odesa, Ukr. 47°21' N, 31°45' E 156
Nova Olinda do Norte, Braz. 3°49' S, 59°2' W 130
Nova Prata, Braz. 28°50' S, 51°35' W 139
Nova Roma, Braz. 13°53' S, 46°59' W 138
Nova Scotia, adm. division, Can. 44°50' N, 65°14' W 111
Nova Sofala, Mozambique 20°10' S, 34°43' E 227
Nova Trento, Braz. 27°20' S, 48°56' W 138
Nova Varoš, Serb. and Mont. 43°27' N, 19°48' E 168
Nova Venécia, Braz. 18°46' S, 40°26' W 138
Nova Viçosa, Braz. 17°54' S, 39°24' W 138
Novafeltria, It. 43°53' N, 12°17' E 167
Novalukoml', Belarus 54°42' N, 29°11' E 166
Novara, It. 45°26' N, 8°36' E 167
Novato, Calif., U.S. 38°7' N, 122°35' W 100
Novaya Lyalya, Russ. 59°1' N, 60°39' E 154
Novaya Shul'ba, Kaz. 50°32' N, 81°19' E 184
Novaya Sibir', Ostrov, island, Russ. 75°1' N, 151°6' E 160
Novaya Vodolaga, Ukr. 49°44' N, 35°53' E 158
Novaya Zemlya, island, Russ. 70°43' N, 57°35' E 169
Nové Zámky, Slovakia 47°59' N, 18°10' E 168
Novelda, Sp. 38°22' N, 0°47' E 164
Novgorod, adm. division, Russ. 58°2' N, 30°16' E 166
Novgorodka, Russ. 57°2' N, 28°33' E 166
Novhorod-Sivers'kyy, Ukr. 51°58' N, 33°18' E 158
Novi Bečej, Serb. and Mont. 45°35' N, 20°8' E 168
Novi Kneževac, Serb. and Mont. 46°2' N, 20°6' E 168
Novi Ligure, It. 44°45' N, 8°47' E 167
Novi Pazar, Bulg. 43°20' N, 27°11' E 158
Novi Pazar, Serb. and Mont. 43°11' N, 20°33' E 180
Novi Pazar, Serb. and Mont. 43°8' N, 20°31' E 16
Novi Sad, Serb. and Mont. 45°14' N, 19°46' E 168
Novigrad, Croatia 45°20' N, 13°34' E 167
Novikovo, Russ. 58°9' N, 80°35' E 169
Novilara, It. 43°51' N, 12°55' E 167
Noville Peninsula, Antarctica 71°26' S, 95°25' W 248
Novillero, Mex. 22°21' N, 105°40' W 114
Novinka, Russ. 59°10' N, 30°20' E 166
Novo Acordo, Braz. 10°9' S, 47°20' W 130
Novo Aripuanã, Braz. 5°9' S, 60°21' W 130
Novo Cruzeiro, Braz. 17°29' S, 41°53' W 138
Novo Hamburgo, Braz. 29°42' S, 51°7' W 139
Novo Horizonte, Braz. 21°29' S, 49°15' W 138
Novo Izborsk, Russ. 57°47' N, 27°55' E 166
Novo Paraíso, Braz. 1°15' N, 60°18' W 123
Novo, river, Braz. 4°47' S, 53°49' W 130
Novoagansk, Russ. 61°57' N, 76°26' E 169
Novoaleksandrovsk, Russ. 45°31' N, 41°6' E 158
Novoaltaysk, Russ. 53°27' N, 84°6' E 184
Novoanninskiy, Russ. 50°28' N, 42°42' E 158
Novobogatīnskoe, Kaz. 47°21' N, 51°11' E 158
Novocheremshansk, Russ. 54°21' N, 50°5' E 154
Novodvinsk, Russ. 64°25' N, 40°48' E 154
Novohrad-Volyns'kyy, Ukr. 50°34' N, 27°35' E 152
Novoīshīmskīy, Kaz. 53°13' N, 66°48' E 184
Novokhovansk, Russ. 55°55' N, 29°43' E 166
Novokuybyshevsk, Russ. 53°6' N, 50°0' E 154
Novokuznetsk, Russ. 53°48' N, 87°8' E 184
Novolazarevskaya, Russia, station, Antarctica 70°47' S, 11°39' E 248
Novomalykla, Russ. 54°10' N, 49°50' E 154
Novomichurinsk, Russ. 53°59' N, 39°49' E 154
Novomikhaylovskoye, Russ. 44°15' N, 38°55' E 156
Novomoskovsk, Russ. 54°3' N, 38°12' E 154
Novomoskovs'k, Ukr. 48°40' N, 35°18' E 158
Novonikolayevskiy, Russ. 50°56' N, 42°20' E 158
Novonikol'skoye, Russ. 49°5' N, 45°4' E 158
Novonikol'skoye, Russ. 59°43' N, 79°17' E 169
Novooleksiyivka, Ukr. 46°15' N, 34°37' E 156
Novoorsk, Russ. 51°23' N, 58°57' E 158
Novopokrovskaya, Russ. 45°58' N, 40°37' E 158
Novopskov, Ukr. 49°34' N, 39°9' E 158
Novorepnoye, Russ. 51°3' N, 48°21' E 158
Novorossiysk, Russ. 44°46' N, 37°41' E 156
Novorybnoye, Russ. 72°45' N, 105°56' E 160
Novorzhev, Russ. 57°1' N, 29°18' E 166
Novosel'ye, Russ. 58°5' N, 28°52' E 166
Novosergiyevka, Russ. 52°3' N, 53°36' E 158
Novoshakhtinsk, Russ. 47°43' N, 39°57' E 158
Novosi Birskiye Ostrova (New Siberian Islands), Russ. 76°14' N, 142°6' E 160
Novosibirsk, Russ. 55°3' N, 83°2' E 184
Novosibirsk, adm. division, Russ. 54°25' N, 77°40' E 184
Novosil', Russ. 52°57' N, 37°1' E 154
Novosil'skiy, Cape, Antarctica 68°20' S, 159°52' E 248
Novosokol'niki, Russ. 56°20' N, 30°13' E 154
Novotitarovskaya, Russ. 45°16' N, 39°1' E 156
Novotroitsk, Russ. 51°13' N, 58°16' E 158
Novoukrayinka, Ukr. 48°21' N, 31°36' E 156
Novouzensk, Russ. 50°29' N, 48°7' E 158
Novovyatsk, Russ. 58°28' N, 49°41' E 154
Novozhilovskaya, Russ. 64°49' N, 51°24' E 154
Novozybkov, Russ. 52°30' N, 31°58' E 154
Novska, Croatia 45°19' N, 16°59' E 168
Novyy Oskol, Russ. 50°46' N, 37°53' E 158
Novyy Bor, Russ. 66°43' N, 52°16' E 154
Novyy Buh, Ukr. 47°41' N, 32°25' E 156
Novyy Buyan, Russ. 53°40' N, 50°5' E 154
Novyy Port, Russ. 67°40' N, 72°54' E 169
Novyy Uoyan, Russ. 56°5' N, 111°38' E 173
Novyy Urengoy, Russ. 65°53' N, 77°10' E 169
Novyy Vasyugan, Russ. 58°34' N, 76°25' E 169
Now Zad, Afghan. 32°23' N, 64°30' E 186
Nowa Sól, Pol. 51°47' N, 15°43' E 152
Nowata, Okla., U.S. 36°41' N, 95°39' W 96
Nowbarān, Iran 35°12' N, 49°40' E 180
Nowgong, India 25°4' N, 79°26' E 197
Nowra, Austral. 34°49' S, 150°36' E 231
Nowshera, Pak. 33°57' N, 72°0' E 186
Nowy Sącz, Pol. 49°40' N, 20°47' E 160
Noxapater, Miss., U.S. 32°58' N, 89°4' W 103
Noxon, Mont., U.S. 47°57' N, 115°47' W 90
Noxubee, river, Ala., U.S. 33°11' N, 88°47' W 103
Noy, river, Laos 17°6' N, 105°20' E 202
Noyabr'sk, Russ. 63°12' N, 75°24' E 169
Noyes, Minn., U.S. 48°57' N, 97°13' W 94
Noyo, Calif., U.S. 39°25' N, 123°49' W 90
Noyo, river, Calif., U.S. 39°20' N, 123°46' W 90
Noyon, Fr. 49°34' N, 3°0' E 163
Nsanje (Port Herald), Malawi 16°56' S, 35°13' E 224
Nsawam, Ghana 5°50' N, 0°21' E 222
Nsélé, Gabon 6°357' N, 10°10' E 218
Nsoc, Equatorial Guinea 1°13' N, 11°14' E 218
Nsontin, Dem. Rep. of the Congo 3°9' S, 17°54' E 218
Nsukka, Nig. 6°51' N, 7°23' E 222
Nsumbu National Park, Zambia 8°52' S, 30°7' E 206
Ntakat, spring, Mauritania 16°49' N, 11°45' W 222
N'Tima, Congo 3°47' S, 12°3' E 218
Ntui, Cameroon 4°25' N, 11°36' E 222
Nu (Salween), river, Asia 31°21' N, 93°34' E 190
Nu'aymah, Syr. 32°38' N, 36°10' E 194
Nuba Mountains, Sudan 10°45' N, 30°5' E 224
Nubia, Lake, Sudan 21°56' N, 30°53' E 182
Nubian Desert, Sudan 20°50' N, 30°59' E 182
Nucet, Rom. 46°30' N, 22°35' E 168
Nucla, Colo., U.S. 38°16' N, 108°33' W 90
Nüden, Mongolia 43°58' N, 110°37' E 198
Nueces, river, Tex., U.S. 28°12' N, 98°46' W 92
Nueltin Lake, Can. 59°37' N, 102°11' W 106
Nueva Esparta, adm. division, Venez. 10°57' N, 64°24' W 130
Nueva Galia, Arg. 35°6' S, 65°13' W 134
Nueva Gerona, Cuba 21°53' N, 82°49' W 116
Nueva, Isla, island, Chile 55°13' S, 66°24' W 134

Nueva Palmira, *Uru.* 33°54' S, 58°20' W **139**
Nueva Rosita, *Mex.* 27°55' N, 101°12' W **92**
Nuevo Berlín, *Uru.* 32°59' S, 57°59' W **139**
Nuevo Casas Grandes, *Mex.* 30°24' N, 107°55' W **92**
Nuevo Delicias, *Mex.* 26°16' N, 102°48' W **114**
Nuevo Ideal, *Mex.* 24°51' N, 105°4' W **114**
Nuevo Laredo, *Mex.* 27°28' N, 99°32' W **96**
Nuevo León, *Mex.* 32°25' N, 115°14' W **101**
Nuevo León, adm. division, *Mex.* 25°9' N, 100°14' W **114**
Nuevo Morelos, *Mex.* 22°30' N, 99°13' W **114**
Nuevo Rocafuerte, *Ecua.* 0°60' N, 75°27' W **136**
Nuevo Rodriguez, *Mex.* 27°8' N, 100°4' W **96**
Nugaaleed, Dooxo, *Somalia* 8°39' N, 47°24' E **216**
Nugruș, Gebel, peak, *Egypt* 24°47' N, 34°29' E **182**
Nuh, Ras, *Pak.* 24°55' N, 62°25' E **182**
Nuia, *Est.* 58°5' N, 25°30' E **166**
Nuijamaa, *Fin.* 60°58' N, 28°34' E **166**
Nuiqsut, *Alas., U.S.* 70°12' N, 151°2' W **98**
Nuits, *Fr.* 47°43' N, 4°11' E **150**
Nukhayb, *Iraq* 32°3' N, 42°15' E **180**
Nukheila (Merga), spring, *Sudan* 19°3' N, 26°20' E **226**
Nuku'alofa, *Tonga* 21°8' S, 175°12' W **241**
Nukumanu Islands, *South Pacific Ocean* 4°52' S, 159°33' E **238**
Nukus, *Uzb.* 42°26' N, 59°39' E **180**
Nulato, *Alas., U.S.* 64°36' N, 158°12' W **98**
Nules, *Sp.* 39°51' N, 0°10' E **164**
Nullarbor Plain, *Austral.* 30°43' S, 125°29' E **230**
Numan, *Nig.* 9°29' N, 12°5' E **216**
Numata, *Japan* 36°38' N, 139°2' E **201**
Numazu, *Japan* 35°5' N, 138°53' E **201**
Numedal, region, *Nor.* 60°8' N, 8°56' E **152**
Numfoor, island, *Indonesia* 1°23' S, 134°21' E **192**
Nummi, *Fin.* 60°23' N, 23°52' E **166**
Numto, *Russ.* 63°30' N, 71°20' E **169**
Nunap Isua (Kap Farvel) 59°20' N, 43°43' W **106**
Nunavik 71°32' N, 56°33' W **106**
Nunavut, adm. division, *Can.* 65°9' N, 74°23' W **106**
Nunchía, *Col.* 5°35' N, 72°14' W **136**
Nuneaton, *U.K.* 52°31' N, 1°27' W **162**
Nuñes, island, *Chile* 53°38' S, 74°58' W **134**
Nungesser Lake, *Can.* 51°31' N, 94°27' W **80**
Nungnain Sum, *China* 45°42' N, 119°0' E **198**
Nungo, *Mozambique* 13°23' S, 37°46' E **224**
Nunim Lake, lake, *Can.* 59°28' N, 102°54' W **108**
Nunivak Island, *Alas., U.S.* 59°24' N, 166°59' W **98**
Nunkini, *Mex.* 20°21' N, 90°13' W **112**
Nunligran, *Russ.* 64°51' N, 175°16' W **98**
Nuñoa, *Peru* 14°31' S, 70°37' W **137**
Nuoro, *It.* 40°19' N, 9°19' E **156**
Nuqayr, spring, *Saudi Arabia* 27°50' N, 48°17' E **196**
Nuquí, *Col.* 5°41' N, 77°16' W **136**
Nura, river, *Kaz.* 50°28' N, 71°12' E **184**
Nurki, Mys, *Russ.* 56°29' N, 138°30' E **160**
Nurlat, *Russ.* 54°26' N, 50°41' E **154**
Nurmes, *Fin.* 63°31' N, 29°7' E **152**
Nurmo, *Fin.* 62°49' N, 22°50' E **154**
Nürnberg, *Ger.* 49°26' N, 11°0' E **143**
Nurobod, *Uzb.* 39°34' N, 66°17' E **197**
Nurota, *Uzb.* 40°33' N, 65°41' E **197**
Nurri, Mount, peak, *Austral.* 31°45' S, 145°48' E **230**
Nushagak Peninsula, *Alas., U.S.* 58°17' N, 160°46' W **98**
Nushki, *Pak.* 29°31' N, 66°3' E **182**
Nut Mountain, *Can.* 52°8' N, 103°23' W **108**
Nuttby Mountain, peak, *Can.* 45°32' N, 63°18' W **111**
Nu'uanu Pali Overlook, site, *Hawai'i, U.S.* 21°20' N, 157°50' W **99**
Nuugaatsiaq 71°35' N, 53°13' W **106**
Nuuk (Godthåb), *Greenland, Den.* 64°14' N, 51°38' W **106**
Nuupas, *Fin.* 66°0' N, 26°19' E **154**
Nuussuaq 70°6' N, 51°42' W **106**
Nuussuaq (Kraulshavn) 74°9' N, 57°1' W **106**
Nuwara Eliya, *Sri Lanka* 6°56' N, 80°47' E **188**
Nuwerus, *S. Af.* 31°8' S, 18°20' E **227**
Nuyno, *Ukr.* 51°31' N, 24°53' E **158**
Nuyts Archipelago, islands, *Great Australian Bight* 32°45' S, 130°56' E **230**
Nwayfadh, *Africa* 24°53' N, 14°50' W **214**
Nxai Pan National Park, *Botswana* 20°3' S, 24°40' E **224**
Ny Ålesund, *Nor.* 78°50' N, 12°1' E **160**
Nyaake, *Liberia* 4°50' N, 7°36' W **222**
Nyac, *Alas., U.S.* 60°53' N, 160°7' W **98**
Nyagan', *Russ.* 62°19' N, 65°34' E **169**
Nyahanga, *Tanzania* 2°22' S, 33°34' E **224**
Nyainqêntanglha Feng, peak, *China* 30°23' N, 90°32' E **197**
Nyainrong, *China* 32°2' N, 92°14' E **188**
Nyakabindi, *Tanzania* 2°37' S, 33°55' E **224**
Nyakanazi, *Tanzania* 3°6' S, 31°15' E **224**
Nyåker, *Nor.* 63°47' N, 19°19' E **152**
Nyakrom, *Ghana* 5°37' N, 0°48' E **222**
Nyaksimvol', *Russ.* 62°29' N, 60°51' E **169**
Nyala, *Sudan* 12°2' N, 24°53' E **224**
Nyalam, *China* 28°11' N, 85°57' E **197**
Nyamandhlovu, *Zimb.* 19°53' S, 28°16' E **224**
Nyamapanda, *Zimb.* 16°56' S, 32°48' E **224**
Nyambiti, *Tanzania* 2°49' S, 33°24' E **218**
Nyamirembe, *Tanzania* 2°33' S, 31°42' E **224**
Nyamtumbo, *Tanzania* 10°31' S, 36°6' E **224**
Nyanding, river, *Sudan* 8°8' N, 32°18' E **224**
Nyandoma, *Russ.* 61°39' N, 40°10' E **154**
Nyanga, *Zimb.* 18°11' S, 32°42' E **224**
Nyanga Nature Reserve, *Congo* 3°2' S, 11°27' E **206**
Nyangwe, *Dem. Rep. of the Congo* 4°12' S, 26°11' E **218**
Nyanje, *Zambia* 14°24' S, 31°47' E **224**
Nyanza Lac, *Burundi* 4°20' S, 29°36' E **224**
Nyarling, river, *Can.* 60°20' N, 114°23' W **108**
Nyashabozh, *Russ.* 65°28' N, 53°52' E **154**
Nyaunglebin, *Myanmar* 17°58' N, 96°42' E **202**
Nyazepetrovsk, *Russ.* 56°3' N, 59°39' E **154**
Nyborg, *Den.* 55°17' N, 10°47' E **150**
Nyborg, *Nor.* 70°10' N, 28°36' E **152**
Nybro, *Nor.* 56°45' N, 15°53' E **152**
Nyda, *Russ.* 66°34' N, 73°2' E **169**
Nye Mountains, *Antarctica* 68°4' S, 48°39' E **248**
Nyeboe Land 81°28' N, 53°44' W **246**
Nyeharelaye, *Belarus* 53°33' N, 27°4' E **152**
Nyékládháza, *Hung.* 47°59' N, 20°48' E **168**
Nyeri, *Kenya* 0°26' N, 36°57' E **224**
Nyerol, *Sudan* 8°40' N, 32°2' E **224**
Nyika National Park, *Malawi* 11°6' S, 34°9' E **224**
Nyika Plateau, *Malawi* 10°39' S, 33°28' E **224**
Nyima, *China* 31°55' N, 87°49' E **188**
Nyimba, *Zambia* 14°35' S, 30°50' E **224**
Nyingchi, *China* 29°36' N, 94°24' E **188**
Nyírábrány, *Hung.* 47°33' N, 22°3' E **168**
Nyírbátor, *Hung.* 47°49' N, 22°8' E **168**
Nyíregyháza, *Hung.* 47°56' N, 21°44' E **168**
Nyiri Desert, *Kenya* 2°23' S, 37°10' E **224**
Nyiru, Mount, peak, *Kenya* 2°16' N, 36°42' E **224**
Nykarleby (Uusikaarlepyy), *Fin.* 63°31' N, 22°32' E **152**
Nykøbing, *Den.* 54°46' N, 11°53' E **152**
Nykøbing, *Den.* 56°47' N, 8°49' E **150**
Nykøbing, *Den.* 55°55' N, 11°39' E **152**
Nyköping, *Nor.* 58°44' N, 16°59' E **152**
Nylstroom see Modimolle, *S. Af.* 24°44' S, 28°24' E **227**
Nynäshamn, *Sw.* 58°53' N, 17°53' E **166**
Nyoma Rap, *India* 33°9' N, 78°39' E **188**
Nyoman, river, *Belarus* 53°52' N, 25°34' E **166**
Nyon, *Switz.* 46°25' N, 6°16' E **167**
Nyonga, *Tanzania* 6°42' S, 32°3' E **224**
Nyrob, *Russ.* 60°44' N, 56°43' E **154**
Nyrud, *Nor.* 69°9' N, 29°12' E **152**
Nyrza, *Russ.* 63°27' N, 43°37' E **154**
Nysa, *Pol.* 50°29' N, 17°20' E **152**
Nyssa, *Oreg., U.S.* 43°52' N, 117°1' W **90**
Nytva, *Russ.* 57°56' N, 55°21' E **154**
Nyukhcha, *Russ.* 63°27' N, 46°28' E **154**
Nyukka, *Russ.* 66°3' N, 32°41' E **152**
Nyuksenitsa, *Russ.* 60°24' N, 44°18' E **154**
Nyunzu, *Dem. Rep. of the Congo* 5°58' S, 27°57' E **224**
Nyurba, *Russ.* 63°22' N, 118°13' E **160**
Nyuvchim, *Russ.* 61°22' N, 50°50' E **154**
Nyzhn'ohirs'kyy, *Ukr.* 45°26' N, 34°41' E **156**
Nzara, *Sudan* 4°41' N, 28°14' E **224**
Nzega, *Tanzania* 4°14' S, 33°11' E **224**
Nzérékoré, *Guinea* 7°38' N, 8°50' W **222**
N'zeto, *Angola* 7°19' S, 12°52' E **218**
Nzi, river, *Côte d'Ivoire* 6°6' N, 4°51' W **222**
Nzo, *Guinea* 7°35' N, 8°20' W **222**
Nzo, river, *Côte d'Ivoire* 6°49' N, 7°36' W **222**
Nzoro, *Dem. Rep. of the Congo* 3°14' N, 29°31' E **224**
Nzoro, river, *Dem. Rep. of the Congo* 3°25' N, 30°25' E **224**
Nzwani, island, *Comoros* 12°36' S, 44°15' E **220**

O

Oacoma, *S. Dak., U.S.* 43°47' N, 99°24' W **90**
Oahe Dam, *S. Dak., U.S.* 44°39' N, 101°32' W **82**
Oahe, Lake, *N. Dak., U.S.* 45°33' N, 100°54' W **80**
O'ahu, island, *Hawai'i, U.S.* 21°43' N, 157°60' W **99**
Oak Bluffs, *Mass., U.S.* 41°27' N, 70°35' W **104**
Oak Creek, *Colo., U.S.* 40°17' N, 106°57' W **90**
Oak Grove, *La., U.S.* 32°50' N, 91°23' W **103**
Oak Harbor, *Ohio, U.S.* 41°30' N, 83°9' W **102**
Oak Harbor, *Wash., U.S.* 48°17' N, 122°38' W **100**
Oak Hill, *Fla., U.S.* 28°51' N, 80°52' W **105**
Oak Hill, *W. Va., U.S.* 37°58' N, 81°9' W **94**
Oak Lake, *Can.* 49°45' N, 100°39' W **90**
Oak Lawn, *Ill., U.S.* 41°43' N, 87°45' W **102**
Oak Park, *Ill., U.S.* 41°53' N, 87°48' W **102**
Oak Ridge, *La., U.S.* 32°36' N, 91°46' W **103**
Oak Ridge, *Tenn., U.S.* 36°0' N, 84°15' W **96**
Oak View, *Calif., U.S.* 34°24' N, 119°19' W **100**
Oakdale, *Calif., U.S.* 37°45' N, 120°52' W **100**
Oakdale, *La., U.S.* 30°47' N, 92°40' W **103**
Oakdale, *Mass., U.S.* 42°23' N, 71°48' W **104**
Oakengates, *U.K.* 52°41' N, 2°26' W **162**
Oakes, *N. Dak., U.S.* 46°7' N, 98°6' W **90**
Oakesdale, *Wash., U.S.* 47°7' N, 117°15' W **90**
Oakham, *U.K.* 52°39' N, 0°44' E **162**
Oakhurst, *Calif., U.S.* 37°20' N, 119°40' W **100**
Oakland, *Calif., U.S.* 37°48' N, 122°16' W **100**
Oakland, *Ill., U.S.* 39°38' N, 88°2' W **102**
Oakland, *Iowa, U.S.* 41°17' N, 95°22' W **90**
Oakland, *Me., U.S.* 44°32' N, 69°44' W **104**
Oakland, *Nebr., U.S.* 41°48' N, 96°28' W **90**
Oakland, *Oreg., U.S.* 43°24' N, 123°18' W **90**
Oakland, *Pa., U.S.* 41°56' N, 75°38' W **94**
Oakland Park, *Fla., U.S.* 26°10' N, 80°9' W **105**
Oakley, *Calif., U.S.* 37°59' N, 121°44' W **100**
Oakley, *Kans., U.S.* 39°7' N, 100°52' W **90**
Oakridge, *Oreg., U.S.* 43°44' N, 122°28' W **90**
Oaktown, *Ind., U.S.* 38°51' N, 87°27' W **102**
Oakura, *N.Z.* 39°10' S, 173°57' E **240**
Oakville, *Conn., U.S.* 41°35' N, 73°5' W **104**
Oakville, *Wash., U.S.* 46°48' N, 123°14' W **100**
Oamaru, *N.Z.* 45°6' S, 170°57' E **240**
Oaro, *N.Z.* 42°33' S, 173°28' E **240**
Ōasa, *Japan* 34°45' N, 132°28' E **201**
Oates Coast, *Antarctica* 69°56' S, 159°4' E **248**
Oatman, *Ariz., U.S.* 35°0' N, 114°23' W **101**
Oaxaca, *Mex.* 17°2' N, 96°46' W **114**
Oaxaca, adm. division, *Mex.* 17°32' N, 97°22' W **114**
Ob', *Russ.* 54°59' N, 82°50' E **184**
Ob' Bank, *Greenland Sea* 80°34' N, 10°39' W **255**
Ob', river, *Russ.* 51°41' N, 83°0' E **172**
Ob' Tablemount, *Indian Ocean* 52°22' S, 41°12' E **255**
Oba, *Can.* 49°5' N, 84°6' W **94**
Oba Lake, *Can.* 48°34' N, 84°44' W **94**
Obabika Lake, lake, *Can.* 47°3' N, 80°43' W **94**
Obak, spring, *Sudan* 18°10' N, 34°51' E **182**
Obala, *Cameroon* 4°12' N, 11°31' E **222**
Obalj, *Bosn. and Herzg.* 43°27' N, 18°20' E **168**
Obama, *Japan* 32°44' N, 130°13' E **201**
Obama, *Japan* 35°28' N, 135°44' E **201**
Obamsca, Lac, lake, *Can.* 50°23' N, 78°51' W **110**
Obamsca, river, *Can.* 50°51' N, 78°50' W **110**
Oban, *U.K.* 56°25' N, 5°28' W **150**
Oban (Halfmoon Bay), *N.Z.* 46°55' S, 168°7' E **240**
Obanazawa, *Japan* 38°36' N, 140°25' E **201**
Obando, *Col.* 3°48' N, 67°51' W **136**
Obed, *Can.* 53°34' N, 117°14' W **108**
Obed Wild and Scenic River, *Tenn., U.S.* 35°51' N, 87°55' W **80**
Oberá, *Arg.* 27°29' S, 55°10' W **139**
Oberdrauburg, *Aust.* 46°45' N, 12°58' E **167**
Oberhausen, *Ger.* 51°28' N, 6°51' E **167**
Oberlin, *Kans., U.S.* 39°49' N, 100°33' W **90**
Oberlin, *La., U.S.* 30°36' N, 92°47' W **103**
Oberlin, *Ohio, U.S.* 41°16' N, 82°13' W **102**
Obernai, *Fr.* 48°27' N, 7°28' E **163**
Obernburg, *Ger.* 49°50' N, 9°9' E **167**
Oberpullendorf, *Aust.* 47°30' N, 16°31' E **168**
Obersuhl, *Ger.* 50°57' N, 10°1' E **167**
Oberursel, *Ger.* 50°12' N, 8°33' E **167**
Oberwesel, *Ger.* 50°6' N, 7°42' E **167**
Obi, *Nig.* 8°20' N, 8°45' E **222**
Obi, island, *Indonesia* 1°21' S, 127°18' E **192**
Obi, Kepulauan, islands, *Indonesia* 2°17' S, 126°42' E **192**
Óbidos, *Braz.* 1°53' S, 55°32' W **130**
Óbidos, *Port.* 39°21' N, 9°11' W **150**
Obigarm, *Taj.* 38°43' N, 69°45' E **197**
Obihiro, *Japan* 42°55' N, 143°9' E **190**
Obili, *Gabon* 0°42' N, 14°22' E **218**
Obil'noye, *Russ.* 47°29' N, 44°20' E **158**
Obion, *Tenn., U.S.* 36°15' N, 89°12' W **96**
Obispo, Punta, *Chile* 26°45' S, 71°27' W **132**
Obispo Trejo, *Arg.* 30°47' S, 63°26' W **139**
Obispos, *Venez.* 8°37' N, 70°8' W **136**
Oblivskaya, *Russ.* 48°31' N, 42°25' E **158**
Oblong, *Ill., U.S.* 39°0' N, 87°54' W **102**
Obluch'ye, *Russ.* 49°6' N, 131°5' E **190**
Obninsk, *Russ.* 55°4' N, 36°40' E **154**
Obo, *Cen. Af. Rep.* 5°21' N, 26°30' E **224**
Obo Liang, *China* 38°48' N, 92°39' E **188**
Oboa, peak, *Uganda* 1°45' N, 34°37' E **224**
Obock, *Djibouti* 11°55' N, 43°20' E **182**
Obokote, *Dem. Rep. of the Congo* 0°52' N, 26°19' E **224**
Obol', *Belarus* 55°23' N, 29°22' E **166**
Obonga Lake, *Can.* 49°58' N, 89°45' W **94**
Obot, *Alban.* 41°59' N, 19°25' E **168**
Obouya, *Congo* 0°57' N, 15°43' E **218**
Oboyan', *Russ.* 51°12' N, 36°21' E **158**
Obozerskiy, *Russ.* 63°27' N, 40°24' E **154**
Obra, river, *Pol.* 52°31' N, 15°33' E **152**
Obre Lake, *Can.* 60°19' N, 103°25' W **108**
Obreja, *Rom.* 45°28' N, 22°16' E **168**
Obrenovac, *Serb. and Mont.* 44°38' N, 20°10' E **168**
Obrian Peak see Trident Peak, *Nev., U.S.* 41°53' N, 118°30' W **90**
O'Brien, *Can.* 47°40' N, 80°45' W **110**
Obruk, *Turk.* 38°8' N, 33°11' E **156**
Observation Peak, *Calif., U.S.* 40°45' N, 120°16' W **90**
Obskaya Guba 67°26' N, 71°48' E **169**
Obuasi, *Ghana* 6°15' N, 1°40' W **222**
Obubra, *Nig.* 6°2' N, 8°19' E **222**
Ob'yachevo, *Russ.* 60°21' N, 49°39' E **154**
Obzor, *Bulg.* 42°49' N, 27°52' E **158**
Oca, Montes de, *Sp.* 42°24' N, 3°38' W **164**
Ocala, *Fla., U.S.* 29°10' N, 82°9' W **105**
Ocampo, *Mex.* 22°49' N, 99°19' W **114**
Ocampo, *Mex.* 21°36' N, 101°29' W **114**
Ocaña, *Col.* 8°12' N, 73°20' W **136**
Ocaña, *Sp.* 39°57' N, 3°30' W **164**
Occidental, Cordillera, *South America* 4°36' N, 76°51' W **122**
Occidental, Grand Erg, *Alg.* 30°22' N, 0°26' E **214**
Ocean Cay, island, *Bahamas* 25°25' N, 79°26' W **105**
Ocean City, *Md., U.S.* 38°20' N, 75°6' W **94**
Ocean City, *Wash., U.S.* 47°3' N, 124°10' W **100**
Ocean Falls, *Can.* 52°22' N, 127°43' W **108**
Ocean Grove, *Mass., U.S.* 41°43' N, 71°13' W **104**
Ocean Island see Kure Atoll, *Hawai'i, U.S.* 28°6' N, 179°12' W **99**
Ocean Lake, lake, *Wyo., U.S.* 43°9' N, 108°57' W **90**
Ocean Park, *Wash., U.S.* 46°28' N, 124°3' W **100**
Ocean Springs, *Miss., U.S.* 30°24' N, 88°50' W **96**
Oceano, *Calif., U.S.* 35°6' N, 120°37' W **100**
Oceanographer Fracture Zone, *North Atlantic Ocean* 34°28' N, 33°24' W **253**
Oceanside, *Calif., U.S.* 33°11' N, 117°23' W **101**
Ochakiv, *Ukr.* 46°41' N, 31°29' E **156**
Och'amch'ire, *Asia* 42°42' N, 41°31' E **195**
Ocher, *Russ.* 57°52' N, 54°49' E **154**
Ōchi, *Japan* 35°4' N, 132°36' E **201**
Ochobo, *Nig.* 7°10' N, 7°59' E **222**
Ochogavía, *Sp.* 42°55' N, 1°6' W **164**
Ochopee, *Fla., U.S.* 25°53' N, 81°18' W **105**
Ochre River, *Can.* 51°4' N, 99°48' W **90**
Ochtrup, *Ger.* 52°13' N, 7°12' E **163**
Ocilla, *Ga., U.S.* 31°35' N, 83°16' W **96**
Ockelbo, *Nor.* 60°53' N, 16°42' E **152**
Ocmulgee, river, *Ga., U.S.* 32°46' N, 83°37' W **80**
Ocnele Mari, *Rom.* 45°5' N, 24°17' E **156**
Ocnița, *Mold.* 48°23' N, 27°26' E **156**
Ocoee, *Fla., U.S.* 28°34' N, 81°33' W **105**
Ocoña, *Peru* 16°27' S, 73°6' W **137**
Ocoña, river, *Peru* 16°2' S, 73°19' W **137**
Oconee, Lake, *Ga., U.S.* 33°21' N, 83°39' W **96**
Oconee, river, *Ga., U.S.* 32°41' N, 83°14' W **80**
Oconomowoc, *Wis., U.S.* 43°6' N, 88°30' W **102**
Oconto, *Wis., U.S.* 44°54' N, 87°52' W **94**
Oconto Falls, *Wis., U.S.* 44°52' N, 88°8' W **94**
Ocoruro, *Peru* 15°4' S, 71°8' W **137**
Ocós, *Guatemala* 14°32' N, 92°12' W **115**
Ocotillo, *Calif., U.S.* 32°44' N, 116°2' W **101**
Ocotillo Wells, *Calif., U.S.* 33°8' N, 116°9' W **101**
Ocotlán, *Mex.* 20°21' N, 102°46' W **114**
Ocoyo, *Peru* 14°3' S, 75°1' W **137**
Ocracoke, *N.C., U.S.* 35°6' N, 75°60' W **96**
Ocracoke Inlet 34°49' N, 75°39' W **80**
Öcsa, *Hung.* 47°17' N, 19°14' E **168**
Octave, river, *Can.* 48°52' N, 78°35' W **94**
Ocumare del Tuy, *Venez.* 10°5' N, 66°47' W **136**
Ocurí, *Bol.* 18°55' S, 65°52' W **137**
Oda, *Eth.* 6°41' N, 41°10' E **224**
Oda, *Ghana* 5°55' N, 0°60' E **222**
Ōda, *Japan* 35°11' N, 132°30' E **201**
Oda, Jebel, peak, *Sudan* 20°17' N, 36°32' E **182**
Ŏdaejin, *N. Korea* 41°21' N, 129°47' E **200**
Odanovce, *Serb. and Mont.* 42°32' N, 21°41' E **168**
Odawara, *Japan* 35°15' N, 139°9' E **201**
Odda, *Nor.* 60°5' N, 6°31' E **152**
Oddur see Xuddur, *Somalia* 4°6' N, 43°55' E **218**
Odebolt, *Iowa, U.S.* 42°18' N, 95°15' W **90**
Odei, river, *Can.* 56°18' N, 98°57' W **108**
Odell, *Ill., U.S.* 41°0' N, 88°31' W **102**
Odell, *Oreg., U.S.* 45°36' N, 121°33' W **100**
Ödemiș, *Turk.* 38°13' N, 27°56' E **156**
Odendaalsrus, *S. Af.* 27°53' S, 26°39' E **227**
Odense, *Den.* 55°23' N, 10°23' E **150**
Odenwald, *Ger.* 49°45' N, 8°35' E **167**
Odesa, *Ukr.* 46°28' N, 30°43' E **156**
Odesdino, *Russ.* 63°28' N, 54°25' E **154**
Odessa, *Tex., U.S.* 31°49' N, 102°22' W **92**
Odessa, *Wash., U.S.* 47°18' N, 118°42' W **90**
Odiel, river, *Sp.* 37°34' N, 6°47' W **164**
Odienné, *Côte d'Ivoire* 9°31' N, 7°34' W **222**
Odin, Mount, peak, *Can.* 50°32' N, 118°14' W **90**
Odolanów, *Pol.* 51°35' N, 17°41' E **152**
Odon, *Ind., U.S.* 38°50' N, 86°60' W **102**
O'Donnell, *Tex., U.S.* 32°57' N, 101°49' W **92**
Odra, river, *Pol.* 51°37' N, 16°16' E **160**
Odra, river, *Sp.* 42°29' N, 4°3' W **164**
Odžaci, *Serb. and Mont.* 45°29' N, 19°16' E **168**
Odžak, *Bosn. and Herzg.* 45°0' N, 18°18' E **168**
Odzala, *Congo* 0°32' N, 14°34' E **218**
Odzala National Park, *Congo* 0°45' N, 14°35' E **206**
Odzi, river, *Zimb.* 19°11' S, 32°22' E **224**
Oecusse see Pante Makasar, *Indonesia* 9°21' S, 124°20' E **192**
Oederan, *Ger.* 50°51' N, 13°10' E **152**
Oeiras, *Braz.* 6°60' S, 42°10' W **132**
Oelde, *Ger.* 51°49' N, 8°7' E **167**
Oelrichs, *S. Dak., U.S.* 43°10' N, 103°15' W **90**
Oelwein, *Iowa, U.S.* 42°40' N, 91°55' W **94**
Oeniadae, ruin(s), *Gr.* 38°23' N, 21°5' E **156**
Oenpelli, *Austral.* 12°22' S, 133°6' E **238**
Oerlenbach, *Ger.* 50°9' N, 10°7' E **167**
Oeta, Mount see Oiti, Óros, peak, *Gr.* 38°47' N, 22°10' E **156**
Of, *Turk.* 40°57' N, 40°17' E **195**
O'Fallon, *Ill., U.S.* 38°34' N, 89°55' W **102**
O'Fallon Creek, river, *Mont., U.S.* 46°49' N, 105°31' W **90**
Ofaqim, *Israel* 31°19' N, 34°37' E **194**
Ofen Pass, *Switz.* 46°38' N, 10°17' E **167**
Offa, *Nig.* 8°12' N, 4°43' E **222**
Offenbach, *Ger.* 50°5' N, 8°46' E **167**
Offutt Air Force Base, *Nebr., U.S.* 41°5' N, 95°60' W **90**
Oficina Dominador, *Chile* 24°23' S, 69°34' W **132**
Oficina, oil field, *Venez.* 8°43' N, 64°27' W **116**
Oficina Santa Fe, *Chile* 21°52' S, 69°37' W **137**
Ofin, river, *Ghana* 6°26' N, 2°2' W **222**
Ofu, island, *United States* 14°11' S, 169°38' W **241**
Ogadēn, region, *Eth.* 6°45' N, 42°8' E **224**
Ōgaki, *Japan* 35°21' N, 136°37' E **201**
Ogallala, *Nebr., U.S.* 41°7' N, 101°44' W **92**
Ogasawara Guntō see Bonin Islands, *North Pacific Ocean* 25°25' N, 143°8' E **238**
Ogbomosho, *Nig.* 8°10' N, 4°16' E **222**
Ogden, *Iowa, U.S.* 42°0' N, 94°2' W **94**
Ogden, *Utah, U.S.* 41°13' N, 111°58' W **90**
Ogden, Mount, peak, *Can.* 58°25' N, 133°32' W **108**
Ogema, *Can.* 49°33' N, 104°56' W **90**
Oggiono, *It.* 45°46' N, 9°19' E **167**
Ogi, *Japan* 37°49' N, 138°16' E **201**
Ogilvie Mountains, *Can.* 64°46' N, 139°9' W **106**
Oglanly, *Turkm.* 39°52' N, 54°22' E **180**
Oglat Beraber, spring, *Alg.* 30°24' N, 3°34' W **214**
Oglat d'Admamlalmat, spring, *Mauritania* 23°25' N, 11°48' W **214**
'Oglât ed Daoud, spring, *Mauritania* 23°31' N, 6°57' W **214**
'Oglât el Fersig, spring, *Mauritania* 21°49' N, 6°21' W **222**
'Oglat el Khnâchîch, spring, *Mali* 21°51' N, 3°59' W **222**
Oglats de Mkhaïzira, spring, *Mauritania* 22°44' N, 10°18' W **214**
Oglesby, *Ill., U.S.* 41°17' N, 89°5' W **102**
Oglethorpe, *Ga., U.S.* 32°17' N, 84°4' W **96**
Oglethorpe, Mount, peak, *Ga., U.S.* 34°28' N, 84°24' W **96**
Ogna, *Nor.* 58°31' N, 5°48' E **150**
Ognev Yar, *Russ.* 58°21' N, 76°30' E **169**
Ognon, river, *Fr.* 47°17' N, 5°59' E **165**
Ogoja, *Nig.* 6°38' N, 8°42' E **222**
Ogoki, *Can.* 51°40' N, 85°52' W **82**
Ogoki Reservoir, lake, *Can.* 50°50' N, 89°14' W **80**
Ogoki, river, *Can.* 51°5' N, 86°10' W **110**
Ögöömör, *Mongolia* 46°47' N, 107°50' E **198**
Ogōri, *Japan* 34°6' N, 131°24' E **200**
Ogou, river, *Togo* 8°48' N, 1°25' E **222**
Ogr, *Sudan* 12°2' N, 27°1' E **218**
Ograđen, *Maced.* 41°25' N, 22°52' E **168**
Ogre, *Latv.* 56°49' N, 24°33' E **166**
Ogre, river, *Latv.* 56°46' N, 25°27' E **166**
'Ogueïlet en Nmâdi, spring, *Mauritania* 19°45' N, 11°1' W **222**
Oguma, *Nig.* 7°51' N, 7°2' E **222**
Ogunquit, *Me., U.S.* 43°14' N, 70°37' W **104**
Ogwashi Uku, *Nig.* 6°17' N, 6°28' E **222**
Ohanet, oil field, *Alg.* 28°46' N, 8°49' E **214**
Ohangoron, *Uzb.* 40°56' N, 69°35' E **197**
Ohau, *N.Z.* 40°41' S, 175°15' E **240**
Óhi, Óros, peak, *Gr.* 38°3' N, 24°23' E **156**
Ohio, *Ill., U.S.* 41°33' N, 89°28' W **102**
Ohio, adm. division, *Ohio, U.S.* 40°15' N, 83°3' W **102**
Ohio City, *Ohio, U.S.* 40°45' N, 84°37' W **102**
Ohio Range, *Antarctica* 85°4' S, 101°32' W **248**
Ohio, river, *U.S.* 37°37' N, 87°7' W **80**
Ōi, river, *Japan* 35°9' N, 138°8' E **201**
Oiapoque, *Braz.* 3°50' N, 51°48' W **130**
Oijärvi, *Fin.* 65°38' N, 25°48' E **152**
Oil City, *La., U.S.* 32°44' N, 93°58' W **103**
Oil City, *Pa., U.S.* 41°24' N, 79°43' W **94**
Oil Islands see Chagos Archipelago, *Indian Ocean* 6°42' S, 71°25' E **188**
Oildale, *Calif., U.S.* 35°25' N, 119°2' W **101**
Oilton, *Okla., U.S.* 36°3' N, 96°35' W **92**
Oilton, *Tex., U.S.* 27°27' N, 98°58' W **92**
Oise, river, *Fr.* 49°51' N, 3°39' E **163**
Ōita, *Japan* 33°13' N, 131°37' E **201**
Ōita, adm. division, *Japan* 33°42' N, 131°34' E **200**
Oiti, Óros (Oeta, Mount), peak, *Gr.* 38°47' N, 22°10' E **156**
Oiticica, *South America* 5°2' S, 41°6' W **132**
Oituz, *Rom.* 46°6' N, 26°23' E **156**
Ojai, *Calif., U.S.* 34°26' N, 119°15' W **101**
Øje, *Nor.* 60°48' N, 13°49' E **152**
Ojeda, *Arg.* 35°18' S, 63°59' W **139**
Ojinaga, *Mex.* 29°33' N, 104°27' W **92**
Ojiya, *Japan* 37°17' N, 138°47' E **201**
Ojo Caliente, *Mex.* 22°33' N, 102°16' W **114**
Ojo de Laguna, *Mex.* 29°26' N, 106°25' W **92**
Ojós, *Sp.* 38°8' N, 1°22' W **164**
Ojos del Salado, Cerro, peak, *Chile* 27°6' S, 68°45' W **132**
Ojuelos de Jalisco, *Mex.* 21°51' N, 101°35' W **114**
Oka, river, *Russ.* 55°43' N, 42°12' E **154**
Oka, river, *Russ.* 53°14' N, 36°17' E **154**
Okaba, *Indonesia* 8°7' S, 139°37' E **192**
Okahandja, *Namibia* 21°59' S, 16°53' E **227**
Okahukura, *N.Z.* 38°49' S, 175°14' E **240**
Okak Islands, *Can.* 57°32' N, 65°21' W **106**
Okakarara, *Namibia* 20°36' S, 17°30' E **227**
Okaloacoochee Slough, marsh, *Fla., U.S.* 26°26' N, 80°42' W **105**
Okanagan Lake, *Can.* 49°50' N, 120°51' W **80**
Okanogan, *Wash., U.S.* 48°21' N, 119°37' W **90**
Okanogan Range, *Wash., U.S.* 48°48' N, 120°27' W **90**
Okány, *Hung.* 46°53' N, 21°21' E **168**
Okaputa, *Namibia* 20°7' S, 16°58' E **227**
Okara, *Pak.* 30°49' N, 73°27' E **186**
Okatjoruu, *Namibia* 19°38' S, 18°34' E **220**
Okaukuejo, *Namibia* 19°9' S, 15°57' E **220**
Okavango Delta, *Botswana* 19°33' S, 23°16' E **224**
Ōkawa, *Japan* 33°12' N, 130°22' E **201**
Okawville, *Ill., U.S.* 38°25' N, 89°33' W **102**
Okaya, *Japan* 36°4' N, 138°2' E **201**
Okayama, *Japan* 34°38' N, 133°53' E **201**
Okayama, adm. division, *Japan* 34°54' N, 133°20' E **201**
Okazaki, *Japan* 34°56' N, 137°10' E **201**
Okcheon, *S. Korea* 36°18' N, 127°34' E **200**
Okeechobee, *Fla., U.S.* 27°15' N, 80°50' W **105**
Okeechobee, Lake, *Fla., U.S.* 26°57' N, 80°59' W **105**
Okeene, *Okla., U.S.* 36°6' N, 98°20' W **92**
Okefenokee Swamp, marsh, *Ga., U.S.* 30°35' N, 83°9' W **80**
Okene, *Nig.* 7°34' N, 6°14' E **222**
Okha, *India* 22°26' N, 69°3' E **186**
Okha, *Russ.* 53°33' N, 142°43' E **160**
Okhaldhunga, *Nepal* 27°20' N, 86°30' E **197**
Okhansk, *Russ.* 57°42' N, 55°19' E **154**
Okhotsk, *Russ.* 59°26' N, 143°20' E **160**
Okhotsk, Sea of 57°51' N, 141°45' E **160**
Okhotskiy Perevoz, *Russ.* 61°52' N, 135°38' E **160**
Okhtyrka, *Ukr.* 50°19' N, 34°55' E **158**
Oki Guntō, islands, *Sea of Japan* 35°59' N, 133°6' E **201**
Okiep, *S. Af.* 29°36' S, 17°52' E **227**
Okinawa, island, *Japan* 26°22' N, 128°16' E **190**
Okino Erabu Shima, island, *Japan* 27°2' N, 128°25' E **190**
Okkang, *N. Korea* 40°18' N, 124°46' E **200**
Oklahoma, adm. division, *Okla., U.S.* 35°37' N, 98°23' W **96**
Oklahoma City, *Okla., U.S.* 35°25' N, 97°36' W **92**
Oklawaha, *Fla., U.S.* 29°2' N, 81°56' W **105**
Okletac, *Serb. and Mont.* 44°5' N, 19°34' E **168**
Okmulgee, *Okla., U.S.* 35°36' N, 95°58' W **94**
Okolona, *Miss., U.S.* 33°59' N, 88°45' W **96**
Okotoks, *Can.* 50°44' N, 113°59' W **90**
Okounfo, *Benin* 8°20' N, 2°37' E **222**
Okoyo, *Congo* 1°27' S, 15°1' E **218**
Okpara, river, *Africa* 7°44' N, 2°37' E **222**
Okp'yŏng, *N. Korea* 39°16' N, 127°20' E **200**
Oksino, *Russ.* 67°34' N, 52°20' E **169**
Oksovskiy, *Russ.* 62°36' N, 39°56' E **154**
Okstindan, peak, *Nor.* 65°59' N, 14°11' E **152**
Oktyabr'sk, *Kaz.* 49°26' N, 57°25' E **158**
Oktyabr'skiy, *Kaz.* 49°39' N, 83°37' E **184**
Oktyabr'skiy, *Russ.* 55°5' N, 60°10' E **154**

Oktyabr'skiy, Russ. 47°55' N, 43°34' E 158
Oktyabr'skiy, Russ. 54°27' N, 53°35' E 154
Oktyabr'skoe, Kaz. 52°8' N, 65°40' E 184
Oktyabr'skoye, Russ. 62°34' N, 66°2' E 160
Oktyabr'skoye, Russ. 52°23' N, 55°37' E 154
Oktyabr'skoye, Russ. 52°21' N, 55°42' E 184
Okučani, Croatia 45°15' N, 17°12' E 168
Ōkuchi, Japan 32°3' N, 130°37' E 201
Okulovka, Russ. 58°24' N, 33°19' E 154
Okunev Nos, Russ. 66°16' N, 52°39' E 154
Okushiri, island, Japan 41°45' N, 138°29' E 190
Okuta, Nig. 9°12' N, 3°15' E 222
Ola, Ark., U.S. 35°1' N, 93°14' W 96
Ola, Russ. 59°37' N, 151°11' E 160
Ólafsvík, Ice. 64°53' N, 23°45' W 246
Olaine, Latv. 56°48' N, 23°57' E 166
Olancha, Calif., U.S. 36°17' N, 118°2' W 101
Olancha Peak, Calif., U.S. 36°15' N, 118°10' W 101
Olanchito, Hond. 15°28' N, 86°35' W 115
Ölands Norra Udde, Sw. 57°23' N, 16°58' E 152
Ölands Södra Udde, Sw. 55°54' N, 16°3' E 152
Olanga, Russ. 66°9' N, 30°35' E 152
Olary, Austral. 32°16' S, 140°20' E 231
Olasan, spring, Eth. 5°17' N, 45°4' E 218
Olascoaga, Arg. 35°15' S, 60°39' W 139
Olathe, Kans., U.S. 38°51' N, 94°49' W 94
Olavarría, Arg. 36°55' S, 60°17' W 139
Oława, Pol. 50°57' N, 17°17' E 152
Olbia, It. 40°55' N, 9°28' E 214
Old Cove Fort, site, Utah, U.S. 38°39' N, 112°38' W 90
Old Crow, Can. 67°32' N, 139°56' W 73
Old Dongola, ruin(s), Sudan 18°12' N, 30°42' E 226
Old Fort, Can. 55°4' N, 126°20' W 108
Old Man of the Mountain, site, N.H., U.S. 44°10' N, 71°44' W 104
Old Mkushi, Zambia 14°22' S, 29°20' E 224
Old Orchard Beach, Me., U.S. 43°30' N, 70°24' W 104
Old Rhodes Key, island, Fla., U.S. 25°22' N, 80°14' W 105
Old Sarum, ruin(s), U.K. 51°5' N, 1°50' W 162
Old Saybrook, Conn., U.S. 41°17' N, 72°23' W 104
Old Slains Castle, site, U.K. 57°20' N, 2°11' W 150
Old Speck Mountain, peak, Me., U.S. 44°33' N, 70°60' W 104
Old Sturbridge, site, Mass., U.S. 42°5' N, 72°8' W 104
Old Sugar Mill, site, Hawai'i, U.S. 21°30' N, 157°53' W 99
Old Town, Fla., U.S. 29°36' N, 82°60' W 105
Old Wives Lake, Can. 50°3' N, 106°39' W 90
Old Woman Mountains, Calif., U.S. 34°26' N, 115°25' W 101
Oldbury, U.K. 52°29' N, 2°1' W 162
Oldeani, Tanzania 3°20' S, 35°34' E 224
Olden, Nor. 61°50' N, 6°49' E 152
Oldenburg, Ger. 53°8' N, 8°13' E 163
Oldenzaal, Neth. 52°18' N, 6°55' E 163
Oldham, U.K. 53°32' N, 2°7' W 162
Olds, Can. 51°49' N, 114°6' W 90
Olduvai Gorge, site, Tanzania 2°57' S, 35°14' E 224
Öldzeyte Suma, Mongolia 44°33' N, 106°10' E 198
Öldziyt, Mongolia 44°39' N, 109°3' E 198
Olean, N.Y., U.S. 42°4' N, 78°27' W 94
Olecko, Pol. 54°1' N, 22°31' E 166
Olekma, river, Russ. 59°23' N, 120°19' E 160
Olekminsk, Russ. 60°23' N, 120°16' E 160
Oleksandriya, Ukr. 50°44' N, 26°20' E 152
Olema, Russ. 64°28' N, 46°2' E 154
Ølen, Nor. 59°35' N, 5°47' E 152
Olenegorsk, Russ. 68°8' N, 33°15' E 152
Olenek, Russ. 68°30' N, 112°22' E 160
Olenek, river, Russ. 66°59' N, 107°5' E 160
Olenekskiy Zaliv 72°54' N, 114°57' E 160
Olenino, Russ. 56°12' N, 33°37' E 154
Olenitsa, Russ. 66°26' N, 35°13' E 152
Oleniy, Ostrov, island, Russ. 72°2' N, 72°25' E 160
Olesno, Pol. 50°52' N, 18°25' E 152
Olevs'k, Ukr. 51°13' N, 27°40' E 152
Ølfjellet, peak, Nor. 66°46' N, 15°4' E 152
Olga, Lac, lake, Can. 49°45' N, 77°35' W 94
Olga, Mount see Kata Tjuta, peak, Austral. 25°21' S, 130°31' E 230
Olgastretet 78°6' N, 20°12' E 160
Ölgiy, Mongolia 48°57' N, 89°50' E 184
Ølgod, Den. 55°48' N, 8°35' E 150
Olhava, Fin. 65°28' N, 25°22' E 152
Oli Qoltyq Sory, marsh, Kaz. 45°20' N, 53°31' E 158
Oli, river, Nig. 9°46' N, 4°0' E 222
Oliete, Sp. 40°59' N, 0°41' E 164
Olifants, river, S. Af. 24°36' S, 30°29' E 227
Olifantshoek, S. Af. 27°58' S, 22°42' E 227
Olimarao Atoll 7°48' N, 143°3' E 192
Ólimbos, Gr. 35°44' N, 27°11' E 156
Ólimbos, Óros (Olympus), peak, Gr. 40°3' N, 22°17' E 156
Olímpia, Braz. 20°43' S, 48°55' W 138
Olinalá, Mex. 17°48' N, 98°51' W 114
Olinda, Braz. 7°60' S, 34°55' W 132
Olinda Entrance 11°17' S, 142°53' E 192
Olite, Sp. 42°28' N, 1°39' W 164
Oliva, Arg. 32°3' S, 63°33' W 139
Oliva, Sp. 38°55' N, 0°8' E 164
Oliva de la Frontera, Sp. 38°16' N, 6°56' W 150
Oliveira, Braz. 20°40' S, 44°51' W 138
Oliver, Can. 49°10' N, 119°34' W 90
Oliver Lake, lake, Can. 56°50' N, 103°50' W 108
Olivet, Mich., U.S. 42°27' N, 84°55' W 102
Olivia, Minn., U.S. 44°46' N, 94°60' W 90
Ol'khovka, Russ. 49°51' N, 44°31' E 158
Olla, La., U.S. 31°53' N, 92°15' W 103
Ollachea, Peru 13°49' S, 70°32' W 137
Ollagüe (Oyahue), Chile 21°14' S, 68°18' W 137
Ollagüe, Volcan, peak, Chile 21°19' S, 68°20' W 137
Ollanta, Peru 9°45' S, 74°2' W 137
Ollerton, U.K. 53°11' N, 1°2' W 162
Olmaliq, Uzb. 40°50' N, 69°35' E 197
Olnes, Alas., U.S. 65°5' N, 147°40' W 98
Olney, Ill., U.S. 38°42' N, 88°1' W 82
Olney, Tex., U.S. 33°21' N, 98°46' W 92
Olney, U.K. 52°9' N, 0°42' E 162
Oloibiri, oil field, Nig. 4°39' N, 6°16' E 222
Olomouc, Czech Rep. 49°35' N, 17°16' E 152
Olomoucký, adm. division, Czech Rep. 49°35' N, 17°16' E 152
Olonets, Russ. 60°56' N, 33°2' E 154
Olongapo, Philippines 14°50' N, 120°17' E 203
Olonzac, Fr. 43°16' N, 2°42' E 164
Oloron, Fr. 43°12' N, 0°36' E 164
Oloru, Nig. 8°39' N, 4°35' E 222
Olosega, island, United States 14°11' S, 169°36' W 241
Olot, Sp. 42°11' N, 2°28' E 164
Olovo, Bosn. and Herzg. 44°7' N, 18°34' E 168
Olovyannaya, Russ. 50°54' N, 115°24' E 190
Olovyannaya, Russ. 66°13' N, 178°56' W 98
Oloy, river, Russ. 66°12' N, 160°20' E 160
Olpe, Ger. 51°1' N, 7°50' E 167
Ølshammar, Nor. 58°45' N, 14°45' E 152
Olsztyn, Pol. 53°46' N, 20°28' E 166
Olt, adm. division, Rom. 44°11' N, 24°12' E 156
Olt, river, Rom. 45°46' N, 24°19' E 156
Olten, Switz. 47°21' N, 7°53' E 156
Olteni, Rom. 44°11' N, 25°18' E 156
Oltenița, Rom. 44°6' N, 26°39' E 156
Olton, Tex., U.S. 34°9' N, 102°8' W 92
Oltu, Turk. 40°34' N, 41°57' E 195
Oltu, river, Turk. 40°43' N, 41°41' E 195
Oluan Pi, Taiwan 21°39' N, 120°53' E 198
Olukonda, Namibia 18°6' S, 16°4' E 220
Ólvega, Sp. 41°45' N, 1°59' W 164
Olvera, Sp. 36°55' N, 5°17' W 164
Olympia, Wash., U.S. 47°1' N, 122°56' W 100
Olympia, ruin(s), Gr. 37°38' N, 21°32' E 156
Olympic Mountains, Wash., U.S. 47°16' N, 123°50' W 100
Olympic National Park, Wash., U.S. 48°0' N, 125°7' W 100
Olympos, peak, Cyprus 34°55' N, 32°50' E 194
Olympus, Mount, peak, Wash., U.S. 47°47' N, 123°45' W 100
Olympus, Mount see Ulu Dağ, peak, Turk. 40°4' N, 29°7' E 156
Olympus see Ólimbos, Óros, peak, Gr. 40°3' N, 22°17' E 156
Olynthus, ruin(s), Gr. 40°16' N, 23°17' E 156
Olyutorskiy, Mys, Russ. 59°44' N, 170°18' E 160
Om', river, Russ. 55°17' N, 77°33' E 184
Oma, China 32°26' N, 83°17' E 188
Oma, Miss., U.S. 31°43' N, 90°9' W 103
Oma, river, Russ. 66°23' N, 46°47' E 154
Ōmachi, Japan 36°30' N, 137°51' E 201
Omae Zaki, Japan 34°29' N, 138°14' E 201
Omaha, Nebr., U.S. 41°15' N, 95°58' W 90
Omaha, Tex., U.S. 33°10' N, 94°45' W 103
Omaha Beach, Fr. 49°17' N, 1°13' W 150
Omak, Wash., U.S. 48°24' N, 119°33' W 90
Omakau, N.Z. 45°5' S, 169°38' E 240
Omakere, N.Z. 40°3' S, 176°49' E 240
Oman 21°52' N, 57°32' E 182
Oman, Gulf of 24°46' N, 57°23' E 172
Oman, Gulf of 24°30' N, 58°46' E 254
Omarama, N.Z. 44°31' S, 169°58' E 240
Omaruru, Namibia 21°27' S, 15°55' E 227
Ombabika, Can. 50°14' N, 87°54' W 94
Ombaïa, Congo 2°24' S, 13°10' E 218
Ombombo, spring, Namibia 18°44' S, 13°55' E 220
Ombwe, Dem. Rep. of the Congo 4°23' S, 25°32' E 224
Omchali, Mys, Turkm. 40°54' N, 53°5' E 158
Omdurman, Sudan 15°36' N, 32°27' E 182
Omegna, It. 45°52' N, 8°24' E 167
Omer, Mich., U.S. 44°3' N, 83°51' W 102
Ometepec, Mex. 16°30' N, 98°28' W 73
Ōmihachiman, Japan 35°6' N, 136°5' E 201
Omihi, N.Z. 43°2' S, 172°52' E 240
Omineca, river, Can. 55°54' N, 126°9' W 108
Omiš, Croatia 43°26' N, 16°42' E 168
Ōmiya, Japan 35°54' N, 139°38' E 201
Ommaney, Cape, Alas., U.S. 56°0' N, 135°20' W 108
Ommen, Neth. 52°31' N, 6°24' E 163
Omo National Park, Eth. 5°39' N, 35°20' E 224
Omo, river, Eth. 5°54' N, 35°55' E 224
Omolon, Russ. 65°10' N, 160°34' E 173
Omolon, river, Russ. 69°30' N, 155°38' E 172
Omoloy, river, Russ. 69°50' N, 132°42' E 160
Omont, Fr. 49°35' N, 4°42' E 163
Omro, Wis., U.S. 44°1' N, 88°45' W 102
Omsk, Russ. 54°58' N, 73°26' E 184
Omsk, adm. division, Russ. 54°44' N, 72°20' E 184
Omsukchan, Russ. 62°29' N, 155°44' E 173
Omu Aran, Nig. 8°9' N, 5°6' E 222
Omul, peak, Rom. 45°26' N, 25°22' E 156
Omulyakhskaya Guba 72°1' N, 138°2' E 160
Ōmura, Japan 32°54' N, 129°58' E 201
Ōmuta, Japan 33°1' N, 130°26' E 201
Omutninsk, Russ. 58°40' N, 52°15' E 154
Oña, Sp. 42°43' N, 3°26' W 164
Onaga, Kans., U.S. 39°28' N, 96°10' W 90
Onakawana, Can. 50°36' N, 81°27' W 110
Onalaska, Tex., U.S. 30°47' N, 95°7' W 103
Onaman Lake, Can. 50°0' N, 87°59' W 110
Onamia, Minn., U.S. 46°3' N, 93°41' W 94
Onaping Lake, Can. 46°56' N, 82°3' W 94
Onarga, Ill., U.S. 40°42' N, 88°1' W 102
Onatchiway, Lac, lake, Can. 48°59' N, 71°46' W 94
Oñati, Sp. 43°1' N, 2°24' W 164
Onavas, Mex. 28°27' N, 109°32' W 92
Onawa, Iowa, U.S. 42°0' N, 96°6' W 90
Oncativo, Arg. 31°55' S, 63°41' W 139
Onda, Sp. 39°58' N, 0°17' E 164
Ondangwa, Namibia 17°56' S, 15°59' E 220
Ondas, river, Braz. 12°42' S, 46°4' W 132
Ondjiva, Angola 17°6' S, 15°39' E 220
Ondo, Nig. 7°7' N, 4°49' E 222
Ondor Sum, China 42°30' N, 112°50' E 198
Öndörhaan, Mongolia 47°22' N, 110°40' E 198
Öndörhushuu, Mongolia 47°59' N, 113°55' E 198
One and Half Degree Channel 0°58' N, 72°7' E 188
Oneco, Conn., U.S. 41°41' N, 71°49' W 104
Oneco, Fla., U.S. 27°27' N, 82°32' W 105
Onega, Russ. 63°55' N, 38°12' E 154
Oneida, N.Y., U.S. 43°5' N, 75°41' W 94
Oneida, Tenn., U.S. 36°29' N, 84°31' W 96
Oneida Lake, N.Y., U.S. 43°14' N, 76°34' W 80
O'Neill, Nebr., U.S. 42°26' N, 98°40' W 90
Oneonta, Ala., U.S. 33°56' N, 86°29' W 96
Oneonta, N.Y., U.S. 42°27' N, 75°5' W 94
Onezhskaya Guba 64°4' N, 36°13' E 154
Onezhskoye Ozero, lake, Russ. 60°31' N, 33°29' E 160
Ongarue, N.Z. 38°43' S, 175°17' E 240
Ongcheon, S. Korea 36°41' N, 128°42' E 200
Ongi, Mongolia 45°28' N, 103°56' E 198
Ongjin, N. Korea 37°55' N, 125°22' E 200
Ongniud Qi, China 42°56' N, 118°59' E 198
Ongoka, Dem. Rep. of the Congo 1°24' S, 26°2' E 224
Ongole, India 15°30' N, 80°4' E 188
Ongtustik Qazaqstan, adm. division, Kaz. 42°4' N, 67°24' E 197
Ongwediva, Namibia 17°55' S, 15°54' E 220
Oni, Ga. 42°33' N, 43°27' E 195
Onib, Sudan 21°26' N, 35°16' E 182
Onitsha, Nig. 6°15' N, 6°46' E 222
Onizuka Center for International Astronomy, site, Hawai'i, U.S. 19°43' N, 155°29' W 99
Önjüül, Mongolia 46°46' N, 105°32' E 198
Onley, Va., U.S. 37°41' N, 75°44' W 94
Onnela, Fin. 69°54' N, 26°59' E 152
Ōno, Japan 35°58' N, 136°29' E 201
Onoda, Japan 33°58' N, 131°11' E 200
Onolimbu, Indonesia 1°3' N, 97°51' E 196
Onomichi, Japan 34°25' N, 133°12' E 201
Onon, Mongolia 49°9' N, 112°41' E 198
Onon, Mongolia 48°32' N, 110°30' E 198
Onon, river, Asia 49°19' N, 112°28' E 198
Onoto, Venez. 9°36' N, 65°12' W 136
Onoway, Can. 53°42' N, 114°13' W 108
Onsen, Japan 35°32' N, 134°29' E 201
Onslow, Austral. 21°39' S, 115°7' E 231
Onsŏng, N. Korea 42°57' N, 129°59' E 200
Onsugok, S. Korea 37°37' N, 126°28' E 200
Ontario, Calif., U.S. 34°3' N, 117°40' W 101
Ontario, Ohio, U.S. 40°44' N, 82°38' W 102
Ontario, Oreg., U.S. 43°58' N, 116°58' W 82
Ontario, adm. division, Can. 51°1' N, 90°29' W 106
Ontario, Lake 43°37' N, 78°57' W 80
Ontojärvi, lake, Fin. 64°19' N, 26°24' E 154
Ontong Java Atoll, islands, South Pacific Ocean 7°9' S, 159°58' E 238
Ontur, Sp. 38°36' N, 1°30' W 164
Onuškis, Lith. 54°27' N, 24°36' E 166
Onyx, Calif., U.S. 35°41' N, 118°15' W 101
Oodaaq Island, 83°32' N, 30°53' W 255
Oodnadatta, Austral. 27°34' S, 135°27' E 231
Oodweyne, Somalia 9°22' N, 45°5' E 216
Ooldea, Austral. 30°28' S, 131°50' E 231
Oolitic, Ind., U.S. 38°53' N, 86°33' W 102
Oona River, Can. 53°57' N, 130°19' W 108
Ooruk-Tam, Kyrg. 41°26' N, 76°39' E 184
Oost Vlieland, Neth. 53°17' N, 5°2' E 163
Oostburg, Wis., U.S. 43°37' N, 87°48' W 102
Oostende (Ostend), Belg. 51°13' N, 2°55' E 163
Oosterhout, Neth. 51°39' N, 4°51' E 167
Ootsa Lake, Can. 53°50' N, 126°3' W 108
Opachuanau Lake, lake, Can. 56°42' N, 100°14' W 108
Opal, Wyo., U.S. 41°47' N, 110°19' W 92
Opala, Dem. Rep. of the Congo 0°38' N, 24°20' E 224
Opari, Sudan 3°53' N, 32°5' E 224
Oparino, Russ. 59°52' N, 48°14' E 154
Opasatica, Lac, lake, Can. 48°1' N, 79°53' W 110
Opasatika Lake, lake, Can. 49°2' N, 83°40' W 94
Opasatika, river, Can. 49°32' N, 82°56' W 94
Opataca, Lac, lake, Can. 50°13' N, 75°49' W 94
Opataouaga, Lac, lake, Can. 50°19' N, 77°24' W 94
Opelika, Ala., U.S. 32°38' N, 85°24' W 96
Opelousas, La., U.S. 30°30' N, 92°6' W 103
Opheim, Mont., U.S. 48°50' N, 106°25' W 90
Ophir, peak, Indonesia 8°475' N, 99°55' E 196
Ophthalmia Range, Austral. 23°24' S, 118°34' E 230
Opienge, Dem. Rep. of the Congo 0°15' N, 27°21' E 224
Opinaca, Réservoir, lake, Can. 52°3' N, 77°47' W 110
Opinaca, river, Can. 52°14' N, 78°18' W 106
Opladen, Ger. 51°4' N, 7°0' E 167
Oploca, Bol. 21°22' S, 65°48' W 137
Opobo, Nig. 4°34' N, 7°32' E 222
Opochka, Russ. 56°41' N, 28°40' E 166
Opoczno, Pol. 51°23' N, 20°15' E 152
Opodepe, Mex. 29°55' N, 110°38' W 92
Opole, Pol. 50°39' N, 17°57' E 152
Opolskie, adm. division, Pol. 50°39' N, 17°57' E 152
Opornyy, Kaz. 46°3' N, 54°37' E 158
Oporto see Porto, Port. 41°8' N, 8°38' W 150
Opotiki, N.Z. 38°2' S, 177°19' E 240
Opp, Ala., U.S. 31°16' N, 86°15' W 96
Oppenheim, Ger. 49°50' N, 8°21' E 167
Oppola, Russ. 61°34' N, 30°19' E 166
Oprişoru, Rom. 44°16' N, 23°6' E 168
Opsa, Belarus 55°32' N, 26°49' E 166
Opua, N.Z. 35°21' S, 174°5' E 240
Opukhliki, Russ. 56°5' N, 30°9' E 166
Opunake, N.Z. 39°28' S, 173°51' E 240
Opuwo, Namibia 18°6' S, 13°50' E 220
Oqtosh, Uzb. 39°55' N, 65°55' E 197
Or, Les Îles d' see Hyères, Îles d', islands, Mediterranean Sea 42°57' N, 6°33' E 165
Or, river, Asia 49°38' N, 58°38' E 158
Ora, oil field, Lib. 28°26' N, 19°15' E 216
Oradea, Rom. 47°3' N, 21°57' E 168
Öræfajökull, glacier, Ice. 63°52' N, 15°30' W 142
Orahovica, Croatia 45°32' N, 17°54' E 168
Oral, Kaz. 51°12' N, 51°24' E 158
Oran, Alg. 35°39' N, 0°38' E 214
Orange, Fr. 44°8' N, 4°47' E 214
Orange, Mass., U.S. 42°35' N, 72°19' W 104
Orange, Tex., U.S. 30°5' N, 93°45' W 103
Orange, Va., U.S. 38°14' N, 78°7' W 94
Orange, Cabo, Braz. 4°26' N, 51°35' W 130
Orange City, Fla., U.S. 28°57' N, 81°19' W 105
Orange City, Iowa, U.S. 42°58' N, 96°5' W 90
Orange Cove, Calif., U.S. 36°37' N, 119°20' W 100
Orange Grove, Tex., U.S. 27°56' N, 97°56' W 96
Orange (Oranje), river, Africa 28°40' S, 18°39' E 227
Orange, river, S. Af. 30°46' S, 26°51' E 227
Orange Walk, Belize 18°5' N, 88°35' W 115
Orangeburg, S.C., U.S. 33°29' N, 80°51' W 96
Orangeville, Can. 43°55' N, 80°6' W 94
Orangeville, Ill., U.S. 42°27' N, 89°39' W 102
Orango, island, Guinea-Bissau 11°1' N, 16°41' W 222
Oranienburg, Ger. 52°45' N, 13°14' E 152
Oranje Gebergte, Suriname 3°12' N, 56°2' W 130
Oranje see Orange, river, Africa 28°40' S, 18°39' E 227
Oranjemund, Namibia 28°31' S, 16°25' E 227
Oranjestad, Aruba, Neth. 12°34' N, 70°2' W 118
Oranzherei, Russ. 45°49' N, 47°35' E 158
Orapa, Botswana 21°16' S, 25°17' E 227
Orari, N.Z. 44°9' S, 171°17' E 240
Oras, Philippines 12°10' N, 125°26' E 203
Orašac, Maced. 42°3' N, 21°48' E 168
Orašje, Bosn. and Herzg. 45°1' N, 18°40' E 168
Oravais (Oravainen), Fin. 63°16' N, 22°21' E 152
Orawia, N.Z. 46°4' S, 167°46' E 240
Orba Co, lake, China 34°28' N, 80°29' E 188
Örbyhus, Nor. 60°13' N, 17°39' E 152
Orcadas, station, Antarctica 60°46' S, 44°52' W 134
Orce, Sp. 37°42' N, 2°29' W 164
Orcera, Sp. 38°18' N, 2°39' W 164
Orchard City, Colo., U.S. 38°50' N, 107°58' W 92
Orchards, Wash., U.S. 45°39' N, 122°34' W 100
Orchies, Fr. 50°28' N, 3°14' E 163
Orchomenus, ruin(s), Gr. 38°29' N, 22°50' E 156
Orcières, Fr. 44°41' N, 6°19' E 167
Orco, river, It. 45°23' N, 7°25' E 167
Orcutt, Calif., U.S. 34°51' N, 120°28' W 100
Ord, Nebr., U.S. 41°35' N, 98°57' W 90
Ord, Mount, peak, Austral. 17°22' S, 125°22' E 230
Ord Mountains, Calif., U.S. 34°40' N, 116°49' W 101
Orda, Russ. 57°11' N, 56°56' E 154
Orderville, Utah, U.S. 37°16' N, 112°38' W 92
Ordu, Turk. 40°58' N, 37°51' E 156
Ordubad, Asia 38°53' N, 46°0' E 195
Orduña, Sp. 43°58' N, 3°2' W 164
Orduña, peak, Sp. 37°19' N, 3°33' W 164
Ordway, Colo., U.S. 38°13' N, 103°46' W 90
Ordzhonīkīdze, Kaz. 52°27' N, 61°41' E 184
Ordzhonikidze, Ukr. 47°41' N, 34°5' E 156
Ore City, Tex., U.S. 32°48' N, 94°44' W 103
Orea, Sp. 40°32' N, 1°43' W 164
Oreana, Ill., U.S. 39°56' N, 88°52' W 102
Orebić, Croatia 42°58' N, 17°9' E 168
Örebro, Nor. 59°16' N, 15°10' E 152
Oredezh, Russ. 58°49' N, 30°20' E 166
Oregon, Ohio, U.S. 41°38' N, 83°29' W 102
Oregon, Wis., U.S. 42°55' N, 89°23' W 102
Oregon, adm. division, Oreg., U.S. 43°43' N, 121°32' W 90
Oregon Caves National Monument, Oreg., U.S. 42°5' N, 123°29' W 90
Oregon Dunes National Recreation Area, Oreg., U.S. 43°59' N, 129°37' W 80
Öregrund, Sw. 60°18' N, 18°22' E 166
Orekhovo-Zuyevo, Russ. 55°49' N, 38°56' E 154
Orel, Russ. 52°55' N, 36°4' E 154
Orel, adm. division, Russ. 52°59' N, 35°55' E 154
Orellana, Peru 6°56' S, 75°14' W 130
Orellana la Vieja, Sp. 39°0' N, 5°32' W 164
Orem, Utah, U.S. 40°18' N, 111°41' W 90
Ören, Turk. 37°1' N, 27°57' E 156
Orenburg, Russ. 51°47' N, 55°9' E 154
Orenburg, adm. division, Russ. 52°50' N, 51°59' E 154
Orense, Arg. 38°41' S, 59°45' W 139
Örenşehir, Turk. 38°59' N, 36°40' E 156
Orford, N.H., U.S. 43°54' N, 72°8' W 104
Orford, U.K. 52°5' N, 1°31' E 163
Orford Ness, U.K. 52°0' N, 1°35' E 163
Orfordville, N.H., U.S. 43°52' N, 72°7' W 104
Orfordville, Wis., U.S. 42°38' N, 89°15' W 102
Organ Peak, N. Mex., U.S. 32°20' N, 106°43' W 82
Organ Pipe Cactus National Monument, Ariz., U.S. 32°2' N, 112°37' W 80
Organt, Kaz. 44°7' N, 66°46' E 184
Organyà, Sp. 42°12' N, 1°18' E 164
Órgiva, Sp. 36°53' N, 3°26' W 164
Orgon, Fr. 43°47' N, 5°1' E 150
Orgun, Afghan. 32°52' N, 69°11' E 186
Orhaneli, Turk. 39°54' N, 28°57' E 156
Orhangazi, Turk. 40°29' N, 29°17' E 158
Orhei, Mold. 47°22' N, 28°50' E 156
Orhi, peak, Fr. 42°58' N, 1°3' W 164
Orhon, adm. division, Mongolia 49°2' N, 104°5' E 198
Orhon, river, Mongolia 48°34' N, 104°41' E 190
Orhontuul, Mongolia 48°54' N, 104°57' E 198
Oria, Sp. 37°29' N, 2°18' W 164
Orick, Calif., U.S. 41°16' N, 124°5' W 92
Oricum see Orikon, ruin(s), Alban. 40°17' N, 19°19' E 156
Orient, N.Y., U.S. 41°8' N, 72°18' W 104
Orient, Wash., U.S. 48°51' N, 118°14' W 90
Orient Point, N.Y., U.S. 41°9' N, 72°20' W 104
Oriental, Cordillera, Peru 5°11' S, 77°46' W 130
Oriental, Grand Erg, Alg. 29°30' N, 4°11' E 214
Orientale, adm. division, Dem. Rep. of the Congo 2°6' N, 26°40' E 218
Oriente, Arg. 38°44' S, 60°37' W 139
Oriente, Braz. 10°1' S, 64°7' W 137
Origny-Sainte-Benoite, Fr. 49°50' N, 3°29' E 163
Orihuela, Sp. 38°4' N, 0°57' E 164
Orikhiv, Ukr. 47°32' N, 35°47' E 156
Orikon (Oricum), ruin(s), Alban. 40°17' N, 19°19' E 156
Orillia, Can. 44°36' N, 79°25' W 94
Orimattila, Fin. 60°47' N, 25°42' E 166
Orinoca, Bol. 18°59' S, 67°15' W 137
Orinoco, river, Venez. 3°9' N, 65°14' W 130
Orissa, adm. division, India 21°55' N, 84°41' E 19
Orissaare, Est. 58°32' N, 23°3' E 166
Oristano, It. 39°54' N, 8°35' E 214
Orivesi, Fin. 61°40' N, 24°18' E 166
Oriximiná, Braz. 1°44' S, 55°54' W 130
Orizaba, Mex. 18°50' N, 97°6' W 114
Orizaba, Pico de, peak, Mex. 18°59' N, 97°20' W 114
Orizona, Braz. 17°4' S, 48°19' W 138
Orjen, peak, Europe 42°33' N, 18°30' E 168
Orkney, S. Af. 26°59' S, 26°38' E 227
Orkney Islands, North Atlantic Ocean 59°28' N, 6°40' W 142
Orland, Calif., U.S. 39°44' N, 122°13' W 90
Orland, Me., U.S. 44°34' N, 68°45' W 94
Orlando, Fla., U.S. 28°32' N, 81°23' W 105
Orlando, Capo d', It. 38°11' N, 13°59' E 156
Orléanais, region, Fr. 48°23' N, 1°15' E 163
Orléans, Fr. 47°54' N, 1°54' E 163
Orleans, Ind., U.S. 38°39' N, 86°27' W 102
Orleans, Mass., U.S. 41°46' N, 69°60' W 104
Orleans, Nebr., U.S. 40°6' N, 99°27' W 90
Orlik, Russ. 52°36' N, 99°50' E 190
Orlová, Czech Rep. 49°50' N, 18°25' E 152
Orlovat, Serb. and Mont. 45°15' N, 20°33' E 168
Orlovka, Russ. 56°55' N, 76°24' E 169
Orlovskiy, Russ. 46°49' N, 41°56' E 158
Orlu, Nig. 5°45' N, 7°10' E 222
Ormara, Pak. 25°12' N, 64°35' E 182
Ormara, Ras, Pak. 25°2' N, 64°39' E 182
Ormea, It. 44°9' N, 7°54' E 167
Ormoc, Philippines 11°2' N, 124°36' E 203
Ormond, N.Z. 38°33' S, 177°55' E 240
Ormond Beach, Fla., U.S. 29°16' N, 81°4' W 105
Ormond by the Sea, Fla., U.S. 29°19' N, 81°4' W 105
Ormož, Slov. 46°24' N, 16°7' E 168
Ormskirk, U.K. 53°34' N, 2°53' W 162
Orne, river, Fr. 49°7' N, 5°44' E 163
Orneta, Pol. 54°5' N, 20°7' E 166
Ornö, island, Sw. 59°0' N, 18°32' E 166
Orno Peak, Colo., U.S. 40°3' N, 107°10' W 90
Örnsköldsvik, Nor. 63°16' N, 18°43' E 152
Oro Blanco, Peru 3°11' S, 73°14' W 136
Oro Grande, Calif., U.S. 34°36' N, 117°21' W 101
Oro Ingenio, Bol. 21°16' S, 66°1' W 137
Oro, river, Mex. 25°55' N, 105°18' W 80
Orobie, Alpi, It. 46°18' N, 9°48' E 167
Orocopia Mountains, Calif., U.S. 33°38' N, 115°55' W 101
Orocué, Col. 4°47' N, 71°21' W 136
Orodara, Burkina Faso 10°57' N, 4°56' W 222
Orofino, Idaho, U.S. 46°29' N, 116°15' W 90
Orokam, Nig. 7°1' N, 7°33' E 222
Oromia, region, Eth. 5°54' N, 38°39' E 224
Oron, Israel 30°54' N, 35°0' E 194
Oron, Nig. 4°49' N, 8°12' E 222
Orono, Me., U.S. 44°52' N, 68°41' W 111
Oronoquekamp, Guyana 2°43' N, 57°32' W 130
Orontes see 'Āşī, river, Syr. 35°40' N, 36°21' E 194
Oropesa, Sp. 40°5' N, 0°7' E 164
Oroquieta, Philippines 8°31' N, 123°46' E 203
Orós, Braz. 6°21' S, 38°53' W 132
Oros Áskio, peak, Gr. 40°23' N, 21°28' E 156
Orosháza, Hung. 46°33' N, 20°40' E 168
Orosi, Calif., U.S. 36°33' N, 119°18' W 100
Orotukan, Russ. 62°13' N, 151°26' E 160
Oroville, Calif., U.S. 39°30' N, 121°35' W 90
Oroyek, Russ. 64°52' N, 153°22' E 160
Oroz Betelu, Sp. 42°54' N, 1°19' W 164
Orqohan, China 49°29' N, 121°22' E 198
Orr, Minn., U.S. 48°2' N, 92°50' W 94
Orrs Island, Me., U.S. 43°45' N, 69°59' W 104
Orrville, Ohio, U.S. 40°49' N, 81°45' W 102
Orsa, Nor. 61°6' N, 14°35' E 152
Orsha, Belarus 54°31' N, 30°31' E 154
Orshanka, Russ. 56°54' N, 47°55' E 154
Orsk, Russ. 51°11' N, 58°36' E 158
Örskär, island, Sw. 60°31' N, 18°12' E 166
Orta, Turk. 40°37' N, 33°6' E 156
Ortaca, Turk. 36°50' N, 28°45' E 156
Ortegal, Cabo, Sp. 43°46' N, 7°54' W 150
Orthez, Fr. 43°29' N, 0°46' E 164
Orting, Wash., U.S. 47°4' N, 122°13' W 100
Ortisei, It. 46°36' N, 11°39' E 167
Orţişoara, Rom. 45°58' N, 21°12' E 168
Ortiz, Mex. 28°17' N, 110°44' W 92
Ortiz, Mex. 28°14' N, 105°33' W 92
Ortiz, Venez. 9°35' N, 67°19' W 136
Ortles, It. 46°22' N, 10°15' E 167
Orto Surt, Russ. 62°34' N, 125°4' E 173
Ortón, river, Bol. 11°2' S, 66°58' W 137
Ortona, It. 42°21' N, 14°23' E 156
Ortonville, Mich., U.S. 42°51' N, 83°28' W 102
Ortonville, Minn., U.S. 45°17' N, 96°27' W 90
Örträsk, Nor. 64°8' N, 18°59' E 152
Orūmīyeh, Iran 37°30' N, 44°58' E 143
Orūmīyeh, Daryācheh-ye (Urmia, Lake), Iran 38°7' N, 45°16' E 195
Orūmīyeh (Urmia), Iran 37°37' N, 45°4' E 195

Orungo, Uganda 2°0' N, 33°28' E 224
Oruro, Bol. 17°59' S, 67°8' W 137
Oruro, adm. division, Bol. 18°53' S, 68°19' W 137
Orwell, Ohio, U.S. 41°31' N, 80°52' W 102
Orwell, Vt., U.S. 43°48' N, 73°19' W 104
Orxon, river, China 48°16' N, 117°47' E 198
Orynyn, Ukr. 48°44' N, 26°25' E 152
Orzinuovi, It. 45°24' N, 9°55' E 167
Os, Nor. 60°11' N, 5°27' E 152
Osa, Russ. 57°15' N, 55°32' E 154
Osage, Iowa, U.S. 43°15' N, 92°49' W 94
Osage, Wyo., U.S. 43°57' N, 104°25' W 90
Osage City, Kans., U.S. 38°36' N, 95°50' W 90
Ōsaka, Japan 34°42' N, 135°32' E 190
Osaka, Japan 35°57' N, 137°17' E 201
Ōsaka, Japan 34°40' N, 135°30' E 201
Ōsaka, adm. division, Japan 34°20' N, 135°21' E 201
Osakarovka, Kaz. 50°34' N, 72°35' E 184
Osakis, Minn., U.S. 45°50' N, 95°11' W 90
Osan, S. Korea 37°8' N, 127°4' E 200
Osawatomie, Kans., U.S. 38°28' N, 94°57' W 94
Osborn Plateau, Indian Ocean 14°42' S, 86°43' E 254
Osborne, Kans., U.S. 39°25' N, 98°43' W 90
Osby, Nor. 56°23' N, 13°57' E 152
Oscar II Coast, Antarctica 65°25' S, 61°36' W 134
Osceola, Iowa, U.S. 41°2' N, 93°45' W 94
Osečina, Serb. and Mont. 44°22' N, 19°35' E 168
Ösel see Saaremaa, island, Est. 58°32' N, 21°21' E 166
Osel'ki, Russ. 60°14' N, 30°26' E 166
Osen, Nor. 64°18' N, 10°31' E 152
Osgood, Ind., U.S. 39°7' N, 85°17' W 102
Osgood Mountains, Nev., U.S. 41°3' N, 117°37' W 90
Osh, Kyrg. 40°31' N, 72°49' E 197
Oshakati, Namibia 17°54' S, 15°48' E 220
Oshawa, Can. 43°53' N, 78°50' W 94
Oshikango, Namibia 17°28' S, 15°52' E 220
Ōshima, Japan 34°44' N, 139°21' E 201
Oshkosh, Nebr., U.S. 41°24' N, 102°22' W 90
Oshkosh, Wis., U.S. 44°1' N, 88°33' W 102
Oshkur'ya, Russ. 66°0' N, 56°40' E 154
Oshogbo, Nig. 7°50' N, 4°35' E 222
Oshta, Russ. 60°49' N, 35°33' E 154
Oshwe, Dem. Rep. of the Congo 3°27' S, 19°29' E 218
Osian, India 26°41' N, 72°55' E 186
Osijek, Croatia 45°32' N, 18°40' E 168
Osilinka, river, Can. 56°4' N, 125°26' W 108
Osinovka, Russ. 56°33' N, 102°11' E 160
Osinovo, Russ. 61°18' N, 89°49' E 169
Oskaloosa, Iowa, U.S. 41°17' N, 92°38' W 94
Öskemen (Ust' Kamenogorsk), Kaz. 49°59' N, 82°38' E 184
Oskoba, Russ. 60°20' N, 100°33' E 160
Oskol, river, Russ. 50°34' N, 37°37' E 158
Oslo, Minn., U.S. 48°10' N, 97°8' W 90
Oslo, Nor. 59°53' N, 10°33' E 152
Oslob, Philippines 9°32' N, 123°23' E 203
Osma, Sp. 41°34' N, 3°6' W 164
Osmancık, Turk. 40°58' N, 34°47' E 156
Osmaniye, Turk. 37°4' N, 36°13' E 156
Os'mino, Russ. 59°1' N, 29°7' E 166
Osmus Saar, island, Est. 59°9' N, 23°14' E 166
Osnabrück, Ger. 52°16' N, 8°2' E 163
Osnaburgh House, Can. 51°8' N, 90°17' W 110
Oso, Wash., U.S. 48°16' N, 121°56' W 100
Oso, river, Dem. Rep. of the Congo 0°60' N, 27°43' E 224
Osogovske Planina, Maced. 42°2' N, 22°2' E 168
Osor, Croatia 44°42' N, 14°23' E 156
Osório, Braz. 29°54' S, 50°17' W 134
Osorno, Chile 40°34' S, 73°9' W 134
Osorno, Sp. 42°24' N, 4°22' W 150
Osoyoos, Can. 49°1' N, 119°30' W 108
Ospika, river, Can. 57°3' N, 124°28' W 108
Osprey, Fla., U.S. 27°12' N, 82°28' W 105
Oss, Neth. 51°45' N, 5°31' E 167
Ossa, Mount, peak, Austral. 41°53' S, 145°50' E 230
Óssa, Óros, peak, Gr. 39°47' N, 22°36' E 156
Ossabaw Island, Ga., U.S. 31°36' N, 81°3' W 112
Osse, river, Nig. 7°44' N, 5°58' E 222
Osselé, Congo 1°26' S, 15°19' E 218
Osseo, Wis., U.S. 44°33' N, 91°13' W 94
Ossian, Ind., U.S. 40°52' N, 85°10' W 102
Ossining, N.Y., U.S. 41°9' N, 73°52' W 104
Ossipee, N.H., U.S. 43°40' N, 71°8' W 104
Ossjøen, lake, Nor. 61°10' N, 11°24' E 152
Ossokmanuan Reservoir, lake, Can. 52°59' N, 66°19' W 111
Ossora, Russ. 59°14' N, 163°0' E 160
Ostaboningue, Lac, lake, Can. 47°1' N, 79°36' W 94
Ostashkov, Russ. 57°7' N, 33°12' E 154
Östavall, Nor. 62°25' N, 15°29' E 152
Ostbevern, Ger. 52°2' N, 7°50' E 167
Ostellato, It. 44°44' N, 11°56' E 167
Ostend see Oostende, Belg. 51°13' N, 2°55' E 163
Østerdalen, Nor. 61°50' N, 10°47' E 152
Östergarnsholme, island, Sw. 57°25' N, 19°1' E 166
Osterode, Ger. 51°44' N, 10°13' E 167
Östersund, Nor. 63°10' N, 14°40' E 152
Osterville, Mass., U.S. 41°37' N, 70°24' W 104
Östhammar, Sw. 60°14' N, 18°18' E 166
Ostheim, Ger. 50°27' N, 10°13' E 167
Ostiglia, It. 45°3' N, 11°8' E 167
Östra Kvarken 63°31' N, 20°16' E 152
Ostrava, Czech Rep. 49°49' N, 18°15' E 152
Ostro, Pol. 53°4' N, 21°33' E 152
Ostróda, Pol. 53°41' N, 19°58' E 152
Ostrov, Russ. 57°21' N, 28°21' E 166
Ostrov, Russ. 58°28' N, 28°37' E 166
Ostrov Russkiy, island, Russ. 76°38' N, 89°18' E 160
Ostrovtsy, Russ. 58°23' N, 27°42' E 166
Ostrožac, Bosn. and Herzg. 43°40' N, 17°50' E 168
Ostuni, It. 40°43' N, 17°35' E 156
O'sullivan Lake, lake, Can. 50°22' N, 87°38' W 110
Osuna, Sp. 37°14' N, 5°7' W 164
Osvaldo Cruz, Braz. 21°47' S, 50°52' W 138
Oswego, N.Y., U.S. 43°26' N, 76°32' W 110
Oswestry, U.K. 52°51' N, 3°4' W 162
Osyka, Miss., U.S. 31°0' N, 90°30' W 103
Ōta, Japan 35°56' N, 136°3' E 201
Ōta, Japan 36°16' N, 139°24' E 201
Ōta, river, Japan 34°29' N, 132°11' E 201
Otaci, Mold. 48°25' N, 27°47' E 152
Ōtake, Japan 34°12' N, 132°13' E 200
Otaki, N.Z. 40°46' S, 175°8' E 240
Otanmäki, Fin. 64°4' N, 27°4' E 152
Otar, Kaz. 43°31' N, 75°12' E 184
Otare, Cerro, peak, Col. 1°43' N, 72°49' W 136
Otaru, Japan 43°12' N, 140°49' E 190
Otatara, N.Z. 46°27' S, 168°18' E 240
Otautau, N.Z. 46°11' S, 167°58' E 240
Otava, Fin. 61°37' N, 27°2' E 166
Otavalo, Ecua. 0°11' N, 78°24' W 136
Otavi, Namibia 19°39' S, 17°19' E 220
Otawara, Japan 36°49' N, 140°1' E 201
Otay, Calif., U.S. 32°36' N, 117°6' W 101
Otchinjau, Angola 16°30' S, 13°56' E 220
Otelec, Rom. 45°36' N, 20°50' E 168
Oțelu Roșu, Rom. 45°30' N, 22°23' E 168
Otematata, N.Z. 44°37' S, 170°11' E 240
Otepää, Est. 58°2' N, 26°29' E 166
Oteros, river, Mex. 27°19' N, 108°36' W 80
Othello, Wash., U.S. 46°48' N, 119°11' W 90
Otherside, river, Can. 59°5' N, 107°21' W 108
Óthris, Óros, Gr. 38°57' N, 22°19' E 156
Oti, river, Ghana 8°32' N, 8°476' E 222
Otinapa, Mex. 24°0' N, 105°1' W 114
Otira, N.Z. 42°50' S, 171°33' E 240
Otis, Colo., U.S. 40°9' N, 102°58' W 90
Otis, Mass., U.S. 42°11' N, 73°6' W 104
Otisco, Ind., U.S. 38°32' N, 85°39' W 102
Otish, Monts, peak, Can. 52°17' N, 70°36' W 111
Otjikondo, Namibia 19°52' S, 15°29' E 220
Otjimbingwe, Namibia 22°19' S, 16°7' E 227
Otjivero, Namibia 22°16' S, 17°51' E 227
Otjiwarongo, Namibia 20°27' S, 16°39' E 227
Otley, U.K. 53°54' N, 1°41' W 162
Otmök, Kyrg. 42°11' N, 73°16' E 197
Otog Qi, China 39°6' N, 107°58' E 198
Otok, Croatia 45°8' N, 18°51' E 168
Otok, Croatia 43°41' N, 16°43' E 168
Otoka, Bosn. and Herzg. 44°57' N, 16°8' E 168
Otorohanga, N.Z. 38°11' S, 175°13' E 240
Otoskwin, river, Can. 51°48' N, 90°58' W 80
Otosquen, Can. 53°16' N, 102°1' W 108
Otradnaya, Russ. 44°22' N, 41°27' E 158
Otradnoye, Russ. 51°59' N, 156°39' E 160
Otradnoye, Russ. 56°13' N, 30°3' E 166
Otradnyy, Russ. 53°24' N, 51°26' E 154
Otranto, Capo d', It. 40°2' N, 18°31' E 156
Otsego, Mich., U.S. 42°26' N, 85°42' W 102
Ōtsu, Japan 35°1' N, 135°51' E 201
Otta, Nig. 6°44' N, 3°13' E 222
Ottawa, Can. 45°22' N, 75°50' W 94
Ottawa, Ill., U.S. 41°20' N, 88°51' W 102
Ottawa, Kans., U.S. 38°34' N, 95°17' W 94
Ottawa, Mo., U.S. 41°20' N, 88°51' W 110
Ottawa, Ohio, U.S. 41°1' N, 84°3' W 102
Ottawa Islands, islands, Can. 59°8' N, 83°8' W 106
Ottenby, Sw. 56°14' N, 16°26' E 152
Otter Creek, Fla., U.S. 29°19' N, 82°47' W 105
Otter Head, Can. 47°53' N, 86°14' W 94
Otter Rapids, Can. 50°11' N, 81°40' W 94
Otterbein, Ind., U.S. 40°29' N, 87°6' W 102
Otterndorf, Ger. 53°48' N, 8°54' E 152
Ottoville, Ohio, U.S. 40°55' N, 84°20' W 102
Otú, Col. 6°55' N, 74°45' W 136
Otukpa, Nig. 7°4' N, 7°40' E 222
Otukpo, Nig. 7°12' N, 8°9' E 222
Otumpa, Arg. 27°20' S, 62°16' W 139
Otynya, Ukr. 48°43' N, 24°49' E 152
Ötztal Alps, Aust. 46°46' N, 10°36' E 167
Ou Nua, Laos 22°16' N, 101°48' E 202
Ou, river, Laos 21°49' N, 102°6' E 202
Ouachita, Lake, Ark., U.S. 34°41' N, 93°59' W 80
Ouachita Mountains, Ark., U.S. 34°26' N, 95°36' W 96
Ouachita, river, La., U.S. 32°16' N, 92°10' W 103
Ouadane, Mauritania 20°57' N, 11°37' W 222
Ouadda, Cen. Af. Rep. 8°4' N, 22°24' E 218
Ouagadougou, Burkina Faso 12°19' N, 1°43' W 222
Ouagama, Lac, lake, Can. 50°37' N, 77°43' W 110
Ouahigouya, Burkina Faso 13°34' N, 2°26' W 222
Ouaka, river, Cen. Af. Rep. 5°11' N, 19°49' E 218
Oualâta, Mauritania 17°18' N, 7°2' W 222
Oualâta, Dahr, Mauritania 17°41' N, 8°22' W 222
Oualidia, Mor. 32°43' N, 9°4' W 214
Ouallam, Niger 14°22' N, 1°59' E 222
Ouan Taredert, oil field, Alg. 27°26' N, 9°29' E 214
Oua-n-Ahaggar, Tassili, Alg. 21°14' N, 4°57' E 222
Ouanda Djallé, Cen. Af. Rep. 8°52' N, 22°48' E 218
Ouandjia, Cen. Af. Rep. 9°17' N, 22°40' E 218
Ouando, Cen. Af. Rep. 5°58' N, 25°45' E 224
Ouango, Cen. Af. Rep. 4°20' N, 22°29' E 218
Ouaouizarht, Mor. 32°12' N, 6°23' W 214
Ouarane, Mauritania 20°48' N, 11°23' W 222
Ouargaye, Burkina Faso 11°31' N, 0°2' W 222
Ouargla, Alg. 31°56' N, 5°20' E 214
Ouarkoye, Burkina Faso 12°6' N, 3°41' W 222
Ouarkziz, Jebel, Mor. 28°10' N, 9°37' W 214
Ouarra, river, Cen. Af. Rep. 5°49' N, 25°48' E 224
Ouarsenis, Djebel, peak, Alg. 35°52' N, 1°34' E 150
Ouas Ouas, spring, Mali 16°6' N, 1°20' E 222
Ouasiemsca, river, Can. 49°43' N, 73°11' W 111
Ouassane, spring, Mauritania 17°56' N, 13°13' W 222
Ouassou, Guinea 10°2' N, 13°45' W 222
Ouche, river, Fr. 47°15' N, 4°48' E 165
Ouchennane, spring, Mali 17°23' N, 1°59' E 222
Ouddorp, Neth. 51°48' N, 3°55' E 163
Oude Rijn, river, Neth. 52°12' N, 4°26' E 163
Oudeïka, spring, Mali 17°27' N, 1°42' W 222
Oudenaarde, Belg. 50°50' N, 3°36' E 163
Oudeschild, Neth. 53°2' N, 4°50' E 163
Oudon, Fr. 47°21' N, 1°19' W 150
Oudtshoorn, S. Af. 33°35' S, 22°11' E 227
Oued Laou, Mor. 35°26' N, 5°6' W 150
Oued Lili, Alg. 35°30' N, 1°16' E 150
Oued Rhiou, Alg. 35°57' N, 0°55' E 164
Oued Taria, Alg. 35°6' N, 9°535' E 150
Oued Tlelat, Alg. 35°32' N, 0°28' E 150
Oueïba, spring, Chad 18°24' N, 23°18' E 226
Oueïta, spring, Chad 17°43' N, 20°42' E 216
Ouella, spring, Niger 14°39' N, 3°53' E 222
Ouellé, Côte d'Ivoire 7°14' N, 4°2' W 222
Ouémé, river, Benin 8°19' N, 2°11' E 222
Ouescapis, Lac, lake, Can. 50°15' N, 77°36' W 94
Ouessa, Burkina Faso 11°3' N, 2°48' W 222
Ouesso, Congo 1°51' N, 16°2' E 218
Ouest, Pointe, Haiti 18°51' N, 74°1' W 116
Ouest, Pointe de l' (Coupé, Cap), Fr. 46°48' N, 56°60' W 111
Ouffet, Belg. 50°26' N, 5°26' E 167
Oufrane, Alg. 28°31' N, 0°10' E 214
Ougarta, Alg. 29°40' N, 2°16' W 214
Ougrée, Belg. 50°35' N, 5°33' E 167
Ouidah, Benin 6°23' N, 2°5' E 222
Oujaf, spring, Mauritania 17°50' N, 7°54' W 222
Oujda, Mor. 34°38' N, 1°55' W 214
Oujeft, Mauritania 20°2' N, 13°4' W 222
Oulad el Abed, Tun. 35°59' N, 10°17' E 156
Oulad Hammou, Mor. 35°7' N, 6°9' W 150
Oulad Saïd, Alg. 29°27' N, 0°15' E 214
Oulainen, Fin. 64°15' N, 24°44' E 152
Ould Mouloud, spring, Alg. 23°46' N, 0°9' E 214
Ouled Amar, Alg. 35°27' N, 5°8' E 150
Ouled Djellal, Alg. 34°23' N, 5°3' E 214
Oulou, river, Cen. Af. Rep. 10°27' N, 22°30' E 218
Oulton Broad, U.K. 52°27' N, 1°41' E 163
Oulton Lake, lake, Can. 60°45' N, 111°53' W 108
Oulu, Fin. 64°59' N, 25°47' E 160
Oulu (Uleåborg), Fin. 65°0' N, 25°25' E 152
Oulx, It. 45°1' N, 6°51' E 167
Oum Chalouba, Chad 15°47' N, 20°45' E 216
Oum er Rbia, Oued, river, Mor. 32°10' N, 8°13' W 142
Oum Hadjer, Chad 13°15' N, 19°40' E 216
Oum Mesgué, Mauritania 16°17' N, 7°15' W 222
Oumache, Alg. 34°40' N, 5°42' E 214
Oumé, Côte d'Ivoire 6°17' N, 5°25' W 222
Oumm el A'sel, spring, Mali 23°32' N, 4°46' W 214
Oumm el Khez, spring, Mauritania 17°7' N, 11°3' W 222
Ounasselkä, Fin. 67°32' N, 24°23' E 152
Oundle, U.K. 52°28' N, 0°29' E 162
Ounianga Kébir, Chad 19°4' N, 20°31' E 216
Ounianga Sérir, spring, Chad 18°54' N, 20°54' E 216
Ounissouli, spring, Niger 17°33' N, 12°3' E 222
Ouolodo, Mali 13°13' N, 7°55' W 222
Ourafane, Niger 14°2' N, 8°8' E 222
Ouray, Utah, U.S. 40°5' N, 109°41' W 90
Ouray, Mount, peak, Colo., U.S. 38°24' N, 106°18' W 90
Ourense, Sp. 42°19' N, 7°53' W 150
Ouri, Chad 21°35' N, 19°13' E 216
Ourinhos, Braz. 22°58' S, 49°52' W 138
Ouro, Braz. 8°13' S, 46°14' W 130
Ouro Preto, Braz. 20°24' S, 43°31' W 138
Ouro Prêto, river, Braz. 10°44' S, 64°28' W 137
Ours, Cap de l', Can. 49°36' N, 62°30' W 111
Oursi, Burkina Faso 14°40' N, 4°238' E 222
Ourthe, river, Belg. 50°11' N, 5°34' E 167
Ouse, river, U.K. 54°4' N, 1°21' W 162
Oust, Fr. 42°51' N, 1°12' E 164
Outardes Quatre, Réservoir, lake, Can. 49°34' N, 70°50' W 94
Outat Oulad el Hajj, Mor. 33°25' N, 3°44' W 214
Outeniqua Mountains, S. Af. 33°49' S, 22°28' E 227
Outer Banks, islands, North Atlantic Ocean 35°28' N, 75°25' W 96
Outer Santa Barbara Channel 33°9' N, 118°41' W 101
Outjo, Namibia 20°7' S, 16°10' E 227
Outlook, Can. 51°29' N, 107°5' W 90
Outokumpu, Fin. 62°43' N, 29°0' E 152
Outram Island, India 12°17' N, 93°14' E 188
Outtaye, Mali 14°28' N, 8°23' W 222
Ovacık, Turk. 39°21' N, 39°12' E 195
Ovada, It. 44°38' N, 8°39' E 167
Oval Peak, Wash., U.S. 48°15' N, 120°31' W 90
Ovalle, Chile 30°35' S, 71°14' W 134
Ovalo, Tex., U.S. 32°10' N, 99°50' W 92
Ovamboland, region, Namibia 19°53' S, 15°29' E 227
Ovana, Cerro, peak, Venez. 4°37' N, 67°4' W 136
Ovar, Port. 40°51' N, 8°40' W 150
Overath, Ger. 50°56' N, 7°16' E 167
Øverbygd, Nor. 69°0' N, 19°7' E 152
Overflowing River, Can. 53°6' N, 101°10' W 108
Overland Park, Kans., U.S. 38°56' N, 94°41' W 94
Overland Pass, Nev., U.S. 40°1' N, 115°36' W 90
Övermark (Ylimarkku), Fin. 62°35' N, 21°25' E 152
Overpelt, Belg. 51°11' N, 5°24' E 167
Överstjuktan, lake, Nor. 65°39' N, 15°22' E 152
Overstrand, U.K. 52°54' N, 1°20' E 162
Overton, Nev., U.S. 36°32' N, 114°27' W 101
Overton, Tex., U.S. 32°16' N, 94°59' W 103
Overton, U.K. 52°57' N, 2°55' W 162
Överum, Nor. 58°0' N, 16°17' E 152
Ovett, Miss., U.S. 31°27' N, 89°1' W 103
Ovid, Colo., U.S. 40°57' N, 102°23' W 90
Ovid, Mich., U.S. 43°0' N, 84°22' W 102
Oviedo, Sp. 43°21' N, 5°51' W 150
Oviši, Latv. 57°29' N, 21°33' E 166
Ovoot, Mongolia 45°20' N, 113°38' E 198
Övör-Ereen, Mongolia 49°16' N, 112°25' E 198
Ovruch, Ukr. 51°19' N, 28°52' E 152
Owaka, N.Z. 46°28' S, 169°42' E 240
Owando, Congo 0°33' N, 15°53' E 218
Owaneco, Ill., U.S. 39°28' N, 89°12' W 102
Owase, Japan 34°3' N, 136°12' E 201
Owbeh, Afghan. 34°26' N, 63°10' E 186
Owego, N.Y., U.S. 42°6' N, 76°17' W 94
Owen Falls Dam, Uganda 0°5' N, 33°1' E 224
Owen Fracture Zone, Arabian Sea 11°9' N, 57°40' E 254
Owen, Mount, peak, N.Z. 41°34' S, 172°28' E 240
Owen River, N.Z. 41°42' S, 172°27' E 240
Owen Sound, Can. 44°34' N, 80°56' W 94
Owen Stanley Range, P.N.G. 8°34' S, 147°0' E 192
Owens Peak, Calif., U.S. 35°44' N, 118°2' W 101
Owensboro, Ky., U.S. 37°45' N, 87°7' W 96
Owensburg, Ind., U.S. 38°55' N, 86°44' W 102
Owensville, Mo., U.S. 38°20' N, 91°30' W 94
Owenton, Ky., U.S. 38°31' N, 84°50' W 102
Owerri, Nig. 5°30' N, 7°0' E 222
Owikeno, Can. 51°41' N, 127°16' W 108
Owl Creek Mountains, Wyo., U.S. 43°36' N, 109°5' W 90
Owlshead Mountains, Calif., U.S. 35°46' N, 116°46' W 101
Owo, Nig. 6°28' N, 7°43' E 222
Owo, Nig. 7°15' N, 5°36' E 222
Owosso, Mich., U.S. 43°0' N, 84°8' W 102
Owschlag, Ger. 54°24' N, 9°35' E 150
Owyhee, Nev., U.S. 41°57' N, 116°6' W 90
Owyhee Mountains, Idaho, U.S. 43°10' N, 116°45' W 90
Owyhee, river, Idaho, U.S. 42°25' N, 117°4' W 106
Ox Mountains, the see Gamph, Slieve, Ire. 54°2' N, 9°28' W 150
Öxarfjördur 66°6' N, 16°60' W 142
Oxbow Dam, U.S. 45°1' N, 116°55' W 90
Oxford, Kans., U.S. 37°15' N, 97°11' W 90
Oxford, Me., U.S. 44°7' N, 70°30' W 104
Oxford, Mich., U.S. 42°48' N, 83°16' W 102
Oxford, Miss., U.S. 34°20' N, 89°31' W 96
Oxford, Nebr., U.S. 40°14' N, 99°39' W 90
Oxford, N.Z. 43°19' S, 172°11' E 240
Oxford, Ohio, U.S. 39°30' N, 84°45' W 102
Oxford, U.K. 51°44' N, 1°16' W 162
Oxford, Wis., U.S. 43°46' N, 89°33' W 102
Oxford House, Can. 54°54' N, 95°17' W 108
Oxford Peak, Idaho, U.S. 42°17' N, 112°10' W 90
Oxnard, Calif., U.S. 34°11' N, 119°12' W 101
Oxus see Ab-e Vakhan, river, Afghan. 37°8' N, 72°26' E 186
Oya, Malaysia 2°47' N, 111°52' E 192
Oyahue see Ollagüe, Chile 21°14' S, 68°18' W 137
Oyan, Kaz. 50°44' N, 50°23' E 158
Øye, Nor. 62°11' N, 6°39' E 152
Oyé Yeska, spring, Chad 18°36' N, 19°31' E 216
Oyem, Gabon 1°35' N, 11°36' E 207
Oyen, Can. 51°22' N, 110°29' W 90
Øygarden Group, islands, Indian Ocean 66°53' S, 57°43' E 248
Oymyakon, Russ. 63°25' N, 142°41' E 160
Oyo, Congo 1°10' S, 15°59' E 218
Oyo, Nig. 7°54' N, 3°57' E 222
Oyo, Sudan 21°56' N, 36°12' E 182
Oyonnax, Fr. 46°15' N, 5°38' E 150
Oyster Bay, N.Y., U.S. 40°52' N, 73°32' W 104
Oyster River, Can. 49°53' N, 125°8' W 100
Oysterville, Wash., U.S. 46°32' N, 124°2' W 100
Oyyl, Kaz. 49°4' N, 54°38' E 158
Özalp, Turk. 38°38' N, 43°57' E 195
Ozamis, Philippines 8°13' N, 123°50' E 203
Ozark, Ala., U.S. 31°27' N, 85°39' W 96
Ozark, Ark., U.S. 35°28' N, 93°51' W 96
Ozark, Mo., U.S. 37°0' N, 93°11' W 96
Ozark National Scenic Riverways, Mo., U.S. 37°0' N, 96°4' W 80
Ozark Plateau, Mo., U.S. 35°31' N, 93°28' W 96
Ozen, Kaz. 43°27' N, 53°3' E 158
Ozernovskiy, Russ. 51°32' N, 156°34' E 160
Ozernoy, Mys, Russ. 57°26' N, 163°12' E 160
Ozernyy, Russ. 55°30' N, 32°29' E 154
Ozernyy, Russ. 51°6' N, 60°57' E 158
Ozernyy, Russ. 66°23' N, 179°3' W 98
Ozersk, Russ. 54°25' N, 21°58' E 166
Ozery, Russ. 54°52' N, 38°30' E 154
Ozgon, Kyrg. 40°45' N, 73°18' E 197
Ozhiski Lake, Can. 51°57' N, 89°4' W 110
Ozhogino, Russ. 68°59' N, 147°39' E 160
Ozieri, It. 40°35' N, 9°1' E 156
Ozinki, Russ. 51°11' N, 49°46' E 158
Ozoli, Latv. 57°38' N, 24°55' E 166
Ozona, Tex., U.S. 30°41' N, 101°12' W 92
Ozorków, Pol. 51°57' N, 19°17' E 152
Ozrinići, Europe 42°44' N, 19°0' E 168
Ōzu, Japan 33°30' N, 132°32' E 201
Ozurget'i, Ga. 41°54' N, 42°0' E 195

P

Pa Kha, Vietnam 22°34' N, 104°16' E 202
Pa Mong Dam, Asia 18°10' N, 101°26' E 202
Pa Sak, river, Thai. 15°27' N, 101°2' E 202
Paakkola, Fin. 66°0' N, 24°40' E 152
Paamiut (Frederikshåb) 62°4' N, 49°33' W 106
Paarl, S. Af. 33°45' S, 18°55' E 227
Paavola, Fin. 64°35' N, 25°9' E 152
Paberžė, Lith. 54°56' N, 25°14' E 166
Pabo, Uganda 2°58' N, 32°7' E 224
Pabradė, Lith. 54°59' N, 25°43' E 166
Pac, Alban. 42°17' N, 20°12' E 168
Pacaás Novos National Park, Braz. 11°14' S, 63°35' W 137
Pacaás Novos, river, Braz. 11°13' S, 65°5' W 137
Pacaás Novos, Serra dos, Braz. 10°27' S, 64°29' W 130
Pacahuaras, river, Bol. 10°25' S, 66°13' W 137
Pacajus, Braz. 4°14' S, 38°30' W 132
Pacanów, Pol. 50°24' N, 21°2' E 152
Pacaraima, Sierra, Venez. 4°3' N, 63°19' W 130
Pacasmayo, Peru 7°23' S, 79°35' W 130
Pacaya, Peru 10°9' S, 74°7' W 137
Paceco, It. 37°58' N, 12°32' E 156
Pacheco Pass, Calif., U.S. 37°4' N, 121°14' W 100
Pachelma, Russ. 53°18' N, 43°20' E 154
Pachena Point, Can. 48°44' N, 125°5' W 100
Pachía, Peru 17°56' S, 70°9' W 137
Pachuca, Mex. 20°6' N, 98°48' W 114
Pachuta, Miss., U.S. 32°1' N, 88°53' W 103
Pacific, Can. 54°44' N, 128°20' W 108
Pacific Beach, Wash., U.S. 47°10' N, 124°11' W 100
Pacific Crest Trail, U.S. 47°55' N, 121°14' W 100
Pacific Grove, Calif., U.S. 36°36' N, 121°56' W 100
Pacific Missile Test Center, Calif., U.S. 34°6' N, 119°10' W 101
Pacific Ocean 35°4' N, 121°60' W 252
Pacific Rim National Park Reserve, Can. 48°38' N, 124°46' W 100
Pacifica, Calif., U.S. 37°37' N, 122°30' W 100
Pacific-Antarctic Ridge, South Pacific Ocean 63°11' S, 161°29' W 255
Pačir, Serb. and Mont. 45°54' N, 19°26' E 168
Packwood, Wash., U.S. 46°35' N, 121°41' W 100
Pacov, Czech Rep. 49°27' N, 14°59' E 152
Padada, Philippines 6°41' N, 125°21' E 203
Padang, Indonesia 3°2' N, 105°42' E 196
Padang, Indonesia 0°55' N, 100°22' E 196
Padang Endau, Malaysia 2°39' N, 103°38' E 196
Padang, island, Indonesia 0°55' N, 101°49' E 196
Padangpanjang, Indonesia 0°28' N, 100°23' E 196
Padangsidempuan, Indonesia 1°23' N, 99°17' E 196
Padany, Russ. 63°17' N, 33°24' E 152
Padas, river, Malaysia 4°40' N, 115°43' E 203
Padasjoki, Fin. 61°20' N, 25°15' E 166
Padauiri, river, Braz. 0°59' N, 64°48' W 130
Padcaya, Bol. 21°52' S, 64°48' W 137
Paddle Prairie, Can. 57°55' N, 117°27' W 108
Paden City, W. Va., U.S. 39°35' N, 80°56' W 102
Paderborn, Ger. 51°43' N, 8°45' E 167
Padeș, peak, Rom. 45°39' N, 22°18' E 168
Padilla, Bol. 19°17' S, 64°21' W 137
Padina, Serb. and Mont. 45°7' N, 20°44' E 168
Padirac, site, Fr. 44°51' N, 1°42' E 165
Padlei, Can. 61°56' N, 96°42' W 73
Padloping Island, Can. 67°11' N, 62°19' W 246
Padova (Padua), It. 45°24' N, 11°52' E 167
Padrauna, India 26°52' N, 83°58' E 197
Padre Island National Seashore, Gulf of Mexico 27°4' N, 97°18' W 96
Padrela, Serra da, Port. 41°35' N, 7°53' W 150
Padsvillye, Belarus 55°10' N, 27°57' E 166
Padua see Padova, It. 45°24' N, 11°52' E 167
Paducah, Ky., U.S. 37°4' N, 88°37' W 96
Paducah, Tex., U.S. 34°0' N, 100°19' W 92
Padul, Sp. 37°1' N, 3°37' W 164
Padun, Russ. 68°37' N, 31°48' E 152
Padwa, India 18°23' N, 82°41' E 188
Paech'ŏn, N. Korea 37°58' N, 126°18' E 200
Paektu-san, peak, N. Korea 41°58' N, 128°4' E 200
Paeroa, N.Z. 37°22' S, 175°40' E 240
Paesana, It. 44°41' N, 7°16' E 167
Paestum, ruin(s), It. 40°24' N, 14°54' E 156
Páez, Col. 2°37' N, 75°59' W 136
Pafos, Cyprus 34°45' N, 32°24' E 194
Pafúri, Mozambique 22°27' S, 31°23' E 227
Paga Conta, Braz. 4°58' S, 54°37' W 130
Pagadian, Philippines 7°52' N, 123°25' E 203
Pagan, island, Pagan 18°7' N, 144°58' E 192
Pagasae, ruin(s), Gr. 39°18' N, 22°49' E 156
Pagashi, river, Can. 51°31' N, 83°51' W 110
Pagato, river, Can. 56°4' N, 102°44' W 108
Page, N. Dak., U.S. 47°9' N, 97°35' W 90
Pagėgiai, Lith. 55°8' N, 21°54' E 166
Pager, river, Uganda 3°18' N, 33°13' E 224
Paghman, Afghan. 34°38' N, 68°57' E 186
Pagiriai, Lith. 55°21' N, 24°20' E 166
Pagnag, China 32°19' N, 91°44' E 188
Pago Pago, American Samoa, U.S. 14°14' S, 170°42' W 241
Pagoda Peak, Colo., U.S. 40°7' N, 107°26' W 90
Pagoda Point, Myanmar 15°59' N, 94°14' E 202
Paguchi Lake, lake, Can. 49°31' N, 92°2' W 94
Pagwa River, Can. 50°1' N, 85°12' W 94
Pagwachuan Lake, lake, Can. 49°40' N, 86°46' W 94
Pah Rah Range, Nev., U.S. 39°42' N, 119°42' W 90
Pahang, river, Malaysia 3°19' N, 102°37' E 196
Paharpur, Pak. 32°5' N, 71°1' E 186
Pahokee, Fla., U.S. 26°49' N, 80°40' W 105
Pahranagat Range, Nev., U.S. 37°6' N, 115°19' W 101
Pahranagat Valley, Nev., U.S. 37°11' N, 115°11' W 101
Pahrock Range, Nev., U.S. 38°1' N, 115°7' W 90
Pah-rum Peak, Nev., U.S. 40°22' N, 119°40' W 90
Pahrump, Nev., U.S. 36°12' N, 115°60' W 101
Pahute Mesa, Nev., U.S. 37°12' N, 116°41' W 92
Pai, Thai. 19°18' N, 98°23' E 202
Paiaguás, Braz. 18°24' S, 57°9' W 132
Paicines, Calif., U.S. 36°43' N, 121°17' W 100
Paide, Est. 58°53' N, 25°33' E 166
Paige, Tex., U.S. 30°11' N, 97°7' W 96
Paihia, N.Z. 35°20' S, 174°4' E 240
Paiján, Peru 7°44' S, 79°18' W 130
Päijänne, lake, Fin. 61°36' N, 25°27' E 166
Pailin City, Cambodia 12°52' N, 102°37' E 202
Paimio, Fin. 60°26' N, 22°41' E 166
Paimpol, Fr. 48°47' N, 3°4' W 150
Painan, Indonesia 1°19' S, 100°34' E 196
Paincourtville, La., U.S. 29°58' N, 91°4' W 103
Paine, Cerro, peak, Chile 50°60' S, 73°13' W 134
Painesville, Ohio, U.S. 41°42' N, 81°15' W 102
Paint Lake, lake, Can. 55°23' N, 98°33' W 108
Paint Rock, Tex., U.S. 31°29' N, 99°56' W 92

Painted Desert, Ariz., U.S. 36°17′ N, 110°60′ W 92
Painter, Mount, peak, Austral. 30°19′ S, 139°7′ E 230
Paintsville, Ky., U.S. 37°49′ N, 82°49′ W 94
Paisley, Oreg., U.S. 42°41′ N, 120°33′ W 90
Paistunturit, peak, Fin. 69°35′ N, 26°13′ E 152
Paita, Peru 4°60′ S, 81°9′ W 130
Pajala, Nor. 67°12′ N, 23°22′ E 152
Pajares, Puerto de, pass, Sp. 43°0′ N, 5°47′ W 150
Pajarito, N. Mex., U.S. 34°59′ N, 106°42′ W 92
Pajaro, Calif., U.S. 36°52′ N, 121°45′ W 100
Pájaro, Col. 11°40′ N, 72°40′ W 136
Pajule, Uganda 2°56′ N, 32°54′ E 224
Pajusti, Est. 59°15′ N, 26°22′ E 166
Pak Nam Chumphon, Thai. 10°22′ N, 99°16′ E 202
Pak Phanang, Thai. 8°22′ N, 100°13′ E 202
Pakaraima Mountains, Guyana 5°59′ N, 60°35′ W 130
Pakaur, India 24°36′ N, 87°50′ E 197
Pakawau, N.Z. 40°38′ S, 172°40′ E 240
Pakbèng, Laos 19°55′ N, 101°11′ E 202
Pakch'ŏn, N. Korea 39°43′ N, 125°36′ E 200
Pakhtusovo, Russ. 74°23′ N, 59°40′ E 160
Paki, Nig. 11°28′ N, 8°10′ E 222
Pakipaki, N.Z. 39°42′ S, 176°46′ E 240
Pakistan 33°52′ N, 73°37′ E 186
Pakleni Otoci, island, Croatia 43°10′ N, 15°56′ E 168
Pakokku, Myanmar 21°24′ N, 95°5′ E 202
Pakotai, N.Z. 35°43′ S, 173°54′ E 240
Pak-Ou, Laos 20°5′ N, 102°13′ E 202
Pakowki Lake, Can. 49°12′ N, 111°36′ W 90
Pakpattan, Pak. 30°22′ N, 73°22′ E 186
Pakrac, Croatia 45°26′ N, 17°12′ E 168
Pakruojis, Lith. 55°58′ N, 23°51′ E 166
Pakwach, Uganda 2°25′ N, 31°28′ E 224
Pakxan, Laos 18°23′ N, 103°40′ E 202
Pal Lahara, India 21°26′ N, 85°12′ E 188
Pala, Calif., U.S. 33°22′ N, 117°6′ W 101
Pala, Chad 9°23′ N, 14°55′ E 216
Pala, Myanmar 12°51′ N, 98°39′ E 202
Palabek, Uganda 3°27′ N, 32°34′ E 224
Palacios, Tex., U.S. 28°42′ N, 96°13′ W 96
Palaeopolis, ruin(s), Gr. 40°28′ N, 25°24′ E 156
Palafrugell, Sp. 41°54′ N, 3°9′ E 164
Palagruža (Pelagosa), island, Croatia 42°25′ N, 16°0′ E 168
Palaichori, Cyprus 34°55′ N, 33°4′ E 194
Palaiseau, Fr. 48°41′ N, 2°14′ E 163
Palamau National Park, India 23°45′ N, 84°9′ E 197
Palamós, Sp. 41°50′ N, 3°7′ E 164
Palana, Russ. 59°7′ N, 160°9′ E 160
Palanan, Philippines 17°4′ N, 122°25′ E 203
Palanga, Lith. 55°54′ N, 21°4′ E 166
Palani, India 10°27′ N, 77°30′ E 188
Palanpur, India 24°10′ N, 72°26′ E 186
Palapag, Philippines 12°33′ N, 125°7′ E 203
Palapye, Botswana 22°30′ S, 27°5′ E 227
Palar, river, India 12°46′ N, 79°11′ E 188
Palatia, ruin(s), Gr. 35°51′ N, 27°9′ E 156
Palatka, Fla., U.S. 29°38′ N, 81°39′ W 105
Palatka, Russ. 60°13′ N, 150°51′ E 160
Palau 5°28′ N, 132°55′ E 242
Palau Trench, North Pacific Ocean 4°9′ N, 133°9′ E 254
Palauig, Philippines 15°26′ N, 119°55′ E 203
Palauk, Myanmar 13°16′ N, 98°38′ E 202
Palaw, Myanmar 12°58′ N, 98°39′ E 202
Palawan, island, Philippines 8°51′ N, 116°11′ E 192
Palawan Trough, South China Sea 9°2′ N, 116°31′ E 254
Palazzo San Gervasio, It. 40°56′ N, 15°59′ E 156
Palazzolo sull'Oglio, It. 45°36′ N, 9°51′ E 167
Paldiski, Est. 59°20′ N, 24°2′ E 166
Pale, Bosn. and Herzg. 43°49′ N, 18°34′ E 168
Pale, ruin(s), Gr. 38°10′ N, 20°18′ E 156
Palel, India 24°27′ N, 94°3′ E 188
Paleleh, Indonesia 1°2′ N, 121°53′ E 192
Paleliu (Beliliou), island, Palau 7°0′ N, 134°15′ E 242
Palembang, Indonesia 2°59′ S, 104°39′ E 192
Palen Mountains, Calif., U.S. 33°47′ N, 115°10′ W 101
Palencia, Sp. 42°0′ N, 4°33′ W 150
Palenque National Park, Mex. 17°29′ N, 92°9′ W 115
Palenque, ruin(s), Mex. 17°28′ N, 92°8′ W 115
Palermo, Col. 0°24′ N, 73°29′ W 136
Palermo, It. 38°8′ N, 13°20′ E 156
Palestina, Chile 23°52′ S, 69°47′ W 132
Palestina, Mex. 29°8′ N, 100°59′ W 92
Palestine, Ill., U.S. 39°0′ N, 87°37′ W 102
Palestine, Tex., U.S. 31°44′ N, 95°38′ W 103
Paletwa, Myanmar 21°19′ N, 92°46′ E 188
Palgrave, Mount, peak, Austral. 23°25′ S, 115°46′ E 230
Palgrave Point, Namibia 20°47′ S, 12°44′ E 220
Pali, India 25°46′ N, 73°21′ E 186
Pali, river, Sri Lanka 9°4′ N, 79°55′ E 188
Palian, Thai. 7°13′ N, 99°40′ E 196
Palić, Serb. and Mont. 46°5′ N, 19°46′ E 168
Palikir, F.S.M. 6°57′ N, 158°10′ E 242
Palimbang, Philippines 6°15′ N, 124°12′ E 203
Palinuro, Capo, It. 39°56′ N, 14°28′ E 156
Palisade, Colo., U.S. 39°7′ N, 108°22′ W 90
Palisade, Nebr., U.S. 40°20′ N, 101°7′ W 90
Palisade Glacier, Calif., U.S. 37°3′ N, 118°46′ W 101
Palizada, Mex. 18°14′ N, 92°8′ W 115
Pälkäne, Fin. 61°20′ N, 24°14′ E 166
Palkino, Russ. 57°32′ N, 28°0′ E 166
Pallasovka, Russ. 50°2′ N, 46°51′ E 158
Pallës, Bishti i, Alban. 41°20′ N, 18°42′ E 156
Palling, Can. 54°21′ N, 125°55′ W 108
Palliser, Cape, N.Z. 41°49′ S, 174°57′ E 240
Palm Bay, Fla., U.S. 28°2′ N, 80°37′ W 105
Palm Beach, Fla., U.S. 26°42′ N, 80°3′ W 105
Palm Beach Gardens, Fla., U.S. 26°50′ N, 80°8′ W 105
Palm Coast, Fla., U.S. 29°30′ N, 81°11′ W 105
Palm Harbor, Fla., U.S. 28°3′ N, 82°45′ W 105
Palm Islands, Coral Sea 18°27′ S, 146°34′ E 230
Palm Point, Nig. 4°9′ N, 5°30′ E 222
Palm Springs, Calif., U.S. 33°51′ N, 116°33′ W 101
Palm Springs, Fla., U.S. 26°38′ N, 80°7′ W 105
Palma, Mozambique 10°46′ S, 40°29′ E 224
Palma, Sp. 39°40′ N, 2°37′ E 143
Palma de Mallorca, Sp. 39°34′ N, 2°39′ E 150
Palma del Río, Sp. 37°42′ N, 5°17′ W 164
Palma, river, Braz. 12°27′ S, 47°55′ W 130
Palma Sola, Venez. 10°33′ N, 68°34′ W 136
Palmachim, spaceport, Israel 31°51′ N, 34°39′ E 194
Palmaner, India 13°12′ N, 78°45′ E 188
Palmanova, It. 45°54′ N, 13°18′ E 167
Palmar Sur, C.R. 8°57′ N, 83°27′ W 115
Palmares, Braz. 10°27′ S, 67°47′ W 137
Palmares, Braz. 8°38′ S, 35°34′ W 132
Palmarito, Venez. 7°38′ N, 70°9′ W 136
Palmas, Braz. 26°28′ S, 52°1′ W 139
Palmas, Braz. 10°11′ S, 48°18′ W 130
Palmas, Cape 4°10′ N, 7°35′ W 222
Palmas de Monte Alto, Braz. 14°19′ S, 43°7′ W 138
Palmdale, Calif., U.S. 34°35′ N, 118°8′ W 101
Palmdale, Fla., U.S. 26°56′ N, 81°19′ W 105
Palmeira das Missões, Braz. 27°54′ S, 53°18′ W 139
Palmeira dos Índios, Braz. 9°25′ S, 36°37′ W 132
Palmeirante, Braz. 7°49′ S, 47°55′ W 130
Palmela, Port. 38°33′ N, 8°55′ W 150
Palmer, Alas., U.S. 61°31′ N, 149°10′ W 98
Palmer, Mass., U.S. 42°9′ N, 72°20′ W 104
Palmer Archipelago, islands, Weddell Sea 63°51′ S, 63°17′ W 134
Palmer Land, region, Antarctica 69°25′ S, 65°11′ W 248
Palmer, river, Austral. 16°10′ S, 142°53′ E 230
Palmer, station, Antarctica 64°48′ S, 63°60′ W 134
Palmerston, Can. 43°49′ N, 80°50′ W 102
Palmerston, N.Z. 45°30′ S, 170°43′ E 240
Palmerston North, N.Z. 40°23′ S, 175°36′ E 240
Palmertown, Conn., U.S. 41°26′ N, 72°8′ W 104
Palmetto, Fla., U.S. 27°31′ N, 82°33′ W 105
Palmillas, Mex. 23°17′ N, 99°34′ W 114
Palmira, Col. 3°29′ N, 76°18′ W 136
Palmira, Venez. 8°49′ N, 72°24′ W 136
Palmitas, Uru. 33°31′ S, 57°48′ W 139
Palmyra, Ill., U.S. 39°25′ N, 89°60′ W 102
Palmyra, Mo., U.S. 39°47′ N, 91°33′ W 94
Palmyras Point, India 20°32′ N, 87°4′ E 188
Palo Alto, Calif., U.S. 37°27′ N, 122°11′ W 100
Palo Duro Canyon, Tex., U.S. 34°39′ N, 101°35′ W 92
Palo Negro, Arg. 29°39′ S, 62°10′ W 139
Palo Negro, Col. 1°29′ N, 72°20′ W 136
Palo Verde, Calif., U.S. 33°25′ N, 114°45′ W 101
Paloh, Indonesia 1°45′ N, 109°17′ E 196
Paloich, Sudan 10°27′ N, 32°32′ E 224
Palojärvi, Fin. 63°22′ N, 28°43′ E 152
Palokoski, Fin. 66°51′ N, 25°23′ E 152
Palomar Mountain, peak, Calif., U.S. 33°21′ N, 116°53′ W 101
Palomas, Mex. 31°41′ N, 107°37′ W 92
Palopo, Indonesia 2°60′ S, 120°10′ E 192
Palos, Cabo de, Sp. 37°38′ N, 0°42′ E 164
Palouse Hills, Wash., U.S. 47°11′ N, 117°57′ W 90
Palouse, river, Wash., U.S. 46°37′ N, 118°22′ W 90
Palpa, Peru 14°35′ S, 75°11′ W 132
Palpa, Peru 11°30′ S, 77°7′ W 130
Palpana, Cerro, peak, Chile 21°34′ S, 68°37′ W 137
Paltamo, Fin. 64°24′ N, 27°45′ E 152
Păltsa, peak, Nor. 69°0′ N, 20°2′ E 152
Palu, Indonesia 0°54′ N, 119°51′ E 238
Palu, Indonesia 0°60′ S, 119°52′ E 192
Palu, Turk. 38°42′ N, 39°56′ E 195
Paluan, Philippines 13°27′ N, 120°28′ E 203
Palwal, India 28°8′ N, 77°19′ E 197
Pama, Burkina Faso 11°14′ N, 0°42′ E 222
Pama, river, Cen. Af. Rep. 4°42′ N, 17°8′ E 218
Pamekasan, Indonesia 7°13′ S, 113°28′ E 192
Pamiers, Fr. 43°6′ N, 1°36′ E 164
Pamir, river, Taj. 37°15′ N, 72°46′ E 184
Pamirs, Taj. 37°33′ N, 72°10′ E 190
Pamoni, Venez. 2°49′ N, 65°54′ W 136
Pampa, Tex., U.S. 35°30′ N, 100°58′ W 92
Pampa de los Guanacos, Arg. 26°15′ S, 61°54′ W 139
Pampa del Indio, Arg. 26°3′ S, 59°55′ W 139
Pampa del Infierno, Arg. 26°30′ S, 61°12′ W 139
Pampa Grande, Bol. 18°7′ S, 64°7′ W 137
Pampaļi, Latv. 56°32′ N, 22°11′ E 166
Pamparato, It. 44°15′ N, 7°55′ E 167
Pampas, Peru 12°20′ S, 74°58′ W 137
Pampeiro, Braz. 30°37′ S, 55°18′ W 139
Pamplona, Col. 7°25′ N, 72°37′ W 136
Pamplona (Iruña), Sp. 42°47′ N, 1°40′ W 164
Pamzal, India 34°13′ N, 78°47′ E 188
Pan de Azúcar, Bol. 21°56′ S, 67°28′ W 137
Pan de Azúcar, Uru. 34°48′ S, 55°16′ W 139
Pana, Ill., U.S. 39°23′ N, 89°5′ W 102
Pana Tinai, island, P.N.G. 11°9′ S, 153°5′ E 230
Panabá, Mex. 21°17′ N, 88°17′ W 112
Panaca, Nev., U.S. 37°47′ N, 114°24′ W 92
Panacea, Fla., U.S. 30°2′ N, 84°23′ W 96
Panadura, Sri Lanka 6°41′ N, 79°56′ E 188
Panahaïkó, Óros, peak, Gr. 38°10′ N, 21°47′ E 156
Panaji, India 15°27′ N, 73°51′ E 188
Panama, Okla., U.S. 35°8′ N, 94°41′ W 96
Panama 8°20′ N, 81°0′ W 115
Panamá, Pan. 8°58′ N, 79°39′ W 115
Panama, Sri Lanka 6°45′ N, 81°48′ E 188
Panamá, Bahía de 8°46′ N, 80°20′ W 115
Panama Basin, North Pacific Ocean 2°47′ N, 83°11′ W 252
Panama City, Fla., U.S. 30°9′ N, 85°40′ W 96
Panamá, Golfo de 7°45′ N, 80°2′ W 115
Panamá Viejo, ruin(s), Golfo de Panamá 8°59′ N, 79°33′ W 115
Panambi, Braz. 28°20′ S, 53°29′ W 139
Panamint Range, Calif., U.S. 36°18′ N, 117°20′ W 101
Panamint Springs, Calif., U.S. 36°20′ N, 117°29′ W 101
Panamint Valley, Calif., U.S. 36°3′ N, 117°25′ W 101
Panay, island, Philippines 10°6′ N, 121°16′ E 192
Pancake Range, Nev., U.S. 38°34′ N, 116°13′ W 90
Pančevo, Europe 44°52′ N, 20°38′ E 156
Pančićev Vrh, peak, Europe 43°15′ N, 20°47′ E 168
Pancorbo, Sp. 42°37′ N, 3°6′ W 164
Pancurbatu, Indonesia 3°29′ N, 98°37′ E 196
Panda, Mozambique 23°60′ S, 34°42′ E 227
Pandan, Philippines 14°3′ N, 124°10′ E 203
Pandan, Philippines 11°41′ N, 122°6′ E 203
Pandėlys, Lith. 56°0′ N, 25°12′ E 166
Pando, Uru. 34°41′ S, 55°57′ W 139
Pando, adm. division, Bol. 10°53′ S, 67°31′ W 137
Pandora Entrance 11°42′ S, 143°12′ E 230
Panetolikó, Óros, peak, Gr. 38°40′ N, 21°30′ E 156
Panevėžys, Lith. 55°42′ N, 24°20′ E 166
Panfilovo, Russ. 50°22′ N, 42°50′ E 158
Panga, Dem. Rep. of the Congo 1°50′ N, 26°23′ E 224
Pangala, Congo 3°20′ S, 14°34′ E 218
Pangani, Tanzania 5°23′ S, 38°59′ E 224
Panganiban (Payo), Philippines 13°56′ N, 124°17′ E 203
Pangéo, Óros, Gr. 40°51′ N, 23°44′ E 156
Panghyŏn, N. Korea 39°52′ N, 125°14′ E 200
Pangi, Dem. Rep. of the Congo 3°14′ S, 26°39′ E 224
Pangkalanbrandan, Indonesia 4°2′ N, 98°18′ E 196
Pangkalanbuun, Indonesia 2°44′ S, 111°31′ E 192
Pangkalankotabaru, Indonesia 0°7′ N, 100°43′ E 196
Pangkalpinang, Indonesia 2°3′ S, 106°2′ E 192
Pangkor, island, Malaysia 4°4′ N, 100°3′ E 196
Pangnirtung, Can. 66°7′ N, 65°46′ W 106
Panguitch, Utah, U.S. 37°48′ N, 112°25′ W 82
Panguma, Sierra Leone 8°9′ N, 11°8′ W 222
Panguru, N.Z. 35°24′ S, 173°22′ E 240
Pangutaran, Philippines 6°20′ N, 120°33′ E 203
Panhandle, Tex., U.S. 35°20′ N, 101°23′ W 92
Pania Mutombo, Dem. Rep. of the Congo 5°13′ S, 23°52′ E 224
Pānī'au, peak, Hawai'i, U.S. 21°55′ N, 160°8′ W 99
Panié, Mount, peak 20°39′ S, 164°24′ E 238
Panipat, India 29°23′ N, 77°0′ E 197
Panj, Taj. 37°14′ N, 69°6′ E 186
Panj, river, Asia 37°40′ N, 71°30′ E 197
Panjab, Afghan. 34°23′ N, 67°6′ E 186
Panjakent, Taj. 39°28′ N, 67°32′ E 197
Panjang, island, Indonesia 2°48′ N, 108°57′ E 196
Panjang, oil field, Strait of Malacca 4°10′ N, 98°14′ E 196
Panjgur, Pak. 26°55′ N, 64°7′ E 182
Pankakoski, Fin. 63°17′ N, 30°8′ E 152
Pankow, Ger. 52°35′ N, 13°25′ E 152
Pankshin, Nig. 9°18′ N, 9°24′ E 222
Panmunjŏm, site, N. Korea 37°56′ N, 126°34′ E 200
Panna, India 24°42′ N, 80°12′ E 197
Pannonhalma, Hung. 47°32′ N, 17°48′ E 168
Panny, river, Can. 57°17′ N, 114°41′ W 108
Pano Lefkara, Cyprus 34°52′ N, 33°18′ E 194
Pano Panagia, Cyprus 34°55′ N, 32°37′ E 194
Pano Platres, Cyprus 34°52′ N, 32°51′ E 194
Panoche Pass, Calif., U.S. 36°37′ N, 121°1′ W 100
Panola, Ala., U.S. 32°58′ N, 88°15′ W 103
Panolik, Russ. 60°23′ N, 101°25′ E 173
Panorama, Braz. 21°19′ S, 51°51′ W 138
Panozero, Russ. 64°57′ N, 32°50′ E 152
P'anp'yŏng, N. Korea 40°26′ N, 125°50′ E 200
Panshi, China 42°55′ N, 126°3′ E 200
Pantanal Matogrossense National Park, Braz. 17°45′ S, 58°17′ W 132
Pantar, island, Indonesia 8°15′ S, 123°28′ E 192
Pante Makasar (Oecusse), Indonesia 9°21′ S, 124°20′ E 192
Pantelleria, island, It. 36°47′ N, 10°43′ E 216
Pantepec, Mex. 20°35′ N, 97°55′ W 114
Pantoja, Peru 0°59′ N, 75°11′ W 136
Pantonlabu, Indonesia 5°7′ N, 97°26′ E 196
Pantyy, Russ. 62°27′ N, 48°55′ E 154
Pánuco, Mex. 22°1′ N, 98°11′ W 114
Pánuco, river, Mex. 21°56′ N, 98°25′ W 114
Panyam, Nig. 9°23′ N, 9°12′ E 222
Panza Range, La, Calif., U.S. 35°22′ N, 120°19′ W 100
Panzhihua, China 26°21′ N, 101°45′ E 190
Panzi, Dem. Rep. of the Congo 7°17′ S, 18°0′ E 218
Pao, river, Thai. 17°1′ N, 103°9′ E 202
Pao, river, Venez. 8°23′ N, 64°24′ W 116
Paola, It. 39°22′ N, 16°2′ E 156
Paola, Kans., U.S. 38°33′ N, 94°52′ W 94
Paoli, Ind., U.S. 38°33′ N, 86°28′ W 102
Paonia, Colo., U.S. 38°51′ N, 107°35′ W 90
Paoua, Cen. Af. Rep. 7°12′ N, 16°25′ E 218
Paouignan, Benin 7°44′ N, 2°12′ E 222
Paoziyan, China 41°19′ N, 125°24′ E 200
Pap, Sudan 6°6′ N, 31°12′ E 224
Pápa, Hung. 47°19′ N, 17°28′ E 168
Pāpā Heiau, site, Hawai'i, U.S. 21°9′ N, 156°48′ W 99
Papakura, N.Z. 37°4′ S, 174°58′ E 240
Papanoa, Mex. 17°16′ N, 101°2′ W 114
Papanoa, Morro de, Mex. 17°15′ N, 101°1′ W 114
Papantla, Mex. 20°26′ N, 97°19′ W 114
Paparoa, N.Z. 36°7′ S, 174°15′ E 240
Papeete, French Polynesia, Fr. 17°32′ S, 149°35′ W 241
Papenburg, Ger. 53°5′ N, 7°23′ E 163
Papigochic, river, Mex. 29°0′ N, 108°1′ W 80
Papíkio, peak, Gr. 41°12′ N, 25°13′ E 156
Papilė, Lith. 56°9′ N, 22°46′ E 166
Papua, Gulf of 8°59′ S, 144°26′ E 192
Papua New Guinea 6°34′ S, 142°53′ E 192
Papuk, Croatia 45°32′ N, 17°20′ E 168
Papun, Myanmar 18°4′ N, 97°26′ E 202
Papuri, river, Braz. 0°36′ N, 70°11′ W 130
Pará, adm. division, Braz. 4°16′ S, 53°14′ W 130
Paracale, Philippines 14°16′ N, 122°47′ E 203
Paracari, river, Braz. 4°42′ S, 57°55′ W 132
Paracas, Peninsula, Peru 13°53′ S, 77°45′ W 130
Paracatu, Braz. 17°16′ S, 46°52′ W 138
Paracatu, river, Braz. 17°25′ S, 46°35′ W 138
Paracel Islands, islands, South China Sea 16°38′ N, 111°40′ E 192
Parachinar, Pak. 33°52′ N, 70°8′ E 186
Parachute, Colo., U.S. 39°27′ N, 108°4′ W 90
Paraćin, Serb. and Mont. 43°51′ N, 21°24′ E 168
Paracuru, Braz. 3°25′ S, 39°7′ W 132
Parád, Hung. 47°54′ N, 20°2′ E 168
Parada, Punta, Peru 15°37′ S, 75°39′ W 132
Paradas, Sp. 37°17′ N, 5°31′ W 150
Paradis, Can. 48°14′ N, 76°35′ W 94
Paradise, Calif., U.S. 39°45′ N, 121°39′ W 90
Paradise, Mich., U.S. 46°37′ N, 85°4′ W 94
Paradise, Mont., U.S. 47°22′ N, 114°49′ W 90
Paradise, Nev., U.S. 36°5′ N, 115°9′ W 101
Paradise Valley, Nev., U.S. 41°29′ N, 117°32′ W 90
Paraf'yanava, Belarus 54°52′ N, 27°35′ E 166
Paragon Lake, lake, Can. 58°16′ N, 97°49′ W 108
Paragould, Ark., U.S. 36°3′ N, 90°29′ W 94
Paraguá, river, Bol. 15°1′ S, 61°6′ W 132
Paragua, river, Venez. 5°37′ N, 63°43′ W 130
Paraguaçu Paulista, Braz. 22°26′ S, 50°39′ W 138
Paraguaçu, river, Braz. 13°10′ S, 40°53′ W 138
Paraguai, river, South America 20°11′ S, 58°21′ W 132
Paraguaipoa, Venez. 11°21′ N, 71°60′ W 136
Paraguaná, Peninsula de, Venez. 12°6′ N, 70°25′ W 116
Paraguaná, Peninsula de, Venez. 12°3′ N, 70°14′ W 136
Paraguarí, Parag. 25°38′ S, 57°9′ W 132
Paraguay 23°21′ S, 59°9′ W 132
Paraíba, adm. division, Braz. 7°3′ S, 38°22′ W 132
Parainen see Pargas, Fin. 60°17′ N, 22°17′ E 166
Paraíso, Braz. 19°3′ S, 53°2′ W 138
Paraíso, Braz. 6°41′ S, 59°1′ W 130
Paraíso, Mex. 18°24′ N, 93°14′ W 115
Paraíso do Tocantins, Braz. 10°15′ S, 48°57′ W 132
Parakhonsk, Belarus 52°13′ N, 26°26′ E 152
Parakou, Benin 9°19′ N, 2°36′ E 222
Paralimni, Cyprus 35°2′ N, 33°58′ E 194
Paramaribo, Suriname 5°42′ N, 55°27′ W 130
Paramé, Fr. 48°39′ N, 1°60′ W 150
Paramera, Sierra de la, Sp. 40°22′ N, 5°33′ W 150
Paramillo National Park, Col. 7°21′ N, 76°14′ W 136
Paramirim, Braz. 13°27′ S, 42°16′ W 138
Paraná, adm. division, Braz. 24°35′ S, 51°41′ W 132
Paraná, Arg. 31°46′ S, 60°31′ W 139
Paranã, Braz. 12°35′ S, 47°50′ W 130
Paraná, river, Arg. 29°37′ S, 58°49′ W 123
Paranaguá, Braz. 25°34′ S, 48°33′ W 138
Paranaíba, Braz. 19°40′ S, 51°13′ W 138
Paranaíba, river, Braz. 19°34′ S, 51°11′ W 138
Paranaiguara, Braz. 18°53′ S, 50°33′ W 138
Paranaíta, river, Braz. 9°31′ S, 56°55′ W 130
Paranapanema, river, Braz. 22°26′ S, 52°17′ W 138
Paranapiacaba, Serra do, Braz. 24°13′ S, 49°11′ W 132
Paranavaí, Braz. 23°4′ S, 52°37′ W 138
Parang, Philippines 5°58′ N, 120°53′ E 203
Parapetí, river, Bol. 20°14′ S, 63°34′ W 137
Parás, Mex. 26°27′ N, 99°31′ W 114
Parati, Braz. 23°13′ S, 44°45′ W 132
Paratinga, Braz. 12°43′ S, 43°11′ W 138
Parauapebas, river, Braz. 6°60′ S, 50°16′ W 130
Parauaquara, Serra, peak, Braz. 1°34′ S, 53°13′ W 130
Paraúna, Braz. 17°4′ S, 50°28′ W 138
Parbati, river, India 24°46′ N, 77°3′ E 197
Parbhani, India 19°15′ N, 76°45′ E 188
Parbig, Russ. 57°11′ N, 81°29′ E 169
Parcines, It. 46°41′ N, 11°4′ E 167
Parczew, Pol. 51°38′ N, 22°53′ E 152
Pardés Hanna-Karkur, Israel 32°28′ N, 34°58′ E 194
Pardilla, Sp. 41°32′ N, 3°43′ W 164
Pardo, river, Braz. 20°59′ S, 53°16′ W 138
Pardo, river, Braz. 15°49′ S, 42°6′ W 138
Pardo, river, Braz. 21°32′ S, 46°54′ W 138
Pardo, river, Braz. 15°29′ S, 45°7′ W 138
Pardubice, Czech Rep. 50°1′ N, 15°47′ E 152
Pardubický, adm. division, Czech Rep. 49°50′ N, 16°5′ E 152
Pare Mountains, Tanzania 3°29′ S, 37°42′ E 224
Parec, Serra dos, Braz. 9°47′ S, 64°10′ W 137
Parechcha, Belarus 53°51′ N, 24°8′ E 166
Parecis, Braz. 13°34′ S, 55°55′ W 123
Parecis, river, Braz. 13°39′ S, 57°13′ W 130
Paren', Russ. 62°24′ N, 162°51′ E 160
Parent, Can. 47°56′ N, 74°38′ W 94
Parent, Lac, lake, Can. 48°44′ N, 77°24′ W 94
Parepare, Indonesia 3°60′ S, 119°37′ E 192
Pargas (Parainen), Fin. 60°17′ N, 22°17′ E 166
Pargny, Fr. 48°45′ N, 4°48′ E 163
Parguaza, Venez. 6°24′ N, 67°5′ W 136
Paria, Bol. 17°52′ S, 67°1′ W 137
Paria, Gulf of 10°13′ N, 62°40′ W 116
Paria, Peninsula de, Venez. 10°47′ N, 62°56′ W 116
Pariacaca, Cerro, peak, Peru 11°58′ S, 76°5′ W 130
Pariaman, Indonesia 0°36′ N, 100°8′ E 196
Paricá, Lago, lake, Braz. 1°54′ S, 66°4′ W 136
Paricutín, Volcán, peak, Mex. 19°28′ N, 102°21′ W 114
Parida, Isla, island, Pan. 7°48′ N, 82°24′ W 115
Parika, Guyana 6°47′ N, 58°27′ W 130
Parikkala, Fin. 61°31′ N, 29°30′ E 166
Parima, river, Braz. 2°30′ N, 63°49′ W 130
Parima, Serra, Braz. 3°17′ N, 64°33′ W 130
Parima-Tapirapecó National Park, Venez. 1°56′ N, 65°41′ W 136
Pariñas, Punta, Peru 4°31′ S, 82°26′ W 130
Parintins, Braz. 2°42′ S, 56°48′ W 130
Paris, Ark., U.S. 35°16′ N, 93°45′ W 96
Paris, Fr. 48°52′ N, 2°17′ E 163
Paris, Ill., U.S. 39°36′ N, 87°42′ W 102
Paris, Ky., U.S. 38°12′ N, 84°16′ W 94
Paris, Me., U.S. 44°16′ N, 70°30′ W 104
Paris, Mo., U.S. 39°28′ N, 92°1′ W 94
Paris, Mo., U.S. 39°36′ N, 87°42′ W 94
Paris, Tenn., U.S. 36°17′ N, 88°20′ W 96
Paris, Tex., U.S. 33°38′ N, 95°32′ W 96
Parismina, C.R. 10°15′ N, 83°22′ W 115
Parit Buntar, Malaysia 5°6′ N, 100°29′ E 196
Parita, Pan. 8°0′ N, 80°32′ W 115
Park Falls, Wis., U.S. 45°55′ N, 90°28′ W 94
Park Range, Colo., U.S. 40°43′ N, 106°47′ W 90
Park Rapids, Minn., U.S. 46°54′ N, 95°5′ W 90
Park River, N. Dak., U.S. 48°21′ N, 97°47′ W 90
Parkajoki, Nor. 67°42′ N, 23°24′ E 152
Parkal, India 18°11′ N, 79°42′ E 188
Parkano, Fin. 62°0′ N, 22°58′ E 166
Parkdale, Ark., U.S. 33°6′ N, 91°33′ W 103
Parker, Ariz., U.S. 34°8′ N, 114°18′ W 101
Parker, S. Dak., U.S. 43°22′ N, 97°8′ W 90
Parker Dam, Calif., U.S. 34°16′ N, 114°10′ W 101
Parker Dam, Calif., U.S. 34°19′ N, 114°16′ W 101
Parkersburg, W. Va., U.S. 39°15′ N, 81°34′ W 102
Parkhill, Can. 43°9′ N, 81°41′ W 102
Parkin, Ark., U.S. 35°14′ N, 90°34′ W 96
Parkland, Wash., U.S. 47°7′ N, 122°26′ W 100
Parks, La., U.S. 30°11′ N, 91°51′ W 103
Parks Lake, lake, Can. 49°25′ N, 87°58′ W 110
Parksley, Va., U.S. 37°46′ N, 75°40′ W 94
Parkston, S. Dak., U.S. 43°22′ N, 97°59′ W 90
Parksville, Can. 49°18′ N, 124°19′ W 100
Parkumäki, Fin. 61°56′ N, 28°27′ E 166
Parkview Mountain, peak, Colo., U.S. 40°18′ N, 106°12′ W 90
Parli, India 18°51′ N, 76°31′ E 188
Parlier, Calif., U.S. 36°36′ N, 119°33′ W 101
Parma, Idaho, U.S. 43°46′ N, 116°57′ W 90
Parma, It. 44°47′ N, 10°20′ E 167
Parma, Mich., U.S. 42°14′ N, 84°36′ W 102
Parma, Ohio, U.S. 41°23′ N, 81°42′ W 94
Parma, river, It. 44°25′ N, 10°3′ E 167
Parnaguá, Braz. 10°16′ S, 44°36′ W 132
Parnaíba, Braz. 2°58′ S, 41°45′ W 132
Parnaíba, river, Braz. 8°21′ S, 45°45′ W 130
Parnamirim, Braz. 8°8′ S, 39°35′ W 132
Parnarama, Braz. 5°43′ S, 43°9′ W 132
Parnassós National Park, Gr. 38°29′ N, 22°26′ E 180
Parnassós, peak, Gr. 38°31′ N, 22°32′ E 156
Parnassus, N.Z. 42°42′ S, 173°17′ E 240
Párnitha National Park, Gr. 38°8′ N, 23°38′ E 156
Párnitha, Óros, peak, Gr. 38°10′ N, 23°38′ E 156
Párnonas, Óros, Gr. 37°22′ N, 22°31′ E 156
Pärnu, Est. 58°23′ N, 24°29′ E 166
Pärnu Jaagupi, Est. 58°36′ N, 24°27′ E 166
Pärnu Laht 58°18′ N, 24°7′ E 166
Pärnu, river, Est. 58°45′ N, 25°16′ E 166
Paroho, lake, S. Korea 38°8′ N, 127°41′ E 200
Páros, Gr. 37°4′ N, 25°9′ E 156
Páros, island, Gr. 36°50′ N, 24°52′ E 180
Parowan, Utah, U.S. 37°50′ N, 112°49′ W 92
Parr, Cape 81°8′ S, 171°43′ E 248
Parral, Chile 36°7′ S, 71°52′ W 134
Parras de la Fuente, Mex. 25°25′ N, 102°12′ W 114
Parris Island, S.C., U.S. 32°5′ N, 80°27′ W 112
Parrish, Fla., U.S. 27°35′ N, 82°25′ W 105
Parrs Halt, Botswana 23°22′ S, 27°16′ E 227
Parry, Cape, Can. 69°59′ N, 124°19′ W 106
Parry, Cape, Can. 70°11′ N, 126°24′ W 98
Parry Islands, Foxe Basin 74°19′ N, 107°51′ W 106
Parry, Kap 76°58′ N, 75°51′ W 106
Parry, Kap, Traill Ø 72°1′ N, 21°53′ W 246
Parry Peninsula, Can. 69°48′ N, 125°21′ W 98
Parry Sound, Can. 45°20′ N, 80°2′ W 94
Parshall, N. Dak., U.S. 47°57′ N, 102°10′ W 90
Parsi, oil field, Iran 31°0′ N, 49°54′ E 180
Parsnip Peak, Nev., U.S. 38°8′ N, 114°25′ W 90
Parsnip Peak, Oreg., U.S. 42°50′ N, 117°11′ W 90
Parsnip, river, Can. 54°34′ N, 122°18′ W 108
Parsons, Kans., U.S. 37°19′ N, 95°16′ W 96
Pårtefjället, peak, Nor. 67°9′ N, 17°29′ E 152
Partridge Bay 53°8′ N, 56°28′ W 111
Partridge, river, Can. 50°50′ N, 80°23′ W 110
Parú, river, Venez. 4°34′ N, 66°7′ W 136
Parucito, river, Venez. 5°2′ N, 66°8′ W 136
Paruro, Peru 13°48′ S, 71°51′ W 137
P'arvani, Tba, lake, Ga. 41°23′ N, 43°28′ E 195
Parvatipuram, India 18°45′ N, 83°26′ E 188
Paryang, China 30°11′ N, 83°20′ E 197
Parychy, Belarus 52°46′ N, 29°29′ E 152
Parys, S. Af. 26°58′ S, 27°27′ E 227
Pasadena, Calif., U.S. 34°8′ N, 118°11′ W 101
Pasadena, Tex., U.S. 29°41′ N, 95°12′ W 103
Pasado, Cabo, Ecua. 0°22′ N, 81°24′ W 130
Pasaje, Ecua. 3°28′ S, 79°49′ W 130
Pasaje (Juramento), river, Arg. 28°44′ S, 62°58′ W 139
P'asanauri, Ga. 42°19′ N, 44°37′ E 195
Pascagoula, Miss., U.S. 30°21′ N, 88°32′ W 103
Paşcani, Rom. 47°14′ N, 26°42′ E 156
Pasco, Wash., U.S. 46°13′ N, 119°5′ W 90
Pasco, adm. division, Peru 10°15′ S, 74°55′ W 137
Pascoag, R.I., U.S. 41°57′ N, 71°43′ W 104
Pascoal, Monte, peak, Braz. 16°53′ S, 39°25′ W 138
Pascua, Isla de see Easter Island, Chile 27°0′ S, 109°0′ W 241
Pasewalk, Ger. 53°30′ N, 13°59′ E 152
Pasfield Lake, Can. 58°24′ N, 105°44′ W 108
Pasha, river, Russ. 59°46′ N, 34°4′ E 154
Pashiya, Russ. 58°26′ N, 58°22′ E 154
Pashskiy Perevoz, Russ. 60°23′ N, 33°8′ E 154
Pasinler, Turk. 39°59′ N, 41°40′ E 195
Pasir Mas, Malaysia 6°3′ N, 102°7′ E 196
Pasir Puteh, Malaysia 5°50′ N, 102°23′ E 196
Paskwachi Bay 57°14′ N, 102°46′ W 108
Pasley, Cape, Austral. 34°26′ S, 123°41′ E 231

Pasni, *Pak.* 25°15' N, 63°26' E **182**
Paso de los Libres, *Arg.* 29°40' S, 57°9' W **139**
Paso de los Toros, *Uru.* 32°46' S, 56°31' W **139**
Paso de Ovejas, *Mex.* 19°16' N, 96°26' W **114**
Paso Robles, *Calif., U.S.* 35°37' N, 120°42' W **100**
Pasorapa, *Bol.* 18°21' S, 64°39' W **137**
Pasque Island, *Mass., U.S.* 41°27' N, 70°53' W **104**
Pass Christian, *Miss., U.S.* 30°18' N, 89°15' W **103**
Passadumkeag Mountain, peak, *Me., U.S.* 45°6' N, 68°28' W **94**
Passat Nunatak, peak, *Antarctica* 71°25' S, 4°12' W **248**
Passau, *Ger.* 48°33' N, 13°28' E **152**
Passero, Capo, *It.* 36°39' N, 15°9' E **216**
Passo Fundo, *Braz.* 28°16' S, 52°27' W **139**
Passos, *Braz.* 20°43' S, 46°37' W **138**
Pastavy, *Belarus* 55°7' N, 26°50' E **166**
Pastaza, river, *Ecua.* 2°3' S, 77°39' W **130**
Pastaza, river, *Peru* 4°29' S, 76°33' W **130**
Pasteur, *Arg.* 35°7' S, 62°14' W **139**
Pasto, *Col.* 1°13' N, 77°17' W **136**
Pastora Peak, *Ariz., U.S.* 36°46' N, 109°14' W **92**
Pastos Bons, *Braz.* 6°38' S, 44°5' W **132**
Pastrana, *Sp.* 40°24' N, 2°56' W **150**
Pasvalys, *Lith.* 56°3' N, 24°22' E **166**
Pasvik, *Nor.* 69°47' N, 30°32' E **152**
Pašvitinys, *Lith.* 56°9' N, 23°47' E **166**
Pásztó, *Hung.* 47°54' N, 19°43' E **168**
Pata, *Cen. Af. Rep.* 8°2' N, 21°28' E **218**
Patagonia, *Ariz., U.S.* 31°31' N, 110°45' W **92**
Patamisk, Lac, lake, *Can.* 52°52' N, 71°43' W **111**
Patan, *India* 23°50' N, 72°7' E **186**
Patan, *India* 17°24' N, 73°55' E **188**
Patan, *India* 23°16' N, 79°43' E **197**
Patan see Lalitpur, *Nepal* 27°36' N, 85°22' E **197**
Patani, *Indonesia* 0°15' N, 128°46' E **192**
Patara Shiraki, *Ga.* 41°17' N, 46°20' E **195**
Patchogue, *N.Y., U.S.* 40°45' N, 73°1' W **104**
Pate Island, *Kenya* 2°16' S, 41°4' E **224**
Pategi, *Nig.* 8°43' N, 5°44' E **222**
Pateley Bridge, *U.K.* 54°5' N, 1°45' W **162**
Patensie, *S. Af.* 33°46' S, 24°48' E **227**
Paternion, *Aust.* 46°43' N, 13°40' E **167**
Paterson, *N.J., U.S.* 40°53' N, 74°11' W **82**
Paterson Range, *Austral.* 21°46' S, 121°56' E **230**
Pathankot, *India* 32°16' N, 75°42' E **186**
Pathein, *Myanmar* 16°44' N, 94°45' E **202**
Pathfinder Dam, *Wyo., U.S.* 42°28' N, 106°49' W **90**
Pathum Thani, *Thai.* 14°1' N, 100°31' E **202**
Pati, river, *Braz.* 3°40' S, 67°54' W **136**
Patiala, *India* 30°19' N, 76°22' E **197**
Pativilca, *Peru* 10°42' S, 77°47' W **130**
Pátmos, *Gr.* 37°18' N, 26°33' E **156**
Patna, *India* 25°33' N, 85°5' E **197**
Patnos, *Turk.* 39°13' N, 42°52' E **195**
Pató, *Col.* 7°27' N, 74°55' W **136**
Patoka, *Ill., U.S.* 38°44' N, 89°6' W **102**
Patoka, *Ind., U.S.* 38°24' N, 87°36' W **94**
Patos, *Braz.* 6°60' S, 37°15' W **132**
Patos de Minas, *Braz.* 18°36' S, 46°30' W **138**
Patos, Lagoa dos, lake, *Braz.* 31°15' S, 51°35' W **139**
Patos, Laguna de, lake, *Mex.* 30°41' N, 107°3' W **92**
Patos, Ponta dos, *Braz.* 2°59' S, 39°40' W **132**
Pátra, *Gr.* 38°12' N, 21°47' E **180**
Patrae see Pátra, *Gr.* 38°14' N, 21°43' E **156**
Patricio Lynch, Isla, island, *Chile* 48°27' S, 77°53' W **134**
Patrick Air Force Base, *Fla., U.S.* 28°14' N, 80°39' W **105**
Patrick, Croagh, peak, *Ire.* 53°44' N, 9°46' W **150**
Patrick Point, peak, *Antarctica* 73°36' S, 66°6' E **248**
Patrimonio, *Braz.* 19°30' S, 48°31' W **138**
Patrington, *U.K.* 53°40' N, 7°419' W **162**
Patriot, *Ind., U.S.* 38°50' N, 84°49' W **102**
Patriot Hills, station, *Antarctica* 81°29' S, 81°27' W **248**
Patrocínio, *Braz.* 18°57' S, 46°58' W **138**
Pattani, *Thai.* 6°50' N, 101°16' E **196**
Patten, *Me., U.S.* 45°59' N, 68°27' W **94**
Patterson, *Calif., U.S.* 37°28' N, 121°9' W **100**
Patterson Lake, lake, *Can.* 57°37' N, 109°54' W **108**
Patterson, Mount, peak, *Calif., U.S.* 38°25' N, 119°24' W **90**
Patterson Mountain, peak, *Calif., U.S.* 36°58' N, 119°6' W **101**
Patti, *India* 31°16' N, 74°53' E **186**
Pattison, *Miss., U.S.* 31°53' N, 90°53' W **103**
Patton Seamounts, *North Pacific Ocean* 54°12' N, 150°21' W **252**
Pattullo, Mount, peak, *Can.* 56°13' N, 129°48' W **108**
Patu, *Braz.* 6°8' S, 37°38' W **132**
Patuakhali, *Bangladesh* 22°18' N, 90°19' E **197**
Patuanak, *Can.* 55°55' N, 107°44' W **108**
Patuca National Park, *Hond.* 14°27' N, 85°53' W **115**
Patuca, river, *Hond.* 14°16' N, 85°54' W **115**
Pătulele, *Rom.* 44°20' N, 22°47' E **168**
Patutahi, *N.Z.* 38°38' S, 177°52' E **240**
Patuxent River Naval Air Test Center, *Md., U.S.* 38°16' N, 76°29' W **94**
Pátzcuaro, *Mex.* 19°28' N, 101°37' W **114**
Pátzcuaro, Laguna de, lake, *Mex.* 19°30' N, 102°3' W **114**
Pau, *Fr.* 43°18' N, 0°22' E **164**
Pau d'Arco, river, *Braz.* 8°20' S, 50°41' W **132**
Paucarbamba, *Peru* 12°27' S, 74°37' W **137**
Paucartambo, *Peru* 13°22' S, 71°36' W **137**
Pauillac, *Fr.* 45°12' N, 0°46' E **150**
Pauini, *Braz.* 7°45' S, 67°2' W **130**
Pauini, river, *Braz.* 2°33' S, 63°52' W **130**
Pauini, river, *Braz.* 7°42' S, 67°48' W **130**
Pauini, river, *Braz.* 8°5' S, 69°34' W **130**
Paulatuk, *Can.* 69°26' N, 124°6' W **98**
Paulding, *Miss., U.S.* 32°0' N, 89°1' W **103**
Paulding, *Ohio, U.S.* 41°7' N, 84°35' W **102**
Pauléoula, *Côte d'Ivoire* 5°45' N, 7°24' W **222**
Paulilatino, *It.* 40°5' N, 8°47' E **156**
Paulina Peak, *Oreg., U.S.* 43°40' N, 121°21' W **90**
Pauline, Mount, peak, *Can.* 53°31' N, 119°59' W **108**
Paulis see Isiro, *Dem. Rep. of the Congo* 2°43' N, 27°39' E **224**
Paulista, *Braz.* 7°56' S, 34°59' W **132**
Paulistana, *Braz.* 8°10' S, 41°9' W **132**
Paull Lake, lake, *Can.* 56°8' N, 105°11' W **108**
Paullo, *It.* 45°25' N, 9°23' E **167**
Paulo Afonso, *Braz.* 9°24' S, 38°16' W **132**
Pauls Valley, *Okla., U.S.* 34°43' N, 97°13' W **92**
Pauma Valley, *Calif., U.S.* 33°18' N, 116°60' W **101**
Paungde, *Myanmar* 18°30' N, 95°29' E **202**
Pauni, *India* 20°45' N, 79°37' E **188**
Pauri, *India* 30°9' N, 78°48' E **197**
Pausa, *Peru* 15°19' S, 73°22' W **137**
Pauto, river, *Col.* 5°21' N, 71°31' W **136**
Pavão, *Braz.* 17°25' S, 41°5' W **138**
Pavda, *Russ.* 59°17' N, 59°29' E **154**
Pāveh, *Iran* 35°4' N, 46°21' E **180**
Pavia, *It.* 45°11' N, 9°9' E **167**
Pavia, *Port.* 38°52' N, 8°2' W **150**
Pavie, *Fr.* 43°36' N, 0°35' E **150**
Pavillion, *Wyo., U.S.* 43°14' N, 108°42' W **90**
Pavilly, *Fr.* 49°34' N, 0°57' E **163**
Pāvilosta, *Latv.* 56°53' N, 21°11' E **166**
Pavino, *Russ.* 59°7' N, 46°9' E **154**
Pavlica, *Serb. and Mont.* 43°20' N, 20°39' E **168**
Pavlodar, *Kaz.* 52°17' N, 76°57' E **184**
Pavlodar, adm. division, *Kaz.* 52°5' N, 74°35' E **184**
Pavlof Volcano, peak, *Alas., U.S.* 55°23' N, 162°4' W **98**
Pavlohrad, *Ukr.* 48°32' N, 35°52' E **158**
Pavlovac, *Croatia* 45°43' N, 17°1' E **168**
Pavlovka, *Russ.* 53°5' N, 51°17' E **154**
Pavlovka, *Russ.* 52°39' N, 47°13' E **158**
Pavlovo, *Russ.* 55°55' N, 43°8' E **154**
Pavlovsk, *Russ.* 50°27' N, 40°6' E **158**
Pavlovskaya, *Russ.* 46°8' N, 39°44' E **158**
Pavullo nel Frignano, *It.* 44°20' N, 10°49' E **167**
Pavy, *Russ.* 58°2' N, 29°30' E **166**
Paw Paw, *Mich., U.S.* 42°13' N, 85°53' W **94**
Pawarenga, *N.Z.* 35°24' S, 173°15' E **240**
Pawcatuck, *Conn., U.S.* 41°22' N, 71°51' W **104**
Pawhuska, *Okla., U.S.* 36°39' N, 96°20' W **92**
Pawlet, *Vt., U.S.* 43°20' N, 73°12' W **104**
Pawleys Island, *S.C., U.S.* 33°25' N, 79°8' W **96**
Pawling, *N.Y., U.S.* 41°33' N, 73°37' W **104**
Pawnee, *Okla., U.S.* 36°18' N, 96°48' W **92**
Pawnee Buttes, peak, *Colo., U.S.* 40°49' N, 104°4' W **90**
Pawnee City, *Nebr., U.S.* 40°5' N, 96°10' W **90**
Pawnee Creek, river, *Colo., U.S.* 40°31' N, 103°60' W **90**
Pawonków, *Pol.* 50°41' N, 18°35' E **152**
Pawtucket, *R.I., U.S.* 41°52' N, 71°24' W **104**
Paxi, *Gr.* 39°11' N, 20°10' E **156**
Paxtakor, *Uzb.* 40°22' N, 67°59' E **197**
Paxton, *Ill., U.S.* 40°27' N, 88°6' W **102**
Paxton, *Mass., U.S.* 42°18' N, 71°56' W **104**
Paxton, *Mo., U.S.* 40°27' N, 88°6' W **94**
Paxton, *Nebr., U.S.* 41°7' N, 101°23' W **90**
Payakumbuh, *Indonesia* 0°13' N, 100°37' E **196**
Payar, *Senegal* 14°24' N, 14°32' W **222**
Payas, peak, *Hond.* 15°43' N, 84°60' W **115**
Payer Mountains, *Antarctica* 71°54' S, 15°30' E **248**
Payerne, *Switz.* 46°49' N, 6°57' E **167**
Payette, *Idaho, U.S.* 44°2' N, 116°53' W **82**
Payne, *Ohio, U.S.* 41°4' N, 84°44' W **102**
Payne, Lac, lake, *Can.* 59°34' N, 75°34' W **106**
Payne, Mount, peak, *Peru* 12°19' S, 73°39' W **137**
Paynesville, *Minn., U.S.* 45°20' N, 94°44' W **90**
Payo see Panganiban, *Philippines* 13°56' N, 124°17' E **203**
Pays de La Loire, adm. division, *Fr.* 47°34' N, 1°59' W **150**
Paysandú, *Uru.* 32°21' S, 58°2' W **139**
Payson, *Ariz., U.S.* 34°13' N, 111°19' W **92**
Payson, *Utah, U.S.* 40°1' N, 111°43' W **90**
Paz, *Braz.* 25°41' S, 52°11' W **138**
Paz de Ariporo, *Col.* 5°50' N, 71°51' W **136**
Paz de Rio, *Col.* 5°59' N, 72°46' W **136**
Paz, river, *Braz.* 9°26' S, 52°2' W **130**
Pazar, *Turk.* 40°16' N, 36°16' E **156**
Pazar, *Turk.* 41°10' N, 40°52' E **195**
Pazar, *Turk.* 40°17' N, 32°42' E **156**
Pazarcık, *Turk.* 37°29' N, 37°19' E **156**
Pazardzhik, *Bulg.* 42°12' N, 24°19' E **156**
Pazña, *Bol.* 18°38' S, 66°56' W **137**
Pčinja, river, *Maced.* 41°46' N, 21°48' E **156**
Pe, *Myanmar* 13°27' N, 98°30' E **202**
Pe Ell, *Wash., U.S.* 46°32' N, 123°18' W **100**
Peabody, *Kans., U.S.* 38°9' N, 97°7' W **94**
Peabody, *Mass., U.S.* 42°31' N, 70°56' W **104**
Peace Dale, *R.I., U.S.* 41°27' N, 71°31' W **104**
Peace Garden, *N. Dak., U.S.* 48°58' N, 100°9' W **90**
Peace River, *Can.* 56°14' N, 117°15' W **108**
Peace, river, *Can.* 57°16' N, 116°57' W **108**
Peace, river, *Fla., U.S.* 27°11' N, 81°54' W **105**
Peach Springs, *Ariz., U.S.* 35°31' N, 113°25' W **101**
Peaima Falls, *Guyana* 6°23' N, 61°16' W **130**
Peaked Mountain, *Me., U.S.* 46°33' N, 68°54' W **94**
Peale, Mount, peak, *Utah, U.S.* 38°25' N, 109°18' W **90**
Peard Bay 70°39' N, 160°16' W **98**
Pearisburg, *Va., U.S.* 37°18' N, 80°44' W **96**
Pearl and Hermes Atoll, islands, *North Pacific Ocean* 26°30' N, 179°37' E **238**
Pearl Peak, *Nev., U.S.* 40°13' N, 115°37' W **90**
Pearl River, *La., U.S.* 30°21' N, 89°45' W **103**
Pearl, river, *Miss., U.S.* 30°46' N, 89°41' W **103**
Pearland, *Tex., U.S.* 29°32' N, 95°17' W **103**
Pearsall, *Tex., U.S.* 28°53' N, 99°6' W **92**
Pearse Canal 54°48' N, 130°40' W **108**
Pearson, *Ga., U.S.* 31°17' N, 82°51' W **96**
Pearston, *S. Af.* 32°36' S, 25°8' E **227**
Peary Land 83°29' N, 42°51' W **72**
Pease, river, *Tex., U.S.* 34°21' N, 100°39' W **80**
Peawanuk, *Can.* 55°3' N, 85°34' W **106**
Pebane, *Mozambique* 17°16' S, 38°11' E **224**
Pebas, *Peru* 3°19' S, 71°51' W **136**
Pebble Beach, *Calif., U.S.* 36°34' N, 121°58' W **100**
Pebble Island, *Pebble Island* 51°9' S, 60°3' W **248**
Peć, *Europe* 42°40' N, 20°17' E **168**
Pecan Island, *La., U.S.* 29°38' N, 92°26' W **103**
Peçanha, *Braz.* 18°34' S, 42°35' W **138**
Pécel, *Hung.* 47°29' N, 19°20' E **168**
Pechenga, *Russ.* 69°32' N, 31°11' E **152**
Pechina, *Sp.* 36°54' N, 2°26' W **164**
Pechora, *Russ.* 65°8' N, 57°11' E **154**
Pechora, river, *Russ.* 65°40' N, 56°56' E **154**
Pechorskaya Guba 68°13' N, 50°14' E **246**
Pechorskaya Nizmennost', *Russ.* 64°53' N, 51°55' E **154**
Pechorskoye More 69°0' N, 53°8' E **246**
Pechory, *Russ.* 57°48' N, 27°36' E **166**
Pecica, *Rom.* 46°10' N, 21°4' E **168**
Peciu Nou, *Rom.* 45°36' N, 21°4' E **168**
Peck, Mount, peak, *Can.* 58°17' N, 124°52' W **108**
Pecka, *Serb. and Mont.* 44°18' N, 19°32' E **168**
Peconic, *N.Y., U.S.* 41°2' N, 72°28' W **104**
Pecora, Capo, *It.* 39°23' N, 7°46' E **156**
Pecos, *N. Mex., U.S.* 35°34' N, 105°41' W **92**
Pecos, *Tex., U.S.* 31°24' N, 103°30' W **92**
Pecos, river, *U.S.* 35°7' N, 105°5' W **92**
Pécs, *Hung.* 46°4' N, 18°13' E **168**
Pécsvárad, *Hung.* 46°8' N, 18°25' E **168**
Peddapalli, *India* 18°36' N, 79°23' E **188**
Pededze, river, *Latv.* 57°11' N, 27°6' E **166**
Pedernales, *Venez.* 9°54' N, 62°16' W **116**
Pedja, river, *Est.* 58°28' N, 26°13' E **166**
Pêdo Pass, *China* 29°24' N, 83°24' E **197**
Pedra Azul, *Braz.* 16°3' S, 41°16' W **138**
Pedra de Amolar, *Braz.* 10°34' S, 46°25' W **130**
Pedras Altas, *Braz.* 31°44' S, 53°32' W **139**
Pedras Negras, *Braz.* 12°49' S, 62°54' W **130**
Pedregal, *Venez.* 11°2' N, 70°8' W **136**
Pedreiras, *Braz.* 4°34' S, 44°41' W **132**
Pedrera, *Sp.* 37°13' N, 4°55' W **164**
Pedriceña, *Mex.* 25°5' N, 103°49' W **114**
Pedro Afonso, *Braz.* 8°59' S, 48°10' W **130**
Pedro Bay, *Alas., U.S.* 59°47' N, 154°7' W **98**
Pedro Cays, islands, *Caribbean Sea* 16°52' N, 77°47' W **115**
Pedro de Valdivia, *Chile* 22°37' S, 69°44' W **137**
Pedro González, Isla, island, *Pan.* 8°23' N, 80°13' W **115**
Pedro Juan Caballero, *Parag.* 22°36' S, 55°46' W **132**
Pedro Luro, *Arg.* 39°31' S, 62°42' W **139**
Pedro Montoya, *Mex.* 21°38' N, 99°49' W **114**
Pedro Muñoz, *Sp.* 39°23' N, 2°57' W **164**
Pedro Osório, *Braz.* 31°52' S, 52°48' W **139**
Pedro R. Fernández, *Arg.* 28°44' S, 58°39' W **139**
Pedroso, Sierra del, *Sp.* 38°27' N, 5°51' W **164**
Pee Dee, river, *S.C., U.S.* 34°48' N, 79°52' W **80**
Peebles, *Ohio, U.S.* 38°56' N, 83°25' W **102**
Peekskill, *N.Y., U.S.* 41°16' N, 73°56' W **104**
Peel, river, *Can.* 65°54' N, 137°18' W **98**
Peene, *U.K.* 51°7' N, 1°14' E **162**
Peeples Valley, *Ariz., U.S.* 34°15' N, 112°44' W **92**
Peerless Lake, *Can.* 56°41' N, 115°8' W **108**
Peetz, *Colo., U.S.* 40°57' N, 103°8' W **90**
Pego, *Sp.* 38°49' N, 0°7' E **164**
Pegtymel', river, *Russ.* 69°51' N, 173°25' E **160**
Pegyshdor, *Russ.* 63°26' N, 50°35' E **154**
Pehčevo, *Maced.* 41°45' N, 22°54' E **168**
Pehuajó, *Arg.* 35°47' S, 61°54' W **139**
Peine, *Ger.* 52°19' N, 10°13' E **152**
Peixe, *Braz.* 12°5' S, 48°35' W **130**
Peixe, river, *Braz.* 27°25' S, 51°52' W **139**
Peixe, river, *Braz.* 14°42' S, 50°46' W **138**
Pek, river, *Serb. and Mont.* 44°34' N, 21°34' E **168**
Pekalongan, *Indonesia* 7°1' S, 109°38' E **192**
Pekan, *Malaysia* 3°30' N, 103°24' E **196**
Pekanbaru, *Indonesia* 0°32' N, 101°27' E **196**
Pekin, *Ill., U.S.* 40°33' N, 89°39' W **102**
Peking see Beijing, *China* 39°52' N, 116°9' E **198**
Pekkala, *Fin.* 66°21' N, 26°52' E **152**
Pelado, peak, *Sp.* 39°44' N, 1°27' W **150**
Pelagie, Isole, islands, *Mediterranean Sea* 35°6' N, 12°12' E **156**
Pelagosa see Palagruža, island, *Croatia* 42°25' N, 16°0' E **168**
Pelahatchie, *Miss., U.S.* 32°18' N, 89°48' W **103**
Pelalawan, *Indonesia* 0°29' N, 102°6' E **196**
Pelat, Mont, peak, *Fr.* 44°16' N, 6°39' E **165**
Peldoaivi, peak, *Fin.* 69°10' N, 26°25' E **152**
Peleaga, peak, *Rom.* 45°21' N, 22°52' E **168**
Pelechuco, *Bol.* 14°52' S, 69°4' W **137**
Peleduy, *Russ.* 59°45' N, 112°45' E **160**
Pelee Island, *Can.* 41°44' N, 82°40' W **102**
Pelée, Montagne, peak, *Martinique* 14°47' N, 61°15' W **116**
Pelendria, *Cyprus* 34°53' N, 32°58' E **194**
Peleng, island, *Indonesia* 1°60' S, 122°52' E **192**
Pelham, *Ga., U.S.* 31°7' N, 84°9' W **96**
Pelham, *Mass., U.S.* 42°23' N, 72°25' W **104**
Pelican, *Alas., U.S.* 57°58' N, 136°14' W **98**
Pelican, *La., U.S.* 31°52' N, 93°36' W **103**
Pelican Lake, lake, *Can.* 52°24' N, 100°48' W **108**
Pelican Mountain, peak, *Can.* 55°36' N, 113°53' W **108**
Pelican Narrows, *Can.* 55°12' N, 102°56' W **108**
Pelican Point, *Namibia* 22°55' S, 13°55' E **220**
Pelican Portage, *Can.* 55°41' N, 112°36' W **108**
Pelican Rapids, *Can.* 52°43' N, 100°44' W **108**
Pelican Rapids, *Minn., U.S.* 46°32' N, 96°5' W **94**
Pelinéo, Óros, peak, *Gr.* 38°33' N, 25°56' E **156**
Pelister National Park, *Maced.* 40°29' N, 21°15' E **180**
Pelister, peak, *Maced.* 40°59' N, 21°7' E **156**
Pelješac, *Croatia* 42°58' N, 17°6' E **168**
Pella, *S. Af.* 29°3' S, 19°9' E **227**
Pellegrini, *Arg.* 36°18' S, 63°9' W **139**
Pello, *Fin.* 66°47' N, 24°0' E **152**
Pelly, *Can.* 51°50' N, 101°56' W **90**
Pelly Crossing, *Can.* 62°53' N, 136°34' W **98**
Pelly, river, *Can.* 61°45' N, 131°16' W **98**
Pelokehn, *Liberia* 5°34' N, 8°8' W **222**
Peloponnesus, *Gr.* 38°2' N, 21°53' E **180**
Peloponnisos, adm. division, *Gr.* 36°51' N, 22°29' E **156**
Peloritani, Monti, *It.* 38°0' N, 14°49' E **156**
Pelotas, *Braz.* 31°44' S, 52°19' W **139**
Pelotas, river, *Braz.* 27°42' S, 51°25' W **139**
Pelplin, *Pol.* 53°55' N, 18°42' E **166**
Pelsart Group, islands, *Indian Ocean* 29°25' S, 112°14' E **230**
Peltovuoma, *Fin.* 68°22' N, 24°11' E **152**
Pelusium, ruin(s), *Egypt* 31°0' N, 32°29' E **194**
Pelvoux, Massif du, *Fr.* 44°50' N, 6°9' E **165**
Pelyatka, *Russ.* 69°59' N, 82°13' E **169**
Pelym, *Russ.* 59°40' N, 63°5' E **154**
Pelym, river, *Russ.* 60°42' N, 62°22' E **154**
Pemache, river, *Can.* 47°29' N, 83°50' W **110**
Pemaquid Point, *Me., U.S.* 43°37' N, 69°34' W **94**
Pematang, *Indonesia* 0°10' N, 102°6' E **196**
Pematangsiantar, *Indonesia* 3°2' N, 99°7' E **196**
Pemba, *Mozambique* 13°2' S, 40°33' E **224**
Pemba, *Zambia* 16°32' S, 27°20' E **224**
Pemba Island, *Tanzania* 5°7' S, 39°54' E **224**
Pemberton, *Can.* 50°19' N, 122°49' W **100**
Pembina, *N. Dak., U.S.* 48°56' N, 97°17' W **90**
Pembina Hills, *Can.* 49°27' N, 98°58' W **90**
Pembina, oil field, *Can.* 53°6' N, 115°14' W **108**
Pembina, river, *North America* 53°4' N, 116°13' W **108**
Pembroke, *Can.* 45°50' N, 77°7' W **110**
Pembroke, *Ga., U.S.* 32°8' N, 81°38' W **96**
Pembroke, *N.H., U.S.* 43°8' N, 71°28' W **104**
Pembroke, Cape, *East Falkland* 51°49' S, 57°42' W **134**
Peña Blanca, Cerro, peak, *Pan.* 8°39' N, 80°40' W **115**
Peña de Francia, Sierra de, *Sp.* 40°32' N, 6°47' W **150**
Peña Grande, *Sp.* 40°28' N, 3°45' W **164**
Penã Negra, Paso de, pass, *Chile* 28°14' S, 69°28' W **132**
Peña, Sierra de, *Sp.* 42°27' N, 0°60' E **164**
Penalva, *Braz.* 3°18' S, 45°13' W **132**
Penápolis, *Braz.* 21°24' S, 50°7' W **138**
Peñarroya, peak, *Sp.* 40°22' N, 0°43' E **164**
Penarth, *U.K.* 51°26' N, 3°10' W **162**
Peñas Blancas, *Nicar.* 11°13' N, 85°36' W **115**
Peñas, Cabo de, *Sp.* 43°39' N, 6°7' W **150**
Peñas de San Pedro, *Sp.* 38°43' N, 1°60' W **150**
Pencarreg, *U.K.* 52°4' N, 4°8' W **162**
Pench National Park, *India* 21°40' N, 79°30' E **197**
Penck, Cape 66°6' S, 84°17' E **248**
Pendé, river, *Cen. Af. Rep.* 6°38' N, 15°51' E **218**
Pendéli, peak, *Gr.* 38°4' N, 23°48' E **156**
Pendembu, *Sierra Leone* 8°3' N, 10°42' W **222**
Pender, *Nebr., U.S.* 42°5' N, 96°43' W **90**
Pender Bay 16°60' S, 122°19' E **230**
Pendjari National Park, *Benin* 11°17' N, 1°27' E **222**
Pendleton, *Ind., U.S.* 39°59' N, 85°44' W **102**
Pendleton, *Oreg., U.S.* 45°38' N, 118°48' W **90**
Pendleton, Mount, peak, *Can.* 59°12' N, 129°29' W **108**
Pendroy, *Mont., U.S.* 48°2' N, 112°19' W **90**
Penebangan, island, *Indonesia* 1°7' S, 108°41' E **196**
Penedo, *Braz.* 10°15' S, 36°36' W **132**
Penetanguishene, *Can.* 44°45' N, 79°56' W **94**
Penge, *Dem. Rep. of the Congo* 5°32' S, 24°36' E **224**
Penglai, *China* 37°47' N, 120°49' E **198**
Pengshui, *China* 29°18' N, 108°14' E **198**
Pengxi, *China* 30°45' N, 105°42' E **198**
Penha do Tapaua, *Braz.* 5°48' S, 64°29' W **130**
Penhold, *Can.* 52°7' N, 113°53' W **90**
Peniche, *Port.* 39°20' N, 9°23' W **214**
Peninga, *Russ.* 63°33' N, 31°35' E **152**
Península de Paria National Park, *Caribbean Sea* 10°37' N, 62°36' W **122**
Peñíscola, *Sp.* 40°21' N, 0°23' E **164**
Penitente, Serra do, *Braz.* 9°3' S, 46°49' W **130**
Pénjamo, *Mex.* 20°25' N, 101°44' W **114**
Penmaenmawr, *U.K.* 53°16' N, 3°55' W **162**
Penmarc'h, Pointe de, *Fr.* 47°29' N, 4°56' W **150**
Penmon, *U.K.* 53°18' N, 4°3' W **162**
Penn Yan, *N.Y., U.S.* 42°40' N, 77°4' W **94**
Penna, Punta della, *It.* 42°11' N, 14°44' E **156**
Pennabilli, *It.* 43°49' N, 12°15' E **167**
Pennant Point, *Can.* 44°20' N, 63°44' W **111**
Pennask Lake, *Can.* 49°56' N, 120°44' W **90**
Pennask Mountain, peak, *Can.* 49°52' N, 120°12' W **90**
Pennell Coast, *Antarctica* 70°51' S, 173°14' E **248**
Pennine Alps, *Switz.* 46°13' N, 7°29' E **165**
Pennines, The, *U.K.* 54°14' N, 2°15' W **162**
Pennino, Monte, peak, *It.* 43°5' N, 12°48' E **156**
Pennsboro, *W. Va., U.S.* 39°16' N, 80°58' W **102**
Pennsylvania, adm. division, *Pa., U.S.* 41°46' N, 79°36' W **94**
Pennville, *Ind., U.S.* 40°29' N, 85°9' W **102**
Penny, *Can.* 53°50' N, 121°17' W **108**
Penny Point 80°25' S, 170°23' E **248**
Pennycutaway, river, *Can.* 56°7' N, 94°14' W **108**
Peno, *Russ.* 56°56' N, 32°47' E **154**
Penobscot Bay 44°8' N, 69°6' W **80**
Penong, *Austral.* 31°57' S, 132°59' E **231**
Penrith, *U.K.* 54°40' N, 2°46' W **162**
Penryn, *Calif., U.S.* 38°51' N, 121°11' W **90**
Pensacola, *Fla., U.S.* 30°24' N, 87°13' W **96**
Pensacola Mountains, *Antarctica* 85°14' S, 76°52' W **248**
Penticton, *Can.* 49°27' N, 119°33' W **106**
Pentland Hills, *U.K.* 55°48' N, 3°57' W **150**
Pentland Skerries, islands, *North Sea* 58°23' N, 2°50' W **150**
Pentwater, *Mich., U.S.* 43°46' N, 86°25' W **102**
Penunjok, Tanjong, *Malaysia* 4°1' N, 103°30' E **196**
Penwell, *Tex., U.S.* 31°43' N, 102°36' W **92**
Penza, *Russ.* 53°9' N, 45°3' E **154**
Penza, adm. division, *Russ.* 53°28' N, 43°26' E **154**
Penzance, *U.K.* 50°7' N, 5°33' W **150**
Peoples Creek, river, *Mont., U.S.* 48°5' N, 109°10' W **108**
Peoria, *Ariz., U.S.* 33°34' N, 112°14' W **92**
Peoria, *Ill., U.S.* 40°40' N, 89°37' W **102**
Peotillos, *Mex.* 22°28' N, 100°37' W **114**
Peotone, *Ill., U.S.* 41°19' N, 87°47' W **102**
Pepe'ekeo, *Hawai'i, U.S.* 19°50' N, 155°7' W **99**
Pepel, *Sierra Leone* 8°37' N, 13°4' W **222**
Pephnos, ruin(s), *Gr.* 36°47' N, 22°13' E **156**
Pequeña, Punta, *Mex.* 26°6' N, 113°34' W **112**
Pequop Mountains, *Nev., U.S.* 40°40' N, 114°44' W **90**
Pera, *Cyprus* 35°1' N, 33°15' E **194**
Perälä, *Fin.* 62°27' N, 21°36' E **152**
Peralada, *Sp.* 42°18' N, 3°1' E **164**
Perales de Alfambra, *Sp.* 40°37' N, 0°60' E **164**
Peramiho, *Tanzania* 10°38' S, 35°28' E **224**
Peranka, *Fin.* 65°21' N, 29°1' E **154**
Peräposio, *Fin.* 66°11' N, 27°52' E **154**
Perast, *Europe* 42°29' N, 18°42' E **168**
Perati, ruin(s), *Aegean Sea* 37°54' N, 23°56' E **156**
Percé, *Can.* 48°30' N, 64°15' W **111**
Perce Point, *Antarctica* 72°48' S, 78°20' W **248**
Perch Bay 58°2' N, 102°23' W **108**
Perche, region, *Fr.* 48°50' N, 0°46' E **163**
Percy Isles, islands, *Coral Sea* 21°39' S, 150°29' E **230**
Perdido, *Ala., U.S.* 30°59' N, 87°37' W **103**
Perdido, Monte, peak, *Sp.* 42°39' N, 1°59' W **164**
Perdido, river, *U.S.* 30°45' N, 87°38' W **103**
Perdizes, *Braz.* 19°22' S, 47°19' W **138**
Perechitsy, *Russ.* 58°48' N, 30°3' E **166**
Perechyn, *Ukr.* 48°43' N, 22°26' E **152**
Pereira, *Col.* 4°45' N, 75°42' W **136**
Pereira Barreto, *Braz.* 20°38' S, 51°6' W **138**
Perelazovskiy, *Russ.* 49°8' N, 42°25' E **158**
Perelyub, *Russ.* 51°51' N, 50°21' E **158**
Peremennyy, Cape, *Antarctica* 65°57' S, 109°36' E **248**
Peremetnoe, *Kaz.* 51°11' N, 50°53' E **158**
Pereslavl' Zalesskiy, *Russ.* 56°44' N, 38°50' E **154**
Perevolotskiy, *Russ.* 51°51' N, 54°12' E **158**
Pereyaslav-Khmel'nyts'kyy, *Ukr.* 50°3' N, 31°33' E **158**
Pérez, Isla, island, *Mex.* 22°17' N, 89°57' W **116**
Perga, ruin(s), *Turk.* 36°59' N, 30°44' E **156**
Pergamino, *Arg.* 33°57' S, 60°34' W **139**
Perham, *Minn., U.S.* 46°34' N, 95°35' W **90**
Perhentian Besar, island, *Malaysia* 5°58' N, 102°37' E **196**
Perho, *Fin.* 63°13' N, 24°21' E **152**
Peri Mirim, *Braz.* 2°41' S, 44°53' W **132**
Periam, *Rom.* 46°2' N, 20°54' E **168**
Péribonka, Lac, lake, *Can.* 49°55' N, 71°53' W **94**
Péribonka, river, *Can.* 48°50' N, 71°20' W **111**
Perico, *Arg.* 24°24' S, 65°7' W **134**
Peridot, *Ariz., U.S.* 33°19' N, 110°27' W **92**
Perigoso, Canal 3°177' S, 50°35' W **130**
Perijá National Park, *Venez.* 9°15' N, 73°18' W **136**
Perijá, Sierra de, *Venez.* 10°10' N, 73°20' W **136**
Perim see Barīm, island, *Yemen* 12°36' N, 42°32' E **182**
Períssa, *Gr.* 36°20' N, 25°27' E **156**
Perito Moreno, *Arg.* 46°35' S, 70°55' W **134**
Perito Moreno National Park, *Arg.* 47°60' S, 72°42' W **122**
Peritoró, *Braz.* 4°17' S, 44°21' W **132**
Perkins, *Okla., U.S.* 35°57' N, 97°2' W **92**
Perkinston, *Miss., U.S.* 30°45' N, 89°7' W **103**
Perkinsville, *Vt., U.S.* 43°22' N, 72°32' W **104**
Perković, *Croatia* 43°40' N, 16°5' E **168**
Perky, *Fla., U.S.* 24°38' N, 81°34' W **105**
Perl, *Ger.* 49°28' N, 6°23' E **163**
Perla, *Ark., U.S.* 34°20' N, 92°47' W **96**
Perlas, Laguna de 12°24' N, 83°56' W **115**
Perlevka, *Russ.* 51°50' N, 38°47' E **158**
Perm', *Russ.* 57°57' N, 56°14' E **154**
Perm', adm. division, *Russ.* 58°50' N, 56°13' E **154**
Permas, *Russ.* 59°19' N, 45°36' E **154**
Pernaja see Pernå, *Fin.* 60°26' N, 26°2' E **166**
Pernambuco, adm. division, *Braz.* 8°41' S, 38°59' W **132**
Pernambuco Plain, *South Atlantic Ocean* 7°10' S, 25°50' W **253**
Pernik, *Bulg.* 42°36' N, 23°2' E **168**
Pernik, adm. division, *Bulg.* 42°31' N, 22°44' E **168**
Perniö, *Fin.* 60°11' N, 23°6' E **166**
Pernitz, *Aust.* 47°54' N, 15°57' E **168**
Peron Islands, *Joseph Bonaparte Gulf* 13°19' S, 128°31' E **230**
Peronit Burnu, *Turk.* 41°23' N, 41°2' E **195**
Péronne, *Fr.* 49°55' N, 2°55' E **163**
Peros Banhos, atoll, *Indian Ocean* 5°16' S, 71°8' E **188**
Perosa Argentina, *It.* 44°57' N, 7°12' E **167**
Perote, *Mex.* 19°31' N, 97°16' W **114**
Perouse Strait, La 45°35' N, 139°41' E **160**
Perow, *Can.* 54°31' N, 126°27' W **108**
Perpignan, *Fr.* 42°41' N, 2°53' E **164**
Perrault Falls, *Can.* 50°19' N, 93°10' W **90**
Perrault Lake, lake, *Can.* 50°14' N, 93°36' W **90**
Perrine, *Fla., U.S.* 25°36' N, 80°22' W **105**
Perris, *Calif., U.S.* 33°47' N, 117°16' W **101**
Perros-Guirec, *Fr.* 48°48' N, 3°28' W **150**
Perry, *Fla., U.S.* 30°5' N, 83°34' W **96**
Perry, *Ga., U.S.* 32°27' N, 83°44' W **96**
Perry, *Iowa, U.S.* 41°49' N, 94°6' W **94**
Perry, *Mich., U.S.* 42°49' N, 84°12' W **102**
Perry, *Ohio, U.S.* 41°44' N, 81°7' W **102**
Perry, *Okla., U.S.* 36°15' N, 97°17' W **92**
Perry, *Utah, U.S.* 41°27' N, 112°1' W **90**

Perry Island, Foxe Basin 67°49' N, 102°21' W 106
Perrysburg, Ohio, U.S. 41°32' N, 83°38' W 102
Perryton, Tex., U.S. 36°22' N, 100°49' W 92
Perşembe, Turk. 41°4' N, 37°45' E 156
Persepolis, ruin(s), Iran 30°2' N, 52°54' E 196
Pershore, U.K. 52°6' N, 2°5' W 162
Persian Gulf 26°40' N, 51°30' E 196
Pertek, Turk. 38°52' N, 39°19' E 195
Perth, Austral. 31°57' S, 115°32' E 230
Perth, Can. 44°54' N, 76°16' W 94
Perth-Andover, Can. 46°43' N, 67°42' W 94
Pertominsk, Russ. 64°47' N, 38°20' E 154
Pertunmaa, Fin. 61°30' N, 26°28' E 166
Peru, Ill., U.S. 41°19' N, 89°8' W 102
Peru, Ind., U.S. 40°45' N, 86°4' W 102
Peru, Me., U.S. 44°30' N, 70°26' W 104
Peru, Mo., U.S. 41°19' N, 89°8' W 94
Peru, Nebr., U.S. 40°28' N, 95°44' W 94
Peru, N.Y., U.S. 44°34' N, 73°34' W 104
Peru 8°44' S, 77°9' W 130
Peru, Vt., U.S. 43°14' N, 72°54' W 104
Peru Basin, South Pacific Ocean 11°59' S, 88°41' W 252
Peru-Chile Trench, South Pacific Ocean 18°8' S, 73°12' W 253
Perugia, It. 43°6' N, 12°23' E 156
Perugorría, Arg. 29°20' S, 58°34' W 139
Péruwelz, Belg. 50°29' N, 3°35' E 163
Pervari, Turk. 37°53' N, 42°32' E 195
Pervomaevka, Kaz. 42°5' N, 69°52' E 197
Pervomaysk, Russ. 54°49' N, 43°49' E 154
Pervomays'k, Ukr. 48°4' N, 30°58' E 156
Pervomayskīy, Kaz. 50°14' N, 81°58' E 184
Pervomayskiy, Russ. 53°15' N, 40°14' E 154
Pervomayskiy, Russ. 59°33' N, 61°23' E 154
Pervomayskiy, Russ. 51°29' N, 55°4' E 158
Pervomayskoye, Russ. 51°26' N, 47°40' E 158
Pervomayskoye, Russ. 57°4' N, 86°21' E 169
Pervoural'sk, Russ. 56°56' N, 59°57' E 154
Pervyy Kuril'skiy Proliv 50°43' N, 153°5' E 160
Pesaro, It. 43°54' N, 12°55' E 167
Pescadero, Calif., U.S. 37°14' N, 122°24' W 100
Pescara, It. 42°27' N, 14°13' E 156
Peschanyy, Mys, Kaz. 43°2' N, 50°52' E 195
Peschici, It. 41°56' N, 16°1' E 168
Peschiera, It. 45°26' N, 10°40' E 167
Pesha, river, Russ. 66°28' N, 48°19' E 154
Peshawar, Pak. 34°0' N, 71°35' E 186
Peshawarun, ruin(s), Afghan. 31°29' N, 61°31' E 186
Peshtigo, Wis., U.S. 45°3' N, 87°47' W 94
Peski, Russ. 51°15' N, 42°29' E 158
Peskovka, Russ. 59°1' N, 52°25' E 154
Pesochnoye, Russ. 57°58' N, 39°7' E 154
Pesotum, Ill., U.S. 39°54' N, 88°17' W 102
Pest, adm. division, Hung. 47°13' N, 18°57' E 156
Peşteana Jiu, Rom. 44°50' N, 23°18' E 168
Pestovo, Russ. 58°37' N, 35°50' E 154
Pestravka, Russ. 52°24' N, 49°56' E 158
Petah Tiqwa, Israel 32°5' N, 34°53' E 194
Petäjävesi, Fin. 62°14' N, 25°11' E 154
Petal, Miss., U.S. 31°19' N, 89°14' W 103
Petalax (Petolahti), Fin. 62°49' N, 21°24' E 154
Petaluma, Calif., U.S. 38°13' N, 122°39' W 100
Petange, Lux. 49°32' N, 5°51' E 163
Petare, Venez. 10°27' N, 66°48' W 116
Petatlán, Mex. 17°29' N, 101°16' W 114
Petatlán, river, Mex. 26°14' N, 107°46' W 80
Petatlán, river, Mex. 17°20' N, 101°31' W 112
Petauke, Zambia 14°16' S, 31°16' E 224
Petén, region, Guatemala 16°4' N, 90°38' W 115
Petenwell Lake, Wis., U.S. 44°6' N, 90°16' W 102
Peter I Island, Antarctica 68°58' S, 90°43' W 248
Peter Lake, Can. 57°11' N, 104°29' W 108
Peter Pond Lake, Can. 55°58' N, 111°17' W 106
Peterbell, Can. 48°36' N, 83°22' W 94
Peterborough, Austral. 32°59' S, 138°49' E 231
Peterborough, Can. 44°18' N, 78°21' W 94
Peterborough, U.K. 52°34' N, 0°15' E 162
Petermann Bjerg, peak 73°3' N, 28°60' W 246
Petermann Gletscher, glacier 78°50' N, 62°8' W 72
Petersberg, Ger. 50°33' N, 9°42' E 167
Petersburg, Alas., U.S. 56°36' N, 132°51' W 106
Petersburg, Ill., U.S. 40°0' N, 89°51' W 102
Petersburg, Ind., U.S. 38°29' N, 87°16' W 102
Petersburg, Mich., U.S. 41°53' N, 83°42' W 102
Petersburg, Tex., U.S. 33°51' N, 101°36' W 96
Petersburg, Va., U.S. 37°11' N, 77°23' W 82
Petersburg, W. Va., U.S. 38°59' N, 79°8' W 94
Petersburg National Battlefield, Va., U.S. 37°12' N, 77°27' W 96
Petersfield, U.K. 51°0' N, 0°56' E 162
Petersham, Mass., U.S. 42°29' N, 72°12' W 104
Petit Port, Alg. 36°11' N, 0°23' E 164
Petit-Louango Faunal Reserve, Gabon 2°20' S, 9°17' E 206
Petitot, river, Can. 59°49' N, 123°28' W 106
Petitot, river, Can. 60°4' N, 122°43' W 108
Petkula, Fin. 67°40' N, 26°41' E 152
Petlad, India 22°27' N, 72°49' E 186
Petlalcingo, Mex. 18°4' N, 97°55' W 114
Peto, Mex. 20°6' N, 88°57' W 115
Petolahti see Petalax, Fin. 62°49' N, 21°24' E 154
Petoskey, Mich., U.S. 45°20' N, 84°60' W 82
Petra, Ostrova, islands, Laptev Sea 75°41' N, 108°52' E 160
Petra, ruin(s), Jordan 30°17' N, 35°23' E 180
Petra Velikogo, Zaliv 42°40' N, 131°45' E 200
Petras, Mount, peak, Antarctica 75°47' S, 127°55' W 248
Petre, Point, Can. 43°38' N, 77°26' W 94
Petriano, It. 43°46' N, 12°43' E 167
Petrich, Bulg. 41°24' N, 23°9' E 180
Petrified Forest National Park, Ariz., U.S. 34°44' N, 109°45' W 92
Petrinja, Croatia 45°26' N, 16°16' E 168
Petrodvorets, Russ. 59°49' N, 29°47' E 166
Petroglyphs, site, Hawai'i, U.S. 19°0' N, 155°50' W 99
Petrolândia, Braz. 9°1' S, 38°15' W 132
Petrólea, Col. 8°29' N, 72°40' W 136
Petrolia, Calif., U.S. 40°19' N, 124°18' W 90
Petrolia, Can. 42°52' N, 82°10' W 102
Petrolia, Tex., U.S. 33°59' N, 98°14' W 92
Petrolina, Braz. 9°20' S, 40°31' W 123
Petrolina de Goiás, Braz. 16°9' S, 49°21' W 138
Petropavlovsk, Kaz. 54°51' N, 69°7' E 184
Petropavlovsk Kamchatskiy, Russ. 53°10' N, 158°42' E 160
Petroşani, Rom. 45°24' N, 23°22' E 168
Petrovac, Serb. and Mont. 42°11' N, 18°57' E 168
Petrovac, Serb. and Mont. 44°23' N, 21°25' E 168
Petrovaradin, Serb. and Mont. 45°14' N, 19°52' E 168
Petrovgrad see Zrenjanin, Serb. and Mont. 45°23' N, 20°22' E 168
Petrovići, Europe 42°46' N, 18°29' E 168
Petrovsk, Russ. 52°19' N, 45°26' E 158
Petrovsk Zabaykal'skiy, Russ. 51°25' N, 108°56' E 190
Petrovskoye, Russ. 57°0' N, 39°11' E 154
Petrozavodsk, Russ. 61°45' N, 34°23' E 154
Petrun', Russ. 66°27' N, 62°54' E 169
Petscapiskau Hill, peak, Can. 54°23' N, 64°34' W 111
Petten, Neth. 52°44' N, 4°39' E 163
Petukhovo, Russ. 55°5' N, 67°57' E 184
Peukankuala, Indonesia 4°6' N, 96°12' E 196
Peumo, Chile 34°22' S, 71°13' W 134
Peunasoe, island, Indonesia 5°31' N, 94°35' E 202
Peuplier, Pointe du, Can. 51°13' N, 79°32' W 110
Peurasuvanto, Fin. 67°48' N, 26°43' E 152
Peureulak, Indonesia 4°50' N, 97°52' E 196
Pevek, Russ. 69°40' N, 170°27' E 160
Pevensey, U.K. 50°49' N, 0°20' E 162
Pewsum, Ger. 53°26' N, 7°4' E 163
Peyia, Cyprus 34°53' N, 32°22' E 194
Peza, river, Russ. 65°37' N, 46°57' E 154
Pézenas, Fr. 43°27' N, 3°24' E 164
Pezmog, Russ. 61°53' N, 51°50' E 154
Pezu, Pak. 32°18' N, 70°47' E 186
Pfungstadt, Ger. 49°48' N, 8°35' E 167
Phaestus, ruin(s), Gr. 35°1' N, 24°42' E 156
Phalasarna, ruin(s), Gr. 35°29' N, 23°29' E 156
Phalodi, India 27°6' N, 72°21' E 186
Phalsbourg, Fr. 48°45' N, 7°14' E 163
Phan, Thai. 19°31' N, 99°43' E 202
Phan Ly, Vietnam 11°13' N, 108°34' E 202
Phan Rang, Vietnam 11°34' N, 108°58' E 202
Phan Thiet, Vietnam 10°56' N, 108°4' E 202
Phanae, ruin(s), Gr. 38°11' N, 25°49' E 156
Phangan, Ko, island, Thai. 9°49' N, 99°43' E 202
Phangnga, Thai. 8°30' N, 98°32' E 202
Pharus see Hvar, island, Croatia 43°3' N, 16°47' E 168
Phato, Thai. 9°47' N, 98°49' E 202
Phatthalung, Thai. 7°38' N, 100°6' E 196
Phayao, Thai. 19°13' N, 99°55' E 202
Phelps, Tex., U.S. 30°41' N, 95°26' W 103
Phelps Lake, lake, Can. 59°10' N, 103°45' W 108
Pheneus, ruin(s), Gr. 37°53' N, 22°14' E 156
Phenix City, Ala., U.S. 32°27' N, 85°1' W 96
Phetchabun, Thai. 16°25' N, 101°8' E 202
Phetchaburi, Thai. 13°7' N, 99°55' E 202
Phiafai, Laos 14°49' N, 105°58' E 202
Phibun Mangsaban, Thai. 15°15' N, 105°14' E 202
Phichai, Thai. 17°18' N, 100°6' E 202
Phichit, Thai. 16°25' N, 100°19' E 202
Philadelphia, Miss., U.S. 32°45' N, 89°7' W 103
Philadelphia, Pa., U.S. 39°57' N, 75°11' W 94
Philadelphia see 'Ammān, Jordan 31°56' N, 35°53' E 194
Philae, ruin(s), Egypt 23°56' N, 32°44' E 182
Philbin Inlet 74°5' S, 113°45' W 248
Philip, S. Dak., U.S. 44°2' N, 101°41' W 90
Philip Smith Mountains, Alas., U.S. 67°56' N, 149°31' W 98
Philippeville, Belg. 50°11' N, 4°32' E 167
Philippi, W. Va., U.S. 39°8' N, 80°3' W 94
Philippi, ruin(s), Gr. 41°0' N, 24°10' E 156
Philippine Basin, Philippine Sea 14°23' N, 128°46' E 254
Philippine Sea 15°8' N, 123°42' E 203
Philippine Trench, Philippine Sea 11°16' N, 127°0' E 254
Philippines 15°0' N, 121°0' E 203
Philippolis, S. Af. 30°16' S, 25°16' E 227
Philippopolis see Plovdiv, Bulg. 42°9' N, 24°45' E 156
Philippopolis see Shahbā', Syr. 32°51' N, 36°37' E 194
Philipstown, S. Af. 30°25' S, 24°27' E 227
Phillip Bay, Port 38°18' S, 143°6' E 230
Phillip Island, island, Austral. 38°56' S, 144°23' E 230
Phillips, Tex., U.S. 35°40' N, 101°22' W 92
Phillips, Wis., U.S. 45°41' N, 90°24' W 94
Phillips, Mount, peak, Austral. 24°29' S, 116°18' E 230
Phillipsburg, Kans., U.S. 39°44' N, 99°20' W 92
Phillipsburg, N.J., U.S. 40°41' N, 75°12' W 110
Philmont, N.Y., U.S. 42°14' N, 73°39' W 104
Philomath, Oreg., U.S. 44°31' N, 123°22' W 90
Philomena, Can. 55°9' N, 111°40' W 108
Phitsanulok, Thai. 16°52' N, 100°12' E 202
Phnom Bokor National Park, Cambodia 10°46' N, 103°34' E 172
Phnom Penh, Cambodia 11°32' N, 104°45' E 202
Pho, Laem, Thai. 6°54' N, 101°24' E 196
Phoenix, Ariz., U.S. 33°25' N, 112°8' W 92
Phoenix Islands, South Pacific Ocean 4°31' S, 173°41' W 238
Phon Phisai, Thai. 18°3' N, 103°6' E 202
Phong Tho, Vietnam 22°32' N, 103°21' E 202
Phôngsali, Laos 21°44' N, 102°5' E 202
Phra Thong, Ko, island, Thai. 8°47' N, 97°49' E 202
Phraaspa, ruin(s), Iran 36°44' N, 47°18' E 195
Phrae, Thai. 18°9' N, 100°9' E 202
Phran Kratai, Thai. 16°40' N, 99°37' E 202
Phrao, Thai. 18°7' N, 100°7' E 190
Phrao, Thai. 19°24' N, 99°11' E 202
Phrom Phiram, Thai. 17°3' N, 100°12' E 202
Phu Cat, Vietnam 14°1' N, 109°4' E 202
Phu Loc, Vietnam 16°17' N, 107°53' E 202
Phu Ly, Vietnam 20°33' N, 105°55' E 198
Phu My, Vietnam 14°12' N, 109°2' E 202
Phu Quoc, Dao, island, Vietnam 9°53' N, 103°33' E 202
Phu Rieng, Vietnam 11°42' N, 106°56' E 202
Phuket, Thai. 7°54' N, 98°23' E 202
Phuket, Ko, island, Thai. 7°38' N, 97°55' E 196
Phum Kompadou, Cambodia 13°48' N, 107°25' E 202
Phuntsholing, Bhutan 26°52' N, 89°20' E 197
Phuoc Long, Vietnam 9°27' N, 105°25' E 202
Phuthaditjhaba, S. Af. 28°33' S, 28°47' E 227
Phutthaisong, Thai. 15°28' N, 102°56' E 202
Phyarpon, Myanmar 16°17' N, 95°39' E 202
Pi, Pol. 53°8' N, 16°44' E 152
Piacenza, It. 45°2' N, 9°40' E 167
Piacouadie, Lac, lake, Can. 51°13' N, 71°36' W 111
Piadena, It. 45°7' N, 10°21' E 167
Piana, Fr. 42°14' N, 8°38' E 156
Pianello Val Tidone, It. 44°56' N, 9°23' E 167
Pianguan, China 39°27' N, 111°29' E 198
Pianoro, It. 44°22' N, 11°20' E 167
Pianosa, It. 42°35' N, 10°5' E 156
Piapot, Can. 49°58' N, 109°7' W 90
Piaseczno, Pol. 52°4' N, 21°1' E 152
Piatã, Braz. 13°13' S, 41°45' W 138
Piatra, Rom. 43°48' N, 25°10' E 156
Piatra Neamţ, Rom. 46°56' N, 26°22' E 156
Piauí, adm. division, Braz. 10°24' S, 45°55' W 130
Piauí, Serra do, Braz. 9°52' S, 42°4' W 132
Piaxtla, river, Mex. 23°54' N, 106°6' W 114
Piazzi, Isla, island, Chile 51°36' S, 73°59' W 134
Pibor Post, Sudan 6°44' N, 33°6' E 224
Pic, river, Can. 48°51' N, 86°10' W 94
Pica, Chile 20°31' S, 69°22' W 137
Picacho, Ariz., U.S. 32°43' N, 111°28' W 92
Picacho Pass, Ariz., U.S. 32°37' N, 111°24' W 92
Picachos, Cerro dos, peak, Mex. 29°21' N, 114°12' W 92
Picardie, adm. division, Fr. 49°35' N, 1°44' E 150
Picardy, region, Fr. 49°58' N, 1°57' E 163
Picassent, Sp. 39°20' N, 0°29' E 164
Picayune, Miss., U.S. 30°31' N, 89°40' W 103
Picerno, It. 40°39' N, 15°38' E 156
Pichanal, Arg. 23°17' S, 64°13' W 134
Picher, Okla., U.S. 36°57' N, 94°51' W 96
Pichhor, India 25°56' N, 78°23' E 197
Pichilemu, Chile 34°25' S, 71°60' W 134
Pichilingue, Mex. 24°17' N, 110°20' W 112
Pickens, Miss., U.S. 32°53' N, 89°59' W 103
Pickerel Lake, Can. 48°33' N, 91°59' W 110
Pickering, U.K. 54°14' N, 0°47' E 162
Pickering Nunatak, peak, Antarctica 71°27' S, 70°58' E 248
Pickle Crow, Can. 51°29' N, 90°4' W 110
Pickle Lake, Can. 51°28' N, 90°11' W 110
Pickton, Tex., U.S. 33°1' N, 95°23' W 103
Pico da Neblina National Park, Braz. 0°7' N, 65°34' W 136
Pico de Orizaba National Park, Mex. 19°0' N, 97°34' W 72
Pico de Tancítaro National Park, Mex. 19°18' N, 102°43' W 72
Pico, island, Port. 38°21' N, 28°24' W 253
Pico Truncado, Arg. 46°45' S, 67°57' W 134
Picos, Braz. 7°6' S, 41°26' W 132
Picton, Can. 44°0' N, 77°9' W 94
Picton, N.Z. 41°19' S, 174°0' E 240
Pictou, Can. 45°41' N, 62°43' W 111
Picture Gorge, site, Oreg., U.S. 44°32' N, 119°43' W 90
Pictured Rocks, Mich., U.S. 46°30' N, 87°10' W 80
Pictured Rocks National Lakeshore, Mich., U.S. 46°12' N, 92°34' W 80
Picuris Peak, N. Mex., U.S. 36°13' N, 105°44' W 92
Pidurutalagala, peak, Sri Lanka 6°58' N, 80°41' E 188
Piedecuesta, Col. 6°58' N, 73°4' W 136
Piedmont, Mo., U.S. 37°9' N, 90°42' W 96
Piedmont, adm. division, It. 44°51' N, 6°58' E 165
Piedra, Calif., U.S. 36°49' N, 119°23' W 100
Piedra del Águila, Arg. 40°2' S, 70°6' W 134
Piedra Lais, Venez. 3°6' N, 65°56' W 136
Piedra Parada, ruin(s), Mex. 16°48' N, 93°33' W 115
Piedra Shotel, Arg. 44°23' S, 70°30' W 134
Piedra Sola, Uru. 32°4' S, 56°19' W 139
Piedrabuena, Sp. 39°2' N, 4°11' W 164
Piedras Blancas, Point, Calif., U.S. 35°41' N, 121°29' W 100
Piedras Negras, Mex. 28°40' N, 100°31' W 92
Piedras Negras, ruin(s), Guatemala 17°11' N, 91°23' W 115
Piedras, Punta, Arg. 35°25' S, 57°9' W 139
Piedras, river, Peru 11°22' S, 70°42' W 137
Piedritas, Arg. 34°47' S, 62°58' W 139
Piedruja, Latv. 55°47' N, 27°26' E 166
Pieksämäki, Fin. 62°16' N, 27°7' E 154
Piendamó, Col. 2°38' N, 76°33' W 136
Pieniężno, Pol. 54°13' N, 20°8' E 166
Pierce, Idaho, U.S. 46°28' N, 115°47' W 90
Pierce, Nebr., U.S. 42°11' N, 97°32' W 90
Piéria, Óros, Gr. 40°7' N, 22°3' E 156
Pierre, S. Dak., U.S. 44°21' N, 100°26' W 90
Pierre Lake, lake, Can. 49°28' N, 81°6' W 94
Pierrefonds, Fr. 49°20' N, 2°58' E 163
Pierrelatte, Fr. 44°22' N, 4°41' E 150
Pierson, Fla., U.S. 29°14' N, 81°28' W 105
Piet Retief, S. Af. 27°1' S, 30°45' E 227
Pietarsaari see Jakobstad, Fin. 63°39' N, 22°39' E 152
Pietermaritzburg, S. Af. 29°35' S, 30°21' E 227
Pietersburg see Polokwane, S. Af. 23°54' S, 29°26' E 227
Pietro Verri, Somalia 3°20' N, 45°39' E 218
Pietrosu, peak, Rom. 47°5' N, 25°4' E 156
Pietrosul, peak, Rom. 47°34' N, 24°32' E 156
Pieve d'Alpago, It. 46°9' N, 12°20' E 167
Pieve di Cadore, It. 46°25' N, 12°20' E 167
Pigailoe (West Fayu Atoll) 8°36' N, 146°3' E 192
Pigeon, Mich., U.S. 43°49' N, 83°16' W 102
Pigeon Cove, Mass., U.S. 42°40' N, 70°38' W 104
Pigeon Lake, Can. 53°2' N, 114°24' W 108
Pigeon Point, Lake Superior 47°46' N, 89°36' W 94
Pigeon, river, Can. 52°13' N, 96°58' W 108
Piggott, Ark., U.S. 36°22' N, 90°12' W 96
Pigüé, Arg. 37°37' S, 62°23' W 139
Pihlava, Fin. 61°32' N, 21°36' E 166
Pihtipudas, Fin. 63°21' N, 25°32' E 154
Pihuamo, Mex. 19°15' N, 103°22' W 114
P'ihyŏn, N. Korea 40°0' N, 124°35' E 200
Pi'ilanihale Heiau, site, Hawai'i, U.S. 20°47' N, 156°6' W 99
Pijijiapan, Mex. 15°40' N, 93°15' W 115
Pikalevo, Russ. 59°33' N, 34°5' E 154
Pikangikum, Can. 51°48' N, 93°57' W 82
Pike, river, Wis., U.S. 45°31' N, 88°3' W 94
Pikelot, island, F.S.M. 8°17' N, 147°41' E 192
Pikes Peak, Colo., U.S. 38°49' N, 105°7' W 90
Piketberg, S. Af. 32°54' S, 18°43' E 227
Piketon, Ohio, U.S. 39°3' N, 83°1' W 102
Pikeville, Ky., U.S. 37°29' N, 82°32' W 96
Pikounda, Congo 0°30' N, 16°38' E 218
Pikwitonei, Can. 55°35' N, 97°12' W 108
Pila, Arg. 36°2' S, 58°10' W 139
Pila, peak, Sp. 38°15' N, 1°14' W 164
Pilani, India 28°21' N, 75°37' E 197
Pilão Arcado, Braz. 9°57' S, 42°32' W 132
Pilar, Arg. 31°26' S, 61°16' W 139
Pilar, Parag. 26°51' S, 58°16' W 139
Pilar, Cabo, Chile 52°46' S, 76°6' W 134
Pilatovica, peak, Europe 43°27' N, 20°54' E 168
Pilaya, river, Bol. 21°13' S, 64°29' W 137
Pilcaniyeu, Arg. 41°9' S, 70°41' W 134
Pilcomayo, river, Bol. 19°19' S, 65°2' W 137
Pil'dozero, Russ. 65°40' N, 33°27' E 152
Pil'gyn, Russ. 69°19' N, 179°3' E 98
Pilibhit, India 28°37' N, 79°47' E 197
Pilio, Gr. 38°45' N, 23°34' E 156
Pilio, Óros, peak, Gr. 39°25' N, 22°58' E 156
Pillcopata, Peru 13°5' S, 71°11' W 137
Pilling, U.K. 53°55' N, 2°55' W 162
Pilón, river, Mex. 25°15' N, 100°31' W 114
Pilón-Laja National Park, Bol. 14°51' S, 66°41' W 137
Pilos, Gr. 36°54' N, 21°41' E 156
Pilot Butte, peak, Oreg., U.S. 44°3' N, 121°20' W 90
Pilot Knob, Mo., U.S. 37°37' N, 90°39' W 96
Pilot Knob, peak, Ark., U.S. 35°33' N, 93°20' W 96
Pilot Knob, peak, Idaho, U.S. 45°52' N, 115°47' W 90
Pilot Mound, Can. 49°12' N, 98°55' W 108
Pilot Peak, Nev., U.S. 38°20' N, 118°4' W 90
Pilot Peak, Nev., U.S. 41°0' N, 114°9' W 90
Pilot Peak, Wyo., U.S. 44°57' N, 109°59' W 90
Pilot Point, Alas., U.S. 57°31' N, 157°38' W 98
Pilottown, La., U.S. 29°11' N, 89°15' W 103
Pilsen see Plzeň, Czech Rep. 49°44' N, 13°23' E 152
Pil'skaya Guba, Russ. 66°47' N, 34°12' E 152
Piltene, Latv. 57°13' N, 21°40' E 166
Pil'tun, Zaliv 52°48' N, 141°39' E 160
Pim, river, Russ. 62°20' N, 71°29' E 169
Pimenta Bueno, Braz. 11°41' S, 61°15' W 130
Piña, Pan. 9°16' N, 80°2' W 130
Pinacate, Cerro del, peak, Mex. 31°44' N, 113°35' W 92
Pinang, island, Malaysia 5°14' N, 99°44' E 196
Pinangah, Malaysia 5°15' N, 116°48' E 203
Pinar del Río, Cuba 22°25' N, 83°43' W 116
Pinar del Río, adm. division, Cuba 22°33' N, 83°55' W 116
Pinar del Río, island, Cuba 23°1' N, 83°27' W 116
Pınarbaşı, Turk. 38°42' N, 36°24' E 156
Pinardville, N.H., U.S. 42°59' N, 71°31' W 104
Pinas, Arg. 31°9' S, 65°28' W 134
Pinatubo, Mount, peak, Philippines 15°5' N, 120°1' E 238
Pinawa, Can. 50°8' N, 95°52' W 90
Pincehely, Hung. 46°41' N, 18°25' E 168
Pincén, Arg. 34°51' S, 63°55' W 139
Pincher, Can. 49°31' N, 113°57' W 90
Pincher Creek, Can. 49°28' N, 113°56' W 90
Pinchi Lake, lake, Can. 54°32' N, 124°49' W 108
Pinckney, Mich., U.S. 42°26' N, 83°57' W 102
Pinconning, Mich., U.S. 43°50' N, 83°59' W 102
Pîncota, Rom. 46°20' N, 21°43' E 168
Pindamonhangaba, Braz. 22°57' S, 45°27' W 138
Pinders Point, Bahamas 26°27' N, 78°42' W 105
Pindi Bhattian, Pak. 31°54' N, 73°14' E 186
Pindi Gheb, Pak. 33°14' N, 72°17' E 186
Píndos, peak, Gr. 39°18' N, 21°28' E 156
Pindus Mountains, Gr. 39°54' N, 20°40' E 156
Pine Bluff, Ark., U.S. 34°12' N, 92°1' W 96
Pine Bluffs, Wyo., U.S. 41°11' N, 104°5' W 90
Pine, Cape, Can. 46°38' N, 54°6' W 111
Pine City, Minn., U.S. 45°47' N, 92°60' W 94
Pine Creek, Austral. 13°51' S, 131°51' E 231
Pine Falls, Can. 50°31' N, 96°17' W 108
Pine Flat, Calif., U.S. 35°52' N, 118°39' W 101
Pine Flat Lake, Calif., U.S. 36°50' N, 119°32' W 101
Pine Forest Range, Nev., U.S. 41°41' N, 119°7' W 90
Pine Hill, Ala., U.S. 31°58' N, 87°35' W 103
Pine Hills, Fla., U.S. 28°34' N, 81°28' W 105
Pine Island, Fla., U.S. 26°37' N, 82°25' W 105
Pine Island Bay 74°36' S, 97°34' W 248
Pine Mountain, Ky., U.S. 37°17' N, 82°36' W 96
Pine Mountain, peak, Calif., U.S. 35°41' N, 121°9' W 100
Pine Mountain, peak, Calif., U.S. 35°33' N, 118°49' W 101
Pine Pass, Can. 55°23' N, 122°41' W 108
Pine Plains, N.Y., U.S. 41°58' N, 73°40' W 104
Pine Point, Can. 60°46' N, 114°19' W 73
Pine Point, Can. 60°46' N, 114°22' W 108
Pine Point, Me., U.S. 43°32' N, 70°21' W 104
Pine River, Can. 51°46' N, 100°33' W 90
Pine River, Can. 55°55' N, 107°28' W 108
Pine River, Minn., U.S. 46°42' N, 94°25' W 90
Pine, river, Can. 55°52' N, 121°7' W 108
Pine, river, Mich., U.S. 44°1' N, 85°19' W 102
Pine Valley, Can. 55°38' N, 122°10' W 108
Pinecrest, Calif., U.S. 38°11' N, 120°1' W 100
Pinedale, Calif., U.S. 36°50' N, 119°48' W 92
Pinega, Russ. 64°43' N, 43°19' E 154
Pinega, river, Russ. 63°44' N, 45°11' E 154
Pinehouse Lake, Can. 55°33' N, 107°14' W 108
Pinehouse Lake, Can. 55°30' N, 106°37' W 108
Pinehurst, Ga., U.S. 32°11' N, 83°46' W 96
Pinehurst, N.C., U.S. 35°11' N, 79°29' W 96
Pineland, Tex., U.S. 31°14' N, 93°58' W 103
Pinellas Park, Fla., U.S. 27°51' N, 82°42' W 105
Pinerolo, It. 44°53' N, 7°20' E 167
Pinetown, S. Af. 29°49' S, 30°46' E 227
Pineville, Ky., U.S. 36°44' N, 83°43' W 96
Pineville, La., U.S. 31°18' N, 92°26' W 103
Piney, Fr. 48°22' N, 4°19' E 163
Piney Buttes, Mont., U.S. 47°27' N, 107°14' W 90
Piney Point, Fla., U.S. 29°46' N, 83°35' W 105
Piney Woods, Miss., U.S. 32°2' N, 89°59' W 103
Ping, river, Thai. 16°8' N, 99°46' E 202
Pingba, China 26°26' N, 106°14' E 198
Pingchang, China 31°35' N, 107°4' E 198
Pingdingshan, China 33°44' N, 113°19' E 198
Pingdu, China 36°49' N, 119°58' E 198
Pinggang, China 42°56' N, 124°50' E 200
Pingguo, China 23°18' N, 107°34' E 198
Pingjiang, China 28°45' N, 113°37' E 198
Pingle, China 24°35' N, 110°41' E 198
Pingli, China 32°29' N, 109°24' E 198
Pingliang, China 35°31' N, 106°39' E 198
Pinglu, China 39°31' N, 112°17' E 198
Pinglu, China 34°53' N, 111°12' E 198
Pingluo, China 38°57' N, 106°33' E 198
Pingnan, China 23°48' N, 110°23' E 198
Pingquan, China 41°2' N, 118°39' E 198
Pingsha, China 22°2' N, 113°12' E 198
Pingtan, China 25°28' N, 119°51' E 198
Pingtang, China 25°50' N, 107°17' E 198
P'ingtung, Taiwan 22°43' N, 120°31' E 198
Pingwu, China 32°28' N, 104°34' E 198
Pingxiang, China 27°41' N, 113°48' E 198
Pingxiang, China 22°5' N, 106°44' E 198
Pingyang, China 27°37' N, 120°33' E 198
Pingyao, China 37°15' N, 112°9' E 198
Pingyi, China 35°28' N, 117°39' E 198
Pingyin, China 36°18' N, 116°26' E 198
Pingyuan, China 24°32' N, 115°52' E 198
Pinhal, Braz. 22°13' S, 46°47' W 138
Pinhão, Braz. 25°42' S, 51°38' W 138
Pinheiro, Braz. 2°31' S, 45°7' W 132
Pinheiro Machado, Braz. 31°37' S, 53°22' W 139
Pinhuã, river, Braz. 7°4' S, 65°60' W 130
Pini, island, Indonesia 0°6' N, 98°51' E 196
Pink Mountain, Can. 57°4' N, 122°36' W 108
Pink, river, Can. 56°39' N, 104°24' W 108
Pinkafeld, Aust. 47°21' N, 16°8' E 168
Pinlaung, Myanmar 20°7' N, 96°42' E 202
Pinlebu, Myanmar 24°1' N, 95°22' E 188
Pinnacles National Monument, Calif., U.S. 36°27' N, 121°20' W 100
Pino Hachado, Paso de, pass, Chile 38°34' S, 70°54' W 134
Pinola, Miss., U.S. 31°52' N, 89°58' W 103
Pinon Hills, Calif., U.S. 34°26' N, 117°39' W 101
Pinos, Mex. 22°17' N, 101°34' W 114
Pinos, Mount, peak, Calif., U.S. 34°48' N, 119°11' W 101
Pinos, Point, Calif., U.S. 36°38' N, 122°3' W 100
Pinos-Puente, Sp. 37°15' N, 3°46' W 150
Pinotepa Nacional, Mex. 16°20' N, 98°2' W 112
Pins, Pointe aux, Can. 42°6' N, 81°50' W 102
Pinsk, Belarus 52°7' N, 26°6' E 152
Pinsk Marshes, Belarus 52°39' N, 25°28' E 142
Pinta, Sierra, Ariz., U.S. 32°27' N, 113°48' W 101
Pinta, Sierra, Mex. 31°26' N, 115°33' W 112
Pintados, Chile 20°37' S, 69°38' W 137
Pintasan, Malaysia 5°27' N, 117°40' E 203
Pinto, Arg. 29°9' S, 62°40' W 139
Pinto, Sp. 40°14' N, 3°42' W 164
Pinto Butte, peak, Can. 49°18' N, 107°30' W 90
Pinto Mountains, Calif., U.S. 34°4' N, 115°57' W 101
Pintoyacu, river, Peru 2°58' S, 74°37' W 136
Pintwater Range, Nev., U.S. 36°42' N, 115°35' W 101
Pinyon Pines, Calif., U.S. 33°35' N, 116°29' W 101
Pinyug, Russ. 60°15' N, 47°45' E 154
Pioche, Nev., U.S. 37°55' N, 114°27' W 92
Piombino, It. 42°56' N, 10°32' E 156
Pioneer, La., U.S. 32°43' N, 91°26' W 103
Pioneer, Ohio, U.S. 41°40' N, 84°33' W 102
Pioneer Fracture Zone, North Pacific Ocean 37°39' N, 139°49' W 252
Pioneer Mountains, Idaho, U.S. 43°34' N, 114°3' W 90
Pioneer Mountains, Mont., U.S. 45°30' N, 113°21' W 90
Pioneer Point, Calif., U.S. 35°47' N, 117°23' W 101
Pioneer Tank, spring, Austral. 31°47' S, 123°48' E 230
Pioner, Ostrov, island, Russ. 79°38' N, 99°4' E 246
Pionki, Pol. 51°29' N, 21°25' E 152
Piorini, Lago, lake, Braz. 3°38' S, 63°31' W 130
Piorini, river, Braz. 2°34' S, 64°7' W 130
Piotrków Trybunalski, Pol. 51°23' N, 19°41' E 152
Piove di Sacco, It. 45°18' N, 12°1' E 167
Pipar, India 26°20' N, 73°33' E 186
Piparia, India 21°55' N, 77°22' E 197
Piper City, Ill., U.S. 40°45' N, 88°12' W 102
Piper, oil field, North Sea 58°26' N, 0°10' E 150
Pipestone, Minn., U.S. 43°58' N, 96°19' W 94
Pipestone Lake, lake, Can. 48°59' N, 94°9' W 90

Pipestone, river, *Can.* 57°57′ N, 106°36′ W **108**
Pipinas, *Arg.* 35°32′ S, 57°21′ W **139**
Pipmuacan, Réservoir, lake, *Can.* 49°28′ N, 71°47′ W **94**
Piqua, *Ohio, U.S.* 40°7′ N, 84°16′ W **102**
Piquiá, *Braz.* 1°49′ S, 66°8′ W **136**
Piquiri, river, *Braz.* 24°58′ S, 52°42′ W **138**
Pira, *Benin* 8°30′ N, 1°44′ E **222**
Piracanjuba, *Braz.* 17°21′ S, 49°2′ W **138**
Piracicaba, *Braz.* 22°45′ S, 47°38′ W **138**
Piracuruca, *Braz.* 3°56′ S, 41°42′ W **132**
Piraeus see Pireás, *Gr.* 37°57′ N, 23°38′ E **156**
Piraí do Sul, *Braz.* 24°34′ S, 49°57′ W **138**
Piraju, *Braz.* 23°15′ S, 49°25′ W **138**
Pirajuí, *Braz.* 22°1′ S, 49°28′ W **138**
Piran, *Slov.* 45°31′ N, 13°35′ E **167**
Pirané, *Arg.* 25°45′ S, 59°6′ W **132**
Pirane, *Europe* 42°17′ N, 20°41′ E **168**
Piranhas, *Braz.* 16°34′ S, 51°49′ W **138**
Piranhas, *Braz.* 9°37′ S, 37°45′ W **132**
Pirapora, *Braz.* 17°22′ S, 44°55′ W **138**
Pirarajá, *Uru.* 33°45′ S, 54°44′ W **139**
Piratuba, *Braz.* 27°27′ S, 51°48′ W **139**
Piray, river, *Bol.* 16°49′ S, 63°37′ W **137**
Pire Goureye, *Senegal* 15°2′ N, 16°34′ W **222**
Pireás, *Gr.* 37°57′ N, 23°36′ E **180**
Pireás (Piraeus), *Gr.* 37°57′ N, 23°38′ E **156**
Pirenópolis, *Braz.* 15°55′ S, 48°60′ W **138**
Pires do Rio, *Braz.* 17°20′ S, 48°17′ W **138**
Pirgos, *Gr.* 37°38′ N, 21°26′ E **216**
Piriá, river, *Braz.* 2°10′ S, 46°28′ W **130**
Piriápolis, *Uru.* 34°53′ S, 55°16′ W **139**
Pirin, *Bulg.* 41°21′ N, 23°26′ E **156**
Pirin National Park, *Bulg.* 41°37′ N, 22°39′ E **180**
Piripiri, *Braz.* 4°17′ S, 41°49′ W **132**
Píritu, *Venez.* 9°22′ N, 69°15′ W **136**
Pirna, *Ger.* 50°58′ N, 13°56′ E **152**
Pirojpur, *Bangladesh* 22°35′ N, 89°58′ E **197**
Pirot, *Serb. and Mont.* 43°8′ N, 22°34′ E **168**
Pirre, Cerro, peak, *Pan.* 7°47′ N, 77°49′ W **136**
Pirsagat, river, *Azerb.* 40°28′ N, 48°40′ E **195**
Pirtleville, *Ariz., U.S.* 31°22′ N, 109°34′ W **92**
Pirttikylä see Pörtom, *Fin.* 62°41′ N, 21°35′ E **154**
Piru, *Calif., U.S.* 34°25′ N, 118°48′ W **101**
Piru, *Indonesia* 3°6′ S, 128°7′ E **192**
Pisa, *It.* 43°44′ N, 10°24′ E **167**
Pisac, *Peru* 13°27′ S, 71°50′ W **137**
Pisagua, *Chile* 19°37′ S, 70°14′ W **137**
Pisarovina, *Croatia* 45°35′ N, 15°51′ E **168**
Pisco, *Peru* 13°45′ S, 76°12′ W **130**
Písek, *Czech Rep.* 49°17′ N, 14°8′ E **152**
Pisgah Crater, *Calif., U.S.* 34°44′ N, 116°23′ W **101**
Pisgah, Mount, peak, *Oreg., U.S.* 44°26′ N, 120°20′ W **90**
Pishan (Guma), *China* 37°39′ N, 78°22′ E **184**
Pishcha, *Ukr.* 51°35′ N, 23°47′ E **158**
Pīshīn, *Iran* 26°4′ N, 61°46′ E **182**
Pishin, *Pak.* 30°34′ N, 67°2′ E **186**
Pishin Lora, river, *Pak.* 29°14′ N, 65°33′ E **186**
Piskom, *Uzb.* 41°53′ N, 70°19′ E **197**
Pismo Beach, *Calif., U.S.* 35°9′ N, 120°39′ W **100**
Pis'moguba, *Russ.* 64°33′ N, 31°50′ E **152**
Pisogne, *It.* 45°48′ N, 10°6′ E **167**
Pissouri, *Cyprus* 34°39′ N, 32°42′ E **194**
Pisté, *Mex.* 20°42′ N, 88°38′ W **116**
Pistoia, *It.* 43°55′ N, 10°55′ E **156**
Pisz, *Pol.* 53°37′ N, 21°46′ E **152**
Piszczac, *Pol.* 51°58′ N, 23°22′ E **152**
Pit, river, *Calif., U.S.* 41°25′ N, 121°5′ W **90**
Pita, *Guinea* 11°3′ N, 12°26′ W **222**
Pitaga, *Can.* 52°26′ N, 65°48′ W **111**
Pitanga, *Braz.* 24°45′ S, 51°47′ W **138**
Pitangui, *Braz.* 19°41′ S, 44°54′ W **138**
Pitcairn Island, *U.K.* 25°5′ S, 130°6′ W **241**
Piteå, *Nor.* 65°19′ N, 21°29′ E **152**
Pitești, *Rom.* 44°52′ N, 24°52′ E **156**
Pithiviers, *Fr.* 48°9′ N, 2°15′ E **163**
Pithora, *India* 21°15′ N, 82°30′ E **188**
Pithoragarh, *India* 29°36′ N, 80°12′ E **197**
Pitkin, *La., U.S.* 30°54′ N, 92°57′ W **103**
Pitkyaranta, *Russ.* 61°31′ N, 31°33′ E **152**
Pitlochrie, *Can.* 55°0′ N, 111°45′ W **108**
Pitlyar, *Russ.* 65°50′ N, 66°4′ E **169**
Pitman, river, *Can.* 57°53′ N, 128°36′ W **108**
Pitomača, *Croatia* 45°57′ N, 17°15′ E **168**
Pitre, Isle au, island, *La., U.S.* 30°1′ N, 89°11′ W **103**
Pitsligo Castle, site, *U.K.* 57°39′ N, 2°13′ W **150**
Pitt Island, *Can.* 53°37′ N, 130°52′ W **98**
Pitt Island, island, *Can.* 53°43′ N, 129°56′ W **106**
Pitt Lake, *Can.* 49°22′ N, 122°43′ W **100**
Pittsboro, *Miss., U.S.* 33°55′ N, 89°20′ W **96**
Pittsburg, *Calif., U.S.* 38°1′ N, 121°54′ W **100**
Pittsburg, *Kans., U.S.* 37°23′ N, 94°42′ W **96**
Pittsburg, *Tex., U.S.* 32°59′ N, 94°59′ W **103**
Pittsburgh, *Pa., U.S.* 40°26′ N, 79°59′ W **94**
Pittsfield, *Mass., U.S.* 42°26′ N, 73°16′ W **104**
Pittsfield, *Mo., U.S.* 39°35′ N, 90°49′ W **94**
Pittsfield, *N.H., U.S.* 43°18′ N, 71°20′ W **104**
Pittsfield, *Vt., U.S.* 43°46′ N, 72°49′ W **104**
Pittsford, *Vt., U.S.* 43°42′ N, 73°2′ W **104**
Pittston, *Pa., U.S.* 41°18′ N, 75°48′ W **94**
Piua Petrii, *Rom.* 44°41′ N, 27°51′ E **156**
Piūí, *Braz.* 20°31′ S, 45°57′ W **138**
Piura, *Peru* 5°6′ S, 80°40′ W **130**
Piura, adm. division, *Peru* 4°50′ S, 81°6′ W **130**
Piute Pass, *Calif., U.S.* 37°14′ N, 118°41′ W **101**
Piute Peak, *Calif., U.S.* 35°26′ N, 118°26′ W **101**
Piute Valley, *Calif., U.S.* 35°1′ N, 114°54′ W **101**
Piva, river, *Europe* 43°8′ N, 18°52′ E **168**
Pivabiska, river, *Can.* 49°53′ N, 83°45′ W **94**
Pivdennyy Buh, river, *Ukr.* 48°3′ N, 30°39′ E **158**
Pivka, *Slov.* 45°41′ N, 14°11′ E **156**
Pivot Mountain, peak, *Can.* 54°0′ N, 133°6′ W **108**
Pixariá Óros, peak, *Gr.* 38°42′ N, 23°34′ E **156**
Pixian, *China* 34°17′ N, 117°58′ E **198**
Pixley, *Calif., U.S.* 35°58′ N, 119°18′ W **100**
Pizacoma, *Peru* 16°57′ S, 69°22′ W **137**
Pizarra, *Sp.* 36°45′ N, 4°43′ W **164**
Pizhma, river, *Russ.* 64°37′ N, 51°1′ E **154**
Placentia, *Can.* 47°12′ N, 53°60′ W **111**
Placentia Point, *Belize* 16°26′ N, 88°21′ W **115**
Placer, *Philippines* 9°40′ N, 125°35′ E **203**
Placerville, *Calif., U.S.* 38°44′ N, 120°47′ W **82**
Placid, Lake, *Fla., U.S.* 27°14′ N, 81°27′ W **105**
Placid Lake, *Mont., U.S.* 47°3′ N, 114°1′ W **90**
Placida, *Fla., U.S.* 26°51′ N, 82°17′ W **105**
Plácido de Castro, *Braz.* 10°19′ S, 67°11′ W **137**
Plačkovica, *Maced.* 41°44′ N, 22°13′ E **168**
Plahn, *Liberia* 5°20′ N, 8°51′ W **222**
Plain, *Wis., U.S.* 43°16′ N, 90°3′ W **102**
Plain, Cape, *South Atlantic Ocean* 34°50′ S, 7°54′ E **253**
Plain City, *Ohio, U.S.* 40°5′ N, 83°17′ W **102**
Plain Dealing, *La., U.S.* 32°53′ N, 93°42′ W **103**
Plainfield, *Conn., U.S.* 41°40′ N, 71°56′ W **104**
Plainfield, *Ind., U.S.* 39°41′ N, 86°24′ W **102**
Plainfield, *Mass., U.S.* 42°30′ N, 72°56′ W **104**
Plainfield, *Vt., U.S.* 44°16′ N, 72°27′ W **104**
Plains, *Kans., U.S.* 37°15′ N, 100°36′ W **92**
Plains, *Mont., U.S.* 47°26′ N, 114°54′ W **90**
Plains, *Pa., U.S.* 41°16′ N, 75°51′ W **110**
Plains, *Tex., U.S.* 33°9′ N, 102°50′ W **92**
Plainview, *Nebr., U.S.* 42°19′ N, 97°49′ W **90**
Plainview, *Tex., U.S.* 34°10′ N, 101°43′ W **92**
Plainwell, *Mich., U.S.* 42°26′ N, 85°37′ W **110**
Plaistow, *N.H., U.S.* 42°49′ N, 71°6′ W **104**
Pláka, *Gr.* 40°0′ N, 25°25′ E **156**
Plakoti, Cape 35°32′ N, 34°1′ E **194**
Plan, *Sp.* 42°34′ N, 0°20′ E **164**
Plana, *Bosn. and Herzg.* 42°57′ N, 18°24′ E **168**
Plana Cays (French Cays), islands, *North Atlantic Ocean* 22°41′ N, 73°33′ W **116**
Plana o Nueva Tabarca, Isla, island, *Sp.* 38°5′ N, 0°28′ E **164**
Planada, *Calif., U.S.* 37°17′ N, 120°20′ W **100**
Planeta Rica, *Col.* 8°25′ N, 75°35′ W **116**
Planinica, *Serb. and Mont.* 43°49′ N, 22°7′ E **168**
Plano, *Ill., U.S.* 41°39′ N, 88°33′ W **102**
Plano, *Tex., U.S.* 33°0′ N, 96°42′ W **96**
Plant City, *Fla., U.S.* 28°1′ N, 82°7′ W **105**
Plantation, *Fla., U.S.* 26°8′ N, 80°15′ W **105**
Plantation Key, island, *Fla., U.S.* 25°16′ N, 80°41′ W **105**
Plantsite, *Ariz., U.S.* 33°2′ N, 109°18′ W **92**
Plaquemine, *La., U.S.* 30°16′ N, 91°15′ W **103**
Plasencia, *Sp.* 40°2′ N, 6°5′ W **150**
Plaški, *Croatia* 45°4′ N, 15°20′ E **156**
Plassen, *Nor.* 61°8′ N, 12°29′ E **152**
Plast, *Russ.* 54°22′ N, 60°43′ E **154**
Plaster City, *Calif., U.S.* 32°47′ N, 115°52′ W **101**
Plaster Rock, *Can.* 46°54′ N, 67°24′ W **111**
Plata, Punta, *Chile* 25°1′ S, 71°10′ W **132**
Plata, Río de la, *South America* 35°34′ S, 57°6′ W **139**
Plataea 479 B.C., battle, *Gr.* 38°11′ N, 23°9′ E **156**
Platanal, *Venez.* 2°22′ N, 64°58′ W **130**
Plátano, river, *Hond.* 15°18′ N, 85°2′ W **116**
Plateau, *Can.* 48°57′ N, 108°46′ W **90**
Plateau Station (closed), site, *Antarctica* 80°37′ S, 36°13′ E **248**
Platen, Kapp, *Nor.* 80°28′ N, 23°58′ E **160**
Plateros, *Mex.* 23°13′ N, 102°52′ W **114**
Plato, *Col.* 9°46′ N, 74°47′ W **136**
Platte, *S. Dak., U.S.* 43°21′ N, 98°51′ W **90**
Platte, river, *Nebr., U.S.* 40°56′ N, 100°48′ W **80**
Platteville, *Wis., U.S.* 42°43′ N, 90°28′ W **94**
Plattsburg, *Mo., U.S.* 39°32′ N, 94°27′ W **94**
Plattsmouth, *Nebr., U.S.* 40°59′ N, 95°53′ W **94**
Plauen, *Ger.* 50°30′ N, 12°8′ E **152**
Plav, *Europe* 42°35′ N, 19°56′ E **168**
Plavča Draga, *Croatia* 45°2′ N, 15°23′ E **156**
Pļaviņas, *Latv.* 56°36′ N, 25°42′ E **166**
Plavnica, *Europe* 42°17′ N, 19°13′ E **168**
Plavsk, *Russ.* 53°40′ N, 37°19′ E **154**
Play Ku, *Vietnam* 14°2′ N, 107°48′ E **192**
Playa Grande, *Mex.* 31°8′ N, 114°56′ W **92**
Playa Lauro Villar, *Mex.* 25°52′ N, 97°10′ W **114**
Playa los Corchos, *Mex.* 21°41′ N, 105°28′ W **114**
Playa Vicente, *Mex.* 17°49′ N, 95°49′ W **114**
Playa Vicente, river, *Mex.* 17°50′ N, 95°40′ W **114**
Playas, *Ecua.* 2°43′ S, 80°22′ W **130**
Pleasant Grove, *Utah, U.S.* 40°21′ N, 111°43′ W **90**
Pleasant Hill, *La., U.S.* 31°47′ N, 93°31′ W **103**
Pleasant Point, *N.Z.* 44°17′ S, 171°8′ E **240**
Pleasant Valley, *N.Y., U.S.* 41°44′ N, 73°51′ W **104**
Pleasanton, *Calif., U.S.* 37°39′ N, 121°52′ W **100**
Pleasanton, *Kans., U.S.* 38°10′ N, 94°42′ W **94**
Pleasanton, *Tex., U.S.* 28°56′ N, 98°30′ W **96**
Pleasantville, *N.J., U.S.* 39°23′ N, 74°33′ W **94**
Plenița, *Rom.* 44°12′ N, 23°13′ E **168**
Plentywood, *Mont., U.S.* 48°45′ N, 104°34′ W **90**
Plentzia, *Sp.* 43°23′ N, 2°58′ W **164**
Plesetsk, *Russ.* 62°43′ N, 40°18′ E **154**
Plesetsk Cosmodrome, spaceport, *Russ.* 62°17′ N, 39°54′ E **160**
Plessisville, *Can.* 46°13′ N, 71°47′ W **94**
Pleternica, *Croatia* 45°16′ N, 17°47′ E **168**
Plétipi, Lac, lake, *Can.* 51°43′ N, 70°26′ W **111**
Plettenberg, *Ger.* 51°13′ N, 7°52′ E **167**
Pleuron, ruin(s), *Gr.* 38°23′ N, 21°18′ E **156**
Pleven, *Bulg.* 43°25′ N, 24°37′ E **156**
Pleven, adm. division, *Bulg.* 43°34′ N, 24°18′ E **156**
Plevna, *Mont., U.S.* 46°23′ N, 104°33′ W **90**
Plibo, *Liberia* 4°38′ N, 7°42′ W **222**
Plješevica, *Croatia* 44°42′ N, 15°49′ E **168**
Pljevlja, *Europe* 43°21′ N, 19°20′ E **168**
Ploče, *Croatia* 43°2′ N, 17°26′ E **168**
Ploiești, *Rom.* 44°57′ N, 26°1′ E **156**
Plomb du Cantal, peak, *Fr.* 45°3′ N, 2°43′ E **165**
Płońsk, *Pol.* 52°32′ N, 19°41′ E **152**
Plopiș, Munții, *Rom.* 47°12′ N, 22°17′ E **168**
Plotnikovo, *Russ.* 56°50′ N, 83°15′ E **169**
Plougastel, *Fr.* 48°22′ N, 4°22′ W **150**
Plovdiv, *Bulg.* 42°5′ N, 24°45′ E **180**
Plovdiv, adm. division, *Bulg.* 42°0′ N, 24°30′ E **156**
Plovdiv (Philippopolis), *Bulg.* 42°9′ N, 24°45′ E **156**
Plugari, *Rom.* 47°28′ N, 27°6′ E **158**
Plum, *Pa., U.S.* 40°29′ N, 79°46′ W **94**
Plum Island, *Mass., U.S.* 42°44′ N, 70°48′ W **104**
Plum Island, *N.Y., U.S.* 41°9′ N, 72°10′ W **104**
Plummer, *Idaho, U.S.* 47°18′ N, 116°54′ W **90**
Plumtree, *Zimb.* 20°30′ S, 27°47′ E **227**
Plungė, *Lith.* 55°55′ N, 21°52′ E **166**
Pluscarden Abbey, site, *U.K.* 57°35′ N, 3°33′ W **150**
Plyeshchanitsy, *Belarus* 54°26′ N, 27°49′ E **166**
Plymouth, *Conn., U.S.* 41°40′ N, 73°3′ W **104**
Plymouth, *Ind., U.S.* 41°20′ N, 86°19′ W **102**
Plymouth, *Mass., U.S.* 41°57′ N, 70°41′ W **104**
Plymouth, *Montserrat* 16°44′ N, 62°14′ W **116**
Plymouth, *N.C., U.S.* 35°51′ N, 76°46′ W **96**
Plymouth, *Ohio, U.S.* 40°58′ N, 82°40′ W **102**
Plymouth, *U.K.* 50°29′ N, 4°11′ W **143**
Plymouth, *Wash., U.S.* 45°56′ N, 119°22′ W **90**
Plymouth, *Wis., U.S.* 43°44′ N, 87°60′ W **102**
Plympton, *Mass., U.S.* 41°57′ N, 70°50′ W **104**
Plyusa, *Russ.* 58°25′ N, 29°20′ E **166**
Plyusa, river, *Russ.* 58°47′ N, 27°53′ E **154**
Plzeň (Pilsen), *Czech Rep.* 49°44′ N, 13°23′ E **152**
Plzeňský, adm. division, *Czech Rep.* 49°46′ N, 12°31′ E **152**
Pnevo, *Russ.* 58°13′ N, 27°33′ E **166**
Pô, *Burkina Faso* 11°9′ N, 1°12′ W **222**
Po di Volano, river, *It.* 44°44′ N, 11°57′ E **167**
Po, river, *It.* 45°7′ N, 9°19′ E **167**
Pobé, *Benin* 7°2′ N, 2°39′ E **222**
Pobeda, Gora, peak, *Russ.* 65°15′ N, 145°7′ E **160**
Pobedy Peak (Jengish Chokusu, Victory Peak), *China* 42°2′ N, 80°3′ E **184**
Pocahontas, *Ark., U.S.* 36°14′ N, 90°59′ W **96**
Pocahontas, *Can.* 53°11′ N, 117°56′ W **108**
Pocahontas, *Ill., U.S.* 38°48′ N, 89°32′ W **102**
Pocahontas, *Iowa, U.S.* 42°43′ N, 94°41′ W **94**
Pocasset, *Mass., U.S.* 41°41′ N, 70°37′ W **104**
Pocatello, *Idaho, U.S.* 42°53′ N, 112°26′ W **90**
Pochala, *Sudan* 7°11′ N, 34°2′ E **224**
Pochep, *Russ.* 52°53′ N, 33°25′ E **154**
Pochinok, *Russ.* 54°24′ N, 32°30′ E **154**
Pochutla, *Mex.* 15°44′ N, 96°28′ W **112**
Pocklington, *U.K.* 53°55′ N, 0°48′ E **162**
Poções, *Braz.* 14°34′ S, 40°21′ W **138**
Pocolo, *Angola* 15°45′ S, 13°41′ E **220**
Pocoma, *Peru* 17°29′ S, 71°23′ W **137**
Poconé, *Braz.* 16°17′ S, 56°39′ W **132**
Pocono Mountains, *Pa., U.S.* 41°21′ N, 75°15′ W **94**
Poços de Caldas, *Braz.* 21°47′ S, 46°35′ W **138**
Podareš, *Maced.* 41°37′ N, 22°32′ E **168**
Podberez'ye, *Russ.* 56°57′ N, 30°40′ E **152**
Podborov'ye, *Russ.* 57°52′ N, 28°35′ E **166**
Podchinnyy, *Russ.* 50°49′ N, 45°13′ E **158**
Poddor'ye, *Russ.* 57°27′ N, 31°6′ E **152**
Podgora, *Croatia* 43°14′ N, 17°4′ E **168**
Podgorac, *Serb.* 43°56′ N, 21°57′ E **168**
Podgorica, *Mont.* 42°25′ N, 19°11′ E **168**
Podgornoye, *Russ.* 57°45′ N, 82°46′ E **169**
Podhum, *Bosn. and Herzg.* 43°42′ N, 16°58′ E **168**
Podil's'ka Vysochyna, *Ukr.* 48°46′ N, 25°47′ E **152**
Podkamennaya Tunguska, river, *Russ.* 61°52′ N, 89°40′ E **160**
Podkarpakie, adm. division, *Pol.* 50°9′ N, 21°13′ E **152**
Podlaskie, adm. division, *Pol.* 54°9′ N, 22°33′ E **166**
Podlesnoye, *Russ.* 51°46′ N, 47°3′ E **158**
Podnovlje, *Bosn. and Herzg.* 44°56′ N, 18°5′ E **168**
Podocarpus National Park, *Ecua.* 4°22′ S, 79°17′ W **122**
Podoleni, *Rom.* 46°47′ N, 26°37′ E **156**
Podol'sk, *Russ.* 55°23′ N, 37°31′ E **154**
Podor, *Senegal* 16°38′ N, 14°60′ W **222**
Podosinovets, *Russ.* 60°17′ N, 47°3′ E **154**
Podporozh'ye, *Russ.* 60°52′ N, 34°12′ E **154**
Podravska Slatina, *Croatia* 45°41′ N, 17°40′ E **168**
Podromanija, *Bosn. and Herzg.* 43°55′ N, 18°45′ E **168**
Podsosan'ye (Zvoz), *Russ.* 63°17′ N, 42°2′ E **154**
Podtesovo, *Russ.* 58°36′ N, 92°11′ E **169**
Podyuga, *Russ.* 61°6′ N, 40°49′ E **154**
Pofadder, *S. Af.* 29°8′ S, 19°22′ E **227**
Poggio Rusco, *It.* 44°59′ N, 11°6′ E **167**
Pogi, *Russ.* 59°31′ N, 30°35′ E **166**
Pogny, *Fr.* 48°51′ N, 4°29′ E **163**
Pogŏ, *N. Korea* 40°42′ N, 128°54′ E **200**
Pogorelets, *Russ.* 65°26′ N, 45°5′ E **154**
Pogost, *Belarus* 52°50′ N, 27°40′ E **152**
Pogromnoye, *Russ.* 52°35′ N, 52°28′ E **154**
P'oha, *N. Korea* 40°58′ N, 129°43′ E **200**
Pohang, *S. Korea* 36°2′ N, 129°22′ E **200**
Pohja see Pojo, *Fin.* 60°5′ N, 23°31′ E **166**
Pohnpei (Ponape), island, *F.S.M.* 6°55′ N, 158°15′ E **242**
Pohorje, *Slov.* 46°25′ N, 15°37′ E **168**
Poiana Mare, *Rom.* 43°55′ N, 23°4′ E **168**
Poiana Ruscă, Munții, *Rom.* 45°36′ N, 22°18′ E **168**
Poie, *Dem. Rep. of the Congo* 2°52′ S, 23°11′ E **218**
Poim, *Russ.* 53°0′ N, 43°7′ E **154**
Poincaré, Lac, lake, *Can.* 51°43′ N, 58°54′ W **111**
Poinsett, Cape, *Antarctica* 65°27′ S, 117°42′ E **248**
Point Baker, *Alas., U.S.* 56°19′ N, 133°32′ W **108**
Point, China, *Calif., U.S.* 32°44′ N, 118°33′ W **101**
Point Coulomb National Park, *Austral.* 17°22′ S, 121°55′ E **238**
Point Edward, *Can.* 42°59′ N, 82°24′ W **102**
Point Hope, *Alas., U.S.* 68°19′ N, 166°40′ W **98**
Point Judith, *R.I., U.S.* 41°21′ N, 71°30′ W **104**
Point Lake, *Can.* 64°58′ N, 113°44′ W **106**
Point Lay, *Alas., U.S.* 69°46′ N, 163°10′ W **73**
Point Pedro, *Sri Lanka* 9°49′ N, 80°14′ E **188**
Point Pelee National Park, *Can.* 41°53′ N, 82°56′ W **102**
Point Pleasant, *W. Va., U.S.* 38°50′ N, 82°9′ W **102**
Point Reyes National Seashore, *Calif., U.S.* 38°16′ N, 127°9′ W **80**
Point Roberts, *Can.* 48°58′ N, 123°4′ W **100**
Pointe a la Hache, *La., U.S.* 29°34′ N, 89°49′ W **103**
Pointe, Lac de la, lake, *Can.* 52°42′ N, 70°54′ W **111**
Pointe-à-Gravois, *Haiti* 17°54′ N, 74°4′ W **116**
Pointe-à-Pitre, *Grande-Terre* 16°15′ N, 61°31′ W **116**
Pointe-au-Pic, *Can.* 47°36′ N, 70°10′ W **94**
Pointe-aux-Anglais, *Can.* 49°40′ N, 67°12′ W **111**
Pointe-Noire, *Congo* 4°49′ S, 11°50′ E **218**
Poipet, *Cambodia* 13°40′ N, 102°37′ E **202**
Poissons, *Fr.* 48°24′ N, 5°12′ E **163**
Poissy, *Fr.* 48°56′ N, 2°3′ E **163**
Poitiers, *Fr.* 46°34′ N, 0°19′ E **150**
Poitou, region, *Fr.* 46°19′ N, 1°0′ E **165**
Poitou-Charentes, adm. division, *Fr.* 46°13′ N, 0°37′ E **150**
Poix, *Fr.* 49°46′ N, 1°58′ E **163**
Poix-Terron, *Fr.* 49°38′ N, 4°39′ E **163**
Pojo, *Bol.* 17°47′ S, 64°53′ W **137**
Pojo (Pohja), *Fin.* 60°5′ N, 23°31′ E **166**
Pokcha, *Russ.* 62°56′ N, 56°11′ E **154**
Pokeno, *N.Z.* 37°15′ S, 175°3′ E **240**
Pokhara, *Nepal* 28°17′ N, 83°58′ E **197**
Pokhvistnevo, *Russ.* 53°38′ N, 52°4′ E **154**
Pokka, *Fin.* 68°9′ N, 25°47′ E **152**
Poko, *Dem. Rep. of the Congo* 3°7′ N, 26°53′ E **224**
Pokrashevo, *Belarus* 53°11′ N, 27°33′ E **152**
Pokrovsk Ural'skiy, *Russ.* 60°7′ N, 59°48′ E **154**
Pokshen'ga, river, *Russ.* 63°31′ N, 43°43′ E **154**
Pokupsko, *Croatia* 45°29′ N, 16°0′ E **168**
Pola, *Philippines* 13°10′ N, 121°25′ E **203**
Pola, *Russ.* 57°54′ N, 31°50′ E **154**
Polače, *Croatia* 42°46′ N, 17°22′ E **168**
Polān, *Iran* 25°32′ N, 61°11′ E **182**
Poland 51°58′ N, 18°31′ E **152**
Polar Plateau, *Antarctica* 88°4′ S, 20°29′ W **248**
Polatlı, *Turk.* 39°34′ N, 32°9′ E **156**
Polatna, *Europe* 43°2′ N, 21°7′ E **168**
Polatsk, *Belarus* 55°29′ N, 28°47′ E **166**
Polch, *Ger.* 50°17′ N, 7°18′ E **163**
Polcirkeln, *Nor.* 66°33′ N, 20°58′ E **152**
Pol-e Khomri, *Afghan.* 35°56′ N, 68°50′ E **186**
Pole Plain, *Arctic Ocean* 83°54′ N, 131°5′ E **255**
Polesella, *It.* 44°58′ N, 11°46′ E **167**
Polessk, *Russ.* 54°50′ N, 21°2′ E **166**
Poletica, Mount, peak, *Alas., U.S.* 59°4′ N, 134°43′ W **98**
Polevskoy, *Russ.* 56°26′ N, 60°13′ E **154**
Poli, *Cameroon* 8°26′ N, 13°14′ E **218**
Poligus, *Russ.* 62°0′ N, 94°40′ E **169**
Polikarpovskoye, *Russ.* 70°41′ N, 82°13′ E **169**
Polillo Islands, *Philippine Sea* 14°33′ N, 121°54′ E **203**
Polis, *Cyprus* 35°2′ N, 32°25′ E **194**
Polje, *Bosn. and Herzg.* 44°59′ N, 17°57′ E **168**
Polkville, *Miss., U.S.* 32°10′ N, 89°42′ W **103**
Pollachi, *India* 10°40′ N, 77°1′ E **188**
Pöllau, *Aust.* 47°18′ N, 15°49′ E **168**
Pollino, Monte, peak, *It.* 39°53′ N, 16°8′ E **156**
Pollock, *La., U.S.* 31°30′ N, 92°26′ W **103**
Pollock, *S. Dak., U.S.* 45°52′ N, 100°19′ W **90**
Pollok, *Tex., U.S.* 31°26′ N, 94°52′ W **103**
Pollos, *Sp.* 41°25′ N, 5°9′ W **150**
Polna, *Russ.* 58°27′ N, 28°8′ E **166**
Polnovat, *Russ.* 63°47′ N, 66°2′ E **169**
Polo, *Ill., U.S.* 41°58′ N, 89°35′ W **102**
Polohy, *Ukr.* 47°26′ N, 36°14′ E **156**
Polokwane (Pietersburg), *S. Af.* 23°54′ S, 29°26′ E **227**
Polom, *Russ.* 59°11′ N, 50°54′ E **154**
Polonne, *Ukr.* 50°5′ N, 27°31′ E **152**
Polson, *Mont., U.S.* 47°38′ N, 114°12′ W **82**
Poltava, *Ukr.* 49°36′ N, 34°29′ E **158**
Poltavka, *Russ.* 54°19′ N, 71°47′ E **184**
Põltsamaa, *Est.* 58°38′ N, 25°55′ E **166**
Polunochnoye, *Russ.* 60°51′ N, 60°26′ E **154**
Polur, *India* 12°32′ N, 79°7′ E **188**
Poluy, *Russ.* 65°5′ N, 69°7′ E **169**
Põlva, *Est.* 58°2′ N, 27°2′ E **166**
Polvadera, *N. Mex., U.S.* 34°12′ N, 106°55′ W **92**
Polyarnoye, *Russ.* 71°1′ N, 149°0′ E **160**
Polyarnyy, *Russ.* 69°11′ N, 33°27′ E **152**
Polyarnyy, *Russ.* 69°8′ N, 178°45′ E **98**
Polyarnyy Krug, *Russ.* 66°26′ N, 32°51′ E **154**
Polyarnyye Zori, *Russ.* 67°19′ N, 32°27′ E **152**
Polynesian Cultural Center, site, *Hawai'i, U.S.* 21°37′ N, 157°58′ W **99**
Polyrrhenia, ruin(s), *Gr.* 35°25′ N, 23°35′ E **156**
Pomabamba, *Peru* 8°52′ S, 77°28′ W **130**
Pomarão, *Port.* 37°33′ N, 7°33′ W **150**
Pomarkku, *Fin.* 61°40′ N, 22°1′ E **166**
Pómaro, *Mex.* 18°17′ N, 103°18′ W **114**
Pomáz, *Hung.* 47°38′ N, 19°1′ E **168**
Pombal, *Braz.* 6°47′ S, 37°48′ W **132**
Pomene, *Mozambique* 22°53′ S, 35°29′ E **220**
Pomerania, region, *Pol.* 54°38′ N, 18°22′ E **166**
Pomeroy, *Ohio, U.S.* 39°1′ N, 82°2′ W **102**
Pomeroy, *Wash., U.S.* 46°28′ N, 117°37′ W **90**
Pomichna, *Ukr.* 48°15′ N, 31°31′ E **156**
Pomona, *Calif., U.S.* 34°3′ N, 117°46′ W **101**
Pomona Park, *Fla., U.S.* 29°29′ N, 81°36′ W **105**
Pomorskie, adm. division, *Pol.* 53°54′ N, 18°28′ E **166**
Pomos Point, *Cyprus* 35°9′ N, 32°27′ E **194**
Pomovaara, peak, *Fin.* 67°54′ N, 26°14′ E **152**
Pomozdino, *Russ.* 62°10′ N, 54°10′ E **154**
Pompano Beach, *Fla., U.S.* 26°14′ N, 80°9′ W **105**
Pompéia, *Braz.* 22°8′ S, 50°12′ W **138**
Pompeii, ruin(s), *It.* 40°45′ N, 14°24′ E **156**
Pompeiopolis, ruin(s), *Turk.* 36°43′ N, 34°26′ E **156**
Pompéu, *Braz.* 19°14′ S, 44°60′ W **138**
Pompeys Pillar, *Mont., U.S.* 45°57′ N, 107°56′ W **90**
Pompeys Pillar National Monument, *Mont., U.S.* 45°58′ N, 108°2′ W **90**
Pomuq, *Uzb.* 39°1′ N, 65°0′ E **197**
Ponape see Pohnpei, island, *F.S.M.* 6°55′ N, 158°15′ E **242**
Ponca City, *Okla., U.S.* 36°40′ N, 97°7′ W **82**
Ponce 18°1′ N, 66°37′ W **116**
Ponce de Leon Bay 25°20′ N, 81°22′ W **105**
Ponchatoula, *La., U.S.* 30°25′ N, 90°26′ W **103**
Poncheville, Lac, lake, *Can.* 50°8′ N, 77°36′ W **94**
Poncin, *Fr.* 46°5′ N, 5°24′ E **156**
Poncitlán, *Mex.* 20°22′ N, 102°57′ W **114**
Pond, *Calif., U.S.* 35°43′ N, 119°21′ W **100**
Pond Creek, *Okla., U.S.* 36°39′ N, 97°48′ W **92**
Pond Inlet, *Can.* 72°36′ N, 77°53′ W **73**
Pondicherry see Puducherry, *India* 11°56′ N, 79°47′ E **188**
Ponferrada, *Sp.* 42°33′ N, 6°37′ W **150**
Pong, *Thai.* 19°12′ N, 100°15′ E **202**
Pongaroa, *N.Z.* 40°34′ S, 176°13′ E **240**
Pongo, river, *Sudan* 7°39′ N, 27°11′ E **224**
Pon'goma, *Russ.* 65°19′ N, 34°15′ E **152**
Ponlei, *Cambodia* 12°26′ N, 104°27′ E **202**
Ponoka, *Can.* 52°40′ N, 113°40′ W **108**
Ponomarevka, *Russ.* 53°18′ N, 54°10′ E **154**
Ponoy, *Russ.* 67°4′ N, 40°59′ E **154**
Ponoy, river, *Russ.* 66°59′ N, 38°23′ E **154**
Pons, *Fr.* 45°34′ N, 0°33′ E **150**
Pont Canavese, *It.* 45°25′ N, 7°36′ E **167**
Pont de Suert, *Sp.* 42°23′ N, 0°44′ E **164**
Ponta Delgada, *Port.* 37°40′ N, 25°51′ W **207**
Ponta Grossa, *Braz.* 25°6′ S, 50°9′ W **138**
Ponta Porã, *Braz.* 22°32′ S, 55°40′ W **132**
Pontalina, *Braz.* 17°34′ S, 49°29′ W **138**
Pont-à-Mousson, *Fr.* 48°54′ N, 6°2′ E **163**
Pontarlier, *Fr.* 46°54′ N, 6°19′ E **156**
Pontassieve, *It.* 43°47′ N, 11°25′ E **167**
Pontax, river, *Can.* 51°50′ N, 77°1′ W **110**
Pontchartrain, Lake, *La., U.S.* 30°10′ N, 90°24′ W **103**
Pontchâteau, *Fr.* 47°26′ N, 2°7′ W **150**
Ponte Branca, *Braz.* 16°25′ S, 52°42′ W **138**
Ponte de Lima, *Port.* 41°45′ N, 8°37′ W **150**
Ponte di Legno, *It.* 46°16′ N, 10°29′ E **167**
Ponte Firme, *Braz.* 18°4′ S, 46°26′ W **138**
Ponte Nova, *Braz.* 20°25′ S, 42°53′ W **138**
Ponteareas, *Sp.* 42°9′ N, 8°31′ W **150**
Pontedecimo, *It.* 44°30′ N, 8°55′ E **167**
Pontedera, *It.* 43°39′ N, 10°36′ E **156**
Pontefract, *U.K.* 53°41′ N, 1°18′ W **162**
Ponteix, *Can.* 49°43′ N, 107°28′ W **90**
Pontevedra, *Sp.* 42°24′ N, 8°39′ W **150**
Pontiac, *Ill., U.S.* 40°52′ N, 88°38′ W **102**
Pontiac, *Mich., U.S.* 42°37′ N, 83°18′ W **102**
Pontiac, *Mo., U.S.* 40°52′ N, 88°38′ W **94**
Pontian Kechil, *Malaysia* 1°29′ N, 103°23′ E **196**
Pontianak, *Indonesia* 3°178′ S, 109°18′ E **196**
Pontoise, *Fr.* 49°3′ N, 2°4′ E **163**
Ponton, *Can.* 54°37′ N, 99°11′ W **108**
Ponton, river, *Can.* 58°26′ N, 116°3′ W **108**
Pontós, *Sp.* 42°10′ N, 2°54′ E **164**
Pontrieux, *Fr.* 48°41′ N, 3°10′ W **150**
Ponts, *Sp.* 41°54′ N, 1°11′ E **164**
Pont-Sainte-Maxence, *Fr.* 49°18′ N, 2°37′ E **163**
Pont-sur-Yonne, *Fr.* 48°16′ N, 3°12′ E **163**
Pontypool, *U.K.* 51°41′ N, 3°3′ W **162**
Ponyri, *Russ.* 52°17′ N, 36°17′ E **158**
Ponziane, Isole, islands, *Tyrrhenian Sea* 40°46′ N, 12°1′ E **156**
Ponzone, *It.* 44°35′ N, 8°29′ E **167**
Poole, *U.K.* 50°43′ N, 1°59′ W **162**
Poondinna, Mount, peak, *Austral.* 27°22′ S, 129°46′ E **230**
Poopó, *Bol.* 18°23′ S, 66°59′ W **137**
Poopó, Lago, lake, *Bol.* 18°59′ S, 67°12′ W **137**
Pöösapea, *Est.* 59°12′ N, 23°29′ E **166**
Popa, Isla, island, *Pan.* 8°52′ N, 82°18′ W **115**
Popayán, *Col.* 2°23′ N, 76°37′ W **136**
Pope, *Latv.* 57°23′ N, 21°50′ E **166**
Poperinge, *Belg.* 50°51′ N, 2°43′ E **163**
Popham Beach, *Me., U.S.* 43°44′ N, 69°48′ W **104**
Popigay, *Russ.* 72°1′ N, 110°58′ E **160**
Poplar, *Calif., U.S.* 36°3′ N, 119°10′ W **101**
Poplar, *Mont., U.S.* 48°5′ N, 105°11′ W **90**
Poplar Bluff, *Mo., U.S.* 36°45′ N, 90°24′ W **96**
Poplar Point, *Can.* 52°54′ N, 97°53′ W **108**
Poplar, river, *Can.* 61°22′ N, 121°44′ W **108**
Poplar, river, *Can.* 52°27′ N, 95°49′ W **108**
Poplarville, *Miss., U.S.* 30°50′ N, 89°33′ W **103**
Popocatépetl, peak, *Mex.* 19°0′ N, 98°40′ W **114**
Popokabaka, *Dem. Rep. of the Congo* 5°41′ S, 16°36′ E **218**
Popovača, *Croatia* 45°34′ N, 16°37′ E **168**
Poppi, *It.* 43°43′ N, 11°44′ E **167**
Poprad, *Slovakia* 49°3′ N, 20°18′ E **152**
Pŏptong, *N. Korea* 38°58′ N, 127°4′ E **200**
Populonia, *It.* 42°58′ N, 10°30′ E **156**
Por Chaman, *Afghan.* 33°10′ N, 63°52′ E **186**
Porangahau, *N.Z.* 40°19′ S, 176°38′ E **240**
Porangatu, *Braz.* 13°30′ S, 49°12′ W **138**
Porazava, *Belarus* 52°56′ N, 24°21′ E **152**
Porbandar, *India* 21°39′ N, 69°37′ E **186**
Porcher Island, *Can.* 54°1′ N, 130°53′ W **98**
Porco, *Bol.* 19°50′ S, 66°1′ W **137**
Porcos, river, *Braz.* 13°5′ S, 45°10′ W **138**
Porcuna, *Sp.* 37°53′ N, 4°12′ W **164**
Porcupine, Cape, *Can.* 53°57′ N, 57°8′ W **111**
Porcupine Hill, peak, *Can.* 53°42′ N, 61°5′ W **111**
Porcupine Mountains, peak, *Mich., U.S.* 46°43′ N, 89°52′ W **94**
Porcupine Plain, *Can.* 52°35′ N, 103°16′ W **108**
Porcupine Plain, *North Atlantic Ocean* 47°55′ N, 15°54′ W **253**
Porcupine, river, *Can.* 66°51′ N, 144°4′ W **106**
Pordenone, *It.* 45°57′ N, 12°39′ E **167**
Pordim, *Bulg.* 43°22′ N, 24°50′ E **156**
Poreč, *Croatia* 45°13′ N, 13°36′ E **167**
Porecatu, *Braz.* 22°47′ S, 51°28′ W **138**
Poretskoye, *Russ.* 55°11′ N, 46°19′ E **154**
Pórfido, Punta, *Arg.* 41°56′ S, 64°57′ W **134**
Porga, *Benin* 11°0′ N, 0°58′ E **222**
Porgho, *Mali* 16°34′ N, 6°356′ W **222**
Pori (Björneborg), *Fin.* 61°26′ N, 21°44′ E **166**
Porirua, *N.Z.* 41°10′ S, 174°51′ E **240**

Porjus, Nor. 66°56′ N, 19°50′ E 152
Porkhov, Russ. 57°44′ N, 29°39′ E 166
Porkkala, Fin. 59°58′ N, 24°24′ E 166
Porlock, U.K. 51°12′ N, 3°35′ W 162
Porog, Russ. 62°1′ N, 56°40′ E 154
Poroma, Bol. 18°30′ S, 65°34′ W 137
Poronaysk, Russ. 49°15′ N, 143°0′ E 190
Poronin, Pol. 49°20′ N, 20°0′ E 152
Poroslyany, Belarus 52°39′ N, 24°21′ E 152
Porosozero, Russ. 62°43′ N, 32°44′ E 152
Poroszló, Hung. 47°38′ N, 20°38′ E 168
Porozhsk, Russ. 63°56′ N, 53°41′ E 154
Porpoise Bay 66°28′ S, 128°20′ E 255
Porsangerhalvøya, Nor. 70°46′ N, 23°56′ E 152
Porsuk, river, Turk. 39°30′ N, 29°57′ E 156
Port Alberni, Can. 49°14′ N, 124°48′ W 100
Port Albert, Can. 43°52′ N, 81°42′ W 102
Port Alexander, Alas., U.S. 56°15′ N, 134°41′ W 108
Port Alfred, S. Af. 33°35′ S, 26°52′ E 227
Port Alice, Can. 50°22′ N, 127°26′ W 90
Port Allen, La., U.S. 30°27′ N, 91°14′ W 103
Port Alsworth, Alas., U.S. 60°11′ N, 154°20′ W 98
Port Angeles, Wash., U.S. 48°5′ N, 123°26′ W 100
Port Antonio, Jam. 18°10′ N, 76°27′ W 115
Port Arthur, Tex., U.S. 29°53′ N, 93°56′ W 103
Port Arthur see Lüshun, China 38°52′ N, 121°16′ E 198
Port Austin, Mich., U.S. 44°2′ N, 82°60′ W 102
Port Barre, La., U.S. 30°32′ N, 91°58′ W 103
Port Bay, Port au 48°38′ N, 59°28′ W 111
Port Beaufort, S. Af. 34°21′ S, 20°46′ E 227
Port Bell, Uganda 0°16′ N, 32°36′ E 224
Port Blair, India 11°44′ N, 92°52′ E 188
Port Blanford, Can. 48°21′ N, 54°11′ W 111
Port Bolivar, Tex., U.S. 29°21′ N, 94°46′ W 103
Port Bouet, Côte d'Ivoire 5°16′ N, 3°59′ W 222
Port Bruce, Can. 42°38′ N, 81°1′ W 102
Port Burwell, Can. 42°38′ N, 80°47′ W 102
Port Burwell, Can. 60°19′ N, 64°39′ W 106
Port Canning, India 22°18′ N, 88°38′ E 197
Port Carling, Can. 45°6′ N, 79°33′ W 94
Port Chalmers, N.Z. 45°48′ S, 170°36′ E 240
Port Charlotte, Fla., U.S. 26°59′ N, 82°5′ W 105
Port Clements, Can. 53°41′ N, 132°11′ W 108
Port Clinton, Ohio, U.S. 41°29′ N, 82°57′ W 102
Port Colborne, Can. 42°52′ N, 79°15′ W 110
Port Coquitlam, Can. 49°15′ N, 122°46′ W 100
Port de Sóller, Sp. 39°47′ N, 2°42′ E 164
Port Dickson, Malaysia 2°35′ N, 101°48′ E 196
Port Eads, La., U.S. 29°1′ N, 89°9′ W 103
Port Edward, Can. 54°13′ N, 130°16′ W 108
Port Edwards, Wis., U.S. 44°20′ N, 89°53′ W 110
Port Elgin, Can. 44°25′ N, 81°23′ W 94
Port Elizabeth, S. Af. 33°56′ S, 25°34′ E 227
Port Étienne see Nouadhibou, Mauritania 20°56′ N, 17°2′ W 222
Port Ewen, N.Y., U.S. 41°53′ N, 73°60′ W 104
Port Fitzroy, N.Z. 36°11′ S, 175°22′ E 240
Port Gamble, Wash., U.S. 47°49′ N, 122°37′ W 100
Port Gibson, Miss., U.S. 31°57′ N, 90°60′ W 103
Port Harcourt, Nig. 4°46′ N, 7°0′ E 222
Port Hardy, Can. 50°43′ N, 127°32′ W 108
Port Hawkesbury, Can. 45°36′ N, 61°22′ W 111
Port Henry, N.Y., U.S. 44°2′ N, 73°29′ W 104
Port Herald see Nsanje, Malawi 16°56′ S, 35°13′ E 224
Port Hope, Can. 43°56′ N, 78°19′ W 94
Port Hope, Mich., U.S. 43°56′ N, 82°44′ W 102
Port Hueneme, Calif., U.S. 34°9′ N, 119°12′ W 101
Port Huron, Mich., U.S. 42°57′ N, 82°28′ W 102
Port Isabel, Tex., U.S. 26°5′ N, 97°13′ W 114
Port Jefferson, N.Y., U.S. 40°56′ N, 73°4′ W 104
Port Jervis, N.Y., U.S. 41°22′ N, 74°42′ W 110
Port Joinville, Fr. 46°43′ N, 2°22′ W 150
Port Kaituma, Guyana 7°47′ N, 59°55′ W 116
Port Katon, Russ. 46°51′ N, 38°44′ E 156
Port Kelang, Malaysia 2°58′ N, 101°26′ E 196
Port Láirge see Waterford, Ire. 52°15′ N, 7°8′ W 150
Port Laoise, Ire. 53°2′ N, 7°18′ W 150
Port Lavaca, Tex., U.S. 28°35′ N, 96°37′ W 96
Port Lions, Alas., U.S. 57°50′ N, 152°56′ W 98
Port Loko, Sierra Leone 8°46′ N, 12°47′ W 222
Port Louis, Mauritius 20°9′ S, 57°30′ E 22
Port Lyautey see Kenitra, Mor. 34°17′ N, 6°37′ W 214
Port Mansfield, Tex., U.S. 26°33′ N, 97°26′ W 114
Port Maria, Jam. 18°21′ N, 76°54′ W 115
Port Mcneill, Can. 50°33′ N, 127°6′ W 90
Port Mcnicoll, Can. 44°44′ N, 79°48′ W 94
Port Moody, Can. 49°15′ N, 122°51′ W 100
Port Moresby, P.N.G. 9°30′ S, 146°47′ E 230
Port Neches, Tex., U.S. 29°58′ N, 93°57′ W 103
Port Neville, Can. 50°29′ N, 126°2′ W 90
Port Nolloth, S. Af. 29°15′ S, 16°52′ E 227
Port O'Connor, Tex., U.S. 28°26′ N, 96°26′ W 96
Port Ontario, N.Y., U.S. 43°33′ N, 76°12′ W 94
Port Orange, Fla., U.S. 29°7′ N, 80°60′ W 105
Port Orchard, Wash., U.S. 47°30′ N, 122°39′ W 100
Port Pirie, Austral. 33°12′ S, 138°0′ E 231
Port Renfrew, Can. 48°32′ N, 124°25′ W 100
Port Royal, S.C., U.S. 32°22′ N, 80°42′ W 96
Port Royal National Historic Site, Can. 44°42′ N, 65°43′ W 111
Port Said see Bûr Sa'îd, Egypt 31°15′ N, 32°18′ E 194
Port Saint Joe, Fla., U.S. 29°48′ N, 85°17′ W 96
Port Saint Johns, S. Af. 31°39′ S, 29°30′ E 227
Port Saint Lucie, Fla., U.S. 27°20′ N, 80°18′ W 105
Port Salerno, Fla., U.S. 27°7′ N, 80°13′ W 105
Port Sanilac, Mich., U.S. 43°25′ N, 82°34′ W 102
Port Saunders, Can. 50°38′ N, 57°18′ W 111
Port Shepstone, S. Af. 30°44′ S, 30°25′ E 227
Port Simpson, Can. 54°32′ N, 130°25′ W 108
Port Stanley, Can. 42°39′ N, 81°14′ W 102
Port Sudan, Sudan 19°38′ N, 37°11′ E 182
Port Sulphur, La., U.S. 29°28′ N, 89°42′ W 103
Port Talbot, Can. 42°38′ N, 81°20′ W 102
Port Talbot, U.K. 51°35′ N, 3°46′ W 162
Port Townsend, Wash., U.S. 48°6′ N, 122°47′ W 100
Port Vladimir, Russ. 69°25′ N, 33°6′ E 152
Port Washington, N.Y., U.S. 40°49′ N, 73°42′ W 104
Port Washington, Wis., U.S. 43°23′ N, 87°53′ W 102
Port Weld, Malaysia 4°50′ N, 100°37′ E 196
Port William, Alas., U.S. 58°29′ N, 152°38′ W 98
Portachuelo, Bol. 17°23′ S, 63°30′ W 132
Portadown, U.K. 54°24′ N, 6°27′ W 150
Portage, Ind., U.S. 41°33′ N, 87°11′ W 102
Portage, Mich., U.S. 42°11′ N, 85°36′ W 102
Portage, Wis., U.S. 43°31′ N, 89°27′ W 102
Portage Creek, Alas., U.S. 58°52′ N, 157°44′ W 98
Portage la Prairie, Can. 49°58′ N, 98°19′ W 108
Portageville, Mo., U.S. 36°25′ N, 89°42′ W 96
Portal, N. Dak., U.S. 48°57′ N, 102°35′ W 90
Portalegre, Port. 39°17′ N, 7°26′ W 150
Portalegre, adm. division, Port. 39°3′ N, 8°10′ W 150
Portales, N. Mex., U.S. 34°10′ N, 103°21′ W 92
Port-à-Piment, Haiti 18°16′ N, 74°8′ W 115
Port-au-Prince, Haiti 18°31′ N, 72°29′ W 116
Port-Bergé see Boriziny, Madagascar 15°35′ S, 47°43′ E 220
Portbou, Sp. 42°25′ N, 3°9′ E 164
Port-Cartier, Can. 50°1′ N, 66°51′ W 111
Port-Cartier, Can. 50°2′ N, 66°54′ W 106
Port-Daniel, Can. 48°10′ N, 64°59′ W 94
Porteirinha, Braz. 15°45′ S, 43°4′ W 138
Portel, Braz. 1°59′ S, 50°48′ W 130
Portela, Braz. 21°39′ S, 41°60′ W 138
Portendick, Mauritania 18°34′ N, 16°7′ W 222
Porter, Me., U.S. 43°47′ N, 70°56′ W 104
Porter, Tex., U.S. 30°4′ N, 95°14′ W 103
Porter Lake, Can. 56°13′ N, 107°56′ W 108
Porter Lake, lake, Can. 61°40′ N, 108°34′ W 108
Porterdale, Ga., U.S. 33°33′ N, 83°54′ W 96
Porterville, Calif., U.S. 36°5′ N, 119°2′ W 101
Porterville, Miss., U.S. 32°40′ N, 88°29′ W 103
Porterville, S. Af. 33°1′ S, 19°1′ E 227
Portete, Bahía de 12°12′ N, 72°32′ W 136
Port-Gentil, Gabon 1°9′ S, 8°53′ E 207
Porthcawl, U.K. 51°28′ N, 3°42′ W 162
Port-İliç, Azerb. 38°51′ N, 48°47′ E 195
Portimão, Port. 37°6′ N, 8°36′ W 214
Portishead, U.K. 51°28′ N, 2°46′ W 162
Portland, Ark., U.S. 33°13′ N, 91°31′ W 103
Portland, Conn., U.S. 41°34′ N, 72°39′ W 104
Portland, Ind., U.S. 40°26′ N, 84°58′ W 102
Portland, Me., U.S. 43°39′ N, 70°16′ W 104
Portland, Mich., U.S. 42°51′ N, 84°55′ W 102
Portland, N. Dak., U.S. 47°28′ N, 97°24′ W 90
Portland, Oreg., U.S. 45°30′ N, 122°43′ W 90
Portland, Tenn., U.S. 36°34′ N, 86°31′ W 96
Portland Inlet 54°43′ N, 131°3′ W 108
Portland Point, Jam. 17°35′ N, 77°7′ W 115
Port-la-Nouvelle, Fr. 43°0′ N, 3°1′ E 164
Port-Menier, Can. 49°48′ N, 64°22′ W 106
Portneuf, Lac, lake, Can. 49°9′ N, 70°56′ W 94
Portneuf-sur-Mer, Can. 48°36′ N, 69°8′ W 111
Porto, Braz. 3°54′ S, 42°44′ W 132
Porto, Fr. 42°16′ N, 8°42′ E 156
Porto, Port. 41°13′ N, 8°32′ W 143
Pôrto Acre, Braz. 9°37′ S, 67°33′ W 137
Porto, adm. division, Port. 41°12′ N, 8°44′ W 150
Porto Alegre, Braz. 21°34′ S, 53°33′ W 132
Porto Alegre, Braz. 8°60′ S, 67°51′ W 137
Porto Alegre, Braz. 4°24′ S, 52°47′ W 130
Porto Alegre, Braz. 30°3′ S, 51°10′ W 139
Porto Amboim, Angola 10°44′ S, 13°47′ E 220
Porto Artur, Braz. 13°5′ S, 55°5′ W 130
Porto de Moz, Braz. 1°45′ S, 52°13′ W 130
Porto de Pedras, Braz. 9°10′ S, 35°20′ W 132
Porto do Son, Sp. 42°42′ N, 8°60′ W 150
Porto dos Gaúchos, Braz. 11°30′ S, 57°23′ W 130
Porto Empedocle, It. 37°18′ N, 13°31′ E 156
Porto Esperança, Braz. 19°37′ S, 57°26′ W 132
Porto Esperidião, Braz. 15°50′ S, 58°31′ W 132
Porto Franco, Braz. 6°23′ S, 47°24′ W 130
Porto Garibaldi, It. 44°40′ N, 12°13′ E 167
Porto Grande, Braz. 0°42′ N, 51°25′ W 130
Porto Levante, It. 45°3′ N, 12°21′ E 167
Porto Levante, It. 38°25′ N, 14°56′ E 156
Porto Lucena, Braz. 27°53′ S, 55°1′ W 132
Porto Murtinho, Braz. 21°42′ S, 57°54′ W 132
Porto Nacional, Braz. 10°43′ S, 48°24′ W 130
Porto (Oporto), Port. 41°8′ N, 8°38′ W 150
Porto San Giorgio, It. 43°10′ N, 13°47′ E 156
Porto Santana, Braz. 1°59′ S, 51°11′ W 130
Porto Santo Stefano, It. 42°26′ N, 11°6′ E 156
Porto São José, Braz. 22°44′ S, 53°12′ W 138
Porto Tolle, It. 44°56′ N, 12°19′ E 167
Porto Velho, Braz. 8°43′ S, 63°53′ W 137
Portobelo, Pan. 9°33′ N, 79°39′ W 115
Portobelo National Park, Pan. 9°33′ N, 79°41′ W 115
Portofino, It. 44°18′ N, 9°12′ E 167
Port-of-Spain, Trinidad and Tobago 10°40′ N, 61°32′ W 118
Portogruaro, It. 45°45′ N, 12°50′ E 167
Portola, Calif., U.S. 39°48′ N, 120°29′ W 90
Pörtom (Pirttikylä), Fin. 62°41′ N, 21°35′ E 154
Portomaggiore, It. 44°41′ N, 11°47′ E 167
Porto-Novo, Benin 6°31′ N, 2°31′ E 222
Portorož, Slov. 45°30′ N, 13°37′ E 167
Porto-Vecchio, Fr. 41°35′ N, 9°17′ E 156
Portovenere, It. 44°3′ N, 9°50′ E 167
Portoviejo, Ecua. 1°11′ S, 80°19′ W 130
Port-Sainte-Marie, Fr. 44°14′ N, 0°23′ E 150
Portsmouth, N.H., U.S. 43°4′ N, 70°46′ W 104
Portsmouth, N.C., U.S. 35°4′ N, 76°5′ W 96
Portsmouth, Ohio, U.S. 38°44′ N, 82°59′ W 102
Portsmouth, R.I., U.S. 41°35′ N, 71°16′ W 104
Portsmouth, U.K. 50°47′ N, 1°6′ W 162
Portsmouth, Va., U.S. 36°49′ N, 76°19′ W 96
Port-sur-Saône, Fr. 47°41′ N, 6°2′ E 156
Portugal 38°56′ N, 8°33′ W 150
Portugués, Peru 8°21′ S, 78°5′ W 130
Portuguesa, adm. division, Venez. 8°51′ N, 69°58′ W 136
Portuguesa, river, Venez. 8°45′ N, 69°2′ W 136
Port-Vendres, Fr. 42°30′ N, 3°5′ E 164
Port-Vila, Vanuatu 17°41′ S, 167°55′ E 243
Porvenir, Bol. 11°15′ S, 68°45′ W 137
Porvenir, Chile 53°14′ S, 70°21′ W 134
Porvoo (Borgå), Fin. 60°23′ N, 25°40′ E 166
Por'ya Guba, Russ. 66°45′ N, 33°48′ E 154
Porz, Ger. 50°53′ N, 7°3′ E 167
Porzuna, Sp. 39°8′ N, 4°9′ W 164
Posadas, Arg. 27°25′ S, 55°55′ W 139
Posadas, Sp. 37°48′ N, 5°6′ W 164
Posadowsky Bay 66°58′ S, 88°27′ E 248
Poshekhon'ye Volodarsk, Russ. 58°29′ N, 39°11′ E 154
Poshkokagan, river, Can. 49°19′ N, 89°35′ W 94
Posht-e Bādām, Iran 32°57′ N, 55°19′ E 180
Posidium, ruin(s), Gr. 35°28′ N, 27°9′ E 156
Posio, Fin. 66°5′ N, 28°7′ E 154
Poso, Indonesia 1°27′ S, 120°44′ E 192
Poso Creek, river, Calif., U.S. 35°37′ N, 119°9′ W 101
Posof, Turk. 41°30′ N, 42°42′ E 195
Pospelkova, Russ. 59°27′ N, 60°53′ E 154
Posse, Braz. 14°8′ S, 46°23′ W 138
Possel, Cen. Af. Rep. 5°4′ N, 19°14′ E 218
Possession Island, Namibia 27°13′ S, 15°14′ E 227
Possession Islands, Ross Sea 71°53′ S, 178°9′ E 248
Post Falls, Idaho, U.S. 47°41′ N, 116°56′ W 90
Post Mills, Vt., U.S. 43°53′ N, 72°17′ W 104
Posta de San Martín, Arg. 33°11′ S, 60°29′ W 139
Poste, Baie du, lake, Can. 50°39′ N, 73°51′ W 110
Postmasburg, S. Af. 28°23′ S, 23°5′ E 227
Posto Alto Maniçauá, Braz. 11°19′ S, 54°44′ W 130
Posto Bobonaza, Peru 2°40′ S, 76°36′ W 136
Posto Cunambo, Peru 2°9′ S, 76°1′ W 136
Poston, Ariz., U.S. 33°58′ N, 114°25′ W 101
Postville, Iowa, U.S. 43°4′ N, 91°34′ W 94
Posušje, Bosn. and Herzg. 43°27′ N, 17°18′ E 168
Pos'yet, Russ. 42°40′ N, 130°49′ E 200
Pot Mountain, peak, Idaho, U.S. 46°41′ N, 115°30′ W 90
Potamós, Gr. 35°52′ N, 23°16′ E 156
Potapovo, Russ. 68°40′ N, 86°26′ E 169
Potchefstroom, S. Af. 26°45′ S, 27°1′ E 227
Poté, Braz. 17°50′ S, 41°53′ W 138
Poteau, Okla., U.S. 35°0′ N, 94°38′ W 96
Poteet, Tex., U.S. 29°1′ N, 98°34′ W 96
Potenza, It. 40°38′ N, 15°48′ E 156
Potenza Picena, It. 43°21′ N, 13°37′ E 156
Potgietersrus see Mokopane, S. Af. 24°9′ S, 28°59′ E 227
Poth, Tex., U.S. 29°3′ N, 98°5′ W 92
P'ot'i, Ga. 42°7′ N, 41°38′ E 195
Potidaea, ruin(s), Aegean Sea 40°11′ N, 23°14′ E 156
Potiskum, Nig. 11°42′ N, 11°5′ E 222
Potlatch, Idaho, U.S. 46°54′ N, 116°56′ W 90
Potlogi, Rom. 44°34′ N, 25°35′ E 156
Potoci, Bosn. and Herzg. 43°23′ N, 17°53′ E 168
Potomac, Ill., U.S. 40°17′ N, 87°48′ W 102
Potosí, Bol. 19°37′ S, 65°37′ W 123
Potosí, Bol. 19°36′ S, 65°44′ W 137
Potosi, Mo., U.S. 37°55′ N, 90°47′ W 94
Potosí, Nicar. 12°58′ N, 87°30′ W 115
Potosí, adm. division, Bol. 20°39′ S, 67°39′ W 137
Potosi Mountain, peak, Nev., U.S. 35°56′ N, 115°32′ W 101
Potosí, river, Mex. 24°45′ N, 100°17′ W 114
Potrerillo, Paso de, pass, Chile 29°24′ S, 69°60′ W 132
Potrerillos, Chile 26°25′ S, 69°30′ W 132
Potsdam, Ger. 52°24′ N, 13°3′ E 152
Potsdam, N.Y., U.S. 44°40′ N, 74°60′ W 94
Pottendorf, Aust. 47°54′ N, 16°22′ E 168
Potter, Nebr., U.S. 41°13′ N, 103°20′ W 90
Pottersville, N.Y., U.S. 43°43′ N, 73°50′ W 104
Potterville, Mich., U.S. 42°36′ N, 84°45′ W 102
Potton, U.K. 52°7′ N, 0°13′ E 162
Pouancé, Fr. 47°43′ N, 1°11′ W 150
Poughkeepsie, N.Y., U.S. 41°41′ N, 73°55′ W 104
Poulan, Ga., U.S. 31°30′ N, 83°48′ W 96
Poulsbo, Wash., U.S. 47°43′ N, 122°39′ W 100
Poultney, Vt., U.S. 43°31′ N, 73°15′ W 104
Poulton le Fylde, U.K. 53°50′ N, 2°60′ W 162
Pouma, Cameroon 3°55′ N, 10°37′ E 222
Pourri, Mont, peak, Fr. 45°31′ N, 6°50′ E 165
Pouso Alegre, Braz. 22°13′ S, 45°56′ W 138
Pouss, Cameroon 10°50′ N, 15°0′ E 216
Poussu, Fin. 65°47′ N, 29°18′ E 152
Poutrincourt, Lac, lake, Can. 49°4′ N, 74°48′ W 94
Povenets, Russ. 62°51′ N, 34°52′ E 154
Povlen, Serb. and Mont. 44°6′ N, 19°31′ E 168
Povorino, Russ. 51°9′ N, 42°12′ E 158
Povors'k, Ukr. 51°16′ N, 25°7′ E 152
Povungnituk, Baie de 59°33′ N, 79°35′ W 106
Poway, Calif., U.S. 32°57′ N, 117°3′ W 101
Powder River, Wyo., U.S. 43°1′ N, 106°59′ W 90
Powder, river, Mont., U.S. 44°58′ N, 105°46′ W 90
Powder River Pass, Wyo., U.S. 44°7′ N, 107°6′ W 90
Powder, river, Wyo., U.S. 45°2′ N, 105°33′ W 80
Powderly, Ky., U.S. 37°13′ N, 87°10′ W 96
Powell, Wyo., U.S. 44°43′ N, 108°46′ W 90
Powell Butte, Oreg., U.S. 44°13′ N, 121°3′ W 90
Powell Lake, Can. 50°2′ N, 124°32′ W 100
Powell Peak, Ariz., U.S. 34°39′ N, 114°28′ W 92
Powell River, Can. 49°52′ N, 124°30′ W 100
Powers Lake, N. Dak., U.S. 48°33′ N, 102°39′ W 90
Powerview, Can. 50°30′ N, 96°14′ W 90
Powhatan, La., U.S. 31°51′ N, 93°13′ W 103
Pownal Center, Vt., U.S. 42°47′ N, 73°14′ W 104
Poxoréo, Braz. 15°52′ S, 54°24′ W 132
Poygan, Lake, Wis., U.S. 44°8′ N, 89°5′ W 102
Poygan, Lake, Wis., U.S. 44°4′ N, 89°16′ W 110
Pöytyä, Fin. 60°45′ N, 22°37′ E 166
Poza Rica, Mex. 20°32′ N, 97°26′ W 114
Pozantı, Turk. 37°24′ N, 34°51′ E 156
Požaranje, Europe 42°22′ N, 21°20′ E 168
Požarevac, Serb. and Mont. 44°37′ N, 21°10′ E 168
Pozas de Santa Ana, Mex. 22°47′ N, 100°29′ W 114
Požega, Serb. and Mont. 43°9′ N, 20°24′ E 168
Pozheg, Russ. 61°58′ N, 54°20′ E 154
Pozhva, Russ. 59°6′ N, 56°5′ E 154
Poznań, Pol. 52°24′ N, 16°55′ E 152
Pozo Alcón, Sp. 37°42′ N, 2°56′ W 164
Pozo Almonte, Chile 20°16′ S, 69°50′ W 137
Pozo Borrado, Arg. 28°55′ S, 61°43′ W 139
Pozo Colorado, Parag. 23°29′ S, 58°52′ W 132
Pozoblanco, Sp. 38°22′ N, 4°52′ W 164
Pozohondo, Sp. 38°43′ N, 1°55′ W 164
Pozos, Mex. 21°12′ N, 100°30′ W 114
Pozzallo, It. 36°44′ N, 14°51′ E 156
Pra, river, Ghana 5°4′ N, 1°41′ W 222
Prača, Bosn. and Herzg. 43°46′ N, 18°45′ E 168
Prachin Buri, Thai. 14°2′ N, 101°22′ E 202
Prachuap Khiri Khan, Thai. 11°48′ N, 99°46′ E 202
Prádena, Sp. 41°7′ N, 3°42′ W 164
Prado, Braz. 17°20′ S, 39°15′ W 132
Praesus, ruin(s), Gr. 35°5′ N, 25°59′ E 156
Prague see Praha, Czech Rep. 50°4′ N, 14°17′ E 152
Praha, adm. division, Czech Rep. 50°0′ N, 14°10′ E 152
Praha (Prague), Czech Rep. 50°4′ N, 14°17′ E 152
Prahova, adm. division, Rom. 45°2′ N, 25°43′ E 156
Prahovo, Serb. and Mont. 44°16′ N, 22°34′ E 168
Prai, Malaysia 5°20′ N, 100°25′ E 196
Praia Grande, Braz. 29°11′ S, 49°56′ W 138
Prainha, Braz. 7°18′ S, 60°32′ W 130
Prainha, Braz. 1°48′ S, 53°32′ W 130
Prairie City, Oreg., U.S. 44°27′ N, 118°44′ W 90
Prairie du Chien, Wis., U.S. 43°1′ N, 91°10′ W 82
Prairie du Sac, Wis., U.S. 43°16′ N, 89°43′ W 102
Prairie River, Can. 52°51′ N, 102°59′ W 108
Prairieton, Ind., U.S. 39°22′ N, 87°28′ W 102
Pran Buri, Thai. 12°21′ N, 99°56′ E 202
Prangli, island, Est. 59°33′ N, 24°48′ E 166
Pranjani, Serb. and Mont. 44°1′ N, 20°11′ E 168
Prapat, Indonesia 2°42′ N, 98°56′ E 196
Prata, Braz. 19°19′ S, 48°57′ W 138
Prata, river, Braz. 18°60′ S, 49°44′ W 138
Prato, It. 43°53′ N, 11°4′ E 167
Pratt, Kans., U.S. 37°38′ N, 98°46′ W 90
Pratt Seamount, North Pacific Ocean 56°10′ N, 142°51′ W 252
Pravdinsk, Russ. 54°27′ N, 20°53′ E 166
Prawle Point, U.K. 50°2′ N, 3°56′ W 150
Prazaroki, Belarus 55°18′ N, 28°13′ E 166
Predazzo, It. 46°18′ N, 11°37′ E 167
Predejane, Serb. and Mont. 42°50′ N, 22°9′ E 168
Predigtstuhl, peak, Ger. 47°40′ N, 12°48′ E 156
Predlitz, Aust. 47°3′ N, 13°55′ E 156
Preeceville, Can. 51°57′ N, 102°40′ W 108
Preetz, Ger. 54°14′ N, 10°17′ E 152
Pregolya, river, Russ. 54°38′ N, 21°24′ E 166
Pregonero, Venez. 7°59′ N, 71°46′ W 136
Pregrada, Croatia 46°10′ N, 15°45′ E 168
Preila, Russ. 55°23′ N, 21°3′ E 166
Preiļi, Latv. 56°17′ N, 26°44′ E 166
Prek Kak, Cambodia 12°14′ N, 105°30′ E 202
Prekovský, adm. division, Slovakia 49°8′ N, 20°7′ E 152
Prelate, Can. 50°51′ N, 109°24′ W 90
Preljina, Serb. and Mont. 43°55′ N, 20°25′ E 168
Prelog, Croatia 46°20′ N, 16°37′ E 168
Premont, Tex., U.S. 27°21′ N, 98°7′ W 92
Prenj, Bosn. and Herzg. 43°34′ N, 17°45′ E 168
Prentice, Wis., U.S. 45°31′ N, 90°19′ W 94
Prentiss, Miss., U.S. 31°35′ N, 89°51′ W 103
Preparis North Channel 14°59′ N, 91°25′ E 188
Preparis South Channel 14°17′ N, 92°20′ E 188
Prepolac, Europe 43°0′ N, 21°13′ E 168
Přerov, Czech Rep. 49°27′ N, 17°26′ E 152
Presa de la Amistad, Mex. 29°23′ N, 101°7′ W 112
Prescott, Ariz., U.S. 34°32′ N, 112°30′ W 112
Prescott, Ark., U.S. 33°47′ N, 93°23′ W 96
Prescott, Can. 44°43′ N, 75°32′ W 94
Prescott, Mich., U.S. 44°11′ N, 83°56′ W 102
Prescott, Wash., U.S. 46°17′ N, 118°19′ W 90
Preseli, Mynydd, peak, U.K. 51°56′ N, 4°51′ W 150
Preševo, Serb. and Mont. 42°17′ N, 21°39′ E 168
Presho, S. Dak., U.S. 43°53′ N, 100°5′ W 90
Presidante Eduardo Frei, station, Antarctica 62°12′ S, 59°5′ W 134
Presidencia Roca, Arg. 26°9′ S, 59°37′ W 139
Presidente de la Plaza, Arg. 26°60′ S, 59°50′ W 139
Presidente Dutra, Braz. 5°17′ S, 44°31′ W 132
Presidente Eduardo Frei, Chile, station, Antarctica 62°12′ S, 59°5′ W 248
Presidente Epitácio, Braz. 21°49′ S, 52°8′ W 138
Presidente Olegário, Braz. 18°25′ S, 46°27′ W 138
Presidente Prudente, Braz. 22°9′ S, 51°25′ W 138
Presidente Roque Sáenz Peña, Arg. 26°47′ S, 60°27′ W 139
Presidente Venceslau, Braz. 21°52′ S, 51°53′ W 138
Presidential Range, N.H., U.S. 44°20′ N, 71°22′ W 104
Presidio, Tex., U.S. 29°32′ N, 104°22′ W 92
Presidio, river, Mex. 23°50′ N, 105°56′ W 114
Presidios, Mex. 25°16′ N, 105°37′ W 114
Presnovka, Kaz. 54°38′ N, 67°9′ E 184
Prešov, Slovakia 48°59′ N, 21°14′ E 152
Prešovský, adm. division, Slovakia 49°10′ N, 21°15′ E 152
Prespa, peak, Bulg. 41°41′ N, 24°45′ E 156
Presque Isle, Me., U.S. 46°41′ N, 68°8′ W 106
Presque Isle, Mich., U.S. 45°19′ N, 83°28′ W 94
Presque Isle, Pa., U.S. 42°9′ N, 80°19′ W 94
Presqu'île d'Ampasindava, Madagascar 13°32′ S, 46°47′ E 220
Pressburg see Bratislava, Slovakia 48°7′ N, 16°57′ E 152
Prestatyn, U.K. 53°20′ N, 3°24′ W 162
Prestea, Ghana 5°25′ N, 2°10′ W 222
Presteigne, U.K. 52°15′ N, 2°60′ W 162
Presto, Bol. 18°55′ S, 64°58′ W 137
Preston, Idaho, U.S. 42°6′ N, 111°53′ W 92
Preston, Minn., U.S. 43°40′ N, 92°6′ W 94
Preston, Mo., U.S. 37°55′ N, 93°13′ W 96
Preston, U.K. 53°46′ N, 2°42′ W 162
Preston City, Conn., U.S. 41°31′ N, 71°59′ W 104
Preston Peak, Calif., U.S. 41°49′ N, 123°42′ W 90
Prestonsburg, Ky., U.S. 37°40′ N, 82°46′ W 94
Prêto, river, Braz. 16°38′ S, 46°44′ W 138
Pretoria (Tshwane), S. Af. 25°48′ S, 28°3′ E 227
Prey Nop, Cambodia 10°39′ N, 103°46′ E 202
Prey Veng, Cambodia 11°29′ N, 105°17′ E 202
Priansus, ruin(s), Gr. 34°58′ N, 25°10′ E 156
Pribilof Islands, Anadyrskiy Zaliv 56°57′ N, 169°25′ W 98
Pribinić, Bosn. and Herzg. 44°37′ N, 17°41′ E 168
Priboj, Serb. and Mont. 42°37′ N, 22°0′ E 168
Priboj, Serb. and Mont. 43°35′ N, 19°31′ E 168
Price, Tex., U.S. 32°7′ N, 94°57′ W 103
Price, Utah, U.S. 39°35′ N, 110°49′ W 90
Price, Cape, India 13°35′ N, 93°8′ E 188
Prichard, Ala., U.S. 30°43′ N, 88°5′ W 103
Pridvorje, Croatia 42°32′ N, 18°20′ E 168
Priego de Córdoba, Sp. 37°26′ N, 4°12′ W 164
Priekule, Lith. 55°34′ N, 21°18′ E 166
Prienai, Lith. 54°38′ N, 23°55′ E 166
Prieska, S. Af. 29°41′ S, 22°43′ E 227
Priest River, Idaho, U.S. 48°10′ N, 116°56′ W 90
Priestly Mountain, peak, Me., U.S. 46°31′ N, 69°30′ W 94
Prieta, Peña, peak, Sp. 42°59′ N, 4°46′ W 150
Prigorodnyy, Kaz. 52°13′ N, 61°19′ E 158
Prijedor, Bosn. and Herzg. 44°58′ N, 16°43′ E 168
Prijepolje, Serb. and Mont. 43°22′ N, 19°39′ E 168
Prilep, Maced. 41°19′ N, 21°35′ E 180
Priluka, Bosn. and Herzg. 43°52′ N, 16°56′ E 168
Prim, Point, Can. 45°58′ N, 63°38′ W 111
Primavera, Braz. 0°57′ N, 47°1′ W 130
Primeira Cruz, Braz. 2°31′ S, 43°25′ W 132
Primero de la Vega, Sp. 36°41′ N, 4°29′ W 164
Primolano, It. 45°58′ N, 11°43′ E 167
Primorsk, Russ. 54°44′ N, 20°0′ E 166
Primorsk, Russ. 60°22′ N, 28°36′ E 166
Primorsko Akhtarsk, Russ. 46°5′ N, 38°10′ E 156
Primošten, Croatia 43°35′ N, 15°55′ E 168
Primrose Lake, Can. 54°46′ N, 110°37′ W 108
Prince Albert, Can. 53°10′ N, 105°46′ W 108
Prince Albert, S. Af. 33°15′ S, 22°2′ E 227
Prince Albert Mountains, Antarctica 75°43′ S, 179°49′ E 248
Prince Albert National Park, Can. 53°40′ N, 106°52′ W 108
Prince Albert Peninsula, Can. 72°24′ N, 124°18′ W 106
Prince Albert Sound 70°23′ N, 110°14′ W 246
Prince Alfred, Cape, Can. 74°7′ N, 132°53′ W 106
Prince Charles Island, Can. 67°18′ N, 84°1′ W 106
Prince Charles's Cave, site 57°26′ N, 6°16′ W 150
Prince Edward Fracture Zone, Indian Ocean 44°27′ S, 35°49′ E 254
Prince Edward Island, Can. 46°35′ N, 62°1′ W 106
Prince Edward Island, adm. division, Can. 46°18′ N, 63°31′ W 111
Prince Edward Islands, Indian Ocean 46°47′ S, 37°53′ E 254
Prince George, Can. 53°44′ N, 122°48′ W 106
Prince Gustaf Adolf Sea 78°44′ N, 105°4′ W 246
Prince of Wales Island, Alas., U.S. 55°18′ N, 135°26′ W 98
Prince of Wales Island, Austral. 11°18′ S, 141°21′ E 192
Prince of Wales Island, Can. 71°17′ N, 103°2′ W 106
Prince of Wales Strait 72°19′ N, 120°33′ W 72
Prince Patrick Island, Can. 75°38′ N, 126°11′ W 106
Prince Regent Inlet 72°52′ N, 90°5′ W 246
Prince Regent Nature Reserve, Austral. 15°39′ S, 124°56′ E 238
Prince Rupert, Can. 54°17′ N, 130°19′ W 108
Prince William Forest Park, Va., U.S. 38°34′ N, 77°27′ W 94
Prince William Sound 60°4′ N, 147°27′ W 98
Princess Anne, Md., U.S. 38°12′ N, 75°41′ W 94
Princess Astrid Coast, Antarctica 71°37′ S, 4°26′ E 248
Princess Martha Coast, Antarctica 75°5′ S, 27°22′ W 248
Princess Ragnhild Coast, Antarctica 70°44′ S, 23°46′ E 248
Princeton, Can. 49°25′ N, 120°32′ W 90
Princeton, Ill., U.S. 41°22′ N, 89°27′ W 102
Princeton, Mo., U.S. 40°23′ N, 93°35′ W 94
Princeton, N.J., U.S. 40°20′ N, 74°40′ W 94
Princeton, Wis., U.S. 43°51′ N, 89°8′ W 102
Princeville, Ill., U.S. 40°55′ N, 89°45′ W 102
Principe Channel 53°21′ N, 130°24′ W 108
Príncipe da Beira, Braz. 12°28′ S, 64°24′ W 137
Príncipe, island, Sao Tome and Principe 1°21′ N, 6°33′ E 214
Prineville, Oreg., U.S. 44°17′ N, 120°50′ W 82
Prins Karls Forland, island, Nor. 78°53′ N, 3°57′ W 246
Prinzapolka, Nicar. 13°22′ N, 83°36′ W 115
Prior, Cabo 43°31′ N, 8°38′ W 150
Priozersk, Russ. 61°2′ N, 30°7′ E 166
Priozerskoye, Russ. 45°15′ N, 44°49′ E 158
Prisaca, Rom. 45°52′ N, 26°47′ E 158
Prislop, Pasul, pass, Rom. 47°36′ N, 24°53′ E 152
Priština, Europe 42°40′ N, 21°10′ E 168
Pritchett, Colo., U.S. 37°22′ N, 102°52′ W 92
Pritzwalk, Ger. 53°10′ N, 12°11′ E 152
Privlaka, Croatia 44°15′ N, 15°6′ E 156
Privodino, Russ. 61°4′ N, 46°34′ E 154
Privolzhsk, Russ. 57°21′ N, 41°17′ E 154

Privolzhskaya Vozvyshennost', *Russ.* 53°31' N, 46°34' E **154**
Privolzhskiy, *Russ.* 51°19' N, 46°6' E **158**
Privolzh'ye, *Russ.* 52°51' N, 48°39' E **154**
Priyutnoye, *Russ.* 46°3' N, 43°20' E **158**
Prizren, *Europe* 42°13' N, 20°43' E **168**
Prizzi, *It.* 37°44' N, 13°26' E **156**
Prnjavor, *Bosn. and Herzg.* 44°51' N, 17°39' E **168**
Prnjavor, *Serb. and Mont.* 44°41' N, 19°23' E **168**
Proberta, *Calif., U.S.* 40°5' N, 122°11' W **90**
Probizhna, *Ukr.* 49°0' N, 25°58' E **152**
Probstzella, *Ger.* 50°32' N, 11°24' E **152**
Proctor, *Minn., U.S.* 46°45' N, 92°15' W **94**
Proctor, *Vt., U.S.* 43°39' N, 73°4' W **104**
Proddatur, *India* 14°44' N, 78°35' E **188**
Prodromi, *Cyprus* 35°1' N, 32°23' E **194**
Progreso, *Mex.* 21°17' N, 89°40' W **116**
Progress, Russia, station, *Antarctica* 69°33' S, 76°34' E **248**
Progresso, *Braz.* 9°47' S, 71°44' W **137**
Prokhladnyy, *Russ.* 43°44' N, 44°0' E **195**
Prokhorkino, *Russ.* 59°30' N, 79°28' E **169**
Prokop'yevsk, *Russ.* 53°53' N, 86°49' E **184**
Prokuplje, *Serb. and Mont.* 43°14' N, 21°35' E **168**
Proletarsk, *Russ.* 46°41' N, 41°35' E **158**
Proletarskiy, *Russ.* 50°46' N, 35°49' E **158**
Prolivy, *Russ.* 67°6' N, 32°14' E **152**
Prolog, *Bosn. and Herzg.* 43°46' N, 16°49' E **168**
Promissão, *Braz.* 18°18' S, 55°40' W **132**
Promyshlennyy, *Kaz.* 51°7' N, 71°35' E **184**
Pronsfeld, *Ger.* 50°9' N, 6°20' E **167**
Prophet River, *Can.* 58°5' N, 122°45' W **108**
Prophet, river, *Can.* 57°34' N, 124°5' W **108**
Prophetstown, *Ill., U.S.* 41°40' N, 89°57' W **102**
Propriá, *Braz.* 10°16' S, 36°52' W **132**
Prorva, *Kaz.* 45°56' N, 53°17' E **158**
Prosek, *Alban.* 41°44' N, 19°56' E **168**
Prosperity, *W. Va., U.S.* 37°49' N, 81°13' W **94**
Prosser, *Wash., U.S.* 46°10' N, 119°47' W **90**
Protection, *Kans., U.S.* 37°11' N, 99°30' W **92**
Protem, *S. Af.* 34°14' S, 20°4' E **227**
Prouts Neck, *Me., U.S.* 43°31' N, 70°20' W **104**
Provencal, *La., U.S.* 31°38' N, 93°13' W **103**
Provence, region, *Fr.* 43°11' N, 5°35' E **165**
Provence-Alpes-Côte D'Azur, adm. division, *Fr.* 43°54' N, 4°52' E **150**
Proves, *It.* 46°28' N, 11°1' E **167**
Providence, *Ky., U.S.* 37°23' N, 87°46' W **96**
Providence, *R.I., U.S.* 41°49' N, 71°27' W **104**
Providence Island, *Seychelles* 9°32' S, 51°7' E **218**
Providence Mountains, *Calif., U.S.* 35°1' N, 115°35' W **101**
Providencia, Isla del, island, *Col.* 13°4' N, 82°8' W **115**
Providência, Serra da, *Braz.* 10°43' S, 61°36' W **130**
Providenciales, island, *Providenciales* 21°54' N, 73°28' W **80**
Provideniya, *Russ.* 64°31' N, 173°8' W **98**
Provincetown, *Mass., U.S.* 42°2' N, 70°12' W **104**
Provins, *Fr.* 48°33' N, 3°17' E **163**
Provo, *Serb. and Mont.* 44°40' N, 19°54' E **168**
Provo, *Utah, U.S.* 40°14' N, 111°38' W **90**
Provost, *Can.* 52°21' N, 110°16' W **108**
Prozor, *Bosn. and Herzg.* 43°47' N, 17°36' E **168**
Prudentópolis, *Braz.* 25°15' S, 50°60' W **138**
Prudhoe Bay, *Alas., U.S.* 70°12' N, 148°22' W **98**
Prud'homme, *Can.* 52°20' N, 105°54' W **108**
Prüm, *Ger.* 50°12' N, 6°24' E **167**
Prüm, river, *Ger.* 50°8' N, 6°17' E **167**
Pruna, *Sp.* 36°58' N, 5°14' W **164**
Prundeni, *Rom.* 44°45' N, 24°14' E **156**
Prusac, *Bosn. and Herzg.* 44°5' N, 17°23' E **168**
Prussia, region, *Pol.* 54°29' N, 19°50' E **166**
Pruszcz Gdański, *Pol.* 54°16' N, 18°36' E **166**
Prut, river, *Ukr.* 48°18' N, 26°2' E **158**
Pryazha, *Russ.* 61°41' N, 33°41' E **154**
Prydz Bay 69°36' S, 73°49' E **248**
Pryluky, *Ukr.* 50°34' N, 32°26' E **158**
Prymors'k, *Ukr.* 46°43' N, 36°17' E **156**
Prymors'ke, *Ukr.* 46°23' N, 35°19' E **156**
Pryor, *Okla., U.S.* 36°17' N, 95°19' W **94**
Pryor Mountains, *Mont., U.S.* 45°17' N, 108°32' W **90**
Prypyats', river, *Belarus* 51°39' N, 29°36' E **158**
Przemyśl, *Pol.* 49°45' N, 22°47' E **152**
Przeradz, *Pol.* 53°46' N, 16°33' E **152**
Przerośl, *Pol.* 54°14' N, 22°38' E **166**
Przeworsk, *Pol.* 50°3' N, 22°32' E **152**
Przytu, *Pol.* 53°22' N, 22°17' E **152**
Psará, *Gr.* 38°32' N, 25°33' E **156**
Psiloreítis see Ídi, Óros, peak, *Gr.* 35°12' N, 24°41' E **156**
Pskov, *Russ.* 57°49' N, 28°22' E **166**
Pskov, adm. division, *Russ.* 57°21' N, 28°27' E **166**
Ps'ol, river, *Ukr.* 49°17' N, 33°25' E **158**
Psunj, peak, *Croatia* 45°22' N, 17°17' E **168**
Ptsich, river, *Belarus* 53°51' N, 27°4' E **152**
Ptuj, *Slov.* 46°25' N, 15°52' E **168**
Pua, *Thai.* 19°14' N, 100°53' E **202**
Puán, *Arg.* 37°35' S, 62°47' W **139**
Puarent', Ozero, lake, *Russ.* 68°44' N, 33°7' E **152**
Pubei, *China* 22°15' N, 109°31' E **198**
Puca Barranca, *Peru* 2°43' S, 73°32' W **136**
Puca Urco, *Peru* 2°22' S, 71°54' W **136**
Pucacuro, river, *Peru* 2°55' S, 75°18' W **136**
Pucallpa, *Peru* 8°25' S, 74°36' W **137**
Pucará, *Bol.* 18°44' S, 64°18' W **137**
Pucará, *Peru* 15°6' S, 70°24' W **137**
Pucarani, *Bol.* 16°24' S, 68°30' W **137**
Pucheng, *China* 34°56' N, 109°34' E **198**
Pucheng, *China* 27°58' N, 118°30' E **198**
Puckett, *Miss., U.S.* 32°4' N, 89°46' W **103**
Pudasjärvi, *Fin.* 65°24' N, 26°52' E **152**
Pudem, *Russ.* 58°18' N, 52°15' E **154**
Pudimoe, *S. Af.* 27°26' S, 24°42' E **227**
Pudino, *Russ.* 57°35' N, 79°26' E **169**
Pudozh, *Russ.* 61°49' N, 36°38' E **154**
Pudu, *Indonesia* 0°25' N, 102°16' E **196**
Puducherry, adm. division, *India* 11°44' N, 79°20' E **188**
Puducherry (Pondicherry), *India* 11°56' N, 79°47' E **188**
Pudukkottai, *India* 10°25' N, 78°48' E **188**
Puebla, *Mex.* 18°59' N, 98°16' W **114**
Puebla, adm. division, *Mex.* 18°51' N, 98°31' W **114**
Puebla de Alcocer, *Sp.* 38°59' N, 5°16' W **164**
Puebla de Don Rodrigo, *Sp.* 39°4' N, 4°38' W **164**
Pueblo, *Colo., U.S.* 38°17' N, 104°39' W **90**
Pueblo Bonito, site, *N. Mex., U.S.* 36°3' N, 108°2' W **92**
Pueblo Mountains, *Oreg., U.S.* 42°14' N, 118°57' W **90**
Pueblo Nuevo, *Mex.* 23°23' N, 105°21' W **114**
Pueblo Nuevo, *Peru* 16°44' S, 72°27' W **137**
Pueblo Nuevo, *Venez.* 11°57' N, 69°57' W **136**
Pueblo Nuevo Tiquisate, *Guatemala* 14°15' N, 91°22' W **115**
Puelches, *Arg.* 38°9' S, 65°56' W **134**
Puente de Ixtla, *Mex.* 18°35' N, 99°21' W **114**
Puente la Reina (Gares), *Sp.* 42°39' N, 1°49' W **164**
Puente-Genil, *Sp.* 37°23' N, 4°47' W **164**
Pu'er, *China* 22°56' N, 101°3' E **202**
Puertecitos, *Mex.* 30°14' N, 114°41' W **92**
Puerto Acosta, *Bol.* 15°34' S, 69°15' W **137**
Puerto Aisén, *Chile* 45°25' S, 72°59' W **123**
Puerto Alegre, *Peru* 8°44' S, 74°14' W **130**
Puerto Alfonso, *Col.* 2°13' S, 71°2' W **136**
Puerto América, *Peru* 4°42' S, 77°3' W **130**
Puerto Ángel, *Mex.* 15°39' N, 96°31' W **112**
Puerto Arista, *Mex.* 15°58' N, 93°50' W **115**
Puerto Armuelles, *Pan.* 8°18' N, 82°51' W **115**
Puerto Asís, *Col.* 0°27' N, 76°32' W **136**
Puerto Aurora, *Peru* 2°12' S, 74°18' W **136**
Puerto Ayacucho, *Venez.* 5°37' N, 67°32' W **136**
Puerto Ayora, *Ecua.* 0°45' N, 90°20' W **130**
Puerto Bahía Negra, *Parag.* 20°12' S, 58°14' W **132**
Puerto Baquerizo Moreno, *Ecua.* 0°57' N, 89°27' W **130**
Puerto Barrios, *Guatemala* 15°42' N, 88°36' W **115**
Puerto Belgrano, *Arg.* 38°53' S, 62°6' W **139**
Puerto Bermúdez, *Peru* 10°19' S, 74°54' W **137**
Puerto Berrío, *Col.* 6°28' N, 74°26' W **136**
Puerto Boy, *Col.* 0°11' N, 74°53' W **136**
Puerto Cabello, *Venez.* 10°27' N, 68°1' W **136**
Puerto Cabezas, *Nicar.* 14°2' N, 83°24' W **115**
Puerto Cahuinari, *Col.* 1°26' S, 70°44' W **136**
Puerto Capaz see El Jabha, *Mor.* 35°12' N, 4°40' W **150**
Puerto Carabuco, *Bol.* 15°44' S, 69°5' W **137**
Puerto Carlos, *Col.* 1°41' S, 71°52' W **136**
Puerto Carlos, *Peru* 12°57' S, 70°15' W **137**
Puerto Carranza, *Col.* 2°38' S, 70°11' W **136**
Puerto Carreño, *Col.* 6°9' N, 67°25' W **136**
Puerto Chicama, *Peru* 7°43' S, 79°26' W **130**
Puerto Coig, *Arg.* 50°54' S, 69°13' W **134**
Puerto Colombia, *Col.* 10°57' N, 74°57' W **136**
Puerto Copal, *Peru* 3°1' S, 74°46' W **136**
Puerto Córdoba, *Col.* 1°20' S, 69°53' W **136**
Puerto Cortés, *Hond.* 15°49' N, 87°56' W **116**
Puerto Cumarebo, *Venez.* 11°27' N, 69°22' W **136**
Puerto Curaray, *Peru* 2°26' S, 74°7' W **136**
Puerto de Lomas, *Peru* 15°34' S, 74°50' W **137**
Puerto de Luna, *N. Mex., U.S.* 34°49' N, 104°37' W **92**
Puerto de Nutrias, *Venez.* 8°5' N, 69°20' W **136**
Puerto de Santa Cruz, *Sp.* 39°18' N, 5°51' W **164**
Puerto Deseado, *Arg.* 47°43' S, 65°55' W **134**
Puerto El Triunfo, *El Salv.* 13°16' N, 88°34' W **115**
Puerto Escondido, *Col.* 9°2' N, 76°15' W **136**
Puerto Escondido, *Mex.* 15°52' N, 97°6' W **112**
Puerto Estrella, *Col.* 12°19' N, 71°20' W **136**
Puerto Francisco de Orellana, *Ecua.* 0°30' N, 77°2' W **136**
Puerto Frey, *Bol.* 14°44' S, 61°10' W **132**
Puerto General Ovando, *Bol.* 9°51' S, 65°39' W **137**
Puerto Grether, *Bol.* 17°14' S, 64°23' W **137**
Puerto Heath, *Bol.* 12°33' S, 68°39' W **137**
Puerto Huitoto, *Col.* 0°16' N, 74°3' W **136**
Puerto Inírida, *Col.* 3°44' N, 67°53' W **136**
Puerto Iradier, *Equatorial Guinea* 1°6' N, 9°43' E **218**
Puerto Jiménez, *C.R.* 8°32' N, 83°19' W **115**
Puerto La Concordia, *Col.* 2°38' N, 72°49' W **136**
Puerto La Cruz, *Venez.* 10°12' N, 64°39' W **130**
Puerto La Esperanza, *Parag.* 21°60' S, 58°3' W **132**
Puerto La Paz, *Arg.* 22°29' S, 62°24' W **132**
Puerto La Victoria, *Parag.* 22°17' S, 57°58' W **132**
Puerto Lápice, *Sp.* 39°19' N, 3°29' W **164**
Puerto Leguízamo, *Col.* 0°11' N, 74°47' W **136**
Puerto Leigue, *Bol.* 14°19' S, 64°53' W **137**
Puerto Lempira, *Hond.* 15°10' N, 83°47' W **115**
Puerto Limón, *Col.* 1°0' N, 76°32' W **136**
Puerto Limón, *C.R.* 9°45' N, 83°4' W **123**
Puerto Limón, *C.R.* 9°59' N, 83°2' W **115**
Puerto Lobos, *Mex.* 30°16' N, 112°51' W **92**
Puerto Lobos (Arroyo Verde), *Arg.* 42°2' S, 65°5' W **134**
Puerto López, *Col.* 4°6' N, 72°59' W **136**
Puerto López (Tucacas), *Col.* 11°56' N, 71°18' W **136**
Puerto Lumbreras, *Sp.* 37°33' N, 1°50' W **164**
Puerto Macaco, *Col.* 2°0' N, 71°5' W **136**
Puerto Madryn, *Arg.* 42°53' S, 64°59' W **123**
Puerto Maldonado, *Peru* 12°39' S, 69°13' W **137**
Puerto Mamoré, *Bol.* 16°43' S, 64°51' W **137**
Puerto Miraña, *Col.* 1°21' S, 70°20' W **136**
Puerto Mirando, *Venez.* 10°46' N, 71°34' W **116**
Puerto Montt, *Chile* 41°29' S, 72°58' W **134**
Puerto Morazán, *Nicar.* 12°50' N, 87°10' W **115**
Puerto Morelos, *Mex.* 20°50' N, 86°56' W **116**
Puerto Mutis see Bahía Solano, *Col.* 6°12' N, 77°25' W **136**
Puerto Napo, *Ecua.* 1°7' S, 77°52' W **136**
Puerto Naré, *Col.* 6°9' N, 74°37' W **136**
Puerto Natales, *Chile* 51°39' S, 72°29' W **134**
Puerto Nuevo, *Col.* 5°43' N, 70°1' W **136**
Puerto Obaldía, *Col.* 8°40' N, 77°25' W **115**
Puerto Olaya, *Col.* 6°29' N, 74°22' W **136**
Puerto Páez, *Venez.* 6°14' N, 67°23' W **136**
Puerto Pardo, *Peru* 12°33' S, 68°48' W **137**
Puerto Patiño, *Bol.* 16°36' S, 65°50' W **137**
Puerto Peñasco, *Mex.* 31°18' N, 113°33' W **92**
Puerto Pinasco, *Parag.* 22°36' S, 57°52' W **132**
Puerto Piracuacito, *Arg.* 28°11' S, 59°10' W **139**
Puerto Píritu, *Venez.* 10°3' N, 65°3' W **116**
Puerto Pizarro, *Col.* 0°16' N, 73°28' W **136**
Puerto Plata, *Dom. Rep.* 19°46' N, 70°41' W **116**
Puerto Portillo, *Peru* 9°46' S, 72°46' W **137**
Puerto Prado, *Peru* 11°11' S, 74°20' W **137**
Puerto Princesa, *Philippines* 9°44' N, 118°45' E **203**
Puerto Príncipe, *Col.* 0°27' N, 75°9' W **136**
Puerto Real, *Sp.* 36°31' N, 6°12' W **164**
Puerto Rico, *Bol.* 11°8' S, 67°35' W **137**
Puerto Rico, *Col.* 2°33' N, 74°14' W **136**
Puerto Rico, adm. division, *U.S.* 18°13' N, 66°29' W **118**
Puerto Rico Trench, *North Atlantic Ocean* 19°41' N, 63°30' W **253**
Puerto Rondón, *Col.* 6°19' N, 71°7' W **136**
Puerto Salgar, *Col.* 5°28' N, 74°38' W **136**
Puerto Salvatierra, *Peru* 3°34' S, 76°31' W **136**
Puerto San Augustín, *Peru* 2°45' S, 71°25' W **136**
Puerto San Julián, *Arg.* 49°17' S, 67°46' W **134**
Puerto Sandino, *Nicar.* 12°10' N, 86°44' W **115**
Puerto Santa Cruz, *Arg.* 49°60' S, 68°33' W **134**
Puerto Saucedo, *Bol.* 14°1' S, 62°50' W **130**
Puerto Siles, *Bol.* 12°47' S, 65°7' W **137**
Puerto Socorro, *Col.* 2°48' S, 69°59' W **136**
Puerto Tejada, *Col.* 3°14' N, 76°25' W **136**
Puerto Tirol, *Arg.* 27°22' S, 59°6' W **139**
Puerto Tres Palmas, *Parag.* 21°43' S, 57°59' W **132**
Puerto Umbría, *Col.* 0°47' N, 76°35' W **136**
Puerto Vallarta, *Mex.* 20°35' N, 105°16' W **114**
Puerto Velarde, *Bol.* 16°31' S, 63°41' W **137**
Puerto Velasco Ibarra, *Ecua.* 1°22' S, 90°33' W **130**
Puerto Villamil, *Ecua.* 0°55' N, 90°57' W **130**
Puerto Villarroel, *Bol.* 16°54' S, 64°49' W **137**
Puerto Villazón, *Bol.* 13°29' S, 61°56' W **130**
Puerto Wilches, *Col.* 7°20' N, 73°52' W **136**
Puertollano, *Sp.* 38°41' N, 4°7' W **164**
Puești, *Rom.* 46°24' N, 27°30' E **156**
Puesto Arturo, *Peru* 1°51' S, 73°20' W **136**
Pugachev, *Russ.* 52°1' N, 48°48' E **158**
Pugal, *India* 28°30' N, 72°49' E **186**
Puget Sound 47°46' N, 123°32' W **80**
Puget-Théniers, *Fr.* 43°57' N, 6°52' E **167**
Puglia, adm. division, *It.* 41°12' N, 15°15' E **156**
Pugŏ, *N. Korea* 42°2' N, 129°58' E **200**
Puhja, *Est.* 58°19' N, 26°18' E **166**
Pui, *Rom.* 45°31' N, 23°6' E **168**
Puig Major, peak, *Sp.* 39°47' N, 2°45' E **164**
Puigcerdà, *Fr.* 42°25' N, 1°55' E **164**
Puigmal d'Err, peak, *Sp.* 42°22' N, 2°3' E **164**
Puig-reig, *Sp.* 41°57' N, 1°52' E **164**
Puiseaux, *Fr.* 48°11' N, 2°28' E **163**
Pujehun, *Sierra Leone* 7°21' N, 11°44' W **222**
Pujiang, *China* 29°30' N, 119°55' E **198**
Pujŏn, *N. Korea* 40°26' N, 127°37' E **200**
Pujŏn, river, *N. Korea* 40°54' N, 127°33' E **200**
Puka, *Est.* 58°3' N, 26°13' E **166**
Puka see Pukë, *Alban.* 42°2' N, 19°53' E **168**
Pukaki, Lake, *N.Z.* 44°7' S, 169°48' E **240**
Pukapuka Atoll (Danger Islands), *South Pacific Ocean* 10°35' S, 167°12' W **238**
Pukapuka, island, *Fr.* 14°46' S, 138°53' W **252**
Pukari, *Russ.* 65°58' N, 30°1' E **152**
Pukaskwa National Park, *Can.* 48°16' N, 88°31' W **94**
Pukatawagan, *Can.* 55°45' N, 101°17' W **108**
Pukchin, *N. Korea* 40°12' N, 125°44' E **200**
Pukch'ŏng, *N. Korea* 40°14' N, 128°21' E **200**
Pukë (Puka), *Alban.* 42°2' N, 19°53' E **168**
Pukeashun Mountain, peak, *Can.* 51°12' N, 119°19' W **90**
Pukehou, *N.Z.* 39°51' S, 176°38' E **240**
Pukekohe, *N.Z.* 37°13' S, 174°53' E **240**
Pukemiro, *N.Z.* 37°38' S, 175°0' E **240**
Pukovac, *Serb. and Mont.* 43°10' N, 21°50' E **168**
Puksa, *Russ.* 62°35' N, 40°20' E **154**
Puksoozero, *Russ.* 62°36' N, 40°34' E **154**
Pula, Capo di, *It.* 38°53' N, 8°59' E **156**
Pulacayo, *Bol.* 20°28' S, 66°40' W **137**
Pulaj, *Alban.* 41°53' N, 19°23' E **168**
Pulap Atoll 7°29' N, 150°1' E **192**
Pular, Cerro, peak, *Chile* 24°12' S, 68°12' W **132**
Pulaski, *N.Y., U.S.* 43°34' N, 76°8' W **94**
Pulaski, *Tenn., U.S.* 35°10' N, 87°1' W **96**
Pulaski, *Va., U.S.* 37°2' N, 80°47' W **96**
Pulaukijang, *Indonesia* 0°42' N, 103°11' E **196**
Pulheim, *Ger.* 51°0' N, 6°47' E **167**
Puli, *Taiwan* 23°52' N, 120°57' E **198**
Pulkkila, *Fin.* 64°16' N, 25°50' E **152**
Pullen Island, island, *Antarctica* 73°2' S, 63°3' W **248**
Pullman, *Mich., U.S.* 42°28' N, 86°5' W **102**
Pullman, *Wash., U.S.* 46°44' N, 117°10' W **90**
Pullo, *Peru* 15°15' S, 73°50' W **137**
Pulog, Mount, peak, *Philippines* 16°35' N, 120°49' E **203**
Pulozero, *Russ.* 68°21' N, 33°18' E **152**
Pulpí, *Sp.* 37°24' N, 1°44' W **164**
Púlpito, Punta, *Mex.* 26°33' N, 111°32' W **112**
Pülümür, *Turk.* 39°29' N, 39°53' E **195**
Puluwat Atoll 6°50' N, 149°57' E **192**
Puma Yumco, lake, *China* 28°40' N, 90°6' E **197**
Pummanki, *Russ.* 69°46' N, 31°53' E **152**
Pumpsaint, *U.K.* 52°1' N, 3°56' W **162**
Puná, *Arg.* 27°47' S, 62°30' W **139**
Puná, Isla, island, *Ecua.* 3°11' S, 80°46' W **130**
Puna, region, *Hawai'i, U.S.* 19°32' N, 155°23' W **99**
Punakha, *Bhutan* 27°37' N, 89°51' E **197**
Punata, *Bol.* 17°35' S, 65°47' W **137**
Punch, *India* 33°46' N, 74°6' E **186**
Punchaw, *Can.* 53°27' N, 123°15' W **108**
Pune, *India* 18°30' N, 73°53' E **188**
Pungan, *Uzb.* 40°47' N, 70°55' E **197**
P'ungch'ŏn see Kwail, *N. Korea* 38°25' N, 125°1' E **200**
Punggi, *S. Korea* 36°51' N, 128°32' E **200**
Punilla, Cordillera de la, *Chile* 29°37' S, 71°36' W **134**
Punitaqui, *Chile* 30°50' S, 71°17' W **134**
Punjab, adm. division, *India* 30°2' N, 74°58' E **197**
Punjab, adm. division, *Pak.* 30°51' N, 71°22' E **186**
Punkaharju, *Fin.* 61°47' N, 29°18' E **166**
Puno, *Peru* 15°53' S, 70°1' W **137**
Puno, adm. division, *Peru* 15°4' S, 70°39' W **137**
Punta Abreojos, *Mex.* 26°44' N, 113°38' W **112**
Punta Alta, *Arg.* 38°49' S, 62°4' W **139**
Punta Arenas, *Chile* 53°6' S, 70°56' W **134**
Punta Cardón, *Venez.* 11°38' N, 70°13' W **136**
Punta de Bombón, *Peru* 17°13' S, 71°46' W **137**
Punta de Díaz, *Chile* 28°3' S, 70°38' W **132**
Punta del Este, *Uru.* 34°58' S, 54°58' W **139**
Punta Gorda, *Fla., U.S.* 26°55' N, 82°2' W **105**
Punta Gorda, *Nicar.* 11°31' N, 83°48' W **115**
Punta Gorda, river, *Nicar.* 11°45' N, 84°16' W **115**
Punta Indio, *Arg.* 35°21' S, 57°18' W **139**
Punta La Marmora, peak, *It.* 39°58' N, 9°14' E **156**
Punta Maldonado, *Mex.* 16°19' N, 98°33' W **112**
Punta Prieta, *Mex.* 28°54' N, 114°21' W **92**
Punta San Francisquito, *Mex.* 28°24' N, 112°54' W **92**
Punta Skala, *Croatia* 44°11' N, 15°8' E **156**
Puntarenas, *C.R.* 9°59' N, 84°50' W **115**
Punto Fijo, *Venez.* 11°41' N, 70°14' W **136**
Puntzi Lake, lake, *Can.* 52°10' N, 124°26' W **108**
Punxsutawney, *Pa., U.S.* 40°56' N, 78°59' W **94**
Puok, *Cambodia* 13°28' N, 103°46' E **202**
Puokio, *Fin.* 64°44' N, 27°16' E **152**
Puolanka, *Fin.* 64°50' N, 27°36' E **152**
Puqi, *China* 29°38' N, 113°51' E **198**
Puquina, *Peru* 16°40' S, 71°11' W **137**
Puquio, *Peru* 14°43' S, 74°9' W **137**
Puračić, *Bosn. and Herzg.* 44°33' N, 18°28' E **168**
Puranpur, *India* 28°31' N, 80°7' E **197**
Purari, river, *P.N.G.* 7°1' S, 144°29' E **192**
Purcell, *Okla., U.S.* 35°0' N, 97°22' W **92**
Purcell Mountains, *Can.* 48°59' N, 116°12' W **108**
Purchena, *Sp.* 37°19' N, 2°22' W **164**
Purdy Islands, *Bismarck Sea* 3°3' S, 144°14' E **192**
Purépero, *Mex.* 19°53' N, 102°1' W **114**
Puri, *Angola* 7°43' S, 15°40' E **218**
Puri, *India* 19°48' N, 85°49' E **188**
Purificación, *Mex.* 19°42' N, 104°39' W **114**
Purikari Neem, *Est.* 59°39' N, 25°21' E **166**
Purmerend, *Neth.* 52°30' N, 4°56' E **163**
Purnema, *Russ.* 64°24' N, 37°21' E **154**
Purnia, *India* 25°45' N, 87°28' E **197**
Purnululu National Park, *Austral.* 17°30' S, 128°16' E **238**
Pursat, *Cambodia* 12°35' N, 103°48' E **202**
Puruándiro, *Mex.* 20°4' N, 101°31' W **114**
Puruê, river, *Braz.* 2°12' S, 68°30' W **136**
Purukcahu, *Indonesia* 0°34' N, 114°29' E **192**
Purulia, *India* 23°20' N, 86°21' E **197**
Purus, river, *Braz.* 9°3' S, 69°52' W **132**
Purvis, *Miss., U.S.* 31°7' N, 89°24' W **103**
Puryŏng, *N. Korea* 42°3' N, 129°41' E **200**
Pusad, *India* 19°53' N, 77°34' E **188**
Pusan see Busan, *S. Korea* 35°6' N, 129°3' E **200**
Pushkin, *Russ.* 59°41' N, 30°21' E **152**
Pushkino, *Russ.* 51°12' N, 46°55' E **158**
Pushkinskiye Gory, *Russ.* 57°1' N, 28°53' E **166**
Pusi, *Peru* 15°30' S, 69°58' W **137**
Püspökladány, *Hung.* 47°18' N, 21°7' E **168**
Püssi, *Est.* 59°20' N, 27°2' E **166**
Pusticamica, Lac, lake, *Can.* 49°19' N, 77°6' W **110**
Pustoshka, *Russ.* 56°19' N, 29°28' E **166**
Pusztamérges, *Hung.* 46°19' N, 19°41' E **168**
Puta, *Azerb.* 40°19' N, 49°38' E **195**
Putahow Lake, lake, *Can.* 59°50' N, 101°15' W **108**
Putao, *Myanmar* 27°23' N, 97°19' E **190**
Putari, Lagoa, lake, *Braz.* 13°3' S, 61°54' W **130**
Putaruru, *N.Z.* 38°3' S, 175°46' E **240**
Putian, *China* 25°26' N, 119°3' E **198**
Putilovo, *Russ.* 59°22' N, 44°35' E **154**
Putina, *Peru* 14°57' S, 69°54' W **137**
Put-in-Bay, *Ohio, U.S.* 41°39' N, 82°48' W **102**
Putla, *Mex.* 17°0' N, 97°56' W **112**
Put'Lenina, *Russ.* 68°28' N, 107°40' E **173**
Putna, *Rom.* 47°52' N, 25°37' E **156**
Putnam, *Conn., U.S.* 41°54' N, 71°55' W **104**
Putnam, *Dem. Rep. of the Congo* 1°25' N, 28°34' E **224**
Putorana, Plato, *Russ.* 68°46' N, 91°28' E **169**
Putorino, *N.Z.* 39°8' S, 177°1' E **240**
Putre, *Chile* 18°14' S, 69°37' W **137**
Putsonderwater, *S. Af.* 29°12' S, 21°50' E **227**
Puttalam, *Sri Lanka* 8°2' N, 79°51' E **188**
Putten, *Neth.* 52°14' N, 5°36' E **163**
Puttur, *India* 12°44' N, 75°12' E **188**
Puttur, *India* 13°27' N, 79°33' E **188**
Putu Range, *Liberia* 5°32' N, 7°50' W **222**
Putumayo, *Ecua.* 9°535' N, 75°53' W **136**
Putumayo, adm. division, *Col.* 0°34' N, 77°9' W **136**
Putumayo, river, *South America* 2°52' S, 73°10' W **122**
Putussibau, *Indonesia* 0°52' N, 112°51' E **192**
Pu'u Kūlua, peak, *Hawai'i, U.S.* 19°31' N, 155°29' W **99**
Pu'u Lehua, peak, *Hawai'i, U.S.* 19°33' N, 155°51' W **99**
Pu'u Maka'ala, peak, *Hawai'i, U.S.* 19°31' N, 155°17' W **99**
Pu'u Mākanaka, peak, *Hawai'i, U.S.* 19°50' N, 155°29' W **99**
Pu'uhonua O Hōnaunau National Historical Park (City of Refuge National Historical Park), *Hawai'i, U.S.* 19°24' N, 155°57' W **99**
Pu'ukoholā Heiau National Historic Site, *Hawai'i, U.S.* 20°1' N, 155°52' W **99**
Puulavesi, lake, *Fin.* 61°41' N, 26°26' E **166**
Puumala, *Fin.* 61°31' N, 28°9' E **166**
Pu'uomahuka Heiau, site, *Hawai'i, U.S.* 21°38' N, 158°6' W **99**
Puvirnituq, *Can.* 60°5' N, 77°15' W **73**
Puxian, *China* 36°24' N, 111°5' E **198**
Puyallup, *Wash., U.S.* 47°9' N, 122°18' W **100**
Puyang, *China* 35°41' N, 114°58' E **198**
Puylaurens, *Fr.* 43°34' N, 2°0' E **150**
Puyo, *Ecua.* 1°36' S, 78°4' W **136**
Puyoô-Bellocq-Ramous, *Fr.* 43°32' N, 0°55' E **164**
Puysegur Point, *N.Z.* 46°21' S, 166°20' E **240**
Pwani, adm. division, *Tanzania* 7°19' S, 38°26' E **224**
Pweto, *Zambia* 8°29' S, 28°52' E **224**
Pwllheli, *U.K.* 52°53' N, 4°25' W **150**
Pyakupur, river, *Russ.* 63°23' N, 73°59' E **169**
Pyalitsa, *Russ.* 66°14' N, 39°28' E **154**
Pyal'ma, *Russ.* 62°24' N, 35°58' E **154**
P'yana, river, *Russ.* 55°26' N, 44°27' E **154**
Pyasina, river, *Russ.* 71°11' N, 90°11' E **160**
Pyasino, Ozero, lake, *Russ.* 69°58' N, 86°36' E **169**
Pyasinskiy Zaliv 73°39' N, 78°4' E **160**
Pyatigorsk, *Russ.* 44°4' N, 43°6' E **158**
Pyatīmarskoe, *Kaz.* 49°31' N, 50°28' E **158**
P'yatykhatky, *Ukr.* 48°24' N, 33°40' E **156**
Pyay, *Myanmar* 18°51' N, 95°14' E **202**
Pydna 168 B.C., battle, *Gr.* 40°22' N, 22°27' E **156**
Pyeongchang, *S. Korea* 37°21' N, 128°23' E **200**
Pyeonghae, *S. Korea* 36°43' N, 129°28' E **200**
Pyeongtaek, *S. Korea* 36°57' N, 127°7' E **200**
Pyetrikaw, *Belarus* 52°8' N, 28°34' E **152**
Pyhäjärvi, lake, *Fin.* 60°59' N, 21°55' E **166**
Pyhäjoki, *Fin.* 64°27' N, 24°13' E **152**
Pyhämaa, *Fin.* 60°56' N, 21°20' E **166**
Pyhäntä, *Fin.* 64°5' N, 26°18' E **152**
Pyhäsalmi, *Fin.* 63°40' N, 25°54' E **152**
Pyhäselkä, *Fin.* 62°24' N, 29°56' E **152**
Pyhätunturi, peak, *Fin.* 66°59' N, 26°56' E **152**
Pyhtää (Pyttis), *Fin.* 60°29' N, 26°33' E **166**
Pyinkayaing, *Myanmar* 15°58' N, 94°25' E **202**
Pyinmanaa, *Myanmar* 19°46' N, 96°10' E **202**
Pyin-U-Lwin, *Myanmar* 22°1' N, 96°27' E **202**
Pylos, ruin(s), *Ionian Sea* 36°56' N, 21°34' E **156**
P'yŏngyang, *N. Korea* 39°1' N, 125°45' E **200**
P'yŏngsan, *N. Korea* 38°20' N, 126°24' E **200**
P'yŏngsan, *N. Korea* 40°36' N, 127°57' E **200**
P'yŏng-sŏng, *N. Korea* 39°13' N, 125°52' E **200**
P'yŏngwŏn, *N. Korea* 39°18' N, 125°37' E **200**
Pyote, *Tex., U.S.* 31°31' N, 103°8' W **92**
Pyramid Lake, *Nev., U.S.* 39°50' N, 120°31' W **80**
Pyramid Mountain, peak, *Can.* 58°52' N, 129°60' W **108**
Pyramid Peak, *Calif., U.S.* 36°22' N, 116°40' W **101**
Pyrds Bay 68°45' S, 74°19' E **255**
Pyrenees, *Sp.* 43°7' N, 1°10' E **165**
Pyrrha, ruin(s), *Gr.* 39°8' N, 26°12' E **156**
Pyryatyn, *Ukr.* 50°12' N, 32°30' E **158**
Pyshchug, *Russ.* 58°52' N, 45°43' E **154**
Pyshma, *Russ.* 56°58' N, 63°13' E **154**
Pytalovo, *Russ.* 57°3' N, 27°52' E **166**
Pýthion, *Gr.* 41°22' N, 26°36' E **156**
Pyttegja, peak, *Nor.* 62°11' N, 7°34' E **152**
Pyttis see Pyhtää, *Fin.* 60°29' N, 26°33' E **166**
Pyu, *Myanmar* 18°30' N, 96°25' E **202**

Qaa, *Leb.* 34°22' N, 36°29' E **194**
Qaanaaq (Thule) 77°32' N, 69°13' W **106**
Qabanbay, *Kaz.* 45°49' N, 80°36' E **184**
Qabb Ilyās, *Leb.* 33°47' N, 35°49' E **194**
Qades, *Afghan.* 34°48' N, 63°26' E **186**
Qāḑub, *Yemen* 12°37' N, 53°50' E **182**
Qā'emshahr, *Iran* 36°30' N, 52°55' E **186**
Qagan Nur, *China* 43°18' N, 112°57' E **198**
Qagan Nur, lake, *China* 43°18' N, 114°17' E **198**
Qagcaka, *China* 32°33' N, 81°52' E **188**
Qahar Youyi Houqi, *China* 41°28' N, 113°11' E **198**
Qahar Youyi Zhongqi, *China* 41°15' N, 112°36' E **198**
Qaharir, oil field, *Oman* 17°55' N, 55°30' E **182**
Qaidam Pendi, *China* 37°41' N, 91°15' E **188**
Qaidam, river, *China* 36°29' N, 97°23' E **188**
Qairouan, *Tun.* 35°40' N, 10°5' E **156**
Qaiyara, oil field, *Iraq* 35°43' N, 43°6' E **180**
Qal 'at al Ḩasā, ruin(s), *Jordan* 30°49' N, 35°53' E **194**
Qala 'en Nahl, *Sudan* 13°36' N, 34°55' E **182**
Qalaa Kebira, *Tun.* 35°53' N, 10°31' E **156**
Qalansīyah, *Yemen* 12°38' N, 53°26' E **182**
Qalat, *Afghan.* 32°8' N, 66°58' E **186**
Qal'at al Aẓlam, ruin(s), *Saudi Arabia* 27°3' N, 35°55' E **180**
Qal'at al Maḑīq, *Syr.* 35°25' N, 36°22' E **194**
Qal'at Bīshah, *Saudi Arabia* 19°59' N, 42°37' E **182**
Qal'at Şahyūn, ruin(s), *Syr.* 35°34' N, 36°0' E **194**
Qal'at Şāliḩ, ruin(s), *Syr.* 35°33' N, 35°59' E **156**
Qal'eh-ye Bar Panj, *Afghan.* 37°32' N, 71°27' E **184**
Qal'eh-ye Now, *Afghan.* 34°57' N, 63°11' E **186**
Qal'eh-ye Saber, *Afghan.* 34°3' N, 69°4' E **186**
Qal'eh-ye Sarkari, *Afghan.* 35°51' N, 67°16' E **186**
Qalhāt, *Oman* 22°40' N, 59°20' E **182**
Qallabat, *Sudan* 12°56' N, 36°6' E **182**
Qalqaman, *Kaz.* 51°57' N, 76°4' E **184**
Qalqīlyah, *West Bank* 32°11' N, 34°58' E **194**
Qaltat Bū as Su'ūd, spring, *Lib.* 27°39' N, 18°13' E **216**
Qalzhat, *Kaz.* 43°32' N, 80°35' E **184**

Qamar, Ghubbat al 15°45′ N, 52°17′ E 182
Qamashi, Uzb. 38°49′ N, 66°27′ E 197
Qamata, S. Af. 31°60′ S, 27°26′ E 227
Qamdo, China 31°10′ N, 97°6′ E 188
Qamīnis, Lib. 31°39′ N, 20°1′ E 216
Qamystybas, Kaz. 46°13′ N, 61°58′ E 184
Qanā, Saudi Arabia 27°44′ N, 41°30′ E 180
Qanawāt, Syr. 32°45′ N, 36°36′ E 194
Qandala, Somalia 11°23′ N, 49°50′ E 216
Qanshenggel, Kaz. 44°18′ N, 75°30′ E 184
Qapqal, China 43°49′ N, 81°18′ E 184
Qapshaghay, Kaz. 43°54′ N, 77°6′ E 184
Qaqortoq (Julianehåb) 60°47′ N, 46°7′ W 106
Qâra, Egypt 29°38′ N, 26°32′ E 180
Qarabey, Kaz. 48°46′ N, 53°2′ E 158
Qarabulaq, Kaz. 44°53′ N, 78°28′ E 184
Qarabulaq, Kaz. 42°32′ N, 69°49′ E 197
Qarabutaq, Kaz. 49°57′ N, 60°7′ E 158
Qaraghandy, Kaz. 49°49′ N, 73°9′ E 184
Qaraghandy, adm. division, Kaz. 48°3′ N, 68°19′ E 184
Qaraghayly, Kaz. 49°20′ N, 75°43′ E 184
Qārah, Syr. 34°9′ N, 36°44′ E 194
Qarah Bagh, Afghan. 33°9′ N, 68°10′ E 186
Qaraoba, Kaz. 47°0′ N, 56°14′ E 158
Qaraqalpakstan, Uzb. 44°49′ N, 56°10′ E 158
Qarasū, Kaz. 52°39′ N, 65°30′ E 184
Qaratal, river, Kaz. 45°59′ N, 77°1′ E 184
Qarataū, Kaz. 43°5′ N, 70°28′ E 184
Qarataū Zhotasy, Kaz. 42°32′ N, 70°38′ E 197
Qaratöbe, Kaz. 49°43′ N, 53°26′ E 158
Qaratoghay, Kaz. 48°24′ N, 84°29′ E 184
Qaraton, Kaz. 46°20′ N, 53°35′ E 158
Qaraūt, Kaz. 48°56′ N, 79°15′ E 184
Qarazhal, Kaz. 48°1′ N, 70°49′ E 184
Qarazhar, Kaz. 47°45′ N, 56°8′ E 158
Qardho, Somalia 9°30′ N, 49°7′ E 216
Qareh, river, Iran 38°31′ N, 47°57′ E 195
Qarghaly, Kaz. 50°18′ N, 57°17′ E 158
Qarn Alam, oil field, Oman 20°59′ N, 57°3′ E 182
Qarokül, lake, Taj. 39°5′ N, 73°10′ E 197
Qarqan, river, China 38°25′ N, 86°14′ E 188
Qarqan, river, China 38°31′ N, 85°47′ E 190
Qarqaraly, Kaz. 49°29′ N, 75°23′ E 184
Qarsaqbay, Kaz. 47°47′ N, 66°37′ E 184
Qarshi, Uzb. 38°51′ N, 65°48′ E 197
Qarṭabā, Leb. 34°5′ N, 35°51′ E 194
Qaryah al 'Ulyā, Saudi Arabia 27°32′ N, 47°40′ E 196
Qaryat abu Nujaym, Lib. 30°34′ N, 15°21′ E 216
Qaryat al Qaddāḩīyah, Lib. 31°21′ N, 15°13′ E 216
Qaryat az Zuwaytīnah, Lib. 30°56′ N, 20°8′ E 216
Qaryat Shumaykh, Lib. 31°21′ N, 13°57′ E 216
Qarynzharyq, desert, Kaz. 42°45′ N, 53°31′ E 180
Qasigianguit (Christianshåb) 68°47′ N, 51°7′ W 106
Qāsim, Syr. 32°59′ N, 36°3′ E 194
Qaskeleng, Kaz. 43°12′ N, 76°39′ E 184
Qaşr al Azraq, ruin(s), Jordan 31°51′ N, 36°46′ E 194
Qaşr al Ḩallābāt, ruin(s), Jordan 32°3′ N, 36°19′ E 194
Qaşr al Ḩammām, ruin(s), Jordan 31°31′ N, 36°8′ E 194
Qaşr al Kharānah, ruin(s), Jordan 31°43′ N, 36°26′ E 194
Qaşr al Mushayyish, ruin(s), Jordan 30°54′ N, 36°5′ E 194
Qaşr 'Amrah, ruin(s), Jordan 31°47′ N, 36°32′ E 194
Qaşr ash Shaqqah, ruin(s), Lib. 30°48′ N, 24°52′ E 180
Qaşr aţ Ţūbah, ruin(s), Jordan 31°18′ N, 36°31′ E 194
Qaşr Bū Hādī, ruin(s), Lib. 31°3′ N, 16°20′ E 216
Qaşr Burqu', ruin(s), Jordan 32°34′ N, 37°48′ E 180
Qaşr Farâfra, Egypt 27°2′ N, 27°58′ E 180
Qaşr Ḩamām, Saudi Arabia 20°47′ N, 45°51′ E 182
Qaşr Ibrîm, ruin(s), Egypt 22°30′ N, 31°51′ E 182
Qaşr-e Qand, Iran 26°11′ N, 60°50′ E 182
Qaşr-e Shīrīn, Iran 34°31′ N, 45°34′ E 180
Qasserine (Kasserine), Tun. 35°9′ N, 8°51′ E 156
Qatar 25°0′ N, 51°0′ E 196
Qattara Depression see Qaţţâra, Munkhafad el, Egypt 29°32′ N, 26°42′ E 180
Qaţţâra, Munkhafad el (Qattara Depression), Egypt 29°32′ N, 26°42′ E 180
Qaţţâra, spring, Egypt 30°10′ N, 27°9′ E 180
Qax, Azerb. 41°25′ N, 46°55′ E 195
Qāyen, Iran 33°44′ N, 59°14′ E 180
Qaynar, Kaz. 49°16′ N, 77°29′ E 184
Qazakh, Azerb. 41°5′ N, 45°21′ E 195
Qazaly, Kaz. 45°49′ N, 62°7′ E 184
Qazaq Shyghanaghy 42°42′ N, 51°45′ E 158
Qazbegi, Ga. 42°38′ N, 44°40′ E 195
Qazımämmäd, Azerb. 40°2′ N, 48°54′ E 195
Qazvīn, Iran 36°18′ N, 49°59′ E 195
Qazyqurt, Kaz. 41°48′ N, 69°27′ E 197
Qeissan, Sudan 10°47′ N, 34°48′ E 224
Qelibia, Tun. 36°51′ N, 11°5′ E 156
Qemult'a, Asia 42°26′ N, 43°47′ E 158
Qena, Egypt 26°12′ N, 32°40′ E 180
Qeqertarsuaq (Disko), island, Qeqertarsuaq 69°31′ N, 62°11′ W 106
Qeqertarsuaq (Godhavn), Qeqertarsuaq 69°15′ N, 53°30′ W 106
Qeqertarsuatsiaat (Fiskenæsset) 63°6′ N, 50°43′ W 106
Qeren Naftali, peak, Israel 33°3′ N, 35°30′ E 194
Qerqenah Islands, Tun. 35°1′ N, 11°13′ E 214
Qertassi see Qirţās, ruin(s), Egypt 23°39′ N, 32°43′ E 182
Qeshm, Iran 26°55′ N, 56°12′ E 196
Qeshm, island, Iran 26°36′ N, 56°3′ E 180
Qeys, island, Iran 26°22′ N, 53°46′ E 180
Qeysar, Afghan. 35°42′ N, 64°14′ E 186
Qezel Owzan, river, Iran 37°3′ N, 48°34′ E 195
Qian Gorlos, China 45°1′ N, 124°48′ E 198
Qian'an, China 44°58′ N, 124°4′ E 198
Qianxi, China 27°3′ N, 106°2′ E 198
Qianxian, China 34°31′ N, 108°15′ E 198
Qianyang, China 27°16′ N, 110°11′ E 198
Qianyang, China 34°38′ N, 107°6′ E 198
Qiaowan, China 40°35′ N, 96°43′ E 188
Qibā', Saudi Arabia 27°22′ N, 44°23′ E 180
Qidaogou, China 41°32′ N, 126°21′ E 200
Qidong, China 31°48′ N, 121°38′ E 198
Qidong, China 26°44′ N, 112°8′ E 198
Qiemo, China 38°12′ N, 85°18′ E 190
Qijiang, China 28°58′ N, 106°38′ E 198
Qikiqtarjuaq (Broughton Island), Can. 67°30′ N, 63°52′ W 73
Qila Ladgasht, Pak. 27°49′ N, 63°0′ E 182
Qila Safed, Pak. 28°58′ N, 61°35′ E 182
Qilian Shan, China 39°14′ N, 96°43′ E 188
Qimen, China 29°51′ N, 117°40′ E 198
Qimusseriarsuaq 75°28′ N, 66°10′ W 106
Qin'an, China 34°51′ N, 105°40′ E 198
Qing, river, China 30°28′ N, 110°40′ E 198
Qing'an, China 46°53′ N, 127°30′ E 198
Qingchengzi, China 40°43′ N, 123°37′ E 200
Qingdao, China 36°5′ N, 120°24′ E 198
Qinggang, China 46°40′ N, 126°7′ E 198
Qinghai, adm. division, China 35°28′ N, 92°33′ E 188
Qinghai Hu, lake, China 36°45′ N, 99°5′ E 190
Qinghe, China 42°32′ N, 124°9′ E 200
Qingjian, China 37°8′ N, 110°11′ E 198
Qingjiang, China 28°1′ N, 115°30′ E 198
Qingshuihe, China 33°42′ N, 97°4′ E 188
Qingshuihe, China 39°54′ N, 111°40′ E 198
Qingtian, China 28°10′ N, 120°17′ E 198
Qingtongxia, China 38°4′ N, 106°3′ E 198
Qingxu, China 37°36′ N, 112°19′ E 198
Qingyang, China 36°2′ N, 107°54′ E 198
Qingyuan, China 42°6′ N, 124°52′ E 200
Qingyuan, China 23°40′ N, 113°2′ E 198
Qinhuangdao, China 39°56′ N, 119°36′ E 198
Qinxian, China 36°45′ N, 112°42′ E 198
Qinzhou, China 21°56′ N, 108°34′ E 198
Qionghai, China 19°14′ N, 110°31′ E 198
Qiqian, China 52°21′ N, 120°47′ E 190
Qiqihar, China 47°21′ N, 123°59′ E 198
Qira, China 37°2′ N, 80°54′ E 184
Qir'awn, Buḩayrat al, lake, Leb. 33°34′ N, 35°35′ E 194
Qirţās (Qertassi), ruin(s), Egypt 23°39′ N, 32°43′ E 182
Qiryat Arba', West Bank 31°32′ N, 35°7′ E 194
Qiryat Ata, Israel 32°47′ N, 35°6′ E 194
Qiryat Gat, Israel 31°36′ N, 34°46′ E 194
Qiryat Mal'akhi, Israel 31°43′ N, 34°43′ E 194
Qiryat Motzkin, Israel 32°49′ N, 35°3′ E 194
Qiryat Shemona, Israel 33°12′ N, 35°34′ E 194
Qishn, Yemen 15°26′ N, 51°39′ E 182
Qitaihe, China 45°49′ N, 130°52′ E 238
Qixia, China 37°16′ N, 120°47′ E 198
Qïyaly, Kaz. 54°11′ N, 69°37′ E 184
Qiyang, China 26°38′ N, 111°48′ E 198
Qızılağac Körfäzi 39°6′ N, 48°36′ E 195
Qizilcha, Uzb. 40°42′ N, 66°11′ E 197
Qizilqum, Uzb. 41°58′ N, 64°9′ E 197
Qiziltepa, Uzb. 40°1′ N, 64°50′ E 197
Qobda, Kaz. 50°8′ N, 55°37′ E 158
Qoghaly, Kaz. 44°25′ N, 78°37′ E 184
Qoghir see K2, peak, Pak. 35°51′ N, 76°25′ E 186
Qom (Qum), Iran 34°39′ N, 50°50′ E 180
Qom, river, Iran 34°17′ N, 50°22′ E 180
Qomolangma see Everest, Mount, peak, China-Nepal 28°0′ N, 86°53′ E 197
Qomsheh, Iran 32°1′ N, 51°51′ E 180
Qonaqkänd, Azerb. 41°3′ N, 48°36′ E 195
Qonggyai, China 29°5′ N, 91°37′ E 197
Qongyrat, Kaz. 46°59′ N, 74°57′ E 184
Qoornoq 64°33′ N, 51°9′ W 106
Qoow, Somalia 11°11′ N, 48°57′ E 216
Qo'qon, Uzb. 40°31′ N, 70°55′ E 197
Qorakül, Uzb. 39°30′ N, 63°51′ E 197
Qorday, Kaz. 43°17′ N, 74°54′ E 184
Qorghalzhyn, Kaz. 50°36′ N, 69°50′ E 184
Qorovulbozor, Uzb. 39°31′ N, 64°51′ E 197
Qorsaq, Kaz. 47°0′ N, 53°18′ E 158
Qorveh, Iran 35°11′ N, 47°44′ E 180
Qoryaale, Somalia 7°28′ N, 49°11′ E 218
Qo'shrabot, Uzb. 40°15′ N, 66°39′ E 197
Qosköl, Kaz. 49°36′ N, 67°3′ E 184
Qosshaghyl, Kaz. 46°54′ N, 53°54′ E 158
Qostanay, Kaz. 53°13′ N, 63°35′ E 184
Qostanay, adm. division, Kaz. 52°2′ N, 60°25′ E 154
Qotanqaraghay, Kaz. 49°10′ N, 85°36′ E 184
Qoton, Somalia 9°30′ N, 50°27′ E 216
Qoţūr, Iran 38°27′ N, 44°23′ E 195
Qoubaiyat, Leb. 34°34′ N, 36°17′ E 194
Qsar Ghilan, Tun. 33°3′ N, 9°35′ E 216
Qsour Essaf, Tun. 35°26′ N, 10°58′ E 156
Qu' Appelle Valley Dam, Can. 50°47′ N, 106°26′ W 90
Quail Mountains, Calif., U.S. 35°39′ N, 117°1′ W 101
Quakenbrück, Ger. 52°40′ N, 7°58′ E 163
Qualicum Beach, Can. 49°20′ N, 124°26′ W 100
Quan Hoa, Vietnam 20°25′ N, 105°7′ E 202
Quanah, Tex., U.S. 34°16′ N, 99°45′ W 92
Quang Ngai, Vietnam 15°7′ N, 108°47′ E 202
Quang Tri, Vietnam 16°44′ N, 107°12′ E 202
Quannan, China 24°41′ N, 114°28′ E 198
Quantz Lake, Can. 51°7′ N, 85°56′ W 110
Quanzhou, China 25°59′ N, 111°4′ E 198
Quanzhou, China 24°58′ N, 118°36′ E 198
Qu'Appelle, Can. 50°32′ N, 103°54′ W 90
Qu'Appelle, river, Can. 50°40′ N, 103°48′ W 108
Quaraí, Braz. 30°25′ S, 56°24′ W 139
Quaraí, river, South America 30°8′ S, 57°11′ W 139
Quartz Hill, Calif., U.S. 34°39′ N, 118°14′ W 101
Quartzite Mountain, peak, Nev., U.S. 37°29′ N, 116°25′ W 92
Quartzsite, Ariz., U.S. 33°39′ N, 114°15′ W 101
Quatsino, Can. 50°32′ N, 127°38′ W 90
Quba, Azerb. 41°20′ N, 48°32′ E 195
Qūchān, Iran 37°4′ N, 58°29′ E 180
Que Son, Vietnam 15°40′ N, 108°13′ E 202
Québec, Can. 46°47′ N, 71°22′ W 94
Quebec, adm. division, Can. 53°50′ N, 76°4′ W 106
Quebracho, Uru. 31°57′ S, 57°52′ W 139
Quebracho Coto, Arg. 26°20′ S, 64°28′ W 132
Quedal, Cabo, Chile 41°11′ S, 75°34′ W 134
Queen Bess, Mount, peak, Can. 51°15′ N, 124°39′ W 90
Queen Charlotte Islands, Hecate Strait 53°6′ N, 132°30′ W 98
Queen Charlotte Sound 51°46′ N, 130°1′ W 108
Queen City, Tex., U.S. 33°8′ N, 94°10′ W 103
Queen Elizabeth Islands, Northwest Passage 76°21′ N, 116°41′ W 106
Queen Elizabeth National Park, Uganda 0°25′ N, 30°10′ E 224
Queen Mary Coast, Antarctica 69°42′ S, 97°55′ E 248
Queen Maud Gulf 67°52′ N, 102°7′ W 106
Queen Maud Land, region, Antarctica 76°48′ S, 8°55′ E 248
Queen Maud Mountains, Antarctica 86°1′ S, 141°33′ W 248
Queen Victoria's Profile, site, Hawai'i, U.S. 21°55′ N, 159°27′ W 99
Queens Channel 75°46′ N, 100°43′ W 106
Queens Sound 51°48′ N, 128°37′ W 108
Queensbury, U.K. 53°46′ N, 1°52′ W 162
Queensland, adm. division, Austral. 23°32′ S, 140°33′ E 231
Queenstown, Austral. 42°3′ S, 145°33′ E 231
Queenstown, N.Z. 45°1′ S, 168°39′ E 240
Queenstown, S. Af. 31°54′ S, 26°45′ E 207
Queenstown, S. Af. 31°53′ S, 26°51′ E 227
Queets, Wash., U.S. 47°31′ N, 124°20′ W 100
Queets, river, Wash., U.S. 47°28′ N, 124°16′ W 100
Queimadas, Braz. 11°2′ S, 39°38′ W 132
Quela, Angola 9°17′ S, 17°4′ E 218
Quelimane, Mozambique 17°55′ S, 36°52′ E 224
Quellón, Chile 43°6′ S, 73°39′ W 134
Quelo, Angola 6°28′ S, 12°48′ E 218
Quemado, N. Mex., U.S. 34°19′ N, 108°29′ W 92
Quemado, Tex., U.S. 28°56′ N, 100°37′ W 92
Quemado de Güines, Cuba 22°47′ N, 80°15′ W 116
Quembo, river, Angola 13°59′ S, 19°30′ E 220
Quemoy see Kinmen, island, China 24°23′ N, 118°32′ E 198
Quemú Quemú, Arg. 36°4′ S, 63°33′ W 139
Quentin, Miss., U.S. 31°29′ N, 90°45′ W 103
Quequén, Arg. 38°31′ S, 58°43′ W 139
Quequeña, Peru 16°36′ S, 71°26′ W 137
Querco, Peru 13°53′ S, 74°52′ W 137
Quercy, Fr. 44°40′ N, 1°10′ E 165
Querétaro, Mex. 20°34′ N, 100°27′ W 114
Querétaro, adm. division, Mex. 20°44′ N, 100°33′ W 114
Quesada, Sp. 37°51′ N, 3°5′ W 164
Queshan, China 32°46′ N, 114°2′ E 198
Quesnel, Can. 52°59′ N, 122°21′ W 106
Quesnel Lake, lake, Can. 52°41′ N, 121°20′ W 108
Quetico Lake, lake, Can. 48°32′ N, 92°24′ W 94
Quetta, Pak. 30°13′ N, 67°5′ E 182
Quetzaltenango, Guatemala 14°50′ N, 91°31′ W 115
Queulat National Park, Chile 44°30′ S, 72°44′ W 122
Queule, Chile 39°18′ S, 73°12′ W 134
Quevedo, Ecua. 1°8′ S, 79°37′ W 130
Quevedo, Península de, Mex. 23°56′ N, 108°18′ W 112
Quévillon, Lac, lake, Can. 49°2′ N, 77°31′ W 94
Quezon, Philippines 9°15′ N, 118°2′ E 203
Quezon City, Philippines 14°43′ N, 121°1′ E 203
Qufār, Saudi Arabia 27°24′ N, 41°40′ E 180
Qufu, China 35°34′ N, 116°54′ E 198
Qui Nhon, Vietnam 13°47′ N, 109°12′ E 202
Quibala, Angola 10°45′ S, 14°58′ E 220
Quibaxe, Angola 8°30′ S, 14°36′ E 220
Quibdó, Col. 5°40′ N, 76°38′ W 136
Quibell, Can. 49°57′ N, 93°26′ W 90
Quiberon, Presqu'île de, Fr. 47°32′ N, 3°9′ W 150
Quicabo, Angola 8°20′ S, 13°47′ E 220
Quick, Can. 54°35′ N, 126°58′ W 108
Quigley, Can. 56°5′ N, 110°55′ W 108
Quiĩama National Park, Angola 9°57′ S, 13°20′ E 206
Quiindy, Parag. 25°60′ S, 57°14′ W 139
Quilá, Mex. 24°23′ N, 107°13′ W 112
Quilán, Isla, island, Chile 43°34′ S, 74°35′ W 134
Quilcene, Wash., U.S. 47°48′ N, 122°53′ W 100
Quilengues, Angola 14°6′ S, 14°3′ E 220
Quill Lake, Can. 52°4′ N, 104°16′ W 108
Quillabamba, Peru 12°50′ S, 72°43′ W 137
Quillacollo, Bol. 17°29′ S, 66°13′ W 137
Quillagua, Chile 21°40′ S, 69°33′ W 137
Quillaicillo, Chile 31°24′ S, 71°37′ W 134
Quillan, Fr. 42°52′ N, 2°9′ E 164
Quilpie, Austral. 26°37′ S, 144°15′ E 231
Quilpué, Chile 33°3′ S, 71°26′ W 134
Quimbele, Angola 6°32′ S, 16°10′ E 218
Quime, Bol. 17°5′ S, 67°18′ W 137
Quimilí, Arg. 27°38′ S, 62°25′ W 139
Quimistán, Hond. 15°22′ N, 88°22′ W 116
Quinault, Wash., U.S. 47°26′ N, 123°51′ W 100
Quinault, river, Wash., U.S. 47°22′ N, 124°9′ W 100
Quince Mil, Peru 13°15′ S, 70°44′ W 137
Quincy, Fla., U.S. 30°34′ N, 84°35′ W 96
Quincy, Mass., U.S. 42°14′ N, 71°1′ W 104
Quincy, Mich., U.S. 41°56′ N, 84°54′ W 102
Quincy, Mo., U.S. 39°55′ N, 91°25′ W 94
Quincy, Oreg., U.S. 46°7′ N, 123°10′ W 100
Quines, Arg. 32°15′ S, 65°48′ W 134
Quinga, Mozambique 15°49′ S, 40°11′ E 224
Quinhagak, Alas., U.S. 59°41′ N, 161°45′ W 106
Quinigua, Serranía, peak, Venez. 4°19′ N, 65°41′ W 136
Quintana Roo, adm. division, Mex. 19°18′ N, 88°58′ W 115
Quintanar de la Orden, Sp. 39°35′ N, 3°2′ W 164
Quinter, Kans., U.S. 39°3′ N, 100°14′ W 90
Quintette Mountain, peak, Can. 54°51′ N, 120°59′ W 108
Quintin, Fr. 48°24′ N, 2°55′ W 150
Quinto, Sp. 41°24′ N, 0°31′ E 164
Quinzau, Angola 6°50′ S, 12°43′ E 218
Quionga, Mozambique 10°37′ S, 40°33′ E 224
Quiquibey, river, Bol. 14°48′ S, 67°39′ W 137
Quiriguá, ruin(s), Guatemala 15°15′ N, 89°10′ W 115
Quirima, Angola 10°49′ S, 18°4′ E 220
Quirinópolis, Braz. 18°35′ S, 50°32′ W 138
Quirke Lake, Can. 46°27′ N, 83°4′ W 94
Quiroga, Arg. 35°18′ S, 61°27′ W 139
Quiroga, Punta, Arg. 42°23′ S, 66°1′ W 134
Quirusillas, Bol. 18°23′ S, 63°57′ W 137
Quisiro, Venez. 10°56′ N, 71°18′ W 136
Quissanga, Mozambique 12°24′ S, 40°30′ E 224
Quissico, Mozambique 24°40′ S, 34°43′ E 227
Quitapa, Angola 10°23′ S, 18°11′ E 220
Quitaque, Tex., U.S. 34°21′ N, 101°4′ W 92
Quiterajo, Mozambique 11°45′ S, 40°27′ E 224
Quitilipi, Arg. 26°53′ S, 60°13′ W 139
Quitman, Ga., U.S. 30°46′ N, 83°34′ W 96
Quitman, La., U.S. 32°20′ N, 92°44′ W 103
Quitman, Miss., U.S. 32°2′ N, 88°43′ W 103
Quitman, Tex., U.S. 32°47′ N, 95°27′ W 103
Quito, Ecua. 0°17′ N, 78°49′ W 130
Quitor, Chile 22°50′ S, 68°14′ W 137
Quitovac, Mex. 31°30′ N, 112°45′ W 92
Quixadá, Braz. 4°56′ S, 39°4′ W 132
Quixaxe, Mozambique 15°16′ S, 40°9′ E 224
Qujiang, China 24°38′ N, 113°34′ E 198
Qulan (Lūgovoy), Kaz. 42°54′ N, 72°44′ E 184
Qulandy, Kaz. 46°6′ N, 59°28′ E 184
Qulbān Layyah, spring, Iraq 29°47′ N, 46°1′ E 196
Qullissat, Qeqertarsuaq 70°3′ N, 53°2′ W 106
Qulsary, Kaz. 46°58′ N, 54°1′ E 158
Qum see Qom, Iran 34°39′ N, 50°50′ E 180
Qumarlêb, China 34°27′ N, 95°24′ E 188
Qumsay, Kaz. 49°27′ N, 58°25′ E 158
Qunayyah, Syr. 34°30′ N, 37°1′ E 194
Quneitra see Al Qunaytirah, Syr. 33°7′ N, 35°49′ E 194
Qŭnghirot, Uzb. 43°1′ N, 58°50′ E 180
Qu'nyido, China 31°18′ N, 97°58′ E 188
Quogue, N.Y., U.S. 40°49′ N, 72°36′ W 104
Quoin Point, S. Af. 35°3′ S, 19°34′ E 227
Quorn, Can. 49°25′ N, 90°54′ W 94
Qurayyāt, Oman 23°16′ N, 58°54′ E 182
Qŭrghonteppa, Taj. 37°49′ N, 68°48′ E 197
Quryq, Kaz. 43°11′ N, 51°41′ E 158
Qûş, Egypt 25°54′ N, 32°44′ E 182
Qusar, Azerb. 41°24′ N, 48°27′ E 195
Quşeir, Egypt 26°8′ N, 34°13′ E 180
Qusmuryn, Kaz. 52°27′ N, 64°37′ E 184
Qusum, China 29°5′ N, 92°12′ E 197
Quthing, Lesotho 30°25′ S, 27°41′ E 227
Quttinirpaaq National Park, Can. 81°58′ N, 73°8′ W 72
Quwo, China 35°40′ N, 111°27′ E 198
Quxian, China 30°51′ N, 106°52′ E 198
Qüxü, China 29°21′ N, 90°39′ E 197
Quy Chau, Vietnam 19°32′ N, 105°7′ E 202
Quzhou, China 36°49′ N, 114°53′ E 198
Quzhou, China 28°56′ N, 118°49′ E 198
Qvareli, Ga. 41°57′ N, 45°48′ E 195
Qyyq, Kaz. 43°46′ N, 70°57′ E 184
Qyzan, Kaz. 44°56′ N, 52°45′ E 158
Qyzylkayyn, Kaz. 45°47′ N, 80°14′ E 184
Qyzylorda, Kaz. 44°49′ N, 65°34′ E 184
Qyzylorda, adm. division, Kaz. 42°40′ N, 66°6′ E 197
Qyzylorda, adm. division, Kaz. 44°54′ N, 61°41′ E 184
Qyzylqaq Köli, lake, Kaz. 53°27′ N, 73°13′ E 184
Qyzylzhar, Kaz. 48°17′ N, 69°38′ E 184

R

Raab, river, Aust. 47°2′ N, 15°40′ E 168
Raahe (Brahestad), Fin. 64°41′ N, 24°27′ E 152
Raanujärvi, Fin. 66°39′ N, 24°41′ E 152
Raate, Fin. 64°47′ N, 29°43′ E 152
Rab, Croatia 44°46′ N, 14°45′ E 156
Raba, Indonesia 8°31′ S, 118°52′ E 192
Rába, river, Hung. 47°26′ N, 17°10′ E 168
Rábahidvég, Hung. 47°4′ N, 16°45′ E 168
Rabai, Kenya 3°54′ S, 39°35′ E 224
Rabak, Sudan 13°6′ N, 32°46′ E 182
Rabast, Cap de, Can. 49°59′ N, 64°15′ W 111
Rabastens, Fr. 43°48′ N, 1°42′ E 150
Rabastens, Fr. 43°23′ N, 0°8′ E 164
Rabat, Mor. 33°53′ N, 7°7′ W 214
Rabaul, P.N.G. 4°15′ S, 152°8′ E 238
Rabbit Ears Pass, Colo., U.S. 40°22′ N, 106°38′ W 90
Rabbit Lake, Can. 53°8′ N, 107°46′ W 108
Rabbit, river, Can. 59°25′ N, 127°17′ W 108
Rabga Pass, China 27°51′ N, 87°33′ E 197
Rābigh, Saudi Arabia 22°48′ N, 39°0′ E 182
Rabrovo, Serb. and Mont. 44°33′ N, 21°32′ E 168
Rabyānah, spring, Lib. 24°16′ N, 21°57′ E 216
Răcăşdia, Rom. 44°59′ N, 21°37′ E 168
Racconigi, It. 44°45′ N, 7°41′ E 167
Raccoon Point, La., U.S. 28°58′ N, 91°7′ W 103
Race, Cape, Can. 46°41′ N, 53°15′ W 111
Race Point, Mass., U.S. 42°3′ N, 70°21′ W 104
Race Point, N.Y., U.S. 41°11′ N, 72°2′ W 104
Race, The 41°11′ N, 72°9′ W 104
Raceland, La., U.S. 29°42′ N, 90°37′ W 103
Rach Gia, Vietnam 10°1′ N, 105°5′ E 202
Raciąż, Pol. 52°46′ N, 20°5′ E 152
Racine, Wis., U.S. 42°42′ N, 87°48′ W 102
Racing, river, Can. 58°36′ N, 125°4′ W 108
Raco, Mich., U.S. 46°22′ N, 84°44′ W 94
Raczki, Pol. 53°58′ N, 22°46′ E 166
Radan, Serb. and Mont. 43°1′ N, 21°22′ E 168
Radashkovichy, Belarus 54°9′ N, 27°14′ E 166
Rădăuţi, Rom. 47°50′ N, 25°55′ E 152
Radcliff, Ky., U.S. 37°50′ N, 85°57′ W 96
Radebeul, Ger. 51°6′ N, 13°37′ E 152
Radford, Va., U.S. 37°6′ N, 80°35′ W 96
Radhanpur, India 23°49′ N, 71°38′ E 186
Radio Beacon, site, Can. 43°55′ N, 60°7′ W 111
Radishchevo, Russ. 52°49′ N, 47°52′ E 154
Radisson, Can. 52°28′ N, 107°23′ W 108
Radisson, Can. 53°44′ N, 77°40′ W 106
Raditsa Krylovka, Russ. 53°17′ N, 34°23′ E 154
Radlinski, Mount, peak, Antarctica 82°22′ S, 102°9′ W 248
Radna, Rom. 46°6′ N, 21°42′ E 168
Radojevo, Serb. and Mont. 45°44′ N, 20°47′ E 168
Radolfzell, Ger. 47°44′ N, 8°57′ E 150
Radom, Pol. 51°23′ N, 21°9′ E 152
Radom, Sudan 9°49′ N, 24°50′ E 224
Radom National Park, Sudan 9°1′ N, 23°41′ E 224
Radomiru, Rom. 44°8′ N, 24°10′ E 156
Radomsko, Pol. 51°4′ N, 19°27′ E 152
Radomyshl', Ukr. 50°29′ N, 29°19′ E 158
Radovići, Europe 42°23′ N, 18°40′ E 168
Radoviš, Maced. 41°38′ N, 22°27′ E 168
Radstock, U.K. 51°17′ N, 2°27′ W 162
Raduzhnyy, Russ. 62°0′ N, 77°39′ E 169
Radviliškis, Lith. 55°47′ N, 23°30′ E 166
Radville, Can. 49°26′ N, 104°19′ W 90
Raḑwá, Jabal, peak, Saudi Arabia 24°32′ N, 38°11′ E 182
Radway, Can. 54°3′ N, 112°57′ W 108
Radziwiłłówka, Pol. 52°22′ N, 23°1′ E 152
Rae Bareli, India 26°13′ N, 81°14′ E 197
Rae Isthmus, Can. 66°53′ N, 90°60′ W 106
Rae, Mount, peak, Can. 50°36′ N, 115°4′ W 90
Rae, river, Can. 68°7′ N, 118°55′ W 98
Rae-Edzo, Can. 62°42′ N, 116°26′ W 106
Raesfeld, Ger. 51°46′ N, 6°51′ E 167
Raetihi, N.Z. 39°27′ S, 175°15′ E 240
Rāf, Jabal, peak, Saudi Arabia 29°12′ N, 39°47′ E 180
Rafaela, Arg. 31°14′ S, 61°27′ W 139
Rafaḩ, Gaza Strip 31°16′ N, 34°15′ E 194
Rafaï, Cen. Af. Rep. 4°58′ N, 23°58′ E 224
Rafalivka, Ukr. 51°18′ N, 25°55′ E 152
Rafḩā', Saudi Arabia 29°41′ N, 43°31′ E 180
Rafsanjān, Iran 30°22′ N, 56°5′ E 196
Raft River Mountains, Utah, U.S. 41°48′ N, 113°46′ W 90
Rafter, Can. 55°38′ N, 101°11′ W 108
Rafz, Switz. 47°36′ N, 8°32′ E 150
Raga, Sudan 8°25′ N, 25°39′ E 224
Raga, river, Sudan 8°11′ N, 25°30′ E 224
Ragachow, Belarus 53°5′ N, 30°9′ E 154
Ragag, Sudan 10°56′ N, 24°45′ E 224
Ragauka, Latv. 56°41′ N, 27°24′ E 166
Ragay Gulf 13°35′ N, 122°30′ E 203
Ragged, Mount, peak, Austral. 33°29′ S, 123°13′ E 230
Raglan, N.Z. 37°51′ S, 174°54′ E 240
Ragley, La., U.S. 30°29′ N, 93°15′ W 103
Raguba, oil field, Lib. 29°1′ N, 18°57′ E 216
Ragunda, Nor. 63°3′ N, 16°23′ E 154
Ragusa, It. 36°54′ N, 14°42′ E 216
Ragusa see Dubrovnik, Croatia 42°38′ N, 18°5′ E 156
Rahad el Berdi, Sudan 11°16′ N, 23°52′ E 224
Raheita, Eritrea 12°43′ N, 43°5′ E 218
Rahib, Jebel, peak, Sudan 17°41′ N, 27°5′ E 226
Rahimyar Khan, Pak. 28°24′ N, 70°18′ E 186
Rahotu, N.Z. 39°20′ S, 173°49′ E 240
Rahuri, India 19°25′ N, 74°38′ E 188
Raíces, Arg. 31°53′ S, 59°14′ W 139
Raichur, India 16°12′ N, 77°20′ E 188
Raiganj, India 25°35′ N, 88°6′ E 197
Raigarh, India 21°54′ N, 83°22′ E 197
Rakiura National Park, N.Z. 47°25′ S, 168°23′ E 240
Railroad Flat, Calif., U.S. 38°20′ N, 120°32′ W 100
Railroad Pass, Nev., U.S. 39°22′ N, 117°25′ W 90
Rainbach, Aust. 48°33′ N, 14°28′ E 156
Rainbow, Calif., U.S. 33°24′ N, 117°10′ W 101
Rainbow Falls, site, Hawai'i, U.S. 19°42′ N, 155°10′ W 99
Rainbow Lake, Can. 58°28′ N, 119°29′ W 108
Rainbow Springs, site, Fla., U.S. 29°6′ N, 82°27′ W 105
Rainer, Minn., U.S. 48°35′ N, 93°21′ W 94
Rainier, Oreg., U.S. 46°4′ N, 122°57′ W 100
Rainier, Mount, peak, Wash., U.S. 46°49′ N, 121°49′ W 100
Rainy Lake, Can. 48°41′ N, 94°17′ W 80
Rainy River, Can. 48°44′ N, 94°34′ W 90
Rainy, river, Can. 48°31′ N, 94°41′ W 82
Raippaluoto see Replot, Fin. 63°13′ N, 21°24′ E 152
Raipur, India 21°15′ N, 81°38′ E 197
Rairakhol, India 21°4′ N, 84°20′ E 188
Ra's, Saudi Arabia 23°33′ N, 38°37′ E 182
Raisduoddarhaldde, peak, Nor. 69°19′ N, 21°11′ E 152
Raisin, Calif., U.S. 36°36′ N, 119°55′ W 101
Raisinghnagar, India 29°31′ N, 73°27′ E 186
Raisio, Fin. 60°28′ N, 22°10′ E 166
Raj Samund, India 25°1′ N, 73°51′ E 186
Raja, Est. 58°46′ N, 26°53′ E 166
Raja, Ujung, Indonesia 3°30′ N, 96°14′ E 196
Rajada, Braz. 8°46′ S, 40°50′ W 132
Rajahmundry, India 17°0′ N, 81°48′ E 190
Rajamäki, Fin. 60°30′ N, 24°44′ E 166
Rajampet, India 14°11′ N, 79°8′ E 188
Rajanpur, Pak. 29°8′ N, 70°21′ E 186
Rajasthan, adm. division, India 26°20′ N, 70°59′ E 188
Rajasthan Canal, India 28°0′ N, 72°30′ E 186
Rajbari, Bangladesh 23°40′ N, 89°36′ E 197

Rajgarh, India 28°38′ N, 75°24′ E 197
Rajin see Najin, N. Korea 42°15′ N, 130°19′ E 200
Rajka, Hung. 47°59′ N, 17°12′ E 168
Rajkot, India 22°17′ N, 70°46′ E 186
Rajshahi, Bangladesh 24°21′ N, 88°33′ E 197
Raka, river, China 29°23′ N, 85°57′ E 197
Rakai, Uganda 0°43′ N, 31°22′ E 224
Rakaia, N.Z. 43°46′ S, 172°0′ E 240
Rakamaz, Hung. 48°6′ N, 21°27′ E 152
Rakaposhi, peak, Pak. 36°7′ N, 74°22′ E 186
Rakaw, Belarus 53°58′ N, 27°2′ E 166
Rakhshan, river, Pak. 26°58′ N, 63°58′ E 186
Rakhyūt, Oman 16°41′ N, 53°18′ E 182
Rakisvaara, peak, Nor. 68°13′ N, 20°6′ E 152
Rakke, Est. 58°58′ N, 26°13′ E 166
Rakops, Botswana 21°3′ S, 24°24′ E 227
Rakoš, Europe 42°46′ N, 20°34′ E 168
Rakovitsa, Bulg. 43°46′ N, 22°27′ E 168
Rakovo, Bulg. 42°5′ N, 22°43′ E 168
Rakow, Ger. 54°2′ N, 13°2′ E 152
Rakula, Russ. 63°42′ N, 41°36′ E 154
Rakulka, Russ. 61°50′ N, 45°19′ E 154
Rakvere, Est. 59°20′ N, 26°19′ E 166
Raleigh, Miss., U.S. 32°1′ N, 89°31′ W 103
Raleigh, N.C., U.S. 35°45′ N, 78°43′ W 96
Ralik Chain, islands, North Pacific Ocean 7°28′ N, 166°35′ E 238
Ralja, Serb. and Mont. 44°33′ N, 20°32′ E 168
Ralls, Tex., U.S. 33°39′ N, 101°23′ W 92
Ralston, Can. 50°15′ N, 111°12′ W 90
Rām Allāh, West Bank 31°53′ N, 35°11′ E 194
Rama, Israel 32°56′ N, 35°22′ E 194
Rama, Nicar. 12°10′ N, 84°10′ W 115
Ramādī Barrage, dam, Iraq 33°39′ N, 42°10′ E 180
Ramage Point 73°23′ S, 115°8′ W 248
Ramah, Colo., U.S. 39°6′ N, 104°11′ W 92
Ramah, N. Mex., U.S. 35°7′ N, 108°29′ W 92
Ramales de la Victoria, Sp. 43°14′ N, 3°30′ W 164
Ramalho, Serra do, Braz. 13°60′ S, 44°39′ W 132
Ramallo, Arg. 33°31′ S, 60°1′ W 139
Raman, Thai. 6°24′ N, 101°22′ E 196
Raman, oil field, Turk. 37°45′ N, 41°29′ E 195
Ramanava, Belarus 53°56′ N, 24°37′ E 166
Ramanuj Ganj, India 23°46′ N, 83°39′ E 197
Ramat Magshimim, Israel 32°51′ N, 35°49′ E 194
Ramatlabama, Botswana 25°38′ S, 25°31′ E 227
Rambau, Lac, lake, Can. 53°39′ N, 70°45′ W 111
Rambouillet, Fr. 48°38′ N, 1°49′ E 163
Rambutyo, island, P.N.G. 2°44′ S, 147°51′ E 192
Ramea, Can. 47°31′ N, 57°24′ W 111
Ramerupt, Fr. 48°30′ N, 4°17′ E 163
Rameshki, Russ. 57°18′ N, 36°1′ E 154
Ramgarh, India 23°35′ N, 85°32′ E 197
Ramgarh, India 27°22′ N, 70°29′ E 186
Ramirez, Isla, island, Chile 51°49′ S, 76°41′ W 134
Rāmis, river, Eth. 8°27′ N, 41°27′ E 224
Ramla, Israel 31°55′ N, 34°52′ E 194
Ramlu, peak, Eritrea 13°22′ N, 41°38′ E 182
Ramnagar, India 25°14′ N, 83°3′ E 197
Ramnagar, India 29°24′ N, 79°6′ E 197
Ramnäs, Nor. 59°46′ N, 16°10′ E 152
Râmnicu Vâlcea, Rom. 45°7′ N, 24°21′ E 156
Ramon′, Russ. 51°52′ N, 39°13′ E 158
Ramon, Har, peak, Israel 30°29′ N, 34°36′ E 194
Ramón Santamarina, Arg. 38°28′ S, 59°21′ W 139
Ramón Trigo, Uru. 32°21′ S, 54°39′ W 139
Ramona, Calif., U.S. 33°2′ N, 116°53′ W 101
Ramonal, Mex. 18°25′ N, 88°34′ W 115
Ramore, Can. 48°26′ N, 80°20′ W 94
Ramos, Mex. 22°48′ N, 101°56′ W 114
Ramos Arizpe, Mex. 25°32′ N, 100°57′ W 114
Ramos, oil field, Arg. 22°41′ S, 64°15′ W 137
Ramos, river, Mex. 25°13′ N, 105°19′ W 114
Ramotswa, Botswana 24°52′ S, 25°47′ E 227
Rampart, Alas., U.S. 65°19′ N, 150°13′ W 98
Ramparts, river, Can. 66°25′ N, 130°46′ W 98
Rampur, India 28°46′ N, 79°3′ E 197
Rampur Hat, India 24°9′ N, 87°48′ E 197
Ramsay, Mich., U.S. 46°28′ N, 90°1′ W 94
Ramsele, Nor. 63°31′ N, 16°29′ E 152
Ramsey, Ill., U.S. 39°8′ N, 89°6′ W 102
Ramsey, N.J., U.S. 41°3′ N, 74°9′ W 104
Ramsey Lake, Can. 47°9′ N, 82°46′ W 110
Ramsgate, U.K. 51°20′ N, 1°24′ E 163
Ramsjö, Nor. 62°11′ N, 15°38′ E 152
Ramu, Kenya 3°50′ N, 41°13′ E 224
Ramu, river, P.N.G. 5°7′ S, 144°53′ E 192
Ramvik, Nor. 62°48′ N, 17°49′ E 152
Rana, Cerro, peak, Col. 3°34′ N, 68°9′ W 136
Ranaghat, India 23°7′ N, 88°35′ E 197
Ranai, Indonesia 3°59′ N, 108°23′ E 196
Ranau, Malaysia 5°57′ N, 116°41′ E 203
Rancagua, Chile 34°11′ S, 70°50′ W 134
Rance, Belg. 50°7′ N, 4°17′ E 163
Rancharia, Braz. 22°14′ S, 50°56′ W 138
Rancheria, river, Can. 60°0′ N, 130°57′ W 108
Ranchester, Wyo., U.S. 44°54′ N, 107°10′ W 90
Ranchi, India 23°22′ N, 85°19′ E 197
Ranchita, Calif., U.S. 33°13′ N, 116°33′ W 101
Rancho California, Calif., U.S. 33°30′ N, 117°11′ W 101
Rancho Cordova, Calif., U.S. 38°35′ N, 121°19′ W 92
Rancho de Caça dos Tapiúnas, Braz. 10°50′ S, 56°2′ W 130
Rancho Mirage, Calif., U.S. 33°43′ N, 116°26′ W 101
Rancho Santa Fe, Calif., U.S. 33°1′ N, 117°13′ W 101
Ranchos de Taos, N. Mex., U.S. 36°20′ N, 105°37′ W 92
Randa, Nig. 9°7′ N, 8°27′ E 222
Randers, Den. 56°27′ N, 10°0′ E 152
Randers Fjord 56°32′ N, 9°59′ E 152
Randijaur, lake, Nor. 66°41′ N, 18°35′ E 152
Randle, Wash., U.S. 46°31′ N, 121°59′ W 100
Randolph, Me., U.S. 44°14′ N, 69°46′ W 104
Randolph, Nebr., U.S. 42°21′ N, 97°21′ W 90
Randolph, N.H., U.S. 44°22′ N, 71°17′ W 104
Randolph, Utah, U.S. 41°40′ N, 111°11′ W 90
Randolph, Vt., U.S. 43°55′ N, 72°41′ W 104
Randolph, Wis., U.S. 43°32′ N, 88°60′ W 102
Randolph Air Force Base, Tex., U.S. 29°28′ N, 98°21′ W 92
Randolph Center, Vt., U.S. 43°56′ N, 72°37′ W 104
Random Lake, Wis., U.S. 43°32′ N, 87°58′ W 102
Randsburg, Calif., U.S. 35°21′ N, 117°41′ W 101
Rånea, Nor. 65°51′ N, 22°16′ E 152
Ranérou, Senegal 15°19′ N, 13°60′ W 222
Ranfurly, N.Z. 45°8′ S, 170°6′ E 240
Rangae, Thai. 6°19′ N, 101°45′ E 196
Rangamati, Bangladesh 22°37′ N, 92°7′ E 188
Rangeley, Me., U.S. 44°57′ N, 70°40′ W 94
Rangely, Colo., U.S. 40°4′ N, 108°48′ W 90
Ranger, Tex., U.S. 32°27′ N, 98°41′ W 92
Rangiora, N.Z. 43°20′ S, 172°34′ E 240
Rangkŭl, Taj. 38°27′ N, 74°25′ E 184
Rangoon see Yangon, Myanmar 16°45′ N, 96°0′ E 202
Rangpur, Bangladesh 25°41′ N, 89°12′ E 197
Rangsang, island, Indonesia 1°1′ N, 103°5′ E 196
Raniganj, India 23°37′ N, 87°7′ E 197
Ranikhet, India 29°40′ N, 79°25′ E 197
Rāniyah, Iraq 36°15′ N, 44°52′ E 195
Rankin, Tex., U.S. 31°12′ N, 101°57′ W 92
Rankin Inlet, Can. 62°50′ N, 92°9′ W 106
Rankūs, Syr. 33°45′ N, 36°22′ E 194
Rann of Kutch 23°59′ N, 69°56′ E 186
Rano, Nig. 11°32′ N, 8°34′ E 222
Ranohira, Madagascar 22°36′ S, 45°22′ E 220
Ranomafana, Madagascar 24°33′ S, 46°59′ E 220
Ranomafana, Madagascar 21°13′ S, 47°23′ E 220
Ranomena, Madagascar 23°24′ S, 47°16′ E 220
Ranong, Thai. 9°54′ N, 98°38′ E 192
Ranongga (Ganongga), island, Solomon Islands 8°5′ S, 156°30′ E 242
Ranot, Thai. 7°48′ N, 100°20′ E 196
Ransiki, Indonesia 1°27′ S, 134°2′ E 192
Ransom, Ill., U.S. 41°9′ N, 88°39′ W 102
Rantasalmi, Fin. 62°2′ N, 28°15′ E 166
Rantau, oil field, Indonesia 4°23′ N, 98°7′ E 196
Rantauprapat, Indonesia 2°6′ N, 99°50′ E 196
Rantoul, Ill., U.S. 40°18′ N, 88°9′ W 102
Rantsila, Fin. 64°30′ N, 25°37′ E 152
Ranua, Fin. 65°53′ N, 26°30′ E 152
Rao, Senegal 15°56′ N, 16°26′ W 222
Raoui, Erg er, Alg. 30°3′ N, 3°41′ W 214
Rapahoe, N.Z. 42°23′ S, 171°17′ E 240
Raper, Cabo 46°54′ S, 77°3′ W 134
Raper, Cape, Can. 69°39′ N, 67°9′ W 106
Rapid City, Can. 50°9′ N, 100°3′ W 90
Rapid City, S. Dak., U.S. 44°3′ N, 103°15′ W 90
Rapid River, Mich., U.S. 45°55′ N, 86°59′ W 94
Rapid, river, Minn., U.S. 48°16′ N, 95°2′ W 90
Räpina, Est. 58°6′ N, 27°27′ E 166
Rapla, Est. 59°0′ N, 24°47′ E 166
Rappahannock, river, Va., U.S. 38°36′ N, 77°58′ W 80
Rápulo, river, Bol. 14°24′ S, 66°30′ W 137
Raqiq, ruin(s), Israel 31°16′ N, 34°39′ E 194
Rara National Park, Nepal 29°29′ N, 81°58′ E 197
Rarotonga, island, N.Z. 21°14′ S, 159°47′ W 241
Ra's Abū Madd, Saudi Arabia 24°44′ N, 37°10′ E 182
Ra's Abū Qumayyiș, Saudi Arabia 24°33′ N, 51°30′ E 196
Ra's al Arḑ, Kuwait 29°19′ N, 48°8′ E 196
Ra's al 'Ayn, Syr. 36°49′ N, 40°7′ E 195
Ra's al Basīt 35°52′ N, 35°13′ E 156
Ra's al Bayyāḑah, Leb. 33°9′ N, 35°0′ E 194
Ra's al Ḩadd, Oman 22°33′ N, 59°46′ E 182
Ra's al Hilāl, Lib. 33°2′ N, 22°7′ E 216
Ra's al Kalb, Yemen 13°55′ N, 48°41′ E 182
Ra's al Khaymah, U.A.E. 25°45′ N, 55°57′ E 196
Ra's al Madrakah, Oman 18°59′ N, 56°39′ E 182
Ra's al Milḩ, Lib. 32°1′ N, 24°56′ E 180
Ra's al Mish'āb, Saudi Arabia 28°9′ N, 48°36′ E 196
Ra's al Qulay'ah, Kuwait 28°53′ N, 48°17′ E 196
Ra's al Unūf, Lib. 30°31′ N, 18°31′ E 216
Ra's 'Āmir, Lib. 33°2′ N, 20°43′ E 216
Ra's an Naqb, Jordan 29°57′ N, 35°32′ E 180
Ra's as Sa'dīyāt, Leb. 33°41′ N, 35°14′ E 194
Ra's ash Shaqq, Leb. 34°19′ N, 35°34′ E 194
Ra's ash Sharbatāt, Oman 17°42′ N, 56°21′ E 182
Ra's aţ Ţarfā, Saudi Arabia 16°55′ N, 41°35′ E 182
Ra's at Tīn, Lib. 32°41′ N, 23°5′ E 180
Ra's az Zawr, Saudi Arabia 27°28′ N, 49°0′ E 196
Ra's Ba'labakk, Leb. 34°15′ N, 36°24′ E 194
Ra's Ḑarbat 'Alī, Oman 16°42′ N, 52°15′ E 182
Rās el 'Ish, Egypt 31°8′ N, 32°17′ E 194
Ras el Ma, Alg. 36°7′ N, 5°31′ E 150
Ras el Ma, Alg. 34°29′ N, 0°48′ E 214
Râs el Mâ, Mali 16°36′ N, 4°38′ W 222
Ra's Fartak, Yemen 15°38′ N, 51°28′ E 182
Rās Ghārib, Egypt 28°21′ N, 33°0′ E 180
Rās Ghārib, oil field, Egypt 27°56′ N, 32°47′ E 182
Ra's Ḩāţibah, Saudi Arabia 21°55′ N, 38°6′ E 182
Ra's Ibn Hāni′, Syr. 35°35′ N, 35°44′ E 194
Ra's Jibsh, Oman 21°28′ N, 58°38′ E 182
Ra's Mirbāţ, Oman 16°48′ N, 54°46′ E 182
Ras Muhammad National Park, Egypt 27°44′ N, 33°47′ E 182
Ra's Musandam, Oman 26°18′ N, 56°29′ E 196
Ra's Shamrah, site, Mediterranean Sea 35°35′ N, 35°41′ E 156
Ra's Shamrah (Ugarit), site, Syr. 35°33′ N, 35°44′ E 194
Ra's Sharwayn, Yemen 15°11′ N, 51°29′ E 182
Ra's Shū'ab, Yemen 12°24′ N, 52°34′ E 182
Ra's Tannūrah, Saudi Arabia 26°39′ N, 50°7′ E 196
Rasa, Punta, Arg. 40°51′ S, 62°17′ W 134
Raseiniai, Lith. 55°22′ N, 23°5′ E 166
Rashaant, Mongolia 45°21′ N, 106°14′ E 198
Rashad, Sudan 11°51′ N, 31°4′ E 216
Rāshayyā, Leb. 33°29′ N, 35°50′ E 194
Rashi, oil field, Iraq 30°9′ N, 47°1′ E 196
Rashīd (Rosetta), Egypt 31°23′ N, 30°21′ E 180
Rasht, Iran 37°15′ N, 49°32′ E 195
Raška, Serb. and Mont. 43°17′ N, 20°36′ E 168
Raška, river, Serb. and Mont. 43°7′ N, 20°35′ E 168
Rasony, Belarus 55°52′ N, 28°50′ E 166
Rasovo, Bulg. 43°42′ N, 23°14′ E 168
Rășcani, Mold. 47°45′ N, 28°37′ E 156
Rasskazovo, Russ. 52°37′ N, 41°49′ E 158
Rastatt, Ger. 48°50′ N, 8°10′ E 150
Rastede, Ger. 53°14′ N, 8°11′ E 163
Rastigaissa, peak, Nor. 69°58′ N, 26°5′ E 152
Rastu, Rom. 43°53′ N, 23°17′ E 168
Rasua Garhi, Nepal 28°18′ N, 85°24′ E 197
Rat, island, Alas., U.S. 51°33′ N, 177°41′ E 160
Rat Islands, Bering Sea 51°41′ N, 174°8′ E 160
Rat Lake, lake, Can. 56°23′ N, 99°38′ W 108
Rat Rapids, Can. 51°10′ N, 90°13′ W 110
Rat, river, Can. 56°8′ N, 99°19′ W 108
Rat, river, Wis., U.S. 45°33′ N, 88°38′ W 94
Rata, N.Z. 39°60′ S, 175°30′ E 240
Rataje, Serb. and Mont. 43°28′ N, 21°7′ E 168
Ratak Chain, islands, North Pacific Ocean 9°43′ N, 169°11′ E 238
Ratamka, Belarus 53°54′ N, 27°21′ E 166
Ratangarh, India 28°3′ N, 74°38′ E 186
Ratanpur, India 22°18′ N, 82°10′ E 197
Ratcliff, Tex., U.S. 31°22′ N, 95°8′ W 103
Rath, India 25°35′ N, 79°34′ E 197
Rätikon, Switz. 46°55′ N, 9°41′ E 167
Ratina, Serb. and Mont. 43°42′ N, 20°44′ E 168
Ratkovac, Europe 42°24′ N, 20°33′ E 168
Ratlam, India 23°18′ N, 75°1′ E 188
Ratnagiri, India 17°0′ N, 73°19′ E 188
Ratne, Ukr. 51°38′ N, 24°32′ E 152
Raton, N. Mex., U.S. 36°53′ N, 104°27′ W 92
Raton Pass, N. Mex., U.S. 36°58′ N, 104°29′ W 92
Ratta, Russ. 63°34′ N, 83°50′ E 169
Rattlesnake Hills, Wash., U.S. 46°30′ N, 120°25′ W 90
Rattlesnake Hills, Wyo., U.S. 42°50′ N, 107°40′ W 90
Rättvik, Nor. 60°52′ N, 15°6′ E 152
Ratz, Mount, peak, Can. 57°23′ N, 132°27′ W 108
Raub, Malaysia 3°47′ N, 101°50′ E 196
Rauch, Arg. 36°47′ S, 59°8′ W 139
Raudal Yupurari (Devils Cataract), fall(s), Col. 0°58′ N, 71°28′ W 136
Raudhatain, oil field, Kuwait 29°51′ N, 47°39′ E 196
Rauer Islands, Indian Ocean 68°54′ S, 74°26′ E 248
Raufarhöfn, Ice. 66°28′ N, 16°5′ W 143
Raul Soares, Braz. 20°7′ S, 42°29′ W 138
Rauma, Fin. 61°7′ N, 21°29′ E 166
Rauna, Latv. 57°19′ N, 25°37′ E 166
Raupunga, N.Z. 39°3′ S, 177°8′ E 240
Raurkela, India 22°14′ N, 84°57′ E 197
Rautas, Nor. 67°59′ N, 19°53′ E 152
Rautavaara, Fin. 63°28′ N, 28°15′ E 152
Rautio, Fin. 64°4′ N, 24°10′ E 154
Rautjärvi, Fin. 61°16′ N, 29°7′ E 166
Ravānsar, Iran 34°43′ N, 46°41′ E 180
Rāvar, Iran 31°12′ N, 56°55′ E 180
Ravelo, Bol. 18°51′ S, 65°36′ W 137
Ravena, N.Y., U.S. 42°28′ N, 73°50′ W 104
Ravenglass, U.K. 54°21′ N, 3°24′ W 162
Ravenna, It. 44°24′ N, 12°11′ E 167
Ravenna, Ky., U.S. 37°40′ N, 83°57′ W 94
Ravenna, Nebr., U.S. 41°1′ N, 98°55′ W 90
Ravenna, Ohio, U.S. 41°8′ N, 81°14′ W 102
Ravensthorpe, Austral. 33°35′ S, 120°1′ E 231
Ravenswood, W. Va., U.S. 38°56′ N, 81°46′ W 94
Ravi, river, Pak. 30°34′ N, 71°52′ E 186
Ravn, Kap 68°9′ N, 28°16′ W 246
Ravna Banja, Serb. and Mont. 42°45′ N, 21°40′ E 168
Ravne, Slov. 46°31′ N, 14°57′ E 156
Ravno, Bosn. and Herzg. 43°50′ N, 17°22′ E 168
Rawa Aopa Watumohai National Park, Indonesia 4°22′ S, 121°38′ E 238
Rāwah, Iraq 34°30′ N, 41°55′ E 180
Rawalpindi, Pak. 33°31′ N, 73°4′ E 186
Rawandoz, Iraq 36°39′ N, 44°31′ E 195
Rawene, N.Z. 35°26′ S, 173°30′ E 240
Rawḑah, Saudi Arabia 19°28′ N, 41°44′ E 182
Rawhide Lake, Can. 46°36′ N, 83°11′ W 94
Rawi, Ko, island, Thai. 6°36′ N, 98°58′ E 196
Rawicz, Pol. 51°36′ N, 16°52′ E 152
Rawley Point, Wis., U.S. 44°7′ N, 87°30′ W 102
Rawlinna, Austral. 30°60′ S, 125°19′ E 231
Rawlins, Wyo., U.S. 41°48′ N, 107°14′ W 90
Rawlinson Range, Austral. 25°29′ S, 127°57′ E 230
Rawson, Arg. 43°16′ S, 65°7′ W 134
Rawtenstall, U.K. 53°42′ N, 2°17′ W 162
Raxaul, India 26°58′ N, 84°48′ E 197
Ray, N. Dak., U.S. 48°19′ N, 103°11′ W 90
Ray, Cape, Can. 47°39′ N, 59°56′ W 111
Raya, peak, Indonesia 0°40′ N, 112°25′ E 192
Rayachoti, India 14°2′ N, 78°46′ E 188
Rayagada, India 19°10′ N, 83°24′ E 188
Rayakoski, Russ. 68°56′ N, 28°44′ E 152
Raychikhinsk, Russ. 49°52′ N, 129°24′ E 190
Rayevskiy, Russ. 54°4′ N, 54°54′ E 154
Raymond, Calif., U.S. 37°13′ N, 119°56′ W 100
Raymond, Can. 49°27′ N, 112°40′ W 90
Raymond, N.H., U.S. 43°2′ N, 71°12′ W 104
Raymond, Wash., U.S. 46°41′ N, 123°44′ W 100
Raymondville, Tex., U.S. 26°28′ N, 97°47′ W 114
Raymore, Can. 51°24′ N, 104°31′ W 90
Rayna, India 23°2′ N, 87°52′ E 197
Rayne, La., U.S. 30°13′ N, 92°17′ W 103
Rayner Peak, Antarctica 67°30′ S, 55°30′ E 248
Raynham Center, Mass., U.S. 41°55′ N, 71°4′ W 104
Rayón, Mex. 29°42′ N, 110°34′ W 92
Rayón, Mex. 21°49′ N, 99°39′ W 114
Rayón National Park, Mex. 19°58′ N, 100°9′ W 112
Rayong, Thai. 12°41′ N, 101°18′ E 202
Rayside-Balfour, Can. 46°35′ N, 81°11′ W 94
Rayville, La., U.S. 32°27′ N, 91°46′ W 103
Raz, Pointe du, Fr. 47°46′ N, 4°59′ W 150
Razan, Iran 35°24′ N, 49°2′ E 180
Ražana, Serb. and Mont. 44°5′ N, 19°54′ E 168
Ražanj, Serb. and Mont. 43°40′ N, 21°32′ E 168
Razbojna, Serb. and Mont. 43°19′ N, 21°10′ E 168
Razgrad, Bulg. 43°33′ N, 26°31′ E 156
Razgrad, adm. division, Bulg. 43°33′ N, 26°7′ E 156
Razhanka, Belarus 53°31′ N, 24°43′ E 158
Razzaza Lake, Iraq 32°54′ N, 42°53′ E 180
Re, Cu Lao, island, Vietnam 15°15′ N, 109°10′ E 202
Readfield, Me., U.S. 44°23′ N, 69°59′ W 104
Reading, Mich., U.S. 41°49′ N, 84°46′ W 102
Reading, Ohio, U.S. 39°13′ N, 84°27′ W 102
Reading, U.K. 51°27′ N, 0°57′ E 162
Readsboro, Vt., U.S. 42°46′ N, 72°58′ W 104
Real, Cordillera, Bol. 17°2′ S, 67°51′ W 132
Real del Castillo, Mex. 31°55′ N, 116°20′ W 92
Realicó, Arg. 35°2′ S, 64°14′ W 134
Ream, Cambodia 10°30′ N, 103°39′ E 202
Rębków, Pol. 51°52′ N, 21°33′ E 152
Rebojo, Cachoeira do, fall(s), Braz. 9°44′ S, 59°8′ W 130
Reboly, Russ. 63°49′ N, 30°47′ E 152
Rebouças, Braz. 25°37′ S, 50°42′ W 138
Rebun, island, Japan 45°31′ N, 139°42′ E 190
Recalada, Isla, island, Chile 53°26′ S, 76°1′ W 134
Recalde, Arg. 36°41′ S, 61°9′ W 139
Recaş, Rom. 45°48′ N, 21°30′ E 168
Recherche, Archipelago of the, islands, Great Australian Bight 34°52′ S, 120°32′ E 230
Rechytsa, Belarus 52°19′ N, 30°26′ E 154
Recife, Braz. 8°4′ S, 34°57′ W 132
Recife, Cape, S. Af. 34°19′ S, 25°42′ E 227
Recklinghausen, Ger. 51°36′ N, 7°12′ E 167
Recoaro Terme, It. 45°43′ N, 11°13′ E 167
Reconquista, Arg. 29°10′ S, 59°39′ W 139
Recreo, Arg. 29°17′ S, 65°6′ W 134
Recsk, Hung. 47°55′ N, 20°7′ E 168
Red Bay, Ala., U.S. 34°26′ N, 88°8′ W 96
Red Bay, Can. 51°44′ N, 56°26′ W 111
Red Bluff, Calif., U.S. 40°11′ N, 122°16′ W 106
Red Cedar Lake, lake, Can. 46°38′ N, 80°30′ W 94
Red Cinder, peak, Calif., U.S. 40°29′ N, 121°20′ W 90
Red Cliff, Wis., U.S. 46°51′ N, 90°49′ W 94
Red Cloud, Nebr., U.S. 40°4′ N, 98°33′ W 90
Red Deer, Can. 52°13′ N, 113°48′ W 108
Red Deer Lake, lake, Can. 52°56′ N, 101°58′ W 108
Red Deer Point, Can. 52°4′ N, 99°51′ W 108
Red Deer, river, Can. 51°41′ N, 115°26′ W 108
Red Devil, Alas., U.S. 61°48′ N, 157°13′ W 73
Red Hill see Pu'u 'Ula'ula, peak, Hawai'i, U.S. 20°42′ N, 156°18′ W 99
Red Hill, site, Va., U.S. 37°0′ N, 78°58′ W 96
Red Hills, Kans., U.S. 37°28′ N, 99°23′ W 90
Red Hook, N.Y., U.S. 41°59′ N, 73°53′ W 104
Red Indian Lake, Can. 48°41′ N, 57°34′ W 111
Red Lake, Can. 51°0′ N, 93°50′ W 90
Red Lake, Can. 50°55′ N, 95°1′ W 80
Red Lake, Minn., U.S. 47°50′ N, 95°1′ W 90
Red Lake Falls, Minn., U.S. 47°50′ N, 96°18′ W 90
Red Lake Road, Can. 49°57′ N, 93°23′ W 90
Red Lick, Miss., U.S. 31°46′ N, 90°58′ W 103
Red Mountain, Calif., U.S. 35°21′ N, 117°38′ W 101
Red Mountain, peak, Calif., U.S. 41°30′ N, 123°60′ W 90
Red Mountain, peak, Mont., U.S. 47°4′ N, 112°49′ W 90
Red Oak, Iowa, U.S. 40°59′ N, 95°12′ W 94
Red Pass, Can. 52°57′ N, 119°3′ W 108
Red, river, Can. 59°17′ N, 128°11′ W 108
Red, river, Can. 49°16′ N, 97°12′ W 90
Red, river, La., U.S. 31°11′ N, 92°26′ W 103
Red, river, Okla., U.S. 33°56′ N, 97°49′ W 80
Red, river, Tenn., U.S. 36°26′ N, 87°15′ W 96
Red Rock, Can. 48°56′ N, 88°16′ W 94
Red Sea 18°15′ N, 39°26′ E 182
Red Sea, adm. division, Sudan 19°37′ N, 35°5′ E 182
Red Sucker Lake, Can. 54°8′ N, 93°38′ W 108
Red Wing, Minn., U.S. 44°32′ N, 92°32′ W 94
Redang, island, Malaysia 5°44′ N, 103°4′ E 196
Redcar, U.K. 54°36′ N, 1°5′ W 162
Redcliff, Can. 50°4′ N, 110°46′ W 90
Redcliff, Zimb. 19°3′ S, 29°47′ E 224
Redcliffe, Mount, peak, Austral. 28°27′ S, 121°20′ E 230
Reddell, La., U.S. 30°39′ N, 92°26′ W 103
Reddick, Fla., U.S. 29°22′ N, 82°12′ W 105
Redding, Calif., U.S. 40°35′ N, 122°24′ W 90
Redding, Conn., U.S. 41°18′ N, 73°23′ W 104
Redditch, U.K. 52°18′ N, 1°57′ W 162
Redeyef, Tun. 34°21′ N, 8°7′ E 214
Redfield, S. Dak., U.S. 44°51′ N, 98°33′ W 90
Redgranite, Wis., U.S. 44°1′ N, 89°6′ W 102
Rédics, Hung. 46°36′ N, 16°29′ E 168
Redig, S. Dak., U.S. 45°15′ N, 103°33′ W 90
Redkey, Ind., U.S. 40°20′ N, 85°9′ W 102
Redknife, river, Can. 60°49′ N, 119°41′ W 108
Redlands, Calif., U.S. 34°3′ N, 117°13′ W 101
Redmon, Ill., U.S. 39°38′ N, 87°52′ W 102
Redmond, Oreg., U.S. 44°16′ N, 121°9′ W 238
Redmond, Wash., U.S. 47°39′ N, 122°7′ W 100
Redon, Fr. 47°39′ N, 2°7′ W 150
Redonda Islands, Strait of Georgia 50°12′ N, 124°55′ W 100
Redonda, Punta, Arg. 41°8′ S, 62°40′ W 134
Redondeados, Mex. 25°51′ N, 106°48′ W 114
Redondo, Port. 38°38′ N, 7°34′ W 150
Redondo Beach, Calif., U.S. 33°50′ N, 118°24′ W 101
Redondo, Pico, peak, Braz. 2°29′ N, 63°33′ W 130
Redoubt Volcano, peak, Alas., U.S. 60°28′ N, 152°55′ W 98
Redvers, Can. 49°34′ N, 101°43′ W 90
Redwater, Can. 53°57′ N, 113°7′ W 108
Redwater, Tex., U.S. 33°21′ N, 94°16′ W 103
Redwood, Miss., U.S. 32°29′ N, 90°48′ W 103
Redwood City, Calif., U.S. 37°29′ N, 122°15′ W 100
Redwood Empire, region, Calif., U.S. 39°43′ N, 123°40′ W 92
Redwood National Park, Calif., U.S. 41°20′ N, 126°3′ W 92
Reed City, Mich., U.S. 43°52′ N, 85°31′ W 102
Reeder, N. Dak., U.S. 46°6′ N, 102°57′ W 90
Reedley, Calif., U.S. 36°35′ N, 119°28′ W 100
Reedsburg, Wis., U.S. 43°32′ N, 90°1′ W 102
Reedsport, Oreg., U.S. 43°41′ N, 124°6′ W 90
Reedsville, Wis., U.S. 44°9′ N, 87°58′ W 102
Reefton, N.Z. 42°7′ S, 171°52′ E 240
Rees, Ger. 51°45′ N, 6°24′ E 167
Reese, Mich., U.S. 43°26′ N, 83°42′ W 102
Reeth, U.K. 54°23′ N, 1°57′ W 162
Reeves, La., U.S. 30°30′ N, 93°4′ W 103
Refahiye, Turk. 39°53′ N, 38°47′ E 180
Reform, Ala., U.S. 33°21′ N, 88°1′ W 103
Refuge Cove, Can. 50°7′ N, 124°50′ W 100
Refugio, Tex., U.S. 28°18′ N, 97°17′ W 96
Regbat, region, Alg. 26°23′ N, 6°14′ W 214
Regência, Braz. 19°40′ S, 39°54′ W 138
Regência, Pontal de, Braz. 19°60′ S, 39°48′ W 138
Regeneração, Braz. 6°16′ S, 42°43′ W 132
Regensburg, Ger. 49°0′ N, 12°6′ E 152
Reggane, Alg. 26°42′ N, 0°8′ E 214
Reggio di Calabria, It. 38°13′ N, 15°40′ E 143
Regina, Can. 50°26′ N, 104°46′ W 90
Régina, South America 4°21′ N, 52°11′ W 130
Registro, Braz. 24°30′ S, 47°48′ W 138
Registro do Araguaia, Braz. 15°45′ S, 51°47′ W 138
Regocijo, Mex. 23°39′ N, 105°9′ W 114
Regozero, Russ. 65°30′ N, 31°17′ E 152
Rehoboth, Namibia 23°18′ S, 17°3′ E 227
Reḥovot, Israel 31°53′ N, 34°48′ E 194
Reïbell see Ksar Chellala, Alg. 35°12′ N, 2°19′ E 150
Reidsville, Ga., U.S. 32°4′ N, 82°7′ W 96
Reidsville, N.C., U.S. 36°21′ N, 79°41′ W 94
Reigate, U.K. 51°14′ N, 0°13′ E 162
Reims, Fr. 49°15′ N, 4°2′ E 163
Reina Adelaida, Archipiélago, islands, Chile 52°7′ S, 78°46′ W 134
Reina, Jardines de la, islands, Caribbean Sea 20°13′ N, 79°3′ W 115
Reinbolt Hills, Antarctica 71°11′ S, 72°8′ E 248
Reindeer Lake, Can. 57°3′ N, 111°32′ W 72
Reine, Nor. 67°55′ N, 13°4′ E 152
Reinga, Cape, N.Z. 34°27′ S, 172°19′ E 240
Reinhardswald, Ger. 51°28′ N, 9°23′ E 167
Reinosa, Sp. 43°0′ N, 4°9′ W 150
Reira, spring, Sudan 15°19′ N, 34°38′ E 182
Reisjärvi, Fin. 63°36′ N, 24°52′ E 154
Reitz, S. Af. 27°50′ S, 28°24′ E 227
Rejaf, Sudan 4°43′ N, 31°33′ E 224
Rekavice, Bosn. and Herzg. 44°40′ N, 17°7′ E 168
Reken, Ger. 51°50′ N, 7°3′ E 167
Rekinniki, Russ. 60°45′ N, 163°30′ E 160
Rekovac, Serb. and Mont. 43°51′ N, 21°6′ E 168
Rėkyva, lake, Lith. 55°51′ N, 23°5′ E 166
Reliance, Can. 62°44′ N, 109°4′ W 106
Reliance, Wyo., U.S. 41°40′ N, 109°11′ W 90
Relizane, Alg. 35°44′ N, 0°33′ E 150
Remada, Tun. 32°21′ N, 10°24′ E 216
Remagen, Ger. 50°34′ N, 7°13′ E 167
Remansão, Braz. 4°28′ S, 49°35′ W 130
Remanso, Braz. 9°34′ S, 42°8′ W 132
Remarkables, The, peak, N.Z. 45°6′ S, 168°45′ E 240
Remate de Males, Braz. 4°25′ S, 70°13′ W 130
Remecó, Arg. 37°39′ S, 63°37′ W 139
Remer, Minn., U.S. 47°2′ N, 93°56′ W 90
Remeshk, Iran 26°48′ N, 58°51′ E 196
Remich, Lux. 49°33′ N, 6°21′ E 163
Remington, Ind., U.S. 40°45′ N, 87°10′ W 102
Rémire, South America 4°54′ N, 52°17′ W 130
Remmel Mountain, peak, Wash., U.S. 48°54′ N, 120°17′ W 90
Remontnoye, Russ. 46°30′ N, 43°34′ E 158
Remscheid, Ger. 51°10′ N, 7°11′ E 167
Remus, Mich., U.S. 43°36′ N, 85°9′ W 102
Rena, Nor. 61°8′ N, 11°19′ E 152
Renascença, Braz. 3°51′ S, 66°30′ W 130
Renaud Island, Antarctica 65°34′ S, 68°9′ W 134
Renca, Arg. 32°47′ S, 65°19′ W 134
Rencēni, Latv. 57°43′ N, 25°23′ E 166
Renda, Latv. 57°3′ N, 22°15′ E 166
Rendakoma, Eth. 14°25′ N, 40°2′ E 182
Rendova, island, Solomon Islands 8°35′ S, 157°15′ E 242
Renfrew, Can. 45°28′ N, 76°43′ W 94
Rengat, Indonesia 0°23′ N, 102°30′ E 196
Renholmen, Nor. 65°0′ N, 21°20′ E 152
Renhuai, China 27°46′ N, 106°24′ E 198
Reni, India 28°40′ N, 75°4′ E 186
Renison, Can. 50°58′ N, 81°9′ W 110
Renk, Sudan 11°44′ N, 32°48′ E 182
Renko, Fin. 60°53′ N, 24°16′ E 166
Rennell, island, Solomon Islands 11°41′ S, 160°19′ E 242
Rennell Sound 53°18′ N, 132°59′ W 108
Rennerod, Ger. 50°36′ N, 8°3′ E 167
Rennes, Fr. 48°6′ N, 1°42′ W 150
Reno, Nev., U.S. 39°32′ N, 119°50′ W 90
Reno, river, It. 44°34′ N, 11°58′ E 167
Rensselaer, Ind., U.S. 40°56′ N, 87°10′ W 102
Rensselaer, N.Y., U.S. 42°37′ N, 73°45′ W 104
Rentería, Sp. 43°17′ N, 1°54′ W 164
Renton, Wash., U.S. 47°28′ N, 122°14′ W 100
Renville, Minn., U.S. 44°46′ N, 95°13′ W 90
Reo, Indonesia 8°26′ S, 120°26′ E 192
Répcelak, Hung. 47°25′ N, 17°1′ E 168
Repino, Russ. 60°10′ N, 29°52′ E 166
Replot (Raippaluoto), Fin. 63°13′ N, 21°24′ E 152
Repossaari, Fin. 61°36′ N, 21°25′ E 166
Repparfjord, Nor. 70°26′ N, 24°19′ E 152
Republic, Mich., U.S. 46°24′ N, 87°58′ W 94
Republic, Ohio, U.S. 41°6′ N, 83°1′ W 102

Republican, river, Nebr., U.S. 40°17' N, 100°48' W 80
Repulse Bay, Can. 66°39' N, 86°29' W 73
Requa, Calif., U.S. 41°32' N, 124°4' W 90
Requena, Peru 5°5' S, 73°50' W 130
Requena, Sp. 39°30' N, 1°7' W 164
Requeña, Venez. 7°58' N, 65°33' W 136
Reşadiye, Turk. 40°23' N, 37°19' E 156
Resavica, Serb. and Mont. 44°1' N, 21°34' E 168
Rescue, Punta, Chile 46°16' S, 76°41' W 134
Resende, Braz. 22°29' S, 44°22' W 138
Reserva, Braz. 24°41' S, 50°55' W 138
Reserve, N. Mex., U.S. 33°41' N, 108°46' W 92
Reshadat, oil field, Persian Gulf 25°57' N, 52°43' E 196
Reshety, Russ. 57°8' N, 28°27' E 166
Resia, It. 46°49' N, 10°32' E 167
Resistencia, Arg. 27°27' S, 59°2' W 139
Reşiţa, Rom. 45°18' N, 21°53' E 168
Resolute, Can. 74°39' N, 94°58' W 73
Resolution Island, Can. 61°20' N, 64°59' W 106
Restigouche, Can. 48°1' N, 66°43' W 94
Reston, Can. 49°32' N, 101°7' W 90
Restrepo, Col. 4°14' N, 73°34' W 136
Reszel, Pol. 54°2' N, 21°8' E 166
Retalhuleu, Guatemala 14°32' N, 91°40' W 115
Retezat, Munţii, Rom. 45°19' N, 22°47' E 168
Rethel, Fr. 49°30' N, 4°21' E 163
Rethondes, Fr. 49°24' N, 2°56' E 163
Reti, Pak. 28°4' N, 69°49' E 186
Retno, Russ. 57°59' N, 30°12' E 166
Rétság, Hung. 47°54' N, 19°9' E 168
Return Point, Antarctica 60°50' S, 47°56' W 134
Réunion, island, Fr. 21°9' S, 55°35' E 254
Reus, Sp. 41°8' N, 1°6' E 164
Reva, S. Dak., U.S. 45°32' N, 103°6' W 90
Reval see Tallinn, Est. 59°23' N, 24°37' E 166
Revda, Russ. 67°58' N, 34°30' E 152
Revda, Russ. 56°47' N, 59°56' E 154
Reveille Peak, Nev., U.S. 37°50' N, 116°13' W 90
Revelle Inlet 68°43' S, 66°33' W 248
Revelstoke, Can. 51°0' N, 118°12' W 90
Révfülöp, Hung. 46°50' N, 17°38' E 168
Revigny, Fr. 48°50' N, 4°59' E 163
Revillagigedo, Islas, islands, North Pacific Ocean 18°28' N, 113°41' W 112
Revin, Fr. 49°55' N, 4°38' E 163
Revivim, Israel 31°1' N, 34°43' E 194
Rewa, India 24°31' N, 81°19' E 197
Rex, Mount, peak, Antarctica 74°52' S, 76°39' W 248
Rexburg, Idaho, U.S. 43°49' N, 111°48' W 90
Rexford, Mont., U.S. 48°52' N, 115°10' W 90
Rexton, Mich., U.S. 46°9' N, 85°15' W 110
Rey, Iran 35°34' N, 51°30' E 180
Rey Bouba, Cameroon 8°38' N, 14°12' E 218
Rey, Isla del, island, Pan. 8°7' N, 79°3' W 115
Rey, river, Cameroon 8°10' N, 14°26' E 218
Reyes, Bol. 14°22' S, 67°25' W 137
Reyes, Point 38°2' N, 123°22' W 90
Reyes, Punta, Col. 2°40' N, 78°24' W 136
Reykjanes Ridge, North Atlantic Ocean 59°58' N, 29°41' W 253
Reykjavík, Ice. 64°4' N, 22°23' W 246
Reynoldsburg, Ohio, U.S. 39°56' N, 82°49' W 102
Rēzekne, Latv. 56°29' N, 27°19' E 166
Rezh, Russ. 57°23' N, 61°22' E 154
Rezh, river, Russ. 57°26' N, 60°57' E 154
Rezovo, Bulg. 41°59' N, 28°1' E 156
Rgotina, Serb. and Mont. 44°0' N, 22°16' E 168
Rhaetian Alps, Switz. 46°22' N, 9°21' E 167
Rhafsaï, Mor. 34°39' N, 4°55' W 214
Rhame, N. Dak., U.S. 46°13' N, 103°40' W 90
Rhamnus, ruin(s), Gr. 38°12' N, 23°56' E 156
Rhayader, U.K. 52°17' N, 3°31' W 162
Rheda-Wiedenbrück, Ger. 51°51' N, 8°17' E 167
Rhede, Ger. 51°50' N, 6°42' E 167
Rheden, Neth. 52°0' N, 6°3' E 167
Rhein, river, Ger. 51°47' N, 6°15' E 167
Rheinbach, Ger. 50°37' N, 6°57' E 167
Rheinbrohl, Ger. 50°29' N, 7°21' E 167
Rheine, Ger. 52°16' N, 7°26' E 163
Rheinland-Palatinate, adm. division, Ger. 49°50' N, 6°34' E 150
Rhemilès, spring, Alg. 28°28' N, 4°22' W 214
Rhens, Ger. 50°16' N, 7°37' E 167
Rheydt, Ger. 51°9' N, 6°26' E 167
Rhinebeck, N.Y., U.S. 41°55' N, 73°55' W 104
Rhinelander, Wis., U.S. 45°38' N, 89°23' W 94
Rhineland-Palatinate, adm. division, Ger. 50°15' N, 6°36' E 167
Rhino Camp, Uganda 2°58' N, 31°23' E 224
Rhinocolura see El 'Arîsh, Egypt 31°6' N, 33°46' E 194
Rhiou, river, Alg. 35°59' N, 0°58' E 150
Rhir, Cap, Mor. 30°41' N, 10°44' W 214
Rho, It. 45°32' N, 9°1' E 167
Rhode Island, adm. division, R.I., U.S. 41°45' N, 71°46' W 104
Rhode Island Sound 41°14' N, 71°13' W 104
Rhodes Peak, Idaho, U.S. 46°38' N, 114°53' W 90
Rhodes see Ródos, Gr. 36°25' N, 28°13' E 156
Rhodes see Ródos, adm. division, Gr. 35°58' N, 27°21' E 156
Rhodes see Ródos, island, Gr. 35°44' N, 27°53' E 156
Rhodope Mountains, Bulg. 41°50' N, 23°44' E 156
Rhön, Ger. 50°36' N, 9°54' E 167
Rhône, river, Europe 46°10' N, 7°16' E 165
Rhône-Alpes, adm. division, Fr. 45°24' N, 5°32' E 156
Rhône-Alpes, adm. division, Fr. 45°41' N, 4°23' E 150
Rhourd el Baguel, oil field, Alg. 31°25' N, 6°40' E 214
Rhyl, U.K. 53°18' N, 3°29' W 162
Riachão, Braz. 7°22' S, 46°41' W 130
Riacho de Santana, Braz. 13°37' S, 42°59' W 138
Riachos, Isla de los, island, Arg. 40°12' S, 62°5' W 134
Rialma, Braz. 15°21' S, 49°34' W 138
Rialto, Calif., U.S. 34°6' N, 117°23' W 101
Rianápolis, Braz. 15°31' S, 49°28' W 138
Riangnom, Sudan 9°53' N, 30°1' E 224
Riaño, Sp. 42°57' N, 5°2' W 150
Riasi, India 33°4' N, 74°51' E 186
Riau, Kepulauan, islands, South China Sea 0°25' N, 103°59' E 196
Riaza, Sp. 41°16' N, 3°29' W 164
Rib Lake, Wis., U.S. 45°19' N, 90°13' W 94
Rib Mountain, peak, Wis., U.S. 44°54' N, 89°47' W 94
Riba de Saelices, Sp. 40°54' N, 2°18' W 164
Ribadavia, Sp. 42°16' N, 8°11' W 150
Ribadeo, Sp. 43°31' N, 7°4' W 150
Riba-roja d'Ebre, Sp. 41°13' N, 0°28' E 164
Ribarska Banja, Serb. and Mont. 43°25' N, 21°32' E 168
Ribas do Rio Pardo, Braz. 20°27' S, 53°49' W 132
Ribáuè, Mozambique 14°57' S, 38°21' E 220
Ribe, Den. 55°19' N, 8°45' E 150
Ribécourt-Dreslincourt, Fr. 49°30' N, 2°55' E 163
Ribeira, Braz. 24°41' S, 48°60' W 138
Ribeira do Pombal, Braz. 10°49' S, 38°34' W 132
Ribeira, river, Braz. 24°43' S, 48°18' W 138
Ribeirão, Braz. 8°30' S, 35°20' W 132
Ribeirão do Salto, Braz. 15°48' S, 40°17' W 138
Ribeirão Preto, Braz. 21°11' S, 47°50' W 138
Ribemont, Fr. 49°47' N, 3°27' E 163
Riberalta, Bol. 11°2' S, 66°7' W 137
Ribes de Freser, Sp. 42°18' N, 2°9' E 164
Riblah, Syr. 34°27' N, 36°33' E 194
Rîbniţa, Mold. 47°44' N, 29°0' E 156
Ricardo Flores Magón, Mex. 29°56' N, 106°58' W 92
Ricaurte, Col. 1°10' S, 70°14' W 136
Riccione, It. 43°58' N, 12°38' E 167
Rice Lake, Wis., U.S. 45°30' N, 91°45' W 94
Rice Mountain, peak, N.H., U.S. 44°50' N, 71°20' W 94
Rice Valley, Calif., U.S. 34°1' N, 114°52' W 101
Rich, Mor. 32°20' N, 4°31' W 214
Rich Creek, Va., U.S. 37°22' N, 80°50' W 96
Rich Hill, Mo., U.S. 38°4' N, 94°22' W 94
Richan, Can. 49°59' N, 92°49' W 94
Richard Collinson Inlet 72°42' N, 114°48' W 106
Richard Toll, Senegal 16°28' N, 15°44' W 222
Richards Island, Can. 69°12' N, 136°58' W 98
Richardson Lake, Can. 58°18' N, 111°58' W 108
Richardson Mountains, Can. 68°35' N, 136°39' W 98
Richardson, river, Can. 58°6' N, 110°60' W 108
Richardton, N. Dak., U.S. 46°52' N, 102°20' W 90
Riche, Pointe, Can. 50°43' N, 58°9' W 111
Richey, Mont., U.S. 47°37' N, 105°6' W 90
Richfield, Utah, U.S. 38°46' N, 112°5' W 92
Richford, Vt., U.S. 44°59' N, 72°41' W 94
Richgrove, Calif., U.S. 35°48' N, 119°7' W 101
Richibucto, Can. 46°40' N, 64°53' W 111
Richland, Wash., U.S. 46°21' N, 119°20' W 246
Richland Center, Wis., U.S. 43°19' N, 90°23' W 94
Richland Springs, Tex., U.S. 31°15' N, 98°57' W 92
Richlands, Va., U.S. 37°5' N, 81°49' W 94
Richmond, Austral. 33°37' S, 150°48' E 231
Richmond, Calif., U.S. 37°56' N, 122°21' W 100
Richmond, Can. 45°39' N, 72°8' W 111
Richmond, Can. 49°9' N, 123°10' W 100
Richmond, Ill., U.S. 42°28' N, 88°18' W 102
Richmond, Ind., U.S. 39°48' N, 84°52' W 102
Richmond, Ky., U.S. 37°43' N, 84°18' W 96
Richmond, Me., U.S. 44°5' N, 69°49' W 104
Richmond, Mass., U.S. 42°21' N, 73°23' W 104
Richmond, Mo., U.S. 39°16' N, 93°58' W 94
Richmond, Mo., U.S. 42°28' N, 88°18' W 94
Richmond, N.H., U.S. 42°44' N, 72°17' W 104
Richmond, S. Af. 29°54' S, 30°15' E 227
Richmond, S. Af. 31°26' S, 23°56' E 227
Richmond, U.K. 54°24' N, 1°45' W 162
Richmond, Vt., U.S. 44°24' N, 72°60' W 104
Richmond, Va., U.S. 37°30' N, 77°33' W 96
Richmond Dale, Ohio, U.S. 39°12' N, 82°49' W 102
Richmond Hill, Can. 43°53' N, 79°26' W 94
Richtersveld National Park, S. Af. 28°14' S, 16°16' E 227
Richton, Miss., U.S. 31°20' N, 88°56' W 103
Richwood, Ohio, U.S. 40°25' N, 83°17' W 102
Ricla, Sp. 41°30' N, 1°25' W 164
Rico, Colo., U.S. 37°41' N, 108°2' W 92
Ridā', Yemen 14°26' N, 44°49' E 182
Ridanna, It. 46°54' N, 11°17' E 167
Riddell Nunataks, Antarctica 70°25' S, 56°25' E 248
Ridder, Kaz. 50°16' N, 83°30' E 190
Ridder (Leninogorsk), Kaz. 50°21' N, 83°32' E 184
Riddle, Idaho, U.S. 42°12' N, 116°7' W 90
Riderwood, Ala., U.S. 32°8' N, 88°20' W 103
Ridge Farm, Ill., U.S. 39°53' N, 87°39' W 102
Ridge, river, Can. 50°24' N, 83°51' W 110
Ridgecrest, Calif., U.S. 35°37' N, 117°41' W 101
Ridgefield, Conn., U.S. 41°17' N, 73°30' W 104
Ridgefield, Wash., U.S. 45°48' N, 122°44' W 100
Ridgeland, Miss., U.S. 32°24' N, 90°9' W 103
Ridgetown, Can. 42°25' N, 81°53' W 102
Ridgeville, Ind., U.S. 40°16' N, 85°2' W 102
Ridgewood, N.J., U.S. 40°58' N, 74°8' W 104
Riding Mountain National Park, Can. 50°49' N, 101°3' W 108
Riding Rocks, islands, North Atlantic Ocean 24°56' N, 79°6' W 116
Riedlingen, Ger. 48°9' N, 9°29' E 156
Rieneck, Ger. 50°5' N, 9°39' E 167
Ries, region, Ger. 48°44' N, 10°30' E 152
Riesco, Isla, island, Chile 52°41' S, 71°24' W 134
Rietavas, Lith. 55°44' N, 21°56' E 166
Rietberg, Ger. 51°47' N, 8°25' E 167
Rietfontein, Namibia 26°46' S, 19°59' E 227
Rievaulx, U.K. 54°15' N, 1°7' W 162
Riffe Lake, Wash., U.S. 46°28' N, 122°21' W 100
Rifle, Colo., U.S. 39°31' N, 107°47' W 90
Rig Rig, Chad 14°16' N, 14°21' E 216
Rīga, Latv. 56°55' N, 24°1' E 166
Riga, Gulf of 57°41' N, 23°20' E 166
Rīgān, Iran 28°38' N, 59°3' E 196
Riggins, Idaho, U.S. 45°24' N, 116°19' W 90
Rigolet, Can. 54°11' N, 58°24' W 111
Riguldi, Est. 59°6' N, 23°31' E 166
Rihand Dam, India 23°55' N, 82°11' E 197
Riihimäki, Fin. 60°44' N, 24°44' E 166
Riipi, Fin. 67°19' N, 26°3' E 152
Riiser-Larsen, Mount, peak, Antarctica 66°44' S, 50°12' E 248
Riisipere, Est. 59°6' N, 24°17' E 166
Riistavesi, Fin. 62°53' N, 28°6' E 154
Riíto, Mex. 32°5' N, 114°55' W 92
Rijau, Nig. 11°4' N, 5°14' E 222
Rijeća, Bosn. and Herzg. 44°1' N, 18°40' E 168
Rijeka (Fiume), Croatia 45°20' N, 14°26' E 156
Rijssen, Neth. 52°18' N, 6°30' E 163
Rila, Bulg. 41°59' N, 23°11' E 168
Rila, Bulg. 42°7' N, 23°8' E 168
Rila National Park, Bulg. 41°47' N, 22°39' E 180
Riley, Kans., U.S. 39°16' N, 96°50' W 90
Rilly, Fr. 49°9' N, 4°2' E 163
Rimāḩ, Jabal ar, peak, Jordan 32°18' N, 36°51' E 194
Rimbey, Can. 52°37' N, 114°14' W 108
Rimbo, Sw. 59°44' N, 18°21' E 166
Rimini, It. 44°2' N, 12°33' E 167
Rîmnicu Sărat, Rom. 45°23' N, 27°3' E 156
Rimouski, Can. 48°26' N, 68°31' W 94
Rimpar, Ger. 49°51' N, 9°57' E 167
Rimrock, Wash., U.S. 46°39' N, 121°8' W 100
Rinbung, China 29°15' N, 89°57' E 197
Rinca, island, Indonesia 9°14' S, 119°36' E 192
Rincão, Braz. 21°33' S, 48°5' W 138
Rînceni, Rom. 46°23' N, 28°7' E 158
Rincon, Ga., U.S. 32°17' N, 81°14' W 96
Rincon, N. Mex., U.S. 32°40' N, 107°5' W 92
Rincón, Cerro, peak, Arg. 24°6' S, 67°30' W 132
Rincon de Guayabitos, Mex. 21°0' N, 105°20' W 114
Rincón de Romos, Mex. 22°13' N, 102°19' W 114
Rincón de Soto, Sp. 42°13' N, 1°51' W 164
Rincón del Atuel, Arg. 34°44' S, 68°23' W 134
Rincón del Bonete, Uru. 32°54' S, 56°26' W 139
Rincón del Bonete, Lago, lake, Uru. 32°30' S, 56°26' W 139
Rincón Hondo, Venez. 7°24' N, 69°6' W 136
Rincona, Sp. 37°11' N, 4°28' W 164
Rinconada, Arg. 22°27' S, 66°13' W 137
Rindge, N.H., U.S. 42°44' N, 72°1' W 104
Ringgold, La., U.S. 32°18' N, 93°17' W 103
Ringim, Nig. 12°9' N, 9°9' E 222
Ringkøbing, Den. 56°5' N, 8°13' E 150
Ringwood, U.K. 50°51' N, 1°47' W 162
Rini, spring, Mauritania 16°57' N, 6°58' W 222
Rinns Point 55°29' N, 6°45' W 150
Rio, Fla., U.S. 27°13' N, 80°15' W 105
Río Abiseo National Park, Peru 7°60' S, 77°34' W 122
Rio Azul, Braz. 25°45' S, 50°48' W 138
Rio Branco, Braz. 9°58' S, 67°49' W 137
Río Branco, Uru. 32°34' S, 53°23' W 139
Rio Branco do Sul, Braz. 25°10' S, 49°21' W 138
Río Bravo, Mex. 26°0' N, 98°8' W 114
Río Bravo del Norte see Rio Grande, river, North America 28°13' N, 99°43' W 80
Rio Brilhante, Braz. 21°50' S, 54°32' W 132
Río Bueno, Chile 40°20' S, 72°59' W 134
Río Caribe, Venez. 10°40' N, 63°7' W 116
Río Chico, Venez. 10°21' N, 65°59' W 136
Rio Claro, Braz. 22°26' S, 47°35' W 138
Río Colorado, Arg. 39°1' S, 64°5' W 139
Río Corrientes, Ecua. 2°22' S, 76°23' W 136
Río Cuarto, Arg. 33°10' S, 64°21' W 134
Rio das Mortes see Manso, river, Braz. 15°20' S, 53°1' W 138
Rio de Contas, Braz. 13°34' S, 41°51' W 138
Rio de Janeiro, Braz. 22°53' S, 43°15' W 138
Rio de Janeiro, adm. division, Braz. 22°4' S, 42°44' W 138
Río de Jesús, Pan. 7°59' N, 81°10' W 115
Rio do Prado, Braz. 16°37' S, 40°34' W 138
Rio do Sul, Braz. 27°17' S, 49°39' W 138
Río Gallegos, Arg. 51°37' S, 69°17' W 134
Río Grande, Arg. 53°50' S, 67°48' W 123
Río Grande, Bol. 20°52' S, 67°16' W 137
Rio Grande, Braz. 32°1' S, 52°11' W 139
Rio Grande, Braz. 32°11' S, 52°10' W 123
Río Grande, Mex. 23°47' N, 103°2' W 114
Rio Grande City, Tex., U.S. 26°24' N, 98°49' W 114
Río Grande de Matagalpa, river, Nicar. 13°21' N, 84°20' W 115
Rio Grande do Norte, adm. division, Braz. 5°27' S, 37°44' W 132
Rio Grande do Sul, adm. division, Braz. 28°37' S, 53°52' W 138
Rio Grande (Río Bravo del Norte), river, North America 28°13' N, 99°43' W 80
Rio Grande Rise, South Atlantic Ocean 31°19' S, 35°27' W 253
Rio Grande Wild and Scenic River, Tex., U.S. 29°51' N, 102°10' W 96
Río Muerto, Arg. 26°19' S, 61°40' W 139
Río Mulatos, Bol. 19°42' S, 66°48' W 137
Río Muni, region, Equatorial Guinea 1°40' N, 9°49' E 218
Rio Negro, Braz. 26°4' S, 49°45' W 138
Rio Pardo, Braz. 29°59' S, 52°25' W 139
Rio Pardo de Minas, Braz. 15°39' S, 42°35' W 138
Río Pico, Arg. 44°12' S, 71°24' W 134
Río Pilcomayo National Park, Arg. 25°17' S, 58°18' W 122
Rio Pomba, Braz. 21°17' S, 43°11' W 138
Río Sucio, Col. 5°25' N, 75°42' W 136
Río Tercero, Arg. 32°13' S, 64°8' W 134
Río Tigre, Ecua. 2°7' S, 76°4' W 136
Rio Tinto, Braz. 6°48' S, 35°5' W 132
Rio Tuba, Philippines 8°33' N, 117°26' E 203
Rio Verde, Braz. 17°50' S, 50°57' W 138
Río Verde, Chile 52°34' S, 71°28' W 134
Río Verde, Mex. 21°53' N, 99°60' W 114
Rio Verde de Mato Grosso, Braz. 18°57' S, 54°53' W 132
Rio Vista, Calif., U.S. 38°9' N, 121°43' W 100
Riobamba, Ecua. 1°47' S, 78°47' W 130
Riogordo, Sp. 36°54' N, 4°18' W 164
Riohacha, Col. 11°29' N, 72°55' W 136
Riom, Fr. 45°54' N, 3°6' E 150
Riomaggiore, It. 44°5' N, 9°45' E 167
Rion-des-Landes, Fr. 43°56' N, 0°57' E 150
Rionegro, Col. 6°10' N, 75°21' W 136
Rioni, river, Ga. 42°29' N, 43°10' E 195
Riosucio, Col. 7°29' N, 77°9' W 136
Riou Lake, lake, Can. 59°2' N, 106°56' W 108
Riozinho, Braz. 9°32' S, 66°51' W 137
Riozinho, river, Braz. 3°7' S, 67°7' W 136
Riozinho, river, Braz. 8°22' S, 52°3' W 130
Ripanj, Serb. and Mont. 44°38' N, 20°30' E 168
Riparius, N.Y., U.S. 43°39' N, 73°55' W 104
Ripley, Calif., U.S. 33°31' N, 114°40' W 101
Ripley, Can. 44°3' N, 81°34' W 102
Ripley, Miss., U.S. 34°42' N, 88°58' W 96
Ripley, Ohio, U.S. 38°43' N, 83°49' W 102
Ripley, U.K. 53°3' N, 1°25' W 162
Ripoll, Sp. 42°12' N, 2°11' E 164
Ripon, Calif., U.S. 37°44' N, 121°8' W 100
Ripon, U.K. 54°8' N, 1°32' W 162
Ripon, Wis., U.S. 43°50' N, 88°50' W 102
Ripple Mountain, peak, Can. 49°0' N, 117°10' W 90
Risaralda, adm. division, South America 5°9' N, 76°8' W 136
Risbäck, Nor. 64°41' N, 15°31' E 154
Rīshahr, Iran 28°50' N, 50°55' E 196
Rishikesh, India 30°8' N, 78°18' E 197
Rishiri, island, Japan 44°52' N, 140°18' E 190
Rishon Leẕiyyon, Israel 31°57' N, 34°47' E 194
Rising Star, Tex., U.S. 32°5' N, 98°59' W 92
Rising Sun, Ind., U.S. 38°56' N, 84°52' W 102
Rissani, Mor. 31°18' N, 4°15' W 214
Risti, Est. 58°59' N, 24°3' E 166
Ristiina, Fin. 61°29' N, 27°14' E 166
Ristna, Est. 58°53' N, 21°42' E 166
Risum-Lindholm, Ger. 54°46' N, 8°52' E 150
Ritscher Upland, Antarctica 74°5' S, 11°15' W 248
Ritter, Mount, peak, Calif., U.S. 37°41' N, 119°15' W 100
Rittman, Ohio, U.S. 40°57' N, 81°47' W 102
Ritva, Fin. 65°29' N, 26°32' E 152
Ritzville, Wash., U.S. 47°6' N, 118°24' W 90
Riva del Garda, It. 45°53' N, 10°50' E 167
Rivadavia, Arg. 35°28' S, 62°58' W 139
Rivadavia, Arg. 33°12' S, 68°29' W 134
Rivarolo Canavese, It. 45°19' N, 7°43' E 167
Rivas, Nicar. 11°26' N, 85°51' W 115
River Cess, Liberia 5°26' N, 9°35' W 222
River Jordan, Can. 48°25' N, 124°2' W 100
River Nile, adm. division, Sudan 18°30' N, 32°31' E 182
Rivera, Arg. 37°12' S, 63°13' W 139
Rivera, Uru. 30°53' S, 55°35' W 139
Riverbank, Calif., U.S. 37°43' N, 120°58' W 100
Riverdale, Calif., U.S. 36°25' N, 119°53' W 100
Riverdale, N. Dak., U.S. 47°28' N, 101°23' W 90
Riverhead, N.Y., U.S. 40°55' N, 72°39' W 104
Riverhurst, Can. 50°54' N, 106°53' W 90
Riverina, region, Austral. 33°35' S, 146°11' E 230
Rivero, Isla, island, Chile 45°34' S, 75°39' W 134
Rivers, Can. 50°2' N, 100°15' W 90
Riversdale, N.Z. 45°56' S, 168°45' E 240
Riversdale, S. Af. 34°5' S, 21°14' E 227
Riverside, Calif., U.S. 33°59' N, 117°24' W 101
Riverside, Tex., U.S. 30°50' N, 95°24' W 103
Riverside, Wash., U.S. 48°29' N, 119°32' W 90
Riverton, Can. 50°58' N, 97°1' W 90
Riverton, Conn., U.S. 41°57' N, 73°1' W 104
Riverton, Ill., U.S. 39°50' N, 89°32' W 102
Riverton, Wyo., U.S. 43°1' N, 108°23' W 90
Riverview, Can. 46°2' N, 64°49' W 111
Rivesaltes, Fr. 42°45' N, 2°51' E 164
Riviera, Ariz., U.S. 35°5' N, 114°37' W 101
Riviera Beach, Fla., U.S. 26°46' N, 80°5' W 105
Riviera, region, Mediterranean Sea 43°21' N, 6°39' E 165
Rivière au Serpent, river, Can. 50°29' N, 71°42' W 110
Rivière aux Rats, river, Can. 49°9' N, 72°14' W 94
Rivière-de-la-Chaloupe, site, Gulf of St. Lawrence 49°8' N, 62°35' W 111
Rivière-du-Loup, Can. 47°48' N, 69°34' W 94
Rivne, Ukr. 50°37' N, 26°13' E 152
Rivoli, It. 45°3' N, 7°30' E 167
Riwaka, N.Z. 41°6' S, 172°59' E 240
Riwoqê, China 31°8' N, 96°33' E 188
Riyadh see Ar Riyāḑ, Saudi Arabia 24°35' N, 46°35' E 186
Riyāq, Leb. 33°51' N, 36°0' E 194
Rize, Turk. 41°2' N, 40°29' E 195
Rizhao, China 35°26' N, 119°27' E 198
Rizokarpaso 35°35' N, 34°22' E 194
Rizzuto, Capo, It. 38°48' N, 17°8' E 156
Rkiz, Lac, lake, Mauritania 16°55' N, 15°26' W 222
Roa, Sp. 41°41' N, 3°57' W 164
Roachdale, Ind., U.S. 39°50' N, 86°48' W 102
Road Town, Tortola 18°27' N, 64°38' W 116
Roan, Nor. 64°10' N, 10°14' E 152
Roan Cliffs, Colo., U.S. 39°38' N, 108°13' W 90
Roan Cliffs, Utah, U.S. 39°29' N, 110°17' W 90
Roan Plateau, Colo., U.S. 39°44' N, 108°50' W 90
Roann, Ind., U.S. 40°54' N, 85°54' W 102
Roanne, Fr. 46°1' N, 4°3' E 150
Roanoke, Ind., U.S. 40°57' N, 85°23' W 102
Roanoke, La., U.S. 30°13' N, 92°46' W 103
Roanoke Island, N.C., U.S. 35°46' N, 75°34' W 80
Roatán, Isla de, island, Hond. 16°13' N, 86°24' W 115
Robaa Ouled Yahia, Tun. 36°5' N, 9°34' E 156
Robāt-e Khān, Iran 33°21' N, 56°4' E 180
Robāţ-e Tork, Iran 33°45' N, 50°51' E 180
Robbins Island, Austral. 41°2' S, 142°8' E 230
Robe, Mount, peak, Austral. 31°41' S, 141°7' E 230
Robeline, La., U.S. 31°40' N, 93°19' W 103
Robert, Cap, Can. 49°29' N, 62°18' W 111
Robert, Cape, Antarctica 66°26' S, 137°47' E 248
Robert Lee, Tex., U.S. 31°53' N, 100°28' W 92
Roberts, Arg. 35°8' S, 61°59' W 139
Roberts, Idaho, U.S. 43°43' N, 112°7' W 90
Roberts, Ill., U.S. 40°37' N, 88°11' W 102
Roberts Butte, peak, Antarctica 72°35' S, 160°47' E 248
Roberts Creek Mountain, peak, Nev., U.S. 39°51' N, 116°23' W 90
Roberts Knoll, peak, Antarctica 71°27' S, 3°40' W 248
Roberts Mountain, peak, Wyo., U.S. 42°54' N, 109°22' W 90
Roberts, Point, Wash., U.S. 48°53' N, 122°45' W 80
Robertsdale, Ala., U.S. 30°32' N, 87°42' W 103
Robertsganj, India 24°40' N, 83°2' E 197
Robertson, S. Af. 33°48' S, 19°53' E 227
Robertson Island, Antarctica 65°11' S, 59°19' W 134
Robertsport, Liberia 6°40' N, 11°22' W 222
Roberval, Can. 48°28' N, 72°15' W 82
Robin Hood's Bay, U.K. 54°26' N, 0°33' E 162
Robinson, Ill., U.S. 39°0' N, 87°44' W 102
Robinson Range, Austral. 26°23' S, 118°37' E 230
Robinsons, Me., U.S. 46°28' N, 67°50' W 111
Roblin, Can. 51°14' N, 101°22' W 90
Roboré, Bol. 18°25' S, 59°43' W 132
Robsart, Can. 49°23' N, 109°17' W 90
Robson, Can. 49°20' N, 117°41' W 90
Robson, Mount, peak, Can. 53°5' N, 119°16' W 108
Roby, Tex., U.S. 32°44' N, 100°23' W 92
Roca Partida, Isla, island, Isla Roca Partida 19°1' N, 112°48' W 112
Roca Partida, Punta, Mex. 18°43' N, 95°14' W 114
Rocamadour, Fr. 44°46' N, 1°38' E 214
Rocas, Atol das, island, Atol das Rocas 4°5' S, 33°47' W 132
Rocchetta Ligure, It. 44°42' N, 9°3' E 167
Rocha, Uru. 34°30' S, 54°20' W 139
Rochdale, Mass., U.S. 42°11' N, 71°55' W 104
Rochdale, U.K. 53°37' N, 2°9' W 162
Rochefort, Belg. 50°9' N, 5°13' E 167
Rochegda, Russ. 62°42' N, 43°27' E 154
Rochelle, Ga., U.S. 31°56' N, 83°28' W 96
Rochelle, Ill., U.S. 41°55' N, 89°5' W 102
Rocher, Lac, lake, Can. 50°28' N, 76°60' W 110
Roches, Lac des, lake, Can. 51°30' N, 120°54' W 90
Rochester, Can. 54°22' N, 113°26' W 108
Rochester, Ill., U.S. 39°44' N, 89°32' W 102
Rochester, Ind., U.S. 41°3' N, 86°13' W 102
Rochester, Minn., U.S. 44°1' N, 92°30' W 94
Rochester, N.H., U.S. 43°18' N, 70°59' W 104
Rochester, N.Y., U.S. 43°9' N, 77°37' W 110
Rochester, Pa., U.S. 40°41' N, 80°17' W 94
Rochester, U.K. 51°22' N, 0°28' E 162
Rochester, Vt., U.S. 43°52' N, 72°49' W 104
Rochester, Wash., U.S. 46°48' N, 123°5' W 100
Rock Falls, Ill., U.S. 41°45' N, 89°42' W 102
Rock Hill, S.C., U.S. 34°55' N, 81°2' W 96
Rock Island, Mo., U.S. 41°29' N, 90°34' W 110
Rock Lake, N. Dak., U.S. 48°45' N, 99°15' W 90
Rock Rapids, Iowa, U.S. 43°24' N, 96°11' W 90
Rock River, Wyo., U.S. 41°44' N, 105°58' W 90
Rock, river, Can. 60°24' N, 127°14' W 108
Rock, river, Wis., U.S. 42°48' N, 89°12' W 102
Rock Sound, Bahamas 24°55' N, 76°10' W 96
Rock Springs, Mont., U.S. 46°47' N, 106°16' W 90
Rock Springs, Wyo., U.S. 41°38' N, 109°14' W 106
Rockall, island, U.K. 57°36' N, 13°41' W 253
Rockdale, Ill., U.S. 41°29' N, 88°7' W 102
Rockefeller Plateau, Antarctica 79°52' S, 104°57' W 248
Rockenhausen, Ger. 49°37' N, 7°48' E 163
Rockford, Ill., U.S. 42°16' N, 89°4' W 102
Rockford, Mich., U.S. 43°7' N, 85°33' W 102
Rockford, Ohio, U.S. 40°40' N, 84°39' W 102
Rockglen, Can. 49°10' N, 105°58' W 90
Rockingham, Austral. 32°19' S, 115°45' E 231
Rockingham, N.C., U.S. 34°55' N, 79°48' W 96
Rockingham, Vt., U.S. 43°11' N, 72°30' W 104
Rockland, Can. 45°32' N, 75°18' W 94
Rockland, Idaho, U.S. 42°35' N, 112°52' W 90
Rockland, Mass., U.S. 42°7' N, 70°55' W 104
Rockledge, Fla., U.S. 28°19' N, 80°44' W 105
Rockport, Calif., U.S. 39°44' N, 123°50' W 90
Rockport, Ind., U.S. 37°52' N, 87°4' W 94
Rockport, Me., U.S. 44°11' N, 69°5' W 94
Rockport, Tex., U.S. 28°0' N, 97°4' W 96
Rockport, Wash., U.S. 48°29' N, 121°36' W 100
Rocksprings, Tex., U.S. 30°0' N, 100°13' W 92
Rockton, Ill., U.S. 42°27' N, 89°5' W 102
Rockville, Ind., U.S. 39°45' N, 87°14' W 102
Rockville, N.Z. 40°46' S, 172°39' E 240
Rockwell City, Iowa, U.S. 42°23' N, 94°38' W 94
Rockwood, Tenn., U.S. 35°52' N, 84°41' W 96
Rocky Ford, Colo., U.S. 38°3' N, 103°44' W 90
Rocky Hill, Conn., U.S. 41°39' N, 72°39' W 104
Rocky Lane, Can. 58°29' N, 116°23' W 108
Rocky Mount, N.C., U.S. 35°55' N, 77°48' W 96
Rocky Mountain House, Can. 52°21' N, 114°53' W 108
Rocky Mountain National Park, Colo., U.S. 40°33' N, 105°37' W 80
Rocky Mountain, peak, Mont., U.S. 47°46' N, 112°52' W 90
Rocky Mountains, Mont., U.S. 45°5' N, 114°26' W 72
Rocky Point, Calif., U.S. 41°9' N, 124°26' W 90
Rocky Point, Namibia 19°6' S, 12°1' E 220

Rocky Point, N.Y., U.S. 40°56' N, 72°56' W 104
Roda de Isabena, Sp. 42°16' N, 0°31' E 164
Rødby, Den. 54°42' N, 11°23' E 152
Roddickton, Can. 50°51' N, 56°7' W 111
Rodel 57°44' N, 6°58' W 150
Rodeo, Arg. 30°13' S, 69°7' W 134
Rodeo, Mex. 25°8' N, 104°35' W 114
Rodeo, N. Mex., U.S. 31°50' N, 109°1' W 92
Rodessa, La., U.S. 32°57' N, 94°1' W 103
Rodez, Fr. 44°21' N, 2°35' E 150
Rodi Garganico, It. 41°55' N, 15°54' E 156
Rodino, Russ. 52°28' N, 80°18' E 184
Rodnei, Munţii, Rom. 47°28' N, 24°19' E 156
Rodney, Can. 42°33' N, 81°41' W 102
Rodniki, Kaz. 49°9' N, 58°22' E 158
Rodniki, Russ. 57°5' N, 41°39' E 154
Rodnīkovka, Kaz. 50°39' N, 57°8' E 158
Rodonit, Kepi i, Alban. 41°27' N, 19°15' E 168
Ródos, Gr. 36°20' N, 28°10' E 180
Ródos (Rhodes), Gr. 36°25' N, 28°13' E 156
Ródos (Rhodes), adm. division, Gr. 35°58' N, 27°21' E 156
Ródos (Rhodes), island, Gr. 35°44' N, 27°53' E 156
Rødøy, Nor. 66°39' N, 13°3' E 152
Rodrigues, Braz. 6°34' S, 73°12' W 130
Rodrigues Fracture Zone, Indian Ocean 19°45' S, 62°11' E 254
Rodrigues, island, Mauritius 19°45' S, 63°25' E 254
Roebourne, Austral. 20°46' S, 117°6' E 231
Roebuck Bay 18°13' S, 120°59' E 230
Roes Welcome Sound 64°30' N, 89°28' W 106
Roeselare, Belg. 50°56' N, 3°7' E 163
Roetgen, Ger. 50°38' N, 6°11' E 167
Rogagua, Lago, lake, Bol. 13°40' S, 67°19' W 137
Rogaguado, Bol. 13°35' S, 64°44' W 137
Rogaguado, Laguna, lake, Bol. 12°56' S, 65°54' W 137
Rogaguado, Laguna, lake, Bol. 12°56' S, 66°43' W 130
Roganville, Tex., U.S. 30°47' N, 93°55' W 103
Rogatica, Bosn. and Herzg. 43°48' N, 19°0' E 168
Rogers, Ark., U.S. 36°18' N, 94°7' W 96
Rogers, Conn., U.S. 41°50' N, 71°55' W 104
Rogers, Tex., U.S. 30°54' N, 97°13' W 96
Rogers City, Mich., U.S. 45°25' N, 83°50' W 94
Rogers, Mount, peak, Va., U.S. 36°38' N, 81°38' W 96
Rogerson, Idaho, U.S. 42°13' N, 114°36' W 90
Rogersville, Tenn., U.S. 36°23' N, 83°1' W 94
Rognan, Nor. 67°5' N, 15°19' E 152
Rogun, Taj. 38°46' N, 69°51' E 197
Roha, India 18°25' N, 73°8' E 188
Rohault, Lac, lake, Can. 49°22' N, 74°51' W 94
Rohia, Tun. 35°39' N, 9°3' E 156
Röhlingen, Ger. 48°56' N, 10°11' E 152
Rohnerville, Calif., U.S. 40°34' N, 124°9' W 92
Rohri, Pak. 27°38' N, 68°59' E 186
Rohtak, India 28°54' N, 76°34' E 188
Rohtasgarh, India 24°36' N, 83°56' E 197
Roi Et, Thai. 16°3' N, 103°41' E 202
Roja, Latv. 57°30' N, 22°46' E 166
Roja, Punta, Sp. 38°26' N, 1°36' E 150
Rojas, Arg. 34°14' S, 60°41' W 139
Rojo, Cabo 17°49' N, 67°45' W 116
Rojo, Cabo, Mex. 21°36' N, 97°23' W 114
Rokan, river, Indonesia 0°57' N, 100°36' E 196
Rokeby National Park, Austral. 14°1' S, 142°34' E 238
Rokel, river, Sierra Leone 8°54' N, 11°46' W 222
Rokhmoyva, Gora, peak, Russ. 66°51' N, 29°2' E 152
Rokiškis, Lith. 55°57' N, 25°34' E 166
Rokytne, Ukr. 51°16' N, 27°11' E 152
Rola Co, lake, China 35°17' N, 87°51' E 188
Rolde, Neth. 52°59' N, 6°37' E 163
Rolette, N. Dak., U.S. 48°38' N, 99°52' W 90
Roll, Ariz., U.S. 32°44' N, 113°59' W 101
Rolla, Can. 55°53' N, 120°10' W 108
Rolla, Mo., U.S. 37°56' N, 91°46' W 96
Rolla, N. Dak., U.S. 48°50' N, 99°38' W 90
Rolle, Switz. 46°29' N, 6°21' E 167
Rolleston, N.Z. 43°35' S, 172°21' E 240
Rolling Fork, Miss., U.S. 32°53' N, 90°53' W 103
Rollins, Mont., U.S. 47°53' N, 114°12' W 90
Rom, Sudan 10°46' N, 32°30' E 182
Roma, Austral. 26°34' S, 148°47' E 231
Roma (Rome), It. 41°52' N, 12°21' E 156
Romain, Cape, S.C., U.S. 32°54' N, 79°32' W 96
Romakloster, Sw. 57°28' N, 18°28' E 166
Roma-Los Saenz, Tex., U.S. 26°26' N, 98°59' W 98
Roman, Rom. 46°56' N, 26°56' E 156
Romanche Fracture Zone, North Atlantic Ocean 0°8' N, 16°37' W 253
Romang, Arg. 29°29' S, 59°50' W 139
Români, Egypt 31°0' N, 32°38' E 194
Romania 45°55' N, 24°6' E 156
Romanija, peak, Bosn. and Herzg. 43°51' N, 18°37' E 168
Roman-Kosh, peak, Ukr. 44°37' N, 34°8' E 156
Romano, Cape, Fla., U.S. 25°54' N, 82°1' W 105
Romano, Cayo, island, Cuba 22°0' N, 77°36' W 116
Romanovce, Maced. 42°4' N, 21°40' E 168
Romanovka, Russ. 53°14' N, 112°47' E 238
Romanovka, Russ. 51°43' N, 42°44' E 158
Romans, Fr. 45°3' N, 5°3' E 150
Romanzof, Cape, Alas., U.S. 61°29' N, 168°48' W 98
Romblon, Philippines 12°35' N, 122°17' E 203
Rome, Ga., U.S. 34°15' N, 85°10' W 96
Rome, N.Y., U.S. 43°13' N, 75°28' W 94
Rome City, Ind., U.S. 41°29' N, 85°23' W 102
Rome see Roma, It. 41°52' N, 12°21' E 156
Romeo, Mich., U.S. 42°47' N, 83°1' W 102
Romford, U.K. 51°34' N, 0°10' E 162
Romilly, Fr. 48°31' N, 3°44' E 163
Romiton, Uzb. 39°56' N, 64°22' E 197
Rommani, Mor. 33°33' N, 6°42' W 143
Romnaes, Mount, peak, Antarctica 71°30' S, 23°33' E 248
Romney Marsh, U.K. 50°59' N, 0°45' E 162
Romny, Ukr. 50°45' N, 33°28' E 158
Romodanovo, Russ. 54°25' N, 45°22' E 154
Romont, Switz. 46°42' N, 6°54' E 167
Romsdal, Nor. 62°26' N, 7°43' E 152
Romsey, U.K. 50°59' N, 1°30' W 162
Røn, Nor. 61°3' N, 9°3' E 152
Ron, Mui, Vietnam 17°57' N, 106°33' E 198
Ronald, Wash., U.S. 47°13' N, 121°2' W 100
Ronan, Mont., U.S. 47°30' N, 114°7' W 90
Roncade, It. 45°37' N, 12°21' E 167
Roncador, Serra do, Braz. 11°42' S, 52°48' W 130
Ronceverte, W. Va., U.S. 37°45' N, 80°28' W 94
Ronchamp, Fr. 47°42' N, 6°37' E 150
Ronda, Sp. 36°44' N, 5°9' W 150
Rondane, peak, Nor. 61°54' N, 9°43' E 152
Rønde, Den. 56°18' N, 10°28' E 150
Rondón, Col. 6°15' N, 71°7' W 136
Rondonia, adm. division, Braz. 10°29' S, 65°14' W 137
Rondonia see Ji-Paraná, Braz. 10°53' S, 61°58' W 130
Rondonópolis, Braz. 16°29' S, 54°37' W 132
Rong, Koh, island, Cambodia 10°41' N, 102°33' E 202
Rong Kwang, Thai. 18°22' N, 100°19' E 202
Rong'an, China 25°16' N, 109°18' E 198
Rongcheng (Yatou), China 37°10' N, 122°26' E 198
Rongjiang, China 25°56' N, 108°27' E 198
Rongshui, China 25°4' N, 109°12' E 198
Rõngu, Est. 58°7' N, 26°13' E 166
Rongxian, China 22°50' N, 110°33' E 198
Ronkonkoma, N.Y., U.S. 40°49' N, 73°9' W 104
Ronne Ice Shelf, Antarctica 77°54' S, 68°27' W 248
Rönnskär, Nor. 64°39' N, 21°15' E 152
Ronse, Belg. 50°44' N, 3°35' E 163
Ronuro, river, Braz. 13°7' S, 54°31' W 130
Roodhouse, Mo., U.S. 39°28' N, 90°22' W 94
Roof Butte, peak, Ariz., U.S. 36°26' N, 109°9' W 92
Roosendaal, Neth. 51°32' N, 4°28' E 167
Roosevelt, Utah, U.S. 40°17' N, 109°60' W 92
Roosevelt Island, Antarctica 78°13' S, 162°49' W 248
Roosevelt, Mount, peak, Can. 58°24' N, 125°29' W 108
Rooslepa, Est. 59°11' N, 23°29' E 166
Root, river, Can. 62°50' N, 124°50' W 98
Root, river, Minn., U.S. 43°32' N, 92°10' W 80
Ropaži, Latv. 56°56' N, 24°40' E 166
Ropcha, Russ. 63°2' N, 52°29' E 154
Roper, river, Austral. 15°13' S, 134°30' E 230
Ropi, Fin. 68°36' N, 21°46' E 152
Ropotovo, Maced. 41°28' N, 21°22' E 168
Roquefort, Fr. 44°1' N, 0°19' E 150
Roquetes, Sp. 40°49' N, 0°29' E 164
Roraima, adm. division, Braz. 2°16' N, 63°20' W 130
Roraima, Mount, peak, Venez. 5°12' N, 60°51' W 130
Rorketon, Can. 51°23' N, 99°35' W 90
Rørstad, Nor. 67°34' N, 15°13' E 152
Rosa, Zambia 9°40' S, 31°21' E 224
Rosa, Monte, peak, Switz. 45°56' N, 7°49' E 165
Rosa, Punta, Mex. 26°31' N, 110°22' W 112
Rosales, Arg. 34°10' S, 63°10' W 139
Rosales, Mex. 28°9' N, 105°33' W 92
Rosalia, Wash., U.S. 47°13' N, 117°22' W 90
Rosamond, Calif., U.S. 34°51' N, 118°11' W 101
Rosamorada, Mex. 22°7' N, 105°12' W 114
Rosario, Arg. 32°57' S, 60°45' W 123
Rosario, Arg. 32°56' S, 60°41' W 139
Rosário, Braz. 2°57' S, 44°16' W 132
Rosario, Mex. 23°0' N, 105°54' W 114
Rosario, Parag. 24°26' S, 57°7' W 132
Rosario, Uru. 34°19' S, 57°19' W 139
Rosario, Venez. 10°18' N, 72°24' W 136
Rosario, Bahía del 29°53' N, 116°22' W 92
Rosario, Cayo del, island, Cuba 21°10' N, 81°60' W 116
Rosario de Lerma, Arg. 24°58' S, 65°36' W 134
Rosario del Tala, Arg. 32°18' S, 59°6' W 139
Rosário do Sul, Braz. 30°16' S, 54°58' W 139
Rosário d'Oeste, Braz. 14°51' S, 56°26' W 132
Rosarito, Mex. 32°20' N, 117°4' W 92
Rosarito, Mex. 26°29' N, 111°40' W 112
Rosas, Col. 2°13' N, 76°45' W 136
Roscoe, Tex., U.S. 32°26' N, 100°34' W 92
Roscoff, Fr. 48°43' N, 3°60' W 150
Roscommon, Ire. 53°38' N, 8°12' W 150
Roscommon, Mich., U.S. 44°29' N, 84°36' W 94
Rose Blanche, Can. 47°36' N, 58°41' W 111
Rose Harbour, Can. 52°6' N, 131°5' W 108
Rose Lake, Can. 54°24' N, 126°4' W 108
Rose Point, Can. 54°8' N, 131°39' W 108
Rose Prairie, Can. 56°29' N, 120°50' W 108
Rose Valley, Can. 52°16' N, 103°48' W 108
Roseau, Dominica 15°16' N, 61°31' W 116
Roseau, Minn., U.S. 48°49' N, 95°49' W 90
Roseau, river, North America 48°57' N, 96°21' W 94
Rosebud, Mont., U.S. 46°15' N, 106°27' W 90
Rosebud Mountains, Mont., U.S. 45°21' N, 107°15' W 90
Rosebud Peak, Nev., U.S. 40°48' N, 118°45' W 90
Roseburg, Oreg., U.S. 43°12' N, 123°20' W 82
Rosebush, Mich., U.S. 43°42' N, 84°46' W 102
Rosedale, Ind., U.S. 39°37' N, 87°17' W 102
Rosée, Belg. 50°13' N, 4°40' E 167
Roseires Dam, Sudan 11°39' N, 34°2' E 182
Roseland, La., U.S. 30°45' N, 90°31' W 103
Roselawn, Ind., U.S. 41°8' N, 87°19' W 102
Roselend, Lac de, lake, Fr. 45°40' N, 6°28' E 165
Rosenberg, Tex., U.S. 29°32' N, 95°49' W 96
Rosendal, Nor. 59°59' N, 5°59' E 152
Rosendale, N.Y., U.S. 41°50' N, 74°7' W 104
Rosepine, La., U.S. 30°54' N, 93°18' W 103
Roseto degli Abruzzi, It. 42°39' N, 14°0' E 156
Rosetown, Can. 51°33' N, 107°60' W 90
Rosetta see Rashîd, Egypt 31°23' N, 30°21' E 180
Roseville, Calif., U.S. 38°44' N, 121°19' W 90
Roseville, Mich., U.S. 42°29' N, 82°57' W 94
Roseville, Ohio, U.S. 39°48' N, 82°5' W 102
Rosharon, Tex., U.S. 29°20' N, 95°27' W 103
Roshchino, Russ. 60°14' N, 29°36' E 166
Rosholt, S. Dak., U.S. 45°51' N, 96°45' W 90
Roshtkala, Taj. 37°13' N, 71°48' E 186
Rosignol, Guyana 6°9' N, 57°35' W 130
Roşiori de Vede, Rom. 44°6' N, 24°56' E 143
Roskilde, Den. 55°37' N, 12°4' E 152
Roslavl', Russ. 53°54' N, 32°55' E 154
Roslyn, Wash., U.S. 47°12' N, 120°60' W 90
Rösrath, Ger. 50°53' N, 7°10' E 163
Ross, N.Z. 42°55' S, 170°49' E 240
Ross Bethio, Senegal 16°17' N, 16°11' W 214
Ross Dam, Wash., U.S. 48°50' N, 121°5' W 82
Ross Ice Shelf, Antarctica 81°35' S, 166°21' W 248
Ross Island, island, Antarctica 77°2' S, 171°48' E 248
Ross Lake National Recreation Area, Wash., U.S. 48°43' N, 121°28' W 100
Ross, Mount, peak, N.Z. 41°29' S, 175°17' E 240
Ross on Wye, U.K. 51°55' N, 2°35' W 162
Ross River, Can. 61°56' N, 132°32' W 98
Ross, river, Can. 62°6' N, 131°21' W 98
Ross Sea 74°54' S, 179°17' E 248
Rossburn, Can. 50°40' N, 100°49' W 90
Rosscarbery, Ire. 51°35' N, 9°2' W 150
Rossel Island, island, P.N.G. 11°15' S, 154°4' E 192
Rosses, The, Ire. 54°46' N, 8°16' W 150
Rossignol, Lac, lake, Can. 52°41' N, 74°1' W 111
Rossini Point 72°60' S, 74°12' W 248
Rossland, Can. 49°3' N, 117°50' W 82
Rosso, Mauritania 16°34' N, 15°52' W 222
Rosso, Capo, Fr. 42°9' N, 7°58' E 156
Rossosh', Russ. 50°13' N, 39°32' E 158
Rossville, Ill., U.S. 40°22' N, 87°39' W 102
Rossville, Ind., U.S. 40°24' N, 86°36' W 102
Røst Bank, Norwegian Sea 67°47' N, 12°7' E 255
Rosthern, Can. 52°39' N, 106°20' W 108
Rostock, Ger. 54°5' N, 12°7' E 152
Rostov, Russ. 57°12' N, 39°19' E 154
Rostov, adm. division, Russ. 47°19' N, 38°14' E 156
Rostov na Donu, Russ. 47°13' N, 39°42' E 156
Rostuša, Maced. 41°36' N, 20°35' E 168
Røsvassbukt, Nor. 65°52' N, 14°4' E 152
Roswell, N. Mex., U.S. 33°23' N, 104°32' W 92
Rota, Sp. 36°37' N, 6°22' W 164
Rotan, Tex., U.S. 32°50' N, 100°29' W 92
Rotenburg, Ger. 51°0' N, 9°43' E 167
Rothaargebirge, Ger. 51°4' N, 8°8' E 167
Rothera, U.K., station, Antarctica 67°32' S, 68°18' W 248
Rotherham, N.Z. 42°44' S, 172°56' E 240
Rotherham, U.K. 53°26' N, 1°22' W 162
Rothschild Island, Antarctica 69°22' S, 77°37' W 248
Roti, island, Indonesia 11°14' S, 122°38' E 192
Rotondo, Monte, peak, Fr. 42°12' N, 8°59' E 156
Rotorua, N.Z. 38°9' S, 176°13' E 240
Rotterdam, Neth. 51°54' N, 4°29' E 167
Rotterdam, N.Y., U.S. 42°48' N, 73°60' W 104
Rottneros, Nor. 59°49' N, 13°5' E 152
Rottnest Island, Austral. 32°39' S, 114°32' E 230
Rottumeroog, island, Neth. 53°29' N, 6°32' E 163
Rottumerplaat, island, Neth. 53°31' N, 5°57' E 163
Roubaix, Fr. 50°41' N, 3°10' E 163
Rouen, Fr. 49°26' N, 1°6' E 163
Rõuge, Est. 57°44' N, 26°53' E 166
Rouge, Pointe 49°20' N, 68°5' W 94
Rouina, Alg. 36°14' N, 1°48' E 150
Roumila, Alg. 37°2' N, 6°20' E 150
Round Mount, peak, Austral. 30°22' S, 152°2' E 230
Round Pond, Me., U.S. 43°57' N, 69°28' W 94
Round Rock, Tex., U.S. 30°29' N, 97°41' W 92
Roundstone, Ire. 53°23' N, 9°57' W 150
Roundup, Mont., U.S. 46°25' N, 108°33' W 90
Roura, South America 4°46' N, 52°20' W 130
Rous, Peninsula, Chile 55°23' S, 71°22' W 134
Rouses Point, N.Y., U.S. 44°58' N, 73°24' W 94
Rouseville, Pa., U.S. 41°27' N, 79°42' W 110
Roussillon, region, Fr. 42°51' N, 2°39' E 165
Rouxville, S. Af. 30°25' S, 26°50' E 227
Rouyn-Noranda, Can. 48°14' N, 79°2' W 110
Rovaniemi, Fin. 66°26' N, 25°38' E 160
Rovde, Nor. 62°9' N, 5°44' E 152
Rovdino, Russ. 61°41' N, 42°35' E 154
Roven'ki, Russ. 49°58' N, 38°54' E 158
Rover, Mount, peak, Can. 66°38' N, 140°60' W 98
Rovereto, It. 45°53' N, 11°3' E 167
Roversi, Arg. 27°35' S, 61°58' W 139
Rovieng, Cambodia 13°21' N, 105°5' E 202
Rovigo, It. 45°4' N, 11°47' E 167
Rovinj, Croatia 45°5' N, 13°38' E 167
Rovišće, Croatia 45°56' N, 16°43' E 168
Rovkuly, Russ. 64°2' N, 30°47' E 152
Rovnoye, Russ. 50°43' N, 46°5' E 158
Rovuma, river, Africa 11°6' S, 37°36' E 224
Rowan Lake, Can. 49°15' N, 94°4' W 94
Rowd-e Lurah, river, Afghan. 31°31' N, 66°49' E 186
Rowletts, Ky., U.S. 37°13' N, 85°54' W 96
Rowley, Mass., U.S. 42°42' N, 70°53' W 104
Rowley Island, Can. 68°35' N, 80°9' W 106
Roxa, island, Guinea-Bissau 11°9' N, 15°37' W 222
Roxas, Philippines 10°18' N, 119°16' E 203
Roxas, Philippines 17°5' N, 121°36' E 203
Roxas, Philippines 11°33' N, 122°43' E 203
Roxas, Philippines 12°36' N, 121°30' E 203
Roxburgh, N.Z. 45°33' S, 169°17' E 240
Roxbury, Vt., U.S. 44°5' N, 72°44' W 104
Roxen, lake, Nor. 58°26' N, 15°14' E 152
Roxo, Cap, Senegal 12°26' N, 17°12' W 222
Roy, Mont., U.S. 47°18' N, 108°58' W 90
Roy, N. Mex., U.S. 35°56' N, 104°13' W 92
Roy, Utah, U.S. 41°9' N, 112°1' W 92
Royal Center, Ind., U.S. 40°51' N, 86°30' W 102
Royal Chitwan National Park, Nepal 27°14' N, 83°51' E 197
Royal Gorge, site, Colo., U.S. 38°27' N, 105°26' W 90
Royal Manas National Park, Bhutan 26°37' N, 91°8' E 197
Royal Natal National Park, S. Af. 28°52' S, 28°0' E 227
Royale, Isle, island, Mich., U.S. 47°37' N, 89°34' W 80
Royalton, Vt., U.S. 43°49' N, 72°34' W 104
Royalty, Tex., U.S. 31°21' N, 102°52' W 92
Royan, Fr. 45°39' N, 1°3' W 150
Roye, Fr. 49°41' N, 2°48' E 163
Røyrvik, Nor. 64°53' N, 13°31' E 152
Royston, Can. 49°38' N, 124°57' W 100
Royston, U.K. 52°2' N, 1°59' W 162
Rožaje, Europe 42°50' N, 20°9' E 168
Rožanj, peak, Serb. and Mont. 44°17' N, 19°24' E 168
Rožanstvo, Serb. and Mont. 43°43' N, 19°50' E 168
Rozdil'na, Ukr. 46°53' N, 30°3' E 156
Rozewie, Przylądek, Pol. 54°51' N, 17°52' E 152
Rozhdestvenskoye, Russ. 58°7' N, 45°38' E 154
Rozhyshche, Ukr. 50°54' N, 25°15' E 152
Rozivka, Ukr. 47°21' N, 37°3' E 156
Rožňava, Slovakia 48°39' N, 20°32' E 152
Roznov, Rom. 46°51' N, 26°29' E 158
Rozoy, Fr. 49°42' N, 4°7' E 163
Roztocze, Pol. 50°37' N, 22°29' E 152
Rrëshen, Alban. 41°47' N, 19°54' E 168
Rtanj, Serb. and Mont. 43°50' N, 21°42' E 168
Rtishchevo, Russ. 52°15' N, 43°48' E 158
Ruabon, U.K. 52°59' N, 3°2' W 162
Ruacaná Falls, Angola 17°54' S, 12°59' E 220
Ruaha, Tanzania 7°23' S, 36°34' E 224
Ruaha National Park, Tanzania 7°47' S, 34°17' E 224
Ruakituri, N.Z. 38°45' S, 177°24' E 240
Ruapehu, Mount, peak, N.Z. 39°20' S, 175°28' E 240
Ruatahuna, N.Z. 38°38' S, 176°58' E 240
Ruatoria, N.Z. 37°55' S, 178°19' E 240
Ruawai, N.Z. 36°9' S, 174°2' E 240
Rubafu, Tanzania 1°5' S, 31°51' E 224
Rubel', Belarus 51°57' N, 27°5' E 152
Rubene, Latv. 57°27' N, 25°13' E 166
Rubeži, Europe 42°46' N, 19°1' E 168
Rubi, river, Dem. Rep. of the Congo 2°33' N, 25°16' E 224
Rubiataba, Braz. 15°11' S, 49°51' W 138
Rubielos de Mora, Sp. 40°10' N, 0°40' E 164
Rubim, Braz. 16°23' S, 40°33' W 138
Rubin, Mount, peak, Antarctica 73°31' S, 64°58' E 248
Rubio, Venez. 7°41' N, 72°23' W 136
Rubio, peak, Sp. 41°25' N, 3°51' W 164
Rubondo Island National Park, Tanzania 2°31' S, 32°6' E 224
Rubtsovsk, Russ. 51°31' N, 81°11' E 184
Ruby, Alas., U.S. 64°33' N, 155°34' W 98
Ruby Beach, site, Wash., U.S. 47°42' N, 124°27' W 100
Ruby Dome, peak, Nev., U.S. 40°36' N, 115°33' W 90
Ruby Mountains, Nev., U.S. 40°30' N, 115°37' W 90
Ruby Range, Mont., U.S. 44°58' N, 112°50' W 90
Rucava, Latv. 56°9' N, 21°8' E 166
Ruch'i, Russ. 66°2' N, 41°6' E 154
Ruch'i Karel'skiye, Russ. 66°59' N, 32°10' E 152
Ruda, Pol. 53°35' N, 22°30' E 152
Rudall River National Park, Austral. 22°34' S, 122°13' E 238
Rudan, Iran 27°26' N, 57°18' E 196
Rudauli, India 26°44' N, 81°45' E 188
Rudawka, Pol. 53°51' N, 23°29' E 166
Rudbar, Afghan. 30°6' N, 62°37' E 186
Rūdbār, Iran 36°50' N, 49°21' E 195
Rudinice, Europe 43°4' N, 18°50' E 168
Rūdiškės, Lith. 54°30' N, 24°48' E 166
Rudky, Ukr. 49°38' N, 23°28' E 152
Rudne, Ukr. 49°50' N, 23°51' E 152
Rudnica, Serb. and Mont. 43°13' N, 20°43' E 168
Rūdnīchnyy, Kaz. 44°39' N, 78°55' E 184
Rudnichnyy, Russ. 59°39' N, 52°32' E 154
Rudnichnyy, Russ. 59°40' N, 60°17' E 154
Rudnik, Serb. and Mont. 44°3' N, 20°26' E 168
Rudnik, Serb. and Mont. 44°8' N, 20°28' E 168
Rudno, Russ. 58°57' N, 28°15' E 166
Rudnya, Russ. 54°57' N, 31°11' E 154
Rūdnyy, Kaz. 52°58' N, 63°5' E 184
Rudo, Bosn. and Herzg. 43°37' N, 19°22' E 168
Rudolf, Lake see Turkana, Lake, Kenya 2°32' N, 34°10' E 206
Rudolph, Ostrov, island, Russ. 81°54' N, 59°19' E 160
Rudong, China 32°18' N, 121°11' E 198
Rudyard, Mich., U.S. 46°13' N, 84°36' W 94
Rudzyensk, Belarus 53°35' N, 27°53' E 152
Rue, Fr. 50°15' N, 1°39' E 163
Rufa'a, Sudan 14°44' N, 33°23' E 182
Rufiji, river, Tanzania 8°14' S, 37°49' E 224
Rufino, Arg. 34°16' S, 62°41' W 139
Rufisque, Senegal 14°45' N, 16°56' W 214
Rufunsa, Zambia 15°4' S, 29°36' E 224
Rugāji, Latv. 57°0' N, 27°4' E 166
Rugby, N. Dak., U.S. 48°20' N, 99°60' W 90
Rugby, U.K. 52°22' N, 1°16' W 162
Rugei, oil field, Kuwait 29°10' N, 46°47' E 196
Rugeley, U.K. 52°45' N, 1°57' W 162
Rugozero, Russ. 64°5' N, 32°42' E 152
Ruhengeri, Rwanda 1°32' S, 29°36' E 224
Ruhla, Ger. 50°53' N, 10°21' E 167
Ruhnu Saar, island, Est. 57°41' N, 23°5' E 166
Ruhr, region, Ger. 51°38' N, 7°7' E 167
Ruhr, river, Ger. 51°21' N, 8°10' E 167
Ruhuhu, river, Tanzania 10°16' S, 34°54' E 224
Ruhuna National Park, Sri Lanka 6°21' N, 81°4' E 172
Rui Barbosa, Braz. 12°18' S, 40°27' W 132
Rui'an, China 27°45' N, 120°39' E 198
Ruidosa, Tex., U.S. 29°58' N, 104°41' W 92
Ruidoso, N. Mex., U.S. 33°19' N, 105°41' W 92
Ruidoso Downs, N. Mex., U.S. 33°19' N, 105°35' W 92
Ruijin, China 25°50' N, 116°0' E 198
Ruinas de Numancia, ruin(s), Sp. 41°48' N, 2°30' W 164
Ruinen, Neth. 52°45' N, 6°21' E 163
Ruiru, Kenya 1°9' S, 36°56' E 224
Ruivo, Pico, peak, Port. 32°38' N, 17°4' W 214
Ruíz, Mex. 21°57' N, 105°8' W 114
Ruj, peak, Bulg. 42°50' N, 22°32' E 168
Rujen, peak, Maced. 42°8' N, 22°28' E 168
Rūjiena, Latv. 57°54' N, 25°18' E 166
Ruker, Mount, peak, Antarctica 73°47' S, 63°43' E 248
Ruki, river, Dem. Rep. of the Congo 1°60' N, 18°32' E 218
Rukungiri, Uganda 0°51' N, 29°55' E 224
Rukwa, adm. division, Tanzania 6°54' S, 30°38' E 224
Rule, Tex., U.S. 33°10' N, 99°54' W 92
Rum Cay, island, Bahamas 23°32' N, 74°47' W 116
Rum, river, Minn., U.S. 45°43' N, 93°41' W 94
Ruma, Serb. and Mont. 45°0' N, 19°49' E 168
Rumāh, Saudi Arabia 25°34' N, 47°11' E 196
Rumaila, oil field, Iraq 30°15' N, 47°23' E 196
Rumaylah, 'Urūqar, Saudi Arabia 23°47' N, 47°58' E 196
Rumaysh, Leb. 33°4' N, 35°21' E 194
Rumbek, Sudan 6°47' N, 29°38' E 224
Rumford, Me., U.S. 44°32' N, 70°33' W 104
Rumia, Pol. 54°34' N, 18°24' E 152
Rumija, peak, Europe 42°5' N, 19°9' E 168
Rumilly, Fr. 45°51' N, 5°56' E 150
Rumney, N.H., U.S. 43°48' N, 71°50' W 104
Rumo, Fin. 63°49' N, 28°31' E 152
Rumonge, Burundi 3°59' S, 29°24' E 218
Rumphi, Malawi 11°1' S, 33°49' E 224
Rumput, peak, Indonesia 1°44' N, 109°35' E 196
Rumuruti, Kenya 0°15' N, 36°32' E 224
Runan, China 33°0' N, 114°19' E 198
Runaway, Cape, N.Z. 37°32' S, 177°29' E 240
Runcorn, U.K. 53°19' N, 2°44' W 162
Runde, river, Zimb. 21°15' S, 31°22' E 227
Rundeng, Indonesia 2°41' N, 97°48' E 196
Rundēni, Latv. 56°15' N, 27°50' E 166
Rundu, Namibia 17°54' S, 19°44' E 220
Rundvik, Nor. 63°30' N, 19°24' E 152
Runere, Tanzania 3°7' S, 33°15' E 224
Runge, Tex., U.S. 28°52' N, 97°43' W 92
Rungu, Dem. Rep. of the Congo 3°12' N, 27°54' E 224
Rungwa, Tanzania 6°58' S, 33°32' E 224
Rungwa Game Reserve, Tanzania 7°5' S, 33°52' E 206
Rungwa, river, Tanzania 7°24' S, 32°3' E 224
Rungwe Mountain, peak, Tanzania 9°5' S, 33°58' E 224
Runib, oil field, Oman 18°45' N, 56°6' E 182
Ruokolahti, Fin. 61°17' N, 28°49' E 166
Ruoqiang, China 39°6' N, 88°12' E 188
Ruovesi, Fin. 61°57' N, 24°0' E 166
Rupanco, Lago, lake, Chile 40°49' S, 73°42' W 134
Rupara, Namibia 17°52' S, 19°7' E 220
Rupat, island, Indonesia 1°59' N, 101°48' E 196
Rupert, Idaho, U.S. 42°38' N, 113°40' W 90
Rupert, Vt., U.S. 43°15' N, 73°14' W 104
Rupert, Baie de 51°24' N, 80°18' W 80
Rupert Creek, river, Can. 57°18' N, 93°20' W 108
Ruponda, Tanzania 10°17' S, 38°41' E 224
Ruppert Coast, Antarctica 75°24' S, 126°21' W 248
Rur, river, Ger. 50°36' N, 6°29' E 167
Rurrenabaque, Bol. 14°30' S, 67°34' W 137
Rusambo, Zimb. 16°36' S, 32°12' E 224
Rušani, Croatia 45°53' N, 17°32' E 168
Rusanova, Russ. 69°32' N, 63°38' E 169
Rusanova, Zaliv 74°43' N, 55°55' E 160
Rusanovo, Russ. 70°35' N, 56°13' E 169
Rusape, Zimb. 18°34' S, 32°8' E 224
Ruse, Bulg. 43°50' N, 25°57' E 156
Ruse, adm. division, Bulg. 43°32' N, 25°31' E 156
Rushan, Taj. 37°57' N, 71°37' E 197
Rushden, U.K. 52°17' N, 0°36' E 162
Rushford, Minn., U.S. 43°48' N, 91°45' W 110
Rushville, Ind., U.S. 39°36' N, 85°28' W 102
Rushville, Mo., U.S. 40°6' N, 90°33' W 94
Rushville, Nebr., U.S. 42°42' N, 102°29' W 90
Rusizi, river, Africa 2°44' S, 29°0' E 224
Rusk, Tex., U.S. 31°46' N, 95°9' W 103
Ruskie Piaski, Pol. 50°48' N, 23°6' E 152
Rusksträsk, Nor. 64°49' N, 18°44' E 152
Rusnė, Lith. 55°18' N, 21°19' E 166
Rusoma, Russ. 64°45' N, 45°53' E 154
Rušonu Ezers, lake, Latv. 56°12' N, 26°49' E 166
Russas, Braz. 4°58' S, 37°59' W 132
Russell, Can. 50°47' N, 101°17' W 90
Russell, Kans., U.S. 38°52' N, 98°52' W 90
Russell, Ky., U.S. 38°31' N, 82°43' W 94
Russell, Cape, Antarctica 74°37' S, 169°23' E 248
Russell Cave National Monument, Ala., U.S. 34°57' N, 85°52' W 96
Russell Fiord 59°52' N, 140°33' W 98
Russell Island, island, Can. 73°57' N, 103°15' W 106
Russell Islands, Solomon Sea 9°5' S, 159°10' E 242
Russell Lake, Can. 57°22' N, 105°59' W 108
Russell Lake, lake, Can. 56°9' N, 102°6' W 108
Russell, Mount, peak, Austral. 23°17' S, 130°14' E 230
Russells Point, Ohio, U.S. 40°27' N, 83°54' W 102
Russellville, Ala., U.S. 34°30' N, 87°43' W 96
Russellville, Ark., U.S. 35°15' N, 93°8' W 96
Russellville, Ky., U.S. 36°50' N, 86°54' W 96
Rüsselsheim, Ger. 49°59' N, 8°24' E 167

Russi, It. 44°22' N, 12°2' E 167
Russia 65°0' N, 97°26' E 160
Russian Fort Elizabeth State Historical Park, Hawai'i, U.S. 21°56' N, 159°42' W 99
Russian Mission, Alas., U.S. 61°46' N, 161°26' W 98
Russian Peak, Calif., U.S. 41°16' N, 123°3' W 90
Russiaville, Ind., U.S. 40°25' N, 86°16' W 102
Russkaya Gavan', Russ. 76°5' N, 62°55' E 160
Russkaya Polyana, Russ. 53°47' N, 73°50' E 184
Russkiy, Ostrov, island, Russ. 77°12' N, 88°39' E 160
Russum, Miss., U.S. 31°52' N, 91°1' W 103
Rust'avi, Ga. 41°32' N, 45°0' E 195
Rustenburg, S. Af. 25°41' S, 27°13' E 227
Ruston, La., U.S. 32°30' N, 92°39' W 103
Rutana, Burundi 3°57' S, 29°59' E 224
RÜtenbrock, Ger. 52°50' N, 7°6' E 163
Ruteng, Indonesia 8°32' S, 120°28' E 238
Ruth, Miss., U.S. 31°22' N, 90°20' W 103
Ruth, Nev., U.S. 39°17' N, 114°60' W 90
Rüthen, Ger. 51°27' N, 8°25' E 167
Rutheron, N. Mex., U.S. 36°43' N, 106°36' W 92
Ruthin, U.K. 53°6' N, 3°17' W 162
Rutland, Ohio, U.S. 39°2' N, 82°8' W 102
Rutland, Vt., U.S. 43°36' N, 72°59' W 104
Rutland Island, India 11°11' N, 91°46' E 188
Rutledge Lake, lake, Can. 61°32' N, 111°30' W 108
Rutledge, river, Can. 61°13' N, 112°19' W 108
Rutshuru, Dem. Rep. of the Congo 1°13' S, 29°26' E 224
Ruurlo, Neth. 52°5' N, 6°27' E 163
Ruvozero, Russ. 66°27' N, 30°44' E 152
Ruvu, Tanzania 6°46' S, 38°43' E 224
Ruvu, river, Tanzania 7°24' S, 38°14' E 218
Ruvuma, adm. division, Tanzania 11°2' S, 35°25' E 224
Ruvuma, river, Africa 11°25' S, 38°25' E 224
Ruwe, Dem. Rep. of the Congo 10°39' S, 25°29' E 224
Ruwenzori, Uganda 0°12' N, 29°58' E 224
Ruwenzori Mountain National Park, Dem. Rep. of the Congo 0°20' N, 29°40' E 206
Ruwer, Ger. 49°46' N, 6°43' E 167
Ruzayevka, Russ. 54°2' N, 44°52' E 154
Ruzhany, Belarus 52°52' N, 24°53' E 152
Rwanda 2°4' S, 29°53' E 224
Rwindi, Dem. Rep. of the Congo 0°47' N, 29°16' E 224
Ryabovo, Russ. 61°33' N, 47°54' E 154
Ryan, Okla., U.S. 34°0' N, 97°57' W 92
Ryasna, Belarus 54°38' N, 29°53' E 166
Ryazan', Russ. 54°36' N, 39°43' E 154
Ryazan', adm. division, Russ. 54°26' N, 39°28' E 154
Ryazhsk, Russ. 53°40' N, 40°4' E 154
Rybach'e, Kaz. 46°29' N, 81°34' E 184
Rybachiy, Russ. 55°9' N, 20°49' E 166
Rybachiy, Poluostrov, Russ. 69°50' N, 28°33' E 152
Rybinsk, Russ. 58°1' N, 38°49' E 154
Rybinskoye Vodokhranilishche, lake, Russ. 58°29' N, 37°45' E 154
Rybnaya Sloboda, Russ. 55°28' N, 50°2' E 154
Rybnik, Pol. 50°4' N, 18°33' E 152
Rycroft, Can. 55°44' N, 118°43' W 108
Ryderwood, Wash., U.S. 46°21' N, 123°3' W 100
Rye, Colo., U.S. 37°55' N, 104°57' W 90
Rye, N.H., U.S. 43°0' N, 70°47' W 104
Rye, N.Y., U.S. 40°58' N, 73°42' W 104
Rye, U.K. 50°57' N, 0°44' E 162
Rye, river, U.K. 54°11' N, 0°58' E 162
Ryegate, Mont., U.S. 46°17' N, 109°17' W 90
Ryfylke, region, Nor. 59°16' N, 5°53' E 152
Rykovo, Russ. 56°9' N, 28°51' E 166
Ryley, Can. 53°16' N, 112°27' W 108
Ryl'sk, Russ. 51°32' N, 34°38' E 158
Rymättylä, Fin. 60°21' N, 21°55' E 166
Ryn, Pol. 53°55' N, 21°32' E 166
Rynda, Russ. 68°51' N, 36°49' E 152
Ryōtsu, Japan 38°6' N, 138°26' E 201
Rypin, Pol. 53°4' N, 19°25' E 152
Rysy, peak, Slovakia 49°10' N, 19°58' E 152
Rytel, Pol. 53°45' N, 17°48' E 152
Ryūjin, Japan 33°57' N, 135°33' E 201
Ryukyu Islands (Nansei Shotō), East China Sea 25°0' N, 125°56' E 190
Ryukyu Trench, Philippine Sea 25°33' N, 129°7' E 254
Rzeszów, Pol. 50°1' N, 22°0' E 152
Rzhev, Russ. 56°14' N, 34°24' E 154

S

's Gravenhage (The Hague), Neth. 52°5' N, 4°18' E 167
's Hertogenbosch, Neth. 51°41' N, 5°18' E 167
Sa, Thai. 18°39' N, 100°42' E 202
Sa Dec, Vietnam 10°16' N, 105°45' E 202
Sa Pobla, Sp. 39°45' N, 3°1' E 164
Sa Vileta, Sp. 39°35' N, 2°37' E 150
Saa, Cameroon 4°20' N, 11°26' E 222
Saacow, Somalia 1°39' N, 42°28' E 224
Sa'ādatābād, Iran 27°58' N, 55°55' E 196
Saales, Fr. 48°20' N, 7°6' E 163
Saanen, Switz. 46°29' N, 7°16' E 167
Saanich, Can. 48°26' N, 123°22' W 100
Saarbrücken, Ger. 49°14' N, 6°58' E 163
Saarburg, Ger. 49°36' N, 6°33' E 163
Sääre, Est. 57°55' N, 22°2' E 166
Saaremaa (Ösel), island, Est. 58°32' N, 21°21' E 166
Saarenkylä, Fin. 63°16' N, 25°2' E 152
Saari, Fin. 61°38' N, 29°45' E 166
Saarijärvi, Fin. 62°42' N, 25°12' E 152
Saariselkä, Fin. 68°5' N, 27°26' E 152
Saarland, adm. division, Ger. 49°21' N, 6°36' E 163
Saarlouis, Ger. 49°18' N, 6°45' E 163
Sa'ata, Sudan 12°41' N, 29°33' E 216
Saatta, Eritrea 16°28' N, 37°22' E 182
Saavedra, Arg. 37°46' S, 62°21' W 139
Sab' Ābār, Syr. 33°43' N, 37°40' E 180
Saba, island, Saba 17°39' N, 63°12' W 116
Šabac, Serb. and Mont. 44°44' N, 19°41' E 168
Sabadell, Sp. 41°33' N, 2°5' E 164
Sabae, Japan 35°56' N, 136°11' E 201
Sabah, region, Malaysia 4°57' N, 115°59' E 203
Sabán, oil field, Venez. 9°7' N, 65°53' W 136
Sabana, Col. 3°48' N, 70°58' W 136
Sabana, Archipiélago de, North Atlantic Ocean 23°19' N, 80°40' W 116
Sabana de La Mar, Dom. Rep. 19°2' N, 69°24' W 116
Sabanalarga, Col. 10°36' N, 74°56' W 115
Sabancuy, Mex. 18°57' N, 91°12' W 115
Sabang, Indonesia 0°9' N, 119°53' E 192
Sabang, Indonesia 5°54' N, 95°19' E 196
Şabanözü, Turk. 40°29' N, 33°16' E 156
Sabará, Braz. 19°52' S, 43°47' W 138
Sabarei, Kenya 4°17' N, 36°56' E 224
Sabasṭīyah, West Bank 32°16' N, 35°11' E 194
Sabattus, Me., U.S. 44°7' N, 70°7' W 104
Sabattus Pond, lake, Me., U.S. 44°9' N, 70°16' W 104
Sabaudia, It. 41°18' N, 13°2' E 156
Sabaya, Bol. 19°3' S, 68°24' W 137
Sabbathday Lake, Me., U.S. 43°59' N, 70°23' W 104
Sabderat, Eritrea 15°23' N, 36°38' E 182
Sabetha, Kans., U.S. 39°53' N, 95°48' W 90
Şabḩā, Jordan 32°19' N, 36°30' E 194
Sabhā, Lib. 27°5' N, 14°26' E 216
Şabḩah, Saudi Arabia 23°13' N, 44°40' E 182
Sabidana, Jebel, peak, Sudan 18°3' N, 36°41' E 182
Sabie, S. Af. 25°6' S, 30°49' E 227
Sabile, Latv. 57°3' N, 22°33' E 166
Sabina, Ohio, U.S. 39°29' N, 83°37' W 102
Sabinal, Mex. 30°55' N, 107°35' W 92
Sabinal, Tex., U.S. 29°18' N, 99°28' W 92
Sabinal, Cayo, island, Cuba 21°41' N, 77°10' W 116
Sabinal, Punta del, Sp. 36°31' N, 2°42' W 164
Sabiñánigo, Sp. 42°30' N, 0°23' E 164
Sabinas Hidalgo, Mex. 26°30' N, 100°11' W 114
Sabine, Tex., U.S. 29°41' N, 93°53' W 103
Sabine Pass, Tex., U.S. 29°43' N, 93°54' W 103
Sabine, river, U.S. 30°33' N, 93°40' W 103
Sabiote, Sp. 38°4' N, 3°18' W 164
Sabitsy, Russ. 58°49' N, 29°17' E 166
Sablayan, Philippines 12°50' N, 120°48' E 203
Sable, Cape, Can. 43°19' N, 65°36' W 111
Sable, Cape, Fla., U.S. 25°12' N, 81°24' W 105
Sable Island, Can. 43°40' N, 61°10' W 106
Sable, Lac du, lake, Can. 54°20' N, 68°9' W 111
Sables, Lac des, lake, Can. 48°14' N, 70°17' W 111
Sabonkafi, Niger 14°37' N, 8°42' E 222
Sabrina Coast, Antarctica 68°56' S, 121°18' E 248
Sabriyah, oil field, Kuwait 29°50' N, 47°49' E 196
Sabtang, island, Philippines 20°13' N, 121°21' E 198
Sabun, river, Russ. 62°8' N, 81°15' E 169
Sabunçu, Azerb. 40°28' N, 50°0' E 180
Şabyā, Saudi Arabia 17°7' N, 42°36' E 182
Sabzawar see Shindand, Afghan. 33°17' N, 62°11' E 186
Sabzevār, Iran 36°16' N, 57°40' E 180
Sac City, Iowa, U.S. 42°24' N, 95°1' W 90
Sacaca, Bol. 18°7' S, 66°24' W 137
Sacajawea Peak, Oreg., U.S. 45°13' N, 117°23' W 90
Sacanta, Arg. 31°42' S, 63°4' W 139
Săcăşeni, Rom. 47°27' N, 22°40' E 168
Sachene, Col. 1°52' N, 74°2' W 136
Sacheon, S. Korea 34°56' N, 128°6' E 200
Sachigo, river, Can. 54°51' N, 90°58' W 106
Sachs Harbour, Can. 71°56' N, 124°42' W 106
Sacile, It. 45°57' N, 12°30' E 167
Sackets Harbor, N.Y., U.S. 43°56' N, 76°8' W 94
Sackville, Can. 45°52' N, 64°23' W 111
Saco, Me., U.S. 43°30' N, 70°27' W 104
Saco, Mont., U.S. 48°26' N, 107°17' W 90
Sacramento, Braz. 19°53' S, 47°30' W 138
Sacramento, Calif., U.S. 38°31' N, 121°35' W 90
Sacramento, Mex. 26°59' N, 101°44' W 82
Sacramento Mountains, N. Mex., U.S. 32°32' N, 105°43' W 92
Sacramento Pass, Nev., U.S. 39°8' N, 114°21' W 90
Sacramento Valley, Calif., U.S. 38°16' N, 121°56' W 100
Sacratif, Cabo, Sp. 36°34' N, 3°28' W 164
Sacromonte National Park, Mex. 19°16' N, 98°58' W 72
Săcueni, Rom. 47°20' N, 22°6' E 168
Sacul, Tex., U.S. 31°49' N, 94°55' W 103
Sacuriuiná, river, Braz. 14°4' S, 57°45' W 130
Şadad, Syr. 34°18' N, 36°55' E 194
Şa'dah, Yemen 16°57' N, 43°45' E 182
Saddat ash Shuqqah, Yemen 18°36' N, 50°29' E 182
Saddle Mountain, peak, Idaho, U.S. 43°54' N, 113°2' W 90
Saddle Mountains, Wash., U.S. 46°44' N, 119°47' W 90
Saddle Peak, India 13°9' N, 92°56' E 188
Saddle Peak, Mont., U.S. 45°46' N, 111°3' W 90
Saddleback Mountain, peak, Me., U.S. 46°24' N, 68°9' W 94
Şadḩ, Oman 17°4' N, 55°4' E 182
Sadiola, Mali 13°55' N, 11°43' W 222
Sadiqabad, Pak. 28°14' N, 70°3' E 186
Sado, island, Japan 38°11' N, 137°23' E 190
Sadovoye, Russ. 47°45' N, 44°27' E 158
Sadská, Czech Rep. 50°8' N, 14°58' E 152
Sa'dun, Sudan 11°18' N, 25°11' E 224
Sädvaluspen, Nor. 66°26' N, 16°43' E 152
Sae Islands, South Pacific Ocean 0°42' N, 144°26' E 192
Saebyŏl, N. Korea 42°49' N, 130°11' E 200
Saelices, Sp. 39°54' N, 2°49' W 164
Şafājah, Saudi Arabia 26°17' N, 38°44' E 180
Safaniya, oil field, Persian Gulf 28°2' N, 48°44' E 196
Şafarābād, Iran 39°2' N, 47°27' E 195
Säffle, Nor. 59°7' N, 12°52' E 152
Safford, Ala., U.S. 32°16' N, 87°22' W 103
Safford, Ariz., U.S. 32°48' N, 109°42' W 112
Saffron Walden, U.K. 52°1' N, 0°14' E 162
Safi, Mor. 32°17' N, 9°13' W 214
Safia, Hamada, Mali 23°5' N, 5°11' W 214
Şāfītā, Syr. 34°49' N, 36°7' E 194
Safonovo, Russ. 55°4' N, 33°16' E 154
Safonovo, Russ. 65°42' N, 47°34' E 154
Safranbolu, Turk. 41°14' N, 32°41' E 156
Şafwān, Iraq 30°6' N, 47°43' E 196
Sag Harbor, N.Y., U.S. 40°59' N, 72°18' W 104
Saga, China 29°23' N, 85°25' E 197
Saga, Japan 33°4' N, 133°4' E 201
Saga, Japan 33°15' N, 130°18' E 201
Saga, adm. division, Japan 33°17' N, 129°52' E 201
Sagae, Japan 38°23' N, 140°16' E 201
Sagaing, Myanmar 21°56' N, 95°56' E 202
Sagamore, Mass., U.S. 41°45' N, 70°33' W 104
Sagamore Beach, Mass., U.S. 41°47' N, 70°32' W 104
Saganaga Lake, Can. 48°12' N, 91°24' W 94
Sagar, India 14°9' N, 75°3' E 188
Sagar (Saugor), India 23°50' N, 78°45' E 188
Sagara, Japan 34°41' N, 138°11' E 201
Sagard, Ger. 54°32' N, 13°33' E 152
Sagarejo, Ga. 41°44' N, 45°17' E 195
Sagarmāthā see Everest, Mount, peak, China-Nepal 28°0' N, 86°53' E 197
Sagastyr, Russ. 73°18' N, 126°45' E 160
Saghyz, Kaz. 48°16' N, 54°55' E 158
Saginaw, Mich., U.S. 43°24' N, 83°56' W 102
Saginaw Bay 43°28' N, 84°8' W 80
Saginaw Point, Mich., U.S. 47°50' N, 88°41' W 94
Saglelpie, Liberia 6°52' N, 8°50' W 222
Saglek Bay 58°17' N, 63°17' W 106
Sagra, peak, Sp. 37°56' N, 2°36' W 164
Sagres, Ponta de, Port. 36°40' N, 8°56' W 150
Sagu, Myanmar 20°19' N, 94°41' E 202
Şagu, Rom. 46°4' N, 21°17' E 168
Saguache, Colo., U.S. 38°5' N, 106°8' W 90
Saguaro National Park, Ariz., U.S. 32°16' N, 113°14' W 80
Saguenay, river, Can. 48°5' N, 71°39' W 80
Sagunto-Sagunt, Sp. 39°40' N, 0°17' E 150
Sagwon, Alas., U.S. 69°23' N, 148°42' W 98
Sa'gya, China 28°53' N, 88°4' E 197
Sagyndyk, Mys, Kaz. 43°50' N, 50°14' E 158
Sahagún, Col. 8°58' N, 75°27' W 136
Sahagún, Sp. 42°22' N, 5°3' W 150
Şaham, Oman 24°8' N, 56°52' E 196
Sahara, Africa 33°57' N, 8°18' E 214
Saharanpur, India 29°56' N, 77°34' E 197
Saharsa, India 25°51' N, 86°34' E 197
Sahasinaka, Madagascar 21°49' S, 47°49' E 220
Sahaswan, India 28°3' N, 78°46' E 197
Sahel, region, Africa 15°2' N, 3°51' W 206
Sahiwal, Pak. 31°58' N, 72°22' E 186
Sahiwal, Pak. 30°39' N, 73°7' E 186
Şaḩrā' Awbārī, Lib. 28°22' N, 10°13' E 142
Şaḩrā' Marzūq, Lib. 24°58' N, 12°3' E 216
Sahtaneh, river, Can. 59°1' N, 122°22' W 108
Sahuaripa, Mex. 29°2' N, 109°14' W 92
Sahuayo, Mex. 20°3' N, 102°44' W 114
Sai Buri, Thai. 6°42' N, 101°38' E 196
Saibi, Indonesia 1°20' S, 98°50' E 196
Sa'id Bundas, Sudan 8°28' N, 24°39' E 224
Saïda, Alg. 34°48' N, 0°9' E 214
Saida (Sidon), Leb. 33°33' N, 35°22' E 194
Sa'īdābād (Sīrjan), Iran 29°29' N, 55°40' E 196
Saidpur, Bangladesh 25°47' N, 88°52' E 197
Saidpur, India 25°32' N, 83°14' E 197
Saidu, Pak. 34°44' N, 72°26' E 186
Saigon see Ho Chi Minh City, Vietnam 10°48' N, 106°40' E 202
Saih Nihayda, oil field, Oman 21°18' N, 57°5' E 182
Saija, Fin. 67°5' N, 28°49' E 152
Saijō, Japan 33°53' N, 133°10' E 201
Saijō, Japan 34°56' N, 133°7' E 201
Saikai National Park, Japan 33°23' N, 129°42' E 201
Saiki, Japan 32°57' N, 131°53' E 201
Saillagouse-Llo, Fr. 42°27' N, 2°1' E 164
Saillolof, Indonesia 1°7' S, 130°44' E 192
Sailu, India 19°25' N, 76°28' E 188
Saima, China 40°58' N, 124°15' E 200
Saimbeyli, Turk. 37°58' N, 36°5' E 156
Sain Alto, Mex. 23°32' N, 103°14' W 114
Şā'īn Dezh, Iran 36°46' N, 46°35' E 195
Saint Agnes Head, U.K. 50°20' N, 5°33' W 150
Saint Alban's, Can. 47°51' N, 55°52' W 111
Saint Albans, U.K. 51°44' N, 0°21' E 162
Saint Albans, Vt., U.S. 44°48' N, 73°6' W 94
Saint Albans Bay, Vt., U.S. 44°48' N, 73°9' W 110
Saint Alban's Head, English Channel 50°16' N, 2°21' W 150
Saint Albert, Can. 53°37' N, 113°39' W 108
Saint André, Cap, Madagascar 16°13' S, 43°55' E 220
Saint Andrew Bay 30°2' N, 86°50' W 80
Saint Andrews, Can. 45°4' N, 67°4' W 94
Saint Andrews, N.Z. 44°32' S, 171°10' E 240
Saint Anne, Ill., U.S. 41°1' N, 87°43' W 102
Saint Ann's Bay, Jam. 18°25' N, 77°14' W 116
Saint Ann's Head, U.K. 51°23' N, 5°31' W 150
Saint Anthony, Can. 51°20' N, 55°38' W 106
Saint Anthony, Idaho, U.S. 43°57' N, 111°41' W 90
Saint Augustine, Fla., U.S. 29°52' N, 81°20' W 105
Saint Augustine, Fla., U.S. 29°52' N, 81°20' W 73
Saint Bees Head, U.K. 54°30' N, 3°46' W 162
Saint Bernard, Philippines 10°17' N, 125°10' E 203
Saint Blaize, Cape, S. Af. 34°33' S, 22°12' E 227
Saint Boniface, Can. 49°52' N, 97°3' W 90
Saint Bride, Mount, peak, Can. 51°30' N, 116°3' W 90
Saint Catharines, Can. 43°8' N, 79°14' W 94
Saint Catherines Island, Ga., U.S. 31°25' N, 81°7' W 112
Saint Catherine's Point 50°16' N, 1°17' W 150
Saint Charles, Idaho, U.S. 42°8' N, 111°24' W 90
Saint Charles, Mich., U.S. 43°16' N, 84°8' W 102
Saint Charles, Minn., U.S. 43°57' N, 92°4' W 94
Saint Charles, Mo., U.S. 38°46' N, 90°31' W 94
Saint Christopher see Saint Kitts, island, Saint Kitts and Nevis 17°21' N, 62°47' W 118
Saint Clair, Mich., U.S. 42°48' N, 82°30' W 94
Saint Clair, Mo., U.S. 38°20' N, 90°60' W 94
Saint Clair, Pa., U.S. 40°42' N, 76°12' W 94
Saint Clair Shores, Mich., U.S. 42°28' N, 82°53' W 102
Saint Cloud, Fla., U.S. 28°15' N, 81°18' W 105
Saint Cloud, Minn., U.S. 45°32' N, 94°21' W 106
Saint Cloud, Minn., U.S. 45°32' N, 94°11' W 90
Saint Croix, Can. 45°33' N, 67°24' W 94
Saint Croix Falls, Wis., U.S. 45°23' N, 92°38' W 94
Saint Croix Island International Historic Site, Me., U.S. 45°6' N, 67°14' W 111
Saint Croix, island, U.S. 17°43' N, 64°47' W 118
Saint Croix National Scenic Riverway, Wis., U.S. 45°54' N, 92°44' W 110
Saint David, Ill., U.S. 40°28' N, 90°4' W 102
Saint David Island, U.K. 32°30' N, 64°41' W 118
Saint David's, U.K. 51°52' N, 5°16' W 150
Saint Edward, Nebr., U.S. 41°33' N, 97°52' W 90
Saint Elias, Mount, peak, Alas., U.S. 60°11' N, 141°6' W 98
Saint Elias Mountains, Can. 59°29' N, 138°43' W 98
Saint Elmo, Ala., U.S. 30°28' N, 88°16' W 103
Saint Elmo, Ill., U.S. 39°1' N, 88°51' W 102
Saint Eustatius, island, Saint Eustatius 17°24' N, 63°48' W 116
Saint Francis, Ark., U.S. 36°26' N, 90°9' W 96
Saint Francis, S. Dak., U.S. 43°8' N, 100°55' W 90
Saint Francis, Wis., U.S. 42°58' N, 87°53' W 102
Saint Francis Bay 34°9' S, 24°27' E 227
Saint Francis, Cape, Can. 47°49' N, 53°40' W 111
Saint Francis, Cape, S. Af. 34°36' S, 24°27' E 227
Saint Francis, river, Ark., U.S. 34°57' N, 90°30' W 80
Saint Francisville, Ill., U.S. 38°35' N, 87°39' W 102
Saint Francisville, La., U.S. 30°45' N, 91°23' W 103
Saint François Mountains, Mo., U.S. 37°20' N, 90°59' W 96
Saint George, Anadyrskiy Zaliv 56°35' N, 169°34' W 98
Saint George, Can. 45°7' N, 66°50' W 94
Saint George, S.C., U.S. 33°10' N, 80°34' W 96
Saint George, Utah, U.S. 37°6' N, 113°33' W 101
Saint George, Cape, Can. 48°23' N, 60°23' W 111
Saint George, Cape, Fla., U.S. 29°29' N, 85°1' W 96
Saint George, Cape, P.N.G. 5°1' S, 152°57' E 192
Saint George's, Can. 48°24' N, 58°28' W 111
Saint George's, Grenada 12°1' N, 61°50' W 116
Saint Georges Bay 45°38' N, 61°49' W 111
Saint George's Channel 52°2' N, 6°25' W 150
Saint Gregory, Cape, Can. 49°26' N, 59°21' W 111
Saint Gregory, Mount, peak, Can. 49°18' N, 58°17' W 111
Saint Helen, Lake, Mich., U.S. 44°19' N, 84°57' W 94
Saint Helena, island, U.K. 15°59' S, 5°45' W 253
Saint Helena, Mount, peak, Calif., U.S. 38°39' N, 122°43' W 90
Saint Helena Sound 32°21' N, 81°48' W 80
Saint Helens, Oreg., U.S. 45°50' N, 122°49' W 100
Saint Helens, U.K. 53°27' N, 2°45' W 162
Saint Helens, Mount, peak, Wash., U.S. 46°11' N, 122°14' W 100
Saint Helier, U.K. 49°11' N, 2°6' W 150
Saint Ignace, Mich., U.S. 45°51' N, 84°44' W 94
Saint Ives, U.K. 52°19' N, 0°3' E 162
Saint James, Mo., U.S. 37°59' N, 91°37' W 94
Saint James, Cape, Can. 51°40' N, 131°26' W 108
Saint James City, Fla., U.S. 26°29' N, 82°5' W 105
Saint John, Can. 45°16' N, 66°5' W 94
Saint John, Kans., U.S. 38°0' N, 98°46' W 90
Saint John, N. Dak., U.S. 48°55' N, 99°44' W 90
Saint John Bay 50°50' N, 57°41' W 111
Saint John, Cape, Can. 50°0' N, 55°30' W 111
Saint John, island, Virgin Is., U.S. 18°21' N, 64°44' W 118
Saint John's, Antigua and Barbuda 17°6' N, 61°59' W 116
Saint Johns, Ariz., U.S. 34°29' N, 109°22' W 92
Saint John's, Can. 47°22' N, 53°3' W 106
Saint John's, Can. 47°32' N, 52°49' W 111
Saint Johns, Mich., U.S. 43°0' N, 84°34' W 102
Saint Joseph, La., U.S. 31°54' N, 91°15' W 103
Saint Joseph, Mich., U.S. 42°5' N, 86°29' W 102
Saint Joseph, Mo., U.S. 39°45' N, 94°54' W 82
Saint Joseph Island, Can. 46°19' N, 84°1' W 80
Saint Joseph, Lake, Can. 50°49' N, 92°26' W 110
Saint Joseph, Lake, Can. 51°12' N, 91°31' W 80
Saint Joseph Point, Fla., U.S. 29°46' N, 86°14' W 96
Saint Kitts and Nevis, islands, Caribbean Sea 17°16' N, 62°41' W 118
Saint Kitts (Saint Christopher), island, Saint Kitts and Nevis 17°21' N, 62°47' W 118
Saint Landrey, La., U.S. 30°50' N, 92°16' W 103
Saint Laurent, Can. 50°24' N, 97°56' W 90
Saint Lawrence, Can. 46°54' N, 55°24' W 111
Saint Lawrence, S. Dak., U.S. 44°30' N, 98°57' W 90
Saint Lawrence, Gulf of 46°56' N, 63°44' W 111
Saint Lawrence Island, Alas., U.S. 62°43' N, 171°35' W 98
Saint Lawrence Islands National Park, Can. 44°20' N, 76°10' W 110
Saint Lawrence River, river, Can. 49°0' N, 69°0' W 111
Saint Lawrence Seaway, Lake Ontario 44°20' N, 75°7' W 80
Saint Leo, Fla., U.S. 28°20' N, 82°15' W 105
Saint Lewis, river, Can. 52°7' N, 57°9' W 111
Saint Louis, Mich., U.S. 43°22' N, 84°37' W 102
Saint Louis, Mo., U.S. 38°37' N, 90°15' W 94
Saint Louis, Mo., U.S. 38°38' N, 90°28' W 73
Saint Lucia, Cape, S. Af. 28°31' S, 31°58' E 227
Saint Lucia 13°53' N, 60°68' W 116
Saint Lucia Channel 14°11' N, 61°40' W 116
Saint Lucie, Fla., U.S. 27°29' N, 80°21' W 105
Saint Lucie Canal, Fla., U.S. 26°59' N, 80°23' W 105
Saint Marks, Fla., U.S. 30°8' N, 84°13' W 96
Saint Martin, island, Fr. 18°3' N, 63°4' W 116
Saint Martin, Lake, Can. 51°40' N, 98°53' W 108
Saint Martinville, La., U.S. 30°6' N, 91°51' W 103
Saint Mary, Cape, Can. 43°50' N, 66°35' W 94
Saint Mary Peak, Austral. 31°33' S, 138°20' E 230
Saint Marys, Can. 43°15' N, 81°8' W 102
Saint Marys, Ga., U.S. 30°43' N, 81°34' W 96
Saint Marys, Kans., U.S. 39°10' N, 96°5' W 92
Saint Marys, Ohio, U.S. 40°31' N, 84°24' W 102
Saint Marys Bay 44°20' N, 66°15' W 111
Saint Mary's, Cape, Can. 46°43' N, 55°22' W 111
Saint Marys City, Md., U.S. 38°10' N, 76°26' W 94
Saint Matthew Island, Alas., U.S. 60°27' N, 172°55' W 98
Saint Matthews, S.C., U.S. 33°39' N, 80°47' W 96
Saint Michael, Alas., U.S. 63°24' N, 162°1' W 106
Saint Michael, Alas., U.S. 63°20' N, 162°11' W 98
Saint Michael's Mount, site, English Channel 50°6' N, 5°35' W 150
Saint Nazianz, Wis., U.S. 44°0' N, 87°56' W 102
Saint Neots, U.K. 52°13' N, 0°15' E 162
Saint Ninian's Cave, site, U.K. 54°41' N, 4°31' W 150
Saint Norbert, Can. 49°48' N, 97°10' W 90
Saint Ouen 49°13' N, 2°14' W 150
Saint Paris, Ohio, U.S. 40°6' N, 83°58' W 102
Saint Paul, Anadyrskiy Zaliv 57°8' N, 170°16' W 98
Saint Paul, Can. 53°58' N, 111°19' W 108
Saint Paul, Minn., U.S. 44°55' N, 93°15' W 94
Saint Paul, Minn., U.S. 44°58' N, 93°28' W 106
Saint Paul, Nebr., U.S. 41°12' N, 98°28' W 90
Saint Paul, Cape, Ghana 5°42' N, 0°57' E 222
Saint Paul Island, Can. 47°15' N, 61°15' W 80
Saint Pauls, N.C., U.S. 34°48' N, 78°60' W 96
Saint Peter, Minn., U.S. 44°18' N, 93°59' W 94
Saint Peter and Saint Paul Rocks, islands, North Atlantic Ocean 0°54' N, 29°27' W 253
Saint Peter Port, U.K. 49°27' N, 2°32' W 150
Saint Peters, Can. 45°39' N, 60°53' W 111
Saint Petersburg, Fla., U.S. 27°47' N, 82°39' W 105
Saint Petersburg see Sankt-Peterburg, Russ. 59°55' N, 30°17' E 166
Saint Pierre and Miquelon, Fr. 47°5' N, 56°49' W 111
Saint Pierre Island, Seychelles 9°16' S, 50°11' E 218
Saint Pierre-Jolys, Can. 49°25' N, 97°1' W 90
Saint Sébastien, Cap, Madagascar 12°29' S, 47°49' E 220
Saint Simons Island, Ga., U.S. 31°8' N, 81°24' W 96
Saint Stephen, Can. 45°11' N, 67°15' W 82
Saint Stephen, S.C., U.S. 33°23' N, 79°56' W 96
Saint Terese, Alas., U.S. 58°28' N, 134°46' W 108
Saint Thomas, Can. 42°47' N, 81°11' W 102
Saint Thomas, N. Dak., U.S. 48°35' N, 97°27' W 90
Saint Thomas, island, U.S. 18°21' N, 64°56' W 118
Saint Vincent, Minn., U.S. 48°55' N, 97°13' W 90
Saint Vincent and the Grenadines 13°15' N, 61°12' W 116
Saint Vincent, Cap, Madagascar 21°58' S, 42°31' E 220
Saint Vincent Island, Fla., U.S. 29°8' N, 85°32' W 112
Saint Vith, Belg. 50°16' N, 6°7' E 167
Saint Walburg, Can. 53°38' N, 109°12' W 108
Saint-Agapit, Can. 46°33' N, 71°26' W 94
Saint-Amand, Fr. 50°26' N, 3°24' E 163
Saint-Amand-Montrond, Fr. 46°43' N, 2°29' E 150
Saint-Augustin, Can. 51°14' N, 58°42' W 106
Saint-Avold, Fr. 49°6' N, 6°42' E 163
Saint-Brice, Fr. 45°52' N, 0°57' E 150
Saint-Brieuc, Fr. 48°30' N, 2°50' W 143
Saint-Denis, Can. 47°28' N, 69°56' W 94
Saint-Denis, Fr. 46°2' N, 1°25' W 150
Saint-Denis, Indian Ocean 20°54' S, 55°25' E 207
Saint-Denis, Réunion 20°55' S, 55°25' E 220
Saint-Dié, Fr. 48°17' N, 6°57' E 163
Saint-Dizier, Fr. 48°39' N, 4°56' E 163
Saint-Dizier, Fr. 48°39' N, 4°57' E 143
Sainte Agathe, Can. 49°33' N, 97°13' W 90
Sainte Anne, Can. 49°38' N, 96°40' W 90
Sainte Marie, Gabon 3°50' S, 11°2' E 218
Sainte Marie, Ill., U.S. 38°55' N, 88°2' W 102
Sainte Marie, Cap, Madagascar 26°14' S, 44°46' E 220
Sainte Marie, Nosy, island, Madagascar 16°50' S, 50°3' E 220
Sainte Rose du Lac, Can. 51°3' N, 99°31' W 90
Sainte-Agathe-des-Monts, Can. 46°2' N, 74°18' W 110

inte-Anne, Lac, lake, *Can.* 50°12' N, 68°19' W **111**
inte-Anne-de-Beaupré, *Can.* 47°0' N, 70°59' W **94**
inte-Anne-de-Madawaska, *Can.* 47°15' N, 68°3' W **111**
inte-Anne-des-Monts, *Can.* 49°6' N, 66°30' W **111**
inte-Anne-du-Lac, *Can.* 46°51' N, 75°22' W **94**
inte-Marie, *Can.* 46°26' N, 71°1' W **94**
inte-Marie, *Martinique* 14°45' N, 61°1' W **116**
inte-Maxime, *Fr.* 43°18' N, 6°37' E **150**
inte-Menehould, *Fr.* 49°5' N, 4°54' E **163**
intes, Les, islands, *Caribbean Sea* 15°44' N, 62°30' W **116**
nt-Étienne, *Fr.* 45°26' N, 4°23' E **150**
nt-Étienne-du-Rouvray, *Fr.* 49°21' N, 1°5' E **163**
nt-Félicien, *Can.* 48°38' N, 72°27' W **94**
nt-Gaudens National Historic Site, *N.H., U.S.* 43°29' N, 72°24' W **104**
nt-Georges, *Can.* 46°37' N, 72°40' W **111**
nt-Georges, *Can.* 46°6' N, 70°40' W **94**
nt-Georges, *South America* 3°54' N, 51°51' W **130**
int-Germain, *Fr.* 48°53' N, 2°5' E **163**
int-Hilaire-de-Riez, *Fr.* 46°43' N, 1°58' W **150**
int-Hyacinthe, *Can.* 45°36' N, 72°59' W **110**
int-Jacques, *Can.* 45°56' N, 73°35' W **94**
int-Jean, *South America* 5°23' N, 54°6' W **130**
int-Jean, Lac, lake, *Can.* 48°35' N, 72°56' W **80**
int-Jean, Lac, lake, *Can.* 48°33' N, 73°30' W **106**
int-Jean-de-Luz, *Fr.* 43°22' N, 1°40' W **164**
int-Jean-de-Maurienne, *Fr.* 45°16' N, 6°19' E **167**
int-Jean-Pied-de-Port, *Fr.* 43°9' N, 1°16' W **164**
int-Jean-sur-Richelieu, *Can.* 45°17' N, 73°17' W **94**
int-Joseph-de-Beauce, *Can.* 46°18' N, 70°53' W **111**
nt-Jovite, *Can.* 46°7' N, 74°36' W **94**
nt-Julien, *Fr.* 46°8' N, 6°4' E **167**
nt-Just-en-Chausée, *Fr.* 49°30' N, 2°26' E **163**
nt-Laurent du Maroni, *South America* 5°23' N, 53°57' W **123**
nt-Laurent du Maroni, *South America* 5°30' N, 54°1' W **130**
int-Léonard, *Can.* 47°9' N, 67°55' W **94**
int-Louis, *Senegal* 15°54' N, 16°22' W **207**
int-Louis, *Senegal* 16°3' N, 16°31' W **222**
int-Lys, *Fr.* 43°30' N, 1°10' E **164**
int-Malo, *Fr.* 48°39' N, 2°1' W **150**
int-Marc, *Haiti* 19°8' N, 72°43' W **116**
int-Marcel, Mont, peak, *South America* 2°21' N, 53°7' W **130**
nt-Martory, *Fr.* 43°8' N, 0°55' E **164**
nt-Mathieu, Pointe de, *Fr.* 47°32' N, 10°13' W **143**
nt-Michel, *Fr.* 49°54' N, 4°8' E **163**
nt-Mihiel, *Fr.* 48°53' N, 5°32' E **163**
nt-Nazaire, *Fr.* 47°16' N, 2°13' W **150**
nt-Nicolas-de-Port, *Fr.* 48°37' N, 6°18' E **163**
nt-Octave-de-Metis, *Can.* 48°35' N, 68°6' W **111**
nt-Omer, *Fr.* 50°45' N, 2°15' E **163**
nt-Pacôme, *Can.* 47°23' N, 69°57' W **94**
nt-Pascal, *Can.* 47°30' N, 69°49' W **111**
nt-Paul, *Fr.* 44°31' N, 6°44' E **167**
nt-Paul, island, *Fr.* 38°36' S, 77°34' E **254**
nt-Paul-de-Fenouillet, *Fr.* 42°48' N, 2°28' E **164**
nt-Pierre 46°46' N, 56°11' W **111**
nt-Pierre, *Fr.* 45°57' N, 1°20' W **150**
nt-Pierre, Pointe, *Can.* 48°32' N, 64°10' W **111**
nt-Pol, *Fr.* 50°21' N, 2°22' E **163**
nt-Pol-de-Léon, *Fr.* 48°41' N, 3°60' W **150**
nt-Pons, *Fr.* 43°28' N, 2°45' E **164**
nt-Quentin, *Fr.* 49°51' N, 3°16' E **163**
nt-Quentin, Pointe de, *Fr.* 50°16' N, 1°11' E **163**
nt-Romain, *Can.* 45°46' N, 71°7' W **94**
nt-Servan, *Fr.* 48°37' N, 2°1' W **150**
nt-Siméon, *Can.* 47°49' N, 69°54' W **94**
nt-Tite, *Can.* 46°43' N, 72°34' W **94**
int-Valéry-sur-Somme, *Fr.* 50°10' N, 1°37' E **163**
nt-Vallier, *Fr.* 43°41' N, 6°50' E **167**
nt-Vincent, *It.* 45°45' N, 7°39' E **167**
nt-Vincent-de-Tyrosse, *Fr.* 43°39' N, 1°20' W **150**
nt-Vivien, *Fr.* 45°25' N, 1°3' W **150**
pan, island, *U.S.* 15°11' N, 145°45' E **242**
ssac, *Fr.* 43°21' N, 2°9' E **164**
tama, adm. division, *Japan* 35°53' N, 138°44' E **201**
to, *Japan* 32°5' N, 131°23' E **201**
ama, *Bol.* 18°8' S, 68°60' W **137**
ama, Nevado, peak, *Bol.* 18°9' S, 68°58' W **137**
ka, *Kenya* 0°10' N, 39°23' E **224**
kai, *Japan* 34°35' N, 135°28' E **201**
kaide, *Japan* 34°18' N, 133°51' E **201**
kaiminato, *Japan* 35°30' N, 133°13' E **201**
kākah, *Saudi Arabia* 29°55' N, 40°15' E **180**
kakawea, Lake, *N. Dak., U.S.* 48°18' N, 102°54' W **90**
kal, *Senegal* 15°52' N, 16°15' W **222**
kalilo, *Tanzania* 8°8' S, 31°59' E **224**
kami, *Can.* 53°36' N, 76°8' W **106**
kami, Lac, lake, *Can.* 53°9' N, 78°17' W **106**
kami, river, *Can.* 53°6' N, 73°14' W **111**
kania, *Dem. Rep. of the Congo* 12°48' S, 28°31' E **224**
kar, *Turkm.* 38°55' N, 63°41' E **197**
karya, river, *Turk.* 40°3' N, 30°33' E **156**
kata, *Japan* 38°50' N, 139°53' E **190**
kçagöze, *Turk.* 37°10' N, 36°52' E **156**
kchu, *N. Korea* 40°22' N, 125°2' E **200**
kha, adm. division, *Russ.* 65°15' N, 125°44' E **160**
Sakhalin, adm. division, *Russ.* 44°21' N, 147°1' E **160**
Sakhalin, Ostrov, island, *Russ.* 50°36' N, 143°44' E **190**
Sakhalinskiy Zaliv 53°48' N, 139°32' E **160**
Sakhar, *Afghan.* 32°54' N, 65°32' E **186**
Şäki, *Azerb.* 41°12' N, 47°9' E **195**
Šakiai, *Lith.* 54°57' N, 23°1' E **166**
Sakinohama, *Japan* 33°24' N, 134°11' E **201**
Sakishima Shotō, islands, *East China Sea* 22°44' N, 124°24' E **238**
Sakmara, *Russ.* 52°1' N, 55°21' E **158**
Sa-koi, *Myanmar* 19°54' N, 97°1' E **202**
Sakon Nakhon, *Thai.* 17°13' N, 103°59' E **202**
Sakora, *Mali* 14°10' N, 9°21' W **222**
Sakrand, *Pak.* 26°10' N, 68°16' E **186**
Sakrivier, *S. Af.* 30°53' S, 20°25' E **227**
Saku, *Japan* 36°13' N, 138°25' E **201**
Saky, *Ukr.* 45°8' N, 33°35' E **156**
Säkylä, *Fin.* 61°2' N, 22°19' E **166**
Sal Mountains, La, *Utah, U.S.* 38°24' N, 109°18' W **90**
Sal, Punta, *Hond.* 15°53' N, 87°37' W **115**
Sal, river, *Russ.* 47°22' N, 43°19' E **184**
Sal, river, *Russ.* 47°12' N, 41°50' E **158**
Sala, *Eritrea* 16°56' N, 37°25' E **182**
Sala, *Nor.* 59°54' N, 16°34' E **152**
Šal'a, *Slovakia* 48°9' N, 17°52' E **152**
Salaberry-de-Valleyfield, *Can.* 45°16' N, 74°9' W **110**
Sălacea, *Rom.* 47°26' N, 22°18' E **168**
Salacgrīva, *Latv.* 57°44' N, 24°20' E **166**
Saladas, *Arg.* 28°16' S, 58°37' W **139**
Saladillo, *Arg.* 35°39' S, 59°47' W **139**
Saladillo, river, *Arg.* 28°47' S, 64°10' W **134**
Salado, river, *Arg.* 29°28' S, 62°14' W **139**
Salado, river, *Arg.* 35°50' S, 57°49' W **139**
Salado, river, *Arg.* 36°1' S, 66°45' W **134**
Salado, river, *Mex.* 26°57' N, 99°51' W **96**
Salaga, *Ghana* 8°33' N, 0°32' E **222**
Salagle, *Somalia* 1°48' N, 42°17' E **224**
Şalaḩ ad Dīn, *Iraq* 36°23' N, 44°8' E **195**
Salahīyah, *Syr.* 35°0' N, 37°3' E **194**
Salahmi, *Fin.* 63°47' N, 26°53' E **152**
Salair, *Russ.* 54°11' N, 85°49' E **184**
Sălaj, adm. division, *Rom.* 47°1' N, 22°45' E **156**
Salal, *Chad* 14°49' N, 17°14' E **216**
Salala, *Sudan* 21°15' N, 36°16' E **182**
Salālah, *Oman* 17°2' N, 54°6' E **182**
Salamanca, *Chile* 31°46' S, 71°1' W **134**
Salamanca, *Mex.* 20°34' N, 101°12' W **114**
Salamanca, *Sp.* 40°58' N, 5°38' W **214**
Salamis 480 B.C., battle, *Aegean Sea* 37°56' N, 23°25' E **156**
Salamis, ruin(s) 35°10' N, 33°51' E **194**
Salang, Kowtal-e, pass, *Afghan.* 35°21' N, 69°5' E **186**
Salangen, *Nor.* 68°51' N, 17°51' E **152**
Salantai, *Lith.* 56°2' N, 21°34' E **166**
Sălard, *Rom.* 47°13' N, 22°1' E **168**
Salardú, *Sp.* 42°42' N, 0°55' E **164**
Salaš, *Serb. and Mont.* 44°6' N, 22°19' E **168**
Salas de Bureba, *Sp.* 42°41' N, 3°29' W **164**
Salas de los Infantes, *Sp.* 42°0' N, 3°17' W **164**
Salaspils, *Latv.* 56°52' N, 24°18' E **166**
Salavat, *Russ.* 53°22' N, 55°51' E **154**
Salaverry, *Peru* 8°13' S, 78°57' W **123**
Salavina, *Arg.* 28°48' S, 63°26' W **139**
Salawati, island, *Indonesia* 1°28' S, 129°43' E **192**
Salay, *Philippines* 8°53' N, 124°50' E **203**
Salay Gómez Ridge, *South Pacific Ocean* 26°4' S, 95°15' W **252**
Sala-y-Gómez, Isla, island, *Chile* 26°25' S, 105°19' W **252**
Salbris, *Fr.* 47°25' N, 2°2' E **150**
Šalčininkai, *Lith.* 54°19' N, 25°22' E **166**
Sălciua de Jos, *Rom.* 46°24' N, 23°27' E **168**
Saldanha, *S. Af.* 32°59' S, 17°55' E **220**
Saldé, *Senegal* 16°9' N, 13°59' W **222**
Saldungaray, *Arg.* 38°13' S, 61°48' W **139**
Saldus, *Latv.* 56°38' N, 22°28' E **166**
Sale, *Austral.* 38°6' S, 147°3' E **231**
Sale, *U.K.* 53°25' N, 2°20' W **162**
Salekhard, *Russ.* 66°29' N, 66°46' E **169**
Salem, *Ark., U.S.* 36°21' N, 91°49' W **96**
Salem, *Conn., U.S.* 41°29' N, 72°17' W **104**
Salem, *Fla., U.S.* 29°52' N, 83°26' W **105**
Salem, *India* 11°37' N, 78°10' E **188**
Salem, *Ind., U.S.* 38°36' N, 86°6' W **102**
Salem, *Mo., U.S.* 37°37' N, 91°32' W **96**
Salem, *Mo., U.S.* 38°36' N, 88°57' W **94**
Salem, *N.H., U.S.* 42°47' N, 71°13' W **104**
Salem, *N.Y., U.S.* 43°10' N, 73°21' W **104**
Salem, *Ohio, U.S.* 40°53' N, 80°51' W **102**
Salem, *Oreg., U.S.* 44°55' N, 123°8' W **90**
Salem, *S. Dak., U.S.* 43°42' N, 97°24' W **90**
Salem, *Sw.* 59°14' N, 17°47' E **166**
Salem, *Va., U.S.* 37°17' N, 80°4' W **96**
Salem, *W. Va., U.S.* 39°16' N, 80°34' W **94**
Sälen, *Nor.* 61°10' N, 13°13' E **152**
Salford, *U.K.* 53°28' N, 2°19' W **162**
Salgótarján, *Hung.* 48°5' N, 19°49' E **168**
Salgueiro, *Braz.* 8°8' S, 39°7' W **132**
Salhus, *Nor.* 60°30' N, 5°16' E **152**
Sali, *Alg.* 26°58' N, 2°118' W **214**
Salida, *Calif., U.S.* 37°42' N, 121°6' W **100**
Salida, *Colo., U.S.* 38°32' N, 106°2' W **82**
Salies-du-Salat, *Fr.* 43°6' N, 0°56' E **164**
Şalīf, *Yemen* 15°18' N, 42°41' E **182**
Salihorsk, *Belarus* 52°47' N, 27°29' E **158**
Salima, *Malawi* 13°46' S, 34°24' E **224**
Salin, *Myanmar* 20°35' N, 94°39' E **202**
Salina, *Kans., U.S.* 38°49' N, 97°38' W **94**
Salina, *Utah, U.S.* 38°57' N, 111°52' W **90**
Salinas, *Braz.* 16°11' S, 42°22' W **138**
Salinas, *Calif., U.S.* 36°40' N, 121°40' W **100**
Salinas, *Ecua.* 2°17' S, 80°56' W **130**
Salinas, *Mex.* 22°36' N, 101°43' W **114**
Salinas de Añana, *Sp.* 42°48' N, 2°59' W **164**
Salinas de G. Mendoza, *Bol.* 19°39' S, 67°43' W **137**
Salinas, Ponta das, *Angola* 12°55' S, 12°20' E **220**
Salinas, Sierra de, *Calif., U.S.* 36°20' N, 121°30' W **100**
Salinas Victoria, *Mex.* 25°57' N, 100°18' W **114**
Saline, *La., U.S.* 32°9' N, 92°59' W **103**
Saline, *Mich., U.S.* 42°9' N, 83°48' W **102**
Saline, river, *Ark., U.S.* 33°9' N, 92°6' W **103**
Saline, river, *Kans., U.S.* 39°0' N, 99°22' W **90**
Saline, river, *La., U.S.* 32°20' N, 93°2' W **103**
Saline Valley, *Calif., U.S.* 36°47' N, 117°55' W **101**
Salines, Point, *Grenada* 11°53' N, 62°36' W **116**
Salinópolis, *Braz.* 0°38' N, 47°19' W **130**
Salisbury, *Conn., U.S.* 41°59' N, 73°26' W **104**
Salisbury, *N.H., U.S.* 43°22' N, 71°44' W **104**
Salisbury, *U.K.* 51°4' N, 1°47' W **162**
Salisbury, *Vt., U.S.* 43°53' N, 73°7' W **104**
Salisbury Island, *Can.* 63°31' N, 76°33' W **106**
Salisbury, Mount, peak, *Alas., U.S.* 69°7' N, 146°30' W **98**
Salisbury Plain, *U.K.* 51°18' N, 2°5' W **162**
Salisbury Sound 57°16' N, 136°9' W **108**
Salish Mountains, *Mont., U.S.* 48°30' N, 115°8' W **90**
Sălişte, *Rom.* 45°48' N, 23°54' E **156**
Şalkhad, *Syr.* 32°29' N, 36°43' E **194**
Salkum, *Wash., U.S.* 46°30' N, 122°39' W **100**
Salla, *Fin.* 66°49' N, 28°39' E **152**
Sallanches, *Fr.* 45°56' N, 6°37' E **167**
Sallent, *Sp.* 41°50' N, 1°54' E **164**
Sallent de Gállego, *Sp.* 42°46' N, 0°20' E **164**
Salliqueló, *Arg.* 36°45' S, 62°57' W **139**
Sallis, *Miss., U.S.* 33°0' N, 89°47' W **103**
Sallisaw, *Okla., U.S.* 35°26' N, 94°47' W **96**
Sallom, *Sudan* 19°23' N, 37°3' E **182**
Salluit, *Can.* 62°11' N, 75°42' W **106**
Salmās, *Iran* 38°17' N, 44°44' E **195**
Salme, *Est.* 58°9' N, 22°14' E **166**
Salmerón, *Sp.* 40°33' N, 2°30' W **164**
Salmi, *Russ.* 61°21' N, 31°56' E **152**
Salmo, *Can.* 49°11' N, 117°17' W **90**
Salmon, *Idaho, U.S.* 45°9' N, 113°54' W **90**
Salmon Arm, *Can.* 50°41' N, 119°17' W **90**
Salmon Falls Creek Reservoir, lake, *Idaho, U.S.* 42°19' N, 118°19' W **80**
Salmon Mountain, peak, *Idaho, U.S.* 45°34' N, 114°56' W **90**
Salmon Mountains, *Calif., U.S.* 41°7' N, 123°27' W **90**
Salmon, river, *Idaho, U.S.* 45°31' N, 116°2' W **106**
Salmon River Mountains, *Idaho, U.S.* 45°9' N, 116°18' W **90**
Salo, *Cen. Af. Rep.* 3°23' N, 16°8' E **218**
Salo, *Fin.* 60°23' N, 23°5' E **166**
Salò, *It.* 45°37' N, 10°31' E **167**
Salobelyak, *Russ.* 57°8' N, 48°5' E **154**
Salole, *Eth.* 4°27' N, 39°33' E **224**
Salome, *Ariz., U.S.* 33°46' N, 113°36' W **101**
Salomon Islands, *Indian Ocean* 5°16' S, 72°22' E **188**
Salon, *Fr.* 43°38' N, 5°5' E **150**
Salonae see Solin, *Croatia* 43°32' N, 16°28' E **168**
Salonga National Park, *Dem. Rep. of the Congo* 2°60' S, 20°3' E **218**
Salonga, river, *Dem. Rep. of the Congo* 1°6' S, 20°36' E **218**
Salonica see Thessaloníki, *Gr.* 40°38' N, 22°57' E **156**
Salonta, *Rom.* 46°48' N, 21°42' E **168**
Salor, river, *Sp.* 39°19' N, 6°20' W **164**
Salou, Cap de, *Sp.* 40°53' N, 1°8' E **164**
Salpausselkä, *Fin.* 61°19' N, 28°51' E **166**
Salsberry Pass, *Calif., U.S.* 35°55' N, 116°26' W **101**
Salses, *Fr.* 42°49' N, 2°53' E **164**
Sălsig, *Rom.* 47°30' N, 23°19' E **168**
Sal'sk, *Russ.* 46°27' N, 41°26' E **158**
Salsomaggiore Terme, *It.* 44°48' N, 9°58' E **167**
Salt, *Sp.* 41°57' N, 2°47' E **164**
Salt Fork Brazos, river, *Tex., U.S.* 33°9' N, 101°34' W **80**
Salt Fork Red, river, *Tex., U.S.* 35°5' N, 100°57' W **112**
Salt Lake, *Calif., U.S.* 36°41' N, 117°58' W **101**
Salt Lake City, *Utah, U.S.* 40°43' N, 111°59' W **90**
Salt River, *Can.* 60°6' N, 112°22' W **108**
Salt, river, *Can.* 59°36' N, 112°15' W **108**
Salt, river, *Mo., U.S.* 39°29' N, 91°35' W **94**
Salt River Range, *Wyo., U.S.* 42°53' N, 111°5' W **90**
Salta, *Arg.* 24°47' S, 65°25' W **132**
Saltburn by the Sea, *U.K.* 54°35' N, 0°59' E **162**
Saltcoats, *Can.* 51°2' N, 102°11' W **90**
Saltdal, *Nor.* 67°4' N, 15°24' E **152**
Saltee Islands, *Ire.* 51°49' N, 6°37' W **150**
Saltfleetby Saint Peter, *U.K.* 53°23' N, 0°10' E **162**
Saltillo, *Mex.* 25°23' N, 101°5' W **114**
Salto, *Arg.* 34°18' S, 60°16' W **139**
Salto, *Uru.* 31°22' S, 57°55' W **139**
Salto Angostura I, fall(s), *Col.* 1°59' N, 73°53' W **136**
Salto Angostura Ii, fall(s), *Col.* 2°11' N, 73°35' W **136**
Salto Angostura Iii, fall(s), *Col.* 2°54' N, 72°16' W **136**
Salto del Guairá, *Parag.* 24°3' S, 54°19' W **132**
Salto Grande, *Braz.* 22°54' S, 49°60' W **138**
Salto, river, *Mex.* 22°12' N, 99°19' W **114**
Saltoluokta, *Nor.* 67°23' N, 18°31' E **152**
Salton City, *Calif., U.S.* 33°16' N, 115°58' W **101**
Salton Sea Beach, *Calif., U.S.* 33°20' N, 115°60' W **101**
Salton Sea, lake, *Calif., U.S.* 33°19' N, 115°53' W **101**
Saltoro Kangri, peak, *Pak.* 35°22' N, 76°45' E **188**
Saltpond, *Ghana* 5°14' N, 1°5' W **222**
Saltsjöbaden, *Sw.* 59°15' N, 18°15' E **166**
Saltspring Island, *Can.* 48°48' N, 123°16' W **100**
Saltvik, *Fin.* 60°15' N, 20°3' E **166**
Saluda, *S.C., U.S.* 34°0' N, 81°47' W **96**
Saluggia, *It.* 45°13' N, 8°0' E **167**
Salûm, *Egypt* 31°33' N, 25°11' E **180**
Salur, *India* 18°31' N, 83°12' E **188**
Saluzzo, *It.* 44°38' N, 7°30' E **167**
Salvacañete, *Sp.* 40°5' N, 1°31' W **164**
Salvador (Bahia), *Braz.* 12°59' S, 38°28' W **132**
Salvador Mazza, *Arg.* 22°5' S, 63°48' W **137**
Salvage Islands see Selvagens, Ilhas, *North Atlantic Ocean* 30°18' N, 16°15' W **214**
Salvaterra, *Braz.* 0°46' N, 48°33' W **130**
Salvatierra, *Mex.* 20°11' N, 100°54' W **114**
Salvatierra, *Sp.* 42°50' N, 2°23' W **150**
Salwá, Dawḩat 24°39' N, 49°59' E **196**
Salween see Nu, river, *Asia* 31°21' N, 93°34' E **190**
Salween see Thanlwin, river, *Asia* 21°45' N, 98°44' E **202**
Salyan, *Azerb.* 39°36' N, 48°58' E **195**
Salyan, *Azerb.* 41°3' N, 49°6' E **180**
Salyersville, *Ky., U.S.* 37°44' N, 83°4' W **96**
Salym, *Russ.* 60°6' N, 71°26' E **169**
Salzbrunn, *Namibia* 24°24' S, 17°57' E **227**
Salzburg, *Aust.* 47°49' N, 13°3' E **156**
Salzgitter, *Ger.* 52°2' N, 10°22' E **152**
Salzkammergut, region, *Aust.* 47°39' N, 12°48' E **156**
Salzkotten, *Ger.* 51°40' N, 8°36' E **167**
Sam, *India* 26°47' N, 70°34' E **186**
Sam Rayburn Reservoir, lake, *Tex., U.S.* 31°3' N, 94°60' W **103**
Sam Son, *Vietnam* 19°45' N, 105°52' E **198**
Sama, river, *Peru* 18°11' S, 70°36' W **137**
Samah, oil field, *Lib.* 28°7' N, 19°0' E **216**
Samāḩ, spring, *Saudi Arabia* 29°2' N, 45°26' E **196**
Samaipata, *Bol.* 18°13' S, 63°52' W **137**
Samâlût, *Egypt* 28°16' N, 30°39' E **180**
Samaná, *Dom. Rep.* 19°12' N, 69°20' W **116**
Samaná, Cabo, *Dom. Rep.* 19°12' N, 69°7' W **116**
Samana Cay, island, *Bahamas* 23°10' N, 74°2' W **116**
Samandaği (Seleucia), *Turk.* 36°4' N, 35°57' E **156**
Samanga, *Tanzania* 8°20' S, 39°13' E **224**
Samaqua, river, *Can.* 49°53' N, 72°31' W **94**
Samar, *Jordan* 32°39' N, 35°48' E **194**
Samar, island, *Philippines* 12°14' N, 125°25' E **192**
Samara, *Russ.* 53°14' N, 50°14' E **154**
Samara, adm. division, *Russ.* 53°31' N, 49°15' E **154**
Samara, river, *Russ.* 52°22' N, 53°17' E **184**
Samarai, *P.N.G.* 10°38' S, 150°40' E **231**
Samaria Mountain, peak, *Idaho, U.S.* 42°4' N, 112°26' W **90**
Samariapo, *Venez.* 5°10' N, 67°44' W **136**
Samarinda, *Indonesia* 0°30' N, 117°7' E **192**
Samarqand, *Uzb.* 39°39' N, 67°0' E **197**
Sāmarrā', *Iraq* 34°17' N, 43°52' E **180**
Samarskoe, *Kaz.* 49°1' N, 83°23' E **184**
Samarskoye, *Russ.* 46°57' N, 39°38' E **156**
Samastipur, *India* 25°50' N, 85°47' E **197**
Samatiguila, *Côte d'Ivoire* 9°49' N, 7°35' W **222**
Samaúma, *Braz.* 0°8' N, 69°16' W **136**
Samaúma, *Braz.* 8°43' S, 67°22' W **130**
Samawah see As Samāwah, *Iraq* 31°15' N, 45°15' E **180**
Samba, *Burkina Faso* 12°40' N, 2°26' W **222**
Samba, *Gabon* 1°4' S, 10°41' E **218**
Samba, *India* 32°33' N, 75°9' E **188**
Sambalpur, *India* 21°29' N, 83°59' E **188**
Sambalpur, *India* 20°18' N, 81°2' E **188**
Sambas, *Indonesia* 1°22' N, 109°17' E **196**
Sambava, *Madagascar* 14°19' S, 50°8' E **220**
Sambhal, *India* 28°32' N, 78°34' E **197**
Sambhar, *India* 26°54' N, 75°13' E **197**
Sambiase, *It.* 38°58' N, 16°15' E **156**
Sambir, *Ukr.* 49°30' N, 23°11' E **152**
Sambolabbo, *Cameroon* 7°3' N, 11°57' E **218**
Samborombón, Bahía 34°27' S, 58°24' W **134**
Samburg, *Russ.* 66°52' N, 78°20' E **169**
Samburu Reserve, *Kenya* 0°29' N, 37°10' E **206**
Samcheok, *S. Korea* 37°27' N, 129°9' E **200**
Samdari, *India* 25°49' N, 72°34' E **186**
Samdŭng, *N. Korea* 38°59' N, 126°12' E **200**
Same, *Tanzania* 4°5' S, 37°44' E **224**
Samedan, *Switz.* 46°33' N, 9°52' E **167**
Samer, *Fr.* 50°38' N, 1°45' E **163**
Samfya, *Zambia* 11°21' S, 29°30' E **224**
Samgi, *N. Korea* 40°27' N, 128°20' E **200**
Samho, *N. Korea* 39°55' N, 127°51' E **200**
Şāmiţah, *Saudi Arabia* 16°35' N, 42°55' E **182**
Sammatti, *Fin.* 60°18' N, 23°48' E **166**
Samnangjin, *S. Korea* 35°24' N, 128°51' E **200**
Samnū, *Lib.* 27°17' N, 14°52' E **216**
Samnye, *S. Korea* 35°54' N, 127°5' E **200**
Samoa, *Calif., U.S.* 40°48' N, 124°11' W **90**
Samoa 13°50' S, 172°8' W **241**
Samoa, islands, *South Pacific Ocean* 13°58' S, 175°18' W **238**
Samoded, *Russ.* 63°37' N, 40°30' E **154**
Samoëns, *Fr.* 46°5' N, 6°43' E **167**
Samokov, *Maced.* 41°40' N, 21°8' E **168**
Samolva, *Russ.* 58°15' N, 27°38' E **166**
Samorogouan, *Burkina Faso* 11°24' N, 4°58' W **222**
Samoš, *Serb. and Mont.* 45°12' N, 20°47' E **168**
Sámos, island, *Gr.* 37°50' N, 26°34' E **180**
Samos, ruin(s), *Gr.* 37°40' N, 26°51' E **156**
Samothráki, island, *Gr.* 40°31' N, 25°17' E **180**
Samoylovka, *Russ.* 51°8' N, 43°44' E **158**
Sampa, *Ghana* 7°58' N, 2°43' W **222**
Sampacho, *Arg.* 33°24' S, 64°43' W **134**
Samparha Koura, *Mali* 14°38' N, 8°5' W **222**
Samper de Calanda, *Sp.* 41°10' N, 0°23' E **164**
Sampit, *Indonesia* 2°32' S, 112°46' E **192**
Samp'o, *N. Korea* 41°1' N, 127°9' E **200**
Sam'po, *N. Korea* 41°13' N, 129°42' E **200**
Sampwe, *Dem. Rep. of the Congo* 9°20' S, 27°23' E **224**
Samrē, *Eth.* 13°10' N, 39°12' E **182**
Samro, Ozero, lake, *Russ.* 58°58' N, 28°36' E **166**
Samrong, *Cambodia* 14°12' N, 103°34' E **202**
Samsŏ, *N. Korea* 41°17' N, 127°39' E **200**
Samsu, *N. Korea* 41°18' N, 128°2' E **200**
Samsun, *Turk.* 41°13' N, 36°13' E **143**
Samsun (Amisus), *Turk.* 41°17' N, 36°20' E **158**
Samthar, *India* 25°51' N, 78°55' E **197**
Samtredia, *Ga.* 42°9' N, 42°22' E **195**
Samuel, Mount, peak, *Austral.* 19°42' S, 133°57' E **230**
Samuhú, *Arg.* 27°30' S, 60°30' W **139**
Samui, Ko, island, *Thai.* 9°15' N, 99°59' E **202**
Samur, river, *Europe* 41°22' N, 47°38' E **195**
Samus', *Russ.* 56°46' N, 84°47' E **169**
Samut Prakan, *Thai.* 13°36' N, 100°36' E **202**
Samut Songkhram, *Thai.* 13°26' N, 100°2' E **202**
San, *Mali* 13°17' N, 4°56' W **222**
San Adrián, Cabo, *Sp.* 43°1' N, 8°54' W **150**
San Agustín, *Col.* 1°53' N, 76°18' W **136**
San Agustin, Cape, *Philippines* 6°17' N, 126°14' E **203**
San Agustín de Valle Fértil, *Arg.* 30°39' S, 67°35' W **134**
San Ambrosio Island, *Chile* 26°14' S, 79°39' W **253**
San Andreas, *Calif., U.S.* 38°11' N, 120°42' W **100**
San Andrés, *Bol.* 15°2' S, 64°28' W **137**
San Andrés, Isla de, island, *Col.* 12°23' N, 82°18' W **115**
San Andrés, Laguna de 22°40' N, 98°25' W **114**
San Andrés Tuxtla, *Mex.* 18°25' N, 95°12' W **114**
San Angelo, *Tex., U.S.* 31°27' N, 100°26' W **92**
San Anselmo, *Calif., U.S.* 37°58' N, 122°35' W **100**
San Antero, *Col.* 9°21' N, 75°46' W **136**
San Antonio, *Bol.* 14°56' S, 64°32' W **137**
San Antonio, *Col.* 1°48' N, 78°19' W **136**
San Antonio, *Peru* 3°45' S, 74°25' W **136**
San Antonio, *Tex., U.S.* 29°25' N, 98°30' W **92**
San Antonio, *Venez.* 3°29' N, 66°46' W **136**
San Antonio Bay 28°9' N, 96°58' W **112**
San Antonio, Cabo, *Arg.* 36°48' S, 57°6' W **139**
San Antonio da Cachoeira, *Braz.* 0°39' N, 52°31' W **130**
San Antonio de Areco, *Arg.* 34°15' S, 59°27' W **139**
San Antonio de Bravo, *Tex., U.S.* 30°11' N, 104°42' W **92**
San Antonio de Caparo, *Venez.* 7°32' N, 71°31' W **136**
San Antonio de las Alazanas, *Mex.* 25°15' N, 100°35' W **114**
San Antonio de los Cobres, *Arg.* 24°11' S, 66°23' W **132**
San Antonio, Lake, *Calif., U.S.* 35°49' N, 121°4' W **100**
San Antonio, Mount, peak, *Calif., U.S.* 34°17' N, 117°42' W **101**
San Antonio Mountain, peak, *Tex., U.S.* 31°56' N, 105°38' W **92**
San Antonio Mountains, *Nev., U.S.* 38°9' N, 117°34' W **90**
San Antonio, Punta, *Mex.* 29°28' N, 116°4' W **92**
San Antonio, river, *Tex., U.S.* 29°18' N, 99°13' W **80**
San Antonio, Sierra de, *Mex.* 30°9' N, 110°53' W **112**
San Ardo, *Calif., U.S.* 36°1' N, 120°55' W **100**
San Asensio, *Sp.* 42°29' N, 2°45' W **164**
San Augustine, *Tex., U.S.* 31°30' N, 94°7' W **103**
San Bartolo, *Peru* 12°28' S, 76°48' W **130**
San Benedetto Po, *It.* 45°2' N, 10°55' E **167**
San Benedicto, Isla, island, *Isla San Benedicto* 19°4' N, 110°53' W **112**
San Benito, *Tex., U.S.* 26°6' N, 97°37' W **114**
San Benito, Islas, islands, *North Pacific Ocean* 28°23' N, 116°19' W **112**
San Benito Mountain, peak, *Calif., U.S.* 36°21' N, 120°42' W **100**
San Bernardino, *Calif., U.S.* 34°6' N, 117°18' W **101**
San Bernardino Mountains, *Calif., U.S.* 34°12' N, 117°25' W **101**
San Bernardino Strait 12°35' N, 123°0' E **192**
San Bernardo, *Chile* 33°36' S, 70°45' W **134**
San Bernardo, *Mex.* 25°59' N, 105°28' W **114**
San Blas, *Mex.* 21°33' N, 105°17' W **114**
San Blas, *Mex.* 27°26' N, 101°45' W **96**
San Blas, Archipiélago de, *North America* 9°22' N, 78°6' W **115**
San Blas, Cape, *Fla., U.S.* 29°33' N, 85°57' W **96**
San Bonifacio, *It.* 45°23' N, 11°17' E **167**
San Borja, *Bol.* 14°51' S, 66°52' W **137**
San Borja, Sierra de, *Mex.* 29°34' N, 115°3' W **112**
San Buenaventura, *Bol.* 14°33' S, 67°38' W **137**
San Candido, *It.* 46°43' N, 12°17' E **167**
San Carlos, *Arg.* 27°45' S, 55°58' W **139**
San Carlos, *Arg.* 25°57' S, 65°57' W **134**
San Carlos, *Chile* 36°24' S, 71°59' W **134**
San Carlos, *Mex.* 29°0' N, 100°54' W **92**
San Carlos, *Mex.* 24°33' N, 98°56' W **114**
San Carlos, *Mex.* 27°59' N, 111°4' W **112**
San Carlos, *Mex.* 24°46' N, 112°6' W **112**
San Carlos, *Nicar.* 11°8' N, 84°46' W **115**
San Carlos, *Philippines* 15°55' N, 120°19' E **203**
San Carlos, *Philippines* 10°27' N, 123°22' E **203**
San Carlos, *Uru.* 34°48' S, 54°56' W **139**
San Carlos, *Venez.* 9°39' N, 68°36' W **136**
San Carlos, *Venez.* 1°56' N, 66°59' W **123**
San Carlos Centro, *Arg.* 31°44' S, 61°4' W **139**
San Carlos de Bolívar, *Arg.* 36°13' S, 61°6' W **139**
San Carlos de Río Negro, *Venez.* 1°52' N, 67°2' W **136**
San Carlos, Mesa de, peak, *Mex.* 29°37' N, 115°25' W **92**
San Carlos, Punta, *Mex.* 29°17' N, 115°44' W **92**
San Cayetano, *Arg.* 38°21' S, 59°37' W **139**
San Clemente, *Calif., U.S.* 33°25' N, 117°38' W **101**
San Clemente, island, *Calif., U.S.* 32°46' N, 118°22' W **101**
San Cosme, *Arg.* 27°22' S, 58°33' W **139**
San Cosme y Damián, *Parag.* 27°18' S, 56°20' W **139**
San Cristóbal, *Arg.* 30°17' S, 61°14' W **139**
San Cristóbal, *Bol.* 21°6' S, 67°10' W **137**
San Cristóbal, *Col.* 2°18' S, 73°2' W **136**
San Cristóbal, *Venez.* 7°44' N, 72°14' W **136**
San Cristóbal, Isla, island, *Ecua.* 0°45' N, 89°16' W **130**

San Cristobal, island, Solomon Islands 10°35′ S, 161°45′ E 242
San Cristóbal Verapaz, Guatemala 15°23′ N, 90°26′ W 115
San Custodio, Venez. 1°35′ N, 66°13′ W 136
San Diego, Calif., U.S. 32°43′ N, 117°11′ W 101
San Diego, Tex., U.S. 27°45′ N, 98°14′ W 92
San Diego, Cabo, Arg. 54°30′ S, 65°11′ W 134
San Donà di Piave, It. 45°38′ N, 12°33′ E 167
San Estanislao, Parag. 24°39′ S, 56°29′ W 132
San Esteban, Hond. 15°17′ N, 85°52′ W 115
San Esteban de Gormaz, Sp. 41°34′ N, 3°13′ W 164
San Esteban de Litera, Sp. 41°54′ N, 0°19′ E 164
San Esteban, island, Mex. 28°29′ N, 112°33′ W 112
San Felice sul Panaro, It. 44°50′ N, 11°8′ E 167
San Felipe, Col. 1°51′ N, 67°5′ W 136
San Felipe, Mex. 21°27′ N, 101°14′ W 114
San Felipe, Tex., U.S. 29°47′ N, 96°6′ W 96
San Felipe, Venez. 10°18′ N, 68°46′ W 136
San Felipe, Cayos de, Caribbean Sea 21°35′ N, 84°7′ W 116
San Felipe, peak, Mex. 17°8′ N, 96°43′ W 114
San Félix, Venez. 8°5′ N, 72°15′ W 136
San Félix Island, Chile 26°7′ S, 80°18′ W 253
San Fermín, Punta, Mex. 30°19′ N, 114°38′ W 92
San Fernando, Calif., U.S. 34°17′ N, 118°27′ W 101
San Fernando, Mex. 24°50′ N, 98°9′ W 114
San Fernando, Philippines 15°1′ N, 120°40′ E 203
San Fernando, Philippines 16°38′ N, 120°20′ E 203
San Fernando, Sp. 36°27′ N, 6°12′ W 164
San Fernando, Trinidad and Tobago 10°16′ N, 61°26′ W 116
San Fernando de Apure, Venez. 7°51′ N, 67°30′ W 136
San Fernando de Atabapo, Venez. 3°59′ N, 67°42′ W 136
San Fernando, river, Mex. 25°12′ N, 98°37′ W 114
San Francisco, Arg. 31°27′ S, 62°6′ W 139
San Francisco, Bol. 15°18′ S, 65°33′ W 137
San Francisco, Calif., U.S. 37°46′ N, 122°26′ W 100
San Francisco, Col. 1°10′ N, 76°58′ W 136
San Francisco, Mex. 30°49′ N, 112°37′ W 92
San Francisco Bay 37°36′ N, 122°19′ W 100
San Francisco, Cabo de, Ecua. 0°33′ N, 81°47′ W 130
San Francisco de Bellocq, Arg. 38°42′ S, 60°2′ W 139
San Francisco de Conchos, Mex. 27°35′ N, 105°18′ W 112
San Francisco de la Paz, Hond. 14°55′ N, 86°4′ W 115
San Francisco de Macorís, Dom. Rep. 19°16′ N, 70°15′ W 116
San Francisco de Paula, Cabo, Arg. 49°56′ S, 67°41′ W 134
San Francisco del Monte de Oro, Arg. 32°36′ S, 66°7′ W 134
San Francisco del Oro, Mex. 26°51′ N, 105°51′ W 112
San Francisco del Rincón, Mex. 21°0′ N, 101°52′ W 114
San Francisco Javier, Sp. 38°41′ N, 1°25′ E 150
San Francisco Mountain, Ariz., U.S. 35°17′ N, 111°58′ W 92
San Francisco Mountain, peak, Ariz., U.S. 35°19′ N, 111°47′ W 112
San Francisco, Paso de, pass, Chile 26°53′ S, 68°22′ W 132
San Gabriel, Ecua. 0°34′ N, 77°60′ W 136
San Gabriel Mountains, Calif., U.S. 34°24′ N, 118°19′ W 101
San Germán 18°4′ N, 67°4′ W 116
San Gervàs, peak, Sp. 42°17′ N, 0°47′ E 164
San Gregorio, Arg. 34°21′ S, 62°2′ W 139
San Gregorio, Uru. 32°36′ S, 55°50′ W 139
San Guillermo, Arg. 30°22′ S, 61°55′ W 139
San Hipólito, Punta, Mex. 26°55′ N, 115°40′ W 112
San Ignacio, Arg. 27°15′ S, 55°33′ W 132
San Ignacio, Belize 17°9′ N, 89°7′ W 115
San Ignacio, Bol. 16°29′ S, 60°60′ W 132
San Ignacio, Bol. 14°58′ S, 65°38′ W 137
San Ignacio, Mex. 23°56′ N, 106°26′ W 114
San Ignacio, Mex. 27°18′ N, 112°55′ W 112
San Ignacio, Parag. 26°51′ S, 56°58′ W 139
San Ignacio, Peru 14°5′ S, 68°58′ W 137
San Ignacio, Peru 5°2′ S, 78°60′ W 130
San Ildefonso, Cape, Philippines 15°40′ N, 122°1′ E 203
San In Kaigan National Park, Japan 35°30′ N, 134°30′ E 201
San Isidro, Peru 4°55′ S, 76°17′ W 130
San Jacinto, Calif., U.S. 33°47′ N, 116°59′ W 101
San Jacinto Mountains, Calif., U.S. 33°47′ N, 116°41′ W 101
San Jaime, Arg. 30°17′ S, 58°21′ W 139
San Javier, Arg. 30°33′ S, 59°58′ W 139
San Javier, Arg. 27°52′ S, 55°9′ W 139
San Javier, Bol. 14°38′ S, 64°42′ W 137
San Javier, Bol. 16°28′ S, 62°37′ W 132
San Javier, Mex. 28°36′ N, 109°45′ W 92
San Javier, Sp. 37°48′ N, 0°51′ E 164
San Javier, Uru. 32°40′ S, 58°5′ W 139
San Jerónimo, Mex. 17°7′ N, 100°28′ W 114
San Jerónimo, Peru 7°52′ S, 74°53′ W 130
San Joaquín, Bol. 13°8′ S, 64°51′ W 137
San Joaquin, Calif., U.S. 36°36′ N, 120°12′ W 100
San Joaquin Valley, Calif., U.S. 35°29′ N, 119°46′ W 100
San Jon, N. Mex., U.S. 35°6′ N, 103°20′ W 92
San Jorge, Arg. 31°54′ S, 61°49′ W 139
San Jorge, Nicar. 11°26′ N, 85°48′ W 115
San Jorge, Bahía de 31°0′ N, 113°17′ W 92
San Jorge, Golfo 46°26′ S, 68°15′ W 134
San Jorge, Golfo 46°19′ S, 69°42′ W 122
San Jorge, Golfo 45°51′ S, 70°25′ W 123
San Jorge, Gulf of 46°6′ S, 66°41′ W 253
San Jorge, river, Col. 7°40′ N, 75°55′ W 115
San José, Arg. 27°45′ S, 55°46′ W 139
San Jose, Calif., U.S. 37°19′ N, 121°54′ W 100
San José, Col. 2°42′ N, 68°3′ W 136
San José, C.R. 9°54′ N, 84°11′ W 115
San José, Guatemala 13°56′ N, 90°50′ W 115
San Jose, Ill., U.S. 40°18′ N, 89°37′ W 102
San José, Peru 14°44′ S, 70°10′ W 137
San José, Peru 3°29′ S, 76°33′ W 136
San Jose, Philippines 12°22′ N, 121°4′ E 203
San Jose, Philippines 15°48′ N, 120°57′ E 203
San Jose, Philippines 10°45′ N, 121°57′ E 203
San José, Sp. 38°55′ N, 1°17′ E 150
San José, Venez. 4°36′ N, 67°49′ W 136
San José de Amacuro, Venez. 8°28′ N, 60°29′ W 116
San José de Chiquitos, Bol. 17°50′ S, 60°44′ W 132
San José de Feliciano, Arg. 30°20′ S, 58°44′ W 139
San José de Jáchal, Arg. 30°15′ S, 68°46′ W 134
San José de Mayo, Uru. 34°21′ S, 56°42′ W 139
San José de Ocuné, Col. 4°15′ N, 70°22′ W 136
San José de Raíces, Mex. 24°33′ N, 100°14′ W 114
San José del Guaviare, Col. 2°32′ N, 72°39′ W 136
San José, Isla, island, Mex. 24°52′ N, 110°30′ W 112
San José, Isla, island, Pan. 7°54′ N, 79°26′ W 115
San José, Punta, Mex. 31°9′ N, 116°39′ W 92
San José, Serranía de, Bol. 18°20′ S, 61°26′ W 132
San Juan, Arg. 31°33′ S, 68°34′ W 134
San Juan, Col. 8°45′ N, 76°32′ W 136
San Juan, Dom. Rep. 18°48′ N, 71°13′ W 116
San Juan, Tex., U.S. 26°13′ N, 98°9′ W 114
San Juan, Trinidad and Tobago 10°39′ N, 61°28′ W 118
San Juan, P.R., U.S. 18°28′ N, 66°6′ W 118
San Juan, adm. division, Arg. 31°19′ S, 70°15′ W 134
San Juan Bautista, Calif., U.S. 36°50′ N, 121°33′ W 100
San Juan Bautista, Parag. 26°40′ S, 57°10′ W 139
San Juan, Cabo, Arg. 54°47′ S, 63°46′ W 134
San Juan, Cabo, Equatorial Guinea 1°10′ N, 9°1′ E 218
San Juan Capistrano, Calif., U.S. 33°30′ N, 117°41′ W 101
San Juan de Alicante, Sp. 38°23′ N, 0°26′ E 164
San Juan de Guadalupe, Mex. 24°35′ N, 102°46′ W 114
San Juan de Lima, Punta, Mex. 18°26′ N, 105°17′ W 112
San Juan de los Cayos, Venez. 11°9′ N, 68°28′ W 136
San Juan de los Lagos, Mex. 21°14′ N, 102°19′ W 114
San Juan de los Morros, Venez. 9°51′ N, 67°23′ W 136
San Juan de Sabinas, Mex. 27°50′ N, 101°7′ W 92
San Juan del Cesar, Col. 10°46′ N, 72°59′ W 136
San Juan del Norte, Nicar. 10°53′ N, 83°42′ W 115
San Juan del Río, Mex. 24°45′ N, 104°27′ W 114
San Juan del Río, Mex. 20°22′ N, 100°1′ W 114
San Juan del Sur, Nicar. 11°14′ N, 85°51′ W 115
San Juan Island National Historical Park, Wash., U.S. 48°35′ N, 123°10′ W 100
San Juan Islands, Hecate Strait 48°16′ N, 122°29′ W 80
San Juan Mountains, Colo., U.S. 38°0′ N, 107°58′ W 90
San Juan Neembucú, Parag. 26°41′ S, 57°59′ W 139
San Juan Nepomuceno, Col. 9°55′ N, 75°6′ W 136
San Juan Nepomuceno, Parag. 26°8′ S, 55°53′ W 139
San Juan, Punta, El Salv. 12°58′ N, 89°31′ W 130
San Juan, Punta, El Salv. 13°1′ N, 88°32′ W 116
San Juan, Punta, Mex. 18°20′ N, 94°54′ W 112
San Juan, river, Can. 48°36′ N, 124°5′ W 100
San Juan, river, Col. 4°14′ N, 77°13′ W 136
San Juan, river, Mex. 25°32′ N, 99°22′ W 114
San Juan, river, Nicar. 10°51′ N, 84°27′ W 115
San Juanico, Punta, Mex. 25°54′ N, 113°36′ W 112
San Juanito, Mex. 27°58′ N, 107°36′ W 112
San Just, Sierra de, Sp. 40°44′ N, 1°2′ W 164
San Justo, Arg. 34°42′ S, 58°33′ W 139
San Justo, Arg. 30°46′ S, 60°34′ W 139
San Lázaro, Cabo, Mex. 24°50′ N, 113°42′ W 112
San Leandro, Calif., U.S. 37°42′ N, 122°9′ W 100
San Leo, It. 43°53′ N, 12°21′ E 167
San Leonardo de Yagüe, Sp. 41°49′ N, 3°5′ W 164
San Lorenzo, Arg. 28°7′ S, 58°46′ W 139
San Lorenzo, Arg. 32°45′ S, 60°44′ W 139
San Lorenzo, Bol. 11°53′ S, 66°52′ W 137
San Lorenzo, Bol. 21°29′ S, 64°47′ W 137
San Lorenzo, Bol. 15°25′ S, 65°52′ W 137
San Lorenzo, Col. 6°59′ N, 71°31′ W 136
San Lorenzo, Ecua. 1°14′ N, 78°58′ W 130
San Lorenzo, Hond. 13°24′ N, 87°27′ W 115
San Lorenzo, Mex. 29°47′ N, 107°7′ W 92
San Lorenzo, Mex. 25°31′ N, 102°11′ W 114
San Lorenzo, Parag. 25°22′ S, 57°30′ W 134
San Lorenzo, Peru 11°28′ S, 69°20′ W 137
San Lorenzo al Mare, It. 43°51′ N, 7°57′ E 167
San Lorenzo, Isla, island, Peru 12°9′ S, 78°36′ W 130
San Lorenzo, island, Mex. 28°34′ N, 113°59′ W 112
San Lorenzo, river, Mex. 25°34′ N, 99°6′ W 114
San Lorenzo, river, Mex. 24°21′ N, 106°55′ W 114
San Lorenzo, ruin(s), Mex. 17°42′ N, 94°52′ W 114
San Lucas, Bol. 20°5′ S, 65°9′ W 137
San Lucas, Calif., U.S. 36°8′ N, 121°2′ W 100
San Lucas, Mex. 22°32′ N, 104°27′ W 114
San Lucas, Cabo, Mex. 22°40′ N, 109°52′ W 112
San Luis, Arg. 33°20′ S, 66°20′ W 134
San Luis, Colo., U.S. 37°11′ N, 105°26′ W 92
San Luis, Guatemala 16°12′ N, 89°28′ W 116
San Luis, Mex. 32°29′ N, 114°47′ W 101
San Luis, adm. division, Arg. 33°41′ S, 66°59′ W 134
San Luis de la Paz, Mex. 21°18′ N, 100°30′ W 114
San Luis de Palenque, Col. 5°23′ N, 71°39′ W 136
San Luis del Cordero, Mex. 25°23′ N, 104°18′ W 114
San Luis del Palmar, Arg. 27°32′ S, 58°32′ W 139
San Luis, Isla, island, Mex. 29°50′ N, 114°25′ W 112
San Luis, Lago de, lake, Bol. 13°53′ S, 64°33′ W 137
San Luis Obispo, Calif., U.S. 35°17′ N, 120°41′ W 100
San Luis Peak, Colo., U.S. 37°58′ N, 107°1′ W 90
San Luis Potosí, Mex. 22°6′ N, 101°3′ W 114
San Luis Potosí, adm. division, Mex. 22°40′ N, 101°25′ W 114
San Luis Río Colorado, Mex. 32°27′ N, 114°48′ W 101
San Luis Valley, Colo., U.S. 38°1′ N, 106°15′ W 90
San Marcial, Punta, Mex. 25°20′ N, 111°2′ W 112
San Marco, Capo, It. 37°24′ N, 12°27′ E 156
San Marcos, Arg. 32°37′ S, 62°29′ W 139
San Marcos, Calif., U.S. 33°8′ N, 117°11′ W 101
San Marcos, Col. 8°39′ N, 75°8′ W 136
San Marcos, Tex., U.S. 29°51′ N, 97°56′ W 96
San Marcos, Isla, island, Mex. 27°12′ N, 112°2′ W 112
San Marino 43°54′ N, 12°11′ E 156
San Marino, San Marino 43°55′ N, 12°24′ E 167
San Martín, Arg. 33°6′ S, 68°29′ W 134
San Martin, Calif., U.S. 37°4′ N, 121°38′ W 100
San Martín, Col. 3°41′ N, 73°43′ W 136
San Martín, Mex. 21°20′ N, 98°39′ W 114
San Martín, adm. division, Peru 6°45′ S, 77°36′ W 130
San Martín, Argentina, station, Antarctica 68°16′ S, 67°5′ W 248
San Martin, Cape, Calif., U.S. 35°47′ N, 121°39′ W 100
San Martín, Isla, island, Mex. 30°27′ N, 117°21′ W 112
San Martín, river, Bol. 15°1′ S, 62°19′ W 132
San Mateo, Calif., U.S. 37°33′ N, 122°20′ W 100
San Mateo, Peru 3°53′ S, 71°37′ W 130
San Mateo, Venez. 9°45′ N, 64°35′ W 116
San Mateo del Mar, Mex. 16°13′ N, 94°59′ W 112
San Mateo Peak, N. Mex., U.S. 33°36′ N, 107°30′ W 92
San Matías, Bol. 16°25′ S, 58°23′ W 132
San Matías, Golfo 41°24′ S, 64°56′ W 134
San Miguel, Arg. 27°60′ S, 57°35′ W 139
San Miguel, Bol. 13°59′ S, 65°25′ W 137
San Miguel, Calif., U.S. 35°45′ N, 120°43′ W 100
San Miguel, Col. 0°16′ N, 76°32′ W 136
San Miguel, El Salv. 13°27′ N, 88°13′ W 115
San Miguel, N. Mex., U.S. 32°9′ N, 106°44′ W 92
San Miguel, Peru 13°2′ S, 74°1′ W 137
San Miguel, Venez. 2°39′ N, 67°28′ W 136
San Miguel Bay 13°48′ N, 122°39′ E 203
San Miguel de Allende, Mex. 20°53′ N, 100°45′ W 114
San Miguel de Horcasitas, Mex. 29°28′ N, 110°44′ W 92
San Miguel de Huachi, Bol. 15°43′ S, 67°15′ W 137
San Miguel de Salinas, Sp. 37°58′ N, 0°48′ E 164
San Miguel de Tucumán, Arg. 26°51′ S, 65°14′ W 132
San Miguel del Monte, Arg. 35°25′ S, 58°48′ W 139
San Miguel, island, Calif., U.S. 34°3′ N, 120°43′ W 100
San Miguel, river, Mex. 29°30′ N, 110°29′ W 92
San Miguel (San Pablo), river, Bol. 14°3′ S, 64°2′ W 137
San Miguel Zapotitlán, Mex. 25°55′ N, 109°4′ W 112
San Miguelito, Bol. 11°40′ S, 68°28′ W 137
San Narciso, Philippines 15°3′ N, 120°5′ E 203
San Nicolás, Arg. 33°23′ S, 60°13′ W 139
San Nicolás, Mex. 24°54′ N, 105°27′ W 114
San Nicolás, Mex. 24°40′ N, 98°48′ W 114
San Nicolas, Philippines 18°11′ N, 120°34′ E 203
San Nicolas, island, Calif., U.S. 33°16′ N, 119°46′ W 101
San Pablo, Arg. 54°14′ S, 66°47′ W 134
San Pablo, Bol. 21°43′ S, 66°37′ W 137
San Pablo, Bol. 15°44′ S, 63°15′ W 137
San Pablo, Philippines 14°3′ N, 121°18′ E 203
San Pablo Bay 38°3′ N, 122°32′ W 100
San Pablo, Punta, Mex. 27°16′ N, 115°54′ W 112
San Pablo see San Miguel, river, Bol. 14°3′ S, 64°2′ W 137
San Patricio, N. Mex., U.S. 33°24′ N, 105°20′ W 92
San Pedro, Arg. 24°22′ S, 64°58′ W 132
San Pedro, Arg. 26°38′ S, 54°11′ W 139
San Pedro, Arg. 33°42′ S, 59°41′ W 139
San Pedro, Belize 17°56′ N, 87°59′ W 116
San Pedro, Bol. 14°23′ S, 64°50′ W 137
San Pedro, Bol. 16°49′ S, 62°32′ W 132
San Pedro, Bol. 16°17′ S, 68°53′ W 137
San Pedro, Mex. 27°0′ N, 109°38′ W 112
San Pedro, Mex. 22°12′ N, 100°48′ W 114
San Pedro, Mex. 29°20′ N, 104°54′ W 92
San Pedro Carchá, Guatemala 15°28′ N, 90°16′ W 115
San Pedro Channel 33°34′ N, 118°43′ W 101
San Pedro Corralitos, Mex. 30°43′ N, 107°41′ W 92
San Pedro de Arimena, Col. 4°35′ N, 71°37′ W 136
San Pedro de Atacama, Chile 22°55′ S, 68°15′ W 137
San Pedro de Curahuara, Bol. 17°41′ S, 68°3′ W 137
San Pedro de las Colonias, Mex. 25°44′ N, 102°59′ W 114
San Pedro de Lloc, Peru 7°25′ S, 79°28′ W 130
San Pedro de Macorís, Dom. Rep. 18°28′ N, 69°17′ W 116
San Pedro del Gallo, Mex. 25°32′ N, 104°18′ W 114
San Pedro del Norte, Nicar. 13°4′ N, 84°44′ W 115
San Pedro del Paraná, Parag. 26°46′ S, 56°13′ W 139
San Pedro del Pinatar, Sp. 37°49′ N, 0°48′ E 164
San Pedro Lagunillas, Mex. 21°13′ N, 104°45′ W 114
San Pedro Mártir, Sierra, Mex. 31°12′ N, 115°38′ W 112
San Pedro, Punta, Chile 25°36′ S, 71°15′ W 132
San Pedro, Sierra de, Sp. 39°20′ N, 6°54′ W 164
San Pedro Sula, Hond. 15°29′ N, 88°1′ W 115
San Quintín, Mex. 30°27′ N, 115°56′ W 92
San Quintín, Cabo, Mex. 30°5′ N, 116°22′ W 92
San Rafael, Arg. 34°33′ S, 68°12′ W 123
San Rafael, Bol. 16°48′ S, 60°36′ W 132
San Rafael, Calif., U.S. 37°57′ N, 122°33′ W 100
San Rafael, Col. 6°1′ N, 69°47′ W 136
San Rafael, Venez. 10°57′ N, 71°47′ W 136
San Rafael, Bahía 28°25′ N, 113°20′ W 92
San Rafael, Cabo, Dom. Rep. 19°2′ N, 68°53′ W 116
San Rafael de Atamaica, Venez. 7°31′ N, 67°24′ W 136
San Rafael Knob, peak, Utah, U.S. 38°48′ N, 110°56′ W 90
San Rafael Mountains, Calif., U.S. 34°47′ N, 120°9′ W 100
San Rafael National Park, Parag. 26°23′ S, 55°42′ W 139
San Ramón, Bol. 13°23′ S, 64°43′ W 137
San Ramón, Uru. 34°18′ S, 55°56′ W 139
San Ramón de la Nueva Orán, Arg. 23°7′ S, 64°22′ W 132
San Remo, It. 43°49′ N, 7°46′ E 150
San, river, Cambodia 13°36′ N, 106°36′ E 202
San Roque, Arg. 28°34′ S, 58°42′ W 139
San Roque, Sp. 36°12′ N, 5°26′ W 164
San Saba, Tex., U.S. 31°10′ N, 98°43′ W 92
San Saba, river, Tex., U.S. 30°35′ N, 100°42′ W 112
San Salvador, Arg. 31°37′ S, 58°31′ W 139
San Salvador, El Salv. 13°40′ N, 89°21′ W 115
San Salvador, Peru 2°26′ S, 71°20′ W 136
San Salvador and Rum Cay, adm. division, Bahamas 24°35′ N, 76°23′ W 96
San Salvador de Jujuy, Arg. 24°13′ S, 65°21′ W 132
San Salvador (Watling), island, Bahamas 23°41′ N, 74°29′ W 116
San Sebastián, Arg. 53°15′ S, 68°30′ W 134
San Sebastián, Cabo, Arg. 53°32′ S, 68°2′ W 134
San Severo, It. 41°41′ N, 15°23′ E 156
San Silvestre, oil field, Venez. 8°21′ N, 70°10′ W 136
San Simeon, Calif., U.S. 35°39′ N, 121°13′ W 100
San Simon, Ariz., U.S. 32°15′ N, 109°13′ W 92
San Sosti, It. 39°39′ N, 16°1′ E 156
San Telmo, Mex. 30°56′ N, 116°6′ W 92
San Tiburcio, Mex. 24°9′ N, 101°28′ W 114
San Vicente, Mex. 31°17′ N, 116°14′ W 92
San Vicente, Mex. 24°8′ N, 100°55′ W 114
San Vicente, Venez. 4°56′ N, 67°45′ W 130
San Vicente de Cañete (Cañete), Peru 13°5′ S, 76°23′ W 130
San Vicente del Caguán, Col. 2°7′ N, 74°48′ W 136
San Vincenzo, It. 38°48′ N, 15°12′ E 156
San Vito al Tagliamento, It. 45°54′ N, 12°51′ E 167
San Ygnacio, Tex., U.S. 27°4′ N, 99°24′ W 96
Şan‘ā’ (Sanaa), Yemen 15°22′ N, 44°3′ E 182
Sanaa see Şan‘ā’, Yemen 15°22′ N, 44°3′ E 182
Sanad, Serb. and Mont. 45°59′ N, 20°7′ E 168
Sanae, South Africa, station, Antarctica 71°48′ S, 3°5′ W 248
Şanāfīr, island, Egypt 27°50′ N, 34°43′ E 180
Sanam, Niger 14°54′ N, 4°20′ E 222
Sanana, island, Indonesia 2°39′ S, 126°5′ E 192
Sanandaj, Iran 35°20′ N, 46°59′ E 180
Sanandita, Bol. 21°40′ S, 63°38′ W 137
Sananduva, Braz. 27°59′ S, 51°49′ W 139
Sanāw, Yemen 17°50′ N, 51°4′ E 182
Sanawad, India 22°10′ N, 76°4′ E 197
Şanawbar, Syr. 35°28′ N, 35°53′ E 194
Sanbornville, N.H., U.S. 43°33′ N, 71°3′ W 104
Sanchahe, China 44°58′ N, 126°1′ E 198
Sanchakou, China 39°55′ N, 78°27′ E 184
Sanchor, India 24°48′ N, 71°46′ E 186
Sanchursk, Russ. 56°54′ N, 47°18′ E 154
Sancti Spíritus, Cuba 21°55′ N, 79°28′ W 116
Sancti Spíritus, adm. division, Cuba 21°50′ N, 79°47′ W 116
Sancti Spíritus, island, Cuba 21°32′ N, 80°49′ W 116
Sancy, Puy de, peak, Fr. 45°31′ N, 2°46′ E 165
Sand Hill, river, Minn., U.S. 47°26′ N, 97°3′ W 94
Sand Hills, Calif., U.S. 32°58′ N, 115°9′ W 101
Sand Hills, Nebr., U.S. 42°16′ N, 101°38′ W 90
Sand Lake, Can. 49°2′ N, 95°16′ W 94
Sand Lake, Mich., U.S. 43°17′ N, 85°31′ W 102
Sand Lake, Minn., U.S. 47°34′ N, 94°27′ W 90
Sand Point, Lake Huron 43°50′ N, 83°40′ W 102
Sand, river, Can. 54°44′ N, 111°6′ W 108
Sand Sea of Calanscio see Kalanshiyū ar Ramlī al Kabīr, Sarīr, Lib. 28°52′ N, 23°25′ E 180
Sand Springs, Mont., U.S. 47°4′ N, 107°29′ W 90
Sand Springs, Okla., U.S. 36°7′ N, 96°6′ W 96
Sandakan, Malaysia 5°53′ N, 118°6′ E 203
Sandalo, Capo, It. 39°3′ N, 7°38′ E 156
Sandaré, Mali 14°41′ N, 10°19′ W 222
Sandbach, U.K. 53°8′ N, 2°22′ W 162
Sandborn, Ind., U.S. 38°53′ N, 87°12′ W 102
Sande, Nor. 62°14′ N, 5°27′ E 152
Sandeid, Nor. 59°33′ N, 5°50′ E 152
Sandercock Nunataks, Antarctica 69°7′ S, 42°3′ E 248
Sanderek, Iran 26°52′ N, 57°30′ E 196
Sanders, Ariz., U.S. 35°12′ N, 109°20′ W 92
Sanders, Ky., U.S. 38°39′ N, 84°57′ W 102
Sanderson, Tex., U.S. 30°8′ N, 102°23′ W 92
Sandersville, Ga., U.S. 32°58′ N, 82°49′ W 96
Sandersville, Miss., U.S. 31°46′ N, 89°3′ W 103
Sandford Lake, lake, Can. 49°5′ N, 92°11′ W 110
Sandgate, U.K. 51°4′ N, 1°8′ E 162
Sandhammaren, Nor. 55°23′ N, 14°12′ E 152
Sandhamn, Sw. 59°16′ N, 18°53′ E 166
Sandia, Peru 14°18′ S, 69°29′ W 137
Sandia Crest, peak, N. Mex., U.S. 35°12′ N, 106°31′ W 92
Sandıklı, Turk. 38°27′ N, 30°15′ E 156
Sandila, India 27°3′ N, 80°30′ E 197
Sandknölen, peak, Nor. 64°6′ N, 14°16′ E 152
Sandnes, Nor. 58°50′ N, 5°45′ E 152
Sandnessjøen, Nor. 66°0′ N, 12°37′ E 152
Sandoa, Dem. Rep. of the Congo 9°42′ S, 22°54′ E 218
Sandoval, Ill., U.S. 38°36′ N, 89°7′ W 102
Sandoval, Boca de 25°0′ N, 97°58′ W 114
Sandovo, Russ. 58°25′ N, 36°30′ E 154
Sandow, Mount, peak, Antarctica 67°28′ S, 100°53′ E 248
Sandoway, Myanmar 18°37′ N, 94°12′ E 173
Sandpoint, Idaho, U.S. 48°15′ N, 116°34′ W 108
Sandringham, U.K. 52°49′ N, 0°31′ E 162
Sands Key, island, Fla., U.S. 25°29′ N, 80°11′ W 105
Sandspit, Can. 53°14′ N, 131°52′ W 108
Sandstad, Nor. 63°30′ N, 9°3′ E 152
Sandstone, Minn., U.S. 46°7′ N, 92°54′ W 94
Sandtop, Cap, Can. 49°13′ N, 61°43′ W 111
Sandu, China 26°0′ N, 107°51′ E 198
Sandusky, Mich., U.S. 43°24′ N, 82°49′ W 102
Sandusky, Ohio, U.S. 41°26′ N, 82°41′ W 94
Sandusky, river, Ohio, U.S. 41°4′ N, 83°8′ W 102
Sandvika, Nor. 59°53′ N, 10°29′ E 152
Sandviken, Nor. 60°37′ N, 16°49′ E 152
Sandwich, Mass., U.S. 41°45′ N, 70°30′ W 104
Sandwich, Mo., U.S. 41°38′ N, 88°37′ W 94
Sandwich Bay 23°21′ S, 13°35′ E 220
Sandwich Mountain, peak, N.H., U.S. 43°53′ N, 71°32′ W 104
Sandwip, Bangladesh 22°30′ N, 91°28′ E 197
Sandy, Nev., U.S. 35°47′ N, 115°37′ W 101
Sandy, U.K. 52°8′ N, 0°18′ E 162
Sandy, Utah, U.S. 40°34′ N, 111°52′ W 90
Sandy Bar, Can. 52°25′ N, 97°23′ W 108
Sandy Bay, Can. 55°31′ N, 102°21′ W 108
Sandy Hook, N.J., U.S. 40°2′ N, 73°56′ W 80
Sandy Lake, Can. 56°58′ N, 107°17′ W 108
Sandy Lake, Can. 53°6′ N, 93°39′ W 80
Sandy Lake, Can. 53°6′ N, 93°25′ W 82
Sandy Narrows, Can. 55°2′ N, 103°4′ W 108
Sandy Point 41°13′ N, 71°29′ W 104
Sandy Point, Bahamas 26°0′ N, 77°24′ W 96
Sånfjället, peak, Nor. 62°15′ N, 13°23′ E 152
Sanford, Fla., U.S. 28°47′ N, 81°17′ W 105
Sanford, Me., U.S. 43°26′ N, 70°47′ W 104
Sanford, Mich., U.S. 43°39′ N, 84°22′ W 102
Sanford, Miss., U.S. 31°28′ N, 89°26′ W 103
Sanford, N.C., U.S. 35°28′ N, 79°12′ W 96
Sanford, Mount, peak, Alas., U.S. 62°11′ N, 144°19′ W 98
Sang Bast, Iran 35°58′ N, 59°46′ E 180
Sanga, Angola 11°8′ S, 15°25′ E 220
Sanga, Burkina Faso 11°11′ N, 0°8′ E 222
Sanga, Mali 14°26′ N, 3°19′ W 222
Sangar, Russ. 64°2′ N, 127°21′ E 160
Sangardo, Guinea 9°23′ N, 10°14′ W 222
Sangaréd, Guinea 11°3′ N, 13°46′ W 222
Sangay National Park, Ecua. 1°58′ S, 78°42′ W 122
Sangay, peak, Ecua. 2°5′ S, 78°29′ W 136
Sangayan, Isla de, island, Peru 14°5′ S, 77°5′ W 130
Sangbé, Cameroon 6°1′ N, 12°28′ E 218
Sangbu, S. Korea 35°33′ N, 128°17′ E 200
Sang-e Masheh, Afghan. 33°16′ N, 67°7′ E 186
Sanger, Calif., U.S. 36°42′ N, 119°34′ W 100
Sanger, Tex., U.S. 33°21′ N, 97°9′ W 92
Sanggan, river, China 39°44′ N, 113°30′ E 198
Sanggou Wan 37°0′ N, 122°2′ E 198
Sanghar, Pak. 26°3′ N, 68°58′ E 186
Sangihe, Kepulauan, islands, Molucca Sea 2°38′ N, 125°59′ E 192
Sangiyn Dalay, Mongolia 46°0′ N, 104°58′ E 198
Sangju, S. Korea 36°23′ N, 128°11′ E 200
Sangkhla, Thai. 15°7′ N, 98°32′ E 202
Sangkulirang, Indonesia 0°56′ N, 117°52′ E 192
Sangla, Pak. 31°45′ N, 73°21′ E 186
Sangni, N. Korea 40°58′ N, 128°7′ E 200
Sangre de Cristo Mountains, N. Mex., U.S. 35°28′ N, 105°41′ W 112
Sangri, China 29°20′ N, 92°10′ E 197
Sangt'ong, N. Korea 40°5′ N, 127°20′ E 200
Sangue, river, Braz. 11°2′ S, 58°36′ W 130
Sanguinaires, Îles, islands, Mediterranean Sea 41°50′ N, 7°26′ E 156
Sangvor, Taj. 38°41′ N, 71°21′ E 197
Sangwŏn, N. Korea 38°50′ N, 126°6′ E 200
Sangzhi, China 29°24′ N, 110°10′ E 198
Sanhecun, China 42°30′ N, 129°42′ E 200
Sanibel Island, Fla., U.S. 26°20′ N, 82°10′ W 105
Sanikiluaq, Can. 56°20′ N, 79°9′ W 73
Saniquellie, Liberia 7°16′ N, 8°41′ W 222
Sanislău, Rom. 47°39′ N, 22°21′ E 168
Sāniyat ad Daffah, spring, Lib. 30°5′ N, 24°13′ E 180
Sanje, Uganda 0°50′ N, 31°29′ E 224
Sanjeong, S. Korea 34°21′ N, 126°33′ E 200
Sanjiang, China 25°52′ N, 109°39′ E 198
Sanjō, Japan 37°38′ N, 138°58′ E 201
Sankaty Head, Mass., U.S. 41°16′ N, 69°58′ W 104
Sankeyushu, China 41°44′ N, 125°21′ E 200
Sankt Augustin, Ger. 50°45′ N, 7°10′ E 167
Sankt Goar, Ger. 50°8′ N, 7°41′ E 167
Sankt Ingbert, Ger. 49°16′ N, 7°6′ E 163
Sankt Michael, Aust. 47°7′ N, 16°15′ E 168
Sankt Moritz, Switz. 46°30′ N, 9°49′ E 167
Sankt Pölten, Aust. 48°11′ N, 15°38′ E 143

ankt Pölten, *Aust.* 48°12′ N, 15°37′ E 152
ankt Ruprecht, *Aust.* 47°10′ N, 15°40′ E 168
ankt Wendel, *Ger.* 49°27′ N, 7°10′ E 163
ankt-Maurice, *Switz.* 46°13′ N, 7°1′ E 167
ankt-Peterburg, adm. division, *Russ.* 59°55′ N, 30°15′ E 166
ankt-Peterburg (Saint Petersburg, Leningrad), *Russ.* 59°55′ N, 30°17′ E 166
ankuru, river, *Dem. Rep. of the Congo* 4°3′ S, 21°26′ E 218
ankuru, river, *Dem. Rep. of the Congo* 5°56′ S, 23°37′ E 224
anlıurfa (Edessa), *Turk.* 37°6′ N, 38°45′ E 180
anlúcar de Barrameda, *Sp.* 36°46′ N, 6°22′ W 164
anmenxia, *China* 34°45′ N, 111°12′ E 198
anming, *China* 26°9′ N, 117°34′ E 198
annazzaro, *It.* 45°6′ N, 8°54′ E 167
annikova, Proliv 74°30′ N, 145°34′ E 246
ano, *Japan* 36°18′ N, 139°36′ E 201
anquianga National Park, *Col.* 2°25′ N, 78°40′ W 122
ans Sault Rapids, fall(s), *Can.* 65°13′ N, 128°46′ W 98
ansanding, *Mali* 13°45′ N, 6°1′ W 222
ansane, *Niger* 13°50′ N, 1°37′ E 222
ansha, *China* 26°58′ N, 120°12′ E 198
anshui, *China* 23°10′ N, 112°55′ E 198
ansui, *China* 27°1′ N, 108°40′ E 198
ant' Antioco, island, *It.* 38°27′ N, 7°30′ E 214
ant Antoni de Portmany, *Sp.* 38°58′ N, 1°17′ E 150
ant Celoni, *Sp.* 41°41′ N, 2°29′ E 164
ant Feliu de Guíxols, *Sp.* 41°46′ N, 3°1′ E 164
ant Jaume d'Enveja, *Sp.* 40°41′ N, 0°43′ E 164
ant Llorenç de Morunys, *Sp.* 42°8′ N, 1°34′ E 164
ant Quirze de Besora, *Sp.* 42°6′ N, 2°13′ E 164
anta, *Peru* 9°2′ S, 78°38′ W 130
anta Amelia, *Guatemala* 16°14′ N, 90°3′ W 115
anta Ana, *Bol.* 15°32′ S, 67°30′ W 137
anta Ana, *Calif., U.S.* 33°45′ N, 117°53′ W 101
anta Ana, *El Salv.* 13°59′ N, 89°33′ W 115
anta Ana, *Mex.* 30°32′ N, 111°6′ W 92
anta Ana, *Philippines* 18°29′ N, 122°9′ E 203
anta Ana, island, *Solomon Islands* 10°50′ S, 162°30′ E 242
anta Ana Mountains, *Calif., U.S.* 33°40′ N, 117°36′ W 101
anta Ana, river, *Venez.* 9°32′ N, 72°47′ W 116
anta Barbara, *Calif., U.S.* 34°25′ N, 119°44′ W 100
anta Bárbara, *Mex.* 26°47′ N, 105°50′ W 112
anta Bárbara, *Peru* 12°53′ S, 75°2′ W 130
anta Bàrbara, *Sp.* 40°42′ N, 0°30′ E 164
anta Bárbara, *Venez.* 3°54′ N, 67°5′ W 136
anta Bárbara, *Venez.* 7°47′ N, 71°12′ W 136
anta Barbara Channel 34°13′ N, 120°27′ W 100
anta Barbara, island, *Calif., U.S.* 33°29′ N, 119°23′ W 101
anta Bárbara, peak, *Sp.* 37°22′ N, 2°53′ W 164
anta Catalina, *Arg.* 21°57′ S, 66°4′ W 137
anta Catalina, *Pan.* 8°46′ N, 81°19′ W 115
anta Catalina, Isla, island, *Mex.* 25°30′ N, 110°46′ W 112
anta Catalina, island, *Calif., U.S.* 33°25′ N, 118°23′ W 101
anta Catalina, island, *Solomon Islands* 10°53′ S, 162°30′ E 242
anta Catarina, *Mex.* 25°39′ N, 100°29′ W 114
anta Catarina, adm. division, *Braz.* 26°54′ S, 53°39′ W 139
anta Catarina, Ilha de, island, *Braz.* 27°57′ S, 48°22′ W 132
nta Clara, *Calif., U.S.* 37°21′ N, 121°57′ W 100
nta Clara, *Col.* 2°45′ S, 69°43′ W 136
nta Clara, *Cuba* 22°26′ N, 79°57′ W 116
nta Clara, *Mex.* 24°27′ N, 103°22′ W 114
nta Clara, *Mex.* 29°16′ N, 107°2′ W 92
nta Clara, *Uru.* 32°55′ S, 54°58′ W 139
nta Clara, *Utah, U.S.* 37°8′ N, 113°39′ W 101
nta Clarita, *Calif., U.S.* 34°25′ N, 118°34′ W 101
nta Claus Mountain, peak, *Can.* 54°11′ N, 61°31′ W 111
nta Clotilde, *Peru* 2°32′ S, 73°41′ W 136
nta Cruz, *Angola* 6°59′ S, 16°17′ E 218
nta Cruz, *Bol.* 17°48′ S, 63°13′ W 137
nta Cruz, *Braz.* 6°1′ S, 72°25′ W 130
nta Cruz, *Calif., U.S.* 36°58′ N, 122°3′ W 100
nta Cruz, *Mex.* 31°12′ N, 110°38′ W 92
nta Cruz, *Philippines* 17°5′ N, 120°27′ E 203
nta Cruz, *Philippines* 13°6′ N, 120°45′ E 203
nta Cruz, *Philippines* 14°16′ N, 121°24′ E 203
nta Cruz, *Philippines* 15°47′ N, 119°55′ E 203
nta Cruz, *Venez.* 8°2′ N, 64°26′ W 130
nta Cruz, adm. division, *Arg.* 48°26′ S, 71°7′ W 134
nta Cruz, adm. division, *Bol.* 17°36′ S, 64°15′ W 137
nta Cruz Cabrália, *Braz.* 16°18′ S, 39°3′ W 132
nta Cruz Channel 33°57′ N, 120°5′ W 101
nta Cruz de la Zarza, *Sp.* 39°59′ N, 3°13′ W 164
nta Cruz de Moya, *Sp.* 39°57′ N, 1°17′ W 164
nta Cruz de Mudela, *Sp.* 38°39′ N, 3°28′ W 164
nta Cruz del Norte, *Cuba* 23°8′ N, 81°55′ W 112
nta Cruz del Sur, *Cuba* 20°43′ N, 77°59′ W 116
nta Cruz do Arai, *Braz.* 0°36′ N, 49°12′ W 130
nta Cruz do Rio Pardo, *Braz.* 22°53′ S, 49°39′ W 138
nta Cruz do Sul, *Braz.* 29°42′ S, 52°23′ W 139
nta Cruz, Isla, island, *Ecua.* 0°40′ N, 90°9′ W 130
nta Cruz, island, *Calif., U.S.* 34°4′ N, 119°42′ W 100
nta Cruz Islands, *Coral Sea* 11°42′ S, 166°19′ E 238
nta Cruz Mountains, *Calif., U.S.* 37°16′ N, 122°4′ W 100
nta Elena, *Arg.* 30°56′ S, 59°46′ W 139
nta Elena, *Ecua.* 2°18′ S, 80°48′ W 130
Santa Elena, *Mex.* 27°57′ N, 103°60′ W 92
Santa Elena, *Venez.* 4°36′ N, 61°7′ W 130
Santa Elena, Cabo, *C.R.* 10°50′ N, 86°60′ W 115
Santa Eulalia, *Sp.* 40°33′ N, 1°19′ W 164
Santa Eulalia del Río, *Sp.* 38°58′ N, 1°32′ E 150
Santa Fe, *Arg.* 31°37′ S, 60°42′ W 139
Santa Fe, *N. Mex., U.S.* 35°40′ N, 106°2′ W 92
Santa Fe, *Philippines* 12°10′ N, 121°59′ E 203
Santa Fé, *Sp.* 37°11′ N, 3°43′ W 164
Santa Fe, adm. division, *Arg.* 30°54′ S, 61°46′ W 139
Santa Filomena, *Braz.* 9°7′ S, 45°54′ W 130
Santa Helena, *Braz.* 24°56′ S, 54°26′ W 132
Santa Helena, *Braz.* 5°13′ S, 56°20′ W 130
Santa Helena de Goiás, *Braz.* 17°49′ S, 50°33′ W 138
Santa Inês, *Braz.* 3°43′ S, 45°26′ W 130
Santa Inês, *Braz.* 13°22′ S, 39°49′ W 138
Santa Inés, Isla, island, *Chile* 53°50′ S, 75°22′ W 134
Santa Inés, peak, *Sp.* 38°31′ N, 5°40′ W 164
Santa Isabel, *Arg.* 36°15′ S, 66°54′ W 134
Santa Isabel, *Arg.* 33°55′ S, 61°40′ W 139
Santa Isabel, *Venez.* 1°20′ N, 65°49′ W 136
Santa Isabel do Morro, *Braz.* 11°32′ S, 50°43′ W 130
Santa Isabel, Ilha Grande de, island, *Braz.* 3°25′ S, 42°32′ W 132
Santa Isabel, island, *Solomon Islands* 8°5′ S, 159°10′ E 242
Santa Juana, *Venez.* 7°0′ N, 67°33′ W 136
Santa Júlia, *Braz.* 7°48′ S, 58°14′ W 130
Santa Julia, *Col.* 1°34′ S, 72°18′ W 136
Santa Juliana, *Braz.* 19°19′ S, 47°32′ W 138
Santa Kurutze Kanpezu, *Sp.* 42°39′ N, 2°21′ W 164
Santa Lucía, *Arg.* 28°59′ S, 59°8′ W 139
Santa Lucía, *Nicar.* 12°30′ N, 85°41′ W 115
Santa Lucía, *Uru.* 34°28′ S, 56°22′ W 139
Santa Lucia Range, *Calif., U.S.* 35°58′ N, 121°22′ W 100
Santa Magdalena, *Arg.* 34°32′ S, 63°54′ W 139
Santa Margarita, *Calif., U.S.* 35°23′ N, 120°38′ W 100
Santa Margarita, Isla, island, *Mex.* 24°9′ N, 112°57′ W 112
Santa María, *Arg.* 26°43′ S, 66°2′ W 132
Santa Maria, *Braz.* 1°45′ S, 58°36′ W 130
Santa Maria, *Braz.* 2°57′ S, 60°25′ W 130
Santa Maria, *Braz.* 29°44′ S, 53°48′ W 139
Santa Maria, *Calif., U.S.* 34°57′ N, 120°27′ W 100
Santa María, *Peru* 1°25′ S, 74°38′ W 136
Santa Maria, *Switz.* 46°35′ N, 10°24′ E 167
Santa Maria, *Zambia* 11°9′ S, 29°58′ E 224
Santa María, Bahía 24°57′ N, 109°16′ W 80
Santa María, Cabo, *Uru.* 34°59′ S, 54°11′ W 139
Santa Maria, Cape, *Bahamas* 23°44′ N, 75°18′ W 80
Santa María, Cayo, island, *Cuba* 22°42′ N, 78°57′ W 116
Santa Maria da Vitória, *Braz.* 13°23′ S, 44°14′ W 138
Santa María de Huerta, *Sp.* 41°15′ N, 2°11′ W 164
Santa María de Ipire, *Venez.* 8°48′ N, 65°20′ W 136
Santa María de los Ángeles, *Mex.* 22°10′ N, 103°12′ W 114
Santa María de Nanay, *Peru* 3°54′ S, 73°45′ W 130
Santa María de Otáez, *Mex.* 24°40′ N, 105°60′ W 114
Santa María del Oro, *Mex.* 25°55′ N, 105°19′ W 114
Santa María del Oro, *Mex.* 21°20′ N, 104°36′ W 114
Santa María del Río, *Mex.* 21°47′ N, 100°44′ W 114
Santa Maria do Suaçuí, *Braz.* 18°12′ S, 42°26′ W 138
Santa María, Isla, island, *Chile* 37°8′ S, 75°29′ W 134
Santa María, Isla, island, *Ecua.* 1°54′ S, 90°21′ W 130
Santa María, river, *Mex.* 21°47′ N, 100°34′ W 114
Santa Marta, *Col.* 11°11′ N, 74°14′ W 136
Santa Marta, *Sp.* 38°36′ N, 6°38′ W 164
Santa Marta Grande, Cabo de, *Braz.* 28°34′ S, 48°43′ W 134
Santa Monica Mountains, *Calif., U.S.* 34°8′ N, 118°55′ W 101
Santa Olalla del Cala, *Sp.* 37°54′ N, 6°15′ W 164
Santa Pola, *Sp.* 38°11′ N, 0°34′ E 164
Santa Rita, *Col.* 4°54′ N, 68°22′ W 136
Santa Rita, *Venez.* 8°6′ N, 66°17′ W 136
Santa Rita, *Venez.* 10°33′ N, 71°32′ W 116
Santa Rita do Araguaia, *Braz.* 17°22′ S, 53°14′ W 138
Santa Rita do Weil, *Braz.* 3°31′ S, 69°20′ W 136
Santa Rita Park, *Calif., U.S.* 37°2′ N, 120°36′ W 100
Santa, river, *Peru* 8°55′ S, 78°46′ W 130
Santa Rosa, *Arg.* 28°3′ S, 67°37′ W 132
Santa Rosa, *Arg.* 36°37′ S, 64°18′ W 139
Santa Rosa, *Arg.* 39°60′ S, 66°33′ W 134
Santa Rosa, *Arg.* 32°21′ S, 65°9′ W 134
Santa Rosa, *Ariz., U.S.* 32°19′ N, 112°2′ W 92
Santa Rosa, *Bol.* 14°13′ S, 66°54′ W 137
Santa Rosa, *Bol.* 11°41′ S, 65°14′ W 137
Santa Rosa, *Bol.* 10°38′ S, 67°24′ W 137
Santa Rosa, *Braz.* 15°6′ S, 47°15′ W 138
Santa Rosa, *Braz.* 27°53′ S, 54°31′ W 139
Santa Rosa, *Calif., U.S.* 38°26′ N, 122°42′ W 90
Santa Rosa, *N. Mex., U.S.* 34°55′ N, 104°41′ W 92
Santa Rosa, *Peru* 14°39′ S, 70°46′ W 137
Santa Rosa, *Peru* 3°48′ S, 76°26′ W 136
Santa Rosa, *Peru* 9°28′ S, 70°33′ W 137
Santa Rosa, *Peru* 3°1′ S, 73°13′ W 136
Santa Rosa, *Venez.* 8°30′ N, 69°43′ W 136
Santa Rosa de Amanadona, *Venez.* 1°25′ N, 66°53′ W 136
Santa Rosa de Cop'an, *Hond.* 14°46′ N, 88°46′ W 115
Santa Rosa de Río Primero, *Arg.* 31°9′ S, 63°22′ W 139
Santa Rosa, island, *Calif., U.S.* 34°3′ N, 120°7′ W 100
Santa Rosa Mountains, *Calif., U.S.* 33°29′ N, 116°21′ W 101
Santa Rosa National Park, *North Pacific Ocean* 10°46′ N, 85°46′ W 115
Santa Rosa Peak, *Nev., U.S.* 41°33′ N, 117°46′ W 90
Santa Rosa Range, *Nev., U.S.* 41°50′ N, 117°39′ W 90
Santa Rosalía, *Mex.* 27°20′ N, 112°17′ W 82
Santa Rosalía, *Venez.* 7°25′ N, 65°42′ W 136
Santa Rosalillita, *Mex.* 28°40′ N, 114°19′ W 92
Santa Sylvina, *Arg.* 27°47′ S, 61°8′ W 139
Santa Teresa, *Arg.* 33°27′ S, 60°46′ W 139
Santa Teresa, *Braz.* 13°42′ S, 49°3′ W 138
Santa Teresa, *Mex.* 25°18′ N, 97°52′ W 114
Santa Teresa, river, *Braz.* 13°39′ S, 49°1′ W 138
Santa Teresinha, *Braz.* 10°28′ S, 50°35′ W 130
Santa Victoria, *Arg.* 22°16′ S, 62°45′ W 132
Santa Victoria, *Arg.* 22°16′ S, 64°59′ W 137
Santa Vitória do Palmar, *Braz.* 33°31′ S, 53°20′ W 139
Santa Ynez, *Calif., U.S.* 34°37′ N, 120°6′ W 100
Santa Ynez Mountains, *Calif., U.S.* 34°32′ N, 120°28′ W 100
Santai, *China* 31°2′ N, 105°0′ E 198
Santalpur, *India* 23°47′ N, 71°12′ E 186
Santana, *Braz.* 12°59′ S, 44°5′ W 138
Santana do Araguaia, *Braz.* 8°52′ S, 49°45′ W 130
Santana do Livramento, *Braz.* 30°53′ S, 55°29′ W 139
Santana, river, *Braz.* 9°60′ S, 51°14′ W 130
Santander, *Col.* 2°58′ N, 76°30′ W 136
Santander, *Sp.* 43°23′ N, 3°59′ W 214
Santander, *Sp.* 43°27′ N, 3°49′ W 164
Santander, adm. division, *Col.* 6°30′ N, 74°20′ W 136
Santander Jiménez, *Mex.* 24°11′ N, 98°30′ W 114
Sant'Angelo Lodigiano, *It.* 45°13′ N, 9°24′ E 167
Santanilla, Islas, islands, *Caribbean Sea* 17°40′ N, 84°22′ W 115
Santanyí, *Sp.* 39°20′ N, 3°7′ E 150
Santarcangelo di Romagna, *It.* 44°3′ N, 12°26′ E 167
Santarém, *Braz.* 2°29′ S, 54°48′ W 130
Santarém, *Port.* 39°13′ N, 8°42′ W 150
Santarém, adm. division, *Port.* 39°17′ N, 8°59′ W 150
Santaren Channel 23°42′ N, 79°35′ W 96
Santee, *Calif., U.S.* 32°50′ N, 116°59′ W 101
Santee Point 33°1′ N, 79°15′ W 96
Santee, river, *S.C., U.S.* 33°36′ N, 80°10′ W 80
Santena, *It.* 44°57′ N, 7°46′ E 167
Santhià, *It.* 45°22′ N, 8°10′ E 167
Santiago, *Bol.* 18°26′ S, 59°34′ W 132
Santiago, *Braz.* 29°12′ S, 54°50′ W 139
Santiago, *Chile* 33°30′ S, 70°56′ W 134
Santiago, *Mex.* 25°24′ N, 100°7′ W 114
Santiago, Cerro, peak, *Pan.* 8°32′ N, 81°48′ W 115
Santiago de Compostela, *Sp.* 42°51′ N, 8°34′ W 150
Santiago de Cuba, *Cuba* 20°1′ N, 75°50′ W 115
Santiago de Cuba, adm. division, *Cuba* 20°11′ N, 76°25′ W 115
Santiago de la Peña, *Mex.* 20°53′ N, 97°24′ W 114
Santiago del Estero, *Arg.* 27°48′ S, 64°19′ W 132
Santiago del Estero, adm. division, *Arg.* 28°2′ S, 63°30′ W 139
Santiago, Isla, island, *Ecua.* 0°21′ N, 90°34′ W 130
Santiago Mountains, *Tex., U.S.* 29°59′ N, 103°28′ W 92
Santiago Papasquiaro, *Mex.* 25°1′ N, 105°28′ W 114
Santiago, Region Metropolitana de, adm. division, *Chile* 33°45′ S, 72°16′ W 134
Santiago, Serranía de, *Bol.* 17°57′ S, 60°30′ W 132
Santiago Tuxtla, *Mex.* 18°27′ N, 95°19′ W 114
Santiaguillo, Laguna de, lake, *Mex.* 24°56′ N, 105°40′ W 81
Santiam Pass, *Oreg., U.S.* 44°24′ N, 121°52′ W 90
Santillana, *Sp.* 43°23′ N, 4°6′ W 164
Santo Amaro, *Braz.* 12°31′ S, 38°44′ W 132
Santo Anastácio, *Braz.* 21°58′ S, 51°42′ W 138
Santo André, *Braz.* 23°39′ S, 46°32′ W 138
Santo ângelo, *Braz.* 28°22′ S, 54°18′ W 139
Santo Antônio, *Braz.* 1°60′ N, 68°29′ W 136
Santo Antônio do Içá, *Braz.* 3°5′ S, 67°58′ W 136
Santo Corazón, *Bol.* 17°60′ S, 58°49′ W 132
Santo Domingo, *Dom. Rep.* 18°26′ N, 70°3′ W 116
Santo Domingo, *Mex.* 23°18′ N, 101°44′ W 114
Santo Domingo de Acobamba, *Peru* 11°49′ S, 74°45′ W 137
Santo Domingo de los Colorados, *Ecua.* 0°16′ N, 79°13′ W 130
Santo Domingo Pueblo, *N. Mex., U.S.* 35°30′ N, 106°22′ W 92
Santo Hipólito, *Braz.* 18°17′ S, 44°16′ W 138
Santo Stefano, *It.* 44°32′ N, 9°26′ E 167
Santo Tomás, *Mex.* 31°32′ N, 116°25′ W 92
Santo Tomás, *Peru* 14°30′ S, 72°5′ W 137
Santo Tomás, Punta, *Mex.* 31°16′ N, 116°60′ W 92
Santo Tomé, *Arg.* 31°41′ S, 60°46′ W 139
Santo Tomé, *Arg.* 28°33′ S, 56°4′ W 139
Santok, *Pol.* 52°45′ N, 15°25′ E 152
Santong, river, *China* 42°4′ N, 125°59′ E 200
Santopitar, peak, *Sp.* 36°47′ N, 4°20′ W 164
Santos, *Braz.* 23°56′ S, 46°21′ W 138
Santos Dumont, *Braz.* 21°28′ S, 43°32′ W 138
Santos Dumont, *Braz.* 6°28′ S, 68°16′ W 130
Santos Plateau, *South Atlantic Ocean* 26°36′ S, 43°17′ W 253
Santos, Sierra de los, *Sp.* 37°57′ N, 5°14′ W 164
Santovenia de Pisuerga, *Sp.* 41°40′ N, 4°42′ W 150
Santuario del Moncayo, peak, *Sp.* 41°46′ N, 1°54′ W 164
Santurtzi, *Sp.* 43°18′ N, 3°2′ W 164
Sanya, *China* 18°13′ N, 109°30′ E 198
Sanyuan, *China* 34°38′ N, 108°56′ E 198
Sanza Pombo, *Angola* 7°21′ S, 15°59′ E 218
São Benedito, river, *Braz.* 9°16′ S, 57°29′ W 132
São Bento, *Braz.* 2°43′ S, 44°47′ W 132
São Borja, *Braz.* 28°41′ S, 56°3′ W 139
São Carlos, *Braz.* 22°2′ S, 47°55′ W 138
São Cristóvão, *Braz.* 11°2′ S, 37°11′ W 132
São Domingos, *Braz.* 19°14′ S, 40°38′ W 138
São Domingos, *Braz.* 13°24′ S, 46°23′ W 138
São Domingos, *Guinea-Bissau* 12°23′ N, 16°9′ W 222
São Fé de Minas, *Braz.* 16°42′ S, 45°25′ W 138
São Félix do Xingu, *Braz.* 6°39′ S, 51°60′ W 130
São Fidélis, *Braz.* 21°41′ S, 41°47′ W 138
São Francisco, *Braz.* 15°58′ S, 44°54′ W 138
São Francisco, *Peru* 10°56′ S, 69°41′ W 137
São Francisco de Sales, *Braz.* 19°53′ S, 49°47′ W 138
São Francisco do Sul, *Braz.* 26°16′ S, 48°34′ W 138
São Francisco, Ilha de, island, *Braz.* 26°22′ S, 48°27′ W 132
São Francisco, river, *Braz.* 14°13′ S, 43°40′ W 138
São Gabriel, *Braz.* 30°22′ S, 54°20′ W 139
São Gabriel da Cachoeira, *Braz.* 0°8′ N, 67°5′ W 136
São Gabriel de Goiás, *Braz.* 15°13′ S, 47°34′ W 138
São Geraldo do Araguaia, *Braz.* 6°21′ S, 48°35′ W 130
São Gonçalo do Abaete, *Braz.* 18°21′ S, 45°52′ W 138
Sao Hill, *Tanzania* 8°23′ S, 35°13′ E 224
São João, *Guinea-Bissau* 11°36′ N, 15°26′ W 222
São João da Aliança, *Braz.* 14°44′ S, 47°31′ W 138
São João da Barra, *Braz.* 21°41′ S, 41°3′ W 138
São João da Boa Vista, *Braz.* 21°58′ S, 46°48′ W 138
São João da Ponte, *Braz.* 15°58′ S, 43°60′ W 138
São João de Cortes, *Braz.* 2°11′ S, 44°30′ W 132
São João del Rei, *Braz.* 21°9′ S, 44°16′ W 138
São João do Araguaia, *Braz.* 5°26′ S, 48°46′ W 130
São João do Paraíso, *Braz.* 15°21′ S, 42°6′ W 138
São João do Piauí, *Braz.* 8°22′ S, 42°14′ W 132
São João, Serra de, *Braz.* 8°22′ S, 62°44′ W 130
São Joaquim, *Braz.* 28°20′ S, 49°57′ W 138
São Joaquim, *Braz.* 2°119′ S, 67°19′ W 136
São Joaquim da Barra, *Braz.* 20°37′ S, 47°53′ W 138
São Joaquim National Park, *Braz.* 28°18′ S, 49°50′ W 138
São José, *Braz.* 9°40′ S, 67°10′ W 137
São José, *Braz.* 27°37′ S, 48°38′ W 138
São José de Anauá, *Braz.* 1°2′ N, 61°27′ W 130
São José do Norte, *Braz.* 32°2′ S, 52°3′ W 139
São José do Rio Pardo, *Braz.* 21°37′ S, 46°56′ W 138
São José do Rio Preto, *Braz.* 20°49′ S, 49°22′ W 138
São José dos Campos, *Braz.* 23°12′ S, 45°51′ W 138
São José dos Pinhais, *Braz.* 25°32′ S, 49°11′ W 138
São Leopoldo, *Braz.* 29°45′ S, 51°12′ W 139
São Lourenço, *Braz.* 22°8′ S, 45°4′ W 138
São Lourenço do Sul, *Braz.* 31°20′ S, 51°58′ W 139
São Luís, *Braz.* 2°33′ S, 44°15′ W 130
São Luís de Montes Belos, *Braz.* 16°33′ S, 50°21′ W 138
São Luís do Tocantins, *Braz.* 14°19′ S, 47°60′ W 138
São Luís Gonzaga, *Braz.* 28°27′ S, 54°59′ W 139
São Luís, Ilha de, island, *Braz.* 2°45′ S, 43°60′ W 132
São Manuel see Teles Pires, river, *Braz.* 9°30′ S, 55°14′ W 122
São Marcelino, *Braz.* 0°53′ N, 67°15′ W 136
São Marcos, river, *Braz.* 18°1′ S, 47°33′ W 138
São Mateus, *Braz.* 18°45′ S, 39°53′ W 138
São Mateus do Sul, *Braz.* 25°52′ S, 50°25′ W 138
São Miguel do Araguaia, *Braz.* 13°22′ S, 50°16′ W 138
São Miguel, river, *Braz.* 12°27′ S, 63°14′ W 132
São Paulo, *Braz.* 23°33′ S, 46°36′ W 138
São Paulo, adm. division, *Braz.* 21°42′ S, 49°43′ W 138
São Paulo de Olivença, *Braz.* 3°31′ S, 68°49′ W 136
São Pedro, *Braz.* 0°19′ N, 66°50′ W 136
São Pedro, *Braz.* 22°34′ S, 47°56′ W 138
São Pedro, *Braz.* 3°6′ S, 68°54′ W 136
São Raimundo do Araguaia, *Braz.* 5°40′ S, 48°14′ W 130
São Raimundo Nonato, *Braz.* 9°2′ S, 42°43′ W 132
São Romão, *Braz.* 5°51′ S, 67°48′ W 130
São Romão, *Braz.* 16°22′ S, 45°8′ W 138
São Roque do Paraguaçu, *Braz.* 12°54′ S, 38°54′ W 132
São Salvador, *Braz.* 7°28′ S, 73°13′ W 130
São Sebastião, *Braz.* 23°48′ S, 45°27′ W 138
São Sebastião do Paraíso, *Braz.* 20°55′ S, 46°59′ W 138
São Sebastião dos Poções, *Braz.* 14°34′ S, 44°24′ W 138
São Sebastião, Ilha de, island, *Braz.* 24°18′ S, 45°10′ W 132
São Sebastião, Ponta, *Mozambique* 22°35′ S, 35°29′ E 220
Sao Tome and Principe 1°0′ N, 7°0′ E 214
São Tomé, island, *Sao Tome and Principe* 0°12′ N, 6°39′ E 214
São Tomé, river, *Braz.* 8°29′ S, 57°57′ W 130
São Tomé & Príncipe 0°10′ N, 6°32′ E 218
São Vicente, *Braz.* 10°38′ S, 69°28′ W 137
São Vicente, *Braz.* 23°60′ S, 46°27′ W 138
São Vicente, Cabo de, *Port.* 36°57′ N, 11°3′ W 214
São Vicente do Sul, *Braz.* 29°42′ S, 54°43′ W 139
Saona, Isla, island, *Dom. Rep.* 17°48′ N, 68°52′ W 116
Saône, river, *Fr.* 45°58′ N, 4°39′ E 165
Saône, river, *Fr.* 47°32′ N, 5°41′ E 165
Saonek, *Indonesia* 0°23′ N, 130°43′ E 192
Saoner, *India* 21°22′ N, 78°54′ E 188
Saous, spring, *Mali* 17°45′ N, 5°296′ W 222
Sap, Tonle, lake, *Cambodia* 13°6′ N, 103°45′ E 202
Sapahaqui, *Bol.* 16°60′ S, 67°55′ W 137
Sapanca, *Turk.* 40°41′ N, 30°16′ E 156
Sapateiro, Lago, lake, *Braz.* 2°18′ S, 67°8′ W 136
Sapele, *Nig.* 5°59′ N, 5°41′ E 222
Şaphane Dağı, peak, *Turk.* 39°2′ N, 29°13′ E 156
Sapo, Serranía del, *Pan.* 7°38′ N, 78°2′ W 136
Sappada, *It.* 46°34′ N, 12°41′ E 167
Sapphire Mountains, *Mont., U.S.* 46°4′ N, 113°55′ W 90
Sappho, *Wash., U.S.* 48°3′ N, 124°18′ W 100
Sapporo, *Japan* 43°14′ N, 141°18′ E 190
Sapri, *It.* 40°5′ N, 15°37′ E 156
Sapt Kosi, river, *India* 26°10′ N, 86°44′ E 197
Sapulpa, *Okla., U.S.* 35°58′ N, 96°6′ W 96
Saqqez, *Iran* 36°17′ N, 46°14′ E 195
Šar Planina, *Maced.* 41°54′ N, 20°43′ E 168
Sara, *Burkina Faso* 11°44′ N, 3°50′ W 222
Sara National Park, *Europe* 42°7′ N, 20°48′ E 168
Sarāb, *Iran* 37°58′ N, 47°32′ E 195
Saraburi, *Thai.* 14°33′ N, 100°57′ E 202
Saraféré, *Mali* 15°48′ N, 3°42′ W 222
Sarahs, *Turkm.* 36°31′ N, 61°13′ E 180
Sarai, *Russ.* 53°41′ N, 40°58′ E 154
Sarajevo, *Bosn. and Herzg.* 43°51′ N, 18°22′ E 168
Sarakhs, *Iran* 36°33′ N, 61°4′ E 180
Saraktash, *Russ.* 51°46′ N, 56°16′ E 158
Sarala, *Côte d'Ivoire* 8°34′ N, 4°40′ W 222
Saraland, *Ala., U.S.* 30°48′ N, 88°4′ W 103
Saralzhyn, *Kaz.* 49°11′ N, 48°54′ E 158
Sarana, *Russ.* 56°29′ N, 57°46′ E 154
Saranac, *Mich., U.S.* 42°54′ N, 85°13′ W 102
Saranac Lake, *N.Y., U.S.* 44°19′ N, 74°9′ W 104
Saranda, *Tanzania* 5°41′ S, 34°56′ E 224
Sarandi, *Braz.* 27°58′ S, 52°56′ W 139
Sarandí del Yí, *Uru.* 33°19′ S, 55°39′ W 139
Sarandí Grande, *Uru.* 33°45′ S, 56°21′ W 139
Sarangani Bay 5°52′ N, 125°4′ E 203
Sarangani Islands, islands, *Philippine Sea* 4°20′ N, 123°17′ E 192
Saranpaul', *Russ.* 64°15′ N, 60°53′ E 169
Saransk, *Russ.* 54°9′ N, 45°7′ E 154
Sarapul, *Russ.* 56°28′ N, 53°47′ E 154
Sarasota, *Fla., U.S.* 27°21′ N, 82°31′ W 105
Saratoga, *Tex., U.S.* 30°17′ N, 94°32′ W 103
Saratoga, *Wyo., U.S.* 41°27′ N, 106°48′ W 90
Saratoga National Historical Park, *N.Y., U.S.* 42°58′ N, 73°42′ W 104
Saratoga Springs, *N.Y., U.S.* 43°4′ N, 73°48′ W 104
Saratoga Table, *Antarctica* 84°9′ S, 45°38′ W 248
Saratok, *Malaysia* 1°45′ N, 111°21′ E 192
Saratov, *Russ.* 51°29′ N, 45°56′ E 158
Saratov, adm. division, *Russ.* 52°44′ N, 47°53′ E 154
Saravan, *Laos* 15°43′ N, 106°22′ E 202
Sarawak, region, *Malaysia* 4°47′ N, 114°58′ E 203
Saray, *Turk.* 41°25′ N, 27°54′ E 156
Saray, *Turk.* 38°39′ N, 44°9′ E 195
Saraya, *Senegal* 12°51′ N, 11°47′ W 222
Sarayacu, *Ecua.* 1°48′ S, 77°31′ W 136
Sarayköy, *Turk.* 37°55′ N, 28°54′ E 156
Sarbāz, *Iran* 26°34′ N, 61°15′ E 182
Sarbīsheh, *Iran* 32°32′ N, 59°48′ E 180
Sárbogárd, *Hung.* 46°52′ N, 18°37′ E 168
Sarca, river, *It.* 46°4′ N, 10°49′ E 167
Sarco, *Chile* 28°49′ S, 71°26′ W 134
Sardão, Cabo, *Port.* 37°26′ N, 9°10′ W 150
Sardarshahr, *India* 28°26′ N, 74°29′ E 186
Sardegna (Sardinia), adm. division, *It.* 39°58′ N, 8°28′ E 156
Sardinal, *C.R.* 10°30′ N, 85°40′ W 115
Sardinia, island, *It.* 40°44′ N, 5°41′ E 143
Sardinia see Sardegna, adm. division, *It.* 39°58′ N, 8°28′ E 156
Sardis, *Miss., U.S.* 34°26′ N, 89°55′ W 96
Sardis Lake, lake, *Okla., U.S.* 34°39′ N, 95°42′ W 96
Sardis, ruin(s), *Turk.* 38°27′ N, 27°55′ E 156
Sar-e Pol, *Afghan.* 36°12′ N, 65°55′ E 186
Sarepta, *La., U.S.* 32°52′ N, 93°27′ W 103
Sargent, *Nebr., U.S.* 41°38′ N, 99°23′ W 90
Sargento Lores, *Peru* 3°48′ S, 74°33′ W 136
Sargo Plateau, *Arctic Ocean* 78°14′ N, 175°5′ W 255
Sargodha, *Pak.* 32°5′ N, 72°45′ E 186
Sarh, *Chad* 9°0′ N, 18°12′ E 207
Sarḩadd, *Afghan.* 36°57′ N, 73°29′ E 186
Sarhro, Jebel, *Mor.* 30°53′ N, 6°8′ W 214
Sārī, *Iran* 36°34′ N, 53°3′ E 180
Sariá, island, *Gr.* 35°52′ N, 26°48′ E 180
Sariã, river, *Braz.* 6°57′ S, 66°15′ W 130
Saric, *Mex.* 31°7′ N, 111°25′ W 92
Sarigan, island, *Sarigan* 16°46′ N, 144°50′ E 192
Sarıgöl, *Turk.* 38°14′ N, 28°40′ E 156
Sarıkamış, *Turk.* 40°20′ N, 42°35′ E 195
Sarikei, *Malaysia* 2°3′ N, 111°33′ E 192
Sarimoy, *Uzb.* 41°4′ N, 62°0′ E 180
Sariñena, *Sp.* 41°47′ N, 0°10′ W 164
Sarinleey, *Somalia* 2°24′ N, 42°16′ E 224
Sarīr, oil field, *Lib.* 27°36′ N, 22°18′ E 216
Sariwŏn, *N. Korea* 38°29′ N, 125°45′ E 200
Sarıyer, *Turk.* 41°10′ N, 29°1′ E 156
Sarız, *Turk.* 38°28′ N, 36°29′ E 156
Sarjektjåkko, peak, *Nor.* 67°26′ N, 17°33′ E 152
Särkelä, *Fin.* 65°39′ N, 27°42′ E 152
Sarkhan, oil field, *Iran* 33°19′ N, 47°42′ E 180
Şarkîkaraağaç, *Turk.* 38°4′ N, 31°22′ E 156
Särkisalo, *Fin.* 62°47′ N, 26°6′ E 154
Şarkışla, *Turk.* 39°20′ N, 36°24′ E 156
Şarköy, *Turk.* 40°36′ N, 27°4′ E 156

Sarles, N. Dak., U.S. 48°55′ N, 99°2′ W 90
Sarman Didinte, Eth. 10°32′ N, 42°28′ E 224
Sărmăşag, Rom. 47°20′ N, 22°51′ E 168
Sarmi, Indonesia 1°50′ S, 138°40′ E 192
Sarmiento, Arg. 45°35′ S, 69°9′ W 134
Särna, Nor. 61°41′ N, 13°5′ E 152
Sarnen, Switz. 46°54′ N, 8°14′ E 167
Sarnia, Can. 42°57′ N, 82°23′ W 102
Sarny, Ukr. 51°19′ N, 26°36′ E 152
Särö, Nor. 57°31′ N, 11°57′ E 152
Saronno, It. 45°37′ N, 9°1′ E 167
Sárospatak, Hung. 48°20′ N, 21°33′ E 152
Sarowbi, Afghan. 34°35′ N, 69°48′ E 186
Sarpa, Russ. 47°2′ N, 45°27′ E 158
Sarpa, Ozero, lake, Russ. 47°12′ N, 45°10′ E 158
Sarqan, Kaz. 45°25′ N, 79°54′ E 184
Sarracín, Sp. 42°14′ N, 3°42′ W 164
Sarralbe, Fr. 49°0′ N, 7°3′ E 163
Sarrebourg, Fr. 48°44′ N, 7°3′ E 163
Sarreguemines, Fr. 49°7′ N, 7°4′ E 163
Sarre-Union, Fr. 48°56′ N, 7°5′ E 163
Sarria, Sp. 42°47′ N, 7°26′ W 214
Sarrión, Sp. 40°7′ N, 0°49′ E 164
Sars, Russ. 56°33′ N, 57°17′ E 154
Sarsang, Iraq 37°5′ N, 43°13′ E 195
Sarsina, It. 43°56′ N, 12°8′ E 167
Sarstoon, river, North America 15°56′ N, 89°29′ W 115
Sartène, Fr. 41°37′ N, 8°59′ E 156
Sarto, Col. 4°54′ N, 70°10′ W 136
Särur, Asia 39°33′ N, 44°57′ E 195
Sárvár, Hung. 47°15′ N, 16°55′ E 168
Sárvíz, river, Hung. 46°33′ N, 18°35′ E 168
Saryaghash, Kaz. 41°23′ N, 69°2′ E 197
Sary-Bee, Kyrg. 40°36′ N, 73°54′ E 197
Sarych, Mys, Ukr. 44°18′ N, 32°56′ E 156
Saryg Sep, Russ. 51°32′ N, 95°43′ E 190
Sarykemer, Kaz. 42°55′ N, 71°25′ E 184
Sarykenggir, river, Kaz. 49°16′ N, 67°24′ E 184
Saryköl, Kaz. 53°19′ N, 65°32′ E 184
Sary-Mogol, Kyrg. 39°40′ N, 72°57′ E 197
Saryözek, Kaz. 44°21′ N, 77°56′ E 184
Saryqamys, Kaz. 45°57′ N, 53°31′ E 158
Saryqopa Köli, lake, Kaz. 50°17′ N, 63°20′ E 184
Sarysay, Kaz. 48°24′ N, 60°32′ E 184
Saryshaghan, Kaz. 46°3′ N, 73°33′ E 184
Sarysu, river, Kaz. 46°27′ N, 67°16′ E 184
Sary-Tash, Kyrg. 39°42′ N, 73°15′ E 197
Saryzhal, Kaz. 49°36′ N, 78°45′ E 184
Saryzhaz, Kaz. 42°54′ N, 79°39′ E 184
Sarzana, It. 44°6′ N, 9°58′ E 167
Sas de Còrdoba, Arg. 31°38′ S, 63°50′ W 139
Sas van Gent, Neth. 51°13′ N, 3°48′ E 163
Sa'sa', Syr. 33°18′ N, 36°1′ E 194
Sásabe, Mex. 31°28′ N, 111°33′ W 92
Sasaginnigak Lake, lake, Can. 51°29′ N, 96°23′ W 108
Sasak, Indonesia 4°238′ N, 99°41′ E 196
Sasaram, India 24°56′ N, 84°0′ E 197
Sasca Montană, Rom. 44°52′ N, 21°44′ E 168
Sásd, Hung. 46°15′ N, 18°6′ E 168
Sasebo, Japan 33°10′ N, 129°43′ E 201
Saser Kangri, peak, India 34°49′ N, 77°37′ E 188
Saskatchewan, adm. division, Can. 53°56′ N, 109°60′ W 106
Saskatoon, Can. 52°8′ N, 106°40′ W 108
Sason, Turk. 38°19′ N, 41°26′ E 195
Sasovo, Russ. 54°18′ N, 41°53′ E 154
Sass, river, Can. 60°13′ N, 113°18′ W 108
Sassafras Mountain, peak, N.C., U.S. 35°2′ N, 82°52′ W 96
Sassan, oil field, Iraq 36°24′ N, 42°15′ E 195
Sassandra, Côte d'Ivoire 4°58′ N, 6°6′ W 222
Sassari, It. 40°43′ N, 8°34′ E 156
Sassello, It. 44°29′ N, 8°29′ E 167
Sassnitz, Ger. 54°31′ N, 13°39′ E 160
Sasstown, Liberia 4°46′ N, 8°26′ W 222
Sassulko, Goz, Cen. Af. Rep. 10°59′ N, 23°22′ E 218
Sassuolo, It. 44°33′ N, 10°47′ E 167
Sástago, Sp. 41°18′ N, 0°22′ E 164
Sastre, Arg. 31°46′ S, 61°49′ W 139
Sasyk-Kel, Taj. 37°39′ N, 73°10′ E 197
Sasykoli, Russ. 47°27′ N, 47°2′ E 158
Sata Misaki, Japan 30°28′ N, 129°42′ E 190
Satadougou Tintiba, Mali 12°39′ N, 11°25′ W 222
Satala, ruin(s), Turk. 40°1′ N, 39°31′ E 195
Satama Sakoura, Côte d'Ivoire 7°53′ N, 4°19′ W 222
Sataniv, Ukr. 49°15′ N, 26°14′ E 152
Satanta, Kans., U.S. 37°25′ N, 100°60′ W 92
Satara, India 17°41′ N, 73°58′ E 188
Satartia, Miss., U.S. 32°39′ N, 90°32′ W 103
Satawan Atoll 5°14′ N, 150°47′ E 192
Sätbaev, Kaz. 47°54′ N, 67°30′ E 184
Satellite Beach, Fla., U.S. 28°9′ N, 80°37′ W 105
Säter, Nor. 60°20′ N, 15°42′ E 152
Satevó, Mex. 27°56′ N, 106°6′ W 82
Saticoy, Calif., U.S. 34°17′ N, 119°10′ W 101
Satilla, river, Ga., U.S. 31°32′ N, 83°4′ W 80
Satipo, Peru 11°15′ S, 74°42′ W 137
Satka, Russ. 55°5′ N, 59°6′ E 154
Satna, India 24°34′ N, 80°49′ E 197
Sato, Japan 37°25′ N, 137°2′ E 201
Sato, Japan 31°50′ N, 129°54′ E 201
Šator, peak, Bosn. and Herzg. 44°9′ N, 16°35′ E 168
Satpura National Park, India 22°30′ N, 78°12′ E 197
Sattahip, Thai. 12°41′ N, 100°53′ E 202
Satu Mare, Rom. 47°47′ N, 22°54′ E 168
Satu Mare, adm. division, Rom. 48°5′ N, 22°59′ E 152
Satun, Thai. 6°35′ N, 100°3′ E 196
Sauce, Arg. 30°4′ S, 58°45′ W 139
Saucier, Miss., U.S. 30°37′ N, 89°7′ W 103
Saúdakent, Kaz. 43°42′ N, 69°55′ E 184
Sauðárkrókur, Ice. 65°43′ N, 19°41′ W 246
Saudi Arabia 23°44′ N, 43°56′ E 182
Sauêruiná, river, Braz. 11°36′ S, 58°51′ W 132
Saugatuck, Mich., U.S. 42°39′ N, 86°11′ W 102
Saugor see Sagar, India 23°50′ N, 78°45′ E 188
Sauk Centre, Minn., U.S. 45°46′ N, 94°57′ W 82
Sauk City, Wis., U.S. 43°15′ N, 89°44′ W 102
Sauk Rapids, Minn., U.S. 45°35′ N, 94°11′ W 90
Sauk, river, Wash., U.S. 48°26′ N, 121°41′ W 100
Saukville, Wis., U.S. 43°22′ N, 87°58′ W 102
Saulkrasti, Latv. 57°16′ N, 24°25′ E 166
Sault Sainte Marie, Can. 46°35′ N, 84°18′ W 106
Sault Sainte Marie, Mich., U.S. 46°29′ N, 84°22′ W 94
Saümalköl, Kaz. 53°18′ N, 68°8′ E 184
Saumlaki, Indonesia 7°58′ S, 131°10′ E 192
Saundatti, India 15°46′ N, 75°6′ E 188
Saunders Coast, South Pacific Ocean 76°48′ S, 132°37′ W 248
Saunders Mount, peak, Antarctica 76°46′ S, 144°52′ W 248
Saunders, Mount, peak, Antarctica 85°40′ S, 163°7′ E 248
Saurimo, Angola 9°38′ S, 20°25′ E 218
Sauris, It. 46°27′ N, 12°42′ E 167
Sautar, Angola 11°6′ S, 18°27′ E 220
Sauterelles, Lac aux, lake, Can. 51°58′ N, 65°8′ W 111
Sava, river, Croatia 45°46′ N, 15°48′ E 168
Savage, Mont., U.S. 47°25′ N, 104°22′ W 90
Savai'i, island, Samoa 13°38′ S, 172°38′ W 241
Savalou, Benin 7°57′ N, 1°57′ E 222
Savanna, Ill., U.S. 42°4′ N, 90°9′ W 102
Savannah, Ga., U.S. 32°3′ N, 81°6′ W 96
Savannah, Mo., U.S. 39°55′ N, 94°50′ W 94
Savannah, river, U.S. 33°27′ N, 82°1′ W 80
Savannakhét, Laos 16°32′ N, 104°46′ E 202
Savanna-la-Mar, Jam. 18°14′ N, 78°8′ W 115
Savant Lake, Can. 50°14′ N, 90°42′ W 110
Savant Lake, Can. 50°14′ N, 90°42′ W 94
Savanur, India 14°58′ N, 75°20′ E 188
Savar Kundla, India 21°21′ N, 71°17′ E 186
Savaştepe, Turk. 39°22′ N, 27°38′ E 156
Savé, Benin 8°4′ N, 2°27′ E 222
Save, river, Africa 21°16′ S, 32°29′ E 207
Save, river, Fr. 43°40′ N, 1°10′ E 165
Sāveh, Iran 35°3′ N, 50°19′ E 180
Savelugu, Ghana 9°37′ N, 0°51′ E 222
Saverdun, Fr. 43°13′ N, 1°33′ E 164
Saverne, Fr. 48°44′ N, 7°21′ E 163
Savigliano, It. 44°37′ N, 7°39′ E 167
Savignano sul Rubicone, It. 44°6′ N, 12°24′ E 156
Savignone, It. 44°33′ N, 8°59′ E 167
Savinobor, Russ. 63°35′ N, 56°27′ E 154
Savio, river, It. 44°8′ N, 12°11′ E 167
Săvîrşin, Rom. 46°1′ N, 22°14′ E 168
Savissivik 75°59′ N, 64°51′ W 246
Savitaipale, Fin. 61°11′ N, 27°40′ E 166
Šavnik, Europe 42°56′ N, 19°5′ E 168
Savona, It. 44°18′ N, 8°28′ E 167
Savonlinna, Fin. 61°51′ N, 28°51′ E 166
Savonranta, Fin. 62°9′ N, 29°11′ E 152
Savoy, Ill., U.S. 40°3′ N, 88°15′ W 102
Savoy, Mass., U.S. 42°33′ N, 73°2′ W 104
Savoy, region, Fr. 45°19′ N, 6°12′ E 165
Şavşat, Turk. 41°15′ N, 42°20′ E 195
Savu Sea 9°59′ S, 121°35′ E 192
Savudrija, Croatia 45°29′ N, 13°30′ E 167
Savukoski, Fin. 67°18′ N, 28°6′ E 152
Savur, Turk. 37°32′ N, 40°56′ E 195
Saw, Myanmar 21°12′ N, 94°5′ E 202
Sawada, Japan 38°0′ N, 138°20′ E 201
Sawahlunto, Indonesia 0°40′ N, 100°47′ E 196
Sawai Madhopur, India 26°0′ N, 76°25′ E 197
Sawankhalok, Thai. 17°19′ N, 99°51′ E 202
Sawara, Japan 35°52′ N, 140°31′ E 201
Sawārah Tūkā, Iraq 37°0′ N, 43°6′ E 195
Sawatch Range, Colo., U.S. 39°21′ N, 106°52′ W 90
Sawdā', Jabal as, Lib. 29°0′ N, 14°26′ E 216
Sawdā', Qurnat as, peak, Leb. 34°18′ N, 36°5′ E 194
Sawe, Indian Ocean 1°31′ N, 97°23′ E 196
Sawi, Thai. 10°13′ N, 99°6′ E 202
Sāwinnū, ruin(s), Lib. 30°59′ N, 20°45′ E 216
Sawkanah, Lib. 29°6′ N, 15°45′ E 216
Sawla, Ghana 9°16′ N, 2°26′ W 222
Sawn Lake, Can. 56°57′ N, 116°29′ W 108
Şawqirah, Oman 18°5′ N, 56°29′ E 182
Şawqirah, Ghubbat 18°31′ N, 56°2′ E 182
Sawtooth Mountains, Minn., U.S. 47°35′ N, 91°23′ W 94
Sawtooth National Recreation Area, Idaho, U.S. 43°42′ N, 121°19′ W 80
Sawtooth Range, Idaho, U.S. 44°7′ N, 115°16′ W 90
Sawu, island, Indonesia 10°33′ S, 122°2′ E 192
Sawyer, Mich., U.S. 41°52′ N, 86°35′ W 102
Sawyer Bay 41°3′ S, 145°0′ E 230
Sax, Sp. 38°31′ N, 0°51′ E 164
Saxmundham, U.K. 52°12′ N, 1°28′ E 163
Saxnäs, Nor. 64°56′ N, 15°17′ E 152
Saxony, adm. division, Ger. 51°7′ N, 12°33′ E 152
Saxony-Anhalt, adm. division, Ger. 52°38′ N, 10°57′ E 152
Saxtons River, Vt., U.S. 43°8′ N, 72°31′ W 104
Say, Niger 13°5′ N, 2°18′ E 222
Sayak, Kaz. 47°0′ N, 77°24′ E 184
Sayanogorsk, Russ. 52°48′ N, 91°19′ E 190
Sayat, Turkm. 38°47′ N, 63°53′ E 197
Saybrook, Ill., U.S. 40°25′ N, 88°32′ W 102
Şaydnāyā, Syr. 33°41′ N, 36°22′ E 194
Sayhūt, Yemen 15°15′ N, 51°15′ E 182
Saylac, Somalia 11°16′ N, 43°27′ E 216
Säyneinen, Fin. 63°10′ N, 28°24′ E 152
Saynshand (Buyant-Uhaa), Mongolia 44°51′ N, 110°9′ E 190
Sayötesh, Kaz. 44°18′ N, 53°33′ E 158
Sayqyn, Kaz. 48°48′ N, 46°47′ E 158
Sayram Hu, lake, China 44°27′ N, 80°40′ E 184
Sayre, Okla., U.S. 35°16′ N, 99°39′ W 92
Sayre, Pa., U.S. 41°58′ N, 76°32′ W 94
Sayrob, Uzb. 38°2′ N, 67°0′ E 197
Sayula, Mex. 19°52′ N, 103°37′ W 114
Sayula, Mex. 17°51′ N, 94°58′ W 114
Sayulita, Mex. 20°51′ N, 105°28′ W 114
Sayville, N.Y., U.S. 40°44′ N, 73°5′ W 104
Sbaa, Alg. 28°14′ N, 0°11′ E 214
Sbikha, Tun. 35°56′ N, 10°1′ E 156
Scafell Pike, peak, U.K. 54°26′ N, 3°15′ W 162
Scalea, It. 39°49′ N, 15°47′ E 156
Scammon Bay, Alas., U.S. 61°50′ N, 165°35′ W 98
Scandia, Kans., U.S. 39°46′ N, 97°47′ W 90
Scandiano, It. 44°36′ N, 10°41′ E 167
Scanzano Ionico, It. 40°15′ N, 16°42′ E 156
Scapegoat Mountain, peak, Mont., U.S. 47°16′ N, 112°55′ W 90
Scappoose, Oreg., U.S. 45°44′ N, 122°52′ W 100
Scaraben, peak, U.K. 58°12′ N, 3°43′ W 150
Scarborough, Me., U.S. 43°34′ N, 70°19′ W 104
Scarborough, U.K. 54°16′ N, 0°26′ E 162
Scardona see Skradin, Croatia 43°49′ N, 15°54′ E 168
Scargill, N.Z. 42°58′ S, 172°57′ E 240
Scauri, It. 36°45′ N, 11°59′ E 156
Sceale Bay 33°7′ S, 132°54′ E 230
Sceaux, Fr. 48°46′ N, 2°18′ E 163
Šćedro, island, Croatia 43°2′ N, 16°29′ E 168
Schagen, Neth. 52°47′ N, 4°46′ E 163
Schaghticoke, N.Y., U.S. 42°54′ N, 73°36′ W 104
Schefferville, Can. 54°51′ N, 67°3′ W 106
Schela, Rom. 45°9′ N, 23°18′ E 168
Schell Creek Range, Nev., U.S. 39°34′ N, 114°51′ W 90
Schenectady, N.Y., U.S. 42°48′ N, 73°57′ W 104
Scherfede, Ger. 51°31′ N, 9°2′ E 167
Scherhorn, peak, Switz. 46°47′ N, 8°47′ E 167
Schertz, Tex., U.S. 29°31′ N, 98°16′ W 92
Schiermonnikoog, island, Neth. 53°25′ N, 6°1′ E 163
Schillighörn 53°39′ N, 7°51′ E 163
Schilpario, It. 46°1′ N, 10°9′ E 167
Schio, It. 45°43′ N, 11°21′ E 167
Schirmeck, Fr. 48°28′ N, 7°12′ E 163
Schleiden, Ger. 50°31′ N, 6°28′ E 167
Schleswig-Holstein, adm. division, Ger. 54°2′ N, 9°4′ E 150
Schlitz, Ger. 50°40′ N, 9°33′ E 167
Schlossbach, Cape, Antarctica 75°51′ S, 61°41′ W 248
Schlüchtern, Ger. 50°20′ N, 9°31′ E 167
Schmallenberg, Ger. 51°9′ N, 8°16′ E 167
Schmelz, Ger. 49°26′ N, 6°51′ E 163
Schmücke, peak, Ger. 51°13′ N, 11°12′ E 152
Schofield, Wis., U.S. 44°54′ N, 89°36′ W 110
Schofield Barracks, Hawai'i, U.S. 21°29′ N, 158°7′ W 99
Schönecken, Ger. 50°9′ N, 6°28′ E 167
Schonungen, Ger. 50°3′ N, 10°17′ E 167
Schoolcraft, Mich., U.S. 42°6′ N, 85°38′ W 102
Schortens, Ger. 53°31′ N, 7°57′ E 163
Schotten, Ger. 50°30′ N, 9°7′ E 167
Schouten Islands, islands, Bismarck Sea 3°8′ S, 142°32′ E 192
Schreiber, Can. 48°48′ N, 87°15′ W 110
Schreiner Peak, Oreg., U.S. 44°52′ N, 122°8′ W 90
Schroeder, Minn., U.S. 47°32′ N, 90°56′ W 110
Schroon Lake, N.Y., U.S. 43°50′ N, 73°47′ W 104
Schubert Inlet 71°7′ S, 72°22′ W 248
Schuler, Can. 50°20′ N, 110°5′ W 90
Schull, Ire. 51°31′ N, 9°33′ W 150
Schumacher, Can. 48°29′ N, 81°17′ W 94
Schüttorf, Ger. 52°19′ N, 7°14′ E 163
Schuyler, Nebr., U.S. 41°26′ N, 97°4′ W 92
Schuylerville, N.Y., U.S. 43°5′ N, 73°36′ W 104
Schwaben, region, Ger. 48°8′ N, 7°50′ E 163
Schwäbische Alb, Ger. 48°9′ N, 8°23′ E 150
Schwalmstadt, Ger. 50°55′ N, 9°12′ E 167
Schwarzwald, region, Ger. 48°6′ N, 7°38′ E 163
Schweich, Ger. 49°49′ N, 6°45′ E 167
Schweinfurt, Ger. 50°2′ N, 10°13′ E 167
Schweizer Reneke, S. Af. 27°11′ S, 25°18′ E 227
Schwerin, Ger. 53°38′ N, 11°25′ E 152
Schwerte, Ger. 51°26′ N, 7°33′ E 167
Schwob Peak, Antarctica 75°50′ S, 127°59′ W 248
Scicli, It. 36°47′ N, 14°42′ E 156
Scilly, Isles of, islands, Celtic Sea 49°48′ N, 6°58′ W 150
Scînteia, Rom. 46°55′ N, 27°34′ E 156
Scione, ruin(s), Gr. 39°56′ N, 23°26′ E 156
Scioto, river, Ohio, U.S. 40°26′ N, 83°16′ W 102
Scipio, Utah, U.S. 39°14′ N, 112°6′ W 90
Scituate, Mass., U.S. 42°11′ N, 70°44′ W 104
Scobey, Mont., U.S. 48°46′ N, 105°26′ W 90
Scooba, Miss., U.S. 32°47′ N, 88°30′ W 103
Scoresby Land 71°45′ N, 24°3′ W 246
Scoresby Sund 70°5′ N, 31°35′ W 72
Scoresbysund see Ittoqqortoormiit 70°26′ N, 21°53′ W 246
Scorpion Bight 32°38′ S, 126°15′ E 230
Scorton, U.K. 54°24′ N, 1°37′ W 162
Scotch Corner, U.K. 54°26′ N, 1°41′ W 162
Scotia, Calif., U.S. 40°28′ N, 124°6′ W 92
Scotia, N.Y., U.S. 42°49′ N, 73°59′ W 104
Scotia Sea 56°22′ S, 49°38′ W 134
Scotland, S. Dak., U.S. 43°6′ N, 97°43′ W 90
Scotland, adm. division, U.K. 56°50′ N, 5°37′ W 150
Scotland Neck, N.C., U.S. 36°7′ N, 77°26′ W 96
Scotlandville, La., U.S. 30°30′ N, 91°12′ W 103
Scotstown, Can. 45°31′ N, 71°17′ W 111
Scott, Can. 52°21′ N, 108°51′ W 108
Scott, La., U.S. 30°13′ N, 92°6′ W 96
Scott Air Force Base, Ill., U.S. 38°31′ N, 89°54′ W 102
Scott Bar Mountains, Calif., U.S. 41°51′ N, 122°60′ W 90
Scott Base, New Zealand, station, Antarctica 77°52′ S, 166°44′ E 248
Scott, Cape, Can. 50°35′ N, 128°45′ W 90
Scott City, Kans., U.S. 38°29′ N, 100°55′ W 90
Scott Coast, Antarctica 76°20′ S, 169°0′ E 248
Scott Island, South Pacific Ocean 67°24′ S, 179°50′ E 255
Scott Islands, North Pacific Ocean 50°18′ N, 130°51′ W 106
Scott, Mount, peak, Oreg., U.S. 42°54′ N, 122°7′ W 90
Scott Mountains, Antarctica 67°31′ S, 49°49′ E 248
Scott Mountains, Calif., U.S. 41°14′ N, 122°55′ W 90
Scott Nunataks, Antarctica 77°13′ S, 156°24′ W 248
Scott Point, Mich., U.S. 45°47′ N, 85°60′ W 94
Scottburgh, S. Af. 30°17′ S, 30°41′ E 227
Scotts Valley, Calif., U.S. 37°3′ N, 122°2′ W 100
Scottsbluff, Nebr., U.S. 41°51′ N, 103°39′ W 82
Scottsboro, Ala., U.S. 34°39′ N, 86°1′ W 96
Scottsburg, Ind., U.S. 38°41′ N, 85°46′ W 102
Scottsville, Ky., U.S. 36°44′ N, 86°12′ W 96
Scottville, Mich., U.S. 43°57′ N, 86°17′ W 102
Scourie, U.K. 58°21′ N, 5°9′ W 150
Scout Mountain, peak, Idaho, U.S. 42°40′ N, 112°24′ W 90
Scranton, Pa., U.S. 41°24′ N, 75°40′ W 94
Scranton, S.C., U.S. 33°54′ N, 79°46′ W 96
Scribner, Nebr., U.S. 41°38′ N, 96°41′ W 90
Scudder, Can. 41°48′ N, 82°38′ W 102
Scugog, Lake, Can. 44°7′ N, 79°16′ W 110
Scullin Monolith, peak, Antarctica 67°52′ S, 66°27′ E 248
Scunthorpe, U.K. 53°34′ N, 0°40′ E 162
Scuol, Switz. 46°48′ N, 10°17′ E 167
Scutari see Shkodër, Alban. 42°4′ N, 19°30′ E 168
Sea Gull Lake, lake, Minn., U.S. 48°5′ N, 91°4′ W 110
Sea Island, Ga., U.S. 31°10′ N, 81°22′ W 96
Sea Lion Islands, Scotia Sea 52°42′ S, 58°40′ W 134
Seabrook, N.H., U.S. 42°53′ N, 70°53′ W 104
Seabrook, Tex., U.S. 29°34′ N, 95°1′ W 103
Seacliff, N.Z. 45°41′ S, 170°37′ E 240
Seadrift, Tex., U.S. 28°24′ N, 96°43′ W 96
Seaford, Del., U.S. 38°38′ N, 75°37′ W 94
Seaford, U.K. 50°46′ N, 0°535′ E 162
Seaforth, Can. 43°33′ N, 81°24′ W 102
Seagraves, Tex., U.S. 32°55′ N, 102°34′ W 92
Seaham, U.K. 54°50′ N, 1°21′ W 162
Seal Bay 71°46′ S, 14°44′ W 248
Seal, Cape, S. Af. 34°21′ S, 23°27′ E 227
Seal Islands, Scotia Sea 60°59′ S, 56°17′ W 134
Seal Nunataks 64°59′ S, 60°8′ W 248
Seal, river, Can. 58°50′ N, 96°21′ W 108
Sealy, Tex., U.S. 29°45′ N, 96°9′ W 96
Seaman, Ohio, U.S. 38°55′ N, 83°34′ W 102
Seaman Range, Nev., U.S. 37°57′ N, 115°22′ W 90
Searchlight, Nev., U.S. 35°27′ N, 114°56′ W 101
Searcy, Ark., U.S. 35°14′ N, 91°47′ W 112
Seascale, U.K. 54°24′ N, 3°29′ W 162
Seaside, Calif., U.S. 36°36′ N, 121°52′ W 100
Seaside, Oreg., U.S. 45°59′ N, 123°54′ W 100
Seaside Park, N.J., U.S. 39°54′ N, 74°6′ W 94
Seattle, Wash., U.S. 47°35′ N, 122°19′ W 100
Seaview, Wash., U.S. 46°18′ N, 124°3′ W 100
Sebago Lake, Me., U.S. 43°50′ N, 70°38′ W 104
Sebago Lake, Me., U.S. 43°45′ N, 70°32′ W 104
Sebanga, oil field, Indonesia 1°16′ N, 101°10′ E 196
Sebastian, Fla., U.S. 27°48′ N, 80°29′ W 105
Sebastian, Cape, Oreg., U.S. 42°18′ N, 124°56′ W 90
Sebastián Elcano, Arg. 30°10′ S, 63°38′ W 139
Sebastián Vizcaíno, Bahía 28°3′ N, 115°1′ W 92
Sebastopol, Calif., U.S. 38°24′ N, 122°50′ W 100
Sebastopol, Miss., U.S. 32°33′ N, 89°21′ W 103
Sebba, Burkina Faso 13°26′ N, 0°30′ E 222
Sébé, river, Gabon 0°56′ N, 13°15′ E 218
Seben, Turk. 40°24′ N, 31°33′ E 156
Seberi, Braz. 27°43′ S, 53°19′ W 139
Seberi, Cerro, peak, Mex. 27°46′ N, 110°21′ W 112
Sebeşului, Munţii, Rom. 45°34′ N, 23°9′ E 168
Sebeta, Rabt, Africa 23°59′ N, 14°47′ W 214
Sebewaing, Mich., U.S. 43°43′ N, 83°26′ W 102
Sebezh, Russ. 56°17′ N, 28°29′ E 166
Sebina, Botswana 20°53′ S, 27°13′ E 227
Sebiş, Rom. 46°23′ N, 22°10′ E 168
Sebring, Fla., U.S. 27°30′ N, 81°26′ W 105
Sečanj, Serb. and Mont. 45°22′ N, 20°47′ E 168
Sechelt, Can. 49°28′ N, 123°46′ W 100
Sechura, Peru 5°30′ S, 80°51′ W 130
Sechura, Desierto de, Peru 6°10′ S, 82°8′ W 130
Seclin, Fr. 50°32′ N, 3°1′ E 163
Second Mesa, Ariz., U.S. 35°46′ N, 110°30′ W 92
Secret Pass, Nev., U.S. 40°50′ N, 115°12′ W 90
Secunderabad, India 17°28′ N, 78°28′ E 188
Securé, river, Bol. 15°44′ S, 65°44′ W 137
Seda, Latv. 57°39′ N, 25°44′ E 166
Seda, Lith. 56°9′ N, 22°4′ E 166
Sedalia, Mo., U.S. 38°41′ N, 93°14′ W 94
Sedan, Fr. 49°42′ N, 4°56′ E 163
Sedano, Sp. 42°42′ N, 3°44′ W 164
Sedbergh, U.K. 54°19′ N, 2°32′ W 162
Seddon, N.Z. 41°43′ S, 174°3′ E 240
Seddon, Kap 75°11′ N, 58°11′ W 106
Seddonville, N.Z. 41°35′ S, 171°58′ E 240
Sedé Boqér, Israel 30°51′ N, 34°47′ E 194
Sedeh, Iran 33°20′ N, 59°16′ E 180
Sederot, Israel 31°31′ N, 34°36′ E 194
Sedgemoor 1685, battle, U.K. 51°8′ N, 2°56′ W 162
Sédhiou, Senegal 12°43′ N, 15°33′ W 222
Sedlare, Serb. and Mont. 44°12′ N, 21°16′ E 168
Sedley, Can. 50°9′ N, 104°2′ W 90
Sedom, Israel 31°4′ N, 35°23′ E 194
Sedro Woolley, Wash., U.S. 48°30′ N, 122°15′ W 100
Šeduva, Lith. 55°44′ N, 23°44′ E 166
Seeheim, Namibia 26°50′ S, 17°46′ E 227
Seeis, Namibia 22°28′ S, 17°34′ E 227
Seekonk, Mass., U.S. 41°48′ N, 71°21′ W 104
Seeley, Calif., U.S. 32°47′ N, 115°42′ W 101
Seelig, Mount, peak, Antarctica 82°14′ S, 102°46′ W 248
Seelow, Ger. 52°32′ N, 14°22′ E 152
Seelyville, Ind., U.S. 39°29′ N, 87°16′ W 102
Seemade, Somalia 7°9′ N, 48°31′ E 218
Sefare, Botswana 22°60′ S, 27°27′ E 227
Sefophe, Botswana 22°16′ S, 27°59′ E 227
Sefrou, Mor. 33°51′ N, 4°53′ W 214
Seg Ozero, lake, Russ. 63°15′ N, 33°33′ E 154
Segag, Eth. 7°32′ N, 42°55′ E 218
Ségala, Mali 14°35′ N, 10°58′ W 222
Segamat, Malaysia 2°33′ N, 102°49′ E 196
Segbana, Benin 10°57′ N, 3°38′ E 222
Segesta, ruin(s), It. 37°54′ N, 12°43′ E 156
Segezha, Russ. 63°45′ N, 34°16′ E 154
Segorbe, Sp. 39°50′ N, 0°30′ E 164
Ségou, Mali 13°25′ N, 6°16′ W 222
Segovia, Sp. 40°55′ N, 4°8′ W 150
Séguédine, Niger 20°17′ N, 12°55′ E 216
Séguéla, Côte d'Ivoire 7°53′ N, 6°40′ W 222
Séguéla, Mali 14°6′ N, 6°44′ W 222
Seguin, Tex., U.S. 29°33′ N, 97°58′ W 92
Segura, Sierra de, Sp. 37°58′ N, 2°57′ W 164
Sehithwa, Botswana 20°26′ S, 22°39′ E 227
Sehnkwehn, Liberia 5°13′ N, 9°22′ W 222
Sehore, India 23°11′ N, 77°5′ E 197
Seibal, ruin(s), Guatemala 16°28′ N, 90°13′ W 115
Seida, Nor. 70°12′ N, 28°6′ E 152
Seiling, Okla., U.S. 36°8′ N, 98°56′ W 92
Seine, river, Fr. 48°9′ N, 4°21′ E 165
Seine, river, Fr. 49°4′ N, 1°35′ E 163
Seini, Rom. 47°44′ N, 23°16′ E 168
Seira, Sp. 42°28′ N, 0°26′ E 164
Sejenane, Tun. 37°4′ N, 9°15′ E 156
Sejny, Pol. 54°5′ N, 23°20′ E 166
Seke, Tanzania 3°19′ S, 33°30′ E 224
Seke Banza, Dem. Rep. of the Congo 5°20′ S, 13°15′ E 218
Seken Seyfüllin, Kaz. 48°50′ N, 72°48′ E 184
Sekenke, Tanzania 4°17′ S, 34°9′ E 224
Sekhira, Tun. 34°21′ N, 10°4′ E 156
Sekikawa, Japan 38°5′ N, 139°33′ E 201
Sekiu, Wash., U.S. 48°14′ N, 124°20′ W 100
Sekondi-Takoradi, Ghana 4°58′ N, 1°45′ W 222
Sekseüil, Kaz. 47°4′ N, 61°9′ E 184
Sekulići, Europe 42°33′ N, 19°9′ E 168
Sela Dingay, Eth. 9°55′ N, 39°37′ E 224
Selama, Malaysia 5°12′ N, 100°43′ E 196
Selaru, island, Indonesia 8°39′ S, 130°27′ E 192
Selatpampang, Indonesia 0°13′ N, 109°8′ E 196
Selawik, Alas., U.S. 66°28′ N, 159°60′ W 98
Selayar, island, Indonesia 6°45′ S, 119°37′ E 192
Selby, S. Dak., U.S. 45°30′ N, 100°3′ W 90
Selby, U.K. 53°47′ N, 1°4′ W 162
Selce, Maced. 42°3′ N, 20°55′ E 168
Selden, Kans., U.S. 39°32′ N, 100°34′ W 90
Selden, N.Y., U.S. 40°52′ N, 73°3′ W 104
Seldovia, Alas., U.S. 59°19′ N, 151°43′ W 98
Selebi Phikwe, Botswana 21°59′ S, 27°52′ E 227
Selečka Planina, Maced. 41°14′ N, 21°7′ E 156
Selendi, Turk. 38°46′ N, 28°51′ E 156
Selenge, adm. division, Mongolia 49°12′ N, 105°4′ E 198
Selenge, river, Mongolia 48°15′ N, 99°37′ E 172
Selenge, river, Mongolia 49°25′ N, 103°10′ E 190
Sélestat, Fr. 48°16′ N, 7°27′ E 163
Seleucia see Samandağı, Turk. 36°4′ N, 35°57′ E 156
Selevac, Serb. and Mont. 44°29′ N, 20°52′ E 168
Seleznevo, Russ. 60°45′ N, 28°37′ E 166
Selfridge, N. Dak., U.S. 46°2′ N, 100°57′ W 90
Selib, Russ. 63°47′ N, 48°28′ E 154
Sélibaby, Mauritania 15°9′ N, 12°13′ W 222
Seliger, Ozero, lake, Russ. 57°16′ N, 32°32′ E 154
Seligman, Ariz., U.S. 35°19′ N, 112°52′ W 92
Selima Oasis, Sudan 21°22′ N, 29°21′ E 226
Selinde, Russ. 57°16′ N, 132°39′ E 173
Selinus, ruin(s), It. 37°34′ N, 12°43′ E 156
Selitrennoye, Russ. 47°9′ N, 47°23′ E 158
Selityarovo, Russ. 61°17′ N, 70°16′ E 169
Selizharovo, Russ. 56°50′ N, 33°38′ E 154
Selje, Nor. 62°3′ N, 5°22′ E 152
Selkirk, Can. 50°8′ N, 96°54′ W 90
Selkirk Mountains, Can. 51°22′ N, 117°56′ W 108
Selles, Fr. 47°16′ N, 1°33′ E 150
Sells, Ariz., U.S. 31°54′ N, 111°52′ W 92
Sellye, Hung. 45°51′ N, 17°51′ E 168
Selma, Ala., U.S. 32°24′ N, 87°1′ W 96
Selma, Calif., U.S. 36°34′ N, 119°37′ W 100
Selma, N.C., U.S. 35°32′ N, 78°18′ W 96
Selmer, Tenn., U.S. 35°9′ N, 88°35′ W 96
Selous Game Reserve, Tanzania 9°29′ S, 36°6′ E 224
Selous, Mount, peak, Can. 62°56′ N, 132°38′ W 98
Sel'tso, Russ. 63°19′ N, 41°23′ E 154
Selty, Russ. 57°19′ N, 52°8′ E 169
Seluan, island, Indonesia 4°1′ N, 107°25′ E 196
Selva, Arg. 29°45′ S, 62°3′ W 139
Selvagens, Ilhas (Salvage Islands), North Atlantic Ocean 30°18′ N, 16°15′ W 214
Selwyn Mountains, Can. 62°26′ N, 129°39′ W 98
Selwyn Range, Austral. 21°1′ S, 139°47′ E 230
Selyatyn, Ukr. 47°51′ N, 25°11′ E 156
Semarang, Indonesia 7°5′ S, 110°15′ E 192
Sembé, Congo 1°38′ N, 14°37′ E 218
Sembo, Eth. 7°32′ N, 36°37′ E 224
Şemdinli, Turk. 37°18′ N, 44°31′ E 195
Semenov, Russ. 56°45′ N, 44°35′ E 154
Semepalatinsk see Semey, Kaz. 50°23′ N, 80°14′ E 184
Semeru, peak, Indonesia 8°5′ S, 112°44′ E 192
Semey (Semepalatinsk), Kaz. 50°23′ N, 80°14′ E 184
Semichi Islands, islands, Alas., U.S. 52°28′ N, 175°7′ E 160
Sémien, Côte d'Ivoire 7°33′ N, 7°9′ W 222
Semiluki, Russ. 51°40′ N, 38°58′ E 158
Seminary, Miss., U.S. 31°33′ N, 89°30′ W 103
Seminole, Okla., U.S. 35°13′ N, 96°41′ W 96
Seminole, Tex., U.S. 32°42′ N, 102°38′ W 92
Sémit, spring, Mali 16°43′ N, 0°41′ E 222
Semizovac, Bosn. and Herzg. 43°55′ N, 18°17′ E 168
Semmé, Senegal 15°11′ N, 12°60′ W 222
Semmens Lake, lake, Can. 54°57′ N, 94°50′ W 108
Semmering, pass, Aust. 47°37′ N, 15°47′ E 168

Semmes, Ala., U.S. 30°46' N, 88°15' W 103
Semna West, ruin(s), Sudan 21°30' N, 30°49' E 182
Semnān, Iran 35°36' N, 53°26' E 180
Semzha, Russ. 66°9' N, 44°11' E 154
Sen, river, Cambodia 13°50' N, 104°36' E 202
Sena, Bol. 11°31' S, 67°11' W 137
Sena, Mozambique 17°27' S, 34°59' E 224
Sena, Sp. 41°42' N, 3°177' W 164
Sena Madureira, Braz. 9°8' S, 68°41' W 137
Senador José Porfírio, Braz. 2°39' S, 51°56' W 130
Senaja, Malaysia 6°50' N, 117°3' E 203
Senanga, Zambia 16°8' S, 23°16' E 220
Senatobia, Miss., U.S. 34°37' N, 89°58' W 96
Sendai, Japan 31°47' N, 130°19' E 201
Sendai, Japan 38°16' N, 140°53' E 201
Senden, Ger. 51°51' N, 7°29' E 167
Sendenhorst, Ger. 51°50' N, 7°49' E 167
Senec, Slovakia 48°13' N, 17°24' E 152
Seneca, Ill., U.S. 41°19' N, 88°38' W 102
Seneca, Kans., U.S. 39°48' N, 96°4' W 90
Seneca, Oreg., U.S. 44°8' N, 118°58' W 90
Seneca, Pa., U.S. 41°23' N, 79°42' W 110
Seneca, S.C., U.S. 34°40' N, 82°58' W 96
Seneca Rocks, site, W. Va., U.S. 38°48' N, 79°31' W 82
Senecaville Lake, Ohio, U.S. 39°52' N, 81°41' W 102
Senegal 15°10' N, 15°27' W 214
Sénégal, river, Africa 16°36' N, 15°57' W 206
Seneki, Ga. 42°16' N, 42°4' E 195
Senetosa, Punta di, Fr. 41°29' N, 7°54' E 156
Senftenberg, Ger. 51°31' N, 13°59' E 152
Sengés, Braz. 24°7' S, 49°29' W 138
Sengiley, Russ. 53°54' N, 48°47' E 154
Senguerr, river, Arg. 45°3' S, 71°6' W 134
Sengwa, river, Zimb. 18°24' S, 28°11' E 224
Senhor do Bonfim, Braz. 10°27' S, 40°11' W 132
Senigallia, It. 43°42' N, 13°12' E 167
Senkobo, Zambia 17°38' S, 25°54' E 224
Senlin Shan, peak, China 43°10' N, 130°35' E 200
Senlis, Fr. 49°12' N, 2°35' E 163
Senmonorom, Cambodia 12°37' N, 107°14' E 202
Sennar, Sudan 13°31' N, 33°34' E 182
Senneterre, Can. 48°24' N, 77°16' W 94
Sénoudébou, Senegal 14°21' N, 12°18' W 222
Senozero, Russ. 66°9' N, 31°44' E 154
Sens, Fr. 48°11' N, 3°17' E 163
Sensuntepeque, El Salv. 13°52' N, 88°38' W 116
Senta, Serb. and Mont. 45°55' N, 20°4' E 168
Sentein, Fr. 42°52' N, 0°55' E 164
Sentinel, Okla., U.S. 35°7' N, 99°10' W 96
Sentinel Peak, Can. 54°53' N, 122°4' W 108
Senyavin Islands, North Pacific Ocean 7°29' N, 156°35' E 238
Seocheon, S. Korea 36°4' N, 126°43' E 200
Seogwipo, S. Korea 33°18' N, 126°35' E 198
Seokjeong, S. Korea 34°53' N, 127°0' E 200
Seomjin, river, S. Korea 35°11' N, 127°28' E 200
Seongnae, S. Korea 36°30' N, 129°26' E 200
Seoni, India 22°5' N, 79°33' E 197
Seoni Malwa, India 22°27' N, 77°28' E 197
Seonsan, S. Korea 36°13' N, 128°19' E 200
Seosan, S. Korea 36°45' N, 126°26' E 200
Seoul, S. Korea 37°33' N, 126°54' E 200
Sepahua, Peru 11°7' S, 73°4' W 137
Separation Point, Can. 53°36' N, 57°26' W 111
Sepatini, river, Braz. 8°4' S, 66°6' W 132
Sept Îles, Les, islands, English Channel 48°57' N, 3°38' W 150
Sept-Îles, Can. 50°11' N, 66°22' W 111
Sepupa, Botswana 18°48' S, 22°10' E 220
Sequim, Wash., U.S. 48°3' N, 123°6' W 100
Serafimovich, Russ. 49°32' N, 42°41' E 158
Seraing, Belg. 50°35' N, 5°30' E 167
Seram, India 17°11' N, 77°18' E 188
Serang, Indonesia 6°13' S, 106°7' E 192
Serasan, island, Indonesia 2°24' N, 108°36' E 196
Seraya, island, Indonesia 2°33' N, 108°11' E 196
Särba, Eth. 13°12' N, 40°32' E 182
Serbia 43°45' N, 20°29' E 168
Sercaia, Rom. 45°50' N, 25°9' E 158
Serdeles see Al 'Uwaynāt, Lib. 25°47' N, 10°33' E 216
Serdo, Eth. 11°54' N, 41°19' E 182
Serdobol see Sortavala, Russ. 61°42' N, 30°39' E 166
Serdobsk, Russ. 52°28' N, 44°13' E 158
Serebryanka, Russ. 57°6' N, 70°43' E 169
Serebryansk, Kaz. 49°42' N, 83°21' E 184
Seredka, Russ. 58°8' N, 28°10' E 166
Şereflikoçhisar, Turk. 38°54' N, 33°32' E 156
Seregno, It. 45°38' N, 9°12' E 167
Seremban, Malaysia 2°45' N, 101°55' E 196
Serena, Ill., U.S. 41°28' N, 88°44' W 102
Serengeti National Park, Tanzania 2°26' S, 34°26' E 224
Serengeti Plain, Tanzania 1°51' S, 35°12' E 224
Serenje, Zambia 13°16' S, 30°14' E 224
Serere, Uganda 1°29' N, 33°25' E 224
Séres, Gr. 41°5' N, 23°31' E 180
Serg Ozero, lake, Russ. 66°45' N, 36°13' E 154
Ser'ga, Russ. 57°47' N, 57°1' E 154
Sergach, Russ. 55°31' N, 45°33' E 154
Sergeant Robinson, Mount, peak, Alas., U.S. 61°33' N, 148°2' W 98
Sergeevka, Kaz. 53°53' N, 67°23' E 184
Sergeyevo, Russ. 57°17' N, 86°6' E 169
Sergino, Russ. 62°37' N, 65°34' E 169
Sergipe, adm. division, Braz. 9°54' S, 37°48' W 132
Sergiyev Posad, Russ. 56°19' N, 38°7' E 154
Seria, Brunei 4°35' N, 114°25' E 192
Serian, Malaysia 1°3' N, 110°33' E 192
Seribudolok, Indonesia 2°56' N, 98°36' E 196
Sérifontaine, Fr. 49°21' N, 1°46' E 163
Sérignan, Fr. 43°16' N, 3°15' E 164
Serik, Turk. 36°54' N, 31°5' E 156
Seringa, Serra da, Braz. 7°36' S, 50°60' W 130
Seripe, Ghana 8°55' N, 2°24' W 222
Serkovo, Russ. 66°35' N, 88°25' E 169
Sermata, island, Indonesia 8°38' S, 128°59' E 192
Sermyle, ruin(s), Gr. 40°13' N, 23°27' E 156
Sernur, Russ. 56°57' N, 49°12' E 154
Séro, Mali 14°49' N, 11°4' W 222
Seroglazovka, Russ. 46°56' N, 47°27' E 158
Serón, Sp. 37°19' N, 2°31' W 164
Seronera, Tanzania 2°28' S, 34°50' E 224
Serov, Russ. 59°38' N, 60°37' E 154
Serowe, Botswana 22°23' S, 26°42' E 227
Serpent's Mouth 9°50' N, 62°13' W 116
Serpukhov, Russ. 54°54' N, 37°22' E 154
Serra Bonita, Braz. 15°16' S, 46°50' W 138
Serra da Bocaina National Park, Braz. 23°22' S, 44°57' W 122
Serra da Canastra National Park, Braz. 20°24' S, 46°53' W 138
Serra da Capivara National Park, Braz. 8°44' S, 42°32' W 122
Serra das Araras, Braz. 15°34' S, 45°24' W 138
Serra do Divisor National Park, Braz. 9°11' S, 73°16' W 137
Serra do Espinhaço, Braz. 17°53' S, 43°58' W 138
Serra do Navio, Braz. 0°57' N, 52°5' W 130
Serra Dourada, Braz. 12°45' S, 43°59' W 138
Serrado Roncador, Braz. 14°7' S, 53°7' W 138
Serranía de la Macarena National Park, Col. 2°33' N, 73°56' W 136
Serranía de La Neblina National Park, Venez. 1°4' N, 66°23' W 136
Serrano, Arg. 34°29' S, 63°33' W 139
Serre, river, Fr. 49°41' N, 3°44' E 163
Serrezuela, Arg. 30°39' S, 65°23' W 134
Serrinha, Braz. 11°40' S, 39°3' W 132
Serro, Braz. 18°38' S, 43°25' W 138
Sertã, Port. 39°47' N, 8°7' W 150
Sertânia, Braz. 8°5' S, 37°16' W 132
Sertanópolis, Braz. 23°5' S, 51°6' W 138
Serti, Nig. 7°30' N, 11°20' E 222
Serui, Indonesia 1°48' S, 136°11' E 192
Serule, Botswana 21°58' S, 27°13' E 227
Sêrxü, China 33°0' N, 98°5' E 188
Seryesik-Atyraū Qumy, Kaz. 46°3' N, 75°39' E 184
Sesa, Dem. Rep. of the Congo 7°2' S, 26°7' E 224
Sese Islands, Uganda 0°34' N, 32°5' E 224
Seseganaga Lake, Can. 49°54' N, 91°13' W 94
Sesfontein, Namibia 19°10' S, 13°36' E 220
Sesheke, Zambia 17°28' S, 24°17' E 224
Seskar, Ostrov, island, Russ. 60°0' N, 28°26' E 166
Seskarö, Sw. 65°43' N, 23°43' E 152
Sessa, Angola 13°57' S, 20°37' E 220
Séssao, spring, Mali 16°59' N, 4°5' E 222
Sestino, It. 43°43' N, 12°16' E 167
Sesto Calende, It. 45°44' N, 8°37' E 167
Sesto Fiorentino, It. 43°50' N, 11°12' E 167
Sesto San Giovanni, It. 45°32' N, 9°14' E 167
Šeštokai, Lith. 54°21' N, 23°26' E 166
Sestola, It. 44°13' N, 10°45' E 167
Sestri Ponente, It. 44°25' N, 8°52' E 167
Sestroretsk, Russ. 60°4' N, 29°55' E 166
Šeta, Lith. 55°16' N, 24°13' E 166
Sete, Angola 14°56' S, 21°44' E 220
Sète, Fr. 43°24' N, 3°40' E 164
Sete Lagoas, Braz. 19°27' S, 44°16' W 138
Sete Quedas, Cachoeira das, fall(s), Braz. 9°42' S, 56°32' W 130
Setenil, Sp. 36°51' N, 5°11' W 164
Setesdal, region, Nor. 58°58' N, 7°4' E 152
Sétif, Alg. 36°13' N, 5°25' E 150
Setit, river, Africa 14°20' N, 37°5' E 182
Seto, Japan 35°10' N, 137°6' E 201
Seto Naikai National Park, Japan 34°16' N, 134°16' E 201
Settat, Mor. 33°2' N, 7°38' W 214
Setté Cama, Gabon 2°32' S, 9°46' E 218
Settle, U.K. 54°4' N, 2°16' W 162
Setúbal, Port. 38°31' N, 8°54' W 150
Setúbal, adm. division, Port. 38°28' N, 8°42' W 150
Seul Choix Point, Mich., U.S. 45°39' N, 86°8' W 110
Seul, Lac, lake, Can. 50°33' N, 93°10' W 80
Seulimeum, Indonesia 5°21' N, 95°33' E 202
Seumanyam, Indonesia 3°47' N, 96°37' E 196
Sevan, Arm. 40°33' N, 44°56' E 195
Sevan National Park, Arm. 40°21' N, 45°12' E 195
Sevana Lich, lake, Arm. 40°14' N, 45°15' E 195
Sevar, Bulg. 43°50' N, 26°36' E 156
Sevaruyo, Bol. 19°26' S, 66°53' W 137
Sevastopol', Ukr. 44°34' N, 33°28' E 156
Seven Heads, Ire. 51°22' N, 8°41' W 150
Seven Sisters Peaks, Can. 54°56' N, 128°18' W 108
Seven Stones, islands, Celtic Sea 50°5' N, 7°11' W 150
Seven Troughs Range, Nev., U.S. 40°36' N, 118°57' W 90
Sevenoaks, U.K. 51°16' N, 0°11' E 162
Severn y ye Uvaly, Russ. 59°38' N, 46°36' E 169
Severnaya Dvina, river, Russ. 62°37' N, 43°16' E 154
Severnaya Osetiya-Alaniya, adm. division, Russ. 42°59' N, 43°49' E 195
Severnaya, river, Russ. 63°21' N, 41°46' E 154
Severnaya, river, Russ. 63°21' N, 40°44' E 246
Severnaya Zemlya (North Land), islands, Russ. 80°22' N, 102°0' E 160
Severnoye, Russ. 56°21' N, 78°15' E 169
Severnoye Ust'ye, Russ. 57°34' N, 30°16' E 166
Severnyy, Russ. 67°39' N, 64°18' E 169
Severnyy Kommunar, Russ. 58°21' N, 54°4' E 154
Severnyy Mayak, Russ. 65°19' N, 43°39' E 154
Severnyye Uvaly, Russ. 60°56' N, 51°45' E 154
Severo Kuril'sk, Russ. 50°35' N, 155°59' E 160
Severo Yeniseyskiy, Russ. 60°23' N, 93°13' E 169
Severobaykal'sk, Russ. 55°49' N, 109°7' E 190
Severodvinsk, Russ. 64°34' N, 39°52' E 154
Severomuysk, Russ. 56°20' N, 113°25' E 190
Severoural'sk, Russ. 60°10' N, 59°55' E 154
Seversk, Russ. 56°39' N, 84°51' E 169
Sevettijärvi, Fin. 69°32' N, 28°35' E 152
Sevier Desert, Utah, U.S. 39°38' N, 112°60' W 90
Sevier, river, Utah, U.S. 38°27' N, 112°24' W 80
Sevilla, Col. 4°14' N, 75°57' W 136
Sevilla, Sp. 37°22' N, 5°58' W 214
Sevilla (Seville), Sp. 37°23' N, 5°60' W 164
Seville, Fla., U.S. 29°18' N, 81°29' W 105
Seville see Sevilla, Sp. 37°23' N, 5°60' W 164
Sevnica, Slov. 46°0' N, 15°18' E 156
Sevsk, Russ. 52°7' N, 34°30' E 158
Seward, Alas., U.S. 60°2' N, 149°33' W 98
Seward, Nebr., U.S. 40°53' N, 97°6' W 90
Seward Peninsula, Alas., U.S. 67°2' N, 167°43' W 160
Seward Peninsula, Alas., U.S. 65°17' N, 165°10' W 98
Sexsmith, Can. 55°20' N, 118°47' W 108
Sexton Mountain Pass, Oreg., U.S. 42°34' N, 123°25' W 90
Seyakha, Russ. 70°8' N, 72°28' E 169
Seychelles 8°7' S, 51°26' E 173
Seydi, Turkm. 39°25' N, 62°55' E 184
Seydişehir, Turk. 37°24' N, 31°51' E 156
Seyitgazi, Turk. 39°27' N, 30°41' E 156
Seym, river, Russ. 51°24' N, 36°36' E 158
Seym, river, Ukr. 51°19' N, 33°0' E 158
Seymchan, Russ. 62°55' N, 152°12' E 160
Seymour, Conn., U.S. 41°23' N, 73°5' W 104
Seymour, Ind., U.S. 38°57' N, 85°54' W 102
Seymour, Tex., U.S. 33°34' N, 99°16' W 92
Seymour, Wis., U.S. 44°30' N, 88°20' W 94
Seymour Island, Antarctica 64°25' S, 56°33' W 134
Seyne, Fr. 44°21' N, 6°19' E 167
Sézanne, Fr. 48°43' N, 3°44' E 163
Sfax, Tun. 34°48' N, 10°46' E 156
Sferracavallo, Capo, It. 39°44' N, 9°42' E 156
Sfîntu Gheorghe, Rom. 45°52' N, 25°47' E 156
Sfizef, Alg. 35°13' N, 0°15' E 150
Sha, river, China 26°5' N, 117°4' E 198
Shaanxi, adm. division, China 37°13' N, 107°48' E 198
Shabasha, Sudan 14°7' N, 32°11' E 226
Shabla, Bulg. 43°33' N, 28°32' E 156
Shabla, Nos, Bulg. 43°34' N, 28°38' E 156
Shabogamo Lake, Can. 53°13' N, 67°3' W 111
Shabunda, Dem. Rep. of the Congo 2°41' S, 27°19' E 224
Shaburovo, Russ. 59°40' N, 62°8' E 154
Shabwah, Yemen 15°21' N, 47°5' E 182
Shache (Yarkant), China 38°27' N, 77°17' E 184
Shackleton Base (historic), site, Weddell Sea 78°21' S, 37°47' W 248
Shackleton Coast, Antarctica 82°30' S, 179°30' E 248
Shadehill Reservoir, lake, S. Dak., U.S. 45°46' N, 102°37' W 90
Shadrinsk, Russ. 56°5' N, 63°40' E 184
Shaduzup, Myanmar 25°56' N, 96°40' E 188
Shadyside, Ohio, U.S. 39°57' N, 80°46' W 94
Sha'f, Syr. 32°36' N, 36°50' E 194
Shafer Peak, Antarctica 73°56' S, 163°9' E 248
Shafter, Calif., U.S. 35°30' N, 119°18' W 100
Shaftesbury, U.K. 51°0' N, 2°12' W 162
Shaftsbury, Vt., U.S. 43°0' N, 73°12' W 104
Shag Rocks, islands, Scotia Sea 54°7' S, 42°46' W 134
Shagamu, Nig. 7°0' N, 3°37' E 222
Shaghan, Kaz. 50°34' N, 79°13' E 184
Shah Bandar, Pak. 24°10' N, 67°58' E 186
Shah Juy, Afghan. 32°31' N, 67°28' E 186
Shah Malan, Afghan. 31°11' N, 64°5' E 186
Shahabad, India 27°38' N, 79°54' E 197
Shahabad, India 25°16' N, 77°10' E 197
Shahbā' (Philippopolis), Syr. 32°51' N, 36°37' E 194
Shahdadkot, Pak. 27°51' N, 67°55' E 186
Shahdol, India 23°18' N, 81°22' E 197
Shahgarh, India 27°6' N, 69°58' E 186
Shaḩḩāt (Cyrene), Lib. 32°50' N, 21°50' E 216
Shahimardan, Uzb. 39°56' N, 71°45' E 197
Shahjahanpur, India 27°51' N, 79°54' E 197
Shahpur, Pak. 28°42' N, 68°22' E 186
Shahpura, India 23°11' N, 80°43' E 197
Shahrak, Afghan. 34°11' N, 64°24' E 186
Shahr-e Bābak, Iran 30°7' N, 55°9' E 196
Shahr-e Kord, Iran 32°19' N, 50°51' E 180
Shahr-e Monjan, Afghan. 36°2' N, 70°58' E 186
Shahrisabz, Uzb. 39°5' N, 66°51' E 197
Shahriston, Taj. 39°46' N, 68°52' E 197
Shahrtuz, Taj. 37°14' N, 68°9' E 186
Shāhrūd, Iran 36°27' N, 54°59' E 180
Shaim, Russ. 60°15' N, 64°16' E 169
Shajapur, India 23°24' N, 76°16' E 197
Shakawe, Botswana 18°25' S, 21°48' E 220
Shaker Heights, Ohio, U.S. 41°26' N, 81°34' W 102
Shakespeare Cliff, U.K. 51°6' N, 1°21' E 163
Shakhbuz, Asia 39°24' N, 45°34' E 195
Shakhtakhty, Asia 39°19' N, 45°7' E 195
Shakhtīnsk, Kaz. 49°44' N, 72°37' E 184
Shakhty, Russ. 47°40' N, 40°9' E 156
Shakhun'ya, Russ. 57°39' N, 46°41' E 154
Shaki, Nig. 8°40' N, 3°23' E 222
Shâkir, Gezîrat, island, Egypt 27°25' N, 32°57' E 180
Shalaamboot, Somalia 1°38' N, 44°41' E 218
Shalakusha, Russ. 62°11' N, 40°18' E 154
Shalë, Alban. 42°18' N, 19°48' E 168
Shali, Russ. 43°6' N, 45°52' E 195
Shaling, China 41°19' N, 123°5' E 200
Shalkar Yega Kara, Ozero, lake, Russ. 50°39' N, 59°7' E 158
Shallowater, Tex., U.S. 33°41' N, 101°59' W 92
Shalqar, Kaz. 50°29' N, 51°49' E 158
Shalqar, Kaz. 47°56' N, 59°36' E 160
Shalqar, Kaz. 47°50' N, 59°39' E 158
Shalqar Köli, lake, Kaz. 50°35' N, 51°20' E 158
Shalqīya, Kaz. 47°15' N, 70°38' E 184
Shal'skiy, Russ. 61°48' N, 36°4' E 154
Shām, Jabal ash, peak, Oman 23°10' N, 57°11' E 182
Shamattawa, Can. 55°59' N, 91°53' W 106
Shambe, Sudan 7°5' N, 30°43' E 224
Shamīl, Iran 27°28' N, 56°53' E 196
Shamkhor, Azerb. 40°49' N, 46°0' E 195
Shammar, Jabal, Saudi Arabia 27°8' N, 40°8' E 180
Shamokin, Pa., U.S. 40°47' N, 76°34' W 94
Shamrock, Fla., U.S. 29°38' N, 83°11' W 105
Shamrock, Tex., U.S. 35°12' N, 100°15' W 92
Shamva, Zimb. 17°21' S, 31°34' E 224
Shanchengzhen, China 42°22' N, 125°27' E 200
Shandon, Calif., U.S. 35°39' N, 120°24' W 100
Shandong, adm. division, China 36°25' N, 116°37' E 198
Shandur Pass, Pak. 36°3' N, 72°31' E 186
Shangalowe, Dem. Rep. of the Congo 10°50' S, 26°30' E 224
Shangaly, Russ. 61°8' N, 43°18' E 154
Shangani, Zimb. 19°48' S, 29°21' E 224
Shangcai, China 33°17' N, 114°17' E 198
Shangcheng, China 31°48' N, 115°23' E 198
Shangchuan Dao, island, China 21°31' N, 112°51' E 198
Shangdu, China 41°35' N, 113°33' E 198
Shanghai, China 31°15' N, 121°27' E 198
Shanghang, China 24°58' N, 116°21' E 198
Shanghekou, China 40°25' N, 124°49' E 200
Shanglin, China 23°29' N, 108°35' E 198
Shangnan, China 33°32' N, 110°55' E 198
Shangombo, Zambia 16°20' S, 22°7' E 220
Shangqiu, China 34°27' N, 115°34' E 198
Shangrao, China 28°27' N, 117°56' E 198
Shangsi, China 22°12' N, 107°57' E 198
Shangxian, China 33°55' N, 109°56' E 198
Shangyi, China 41°5' N, 113°58' E 198
Shangyou, China 25°50' N, 114°30' E 198
Shangyou Shuiku, lake, China 40°24' N, 79°49' E 184
Shangzhi, China 45°12' N, 127°53' E 198
Shani, Nig. 10°12' N, 12°5' E 218
Shanidar Cave, ruin(s), Iraq 36°48' N, 44°8' E 195
Shaniko, Oreg., U.S. 44°59' N, 120°46' W 90
Shannock, R.I., U.S. 41°26' N, 71°39' W 104
Shannon, Ill., U.S. 42°8' N, 89°44' W 102
Shannon, Ire. 52°52' N, 8°49' W 143
Shannon, Miss., U.S. 34°6' N, 88°43' W 96
Shannon, N.Z. 40°35' S, 175°25' E 240
Shannon Airport, Ire. 52°40' N, 9°8' W 150
Shannon, island, Shannon 75°18' N, 17°23' W 246
Shannon, Lake, Wash., U.S. 48°35' N, 121°58' W 100
Shantarskiye Ostrova, islands, Russ. 54°31' N, 138°48' E 160
Shantou (Swatow), China 23°23' N, 116°40' E 198
Shanwa, Tanzania 3°8' S, 33°45' E 224
Shanxi, adm. division, China 38°43' N, 111°16' E 198
Shanxian, China 34°49' N, 116°5' E 198
Shanyang, China 33°33' N, 109°54' E 198
Shanyin, China 39°29' N, 112°51' E 198
Shanyincheng, China 39°24' N, 112°56' E 198
Shaoguan, China 24°52' N, 113°32' E 198
Shaowu, China 27°14' N, 117°27' E 198
Shaoxing, China 29°59' N, 120°34' E 198
Shaoyang, China 27°15' N, 111°29' E 198
Shap, U.K. 54°32' N, 2°41' W 162
Shapa, China 21°32' N, 111°28' E 198
Shapleigh, Me., U.S. 43°33' N, 70°52' W 104
Shaqlāwah, Iraq 36°24' N, 44°16' E 195
Shaqqā, Syr. 32°53' N, 36°41' E 194
Shaqrā', Saudi Arabia 25°12' N, 45°18' E 182
Shaqrā', Yemen 13°24' N, 45°41' E 182
Shar, Kaz. 49°37' N, 81°1' E 184
Shār, Jabal, peak, Saudi Arabia 27°36' N, 35°40' E 180
Shar Space Launch Center, spaceport, India 13°36' N, 80°5' E 188
Sharafkhāneh, Iran 38°17' N, 45°26' E 195
Sharbaqty, Kaz. 52°30' N, 78°11' E 184
Sharbatāt, Oman 17°53' N, 56°18' E 182
Shardara, Kaz. 41°16' N, 67°54' E 197
Sharg'un, Uzb. 38°21' N, 68°0' E 197
Sharhulsan, Mongolia 44°37' N, 104°1' E 198
Sharjah, U.A.E. 25°21' N, 55°24' E 196
Shark Bay 25°46' S, 113°18' E 230
Sharkan, Russ. 57°15' N, 53°54' E 154
Sharkovshchyna, Belarus 55°22' N, 27°24' E 166
Sharlawuk, Turkm. 38°14' N, 55°42' E 180
Sharlyk, Russ. 52°55' N, 54°46' E 154
Sharon, Conn., U.S. 41°52' N, 73°29' W 104
Sharon, Mass., U.S. 42°7' N, 71°11' W 104
Sharon, Pa., U.S. 41°13' N, 80°31' W 94
Sharon, Vt., U.S. 43°47' N, 72°28' W 104
Sharon, Wis., U.S. 42°30' N, 88°44' W 102
Sharon Springs, Kans., U.S. 38°53' N, 101°46' W 90
Sharp Top, peak, Oreg., U.S. 42°50' N, 120°34' W 90
Sharpe, Lake, S. Dak., U.S. 43°9' N, 99°14' W 80
Sharuhen, ruin(s), Israel 31°15' N, 34°26' E 194
Shar'ya, Russ. 58°20' N, 45°34' E 154
Sharypovo, Russ. 55°34' N, 89°15' E 169
Shasha, Eth. 6°28' N, 35°55' E 224
Shashe, river, Africa 21°47' S, 28°27' E 227
Shashemenē, Eth. 7°12' N, 38°32' E 224
Shashi, China 30°22' N, 112°18' E 198
Shass Mountain, peak, Can. 54°25' N, 124°58' W 108
Shasta, Mount, peak, Calif., U.S. 41°24' N, 122°18' W 90
Shatsk, Belarus 53°25' N, 27°42' E 152
Shatsk, Russ. 54°0' N, 41°39' E 154
Shats'k, Ukr. 51°27' N, 23°54' E 152
Shatskiy Rise, North Pacific Ocean 34°16' N, 160°36' E 252
Shattuck, Okla., U.S. 36°15' N, 99°53' W 92
Shatura, Russ. 55°33' N, 39°31' E 154
Shaumyan, Azerb. 40°26' N, 46°33' E 195
Shaumyani, Ga. 41°20' N, 44°44' E 195
Shaunavon, Can. 49°37' N, 108°26' W 90
Shaver Lake, Calif., U.S. 37°6' N, 119°20' W 100
Shaverki, Russ. 63°14' N, 31°27' E 154
Shavikilde, peak, Ga. 42°14' N, 45°35' E 195
Shaw, Miss., U.S. 33°35' N, 90°47' W 96
Shaw Air Force Base, S.C., U.S. 33°57' N, 80°33' W 96
Shaw Island, Austral. 20°22' S, 149°7' E 230
Shawan, China 44°20' N, 85°39' E 184
Shawano, Wis., U.S. 44°46' N, 88°37' W 94
Shawinigan, Can. 46°33' N, 72°46' W 94
Shawinigan-Sud, Can. 46°30' N, 72°45' W 94
Shawnee, Ohio, U.S. 39°35' N, 82°13' W 102
Shawnee, Wyo., U.S. 42°44' N, 105°1' W 90
Shawnigan Lake, Can. 48°38' N, 123°37' W 100
Shaxian, China 26°24' N, 117°44' E 198
Shaxrixon, Uzb. 40°41' N, 72°4' E 197
Shaybah, oil field, Saudi Arabia 22°23' N, 53°55' E 182
Shaybārā, island, Saudi Arabia 25°25' N, 36°3' E 182
Shâyib el Banât, Gebel, peak, Egypt 26°58' N, 33°22' E 180
Shaykh, Jabal ash (Hermon, Mount), peak, Leb. 33°24' N, 35°49' E 194
Shaykh Miskīn, Syr. 32°50' N, 36°10' E 194
Shaykh 'Uthmān, Yemen 12°52' N, 44°59' E 182
Shayman, Taj. 37°29' N, 74°51' E 184
Shayrāt, Syr. 34°29' N, 36°57' E 194
Shaytanovka, Russ. 62°2' N, 58°6' E 154
Shchekino, Russ. 53°59' N, 37°33' E 154
Shchel'yabozh, Russ. 66°17' N, 56°23' E 154
Shchel'yayur, Russ. 65°18' N, 53°26' E 154
Shchigry, Russ. 51°49' N, 36°57' E 158
Shchuch'ye, Russ. 67°6' N, 68°36' E 169
Shchūchīnsk, Kaz. 52°52' N, 70°14' E 184
Shchurovo, Russ. 55°1' N, 38°49' E 154
Shchurovychi, Ukr. 50°16' N, 25°0' E 152
Shchyrets', Ukr. 49°38' N, 23°50' E 152
Shchytkavichy, Belarus 53°13' N, 27°58' E 154
Shebar, Kowtal-e, pass, Afghan. 34°57' N, 68°9' E 186
Shebekino, Russ. 50°24' N, 36°56' E 158
Shebele, river, Eth. 5°47' N, 42°0' E 207
Sheberghan, Afghan. 36°40' N, 65°46' E 186
Sheboya, Peru 9°59' S, 74°8' W 137
Sheboygan, Wis., U.S. 43°45' N, 87°44' W 102
Shediac, Can. 46°12' N, 64°32' W 111
Shedin Peak, Can. 55°56' N, 127°36' W 108
Shedok, Russ. 44°12' N, 40°44' E 158
Sheenjek, river, Alas., U.S. 66°50' N, 144°27' W 98
Sheep Hole Mountains, Calif., U.S. 34°21' N, 115°45' W 101
Sheep Mountain, peak, Colo., U.S. 39°54' N, 107°13' W 90
Sheep Mountain, peak, Mont., U.S. 45°4' N, 110°46' W 90
Sheep Peak, Nev., U.S. 36°34' N, 115°18' W 101
Sheep Range, Nev., U.S. 36°44' N, 115°13' W 101
Sheepeater Mountain, peak, Idaho, U.S. 45°22' N, 115°25' W 90
Sheep's Head, Ire. 51°22' N, 10°11' W 150
Sheerness, U.K. 51°25' N, 0°45' E 162
Sheet Harbour, Can. 44°56' N, 62°32' W 111
Sheffield, Ala., U.S. 34°45' N, 87°41' W 96
Sheffield, Ill., U.S. 41°21' N, 89°44' W 102
Sheffield, Mass., U.S. 42°6' N, 73°22' W 104
Sheffield, Tex., U.S. 30°40' N, 101°49' W 92
Sheffield, U.K. 53°22' N, 1°28' W 162
Sheguiandah, Can. 45°54' N, 81°55' W 94
Sheikh Idris, Sudan 11°45' N, 33°28' E 182
Sheksna, Russ. 59°11' N, 38°29' E 154
Shelagskiy, Mys, Russ. 69°48' N, 174°42' E 160
Shelburn, Ind., U.S. 39°10' N, 87°24' W 102
Shelburne, Can. 43°44' N, 65°20' W 111
Shelburne, Vt., U.S. 44°22' N, 73°15' W 104
Shelburne Falls, Vt., U.S. 42°41' N, 73°13' W 104
Shelby, Ind., U.S. 41°11' N, 87°21' W 102
Shelby, Mich., U.S. 43°36' N, 86°21' W 102
Shelby, Mont., U.S. 48°28' N, 111°51' W 90
Shelby, Ohio, U.S. 40°51' N, 82°39' W 102
Shelbyville, Ill., U.S. 39°23' N, 88°48' W 102
Shelbyville, Ind., U.S. 39°30' N, 85°46' W 102
Shelbyville, Tex., U.S. 31°44' N, 94°5' W 103
Sheldon, Ill., U.S. 40°45' N, 87°34' W 102
Sheldon, Iowa, U.S. 43°10' N, 95°51' W 94
Sheldrake, Can. 50°16' N, 64°54' W 111
Shelikhova, Zaliv 61°11' N, 158°34' E 160
Shelikof Strait 58°3' N, 154°5' W 98
Shell Beach, Guyana 8°8' N, 59°42' W 116
Shell Lake, Can. 53°17' N, 107°1' W 108
Shell Lake, Wis., U.S. 45°44' N, 91°57' W 94
Shell Mountain, peak, Calif., U.S. 40°5' N, 123°10' W 90
Shellbrook, Can. 53°13' N, 106°24' W 108
Shellem, Nig. 9°57' N, 12°2' E 218
Shellman, Ga., U.S. 31°45' N, 84°37' W 96
Shellrock Peak, Idaho, U.S. 44°56' N, 115°1' W 90
Shelokhovskaya, Russ. 61°54' N, 39°3' E 154
Shelter Island, N.Y., U.S. 41°3' N, 72°21' W 104
Shelton, Conn., U.S. 41°18' N, 73°6' W 104
Shelton, Wash., U.S. 47°11' N, 123°7' W 100
Sheltozero, Russ. 61°20' N, 35°25' E 154
Shemakha, Azerb. 40°37' N, 48°37' E 195
Shemgang, Bhutan 27°7' N, 90°45' E 197
Shemonaīkha, Kaz. 50°38' N, 81°55' E 184
Shëmri, Alban. 42°6' N, 20°13' E 168
Shenandoah, Pa., U.S. 40°49' N, 76°13' W 94
Shenandoah Mountain, Va., U.S. 38°29' N, 79°32' W 94
Shenandoah National Park, Va., U.S. 37°29' N, 79°36' W 80
Shenchi, China 39°4' N, 112°10' E 198
Shendam, Nig. 8°53' N, 9°29' E 222
Shendi, Sudan 16°39' N, 33°24' E 182
Shenge, Sierra Leone 7°54' N, 12°57' W 222
Shëngjin, Alban. 41°49' N, 19°34' E 168
Shengli Daban, pass, China 43°6' N, 86°48' E 184
Shengxian, China 29°39' N, 120°44' E 198
Shenkursk, Russ. 62°4' N, 42°58' E 154
Shenmu, China 38°51' N, 110°31' E 198
Shennongjia, China 31°44' N, 110°45' E 198

Shenqiu, China 33°27' N, 115°6' E 198
Shenton, Mount, peak, Austral. 28°1' S, 123°11' E 230
Shenyang, China 41°49' N, 123°28' E 200
Shenzhen, China 22°34' N, 114°7' E 198
Sheopur, India 25°41' N, 76°43' E 197
Shepard Island, Antarctica 73°49' S, 134°36' W 248
Shepetivka, Ukr. 50°10' N, 27°4' E 152
Shepherd, Mich., U.S. 43°30' N, 84°42' W 102
Shepherd, Tex., U.S. 30°29' N, 94°59' W 103
Shepparton, Austral. 36°23' S, 145°27' E 231
Sherada, Eth. 7°17' N, 36°29' E 224
Sherborne, U.K. 50°56' N, 2°31' W 162
Sherbro Island, Sierra Leone 7°8' N, 12°52' W 222
Sherbrooke, Can. 45°24' N, 71°56' W 94
Sherburn, Minn., U.S. 43°38' N, 94°44' W 90
Sherda, spring, Chad 20°10' N, 16°43' E 216
Shereiq, Sudan 18°44' N, 33°36' E 182
Sherghati, India 24°33' N, 84°49' E 197
Shergui Island, Tun. 34°39' N, 11°21' E 216
Sheridan, Ill., U.S. 41°31' N, 88°41' W 102
Sheridan, Ind., U.S. 40°7' N, 86°13' W 102
Sheridan, Mich., U.S. 43°12' N, 85°5' W 102
Sheridan, Wyo., U.S. 44°47' N, 106°56' W 90
Sheridan, Cape, Can. 81°51' N, 73°43' W 246
Sheringham, U.K. 52°56' N, 1°12' E 162
Sherkaly, Russ. 62°48' N, 65°41' E 169
Sherman, Me., U.S. 45°51' N, 68°25' W 94
Sherman, Tex., U.S. 33°37' N, 96°36' W 96
Sherman Island, island, Antarctica 72°20' S, 100°58' W 248
Sherman Mountain, peak, Nev., U.S. 40°6' N, 115°40' W 90
Sherman Peak, Calif., U.S. 36°0' N, 118°26' W 101
Sherman Peak, Idaho, U.S. 42°28' N, 111°38' W 90
Sherman Peak, Idaho, U.S. 44°31' N, 114°44' W 90
Sherobod, Uzb. 37°39' N, 67°1' E 197
Sherridon, Can. 55°6' N, 101°6' W 108
Sherwood, N. Dak., U.S. 48°57' N, 101°40' W 108
Sherwood Forest, U.K. 53°14' N, 1°13' W 162
Sherwood Lake, Can. 60°48' N, 104°14' W 108
Sherwood Peak, Calif., U.S. 39°30' N, 123°36' W 90
Sheshea, river, Peru 9°26' S, 73°51' W 137
Sheslay, river, Can. 58°27' N, 132°15' W 108
Shestakovo, Russ. 58°55' N, 50°9' E 154
Shethanei Lake, Can. 58°47' N, 98°24' W 108
Shetland Islands, North Atlantic Ocean 61°2' N, 3°52' W 72
Shetlands Islands, U.K. 60°53' N, 3°18' W 142
Shetpe, Kaz. 44°9' N, 52°6' E 158
Shetrunja, peak, India 21°26' N, 71°41' E 186
Shewa Gīmīra, Eth. 6°59' N, 35°49' E 224
Shexian, China 29°52' N, 118°26' E 198
Sheyang, China 33°45' N, 120°15' E 198
Sheyenne, N. Dak., U.S. 47°48' N, 99°8' W 90
Sheyenne, river, N. Dak., U.S. 47°40' N, 98°56' W 90
Sheyenne, river, N. Dak., U.S. 46°26' N, 97°38' W 90
Sheykhabad, Afghan. 34°6' N, 68°45' E 186
Shḫīm, Leb. 33°38' N, 35°29' E 194
Shibām, Yemen 15°54' N, 48°36' E 182
Shibata, Japan 37°57' N, 139°20' E 201
Shibîn el Kôm, Egypt 30°34' N, 30°57' E 180
Shibing, China 27°0' N, 108°4' E 198
Shibukawa, Japan 36°29' N, 138°59' E 201
Shibushi, Japan 31°27' N, 131°5' E 201
Shicheng, China 26°21' N, 116°16' E 198
Shidao, China 36°55' N, 122°25' E 198
Shiderti, Kaz. 51°40' N, 74°27' E 184
Shidler, Okla., U.S. 36°45' N, 96°40' W 92
Shiega, Ghana 10°42' N, 0°44' E 222
Shīeli, Kaz. 44°9' N, 66°44' E 184
Shi'erdaogou, China 41°30' N, 127°35' E 200
Shifnal, U.K. 52°39' N, 2°22' W 162
Shiga, Japan 37°1' N, 136°46' E 201
Shiga, adm. division, Japan 35°12' N, 135°52' E 201
Shiguaigou, China 40°42' N, 110°17' E 198
Shiḫan, Yemen 17°41' N, 52°27' E 182
Shihezi, China 44°17' N, 86°1' E 184
Shiikh, Somalia 9°55' N, 45°12' E 216
Shijiazhuang, China 38°5' N, 114°30' E 198
Shikag Lake, lake, Can. 49°41' N, 91°15' W 94
Shikarpur, Pak. 27°53' N, 68°42' E 186
Shikoku, island, Japan 32°22' N, 133°0' E 190
Shilabo, Eth. 6°5' N, 44°45' E 218
Shildon, U.K. 54°38' N, 1°40' W 162
Shīli, Kaz. 50°34' N, 62°34' E 184
Shiliguri, India 26°43' N, 88°28' E 190
Shilik, Kaz. 43°34' N, 78°12' E 184
Shiliu see Changjiang, China 19°13' N, 109°2' E 198
Shiliyn Bogd Uul, peak, Mongolia 45°26' N, 114°24' E 198
Shilka, Russ. 51°54' N, 116°0' E 238
Shilka, river, Russ. 52°45' N, 119°25' E 190
Shilla, peak, Nepal 32°22' N, 78°4' E 188
Shillong, India 25°32' N, 91°52' E 197
Shiloh, ruin(s), West Bank 32°2' N, 35°15' E 194
Shilou, China 37°2' N, 110°47' E 198
Shilovo, Russ. 54°17' N, 40°50' E 154
Shimabara, Japan 32°46' N, 130°20' E 201
Shimada, Japan 34°50' N, 138°11' E 201
Shimane, adm. division, Japan 34°32' N, 131°43' E 200
Shimanovsk, Russ. 52°4' N, 127°46' E 190
Shimen, China 29°36' N, 111°24' E 198
Shimizu, Japan 35°0' N, 138°28' E 201
Shimminato, Japan 36°46' N, 137°5' E 201
Shimoda, Japan 32°57' N, 132°58' E 201
Shimoda, Japan 34°41' N, 138°58' E 201
Shimoga, India 13°55' N, 75°33' E 188
Shimokoshiki, Japan 31°38' N, 129°43' E 201
Shimoni, Kenya 4°35' S, 39°22' E 224
Shimonoseki, Japan 33°58' N, 130°56' E 200
Shimotsu, Japan 34°7' N, 135°8' E 201
Shimozero, Russ. 60°29' N, 35°37' E 154
Shimsk, Russ. 58°13' N, 30°44' E 152
Shīn, Syr. 34°46' N, 36°26' E 194
Shināș, Oman 24°45' N, 56°25' E 196
Shindand (Sabzawar), Afghan. 33°17' N, 62°11' E 186
Shiner, Tex., U.S. 29°25' N, 97°11' W 96
Shingū, Japan 33°41' N, 135°58' E 201
Shinjō, Japan 38°46' N, 140°18' E 201
Shinkafi, Nig. 13°3' N, 6°30' E 222
Shinkay, Afghan. 31°54' N, 67°21' E 186
Shinkolobwe, Dem. Rep. of the Congo 11°3' S, 26°36' E 224
Shinnston, W. Va., U.S. 39°23' N, 80°18' W 94
Shinonoi, Japan 36°35' N, 138°9' E 201
Shinshār, Syr. 34°36' N, 36°43' E 194
Shinyanga, Tanzania 3°42' S, 33°26' E 224
Shinyanga, adm. division, Tanzania 3°36' S, 31°46' E 224
Shiogama, Japan 38°19' N, 141°0' E 201
Shiono Misaki, Japan 33°17' N, 135°45' E 201
Shionomachi, Japan 38°19' N, 139°33' E 201
Ship Island, Miss., U.S. 30°9' N, 88°55' W 103
Shiping, China 23°41' N, 102°26' E 202
Shipitsino, Russ. 61°17' N, 46°32' E 154
Shipki La, pass, China 31°51' N, 78°43' E 188
Shipley, U.K. 53°49' N, 1°47' W 162
Shippagan, Can. 47°44' N, 64°44' W 94
Shiprock, N. Mex., U.S. 36°46' N, 108°42' W 82
Shipu, China 29°12' N, 121°52' E 198
Shipunovo, Russ. 52°15' N, 82°24' E 184
Shiqian, China 27°30' N, 108°14' E 198
Shiqiao, China 31°21' N, 107°4' E 198
Shiqijie, China 42°56' N, 128°29' E 200
Shiquan, China 33°4' N, 108°15' E 198
Shiquanhe, China 32°29' N, 79°48' E 188
Shir Khan, Afghan. 37°9' N, 68°40' E 186
Shīr Kūh, peak, Iran 31°35' N, 54°0' E 180
Shirakawa, Japan 37°6' N, 140°12' E 201
Shirase Coast, Antarctica 79°5' S, 139°50' W 248
Shirati, Tanzania 1°11' S, 34°0' E 224
Shīrāz, Iran 29°40' N, 52°29' E 196
Shirbîn, Egypt 31°12' N, 31°30' E 180
Shire, river, Malawi 15°60' S, 34°49' E 224
Shireet, Mongolia 45°42' N, 112°21' E 198
Shiren, China 41°57' N, 126°38' E 200
Shiringushi, Russ. 53°47' N, 42°44' E 154
Shirley, Ind., U.S. 39°52' N, 85°34' W 102
Shirley, N.Y., U.S. 40°48' N, 72°53' W 104
Shirley, Mount, peak, Antarctica 75°30' S, 141°18' W 248
Shirley Mountains, Wyo., U.S. 42°8' N, 106°39' W 90
Shiroishi, Japan 38°0' N, 140°37' E 201
Shirone, Japan 37°45' N, 139°0' E 201
Shirotori, Japan 35°52' N, 136°53' E 201
Shīrvān, Iran 37°27' N, 57°56' E 180
Shiryayevo, Russ. 59°58' N, 46°17' E 154
Shishaldin Volcano, peak, Alas., U.S. 54°39' N, 164°14' W 98
Shishmaref, Alas., U.S. 66°12' N, 166°3' W 98
Shishou, China 29°39' N, 112°24' E 198
Shitai, China 30°12' N, 117°26' E 198
Shiv, India 26°11' N, 71°17' E 186
Shivpuri, India 25°26' N, 77°39' E 197
Shiwa Ngandu, Zambia 11°10' S, 31°44' E 224
Shixian, China 43°5' N, 129°47' E 200
Shiyan, China 32°39' N, 110°48' E 198
Shizhu, China 29°59' N, 108°9' E 198
Shizui, China 43°3' N, 126°9' E 200
Shizuishan, China 39°19' N, 106°44' E 198
Shizuishan (Dawukou), China 39°4' N, 106°25' E 198
Shizuoka, Japan 34°57' N, 138°23' E 201
Shizuoka, adm. division, Japan 35°4' N, 137°51' E 201
Shklow, Belarus 54°14' N, 30°19' E 154
Shkodër (Scutari), Alban. 42°4' N, 19°30' E 168
Shkunovka, Russ. 50°45' N, 55°23' E 158
Shmoylovo, Russ. 57°35' N, 28°52' E 166
Shoal Lake, Can. 50°27' N, 100°36' W 90
Shoals, Ind., U.S. 38°39' N, 86°47' W 102
Shoals, Isles of, islands, Gulf of Maine 42°56' N, 70°34' W 104
Shoalwater, Cape, Wash., U.S. 46°38' N, 124°24' W 100
Shōbara, Japan 34°50' N, 133°2' E 201
Shocha, Russ. 63°9' N, 46°50' E 154
Shoe Cove Point, Can. 48°56' N, 53°37' W 111
Shoeburyness, U.K. 51°31' N, 0°47' E 162
Shokal'skogo, Proliv 78°34' N, 90°29' E 160
Sholapur, India 17°40' N, 75°52' E 188
Shollar, Azerb. 41°37' N, 48°39' E 195
Shombozero, Russ. 65°18' N, 32°18' E 152
Shomvukva, Russ. 63°41' N, 51°50' E 154
Shonga, Nig. 9°5' N, 5°7' E 222
Shonzhy, Kaz. 43°31' N, 79°28' E 184
Shoqpar, Kaz. 43°49' N, 74°21' E 184
Sho'rchi, Uzb. 37°42' N, 67°31' E 197
Shoreham, Vt., U.S. 43°53' N, 73°19' W 104
Shoreham by Sea, U.K. 50°50' N, 0°17' E 162
Shorewood, Wis., U.S. 43°4' N, 87°53' W 102
Shorobe, Botswana 19°46' S, 23°42' E 224
Shortland, island, Solomon Islands 7°5' S, 155°40' E 242
Shortland Islands, Solomon Sea 7°0' S, 155°49' E 242
Shoshone, Calif., U.S. 35°58' N, 116°17' W 101
Shoshone Mountains, Nev., U.S. 38°54' N, 117°37' W 90
Shoshone Range, Nev., U.S. 40°34' N, 116°58' W 90
Shoshong, Botswana 23°1' S, 26°27' E 227
Shoshoni, Wyo., U.S. 43°14' N, 108°7' W 90
Shostka, Ukr. 51°49' N, 33°33' E 158
Shotor Khun Kowtal, pass, Afghan. 34°25' N, 64°54' E 186
Shoval, Israel 31°24' N, 34°43' E 194
Showak, Sudan 14°22' N, 35°46' E 182
Shoyna, Russ. 67°47' N, 44°12' E 169
Shpola, Ukr. 49°1' N, 31°32' E 158
Shreve, Ohio, U.S. 40°40' N, 82°2' W 102
Shreveport, La., U.S. 32°29' N, 93°46' W 103
Shrewsbury, U.K. 52°42' N, 2°45' W 162
Shri Mohangarh, India 27°15' N, 71°14' E 186
Shrub Oak, N.Y., U.S. 41°18' N, 73°51' W 104
Shū, Kaz. 43°35' N, 73°45' E 190
Shū, river, Kaz. 44°51' N, 70°15' E 190
Shuangcheng, China 45°22' N, 126°19' E 198
Shuangchengzi, China 40°18' N, 99°45' E 190
Shuangjiang, China 23°29' N, 99°48' E 202
Shuangliao, China 43°31' N, 123°27' E 198
Shuangyang, China 43°32' N, 125°42' E 198
Shuangyashan, China 46°41' N, 131°11' E 238
Shubararköl, Kaz. 49°7' N, 68°46' E 184
Shubarquduyq, Kaz. 49°8' N, 56°26' E 158
Shubarshī, Kaz. 48°35' N, 57°17' E 158
Shubuta, Miss., U.S. 31°51' N, 88°42' W 103
Shucheng, China 31°26' N, 116°56' E 198
Shudino, Russ. 61°41' N, 48°9' E 154
Shufu, China 39°22' N, 75°44' E 184
Shugozero, Russ. 59°55' N, 34°16' E 154
Shukpa Kunzang, India 34°22' N, 78°21' E 188
Shuksan, Mount, peak, Wash., U.S. 48°48' N, 121°38' W 100
Shulan, China 44°25' N, 126°58' E 198
Shulaps Peak, Can. 50°57' N, 122°37' W 90
Shule, China 39°23' N, 76°3' E 184
Shullsburg, Wis., U.S. 42°34' N, 90°14' W 102
Shumagin Islands, Gulf of Alaska 54°23' N, 161°29' W 98
Shumanay, Uzb. 42°35' N, 58°59' E 180
Shumen (Kolarovgrad), Bulg. 43°16' N, 26°55' E 156
Shumerlya, Russ. 55°29' N, 46°29' E 154
Shumikha, Russ. 55°13' N, 63°16' E 184
Shumilina, Belarus 55°21' N, 29°41' E 166
Shunchang, China 26°50' N, 117°47' E 198
Shun'ga, Russ. 62°34' N, 34°59' E 154
Shungnak, Alas., U.S. 66°47' N, 157°12' W 98
Shungopavi, Ariz., U.S. 35°48' N, 110°31' W 92
Shuozhou, China 39°18' N, 112°26' E 198
Shupenzë, Alban. 41°31' N, 20°25' E 168
Shuqualak, Miss., U.S. 32°57' N, 88°34' W 103
Shūr Gaz, Iran 29°9' N, 59°21' E 180
Shuraabad, Azerb. 40°49' N, 49°27' E 195
Shūrāb, Iran 33°42' N, 56°32' E 180
Shurma, Russ. 56°56' N, 50°24' E 154
Shurob, Taj. 40°4' N, 70°32' E 197
Shurugwi, Zimb. 19°40' S, 29°58' E 224
Shuryshkary, Russ. 65°56' N, 65°25' E 169
Shūsf, Iran 31°47' N, 60°5' E 180
Shushan, N.Y., U.S. 43°5' N, 73°21' W 104
Shushenskoye, Russ. 53°19' N, 92°2' E 184
Shūshtar, Iran 32°1' N, 48°55' E 180
Shuya, Russ. 56°50' N, 41°21' E 154
Shuya, Russ. 61°58' N, 34°19' E 154
Shuyak Island, Alas., U.S. 58°22' N, 152°19' W 98
Shuyang, China 34°8' N, 118°50' E 198
Shuyskoye, Russ. 59°21' N, 40°58' E 154
Shwebo, Myanmar 22°33' N, 95°44' E 202
Shwegu, Myanmar 24°10' N, 96°45' E 188
Shwegyin, Myanmar 17°56' N, 96°52' E 202
Shweli, river, Asia 23°29' N, 97°5' E 202
Shyghys Qazaqstan, adm. division, Kaz. 48°56' N, 80°14' E 184
Shymkent, Kaz. 42°17' N, 69°34' E 197
Shyngghyrlau, Kaz. 51°5' N, 54°3' E 158
Shyok, river, India 35°1' N, 76°45' E 188
Siabu, Indonesia 1°1' N, 99°29' E 196
Sīah Chashmeh, Iran 39°4' N, 44°26' E 195
Sialkot, Pak. 32°27' N, 74°33' E 186
Sian see Xi'an, China 34°6' N, 108°48' E 190
Sianów, Pol. 54°13' N, 16°18' E 152
Siantan, island, Indonesia 3°6' N, 106°18' E 196
Siapa, river, Venez. 1°57' N, 66°5' W 136
Siargao, island, Philippines 9°56' N, 126°9' E 192
Siasconset, Mass., U.S. 41°15' N, 69°59' W 104
Siasi, Philippines 5°35' N, 120°49' E 203
Siaton, Philippines 9°4' N, 123°2' E 203
Šiaulėnai, Lith. 55°40' N, 23°24' E 166
Šiauliai, Lith. 55°55' N, 23°17' E 166
Sibâ'i, Gebel el, peak, Egypt 25°42' N, 34°3' E 182
Sibari, It. 39°45' N, 16°27' E 156
Sibay, Russ. 52°44' N, 58°37' E 154
Sibaya, Lake, S. Af. 27°21' S, 32°5' E 227
Sibbald, Cape, Antarctica 73°46' S, 172°14' E 248
Sibbo (Sipoo), Fin. 60°22' N, 25°13' E 166
Šibenik, Croatia 43°44' N, 15°53' E 168
Siberia, region, Russ. 68°9' N, 99°54' E 172
Siberut, island, Indonesia 1°23' S, 99°7' E 196
Siberut National Park, Indonesia 1°17' S, 98°20' E 172
Siberut, Selat 0°52' N, 98°4' E 196
Sibi, Pak. 29°37' N, 67°53' E 186
Sibigo, Indonesia 2°49' N, 95°53' E 196
Sibiloi National Park, Kenya 3°55' N, 36°36' E 224
Sibirskiy, Russ. 60°36' N, 69°51' E 169
Sibiryakova, Ostrov, island, Russ. 72°47' N, 79°54' E 160
Sibiti, Congo 3°42' S, 13°18' E 218
Sibiu, Rom. 45°49' N, 24°8' E 156
Sibiu, adm. division, Rom. 45°38' N, 23°39' E 156
Sibley, La., U.S. 32°31' N, 93°18' W 103
Sibolga, Indonesia 1°46' N, 98°48' E 196
Siborongborong, Indonesia 2°14' N, 98°59' E 196
Şibot, Rom. 45°56' N, 23°20' E 168
Sibsagar, India 27°0' N, 94°38' E 188
Sibsey, U.K. 53°2' N, 2°119' E 162
Sibu, Malaysia 2°18' N, 111°51' E 192
Sibu, island, Malaysia 2°9' N, 104°6' E 196
Sibuco, Philippines 7°20' N, 122°4' E 203
Sibut, Cen. Af. Rep. 5°42' N, 19°5' E 218
Sibuyan Sea 12°34' N, 122°29' E 203
Siby, Mali 12°23' N, 8°20' W 222
Sicapoo, Mount, peak, Philippines 18°1' N, 120°51' E 203
Sicasica, Bol. 17°24' S, 67°48' W 137
Sichuan, adm. division, China 31°1' N, 105°8' E 198
Sicié, Cap, Fr. 42°57' N, 5°44' E 165
Sicilia (Sicily), adm. division, It. 37°28' N, 13°21' E 156
Sicily Island, La., U.S. 31°49' N, 91°41' W 103
Sicily, island, It. 36°26' N, 14°37' E 156
Sicilia see Sicily, adm. division, Sicily 38°18' N, 12°49' E 156
Sico, river, Hond. 15°38' N, 85°43' W 115
Sicuani, Peru 14°19' S, 71°12' W 137
Sicyon, ruin(s), Gr. 37°58' N, 22°38' E 156
Šid, Serb. and Mont. 45°7' N, 19°13' E 168
Sidaogou, China 41°48' N, 127°5' E 200
Sidaouet, Niger 18°32' N, 8°4' E 222
Sidas, Indonesia 0°23' N, 109°42' E 196
Siddhapur, India 23°56' N, 72°22' E 186
Side, ruin(s), Mediterranean Sea 36°43' N, 31°17' E 156
Sideby (Siipyy), Fin. 62°1' N, 21°19' E 166
Sideia, island, P.N.G. 10°56' S, 150°17' E 192
Sidéradougou, Burkina Faso 10°39' N, 4°16' W 222
Sidi Aïch, Alg. 36°36' N, 4°42' E 150
Sidi Aïssa, Alg. 35°52' N, 3°46' E 150
Sidi Akacha, Alg. 36°27' N, 1°18' E 150
Sidi Ali, Alg. 36°5' N, 0°25' E 150
Sidi Amar, Alg. 36°32' N, 2°18' E 150
Sîdi Barrâni, Egypt 31°39' N, 25°57' E 180
Sidi Bel Abbès, Alg. 35°10' N, 0°38' E 150
Sidi Bel Atar, Alg. 36°1' N, 0°16' E 164
Sidi Bernous, Djebel, peak, Alg. 36°20' N, 1°31' E 150
Sidi bou Haous, Alg. 32°4' N, 2°3' E 214
Sidi Bouzid, Tun. 35°2' N, 9°29' E 156
Sidi Daoud, Alg. 36°50' N, 3°51' E 150
Sidi el Hadj bou Haous, Alg. 31°38' N, 2°0' E 214
Sidi el Hadj Zaoui, Alg. 28°17' N, 4°36' E 214
Sidi Hosni, Alg. 35°28' N, 1°35' E 150
Sidi Ifni, Mor. 29°21' N, 10°10' W 214
Sidi Kada, Alg. 35°19' N, 0°19' E 150
Sidi Lakhdar, Alg. 36°9' N, 0°26' E 164
Sîdi ʿOmar, Egypt 31°24' N, 24°55' E 180
Siding Spring Observatory, Austral. 31°21' S, 148°51' E 230
Sidlaw Hills, U.K. 56°22' N, 3°17' W 150
Sidley, Mount, peak, Antarctica 76°57' S, 125°31' W 248
Sidney, Can. 48°38' N, 123°24' W 100
Sidney, Iowa, U.S. 40°44' N, 95°39' W 90
Sidney, Mont., U.S. 47°40' N, 104°11' W 90
Sidney, Nebr., U.S. 41°8' N, 102°60' W 90
Sidney, N.Y., U.S. 42°18' N, 75°24' W 94
Sidney, Ohio, U.S. 40°17' N, 84°9' W 102
Sido, Mali 11°41' N, 7°36' W 222
Sidoktaya, Myanmar 20°27' N, 94°13' E 202
Sidon, Miss., U.S. 33°23' N, 90°13' W 103
Sidon see Saida, Leb. 33°33' N, 35°22' E 194
Sidorovsk, Russ. 66°34' N, 82°24' E 169
Sidra, Gulf of 31°40' N, 16°32' E 142
Sidra see Surt, Lib. 31°12' N, 16°32' E 216
Siedlce, Pol. 52°10' N, 22°16' E 152
Siegal, Mount, peak, Nev., U.S. 38°53' N, 119°36' W 90
Siegburg, Ger. 50°48' N, 7°11' E 167
Siegen, Ger. 50°53' N, 8°1' E 167
Siem Pang, Cambodia 14°9' N, 106°19' E 202
Siem Reap, Cambodia 13°24' N, 103°51' E 202
Siempurgo, Côte d'Ivoire 9°31' N, 6°13' W 222
Siena, It. 43°20' N, 11°19' E 214
Sieppijärvi, Fin. 67°8' N, 23°56' E 152
Sieradz, Pol. 51°35' N, 18°43' E 152
Sierck, Fr. 49°25' N, 6°21' E 163
Sierra Blanca, Tex., U.S. 31°9' N, 105°22' W 92
Sierra Colorada, Arg. 40°35' S, 67°46' W 134
Sierra de San Pedro Mártir National Park, Mex. 30°58' N, 115°45' W 238
Sierra Gorda, Chile 22°54' S, 69°22' W 137
Sierra Grande, Arg. 41°35' S, 65°22' W 134
Sierra Leone 8°30' N, 12°17' W 214
Sierra Leone Rise, North Atlantic Ocean 5°17' N, 20°42' W 253
Sierra Madre Mountains, Calif., U.S. 34°57' N, 120°5' W 100
Sierra Madre Occidental, Mex. 25°42' N, 106°57' W 114
Sierra Madre Oriental, Mex. 23°10' N, 100°33' W 114
Sierra Mojada, Mex. 27°18' N, 103°42' W 112
Sierra Nevada de Santa Marta National Park, Col. 11°19' N, 74°8' W 130
Sierra Nevada National Park, Venez. 8°41' N, 71°26' W 136
Sierra Vista, Ariz., U.S. 31°33' N, 110°18' W 92
Sierre, Switz. 46°18' N, 7°31' E 167
Sieruela, Sp. 38°58' N, 5°3' W 164
Siesta Key, island, Fla., U.S. 27°10' N, 82°37' W 105
Siete Aguas, Sp. 39°28' N, 0°56' E 164
Şieu, Rom. 47°0' N, 24°36' E 156
Sif Fatima, spring, Alg. 31°6' N, 8°40' E 214
Sifié, Côte d'Ivoire 7°54' N, 6°56' W 222
Sifnos, island, Gr. 36°51' N, 24°9' E 180
Sifton, Can. 51°22' N, 100°8' W 90
Sifton Pass, Can. 57°53' N, 126°10' W 108
Sig, Russ. 65°34' N, 34°9' E 152
Sigdal, Nor. 60°3' N, 9°37' E 152
Sigean, Fr. 43°1' N, 2°56' E 164
Sigep, Indonesia 0°59' N, 98°49' E 196
Sighnaghi, Ga. 41°37' N, 45°55' E 195
Siglan, Russ. 59°17' N, 152°31' E 173
Sigli, Indonesia 5°23' N, 95°55' E 196
Siglufjörður, Ice. 66°10' N, 19°5' W 143
Sigmaringen, Ger. 48°4' N, 9°12' E 152
Signal, site, Can. 48°18' N, 76°55' W 94
Signal Hill, peak, Austral. 21°59' S, 139°52' E 230
Signal Peak, Ariz., U.S. 33°21' N, 114°8' W 101
Signy Island, Antarctica 60°60' S, 46°55' W 134
Signy-le-Petit, Fr. 49°53' N, 4°17' E 163
Sigourney, Iowa, U.S. 41°20' N, 92°12' W 94
Sigovo, Russ. 62°39' N, 87°2' E 169
Sigre, river, Hond. 15°21' N, 84°51' W 115
Sigüenza, Sp. 41°3' N, 2°40' W 164
Siguiri, Guinea 11°27' N, 9°11' W 222
Sigulda, Latv. 57°8' N, 24°51' E 166
Sihor, India 21°42' N, 71°56' E 186
Sihora, India 23°29' N, 80°7' E 197
Siikainen, Fin. 61°51' N, 21°47' E 166
Siilinjärvi, Fin. 63°3' N, 27°38' E 152
Siipyy see Sideby, Fin. 62°1' N, 21°19' E 166
Siirt, Turk. 37°54' N, 41°57' E 195
Sikanni Chief, Can. 57°15' N, 122°44' W 108
Sikanni Chief, river, Can. 57°26' N, 122°27' W 108
Sikar, India 27°36' N, 75°10' E 197
Sikasso, Mali 11°19' N, 5°41' W 222
Sikeå, Nor. 64°9' N, 20°55' E 152
Sikes, La., U.S. 32°3' N, 92°13' W 103
Sikeston, Mo., U.S. 36°51' N, 89°35' W 96
Sikhote Alin', Khrebet 43°1' N, 132°36' E 200
Sikinos, island, Gr. 36°44' N, 24°37' E 180
Sikkim, adm. division, India 27°29' N, 88°6' E 197
Siklós, Hung. 45°50' N, 18°17' E 168
Siknäs, Nor. 65°50' N, 22°40' E 152
Sikonda, Hung. 46°9' N, 18°14' E 168
Sikonge, Tanzania 5°36' S, 32°47' E 224
Siksjö, Nor. 64°21' N, 17°47' E 152
Siktyakh, Russ. 69°51' N, 124°43' E 160
Sikuati, Malaysia 6°54' N, 116°40' E 203
Sila, La, It. 39°31' N, 16°21' E 156
Silacayoapan, Mex. 17°29' N, 98°9' W 114
Šilalė, Lith. 55°29' N, 22°10' E 166
Silame, Nig. 13°2' N, 4°51' E 222
Silandro, It. 46°37' N, 10°47' E 167
Silao, Mex. 20°54' N, 101°26' W 114
Silas, Ala., U.S. 31°46' N, 88°20' W 103
Šilderi, Latv. 56°51' N, 22°10' E 166
Şile, Turk. 41°10' N, 29°36' E 156
Silesia, region, Pol. 49°36' N, 17°59' E 152
Silet, Alg. 22°39' N, 4°37' E 214
Siletitengi Köli, lake, Kaz. 53°9' N, 72°22' E 184
Siliana, Alg. 36°32' N, 6°17' E 150
Silifke, Turk. 36°20' N, 33°55' E 156
Silil, spring, Somalia 10°52' N, 43°18' E 182
Siling Co, lake, China 31°37' N, 88°26' E 188
Silistra, Bulg. 44°5' N, 27°15' E 156
Silistra, adm. division, Bulg. 43°56' N, 26°22' E 156
Silivri, Turk. 41°5' N, 28°14' E 156
Silkeborg, Den. 56°8' N, 9°31' E 150
Silla, Sp. 39°21' N, 0°24' E 164
Sillamäe, Est. 59°22' N, 27°43' E 166
Silli, Burkina Faso 11°35' N, 2°30' W 222
Silliman, Mount, peak, Calif., U.S. 36°37' N, 118°44' W 101
Silloth, U.K. 54°52' N, 3°23' W 162
Silo, peak, Gr. 41°9' N, 25°51' E 156
Silogui, Indonesia 1°12' S, 98°58' E 196
Silopi, Turk. 37°14' N, 42°17' E 195
Silsbee, Tex., U.S. 30°19' N, 94°11' W 103
Silt Lake, Can. 60°2' N, 119°18' W 108
Siltou, spring, Chad 16°51' N, 15°42' E 216
Siluas, Indonesia 1°17' N, 109°49' E 196
Šilutė, Lith. 55°22' N, 21°28' E 166
Silvan, Turk. 38°8' N, 41°3' E 195
Silvânia, Braz. 16°42' S, 48°37' W 138
Silvassa, India 20°16' N, 73°3' E 186
Silver Bay, Minn., U.S. 47°17' N, 91°17' W 110
Silver City, Idaho, U.S. 43°1' N, 116°46' W 90
Silver City, Miss., U.S. 33°4' N, 90°31' W 103
Silver City, Nev., U.S. 39°15' N, 119°39' W 90
Silver City, N. Mex., U.S. 32°45' N, 108°18' W 112
Silver Cliff, Colo., U.S. 38°8' N, 105°26' W 90
Silver Creek, Miss., U.S. 31°34' N, 89°59' W 103
Silver Lake, Ind., U.S. 41°3' N, 85°53' W 102
Silver Lake, N.H., U.S. 43°53' N, 71°11' W 104
Silver Peak, Nev., U.S. 37°45' N, 117°39' W 92
Silver Run Peak, Mont., U.S. 45°5' N, 109°37' W 90
Silver Springs, Fla., U.S. 29°12' N, 82°4' W 105
Silver Star Mountain, peak, Can. 50°21' N, 119°9' W 90
Silver Zone Pass, Nev., U.S. 40°56' N, 114°21' W 90
Silverthrone, Mount, peak, Alas., U.S. 63°6' N, 150°53' W 98
Silverthrone Mountain, peak, Can. 51°29' N, 126°10' W 108
Silverton, Colo., U.S. 37°48' N, 107°40' W 82
Silverton, Tex., U.S. 34°27' N, 101°19' W 92
Silves, Braz. 2°52' S, 58°14' W 130
Silvretta, Aust. 46°49' N, 9°58' E 167
Silwa Baḥari, Egypt 24°42' N, 32°55' E 182
Sim, Russ. 54°59' N, 57°39' E 154
Sim, Cap, Mor. 31°25' N, 10°40' W 214
Simaleke-hilir, Indonesia 1°10' S, 98°37' E 196
Sim'ān, Jabal, Syr. 36°31' N, 36°38' E 156
Simao, China 22°37' N, 101°12' E 202
Şīmareh, river, Iran 33°25' N, 46°51' E 180
Simav, Turk. 39°4' N, 28°58' E 156
Simav, river, Turk. 39°17' N, 28°15' E 156
Simba, Dem. Rep. of the Congo 0°36' N, 22°56' E 218
Simbo, island, Solomon Islands 8°17' S, 156°30' E 242
Simcoe, Can. 42°49' N, 80°18' W 94
Simcoe, Lake, Can. 44°27' N, 79°55' W 80
Simcoe Mountains, peak, Wash., U.S. 45°57' N, 120°55' W 90
Simdega, India 22°35' N, 84°30' E 197
Simeria, Rom. 45°50' N, 23°1' E 168
Simeulue, island, Indonesia 2°43' N, 95°5' E 196
Simferopol', Ukr. 44°57' N, 34°1' E 156
Simhana, China 39°40' N, 73°57' E 197
Simi, Gr. 36°36' N, 27°49' E 156
Simi Valley, Calif., U.S. 34°16' N, 118°46' W 101
Simikot, Nepal 29°59' N, 81°51' E 197
Simin Han, Bosn. and Herzg. 44°32' N, 18°44' E 168
Simiti, Col. 7°57' N, 73°59' W 136
Simla, Colo., U.S. 39°8' N, 104°6' W 92
Simla, Nepal 31°8' N, 77°9' E 197
Şimleu Silvaniei, Rom. 47°14' N, 22°50' E 168
Simme, river, Switz. 46°34' N, 7°25' E 165
Simmern, Ger. 49°58' N, 7°30' E 167
Simmesport, La., U.S. 30°57' N, 91°50' W 103
Simojärvi, Fin. 65°55' N, 27°7' E 152
Simojovel, Mex. 17°9' N, 92°44' W 115
Simola, Fin. 60°54' N, 28°7' E 166
Simón Bolívar, Mex. 24°39' N, 103°15' W 114

Simonette, river, Can. 54°1' N, 118°37' W 108
Simonhouse, Can. 54°26' N, 101°24' W 108
Simon's Town, S. Af. 34°12' S, 18°25' E 227
Simontornya, Hung. 46°45' N, 18°32' E 168
Simpang, Indonesia 0°9' N, 103°16' E 196
Simpang, Indonesia 1°15' S, 104°5' E 196
Simpele, Fin. 61°25' N, 29°20' E 166
Simplicio Mendes, Braz. 7°51' S, 41°55' W 132
Simplon Pass, Switz. 46°15' N, 8°1' E 167
Simpson, La., U.S. 31°14' N, 93°1' W 103
Simpson, Pa., U.S. 41°34' N, 75°29' W 94
Simpson Desert, Austral. 25°28' S, 135°47' E 230
Simpson Hill, peak, Austral. 26°34' S, 126°21' E 230
Simpson Lake, Can. 60°47' N, 129°44' W 108
Simpson Park Mountains, Nev., U.S. 39°45' N, 116°58' W 90
Simpson Peninsula, Can. 68°27' N, 91°51' W 106
Simrishamn, Nor. 55°32' N, 14°20' E 152
Sims Lake, Can. 53°59' N, 66°28' W 111
Simsboro, La., U.S. 32°31' N, 92°49' W 103
Simushir, island, Russ. 46°43' N, 152°15' E 190
Sina, Peru 14°34' S, 69°16' W 137
Sinabang, Indonesia 2°29' N, 96°20' E 196
Sinabung, peak, Indonesia 3°11' N, 98°17' E 196
Sinai, Egypt 30°23' N, 33°2' E 194
Sinai, Mount see Mûsa, Gebel, peak, Egypt 28°30' N, 33°54' E 226
Sinaí, Morro do, Braz. 10°41' S, 55°37' W 130
Sinaloa, adm. division, Mex. 23°42' N, 106°50' W 114
Sinaloa, river, Mex. 25°46' N, 108°25' W 80
Sinamaica, Venez. 11°6' N, 71°53' W 136
Sinan, China 27°56' N, 108°13' E 198
Sînandrei, Rom. 45°52' N, 21°10' E 168
Sinanju, N. Korea 39°35' N, 125°36' E 200
Sīnāwin, Lib. 31°4' N, 10°37' E 216
Sinbang-ni, N. Korea 41°5' N, 127°28' E 200
Sincelejo, Col. 9°16' N, 75°26' W 136
Sincennes, Lac, lake, Can. 47°27' N, 74°27' W 94
Sinch'ang, N. Korea 40°7' N, 128°28' E 200
Sinch'ang, N. Korea 39°23' N, 126°7' E 200
Sinchiyacu, Peru 3°11' S, 76°44' W 136
Sinch'ŏn, N. Korea 38°21' N, 125°29' E 200
Sinclair, Wyo., U.S. 41°46' N, 107°6' W 90
Sinclair, Lake, Ga., U.S. 33°12' N, 83°57' W 112
Sindangan, Philippines 8°16' N, 123°0' E 203
Sindara, Gabon 1°4' S, 10°37' E 218
Sindeni, Tanzania 5°18' S, 38°15' E 224
Sindèr, Niger 14°14' N, 1°14' E 222
Sindeya, Russ. 60°5' N, 61°29' E 154
Sindh, adm. division, Pak. 25°54' N, 68°3' E 186
Sindi, Est. 58°22' N, 24°39' E 166
Sindi, Sudan 14°22' N, 25°48' E 226
Sindri, India 23°40' N, 86°30' E 197
Sinegorskiy, Russ. 47°56' N, 40°49' E 158
Sines, Port. 37°57' N, 8°52' W 150
Sines, Cabo de, Port. 37°42' N, 9°11' W 150
Sinfra, Côte d'Ivoire 6°31' N, 5°55' W 222
Sing Buri, Thai. 14°53' N, 100°23' E 202
Singa, Sudan 13°8' N, 33°56' E 182
Singapore, Singapore 1°16' N, 103°43' E 196
Singer, La., U.S. 30°38' N, 93°25' W 103
Sîngerei, Mold. 47°38' N, 28°8' E 158
Singida, Tanzania 4°49' S, 34°43' E 224
Singida, adm. division, Tanzania 5°60' S, 34°4' E 224
Singing Tower, site, Fla., U.S. 27°55' N, 81°36' W 105
Singkawang, Indonesia 0°55' N, 108°58' E 196
Singkep, island, Indonesia 0°38' N, 104°36' E 196
Singkil, Indonesia 2°19' N, 97°46' E 196
Singkuang, Indonesia 1°6' N, 98°57' E 196
Singleton, Mount, peak, Austral. 22°5' S, 130°37' E 230
Singö, island, Sw. 60°10' N, 18°46' E 166
Singoli, India 24°58' N, 75°18' E 188
Singtam, India 27°17' N, 88°29' E 197
Singu, Myanmar 22°34' N, 96°0' E 202
Singus, ruin(s), Gr. 40°9' N, 23°41' E 156
Sin'gye, N. Korea 38°30' N, 126°32' E 200
Singye Dzong, Bhutan 28°0' N, 91°18' E 197
Sinhŭng, N. Korea 40°11' N, 127°36' E 200
Sini Vrŭkh, peak, Bulg. 41°49' N, 24°56' E 156
Sinianka-Minia Game Reserve, Chad 10°5' N, 17°4' E 218
Şinifḩah, Jordan 30°50' N, 35°33' E 194
Sinj, Croatia 43°42' N, 16°37' E 168
Sinjajevina, Europe 43°0' N, 19°6' E 168
Sinjār, Iraq 36°20' N, 41°53' E 195
Sinkat, Sudan 18°51' N, 36°48' E 182
Sinkiang, region 38°43' N, 73°57' E 197
Sinkiang, region, China 46°12' N, 83°11' E 184
Sinking Spring, Ohio, U.S. 39°3' N, 83°24' W 102
Sin-le-Noble, Fr. 50°20' N, 3°7' E 163
Sinnamary, South America 5°23' N, 52°57' W 130
Sinnar, adm. division, Sudan 12°44' N, 33°18' E 182
Sinntal, Ger. 50°18' N, 9°38' E 167
Sinnûris, Egypt 29°25' N, 30°50' E 180
Sinop, Braz. 11°55' S, 55°35' W 130
Sinop, Turk. 41°53' N, 34°57' E 143
Sinop Burnu, Turk. 42°1' N, 35°14' E 156
Sinop (Sinope), Turk. 42°1' N, 35°8' E 156
Sinope see Sinop, Turk. 42°1' N, 35°8' E 156
Sinp'a see Kimjŏngsuk, N. Korea 41°24' N, 127°48' E 200
Sinp'o, N. Korea 40°1' N, 128°13' E 200
Sinsang, N. Korea 39°39' N, 127°25' E 200
Sinsk, Russ. 61°9' N, 126°40' E 160
Sint Andries, Belg. 51°11' N, 3°11' E 163
Sint Georgen, Ger. 48°7' N, 8°19' E 152
Sint Mang, Ger. 47°43' N, 10°20' E 152
Sint Maarten, island, Neth. 18°2' N, 63°4' W 116
Sint Truiden, Belg. 50°48' N, 5°11' E 167
Sîntana, Rom. 46°20' N, 21°31' E 168
Sintang, Indonesia 4°238' N, 111°27' E 192
Sinton, Tex., U.S. 28°1' N, 97°30' W 96
Sintuya, Peru 12°44' S, 71°17' W 137
Sinú, river, Col. 7°52' N, 76°16' W 136
Sinŭiju, N. Korea 40°3' N, 124°23' E 200
Sinujiif, Somalia 8°32' N, 48°59' E 216
Sinwŏn, N. Korea 38°12' N, 125°43' E 200
Sinyaya, river, Latv. 56°26' N, 28°2' E 166
Sinzig, Ger. 50°32' N, 7°15' E 163
Sió, river, Hung. 46°48' N, 18°13' E 168
Sióagárd, Hung. 46°23' N, 18°39' E 168
Siocon, Philippines 7°45' N, 122°8' E 203
Siófok, Hung. 46°54' N, 18°5' E 168
Sioma, Zambia 16°41' S, 23°30' E 224
Sioma Ngwezi National Park, Zambia 17°7' S, 23°42' E 224
Sion, Switz. 46°14' N, 7°20' E 167
Siorapaluk 77°50' N, 70°37' W 246
Sioux City, Iowa, U.S. 42°29' N, 96°26' W 82
Sioux Falls, S. Dak., U.S. 43°31' N, 96°44' W 90
Sioux Lookout, Can. 50°5' N, 91°51' W 82
Sioux Narrows, Can. 49°25' N, 94°7' W 90
Sioux Rapids, Iowa, U.S. 42°52' N, 95°10' W 90
Sipalay, Philippines 9°45' N, 122°24' E 203
Šipan, island, Croatia 42°44' N, 17°54' E 168
Sipapo, Cerro, peak, Venez. 4°51' N, 67°15' W 136
Sipapo, river, Venez. 4°35' N, 67°40' W 136
Siphaqeni, S. Af. 31°5' S, 29°29' E 227
Siping, China 43°8' N, 124°22' E 200
Sipirok, Indonesia 1°37' N, 99°17' E 196
Sipiwesk, Can. 55°28' N, 97°25' W 108
Siple Coast, Antarctica 82°60' S, 148°28' W 248
Siple Island, Antarctica 72°30' S, 127°21' W 248
Siple, Mount, peak, Antarctica 73°20' S, 126°3' W 248
Šipovo, Bosn. and Herzg. 44°17' N, 17°4' E 168
Sippo see Sibbo, Fin. 60°22' N, 25°13' E 166
Šiprage, Bosn. and Herzg. 44°27' N, 17°33' E 168
Sipsey, river, Ala., U.S. 33°25' N, 87°46' W 103
Sipura, island, Indonesia 2°5' S, 99°22' E 192
Siqueros, Mex. 23°18' N, 106°15' W 114
Siquia, river, Nicar. 12°31' N, 84°32' W 115
Siquijor, Philippines 9°13' N, 123°29' E 203
Siquisique, Venez. 10°31' N, 69°46' W 136
Sir Alexander, Mount, peak, Can. 53°55' N, 120°29' W 108
Şīr Banī Yās, island, U.A.E. 24°23' N, 52°28' E 182
Sir Douglas, Mount, peak, Can. 50°43' N, 115°25' W 90
Sir Edward Pellew Group, islands, Austral. 15°27' S, 136°56' E 230
Sir Francis Drake, Mount, peak, Can. 50°48' N, 124°54' W 90
Sir Graham Moore Islands, Austral. 13°44' S, 124°3' E 230
Sir James Macbrien, Mount, peak, Can. 61°57' N, 129°1' W 72
Sir Sandford, Mount, peak, Can. 51°40' N, 117°58' W 90
Sir Thomas, Mount, peak, Austral. 27°13' S, 129°31' E 230
Sira, India 13°44' N, 76°56' E 188
Siracusa, It. 37°3' N, 15°14' E 216
Siracusa (Syracuse), It. 37°3' N, 15°17' E 156
Sirajganj, Bangladesh 24°22' N, 89°39' E 197
Şiran, Turk. 40°12' N, 39°8' E 195
Sirba, river, Burkina Faso 12°25' N, 0°32' E 222
Sirdaryo, Uzb. 40°50' N, 68°39' E 197
Sīrē, Eth. 8°14' N, 39°27' E 224
Sīrē, Eth. 9°1' N, 36°53' E 224
Sireniki, Russ. 64°30' N, 173°50' W 98
Sirghāyā, Syr. 33°48' N, 36°9' E 194
Siri, Cape, P.N.G. 11°54' S, 153°3' E 192
Siri, Gebel, peak, Egypt 22°6' N, 31°3' E 182
Sīrīk, Iran 26°32' N, 57°9' E 196
Sirino, Monte, peak, It. 40°7' N, 15°44' E 156
Sīrjan see Sa'īdābād, Iran 29°29' N, 55°40' E 196
Sirkka, Fin. 67°48' N, 24°47' E 152
Sirma, Nor. 70°1' N, 27°21' E 152
Sirmilik National Park, Can. 73°2' N, 83°20' W 72
Şırnak, Turk. 37°30' N, 42°23' E 195
Siro, Jebel, peak, Sudan 14°22' N, 24°16' E 226
Sirohi, India 24°52' N, 72°52' E 186
Široki Brijeg, Bosn. and Herzg. 43°24' N, 17°35' E 168
Sirombu, Indonesia 1°0' N, 97°23' E 196
Sīrrī, island, Iran 25°47' N, 54°21' E 180
Sirsa, India 29°32' N, 75°4' E 186
Sirur, India 18°49' N, 74°23' E 188
Şirvan, Turk. 38°1' N, 42°0' E 195
Širvintos, Lith. 55°1' N, 24°56' E 166
Sisak, Croatia 45°27' N, 16°22' E 168
Sisal, Mex. 21°9' N, 90°6' W 116
Sishen, S. Af. 27°47' S, 23°3' E 227
Sisian, Arm. 39°32' N, 46°2' E 195
Sisib Lake, lake, Can. 52°34' N, 99°41' W 108
Sisimiut (Holsteinsborg) 66°56' N, 53°43' W 106
Siskiyou Mountains, Calif., U.S. 41°51' N, 123°44' W 90
Sisophon, Cambodia 13°37' N, 102°58' E 202
Sisquoc, Calif., U.S. 34°52' N, 120°19' W 100
Sisseton, S. Dak., U.S. 45°38' N, 97°5' W 90
Sissonne, Fr. 49°34' N, 3°53' E 163
Sīstān, Daryācheh-ye, lake, Iran 30°44' N, 60°36' E 186
Sīstān, region, Iran 32°6' N, 59°49' E 180
Sister Bay, Wis., U.S. 45°11' N, 87°7' W 110
Sistersville, W. Va., U.S. 39°32' N, 80°60' W 102
Sitampiky, Madagascar 16°41' S, 46°8' E 220
Sitapur, India 27°33' N, 80°42' E 197
Siteki, Swaziland 26°23' S, 31°56' E 227
Sitges, Sp. 41°14' N, 1°48' E 164
Sithonia, Gr. 40°12' N, 23°39' E 156
Sitia, Gr. 35°9' N, 26°6' E 180
Sitidgi Lake, Can. 68°28' N, 134°8' W 98
Sítio da Abadia, Braz. 14°51' S, 46°15' W 138
Sítio do Mato, Braz. 13°5' S, 43°30' W 138
Sitka, Alas., U.S. 57°6' N, 135°14' W 73
Sitka National Historical Park, Alas., U.S. 57°2' N, 135°18' W 108
Sitkalidak Island, Alas., U.S. 56°43' N, 153°12' W 106
Sitkovo, Russ. 69°7' N, 86°19' E 169
Sitra, spring, Egypt 28°43' N, 26°53' E 180
Sittard, Neth. 51°0' N, 5°50' E 167
Sittingbourne, U.K. 51°19' N, 0°43' E 162
Sittong, river, Myanmar 19°24' N, 96°14' E 202
Sittwe, Myanmar 20°12' N, 92°52' E 188
Siuna, Nicar. 13°44' N, 84°46' W 115
Siuri, India 23°51' N, 87°31' E 197
Siv. Donets, river, Ukr. 49°25' N, 36°31' E 158
Sivac, Serb. and Mont. 45°41' N, 19°23' E 168
Sivas, Turk. 39°45' N, 37°0' E 156
Siverek, Turk. 37°43' N, 39°19' E 195
Siverić, Croatia 43°52' N, 16°11' E 168
Siverskiy, Russ. 59°20' N, 30°5' E 166
Sivil, peak, Sp. 42°12' N, 6°356' W 164
Sivrihisar, Turk. 39°27' N, 31°31' E 156
Sivuchiy, Mys, Russ. 56°56' N, 162°44' E 160
Sivulya, Hora, peak, Ukr. 48°31' N, 24°2' E 152
Sīwa, Egypt 29°13' N, 25°33' E 180
Siwan, India 26°11' N, 84°21' E 197
Sixaola, Pan. 9°30' N, 82°37' W 115
Sixian, China 33°30' N, 117°53' E 198
Siyal Islands, Red Sea 22°17' N, 35°39' E 182
Siyäzän, Azerb. 41°4' N, 49°5' E 195
Siziwang Qi, China 41°33' N, 111°46' E 198
Sjenica, Serb. and Mont. 43°15' N, 19°59' E 168
Sjoa, Nor. 61°41' N, 9°34' E 152
Sjoutnäs, Nor. 64°35' N, 14°54' E 152
Sjøvegan, Nor. 68°53' N, 17°50' E 152
Skadovs'k, Ukr. 46°8' N, 32°54' E 156
Skaftung, Fin. 62°6' N, 21°18' E 152
Skagen, Den. 57°42' N, 10°33' E 150
Skagens Odde, Den. 57°30' N, 10°37' E 150
Skagerrak, strait 57°52' N, 7°50' E 152
Skaget, peak, Nor. 61°16' N, 9°3' E 152
Skagit, river, Wash., U.S. 48°31' N, 122°3' W 100
Skagway, Alas., U.S. 59°26' N, 135°19' W 108
Skaistkalne, Latv. 56°23' N, 24°38' E 166
Skala-Podil's'ka, Ukr. 48°50' N, 26°11' E 156
Skamokawa, Wash., U.S. 46°15' N, 123°27' W 100
Skånevik, Nor. 59°43' N, 5°54' E 152
Skänninge, Nor. 58°22' N, 15°3' E 152
Skærbæk, Den. 55°9' N, 8°44' E 150
Skardu, Pak. 35°17' N, 75°39' E 186
Skærfjorden 77°13' N, 24°16' W 246
Skärhamn, Sw. 57°59' N, 11°33' E 150
Skarnes, Nor. 60°14' N, 11°41' E 152
Skarvdalsegga, peak, Nor. 62°4' N, 7°55' E 152
Skattkärr, Nor. 59°24' N, 13°38' E 152
Skaudvilė, Lith. 55°24' N, 22°34' E 166
Skaymat, Africa 24°29' N, 15°7' W 214
Skebo, Sw. 59°57' N, 18°33' E 166
Skeena Crossing, Can. 55°4' N, 127°48' W 108
Skeena Mountains, Can. 56°49' N, 129°31' W 98
Skeena, river, Can. 55°21' N, 127°45' W 108
Skegness, U.K. 53°8' N, 0°20' E 162
Skeldon, Guyana 5°46' N, 57°12' W 130
Skeleton Coast Park, Namibia 17°59' S, 10°48' E 220
Skeleton Coast, region, Namibia 17°31' S, 11°47' E 220
Skellefteå, Nor. 64°45' N, 20°53' E 152
Skelleftehamn, Nor. 64°40' N, 21°14' E 152
Skender Vakuf, Bosn. and Herzg. 44°29' N, 17°22' E 168
Skępe, Pol. 52°51' N, 19°21' E 152
Skerries, Ire. 53°33' N, 6°8' W 150
Ski, Nor. 59°43' N, 10°51' E 152
Skiatook, Okla., U.S. 36°21' N, 95°60' W 96
Skibo Castle, site, U.K. 57°51' N, 4°16' W 150
Skibotn, Nor. 69°23' N, 20°21' E 152
Skidal', Belarus 53°35' N, 24°14' E 152
Skiddaw, peak, U.K. 54°38' N, 3°11' W 162
Skidmore, Tex., U.S. 28°14' N, 97°41' W 92
Skidmore, Mount, peak, Antarctica 80°29' S, 29°26' W 248
Skien, Nor. 59°13' N, 9°32' E 160
Skihist Mountain, peak, Can. 50°10' N, 121°59' W 108
Skillingaryd, Nor. 57°25' N, 14°4' E 152
Skipskjolen, peak, Nor. 70°20' N, 29°32' E 152
Skipton, U.K. 53°57' N, 2°1' W 162
Skiros, island, Gr. 38°57' N, 24°31' E 180
Skive, Den. 56°33' N, 9°0' E 150
Skjåk, Nor. 61°52' N, 8°21' E 152
Skjern, Den. 55°56' N, 8°27' E 150
Skjern Å, river, Den. 55°50' N, 8°41' E 152
Skjervøy, Nor. 70°1' N, 20°59' E 152
Sklad, Russ. 71°53' N, 123°21' E 160
Sklinna, islands, Norwegian Sea 65°8' N, 9°53' E 152
Skodje, Nor. 62°29' N, 6°42' E 152
Skokie, Ill., U.S. 42°1' N, 87°44' W 102
Skokowa, Pol. 51°23' N, 16°52' E 152
Skole, Ukr. 49°2' N, 23°31' E 152
Skönvik, Nor. 62°26' N, 17°17' E 152
Skopin, Russ. 53°50' N, 39°30' E 154
Skopje, Maced. 41°58' N, 21°21' E 168
Skotoúsa, Gr. 41°7' N, 23°23' E 156
Skövde, Nor. 58°22' N, 13°48' E 152
Skovorodino, Russ. 53°52' N, 123°53' E 190
Skowhegan, Me., U.S. 44°43' N, 69°44' W 82
Skrad, Croatia 45°25' N, 14°53' E 156
Skradin (Scardona), Croatia 43°49' N, 15°54' E 168
Skrīveri, Latv. 56°37' N, 25°7' E 166
Skrunda, Latv. 56°39' N, 21°58' E 166
Skudeneshavn, Nor. 59°9' N, 5°15' E 152
Skulerud, Nor. 59°40' N, 11°32' E 152
Skull Mountain, peak, Nev., U.S. 36°46' N, 116°13' W 101
Skultuna, Nor. 59°42' N, 16°25' E 152
Skuodas, Lith. 56°15' N, 21°32' E 166
Skutskär, Sw. 60°38' N, 17°23' E 166
Skvyra, Ukr. 49°44' N, 29°47' E 158
Skwentna, Alas., U.S. 61°48' N, 151°17' W 98
Skykomish, Wash., U.S. 47°41' N, 121°22' W 100
Skykomish, river, Wash., U.S. 47°48' N, 121°58' W 100
Slagelse, Den. 55°23' N, 11°22' E 152
Slagle, La., U.S. 31°11' N, 93°9' W 103
Slains Castle, site, U.K. 57°24' N, 1°57' W 150
Slakovci, Croatia 45°13' N, 18°55' E 168
Slano, Croatia 42°46' N, 17°52' E 168
Slantsy, Russ. 59°5' N, 28°0' E 166
Slaný, Czech Rep. 50°13' N, 14°4' E 152
Śląskie, adm. division, Pol. 50°19' N, 18°25' E 152
Slate Islands, Can. 48°29' N, 87°23' W 94
Slate Mountain, peak, Calif., U.S. 40°48' N, 120°57' W 90
Slate Range, Calif., U.S. 35°49' N, 117°22' W 101
Slater, Mo., U.S. 39°12' N, 93°4' W 94
Slatersville, R.I., U.S. 41°59' N, 71°35' W 104
Slatina, Bosn. and Herzg. 44°49' N, 17°16' E 168
Slatina, Bosn. and Herzg. 44°57' N, 18°26' E 168
Slatina, Rom. 44°27' N, 24°21' E 156
Slatina Timiş, Rom. 45°15' N, 22°16' E 168
Slatinski Drenovac, Croatia 45°32' N, 17°42' E 168
Slaton, Tex., U.S. 33°25' N, 101°39' W 92
Slave Coast, region, Nig. 5°48' N, 5°8' E 222
Slave Lake, Can. 55°17' N, 114°47' W 108
Slave Point, Can. 61°1' N, 115°56' W 108
Slave, river, Can. 59°1' N, 111°30' W 106
Slavgorod, Belarus 53°23' N, 31°1' E 154
Slavgorod, Russ. 52°59' N, 78°47' E 184
Slavinja, Serb. and Mont. 43°8' N, 22°52' E 168
Slavkovichi, Russ. 57°37' N, 29°4' E 166
Slavonia, region, Croatia 45°20' N, 16°50' E 168
Slavonice, Czech Rep. 48°59' N, 15°21' E 152
Slavonski Kobaš, Croatia 45°6' N, 17°44' E 168
Slavuta, Ukr. 50°18' N, 26°53' E 152
Slavyanka, Russ. 42°51' N, 131°22' E 200
Slavyansk na Kubani, Russ. 45°17' N, 38°13' E 156
Slayton, Minn., U.S. 43°57' N, 95°45' W 94
Sleaford, U.K. 52°59' N, 0°25' E 162
Sleat, Point of 56°43' N, 6°3' W 150
Sled Lake, lake, Can. 54°22' N, 107°42' W 108
Sleeper Islands, islands, Can. 57°9' N, 82°37' W 106
Sleepy Eye, Minn., U.S. 44°16' N, 94°44' W 94
Ślesin, Pol. 53°10' N, 17°42' E 152
Slide Mountain, peak, N.Y., U.S. 41°58' N, 74°29' W 94
Slidell, La., U.S. 30°14' N, 89°47' W 103
Sliedrecht, Neth. 51°49' N, 4°45' E 167
Slievemore, peak, Ire. 53°59' N, 10°10' W 150
Slievenamon, peak, Ire. 52°24' N, 7°40' W 150
Sligo, Ire. 54°15' N, 8°29' W 150
Slim Buttes, peak, S. Dak., U.S. 45°21' N, 103°16' W 90
Slinger, Wis., U.S. 43°19' N, 88°17' W 102
Slingerlands, N.Y., U.S. 42°37' N, 73°53' W 104
Slite, Sw. 57°42' N, 18°47' E 166
Sliven, Bulg. 42°40' N, 26°18' E 156
Sliven, adm. division, Bulg. 42°40' N, 25°52' E 156
Slivnica, Serb. and Mont. 42°58' N, 22°45' E 168
Slivnitsa, Bulg. 42°51' N, 23°2' E 168
Sljeme, peak, Croatia 45°54' N, 15°55' E 168
Sloan, Nev., U.S. 35°56' N, 115°14' W 101
Slobodchikovo, Russ. 61°45' N, 48°16' E 154
Slobodskoy, Russ. 58°46' N, 50°10' E 169
Slobozia, Rom. 44°34' N, 27°21' E 156
Slocan, Can. 49°45' N, 117°28' W 90
Sloka, Latv. 56°57' N, 23°37' E 166
Słomniki, Pol. 50°14' N, 20°6' E 152
Slonim, Belarus 53°4' N, 25°18' E 152
Slotten, Nor. 70°44' N, 24°33' E 152
Slottsbron, Nor. 59°18' N, 13°3' E 152
Slough, U.K. 51°31' N, 0°37' E 162
Slovakia 48°50' N, 18°49' E 152
Sloveni, Belarus 54°20' N, 29°35' E 166
Slovenia 46°4' N, 14°46' E 156
Slov''yans'k, Ukr. 48°51' N, 37°37' E 158
Sludka, Russ. 61°56' N, 50°12' E 154
Sludka, Russ. 59°22' N, 49°43' E 154
Sluis, Neth. 51°18' N, 3°23' E 163
Slumbering Hills, Nev., U.S. 41°16' N, 118°18' W 90
Slŭnchev Bryag, Bulg. 42°41' N, 27°42' E 156
Słupca, Pol. 52°17' N, 17°52' E 152
Słupsk, Pol. 54°21' N, 16°40' E 152
Slussfors, Nor. 65°26' N, 16°14' E 152
Slutsk, Belarus 53°0' N, 27°33' E 152
Slyudyanka, Russ. 51°32' N, 103°50' E 190
Smackover, Ark., U.S. 33°20' N, 92°44' W 103
Smalininkai, Lith. 55°4' N, 22°35' E 166
Small Lake, lake, Can. 57°40' N, 97°46' W 108
Small Point, Me., U.S. 43°38' N, 69°52' W 104
Smalltree Lake, lake, Can. 61°0' N, 105°43' W 108
Smallwood Reservoir, lake, Can. 53°25' N, 70°28' W 106
Smalyavichy, Belarus 54°1' N, 28°5' E 166
Smara, Africa 26°45' N, 11°43' W 214
Smarhon', Belarus 54°29' N, 26°22' E 166
Smederevo, Serb. and Mont. 44°39' N, 20°55' E 168
Smedjebacken, Nor. 60°6' N, 15°23' E 152
Smeïda see Taoudenni, Mali 22°41' N, 3°59' W 214
Śmigiel, Pol. 52°0' N, 16°31' E 152
Smila, Ukr. 49°15' N, 31°48' E 160
Smilavichy, Belarus 53°46' N, 28°2' E 152
Smilde, Neth. 52°56' N, 6°28' E 163
Smiltene, Latv. 57°25' N, 25°52' E 166
Smirnovo, Kaz. 54°30' N, 69°26' E 184
Smith, Can. 55°8' N, 114°3' W 108
Smith Arm 66°9' N, 124°31' W 98
Smith Bay 70°51' N, 155°33' W 98
Smith Bay 76°54' N, 81°57' W 106
Smith Canyon, Colo., U.S. 37°23' N, 103°35' W 92
Smith Center, Kans., U.S. 39°46' N, 98°47' W 90
Smith Island, Antarctica 62°54' S, 63°41' W 134
Smith Island, Can. 60°21' N, 80°16' W 106
Smith, Mount, peak, Eth. 6°15' N, 36°15' E 224
Smith River, Can. 59°52' N, 126°26' W 108
Smith Sound 51°10' N, 128°2' W 108
Smith Sound 78°12' N, 79°48' W 246
Smithboro, Ill., U.S. 38°53' N, 89°21' W 102
Smithdale, Miss., U.S. 31°19' N, 90°41' W 103
Smithers, Can. 54°44' N, 127°15' W 106
Smithers, W. Va., U.S. 38°10' N, 81°19' W 94
Smithfield, N.C., U.S. 35°30' N, 78°21' W 96
Smithfield, S. Af. 30°12' S, 26°32' E 227
Smiths Falls, Can. 44°54' N, 75°58' W 82
Smithtown, N.Y., U.S. 40°51' N, 73°12' W 104
Smithville, W. Va., U.S. 39°4' N, 81°6' W 102
Smoke Creek Desert, Nev., U.S. 40°32' N, 120°5' W 90
Smokey, Cape, Can. 46°30' N, 60°22' W 111
Smokvica, Croatia 42°54' N, 16°52' E 168
Smoky Falls, Can. 50°3' N, 82°11' W 94
Smoky Hill, river, Kans., U.S. 38°41' N, 99°5' W 90
Smoky Hills, Kans., U.S. 39°16' N, 99°19' W 90
Smoky Lake, Can. 54°6' N, 112°28' W 108
Smoky Mountains, Idaho, U.S. 43°40' N, 114°50' W 90
Smoky, river, Can. 53°52' N, 119°16' W 108
Smoky, river, Can. 55°21' N, 118°10' W 108
Smolensk, Russ. 54°48' N, 32°7' E 154
Smolensk, adm. division, Russ. 54°59' N, 31°37' E 154
Smolijana, Bosn. and Herzg. 44°37' N, 16°25' E 168
Smólikas, peak, Gr. 40°4' N, 20°51' E 156
Smolyan, Bulg. 41°35' N, 24°40' E 156
Smolyan, adm. division, Bulg. 41°37' N, 24°7' E 156
Smolyanovtsi, Bulg. 43°31' N, 22°59' E 168
Smooth Rock Falls, Can. 49°17' N, 81°38' W 94
Smyley Island, Antarctica 72°41' S, 82°11' W 248
Smyrna see İzmir, Turk. 38°24' N, 27°8' E 156
Snaefell, peak 54°14' N, 4°33' W 150
Snaght, Slieve, peak, Ire. 55°10' N, 7°27' W 150
Snake Falls, Can. 50°50' N, 93°26' W 90
Snake Range, Nev., U.S. 39°18' N, 114°25' W 90
Snake River, Can. 59°5' N, 122°26' W 108
Snake, river, Can. 65°50' N, 133°4' W 98
Snake River Plain, Idaho, U.S. 43°24' N, 116°24' W 90
Snake, river, U.S. 43°5' N, 116°27' W 90
Snappertuna, Fin. 59°59' N, 23°39' E 166
Snare Lake, Can. 58°25' N, 108°18' W 108
Snare, river, Can. 58°23' N, 107°39' W 108
Snåsa, Nor. 64°13' N, 12°20' E 152
Sneek, Neth. 53°1' N, 5°40' E 163
Snelland, U.K. 53°18' N, 0°24' E 162
Snelling, Calif., U.S. 37°31' N, 120°28' W 100
Snettisham, U.K. 52°52' N, 0°30' E 162
Snezhnogorsk, Russ. 68°6' N, 87°36' E 169
Snezhnoye, Russ. 65°27' N, 173°3' E 160
Sněžka, peak, Czech Rep. 50°43' N, 15°37' E 152
Snihurivka, Ukr. 47°5' N, 32°48' E 156
Snilfjord, Nor. 63°23' N, 9°30' E 152
Snipe Keys, islands, Gulf of Mexico 24°43' N, 81°46' W 105
Snøhetta, peak, Nor. 62°18' N, 9°9' E 152
Snohomish, Wash., U.S. 47°54' N, 122°6' W 100
Snonuten, peak, Nor. 59°29' N, 6°45' E 152
Snoqualmie, Wash., U.S. 47°30' N, 121°50' W 100
Snoqualmie Pass, Wash., U.S. 47°24' N, 121°25' W 100
Snov, river, Ukr. 51°34' N, 31°44' E 158
Snover, Mich., U.S. 43°27' N, 82°58' W 102
Snow Hill Island, Antarctica 64°55' S, 56°59' W 134
Snow Island, Antarctica 62°42' S, 61°37' W 134
Snow Lake, Can. 54°52' N, 100°3' W 108
Snow, Mount, peak, Vt., U.S. 42°57' N, 72°57' W 104
Snow Mountain, peak, Calif., U.S. 39°22' N, 122°51' W 90
Snow Mountain, peak, Me., U.S. 45°16' N, 70°48' W 94
Snow Peak, Wash., U.S. 48°33' N, 118°33' W 90
Snowbird Lake, Can. 60°37' N, 103°28' W 108
Snowden, Can. 53°29' N, 104°40' W 108
Snowdon, peak, U.K. 53°4' N, 4°6' W 162
Snowflake, Ariz., U.S. 34°30' N, 110°5' W 92
Snowmass Mountain, peak, Colo., U.S. 39°7' N, 107°10' W 90
Snowshoe Peak, Mont., U.S. 48°11' N, 115°46' W 90
Snowy Mountains, Austral. 36°23' S, 147°16' E 230
Snuol, Cambodia 12°6' N, 106°24' E 202
Snyder, Colo., U.S. 40°19' N, 103°37' W 90
Snyder, Okla., U.S. 34°38' N, 98°58' W 92
Snyder, Tex., U.S. 32°41' N, 100°54' W 92
Soala see Sokolo, Mali 14°45' N, 6°7' W 222
Soanierana-Ivongo, Madagascar 16°54' S, 49°33' E 220
Soatá, Col. 6°19' N, 72°42' W 136
Soavinandriana, Madagascar 19°11' S, 46°44' E 220
Soba, Nig. 10°57' N, 8°5' E 222
Sobat, river, Sudan 8°53' N, 32°30' E 224
Soberania National Park, Pan. 9°9' N, 79°51' W 115
Sobernheim, Ger. 49°46' N, 7°39' E 167
Sobinka, Russ. 55°58' N, 40°1' E 154
Sobolev, Russ. 51°54' N, 51°41' E 158
Sobozo, spring, Niger 21°10' N, 14°47' E 222
Sobral, Braz. 3°41' S, 40°23' W 132
Sobti, spring, Mali 22°45' N, 1°46' W 214
Soc Trang, Vietnam 9°36' N, 105°57' E 202
Sočanica, Europe 43°3' N, 20°50' E 168
Socha, Col. 5°59' N, 72°41' W 136
Sochaczew, Pol. 52°13' N, 20°14' E 152
Sochi, Russ. 43°36' N, 39°46' E 195
Society Islands, South Pacific Ocean 17°21' S, 152°59' W 238
Socompa, Chile 24°25' S, 68°21' W 132
Socorro, N. Mex., U.S. 34°2' N, 106°53' W 82
Socorro, Isla, island, Isla Socorro 18°28' N, 110°60' W 112
Socotra (Suquṭrā), island, Yemen 12°19' N, 54°12' E 182
Socovos, Sp. 38°20' N, 1°59' W 164
Socuéllamos, Sp. 39°17' N, 2°48' W 164
Soda Creek, Can. 52°20' N, 122°16' W 108
Soda Lake, Calif., U.S. 35°12' N, 120°2' W 100

Soda Mountains, Calif., U.S. 35°16′ N, 116°20′ W 101
Soda Peak, Wash., U.S. 45°51′ N, 122°6′ W 100
Sodankylä, Fin. 67°25′ N, 26°33′ E 152
Söderhamn, Nor. 61°18′ N, 17°0′ E 152
Södertälje, Nor. 59°10′ N, 17°34′ E 152
Sodiri, Sudan 14°23′ N, 29°8′ E 226
Sodo, Eth. 6°49′ N, 37°46′ E 224
Södra Kvarken 60°17′ N, 18°40′ E 166
Södra Storfjället, peak, Nor. 65°36′ N, 14°36′ E 152
Södra Sunderbyn, Nor. 65°39′ N, 21°56′ E 152
Södra Vi, Nor. 57°44′ N, 15°46′ E 152
Sodus, Mich., U.S. 42°1′ N, 86°22′ W 102
Soekmekaar see Morebeng, S. Af. 23°30′ S, 29°56′ E 227
Soela Väin 58°37′ N, 22°8′ E 166
Soest, Ger. 51°34′ N, 8°6′ E 167
Sofala, adm. division, Mozambique 18°26′ S, 34°1′ E 224
Sofara, Mali 14°1′ N, 4°15′ W 222
Sofi, Sudan 14°8′ N, 35°51′ E 226
Sofi, Tanzania 8°47′ S, 36°9′ E 224
Sofia see Sofiya, Bulg. 42°41′ N, 23°12′ E 156
Sofiya, adm. division, Bulg. 42°51′ N, 22°47′ E 168
Sofiya (Sofia), Bulg. 42°41′ N, 23°12′ E 156
Sofiya-Grad, adm. division, Bulg. 42°35′ N, 23°7′ E 156
Sofporog, Russ. 65°48′ N, 31°28′ E 152
Sof'yanga, Russ. 65°52′ N, 31°17′ E 152
Soga, Tanzania 6°47′ S, 38°55′ E 224
Sogamoso, Col. 5°41′ N, 72°56′ W 136
Sogata, Eth. 5°41′ N, 35°8′ E 224
Sögel, Ger. 52°50′ N, 7°32′ E 163
Sogod, Philippines 10°24′ N, 125°0′ E 203
Sogolle, spring, Chad 15°20′ N, 15°20′ E 216
Sogra, Russ. 62°49′ N, 47°28′ E 169
Sogra, Russ. 62°39′ N, 46°16′ E 154
Söğüt, Turk. 40°0′ N, 30°10′ E 180
Söğüt Gölü, lake, Turk. 37°4′ N, 29°39′ E 156
Sogxian, China 31°51′ N, 93°40′ E 188
Sohâg, Egypt 26°33′ N, 31°35′ E 180
Soham, U.K. 52°19′ N, 0°20′ E 162
Soheuksando, island, S. Korea 34°7′ N, 124°32′ E 198
Sohm Plain, North Atlantic Ocean 37°43′ N, 53°36′ W 253
Söhüng, N. Korea 38°28′ N, 126°10′ E 200
Soignies, Belg. 50°35′ N, 4°4′ E 163
Şoimuş, Rom. 45°55′ N, 22°55′ E 168
Soissons, Fr. 49°22′ N, 3°18′ E 163
Sōja, Japan 34°40′ N, 133°45′ E 201
Sojat, India 25°54′ N, 73°42′ E 186
Sok, river, Russ. 53°53′ N, 51°16′ E 154
Sokcho, S. Korea 38°13′ N, 128°34′ E 200
Söke, Turk. 37°44′ N, 27°22′ E 156
Sokhumi (Sukhum), Rep. of Georgia 43°0′ N, 41°55′ E 195
Soko Banja, Serb. and Mont. 43°38′ N, 21°51′ E 168
Sokodé, Togo 8°57′ N, 1°8′ E 214
Sokol, Russ. 59°28′ N, 40°12′ E 154
Sokolac, Bosn. and Herzg. 43°56′ N, 18°49′ E 168
Sokolarci, Maced. 41°54′ N, 22°17′ E 168
Sokółka, Pol. 53°24′ N, 23°29′ E 152
Sokolo (Soala), Mali 14°45′ N, 6°7′ W 222
Sokolovka, Kaz. 55°9′ N, 69°11′ E 184
Sokolovo, Russ. 65°21′ N, 57°1′ E 154
Sokol'skoye, Russ. 57°8′ N, 43°13′ E 154
Sokoto, Nig. 13°1′ N, 5°13′ E 222
Soksa, N. Korea 40°38′ N, 127°17′ E 200
Sokuluk, Kyrg. 42°51′ N, 74°23′ E 184
Sol, Costa del, Sp. 36°34′ N, 4°40′ W 164
Sol de Julio, Arg. 29°33′ S, 63°27′ W 139
Sol, river, Braz. 6°42′ S, 67°47′ W 130
Solana Beach, Calif., U.S. 32°59′ N, 117°17′ W 101
Solano, Venez. 1°56′ N, 66°56′ W 136
Solano, Punta, Col. 6°16′ N, 77°53′ W 136
Solberg, Nor. 63°47′ N, 17°38′ E 152
Solberget, peak, Nor. 63°47′ N, 17°27′ E 152
Solec, Pol. 51°8′ N, 21°45′ E 152
Soledad, Arg. 30°38′ S, 60°55′ W 139
Soledad, Calif., U.S. 36°25′ N, 121°20′ W 100
Soledad, Col. 10°52′ N, 74°48′ W 136
Soledad, Peru 3°32′ S, 77°49′ W 136
Soledad, Venez. 8°11′ N, 63°33′ W 116
Soledad de Doblado, Mex. 19°3′ N, 96°25′ W 114
Soledad Pass, Calif., U.S. 34°30′ N, 118°9′ W 101
Soledade, Braz. 28°50′ S, 52°32′ W 139
Soledade, Braz. 6°38′ S, 69°9′ W 130
Solhan, Turk. 38°57′ N, 41°3′ E 195
Solliera, It. 44°44′ N, 10°55′ E 167
Soligalich, Russ. 59°5′ N, 42°16′ E 154
Solignano, It. 44°38′ N, 9°58′ E 156
Solikamsk, Russ. 59°38′ N, 56°45′ E 154
Solimões (Amazonas), river, Braz. 2°50′ S, 66°35′ W 122
Solin (Salonae), Croatia 43°32′ N, 16°28′ E 168
Solingen, Ger. 51°9′ N, 7°5′ E 167
Sollefteå, Nor. 63°9′ N, 17°15′ E 152
Solling, Ger. 51°43′ N, 9°23′ E 167
Sol'lletsk, Russ. 51°9′ N, 55°2′ E 158
Solms, Ger. 50°31′ N, 8°24′ E 167
Solna, Sw. 59°22′ N, 17°58′ E 166
Solnechnogorsk, Russ. 56°9′ N, 37°0′ E 154
Solobkivtsi, Ukr. 49°3′ N, 26°54′ E 152
Solodcha, Russ. 49°37′ N, 44°18′ E 158
Solok, Indonesia 0°47′ N, 100°39′ E 196
Sololo, Kenya 3°27′ N, 38°34′ E 224
Solomennoye, Russ. 61°50′ N, 34°19′ E 154
Solomon, Can. 53°21′ N, 117°56′ W 108
Solomon, Kans., U.S. 38°53′ N, 97°22′ W 90
Solomon Islands 10°21′ S, 162°22′ E 242
Solomon Islands, South Pacific Ocean 10°55′ S, 162°35′ E 238
Solomon, river, Kans., U.S. 39°41′ N, 99°17′ W 90
Solomon Sea 6°43′ S, 150°46′ E 238
Solon Springs, Wis., U.S. 46°21′ N, 91°50′ W 94
Solotcha, Russ. 54°47′ N, 39°49′ E 154
Solothurn, Switz. 47°12′ N, 7°31′ E 150
Solovetskiye Ostrova, islands, Beloye More 64°40′ N, 35°18′ E 154
Solsona, Sp. 41°59′ N, 1°31′ E 164
Solstad, Nor. 65°10′ N, 12°8′ E 152
Solt, Hung. 46°47′ N, 19°1′ E 168
Šolta, island, Croatia 43°18′ N, 16°9′ E 168
Soltan Bagh, Afghan. 33°19′ N, 68°39′ E 186
Soltānābād, Iran 36°24′ N, 57°56′ E 180
Soltānābād, Iran 31°2′ N, 49°44′ E 186
Soltan-e Bakva, Afghan. 32°18′ N, 62°58′ E 186
Soltüstik Qazaqstan, adm. division, Kaz. 53°58′ N, 67°52′ E 184
Soltvadkert, Hung. 46°34′ N, 19°25′ E 168
Solund, Nor. 61°4′ N, 4°50′ E 152
Solunska Glava, peak, Maced. 41°41′ N, 21°21′ E 168
Soluntum, ruin(s), It. 38°5′ N, 13°25′ E 156
Sol'vychegodsk, Russ. 61°21′ N, 46°59′ E 154
Solwezi, Zambia 12°13′ S, 26°24′ E 224
Solyanka, Russ. 51°28′ N, 50°7′ E 158
Soma, Turk. 39°10′ N, 27°35′ E 156
Somabhula, Zimb. 19°43′ S, 29°40′ E 224
Somali Basin, Indian Ocean 0°21′ N, 51°48′ E 254
Somali, region, Eth. 4°34′ N, 42°4′ E 224
Somalia 4°7′ N, 45°14′ E 218
Somaliland, special sovereignty, Somalia 10°26′ N, 42°54′ E 216
Sombor, Serb. and Mont. 45°45′ N, 19°7′ E 168
Sombrerete, Mex. 23°36′ N, 103°39′ W 112
Sombrero, island, Sombrero 18°38′ N, 63°21′ W 116
Somero, Fin. 60°35′ N, 23°29′ E 166
Somers, Mont., U.S. 48°3′ N, 114°15′ W 108
Somers Point, N.J., U.S. 39°19′ N, 74°36′ W 94
Somerset, Can. 49°23′ N, 98°40′ W 94
Somerset, Colo., U.S. 38°56′ N, 107°28′ W 90
Somerset, Ky., U.S. 37°4′ N, 84°36′ W 96
Somerset, Mass., U.S. 41°46′ N, 71°8′ W 104
Somerset, Ohio, U.S. 39°48′ N, 82°19′ W 102
Somerset, Pa., U.S. 40°0′ N, 79°5′ W 94
Somerset Center, Mich., U.S. 42°2′ N, 84°26′ W 102
Somerset East, S. Af. 32°45′ S, 25°33′ E 227
Somerset Island, Can. 71°22′ N, 92°26′ W 106
Somerton, Ariz., U.S. 32°35′ N, 114°43′ W 101
Somerville, Mass., U.S. 42°23′ N, 71°6′ W 104
Somerville, Tenn., U.S. 35°14′ N, 89°21′ W 96
Somerville, Tex., U.S. 30°19′ N, 96°32′ W 96
Sommepy-Tahure, Fr. 49°15′ N, 4°32′ E 163
Sommesous, Fr. 48°44′ N, 4°12′ E 163
Somogy, adm. division, Hung. 46°31′ N, 17°13′ E 156
Somonauk, Ill., U.S. 41°37′ N, 88°42′ W 102
Somotillo, Nicar. 13°1′ N, 86°53′ W 115
Sompa, Est. 59°20′ N, 27°20′ E 166
Somuncurá, Meseta de, Arg. 41°27′ S, 69°4′ W 134
Son, Con, islands, South China Sea 8°29′ N, 106°16′ E 202
Son Ha, Vietnam 15°3′ N, 108°33′ E 202
Son Hoa, Vietnam 13°4′ N, 108°58′ E 202
Son Islands, Con, South China Sea 6°2′ N, 107°2′ E 238
Son, river, India 24°23′ N, 82°1′ E 197
Son, river, India 25°22′ N, 84°42′ E 197
Son, river, India 23°50′ N, 81°25′ E 190
Son Tay, Vietnam 21°7′ N, 105°29′ E 202
Sŏnbong, N. Korea 42°20′ N, 130°25′ E 200
Sŏnch'ŏn, N. Korea 39°47′ N, 124°53′ E 200
Soncillo, Sp. 42°57′ N, 3°48′ W 164
Soncino, It. 45°24′ N, 9°51′ E 167
Sondalo, It. 46°19′ N, 10°17′ E 167
Sondheimer, La., U.S. 32°32′ N, 91°10′ W 103
Sondrio, It. 46°10′ N, 9°51′ E 167
Song, Nig. 9°49′ N, 12°36′ E 216
Song Cau, Vietnam 13°28′ N, 109°11′ E 202
Song Ma, Vietnam 21°4′ N, 103°42′ E 202
Songea, Tanzania 10°42′ S, 35°39′ E 224
Songeons, Fr. 49°32′ N, 1°51′ E 163
Songhua Hu, lake, China 43°3′ N, 126°28′ E 200
Songhua, river, China 46°3′ N, 129°18′ E 190
Songjiang, China 30°59′ N, 121°13′ E 198
Songjianghe, China 42°8′ N, 127°30′ E 200
Sŏngjin see Kimch'aek, N. Korea 40°38′ N, 129°11′ E 200
Songkhla, Thai. 7°10′ N, 100°35′ E 196
Songkhram, river, Thai. 18°7′ N, 103°29′ E 202
Song-Köl, lake, Kyrg. 41°49′ N, 74°39′ E 184
Songling, China 48°1′ N, 121°5′ E 198
Songnim, N. Korea 38°44′ N, 125°39′ E 200
Songo, Angola 7°23′ S, 14°51′ E 218
Songo Songo Island, Tanzania 8°29′ S, 39°25′ E 224
Songshuzhen, China 42°2′ N, 127°6′ E 200
Songxi, China 27°35′ N, 118°47′ E 198
Songxian, China 34°10′ N, 112°4′ E 198
Songzi, China 30°10′ N, 111°45′ E 198
Sonhat, India 23°29′ N, 82°32′ E 197
Sonid Youqi, China 42°51′ N, 112°35′ E 198
Sonid Zuoqi, China 43°49′ N, 113°43′ E 198
Sonipat, India 28°57′ N, 77°1′ E 188
Sonkovo, Russ. 57°45′ N, 37°9′ E 154
Sonmiani, Pak. 25°25′ N, 66°32′ E 186
Sonmiani Bay 25°14′ N, 65°37′ E 186
Sonoita, Mex. 31°52′ N, 112°51′ W 92
Sonoita, river, Mex. 31°15′ N, 113°23′ W 92
Sonoma, Calif., U.S. 38°17′ N, 122°28′ W 100
Sonoma Peak, Nev., U.S. 40°50′ N, 117°42′ W 90
Sonoma Range, Nev., U.S. 40°45′ N, 117°50′ W 90
Sonora, Calif., U.S. 37°58′ N, 120°23′ W 100
Sonora, Tex., U.S. 30°32′ N, 100°38′ W 92
Sonora, adm. division, Mex. 30°11′ N, 111°25′ W 92
Sonora Pass, Calif., U.S. 38°19′ N, 119°39′ W 100
Sonora Peak, Calif., U.S. 38°21′ N, 119°41′ W 100
Sonoran Desert, Ariz., U.S. 33°27′ N, 115°27′ W 101
Sonqor, Iran 34°45′ N, 47°35′ E 180
Sonsón, Col. 5°40′ N, 75°16′ W 136
Sonsonate, El Salv. 13°44′ N, 89°44′ W 115
Sonsoro, Benin 11°7′ N, 2°46′ E 222
Sonsorol Islands, Philippine Sea 5°19′ N, 129°32′ E 192
Sonta, Serb. and Mont. 45°35′ N, 19°6′ E 168
Sontra, Ger. 51°4′ N, 9°56′ E 167
Sooke, Can. 48°21′ N, 123°43′ W 100
Sopachuy, Bol. 19°30′ S, 64°36′ W 137
Soperton, Ga., U.S. 32°22′ N, 82°36′ W 96
Sopo, river, Sudan 7°50′ N, 25°52′ E 224
Sopochnoye, Russ. 56°1′ N, 156°4′ E 160
Sopot, Pol. 54°25′ N, 18°33′ E 166
Sopron, Hung. 47°40′ N, 16°36′ E 168
Šopsko Rudare, Maced. 42°4′ N, 22°0′ E 168
Sopur, India 34°18′ N, 74°30′ E 186
Soquel, Calif., U.S. 37°0′ N, 121°57′ W 100
Sør Flatanger, Nor. 64°26′ N, 10°46′ E 152
Sør Varanger, region, Nor. 69°54′ N, 29°6′ E 152
Sorata, Bol. 15°46′ S, 68°43′ W 137
Soratte, Monte, peak, It. 42°13′ N, 12°25′ E 156
Sorbas, Sp. 37°5′ N, 2°8′ W 164
Sore, Fr. 44°19′ N, 0°35′ E 150
Sorel, Can. 46°1′ N, 73°6′ W 110
Soresina, It. 45°17′ N, 9°50′ E 167
Sørfjord, Nor. 66°29′ N, 13°17′ E 152
Sorgun, Turk. 39°49′ N, 35°10′ E 156
Soria, Sp. 41°45′ N, 2°30′ W 164
Soriano, Uru. 33°25′ S, 58°16′ W 139
Sorkwity, Pol. 53°49′ N, 21°10′ E 166
Sorø, Den. 55°26′ N, 11°34′ E 152
Sorocaba, Braz. 23°30′ S, 47°30′ W 138
Sorochinsk, Russ. 52°25′ N, 53°9′ E 154
Sorol Atoll 8°24′ N, 141°13′ E 192
Sorong, Indonesia 0°52′ N, 131°12′ E 192
Soroti, Uganda 1°41′ N, 33°35′ E 224
Soroti Station, Uganda 1°45′ N, 33°37′ E 224
Sorotona, Côte d'Ivoire 7°59′ N, 7°9′ W 222
Sørøyane, islands, Nor. 62°10′ N, 4°15′ E 152
Sorqudyq, Kaz. 46°30′ N, 59°4′ E 158
Sørreisa, Nor. 69°10′ N, 18°5′ E 152
Sorrento, La., U.S. 30°9′ N, 90°52′ W 103
Sorsatunturi, peak, Fin. 67°23′ N, 29°27′ E 152
Sorsele, Nor. 65°31′ N, 17°32′ E 152
Sorsk, Russ. 54°2′ N, 90°14′ E 184
Sorsogon, Philippines 13°0′ N, 124°0′ E 203
Sort, Sp. 42°24′ N, 1°6′ E 164
Sortavala, Russ. 61°38′ N, 30°35′ E 160
Sortavala (Serdobol), Russ. 61°42′ N, 30°39′ E 166
Sortland, Nor. 68°41′ N, 15°24′ E 152
Sørumsand, Nor. 59°58′ N, 11°14′ E 152
Sørvær, Nor. 70°37′ N, 22°0′ E 152
Sõrve Poolsaar, Est. 58°4′ N, 21°39′ E 166
Sõrve Säär, Est. 57°47′ N, 21°52′ E 166
Sørvika, Nor. 62°25′ N, 11°51′ E 152
Sos del Rey Católico, Sp. 42°29′ N, 1°13′ W 164
Sosaq, Kaz. 44°9′ N, 68°28′ E 184
Soscumica, Lac, lake, Can. 50°15′ N, 78°17′ W 110
Sosna, river, Russ. 52°20′ N, 38°2′ E 158
Sosnogorsk, Russ. 63°35′ N, 54°0′ E 154
Sosnovets, Russ. 64°26′ N, 34°20′ E 152
Sosnovka, Russ. 66°30′ N, 40°25′ E 154
Sosnovka, Russ. 56°15′ N, 51°21′ E 154
Sosnovka, Russ. 53°12′ N, 41°18′ E 154
Sosnovka, Russ. 56°11′ N, 47°11′ E 154
Sosnovo, Russ. 60°33′ N, 30°15′ E 166
Sosnovyy Bor, Russ. 59°54′ N, 29°7′ E 166
Sosnowica, Pol. 51°30′ N, 23°4′ E 152
Soso, Miss., U.S. 31°45′ N, 89°16′ W 103
Sospel, Fr. 43°52′ N, 7°26′ E 150
Sospirolo, It. 46°7′ N, 12°3′ E 167
Sosso, Cen. Af. Rep. 3°58′ N, 15°32′ E 218
Sos'va, Russ. 59°12′ N, 61°45′ E 154
Sos'va, Russ. 63°42′ N, 61°56′ E 169
Sotataival, Fin. 67°44′ N, 28°52′ E 152
Soteir, spring, Sudan 17°3′ N, 30°27′ E 182
Sotério, river, Braz. 11°36′ S, 64°36′ W 137
Sotik, Kenya 0°41′ N, 35°4′ E 224
Sotkamo, Fin. 64°7′ N, 28°22′ E 152
Soto la Marina, Mex. 23°44′ N, 98°12′ W 114
Sotsgorodok, Russ. 50°8′ N, 38°4′ E 158
Sottunga 60°6′ N, 20°40′ E 166
Sotuélamos, Sp. 39°2′ N, 2°35′ W 164
Sotuf, Adrar, Africa 21°9′ N, 15°55′ W 222
Souanké, Congo 2°2′ N, 14°2′ E 218
Soubré, Côte d'Ivoire 5°46′ N, 6°37′ W 222
Soudan, Minn., U.S. 47°48′ N, 92°14′ W 94
Souffay, Congo 2°4′ N, 14°54′ E 218
Souilly, Fr. 49°1′ N, 5°17′ E 163
Souk Ahras, Alg. 36°17′ N, 7°58′ E 156
Souk el Arba du Rharb, Mor. 34°42′ N, 6°2′ W 214
Soulac-sur-Mer, Fr. 45°30′ N, 1°9′ W 150
Soultz-sous-Forêts, Fr. 48°56′ N, 7°52′ E 163
Soumoulou, Fr. 43°15′ N, 0°11′ E 164
Sounding Lake, Can. 52°10′ N, 110°55′ W 108
Soúnion, ruin(s), Gr. 37°38′ N, 23°55′ E 156
Sountel, spring, Niger 16°50′ N, 11°37′ E 222
Souppes, Fr. 48°10′ N, 2°43′ E 163
Sour, Alg. 35°59′ N, 0°19′ E 164
Sour Lake, Tex., U.S. 30°7′ N, 94°25′ W 103
Soûr (Tyre), Leb. 33°16′ N, 35°12′ E 194
Soure, Braz. 0°42′ N, 48°31′ W 130
Soure, Port. 40°3′ N, 8°38′ W 150
Souris, Can. 46°21′ N, 62°15′ W 111
Souris, Can. 49°38′ N, 100°15′ W 90
Souris, river, Can.-U.S. 49°11′ N, 101°9′ W 80
Sous, Oued, river, Mor. 30°2′ N, 9°37′ W 142
Sousa, Braz. 6°48′ S, 38°9′ W 132
Sousse, Tun. 35°49′ N, 10°35′ E 156
South Africa 29°13′ S, 23°21′ E 227
South America 37°0′ S, 58°0′ W 123
South Andaman, island, India 12°10′ N, 91°34′ E 188
South Atlantic Ocean 66°37′ S, 30°53′ W 253
South Aulatsivik Island, Can. 56°52′ N, 64°48′ W 106
South Australia, adm. division, Austral. 29°25′ S, 133°4′ E 231
South Australian Basin, Great Australian Bight 37°26′ S, 128°11′ E 254
South Baldy, peak, N. Mex., U.S. 33°58′ N, 107°16′ W 92
South Baldy, peak, Wash., U.S. 48°24′ N, 117°13′ W 90
South Barre, Mass., U.S. 42°22′ N, 72°6′ W 104
South Barre, Vt., U.S. 44°10′ N, 72°31′ W 104
South Barrule, peak 54°8′ N, 4°47′ W 150
South Bay, Fla., U.S. 26°39′ N, 80°43′ W 105
South Baymouth, Can. 45°34′ N, 81°60′ W 94
South Beloit, Ill., U.S. 42°28′ N, 89°3′ W 102
South Bend, Ind., U.S. 41°39′ N, 86°15′ W 102
South Bend, Wash., U.S. 46°38′ N, 123°47′ W 100
South Bentinck Arm 52°4′ N, 127°5′ W 108
South Berwick, Me., U.S. 43°13′ N, 70°49′ W 104
South Bimini, island, Bahamas 25°39′ N, 79°34′ W 105
South Bruny Island, island, Austral. 43°8′ S, 145°12′ E 230
South Burlington, Vt., U.S. 44°27′ N, 73°10′ W 104
South Carolina, adm. division, S.C., U.S. 34°13′ N, 81°30′ W 96
South Cat Cay, island, Bahamas 25°30′ N, 79°34′ W 105
South Chatham, N.H., U.S. 44°6′ N, 71°1′ W 104
South China Sea 9°35′ N, 110°49′ E 192
South Cle Elum, Wash., U.S. 47°9′ N, 120°58′ W 100
South Dakota, adm. division, S. Dak., U.S. 44°43′ N, 101°5′ W 90
South Daytona, Fla., U.S. 29°10′ N, 81°1′ W 105
South Deerfield, Mass., U.S. 42°28′ N, 72°37′ W 104
South Dorset, Vt., U.S. 43°13′ N, 73°5′ W 104
South Dos Palos, Calif., U.S. 36°57′ N, 120°40′ W 101
South Downs, region, U.K. 50°55′ N, 1°10′ W 162
South Egremont, Mass., U.S. 42°9′ N, 73°25′ W 104
South Elgin, Ill., U.S. 41°59′ N, 88°19′ W 102
South Fiji Basin, South Pacific Ocean 27°11′ S, 176°32′ E 252
South Fork Kern, river, Calif., U.S. 36°17′ N, 118°16′ W 101
South Fork Moreau, river, S. Dak., U.S. 45°6′ N, 104°14′ W 90
South Fork Mountain, Calif., U.S. 40°32′ N, 123°50′ W 90
South Fulton, Tenn., U.S. 36°28′ N, 88°52′ W 96
South Georgia, island, U.K. 54°19′ S, 39°36′ W 134
South Govç, adm. division, Mongolia 43°16′ N, 104°29′ E 198
South Hadley, Mass., U.S. 42°15′ N, 72°35′ W 104
South Hamilton, Mass., U.S. 42°36′ N, 70°53′ W 104
South Hangay, adm. division, Mongolia 45°20′ N, 102°36′ E 198
South Haven, Mich., U.S. 42°23′ N, 86°16′ W 102
South Head, Can. 49°4′ N, 59°4′ W 111
South Henik Lake, lake, Can. 61°26′ N, 99°59′ W 106
South Horr, Kenya 2°12′ N, 36°53′ E 224
South Indian Basin, Indian Ocean 59°4′ S, 115°12′ E 255
South Indian Lake, Can. 56°46′ N, 98°54′ W 108
South Island National Park, Kenya 2°31′ N, 36°32′ E 224
South Jacksonville, Mo., U.S. 39°41′ N, 90°15′ W 94
South Knife Lake, lake, Can. 58°11′ N, 97°8′ W 108
South Korea 35°16′ N, 126°48′ E 238
South Lee, Mass., U.S. 42°16′ N, 73°18′ W 104
South Loup, river, Nebr., U.S. 41°19′ N, 100°42′ W 80
South Luangwa National Park, Zambia 13°7′ S, 31°5′ E 224
South Male Atoll, Maldives 3°43′ N, 72°38′ E 188
South Mansfield, La., U.S. 31°59′ N, 93°44′ W 103
South Milwaukee, Wis., U.S. 42°54′ N, 87°53′ W 102
South Molton, U.K. 51°1′ N, 3°50′ W 162
South Mountain, peak, Idaho, U.S. 42°44′ N, 116°60′ W 90
South Nahanni, river, Can. 61°12′ N, 124°28′ W 246
South Negril Point, Jam. 18°15′ N, 79°22′ W 115
South Orkney Islands, Scotia Sea 60°22′ S, 46°55′ W 134
South Orleans, Mass., U.S. 41°44′ N, 69°60′ W 104
South Ossetia 42°27′ N, 43°41′ E 195
South Ossetia, special sovereignty, Asia 42°13′ N, 43°45′ E 195
South Pacific Ocean 31°20′ S, 86°12′ W 252
South Paris, Me., U.S. 44°13′ N, 70°32′ W 104
South Pass, Wyo., U.S. 42°21′ N, 108°55′ W 90
South Point, Can. 46°43′ N, 60°17′ W 111
South Point, Mich., U.S. 44°42′ N, 83°39′ W 94
South Point see Kalae, Hawai'i, U.S. 18°40′ N, 155°43′ W 99
South Porcupine, Can. 48°27′ N, 81°10′ W 106
South Portland, Me., U.S. 43°38′ N, 70°15′ W 104
South River, Can. 45°50′ N, 79°22′ W 82
South Royalton, Vt., U.S. 43°48′ N, 72°32′ W 104
South Ryegate, Vt., U.S. 44°11′ N, 72°9′ W 104
South Saskatchewan, river, Can. 50°21′ N, 110°52′ W 106
South Seal, river, Can. 57°49′ N, 99°40′ W 108
South Shaftsbury, Vt., U.S. 42°56′ N, 73°14′ W 104
South Shetland Islands, Drake Passage 62°7′ S, 56°55′ W 134
South Shore, Ky., U.S. 38°42′ N, 82°58′ W 102
South Shoshone Peak, Nev., U.S. 39°3′ N, 117°39′ W 90
South Sioux City, Nebr., U.S. 42°26′ N, 96°25′ W 90
South Superior, Wyo., U.S. 41°44′ N, 108°57′ W 92
South Tamworth, N.H., U.S. 43°49′ N, 71°18′ W 104
South Tasman Rise, South Pacific Ocean 47°59′ S, 148°46′ E 252
South Wabasca Lake, Can. 55°53′ N, 114°29′ W 108
South Weare, N.H., U.S. 43°3′ N, 71°43′ W 104
South Wellesley Islands, Austral. 17°51′ S, 139°47′ E 230
South Wellfleet, Mass., U.S. 41°55′ N, 69°60′ W 104
South Wellington, Can. 49°5′ N, 123°53′ W 100
South West Island, Austral. 16°26′ S, 135°45′ E 230
South Weymouth Naval Air Station, Mass., U.S. 42°8′ N, 70°58′ W 104
South Whitley, Ind., U.S. 41°4′ N, 85°38′ W 102
South Windham, Conn., U.S. 41°40′ N, 72°11′ W 104
South Windsor, Conn., U.S. 41°48′ N, 72°38′ W 104
South Woodbury, Vt., U.S. 44°24′ N, 72°26′ W 104
South Woodstock, Conn., U.S. 41°55′ N, 71°58′ W 104
South Woodstock, Vt., U.S. 43°33′ N, 72°33′ W 104
South Yarmouth, Mass., U.S. 41°39′ N, 70°12′ W 104
South Yolla Bolly Mountains, peak, Calif., U.S. 40°1′ N, 122°57′ W 90
South Zanesville, Ohio, U.S. 39°53′ N, 82°1′ W 102
Southampton, N.Y., U.S. 40°53′ N, 72°24′ W 104
Southampton, U.K. 50°54′ N, 1°25′ W 162
Southampton, Cape, Can. 61°57′ N, 87°52′ W 106
Southampton Island, Can. 65°3′ N, 90°41′ W 106
Southaven, Miss., U.S. 34°57′ N, 90°1′ W 96
Southbank, Can. 53°59′ N, 125°47′ W 108
Southbridge, Mass., U.S. 42°4′ N, 72°3′ W 104
Southbury, Conn., U.S. 41°28′ N, 73°13′ W 104
Southeast Indian Ridge, Indian Ocean 47°18′ S, 98°12′ E 254
Southeast Pacific Basin, South Pacific Ocean 47°50′ S, 90°49′ W 252
Southeast Point 41°5′ N, 71°26′ W 104
Southend, Can. 56°20′ N, 103°17′ W 108
Southend-on-Sea, U.K. 51°32′ N, 0°42′ E 162
Southern Alps, N.Z. 44°16′ S, 168°19′ E 240
Southern Darfur, adm. division, Sudan 10°34′ N, 23°30′ E 224
Southern Indian Lake, Can. 57°40′ N, 100°23′ W 108
Southern Indian Lake, lake, Can. 56°10′ N, 100°54′ W 106
Southern Kordofan, adm. division, Sudan 11°5′ N, 29°45′ E 224
Southern National Park, Sudan 6°25′ N, 27°55′ E 224
Southern Uplands, U.K. 55°19′ N, 4°36′ W 150
Southey, Can. 50°56′ N, 104°31′ W 90
Southfield, Mass., U.S. 42°5′ N, 73°15′ W 104
Southington, Conn., U.S. 41°35′ N, 72°53′ W 104
Southminster, U.K. 51°40′ N, 0°49′ E 162
Southold, N.Y., U.S. 41°4′ N, 72°26′ W 104
Southport, Fla., U.S. 30°17′ N, 85°38′ W 96
Southport, N.Y., U.S. 42°3′ N, 76°50′ W 94
Southport, N.C., U.S. 33°55′ N, 78°2′ W 96
Southport, U.K. 53°38′ N, 3°1′ W 162
Southwell, U.K. 53°4′ N, 0°58′ E 162
Southwest Indian Ridge, Indian Ocean 39°49′ S, 48°6′ E 254
Southwest Pacific Basin, South Pacific Ocean 40°58′ S, 149°1′ W 252
Southwest Point, Bahamas 25°45′ N, 77°12′ W 96
Southwold, U.K. 52°19′ N, 1°40′ E 163
Soutpansberg, peak, S. Af. 23°2′ S, 29°20′ E 227
Souvannakhili, Laos 15°25′ N, 105°48′ E 202
Soveja, Rom. 45°59′ N, 26°39′ E 158
Sovetsk, Russ. 55°4′ N, 21°52′ E 166
Sovetsk, Russ. 57°35′ N, 49°3′ E 154
Sovetskaya Gavan', Russ. 48°54′ N, 140°9′ E 238
Sovetskaya Rechka, Russ. 66°41′ N, 83°37′ E 169
Sovetskiy, Russ. 60°30′ N, 28°41′ E 166
Sovetskiy, Russ. 61°26′ N, 63°15′ E 169
Sovetskoye, Russ. 47°16′ N, 44°28′ E 158
Soy, Belg. 50°16′ N, 5°30′ E 167
Soyala, Russ. 64°13′ N, 43°21′ E 154
Soyana, river, Russ. 65°35′ N, 42°11′ E 154
Soymigora, Russ. 63°9′ N, 31°50′ E 154
Soyo, Angola 6°12′ S, 12°20′ E 218
Soyopa, Mex. 28°45′ N, 109°40′ W 92
Sozh, river, Belarus 52°3′ N, 30°59′ E 158
Sozimskiy, Russ. 59°44′ N, 52°17′ E 154
Sozopol (Apollonia), Bulg. 42°25′ N, 27°42′ E 156
Spa, Belg. 50°30′ N, 5°52′ E 167
Spa, Pol. 51°32′ N, 20°8′ E 152
Spaatz Island, Antarctica 74°21′ S, 75°18′ W 248
Spackenkill, N.Y., U.S. 41°38′ N, 73°56′ W 104
Spain 40°34′ N, 3°17′ W 150
Spalatum see Split, Croatia 43°30′ N, 16°26′ E 168
Spalding, Nebr., U.S. 41°40′ N, 98°22′ W 90
Spalding, U.K. 52°47′ N, 0°9′ E 162
Spanish Fork, Utah, U.S. 40°5′ N, 111°37′ W 90
Spanish Head 53°51′ N, 5°7′ W 150
Spanish Peak, Oreg., U.S. 44°22′ N, 119°51′ W 90
Spanish Peaks, Colo., U.S. 37°9′ N, 104°56′ W 92
Spanish Town, Jam. 17°59′ N, 76°59′ W 115
Spann, Mount, peak, Antarctica 82°4′ S, 42°47′ W 248
Sparkman, Ark., U.S. 33°54′ N, 92°51′ W 96
Sparks, Ga., U.S. 31°9′ N, 83°26′ W 96
Sparks Lake, lake, Can. 61°11′ N, 110°10′ W 108
Sparland, Ill., U.S. 41°0′ N, 89°28′ W 102
Sparta, Can. 42°41′ N, 81°5′ W 102
Sparta, Ga., U.S. 33°16′ N, 82°58′ W 96
Sparta, Mo., U.S. 38°6′ N, 89°42′ W 94
Sparta, Tenn., U.S. 35°55′ N, 85°28′ W 96
Sparta, Wis., U.S. 43°57′ N, 90°49′ W 94
Spartanburg, S.C., U.S. 34°57′ N, 81°56′ W 96
Spartel, Cap, Mor. 35°50′ N, 7°13′ W 214
Spartivento, Capo, It. 37°51′ N, 16°6′ E 156
Spartivento, Capo, It. 38°47′ N, 8°52′ E 156

Sparwood, Can. 49°44′ N, 114°53′ W 90
Spas Demensk, Russ. 54°28′ N, 34°3′ E 154
Spas Klepiki, Russ. 55°9′ N, 40°11′ E 154
Spasporub, Russ. 60°39′ N, 48°57′ E 154
Spassk, Russ. 52°47′ N, 87°48′ E 184
Spassk Dal'niy, Russ. 44°38′ N, 132°48′ E 160
Spatsizi, river, Can. 57°14′ N, 128°35′ W 108
Spearfish, S. Dak., U.S. 44°28′ N, 103°53′ W 82
Spearman, Tex., U.S. 36°10′ N, 101°12′ W 92
Spearsville, La., U.S. 32°54′ N, 92°36′ W 103
Specter Range, Nev., U.S. 36°41′ N, 116°17′ W 101
Speedway, Ind., U.S. 39°47′ N, 86°14′ W 102
Speedwell Island, Speedwell Island 52°55′ S, 59°49′ W 248
Speicher, Ger. 49°56′ N, 6°39′ E 167
Speightstown, Barbados 13°12′ N, 59°37′ W 116
Spencer, Idaho, U.S. 44°20′ N, 112°10′ W 90
Spencer, Ind., U.S. 39°17′ N, 86°47′ W 102
Spencer, Iowa, U.S. 43°8′ N, 95°9′ W 90
Spencer, Nebr., U.S. 42°51′ N, 98°43′ W 90
Spencer, W. Va., U.S. 38°48′ N, 81°23′ W 94
Spencer, Cape, Austral. 35°9′ S, 136°35′ E 231
Spencer Gulf 34°27′ S, 135°22′ E 230
Spencerville, Ohio, U.S. 40°41′ N, 84°21′ W 102
Spences Bridge, Can. 50°24′ N, 121°21′ W 108
Spennymoor, U.K. 54°42′ N, 1°37′ W 162
Sperlonga, It. 41°16′ N, 13°26′ E 156
Sperone, Capo, It. 38°54′ N, 7°43′ E 156
Sperrin Mountains, U.K. 54°46′ N, 7°48′ W 150
Spessart, Ger. 50°7′ N, 9°7′ E 167
Spezand, Pak. 29°58′ N, 66°59′ E 186
Spicer Islands, islands, Can. 67°44′ N, 80°35′ W 106
Spickard, Mount, peak, Wash., U.S. 48°57′ N, 121°17′ W 100
Spieden, Cape 66°10′ S, 129°48′ E 248
Spiess Seamount, South Atlantic Ocean 55°29′ S, 1°19′ W 255
Spiez, Switz. 46°41′ N, 7°40′ E 167
Spike Mountain, peak, Alas., U.S. 67°26′ N, 142°2′ W 98
Spilsby, U.K. 53°10′ N, 9°535′ E 162
Spin Buldak, Afghan. 31°1′ N, 66°27′ E 186
Spincourt, Fr. 49°19′ N, 5°39′ E 163
Spind, Nor. 58°5′ N, 6°54′ E 150
Špionica, Bosn. and Herzg. 44°45′ N, 18°31′ E 168
Spirit Lake, Iowa, U.S. 43°24′ N, 95°7′ W 90
Spirit Lake, Wash., U.S. 46°15′ N, 122°19′ W 100
Spirit River, Can. 55°46′ N, 118°50′ W 108
Spiritwood, Can. 53°21′ N, 107°28′ W 108
Spiro, Okla., U.S. 35°12′ N, 94°38′ W 96
Spirovo, Russ. 57°24′ N, 35°0′ E 154
Spišská Nová Ves, Slovakia 48°56′ N, 20°33′ E 152
Spitsbergen Fracture Zone, Greenland Sea 81°13′ N, 3°8′ W 255
Spitsbergen, island, Nor. 77°10′ N, 3°50′ E 160
Spittal, Aust. 46°48′ N, 13°29′ E 167
Splendora, Tex., U.S. 30°12′ N, 95°10′ W 103
Split, Cape, Can. 45°20′ N, 64°27′ W 111
Split Lake, Can. 56°14′ N, 96°11′ W 108
Split Peak, Nev., U.S. 41°48′ N, 118°31′ W 90
Split (Spalatum), Croatia 43°30′ N, 16°26′ E 168
Splügen, Switz. 46°33′ N, 9°17′ E 167
Splügen Pass, Switz. 46°31′ N, 9°19′ E 167
Spogi, Latv. 56°3′ N, 26°43′ E 166
Spokane, Wash., U.S. 47°40′ N, 117°27′ W 90
Spokane, Mount, peak, Wash., U.S. 47°53′ N, 117°12′ W 90
Spokane, river, Wash., U.S. 47°57′ N, 118°41′ W 80
Spooner, Wis., U.S. 45°49′ N, 91°54′ W 94
Sporyy Navolok, Mys, Russ. 75°20′ N, 44°26′ E 172
Spotted Range, Nev., U.S. 36°45′ N, 115°53′ W 101
Sprague, Can. 49°1′ N, 95°36′ W 90
Sprague, Wash., U.S. 47°16′ N, 117°59′ W 90
Spranger, Mount, peak, Can. 52°53′ N, 120°50′ W 108
Spratly Islands, South China Sea 11°51′ N, 112°52′ E 238
Spray, Oreg., U.S. 44°49′ N, 119°48′ W 90
Spremberg, Ger. 51°34′ N, 14°21′ E 152
Spring, Tex., U.S. 30°3′ N, 95°25′ W 103
Spring Butte, peak, Oreg., U.S. 43°30′ N, 121°26′ W 90
Spring Glen, Utah, U.S. 39°39′ N, 110°51′ W 92
Spring Green, Wis., U.S. 43°10′ N, 90°4′ W 102
Spring Grove, Minn., U.S. 43°33′ N, 91°39′ W 94
Spring Hill, Fla., U.S. 28°26′ N, 82°36′ W 105
Spring Lake, Mich., U.S. 43°3′ N, 86°10′ W 94
Spring Mountains, Nev., U.S. 36°22′ N, 115°51′ W 101
Spring Point, Can. 59°24′ N, 109°46′ W 108
Spring Valley, N.Y., U.S. 41°6′ N, 74°3′ W 104
Springbok, S. Af. 29°41′ S, 17°52′ E 227
Springdale, Ark., U.S. 36°10′ N, 94°9′ W 96
Springdale, Can. 49°30′ N, 56°6′ W 111
Springdale, Ohio, U.S. 39°16′ N, 84°29′ W 102
Springer, N. Mex., U.S. 36°21′ N, 104°36′ W 92
Springer Mountain, peak, Ga., U.S. 34°37′ N, 84°17′ W 96
Springfield, Colo., U.S. 37°23′ N, 102°37′ W 92
Springfield, Fla., U.S. 30°8′ N, 85°36′ W 96
Springfield, Idaho, U.S. 43°5′ N, 112°41′ W 90
Springfield, Ill., U.S. 39°47′ N, 89°41′ W 102
Springfield, La., U.S. 30°24′ N, 90°33′ W 103
Springfield, Mass., U.S. 42°6′ N, 72°36′ W 104
Springfield, Minn., U.S. 44°13′ N, 94°60′ W 90
Springfield, Mo., U.S. 37°12′ N, 93°18′ W 96
Springfield, Mo., U.S. 39°46′ N, 89°45′ W 94
Springfield, N.Z. 43°21′ S, 171°55′ E 240
Springfield, Ohio, U.S. 39°54′ N, 83°48′ W 102
Springfield, Oreg., U.S. 44°2′ N, 123°1′ W 90
Springfield, S. Dak., U.S. 42°50′ N, 97°55′ W 90
Springfield, Tenn., U.S. 36°30′ N, 86°52′ W 94
Springfield, Vt., U.S. 43°17′ N, 72°29′ W 104
Springfontein, S. Af. 30°16′ S, 25°42′ E 227
Springhill, Can. 45°38′ N, 64°5′ W 111
Springhill, La., U.S. 32°59′ N, 93°28′ W 103
Springport, Mich., U.S. 42°22′ N, 84°42′ W 102
Springvale, Me., U.S. 43°27′ N, 70°49′ W 104
Springview, Nebr., U.S. 42°48′ N, 99°46′ W 90
Springville, Calif., U.S. 36°8′ N, 118°50′ W 101
Spruce Home, Can. 53°23′ N, 105°46′ W 108
Spruce Knob, peak, W. Va., U.S. 38°41′ N, 79°37′ W 94
Spruce Knob-Seneca Rocks National Recreation Area, W. Va., U.S. 38°49′ N, 87°57′ W 80
Spruce Mountain, peak, Nev., U.S. 40°32′ N, 114°54′ W 90
Spruce Pine, N.C., U.S. 35°55′ N, 82°5′ W 96
Spry, Pa., U.S. 39°54′ N, 76°41′ W 94
Spulico, Capo, It. 39°57′ N, 16°40′ E 156
Spur, Tex., U.S. 33°27′ N, 100°51′ W 92
Spurger, Tex., U.S. 30°40′ N, 94°11′ W 103
Spurn Head, U.K. 53°30′ N, 0°7′ E 162
Spuž, Europe 42°31′ N, 19°13′ E 168
Spuzzum, Can. 49°41′ N, 121°26′ W 100
Squamish, Can. 49°42′ N, 123°8′ W 100
Squamish, river, Can. 50°7′ N, 123°20′ W 100
Square Islands, Can. 52°43′ N, 55°51′ W 111
Squires, Mount, peak, Austral. 26°15′ S, 127°12′ E 230
Squirrel, river, Can. 50°25′ N, 84°20′ W 110
Srbac, Bosn. and Herzg. 45°5′ N, 17°31′ E 168
Srbica, Europe 42°44′ N, 20°46′ E 168
Srbobran, Serb. and Mont. 45°33′ N, 19°47′ E 168
Sre Umbell, Cambodia 11°6′ N, 103°45′ E 202
Srebrenica, Bosn. and Herzg. 44°6′ N, 19°19′ E 168
Sredinnyy Khrebet, Russ. 57°35′ N, 160°3′ E 160
Srednekolymsk, Russ. 67°27′ N, 153°21′ E 160
Sredneye Bugayevo, Russ. 66°0′ N, 52°28′ E 154
Srednyaya Olekma, Russ. 55°20′ N, 120°33′ E 190
Sremska Mitrovica, Serb. and Mont. 44°58′ N, 19°37′ E 168
Sremska Rača, Serb. and Mont. 44°54′ N, 19°19′ E 168
Sremski Karlovci, Serb. and Mont. 45°11′ N, 19°55′ E 168
Sretensk, Russ. 52°17′ N, 117°45′ E 190
Sri Kalahasti, India 13°46′ N, 79°40′ E 188
Sri Lanka 7°26′ N, 80°15′ E 188
Sri Madhopur, India 27°28′ N, 75°37′ E 197
Srikakulam, India 18°17′ N, 83°55′ E 188
Srinagar, India 34°7′ N, 74°48′ E 186
Srivardhan, India 18°5′ N, 73°0′ E 188
Srnetica, Bosn. and Herzg. 44°26′ N, 16°35′ E 168
Srokowo, Pol. 54°11′ N, 21°31′ E 166
Srpska Crnja, Serb. and Mont. 45°43′ N, 20°42′ E 168
Srpski Itebej, Serb. and Mont. 45°34′ N, 20°43′ E 168
Ssanggyo, N. Korea 37°46′ N, 125°26′ E 200
Staaten River National Park, Austral. 16°39′ S, 142°26′ E 238
Staberhuk, Kattegat 54°18′ N, 10°48′ E 152
Stack, Ben, peak, U.K. 58°19′ N, 5°5′ W 150
Stade, Ger. 53°36′ N, 9°28′ E 150
Städjan, peak, Nor. 61°54′ N, 12°44′ E 152
Stadskanaal, Neth. 52°59′ N, 6°57′ E 163
Stadtallendorf, Ger. 50°49′ N, 9°0′ E 167
Stadtkyll, Ger. 50°20′ N, 6°32′ E 167
Stadtlohn, Ger. 51°59′ N, 6°54′ E 167
Stafford, Kans., U.S. 37°56′ N, 98°36′ W 90
Stafford, U.K. 52°47′ N, 2°7′ W 162
Stafford Springs, Conn., U.S. 41°57′ N, 72°19′ W 104
Staffordsville, Ky., U.S. 37°49′ N, 82°51′ W 94
Stage Road Pass, Oreg., U.S. 42°43′ N, 123°22′ W 90
Stagira, ruin(s), Gr. 40°31′ N, 23°38′ E 156
Stagnone, Isole dello, islands, Mediterranean Sea 37°35′ N, 11°52′ E 156
Staicele, Latv. 57°51′ N, 24°44′ E 166
Staigue Fort, site, Ire. 51°47′ N, 10°7′ W 150
Staines, U.K. 51°26′ N, 0°31′ E 162
Staithes, U.K. 54°33′ N, 0°48′ E 162
Stalać, Serb. and Mont. 43°41′ N, 21°25′ E 168
Staldzene, Latv. 57°25′ N, 21°35′ E 166
Stalham, U.K. 52°46′ N, 1°31′ E 163
Stalingrad see Volgograd, Russ. 48°46′ N, 44°28′ E 158
Stallo, Miss., U.S. 32°53′ N, 89°6′ W 103
Stallworthy, Cape, Can. 81°41′ N, 95°15′ W 246
Stalowa Wola, Pol. 50°33′ N, 22°2′ E 152
Stamford, Conn., U.S. 41°2′ N, 73°33′ W 104
Stamford, N.Y., U.S. 42°24′ N, 74°39′ W 110
Stamford, Tex., U.S. 32°55′ N, 99°49′ W 92
Stamford, U.K. 52°39′ N, 0°29′ E 162
Stamford Bridge, U.K. 53°59′ N, 0°55′ E 162
Stamovo, Bulg. 42°26′ N, 25°50′ E 156
Stampriet, Namibia 24°18′ S, 18°23′ E 227
Stamps, Ark., U.S. 33°21′ N, 93°31′ W 103
Stanberry, Mo., U.S. 40°12′ N, 94°32′ W 94
Standerton, S. Af. 26°57′ S, 29°13′ E 227
Standish, Me., U.S. 43°43′ N, 70°33′ W 104
Standish, Mich., U.S. 43°58′ N, 83°58′ W 102
Standish Ranges, Austral. 21°44′ S, 138°59′ E 230
Stanfield, Oreg., U.S. 45°46′ N, 119°14′ W 90
Stanford, Ky., U.S. 37°31′ N, 84°40′ W 94
Stanford, Mont., U.S. 47°7′ N, 110°14′ W 90
Stånga, Sw. 57°16′ N, 18°27′ E 166
Stanger, S. Af. 29°21′ S, 31°15′ E 227
Staniard Creek, Bahamas 24°50′ N, 77°55′ W 96
Stanišić, Serb. and Mont. 45°55′ N, 19°9′ E 168
Staňkov, Czech Rep. 49°33′ N, 13°4′ E 152
Stanley, Can. 46°16′ N, 66°45′ W 111
Stanley, Falk. Is., U.K. 51°42′ S, 57°52′ W 134
Stanley, Idaho, U.S. 44°12′ N, 114°56′ W 90
Stanley, N. Dak., U.S. 48°17′ N, 102°24′ W 90
Stanley, Wis., U.S. 44°57′ N, 90°56′ W 94
Stanley Falls see Boyoma Falls, Dem. Rep. of the Congo 0°14′ N, 25°9′ E 224
Stanley Mission, Can. 55°25′ N, 104°30′ W 108
Stanley, Mount, peak, Austral. 22°50′ S, 130°28′ E 230
Stanley, Mount, peak, Austral. 40°6′ S, 143°46′ E 230
Stanley Peak, Can. 51°11′ N, 116°6′ W 90
Stanleyville see Kisangani, Dem. Rep. of the Congo 0°33′ N, 25°16′ E 224
Stanovoy Khrebet, Russ. 54°46′ N, 122°14′ E 190
Stanton, Mich., U.S. 43°17′ N, 85°5′ W 102
Stanton, Tex., U.S. 32°7′ N, 101°47′ W 92
Stanwick, U.K. 52°20′ N, 0°33′ E 162
Stanwood, Wash., U.S. 48°13′ N, 122°23′ W 100
Staphorst, Neth. 52°39′ N, 6°12′ E 163
Staples, Minn., U.S. 46°20′ N, 94°48′ W 90
Stapleton, Nebr., U.S. 41°28′ N, 100°31′ W 90
Star, Miss., U.S. 32°5′ N, 90°2′ W 103
Star City, Ark., U.S. 33°56′ N, 91°51′ W 96
Star City, Ind., U.S. 40°58′ N, 86°34′ W 102
Star Peak, Nev., U.S. 40°31′ N, 118°16′ W 90
Star Valley, Wyo., U.S. 42°38′ N, 111°3′ W 90
Stara Moravica, Serb. and Mont. 45°52′ N, 19°28′ E 168
Stara Pazova, Serb. and Mont. 44°58′ N, 20°9′ E 168
Stara Ushytsya, Ukr. 48°34′ N, 27°5′ E 152
Stara Vyzhivka, Ukr. 51°25′ N, 24°25′ E 152
Stara Zagora, Bulg. 42°25′ N, 25°36′ E 156
Stara Zagora, adm. division, Bulg. 42°39′ N, 25°6′ E 156
Staraya, Russ. 70°56′ N, 112°20′ E 173
Staraya Poltavka, Russ. 50°28′ N, 46°26′ E 158
Staraya Russa, Russ. 57°56′ N, 31°23′ E 152
Starbuck, Wash., U.S. 46°30′ N, 118°8′ W 90
Stare Pole, Pol. 54°3′ N, 19°11′ E 166
Stargard Szczeciński, Pol. 53°19′ N, 15°1′ E 152
Stari Bar, Europe 42°6′ N, 19°8′ E 168
Stari Mikanovci, Croatia 45°15′ N, 18°33′ E 168
Starigrad, Croatia 43°10′ N, 16°35′ E 168
Staritsa, Belarus 53°14′ N, 27°15′ E 154
Staritsa, Russ. 56°28′ N, 34°56′ E 154
Starke, Fla., U.S. 29°56′ N, 82°8′ W 96
Starks, La., U.S. 30°17′ N, 93°40′ W 103
Starksboro, Vt., U.S. 44°13′ N, 73°4′ W 104
Starkville, Colo., U.S. 37°7′ N, 104°33′ W 92
Starkville, Miss., U.S. 33°26′ N, 88°48′ W 103
Starobaltachevo, Russ. 56°1′ N, 55°56′ E 154
Starobil's'k, Ukr. 49°18′ N, 38°53′ E 158
Starobin, Belarus 52°42′ N, 27°27′ E 152
Starodub, Russ. 52°31′ N, 32°51′ E 154
Starokostyantyniv, Ukr. 49°44′ N, 27°12′ E 152
Starominskaya, Russ. 46°32′ N, 39°1′ E 156
Staropol'ye, Russ. 59°1′ N, 28°34′ E 166
Starorybnoye, Russ. 72°48′ N, 104°49′ E 173
Staroshcherbinovskaya, Russ. 46°37′ N, 38°38′ E 156
Staroye Syalo, Belarus 55°17′ N, 29°58′ E 166
Start Point, English Channel 50°2′ N, 3°37′ W 150
Starvyy Karabutak, Kaz. 49°49′ N, 59°54′ E 158
Staryy Biryuzyak, Russ. 44°45′ N, 46°47′ E 158
Staryy Krym, Ukr. 45°1′ N, 35°0′ E 156
Staryy Kryvyn, Ukr. 50°21′ N, 26°42′ E 152
Staryy Nadym, Russ. 65°36′ N, 72°50′ E 169
Staryy Oskol, Russ. 51°17′ N, 37°45′ E 158
Staryy Sambir, Ukr. 49°23′ N, 22°55′ E 152
Staszów, Pol. 50°33′ N, 21°10′ E 152
State Line, Miss., U.S. 31°24′ N, 88°28′ W 103
Staten Island, N.Y., U.S. 40°27′ N, 74°6′ W 104
Staten Island see de los Estados, Isla, Arg. 55°28′ S, 64°48′ W 134
Statesboro, Ga., U.S. 32°25′ N, 81°47′ W 112
Station 10, Sudan 19°41′ N, 33°8′ E 182
Station 5, Sudan 21°2′ N, 32°19′ E 182
Station 6, Sudan 20°44′ N, 32°30′ E 182
Staunton, Ill., U.S. 39°0′ N, 89°47′ W 102
Staunton, Va., U.S. 38°8′ N, 79°5′ W 94
Stavanger, Nor. 58°56′ N, 5°43′ E 152
Stave Lake, Can. 49°18′ N, 122°30′ W 100
Stavelot, Belg. 50°23′ N, 5°56′ E 167
Stavely, Can. 50°10′ N, 113°39′ W 90
Staveren, Neth. 52°53′ N, 5°22′ E 163
Stavnoye, Ukr. 48°56′ N, 22°42′ E 156
Stavropol', Russ. 45°3′ N, 41°58′ E 158
Stavropol', adm. division, Russ. 45°26′ N, 41°12′ E 160
Stawiski, Pol. 53°22′ N, 22°8′ E 154
Stayner, Can. 44°24′ N, 80°6′ W 110
Steamboat, Can. 58°40′ N, 123°45′ W 108
Steamboat Mountain, peak, Wyo., U.S. 41°57′ N, 109°2′ W 90
Stederdorf, Ger. 52°21′ N, 10°13′ E 150
Steele, N. Dak., U.S. 46°50′ N, 99°56′ W 108
Steele Island, island, Antarctica 71°8′ S, 60°19′ W 248
Steelpoort, S. Af. 24°46′ S, 30°11′ E 227
Steelton, Pa., U.S. 40°13′ N, 76°51′ W 94
Steelville, Mo., U.S. 37°57′ N, 91°21′ W 96
Steen River, Can. 59°39′ N, 117°11′ W 108
Steen, river, Can. 59°17′ N, 118°21′ W 108
Steens Mountain, Oreg., U.S. 43°21′ N, 118°14′ W 90
Steensby Inlet 69°57′ N, 81°26′ W 106
Steenstrup Gletscher, glacier 74°42′ N, 64°7′ W 106
Steenwijk, Neth. 52°46′ N, 6°6′ E 163
Steep Rock, Can. 51°26′ N, 98°48′ W 90
Steep Rock Lake, Can. 48°49′ N, 91°38′ W 94
Steers Head 81°45′ S, 164°32′ W 248
Stefansson Island, island, Can. 73°43′ N, 112°11′ W 106
Stege, Den. 54°59′ N, 12°17′ E 152
Steger, Ill., U.S. 41°27′ N, 87°38′ W 102
Steigen, Nor. 67°55′ N, 14°58′ E 152
Steigerwald, Ger. 49°45′ N, 10°17′ E 167
Stein Pass, Ger. 47°39′ N, 12°45′ E 152
Stein, river, Can. 50°10′ N, 122°21′ W 90
Steinau, Ger. 50°18′ N, 9°27′ E 167
Steinbach, Can. 49°31′ N, 96°42′ W 90
Steinfeld, Ger. 52°36′ N, 8°13′ E 163
Steinfort, Lux. 49°39′ N, 5°55′ E 163
Steinfurt, Ger. 52°8′ N, 7°19′ E 163
Steinhatchee, Fla., U.S. 29°40′ N, 83°24′ W 105
Steinhausen, Namibia 21°49′ S, 18°15′ E 227
Steinkjer, Nor. 63°57′ N, 11°44′ E 160
Steinkopf, S. Af. 29°15′ S, 17°42′ E 227
Stellaland, region, S. Af. 27°19′ S, 24°2′ E 227
Stelle, Ger. 53°22′ N, 10°6′ E 152
Stellenbosch, S. Af. 33°55′ S, 18°48′ E 227
Stelvio, Passo dello, It. 46°31′ N, 10°26′ E 167
Stenay, Fr. 49°29′ N, 5°11′ E 163
Stende, Latv. 57°8′ N, 22°32′ E 166
Stenstorp, Nor. 58°15′ N, 13°41′ E 152
Stenträsk, Nor. 66°19′ N, 19°50′ E 152
Stepanakert (Xankändi), Asia 39°48′ N, 46°43′ E 195
Step'anavan, Arm. 41°0′ N, 44°21′ E 195
Stepanci, Maced. 41°29′ N, 21°38′ E 168
Stephen, Minn., U.S. 48°26′ N, 96°53′ W 94
Stephens, Ark., U.S. 33°23′ N, 93°5′ W 103
Stephens Lake, lake, Can. 56°42′ N, 94°17′ W 108
Stephens Passage 57°46′ N, 134°48′ W 108
Stephens, Port 32°50′ S, 150°48′ E 230
Stephenson, Mich., U.S. 45°24′ N, 87°36′ W 94
Stephenson, Mount, peak, Antarctica 69°49′ S, 70°21′ W 248
Stephenville, Can. 48°31′ N, 58°39′ W 106
Stephenville, Tex., U.S. 32°13′ N, 98°13′ W 92
Stepnogorsk, Kaz. 52°23′ N, 71°54′ E 184
Stepnoye, Russ. 44°15′ N, 44°32′ E 158
Stepnyak, Kaz. 52°49′ N, 70°47′ E 184
Stepojevac, Serb. and Mont. 44°30′ N, 20°18′ E 168
Steptoe Butte, peak, Wash., U.S. 46°59′ N, 117°24′ W 900
Stereá Eláda, adm. division, Gr. 38°54′ N, 22°26′ E 156
Sterling, Colo., U.S. 40°37′ N, 103°14′ W 90
Sterling, Ill., U.S. 41°47′ N, 89°42′ W 102
Sterling, Kans., U.S. 38°12′ N, 98°13′ W 90
Sterling, Mich., U.S. 44°1′ N, 84°2′ W 102
Sterling, Mo., U.S. 41°47′ N, 89°42′ W 94
Sterling, N. Dak., U.S. 46°48′ N, 100°18′ W 90
Sterling City, Tex., U.S. 31°49′ N, 100°60′ W 92
Sterlington, La., U.S. 32°40′ N, 92°5′ W 103
Sterlitamak, Russ. 53°39′ N, 55°53′ E 154
Stettler, Can. 52°19′ N, 112°42′ W 108
Stevenage, U.K. 51°54′ N, 0°13′ E 162
Stevens Point, Wis., U.S. 44°31′ N, 89°35′ W 94
Stevenson, Wash., U.S. 45°41′ N, 121°54′ W 100
Stevenson Lake, lake, Can. 53°54′ N, 96°43′ W 108
Stevenson Mountain, peak, Oreg., U.S. 44°33′ N, 120°32′ W 90
Stevensville, Mich., U.S. 42°0′ N, 86°30′ W 102
Stewardson, Ill., U.S. 39°15′ N, 88°39′ W 102
Stewart, Can. 55°56′ N, 130°1′ W 108
Stewart, Miss., U.S. 33°25′ N, 89°26′ W 103
Stewart, Ohio, U.S. 39°18′ N, 81°54′ W 102
Stewart Crossing, Can. 63°27′ N, 136°41′ W 98
Stewart, Isla, island, Chile 54°51′ S, 72°56′ W 134
Stewart Islands, South Pacific Ocean 7°60′ S, 163°3′ E 238
Stewart River, Can. 63°21′ N, 139°26′ W 98
Steynsburg, S. Af. 31°18′ S, 25°47′ E 227
Steyr, Aust. 48°2′ N, 14°24′ E 152
Steytlerville, S. Af. 33°20′ S, 24°18′ E 227
Stia, It. 43°48′ N, 11°41′ E 167
Stickney, S. Dak., U.S. 43°34′ N, 98°26′ W 90
Stiene, Latv. 57°23′ N, 24°33′ E 166
Stiens, Neth. 53°15′ N, 5°44′ E 163
Stigler, Okla., U.S. 35°13′ N, 95°9′ W 96
Stih, Hora, peak, Ukr. 48°35′ N, 23°12′ E 152
Stikine, river, Can. 57°15′ N, 131°59′ W 108
Stikine, river, Can. 58°11′ N, 130°31′ W 98
Stikine, river, Can. 58°0′ N, 129°22′ W 108
Stillman Valley, Ill., U.S. 42°6′ N, 89°11′ W 102
Stillwater, Can. 49°46′ N, 124°17′ W 100
Stillwater, Minn., U.S. 45°2′ N, 92°50′ W 94
Stillwater, N.Y., U.S. 42°56′ N, 73°40′ W 104
Stillwater, Okla., U.S. 36°5′ N, 97°2′ W 92
Stillwater Range, Nev., U.S. 39°59′ N, 118°14′ W 90
Stilo, Punta, It. 38°27′ N, 16°35′ E 156
Stilton, U.K. 52°29′ N, 0°17′ E 162
Stilwell, Okla., U.S. 35°46′ N, 94°38′ W 96
Štimlje, Europe 42°27′ N, 21°3′ E 168
Stine Mountain, peak, Mont., U.S. 45°41′ N, 113°11′ W 90
Stinear, Mount, peak, Antarctica 73°18′ S, 66°2′ E 248
Stinkingwater Pass, Oreg., U.S. 43°42′ N, 118°32′ W 90
Stinnett, Tex., U.S. 35°47′ N, 101°27′ W 92
Stinson Lake, N.H., U.S. 43°51′ N, 71°50′ W 104
Štip, Maced. 41°44′ N, 22°11′ E 168
Stiring-Wendel, Fr. 49°12′ N, 6°55′ E 163
Stirling Island, Solomon Islands 7°20′ S, 155°30′ E 242
Stirling, Mount, peak, Nev., U.S. 36°26′ N, 116°1′ W 101
Stobi, ruin(s), Maced. 41°31′ N, 21°54′ E 168
Stock Route, Austral. 19°46′ S, 126°40′ E 231
Stockbridge, Mass., U.S. 42°16′ N, 73°20′ W 104
Stockbridge, Mich., U.S. 42°25′ N, 84°11′ W 102
Stockbridge, U.K. 51°6′ N, 1°29′ W 162
Stockbridge, Vt., U.S. 43°47′ N, 72°46′ W 104
Stockdale, Tex., U.S. 29°13′ N, 97°57′ W 96
Stockholm, Sw. 59°19′ N, 17°55′ E 166
Stockport, U.K. 53°23′ N, 2°10′ W 162
Stockton, Ala., U.S. 30°58′ N, 87°51′ W 103
Stockton, Calif., U.S. 37°57′ N, 121°17′ W 100
Stockton, Ill., U.S. 42°20′ N, 90°1′ W 102
Stockton, Kans., U.S. 39°26′ N, 99°17′ W 90
Stockton, Mo., U.S. 37°40′ N, 93°48′ W 94
Stockton on Tees, U.K. 54°34′ N, 1°20′ W 162
Stockwell, Ind., U.S. 40°16′ N, 86°46′ W 102
Stoddard, N.H., U.S. 43°4′ N, 72°8′ W 104
Stöde, Nor. 62°24′ N, 16°33′ E 152
Stogovo, Maced. 41°28′ N, 20°32′ E 168
Stoke, N.Z. 41°21′ S, 173°14′ E 240
Stoke Ferry, U.K. 52°34′ N, 0°31′ E 162
Stoke on Trent, U.K. 53°0′ N, 2°11′ W 162
Stokes, Bahía 54°9′ S, 73°50′ W 134
Stokes, Mount, peak, N.Z. 41°8′ S, 174°2′ E 240
Stokesay, U.K. 52°25′ N, 2°50′ W 162
Stoksund, Nor. 64°2′ N, 10°4′ E 152
Stolac, Bosn. and Herzg. 43°3′ N, 17°57′ E 168
Stolberg, Ger. 50°46′ N, 6°12′ E 167
Stolbovo, Russ. 55°59′ N, 30°1′ E 166
Stolbovoy, Ostrov, island, Russ. 73°52′ N, 128°4′ E 160
Stolin, Belarus 51°53′ N, 26°49′ E 152
Stöllet, Nor. 60°23′ N, 13°16′ E 152
Stolnici, Rom. 44°35′ N, 24°47′ E 156
Stone, U.K. 52°54′ N, 2°8′ W 162
Stone Lake, lake, Can. 50°34′ N, 87°51′ W 110
Stonehenge, site, U.K. 51°9′ N, 1°51′ W 162
Stoner, Can. 53°38′ N, 122°40′ W 108
Stonewall, Can. 50°7′ N, 97°19′ W 108
Stonewall, La., U.S. 32°16′ N, 93°50′ W 103
Stonewall, Miss., U.S. 32°7′ N, 88°46′ W 103
Stonglandet, Nor. 69°5′ N, 17°12′ E 152
Stonington, Ill., U.S. 39°37′ N, 89°12′ W 102
Stony Brook, N.Y., U.S. 40°55′ N, 73°9′ W 104
Stony Creek, N.Y., U.S. 43°25′ N, 73°57′ W 104
Stony Lake, Can. 58°53′ N, 99°17′ W 108
Stony Plain, Can. 53°31′ N, 114°3′ W 108
Stony Point, N.C., U.S. 43°39′ N, 76°34′ W 94
Stony Point, N.Y., U.S. 41°13′ N, 73°60′ W 104
Stony Rapids, Can. 59°10′ N, 105°60′ W 106
Stony River, Alas., U.S. 61°48′ N, 156°33′ W 98
Stooping, river, Can. 51°19′ N, 82°32′ W 110
Støren, Nor. 63°0′ N, 10°18′ E 152
Storfjord, Nor. 69°16′ N, 19°59′ E 152
Storfjorden 77°20′ N, 7°31′ E 172
Storkerson Bay 72°55′ N, 128°56′ W 106
Storlien, Nor. 63°18′ N, 12°7′ E 152
Storm Berg, peak, S. Af. 31°22′ S, 26°27′ E 227
Storm King Mountain, peak, Colo., U.S. 37°55′ N, 106°29′ W 90
Storm Lake, Iowa, U.S. 42°38′ N, 95°13′ W 90
Storozhevsk, Russ. 61°56′ N, 52°20′ E 154
Storr, The, peak 57°29′ N, 6°18′ W 150
Storriten, peak, Nor. 68°6′ N, 17°7′ E 152
Storrs, Conn., U.S. 41°48′ N, 72°16′ W 104
Storsjö, Nor. 62°47′ N, 13°2′ E 152
Storskavlen, peak, Nor. 60°44′ N, 7°10′ E 152
Storuman, Nor. 65°5′ N, 17°6′ E 152
Storvätteshågna, peak, Nor. 62°7′ N, 12°21′ E 152
Storvik, Nor. 60°34′ N, 16°28′ E 152
Story, Wyo., U.S. 44°34′ N, 106°53′ W 90
Story City, Iowa, U.S. 42°11′ N, 93°36′ W 94
Stoughton, Can. 49°40′ N, 103°4′ W 90
Stoughton, Wis., U.S. 42°54′ N, 89°12′ W 102
Stour, river, U.K. 51°58′ N, 0°47′ E 162
Stourbridge, U.K. 52°27′ N, 2°9′ W 162
Stourport on Severn, U.K. 52°20′ N, 2°16′ W 162
Stovepipe Wells, Calif., U.S. 36°36′ N, 117°10′ W 101
Stow, Ohio, U.S. 41°8′ N, 81°26′ W 94
Stow on the Wold, U.K. 51°55′ N, 1°44′ W 162
Stowbtsy, Belarus 53°29′ N, 26°45′ E 154
Stowe, Vt., U.S. 44°27′ N, 72°42′ W 104
Stowell, Tex., U.S. 29°46′ N, 94°24′ W 103
Stowmarket, U.K. 52°11′ N, 0°59′ E 162
Stoyaniv, Ukr. 50°22′ N, 24°39′ E 158
Stradella, It. 45°4′ N, 9°17′ E 167
Strait 69°45′ N, 84°55′ W 106
Straldzha, Bulg. 42°36′ N, 26°41′ E 158
Stralsund, Ger. 54°16′ N, 13°4′ E 160
Strand, S. Af. 34°6′ S, 18°51′ E 227
Strandebarm, Nor. 60°16′ N, 5°59′ E 152
Strasbourg, Can. 51°3′ N, 104°57′ W 90
Strasbourg, Fr. 48°34′ N, 7°44′ E 163
Strasburg, N. Dak., U.S. 46°7′ N, 100°11′ W 90
Strasburg, Ohio, U.S. 40°35′ N, 81°32′ W 102
Strasburg, Va., U.S. 38°59′ N, 78°22′ W 94
Strășeni, Mold. 47°7′ N, 28°38′ E 156
Strata Florida, U.K. 52°16′ N, 3°50′ W 162
Stratford, Calif., U.S. 36°11′ N, 119°50′ W 100
Stratford, Can. 43°21′ N, 80°58′ W 102
Stratford, Conn., U.S. 41°11′ N, 73°9′ W 104
Stratford, Tex., U.S. 36°19′ N, 102°5′ W 92
Stratford upon Avon, U.K. 52°11′ N, 1°44′ W 162
Strathcona, Mount, peak, Antarctica 67°24′ S, 99°40′ E 248
Strathmore, Calif., U.S. 36°9′ N, 119°5′ W 101
Strathmore, Can. 51°2′ N, 113°25′ W 90
Strathmore, U.K. 56°24′ N, 3°37′ W 150
Strathnaver, Can. 53°20′ N, 122°33′ W 108
Strathroy, Can. 42°56′ N, 81°36′ W 102
Stratobowl, S. Dak., U.S. 43°58′ N, 103°25′ W 90
Stratonicea, ruin(s), Gr. 40°30′ N, 23°42′ E 156
Stratton, Colo., U.S. 39°17′ N, 102°36′ W 90
Stratton, Me., U.S. 45°8′ N, 70°27′ W 111
Stratton, Nebr., U.S. 40°8′ N, 101°14′ W 90
Stratus, ruin(s), Gr. 38°40′ N, 21°12′ E 156
Straubing, Ger. 48°52′ N, 12°34′ E 152
Straw Peak, Calif., U.S. 35°37′ N, 117°14′ W 101
Strawberry, Calif., U.S. 38°12′ N, 120°2′ W 100
Strawberry Mountain, peak, Oreg., U.S. 44°18′ N, 118°48′ W 90
Strawn, Ill., U.S. 40°38′ N, 88°24′ W 102
Strawn, Tex., U.S. 32°32′ N, 98°31′ W 92
Strážske, Slovakia 48°51′ N, 21°50′ E 156
Streaky Bay, Austral. 32°51′ S, 134°11′ E 231
Streatfield Lake, lake, Can. 52°7′ N, 86°30′ W 110
Streator, Ill., U.S. 41°7′ N, 88°50′ W 102
Středočeský, adm. division, Czech Rep. 49°52′ N, 13°50′ E 152
Streeter, N. Dak., U.S. 46°38′ N, 99°23′ W 90
Strehaia, Rom. 44°37′ N, 23°12′ E 168
Strekov, Slovakia 47°53′ N, 18°26′ E 168
Strel'na, Russ. 66°5′ N, 38°28′ E 154
Strel'skaya, Russ. 59°28′ N, 47°40′ E 154
Strenči, Latv. 57°37′ N, 25°40′ E 166
Stresa, It. 45°53′ N, 8°32′ E 167
Strezhevoy, Russ. 60°41′ N, 77°21′ E 169
Strickland, river, P.N.G. 7°53′ S, 141°4′ E 192
Strilki, Ukr. 49°18′ N, 22°53′ E 152
Strimasund, Nor. 66°3′ N, 14°54′ E 152
Strizhi, Russ. 58°23′ N, 49°2′ E 154
Strizivojna, Croatia 45°13′ N, 18°24′ E 168
Strmica, Croatia 44°8′ N, 16°14′ E 168
Stroeder, Arg. 40°12′ S, 62°36′ W 134
Strofádes, Nísoi, islands, Ionian Sea 37°9′ N, 20°20′ E 156
Ströhen, Ger. 52°32′ N, 8°41′ E 163
Stromberg, Ger. 49°57′ N, 7°46′ E 167

Stromsburg, Nebr., U.S. 41°6' N, 97°37' W 90
Strömsnäsbruk, Nor. 56°32' N, 13°43' E 152
Strömstad, Nor. 58°56' N, 11°12' E 152
Strömsund, Nor. 63°51' N, 15°33' E 152
Strong, Ark., U.S. 33°5' N, 92°22' W 103
Stroud, Okla., U.S. 35°42' N, 96°40' W 92
Stroud, U.K. 51°44' N, 2°13' W 162
Stroudsburg, Pa., U.S. 40°59' N, 75°13' W 94
Štrpce, Europe 42°15' N, 21°2' E 168
Struer, Den. 56°28' N, 8°34' E 150
Strugi-Krasnyye, Russ. 58°16' N, 29°6' E 166
Strumica, Maced. 41°26' N, 22°37' E 168
Struthers, Ohio, U.S. 41°2' N, 80°36' W 94
Stružec, Croatia 45°30' N, 16°32' E 168
Strydenburg, S. Af. 29°58' S, 23°40' E 227
Stryker, Ohio, U.S. 41°29' N, 84°25' W 102
Stryy, Ukr. 49°14' N, 23°50' E 152
Strzelce Opolskie, Pol. 50°31' N, 18°19' E 152
Stuart, Fla., U.S. 27°11' N, 80°14' W 105
Stuart, Iowa, U.S. 41°30' N, 94°20' W 94
Stuart, Nebr., U.S. 42°34' N, 99°9' W 90
Stuart, Va., U.S. 36°38' N, 80°17' W 94
Stuart Bluff Range, Austral. 22°37' S, 131°45' E 231
Stuart Island, Alas., U.S. 63°34' N, 163°8' W 98
Stuart Lake, lake, Can. 54°8' N, 124°56' W 106
Stuart Range, Austral. 28°48' S, 134°5' E 230
Stuart, river, Can. 54°16' N, 124°4' W 108
Stubbenkammer 54°29' N, 13°54' E 152
Stubica, Serb. and Mont. 43°56' N, 21°29' E 168
Štubik, Serb. and Mont. 44°16' N, 22°21' E 168
Studholme Junction, N.Z. 44°45' S, 171°7' E 240
Stugun, Nor. 63°10' N, 15°39' E 154
Stumpy Point, N.C., U.S. 35°43' N, 75°46' W 96
Stupart, river, Can. 55°25' N, 94°34' W 108
Stupino, Russ. 54°53' N, 38°2' E 154
Sturbridge, Mass., U.S. 42°6' N, 72°5' W 104
Sturgeon Bay 51°59' N, 98°31' W 108
Sturgeon Falls, Can. 46°22' N, 79°53' W 94
Sturgeon Lake, Can. 50°1' N, 91°23' W 110
Sturgeon Landing, Can. 54°17' N, 101°52' W 108
Sturgeon Point, Mich., U.S. 44°32' N, 83°15' W 110
Sturgeon, river, Can. 50°14' N, 94°26' W 90
Sturgis, Can. 51°55' N, 102°33' W 90
Sturgis, Ky., U.S. 37°32' N, 87°59' W 96
Sturgis, Mich., U.S. 41°47' N, 85°25' W 102
Sturgis, Miss., U.S. 33°19' N, 89°3' W 103
Sturgis, S. Dak., U.S. 44°23' N, 103°31' W 90
Štúrovo, Slovakia 47°48' N, 18°42' E 168
Sturt Stony Desert, Austral. 26°37' S, 139°38' E 230
Sturtevant, Wis., U.S. 42°41' N, 87°54' W 102
Stuttgart, Ark., U.S. 34°30' N, 91°36' W 82
Stuttgart, Ger. 48°47' N, 9°11' E 150
Styx, river, Ala., U.S. 30°49' N, 87°44' W 103
Suakin, Sudan 19°5' N, 37°16' E 182
Suakin Archipelago, islands, Red Sea 18°49' N, 37°56' E 182
Suao, Taiwan 24°27' N, 121°45' E 198
Suaqui Grande, Mex. 28°24' N, 109°54' W 92
Suardi, Arg. 30°29' S, 61°56' W 139
Subačius, Lith. 55°45' N, 24°46' E 166
Subaşı Dağı, peak, Turk. 38°22' N, 41°30' E 195
Subata, Latv. 56°0' N, 25°54' E 166
Subcetate, Rom. 45°36' N, 23°0' E 168
Subei, China 39°30' N, 94°57' E 188
Subeita, ruin(s), Israel 30°53' N, 34°35' E 194
Subi, island, Indonesia 3°3' N, 108°52' E 196
Sublette, Ill., U.S. 41°38' N, 89°14' W 102
Sublette, Kans., U.S. 37°28' N, 100°51' W 92
Sublime, Point, peak, Ariz., U.S. 36°10' N, 112°18' W 92
Subotica, Serb. and Mont. 46°5' N, 19°40' E 168
Subugo, peak, Kenya 1°40' S, 35°44' E 224
Suceava, Rom. 47°38' N, 26°15' E 152
Suceava, adm. division, Rom. 47°27' N, 25°9' E 156
Sučevići, Croatia 44°16' N, 16°4' E 168
Suchdol, Czech Rep. 48°53' N, 14°52' E 152
Suchixtepec, Mex. 16°4' N, 96°28' W 112
Suchowola, Pol. 51°42' N, 22°43' E 152
Sucio, river, Col. 7°26' N, 77°3' W 136
Sucre, Bol. 19°3' S, 65°22' W 137
Sucre, Col. 8°52' N, 74°44' W 136
Sucre, Col. 1°48' N, 75°40' W 136
Sucre, adm. division, Col. 8°42' N, 75°15' W 136
Sucre, adm. division, Venez. 10°19' N, 63°47' W 116
Sucuaro, Col. 4°32' N, 68°50' W 136
Sucunduri, river, Braz. 5°30' S, 59°32' W 130
Sucunduri, river, Braz. 9°5' S, 58°59' W 132
Sućuraj, Croatia 43°6' N, 17°9' E 168
Sucuriú, river, Braz. 18°42' S, 53°20' W 138
Sud Kivu, adm. division, Dem. Rep. of the Congo 3°59' S, 28°18' E 218
Sud, Pointe du, Can. 48°58' N, 62°57' W 111
Suda, Russ. 59°7' N, 37°29' E 154
Suda, river, Russ. 59°33' N, 36°18' E 154
Sudak, Ukr. 44°51' N, 34°54' E 156
Sudan 13°26' N, 24°57' E 207
Sudan, Tex., U.S. 34°3' N, 102°32' W 92
Suday, Russ. 58°59' N, 43°9' E 154
Sudbury, Can. 46°29' N, 80°60' W 94
Sudbury, Mass., U.S. 42°22' N, 71°26' W 104
Sudbury, U.K. 52°2' N, 0°43' E 162
Suddie, Guyana 7°3' N, 58°33' W 130
Sudeten, Pol. 50°58' N, 14°40' E 152
Sud-Kivu, adm. division, Dem. Rep. of the Congo 3°17' N, 27°56' E 218
Sud-Ouest, Pointe du, Can. 49°20' N, 64°50' W 111
Sudr, Egypt 29°38' N, 32°42' E 180
Suðuroy, island, Suduroy 61°26' N, 10°6' W 142
Sudzha, Russ. 51°10' N, 35°18' E 158
Sue, Mys, Kaz. 41°34' N, 52°11' E 158
Sue, river, Sudan 7°1' N, 28°7' E 224
Sueca, Sp. 39°11' N, 0°19' E 150
Suehn, Liberia 6°31' N, 10°43' W 222
Sueyoshi, Japan 31°39' N, 131°1' E 201
Suez Canal, Egypt 30°19' N, 32°20' E 206
Suez see El Suweis, Egypt 30°1' N, 32°26' E 180
Sūf, Jordan 32°18' N, 35°50' E 194
Şufaynah, Saudi Arabia 23°5' N, 40°36' E 182
Suffield, Can. 50°12' N, 111°10' W 90
Suffield, Conn., U.S. 41°58' N, 72°39' W 104
Suffolk, Va., U.S. 36°43' N, 76°35' W 96
Şūfiān, Iran 38°18' N, 46°0' E 195
Sugar City, Colo., U.S. 38°14' N, 103°40' W 90
Sugar City, Idaho, U.S. 43°52' N, 111°45' W 90
Sugar Hill, N.H., U.S. 44°12' N, 71°48' W 104
Sugarbush Hill, peak, Wis., U.S. 45°31' N, 88°55' W 94
Sugarcreek, Ohio, U.S. 40°29' N, 81°37' W 102
Sugarloaf Key, island, Fla., U.S. 24°44' N, 81°39' W 105
Sugarloaf Mountain, peak, Me., U.S. 45°0' N, 70°23' W 94
Sugarloaf Mountain, peak, N.H., U.S. 44°43' N, 71°33' W 94
Suggi Lake, lake, Can. 54°20' N, 103°12' W 108
Suğla Gölü, lake, Turk. 37°18' N, 31°44' E 180
Sugut, river, Malaysia 6°0' N, 117°8' E 203
Sugut, Tanjong, Malaysia 6°25' N, 117°46' E 203
Suhai Hu, lake, China 38°49' N, 93°36' E 188
Şuḩār, Oman 24°19' N, 56°44' E 196
Sühbaatar, Mongolia 50°14' N, 106°13' E 198
Sühbaatar, adm. division, Mongolia 46°0' N, 111°56' E 198
Suheli Par 10°5' N, 71°16' E 188
Suhopolje, Croatia 45°46' N, 17°29' E 168
Şuhut, Turk. 38°31' N, 30°32' E 156
Sui, Pak. 28°38' N, 69°18' E 186
Šuica, Bosn. and Herzg. 43°49' N, 17°10' E 168
Suichang, China 28°36' N, 119°15' E 198
Suichuan, China 26°20' N, 114°33' E 198
Suide, China 37°28' N, 110°14' E 198
Suihua, China 46°38' N, 127°2' E 198
Suileng, China 47°14' N, 127°11' E 198
Suining, China 33°53' N, 117°58' E 198
Suining, China 26°38' N, 110°11' E 198
Suippes, Fr. 49°8' N, 4°32' E 163
Suisun City, Calif., U.S. 38°13' N, 122°3' W 100
Suixi, China 33°51' N, 116°48' E 198
Suixi, China 21°23' N, 110°14' E 202
Suiyang, China 27°57' N, 107°10' E 198
Suizhong, China 40°19' N, 120°19' E 198
Suizhou, China 31°45' N, 113°20' E 198
Sujangarh, India 27°42' N, 74°29' E 186
Sukabumi, Indonesia 6°59' S, 106°51' E 192
Sukagawa, Japan 37°17' N, 140°21' E 201
Sukau, Malaysia 5°33' N, 118°16' E 203
Sukch'ŏn, N. Korea 39°24' N, 125°38' E 200
Sukeva, Fin. 63°49' N, 27°21' E 152
Sŭkh, Uzb. 40°0' N, 71°7' E 197
Sukhaya Tunguska, Russ. 65°3' N, 88°4' E 169
Sukhinichi, Russ. 54°3' N, 35°24' E 154
Sukhona, river, Russ. 60°0' N, 42°51' E 160
Sukhona, river, Russ. 60°19' N, 44°4' E 154
Sukhothai, Thai. 17°4' N, 99°49' E 202
Sukhoy Nos, Mys, Russ. 73°37' N, 46°36' E 160
Sukhum see Sokhumi, Rep. of Georgia 43°0' N, 41°55' E 195
Sukkertoppen see Maniitsoq 65°26' N, 52°60' W 106
Sukkur, Pak. 27°45' N, 68°55' E 186
Sukon, Ko, island, Thai. 7°0' N, 98°57' E 196
Suksun, Russ. 57°9' N, 57°26' E 154
Sukumo, Japan 32°56' N, 132°41' E 201
Sukunka, river, Can. 55°9' N, 121°33' W 108
Šula, Europe 43°23' N, 19°4' E 168
Sula, Kepulauan, islands, Banda Sea 1°49' S, 124°12' E 192
Sula, river, Russ. 66°58' N, 50°14' E 169
Sula, river, Ukr. 50°48' N, 33°36' E 158
Sulaco, river, Hond. 15°4' N, 87°41' W 115
Sulak, Russ. 43°18' N, 47°35' E 195
Sulak, Russ. 51°50' N, 48°23' E 184
Sulanheer, Mongolia 42°42' N, 109°24' E 198
Sulat, Philippines 11°48' N, 125°26' E 203
Sulawesi (Celebes), island, Indonesia 0°39' N, 123°14' E 192
Sulb, ruin(s), Sudan 20°23' N, 30°12' E 226
Sulechów, Pol. 52°5' N, 15°38' E 152
Suleya, Russ. 55°14' N, 58°46' E 154
Süleymanlı, Turk. 37°52' N, 36°49' E 156
Sulgrave, U.K. 52°5' N, 1°13' W 162
Sulima, Sierra Leone 6°57' N, 11°32' W 222
Sulina, Rom. 45°9' N, 29°38' E 156
Sulitjelma, peak, Nor. 67°7' N, 16°13' E 152
Sulkava, Fin. 61°46' N, 28°21' E 166
Sull Basin, Sulu Sea 8°31' N, 120°28' E 254
Sullivan, Ill., U.S. 39°35' N, 88°37' W 102
Sullivan, Ind., U.S. 39°5' N, 87°25' W 102
Sullivan, Mo., U.S. 38°12' N, 91°10' W 94
Sullivan Bay, Can. 50°51' N, 126°47' W 90
Sullivan Lake, Can. 52°1' N, 112°19' W 90
Sulphur, La., U.S. 30°12' N, 93°23' W 103
Sulphur, Okla., U.S. 34°29' N, 96°58' W 92
Sulphur Point, Can. 60°56' N, 114°51' W 108
Sulphur, river, Tex., U.S. 33°23' N, 95°13' W 103
Sulphur Springs, Tex., U.S. 33°7' N, 95°36' W 103
Sultan Kheyl, Afghan. 33°50' N, 68°42' E 186
Sultanhanı, Turk. 38°14' N, 33°33' E 156
Sultanpur, India 26°14' N, 82°3' E 197
Sul'tsa, Russ. 63°28' N, 46°0' E 154
Sulu Archipelago, islands, Sulu Sea 5°31' N, 121°16' E 203
Sulu Sea 7°57' N, 119°4' E 192
Sülüklü, Turk. 38°52' N, 32°22' E 156
Suluova, Turk. 40°48' N, 35°41' E 156
Sulūq, Lib. 31°39' N, 20°15' E 216
Sulütöbe, Kaz. 44°39' N, 66°1' E 184
Sulz, Ger. 48°21' N, 8°36' E 150
Sumaco Napo Galeras National Park, Ecua. 0°49' N, 78°13' W 136
Sumampa, Arg. 29°22' S, 63°30' W 139
Sumapaz National Park, Col. 3°40' N, 74°55' W 136
Sumarokovo, Russ. 61°36' N, 89°38' E 169
Sumas, Wash., U.S. 48°59' N, 122°17' W 100
Sumatra, island, Indonesia 4°43' S, 105°52' E 192
Šumava, Czech Rep. 49°13' N, 13°12' E 152
Sumba, island, Indonesia 10°3' S, 117°57' E 192
Sumbar, river, Turkm. 38°12' N, 55°30' E 180
Sumbawa, island, Indonesia 8°13' S, 117°31' E 192
Sumbawanga, Tanzania 7°56' S, 31°37' E 224
Sumbay, Peru 15°60' S, 71°22' W 137
Sumbe, Angola 11°15' S, 13°53' E 220
Sumbuya, Sierra Leone 7°39' N, 11°58' W 222
Sumé, Braz. 7°39' S, 36°53' W 132
Sümeg, Hung. 46°57' N, 17°17' E 168
Sumeih, Sudan 9°47' N, 27°34' E 224
Sumiton, Ala., U.S. 33°44' N, 87°3' W 96
Sümiyn Bulag, Mongolia 49°38' N, 114°59' E 198
Sumkino, Russ. 58°3' N, 68°14' E 169
Summer Lake, Oreg., U.S. 42°45' N, 121°49' W 80
Summerfield, La., U.S. 32°53' N, 92°50' W 103
Summerfield, Ohio, U.S. 39°47' N, 81°20' W 102
Summerland, Calif., U.S. 34°25' N, 119°37' W 101
Summerland, Can. 49°36' N, 119°40' W 108
Summerland Key, Fla., U.S. 24°39' N, 81°27' W 105
Summerside, Can. 46°23' N, 63°47' W 111
Summersville, W. Va., U.S. 38°16' N, 80°52' W 94
Summerville, S.C., U.S. 33°0' N, 80°11' W 96
Summit, Miss., U.S. 31°16' N, 90°28' W 103
Summit, Sudan 18°47' N, 36°48' E 182
Summit Lake, Can. 58°39' N, 124°39' W 108
Summit Lake, Can. 54°16' N, 122°37' W 108
Summit Mountain, peak, Nev., U.S. 39°21' N, 116°33' W 90
Summitville, Ind., U.S. 40°20' N, 85°39' W 102
Sumner, Lake, N. Mex., U.S. 34°36' N, 105°23' W 80
Sumner Strait 56°10' N, 134°28' W 108
Sumoto, Japan 34°20' N, 134°52' E 201
Sumprabum, Myanmar 26°35' N, 97°32' E 188
Sumqayıt, Azerb. 40°36' N, 49°36' E 195
Sumrall, Miss., U.S. 31°24' N, 89°33' W 103
Sumsa, Fin. 64°14' N, 29°50' E 152
Sumskiy Posad, Russ. 64°14' N, 35°22' E 154
Sumter, S.C., U.S. 33°54' N, 80°23' W 82
Sumy, Ukr. 50°55' N, 34°46' E 158
Sun, La., U.S. 30°38' N, 89°54' W 103
Sun City, Calif., U.S. 33°43' N, 117°13' W 101
Sun City, S. Af. 25°20' S, 27°0' E 227
Sun Kosi, river, Nepal 27°20' N, 85°44' E 197
Sun Prairie, Wis., U.S. 43°11' N, 89°14' W 102
Sun, river, Mont., U.S. 47°24' N, 112°20' W 90
Sun, river, Mont., U.S. 47°55' N, 113°15' W 80
Suna, Russ. 57°50' N, 50°10' E 154
Suna, river, Russ. 62°38' N, 32°38' E 152
Sunan, N. Korea 39°11' N, 125°42' E 200
Sunapee, N.H., U.S. 43°23' N, 72°5' W 104
Sunburst, Mont., U.S. 48°52' N, 111°57' W 90
Sunbury, Ohio, U.S. 40°14' N, 82°52' W 102
Sunbury, Pa., U.S. 40°51' N, 76°48' W 94
Sunchales, Arg. 30°58' S, 61°34' W 139
Suncho Corral, Arg. 27°57' S, 63°27' W 139
Sunch'ŏn, N. Korea 39°21' N, 126°1' E 200
Sund, Fin. 60°14' N, 20°5' E 166
Sundance, Wyo., U.S. 44°22' N, 104°23' W 90
Sundargarh, India 22°6' N, 84°4' E 197
Sunderland, U.K. 54°54' N, 1°24' W 162
Sunderland, Vt., U.S. 43°6' N, 73°6' W 104
Sundern, Ger. 51°19' N, 8°0' E 167
Sündiken Dağ, peak, Turk. 39°57' N, 31°2' E 156
Sundown, Tex., U.S. 33°26' N, 102°30' W 92
Sundridge, Can. 45°45' N, 79°25' W 94
Sundsvall, Nor. 62°22' N, 17°15' E 152
Sunflower, Mount, peak, Kans., U.S. 39°0' N, 102°7' W 90
Sungai Petani, Malaysia 5°37' N, 100°29' E 196
Sungaidareh, Indonesia 0°57' N, 101°31' E 196
Sungaiguntung, Indonesia 0°19' N, 103°37' E 196
Süngam, N. Korea 41°39' N, 129°40' E 200
Sungikai, Sudan 12°19' N, 29°47' E 218
Sungurlu, Turk. 40°9' N, 34°23' E 156
Suni, Sudan 13°3' N, 24°27' E 226
Sunja, Croatia 45°21' N, 16°33' E 168
Sunjiapuzi, China 42°0' N, 126°38' E 200
Sunman, Ind., U.S. 39°13' N, 85°6' W 102
Sunne, Nor. 59°51' N, 13°6' E 152
Sunnhordland, region, North Sea 59°51' N, 5°0' E 152
Sunniland, Fla., U.S. 26°15' N, 81°21' W 105
Sunnmøre, region, Nor. 62°8' N, 5°42' E 152
Sunnyvale, Calif., U.S. 37°22' N, 122°2' W 100
Sunray, Tex., U.S. 36°0' N, 101°50' W 92
Sunrise, Wyo., U.S. 42°19' N, 104°42' W 90
Sunrise Peak, Wash., U.S. 46°18' N, 121°48' W 100
Sunsas, Serranía de, Bol. 18°7' S, 59°38' W 132
Sunset, La., U.S. 30°23' N, 92°5' W 103
Sunset Peak, Mont., U.S. 44°50' N, 112°13' W 90
Sunset Prairie, Can. 55°49' N, 120°48' W 108
Suntar, Russ. 62°9' N, 117°28' E 160
Suntaži, Latv. 56°52' N, 24°55' E 166
Suntsar, Pak. 25°26' N, 62°2' E 182
Sunwu, China 49°24' N, 127°21' E 198
Sunyani, Ghana 7°21' N, 2°22' W 222
Suō Nada 33°46' N, 131°13' E 200
Suolahti, Fin. 62°33' N, 25°49' E 152
Suomenniemi, Fin. 61°19' N, 27°26' E 166
Suomenselkä, Fin. 61°47' N, 23°16' E 166
Suomussalmi, Fin. 64°53' N, 29°3' E 152
Suonenjoki, Fin. 62°36' N, 27°4' E 152
Suorsa Pää, peak, Fin. 68°32' N, 28°16' E 152
Suorva, Nor. 67°32' N, 18°15' E 152
Suoyarvi, Russ. 62°6' N, 32°22' E 152
Superior, Ariz., U.S. 33°17' N, 111°6' W 92
Superior, Nebr., U.S. 40°0' N, 98°5' W 90
Superior, Wis., U.S. 46°42' N, 92°5' W 94
Superior, Wyo., U.S. 41°46' N, 108°58' W 90
Superior, Lake 47°32' N, 89°30' W 110
Superstition Mountains, Ariz., U.S. 33°22' N, 111°40' W 92
Supetar, Croatia 43°22' N, 16°32' E 168
Süphan Dağı, peak, Turk. 38°54' N, 42°45' E 195
Supiori, island, Indonesia 0°31' N, 135°18' E 192
Sūq Suwayq, Saudi Arabia 24°21' N, 38°27' E 182
Suqa el Gamal, Sudan 12°48' N, 27°39' E 216
Suquṭrá see Socotra, island, Yemen 12°19' N, 54°12' E 182
Şūr, Oman 22°31' N, 59°32' E 182
Sur, Point, Calif., U.S. 36°13' N, 121°58' W 100
Sur, Punta, Arg. 37°5' S, 56°40' W 134
Sura, river, Russ. 53°23' N, 45°15' E 154
Sura, river, Russ. 53°16' N, 46°16' E 154
Surab, Pak. 28°29' N, 66°19' E 186
Surabaya, Indonesia 7°19' S, 112°37' E 192
Surahammar, Nor. 59°42' N, 16°11' E 152
Sūrak, Iran 25°41' N, 58°49' E 196
Surakarta, Indonesia 7°30' S, 110°35' E 192
Surama, Venez. 6°57' N, 63°19' W 130
Şūrān, Syr. 35°17' N, 36°44' E 194
Surar, Eth. 7°30' N, 40°53' E 224
Surat, India 21°11' N, 72°51' E 186
Surat Thani (Ban Don), Thai. 9°7' N, 99°20' E 202
Suraxanı, Azerb. 40°26' N, 50°1' E 195
Surazh, Russ. 52°59' N, 32°25' E 154
Surduc, Rom. 47°15' N, 23°22' E 168
Surdulica, Serb. and Mont. 42°41' N, 22°10' E 168
Surendranagar, India 22°39' N, 71°39' E 186
Surfside, Mass., U.S. 41°14' N, 70°6' W 104
Surgidero de Batabanó, Cuba 22°42' N, 82°16' W 112
Surgut, Russ. 61°15' N, 73°19' E 169
Surgut, Russ. 53°55' N, 51°6' E 154
Surgutikha, Russ. 63°49' N, 87°18' E 169
Surianu, peak, Rom. 45°34' N, 23°25' E 156
Surigao, Philippines 9°47' N, 125°30' E 203
Surimena, Col. 3°51' N, 73°16' W 136
Surin, Thai. 14°53' N, 103°28' E 202
Surin Nua, Ko, island, Thai. 9°22' N, 96°58' E 202
Suriname 4°0' N, 55°51' W 122
Sürmene, Turk. 40°55' N, 40°5' E 195
Surovikino, Russ. 48°37' N, 42°45' E 158
Surovni, Belarus 55°31' N, 29°38' E 166
Surprise Lake, lake, Can. 59°37' N, 134°3' W 108
Surrey, Can. 49°11' N, 122°54' W 100
Sursee, Switz. 47°10' N, 8°7' E 156
Sursk, Russ. 53°2' N, 45°45' E 154
Surskoye, Russ. 54°29' N, 46°44' E 154
Surt (Sidra), Lib. 31°12' N, 16°32' E 216
Surtanahu, Pak. 26°22' N, 70°3' E 186
Surte, Nor. 57°50' N, 12°1' E 152
Surtsey, island, Iceland 63°16' N, 20°29' W 253
Surud Cad, Buuraha, peak, Somalia 10°38' N, 47°9' E 218
Surumu, river, Braz. 4°11' N, 61°30' W 130
Susa, It. 45°7' N, 7°2' E 167
Susa, Japan 34°36' N, 131°36' E 200
Sušac, island, Croatia 42°46' N, 16°25' E 168
Sūsah (Apollonia), Lib. 32°52' N, 21°59' E 143
Susaki, Japan 33°23' N, 133°16' E 201
Süsangerd, Iran 31°29' N, 48°15' E 216
Susanino, Russ. 58°8' N, 41°38' E 154
Suşehri (Nicopolis), Turk. 40°8' N, 38°5' E 180
Susitna, Alas., U.S. 61°31' N, 150°30' W 98
Susitna, river, Alas., U.S. 62°30' N, 147°57' W 98
Suslonger, Russ. 56°18' N, 48°14' E 154
Susoh, Indonesia 3°44' N, 96°48' E 196
Suspiro, Braz. 30°39' S, 54°23' W 139
Susques, Arg. 23°25' S, 66°32' W 132
Sussex, Can. 45°42' N, 65°31' W 94
Sustut Peak, Can. 56°33' N, 126°42' W 108
Sustut, river, Can. 56°15' N, 127°9' W 108
Susuman, Russ. 62°56' N, 147°27' E 160
Susurluk, Turk. 39°54' N, 28°8' E 156
Susz, Pol. 53°43' N, 19°20' E 152
Sutak, India 33°7' N, 77°34' E 188
Sutatenza, Col. 5°2' N, 73°24' W 136
Sütçüler, Turk. 37°29' N, 30°58' E 156
Sutherland, Nebr., U.S. 41°9' N, 101°9' W 90
Sutherland, S. Af. 32°23' S, 20°38' E 227
Sutherlin, Oreg., U.S. 43°22' N, 123°20' W 90
Sutjesca National Park, Bosn. and Herzg. 43°16' N, 18°28' E 168
Sutlej, river, Pak. 29°35' N, 72°12' E 186
Sutorman, Europe 42°10' N, 19°7' E 168
Sutter Buttes, peak, Calif., U.S. 39°11' N, 121°55' W 90
Sutter Creek, Calif., U.S. 38°22' N, 120°49' W 100
Sutton, Nebr., U.S. 40°35' N, 97°51' W 90
Sutton Coldfield, U.K. 52°33' N, 1°50' W 162
Sutton on Sea, U.K. 53°18' N, 0°16' E 162
Sutton, river, Can. 54°19' N, 84°35' W 106
Sutwik Island, Alas., U.S. 56°8' N, 157°43' W 98
Suure-Jaani, Est. 58°31' N, 25°27' E 166
Suva, Fiji Islands 18°12' S, 178°26' E 242
Suva Gora, Maced. 41°54' N, 21°2' E 168
Suva Planina, Serb. and Mont. 43°14' N, 21°58' E 168
Suvadiva Atoll (Huvadu), Maldives 0°39' N, 72°35' E 188
Suvainiškis, Lith. 56°9' N, 25°15' E 166
Suvorov, Russ. 54°8' N, 36°29' E 154
Suwa, Eritrea 14°12' N, 41°8' E 182
Suwa, Japan 36°3' N, 138°8' E 201
Suwałki, Pol. 54°6' N, 22°57' E 166
Suwannaphum, Thai. 15°35' N, 103°47' E 202
Suwannee, Fla., U.S. 29°19' N, 83°9' W 105
Suwannee, river, Fla., U.S. 29°20' N, 83°1' W 105
Suwannee Sound 29°11' N, 83°18' W 105
Şuwaylih, Jordan 32°1' N, 35°50' E 194
Suwon, S. Korea 37°16' N, 127°1' E 200
Suydam, Mount, peak, Antarctica 84°32' S, 67°31' W 248
Suyevat, Russ. 61°36' N, 60°30' E 154
Süyqbulaq, Kaz. 49°50' N, 80°48' E 184
Suyutkino, Russ. 44°10' N, 47°12' E 158
Suzaka, Japan 36°39' N, 138°18' E 201
Suzhou, China 31°22' N, 120°38' E 198
Suzhou, China 39°31' N, 98°39' E 173
Suzhou, China 33°38' N, 116°56' E 198
Suzu (Iida), Japan 37°26' N, 137°15' E 201
Suzu Misaki, Japan 37°32' N, 137°21' E 201
Suzuka, Japan 34°52' N, 136°36' E 201
Suzun, Russ. 53°47' N, 82°27' E 184
Suzzara, It. 44°59' N, 10°45' E 167
Svalbard, islands, Barents Sea 76°55' N, 20°18' E 246
Svalbard, islands, Barents Sea 78°21' N, 22°28' E 255
Svaneke, Den. 55°7' N, 15°7' E 152
Svanstein, Nor. 66°39' N, 23°49' E 152
Svarta (Mustio), Fin. 60°8' N, 23°51' E 166
Svatove, Ukr. 49°25' N, 38°12' E 158
Svatsum, Nor. 61°18' N, 9°50' E 152
Svay Chek, Cambodia 13°53' N, 103°1' E 202
Svay Rieng, Cambodia 11°5' N, 105°46' E 202
Svealand, region, Sw. 60°4' N, 17°28' E 166
Svecha, Russ. 58°16' N, 47°30' E 154
Svėdasai, Lith. 55°40' N, 25°21' E 166
Švėkšna, Lith. 55°31' N, 21°36' E 166
Švenčionėliai, Lith. 55°10' N, 26°0' E 166
Švenčionys, Lith. 55°9' N, 26°11' E 166
Svendborg, Den. 55°3' N, 10°36' E 152
Šventoji, Lith. 56°1' N, 21°6' E 166
Sverdlovs'k, Ukr. 48°6' N, 39°41' E 158
Sverdlovsk, adm. division, Russ. 58°42' N, 60°3' E 154
Sverdrup Islands, Foxe Basin 77°45' N, 99°50' W 106
Sverdrup Mountains, Antarctica 72°33' S, 2°60' W 248
Svēte, river, Latv. 56°22' N, 23°26' E 166
Sveti Đorđe, Europe 41°57' N, 19°20' E 168
Sveti Nikola, Europe 41°53' N, 19°21' E 168
Sveti Nikola, Prokhod, pass, Bulg. 43°27' N, 22°34' E 168
Sveti Nikole, Maced. 41°51' N, 21°57' E 168
Sveti Stefan, Europe 42°14' N, 18°53' E 168
Světlá, Czech Rep. 49°40' N, 15°24' E 152
Svetlaya, Russ. 46°36' N, 138°10' E 190
Svetlogorsk, Russ. 54°55' N, 20°9' E 166
Svetlogorsk, Russ. 66°47' N, 88°30' E 169
Svetlograd, Russ. 45°18' N, 42°42' E 158
Svetlyy, Russ. 54°40' N, 20°6' E 166
Svetogorsk, Russ. 61°6' N, 28°51' E 166
Svetozar Miletić, Serb. and Mont. 45°50' N, 19°12' E 168
Svilaja, Croatia 43°48' N, 16°18' E 168
Svilajnac, Serb. and Mont. 44°14' N, 21°11' E 168
Svilengrad, Bulg. 41°46' N, 26°11' E 158
Svir, Belarus 54°50' N, 26°22' E 166
Svir', river, Russ. 60°32' N, 33°2' E 154
Sviritsa, Russ. 60°28' N, 32°51' E 154
Svir'stroy, Russ. 60°48' N, 33°48' E 154
Svislach, Belarus 53°2' N, 24°5' E 152
Svitavy, Czech Rep. 49°45' N, 16°29' E 152
Svobodny Cosmodrome, spaceport, Russ. 51°43' N, 128°9' E 190
Svobodnyy, Russ. 51°27' N, 128°5' E 238
Svodna, Bosn. and Herzg. 45°3' N, 16°31' E 168
Svolvær, Nor. 68°16' N, 14°14' E 160
Svrljig, Serb. and Mont. 43°24' N, 22°7' E 168
Svrljiške Planina, Serb. and Mont. 43°16' N, 22°16' E 168
Svyataya Anna Fan, Arctic Ocean 84°7' N, 59°47' E 255
Svyataya Anna Trough, Kara Sea 80°7' N, 71°25' E 255
Svyatitsa, Belarus 52°44' N, 26°1' E 154
Svyatoy Nos, Mys, Russ. 72°24' N, 133°19' E 160
Svyetlahorsk, Belarus 52°34' N, 29°48' E 154
Swa Tenda, Dem. Rep. of the Congo 7°12' S, 17°5' E 218
Swadlincote, U.K. 52°45' N, 1°34' W 162
Swaffham, U.K. 52°38' N, 0°41' E 162
Swain Post, Can. 51°17' N, 92°40' W 110
Swains Island, U.S. 11°4' S, 171°10' W 252
Swainsboro, Ga., U.S. 32°35' N, 82°21' W 96
Swakopmund, Namibia 22°31' S, 14°28' E 207
Swale, river, U.K. 54°23' N, 1°51' W 162
Swampscott, Mass., U.S. 42°28' N, 70°56' W 104
Swan Hills, Can. 54°43' N, 115°35' W 108
Swan Lake, S. Dak., U.S. 45°14' N, 100°18' W 90
Swan Lake, lake, Can. 55°45' N, 129°7' W 108
Swan Range, Mont., U.S. 47°43' N, 113°44' W 90
Swan River, Can. 52°4' N, 101°15' W 108
Swan, river, Can. 52°16' N, 102°16' W 108
Swanquarter, N.C., U.S. 35°24' N, 76°21' W 96
Swansea (Abertawe), U.K. 51°37' N, 3°57' W 162
Swanton, Ohio, U.S. 41°35' N, 83°53' W 102
Swanzey, N.H., U.S. 42°52' N, 72°18' W 104
Swartmodder, S. Af. 28°5' S, 20°34' E 227
Swartruggens, S. Af. 25°41' S, 26°41' E 227
Swartz, La., U.S. 32°33' N, 91°59' W 103
Swarzędz, Pol. 52°24' N, 17°4' E 152
Swasey Peak, Utah, U.S. 39°22' N, 113°23' W 90
Swat, river, Pak. 34°46' N, 72°20' E 186
Swatow see Shantou, China 23°23' N, 116°40' E 198
Swaziland 26°31' S, 31°28' E 227
Sweden 63°13' N, 16°14' E 152
Swedru, Ghana 5°32' N, 0°44' E 222
Sweeney Mountains, Antarctica 74°37' S, 74°59' W 248
Sweet Home, Oreg., U.S. 44°22' N, 122°44' W 90
Sweetgrass, Mont., U.S. 48°58' N, 111°59' W 90
Sweetwater, Tenn., U.S. 35°35' N, 84°28' W 96
Sweetwater, Tex., U.S. 32°27' N, 100°24' W 96
Sweetwater Summit, pass, Nev., U.S. 38°30' N, 119°14' W 100
Świdwin, Pol. 53°45' N, 15°47' E 152
Świebodzin, Pol. 52°15' N, 15°31' E 152
Świętokrzyskie, Pol. 51°5' N, 19°47' E 152
Świętokrzyskie, adm. division, Pol. 50°51' N, 19°47' E 152
Swift Current, Can. 50°17' N, 107°49' W 90
Swift River, Can. 60°2' N, 131°13' W 108
Swift, river, Can. 59°57' N, 131°54' W 108
Swindon, U.K. 51°33' N, 1°47' W 162
Świnoujście, Pol. 53°54' N, 14°14' E 152
Switz City, Ind., U.S. 39°1' N, 87°3' W 102
Switzerland 46°48' N, 7°57' E 156
Syamzha, Russ. 60°3' N, 41°9' E 154
Syanno, Belarus 54°48' N, 29°46' E 166
Syas', river, Russ. 59°47' N, 32°43' E 154
Syas'stroy, Russ. 60°7' N, 32°41' E 154

Syava, Russ. 58°0' N, 46°21' E 154
Sycamore, Ga., U.S. 31°39' N, 83°38' W 96
Sycamore, Ill., U.S. 41°59' N, 88°41' W 102
Sycamore, Ohio, U.S. 40°56' N, 83°10' W 102
Sycewice, Pol. 54°25' N, 16°51' E 152
Sychevka, Russ. 55°49' N, 34°21' E 154
Sydney, Austral. 33°56' S, 150°50' E 230
Sydney, Can. 46°8' N, 60°11' W 111
Sydney Lake, Can. 50°40' N, 94°47' W 90
Syelishcha, Belarus 53°0' N, 27°23' E 154
Syghyndy, Kaz. 43°45' N, 51°4' E 195
Syktyvkar, Russ. 61°44' N, 50°56' E 154
Sylacauga, Ala., U.S. 33°9' N, 86°20' W 112
Sylarna, peak, Nor. 62°59' N, 12°5' E 152
Sylhet, Bangladesh 24°53' N, 91°53' E 197
Sylte, Nor. 62°50' N, 7°15' E 152
Sylva, Russ. 58°1' N, 56°46' E 154
Sylvan Lake, Can. 52°18' N, 114°7' W 108
Sylvan Pass, Wyo., U.S. 44°27' N, 110°8' W 90
Sylvania, Ga., U.S. 32°43' N, 81°39' W 96
Sylvania, Ohio, U.S. 41°42' N, 83°42' W 102
Sylvester, Tex., U.S. 32°43' N, 100°17' W 92
Sylvester, Mount, peak, Can. 48°9' N, 55°11' W 111
Sylvia, Mount, peak, Can. 58°5' N, 124°32' W 108
Sym, Russ. 60°19' N, 88°25' E 169
Sym, river, Russ. 60°42' N, 87°3' E 169
Synel'nykove, Ukr. 48°18' N, 35°32' E 158
Syngyrli, Mys, Kaz. 41°54' N, 51°54' E 158
Synnfjell, peak, Nor. 61°3' N, 9°40' E 152
Synnot, Mount, peak, Austral. 16°43' S, 125°3' E 230
Synya, Russ. 65°23' N, 58°1' E 154
Syowa, Japan, station, Antarctica 68°60' S, 39°36' E 248
Syr Darya, river, Kaz. 44°30' N, 65°40' E 184
Syracuse, Ind., U.S. 41°25' N, 85°45' W 102
Syracuse, Kans., U.S. 37°59' N, 101°45' W 90
Syracuse, Nebr., U.S. 40°38' N, 96°11' W 90
Syracuse, N.Y., U.S. 43°3' N, 76°10' W 94
Syracuse see Siracusa, It. 37°3' N, 15°17' E 156
Syria 34°59' N, 38°11' E 180
Syrian Desert, Iraq 32°22' N, 37°50' E 180
Syrian Gates, pass, Turk. 36°28' N, 36°12' E 156
Syrna, island, Gr. 36°13' N, 26°43' E 180
Sysert', Russ. 56°30' N, 60°50' E 154
Sysmä, Fin. 61°29' N, 25°38' E 166
Sysola, river, Russ. 61°2' N, 50°31' E 154
Systyg Khem, Russ. 52°52' N, 95°43' E 190
Sytomino, Russ. 61°18' N, 71°21' E 169
Syumsi, Russ. 57°5' N, 51°42' E 154
Syuneysale, Russ. 66°54' N, 71°23' E 169
Syutkya, peak, Bulg. 41°52' N, 23°56' E 156
Syzran', Russ. 53°11' N, 48°33' E 154
Szabadszállás, Hung. 46°51' N, 19°13' E 168
Szabolcs-Szatmár-Bereg, adm. division, Hung. 48°6' N, 21°43' E 156
Szamotuły, Pol. 52°36' N, 16°34' E 152
Szarvas, Hung. 46°52' N, 20°33' E 168
Szczebra, Pol. 53°55' N, 22°57' E 166
Szczecin, Pol. 53°25' N, 14°33' E 152
Szczecinek, Pol. 53°42' N, 16°42' E 152
Szczuczyn, Pol. 53°33' N, 22°14' E 152
Szeged, Hung. 46°15' N, 20°8' E 168
Szeghalom, Hung. 47°1' N, 21°9' E 168
Szegvár, Hung. 46°35' N, 20°14' E 168
Székesfehérvár, Hung. 47°11' N, 18°25' E 168
Szekszárd, Hung. 46°20' N, 18°42' E 168
Szentendre, Hung. 47°39' N, 19°6' E 168
Szentes, Hung. 46°39' N, 20°16' E 168
Szentgotthárd, Hung. 46°56' N, 16°16' E 168
Szentl orinc, Hung. 46°2' N, 17°59' E 168
Szepietowo, Pol. 52°51' N, 22°31' E 152
Szigetvár, Hung. 46°2' N, 17°48' E 168
Szikszó, Hung. 48°12' N, 20°56' E 152
Szob, Hung. 47°48' N, 18°54' E 168
Szolnok, Hung. 47°11' N, 20°11' E 168
Szombathely, Hung. 47°14' N, 16°39' E 168
Sz ony, Hung. 47°44' N, 18°10' E 168
Sz oreg, Hung. 46°12' N, 20°12' E 168
Sztum, Pol. 53°54' N, 19°0' E 166
Sztutowo, Pol. 54°19' N, 19°9' E 166
Szulok, Hung. 46°3' N, 17°32' E 168
Szypliszki, Pol. 54°14' N, 23°5' E 166

T

Ta La, Vietnam 11°26' N, 107°26' E 202
Taalintehdas see Dalsbruk, Fin. 60°1' N, 22°31' E 166
Taavetti, Fin. 60°54' N, 27°31' E 166
Tab, Hung. 46°43' N, 18°1' E 168
Tabacal, Arg. 23°14' S, 64°16' W 132
Ţābah, Saudi Arabia 27°3' N, 42°11' E 180
Tabalak, Niger 15°3' N, 6°0' E 222
Tabane Lake, lake, Can. 60°33' N, 102°21' W 108
Tabankort, spring, Mali 17°49' N, 0°15' E 222
Tabanovce, Maced. 42°11' N, 21°42' E 168
Ţabaqat Faḩl, Jordan 32°26' N, 35°36' E 194
Tabar Islands, islands, P.N.G. 2°35' S, 152°4' E 192
Ţabas, Iran 33°35' N, 56°54' E 180
Ţabas, Iran 32°49' N, 60°13' E 180
Tabasará, Serranía de, Pan. 8°29' N, 81°39' W 115
Tabasco, Mex. 21°51' N, 102°55' W 114
Tabasco, adm. division, Mex. 18°12' N, 93°42' W 115
Tabatinga, Serra da, Braz. 10°53' S, 45°27' W 130
Tabelbala, Alg. 29°25' N, 3°15' W 143
Tabelkoza, Alg. 29°44' N, 0°44' E 214
Tabelot, Niger 17°34' N, 8°55' E 222
Taber, Can. 49°46' N, 112°8' W 90
Tabernas, Sp. 37°2' N, 2°24' W 164
Tabili, Dem. Rep. of the Congo 0°6' N, 27°59' E 224
Tablas Strait 12°28' N, 121°16' E 203
Tablat, Alg. 36°24' N, 3°19' E 150
Table, Cap de la, Can. 49°21' N, 61°51' W 111
Table Head, Can. 51°59' N, 55°45' W 111
Table Hill, peak, Austral. 14°33' S, 129°35' E 230
Table Mountain, peak, Alas., U.S. 68°12' N, 144°2' W 98
Table Mountain, peak, S. Dak., U.S. 45°51' N, 103°46' W 90
Table Point, Can. 50°23' N, 58°21' W 111
Table Rock, Nebr., U.S. 40°9' N, 96°5' W 94
Taboose Pass, Calif., U.S. 36°59' N, 118°26' W 101
Tábor, Czech Rep. 49°25' N, 14°38' E 152
Tabor, Russ. 71°9' N, 150°45' E 160
Tabor City, N.C., U.S. 34°8' N, 78°54' W 96
Tabora, Tanzania 5°2' S, 32°49' E 224
Tabora, adm. division, Tanzania 5°32' S, 31°41' E 224
Tabory, Russ. 58°31' N, 64°28' E 154
Taboshar, Taj. 40°35' N, 69°37' E 197
Tabou, Côte d'Ivoire 4°33' N, 7°22' W 222
Tabrīz, Iran 38°4' N, 46°16' E 195
Tabūk, Saudi Arabia 28°23' N, 36°34' E 180
Tabuleiro, Braz. 5°7' S, 58°28' W 130
Tabusintac Bay 47°18' N, 65°36' W 111
Tabusintac, river, Can. 47°18' N, 65°51' W 94
Tabuyung, Indonesia 0°51' N, 98°59' E 196
Täby, Sw. 59°29' N, 18°2' E 166
Tacalé, Braz. 1°37' N, 54°46' W 130
Tacámbaro, Mex. 19°13' N, 101°28' W 114
Tacaná, Volcán, peak, Mex. 15°8' N, 92°14' W 115
Tacheng, China 46°41' N, 83°5' E 184
Tachichilte, Isla de, island, Mex. 24°40' N, 109°13' W 112
Tachikawa, Japan 35°41' N, 139°25' E 201
Táchira, adm. division, Venez. 7°32' N, 72°29' W 136
Tacloban, Philippines 11°13' N, 125°0' E 203
Tacna, Ariz., U.S. 32°41' N, 113°58' W 101
Tacna, Col. 2°25' S, 70°38' W 136
Tacna, Peru 18°2' S, 70°14' W 137
Tacna, adm. division, Peru 17°46' S, 70°53' W 137
Taco Pozo, Arg. 25°38' S, 63°16' W 132
Tacoma, Wash., U.S. 47°13' N, 122°26' W 100
Tacuarembó, Uru. 31°45' S, 55°59' W 139
Tacubaya, Mex. 25°38' N, 103°2' W 114
Tacupeto, Mex. 28°47' N, 109°9' W 92
Tadami, Japan 37°21' N, 139°18' E 201
Tadcaster, U.K. 53°53' N, 1°15' W 162
Tadebyayakha, Russ. 70°26' N, 74°21' E 169
Tadélaka, spring, Niger 15°29' N, 7°57' E 222
Tademaït, Plateau du, Alg. 28°24' N, 1°10' E 214
Tadjakant, Mauritania 18°36' N, 14°34' W 222
Tadjetaret, spring, Alg. 22°39' N, 7°52' E 214
Tadjmout, Alg. 25°32' N, 3°42' E 214
Tadjoura, Djibouti 11°43' N, 42°54' E 216
Tadmor, N.Z. 41°28' S, 172°46' E 240
Tadmur, Syr. 34°32' N, 38°19' E 180
Tadoba National Park, India 20°18' N, 79°12' E 188
Tadoule Lake, Can. 58°32' N, 99°4' W 108
Tadoussac, Can. 48°8' N, 69°43' W 94
Taean, S. Korea 36°44' N, 126°18' E 200
T'aech'ŏn, N. Korea 39°55' N, 125°29' E 200
Taedong, N. Korea 40°37' N, 125°27' E 200
Taedong, river, N. Korea 39°51' N, 126°37' E 200
Taegu see Daegu, S. Korea 35°51' N, 128°37' E 200
Taegwan, N. Korea 40°11' N, 125°10' E 200
Taehŭng, N. Korea 40°5' N, 126°56' E 200
Taejŏn see Daejeon, S. Korea 36°18' N, 127°27' E 200
Taenarum see Akrotírio Ténaro, Gr. 36°13' N, 21°38' E 156
T'aet'an, N. Korea 38°2' N, 125°18' E 200
Tafalla, Sp. 42°31' N, 1°41' W 164
Tafara, Mali 15°38' N, 11°22' W 222
Tafarit, Cap, Mauritania 20°0' N, 16°12' W 222
Ţafas, Syr. 32°43' N, 36°3' E 194
Tafi Viejo, Arg. 26°46' S, 65°16' W 134
Tafiré, Côte d'Ivoire 9°4' N, 5°10' W 222
Tafraout, Mor. 29°43' N, 8°59' W 214
Taft, Calif., U.S. 35°8' N, 119°29' W 100
Taft, Tex., U.S. 27°57' N, 97°23' W 96
Taftān, Kūh-e, peak, Iran 28°37' N, 61°7' E 182
Tagama, region, Niger 15°46' N, 7°16' E 222
Taganrog, Russ. 47°14' N, 38°51' E 156
Taganrogskiy Zaliv 47°0' N, 38°41' E 158
Tagant, region, Mauritania 17°21' N, 12°13' W 222
Tagarma, China 38°1' N, 75°5' E 184
Tagawa, Japan 33°37' N, 130°49' E 201
Tagbilaran, Philippines 9°40' N, 123°52' E 203
Taggafadi, Niger 18°31' N, 9°14' E 222
Taggia, It. 43°51' N, 7°50' E 167
Taghit, Alg. 30°58' N, 1°60' W 214
Tagil, river, Russ. 58°14' N, 61°20' E 154
Tagish, Can. 60°20' N, 134°22' W 108
Taglio di Po, It. 45°0' N, 12°10' E 167
Tagnout Chaggueret, spring, Mali 21°15' N, 0°48' E 222
Tagounit, Mor. 29°57' N, 5°39' W 214
Tagtabazar, Turkm. 35°55' N, 62°56' E 186
Tagua, Bol. 19°54' S, 67°44' W 137
Taguedoufat, spring, Niger 16°8' N, 8°24' E 222
Tagula, island, P.N.G. 11°20' S, 153°16' E 192
Tagum, Philippines 7°30' N, 125°47' E 203
Tagus see Tajo, river, Sp. 39°56' N, 6°57' W 214
Tahaetkun Mountain, peak, Can. 50°15' N, 119°49' W 90
Tahakopa, N.Z. 46°31' S, 169°22' E 240
Tahala, Mor. 34°6' N, 4°25' W 214
Tahan, peak, Malaysia 4°37' N, 102°8' E 196
Tahat, Mount, peak, Alg. 23°15' N, 5°23' E 214
Ţāherī, Iran 27°43' N, 52°22' E 196
Tahiti, island, French Polynesia, Fr. 17°38' S, 149°25' W 241
Tahkoluoto, Fin. 61°37' N, 21°25' E 166
Tahkuna Nina, Est. 59°5' N, 22°35' E 166
Tahlequah, Okla., U.S. 35°53' N, 94°59' W 96
Tahltan, Can. 58°1' N, 131°1' W 108
Tahltan Lake, Can. 57°56' N, 132°22' W 108
Tahoe City, Calif., U.S. 39°10' N, 120°10' W 90
Tahoka, Tex., U.S. 33°8' N, 101°49' W 92
Taholah, Wash., U.S. 47°18' N, 124°17' W 100
Tahoua, Niger 14°54' N, 5°17' E 222
Tahquamenon, river, Mich., U.S. 46°27' N, 86°7' W 94
Tahsis, Can. 49°55' N, 126°40' W 90
Tahtalı Dağ, peak, Turk. 38°45' N, 36°42' E 156
Tahtalıdağı, peak, Turk. 36°30' N, 30°22' E 156
Tahuamanu, river, Bol. 11°13' S, 68°47' W 137
Tahuamanu, river, Peru 11°7' S, 70°52' W 137
Tahuna, Indonesia 3°41' N, 125°26' E 192
Taï, Côte d'Ivoire 5°49' N, 7°28' W 222
Tai Hu, lake, China 31°13' N, 120°0' E 198
Taï National Park, Côte d'Ivoire 5°49' N, 7°11' W 222
Tai'an, China 36°12' N, 117°8' E 198
Taibai, China 34°0' N, 107°19' E 198
Taibei see T'aipei, Taiwan 24°58' N, 121°21' E 198
Taibilla, Sierra de, Sp. 37°57' N, 2°28' W 164
Taibus Qi, China 41°52' N, 115°15' E 198
T'aichung, Taiwan 24°7' N, 120°41' E 198
Taigbe, Sierra Leone 7°25' N, 12°23' W 222
Taigetos, Óros, Gr. 37°10' N, 22°10' E 156
Taigu, China 37°26' N, 112°30' E 198
Taihape, N.Z. 39°42' S, 175°46' E 240
Taihe, China 26°47' N, 114°50' E 198
Taihe, China 33°12' N, 115°36' E 198
Taihu, China 30°26' N, 116°15' E 198
Taikkyee, Myanmar 17°20' N, 95°56' E 202
Tailai, China 46°18' N, 123°27' E 198
Taim, Braz. 32°30' S, 52°38' W 139
Taïmana, Mali 13°55' N, 6°45' W 222
Tain, Fr. 45°4' N, 4°50' E 150
T'ainan, Taiwan 22°59' N, 120°12' E 198
Taining, China 26°56' N, 117°7' E 198
Taiobeiras, Braz. 15°49' S, 42°15' W 138
Taipale, Fin. 62°38' N, 29°9' E 152
T'aipei (Taibei), Taiwan 24°58' N, 121°21' E 198
Taiping, Malaysia 4°51' N, 100°44' E 196
Taiping Ling, peak, China 47°35' N, 120°26' E 198
Taipingshao, China 40°53' N, 125°12' E 200
Taipudia, India 27°49' N, 94°35' E 188
Taira, Japan 37°2' N, 140°52' E 201
Tairua, N.Z. 36°60' S, 175°50' E 240
Taisha, Japan 35°22' N, 132°41' E 201
Taishan, China 22°16' N, 112°43' E 198
Taitao, Cabo, Chile 45°60' S, 76°26' W 134
Taitao, Península de, South America 46°27' S, 75°28' W 134
T'aitung, Taiwan 22°44' N, 121°6' E 198
Taivalkoski, Fin. 65°34' N, 28°13' E 152
Taivassalo, Fin. 60°33' N, 21°36' E 166
Taiwan 23°41' N, 120°53' E 198
Taiwan, island, Taiwan 24°25' N, 121°54' E 198
Taiwan Strait 23°49' N, 118°3' E 198
Taiyara, Sudan 13°8' N, 30°45' E 226
Taiyuan, China 37°52' N, 112°35' E 198
Taiyuan Space Launch Center, spaceport, China 37°33' N, 112°32' E 198
Taizhou, China 32°30' N, 119°55' E 198
Ta'izz, Yemen 13°35' N, 44°1' E 182
Tajarḩī, Lib. 24°21' N, 14°12' E 216
Tajerouine, Tun. 35°53' N, 8°33' E 156
Tajikistan 38°32' N, 69°13' E 184
Tajima, Japan 37°11' N, 139°46' E 201
Tajimi, Japan 35°18' N, 137°10' E 201
Tajo, river, Sp. 40°5' N, 3°6' W 164
Tajo (Tagus), river, Sp. 39°56' N, 6°57' W 214
Tajrīsh, Iran 35°52' N, 51°35' E 180
Tajumulco, Volcán, peak, Guatemala 15°0' N, 91°60' W 115
Tak, Thai. 16°52' N, 99°7' E 202
Takāb, Iran 36°27' N, 47°5' E 195
Takaba, Kenya 3°20' N, 40°10' E 224
Takahashi, Japan 34°48' N, 133°37' E 201
Takahe, Mount, peak, Antarctica 76°12' S, 111°45' W 248
Takajō, Japan 31°47' N, 131°7' E 201
Takaka, N.Z. 40°54' S, 172°50' E 240
Takamatsu, Japan 34°20' N, 134°2' E 201
Takamori, Japan 32°48' N, 131°7' E 201
Takanabe, Japan 32°7' N, 131°29' E 201
Takaoka, Japan 36°44' N, 137°1' E 201
Takapau, N.Z. 40°4' S, 176°22' E 240
Takasaki, Japan 36°18' N, 139°0' E 201
Takatsu, Japan 34°40' N, 131°48' E 200
Takaungu, Kenya 3°43' S, 39°51' E 224
Tā-kaw, Myanmar 21°15' N, 98°39' E 202
Takayama, Japan 36°8' N, 137°16' E 201
Takefu, Japan 35°53' N, 136°10' E 201
Takengon, Indonesia 4°38' N, 96°49' E 196
Takeo, Cambodia 10°58' N, 104°47' E 202
Takeo, Japan 33°11' N, 130°1' E 201
Tākestān, Iran 36°6' N, 49°39' E 180
Taketa, Japan 32°57' N, 131°24' E 201
Takhiatosh, Uzb. 42°20' N, 59°36' E 180
Takhini, Can. 60°51' N, 135°25' W 108
Takhta, Russ. 45°51' N, 41°58' E 158
Takiéta, Niger 13°41' N, 8°31' E 222
Takijuq Lake, Can. 66°22' N, 115°33' W 106
Takipy, Can. 55°24' N, 100°58' W 108
Takla Lake, Can. 55°9' N, 126°12' W 108
Takla Landing, Can. 55°28' N, 125°59' W 108
Taklimakan Shamo, China 39°27' N, 77°39' E 184
Takotna, Alas., U.S. 62°59' N, 156°4' W 98
Taksa Bor, Russ. 67°4' N, 34°40' E 152
Taku, river, Can. 58°39' N, 133°35' W 108
Takua Pa, Thai. 8°53' N, 98°20' E 202
Takum, India 27°48' N, 93°37' E 188
Takum, Nig. 7°13' N, 9°57' E 222
Takwa, river, Can. 51°32' N, 72°10' W 110
Tal, Pak. 35°28' N, 72°14' E 186
Tala, Mex. 20°38' N, 103°40' W 114
Tala, Tun. 35°32' N, 8°38' E 156
Talachyn, Belarus 54°24' N, 29°42' E 166
Talaimannar, Sri Lanka 9°6' N, 79°42' E 188
Talak, region, Niger 18°15' N, 4°51' E 222
Talara, Peru 4°37' S, 81°13' W 123
Talas, Kyrg. 42°27' N, 72°33' E 197
Talas, river, Kyrg. 42°37' N, 71°44' E 197
Talâta, Egypt 30°35' N, 32°20' E 194
Talata Mafara, Nig. 12°33' N, 6°2' E 222
Talaud, Kepulauan, islands, Philippine Sea 4°1' N, 127°6' E 192
Talavera de la Reina, Sp. 39°57' N, 4°51' W 150
Talavera la Real, Sp. 38°52' N, 6°48' W 164
Talayón, peak, Sp. 37°32' N, 1°34' W 164
Talayuelas, Sp. 39°51' N, 1°17' W 164
Talbahat, India 25°2' N, 78°27' E 197
Talbert, Sillon de, English Channel 48°54' N, 3°10' W 150
Talbot, Cape, Austral. 13°51' S, 123°45' E 172
Talbot, Mount, peak, Austral. 26°10' S, 126°25' E 230
Talca, Chile 35°25' S, 71°41' W 134
Talcahuano, Chile 36°45' S, 73°7' W 134
Talco, Tex., U.S. 33°20' N, 95°6' W 103
Taldyq, Kaz. 49°18' N, 59°52' E 158
Taldyqorghan, Kaz. 44°59' N, 78°22' E 184
Taleex, Somalia 9°10' N, 48°25' E 216
Talgarth, U.K. 51°59' N, 3°13' W 162
Talguharai, Sudan 18°14' N, 35°52' E 182
Tali Post, Sudan 5°54' N, 30°48' E 224
Taliabu, island, Indonesia 2°22' S, 124°26' E 192
Talibong, Ko, island, Thai. 7°10' N, 98°36' E 196
Talitsa, Russ. 61°8' N, 60°28' E 154
Talitsa, Russ. 58°2' N, 51°32' E 154
Talitsa, Russ. 56°59' N, 63°44' E 154
Talkot, Nepal 29°33' N, 81°18' E 197
Tall Abū Ẓahir, Iraq 36°50' N, 42°23' E 195
Tall 'Afar, Iraq 36°22' N, 42°19' E 195
Tall as Sulṭān, ruin(s), West Bank 31°52' N, 35°24' E 194
Tall Birāk, Syr. 36°39' N, 41°6' E 195
Tall Bīsah, Syr. 34°50' N, 36°43' E 194
Tall Ḩalaf, ruin(s), Syr. 36°46' N, 40°1' E 195
Tall Kalakh, Syr. 34°40' N, 36°16' E 194
Tall Kayf, Iraq 36°30' N, 43°1' E 195
Tall Kūjik, Syr. 36°48' N, 42°1' E 195
Tall Tamir, Syr. 36°38' N, 40°25' E 195
Tall Trees Grove, site, Calif., U.S. 41°12' N, 124°4' W 90
Tallahassee, Fla., U.S. 30°24' N, 84°23' W 96
Tallaringa Well, spring, Austral. 28°60' S, 133°24' E 230
Tallassee, Ala., U.S. 32°31' N, 85°54' W 96
Tällberg, Nor. 60°48' N, 14°59' E 152
Talley, U.K. 51°58' N, 3°59' W 162
Tallinn, Est. 59°11' N, 23°47' E 160
Tallinn (Reval), Est. 59°23' N, 24°37' E 166
Tallmadge, Ohio, U.S. 41°5' N, 81°26' W 102
Tallulah, La., U.S. 32°23' N, 91°12' W 103
Talmage, Calif., U.S. 39°8' N, 123°10' W 90
Talmine, Alg. 29°21' N, 0°29' E 214
Talnakh, Russ. 69°28' N, 88°34' E 169
Tal'ne, Ukr. 48°51' N, 30°49' E 158
Talo, peak, Eth. 10°38' N, 37°55' E 224
Talodi, Sudan 10°35' N, 30°24' E 224
Taloga, Okla., U.S. 36°1' N, 98°58' W 92
Talon, Russ. 59°47' N, 148°39' E 173
Taloqan, Afghan. 36°45' N, 69°31' E 186
Talorha, Mauritania 18°52' N, 12°23' W 222
Talos Dome, Antarctica 73°6' S, 161°47' E 248
Taloyoak, Can. 69°25' N, 93°20' W 106
Talpa de Allende, Mex. 20°26' N, 104°50' W 114
Talshand, Mongolia 45°20' N, 97°55' E 190
Talsi, Latv. 57°14' N, 22°34' E 166
Talsint, Mor. 32°34' N, 3°27' W 214
Taltal, Chile 25°25' S, 70°30' W 132
Taltson, river, Can. 60°34' N, 111°59' W 108
Talu, Indonesia 0°14' N, 100°0' E 196
Taluk, Indonesia 0°30' N, 101°33' E 196
Talvik, Nor. 70°2' N, 22°54' E 152
Talybont, U.K. 52°28' N, 3°59' W 162
Talyllyn, U.K. 52°38' N, 3°53' W 162
Tam Ky, Vietnam 15°34' N, 108°29' E 202
Tam Quan, Vietnam 14°34' N, 109°1' E 202
Tamada, spring, Alg. 21°37' N, 3°10' E 222
Tamala, Russ. 52°32' N, 43°14' E 158
Tamalameque, Col. 8°51' N, 73°48' W 136
Tamale, Ghana 9°24' N, 0°52' E 222
Tamale Port see Yapei, Ghana 9°10' N, 1°11' W 222
Taman', Russ. 45°13' N, 36°40' E 156
Taman Negara National Park, Malaysia 4°30' N, 102°51' E 196
Tamana, Japan 32°55' N, 130°33' E 201
Tamanar, Mor. 30°59' N, 9°41' W 214
Tamánco, Peru 5°48' S, 74°18' W 130
Tamano, Japan 34°29' N, 133°55' E 201
Tamanrasset, Alg. 22°48' N, 5°18' E 207
Támara, Col. 5°47' N, 72°10' W 136
Tamarugal, Pampa del, Chile 20°34' S, 69°24' W 132
Tamashima, Japan 34°32' N, 133°39' E 201
Tamási, Hung. 46°38' N, 18°16' E 168
Tamaulipas, adm. division, Mex. 24°20' N, 99°35' W 114
Tamaulipas, Sierra de, Mex. 23°9' N, 98°45' W 112
Tamaya, river, Peru 8°59' S, 74°11' W 137
Tamayya, Africa 23°56' N, 15°42' W 214
Tamazula, Mex. 19°39' N, 103°15' W 114
Tamazula, Mex. 24°55' N, 106°57' W 114
Tamazulapan, Mex. 17°38' N, 97°34' W 114
Tamazunchale, Mex. 21°12' N, 98°48' W 114
Tambach, Kenya 0°35' N, 35°33' E 224
Tambacounda, Senegal 13°46' N, 13°43' W 222
Tambaga, Mali 13°0' N, 9°53' W 222
Tambaqui, Braz. 5°15' S, 62°50' W 130
Tambelan Besar, island, Indonesia 0°49' N, 106°57' E 196
Tambey, Russ. 71°30' N, 71°56' E 173
Tambo de Mora, Peru 13°32' S, 76°12' W 130
Tambo, river, Peru 10°48' S, 73°53' W 137
Tambo, river, Peru 17°4' S, 71°21' W 137
Tamboril, Braz. 4°50' S, 40°22' W 132
Tambov, Russ. 52°41' N, 41°19' E 154
Tambov, adm. division, Russ. 53°5' N, 40°14' E 154
Tambunan, Malaysia 5°41' N, 116°20' E 203
Tambura, Sudan 5°34' N, 27°29' E 218
Tamchaket, Mauritania 17°16' N, 10°44' W 222
Tamel Aike, Arg. 48°18' S, 70°57' W 134
Tamesí, river, Mex. 22°26' N, 98°27' W 114
Tamesna, region, Niger 18°45' N, 4°10' E 222
Tamgak, Adrar, peak, Niger 19°11' N, 8°37' E 222
Tamgrout, Mor. 30°19' N, 5°45' W 214
Tamgué, Guinea 12°18' N, 12°21' W 222
Tamiahua, Mex. 21°14' N, 97°27' W 114
Tamiahua, Laguna de 21°29' N, 98°2' W 114
Tamil Nadu, adm. division, India 9°23' N, 77°23' E 188
Tamīnah, Lib. 32°16' N, 15°3' E 216
Tamins, Switz. 46°50' N, 9°23' E 167
Tamitatoala (Batovi), river, Braz. 14°11' S, 53°58' W 132
Tamitsa, Russ. 64°10' N, 38°5' E 154
Tammerfors see Tampere, Fin. 61°29' N, 23°43' E 166
Tammisaari see Ekenäs, Fin. 59°58' N, 23°26' E 166
Tampa, Fla., U.S. 27°58' N, 82°26' W 105
Tampa Bay 27°37' N, 83°17' W 80
Tampere, Fin. 61°23' N, 23°51' E 160
Tampere (Tammerfors), Fin. 61°29' N, 23°43' E 166
Tampico, Ill., U.S. 41°37' N, 89°48' W 102
Tampico, Mex. 22°11' N, 97°51' W 112
Tampin, Malaysia 2°29' N, 102°12' E 196
Tamrida see Hadiboh, Yemen 12°37' N, 53°49' E 173
Tamsagbulag, Mongolia 47°13' N, 117°15' E 198
Tamsalu, Est. 59°7' N, 26°5' E 166
Tamshiyacu, Peru 4°1' S, 73°6' W 130
Tamu, Myanmar 24°10' N, 94°19' E 188
Tamuín, Mex. 21°59' N, 98°46' W 114
Tamuning, U.S. 13°28' N, 144°46' E 242
Tamur, river, Nepal 26°56' N, 87°39' E 197
Tamworth, N.H., U.S. 43°51' N, 71°17' W 104
Tamworth, U.K. 52°39' N, 1°42' W 162
Tan An, Vietnam 10°32' N, 106°25' E 202
Tan Quang, Vietnam 22°30' N, 104°51' E 202
Tana, Nor. 70°27' N, 28°15' E 152
Tana, Lake, Eth. 11°57' N, 35°26' E 206
Tana, river, Europe 68°26' N, 25°33' E 160
Tana, river, Kenya 1°37' S, 40°7' E 224
Tanabe, Japan 33°43' N, 135°23' E 201
Tanacross, Alas., U.S. 63°14' N, 143°23' W 98
Tanafjorden 70°37' N, 25°20' E 160
Tanaga, island, Alas., U.S. 51°25' N, 178°58' W 160
Tanagra, ruin(s), Gr. 38°19' N, 23°26' E 156
Tanagura, Japan 37°1' N, 140°23' E 201
Tanah Merah, Malaysia 5°48' N, 102°7' E 196
Tanahbala, island, Indonesia 0°38' N, 97°40' E 196
Tanahgrogot, Indonesia 1°56' S, 116°11' E 192
Tanahmasa, island, Indonesia 0°18' N, 98°33' E 196
Tanahmerah, Indonesia 3°44' N, 117°33' E 192
Tanahmerah, Indonesia 6°14' S, 140°17' E 192
Tanakpur, India 29°4' N, 80°3' E 197
Tanalyk, river, Russ. 52°38' N, 58°2' E 154
Tanama, river, Russ. 69°45' N, 78°33' E 169
Tanami Desert, Austral. 19°13' S, 130°40' E 230
Tanami, Mount, peak, Austral. 19°59' S, 129°25' E 230
Tanana, Alas., U.S. 65°3' N, 152°16' W 98
Tanana, river, Alas., U.S. 63°31' N, 144°53' W 98
Tancheng, China 34°36' N, 118°23' E 198
Tanch'ŏn, N. Korea 40°26' N, 128°56' E 200
Tanda, India 26°31' N, 82°38' E 197
Ţăndărei, Rom. 44°38' N, 27°39' E 156
Tandaué, river, Angola 15°55' S, 16°59' E 220
Tandik, Malaysia 6°37' N, 116°52' E 203
Tandil, Arg. 37°20' S, 59°11' W 139
Tandil, Sierra del, Arg. 37°52' S, 59°49' W 134
Tando Allahyar, Pak. 25°29' N, 68°45' E 186
Tando Muhammad Khan, Pak. 25°10' N, 68°34' E 186
Tandur, India 19°9' N, 79°28' E 188
Tandur, India 17°16' N, 77°34' E 188
Tanega Shima, island, Japan 30°14' N, 131°3' E 190
Tanegashima Space Center, spaceport, Japan 30°37' N, 130°50' E 190
Tanezrouft, region, Alg. 21°41' N, 2°31' W 222
Tang Paloch, Cambodia 12°3' N, 104°21' E 202
Tanga, Tanzania 5°6' S, 39°4' E 224
Tanga, adm. division, Tanzania 5°32' S, 37°29' E 224
Tangail, Bangladesh 24°13' N, 89°54' E 197
Tangaza, Nig. 13°21' N, 4°55' E 222
Tange Promontory, Antarctica 67°10' S, 40°56' E 248
Tanger (Tangier), Mor. 35°47' N, 5°46' W 150
Tanggu, China 39°4' N, 117°40' E 198
Tanggula Shan, China 32°34' N, 90°26' E 188
Tanggula Shankou, pass, China 32°52' N, 91°57' E 188
Tanggulashan (Tuotuoheyan), China 34°10' N, 92°24' E 188
Tanghe, China 32°38' N, 112°53' E 198
Tangi, India 19°53' N, 85°23' E 188
Tangier see Tanger, Mor. 35°47' N, 5°46' W 150
Tangipahoa, La., U.S. 30°52' N, 90°31' W 103
Tanglewood, site, Mass., U.S. 42°20' N, 73°21' W 104
Tangmai, China 30°6' N, 95°7' E 188
Tango, Japan 35°42' N, 135°6' E 201
Tangra Yumco, lake, China 30°46' N, 85°46' E 197
Tangse, Indonesia 5°3' N, 95°55' E 196
Tangshan, China 39°34' N, 118°10' E 198
Tanguiéta, Benin 10°38' N, 1°16' E 222
Tanguro, river, Braz. 12°42' S, 52°30' W 138
Tanh Linh, Vietnam 11°6' N, 107°41' E 202
Tanimbar, Kepulauan, islands, Banda Sea 10°2' S, 131°4' E 238
Tanimbar, Kepulauan, islands, Indonesia 7°56' S, 132°5' E 192
Taninges, Fr. 46°6' N, 6°35' E 167
Tanintharyi, Myanmar 12°3' N, 98°59' E 202
Taniyama, Japan 31°29' N, 130°30' E 201
Tanjay, Philippines 9°31' N, 123°7' E 203

Tanjung Puting National Park, *Indonesia* 3°4' S, 111°39' E **238**
Tanjungbalai, *Indonesia* 2°59' N, 99°48' E **196**
Tanjungpandan, *Indonesia* 2°45' S, 107°40' E **192**
Tanjungpinang, *Indonesia* 0°54' N, 104°29' E **196**
Tanjungpura, *Indonesia* 3°56' N, 98°24' E **196**
Tanjungredep, *Indonesia* 2°10' N, 117°18' E **192**
Tanjungselor, *Indonesia* 2°53' N, 117°16' E **192**
Tank, *Pak.* 32°10' N, 70°25' E **186**
Tankābon, *Iran* 36°47' N, 50°54' E **180**
Tankapirtti, *Fin.* 68°15' N, 27°15' E **152**
Ta-n-Kena, *Alg.* 26°33' N, 9°36' E **214**
Tankovo, *Russ.* 60°38' N, 89°47' E **169**
Tann, *Ger.* 50°38' N, 10°1' E **167**
Tännäs, *Nor.* 62°26' N, 12°39' E **152**
Tannersville, *N.Y., U.S.* 42°11' N, 74°9' W **104**
Tannila, *Fin.* 65°27' N, 26°0' E **152**
Tannin, *Can.* 49°39' N, 91°1' W **94**
Tannur, ruin(s), *Jordan* 30°57' N, 35°40' E **194**
Tano, river, *Ghana* 6°13' N, 2°45' W **222**
Tanobato, *Indonesia* 0°46' N, 99°32' E **196**
Tanot, *India* 27°47' N, 70°19' E **186**
Tanoûchert, spring, *Mauritania* 20°46' N, 11°51' W **222**
Tanoudert, *Mauritania* 20°10' N, 16°10' W **222**
Tânout, *Niger* 14°57' N, 8°50' E **222**
Tanquián, *Mex.* 21°35' N, 98°40' W **114**
Ţanţa, *Egypt* 30°46' N, 30°58' E **180**
Tantabin, *Myanmar* 18°50' N, 96°26' E **202**
Tantallon Castle, site, *U.K.* 56°2' N, 2°45' W **150**
Tan-Tan, *Mor.* 28°25' N, 11°9' W **214**
Tantonville, *Fr.* 48°27' N, 6°8' E **163**
Tantoyuca, *Mex.* 21°19' N, 98°14' W **114**
Tanus, *Fr.* 44°6' N, 2°18' E **150**
Tanyang, *S. Korea* 36°55' N, 128°20' E **200**
Tanzania 6°44' S, 33°1' E **224**
Tao, Ko, island, *Thai.* 10°6' N, 99°39' E **202**
Tao'er, river, *China* 45°25' N, 123°5' E **198**
Taojiang, *China* 28°31' N, 112°5' E **198**
Taokest, peak, *Mauritania* 18°6' N, 9°32' W **222**
Taole, *China* 38°47' N, 106°44' E **198**
Taonan, *China* 45°19' N, 122°47' E **198**
Taos, *N. Mex., U.S.* 36°24' N, 105°34' W **92**
Taoudenni (Smeïda), *Mali* 22°41' N, 3°59' W **214**
Taoujafet, spring, *Mauritania* 18°53' N, 11°50' W **222**
Taourirt, *Alg.* 26°43' N, 0°13' E **214**
Taourirt, *Mor.* 34°27' N, 2°51' W **214**
Taoussa, *Mali* 16°56' N, 0°33' E **222**
Taouz, *Mor.* 30°57' N, 3°58' W **214**
Taoyuan, *China* 28°54' N, 111°28' E **198**
T'aoyüan, *Taiwan* 24°58' N, 121°14' E **198**
Tapa, *Est.* 59°14' N, 25°56' E **166**
Tapachula, *Mex.* 14°54' N, 92°16' W **115**
Tapah, *Malaysia* 4°11' N, 101°16' E **196**
Tapajós, river, *Braz.* 4°53' S, 55°51' W **123**
Tapaktuan, *Indonesia* 3°17' N, 97°11' E **196**
Tapalquén, *Arg.* 36°22' S, 60°5' W **139**
Tapanui, *N.Z.* 45°57' S, 169°17' E **240**
Tapauá, river, *Braz.* 6°23' S, 65°55' W **130**
Tapawera, *N.Z.* 41°23' S, 172°50' E **240**
Tapera, *Braz.* 28°37' S, 52°55' W **139**
Tapera, river, *Braz.* 0°22' N, 61°45' W **130**
Tapes, *Braz.* 30°40' S, 51°27' W **139**
Tapeta, *Liberia* 6°20' N, 8°54' W **222**
Taphan Hin, *Thai.* 16°19' N, 100°27' E **202**
Tapi, river, *India* 21°17' N, 73°33' E **186**
Tapiola, *Fin.* 60°9' N, 24°48' E **166**
Tápiószele, *Hung.* 47°20' N, 19°53' E **168**
Tapira, *Braz.* 1°20' N, 68°3' W **136**
Tapirapecó, Sierra, *Venez.* 1°27' N, 65°2' W **130**
Tapley Mountains, *Antarctica* 84°46' S, 134°49' W **248**
Tapol, *Chad* 8°31' N, 15°34' E **218**
Tapolca, *Hung.* 46°52' N, 17°27' E **168**
Tappahannock, *Va., U.S.* 37°55' N, 76°53' W **94**
Tapuaenuku, peak, *N.Z.* 42°2' S, 173°35' E **240**
Tapul, *Philippines* 5°45' N, 120°53' E **203**
Tapurucuará, *Braz.* 0°27' N, 65°6' W **130**
Ţaqah, *Oman* 17°3' N, 54°22' E **182**
Taquara, *Braz.* 29°39' S, 50°48' W **139**
Taquari, *Braz.* 17°52' S, 53°18' W **138**
Taquari, river, *Braz.* 18°45' S, 57°2' W **132**
Tar, *Croatia* 45°18' N, 13°37' E **167**
Tar, river, *N.C., U.S.* 36°12' N, 78°32' W **80**
Tara, *Russ.* 56°50' N, 74°26' E **169**
Tara, *Zambia* 16°57' S, 26°45' E **224**
Tara, Hill of, peak, *Ire.* 53°33' N, 6°44' W **150**
Tara National Park, *Serb. and Mont.* 43°49' N, 19°20' E **168**
Tara, river, *Russ.* 56°17' N, 76°25' E **169**
Taraba, river, *Nig.* 7°55' N, 10°57' E **222**
Tarabuco, *Bol.* 19°8' S, 64°58' W **137**
Ţarābulus (Tripoli), *Leb.* 34°22' N, 35°53' E **216**
Ţarābulus (Tripoli), *Lib.* 32°37' N, 12°35' E **216**
Taraclia, *Mold.* 46°33' N, 29°7' E **156**
Taraco, *Peru* 15°21' S, 69°58' W **137**
Taradale, *N.Z.* 39°32' S, 176°50' E **240**
Taragi, *Japan* 32°15' N, 130°56' E **201**
Taragma, *Sudan* 16°42' N, 33°36' E **182**
Tarairi, *Bol.* 21°9' S, 63°31' W **137**
Tarakan, *Indonesia* 3°22' N, 117°29' E **192**
Taran, Mys, *Russ.* 54°56' N, 19°42' E **166**
Taranaki, Mount (Egmont, Mount), peak, *N.Z.* 39°20' S, 173°58' E **240**
Tarancón, *Sp.* 40°0' N, 3°1' W **164**
Tarangire National Park, *Tanzania* 4°20' S, 35°41' E **224**
Taranto, *It.* 40°27' N, 17°13' E **156**
Tarapacá, *Chile* 19°56' S, 69°35' W **137**
Tarapacá, *Col.* 2°56' S, 69°44' W **136**
Tarapacá, adm. division, *Chile* 19°30' S, 70°16' W **137**
Tarapoto, *Peru* 6°31' S, 76°21' W **123**
Taraquá, *Braz.* 7°416' N, 68°25' W **136**
Tarare, *Fr.* 45°53' N, 4°25' E **150**
Tarasa Dwip, island, *India* 8°24' N, 91°59' E **188**
Tarascon, *Fr.* 42°50' N, 1°35' E **150**
Tarasovo, *Russ.* 66°16' N, 46°43' E **154**
Tarasp, *Switz.* 46°45' N, 10°13' E **167**
Tarat, *Alg.* 26°7' N, 9°22' E **214**
Tarata, *Bol.* 17°39' S, 65°53' W **137**
Tarata, *Peru* 17°33' S, 70°3' W **137**
Taratakbuluh, *Indonesia* 0°25' N, 101°26' E **196**
Tarauacá, *Braz.* 8°12' S, 70°48' W **130**
Tarauacá, river, *Braz.* 7°43' S, 70°59' W **130**
Tarawa (Bairiki), *Kiribati* 1°15' N, 169°58' E **242**
Tarawa, island, *Kiribati* 1°30' N, 173°0' E **242**
Tarawera, *N.Z.* 39°3' S, 176°34' E **240**
Tarawera, Mount, peak, *N.Z.* 38°15' S, 176°27' E **240**
Taraz, *Kaz.* 42°52' N, 71°21' E **197**
Tarazit, Massif de, *Niger* 19°41' N, 7°25' E **222**
Tarazit, spring, *Niger* 20°3' N, 8°18' E **222**
Tarazona, *Sp.* 41°53' N, 1°45' W **164**
Tarazona de la Mancha, *Sp.* 39°15' N, 1°56' W **164**
Tarbagatay Zhotasy, *Kaz.* 47°15' N, 81°21' E **184**
Tarbaj, *Kenya* 2°8' N, 40°5' E **224**
Tarbes, *Fr.* 43°13' N, 0°4' E **164**
Tarboro, *N.C., U.S.* 35°54' N, 77°34' W **96**
Tarcău, Munţii, *Rom.* 46°42' N, 25°42' E **156**
Tarcento, *It.* 46°12' N, 13°14' E **167**
Tarčin, *Bosn. and Herzg.* 43°48' N, 18°6' E **168**
Tarcoola, *Austral.* 30°44' S, 134°34' E **231**
Tardajos, *Sp.* 42°20' N, 3°50' W **164**
Tardienta, *Sp.* 41°58' N, 0°32' E **164**
Tärendö, *Nor.* 67°9' N, 22°35' E **152**
Tareraimbu, Cachoeria do, fall(s), *Braz.* 7°51' S, 53°36' W **130**
Tarfaya (Villa Bens), *Mor.* 27°55' N, 12°54' W **214**
Targane, spring, *Niger* 16°32' N, 5°43' E **222**
Targhee Pass, *Mont., U.S.* 44°39' N, 111°17' W **90**
Târgu Mureş, *Rom.* 46°33' N, 24°33' E **156**
Tarhaouhaout (Fort Motylinski), *Alg.* 22°38' N, 5°55' E **214**
Tarhmert, *Niger* 18°45' N, 8°51' E **222**
Tarhūnī, Jabal at, peak, *Lib.* 22°9' N, 22°14' E **216**
Tariana, *Braz.* 0°24' N, 68°46' W **136**
Târié, spring, *Mauritania* 20°8' N, 11°37' W **222**
Ţarīf, *U.A.E.* 24°1' N, 53°44' E **196**
Tarifa, *Sp.* 36°0' N, 5°37' W **164**
Tarifa, Punta de, *Sp.* 35°51' N, 5°36' W **164**
Tariffville, *Conn., U.S.* 41°53' N, 72°47' W **104**
Tarija, *Bol.* 21°34' S, 64°44' W **137**
Tarija, adm. division, *Bol.* 21°51' S, 64°52' W **137**
Tarik Ibn Ziad, *Alg.* 35°59' N, 2°9' E **150**
Tarīm, *Yemen* 16°5' N, 49°1' E **182**
Tarim, river, *China* 40°9' N, 80°48' E **190**
Tarime, *Tanzania* 1°20' S, 34°26' E **224**
Taringamotu, *N.Z.* 38°51' S, 175°16' E **240**
Taritatu, river, *Indonesia* 2°42' S, 138°14' E **192**
Tarka, *Niger* 14°36' N, 7°54' E **222**
Tarkastad, *S. Af.* 32°2' S, 26°14' E **227**
Tarkhankut, Mys, *Ukr.* 45°24' N, 31°29' E **156**
Tarkhoj, *Afghan.* 35°22' N, 66°36' E **186**
Tarkio, *Mo., U.S.* 40°25' N, 95°23' W **90**
Tarko Sale, *Russ.* 64°52' N, 77°50' E **169**
Tarkwa, *Ghana* 5°19' N, 1°56' W **222**
Tarlac, *Philippines* 15°30' N, 120°35' E **203**
Tarm, *Den.* 55°53' N, 8°29' E **150**
Tarma, *Peru* 3°23' S, 71°45' W **136**
Tarn, Bahia 47°57' S, 75°13' W **134**
Tarn, river, *Fr.* 43°47' N, 1°35' E **165**
Tarnak, river, *Afghan.* 31°51' N, 66°45' E **186**
Tarnogskiy Gorodok, *Russ.* 60°27' N, 43°38' E **154**
Tarnów, *Pol.* 50°0' N, 20°59' E **152**
Tarnya, *Russ.* 62°5' N, 42°24' E **154**
Ţārom, *Iran* 28°8' N, 55°43' E **196**
Tarou, spring, *Chad* 20°41' N, 19°14' E **216**
Tarpon Springs, *Fla., U.S.* 28°8' N, 82°44' W **105**
Tarporley, *U.K.* 53°9' N, 2°38' W **162**
Tarragona, *Sp.* 41°7' N, 1°15' E **164**
Tarras, *N.Z.* 44°50' S, 169°25' E **240**
Tàrrega, *Sp.* 41°38' N, 1°8' E **164**
Tarrekaise, peak, *Nor.* 67°1' N, 17°14' E **152**
Tarrytown, *N.Y., U.S.* 41°3' N, 73°52' W **104**
Tarsus, *Turk.* 36°53' N, 34°53' E **156**
Tart, *China* 37°4' N, 92°51' E **188**
Tartagal, *Arg.* 28°37' S, 59°53' W **139**
Tartagal, *Arg.* 22°29' S, 63°53' W **137**
Tartar Strait 47°18' N, 139°16' E **238**
Tartas, river, *Russ.* 56°24' N, 78°32' E **169**
Tartu, *Est.* 58°21' N, 26°40' E **166**
Ţarţūs (Tortosa), *Syr.* 34°53' N, 35°53' E **194**
Tarumizu, *Japan* 31°28' N, 130°43' E **201**
Tarusa, *Russ.* 54°42' N, 37°10' E **154**
Tarutao, Ko, island, *Thai.* 6°38' N, 99°41' E **196**
Tarutung, *Indonesia* 2°0' N, 98°56' E **196**
Tarvisio, *It.* 46°30' N, 13°34' E **156**
Tasa, *N. Korea* 39°49' N, 124°23' E **200**
Tasajera, Sierra de la, *Mex.* 29°34' N, 105°52' W **112**
Tasāwah, *Lib.* 26°2' N, 13°31' E **216**
Taschereau, *Can.* 48°40' N, 78°43' W **110**
Tascosa, *Tex., U.S.* 35°28' N, 102°14' W **92**
Taseko Mountain, peak, *Can.* 51°13' N, 123°36' W **90**
Taseko, river, *Can.* 51°45' N, 123°40' W **108**
Tashanta, *Russ.* 49°41' N, 89°10' E **184**
Tashigang, *Bhutan* 27°16' N, 91°33' E **188**
Tashk, Daryācheh-ye, lake, *Iran* 29°46' N, 53°13' E **196**
Tashkent see Toshkent, *Uzb.* 41°18' N, 69°10' E **197**
Tash-Kömür, *Kyrg.* 41°23' N, 72°15' E **197**
Tashla, *Russ.* 51°46' N, 52°44' E **158**
Tashota, *Can.* 50°14' N, 87°40' W **94**
Tashtagol, *Russ.* 52°48' N, 88°0' E **184**
Tashtyp, *Russ.* 52°49' N, 89°56' E **184**
Tasiilaq 65°39' N, 37°48' W **106**
Tasikmalaya, *Indonesia* 7°21' S, 108°12' E **238**
Tasiusaq 73°22' N, 56°3' W **106**
Tåsjö, *Nor.* 64°12' N, 15°56' E **152**
Tåsjön, lake, *Nor.* 64°20' N, 15°12' E **152**
Task, *Niger* 14°54' N, 10°43' E **222**
Taskan, *Russ.* 63°14' N, 150°29' E **160**
Tasker, *Niger* 15°12' N, 10°46' E **222**
Taskesken, *Kaz.* 47°14' N, 80°45' E **184**
Taskinigup Falls, *Can.* 55°24' N, 98°60' W **108**
Taşköprü, *Turk.* 41°30' N, 34°12' E **156**
Tasman, *N.Z.* 41°14' S, 173°2' E **240**
Tasman Fracture Zone, *South Pacific Ocean* 52°43' S, 147°43' E **255**
Tasman Peninsula, *Austral.* 42°49' S, 147°14' E **230**
Tasman Plain, *Tasman Sea* 35°46' S, 153°34' E **252**
Tasman Sea 37°36' S, 153°44' E **231**
Tasmania, adm. division, *Austral.* 42°4' S, 145°43' E **231**
Tăşnad, *Rom.* 47°27' N, 22°36' E **168**
Taşova, *Turk.* 40°47' N, 36°19' E **156**
Tass, *Hung.* 47°1' N, 19°2' E **168**
Tassara, *Niger* 16°49' N, 5°29' E **222**
Tassialouc, Lac, lake, *Can.* 58°58' N, 76°3' W **106**
Tassili-n-Ajjer National Park, *Alg.* 25°43' N, 7°49' E **214**
Tassili-n-Ajjer, region, *Alg.* 25°32' N, 7°10' E **214**
Tasso Fragoso, *Braz.* 8°30' S, 45°46' W **130**
Tast, Lac du, lake, *Can.* 50°58' N, 77°53' W **110**
Tasty-Taldy, *Kaz.* 50°43' N, 66°37' E **184**
Tata, *Mor.* 29°45' N, 7°59' W **214**
Tatabánya, *Hung.* 47°32' N, 18°26' E **168**
Tatalin, river, *China* 37°33' N, 96°17' E **188**
Tatar Strait 48°40' N, 136°53' E **172**
Tatarbunary, *Ukr.* 45°49' N, 29°35' E **156**
Tatarsk, *Russ.* 55°10' N, 75°59' E **184**
Tatarskiy Proliv 50°55' N, 141°25' E **190**
Tatarstan, adm. division, *Russ.* 55°18' N, 48°59' E **154**
Tatau, island, *P.N.G.* 2°42' S, 151°9' E **192**
Tate, *Ga., U.S.* 34°24' N, 84°24' W **96**
Tatebayashi, *Japan* 36°14' N, 139°32' E **201**
Tateyama, *Japan* 34°58' N, 139°52' E **201**
Tathlina Lake, *Can.* 60°31' N, 118°6' W **108**
Tathlīth, *Saudi Arabia* 19°30' N, 43°30' E **182**
Tatishchevo, *Russ.* 51°39' N, 45°35' E **158**
Tatkon, *Myanmar* 20°8' N, 96°14' E **202**
Tatlatui Lake, *Can.* 56°53' N, 127°53' W **108**
Tatlayoko Lake, *Can.* 51°34' N, 125°6' W **108**
Tatman Mountain, peak, *Wyo., U.S.* 44°16' N, 108°33' W **90**
Tatnam, Cape, *Can.* 57°19' N, 90°49' W **106**
Tatoosh Island, *Wash., U.S.* 48°17' N, 124°55' W **100**
Tatrang, *China* 38°35' N, 85°50' E **184**
Tatrart, spring, *Mauritania* 17°32' N, 10°21' W **222**
Tatry, *Pol.* 49°7' N, 19°22' E **152**
Tatsamenie Lake, *Can.* 58°19' N, 133°15' W **108**
Tattershall, *U.K.* 53°4' N, 0°12' E **162**
Tätti, *Kaz.* 43°12' N, 73°20' E **184**
Tatuí, *Braz.* 23°22' S, 47°50' W **138**
Tatuke, *Liberia* 5°9' N, 8°17' W **222**
Tatum, *N. Mex., U.S.* 33°14' N, 103°19' W **92**
Tatum, *Tex., U.S.* 32°18' N, 94°32' W **103**
Tatvan, *Turk.* 38°30' N, 42°14' E **195**
Tau, island, *U.S.* 14°14' S, 169°29' W **241**
Tauá, *Braz.* 6°2' S, 40°24' W **132**
Tauapeçaçu, *Braz.* 2°41' S, 60°57' W **130**
Taubaté, *Braz.* 23°3' S, 45°34' W **138**
Tauern, Hohe, *Aust.* 46°51' N, 12°14' E **167**
Taulabé National Monument, *Hond.* 14°42' N, 88°3' W **115**
Taum Sauk Mountain, peak, *Mo., U.S.* 37°32' N, 90°48' W **96**
Taumarunui, *N.Z.* 38°54' S, 175°17' E **240**
Taumatawhakatangihangakoauauotamateapokai-whenuakitanatahu, peak, *N.Z.* 40°21' S, 176°29' E **240**
Taung, *S. Af.* 27°33' S, 24°47' E **227**
Taunggok, *Myanmar* 18°51' N, 94°15' E **202**
Taungoo, *Myanmar* 18°58' N, 96°23' E **202**
Taungup Pass, *Myanmar* 18°40' N, 94°45' E **202**
Taunsa, *Pak.* 30°42' N, 70°40' E **186**
Taunsa Barrage, dam, *Pak.* 30°13' N, 70°38' E **186**
Taunton, *Mass., U.S.* 41°54' N, 71°6' W **104**
Taunton, *U.K.* 51°0' N, 3°7' W **162**
Taunus, *Ger.* 50°18' N, 7°54' E **167**
Taunusstein, *Ger.* 50°8' N, 8°11' E **167**
Taupo, *N.Z.* 38°43' S, 176°7' E **240**
Tauragė, *Lith.* 55°15' N, 22°17' E **166**
Tauramena, *Col.* 5°1' N, 72°45' W **136**
Taureau, Réservoir, lake, *Can.* 46°45' N, 74°23' W **94**
Taurus see Toros Dağlar, *Turk.* 36°29' N, 32°7' E **156**
Taūshyq, *Kaz.* 44°17' N, 51°18' E **158**
Tauste, *Sp.* 41°55' N, 1°16' W **164**
Tauyskaya Guba 59°1' N, 147°41' E **160**
Tavankut, *Serb. and Mont.* 46°2' N, 19°29' E **168**
Tavares, *Braz.* 31°13' S, 50°60' W **139**
Tavares, *Fla., U.S.* 28°48' N, 81°45' W **105**
Tavas, *Turk.* 37°34' N, 29°3' E **156**
Tavda, *Russ.* 57°58' N, 65°19' E **160**
Tavda, river, *Russ.* 59°37' N, 62°54' E **154**
Tavernes de la Valldigna, *Sp.* 39°4' N, 0°16' E **164**
Tavernier, *Fla., U.S.* 25°1' N, 80°32' W **105**
Taveta, *Kenya* 3°25' S, 37°40' E **218**
Taveta, *Tanzania* 9°2' S, 35°32' E **224**
Taviche, *Mex.* 16°43' N, 96°35' W **112**
Tavistock, *Can.* 43°19' N, 80°49' W **102**
Tavoy Point, *Myanmar* 13°31' N, 97°43' E **202**
Tavricheskoye, *Russ.* 54°32' N, 73°36' E **184**
Tavşanlı, *Turk.* 39°33' N, 29°30' E **156**
Tawai, *India* 27°46' N, 96°46' E **188**
Tawake, *Liberia* 5°10' N, 7°38' W **222**
Tawang, *India* 27°36' N, 91°51' E **197**
Tawau, *Malaysia* 4°19' N, 117°53' E **192**
Taweisha, *Sudan* 12°14' N, 26°39' E **216**
Tawi Tawi, island, *Philippines* 5°14' N, 119°31' E **192**
Tawu, *Taiwan* 22°22' N, 120°52' E **198**
Ţāwūq, *Iraq* 35°9' N, 44°26' E **180**
Tāwurghā', *Lib.* 32°5' N, 15°8' E **216**
Taxco, *Mex.* 18°32' N, 99°37' W **114**
Taxila, ruin(s), *Pak.* 33°43' N, 72°38' E **186**
Taxkorgan, *China* 37°48' N, 75°9' E **184**
Tay Ninh, *Vietnam* 11°18' N, 106°4' E **202**
Tay, river, *Can.* 62°38' N, 133°39' W **98**
Tayabas Bay 13°36' N, 121°40' E **203**
Tayarte, spring, *Alg.* 23°6' N, 0°20' E **214**
Tayeeglow, *Somalia* 4°1' N, 44°31' E **218**
Tayga, *Russ.* 56°3' N, 85°46' E **169**
Taygonos, Poluostrov, *Russ.* 62°44' N, 159°36' E **160**
Tayildara, *Taj.* 38°40' N, 70°31' E **197**
Taylakova, *Russ.* 59°11' N, 74°0' E **169**
Taylor, *Ariz., U.S.* 34°28' N, 110°5' W **92**
Taylor, *Ark., U.S.* 33°6' N, 93°28' W **103**
Taylor, *Tex., U.S.* 30°33' N, 97°24' W **96**
Taylor, Mount, peak, *N. Mex., U.S.* 35°14' N, 107°42' W **92**
Taylor Mountain, peak, *Idaho, U.S.* 44°52' N, 114°17' W **90**
Taylor Mountains, peak, *Alas., U.S.* 60°47' N, 157°45' W **98**
Taylors Head, *Can.* 44°41' N, 62°34' W **111**
Taylorsville, *Ind., U.S.* 39°17' N, 85°57' W **102**
Taylorsville, *Miss., U.S.* 31°50' N, 89°26' W **103**
Taylorville, *Ill., U.S.* 39°32' N, 89°18' W **102**
Taymā', *Saudi Arabia* 27°36' N, 38°28' E **180**
Taymura, river, *Russ.* 63°11' N, 99°3' E **160**
Taymylyr, *Russ.* 72°29' N, 122°5' E **160**
Taymyr, adm. division, *Russ.* 68°43' N, 85°44' E **169**
Taymyr, Ozero, lake, *Russ.* 74°33' N, 99°13' E **160**
Taymyr, Poluostrov, *Russ.* 75°28' N, 84°4' E **160**
Taypaq, *Kaz.* 48°57' N, 51°47' E **158**
Tayshet, *Russ.* 55°57' N, 98°2' E **160**
Taytay, *Philippines* 10°47' N, 119°31' E **203**
Ţayyebāt, *Iran* 34°50' N, 60°47' E **180**
Tayynsha, *Kaz.* 53°49' N, 69°25' E **160**
Taz, river, *Russ.* 64°55' N, 81°39' E **169**
Taz, river, *Russ.* 63°43' N, 84°32' E **169**
Taza, *Mor.* 34°15' N, 4°4' W **214**
Tazadite, spring, *Mali* 24°32' N, 4°56' W **214**
Taze, *Myanmar* 22°57' N, 95°25' E **202**
Tazin Lake, *Can.* 59°50' N, 110°4' W **108**
Tazin, river, *Can.* 59°41' N, 108°48' W **108**
Tazin, river, *Can.* 60°21' N, 110°59' W **108**
Tāzirbū, *Lib.* 25°47' N, 21°2' E **216**
Tazolé, *Niger* 17°12' N, 9°10' E **222**
Tazouikert, spring, *Mali* 21°32' N, 1°19' W **222**
Tazovskaya Guba 68°46' N, 74°22' E **169**
Tazovskiy, *Russ.* 67°21' N, 78°43' E **169**
Tazzaït, spring, *Alg.* 26°57' N, 5°55' E **214**
Tazzarine, *Mor.* 30°46' N, 5°34' W **214**
T'bilisi, *Ga.* 41°42' N, 44°42' E **195**
Tbilisskaya, *Russ.* 45°22' N, 40°7' E **158**
Tchamba, *Togo* 8°56' N, 1°22' E **222**
Tchaourou, *Benin* 8°54' N, 2°35' E **222**
Tchentlo Lake, *Can.* 55°11' N, 125°26' W **108**
Tchibanga, *Gabon* 2°58' S, 10°56' E **207**
Tchié, spring, *Chad* 17°6' N, 18°53' E **216**
Tchin-Tabaradène, *Niger* 15°45' N, 5°38' E **222**
Tchula, *Miss., U.S.* 33°9' N, 90°14' W **103**
Te Anau, *N.Z.* 45°26' S, 167°44' E **240**
Te Anau, Lake, *N.Z.* 45°12' S, 167°25' E **240**
Te Araroa, *N.Z.* 37°40' S, 178°20' E **240**
Te Aroha, *N.Z.* 37°33' S, 175°43' E **240**
Te Hapua, *N.Z.* 34°32' S, 172°54' E **240**
Te Kaha, *N.Z.* 37°46' S, 177°41' E **240**
Te Kao, *N.Z.* 34°40' S, 172°57' E **240**
Te Karaka, *N.Z.* 38°29' S, 177°51' E **240**
Te Kauwhata, *N.Z.* 37°25' S, 175°9' E **240**
Te Kopuru, *N.Z.* 36°3' S, 173°55' E **240**
Te Kuiti, *N.Z.* 38°23' S, 175°8' E **240**
Te Pohue, *N.Z.* 39°16' S, 176°42' E **240**
Te Puia Springs, *N.Z.* 38°3' S, 178°18' E **240**
Te Puke, *N.Z.* 37°48' S, 176°19' E **240**
Te Teko, *N.Z.* 38°3' S, 176°47' E **240**
Tea, river, *Braz.* 0°37' N, 65°37' W **136**
Teacapan, *Mex.* 22°33' N, 105°44' W **114**
Teague, *Tex., U.S.* 31°36' N, 96°17' W **96**
Teapa, *Mex.* 17°32' N, 92°57' W **115**
Teapot Dome, peak, *Wyo., U.S.* 43°13' N, 106°16' W **90**
Tearce, *Maced.* 42°4' N, 21°3' E **168**
Teba, *Sp.* 36°59' N, 4°56' W **164**
Ţebea, *Rom.* 46°10' N, 22°45' E **168**
Teberda, *Russ.* 43°27' N, 41°42' E **195**
Tébessa, *Alg.* 35°23' N, 8°8' E **156**
Tebicuary, river, *Parag.* 26°29' S, 58°1' W **139**
Tebingtinggi, *Indonesia* 3°19' N, 99°8' E **196**
Tebingtinggi, island, *Indonesia* 0°36' N, 102°10' E **196**
Teboursouq, *Tun.* 36°26' N, 9°14' E **216**
Tebra, river, *Latv.* 56°53' N, 21°20' E **152**
Tebulosmta, peak, *Russ.* 42°34' N, 45°21' E **195**
Tecalitlán, *Mex.* 19°27' N, 103°18' W **114**
Tecate, *Mex.* 32°34' N, 116°39' W **101**
Techa, river, *Russ.* 55°37' N, 61°59' E **154**
Tecolote, *Mex.* 32°34' N, 114°60' W **101**
Tecolotlán, *Mex.* 20°12' N, 104°3' W **114**
Tecomán, *Mex.* 18°54' N, 103°53' W **112**
Tecopa, *Calif., U.S.* 35°50' N, 116°14' W **101**
Tecopa Hot Springs, *Calif., U.S.* 35°52' N, 116°14' W **101**
Tecoripa, *Mex.* 28°36' N, 109°56' W **92**
Tecozautla, *Mex.* 20°31' N, 99°38' W **114**
Tecpan, *Mex.* 17°11' N, 100°38' W **114**
Tecuala, *Mex.* 22°23' N, 105°29' W **114**
Tecumseh, *Can.* 42°17' N, 82°53' W **102**
Tecumseh, *Mich., U.S.* 42°0' N, 83°57' W **102**
Ted Ceidaar Dabole, *Somalia* 4°21' N, 43°56' E **218**
Teerijärvi see Terjärv, *Fin.* 63°32' N, 23°29' E **154**
Tefé, *Braz.* 3°29' S, 64°46' W **123**
Tefé, river, *Braz.* 3°50' S, 65°20' W **130**
Tefenni, *Turk.* 37°17' N, 29°46' E **156**
Tegalhusi, *Sudan* 15°29' N, 36°14' E **182**
Tegea, ruin(s), *Gr.* 37°27' N, 22°19' E **156**
Tegelen, *Neth.* 51°20' N, 6°8' E **167**
Tegina, *Nig.* 10°3' N, 6°11' E **222**
Tégouma, spring, *Niger* 15°42' N, 9°15' E **222**
Tegucigalpa, *Hond.* 14°3' N, 87°21' W **115**
Teguidda-n-Tessoumt, *Niger* 17°26' N, 6°38' E **222**
Tegul'det, *Russ.* 57°18' N, 88°16' E **169**
Tehachapi, *Calif., U.S.* 35°8' N, 118°28' W **101**
Tehachapi Mountains, *Calif., U.S.* 34°56' N, 118°40' W **101**
Tehachapi Pass, *Calif., U.S.* 35°6' N, 118°18' W **101**
Tehama, *Calif., U.S.* 40°1' N, 122°8' W **92**
Tehamiyam, *Sudan* 18°19' N, 36°28' E **182**
Tehek Lake, *Can.* 65°13' N, 97°17' W **106**
Téhini, *Côte d'Ivoire* 9°36' N, 3°41' W **222**
Tehrān, *Iran* 35°41' N, 51°20' E **180**
Tehuacán, *Mex.* 18°25' N, 97°25' W **114**
Tehuantepec, Istmo de, *Mex.* 17°38' N, 95°8' W **114**
Tehuantepec, Golfo de 15°10' N, 96°44' W **73**
Teide, Pico de, peak, *Sp.* 28°12' N, 16°47' W **214**
Teifi, river, *U.K.* 52°6' N, 4°40' W **150**
Teisko, *Fin.* 61°40' N, 23°47' E **166**
Teixeiro, *Sp.* 43°5' N, 8°4' W **150**
Tejen, *Turkm.* 37°23' N, 60°30' E **180**
Tejo, river, *Braz.* 9°12' S, 72°23' W **137**
Tejo, river, *Port.* 39°28' N, 8°16' W **150**
Tejon Pass, *Calif., U.S.* 34°47' N, 118°53' W **101**
Teju, *India* 27°54' N, 96°11' E **188**
Tejupan, Punta, *Mex.* 18°21' N, 103°32' W **114**
Tejupilco, *Mex.* 18°52' N, 100°9' W **114**
Tekamah, *Nebr., U.S.* 41°45' N, 96°13' W **90**
Tekax, *Mex.* 20°11' N, 89°18' W **112**
Tekes, *China* 43°11' N, 81°50' E **184**
Tekes, river, *Asia* 42°55' N, 80°31' E **184**
Tekezē, river, *Eth.* 13°44' N, 38°33' E **182**
Tekiliktag, peak, *China* 36°31' N, 80°15' E **184**
Tekirdağ, *Turk.* 40°58' N, 27°30' E **156**
Tekirova, *Turk.* 36°29' N, 30°29' E **156**
Tekkali, *India* 18°37' N, 84°13' E **188**
Tekman, *Turk.* 39°37' N, 41°30' E **195**
Teknaf, *Bangladesh* 20°52' N, 92°16' E **188**
Tekoa, *Wash., U.S.* 47°13' N, 117°6' W **90**
Tekro, spring, *Chad* 19°29' N, 20°56' E **216**
Tel Aviv-Yafo, *Israel* 32°2' N, 34°45' E **194**
Tel Jemmeh, ruin(s), *Israel* 31°22' N, 34°24' E **194**
Tela, *Hond.* 15°45' N, 87°26' W **115**
Télabit, *Mali* 19°4' N, 0°56' E **222**
Telaga, island, *Indonesia* 3°10' N, 105°42' E **196**
Telataipale, *Fin.* 61°37' N, 28°36' E **166**
T'elavi, *Ga.* 41°55' N, 45°28' E **195**
Tele, river, *Dem. Rep. of the Congo* 2°29' N, 24°31' E **224**
Telegraph Creek, *Can.* 57°55' N, 131°12' W **108**
Telêmaco Borba, *Braz.* 24°25' S, 50°38' W **138**
Telemark, region, *Nor.* 59°13' N, 7°55' E **152**
Teleneşti, *Mold.* 47°29' N, 28°21' E **156**
Teleorman, adm. division, *Rom.* 43°47' N, 24°43' E **156**
Telerhteba, Djebel, peak, *Alg.* 24°11' N, 6°46' E **214**
Teles Pires (São Manuel), river, *Braz.* 9°30' S, 55°14' W **122**
Telescope Peak, *Calif., U.S.* 36°9' N, 117°8' W **101**
Teletskoye Ozero, lake, *Russ.* 51°38' N, 86°38' E **184**
Telfel, spring, *Mali* 19°9' N, 3°39' W **222**
Telford, *U.K.* 52°40' N, 2°29' W **162**
Telgte, *Ger.* 51°58' N, 7°46' E **167**
Télimélé, *Guinea* 10°54' N, 13°5' W **222**
Telixtlahuaca, *Mex.* 17°15' N, 96°51' W **114**
Teljo, Jebel, peak, *Sudan* 14°40' N, 25°52' E **226**
Telkwa, *Can.* 54°40' N, 127°7' W **108**
Tell City, *Ind., U.S.* 37°56' N, 86°45' W **96**
Tell el 'Amârna, ruin(s), *Egypt* 27°39' N, 30°48' E **180**
Tell Tayinat, ruin(s), *Turk.* 36°14' N, 36°16' E **156**
Tellicherry (Thalassery), *India* 11°45' N, 75°29' E **188**
Tellier, *Arg.* 47°37' S, 66°4' W **134**
Telluride, *Colo., U.S.* 37°56' N, 107°50' W **92**
Telo, *Indonesia* 2°118' S, 98°15' E **196**
Teloloapan, *Mex.* 18°20' N, 99°53' W **114**
Telsen, *Arg.* 42°28' S, 66°51' W **134**
Telšiai, *Lith.* 55°59' N, 22°14' E **166**
Teluk Intan, *Malaysia* 4°1' N, 101°1' E **196**
Telukbutun, *Indonesia* 4°14' N, 108°13' E **196**
Telukdalem, *Indonesia* 0°37' N, 97°48' E **196**
Tema, *Ghana* 5°41' N, 1°60' E **222**
Temagami, Lake, *Can.* 46°59' N, 80°43' W **110**
Tembenchi, *Russ.* 64°56' N, 99°16' E **246**
Tembenchi, river, *Russ.* 66°3' N, 94°53' E **169**
Témbi, *Gr.* 39°46' N, 22°18' E **156**
Tembilahan, *Indonesia* 0°18' N, 103°8' E **196**
Temblor Range, *Calif., U.S.* 35°28' N, 120°5' W **100**
Teme, river, *U.K.* 52°17' N, 2°29' W **162**
Temecula, *Calif., U.S.* 33°29' N, 117°10' W **101**
Temerin, *Serb. and Mont.* 45°23' N, 19°53' E **168**
Temerloh, *Malaysia* 3°28' N, 102°23' E **196**
Temiang, island, *Indonesia* 2°57' N, 106°9' E **196**
Temir, *Kaz.* 49°8' N, 57°7' E **158**
Temir, *Kaz.* 42°48' N, 68°26' E **197**
Temirgoyevskaya, *Russ.* 45°6' N, 40°15' E **158**
Temirtaū, *Kaz.* 50°10' N, 73°2' E **190**
Temirtaū, *Kaz.* 50°5' N, 72°53' E **184**
Temirtau, *Russ.* 53°9' N, 87°35' E **184**
Témiscamie, Lac, lake, *Can.* 51°6' N, 72°55' W **110**
Témiscaming, *Can.* 46°44' N, 79°6' W **94**
Temnikov, *Russ.* 54°38' N, 43°16' E **154**
Temósachic, *Mex.* 28°57' N, 107°50' W **92**
Tempe, *Ariz., U.S.* 33°24' N, 111°58' W **112**
Tempestad, *Peru* 1°20' S, 74°56' W **136**
Temple, *N.H., U.S.* 42°48' N, 71°51' W **104**
Temple, *Okla., U.S.* 34°14' N, 98°14' W **92**
Temple, *Tex., U.S.* 31°5' N, 97°20' W **96**
Temple Bar, *Ariz., U.S.* 36°0' N, 114°20' W **101**
Temple, Mount, peak, *Can.* 51°20' N, 116°17' W **90**
Templeman, Mount, peak, *Can.* 50°40' N, 117°19' W **90**
Templeton, *Calif., U.S.* 35°33' N, 120°44' W **100**
Templeton, *Mass., U.S.* 42°33' N, 72°5' W **104**
Tempoal, *Mex.* 21°31' N, 98°26' W **114**
Tempué, *Angola* 13°30' S, 18°50' E **220**
Temryuk, *Russ.* 45°18' N, 37°24' E **156**
Temryukskiy Zaliv 45°23' N, 37°2' E **158**
Temse, *Belg.* 51°7' N, 4°12' E **163**
Temuco, *Chile* 38°43' S, 72°39' W **134**
Temuka, *N.Z.* 44°15' S, 171°18' E **240**
Ten Degree Channel 9°44' N, 91°13' E **188**
Ten Sleep, *Wyo., U.S.* 44°1' N, 107°26' W **90**
Ten Thousand Islands, *Gulf of Mexico* 25°48' N, 81°41' W **105**
Tena, *Ecua.* 1°4' S, 77°55' W **136**

enabo, Mount, peak, *Nev., U.S.* 40°9' N, 116°42' W **90**
enaha, *Tex., U.S.* 31°55' N, 94°15' W **103**
enakee Springs, *Alas., U.S.* 57°48' N, 135°11' W **108**
enala, *Fin.* 60°2' N, 23°17' E **166**
enamaxtlán, *Mex.* 20°11' N, 104°10' W **114**
enancingo, *Mex.* 18°56' N, 99°38' W **114**
enay, *Fr.* 45°55' N, 5°30' E **156**
enbury, *U.K.* 52°17' N, 2°36' W **162**
endaho, *Eth.* 11°39' N, 40°56' E **182**
ende, *Fr.* 44°5' N, 7°34' E **167**
endelti, *Sudan* 13°0' N, 31°52' E **182**
endō, *Japan* 38°22' N, 140°22' E **201**
endoy Mountains, *Mont., U.S.* 44°49' N, 113°6' W **90**
endrara, *Mor.* 33°5' N, 1°60' W **214**
endürek Dağı, peak, *Turk.* 39°20' N, 43°50' E **195**
enekert, spring, *Mali* 17°48' N, 3°9' E **222**
énenkou, *Mali* 14°28' N, 4°57' W **222**
énéré, *Niger* 19°23' N, 9°29' E **222**
énéré du Tafassâsset, region, *Niger* 20°49' N, 9°47' E **222**
énéré, 'Erg du, *Niger* 17°10' N, 9°47' E **222**
enerife, island, *Sp.* 28°32' N, 16°3' W **214**
énès, *Alg.* 36°30' N, 1°18' E **150**
enexpa, *Mex.* 17°10' N, 100°43' W **114**
eng'aopu, *China* 41°5' N, 122°48' E **200**
engchong, *China* 25°3' N, 98°26' E **190**
engge, *Kaz.* 43°16' N, 52°46' E **158**
engiz, oil field, *Kaz.* 46°7' N, 53°23' E **158**
engizy Köli, lake, *Kaz.* 50°11' N, 68°11' E **184**
engxian, *China* 35°5' N, 117°9' E **198**
engxian, *China* 23°16' N, 110°51' E **198**
eniente Origone, *Arg.* 39°6' S, 62°35' W **139**
enino, *Wash., U.S.* 46°50' N, 122°52' W **100**
enke, *Dem. Rep. of the Congo* 10°36' S, 26°10' E **224**
enkeli, *Russ.* 70°10' N, 140°46' E **160**
enkergynpil'gyn, Laguna 68°29' N, 178°36' E **98**
en'ki, *Russ.* 55°24' N, 48°54' E **154**
enkodogo, *Burkina Faso* 11°46' N, 0°22' E **222**
enlaa, *India* 7°1' N, 93°58' E **188**
ennant Creek, *Austral.* 19°38' S, 134°13' E **231**
ennessee, adm. division, *Tenn., U.S.* 35°41' N, 87°31' W **96**
ennessee Pass, *Colo., U.S.* 39°20' N, 106°19' W **90**
enojoki, river, *Europe* 68°54' N, 25°39' E **160**
enosique, *Mex.* 17°28' N, 91°26' W **116**
enryū, river, *Japan* 35°7' N, 137°41' E **201**
ensas, river, *La., U.S.* 32°8' N, 91°21' W **103**
ensaw, *Ala., U.S.* 31°8' N, 87°48' W **103**
entane, *Mauritania* 19°55' N, 13°3' W **222**
eocaltiche, *Mex.* 21°25' N, 102°34' W **114**
eodelina, *Arg.* 34°12' S, 61°34' W **139**
eófilo Otoni, *Braz.* 17°49' S, 41°32' W **138**
eofipol', *Ukr.* 49°49' N, 26°24' E **152**
eolo, *It.* 45°20' N, 11°40' E **167**
eora, *It.* 40°52' N, 15°16' E **156**
eotepec, Cerro, peak, *Mex.* 17°26' N, 100°13' W **114**
eotihuacan, ruin(s), *Mex.* 19°40' N, 98°57' W **114**
epache, *Mex.* 29°31' N, 109°31' W **92**
epalcatepec, *Mex.* 19°10' N, 102°52' W **114**
epalcatepec, river, *Mex.* 19°0' N, 102°44' W **114**
epatitlán, *Mex.* 20°48' N, 102°47' W **114**
epe Gawra, ruin(s), *Iraq* 36°32' N, 43°7' E **195**
epe Musyan, ruin(s), *Iran* 32°34' N, 47°9' E **180**
epe, peak, *Europe* 42°43' N, 21°31' E **168**
epechitlán, *Mex.* 21°38' N, 103°19' W **114**
epecoacuilco, *Mex.* 18°16' N, 99°29' W **114**
epehuanes, *Mex.* 25°21' N, 105°42' W **114**
epeji de Ocampo, *Mex.* 19°52' N, 99°20' W **114**
epetongo, *Mex.* 22°27' N, 103°8' W **114**
epic, *Mex.* 21°29' N, 104°57' W **114**
epich, *Mex.* 20°17' N, 88°14' W **115**
epoca, Cabo, *Mex.* 30°4' N, 113°3' W **92**
eposcolula, *Mex.* 17°29' N, 97°31' W **114**
equila, *Mex.* 20°53' N, 103°49' W **114**
equisquiapan, *Mex.* 20°30' N, 99°54' W **114**
er Apel, *Neth.* 52°52' N, 7°4' E **163**
'er, river, *Eth.* 7°14' N, 41°49' E **224**
éra, *Niger* 13°59' N, 0°46' E **222**
eradomari, *Japan* 37°37' N, 138°47' E **201**
erakeka, *Sudan* 5°25' N, 31°43' E **224**
eramo, *It.* 42°39' N, 13°42' E **156**
ercan, *Turk.* 39°47' N, 40°22' E **195**
eregova, *Rom.* 45°7' N, 22°18' E **168**
erek, river, *Russ.* 43°24' N, 46°17' E **195**
erekhovka, *Belarus* 52°10' N, 31°30' E **158**
erekli Mekteb, *Russ.* 44°9' N, 45°53' E **158**
erekty, *Kaz.* 48°22' N, 85°39' E **184**
erempa, *Indonesia* 3°14' N, 106°12' E **196**
erengözek, *Kaz.* 45°2' N, 64°59' E **184**
erenos, *Braz.* 20°24' S, 54°51' W **132**
ereressene, spring, *Mali* 16°55' N, 2°39' E **222**
eresa Cristina, *Braz.* 24°52' S, 51°6' W **138**
eresina, *Braz.* 5°3' S, 42°48' W **132**
eresinha, *Braz.* 0°57' N, 52°1' W **130**
eresita, *Peru* 12°35' S, 73°47' W **137**
erezino Polje, *Croatia* 45°56' N, 17°27' E **168**
ergnier, *Fr.* 49°39' N, 3°17' E **163**
erhazza, ruin(s), *Mali* 23°34' N, 5°9' W **214**
eriberka, *Russ.* 69°10' N, 35°9' E **152**
eriberskiy, Mys, *Russ.* 69°1' N, 35°15' E **152**
erisaqqan, river, *Kaz.* 51°22' N, 67°25' E **184**
erjärv (Teerijärvi), *Fin.* 63°32' N, 23°29' E **154**
erkezi, spring, *Chad* 18°24' N, 21°28' E **216**
ermas de Río Hondo, *Arg.* 27°29' S, 64°52' W **134**
erme, *Turk.* 41°12' N, 36°57' E **156**
ermini Imerese, *It.* 37°58' N, 13°41' E **156**
erminus Mountain, peak, *Can.* 58°46' N, 127°12' W **108**
ermit, *Niger* 16°5' N, 11°11' E **222**
ermit, Massif de, *Niger* 16°8' N, 10°42' E **222**
ermit, spring, *Niger* 15°58' N, 11°15' E **206**
Termita, *Russ.* 45°5' N, 45°14' E **158**
Termit-Kaoboul, *Niger* 15°37' N, 11°26' E **222**
Termiz, *Uzb.* 37°14' N, 67°16' E **186**
Termoli, *It.* 41°59' N, 14°59' E **156**
Termópilas, *Peru* 10°41' S, 73°53' W **137**
Ternate, *Indonesia* 0°41' N, 127°25' E **192**
Terneuzen, *Neth.* 51°19' N, 3°50' E **163**
Terney, *Russ.* 45°6' N, 136°31' E **190**
Terni, *It.* 42°34' N, 12°39' E **156**
Ternitz, *Aust.* 47°43' N, 16°0' E **168**
Ternopil', *Ukr.* 49°31' N, 25°35' E **152**
Terpeniya, Mys, *Russ.* 48°8' N, 144°42' E **190**
Terpeniya, Zaliv 47°55' N, 142°48' E **190**
Terra Bella, *Calif., U.S.* 35°58' N, 119°3' W **101**
Terra Nova Bay, Italy, station, *Antarctica* 74°45' S, 163°39' E **248**
Terra Nova National Park, *Can.* 48°30' N, 54°55' W **111**
Terrace, *Can.* 54°31' N, 128°36' W **108**
Terrace Bay, *Can.* 48°47' N, 87°6' W **94**
Terracina, *It.* 41°18' N, 13°14' E **156**
Terralba, *It.* 39°42' N, 8°37' E **214**
Terrassa, *Sp.* 41°33' N, 2°1' E **164**
Terre Haute, *Ind., U.S.* 39°27' N, 87°25' W **102**
Terrebonne Bay 29°1' N, 90°39' W **96**
Terrecht, region, *Mali* 20°26' N, 0°55' E **222**
Terrell, *Tex., U.S.* 32°45' N, 96°18' W **112**
Terry, *Miss., U.S.* 32°4' N, 90°18' W **103**
Terry, *Mont., U.S.* 46°46' N, 105°20' W **90**
Terry Peak, *S. Dak., U.S.* 44°18' N, 103°55' W **90**
Terschelling, island, *Neth.* 53°27' N, 5°7' E **163**
Tertenia, *It.* 39°40' N, 9°33' E **156**
Teru, *Pak.* 36°8' N, 72°48' E **186**
Teruel, *Sp.* 40°19' N, 1°9' W **214**
Tervo, *Fin.* 62°55' N, 26°41' E **152**
Tešanj, *Bosn. and Herzg.* 44°36' N, 17°59' E **168**
Teshi, *Ghana* 5°37' N, 7°415' W **222**
Teshi, river, *Nig.* 9°17' N, 4°3' E **222**
Tešica, *Serb. and Mont.* 43°25' N, 21°45' E **168**
Teslić, *Bosn. and Herzg.* 44°36' N, 17°50' E **168**
Teslin, *Can.* 60°13' N, 132°47' W **108**
Teslin Lake, *Can.* 59°45' N, 132°58' W **108**
Teslin, river, *Can.* 59°16' N, 132°5' W **108**
Tesouro, *Braz.* 16°7' S, 53°33' W **132**
Tesovo Netyl'skiy, *Russ.* 58°56' N, 31°8' E **152**
Tessalit, *Mali* 20°12' N, 0°58' E **222**
Tessaoua, *Niger* 13°47' N, 7°57' E **222**
Tessenberg, *Aust.* 46°45' N, 12°28' E **167**
Tessenei, *Eritrea* 15°6' N, 36°39' E **182**
Tessier, Lac, lake, *Can.* 48°10' N, 75°44' W **94**
Tessounfat, spring, *Mali* 20°51' N, 0°37' E **222**
Tét, *Hung.* 47°30' N, 17°31' E **168**
Tetas, Punta, *Chile* 23°28' S, 71°8' W **132**
Tétat ed Douaïr, *Alg.* 35°59' N, 2°53' E **150**
Tete, *Mozambique* 16°13' S, 33°34' E **224**
Tete, adm. division, *Mozambique* 15°27' S, 31°58' E **224**
Tête Jaune Cache, *Can.* 52°57' N, 119°26' W **108**
Tetepare, island, *Solomon Islands* 8°45' S, 157°30' E **242**
Tetford, *U.K.* 53°15' N, 2°119' E **162**
Tethul, river, *Can.* 60°30' N, 112°25' W **108**
Tetlin, *Alas., U.S.* 63°9' N, 142°29' W **98**
Tetney, *U.K.* 53°29' N, 0°1' E **162**
Teton Pass, *Wyo., U.S.* 43°30' N, 110°58' W **90**
Teton Range, *Wyo., U.S.* 43°29' N, 110°59' W **90**
Teton, river, *Mont., U.S.* 47°56' N, 111°43' W **90**
Tétouan (Tetuán), *Mor.* 35°35' N, 5°23' W **150**
Tetovo, *Maced.* 42°1' N, 20°58' E **168**
Tetrino, *Russ.* 66°5' N, 38°6' E **154**
Tetuán see Tétouan, *Mor.* 35°35' N, 5°23' W **150**
Tetyushi, *Russ.* 54°56' N, 48°44' E **154**
Teuco, river, *Arg.* 24°41' S, 61°45' W **132**
Teul, *Mex.* 21°27' N, 103°29' W **114**
Teulada, Capo, *It.* 38°48' N, 7°59' E **156**
Teulon, *Can.* 50°23' N, 97°18' W **90**
Teutopolis, *Ill., U.S.* 39°7' N, 88°29' W **102**
Teutschenthal, *Ger.* 51°27' N, 11°48' E **152**
Teuva, *Fin.* 62°28' N, 21°41' E **152**
Teverya (Tiberias), *Israel* 32°47' N, 35°31' E **194**
Tewantin, *Austral.* 26°26' S, 153°2' E **231**
Tewkesbury, *U.K.* 51°59' N, 2°9' W **162**
Texada Island, *Can.* 49°38' N, 124°16' W **100**
Texarkana, *Ark., U.S.* 33°24' N, 94°3' W **103**
Texas, adm. division, *Tex., U.S.* 31°8' N, 101°3' W **82**
Texas City, *Tex., U.S.* 29°21' N, 94°54' W **103**
Texas Point, *Tex., U.S.* 29°34' N, 93°54' W **103**
Texcoco, *Mex.* 19°27' N, 99°15' W **112**
Texel, island, *Neth.* 53°5' N, 4°33' E **163**
Texhoma, *Okla., U.S.* 36°30' N, 101°47' W **92**
Texico, *Tex., U.S.* 34°23' N, 103°4' W **92**
Texline, *Tex., U.S.* 36°22' N, 103°2' W **92**
Texon, *Tex., U.S.* 31°11' N, 101°41' W **92**
Teya, *Russ.* 60°20' N, 92°46' E **169**
Teykovo, *Russ.* 56°52' N, 40°27' E **154**
Teylan, *Afghan.* 35°34' N, 64°49' E **186**
Teziutlán, *Mex.* 19°48' N, 97°23' W **114**
Tezontepec, *Mex.* 19°50' N, 98°48' W **114**
Tezpur, *India* 26°43' N, 92°45' E **188**
Tezzeron Lake, *Can.* 54°38' N, 125°6' W **108**
Tfaritiy, *Africa* 26°11' N, 10°34' W **214**
Tha Li, *Thai.* 17°39' N, 101°23' E **202**
Tha, river, *Laos* 21°6' N, 101°15' E **202**
Tha Sala, *Thai.* 8°40' N, 99°56' E **202**
Thaba Nchu, *S. Af.* 29°14' S, 26°48' E **227**
Thabaung, *Myanmar* 17°4' N, 94°46' E **202**
Thabazimbi, *S. Af.* 24°38' S, 27°23' E **227**
Thādiq, *Saudi Arabia* 25°16' N, 45°53' E **182**
Thaga Pass, *India* 31°26' N, 79°8' E **188**
Thagyettaw, *Myanmar* 13°46' N, 98°8' E **202**
Thai Binh, *Vietnam* 20°27' N, 106°20' E **198**
Thai Hoa, *Vietnam* 19°20' N, 105°26' E **202**
Thai Nguyen, *Vietnam* 21°35' N, 105°50' E **198**
Thailand 15°33' N, 101°6' E **202**
Thailand, Gulf of 9°44' N, 101°14' E **202**
Thal, *Pak.* 33°22' N, 70°38' E **186**
Thalabarivat, *Cambodia* 13°35' N, 105°56' E **202**
Thalassery see Tellicherry, *India* 11°45' N, 75°29' E **188**
Thamad Bū Ḥashīshah, spring, *Lib.* 26°23' N, 18°44' E **216**
Thamarīt, *Oman* 17°38' N, 54°1' E **182**
Thames, *N.Z.* 37°10' S, 175°34' E **240**
Thames, river, *Can.* 42°16' N, 82°26' W **102**
Thamesville, *Can.* 42°32' N, 81°57' W **102**
Thamūd, *Yemen* 17°18' N, 49°55' E **182**
Thane, *India* 19°12' N, 72°56' E **188**
Thanggu, *India* 27°53' N, 88°36' E **197**
Thanh Hoa, *Vietnam* 19°48' N, 105°44' E **202**
Thanh Tri, *Vietnam* 9°26' N, 105°43' E **202**
Thanlwin (Salween), river, *Asia* 21°45' N, 98°44' E **202**
Thann, *Fr.* 47°48' N, 7°5' E **150**
Thaon-les-Vosges, *Fr.* 48°14' N, 6°25' E **163**
Thap Lan National Park, *Thai.* 14°1' N, 102°29' E **202**
Tharabwin, *Myanmar* 12°19' N, 99°3' E **202**
Tharad, *India* 24°24' N, 71°41' E **186**
Tharrawaddy, *Myanmar* 17°40' N, 95°47' E **202**
Tharros, ruin(s), *It.* 39°52' N, 8°21' E **156**
Tharthār Lake, *Iraq* 33°57' N, 42°50' E **180**
Thássos, island, *Gr.* 40°26' N, 24°36' E **180**
That Khe, *Vietnam* 22°18' N, 106°30' E **198**
That Phanom, *Thai.* 16°58' N, 104°42' E **202**
Thatcher, *Ariz., U.S.* 32°50' N, 109°45' W **92**
Thaton, *Myanmar* 16°56' N, 97°21' E **202**
Thatta, *Pak.* 24°45' N, 67°55' E **186**
Thaungdut, *Myanmar* 24°25' N, 94°37' E **188**
Thawatti, *Myanmar* 19°31' N, 96°12' E **202**
Thaxted, *U.K.* 51°56' N, 0°21' E **162**
Thayawthadangyi Kyun, island, *Myanmar* 12°20' N, 96°28' E **202**
Thayer, *Ill., U.S.* 39°32' N, 89°45' W **102**
Thayer, *Mo., U.S.* 36°31' N, 91°33' W **96**
Thayetchaung, *Myanmar* 13°52' N, 98°16' E **202**
The Alley, *Jam.* 17°47' N, 77°16' W **115**
The Brothers see Al Ikhwān, islands, *Yemen* 11°24' N, 52°52' E **182**
The Caterthuns, ruin(s), *U.K.* 56°46' N, 2°53' W **150**
The Curragh, site, *Ire.* 53°8' N, 6°56' W **150**
The Dalles, *Oreg., U.S.* 45°34' N, 121°11' W **90**
The English Company's Islands, *Arafura Sea* 11°39' S, 136°42' E **230**
The Four Archers, site, *Austral.* 15°30' S, 135°13' E **230**
The Hague see 's Gravenhage, *Neth.* 52°5' N, 4°18' E **167**
The Mumbles, *U.K.* 51°34' N, 3°60' W **162**
The Ovens, site, *Can.* 44°18' N, 64°23' W **111**
The Pas, *Can.* 53°47' N, 101°17' W **108**
The Plains, *Ohio, U.S.* 39°21' N, 82°8' W **102**
The Rivals see Yr Eifl, peak, *U.K.* 52°57' N, 4°32' W **150**
The Slot see New Georgia Sound 8°11' S, 158°30' E **242**
The Two Rivers, *Can.* 55°45' N, 103°15' W **108**
The Valley, *Anguilla* 18°13' N, 63°4' W **116**
The Woodlands, *Tex., U.S.* 30°10' N, 95°28' W **103**
Theano Point, *Can.* 47°10' N, 84°40' W **110**
Thebes, ruin(s), *Egypt* 25°40' N, 32°2' E **206**
Thedford, *Can.* 43°9' N, 81°51' W **102**
Thedford, *Nebr., U.S.* 41°58' N, 100°35' W **90**
Thekulthili Lake, *Can.* 61°2' N, 110°46' W **108**
Thelon, river, *Can.* 63°20' N, 104°51' W **106**
Thenon, *Fr.* 45°8' N, 1°4' E **150**
Theo, Mount, peak, *Austral.* 21°23' S, 131°9' E **230**
Théodat, Lac, lake, *Can.* 50°53' N, 76°41' W **110**
Theodore Roosevelt National Park, Elkhorn Ranch Site, *N. Dak., U.S.* 47°12' N, 103°45' W **90**
Theodore Roosevelt National Park, North Unit, *N. Dak., U.S.* 47°17' N, 105°57' W **80**
Theodore Roosevelt, river, *Braz.* 11°28' S, 60°30' W **130**
Thepha, *Thai.* 6°51' N, 100°56' E **196**
Thera, ruin(s), *Gr.* 36°20' N, 25°23' E **156**
Therien, *Can.* 54°13' N, 111°17' W **108**
Thermal, *Calif., U.S.* 33°38' N, 116°9' W **101**
Thermiá, ruin(s), *Gr.* 41°27' N, 24°20' E **156**
Thermopolis, *Wyo., U.S.* 43°38' N, 108°13' W **90**
Thermopylae 480 B.C., battle, *Gr.* 38°47' N, 22°27' E **156**
Thermum, ruin(s), *Gr.* 38°33' N, 21°36' E **156**
Thessalia, adm. division, *Gr.* 39°19' N, 21°28' E **156**
Thessalon, *Can.* 46°16' N, 83°34' W **94**
Thessaloníki (Salonica), *Gr.* 40°38' N, 22°57' E **156**
Thetford, *U.K.* 52°25' N, 0°45' E **162**
Thetford Mines, *Can.* 46°4' N, 71°18' W **111**
Theux, *Belg.* 50°31' N, 5°48' E **167**
Thiaucourt, *Fr.* 48°57' N, 5°50' E **163**
Thibodaux, *La., U.S.* 29°46' N, 90°50' W **103**
Thicket Portage, *Can.* 55°18' N, 97°42' W **108**
Thief River Falls, *Minn., U.S.* 48°6' N, 96°13' W **90**
Thielsen, Mount, peak, *Oreg., U.S.* 43°8' N, 122°9' W **90**
Thiene, *It.* 45°42' N, 11°28' E **167**
Thiès, *Senegal* 14°48' N, 16°41' W **222**
Thignica, ruin(s), *Tun.* 36°31' N, 9°15' E **156**
Thika, *Kenya* 1°3' S, 37°4' E **224**
Thilogne, *Senegal* 15°57' N, 13°40' W **222**
Thimphu, *Bhutan* 27°32' N, 89°31' E **197**
Thinahtea Lake, *Can.* 59°40' N, 121°4' W **108**
Thio, *Eritrea* 14°38' N, 40°54' E **182**
Thionville, *Fr.* 49°22' N, 6°9' E **163**
Thiou, *Burkina Faso* 13°47' N, 2°42' W **222**
Thíra, island, *Gr.* 36°11' N, 25°9' E **180**
Thirsk, *U.K.* 54°14' N, 1°21' W **162**
Thiruvananthapuram see Trivandrum, *India* 8°28' N, 76°56' E **188**
Thisted, *Den.* 56°57' N, 8°40' E **150**
Thistle Island, island, *Austral.* 35°8' S, 134°33' E **230**
Thíva, *Gr.* 38°20' N, 23°20' E **180**
Thiviers, *Fr.* 45°24' N, 0°55' E **150**
Thlewiaza, river, *Can.* 60°54' N, 99°1' W **108**
Tho Chu, Dao, island, *Vietnam* 9°2' N, 103°21' E **202**
Thoa, river, *Can.* 60°39' N, 108°55' W **108**
Thoen, *Thai.* 17°37' N, 99°10' E **202**
Thohoyandou, *S. Af.* 22°58' S, 30°25' E **227**
Tholey, *Ger.* 49°29' N, 7°5' E **163**
Thomas, *Okla., U.S.* 35°43' N, 98°44' W **92**
Thomas Mountains, *Antarctica* 76°11' S, 75°43' W **248**
Thomaston, *Ala., U.S.* 32°15' N, 87°37' W **103**
Thomaston, *Ga., U.S.* 32°53' N, 84°19' W **96**
Thomaston, *Me., U.S.* 44°4' N, 69°12' W **94**
Thomasville, *Ala., U.S.* 31°55' N, 87°44' W **103**
Thomasville, *Ga., U.S.* 30°49' N, 83°59' W **96**
Thomasville, *N.C., U.S.* 35°52' N, 80°6' W **96**
Thompson, *Can.* 55°44' N, 97°51' W **108**
Thompson, *Utah, U.S.* 38°58' N, 109°43' W **90**
Thompson Lake, *Me., U.S.* 44°1' N, 70°41' W **104**
Thompson Peak, *Calif., U.S.* 40°59' N, 123°9' W **90**
Thompson Peak, *Mont., U.S.* 47°43' N, 114°56' W **90**
Thompson Point, *Can.* 58°14' N, 92°60' W **108**
Thompson, river, *Can.* 49°56' N, 121°12' W **80**
Thomson, *Ill., U.S.* 41°57' N, 90°6' W **102**
Thomson, Mount, peak, *Austral.* 24°1' S, 115°37' E **230**
Thon Buri, *Thai.* 13°39' N, 100°25' E **202**
Thongwa, *Myanmar* 16°46' N, 96°35' E **202**
Thonotosassa, *Fla., U.S.* 28°4' N, 82°18' W **105**
Thorenc, *Fr.* 43°47' N, 6°49' E **167**
Thorhild, *Can.* 54°9' N, 113°8' W **108**
Thornaby on Tees, *U.K.* 54°33' N, 1°19' W **162**
Thornapple, river, *Mich., U.S.* 42°40' N, 85°22' W **102**
Thornbury, *Can.* 44°33' N, 80°27' W **94**
Thornbury, *N.Z.* 46°18' S, 168°6' E **240**
Thornbury, *U.K.* 51°37' N, 2°31' W **162**
Thorndale, *Tex., U.S.* 30°35' N, 97°12' W **96**
Thorne, *U.K.* 53°36' N, 0°59' E **162**
Thorne Bay, *Alas., U.S.* 55°42' N, 132°35' W **98**
Thornton, *Calif., U.S.* 38°13' N, 121°26' W **100**
Thornton, *W. Va., U.S.* 39°20' N, 79°57' W **94**
Thorp, *Wash., U.S.* 47°2' N, 120°42' W **90**
Thorp, *Wis., U.S.* 44°57' N, 90°49' W **94**
Thouars, *Fr.* 46°59' N, 0°14' E **150**
Thousand Oaks, *Calif., U.S.* 34°11' N, 118°53' W **101**
Thrapston, *U.K.* 52°23' N, 0°31' E **162**
Three Brothers, islands, *Indian Ocean* 5°55' S, 69°39' E **188**
Three Brothers Mountain, peak, *Can.* 49°8' N, 120°51' W **90**
Three Cocks, *U.K.* 52°1' N, 3°12' W **162**
Three Fingered Jack, peak, *Oreg., U.S.* 44°27' N, 121°56' W **90**
Three Forks, *Mont., U.S.* 45°52' N, 111°34' W **90**
Three Hills, *Can.* 51°43' N, 113°17' W **90**
Three Lakes, *Wis., U.S.* 45°48' N, 89°10' W **94**
Three Oaks, *Mich., U.S.* 41°47' N, 86°36' W **102**
Three Pagodas Pass, *Thai.* 15°19' N, 98°24' E **202**
Three Points, *Calif., U.S.* 34°44' N, 118°37' W **101**
Three Points, Cape 4°29' N, 3°5' W **222**
Three Rivers, *Calif., U.S.* 36°26' N, 118°55' W **101**
Three Rivers, *Mass., U.S.* 42°10' N, 72°23' W **104**
Three Rivers, *Mich., U.S.* 41°56' N, 85°38' W **102**
Three Rivers, *Tex., U.S.* 28°27' N, 98°11' W **92**
Three Sisters, *S. Af.* 31°53' S, 23°5' E **227**
Three Sisters Islands, *Solomon Sea* 10°11' S, 161°55' E **242**
Three Sisters, peak, *Oreg., U.S.* 44°4' N, 121°51' W **90**
Thrissur see Trichur, *India* 10°31' N, 76°11' E **188**
Throckmorton, *Tex., U.S.* 33°10' N, 99°11' W **92**
Throssell Range, *Austral.* 21°43' S, 120°55' E **230**
Thu, Cu Lao, island, *Vietnam* 10°16' N, 108°52' E **202**
Thugga, ruin(s), *Tun.* 36°24' N, 9°7' E **156**
Thuin, *Belg.* 50°20' N, 4°17' E **163**
Thulaythīwāt, Tilāl ath, peak, *Jordan* 30°58' N, 36°38' E **194**
Thule Air Base 76°28' N, 69°3' W **106**
Thule see Qaanaaq 77°32' N, 69°13' W **106**
Thuli, river, *Zimb.* 21°21' S, 28°59' E **227**
Thun, *Switz.* 46°44' N, 7°36' E **167**
Thunder Bay, *Can.* 48°24' N, 89°14' W **94**
Thunder Hills, *Can.* 54°19' N, 106°33' W **108**
Thuner See, lake, *Switz.* 46°42' N, 7°28' E **165**
Thung Song, *Thai.* 8°10' N, 99°41' E **202**
Thüringer Wald, *Ger.* 50°54' N, 10°1' E **167**
Thuringia, adm. division, *Ger.* 50°46' N, 9°58' E **167**
Thurston Island, *Antarctica* 72°13' S, 98°45' W **255**
Thusis, *Switz.* 46°42' N, 9°25' E **167**
Thutade Lake, *Can.* 56°46' N, 127°52' W **108**
Thyborøn, *Den.* 56°41' N, 8°10' E **150**
Thynne, Mount, peak, *Can.* 49°41' N, 120°57' W **100**
Thyou, *Burkina Faso* 11°55' N, 2°14' W **222**
Tiago, *Braz.* 0°59' N, 57°1' W **130**
Tian Head, *Can.* 53°38' N, 133°34' W **108**
Tian Shan 40°8' N, 71°21' E **197**
Tianbaoshan, *China* 42°57' N, 128°56' E **200**
Tiandeng, *China* 23°3' N, 107°6' E **198**
Tiandong, *China* 23°33' N, 107°6' E **198**
Tian'e, *China* 25°0' N, 107°9' E **198**
Tianguá, *Braz.* 3°43' S, 40°60' W **132**
Tianjin, *China* 38°52' N, 117°15' E **190**
Tianjin, adm. division, *China* 39°47' N, 117°15' E **190**
Tianjin (Tientsin), *China* 39°3' N, 117°9' E **198**
Tianjun, *China* 37°18' N, 99°0' E **188**
Tianlin, *China* 24°16' N, 106°14' E **198**
Tianmen, *China* 30°40' N, 113°10' E **198**
Tianshan see Ar Horqin Qi, *China* 43°55' N, 120°7' E **198**
Tianshifu, *China* 41°14' N, 124°19' E **200**
Tianshui, *China* 34°36' N, 105°42' E **198**
Tianyang, *China* 23°45' N, 106°51' E **198**
Tianzhu, *China* 26°56' N, 109°11' E **198**
Tiaret, *Alg.* 35°21' N, 1°19' E **150**
Tiaret, spring, *Tun.* 30°56' N, 10°6' E **214**
Tiaski, *Senegal* 15°40' N, 14°18' W **222**
Tiassalé, *Côte d'Ivoire* 5°49' N, 4°53' W **222**
Tib, Ras el, *Tun.* 36°57' N, 10°31' E **156**
Tibagi, *Braz.* 24°31' S, 50°27' W **138**
Tibagi, river, *Braz.* 23°51' S, 50°44' W **138**
Tibasti, Sarīr, *Lib.* 22°48' N, 15°52' E **216**
Tibati, *Cameroon* 6°23' N, 12°36' E **218**
Tibbie, *Ala., U.S.* 31°21' N, 88°15' W **103**
Tibé, Pic de, peak, *Guinea* 8°49' N, 8°58' W **222**
Tiber Dam, *Mont., U.S.* 48°8' N, 111°8' W **90**
Tiberias see Teverya, *Israel* 32°47' N, 35°31' E **194**
Tibesti, *Chad* 19°48' N, 17°13' E **216**
Tibet, Plateau of, *China* 33°55' N, 81°5' E **172**
Tibeysale, *Russ.* 67°3' N, 79°31' E **169**
Tibidabo, peak, *Sp.* 41°24' N, 2°6' E **164**
Tibiri, *Niger* 13°5' N, 3°55' E **222**
Tibiri, *Niger* 13°34' N, 7°3' E **222**
Ţibleş, Munţii, *Rom.* 47°31' N, 23°48' E **156**
Ţibleş, peak, *Rom.* 47°30' N, 24°11' E **156**
Tibnine, *Leb.* 33°11' N, 35°24' E **194**
Tibrikot, *Nepal* 29°0' N, 82°50' E **197**
Tibú, *Col.* 8°37' N, 72°42' W **136**
Tiburon, *Calif., U.S.* 37°52' N, 122°29' W **100**
Tiburón, Cabo, *Col.* 8°41' N, 77°31' W **136**
Tiburón, Isla, island, *Mex.* 28°30' N, 112°28' W **80**
Tichégami, river, *Can.* 51°50' N, 73°58' W **110**
Tîchît, *Mauritania* 18°28' N, 9°30' W **222**
Tîchît, Dahr, *Mauritania* 18°36' N, 10°27' W **214**
Ticonderoga, *N.Y., U.S.* 43°50' N, 73°26' W **104**
Ticouapé, *Can.* 48°42' N, 72°30' W **94**
Ticul, *Mex.* 20°23' N, 89°33' W **115**
Tide Lake, *Can.* 50°33' N, 111°32' W **108**
Tidikelt, region, *Alg.* 26°28' N, 1°9' E **214**
Tidjidit, Erg, *Alg.* 23°32' N, 0°8' E **214**
Tidjikdja, *Mauritania* 18°30' N, 11°27' W **207**
Tidra, Île, island, *Mauritania* 19°47' N, 16°46' W **222**
Tiébissou, *Côte d'Ivoire* 7°5' N, 5°14' W **222**
Tiechang, *China* 41°40' N, 126°13' E **200**
Tiehnpo, *Liberia* 5°13' N, 8°6' W **222**
Tiel, *Neth.* 51°53' N, 5°25' E **167**
Tiel, *Senegal* 14°55' N, 15°2' W **222**
Tieli, *China* 47°3' N, 128°3' E **198**
Tieling, *China* 42°17' N, 123°51' E **200**
Tielt, *Belg.* 51°0' N, 3°19' E **163**
Tien Yen, *Vietnam* 21°20' N, 107°21' E **198**
Tienen, *Belg.* 50°48' N, 4°55' E **167**
Tiensuu, *Fin.* 65°35' N, 25°59' E **152**
Tientsin see Tianjin, *China* 39°3' N, 117°9' E **198**
Tiéré, *Mali* 11°54' N, 5°26' W **222**
Tiermas, *Sp.* 42°37' N, 1°7' W **164**
Tieroko, peak, *Chad* 20°46' N, 17°43' E **216**
Tierp, *Sw.* 60°20' N, 17°29' E **166**
Tierra Blanca, *Mex.* 18°26' N, 96°20' W **114**
Tierra Colorada, *Mex.* 17°9' N, 99°32' W **114**
Tierra del Fuego, Isla Grande de, island, *Arg.-Chile* 53°3' S, 68°33' W **248**
Tierra del Fuego-Antártida E Islas Atlántico Sur, adm. division, *Arg.* 53°44' S, 70°49' W **134**
Tietê, river, *Braz.* 23°28' S, 46°16' W **138**
Tiffany Mountain, peak, *Wash., U.S.* 48°38' N, 120°1' W **90**
Tiffin, *Ohio, U.S.* 41°6' N, 83°11' W **102**
Tifristós, peak, *Gr.* 38°56' N, 21°44' E **156**
Tifton, *Ga., U.S.* 31°27' N, 83°31' W **96**
Tigharry 57°37' N, 7°29' W **150**
Tighennif, *Alg.* 35°24' N, 0°20' E **150**
Tigil', *Russ.* 57°51' N, 158°45' E **160**
Tignère, *Cameroon* 7°20' N, 12°39' E **218**
Tigray, region, *Eth.* 13°57' N, 36°41' E **182**
Tigre, river, *Peru* 3°48' S, 74°47' W **136**
Tigre, river, *Venez.* 8°56' N, 63°10' W **116**
Tigris (Dicle, Dijlah), river, *Iraq* 32°8' N, 46°36' E **180**
Tiguent, *Mauritania* 17°17' N, 16°7' W **222**
Tiguentourine, oil field, *Alg.* 27°44' N, 9°4' E **214**
Tiguidit, Falaise de, region, *Niger* 16°40' N, 6°58' E **222**
Tigyaing, *Myanmar* 23°45' N, 96°3' E **202**
Tîh, Gebel el, *Egypt* 29°35' N, 33°0' E **180**
Tihany, *Hung.* 46°54' N, 17°53' E **168**
Tihosuco, *Mex.* 20°12' N, 88°26' W **115**
Tihuatlán, *Mex.* 20°41' N, 97°33' W **114**
Tijamré, spring, *Mauritania* 20°18' N, 11°16' W **222**
Tijesno, *Croatia* 43°47' N, 15°38' E **156**
Tijola, *Sp.* 37°19' N, 2°26' W **164**
Tîjti, spring, *Mauritania* 17°52' N, 7°15' W **222**
Tijuana, *Mex.* 32°31' N, 117°4' W **101**
Tijucas, *Braz.* 27°16' S, 48°39' W **138**
Tijucas do Sul, *Braz.* 25°57' S, 49°12' W **138**
Tikal National Park, *Guatemala* 17°13' N, 90°10' W **115**
Tikamgarh, *India* 24°44' N, 78°50' E **197**
Tikanlik, *China* 40°40' N, 87°40' E **188**
Tikaré, *Burkina Faso* 13°16' N, 1°44' W **222**
Tikattane, *Mauritania* 19°2' N, 16°15' W **222**
Tikhmanga, *Russ.* 61°14' N, 38°31' E **154**
Tikhoretsk, *Russ.* 45°52' N, 40°5' E **158**
Tikhtozero, *Russ.* 65°33' N, 30°31' E **154**
Tikhvin, *Russ.* 59°38' N, 33°32' E **154**
Tikitiki, *N.Z.* 37°48' S, 178°23' E **240**
Tikkurila, *Fin.* 60°16' N, 24°58' E **166**
Tiko, *Cameroon* 4°5' N, 9°21' E **222**
Tikshozero, *Russ.* 64°6' N, 31°47' E **152**
Tikshozero, *Russ.* 66°0' N, 32°23' E **152**
Tiksi, *Russ.* 71°22' N, 128°46' E **160**
Tilaiya Dam, *India* 24°20' N, 85°35' E **197**
Tilamuta, *Indonesia* 0°34' N, 122°17' E **192**
Tilatou, *Alg.* 35°19' N, 5°47' E **150**
Tilburg, *Neth.* 51°33' N, 5°4' E **163**
Tilbury, *Can.* 42°15' N, 82°27' W **102**
Tilbury, *U.K.* 51°27' N, 0°21' E **162**
Til-Châtel, *Fr.* 47°30' N, 5°9' E **150**
Tilden, *Nebr., U.S.* 42°1' N, 97°50' W **90**
Tileagd, *Rom.* 47°3' N, 22°14' E **168**
Tilemsoun, *Mor.* 28°13' N, 10°57' W **214**
Tilichiki, *Russ.* 60°28' N, 165°53' E **160**
Tillabéri, *Niger* 14°12' N, 1°26' E **222**
Tillamook, *Oreg., U.S.* 45°27' N, 123°51' W **90**
Tillamook Head, *Oreg., U.S.* 45°56' N, 124°9' W **100**
Tillanchang Dwip, island, *India* 8°34' N, 93°43' E **188**

Tillia, Niger 15°53′ N, 4°35′ E 222
Tilloo Cay, island, Bahamas 26°33′ N, 76°56′ W 116
Tillson, N.Y., U.S. 41°49′ N, 74°5′ W 104
Tillsonburg, Can. 42°51′ N, 80°43′ W 102
Tilos, island, Gr. 36°24′ N, 27°25′ E 180
Tilpa, Austral. 30°56′ S, 144°26′ E 231
Tilrhemt, Alg. 33°11′ N, 3°21′ E 214
Tiltagals, Latv. 56°33′ N, 26°39′ E 166
Tilton, Ill., U.S. 40°5′ N, 87°40′ W 102
Tilton, N.H., U.S. 43°26′ N, 71°36′ W 104
Tilža, Latv. 56°53′ N, 27°21′ E 166
Tim, Russ. 51°34′ N, 37°9′ E 158
Ţima, Egypt 26°55′ N, 31°21′ E 180
Timanskiy Kryazh, Russ. 65°21′ N, 50°38′ E 154
Timaru, N.Z. 44°24′ S, 171°13′ E 240
Timashevo, Russ. 53°22′ N, 51°5′ E 154
Timashevsk, Russ. 45°40′ N, 38°58′ E 156
Timbáki, Gr. 35°2′ N, 24°44′ E 180
Timbalier Bay 29°8′ N, 90°33′ W 103
Timbalier Island, La., U.S. 28°57′ N, 90°34′ W 103
Timbédra, Mauritania 16°16′ N, 8°12′ W 222
Timber, Oreg., U.S. 45°42′ N, 123°19′ W 100
Timber Bay, Can. 54°9′ N, 105°40′ W 108
Timber Lake, S. Dak., U.S. 45°25′ N, 101°6′ W 90
Timber Mountain, peak, Calif., U.S. 41°37′ N, 121°23′ W 90
Timber Mountain, peak, Nev., U.S. 37°2′ N, 116°30′ W 101
Timbío, Col. 2°17′ N, 76°43′ W 136
Timbiquí, Col. 2°41′ N, 77°45′ W 136
Timbo, Guinea 10°37′ N, 11°52′ W 222
Timbo, Liberia 5°31′ N, 9°42′ W 222
Timbuktu see Tombouctou, Mali 16°44′ N, 3°2′ W 222
Timeïaouine, spring, Alg. 20°28′ N, 1°48′ E 222
Timellouline, spring, Alg. 29°15′ N, 8°55′ E 214
Timerein, Sudan 16°58′ N, 36°29′ E 182
Timétrine, region, Mali 19°15′ N, 1°20′ W 222
Timfi, Óros, peak, Gr. 39°58′ N, 20°43′ E 156
Timgad, ruin(s), Alg. 35°25′ N, 6°21′ E 150
Tîmia, Niger 18°3′ N, 8°39′ E 222
Timiş, adm. division, Rom. 45°49′ N, 20°44′ E 156
Timimoun, Alg. 29°6′ N, 0°13′ E 207
Timiris, Cap (Mirik), Mauritania 19°28′ N, 16°53′ W 222
Timiryazevskiy, Russ. 56°28′ N, 84°44′ E 169
Timiskaming, Lake, Can. 47°15′ N, 80°13′ W 94
Timişoara, Rom. 45°46′ N, 21°14′ E 168
Timkapaul', Russ. 61°29′ N, 62°16′ E 169
Timmiarmiut 62°33′ N, 42°19′ W 106
Timmins, Can. 48°29′ N, 81°16′ W 82
Timms Hill, peak, Wis., U.S. 45°25′ N, 90°16′ W 94
Timon, Braz. 5°6′ S, 42°53′ W 132
Timor, island, Indonesia 9°36′ S, 122°49′ E 192
Timor Sea 11°14′ S, 126°40′ E 192
Timor-Leste (East Timor) 9°0′ S, 125°0′ E 192
Timote, Arg. 35°20′ S, 62°15′ W 139
Timpanogos Cave National Monument, Utah, U.S. 40°25′ N, 111°46′ W 90
Timpson, Tex., U.S. 31°53′ N, 94°23′ W 103
Timrå, Nor. 62°28′ N, 17°17′ E 152
Tin Férafé, spring, Mali 15°6′ N, 0°53′ E 222
Tin Fouye, oil field, Alg. 28°31′ N, 7°20′ E 214
Tin Mountain, peak, Calif., U.S. 36°52′ N, 117°33′ W 92
Tîna, Khalîg el 31°3′ N, 32°35′ E 194
Tina, Mont, peak, Dem. Rep. of the Congo 2°56′ N, 28°32′ E 224
Tinaca Point, Philippines 5°25′ N, 125°1′ E 203
Tinaco, Venez. 9°41′ N, 68°28′ W 136
Ti-n-Assamert, spring, Mali 16°12′ N, 0°30′ E 222
Ti-n-Brahim, spring, Mauritania 19°31′ N, 15°58′ W 222
Tinca, Rom. 46°46′ N, 21°58′ E 168
Tinde see Jomu, Tanzania 3°53′ S, 33°11′ E 224
Ti-n-Deïla, spring, Mauritania 17°59′ N, 15°32′ W 222
Tindel, spring, Mauritania 17°0′ N, 12°57′ W 222
Tindouf, Alg. 27°43′ N, 8°9′ W 143
Tiné, Chad 14°59′ N, 22°47′ E 216
Ti-n-Ekkart, spring, Mali 16°14′ N, 3°17′ E 222
Ti-n-Essako, spring, Mali 18°25′ N, 2°29′ E 222
Ti-n-Ethisane, spring, Mali 19°2′ N, 0°50′ E 222
Tinfouchy, spring, Alg. 28°53′ N, 5°49′ W 214
Tinfunque National Park, Parag. 24°3′ S, 60°28′ W 122
Tinggi, island, Malaysia 2°21′ N, 103°58′ E 196
Tingo María National Park, Peru 9°13′ S, 76°11′ W 130
Tingréla, Côte d'Ivoire 10°30′ N, 6°25′ W 222
Tingri (Xêgar), China 28°40′ N, 87°3′ E 197
Tingsryd, Nor. 56°31′ N, 14°59′ E 152
Tingstäde, Sw. 57°44′ N, 18°36′ E 166
Tinkisso, river, Guinea 11°27′ N, 10°6′ W 222
Tinn, Nor. 59°58′ N, 8°44′ E 152
Tinniswood, Mount, peak, Can. 50°18′ N, 123°52′ W 100
Tinogasta, Arg. 28°5′ S, 67°34′ W 132
Tinombo, Indonesia 0°24′ N, 120°13′ E 192
Ti-n-Orfane, Mali 16°30′ N, 2°15′ W 222
Tiñoso, Cabo, Sp. 37°25′ N, 1°15′ W 164
Ti-n-Rerhoh, spring, Alg. 20°45′ N, 4°1′ E 222
Tinrhert, Hamada de, Lib. 28°3′ N, 6°55′ E 206
Tinsley, Miss., U.S. 32°42′ N, 90°28′ W 103
Tinsukia, India 27°29′ N, 95°22′ E 188
Tintagel (King Arthur's Castle), site, U.K. 50°39′ N, 4°49′ W 150
Tintane, spring, Mauritania 20°51′ N, 16°32′ W 222
Ti-n-Taourdi, spring, Alg. 22°46′ N, 8°0′ E 214
Tintina, Arg. 27°1′ S, 62°43′ W 139
Tinto Hills, peak, U.K. 55°34′ N, 3°47′ W 150
Ti-n-Toumma, region, Niger 16°27′ N, 12°0′ E 222
Tinui, N.Z. 40°54′ S, 176°5′ E 240
Ti-n-Zaouâtene (Fort Pierre Bordes), Alg. 19°58′ N, 2°57′ E 222
Tioga, La., U.S. 31°22′ N, 92°26′ W 103
Tioga, N. Dak., U.S. 48°23′ N, 102°57′ W 90
Tioga Pass, Calif., U.S. 37°54′ N, 119°16′ W 100
Tioman, peak, Malaysia 2°47′ N, 104°4′ E 196
Tionaga, Can. 48°5′ N, 82°6′ W 94
Tip Top Mountain, peak, Can. 48°16′ N, 86°4′ W 94
Tipitapa, Nicar. 12°9′ N, 86°4′ W 115
Tipp City, Ohio, U.S. 39°57′ N, 84°10′ W 102
Tippecanoe, Ind., U.S. 41°11′ N, 86°7′ W 102
Tipton, Calif., U.S. 36°3′ N, 119°20′ W 100
Tipton, Ind., U.S. 40°17′ N, 86°2′ W 102
Tipton, Iowa, U.S. 41°45′ N, 91°8′ W 110
Tipton, Mich., U.S. 42°0′ N, 84°4′ W 102
Tipton, Okla., U.S. 34°28′ N, 99°9′ W 92
Tipton, Mount, peak, Ariz., U.S. 35°31′ N, 114°13′ W 101
Tipuani, Bol. 15°35′ S, 67°60′ W 137
Tiputini, river, Ecua. 1°6′ S, 77°6′ W 136
Tiquicheo, Mex. 18°52′ N, 100°45′ W 114
Tiquié, river, Braz. 0°7′ N, 69°41′ W 136
Tir Pol, Afghan. 34°38′ N, 61°20′ E 180
Tiracambu, Serra do, Braz. 3°36′ S, 46°54′ W 130
Tīrān, island, Egypt 27°57′ N, 34°5′ E 180
Tirana see Tiranë, Alban. 41°19′ N, 19°41′ E 156
Tiranë (Tirana), Alban. 41°19′ N, 19°41′ E 156
Tirano, It. 46°12′ N, 10°9′ E 167
Tiraspol, Mold. 46°49′ N, 29°37′ E 156
Tirat Karmel, Israel 32°45′ N, 34°58′ E 194
Tire, Turk. 38°3′ N, 27°42′ E 156
Tiream, Rom. 47°37′ N, 22°29′ E 168
Tirebolu, Turk. 41°0′ N, 38°46′ E 195
Tirest, spring, Mali 20°21′ N, 1°6′ E 222
Tîrgovişte, Rom. 44°57′ N, 25°26′ E 156
Tîrgu Jiu, Rom. 45°1′ N, 23°18′ E 168
Tîrguşor, Rom. 44°28′ N, 28°24′ E 158
Tirich Mir, peak, Pak. 36°16′ N, 71°41′ E 186
Tiririne, spring, Alg. 23°34′ N, 8°31′ E 214
Tirlyanskiy, Russ. 54°14′ N, 58°28′ E 154
Tîrnova, Mold. 48°9′ N, 27°39′ E 152
Tîrnova, Rom. 45°19′ N, 21°59′ E 168
Tiroungoulou, Cen. Af. Rep. 9°34′ N, 22°8′ E 216
Tirthahalli, India 13°42′ N, 75°14′ E 188
Tiruchchirappalli, India 10°48′ N, 78°41′ E 188
Tirunelveli, India 8°44′ N, 77°40′ E 188
Tiruntán, Peru 7°56′ S, 74°56′ W 130
Tiryns, ruin(s), Gr. 37°35′ N, 22°42′ E 156
Tisaiyanvilai, India 8°20′ N, 77°49′ E 188
Tisdale, Can. 52°50′ N, 104°4′ W 108
Tishomingo, Okla., U.S. 34°13′ N, 96°40′ W 92
Tiskilwa, Ill., U.S. 41°17′ N, 89°31′ W 102
Tissamaharama, Sri Lanka 6°17′ N, 81°18′ E 188
Tissemsilt, Alg. 35°36′ N, 1°49′ E 150
Tissint, Mor. 29°53′ N, 7°20′ W 214
Tista, river, India 25°59′ N, 89°9′ E 197
Tisul', Russ. 55°43′ N, 88°25′ E 169
Tisza, river, Hung. 46°31′ N, 20°4′ E 156
Tiszacsege, Hung. 47°40′ N, 20°58′ E 168
Tiszaföldvár, Hung. 46°59′ N, 20°15′ E 168
Tiszafüred, Hung. 47°37′ N, 20°45′ E 168
Tiszakürt, Hung. 46°53′ N, 20°8′ E 168
Tiszanána, Hung. 47°32′ N, 20°32′ E 168
Tiszaug, Hung. 46°50′ N, 20°2′ E 168
Tiszaújváros, Hung. 47°53′ N, 21°2′ E 168
Tit, Alg. 26°56′ N, 1°30′ E 214
Titaf, Alg. 27°27′ N, 0°12′ E 214
Titan Dome, Antarctica 88°11′ S, 165°43′ W 248
Titel, Serb. and Mont. 45°12′ N, 20°17′ E 168
Titicaca, Lago, lake, Peru 15°34′ S, 70°43′ W 122
Titu, Rom. 44°40′ N, 25°31′ E 158
Titule, Dem. Rep. of the Congo 3°12′ N, 25°32′ E 224
Titusville, Fla., U.S. 28°36′ N, 80°50′ W 105
Titusville, Pa., U.S. 41°37′ N, 79°41′ W 94
Tivaouane, Senegal 14°57′ N, 16°38′ W 222
Tivat, Europe 42°26′ N, 18°41′ E 168
Tiverton, U.K. 50°54′ N, 3°28′ W 162
Tivissa, Sp. 41°2′ N, 0°44′ E 164
Tivoli, N.Y., U.S. 42°3′ N, 73°55′ W 104
Tiwai Point, N.Z. 46°35′ S, 168°23′ E 240
Tiwanacu, Bol. 16°38′ S, 68°43′ W 137
Tixtla, Mex. 17°32′ N, 99°23′ W 114
Tizayuca, Mex. 19°49′ N, 98°57′ W 114
Tizi Ouzou, Alg. 36°42′ N, 4°3′ E 150
Tizimín, Mex. 21°7′ N, 88°11′ W 116
Tiznit, Mor. 29°42′ N, 9°45′ W 214
Tjåmotis, Nor. 66°54′ N, 18°39′ E 152
Tlacotalpan, Mex. 18°37′ N, 95°40′ W 114
Tlahualilo de Zaragoza, Mex. 26°6′ N, 103°27′ W 114
Tlajomulco, Mex. 20°27′ N, 103°28′ W 114
Tlalnepantla, Mex. 19°31′ N, 99°11′ W 114
Tlapa, Mex. 17°31′ N, 98°34′ W 114
Tlapacoyan, Mex. 19°57′ N, 97°13′ W 114
Tlaquepaque, Mex. 20°37′ N, 103°19′ W 112
Tlaxcala, Mex. 19°15′ N, 98°19′ W 114
Tlaxcala, adm. division, Mex. 19°30′ N, 98°38′ W 114
Tlaxiaco, Mex. 17°15′ N, 97°42′ W 114
Tlell, Can. 53°36′ N, 131°59′ W 108
Tlemcen, Alg. 34°51′ N, 1°18′ W 214
Tleta, Alg. 36°47′ N, 5°52′ E 150
Tlīsan, spring, Lib. 28°27′ N, 17°28′ E 216
Tlyarata, Russ. 42°3′ N, 46°22′ E 195
Tmassah, Lib. 26°22′ N, 15°46′ E 216
Tni Haïa, spring, Alg. 24°20′ N, 2°45′ W 214
Toad River, Can. 58°50′ N, 125°15′ W 108
Toadlena, N. Mex., U.S. 36°13′ N, 108°53′ W 92
Toahayana, Mex. 26°8′ N, 107°42′ W 112
Toamasina, Madagascar 18°8′ S, 49°22′ E 220
Toana Range, Nev., U.S. 40°45′ N, 114°29′ W 90
Toano, It. 44°22′ N, 10°33′ E 167
Toast, N.C., U.S. 36°28′ N, 80°39′ W 96
Toay, Arg. 36°41′ S, 64°23′ W 134
Toba, Japan 34°27′ N, 136°51′ E 201
Toba, Danau, lake, Indonesia 2°47′ N, 98°39′ E 196
Toba Inlet 50°19′ N, 124°52′ W 90
Toba, river, Can. 50°35′ N, 124°16′ W 108
Tobacco Root Mountains, Mont., U.S. 45°25′ N, 112°19′ W 90
Tobago, island, Trinidad and Tobago 11°13′ N, 60°39′ W 118
Tobarra, Sp. 38°35′ N, 1°42′ W 164
Tobelo, Indonesia 1°41′ N, 127°54′ E 192
Tobermory 56°37′ N, 6°5′ W 150
Tobermory, Can. 45°13′ N, 81°40′ W 94
Tobin, Mount, peak, Nev., U.S. 40°22′ N, 117°37′ W 90
Tobli, Liberia 6°16′ N, 8°33′ W 222
Toboali, Indonesia 3°3′ S, 106°26′ E 192
Tobol, river, Russ. 56°41′ N, 66°37′ E 169
Tobol'sk, Russ. 58°14′ N, 68°22′ E 169
Tobruk, Lib. 31°52′ N, 23°50′ E 207
Tobruk see Ţubruq, Lib. 32°3′ N, 23°57′ E 216
Tobseda, Russ. 68°31′ N, 52°47′ E 160
Toby, Mount, peak, Mass., U.S. 42°28′ N, 72°34′ W 104
Tobyl, Kaz. 52°41′ N, 62°39′ E 184
Tobyl, river, Kaz. 53°48′ N, 63°50′ E 184
Tobysh, river, Russ. 66°21′ N, 50°21′ E 154
Tocantinia, Braz. 9°36′ S, 48°23′ W 130
Tocantinópolis, Braz. 6°19′ S, 47°28′ W 130
Tocantins, adm. division, Braz. 12°57′ S, 48°39′ W 138
Tocantins, river, Braz. 5°23′ S, 56°13′ W 132
Tocantins, river, Braz. 11°43′ S, 48°39′ W 130
Toccoa, Ga., U.S. 34°33′ N, 83°20′ W 96
Tochigi, adm. division, Japan 36°37′ N, 139°24′ E 201
Tochio, Japan 37°28′ N, 138°59′ E 201
Toco, Chile 22°5′ S, 69°41′ W 137
Toconao, Chile 23°12′ S, 68°2′ W 132
Tocopilla, Chile 22°8′ S, 70°13′ W 137
Tocuyo de la Costa, Venez. 11°1′ N, 68°25′ W 136
Tocuyo, river, Venez. 10°43′ N, 69°31′ W 136
Todal, Nor. 62°48′ N, 8°44′ E 152
Todd, Alas., U.S. 57°29′ N, 135°5′ W 108
Todenyang, Kenya 4°27′ N, 35°53′ E 224
Todireni, Rom. 47°36′ N, 27°5′ E 156
Todmorden, U.K. 53°43′ N, 2°6′ W 162
Todo Santos, Peru 1°16′ S, 73°47′ W 136
Todorovo, Bulg. 43°43′ N, 26°55′ E 156
Todos Santos, Bol. 16°49′ S, 65°10′ W 137
Todos Santos, Mex. 23°26′ N, 110°13′ W 112
Toe Head 57°49′ N, 7°32′ W 150
Tofield, Can. 53°21′ N, 112°40′ W 108
Tofino, Can. 49°6′ N, 125°52′ W 82
Töfsingdalens National Park, Nor. 62°11′ N, 12°23′ E 152
Tōgane, Japan 35°30′ N, 140°19′ E 201
Togi, Japan 37°7′ N, 136°44′ E 201
Togiak, Alas., U.S. 59°3′ N, 160°25′ W 106
Togian, Kepulauan, islands, Indonesia 0°10′ N, 122°30′ E 192
Togliatti see Tol'yatti, Russ. 53°30′ N, 49°34′ E 154
Togni, Sudan 18°2′ N, 35°9′ E 182
Tognuf, Eritrea 16°8′ N, 37°23′ E 182
Togo, Can. 51°24′ N, 101°37′ W 90
Togo 8°41′ N, 1°2′ E 214
Togobala, Guinea 9°16′ N, 7°57′ W 222
Togtoh, China 40°17′ N, 111°8′ E 198
Togur, Russ. 58°21′ N, 82°43′ E 169
Togüsken, Kaz. 43°34′ N, 67°24′ E 184
Togwotee Pass, Wyo., U.S. 43°44′ N, 110°3′ W 90
Togyz, Kaz. 47°36′ N, 60°30′ E 184
Tohatchi, N. Mex., U.S. 35°51′ N, 108°46′ W 92
Tohma, river, Turk. 38°58′ N, 37°29′ E 156
Tohogne, Belg. 50°22′ N, 5°29′ E 167
Toholampi, Fin. 63°45′ N, 24°11′ E 152
Töhöm, Mongolia 44°26′ N, 108°17′ E 198
Toibalawe, India 10°35′ N, 92°39′ E 188
Toijala, Fin. 61°9′ N, 23°52′ E 166
Toinya, Sudan 6°16′ N, 29°42′ E 224
Toiyabe Range, Nev., U.S. 39°23′ N, 117°19′ W 90
Tok, river, Russ. 52°40′ N, 52°27′ E 154
Tōkamachi, Japan 37°6′ N, 138°45′ E 201
Tokar, Sudan 18°26′ N, 37°41′ E 182
Tokara Rettō, islands, East China Sea 29°46′ N, 128°15′ E 190
Tokat, Turk. 40°18′ N, 36°34′ E 156
Tŏkch'ŏn, N. Korea 39°44′ N, 126°18′ E 200
Tokeland, Wash., U.S. 46°41′ N, 123°59′ W 100
Tokelau, islands, N.Z. 8°1′ S, 173°11′ W 238
Tokewanna Peak, Utah, U.S. 40°47′ N, 110°42′ W 90
Tokhtamysh, Taj. 37°49′ N, 74°40′ E 184
Toki, Japan 35°21′ N, 137°13′ E 201
Tokmak, Ukr. 47°12′ N, 35°45′ E 156
Tokmok, Kyrg. 42°48′ N, 75°17′ E 184
Toko, N.Z. 39°21′ S, 174°22′ E 240
Tokomaru Bay, N.Z. 38°8′ S, 178°17′ E 240
Tokoroa, N.Z. 38°15′ S, 175°52′ E 240
Toksova, Russ. 60°9′ N, 30°31′ E 166
Toksu see Xinhe, China 41°35′ N, 82°38′ E 184
Toktogul Reservoir, lake, Kyrg. 41°50′ N, 72°37′ E 197
Tokuno Shima, island, Japan 27°22′ N, 129°2′ E 190
Tokushima, Japan 34°4′ N, 134°32′ E 201
Tokushima, adm. division, Japan 33°53′ N, 133°42′ E 201
Tokuyama, Japan 34°4′ N, 131°50′ E 200
Tōkyō, Japan 35°39′ N, 139°40′ E 201
Tōkyō, adm. division, Japan 35°38′ N, 139°16′ E 201
Tolaga Bay, N.Z. 38°21′ S, 178°17′ E 240
Tôlañaro, Madagascar 24°56′ S, 46°58′ E 207
Tolbo, Mongolia 48°22′ N, 90°16′ E 184
Tolchin, Mount, peak, Antarctica 85°6′ S, 67°14′ W 248
Tōle Bī, Kaz. 43°36′ N, 73°47′ E 184
Toledo, Braz. 24°41′ S, 53°46′ W 132
Toledo, Braz. 5°56′ S, 73°6′ W 130
Toledo, Ill., U.S. 39°16′ N, 88°15′ W 102
Toledo, Iowa, U.S. 41°59′ N, 92°35′ W 94
Toledo, Ohio, U.S. 41°38′ N, 83°32′ W 102
Toledo, Sp. 39°52′ N, 4°2′ W 164
Toledo, Wash., U.S. 46°25′ N, 122°52′ W 100
Toledo Bend Reservoir, lake, La., U.S. 31°49′ N, 93°56′ W 103
Toledo, Montes de, Sp. 39°29′ N, 4°52′ W 164
Tolentino, It. 43°12′ N, 13°16′ E 156
Tolentino, Mex. 22°14′ N, 100°34′ W 114
Tolhuaca National Park, Chile 38°8′ S, 71°55′ W 134
Tol'yatti (Togliatti), Russia 53°30′ N, 49°34′ E 154
Toli, China 45°47′ N, 83°40′ E 184
Toliara, Madagascar 23°18′ S, 43°50′ E 207
Tolima, adm. division, Col. 4°1′ N, 75°40′ W 136
Tolitoli, Indonesia 1°5′ N, 120°45′ E 192
Tol'ka, Russ. 63°57′ N, 82°2′ E 169
Tolkaboua, Burkina Faso 10°11′ N, 2°59′ W 222
Tolkmicko, Pol. 54°18′ N, 19°32′ E 166
Tollhouse, Calif., U.S. 37°1′ N, 119°25′ W 100
Tollimarjon, Uzb. 38°17′ N, 65°33′ E 197
Tollya, Zaliv 76°15′ N, 98°2′ E 160
Tolmachevo, Russ. 58°51′ N, 29°52′ E 166
Tolmin, Slov. 46°11′ N, 13°44′ E 167
Tolna, Hung. 46°25′ N, 18°46′ E 168
Tolna, adm. division, Hung. 46°26′ N, 18°4′ E 156
Tolo, Teluk 2°28′ S, 121°52′ E 192
Tolono, Ill., U.S. 39°58′ N, 88°16′ W 102
Tolosa, Sp. 43°8′ N, 2°3′ W 164
Tolstoi, Can. 49°5′ N, 96°49′ W 90
Toltén, Chile 39°12′ S, 73°13′ W 134
Tolti, Pak. 35°0′ N, 76°6′ E 186
Tolú, Col. 9°31′ N, 75°34′ W 136
Toluca, Ill., U.S. 41°0′ N, 89°8′ W 102
Toluca, Mex. 19°14′ N, 99°43′ W 114
Toluca, Mo., U.S. 41°0′ N, 89°8′ W 94
Tom Burke, S. Af. 23°5′ S, 27°59′ E 227
Tom, Mount, peak, Mass., U.S. 42°14′ N, 72°41′ W 104
Tom Price, Austral. 22°41′ S, 117°49′ E 238
Tom', river, Russ. 55°15′ N, 85°0′ E 160
Tom White, Mount, peak, Alas., U.S. 60°38′ N, 143°50′ W 98
Tomah, Wis., U.S. 43°58′ N, 90°30′ W 94
Tomahawk, Wis., U.S. 45°27′ N, 89°43′ W 94
Tomales Point, Calif., U.S. 38°13′ N, 122°57′ W 90
Tomar, Braz. 0°25′ N, 63°54′ W 130
Tómaros, peak, Gr. 39°28′ N, 20°43′ E 156
Tomás Barrón, Bol. 17°41′ S, 67°29′ W 137
Tomás Gomensoro, Uru. 30°24′ S, 57°27′ W 139
Tomaševo, Europe 43°4′ N, 19°39′ E 168
Tomashevka, Belarus 51°32′ N, 23°35′ E 152
Tomatin, U.K. 57°20′ N, 3°60′ W 150
Tomatlán, Mex. 19°56′ N, 105°17′ W 114
Tomatlán, river, Mex. 19°46′ N, 105°21′ W 114
Tombador, Serra do, Braz. 10°46′ S, 58°16′ W 130
Tombe, Sudan 5°47′ N, 31°39′ E 224
Tombigbee, river, Ala., U.S. 31°46′ N, 88°8′ W 103
Tomboco, Angola 6°51′ S, 13°17′ E 218
Tombos, Braz. 20°54′ S, 42°3′ W 138
Tombouctou (Timbuktu), Mali 16°44′ N, 3°2′ W 222
Tombstone, Ariz., U.S. 31°41′ N, 110°4′ W 112
Tombstone Mountain, peak, Can. 64°19′ N, 138°47′ W 98
Tombua, Angola 15°52′ S, 11°50′ E 220
Tomdibuloq, Uzb. 41°45′ N, 64°39′ E 197
Tomé, Chile 36°35′ S, 72°57′ W 134
Tomelloso, Sp. 39°9′ N, 3°2′ W 164
Tomini, Teluk 0°22′ N, 120°27′ E 192
Tomislavgrad, Bosn. and Herzg. 43°40′ N, 17°12′ E 168
Tommot, Russ. 58°59′ N, 126°27′ E 160
Tomo, river, Col. 5°29′ N, 68°18′ W 136
Tomorit, Maja e, peak, Alban. 40°41′ N, 20°4′ E 156
Tompa, Hung. 46°11′ N, 19°32′ E 168
Tompkinsville, Ky., U.S. 36°41′ N, 85°42′ W 96
Tomsino, Russ. 56°26′ N, 28°32′ E 166
Tomsk, Russ. 56°30′ N, 85°3′ E 169
Tomsk, adm. division, Russ. 58°34′ N, 80°3′ E 169
Tonalá, Mex. 16°4′ N, 93°46′ W 115
Tonale, Passo del, It. 46°16′ N, 10°34′ E 167
Tonami, Japan 36°37′ N, 136°56′ E 201
Tonantins, Braz. 2°45′ S, 67°46′ W 136
Tonantins, river, Braz. 2°26′ S, 68°35′ W 136
Tonasket, Wash., U.S. 48°41′ N, 119°27′ W 90
Tonbridge, U.K. 51°11′ N, 0°16′ E 162
Tondi Kiwindi, Niger 14°40′ N, 1°51′ E 222
Tondou, Massif du, Cen. Af. Rep. 7°50′ N, 23°43′ E 224
Toney Mount, peak, Antarctica 75°44′ S, 115°16′ W 248
Tonga 22°46′ S, 174°39′ W 238
Tonga, Sudan 9°30′ N, 31°3′ E 224
Tonga, islands, South Pacific Ocean 20°25′ S, 173°49′ W 238
Tonga Trench, South Pacific Ocean 21°53′ S, 172°51′ W 252
Tong'an, China 24°43′ N, 118°9′ E 198
Tongatapu Group, islands, Tonga 22°46′ S, 174°39′ W 238
Tongatapu, island, Tonga 21°11′ S, 175°11′ W 241
Tongcheng, China 31°3′ N, 116°56′ E 198
Tongchuan, China 35°7′ N, 109°9′ E 198
Tongdao, China 26°9′ N, 109°45′ E 198
Tongeren, Belg. 50°46′ N, 5°27′ E 167
Tonghe, China 46°0′ N, 128°45′ E 198
Tonghua, China 41°42′ N, 125°54′ E 200
Tonghua (Kuaidamao), China 41°41′ N, 125°45′ E 200
Tongjiang, China 31°59′ N, 107°14′ E 198
Tongjosŏn-man 39°23′ N, 128°10′ E 200
Tongliang, China 29°50′ N, 106°4′ E 198
Tongliao, China 43°35′ N, 122°17′ E 198
Tongling, China 30°53′ N, 117°48′ E 198
Tonglu, China 29°47′ N, 119°37′ E 198
Tongnae, S. Korea 35°11′ N, 129°6′ E 200
Tongobory, Madagascar 23°28′ S, 44°18′ E 220
Tongren, China 27°45′ N, 109°13′ E 198
Tongshi, China 18°43′ N, 109°29′ E 198
Tongtian, river, China 33°51′ N, 93°30′ E 190
Tongue of the Ocean 23°55′ N, 77°32′ W 96
Tongue, river, Mont., U.S. 45°47′ N, 106°6′ W 90
Tongwei, China 35°14′ N, 105°12′ E 198
Tongxian, China 39°52′ N, 116°38′ E 198
Tongxin, China 37°1′ N, 105°53′ E 198
Tongyeong, S. Korea 34°50′ N, 128°26′ E 200
Tongyu, China 44°47′ N, 123°4′ E 198
Tongyuanpu, China 40°47′ N, 123°57′ E 200
Tongzi, China 28°8′ N, 106°48′ E 198
Tonica, Ill., U.S. 41°12′ N, 89°4′ W 102
Tonichi, Mex. 28°35′ N, 109°33′ W 92
Tönisvorst, Ger. 51°18′ N, 6°30′ E 167
Tonj, Sudan 7°16′ N, 28°45′ E 224
Tonj see Ibba, river, Sudan 6°16′ N, 28°21′ E 224
Tonk, India 26°9′ N, 75°48′ E 197
Tonkawa, Okla., U.S. 36°39′ N, 97°18′ W 92
Tonkin, Gulf of 19°38′ N, 107°25′ E 190
Tonneins, Fr. 44°23′ N, 0°17′ E 150
Tonopah, Nev., U.S. 38°4′ N, 117°15′ W 92
Tonota, Botswana 21°30′ S, 27°26′ E 227
Tønsberg, Nor. 59°16′ N, 10°26′ E 152
Tonsina, Alas., U.S. 61°38′ N, 145°11′ W 98
Tonto National Monument, Ariz., U.S. 33°37′ N, 111°10′ W 92
Tonya, Turk. 40°52′ N, 39°15′ E 195
Tooele, Utah, U.S. 40°32′ N, 112°14′ W 106
Toora Khem, Russ. 52°29′ N, 96°34′ E 190
Toore, Somalia 1°21′ N, 44°22′ E 218
Tootsi, Est. 58°34′ N, 24°47′ E 166
Topaz Mountain, peak, Utah, U.S. 39°41′ N, 113°11′ W 90
Topeka, Kans., U.S. 38°59′ N, 95°48′ W 90
Topia, Mex. 25°9′ N, 106°33′ W 114
Topki, Russ. 55°15′ N, 85°43′ E 169
Topley, Can. 54°31′ N, 126°20′ W 108
Topley Landing, Can. 54°48′ N, 126°11′ W 108
Topli Do, Serb. and Mont. 43°20′ N, 22°40′ E 168
Topocalma, Punta, Chile 34°15′ S, 73°58′ W 134
Topock, Ariz., U.S. 34°42′ N, 114°28′ W 101
Topola, Serb. and Mont. 44°15′ N, 20°40′ E 168
Topolobampo, Bahía de 25°32′ N, 110°21′ W 80
Topolovăţu Mare, Rom. 45°47′ N, 21°38′ E 168
Toppenish, Wash., U.S. 46°21′ N, 120°20′ W 90
Topsfield, Mass., U.S. 42°38′ N, 70°58′ W 104
Topsham, Me., U.S. 43°55′ N, 69°58′ W 104
Toquepala, Peru 17°18′ S, 70°35′ W 137
Toquima Range, Nev., U.S. 39°28′ N, 116°59′ W 90
Tor, Eth. 7°48′ N, 33°32′ E 224
Tor Bay 45°10′ N, 61°39′ W 111
Torà, Sp. 41°48′ N, 1°23′ E 164
Toragay, oil field, Azerb. 40°9′ N, 49°21′ E 195
Toranou, Côte d'Ivoire 8°48′ N, 7°47′ W 222
Torata, Peru 17°7′ S, 70°51′ W 137
Torbalı, Turk. 38°10′ N, 27°20′ E 156
Torbat-e Ḩeydarīyeh, Iran 35°17′ N, 59°13′ E 180
Torbat-e Jām, Iran 35°16′ N, 60°34′ E 180
Torbay, U.K. 50°27′ N, 3°34′ W 150
Torbert, Mount, peak, Antarctica 83°32′ S, 55°58′ W 248
Torch, river, Can. 53°33′ N, 104°9′ W 108
Torchiara, It. 40°19′ N, 15°2′ E 156
Torda, Serb. and Mont. 45°35′ N, 20°26′ E 168
Tordesilos, Sp. 40°39′ N, 1°35′ W 164
Töre, Nor. 65°54′ N, 22°39′ E 152
Töreboda, Nor. 58°41′ N, 14°7′ E 152
Torelló, Sp. 42°2′ N, 2°15′ E 164
Torere, N.Z. 37°59′ S, 177°30′ E 240
Torez, Ukr. 47°59′ N, 38°37′ E 158
Torgau, Ger. 51°34′ N, 12°59′ E 152
Torghay, Kaz. 49°46′ N, 63°35′ E 184
Torghay, river, Kaz. 48°34′ N, 62°27′ E 184
Torhout, Belg. 51°3′ N, 3°6′ E 163
Torija, Sp. 40°44′ N, 3°2′ W 164
Torino (Turin), It. 45°4′ N, 7°40′ E 167
Torit, Sudan 4°24′ N, 32°33′ E 224
Torixoreu, Braz. 16°13′ S, 52°31′ W 138
Torkovichi, Russ. 58°53′ N, 30°26′ E 166
Torma, Est. 58°47′ N, 26°43′ E 166
Tormac, Rom. 45°31′ N, 21°30′ E 168
Tornado Mountain, peak, Can. 49°56′ N, 114°45′ W 90
Torneå see Tornio, Fin. 65°51′ N, 24°7′ E 154
Torneträsk, lake, Nor. 67°53′ N, 19°22′ E 152
Torngat Mountains, Can. 59°30′ N, 64°3′ W 106
Tornillo, Tex., U.S. 31°26′ N, 106°5′ W 92
Tornio (Torneå), Fin. 65°51′ N, 24°7′ E 154
Tornquist, Arg. 38°6′ S, 62°15′ W 139
Toro, Nig. 10°2′ N, 9°3′ E 222
Toro, Sp. 41°31′ N, 5°25′ W 150
Toro Doum, spring, Chad 16°31′ N, 16°37′ E 216
Toro Peak, Calif., U.S. 33°31′ N, 116°28′ W 101
Torodi, Niger 13°18′ N, 1°42′ E 222
Torodo, Mali 14°33′ N, 8°52′ W 222
Törökszentmiklos, Hung. 47°10′ N, 20°26′ E 168
Torom, Russ. 54°20′ N, 135°47′ E 190
Torone, ruin(s), Gr. 40°0′ N, 23°43′ E 156
Toronto, Can. 43°39′ N, 79°29′ W 94
Toronto, Kans., U.S. 37°46′ N, 95°57′ W 94
Toropalca, Bol. 20°25′ S, 65°49′ W 137
Toropets, Russ. 56°29′ N, 31°39′ E 154
Tororo, Uganda 0°39′ N, 34°12′ E 224
Toros Dağlar (Taurus), Turk. 36°29′ N, 37°7′ E 156
Toros Dağları, Turk. 36°26′ N, 32°15′ E 180
Torotoro, Bol. 18°7′ S, 65°50′ W 137
Torquato Severo, Braz. 31°4′ S, 54°14′ W 139
Torra Bay, Namibia 20°17′ S, 13°15′ E 220
Torrance, Calif., U.S. 33°50′ N, 118°21′ W 101
Torre Astura, It. 41°25′ N, 12°44′ E 156
Torre de Moncorvo, Port. 41°9′ N, 7°4′ W 150
Torre Pacheco, Sp. 37°43′ N, 0°58′ E 164
Torreblanca, Sp. 40°12′ N, 0°10′ E 164
Torre-Cardela, Sp. 37°31′ N, 3°21′ W 164
Torrecilla en Cameros, Sp. 42°15′ N, 2°38′ W 164
Torredelcampo, Sp. 37°46′ N, 3°54′ W 164
Torredonjimeno, Sp. 37°46′ N, 3°58′ W 164
Torrelaguna, Sp. 40°49′ N, 3°32′ W 164
Torremolinos, Sp. 36°37′ N, 4°31′ W 164
Torrent, Arg. 28°49′ S, 56°28′ W 139
Torrent, Sp. 39°26′ N, 0°28′ E 164
Torrenueva, Sp. 38°39′ N, 3°22′ W 164
Torreón, Mex. 25°31′ N, 103°26′ W 114
Torreón de Cañas, Mex. 26°22′ N, 105°16′ W 114
Torres, Mex. 28°45′ N, 110°46′ W 92
Torres del Paine National Park, Chile 51°6′ S, 73°25′ W 122

Torres Islands, South Pacific Ocean 14°42′ S, 164°17′ E 238
Torres Strait 9°40′ S, 141°19′ E 231
Torrevieja, Sp. 37°58′ N, 0°41′ W 164
Torrijo, Sp. 41°29′ N, 1°53′ W 164
Torrijos, Sp. 39°59′ N, 4°17′ W 150
Torrington, Conn., U.S. 41°47′ N, 73°8′ W 104
Torrington, Wyo., U.S. 42°4′ N, 104°11′ W 90
Torroella de Montgrí, Sp. 42°2′ N, 3°7′ E 164
Torrox, Sp. 36°45′ N, 3°58′ W 164
Torsås, Nor. 56°25′ N, 15°58′ E 152
Tórshavn 62°10′ N, 6°53′ W 143
Torsken, Nor. 69°21′ N, 17°8′ E 152
Tortola, island, British Virgin Is., U.K. 18°26′ N, 64°38′ W 118
Tortolì, It. 39°55′ N, 9°36′ E 214
Tortona, It. 44°53′ N, 8°52′ E 167
Tortosa, Sp. 40°50′ N, 0°34′ E 214
Tortosa, Cap de, Sp. 40°29′ N, 0°59′ E 143
Tortosa see Ţarţūs, Syr. 34°53′ N, 35°53′ E 194
Tortue, Île de la, island, Haiti 20°9′ N, 73°9′ W 116
Tortuguero, C.R. 10°33′ N, 83°32′ W 115
Tortum, Turk. 40°19′ N, 41°34′ E 195
Ţorūd, Iran 35°26′ N, 55°6′ E 180
Torul, Turk. 40°35′ N, 39°18′ E 195
Tõrva, Est. 57°59′ N, 25°54′ E 166
Torzhok, Russ. 57°0′ N, 34°57′ E 154
Tosa, Japan 33°30′ N, 133°25′ E 201
Tosa Wan 33°16′ N, 133°37′ E 201
Tosamaganga, Tanzania 7°50′ S, 35°35′ E 224
T'osan, N. Korea 38°17′ N, 126°43′ E 200
Tosanachi, Mex. 28°32′ N, 108°3′ W 92
Tosashimizu, Japan 32°46′ N, 132°55′ E 201
Tosayamada, Japan 33°37′ N, 133°40′ E 201
Tosca, S. Af. 26°9′ S, 23°51′ E 227
Tosca, Punta, Mex. 24°19′ N, 112°36′ W 112
Toshkent (Tashkent), Uzb. 41°18′ N, 69°10′ E 197
Toson Hu, lake, China 37°3′ N, 96°15′ E 188
Tossa de Mar, Sp. 41°43′ N, 2°55′ E 164
Tostado, Arg. 29°13′ S, 61°48′ W 139
Tõstamaa, Est. 58°19′ N, 23°56′ E 166
Tostuya, Russ. 73°10′ N, 113°42′ E 173
Tosu, Japan 33°22′ N, 130°31′ E 201
Tosya, Turk. 41°1′ N, 34°1′ E 156
Toszek, Pol. 50°26′ N, 18°31′ E 152
Totana, Sp. 37°46′ N, 1°31′ W 164
Totara, N.Z. 45°9′ S, 170°52′ E 240
Totatiche, Mex. 21°55′ N, 103°27′ W 114
Toten, region, Nor. 60°41′ N, 10°37′ E 152
Toteng, Botswana 20°23′ S, 22°57′ E 227
Tôtes, Fr. 49°40′ N, 1°2′ E 163
Tótkomlós, Hung. 46°24′ N, 20°45′ E 168
Tot'ma, Russ. 59°58′ N, 42°48′ E 154
Totness (Coronie), Suriname 5°49′ N, 56°18′ W 130
Tôto, Angola 7°11′ S, 14°18′ E 218
Totogan Lake, lake, Can. 52°3′ N, 89°35′ W 110
Totokro, Côte d'Ivoire 7°10′ N, 5°8′ W 222
Totolapan, Mex. 18°7′ N, 100°23′ W 114
Totora, Bol. 17°47′ S, 65°9′ W 137
Totoras, Arg. 32°37′ S, 61°9′ W 139
Totskoye, Russ. 52°31′ N, 52°43′ E 154
Tottori, Japan 35°27′ N, 134°14′ E 201
Tottori, adm. division, Japan 35°19′ N, 133°25′ E 201
Touba, Côte d'Ivoire 8°12′ N, 7°41′ W 222
Touba, Senegal 14°52′ N, 15°49′ W 222
Toubakouta, Senegal 13°48′ N, 16°22′ W 222
Toubkal, Jebel, peak, Mor. 31°3′ N, 8°6′ W 214
Toueïla, spring, Mauritania 18°24′ N, 15°46′ W 222
Touerat, spring, Mali 17°57′ N, 3°16′ W 222
Toufourine, spring, Mali 24°38′ N, 4°43′ W 214
Tougan, Burkina Faso 13°4′ N, 3°6′ W 222
Touggourt, Alg. 32°58′ N, 5°58′ E 207
Tougouri, Burkina Faso 13°18′ N, 0°34′ E 222
Tougouya, Burkina Faso 13°27′ N, 2°5′ W 222
Tougué, Guinea 11°26′ N, 11°42′ W 222
Touila, spring, Mauritania 25°56′ N, 6°22′ W 214
Toukoto, Mali 13°29′ N, 9°52′ W 222
Toul, Fr. 48°39′ N, 5°52′ E 163
Toulépleu, Côte d'Ivoire 6°27′ N, 8°24′ W 222
Touliu, Taiwan 23°40′ N, 120°31′ E 198
Toulon, Fr. 43°7′ N, 5°55′ E 150
Toulon, Ill., U.S. 41°5′ N, 89°52′ W 102
Toulouse, Fr. 43°35′ N, 1°27′ E 164
Toumania, Guinea 10°24′ N, 10°50′ W 222
Toumbélaga, spring, Niger 15°52′ N, 7°48′ E 222
Toummo, Lib. 22°39′ N, 14°11′ E 216
Toumodi, Côte d'Ivoire 6°28′ N, 5°2′ W 222
Toungad, Mauritania 20°4′ N, 13°9′ W 222
Toungo, Nig. 8°3′ N, 12°2′ E 218
Touraine, region, Fr. 47°35′ N, 0°56′ E 165
Tourassine, ruin(s), Mauritania 24°40′ N, 11°36′ W 214
Tourba, Chad 12°53′ N, 15°17′ E 216
Tourbe, Pointe de la, Can. 49°14′ N, 64°15′ W 111
Tourcoing, Fr. 50°43′ N, 3°9′ E 163
Tourine, spring, Mauritania 22°31′ N, 11°53′ W 214
Tournai, Belg. 50°35′ N, 3°23′ E 163
Tournan, Fr. 48°44′ N, 2°46′ E 163
Tournus, Fr. 46°34′ N, 4°53′ E 150
Touros, Braz. 5°14′ S, 35°29′ W 132
Touroua, Cameroon 9°0′ N, 12°58′ E 216
Tours, Fr. 47°23′ N, 0°41′ E 150
Toury, Fr. 48°11′ N, 1°55′ E 163
Touside, Pic, peak, Chad 21°1′ N, 16°19′ E 216
Tovar, Venez. 8°20′ N, 71°48′ W 136
Tovarkovskiy, Russ. 53°39′ N, 38°13′ E 154
Tovik, Nor. 68°40′ N, 16°54′ E 152
Tovste, Ukr. 48°50′ N, 25°43′ E 156
Tovuz, Azerb. 40°58′ N, 45°35′ E 195
Towanda, Pa., U.S. 41°45′ N, 76°28′ W 94
Towcester, U.K. 52°7′ N, 0°60′ E 162
Tower, Minn., U.S. 47°47′ N, 92°17′ W 110
Tower Hill, Ill., U.S. 39°22′ N, 88°58′ W 102
Tower Island, Antarctica 63°32′ S, 61°29′ W 134
Tower Mountain, peak, Oreg., U.S. 45°2′ N, 118°40′ W 90
Towne Pass, Calif., U.S. 36°23′ N, 117°18′ W 101
Towner, N. Dak., U.S. 48°19′ N, 100°25′ W 90
Townsend, Mass., U.S. 42°39′ N, 71°43′ W 104
Townsend, Mont., U.S. 46°17′ N, 111°30′ W 90
Townsend, Va., U.S. 37°10′ N, 75°58′ W 96
Townshend, Vt., U.S. 43°2′ N, 72°41′ W 104
Townshend Island, island, Austral. 22°30′ S, 150°37′ E 230
Towot, Sudan 6°12′ N, 34°22′ E 224
Towraghondi, Afghan. 35°13′ N, 62°15′ E 186
Towrzi, Afghan. 30°10′ N, 66°2′ E 186
Towuti, Danau, lake, Indonesia 2°51′ S, 120°29′ E 192
Toxkan, river, China 40°55′ N, 76°50′ E 184
Toyah, Tex., U.S. 31°17′ N, 103°48′ W 92
Toyahvale, Tex., U.S. 30°55′ N, 103°47′ W 92
Toyama, Japan 36°41′ N, 137°14′ E 201
Toyama, adm. division, Japan 36°32′ N, 136°50′ E 201
Toyama Wan 36°50′ N, 137°8′ E 201
Toyohashi, Japan 34°44′ N, 137°23′ E 201
Toyooka, Japan 35°31′ N, 134°47′ E 201
Toyoura, Japan 34°9′ N, 130°56′ E 200
To'ytepa, Uzb. 41°2′ N, 69°21′ E 197
Tozeur, Tun. 33°54′ N, 8°1′ E 143
Tozeur, spring, Chad 18°9′ N, 18°22′ E 216
Tpig, Russ. 41°45′ N, 47°36′ E 195
Tqvarch'eli, Asia 42°49′ N, 41°41′ E 195
Traben-Trarbach, Ger. 49°57′ N, 7°7′ E 167
Trablous (Tripoli), Leb. 34°26′ N, 35°50′ E 194
Trabzon, Turk. 40°58′ N, 39°41′ E 195
Trachonas 35°12′ N, 33°20′ E 194
Tracy, Calif., U.S. 37°44′ N, 121°27′ W 100
Tracy, Can. 46°0′ N, 73°10′ W 111
Tracy, Minn., U.S. 44°12′ N, 95°38′ W 90
Tracy Arm 57°52′ N, 134°8′ W 108
Tradate, It. 45°43′ N, 8°54′ E 167
Trade Lake, lake, Can. 55°19′ N, 104°14′ W 108
Trade Town, Liberia 5°41′ N, 9°51′ W 222
Trädet, Nor. 57°58′ N, 13°32′ E 152
Trading, river, Can. 51°33′ N, 89°29′ W 110
Traeger Hills, peak, Austral. 23°53′ S, 124°26′ E 230
Traer, Iowa, U.S. 42°10′ N, 92°28′ W 94
Trafalgar, Ind., U.S. 39°24′ N, 86°9′ W 102
Trafalgar, Cabo, Sp. 36°5′ N, 6°14′ W 164
Trafford, Lake, Fla., U.S. 26°25′ N, 81°37′ W 105
Tragacete, Sp. 40°19′ N, 1°52′ W 164
Traian, Rom. 45°10′ N, 27°44′ E 156
Tráighlí see Tralee, Ire. 52°16′ N, 9°42′ W 150
Trail, Can. 49°6′ N, 117°44′ W 90
Traill Ø, island, Traill Ø 72°17′ N, 28°9′ W 246
Trainor Lake, Can. 60°26′ N, 120°43′ W 108
Traíra Tarairá, river, South America 5°296′ S, 69°56′ W 136
Trakai National Park, Lith. 54°37′ N, 24°35′ E 166
Tralake, Miss., U.S. 33°14′ N, 90°48′ W 103
Tralee (Tráighlí), Ire. 52°16′ N, 9°42′ W 150
Tramonti di Sopra, It. 46°18′ N, 12°47′ E 167
Træna, islands, Norwegian Sea 66°33′ N, 11°1′ E 152
Tranås, Nor. 58°2′ N, 14°58′ E 152
Tranebjerg, Den. 55°49′ N, 10°34′ E 150
Trang, Thai. 7°35′ N, 99°38′ E 196
Trangan, island, Indonesia 7°9′ S, 133°3′ E 192
Tranqueras, Uru. 31°13′ S, 55°43′ W 139
Tranquillity, Calif., U.S. 36°38′ N, 120°16′ W 100
Tranquitas, oil field, Arg. 22°41′ S, 63°60′ W 137
Transantarctic Mountains, Antarctica 81°39′ S, 40°42′ W 248
Transcona, Can. 49°52′ N, 96°58′ W 90
Transdniester, special sovereignty, Mold. 48°6′ N, 27°46′ E 152
Transit Hill, peak, Austral. 15°21′ S, 129°21′ E 230
Transylvania, region, Rom. 46°2′ N, 22°9′ E 168
Transylvanian Alps, Rom. 44°55′ N, 22°35′ E 168
Trapper Peak, Mont., U.S. 45°51′ N, 114°26′ W 80
Trarza, region, Mauritania 17°53′ N, 15°24′ W 222
Trascău, Munţii, Rom. 46°14′ N, 23°13′ E 168
Trasury Islands, Solomon Sea 7°20′ S, 155°30′ E 242
Trat, Thai. 12°15′ N, 102°31′ E 202
Trauira, Ilha da, island, Braz. 1°34′ S, 46°34′ W 130
Travemünde, Ger. 53°58′ N, 10°52′ E 150
Traver, Calif., U.S. 36°27′ N, 119°30′ W 100
Travers Reservoir, lake, Can. 50°9′ N, 113°19′ W 90
Travis Air Force Base, Calif., U.S. 38°14′ N, 121°59′ W 100
Travnik, Bosn. and Herzg. 44°14′ N, 17°41′ E 168
Trawsfynydd, U.K. 52°54′ N, 3°54′ W 162
Trbunje, Serb. and Mont. 43°15′ N, 21°16′ E 168
Trebinje, Bosn. and Herzg. 42°43′ N, 18°19′ E 168
Trebujena, Sp. 36°51′ N, 6°11′ W 164
Trecate, It. 45°25′ N, 8°43′ E 167
Trecenta, It. 45°1′ N, 11°28′ E 167
Treetops, site, Kenya 0°24′ N, 36°41′ E 224
Treffurt, Ger. 51°8′ N, 10°14′ E 167
Tregaron, U.K. 52°12′ N, 3°55′ W 162
Tregrosse Islets, islands, Coral Sea 18°3′ S, 149°35′ E 230
Treinta-y-Tres, Uru. 33°13′ S, 54°22′ W 139
Treis-Karden, Ger. 50°10′ N, 7°18′ E 167
Treklyano, Bulg. 42°32′ N, 22°36′ E 168
Trelawney, Zimb. 17°31′ S, 30°28′ E 224
Trelleborg, Nor. 55°22′ N, 13°8′ E 152
Tremblant, Mount, peak, Can. 46°13′ N, 74°40′ W 94
Tremiti, Isole, islands, Adriatic Sea 42°11′ N, 15°36′ E 156
Tremont, Ill., U.S. 40°30′ N, 89°30′ W 102
Tremp, Sp. 42°9′ N, 0°52′ E 164
Trenary, Mich., U.S. 46°11′ N, 86°58′ W 94
Trenche, river, Can. 48°43′ N, 73°43′ W 94
Trenčianský, adm. division, Slovakia 48°52′ N, 18°3′ E 156
Trenčín, Slovakia 48°52′ N, 18°3′ E 152
Trenque Lauquen, Arg. 35°57′ S, 62°42′ W 139
Trent, river, U.K. 53°33′ N, 0°46′ E 162
Trent, river, U.K. 53°1′ N, 2°10′ W 162
Trentino-Alto Adige, adm. division, It. 46°32′ N, 10°41′ E 167
Trento, It. 46°4′ N, 11°8′ E 167
Trenton, Can. 44°6′ N, 77°35′ W 110
Trenton, Fla., U.S. 29°36′ N, 82°50′ W 105
Trenton, Mich., U.S. 42°8′ N, 83°12′ W 102
Trenton, Nebr., U.S. 40°10′ N, 101°1′ W 90
Trenton, N.J., U.S. 40°11′ N, 74°53′ W 94
Trepassey, Can. 46°43′ N, 53°22′ W 111
Trepča, Europe 42°56′ N, 20°55′ E 168
Tres Arboles, Uru. 32°26′ S, 56°43′ W 139
Tres Arroyos, Arg. 38°23′ S, 60°14′ W 139
Três Corações, Braz. 21°42′ S, 45°14′ W 138
Tres Cruces, Cerro, peak, Mex. 15°26′ N, 92°32′ W 115
Tres Esquinas, Col. 0°43′ N, 75°14′ W 136
Tres Isletas, Arg. 26°20′ S, 60°25′ W 139
Três Lagoas, Braz. 20°47′ S, 51°44′ W 138
Tres Lagos, Arg. 49°36′ S, 71°30′ W 134
Tres Lomas, Arg. 36°28′ S, 62°51′ W 139
Três Marias Dam, Braz. 18°6′ S, 45°17′ W 138
Tres Montes, Península, Chile 47°7′ S, 77°36′ W 134
Três Passos, Braz. 27°28′ S, 53°58′ W 139
Tres Picos, Arg. 38°18′ S, 62°14′ W 139
Tres Pinos, Calif., U.S. 36°47′ N, 121°20′ W 100
Três Pontas, Braz. 21°24′ S, 45°29′ W 138
Tres Pozos, Arg. 28°23′ S, 62°15′ W 139
Tres Puntas, Cabo, Arg. 47°1′ S, 65°54′ W 134
Tres Puntas, Cabo de, Guatemala 15°59′ N, 88°44′ W 115
Três Rios, Braz. 22°5′ S, 43°14′ W 138
Tres Valles, Mex. 18°14′ N, 96°8′ W 114
Tres Zapotes, ruin(s), Mex. 18°26′ N, 95°32′ W 114
Treskavica, Bosn. and Herzg. 43°39′ N, 18°12′ E 168
Trespaderne, Sp. 42°47′ N, 3°25′ W 164
Tretower, U.K. 51°52′ N, 3°11′ W 162
Treungen, Nor. 58°59′ N, 8°29′ E 152
Trêve, Lac la, lake, Can. 49°55′ N, 76°5′ W 94
Treviglio, It. 45°30′ N, 9°35′ E 167
Treviño, Sp. 42°43′ N, 2°45′ W 164
Treviso, It. 45°39′ N, 12°13′ E 167
Trgovište, Serb. and Mont. 42°22′ N, 22°6′ E 168
Tría, islands, Aegean Sea 36°9′ N, 26°46′ E 156
Triánda (Ialysus), Gr. 36°24′ N, 28°10′ E 156
Triangle, Zimb. 21°3′ S, 31°33′ E 227
Triángulo Oeste, islands, Gulf of Mexico 21°5′ N, 93°24′ W 112
Triángulo Sur, islands, Gulf of Mexico 20°49′ N, 92°7′ W 112
Triberg, Ger. 48°7′ N, 8°14′ E 152
Tribune, Kans., U.S. 38°28′ N, 101°46′ W 90
Tricase, It. 39°55′ N, 18°21′ E 156
Trichur (Thrissur), India 10°31′ N, 76°11′ E 188
Trident Peak (Obrian Peak), Nev., U.S. 41°53′ N, 118°30′ W 90
Trie, Fr. 43°19′ N, 0°21′ E 164
Trier, Ger. 49°45′ N, 6°39′ E 163
Trieste, It. 45°38′ N, 13°45′ E 167
Trigal, Bol. 18°18′ S, 64°14′ W 137
Triglav, peak, Slov. 46°22′ N, 13°46′ E 156
Trigo Mountains, Ariz., U.S. 33°7′ N, 114°37′ W 101
Trijebovo, Bosn. and Herzg. 44°30′ N, 17°4′ E 168
Tríkala, Gr. 39°32′ N, 21°46′ E 180
Trikomo 35°17′ N, 33°53′ E 194
Trikora, Puncak, peak, Indonesia 4°10′ S, 138°25′ E 192
Trilby, Fla., U.S. 28°26′ N, 82°14′ W 105
Trilj, Croatia 43°37′ N, 16°42′ E 168
Trillo, Sp. 40°42′ N, 2°36′ W 164
Trilsbeck Lake, lake, Can. 50°56′ N, 84°38′ W 110
Trincomalee, Sri Lanka 8°34′ N, 81°14′ E 188
Trindade, Braz. 16°41′ S, 49°30′ W 138
Trindade, island, Braz. 20°45′ S, 30°23′ W 132
Trinidad, Bol. 14°49′ S, 64°48′ W 137
Trinidad, Colo., U.S. 37°10′ N, 104°29′ W 92
Trinidad, Uru. 33°32′ S, 56°54′ W 139
Trinidad and Tobago 10°41′ N, 61°3′ W 118
Trinidad Head, Calif., U.S. 40°52′ N, 124°27′ W 90
Trinidad, Isla, island, Arg. 39°21′ S, 61°52′ W 134
Trinidad, island, Trinidad and Tobago 10°8′ N, 60°56′ W 116
Trinidad, island, Trinidad and Tobago 10°25′ N, 61°14′ W 118
Trinity, Tex., U.S. 30°55′ N, 95°23′ W 103
Trinity Bay 47°57′ N, 54°30′ W 106
Trinity Island, island, Antarctica 64°12′ S, 61°28′ W 248
Trinity Islands, Alas., U.S. 55°55′ N, 155°52′ W 98
Trinity Mountains, Calif., U.S. 40°56′ N, 122°47′ W 90
Trinity Range, Nev., U.S. 40°23′ N, 118°49′ W 90
Trinity, river, Calif., U.S. 40°38′ N, 123°37′ W 80
Trinity, river, Tex., U.S. 30°26′ N, 94°56′ W 103
Trinkitat, Sudan 18°37′ N, 37°41′ E 182
Trino, It. 45°12′ N, 8°17′ E 167
Trinway, Ohio, U.S. 40°8′ N, 82°1′ W 102
Trion, Ga., U.S. 34°31′ N, 85°19′ W 96
Triora, It. 43°59′ N, 7°46′ E 167
Trípoli, Gr. 37°31′ N, 22°22′ E 156
Tripoli see Ţarābulus, Lib. 32°37′ N, 12°35′ E 216
Tripoli see Trablous, Leb. 34°26′ N, 35°50′ E 194
Tripolitania, region, Lib. 30°23′ N, 11°4′ E 214
Tripp, S. Dak., U.S. 43°11′ N, 97°58′ W 90
Tripura, adm. division, India 23°47′ N, 91°18′ E 197
Tristan da Cunha Group, islands, South Atlantic Ocean 36°47′ S, 14°34′ W 206
Tristao, Îles, islands, North Atlantic Ocean 10°23′ N, 15°45′ W 222
Triunfo, river, Braz. 6°38′ S, 53°18′ W 130
Trivandrum (Thiruvananthapuram), India 8°28′ N, 76°56′ E 188
Trivento, It. 41°46′ N, 14°32′ E 156
Trn, Bosn. and Herzg. 44°50′ N, 17°13′ E 168
Trnava, Slovakia 48°22′ N, 17°35′ E 152
Trnavský, adm. division, Slovakia 48°34′ N, 16°56′ E 152
Trnovo, Bosn. and Herzg. 43°39′ N, 18°27′ E 168
Trobriand Islands, P.N.G. 8°14′ S, 150°59′ E 238
Trobriand Islands, Solomon Sea 7°51′ S, 149°6′ E 192
Trochu, Can. 51°51′ N, 113°14′ W 90
Troebratskīy, Kaz. 54°19′ N, 66°7′ E 184
Troezen, ruin(s), Gr. 37°29′ N, 23°16′ E 156
Trofimovka, Kaz. 53°27′ N, 76°59′ E 184
Trofors, Nor. 65°32′ N, 13°19′ E 152
Troilus, Lac, lake, Can. 50°53′ N, 75°5′ W 110
Troisdorf, Ger. 50°49′ N, 7°8′ E 167
Trois-Pistoles, Can. 48°6′ N, 69°9′ W 94
Trois-Ponts, Belg. 50°24′ N, 4°42′ E 167
Trois-Rivières, Can. 46°20′ N, 72°34′ W 94
Troisvierges, Lux. 50°7′ N, 6°0′ E 167
Troitsk, Russ. 54°9′ N, 61°32′ E 154
Troitskiy, Russ. 57°5′ N, 63°42′ E 154
Troitsko Pechorsk, Russ. 62°42′ N, 56°7′ E 154
Troitskoye, Russ. 46°22′ N, 44°11′ E 158
Troitskoye, Russ. 52°19′ N, 56°16′ E 154
Troitskoye, Russ. 53°1′ N, 84°43′ E 184
Troll, Norway, station, Antarctica 71°50′ S, 2°56′ E 248
Trolla, spring, Chad 15°26′ N, 14°48′ E 216
Troll-heimen, Nor. 62°57′ N, 8°39′ E 152
Trombas, Braz. 13°29′ S, 48°47′ W 138
Tromelin Island, Fr. 15°58′ S, 54°27′ E 254
Tromsø, Nor. 69°38′ N, 18°53′ E 152
Tron, peak, Nor. 62°9′ N, 10°34′ E 152
Trona, Calif., U.S. 35°45′ N, 117°24′ W 101
Troncon, Mex. 23°29′ N, 104°20′ W 114
Trondheim, Nor. 63°23′ N, 10°27′ E 152
Trondheimsfjorden 63°25′ N, 5°22′ E 142
Trones, Nor. 64°45′ N, 12°50′ E 152
Trönninge, Nor. 56°38′ N, 12°57′ E 152
Troodos Mountains, Cyprus 34°58′ N, 32°24′ E 194
Tropea, It. 38°41′ N, 15°53′ E 156
Tropic, Utah, U.S. 37°37′ N, 112°4′ W 92
Tropojë, Alban. 42°24′ N, 20°9′ E 168
Trosa, Nor. 58°54′ N, 17°29′ E 152
Trosh, Russ. 66°22′ N, 55°59′ E 154
Troškūnai, Lith. 55°35′ N, 24°52′ E 166
Trostan, peak, U.K. 55°1′ N, 6°16′ W 150
Trostyanets', Ukr. 50°28′ N, 34°57′ E 158
Trotternish, region 57°35′ N, 6°46′ W 150
Trotwood, Ohio, U.S. 39°47′ N, 84°19′ W 102
Troup, Tex., U.S. 32°8′ N, 95°8′ W 103
Troup Head 57°42′ N, 2°42′ W 150
Trout, La., U.S. 31°41′ N, 92°12′ W 103
Trout Creek, Can. 45°59′ N, 79°21′ W 94
Trout Lake, Can. 50°39′ N, 117°33′ W 90
Trout Lake, Can. 51°10′ N, 93°47′ W 110
Trout Lake, Can. 60°25′ N, 121°11′ W 108
Trout Lake, Minn., U.S. 47°55′ N, 92°47′ W 94
Trout Lake, Wash., U.S. 45°58′ N, 121°32′ W 100
Trout Lake, lake, Can. 51°6′ N, 94°18′ W 106
Trout Peak, Wyo., U.S. 44°34′ N, 109°37′ W 90
Trout, river, Can. 60°58′ N, 120°45′ W 108
Trout, river, Can. 56°18′ N, 114°30′ W 108
Troutdale, Oreg., U.S. 45°32′ N, 122°25′ W 90
Trouville, Fr. 49°21′ N, 8°475′ E 150
Trowbridge, U.K. 51°18′ N, 2°12′ W 162
Troy, Ala., U.S. 31°48′ N, 85°59′ W 96
Troy, Mich., U.S. 42°34′ N, 83°9′ W 102
Troy, Mo., U.S. 38°58′ N, 90°59′ W 94
Troy, Mont., U.S. 48°26′ N, 115°54′ W 90
Troy, N.H., U.S. 42°49′ N, 72°12′ W 104
Troy, N.Y., U.S. 42°43′ N, 73°42′ W 104
Troy, N.C., U.S. 35°21′ N, 79°55′ W 96
Troy, Ohio, U.S. 40°1′ N, 84°13′ W 102
Troy Peak, Nev., U.S. 38°18′ N, 115°35′ W 90
Troy, ruin(s), Turk. 39°56′ N, 26°7′ E 156
Troyes, Fr. 48°17′ N, 4°4′ E 163
Trozadero, Peru 2°60′ S, 76°47′ W 136
Trpezi, Europe 42°53′ N, 20°0′ E 168
Trubar, Bosn. and Herzg. 44°21′ N, 16°13′ E 168
Trubchevsk, Russ. 52°33′ N, 33°49′ E 158
Truckee, Calif., U.S. 39°19′ N, 120°12′ W 90
Trudfront, Russ. 45°53′ N, 47°40′ E 158
Trufant, Mich., U.S. 43°17′ N, 85°21′ W 102
Trujillo, Hond. 15°54′ N, 85°59′ W 115
Trujillo, Peru 8°8′ S, 79°2′ W 130
Trujillo, Sp. 39°27′ N, 5°53′ W 164
Trujillo, Venez. 9°20′ N, 70°27′ W 136
Trujillo, adm. division, Venez. 9°26′ N, 71°6′ W 136
Trujillo Alto, U.S. 18°21′ N, 66°0′ W 118
Truk Islands see Chuuk, islands, F.S.M. 7°44′ N, 152°5′ E 242
Trumbull, Conn., U.S. 41°14′ N, 73°12′ W 104
Trumbull, Mount, peak, Ariz., U.S. 36°23′ N, 113°12′ W 92
Trumon, Indonesia 2°51′ N, 97°36′ E 196
Trŭn, Bulg. 42°49′ N, 22°37′ E 168
Truro, Can. 45°21′ N, 63°17′ W 111
Truro, Mass., U.S. 41°59′ N, 70°4′ W 104
Truşeşti, Rom. 47°45′ N, 27°1′ E 152
Trutch, Can. 57°44′ N, 122°57′ W 108
Truth or Consequences, N. Mex., U.S. 33°8′ N, 107°15′ W 92
Trutnov, Czech Rep. 50°33′ N, 15°54′ E 152
Truxton, Ariz., U.S. 35°29′ N, 113°33′ W 101
Trwyn Cilan, U.K. 52°36′ N, 4°52′ W 150
Tryphena, N.Z. 36°19′ S, 175°27′ E 240
Trysil, Nor. 61°19′ N, 12°15′ E 152
Trzcianka, Pol. 53°1′ N, 16°27′ E 152
Trzebież, Pol. 53°39′ N, 14°31′ E 152
Trzemeszno, Pol. 52°33′ N, 17°49′ E 152
Tsacha Lake, Can. 52°59′ N, 125°26′ W 108
Tsada, Cyprus 34°50′ N, 32°28′ E 194
Tsagaanders, Mongolia 48°5′ N, 114°21′ E 198
Tsagaangol, Mongolia 49°1′ N, 89°3′ E 184
Tsagaannuur, Mongolia 49°28′ N, 89°39′ E 184
Tsagan Aman, Russ. 47°30′ N, 46°37′ E 158
Ts'ageri, Ga. 42°36′ N, 42°42′ E 195
Tsagveri, Ga. 41°48′ N, 43°27′ E 195
Tsaka La, pass, India 33°20′ N, 78°50′ E 188
Tsalka, Ga. 41°34′ N, 44°3′ E 195
Tsao see Tsau, Botswana 20°13′ S, 22°23′ E 227
Tsapel'ka, Russ. 58°2′ N, 28°57′ E 166
Tsaratanana, Massif du, Madagascar 14°17′ S, 48°37′ E 220
Tsarevo, Bulg. 42°10′ N, 27°51′ E 158
Tsau (Tsao), Botswana 20°13′ S, 22°23′ E 227
Tsavo, Kenya 3°3′ S, 38°29′ E 224
Tsavo National Park, Kenya 2°59′ S, 39°7′ E 218
Tsavo, river, Kenya 3°15′ S, 37°42′ E 224
Tsawisis, Namibia 26°16′ S, 18°8′ E 227
Tsayta Lake, lake, Can. 55°23′ N, 125°57′ W 108
Tschaukaib, Namibia 26°37′ S, 15°36′ E 227
Tschida, Lake, N. Dak., U.S. 46°33′ N, 102°24′ W 90
Tselina, Russ. 46°33′ N, 40°59′ E 158
Tsenogora, Russ. 64°55′ N, 46°34′ E 154
Tserovo, Bulg. 42°21′ N, 24°3′ E 156
Tses, Namibia 25°53′ S, 18°3′ E 227
Tsetsegnuur, Mongolia 46°32′ N, 93°6′ E 190
Tsetseng, Botswana 23°32′ S, 23°6′ E 227
Tsetserleg, Mongolia 47°28′ N, 101°24′ E 198
Tsévié, Togo 6°28′ N, 1°12′ E 222
Tshabong, Botswana 26°4′ S, 22°27′ E 227
Tshane, Botswana 24°3′ S, 21°53′ E 227
Tshela, Dem. Rep. of the Congo 5°1′ S, 12°52′ E 218
Tshibamba, Dem. Rep. of the Congo 9°7′ S, 22°31′ E 218
Tshikapa, Dem. Rep. of the Congo 6°25′ S, 20°50′ E 218
Tshilenge, Dem. Rep. of the Congo 6°17′ S, 23°45′ E 224
Tshilongo, Dem. Rep. of the Congo 10°31′ S, 26°0′ E 224
Tshinota, Dem. Rep. of the Congo 7°2′ S, 20°55′ E 218
Tshinsenda, Dem. Rep. of the Congo 12°18′ S, 27°56′ E 224
Tshisenga, Dem. Rep. of the Congo 7°17′ S, 22°0′ E 218
Tsholotsho, Zimb. 19°47′ S, 27°45′ E 224
Tshootsha, Botswana 22°5′ S, 20°54′ E 227
Tshopo, river, Dem. Rep. of the Congo 0°26′ N, 26°42′ E 224
Tshuapa, river, Dem. Rep. of the Congo 2°15′ S, 24°11′ E 224
Tshumbe, Dem. Rep. of the Congo 4°10′ S, 24°21′ E 218
Tshwane see Pretoria, S. Af. 25°48′ S, 28°3′ E 227
Tsiigehtchic, Can. 67°25′ N, 133°35′ W 98
Tsil'ma, river, Russ. 65°29′ N, 51°1′ E 154
Tsimanampetsotsa, Lac, lake, Madagascar 24°15′ S, 42°16′ E 220
Tsimkavichy, Belarus 53°4′ N, 27°0′ E 152
Tsimlyansk, Russ. 47°37′ N, 41°58′ E 158
Tsinjomitondraka, Madagascar 15°40′ S, 47°9′ E 220
Tsintsabis, Namibia 18°43′ S, 17°58′ E 220
Tsiombe, Madagascar 25°17′ S, 45°32′ E 220
Tsipikan, Russ. 54°57′ N, 113°20′ E 190
Tsiteli Tskaro, Ga. 41°24′ N, 46°8′ E 180
Tsitondroina, Madagascar 21°16′ S, 46°0′ E 220
Tsitsikamma Forest and Coastal National Park, Indian Ocean 34°5′ S, 23°29′ E 206
Tsivory, Madagascar 24°3′ S, 46°6′ E 220
Ts'khinvali, Asia 42°11′ N, 43°53′ E 195
Tsna, river, Russ. 53°52′ N, 41°47′ E 154
Tsnori, Ga. 41°36′ N, 45°57′ E 195
Tsomog, Mongolia 45°53′ N, 109°8′ E 198
Tsoohor, Mongolia 43°16′ N, 104°5′ E 198
Tsu, Japan 34°42′ N, 136°31′ E 201
Tsu Lake, lake, Can. 60°38′ N, 112°18′ W 108
Tsubame, Japan 37°39′ N, 138°56′ E 201
Tsubata, Japan 36°40′ N, 136°43′ E 201
Tsuchiura, Japan 36°5′ N, 140°12′ E 201
Tsugaru Kaikyō 41°4′ N, 138°25′ E 190
Tsukumi, Japan 33°3′ N, 131°51′ E 201
Tsuma, Japan 36°12′ N, 133°14′ E 201
Tsumeb, Namibia 19°16′ S, 17°41′ E 220
Tsumis Park, Namibia 23°42′ S, 17°25′ E 227
Tsumkwe, Namibia 19°38′ S, 20°35′ E 220
Tsunō, Japan 32°14′ N, 131°33′ E 201
Tsuru, Japan 35°32′ N, 138°54′ E 201
Tsuruga, Japan 35°37′ N, 136°4′ E 201
Tsurugi, Japan 36°27′ N, 136°37′ E 201
Tsuruoka, Japan 38°43′ N, 139°50′ E 201
Tsurusaki, Japan 33°14′ N, 131°41′ E 201
Tsushima, Japan 35°9′ N, 136°44′ E 201
Tsushima, Japan 33°6′ N, 132°31′ E 201
Tsushima Strait 33°56′ N, 125°37′ E 198
Tsutsu, Japan 34°7′ N, 129°11′ E 200
Tsuyama, Japan 35°4′ N, 134°0′ E 201
Tsyp Navolok, Russ. 69°42′ N, 33°5′ E 152
Tsyurupyns'k, Ukr. 46°37′ N, 32°43′ E 156
Tua, Dem. Rep. of the Congo 3°42′ S, 16°36′ E 218
Tuai, N.Z. 38°51′ S, 177°9′ E 240
Tuakau, N.Z. 37°17′ S, 174°58′ E 240
Tual, Indonesia 5°46′ S, 132°37′ E 192
Tuan Giao, Vietnam 21°45′ N, 103°19′ E 202
Tuangku, island, Indonesia 2°9′ N, 97°18′ E 196
Tuapí, Nicar. 14°8′ N, 83°19′ W 115
Tuapse, Russ. 44°6′ N, 39°4′ E 156
Tuaran, Malaysia 6°12′ N, 116°14′ E 203
Tuba City, Ariz., U.S. 36°8′ N, 111°15′ W 92
Tuban, Indonesia 7°3′ S, 111°53′ E 192
Tubarão, Braz. 28°32′ S, 48°60′ W 138
Ţūbās, West Bank 32°19′ N, 35°21′ E 194
Tubinskiy, Russ. 52°54′ N, 58°10′ E 154
Tubmanburg, Liberia 6°47′ N, 10°53′ W 222
Tubod, Philippines 8°3′ N, 123°48′ E 203
Ţubruq (Tobruk), Lib. 32°3′ N, 23°57′ E 216
Tubuai Islands see Austral Islands, South Pacific Ocean 21°30′ S, 152°33′ W 238
Tubutama, Mex. 30°53′ N, 111°29′ W 92
Tucacas, Venez. 10°47′ N, 68°21′ W 136
Tucacas see Puerto López, Col. 11°56′ N, 71°18′ W 136
Tucano, Braz. 10°58′ S, 38°49′ W 132
Tucavaca, Bol. 18°39′ S, 58°58′ W 132
Tuchomie, Pol. 54°7′ N, 17°21′ E 152
Tuckerman, Ark., U.S. 35°43′ N, 91°13′ W 96
Tuckernuck Island, Mass., U.S. 41°16′ N, 70°36′ W 104
Tuckerton, N.J., U.S. 39°35′ N, 74°21′ W 94
Tucki Mountain, peak, Calif., U.S. 36°29′ N, 117°13′ W 92

Tucson, *Ariz., U.S.* 32°14′ N, 110°58′ W **92**
Tucumán, adm. division, *Arg.* 26°30′ S, 66°11′ W **132**
Tucumcari, *N. Mex., U.S.* 35°10′ N, 103°44′ W **92**
Tucupita, *Venez.* 9°5′ N, 62°5′ W **116**
Tucuruí, *Braz.* 3°44′ S, 49°46′ W **130**
Tuczno, *Pol.* 53°11′ N, 16°9′ E **152**
Tudela, *Sp.* 42°3′ N, 1°37′ W **164**
Tudulinna, *Est.* 59°1′ N, 27°1′ E **166**
Ţufayḩ, *Saudi Arabia* 26°49′ N, 49°39′ E **196**
Tuffé, *Fr.* 48°6′ N, 0°30′ E **150**
Tufts Plain, *North Pacific Ocean* 44°55′ N, 143°12′ W **252**
Tughyl, *Kaz.* 47°42′ N, 84°11′ E **184**
Tuguegarao, *Philippines* 17°38′ N, 121°42′ E **203**
Tugur, *Russ.* 53°46′ N, 136°38′ E **190**
Tui, *Sp.* 42°2′ N, 8°41′ W **214**
Tuichi, river, *Bol.* 14°14′ S, 68°23′ W **137**
Tuitán, *Mex.* 23°59′ N, 104°15′ W **114**
Tukan, *Russ.* 53°52′ N, 57°26′ E **154**
Tukayyid, spring, *Iraq* 29°45′ N, 45°38′ E **196**
Tukchi, *Russ.* 57°28′ N, 139°21′ E **173**
Tukhkala, *Russ.* 65°41′ N, 30°41′ E **152**
Tukhlya, *Ukr.* 48°52′ N, 23°30′ E **152**
Tukita, *Can.* 64°53′ N, 125°16′ W **106**
Tükrah, *Lib.* 32°31′ N, 20°34′ E **216**
Tuktoyaktuk, *Can.* 69°24′ N, 133°11′ W **73**
Tuktut Nogait National Park, *Can.* 68°46′ N, 123°49′ W **98**
Tukums, *Latv.* 56°58′ N, 23°7′ E **166**
Tukuyu, *Tanzania* 9°17′ S, 33°39′ E **224**
Tula, *Mex.* 22°58′ N, 99°43′ W **114**
Tula, *Mex.* 20°1′ N, 99°27′ W **112**
Tula, *Russ.* 54°10′ N, 37°36′ E **154**
Tula, adm. division, *Russ.* 53°58′ N, 36°48′ E **154**
Tula de Allende, *Mex.* 20°0′ N, 99°21′ W **114**
Tulak, *Afghan.* 33°56′ N, 63°38′ E **186**
Tulameen, *Can.* 49°32′ N, 120°47′ W **90**
Tulancingo, *Mex.* 20°2′ N, 98°22′ W **114**
Tulare, *Calif., U.S.* 36°13′ N, 119°21′ W **100**
Tulare, *Serb. and Mont.* 42°48′ N, 21°27′ E **168**
Tularosa Valley, *N. Mex., U.S.* 33°7′ N, 106°27′ W **92**
Tulcán, *Ecua.* 0°44′ N, 77°57′ W **136**
Tulcea, *Rom.* 45°10′ N, 28°47′ E **156**
Tulcea, adm. division, *Rom.* 44°58′ N, 28°9′ E **156**
Tul'chyn, *Ukr.* 48°40′ N, 28°57′ E **156**
Tülen Araldary, islands, *Caspian Sea* 44°43′ N, 49°2′ E **180**
Tuli, *Zimb.* 21°55′ S, 29°14′ E **227**
Tulia, *Tex., U.S.* 34°30′ N, 101°47′ W **92**
Tulita, *Can.* 64°56′ N, 125°23′ W **98**
Tulivaara, *Russ.* 63°37′ N, 30°26′ E **154**
Ţūlkarm, *West Bank* 32°18′ N, 35°1′ E **194**
Tülkibas, *Kaz.* 42°28′ N, 70°19′ E **197**
Tullahoma, *Tenn., U.S.* 35°21′ N, 86°13′ W **96**
Tullamore, *Ire.* 53°15′ N, 7°30′ W **150**
Tulloch Reservoir, lake, *Calif., U.S.* 37°52′ N, 120°46′ W **100**
Tullos, *La., U.S.* 31°48′ N, 92°20′ W **103**
Tully Lake, *Mass., U.S.* 42°38′ N, 72°21′ W **104**
Tulpan, *Russ.* 61°23′ N, 57°22′ E **154**
Tulsa, *Okla., U.S.* 36°8′ N, 95°59′ W **96**
Tulsequah, *Can.* 58°36′ N, 133°36′ W **108**
Tuluá, *Col.* 4°4′ N, 76°13′ W **136**
Tuluksak, *Alas., U.S.* 61°4′ N, 160°59′ W **98**
Tulum National Park, *Mex.* 20°8′ N, 87°35′ W **115**
Tulum, ruin(s), *Mex.* 20°11′ N, 87°36′ W **115**
Tulun, *Russ.* 54°40′ N, 100°27′ E **160**
Tuma, *Russ.* 55°8′ N, 40°34′ E **154**
Tuma, river, *Nicar.* 13°20′ N, 85°36′ W **115**
Tumaco, *Col.* 1°39′ N, 78°37′ W **123**
Tumanskaya, *Russ.* 64°3′ N, 178°9′ E **73**
Tumany, *Russ.* 60°57′ N, 155°46′ E **160**
Tumba, *Dem. Rep. of the Congo* 3°10′ S, 23°35′ E **224**
Tumbes, *Peru* 3°39′ S, 80°25′ W **130**
Tumble Mountain, peak, *Mont., U.S.* 45°17′ N, 110°6′ W **90**
Tumbledown Mountain, peak, *Me., U.S.* 45°26′ N, 70°33′ W **94**
Tumbler Ridge, *Can.* 55°3′ N, 120°60′ W **108**
Tumcha, *Russ.* 66°34′ N, 30°46′ E **152**
Tumd Youqi, *China* 40°31′ N, 110°31′ E **198**
Tumd Zuoqi, *China* 40°44′ N, 111°8′ E **198**
Tumeka Lake, *Can.* 57°11′ N, 130°21′ W **108**
Tumen, *China* 42°57′ N, 129°49′ E **200**
Tumen, river, *Asia* 42°2′ N, 128°35′ E **200**
Tumeremo, *Venez.* 7°18′ N, 61°30′ W **130**
Tumiã, river, *Braz.* 8°15′ S, 66°37′ W **132**
Tumiritinga, *Braz.* 18°60′ S, 41°39′ W **138**
Tumpat, *Malaysia* 6°11′ N, 102°8′ E **196**
Tumu, *Ghana* 10°51′ N, 1°60′ W **222**
Tumucumaque National Park, *Braz.* 1°51′ N, 56°1′ W **130**
Tumucumaque, Serra de, *Braz.* 0°45′ N, 55°55′ W **130**
Tumupasa, *Bol.* 14°11′ S, 67°55′ W **137**
Tumusla, *Bol.* 20°32′ S, 65°41′ W **137**
Tumwater, *Wash., U.S.* 46°59′ N, 122°55′ W **100**
Tuna, *Ghana* 9°29′ N, 2°27′ W **222**
Tunapuna, *Trinidad and Tobago* 10°37′ N, 61°24′ W **118**
Tunas, *Braz.* 25°1′ S, 49°6′ W **138**
Tunas, Sierra de las, *Mex.* 30°5′ N, 107°50′ W **112**
Tunbridge, *Vt., U.S.* 43°53′ N, 72°30′ W **104**
Tunbridge Wells, *U.K.* 51°7′ N, 0°15′ E **162**
Tunceli, *Turk.* 39°5′ N, 39°31′ E **195**
Tunchang, *China* 19°21′ N, 110°4′ E **202**
Tünchel, *Mongolia* 48°50′ N, 106°42′ E **198**
Tundubai, *Sudan* 14°47′ N, 22°42′ E **216**
Tundubai, spring, *Sudan* 18°25′ N, 28°30′ E **226**
Tunduma, *Tanzania* 9°19′ S, 32°46′ E **224**
Tunduru, *Tanzania* 11°7′ S, 37°22′ E **224**
Tunel, *Pol.* 50°25′ N, 19°58′ E **152**
Tunga, *Nig.* 8°2′ N, 9°21′ E **222**
Tŭngam, *N. Korea* 37°44′ N, 125°26′ E **200**
Tungaru, *Sudan* 10°12′ N, 30°45′ E **224**
Tungelsta, *Sw.* 59°6′ N, 18°2′ E **166**
Tungkang, *Taiwan* 22°29′ N, 120°30′ E **198**
Tungsten, *Can.* 62°1′ N, 128°21′ W **98**
Tunguska Podkamennaya, *Russ.* 61°35′ N, 90°11′ E **169**
Tuni, *India* 17°21′ N, 82°32′ E **188**
Tunica, *Miss., U.S.* 34°39′ N, 90°24′ W **96**
Tunis, *Tun.* 36°46′ N, 10°3′ E **156**
Tunisia 34°0′ N, 9°0′ E **214**
Tunja, *Col.* 5°32′ N, 73°23′ W **136**
Tunkinsky National Park, *Russ.* 51°26′ N, 101°42′ E **172**
Tŭnkovo, *Bulg.* 41°42′ N, 25°45′ E **156**
Tuntutuliak, *Alas., U.S.* 60°20′ N, 162°38′ W **98**
Tununak, *Alas., U.S.* 60°29′ N, 165°20′ W **98**
Tunuyán, *Arg.* 33°35′ S, 69°3′ W **134**
Tuolumne, *Calif., U.S.* 37°57′ N, 120°15′ W **100**
Tuong Duong, *Vietnam* 19°15′ N, 104°23′ E **202**
Tuotuo, river, *China* 34°3′ N, 91°7′ E **188**
Tuotuoheyan see Tanggulashan, *China* 34°10′ N, 92°24′ E **188**
Tup, *Kyrg.* 42°43′ N, 78°21′ E **184**
Tupã, *Braz.* 21°56′ S, 50°29′ W **138**
Tupaciguara, *Braz.* 18°36′ S, 48°45′ W **138**
Tupanciretã, *Braz.* 29°6′ S, 53°50′ W **139**
Tuparro, river, *Col.* 4°42′ N, 69°28′ W **136**
Tupelo, *Miss., U.S.* 34°15′ N, 88°44′ W **112**
Tupi, *Philippines* 6°13′ N, 125°1′ E **203**
Tupinambarana, Ilha, *Braz.* 3°24′ S, 58°32′ W **130**
Tupiraçaba, *Braz.* 14°34′ S, 48°36′ W **138**
Tupitsyno, *Russ.* 58°34′ N, 28°21′ E **166**
Tupiza, *Bol.* 21°29′ S, 65°46′ W **137**
Tupper, *Can.* 55°31′ N, 120°4′ W **108**
Tupper Lake, *N.Y., U.S.* 44°13′ N, 74°29′ W **94**
Tüpqaraghan Tübegi, *Kaz.* 44°24′ N, 50°30′ E **180**
Tuquan, *China* 45°23′ N, 121°32′ E **198**
Túquerres, *Col.* 1°6′ N, 77°39′ W **136**
Túr, river, *Hung.* 48°0′ N, 22°23′ E **168**
Tura, *Hung.* 47°35′ N, 19°36′ E **168**
Tura, *India* 25°26′ N, 90°11′ E **188**
Tura, *Russ.* 64°22′ N, 100°29′ E **173**
Tura, *Russ.* 64°22′ N, 100°29′ E **160**
Tura, *Tanzania* 5°28′ S, 33°50′ E **224**
Tura, river, *Russ.* 58°20′ N, 62°52′ E **154**
Turabah, *Saudi Arabia* 21°12′ N, 41°40′ E **182**
Turabah, spring, *Saudi Arabia* 28°12′ N, 42°53′ E **180**
Turan Lowland, *Uzb.* 40°50′ N, 57°48′ E **180**
Turangi, *N.Z.* 39°1′ S, 175°47′ E **240**
Turar Ryskulov, *Kaz.* 42°30′ N, 70°20′ E **197**
Turaw, *Belarus* 52°4′ N, 27°44′ E **152**
Ţurayf, *Saudi Arabia* 31°39′ N, 38°38′ E **180**
Turba, *Est.* 59°3′ N, 24°11′ E **166**
Turbaco, *Col.* 10°19′ N, 75°25′ W **136**
Turbacz, peak, *Pol.* 49°31′ N, 20°1′ E **152**
Turbat, *Pak.* 25°56′ N, 63°6′ E **182**
Turbe, *Bosn. and Herzg.* 44°15′ N, 17°35′ E **168**
Turbo, *Col.* 8°7′ N, 76°43′ W **136**
Turco, *Bol.* 18°14′ S, 68°13′ W **137**
Turda, spring, *Sudan* 10°22′ N, 28°33′ E **224**
Turégano, *Sp.* 41°9′ N, 4°1′ W **164**
Turenki, *Fin.* 60°54′ N, 24°38′ E **166**
Tureta, *Nig.* 12°35′ N, 5°35′ E **222**
Turgeon, river, *Can.* 49°32′ N, 79°47′ W **94**
Türgovishte, *Bulg.* 43°14′ N, 26°34′ E **156**
Türgovishte, adm. division, *Bulg.* 43°1′ N, 25°52′ E **156**
Turgut, *Turk.* 38°37′ N, 31°47′ E **156**
Turhal, *Turk.* 40°23′ N, 36°6′ E **156**
Türi, *Est.* 58°47′ N, 25°25′ E **166**
Turiaçu, *Braz.* 1°40′ S, 45°25′ W **130**
Turin, *Can.* 49°57′ N, 112°33′ W **90**
Turin see Torino, *It.* 45°4′ N, 7°40′ E **167**
Turinsk, *Russ.* 58°2′ N, 63°35′ E **154**
Turinskaya Sloboda, *Russ.* 57°36′ N, 64°21′ E **154**
Turjak, *Bosn. and Herzg.* 45°0′ N, 17°10′ E **168**
Turkana, Lake (Rudolph, Lake), *Kenya* 2°32′ N, 34°10′ E **206**
Turkestan Range, *Uzb.* 39°30′ N, 68°9′ E **184**
Túrkeve, *Hung.* 47°6′ N, 20°45′ E **168**
Turkey, *Tex., U.S.* 34°22′ N, 100°55′ W **96**
Turkey 38°54′ N, 33°55′ E **180**
Turki, *Russ.* 51°57′ N, 43°17′ E **158**
Türkistan, *Kaz.* 43°17′ N, 68°13′ E **184**
Türkmenabat (Chärjew), *Turkm.* 39°4′ N, 63°35′ E **184**
Türkmenbaşy, *Turkm.* 40°0′ N, 52°58′ E **180**
Turkmenistan 39°37′ N, 57°48′ E **184**
Turks and Caicos Islands, *U.K.* 21°58′ N, 72°29′ W **116**
Turks Islands, *North Atlantic Ocean* 21°27′ N, 70°58′ W **116**
Turku, *Fin.* 60°27′ N, 22°0′ E **160**
Turku (Åbo), *Fin.* 60°27′ N, 22°15′ E **166**
Turmalina, *Braz.* 17°16′ S, 42°46′ W **138**
Turnagain, Cape, *N.Z.* 40°43′ S, 176°35′ E **240**
Turnberry, *Can.* 53°26′ N, 101°42′ W **108**
Turneffe Islands, *Caribbean Sea* 17°35′ N, 87°42′ W **115**
Turner, *Me., U.S.* 44°15′ N, 70°16′ W **104**
Turner, *Mont., U.S.* 48°49′ N, 108°25′ W **90**
Turner Mountain, peak, *Calif., U.S.* 40°17′ N, 121°43′ W **90**
Turners Falls, *Mass., U.S.* 42°35′ N, 72°34′ W **104**
Turnertown, *Tex., U.S.* 32°11′ N, 94°58′ W **103**
Turnhout, *Belg.* 51°19′ N, 4°56′ E **167**
Turnu, *Rom.* 46°16′ N, 21°6′ E **168**
Turnu Roşu, Pasul, pass, *Rom.* 45°34′ N, 24°14′ E **156**
Turobin, *Pol.* 50°48′ N, 22°44′ E **152**
Turpan, *China* 43°3′ N, 89°14′ E **190**
Turpan Depression, *China* 42°8′ N, 91°23′ E **190**
Turquino, Pico, peak, *Cuba* 19°58′ N, 76°56′ W **115**
Turre, *Sp.* 37°8′ N, 1°54′ W **164**
Tursunzoda, *Taj.* 38°31′ N, 68°19′ E **197**
Turt, *Mongolia* 51°22′ N, 100°56′ E **190**
Turţ, *Rom.* 47°59′ N, 23°13′ E **168**
Turtas, river, *Russ.* 58°37′ N, 69°48′ E **169**
Türtkŭl, *Uzb.* 41°32′ N, 61°0′ E **180**
Turtle Creek Point, *Fla., U.S.* 29°2′ N, 83°11′ W **105**
Turtle Islands, *North Atlantic Ocean* 7°30′ N, 13°42′ W **222**
Turtle Mountain, peak, *N. Dak., U.S.* 48°59′ N, 100°31′ W **90**
Turtle Mountains, *Calif., U.S.* 34°14′ N, 114°53′ W **101**
Turtle, river, *Can.* 49°6′ N, 92°32′ W **110**
Turtleford, *Can.* 53°23′ N, 108°58′ W **108**
Turugart Pass, *Kyrg.* 40°33′ N, 75°23′ E **184**
Turugart, pass, *China* 40°31′ N, 75°21′ E **184**
Turukhansk, *Russ.* 65°45′ N, 88°6′ E **169**
Turukta, *Russ.* 60°39′ N, 116°3′ E **160**
Turvo, *Braz.* 28°59′ S, 49°43′ W **138**
Turvo, river, *Braz.* 16°24′ S, 50°11′ W **138**
Tur'ya, *Russ.* 62°50′ N, 50°41′ E **154**
Turysh, *Kaz.* 45°27′ N, 56°5′ E **158**
Turza Wielka, *Pol.* 53°18′ N, 20°4′ E **152**
Tuscaloosa, *Ala., U.S.* 33°11′ N, 87°34′ W **103**
Tuscany, adm. division, *It.* 44°2′ N, 10°22′ E **167**
Tuscarora, *Nev., U.S.* 41°19′ N, 116°14′ W **90**
Tuscarora Mountains, *Nev., U.S.* 40°44′ N, 116°22′ W **90**
Tuscola, *Ill., U.S.* 39°48′ N, 88°17′ W **102**
Tuscola, *Tex., U.S.* 32°12′ N, 99°48′ W **92**
Tuscumbia, *Ala., U.S.* 34°43′ N, 87°42′ W **96**
Tuskegee, *Ala., U.S.* 32°24′ N, 85°41′ W **96**
Tustin, *Mich., U.S.* 44°6′ N, 85°28′ W **102**
Tustna, *Nor.* 63°12′ N, 8°7′ E **152**
Tutak, *Turk.* 39°30′ N, 42°41′ E **195**
Tutayev, *Russ.* 57°52′ N, 39°30′ E **154**
Tuticorin, *India* 8°47′ N, 78°6′ E **188**
Tutin, *Serb. and Mont.* 42°59′ N, 20°20′ E **168**
Tutira, *N.Z.* 39°13′ S, 176°53′ E **240**
Tutoko, Mount, peak, *N.Z.* 44°38′ S, 167°56′ E **240**
Tutonchany, *Russ.* 64°14′ N, 93°42′ E **169**
Tutshi Lake, lake, *Can.* 59°53′ N, 135°14′ W **108**
Tutuaca, river, *Mex.* 29°32′ N, 108°48′ W **80**
Tutuala, *Timor-Leste* 8°31′ S, 127°6′ E **192**
Tutubu, *Tanzania* 5°29′ S, 32°41′ E **218**
Tutuila, *American Samoa, U.S.* 14°20′ S, 170°45′ W **241**
Tututepec, *Mex.* 16°6′ N, 97°37′ W **112**
Tuul, river, *Mongolia* 47°17′ N, 105°0′ E **198**
Tuupovaara, *Fin.* 62°28′ N, 30°37′ E **152**
Tuusniemi, *Fin.* 62°48′ N, 28°26′ E **152**
Tuvalu 9°0′ S, 179°0′ E **241**
Tuve, Mount, peak, *Antarctica* 73°50′ S, 80°43′ W **248**
Ţuwayq, Jabal, *Saudi Arabia* 24°12′ N, 46°21′ E **196**
Tuxford, *U.K.* 53°13′ N, 0°54′ E **162**
Tuxpan, *Mex.* 20°56′ N, 97°24′ W **114**
Tuxpan, *Mex.* 19°32′ N, 103°23′ W **114**
Tuxpan, *Mex.* 21°55′ N, 105°19′ W **114**
Tuxtepec, *Mex.* 18°5′ N, 96°7′ W **114**
Tuxtla Gutiérrez, *Mex.* 16°42′ N, 93°14′ W **115**
Tuy An, *Vietnam* 13°17′ N, 109°12′ E **202**
Tuy Hoa, *Vietnam* 13°4′ N, 109°18′ E **202**
Tuya Lake, *Can.* 59°3′ N, 131°11′ W **108**
Tuya, river, *Can.* 58°24′ N, 130°35′ W **108**
Tuyen Hoa, *Vietnam* 17°51′ N, 106°12′ E **198**
Tuyen Quang, *Vietnam* 21°49′ N, 105°11′ E **202**
Tuymazy, *Russ.* 54°34′ N, 53°45′ E **154**
Tüysarkān, *Iran* 34°30′ N, 48°23′ E **180**
Tuz Gölü, lake, *Turk.* 38°40′ N, 33°18′ E **156**
Tuzantla, *Mex.* 19°2′ N, 100°23′ W **114**
Tuzi, *Europe* 42°21′ N, 19°19′ E **168**
Tuzigoot National Monument, *Ariz., U.S.* 34°46′ N, 112°5′ W **92**
Tuzla, *Bosn. and Herzg.* 44°32′ N, 18°39′ E **168**
Tuzla Gölü, lake, *Turk.* 38°59′ N, 35°27′ E **156**
Tuzluca, *Turk.* 40°3′ N, 43°39′ E **195**
Tvedestrand, *Nor.* 58°37′ N, 8°53′ E **152**
Tver', *Russ.* 56°50′ N, 35°54′ E **154**
Tver', adm. division, *Russ.* 56°49′ N, 33°43′ E **154**
Tvervik, *Nor.* 67°2′ N, 14°31′ E **152**
Twain Harte, *Calif., U.S.* 38°1′ N, 120°15′ W **100**
Twee Rivieren, *S. Af.* 26°28′ S, 20°31′ E **227**
Tweedy Mountain, peak, *Mont., U.S.* 45°27′ N, 113°2′ W **90**
Twelve Bens, The, peak, *Ire.* 53°30′ N, 9°56′ W **150**
Twentynine Palms, *Calif., U.S.* 34°8′ N, 116°3′ W **101**
Twifu Praso, *Ghana* 5°37′ N, 1°32′ W **222**
Twillingate, *Can.* 49°38′ N, 54°46′ W **111**
Twin Falls, *Idaho, U.S.* 42°34′ N, 114°28′ W **90**
Twin Lakes, *Can.* 57°25′ N, 117°31′ W **108**
Twin Lakes, *Nebr., U.S.* 42°17′ N, 102°55′ W **90**
Twin Lakes Mountain, peak, *Oreg., U.S.* 43°12′ N, 122°42′ W **90**
Twin Mountain, *N.H., U.S.* 44°16′ N, 71°33′ W **104**
Twin Mountain, peak, *Oreg., U.S.* 44°54′ N, 118°15′ W **90**
Twin Peaks, *Idaho, U.S.* 44°35′ N, 114°33′ W **90**
Twin Valley, *Minn., U.S.* 47°14′ N, 96°17′ W **90**
Twining, *Mich., U.S.* 44°6′ N, 83°49′ W **102**
Twisp, *Wash., U.S.* 48°20′ N, 120°9′ W **90**
Twitya, river, *Can.* 63°42′ N, 129°33′ W **98**
Twizel, *N.Z.* 44°16′ S, 170°6′ E **240**
Two Buttes, *Colo., U.S.* 37°33′ N, 102°24′ W **92**
Two Buttes, peak, *Colo., U.S.* 37°38′ N, 102°38′ W **90**
Two Creeks, *Can.* 54°17′ N, 116°21′ W **108**
Two Harbors, *Minn., U.S.* 47°1′ N, 91°41′ W **94**
Two Hills, *Can.* 53°42′ N, 111°45′ W **108**
Two Ocean Pass, *Wyo., U.S.* 44°1′ N, 110°10′ W **90**
Two Rivers, *Wis., U.S.* 44°9′ N, 87°35′ W **102**
Two Top Peak, *S. Dak., U.S.* 44°57′ N, 103°41′ W **90**
Twofold Bay 37°24′ S, 149°35′ E **230**
Tyab, *Iran* 26°58′ N, 57°1′ E **196**
Tyanya, *Russ.* 59°0′ N, 119°43′ E **160**
Tydal, *Nor.* 63°3′ N, 11°34′ E **152**
Tyee, *Queen Charlotte Sound* 57°2′ N, 134°32′ W **108**
Tygda, *Russ.* 53°9′ N, 126°19′ E **190**
Tyin, *Nor.* 61°13′ N, 8°12′ E **152**
Tyler, *Minn., U.S.* 44°15′ N, 96°10′ W **90**
Tyler, *Tex., U.S.* 32°20′ N, 95°18′ W **103**
Tylertown, *Miss., U.S.* 31°6′ N, 90°9′ W **103**
Tym, river, *Russ.* 60°2′ N, 83°35′ E **169**
Tymsk, *Russ.* 59°19′ N, 80°23′ E **169**
Tynda, *Russ.* 55°10′ N, 124°44′ E **190**
Tyndall, *S. Dak., U.S.* 42°58′ N, 97°53′ W **90**
Tyndaris, ruin(s), *It.* 38°7′ N, 14°55′ E **156**
Tynset, *Nor.* 62°17′ N, 10°45′ E **152**
Tyre see Soûr, *Leb.* 33°16′ N, 35°12′ E **194**
Tyree, Mount, peak, *Antarctica* 78°25′ S, 87°7′ W **248**
Tyrnyauz, *Russ.* 43°24′ N, 42°56′ E **195**
Tyrol, region, *It.* 46°1′ N, 10°30′ E **167**
Tyrone, *N. Mex., U.S.* 32°43′ N, 108°17′ W **92**
Tyrone, *Okla., U.S.* 36°56′ N, 101°6′ W **92**
Tyrrhenian Sea 40°7′ N, 11°28′ E **156**
Tyrvää, *Fin.* 61°21′ N, 22°51′ E **166**
Tysvær, *Nor.* 59°18′ N, 5°28′ E **152**
Tytuvėnai, *Lith.* 55°36′ N, 23°9′ E **166**
Tyubelyakh, *Russ.* 65°18′ N, 142°53′ E **160**
Tyugyuren, *Russ.* 67°12′ N, 142°36′ E **173**
Tyukalinsk, *Russ.* 55°52′ N, 72°13′ E **184**
Tyukyun, river, *Russ.* 65°42′ N, 118°13′ E **160**
Tyulenovo, *Bulg.* 43°31′ N, 28°35′ E **156**
Tyul'gan, *Russ.* 52°22′ N, 56°2′ E **154**
Tyul'kino, *Russ.* 59°47′ N, 56°30′ E **154**
Tyumen', *Russ.* 57°7′ N, 65°32′ E **184**
Tyumen', adm. division, *Russ.* 55°59′ N, 66°44′ E **184**
Tyung, river, *Russ.* 66°37′ N, 116°51′ E **160**
Tyungur, *Russ.* 50°12′ N, 86°38′ E **184**
Tyva, adm. division, *Russ.* 50°56′ N, 89°32′ E **184**
Tyvoll, *Nor.* 62°43′ N, 11°21′ E **152**
Tywyn, *U.K.* 52°34′ N, 4°5′ W **162**
Tzintzuntzan, ruin(s), *Mex.* 19°34′ N, 101°37′ W **114**

U

U. P. Mammoth Kill Site, *Wyo., U.S.* 41°30′ N, 107°43′ W **90**
Uacari, *Braz.* 1°12′ N, 69°26′ W **136**
Üälīkhanov, *Kaz.* 52°47′ N, 71°52′ E **184**
Uamba, *Angola* 7°21′ S, 16°9′ E **218**
Uarandab, *Eth.* 7°8′ N, 44°6′ E **218**
Uarirambá, *Braz.* 1°40′ N, 69°26′ W **136**
Uatumã, river, *Braz.* 0°2′ N, 59°58′ W **130**
Uauá, *Braz.* 9°50′ S, 39°32′ W **132**
Uaupés, river, *Braz.* 0°7′ N, 67°56′ W **136**
Uaxactún, ruin(s), *Guatemala* 17°20′ N, 89°46′ W **115**
Ub, *Serb. and Mont.* 44°26′ N, 20°4′ E **168**
Ubá, *Braz.* 21°7′ S, 42°55′ W **138**
Uba, *Nig.* 10°29′ N, 13°12′ E **216**
Übach-Palenberg, *Ger.* 50°55′ N, 6°7′ E **167**
Ubaitaba, *Braz.* 14°20′ S, 39°18′ W **132**
Ubangi, river, *Africa* 4°24′ N, 19°9′ E **206**
Ubari see Awbārī, *Lib.* 26°37′ N, 12°45′ E **216**
Ubatã, *Braz.* 14°15′ S, 39°28′ W **138**
Úbeda, *Sp.* 38°0′ N, 3°22′ W **164**
Ubehebe Crater, *Calif., U.S.* 37°1′ N, 117°27′ W **101**
Uberaba, *Braz.* 19°44′ S, 47°56′ W **138**
Uberlândia, *Braz.* 18°55′ S, 48°20′ W **138**
Ubiaja, *Nig.* 6°41′ N, 6°22′ E **222**
Ubiatã, *Braz.* 24°33′ S, 53°1′ W **138**
Ubierna, *Sp.* 42°28′ N, 3°43′ W **164**
Ubinas, *Peru* 16°25′ S, 70°52′ W **137**
Ubly, *Mich., U.S.* 43°42′ N, 82°55′ W **102**
Ubombo, *S. Af.* 27°32′ S, 32°9′ E **227**
Ubon Ratchathani, *Thai.* 15°14′ N, 104°53′ E **202**
Ubrique, *Sp.* 36°40′ N, 5°27′ W **164**
Ubundu, *Dem. Rep. of the Congo* 0°24′ N, 25°30′ E **224**
Ucacha, *Arg.* 33°3′ S, 63°30′ W **139**
Üçajy, *Turkm.* 38°4′ N, 62°45′ E **184**
Ucar, *Azerb.* 40°31′ N, 47°38′ E **195**
Ucayali, adm. division, *Peru* 10°3′ S, 73°40′ W **137**
Ucayali, river, *Peru* 6°29′ S, 75°37′ W **122**
Uchab, *Namibia* 19°44′ S, 17°47′ E **220**
Uchaly, *Russ.* 54°22′ N, 59°24′ E **154**
Uchami, *Russ.* 63°49′ N, 96°31′ E **169**
Uchami, river, *Russ.* 62°30′ N, 94°55′ E **160**
Uchami, river, *Russ.* 62°38′ N, 93°54′ E **169**
Uchi Lake, *Can.* 51°4′ N, 92°34′ W **110**
Uchiko, *Japan* 33°33′ N, 132°38′ E **201**
Uchiza, *Peru* 8°26′ S, 76°24′ W **130**
Uchqo'rg'on, *Uzb.* 41°12′ N, 71°59′ E **197**
Uchquduq, *Uzb.* 42°6′ N, 63°37′ E **197**
Uchsay, *Uzb.* 43°48′ N, 58°56′ E **180**
Uchur, river, *Russ.* 56°55′ N, 130°38′ E **160**
Ucluelet, *Can.* 48°56′ N, 125°34′ W **90**
Ucuriş, *Rom.* 46°37′ N, 21°57′ E **168**
Uda, river, *Russ.* 53°59′ N, 133°25′ E **190**
Udachnoye, *Russ.* 47°45′ N, 46°51′ E **184**
Udachnyy, *Russ.* 66°22′ N, 112°38′ E **173**
Udainagar, *India* 22°31′ N, 76°13′ E **197**
Udaipur, *India* 24°33′ N, 73°41′ E **186**
Udala, *India* 21°35′ N, 86°33′ E **188**
Uddevalla, *Nor.* 58°20′ N, 11°56′ E **152**
Uder, *Ger.* 51°21′ N, 10°3′ E **167**
Udhampur, *India* 32°54′ N, 75°10′ E **186**
Udi, *Nig.* 6°19′ N, 7°23′ E **222**
Udine, *It.* 46°4′ N, 13°15′ E **167**
Udintsev Fracture Zone, *South Pacific Ocean* 52°14′ S, 155°38′ W **252**
Udmurtiya, adm. division, *Russ.* 57°3′ N, 51°20′ E **154**
Udobnaya, *Russ.* 44°11′ N, 41°30′ E **158**
Udomlya, *Russ.* 57°51′ N, 35°5′ E **154**
Udorn see Udon Thani, *Thai.* 17°26′ N, 102°46′ E **202**
Udovo, *Maced.* 41°21′ N, 22°26′ E **156**
Udzungwa Mountain National Park, *Tanzania* 7°50′ S, 36°22′ E **206**
Uebonti, *Indonesia* 0°59′ N, 121°35′ E **192**
Ueda, *Japan* 36°24′ N, 138°17′ E **201**
Uele, river, *Dem. Rep. of the Congo* 3°32′ N, 28°10′ E **224**
Uelen, *Russ.* 66°7′ N, 169°51′ W **98**
Uel'kal', *Russ.* 65°34′ N, 179°24′ W **98**
Uelsen, *Ger.* 52°29′ N, 6°53′ E **163**
Ueno, *Japan* 34°44′ N, 136°7′ E **201**
Uere, river, *Dem. Rep. of the Congo* 3°44′ N, 25°23′ E **224**
Ufa, *Russ.* 54°45′ N, 56°0′ E **154**
Ufa, river, *Russ.* 56°29′ N, 58°7′ E **154**
Uftyuga, river, *Russ.* 61°36′ N, 46°15′ E **154**
Ugāle, *Latv.* 57°15′ N, 22°1′ E **166**
Ugalla Game Reserve, *Tanzania* 6°5′ S, 31°39′ E **224**
Ugalla, river, *Tanzania* 5°55′ S, 31°20′ E **224**
Ugam-Chatkal National Park, *Uzb.* 41°38′ N, 70°0′ E **197**
Uganda 1°13′ N, 32°13′ E **224**
Uganik, *Gulf of Alaska* 57°45′ N, 153°38′ W **98**
Ugarit see Ra's Shamrah, site, *Syr.* 35°33′ N, 35°44′ E **194**
Ugleural'skiy, *Russ.* 58°57′ N, 57°36′ E **154**
Uglich, *Russ.* 57°27′ N, 38°20′ E **154**
Ugljane, *Croatia* 43°33′ N, 16°44′ E **168**
Uglovka, *Russ.* 58°15′ N, 33°34′ E **154**
Ugol'nyye Kopi, *Russ.* 64°47′ N, 177°47′ E **73**
Ugoma, *Dem. Rep. of the Congo* 4°28′ S, 28°25′ E **224**
Ugra, river, *Russ.* 54°44′ N, 35°45′ E **154**
Ugut, *Russ.* 60°27′ N, 74°6′ E **169**
Uhlenhorst, *Namibia* 23°42′ S, 17°53′ E **227**
Uhrichsville, *Ohio, U.S.* 40°23′ N, 81°22′ W **102**
Uig 58°11′ N, 7°1′ W **150**
Uíge, *Angola* 7°37′ S, 15°4′ E **218**
Uíge, adm. division, *Angola* 7°15′ S, 14°43′ E **218**
Uijeongbu, *S. Korea* 37°43′ N, 127°2′ E **200**
Uilpata, peak, *Russ.* 42°42′ N, 43°48′ E **195**
Uimaharju, *Fin.* 62°53′ N, 30°13′ E **152**
Uinta Mountains, *Utah, U.S.* 40°23′ N, 110°42′ W **90**
Uiseong, *S. Korea* 36°19′ N, 128°42′ E **200**
Uitenhage, *S. Af.* 33°46′ S, 25°25′ E **220**
Uithuizen, *Neth.* 53°24′ N, 6°40′ E **163**
Újfehértó, *Hung.* 47°47′ N, 21°41′ E **168**
Uji, *Japan* 34°51′ N, 135°51′ E **201**
Ujiie, *Japan* 36°40′ N, 139°58′ E **201**
Ujiji, *Tanzania* 4°57′ S, 29°40′ E **224**
Ujjain, *India* 23°10′ N, 75°47′ E **197**
Újszász, *Hung.* 47°17′ N, 20°5′ E **168**
Ujung Kulon National Park, *Indian Ocean* 7°5′ S, 104°54′ E **172**
Ujungpandang (Makassar), *Indonesia* 5°11′ S, 119°25′ E **192**
Uka, *Russ.* 57°50′ N, 161°48′ E **160**
Ukhiya, *Bangladesh* 21°16′ N, 92°7′ E **188**
Ukhrul, *India* 25°9′ N, 94°22′ E **188**
Ukhta, *Russ.* 63°31′ N, 53°44′ E **169**
Ukhvala, *Belarus* 54°5′ N, 29°16′ E **166**
Ukia, *Tanzania* 7°43′ S, 31°46′ E **224**
Ukiah, *Calif., U.S.* 39°8′ N, 123°14′ W **90**
Ukmergė, *Lith.* 55°15′ N, 24°43′ E **166**
Ukraine 49°12′ N, 31°23′ E **158**
Uktym, *Russ.* 62°38′ N, 49°0′ E **154**
Uku, *Angola* 11°27′ S, 14°19′ E **220**
Ukulahu, island, *Maldives* 4°11′ N, 71°57′ E **188**
Ukuma, *Angola* 12°53′ S, 15°2′ E **220**
Ukwaa, *Sudan* 6°41′ N, 34°37′ E **224**
Ula, *Turk.* 37°5′ N, 28°24′ E **156**
Ulaanbaatar (Ulan Bator), *Mongolia* 47°56′ N, 106°41′ E **198**
Ulaangom, *Mongolia* 49°57′ N, 92°3′ E **184**
Ulaanjirem, *Mongolia* 45°5′ N, 105°45′ E **190**
Ulaan-Uul, *Mongolia* 44°8′ N, 111°15′ E **198**
Ulaga, *Russ.* 66°15′ N, 131°36′ E **160**
Ulan, *China* 36°55′ N, 98°27′ E **188**
Ulan Bator see Ulaanbaatar, *Mongolia* 47°56′ N, 106°41′ E **198**
Ulan Erge, *Russ.* 46°15′ N, 44°51′ E **158**
Ulan Khol, *Russ.* 45°25′ N, 46°48′ E **158**
Ulan Ude, *Russ.* 51°54′ N, 107°30′ E **190**
Ulan Ul Hu, lake, *China* 34°51′ N, 89°56′ E **188**
Ulanbel, *Kaz.* 44°45′ N, 71°9′ E **184**
Ulang, river, *Nicar.* 14°37′ N, 83°51′ W **115**
Ulanhot, *China* 46°5′ N, 122°5′ E **198**
Ulaş, *Turk.* 39°25′ N, 37°2′ E **156**
Ulaya, *Tanzania* 7°3′ S, 36°55′ E **224**
Ülbi, *Kaz.* 50°16′ N, 83°23′ E **184**
Ulbio, *Braz.* 10°20′ S, 70°24′ W **137**
Ulcinj, *Europe* 41°55′ N, 19°12′ E **168**
Uldz, *Mongolia* 48°38′ N, 112°2′ E **198**
Uldz, river, *Mongolia* 49°24′ N, 113°23′ E **198**
Uleåborg see Oulu, *Fin.* 65°0′ N, 25°25′ E **152**
Ulen, *Minn., U.S.* 47°3′ N, 96°17′ W **90**
Ulfborg, *Den.* 56°16′ N, 8°17′ E **150**
Uliastay, *Mongolia* 47°48′ N, 96°47′ E **190**
Ulindi, river, *Dem. Rep. of the Congo* 1°43′ S, 26°5′ E **224**
Ulithi Atoll, *F.S.M.* 9°6′ N, 138°40′ E **192**
Uljin, *S. Korea* 36°59′ N, 129°24′ E **200**
Uljma, *Serb. and Mont.* 45°2′ N, 21°10′ E **168**
Ülken, *Kaz.* 45°12′ N, 73°57′ E **184**
Ülken Borsyq Qumy, *Kaz.* 46°18′ N, 58°51′ E **184**
Ülkennaryn, *Kaz.* 49°13′ N, 84°31′ E **184**
Ulla, *Belarus* 55°12′ N, 29°15′ E **166**
Ullared, *Nor.* 57°9′ N, 12°42′ E **152**
Ulldecona, *Sp.* 40°35′ N, 0°26′ E **164**
Ulleung, *S. Korea* 37°31′ N, 130°55′ E **200**
Ulloma, *Bol.* 17°37′ S, 68°29′ W **137**
Ullswater, lake, *U.K.* 54°34′ N, 2°59′ W **162**
Ulm, *Ger.* 48°24′ N, 9°59′ E **152**
Ulmen, *Ger.* 50°12′ N, 6°59′ E **163**
Ulmeni, *Rom.* 47°27′ N, 23°19′ E **168**
Ulmer, Mount, peak, *Antarctica* 77°32′ S, 87°5′ W **248**
Ulog, *Bosn. and Herzg.* 43°24′ N, 18°17′ E **168**
Ulrichstein, *Ger.* 50°34′ N, 9°12′ E **167**
Ulsan, *S. Korea* 35°33′ N, 129°21′ E **200**
Ulsteinvik, *Nor.* 62°20′ N, 5°52′ E **152**

u Dağ (Olympus, Mount), peak, *Turk.* 40°4' N, 29°7' E **156**
ubat Gölü, lake, *Turk.* 40°4' N, 28°7' E **156**
uborlu, *Turk.* 38°5' N, 30°28' E **156**
ugan Bay 10°1' N, 118°25' E **203**
ugqat, *China* 39°49' N, 74°21' E **197**
uguru Mountains, *Tanzania* 7°28' S, 37°2' E **224**
lukışla, *Turk.* 37°32' N, 34°28' E **156**
lul, island, *F.S.M.* 8°19' N, 149°8' E **192**
lundi, *S. Af.* 28°17' S, 31°33' E **227**
lungur Hu, lake, *China* 47°14' N, 86°46' E **184**
lungur, river, *China* 46°35' N, 87°38' E **184**
lupō Heiau, site, *Hawai'i, U.S.* 21°22' N, 157°47' W **99**
Uluru (Ayers Rock), peak, *Austral.* 25°23' S, 130°52' E **230**
lus, *Turk.* 41°36' N, 32°38' E **158**
luyul, river, *Russ.* 57°34' N, 85°49' E **169**
Ulverston, *U.K.* 54°12' N, 3°6' W **162**
lvöhamn, *Sw.* 63°0' N, 18°38' E **152**
lvvik, *Nor.* 62°40' N, 17°50' E **152**
ly Balkan Gershi, *Turkm.* 39°30' N, 54°0' E **180**
Ul'ya, *Russ.* 58°57' N, 141°46' E **160**
Ul'yanovka, *Russ.* 59°30' N, 30°46' E **166**
Ul'yanovsk, *Russ.* 54°19' N, 48°24' E **154**
Ul'Yanovsk, adm. division, *Russ.* 53°58' N, 46°12' E **154**
Ül'yanovskīy, *Kaz.* 50°4' N, 73°47' E **184**
Ulysses, *Kans., U.S.* 37°34' N, 101°22' W **90**
Ūlytaū, *Kaz.* 48°25' N, 66°48' E **184**
Ulyzhylanshyq, river, *Kaz.* 49°32' N, 64°32' E **184**
Umag, *Croatia* 45°25' N, 13°32' E **167**
Umala, *Bol.* 17°22' S, 67°59' W **137**
Umán, *Mex.* 20°51' N, 89°46' W **116**
Uman', *Ukr.* 48°44' N, 30°23' E **158**
Umaria, *India* 23°30' N, 80°50' E **197**
Umarkot, *Pak.* 25°22' N, 69°44' E **186**
Umasi La, pass, *India* 33°26' N, 76°36' E **186**
Umatilla, *Oreg., U.S.* 45°53' N, 119°22' W **90**
Umb Ozero, lake, *Russ.* 67°35' N, 34°0' E **152**
Umba, *Russ.* 66°40' N, 34°16' E **152**
Umbelasha, river, *Sudan* 9°29' N, 24°3' E **224**
Umberto Primo, *Arg.* 30°54' S, 61°21' W **139**
Umboi, island, *P.N.G.* 5°59' S, 147°5' E **192**
Umbria, adm. division, *It.* 42°41' N, 11°58' E **156**
Umbukta, *Nor.* 66°9' N, 14°35' E **152**
Umčari, *Serb. and Mont.* 44°34' N, 20°44' E **168**
Umeå, *Nor.* 63°49' N, 20°15' E **152**
Umfors, *Nor.* 65°57' N, 15°2' E **152**
Umm al 'Abīd, *Lib.* 27°30' N, 15°1' E **216**
Umm al Arānib, *Lib.* 26°9' N, 14°45' E **216**
Umm al Qaywayn, *U.A.E.* 25°33' N, 55°33' E **196**
Umm az Zumūl, spring, *Saudi Arabia* 22°36' N, 55°20' E **182**
Umm Badr, spring, *Sudan* 14°10' N, 27°56' E **226**
Umm Bel, *Sudan* 13°31' N, 28°3' E **226**
Umm Buru, spring, *Sudan* 15°1' N, 23°45' E **226**
Umm Busha, *Sudan* 13°25' N, 30°35' E **226**
Umm Dam, *Sudan* 13°46' N, 30°58' E **226**
Umm Gudair, oil field, *Kuwait* 28°49' N, 47°39' E **196**
Umm Hagar, *Eritrea* 14°16' N, 36°37' E **182**
Umm Haraz, *Sudan* 11°57' N, 23°10' E **216**
Umm Keddada, *Sudan* 13°35' N, 26°39' E **226**
Umm Lahai, spring, *Sudan* 15°38' N, 25°50' E **226**
Umm Lajj, *Saudi Arabia* 25°4' N, 37°15' E **182**
Umm Qaşr, *Iraq* 30°2' N, 47°55' E **196**
Umm Qays, *Jordan* 32°39' N, 35°40' E **194**
Umm Qozein, spring, *Sudan* 14°15' N, 27°16' E **226**
Umm Rahau, *Sudan* 18°53' N, 32°0' E **182**
Umm Ruwaba, *Sudan* 12°52' N, 31°11' E **216**
Umm Sa'īd, *Qatar* 24°58' N, 51°33' E **196**
Umm Saiyala, *Sudan* 14°24' N, 31°9' E **226**
Umm Shalil, *Sudan* 10°50' N, 23°41' E **224**
Umm Shanqa, *Sudan* 13°12' N, 27°11' E **226**
Umm Urūmah, island, *Saudi Arabia* 25°48' N, 35°31' E **182**
Umniati, *Zimb.* 18°41' S, 29°46' E **224**
Umpulo, *Angola* 12°43' S, 17°39' E **220**
Umreth, *India* 22°38' N, 73°5' E **186**
Umtanum Ridge, *Wash., U.S.* 46°50' N, 120°53' W **90**
Umtata, *S. Af.* 31°35' S, 28°41' E **227**
Umuahia, *Nig.* 5°33' N, 7°30' E **222**
Umuarama, *Braz.* 23°47' S, 53°27' W **138**
Umzimkulu, *S. Af.* 30°16' S, 29°58' E **227**
Umzimvubu, *S. Af.* 31°31' S, 29°24' E **207**
Umzinto, *S. Af.* 30°19' S, 30°36' E **227**
Una, *Russ.* 64°36' N, 38°5' E **154**
Una, river, *Bosn. and Herzg.* 44°39' N, 16°0' E **168**
Unac, river, *Bosn. and Herzg.* 44°22' N, 16°24' E **168**
Unadilla, *Ga., U.S.* 32°15' N, 83°45' W **96**
Unaí, *Braz.* 16°24' S, 46°54' W **138**
Unalakleet, *Alas., U.S.* 63°50' N, 160°39' W **106**
Unalaska, *Alas., U.S.* 53°51' N, 166°33' W **238**
Unalaska Island, *Alas., U.S.* 53°58' N, 168°29' W **98**
Unango, *Mozambique* 12°52' S, 35°25' E **224**
Unari, *Fin.* 67°8' N, 25°42' E **152**
'Unayzah, *Jordan* 30°28' N, 35°47' E **194**
'Unayzah, *Saudi Arabia* 26°5' N, 43°59' E **182**
'Unayzah, Jabal, peak, *Iraq* 32°9' N, 39°13' E **180**
Uncastillo, *Sp.* 42°21' N, 1°8' W **164**
Uncasville, *Conn., U.S.* 41°25' N, 72°7' W **104**
Uncía, *Bol.* 18°29' S, 66°39' W **137**
Uncompahgre Peak, *Colo., U.S.* 38°3' N, 107°32' W **90**
Underberg, *S. Af.* 29°49' S, 29°30' E **227**
Underhill, *Vt., U.S.* 44°31' N, 72°57' W **104**
Underwood, *N. Dak., U.S.* 47°26' N, 101°9' W **90**
Ŭndŏk, *N. Korea* 42°32' N, 130°19' E **200**
Unduksa, *Russ.* 65°39' N, 34°4' E **152**
Unecha, *Russ.* 52°49' N, 32°44' E **154**
Uneiuxi, river, *Braz.* 1°8' S, 66°18' W **136**
Ungava Bay 59°10' N, 68°2' W **106**
Unggi, *N. Korea* 42°29' N, 130°25' E **190**
Unggok, *S. Korea* 34°36' N, 126°2' E **200**
Unhŭng, *N. Korea* 41°17' N, 128°31' E **200**
União, *Braz.* 4°36' S, 42°52' W **132**
União, *Braz.* 9°18' S, 70°58' W **137**
União da Vitória, *Braz.* 26°15' S, 51°8' W **139**
Unicoi, *Tenn., U.S.* 36°11' N, 82°21' W **96**
Unimak Island, *Alas., U.S.* 55°1' N, 164°53' W **98**
Union, *La., U.S.* 30°4' N, 90°54' W **103**
Union, *Miss., U.S.* 32°34' N, 89°7' W **103**
Union, *N.H., U.S.* 43°29' N, 71°3' W **104**
Union, *Oreg., U.S.* 45°12' N, 117°52' W **90**
Union, *S.C., U.S.* 34°42' N, 81°38' W **96**
Union, *Wash., U.S.* 47°19' N, 123°6' W **100**
Union Bay, *Can.* 49°34' N, 124°54' W **100**
Union City, *Ind., U.S.* 40°11' N, 84°49' W **102**
Union City, *Mich., U.S.* 42°4' N, 85°8' W **102**
Union City, *Tenn., U.S.* 36°24' N, 89°3' W **96**
Unión de Tula, *Mex.* 19°56' N, 104°17' W **114**
Union Grove, *Wis., U.S.* 42°41' N, 88°4' W **102**
Union, islands, *Caribbean Sea* 12°47' N, 61°42' W **116**
Union Pass, *Wyo., U.S.* 43°28' N, 109°51' W **90**
Union Springs, *Ala., U.S.* 32°8' N, 85°43' W **96**
Uniondale, *S. Af.* 33°40' S, 23°6' E **227**
Uniontown, *Ala., U.S.* 32°27' N, 87°32' W **103**
Uniontown, *Pa., U.S.* 39°54' N, 79°45' W **94**
Unionville, *Mich., U.S.* 43°38' N, 83°28' W **102**
United Arab Emirates 24°7' N, 54°35' E **196**
United Kingdom 51°54' N, 2°36' W **150**
United States 39°40' N, 101°22' W **82**
United States Naval Base Guantánamo Bay, *Cuba* 19°53' N, 75°14' W **115**
Unity, *Can.* 52°26' N, 109°10' W **108**
Unity, adm. division, *Sudan* 8°46' N, 29°13' E **224**
Universales, Montes, *Sp.* 40°18' N, 1°37' W **164**
University Park, *Iowa, U.S.* 41°16' N, 92°36' W **94**
Unknown Lake, *Can.* 58°19' N, 105°10' W **108**
Unna, *Ger.* 51°32' N, 7°41' E **167**
Unnao, *India* 26°32' N, 80°29' E **197**
Ŭnnyul, *N. Korea* 38°29' N, 125°12' E **200**
Unsan, *N. Korea* 40°5' N, 125°52' E **200**
Unuk, river, *Can.* 56°12' N, 131°1' W **108**
Ünye, *Turk.* 41°7' N, 37°16' E **156**
Unzen-Amakusa National Park, *Japan* 32°27' N, 130°11' E **201**
Unzha, *Russ.* 58°0' N, 44°2' E **154**
Uozu, *Japan* 36°49' N, 137°24' E **201**
Upemba National Park, *Dem. Rep. of the Congo* 9°6' S, 25°37' E **224**
Upernavik 72°49' N, 56°14' W **106**
Upernavik Kujalleq 72°9' N, 55°36' W **106**
Upham, *N. Dak., U.S.* 48°34' N, 100°45' W **90**
Upía, river, *Col.* 4°38' N, 73°10' W **136**
Upington, *S. Af.* 28°25' S, 21°13' E **227**
Upland, *Calif., U.S.* 34°5' N, 117°40' W **101**
Upoloksha, *Russ.* 67°32' N, 31°56' E **152**
Upolu, island, *Samoa* 13°56' S, 171°50' W **241**
Upper Arlington, *Ohio, U.S.* 40°0' N, 83°3' W **102**
Upper Delaware Scenic and Recreational River, *N.Y., U.S.* 41°45' N, 82°49' W **80**
Upper Foster Lake, lake, *Can.* 56°48' N, 105°45' W **108**
Upper Goose Lake, lake, *Can.* 51°42' N, 93°24' W **110**
Upper Laberge, *Can.* 60°57' N, 135°7' W **98**
Upper Lake, *Calif., U.S.* 41°45' N, 120°35' W **90**
Upper Liard, *Can.* 60°3' N, 128°59' W **108**
Upper Missouri River Breaks National Monument, *Mont., U.S.* 47°43' N, 110°27' W **90**
Upper Nile, adm. division, *Sudan* 11°36' N, 32°24' E **182**
Upper Roslyn Lake, lake, *Can.* 49°14' N, 88°9' W **94**
Upper Sandusky, *Ohio, U.S.* 40°48' N, 83°18' W **102**
Uppingham, *U.K.* 52°35' N, 0°44' E **162**
Upplands Väsby, *Sw.* 59°31' N, 17°52' E **166**
Uppsala, *Sw.* 59°51' N, 17°38' E **166**
Uprang, *China* 36°36' N, 75°56' E **186**
Upstart Bay 19°49' S, 146°34' E **230**
Upton, *Wyo., U.S.* 44°5' N, 104°37' W **90**
Uqturpan see Wushi, *China* 41°9' N, 79°17' E **184**
Urabá, Golfo de 8°18' N, 77°25' W **136**
Urad Houqi, *China* 41°30' N, 107°3' E **198**
Urad Qianqi, *China* 40°41' N, 108°38' E **198**
Urad Zhongqi, *China* 41°33' N, 108°33' E **198**
Ural Mountains, *Russ.* 63°37' N, 58°26' E **154**
Ural, river, *Kaz.-Russ.* 52°59' N, 58°53' E **154**
Urambo, *Tanzania* 5°3' S, 32°4' E **224**
Urandi, *Braz.* 14°48' S, 42°40' W **138**
Urania, *La., U.S.* 31°51' N, 92°18' W **103**
Uranium City, *Can.* 59°33' N, 108°42' W **106**
Uraricoera, *Braz.* 3°27' N, 61°1' W **130**
Uravan, *Colo., U.S.* 38°23' N, 108°44' W **90**
Urawa, *Japan* 35°51' N, 139°39' E **201**
Uray, *Russ.* 60°6' N, 65°2' E **169**
'Uray'irah, *Saudi Arabia* 25°56' N, 48°53' E **182**
Urbana, *Ark., U.S.* 33°8' N, 92°27' W **103**
Urbana, *Ill., U.S.* 40°5' N, 88°13' W **102**
Urbana, *Ohio, U.S.* 40°6' N, 83°45' W **102**
Urbandale, *Iowa, U.S.* 41°37' N, 93°43' W **94**
Urbania, *It.* 43°40' N, 12°32' E **156**
Urbano Santos, *Braz.* 3°13' S, 43°25' W **132**
Urbel, river, *Sp.* 42°40' N, 3°57' W **164**
Urbino, *It.* 43°43' N, 12°38' E **167**
Urbión, Picos de, *Sp.* 42°5' N, 2°58' W **164**
Urcos, *Peru* 13°45' S, 71°40' W **137**
Urda, *Sp.* 39°24' N, 3°43' W **164**
Urdos, *Fr.* 42°52' N, 0°33' E **164**
Ure, river, *U.K.* 54°16' N, 1°49' W **162**
Urechcha, *Belarus* 52°56' N, 27°51' E **152**
Ureliki, *Russ.* 64°24' N, 173°17' W **98**
Uren', *Russ.* 57°27' N, 45°51' E **154**
Urengoy, *Russ.* 65°54' N, 78°30' E **169**
Urenui, *N.Z.* 39°1' S, 174°26' E **240**
Ures, *Mex.* 29°25' N, 110°24' W **92**
Urgut, *Uzb.* 39°22' N, 67°18' E **197**
Uri, *India* 34°3' N, 74°4' E **188**
Uriah, *Ala., U.S.* 31°17' N, 87°30' W **103**
Uriah, Mount, peak, *N.Z.* 42°3' S, 171°33' E **240**
Uribe, *Col.* 3°13' N, 74°25' W **136**
Uribia, *Col.* 11°41' N, 72°17' W **136**
Urimán, *Venez.* 5°23' N, 62°43' W **130**
Uriondo, *Bol.* 21°42' S, 64°46' W **137**
Urique, river, *Mex.* 27°18' N, 107°56' W **80**
Uritsk, *Russ.* 59°49' N, 30°8' E **166**
Urjala, *Fin.* 61°4' N, 23°31' E **166**
Urk, *Neth.* 52°40' N, 5°35' E **163**
Úrkút, *Hung.* 47°4' N, 17°38' E **168**
Urkut, *Somalia* 3°29' N, 42°44' E **218**
Urla, *Turk.* 38°18' N, 26°44' E **156**
Urman, *Russ.* 54°53' N, 56°56' E **154**
Urmia, Lake see Orūmīyeh, Daryācheh-ye, *Iran* 38°7' N, 45°16' E **195**
Urmia see Orūmīyeh, *Iran* 37°37' N, 45°4' E **195**
Uroševac, *Europe* 42°22' N, 21°9' E **168**
Ŭroteppa see Istaravshan, *Taj.* 39°53' N, 69°0' E **197**
Urroz, *Sp.* 42°46' N, 1°29' W **164**
Ursus, *Pol.* 52°11' N, 20°50' E **152**
Urszulin, *Pol.* 51°23' N, 23°11' E **152**
Urt Moron, river, *China* 37°3' N, 93°7' E **188**
Uruaçu, *Braz.* 14°33' S, 49°12' W **138**
Uruana, *Braz.* 15°33' S, 49°41' W **138**
Uruapan, *Mex.* 19°24' N, 102°4' W **114**
Urubamba, *Peru* 13°19' S, 72°8' W **130**
Urubamba, river, *Peru* 10°42' S, 73°24' W **137**
Urubaxi, river, *Braz.* 1°30' S, 64°53' W **130**
Urubuquara, Serra, peak, *Braz.* 3°34' S, 52°27' W **130**
Uruçanga, *Braz.* 28°32' S, 49°19' W **138**
Urucará, *Braz.* 2°31' S, 57°46' W **130**
Urucu, river, *Braz.* 4°18' S, 64°15' W **130**
Uruçuí, *Braz.* 7°17' S, 44°34' W **132**
Uruçuí, Serra do, *Braz.* 9°25' S, 45°41' W **130**
Urucuia, *Braz.* 16°8' S, 45°45' W **138**
Urucuia, river, *Braz.* 15°33' S, 46°47' W **138**
Urucurituba, *Braz.* 2°40' S, 57°39' W **130**
Urugi, *Japan* 35°17' N, 137°44' E **201**
Uruguai, river, *Braz.* 27°14' S, 54°6' W **139**
Uruguaiana, *Braz.* 29°48' S, 57°5' W **139**
Uruguay 32°54' S, 55°57' W **139**
Uruguay, river, *South America* 27°36' S, 55°4' W **134**
Urukthapel (Ngeruktabel), island, *Palau* 7°13' N, 134°24' E **242**
Ürümqi, *China* 43°46' N, 87°37' E **184**
Urung, *Indonesia* 2°39' N, 96°4' E **196**
Urup, island, *Russ.* 45°21' N, 148°49' E **190**
Urupá, river, *Braz.* 11°13' S, 62°43' W **130**
Urussu, *Russ.* 54°37' N, 53°25' E **154**
Urutaí, *Braz.* 17°29' S, 48°11' W **138**
Uruti, *N.Z.* 38°59' S, 174°32' E **240**
Uruwira, *Tanzania* 6°24' S, 31°22' E **224**
Urville, Tanjung d', *Indonesia* 1°31' S, 137°53' E **192**
Uryupinsk, *Russ.* 50°47' N, 41°57' E **158**
Ürzhar, *Kaz.* 47°4' N, 81°35' E **184**
Urzhum, *Russ.* 57°8' N, 50°1' E **154**
Us Nuur, Har, lake, *Mongolia* 48°7' N, 91°1' E **190**
Usa, *Japan* 33°28' N, 133°26' E **201**
Usa, river, *Russ.* 66°8' N, 58°13' E **160**
Uşak, *Turk.* 38°40' N, 29°24' E **156**
Usakos, *Namibia* 22°2' S, 15°36' E **227**
Usambara Mountains, peak, *Tanzania* 4°33' S, 38°15' E **224**
Usarp Mountains, *Antarctica* 71°32' S, 161°30' E **248**
Ušće, *Serb. and Mont.* 43°27' N, 20°37' E **168**
Used, *Sp.* 41°3' N, 1°33' W **164**
Useko, *Tanzania* 5°6' S, 32°33' E **224**
Ushachy, *Belarus* 55°10' N, 28°33' E **166**
Ushakova, Ostrov, island, *Russ.* 80°20' N, 74°7' E **160**
Üsharal, *Kaz.* 46°11' N, 80°54' E **184**
'Ushayrah, *Saudi Arabia* 21°43' N, 40°39' E **182**
Ushetu, *Tanzania* 4°10' S, 32°16' E **224**
Ushibuka, *Japan* 32°12' N, 130°1' E **201**
Üshtöbe, *Kaz.* 45°14' N, 77°58' E **184**
Ushtobe, *Kaz.* 45°18' N, 78°3' E **173**
Ushuaia, *Arg.* 54°43' S, 68°18' W **134**
Ushumun, *Russ.* 52°45' N, 126°37' E **190**
Usinge, *Tanzania* 5°6' S, 31°16' E **224**
Usingen, *Ger.* 50°19' N, 8°32' E **167**
Usinsk, *Russ.* 65°58' N, 57°27' E **154**
Usk, *Can.* 54°38' N, 128°27' W **108**
Usk, river, *U.K.* 51°54' N, 3°17' W **162**
Uska, *India* 27°11' N, 83°5' E **197**
Uskoplje see Gornji Vakuf, *Bosn. and Herzg.* 43°55' N, 17°33' E **168**
Üsküdar, *Turk.* 41°1' N, 29°1' E **156**
Uslar, *Ger.* 51°39' N, 9°38' E **167**
Usman', *Russ.* 52°0' N, 39°36' E **158**
Usmas Ezers, lake, *Latv.* 57°10' N, 21°57' E **166**
Usogorsk, *Russ.* 63°25' N, 48°43' E **154**
Usol'ye, *Russ.* 59°25' N, 56°35' E **154**
Usol'ye Sibirskoye, *Russ.* 52°47' N, 103°33' E **173**
Usove, *Ukr.* 51°20' N, 28°5' E **152**
Üspenka, *Kaz.* 52°54' N, 77°22' E **184**
Uspenovka, *Kaz.* 43°12' N, 74°29' E **184**
U.S.S. Arizona Memorial, *Pacific Ocean* 21°21' N, 157°60' W **99**
Usson, *Fr.* 42°44' N, 2°5' E **164**
Ussuriysk, *Russ.* 43°53' N, 132°4' E **190**
Ust' Alekseyevo, *Russ.* 60°28' N, 46°31' E **154**
Ust' Baikha, *Russ.* 65°48' N, 86°14' E **169**
Ust' Barguzin, *Russ.* 53°29' N, 109°8' E **190**
Ust' Bol'sheretsk, *Russ.* 52°58' N, 156°14' E **160**
Ust' Buzulukskaya, *Russ.* 50°7' N, 42°5' E **158**
Ust' Chaun, *Russ.* 68°42' N, 170°21' E **160**
Ust' Chernaya, *Russ.* 60°27' N, 52°41' E **154**
Ust' Ilimsk, *Russ.* 57°46' N, 102°17' E **160**
Ust' Ilych, *Russ.* 62°31' N, 56°48' E **154**
Ust' Ishim, *Russ.* 57°35' N, 71°1' E **160**
Ust' Izes, *Russ.* 55°57' N, 76°55' E **184**
Ust' Izhma, *Russ.* 65°17' N, 52°58' E **154**
Ust' Kalmanka, *Russ.* 52°7' N, 83°28' E **184**
Ust' Kamchatsk, *Russ.* 56°18' N, 162°17' E **160**
Ust' Kamenogorsk see Öskemen, *Kaz.* 49°59' N, 82°38' E **184**
Ust' Kan, *Russ.* 51°2' N, 84°50' E **184**
Ust' Kara, *Russ.* 69°11' N, 65°7' E **169**
Ust' Katav, *Russ.* 54°56' N, 58°14' E **154**
Ust' Khayryuzovo, *Russ.* 57°10' N, 156°50' E **160**
Ust' Kosa, *Russ.* 60°12' N, 55°15' E **154**
Ust' Kozha, *Russ.* 63°37' N, 38°43' E **154**
Ust' Kulom, *Russ.* 61°41' N, 53°46' E **154**
Ust' Kurenga, *Russ.* 57°26' N, 75°32' E **169**
Ust' Kureyka, *Russ.* 66°25' N, 87°23' E **169**
Ust' Kut, *Russ.* 56°55' N, 105°58' E **160**
Ust' Kuyga, *Russ.* 70°5' N, 135°32' E **160**
Ust' Labinsk, *Russ.* 45°15' N, 39°39' E **158**
Ust' Luga, *Russ.* 59°38' N, 28°14' E **166**
Ust' Lyzha, *Russ.* 65°42' N, 56°38' E **154**
Ust' Maya, *Russ.* 60°29' N, 134°29' E **160**
Ust' Mil', *Russ.* 59°45' N, 132°55' E **160**
Ust' Nem, *Russ.* 61°38' N, 54°48' E **154**
Ust' Nera, *Russ.* 64°31' N, 143°13' E **160**
Ust' Nyukzha, *Russ.* 56°25' N, 121°35' E **160**
Ust' Olenek, *Russ.* 72°53' N, 119°39' E **160**
Ust' Ordynskiy, *Russ.* 52°51' N, 104°47' E **190**
Ust' Ordynskiy Buryat, adm. division, *Russ.* 53°23' N, 102°46' E **160**
Ust' Ozernoye, *Russ.* 58°53' N, 87°48' E **169**
Ust' Paden'ga, *Russ.* 61°51' N, 42°37' E **154**
Ust' Pinega, *Russ.* 64°10' N, 42°2' E **154**
Ust' Pit, *Russ.* 58°59' N, 91°53' E **169**
Ust' Port, *Russ.* 69°44' N, 84°25' E **169**
Ust' Shchugor, *Russ.* 64°18' N, 57°30' E **154**
Ust' Shonosha, *Russ.* 61°11' N, 41°16' E **154**
Ust' Tara, *Russ.* 56°40' N, 74°46' E **169**
Ust' Tareya, *Russ.* 73°22' N, 90°50' E **160**
Ust' Tigil', *Russ.* 57°56' N, 158°12' E **173**
Ust' Tsil'ma, *Russ.* 65°26' N, 52°11' E **154**
Ust' Ulagan, *Russ.* 50°41' N, 87°57' E **184**
Ust' Uls, *Russ.* 60°35' N, 58°28' E **154**
Ust' Un'ya, *Russ.* 61°49' N, 57°51' E **154**
Ust' Ura, *Russ.* 63°7' N, 44°48' E **154**
Ust' Usa, *Russ.* 65°59' N, 56°59' E **154**
Ust' Vayen'ga, *Russ.* 63°0' N, 42°44' E **154**
Ust' Voya, *Russ.* 64°28' N, 57°37' E **154**
Ust' Voyampolka, *Russ.* 58°30' N, 159°20' E **160**
Ust' Vym', *Russ.* 62°15' N, 50°25' E **154**
Ust' Yegralyaga, *Russ.* 62°27' N, 59°4' E **154**
Ust' Yudoma, *Russ.* 59°14' N, 135°9' E **160**
Ustaoset, *Nor.* 60°30' N, 8°0' E **152**
Ust'-Dolyssy, *Russ.* 56°9' N, 29°42' E **166**
Ústecký, adm. division, *Czech Rep.* 50°30' N, 13°50' E **152**
Ústí nad Labem, *Czech Rep.* 50°39' N, 14°2' E **152**
Ustica, *It.* 38°42' N, 13°11' E **156**
Ustiprača, *Bosn. and Herzg.* 43°42' N, 19°6' E **168**
Ustrem, *Russ.* 64°18' N, 65°28' E **169**
Ust'ye, *Russ.* 59°38' N, 39°40' E **154**
Ustyluh, *Ukr.* 50°51' N, 24°9' E **158**
Ustyurt Plateau, *Uzb.* 42°38' N, 55°45' E **158**
Ustyuzhna, *Russ.* 58°49' N, 36°29' E **154**
Usu, *China* 44°27' N, 84°41' E **184**
Usuki, *Japan* 33°7' N, 131°47' E **201**
Usure, *Tanzania* 4°39' S, 34°19' E **224**
Us'va, *Russ.* 58°41' N, 57°39' E **154**
Usvyaty, *Russ.* 55°44' N, 30°49' E **154**
Utah, adm. division, *Utah, U.S.* 39°29' N, 112°5' W **92**
Utah Beach, *Fr.* 49°24' N, 1°36' W **150**
Utajärvi, *Fin.* 64°44' N, 26°23' E **152**
'Utaybah, *Syr.* 33°29' N, 36°36' E **194**
Utegi, *Tanzania* 1°23' S, 34°13' E **224**
Utembo, river, *Angola* 16°30' S, 21°27' E **220**
Utena, *Lith.* 55°29' N, 25°35' E **166**
Utete, *Tanzania* 7°60' S, 38°46' E **224**
Uthai Thani, *Thai.* 15°21' N, 100°2' E **202**
Uthal, *Pak.* 25°45' N, 66°38' E **186**
Uthina, ruin(s), *Tun.* 36°36' N, 10°5' E **156**
Utiariti, *Braz.* 13°3' S, 58°21' W **130**
Utica, *Ill., U.S.* 41°20' N, 89°1' W **102**
Utica, *Miss., U.S.* 32°6' N, 90°38' W **103**
Utica, *Mo., U.S.* 41°20' N, 89°1' W **110**
Utica, *N.Y., U.S.* 43°6' N, 75°14' W **94**
Utica, *Ohio, U.S.* 40°13' N, 82°26' W **102**
Utica, ruin(s), *Tun.* 37°3' N, 9°57' E **156**
Utiel, *Sp.* 39°34' N, 1°13' W **164**
Utiku, *N.Z.* 39°47' S, 175°50' E **240**
Utikuma, river, *Can.* 56°5' N, 115°18' W **108**
Utila, Isla de, island, *Hond.* 16°8' N, 87°17' W **115**
Utkholok, *Russ.* 57°35' N, 157°8' E **173**
Uto, *Japan* 32°41' N, 130°41' E **201**
Utö, island, *Sw.* 58°54' N, 18°19' E **166**
Utonkon, *Nig.* 6°55' N, 8°3' E **222**
Utraula, *India* 27°17' N, 82°23' E **197**
Utrecht, *Neth.* 52°4' N, 5°6' E **167**
Utrecht, *S. Af.* 27°40' S, 30°18' E **227**
Utrera, *Sp.* 37°11' N, 5°48' W **164**
Utroya, river, *Russ.* 57°8' N, 28°15' E **166**
Utsunomiya, *Japan* 36°33' N, 139°52' E **201**
Utta, *Russ.* 46°20' N, 45°55' E **158**
Uttar Pradesh, adm. division, *India* 27°12' N, 79°59' E **197**
Uttaradit, *Thai.* 17°39' N, 100°5' E **202**
Uttaranchal, adm. division, *India* 29°54' N, 78°19' E **197**
Uttoxeter, *U.K.* 52°53' N, 1°53' W **162**
Utuado 18°15' N, 66°44' W **116**
Utubulak, *China* 46°51' N, 86°26' E **184**
Utukok, river, *Alas., U.S.* 69°53' N, 161°22' W **98**
Uubulan, *Mongolia* 48°36' N, 101°54' E **198**
Uummannaq 70°36' N, 52°9' W **106**
Uummannaq, island, *Uummannaq* 62°51' N, 41°19' W **106**
Uummannaq Kangerlua 70°45' N, 56°41' W **106**
Uurainen, *Fin.* 62°29' N, 25°25' E **152**
Uusikaarlepyy see Nykarleby, *Fin.* 63°31' N, 22°32' E **152**
Uusikaupunki, *Fin.* 60°47' N, 21°24' E **166**
Uva, *Russ.* 56°57' N, 52°15' E **154**
Uvá, river, *Col.* 3°38' N, 70°3' W **136**
Uvac, river, *Serb. and Mont.* 43°33' N, 19°38' E **168**
Uvalde, *Tex., U.S.* 29°11' N, 99°47' W **92**
Uvarovo, *Russ.* 51°57' N, 42°9' E **158**
Uvat, *Russ.* 59°4' N, 68°52' E **169**
Uvel'skiy, *Russ.* 54°29' N, 61°19' E **154**
Uvinza, *Tanzania* 5°4' S, 30°20' E **224**
Uvira, *Dem. Rep. of the Congo* 3°27' S, 29°4' E **224**
Uvs, adm. division, *Mongolia* 49°54' N, 90°12' E **184**
Uvs Nuur, lake, *Mongolia* 50°29' N, 90°48' E **172**
Uwajima, *Japan* 33°12' N, 132°33' E **201**
'Uweinat, Jebel (Al 'Uwaynāt), peak, *Sudan* 21°51' N, 24°58' E **226**
Uwi, island, *Indonesia* 1°5' N, 107°5' E **196**
Uxbridge, *Mass., U.S.* 42°4' N, 71°39' W **104**
Uxin Qi (Dabqig), *China* 38°24' N, 108°59' E **198**
Uxmal, ruin(s), *Mex.* 20°17' N, 89°54' W **115**
Uy, river, *Russ.* 54°11' N, 60°11' E **154**
Uyar, *Russ.* 55°40' N, 94°17' E **160**
Üydzin, *Mongolia* 44°7' N, 107°1' E **198**
Uyo, *Nig.* 5°3' N, 7°56' E **222**
Uyowa, *Tanzania* 4°33' S, 32°1' E **224**
Uyuni, *Bol.* 20°33' S, 66°55' W **137**
Uza, river, *Russ.* 52°48' N, 45°39' E **158**
Užava, *Latv.* 57°14' N, 21°27' E **166**
Užava, river, *Latv.* 57°8' N, 21°24' E **166**
Uzbekistan 41°0' N, 63°0' E **184**
Uzbel Shankou, pass, *China* 38°39' N, 73°48' E **197**
Uzcudún, *Arg.* 44°13' S, 66°7' W **134**
Uzdin, *Serb. and Mont.* 45°12' N, 20°37' E **168**
Uzhur, *Russ.* 55°21' N, 89°52' E **169**
Užice, *Serb. and Mont.* 43°51' N, 19°50' E **168**
Uzlovaya, *Russ.* 53°57' N, 38°8' E **154**
Üzümlü, *Turk.* 36°44' N, 29°13' E **156**
Uzunköprü, *Turk.* 41°14' N, 26°39' E **156**
Užventis, *Lith.* 55°46' N, 22°39' E **166**
Uzynaghash, *Kaz.* 43°14' N, 76°16' E **184**
Uzynköl, *Kaz.* 53°57' N, 64°52' E **184**

V

Vääksy, *Fin.* 61°9' N, 25°32' E **166**
Vaal, river, *S. Af.* 26°51' S, 29°39' E **227**
Vaala, *Fin.* 64°33' N, 26°48' E **152**
Vaals, *Neth.* 50°46' N, 6°0' E **167**
Vääna, *Est.* 59°22' N, 24°23' E **166**
Vaasa, *Fin.* 63°4' N, 21°42' E **160**
Vaasa (Vasa), *Fin.* 63°5' N, 21°37' E **152**
Vabalninkas, *Lith.* 55°58' N, 24°43' E **166**
Vác, *Hung.* 47°45' N, 19°10' E **168**
Vacaria, *Braz.* 28°28' S, 50°55' W **139**
Vacaville, *Calif., U.S.* 38°21' N, 121°60' W **100**
Vacha, *Ger.* 50°49' N, 10°1' E **167**
Väddö, *Sw.* 60°0' N, 18°49' E **166**
Vader, *Wash., U.S.* 46°23' N, 122°58' W **100**
Vadheim, *Nor.* 61°12' N, 5°49' E **152**
Vadodara, *India* 22°17' N, 73°13' E **186**
Vadsø, *Nor.* 70°10' N, 29°50' E **160**
Vaduz, *Liech.* 47°6' N, 9°22' E **156**
Vaga, river, *Russ.* 61°42' N, 42°48' E **154**
Vagan, *Bosn. and Herzg.* 44°10' N, 17°9' E **168**
Vagay, river, *Russ.* 56°29' N, 68°53' E **169**
Vågen, *Nor.* 64°39' N, 13°43' E **152**
Vaiden, *Miss., U.S.* 33°17' N, 89°45' W **103**
Väike Maarja, *Est.* 59°5' N, 26°15' E **166**
Vailly, *Fr.* 49°24' N, 3°30' E **163**
Vainikkala, *Fin.* 60°51' N, 28°18' E **166**
Vaiņode, *Latv.* 56°25' N, 21°50' E **166**
Vakh, river, *Russ.* 60°45' N, 79°42' E **160**
Vakh, river, *Russ.* 61°22' N, 83°43' E **169**
Vakhsh, river, *Taj.* 37°50' N, 68°58' E **197**
Vakhtan, *Russ.* 57°56' N, 46°45' E **154**
Vál, *Hung.* 47°20' N, 18°39' E **168**
Val Grande National Park, *It.* 45°57' N, 8°7' E **167**
Val Marie, *Can.* 49°13' N, 107°45' W **90**
Val Verde Park, *Calif., U.S.* 34°27' N, 118°41' W **101**
Vala, river, *Russ.* 56°41' N, 52°16' E **154**
Valaam, *Russ.* 61°21' N, 30°58' E **166**
Valaichchenai, *Sri Lanka* 7°54' N, 81°34' E **188**
Valamaz, *Russ.* 57°32' N, 52°8' E **154**
Valatie, *N.Y., U.S.* 42°24' N, 73°41' W **104**
Valberg, *Nor.* 68°11' N, 13°56' E **152**
Vălcani, *Rom.* 46°0' N, 20°23' E **168**
Valcarlos see Luzaide, *Fr.* 43°5' N, 1°19' W **164**
Vâlcea, adm. division, *Rom.* 44°57' N, 23°47' E **156**
Valcheta, *Arg.* 40°39' S, 66°11' W **134**
Valday, *Russ.* 57°57' N, 33°15' E **154**
Valdayskaya Vozvyshennost', *Russ.* 56°12' N, 30°12' E **152**
Valdemārpils, *Latv.* 57°21' N, 22°34' E **166**
Valdepeñas, *Sp.* 38°45' N, 3°23' W **164**
Valderrobres, *Sp.* 40°51' N, 0°8' E **164**
Valders, *Wis., U.S.* 44°3' N, 87°53' W **102**
Valdés, Peninsula, *Arg.* 42°42' S, 64°40' W **134**
Valdez, *Ecua.* 1°10' N, 79°11' W **130**
Valdivia, *Chile* 39°47' S, 73°17' W **134**
Valdivia, *Col.* 7°4' N, 75°28' W **136**
Valdivia, *Sp.* 39°1' N, 5°42' W **164**
Val-d'Or, *Can.* 48°7' N, 77°48' W **94**
Valdosta, *Ga., U.S.* 30°49' N, 83°17' W **96**
Valdres, region, *Nor.* 60°44' N, 8°54' E **152**
Vale, *Oreg., U.S.* 43°59' N, 117°16' W **90**
Valea lui Mihai, *Rom.* 47°31' N, 22°8' E **168**
Valea Vişeului, *Rom.* 47°54' N, 24°10' E **156**
Valemount, *Can.* 52°49' N, 119°16' W **108**
Valença, *Braz.* 13°23' S, 39°9' W **132**
Valença, *Port.* 41°56' N, 8°40' W **214**
Valence, *Fr.* 44°56' N, 4°55' E **143**
Valencia, *Calif., U.S.* 34°23' N, 118°34' W **101**
Valencia, *Sp.* 39°28' N, 0°23' E **164**
Valencia, *Venez.* 10°9' N, 67°59' W **136**
Valencia, adm. division, *Sp.* 40°10' N, 0°26' E **164**
Valencia, Golfo de 39°40' N, 0°51' E **150**
Valenciennes, *Fr.* 50°20' N, 3°32' E **163**
Valentine, *Ariz., U.S.* 35°24' N, 113°40' W **101**

Valentine, Nebr., U.S. 42°50' N, 100°34' W 90
Valentine, Tex., U.S. 30°33' N, 104°29' W 92
Valentine, Cape, Antarctica 61°6' S, 54°60' W 134
Valenza, It. 45°0' N, 8°38' E 167
Våler, Nor. 60°40' N, 11°49' E 152
Valera, Venez. 9°17' N, 70°39' W 136
Valestrand, Nor. 59°40' N, 5°26' E 152
Valets, Lac, lake, Can. 48°30' N, 76°55' W 94
Valga, Est. 57°45' N, 26°3' E 166
Valier, Mo., U.S. 38°0' N, 89°3' W 94
Valier, Mont., U.S. 48°17' N, 112°16' W 90
Valjala, Est. 58°24' N, 22°46' E 166
Valjevo, Serb. and Mont. 44°16' N, 19°52' E 168
Valjok, Nor. 69°41' N, 25°54' E 152
Valka, Latv. 57°45' N, 25°59' E 166
Valkeakoski, Fin. 61°16' N, 23°59' E 166
Valkenswaard, Neth. 51°20' N, 5°26' E 167
Valkyrie Dome, Antarctica 76°20' S, 28°43' E 248
Valla, Nor. 59°1' N, 16°20' E 152
Valladares, Mex. 26°54' N, 100°39' W 96
Valladolid, Mex. 20°41' N, 88°13' W 116
Valladolid, Sp. 41°38' N, 4°44' W 150
Valladolid de los Bimviles, Equatorial Guinea 1°50' N, 10°42' E 218
Vallard, Lac, lake, Can. 52°49' N, 69°26' W 111
Valle, Nor. 59°11' N, 7°32' E 152
Valle Crucis Abbey, site, U.K. 52°59' N, 3°13' W 162
Valle D'Aosta, adm. division, It. 45°49' N, 7°2' E 165
Valle de Banderas, Mex. 20°47' N, 105°17' W 114
Valle de Bravo, Mex. 19°9' N, 100°8' W 114
Valle de la Pascua, Venez. 9°12' N, 66°2' W 136
Valle de Santiago, Mex. 20°22' N, 101°11' W 114
Valle de Zaragoza, Mex. 27°26' N, 105°49' W 112
Valle del Cauca, adm. division, Col. 3°59' N, 78°23' W 130
Valle del Cauca, adm. division, Col. 3°38' N, 76°58' W 136
Valle Fértil, Sierra del, Arg. 30°20' S, 68°17' W 134
Valle Hermoso, Mex. 25°40' N, 97°48' W 114
Vallecillo, Mex. 26°39' N, 99°58' W 114
Vallecito Mountains, Calif., U.S. 33°5' N, 116°22' W 101
Valledupar, Col. 10°26' N, 73°15' W 136
Vallegrande, Bol. 18°32' S, 64°12' W 137
Vallejo, Calif., U.S. 38°5' N, 122°15' W 100
Vallendar, Ger. 50°24' N, 7°37' E 167
Valletta, Malta 35°52' N, 14°23' E 156
Valley, Miss., U.S. 32°45' N, 90°30' W 103
Valley City, N. Dak., U.S. 46°54' N, 98°2' W 90
Valley Falls, R.I., U.S. 41°54' N, 71°24' W 104
Valley Head, Philippines 17°53' N, 122°13' E 203
Valley Mills, Tex., U.S. 31°38' N, 97°28' W 92
Valley Park, Miss., U.S. 32°38' N, 90°53' W 103
Valley Pass, Nev., U.S. 41°8' N, 114°26' W 90
Valley Springs, Calif., U.S. 38°11' N, 120°51' W 100
Valleyview, Can. 55°3' N, 117°19' W 108
Vallibona, Sp. 40°35' N, 6°357' E 164
Vallo della Lucania, It. 40°14' N, 15°16' E 156
Vallorbe, Switz. 46°42' N, 6°23' E 167
Valls, Sp. 41°17' N, 1°15' E 164
Valmeyer, Mo., U.S. 38°16' N, 90°19' W 94
Valmiera, Latv. 57°31' N, 25°23' E 166
Valmy, Fr. 49°5' N, 4°48' E 163
Valozhyn, Belarus 54°4' N, 26°31' E 166
Valparaiso, Braz. 21°16' S, 50°55' W 138
Valparaíso, Chile 33°5' S, 71°40' W 134
Valparaiso, Col. 1°10' N, 75°44' W 136
Valparaiso, Ind., U.S. 41°27' N, 87°3' W 102
Valparaíso, Mex. 22°46' N, 103°35' W 114
Valparaíso, adm. division, Chile 33°23' S, 71°33' W 134
Valpovo, Croatia 45°38' N, 18°24' E 168
Vals, Fr. 44°40' N, 4°21' E 150
Vals, Tanjung, Indonesia 8°24' S, 136°6' E 192
Valsad, India 20°35' N, 72°56' E 188
Valsjöbyn, Nor. 64°4' N, 14°5' E 152
Valstagna, It. 45°52' N, 11°41' E 167
Valtimo, Fin. 63°39' N, 28°48' E 152
Valuyevka, Russ. 46°39' N, 43°40' E 158
Valuyki, Russ. 50°13' N, 38°4' E 158
Valvær, islands, Norwegian Sea 66°51' N, 11°54' E 152
Valverde del Camino, Sp. 37°34' N, 6°46' W 164
Valyntsy, Belarus 55°42' N, 28°10' E 166
Vammala, Fin. 61°19' N, 22°53' E 166
Vámospércs, Hung. 47°31' N, 21°54' E 168
Vampula, Fin. 60°59' N, 22°41' E 166
Van, Tex., U.S. 32°30' N, 95°37' W 103
Van, Turk. 38°27' N, 43°18' E 195
Van Alstyne, Tex., U.S. 33°25' N, 96°35' W 96
Van Blommestein Meer, lake, Suriname 4°38' N, 56°23' W 130
Van Buren, Ark., U.S. 35°24' N, 94°21' W 96
Van Buren, Ind., U.S. 40°36' N, 85°30' W 102
Van Buren, Me., U.S. 47°8' N, 67°57' W 94
Van Gölü, lake, Turk. 38°34' N, 42°36' E 195
Van Hoa, Vietnam 21°11' N, 107°33' E 198
Van Horn, Tex., U.S. 31°1' N, 104°51' W 82
Van, Lake, Turk. 38°10' N, 41°15' E 206
Van Ninh, Vietnam 12°42' N, 109°12' E 202
Van Tassell, Wyo., U.S. 42°40' N, 104°5' W 90
Van Wert, Ohio, U.S. 40°51' N, 84°36' W 102
Van Yen, Vietnam 21°6' N, 104°41' E 202
Vanadzor, Arm. 40°47' N, 44°28' E 195
Vanaja, Fin. 60°58' N, 24°29' E 166
Vananda, Can. 49°44' N, 124°32' W 100
Vanavara, Russ. 60°22' N, 102°12' E 160
Vanceboro, Me., U.S. 45°33' N, 67°28' W 94
Vanceburg, Ky., U.S. 38°34' N, 83°19' W 102
Vancorum, Colo., U.S. 38°14' N, 108°37' W 90
Vancouver, Can. 49°16' N, 123°7' W 100
Vancouver, Wash., U.S. 45°37' N, 122°41' W 100
Vancouver Island, Can. 49°11' N, 123°48' W 100
Vandalia, Ill., U.S. 38°57' N, 89°6' W 102
Vandalia, Ohio, U.S. 39°52' N, 84°12' W 102
Vandenberg Air Force Base, Calif., U.S. 34°43' N, 120°38' W 100
Vandenberg Village, Calif., U.S. 34°42' N, 120°29' W 100
Vanderlin Island, Austral. 15°49' S, 137°10' E 230
Vändra, Est. 58°38' N, 25°1' E 166
Vandúzi, Mozambique 18°60' S, 33°17' E 224
Vandysh, Russ. 61°20' N, 40°12' E 154
Vanegas, Mex. 23°49' N, 100°53' W 114
Vänern, lake, Sw. 58°24' N, 11°45' E 160
Vänersborg, Sw. 57°33' N, 12°11' E 172
Vang, Mount, peak, Antarctica 73°58' S, 69°22' W 248
Vanga, Kenya 4°38' S, 39°12' E 224
Vangaindrano, Madagascar 23°22' S, 47°35' E 220
Vangozero, Russ. 65°34' N, 33°18' E 152
Vanguard, Can. 49°54' N, 107°18' W 90
Vangunu, island, Solomon Islands 8°41' S, 158°0' E 242
Vangviang, Laos 18°56' N, 102°27' E 202
Vanikolo Islands, Solomon Islands 12°49' S, 164°8' E 238
Vanino, Russ. 49°4' N, 140°3' E 190
Vaniyambadi, India 12°40' N, 78°37' E 188
Vanj, Taj. 38°21' N, 71°23' E 197
Vankarem, Russ. 67°44' N, 175°59' W 98
Vännäs, Nor. 63°54' N, 19°44' E 152
Vannes, Fr. 47°40' N, 2°51' W 143
Vanoise, Massif de la, Fr. 45°18' N, 6°25' E 165
Vanrhynsdorp, S. Af. 31°37' S, 18°41' E 227
Vansbro, Nor. 60°29' N, 14°9' E 152
Vanscoy, Can. 52°0' N, 106°59' W 90
Vansittart Bay 14°4' S, 125°1' E 230
Vansittart Island, island, Can. 66°8' N, 84°9' W 106
Vanua Levu, island, Fiji Islands 16°41' S, 179°10' E 242
Vanuatu 17°41' S, 167°55' E 243
Vanwyksvlei, S. Af. 30°22' S, 21°48' E 227
Vanzetur, Russ. 63°31' N, 64°52' E 169
Vanzevat, Russ. 64°15' N, 66°15' E 169
Vanzhil' Kynak, Russ. 60°23' N, 84°17' E 169
Vanzylsrus, S. Af. 26°52' S, 22°3' E 227
Var, river, Fr. 43°54' N, 7°7' E 165
Vara, Nor. 58°14' N, 12°55' E 152
Varades, Fr. 47°23' N, 1°2' W 150
Varakļāni, Latv. 56°36' N, 26°45' E 166
Varalé, Côte d'Ivoire 9°39' N, 3°18' W 222
Varāmīn, Iran 35°21' N, 51°40' E 180
Varanasi (Banaras), India 25°18' N, 82°57' E 197
Varangerfjorden 69°48' N, 26°7' E 142
Varangerhalvøya, Nor. 70°11' N, 28°10' E 152
Varapayeva, Belarus 55°8' N, 27°10' E 166
Varaždin, Croatia 46°19' N, 16°20' E 168
Varazze, It. 44°21' N, 8°34' E 167
Vardar, river, Maced. 41°21' N, 22°7' E 180
Varde, Den. 55°37' N, 8°27' E 150
Vårdö, Fin. 60°14' N, 20°21' E 166
Vardø, Nor. 70°20' N, 31°16' E 160
Varel, Ger. 53°23' N, 8°9' E 163
Varėna, Lith. 54°13' N, 24°34' E 166
Varengeville, Fr. 49°54' N, 0°58' E 163
Varennes, Fr. 49°13' N, 5°0' E 163
Vareš, Bosn. and Herzg. 44°10' N, 18°18' E 168
Varese, It. 45°49' N, 8°50' E 167
Varese, It. 44°22' N, 9°37' E 167
Vårgårda, Nor. 58°1' N, 12°46' E 152
Varginha, Braz. 21°35' S, 45°27' W 138
Varilhes, Fr. 43°2' N, 1°37' E 164
Varitino, Russ. 57°10' N, 29°33' E 166
Varkaus, Fin. 62°18' N, 27°48' E 152
Värmlandsnäs, Nor. 58°49' N, 12°24' E 152
Varna, Bulg. 43°12' N, 27°55' E 156
Varna, Russ. 53°26' N, 60°48' E 154
Varna, adm. division, Bulg. 42°56' N, 27°20' E 156
Varnado, La., U.S. 30°52' N, 89°50' W 103
Värnamo, Nor. 57°11' N, 14°0' E 152
Varnavino, Russ. 57°24' N, 45°3' E 154
Varnek, Russ. 69°47' N, 60°9' E 169
Varniai, Lith. 55°45' N, 22°22' E 166
Varonichy, Belarus 54°59' N, 28°36' E 166
Varosha 35°6' N, 33°56' E 194
Városl od, Hung. 47°8' N, 17°39' E 168
Várpalota, Hung. 47°11' N, 18°9' E 168
Värska, Est. 57°56' N, 27°37' E 166
Varstu, Est. 57°37' N, 26°38' E 166
Vårtejeni, Mold. 47°59' N, 28°33' E 152
Vartius, Fin. 64°29' N, 29°57' E 152
Varto, Turk. 39°10' N, 41°27' E 195
Varvarin, Serb. and Mont. 43°43' N, 21°21' E 168
Várzea da Palma, Braz. 17°34' S, 44°43' W 138
Várzea Grande, Braz. 15°38' S, 56°13' W 132
Várzea, river, Braz. 27°27' S, 53°7' W 139
Varzelândia, Braz. 15°44' S, 44°4' W 138
Varzi, It. 44°49' N, 9°12' E 167
Varzino, Russ. 68°19' N, 38°20' E 169
Varzo, It. 46°13' N, 8°16' E 167
Varzob, Taj. 38°43' N, 68°49' E 197
Varzuga, Russ. 66°22' N, 36°28' E 154
Vas, adm. division, Hung. 47°0' N, 16°31' E 156
Vasa see Vaasa, Fin. 63°5' N, 21°37' E 152
Vasalemma, Est. 59°13' N, 24°15' E 166
Vaşcău, Rom. 46°28' N, 22°31' E 168
Vashka, river, Russ. 64°11' N, 46°16' E 154
Vasilevo, Maced. 41°29' N, 22°37' E 168
Vasiliko, Cyprus 34°43' N, 33°17' E 194
Vasilishki, Belarus 53°46' N, 24°50' E 152
Vasil'ki, Russ. 56°27' N, 29°28' E 166
Vasil'yevo, Russ. 55°49' N, 48°45' E 154
Vasis, Russ. 57°23' N, 74°47' E 169
Vaskelovo, Russ. 60°22' N, 30°25' E 166
Vasknarva, Est. 58°59' N, 27°42' E 166
Vaskút, Hung. 46°6' N, 18°59' E 168
Vaslui, Rom. 46°38' N, 27°44' E 156
Vaslui, adm. division, Rom. 46°32' N, 27°23' E 156
Vassar, Mich., U.S. 43°21' N, 83°35' W 102
Vassilítsa, Óros, peak, Gr. 40°1' N, 21°0' E 156
Västerås, Nor. 59°36' N, 16°32' E 152
Västervik, Nor. 57°44' N, 16°36' E 152
Vasto, It. 42°6' N, 14°42' E 156
Vasvár, Hung. 47°2' N, 16°49' E 168
Vasyl'kiv, Ukr. 50°12' N, 30°27' E 158
Vasyl'kivka, Ukr. 48°14' N, 36°6' E 158
Vasyugan, river, Russ. 59°10' N, 77°11' E 169
Vata, Rom. 46°11' N, 22°37' E 168
Vathí, Gr. 37°44' N, 26°59' E 156
Váthia, Gr. 36°28' N, 22°27' E 156
Vatican City 41°54' N, 12°26' E 156
Vatili 35°7' N, 33°38' E 194
Vatin, Serb. and Mont. 45°13' N, 21°17' E 168
Vatnajökull, glacier, Ice. 64°28' N, 24°60' W 142
Vatneyri, Ice. 65°37' N, 23°57' W 143
Vatomandry, Madagascar 19°20' S, 48°57' E 220
Vatry, Fr. 48°48' N, 4°14' E 163
Vatutin, Ukr. 49°2' N, 31°10' E 158
Vaucouleurs, Fr. 48°36' N, 5°39' E 163
Vaughn, Mont., U.S. 47°32' N, 111°34' W 90
Vaupés, adm. division, Col. 0°39' N, 71°23' W 136
Vauxhall, Can. 50°3' N, 112°7' W 90
Vavincourt, Fr. 48°49' N, 5°12' E 163
Vavla, Cyprus 34°50' N, 33°16' E 194
Vavoua, Côte d'Ivoire 7°19' N, 6°29' W 222
Vavozh, Russ. 56°46' N, 51°55' E 154
Vawa, Tanzania 9°6' S, 32°55' E 224
Vawkavysk, Belarus 53°9' N, 24°29' E 154
Vaxholm, Sw. 59°23' N, 18°18' E 166
Växjö, Sw. 56°51' N, 14°50' E 160
Vaygach, Ostrov, island, Russ. 70°25' N, 59°19' E 169
Vazante, Braz. 18°2' S, 46°56' W 138
Vazhgort, Russ. 64°5' N, 46°54' E 154
Veazie, Me., U.S. 44°50' N, 68°43' W 94
Veblen, S. Dak., U.S. 45°50' N, 97°19' W 90
Vecāki, Latv. 57°4' N, 24°6' E 166
Vecchiano, It. 43°47' N, 10°23' E 167
Vecsés, Hung. 47°23' N, 19°18' E 168
Vedeno, Russ. 42°54' N, 46°5' E 195
Vedia, Arg. 34°29' S, 61°34' W 139
Veedersburg, Ind., U.S. 40°6' N, 87°17' W 102
Vega, Nor. 65°39' N, 11°56' E 152
Vega, Tex., U.S. 35°13' N, 102°25' W 92
Vega de Alatorre, Mex. 19°59' N, 96°38' W 114
Vega Island, Antarctica 63°58' S, 57°4' W 134
Vegesack, Ger. 53°10' N, 8°38' E 163
Veghel, Neth. 51°36' N, 5°32' E 167
Vegreville, Can. 53°29' N, 112°6' W 108
Vehmaa, Fin. 60°40' N, 21°38' E 166
Vehmasjärvi, Fin. 63°35' N, 27°53' E 152
Veines, Nor. 70°37' N, 26°34' E 152
Veio, ruin(s), It. 42°0' N, 12°16' E 156
Vejen, Den. 55°28' N, 9°8' E 152
Vejer de la Frontera, Sp. 36°14' N, 5°58' W 164
Vejle, Den. 55°42' N, 9°31' E 150
Vel', river, Russ. 63°42' N, 55°26' E 154
Vela, Cabo de la, Col. 12°6' N, 72°55' W 116
Vela Luka, Croatia 42°56' N, 16°42' E 168
Velarde, N. Mex., U.S. 36°9' N, 105°58' W 92
Velardeña, Mex. 25°2' N, 103°43' W 114
Velas, Cabo, C.R. 10°24' N, 86°30' W 115
Velasco, Sierra de, Arg. 28°27' S, 67°31' W 132
Velay, Monts du, Fr. 45°4' N, 3°39' E 165
Velázquez, Uru. 34°3' S, 54°18' W 139
Velbert, Ger. 51°20' N, 7°2' E 167
Velebit, Croatia 44°16' N, 15°50' E 168
Veles, Maced. 41°43' N, 21°47' E 168
Vélez, Col. 6°0' N, 73°42' W 136
Vélez Blanco, Sp. 37°41' N, 2°5' W 164
Velež, peak, Bosn. and Herzg. 43°19' N, 17°58' E 168
Vélez Rubio, Sp. 37°38' N, 2°4' W 164
Velhas, river, Braz. 18°49' S, 44°7' W 138
Velia, ruin(s), It. 40°9' N, 15°5' E 156
Velika, Croatia 45°27' N, 17°39' E 168
Velika Drenova, Serb. and Mont. 43°37' N, 21°8' E 168
Velika Gorica, Croatia 45°43' N, 16°4' E 168
Velika Kladuša, Bosn. and Herzg. 45°10' N, 15°48' E 168
Velika Kruša, Europe 42°19' N, 20°38' E 168
Velika Ljubuša, peak, Bosn. and Herzg. 43°44' N, 17°21' E 168
Velika Plana, Serb. and Mont. 44°19' N, 21°2' E 168
Velikaya, river, Russ. 64°12' N, 176°12' E 160
Velikaya, river, Russ. 57°32' N, 28°7' E 166
Veliki Drvenik, island, Croatia 43°27' N, 15°54' E 168
Veliki Popović, Serb. and Mont. 44°6' N, 21°20' E 168
Veliki Snežnik, peak, Slov. 45°35' N, 14°20' E 156
Veliki Troglav, peak, Bosn. and Herzg. 43°56' N, 16°33' E 168
Veliki Zdenci, Croatia 45°39' N, 17°5' E 168
Velikiy Novgorod, Russ. 58°30' N, 31°21' E 152
Velikiy Ustyug, Russ. 60°47' N, 46°24' E 154
Velikiye Luki, Russ. 56°20' N, 30°38' E 152
Veliko Gradište, Serb. and Mont. 44°45' N, 21°30' E 168
Veliko Orašje, Serb. and Mont. 44°22' N, 21°3' E 168
Veliko Tŭrnovo, Bulg. 43°4' N, 25°38' E 156
Veliko Tŭrnovo, adm. division, Bulg. 43°17' N, 25°17' E 156
Velikoye Ozero, Russ. 62°32' N, 37°44' E 154
Vélingara, Senegal 13°9' N, 14°9' W 222
Vélingara, Senegal 15°0' N, 14°43' W 222
Velino, Monte, peak, It. 42°8' N, 13°19' E 156
Velizh, Russ. 55°35' N, 31°13' E 154
Velizhany, Russ. 57°32' N, 65°49' E 169
Vel'ká Ida, Slovakia 48°35' N, 21°9' E 156
Vella Lavella, island, Solomon Islands 7°45' S, 156°34' E 242
Vellberg, Ger. 49°5' N, 9°52' E 152
Vellore, India 12°54' N, 79°8' E 188
Vel'mo, river, Russ. 60°32' N, 93°42' E 169
Velp, Neth. 51°59' N, 5°57' E 167
Vels, Russ. 60°44' N, 58°50' E 154
Vel'sk, Russ. 61°2' N, 42°2' E 154
Velva, N. Dak., U.S. 48°1' N, 100°58' W 90
Vema Fracture Zone, North Atlantic Ocean 12°13' N, 44°53' W 253
Vemdalen, Nor. 62°26' N, 13°49' E 152
Venable Ice Shelf, Antarctica 73°35' S, 92°3' W 248
Venado, Mex. 22°54' N, 101°6' W 114
Venado, Isla del, island, Nicar. 11°52' N, 83°41' W 115
Venado Tuerto, Arg. 33°45' S, 61°57' W 139
Venamo, Cerro, peak, Venez. 5°54' N, 61°32' W 130
Venango, Nebr., U.S. 40°45' N, 102°3' W 90
Venaria, It. 45°7' N, 7°37' E 167
Venceslau Braz, Braz. 23°51' S, 49°49' W 138
Vendenga, Russ. 63°33' N, 47°50' E 154
Vendeuvre, Fr. 48°13' N, 4°27' E 163
Venecia, Col. 5°58' N, 75°44' W 136
Venejärvi, Fin. 67°15' N, 24°13' E 152
Veneto, adm. division, It. 45°41' N, 11°27' E 167
Venev, Russ. 54°21' N, 38°18' E 154
Venezia (Venice), It. 45°25' N, 12°19' E 167
Venezuela 7°0' N, 66°0' W 130
Venezuela, Golfo de 11°18' N, 71°31' W 136
Vengerovo, Russ. 55°38' N, 76°52' E 184
Veniaminof, Mount, peak, Alas., U.S. 56°11' N, 159°26' W 98
Venice, Fla., U.S. 27°6' N, 82°25' W 105
Venice, La., U.S. 29°16' N, 89°22' W 103
Venice, Gulf of 44°47' N, 12°35' E 167
Venice see Venezia, It. 45°25' N, 12°19' E 167
Venlo, Neth. 51°22' N, 6°10' E 167
Vennesund, Nor. 65°13' N, 12°4' E 152
Venray, Neth. 51°31' N, 5°57' E 167
Venta del Olivo, Sp. 38°19' N, 1°29' W 164
Venta, river, Lith. 55°46' N, 22°51' E 166
Ventana, Sierra de la, Arg. 38°15' S, 62°54' W 134
Ventavon, Fr. 44°22' N, 5°54' E 156
Ventersdorp, S. Af. 26°21' S, 26°47' E 227
Ventotene, It. 40°48' N, 13°25' E 156
Ventoux, Mont, peak, Fr. 44°9' N, 5°15' E 165
Vents, Lac des, lake, Can. 49°28' N, 75°25' W 94
Ventspils, Latv. 57°21' N, 21°31' E 166
Ventuari, river, Venez. 5°7' N, 65°59' W 136
Ventuari, river, Venez. 4°1' N, 66°50' W 136
Ventura, Calif., U.S. 34°17' N, 119°19' W 100
Venus, Fla., U.S. 27°4' N, 81°22' W 105
Venustiano Carranza, Mex. 16°19' N, 92°35' W 115
Venustiano Carranza, Mex. 19°45' N, 103°46' W 114
Venustiano Carranza, Presa, lake, Mex. 27°32' N, 101°46' W 80
Vepriai, Lith. 55°9' N, 24°32' E 166
Vera, Arg. 29°26' S, 60°12' W 139
Vera, Okla., U.S. 36°26' N, 95°53' W 96
Vera, Sp. 37°14' N, 1°52' W 164
Vera y Pintado, Arg. 30°7' S, 60°21' W 139
Veracruz, Mex. 19°9' N, 96°9' W 114
Veracruz, adm. division, Mex. 19°32' N, 97°21' W 114
Verba, Ukr. 50°15' N, 25°35' E 152
Verbania, It. 45°56' N, 8°33' E 167
Vercelli, It. 45°19' N, 8°24' E 167
Verçinin Tepesi, peak, Turk. 40°42' N, 40°51' E 195
Verdalsøra, Nor. 63°47' N, 11°29' E 152
Verde, Laguna, lake, Arg. 42°38' S, 69°8' W 134
Verde, Peninsula, Arg. 39°35' S, 62°4' W 139
Verde, river, Braz. 19°2' S, 53°33' W 132
Verde, river, Mex. 26°39' N, 107°18' W 80
Verde, river, Parag. 22°60' S, 59°40' W 132
Verdi Inlet 71°43' S, 77°30' W 248
Verdigre, Nebr., U.S. 42°35' N, 98°4' W 90
Verdon, river, Fr. 43°54' N, 6°34' E 165
Verdun, Fr. 49°10' N, 5°23' E 163
Vereeniging, S. Af. 26°42' S, 27°54' E 227
Vereshchagino, Russ. 64°9' N, 87°41' E 169
Vereshchagino, Russ. 58°6' N, 54°43' E 154
Verga, Cap, Guinea 10°10' N, 15°6' W 222
Vergara, Chile 22°28' S, 69°39' W 137
Vergara, Uru. 32°57' S, 53°58' W 139
Vergato, It. 44°16' N, 11°4' E 167
Vergel Ondara, Sp. 38°48' N, 1°59' E 164
Vergennes, Vt., U.S. 44°9' N, 73°16' W 104
Véria, Gr. 40°31' N, 22°12' E 180
Verín, Sp. 41°55' N, 7°28' W 150
Veríssimo, Braz. 19°42' S, 48°20' W 138
Verkhneimbatsk, Russ. 63°8' N, 88°0' E 169
Verkhnetulomskiy, Russ. 68°39' N, 31°38' E 152
Verkhneural'sk, Russ. 53°51' N, 59°12' E 154
Verkhnevilyuysk, Russ. 63°26' N, 120°13' E 173
Verkhniy Baskunchak, Russ. 48°13' N, 46°37' E 158
Verkhniy Mamon, Russ. 50°12' N, 40°19' E 158
Verkhniy Tagil, Russ. 57°25' N, 59°55' E 154
Verkhniy Ufaley, Russ. 56°3' N, 60°16' E 154
Verkhnyaya Inta, Russ. 66°0' N, 60°16' E 154
Verkhnyaya Pesha, Russ. 66°34' N, 47°51' E 154
Verkhnyaya Pyshma, Russ. 56°58' N, 60°36' E 154
Verkhnyaya Salda, Russ. 58°4' N, 60°34' E 154
Verkhnyaya Sinyachikha, Russ. 57°59' N, 61°36' E 154
Verkhnyaya Taymyra, river, Russ. 72°53' N, 91°25' E 160
Verkhnyaya Tura, Russ. 58°23' N, 59°52' E 154
Verkhnyaya Zolotitsa, Russ. 65°41' N, 40°3' E 154
Verkholuz'ye, Russ. 59°55' N, 48°36' E 154
Verkhoshizhem'ye, Russ. 58°0' N, 49°6' E 154
Verkhotur'ye, Russ. 58°53' N, 60°50' E 154
Verkhovazh'ye, Russ. 60°45' N, 42°0' E 154
Verkhov'ye, Russ. 52°47' N, 37°15' E 158
Verkhoyansk, Russ. 67°27' N, 133°35' E 160
Verkhoyanskiy Khrebet, Russ. 64°49' N, 117°28' E 160
Verkhozim, Russ. 52°54' N, 46°26' E 154
Vermelho, river, Braz. 15°20' S, 51°16' W 138
Vermeş, Rom. 45°32' N, 21°40' E 168
Vermilion, Can. 53°19' N, 110°49' W 108
Vermilion, Ohio, U.S. 41°24' N, 82°22' W 102
Vermilion Bay 29°42' N, 92°3' W 103
Vermilion Bay, Can. 49°51' N, 93°24' W 82
Vermilion Range, Minn., U.S. 48°0' N, 91°38' W 94
Vermillion, S. Dak., U.S. 42°45' N, 96°57' W 90
Vermillon, river, Can. 47°18' N, 73°23' W 94
Vérmio, Óros, Gr. 40°47' N, 21°55' E 156
Vermont, adm. division, Vt., U.S. 43°48' N, 73°7' W 104
Vermontville, N.Y., U.S. 44°26' N, 74°5' W 104
Vermosh, Alban. 42°35' N, 19°42' E 168
Vernadsky, station, Antarctica 65°23' S, 64°14' W 134
Verneuil, Fr. 48°44' N, 0°54' E 163
Vérno, Óros, peak, Gr. 40°38' N, 21°18' E 156
Vernon, Ala., U.S. 33°44' N, 88°6' W 96
Vernon, Can. 50°15' N, 119°15' W 90
Vernon, Fr. 49°5' N, 1°27' E 163
Vernon, Ill., U.S. 38°48' N, 89°5' W 102
Vernon, Ind., U.S. 38°59' N, 85°36' W 102
Vernon, Tex., U.S. 34°8' N, 99°18' W 92
Vernon, Vt., U.S. 42°46' N, 72°32' W 104
Vernonia, Oreg., U.S. 45°51' N, 123°13' W 100
Vero Beach, Fla., U.S. 27°38' N, 80°24' W 105
Verona, Ill., U.S. 41°12' N, 88°30' W 102
Verona, It. 45°25' N, 11°0' E 167
Verona, Ky., U.S. 38°48' N, 84°40' W 102
Verona, Mich., U.S. 43°47' N, 82°53' W 102
Verona, Wis., U.S. 42°58' N, 89°32' W 102
Verónica, Arg. 35°24' S, 57°21' W 139
Verrabotn, Nor. 63°47' N, 10°32' E 152
Verrès, It. 45°40' N, 7°42' E 167
Verret, Lake, La., U.S. 29°50' N, 91°21' W 103
Versailles, Fr. 48°48' N, 2°8' E 163
Versailles, Ky., U.S. 38°2' N, 84°44' W 94
Versailles, Ohio, U.S. 40°12' N, 84°29' W 102
Vershina, Russ. 60°57' N, 62°5' E 154
Vershino Darasunskiy, Russ. 52°23' N, 115°29' E 190
Vershire, Vt., U.S. 43°58' N, 72°20' W 104
Versmold, Ger. 52°2' N, 8°10' E 167
Vert, Cap, Senegal 14°45' N, 17°37' W 222
Verte, river, Can. 47°48' N, 68°34' W 94
Vértes, Hung. 47°23' N, 18°11' E 168
Verviers, Belg. 50°35' N, 5°51' E 167
Vervins, Fr. 49°50' N, 3°54' E 163
Verwood, U.K. 50°52' N, 1°53' W 162
Verzy, Fr. 49°9' N, 4°9' E 163
Vesanto, Fin. 62°55' N, 26°22' E 152
Veselí nad Moravou, Czech Rep. 48°57' N, 17°23' E 152
Veselovskoye, Russ. 53°57' N, 78°43' E 184
Veselyy, Russ. 47°2' N, 40°42' E 158
Veshenskaya, Russ. 49°37' N, 41°36' E 158
Veslyana, Russ. 63°1' N, 51°0' E 154
Veslyana, river, Russ. 60°28' N, 52°52' E 154
Vesnitsk, Belarus 55°4' N, 28°19' E 166
Vesoul, Fr. 47°37' N, 6°8' E 150
Vesterålen, islands, Norwegian Sea 68°51' N, 14°50' E 152
Vesterø Havn, Den. 57°16' N, 10°55' E 152
Vestfjorden 67°53' N, 11°40' E 142
Vestfold Hills, Antarctica 68°26' S, 79°17' E 248
Vestmannaeyjar, islands, Ice. 62°44' N, 26°60' W 142
Vestnes, Nor. 62°36' N, 7°4' E 152
Vestone, It. 45°43' N, 10°23' E 167
Vesuvio, peak, It. 40°44' N, 14°15' E 143
Ves'yegonsk, Russ. 58°37' N, 37°17' E 154
Veszprém, Hung. 47°5' N, 17°55' E 168
Veszprém, adm. division, Hung. 47°8' N, 17°13' E 156
Veszprémvarsány, Hung. 47°25' N, 17°51' E 168
Vetluga, Russ. 57°51' N, 45°49' E 154
Vetluga, river, Russ. 57°33' N, 45°22' E 154
Vetluzhskiy, Russ. 57°8' N, 45°10' E 154
Vetly, Ukr. 51°52' N, 25°6' E 152
Vetto, It. 44°28' N, 10°19' E 167
Vettore, Monte, peak, It. 42°49' N, 13°10' E 156
Veules-les-Roses, Fr. 49°51' N, 0°46' E 163
Veum, Nor. 59°17' N, 8°5' E 152
Veurne (Furnes), Belg. 51°4' N, 2°40' E 150
Vevay, Ind., U.S. 38°44' N, 85°4' W 102
Vevelstad, Nor. 65°41' N, 12°27' E 152
Veveno, river, Sudan 6°5' N, 32°27' E 224
Vevey, Switz. 46°28' N, 6°50' E 167
Vévi, Gr. 40°46' N, 21°36' E 156
Veynes, Fr. 44°32' N, 5°48' E 150
Vézelise, Fr. 48°29' N, 6°4' E 163
Vezhen, peak, Bulg. 42°44' N, 24°20' E 156
Vezirköprü, Turk. 41°8' N, 35°27' E 156
Viacha, Bol. 16°42' S, 68°21' W 137
Viadana, It. 44°55' N, 10°32' E 167
Viale, Arg. 31°52' S, 60°2' W 139
Viamonte, Arg. 33°46' S, 63°4' W 139
Viana, Braz. 3°14' S, 45°4' W 132
Viana do Castelo, Port. 41°41' N, 8°50' W 150
Viana Do Castelo, adm. division, Port. 41°59' N, 8°49' W 150
Vianden, Lux. 49°55' N, 6°11' E 167
Viangchan (Vientiane), Laos 17°56' N, 102°32' E 202
Viareggio, It. 43°52' N, 10°15' E 167
Viaur, river, Fr. 44°5' N, 2°10' E 165
Vibank, Can. 50°19' N, 103°57' W 108
Viborg, Den. 56°26' N, 9°23' E 150
Vic, Sp. 41°55' N, 2°14' E 164
Vicálvaro, Sp. 40°23' N, 3°35' W 164
Vicdessos, Fr. 42°46' N, 1°28' E 164
Vicente Guerrero, Mex. 30°45' N, 115°59' W 112
Vicente Guerrero, Mex. 23°44' N, 103°59' W 114
Vicente Guerrero, Presa, lake, Mex. 23°56' N, 99°20' W 114
Vicente Pérez Rosales National Park, Chile 41°13' S, 72°34' W 122
Vicenza, It. 45°33' N, 11°33' E 167
Vic-Fézensac, Fr. 43°45' N, 0°17' E 150
Vichada, adm. division, Col. 4°52' N, 70°21' W 136
Vichada, river, Col. 4°55' N, 68°23' W 136
Vichadero, Uru. 31°48' S, 54°42' W 139
Vichuga, Russ. 57°11' N, 41°56' E 154
Vichy, Fr. 46°5' N, 3°7' E 143
Vici, Okla., U.S. 36°8' N, 99°18' W 96
Vick, La., U.S. 31°13' N, 92°6' W 103
Vicksburg, Mich., U.S. 42°7' N, 85°32' W 102
Vicksburg, Miss., U.S. 32°18' N, 90°53' W 103

Vicksburg National Military Park, La., U.S. 32°20' N, 90°56' W 103
Viçosa, Braz. 20°45' S, 42°53' W 138
Vicovu de Sus, Rom. 47°55' N, 25°40' E 158
Victor, Idaho, U.S. 43°35' N, 111°6' W 90
Victor Harbor, Austral. 35°33' S, 138°36' E 231
Victor, Mount, peak, Antarctica 72°39' S, 30°58' E 248
Víctor Rosales, Mex. 22°57' N, 102°42' W 114
Victoria, Arg. 32°36' S, 60°10' W 139
Victoria, Can. 48°24' N, 123°23' W 100
Victoria, Chile 38°14' S, 72°20' W 134
Victoria, Guinea 10°51' N, 14°34' W 222
Victoria, Ill., U.S. 41°1' N, 90°7' W 102
Victoria, Philippines 15°34' N, 120°40' E 203
Victoria, Seychelles 4°53' S, 54°51' E 172
Victoria, Tex., U.S. 28°47' N, 96°60' W 96
Victoria, Va., U.S. 36°59' N, 78°14' W 96
Victoria, adm. division, Austral. 36°44' S, 141°23' E 231
Victoria Beach, Can. 50°40' N, 96°33' W 90
Victoria Falls, Zimb. 17°21' S, 20°52' E 207
Victoria Falls National Park, Zimb. 18°3' S, 25°44' E 224
Victoria, Grand lac, lake, Can. 47°33' N, 78°19' W 94
Victoria, Isla, island, Chile 45°18' S, 73°44' W 134
Victoria Island, Can. 70°18' N, 121°1' W 106
Victoria, Lake, Africa 1°23' S, 30°40' E 218
Victoria Land, region, Antarctica 74°59' S, 162°2' E 248
Victoria, Mount, peak, Myanmar 21°27' N, 93°33' E 190
Victoria, Mount, peak, P.N.G. 8°54' S, 147°21' E 192
Victoria Strait 68°57' N, 101°27' W 106
Victoria West, S. Af. 31°24' S, 23°5' E 227
Victoriaville, Can. 46°3' N, 71°59' W 94
Victorica, Arg. 36°14' S, 65°25' W 134
Victorino, Venez. 2°49' N, 67°49' W 136
Victorio Peak, Tex., U.S. 31°17' N, 104°57' W 92
Victorville, Calif., U.S. 34°32' N, 117°19' W 101
Victory Peak see Pobedy Peak, China 42°2' N, 80°3' E 184
Vidal, Calif., U.S. 34°7' N, 114°31' W 101
Vidal, Peru 2°38' S, 73°29' W 136
Vidal Gormaz, Isla, island, Chile 52°17' S, 76°29' W 134
Vidalia, Ga., U.S. 32°12' N, 82°25' W 96
Videira, Braz. 27°1' S, 51°9' W 139
Videla, Arg. 30°57' S, 60°41' W 139
Videle, Rom. 44°17' N, 25°32' E 158
Vidin, Bulg. 43°59' N, 22°51' E 168
Vidin, adm. division, Bulg. 43°42' N, 22°24' E 168
Vidisha (Bhilsa), India 23°32' N, 77°51' E 197
Viditsa, Russ. 61°10' N, 32°28' E 152
Vidor, Tex., U.S. 30°6' N, 94°1' W 103
Vidriži, Latv. 57°19' N, 24°36' E 166
Vidsel, Nor. 65°50' N, 20°28' E 152
Vidzibor, Belarus 51°58' N, 26°47' E 152
Vidzy, Belarus 55°24' N, 26°37' E 166
Vidz'yuyar, Russ. 60°52' N, 51°19' E 154
Vie, river, Fr. 46°36' N, 1°55' W 150
Viedma, Arg. 40°51' S, 63°1' W 134
Viedma, Lago, lake, Arg. 49°34' S, 73°52' W 134
Vieja, Sierra, Tex., U.S. 30°42' N, 105°1' W 92
Viejo, Cerro, peak, Mex. 30°16' N, 112°23' W 92
Viekšniai, Lith. 56°15' N, 22°31' E 166
Vielha, Sp. 42°41' N, 0°47' E 164
Vielsalm, Belg. 50°16' N, 5°55' E 167
Vienna, Ga., U.S. 32°5' N, 83°48' W 96
Vienna, Mo., U.S. 37°25' N, 88°53' W 96
Vienna, W. Va., U.S. 39°19' N, 81°33' W 102
Vienna see Wien, Aust. 48°10' N, 16°14' E 152
Vienne, Fr. 45°31' N, 4°52' E 150
Vientiane, Laos 17°53' N, 101°53' E 172
Vientiane see Viangchan, Laos 17°56' N, 102°32' E 202
Vieques, island, U.S. 18°8' N, 65°26' W 118
Viersen, Ger. 51°15' N, 6°23' E 167
Viesca, Mex. 25°21' N, 102°48' W 114
Vieste, It. 41°52' N, 16°10' E 156
Vieste, Latv. 56°20' N, 25°34' E 166
Vietnam 21°0' N, 105°0' E 202
Vieux-Fort, Can. 51°25' N, 57°49' W 111
Vievis, Lith. 54°45' N, 24°48' E 166
Vif, Fr. 45°2' N, 5°39' E 150
Vigan, Philippines 17°33' N, 120°24' E 203
Vigeois, Fr. 45°22' N, 1°30' E 150
Vigevano, It. 45°18' N, 8°50' E 167
Vigia, Cabo, Arg. 48°46' S, 66°49' W 134
Vigía Chico, Mex. 19°46' N, 87°38' W 116
Vignacourt, Fr. 50°0' N, 2°11' E 163
Vignal, Lac, lake, Can. 53°15' N, 68°51' W 111
Vignale, It. 45°0' N, 8°24' E 167
Vignemale, Pic de, peak, Fr. 42°46' N, 0°11' E 164
Vignola, It. 44°29' N, 11°0' E 167
Vigo, Sp. 42°13' N, 8°45' W 150
Vigone, It. 44°50' N, 7°29' E 167
Vihanti, Fin. 64°29' N, 24°58' E 152
Vihorlat, peak, Slovakia 48°53' N, 22°0' E 152
Viiala, Fin. 61°12' N, 23°43' E 166
Viiksimo, Fin. 64°13' N, 30°26' E 154
Viipuri see Vyborg, Russ. 60°41' N, 28°45' E 166
Viiri, Fin. 66°23' N, 26°38' E 152
Vijayadurg, India 16°31' N, 73°19' E 188
Vijayanagar, ruin(s), India 15°16' N, 76°17' E 188
Vijayawada, India 16°34' N, 80°33' E 190
Vik, Ice. 63°28' N, 18°59' W 143
Vika, Fin. 66°35' N, 26°23' E 152
Vikhren, peak, Bulg. 41°45' N, 23°19' E 156
Viking, Can. 53°5' N, 111°48' W 108
Vikna, islands, Norwegian Sea 64°56' N, 9°48' E 152
Vikulovo, Russ. 56°47' N, 70°37' E 169
Vila Bittencourt, Braz. 1°21' S, 69°23' W 136
Vila Conceição, Braz. 0°8' N, 63°55' W 130
Vila Coutinho, Mozambique 14°34' S, 34°18' E 224
Vila da Maganja, Mozambique 17°19' S, 37°31' E 224
Vila de Moura, Port. 38°7' N, 7°29' W 214
Vila de Sagres, Port. 37°0' N, 8°57' W 150
Vila do Conde, Port. 41°20' N, 8°45' W 150
Vila Gamito, Mozambique 14°11' S, 33°0' E 224
Vila Gomes da Costa, Mozambique 24°19' S, 33°39' E 227
Vila Junqueiro, Mozambique 15°29' S, 36°58' E 224
Vila Luísa, Mozambique 25°42' S, 32°40' E 227
Vila Machado, Mozambique 19°20' S, 34°13' E 224
Vila Murtinho, Braz. 10°23' S, 65°17' W 137
Vila Nova de Foz Côa, Port. 41°4' N, 7°10' W 150
Vila Nova de Gaia, Port. 41°6' N, 8°39' W 150
Vila Paiva de Andrada, Mozambique 18°40' S, 34°4' E 224
Vila Real, Port. 41°17' N, 7°46' W 150
Vila Real, adm. division, Port. 41°23' N, 7°55' W 150
Vila Real de Santo António, Port. 37°12' N, 7°36' W 214
Vila Vasco da Gama, Mozambique 14°54' S, 32°15' E 224
Vila Velha, Braz. 3°15' N, 51°15' W 130
Vila Velha (Espírito Santo), Braz. 20°25' S, 40°21' W 138
Vilafranca del Penedès, Sp. 41°20' N, 1°41' E 164
Viļaka, Latv. 57°10' N, 27°37' E 166
Vilaller, Sp. 42°26' N, 0°42' E 164
Vilán, Cabo, Sp. 43°10' N, 9°27' W 150
Viļāni, Latv. 56°32' N, 26°56' E 166
Vilanova i la Geltrú, Sp. 41°12' N, 1°43' E 164
Vilar Formoso, Port. 40°36' N, 6°52' W 150
Vilcabamba, Cordillera, Peru 12°60' S, 73°16' W 130
Vilcabamba, ruin(s), Peru 13°7' S, 73°25' W 137
Vileyka, Belarus 54°30' N, 26°54' E 166
Vil'gort, Russ. 60°35' N, 56°25' E 154
Vil'gort, Russ. 61°37' N, 50°49' E 154
Vilhelmina, Nor. 64°37' N, 16°38' E 152
Vilhena, Braz. 12°42' S, 60°9' W 130
Viliya, Ukr. 50°11' N, 26°17' E 152
Viliya, river, Belarus 54°49' N, 25°58' E 166
Viljandi, Est. 58°20' N, 25°33' E 166
Vilkaviškis, Lith. 54°40' N, 23°1' E 166
Vil'kitskogo, Proliv 76°58' N, 84°44' E 172
Villa Abecia, Bol. 20°60' S, 65°24' W 137
Villa Ahumada, Mex. 30°36' N, 106°32' W 92
Villa Alberdi, Arg. 27°35' S, 65°37' W 134
Villa Ana, Arg. 28°28' S, 59°37' W 139
Villa Ángela, Arg. 27°34' S, 60°43' W 139
Villa Bella, Bol. 10°29' S, 65°24' W 137
Villa Bens see Tarfaya, Mor. 27°55' N, 12°54' W 214
Villa Berthet, Arg. 27°16' S, 60°25' W 139
Villa Cañás, Arg. 34°1' S, 61°37' W 139
Villa Clara, adm. division, Cuba 22°39' N, 80°15' W 116
Villa Clara, island, Cuba 23°7' N, 80°39' W 116
Villa Constitución, Arg. 33°16' S, 60°19' W 139
Villa Cuauhtémoc, Mex. 22°9' N, 97°49' W 114
Villa de Cos, Mex. 23°17' N, 102°21' W 114
Villa de Guadalupe, Mex. 23°20' N, 100°46' W 114
Villa de Hidalgo, Mex. 22°24' N, 100°41' W 114
Villa de María, Arg. 29°54' S, 63°42' W 139
Villa de San Antonio, Hond. 14°20' N, 87°36' W 115
Villa del Río, Sp. 37°59' N, 4°19' W 164
Villa del Rosario, Arg. 31°37' S, 63°32' W 139
Villa Dolores, Arg. 31°56' S, 65°9' W 134
Villa Elisa, Arg. 32°9' S, 58°23' W 139
Villa Escobedo, Mex. 27°1' N, 105°47' W 112
Villa Florida, Parag. 26°26' S, 57°6' W 139
Villa Grove, Ill., U.S. 39°52' N, 88°11' W 102
Villa Guerrero, Mex. 21°57' N, 103°35' W 114
Villa Guillermina, Arg. 28°13' S, 59°29' W 139
Villa Hayes, Parag. 25°5' S, 57°33' W 132
Villa Hernandarias, Arg. 31°15' S, 59°58' W 139
Villa Hidalgo, Mex. 26°14' N, 104°54' W 114
Villa Ingavi (Caiza), Bol. 21°47' S, 63°33' W 137
Villa Iris, Arg. 38°12' S, 63°13' W 139
Villa Jesus María, Mex. 28°11' N, 114°3' W 92
Villa Juan José Pérez, Bol. 15°16' S, 69°4' W 137
Villa Juárez, Mex. 22°18' N, 100°16' W 114
Villa Mainero, Mex. 24°33' N, 99°38' W 114
Villa María, Arg. 32°25' S, 63°14' W 139
Villa Martín, Bol. 20°47' S, 67°41' W 137
Villa Minetti, Arg. 28°37' S, 61°39' W 139
Villa Nueva, Arg. 32°29' S, 63°15' W 139
Villa Ocampo, Arg. 28°28' S, 59°22' W 139
Villa Ocampo, Mex. 26°26' N, 105°30' W 114
Villa O'Higgins, Chile 48°28' S, 72°38' W 134
Villa Ojo de Agua, Arg. 29°27' S, 63°45' W 139
Villa Oliva, Parag. 25°60' S, 57°50' W 139
Villa Opicina, It. 45°41' N, 13°46' E 156
Villa Orestes Pereyra, Mex. 26°28' N, 105°40' W 114
Villa Pesqueira, Mex. 29°6' N, 109°57' W 92
Villa Ramírez, Arg. 32°10' S, 60°12' W 139
Villa Regina, Arg. 39°7' S, 67°7' W 134
Villa San José, Arg. 32°12' S, 58°12' W 139
Villa Serrano, Bol. 19°5' S, 64°25' W 137
Villa Talavera, Bol. 19°48' S, 65°23' W 137
Villa Tunari, Bol. 16°60' S, 65°28' W 137
Villa Unión, Arg. 29°25' S, 62°47' W 139
Villa Unión, Arg. 29°18' S, 68°12' W 134
Villa Unión, Mex. 23°10' N, 106°14' W 114
Villa Unión, Mex. 23°58' N, 104°3' W 114
Villa Unión, Mex. 28°12' N, 100°45' W 92
Villa Vaca Guzmán, Bol. 19°57' S, 63°48' W 137
Villacañas, Sp. 39°37' N, 3°20' W 164
Villacarrillo, Sp. 38°6' N, 3°5' W 164
Villach, Aust. 46°36' N, 13°50' E 156
Villada, Sp. 42°14' N, 4°58' W 150
Villadossola, It. 46°3' N, 8°14' E 167
Villafeliche, Sp. 41°12' N, 1°30' W 164
Villafranca, Sp. 42°16' N, 1°45' W 164
Villafranca de los Barros, Sp. 38°34' N, 6°20' W 164
Villafranca del Cid, Sp. 40°25' N, 0°17' E 164
Villafranca di Verona, It. 45°21' N, 10°51' E 167
Villagrán, Mex. 24°28' N, 99°30' W 114
Villaguay, Arg. 31°51' S, 59°1' W 139
Villaharta, Sp. 38°7' N, 4°55' W 164
Villahermosa, Mex. 17°56' N, 93°2' W 115
Villahermosa, Sp. 38°45' N, 2°52' W 164
Villajoyosa (La Villa Joiosa), Sp. 38°29' N, 0°14' E 164
Villaldama, Mex. 26°29' N, 100°27' W 114
Villalonga, Arg. 39°54' S, 62°36' W 139
Villamartín, Sp. 36°52' N, 5°39' W 164
Villamontes, Bol. 21°15' S, 63°33' W 137
Villanueva, Mex. 22°21' N, 102°54' W 114
Villanueva, N. Mex., U.S. 35°16' N, 105°22' W 92
Villanueva de Castellón, Sp. 39°4' N, 0°31' E 164
Villanueva de la Concepción, Sp. 36°55' N, 4°33' W 164
Villanueva de la Jara, Sp. 39°26' N, 1°58' W 164
Villanueva de la Serena, Sp. 38°58' N, 5°48' W 164
Villanueva de los Infantes, Sp. 38°44' N, 3°2' W 164
Villanueva del Arzobispo, Sp. 38°10' N, 2°60' W 164
Villanueva del Duque, Sp. 38°23' N, 5°1' W 164
Villanueva del Río y Minas, Sp. 37°39' N, 5°43' W 164
Villány, Hung. 45°52' N, 18°27' E 168
Villapalacios, Sp. 38°34' N, 2°38' W 164
Villaputzu, It. 39°27' N, 9°35' E 156
Villaquejida, Sp. 42°8' N, 5°36' W 150
Villar del Rey, Sp. 39°8' N, 6°51' W 164
Villarcayo, Sp. 42°55' N, 3°34' W 164
Villarino, Punta, Arg. 40°60' S, 64°58' W 134
Villarrica, Parag. 25°45' S, 56°27' W 132
Villarrica National Park, Chile 39°24' S, 72°10' W 134
Villarrobledo, Sp. 39°15' N, 2°37' W 164
Villarroya de la Sierra, Sp. 41°28' N, 1°48' W 164
Villasayas, Sp. 41°20' N, 2°37' W 164
Villavicencio, Col. 4°8' N, 73°40' W 136
Villaviciosa de Córdoba, Sp. 38°4' N, 5°1' W 164
Villavieja, Col. 3°13' N, 75°13' W 136
Villazón, Bol. 22°7' S, 65°39' W 137
Villé, Fr. 48°19' N, 7°17' E 163
Ville Platte, La., U.S. 30°40' N, 92°17' W 103
Villebon, Lac, lake, Can. 47°54' N, 77°50' W 94
Villefranche, Fr. 45°59' N, 4°43' E 150
Villefranche, Fr. 47°17' N, 1°46' E 150
Villefranche-de-Lauragais, Fr. 43°23' N, 1°43' E 164
Villel, Sp. 40°13' N, 1°13' W 164
Villemaur, Fr. 48°15' N, 3°45' E 163
Villena, Sp. 38°37' N, 0°53' E 164
Villenauxe, Fr. 48°35' N, 3°32' E 163
Villeneuve-Saint-Georges, Fr. 48°43' N, 2°26' E 163
Villers-Bretonneux, Fr. 49°52' N, 2°30' E 163
Villerupt, Fr. 49°27' N, 5°55' E 163
Villiers, S. Af. 27°7' S, 28°36' E 227
Villisca, Iowa, U.S. 40°56' N, 94°59' W 94
Villupuram, India 11°56' N, 79°30' E 188
Vilna, Can. 54°6' N, 111°56' W 108
Vilnius, Lith. 54°38' N, 25°12' E 166
Vilppula, Fin. 62°1' N, 24°25' E 166
Vilsandi Saar, island, Est. 58°23' N, 21°35' E 166
Vilshofen, Ger. 48°37' N, 13°11' E 152
Vilusi, Europe 42°42' N, 18°35' E 168
Vilvoorde, Belg. 50°55' N, 4°26' E 167
Vilyuy, river, Russ. 62°48' N, 120°41' E 172
Vilyuy, river, Russ. 64°45' N, 108°36' E 160
Vilyuy, river, Russ. 63°0' N, 115°4' E 160
Vilyuysk, Russ. 63°38' N, 121°30' E 160
Vilyuyskoye Plato, Russ. 66°22' N, 99°40' E 172
Vilyuyskoye Vodokhranilishche, lake, Russ. 63°5' N, 101°50' E 172
Vimioso, Port. 41°34' N, 6°32' W 150
Vimpeli, Fin. 63°9' N, 23°46' E 152
Vina, Calif., U.S. 39°56' N, 122°4' W 90
Vina, Serb. and Mont. 43°37' N, 22°8' E 168
Vinalhaven, Me., U.S. 44°2' N, 68°50' W 94
Vinaròs, Sp. 40°27' N, 0°27' E 150
Vinça, Fr. 42°39' N, 2°29' E 164
Vincennes, Ind., U.S. 38°40' N, 87°31' W 102
Vincent Lake, lake, Can. 50°34' N, 91°27' W 110
Vinchina, Arg. 28°46' S, 68°14' W 134
Vindeln, Nor. 64°11' N, 19°43' E 152
Vindrey, Russ. 54°15' N, 43°0' E 154
Vinegar Hill, peak, Oreg., U.S. 44°41' N, 118°39' W 90
Vineta, Namibia 22°34' S, 14°30' E 220
Vineyard Sound 41°24' N, 70°48' W 104
Vinga, Rom. 46°1' N, 21°12' E 168
Vinh, Vietnam 18°42' N, 105°38' E 202
Vinh Chau, Vietnam 9°21' N, 105°59' E 202
Vinh Long, Vietnam 10°13' N, 105°57' E 202
Vinica, Maced. 41°53' N, 22°30' E 168
Vinita, Okla., U.S. 36°37' N, 95°10' W 96
Vinje, Nor. 59°38' N, 7°51' E 152
Vinjeøra, Nor. 63°12' N, 8°58' E 152
Vînju Mare, Rom. 44°25' N, 22°53' E 168
Vinkovci, Croatia 45°16' N, 18°46' E 168
Vinnytsya, Ukr. 49°12' N, 28°37' E 152
Vinson Massif, peak, Antarctica 78°33' S, 86°54' W 248
Vinton, Iowa, U.S. 42°9' N, 92°2' W 110
Vinton, La., U.S. 30°11' N, 93°36' W 103
Violet Grove, Can. 53°8' N, 115°4' W 108
Vipiteno, It. 46°54' N, 11°25' E 167
Vir, Taj. 37°42' N, 72°11' E 197
Virac, Philippines 13°33' N, 124°13' E 203
Virachei, Cambodia 14°0' N, 106°46' E 202
Virachey National Park, Cambodia 14°12' N, 106°23' E 202
Viramgam, India 23°5' N, 72°3' E 186
Virandozero, Russ. 64°1' N, 36°7' E 154
Viranşehir, Turk. 37°12' N, 39°46' E 195
Virbalis, Lith. 54°38' N, 22°48' E 166
Virden, Can. 49°51' N, 100°57' W 90
Virden, Ill., U.S. 39°29' N, 89°46' W 102
Virden, Mo., U.S. 39°29' N, 89°46' W 94
Vire, Fr. 48°50' N, 0°54' E 150
Vireši, Latv. 57°27' N, 26°21' E 166
Vîrfurile, Rom. 46°18' N, 22°33' E 168
Virgem da Lapa, Braz. 16°48' S, 42°23' W 138
Virgin Gorda, island, U.K. 18°28' N, 64°26' W 118
Virgin Islands, Caribbean Sea 18°4' N, 64°50' W 118
Virgin Islands, adm. division, U.S. 18°20' N, 64°50' W 118
Virgin Mountains, Nev., U.S. 36°39' N, 114°12' W 101
Virgin, river, Can. 57°0' N, 108°9' W 108
Virgin, river, Nev., U.S. 36°39' N, 114°20' W 101
Virginia, Minn., U.S. 47°31' N, 92°35' W 82
Virginia, S. Af. 28°11' S, 26°51' E 227
Virginia, adm. division, Va., U.S. 37°56' N, 79°15' W 94
Virginia Beach, Va., U.S. 36°50' N, 75°60' W 96
Virginia Falls, Can. 61°52' N, 128°14' W 98
Virgolândia, Braz. 18°29' S, 42°18' W 138
Virje, Croatia 46°3' N, 16°58' E 168
Virmutjoki, Fin. 61°20' N, 28°44' E 166
Virojoki, Fin. 60°34' N, 27°40' E 166
Virolahti, Fin. 60°30' N, 27°40' E 166
Virovitica, Croatia 45°49' N, 17°24' E 168
Virpazar, Europe 42°15' N, 19°5' E 168
Virrat, Fin. 62°12' N, 23°43' E 154
Vîrşolţ, Rom. 47°12' N, 22°55' E 168
Virtaniemi, Russ. 68°53' N, 28°27' E 152
Virton, Belg. 49°34' N, 5°32' E 163
Virtsu, Est. 58°33' N, 23°30' E 166
Virú, Peru 8°28' S, 78°46' W 130
Viru Roela, Est. 59°9' N, 26°35' E 166
Viru-Jaagupi, Est. 59°14' N, 26°27' E 166
Virunga, Dem. Rep. of the Congo 1°1' S, 29°0' E 224
Virunga National Park, Dem. Rep. of the Congo 0°40' N, 29°47' E 224
Vis, Croatia 43°2' N, 16°10' E 168
Vis (Lissa), island, Croatia 42°57' N, 16°5' E 168
Visaginas, Lith. 55°34' N, 26°23' E 166
Visalia, Calif., U.S. 36°20' N, 119°18' W 100
Visayan Sea 11°27' N, 123°36' E 203
Visbek, Ger. 52°50' N, 8°19' E 163
Visby, Sw. 57°37' N, 18°17' E 166
Visconde do Rio Branco, Braz. 2°54' S, 69°39' W 136
Viscount Melville Sound 74°17' N, 105°54' W 255
Visé, Belg. 50°44' N, 5°42' E 167
Višegrad, Bosn. and Herzg. 43°47' N, 19°18' E 168
Visegrád, Hung. 47°46' N, 18°59' E 168
Viseu, Braz. 1°13' S, 46°10' W 130
Viseu, Port. 40°39' N, 7°56' W 150
Viseu, adm. division, Port. 40°41' N, 8°16' W 150
Vishakhapatnam, India 17°44' N, 83°18' E 188
Vishera, river, Russ. 61°4' N, 58°44' E 154
Viški, Latv. 56°1' N, 26°46' E 166
Vislanda, Nor. 56°46' N, 14°25' E 152
Viso del Marqués, Sp. 38°30' N, 3°34' W 164
Viso, Monte, peak, It. 44°39' N, 7°4' E 165
Visoko, Bosn. and Herzg. 43°58' N, 18°9' E 168
Visp, Switz. 46°17' N, 7°53' E 167
Vista, Calif., U.S. 33°12' N, 117°16' W 101
Vista Alegre, Braz. 4°21' S, 56°17' W 130
Vista Alegre, Braz. 6°18' S, 68°10' W 130
Vista Alegre, Braz. 1°27' N, 68°14' W 136
Vista, Cerro, peak, N. Mex., U.S. 36°13' N, 105°29' W 92
Vital Lake, lake, Can. 61°31' N, 108°33' W 108
Vitån, river, Nor. 66°17' N, 21°49' E 152
Viterbo, It. 42°25' N, 12°5' E 214
Viti Levu, island, Fiji Islands 17°50' S, 178°0' E 242
Vitichi, Bol. 20°16' S, 65°29' W 137
Vitim, Russ. 59°27' N, 112°22' E 160
Vitim, river, Russ. 53°53' N, 114°38' E 190
Vitina, Bosn. and Herzg. 43°13' N, 17°29' E 168
Vitomirica, Europe 42°41' N, 20°20' E 168
Vitor, Chile 18°48' S, 70°22' W 137
Vitor, Peru 16°29' S, 71°48' W 137
Vitória, Braz. 20°17' S, 40°18' W 138
Vitória, Braz. 2°56' S, 52°3' W 130
Vitória da Conquista, Braz. 14°52' S, 40°52' W 138
Vitória Seamount, South Atlantic Ocean 20°20' S, 36°60' W 253
Vitoria-Gasteiz, Sp. 42°50' N, 2°41' W 164
Vitorog, peak, Bosn. and Herzg. 44°6' N, 17°2' E 168
Vitry-le-François, Fr. 48°43' N, 4°35' E 163
Vitsyebsk, Belarus 55°12' N, 30°20' E 152
Vittangi, Nor. 67°40' N, 21°37' E 152
Vittel, Fr. 48°12' N, 5°58' E 163
Vittoria, It. 36°57' N, 14°31' E 156
Vittorio Veneto, It. 45°58' N, 12°16' E 167
Vitvattnet, Nor. 66°3' N, 23°9' E 152
Vityaz Trench, South Pacific Ocean 11°20' S, 174°17' E 252
Viveiro, Sp. 43°36' N, 7°38' W 214
Viver, Sp. 39°55' N, 0°36' E 164
Vivi, Ozero, lake, Russ. 66°19' N, 92°55' E 169
Vivi, river, Russ. 65°5' N, 96°4' E 169
Vivian, La., U.S. 32°51' N, 93°59' W 103
Vivoratá, Arg. 37°41' S, 57°42' W 139
Vizcachas, Meseta de las, Arg. 50°35' S, 73°58' W 134
Vizcaíno, Cape, Calif., U.S. 39°45' N, 124°16' W 90
Vizcaíno, Desierto de, Mex. 27°41' N, 113°54' W 112
Vizcaíno, Sierra, Mex. 27°31' N, 114°24' W 112
Vize, Turk. 41°34' N, 27°45' E 156
Vizhas, Russ. 66°38' N, 45°50' E 154
Vizhay, Russ. 61°14' N, 60°13' E 154
Vizhevo, Russ. 64°41' N, 43°55' E 154
Vizianagaram, India 18°5' N, 83°24' E 188
Vizinga, Russ. 61°6' N, 50°6' E 154
Vlădeasa, peak, Rom. 46°44' N, 22°46' E 168
Vladičin Han, Serb. and Mont. 42°42' N, 22°3' E 168
Vladikavkaz, Russ. 43°0' N, 44°44' E 195
Vladimir, Russ. 56°9' N, 40°19' E 154
Vladimir, adm. division, Russ. 56°2' N, 39°15' E 154
Vladimirci, Serb. and Mont. 44°35' N, 19°46' E 168
Vladimirovac, Serb. and Mont. 45°1' N, 20°52' E 168
Vladimirovka, Russ. 60°48' N, 30°28' E 166
Vladimirskiy Tupik, Russ. 55°40' N, 33°25' E 154
Vladivostok, Russ. 43°8' N, 131°54' E 200
Vlasenica, Bosn. and Herzg. 44°11' N, 18°55' E 168
Vlašić, Bosn. and Herzg. 44°18' N, 17°21' E 168
Vlasinje, Bosn. and Herzg. 44°26' N, 17°12' E 168
Vlaški Drenovac, Europe 42°27' N, 20°38' E 168
Vlasotince, Serb. and Mont. 42°57' N, 22°7' E 168
Vlčany, Slovakia 48°0' N, 17°57' E 168
Vlieland, island, Neth. 53°18' N, 4°49' E 163
Vlissingen (Flushing), Neth. 51°27' N, 3°34' E 163
Vltava, river, Czech Rep. 49°29' N, 14°4' E 152
Vobkent, Uzb. 40°1' N, 64°33' E 197
Voćin, Croatia 45°37' N, 17°31' E 168
Voden, Bulg. 42°4' N, 26°54' E 156
Vodil, Uzb. 40°9' N, 71°44' E 197
Vodl Ozero, lake, Russ. 62°16' N, 36°18' E 154
Vodnyy, Russ. 63°31' N, 53°28' E 154
Voerde, Ger. 51°36' N, 6°40' E 167
Vogan, Togo 6°21' N, 1°30' E 222
Vogelsberg, Ger. 50°40' N, 8°44' E 167
Voghera, It. 44°58' N, 9°0' E 167
Võhandu, river, Est. 57°46' N, 27°7' E 166
Vohipeno, Madagascar 22°21' S, 47°53' E 220
Võhma, Est. 58°36' N, 25°32' E 166
Võhma, Est. 58°31' N, 22°20' E 166
Vöhringen, Ger. 48°16' N, 10°4' E 152
Voi, Kenya 3°23' S, 38°35' E 224
Void-Vacon, Fr. 48°41' N, 5°36' E 163
Voikoski, Fin. 61°14' N, 26°47' E 166
Vóïo, Óros, peak, Gr. 40°16' N, 20°59' E 156
Voislova, Rom. 45°31' N, 22°27' E 168
Voiteg, Rom. 45°28' N, 21°14' E 156
Vojmån, Nor. 64°47' N, 16°48' E 152
Vojmsjön, lake, Nor. 64°51' N, 16°2' E 152
Vojvodina, region, Serb. and Mont. 45°21' N, 19°4' E 168
Voknavolok, Russ. 64°56' N, 30°33' E 152
Voláda, Gr. 35°32' N, 27°11' E 156
Volán Domuyo, peak, Arg. 36°44' S, 70°47' W 122
Volborg, Mont., U.S. 45°49' N, 105°40' W 90
Volcán, Arg. 23°54' S, 65°29' W 132
Volcán Isluga National Park, Chile 19°20' S, 69°19' W 122
Volcán Masaya National Park, Nicar. 11°56' N, 86°13' W 115
Volcán Nevado de Colima National Park, Mex. 19°27' N, 103°57' W 72
Volcán Poás National Park, C.R. 10°11' N, 84°19' W 115
Volcano Islands (Kazan Rettō), islands, Philippine Sea 23°11' N, 139°38' E 190
Volcano Peak, Calif., U.S. 35°57' N, 117°53' W 101
Volchansk, Russ. 59°57' N, 60°3' E 154
Voldi, Est. 58°32' N, 26°35' E 166
Vol'dino, Russ. 62°15' N, 54°8' E 154
Volga, Russ. 57°57' N, 38°22' E 154
Volga, S. Dak., U.S. 44°17' N, 96°57' W 90
Volga, river, Russ. 55°48' N, 44°12' E 160
Volga-Don Canal, Russ. 48°33' N, 43°47' E 158
Volgodonsk, Russ. 47°30' N, 42°2' E 158
Volgograd, adm. division, Russ. 49°28' N, 42°54' E 158
Volgograd (Stalingrad), Russ. 48°46' N, 44°28' E 158
Volgogradskoye Vodokhranilishche, lake, Russ. 50°16' N, 45°9' E 158
Volgorechensk, Russ. 57°27' N, 41°16' E 154
Volimes, Gr. 37°52' N, 20°39' E 156
Volintiri, Mold. 46°26' N, 29°35' E 156
Volkach, Ger. 49°51' N, 10°13' E 167
Volkhov, Russ. 59°55' N, 32°25' E 154
Volkhov, river, Russ. 58°34' N, 31°39' E 154
Volksrust, S. Af. 27°22' S, 29°50' E 227
Vollenhove, Neth. 52°40' N, 5°58' E 163
Volma, Belarus 53°52' N, 26°57' E 166
Volnovakha, Ukr. 47°36' N, 37°29' E 156
Volochanka, Russ. 71°2' N, 94°36' E 160
Volochys'k, Ukr. 49°30' N, 26°11' E 152
Volodarsk, Russ. 56°13' N, 43°11' E 154
Volodskaya, Russ. 62°22' N, 41°56' E 154
Vologda, Russ. 59°10' N, 39°48' E 154
Vologda, adm. division, Russ. 59°52' N, 39°27' E 154
Voloki, Belarus 54°35' N, 28°11' E 166
Volokonovka, Russ. 50°29' N, 37°51' E 158
Volonga, Russ. 67°3' N, 47°52' E 169
Vólos, Gr. 39°24' N, 22°55' E 180
Voloshka, Russ. 61°19' N, 40°2' E 154
Voloshovo, Russ. 58°42' N, 29°17' E 166
Volosovo, Russ. 59°26' N, 29°28' E 166
Volovo, Russ. 53°32' N, 38°0' E 154
Voloyarvi, Russ. 60°17' N, 30°46' E 166
Vol'sk, Russ. 52°5' N, 47°22' E 158
Volta, Calif., U.S. 37°5' N, 120°56' W 100
Volta, Lake, Ghana 8°15' N, 1°21' W 214
Volta Redonda, Braz. 22°27' S, 44°6' W 138
Volterra, It. 43°24' N, 10°50' E 156
Volubilis, ruin(s), Mor. 34°6' N, 5°46' W 214
Voluntown, Conn., U.S. 41°34' N, 71°52' W 104
Volzhsk, Russ. 55°52' N, 48°25' E 154
Volzhskiy, Russ. 48°49' N, 44°50' E 184
Vonavona, island, Solomon Islands 8°17' S, 157°0' E 242
Vonda, Can. 52°19' N, 106°5' W 108
Vondrozo, Madagascar 22°49' S, 47°19' E 220
Võnnu, Est. 58°16' N, 27°3' E 166
Voo, Kenya 1°41' S, 38°20' E 224
Voranava, Belarus 54°8' N, 25°18' E 166
Vorder-rhein, river, Switz. 46°40' N, 8°52' E 167
Vordingborg, Den. 55°0' N, 11°55' E 152
Vóreio Egéo, adm. division, Gr. 38°45' N, 26°0' E 156
Vorga, Russ. 53°42' N, 32°45' E 154

Vóries Sporádes, islands, Aegean Sea 39°8' N, 23°37' E 180
Voring Plateau, Norwegian Sea 67°13' N, 4°23' E 255
Vorkuta, Russ. 67°25' N, 64°4' E 169
Vorlich, Ben, peak, U.K. 56°20' N, 4°20' W 150
Vormsi, island, Est. 59°3' N, 23°1' E 166
Vorogovo, Russ. 60°57' N, 89°25' E 169
Vorona, river, Russ. 52°8' N, 42°26' E 158
Voronech', Belarus 55°18' N, 28°35' E 166
Voronezh, Russ. 51°38' N, 39°11' E 158
Voronezh, adm. division, Russ. 50°50' N, 38°58' E 158
Voronezh, river, Russ. 52°21' N, 39°31' E 158
Vorontsovka, Russ. 59°37' N, 60°12' E 154
Vorontsovo, Russ. 57°18' N, 28°42' E 166
Vorontsovo, Russ. 71°40' N, 83°35' E 160
Voron'ye, Russ. 68°28' N, 35°20' E 152
Vorposten Peak, Antarctica 71°31' S, 14°56' E 248
Vorskla, river, Ukr. 49°36' N, 34°40' E 158
Vørterkaka Nunatak, peak, Antarctica 72°42' S, 27°23' E 248
Võrts Järv, lake, Est. 58°19' N, 25°43' E 166
Võru, Est. 57°49' N, 27°0' E 166
Vorukh, Taj. 39°50' N, 70°34' E 197
Vosburg, S. Af. 30°35' S, 22°49' E 227
Vose, Taj. 37°46' N, 69°41' E 197
Vosges, Fr. 48°57' N, 6°56' E 163
Voskresensk, Russ. 55°19' N, 38°43' E 154
Voskresenskoye, Russ. 56°48' N, 45°28' E 154
Voskresenskoye, Russ. 59°25' N, 37°56' E 154
Voskresenskoye, Russ. 53°8' N, 56°4' E 154
Voss, Nor. 60°37' N, 6°22' E 152
Vostochnaya Guba, Russ. 67°24' N, 32°38' E 152
Vostok, Russia, station, Antarctica 78°31' S, 107°1' E 248
Võsu, Est. 59°33' N, 25°56' E 166
Votaw, Tex., U.S. 30°24' N, 94°41' W 103
Votice, Czech Rep. 49°38' N, 14°37' E 152
Votkinsk, Russ. 57°0' N, 53°55' E 154
Votuporanga, Braz. 20°25' S, 49°59' W 138
Voulgára, peak, Gr. 39°5' N, 21°50' E 156
Voulx, Fr. 48°14' N, 2°59' E 163
Vounása, peak, Gr. 39°56' N, 21°41' E 156
Voúrnios, Óros, Gr. 40°3' N, 21°16' E 156
Vouziers, Fr. 49°23' N, 4°43' E 163
Vovchans'k, Ukr. 50°16' N, 36°57' E 158
Voves, Fr. 48°15' N, 1°38' E 163
Vovodo, river, Cen. Af. Rep. 5°59' N, 24°33' E 218
Vowchyn, Belarus 52°17' N, 23°17' E 152
Voyageurs National Park, Minn., U.S. 48°14' N, 94°58' W 94
Voynitsa, Russ. 65°9' N, 30°18' E 152
Voyvozh, Russ. 62°54' N, 55°5' E 154
Vozhayel', Russ. 62°50' N, 51°22' E 154
Vozhe, Ozero, lake, Russ. 60°35' N, 38°36' E 154
Vozhega, Russ. 60°27' N, 40°10' E 154
Vozhgora, Russ. 64°34' N, 48°21' E 154
Vozhma, Russ. 58°55' N, 46°47' E 154
Vozh'yel', Russ. 63°14' N, 49°37' E 154
Voznesens'k, Ukr. 47°36' N, 31°21' E 156
Voznesen'ye, Russ. 61°1' N, 35°30' E 154
Vozvyahenka, Kaz. 54°28' N, 70°52' E 184
Vrachionas, peak, Gr. 37°49' N, 20°39' E 156
Vrancea, adm. division, Rom. 45°41' N, 26°29' E 156
Vrancei, Munţii, Rom. 45°49' N, 25°55' E 156
Vrang, Taj. 37°1' N, 72°22' E 186
Vrangelya, Ostrov (Wrangel Island), island, Russ. 71°29' N, 175°23' E 160
Vranica, peak, Bosn. and Herzg. 43°56' N, 17°40' E 168
Vranje, Serb. and Mont. 42°33' N, 21°54' E 168
Vranjska Banja, Serb. and Mont. 42°32' N, 22°1' E 168
Vratsa, Bulg. 43°12' N, 23°33' E 156
Vratsa, adm. division, Bulg. 43°18' N, 23°27' E 156
Vrbanja, Croatia 44°58' N, 18°55' E 168
Vrbas, Serb. and Mont. 45°33' N, 19°38' E 168
Vrbnik, Croatia 44°0' N, 16°9' E 168
Vrbnik, Croatia 45°4' N, 14°39' E 156
Vrboska, Croatia 43°9' N, 16°40' E 156
Vrbovec, Croatia 45°53' N, 16°25' E 168
Vrčin, Serb. and Mont. 44°40' N, 20°33' E 168
Vrdnik, Serb. and Mont. 45°7' N, 19°47' E 168
Vrede, S. Af. 27°27' S, 29°8' E 227
Vreden, Ger. 52°2' N, 6°49' E 167
Vredenburg, S. Af. 32°55' S, 17°58' E 227
Vrginmost, Croatia 45°20' N, 15°52' E 168
Vrgorac, Croatia 43°11' N, 17°22' E 168
Vrlika, Croatia 43°55' N, 16°24' E 168
Vrnograč, Bosn. and Herzg. 45°9' N, 15°57' E 168
Vršac, Serb. and Mont. 45°7' N, 21°18' E 168
Vrtoče, Bosn. and Herzg. 44°38' N, 16°10' E 168
Vryburg, S. Af. 26°59' S, 24°42' E 227
Vryheid, S. Af. 27°48' S, 30°45' E 227
Vsevolodo Blagodatskiy, Russ. 60°28' N, 59°59' E 154
Vsheli, Russ. 58°10' N, 29°50' E 166
Vu Liet, Vietnam 18°42' N, 105°22' E 202
Vučitrn, Europe 42°49' N, 20°58' E 168
Vučja Luka, Bosn. and Herzg. 43°55' N, 18°31' E 168
Vučje, Serb. and Mont. 42°51' N, 21°54' E 168
Vught, Neth. 51°38' N, 5°17' E 167
Vuka, river, Croatia 45°27' N, 18°32' E 168
Vuktyl, Russ. 63°54' N, 57°28' E 154
Vulcan, Can. 50°24' N, 113°16' W 90
Vulcan, Rom. 45°22' N, 23°18' E 168
Vulci, ruin(s), It. 42°23' N, 11°31' E 156
Vung Tau, Vietnam 10°21' N, 107°4' E 202
Vuntut National Park, Can. 68°11' N, 139°49' W 98
Vuoggatjålme, Nor. 66°33' N, 16°21' E 152
Vuohijärvi, Fin. 61°4' N, 26°47' E 166
Vuohijärvi, lake, Fin. 61°7' N, 26°20' E 166
Vuokatti, Fin. 64°7' N, 28°13' E 152
Vuollerim, Nor. 66°25' N, 20°36' E 152
Vuonislahti, Fin. 63°8' N, 29°59' E 152
Vuotso, Fin. 68°5' N, 27°6' E 152
Vurnary, Russ. 55°28' N, 47°1' E 154
Vyartsilya, Russ. 62°10' N, 30°41' E 152
Vyatka, river, Russ. 59°20' N, 52°0' E 154
Vyatskiye Polyany, Russ. 56°11' N, 51°11' E 154
Vyazemskiy, Russ. 47°31' N, 134°46' E 190
Vyaz'ma, Russ. 55°13' N, 34°21' E 154
Vyazniki, Russ. 56°14' N, 42°9' E 154
Vybor, Russ. 57°13' N, 29°7' E 166
Vyborg (Viipuri), Russ. 60°41' N, 28°45' E 166
Vyborovo, Russ. 58°19' N, 29°0' E 166
Vychegda, river, Russ. 61°31' N, 48°11' E 154
Vyderta, Ukr. 51°43' N, 25°1' E 152
Vyerkhnyadzvinsk, Belarus 55°46' N, 27°56' E 166
Vyetryna, Belarus 55°24' N, 28°26' E 166
Vyg Ozero, lake, Russ. 63°48' N, 33°40' E 152
Vyksa, Russ. 55°18' N, 42°12' E 154
Vylkove, Ukr. 45°26' N, 29°35' E 156
Vylok, Ukr. 48°6' N, 22°50' E 168
Vym', river, Russ. 62°41' N, 50°53' E 154
Vym', river, Russ. 63°22' N, 51°36' E 154
Vymsk, Russ. 60°24' N, 48°19' E 154
Vyritsa, Russ. 59°24' N, 30°17' E 166
Vyshhorod, Ukr. 50°32' N, 30°35' E 158
Vyshniy Volochek, Russ. 57°34' N, 34°38' E 154
Vysočina, adm. division, Czech Rep. 49°10' N, 15°21' E 152
Vysokaye, Belarus 52°21' N, 23°20' E 152
Vysokovsk, Russ. 56°17' N, 36°31' E 154
Vysotsk, Russ. 60°36' N, 28°34' E 166
Vysotskoye, Russ. 56°49' N, 29°1' E 166
Vytegra, Russ. 61°1' N, 36°30' E 154

"W" National Park, Benin 11°49' N, 2°27' E 222
Wa, Ghana 10°2' N, 2°30' W 222
Wa, Pol. 50°45' N, 16°16' E 152
Waajid, Somalia 3°47' N, 43°16' E 218
Waal, river, Neth. 51°54' N, 5°35' E 167
Waalwijk, Neth. 51°41' N, 5°5' E 167
Waas, Mount, peak, Utah, U.S. 38°31' N, 109°19' W 90
Wa'at, Sudan 8°8' N, 32°7' E 224
Wababimiga Lake, Can. 50°18' N, 87°9' W 94
Wabakimi Lake, Can. 50°34' N, 90°20' W 110
Wabana, Can. 47°38' N, 52°56' W 111
Wabasca, river, Can. 56°15' N, 113°42' W 108
Wabasca-Desmarais, Can. 55°59' N, 113°52' W 108
Wabash, Ind., U.S. 40°48' N, 85°50' W 102
Wabash, river, Ind., U.S. 40°48' N, 85°14' W 102
Wabasha, Minn., U.S. 44°21' N, 92°3' W 110
Wabassi, river, Can. 51°46' N, 87°39' W 110
Wabasso, Fla., U.S. 27°44' N, 80°27' W 105
Wabē Gestro, river, Eth. 5°53' N, 41°38' E 224
Wabē Shebelē, river, Eth. 7°25' N, 39°36' E 224
Wabern, Ger. 51°6' N, 9°21' E 167
Wabimeig Lake, Can. 51°26' N, 86°15' W 110
Waboose Dam, Can. 50°51' N, 87°60' W 110
Wabowden, Can. 54°54' N, 98°38' W 108
Wabuk Point, Can. 55°18' N, 87°23' W 106
W.A.C. Bennett Dam, Can. 55°51' N, 123°2' W 108
Waccasassa Bay 29°6' N, 82°54' W 105
Wächtersbach, Ger. 50°15' N, 9°17' E 167
Waco, Can. 51°26' N, 65°36' W 111
Waco, Tex., U.S. 31°31' N, 97°8' W 96
Waconichi, Lac, lake, Can. 50°5' N, 74°39' W 94
Wad Abu Nahl, Sudan 13°6' N, 34°53' E 182
Wad Banda, Sudan 13°4' N, 27°56' E 216
Wad el Haddad, Sudan 13°48' N, 33°30' E 182
Wad Hamid, Sudan 16°27' N, 32°45' E 182
Wad Medani, Sudan 14°23' N, 33°29' E 182
Wadamago, Somalia 8°52' N, 46°15' E 216
Wadayama, Japan 35°19' N, 134°48' E 201
Waddān, Lib. 29°10' N, 16°6' E 216
Waddenzee 53°5' N, 4°54' E 163
Waddington, N.Y., U.S. 44°51' N, 75°13' W 94
Waddington, Mount, peak, Can. 51°22' N, 125°21' W 90
Wadena, Can. 51°56' N, 103°48' W 90
Wadena, Minn., U.S. 46°25' N, 95°9' W 94
Wadersloh, Ger. 51°44' N, 8°14' E 167
Wādī al Masīlah, river, Yemen 16°12' N, 49°33' E 182
Wādī as Sīr, Jordan 31°56' N, 35°48' E 194
Wādī Gimāl, Gezîrat, island, Egypt 24°30' N, 33°51' E 182
Wadi Halfa, Sudan 21°46' N, 31°20' E 182
Wādīas Sir bān, Saudi Arabia 31°38' N, 37°3' E 194
Wadsworth, Nev., U.S. 39°38' N, 119°19' W 90
Wadsworth, Ohio, U.S. 41°0' N, 81°44' W 102
Wadu, island, Maldives 5°44' N, 72°17' E 188
Waelder, Tex., U.S. 29°40' N, 97°18' W 96
Waesche, Mount, peak, Antarctica 77°3' S, 126°15' W 248
Wafangdian, China 39°39' N, 121°59' E 198
Wafania, Dem. Rep. of the Congo 1°23' S, 20°19' E 218
Wafra, oil field, Kuwait 28°34' N, 47°52' E 196
Wagenia Fisheries, site, Dem. Rep. of the Congo 0°25' N, 25°17' E 224
Wageningen, Neth. 51°58' N, 5°39' E 167
Wager Bay 65°25' N, 90°48' W 106
Wager, Isla, island, Chile 47°34' S, 75°43' W 134
Waglisla, Can. 52°10' N, 128°10' W 108
Wagner, S. Dak., U.S. 43°3' N, 98°19' W 90
Wagner Nunatak, peak, Antarctica 83°59' S, 68°23' W 248
Wagon Mound, N. Mex., U.S. 36°0' N, 104°43' W 92
Wagontire Mountain, peak, Oreg., U.S. 43°20' N, 119°58' W 90
Wah Wah Range, Utah, U.S. 38°29' N, 113°52' W 90
Waha, oil field, Lib. 28°2' N, 19°46' E 216
Waha'ula Heiau, site, Hawai'i, U.S. 19°19' N, 155°5' W 99
Wahoo, Nebr., U.S. 41°12' N, 96°38' W 90
Wahpeton, N. Dak., U.S. 46°15' N, 96°38' W 90
Wai, India 17°58' N, 73°55' E 188
Wai'ale'ale, peak, Hawai'i, U.S. 22°4' N, 159°33' W 99
Wāīas Sir'ān, Jordan 31°26' N, 36°56' E 194
Waiau, N.Z. 42°40' S, 173°3' E 240
Waiau, river, N.Z. 45°42' S, 167°34' E 240
Waigeo, island, Indonesia 7°416' N, 130°3' E 192
Waihi, N.Z. 37°23' S, 175°50' E 240
Waihola, N.Z. 46°3' S, 170°7' E 240
Waikabubak, Indonesia 9°39' S, 119°20' E 192
Waikanae, N.Z. 40°54' S, 175°4' E 240
Waikawa, N.Z. 46°38' S, 169°6' E 240
Waikiwi, N.Z. 46°24' S, 168°20' E 240
Waikouaiti, N.Z. 45°35' S, 170°40' E 240
Waimamaku, N.Z. 35°34' S, 173°28' E 240
Waimangaroa, N.Z. 41°45' S, 171°45' E 240
Waimarama, N.Z. 39°49' S, 176°58' E 240
Waimate, N.Z. 44°45' S, 171°2' E 240
Wainfleet All Saints, U.K. 53°7' N, 0°14' E 162
Waingapu, Indonesia 9°41' S, 120°4' E 192
Waini Point, Guyana 8°25' N, 59°51' W 116
Wainwright, Alas., U.S. 70°37' N, 160°3' W 246
Wainwright, Can. 52°50' N, 110°51' W 108
Waiohonu Petroglyphs, site, Hawai'i, U.S. 20°42' N, 156°3' W 99
Wai'oli Mission, site, Hawai'i, U.S. 22°11' N, 159°33' W 99
Waiotira, N.Z. 35°57' S, 174°12' E 240
Waiouru, N.Z. 39°30' S, 175°40' E 240
Waipahi, N.Z. 46°9' S, 169°14' E 240
Waipara, N.Z. 43°4' S, 172°45' E 240
Waipawa, N.Z. 39°58' S, 176°35' E 240
Waipu, N.Z. 35°60' S, 174°26' E 240
Waipukurau, N.Z. 40°1' S, 176°35' E 240
Wairau Valley, N.Z. 41°36' S, 173°31' E 240
Wairoa, N.Z. 39°4' S, 177°23' E 240
Waitahanui, N.Z. 38°48' S, 176°5' E 240
Waitakaruru, N.Z. 37°16' S, 175°24' E 240
Waitara, N.Z. 39°2' S, 174°13' E 240
Waitati, N.Z. 45°46' S, 170°34' E 240
Waite, Cape, Antarctica 72°42' S, 103°44' W 248
Waitemata, N.Z. 36°52' S, 174°37' E 240
Waitoa, N.Z. 37°36' S, 175°39' E 240
Waitomo Caves, site, N.Z. 38°18' S, 175°2' E 240
Waitotara, N.Z. 39°49' S, 174°43' E 240
Wajima, Japan 37°23' N, 136°53' E 201
Wajir, Kenya 1°42' N, 40°2' E 224
Waka, Dem. Rep. of the Congo 0°50' N, 20°3' E 218
Waka, Dem. Rep. of the Congo 0°58' N, 20°13' E 218
Waka, Eth. 7°5' N, 37°18' E 224
Wakami Lake, Can. 47°27' N, 83°25' W 94
Wakasa, Japan 35°18' N, 134°22' E 201
Wakasa Wan 35°32' N, 135°31' E 201
Wakaw, Can. 52°39' N, 105°45' W 108
Wakayama, Japan 34°12' N, 135°10' E 201
Wakayama, adm. division, Japan 34°13' N, 135°16' E 201
Wake Forest, N.C., U.S. 35°58' N, 78°31' W 96
Wake Island, U.S. 19°19' N, 166°31' E 252
Wakeeney, Kans., U.S. 39°0' N, 99°54' W 90
Wakefield, Kans., U.S. 39°11' N, 97°2' W 90
Wakefield, Mich., U.S. 46°28' N, 89°57' W 94
Wakefield, Nebr., U.S. 42°15' N, 96°52' W 94
Wakefield, R.I., U.S. 41°26' N, 71°30' W 104
Wakefield, U.K. 53°41' N, 1°30' W 162
Wakema, Myanmar 16°36' N, 95°9' E 202
Wakenaam Island, Guyana 6°59' N, 58°35' W 130
Wakkanai, Japan 45°18' N, 141°48' E 190
Wakkerstroom, S. Af. 27°20' S, 30°7' E 227
Wakuach, Lac, lake, Can. 55°34' N, 69°29' W 106
Wakulla Springs, site, Fla., U.S. 30°12' N, 84°23' W 96
Walachia, region, Rom. 44°28' N, 22°46' E 168
Walberswick, U.K. 52°18' N, 1°39' E 163
Walcott, Can. 54°30' N, 126°54' W 108
Walcott Inlet 16°45' S, 123°56' E 230
Waldbröl, Ger. 50°52' N, 7°36' E 167
Waldeck, Ger. 51°12' N, 9°4' E 167
Walden, Vt., U.S. 44°26' N, 72°14' W 104
Waldfischbach-Burgalben, Ger. 49°16' N, 7°38' E 163
Waldheim, Can. 52°37' N, 106°39' W 108
Waldo, Ark., U.S. 33°20' N, 93°18' W 103
Waldo, Fla., U.S. 29°47' N, 82°11' W 105
Waldport, Oreg., U.S. 44°23' N, 124°3' W 90
Waldron, Ark., U.S. 34°52' N, 94°6' W 96
Waldron, Ind., U.S. 39°27' N, 85°40' W 102
Waldron, Cape, Antarctica 66°15' S, 119°43' E 248
Wales, Alas., U.S. 65°31' N, 168°7' W 98
Wales, Mass., U.S. 42°3' N, 72°11' W 104
Wales, adm. division, U.K. 52°21' N, 3°52' W 162
Wales Island, island, Can. 67°38' N, 89°20' W 106
Walewale, Ghana 10°21' N, 0°49' E 222
Walgreen Coast, Antarctica 75°29' S, 102°49' W 248
Walhalla, Mich., U.S. 43°56' N, 86°7' W 102
Walhalla, N. Dak., U.S. 48°54' N, 97°56' W 90
Walhalla, S.C., U.S. 34°45' N, 83°5' W 96
Walikale, Dem. Rep. of the Congo 1°30' S, 28°5' E 224
Walker, La., U.S. 30°29' N, 90°52' W 103
Walker, Mich., U.S. 42°59' N, 85°43' W 102
Walker, Minn., U.S. 47°4' N, 94°37' W 90
Walker, Lac, lake, Can. 50°24' N, 67°30' W 111
Walker Lake, Nev., U.S. 38°38' N, 119°38' W 80
Walker Lake, lake, Can. 54°36' N, 97°31' W 108
Walker Pass, Calif., U.S. 35°39' N, 118°3' W 101
Walkerton, Can. 44°7' N, 81°9' W 102
Walkerton, Ind., U.S. 41°28' N, 86°29' W 102
Walkerville, Mich., U.S. 43°42' N, 86°7' W 102
Wall, S. Dak., U.S. 43°59' N, 102°16' W 90
Wall, Mount, peak, Austral. 22°50' S, 116°37' E 230
Walla Walla, Wash., U.S. 46°4' N, 118°22' W 106
Wallabi Group, islands, Indian Ocean 28°15' S, 113°42' E 230
Wallaby Plateau, Indian Ocean 22°32' S, 104°34' E 254
Wallace, Idaho, U.S. 47°26' N, 115°54' W 82
Wallace, Nebr., U.S. 40°50' N, 101°11' W 90
Wallace, N.C., U.S. 34°44' N, 77°60' W 96
Wallace Mountain, peak, Can. 54°55' N, 115°56' W 108
Wallaceburg, Can. 42°34' N, 82°22' W 102
Wallaroo, Austral. 33°55' S, 137°39' E 231
Wallasey, U.K. 53°25' N, 3°2' W 162
Walldorf, Ger. 50°36' N, 10°23' E 167
Wallenhorst, Ger. 52°20' N, 7°59' E 163
Wallingford, Conn., U.S. 41°27' N, 72°50' W 104
Wallingford, Vt., U.S. 43°28' N, 72°59' W 104
Wallis, Îles, islands, South Pacific Ocean 14°55' S, 177°49' W 238
Wallops Island, Va., U.S. 37°25' N, 75°20' W 80
Wallowa Mountains, Oreg., U.S. 45°28' N, 117°49' W 90
Walmer, U.K. 51°12' N, 1°23' E 163
Walnum, Mount, peak, Antarctica 72°8' S, 23°50' E 248
Walnut, Ill., U.S. 41°33' N, 89°36' W 102
Walnut Cove, N.C., U.S. 36°18' N, 80°10' W 94
Walnut Grove, Calif., U.S. 38°13' N, 121°32' W 100
Walnut Grove, Miss., U.S. 32°34' N, 89°28' W 103
Walnut Ridge, Ark., U.S. 36°3' N, 90°58' W 96
Walong, India 28°10' N, 97°0' E 188
Walpi, Ariz., U.S. 35°49' N, 110°24' W 92
Walpole, Mass., U.S. 42°5' N, 71°16' W 104
Walpole, N.H., U.S. 43°4' N, 72°26' W 104
Walsall, U.K. 52°35' N, 1°60' W 162
Walsenburg, Colo., U.S. 37°37' N, 104°48' W 92
Walsh, Colo., U.S. 37°22' N, 102°17' W 92
Walsingham, U.K. 52°53' N, 0°52' E 163
Walt Disney World, Fla., U.S. 28°23' N, 81°34' W 105
Walterboro, S.C., U.S. 32°54' N, 80°41' W 96
Walters Shoal, Indian Ocean 33°25' S, 43°32' E 254
Waltham, Mass., U.S. 42°22' N, 71°15' W 104
Walton, Ind., U.S. 40°39' N, 86°14' W 102
Walton, Ky., U.S. 38°51' N, 84°36' W 102
Walton, N.Y., U.S. 42°10' N, 75°9' W 94
Walton on the Naze, U.K. 51°50' N, 1°15' E 163
Walvis Bay, Namibia 22°60' S, 14°33' E 207
Walvis Ridge, South Atlantic Ocean 26°7' S, 5°31' E 253
Walyahmoning Rock, peak, Austral. 30°41' S, 118°32' E 230
Wamac, Ill., U.S. 38°29' N, 89°8' W 102
Wamba, Dem. Rep. of the Congo 1°37' S, 22°28' E 218
Wamba, Dem. Rep. of the Congo 2°9' N, 27°57' E 218
Wamba, Nig. 8°55' N, 8°35' E 222
Wampú, river, Hond. 15°0' N, 85°36' W 115
Wampusirpi, Hond. 15°11' N, 84°38' W 115
Wamsutter, Wyo., U.S. 41°40' N, 107°58' W 90
Wana, Pak. 32°19' N, 69°40' E 188
Wan'an, China 26°28' N, 114°46' E 198
Wandel Sea 82°11' N, 24°59' W 246
Wandering River, Can. 55°9' N, 112°27' W 108
Wando, S. Korea 34°17' N, 126°47' E 200
Wanfried, Ger. 51°11' N, 10°10' E 167
Wang Kai, Sudan 9°3' N, 29°29' E 224
Wang, river, Thai. 17°37' N, 99°18' E 202
Wanganui, N.Z. 39°57' S, 175°2' E 240
Wangcang, China 32°17' N, 106°21' E 198
Wangda see Zogang, China 29°42' N, 97°53' E 188
Wangdiphodrang, Bhutan 27°30' N, 89°54' E 197
Wangdu, China 38°40' N, 115°6' E 198
Wangkui, China 46°50' N, 126°30' E 198
Wangmo, China 25°10' N, 106°6' E 198
Wangou, China 42°4' N, 126°56' E 200
Wangpan Yang 30°22' N, 120°37' E 198
Wanham, Can. 55°43' N, 118°22' W 108
Wani, India 20°2' N, 78°57' E 188
Wanie Rukula, Dem. Rep. of the Congo 0°12' N, 25°35' E 224
Wankaner, India 22°35' N, 70°56' E 186
Wanning, China 18°48' N, 110°19' E 198
Wanow, Afghan. 32°37' N, 65°55' E 186
Wantage, U.K. 51°35' N, 1°26' W 162
Wantagh, N.Y., U.S. 40°40' N, 73°30' W 104
Wanxian, China 30°47' N, 108°17' E 198
Wanyuan, China 32°5' N, 108°7' E 198
Wanzai, China 28°5' N, 114°27' E 198
Wapakoneta, Ohio, U.S. 40°33' N, 84°11' W 102
Wapata Lake, lake, Can. 58°46' N, 106°16' W 108
Wapawekka Lake, lake, Can. 54°54' N, 105°23' W 108
Wapella, Can. 50°17' N, 101°60' W 90
Wapello, Iowa, U.S. 41°10' N, 91°12' W 110
Wapesi, river, Can. 50°25' N, 92°17' W 110
Wapiti, river, Can. 54°43' N, 119°50' W 108
Wapou, Côte d'Ivoire 4°38' N, 7°12' W 222
Wappingers Falls, N.Y., U.S. 41°35' N, 73°56' W 104
Wapta Icefield, glacier, Can. 51°44' N, 116°60' W 108
Wapusk National Park, Can. 57°35' N, 93°37' W 108
War, W. Va., U.S. 37°18' N, 81°42' W 96
War Galoh, Somalia 6°15' N, 47°36' E 218
Warab, Sudan 8°2' N, 28°35' E 224
Warab, adm. division, Sudan 7°50' N, 28°24' E 224
Warangal, India 17°59' N, 79°33' E 188
Warburg, Ger. 51°29' N, 9°8' E 167
Ward, N.Z. 41°51' S, 174°7' E 240
Ward Cove, Alas., U.S. 55°26' N, 131°46' W 108
Ward Hill, peak 58°52' N, 3°28' W 150
Ward, Mount, peak, Antarctica 71°45' S, 66°36' W 248
Ward Mountain, peak, Nev., U.S. 39°5' N, 114°60' W 90
Warden, S. Af. 27°53' S, 28°55' E 227
Warden, Wash., U.S. 46°56' N, 119°3' W 90
Wardenburg, Ger. 53°4' N, 8°12' E 163
Wardha, India 20°43' N, 78°36' E 188
Ward's Stone, peak, U.K. 54°1' N, 2°40' W 162
Wardsboro, Vt., U.S. 43°2' N, 72°48' W 104
Ware, Can. 57°26' N, 125°37' W 108
Ware, Mass., U.S. 42°15' N, 72°15' W 104
Ware Shoals, S.C., U.S. 34°23' N, 82°16' W 96
Waregem, Belg. 50°53' N, 3°26' E 163
Wareham, Mass., U.S. 41°45' N, 70°45' W 104
Warehouse Point, Conn., U.S. 41°55' N, 72°37' W 104
Waremme, Belg. 50°41' N, 5°14' E 167
Waren, Indonesia 2°27' S, 136°18' E 192
Warendorf, Ger. 51°57' N, 7°59' E 167
Warffum, Neth. 53°23' N, 6°34' E 163
Warka, Pol. 51°47' N, 21°11' E 152
Warkworth, U.K. 55°20' N, 1°37' W 150
Warlubie, Pol. 53°35' N, 18°37' E 152
Warm Springs, Ga., U.S. 32°53' N, 84°41' W 96
Warman, Can. 52°17' N, 106°34' W 108
Warmbad, Namibia 28°28' S, 18°45' E 227
Warmbaths see Bela-Bela, S. Af. 24°55' S, 28°16' E 227
Warmeriville, Fr. 49°21' N, 4°13' E 163
Warmińsko-Mazurskie, adm. division, Pol. 53°57' N, 19°25' E 152
Warminster, U.K. 51°12' N, 2°12' W 162
Warner, Can. 49°16' N, 112°12' W 90
Warner, N.H., U.S. 43°16' N, 71°49' W 104
Warner, Mount, peak, Can. 51°4' N, 123°17' W 90
Warner Mountains, Calif., U.S. 41°1' N, 120°16' W 90
Warner Robins, Ga., U.S. 32°32' N, 83°36' W 112
Warner Valley, Oreg., U.S. 42°48' N, 119°59' W 90
Warnes, Arg. 34°54' S, 60°30' W 139
Warora, India 20°13' N, 79°0' E 188
Warralu, Sudan 8°10' N, 27°17' E 224
Warrego Range, Austral. 25°4' S, 145°24' E 230
Warren, Ark., U.S. 33°35' N, 92°5' W 96
Warren, Ill., U.S. 42°29' N, 89°59' W 102
Warren, Ind., U.S. 40°40' N, 85°25' W 102
Warren, Mich., U.S. 42°30' N, 83°3' W 102
Warren, Minn., U.S. 48°9' N, 96°47' W 90
Warren, Ohio, U.S. 41°13' N, 80°48' W 102
Warren, Oreg., U.S. 45°48' N, 122°52' W 100
Warren, Pa., U.S. 41°51' N, 79°10' W 94
Warren, R.I., U.S. 41°43' N, 71°17' W 104
Warren, Tex., U.S. 30°36' N, 94°24' W 103
Warren, Vt., U.S. 44°6' N, 72°52' W 104
Warren Landing, Can. 53°41' N, 97°56' W 108
Warren Peak, Calif., U.S. 41°21' N, 120°19' W 90
Warren Point, Can. 69°43' N, 134°16' W 98
Warrender, Cape, Can. 74°24' N, 80°17' W 106
Warrensburg, N.Y., U.S. 43°29' N, 73°47' W 104
Warrenton, Ga., U.S. 33°23' N, 82°40' W 96
Warrenton, Oreg., U.S. 46°9' N, 123°55' W 100
Warrenton, S. Af. 28°11' S, 24°50' E 227
Warri, Nig. 5°32' N, 5°42' E 222
Warrington, U.K. 53°23' N, 2°36' W 162
Warrnambool, Austral. 38°21' S, 142°29' E 231
Warroad, Minn., U.S. 48°53' N, 95°22' W 90
Warsaw, Ind., U.S. 41°13' N, 85°51' W 102
Warsaw, Ky., U.S. 38°45' N, 84°54' W 102
Warsaw, N.C., U.S. 34°59' N, 78°6' W 96
Warsaw, Ohio, U.S. 40°20' N, 82°1' W 102
Warsaw see Warszawa, Pol. 52°12' N, 20°50' E 152
Warshiikh, Somalia 2°15' N, 45°53' E 218
Warsop, U.K. 53°12' N, 1°9' W 162
Warstein, Ger. 51°26' N, 8°20' E 167
Warszawa (Warsaw), Pol. 52°12' N, 20°50' E 152
Warton, U.K. 53°44' N, 2°54' W 162
Warwick, Austral. 28°12' S, 152°3' E 231
Warwick, R.I., U.S. 41°41' N, 71°23' W 104
Warwick, U.K. 52°16' N, 1°36' W 162
Wasagu, Nig. 11°20' N, 5°51' E 222
Wasam, Pak. 36°32' N, 72°53' E 186
Wasatch Range, Utah, U.S. 39°56' N, 111°51' W 90
Wasco, Calif., U.S. 35°36' N, 119°21' W 100
Wasco, Oreg., U.S. 45°34' N, 120°43' W 90
Wase, Nig. 9°5' N, 9°58' E 222
Wase, river, Nig. 9°8' N, 9°47' E 222
Waseca, Minn., U.S. 44°3' N, 93°33' W 82
Wash, The 52°55' N, 0°9' E 162
Washakie Needles, peak, Wyo., U.S. 43°44' N, 109°17' W 90
Washburn, Ill., U.S. 40°54' N, 89°18' W 102
Washburn, N. Dak., U.S. 47°17' N, 101°4' W 108
Washburn, Mount, peak, Wyo., U.S. 44°46' N, 110°31' W 90
Washington, D.C., U.S. 38°52' N, 77°9' W 94
Washington, Ga., U.S. 33°43' N, 82°45' W 96
Washington, Ill., U.S. 40°41' N, 89°25' W 102
Washington, Ind., U.S. 38°39' N, 87°10' W 102
Washington, Kans., U.S. 39°48' N, 97°3' W 90
Washington, Ky., U.S. 38°36' N, 83°49' W 102
Washington, Md., U.S. 38°38' N, 77°41' W 72
Washington, Miss., U.S. 31°34' N, 91°18' W 96
Washington, Mo., U.S. 38°32' N, 90°60' W 94
Washington, N.H., U.S. 43°10' N, 72°7' W 104
Washington, N.C., U.S. 35°33' N, 77°4' W 96
Washington, Pa., U.S. 40°8' N, 80°15' W 82
Washington, R.I., U.S. 41°40' N, 71°35' W 104
Washington, Utah, U.S. 37°7' N, 113°31' W 101
Washington, Wis., U.S. 45°23' N, 86°55' W 94
Washington, adm. division, Wash., U.S. 47°10' N, 122°22' W 90
Washington, Cape, Antarctica 74°14' S, 172°22' E 248
Washington Court House, Ohio, U.S. 39°32' N, 83°26' W 102
Washington Depot, Conn., U.S. 41°38' N, 73°20' W 104
Washington Land 80°27' N, 66°2' W 246

Washington, Mount, peak, N.H., U.S. 44°15' N, 71°20' W 104
Washington, Mount, peak, Oreg., U.S. 44°18' N, 121°56' W 90
Washita, river, Okla., U.S. 35°38' N, 99°16' W 80
Washita, river, Tex., U.S. 35°36' N, 100°25' W 96
Washtucna, Wash., U.S. 46°44' N, 118°20' W 90
Wasior, Indonesia 2°39' S, 134°28' E 192
Wasipe, Ghana 8°33' N, 2°14' W 222
Waskaganish, Can. 51°27' N, 78°42' W 82
Waskaiowaka Lake, Can. 56°28' N, 97°29' W 108
Waskesiu Lake, Can. 53°55' N, 106°2' W 108
Waskom, Tex., U.S. 32°29' N, 94°5' W 103
Wasselonne, Fr. 48°37' N, 7°26' E 163
Wasserkuppe, peak, Ger. 50°29' N, 9°54' E 167
Wassuk Range, Nev., U.S. 38°57' N, 118°59' W 90
Wassy, Fr. 48°30' N, 4°56' E 163
Waswanipi, Lac, lake, Can. 49°22' N, 77°51' W 80
Waţā al Khān, Syr. 35°40' N, 36°3' E 194
Watamu Marine National Park, Kenya 3°20' S, 39°58' E 224
Watapi Lake, lake, Can. 55°18' N, 110°3' W 108
Watari, Japan 38°2' N, 140°51' E 201
Watch Hill, R.I., U.S. 41°18' N, 71°52' W 104
Watchet, U.K. 51°10' N, 3°19' W 162
Water Cays, islands, North Atlantic Ocean 23°36' N, 79°7' W 80
Waterboro, Me., U.S. 43°32' N, 70°43' W 104
Waterbury, Conn., U.S. 41°33' N, 73°3' W 104
Waterbury, Vt., U.S. 44°19' N, 72°46' W 104
Waterbury Center, Vt., U.S. 44°22' N, 72°44' W 104
Waterbury Lake, lake, Can. 58°2' N, 105°7' W 108
Wateree Lake, S.C., U.S. 34°20' N, 81°49' W 80
Waterford, Calif., U.S. 37°38' N, 120°47' W 100
Waterford, Conn., U.S. 41°20' N, 72°9' W 104
Waterford, Wis., U.S. 42°46' N, 88°14' W 102
Waterford (Port Láirge), Ire. 52°15' N, 7°8' W 150
Waterfound, river, Can. 58°27' N, 104°45' W 108
Waterloo, Can. 45°20' N, 72°33' W 94
Waterloo, Can. 43°27' N, 80°32' W 94
Waterloo, Ind., U.S. 41°25' N, 85°2' W 102
Waterloo, Iowa, U.S. 42°28' N, 92°22' W 94
Waterloo, Mo., U.S. 38°19' N, 90°9' W 94
Waterloo, Sierra Leone 8°20' N, 13°4' W 222
Waterloo, Wis., U.S. 43°10' N, 88°60' W 102
Waterman, Ill., U.S. 41°45' N, 88°48' W 102
Waterman, Isla, island, Chile 55°22' S, 71°46' W 134
Waterproof, La., U.S. 31°47' N, 91°24' W 103
Watersmeet, Mich., U.S. 46°16' N, 89°11' W 94
Waterton Lakes National Park, Can. 49°4' N, 113°35' W 80
Watertown, Conn., U.S. 41°36' N, 73°7' W 104
Watertown, N.Y., U.S. 43°58' N, 75°55' W 94
Watertown, S. Dak., U.S. 44°52' N, 97°7' W 90
Watertown, Wis., U.S. 43°10' N, 88°43' W 102
Waterval Bo, S. Af. 25°40' S, 30°17' E 227
Waterville, Kans., U.S. 39°40' N, 96°45' W 90
Waterville, Me., U.S. 44°32' N, 69°39' W 104
Waterville, Minn., U.S. 44°11' N, 93°35' W 94
Waterville, Ohio, U.S. 41°29' N, 83°44' W 102
Waterville, Wash., U.S. 47°38' N, 120°5' W 90
Waterville Valley, N.H., U.S. 43°57' N, 71°31' W 104
Watervliet, Mich., U.S. 42°10' N, 86°15' W 102
Watervliet, N.Y., U.S. 42°43' N, 73°44' W 104
Watford, Can. 42°56' N, 81°52' W 102
Watford, U.K. 51°39' N, 0°25' E 162
Watford City, N. Dak., U.S. 47°47' N, 103°18' W 90
Wathaman Lake, lake, Can. 56°56' N, 104°28' W 108
Wathena, Kans., U.S. 39°44' N, 94°57' W 94
Watino, Can. 55°41' N, 117°41' W 108
Watling see San Salvador, island, Bahamas 23°41' N, 74°29' W 116
Watonga, Okla., U.S. 35°49' N, 98°24' W 92
Watrous, Can. 51°41' N, 105°29' W 90
Watrous, N. Mex., U.S. 35°46' N, 104°59' W 92
Watsa, Dem. Rep. of the Congo 2°59' N, 29°31' E 224
Watseka, Ill., U.S. 40°45' N, 87°44' W 102
Watsi Kengo, Dem. Rep. of the Congo 0°47' N, 20°31' E 218
Watson, Can. 52°7' N, 104°32' W 108
Watson Lake, Can. 60°6' N, 128°46' W 98
Watsonville, Calif., U.S. 36°54' N, 121°46' W 100
Watton, U.K. 52°33' N, 0°51' E 162
Wattwil, Switz. 47°19' N, 9°5' E 156
Wau, P.N.G. 7°22' S, 146°41' E 192
Wau, Sudan 7°39' N, 27°58' E 224
Wau, river, Sudan 6°8' N, 27°1' E 224
Waubay, S. Dak., U.S. 45°18' N, 97°19' W 90
Wauchula, Fla., U.S. 27°33' N, 81°49' W 105
Waucoba Mountain, peak, Calif., U.S. 37°1' N, 118°3' W 101
Waugh, Can. 49°37' N, 95°13' W 90
Waukena, Calif., U.S. 36°8' N, 119°31' W 100
Waukesha, Wis., U.S. 43°1' N, 88°14' W 102
Waupaca, Wis., U.S. 44°20' N, 89°6' W 94
Waupun, Wis., U.S. 43°37' N, 88°44' W 102
Wauregan, Conn., U.S. 41°44' N, 71°55' W 104
Waurika, Okla., U.S. 34°8' N, 97°59' W 96
Wausa, Nebr., U.S. 42°29' N, 97°33' W 90
Wausau, Wis., U.S. 44°56' N, 89°37' W 94
Wauseon, Ohio, U.S. 41°32' N, 84°9' W 102
Wautoma, Wis., U.S. 44°4' N, 89°18' W 102
Wauwinet, Mass., U.S. 41°19' N, 69°60' W 104
Waveland, Miss., U.S. 30°16' N, 89°23' W 103
Waverley, N.Z. 39°47' S, 174°37' E 240
Waverly, Ill., U.S. 39°34' N, 89°58' W 102
Waverly, Iowa, U.S. 42°42' N, 92°29' W 94
Waverly, Nebr., U.S. 40°54' N, 96°33' W 90
Waverly, N.Y., U.S. 42°0' N, 76°33' W 110
Waverly, Ohio, U.S. 39°6' N, 82°60' W 102
Waverly, Va., U.S. 37°2' N, 77°6' W 96
Wavre, Belg. 50°42' N, 4°36' E 167
Wāw al Kabīr, Lib. 25°20' N, 16°43' E 216
Wāw an Nāmūs, spring, Lib. 24°58' N, 17°46' E 216
Wawa, Can. 47°59' N, 84°47' W 94
Wawa, Nig. 9°54' N, 4°24' E 222
Wawa, river, Nicar. 14°1' N, 84°24' W 115
Wawagosic, river, Can. 50°6' N, 79°5' W 94
Wawona, Calif., U.S. 37°32' N, 119°40' W 100
Waxahachie, Tex., U.S. 32°23' N, 96°51' W 96
Waxweiler, Ger. 50°5' N, 6°22' E 167
Waxxari, China 38°46' N, 87°29' E 188
Way Archipelago, islands, Antarctica 66°37' S, 147°19' E 248
Way Kambas National Park, Indonesia 5°4' S, 105°20' E 172
Wayagamac, Lac, lake, Can. 47°20' N, 73°14' W 94
Waycross, Ga., U.S. 31°11' N, 82°23' W 112
Wayland, Mich., U.S. 42°39' N, 85°39' W 102
Wayne, Can. 51°24' N, 112°42' W 90
Wayne, Me., U.S. 44°20' N, 70°4' W 104
Wayne, Nebr., U.S. 42°12' N, 97°1' W 90
Wayne, Ohio, U.S. 41°17' N, 83°29' W 102
Waynesboro, Ga., U.S. 33°4' N, 82°2' W 96
Waynesboro, Miss., U.S. 31°40' N, 88°38' W 103
Waynesboro, Tenn., U.S. 35°19' N, 87°45' W 96
Waynesboro, Va., U.S. 38°4' N, 78°54' W 94
Waynoka, Okla., U.S. 36°34' N, 98°54' W 92
Wayside, Miss., U.S. 33°14' N, 91°2' W 103
Waza, Cameroon 11°24' N, 14°35' E 216
Waza National Park, Cameroon 11°12' N, 14°21' E 206
Wazay, Afghan. 33°18' N, 69°27' E 186
Wāzin, Lib. 31°57' N, 10°42' E 214
Wazirabad, Pak. 32°24' N, 74°8' E 186
We, island, Indonesia 5°52' N, 95°22' E 196
Weagamow Lake, Can. 52°59' N, 91°20' W 82
Weald, The, region, U.K. 51°0' N, 0°17' E 162
Weare, N.H., U.S. 43°5' N, 71°45' W 104
Wearhead, U.K. 54°45' N, 2°14' W 162
Weatherford, Okla., U.S. 35°30' N, 98°43' W 92
Weatherford, Tex., U.S. 32°46' N, 97°48' W 112
Weaver Lake, lake, Can. 52°42' N, 97°13' W 108
Webb, Can. 50°10' N, 108°13' W 90
Webb City, Okla., U.S. 36°47' N, 96°42' W 92
Webbwood, Can. 46°16' N, 81°53' W 94
Weber Inlet 72°27' S, 74°30' W 248
Weber Ridge, peak, Antarctica 84°21' S, 65°15' W 248
Webster, Fla., U.S. 28°36' N, 82°4' W 105
Webster, Mass., U.S. 42°2' N, 71°53' W 104
Webster, N.H., U.S. 43°19' N, 71°44' W 104
Webster, S. Dak., U.S. 45°18' N, 97°32' W 90
Webster City, Iowa, U.S. 42°26' N, 93°50' W 94
Weda, Indonesia 0°22' N, 127°46' E 192
Weddell Island, Falk. Is., U.K. 51°50' S, 64°6' W 134
Weddell Plain, South Atlantic Ocean 62°46' S, 4°49' W 255
Weddell Sea 65°39' S, 58°34' W 134
Wedge Mountain, peak, Can. 50°7' N, 122°53' W 108
Weed, Calif., U.S. 41°25' N, 122°24' W 92
Weed Patch, Calif., U.S. 35°13' N, 118°56' W 101
Weed Patch Hill, peak, Ind., U.S. 39°8' N, 86°16' W 102
Weekapaug, R.I., U.S. 41°19' N, 71°46' W 104
Weekes, Can. 52°33' N, 102°54' W 108
Weeki Wachee, Fla., U.S. 28°31' N, 82°34' W 105
Weeki Wachee Spring, site, Fla., U.S. 28°29' N, 82°37' W 105
Weems, Mount, peak, Antarctica 77°25' S, 87°1' W 248
Weende, Ger. 51°33' N, 9°56' E 167
Weener, Ger. 53°10' N, 7°21' E 163
Weert, Neth. 51°14' N, 5°41' E 167
Weeze, Ger. 51°37' N, 6°12' E 167
Wegīdī, Eth. 9°25' N, 38°23' E 224
Wei, river, China 34°27' N, 109°55' E 198
Weichang, China 41°54' N, 117°43' E 198
Weiden, Ger. 49°40' N, 12°9' E 152
Weidman, Mich., U.S. 43°40' N, 84°58' W 102
Weifang, China 36°42' N, 119°5' E 198
Weihai, China 37°29' N, 122°8' E 198
Weilburg, Ger. 50°29' N, 8°15' E 167
Weilmünster, Ger. 50°27' N, 8°22' E 167
Weimar, Tex., U.S. 29°41' N, 96°47' W 96
Weinan, China 34°30' N, 109°28' E 198
Weipa, Austral. 12°41' S, 142°4' E 238
Weir, Miss., U.S. 33°14' N, 89°17' W 103
Weir, river, Can. 56°58' N, 93°45' W 108
Weirsdale, Fla., U.S. 28°58' N, 81°55' W 105
Weirton, W. Va., U.S. 40°23' N, 80°37' W 94
Weiser, Idaho, U.S. 44°15' N, 116°59' W 90
Weishan, China 34°47' N, 117°11' E 198
Weisshorn, peak, Switz. 46°6' N, 7°39' E 165
Weissmies, peak, Switz. 46°7' N, 8°0' E 167
Weitra, Aust. 48°42' N, 14°54' E 156
Weitzel Lake, lake, Can. 57°39' N, 107°11' W 108
Weixin, China 27°49' N, 105°3' E 198
Weiya, China 42°7' N, 94°41' E 190
Weizhou Dao, island, China 20°44' N, 108°55' E 198
Wekusko, Can. 54°30' N, 99°46' W 108
Wekusko Lake, lake, Can. 54°39' N, 100°27' W 108
Wel Jara, spring, Kenya 0°28' N, 40°53' E 224
Welaka, Fla., U.S. 29°28' N, 81°40' W 105
Welbeck Abbey, site, U.K. 53°16' N, 1°10' W 162
Welch, W. Va., U.S. 37°26' N, 81°36' W 96
Welcome Mount, peak, Antarctica 72°13' S, 160°40' E 248
Weldiya, Eth. 11°48' N, 39°33' E 182
Weldon, Calif., U.S. 35°39' N, 118°18' W 101
Weldon, Ill., U.S. 40°6' N, 88°45' W 102
Weldon, N.C., U.S. 36°24' N, 77°36' W 96
Weldon, Tex., U.S. 31°0' N, 95°34' W 103
Welel, Tulu, peak, Eth. 8°51' N, 34°44' E 224
Welk'īt'ē, Eth. 8°15' N, 37°48' E 224
Welkom, S. Af. 28°1' S, 26°41' E 227
Welland, Can. 42°52' N, 79°22' W 82
Wellesley, Mass., U.S. 42°17' N, 71°18' W 104
Wellesley Islands, Gulf of Carpentaria 16°33' S, 137°4' E 230
Wellfleet, Mass., U.S. 41°56' N, 70°3' W 104
Wellingborough, U.K. 52°18' N, 0°42' E 162
Wellington, Colo., U.S. 40°42' N, 105°1' W 90
Wellington, Ill., U.S. 40°31' N, 87°41' W 102
Wellington, N.Z. 41°18' S, 174°39' E 240
Wellington, Ohio, U.S. 41°9' N, 82°13' W 102
Wellington, S. Af. 33°38' S, 18°59' E 227
Wellington, Tex., U.S. 34°50' N, 100°14' W 96
Wellington, U.K. 50°58' N, 3°13' W 162
Wellington Channel 74°55' N, 95°14' W 106
Wellington, Isla, island, Chile 49°48' S, 74°23' W 134
Wells, Can. 53°5' N, 121°36' W 108
Wells, Me., U.S. 43°19' N, 70°35' W 104
Wells, Mich., U.S. 45°46' N, 87°5' W 94
Wells, Nev., U.S. 41°6' N, 114°58' W 90
Wells, Tex., U.S. 31°28' N, 94°57' W 103
Wells, Vt., U.S. 43°24' N, 73°13' W 104
Wells next the Sea, U.K. 52°56' N, 0°51' E 162
Wells River, Vt., U.S. 44°8' N, 72°4' W 104
Wellsboro, Pa., U.S. 41°44' N, 77°19' W 82
Wellsford, N.Z. 36°18' S, 174°31' E 240
Wellston, Mich., U.S. 44°12' N, 85°57' W 102
Wellston, Ohio, U.S. 39°6' N, 82°32' W 102
Wellsville, N.Y., U.S. 42°7' N, 77°58' W 94
Wellsville, Ohio, U.S. 40°35' N, 80°39' W 94
Wellton, Ariz., U.S. 32°39' N, 114°10' W 101
Welmel, river, Eth. 6°7' N, 40°6' E 224
Wels, Aust. 48°9' N, 14°1' E 152
Welsh, La., U.S. 30°13' N, 92°50' W 96
Welshpool, U.K. 52°39' N, 3°9' W 162
Welwel, Eth. 7°6' N, 45°23' E 218
Welwyn Garden City, U.K. 51°49' N, 0°14' E 162
Wem, U.K. 52°51' N, 2°43' W 162
Wembley, Can. 55°10' N, 119°9' W 108
Wenatchee, Wash., U.S. 47°24' N, 120°19' W 90
Wenatchee Mountains, Wash., U.S. 47°34' N, 121°49' W 100
Wenchang, China 19°36' N, 110°43' E 198
Wencheng, China 27°45' N, 120°3' E 198
Wenchi, Ghana 7°45' N, 2°8' W 222
Wendelstein, peak, Ger. 47°40' N, 11°55' E 156
Wenden, Ariz., U.S. 33°48' N, 113°33' W 101
Wendeng, China 37°11' N, 122°6' E 198
Wendo, Eth. 6°38' N, 38°21' E 224
Wendover, Utah, U.S. 40°43' N, 114°1' W 82
Wenduine, Belg. 51°16' N, 3°4' E 163
Wenebegon Lake, Can. 47°21' N, 83°46' W 94
Wengyuan, China 24°14' N, 114°6' E 198
Wenling, China 28°19' N, 121°24' E 198
Wenona, Ill., U.S. 41°3' N, 89°4' W 102
Wenquan, China 33°4' N, 91°54' E 188
Wenquan, China 44°50' N, 80°57' E 184
Wenshan, China 23°25' N, 104°18' E 202
Wensu, China 41°16' N, 80°15' E 184
Wentworth, N.H., U.S. 43°51' N, 71°55' W 104
Wentzel Lake, lake, Can. 59°0' N, 115°2' W 108
Wentzel, river, Can. 58°53' N, 114°49' W 108
Wenxian, China 32°56' N, 104°40' E 198
Wenzhou, China 27°57' N, 120°44' E 198
Weobley, U.K. 52°9' N, 2°54' W 162
Wepener, S. Af. 29°45' S, 27°0' E 227
Wepusko Bay 56°59' N, 102°57' W 108
Werbkowice, Pol. 50°44' N, 23°46' E 152
Werda, Botswana 25°17' S, 23°14' E 227
Werdau, Ger. 50°44' N, 12°23' E 152
Werder, Eth. 7°0' N, 45°17' E 218
Werder, Ger. 52°22' N, 12°56' E 152
Werdohl, Ger. 51°15' N, 7°45' E 167
Were Īlu, Eth. 10°35' N, 39°31' E 224
Werl, Ger. 51°33' N, 7°54' E 167
Wermelskirchen, Ger. 51°8' N, 7°13' E 167
Werne, Ger. 51°39' N, 7°37' E 167
Werneck, Ger. 49°59' N, 10°5' E 167
Werota, Eth. 11°45' N, 37°31' E 182
Wertheim, Ger. 49°44' N, 9°30' E 167
Wervik, Belg. 50°47' N, 3°1' E 163
Wesel, Ger. 51°39' N, 6°36' E 167
Wesergebirge, Ger. 52°6' N, 8°54' E 150
Weskan, Kans., U.S. 38°51' N, 101°58' W 90
Weslaco, Tex., U.S. 26°9' N, 98°1' W 96
Wesleyville, Pa., U.S. 42°7' N, 80°2' W 110
Wessel Islands, Arafura Sea 10°56' S, 135°48' E 192
Wesseling, Ger. 50°48' N, 6°58' E 167
Wessex, region, U.K. 51°28' N, 2°20' W 162
Wessington, S. Dak., U.S. 44°26' N, 98°43' W 90
Wessington Springs, S. Dak., U.S. 44°3' N, 98°34' W 90
Wesson, Ark., U.S. 33°5' N, 92°47' W 103
Wesson, Miss., U.S. 31°41' N, 90°25' W 103
West, Miss., U.S. 33°10' N, 89°48' W 103
West, Tex., U.S. 31°46' N, 97°5' W 92
West Acton, Mass., U.S. 42°28' N, 71°29' W 104
West Allis, Wis., U.S. 43°0' N, 88°2' W 102
West Baldwin, Me., U.S. 43°49' N, 70°47' W 104
West Bank 31°59' N, 35°17' E 194
West Bank, special sovereignty, West Bank 31°22' N, 35°0' E 194
West Bay 29°12' N, 95°8' W 103
West Bay 28°59' N, 89°38' W 103
West Bay, Fla., U.S. 30°17' N, 85°52' W 96
West Bend, Wis., U.S. 43°24' N, 88°13' W 102
West Bengal, adm. division, India 24°8' N, 87°45' E 197
West Berlin, Vt., U.S. 44°11' N, 72°38' W 104
West Beskids, Pol. 49°32' N, 18°33' E 152
West Bethel, Me., U.S. 44°23' N, 70°52' W 104
West Boylston, Mass., U.S. 42°21' N, 71°48' W 104
West Braintree, Vt., U.S. 43°58' N, 72°46' W 104
West Branch, Iowa, U.S. 41°40' N, 91°21' W 110
West Branch, Mich., U.S. 44°17' N, 84°14' W 94
West Bridgford, U.K. 52°55' N, 1°7' W 162
West Bromwich, U.K. 52°30' N, 1°60' W 162
West Burlington, Iowa, U.S. 40°49' N, 91°10' W 110
West Butte, peak, Mont., U.S. 48°54' N, 111°38' W 90
West Buxton, Me., U.S. 43°39' N, 70°36' W 104
West Caicos, island, West Caicos 21°35' N, 72°57' W 116
West Camp, N.Y., U.S. 42°6' N, 73°57' W 104
West Campton, N.H., U.S. 43°50' N, 71°41' W 104
West Caroline Basin, North Pacific Ocean 3°16' N, 136°56' E 254
West Carrollton City, Ohio, U.S. 39°39' N, 84°15' W 102
West Castleton, Vt., U.S. 43°39' N, 73°15' W 104
West Chicago, Ill., U.S. 41°52' N, 88°12' W 102
West Coal, river, Can. 61°12' N, 128°15' W 108
West Cornwall, Conn., U.S. 41°52' N, 73°22' W 104
West Danville, Vt., U.S. 44°24' N, 72°12' W 104
West Des Moines, Iowa, U.S. 41°33' N, 93°44' W 94
West Dummerston, Vt., U.S. 42°55' N, 72°38' W 104
West Elk Peak, Colo., U.S. 38°42' N, 107°17' W 90
West End, Bahamas 26°40' N, 78°57' W 105
West End Point, Bahamas 26°41' N, 78°58' W 105
West End Point, Little Cayman 19°42' N, 81°6' W 115
West Falkland, island, Falk. Is., U.K. 51°34' S, 62°18' W 134
West Fayu Atoll see Pigailoe 8°36' N, 146°3' E 192
West Frankfort, Mo., U.S. 37°53' N, 88°55' W 96
West Glacier, Mont., U.S. 48°27' N, 113°59' W 108
West Gouldsboro, Me., U.S. 44°27' N, 68°6' W 111
West Granville, Mass., U.S. 42°4' N, 72°57' W 104
West Group, islands, Great Australian Bight 33°43' S, 120°1' E 230
West Ham, U.K. 51°30' N, 1°59' E 162
West Hartford, Conn., U.S. 41°45' N, 72°45' W 104
West Haven, Conn., U.S. 41°16' N, 72°57' W 104
West Hazleton, Pa., U.S. 40°57' N, 76°1' W 94
West Helena, Ark., U.S. 34°32' N, 90°40' W 96
West Hurley, N.Y., U.S. 41°59' N, 74°7' W 104
West Ice Shelf, Antarctica 66°37' S, 86°47' E 248
West Island, Austral. 15°45' S, 135°31' E 231
West Jefferson, Ohio, U.S. 39°55' N, 83°16' W 102
West Keal, U.K. 53°8' N, 0°2' E 162
West Lafayette, Ohio, U.S. 40°16' N, 81°45' W 102
West Liberty, Ky., U.S. 37°55' N, 83°16' W 94
West Liberty, Ohio, U.S. 40°15' N, 83°46' W 102
West Lorne, Can. 42°35' N, 81°36' W 102
West Lunga National Park, Zambia 12°45' S, 24°52' E 224
West Lunga National Park, Zambia 13°10' S, 24°22' E 206
West Lunga, river, Zambia 12°14' S, 24°21' E 220
West Mariana Basin, Philippine Sea 17°0' N, 138°57' E 254
West Milton, Ohio, U.S. 39°56' N, 84°20' W 102
West Monroe, La., U.S. 32°29' N, 92°9' W 103
West Newfield, Me., U.S. 43°38' N, 70°56' W 104
West Nicholson, Zimb. 21°2' S, 29°18' E 227
West Ossipee, N.H., U.S. 43°49' N, 71°13' W 104
West Palm Beach, Fla., U.S. 26°43' N, 80°5' W 105
West Paris, Me., U.S. 44°19' N, 70°35' W 104
West Park, N.Y., U.S. 41°47' N, 73°59' W 104
West Pawlet, Vt., U.S. 43°21' N, 73°16' W 104
West Peru, Me., U.S. 44°30' N, 70°29' W 104
West Pittston, Pa., U.S. 41°19' N, 75°49' W 94
West Plains, Mo., U.S. 36°43' N, 91°52' W 96
West Point 43°55' N, 60°58' W 111
West Point, Calif., U.S. 38°23' N, 120°33' W 100
West Point, Can. 46°37' N, 64°23' W 111
West Point, Ky., U.S. 37°59' N, 85°58' W 94
West Point, Me., U.S. 43°45' N, 69°52' W 104
West Point, Miss., U.S. 33°35' N, 88°39' W 96
West Point, N.Y., U.S. 41°23' N, 73°59' W 104
West Point, Va., U.S. 37°32' N, 76°48' W 94
West Portsmouth, Ohio, U.S. 38°45' N, 83°2' W 102
West Quoddy Head, Me., U.S. 44°44' N, 66°55' W 111
West Rumney, N.H., U.S. 43°48' N, 71°53' W 104
West Salem, Ill., U.S. 38°31' N, 88°1' W 102
West Southport, Me., U.S. 43°49' N, 69°41' W 104
West Spanish Peak, Colo., U.S. 37°19' N, 105°4' W 80
West Tanfield, U.K. 54°12' N, 1°35' W 162
West Tavaputs Plateau, Utah, U.S. 39°48' N, 110°44' W 90
West Terre Haute, Ind., U.S. 39°27' N, 87°27' W 102
West Terschelling, Neth. 53°21' N, 5°12' E 163
West Thornton, N.H., U.S. 43°56' N, 71°42' W 104
West Topsham, Vt., U.S. 44°6' N, 72°19' W 104
West Townsend, Mass., U.S. 42°40' N, 71°45' W 104
West Union, Ill., U.S. 39°12' N, 87°40' W 102
West Union, Iowa, U.S. 42°57' N, 91°47' W 110
West Virginia, adm. division, W. Va., U.S. 38°34' N, 81°18' W 94
West Wareham, Mass., U.S. 41°47' N, 70°46' W 104
West Webster, N.Y., U.S. 43°12' N, 77°30' W 94
West Wendover, Nev., U.S. 40°43' N, 114°4' W 90
West Woodstock, Vt., U.S. 43°36' N, 72°34' W 104
West Yarmouth, Mass., U.S. 41°38' N, 70°15' W 104
Westbrook, Conn., U.S. 41°16' N, 72°27' W 104
Westbrook, Me., U.S. 43°40' N, 70°22' W 104
Westbrook, Tex., U.S. 32°21' N, 101°1' W 92
Westbury, U.K. 51°15' N, 2°11' W 162
Westend, Calif., U.S. 35°41' N, 117°24' W 101
Westerburg, Ger. 50°33' N, 7°58' E 167
Westerlo, N.Y., U.S. 42°30' N, 74°4' W 104
Westerly, R.I., U.S. 41°22' N, 71°50' W 104
Western Australia, adm. division, Austral. 25°2' S, 118°22' E 231
Western Bahr Al Ghazal, adm. division, Sudan 7°22' N, 25°15' E 224
Western Cape, adm. division, S. Af. 32°60' S, 19°18' E 227
Western Darfur, adm. division, Sudan 14°27' N, 23°55' E 226
Western Desert, Egypt 29°2' N, 24°32' E 142
Western Equatoria, adm. division, Sudan 5°29' N, 27°18' E 224
Western Ghats, India 21°0' N, 73°17' E 186
Western Head, Can. 49°34' N, 58°48' W 111
Western Kordofan, adm. division, Sudan 10°39' N, 27°40' E 224
Western Port 38°38' S, 143°33' E 230
Western Sahara, special sovereignty, Mor. 21°39' N, 13°57' W 222
Western Thebes, ruin(s), Egypt 25°43' N, 32°25' E 182
Westerschelde 51°21' N, 3°54' E 163
Westerville, Ohio, U.S. 40°7' N, 82°55' W 102
Westerwald, Ger. 50°33' N, 7°25' E 167
Westfield, N.Y., U.S. 42°19' N, 79°35' W 110
Westfield, Tex., U.S. 30°0' N, 95°25' W 103
Westfield, Wis., U.S. 43°53' N, 89°30' W 102
Westhampton Beach, N.Y., U.S. 40°48' N, 72°39' W 104
Westhope, N. Dak., U.S. 48°53' N, 101°3' W 90
Westlake, La., U.S. 30°13' N, 93°16' W 103
Westland (Tai Poutini) National Park, N.Z. 43°26' S, 168°39' E 240
Westley, Calif., U.S. 37°32' N, 121°13' W 100
Westlock, Can. 54°9' N, 113°52' W 108
Westminster, Colo., U.S. 39°50' N, 105°3' W 90
Westminster, Vt., U.S. 43°3' N, 72°28' W 104
Westmorland, Calif., U.S. 33°2' N, 115°38' W 101
Weston, Malaysia 5°14' N, 115°36' E 203
Weston, Mo., U.S. 39°24' N, 94°55' W 94
Weston, Oreg., U.S. 45°47' N, 118°26' W 90
Weston, Vt., U.S. 43°17' N, 72°48' W 104
Weston, W. Va., U.S. 39°2' N, 80°28' W 94
Weston super Mare, U.K. 51°19' N, 2°58' W 162
Westonzoyland, U.K. 51°6' N, 2°56' W 162
Westover, W. Va., U.S. 39°37' N, 79°59' W 94
Westoverledingen, Ger. 53°9' N, 7°27' E 163
Westpoint, Ind., U.S. 40°20' N, 87°3' W 102
Westport, Calif., U.S. 39°38' N, 123°47' W 90
Westport, Conn., U.S. 41°8' N, 73°22' W 104
Westport, Ind., U.S. 39°10' N, 85°34' W 102
Westport, N.Y., U.S. 44°10' N, 73°28' W 104
Westport, N.Z. 41°47' S, 171°38' E 240
Westport, Wash., U.S. 46°52' N, 124°7' W 100
Westport Point, Mass., U.S. 41°31' N, 71°6' W 104
Westray, Can. 53°35' N, 101°23' W 108
Westree, Can. 47°25' N, 81°33' W 94
Westville, Ill., U.S. 40°2' N, 87°38' W 102
Westward Ho!, U.K. 51°2' N, 4°13' W 150
Westwego, La., U.S. 29°54' N, 90°9' W 103
Westwood, Calif., U.S. 40°18' N, 120°60' W 92
Wesuwe, Ger. 52°45' N, 7°12' E 163
Wetar, island, Indonesia 7°40' S, 126°18' E 192
Wetaskiwin, Can. 52°57' N, 113°23' W 108
Wete, Tanzania 5°1' S, 39°45' E 224
Wetetnagami, Lac, lake, Can. 48°53' N, 76°59' W 94
Wetherby, U.K. 53°56' N, 1°23' W 162
Wethersfield, Conn., U.S. 41°42' N, 72°41' W 104
Wetter, Ger. 50°53' N, 8°42' E 167
Wetteren, Belg. 50°59' N, 3°53' E 163
Wettringen, Ger. 52°12' N, 7°19' E 163
Wetumka, Okla., U.S. 35°13' N, 96°14' W 96
Wetzlar, Ger. 50°33' N, 8°29' E 167
Wevertown, N.Y., U.S. 43°37' N, 73°58' W 104
Wewak, P.N.G. 3°36' S, 143°37' E 238
Wewoka, Okla., U.S. 35°7' N, 96°29' W 92
Wexford, Ire. 52°20' N, 6°29' W 150
Weybourne, U.K. 52°56' N, 1°8' E 162
Weybridge, Vt., U.S. 44°3' N, 73°13' W 104
Weyburn, Can. 49°39' N, 103°52' W 90
Weymouth, Mass., U.S. 42°13' N, 70°57' W 104
Weymouth Bay 12°36' S, 142°4' E 230
Whakapara, N.Z. 35°33' S, 174°16' E 240
Whakapunake, peak, N.Z. 38°50' S, 177°31' E 240
Whakatane, N.Z. 37°59' S, 177°0' E 240
Whale Bay 56°34' N, 135°35' W 108
Whale Cay, island, Bahamas 25°27' N, 78°38' W 80
Whale Cove, Can. 62°28' N, 92°59' W 73
Whangara, N.Z. 38°33' S, 178°12' E 240
Whangarei, N.Z. 35°46' S, 174°18' E 240
Wharfe, river, U.K. 53°55' N, 1°21' W 162
Wharton, Tex., U.S. 29°18' N, 96°6' W 96
Wharton Basin, Indian Ocean 20°5' S, 100°10' E 254
Wharton, Mount, peak, Antarctica 81°1' S, 158°48' E 248
Wharton, Peninsula, Chile 49°34' S, 76°33' W 134
Whataroa, N.Z. 43°17' S, 170°21' E 240
Whatcom, Lake, Wash., U.S. 48°41' N, 122°34' W 100
Whatley, Ala., U.S. 31°38' N, 87°42' W 103
Whatshan Lake, lake, Can. 50°0' N, 118°40' W 90
Wheatland, Ind., U.S. 38°39' N, 87°19' W 102
Wheatland, Wyo., U.S. 42°3' N, 104°58' W 90
Wheatley, Can. 42°6' N, 82°28' W 102
Wheaton, Ill., U.S. 41°51' N, 88°6' W 102
Wheaton, Minn., U.S. 45°47' N, 96°30' W 90
Wheeler, Kans., U.S. 39°45' N, 101°43' W 90

Wheeler, *Oreg., U.S.* 45°40' N, 123°53' W **100**
Wheeler, *Tex., U.S.* 35°26' N, 100°17' W **92**
Wheeler Mountain, peak, *Nev., U.S.* 41°16' N, 116°7' W **90**
Wheeler Peak, *Nev., U.S.* 38°58' N, 114°23' W **90**
Wheeler Peak, *N. Mex., U.S.* 36°32' N, 105°29' W **92**
Wheeling, *W. Va., U.S.* 40°3' N, 80°43' W **94**
Wheelwright, *Arg.* 33°49' S, 61°12' W **139**
Whinham, Mount, peak, *Austral.* 26°5' S, 129°59' E **230**
Whipple, Mount, peak, *Can.* 56°36' N, 131°44' W **108**
Whipple Observatory, site, *Ariz., U.S.* 31°41' N, 110°57' W **92**
Whirlwind Lake, *Can.* 60°15' N, 109°15' W **108**
Whiskey Jack Lake, *Can.* 58°24' N, 102°28' W **108**
Whistler, *Can.* 50°7' N, 122°59' W **100**
Whitby, *U.K.* 54°29' N, 0°38' E **162**
Whitchurch, *U.K.* 52°58' N, 2°41' W **162**
Whitchurch, *U.K.* 51°13' N, 1°21' W **162**
White Bay 49°57' N, 56°42' W **111**
White Butte, peak, *N. Dak., U.S.* 46°22' N, 103°23' W **90**
White Cap Mountain, peak, *Me., U.S.* 45°32' N, 69°20' W **94**
White Castle, *La., U.S.* 30°9' N, 91°9' W **103**
White City, *Fla., U.S.* 27°23' N, 80°20' W **105**
White Cloud, *Mich., U.S.* 43°33' N, 85°47' W **102**
White Deer, *Tex., U.S.* 35°24' N, 101°11' W **92**
White Hall, *Ark., U.S.* 34°16' N, 92°5' W **96**
White Heath, *Ill., U.S.* 40°4' N, 88°30' W **102**
White Hills, *Ariz., U.S.* 35°47' N, 114°27' W **101**
White Horse Beach, *Mass., U.S.* 41°55' N, 70°35' W **104**
White Horse Pass, *Nev., U.S.* 40°20' N, 114°15' W **90**
White Island, *Antarctica* 78°9' S, 175°55' E **248**
White Island, *Antarctica* 66°45' S, 45°32' E **248**
White Island, island, *Can.* 66°2' N, 88°7' W **246**
White Lake, *La., U.S.* 29°41' N, 92°41' W **103**
White Mount Peak, *Calif., U.S.* 37°37' N, 118°21' W **92**
White Mountain, *Alas., U.S.* 64°40' N, 163°26' W **98**
White Mountains, *Calif., U.S.* 37°10' N, 118°10' W **80**
White Mountains, *Calif., U.S.* 37°46' N, 118°28' W **90**
White Mountains, *N.H., U.S.* 44°2' N, 71°60' W **104**
White Mountains National Park, *Austral.* 20°38' S, 144°43' E **238**
White Nile, adm. division, *Sudan* 13°33' N, 31°53' E **182**
White Nile Dam, *Sudan* 14°56' N, 31°53' E **226**
White Oak, *Tex., U.S.* 32°32' N, 94°52' W **103**
White Otter Lake, lake, *Can.* 49°3' N, 92°29' W **94**
White Pigeon, *Mich., U.S.* 41°47' N, 85°38' W **102**
White Pine Peak, *Utah, U.S.* 38°50' N, 112°18' W **90**
White Pine Range, *Nev., U.S.* 39°4' N, 115°37' W **90**
White Plains, *N.Y., U.S.* 41°1' N, 73°47' W **104**
White River, *Can.* 48°35' N, 85°16' W **94**
White River, *S. Dak., U.S.* 43°34' N, 100°45' W **90**
White, river, *Ark., U.S.* 36°2' N, 92°6' W **80**
White, river, *Ark., U.S.* 34°42' N, 91°43' W **80**
White, river, *Can.* 48°30' N, 86°2' W **94**
White, river, *Can.* 63°13' N, 140°3' W **98**
White, river, *Colo., U.S.* 40°8' N, 108°49' W **90**
White, river, *Colo., U.S.* 39°50' N, 108°56' W **80**
White River Junction, *Vt., U.S.* 43°38' N, 72°20' W **104**
White, river, *Nebr., U.S.* 42°55' N, 103°10' W **90**
White River Plateau, *Colo., U.S.* 39°50' N, 107°54' W **90**
White, river, *S. Dak., U.S.* 43°41' N, 102°24' W **82**
White, river, *S. Dak., U.S.* 43°34' N, 99°56' W **90**
White, river, *Tex., U.S.* 34°5' N, 101°57' W **112**
White, river, *Utah, U.S.* 39°50' N, 109°27' W **90**
White Rock, *Can.* 49°2' N, 122°48' W **100**
White Rock Peak, *Nev., U.S.* 38°14' N, 114°11' W **90**
White Rock, peak, *Oreg., U.S.* 43°6' N, 123°7' W **90**
White Salmon, *Wash., U.S.* 45°43' N, 121°30' W **100**
White Sands National Monument, *N. Mex., U.S.* 32°54' N, 106°5' W **80**
White Sea see Beloye More 63°17' N, 35°24' E **160**
White Volta, river, *Ghana* 9°39' N, 0°54' E **222**
Whitecap Mountain, peak, *Can.* 50°42' N, 122°36' W **90**
Whiteclay Lake, lake, *Can.* 50°49' N, 89°14' W **110**
Whitecourt, *Can.* 54°7' N, 115°42' W **108**
Whiteface Mountain, peak, *N.Y., U.S.* 44°21' N, 73°56' W **104**
Whiteface, river, *Minn., U.S.* 47°4' N, 92°51' W **94**
Whitefield, *Me., U.S.* 44°9' N, 69°39' W **104**
Whitefield, *N.H., U.S.* 44°22' N, 71°37' W **104**
Whitefish, *Mont., U.S.* 48°23' N, 114°21' W **90**
Whitefish Bay, *Wis., U.S.* 43°6' N, 87°55' W **102**
Whitefish Lake, lake, *Can.* 48°12' N, 90°30' W **110**
Whitefish Point, *Mich., U.S.* 46°35' N, 84°56' W **94**
Whitefish Range, *Mont., U.S.* 48°59' N, 114°56' W **90**
Whitefish, river, *Can.* 60°42' N, 125°12' W **108**
Whitehall, *Mich., U.S.* 43°22' N, 86°21' W **102**
Whitehall, *Mont., U.S.* 45°51' N, 112°6' W **90**
Whitehall, *N.Y., U.S.* 43°32' N, 73°26' W **104**
Whitehall, *Ohio, U.S.* 39°57' N, 82°53' W **102**
Whitehall, *Wis., U.S.* 44°21' N, 91°20' W **94**
Whitehaven, *U.K.* 54°33' N, 3°35' W **162**
Whitehorse, *Can.* 60°43' N, 135°20' W **98**
Whitehouse, *Tex., U.S.* 32°12' N, 95°14' W **103**
Whitemouth, *Can.* 49°55' N, 95°59' W **90**
Whitemud, river, *Can.* 56°32' N, 118°28' W **108**
Whiten Head, *U.K.* 58°36' N, 4°54' W **150**
Whiteriver, *Ariz., U.S.* 33°50' N, 109°58' W **92**
Whitesand, river, *Can.* 59°50' N, 115°54' W **108**
Whitesboro, *Tex., U.S.* 33°38' N, 96°55' W **92**
Whitesburg, *Ky., U.S.* 37°7' N, 82°49' W **94**
Whitetail, *Mont., U.S.* 48°52' N, 105°12' W **90**
Whiteville, *N.C., U.S.* 34°19' N, 78°43' W **96**
Whiteville, *Tenn., U.S.* 35°18' N, 89°9' W **96**
Whitewater, *Mont., U.S.* 48°44' N, 107°37' W **90**
Whitewater, *Wis., U.S.* 42°50' N, 88°45' W **102**
Whitewater Bay 25°16' N, 81°13' W **105**
Whitewater Lake, *Can.* 50°42' N, 89°52' W **110**
Whitewood, *Can.* 50°19' N, 102°17' W **90**
Whitianga, *N.Z.* 36°50' S, 175°40' E **240**
Whiting, *Vt., U.S.* 43°51' N, 73°13' W **104**
Whiting, river, *Can.* 58°2' N, 133°46' W **108**
Whitingham, *Vt., U.S.* 42°47' N, 72°54' W **104**
Whitley Gardens, *Calif., U.S.* 35°39' N, 120°32' W **101**
Whitman, *Nebr., U.S.* 42°1' N, 101°32' W **90**
Whitmire, *S.C., U.S.* 34°29' N, 81°37' W **96**
Whitney, Lake, *Tex., U.S.* 31°56' N, 98°22' W **80**
Whitney, Mount, peak, *Calif., U.S.* 36°34' N, 118°20' W **101**
Whitstable, *U.K.* 51°21' N, 1°2' E **162**
Whitsunday Island National Park, *Austral.* 20°21' S, 148°39' E **238**
Whittemore, *Mich., U.S.* 44°13' N, 83°48' W **102**
Whittier, *Alas., U.S.* 60°40' N, 148°51' W **98**
Whittier, *Calif., U.S.* 33°58' N, 118°3' W **101**
Whittle, Cap, *Can.* 50°6' N, 60°13' W **111**
Whittlesey, *U.K.* 52°32' N, 0°8' E **162**
Wholdaia Lake, *Can.* 60°42' N, 105°15' W **108**
Whyalla, *Austral.* 32°60' S, 137°33' E **231**
Wiarton, *Can.* 44°43' N, 81°9' W **94**
Wibaux, *Mont., U.S.* 46°57' N, 104°13' W **90**
Wichita, *Kans., U.S.* 37°39' N, 97°20' W **90**
Wichita Falls, *Tex., U.S.* 33°52' N, 98°30' W **92**
Wichita, river, *Tex., U.S.* 33°47' N, 99°19' W **80**
Wick, *U.K.* 58°27' N, 3°9' W **143**
Wickede, *Ger.* 51°30' N, 7°52' E **167**
Wickenburg, *Ariz., U.S.* 33°58' N, 112°47' W **112**
Wickford see North Kingstown, *R.I., U.S.* 41°34' N, 71°28' W **104**
Wickliffe, *Ky., U.S.* 36°58' N, 89°4' W **96**
Wickliffe, *Ohio, U.S.* 41°35' N, 81°28' W **102**
Wicklow, *Ire.* 52°58' N, 6°4' W **150**
Wicklow Mountains, *Ire.* 53°1' N, 6°59' W **150**
Wickrath, *Ger.* 51°7' N, 6°24' E **167**
Widerøe, Mount, peak, *Antarctica* 72°7' S, 22°53' E **248**
Widnes, *U.K.* 53°21' N, 2°44' W **162**
Wiehl, *Ger.* 50°56' N, 7°32' E **167**
Wielbark, *Pol.* 53°23' N, 20°55' E **152**
Wielkopolskie, adm. division, *Pol.* 52°11' N, 15°54' E **152**
Wien (Vienna), *Aust.* 48°10' N, 16°14' E **152**
Wiener Neustadt, *Aust.* 47°48' N, 16°14' E **168**
Wierden, *Neth.* 52°21' N, 6°35' E **163**
Wiergate, *Tex., U.S.* 30°59' N, 93°43' W **103**
Wiesbaden, *Ger.* 50°4' N, 8°13' E **167**
Wiesmoor, *Ger.* 53°24' N, 7°44' E **163**
Wieżyca, peak, *Pol.* 54°13' N, 18°2' E **152**
Wigan, *U.K.* 53°32' N, 2°38' W **162**
Wiggins, *Miss., U.S.* 30°50' N, 89°6' W **103**
Wignes Lake, *Can.* 60°11' N, 106°37' W **108**
Wigton, *U.K.* 54°49' N, 3°10' W **162**
Wikieup, *Ariz., U.S.* 34°43' N, 113°37' W **101**
Wil, *Switz.* 47°27' N, 9°2' E **156**
Wilberforce, Cape, *Austral.* 11°50' S, 136°37' E **192**
Wilbur, *Wash., U.S.* 47°44' N, 118°42' W **90**
Wilcox, *Can.* 50°5' N, 104°45' W **90**
Wilczek, Zemlya, islands, *Russ.* 79°47' N, 64°40' E **160**
Wild, Cape, *Antarctica* 67°58' S, 152°38' E **248**
Wild Rice, river, *Minn., U.S.* 46°57' N, 96°45' W **94**
Wild Rose, *Wis., U.S.* 44°10' N, 89°16' W **102**
Wildcat Peak, *Nev., U.S.* 39°0' N, 116°55' W **90**
Wilder, *Vt., U.S.* 43°40' N, 72°19' W **104**
Wildflicken, *Ger.* 50°23' N, 9°55' E **167**
Wildomar, *Calif., U.S.* 33°36' N, 117°17' W **101**
Wildon, *Aust.* 46°52' N, 15°28' E **156**
Wildrose, *N. Dak., U.S.* 48°37' N, 103°12' W **90**
Wildspitze, peak, *Aust.* 46°53' N, 10°48' E **167**
Wildwood, *Can.* 53°35' N, 115°16' W **108**
Wildwood, *Fla., U.S.* 28°51' N, 82°3' W **105**
Wildwood, *N.J., U.S.* 38°59' N, 74°50' W **94**
Wiley, *Colo., U.S.* 38°9' N, 102°43' W **90**
Wilhelm, Mount, peak, *P.N.G.* 5°48' S, 144°54' E **192**
Wilhelmina Gebergte, *Suriname* 3°44' N, 56°34' W **130**
Wilhelmshaven, *Ger.* 53°31' N, 8°8' E **163**
Wilhelmstal, *Namibia* 21°53' S, 16°12' E **227**
Wilkes, U.S., station, *Antarctica* 66°5' S, 110°43' E **248**
Wilkesboro, *N.C., U.S.* 36°8' N, 81°10' W **96**
Wilkesland, region, *Antarctica* 69°56' S, 132°51' E **248**
Wilkie, *Can.* 52°25' N, 108°43' W **108**
Wilkinson, *Miss., U.S.* 31°13' N, 91°14' W **103**
Will, Mount, peak, *Can.* 57°31' N, 128°55' W **108**
Willacoochee, *Ga., U.S.* 31°20' N, 83°3' W **96**
Willapa, *Wash., U.S.* 46°40' N, 123°40' W **100**
Willapa Bay 46°32' N, 125°1' W **80**
Willapa Bay, *Wash., U.S.* 46°40' N, 124°4' W **100**
Willapa Hills, *Wash., U.S.* 46°20' N, 123°12' W **100**
Willard, *N. Mex., U.S.* 34°35' N, 106°2' W **92**
Willard, *Ohio, U.S.* 41°2' N, 82°44' W **102**
Willaumez Peninsula, *P.N.G.* 5°15' S, 149°24' E **192**
Willcox, *Ariz., U.S.* 32°14' N, 109°51' W **112**
Willebroek, *Belg.* 51°2' N, 4°21' E **163**
Willemstad, *Neth. Antilles, Neth.* 51°41' N, 4°25' E **167**
William Lake, lake, *Can.* 53°49' N, 99°46' W **108**
William Point, *Can.* 58°55' N, 109°47' W **108**
William, river, *Can.* 58°9' N, 108°60' W **108**
Williams, *Ariz., U.S.* 35°13' N, 112°11' W **82**
Williams, *Calif., U.S.* 39°9' N, 122°10' W **90**
Williams, *Ind., U.S.* 38°48' N, 86°39' W **102**
Williams, *Minn., U.S.* 48°44' N, 94°58' W **90**
Williams Bay, *Wis., U.S.* 42°34' N, 88°33' W **102**
Williams Island, *Bahamas* 24°33' N, 78°35' W **105**
Williams Lake, *Can.* 51°46' N, 91°23' W **110**
Williams Lake, *Can.* 52°6' N, 122°5' W **106**
Williams Lake, *Can.* 52°8' N, 122°7' W **108**
Williams, Point, *Antarctica* 67°54' S, 68°26' E **248**
Williamsburg, *Ky., U.S.* 36°44' N, 84°10' W **96**
Williamsburg, *Mass., U.S.* 42°23' N, 72°43' W **104**
Williamsburg, *Ohio, U.S.* 39°3' N, 84°4' W **102**
Williamsburg, *Va., U.S.* 37°16' N, 76°43' W **94**
Williamsfield, *Ill., U.S.* 40°54' N, 90°2' W **102**
Williamson, *W. Va., U.S.* 37°40' N, 82°17' W **96**
Williamson, Mount, peak, *Calif., U.S.* 36°39' N, 118°21' W **101**
Williamsport, *Ind., U.S.* 40°16' N, 87°18' W **102**
Williamsport, *Ohio, U.S.* 39°34' N, 83°7' W **102**
Williamsport, *Pa., U.S.* 41°14' N, 77°1' W **94**
Williamstown, *Ky., U.S.* 38°37' N, 84°34' W **102**
Williamstown, *Vt., U.S.* 44°7' N, 72°33' W **104**
Williamstown, *W. Va., U.S.* 39°23' N, 81°28' W **102**
Williamsville, *Ill., U.S.* 39°56' N, 89°33' W **102**
Willich, *Ger.* 51°15' N, 6°33' E **167**
Willimantic, *Conn., U.S.* 41°42' N, 72°13' W **104**
Willingdon, Mount, peak, *Can.* 51°46' N, 116°20' W **90**
Willis, *Tex., U.S.* 30°24' N, 95°28' W **103**
Willis Islands, *Scotia Sea* 53°50' S, 39°43' W **134**
Willis Islets, islands, *Coral Sea* 15°9' S, 149°13' E **230**
Williston, *Fla., U.S.* 29°22' N, 82°28' W **105**
Williston, *N. Dak., U.S.* 48°7' N, 103°39' W **90**
Williston, *S. Af.* 31°19' S, 20°53' E **227**
Williston Lake, *Can.* 55°59' N, 124°26' W **108**
Willits, *Calif., U.S.* 39°24' N, 123°22' W **90**
Willmar, *Minn., U.S.* 45°6' N, 95°3' W **90**
Willoughby, *U.K.* 53°13' N, 0°12' E **162**
Willow, *Alas., U.S.* 61°44' N, 150°4' W **98**
Willow Bunch, *Can.* 49°22' N, 105°38' W **90**
Willow City, *N. Dak., U.S.* 48°34' N, 100°19' W **94**
Willow Hill, *Ill., U.S.* 38°58' N, 88°1' W **102**
Willow Island, *Nebr., U.S.* 40°53' N, 100°5' W **90**
Willow Reservoir, lake, *Wis., U.S.* 45°42' N, 90°22' W **94**
Willow River, *Can.* 54°2' N, 122°31' W **108**
Willow Springs, *Mo., U.S.* 36°58' N, 91°59' W **96**
Willowick, *Ohio, U.S.* 41°37' N, 81°28' W **102**
Willowmore, *S. Af.* 33°17' S, 23°29' E **227**
Willows, *Calif., U.S.* 39°31' N, 122°13' W **92**
Wills Point, *Tex., U.S.* 32°41' N, 96°1' W **96**
Willsboro, *N.Y., U.S.* 44°21' N, 73°25' W **104**
Wilmer, *Ala., U.S.* 30°49' N, 88°21' W **103**
Wilmer, *Can.* 50°32' N, 116°4' W **108**
Wilmette, *Ill., U.S.* 42°4' N, 87°42' W **102**
Wilmington, *Del., U.S.* 39°43' N, 75°33' W **94**
Wilmington, *Ill., U.S.* 41°18' N, 88°8' W **102**
Wilmington, *N.Y., U.S.* 44°23' N, 73°50' W **104**
Wilmington, *N.C., U.S.* 34°14' N, 77°55' W **73**
Wilmington, *Ohio, U.S.* 39°26' N, 83°49' W **102**
Wilmington, *Vt., U.S.* 42°51' N, 72°52' W **104**
Wilmot, *Ark., U.S.* 33°2' N, 91°35' W **103**
Wilmot, *S. Dak., U.S.* 45°23' N, 96°53' W **90**
Wilmot Flat, *N.H., U.S.* 43°25' N, 71°54' W **104**
Wilmslow, *U.K.* 53°19' N, 2°14' W **162**
Wilpattu National Park, *Sri Lanka* 8°19' N, 79°37' E **172**
Wilsall, *Mont., U.S.* 45°58' N, 110°40' W **90**
Wilseyville, *Calif., U.S.* 38°22' N, 120°32' W **100**
Wilson, *Ark., U.S.* 35°33' N, 90°3' W **96**
Wilson, *Kans., U.S.* 38°48' N, 98°29' W **92**
Wilson, *La., U.S.* 30°54' N, 91°7' W **103**
Wilson, *N.C., U.S.* 35°42' N, 77°56' W **96**
Wilson, *Okla., U.S.* 34°8' N, 97°25' W **92**
Wilson, *Tex., U.S.* 33°18' N, 101°44' W **92**
Wilson Creek, *Wash., U.S.* 47°25' N, 119°8' W **90**
Wilson Creek Range, *Nev., U.S.* 38°23' N, 114°38' W **90**
Wilson Inlet 35°22' S, 116°46' E **230**
Wilson, Mount, peak, *Colo., U.S.* 37°49' N, 108°4' W **92**
Wilson, Mount, peak, *Nev., U.S.* 38°13' N, 114°28' W **90**
Wilson, Mount, peak, *Oreg., U.S.* 45°2' N, 121°45' W **90**
Wilsonville, *Ill., U.S.* 39°3' N, 89°51' W **102**
Wilton, *Conn., U.S.* 41°11' N, 73°27' W **104**
Wilton, *N.H., U.S.* 42°50' N, 71°45' W **104**
Wilton, *N. Dak., U.S.* 47°8' N, 100°49' W **90**
Wilton, *U.K.* 51°5' N, 1°53' W **162**
Wilton, river, *Austral.* 13°31' S, 133°56' E **231**
Wiluna, *Austral.* 26°36' S, 120°13' E **231**
Wimauma, *Fla., U.S.* 27°43' N, 82°17' W **105**
Wimbledon, *U.K.* 51°25' N, 0°13' E **162**
Wimereux, *Fr.* 50°46' N, 1°37' E **163**
Winam 0°21' N, 34°13' E **224**
Winamac, *Ind., U.S.* 41°2' N, 86°37' W **102**
Winburg, *S. Af.* 28°33' S, 26°58' E **227**
Wincanton, *U.K.* 51°3' N, 2°25' W **162**
Winchelsea, *U.K.* 50°55' N, 0°43' E **162**
Winchelsea Island, *Austral.* 13°36' S, 136°22' E **230**
Winchendon, *Mass., U.S.* 42°40' N, 72°4' W **104**
Winchester, *Calif., U.S.* 33°42' N, 117°6' W **101**
Winchester, *Ind., U.S.* 40°10' N, 84°59' W **102**
Winchester, *N.H., U.S.* 42°45' N, 72°23' W **104**
Winchester, *Ohio, U.S.* 38°55' N, 83°38' W **102**
Winchester, *U.K.* 51°3' N, 1°19' W **162**
Winchester, *Va., U.S.* 39°10' N, 78°10' W **94**
Winchester Bay 43°35' N, 125°28' W **80**
Wind Cave National Park, *S. Dak., U.S.* 43°29' N, 103°16' W **80**
Wind Point, *Wis., U.S.* 42°46' N, 87°46' W **102**
Wind, river, *Can.* 65°23' N, 135°18' W **98**
Wind River Peak, *Wyo., U.S.* 42°42' N, 109°13' W **90**
Wind River Range, *Wyo., U.S.* 42°39' N, 109°21' W **90**
Wind, river, *Wyo., U.S.* 43°22' N, 109°9' W **80**
Windeck, *Ger.* 50°48' N, 7°36' E **167**
Winder, *Ga., U.S.* 33°58' N, 83°44' W **96**
Windermere, *U.K.* 54°22' N, 2°54' W **162**
Windfall, *Can.* 54°9' N, 116°18' W **108**
Windfall, *Ind., U.S.* 40°21' N, 85°58' W **102**
Windham, *Conn., U.S.* 41°41' N, 72°10' W **104**
Windhoek, *Namibia* 22°34' S, 16°56' E **227**
Windigo, river, *Can.* 48°22' N, 73°33' W **94**
Windmill Islands, *Indian Ocean* 66°40' S, 114°44' E **248**
Windom, *Minn., U.S.* 43°51' N, 95°7' W **90**
Windom Peak, *Colo., U.S.* 37°36' N, 107°41' W **92**
Window Rock, *Ariz., U.S.* 35°41' N, 109°3' W **92**
Winds, Bay of 66°11' S, 99°28' E **248**
Windsor, *Can.* 45°34' N, 72°1' W **94**
Windsor, *Can.* 42°18' N, 83°1' W **102**
Windsor, *Can.* 44°59' N, 64°8' W **111**
Windsor, *Colo., U.S.* 40°28' N, 104°55' W **90**
Windsor, *Conn., U.S.* 41°50' N, 72°39' W **104**
Windsor, *Ill., U.S.* 39°25' N, 88°36' W **102**
Windsor, *Mo., U.S.* 38°31' N, 93°31' W **94**
Windsor, *N.C., U.S.* 35°59' N, 76°60' W **96**
Windsor, *U.K.* 51°28' N, 0°37' E **162**
Windsor, *Vt., U.S.* 43°28' N, 72°24' W **104**
Windsorton, *S. Af.* 28°21' S, 24°39' E **227**
Windward Islands, *Caribbean Sea* 13°41' N, 61°20' W **116**
Windy Lake, *Can.* 60°18' N, 100°44' W **108**
Windy Peak, *Wash., U.S.* 48°54' N, 120°3' W **90**
Windy Point, *Can.* 50°56' N, 55°48' W **111**
Winefred Lake, *Can.* 55°25' N, 111°16' W **108**
Winfall, *N.C., U.S.* 36°13' N, 76°29' W **96**
Winfield, *Can.* 52°56' N, 114°27' W **108**
Winfield, *Tex., U.S.* 33°9' N, 95°7' W **103**
Wingham, *Can.* 43°53' N, 81°19' W **102**
Winifred, *Mont., U.S.* 47°31' N, 109°23' W **90**
Winifreda, *Arg.* 36°15' S, 64°15' W **139**
Winisk Lake, *Can.* 52°49' N, 88°29' W **80**
Winisk, river, *Can.* 54°27' N, 86°26' W **106**
Wink, *Tex., U.S.* 31°43' N, 103°9' W **92**
Winkleigh, *U.K.* 50°51' N, 3°57' W **162**
Winkler, *Can.* 49°10' N, 97°56' W **94**
Winlock, *Wash., U.S.* 46°28' N, 122°56' W **100**
Winn, *Me., U.S.* 45°28' N, 68°23' W **94**
Winneba, *Ghana* 5°22' N, 0°40' E **222**
Winnebago, *Ill., U.S.* 42°15' N, 89°15' W **102**
Winnebago, *Minn., U.S.* 43°45' N, 94°10' W **94**
Winnebago, Lake, *Wis., U.S.* 43°50' N, 88°27' W **102**
Winneconne, *Wis., U.S.* 44°6' N, 88°45' W **102**
Winner, *S. Dak., U.S.* 43°21' N, 99°52' W **90**
Winnetka, *Ill., U.S.* 42°6' N, 87°44' W **102**
Winnfield, *La., U.S.* 31°54' N, 92°39' W **103**
Winnibigoshish, Lake, *Minn., U.S.* 47°21' N, 96°1' W **80**
Winnie, *Tex., U.S.* 29°48' N, 94°23' W **103**
Winnipeg, *Can.* 49°53' N, 97°19' W **90**
Winnipeg Beach, *Can.* 50°29' N, 97°2' W **90**
Winnipeg, Lake, *Can.* 53°1' N, 98°32' W **80**
Winnipegosis, *Can.* 51°39' N, 99°57' W **90**
Winnipegosis, Lake, *Can.* 52°3' N, 99°36' W **80**
Winnisquam, *N.H., U.S.* 43°30' N, 71°32' W **104**
Winnsboro, *La., U.S.* 32°9' N, 91°44' W **103**
Winnsboro, *S.C., U.S.* 34°21' N, 81°5' W **96**
Winnsboro, *Tex., U.S.* 32°57' N, 95°17' W **103**
Winokapau Lake, *Can.* 53°13' N, 63°41' W **111**
Winona, *Kans., U.S.* 39°3' N, 101°15' W **90**
Winona, *Minn., U.S.* 44°2' N, 91°38' W **94**
Winona, *Miss., U.S.* 33°27' N, 89°44' W **103**
Winona, *Tex., U.S.* 32°29' N, 95°10' W **103**
Winona Lake, *Ind., U.S.* 41°12' N, 85°49' W **94**
Winschoten, *Neth.* 53°8' N, 7°1' E **163**
Winsen, *Ger.* 53°22' N, 10°12' E **150**
Winsford, *U.K.* 53°11' N, 2°32' W **162**
Winslow, *Ariz., U.S.* 35°1' N, 110°41' W **92**
Winslow, *Me., U.S.* 44°32' N, 69°38' W **94**
Winstead, *S. Af.* 28°51' S, 22°8' E **227**
Winsted, *Conn., U.S.* 41°55' N, 73°4' W **104**
Winter Harbour, *Can.* 50°30' N, 128°4' W **90**
Winter Haven, *Fla., U.S.* 28°1' N, 81°44' W **105**
Winter Park, *Fla., U.S.* 28°35' N, 81°22' W **105**
Winterberg, *Ger.* 51°11' N, 8°32' E **167**
Winterhaven, *Calif., U.S.* 32°44' N, 114°40' W **101**
Wintering Lake, lake, *Can.* 49°23' N, 87°51' W **94**
Winters, *Tex., U.S.* 31°56' N, 99°58' W **96**
Winterswijk, *Neth.* 51°58' N, 6°43' E **167**
Winterton on Sea, *U.K.* 52°43' N, 1°41' E **163**
Winterville, *Miss., U.S.* 33°29' N, 91°3' W **103**
Winthrop, *Mass., U.S.* 42°22' N, 70°60' W **104**
Winthrop, *Minn., U.S.* 44°32' N, 94°23' W **90**
Winthrop, *Wash., U.S.* 48°27' N, 120°10' W **108**
Winthrop Harbor, *Ill., U.S.* 42°28' N, 87°50' W **102**
Winton, *Austral.* 22°25' S, 143°2' E **238**
Winton, *Calif., U.S.* 37°23' N, 120°38' W **100**
Winton, *Minn., U.S.* 47°54' N, 91°49' W **94**
Winton, *N.Z.* 46°9' S, 168°18' E **240**
Wipperfürth, *Ger.* 51°7' N, 7°23' E **163**
Wis, river, *Pol.* 53°7' N, 18°11' E **142**
Wis, river, *Pol.* 50°1' N, 20°37' E **152**
Wisbech, *U.K.* 52°39' N, 0°9' E **162**
Wiscasset, *Me., U.S.* 44°0' N, 69°41' W **94**
Wisconsin, adm. division, *Wis., U.S.* 44°20' N, 91°11' W **94**
Wisconsin Dells, *Wis., U.S.* 43°37' N, 89°46' W **102**
Wisconsin, Lake, *Wis., U.S.* 43°21' N, 89°53' W **102**
Wisconsin Range, *Antarctica* 84°42' S, 105°9' W **248**
Wisconsin Rapids, *Wis., U.S.* 44°23' N, 89°50' W **110**
Wisconsin, river, *Wis., U.S.* 42°45' N, 91°14' W **80**
Wise Bay 82°34' S, 170°4' E **248**
Wiseman, *Alas., U.S.* 67°18' N, 150°16' W **98**
Wishek, *N. Dak., U.S.* 46°14' N, 99°35' W **90**
Wishram, *Wash., U.S.* 45°39' N, 120°58' W **100**
Wisner, *La., U.S.* 31°58' N, 91°39' W **103**
Wissen, *Ger.* 50°46' N, 7°43' E **167**
Wistaria, *Can.* 53°51' N, 126°18' W **108**
Witbank, *S. Af.* 25°53' S, 29°11' E **227**
Witdraai, *S. Af.* 27°1' S, 20°41' E **227**
Witham, *U.K.* 51°48' N, 0°38' E **162**
Witherbee, *N.Y., U.S.* 44°5' N, 73°33' W **104**
Withernsea, *U.K.* 53°43' N, 3°179' E **162**
Witney, *U.K.* 51°47' N, 1°29' W **162**
Witry-lès-Reims, *Fr.* 49°17' N, 4°7' E **163**
Witt, *Ill., U.S.* 39°14' N, 89°21' W **102**
Wittdün, *Ger.* 54°37' N, 8°23' E **150**
Witten, *Ger.* 51°25' N, 7°19' E **167**
Witten, *S. Dak., U.S.* 43°25' N, 100°6' W **90**
Wittenberge, *Ger.* 53°3' N, 11°43' E **160**
Wittlich, *Ger.* 49°59' N, 6°54' E **167**
Wittmund, *Ger.* 53°34' N, 7°47' E **163**
Wittow, *Ger.* 54°38' N, 13°6' E **152**
Witu, *Kenya* 2°23' S, 40°26' E **224**
Witu Islands, islands, *Bismarck Sea* 4°24' S, 148°22' E **192**
Witvlei, *Namibia* 22°24' S, 18°32' E **227**
Witzenhausen, *Ger.* 51°20' N, 9°51' E **167**
Wivenhoe, *Can.* 56°11' N, 95°11' W **108**
Wiwŏn, *N. Korea* 40°53' N, 126°2' E **200**
Wiżajny, *Pol.* 54°21' N, 22°52' E **166**
Włocławek, *Pol.* 52°38' N, 19°4' E **152**
Włodawa, *Pol.* 51°32' N, 23°31' E **152**
Woburn, *Mass., U.S.* 42°28' N, 71°10' W **104**
Woc, *Pol.* 54°16' N, 18°45' E **166**
Wofford Heights, *Calif., U.S.* 35°43' N, 118°28' W **101**
Wokam, island, *Indonesia* 5°44' S, 134°34' E **192**
Woking, *Can.* 55°34' N, 118°47' W **108**
Woking, *U.K.* 51°18' N, 0°35' E **162**
Wokingham, *U.K.* 51°22' N, 0°52' E **162**
Wolcott, *Ind., U.S.* 40°45' N, 87°3' W **102**
Wolds, The, *U.K.* 53°56' N, 0°40' E **162**
Woleai Atoll, *F.M.S.* 7°26' N, 141°37' E **192**
Wolf Creek, *Mont., U.S.* 46°58' N, 112°3' W **90**
Wolf Creek Pass, *Colo., U.S.* 37°29' N, 106°49' W **90**
Wolf Lake, *Can.* 60°38' N, 132°17' W **108**
Wolf Lake, *Mich., U.S.* 43°14' N, 86°7' W **102**
Wolf Mountains, *Mont., U.S.* 45°9' N, 107°18' W **90**
Wolf, river, *Miss., U.S.* 30°33' N, 89°23' W **103**
Wolf, river, *Wis., U.S.* 45°17' N, 88°60' W **94**
Wolfau, *Aust.* 47°15' N, 16°5' E **168**
Wolfeboro, *N.H., U.S.* 43°34' N, 71°13' W **104**
Wolfeboro Falls, *N.H., U.S.* 43°35' N, 71°13' W **104**
Wolfen, *Ger.* 51°40' N, 12°16' E **152**
Wolfforth, *Tex., U.S.* 33°29' N, 102°1' W **92**
Wolfhagen, *Ger.* 51°19' N, 9°10' E **167**
Wolfsburg, *Ger.* 52°25' N, 10°47' E **152**
Wolfstein, *Ger.* 49°34' N, 7°36' E **163**
Wolin, *Pol.* 53°51' N, 14°36' E **152**
Wollaston Forland 74°31' N, 18°52' W **246**
Wollaston, Islas, islands, *Chile* 56°6' S, 67°3' W **134**
Wollaston Lake, *Can.* 57°56' N, 103°5' W **73**
Wollaston Peninsula, *Can.* 69°41' N, 121°29' W **106**
Wollongong, *Austral.* 34°24' S, 150°50' E **231**
Wöllstein, *Ger.* 49°48' N, 7°57' E **167**
Wolmaransstad, *S. Af.* 27°13' S, 25°58' E **227**
Wolseley, *Can.* 50°25' N, 103°17' W **90**
Wolsingham, *U.K.* 54°44' N, 1°54' W **162**
Wolsztyn, *Pol.* 52°7' N, 16°7' E **152**
Wolvega, *Neth.* 52°52' N, 6°0' E **163**
Wolverhampton, *U.K.* 52°35' N, 2°9' W **162**
Wolverine, river, *Can.* 57°46' N, 116°59' W **108**
Wolverton, *U.K.* 52°3' N, 0°49' E **162**
Wondong, *S. Korea* 34°21' N, 126°42' E **200**
Wonewoc, *Wis., U.S.* 43°38' N, 90°12' W **102**
Wonga Wongué National Park, *Gabon* 0°29' N, 9°13' E **206**
Wonju, *S. Korea* 37°19' N, 127°57' E **200**
Wonotobo Vallen, fall(s), *Suriname* 4°22' N, 58°6' W **130**
Wonowon, *Can.* 56°43' N, 121°48' W **108**
Wŏnsan, *N. Korea* 39°8' N, 127°24' E **200**
Wonyulgunna Hill, peak, *Austral.* 24°53' S, 119°34' E **230**
Wood Buffalo National Park, *Can.* 59°16' N, 114°1' W **72**
Wood Lake, *Nebr., U.S.* 42°37' N, 100°15' W **90**
Wood Lake, lake, *Can.* 55°13' N, 103°45' W **108**
Wood, Mount, peak, *Mont., U.S.* 45°14' N, 109°53' W **90**
Wood River, *Nebr., U.S.* 40°48' N, 98°37' W **90**
Wood, river, *Can.* 49°22' N, 107°21' W **80**
Woodah, Isle, island, *Austral.* 13°20' S, 134°37' E **230**
Woodall Mountain, peak, *Miss., U.S.* 34°43' N, 88°18' W **96**
Woodbine, *Ky., U.S.* 36°53' N, 84°6' W **96**
Woodbridge, *Calif., U.S.* 38°8' N, 121°19' W **100**
Woodbridge, *U.K.* 52°5' N, 1°17' E **162**
Woodburn, *Ind., U.S.* 41°6' N, 84°51' W **102**
Woodburn, *Oreg., U.S.* 45°7' N, 122°51' W **90**
Woodbury, *Conn., U.S.* 41°32' N, 73°13' W **104**
Woodbury, *N.J., U.S.* 39°50' N, 75°11' W **94**
Woodcock, Mount, peak, *Austral.* 19°17' S, 133°51' E **230**
Woodhall Spa, *U.K.* 53°9' N, 0°13' E **162**
Woodlake, *Calif., U.S.* 36°25' N, 119°7' W **101**
Woodland, *Calif., U.S.* 38°40' N, 121°47' W **90**
Woodland, *Wash., U.S.* 45°53' N, 122°46' W **100**
Woodlark, island, *P.N.G.* 9°5' S, 153°2' E **192**
Woodmont, *Conn., U.S.* 41°13' N, 72°60' W **104**
Woodpecker, *Can.* 53°30' N, 122°39' W **108**
Woodridge, *Can.* 49°15' N, 96°9' W **90**

Woodroffe, Mount, peak, *Austral.* 26°23' S, 131°32' E **230**
Woodruff, *Utah, U.S.* 41°31' N, 111°10' W **90**
Woods, Lake of the, *Can.* 49°4' N, 96°1' W **106**
Woodsboro, *Tex., U.S.* 28°13' N, 97°19' W **96**
Woodsfield, *Ohio, U.S.* 39°44' N, 81°7' W **102**
Woodstock, *Can.* 43°7' N, 80°44' W **102**
Woodstock, *Can.* 46°9' N, 67°36' W **94**
Woodstock, *Ill., U.S.* 42°18' N, 88°26' W **102**
Woodstock, *N.Y., U.S.* 42°2' N, 74°8' W **104**
Woodstock, *U.K.* 51°50' N, 1°22' W **162**
Woodstock, *Vt., U.S.* 43°37' N, 72°31' W **104**
Woodsville, *N.H., U.S.* 44°8' N, 72°3' W **104**
Woodville, *Calif., U.S.* 36°5' N, 119°13' W **101**
Woodville, *Ga., U.S.* 33°39' N, 83°7' W **96**
Woodville, *Miss., U.S.* 31°4' N, 91°18' W **103**
Woodville, *Tex., U.S.* 30°45' N, 94°26' W **103**
Woodward, *Okla., U.S.* 36°24' N, 99°23' W **96**
Woodworth, *La., U.S.* 31°8' N, 92°31' W **103**
Woody, *Calif., U.S.* 35°42' N, 118°51' W **101**
Woody Point, *Can.* 49°30' N, 57°56' W **111**
Woollard, Mount, peak, *Antarctica* 80°27' S, 95°39' W **248**
Woollett, Lac, lake, *Can.* 51°22' N, 74°22' W **110**
Woolpit, *U.K.* 52°13' N, 0°53' E **162**
Woolwich, *Me., U.S.* 43°55' N, 69°49' W **104**
Woolwich, *U.K.* 51°29' N, 6°357' E **162**
Woomera, *Austral.* 31°13' S, 136°55' E **231**
Woonsocket, *S. Dak., U.S.* 44°2' N, 98°18' W **90**
Wooster, *Ohio, U.S.* 40°47' N, 81°56' W **102**
Woosung, *Ill., U.S.* 41°53' N, 89°33' W **102**
Worbis, *Ger.* 51°25' N, 10°21' E **167**
Worcester, *Mass., U.S.* 42°16' N, 71°48' W **104**
Worcester, *S. Af.* 33°38' S, 19°23' E **227**
Worcester, *U.K.* 52°11' N, 2°12' W **162**
Worden, *Mont., U.S.* 45°57' N, 108°10' W **90**
Wordie Nunatak, peak, *Antarctica* 66°19' S, 51°16' E **248**
Workington, *U.K.* 54°38' N, 3°33' W **162**
Worksop, *U.K.* 53°17' N, 1°8' W **162**
Worland, *Wyo., U.S.* 44°0' N, 107°56' W **90**
World's View Hill, site, *Zimb.* 20°31' S, 28°29' E **227**
Wormeldange, *Lux.* 49°37' N, 6°24' E **163**
Woronoco, *Mass., U.S.* 42°9' N, 72°51' W **104**
Wörrstadt, *Ger.* 49°49' N, 8°6' E **167**
Worsley, *Can.* 56°33' N, 119°8' W **108**
Wörth, *Ger.* 49°47' N, 9°10' E **167**
Wortham, *Tex., U.S.* 31°45' N, 96°28' W **96**
Worthing, *U.K.* 50°49' N, 0°23' E **162**
Worthington, *Ind., U.S.* 39°6' N, 86°59' W **102**
Worthington, *Minn., U.S.* 43°35' N, 95°37' W **90**
Worthington, *Ohio, U.S.* 40°5' N, 82°60' W **102**
Worthington Peak, *Nev., U.S.* 37°54' N, 115°42' W **90**
Worthville, *Ky., U.S.* 38°36' N, 85°4' W **102**
Wosi, *Indonesia* 0°10' N, 127°46' E **192**
Woumbou, *Cameroon* 5°15' N, 14°14' E **218**
Wounta, Laguna de, lake, *Nicar.* 13°34' N, 84°18' W **115**
Wour, *Chad* 21°21' N, 15°57' E **216**
Wowoni, island, *Indonesia* 4°20' S, 123°14' E **192**
Woyla, river, *Indonesia* 4°21' N, 96°4' E **196**
Wragby, *U.K.* 53°16' N, 0°19' E **162**
Wrangel Island see Vrangelya, Ostrov, island, *Russ.* 71°29' N, 175°23' E **160**
Wrangel Plain, *Arctic Ocean* 81°41' N, 157°4' E **255**
Wrangell, *Alas., U.S.* 56°28' N, 132°25' W **108**
Wrangell Mountains, *Alas., U.S.* 61°51' N, 144°32' W **98**
Wrangell-Saint Elias National Park and Preserve, *Alas., U.S.* 62°15' N, 143°49' W **98**
Wray, *Colo., U.S.* 40°3' N, 102°14' W **90**
Wreck Point, *S. Af.* 29°7' S, 16°12' E **227**
Wrekin, The, peak, *U.K.* 52°39' N, 2°36' W **162**
Wren, *Ala., U.S.* 34°25' N, 87°17' W **96**
Wrens, *Ga., U.S.* 33°11' N, 82°24' W **96**
Wrexham, *U.K.* 53°2' N, 2°59' W **162**
Wright, *Philippines* 11°47' N, 125°1' E **203**
Wright, *Wyo., U.S.* 43°42' N, 105°32' W **90**
Wright Hill, peak, *Antarctica* 79°36' S, 159°27' E **248**
Wright, Mont, peak, *Can.* 52°43' N, 67°27' W **111**
Wright Patman Lake, *Ark., U.S.* 33°1' N, 94°59' W **80**
Wright-Patterson Air Force Base, *Ohio, U.S.* 39°48' N, 84°6' W **102**
Wrightsville Beach, *N.C., U.S.* 34°12' N, 77°49' W **96**
Wrightwood, *Calif., U.S.* 34°21' N, 117°39' W **101**
Wrigley, *Can.* 63°19' N, 123°21' W **98**
Wrigley Gulf 73°35' S, 126°58' W **248**
Wrington, *U.K.* 51°21' N, 2°46' W **162**
Wroc, *Pol.* 51°6' N, 17°0' E **152**
Wrong Lake, lake, *Can.* 52°34' N, 96°38' W **108**
Wronki, *Pol.* 52°42' N, 16°23' E **152**
Wroxeter, *Can.* 43°51' N, 81°11' W **102**
Wroxham, *U.K.* 52°43' N, 1°24' E **163**
Wroxton, *Can.* 51°12' N, 101°54' W **90**
Wroxton, *U.K.* 52°4' N, 1°25' W **162**
Wu, river, *China* 28°38' N, 108°25' E **198**
Wu, river, *China* 27°14' N, 108°4' E **190**
Wu'an, *China* 36°42' N, 114°13' E **198**
Wubu, *China* 37°27' N, 110°40' E **198**
Wuchang, *China* 44°55' N, 127°8' E **198**
Wuchuan, *China* 41°7' N, 111°33' E **198**
Wuchuan, *China* 28°26' N, 108°1' E **198**
Wuchuan, *China* 21°24' N, 110°47' E **198**
Wuda, *China* 39°33' N, 106°44' E **198**
Wudalianchi, *China* 48°38' N, 126°10' E **198**
Wudaogou, *China* 42°5' N, 125°51' E **200**
Wudaoliang, *China* 35°13' N, 93°2' E **188**
Wudi, *China* 37°45' N, 117°35' E **198**
Wudu, *China* 33°25' N, 104°54' E **198**
Wufeng, *China* 30°14' N, 110°40' E **198**
Wugang, *China* 26°44' N, 110°34' E **198**
Wugong, *China* 34°17' N, 108°11' E **198**
Wuhai, *China* 39°39' N, 106°50' E **198**
Wuhan, *China* 30°30' N, 114°21' E **198**
Wuhe, *China* 33°9' N, 117°55' E **198**
Wuhu, *China* 31°23' N, 118°26' E **198**
Wüjang, *China* 33°36' N, 79°54' E **188**
Wukari, *Nig.* 7°49' N, 9°48' E **222**
Wulff Land 81°57' N, 58°19' W **246**
Wuli, *China* 34°22' N, 92°45' E **188**
Wulian, *China* 35°44' N, 119°13' E **198**
Wulongbei, *China* 40°15' N, 124°15' E **200**
Wum, *Cameroon* 6°19' N, 10°3' E **222**
Wuming, *China* 23°8' N, 108°18' E **198**
Wun Shwai, *Sudan* 8°1' N, 29°24' E **224**
Wuning, *China* 29°18' N, 115°1' E **198**
Wünnenberg, *Ger.* 51°30' N, 8°43' E **167**
Wunstorf, *Ger.* 52°25' N, 9°26' E **152**
Wuping, *China* 25°4' N, 116°4' E **198**
Wuppertal, *Ger.* 51°16' N, 7°10' E **167**
Wuqi, *China* 36°57' N, 108°14' E **198**
Wuqia, *China* 39°45' N, 75°6' E **184**
Wuqing, *China* 39°25' N, 117°0' E **198**
Wurno, *Nig.* 13°14' N, 5°27' E **222**
Würselen, *Ger.* 50°49' N, 6°7' E **163**
Würzburg, *Ger.* 49°47' N, 9°56' E **167**
Wusa'a, *Sudan* 13°0' N, 32°31' E **182**
Wushan, *China* 31°6' N, 109°51' E **198**
Wushi (Uqturpan), *China* 41°9' N, 79°17' E **184**
Wutai, *China* 38°41' N, 113°11' E **198**
Wuvulu Island, *P.N.G.* 2°23' S, 142°45' E **192**
Wuwei, *China* 38°0' N, 102°55' E **190**
Wuwei, *China* 31°17' N, 117°47' E **198**
Wuxi, *China* 31°23' N, 109°36' E **198**
Wuxi, *China* 31°37' N, 120°18' E **198**
Wuxue, *China* 29°54' N, 115°33' E **198**
Wuyi Shan, *China* 26°4' N, 116°25' E **198**
Wuyiling, *China* 48°37' N, 129°21' E **198**
Wuyuan, *China* 41°4' N, 108°19' E **198**
Wuzhai, *China* 38°54' N, 111°49' E **198**
Wuzhong, *China* 38°1' N, 106°12' E **198**
Wuzhou, *China* 23°34' N, 111°21' E **198**
Wyandotte, *Mich., U.S.* 42°11' N, 83°11' W **102**
Wyanet, *Ill., U.S.* 41°22' N, 89°34' W **102**
Wye, river, *U.K.* 52°15' N, 3°30' W **162**
Wyemandoo, peak, *Austral.* 28°36' S, 118°19' E **230**
Wylatowo, *Pol.* 52°36' N, 17°55' E **152**
Wymondham, *U.K.* 52°34' N, 1°6' E **163**
Wymore, *Nebr., U.S.* 40°5' N, 96°40' W **90**
Wyndham, *Austral.* 15°29' S, 128°14' E **238**
Wyndmere, *N. Dak., U.S.* 46°15' N, 97°10' W **90**
Wynne, *Ark., U.S.* 35°12' N, 90°49' W **96**
Wynnewood, *Okla., U.S.* 34°37' N, 97°9' W **96**
Wynyard, *Can.* 51°45' N, 104°11' W **90**
Wyoming, *Can.* 42°56' N, 82°7' W **102**
Wyoming, *Ill., U.S.* 41°3' N, 89°47' W **102**
Wyoming, adm. division, *Wyo., U.S.* 42°49' N, 108°38' W **90**
Wyoming Peak, *Wyo., U.S.* 42°36' N, 110°43' W **90**
Wyoming Range, *Wyo., U.S.* 42°46' N, 110°47' W **90**
Wysox, *Pa., U.S.* 41°46' N, 76°25' W **110**
Wytheville, *Va., U.S.* 36°56' N, 81°6' W **96**
Wyville Thomson Ridge, *North Atlantic Ocean* 59°30' N, 10°10' W **253**
Wyvis, Ben, peak, *U.K.* 57°39' N, 4°41' W **150**

X

X, Rock, *Antarctica* 66°2' S, 138°54' E **248**
Xá Muteba, *Angola* 9°33' S, 17°49' E **218**
Xaafuun, *Somalia* 10°21' N, 51°18' E **216**
Xaafuun, Raas, *Somalia* 10°26' N, 51°28' E **216**
Xàbia see Jávea, *Sp.* 38°47' N, 0°9' E **164**
Xaçmaz, *Azerb.* 41°27' N, 48°49' E **195**
Xaignabouri, *Laos* 19°16' N, 101°43' E **202**
Xainza, *China* 30°57' N, 88°37' E **197**
Xaitongmoin, *China* 29°27' N, 88°9' E **188**
Xai-Xai, *Mozambique* 25°3' S, 33°39' E **227**
Xalapa, *Mex.* 19°28' N, 96°59' W **114**
Xalin, *Somalia* 9°5' N, 48°37' E **216**
Xam Nua, *Laos* 20°27' N, 104°0' E **202**
Xamure, *Somalia* 7°11' N, 48°56' E **218**
Xamure, spring, *Somalia* 7°12' N, 48°55' E **216**
Xangongo, *Angola* 16°45' S, 15°0' E **220**
Xankändi see Stepanakert, *Asia* 39°48' N, 46°43' E **195**
Xanten, *Ger.* 51°39' N, 6°27' E **167**
Xánthi, *Gr.* 41°8' N, 24°54' E **180**
Xanthus, ruin(s), *Turk.* 36°19' N, 29°12' E **156**
Xanxerê, *Braz.* 26°52' S, 52°25' W **138**
Xapecó, *Braz.* 27°4' S, 52°36' W **139**
Xapecó, river, *Braz.* 26°39' S, 52°30' W **139**
Xapuri, *Braz.* 10°42' S, 68°32' W **137**
Xapuri, river, *Braz.* 10°43' S, 69°13' W **137**
Xar Moron, river, *China* 43°17' N, 119°27' E **198**
Xarardheere, *Somalia* 4°38' N, 47°53' E **218**
Xassengue, *Angola* 10°26' S, 18°33' E **220**
Xátiva, *Sp.* 38°58' N, 0°31' E **164**
Xavantina, *Braz.* 21°15' S, 52°50' W **138**
Xayar, *China* 41°14' N, 82°51' E **184**
Xcalak National Park, *Mex.* 18°20' N, 88°6' W **72**
Xêgar see Tingri, *China* 28°40' N, 87°3' E **197**
Xèng, river, *Laos* 20°10' N, 102°44' E **202**
Xenia, *Ill., U.S.* 38°37' N, 88°38' W **102**
Xenia, *Ohio, U.S.* 39°41' N, 83°56' W **102**
Xépôn, *Laos* 16°41' N, 106°15' E **202**
Xeriuini, river, *Braz.* 0°50' N, 62°15' W **130**
Xhora, *S. Af.* 31°59' S, 28°39' E **227**
Xi Ujimqin Qi, *China* 44°36' N, 117°36' E **198**
Xiachuan Dao, island, *China* 21°17' N, 112°22' E **198**
Xiajiang, *China* 27°35' N, 115°3' E **198**
Xiamen (Amoy), *China* 24°25' N, 118°6' E **198**
Xi'an, *China* 34°17' N, 108°57' E **198**
Xianfeng, *China* 29°41' N, 109°8' E **198**
Xiang, river, *China* 26°33' N, 112°13' E **198**
Xiangfan, *China* 32°6' N, 112°2' E **198**
Xianggang see Hong Kong, island, *China* 21°55' N, 114°15' E **198**
Xianghuang Qi (Hobot Xar), *China* 42°11' N, 113°53' E **198**
Xiangkhoang, *Laos* 19°20' N, 103°23' E **202**
Xiangning, *China* 35°57' N, 110°48' E **198**
Xiangshan, *China* 29°26' N, 121°52' E **198**
Xiangtan, *China* 27°54' N, 112°51' E **198**
Xiangyin, *China* 28°42' N, 112°50' E **198**
Xianju, *China* 28°53' N, 120°43' E **198**
Xiantao, *China* 30°19' N, 113°26' E **198**
Xianyou, *China* 25°22' N, 118°42' E **198**
Xiaogan, *China* 30°55' N, 113°55' E **198**
Xiaojiang, *China* 27°33' N, 120°28' E **198**
Xiaoshan, *China* 30°8' N, 120°18' E **198**
Xiaoyi, *China* 37°7' N, 111°46' E **198**
Xiapu, *China* 26°53' N, 119°59' E **198**
Xichang, *China* 27°53' N, 102°16' E **190**
Xichang Space Launch Center, spaceport, *China* 28°13' N, 101°49' E **190**
Xichú, *Mex.* 21°23' N, 100°5' W **114**
Xichuan, *China* 33°10' N, 111°31' E **198**
Xicoténcatl, *Mex.* 22°58' N, 98°56' W **114**
Xicotepec de Juárez, *Mex.* 20°16' N, 97°57' W **114**
Xié, river, *Braz.* 1°12' N, 67°15' W **136**
Xiejia, *China* 42°23' N, 125°43' E **200**
Xifeng, *China* 42°45' N, 124°39' E **200**
Xifeng, *China* 35°47' N, 107°39' E **198**
Xigazê, *China* 29°13' N, 88°53' E **190**
Xihe, *China* 33°59' N, 105°16' E **198**
Xiis, *Somalia* 10°47' N, 46°52' E **216**
Xiji, *China* 36°0' N, 105°43' E **198**
Xijir Ulan Hu, lake, *China* 35°9' N, 89°12' E **188**
Xiliao, river, *China* 43°45' N, 122°32' E **198**
Xilinhot, *China* 43°56' N, 116°8' E **198**
Xilitla, *Mex.* 21°23' N, 98°58' W **114**
Ximeng, *China* 22°43' N, 99°25' E **202**
Xin Barag Youqi, *China* 48°39' N, 116°47' E **198**
Xin Barag Zuoqi, *China* 48°10' N, 118°13' E **198**
Xin Hot see Abag Qi, *China* 44°1' N, 114°56' E **198**
Xinavane, *Mozambique* 25°2' S, 32°47' E **227**
Xinbin, *China* 41°43' N, 125°4' E **200**
Xincai, *China* 32°46' N, 114°53' E **198**
Xincheng, *China* 38°32' N, 106°11' E **198**
Xinchengzi, *China* 42°4' N, 123°33' E **200**
Xinfeng, *China* 25°24' N, 114°54' E **198**
Xinfeng, *China* 24°1' N, 114°10' E **198**
Xing'an, *China* 25°33' N, 110°37' E **198**
Xingcheng, *China* 40°39' N, 120°46' E **198**
Xingdi, *China* 41°17' N, 87°58' E **188**
Xinge, *Angola* 9°47' S, 19°11' E **220**
Xinghe, *China* 40°51' N, 113°54' E **198**
Xinghua, *China* 32°56' N, 119°53' E **198**
Xingning, *China* 24°6' N, 115°43' E **198**
Xingshan, *China* 31°22' N, 110°44' E **198**
Xingtai, *China* 37°1' N, 114°31' E **198**
Xingu, river, *Braz.* 5°8' S, 54°18' W **122**
Xingxian, *China* 38°28' N, 111°3' E **198**
Xingyi, *China* 25°1' N, 105°8' E **190**
Xingzi, *China* 29°27' N, 115°59' E **198**
Xinhe, *China* 37°31' N, 115°13' E **198**
Xinhe (Toksu), *China* 41°35' N, 82°38' E **184**
Xinhuang, *China* 27°20' N, 109°17' E **198**
Xinhui, *China* 22°26' N, 113°1' E **198**
Xining, *China* 36°30' N, 101°51' E **190**
Xinji, *China* 37°56' N, 115°15' E **198**
Xinjiang, *China* 35°38' N, 111°12' E **198**
Xinjiang, adm. division, *China* 41°27' N, 81°29' E **184**
Xinjin, *China* 39°25' N, 122°2' E **198**
Xinmin, *China* 41°59' N, 122°49' E **200**
Xinning, *China* 26°28' N, 110°48' E **198**
Xinpu see Lianyungang, *China* 34°38' N, 119°14' E **198**
Xinshao, *China* 27°21' N, 111°28' E **198**
Xinwen, *China* 35°53' N, 117°43' E **198**
Xinxiang, *China* 35°12' N, 113°48' E **198**
Xinxing, *China* 22°43' N, 112°9' E **198**
Xinyang, *China* 32°9' N, 114°6' E **198**
Xinye, *China* 32°31' N, 112°26' E **198**
Xinyi, *China* 34°19' N, 118°20' E **198**
Xinyu, *China* 27°46' N, 114°52' E **198**
Xinyuan, *China* 43°25' N, 83°25' E **184**
Xinzhou, *China* 38°24' N, 112°45' E **198**
Xique Xique, *Braz.* 10°51' S, 42°43' W **132**
Xiruá, river, *Braz.* 7°19' S, 68°34' W **130**
Xishui, *China* 30°27' N, 115°13' E **198**
Xishui, *China* 28°20' N, 106°11' E **198**
Xiushan, *China* 28°25' N, 108°59' E **198**
Xiushui, *China* 29°4' N, 114°30' E **198**
Xiuyan, *China* 40°16' N, 123°15' E **200**
Xiuying, *China* 19°59' N, 110°12' E **198**
Xixia, *China* 33°21' N, 111°30' E **198**
Xixian, *China* 32°22' N, 114°41' E **198**
Xixiang, *China* 33°4' N, 107°44' E **198**
Xizang, adm. division, *China* 29°28' N, 87°1' E **197**
Xizhong Dao, island, *China* 39°8' N, 121°11' E **198**
Xochihuehuetlán, *Mex.* 17°54' N, 98°28' W **114**
Xorkol, *China* 38°52' N, 91°10' E **188**
Xpuhil, ruin(s), *Mex.* 18°31' N, 89°33' W **115**
Xuan Loc, *Vietnam* 10°56' N, 107°14' E **202**
Xuan'en, *China* 30°1' N, 109°28' E **198**
Xuanhan, *China* 31°21' N, 107°36' E **198**
Xuanhua, *China* 40°38' N, 115°5' E **198**
Xuanzhou, *China* 30°54' N, 118°46' E **198**
Xuchang, *China* 34°3' N, 113°49' E **198**
Xudat, *Azerb.* 41°37' N, 48°41' E **195**
Xuddur (Oddur), *Somalia* 4°6' N, 43°55' E **218**
Xudun, *Somalia* 9°3' N, 47°29' E **216**
Xui, *Uru.* 33°40' S, 53°29' W **139**
Xulun Hoh see Zhenglan Qi, *China* 42°13' N, 116°2' E **198**
Xümatang, *China* 33°52' N, 97°21' E **188**
Xunwu, *China* 24°52' N, 115°37' E **198**
Xunyang, *China* 32°53' N, 109°22' E **198**
Xunyi, *China* 35°10' N, 108°18' E **198**
Xupu, *China* 27°56' N, 110°35' E **198**
Xuwen, *China* 20°18' N, 110°9' E **198**
Xuyong, *China* 28°9' N, 105°28' E **198**
Xuzhou, *China* 34°16' N, 117°7' E **198**
Xylofagou, *Cyprus* 34°58' N, 33°50' E **194**

Yaak, *Mont., U.S.* 48°49' N, 115°43' W **90**
Yaak, river, *Can.* 48°43' N, 116°2' W **90**
Ya'an, *China* 30°2' N, 103°1' E **190**
Yabassi, *Cameroon* 4°25' N, 9°58' E **222**
Yabēlo, *Eth.* 4°51' N, 38°8' E **224**
Yablunyts'kyy, Pereval, pass, *Ukr.* 48°17' N, 24°27' E **152**
Yabrīn, spring, *Saudi Arabia* 23°11' N, 48°57' E **182**
Yabrūd, *Syr.* 33°58' N, 36°38' E **194**
Yachi, river, *China* 26°59' N, 106°14' E **198**
Yacimiento Río Turbio, *Arg.* 51°35' S, 72°21' W **134**
Yaco, *Bol.* 17°13' S, 67°34' W **137**
Yaco, river, *Peru* 10°47' S, 70°49' W **137**
Yacolt, *Wash., U.S.* 45°51' N, 122°25' W **100**
Yacuma, river, *Bol.* 14°6' S, 66°36' W **137**
Yadgir, *India* 16°46' N, 77°8' E **188**
Yaenengu, *Dem. Rep. of the Congo* 2°27' N, 23°11' E **218**
Yag, river, *China* 34°0' N, 93°55' E **188**
Yağca, *Turk.* 37°1' N, 30°32' E **156**
Yagodnoye, *Russ.* 62°34' N, 149°33' E **160**
Yagoua, *Cameroon* 10°22' N, 15°14' E **216**
Yagradagzê Shan, peak, *China* 35°8' N, 95°34' E **188**
Yaguarón, river, *South America* 31°60' S, 54°1' W **139**
Yaguas, river, *Peru* 3°11' S, 71°2' W **136**
Yahia Lehouas, *Alg.* 35°36' N, 4°55' E **150**
Yahk, *Can.* 49°5' N, 116°7' W **90**
Yahualica, *Mex.* 21°9' N, 102°54' W **114**
Yahuma, *Dem. Rep. of the Congo* 1°5' N, 23°5' E **218**
Yahyalı, *Turk.* 38°5' N, 35°21' E **156**
Yainax Butte, peak, *Oreg., U.S.* 42°19' N, 121°20' W **90**
Yaita, *Japan* 36°47' N, 139°56' E **201**
Yaizu, *Japan* 34°51' N, 138°18' E **201**
Yakeshi, *China* 49°15' N, 120°43' E **198**
Yakima, *Wash., U.S.* 46°35' N, 120°30' W **90**
Yakkabogʻ, *Uzb.* 39°1' N, 66°41' E **197**
Yakmach, *Pak.* 28°43' N, 63°48' E **182**
Yakoma, *Dem. Rep. of the Congo* 4°2' N, 22°21' E **218**
Yakossi, *Cen. Af. Rep.* 5°37' N, 23°22' E **218**
Yakotoko, *Cen. Af. Rep.* 5°20' N, 25°16' E **224**
Yaksha, *Russ.* 61°49' N, 56°50' E **154**
Yaku Shima, island, *Japan* 29°39' N, 130°35' E **190**
Yakusu, *Dem. Rep. of the Congo* 0°35' N, 25°1' E **224**
Yakutsk, *Russ.* 62°2' N, 129°36' E **160**
Yala, *Ghana* 10°7' N, 1°52' W **222**
Yala, *Sri Lanka* 6°22' N, 81°31' E **188**
Yala, *Thai.* 6°30' N, 101°16' E **196**
Yalagüina, *Nicar.* 13°28' N, 86°28' W **115**
Yale, *Can.* 49°34' N, 121°26' W **100**
Yale, *Mich., U.S.* 43°8' N, 82°47' W **102**
Yale, *Okla., U.S.* 36°5' N, 96°41' W **92**
Yale Dam, *Wash., U.S.* 45°59' N, 122°25' W **100**
Yali, *Dem. Rep. of the Congo* 1°59' N, 21°5' E **218**
Yaligimba, *Dem. Rep. of the Congo* 2°11' N, 22°54' E **218**
Yalinga, *Cen. Af. Rep.* 6°30' N, 23°19' E **218**
Yalkubul, Punta, *Mex.* 21°34' N, 89°27' W **116**
Yalova, *Turk.* 40°38' N, 29°15' E **156**
Yalta, *Ukr.* 44°30' N, 34°5' E **156**
Yalu, river, *Asia* 41°46' N, 128°2' E **200**
Yalutorovsk, *Russ.* 56°40' N, 66°11' E **169**
Yalvaç, *Turk.* 38°17' N, 31°9' E **156**
Yamada, *Japan* 33°33' N, 130°45' E **201**
Yamaga, *Japan* 33°0' N, 130°41' E **201**
Yamagata, *Japan* 38°15' N, 140°20' E **201**
Yamagata, adm. division, *Japan* 38°22' N, 139°45' E **201**
Yamaguchi, *Japan* 34°11' N, 131°29' E **200**
Yamaguchi, adm. division, *Japan* 34°6' N, 131°0' E **200**
Yamal, Poluostrov, *Russ.* 70°23' N, 70°9' E **169**
Yamal-Nenets, adm. division, *Russ.* 66°22' N, 74°2' E **160**
Yamanaka, *Japan* 36°14' N, 136°22' E **201**
Yamanashi, adm. division, *Japan* 35°30' N, 138°17' E **201**
Yamato Mountains, *Antarctica* 71°23' S, 36°56' E **248**
Yambio, *Sudan* 4°32' N, 28°24' E **224**
Yambol, *Bulg.* 42°29' N, 26°30' E **156**
Yambol, adm. division, *Bulg.* 42°12' N, 26°17' E **156**
Yamburg, *Russ.* 68°18' N, 77°12' E **169**
Yamdena, island, *Indonesia* 7°13' S, 131°2' E **192**
Yamethinn, *Myanmar* 20°26' N, 96°7' E **202**
Yamkino, *Russ.* 57°53' N, 29°17' E **166**
Yamm, *Russ.* 58°24' N, 28°4' E **166**
Yammaw, *Myanmar* 26°15' N, 97°42' E **188**
Yamoussoukro, *Côte d'Ivoire* 6°44' N, 5°24' W **222**
Yampa, river, *Colo., U.S.* 40°33' N, 108°7' W **92**
Yampil', *Ukr.* 48°14' N, 28°20' E **156**
Yampol', *Ukr.* 49°57' N, 26°16' E **152**
Yamsay Mountain, peak, *Oreg., U.S.* 42°55' N, 121°27' W **90**
Yamsk, *Russ.* 59°35' N, 153°56' E **160**
Yamuna, river, *India* 29°23' N, 77°4' E **190**
Yamzho Yumco, lake, *China* 28°59' N, 90°26' E **197**
Yana, *Sierra Leone* 9°43' N, 12°22' W **222**
Yana, river, *Russ.* 69°54' N, 135°39' E **160**
Yanachaga Chemillén National Park, *Peru* 10°31' S, 75°37' W **122**
Yanagawa, *Japan* 33°9' N, 130°24' E **201**
Yanai, *Japan* 33°58' N, 132°7' E **201**
Yanam, *India* 16°45' N, 82°5' E **190**
Yan'an, *China* 36°33' N, 109°28' E **198**
Yanaoca, *Peru* 14°15' S, 71°25' W **137**
Yanaul, *Russ.* 56°16' N, 55°4' E **154**
Yanbu'al Baḩr, *Saudi Arabia* 24°5' N, 38°4' E **182**
Yanchang, *China* 36°36' N, 110°3' E **198**
Yancheng, *China* 33°21' N, 120°6' E **198**
Yanchi, *China* 37°46' N, 107°20' E **198**
Yanchuan, *China* 36°50' N, 110°10' E **198**
Yandoon, *Myanmar* 17°3' N, 95°37' E **202**
Yanfolila, *Mali* 11°11' N, 8°10' W **222**
Yangambi, *Dem. Rep. of the Congo* 0°47' N, 24°25' E **224**
Yangarey, *Russ.* 68°43' N, 61°29' E **169**
Yangasso, *Mali* 13°4' N, 5°20' W **222**
Yangbajain, *China* 30°11' N, 90°29' E **197**
Yangchun, *China* 22°8' N, 111°47' E **198**
Yangdŏk, *N. Korea* 39°12' N, 126°40' E **200**
Yanggu, *S. Korea* 38°7' N, 127°59' E **200**
Yanghe, *China* 40°4' N, 123°25' E **200**
Yangi-Nishon, *Uzb.* 38°37' N, 65°40' E **197**
Yangiqishloq, *Uzb.* 40°25' N, 67°13' E **197**
Yangiyer, *Uzb.* 40°12' N, 68°51' E **197**
Yangiyŭl, *Uzb.* 41°9' N, 69°4' E **197**
Yangjiang, *China* 21°50' N, 111°59' E **198**
Yangon (Rangoon), *Myanmar* 16°45' N, 96°0' E **202**
Yangory, *Russ.* 62°46' N, 37°48' E **154**
Yangou Gala, *Cen. Af. Rep.* 7°21' N, 20°11' E **218**
Yangquan, *China* 37°52' N, 113°36' E **198**
Yangsan, *S. Korea* 35°20' N, 129°3' E **200**
Yangshan, *China* 24°29' N, 112°39' E **198**
Yangshuo, *China* 24°45' N, 110°26' E **198**
Yangtze, lake, *China* 30°23' N, 106°28' E **172**
Yangtze, river, *China* 27°59' N, 104°57' E **172**
Yangtze see Jinsha, river, *China* 25°47' N, 103°15' E **190**
Yangtze, Source of the, *China* 33°16' N, 90°53' E **188**
Yangudi Rassa National Park, *Eth.* 10°46' N, 41°7' E **224**
Yangxian, *China* 33°13' N, 107°31' E **198**
Yangxin, *China* 29°51' N, 115°6' E **198**
Yangyang, *S. Korea* 38°5' N, 128°37' E **200**
Yangyuan, *China* 40°7' N, 114°8' E **198**
Yangzhou, *China* 32°25' N, 119°27' E **198**
Yangzishao, *China* 42°25' N, 126°7' E **200**
Yanhe, *China* 28°32' N, 108°25' E **198**
Yanis'yarvi, Ozero, lake, *Russ.* 61°52' N, 29°54' E **152**
Yanji, *China* 42°55' N, 129°27' E **200**
Yanji (Longjing), *China* 42°46' N, 129°24' E **200**
Yankari National Park, *Nig.* 9°47' N, 9°50' E **222**
Yankeetown, *Fla., U.S.* 29°2' N, 82°44' W **105**
Yankovichi, *Belarus* 55°47' N, 28°48' E **166**
Yankton, *S. Dak., U.S.* 42°51' N, 97°24' W **90**
Yanonge, *Dem. Rep. of the Congo* 0°33' N, 24°39' E **224**
Yanqi, *China* 42°8' N, 86°39' E **184**
Yanrakynnot, *Russ.* 64°59' N, 172°39' W **98**
Yanshan, *China* 38°4' N, 117°13' E **198**
Yanshan, *China* 23°32' N, 104°20' E **202**
Yanshan, *China* 28°16' N, 117°38' E **198**
Yanshou, *China* 45°30' N, 128°21' E **198**
Yanskiy, *Russ.* 68°22' N, 135°8' E **160**
Yantai, *China* 37°32' N, 121°21' E **198**
Yantarnyy, *Russ.* 54°51' N, 19°56' E **166**
Yao, *Japan* 34°38' N, 135°35' E **201**
Yaoundé, *Cameroon* 3°55' N, 11°24' E **222**
Yaoxian, *China* 34°59' N, 109°0' E **198**
Yap Islands, *Philippine Sea* 9°43' N, 136°10' E **192**
Yap Trench, *North Pacific Ocean* 7°20' N, 137°57' E **254**
Yapacana National Park, *Venez.* 3°44' N, 66°47' W **136**
Yapacani, river, *Bol.* 15°52' S, 64°33' W **137**
Yapei (Tamale Port), *Ghana* 9°10' N, 1°11' W **222**
Yapele, *Dem. Rep. of the Congo* 0°12' N, 24°25' E **224**
Yapen, island, *Indonesia* 1°32' S, 135°43' E **192**
Yapeyú, *Arg.* 29°26' S, 56°53' W **139**
Yaptiksale, *Russ.* 69°20' N, 72°36' E **169**
Yaqui, river, *Mex.* 28°10' N, 110°3' W **112**
Yaquina Head, *Oreg., U.S.* 44°29' N, 124°22' W **90**
Yar, *Russ.* 58°13' N, 52°9' E **154**
Yar Sale, *Russ.* 66°49' N, 70°48' E **169**
Yaracuy, adm. division, *Venez.* 10°25' N, 69°4' W **136**
Yaraka, *Austral.* 24°54' S, 144°4' E **231**
Yaralıgöz, peak, *Turk.* 41°45' N, 34°1' E **156**
Yaransk, *Russ.* 57°18' N, 47°57' E **154**
Yarda, spring, *Chad* 18°31' N, 18°58' E **216**
Yardımcı Burnu, *Turk.* 36°6' N, 30°26' E **156**
Yardymly, *Azerb.* 38°54' N, 48°14' E **195**
Yarega, *Russ.* 63°26' N, 53°35' E **154**
Yaren, *Nauru* 0°33' N, 166°55' E **242**
Yarenga, *Russ.* 62°43' N, 49°33' E **154**
Yarensk, *Russ.* 62°10' N, 49°11' E **154**
Yarí, river, *Col.* 0°20' N, 72°50' W **136**
Yarīm, *Yemen* 14°17' N, 44°24' E **182**
Yarkant, river, *China* 37°58' N, 76°14' E **184**
Yarkant see Shache, *China* 38°27' N, 77°17' E **184**
Yarkul', *Russ.* 54°36' N, 77°17' E **184**
Yarma, *Turk.* 37°49' N, 32°53' E **156**
Yarmouth, *Can.* 43°48' N, 66°8' W **94**
Yarmouth, *Me., U.S.* 43°47' N, 70°12' W **104**
Yarnema, *Russ.* 62°59' N, 39°23' E **154**
Yaroslavl', *Russ.* 57°34' N, 39°48' E **154**
Yaroslavl', adm. division, *Russ.* 57°40' N, 37°38' E **154**
Yaroto, Ozera, lake, *Russ.* 67°59' N, 70°25' E **169**
Yarozero, *Russ.* 60°27' N, 38°35' E **154**
Yartsevo, *Russ.* 60°9' N, 90°14' E **169**
Yarumal, *Col.* 6°58' N, 75°26' W **136**
Yary, *Russ.* 68°50' N, 66°41' E **169**
Yashalta, *Russ.* 46°18' N, 42°6' E **158**
Yashchera, *Russ.* 59°8' N, 29°54' E **166**
Yashi, *Nig.* 12°21' N, 7°55' E **222**
Yashichu, *China* 37°25' N, 75°22' E **184**
Yashikera, *Nig.* 9°44' N, 3°29' E **222**
Yashkino, *Russ.* 52°41' N, 53°30' E **154**
Yashkul', *Russ.* 46°8' N, 45°18' E **158**
Yasnoye, *Russ.* 55°11' N, 21°31' E **166**

Yasnyy, *Russ.* 51°5′ N, 59°53′ E **158**
Yasothon, *Thai.* 15°48′ N, 104°9′ E **202**
Yasugi, *Japan* 35°24′ N, 133°15′ E **201**
Yāsūj, *Iran* 30°39′ N, 51°35′ E **180**
Yasun Burnu, *Turk.* 41°10′ N, 37°6′ E **156**
Yasuní National Park, *Ecua.* 0°57′ N, 76°27′ W **136**
Yata, *Bol.* 13°20′ S, 66°48′ W **137**
Yata, *Braz.* 10°40′ S, 65°21′ W **137**
Yata, river, *Bol.* 11°14′ S, 65°43′ W **137**
Yata, river, *Cen. Af. Rep.* 10°13′ N, 23°2′ E **218**
Yatakala, *Niger* 14°47′ N, 0°22′ E **222**
Yates Center, *Kans., U.S.* 37°51′ N, 95°44′ W **96**
Yates City, *Ill., U.S.* 40°45′ N, 90°1′ W **102**
Yates, river, *Can.* 59°31′ N, 116°31′ W **108**
Yatina, *Bol.* 20°46′ S, 64°45′ W **137**
Yatou see Rongcheng, *China* 37°10′ N, 122°26′ E **198**
Yatsushiro, *Japan* 32°30′ N, 130°36′ E **201**
Yatta Plateau, *Kenya* 1°52′ S, 37°52′ E **224**
Yauca, *Peru* 15°42′ S, 74°31′ W **137**
Yauca, river, *Peru* 15°13′ S, 74°7′ W **137**
Yauna Moloca, *Col.* 0°55′ N, 70°9′ W **136**
Yaupi, *Ecua.* 2°55′ S, 77°53′ W **136**
Yauri (Espinar), *Peru* 14°51′ S, 71°24′ W **137**
Yautepec, *Mex.* 18°51′ N, 99°2′ W **114**
Yavarate, *Col.* 0°38′ N, 69°13′ W **136**
Yavari Mirim, river, *Peru* 5°10′ S, 73°8′ W **130**
Yavaros, *Mex.* 26°42′ N, 109°33′ W **112**
Yavatmal, *India* 20°23′ N, 78°7′ E **188**
Yavero, river, *Peru* 12°25′ S, 72°51′ W **137**
Yavi, *Arg.* 22°10′ S, 65°30′ W **137**
Yavita, *Venez.* 2°53′ N, 67°28′ W **136**
Yavlenka, *Kaz.* 54°17′ N, 68°22′ E **184**
Yavne, *Israel* 31°51′ N, 34°44′ E **194**
Yavoriv, *Ukr.* 49°56′ N, 23°22′ E **152**
Yavr, river, *Russ.* 68°14′ N, 29°36′ E **152**
Yawatahama, *Japan* 33°26′ N, 132°25′ E **201**
Yawnghwe, *Myanmar* 20°40′ N, 96°57′ E **202**
Yawri Bay 8°3′ N, 13°19′ W **222**
Yaxchilán, ruin(s), *Mex.* 16°50′ N, 91°7′ W **115**
Yaya, *Russ.* 56°11′ N, 86°22′ E **169**
Yaynangyoung, *Myanmar* 20°28′ N, 94°54′ E **202**
Yayuan, *China* 41°42′ N, 126°9′ E **200**
Yayva, *Russ.* 59°19′ N, 57°21′ E **154**
Yazd, *Iran* 31°53′ N, 54°26′ E **180**
Yazdān, *Iran* 33°34′ N, 60°53′ E **180**
Yazevets, *Russ.* 65°44′ N, 46°27′ E **154**
Yazhma, *Russ.* 66°57′ N, 44°43′ E **154**
Yazılıkaya, *Turk.* 39°11′ N, 30°42′ E **156**
Yazlıca Dağı, peak, *Turk.* 37°45′ N, 42°27′ E **195**
Yazno, *Russ.* 56°2′ N, 29°18′ E **166**
Yazoo City, *Miss., U.S.* 32°50′ N, 90°26′ W **103**
Yazoo, river, *Miss., U.S.* 32°33′ N, 90°50′ W **103**
Yazykovo, *Russ.* 54°16′ N, 47°27′ E **154**
Ybakoura, spring, *Chad* 22°6′ N, 15°44′ E **216**
Ye, *Myanmar* 15°15′ N, 97°50′ E **202**
Yebbi Bou, *Chad* 21°0′ N, 18°8′ E **216**
Yebyu, *Myanmar* 14°16′ N, 98°8′ E **202**
Yecheng (Kargilik), *China* 37°52′ N, 77°31′ E **184**
Yecheon, *S. Korea* 36°38′ N, 128°26′ E **200**
Yecla, *Sp.* 38°36′ N, 1°7′ W **164**
Yécora, *Mex.* 28°22′ N, 108°58′ W **92**
Yédri, spring, *Chad* 22°11′ N, 17°25′ E **216**
Yeed, *Somalia* 4°28′ N, 43°5′ E **218**
Yefremov, *Russ.* 53°8′ N, 38°4′ E **154**
Yeggueba, spring, *Niger* 19°52′ N, 12°53′ E **222**
Yegorovskaya, *Russ.* 65°43′ N, 52°3′ E **154**
Yegor'yevsk, *Russ.* 55°22′ N, 39°1′ E **154**
Yegozero, *Russ.* 62°44′ N, 36°38′ E **154**
Yegros, *Parag.* 26°23′ S, 56°24′ W **139**
Yeguas, Sierra de, *Sp.* 37°8′ N, 4°58′ W **164**
Yei, *Sudan* 4°3′ N, 30°40′ E **224**
Yei, river, *Sudan* 5°11′ N, 30°17′ E **224**
Yeji, *Ghana* 8°11′ N, 0°43′ E **222**
Yekaterinburg, *Russ.* 56°49′ N, 60°35′ E **154**
Yekaterinovka, *Russ.* 52°1′ N, 44°23′ E **158**
Yekepa, *Liberia* 7°26′ N, 8°34′ W **222**
Yekhrimyanvara, *Russ.* 64°32′ N, 30°9′ E **152**
Yekī, *Eth.* 7°10′ N, 35°17′ E **224**
Yekia Sahal, spring, *Chad* 16°14′ N, 17°38′ E **216**
Yelabuga, *Russ.* 55°46′ N, 52°6′ E **154**
Yelan', *Russ.* 50°56′ N, 43°46′ E **158**
Yelan Kolenovskiy, *Russ.* 51°8′ N, 41°14′ E **158**
Yelapa, *Mex.* 20°28′ N, 105°29′ W **114**
Yelat'ma, *Russ.* 54°56′ N, 41°44′ E **154**
Yelets, *Russ.* 52°37′ N, 38°27′ E **158**
Yeletskiy, *Russ.* 67°3′ N, 64°0′ E **169**
Yelizarovo, *Russ.* 61°22′ N, 68°18′ E **169**
Yelizavety, Mys, *Russ.* 54°19′ N, 142°29′ E **160**
Yelkhovka, *Russ.* 53°50′ N, 50°16′ E **154**
Yellandu, *India* 17°34′ N, 80°18′ E **188**
Yellow Butte, peak, *Oreg., U.S.* 43°31′ N, 123°29′ W **90**
Yellow Grass, *Can.* 49°47′ N, 104°10′ W **90**
Yellow Sea 36°17′ N, 121°47′ E **190**
Yellow see Huang, river, *China* 37°14′ N, 104°6′ E **198**
Yellowknife, *Can.* 62°27′ N, 114°50′ W **106**
Yellowstone, river, *Mont., U.S.* 47°11′ N, 104°31′ W **90**
Yelm, *Wash., U.S.* 46°55′ N, 122°37′ W **90**
Yel'nya, *Russ.* 54°36′ N, 33°14′ E **154**
Yeloguy, river, *Russ.* 61°32′ N, 85°41′ E **169**
Yel'sk, *Belarus* 51°47′ N, 29°14′ E **152**
Yelva, river, *Russ.* 63°26′ N, 50°49′ E **154**
Yelverton Bay 81°31′ N, 98°43′ W **72**
Yelwa, *Nig.* 10°52′ N, 4°45′ E **222**
Yemanzhelinsk, *Russ.* 54°45′ N, 61°21′ E **154**
Yemaotai, *China* 42°20′ N, 122°54′ E **200**
Yemassee, *S.C., U.S.* 32°41′ N, 80°51′ W **96**
Yembo, *Eth.* 8°17′ N, 35°56′ E **224**
Yemel'yanovka, *Russ.* 63°54′ N, 30°56′ E **152**
Yemen 15°57′ N, 48°3′ E **182**
Yemetsk, *Russ.* 63°29′ N, 41°48′ E **154**
Yemtsa, *Russ.* 63°4′ N, 40°22′ E **154**
Yen, *Cameroon* 2°28′ N, 12°42′ E **218**
Yen Bai, *Vietnam* 21°44′ N, 104°52′ E **202**
Yena, *Russ.* 67°36′ N, 31°9′ E **152**
Yenakiyeve, *Ukr.* 48°12′ N, 38°12′ E **158**
Yenanma, *Myanmar* 19°46′ N, 94°49′ E **202**
Yendéré, *Burkina Faso* 10°12′ N, 4°59′ W **222**
Yendi, *Ghana* 9°24′ N, 4°237′ W **222**
Yenge, river, *Dem. Rep. of the Congo* 1°46′ S, 21°21′ E **218**
Yengisar, *China* 38°55′ N, 76°9′ E **184**
Yéni, *Niger* 13°27′ N, 3°0′ E **222**
Yeniçağa, *Turk.* 40°47′ N, 32°0′ E **156**
Yenice, *Turk.* 39°18′ N, 32°41′ E **156**
Yeniceoba, *Turk.* 38°51′ N, 32°46′ E **156**
Yenisey, river, *Russ.* 51°38′ N, 92°28′ E **190**
Yeniseysk, *Russ.* 58°21′ N, 92°10′ E **160**
Yeniseyskiy Zaliv 72°20′ N, 75°5′ E **160**
Yenyuka, *Russ.* 57°53′ N, 121°44′ E **160**
Yeo, river, *U.K.* 51°0′ N, 2°45′ W **162**
Yeoju, *S. Korea* 37°17′ N, 127°38′ E **200**
Yeola, *India* 20°1′ N, 74°29′ E **188**
Yeoncheon, *S. Korea* 38°5′ N, 127°5′ E **200**
Yeongam, *S. Korea* 34°46′ N, 126°41′ E **200**
Yeongdeok, *S. Korea* 36°24′ N, 129°25′ E **200**
Yeongdong, *S. Korea* 36°9′ N, 127°47′ E **200**
Yeonggwang, *S. Korea* 35°14′ N, 126°30′ E **200**
Yeongju, *S. Korea* 36°48′ N, 128°38′ E **200**
Yeongwol, *S. Korea* 37°11′ N, 128°28′ E **200**
Yeoryang, *S. Korea* 37°22′ N, 129°15′ E **200**
Yeosu, *S. Korea* 34°45′ N, 127°45′ E **200**
Yeovil, *U.K.* 50°56′ N, 2°38′ W **162**
Yepes, *Sp.* 39°54′ N, 3°38′ W **164**
Yepómera, *Mex.* 29°2′ N, 107°51′ W **92**
Yerakhtur, *Russ.* 54°40′ N, 41°5′ E **154**
Yerbent, *Turkm.* 39°16′ N, 58°35′ E **180**
Yerbogachen, *Russ.* 61°19′ N, 108°10′ E **160**
Yerema, *Russ.* 60°24′ N, 107°56′ E **173**
Yerevan, *Arm.* 40°8′ N, 44°24′ E **195**
Yerington, *Nev., U.S.* 38°59′ N, 119°11′ W **90**
Yerköy, *Turk.* 39°37′ N, 34°28′ E **156**
Yermak Plateau, *Greenland Sea* 80°41′ N, 6°9′ E **255**
Yermak Point, *Antarctica* 70°15′ S, 160°38′ E **248**
Yermakovo, *Russ.* 66°31′ N, 86°5′ E **169**
Yermilovka, *Russ.* 57°39′ N, 72°59′ E **169**
Yermitsa, *Russ.* 66°56′ N, 52°14′ E **169**
Yermo, *Calif., U.S.* 34°54′ N, 116°50′ W **101**
Yermo, *Mex.* 26°23′ N, 104°3′ W **114**
Yeroham, *Israel* 30°58′ N, 34°54′ E **194**
Yeropol, *Russ.* 65°21′ N, 168°41′ E **160**
Yershov, *Russ.* 51°19′ N, 48°18′ E **158**
Yershovo, *Russ.* 57°57′ N, 28°11′ E **166**
Yerushalayim see Jerusalem, *Israel* 31°46′ N, 35°9′ E **194**
Yesan, *S. Korea* 36°40′ N, 126°51′ E **200**
Yeşilırmak, river, *Turk.* 41°22′ N, 36°28′ E **156**
Yeşilova, *Turk.* 37°29′ N, 29°45′ E **156**
Yeşilyazı, *Turk.* 39°19′ N, 39°4′ E **195**
Yessey, *Russ.* 68°28′ N, 102°1′ E **160**
Yeste, *Sp.* 38°21′ N, 2°19′ W **164**
Yetti, region, *Mauritania* 26°6′ N, 8°10′ W **214**
Ye-u, *Myanmar* 22°46′ N, 95°24′ E **202**
Yevgashchino, *Russ.* 56°24′ N, 74°39′ E **169**
Yevlax, *Azerb.* 40°36′ N, 47°8′ E **195**
Yevpatoriya, *Ukr.* 45°12′ N, 33°19′ E **156**
Yevstratovskiy, *Russ.* 50°9′ N, 39°49′ E **158**
Yexian, *China* 37°11′ N, 119°57′ E **198**
Yeysk, *Russ.* 46°41′ N, 38°11′ E **156**
Yezerishche, *Belarus* 55°49′ N, 30°3′ E **166**
Ygatimí, *Parag.* 24°7′ S, 55°39′ W **132**
Yi, river, *China* 35°6′ N, 118°35′ E **198**
Yi, river, *Uru.* 33°33′ S, 56°20′ W **139**
Yi'an, *China* 47°57′ N, 125°20′ E **198**
Yibin, *China* 28°39′ N, 104°21′ E **190**
Yibug Caka, lake, *China* 32°51′ N, 85°54′ E **188**
Yichang, *China* 30°42′ N, 111°22′ E **198**
Yicheng, *China* 31°41′ N, 112°12′ E **198**
Yichuan, *China* 36°3′ N, 110°9′ E **198**
Yichun, *China* 27°45′ N, 114°23′ E **198**
Yichun, *China* 47°43′ N, 128°58′ E **198**
Yifag, *Eth.* 12°2′ N, 37°44′ E **182**
Yigo, *U.S.* 13°31′ N, 144°52′ E **242**
Yijun, *China* 35°24′ N, 109°3′ E **198**
Yila, *Liberia* 6°46′ N, 9°13′ W **222**
Yilan, *China* 46°19′ N, 129°44′ E **190**
Yıldız Dağları, peak, *Turk.* 41°46′ N, 27°31′ E **156**
Yıldızeli, *Turk.* 39°51′ N, 36°35′ E **156**
Yilehuli Shan, *China* 51°24′ N, 118°51′ E **190**
Yiliang, *China* 24°50′ N, 102°55′ E **190**
Yinan, *China* 35°32′ N, 118°29′ E **198**
Yinchuan, *China* 38°29′ N, 106°21′ E **198**
Yingcheng, *China* 30°56′ N, 113°31′ E **198**
Yingcheng, *China* 44°7′ N, 125°56′ E **198**
Yingchengzi, *China* 43°11′ N, 125°29′ E **200**
Yingde, *China* 24°4′ N, 113°20′ E **198**
Yingkou, *China* 40°39′ N, 122°12′ E **198**
Yingshan, *China* 31°34′ N, 113°49′ E **198**
Yingshang, *China* 32°36′ N, 116°14′ E **198**
Yingxian, *China* 39°32′ N, 113°13′ E **198**
Yining, *China* 43°51′ N, 81°28′ E **184**
Yinmabin, *Myanmar* 22°8′ N, 94°52′ E **202**
Yi'ong, river, *China* 30°27′ N, 93°53′ E **188**
Yirga 'Alem, *Eth.* 6°45′ N, 38°20′ E **224**
Yirol, *Sudan* 6°34′ N, 30°30′ E **224**
Yirshi, *China* 47°16′ N, 119°48′ E **198**
Yishan, *China* 24°26′ N, 108°40′ E **198**
Yishui, *China* 35°45′ N, 118°40′ E **198**
Yitong, *China* 43°19′ N, 125°14′ E **198**
Yitulihe, *China* 50°41′ N, 121°36′ E **238**
Yiwu, *China* 29°18′ N, 120°3′ E **198**
Yixian, *China* 41°31′ N, 121°17′ E **198**
Yixing, *China* 31°21′ N, 119°48′ E **198**
Yiyang, *China* 28°41′ N, 112°22′ E **198**
Yiyuan, *China* 36°11′ N, 118°8′ E **198**
Yliämaa, *Fin.* 60°47′ N, 27°58′ E **166**
Yläne, *Fin.* 60°52′ N, 22°24′ E **166**
Yli Ii, *Fin.* 65°22′ N, 25°47′ E **152**
Ylihärmä, *Fin.* 63°7′ N, 22°45′ E **152**
Ylikiiminki, *Fin.* 65°1′ N, 26°6′ E **152**
Ylimarkku see Övermark, *Fin.* 62°35′ N, 21°25′ E **152**
Ylitornio, *Fin.* 66°19′ N, 23°41′ E **152**
Ylivieska, *Fin.* 64°3′ N, 24°28′ E **152**
Ylivuokki, *Fin.* 64°38′ N, 29°42′ E **154**
Yllästunturi, peak, *Fin.* 67°33′ N, 24°4′ E **152**
Ÿnderbor, *Kaz.* 48°23′ N, 51°31′ E **158**
Yndin, *Russ.* 61°22′ N, 55°11′ E **154**
Yoakum, *Tex., U.S.* 29°17′ N, 97°9′ W **96**
Yobuko, *Japan* 33°31′ N, 129°54′ E **201**
Yog Point, *Philippines* 14°6′ N, 124°13′ E **203**
Yogyakarta, *Indonesia* 7°49′ S, 110°19′ E **238**
Yoho National Park, *Can.* 51°20′ N, 116°51′ W **238**
Yojoa, Lago de, lake, *Hond.* 14°50′ N, 88°31′ W **116**
Yok Don National Park, *Vietnam* 12°50′ N, 107°15′ E **238**
Yōka, *Japan* 35°23′ N, 134°44′ E **201**
Yokadouma, *Cameroon* 3°40′ N, 15°5′ E **218**
Yokkaichi, *Japan* 34°57′ N, 136°38′ E **201**
Yoko, *Cameroon* 5°30′ N, 12°20′ E **218**
Yokohama, *Japan* 35°26′ N, 139°37′ E **201**
Yokosuka, *Japan* 35°15′ N, 139°39′ E **201**
Yola, *Nig.* 9°12′ N, 12°30′ E **216**
Yolombo, *Dem. Rep. of the Congo* 1°37′ S, 23°11′ E **218**
Yolöten, *Turkm.* 37°16′ N, 62°20′ E **186**
Yom, river, *Thai.* 18°0′ N, 99°38′ E **202**
Yombiro, *Guinea* 9°3′ N, 10°20′ W **222**
Yomra, *Turk.* 40°57′ N, 39°50′ E **195**
Yon, river, *Fr.* 46°36′ N, 1°35′ W **150**
Yonago, *Japan* 35°24′ N, 133°21′ E **201**
Yonaguni Jima, island, *Japan* 24°16′ N, 122°27′ E **198**
Yŏnan, *N. Korea* 37°54′ N, 126°9′ E **200**
Yonezawa, *Japan* 37°54′ N, 140°5′ E **201**
Yongama, *Dem. Rep. of the Congo* 2°119′ S, 24°34′ E **224**
Yongamp'o, *N. Korea* 39°55′ N, 124°19′ E **200**
Yong'an, *China* 25°57′ N, 117°25′ E **198**
Yŏngbyŏn, *N. Korea* 39°49′ N, 125°48′ E **200**
Yongch'ŏn, *N. Korea* 39°58′ N, 124°24′ E **200**
Yongchuan, *China* 29°19′ N, 105°55′ E **198**
Yongchun, *China* 25°19′ N, 118°17′ E **198**
Yongfu, *China* 25°0′ N, 110°3′ E **198**
Yŏngjŏ, *N. Korea* 41°23′ N, 127°4′ E **200**
Yongkang, *China* 28°55′ N, 120°3′ E **198**
Yongning, *China* 22°41′ N, 108°30′ E **198**
Yongning, *China* 38°18′ N, 106°15′ E **198**
Yongo, *Dem. Rep. of the Congo* 1°37′ S, 21°50′ E **218**
Yongshun, *China* 29°1′ N, 109°51′ E **198**
Yongtai, *China* 25°52′ N, 118°57′ E **198**
Yongxin, *China* 27°0′ N, 114°16′ E **198**
Yongxing, *China* 26°7′ N, 112°55′ E **198**
Yongxiu, *China* 29°4′ N, 115°46′ E **198**
Yongzhou, *China* 26°15′ N, 111°36′ E **198**
Yonkers, *N.Y., U.S.* 40°56′ N, 73°54′ W **104**
Yonne, river, *Fr.* 48°22′ N, 3°1′ E **163**
Yŏnp'o, *N. Korea* 39°47′ N, 127°30′ E **200**
Yŏnsa, *N. Korea* 41°52′ N, 129°0′ E **200**
Yŏnsan, *N. Korea* 38°51′ N, 126°14′ E **200**
Yonza, *Bol.* 20°39′ S, 68°3′ W **137**
Yopal, *Col.* 5°16′ N, 72°19′ W **136**
Yopurga, *China* 39°16′ N, 76°40′ E **184**
Yoqne'am, *Israel* 32°39′ N, 35°5′ E **194**
York, *Ala., U.S.* 32°28′ N, 88°19′ W **103**
York, *Nebr., U.S.* 40°51′ N, 97°36′ W **90**
York, *Pa., U.S.* 39°57′ N, 76°43′ W **94**
York, *U.K.* 53°58′ N, 1°5′ W **162**
York, Cape, *Austral.* 10°37′ S, 142°35′ E **192**
York Factory National Historic Site, *Can.* 57°1′ N, 92°24′ W **108**
York Harbor, *Me., U.S.* 43°8′ N, 70°39′ W **104**
York, Kap 75°35′ N, 70°18′ W **106**
York Peninsula, Cape, *Austral.* 11°46′ S, 141°22′ E **192**
York, river, *Va., U.S.* 37°40′ N, 77°21′ W **80**
York Village, *Me., U.S.* 43°8′ N, 70°40′ W **104**
Yorkton, *Can.* 51°12′ N, 102°29′ W **90**
Yorktown, *Ark., U.S.* 34°0′ N, 91°50′ W **96**
Yorktown, *Tex., U.S.* 28°58′ N, 97°30′ W **92**
Yorktown, *Va., U.S.* 37°13′ N, 76°32′ W **94**
Yoro, *Hond.* 15°8′ N, 87°7′ W **115**
Yoro, *Mali* 14°17′ N, 2°11′ W **222**
Yorosso, *Mali* 12°23′ N, 4°48′ W **222**
Yortan Tepe, ruin(s), *Turk.* 38°58′ N, 27°20′ E **156**
Yosemite National Park, *Calif., U.S.* 37°52′ N, 119°49′ W **100**
Yosemite Valley, *Calif., U.S.* 37°41′ N, 119°34′ W **100**
Yosemite Village, *Calif., U.S.* 37°45′ N, 119°36′ W **100**
Yoshida, *Japan* 34°39′ N, 132°42′ E **201**
Yoshii, river, *Japan* 35°4′ N, 133°55′ E **201**
Yoshino-Kumano National Park, *Japan* 33°57′ N, 135°45′ E **201**
Yoshiwara, *Japan* 35°9′ N, 138°42′ E **201**
Yoshkar Ola, *Russ.* 56°38′ N, 47°52′ E **154**
Yost, *Utah, U.S.* 41°57′ N, 113°32′ W **90**
Yotala, *Bol.* 19°11′ S, 65°18′ W **137**
You, river, *China* 23°34′ N, 107°15′ E **198**
Youbou, *Can.* 48°53′ N, 124°14′ W **100**
Youhao, *China* 47°54′ N, 128°48′ E **198**
Youkou, *Côte d'Ivoire* 5°14′ N, 7°18′ W **222**
Youkounkoun, *Guinea* 12°32′ N, 13°9′ W **214**
Young, *Uru.* 32°43′ S, 57°39′ W **139**
Young, Mount, peak, *Austral.* 15°14′ S, 135°37′ E **230**
Youngstown, *Can.* 51°32′ N, 111°12′ W **90**
Youngstown, *Ohio, U.S.* 41°5′ N, 80°38′ W **110**
Younts Peak, *Wyo., U.S.* 43°57′ N, 109°57′ W **90**
Yountville, *Calif., U.S.* 38°24′ N, 122°22′ W **100**
Youshashan, *China* 38°11′ N, 90°59′ E **188**
Youssoufia, *Mor.* 32°16′ N, 8°33′ W **214**
Youxian, *China* 27°3′ N, 113°18′ E **198**
Youyang, *China* 28°50′ N, 108°45′ E **198**
Youyu, *China* 39°54′ N, 112°17′ E **190**
Yovan, *Taj.* 38°21′ N, 69°7′ E **197**
Yovkovo, *Bulg.* 43°47′ N, 28°6′ E **158**
Yoxford, *U.K.* 52°15′ N, 1°30′ E **163**
Yozgat, *Turk.* 39°48′ N, 34°48′ E **156**
Ypé Jhú, *Parag.* 23°57′ S, 55°28′ W **132**
Ypres see Ieper, *Belg.* 50°50′ N, 2°53′ E **163**
Ypsilanti, *Mich., U.S.* 42°13′ N, 83°38′ W **102**
Yr Eifl (The Rivals), peak, *U.K.* 52°57′ N, 4°32′ W **150**
Yreka, *Calif., U.S.* 41°42′ N, 122°39′ W **106**
Yrghyz, *Kaz.* 48°37′ N, 61°15′ E **184**
Yrghyz, river, *Kaz.* 48°49′ N, 60°3′ E **158**
Ysabel Channel 2°11′ S, 148°53′ E **192**
Ystad, *Nor.* 55°25′ N, 13°48′ E **152**
Ystrad Mynach, *U.K.* 51°38′ N, 3°14′ W **162**
Ysyk-Köl, lake, *Kyrg.* 42°29′ N, 77°1′ E **184**
Yu, river, *China* 22°32′ N, 109°18′ E **198**
Yü Shan, peak, *Taiwan* 23°31′ N, 120°56′ E **198**
Yuan, river, *China* 28°32′ N, 110°33′ E **198**
Yuanbaoshan, *China* 42°13′ N, 119°15′ E **198**
Yuanjiang, *China* 23°33′ N, 101°53′ E **202**
Yüanli, *Taiwan* 24°26′ N, 120°41′ E **198**
Yüanlin, *Taiwan* 23°52′ N, 120°35′ E **198**
Yuanqu, *China* 35°21′ N, 111°40′ E **198**
Yuba Pass, *Calif., U.S.* 39°37′ N, 120°29′ W **90**
Yūbari, *Japan* 43°5′ N, 142°3′ E **190**
Yubdo, *Eth.* 8°57′ N, 35°26′ E **224**
Yubineto, river, *Peru* 0°38′ N, 74°56′ W **136**
Yucaipa, *Calif., U.S.* 34°2′ N, 117°3′ W **101**
Yucatán, adm. division, *Mex.* 19°0′ N, 90°49′ W **112**
Yucca, *Ariz., U.S.* 34°52′ N, 114°10′ W **101**
Yucca Flat, *Nev., U.S.* 37°9′ N, 116°8′ W **101**
Yucca House National Monument, *Colo., U.S.* 37°14′ N, 108°46′ W **92**
Yucca Mountain, peak, *Nev., U.S.* 36°56′ N, 116°32′ W **101**
Yucca Valley, *Calif., U.S.* 34°7′ N, 116°28′ W **101**
Yucheng, *China* 36°57′ N, 116°42′ E **198**
Yuci, *China* 37°41′ N, 112°42′ E **198**
Yucuyácua, Cerro, peak, *Mex.* 17°7′ N, 97°43′ W **114**
Yudino, *Russ.* 55°48′ N, 48°53′ E **154**
Yueyang, *China* 29°22′ N, 113°6′ E **198**
Yug, *Russ.* 57°43′ N, 56°8′ E **154**
Yug, river, *Russ.* 60°31′ N, 46°57′ E **154**
Yugan, *China* 28°41′ N, 116°38′ E **198**
Yugorenok, *Russ.* 59°54′ N, 137°38′ E **160**
Yugyd Va National Park, *Russ.* 65°15′ N, 59°11′ E **169**
Yuhuan Dao, island, *China* 28°16′ N, 120°24′ E **198**
Yukhnov, *Russ.* 54°43′ N, 35°16′ E **154**
Yukon, river, *Can.-U.S.* 64°54′ N, 154°10′ W **98**
Yukon, adm. division, *Can.* 63°10′ N, 137°18′ W **98**
Yukon-Charley Rivers National Preserve, *Alas., U.S.* 65°8′ N, 143°40′ W **98**
Yüksekova, *Turk.* 37°34′ N, 44°12′ E **195**
Yukspor, Gora, peak, *Russ.* 68°9′ N, 32°14′ E **152**
Yukuhashi, *Japan* 33°42′ N, 130°59′ E **200**
Yula, river, *Russ.* 63°38′ N, 44°14′ E **154**
Yuldybayevo, *Russ.* 52°20′ N, 57°47′ E **154**
Yuli, *China* 41°24′ N, 86°16′ E **184**
Yuli, *Nig.* 9°43′ N, 10°17′ E **222**
Yüli, *Taiwan* 23°20′ N, 121°15′ E **198**
Yulin, *China* 22°38′ N, 110°6′ E **198**
Yulin, *China* 38°22′ N, 109°48′ E **198**
Yuma, *Ariz., U.S.* 32°42′ N, 114°37′ W **101**
Yuma, *Colo., U.S.* 40°7′ N, 102°44′ W **90**
Yuma, *Russ.* 65°6′ N, 33°15′ E **152**
Yuma Desert, *Ariz., U.S.* 32°17′ N, 114°46′ W **92**
Yumaguzino, *Russ.* 52°55′ N, 56°16′ E **154**
Yumari, Cerro, peak, *Venez.* 4°20′ N, 66°52′ W **136**
Yumbe, *Uganda* 3°27′ N, 31°16′ E **224**
Yumbi, *Dem. Rep. of the Congo* 1°56′ S, 16°31′ E **218**
Yumen, *China* 39°54′ N, 97°41′ E **190**
Yumin, *China* 45°59′ N, 82°57′ E **184**
Yumurtalık, *Turk.* 36°46′ N, 35°45′ E **156**
Yunan, *China* 23°12′ N, 111°27′ E **198**
Yuncheng, *China* 35°2′ N, 110°57′ E **198**
Yunguyo, *Peru* 16°20′ S, 69°6′ W **137**
Yūnīn, *Leb.* 34°4′ N, 36°17′ E **194**
Yunnan, adm. division, *China* 23°6′ N, 100°55′ E **202**
Yunotsu, *Japan* 35°5′ N, 132°22′ E **201**
Yunquera de Henares, *Sp.* 40°44′ N, 3°11′ W **164**
Yunxi, *China* 32°59′ N, 110°26′ E **198**
Yunxian, *China* 32°54′ N, 110°49′ E **198**
Yunyang, *China* 31°1′ N, 108°37′ E **198**
Yup'yŏng, *N. Korea* 41°47′ N, 128°51′ E **200**
Yuquan, *China* 45°23′ N, 127°7′ E **198**
Yura, river, *Bol.* 19°58′ S, 66°13′ W **137**
Yurécuaro, *Mex.* 20°19′ N, 102°17′ W **114**
Yurga, *Russ.* 55°42′ N, 84°54′ E **169**
Yuribey, *Russ.* 71°3′ N, 77°2′ E **169**
Yurimaguas, *Peru* 5°55′ S, 76°9′ W **130**
Yurkino, *Russ.* 68°46′ N, 32°0′ E **152**
Yurla, *Russ.* 59°19′ N, 54°21′ E **154**
Yuroma, *Russ.* 65°11′ N, 45°34′ E **154**
Yurovsk, *Russ.* 59°25′ N, 69°8′ E **169**
Yur'ya, *Russ.* 59°3′ N, 49°19′ E **154**
Yur'yev Pol'skiy, *Russ.* 56°30′ N, 39°39′ E **154**
Yur'yevets, *Russ.* 57°17′ N, 43°3′ E **154**
Yuryuzan', *Russ.* 54°51′ N, 58°30′ E **154**
Yuscarán, *Hond.* 13°54′ N, 86°49′ W **115**
Yushan, *China* 28°45′ N, 118°14′ E **198**
Yushkozero, *Russ.* 64°44′ N, 32°3′ E **152**
Yushu, *China* 44°48′ N, 126°31′ E **198**
Yusta, *Russ.* 47°5′ N, 46°17′ E **158**
Yusufeli, *Turk.* 40°55′ N, 41°37′ E **195**
Yus'va, *Russ.* 58°57′ N, 55°1′ E **154**
Yutian, *China* 36°54′ N, 81°34′ E **190**
Yutian, *China* 39°53′ N, 117°47′ E **198**
Yutian (Keriya), *China* 36°55′ N, 81°36′ E **184**
Yuty, *Parag.* 26°31′ S, 56°10′ W **139**
Yuxi, *China* 24°21′ N, 102°36′ E **190**
Yuxian, *China* 38°6′ N, 113°25′ E **198**
Yuzawa, *Japan* 36°56′ N, 138°48′ E **201**
Yuzha, *Russ.* 56°34′ N, 41°59′ E **154**
Yuzhno Sakhalinsk, *Russ.* 46°59′ N, 142°35′ E **190**
Yuzhnoural'sk, *Russ.* 54°27′ N, 61°12′ E **154**
Yuzhnyy, *Kaz.* 49°17′ N, 72°58′ E **184**
Yuzhnyy, *Russ.* 45°46′ N, 45°36′ E **158**
Yuzhnyy, Mys, *Russ.* 57°36′ N, 153°7′ E **160**
Yuzhong, *China* 35°54′ N, 104°8′ E **198**
Yverdon, *Switz.* 46°46′ N, 6°38′ E **167**
Yvetot, *Fr.* 49°36′ N, 0°45′ E **163**

Z

Za, river, *China* 33°3′ N, 95°13′ E **188**
Zaamin National Park, *Uzb.* 39°33′ N, 68°6′ E **197**
Zaanstad, *Neth.* 52°26′ N, 4°49′ E **163**
Zab, *Pol.* 53°0′ N, 23°19′ E **154**
Zāb al Kabīr (Great Zab), river, *Iraq* 36°32′ N, 43°40′ E **195**
Zabalats', *Belarus* 53°56′ N, 24°47′ E **166**
Žabalj, *Serb. and Mont.* 45°22′ N, 20°3′ E **168**
Žabari, *Serb. and Mont.* 44°21′ N, 21°12′ E **168**
Zabaykal'sk, *Russ.* 49°41′ N, 117°22′ E **198**
Zaberezh', *Belarus* 53°56′ N, 26°13′ E **166**
Zabīd, *Yemen* 14°10′ N, 43°17′ E **182**
Zablaće, *Serb. and Mont.* 43°50′ N, 20°26′ E **168**
Žabljak, *Europe* 43°9′ N, 19°7′ E **168**
Zabok, *Croatia* 46°2′ N, 15°53′ E **168**
Zābol, *Iran* 31°1′ N, 61°34′ E **186**
Zābolī, *Iran* 27°6′ N, 61°43′ E **182**
Zabolottsi, *Ukr.* 50°0′ N, 24°58′ E **152**
Zabolottya, *Ukr.* 51°36′ N, 24°14′ E **152**
Zabré, *Burkina Faso* 11°10′ N, 0°41′ E **222**
Zabrežje, *Serb. and Mont.* 44°40′ N, 20°12′ E **168**
Zabu, *Egypt* 28°22′ N, 28°55′ E **180**
Zabūrūn'e, *Kaz.* 46°45′ N, 50°9′ E **158**
Zacapa, *Guatemala* 14°58′ N, 89°34′ W **115**
Zacapu, *Mex.* 19°47′ N, 101°48′ W **114**
Zacatecas, *Mex.* 22°45′ N, 102°40′ W **114**
Zacatecas, adm. division, *Mex.* 23°33′ N, 103°44′ W **114**
Zacatepec, *Mex.* 17°10′ N, 95°51′ W **114**
Zaccar Rherbi, Djebel, peak, *Alg.* 36°19′ N, 2°8′ E **150**
Zachary, *La., U.S.* 30°38′ N, 91°11′ W **103**
Zachodnio-Pomorskie, adm. division, *Pol.* 53°37′ N, 14°39′ E **152**
Zacoalco, *Mex.* 20°14′ N, 103°34′ W **114**
Zacualtipán, *Mex.* 20°38′ N, 98°39′ W **114**
Zadar, *Croatia* 44°8′ N, 15°16′ E **143**
Zadar (Zara), *Croatia* 44°6′ N, 15°14′ E **156**
Zadawa, *Nig.* 11°28′ N, 10°18′ E **222**
Zadetkale Kyun, island, *Myanmar* 10°1′ N, 97°11′ E **202**
Zadetkyi Kyun, island, *Myanmar* 9°32′ N, 98°6′ E **202**
Zadoi, *China* 33°4′ N, 95°4′ E **188**
Zadonsk, *Russ.* 52°19′ N, 38°51′ E **158**
Za'farâna, *Egypt* 29°6′ N, 32°36′ E **180**
Zafarobod, *Uzb.* 40°32′ N, 65°0′ E **197**
Zafirovo, *Bulg.* 43°59′ N, 26°48′ E **158**
Zafóra, islands, *Aegean Sea* 36°4′ N, 25°55′ E **156**
Zafra, *Sp.* 38°25′ N, 6°27′ W **164**
Zafrilla, *Sp.* 40°11′ N, 1°37′ W **164**
Żagań, *Pol.* 51°36′ N, 15°18′ E **152**
Žagarė, *Lith.* 56°21′ N, 23°15′ E **166**
Zagazig, *Egypt* 30°36′ N, 31°29′ E **180**
Zaghouan, *Tun.* 36°23′ N, 10°9′ E **156**
Zagnanado, *Benin* 7°15′ N, 2°20′ E **222**
Zagne, *Côte d'Ivoire* 6°8′ N, 7°29′ W **222**
Zagor, *Bosn. and Herzg.* 43°40′ N, 18°34′ E **168**
Zagora, *Mor.* 30°19′ N, 5°54′ W **214**
Zagreb, *Croatia* 45°47′ N, 15°55′ E **168**
Zagros Mountains see Zāgros, Kūhhā-ye, *Iran* 36°37′ N, 45°23′ E **195**
Žagubica, *Serb. and Mont.* 44°12′ N, 21°47′ E **168**
Zagvozd, *Croatia* 43°22′ N, 17°2′ E **168**
Za'gya, river, *China* 32°20′ N, 89°27′ E **188**
Zahana, *Alg.* 35°30′ N, 0°25′ E **150**
Zaháro, *Gr.* 37°29′ N, 21°38′ E **156**
Zāhedān, *Iran* 29°29′ N, 60°53′ E **182**
Zaḩlah, *Leb.* 33°50′ N, 35°54′ E **194**
Zahrān, *Saudi Arabia* 17°41′ N, 43°24′ E **182**
Zahrisht, *Alban.* 42°12′ N, 20°20′ E **168**
Zaidín, *Sp.* 41°35′ N, 0°16′ E **164**
Zainsk, *Russ.* 55°18′ N, 52°7′ E **184**
Zaire, adm. division, *Angola* 7°36′ S, 13°1′ E **218**
Zaječar, *Serb. and Mont.* 43°53′ N, 22°17′ E **168**
Zajta, *Hung.* 47°53′ N, 22°48′ E **168**
Zaka, *Zimb.* 20°20′ S, 31°29′ E **227**
Zakamensk, *Russ.* 50°22′ N, 103°22′ E **190**
Zákány, *Hung.* 46°16′ N, 16°57′ E **168**
Zakataly, *Azerb.* 41°38′ N, 46°37′ E **195**
Zakho, *Iraq* 37°8′ N, 42°34′ E **195**
Zakhodnyaya Dzvina, river, *Belarus* 54°48′ N, 30°6′ E **154**
Zakhrebetnoye, *Russ.* 68°57′ N, 36°27′ E **152**
Zákinthos, *Gr.* 37°45′ N, 20°51′ E **216**
Zákinthos, island, *Gr.* 37°48′ N, 19°27′ E **216**
Zakīyah, *Syr.* 33°19′ N, 36°8′ E **194**
Zakouma National Park, *Chad* 10°24′ N, 19°17′ E **218**
Zakum, oil field, *Persian Gulf* 24°46′ N, 53°41′ E **196**
Zakwaski Mountain, peak, *Can.* 50°8′ N, 121°24′ W **108**
Zala, *Angola* 7°52′ S, 14°2′ E **218**
Zala, adm. division, *Hung.* 46°34′ N, 16°29′ E **156**
Zalaegerszeg, *Hung.* 46°49′ N, 16°51′ E **168**
Zalalöv o, *Hung.* 46°50′ N, 16°36′ E **168**
Zalamea la Real, *Sp.* 37°40′ N, 6°40′ W **164**
Zalanga, *Nig.* 10°36′ N, 10°10′ E **222**
Zalangoye, *Congo* 1°22′ N, 14°48′ E **218**
Zalantun, *China* 48°2′ N, 122°47′ E **198**
Zalau, *Nig.* 10°22′ N, 8°59′ E **222**
Zalău, *Rom.* 47°10′ N, 23°4′ E **168**
Žalec, *Slov.* 46°15′ N, 15°8′ E **156**
Z̧alim, *Saudi Arabia* 22°41′ N, 42°11′ E **182**
Zalingei, *Sudan* 12°52′ N, 23°29′ E **216**
Zalishchyky, *Ukr.* 48°38′ N, 25°44′ E **152**
Zalṭan, oil field, *Lib.* 28°47′ N, 19°44′ E **216**
Zalve, *Latv.* 56°19′ N, 25°14′ E **166**
Zama, *Miss., U.S.* 32°56′ N, 89°22′ W **103**
Zama Lake, *Can.* 58°46′ N, 119°27′ W **108**
Zamarte, *Pol.* 53°35′ N, 17°29′ E **152**
Žamberk, *Czech Rep.* 50°4′ N, 16°27′ E **152**
Zambezi, *Zambia* 13°33′ S, 23°9′ E **220**
Zambezi National Park, *Zimb.* 18°30′ S, 25°12′ E **224**

Zambezi, river, Zambia 16°33′ S, 23°28′ E 220
Zambézia, adm. division, Mozambique 16°33′ S, 35°52′ E 224
Zambia 15°2′ S, 26°18′ E 220
Zamboanga, Philippines 6°58′ N, 122°3′ E 203
Zamboanguita, Philippines 9°9′ N, 123°11′ E 203
Zâmbuè, Mozambique 15°9′ S, 30°47′ E 224
Zamezhnaya, Russ. 65°0′ N, 51°50′ E 154
Zamoge, Eth. 12°56′ N, 37°19′ E 182
Zamora, Ecua. 4°2′ S, 78°60′ W 130
Zamora, Mex. 19°59′ N, 102°17′ W 114
Zamora, Sp. 41°30′ N, 5°46′ W 150
Zamość, Pol. 50°42′ N, 23°14′ E 152
Zamošša, Belarus 55°30′ N, 27°3′ E 166
Zamostoch'ye, Belarus 53°51′ N, 28°26′ E 166
Zamsheva, Russ. 59°4′ N, 89°14′ E 169
Zamuro, Sierra del, Venez. 4°48′ N, 63°53′ W 130
Zam'yany, Russ. 46°46′ N, 47°35′ E 158
Zanda, China 31°29′ N, 79°47′ E 188
Zandvoort, Neth. 52°22′ N, 4°31′ E 163
Zanesville, Ohio, U.S. 39°56′ N, 82°1′ W 102
Zangeza Bay 57°56′ N, 102°46′ W 108
Zanjān, Iran 36°42′ N, 48°29′ E 195
Zanjón, river, Mex. 29°24′ N, 110°58′ W 80
Zantiguila, Mali 11°37′ N, 5°21′ W 222
Zanzibar, Tanzania 6°7′ S, 39°16′ E 224
Zanzibar Island, Tanzania 6°36′ S, 39°36′ E 224
Zaouatallaz, Alg. 24°53′ N, 8°24′ E 214
Zaouiet Azmour, Tun. 36°55′ N, 11°0′ E 156
Zaoyang, China 32°6′ N, 112°43′ E 198
Zaozhuang, China 34°54′ N, 117°33′ E 198
Zapadnaya Dvina, Russ. 56°15′ N, 32°4′ E 154
Zapadno Sibirskaya Ravnina 61°31′ N, 62°50′ E 154
Zapala, Arg. 38°54′ S, 70°2′ W 123
Zapata, Tex., U.S. 26°53′ N, 99°16′ W 96
Zapata, Peninsula de, Cuba 22°23′ N, 82°2′ W 116
Zapatoca, Col. 6°47′ N, 73°16′ W 136
Zapiga, Chile 19°38′ S, 70°4′ W 137
Zapiola Ridge, South Atlantic Ocean 45°8′ S, 42°14′ W 253
Zapolyarnyy, Russ. 69°25′ N, 30°49′ E 152
Zapol'ye, Russ. 58°38′ N, 29°11′ E 166
Zaporizhzhya, Ukr. 47°48′ N, 35°11′ E 156
Zaporozhskoye, Russ. 60°33′ N, 30°32′ E 166
Zapotiltic, Mex. 19°36′ N, 103°26′ W 114
Zapug, China 33°16′ N, 80°51′ E 188
Zar, spring, Mauritania 18°0′ N, 14°39′ W 222
Zara, Turk. 39°54′ N, 37°44′ E 156
Zara see Zadar, Croatia 44°6′ N, 15°14′ E 156
Zarafshon, Taj. 39°8′ N, 68°39′ E 197
Zarafshon, Uzb. 41°31′ N, 64°14′ E 197
Zarafshon Range, Taj. 39°13′ N, 66°58′ E 184
Zarafshon, river, Taj. 39°20′ N, 69°7′ E 197
Zaragoza, Col. 7°28′ N, 74°49′ W 136
Zaragoza, Mex. 31°36′ N, 106°23′ W 112
Zaragoza, Mex. 28°28′ N, 100°56′ W 92
Zaragoza, Mex. 23°57′ N, 99°46′ W 114
Zaragoza, Mex. 22°0′ N, 100°45′ W 114
Zaragoza, Sp. 41°38′ N, 0°55′ E 164
Zaragoza, Sp. 41°34′ N, 0°60′ E 214
Zarand, Iran 30°46′ N, 56°38′ E 180
Zarand, Munții, Rom. 46°8′ N, 22°4′ E 168
Zaranou, Côte d'Ivoire 6°23′ N, 3°23′ W 222
Zarasai, Lith. 55°44′ N, 26°16′ E 166
Zárate, Arg. 34°6′ S, 59°1′ W 139
Zarautz, Sp. 43°15′ N, 2°12′ W 164
Zaraysk, Russ. 54°45′ N, 38°52′ E 154
Zaraza, Venez. 9°20′ N, 65°21′ W 136
Zarcilla de Ramos, Sp. 37°50′ N, 1°53′ W 164
Zard Kūh, peak, Iran 32°21′ N, 49°58′ E 180
Zarech'ye, Belarus 54°8′ N, 29°49′ E 166
Zarghun Shahr, Afghan. 32°49′ N, 68°26′ E 186
Zaria, Nig. 11°2′ N, 7°43′ E 222
Zarichne, Ukr. 51°48′ N, 26°7′ E 152
Zaris Berge, Namibia 24°22′ S, 16°10′ E 227
Zarit, spring, Mali 16°4′ N, 3°50′ E 222
Żarnów, Pol. 51°14′ N, 20°11′ E 152
Zarqan, Iran 29°46′ N, 52°47′ E 196
Zarrarah, oil field, U.A.E. 22°42′ N, 54°2′ E 182
Zarubikha, Russ. 69°18′ N, 34°14′ E 152
Zarubino, Russ. 42°38′ N, 131°4′ E 200
Zaruma, Ecua. 3°49′ S, 79°37′ W 130
Żary, Pol. 51°37′ N, 15°8′ E 152
Zarya, Poluostrov, Russ. 75°5′ N, 70°47′ E 172
Zarzaïtine, oil field, Alg. 28°5′ N, 9°40′ E 214
Zarzal, Col. 4°21′ N, 76°6′ W 136
Zarzis, Tun. 33°31′ N, 11°5′ E 214
Zashaghan, Kaz. 51°9′ N, 51°20′ E 158
Zasheyek, Russ. 66°15′ N, 31°4′ E 152
Zaskevichi, Belarus 54°23′ N, 26°35′ E 166
Zaslawye, Belarus 54°0′ N, 27°14′ E 166
Zaslonava, Belarus 54°51′ N, 28°59′ E 166
Zastron, S. Af. 30°18′ S, 27°4′ E 227
Zatish'ye, Russ. 66°10′ N, 158°50′ E 160
Zatobyl, Kaz. 53°11′ N, 63°42′ E 184
Zatoka, Ukr. 46°4′ N, 30°28′ E 156
Zaturtsi, Ukr. 50°45′ N, 24°50′ E 152
Zavala, Bosn. and Herzg. 42°49′ N, 17°58′ E 168
Zavalla, Tex., U.S. 31°9′ N, 94°26′ W 103
Zavetnoye, Russ. 47°3′ N, 43°49′ E 158
Zavidovići, Bosn. and Herzg. 44°27′ N, 18°7′ E 168
Zavlaka, Serb. and Mont. 44°27′ N, 19°29′ E 168
Zavolzhsk, Russ. 57°32′ N, 42°9′ E 154
Zav'yalovo, Russ. 56°47′ N, 53°24′ E 154
Zāwiyat al Mukhaylá, Lib. 32°11′ N, 22°17′ E 216
Zāwiyat Masūs, Lib. 31°33′ N, 21°0′ E 216
Zâwyet Shammâs, Egypt 31°28′ N, 26°27′ E 180
Zayāki Jangal, Pak. 27°52′ N, 65°49′ E 182
Zaymah, Saudi Arabia 21°36′ N, 40°8′ E 182
Zaysan, Kaz. 47°27′ N, 84°52′ E 184
Zaysan Köli, lake, Kaz. 47°57′ N, 83°47′ E 184
Zayü, China 28°37′ N, 97°30′ E 188
Zboriv, Ukr. 49°40′ N, 25°7′ E 152
Ždala, Croatia 46°9′ N, 17°7′ E 168
Zdolbuniv, Ukr. 50°31′ N, 26°14′ E 152
Zdziechowice, Pol. 50°47′ N, 22°7′ E 152
Zéalé, Côte d'Ivoire 6°51′ N, 8°9′ W 222
Zebla, Jebel, peak, Tun. 36°48′ N, 9°11′ E 156
Zednes, peak, Mauritania 23°44′ N, 10°46′ W 214
Zeeland, Mich., U.S. 42°48′ N, 86°1′ W 102
Ze'elim, Israel 31°12′ N, 34°31′ E 194
Zeerust, S. Af. 25°34′ S, 26°3′ E 227
Zefat, Israel 32°58′ N, 35°29′ E 194
Zegra, Europe 42°21′ N, 21°30′ E 168
Zeidab, Sudan 17°25′ N, 33°54′ E 182
Zeil, Mount, peak, Austral. 23°27′ S, 132°11′ E 230
Zeist, Neth. 52°5′ N, 5°14′ E 163
Zeitûn, Egypt 29°9′ N, 25°47′ E 180
Zejmen, Alban. 41°42′ N, 19°41′ E 168
Zela see Zile, Turk. 40°19′ N, 35°53′ E 156
Zelenchukskaya, Russ. 43°51′ N, 41°27′ E 195
Zelenikovo, Maced. 41°53′ N, 21°34′ E 168
Zelenoborskiy, Russ. 66°48′ N, 32°19′ E 152
Zelenoe, Kaz. 48°2′ N, 51°34′ E 158
Zelenogorsk, Russ. 60°11′ N, 29°42′ E 166
Zelenogradsk, Russ. 54°56′ N, 20°27′ E 166
Zelenokumsk, Russ. 44°22′ N, 43°55′ E 158
Zelfana, Alg. 32°27′ N, 4°5′ E 214
Zelina, Croatia 45°58′ N, 16°15′ E 168
Željin, Serb. and Mont. 43°29′ N, 20°39′ E 168
Zell, Ger. 49°48′ N, 9°51′ E 167
Zell, Ger. 50°1′ N, 7°10′ E 167
Zellingen, Ger. 49°53′ N, 9°49′ E 167
Zellwood, Fla., U.S. 28°43′ N, 81°37′ W 105
Zeltiņi, Latv. 57°20′ N, 26°45′ E 166
Zel'va, Belarus 53°8′ N, 24°48′ E 152
Želva, Lith. 55°13′ N, 25°5′ E 166
Zemaitija National Park, Lith. 55°58′ N, 21°54′ E 166
Zemē, Eth. 9°53′ N, 37°45′ E 224
Zemen, Bulg. 42°29′ N, 22°45′ E 168
Zemetchino, Russ. 53°27′ N, 42°34′ E 154
Zemio, Cen. Af. Rep. 5°4′ N, 25°6′ E 224
Zemlya Frantsa Iosifa, islands, Barents Sea 82°32′ N, 4°43′ E 173
Zemlya Frantsa Iosifa see Franz Josef Land, islands, Barents Sea 82°32′ N, 4°43′ E 172
Zemongo, Cen. Af. Rep. 7°4′ N, 24°54′ E 224
Zempoala (Cempoala), ruin(s), Mex. 19°23′ N, 96°28′ W 114
Zempoaltepec, Cerro, peak, Mex. 17°8′ N, 96°2′ W 114
Zemun, Serb. and Mont. 44°49′ N, 20°25′ E 168
Zencirli, site, Turk. 37°6′ N, 36°36′ E 156
Zengfeng Shan, peak, China 42°22′ N, 128°42′ E 200
Zenica, Bosn. and Herzg. 44°12′ N, 17°52′ E 168
Zenobia Peak, Colo., U.S. 40°35′ N, 108°57′ W 90
Zenobia, ruin(s), Syr. 35°39′ N, 39°45′ E 180
Zentsūji, Japan 34°14′ N, 133°47′ E 201
Zenza do Itombe, Angola 9°17′ S, 14°14′ E 218
Zenzontepec, Mex. 16°32′ N, 97°31′ W 112
Zepa, Bosn. and Herzg. 43°56′ N, 19°8′ E 168
Žepče, Bosn. and Herzg. 44°26′ N, 18°2′ E 168
Zephyrhills, Fla., U.S. 28°13′ N, 82°11′ W 105
Zepu, China 38°12′ N, 77°18′ E 184
Żerczyce, Pol. 52°28′ N, 23°3′ E 152
Zerendi, Kaz. 52°53′ N, 69°9′ E 184
Zerf, Ger. 49°35′ N, 6°41′ E 163
Zerhamra, Alg. 29°57′ N, 2°29′ W 214
Zerind, Rom. 46°38′ N, 21°32′ E 168
Zermatt, Switz. 46°1′ N, 7°44′ E 167
Zernez, Switz. 46°42′ N, 10°5′ E 167
Zernograd, Russ. 46°50′ N, 40°18′ E 158
Zerqan, Alban. 41°30′ N, 20°21′ E 168
Zestap'oni, Ga. 42°3′ N, 43°2′ E 195
Zetel, Ger. 53°25′ N, 7°59′ E 163
Zevio, It. 45°21′ N, 11°7′ E 167
Zeya, Russ. 53°51′ N, 127°9′ E 190
Zeysk, Russ. 54°51′ N, 129°16′ E 173
Zgharta, Leb. 34°23′ N, 35°54′ E 156
Zgierz, Pol. 51°50′ N, 19°25′ E 152
Zhabinka, Belarus 52°12′ N, 24°0′ E 152
Zhabye, Ukr. 48°9′ N, 24°48′ E 152
Zhag'yab, China 30°37′ N, 97°35′ E 188
Zhalangash, Kaz. 43°2′ N, 78°38′ E 184
Zhalauly, Kaz. 48°1′ N, 61°12′ E 184
Zhaldama, Kaz. 50°26′ N, 65°39′ E 184
Zhalpaqtal, Kaz. 49°40′ N, 49°28′ E 158
Zhaltyr, Kaz. 51°38′ N, 69°51′ E 184
Zhambyl, Kaz. 47°9′ N, 71°8′ E 184
Zhambyl, adm. division, Kaz. 42°45′ N, 70°19′ E 197
Zhanadarīya, Kaz. 44°43′ N, 64°45′ E 184
Zhanang, China 29°16′ N, 91°18′ E 197
Zhanaqala, Kaz. 44°46′ N, 63°11′ E 184
Zhanbike, Kaz. 47°2′ N, 55°7′ E 158
Zhanga Qazan, Kaz. 48°57′ N, 49°35′ E 158
Zhangaly, Kaz. 47°2′ N, 50°46′ E 158
Zhangaözen, Kaz. 43°20′ N, 52°46′ E 158
Zhangaqala, Kaz. 49°13′ N, 50°19′ E 158
Zhangaqīma, Kaz. 51°36′ N, 67°35′ E 184
Zhangbei, China 41°11′ N, 114°40′ E 198
Zhangjiajuan, China 40°33′ N, 95°1′ E 188
Zhangjiakou, China 40°48′ N, 114°51′ E 198
Zhangping, China 25°18′ N, 117°24′ E 198
Zhangpu, China 24°4′ N, 117°36′ E 198
Zhangwu, China 42°24′ N, 122°34′ E 200
Zhangye, China 38°51′ N, 100°33′ E 190
Zhangzhou, China 24°29′ N, 117°36′ E 198
Zhangzi, China 36°6′ N, 112°51′ E 198
Zhanhua, China 37°44′ N, 118°10′ E 198
Zhanibek, Kaz. 49°24′ N, 46°50′ E 158
Zhanjiang, China 21°10′ N, 110°20′ E 198
Zhansügirov, Kaz. 45°21′ N, 79°28′ E 184
Zhäntöbe, Kaz. 44°43′ N, 68°50′ E 184
Zhanyi, China 25°41′ N, 103°44′ E 190
Zhao'an, China 23°42′ N, 117°9′ E 198
Zhaodong, China 46°3′ N, 125°57′ E 198
Zhaosu, China 43°7′ N, 81°1′ E 184
Zhaotong, China 27°19′ N, 103°38′ E 190
Zhaoyuan, China 45°29′ N, 125°6′ E 198
Zhaozhou, China 45°41′ N, 125°17′ E 198
Zhapo, China 21°35′ N, 111°52′ E 198
Zhaqsy, Kaz. 51°55′ N, 67°20′ E 184
Zharbulaq, Kaz. 46°4′ N, 82°4′ E 184
Zharkamys, Kaz. 47°56′ N, 56°21′ E 158
Zharkent, Kaz. 44°8′ N, 79°58′ E 184
Zharkovskiy, Russ. 55°52′ N, 32°20′ E 154
Zharma, Kaz. 48°47′ N, 80°51′ E 184
Zharman Köli, lake, Kaz. 51°32′ N, 63°36′ E 184
Zharmysh, Kaz. 44°8′ N, 52°24′ E 158
Zhashui, China 33°42′ N, 109°7′ E 198
Zhaslyk, Uzb. 43°53′ N, 57°41′ E 158
Zhaxi Co, lake, China 32°5′ N, 84°27′ E 188
Zhayylma, Kaz. 51°33′ N, 61°39′ E 184
Zhayyq, river, Kaz. 50°40′ N, 51°12′ E 158
Zhdanov, Azerb. 39°47′ N, 47°36′ E 195
Zhecheng, China 34°3′ N, 115°16′ E 198
Zhejiang, adm. division, China 28°7′ N, 120°50′ E 198
Zhelezīnka, Kaz. 53°38′ N, 75°13′ E 184
Zheleznodorozhnyy, Russ. 54°20′ N, 21°16′ E 166
Zheleznodorozhnyy, Russ. 62°33′ N, 50°59′ E 154
Zheleznogorsk, Russ. 52°17′ N, 35°20′ E 158
Zheleznovodsk, Russ. 44°10′ N, 43°3′ E 158
Zhem, river, Kaz. 47°13′ N, 55°32′ E 160
Zhen'an, China 33°25′ N, 109°7′ E 198
Zhenba, China 32°32′ N, 107°53′ E 198
Zhenfeng, China 25°21′ N, 105°42′ E 198
Zheng'an, China 28°35′ N, 107°22′ E 198
Zhenghe, China 27°23′ N, 118°51′ E 198
Zhenglan Qi (Xulun Hoh), China 42°13′ N, 116°2′ E 198
Zhengxiangbai Qi, China 42°15′ N, 115°3′ E 198
Zhengzhou (Chengchow), China 34°46′ N, 113°36′ E 198
Zhenjiang, China 32°10′ N, 119°25′ E 198
Zhenlai, China 45°48′ N, 123°11′ E 198
Zhenning, China 26°5′ N, 105°44′ E 198
Zhenping, China 31°58′ N, 109°30′ E 198
Zhenping, China 33°4′ N, 112°16′ E 198
Zhenyuan, China 23°50′ N, 100°50′ E 202
Zhenyuan, China 27°3′ N, 108°26′ E 198
Zhenyuan, China 35°43′ N, 107°13′ E 198
Zherdevka, Russ. 51°52′ N, 41°21′ E 158
Zherino, Belarus 54°50′ N, 29°24′ E 166
Zheshart, Russ. 62°4′ N, 49°36′ E 154
Zhetibay, Kaz. 43°33′ N, 52°4′ E 158
Zhetiger, Kaz. 43°40′ N, 77°6′ E 184
Zhetiqara, Kaz. 52°11′ N, 61°13′ E 158
Zhezdi, Kaz. 48°2′ N, 67°1′ E 184
Zhezkent, Kaz. 50°54′ N, 81°24′ E 184
Zhezqazghan, Kaz. 47°46′ N, 67°31′ E 190
Zhicheng, China 30°18′ N, 111°28′ E 198
Zhidan, China 36°49′ N, 108°45′ E 198
Zhidoi, China 33°54′ N, 95°38′ E 188
Zhigalovo, Russ. 54°44′ N, 104°58′ E 160
Zhigansk, Russ. 66°44′ N, 123°6′ E 160
Zhigulevsk, Russ. 53°26′ N, 49°37′ E 158
Zhijiang, China 27°28′ N, 109°42′ E 198
Zhilichi, Belarus 53°28′ N, 24°8′ E 152
Zhilikhovo, Belarus 52°55′ N, 27°3′ E 152
Zhilinda, Russ. 70°9′ N, 113°46′ E 160
Zhirnovsk, Russ. 50°58′ N, 44°47′ E 158
Zhitkovo, Russ. 60°41′ N, 29°19′ E 166
Zhizdra, Russ. 53°41′ N, 34°49′ E 154
Zhlobin, Belarus 52°52′ N, 30°6′ E 154
Zhmerynka, Ukr. 49°3′ N, 28°19′ E 152
Zhob, Pak. 31°20′ N, 69°30′ E 186
Zhob, river, Pak. 30°50′ N, 68°17′ E 186
Zhodzina, Belarus 54°7′ N, 28°20′ E 166
Zhokhova, island, Russ. 76°1′ N, 152°19′ E 255
Zholymbet, Kaz. 51°45′ N, 71°44′ E 184
Zhongba, China 29°41′ N, 84°13′ E 197
Zhongdian, China 27°52′ N, 99°40′ E 190
Zhongning, China 37°30′ N, 105°38′ E 198
Zhongshan, China 24°28′ N, 111°17′ E 198
Zhongshan, China, station, Antarctica 69°24′ S, 76°11′ E 248
Zhongwei, China 37°32′ N, 105°9′ E 198
Zhongxian, China 30°21′ N, 107°57′ E 198
Zhongxiang, China 31°8′ N, 112°34′ E 198
Zhosaly, Kaz. 45°29′ N, 64°5′ E 184
Zhoukou, China 33°34′ N, 114°43′ E 198
Zhoushan Dao, island, China 30°5′ N, 122°19′ E 198
Zhovten', Ukr. 49°1′ N, 24°46′ E 152
Zhovti Vody, Ukr. 48°23′ N, 33°29′ E 156
Zhovtneve, Ukr. 46°53′ N, 32°1′ E 156
Zhuanghe, China 39°42′ N, 122°57′ E 200
Zhuanglang, China 35°11′ N, 106°2′ E 198
Zhucheng, China 36°3′ N, 119°26′ E 198
Zhugqu, China 33°40′ N, 104°15′ E 198
Zhuji, China 29°44′ N, 120°10′ E 198
Zhukovka, Russ. 53°29′ N, 33°49′ E 154
Zhumysker, Kaz. 47°5′ N, 51°48′ E 158
Zhuolu, China 40°23′ N, 115°10′ E 198
Zhuozhou, China 39°29′ N, 115°57′ E 198
Zhuozi, China 40°55′ N, 112°36′ E 198
Zhuozi Shan, peak, China 39°39′ N, 106°54′ E 198
Zhuryn, Kaz. 49°18′ N, 57°33′ E 158
Zhushan, China 32°16′ N, 110°14′ E 198
Zhuxi, China 32°20′ N, 109°42′ E 198
Zhuzhou, China 27°50′ N, 113°12′ E 198
Zhympity, Kaz. 50°15′ N, 52°37′ E 158
Zhytomyr, Ukr. 50°15′ N, 28°40′ E 152
Zi, river, China 32°39′ N, 96°11′ E 188
Zi, river, China 28°25′ N, 111°8′ E 198
Zibak, Afghan. 36°32′ N, 71°25′ E 186
Zibo, China 36°49′ N, 118°6′ E 198
Zichang, China 37°7′ N, 109°39′ E 198
Zierikzee, Neth. 51°39′ N, 3°55′ E 163
Žiežmariai, Lith. 54°49′ N, 24°25′ E 166
Zigana Geçidi, pass, Turk. 40°37′ N, 39°21′ E 195
Zigey, Chad 14°43′ N, 15°46′ E 216
Zigong, China 29°25′ N, 104°50′ E 198
Zigui, China 31°2′ N, 110°40′ E 198
Ziguinchor, Senegal 12°31′ N, 16°13′ W 222
Zihuatanejo, Mex. 17°36′ N, 101°33′ W 114
Zikhron Ya'aqov, Israel 32°33′ N, 34°57′ E 194
Zilair, Russ. 52°12′ N, 57°21′ E 154
Zile (Zela), Turk. 40°19′ N, 35°53′ E 156
Žilina, Slovakia 49°13′ N, 18°45′ E 152
Žilinský, adm. division, Slovakia 49°13′ N, 18°45′ E 152
Zillah, Lib. 28°32′ N, 17°33′ E 216
Zillah, Wash., U.S. 46°23′ N, 120°17′ W 90
Zilupe, Latv. 56°22′ N, 28°6′ E 166
Zima, Russ. 53°59′ N, 101°50′ E 190
Zimapán, Mex. 20°42′ N, 99°23′ W 114
Zimatlán, Mex. 16°51′ N, 96°45′ W 112
Zimba, Zambia 17°19′ S, 26°9′ E 224
Zimbabwe 19°5′ S, 29°8′ E 220
Zimmi, Sierra Leone 7°16′ N, 11°18′ W 222
Zimnicea, Rom. 43°41′ N, 25°20′ E 180
Zimovniki, Russ. 47°5′ N, 42°21′ E 158
Zina, Cameroon 11°16′ N, 14°56′ E 216
Zinapécuaro, Mex. 19°51′ N, 100°49′ W 114
Zinave National Park, Mozambique 21°47′ S, 33°31′ E 227
Zinder, Niger 13°46′ N, 8°59′ E 222
Zinguinasso, Côte d'Ivoire 10°3′ N, 6°22′ W 222
Zinjibār, Yemen 13°7′ N, 45°19′ E 182
Zion, Ill., U.S. 42°27′ N, 87°49′ W 102
Zion National Park, Utah, U.S. 37°15′ N, 114°31′ W 80
Zionsville, Ind., U.S. 39°57′ N, 86°17′ W 102
Zipaquirá, Col. 5°2′ N, 73°60′ W 136
Zirc, Hung. 47°15′ N, 17°53′ E 168
Žirče, Serb. and Mont. 43°1′ N, 20°22′ E 168
Zirkel, Mount, peak, Colo., U.S. 40°49′ N, 106°44′ W 90
Zirkūh, island, U.A.E. 24°45′ N, 52°44′ E 182
Zitácuaro, Mex. 19°24′ N, 100°23′ W 114
Zitlala, Mex. 17°40′ N, 99°11′ W 114
Zitong, China 31°41′ N, 105°8′ E 198
Zitundo, Mozambique 26°37′ S, 32°53′ E 227
Živinice, Bosn. and Herzg. 44°28′ N, 18°38′ E 168
Zixi, China 27°39′ N, 117°2′ E 198
Zixing, China 26°0′ N, 113°21′ E 198
Ziya, river, China 38°30′ N, 116°41′ E 198
Ziyang, China 30°8′ N, 104°35′ E 198
Ziyang, China 32°34′ N, 108°33′ E 198
Ziyuan, China 26°2′ N, 110°41′ E 198
Ziyun, China 25°43′ N, 106°6′ E 198
Zizhou, China 37°37′ N, 110°5′ E 198
Zlatar, Croatia 46°6′ N, 16°4′ E 168
Zlatna, Rom. 46°7′ N, 23°15′ E 168
Zlatoust, Russ. 55°12′ N, 59°40′ E 154
Zlín, Czech Rep. 49°12′ N, 17°41′ E 152
Zlínský, adm. division, Czech Rep. 49°19′ N, 17°33′ E 152
Zlot, Serb. and Mont. 44°1′ N, 21°59′ E 168
Zmeinogorsk, Russ. 51°10′ N, 82°17′ E 184
Żmigród, Pol. 51°28′ N, 16°55′ E 152
Zmiyev, Ukr. 49°40′ N, 36°18′ E 158
Znamenka, Kaz. 50°2′ N, 79°31′ E 184
Znamensk, Russ. 54°35′ N, 21°12′ E 166
Znam'yanka, Ukr. 48°43′ N, 32°39′ E 158
Zobia, Dem. Rep. of the Congo 3°0′ N, 25°58′ E 224
Zóbuè, Mozambique 15°35′ S, 34°24′ E 224
Zocca, It. 44°21′ N, 10°59′ E 167
Zodoke, Liberia 4°44′ N, 8°8′ W 214
Zoetermeer, Neth. 52°4′ N, 4°30′ E 163
Zofar, Israel 30°28′ N, 35°9′ E 194
Zogang (Wangda), China 29°42′ N, 97°53′ E 188
Zohor, Slovakia 48°18′ N, 16°59′ E 152
Zolfo Springs, Fla., U.S. 27°30′ N, 81°47′ W 105
Zolochiv, Ukr. 50°19′ N, 35°58′ E 158
Zolochiv, Ukr. 49°48′ N, 24°54′ E 152
Zolotarevka, Russ. 53°3′ N, 45°19′ E 154
Zolotonosha, Ukr. 49°38′ N, 32°3′ E 158
Zomba, Malawi 15°22′ S, 35°20′ E 224
Zongga see Gyirong, China 28°59′ N, 85°16′ E 197
Zongo, Dem. Rep. of the Congo 4°16′ N, 18°36′ E 218
Zonguldak, Turk. 41°27′ N, 31°48′ E 156
Zonhoven, Belg. 50°59′ N, 5°22′ E 167
Zoo Baba, spring, Niger 18°12′ N, 13°3′ E 222
Zoquiapan y Anexas National Park, Mex. 19°14′ N, 99°2′ W 72
Zor Dağ, peak, Turk. 39°43′ N, 43°53′ E 195
Zorita, Sp. 39°17′ N, 5°42′ W 164
Zorritos, Peru 3°45′ S, 80°40′ W 130
Żory, Pol. 50°3′ N, 18°41′ E 152
Zorzor, Liberia 7°41′ N, 9°28′ W 222
Zouar, Chad 20°28′ N, 16°31′ E 216
Zoug, Africa 21°37′ N, 14°9′ W 222
Zouîrat, Mauritania 22°46′ N, 12°27′ W 214
Zoushi, China 29°4′ N, 111°35′ E 198
Zoutkamp, Neth. 53°20′ N, 6°18′ E 163
Zouxian, China 35°24′ N, 117°0′ E 198
Zrenjanin (Petrovgrad), Serb. and Mont. 45°23′ N, 20°22′ E 168
Zrin, Croatia 45°11′ N, 16°24′ E 168
Zrze, Europe 42°22′ N, 20°34′ E 168
Zsira, Hung. 47°27′ N, 16°41′ E 168
Zubia, Sp. 37°7′ N, 3°35′ W 164
Zubovo, Russ. 60°16′ N, 37°0′ E 154
Zubtsov, Russ. 56°11′ N, 34°39′ E 154
Zudañez, Bol. 19°2′ S, 64°48′ W 137
Zuénoula, Côte d'Ivoire 7°21′ N, 6°3′ W 222
Zuera, Sp. 41°52′ N, 0°48′ E 164
Zufre, Sp. 37°49′ N, 6°21′ W 164
Zugdidi, Ga. 42°30′ N, 41°52′ E 195
Zugspitze, peak, Aust. 47°23′ N, 10°54′ E 156
Zuidhorn, Neth. 53°14′ N, 6°24′ E 163
Zújar, Sp. 37°32′ N, 2°51′ W 164
Zula, Eritrea 15°12′ N, 39°39′ E 182
Zulia, adm. division, Venez. 9°34′ N, 73°2′ W 136
Zülpich, Ger. 50°41′ N, 6°38′ E 167
Zululand, region, S. Af. 27°12′ S, 31°44′ E 227
Zumaia, Sp. 43°17′ N, 2°15′ W 150
Žumberačka Gora, Slov. 45°39′ N, 14°43′ E 156
Zumbo, Mozambique 15°37′ S, 30°28′ E 224
Zumpango, Mex. 19°45′ N, 99°3′ W 114
Zunape, Col. 4°12′ N, 70°28′ W 136
Zungeru, Nig. 9°47′ N, 6°9′ E 222
Zunhua, China 40°14′ N, 117°56′ E 198
Zuni, N. Mex., U.S. 35°4′ N, 108°51′ W 92
Zunyi, China 27°40′ N, 106°53′ E 198
Zuo, river, China 22°21′ N, 107°31′ E 198
Zuoz, Switz. 46°36′ N, 9°56′ E 167
Županja, Croatia 45°4′ N, 18°41′ E 168
Zūq Mīkhā'īl, Leb. 33°58′ N, 35°36′ E 194
Žur, Europe 42°10′ N, 20°36′ E 168
Zūrābād, Iran 38°47′ N, 44°32′ E 195
Żurawica, Pol. 49°48′ N, 22°47′ E 152
Zureiqa, Sudan 13°32′ N, 32°1′ E 226
Zurich, Can. 43°25′ N, 81°37′ W 102
Zürich, Switz. 47°22′ N, 8°31′ E 150
Zuru, Nig. 11°24′ N, 5°12′ E 222
Zutiua, river, Braz. 5°8′ S, 46°19′ W 130
Zuwārah, Lib. 32°57′ N, 12°2′ E 216
Zuyevka, Russ. 58°24′ N, 51°15′ E 154
Zvenyhorodka, Ukr. 49°5′ N, 31°6′ E 158
Zvishavane, Zimb. 20°20′ S, 30°2′ E 227
Zvolen, Slovakia 48°34′ N, 19°7′ E 156
Zvonce, Serb. and Mont. 42°55′ N, 22°34′ E 168
Zvornik, Bosn. and Herzg. 44°24′ N, 19°5′ E 168
Zvoz see Podsosan'ye, Russ. 63°17′ N, 42°2′ E 154
Zwedru, Liberia 5°57′ N, 8°9′ W 222
Zweibrücken, Ger. 49°14′ N, 7°21′ E 163
Zwickau, Ger. 50°43′ N, 12°29′ E 152
Zwijndrecht, Neth. 51°48′ N, 4°39′ E 167
Zwinge, Ger. 51°32′ N, 10°22′ E 167
Zwoleń, Pol. 51°21′ N, 21°34′ E 152
Zwolle, La., U.S. 31°36′ N, 93°39′ W 103
Zwolle, Neth. 52°31′ N, 6°5′ E 163
Zyembin, Belarus 54°21′ N, 28°11′ E 166
Zygi, Cyprus 34°43′ N, 33°19′ E 194
Żyrardów, Pol. 52°2′ N, 20°24′ E 152
Zyrya, Azerb. 40°22′ N, 50°16′ E 195
Zyryanka, Russ. 65°51′ N, 150°31′ E 160
Zyryanovo, Russ. 63°39′ N, 87°27′ E 169
Zyryanovsk, Kaz. 49°45′ N, 84°18′ E 184

CONSULTANTS

PHYSICAL and POLITICAL MAPS and EDITORIAL CONTENT

United States Government

Central Intelligence Agency
Departments of economic development in each state
Library of Congress, *Geography and Map Division*
National Aeronautics and Space Administration (NASA)
Earth Observatory System (EOS)
Goddard Space Flight Center (GSFC)
Marshall Space Flight Center (MSFC)
National Geospatial-Intelligence Agency (NGA)
Hydrographic and Topographic Center
Naval Research Laboratory
U.S. Board on Geographic Names (BGN)
U.S. Department of Agriculture (USDA)
U.S. Department of Commerce
Bureau of Census
Bureau of Economic Affairs
National Oceanic and Atmospheric Administration (NOAA)
National Marine Fisheries Service (NMFS)
National Environmental Satellite, Data, and Information Service (NESDIS)
National Climatic Data Center (NCDC)
National Geophysical Data Center (NGDC)
National Ocean Service (NOS)
U.S. Department of Defense
Air Force Space and Missile systems Center (SMC)
Defense Meteorological Satellite Program (DMSP)
U.S. Department of Interior
Bureau of Land Management (BLM)
Geological Survey (USGS)
National Biological Survey
EROS Data Center
National Park Service
National Wetlands Research Center
Office of Territories
U.S. Department of State
U.S. Naval Oceanographic Office
U.S. Navy/NOAA Joint Ice Center

Government of Canada

Department of Energy, Mines and Resource
Canadian Permanent Committee on Geographic Names
Government du Québec
Commission de toponymie
Offices of provincial premiers and of commissioners of the territories
Statistics Canada

Other

Embassies and statistical agencies of foreign nations
International Astronomical Union
Working Group for Planetary System Nomenclature
International Telecommunication Union (ITU)
Norwegian Polar Institute
Population Reference Bureau (PRB)
Scripps Institution of Oceanography
State Economic Agencies
United Nations (UN)
Cartography Unit, Map Library, Department of Technical Cooperation, Documentation, Reference and Terminology Section
Department of Economic and Social Affairs, Statistics Division
Environmental Program (UNEP), World Conservation Monitoring Centre (WCMC), Protected Areas Program
Food and Agriculture Organization (FAO)
Global Resources Information Database (GRID)
United Nations High Commission on Refugees (UNHCR)
University of Cambridge, *Scott Polar Research Institute*
Wildlife Conservation Society (WCS), *Human Footprint Project*
World Bank
Map Library, Statistical Office
World Development Indicators
World Health Organization (WHO)
World Resources Institute (WRI), *Global Forest Watch*
World Wildlife Fund (WWF)

WORLD THEMATIC MAPS and EDITORIAL CONTENT

OVERALL CONSULTANTS

HARM J. DE BLIJ, *John A. Hannah Professor of Geography, Michigan State University*
ROGER M. DOWNS, *Pennsylvania State University*

THEMATIC CONSULTANTS

World From Above
ROBERT STACEY, *WorldSat International Inc.*

Geospatial Concepts
STEVEN STEINBERG, *Humboldt State University*

Tectonics
SETH STEIN, *Northwestern University*

Geomorphology
STEPHEN CUNHA, *Humboldt State University*

Earth's Surface
PETER SLOSS, *NOAA*

JONATHAN T. OVERPECK, *Department of Geosciences, The University of Arizona*

JEREMY L. WEISS, *Department of Geosciences, The University of Arizona*

Climate and Weather
JOHN OLIVER, *Indiana State University*

Biosphere
GENE CARL FELDMAN, *SeaWIFs, NASA/Goddard Space Flight Center*

Water
AARON WOLF, *Oregon State University*

Land Cover
PAUL DAVIS, *University of Maryland, Global Land Cover Facility*

Biodiversity
JOHN KUPTER, *University of South Carolina*

Land Use
NAVIN RAMANKUTTY, *University of Wisconsin, Madison*

Human Population and Population Trends
CARL HAUB, *Population Reference Bureau*

Cultures
BERNARD COMRIE, *Max Planck Institute for Revolutionary Anthropology*
DENNIS COSGROVE, *University of California, Los Angeles*

Health & Literacy
MICHAEL REICH, *Harvard University*

Economy
AMY GLASMEIER, *Pennsylvania State University*

Food
GIL LATZ, *Portland State University*

Trade & Globalization
AMY GLASMEIER, *Pennsylvania State University*

Transportation
JEAN-PAUL RODRIGUE, *Hofstra University*

Communication
GREG DOWNEY, *University of Wisconsin, Madison*

Energy
BARRY D. SOLOMON, *Michigan Technological University*

Defense & Conflict
ALEXANDER MURPHY, *University of Oregon*

Environment
TANIA DEL MAR LÓPEZ MARRERO, *Pennsylvania State University*

Protected Lands
PHILIP DEARDEN, *University of Victoria*
ERIC SANDERSON, *Wildlife Conservation Society*

Geographic Comparisons
DAVID DIVINS, *NOAA/NGDC*
ROBERT FISHER, *Scripps Institute of Oceanography*
CARL HAUB, *Population Reference Bureau*
MARTIN JAKOBSSON, *University of New Hampshire*
CHARLES O'REILLY, *Canadian Hydrographic Service*
RON SALVASON, *Canadian Hydrographic Service*
HANS WERNER SCHENKE, *Alfred Wegener Institute for Polar and Marine Research*

CREDITS and SOURCES

Abbreviations: Advanced Very High Resolution Radiometer (AVHRR); Digital Elevation Model (DEM); Moderate Resolution Imaging Spectroradiometer (MODIS); Shuttle Radar Topography Mission (SRTM).

Cover
(Photo: Mt. Everest) Jim Surette; (Photo: Panda from Wolong Nature Reserve, China) Daniel J. Cox, Natural Exposures; (Photo: Tree frog from Gunung Palung National Park, Indonesia) Tim Laman; (Political Maps) National Geographic Maps; (Ocean Circulation) Don Foley; (Lights at Night Data) NOAA/NGDC; DMSP; (Human Footprint) Human Footprint Project, ©WCS and Center for International Earth Science Information Network (CIESIN), Columbia University; (Surface Elevation) ETOPO2 data rendered by Peter W. Sloss, Ph.D., NOAA, NGDC.

Preface: (Map: World) MODIS, ETOPO-2, Lights at Night data; *NOAA/NGDC; DMSP.*

CHAPTER OPENERS

The World, pages 18-19: (Map: World) Human Footprint Project *© Wildlife Conservation Society (WCS) and Center for International Earth Science Information Network (CIESIN)* 2006; Project leads: Eric Sanderson, Kent Redford, *WCS;* Marc Levy, *CIESIN;* Funding: *Center for Environmental Research and Conservation (CERC) at Columbia University, ESRI Conservation Program, Prospect Hill Foundation.*

The Human Footprint Project illustrates the application of geographic information systems (GIS) as a way to combine diverse geographic data to reveal new patterns on the land. The authors of the study from the Wildlife Conservation Society and Columbia University combined nine global data layers to create this "human footprint" map. The layers covered the following themes: human population density, human land use and infrastructure, and human access. They concluded that 83% of the earth's land surface is influenced directly by human beings, whether through human land uses, human access from roads, railways, or major rivers, electrical infrastructure (indicated by lights detected at night), or direct occupancy by human populations at densities above one person per square kilometer. The researchers scored each of the variables on a one to ten scale, summed the numbers, and mapped the results. The lower the score, the lesser the degree of human influence. Antarctica was not mapped in the original study, but human influence there is known to be quite low, so it is shown in a uniform green color.

Continental Images: North America, pages 70-71; South America, pages 120-121; Europe, pages 140-141; Asia, pages 170-171; Africa, pages 204-205; Australia & Oceania, pages 228-229; Polar Regions, pages 244-245: (All Imagery) Landsat, AVHRR, Lights at Night data rendered by Robert Stacey, *WorldSat International Inc.; NOAA/NGDC; DMSP.*

To "paint" the images of continents, polar regions, and oceans which open the chapters, data from multiple passes of numerous satellites, Space Shuttle, and sonar soundings—recorded at varying scales and levels of resolution—were combined digitally to form mosaics. This level of detail, rendered cloud free, captured nighttime lights of populated areas, flares from natural gas burning above oil wells, and lights from fishing fleets. The images were further enhanced and blended to approximate true color. Shaded relief, as if the sun were shining from the northwest, was added for realism, and elevation was exaggerated twenty times to make variations in elevation easily visible. The images were then reproduced as if viewed from space.

Oceans, pages 250-251: (All Globes) Gregory W. Shirah, *NASA/GSFC Scientific Visualization Studio;* David W. Pierce, *Scripps Institution of Oceanography.*

The speed and direction of ocean currents can be computed from small variations in the height of the sea surface just as the speed and direction of the wind is computed from surface air pressure differences. Satellite-derived images depict a ten-year average of the hills and valleys, or shape, of the changing ocean surface. These undulations range over a few meters in height, and flow occurs along the color contours. The vectors (white arrows) show ocean velocity caused exclusively by the effect of wind on the top layer of the ocean (called the Ekman Drift). Estimates of the Ekman Drift are used by ocean researchers to determine the shape of the sea surface and as a component of the overall surface current (which also includes thermal, saline, tidal, and wave-driven components).

WORLD THEMATIC SECTION

World From Above, pages 14-15: (Aerial Photographs: Washington, D.C.) National Capital Planning Commission and District of Columbia, processed by *Photo Science, Gaithersburg, Maryland;* (Radar Imagery, Rio de Janeiro) Radar data by *Canadian Space Agency,* processed by *Radarsat International;* (Imagery: Rio de Janeiro) Landsat/Thermal, Near Infrared, Visible data from *Brazilian Ministry of Science and Technology's National Institute for Space Research,* processed by Stephen W. Stetson, *Systems for World Surveillance;* (Globes) Nimbus satellite data processed by *Laboratory for Oceans and Ice, NASA/GSFC;* (Map: North America) Landsat, AVHRR, and Lights at Night data rendered by Robert Stacey, *WorldSat International Inc.; NOAA/NGDC; DMSP;* (Imagery: Beaufort Sea) Landsat, SPOT, and RADARSAT data processed by *Canada Centre for Remote Sensing;* (Imagery: North Carolina Flooding in 1999) RADARSAT ScanSAR data processed by *Canada Centre for Remote Sensing;* (Imagery: Southern California Wildfire) Landsat-5 data courtesy of *USGS;* (Imagery: Ancient Footpaths, Arenal, Costa Rica) *NASA/MSFC.*

Geospatial Concepts, pages 16-17: (Map series: California) *© National Geographic Society;* (GIS Application: Urban Planning) *Community Cartography;* (GIS Application Sample: TransCAD Transportation Planning) *Caliper Corporation;* (GIS Application: Emergency Management) CalMAST and the San Bernadino County Sheriff used *ESRI's* ArcGIS technology to visualize a 3-D flyover of the Old and Grand Prix Fire perimeters (data provided courtesy of CalMAST and *USGS*); (GIS Application: Demographic/Census) Courtesy of *CBS News* and *ESRI;* (GIS Application: Health) Copyright © 2001-2005 *ESRI.* All rights reserved. Used by permission; (GIS Application: Conservation) *National Zoological Park, Smithsonian Institution.*

Tectonics, pages 24-25: (Map series: Paleogeography) Christopher R. Scotese, *PALEOMAP project* ; (Map: Earth Tectonics) Seth Stein, *Northwestern University; USGS Earthquake Hazard Program; Global Volcanism Program, Smithsonian Institution;* (Artwork: *"Tectonic Block Diagrams"*) Susan Sanford.

Geomorphology, pages 26-27: (Artwork: *"Eolian Landforms"*) Chris Orr; (Map: World Landforms) © *National Geographic Society*; (Photo: Crater Lake, Oregon) James Balog; (Photo: Misti Volcano, Peru) Stefano Scata, *Getty Images;* (Photo: Mount Fuji, Japan) George Mobley; (Photo: Isle of Skye, Scotland) Wilfried Krecicwost, *Getty Images;* (Photo: Southern China) James Blair; (Photo: Namibia) *Natphotos/Getty Images;* (Photo: Blyde River Canyon, South Africa) *Natphotos/Getty Images*; (Photo: Victoria, Australia) Rob Brander; (Photo:, Kejimkujik Lake, Nova Scotia) Douglas Grant, *Parks Canada*; (Photo: Mississippi River Delta, Louisiana) *SPOT Image/Photo Researchers;* (*CNES*); (Photo: Meteor Crater, Arizona) Adriel Heisey; (Artwork: *"Fluvial Landforms" and "Glacial Landforms"*) Steven Fick; (Maps: Eolian Landforms, Watersheds, Ice Age) © *National Geographic Society.*

Earth's Surface, pages 28-29: (Map series: Sea level changes) © *National Geographic Society*; Jonathan T. Overpeck, Jeremy L. Weiss, *Department of Geosciences, The University of Arizona*; (Map: Surface Elevation and Cross-section) ETOPO2 data rendered by Peter W. Sloss, Ph.D., *NOAA, NGDC.*

Climate, pages 30-31: (Artwork: *"Hadley Cells"*) Don Foley, NASA; (Artwork: *"The Seasons"*) Shusei Nagaoka; (Map: Modified Köppen Classification) © H. J. de Blij, P. O. Muller, and *John Wiley & Sons, Inc.*; (Map series: Seasonal Temperature) Barbara Summey, *NASA/GSFC Visualization Analysis Laboratory;* (Map: Mean Annual Precipitation) Data from *NOAA/NESDIS/NCDC/Satellite Data Services Division (SDSD)* compiled by *UNEP-GRID.*

Weather, pages 32-33: (Maps: Air pressure and Winds) *NOAA/Cooperative Institute for Research in Environmental Sciences (CIRES) Climate Diagnostic Center; National Centers for Environmental Prediction (NCEP)/National Center for Atmospheric Research (NCAR)* Reanalysis Project Data; (Map: Oceans and Cyclones) *NASA; NOAA;* (Globes: El Niño/La Niña) TOPEX/Poseidon satellite data from *NASA, Jet Propulsion Laboratory (JPL), California Institute of Technology;* (Artwork: *"Cyclonic Activity"*) Don Foley; (Artwork: *"How Weather Happens"*) Robert Hynes.

Biosphere, pages 34-35: (Map: Biosphere) Gene Carl Feldman, *SeaWIFs, NASA/Goddard Space Flight Center;* (Map: Ocean Circulation) Don Foley; (Artwork: *"Our Layered Ocean"*) Don Foley; (Artwork: *"Water and Carbon Cycle"*) Edward S. Gazsi.

Water, pages 36-37: (Graph: Water by Volume) Peter Gleick, *The Pacific Institute*; (Map: Primary Watersheds) *World Resources Institute*; Peter Gleick, *The Pacific Institute*; (Artwork: *"Hydrologic Cycle"*) Don Foley; (Map: Access to Fresh Water) *World Health Organization*; (Graph: Water Withdrawals) *AQUASTAT-FAO.*

Land Cover, pages 38-39: (Graph and Map: Global Land Cover) Paul Davis, *The Global Land Cover Facility, University of Maryland Institute for Advanced Computer Studies*, *see description below; (Photo: Evergreen Needleleaf Forest) Tom and Pat Leeson, *Photo Researchers*; (Photo: Evergreen Broadleaf Forest) Michael Nichols, *National Geographic Society Image Collection*; (Photo: Deciduous Needleleaf Forest) Stephen Krasemann, *PhotoResearchers*; (Photo: Deciduous Broadleaf Forest) Rod Planck, *Photo Researchers*; (Photo: Mixed Forest) Jim Steinberg, *Photo Researchers*; (Photo: Woodland) Matthew Hansen; (Photo: Wooded Grassland) Gregory Dimijian, *Photo Researchers*; (Photo: Closed Shrubland) Sharon G. Johnson; (Photo: Open Shrubland) Georg Gerster, *Photo Researchers*; (Photo: Grassland) Rod Planck, *Photo Researchers;* (Photo: Cropland) Jim Richardson; (Photo: Barren/Desert) George Steinmetz; (Photo: Built-up) Steve McCurry; (Photo: Barren/Polar Ice) B.&C. Alexander, *Photo Researchers.*

**This land cover classification was created using imagery from the NOAA AVHRR satellites and the NASA Landsat satellites. Using remote sensing, the imagery measures radiation occurring on the planet surface. Data from these measurements are grouped by scientists into classes representing particular land cover types. For example a type of forest will have values in a discrete range, and grasslands will have different values in a different range. Interpretation of values from single images can be very subjective, so scientists analyzed values from a series of global images collected over several years, resulting in an objective classification. It is important to note that this land cover classification explains what the Earth's land cover was when the imagery was collected. Land cover change occurs from natural and human causes.*

Biodiversity, pages 40-41: (Maps: Terrestrial and Aquatic Ecoregions) *Conservation Science Program, World Wildlife Fund—U.S.*; (Graph: Threatened Mammals and Birds) *IUCN Red List*; (Map: Biodiversity Hotspots and Status of Biodiversity) *Conservation International*; (Photo: The Bering Sea) Stephen Krasemann, *Getty Images*; (Photo: Southeastern United States Rivers and Streams) *Kevin Schafer Photography*; (Photo: The Amazon River and Flooded Forests) Flip Nicklin, *Minden Pictures*; (Photo: Rift Valley Lakes) John Ginstina, *Getty Images;* (Photo: Eastern Himalayan Broadleaf and Conifer Forests) ZSSD, *Minden Pictures;* (Photo: Sulu-Sulawesi Seas) Fred Bavendam, *Minden Pictures.*

Land Use, pages 42-43: (Map: Land Use) Jonathan Foley, Navin Ramankutty, Billie Leff, *Center for Sustainability and the Global Environment, University of Wisconsin, Madison*; (Imagery *Left to Right*) Bolivia Deforestation; Black Hills, South Dakota Fire Damage; Saudi Arabia Agricultural Development; Aral Sea Shoreline Changes) Landsat-5 satellite data courtesy of *USGS.*

Human Population, pages 44-45: (Photo: Philippines) Karen Kasmauski, *National Geographic Society Image Collection*; (Map: Population Density) *LandScan, Oak Ridge National Laboratory, Department of Energy;* (Cartogram: World Population) *CIA, The World Factbook; PRB;* (Graph: Regional Population Growth) © *National Geographic Society*; (Graphs: Population Pyramids), International Data Base (IDB), *U.S. Census Bureau.*

Population Trends, pages 46-47: (Maps: Fertility, Infant Mortality, Life Expectancy) *PRB*; (Maps and Charts: Migrant Population, Urban Population Growth, Most Populated Places) *United Nations Department of Economic & Social Affairs: Population Division.* Used by permission.

Cultures, pages 48-49: (Maps and Graphs: World Language, World Religion, Indigenous Languages) © *National Geographic Society;* (Graph: Regional Religion Adherence) *Encyclopedia Britannica*; (Graph: Religious Adherence) © *Adherents.com*; (Imagery *left to right*: Jerusalem, Israel; Mecca, Saudi Arabia; Allahabad, India) IKONOS satellite data courtesy of *Space Imaging.*

Health & Literacy, pages 50-51: (Maps and Graph: Causes of Death, Cardiovascular Deaths, Physicians) *WHO*; (Map: HIV/AIDS) *The Joint United Nations Programme on HIV/AIDS;* (Map: Malaria endemicity*) Robert Snow, *Malaria Atlas Project; Funded by the Wellcome Trust UK;* (Maps: Calorie Supply and Undernourished) *SOFI, UN; WHO*; *The Joint United Nations Programme on HIV/AIDS;* (Map and Graph: Literacy Rate) *CIA, The World Factbook.*

**Endemicity defines the intensity of Plasmodium falciparum transmission and is measured by the percentage of children infected with the parasite at any moment in time.*

Economy, pages 52-53: (Cartogram, Map, Graphs: GDP, GNI, Industry Sector) *CIA, The World Factbook, World Bank*; (Map: Labor Migration, GDP) *World Bank, Institute for the Study of International Migration, Georgetown University.*

Food, pages 54-55: (Maps: Cereals, Roots and Tubers, Sugar-bearing Crops, Pulses, Oil-bearing Crops) Jonathan Foley, Navin Ramankutty, Billie Leff, *Center for Sustainability and the Global Environment, Nelson Institute for Environmental Studies, University of Wisconsin-Madison; FAO;* (Map: Livestock) *Global Livestock Production Health Atlas (GLiPHA), FAO*; (Photo: Corn) Richard Olsenius, *National Geographic Society Image Collection*; (Photo: Wheat) Jim Richardson; (Photo: Rice) Steven L. Raymer, *National Geographic Society Image Collection*; (Graph: World Diets and Chart of World Crop Production by Region) FAOSTAT-FAO; (Map: Fisheries and Aquaculture) Reg Watson and Daniel Pauly, *Fisheries Centre, University of British Columbia; SOFIA, FAO;* (Map: Biotech Cropland) Clive James, Ph.D., *International Service for the Acquisition of Agri-Biotech Applications (ISAAA).*

Trade & Globalization, pages 56-57: (Maps and Graphs: Regional Trade Blocs, World Debt, Imports, Exports) *CIA, The World Factbook*; (Map: Trade Flow) *World Bank, CIA, The World Factbook; World Trade Organization; USGS Minerals Yearbook; United Nations Conference on Trade and Development; FAO;* (Graph: Trade) *World Trade Organization.*

Transportation, pages 58-59: (Map: Airline Passenger Volume) *International Civil Aviation Organization*; (Map: Transportation Routes) © *National Geographic Society; American Association of Port Authorities; Bureau of Transportation Statistics, U.S. Department of Transportation;* (Chart: World's Largest Airports) *Airports Council International;* (Chart: World's Largest Ports) *American Association of Port Authorities.*

Communication, pages 60-61: (Map: Satellite Capacity) *Telegeography Research Group, PriMetrica, Inc*. 2004; (Map of the Internet) Hal Burch and Bill Cheswick, *Lumeta Corporation* Patent(s) Pending & Copyright © *Lumeta Corporation* 2006. All Rights Reserved; (Map: Internet Explosion) Reproduced with the kind permission of *ITU;* (Map: Computer Virus/Code Red Worm) David Moore, *Cooperative Association for Internet Data Analysis (CAIDA)*, Copyright © 2001 *The Regents of the University of California*; (Map: Connecting the Planet) Reproduced with the kind permission of *ITU; Telegeography Research Group, PriMetrica, Inc*. 2004, *www.primetrica.com;* Buckminster Fuller Projection courtesy of the *Buckminster Fuller Institute.*

Energy, pages 62-63: (Photo: Hydropower) Jim Richardson; (Photo: Nuclear) Mark Burnett, *Photo Researchers;* (Photo: Solar) Courtesy *National Renewable Energy Lab*; (Photo: Wind) John Mead, *Science Photo Library/Photo Researchers*; (Photo: Geothermal) *Science Photo Library/Photo Researchers;* (Map: Annual Energy consumption) Energy Infrastructure data courtesy of the *Petroleum Economist Ltd, London; BP Statistical Review of World Energy; Energy Information Administration, U.S. Department of Energy; USGS Mineral Resources Program; International Iron and Steel Institute; FAO*; (Map: Geothermal and Photovoltaic/Solar Electric Power Plants) *The Geothermal Energy Association*; Barry Soloman, *Michigan Technological University; Sandia National Laboratories; Windpower Monthly News Magazine*; © Denis Lenardic, *pvresources.com-photovoltaic technologies and applications*; (Map, Chart: Flow of Oil) *BP Statistical Review of World Energy.*

Defense & Conflict, pages 64-65: (Photo: Srebrenica Refugees) Chris Rainier, *Corbis;* (Map: Regime Type and Active Military) Monty G. Marshall, *Center for Systemic Peace; International Institute of Strategic Studies*; (Graph: Refugees and Uprooted People by Country) *United Nations High Commission on Refugees*; (Map: Defense Spending and Military Services) *CIA, The World Factbook; International Institute of Strategic Studies*; (Maps: Biological, Nuclear, and Chemical Weapons) © *National Geographic Society; Center for Nonproliferation Studies, Monterey Institute of International Studies; Carnegie Endowment for International Peace; Henry Stimson Center; U.S. Department of Energy;* Ken Alibeck.

Environment, pages 66-67: (Graph: Atmospheric Carbon Dioxide) Gene Carl Feldman, *SeaWIFs, NASA/GSFC*; (Map: Habitat Loss) Lara Hansen, Adam Markham, *WWF*; Jay Malcom, University of Toronto; (Photo: Logging) *Photodisc/Getty Images;* (Map: Vanishing Forests) *Global Forest Watch, WRI*; (Photo: Coral) Bruce Fouke and Michael Fortwengler; (Map: Threatened Oceans) *NOAA/NMFS; UNEP-WCMC*; (Photo: Desertification) Bruce Dale, *National Geographic Society Image Collection;* (Map: Risk of Desertification) *USDA Global Desertification Vulnerability Map;* (Map: Polar Ice Cap) *National/Naval Ice Center*; © *National Geographic Society*; (Map: Environmental Stress Factors) © *National Geographic Society*, (Globes: Atmospheric Ozone) *NASA.*

Protected Lands, pages 68-69: (Graph: Protected Areas Worldwide) © *National Geographic Society; UNEP-WCMC*; (Map: Wildest Biomes) © *Wildlife Conservation Society (WCS) and Center for International Earth Science Information Network (CIESIN)*; (Photo: Hawai'i Volcanoes N.P., U.S.) Bryan Lowry, *Seapics.com*; (Photo: Galápagos, N.P., Ecuador) Cristina G. Mittermeier; (Photo: Arches N.P., Western U.S.) Art Wolfe; (Photo: Madidi N.P., Bolivia) Joel Sartore; (Photo: Amazon Basin, Brazil) Michael Nichols; (Photo: Arctic Regions) Flip Nicklin; (Photo: Sareks N.P., Sweden) Jan-Peter Lahall; (Photo: African Reserves) Beverly Joubert, *National Geographic Television and Film*; (Photo: Wolong Nature Reserve, China) Daniel J. Cox, *Natural Exposures*; (Photo: Kamchatka Peninsula, Russia) Sarah Leen; (Photo: Gunung Palung N.P., Indonesia) Tim Laman; (Photo: Australia and New Zealand) Art Wolfe; (Map: Protected Areas Worldwide) *WDPA Consortium*, World Database on Protected Areas. Copyright © *World Conservation Union (IUCN); UNEP-WCMC.*

CONTINENTAL THEMATIC SECTION

Natural World: North America, pages 74-75; United States, pages 84-85; South America, pages 124-125; Europe, pages 144-145; Asia, pages 174-175; Africa, pages 208-209; Australia & Oceania, pages 232-233: (Map: Land Cover) Paul Davis, *The Global Land Cover Facility, University of Maryland Institute for Advanced Computer Studies*; (Map: Climate Modified Köppen) © H. J. de Blij, P. O. Muller, and *John Wiley & Sons, Inc.*; (Map: Natural Hazards) © *National Geographic Society; USGS Earthquake Hazard Program; Global Volcanism Program, Smithsonian Institution;* Lights at Night data, *DMSP*; (Map: Watershed Basins) Aaron Wolf, *Oregon State University;* (Climagraphs) *National Climatic Data Center, NOAA;* (Map: U.S. Federal Lands) *National Park Service, Bureau of Land Management; USDA Forest Service; U.S. Fish and Wildlife Service; Bureau of Indian Affairs; Department of Defense; Department of Energy; NOAA.*

Human World: North America, pages 76-77; United States, pages 86-87; South America, pages 126-127; Europe, pages 146-147; Asia, pages 176-177; Africa, pages 210-211; Australia & Oceania, pages 234-235: (Map: Population Density) *LandScan, Oak Ridge National Laboratory, Department of Energy;* (Map: Percent Population Change 2000-2030) *PRB;* (Map: Percent Urban Population) *United Nations Department of Economic & Social Affairs: Population Division.* Used by permission; (Map: Language) © *National Geographic Society;* (Age/Sex Pyramids) International Data Base (IDB), *U.S. Census Bureau*; (Map: Percent Change in U.S. Population 2000-2005; U.S. Population Density by County; Ancestry by County) *U. S. Census Bureau*; (Map: Reported Church Membership in the U.S. by County) Data for Major Religious Families by Counties of the United States, 2000 from "Religious Congregations and Membership in the United States 2000," Dale E. Jones, et. al. Nashville, TN: *Glenmary Research Center.* © 2002 *Association of Statisticians of American Religious Bodies.* All rights reserved.

Economic World: North America, pages 78-79; United States, pages 88-89; South America, pages 128-129; Europe, pages 148-149; Asia, pages 178-179; Africa, pages 212-213; Australia & Oceania, pages 236-237: (Map: Land Use) Jonathan Foley, Navin Ramankutty, Billie Leff, *Center for Sustainability and the Global Environment, University of Wisconsin, Madison*; (Map: Per Capita Energy Consumption) *PRB;* (Maps: GDP Per Sector) *CIA, The World Factbook* (Map: People Living on Less than $2 per day) *World Bank, World Development Indicators*; (Graph: Imports/Exports) *The Europa World Year Book;* (Map: U.S. Manufacturing by County, Agricultural Land by County, Service Employment by County, Income by County, Employment by Region) *U.S. Census Bureau.*

WORLD FACTS SECTION

Demographic and Socioeconomic Information, pages 258-269: (Capital, Language, Religion, Area sq. km/sq. mi) © *National Geographic Society;* (Population Mid-2005, Projected Pop. Change 2005-2050, Pop. Density, Urban Pop., Natural Increase, Total Fertility/Infant Mortality Rate, Percent of Pop. Age <15/ >65, Life Expectancy, HIV/AIDS Pop. Age 15-49) *PRB;* (GDP Mid-2005) *CIA, The World Factbook*; (Services/Industry/Agriculture as % of GDP Sector, Total Estimated Value of Imports/Exports, Percent of Pop. with Access to Electricity, Telephone Mainlines) *World Bank, World Development Indicators;* (Arable and Permanent Cropland Area, Forested Area as % of Land Area) *FAO;* (Protected Areas as % of Land Area) *UNEP-WCMC;* (Average Annual Deforestation, Carbon Dioxide Emissions) *World Bank, World Development Indicators.*

Geographic Information: Comparisons & Conversions, pages 270-271: (Statistical Information) *PRB; National Park Service; Grand Canyon Information*; Helen Brachmanski, *Great Barrier Reef Marine Park Authority; Atlas of Canada; International Hydrographic Organization*; Ronald Mair, *New Zealand Statistical Office; The Columbia Gazetteer of the World; Encyclopedia Britannica; The World Almanac and Book of Facts; Geodata: The World Geographical Encyclopedia;* (Urban Population) *United Nations Department of Economic & Social Affairs: Population Division.* Used by permission.

ADDITIONAL SOURCES

BP Statistical Review of World Energy. London: BP p.l.c., 2005. Available online at www.bp.com.

Busby, Rebecca L., ed. *International Petroleum Encyclopedia.* Tulsa, Oklahoma: Penwell Corporation, 2005.

Central Intelligence Agency. *The World Factbook.* Washington, D.C.: GPO, 2006. Available online at www.cia.gov/cia/publications/factbook/index.html.

Cohen, Saul. *The Columbia Gazetteer of the World.* New York: Columbia University Press, 1998.

Comrie, Bernard. *The World's Major Languages.* London: Croom Helm, 1997.

Crystal, David. *The Cambridge Encyclopedia of Language.* New York: Cambridge University Press, 1977.

de Blij, H. J. and Peter O. Muller. *Geography: Realms, Regions, and Concepts,* 12th ed. New York: John Wiley & Sons, Inc., 2006.

de Blij, H. J., Peter O. Muller, and Richard S. Williams, Jr. *Physical Geography: The Global Environment.* 3rd ref. ed. New York: Oxford University Press, 2004.

Encyclopedia Britannica. Chicago, Illinois: Encyclopedia Britannica, Inc., 2006. Available online at www.britannica.com.

Energy Information Administration. *International Energy Annual (IEA).* Washington, D.C.: Department of Energy, 2003. Available online at www.eia.doe.gov/iea.

FAO. *Review of Water Resources by Country.* Rome: FAO, 2003. Available online at www.fao.org/ag/agl/aglw/aquastat/water_res.

——.*Statistical Yearbook: 2004.* Rome: FAO, 2005. Available online at www.fao.org/WAICENT/FAOINFO/ECONOMIC/ESS/yearbook. Data from FAOSTAT available online at faostat.fao.org.

——.*The State of Food Insecurity in the World (SOFI): Eradicating World Hunger-Key to achieving the Millennium Development Goals.* Rome: FAO, 2004. Available online at www.fao.org/SOF/sofi.

——.*The State of World Fisheries and Aquaculture (SOFIA).* Rome: FAO, 2004. Available online at www.fao.org/sof/sofia/index_en.htm.

——.*The State of the World's Forests, 2005.* Rome: FAO, 2005. Available online at www.fao.org/forestry/fo/sofo/sofo-e.st.

Foley, J. A., R. DeFries, G. P. Asner, C. Barford, G. Bonan, S. R. Carpenter, F. S. Chapin, M. T. Coe, G. C. Daily, H. K. Gibbs, J. H. Helkowski, T. Holloway, E. A. Howard, C. J. Kucharik, C. Monfreda, J. A. Patz, I. C. Prentice, N. Ramankutty, and P. K. Snyder."Global Consequences of Land Use," *Science* (22 July 2005), 570-574.

Gleick, Peter. *The World's Water, 2006-2007: The Biennial Report on Freshwater Resources.* Washington, D.C.: Island Press, 2006.

Goddard, Ives, Vol. ed. *Handbook of North American Indians. Vol. 17, Languages.* Washington, D.C.: Smithsonian Institution, 1996.

Hansen, M., R. DeFries, J. R. G. Townshend, and R. Sohlberg. *1-Km Land Cover Classification Derived from AVHRR.* College Park, Maryland: The Global Land Cover Facility, 1998. Description available online at glcf.umiacs.umd.edu.

James, Clive. "Global Status of Commercialized Biotech/GM Crops: 2005," *ISAAA Briefs, no. 34* (2005). Available online at www.isaaa.org.

Jones, Dale E., Sherri Doty, Clifford Grammich, James E. Horsch, Richard Houseal, Mac Lynn, John P. Marcum, Kenneth M. Sanchagrin, and Richard H. Taylor. *Religious Congregations and Membership in the United States 2000: An Enumeration by Region, State and County Based on Data Reported by 149 Religious Bodies.* Nashville, TN: Glenmary Research Center, 2002.

Langton, Christopher, ed. *The Military Balance, 2005-06.* Washington, D.C.: International Institute for Strategic Studies, 2005.

Leff, B., N. Ramankutty, and J. A. Foley. "Geographic distribution of major crops across the world," *Global Biogeochemical Cycles* (16 January 2004), GB1009. Available online at www.agu.org/pubs/back/gb/2004/index.php?month=January.

Mackay, J, and G. Mensah, eds. *Atlas of Heart Disease and Stroke,* Geneva, Switzerland: World Health Organization, 2004. Available online at www.who.int/cardiovascular_diseases/resources/atlas/en.

Maher, Joanne and Philip McIntyre, eds. *The Europa World Year Book.* London: Europa Publications, 2004.

McCoy, John, ed. *Geo-Data: The World Geographical Encyclopedia.* Farmington Hills, MI: Thomson Gale, 2003.

Morrell, Virginia. "California's Wild Crusade," *National Geographic* (February 2006), 2-35.

Moseley, Christopher and R. E. Asher, eds. *Atlas of the World's Languages.* London: Routledge, 1994.

National Geographic. "Humans and Habitats: Cultural Extinctions Loom," *National Geographic* (September 2001), *EarthPulse* feature.

National Geographic Maps. "Challenges for Humanity: A Thirsty Planet." Supplement map, *National Geographic* (September 2002).

——."Danger Zones: Earthquake Risk-A Global View." Supplement map, *National Geographic* (April 2006).

——."Earth At Night." Supplement map, *National Geographic* (November 2004).

——."Millennium in Maps: Biodiversity." Supplement map, *National Geographic* (February 1999).

——."Millennium in Maps: Cultures." Supplement map, *National Geographic* (June 1999).

——."State of the Planet: A World Transformed." Supplement map, *National Geographic* (September 2002).

Oliver, John E. and John Hidore. *Climatology: An Atmospheric Science.* New York: Prentice Hall, 2001.

Olson, D. M. and E. Dinerstein.1998. "The Global 200: A representation approach to conserving the earth's most biologically valuable ecoregions," *Conservation Biology* (1998), 502-515.

Olson, D. M., E. Dinerstein, E. D. Wikramanayake, N. D. Burgess, G. V. N. Powell, E. C. Underwood, J. A. D'Amico, I. Itoua, H. E. Strand, J. C. Morrison, C. J. Loucks, T. F. Allnutt, T. H. Ricketts, Y. Kura, J. F. Lamoreux, W. W. Wettengel, P. Hedao, and K. R. Kassem. "Terrestrial Ecoregions of the World: A New Map of Life on Earth," *BioScience* (2001), 933-938.

Overpeck J. T., B. L. Otto-Bliesner, G. H. Miller, D. R. Muhs, R. B. Alley, and J. T. Kiehl. "Paleoclimatic evidence for future ice-sheet instability and rapid sea-level rise," *Science* (24 March 2006), 1747-50.

Population Reference Bureau. *2005 World Population Data Sheet.* Washington, D.C.: PRB, 2006. Available online at www.prb.org.

Ramankutty, N. and J. A. Foley. "Characterizing patterns of global land use: An analysis of global croplands data," *Global Biogeochemical Cycles* (1998), 667-685.

Sarmiento, Jorge L. and Nicolas Gruber. "Sinks for Anthropogenic Carbon," *Physics Today* (August 2002), 30-36.

Scotese, C.R. *Atlas of Earth History, Volume 1, Paleogeography.* Arlington, Texas: PALEOMAP Project, 2001.

Simons, Lewis M. "Weapons of Mass Destruction," *National Geographic* (February 2006), 2-35.

Snow, R. W., C. A. Guerra, A. M. Noor, H. Y. Myint, and S. I. Hay. "The global distribution of clinical episodes of *Plasmodium falciparum* malaria," *Nature* (March 10, 2005), 214-217.

The World Almanac and Book of Facts. New York: World Almanac Education Group, 2006.

UNEP. *One Planet Many People: Atlas of Our Changing Environment.* UNEP/DEWAL/GRID, 2005. Available online at grid2.cr.usgs.gov/OnePlanetManyPeople/index.php.

UNEP. *World Atlas of Desertification.* London: Edward Arnold, 1992.

United Nations, Department of Economic and Social Affairs, Population Division. *International Migration, 2002.* New York, NY: October 2002. Available online at www.un.org/esa/population/publications.

United Nations, Department of Economic and Social Affairs, Population Division. *World Population Prospects: The 2004 Revision.* New York, NY: United Nations, 2005. Available online at esa.un.org/unpp.

United Nations. *World Urbanization Prospects: The 2003 Revision.* New York, NY: United Nations, 2004. Available online at www.un.org/esa/population/unpop.htm.

United States Geological Survey. *Minerals Yearbook, Vol. III, International.* Washington, D.C.: U.S. Department of the Interior, 2003. Available online at minerals.usgs.gov.minerals/pubs.

Watson, R, J. Alder, A. Kitchingman, and D. Pauly. "Catching some needed attention," *Marine Policy* (2005) 281-284.

Watson, R., A. Kitchingman, A. Gelchu, and D. Pauly. "Mapping global fisheries: sharpening our focus," *Fish and Fisheries* (2004), 168-177.

WDPA Consortium. *World Database on Protected Areas.* Cambridge, U.K.: World Conservation Union (IUCN) and UNEP-World Conservation Monitoring Centre (UNEP-WCMC), 2004. Available online at www.wcmc.org.uk/data/database.un_combo.html.

Wilford, John Noble. "Revolutions in Mapping," *National Geographic* (February 1998), 6-39.

World Bank. *World Development Indicators.* Washington, D.C.: The World Bank Group, 2005. Available online at www.worldbank.org/data.

World Health Organization (WHO), UNICEF, and Roll Back Malaria (RBM). *World Malaria Report, 2005.* WHO: Geneva, Switzerland, 2005. Available online at www.rbm.who.int/wmr2005.

World Trade Organization. *International Trade Statistics.* Geneva, Switzerland: World Trade Organization, 2005. Available online at www.wto.org.

ONLINE SOURCES

Central Intelligence Agency
www.cia.gov

Conservation International
www.conservation.org

El Niño/La Niña (TOPEX/Poseidon and Jason-1 data)
sealevel.jpl.nasa.gov

Energy Information Agency
www.eia.doe.gov

Food and Agriculture Organization of the UN (FAO)
www.fao.org

International Telecommunication Union (ITU)
www.itu.int

National Aeronautics and Space Administration
www.nasa.gov

National Atmospheric and Oceanic Administration
www.noaa.gov

National Climatic Data Center
www.ncdc.noaa.gov

National Park Service
www.nps.gov

Ozone hole
www.gsfc.nasa.gov

Pacific Institute-The World's Water
www.worldwater.org

Population Reference Bureau
www.prb.org

The Smithsonian Global Volcanism Program
www.volcano.si.edu

United Nations
www.un.org

UNEP Global Resources Information Database (GRID)
www.grid.unep.ch/data/index

UNEP-World Conservation Monitoring Centre
www.unep-wcmc.org

UNESCO
www.unesco.org

U.S. Geological Survey
www.usgs.gov

World Bank
www.worldbank.org

World Conservation Union
www.iucn.org

World Health Organization
www.who.int

World Resources Institute
www.wri.org

World Wildlife Fund
www.worldwildlife.org

COLLEGE ATLAS OF THE WORLD

NATIONAL GEOGRAPHIC SOCIETY

John M. Fahey, Jr.	*President and Chief Executive Officer*
Gilbert M. Grosvenor	*Chairman of the Board*
Nina D. Hoffman	*Executive Vice President, and President, Book Publishing Group*

Prepared by NATIONAL GEOGRAPHIC MAPS

Frances A. Marshall	*President, National Geographic Maps*
Allen Carroll	*Chief Cartographer*
Daniel J. Ortiz	*Vice President, Consumer Products*
Kevin P. Allen	*Director of Map Services*
Kris Viesselman	*Director of Design*

NATIONAL GEOGRAPHIC MAPS ATLAS STAFF

Richard W. Bullington	*Project Manager, NGMaps Atlas Development*
Michael J. Horner	*Supervisor, NGMaps Database Editorial*
Juan José Valdés	*Project Manager, Editorial*
Billie Leff	*Project Manager, GIS*
Sally Suominen-Summerall	*Art Director*
Dierdre Bevington-Attardi	*Project Manager, Research*
Kaitlin M. Yarnall	*Supervisor of Map Research*
Glenn C. Caillouet	*Supervisor of Map Production*
Maureen J. Flynn, Eric A. Lindstrom, David Byers Miller, Jr.	*Map Editors*
Kristine L. French, Katherine R. Krezel, Linda R. Kriete	*Research Cartographers*
Jess D. Elder, Michael E. Jones, Windy A. Robertson, Andrew L. Wunderlich	*GIS Analysts*
Geoffrey W. Hatchard, Dianne C. Hunt, Micki Anne Laws, Stephen P. Wells	*Production Cartographers*
Robert E. Pratt	*Designer*
Debbie J. Gibbons	*Project Manager, Large Format Mapping*
Eric A. Lindstrom	*Map Librarian*
Denise Shaffer	*Executive Assistant*
William C. Gordon, Raya Guruswamy, Jennifer A. Hogue	*Interns*

ADDITIONAL STAFF

TEXT

Cynthia Barry	*Text Editor*
Cynthia Barry, David Jeffery, David Byers Miller, Jr., Priit J. Vesilind, Amy Jo Woodruff	*Contributing Writers*

PRODUCTION SERVICES

Christopher A. Liedel	*Executive Vice President and Chief Financial Officer*
Phillip L. Schlosser	*Vice President, Manufacturing and Quality Management*
Edward J. Holland	*Manager of Print Quality Control*

Printed and bound by RR Donnelley & Sons Company
Willard, Ohio

Printed in the U.S.A.